THOMSON ONE | Business School Edition

Real-world financial research and analysis for students!

Thomson ONE – Business School Edition (BSE) gives students the opportunity to use an educational version of the Internet-based database that financial analysts and professionals around the world use every day to conduct research. This research tool gives students the practical real-world experience they will need for their financial careers.

Thomson ONE – BSE is easy to use and includes access to many resources. One of the key strengths Thomson ONE – BSE provides is the ability to access **10-year financial statements that can be downloaded to Excel** for easy manipulation or review. Other beneficial resources include one click Peer Set analysis, indices that can be manipulated or compared, and data for international and domestic companies.

If research projects or end-of-chapter Thomson ONE – BSE problems are assigned, students can use Thomson ONE – BSE to complete these assignments.

Get started today with Thomson ONE – BSE!

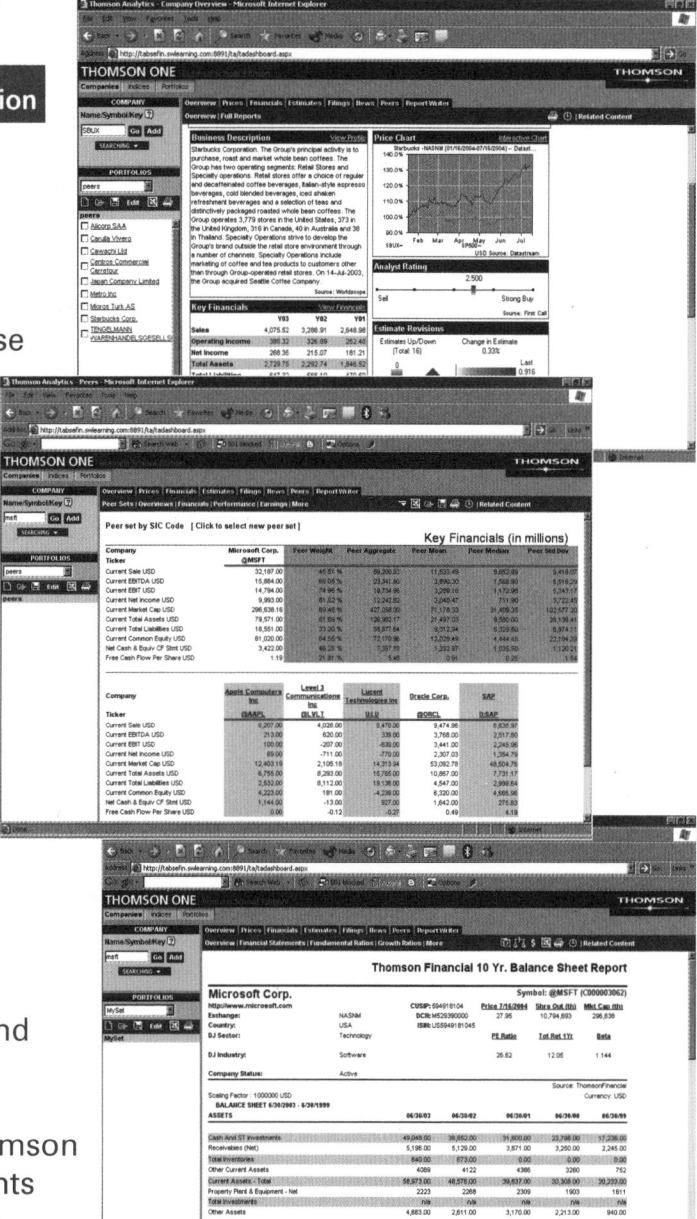

CORPORATE FINANCE

SECOND EDITION

Scott B. Smart
Indiana University

William L. Megginson
University of Oklahoma

Lawrence J. Gitman
San Diego State University

THOMSON
™
SOUTH-WESTERN

Australia • Canada • Mexico • Singapore • Spain • United Kingdom • United States

To Our Families
—SBS, WLM, LJG

Corporate Finance

Second Edition

Scott B. Smart, William L. Megginson, Lawrence J. Gitman

VP/Editorial Director:
Jack W. Calhoun

Editor-in-Chief:
Alex von Rosenberg

Publisher:
Steve Momper

Sr. Developmental Editor:
Susanna C. Smart

Sr. Production Project Manager:
Cliff Kallemeyn

Technology Project Editor:
Matthew McKinney

Web Coordinator:
Karen Schaffer

Art Director:
Bethany Casey

Sr. Manufacturing Coordinator:
Sandee Milewski

Production House:
G&S Book Services
Austin, TX

Printer:
Quebecor World
Taunton, MA

BRIEF CONTENTS

CONTENTS

Smart Ethics Video
Frank Popoff, Chairman of the Board
(retired), Dow Chemical, page 51

Smart Concepts
page 53

Smart Ideas Video
Michael Brennan, UCLA, page 55

Smart Solutions
Problem 2-3, page 60

Smart Concepts
page 94

Smart Ethics Video
Kent Womack, Dartmouth College,
page 95

PART 2: VALUATION, RISK, AND RETURN   122

Smart Practices Video
Jon Olson, Vice President of Finance, Intel Corp. (former). Currently, Chief Financial Officer, Xilinx Corp., page 256

Smart Practices Video
Daniel Carter, Executive Vice President, Chief Financial Officer, Charlotte Russe, page 258

Smart Practices Video
Daniel Carter, Executive Vice President, Chief Financial Officer, Charlotte Russe, page 259

Smart Practices Video
Chris Muscarella, Professor of Finance and L.W. "Roy" and Mary Lois Clark Teaching Fellow, page 264

Smart Concepts
page 279

Smart Practices Video
Beth Acton, Vice President and Treasurer of Ford Motor Co. (former). Currently, Chief Financial Officer, Comerica, page 284

Smart Solutions
Problem 7-9, page 290
Problem 7-29, page 295

Smart Practices Video
Paul Savastano, Director of Information Technology, Sprint Corp., page 307

Smart Concepts
page 308

Smart Ethics Video
Scott Lee, Texas A&M University, page 309

Smart Ideas Video
Mitchell Petersen, Northwestern University, page 455

Smart Practices Video
Keith Woodward, Vice President of Finance, General Mills, page 461

Smart Concepts
page 470

Smart Solutions
Problem 12-15, page 481

Smart Ideas Video
Robert Bruner, University of Virginia, page 490

Smart Ideas Video
Sheridan Titman, University of Texas at Austin, page 491

Smart Practices Video
David Baum, Co-head of MGA for Goldman Sachs in the Americas, page 572

Smart Practices Video
Jay Goodgold, Managing Director, Equities Division, Goldman Sachs, page 575

Smart Ethics Video
Jay Ritter, University of Florida, page 578

Smart Ethics Video
Jay Ritter, University of Florida, page 591

Smart Ethics Video
Jay Ritter, University of Florida, page 592

Smart Ideas Video
Annette Poulsen, University of
Georgia, page 619

Smart Ideas Video
Ed Altman, New York University,
page 621

PART 6: OPTIONS, DERIVATIVES, AND INTERNATIONAL FINANCIAL MANAGEMENT   648

Smart Ideas Video
Myron Scholes, Stanford University,
and Chairman of Oak Hill Platinum
Partners, page 653

Smart Concepts
page 658

Smart Ethics Video
John Eck, President of Broadcast and
Network Operations, NBC, page 671

Smart Concepts
page 679

Smart Ideas Video
Myron Scholes, Stanford University,
and Chairman of Oak Hill Platinum
Partners, page 684

Smart Practices Video
Daniel Carter, Chief Financial Officer of Charlotte Russe, page 850

Smart Concepts
page 854

Smart Concepts
page 860

Smart Solutions
Problem 23-1, page 864
Problem 23-16, page 868

WEB CHAPTERS

ABOUT THE AUTHORS

SCOTT B. SMART

Scott Smart has been a member of the Finance Department at Indiana University since 1990. He has published articles in scholarly journals such as the *Journal of Finance,* the *Journal of Financial Economics,* and the *Review of Economics and Statistics.* His research has been cited by the *Wall Street Journal, Business Week,* and other major newspapers and periodicals. Professor Smart holds a Ph.D. from Stanford University and has been recognized as a master teacher, winning more than a dozen teaching awards, all at the graduate level. His consulting clients include Intel and Unext.

WILLIAM L. MEGGINSON

Bill Megginson is Professor and Rainbolt Chair in Finance at the University of Oklahoma. He is also a voting member of the Italian Ministry of Economics and Finance's Global Advisory Committee on Privatization. He has published refereed articles in several top academic journals, including the *Journal of Economic Literature,* the *Journal of Finance,* the *Journal of Financial Economics,* the *Journal of Financial and Quantitative Analysis,* and *Foreign Policy.* Dr. Megginson has a Ph.D. in finance from Florida State University. He has visited 63 countries and has served as a privatization consultant for the New York Stock Exchange, the OECD, the IMF, the World Federation of Exchanges, and the World Bank.

LAWRENCE J. GITMAN

Lawrence J. Gitman, emeritus professor of finance at San Diego State University, is a prolific textbook author and has published numerous articles in various finance-related journals. He is past president of the San Diego chapter of the Financial Executives Institute, the Midwest Finance Association, and the Academy of Financial Services. He also served as Vice President for Financial Education of the Financial Management Association. He received his bachelor's degree from Purdue University, his M.B.A. from the University of Dayton, and his Ph.D. from the University of Cincinnati.

PREFACE

Corporate Finance 2/e has landed. Thanks to the support of many instructors who took the risk of adopting our first edition, we are pleased to present the new and improved second edition of *Corporate Finance*. Clearly, it is tough to launch a new textbook into a very competitive market having some excellent and entrenched texts. Well, Houston: The launch has been a success! Our goal for this book is to build on the success of the first edition, incorporating the feedback we have received from users over the last three years. Based on that feedback, we believe we have created the most effective teaching/learning tool available in this market.

Professors who teach corporate finance at the M.B.A. level consistently tell us they want a book that has modern content, global integration, strong emphasis on practice, and cutting-edge technology. At the same time, however, they want a book that adds value along these dimensions while minimizing the costs of switching from the books they currently use. *Corporate Finance* 2/e is a fresh, easy-to-use, thoroughly modern text that anchors student learning in the latest corporate finance theory and practice.

OBJECTIVE AND PRIMARY GOALS OF TEXT

The overriding objective that guided our work in developing *Corporate Finance* 2/e was to create a focused, topically cutting-edge text grounded in modern theory. We wanted the book to have a truly global perspective and to reach students through the use of innovative and engaging technologies. Above all, our desire was that students would take away from the book a deeper understanding of the connection between financial theory and practice. To achieve these objectives, we focused our energies on five primary goals.

Goal 1: Focus on Important Topics. This goal drove the development and revision of the overall text structure as well as the topics covered within each chapter. With this goal in mind, we designed a book that covers classic corporate finance concepts, such as risk and return, capital budgeting, and capital structure, as well as emerging theories that we feel are likely to have an impact in the business world as current students progress in their careers. Even seasoned corporate finance instructors will discover something new here. It is our view that the best educational experience for students is one that both allows them to learn the basic tools and techniques of corporate finance and exposes them to emerging discoveries from research.

Goal 2: Make Theory Discussions Intuitive and Practical. We feel it's important to expose M.B.A. students to cutting-edge thinking in corporate finance. The art of doing this in an intuitively appealing and practical manner rests on the ability to synthesize, interpret, and communicate complex ideas in a way that readers can easily digest. We strive to provide students with a smooth bridge between theory and practice by highlighting examples in a feature that we call "Applying the Model." These illustrations help students see how to put theory into action. Similarly, each chapter's Opening Focus relates a story from the business world that stresses the practical relevance of one or more of the chapter's main ideas.

Goal 3: Provide a Truly Global Perspective. We incorporate a seamless global perspective throughout the text rather than confine global issues to a single chapter that few instructors have time to cover. Every chapter has a unique Comparative Corporate Finance (CCF) feature designed to compare corporate finance practices around the world. For example, Chapter 5's CCF examines historic returns on various types of investments in nine different countries. In addition, more than half of the Opening Focus examples which begin each chapter involve non-U.S. companies or markets. In Chapter 2, for instance, the Opening Focus explains the actions of Denmark's Bang & Olufsen's new CEO to improve the firm's poor financial results. Most important, many chapters have extended coverage of international material, such as Chapter 11's discussion of research on law and finance. As a result, our book offers students a more global view of corporate finance than does any other corporate finance text.

Goal 4: Maintain High Reader Interest. To maintain high reader interest, we use a relaxed, conversational writing style. We know that it is crucial for students to develop sharp quantitative skills to succeed in our field. Nevertheless, when we present mathematical topics, such as the variance of a portfolio of assets or pricing an option using Black and Scholes, we do more than simply present the equations along with "plug and chug" examples. We convey the intuition beneath the surface, urging readers to contemplate not just how an equation works, but also why it works. Writing clearly, incorporating real examples, and asking students interesting questions are some of the ways that we try to make the quantitative material more approachable.

Goal 5: Use Technology to Clarify and Motivate. We developed Smart Finance, an integrated technology package, to engage, motivate, and at times entertain students, while helping them master financial concepts on their own time and at their own pace. It also allows students to hear firsthand about exciting recent developments in financial research and to learn from business professionals why the material contained in the text is relevant. The flash animated concept reviews and problem solutions let students review some of the more difficult concepts at any time and as many times as they like. Nearly 100 short video interviews with leading scholars and practitioners give students access to "virtual guest speakers" and help build the bridge between theory and practice that we feel is so important. Use by in-residence and online M.B.A. students as well as in executive M.B.A. programs has generated almost unanimous praise for these features. In fact, the most common complaint we have heard from students is, "Why can't we see more of this?"

ORGANIZATION OF THE TEXT

We divided the text into 9 parts with 25 chapters plus 2 additional web chapters. The nine part titles are:

    Part 1: Introduction
    Part 2: Valuation, Risk, and Return
    Part 3: Capital Budgeting
    Part 4: Capital Structure and Dividend Policy
    Part 5: Long-Term Financing
    Part 6: Options, Derivatives, and International Financial Management
    Part 7: Short-Term Financing Decisions

Part 8: Special Topics
Part 9: Web Chapters

This structure evolved from a number of iterations and refinements based on user feedback. Classroom tests using this structure confirm its effectiveness. Of course, those professors who prefer an alternative structure will find the text is flexible in that alternative sequences generally work well.

Part 1 includes three introductory chapters that provide background and review. Included are discussions of the scope of corporate finance, coverage of financial statement and cash flow analysis, and a chapter on the time value of money. Because of differences in course prerequisites, some professors may assign these chapters and cover them in class while others may include them as review that students can use to confirm their understanding of those course prerequisites. The chapters work well in both of these situations. Part 2 includes three chapters—one on bond and stock valuation and two on risk and return. These chapters provide students with a solid understanding of risk, return, and value that serves as the conceptual base upon which subsequent discussions are built.

Part 3 includes three chapters devoted to capital budgeting processes and techniques, cash flow and capital budgeting, and cost of capital and project risk. Part 4 on capital structure and dividend policy includes six chapters. They cover market efficiency, an overview of long-term financing, capital structure theory and taxes, nontax determinants of corporate leverage, the link between capital structure and capital budgeting; and dividend policy. Part 5 includes two chapters on long-term financing. They focus on investment banking and the public sale of equity securities and long-term debt and leasing.

Part 6 includes three chapters—two on options (options basics and Black and Scholes and beyond) and one on international financial management. Part 7 contains three short-term financing chapters, one on strategic and operational financial planning and two on short-term financial management. Part 8 includes two special topics chapters—one on mergers, acquisitions, and corporate governance and the other on bankruptcy and financial distress. Finally, Part 9 includes two web chapters, one covering entrepreneurial finance and venture capital and another on risk management and financial engineering. These chapters are available at the text website http://www.thomsonedu.com/finance/smartfinance and are not printed in the book.

MAJOR IMPROVEMENTS IN THE SECOND EDITION

We are committed to continuous improvement of *Corporate Finance* 2/e. In the second edition we tweaked the text structure and improved and updated the content of many chapters.

STRUCTURAL IMPROVEMENTS

While the printed text continues to include eight major parts and 25 chapters, we moved two chapters to the web—Chapter 26: Entrepreneurial Finance and Venture Capital and Chapter 27: Risk Management and Financial Engineering. Because most adopters considered these to be enrichment chapters, we now make them available on the web in order to control the length and cost of the printed text.

In response to requests for coverage of more advanced valuation techniques, such as adjusted present value, we added a brand-new chapter—Chapter 14: The Link Between Capital Structure and Capital Budgeting. Another new chapter resulted from splitting and improving the discussion of short-term financial management, which is now covered in Chapter 22: Cash Conversion, Inventory, and Receivables Management and Chapter 23: Liquidity Management. The new chapters provide a more balanced and logical discussion of the key aspects of short-term financial management.

CHAPTER CONTENT IMPROVEMENTS

All chapters, including the Applying the Model examples, were updated with the most current data. In addition, most Opening Focus elements were replaced with more current examples. Most of the Comparative Corporate Finance boxes were updated as well. Also, we added a number of new end-of-chapter problems to each of the more quantitative chapters, particularly Chapters 2 through 9. Some of the key chapter improvements—all made to improve student understanding—include:

Chapter 3 on Time Value of Money. We added computations to time lines and incorporated an appendix from the first edition into the body of the chapter.

Chapter 4 on Valuation. New discussions of bond issuers, bond ratings, and bond price quotations now precede the discussion of bond pricing and a new discussion of stock price quotations now begins the discussion of stock valuation.

Chapter 7 on Capital Budgeting Process and Techniques. This chapter now includes computations on time lines and a new discussion of the modified internal rate of return.

Chapter 12 on Capital Structure Theory and Taxes. This chapter now begins with a detailed discussion, supported by simple tables and figures, of how using financial leverage increases both expected return and risk for corporations.

Chapter 16 on Investment Banking and the Public Sale of Equity Securities. The discussion of international common stock issuance practices was expanded, highlighting the global trend toward use of U.S.-style book-building techniques.

Chapter 20 on International Financial Management This chapter now incorporates greater discussion of the rise of China and India as major trading and industrial powers, including a new Opening Focus describing CNOOC's failed attempt to acquire Unocal during 2005.

Chapter 21 on Strategic and Operational Financial Planning. The discussion of sustainable growth was expanded to include popular growth targets such as ROI and EVA®.

Chapter 22 on Cash Conversion, Inventory, and Receivables Management. This chapter now includes a completely new part describing the fundamentals of inventory management.

Chapter 24 on Mergers, Acquisitions, and Corporate Governance. This chapter has been completely restructured to emphasize the most modern, global corporate governance concepts and to incorporate recent research on the agency costs of overvalued equity and empirical evidence showing that acquiring firms frequently overpay in high-profile acquisitions.

THE END RESULT

In the final analysis, a textbook must cover the topics that professors believe are important and it must do so using a level of rigor appropriate for its readers—in this case, graduate students. Beyond that, professors want a book that students can and will use as a resource to succeed in the classroom and in the workplace. We believe that *Corporate Finance* 2/e delivers the best our profession has to offer in terms of modern theory and practice and effectively engages students in learning, both in a linear fashion on the written page and interactively using the computer. We hope you'll try it. We are confident that if you do, both you and your students will be glad you did.

TEXT SUPPLEMENTS

FOR INSTRUCTORS

Instructor's Manual with Test Bank. Prepared by Pamela Hall, Western Washington University. Designed to support novice instructors and finance veterans alike, this comprehensive Instructor's Manual includes chapter overviews, lecture guides organized by section, enrichment exercises, answers to concept review questions, answers to end-of-chapter questions, solutions for end-of-chapter problems, and the test bank. (0-324-32235-6)

ExamView. ExamView Computerized Testing Software contains all of the questions in the printed test bank. This program is an easy-to-use test creation software compatible with Microsoft Windows. Instructors can add or edit questions, instructions, and answers, and select questions randomly, by number, or by previewing them on the screen. Instructors can also create and administer quizzes online, whether over the Internet, a local area network (LAN), or a wide area network (WAN). (0-324-38122-0)

PowerPoint Slides. PowerPoint slides are available for instructors for enhancing their lectures, and a brief student version is available for use by students as an aid to note-taking. Available as a download from the product support website at http://www.thomsonedu.com/finance/smartfinance.

Instructor's Resource CD-ROM (IRCD). A CD-ROM is available to instructors and contains electronic versions of all print instructor supplements—Instructor's Manual, Test Bank in Microsoft Word and in ExamView, PowerPoint slides—as well as a Resource Integration Guide to help coordinate and integrate all of the text supplements. (0-324-38118-2)

ThomsonNOW for SmartFinance. ThomsonNOW for Smart Finance (http://www.thomsonedu.com/finance/smartfnance) takes the best of current technology tools, including online homework management and course support materials, to support your course goals and save you significant preparation and grading time. It includes Smart Concepts, Smart Solutions, Smart Ideas Videos, Smart Practices Videos, Smart Ethics Videos, Smart Excel Animations, and Smart Quizzing, as described below.

FOR STUDENTS

ThomsonNOW for SmartFinance. SmartFinance is a robust set of educational online tools (http://www.thomsonedu.com/finance/smartfinance) for course study, test preparation, and enrichment of chapter topics that contain the following:

**SMART
IDEAS
VIDEO**

Diane Denis, Purdue University

"At this point it's fairly well
documented that diversified firms
don't seem to do as well as
undiversified firms."

See the entire interview at
SMARTFinance

**SMART
PRACTICES
VIDEO**

**Paul Savastano,
Director of Information
Technology, Sprint Corp.**

"So the challenge becomes, how
do you quantify the benefits
when a big piece of the
investment is going to be for
things that people never see?"

See the entire interview at
SMARTFinance

**SMART
ETHICS
VIDEO**

**Utpal Bhattacharya,
Indiana University**

"The cost of equity goes up if
insider trading laws are not
enforced."

See the entire interview at
SMARTFinance

Smart Concepts. These animated concept review tutorials, organized by chapter, explain key topics step by step, offering students opportunities to review more difficult chapter material at their own pace and at convenient times. Students can also decide how much or what parts of the review they want to cover. An icon in the text directs students to http://smartfinance.swlearning.com to explore.

Smart Solutions. The Smart Solutions feature helps improve students' problem-solving skills by demonstrating animated solution steps and offering coaching about how to identify the right technique to apply to particular problems. An icon in the text directs students to http://smartfinance.swlearning.com to explore Smart Solutions.

Smart Ideas Videos. Introduce your students to the leading academic researchers behind the theory or concepts you are discussing in class with Smart Ideas Videos. Each clip runs approximately 2 to 3 minutes. Video clips feature John Graham (Duke University), Robert Schiller (Yale), Elroy Dimson (London School of Business), Andrew Karolyi (Ohio State University), Kenneth French (Dartmouth College), and many, many more. An icon in the text directs students to http://smartfinance.swlearning.com to view these short video clips, which instructors can also embed in their PowerPoint presentations.

Smart Practices Videos. Business and industry leaders discuss how they maximize their companies' financial performance using cutting-edge practices. These videos can help show students why corporate finance is a vital topic regardless of their functional areas. Presidents and CFOs of major corporations, such as Andy Bryant, CFO of Intel Corp., as well as corporate recruiters, are featured interviewees. An icon in the text directs students to http://smartfinance.swlearning.com, or instructors can embed these 2- to 3-minute video clips within their PowerPoint lectures.

Smart Ethics Videos. These videos show how both academics and business executives view ethics and the impact that ethical or unethical behavior can have on the company's bottom line. An icon in the text directs students to http://smartfinance.swlearning.com to view these clips, or instructors can embed these 2- to 3-minute video clips within their PowerPoint presentations.

Smart Excel Animations. Excel animations walk students through problems or through particularly challenging aspects of problems that can be solved more easily with Excel. Additionally, appendixes for several chapters are provided online to show how to use Excel to solve chapter problems.

Smart Quizzing. The Smart Finance website provides true/false and multiple-choice quiz questions for each chapter to test student knowledge. Each answer yields a response confirming correctness or explaining errors.

ThomsonONE-BSE. Thomson ONE–Business School Edition is a web-based portal product that provides integrated access to Thomson Financial content for the purpose of financial analysis. This is an educational version of the same financial resources used by Wall Street analysts on a daily basis. An access card for Thomson ONE–BSE is provided with each new textbook. If your text is used and does not contain an access card, access may be purchased at http://tobsefin.swlearning.com.

ACKNOWLEDGMENTS

Most people realize that creating a textbook is a collaborative venture. As authors, we truly appreciate all the people who helped plan, edit, produce, and launch our book. Although only three people are listed as authors on the title page, we wish to acknowledge the debt we owe to those who have worked so closely with us.

First, we thank Mike Roche and Kristin Sandberg, who signed us to our original contract. Over the years, numerous other publishing company professionals have helped mold this book. This list includes Heather MacMaster, Trish Taylor, Steve Momper, Susan Smart, and Jason Krall. Thanks are also due freelance editor Ann Torbert. Several people made written contributions to the book and its supplements. We are particularly grateful to Lance Nail, David Whidbee, John Yeoman, Dubos Masson, and Richard Shockley for their written contributions to specific chapters, Pamela Hall for the end-of-chapter mini-cases, Tom Arnold for the many new end-of-chapter problems, and Bill Chittenden for the ThomsonONE problems. We also thank Pamela Hall for revising the Instructor's Manual; Nicholas Wonder, Andreas Rauterkus, and David Beard for the test bank; and Yee-Tien Fu and Art Lathrop's contributions to the PowerPoint slides. Finally, Bill Megginson wishes to extend special thanks to the students at the University of Oklahoma where he used early drafts of this book. Even though students received the text free of charge, they paid a price to help us remove errors from earlier drafts.

Technology is an extremely important part of this book, and we wish to express our deep appreciation to Thomson South-Western for their financial and professional support. In particular, we have been honored to work with technical professionals as competent and supportive as Thomson's Vicky True, John Barans, and Matt McKinney. Many other people have also contributed to creating what we believe to be an outstanding technology package. This list begins with Jack Koning, who made truly amazing contributions in developing the flash animations, and Don Mitchell, whose audio work made the animations come to life.

Though it would be nice to pretend that our skills as authors are so advanced that we did not have to make repeated passes at writing the chapters you see today, in fact this book has benefited immeasurably from the feedback we have received from reviewers. We would like to thank the following people for their insightful comments and constructive criticism of the text:

John Affleck-Graves
University of Notre Dame

Daniel J. Borgia
Florida Gulf Coast University

Ivan Brick
Rutgers University

Arturo Bris
Yale School of Management

Amy Burnett
St. Edwards University

Chao Chen
California State University–Northridge

James Cotter
Wake Forest University

Arnold Cowan
Iowa State University

Pete Crabb
Northwest Nazarene University

Charles Cuny
Texas A&M University

Karen Denning
West Virginia University

James S. Doran
University of Texas

Daniel Ebels
University of Michigan

Lawrence Glosten
Columbia University

John Graham
Duke University

John Hall
University of Arkansas–Little Rock

Joel Harper
Florida Atlantic University

Del Hawley
University of Mississippi

Shady Kholdy
California Polytechnic University–Pomona

Praveen Kumar
University of Houston

Chun-I Lee
Loyola Marymount University

David Lins
University of Illinois–Champaign

Ike Mathur
Southern Illinois University–Carbondale

Vassil Mihov
Texas Christian University

David B. Milton
Bentley College

Roger Morin
Georgia State University

Charles Mossman
University of Manitoba

Jim Musumeci
Southern Illinois University–Carbondale

Narendar V. Rao
Northeastern Illinois University

Ramesh Rao
Oklahoma State University

Bill Reese
Tulane University

Patricia Ryan
Colorado State University

James Schallheim
University of Utah

James Seward
University of Wisconsin–Madison

Dennis Sheehan
Penn State University

Betty Simkins
Oklahoma State University

Mark Simonson
Arizona State University

Alex Tang
Morgan State University

Olaf Thorp
Babson College

Harry Turtle
Washington State University

Joseph Vu
DePaul University

Susan White
University of Maryland

David A. Zalewski
Providence College

In addition to comprehensive reviews, a survey was conducted to provide feedback to improve this edition. We would like to thank our survey participants for their valuable input:

Indudeep Chhachhi
Western Kentucky University

Elroy Dimson
London Business School

Lawrence R.Glosten
Columbia University

Richard Gritta
University of Portland

J. Christopher Hughen
Bowling Green State University

Steve Jordan
University of Virginia

Kathleen Kahle
University of Arizona

Andrew Karolyi
Ohio State University

Nikolay Kosturov
University of Oklahoma

Jim Linck
University of Georgia

John Longo
Rutgers University

Evgeny Lyandres
Rice University

Ike Mathur
Southern Illinois University

Felix Meschke
Arizona State University

Charles E. Mossman
University of Manitoba

Ralph A. Pope
Cal State/Sacramento University

Raghu Rajan
University of Chicago

Lee Redding
University of Michigan

Bill Reese
Tulane University

Andrew Spieler
Hofstra University

Ron Sverdlove
Rutgers University

Alex Tang
Morgan State University

Sorin Tuluca
Fairleigh Dickinson University

Kam-Ming Wan
University of Texas, Dallas

Mukunthan Santhanakrishnan
Idaho State University

Rohan Williamson
Georgetown University

We would like to thank the following instructors for sharing their experience with support pieces and assisting us in the development of the test bank, instructor's manual, solutions manual, and PowerPoint presentation slides for the first edition, carried over to this second edition.

Shyam Bhandari
Bradley University

Kenneth Kim
University of Wisconsin–Milwaukee

John Crocket
George Mason University

Hany Shawky
University at Albany

J. David Diltz
University of Texas–Arlington

Tie Su
University of Miami

A key feature of our book is that we integrate video clips of academics and finance professionals throughout the text. The following academics provided critical contributions to this text by explaining their important contributions to modern financial thought. Our interviews with them appear in Smart Ideas Videos and Smart Ethics Videos.

Anup Agrawal
University of Alabama

Andrew Karolyi
Ohio State University

Franklin Allen
University of Pennsylvania

Laurie Krigman
Babson College

Ed Altman
New York University

Scott Lee
Texas A&M University

Utpal Bhattacharya
Indiana University

Ike Mathur
Southern Illinois University–Carbondale

Michael Brennan
UCLA

David Mauer
Southern Methodist University

James Brickley
University of Rochester

Mitchell Petersen
Northwestern University

Robert Bruner
University of Virginia

Annette Poulsen
University of Georgia

Jennifer Conrad
University of North Carolina

Manju Puri
Stanford University

Francesca Cornelli
London Business School

Raghu Rajan
University of Chicago

David Denis
Purdue University

Jay Ritter
University of Florida

Diane Denis
Purdue University

Myron Scholes
Stanford University and Chairman of Oak Hill Platinum Partners

Elroy Dimson
London School of Business

Lemma Senbet
University of Maryland

Kenneth French
Dartmouth College

William Sharpe
Stanford University and cofounder of Financial Engines

Jon Garfinkel
University of Iowa

Steven Kaplan
University of Chicago

Robert Shiller
Yale University

Laura Starks
University of Texas

Avanidhar Subrahmanyam
UCLA

Anjan Thakor
University of Michigan

Sheridan Titman
University of Texas

Greg Udell
Indiana University

Theo Vermaelen
INSEAD

Rohan Williamson
Georgetown University

Kent Womack
Dartmouth College

We are also grateful to the following individuals who shared their insights based on their experience practicing corporate finance. Our interviews with them appear in Smart Practices Videos and Smart Ethics Videos.

Beth Acton
*Vice President and Treasurer (former),
    Ford Motor Company, currently Chief
    Financial Officer, Comerica*

David Baum
*Cohead of M&A for the Americas,
    Goldman Sachs*

Andy Bryant
*Executive Vice President of Finance and
    Enterprise Systems, Chief Financial
    Officer, Intel Corp.*

Beverly Caen-Kauffman
*President and CEO, Caen Lota Consulting–
    Executive Recruiting*

Dan Carter
*Executive Vice President, Chief Financial
    Officer, Charlotte Russe*

David Childress
*Asset Liability Manager, Ford Motor
    Company*

Tom Cole
Leveraged Finance Group, Deutsche Bank

Ron Dollens
*Chief Executive Officer (retired), Guidant
    Corp.*

John Eck
*President of Broadcast and Network
    Operations, NBC*

Jay Goodgold
*Managing Director, Equities Division,
    Goldman Sachs*

David Haeberle
*Chief Executive Officer, Command Equity
    Group*

Jeff Kauffman
*Portfolio Manager, Blue Collar Fund,
    George Weiss Associates*

Vince LoForti
*Chief Financial Officer, Overland
    Storage Inc.*

Ben Lytle
Chairman Emeritus, Anthem Inc.

David Nickel
*Controller for Legal and Risk Management,
    Intel Corp.*

Jon Olson
Chief Financial Officer, Xilinx Corp.

Frank Popoff
*Chairman of the Board (retired), Dow
    Chemical*

Todd Richter
*Managing Director, Head of Equity
    Healthcare Research, Bank of America
    Securities*

Pam Roberts
*Executive Director of Corporate Services,
    Cummins Inc.*

Paul Savastano
*Director of Information Technology,
    Sprint Corp.*

Jackie Sturm
*Director of Finance for Technology and
    Manufacturing, Intel Corp.*

Keith Woodward
Vice President of Finance, General Mills

Last but certainly not least, the authors wish to thank their families and friends who provided invaluable support and assistance.

SBS, WLM, LJG
April 2006

CORPORATE FINANCE

SECOND EDITION

PART 1: Introduction

Welcome to the study of *corporate finance*. In this book, we explain the theory and practice of corporate finance using a profit-seeking public company as our laboratory. Clearly the theories and practices that we present are applicable with minor modification to any organization—large or small, profit-seeking or not-for-profit, public or private. Because the careers of most MBAs are focused on managing the firm, the primary emphasis in this text is on the concepts and techniques used by financial managers to make decisions consistent with the owners' goals. This part of the text includes three introductory chapters that set the stage for the study of corporate finance. They describe the scope of corporate finance and review two key tools that are used widely in finance—financial statement and cash flow analysis, and the time value of money.

Chapter 1 begins with a description of corporate finance, its core principles—such as compensation for risk—and the five basic corporate finance functions—financing, capital budgeting, financial management, corporate governance, and risk management. Then it presents a brief review of the legal forms of business organizations, placing greatest emphasis on the competitive advantages and characteristics of corporations. Finally, the chapter focuses on the goals of the corporate financial manager, and the related issues of agency costs and ethics.

Chapter 2 provides a broad overview of the most important source of accounting information: a firm's financial statements. Its focus is not on how accountants construct these statements, but rather on why these statements are important to financial managers. Next, we describe why and how finance places primary emphasis on measures of cash flow rather than on financial-statement-based measures of earnings, such as net income or earnings per share. Finally, we demonstrate how companies use the information from financial statements to calculate various ratios to analyze financial performance over time, or to benchmark their results against those achieved by other firms.

Chapter 3 introduces one of the most fundamental concepts in finance: the time value of money. Simply put, *time value of money* means that a dollar today is worth more than a dollar in the future. Because most business decisions involve costs and benefits that are spread out over many months or years, financial managers routinely apply time value of money techniques in decision making. This chapter describes and demonstrates the time value of money techniques commonly used by financial managers to make valid cost/benefit comparisons when cash flows occur at different times.

Resurrecting memories of the heady 1990s "dot-com" era, the stock of Chinese search-engine company Baidu.com soared more than 350 percent on its first trading day in August 2005. Investors who were fortunate enough to buy shares in Baidu's initial public offering (IPO) at the $27.50 price saw the stock gain roughly $95 in a single day, to close at $122.54. At that price, the firm's market capitalization (shares outstanding times price per share) reached approximately $4 billion, or nearly 300 times Baidu's 2004 revenues. Even Google, the U.S. search-engine firm whose stock had risen from its year-earlier IPO price of $85 to almost $300 (making more than half of its employees millionaires along the way), was worth just 26 times 2004 sales.

The market's enthusiastic reception of Baidu pointed to a bright outlook for the Beijing-based company. But many commentators questioned whether Baidu's future would unfold more along the lines of infamous Internet stocks such as TheGlobe.com, whose stock shot up 606 percent on its first day, only to fall to zero a few years later.

Just a month after the Baidu IPO, Chicago-based CoolSavings Inc. took essentially the opposite path that Baidu had chosen. A provider of Internet marketing services to publishers and advertisers, CoolSavings announced that it would de-list its stock from the Nasdaq market and convert back to private ownership after five years as a public company. According to the company's CFO, David Arney, among the factors leading the firm to go private were the substantial regulatory costs of remaining public. Arney explained that as a private firm, CoolSavings could save $1 million annually in legal, audit, and insurance fees, including $200,000 in spending required to comply with the Sarbanes-Oxley Act of 2002.

The Sarbanes-Oxley legislation, passed in response to corporate scandals at Enron, WorldCom, and other companies, appeared to have triggered a small boom in going-private transactions, especially among smaller firms for whom the added compliance costs overwhelmed other benefits of remaining public. Some companies chose to switch the markets on which their stocks traded rather than go private. The London Stock Exchange's "AIM," a market for small, growing firms, saw its listings of non-UK companies double in the twelve months ending in June 2005.

The decisions of Baidu and CoolSavings suggest that there are important costs and benefits associated with being a public or private firm. In this chapter we describe the most common ways that business owners can organize their firms, and we describe the functions that financial managers perform, no matter what organizational form their employer chooses. We begin by answering a simple question, "What is corporate finance?"

Sources: (1) Josh Freidman and Don Lee, "Beijing Firm's Stock Sales Echoes Dot Com Boom," Los Angeles Times (August 6, 2005); (2) Carrie Kirby, "Baidu.com IPO Rockets," San Francisco Chronicle (August 6, 2005); (3) Shruti Date Singh, "Going Private Saves Firm a Cool $1 Million," Crain's Chicago Business (September 19, 2005); (4) Collen Marie O'Connor, "Sarbanes-Oxley: Frying the Small Fry," Investment Dealers Digest (June 27, 2005); (5) http://www.TheDeal.com (accessed 10/6/05).

SMARTFinance
Use the learning tools at www
thomsonedu com/finance/smartfinance

1.1 WHAT IS CORPORATE FINANCE?

Corporate finance is defined generally as the activities involved in managing cash flows in a business environment. The example in the Opening Focus provides important insights into corporate finance theory and practice. Like Baidu.com and CoolSavings, companies everywhere must choose an organizational structure to make the best use of the capital at their disposal, while balancing the objectives of corporate shareholders, managers, and other stakeholders. In this book, we describe the roles that finance professionals play in helping firms of all stripes make wise financial decisions. We emphasize not only *what* financial managers do, but also *why* they do it. In other words, we believe that it is important for students to understand not only how finance is practiced in the business world, but also the theory that shapes everyday practices.

To begin, we describe the principles that form the core of modern financial theory. We follow that with a description of the primary functions that financial managers perform in all types of business.

THE CORE PRINCIPLES OF FINANCE

The Time Value of Money Suppose you win $100 in a contest and are given the choice of receiving your cash prize immediately or in one year. Which would you choose? Most people would rather have the money immediately rather than wait for it. That is not merely a matter of impatience. Rather, it reflects the reality that if you have $100 in hand today, you can invest the money in an interest-bearing asset, accumulating more than $100 in a year's time. Thus we have the first core principle of finance:

> *The opportunity to earn a return on invested funds means that a dollar today is worth more than a dollar in the future.*

This principle is important because most business decisions involve a trade-off between spending money today and receiving money in the future. That is precisely the trade-off that companies face when they invest funds to build new manufacturing facilities, broadcast commercials on television, or hire new employees. In evaluating any of these decisions, financial managers help firms determine how much money must come back to the firm over time to justify today's expenditures. Financial experts rely on the time value of money techniques discussed in Chapters 3 and 4 to make these judgments. Time value of money tools allow managers to make valid comparisons between cash outflows and inflows that occur at different times. Those comparisons are an essential component of the investment evaluation process.

Compensation for Risk Now consider another proposition. You have just won $100 dollars, but you have the opportunity to double your money. The flip of a coin will determine the outcome. If the coin comes up heads, you win $200, but if it comes up tails you win nothing. Would you take the risk and go for $200 or would you count yourself lucky to walk away with $100?

In this situation, most people choose the certain $100 prize over the 50-50 chance at $200. Given that you have an equal likelihood of winning $200 or winning nothing, elementary statistics tells us that the expected value of the coin flip gamble is

$100. But why take that risk when you can get $100 for sure? To entice people to play this game, we might increase the prize for flipping a "heads" to something above $200, or we might change the game so that the probability of winning the $200 prize is greater than 50 percent. In either case, getting people to accept the gamble means changing the game so that the expected payoff exceeds $100, the value of the sure thing. This leads to the second core finance principle:

Investors expect compensation for bearing risk.

There are many business applications of this principle. For example, suppose a consumer-products firm is weighing two investment proposals, both of which require an investment of $10 million. The first proposal is to invest money to begin distribution in Canada of an existing product line that has had proven success in the U.S. market. The second proposal calls for investing $10 million in basic research and development (R&D) to develop new products in a market niche where the company currently has no presence.

Intuitively, the second investment seems riskier than the first. If that intuition is correct, then the company's investors will demand a higher return on the R&D project. Accordingly, in evaluating the two projects, financial managers must recognize that the R&D project must generate higher future cash flows than the alternative project to justify spending $10 million. Chapters 5 through 9 illustrate how to quantify the risk-return trade-off and to evaluate investment projects with very different risk profiles.

Don't Put Your Eggs in One Basket In 1990, Harry Markowitz shared the Nobel Prize in Economics for his work showing how investors could improve the performance of their investment portfolios through diversification. His insights contributed to a boom in the mutual fund business, an industry built on the idea of pooling the money of many investors to allow them to achieve greater diversification together than they could using their own limited funds. Most people understand that they can reduce the risk of their investments by diversifying, but Markowitz's insight went deeper than that. He showed how diversification could actually improve the performance of a portfolio relative to its risk. Thus, Markowitz was an early pioneer in developing the third core finance principle:

Investors can achieve a more favorable trade-off between risk and return by diversifying their portfolios.

Chapters 5 and 6 explore the risk/return relationship and illustrate the characteristics of investment alternatives that influence the design of "optimal" portfolios (those that earn the highest possible returns for a given level of risk).

Markets Are Smart On January 28, 1986, the world was shocked as the spacecraft *Challenger* exploded shortly after launching. Months later, a presidential commission reported its finding that cold temperatures at launch time compromised the integrity of O-rings in the rocket boosters, which led to the explosion. Physicist Richard Feynman famously demonstrated the problem by dunking a piece of O-ring rubber into ice water and showing that when it was cold it was slow to return to its original shape.

Several companies had valuable contracts to produce various components of the space shuttle. These companies included Rockwell International, Lockheed, Martin Marietta, and Morton Thiokol. Stock prices of all three firms fell when the shuttle exploded. But while the prices of Rockwell, Lockheed, and Martin Marietta dropped about 2.5 percent, Morton Thiokol's stock fell almost 12 percent, with much of that drop taking place within 20 minutes of the accident. What was Morton Thiokol's role in the space shuttle program? It made the solid rocket boosters. In other words, prices in the market quickly reflected—accurately, it turned out—investors' perceptions of which company made the component that was critical in causing the Challenger's demise.[1] This illustrates the fourth core principle of finance:

Competition for information tends to make markets efficient.

The term "efficient markets" here simply means that prices of stocks, bonds, and other financial assets reflect all the information that investors have access to. If markets are "informationally efficient," then only *new* information (by definition, information that no one knows or can reliably predict) moves stock prices. Therefore, in an efficient market it is very difficult for any individual, or even a professional money manager, to do a better-than-average job of predicting which stocks will perform particularly well and which ones will disappoint investors. Chapter 10 surveys much of the surprising and, to some, counterintuitive evidence that markets are extremely smart. This evidence leads to the conclusion that markets are, in fact, so smart that most investors are well advised to avoid trying to pick winners and losers in the stock market and should instead simply buy and hold a diversified portfolio.

No Arbitrage The term *arbitrage* refers to a trading strategy in which an investor simultaneously buys and sells the same asset in different markets at different prices to earn an instant, risk-free profit. For example, suppose a currency trader learns that in New York she can exchange $2 for £1, but in London £1 will buy just $1.90. If the trader is clever, she will recognize that there is a profit opportunity here. She might convert £1 million into $2 million in New York, then transfer those funds to the London market and convert them there into £1,052,632. Without taking any risk at all, she earns a £52,632 profit, and she will keep repeating that trade until the exchange rate between dollars and pounds is the same in New York and London. Because opportunities like this one are almost always too good to be true, we have the fifth core finance principle:

Arbitrage opportunities are extremely scarce.

The notion that arbitrage opportunities should be very hard to find, and should not last very long if they are uncovered, has many applications in modern finance. Chapters 12 and 13 illustrate how the "no-arbitrage principle" influences modern thinking about the costs and benefits of debt versus equity financing. Chapter 15 applies similar logic to firms' dividend decisions. Chapters 18 through 20 explain how the no-arbitrage principle allows us to value complex financial instruments such as stock options and forward currency contracts. In fact, the no-arbitrage principle may be simultaneously the most powerful of all the core principles and the least understood.

As you study this book, you will see one or more of these key ideas in almost every chapter. But our goal is not simply to present theoretical concepts. Instead, we want to show how those core ideas influence what financial experts do on a day-to-day basis. As an initial step in achieving that goal, we now turn to a description of the primary finance functions found in most large businesses.

---

[1] For a full description of the stock market's reaction to the Challenger disaster, see Maloney and Mulherin (2003).

THE FIVE BASIC CORPORATE FINANCE FUNCTIONS

The practice of corporate finance involves five basic, related functions:

1. Raising capital to support a company's operations and investment programs—the **financing function.**
2. Selecting the best projects in which to invest the firm's resources, based on each project's perceived risk and expected return—the **capital budgeting function.**
3. Managing the firm's internal cash flows and its mix of debt and equity financing (borrowing money and selling stock) to maximize the firm's value and to ensure its survival—the **financial management function.**
4. Developing a corporate governance structure that ensures that managers act ethically and in stockholders' interests—the **corporate governance function.**
5. Managing the firm's exposure to risk, in order to maintain the optimum risk-return trade-off and therefore maximize shareholder value—the **risk-management function.**

On a daily basis, financial managers spend their time engaged in one or more of these five activities. In order to build a successful career in corporate finance, you will need a deep understanding of the five functions. Understanding the five finance functions is important even for students interested in marketing, operations, human resources, or other functional areas. Understanding finance's role in a corporation matters because most firms ask their employees to accomplish tasks in cross-functional teams. Often finance acts as a "gatekeeper": A marketing manager wanting to launch a new advertising campaign or an engineer seeking to modernize production facilities needs to understand how financial managers will evaluate these proposals.

Financing Businesses raise money in one of two ways: either *externally* from investors or creditors, or *internally* by retaining operating cash flows. Most companies raise the bulk of the funding they require each year internally.

Access to external financing influences the organizational forms that managers choose for their enterprises. Sole proprietorships and partnerships, for example, face limited external funding opportunities. The choices for corporations are much richer, and some enterprises choose to form as corporations in order to tap that larger capital pool. (See section 1.2 for more on the legal forms of business organization.)

Corporations can raise capital either by selling an ownership interest or by borrowing money from creditors. In business terms, an ownership interest (e.g., a security such as stock) is called **equity,** and money borrowed from creditors is termed **debt.** In their early years, corporations usually must raise equity capital privately, often from professional investors such as **venture capitalists,** who specialize in high-risk/high-return investments in fast-growing firms. After a corporation "goes public" by selling its stock through an **initial public offering (IPO),** it has the option to raise cash by selling more stock later.

When a corporation sells securities to investors, it raises capital in a **primary market transaction.** In such a transaction, money flows from investors to firms, and firms then invest the money to exploit investment opportunities. Investors who hold firms' securities can trade them with other investors. Such **secondary market transactions** (trades between investors) generate no cash for the firm, but the existence of an active secondary market does make firms' securities more attractive to investors.

SMART ETHICS VIDEO

Tom Cole, Deutsche Bank, Leveraged Finance Group
"To be good at finance you have to understand how businesses work."

See the entire interview at **SMARTFinance**

Figure 1.1
The Total Value of
Primary (Capital-Raising)
Corporate Security
Issues, 1990–2004
This figure describes the
growth in the volume of security offerings sold directly
to investors through capital
market issues around the
world since 1990. Offerings
by U.S. issuers typically account for two-thirds or more
of the global total. These
data are from the annual
league tables (rankings of investment banks) published by
Investment Dealers' Digest in
early January, and include issues by corporations, housing
finance authorities, and other
nonsovereign issuers, but exclude government bond offerings and syndicated bank
loans. The $5.6 trillion total
for 2004 was a record.

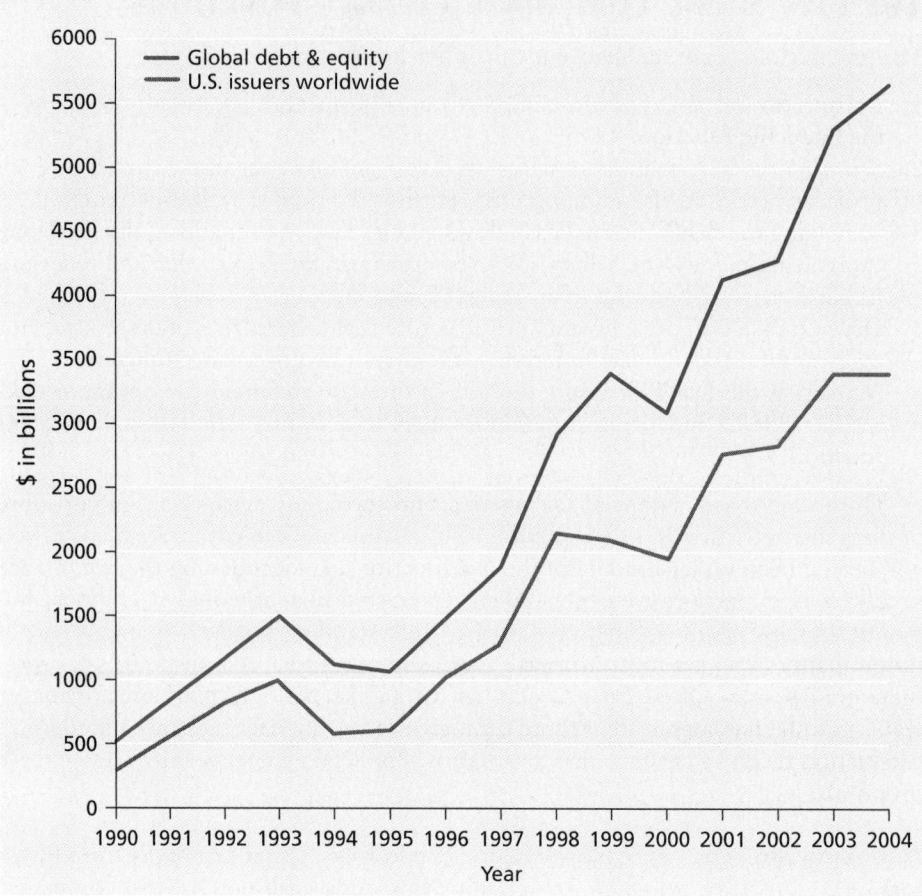

Figure 1.1 details the dramatic growth in the total value of primary-market security offerings sold by corporations and other entities from 1990–2004. The total
value of security offerings worldwide increased from $504 billion in 1990 to more
than $5.6 *trillion* in 2004. The figure also points out the importance of U.S. capital
markets in global finance. From 1990–2004, U.S. issuers accounted for about two-
thirds of worldwide security issues. To put these "market share" numbers in perspective, the United States represents only about one-quarter of world gross domestic product (GDP) and just one-eighth of the total value of world trade (exports plus
imports).

Corporations can obtain debt financing either by selling bonds directly to investors or by borrowing money from a commercial bank or other financial intermediary. The largest and most creditworthy firms raise large amounts of short-term funding by issuing **commercial paper** directly to investors in the **money market,** the
market for debt instruments maturing in one year or less. Longer-term debt instruments include **notes** (debt with original maturities of less than seven years) and various types of corporate **bonds** (debt with original maturities of more than seven
years). Most corporations also borrow at least some money from commercial banks.
The importance of bank financing, relative to capital market financing, has been
declining for large U.S. corporations for several decades. However, bank financing

remains important for smaller businesses.[2] Commercial banking also continues to be an important source of financing in most countries.

Capital Budgeting For two reasons, **capital budgeting**—selecting the best projects in which to invest the firm's resources—is arguably the most important financial function. First, the scale of capital investment projects is usually quite large. Second, companies can prosper in a competitive economy only by seeking out the most promising new products, processes, and services to deliver to customers. Companies such as Intel, General Electric, Deutsche Telekom, and Toyota regularly make huge capital investments, the outcomes of which drive the value of their firms and the wealth of their owners. For these and other companies, the annual capital investment budget can run to several billion dollars.

The capital budgeting process has three steps: (1) identifying potential investments, (2) analyzing those investments to identify which will create shareholder value, and (3) implementing and monitoring the investments selected in step 2. The long-term success of almost any firm depends on mastering these three steps, and the consequences of a flawed capital budgeting process are serious indeed.

Financial Management The finance function is charged with managing the firm's operating cash flows as efficiently as possible. A key element of this management process is **the capital structure decision**—that is, deciding what mix of debt and equity securities the firm should issue to finance its operations. In addition, firms expect the finance staff to ensure that the firm has adequate working capital available to operate smoothly day to day.

Managing working capital involves obtaining seasonal financing, building inventories sufficient to meet customer needs, paying suppliers, collecting from customers, and investing surplus cash. Managing working capital effectively requires not only technical and analytical skills, but also people skills. Almost every component of working capital management involves building and maintaining relationships with customers, suppliers, lenders, and others.

Corporate Governance The existence of a corporate governance function is of overarching importance to the modern corporation. Good management does not develop in a vacuum. Instead, it results from a corporate governance system that hires and promotes qualified, honest people, and structures employees' financial incentives to motivate them to maximize firm value. Some of these issues will be covered in more depth in a later chapter.

An optimal corporate governance system is extremely difficult to develop in practice, not least because the incentives of stockholders, managers, and other stakeholders often conflict. A firm's stockholders want managers to work hard and to protect shareholders' interests, but it is rarely profitable for any *individual* stockholder to expend time and resources monitoring managers to see if they are acting appropriately. An individual stockholder would personally bear all the costs of monitoring

---

[2.] A very informative discussion of the changing role of commercial banking in American corporate financing is provided in Boyd and Gertler (1994). These authors show that although bank lending to corporations has been declining in importance, the demand for other banking products and services (such as electronic funds transfers and risk-management products) has been increasing more rapidly. Additionally, U.S. corporations remain the primary consumers of syndicated loans, which are large lines of credit arranged by consortiums of up to 200 commercial banks. According to Capital DATA Ltd.'s *Loanware* database, over $1.7 trillion worth of syndicated loans were arranged worldwide during 1999 (the total probably exceeded $2 trillion in 2000 and 2001), and U.S. borrowers accounted for over 60 percent of this total.

management, but the benefit of his or her activities would accrue to all shareholders. This is an example of a **collective-action problem** that is pervasive in most relationships between stockholders and managers. Likewise, managers may feel the need to increase the wealth of owners, but they also want to protect their own jobs. Managers rationally do not wish to work harder than necessary if others will reap most of the benefits. Finally, managers and shareholders may together decide to run a company to benefit themselves at the expense of creditors or other stakeholders who do not have a direct say in corporate governance.

As you might expect, a variety of mechanisms designed to mitigate these problems exist. A strong **board of directors** is an essential element in any well-functioning governance system, because it is the board's duty to hire, fire, pay, and promote senior managers. The board develops *fixed* (salary) and *contingent* (bonus and stock-based) compensation packages to align managers' and shareholders' incentives. Auditors play a governance role by certifying the validity of firms' financial statements. The **Securities and Exchange Commission (SEC),** a federal agency established in 1934, oversees the fair reporting of financial information to investors in public companies (those whose shares are listed for trading in a public securities market). In the United States, accounting scandals and concerns about auditors' conflicts of interest prompted the SEC to require the CFOs of large firms to personally certify their firms' earnings numbers.

Despite the efforts of the SEC, corporate scandals near the turn of the century revealed numerous shortcomings in U.S. corporate governance practices. In response, Congress passed the **Sarbanes-Oxley Act of 2002.** This act imposed a host of new requirements on firms, including restrictions on board membership, executive compensation, relationships with auditors, and many others. The Act also required firms to provide extensive documentation of the internal controls they put in place to protect investors from fraud. As the Opening Focus explained, the costs of compliance with this Act prompted many small firms to choose private over public ownership or to raise capital in markets outside the United States. Just as companies struggle to develop an effective corporate governance system, so do countries. Governments establish legal frameworks that either encourage or discourage the development of competitive businesses and efficient financial markets. For example, a legal system should permit efficiency-enhancing mergers and acquisitions but block business combinations that significantly restrict competition. It should provide protection for creditors and minority shareholders that limits the opportunities for managers or majority shareholders to expropriate wealth.

The financial systems in the United States, Western Europe, and Asia differ fundamentally from each other, even though most large economic powers are capitalist democracies. Historically, the United States, Britain, and Canada have witnessed far more mergers and acquisitions (M&A's) than have other developed countries, but this is changing rapidly. As Figure 1.2 reveals, M&A activity worldwide varies dramatically over time. A substantial fraction of the recent growth in takeover activity has come from Europe. Roughly one-third of the total value of M&A's worldwide now involves European firms. European M&A activity could soon surpass that in the United States as continental firms adapt to the increasingly competitive business environment brought about by the adoption of the euro (€) and the integration of the Atlantic economies.[3]

[3.] An excellent discussion of how the political process has influenced corporate governance in the United States is provided in Roe (1997). For a comparison of corporate finance and governance in Japan, Germany, and the United States, see Prowse (1996). Also see the video clip from David Baum, head of M&A at Goldman Sachs, in Chapter 24.

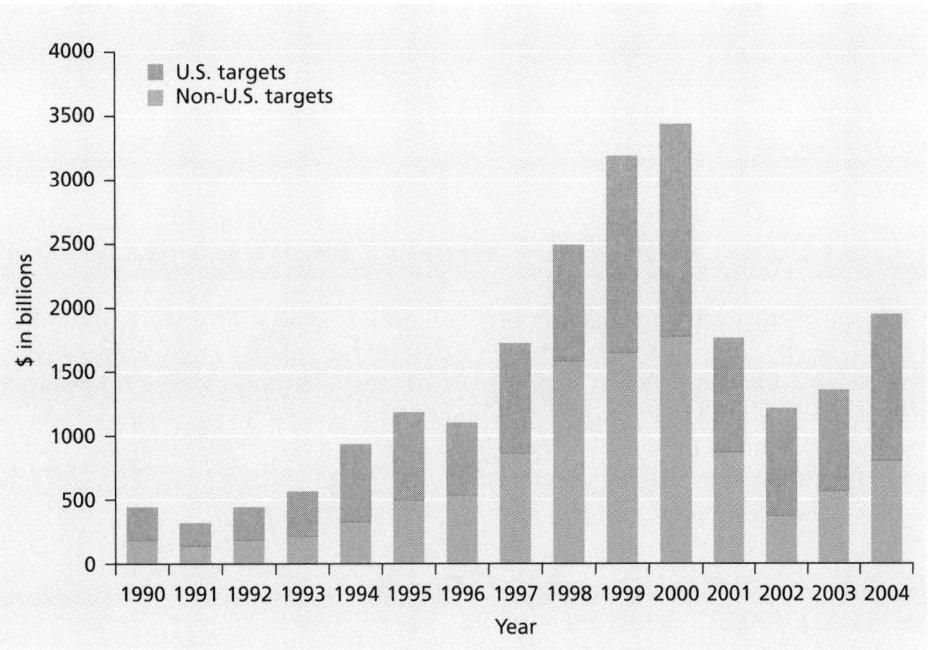

Figure 1.2
Global Value of
Announced Mergers
and Acquisitions,
1990–2004 ($US
Billions)
Sources: Thomson Financial
Securities Data, as reported
in "The Great Merger Wave
Breaks," *The Economist*
(January 27, 2001), pp. 59–
60; and *Investment Dealers'
Digest* (January 2005).

Risk Management Historically, risk management involved identifying a firm's risk exposures and using insurance products or self-insurance to manage those exposures. The risk-management function now includes identifying, measuring, and managing all types of risk exposures. Common examples include losses that can result from adverse interest-rate movements, changes in commodity prices, and fluctuations in currency values. The techniques for managing these risks are among the most sophisticated of all corporate finance practices. The risk-management task begins with quantifying the sources and size of a firm's risk exposure and deciding whether to simply accept these risks or to manage them.

Some risks are easily insurable, such as the risk of loss due to fire, employee theft, or product liability. Firms can reduce some risks by *diversifying*. For example, rather than use a sole supplier for a key production input, a company might choose to contract with several suppliers, even if doing so means purchasing the input above the lowest attainable price.

However, modern risk management focuses on market-driven risks. Today risk managers use complex financial instruments to **hedge,** or offset, market risks such as interest-rate and currency fluctuations. The four most common instruments in the risk manager's arsenal are *forwards, futures, options,* and *swaps.*

SMART CONCEPTS
See the concept
explained
step-by-step at
SMARTFinance

Each year tens of thousands of MBA students select finance as their major. We believe that the popularity of finance stems from the exciting and rewarding career opportunities available to students who master the five basic functions outlined here. Although this book stresses the roles that financial managers play in large corporations, successful careers in finance are by no means limited to the Fortune 500 firms. In the next section, we discuss the pros and cons of different organizational forms that business owners and managers may adopt, both in the U.S. and abroad.

1. What are the core principles of finance?

2. What are the five basic corporate finance functions? Describe some ways in which managers might use the core principles of finance in performing these basic functions.

1.2 LEGAL FORMS OF BUSINESS ORGANIZATION

Companies exist so that people can organize to pursue profit-making ventures in a formal, legally secure manner. Although there are various ways to organize a company, only a handful of forms have proven viable. Variations of these forms occur throughout the world. This section examines how companies organize themselves legally and discusses the costs and benefits of each major form. We begin with the organizational forms available to businesses in the United States. After that, we briefly examine the most important organizational forms used by non-U.S. businesses.

BUSINESS ORGANIZATIONAL FORMS IN THE UNITED STATES

The three key legal forms of business organization in the United States have historically been the sole proprietorship, the partnership, and the corporation. These have recently been joined by a fourth type, the limited liability company (LLC). The sole proprietorship is the most common form of organization. The corporation is by far the dominant form in terms of aggregate sales and profits. In addition to these key forms, there are two very important "hybrid" organizational forms, the limited partnership and the S corporation. We will examine all these forms, beginning with the sole proprietorship.

Sole Proprietorships As the name implies, a **sole proprietorship** is a business with a single owner. In fact, there is no legal distinction between the business and the owner. The business is the owner's personal property, it exists only as long as the owner lives and chooses to operate it, and all business assets belong to the owner personally. Furthermore, the owner bears personal liability for all debts of the company and pays income taxes on the business's earnings. Sole proprietorships are by far the most common type of business in the United States, accounting for over 74 percent of all business tax returns filed each year. However, proprietorships receive less than 6 percent of business income and employ less than 10 percent of the work force.

Simplicity and ease of operation constitute the principal benefits of the proprietorship. However, this organizational form suffers from weaknesses that in most cases limit the firm's long-run growth potential. These include the following:

1. *Limited life.* By definition, a proprietorship ceases to exist when the founder retires or dies. Although the founder/entrepreneur can pass the assets of the business on to his or her children (or sell them to a third party), most of what makes the business valuable on a continuing basis, such as business contracts and relationships, are tied to the proprietor personally. Furthermore, changes in ownership of successful companies can trigger potentially devastating estate-tax liabilities.
2. *Limited access to capital.* A proprietorship can obtain operating capital from only two sources: reinvested profits and personal borrowing by the entrepreneur. In practice, both of these sources are easily exhausted.

3. *Unlimited personal liability.* A sole proprietor is personally liable for all the debts of the business, including judgments awarded a plaintiff in a successful lawsuit. The United States is the most litigious society in history (each year some 20 *million* lawsuits are filed in state courts alone), and a single jury verdict can destroy a lifetime's accomplishments and impoverish even the most successful business family.

Partnerships A (general) **partnership** is essentially a proprietorship with two or more owners who have joined together their skills and personal wealth. As in a sole proprietorship, there is no legal distinction between the business and its owners, each of whom can execute contracts binding on the other(s), and each of whom is personally liable for all the debts of the partnership. This sharing of legal responsibility is known as **joint and several liability.**

Though no legal requirement exists that requires the owners to formalize the terms of their partnership in a written *partnership agreement,* most partnerships create such a document. In the absence of a partnership agreement, the business dissolves whenever one of the partners retires or dies. Furthermore, unless there is a partnership agreement specifying otherwise, each partner shares equally in business income, and each has equal management authority. As with a proprietorship, partnership income is taxed only once, at the personal level.

In addition to the tax benefits and ease of formation that partnerships share with proprietorships, the partnership allows a large number of people to pool their capital and expertise to form a much larger enterprise. Partnerships enjoy more flexibility than proprietorships in that the business need not automatically terminate following the retirement or death of one partner. Industries in which partnerships are usually the dominant form of organization include accounting, consulting, engineering, law, and medicine.

The drawbacks of the partnership form resemble those of the sole proprietorship and include the following:

1. *Limited life.* The life of the firm can be limited, particularly if only a few partners are involved. Problems may also result from the instability inherent in long-term, multiperson business associations.
2. *Limited access to capital.* The firm is still limited to retained profits and personal borrowings.
3. *Unlimited personal liability.* This disadvantage is made all the worse by the fact that the partners are subject to joint and several liability.

As firms grow larger, the competitive disadvantages of the proprietorship and partnership organizational forms tend to become extremely burdensome. Almost all successful companies eventually adopt the corporate organizational form.

In many ways, a **limited partnership (LP)** combines the best features of the (general) partnership and the corporate organizational forms. In any limited partnership, there must be one or more **general partners,** each of whom has unlimited personal liability. Because the general partners operate the business and they alone are legally exposed, the general partners usually receive a greater than-proportional (based on their capital contribution) share of partnership income. Most of the participants in the partnership are **limited partners.** They have the limited liability of corporate shareholders, but their share of the profits from the business is taxed as partnership income. The limited partners, however, must be totally passive. They contribute capital to the partnership, but they cannot have their names associated with the business, and they cannot take any active role in the operation of the business, even as

employees. In return for this passivity, the limited partners do not face personal liability for the debts of the business. This means that limited partners can lose their equity investment in the business, but successful plaintiffs (or the tax authorities) cannot look to the limited partners personally for payment of their claims. Best of all,
limited partners share in partnership income, which is taxed as ordinary personal income for the partners.

Limited partnerships are ideal vehicles for funding long-term investments that
generate large noncash operating losses in the early years of the business, because
these losses *flow through* directly to the limited partners. This means the limited partners can (under specified conditions) use the tax losses to offset taxable income from
other sources. Disadvantages of LPs include illiquidity and difficulties with monitoring and disciplining the general partner(s). In some cases, registering an LP with the
SEC allows secondary-market trading of partnership interests, reducing or eliminating the illiquidity problem.

Corporations In U.S. law, a **corporation** is a separate legal entity with many of the
economic rights and responsibilities enjoyed by individuals. A corporation can sue
and be sued, it can own property and execute contracts in its own name, and it can
be tried and convicted for crimes committed by its employees.

The corporate organizational form has several key competitive advantages over
other forms, including the following:

1. *Unlimited life.* Once created, a corporation has a perpetual life unless it is explicitly terminated.
2. *Limited liability.* The firm's shareholders cannot be held personally liable for the
   firm's debts.
3. *Separable contracting.* Corporations can contract individually with managers,
   suppliers, customers, and ordinary employees, and each individual contract can
   be renegotiated, modified, or terminated without affecting other stakeholders.
4. *Unlimited access to capital.* The company itself, rather than its owners, can borrow money from creditors, and it can also issue various classes of preferred and
   common stock to equity investors. Furthermore, the ownership claims themselves (shares of common stock) can be freely traded among investors without obtaining the permission of other investors if the corporation is a **public company**—
   one whose shares are listed for trading in a public securities market.

A corporation, as a legal entity, is owned by the **shareholders** who hold its
shares of stock. Shares of stock carry voting rights, and shareholders vote at an annual meeting to elect the firm's directors. The directors include key corporate personnel as well as outsiders who are typically successful private businesspeople or
executives of other major corporations. The **board of directors** is responsible for
hiring and firing managers and setting overall corporate policies. The rules dictating
voting procedures and other parameters of corporate governance appear in the
firm's **corporate charter,** the legal document created at the corporation's inception to
govern the firm's operations. The charter can be changed only by a vote of the
shareholders.

Also, in contrast to the practice in almost all other countries, incorporation in the
United States is executed at the state rather than at the national level and is governed
primarily by state rather than federal law. Nonetheless, all 50 states have broadly
similar rules for incorporation and corporate governance, as described in Easterbrook and Fischel (1983). At the federal level, of course, the SEC regulates financial
reporting of public corporations.

Corporations may issue two forms of stock—*common* and *preferred*—each with slightly different rights and privileges. Shareholders of common and preferred stock, as owners of the firm's equity securities, are often called **equity claimants.** Shareholders of preferred stock typically have precedence to the corporation's earnings. In exchange, they generally do not have the right to vote and bear less risk than shareholders of common stock. Therefore, we refer to common stockholders as the firm's ultimate owners. Common stockholders vote periodically to elect the members of the board of directors, including the executive officer, and to amend the firm's corporate charter.

It is important to note the division between owners and managers in a large corporation. The **president** or **chief executive officer (CEO)** is responsible for managing day-to-day operations and carrying out the policies established by the board. The board expects regular reports from the CEO regarding the firm's current status and future direction. The CEO and the board, though, serve at the will of the shareholders. The separation between owners and managers leads to **agency costs,** the costs that arise due to the conflicts of interest between shareholders and managers. These costs and the agency problems that cause them are discussed in greater depth later in this chapter (see section 1.3).

Although corporations dominate economic life around the world, this form has some competitive disadvantages. Many governments tax corporate income at both company and personal levels. In the United States, this treatment, commonly called the **double-taxation problem,** has traditionally been the single greatest disadvantage of the corporate form. But the Jobs and Growth Tax Relief Reconciliation Act of 2003 substantially reduced this problem by lowering personal tax rates on dividends and capital gains.

Table 1.1 illustrates the double-taxation problem by comparing the tax burden faced by investors in a corporation versus the taxes owed by the owners of a partnership. Both businesses earn $100,000 of pre-tax income. We assume that the corporation in our example is taxed at the top corporate income tax rate of 35 percent ($T_c = 0.35$), and the partnership's investors face the top personal income top rate, which is also 35 percent ($T_p = 0.35$). For tax purposes, the law now allows the corporation's shareholders to treat dividends received as capital gains, and we will assume shareholders face the top personal capital gains tax rate of 15 percent ($T_{cg} = 0.15$). As the law currently stands, the partners receive after-tax disposable income of $65,000 [$100,000 × (1 − 0.35)], and shareholders receive net disposable income of $55,250 [$100,000 × (1 − 0.35) × (1 − 0.15)]. As this example shows, a partnership (or proprietorship) enjoys a small tax advantage over a corporation.[4]

In contrast to a regular corporation, an **S corporation** (previously called a *Subchapter S corporation*) allows shareholders to be taxed as partners while still retaining their limited liability status as corporate shareholders. This type of company is an ordinary corporation (or *C corporation*), in which the shareholders have elected to be treated as S corporation shareholders. To be eligible for S status, a firm must meet several requirements: it must have 75 or fewer shareholders, the shareholders must be individuals or certain types of trusts (not corporations), the S corporation cannot issue more than one class of equity security, and it cannot be a *holding company* (cannot hold a controlling fraction of the stock in another company).

[4.] A short article describing the key provisions of the Jobs and Growth Tax Relief Reconciliation Act of 2003 can be obtained upon request from the accounting firm Grant Thornton (http://www.gt.com). The Internal Revenue Service's website (http://www.irs.gov) also presents a summary of the Act's provisions.

Table 1.1
Taxation of Business
Income for Corporations
and Partnerships *After*
Passage of the Jobs and
Growth Tax Relief
Reconciliation Act of
2003

	Corporation	Partnership
Operating income	$100,000	$100,000
Less: Corporate profits tax ($T_c = 0.35$)	35,000	0
Net income	65,000	$100,000
Cash dividends or partnership distributions	65,000	$100,000
Less: Personal tax on dividends ($T_{cg} = 0.15$)	9,750	
Less: Personal tax on partnership income ($T_p = 0.35$)		35,000
After-tax disposable income	$ 55,250	$ 65,000

If a corporation meets these requirements, then S corporation status allows the company's operating income to escape separate taxation at the corporate level.[5] Instead, each shareholder claims as personal income a proportionate fraction of total company profits and pays tax on this profit at his or her personal tax rate. As with a limited partnership, S corporation status yields the limited-liability benefit of the corporate form along with the favorable taxation of the partnership form. In addition, an S corporation can easily switch back to being a regular C corporation whenever company growth causes it to outgrow the 75-shareholder ceiling or if it needs to issue multiple classes of equity securities. Given the inherent flexibility of this type of organization, it is quite common for successful companies to begin life as S corporations and to retain S status until they decide to go public, which forces them to become regular corporations.

Limited-Liability Companies The **limited liability company (LLC)** combines the partnership's pass-through taxation with the S corporation's limited liability. All 50 U.S. states allow LLCs, which are very easy to set up. The IRS allows an LLC's owners to elect taxation as either a partnership or a corporation, and many states allow one-person LLCs as well as a choice of a finite or infinite life. Even though LLCs can be taxed as partnerships, their owners face no personal liability for the other partners' malpractice, making this type of company especially attractive for professional-service firms. Given the limited liability feature and the flexibility of LLCs, we expect them to continue gaining significant "organizational market share" in coming years.

FORMS OF BUSINESS ORGANIZATION USED BY NON-U.S. COMPANIES

Although a comprehensive survey of international forms of business organization is beyond the scope of this chapter, this section will survey the most important organizational patterns observed in many industrialized economies. Even a cursory glance at non-U.S. systems shows striking, universal patterns. In almost all capitalist economies, some form of joint-stock, limited-liability business structure exists—with freely tradable equity claims—and in most societies, these companies dominate economic life.

[5.] According to the 2002 *Statistical Abstract of the United States,* over 53 percent (2.558 million of 4.849 million) of all corporations filing tax returns were S corporations in 1998, which indicates both the popularity of this organizational form and the relatively small *average* size of U.S. businesses.

Limited Liability Companies in Other Industrialized Countries Limited liability companies go by different names in different countries:

> Britain: public limited companies (PLC)
> Germany: *Aktiengesellschaft* (AG)
> France: *Société Générale*
> Spain, Mexico, and elsewhere in Latin America: *Sociedad Anónima* (SA)

While details vary, all of these structures resemble the publicly traded corporations described previously. Key differences between international and U.S. companies revolve around tax treatment of business income and public disclosure requirements. Tax rules are typically, though not always, more punitive in the United States than abroad. Disclosure requirements are invariably greater for U.S. than for non-U.S. companies.

Many countries also make a distinction between limited liability companies meant to be traded publicly and those meant to be privately held. In Germany, *Gesellschaft mit beschränkten Haftung* (GmbH) are privately owned and unlisted limited liability stock companies; in France, such companies are called *Société à Responsibilité Limitée* (SARL). Private companies, and particularly family-owned firms, form the backbone of almost all market economies. For example, the German postwar "economic miracle" was not propelled by giant companies but rather by midsize, export-oriented companies that pursued niche market strategies at home and abroad. These *Mittelstand* (middle market) firms still account for some three-quarters of all German economic activity. A similar set of relatively small, entrepreneurial companies has helped propel Taiwan, Singapore, and other Asian nations to growth rates that until recently were consistently higher than those achieved in the West.[6]

State-Owned Enterprises and Privatization in Non-U.S. Economies By far the biggest difference between the corporate organizational system of the United States and that of other countries is the almost total absence of **state-owned enterprises (SOEs)** in the United States. SOEs are companies owned and operated by the government that conduct business activities in areas outside what many would consider purely governmental affairs. As examples, the state has historically owned and operated the telephone, television, electric utility, airline, and railroad companies in many European countries, as well as throughout most of the developing world. The state has typically allowed little or no private-sector competition in these industries, and this has generally yielded relatively poor levels of service. Not surprisingly, the state still has great influence over many industrial sectors in the transition-economy countries of Eastern Europe and the former Soviet Union.

However, the role of the state in economies around the world is being transformed by the spread of **privatization** programs. In such programs, the state sells off to private companies or to individual private investors all or part of its holdings in SOEs. Although the first major privatization program of the modern era was initiated by the (West) German government of Konrad Adenauer in the early 1960s,

---

[6.] Interestingly, a key feature of the corporate governance systems adopted by most of the dynamic Asian capitalist economies (including Japan, Korea, Taiwan, and Thailand) during their take-off phase was an explicit restriction on foreign (particularly American) ownership in key industries. Development of these sectors was considered to be so important that it could not be left in the hands of potential competitors, and the very high national savings rates and native entrepreneurial talent of these countries' citizens allowed this policy of excluding foreign direct investment to be successful. In contrast, Singapore and Hong Kong took exactly the opposite tack of welcoming foreign investment and achieved equally impressive growth rates, without the distortions inherent in a nationalistic investment and corporate ownership strategy.

Figure 1.3
Annual Privatization
Revenues for Divesting
Governments
Worldwide, 1988–2004
($US Billions)
Source: Privatisation International, as reported in William L. Megginson and Jeffry M. Netter, "From State to Market: A Survey of Empirical Studies on Privatization," *Journal of Economic Literature* 39 (June 2001), pp. 321–389 (updated by author using data from Securities Data Corporation).

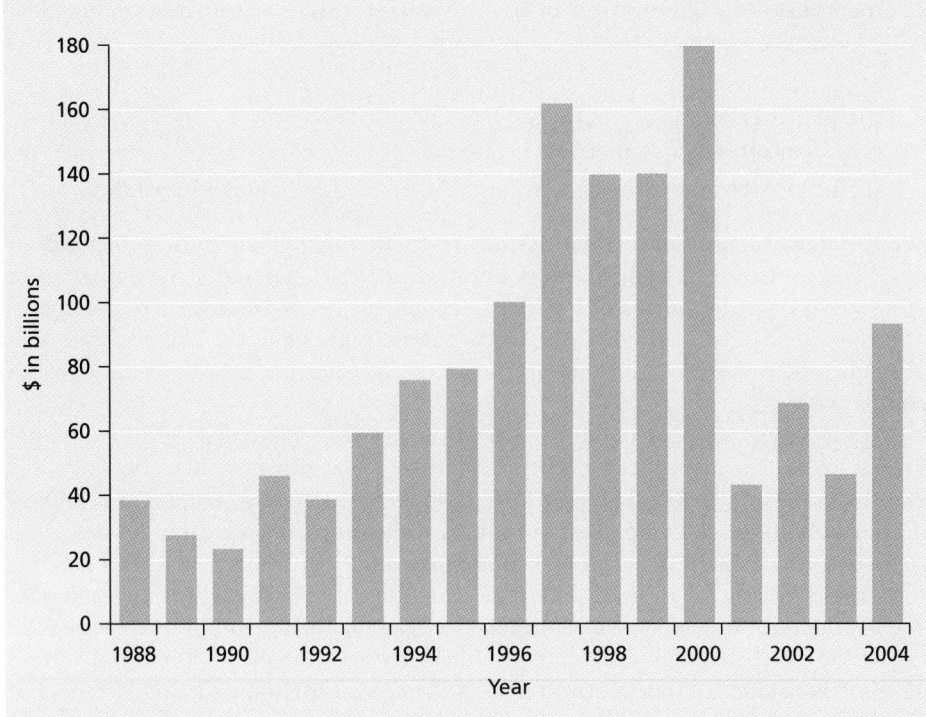

the Conservative government of Britain's Margaret Thatcher launched the current popularity of privatizations. In fact, these were called "denationalizations" until Thatcher gave them the more user-friendly name. After a tentative start, the Conservatives privatized all or part of the aerospace, telecommunications, automobile, airline, steel, oil and gas, electric and water utility, and air and seaport operating industries, raising over $80 billion in the process and transforming the role of the state in the British economy in little more than a decade.

Prompted by the British success, governments around the world launched privatization programs that have to date raised over $1.2 trillion, with virtually all this money flowing to the selling governments rather than to the firms being privatized. Experts predict that privatization programs will continue to raise over $100 billion per year for the foreseeable future. Figure 1.3 shows how much money governments raised through privatization programs between 1988 and 2004.[7]

Concept Review Questions

3. What are the costs and benefits of each of the three major organizational forms? Why do you think the various "hybrid" forms of business organization have proven so successful?

4. Comment on the following statement: "Sooner or later, all successful private companies that are organized as proprietorships or partnerships must become corporations."

[7.] A brief history of privatization programs involving public share offerings is provided in Megginson, Nash, and van Randenborgh (1996). This paper also documents that the financial and operating performance of former state-owned enterprises improved significantly after they were privatized.

1.3   GOALS OF THE CORPORATE FINANCIAL MANAGER

In widely held corporations, the owners typically do not manage the firm. Traditionally, finance teaches that managers should act according to the interests of the firm's owners—its stockholders. In the sections that follow, we discuss what the proper goals of a corporate manager *should* be. We first evaluate profit maximization and then describe wealth maximization. Next, we discuss the *agency costs* arising from potential conflicts between the goals of stockholders and the actions of management. Finally, we consider the role of ethics in corporate finance.

WHAT SHOULD A FINANCIAL MANAGER TRY TO MAXIMIZE?

What should a financial manager try to maximize: corporate profits, shareholder wealth, or something else? In the sections that follow, we hope to convince you that managers should seek to maximize shareholder wealth.

Maximize Profit? Some people believe that the manager's objective is to maximize profits. To achieve this goal, the financial manager takes only those actions that are expected to make a positive contribution to the firm's overall profits. Thus, for each alternative being considered, the financial manager should select the one with the highest expected monetary return. From a practical standpoint, this objective would translate into maximizing earnings per share (EPS).

Although it seems a plausible objective for corporate managers, profit maximization suffers from several flaws. First, EPS figures are inherently backward-looking, reflecting what has happened in the past rather than what will happen in the future. Second, even if managers strive to maximize profits over a period of time, they should not ignore the timing of those profits. A large profit that arrives many years in the future may be less valuable than a smaller one earned today. (Remember the first core principle of finance, the time value of money.) Third, to maximize profits, the manager has to know how to measure them, and conventional barometers of profit rely on accounting principles rather than simply on the measurement of cash flow.

Finally, and perhaps most decisively, focusing only on earnings ignores their variability, or risk. When comparing two investment opportunities, managers should not always choose the one they expect to generate the highest profits. They must consider the risks of the investments as well. As discussed earlier, the third core principle in corporate finance is that a trade-off exists between risk and return. *Risk and return are in fact the key determinants of share prices.* However, they affect share prices differently. Higher cash flow generally leads to higher share prices, while higher risk results in lower share prices. In general, stockholders are **risk-averse,** meaning that they want to avoid risk and must be compensated (with a higher expected return) for the risks they accept.

Maximize Shareholder Wealth? Modern finance asserts that the proper goal of the firm is to maximize the wealth of the shareholders, as measured by the firm's stock. The stock price reflects the timing, magnitude, and risk of the *cash flows* that investors expect a firm to generate over time. When considering alternative strategies, financial managers should undertake only those actions that they expect will increase the firm's share price.

Why does finance preach the wisdom of maximizing share value as the primary corporate objective? Why not focus instead on satisfying the desires of corporate **stakeholders** such as customers, employees, suppliers, and creditors? Both theoretical and empirical arguments support our assertion that managers should focus on shareholder-wealth maximization. A firm's shareholders are sometimes called its **residual claimants,** meaning that they can exert claims only on the firm's cash flows that remain after all other claimants are satisfied in full. It may help to visualize a queue with all the firm's stakeholders standing in line to receive their share of the firm's cash flows. Shareholders stand at the end of this line. If the firm cannot pay its employees, suppliers, creditors, and the tax authorities, then shareholders receive nothing. Shareholders earn a return on their investment only after other stakeholders' claims have been met. In other words, maximizing shareholder returns usually implies that the firm must also satisfy customers, employees, suppliers, creditors, and other stakeholders first.[8]

Furthermore, by accepting their position as residual claimants, shareholders agree to bear more risk than other stakeholders do. If firms did not operate with the goal of shareholder-wealth maximization in mind, shareholders would have little incentive to accept the risks necessary for a business to thrive. To understand this point, consider how a firm would operate if it were run in the interests of its creditors. Given that creditors receive only a fixed return, would such a firm ever make risky investments, no matter how profitable? Only shareholders have the proper incentives to make risky, value-increasing investments.

Focus on Stakeholders? Although shareholder-wealth maximization should be the primary goal of managers, in recent years many firms have broadened their focus to include the interests of other stakeholders. A firm with a *stakeholder focus* consciously avoids actions that would harm stakeholders by transferring their wealth to shareholders. The goal is not so much to maximize stakeholder wealth as to preserve it.

The stakeholder view is often considered part of the firm's "social responsibility." It is expected to provide long-run benefit to shareholders by maintaining positive stakeholder relationships. Such relationships should minimize stakeholder turnover, conflicts, and litigation. Presumably, the firm can better achieve its goal of shareholder-wealth maximization with the cooperation of, rather than conflict with, its other stakeholders. In most cases, stakeholder-wealth maximization is consistent with shareholder-wealth maximization.

However, conflict between these two objectives is probably inevitable, and in that case the firm should ultimately be run in the shareholders' interests. Interestingly, even though U.S. corporations are generally expected to act in a socially responsible way, they are rarely under binding legal or regulatory compunction to do so. The situation is much different in many Western European countries, where corporations are viewed as agents of social welfare almost as much as vehicles for private wealth creation.[9]

[8.] Admittedly, this statement is overly simplistic, and conflicts of interest can exist between a firm's shareholders and its other constituents. Even so, from a legal perspective, shareholders profit only when the firm meets its contractual obligations to other stakeholders.

[9.] A positive take of the European "social market model" is provided in Hentzler (1992). A description and analysis of the role of stakeholders in U.S. financial management are provided in Cornell and Shapiro (1987).

How Can Agency Costs Be Controlled in Corporate Finance?

The control of the modern corporation usually rests in the hands of professional, nonowner managers. We have argued that financial managers should pursue the goal of shareholder wealth maximization. Thus, managers act as *agents* of the owners who have hired them and given them decision-making authority. Technically, any manager who owns less than 100 percent of the firm's stock is to some degree an agent of the other owners.

In practice, managers also care about their personal wealth, job security, lifestyle, prestige, and perquisites such as country club ownerships, limousines, and posh offices—provided at company expense. Such concerns cause managers to pursue objectives other than shareholder-wealth maximization. Shareholders recognize the potential for managers' self-interested behavior, and they use a variety of tools to limit this behavior. The term *agency costs* refers to costs that arise as a result of these conflicts between owners and managers.

Types of Agency Costs The conflict between owners and managers gives rise to **agency problems.** Shareholders can attempt to overcome agency problems by various means: (1) relying on market forces to exert managerial discipline, (2) incurring monitoring and bonding costs necessary to supervise managers, and (3) structuring executive compensation packages that align the interests of managers and stockholders.

Several market forces constrain the opportunistic behavior of a firm's managers. In recent years, large investors have become more active in management. This is particularly true for *institutional investors* such as mutual funds, life insurance companies, and pension funds, which often hold large blocks of a firm's stock. Activist institutional investors use their influence to put pressure on underperforming management teams, occasionally applying enough pressure to replace the CEO.

An even more powerful form of market discipline is the **hostile takeover.** A hostile takeover involves the acquisition of one firm (the *target*) by another (the *acquirer*) through an open-market bid for a majority of the target's shares. By definition, a takeover attempt is hostile if the target firm's senior managers do not support (or, more likely, actively resist) the acquisition. The forces that drive hostile takeovers vary, but poor financial performance is a common trait among targets of hostile bids. Bidders in hostile deals may believe that they can improve the value of the target company, and thereby make a profit on their investment, by replacing incumbent management. Managers naturally see this as a threat and erect a variety of barriers to thwart potential acquirers. Nevertheless, the constant threat of a takeover provides additional motivation for managers to act in the best interests of the firm's owners.

In addition to these market forces, other devices exist that encourage managers to behave in shareholders' interests or that limit the consequences when managers misbehave. *Monitoring expenditures* pay for audits and control procedures that alert shareholders if managers pursue their own interests too aggressively.[10] *Bonding*

[10.] But you may ask, "Who monitors the monitors?" In the wake of Enron's bankruptcy, Enron's auditor, Arthur Andersen, experienced the consequences of failing to alert shareholders to the company's problems. Arthur Andersen's audit clients abandoned the firm in droves, and many of the firm's partners quit, and it closed its accounting/auditing services, coming back as a consulting firm, Accenture. Thus, the market imposed discipline on the auditors for their failure to impose discipline on Enron.

COMPARATIVE CORPORATE FINANCE

The Growth of Stock Market Capitalization

The world's stock markets have increased phenomenally in value and importance during the past 20 years. This growth is revealed graphically in the figure below, which traces the rise in the total value of the world's stock markets from 1983 to February 2005. This 22-year period saw total worldwide market capitalization increase from less than $3.4 trillion to about $37 trillion in 2005. The market value of U.S. stocks increased by more than seven times during this period, but non-U.S. markets experienced even faster growth. At its 2005 peak, the total worldwide stock market capitalization was roughly equal to world GDP. Trading volume, measured in dollars rather than in the number of shares traded, increased even faster.

Sources: World Bank (http://www.worldbank.org) and World Federation of Exchanges (http://www.world-exchanges.org).

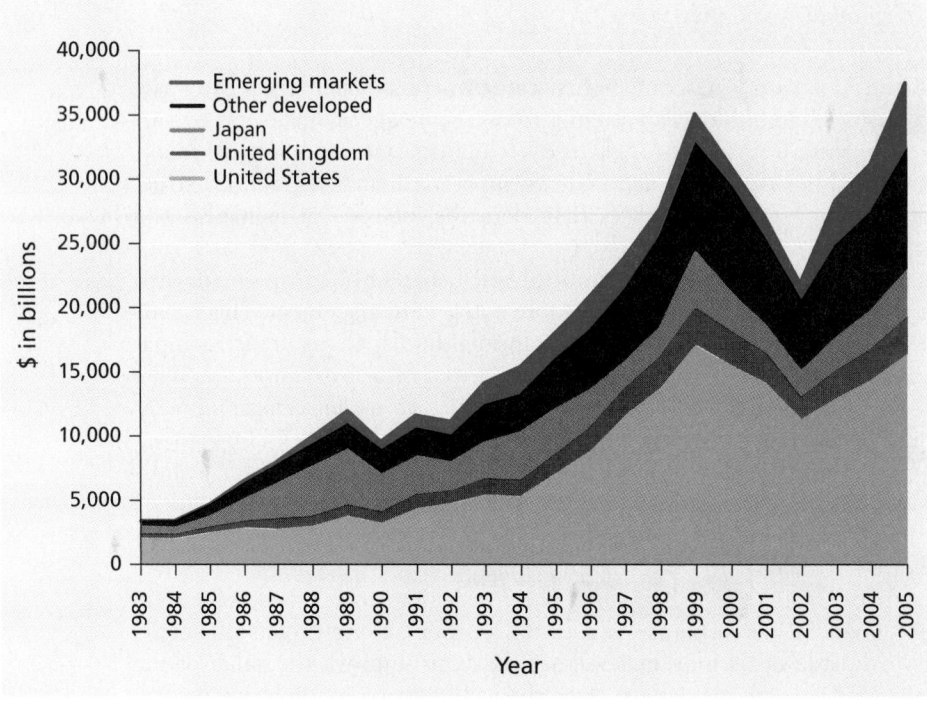

expenditures protect against the potential consequences of dishonest acts by managers. Directors can make bonding expenditures, or managers can themselves make these expenditures to reassure the firm's directors of their benevolent intentions. This can be done, for example, by accepting a portion of their total pay in the form of delayed (and potentially forfeitable) compensation.

Use of Compensation Contracts to Control Agency Costs One of the most popular, powerful, and expensive methods of overcoming agency costs and aligning managerial and stockholder interests is through **executive compensation plans.** The objective is to design such plans to give managers the incentive to act in the best interests of the owners. In addition, the resulting compensation packages allow firms to compete for, hire, and retain the best managers available. For this reason, such pay packages are often called "golden handcuffs" because they tie good managers to the firm.

Incentive compensation plans attempt to directly tie managerial wealth to the firm's share price. This primarily involves making outright grants of stock to top managers or, more commonly, giving them **stock options.** These options give the manager the right to purchase stock at a fixed price, usually the market price of the stock at the time the manager receives the options. The key idea is that managers will have an incentive to take actions that maximize the stock price, because this will increase their wealth along with that of the other shareholders.

Although experts agree that an effective way to motivate management is to tie compensation to performance, many have scrutinized the execution of compensation plans in recent years. Individual and institutional investors, as well as the SEC, have publicly questioned the appropriateness of multi-million-dollar compensation packages that some corporate executives receive. Average levels of CEO compensation in other developed countries tend to be much lower.

While large pay packages may be justified by exceptional increases in shareholder wealth, academic studies generally find only a modest, positive relationship between CEO compensation and share price. These packages are also extremely controversial when managers of poorly performing companies still receive very large payouts. For example, while the U.S. stock market (especially Nasdaq) suffered one of its worst yearly declines in decades during 2000, the average total compensation of 365 CEOs of the companies in *Business Week*'s survey rose by 18 percent, to $13.1 million. Contributing to the publicity surrounding the annual survey of these awards is the relatively recent SEC requirement that publicly traded companies must disclose both the amount of and the method used to determine compensation to their highest-paid executives.

WHAT IS THE IMPORTANCE OF ETHICS IN CORPORATE FINANCE?

In recent years, the media and others have questioned the legitimacy of actions taken by certain businesses. Examples include the $100 million fine paid in early 2002 by Merrill Lynch to the State of New York for intentionally misleading investors with regard to buy and sell recommendations; the July 2002 arrest and charging of Adelphia founder, John Rigas, and his sons, Timothy and Michael, for looting about $2.3 billion from the cable-television company; and the June 2002 insider-trading arrest of Samuel Waksal, founder and CEO of the biotech firm ImClone Systems, who had leaked information to family and friends on the failure of the FDA to approve its marketing application for the cancer drug Erbitux prior to the public release of that information.[11] Clearly, these and other similar actions, such as those involving Enron, Global Crossing, Tyco, and WorldCom, have focused attention on the question of **ethics,** or standards of conduct in business dealings.

[11.] See Ang (1993) and Chambers and Lacey (1996) for examinations of the importance of ethics in corporate finance.

Today, the financial community is developing and enforcing ethical standards, primarily due to the widespread publicity surrounding numerous ethical violations and their perpetrators that began with the Enron collapse in late 2001. The goal of these standards is to motivate businesspeople and investors to adhere to both the letter and the spirit of laws and regulations concerned with all aspects of business and professional practice. In addition, Congress passed the Sarbanes-Oxley Act of 2002, a law that requires firms to provide extensive documentation of the internal controls they put in place to protect investors from fraud.

More and more firms are now directly addressing the issue of ethics by establishing corporate ethics policies and guidelines and by requiring employee compliance with them. Frequently, employees are required to sign a formal pledge to uphold the firm's ethics policies. Such policies typically apply to employee actions in dealing with all corporate stakeholders, including the public at large.[12] *Ethical behavior is therefore viewed as necessary for achieving the firm's goal of owner wealth maximization.*

Concept Review Questions

5. What are *agency costs?* Why do these tend to increase in severity as a corporation grows larger?

6. What are the relative advantages and disadvantages of using sophisticated management compensation packages to align the interests of managers and shareholders?

7. Why are ethics important in corporate finance? What is the likely consequence of unethical behavior by a corporation and its managers?

1.4 SUMMARY

- The practice of corporate finance rests on a foundation of certain core principles and involves five basic, related sets of activities: financing, capital budgeting, financial management, corporate governance, and risk management.
- The three key legal forms of business organization in the United States are sole proprietorships, partnerships, and corporations. Sole proprietorships are most common, but corporations dominate economically. A new, fourth form, the limited liability company, has recently become popular due to its flexibility and the favorable tax treatment it offers.
- Limited liability companies exist in virtually every country, and those in developed countries share many of the same basic traits. Many countries also have a large number of state-owned enterprises, though most governments have launched privatization programs to sell their ownership stakes to private investors.
- The goal of the firm's managers should be to maximize shareholder wealth rather than maximize profits. Maximizing profits focuses on the past, not the future, ignores the timing of profits, relies on accounting values rather than future cash flows, and ignores risk. Shareholder-wealth maximization is socially optimal because shareholders are residual claimants who profit only after all other claims are paid in full.

[12.] Unfortunately, these steps are hardly enough. Enron had a detailed conflict-of-interest policy in place, but then waived it so that its executives could set up the special-purpose entities that subsequently caused Enron's failure. The result of a lack of effective ethics policies at Enron and numerous other firms has been an increased level of government oversight and regulation.

- Agency costs that result from the separation of ownership and control must be addressed satisfactorily for companies to prosper. These costs can be overcome (or at least reduced) by relying on the workings of the market for corporate control, incurring monitoring and bonding costs, and using executive compensation contracts that (theoretically) align the interests of shareholders and managers.

INTERNET RESOURCES

Note: *This textbook includes numerous Internet links throughout, both within the text discussions and at the end of each chapter. Such links may change or be eliminated during the life of this edition. If you encounter a "dead" link, please go to the book's website (http://smart .swcollege.com) to obtain updated links.*

http://money.cnn.com (CNN Money); www.yahoo.com (Yahoo)—Among the best websites for general U.S. business information

www.ft.com (*Financial Times*)—One of the best websites for international business information

www.careers.com (CareerBuilder); www.monster.com (Monster); www.usnews.com (*U.S. News & World Report*); www.careers.wsj.com (WSJ Career Journal)— Websites for career-related facts and figures

www.schwab.com (Charles Schwab); www.etrade.com (E*Trade); www.bankone.com (Bank One)—Excellent websites maintained by brokerage houses and Internet banking firms

KEY TERMS

agency costs	initial public offering (IPO)
agency problems	joint and several liability
board of directors	limited liability company (LLC)
bonds	limited partners
capital budgeting function	limited partnership
capital structure decision	money market
chief executive officer (CEO)	notes
collective action problem	partnership
commercial paper	president
corporate charter	primary market transaction
corporate finance	privatization
corporate governance function	public company
corporation	residual claimants
debt	risk-averse
double-taxation problem	risk-management function
equity	S corporation
equity claimants	Sarbanes-Oxley Act of 2002
ethics	secondary market transactions
executive compensation	shareholders
financial management function	sole proprietorship
financing function	stakeholder
general partners	state-owned enterprises (SOEs)
hedge	stock options
hostile takeover	venture capitalists

QUESTIONS

1-1. Why must a financial manager have an integrated understanding of the five basic finance functions? Why is the corporate governance function considered a finance function? Has the risk-management function become more important in recent years?

1-2. Which of the five core principles of finance relate to the five basic finance functions? Based on the descriptions provided in the chapter, in what ways do these core principles relate to the basic finance functions?

1-3. Enter the home page of the Careers in Business website (www.careers-in-business.com), and page through the finance positions listed and their corresponding salaries. What skill sets or job characteristics lead to the variation in salaries? Which of these positions generally require prior work experience?

1-4. What are the advantages and disadvantages of the different legal forms of business organization? Could the limited liability advantage of a corporation also lead to an agency problem? Why? What legal form would an upstart entrepreneur likely prefer?

1-5. Describe the differences between businesses in the United States and those in foreign countries with respect to taxation, financial disclosure, and ownership structure. Is privatization reducing or increasing these differences?

1-6. Can there be a difference between profit maximization and shareholder-wealth maximization? If so, what could cause this difference? Which of the two should be the goal of the firm and its management?

1-7. Define a corporate *stakeholder*. Which groups are considered to be stakeholders? Would shareholders also be considered stakeholders? Compare the shareholder-wealth maximization principle to the stakeholder-wealth preservation principle in terms of economic systems.

1-8. What is meant by an *agency cost* or *agency problem*? Do these interfere with shareholder-wealth maximization? Why? What mechanisms minimize these costs/problems? Are executive compensation contracts effective in mitigating these costs/problems?

1-9. Are ethics critical to the financial manager's goal of shareholder-wealth maximization? How are the two related? Is the establishment of corporate ethics policies and guidelines, and requiring employee compliance with them, enough to ensure ethical behavior by employees?

PROBLEMS

SMART SOLUTIONS
See the problem and solution explained step-by-step at
SMARTFinance

Legal Forms of Business Organization

1-1.   **a.** Calculate the tax disadvantage to organizing a U.S. business as a corporation versus as a partnership under the following conditions. Assume that all earnings will be paid out as cash dividends. Operating income will be $500,000. The corporate-profits tax rate is 35 percent, the average personal tax rate for the partners is 35 percent, and the capital gains tax rate on dividend income is 15 percent.

   b. Then recalculate the tax disadvantage using the same income but with the maximum tax rates that existed before 2003. These rates were 35 percent on corporate profits and 38.6 percent on personal investment income.

Goals of the Corporate Financial Manager

1-2. Consider the following simple corporate example with one stockholder and one manager. There are two mutually exclusive projects in which the manager may invest and two possible manager compensation plans that the stockholder may choose to employ. The manager may be paid a flat $300,000 or receive 10 percent of corporate profits. The stockholder receives all profits net of manager compensation. (a) Which project maximizes shareholder wealth? (b) Which compensation contract does the manager prefer if this project is chosen? (c) Which project will the manager choose under a flat compensation arrangement? (d) Under a profit-sharing arrangement? (e) Which compensation contract aligns the interests of the stockholder and manager so that the manager will act in the best interest of the stockholder?

  a. Which project maximizes shareholder wealth? Which compensation contract does the manager prefer if this project is chosen?
  b. Which project will the manager choose under a flat compensation arrangement?
  c. Which compensation contract aligns the interests of the stockholder and the manager so that the manager will act in the best interest of the stockholder?
  d. What does this tell you about the structure of the management pay contracts?

Project #1		Project #2	
Probability	Gross Profit	Probability	Gross Profit
33.33%	$ 0	50.0%	$600,000
33.33%	$3,000,000	50.0%	$900,000
33.33%	$9,000,000		

THOMSON ONE BUSINESS SCHOOL EDITION

Access financial information from the Thomson ONE–Business School Edition website for the following problem(s). Go to http://tobsefin.swlearning.com/. If you have already registered your access serial number and have a username and password, click **Enter.** Otherwise, click **Register** and follow the instructions to create a username and password. Register your access serial number and then click **Enter** on the aforementioned website. When you click Enter, you will be prompted for your username and password (please remember that the password is case sensitive). Enter them in the respective boxes and then click **OK** (or hit **Enter**). From the ensuing page, click **Click Here to Access Thomson ONE–Business School Edition Now!** This opens up a new window that gives you access to the Thomson ONE–Business School Edition database. You can retrieve a company's financial information by entering its ticker symbol [provided for each company in the problem(s)] in the box below "Name/Symbol/Key." For further instructions on using the Thomson ONE–Business School Edition database, please refer to "A Guide for Using Thomson ONE–Business School Edition."

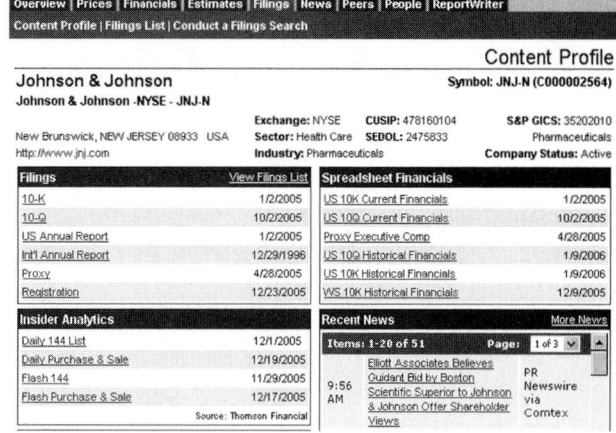

1-3. Examine the insider activities of Johnson & Johnson (ticker symbol, JNJ). Under the Filings tab, click on the Daily 144 List in the Insider Analytics box. Does there appear to be a preponderance of proposed buying or selling of JNJ shares? Does this suggest an agency problem exists?

Chapter 2

Financial Statement and Cash Flow Analysis

SMARTFinance
Use the learning tools at www
.thomsonedu.com/finance/smartfinance

30

> ## OPENING FOCUS
> ### Bang & Olufsen's Rising Profits Are Music to Investors' Ears

Founded in 1925 by two young engineers, Peter Bang and Svend Olufsen, Denmark's Bang & Olufsen (B&O) made sleek and expensive audio-video equipment that for nearly 75 years was the epitome of cool. Then B&O stalled. Its gear was suddenly out-of-tune in the era of the iPod. In 2001, after six years at Danish toymaker LEGO Group, Torben Bellegaard Sorensen became B&O's chief executive officer (CEO). When he arrived at B&O, the company was plagued by inefficiencies and complacent management and was turning in lousy numbers. Its business risked slipping into irrelevance.

To pump up the volume, Sorensen quickly pared B&O's staff from 3,000 to 2,200 and closed dozens of B&O stores. He also moved to repair B&O's image by rolling out high-performance products like the BeoLab 5 series—$16,000 speakers that incorporated a technical breakthrough called the "acoustic lens." In 2005, B&O unveiled a car stereo developed with German automaker Audi that features a head-pounding 14 speakers, including two acoustic lenses that rise silently out of the dashboard when the car starts up. B&O also sought ways to put its products in front of upscale audiences: B&O technicians at the MGM Grand in Las Vegas rewired penthouse hotel suites with B&O sound systems and flat-panel TVs. At the same time, B&O began courting yachtmakers, jet-leasing companies, and developers of high-end real estate to use its products. All of these initiatives were part of Sorensen's strategy to get more people in touch with the B&O brand.

Sorensen's efforts are now paying off, as investors tune back in. B&O's shares in March 2005 were up 23 percent over the preceding 12 months, twice the rise of Copenhagen's stock index in that same period. The company forecast net profits of $46 million for the fiscal year ended May 2005, on revenue growth of 3.5 percent (to $665 million)—the first increase since 2002. B&O forecasts a revenue increase of 6.8 percent in the following year.

Sorensen continues to play the growth tune, with more innovative new-product introductions to come. In addition, he is planning to move some production out of Denmark and shift 200 jobs to a new plant in the Czech Republic to save B&O about $7 million per year. Clearly, Sorensen's product and financial initiatives are music to investors' ears.

Source: Andy Reinhardt, "The Crisp, Clear Sound of Rising Profits," Business Week *(March 14, 2005), p. 60.*

A ccounting is called the language of business. As you will see in this chapter, corporate finance relies heavily on accounting concepts and language. You also will see that the primary focus of finance professionals and accountants differs significantly. Accountants apply *generally accepted accounting principles* (*GAAP*) to construct financial statements that fairly portray a company's past performance. Accountants generally construct these statements using an **accrual-based approach.** This means that accountants record revenues at the point of sale and costs when they are incurred, not necessarily when a firm receives or pays out cash.

In contrast to accountants, finance professionals use a **cash flow approach** that focuses on current and prospective inflows and outflows of cash. The financial manager must convert relevant accounting and tax information into cash inflows and cash outflows. After adjusting for timing differences and risk factors, companies and investors can use this information for analysis and decision making.

This chapter describes how finance professionals use accounting information to analyze the firm's cash flows and financial performance. We begin with a brief review of the four major financial statements. Next, we use these statements to demonstrate some of the key concepts involved in cash flow analysis. We give special emphasis to the effect of depreciation and other noncash charges on cash flows and the various inflows and outflows of cash to the firm. Finally, we discuss some popular financial ratios used to analyze the firm's financial performance.

SMART PRACTICES VIDEO

Jon Olson, Vice President of Finance, Intel Corp. (former). Currently, Chief Financial Officer, Xilinx Corp.

"At Intel, accounting is a fundamental requirement of a financial analyst."

See the entire interview at **SMARTFinance**

2.1   FINANCIAL STATEMENTS

Although our discussion in this chapter is based on U.S. accounting statements and conventions, the principles covered are quite general. Many national governments require public companies to generate financial statements based on widely accepted accounting rules. In the United States, these rules are the GAAP developed by the Financial Accounting Standards Board (FASB). The FASB is a nongovernmental, professional standards body that examines controversial accounting topics and issues standards that almost have the force of law, at least in terms of their impact on accounting practices.

The Securities and Exchange Commission (SEC) regulates publicly traded U.S. companies, as well as the nation's stock and bond markets. Every other industrialized country has an agency similar to the SEC, and most developed countries mandate that companies generate financial statements following international accounting standards (IAS). These are broadly similar to GAAP, although GAAP rules tend to place greater emphasis on public information disclosure than do IAS rules. Also, in response to the accounting scandals of 2001 and 2002, the Sarbanes-Oxley Act of 2002 (SOX) established the Public Company Accounting Oversight Board (PCAOB), which effectively gives the SEC authority to oversee the accounting profession's activities.

To date, the SEC has adamantly insisted that all non-U.S. companies report results based on GAAP if they want to sell their securities on a U.S. stock exchange. However, the FASB has some joint projects underway with the International Accounting Standards Board (IASB), an independent, privately funded standard-setting body whose mission is to develop a single set of accounting standards that can be used worldwide. The FASB and IASB are working together toward convergence of U.S. GAAP and international accounting standards.

The SEC requires four key financial statements: (1) the balance sheet, (2) the income statement, (3) the statement of retained earnings, and (4) the statement of cash flows.[1] Our chief concern in this section is to review the information these statements present. Here, we present the financial statements from the 2007 stockholders' report of the Global Petroleum Corporation (GPC). Though fictional, GPC's accounts are based on the actual statements of the five largest international petroleum companies. Therefore, the values constructed for GPC mirror those of a globally active oil company.

BALANCE SHEET

A firm's balance sheet presents a "snapshot" view of the company's financial position at a specific point in time. By definition, a firm's assets must equal the combined value of its liabilities and stockholders' equity. Phrased differently, creditors and equity investors finance all of a firm's assets.

A balance sheet shows assets and separate classifications for the claims of creditors and shareholders. Sometimes balance sheets present assets on the left and liabilities and owners' equity accounts on the right—a format called the *account form.* Just as often, balance sheets will be in *report form,* with assets first, followed by liabilities and owners' equity. Whatever the format, assets and liabilities appear in descending order of *liquidity,* or the length of time it takes to convert accounts into cash in the normal course of business. The most liquid asset, cash, appears first, and the least liquid, fixed assets, comes last. Similarly, accounts payable represents the obligations the firm must pay with cash within the next year. The last entry on the balance sheet, stockholders' equity, quite literally never matures.

Table 2.1 presents Global Petroleum Corporation's balance sheet as of December 31, 2007. As is standard practice in annual reports, the table also shows the prior year's (2006) accounts for comparison. The following accounts appear among GPC's assets:

- *Cash and cash equivalents* are assets such as checking account balances at commercial banks that can be used directly as means of payment.
- *Marketable securities* represent very liquid, short-term investments, which financial analysts view as a form of "near cash."
- *Accounts receivable* represent the amount customers owe the firm from sales made on credit.
- *Inventories* include raw materials, work in process (partially finished goods), and finished goods held by the firm.
- *Gross property, plant, and equipment* is the original cost of all real property, structures, and long-lived equipment owned by the firm.
- *Net property, plant, and equipment* represents the difference between this original value and *accumulated depreciation*—the cumulative expense recorded for the depreciation of fixed assets since their purchase. Governments allow companies to depreciate (to charge against taxable earnings) a fraction of a fixed asset's cost each year. This charge reflects a decline in the asset's economic value over time. The one fixed asset that is not depreciated is land, because it generally does not decline in value over time.
- Finally, *intangible assets* include items such as patents, trademarks, copyrights, or (in the case of petroleum companies) mineral rights entitling the company to

---

[1.] The SEC requires *publicly held corporations*—those whose stock is traded on either an organized securities exchange or the over-the-counter exchange and/or those with more than $5 million in assets and 500 or more stockholders—to provide their stockholders with an annual stockholders' report that includes these statements. We use these statement titles consistently throughout the text. However, in practice, companies frequently use various, different statement titles.

Table 2.1
Balance Sheet for Global Petroleum Corporation

Global Petroleum Corporation Balance Sheets at December 31, 2006 and 2007 ($ in millions)					
Assets	2007	2006	Liabilities and Stockholders' Equity	2007	2006
Current assets			Current liabilities		
Cash and cash equivalents	$ 440	$ 213	Accounts payable	$1,697	$1,304
Marketable securities	35	28	Notes payable	477	587
Accounts receivable	1,619	1,203	Accrued expenses	440	379
Inventories	615	530	Total current liabilities	$2,614	$2,270
Other (mostly prepaid expenses)	170	176	Long-term liabilities		
Total current assets	$2,879	$2,150	Deferred taxes	$ 907	$ 793
Fixed assets			Long-term debt	1,760	1,474
Gross property, plant, and equipment	$9,920	$9,024	Total long-term liabilities	$2,667	$2,267
Less: Accumulated depreciation	3,968	3,335	Total liabilities	$5,281	$4,537
			Stockholders' equity		
Net property, plant, and equipment	$5,952	$5,689	Preferred stock	$ 30	$ 30
			Common stock ($1 par value)	373	342
Intangible assets and others	758	471	Paid-in-capital in excess of par	248	229
Net fixed assets	$6,710	$6,160	Retained earnings	4,271	3,670
Total assets	$9,589	$8,310	Less: Treasury stock	614	498
			Total stockholders' equity	$4,308	$3,773
			Total liabilities and stockholders' equity	$9,589	$8,310

extract oil and gas on specific properties. Although intangible assets are usually nothing more than legal rights, they are often extremely valuable, as the discussion of the market value of global brands in this chapter's Comparative Corporate Finance insert vividly demonstrates.

Now turn your attention to the liabilities and owners' equity parts of the balance sheet. Current liabilities include the following accounts:

- *Accounts payable,* amounts owed for credit purchases by the firm.
- *Notes payable,* outstanding short-term loans, typically from commercial banks.
- *Accrued expenses,* costs incurred by the firm that have not yet been paid. Examples of accruals include taxes owed to the government and wages due employees.

Accounts payable and accruals are often called *spontaneous liabilities* because they tend to change directly with changes in sales.

Next is the long-term liabilities section. There are two main categories of long-term liabilities: deferred taxes and long-term debt.

- In the United States and many other countries, laws permit firms to construct two sets of financial statements, one for reporting to the public and one for tax

COMPARATIVE CORPORATE FINANCE

Assessing the Market Value of Global Brands

Rank	Brand	2005 Brand Value ($ in millions)	2004 Brand Value ($ in millions)	Percent Change	Country of Ownership
1	Coca-Cola	67,525	67,394	0	U.S.
2	Microsoft	59,941	61,372	−2	U.S.
3	IBM	53,376	53,791	−1	U.S.
4	GE	46,996	44,111	7	U.S.
5	Intel	35,588	33,499	6	U.S.
6	Nokia	26,452	24,041	10	Finland
7	Disney	26,441	27,113	−2	U.S.
8	McDonald's	26,014	25,001	4	U.S.
9	Toyota	24,837	22,673	10	Japan
10	Marlboro	21,189	22,128	−4	U.S.
11	Mercedes-Benz	20,006	21,331	−6	Germany
12	Citi	19,967	19,971	0	U.S.
13	Hewlett-Packard	18,866	20,978	−10	U.S.
14	American Express	18,559	17,683	5	U.S.
15	Gillette	17,534	16,723	5	U.S.
16	BMW	17,126	15,886	8	Germany
17	Cisco	16,592	15,948	4	U.S.
18	Louis Vuitton	16,077	NA	NA	France
19	Honda	15,788	14,874	6	Japan
20	Samsung	14,956	12,553	19	S. Korea
21	Dell	13,231	11,500	15	U.S.
22	Ford	13,159	14,475	−9	U.S.
23	Pepsi	12,399	12,066	3	U.S.
24	Nescafe	12,241	11,892	3	Switzerland
25	Merrill Lynch	12,018	11,499	5	U.S.

How much is a global brand name worth? Interbrand Corporation, a New York–based consulting firm, calculates value annually, and *Business Week* publishes the rankings. The table above details Interbrand's 2005 list of the 25 most valuable brands in 2005. (The table also lists the values of these brands in 2004, which makes it clear that the global business environment increased considerably in 2005.) The total brand values are large and are dominated by brands of U.S.-based companies. Additionally, the rankings are remarkably stable from year to year; the 2004 ranking listed the same top 5 in order, and only two new brands entered the top 25 during 2005.

Although U.S. companies are not required to disclose estimated brand values in their financial statements, large publicly traded British and Australian firms must do so. Brand values do, however, have a significant effect on U.S. accounting rules in one important area—accounting for the "goodwill" created when one firm acquires another for more than the acquired firm's book value. This premium over book value represents the higher market (versus book) value of intangible assets such as patents, copyrights, and trademarks, as well as brand names and business relationships that are not accounted for at all.

Until 2001, goodwill was treated as an expense to be charged against the acquiring firm's earnings over a period of years. Now, however, the Financial Accounting Standards Board requires firms to periodically assess the fair value of assets that they purchase through acquisitions. If the fair value of those assets declines significantly over time, firms must recognize "goodwill impairment," meaning that some of the value of their intangible assets has vanished. Charges arising from goodwill impairment can have a dramatic effect on reported earnings.

Source: Interbrand Corporation, as reported in Robert Berner and David Kiley, "Global Brands," *Business Week* (August 1, 2005), pp. 86–94.

purposes. For example, when a firm purchases a long-lived asset, it can choose to depreciate this asset rapidly for tax purposes, resulting in large, immediate tax write-offs. When the firm constructs financial statements for release to the public, however, it may choose a different depreciation method, perhaps one that results in higher reported earnings in the early years of the asset's life. The **deferred taxes** entry is a long-term liability that reflects the difference between the taxes that firms actually pay and the tax liabilities they report on their public financial statements.

- **Long-term debt** represents debt that matures more than one year in the future.

The stockholder's equity section provides information about the claims against the firm held by investors who own preferred and common shares. It shows the following accounts:

- The **preferred stock** entry shows the proceeds from the sale of preferred stock ($30 million for GPC). This form of ownership has preference over common stock when the firm distributes income and assets.
- Next, two entries show the amount paid in by the original purchasers of **common stock**: The common stock entry equals the number of outstanding common shares multiplied by the **par value** per share. **Paid-in-capital in excess of par** equals the number of shares outstanding multiplied by the original selling price of the shares, net of the par value. The combined value of common stock and paid-in-capital equals the proceeds the firm received when it originally sold shares to investors.
- **Retained earnings** are the cumulative total of the earnings that the firm has reinvested since its inception. Be sure you know that retained earnings are not a reservoir of unspent cash. The retained earnings "vault" is empty because the firm has already reinvested the earnings in new assets.
- Finally, the **Treasury stock** entry records the value of common shares that the firm currently holds in reserve. Usually, Treasury stock appears on the balance sheet because the firm has reacquired previously issued stock through a share repurchase program.

GPC's balance sheet in Table 2.1 shows that the firm's total assets increased by $1,279 million from 2006 to 2007. Other significant changes in GPC's balance sheet include sizable increases in cash, accounts receivable, and intangible assets, coupled with a massive ($896 million) increase in gross property, plant, and equipment. Balancing these increases in asset accounts is an increase of $393 million in accounts payable plus $601 million in new retained earnings. In other words, GPC financed increases in asset accounts mainly by borrowing more from suppliers (accounts payable) and by reinvesting profits (retained earnings). We will discover additional insights into these changes when we look more closely at the statement of cash flows.

INCOME STATEMENT

Table 2.2 presents Global Petroleum Corporation's income statement for the year ended December 31, 2007. As with the balance sheet, GPC's income statement includes data from 2006 for comparison.[2]

[2.] When reporting to shareholders, firms typically also include a **common-size income statement** that expresses all income-statement entries as a percentage of sales.

Global Petroleum Corporation Income Statements for the Years Ended December 31, 2006 and 2007 ($ in millions)		
	2007	2006
Sales revenue	$12,843	$9,110
Less: Cost of goods sold[a]	8,519	5,633
Gross profit	$ 4,324	$3,477
Less: Operating and other expenses	1,544	1,521
Less: Selling, general, and administrative expenses	616	584
Less: Depreciation	633	608
Operating profit	$ 1,531	$ 764
Plus: Other income	140	82
Earnings before interest and taxes (EBIT)	$ 1,671	$ 846
Less: Interest expense	123	112
Pretax income	$ 1,548	$ 734
Less: Taxes		
Current	367	158
Deferred	232	105
Total taxes	599	263
Net income (net profit after tax)	$ 949	$ 471
Less: Preferred stock dividends	3	3
Earnings available for common stockholders	$ 946	$ 468
Less: Dividends	345	326
To retained earnings	$ 601	$ 142
Per-share data[b]		
Earnings per share (EPS)	$ 5.29	$ 2.52
Dividends per share (DPS)	$ 1.93	$ 1.76
Price per share	$ 76.25	$71.50

[a]Annual purchases have historically represented about 80 percent of cost of goods sold. Using this relationship, its credit purchases in 2007 were $6,815 and in 2006, they were $4,506.
[b]Based on 178,719,400 and 185,433,100 shares outstanding as of December 31, 2007 and 2006, respectively.

In the vocabulary of accounting, income (also called *profit, earnings,* or *margin*) equals revenue minus expenses. A firm's income statement, however, has several measures of "income" appearing at different points:

- *Gross profit* is the first income measure. It is the amount by which *sales revenue* exceeds the *cost of goods sold* (the direct cost of producing or purchasing the goods sold).
- Next, a firm deducts from gross profits various operating expenses, including selling expense, general and administrative expense, and depreciation expense.[3] The resulting *operating profit* ($1,531 million for GPC) represents the profits earned from the sale of products, although this amount does not include financial and tax costs.
- *Other income,* earned on transactions directly related to producing and/or selling the firm's products, is added to operating income to yield *earnings before*

[3.] Companies frequently include depreciation expense in manufacturing costs—cost of goods sold—when calculating gross profits. In this text we show depreciation as an expense, to isolate its effect on cash flows.

interest and taxes (*EBIT*). When a firm has no "other income," its operating profit and *EBIT* are equal.

- Next, the firm subtracts *interest expense*—representing the cost of debt financing—from *EBIT* to find its *pretax income*. For example, GPC subtracts $123 million of interest expense from EBIT to find pretax income of $1,548 million.

- The final step is to subtract taxes from pretax income to arrive at *net income,* or *net profits after taxes* ($949 million for GPC). Net income is the proverbial "bottom line" and the single most important accounting number for both corporate managers and external financial analysts.

Note in Table 2.2 that GPC incurred a total tax liability of $599 million during 2007, but only the $367 million *current* portion must be paid immediately.[4] Although the remaining $232 million in deferred taxes must be paid eventually, these are noncash expenses for year 2007.

Based on its income statement, GPC had an average tax rate during 2007 of about 39 percent ($599 million in taxes ÷ $1,548 million of pretax income). For financial decision-making purposes, the financial manager would focus on the firm's *marginal tax rate*—the rate applicable to the next dollar of earnings. Throughout this text, the assumed tax rates are always marginal tax rates.

The next entries in the income statement indicate distributions of net income for various purposes:

- If a firm has preferred stock, it deducts preferred stock dividends from net income. For example, GPC paid $3 million in dividends on its $30 million of preferred stock outstanding during both 2006 and 2007.

- Net income net of preferred stock dividends is **earnings available for common stockholders.** Dividing earnings available for common stockholders by the number of shares of common stock outstanding results in **earnings per share (*EPS*).** *EPS* represents the amount earned during the period on each outstanding share of common stock. GPC's earnings per share for 2007 is $5.29, which represents a significant increase from the *EPS* of $2.52 in 2006. Actual *EPS* for the past 12 months, such as those shown on GPC's income statement, are sometimes called *trailing EPS.* Estimates of earnings for the next 12 months are often called *leading EPS.*

- The final entry in the income statement is the cash **dividend per share (*DPS*)** paid to common stockholders. GPC's DPS during 2007 is $1.93, up slightly from the dividend of $1.76 per share paid in 2006.

STATEMENT OF RETAINED EARNINGS

The third key financial statement, the statement of retained earnings,[5] reconciles the net income earned during a given year, and any cash dividends paid, with the change in retained earnings between the start and end of that year. Table 2.3 presents this statement for Global Petroleum Corporation for the year ended December 31, 2007. A review of the statement shows that the company began the year with $3,670 million in retained earnings and had net income after taxes of $949 million. From its net

---

[4.] Corporations are subject to corporate tax rates that for federal purposes are progressive and range between 15 percent and 39 percent. Personal tax rates too are subject to a progressive schedule; for federal purposes the personal tax rate ranges from 10 percent to 35 percent.

[5.] The *statement of retained earnings* is a simplified form of the *statement of stockholders' equity,* which summarizes all of the transactions that affected the firm's equity account during the year.

Global Petroleum Corporation Statement of Retained Earnings for the Year Ended December 31, 2007 ($ in millions)		
Retained earnings balance (January 1, 2007)		$3,670
Plus: Net income (for 2007)		949
Less: Cash dividends (paid during 2007)		
Preferred stock	$ 3	
Common stock	345	
Total dividends paid		$ 348
Retained earnings balance (December 31, 2007)		$4,271

income GPC paid a total of $348 million in preferred and common stock dividends. At year-end, retained earnings were $4,271 million. Thus, the net increase for GPC is $601 million ($949 million net income − $348 million in dividends) in 2007.

Note two points about GPC's retained earnings between 2006 and 2007: First, 2007 was a very good year for GPC in terms of increased sales and profits. GPC's net income more than doubled, rising from $471 million in 2006 to $949 million in 2007. Thus, it is not surprising that the amount of earnings retained in the firm during 2007 ($601 million) was much larger than in 2006 ($142 million).[6]

Second, note that GPC's increased dividend payment was far smaller proportionally than was the increase in net income. Another way to phrase this is to say that GPC's **dividend payout ratio**—the fraction of current earnings available for common stockholders paid out as dividends—declined. Specifically, its dividend payout ratio declined from 69.7 percent ($326 million ÷ $468 million) in 2006 to 36.5 percent ($345 million ÷ $946 million) in 2007.

STATEMENT OF CASH FLOWS

The statement of cash flows provides a summary of a firm's cash flows over the year. This statement isolates the firm's operating, investment, and financing cash flows and reconciles them with changes in its cash and marketable securities during the year. Table 2.5 presents GPC's statement of cash flows for the year ended December 31, 2007. In section 2.2 we will present some important cash flow concepts and measures and then show how to use those data to prepare the statement of cash flows.

NOTES TO FINANCIAL STATEMENTS

Besides the four key financial statements themselves, the "notes" to financial statements can be very useful to financial managers and analysts. A public company's financial statements include explanatory notes keyed to the relevant accounts in the statements. These notes provide detailed information on the accounting policies, calculations, and transactions underlying entries in the financial statements. For

---

[6] Also note that the two broadest measures of income (*EBIT* and net income) increased proportionally far more than did sales revenue. Whereas sales increased by 41 percent (from $9,110 million to $12,843 million), *EBIT* and net income increased by 98 percent and 101 percent, respectively. This suggests that the firm's extensive use of fixed-cost assets (refineries, pipelines, tankers, etc.) imparts a high degree of *operating leverage*, meaning that a given percentage increase (decrease) in sales yields a much larger percentage increase (decrease) in operating profits (same as *EBIT*). Chapter 9 discusses more fully the concept of operating leverage.

example, the notes to General Motors' 2004 financial statements cover 35 of the 108 pages in its annual report.

Notes typically provide additional information about a firm's revenue recognition practices, income taxes, fixed assets, leases, and employee compensation plans. Professional security analysts find this information particularly useful. They routinely scour the notes to the firm's financial statements to evaluate the firm's performance and value.

Concept Review Questions

1. Are balance sheets and income statements prepared with the same purpose in mind? How are these two statements different, and how are they related?

2. Which statements are of greatest interest to creditors? Which would be of greatest interest to stockholders?

3. Why are the notes to financial statements important to professional security analysts?

2.2 CASH FLOW ANALYSIS

Although financial managers are interested in the information in the firm's accrual-based financial statements, their primary focus is on cash flows. Without adequate cash to pay obligations on time, to fund operations and growth, and to compensate owners, the firm will fail. The financial manager and other interested parties can gain insight into the firm's cash flows over a given period of time by both using some popular measures of cash flow and analyzing the firm's statement of cash flows.

THE FIRM'S CASH FLOWS

In the process of evaluating a firm's cash flows, analysts view cash and marketable securities as perfect substitutes. Both represent a reservoir of liquidity that increases with *cash inflows* and decreases with *cash outflows*.

A firm's total cash flows can be conveniently divided into (1) operating flows, (2) investment flows, and (3) financing flows. The **operating flows** are cash inflows and outflows directly related to the production and sale of products or services. **Investment flows** are cash flows associated with the purchase or sale of fixed assets and business equity. Clearly, purchases result in cash outflows, whereas sales generate cash inflows. The **financing flows** result from debt and equity financing transactions. Taking on new debt (short-term or long-term) results in a cash inflow; repaying existing debt represents a cash outflow. Similarly, the sale of stock results in a cash inflow; the repurchase of stock or payment of cash dividends generates a cash outflow. In combination, the operating, investment, and financing cash flows in a given period affect the firm's cash and marketable securities balances.

Monitoring cash flow is important for financial managers employed by the firm and for outside analysts trying to estimate the firm's worth. Managers and analysts track a variety of cash flow measures. Among these, one of the most important is free cash flow.

Free Cash Flow Free cash flow (*FCF*) is the amount of cash flow available to investors—the providers of debt and equity capital. It represents the net amount of cash flow remaining after the firm has met all operating needs and paid for investments—both long-term (fixed) and short-term (current). Free cash flow for a given period can be calculated in two steps.

First, we find the firm's **net operating profits after taxes (NOPAT)**, the firm's earning before interest and after taxes:[7]

$$NOPAT = EBIT \times (1 - T) \qquad \text{(Eq. 2.1)}$$

where

$EBIT$ = earnings before interest and taxes
T = corporate tax rate

By adding back depreciation to $NOPAT$, we get **operating cash flow (OCF)**, which is the amount of cash flow generated by the firm's operations.

$$OCF = NOPAT + \text{Depreciation} \qquad \text{(Eq. 2.2)}$$

Note that because depreciation is a noncash charge, we add it back to determine OCF. **Noncash charges,** such as depreciation, amortization, and depletion allowances, are expenses that appear on the income statement but do not involve an actual outlay of cash. Almost all firms list depreciation on their income statements, so we focus on depreciation in our presentation. But when amortization or depletion occur in a firm's financial statements, you would treat them in a similar manner.

Substituting Equation 2.1 for $NOPAT$ into Equation 2.2, we get a single equation for OCF:

$$OCF = [EBIT \times (1 - T)] + \text{Depreciation} \qquad \text{(Eq. 2.3)}$$

Substituting the values from GPC's 2007 income statement (from Table 2.2) and assuming a 39% tax rate (T = 39%), we get GPC's operating cash flow:

$$OCF = \$1,671 \times (1.00 - 0.39) + \$633 = \$1,019 + \$633 = \$1,652$$

GPC's OCF is $1,652 million.

Next, we convert operating cash flow to free cash flow (FCF). To do so, we deduct the firm's net investments (denoted by the "change" symbol Δ) in fixed and current assets from operating cash flow, as shown in the following equation:

$$FCF = OCF - \Delta FA - (\Delta CA - \Delta A/P - \Delta \text{accruals}) \qquad \text{(Eq. 2.4)}$$

where

ΔFA = change in gross fixed assets + change in intangible assets and others,

ΔCA = change in current assets = change in fixed assets,

[7.] A related indicator of a firm's financial performance is *earnings before interest, taxes, depreciation, and amortization (EBITDA)*. Analysts use *EBITDA* to compare profitability of companies because it measures revenue minus all expenses other than interest, taxes, depreciation, and amortization. It thereby eliminates the effects of financing and accounting decisions. *EBITDA* is a good measure of profitability, but does not measure cash flows.

$\Delta A/P$ = change in accounts payable, and

Δaccruals = change in accrued liabilities.

Spontaneous current liability changes occur automatically with changes in sales. Therefore they must be deducted from current assets to find the net change in short-term investment. From the preceding calculation, we know that GPC's *OCF* in 2007 was $1,652 million. Using GPC's 2006 and 2007 balance sheets (Table 2.1), we can calculate the changes in gross fixed assets, current assets, accounts payable, and accruals between 2006 and 2007:

$$\Delta FA = (\$9,920 - \$9,024) + (\$758 - \$471) = \$896 + \$287 = \$1,183$$

$$\Delta CA = \$2,879 - \$2,150 = \$729$$

$$\Delta A/P = \$1,697 - \$1,304 = \$393$$

$$\Delta \text{accruals} = \$440 - \$379 = \$61$$

Substituting these values into Equation 2.4, we get the following:

$$FCF = \$1,652 - \$1,183 - (\$729 - \$393 - \$61)$$

$$= \$1,652 - \$1,183 - \$275$$

$$= \$194$$

Reviewing the second line of the *FCF* calculation above, we see that after subtracting $1,183 million in fixed asset investment and $275 million in current asset investment net of accounts payable and accruals, GPC has free cash flow in 2007 of $194 million. In other words, in 2007 the firm had $194 million available to pay its investors.

We will use free cash flow in Chapter 4 to estimate the value of a firm. At this point, suffice it to say that *FCF* is an important measure of cash flow used by corporate finance professionals.

Inflows and Outflows of Cash Table 2.4 classifies the basic inflows and outflows of cash of corporations (assuming other things are held constant). For example, a $1,000 increase in accounts payable would be an *inflow of cash*. A $2,500 increase in inventory would be an *outflow of cash*.

A few additional points about the classifications in Table 2.4 are worth noting:

1. A *decrease* in an asset (such as inventory) is an *inflow of cash* because cash that has been tied up in the asset is released. Managers can use that amount for some other purpose, such as repaying a loan. In contrast, an *increase* in inventory (or any other asset) is an *outflow of cash* because additional inventory ties up more of the firm's cash. Similar logic explains why an increase in any liability is an inflow of cash, and a decrease in any liability is an outflow of cash.

2. Our earlier discussion noted why depreciation and other noncash charges are considered cash inflows. Logic suggests that if net income is a cash inflow, then a *net loss* (negative net profits after taxes) is a cash outflow. The firm must balance its losses with an inflow of cash, such as selling off some of its fixed assets (reducing an asset) or increasing external borrowing (increasing a liability). Can a firm have a *net loss* (negative *NOPAT*) and still have positive operating cash flow (*OCF*)? Yes, as Equation 2.2 indicates, this can occur when depreciation and other noncash charges during the period are greater than the net loss. The statement of cash flows therefore treats net income (or net losses) and depreciation and other noncash charges as separate entries.

Table 2.4
The Inflows and
Outflows of Corporate
Cash

Inflows	Outflows
Decrease in any asset	Increase in any asset
Increase in any liability	Decrease in any liability
Net income (profit after tax)	Net loss
Depreciation and other noncash charges	Dividends paid
Sale of common or preferred stock	Repurchase or retirement of stock

---

APPLYING THE MODEL 2.1

On September 30, 2005, and on June 30, 2005, Procter & Gamble Co.® (P&G) (ticker symbol, PG) reported the following balances in certain current asset and liabilities accounts ($ in millions).

Account	September 30, 2005	June 30, 2005
Cash	$ 6,310	$ 6,389
Short-term investments	1,749	1,744
Accounts receivable	5,539	5,266
Inventory	5,161	5,006
Accounts payable	12,305	13,598
Short-term debt	8,749	11,441

In terms of current assets, cash declined during the third quarter of 2005, providing an inflow of cash for P&G. Short-term investments, accounts receivable, and inventory increased during the quarter, representing cash outflows. It may seem strange to think of a *decrease* in cash balances as a *source* of cash, but that simply means that P&G used some of its cash flow to "invest in other current assets" such as short-term investments, accounts receivable, and inventory. On the liabilities side, accounts payable and short-term debt declined, both representing an outflow of cash for P&G.

DEVELOPING THE STATEMENT OF CASH FLOWS

Accountants construct the statement of cash flows by using the income statement for a given year, along with the beginning- and end-of-year balance sheets. The procedure involves classifying balance sheet changes as inflows or outflows of cash; obtaining income statement data; classifying the relevant values into operating, investment, and financing cash flows; and presenting them in the proper format.[8]

Global Petroleum Corporation's statement of cash flows for the year ended December 31, 2007, appears in Table 2.5. Note that the statement assigns positive values to all cash inflows and negative values to all cash outflows. Notice, too, under the investment activities section that the statement records the increase in *gross* fixed assets, rather than *net* fixed assets, as a cash outflow. Depreciation accounts for the difference between changes in gross and net fixed assets, but depreciation expense

---

[8.] For a description and demonstration of the detailed procedures for developing the statement of cash flows, see any recently published financial accounting text, such as Chapter 14 of *Corporate Financial Accounting*, 8th ed., by Warren, Reeve, and Fess (Mason, Ohio: South-Western Publishing, 2005).

Table 2.5
Statement of Cash
Flows for Global
Petroleum Corporation

Global Petroleum Corporation Statement of Cash Flows for the Year Ended December 31, 2007 ($ in millions)

Cash flow from operating activities		
Net income (net profit after tax)	$949	
Depreciation	633	
Increase in accounts receivable	(416)	
Increase in inventories	(85)	
Decrease in other current assets	6	
Increase in accounts payable	393	
Increase in accrued expenses	61	
Cash provided by operating activities		$1,541
Cash flow from investment activities		
Increase in gross fixed assets	($896)	
Increase in intangible and other assets	(287)	
Cash provided (consumed) by investment activities		($1,183)
Cash flow from financing activities		
Decrease in notes payable	($110)	
Increase in deferred taxes	114	
Increase in long-term debt	286	
Changes in stockholders' equity	(66)	
Dividends paid	(348)	
Cash provided (consumed) by financing activities		($ 124)
Net increase in cash and marketable securities		$ 234

appears in the operating activities section of the statement. Thus, the focus on changes in gross fixed assets avoids double-counting depreciation in the statement. For a similar reason, the statement does not show a specific entry for the change in retained earnings as an inflow (or outflow) of cash. Instead, the factors that determine the change in retained earnings—profits or losses and dividends—appear as separate entries in the statement.

By adding up the items in each category—operating, investment, and financing activities—we obtain the net increase (decrease) in cash and marketable securities for the year. As a check, this value should reconcile with the actual yearly change in cash and marketable securities, obtained from the beginning- and end-of-year balance sheets.

By applying this procedure to GPC's 2007 income statement and 2006 and 2007 balance sheets, we obtain the firm's 2007 statement of cash flows (see Table 2.5). It shows that GPC experienced a $234 million increase in cash and marketable securities in 2007. Looking at GPC's 2006 and 2007 balance sheets in Table 2.1, we see that the firm's cash increased by $227 million, and its marketable securities increased by $7 million. The $234 million net increase in cash and marketable securities from the statement of cash flows reconciles with the total change of $234 million in these accounts during 2007. GPC's statement of cash flows therefore reconciles with the balance sheet changes.

INTERPRETING THE STATEMENT

The statement of cash flows allows the financial manager and other interested parties to analyze the firm's cash flow over a period of time. Unusual changes in either the major categories of cash flow or in specific items offer clues to problems that a firm may be experiencing. For example, an unusually large increase in accounts receivable or inventories, resulting in major cash outflows, may signal credit or inventory problems, respectively.

Financial managers and analysts can also prepare a statement of cash flows developed from projected, or pro forma, financial statements. They use this approach to determine whether the firm will require additional external financing or will generate excess cash that can be reinvested or distributed to shareholders.

Analysis of Global Petroleum Corporation's statement of cash flows for 2007 indicates no major problems for the company. GPC used the $1,541 million of cash from operating activities primarily to purchase an additional $896 million in property, plant, and equipment and increase intangibles and other fixed assets by $287 million. Financing activities were basically a wash: Increases in deferred taxes and long-term debt contributed a combined cash inflow of $400 million. Roughly offsetting these inflows of cash were outflows from a reduction of notes payable ($110 million), payment of common and preferred stock dividends ($348 million), and a net reduction in common stock outstanding of $66 million. In addition to cash provided by net income ($949 million) and depreciation ($633 million), GPC realized major cash inflows by increasing accounts payable ($393 million) and long-term debt ($286 million). The $1,183 million increase in fixed, intangible, and other assets was unusually large, by recent standards, but consistent with the significant growth in revenue that occurred during 2007.

One financially encouraging step taken by GPC in 2007 was to increase its net working capital by $385 million. **Net working capital** is defined as current assets minus current liabilities. It is a measure of the firm's overall liquidity; higher values reflect greater solvency, and vice versa. GPC's net working capital at the end of 2006 was −$120 million. As of December 31, 2007, its net working capital had risen to a positive level of $265 million. GPC engineered this $385 million increase by increasing its investment in current assets by $729 million while increasing its current liabilities by only $344 million. *Cash and marketable securities, accounts receivable,* and *inventories* increased by $234 million, $416 million, and $85 million, respectively, while the *other* current assets decreased by $6 million. Large increases occurred in two of the three categories of current liabilities—accounts payable ($393 million) and accrued expenses ($61 million)—and they were partially offset by a $110 million decline in notes payable. In general, it appears that GPC is growing and is managing its cash flows reasonably well.

Concept Review Questions

4. How do depreciation and other noncash charges act as sources of cash inflow to the firm? Why does a depreciation allowance exist in the tax laws? For a profitable firm, is it better to depreciate an asset quickly or slowly for tax purposes? Explain.

5. What is *operating cash flow (OCF)*? How does it relate to *net operating profits after taxes (NOPAT)*? What is *free cash flow (FCF)*, and how is it related to *OCF*?

6. Why is the financial manager likely to have great interest in the firm's statement of cash flows? What type of information can interested parties obtain from this statement?

2.3 ANALYZING FINANCIAL PERFORMANCE USING RATIO ANALYSIS

Analysis of a firm's financial statements is of interest to shareholders, creditors, and the firm's own management. In many cases, the constituents of a firm want to compare its financial condition to that of similar firms, but doing so can be very tricky. For example, suppose you are introduced to a man named Bill who tells you that he runs a company that earned a profit of $10 million last year. Would you be impressed by that feat? What if you knew that Bill's last name was Gates? Most people would agree that a profit of $10 million would be a great disappointment for Microsoft, the firm run by Bill Gates; Microsoft's annual profit is typically in the billions.

The point here is that the amount of sales, profits, and other items that appear on a firm's financial statements are difficult to interpret unless we have some way to put the numbers in perspective. To analyze financial statements, we need relative measures that in effect normalize size differences. Effective analysis of financial statements is thus based on the use of *ratios* or *relative values*. **Ratio analysis** involves calculating and interpreting financial ratios to assess the firm's performance and status.

USING FINANCIAL RATIOS

Different constituents will focus on different types of financial ratios. The firm's creditors are primarily interested in ratios that measure the firm's short-term liquidity and its ability to make interest and principal payments. A secondary concern of creditors is profitability; they want assurance that the business is healthy and will continue to be successful. Present and prospective shareholders focus on ratios that measure the firm's current and future levels of risk and return, because these two dimensions directly affect share price. The firm's managers use ratios to generate an overall picture of the company's financial health and to monitor its performance from period to period. They carefully examine unexpected changes to isolate developing problems.

An additional complication of ratio analysis is that a normal ratio in one industry may be highly unusual in another. For example, the net profit margin ratio measures the net income generated by each dollar of sales. (We will show the computation of this ratio later.) Net profit margins vary dramatically across industries. An outstanding net profit margin in the retail grocery industry could look paltry in the software business.

Therefore, when making subjective judgments about the health of a given company, analysts usually compare the firm's ratios to two benchmarks. First, analysts compare the financial ratios in the current year with previous years' ratios. They hope to identify trends that help them evaluate the firm's prospects. Second, analysts compare the ratios of one company with those of other "benchmark" firms in the same industry (or to an industry average obtained from a trade association or third-party provider).

We will use the 2007 and 2006 balance sheets and income statements for Global Petroleum Corporation, presented earlier in Tables 2.1 and 2.2, to demonstrate ratio calculations. (To simplify the presentation, we have deleted the *millions* after GPC's values.) The ratios presented in this chapter can be applied to nearly any company. Of course, many companies in different industries use ratios that focus on aspects peculiar to their industry.[9] We will cover the most common financial ratios, grouped into five categories: *liquidity, activity, debt, profitability,* and *market* ratios.

LIQUIDITY RATIOS

Liquidity ratios measure a firm's ability to satisfy its short-term obligations *as they come due.* Because a common precursor to financial distress or bankruptcy is low or declining liquidity, liquidity ratios are good leading indicators of cash flow problems. The two basic measures of liquidity are the *current ratio* and the *quick (acid-test) ratio.*

The **current ratio,** one of the most commonly cited financial ratios, measures the firm's ability to meet its short-term obligations. It is defined as current assets *divided* by current liabilities. (It thus presents in ratio form what *net working capital* measures by *subtracting* current liabilities from current assets.) GPC's current ratio on December 31, 2007, is computed as follows:

$$\text{Current ratio} = \frac{\text{current assets}}{\text{current liabilities}} = \frac{\$2,879}{\$2,614} = 1.10$$

How high should the current ratio be? The answer depends on the type of business and on the costs and benefits of having too much versus too little liquidity. For example, a current ratio of 1.0 would be acceptable for a utility but might be unacceptable for a manufacturer. The more predictable a firm's cash flows, the lower the acceptable current ratio. Because the business of oil exploration and development has notoriously unpredictable annual cash flows, GPC's current ratio of 1.10 indicates that GPC takes a fairly aggressive approach to managing its liquidity.

The **quick (acid-test) ratio** is similar to the current ratio except that it *excludes* inventory, which is usually the least-liquid current asset.[10] The generally low liquidity of inventory results from two factors: First, many types of inventory cannot be easily sold because they are partially completed items, special-purpose items, and the like. Second, inventory is typically sold on credit, and so it becomes an account receivable before being converted into cash. The quick ratio is calculated as follows:

$$\text{Quick ratio} = \frac{\text{current assets} - \text{inventory}}{\text{current liabilities}} = \frac{\$2,879 - \$615}{\$2,614} = 0.866$$

The quick ratio for GPC in 2007 is 0.866.

The quick ratio provides a better measure of overall liquidity only when a firm's inventory cannot be easily converted into cash. If inventory is liquid, the current ratio is a preferred measure. Because GPC's inventory is mostly petroleum and refined products that can be readily converted into cash, the firm's managers will probably focus on the current ratio.

[9.] For example, airlines pay close attention to the ratio of revenues to passenger miles flown. Retailers diligently track the growth in same-store sales from one year to the next.

[10.] An alternate and more precise definition of the *quick (acid-test) ratio* is (cash + marketable securities + accounts receivable) ÷ current liabilities. This definition eliminates inventory as well as prepaid and other current assets from the numerator. For convenience, though, we use the more common approximation shown in the text above.

ACTIVITY RATIOS

Activity ratios measure the speed with which the firm converts various accounts into sales or cash. Analysts use activity ratios as guides to assess how efficiently the firm manages its assets and its accounts payable.

Inventory turnover provides a measure of how quickly a firm sells its goods. GPC's 2007 *inventory turnover ratio* appears below:

$$\text{Inventory turnover} = \frac{\text{cost of goods sold}}{\text{inventory}} = \frac{\$8,519}{\$615} = 13.85$$

Notice that we used cost of goods sold rather than sales in the numerator because firms value inventory at cost on the firm's balance sheet. Also note that in the denominator we use the *ending* inventory balance of $615. If inventories are growing over time or exhibit seasonal patterns, analysts sometimes use the *average* level of inventory throughout the year rather than the ending balance to calculate this ratio.

The resulting turnover of 13.85 indicates that the firm basically sells out its inventory 13.85 times each year, or slightly more than once each month. This value is most meaningful when compared with that of other firms in the same industry or with the firm's past inventory turnover. An inventory turnover of 20.0 is not unusual for a grocery store, whereas a common inventory turnover for an aircraft manufacturer is 4.0. GPC's inventory turnover is in line with that for other oil and gas companies, and slightly above the firm's own historic norms.

We can easily convert inventory turnover into an **average age of inventory** by dividing the turnover figure into 365 (the number of days in a year). For GPC, the average age of inventory is 26.4 days (365 ÷ 13.85). This result means that GPC's inventory balance turns over about every 26 days.

APPLYING THE MODEL 2.2

Inventory ratios, like most other financial ratios, vary a great deal from one industry to another. For example, on September 30, 2005, Intel Corp. reported inventory of $2.82 billion and cost of goods sold of $16.10 billion for the four quarters ended September 30, 2005. This implies an inventory turnover ratio for Intel of about 5.7, and an average age of inventory of about 64 days. With the rapid pace of technological change in the semiconductor industry, Intel cannot afford to hold inventory too long.

In contrast, for the four quarters ending September 30, 2005, Cruzan International, Inc., a publicly traded producer and marketer of rum, brandy, wine, and spirits, reported cost of goods sold of $71.8 million and inventory of $31.3 million. Cruzan's inventory turnover ratio is thus 2.29 and its average age of inventory about 159 days.

Clearly, the differences in these inventory ratios reflect differences in the economic circumstances of the industries. Whereas the value of semiconductors declines as they age, just the opposite occurs in the rum, brandy, wine, and spirit business, at least up to a point.

The **average collection period,** or *average age of accounts receivable,* is useful in evaluating credit and collection policies.[11] To compute this measure, we divide the firm's

---

[11.] The average collection period is sometimes called the *days' sales outstanding (DSO).* As with the inventory turnover ratio, the average collection period can be calculated using end-of-year accounts receivable or the average receivables balance for the year. We discuss the evaluation and establishment of credit and collection policies in Chapter 22.

average daily sales into the accounts receivable balance. As shown below, on average, it takes GPC 46.0 days to receive payment from a credit sale.

$$\text{Average daily sales} = \frac{\text{annual sales}}{365} = \frac{\$12,843}{365} = \$35.19$$

$$\text{Average collection period} = \frac{\text{accounts receivable}}{\text{average daily sales}} = \frac{\$1,619}{\$35.19} = 46.0 \text{ days}$$

The average collection period is meaningful only in relation to the firm's credit terms. If GPC extends 30-day credit terms to customers, an average collection period of 46.0 days may indicate a poorly managed credit or collection department, or both. Or, the longer collection period could be the result of an intentional relaxation of credit-term enforcement in response to competitive pressures. If the firm had offered customers 45-day credit terms, the 46.0-day average collection period would be quite acceptable. Clearly, one would need additional information to evaluate the effectiveness of the firm's credit and collection policies.

Firms use the **average payment period** to evaluate their payment performance. It measures the average length of time it takes a firm to pay its suppliers. The average payment period equals the firm's average daily purchases divided into the accounts payable balance.

To calculate average daily purchases, an analyst may have to estimate the firm's annual purchases, often by taking a specified percentage of cost of goods sold. This estimate is necessary because annual purchases are not reported on a firm's published financial statements. Instead, they are embodied in its cost of goods sold. GPC's annual purchases in 2007 were estimated at 80 percent of cost of goods sold, as shown in footnote *a* to its income statement in Table 2.2.

Using the annual purchase estimate of $6,815, GPC's average payment period in 2007 indicates that the firm usually takes 90.9 days to pay its bills.

$$\text{Average daily purchases} = \frac{\text{annual purchases}}{365} = \frac{\$6,815}{365} = \$18.67$$

$$\text{Average payment period} = \frac{\text{accounts payable}}{\text{average daily purchases}} = \frac{\$1,697}{\$18.67} = 90.9 \text{ days}$$

Like the average collection period, the average payment period is meaningful only in light of the actual credit terms the firm's suppliers offer. If GPC's suppliers, on average, extend 60-day credit terms, the firm's average payment period of 90.9 days indicates that the firm is generally slow in paying its bills. Paying suppliers 30 days later than they expect could damage the firm's ability to obtain additional credit and could raise the cost of any credit that it may obtain.

On the other hand, if suppliers grant GPC average credit terms of 90 days, its 90.9-day average payment period would be very good. Clearly, an analyst would need further information to draw definitive conclusions about the firm's overall payment policies from the average payment period measure.

The **fixed asset turnover** measures the efficiency with which a firm uses its *fixed assets*. The ratio tells analysts how many dollars of sales the firm generates per dollar of investment in fixed assets. The ratio equals sales divided by net fixed assets:

$$\text{Fixed asset turnover} = \frac{\text{sales}}{\text{net fixed assets}} = \frac{\$12,843}{\$6,710} = 1.91$$

GPC's fixed asset turnover in 2007 is 1.91. This means that the company turns over its net fixed assets 1.91 times a year. Stated another way, GPC generates almost $2 in sales for every dollar of fixed assets. As with other ratios, the "normal" level of fixed asset turnover varies widely from one industry to another.

When using this ratio and the total asset turnover ratio (described next), an analyst must be aware that the calculations use the *historical costs* of fixed assets. Because some firms have significantly newer or older assets than do others, comparing fixed asset turnovers of those firms can be misleading. Firms with newer assets tend to have lower turnovers than those with older assets, which have lower book (accounting) values. A naive comparison of fixed asset turnover ratios for different firms may lead an analyst to conclude that one firm operates more efficiently than another, when in fact the firm that appears to be more efficient simply has older (i.e., more fully depreciated) assets on its books.

The **total asset turnover** ratio indicates the efficiency with which a firm uses *all its assets* to generate sales. Like the fixed asset turnover ratio, total asset turnover indicates how many dollars of sales a firm generates per dollar of asset investment. All other factors being equal, analysts favor a high turnover ratio: it indicates that a firm generates more sales (and ideally more cash flow for investors) from a given investment in assets.

GPC's total asset turnover in 2007 equals 1.34, calculated as follows:

$$\text{Total asset turnover} = \frac{\text{sales}}{\text{total assets}} = \frac{\$12,843}{\$9,589} = 1.34$$

DEBT RATIOS

Firms finance their assets from two broad sources, equity and debt. Equity comes from stockholders; debt comes in many forms and from many different lenders. Firms borrow from suppliers, from banks, and from widely scattered investors who buy publicly traded bonds. *Debt ratios* measure the extent to which a firm uses money from creditors rather than stockholders to finance its operations. Because creditors' claims must be satisfied before firms can distribute earnings to stockholders, current and prospective investors pay close attention to the debt on the balance sheet. Lenders share these concerns. The more indebted the firm, the higher the probability that it will be unable to satisfy the claims of all its creditors.

Fixed-cost sources of financing, such as debt and preferred stock, create **financial leverage** that magnifies both the risk and the expected return on the firm's securities.[12] In general, the more debt a firm uses in relation to its total assets, the greater its financial leverage. That is, the more a firm borrows, the riskier its outstanding stock and bonds, and the higher the return that investors require on those securities. In Chapters 12 and 13 we discuss in detail the effect of debt on the firm's risk, return, and value. Here, we focus on the use of debt ratios to assess a firm's indebtedness and its ability to meet the fixed payments associated with debt.

Broadly speaking, there are two types of debt ratios. One type focuses on *balance sheet* measures of outstanding debt relative to other sources of financing. The other type, known as **coverage ratios,** focuses more on *income statement* measures of the firm's ability to generate sufficient cash flow to make scheduled interest and principal

---

[12.] By *fixed cost* we mean that the cost of this financing source does not vary over time in response to changes in the firm's revenue and cash flow. For example, when a firm borrows money at a variable rate, the interest cost of that loan is *not* fixed through time, but the firm's *obligation* to make interest payments is "fixed" regardless of the level of the firm's revenue and cash flow.

payments. Investors and credit-rating agencies use both types of ratios to assess a firm's creditworthiness.

The **debt ratio** measures the proportion of total assets financed by the firm's creditors. The higher this ratio, the greater is the firm's reliance on borrowed money to finance its activities. The ratio equals total liabilities divided by total assets. GPC's debt ratio in 2007 is 0.551, or 55.1 percent:

$$\text{Debt ratio} = \frac{\text{total liabilities}}{\text{total assets}} = \frac{\$5,281}{\$9,589} = 0.551 = 55.1\%$$

This figure indicates that the company has financed more than half of its assets with debt.

A close cousin of the debt ratio is the **assets-to-equity (A/E) ratio,** sometimes called the **equity multiplier:**

$$\text{Assets-to-equity ratio} = \frac{\text{total assets}}{\text{common stock equity}} = \frac{\$9,589}{\$4,278} = 2.24$$

This is calculated as total assets divided by common stock equity. Note that the denominator of this ratio uses only common stock equity of $4,278 ($4,308 of total equity − $30 of preferred stock equity). The resulting value indicates that GPC's assets in 2007 are 2.24 times greater than its equity. This value seems reasonable given that the debt ratio indicates slightly more than half (55.1%) of GPC's assets in 2007 are financed with debt. The high equity multiplier indicates high debt and low equity, while a low equity multiplier indicates low debt and high equity.

An alternative measure of the firm's leverage, which focuses solely on the firm's long-term debt, is the **debt-to-equity ratio.** It is calculated as long-term debt divided by stockholders' equity. The 2007 value of this ratio for GPC is as follows:

$$\text{Debt-to-equity ratio} = \frac{\text{long-term debt}}{\text{stockholders' equity}} = \frac{\$1,760}{\$4,308} = 0.409 = 40.9\%$$

GPC's long-term debts are therefore only 40.9 percent as large as its stockholders' equity.

A word of caution: Both the debt ratio and the debt-to-equity ratio use book values of debt, equity, and assets. Analysts should be aware that the *market values* of these variables may differ substantially from book values.

The **times interest earned ratio** measures the firm's ability to make contractual interest payments. It equals earnings before interest and taxes divided by interest expense. A higher ratio indicates a greater capacity to meet scheduled payments. The times interest earned ratio for GPC in 2007 equals 13.59, indicating that the firm could experience a substantial decline in earnings and still meet its interest obligations:

$$\text{Times interest earned} = \frac{\text{earnings before interest and taxes}}{\text{interest expense}} = \frac{\$1,671}{\$123} = 13.59$$

PROFITABILITY RATIOS

Several measures of profitability relate a firm's earnings to its sales, assets, or equity. *Profitability ratios* are among the most closely watched and widely quoted financial ratios. Many firms link employee bonuses to profitability ratios, and stock prices react sharply to unexpected changes in these measures.

The **gross profit margin** measures the percentage of each sales dollar remaining after the firm has paid for its goods. The higher the gross profit margin, the better. GPC's gross profit margin in 2007 was 33.7 percent:

$$\text{Gross profit margin} = \frac{\text{gross profit}}{\text{sales}} = \frac{\$4,324}{\$12,843} = 0.337 = 33.7\%$$

The **operating profit margin** measures the percentage of each sales dollar remaining after deducting all costs and expenses *other than* interest and taxes. As with the gross profit margin, the higher the operating profit margin, the better. This ratio tells analysts what a firm's bottom line looks like before deductions for payments to creditors and tax authorities. GPC's operating profit margin in 2007 is 11.9 percent:

$$\text{Operating profit margin} = \frac{\text{operating profit}}{\text{sales}} = \frac{\$1,531}{\$12,843} = 0.119 = 11.9\%$$

The **net profit margin** measures the percentage of each sales dollar remaining after deducting all costs and expenses, *including* interest, taxes, and preferred stock dividends. GPC's net profit margin of 7.4 percent in 2007 is calculated as follows:[13]

$$\text{Net profit margin} = \frac{\text{earnings available for common stockholders}}{\text{sales}}$$

$$= \frac{\$946}{\$12,843} = 0.074 = 7.4\%$$

For the quarter ending in September 2005, Microsoft reported a net profit margin of 32.2 percent, more than 10 times larger than the 3.1 percent net profit margin reported by Wal-Mart one month later. This example shows how net profit margins vary widely across industries.

Probably the most closely watched financial ratio of them all is *earnings per share* (*EPS*). The earnings per share measure represents the number of dollars earned on behalf of each outstanding share of common stock. The investing public closely watches *EPS* figures and considers them an important indicator of corporate success. Many firms tie management bonuses to specific *EPS* targets. Earnings per share are calculated as follows:

$$\text{Earnings per share} = \frac{\text{earnings available for common stockholders}}{\text{number of shares of common stock outstanding}}$$

$$= \frac{\$946}{178.7} = \$5.29$$

The value of GPC's earnings per share in 2007 is $5.29.[14] This figure represents the dollar amount *earned* on behalf of each share of common stock outstanding. Note

SMART ETHICS VIDEO

Frank Popoff, Chairman of the Board (retired), Dow Chemical
"Overstating or understating the performance of the enterprise is anathema . . . it's just not done."

See the entire interview at
SMARTFinance

[13.] Some analysts calculate (1) the net profit margin by excluding the financing costs associated with debt and (2) preferred stock dividends by using in the numerator *NOPAT* rather than earnings available for common stockholders. Applying this formula results in a measure of after-tax operating profits. Here we use the more comprehensive measure of overall profits on sales.

[14.] We state all per-share values strictly in dollars and cents, as do company reports. Per-share values are not stated in millions, as are the dollar values used to calculate these and other ratios.

that *EPS* is not the same as dividends. The amount of earnings actually *distributed* to each shareholder is the *dividend per share,* which as noted in GPC's income statement (Table 2.2), rose to $1.93 in 2007 from $1.76 in 2006.

The **return on total assets (*ROA*)**, often called the *return on investment (ROI)*, measures management's overall effectiveness in using the firm's assets to generate returns to common stockholders.[15] The return on total assets for GPC in 2007 equals 9.9 percent:[16]

$$\text{Return on total assets} = \frac{\text{earnings available for common stockholders}}{\text{total assets}}$$

$$= \frac{\$946}{\$9,589} = 0.099 = 9.9\%$$

A closely related measure of profitability is the **return on common equity (*ROE*),** which captures the return earned on the common stockholders' (owners') investment in the firm. For a firm that uses only common stock to finance its operations, the *ROE* and *ROA* figures will be identical. With debt or preferred stock on the balance sheet, these ratios will usually differ. When the firm earns a profit, even after making interest payments to creditors and paying dividends to preferred stockholders, then the firm's use of leverage magnifies the return earned by common stockholders, and *ROE* will exceed *ROA*. Conversely, if the firm's earnings fall short of the amount it must pay to lenders and preferred stockholders, then leverage causes *ROE* to be less than *ROA*. For GPC, the return on common equity for 2007 is 22.1 percent, substantially above GPC's return on total assets:

$$\text{Return on common equity} = \frac{\text{earnings available for common stockholders}}{\text{common stock equity}}$$

$$= \frac{\$946}{\$4,278} = 0.221 = 22.1\%$$

DuPont System of Analysis Financial analysts sometimes conduct a deeper analysis of the *ROA* and *ROE* ratios using the **DuPont system.** This approach uses both income statement and balance sheet information to break the *ROA* and *ROE* ratios into component pieces. It highlights the influence of the net profit margin, total asset turnover, and financial leverage on a firm's profitability. In the DuPont system, the return on total assets equals the product of the net profit margin and total asset turnover:

$$ROA = \text{net profit margin} \times \text{total asset turnover}$$

By definition, the net profit margin equals earnings available for common stockholders divided by sales, and total asset turnover equals sales divided by total assets.

---

[15] Naturally, all other things being equal, firms prefer a high *ROA*. However, as we will see later, analysts must be cautious when interpreting financial ratios. We recall an old Dilbert comic strip in which Wally suggests boosting his firm's *ROA* by firing the security staff. The reduction in expenses would boost the numerator while the reduction in security would lower the denominator.

[16] Some analysts prefer to use in the numerator *NOPAT* rather than *earnings available for common stockholders,* to more clearly focus the ratio on the productivity of assets without regard to their cost of financing. Here we use the more general formula for *ROA*.

When we multiply these two ratios together, the sales figure cancels, resulting in the familiar *ROA* measure:

$$ROA = \frac{\text{earnings available for common stockholders}}{\text{sales}} \times \frac{\text{sales}}{\text{total assets}}$$

$$= \frac{\$946}{\$12,843} \times \frac{\$12,843}{\$9,589} = 0.074 \times 1.34 = 0.099 = 9.9\%$$

$$ROA = \frac{\text{earnings available for common stockholders}}{\text{total assets}} = \frac{\$946}{\$9,589} = 0.099 = 9.9\%$$

Naturally, the *ROA* value for GPC in 2007 obtained using the DuPont system is the same value we calculated before. Now, though, seeing its two component parts, we can think of the *ROA* as a product of how much profit the firm earns on each dollar of sales and of the efficiency with which the firm uses its assets to generate sales. Holding the net profit margin constant, an increase in total asset turnover increases the firm's *ROA*. Similarly, holding total asset turnover constant, an increase in the net profit margin increases *ROA*.

We can push the DuPont system one step further by multiplying the *ROA* times the *assets-to-equity (A/E) ratio*, or the *equity multiplier*. The product of these two ratios equals the return on common equity. For a firm that uses no debt and has no preferred stock, the ratio of assets to equity equals 1.0, so the *ROA* equals the *ROE*. For all other firms, the ratio of assets to equity exceeds 1. It is in this sense that the ratio of assets to equity represents a leverage multiplier.

$$ROE = ROA \times A/E$$

We can apply this version of the DuPont system to GPC to recalculate its return on common equity in 2007:

$$ROE = \frac{\text{earnings available for common stockholders}}{\text{total assets}} \times \frac{\text{total assets}}{\text{common stock equity}}$$

$$= \frac{\$946}{\$9,589} \times \frac{\$9,589}{\$4,278} = 0.099 \times 2.24 = 0.221 = 22.1\%$$

$$ROE = \frac{\text{earnings available for common stockholders}}{\text{common stock equity}} = \frac{\$946}{\$4,278}$$

$$= 0.221 = 22.1\%$$

SMART CONCEPTS
See the concept explained step-by-step at
SMARTFinance

Notice that for GPC, the ratio of assets to equity is 2.24. This means that GPC's return on common equity is more than twice as large as its return on total assets. Of course, using financial leverage has its risks. Notice what would happen if GPC's return on total assets were a negative number rather than a positive one: The financial leverage multiplier would cause GPC's return on common equity to be even more negative than its *ROA*.

The advantage of the DuPont system is that it allows the firm to break its return on common equity into three components tied to the financial statements: (1) a profit-on-sales component (net profit margin) that ties directly to the income statement, (2) an efficiency-of-asset-use component (total asset turnover) that ties directly to the balance sheet, and (3) a financial-leverage-use component (assets-to-equity ratio) that also ties directly to the balance sheet. Analysts can then study the effect of each of these factors on the overall return to common stockholders, as demonstrated in the following Applying the Model.[17]

APPLYING THE MODEL 2.3

The 2007 ratio values for the *ROE, ROA,* assets-to-equity ratio, total asset turnover, and net profit margin calculated earlier for GPC are shown below, along with the 2007 industry averages for globally active oil companies.

Ratio	GPC	Industry Average
Return on common equity (*ROE*)	22.1%	19.7%
Return on total assets (*ROA*)	9.9%	12.1%
Assets-to-equity (A/E) ratio	2.24	1.63
Total asset turnover	1.34	1.42
Net profit margin	7.4%	8.5%

We begin the analysis of GPC's 2007 performance with its return on common equity of 22.1 percent, which is noticeably above the industry average of 19.7 percent. To learn why GPC's *ROE* outperformed the industry, we look at two components of *ROE: ROA* and the assets-to-equity (A/E) ratio. We see that GPC's *ROA* of 9.9 percent was well below the industry average of 12.1 percent. But because of GPC's greater use of leverage—an A/E ratio of 2.24 for GPC versus 1.63 for the industry—GPC was able to generate a higher ROE than the average firm.

Looking further at the two components of *ROA* (the net profit margin and the total asset turnover), we see that GPC's total asset turnover of 1.34 is very close to the industry average of 1.42. However, its net profit margin of 7.4 percent is below the industry average of 8.6 percent, which caused GPC's *ROA* to be below the industry average. Clearly, GPC was unable to manage its costs and generate profit on sales comparable to its competitors.

Summarizing, GPC compensated for its below-average *ROA* by using significantly more leverage than its competitors. Clearly, GPC took greater risk to compensate for low profits on sales. The firm should focus on its income statement to improve its profitability and may want to reduce its leverage to moderate its risk. It appears that GPC has problems in both its income statement (net profit margin) and its balance sheet (assets-to-equity ratio).

[17.] Keep in mind that the ratios in the DuPont system are interdependent and that the equation is just a mathematical identity. It is easy to draw questionable conclusions about lines of causality using the DuPont system. For example, consider this farcical version of the formula:

$$ROE = \frac{\text{earnings available for common stockholders}}{\text{sales}} \times \frac{\text{sales}}{\text{assets}} \times \frac{\text{assets}}{\text{CEO age}} \times \frac{\text{CEO age}}{\text{common stock equity}}$$

In this equation, we might interpret the third term on the right as the efficiency with which a CEO of a given age manages the firm's assets. If a younger CEO manages the same quantity of assets, this ratio would increase, and holding all other factors constant, we could say that the firm's *ROE* would increase. This is clearly silly, but mathematically this expression ultimately gives you the firm's *ROE*.

MARKET RATIOS

Market ratios relate the firm's market value, as measured by its current share price, to certain accounting values. These ratios provide insight into how investors think the firm is performing. They reflect the common stockholders' assessment of the firm's past and expected future performance. Here we consider two popular market ratios, one that focuses on earnings and the other that considers book value.

The **price/earnings (P/E) ratio** measures the amount investors are willing to pay for each dollar of the firm's earnings. Investors often use the P/E ratio, the most widely quoted market ratio, as a barometer of a firm's long-term growth prospects and of investor confidence in the firm's future performance. A high P/E ratio indicates investors' belief that a firm will achieve rapid earnings growth in the future; hence, companies with high P/E ratios are referred to as *growth stocks*. Simply stated, investors who believe that future earnings are going to be higher than current earnings are willing to pay a lot for today's earnings, and vice versa.

Using the per-share price of $76.25 for Global Petroleum Corporation on December 31, 2007, and its 2007 *EPS* of $5.29, the P/E ratio at year-end 2007 is:

$$\text{Price/earnings (P/E) ratio} = \frac{\text{market price per share of common stock}}{\text{earnings per share}} = \frac{\$76.25}{\$5.29}$$

$$= 14.41$$

This figure indicates that investors were paying $14.41 for each $1.00 of GPC's earnings. GPC's price/earnings ratio one year before (on December 31, 2006) had been almost twice as high at 28.37 ($71.50 per share stock price ÷ $2.52 earnings per share).

The **market/book (M/B) ratio** provides another assessment of how investors view the firm's performance. It relates the market value of the firm's shares to their book value. The stocks of firms that investors expect to perform well in the future—improving profits, growing market share, launching successful products, and so forth—typically sell at higher M/B ratios than those firms with less attractive prospects. Firms that investors expect to earn high returns relative to their risk typically sell at higher M/B multiples than those expected to earn low returns relative to risk.

To calculate the M/B ratio for GPC in 2007, we first need to find *book value per share* of common stock:

$$\text{Book value per share} = \frac{\text{common stock equity}}{\text{number of shares of common stock outstanding}}$$

$$= \frac{\$4,278}{178.7} = \$23.94$$

We then compute the M/B ratio by dividing the book value into the current price of the firm's stock:

$$\text{Market/book (M/B) ratio} = \frac{\text{market value per share of common stock}}{\text{book value per share of common stock}}$$

$$= \frac{\$76.25}{\$23.94} = 3.19$$

SMART IDEAS VIDEO

Michael Brennan, UCLA
"In no markets is the role of information more important than it is in financial markets."

See the entire interview at
SMARTFinance

Investors are currently paying $3.19 for each $1.00 of book value of GPC's stock. Clearly, investors expect GPC to continue to grow in the future: they are willing to pay more than book value for the firm's shares.

7. Which of the categories and individual ratios described in this chapter would be of greatest interest to each of the following parties?

    a. Existing and prospective creditors (lenders)

    b. Existing and prospective shareholders

    c. The firm's management

8. How could analysts use the availability of cash inflow and cash outflow data to improve on the accuracy of the liquidity and debt coverage ratios presented previously? What specific ratio measures would you calculate to assess the firm's liquidity and debt coverage, using cash flow rather than financial statement data?

9. Assume that a firm's total assets and sales remain constant. Would an increase in each of the ratios below be associated with a cash inflow or a cash outflow?

    a. Current ratio   **d.** Average payment period

    b. Inventory turnover   **e.** Debt ratio

    c. Average collection period   **f.** Net profit margin

10. Use the DuPont system to explain why a slower-than-average inventory turnover could cause a firm with an above-average net profit margin and an average degree of financial leverage to have a below-average return on common equity.

11. How can you reconcile investor expectations for a firm with an above-average M/B ratio and a below-average P/E ratio? Could the age of the firm have any effect on this ratio comparison?

2.4 SUMMARY

- The four key financial statements are (1) the balance sheet, (2) the income statement, (3) the statement of retained earnings, and (4) the statement of cash flows. Companies typically include with these statements detailed notes describing the technical aspects of the financial statements.
- A firm's total cash flows can be conveniently divided into (1) operating flows, (2) investment flows, and (3) financing flows. Operating cash flow (*OCF*) measures the amount of cash flow the firms generates from its operations. It is calculated by adding any noncash charges (the main one being depreciation) to the firm's net operating profits after taxes (*NOPAT*). *NOPAT* equals earnings before interest and taxes (*EBIT*) multiplied by 1 minus the tax rate.
- More important to financial analysts is free cash flow (*FCF*), the amount of cash flow available to investors. Free cash flow equals operating cash flow less the firm's net investments in fixed and current assets.
- The statement of cash flows summarizes the firm's cash flows over a specified period of time, typically one year. It presents operating, investment, and financing cash flows. When interpreting the statement, an analyst typically looks for

unusual change in either the major categories of cash flow or in specific items to find clues to problems that the firm may be experiencing.

- Financial ratios are a convenient tool for analyzing the firm's financial statements to assess its performance over the given period. Analysts use various financial ratios to assess a firm's liquidity, activity, debt, profitability, and market value. The DuPont system uses both income statement and balance sheet data to assess a firm's profitability, particularly the returns earned on both the total asset investment and the owners' common stock equity in the firm.

INTERNET RESOURCES

Note: *This textbook includes numerous Internet links throughout the text, both within the discussions and at the end of each chapter. Because some links will likely change or be eliminated during the life of this edition, please go to this book's website (http://smart.swcollege.com) to obtain updated links in the event you encounter a dead link.*

http://www.sec.gov — SEC site containing the document search and retrieval engine, EDGAR; useful for obtaining up-to-date financial statements for publicly traded U.S. firms

http://www.quicken.com — Offers a fairly extensive ratio analysis of a given company; simply type in a ticker symbol

http://www.yahoo.com — Contains a link to Yahoo! Finance for retrieval of recent financial statements and a wide variety of other financial information for any listed U.S. firm and many foreign firms

Use the learning tools at http://smartfinance.swlearning.com

KEY TERMS

accrual-based approach	financial leverage
activity ratios	financing flows
assets-to-equity (A/E) ratio	fixed asset turnover
average age of inventory	free cash flow (*FCF*)
average collection period	gross profit margin
average payment period	inventory turnover
cash flow approach	investment flows
cash flow from operations	liquidity ratios
common stock	long-term debt
common-size income statement	market/book (M/B) ratio
coverage ratio	net operating profits after taxes (*NOPAT*)
current ratio	net profit margin
debt ratio	net working capital
debt-to-equity ratio	noncash charges
deferred taxes	operating cash flow (*OCF*)
dividend payout ratio	operating flows
dividend per share (*DPS*)	operating profit margin
DuPont system	paid-in-capital
earnings available for common stockholders	par value
earnings per share (*EPS*)	preferred stock
equity multiplier	price/earnings (P/E) ratio

quick (acid-test) ratio   return on total assets (*ROA*)
ratio analysis   times interest earned ratio
retained earnings   total asset turnover
return on common equity (*ROE*)   treasury stock

QUESTIONS

2-1. What information (explicit and implicit) can be derived from financial statement analysis? Does the standardization required by GAAP add greater validity to comparisons of financial data between companies and industries?

2-2. What role does the Sarbanes-Oxley Act of 2002 (SOX) play in financial reporting? Are there possible shortcomings to relying solely on financial statement analysis to value companies?

2-3. Distinguish between the types of financial information contained in the various financial statements. Which statements provide information on a company's performance over a reporting period? Which present data on a company's current position? What sorts of valuable information may be found in the notes to financial statements? Describe a situation in which the information in the notes would be essential to making an informed decision about the value of a corporation.

2-4. If you were a commercial credit analyst charged with the responsibility of making an accept/reject decision on a company's loan request, with which financial statement would you be most concerned? Which financial statement is most likely to provide pertinent information about a company's ability to repay its debt?

2-5. Suppose someone were to define operating cash flow as net income plus depreciation plus interest expense*(1 − tax rate). Is this definition equal to the definition of operating cash flow in this text (assuming the firm pays interest on debt)? If not, reduce the difference between the two definitions to a simple calculation. (*Hint:* Consider the tax advantages of debt.) Further, are the two definitions the same if the firm is composed entirely of equity (i.e., there is no debt, which means there is no interest expense)?

2-6. Suppose a supplier allows payment for inventory 30 days from delivery and the firm is able to sell all of the inventory within 15 days of delivery. How does this affect free cash flow?

2-7. Firm Q has a low times interest earned ratio relative to industry. However, corporate officers indicate that the ratio is low because Firm Q depreciates assets faster than the industry norm. Is this a credible reason? Would viewing the firm's gross profit margin be revealing in this situation?

2-8. You have determined that for Firm X, {$\Delta CA - \Delta A/P - \Delta accruals$} is negative. Does this affect the firm's operating cash flow and free cash flow positively, negatively, or not at all?

2-9. Suppose a firm has very volatile sales and consequently does not finance with much debt. Relatively speaking (i.e., you expect a ratio to be high or low), what does this mean in regard to the times interest earned ratio, the debt-to-equity ratio, and the equity multiplier?

2-10. How is the DuPont system useful in analyzing a firm's *ROA* and *ROE?* What information can analysts infer by breaking *ROE* into contributing ratios? What is the mathematical relationship between each of the individual components (net profit margin, total asset turnover, and assets-to-equity ratio) and *ROE?* Can *ROE* be raised without affecting *ROA?* How?

PROBLEMS

Financial Statements

2-1.   Use the financial statements below to answer the questions about S&M Manufacturing's financial position at the end of the calendar year 2007.

S&M Manufacturing, Inc.
Balance Sheet at December 31, 2007 ($000)

Assets		Liabilities and Equity	
Current assets		Current liabilities	
Cash	$ 140,000	Accounts payable	$ 480,000
Marketable securities	260,000	Notes payable	500,000
Accounts receivable	650,000	Accruals	80,000
Inventories	800,000	Total current	$1,060,000
Total current assets	$1,850,000	liabilities	
Fixed assets		Long-term debt	
Gross fixed assets	$3,780,000	Bonds outstanding	$1,300,000
Less: Accumulated	1,220,000	Bank debt (long-term)	260,000
depreciation		Total long-term debt	$1,560,000
Net fixed assets	$2,560,000	Stockholders' equity	
Total assets	$4,410,000	Preferred stock	$ 180,000
		Common stock (at par)	200,000
		Paid-in capital	810,000
		in excess of par	
		Retained earnings	600,000
		Total stockholders' equity	$1,790,000
		Total liabilities and equity	$4,410,000

S&M Manufacturing, Inc.
Income Statement for Year Ended December 31, 2007 ($000)

Sales revenue		$6,900,000
Less: Cost of goods sold		4,200,000
Gross profits		$2,700,000
Less: Operating expenses		
Sales expense	$ 750,000	
General and administrative expense	1,150,000	
Leasing expense	210,000	
Depreciation expense	235,000	
Total operating expenses		2,345,000
Earnings before interest and taxes		$ 355,000
Less: Interest expense		85,000
Net profit before taxes		$ 270,000
Less: Taxes		81,000
Net profits after taxes		$ 189,000
Less: Preferred stock dividends		10,800
Earnings available for common stockholders		$ 178,200
Less: Dividends		75,000
To retained earnings		$ 103,200
Per share data		
Earnings per share (EPS)	$1.43	
Dividends per share (DPS)	$0.60	
Price per share	$15.85	

a. How much cash and near cash does S&M have at year-end 2007?

b. What was the original cost of all of the firm's real property that is currently owned?

c. How much in total liabilities did the firm have at year-end 2007?

d. How much did S&M owe for credit purchases at year-end 2007?

e. How much did the firm sell during 2007?

f. How much equity did the common stockholders have in the firm at year-end 2007?

g. What is the cumulative total of earnings reinvested in the firm from its inception through the end of 2007?

h. How much operating profit did the firm earn during 2007?

i. What is the total amount of dividends paid out by the firm during the year 2007?

j. How many shares of common stock did S&M have outstanding at year-end 2007?

2-2. Obtain financial statements for Microsoft for the last five years either from its website (http://www.microsoft.com) or from the SEC's online EDGAR site (http://www .sec.gov/edgar/searchedgar/webusers.htm). First, look at the statements without reading the notes. Then, read the notes carefully, concentrating on those regarding executive stock options. Do you have a different perspective after analyzing these notes?

Cash Flow Analysis

2-3. Given the balance sheets and selected data from the income statement of SMG Industries that follow, answer parts (a)–(d).

a. Calculate the firm's *net operating profits after taxes* (*NOPAT*) for the year ended December 31, 2007, using Equation 2.1.

b. Calculate the firm's *operating cash flow* (*OCF*) for the year ended December 31, 2007, using Equation 2.2.

c. Calculate the firm's *free cash flow* (*FCF*) for the year ended December 31, 2007, using Equation 2.4.

d. Interpret, compare, and contrast your cash flow estimates in parts (b) and (c).

SMG Industries Balance Sheets ($ in millions)

	December 31	
Assets	**2007**	**2006**
Cash	$ 3,500	$ 3,000
Marketable securities	3,800	3,200
Accounts receivable	4,000	3,800
Inventories	4,900	4,800
Total current assets	$16,200	$14,800
Gross fixed assets	$31,500	$30,100
Less: Accumulated depreciation	14,700	13,100
Net fixed assets	$16,800	$17,000
Total assets	$33,000	$31,800
Liabilities and Stockholders' Equity		
Accounts payable	$ 3,600	$ 3,500
Notes payable	4,800	4,200
Accruals	1,200	1,300
Total current liabilities	$ 9,600	$ 9,000
Long-term debt	$ 6,000	$ 6,000
Common stock	$11,000	$11,000
Retained earnings	6,400	5,800
Total stockholders' equity	$17,400	$16,800
Total liabilities and stockholders' equity	$33,000	$31,800

Income Statement Data (2007, $ in millions)

Depreciation expense	$1,600
Earnings before interest and taxes (EBIT)	4,500
Taxes	1,300
Net profits after taxes	2,400

2-4. Classify each of the following items as an inflow (I) or an outflow (O) of cash, or as neither (N).

Item	Change ($)	Item	Change ($)
Cash	+600	Accounts receivable	−900
Accounts payable	−1,200	Net profits	+700
Notes payable	+800	Depreciation	+200
Long-term debt	−2,500	Repurchase of stock	+500
Inventory	+400	Cash dividends	+300
Fixed assets	+600	Sale of stock	+1,300

Analyzing Financial Performance Using Ratio Analysis

2-5. A *common-size income statement* for Aluminum Industries' 2006 operations follows. Using the firm's 2007 income statement presented in Problem 2-12, develop the 2007 common-size income statement (see footnote 2), and compare it with the 2006 statement. Which areas require further analysis and investigation?

Aluminum Industries, Inc. Common-Size Income Statement for the Year Ended December 31, 2006

Sales revenue ($35,000,000)		100.0%
Less: Cost of goods sold		65.9
Gross profit		34.1%
Less: Operating expenses		
Selling expense	12.7%	
General and administrative expenses	6.3	
Lease expense	0.6	
Depreciation expense	3.6	
Total operating expense		23.2
Operating profit		10.9%
Less: Interest expense		1.5
Net profit before taxes		9.4%
Less: Taxes (rate = 40%)		3.8
Net profits after taxes		5.6%

2-6. Assume current liabilities are $10,000.00, the current ratio is 2.0, and the quick ratio is 1.0. How much does the firm have in inventory and how much does the firm have in current assets?

2-7. Suppose a firm's inventory turnover is 4.5 annually and its average collection period is 90 days. Assuming a 365-day year, how many days (on average) is it between receiving inventory and collecting payment from selling the inventory?

2-8. A firm's return on assets is 6% and its return on equity is 9%. What is the firm's debt ratio?

2-9. A firm has earnings available for common stockholders of $15 million with an asset base of $1.25 billion and with equity of $75 million. Assuming equity does not change, how is the firm's return on assets and return on equity affected should the asset base be reduced to $1 billion? Demonstrate by calculating *ROA* and *ROE* before and after the asset base reduction.

2-10. The partially complete 2007 balance sheet and income statement for Challenge Industries are given on the following page, followed by selected ratio values for the firm based on its completed 2007 financial statements. Use the ratios along with the partial statements to complete the financial statements. *Hint:* Use the ratios in the order listed to calculate the missing statement values that need to be installed in the partial statements.

Challenge Industries, Inc.
Balance Sheet at December 31, 2007 ($ in thousands)

Assets		Liabilities and Equity	
Current assets		Current liabilities	
Cash	$ 52,000	Accounts payable	$150,000
Marketable securities	60,000	Notes payable	?
Accounts receivable	200,000	Accruals	80,000
Inventories	?	Total current liabilities	?
Total current assets	?	Long-term debt	$425,000
Fixed assets (gross)	?	Total liabilities	?
Less: Accumulated depreciation	240,000	Stockholders' equity	
		Preferred stock	?
Net fixed assets	?	Common stock (at par)	150,000
Total assets	?	Paid-in capital in excess of par	?
		Retained earnings	390,000
		Total stockholders' equity	?
		Total liabilities and stockholders' equity	?

Challenge Industries, Inc.
Income Statement for the Year Ended December 31, 2007 ($ in thousands)

Sales revenue		$4,800,000
Loss: Cost of goods sold		?
Gross profits		?
Less: Operating expenses		
Sales expense	$690,000	
General and administrative expense	750,000	
Depreciation expense	120,000	
Total operating expenses		1,560,000
Earnings before interest and taxes		?
Less: Interest expense		35,000
Earnings before taxes		?
Less: Taxes		?
Net income (Net profits after taxes)		?
Less: Preferred dividends		15,000
Earnings available for common stockholders		?
Less: Dividends		60,000
To retained earnings		?

Challenge Industries, Inc.
Ratios for the Year Ended December 31, 2007

Ratio	Value
Total asset turnover	2.00
Gross profit margin	40%
Inventory turnover	10
Current ratio	1.60
Net profit margin	3.75%
Return on common equity	12.5%

2-11. Manufacturers Bank is evaluating Aluminum Industries, Inc., which has requested a $3 million loan, to assess the firm's financial leverage and risk. On the basis of the debt ratios for Aluminum, along with the industry averages and Aluminum's recent financial statements (which follow), evaluate and recommend appropriate action on the loan request.

Aluminum Industries, Inc. Income Statement for the Year Ended December 31, 2007

Sales revenue		$30,000,000
Less: Cost of goods sold		21,000,000
Gross profit		$ 9,000,000
Less: Operating expenses		
Selling expense	$3,000,000	
General and administrative expenses	1,800,000	
Lease expense	200,000	
Depreciation expense	1,000,000	
Total operating expense		$6,000,000
Operating profit		$3,000,000
Less: Interest expense		1,000,000
Net profit before taxes		$2,000,000
Less: Taxes (rate = 40%)		800,000
Net profits after taxes		$1,200,000

Aluminum Industries, Inc. Balance Sheet as of December 31, 2007

Assets		Liabilities and Stockholders' Equity	
Current assets		Current liabilities	
Cash	$ 1,000,000	Accounts payable	$ 8,000,000
Marketable securities	3,000,000	Notes payable	8,000,000
Accounts receivable	12,000,000	Accruals	500,000
Inventories	7,500,000	Total current liabilities	$16,500,000
Total current assets	$23,500,000	Long-term debt (including financial leases)	$20,000,000
Gross fixed assets (at cost)		Stockholders' equity	
Land and buildings	$11,000,000	Preferred stock (25,000 shares, $4 dividend)	$ 2,500,000
Machinery and equipment	20,500,000		
Furniture and fixtures	8,000,000	Common stock (1 million shares, $5 par)	5,000,000
Gross fixed assets	$39,500,000		
Less: Accumulated depreciation	13,000,000	Paid-in capital in excess of par value	4,000,000
Net fixed assets	$26,500,000		
Total assets	$50,000,000	Retained earnings	2,000,000
		Total stockholders' equity	$13,500,000
		Total liabilities & stockholders' equity	$50,000,000

Industry Averages	
Debt ratio	0.51
Debt-equity ratio	1.07
Times interest earned ratio	7.30

2-12. A firm's price/earnings ratio is 20.0 with earnings available for common stockholders of $45 million. Assuming there are 27 million shares outstanding, what is the firm's stock price?

2-13. Tracey White, owner of the Buzz Coffee Shop chain, has decided to expand her operations. Her 2007 financial statements follow. Tracey can buy two additional coffeehouses for $3 million, and she has the choice of completely financing these new coffeehouses with either a 10 percent (annual interest) loan or the issuance of new common stock. She also expects these new shops to generate an additional $1 million in sales. Assuming a 40 percent tax rate and no other changes, should Tracey buy the two coffeehouses? Why or why not? Which financing option results in the better *ROE?*

Buzz Coffee Shops, Inc. 2007 Financial Statements

Balance Sheet		Income Statement	
Current assets	$ 250,000	Sales	$500,000
Fixed assets	750,000	−Costs and expenses @40%	200,000
Total assets	$1,000,000	Earnings before interest and taxes (*EBIT*)	$300,000
Current liabilities	$ 300,000	−Interest expense	0
Long-term debt	0	Net profit before taxes	$300,000
Total liabilities	$ 300,000	−Taxes @40%	120,000
Common equity	$ 700,000	Net income	$180,000
Total liabilities and stockholders' equity	$1,000,000		

Use the following information for Problems 2-15 and 2-16.

Income Statements for the Year Ended December 31, 2007

	Heavy Metal Manufacturing (HMM)	Metallic Stamping Inc. (MS)	High-Tech Software Co. (HTS)
Sales	$75,000,000	$50,000,000	$100,000,000
−Operating expenses	65,000,000	40,000,000	60,000,000
Operating profit	$10,000,000	$10,000,000	$ 40,000,000
−Interest expenses	3,000,000	3,000,000	0
Earnings before taxes	$ 7,000,000	$ 7,000,000	$ 40,000,000
−Taxes (rate = 40%)	2,800,000	2,800,000	16,000,000
Net income	$ 4,200,000	$ 4,200,000	$ 24,000,000

Balance Sheets as of December 31, 2007

	Heavy Metal Manufacturing (HMM)	Metallic Stamping Inc. (MS)	High-Tech Software Co. (HTS)
Current assets	$ 10,000,000	$ 5,000,000	$ 20,000,000
Net fixed assets	90,000,000	75,000,000	80,000,000
Total assets	$100,000,000	$80,000,000	$100,000,000
Current liabilities	$ 20,000,000	$10,000,000	$ 10,000,000
Long-term debt	40,000,000	40,000,000	0
Total liabilities	$ 60,000,000	$50,000,000	$ 10,000,000
Common stock	$ 15,000,000	$10,000,000	$ 25,000,000
Retained earnings	25,000,000	20,000,000	65,000,000
Total common equity	$ 40,000,000	$30,000,000	$ 90,000,000
Total liabilities and common equity	$100,000,000	$80,000,000	$100,000,000

2-14. Use the DuPont system to compare the two heavy metal companies shown above (HHM and MS) during 2007.

    a. Which of the two has a higher return on common equity? What is the cause of the difference between the two?

    b. Calculate the return on common equity of the software company HTS. Why is this value so different from those of the heavy metal companies calculated in part (a)?

    c. Compare the leverage levels between the industries. Which industry receives a greater contribution from return on total assets? Which industry receives a greater contribution from the financial leverage as measured by the assets-to-equity (A/E) ratio?

    d. Can you make a meaningful DuPont comparison across industries? Why or why not?

2-15. Referring back to Problem 2-15, perform the same analysis with real data. Download last year's financial data from Ford Motor Company (http://www2.ford.com), General Motors (http://www.gm.com), and Microsoft (http://www.microsoft.com). Which ratios demonstrate the greatest difference between Ford and General Motors? Which of the two is more profitable? Which ratios drive the greater profitability?

2-16. Use the following financial data for Greta's Gadgets, Inc., to determine the effect of using additional debt financing to purchase additional assets. Assume that an additional $1 million of assets is purchased with 100 percent debt financing with a 10 percent annual interest rate.

Greta's Gadgets, Inc.

Income Statement for the Year Ended December 31, 2007		Balance Sheet as of December 31, 2007	
		Assets	
Sales	$4,000,000	Current assets	$ 0
− Costs and expenses @90%	3,600,000	Fixed assets	2,000,000
Earnings before interest & taxes	$ 400,000	Total assets	$2,000,000
		Liabilities and Stockholders' Equity	
− Interest (.10 × $1,000,000)	100,000		
Earnings before taxes	$ 300,000	Current liabilities	$ 0
− Taxes @40%	120,000	Long-term debt @10%	1,000,000
Net income	$ 180,000	Total liabilities	$1,000,000
		Common stock equity	$1,000,000
		Total liabilities and stockholders' equity	$2,000,000

a. Calculate the current (2007) net profit margin, total asset turnover, assets-to-equity ratio, return on total assets, and return on common equity for Greta's.

b. Now, assuming no other changes, determine the impact of purchasing the $1 million in assets using 100 percent debt financing with a 10 percent annual interest rate. Further, assume that the newly purchased assets generate an additional $2 million in sales and that the costs and expenses remain at 90 percent of sales. For purposes of this problem, further assume a tax rate of 40 percent. What is the effect on the ratios calculated in part (a)? Is the purchase of these assets justified on the basis of the return on common equity?

c. Assume that the newly purchased assets in part (b) generate only an extra $500,000 in sales. Is the purchase justified in this case?

d. Which component ratio(s) of the DuPont system is (are) not affected by the change in sales? What does this imply about the use of financial leverage?

2-17. The financial statements of Access Corporation for the year ended December 31, 2007, follow.

Access Corporation Income Statement for the Year Ended December 31, 2007

Sales revenue		$160,000
Less: Cost of goods sold [a]		106,000
Gross profit		$ 54,000
Less: Operating expenses		
Selling expense	$16,000	
General and administrative expense	10,000	
Lease expense	1,000	
Depreciation expense	10,000	
Total operating expense		37,000
Operating profit		$ 17,000
Less: Interest expense		6,100
Net profit before taxes		$ 10,900
Less: Taxes @40%		4,360
Net profits after taxes		$ 6,540

[a] Access Corporation's annual purchases are estimated to equal 75 percent of cost of goods sold.

Access Corporation Balance Sheet as of December 31, 2007

Assets		Liabilities and Stockholders' Equity	
Cash	$ 500	Accounts payable	$ 22,000
Marketable securities	1,000	Notes payable	47,000
Accounts receivable	25,000	Total current liabilities	$ 69,000
Inventories	45,500	Long-term debt	$ 22,950
Total current assets	$ 72,000	Total liabilities	$ 91,950
Land	$ 26,000	Common stock [a]	$ 31,500
Buildings and equipment	90,000	Retained earnings	26,550
Less: Accumulated		Total liabilities and	$150,000
depreciation	38,000	stockholders' equity	
Net fixed assets	$ 78,000		
Total assets	$150,000		

[a] The firm's 3,000 outstanding shares of common stock closed 2007 at a price of $25 per share.

a. Use the preceding financial statements to complete the following table. Assume that the industry averages given in the table are applicable for both 2006 and 2007.

b. Analyze Access Corporation's financial condition as it relates to (1) liquidity, (2) activity, (3) debt, (4) profitability, and (5) market value. Summarize the company's overall financial condition.

Access Corporation's Financial Ratios

Ratio	Industry Average	Actual 2006	Actual 2007
Current ratio	1.80	1.84	_____
Quick (acid-test) ratio	.70	.78	_____
Inventory turnover	2.50	2.59	_____
Average collection period[a]	37 days	36 days	_____
Average payment period[a]	72 days	78 days	_____
Debt-to-equity ratio	50%	51%	_____
Times interest earned ratio	3.8	4.0	_____
Gross profit margin	38%	40%	_____
Net profit margin	3.5%	3.6%	_____
Return on total assets (ROA)	4.0%	4.0%	_____
Return on common equity (ROE)	9.5%	8.0%	_____
Market/book (M/B) ratio	1.1	1.2	_____

[a]Based on a 365-day year and on end-of-year figures.

2-18. Given the following financial statements, historical ratios, and industry averages, calculate the MBA Company's financial ratios for 2007. Analyze its overall financial situation both in comparison with industry averages and over the period 2005–2007. Break your analysis into an evaluation of the firm's liquidity, activity, debt, profitability, and market value.

MBA Company Income Statement for the Year Ended December 31, 2007

Sales revenue		$10,000,000
Less: Cost of goods sold[a]		7,500,000
Gross profit		$ 2,500,000
Less: Operating expenses		
Selling expense	$300,000	
General and administrative expense	650,000	
Lease expense	50,000	
Depreciation expense	200,000	
Total operating expense		1,200,000
Operating profit (EBIT)		$ 1,300,000
Less: Interest expense		200,000
Net profits before taxes		$ 1,100,000
Less: Taxes (rate = 40%)		440,000
Net profits after taxes		$ 660,000
Less: Preferred stock dividends		50,000
Earnings available for common stockholders		$ 610,000
Earnings per share (EPS)		$ 3.05

[a]Annual credit purchases of $6.2 million were made during the year.

MBA Company Balance Sheet as of December 31, 2007

Assets			Liabilities and Stockholders' Equity		
Current assets			Current liabilities		
Cash	$	200,000	Accounts payable	$	900,000
Marketable securities		50,000	Notes payable		200,000
Accounts receivable		800,000	Accruals		100,000
Inventories		950,000	Total current liabilities		$ 1,200,000
Total current assets		$ 2,000,000	Long-term debt (including		$ 3,000,000
Gross fixed assets		$12,000,000	financial leases)		
(at cost)			Stockholders' equity		
Less: Accumulated		3,000,000	Preferred stock (25,000 shares,	$	1,000,000
depreciation			$2 dividend)		
Net fixed assets		$ 9,000,000	Common stock		600,000
Other assets		$ 1,000,000	(200,000 shares, $3 par)[a]		
Total assets		$12,000,000	Paid-in capital in excess of par		5,200,000
			Retained earnings		1,000,000
			Total stockholders' equity		$ 7,800,000
			Total liabilities and stock-holders' equity		$12,000,000

[a]On December 31, 2007, the firm's common stock closed at a price of $27.50 per share.

Historical and Industry Average Ratios for MBA Company

Ratio	Actual 2005	Actual 2006	Industry Average 2007
Current ratio	1.40	1.55	1.85
Quick (acid-test) ratio	1.00	0.92	1.05
Inventory turnover	9.52	9.21	8.60
Average collection period[a]	45.0 days	36.4 days	35.0 days
Average payment period[a]	58.5 days	60.8 days	45.8 days
Fixed asset turnover	1.08	1.05	1.07
Total asset turnover	0.74	0.80	0.74
Debt ratio	0.20	0.20	0.30
Debt-to-equity ratio	0.25	0.27	0.39
Times interest earned ratio	8.2	7.3	8.0
Gross profit margin	0.30	0.27	0.25
Operating profit margin	0.12	0.12	0.10
Net profit margin	0.067	0.067	0.058
Return on total assets (ROA)	0.049	0.054	0.043
Return on common equity (ROE)	0.066	0.073	0.072
Earnings per share (EPS)	$1.75	$2.20	$1.50
Price/earnings (P/E) ratio	12.0	10.5	11.2
Market/book (M/B) ratio	1.20	1.05	1.10

[a]Based on a 365-day year and on end-of-year figures.

2-19. Choose a company that you would like to analyze and obtain its financial statements. Now, select another firm from the same industry and obtain its financial data from the Internet. Perform a complete ratio analysis on each firm. How well does your selected company compare with its industry peer? Which components of your firm's *ROE* are superior, and which are inferior?

THOMSON ONE BUSINESS SCHOOL EDITION

Access financial information from the Thomson ONE–Business School Edition website for the following problem(s). Go to http://tobsefin.swlearning.com/. If you have already registered your access serial number and have a username and password, click **Enter.** Otherwise, click **Register** and follow the instructions to create a username and password. Register your access serial number and then click **Enter** on the aforementioned website. When you click Enter, you will be prompted for your username and password (please remember that the password is case sensitive). Enter them in the respective boxes and then click **OK** (or hit **Enter**). From the ensuing page, click **Click Here to Access Thomson ONE–Business School Edition Now!** This opens up a new window that gives you access to the Thomson ONE–Business School Edition database. You can retrieve a company's financial information by entering its ticker symbol [provided for each company in the problem(s)] in the box below "Name/Symbol/Key." For further instructions on using the Thomson ONE–Business School Edition database, please refer to "A Guide for Using Thomson ONE–Business School Edition."

2-20.   Compare the profitability of Wal-Mart Stores Inc. (ticker symbol, WMT) and Target Corp. (ticker symbol, TGT) for the latest year. Using the return on assets (*ROA*) and return on equity (*ROE*) measures, determine which firm is more profitable. Use the DuPont system to determine what drives the difference in the profitability of the two.

2-21.   Analyze the cash flows of Southwest Airlines (ticker symbol, LUV) over the last five years. Calculate the operating cash flow (using Equation 2.2) and the free cash flow (using Equation 2.3) for each of the last five years. Do the operating cash flows you calculated match the Net Cash Flow from Operating Activities on the 5-Year Annual Cash Flow Statement? If they are different, why are they different?

MINI-CASE: FINANCIAL STATEMENT AND CASH FLOW ANALYSIS

Jaedan Industries has the following account balances as of December 31, 2007. The firm's dividend payout ratio is 25% and the tax rate is 34%. The firm's stock price on December 31, 2006 was $42.89 and on December 31, 2007 it is $56.82. Construct an income statement, balance sheet, statement of retained earnings, and statement of cash flows for 2007. Also determine the firm's free cash flow and calculate the liquidity, activity, debt, profitability, and market ratios for Jaedan Industries. Perform a DuPont analysis and compare the firm to the industry ratios. Highlight any financial strengths and weaknesses that Jaedan Industries may have.

Sales	$42,000,000
Cost of goods sold (COGS)	63%
Portion of COGS that represent purchases	75%
Selling, general, and administrative expenses	$1,621,000
Depreciation	$800,000
Interest rate on short- and long-term debt	10%
Cash balance	$3,689,000
Accounts receivable	$5,423,000
Marketable securities	$1,836,000
Inventory	$4,118,000
Fixed assets	$14,811,000
Accumulated depreciation (does not include depreciation for 2007)	$5,160,000
Accounts payable	$3,136,000
Notes payable	$706,000
Accruals	$500,000
Long-term bonds outstanding	$3,046,000
Preferred stock (at par)	$100,000
Retained earnings (does not include retained earnings for 2007)	$1,628,819
Common stock (at par)	$4,000,000
Paid-in capital in excess of par	$4,500,000
Tax rate	34%
Dividend payout ratio (common stock)	25%
Dividends on preferred stock	8% of par
Number of shares of common stock outstanding	1 million
Terms of trade on accounts receivable	35 days
Terms of trade on accounts payable	45 days

To aid in your calculations, the financial statements from 2006 are included below:

Jaedan Industries
Income Statement
for the Year Ending December 31, 2006

Sales	$38,578,155
Less: Cost of goods sold	27,004,709
Gross profit	$11,573,447
Less: Operating expenses:	
Selling, general, and administrative expenses	$ 1,000,000
Depreciation	700,000
Earnings before interest and taxes	$ 9,873,447
Less: Interest expense	375,000
Earnings before taxes	$ 9,498,447
Less: Taxes	3,229,472
Net income	$ 6,268,975
Less: Dividends paid	1,575,244
To retained earnings	$ 4,693,731

Jaedan Industries
Balance Sheet
December 31, 2006

Assets		Liabilities and Equity	
Cash	$ 871,319	Accounts payable	$ 2,946,000
Marketable securities	3,587,000	Notes payable	684,000
Accounts receivable	2,867,500	Accruals	350,000
Inventories	3,210,000	Total current liabilities	$ 3,980,000
Total current assets	$10,535,819	Long-term debt	$ 3,046,000
Fixed assets	$11,879,000	Preferred stock	$ 100,000
Less: Accumulated	5,160,000	Common stock (at par)	4,000,000
Depreciation		Paid-in capital in excess of par	4,500,000
Net fixed assets	$ 6,719,000	Retained earnings	1,628,819
Total assets	$17,254,819	Total liabilities and equity	$17,254,819

The ratios for the industry for 2006 and 2007 are:

Industry Ratios

	2006	2007
Liquidity Ratios		
Current ratio	2.89	3.26
Quick ratio	1.42	2.19
Activity Ratios		
Inventory turnover	6.71	6.59
Average collection period	35.12	36.17
Average payment period	50.73	49.63
Fixed asset turnover	4.32	4.76
Total asset turnover	2.14	2.33
Debt Ratios		
Debt ratio	41.93%	39.36%
Assets-to-equity ratio	165.82%	163.13%
Debt-to-equity ratio	31.26%	30.23%
Times interest earned	15.72	16.81
Profitability Ratios		
Gross profit margin	22.19%	23.74%
Operating profit margin	19.32%	20.89%
Net profit margin	15.11%	17.97%
Earnings per share	$4.36	$4.58
Return on total assets	32.34%	41.87%
Return on common equity	53.63%	68.30%
Market Ratios		
Price/earnings ratio	5.41	5.97
Market/book ratio	4.19	4.32

Chapter 3

Time Value of Money

SMARTFinance

Why Is a "$340 Million Jackpot" Really Worth Only $164 Million?

The Powerball lottery is a game of chance in which participants pay one dollar for a lottery ticket, select six numbers, and then hope that their numbers will be picked in a random, televised drawing. The lottery operates in the interests of 23 participating U.S. state governments, and over half of the total proceeds from ticket sales flow into the states' operating budgets. Remaining proceeds cover expenses and pay off lucky winners.

The odds against winning these state-sponsored lotteries are astronomically high, yet the lottery is very popular. Demand for lottery tickets rises to a near frenzy if several weeks pass without a winner, because the jackpot grows until someone selects all six winning numbers. The middle of October, 2005, was such a period; it resulted in the largest individual win ever—$340 million. Despite odds of more than 146,000,000:1 against winning, people dreamed of hitting the jackpot, which would pay a 29-year, 30-payment annuity of $11.3 million. Based on this stream of payouts, Powerball officials touted the jackpot's value at $340 million (30 payments × $11.3 million = $340 million).

What few people noticed about this jackpot was the winner's option to exchange this stream of annual cash flows (which we will define in this chapter as a 30-year annuity due) for an immediate single lump-sum payment of $164 million. Why would anyone exchange a "$340 million jackpot" for a "mere" $164 million payment? Because the winner would receive $164 million right away rather than have to wait 30 years for lottery officials to dribble out the entire jackpot. With $164 million in hand, the winner could invest the money and earn interest on it.

Clearly this means that having $164 million on hand today is more valuable than having it at some point in the future. But how much more valuable? Does the opportunity to earn interest mean that $164 million today is worth more than $340 million spread over 30 years?

The answer depends on the interest rate. To compare the $164 million lump sum payment to the $340 million stream of payments, we must calculate how much that stream is worth today—its "present value." For example, suppose an investor could earn 5 percent interest on a relatively safe investment such as U.S. government bonds. If he invested $10 million today at 5 percent interest, he would have $10.5 million one year later. Thus, we can say that $10 million is the present value of a $10.5 million payment that arrives one year in the future. Similarly, if another person invested $8.23 million at 5 percent today, she would have $10.5 million after 5 years. Thus, $8.23 million is the present value of a $10.5 million payment arriving in 5 years.

We can apply this process to an entire cash flow stream in order to answer the question about whether to take the lottery payout now or over the next 30 years. If we assume that the interest rate on an alternative investment is 6 percent, the present value of 30 annual $11.3 million payments (with the first payment arriving immediately) equals $164.9 million. Phrased differently, any investor who could earn 6 percent on low-risk investments should be almost indifferent between the $164 million lump sum and the "$340 million jackpot." At interest rates above 6 percent, the immediate lump sum becomes more attractive; at interest rates below 6 percent, the stream of annual payments is more appealing.

Both as a profession and as an academic discipline, finance is primarily concerned with the *voluntary transfer of wealth* between individuals and across time. The transfer of wealth *between individuals* occurs in financial markets. This transfer can involve creditors lending money to borrowers in exchange for future repayment with interest, or investors purchasing an ownership claim in an entrepreneur's venture in exchange for a share in future profits.

Likewise, transferring wealth *across time* can take two forms. The first involves determining what the value of an investment made today will be worth at a specific future date. The second determines the value today of a cash flow to be received at a specific date in the future. We refer to the first as determining the **future value** of an investment and the second as determining the **present value** of a future cash flow.

These wealth transfers are voluntary "trades" of cash today for promises of greater payments in the future. These trades make all parties better off. In the language of economics, borrowing and lending using financial markets increases economic welfare by helping both borrowers and savers. By forgoing some consumption today in order to lend or invest money, a saver can increase consumption in future periods.

The opportunity to receive cash today in exchange for a promise to repay that cash, plus interest, in the future also makes borrowers better off. Borrowers might be individuals, such as new college graduates, who wish to obtain financing for new cars and are willing to commit a portion of their future income to these loans. Or, "borrowers" might be entrepreneurs with great business plans and managerial talents who need equity financing to turn their dreams into solid businesses. Perhaps the most relevant example of how borrowing can improve personal welfare is the bargain graduate students make with lenders. Students borrow (often sizable) sums of money to finance their educations, and the knowledge they gain increases their lifetime earnings potential by more than enough to repay the debt. In sum, financial markets improve the welfare of savers, entrepreneurs, and ordinary citizens by allowing borrowing, lending, and investing to occur most efficiently.

We have several objectives in this chapter. The first is to introduce the concepts of the time value of money and to briefly describe how the opportunity to borrow and lend enables people with different consumption preferences to transact to their mutual benefit. Second, we show how to compute *future values*, beginning with the future value of a single investment made today and then examining more complex cash flow streams. Third, we demonstrate how to compute the *present values* of future cash flows, again beginning with a single cash flow and then examining streams of future cash flows. The chapter concludes with special applications of time value techniques that financial managers commonly employ.

3.1 THE NOTION OF TIME VALUE OF MONEY

We have asserted that financial markets are economically valuable because they allow savers and borrowers to transact efficiently. We will illustrate the key ideas with a simple example.[1]

[1.] Irving Fisher (1930) first presented the basic ideas of time value and the net present value rule of investment. Hirshleifer (1958), Fama and Miller (1972), and Fama and Jensen (1985) further developed and applied Fisher's ideas in a modern corporate setting.

Consider how financial interaction might improve the lots of two people who both have MBA degrees from the same school, but who are at much different stages in their careers. Sally Peak earned her MBA almost 30 years ago and is now a successful investment banker in her mid-50s. She hopes to work for another 10 years and then retire to a life of travel, comfort, and spoiling her grandchildren. Samuel Start has just graduated at the top of his class and has landed a well-paying job with a prestigious consulting firm. Samuel's future looks very bright. He and his wife are eager to purchase a home and start a family even as they both begin promising careers.

THE ROLE OF FINANCIAL MARKETS

How can financial markets meet the differing consumption preferences of Sally and Samuel? When we analyze these needs separately, the answer is obvious: Sally, now at the peak of her career, earns more than she consumes. In 10 years, when she retires, she will live off her accumulated savings. Therefore, Sally would like to find an opportunity to lend or invest part of her current income at an attractive return so that she will have more income to consume when she retires. Samuel's situation is the mirror image of Sally's. Although his earnings *potential* is great, his current needs for income exceed his current earnings. Samuel would like to increase the amount of money he can spend today by borrowing. Further, because of his promising career prospects, potential lenders would consider Samuel an excellent credit risk.

Now assume that Sally and Samuel meet (perhaps at an alumni dinner) and begin discussing their financial plans and needs. A mutually beneficial financial exchange might emerge. Sally would agree to lend Samuel enough money today so that Samuel could buy a house; Samuel would agree to repay this loan in full, with interest, over the next 10 years. As evidence of their agreement, the two parties would probably sign a contract disclosing the terms of the loan and establishing a repayment schedule. Assuming this contract met appropriate standards, the agreement would be legally enforceable, and either party would have legal recourse in the event of a dispute. The agreement might even be written in such a way that Samuel would promise to make interest and principal payments to any investor who owned the contract, rather than specifically to Sally. This would allow Sally to sell the contract to a third party in case she did not wish to remain Samuel's creditor for the contract's full 10 years.

The transactions between Samuel and Sally accomplish several economic objectives. They allow Samuel to borrow against future earnings to buy a house today. They also allow Sally to increase the amount of money she will have on hand when she retires, by making a relatively safe loan at an attractive interest rate. Because the loan is backed by a legally enforceable contract, each party enjoys protection from the other's exploitation. Finally, Sally's ability to sell the loan to another investor means that she has **liquidity,** the ability to resell an investment easily and at low cost. Both Sally and Samuel benefit from these exchanges. The overall economy benefits as well because the money Sally saves today will be channeled into Samuel's productive investment.

We can, of course, generalize these basic principles of lending and borrowing. If there are a large number of savers and borrowers, then Sally and Samuel do not have to meet each other to achieve their separate objectives. As long as Sally finds a creditworthy borrower and Samuel finds a lender with surplus cash, Sally can profitably save for her retirement and Samuel can borrow enough to jump-start his personal and professional life. Once again, we can express this concept in economic terms: Financial markets allow both savers and borrowers to achieve their desired pattern of *intertemporal consumption,* or consumption over time.

Financial Intermediaries. Our simple analogy can be pushed further, to eliminate the need for Sally to search for an individual borrower or for Samuel to search for an individual lender. Assume that companies called "banks" develop to serve the role of **financial intermediaries.** These companies eliminate the need for savers and borrowers to deal directly with each other; instead, both parties need deal only with the intermediaries. For example, banks can pay savers interest on their deposits with the bank while offering borrowers attractive rates of interest on a variety of loans. As long as they charge borrowers a higher rate than they offer depositors, banks can realize a profit from this interest *spread*. Savers have their choice of lending directly to a final borrower or lending to a financial intermediary (who then finds a final borrower). Borrowers have the same opportunity of borrowing directly from an ultimate saver or borrowing from an intermediary.

Competition and Financial Costs. Competition between potential borrowers and lenders determines the marketwide interest rate, or **equilibrium interest rate.** This is the rate that "clears the market," that equates total savings and investment within an economy. Competition also ensures that riskier borrowers—those who are more likely not to repay their loans—will have to pay a higher interest rate than will more creditworthy borrowers.

A Corporate Perspective. We will see in subsequent chapters that this "pricing" of risk is fundamental to all financial decision making, by individuals as well as by firms. Companies evaluate prospective investment opportunities by assessing whether their expected return, adjusted for project risk, exceeds the firm's *required return*. This is the return the firm itself must promise debt and equity investors; it is also referred to as the corporation's *cost of capital,* or *opportunity cost.*

The fact that corporations receive their financing from financial markets also means that companies can follow the simple investment rule of accepting projects that maximize the value of the firm, rather than accepting projects that appeal to the consumption preferences of individual investors. As an illustration, consider Lambda Corporation, a publicly traded firm with an opportunity to invest in a project that promises a handsome payoff—but not until several years in the future. Investors who trade in Lambda's securities value its shares by predicting what the firm's cash flows will be over time and then determining the present value of that stream today. This valuation process is called **capitalizing** a cash flow stream. We describe the specific techniques used to determine present values later in this chapter.

For now, we simply need to state that market participants calculate the present value of a future cash flow. They do so by determining how much they would need to invest today, at a given interest rate, to equal that cash flow's value in the future. Because Lambda's investment project looks very profitable, the present value of the stream of future cash flows it will generate is greater than the cost of funding the investment today. We will define such a project as having a positive **net present value** (**NPV**). By this, we mean that the present value of the cash inflows (the future profits) exceeds the present value of the cash outflows (today's investment).

Now assume that Lambda Corporation has two controlling shareholders, as well as many smaller investors who trade in its shares. The older of the controlling shareholders expects to retire in two years; the other plans to continue working for a decade or more. In the absence of well-functioning financial markets, these two shareholders might disagree about whether the company should accept the attractive, but long-lived, project. The older shareholder wishes to maximize short-term returns, while the other shareholder has a longer investment horizon.

COMPARATIVE CORPORATE FINANCE

Save Money? Not Me—I'm an American!

This chapter presents the basic valuation rules that economic agents use in determining whether to save or consume their income. Are there differences in the savings patterns of citizens in the major industrialized countries? And have these patterns changed over time?

As the chart below shows, personal savings rates are strikingly different both between countries and within the same country at different points in time. Italy has the highest estimated national savings rate (12%) among rich countries in 2004, closely followed by France and Germany. The ranking was similar ten years earlier in 1994, but Italy's near 20 percent savings rate was well above that of about 11 percent in France, Germany, and Japan.

Although economists are divided about the determinants of varying national savings rates, it seems likely that economic, demographic, and cultural factors all play important roles in explaining the international differences.

The chart also shows that savings rates generally declined between 1991 and 2004 for all six countries shown. This was clearly true for the United States. While never high, the U.S. savings rate was 7 percent in 1991; by 2004, the savings rate of U.S. households was only about 1 percent.

Why did people stop saving during a decade that encompassed the longest economic expansion in U.S. history and that saw the stock market more than triple in value? An even more perplexing question is, how did U.S. corporations finance the $10 trillion or so of capital investments they made between 1991 and 2004? There are several partial explanations for this strange mix of a booming economy and a seemingly extravagant population. In part, the prosperity of this period reduced the need for people to save as much out of their income;

the rising values of their homes and stock portfolios—the famous "wealth effect"—made it possible to finance future consumption with less saving from current income. Record inflows of foreign capital also helped fund the investment programs of U.S. corporations, as did the U.S government's switch from budget deficit to surplus during the late 1990s.

These are all only partial answers, however. In truth, economists really do not understand why the U.S. savings rate has fallen so low or why the consequences of this decline have thus far been so muted.

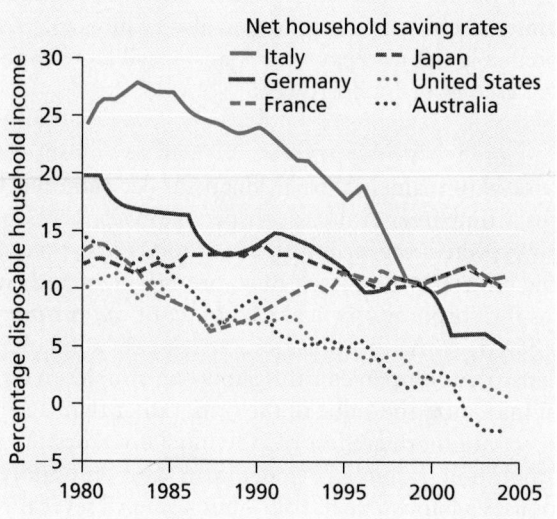

Source: "The Shift Away from Thrift," *The Economist* (April 7, 2005), economist.com.

Financial markets eliminate this potential conflict: Investors in the market will capitalize the project's expected value (i.e., the stock price will rise to reflect the value of the investment) as soon as the firm commits to the investment. The controlling shareholder who wishes to retire in two years thus benefits from the investment; he can sell his shares immediately at a higher price. The other controlling shareholder naturally benefits as well; her shares, which she plans to retain, have increased in price by the net present value of the investment opportunity.

This principle that corporations should accept only positive-*NPV* investment projects, regardless of which investors are financing those projects, is referred to as the **separation of investment and financing**. In following this principle, companies need to focus only on satisfying the impersonal demands of the financial market, not the personal preferences of investors.

Back to a Core Principle. In our discussion thus far, we have finessed one of the core principles of finance introduced in Chapter 1: The opportunity to earn a return on invested funds means that a dollar today is worth more than a dollar (or euro, pound, franc, or yen) in the future. The remainder of this chapter addresses this issue of **time value of money**. Section 3.2 describes how to compute the *future value* of a lump sum invested today at a given interest rate. The counterpart of computing future value is determining what the *present value* is today of a cash flow to be received in the future, if investors can earn a given return on investments of comparable risk. We present the technique for calculating the present value of a lump sum in Section 3.3. Sections 3.4 and 3.5 describe the procedures for calculating the future value and present value, respectively, of a *stream of cash flows*. Section 3.6 demonstrates some *special applications* of present and future value concepts.

---

1. How do financial markets improve the financial prospects of both savers and borrowers? What is required for this to occur?

2. What does *net present value (NPV)* mean? How does the *separation of investment and financing decisions* affect the use of *NPV*?

Concept Review Questions

3.2 FUTURE VALUE OF A LUMP SUM

THE CONCEPT OF FUTURE VALUE

By consuming less than 100 percent of their present income, investors can earn interest on their savings and thereby enjoy higher future consumption. A person who invests $100 today at 5 percent interest expects to receive $105 in one year, representing $5 interest plus the return of the $100 originally invested. In this example, we say that $105 is the *future value* of $100 invested at 5 percent for one year.

We can calculate the future value of an investment over a specified period of time by applying either *simple interest* or *compound interest*. **Simple interest** is interest paid only on the initial principal of an investment. **Principal** refers to the amount of money on which the interest is paid. To demonstrate, if the investment in our previous example pays 5 percent simple interest, then the future value in any year equals $100 plus the product of the annual interest payment and the number of years. In this case, its value would be $110 at the end of year 2 [$100 + (2 × $5)], $115 at the end of year 3 [$100 + (3 × $5)], $120 at the end of year 4 [$100 + (4 × $5)], and so on.

Compound interest is interest earned on both the principal amount and the interest earned in previous periods. To demonstrate compound interest, assume that you can deposit $100 into a risk-free account paying 5 percent interest annually. (For simplicity, we first assume that interest compounds annually; in later sections we show how to compute future values using semiannual, quarterly, and even continuous compounding periods.) At the end of year 1, your account will have a balance of $105. This sum represents the initial principal of $100 plus 5 percent ($5) in interest (the same as for the simple interest calculation for year 1). This future value is calculated as follows:

Future value at end of year 1 = $100 × (1 + 0.05) = $105

If you leave this money in the account to earn compound interest for another year, you will be paid interest at the rate of 5 percent on the *new principal* of $105. In other words, the bank will pay 5 percent interest both on the original principal of $100 and on the first year's interest of $5. At the end of this second year, there will be $110.25 in your account. This amount represents the principal at the beginning of year 2

[Handwritten margin notes:]

$$FV = PV(1+r)^n$$

r and n are units of time and must be the same unit

in excel ✱

= FV(rate, n, payment, PV, type)

payment = 0 if you don't contribute more after the PV

PV = initial amount (but a negative #)

type = 0 if no payments

to find interest.
    rate in excel:

= rate (n, payment,
    PV, FV, type,
    guess)

either ·PV or FV
has to be
negative or excel
returns an error

($105) plus 5 percent of the $105 ($5.25) in interest. The future value at the end of the second year is computed as follows:

Future value at end of year 2 = $105 × (1 + 0.05) = $110.25

Substituting the first equation into the second one yields the following:

Future value at end of year 2 = $100 × (1 + 0.05) × (1 + 0.05)

$$= \$100 \times (1 + 0.05)^2$$

$$= \$110.25$$

Therefore, $100 deposited at 5 percent *compound* annual interest will be worth $110.25 at the end of two years.

It is important to recognize the difference in future values that results from compound versus simple interest. Although the difference between the account balances for simple versus compound interest in this example ($110 versus $110.25) seems rather trivial, the difference quite literally grows exponentially over time. With simple interest this account would have a balance of $250 after 30 years [$100 + (30 × $5)]; with compound interest the account balance would be $432.19 in 30 years.

THE EQUATION FOR FUTURE VALUE

Financial analysts routinely use compound interest. Therefore, throughout this book we generally use compound rather than simple interest. Equation 3.1 gives the general algebraic formula for calculating the future value, at the end of *n* years, of a lump sum invested today at an interest rate of *r* percent per period:

$$FV = PV \times (1 + r)^n \qquad \text{(Eq. 3.1)}$$

where FV = future value of an investment,

PV = present value of an investment (the lump sum),

r = interest rate per period (typically 1 year),

n = number of periods (typically years) that the lump sum is invested.

Applying the Model 3.1 illustrates how you might use the concept of future value to evaluate an investment in a bank certificate of deposit (CD).

APPLYING THE MODEL 3.1

Assume that you have two investment opportunities. One is to invest $100 in an open-ended savings account paying 5 percent interest. The other is to invest $100 in a CD paying 6 percent interest. You would like to know how much your $100 CD investment will be worth at the end of five years.

Substituting PV = $100, r = 0.06, and n = 5 into Equation 3.1 gives the future value at the end of year 5, expressed as FV:

$$FV = \$100 \times (1 + 0.06)^5 = \$100 \times (1.3382) = \$133.82$$

Your CD will have an account balance of $133.82 at the end of the fifth year. This is presented graphically, as a **time line**, in Figure 3.1.

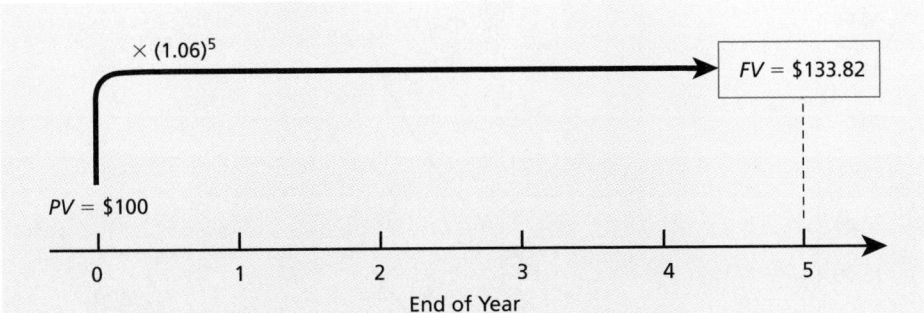

Figure 3.1
Time Line for the Future Value of $100 Invested for Five Years at a 6% Interest Rate

Table 3.1
Format of a Future Value Factor (*FVF*) Table

Period	Interest Rate (*r*)					
	1%	2%	3%	4%	5%	6%
1	1.010	1.020	1.030	1.040	1.050	1.060
2	1.020	1.040	1.061	1.082	1.102	1.124
3	1.030	1.061	1.093	1.125	1.158	1.191
4	1.041	1.082	1.126	1.170	1.216	1.262
5	1.051	1.104	1.159	1.217	1.276	1.338
6	1.062	1.126	1.194	1.265	1.340	1.419
7	1.072	1.149	1.230	1.316	1.407	1.504

In addition to algebra, there are three popular methods for simplifying future value calculations. One method is to use a future value factor (*FVF*) *table*, such as Table A1 in Appendix A at the end of the book. Such a table provides future value factors ($FVF_{r\%,n}$) for various interest rates (*r*) and holding periods (*n*). We have reproduced a portion of Table A1 as Table 3.1.[2] To find the future value factor for 6 percent interest and a 5-year holding period ($FVF_{6\%,5}$), simply move across the interest rates on the horizontal axis of the table until you reach the column labeled "6%," and then move vertically down this column until you find the row labeled "Period 5." Thus you find that $FVF_{6\%,5}$ is equal to 1.338, and you would multiply this number by $100 to compute *FV*. Not surprisingly, this matches the previous *FV* = $133.80 except for a small rounding difference.

A second method is to use a *financial calculator*. To compute *FV* in the example, you would simply input the number of years (5), the interest rate (6), the amount of the initial deposit ($100), and then calculate the future value of $133.82.[3] The third popular method of simplifying time value calculations involves use of a *financial spreadsheet* such as Excel. Figure 3.2 shows a simplified spreadsheet illustrating the key inputs, the cell formula for the output, and the future value of $133.82.[4]

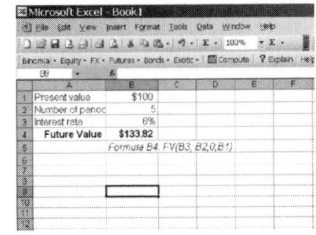

Figure 3.2
An Excel Spreadsheet Used to Solve a Time Value of Interest Problem, in this Case, Future Value

---

[2.] A complete table of future value factors is included in Appendix A at the back of this book. Similarly, complete tables of other factors excerpted in this chapter are included in Appendix A.

[3.] Demonstration of the calculator keystrokes for the TI BAII PLUS calculator and a simplified Excel spreadsheet for this problem and most other problems in this chapter are included in Chapter 3 of Megginson and Smart's undergraduate version of this book, *Introduction to Corporate Finance* (Mason OH: Thomson South-Western, 2006).

[4.] A useful approximation for finding the amount of time it will take for an initial deposit to double in value at a stated interest rate is the *Rule of 72*. The **Rule of 72** states that the approximate amount of time (*n*) required to double an initial deposit at an interest rate (*r*) is:

$$n \approx 72/r$$

For example, if we wanted to find how long it would take to double an initial deposit into an account paying 7% annual interest, substituting *r* = 7 into the above equation, we get *n* = 10.3 years (72/7 = 10.3). Regardless of the amount of the initial deposit, it will take approximately 10.3 years to double it if it earns a 7% annual rate of interest.

Figure 3.3
The Power of
Compound Interest:
Future Value of $1
Invested at Different
Interest Rates

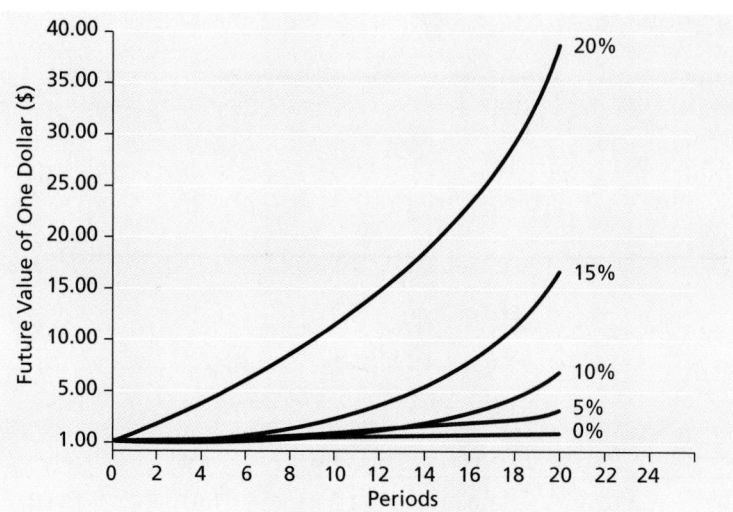

A GRAPHIC VIEW OF FUTURE VALUE

Remember that we measure future value at the *end* of the given period. Figure 3.3 shows the relationship between various interest rates, the number of periods interest is earned, and the future value of $1. The figure shows two key points about future value: (1) the higher the interest rate, the higher the future value, and (2) the longer the period of time, the higher the future value. Note that for an interest rate of 0 percent, the future value always equals the present value ($1), but for any interest rate greater than zero, the future value is greater than the present value of $1.

Concept Review Questions

3. Assuming compounding occurs once per year, will a deposit made in an account paying compound interest yield a higher future value after one period than an equal-size deposit in an account paying simple interest? What about future values for investments held longer than one period?

4. How would (a) a *decrease* in the interest rate or (b) an *increase* in the holding period of a deposit affect its future value? Why?

PV

$$PV = \frac{FV}{(1+r)^n}$$

3.3 PRESENT VALUE OF A LUMP SUM

So far we have examined how to project the amount of cash that will build over time as an initial investment earns interest. Now we reverse that focus, to ask what an investor would be willing to pay today in exchange for a lump-sum payment at some point in the future. In other words, we want to know the *present value* of the future payment.

In the Opening Focus, we were trying to determine the present value of the lottery's 30-year *stream* of $11.3 million annual payments, assuming investment of the cash at a 6 percent interest rate. In this section, we focus on the simpler problem of calculating the present value of a single future cash payment.

THE CONCEPT OF PRESENT VALUE

In finance, we use the term **discounting** to describe the process of calculating present values. Discounting answers this question: If I can earn r percent on my money, what is the most I would be willing to pay *now* for an opportunity to receive FV dollars n periods from today? This process is actually the *inverse* of compounding interest:

> In *compounding*, we find the future value of present dollars invested at a given rate.
>
> In *discounting*, we find the present value of a future amount, assuming an opportunity to earn a given return (r), on the money.[5]

To see how this works, suppose that an investment will pay you $300 one year from now. How much would you be willing to spend today to acquire this investment if you can earn 6 percent on an alternative investment of equal risk? To answer this question, you must determine how many dollars you would have to invest at 6 percent today to have $300 one year from now. Let PV equal this unknown amount, and use the same notation as in the future value discussion:

$$PV \times (1 + 0.06) = \$300$$

Solving this equation for PV gives us the following:

$$PV = \frac{\$300}{(1 + 0.06)} = \$283.02$$

The present value of $300 one year from today is $283.02. That is, investing $283.02 today at a 6 percent interest rate would result in $300 at the end of one year. Therefore, you would be willing to pay no more than $283.02 for the investment that pays you $300 in one year.

in excel:

= PV(r, n, payment, FV, type)

THE EQUATION FOR PRESENT VALUE

We can solve Equation 3.1 for PV in order to find the present value of a lump sum. The present value (PV) of some future amount (FV) to be received n periods from now, assuming an opportunity cost of r, is given by Equation 3.2:

$$PV = \frac{FV}{(1 + r)^n} = FV \times \left[\frac{1}{(1 + r)^n}\right] \qquad \text{(Eq. 3.2)}$$

FV is negative or excel will return a negative PV

Applying the Model 3.2 illustrates application of Equation 3.2, using a corporate investment opportunity as an example.

---

[5] This interest rate is variously referred to as the *discount rate, required return, cost of capital, hurdle rate,* or *opportunity cost.*

APPLYING THE MODEL 3.2

Pam Verity, the financial manager of the Wildcatter Oil Drilling Company, can purchase the right to receive a $1,700 royalty payment eight years from now. This offer came from Sam Long, the owner of Petroleum Land Management Company. Pam believes her company's opportunity cost should be 8 percent on investments of this level of risk. (This is the amount of return she believes she can earn on other similar-risk investments.) How much should Pam be willing to pay for the right to receive this royalty payment? Substituting $FV = \$1,700$, $n = 8$, and $r = 0.08$ into Equation 3.2 yields the following:

$$PV = \frac{\$1,700}{(1 + 0.08)^8} = \frac{\$1,700}{(1.85093)} = \$918.46$$

Pam finds that the present value of this $1,700 royalty payment is $918.46. If Sam offers this investment opportunity at a price of $918.46 or less, Pam should accept the offer; otherwise, she should reject it. Figure 3.4 shows this process in a time line.

As with future values, there are three popular methods for simplifying present value calculations. One method is to use a present value factor (*PVF*) table, such as Table A2 in Appendix A. A portion of Table A2 appears here as Table 3.2. You can find present value factors for specific discount rates and compounding periods ($PVF_{r\%,n}$) just

Figure 3.4
Time Line for the Present Value of $1,700 to Be Received in Eight Years at an 8% Discount Rate

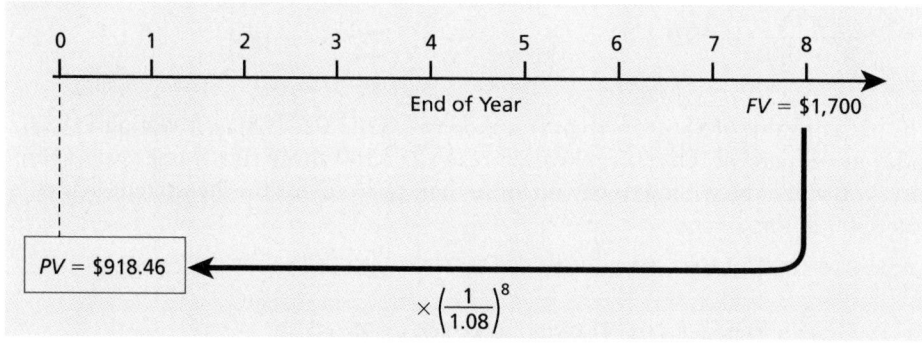

Table 3.2
Format of a Present Value Factor (*PVF*) Table

Period	\multicolumn{8}{c}{Interest Rate (r)}
	1%	2%	3%	4%	5%	6%	7%	8%
1	0.990	0.980	0.971	0.962	0.952	0.943	0.935	0.926
2	0.980	0.961	0.943	0.925	0.907	0.890	0.873	0.857
3	0.971	0.942	0.915	0.889	0.864	0.840	0.816	0.794
4	0.961	0.924	0.888	0.855	0.823	0.792	0.763	0 735
5	0.951	0.906	0.863	0.822	0.784	0.747	0.713	0.681
6	0.942	0.888	0.837	0.790	0.746	0.705	0.666	0.630
7	0.933	0.871	0.813	0.760	0.711	0.665	0.623	0.583
8	0.923	0.853	0.789	0.731	0.677	0.627	0.582	0.540

as you did for future values. For the current example, $PVF_{8\%,8}$, the table indicates that the present value of $1 discounted for 8 years at 8 percent is $0.540 (the intersection of the 8-percent column and the 8-year row). Multiply that figure by $1,700 to find the present value of the royalty payment, $918 (rounding to the nearest dollar). Using financial calculators or spreadsheets are two other popular methods for simplifying present value calculations for a lump sum.

A GRAPHIC VIEW OF PRESENT VALUE

For investors who expect to receive cash in the future, Figure 3.5 contains two important messages. First, the present value of a future cash payment declines the longer investors must wait to receive it. Second, the present value declines as the discount rate rises. Note that for a discount rate of 0 percent, the present value always equals the future value ($1). However, for any discount rate greater than zero, the present value falls below the future value.

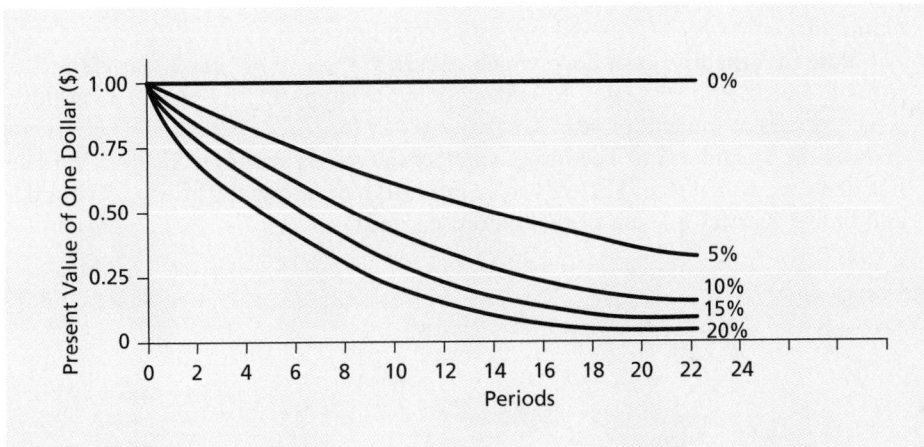

Figure 3.5
The Power of Discounting: Present Value of $1 Discounted at Different Interest Rates

---

Concept Review Questions

5. How are the present value and the future value of a lump sum related—both definitionally and mathematically? Notice that for a given interest rate (r) and a given investment time horizon (n), $PVF_{r,n}$ and $FVF_{r,n}$ are inverses of each other. Why?

6. How would (a) an *increase* in the discount rate or (b) a *decrease* in the time period until the cash flow is received affect the present value? Why?

3.4 FUTURE VALUE OF CASH FLOW STREAMS *annuity*

Financial managers frequently need to evaluate *streams* of cash flows that occur in future periods. Though this is mechanically more complicated than computing the future or present value of a single cash flow, the same basic techniques apply.

Two types of cash flow streams are possible: the mixed stream and the annuity. A **mixed stream** is a series of unequal payments reflecting no particular pattern. An **annuity** is a stream of equal periodic cash flows over a stated period of time. Either of these cash flow patterns can represent *inflows* of returns earned on investments or *outflows* of funds invested to earn future returns. Because certain shortcuts are possible when evaluating an annuity, we discuss mixed streams and annuities separately.

FINDING THE FUTURE VALUE OF A MIXED STREAM

The future value of any *stream* of cash flows measured at the end of a specified year is merely the sum of the future values of the individual cash flows at that year's end. This future value is sometimes called the *terminal value*. Applying the Model 3.3 demonstrates such a calculation.

APPLYING THE MODEL 3.3

Assume that we wish to determine the balance in an investment account earning 9 percent annual interest, given the following five end-of-year deposits: $400 in year 1, $800 in year 2, $500 in year 3, $400 in year 4, and $300 in year 5. These cash flows appear on the time line in Figure 3.6, which also depicts the future value calculation for this mixed stream of cash flows.

Note that the first cash flow, which occurs at the end of year 1, earns interest for four years (end of year 1 to end of year 5). Similarly, the second cash flow, which occurs at the end of year 2, earns interest for three years (end of year 2 to end of year 5), and so on. The future value of the mixed stream is $2,930.70.[6] The five deposits, which total $2,400 before interest, have grown by nearly $531 at the end of five years as a result of the interest earned.

Figure 3.6
Time Line for the Future Value at the End of Five Years of a Mixed Cash Flow Stream Invested at a 9% Interest Rate

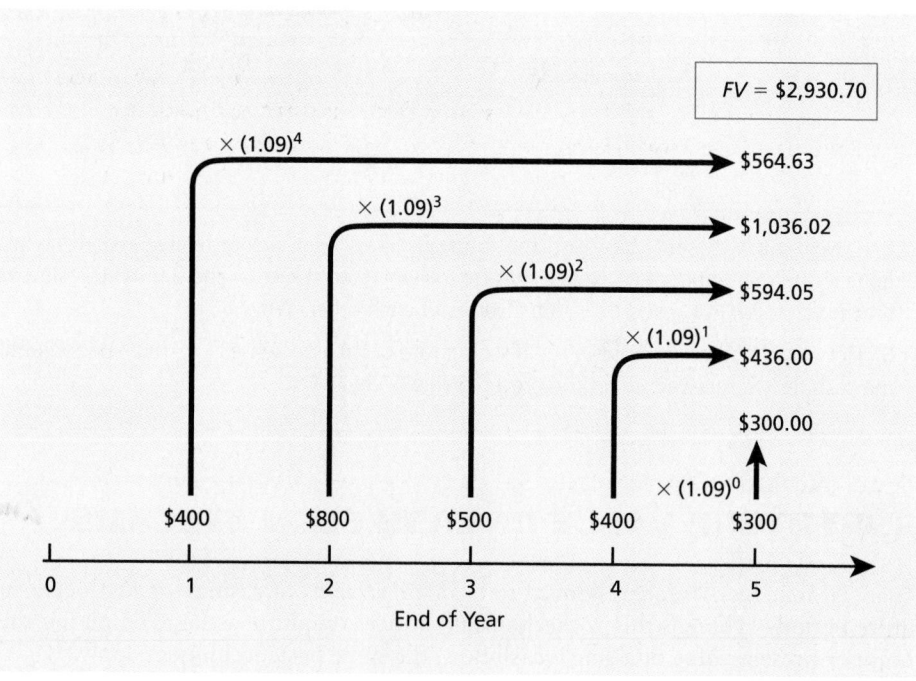

Letting CF_t represent the cash flow at the end of year t, the future value of an n-year mixed stream of cash flows (FV) can be expressed as shown in Equation 3.3:

$$FV = CF_1 \times (1 + r)^{n-1} + CF_2 \times (1 + r)^{n-2} + \cdots$$
$$+ CF_n \times (1 + r)^{n-n}$$

(Eq. 3.3)

Substituting the annual cash flows and the 9 percent interest rate into Equation 3.3, we would calculate the value for each year (shown to the right of the time line). These values would total $2,930.70.

We can simplify the notation for Equation 3.3, as shown in Equation 3.3a, by using the Greek summation symbol, Σ. Doing so would give us a shorthand way of saying that the future value of this n-year mixed stream is equal to the sum of the future values of individual cash flows from periods 1, 2, 3, . . . , n:

$$FV = \sum_{t=1}^{n} CF_t \times (1 + r)^{n-t}$$

(Eq. 3.3a)

Though summations economize on the notation needed to express most of the equations presented in this chapter, for clarity we present equations in their "noncondensed" format wherever possible, and we use the summation notation sparingly. Mathematical purists can construct the more succinct formulations.

TYPES OF ANNUITIES

Before looking at future value computations for annuities, we distinguish between the two basic types of annuities: the ordinary annuity and the annuity due. An **ordinary annuity** is an annuity for which the payments occur *at the end of each period*. An **annuity due** is one for which the payments occur *at the beginning of each period.*

To demonstrate these differences, assume that you want to choose the better of two annuities as a personal investment opportunity. Both are five-year, $1,000 annuities, but annuity A is an ordinary annuity, and annuity B is an annuity due. Although the amount of each annuity totals $5,000, the timing of the cash flows differs; each cash flow arrives one year sooner with the annuity due than with the ordinary annuity. As you might expect from your knowledge of the time value of money core principle, for any positive interest rate, *the future value of an annuity due is always greater than the future value of an otherwise identical ordinary annuity.*[7] Why? Because you have a longer time to earn interest on the annuity due.

FINDING THE FUTURE VALUE OF AN ORDINARY ANNUITY

We can calculate the future value of an ordinary annuity using the same method demonstrated earlier for a mixed stream.

APPLYING THE MODEL 3.4

Assume that you wish to save money on a regular basis to finance an exotic vacation in five years. You are confident that, with sacrifice and discipline, you can force yourself to deposit $1,000 annually at the *end of each* of the next five years

---

[7.] Because ordinary annuities arise frequently in corporate finance, we use the term "annuity" throughout this book to refer to ordinary annuities unless otherwise specified.

into a savings account paying 7 percent annual interest. The time line in Figure 3.7 depicts this situation graphically.

We can use Equation 3.3 to compute the future value (FV) of this annuity. We simply use the assumed interest rate (r) of 7 percent and plug in the known values of each of the five yearly ($n = 5$) cash flows (CF_1 to CF_5), as follows:

$$FV = CF_1 \times (1 + r)^{n-1} + CF_2 \times (1 + r)^{n-2} + \cdots + CF_n \times (1 + r)^{n-n}$$

$$FV = CF_1 \times (1 + r)^{5-1} + CF_2 \times (1 + r)^{5-2} + \cdots + CF_5 \times (1 + r)^{5-5}$$

$$= \$1,000(1.07)^4 + \$1,000(1.07)^3 + \$1,000(1.07)^2 + \$1,000(1.07)^1 + \$1,000(1.07)^0$$

$$= \$1,310.80 + \$1,225.04 + \$1,144.90 + \$1,070 + \$1,000 = \$5,750.74$$

The year-1 cash flow of $1,000 earns 7 percent interest for four years, the year-2 cash flow earns 7 percent interest for three years, and so on. The future value of the ordinary annuity is $5,750.74.

Making this calculation for a longer annuity would become cumbersome. Fortunately, a shortcut formula exists that simplifies the future value calculation of an ordinary annuity. Using the symbol PMT to represent the annuity's annual payment, Equation 3.4 gives the future value of an annuity that lasts for n years (FV), assuming an interest rate of r percent:

$$FV = PMT \times \left\{ \frac{[(1 + r)^n - 1]}{r} \right\} \qquad \text{(Eq. 3.4)}$$

[handwritten annotations in margin: in excel: = FV (r, n, payment, PV, type) payment = negative # type = 0 if ordinary annuity, 1 if annuity due]

[handwritten below equation: FV of ordinary annuity (assumes payment at end of each period)]

Figure 3.7
Time Line for the Future Value at the End of Five Years of an Ordinary Annuity of $1,000 Per Year Invested at a 7% Interest Rate

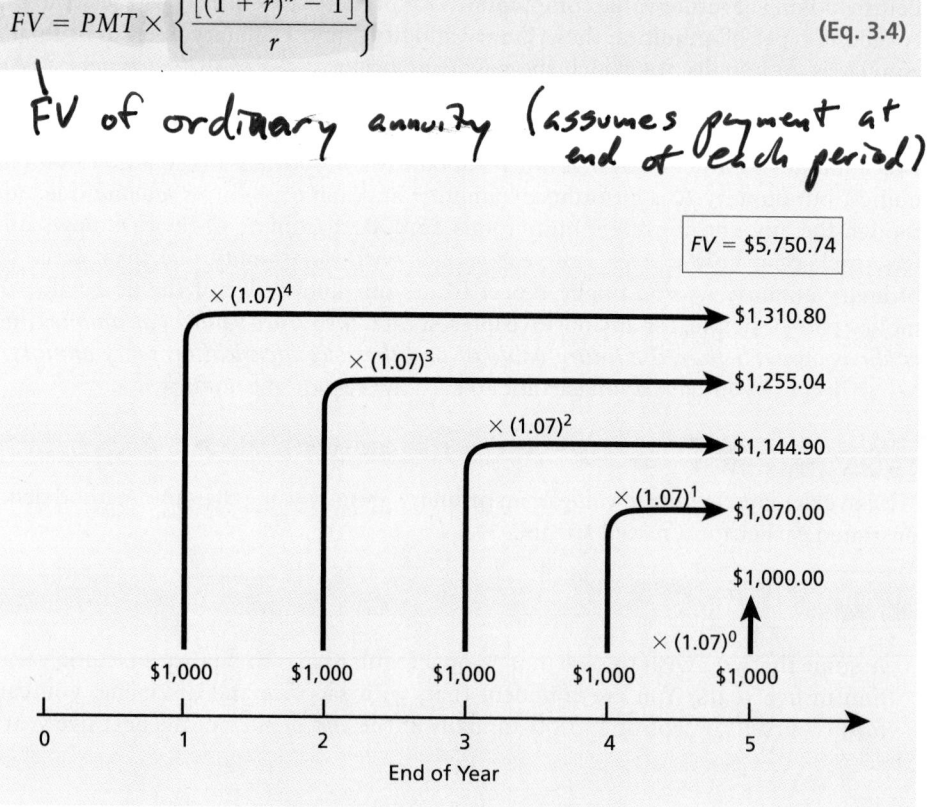

We can demonstrate that Equation 3.4 yields the same answer we obtained in the previous model by plugging in the values, $PMT = \$1{,}000$, $n = 5$, and $r = 0.07$:

$$FV = \$1{,}000 \times \left\{ \frac{[(1.07)^5 - 1]}{0.07} \right\} = \$1{,}000 \times \left[\frac{(1.40255 - 1)}{0.07} \right]$$

$$= \$1{,}000 \times 5.7507 = \$5{,}750.74$$

Once again, we find the future value of this ordinary annuity to be $5,750.74.

Instead of using algebra, we could use a table, such as Table A3 in Appendix A, that details future value factors for ordinary annuities. These are generically labeled $FVFA_{r\%,n}$. In our example, the factor corresponding to $r = 0.07$ and $n = 5$ ($FVFA_{7\%,5}$) equals 5.751. We multiply this factor by the $1,000 to compute FV, which is $5,751. Alternatives we could use to simplify future value calculations for annuities are financial calculators or spreadsheets.

FINDING THE FUTURE VALUE OF AN ANNUITY DUE

The calculations to find the future value of an annuity due involve only a slight change to those already used for an ordinary annuity. For the annuity due, the question is, how much money will you have at the end of five years to finance an exotic vacation if you deposit $1,000 annually at the *beginning of each* year into a savings account paying 7 percent annual interest?

Figure 3.8 depicts this scenario graphically on a time line. Note that the ends of years 0 through 4 are respectively equivalent to the beginnings of years 1 through 5. As

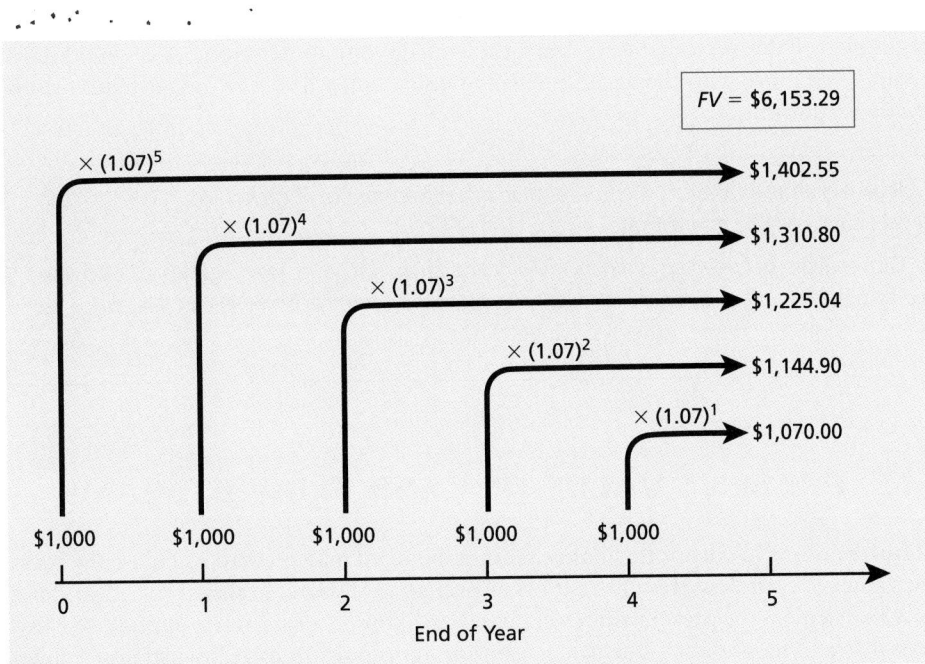

Figure 3.8
Time Line for the Future Value at the End of Five Years of an Annuity Due of $1,000 Per Year Invested at a 7% Interest Rate

expected, the $6,153.29 future value of the annuity due is greater than the $5,750.74 future value of the comparable ordinary annuity. Because the cash flows of the annuity due occur at the beginning of the year, the cash flow of $1,000 at the beginning of year 1 earns 7 percent interest for five years, the cash flow of $1,000 at the beginning of year 2 earns 7 percent interest for four years, and so on. Comparing this to the ordinary annuity, you can see that each $1,000 cash flow of the annuity due earns interest for one more year than the comparable ordinary annuity cash flow. As a result, the future value of the annuity due is greater than the future value of the comparable ordinary annuity.

We can convert the equation for the future value of an ordinary annuity, Equation 3.4, into an expression for the future value of an annuity due, FV (annuity due). To do so, we must take into account that each cash flow of an annuity due earns an additional year of interest. Therefore, we simply multiply the Equation 3.4 formula by $(1 + r)$, as shown in Equation 3.5:

payment at start of each period

$$FV(\text{annuity due}) = PMT \times \left\{ \frac{[(1 + r)^n - 1]}{r} \right\} \times (1 + r) \qquad \text{(Eq. 3.5)}$$

Equation 3.5 demonstrates that the future value of an annuity due always exceeds the future value of a similar ordinary annuity (for any positive interest rate)—by a factor of 1 plus the interest rate. We can check this by comparing the results from the two different five-year vacation savings plans. We determined that, given a 7 percent interest rate, at the end of year 5, the future value of the ordinary annuity was $5,750.74 and the future value of the annuity due was $6,153.29. Multiplying the future value of the ordinary annuity by 1 plus the interest rate yields the future value of the annuity due:

$$FV(\text{annuity due}) = \$5,750.74 \times (1.07) = \$6,153.29$$

The future value of the annuity due is greater because its cash flow occurs at the beginning of the period, rather than the end. In our illustration, you would earn about $400 more with the annuity due and could enjoy a somewhat more luxurious exotic vacation.

Concept Review Questions

7. How would you calculate *the future value of a mixed stream of cash flows,* given the cash flows and applicable interest rate?

8. Differentiate between an *ordinary annuity* and an *annuity due.* How would you calculate the future value of an ordinary annuity? How (for the same cash flows) can that value be converted into the future value of an annuity due?

3.5 PRESENT VALUE OF CASH FLOW STREAMS

Many decisions in corporate finance require financial managers to calculate the present values of cash flow streams that occur over several years. In this section, we show how to calculate the present values of mixed cash flow streams and annuities. We also demonstrate the present value calculation for an important cash flow stream known as a *perpetuity.*

FINDING THE PRESENT VALUE OF A MIXED STREAM

The present value of any cash flow stream is merely the sum of the present values of the individual cash flows. To calculate the present values of all kinds of cash flow streams, we can apply the same techniques we used to calculate present values of lump sums.

APPLYING THE MODEL 3.6

Assume that shortly after graduation you receive an inheritance that you use to purchase a small bed-and-breakfast inn as an investment (and a weekend escape). Your plan is to sell the inn after five years. The inn is an old mansion, so you know that appliances, furniture, and other equipment will wear out and need to be replaced or repaired on a regular basis. You estimate these expenses over the five years of your ownership as follows: $4,000 during year 1, $8,000 during year 2, $5,000 during year 3, $4,000 during year 4, and $3,000 during year 5. For simplicity, assume that the expense payments will be made at the end of each year.

Because you have some of your inheritance left over after purchasing the inn (the deceased was indeed generous), you want to set aside a lump sum today from which you can make annual withdrawals to meet the estimated expenses when they come due, as shown on the time line in Figure 3.9. Suppose you can invest the lump sum in a bank account that pays 9 percent interest. To determine the amount of money you need to put in the account, you must calculate the present value of the stream of future expenses, using 9 percent as the discount rate.

We can use present value factor tables such as Table A2, a financial calculator, or an Excel spreadsheet to determine the present value factors corresponding to each annual cash flow. We then add together the present value of each year's cash flows and find that the present value of the mixed stream is $19,047.58. This is the lump-sum amount you will need to set aside today to fund the estimated expenses over the five years.

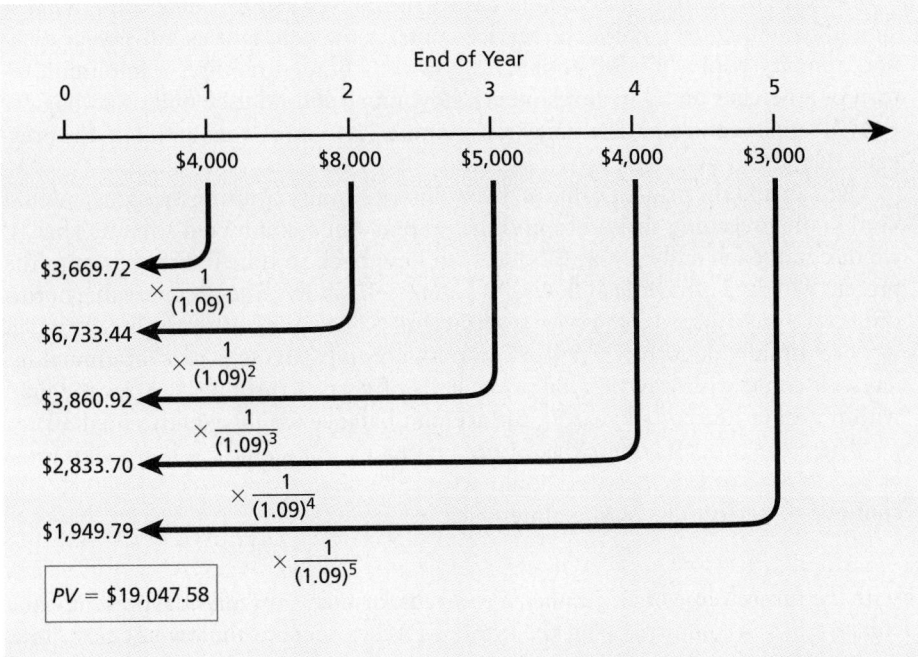

Figure 3.9
Time Line for the Present Value of a Five-Year Mixed Stream Discounted at a 9% Interest Rate

As you no doubt suspect, there is a general formula for computing the present value of a stream of future cash flows. Continuing to let CF_t represent the cash flow at the end of year t, we can express the present value of an n-year mixed stream of cash flows (PV) as Equation 3.6:

$$PV = \left[CF_1 \times \frac{1}{(1+r)^1} \right] + \left[CF_2 \times \frac{1}{(1+r)^2} \right] + \cdots + \left[CF_n \times \frac{1}{(1+r)^n} \right]$$

$$= \sum_{t=1}^{n} CF_t \times \frac{1}{(1+r)^t} \qquad \text{(Eq. 3.6)}$$

If we substitute into Equation 3.6 the cash flows shown on the time line in Figure 3.9 and the 9 percent discount rate, we obtain the present value figure $19,047.58.

FINDING THE PRESENT VALUE OF AN ORDINARY ANNUITY

We can find the present value of an ordinary annuity in a way similar to that for a mixed stream: Discount each payment and then add up each payment's present value to find the annuity's present value.

APPLYING THE MODEL 3.7

Assume that a principal equipment supplier has approached Braden Company, a producer of plastic toys, with an intriguing offer for a service contract. The supplier, the Extruding Machines Corporation (EMC), offers to take over all of Braden's equipment repair and servicing for five years in exchange for a one-time payment today. Braden's managers know that their company spends $7,000 on maintenance at the end of every year, so EMC's service contract would reduce Braden's cash outflows by this $7,000 annually for five years.

Because these are equal annual cash benefits, Braden can determine what it should be willing to pay for the service contract by valuing it as a five-year ordinary annuity with a $7,000 annual cash flow. If Braden requires a minimum return of 8 percent on all its investments, how much should it be willing to pay for EMC's service contract? The time line in Figure 3.10 shows calculation of the present value of this annuity.

We can find the present value of this ordinary annuity by using the same method used in the preceding section to find the present value of a mixed stream. That is, we discount each end-of-year $7,000 cash flow back to time 0 and then sum the present values of all five cash flows. As Figure 3.10 shows, the present value of this ordinary annuity (EMC's service contract) is $27,948.97. Effectively, if Braden were to initially deposit $27,948.97 into an account paying 8 percent annual interest, it could withdraw $7,000 at the ends of years 1 through 5. After the final withdrawal (at the end of year 5), the account balance would exactly equal $0.

Therefore, if EMC offers the service contract to Braden for a lump-sum price of $27,948.97 or less, Braden should accept the offer. Otherwise, Braden should continue to perform its own maintenance.

As with the future value of an annuity, a shortcut formula simplifies the present value calculation for an annuity. Using the symbol PMT to denote the annual cash flow,

Figure 3.10
Time Line for the
Present Value of a
Five-Year Ordinary
Annuity Discounted
at an 8% Interest Rate

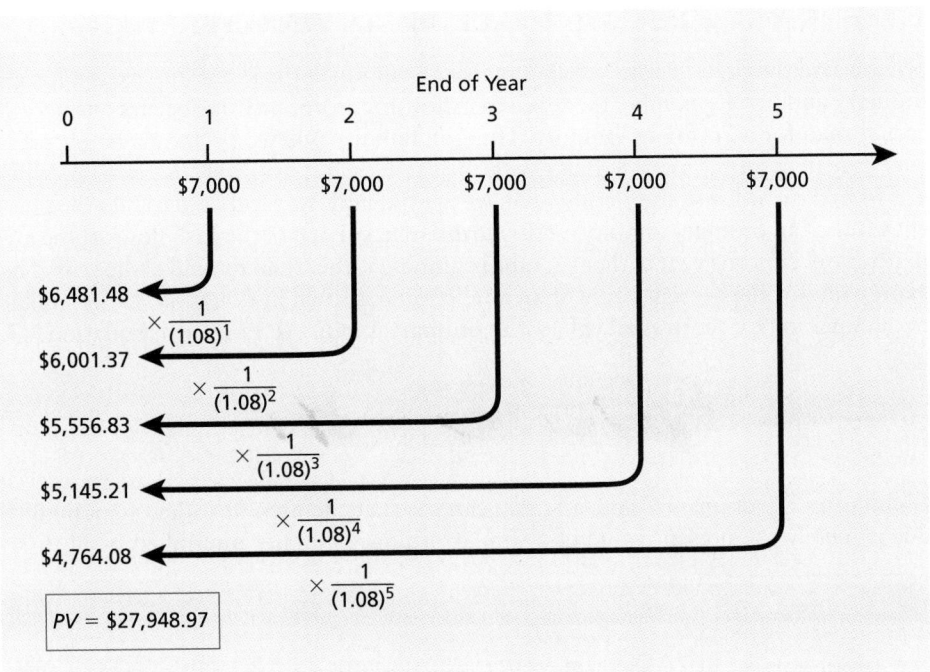

we can use the formula in Equation 3.7 for the present value of an *n*-year ordinary annuity (*PV*):

$$PV = \frac{PMT}{r} \times \left[1 - \frac{1}{(1+r)^n} \right] \qquad \text{(Eq. 3.7)}$$

APPLYING THE MODEL 3.8

We can use Equation 3.7 to calculate the present value of the service contract EMC has offered to Braden Company. Substituting in $n = 5$ years, $r = 0.08$, and $PMT = \$7,000$, we once again find the present value (*PV*) of this ordinary annuity to be $27,948.97, as shown below:

$$PV = \frac{\$7,000}{0.08} \times \left[1 - \frac{1}{(1.08)^5} \right] = \frac{\$7,000}{0.08} \times [1 - 0.6806] = \$27,948.97$$

By now, you know we can simplify these computations using a present value factor table. Many students find it easier to understand Equation 3.7 when the right-hand side of the equation is expressed simply as the annual cash flow (*PMT*) times the present value factor for an annuity paying *r* percent for *n* years, or $PVFA_{r\%,n}$. Table A4 in Appendix A gives present value factors for ordinary annuities at various discount rates for different holding periods. From Table A4 we get $PVFA_{8\%,5} = 3.993$. When multiplied by the $7,000 annual cash flow, that factor results in a present value of $27,951, approximately equal to the present value obtained using more precise computations.

FINDING THE PRESENT VALUE OF AN ANNUITY DUE

We can find the present value of an annuity due in much the same way we did for an ordinary annuity. Remember that each cash flow for an annuity due occurs one period earlier than for an ordinary annuity. Thus, an annuity due would have a larger present value than an ordinary annuity with the same cash flows, discount rate, and life.

To find the value of the annuity due, we use the same method used to find the present value of an ordinary annuity, with one difference: Each of the cash flows of the annuity due occurs one year earlier—at the beginning rather than the end of the year. The expression for the present value of an annuity due, shown in Equation 3.8, is similar to the equation for the present value of an ordinary annuity (PV) given in Equation 3.7.

$$PV(\text{annuity due}) = \frac{PMT}{r} \times \left[1 - \frac{1}{(1 + r)^n}\right] \times (1 + r) \qquad \text{(Eq. 3.8)}$$

Comparing Equations 3.7 and 3.8, you can see that the present value of an annuity due is merely the present value of a similar ordinary annuity multiplied by $(1 + r)$.

APPLYING THE MODEL 3.9

To demonstrate, assume that Braden Company in the previous illustration wishes to determine the present value of the five-year, $7,000 service contract at an 8 percent discount rate, and assume that each of the cash flows occurs *at the beginning of the year*. To convert EMC's service-contract offer into an annuity due, we simply assume that EMC would have had to pay its annual maintenance cost of $7,000 at the *beginning* of each of the next five years. Braden is still evaluating what amounts to a five-year annuity; the company will instead pay out each annual cash flow one year earlier.

The present value of this annuity due is simply $(1 + r)$ times the value of the ordinary annuity: $PV(\text{annuity due}) = \$27,948.97 \times (1.08) = \$30,184.89$. If Braden paid its maintenance costs at the start of each year, the most it would be willing to pay EMC for the service contract would increase by more than $2,000, to $30,184.89.

FINDING THE PRESENT VALUE OF A PERPETUITY

A **perpetuity** is an annuity with an infinite life; it promises to pay the same amount at the end of every year *forever*. One of the first, and certainly the most famous, perpetuities in modern history was the massive "consol" bond issue sold by the British government after the Napoleonic Wars ended in 1815. This bond issue got its name from the fact that it consolidated all the existing British war debts into a single issue that paid a constant annual amount of interest into perpetuity. The issue itself never matured, meaning that the principal was never to be repaid.

Currently, not many corporations or governments issue perpetual bonds.[8] Perhaps the simplest modern example of a perpetuity is preferred stock issued by corporations. Preferred shares promise investors a constant annual (or quarterly) dividend payment forever. Though "forever" is a difficult time period to measure, we simply express the

---

[8] Some examples come close to being perpetuities. In July 1993, the Walt Disney Company sold $300 million of bonds that matured in the year 2093, 100 years after they were issued. The market dubbed these "Sleeping Beauty bonds" because their maturity matched the amount of time that Sleeping Beauty slept before being kissed by Prince Charming in the classic story.

lifetime (n) of this security as infinity (∞), and modify our basic valuation formulation for an annuity accordingly. We wish to determine the present value of an annuity (PV) that pays a constant annual dividend amount (PMT) for a perpetual number of years ($n = \infty$) discounted at a rate r. Here, the Greek summation notation is helpful in expressing the formula in Equation 3.9:

$$PV = PMT \times \sum_{t=1}^{\infty} \frac{1}{(1 + r)^t} \qquad \text{(Eq. 3.9)}$$

Fortunately, Equation 3.9 also comes in a simplified version, which states that the present value of a perpetuity equals the annual, end-of-year payment divided by the discount rate (in decimal form). Equation 3.10 gives this straightforward expression for the present value of a perpetuity (PV):

$$PV = PMT \times \frac{1}{r} = \frac{PMT}{r} \qquad \text{(Eq. 3.10)}$$

APPLYING THE MODEL 3.10

Assume that you wish to find the present value of the dividend stream associated with a preferred stock issued by Alpha and Omega Service Company. A&O, as the company is commonly known, promises to pay $10 per year on its preferred shares. Security analysts believe that the firm's business and financial risk merits a required return of 12.5 percent. Substituting the values $PMT = \$10$ per year and $r = 0.125$ into Equation 3.10, we find the following:

$$PV = \frac{\$10}{0.125} = \$80$$

The present value of A&O's preferred stock dividends, valued as an annuity with a perpetual life, is $80 per share. In other words, the right to receive $10 at the end of every year for an indefinite period is worth $80 today if a person can earn 12.5 percent on investments of similar risk. The reason is that if the person had $80 today and earned 12.5 percent interest on it each year, $10 a year (0.125 × $80) could be withdrawn indefinitely without ever touching the initial $80.

FINDING THE PRESENT VALUE OF A GROWING PERPETUITY

By definition, perpetuities pay a constant periodic amount forever. However, few aspects of modern life are constant, and most of the cash flows we care about have a tendency to grow over time. This is true for items of income such as wages and salaries, dividend payments from corporations, and Social Security payments from governments.[9] Inflation is one, but only one, factor driving the increase in cash flows over time. Because of this tendency for cash flows to grow over time, we must therefore examine how to adjust the present value of a perpetuity formula to account for expected growth in future cash flows.

[9.] Unfortunately, this is also true for expense items such as rent and utility expenses, car prices, and tuition payments.

Suppose we want to calculate the present value (PV) of a stream of cash flows growing forever ($n = \infty$) at rate g. Given an opportunity cost of r, the present value of the **growing perpetuity** is given by equation 3.11, which is sometimes called the **Gordon Growth model**:[10]

$$PV = \frac{CF_1}{r - g} \qquad r > g \qquad \text{(Eq. 3.11)}$$

Note that the numerator in Equation 3.11 is CF_1, the first year's cash flow. This cash flow is expected to grow at a constant annual rate (g) from now to the end of time. We can determine the cash flow for any specific future year (t) by applying the growth rate (g) as follows:

$$CF_t = CF_1 \times (1 + g)^{t-1}$$

APPLYING THE MODEL 3.11

Assume that Gil Bates is a philanthropist wishing to endow a medical foundation with sufficient money to fund ongoing research. Gil is particularly impressed with the research proposal submitted by the Smith Cancer Institute (SCI). The Institute requests an endowment sufficient to cover its expenses for medical equipment. Next year these expenses will total $10 million, and they will grow by 3 percent per year in perpetuity afterwards.

Assume the Institute can earn an 11 percent return on Gil's contribution. How much must Gil contribute to finance the Institute's medical equipment expenditures in perpetuity? Equation 3.11 tells us that the present value of these expenses equals $125 million, computed as follows:

$$PV = \frac{\$10,000,000}{0.11 - 0.03} = \frac{\$10,000,000}{0.08} = \$125,000,000$$

Gil would have to make an investment of "only" $90,909,091 ($10,000,000 ÷ 0.11, using Equation 3.10) to fund a nongrowing perpetuity of $10 million per year. The additional investment of about $34.1 million supports the 3 percent annual growth in the payout to SCI.

SMART CONCEPTS
See the concept explained step-by-step at
SMARTFinance

Concept Review Questions

9. How would you calculate the present value of a *mixed stream* of cash flows, given the cash flows and an applicable required return?

10. Given the present value of an *ordinary annuity* and the applicable required return, how can this value be easily converted into the present value of an otherwise identical *annuity due*? What is the fundamental difference between the cash flow streams of these two annuities?

11. What is a *perpetuity,* and how can you conveniently calculate its present value? How do you find the present value of a *growing perpetuity*?

---

[10] For this formula to work, the discount rate must be greater than the growth rate. When cash flows grow at a rate equal to or greater than the discount rate, the present value of the stream would be infinite.

3.6 SPECIAL APPLICATIONS OF TIME VALUE

Financial managers frequently apply future value and present value techniques to determine the values of other variables. In these cases, the manager or analyst knows the future or present values, and solves the equations presented earlier for the unknown variables. Examples of unknown variables in these instances are the cash flow (*CF* or *PMT*), interest or discount rate (*r*), or number of time periods (*n*).

Here we consider six of the more common time value applications and refinements: (1) compounding more frequently than annually; (2) stated versus effective annual interest rates; (3) calculation of deposits needed to accumulate a future sum; (4) loan amortization; (5) implied interest or growth rates; and (6) number of compounding periods.

COMPOUNDING MORE FREQUENTLY THAN ANNUALLY

In many applications, interest compounds more frequently than once a year. Financial institutions compound interest semiannually, quarterly, monthly, weekly, daily, or even continuously. This section explores how the present and future value techniques change if interest compounds more than once a year.

Semiannual Compounding. **Semiannual compounding** of interest involves two compounding periods within the year. Instead of the stated interest rate being paid once per year, one-half of the rate is paid twice a year.

To demonstrate, consider an opportunity to deposit $100 in a savings account paying 8 percent interest with semiannual compounding. After the first six months, your account grows by 4 percent, to $104. Six months later, the account again grows by 4 percent, to $108.16. Notice that after one year, the total increase in the account value is $8.16, or 8.16 percent ($8.16 ÷ $100). This return slightly exceeds the stated rate of 8 percent because semiannual compounding allows you to earn *interest on interest* during the year. Table 3.3 shows the growth of the account value every six months for the first two years. At the end of two years, the account value reaches $116.99.

Quarterly Compounding. As the name implies, **quarterly compounding** describes a situation in which interest compounds four times per year. An investment with quarterly compounding pays one-fourth of the stated interest rate every three months.

To demonstrate, assume that after further investigation, you find an institution that will pay 8 percent interest compounded quarterly. After three months, your $100 deposit grows by 2 percent, to $102. Three months later the balance again increases 2 percent, to $104.04. By the end of the year, the balance reaches $108.24.

Period (months)	Beginning Principal (1)	Future Value Factor (2)	Future Value at End of Period [(1) × (2)] (3)
6	$100.00	1.04	$104.00
12	104.00	1.04	108.16
18	108.16	1.04	112.49
24	112.49	1.04	116.99

Table 3.3
The Future Value from Investing $100 at 8 Percent Interest Compounded Semiannually over Two Years

Table 3.4 tracks the growth in the account every three months for two years. At the end of two years, the account is worth $117.16.

Table 3.5 compares values for your $100 deposit at the end of years 1 and 2, given annual, semiannual, and quarterly compounding at the 8 percent rate. As you should expect by now, *the more frequently interest compounds, the greater the amount of money that accumulates.*

A General Equation. We can generalize the preceding examples in a simple equation. Suppose that you invest a lump sum, denoted by *PV*, at *r* percent per year for *n* years. If *m* equals the number of times per year that interest compounds, then the future value grows as shown in the following equation:

$$FV = PV \times \left(1 + \frac{r}{m}\right)^{m \times n}$$

(Eq. 3.12)

Notice that if *m* = 1, Equation 3.12 reduces to Equation 3.1. The next several examples verify that this equation yields the same ending account values after two years as shown in Tables 3.3 and 3.4.

APPLYING THE MODEL 3.12

We have calculated the amount that you would have at the end of two years if you deposited $100 at 8 percent interest compounded semiannually and quarterly. For semiannual compounding, *m* = 2 in Equation 3.12; for quarterly compounding,

Table 3.4
The Future Value from Investing $100 at 8 Percent Interest Compounded Quarterly over Two Years

Period (months)	Beginning Principal (1)	Future Value Factor (2)	Future Value at End of Period [(1) × (2)] (3)
3	$100.00	1.02	$102.00
6	102.00	1.02	104.04
9	104.04	1.02	106.12
12	106.12	1.02	108.24
15	108.24	1.02	110.40
18	110.40	1.02	112.61
21	112.61	1.02	114.86
24	114.86	1.02	117.16

Table 3.5
The Future Value from Investing $100 at 8 Percent Interest for Years 1 and 2 Given Various Compounding Periods

| End of Year | Compounding Period | | |
	Annual	Semiannual	Quarterly
1	$108.00	$108.16	$108.24
2	116.64	116.99	117.16

$m = 4$. Substituting the appropriate values for semiannual and quarterly compounding into Equation 3.12 yields the following results:

For semiannual compounding:

$$FV = \$100 \times \left(1 + \frac{0.08}{2}\right)^{2 \times 2} = \$100 \times (1 + 0.04)^4 = \$116.99$$

For quarterly compounding:

$$FV = \$100 \times \left(1 + \frac{0.08}{4}\right)^{4 \times 2} = \$100 \times (1 + 0.02)^8 = \$117.16$$

These results agree with the values for FV_2 in Tables 3.3 and 3.4. If interest is compounded monthly, weekly, or daily, m would equal 12, 52, or 365, respectively.

Continuous Compounding. As we switch from annual, to semiannual, to quarterly compounding, the interval during which interest compounds gets shorter and the number of compounding periods per year gets larger. In principle, there is almost no limit to this process—interest could be compounded daily, hourly, or second by second. **Continuous compounding,** the most extreme case, occurs when interest compounds literally at every moment. In this case, m in Equation 3.12 would approach infinity, and Equation 3.12 converges to this expression:

$$FV(\text{continuous compounding}) = PV \times (e^{r \times n}) \qquad \text{(Eq. 3.13)}$$

The number e is an irrational number, like the number π from geometry; it is useful in mathematical applications involving quantities that grow continuously over time. The value of e is approximately 2.7183.[11] As before, increasing the frequency of compounding, in this case by compounding as frequently as possible, increases the future value of an investment.

APPLYING THE MODEL 3.13

To find the value at the end of two years of your $100 deposit in an account paying 8 percent annual interest compounded continuously, we substitute $PV = \$100$, $r = 0.08$, and $n = 2$ into Equation 3.13:

$$FV(\text{continuous compounding}) = \$100 \times (e^{0.08 \times 2}) = \$100 \times 2.7183^{0.16}$$
$$= \$100 \times 1.1735 = \$117.35$$

The future value with continuous compounding equals $117.35. As expected, that amount is larger than the future value of interest compounded semiannually ($116.99) or quarterly ($117.16).[12]

---

[11] In one of the more esoteric uses of the Internet, the first 2 million digits of the number e appear at the URL http://antwrp.gsfc.nasa.gov/htmltest/rjn_dig.html. Only the first million will be covered on the exam.

[12] The Excel function for continuous compounding is "=exp(argument)." For example, suppose you want to calculate the future value of $100 compounded continuously for five years at 8 percent. To find this value in Excel, first calculate the value of $e^{(.08 \times 5)}$ using "=exp(.08*5)" and then multiply the result by $100.

STATED VERSUS EFFECTIVE ANNUAL INTEREST RATES

Consumers and businesses must make objective comparisons of loan costs or investment returns over different compounding periods. To put interest rates on a common basis for comparison, we distinguish between *stated* and *effective annual interest rates*. The **stated annual rate** is the contractual annual rate charged by a lender or promised by a borrower. The **effective annual rate (*EAR*)**, or the *true annual return*, is the annual rate of interest *actually* paid or earned. Why the difference? The effective annual rate reflects the impact of compounding frequency; the stated annual rate does not. We can best illustrate the differences between stated and effective rates with numerical examples.

Using the notation introduced earlier, we can calculate the effective annual rate by substituting values for the stated annual rate (r) and the compounding frequency (m) into Equation 3.14:

$$EAR = \left(1 + \frac{r}{m}\right)^m - 1$$

(Eq. 3.14)

We can demonstrate application of this equation in Applying the Model 3.14.

APPLYING THE MODEL 3.14

You want to take out a loan for purchase of equipment for a small business you are starting. A community bank offers you a small loan with an 8 percent stated annual rate. You are so excited at actually getting the loan that you forget to ask the bank officer about the compounding period. Before you call the bank to ask, you do some calculations on your own. You wish to find the effective annual rate associated with an 8 percent stated annual rate ($r = 0.08$) when interest is compounded annually ($m = 1$); semiannually ($m = 2$); and quarterly ($m = 4$). Substituting these values into Equation 3.14 produces the following:

For annual compounding:

$$EAR = \left(1 + \frac{0.08}{1}\right)^1 - 1 = (1 + 0.08)^1 - 1$$
$$= 1.08 - 1 = 0.08 = 8.0\%$$

For semiannual compounding:

$$EAR = \left(1 + \frac{0.08}{2}\right)^2 - 1 = (1 + 0.04)^2 - 1$$
$$= 1.0816 - 1 = 0.0816 = 8.16\%$$

For quarterly compounding:

$$EAR = \left(1 + \frac{0.08}{4}\right)^4 - 1 = (1 + 0.02)^4 - 1$$
$$= 1.0824 - 1 = 0.0824 = 8.24\%$$

The results mean that 8 percent compounded semiannually is equivalent to 8.16% compounded annually and 8 percent compounded quarterly is equivalent to

8.24 percent compounded annually. These values demonstrate two important points: (1) the stated and effective rates are equivalent for annual compounding, and (2) the effective annual rate increases with increasing compounding frequency. You now feel better prepared with information about the interest rate before you call the bank.

Not surprisingly, the maximum effective annual rate for a given stated annual rate occurs when interest compounds continuously. The effective annual rate for this extreme case can be found by using the following equation:

$$EAR(\text{continuous compounding}) = e^r - 1 \qquad \text{(Eq. 3.14a)}$$

For the 8 percent stated annual rate ($r = 0.08$), substitution into Equation 3.14a results in an effective annual rate of 8.33 percent, as follows:

$$e^{.08} - 1 = 1.0833 - 1 = .0833 = 8.33\%$$

At the consumer level in the United States, "truth-in-lending laws" *require disclosure* on credit cards and loans of the **annual percentage rate (APR)**. The *APR* is the *stated annual rate* charged on the credit account or loan. It is calculated as the periodic rate (the interest rate per period) multiplied by the number of periods in one year. For example, a bank credit card that charges 1.5 percent per month would have an *APR* of 18 percent (1.5% per month × 12 months per year). In this example, is the 18 percent *APR* the actual cost of the credit card? No necessarily—which is why you must read the fine print on credit card agreements. To find the actual cost of this credit card account, you need to calculate the **annual percentage yield (APY)**. The *APY* is the same as the *effective annual rate*, which (as discussed earlier) reflects the impact of compounding frequency.[13] For this credit card example, 1.5 percent per month interest has an *APY* of $[(1.015)^{12} - 1] = 0.1956$, or 19.56 percent. If the stated rate is 1.75 percent per month, as is the case with many U.S. credit card accounts, the *APY* is a whopping 23.14 percent. If you are carrying a positive credit card balance with an interest rate like this, you will want to pay it off as soon as possible!

DEPOSITS NEEDED TO ACCUMULATE A FUTURE SUM

Suppose that a firm or a person wishes to determine the annual deposit needed to accumulate a certain amount of money at some point in the future. For example, assume that you want to buy a house five years from now and estimate that an initial down payment of $20,000 will be required. You wish to make equal end-of-year deposits into an account paying annual interest of 6 percent, so you must determine what size annuity will result in a lump sum of $20,000 at the end of year 5. We can derive the solution from the equation for the future value of an ordinary annuity.

Earlier, we applied Equation 3.4 to find the future value of an *n*-year ordinary annuity (*FV*). Solving that equation for *PMT* (which in this case is the annual deposit), we get Equation 3.15:

$$PMT = \frac{FV}{\left\{\dfrac{[(1 + r)^n - 1]}{r}\right\}} \qquad \text{(Eq. 3.15)}$$

---

[13] Note that the U.S. "truth-in-savings laws" *require disclosure* of the APY on savings deposits. Clearly, under current law, interest rates on savings are quoted in a more financially accurate way (*APY*) than are the rates charged on credit cards and loans (*APR*).

Once this is done, we have only to substitute the known values of *FV*, *r*, and *n* into the right-hand side of the equation to find the annual deposit required.

APPLYING THE MODEL 3.15

To demonstrate, the calculation to determine the equal annual end-of-year deposits required to accumulate $20,000 (*FV*) at the end of five years (*n* = 5), given an interest rate of 6 percent (*r* = 6%), is as follows:

$$PMT = \frac{\$20,000}{\left\{ \dfrac{[(1.06)^5 - 1]}{0.06} \right\}} = \$3,547.93$$

Instead of using algebra, you can use the future value annuity factor to calculate the amount of deposit. The denominator of Equation 3.15 is equivalent to the future value factor for a 6 percent, five-year annuity, which Table A3 shows as $FVFA_{6\%,5} = 5.637$. Dividing the future amount needed (*FV* = $20,000) by this factor again gives (except for rounding) an annual cash flow of $3,547.99. Alternatively you could use either a financial calculator or spreadsheet to find the amount of the annual deposit.

LOAN AMORTIZATION

Loan amortization refers to a borrower making equal periodic payments over time to fully repay a loan. For instance, with a conventional 30-year home mortgage, the borrower makes the same payment each month for 30 years until the mortgage is completely repaid. To *amortize* a loan (i.e., to calculate the periodic payment that pays off the loan), you must know the total amount of the loan (the amount borrowed), the term of the loan, the frequency of periodic payments, and the interest rate.

In time value of money terms, the loan amortization process involves finding a level stream of payments (over the term of the loan) with a present value (calculated at the loan interest rate) equal to the amount borrowed. Lenders use a **loan amortization schedule** to determine these payments and the allocation of each payment to interest and principal.

For example, suppose that you borrow $25,000 at 8 percent annual interest for five years to purchase a new car. To demonstrate the basic approach, we first amortize this loan assuming that you make payments at the end of years 1 through 5. We will then modify the annual formula to compute the more typical monthly auto loan payments. To find the size of the annual payments, the lender determines the amount of a five-year annuity discounted at 8 percent that has a present value of $25,000. This process is actually the inverse of finding the present value of an annuity.

Earlier, we found the present value (*PV*) of an *n*-year ordinary annuity using Equation 3.7. Solving that equation for *PMT*, the annual loan payment, we get Equation 3.16:

$$PMT = \frac{PV}{\left\{ \dfrac{1}{r} \times \left[1 - \dfrac{1}{(1 + r)^n} \right] \right\}} \qquad \text{(Eq. 3.16)}$$

APPLYING THE MODEL 3.16

To find the annual payment required on the five-year, $25,000 loan with an 8 percent annual rate, we have only to substitute the known values of $PV = \$25,000$, $r = 0.08$, and $n = 5$ into the right-hand side of the equation:

$$PMT = \frac{\$25,000}{\left\{ \frac{1}{0.08} \times \left[1 - \frac{1}{(1.08)^5} \right] \right\}} = \$6,261.41$$

Thus, you will need five annual payments of $6,261.41 to fully amortize this $25,000 loan.

As before, we can also calculate the annual cash flow (PMT) using present value tables. The denominator of Equation 3.16 is equal to the present value factor of an r percent, n-year annuity ($PVFA_{r\%,n}$). Table A4 shows $PVFA_{8\%,5} = 3.993$. Thus, we confirm that the payment required to fully amortize this loan is $6,260.96 (slight rounding difference) per year ($PMT = \$25,000 \div 3.993$). Alternatively, we can find the amount of the annual loan payment by using either a financial calculator or spreadsheet.

Each loan payment consists partly of interest and partly of the loan principal. Columns 3 and 4 of the *loan amortization schedule* in Table 3.6 show the allocation of each loan payment of $6,261.41 to interest and principal. Notice that the portion of each payment representing interest (column 3) declines over the repayment period, and the portion going to principal repayment (column 4) increases. This pattern is typical of amortized loans. With level payments, the interest component declines as the principal falls, leaving a larger portion of each subsequent payment to repay principal.

Computing amortized loan payments is the present value formulation that people use most frequently in their personal lives. In addition to calculating auto loan payments, most people also use it to compute home mortgage payments. Lenders typically require monthly payments on these consumer loans, not the annual payment we have just showed. We will now demonstrate how to do the amortization calculations using monthly payments. First, Equation 3.16a is simply a modified version of Equation 3.16:

$$PMT = \frac{r}{[(1 + r)^n - 1]} \times (1 + r)^n \times PV \qquad \text{(Eq. 3.16a)}$$

Table 3.6
Loan Amortization Schedule for $25,000 Principal, 8 Percent Interest Rate, Five-Year Repayment Period

| End of Year | Loan Payment (1) | Beginning-of-Year Principal (2) | Payments | | End-of-Year Principal [(2) − (4)] (5) |
			Interest [0.08 × (2)] (3)	Principal [(1) − (3)] (4)	
1	$6,261.41	$25,000.00	$2,000.00	$4,261.41	$20,738.59
2	6,261.41	20,738.59	1,659.09	4,602.32	16,136.27
3	6,261.41	16,136.27	1,290.90	4,970.51	11,165.76
4	6,261.41	11,165.76	893.26	5,368.15	5,797.61
5	6,261.41	5,797.61	463.81	5,797.60	.01*

*This value should be zero, but due to rounding, an insignificant difference of 1 cent exists.

Second, we can generalize this formula to more frequent compounding periods by dividing the interest rate by m and multiplying the number of compounding periods by m. This changes the equation as follows:

$$PMT = \frac{\frac{r}{m}}{\left[\left(1 + \frac{r}{m}\right)^{m \times n} - 1\right]} \times \left(1 + \frac{r}{m}\right)^{m \times n} \times PV \qquad \text{(Eq. 3.16b)}$$

APPLYING THE MODEL 3.17

We can use Equation 3.16b to calculate what your *monthly* car payment will be if you borrow $25,000 for five years at 8 percent annual interest. *PV* will again be the $25,000 amount borrowed, but the periodic interest rate ($r \div m$) will be 0.00667, or 0.667 percent per month (0.08 per year ÷ 12 months per year). There will be $m \times n = 60$ compounding periods (12 months/year × 5 years = 60 months). Substituting these values into Equation 3.16b yields a monthly auto loan payment of $506.96:

$$PMT = \frac{\frac{0.08}{12}}{\left[\left(1 + \frac{0.08}{12}\right)^{12 \times 5} - 1\right]} \times \left(1 + \frac{0.08}{12}\right)^{12 \times 5} \times \$25,000$$

$$= \frac{0.00667}{[(1.00667)^{60} - 1]} \times (1.00667)^{60} \times \$25,000$$

$$= \$506.96$$

To test your command of the monthly payment formula, compute the monthly mortgage payment for a home purchased using a 30-year, $100,000 loan with a fixed 7.5 percent annual interest rate. Note that there will be no fewer than 360 compounding periods (30 years × 12 months/year).[14]

IMPLIED INTEREST OR GROWTH RATES

Analysts often need to calculate the compound annual interest or *growth rate* (annual rate of change in values) of a series of cash flows. The calculations required for finding interest rates and growth rates, given known cash flow streams, are the same. We examine each of three possible cash flow patterns: lump sums, annuities, and mixed streams.

Lump Sums. The simplest situation is one in which a person wishes to find the interest or growth rate of a single cash flow over time. As an example, assume that you invested $1,000 in a stock mutual fund in December 2002, and this investment now, in December 2007, is worth $2,150. What was your compound annual rate of return over this five-year period?

As it happens, this is easy to determine, because we are unconcerned about the investment's value during any of the intervening years. We simply wish to determine

---

[14.] To find the solution, just enter the formula "=pmt(.00625,360,100000)" in Excel. The first argument in this function is the monthly interest rate, 7.5 percent divided by 12.

what compound rate of return (r) converted a $1,000 investment ($PV$) into a future amount ($FV$) worth $2,150 in five years ($n$). Note that the number of years of growth (or interest) is the difference between the latest and earliest year number. In this case, $n = 2007 - 2002 = 5$ years. Although the period 2002 through 2007 includes six years, there are only five years of growth: the earliest year (2002) serves as the base year (i.e., time 0) and is then followed by five years of change (2002 to 2003, 2003 to 2004, 2004 to 2005, 2005 to 2006, and 2006 to 2007).

Finding r involves manipulating Equation 3.1 so that we have the value to be determined, in this case $(1 + r)^n$, on the left-hand side of the equation and the two known values, FV and PV, on the right-hand side of the equation, as shown in Equation 3.17:

$$(1 + r)^n = \frac{FV}{PV} \qquad \text{(Eq. 3.17)}$$

Substituting in the known values, we obtain the following:

$$(1 + r)^5 = \frac{\$2,150}{\$1,000} = 2.150$$

This says that 1 plus the rate of return $(1 + r)$, compounded for five years ($n = 5$), equals 2.150. Our final step is to calculate the fifth root of 2.150. We can do this simply by raising 2.150 to the one-fifth power using the y^x key on a financial calculator, and then subtracting 1:

$$r = (2.150)^{0.20} - 1 = 1.1654 - 1 = 0.1654 = 16.54\% \text{ per year}$$

Alternatively, we could use a financial calculator or spreadsheet to more directly solve for a growth or interest rate of a lump sum.

Annuities. Sometimes people need to find the interest rate associated with an annuity, such as the equal annual end-of-year payments on a loan. To demonstrate, assume that your friend John Jacobs can borrow $2,000 to be repaid in equal annual end-of-year amounts of $514.18 for the next five years. He wants to find the interest rate on the loan and asks for your assistance.

You realize that John is really asking an annuity valuation question, so you use a variant of the present value of an annuity formula shown in Equation 3.7:

$$PV = PMT \times \left\{ \frac{1}{r} \times \left[1 - \frac{1}{(1 + r)^n} \right] \right\}$$

You are trying to determine the interest rate (r) that will equate the present value of a five-year annuity ($PV = \$2,000$) to a stream of five equal annual payments ($PMT = \$514.18$ per year). Because you know PV and PMT, you can rearrange Equation 3.7, putting the unknown value on the left-hand side and the known values on the right:

$$\left\{ \left[\frac{1}{r} \right] \times \left[1 - \frac{1}{(1 + r)^n} \right] \right\} = \frac{PV}{PMT} = \frac{\$2,000}{\$514.18} = 3.8897$$

The term on the left-hand side is very difficult to solve directly, but there is an easy shortcut. We can also express Equation 3.7 using present value factors as the annual cash flow (PMT) times the present value factor for an annuity paying r percent for

n years, or $PVFA_{r\%,n}$. That value is the unknown value on the left-hand side of the preceding equation. Substituting, we get the following:

$$PVFA_{r\%,5} = \frac{PV}{PMT} = \frac{\$2,000}{\$514.18} = 3.8897$$

We can then solve this equation by determining the appropriate five-year $PVFA$ having a value of 3.8897. Table A4 in Appendix A shows that $PVFA_{9\%,5} = 3.890$, so we can tell John that he is being charged about 9 percent on his loan.

Of course, a financial calculator or spreadsheet could be used to more directly solve for a growth or interest rate of an annuity.

Mixed Streams. As demonstrated in the previous discussion, finding the unknown interest or growth rate for a lump sum or an annuity is relatively simple using formulas, present value tables, or a financial calculator or spreadsheet. However, finding the unknown interest or growth rate for *a mixed stream* is very difficult using formulas or present value tables. It can be accomplished by an iterative trial-and-error approach, in which we find the interest rate that would cause the present value of the stream's inflows to just equal the present value of its outflows. This calculation is often referred to as finding the *yield-to-maturity* or *internal rate of return (IRR)*.

A much more attractive way to make this type of calculation is to use a financial calculator or spreadsheet that has the IRR function built into it. With such an approach, an analyst can input (with all outflows input as negative numbers) all the cash flows—both outflows and inflows—and then use the IRR function to calculate the unknown interest rate. This approach is discussed and demonstrated in Chapter 4 with regard to bonds and in Chapter 7 with regard to its use in capital budgeting.

NUMBER OF COMPOUNDING PERIODS

Occasionally, for either a lump sum or an annuity, the financial analyst wishes to calculate the unknown number of time periods necessary to achieve a given cash flow goal. We consider this calculation here for both lump sums and annuities.

Lump Sums. If we know the present (PV) and future (FV) amounts along with the interest rate (r), we can calculate the number of periods (n) necessary for a present amount to grow to equal the future amount.

For example, assume that you plan to deposit $1,000 in an investment that is expected to earn an 8 percent annual rate of interest, and you wish to determine how long it will take to triple your money (to accumulate $3,000). Stated differently, at an 8 percent annual interest rate, how many years (n) will it take for $1,000 ($PV$) to grow to $3,000 ($FV$)? We can express this problem simply by rearranging the basic future value formula, Equation 3.1, to express the unknown value, n, on the left-hand side and then plugging in the known values, FV, PV, and r:

$$FV = PV \times (1 + r)^n$$

$$(1 + 0.08)^n = \frac{FV}{PV} = \frac{\$3,000}{\$1,000} = 3.000$$

$$(1.08)^n = 3.000$$

Now what? How do we find the exponent value (n) that will turn 1.08 into 3.000? We do so by taking natural logarithms of both sides of this formula, and then expressing the unknown number of years (n) as a ratio of two log values, as follows:

$$\ln(1.08)^n = \ln(3.000)$$

$$n = \frac{\ln(3.000)}{\ln(1.08)} = \frac{1.0986}{0.0770} = 14.275$$

The result is 14.275 years. This means that at an 8 percent annual rate of interest, it will take about 14.3 years for your $1,000 deposit to triple in value to $3,000. We could also use a financial calculator or spreadsheet to more directly solve for the unknown number of periods for a lump sum.

Annuities. Occasionally we want to determine the unknown life of an annuity that is intended to achieve a specified objective, such as to repay a loan of a given amount with a stated interest rate and equal annual end-of-year payments.

To demonstrate, assume that you can borrow $20,000 at a 12 percent annual interest rate with annual end-of-year payments of $3,000. You wish to determine how long it will take to fully repay the loan's interest and principal. In other words, how many years (n) will it take to repay a $20,000 ($PV$), 12 percent ($r$), loan if the payments of $3,000 ($PMT$) are made at the end of each year?

You have probably already deduced that this is similar to the problem we addressed earlier of determining the unknown interest rate in an annuity. The difference is that now we know that $r = 12$ percent, and we want to determine the number of years (n). We once again rearrange the equation that expresses the present value of an annuity (PV) as the product of its payment (PMT) and the present value factor for an annuity paying r percent for n years ($PVFA_{r\%,n}$).

$$PVFA_{12\%,n} = \frac{PV}{CF} = \frac{\$20,000}{\$3,000} = 6.667$$

We can solve this by finding the 12 percent $PVFA$ value in Table A4 that most closely corresponds to 6.667, which is between 14 years ($PVFA_{12\%,14} = 6.628$) and 15 years ($PVFA_{12\%,15} = 6.811$). Using a financial calculator or spreadsheet, we find the exact number of years to be 14.20. This means that you will have to repay $3,000 at the end of each year for 14 years and about $600 (0.20 × $3,000) at the end of 14.20 years in order to fully repay the $20,000 loan at 12 percent.

---

12. What effect does increasing compounding frequency have on the (a) future value of a given deposit and (b) its *effective annual rate (EAR)?*

13. Under what condition would the stated annual rate equal the effective annual rate (EAR) for a given deposit? How do these rates relate to the *annual percentage rate (APR)* and *annual percentage yield (APY)?*

14. How would you determine the size of the annual end-of-year deposits needed to accumulate a given future sum at the end of a specified future period? What impact does the magnitude of the interest rate have on the size of the deposits needed?

15. What relationship exists between the calculation of the present value of an annuity and amortization of a loan? How can you find the amount of interest paid each year under an amortized loan?

Concept Review Questions

16. How can you find the interest or growth rate for (a) a lump sum amount, (b) an annuity, and (c) a mixed stream?

17. How can you find the number of time periods needed to repay (a) a single-payment loan and (b) an installment loan requiring equal annual end-of-year payments?

3.7 SUMMARY

- In order to compare decision alternatives, financial managers use future value and present value techniques to equate cash flows occurring at different times. Managers rely primarily on present value techniques and commonly use financial calculators or spreadsheet programs to streamline their computations.
- The future value of a lump sum calculation applies compound interest to the present value (the initial investment) over the period of concern. The higher the interest rate and the longer the period of time, the higher the cash flow's future value.
- The present value of a lump sum is the amount of money today that is equivalent to the given future amount, considering the rate of return that can be earned. Its calculation discounts the future value at the given interest rate. The higher the interest rate and the further in the future the cash flow occurs, the lower its present value.
- The future value of any cash flow stream—mixed stream, ordinary annuity, or annuity due—is the sum of the future values of the individual cash flows. Future values of annuities have the same cash flow each period and so are easy to calculate; future values of mixed streams are more difficult to find. The future value of an ordinary annuity (end-of-period cash flows) can be converted into the future value of an annuity due (beginning-of-period cash flows) by multiplying it by 1 plus the interest rate.
- The present value of a cash flow stream is the sum of the present values of the individual cash flows. Present values of annuities, which have the same cash flow each period, are easier to find than the present values of mixed streams. The present value of an ordinary annuity can be converted to the present value of an annuity due by multiplying it by 1 plus the interest rate. The present value of an ordinary perpetuity—an infinite-lived annuity—is found by dividing the amount of the annuity by the interest rate.
- Some special applications of time value include compounding interest more frequently than annually, stated and effective annual rates of interest, deposits needed to accumulate a future sum, loan amortization, implied interest or growth rates, and number of compounding periods. The more frequently interest is compounded at a stated annual rate, the larger the future amount that will be accumulated and the higher the effective annual rate.
- The annual deposit needed to accumulate a given future sum is found by manipulating the future value of an annuity equation. Loan amortization involves manipulating the present value of an annuity equation to determine the equal periodic payments necessary to fully repay loan principal and interest over a given time at a given interest rate. An amortization schedule allocates each payment to principal and interest.
- Implied interest or growth rates can be found using the basic future value equations for lump sums and annuities; for mixed streams, they require an iterative trial-and-error approach. Given present and future cash flows and the applicable

interest rate, the unknown number of periods can be found using the basic equations for future values of lump sums and annuities. Using a financial calculator or spreadsheet greatly simplifies these calculations.

INTERNET RESOURCES

Note: *For updates to links, please go to the book's website at* http://smart.swcollege.com.

http://www.bankrate.com—Offers a variety of automated present and future value calculations, such as a loan amortization calculator and a tool that compares rebates and low-rate financing deals on automobiles

http://www.tcalc.com—Contains numerous financial calculators that can be purchased and added to a website

http://www.moneychimp.com—Try the "How Finance Works" link to learn about many applications of present and future value mathematics; has a number of useful interactive graphs

http://www.financialplayerscenter.com—Provides helpful tutorials on time value concepts

Use the learning tools at http://smartfinance.swcollege.com

KEY TERMS

annual percentage rate (*APR*)
annual percentage yield (*APY*)
annuity
annuity due
capitalizing
compound interest
continuous compounding
discounting
effective annual rate (*EAR*)
equilibrium interest rate
financial intermediaries
future value
Gordon growth model
growing perpetuity
liquidity
loan amortization

loan amortization schedule
mixed stream
net present value (*NPV*)
ordinary annuity
perpetuity
present value
principal
quarterly compounding
Rule of 72
semiannual compounding
separation of investment and financing
simple interest
stated annual rate
time line
time value of money

QUESTIONS

3-1.   The price of a security is the sum of all of the discounted future cash flows associated with the security. Assuming the future cash flows do not change and the price of the security increases, is the discount rate for the security increasing, decreasing, or stable?

3-2.   A particular business deal allows you the choice of receiving $1,000 today or receiving $2,000 ten years from today. How would your choice change based on your ability to invest money at a very low rate of interest or a very high rate of interest?

3-3. If a firm's required return were 0 percent, would time value of money matter? As these returns rise above 0 percent, what impact would the increasing return have on future value? On present value?

3-4. If a series of cash flows are valued using the future value of an annuity, will the valuation of the cash flows increase or decrease as the interest rate increases? What is the answer if the cash flows are valued using the present value of an annuity?

3-5. What happens to the present value of a cash flow stream when the discount rate increases? Place this in the context of an investment. If the required return on an investment goes up but the expected cash flows do not change, would you be willing to pay the same price for the investment or would you pay more or less for this investment than before interest rates changed?

3-6. Look at the formula for the present value of an annuity. What happens to the numerator as the number of periods increases? What distinguishes an annuity from a *perpetuity*? Why is there no future value of a perpetuity?

3-7. When considering the EAR, does it increase or decrease as the number of compounding periods per year increase?

3-8. When considering repaying a loan, an increase in which of the following variables will increase the periodic loan payment: interest rate, number of periods, loan amount?

3-9. If you assume interest rates are expected to increase, would you prefer a loan with a fixed interest rate for the life of the loan, or a loan with a variable rate that will increase with interest rates throughout the life of the loan (assume both loans start with the same interest rate)? Would your answer change if the variable rate loan started at a much lower rate (consider the two situations of interest rates rising slowly or quickly in your answer)?

3-10. Suppose you need to know the discount rate that sets a series of periodic future cash flows equal to an amount "X" in today's dollars. Assuming the series is evaluated as the present value of an annuity, is there a direct solution for finding the discount rate?

3-11. A person plans to retire in one year, and expects to live off of $50,000 annually until death. The person currently has $700,000 in savings that earns 10% interest annually. How long will the savings accommodate this retirement plan?

PROBLEMS

Future Value of a Lump Sum

3-1. You have $1,500 to invest today at 7 percent interest compounded annually.
   a. How much will you have accumulated in the account at the end of the following number of years?
      1. Three years
      2. Six years
      3. Nine years
   b. Use your findings in part (a) to calculate the amount of interest earned in
      1. the first three years (years 1 to 3)
      2. the second three years (years 4 to 6)
      3. the third three years (years 7 to 9)
   c. Compare and contrast your findings in part (b). Explain why the amount of interest earned increases in each succeeding three-year period.

Present Value of a Lump Sum

3-2. An Indiana state savings bond can be converted to $100 at maturity six years from purchase. If the state bonds are to be competitive with U.S. savings bonds, which pay 8 percent annual interest (compounded annually), at what price must the state sell its bonds? Assume no cash payments on savings bonds prior to redemption.

3-3. You just won a lottery that promises to pay you $1 million exactly 10 years from today. Because the state in which you live guarantees the $1 million payment, opportunities exist to sell the claim today for an immediate lump-sum cash payment.

    a. What is the least you will sell your claim for if you could earn the following rates of return on similar-risk investments during the 10-year period?
        1. 6 percent
        2. 9 percent
        3. 12 percent
    b. Rework part (a) under the assumption that the $1 million payment will be received in 15 rather than 10 years.
    c. Based on your findings in parts (a) and (b), discuss the effect of both the size of the rate of return and the time until receipt of payment on the present value of a future sum.

Future Value of Cash Flow Streams

3-4. Dixon Shuttleworth has been offered the choice of three retirement-planning investments. The first investment offers a 5 percent return for the first five years, a 10 percent return for the next five years, and a 20 percent return thereafter. The second investment offers 10 percent for the first 10 years and 15 percent thereafter. The third investment offers a constant 12 percent rate of return. Determine, for each of the given number of years, which of these investments is the best for Dixon if each of these investments requires him to pay the same amount today and he plans to retire in the following number of years.

    a. 15 years
    b. 20 years
    c. 30 years

3-5. Lauren Blanding's employer offers workers a two-month paid sabbatical every seven years. Lauren, who just started working for the firm, plans to spend her sabbatical touring Europe at an estimated cost of $25,000. To finance her trip, Lauren plans to make six annual deposits of $2,500 each, starting one year from now, into an investment account earning 8% interest.

    a. Will Lauren's account balance in seven years be enough to pay for her trip?
    b. Suppose Lauren increases her annual contribution to $3,150. How large will her account balance be in seven years?

3-6. Robert Williams is considering an offer to sell his medical practice, allowing him to retire five years early. He has been offered $500,000 for his practice and can invest this amount in an account earning 10 percent per year, compounded annually. If the practice is expected to generate the following cash flows, should Robert accept this offer and retire now? (*Hint:* Be sure to consider the fact that if Robert retires early, he no longer needs to work.)

End of Year	Cash Flow
1	$150,000
2	150,000
3	125,000
4	125,000
5	100,000

3-7.   Gina Coulson has just contracted to sell a small parcel of land that she inherited a few years ago. The buyer is willing to pay $24,000 at closing of the transaction or will pay the amounts shown in the following table at the *beginning* of each of the next five years. Because Gina doesn't really need the money today, she plans to let it accumulate in an account that earns 7 percent annual interest. Given her desire to buy a house at the end of five years after closing on the sale of the lot, she decides to choose the payment alternative—$24,000 lump sum or mixed stream of payments in the following table—that provides the highest future value at the end of five years.

Mixed Stream	
Beginning of Year (t)	Cash Flow (CF_t)
1	$ 2,000
2	4,000
3	6,000
4	8,000
5	10,000

   a. What is the future value of the lump sum at the end of year 5?
   b. What is the future value of the mixed stream at the end of year 5?
   c. Based on your findings in parts (a) and (b), which alternative should Gina take?
   d. If Gina could earn 10 percent rather than 7 percent on the funds, would your recommendation in part (c) change? Explain.

3-8.   For the following questions, assume an annual annuity of $1,000 and a required return of 12 percent.

   a. What is the future value of an *ordinary annuity* for 10 years?
   b. If you earned an additional year's worth of interest on this annuity, what would be the future value?
   c. What is the future value of a 10-year *annuity due*?
   d. What is the relationship between your answers in parts (b) and (c)? Explain.

3-9.   Starratt Alexander is considering investing specified amounts in each of four investment opportunities described below. For each opportunity, determine the amount of money Starratt will have at the end of the given investment horizon.

   Investment A: Invest a lump sum of $2,750 today in an account that pays 6 percent annual interest and leave the funds on deposit for exactly 15 years.

   Investment B: Invest the following amounts at the *beginning* of each of the next five years in a venture that will earn 9 percent annually and measure the accumulated value at the end of exactly five years.

Beginning of Year	Amount
1	$ 900
2	1,000
3	1,200
4	1,500
5	1,800

   Investment C: Invest $1,200 at the *end of each year* for the next 10 years in an account that pays 10 percent annual interest, and determine the account balance at the end of year 10.

   Investment D: Make the same investment as in investment C, but place the $1,200 in the account at the *beginning of each year.*

3-10. Kim Edwards and Chris Phillips are both newly minted 30-year old MBAs. Kim plans to invest $1,000 per month into her 401(k) beginning next month; Chris intends to invest $2,000 per month, but he does not plan to begin investing until 10 years after Kim begins investing. Both Kim and Chris will retire at age 67, and the 401(k) plan averages a 12 percent annual return, compounded monthly. Who will have more 401(k) money at retirement?

Present Value of Cash Flow Streams

3-11. Given the mixed streams of cash flows shown in the following table, answer parts (a) and (b):

Year	Cash Flow Stream A	B
1	$ 50,000	$ 10,000
2	40,000	20,000
3	30,000	30,000
4	20,000	40,000
5	10,000	50,000
Totals	$150,000	$150,000

a. Find the present value of each stream, using a 15 percent discount rate.

b. Compare the calculated present values, and discuss them in light of the fact that the undiscounted total cash flows amount to $150,000 in each case.

3-12. As part of your personal budgeting process, you have determined that in each of the next five years you will have budget shortfalls. In other words, you will need the amounts shown in the following table at the end of the given year to balance your budget—that is, inflows equal outflows. You expect to be able to earn 8 percent on your investments during the next five years and wish to fund the budget shortfalls over these years with a single initial deposit.

End of Year	Budget Shortfall
1	$ 5,000
2	4,000
3	6,000
4	10,000
5	3,000

a. How large must the lump-sum deposit be today into an account paying 8 percent annual interest to provide for full coverage of the anticipated budget shortfall?

b. What effect would an increase in your earnings rate have on the amount calculated in part (a)? Explain.

3-13. Ron Nail has just received two offers for his seaside home. The first offer is for $1 million today. The second offer is for an owner-financed sale with a payment schedule as follows:

End of Year	Payment
0 (today)	$200,000
1	$200,000
2	$200,000
3	$200,000
4	$200,000
5	$300,000

Assuming no differential tax treatment between the two options and that Ron earns a rate of 8 percent on his investments, which offer should he take?

3-14. A bond has an $80 annual coupon for the next ten years with a par payment also received at the maturity of the bond. You intend to sell the coupon portion of the bond (known as a strip). Assuming a 7% annual discount rate, what is the value of the strip today?

3-15. Assume that you just won the state lottery. Your prize can be taken either in the form of $40,000 at the end of each of the next 25 years (i.e., $1 million over 25 years) or as a lump sum of $500,000 paid immediately.

   a. If you expect to be able to earn 5 percent annually on your investments over the next 25 years, ignoring taxes and other considerations, which alternative should you take? Why?

   b. Would your decision in part (a) be altered if you could earn 7 percent rather than 5 percent on your investments over the next 25 years? Why?

   c. On a strict economic basis, at approximately what earnings rate would you be indifferent when choosing between the two plans?

3-16. For the following questions, assume an end-of-year cash flow of $250 and a 10 percent discount rate.

   a. What is the present value of a single cash flow?
   b. What is the present value of a 5-year annuity?
   c. What is the present value of a 10-year annuity?
   d. What is the present value of a 100-year annuity?
   e. What is the present value of a $250 perpetuity?
   f. Do you detect a relationship between the number of periods of an annuity and its resemblance to a perpetuity?

3-17. Use the following table of cash flows to answer parts (a)–(c). Assume an 8 percent discount rate.

End of Year	Cash Flow
1	$10,000
2	$10,000
3	$10,000
4	$12,000
5	$12,000
6	$12,000
7	$12,000
8	$15,000
9	$15,000
10	$15,000

   a. Solve for the present value of the cash flow stream by summing the present value of each individual cash flow.

   b. Now, solve for the present value by summing the present value of the three separate annuities (one current and two deferred).

   c. Which method is better for a long series of cash flows with embedded annuities?

3-18. Joan Wallace, corporate finance specialist for Big Blazer Bumpers, has been given the task of funding an account to cover anticipated future warranty costs. Warranty costs are expected to be $5 million per year for three years, with the first costs expected to occur four years from today. How much will Joan have to place into an account today earning 10 percent per year to cover these expenses?

3-19.   Landon Lowman, star quarterback of the university football team, is thinking about forgoing his last two years of eligibility and making himself available for the professional football draft. Scouts estimate that Landon could receive a signing bonus of $1 million today along with a five-year contract for $3 million per year (payable at the end of the year). They further estimate that he could negotiate a contract for $5 million per year for the remaining seven years of his career.

The scouts believe, however, that Landon will be a much higher draft pick if he improves by playing out his eligibility. If he stays at the university, he is expected to receive a $2 million signing bonus in two years along with a 5-year contract for $5 million per year. After that, the scouts expect Landon to obtain a five-year contract for $6 million per year to take him into retirement.

Assume that Landon can earn a 10 percent return over this time. Should Landon stay or go?

3-20.   Kate Snead had been offered four investment opportunities, all equally priced at $45,000. Because the opportunities differ in risk, Kate's required returns (i.e., applicable discount rates) are not the same for each opportunity. The cash flows and required returns for each opportunity are summarized below.

Opportunity	Cash Flows		Required Return
A	$7,500 at the end of 5 years		12%
B	Year	Amount	15%
	1	$10,000	
	2	12,000	
	3	18,000	
	4	10,000	
	5	13,000	
	6	9,000	
C	$5,000 at the *end of each* year for the next 30 years.		10%
D	$7,000 at the *beginning of each year* for the next 20 years.		18%

   a. Find the present value of each of the four investment opportunities.
   b. Which, if any, opportunities are acceptable?
   c. Which opportunity should Kate take?

3-21.   Assume you wish to establish a college scholarship of $2,000 paid at the end of each year for a deserving student at the high school you attended. You would like to make a lump-sum gift to the high school to fund the scholarship into perpetuity. The school's treasurer assures you that they will earn 7.5 percent annually forever.

   a. How much must you give the high school today to fund the proposed scholarship program?
   b. If you wanted to allow the amount of the scholarship to increase annually after the first award (end of year 1) by 3 percent per year, how much must you give the school today to fund the scholarship program?
   c. Compare, contrast, and discuss the difference in your response to parts (a) and (b).

3-22.   Matt Sedgwick, facilities and operations manager for the Birmingham Buffalo professional football team, has come up with an idea for generating income. Matt wants to expand the stadium by building skyboxes sold with lifetime (perpetual) season tickets. Each skybox will be guaranteed 10 season tickets at a cost of $200 per ticket per year for life. If each skybox costs $100,000 to build, what is the minimum selling price that Matt will have to charge for the skyboxes to break even, if the required return is 10 percent?

Special Applications of Time Value

3-23. Assume that you deposit $10,000 today into an account paying 6 percent annual interest and leave it on deposit for exactly eight years.

a. How much will be in the account at the end of eight years if interest is compounded as follows?
1. Annually
2. Semiannually
3. Monthly
4. Continuously

b. Calculate the *effective annual rate* (*EAR*) for (1) through (4) above.

c. Based on your findings in parts (a) and (b), what is the general relationship between the frequency of compounding and *EAR*?

3-24. You plan to invest $2,000 in an individual retirement arrangement (IRA) today at a *stated interest rate* of 8 percent, which is expected to apply to all future years.

a. How much will you have in the account at the end of 10 years if interest is compounded as follows?
1. Annually
2. Semiannually
3. Daily (assume a 360-day year)
4. Continuously

b. What is the *effective annual rate* (*EAR*) for each compounding period in part (a)?

c. How much greater will your IRA account balance be at the end of 10 years if interest is compounded continuously rather than annually?

d. How does the compounding frequency affect the future value and effective annual rate for a given deposit? Explain in terms of your findings in parts (a)–(c).

3-25. Jason Spector has shopped around for the best interest rates for his investment of $10,000 over the next year. He has found the following:

Stated Rate	Compounding
6.10%	Annual
5.90%	Semiannual
5.85%	Monthly

a. Which investment offers Jason the highest *effective annual rate* (*EAR*)?

b. Now, assume that Jason wishes to invest his money for only six months and the stated annual compounded rate of 6.10 percent is not available. Which of the remaining investments should Jason choose?

3-26. Calculate the *EAR* for the following stated interest rates and determine which proposed rate is the best for investing:

a. 12% compounded monthly
b. 12.5% compounded quarterly
c. 13% compounded semiannually
d. 13.25% compounded annually

3-27. Answer parts (a)–(c) for each of the following cases.

Case	Amount of Initial Deposit ($)	Stated Annual Rate, r (%)	Compounding Frequency, m (times/year)	Deposit Period (years)
A	2,500	6	2	5
B	50,000	12	6	3
C	1,000	5	1	10
D	20,000	16	4	6

   a. Calculate the future value at the end of the specified deposit period.
   b. Determine the *effective annual rate* (*EAR*).
   c. Compare the stated annual rate (*r*) to the effective annual rate (*EAR*). What relationship exists between compounding frequency and the stated and effective annual rates?

3-28. Tara Cutler is newly married and is now preparing a surprise gift of a trip to Europe for her husband on their tenth anniversary. Tara plans to invest $5,000 per year until that anniversary and plans to make her first $5,000 investment on their first anniversary. If she earns an 8 percent rate on her investments, how much will she have saved for their trip if the interest is compounded in each of the following ways?

   a. Annually
   b. Quarterly
   c. Monthly

3-29. Melissa Gould wants to invest today in order to assure adequate funds for her son's college education. She estimates that her son will need $20,000 at the end of 18 years; $25,000 at the end of 19 years; $30,000 at the end of 20 years; and $40,000 at the end of 21 years. How much will Melissa have to invest in a fund today if the fund earns the following interest rate?

   a. 6 percent per year with annual compounding
   b. 6 percent per year with quarterly compounding
   c. 6 percent per year with monthly compounding

3-30. John Tye has just been hired as the new corporate finance analyst at I-Ell Enterprises and has received his first assignment. John is to take the $25 million in cash received from a recent divestiture and use part of these proceeds to retire an outstanding $10 million bond issue and the remainder to repurchase common stock. However, the bond issue cannot be retired for another two years. If John can place the funds necessary to retire this $10 million debt into an account earning 6 percent compounded *monthly*, how much of the $25 million remains to repurchase stock?

3-31. Find the present value of a 3-year, $20,000 ordinary annuity deposited into an account that pays 12 percent interest, compounded *monthly*. Solve for the present value of the annuity in the following ways:

   a. As three single cash flows discounted at the stated rate of interest
   b. As three single cash flows discounted at the appropriate effective annual rate of interest
   c. As a 3-year annuity discounted at the effective annual rate of interest

3-32. You intend to retire twenty years from today with $800,000 in savings. Assuming you earn 8% annual interest on your investments and intend to make annual payments into your retirement account starting next year, what is the minimum payment you can make to realize your retirement goal?

3-33. To supplement your planned retirement in exactly 42 years, you estimate that you need to accumulate $220,000 by the end of 42 years from today. You plan to make equal annual end-of-year deposits into an account paying 8 percent annual interest.

   a. How large must the annual deposits be to create the $220,000 fund by the end of 42 years?
   b. If you can afford to deposit only $600 per year into the account, how much will you have accumulated by the end of the forty-second year?

3-34. Determine the annual payment required to fund a future liability of $12,000 per year. You will fund this future liability over the next five years, with the first payment to occur one year from today. The future $12,000 liability will last for four years, with the first payment to occur seven years from today. If you can earn 8 percent on this account, how much will you have to deposit each year over the next five years to fund the future liability?

3-35. Mary Sullivan, capital outlay manager for Waxy Widgets, has been instructed to establish a contingency fund to cover the expenses over the next two years (24 months) associated with repairing defective widgets from a new production process. Waxy Widgets' controller wants to make equal monthly cash deposits into this fund. If Mary faces the following monthly repair costs and has $1 million to start the fund today, what will be her *monthly payments* into the fund in order to assume that all repair costs will be covered? Mary will make her first payment one month from today, and the fund will earn 6 percent, compounded monthly.

Months	Repair Costs per Month
1–4	$500,000
5–12	$250,000
13–24	$100,000

3-36. Craig and LaDonna Allen are trying to establish a college fund for their son Spencer, who turned three today. They plan for Spencer to withdraw $10,000 on his eighteenth birthday and $11,000, $12,000, and $15,000 on his subsequent birthdays. They plan to fund these withdrawals with a 10-year annuity, with the first payment to occur one year from today, and expect to earn an average annual return of 8 percent.

   a. How much will the Allens have to contribute each year to achieve their goal?
   b. Create a schedule showing the cash inflows (including interest) and outflows of this fund. How much remains after the $15,000 payment is made on Spencer's twenty-first birthday?

3-37. Joan Messineo borrowed $15,000 at a 14 percent annual interest rate to be repaid over three years. The loan is amortized into three equal annual end-of-year payments.

   a. Calculate the annual end-of-year loan payment.
   b. Prepare a *loan amortization schedule* showing the interest and principal breakdown of each of the three loan payments.
   c. Explain why the interest portion of each payment declines with the passage of time.

3-38. You are planning to purchase a building for $40,000, and you have $10,000 to apply as a down payment. You may borrow the remainder under the following terms: a 10-year loan with semiannual repayments and a stated interest rate of 6 percent. You intend to make $6,000 payments, applying the excess over your required payment to the reduction of the principal balance.

   a. Given these terms, how long (in years) will it take you to fully repay your loan?
   b. What will be your total interest cost?
   c. What would your interest cost be if you made no prepayments and repaid your loan by strictly adhering to its terms?

3-39. Use a spreadsheet to create amortization schedules for the following five scenarios. What happens to the total interest paid under each scenario?

   a. Scenario 1:
   Loan amount: $1 million
   Annual interest rate: 5 percent
   Term: 360 months
   Prepayment: $0
   b. Scenario 2: Same as 1, except annual interest rate is 7 percent
   c. Scenario 3: Same as 1, except term is 180 months
   d. Scenario 4: Same as 1, except prepayment is $250 per month
   e. Scenario 5: Same as 1, except loan amount is $125,000

3-40.   Suppose you make monthly mortgage payments of $2,545 and have ten years left on the mortgage (next payment due next month). Assuming a 6.6% stated annual interest rate for the mortgage, how much would you need today to pay off the mortgage? (*Hint:* Sum the present value of the remaining payments.) Also, what would be the amount of interest you owe on the next mortgage payment?

3-41.   Go to the home page of the Bankrate.com (http://www.bankrate.com), and obtain current average mortgage rates. With this information, go to Interest.com's mortgage calculator (http://www.interest.com/hugh/calc/simple.org). Provide the requested variables to create an amortization schedule. Now, re-create the schedule with different prepayment amounts. What impact does the prepayment have on total interest and the term of the loan?

3-42.   To analyze various retirement-planning options, check out the financial calculator at Bloomberg (http://www.bloomberg.com). Determine the effect of waiting versus immediate planning for retirement. What is the impact of changing interest-rate assumptions on your retirement "nest egg"?

3-43.   For excellent qualitative discussions of the value of compounded interest on saving for future (retirement) obligations, see the following websites:

http://www.prudential.com/retirement (Prudential Financial)

http://www.vanguard.com (The Vanguard Group)

http://www.fid-inv.com (Fidelity Investments)

http://www.bloomberg.com (Bloomberg)

What can you conclude about the timing of cash flows and future values available for retirement, considering the information provided on these websites?

3-44.   Find the rates of return required to do the following:

   a. Double an investment in 4 years
   b. Double an investment in 10 years
   c. Triple an investment in 4 years
   d. Triple an investment in 10 years

3-45.   You are given the series of cash flows shown in the following table.

	Cash Flows		
Year	A	B	C
1	$500	$1,500	$2,500
2	560	1,550	2,600
3	640	1,610	2,650
4	720	1,680	2,650
5	800	1,760	2,800
6		1,850	2,850
7		1,950	2,900
8			2,060
9			2,170
10			2,280

   a. Calculate the compound annual growth rate associated with each cash flow stream.
   b. If year-1 values represent initial deposits in a savings account paying annual interest, what is the annual rate of interest earned on each account?

    c. Compare and discuss the growth rate and interest rate found in parts (a) and (b), respectively.

3-46. Which investment below produces the best annual return?

    a. Purchase a security for $100.00 and then sell the security three years later for $119.10.

    b. Purchase a security for $50.00 and sell the security for $55.00 after one year.

    c. Purchase a security for $200.00 and sell the security for $237.62 after two years.

    d. Purchase a security for $150.00 and sell the security for $300.00 after ten years.

3-47. Imagine that you are a professional personal financial planner. One of your clients asks you the following questions. Use the time value of money techniques to develop appropriate responses to each question.

    a. "I borrowed $75,000, and am required to repay it in six equal (annual) end-of-year installments of $3,344. What rate of interest am I paying?"

    b. "I need to save $37,000 over the next 15 years to fund my three-year-old daughter's college education. If I make equal annual end-of-year deposits into an account that earns 7 percent annual interest, how large must this deposit be?"

3-48. Log on to MSN Money (http://www.investor.msn.com), and select five stocks to analyze. Use their rates of return over the last five years to determine the value of $1,000 invested in each stock five years ago. What is the compound annual rate of return for each of the five stocks over the 5-year period?

SMART
SOLUTIONS
See the problem and
solution explained
step-by-step at
SMARTFinance

3-49. The viatical industry offers a rather grim example of present value concepts. A firm in this business, called a viator, purchases the rights to the benefits from a life insurance contract from a terminally ill client. The viator may then sell claims on the insurance payout to other investors. The industry began in the early 1990s as a way to help AIDS patients capture some of the proceeds from their life insurance policies for living expenses.

    Suppose a patient has a life expectancy of 18 months and a life insurance policy with a death benefit of $100,000. A viator pays $80,000 for the right to the benefit, and then sells that claim to another investor for $80,500.

    a. From the point of view of the patient, this contract is like taking out a loan. What is the compound annual interest rate on the loan if the patient lives exactly 18 months? What if the patient lives 36 months?

    b. From the point of view of the investor, this transaction is like lending money. What is the compound annual interest rate earned on the loan if the patient lives 18 months? What if the patient lives just 12 months?

3-50. Determine the length of time required to double the value of an investment, given the following rates of return.

    a. 4 percent

    b. 10 percent

    c. 30 percent

    d. 100 percent

3-51. You are the pension fund manager for Tanju's Toffees, and your CFO has just made a request of you. The CFO wants to know the minimum annual return required on the pension fund in order to make all required payments over the next five years and not diminish the current asset base. The fund currently has assets of $500 million.

    a. Determine the rate of return if outflows are expected to exceed inflows by $50 million per year.

    b. Determine the rate of return with the following fund cash flows.

End of Year	Inflows	Outflows
1	$55,000,000	$100,000,000
2	60,000,000	110,000,000
3	60,000,000	120,000,000
4	60,000,000	135,000,000
5	64,000,000	145,000,000

c. Consider the cash flows in part (b). What will happen to your asset base if you earn 10 percent? 20 percent?

3-52. Jill Chew wishes to choose the best of four immediate retirement annuities available to her. In each case, in exchange for paying a single premium today, she will receive equal annual end-of-year cash benefits for a specified number of years. She considers the annuities to be equally risky and is not concerned about their differing lives. Her decision will be based solely on the rate of return she will earn on each annuity. The key terms of each of the four annuities are shown in the following table.

Annuity	Premium Paid Today	Annual Benefit	Life (years)
A	$30,000	$3,100	20
B	25,000	3,900	10
C	40,000	4,200	15
D	35,000	4,000	12

a. Calculate to the nearest 1 percent the rate of return on each of the four annuities Jill is considering.
b. Given Jill's stated decision criterion, which annuity would you recommend?

3-53. Determine which of the following three investments offers you the highest rate of return on your $1,000 investment over the next five years.
Investment 1: $2,000 lump sum to be received in five years
Investment 2: $300 at the end of each of the next five years
Investment 3: $250 at the beginning of each of the next five years

a. Which investment offers the highest return?
b. Which offers the highest return if the payouts are doubled (i.e., $4,000, $600, and $500)?
c. What causes the big change in the returns on the annuities?

3-54. Consider the following three investments of equal risk. Which offers the greatest rate of return?

End of Year	Investment		
	A	B	C
0	−$10,000	−$20,000	−$25,000
1	0	9,500	20,000
2	0	9,500	30,000
3	24,600	9,500	−12,600

3-55. You plan to start saving for your son's college education. He will begin college when he turns 18 years old and will need $4,000 at that time and in each of the following three years. You will make a deposit at the end of this year in an account that pays 6 percent compounded annually, and an identical deposit at the end of each year, with the last deposit occurring when he turns 18. If an annual deposit of $1,484 will allow you to reach your goal, how old is your son now?

THOMSON ONE BUSINESS SCHOOL EDITION

Access financial information from the Thomson ONE–Business School Edition website for the following problem(s). Go to http://tobsefin.swlearning.com/. If you have already registered your access serial number and have a username and password, click **Enter**. Otherwise, click **Register** and follow the instructions to create a username and password. Register your access serial number and then click **Enter** on the aforementioned website. When you click Enter, you will be prompted for your username and password (please remember that the password is case sensitive). Enter them in the respective boxes and then click **OK** (or hit **Enter**). From the ensuing page, click **Click Here to Access Thomson ONE–Business School Edition Now!** This opens up a new window that gives you access to the Thomson ONE–Business School Edition database. You can retrieve a company's financial information by entering its ticker symbol [provided for each company in the problem(s)] in the box below "Name/Symbol/Key." For further instructions on using the Thomson ONE–Business School Edition database, please refer to "A Guide for Using Thomson ONE–Business School Edition."

3-56. What is the current price per share (previous close) of Amazon (ticker symbol, AMZN)? What is the three-year total return for Amazon? If Amazon were to continue at this same growth rate, what will be the value of a share of Amazon in three years? If you owned 1,000 shares of Amazon, how much would they have been worth three years ago (assuming the same growth rate)?

3-57. What are the annual growth rates in total assets for Bank of America (ticker symbol, BAC) and Citigroup (ticker symbol, C) over the last four years? What are the annual growth rates in total interest income for both firms? If total assets and total interest income were to continue to grow at the rates you calculated for the next five years, what would total assets and interest income be for both firms?

MINI-CASE: TIME VALUE OF MONEY

It is December 31, 2007, and Camille Henley, age 35, is in the process of reviewing her retirement savings and planning for her retirement at age 60. She currently has $55,000 saved (which includes the deposit she just made today) and she invests $2,000 per year (at the end of the year) in a retirement account that earns about 10% annually. She has decided that she is comfortable living on $40,000 per year (in today's dollars) and she thinks she can continue to live on that amount, as long as it is adjusted annually for inflation. Inflation is expected to average 2.86% per year for the foreseeable future. After researching information on average life expectancy for females of her background, her plan will assume she lives to age 88. She will withdraw the amount needed for each year during retirement at the beginning of the year. So, on December 31 at age 60, she will make her last deposit of $2,000 and the following day (January 1) she will withdraw her first installment for retirement.

1. If Camille continues on her current plan, will she be able to accomplish it?

2. How would the situation change if Camille were to start placing her $2,000 annual savings into her retirement account on January 1st of each year rather than December 31 of each year? Assume the investment still pays interest at the end of the year.

3. If Camille resumes making her deposits at the end of the year, how much would she have to save each year to accomplish her objective?

4.   Assume that Camille continues with her current plan. What interest rate would she have to earn on her investment to make it work?

5.   If Camille wishes to leave a $50,000 perpetuity to her alma mater, starting one year from the year she turns 88, how much extra money would she need to have on December 31 of the year she turns 88? Assume the investment will earn 10%.

6.   Rework question 5, assuming that Camille wants the university investment to grow by 5% per year.

PART 2: Valuation, Risk, and Return

Above all, finance is about valuing things. The things that financial analysts value range from financial assets, such as stocks and bonds, to physical assets, such as new manufacturing facilities. The three chapters in this section introduce the concepts and techniques that are critical in the valuation process.

Chapter 3 introduced the notion that "time is money." In Chapter 4, we apply time value of money concepts to estimate the prices of bonds, preferred stock, and common stock. To become an expert at valuing these securities, you must first understand their basic characteristics—such as when each type of instrument pays cash to investors and what rights investors have in the event that the cash flows they are promised do not materialize. Once you know what cash flows to expect from a particular security, estimating the price of that security becomes a relatively straightforward exercise in applying the time value of money mathematics you've just learned.

Of course, investors know that the cash flows they expect from an investment and the cash flows they actually receive can be quite different. This is the notion of risk, the subject of Chapters 5 and 6. In Chapter 5, we begin by showing some historical evidence, from the United States and many other countries, suggesting that in financial markets, a tradeoff exists between risk and return. To be specific, assets that require investors to accept more risk must offer investors the expectation of higher returns. We devote much of this chapter to carefully defining the terms risk and return. A somewhat counterintuitive lesson emerging from this chapter is that how we define risk depends on whether we are trying to measure the risk of a single asset, such as a share of IBM stock, or a whole portfolio of assets, such as the Standard & Poor's 500.

Chapter 6 delves deeper into the connection between risk and return, and introduces perhaps the most famous financial model of all time, the capital asset pricing model, or CAPM. The CAPM suggests that the expected return on any asset depends on three variables: the risk-free interest rate, the expected return on the overall market portfolio, and the systematic risk of the asset, as measured by beta. Beta captures the extent to which an individual asset's returns are correlated with returns on other assets. Though there are a number of alternative models that attempt to measure the expected returns on risky assets such as stocks, none have gained as much acceptance, especially in the realm of corporate finance, as the CAPM.

What could 1970s glamour-rock icon David Bowie possibly have in common with the Prudential Insurance Company? Known through its advertising campaign as "the Rock," Prudential spent years cultivating an image of financial conservatism and security. Meanwhile, David Bowie was rising to stardom by releasing albums such as *The Rise and Fall of Ziggy Stardust and the Spiders from Mars,* and starring in cult films such as *The Man Who Fell to Earth.* Prudential and the orange-haired, androgynous Bowie seemed unlikely bedfellows. But in early 1997, Bowie made financial history by becoming the first rock star to issue bonds backed by the royalties on his albums. These "Bowie Bonds" promised to pay interest at a rate of 7.9 percent over 10 years using cash flow generated from the 25 albums that Bowie recorded prior to 1990. Recognizing the earning power of Bowie's music, Moody's Investor Services, one of the world's leading credit rating firms, assigned an investment-grade rating to the Bowie Bonds. Prudential purchased the entire bond issue for $55 million. For Prudential, the bonds offered an attractive interest rate (10-year Treasury bonds were paying about 6.4 percent interest at the time), as well as free publicity. For Bowie, the transaction offered a way to immediately capture the present value ($55 million) of 10 years of future royalties. Other prominent musicians such as James Brown, the Isley Brothers, the Bee Gees, Iron Maiden, Rod Stewart, Michael Jackson, and even the famed wax museum in London, Madame Tussaud's, followed suit by issuing their own future-cash-flow backed bonds.

But purchasers of these bonds failed to anticipate the Internet's impact on CD sales. With the rise of Napster and other file-sharing services in the late 1990s, royalties paid to recording artists dropped sharply, so much so that, in 2004, Moody's lowered its rating on Bowie Bonds to just one notch above "junk" status. Ironically, by 2005, another technological development, the rise of Apple's iTunes electronic music distribution service, showed promise of reversing the long slide in music sales.

The up and down saga of Bowie Bonds illustrates a basic financial principle—the value of any financial asset depends on the cash flows that the asset will distribute over time. This chapter explains how to apply this principle to price bonds and stocks.

Source: Kerry Capell, "Care to Buy Some David Bowie Bonds?" Business Week (International Edition, March 11, 2002); "Rating Cut and Debt Backed by Musician," The New York Times, March 23, 2004, Section C, p. 11; and Karen Richardson, "Failed Bowie Bonds Might Perform Encore," The Seattle Times, August, 24, 2005, p. E1.

In the popular imagination, finance is closely associated with markets for stocks, bonds, and other securities. References to the closing level of the Dow Jones Industrial Average, the Nikkei 225, the Financial Times Stock Exchange 100, and many other stock indexes form part of the daily routine for citizens of the world's largest economies, and most come to understand that these numbers can have a profound influence on their personal and professional lives. As more and more countries adopt market-oriented economic policies, the number of people whose lives are touched by security markets reaches into the billions. However, relatively few people understand the fundamental forces that determine security prices. Though we do not wish to understate the complexities of security valuation, a relatively straightforward framework exists that investors can use to value many types of financial assets, including bonds and stocks. This framework states that *the value of any asset equals the present value of all future benefits accruing to the asset's owner.*

Our primary objective in this chapter is to describe the models commonly used to value debt and equity securities, beginning with the simplest discounted cash flow models. Why do corporate managers need to understand how to price bonds and stocks? First, firms must occasionally approach the bond and stock markets to raise capital for new investments. Understanding how investors in these markets value the firm's securities helps managers determine how to finance new projects. Second, firms periodically make investments by acquiring privately held companies, just as they unload past investments by selling divisions. In either case, knowing how the market values a firm guides a manager's expectations regarding the appropriate price for an acquisition or divestiture. Third, a company's stock price provides an external, independent performance assessment of top management, one that a diligent board of directors watches closely. Surely managers who will be judged (and compensated) based on their firm's stock price need to understand the determinants of that price. Fourth, finance theory suggests that the objective of corporate management should be to maximize the stock price. How can managers take actions to maximize the stock price if they don't know what causes stock prices to be high or low?

This chapter presents an introduction to security valuation. We begin by laying out the principles of valuation, principles that can be applied to a wide variety of problems. Next, we use these principles by demonstrating both simple and advanced methods for valuing bonds. We then describe procedures for valuing stocks. Both bond and stock valuation make heavy use of the time value of money techniques covered in Chapter 3. These models enable analysts to make surprisingly accurate value estimates for several types of securities. However, when these models fail, analysts sometimes revert to rules of thumb or comparative valuation techniques to estimate security prices. We conclude the chapter with a brief overview of these comparative techniques, highlighting their strengths and weaknesses.

4.1 VALUATION FUNDAMENTALS

In a market economy, ownership of an asset confers the rights to the benefit stream generated by the asset. These benefits may be tangible, like the interest payments on a government bond, or intangible, like the pleasure experienced from viewing a beautiful painting. In either case, *the value of any asset equals the present value of all its future benefits.* Finance theory focuses primarily on tangible benefits, typically the cash flows paid by an asset over time. The value of a bond equals the present value of future interest and principal payments to be paid by the borrower (issuer) to the lender (bondholder). The value of common stock equals the present value of future dividends and other cash payments that investors expect firms to distribute to them. The value of an apartment complex equals the present value of future rent payments less the cost of operating and maintaining the property. In each case, the asset's worth is determined by the value today of the benefits the asset is expected to convey to its owner in the future.

This implies that pricing an asset requires knowledge of both its future benefits and the appropriate discount rate that converts future benefits into a present value. For some assets, such as U.S. government bonds, investors know with a high degree of certainty what will be the future benefit stream. For investments such as common stock, which give investors an ownership stake in a company, estimating the future benefit stream is quite challenging. Investors must consider how much cash the firm will generate now and in the future, how much of that cash the firm will reinvest to finance growth, and how much it will distribute to shareholders via dividends, share repurchases, or other means. Generally, *the greater the uncertainty about an asset's future benefits, the higher the discount rate investors will apply when discounting those benefits to the present.*

Consequently, the valuation process links an asset's risk and return to determine its price. Holding future benefits (returns) constant, an inverse relationship exists between risk and value. If two investments promise identical cash payments in the future, investors will pay a higher price for the one with the more credible promise. However, holding risk constant, a positive relationship exists between future benefits and value. Confronted with two equally risky assets, investors will pay more to acquire one of these if it offers higher future cash flows than the other. In equilibrium, riskier assets must offer higher returns to attract investors.[1]

THE FUNDAMENTAL VALUATION MODEL

Chapters 5 and 6 present an in-depth analysis of the relationship between risk and return. For now, take as given the market's required rate of return on a specific investment. How does the market use that rate to determine the prices of different types of securities? Equation 4.1 mathematically expresses the fundamental valuation model as follows:

$$P_0 = \frac{CF_1}{(1+r)^1} + \frac{CF_2}{(1+r)^2} + \cdots + \frac{CF_n}{(1+r)^n} \quad \textbf{(Eq. 4.1)}$$

critical to match up r and n

In this equation, P_0 represents the asset's price today (at time 0), CF_t represents the asset's expected cash flow at time t, and r is the required return—the discount rate that reflects the asset's risk. The letter n stands for the asset's life, the period over which it distributes cash flows to investors, usually measured in years. As you will see, n may be a finite number, as in the case of a bond that matures in a certain number of years, or it may be infinite, as in the case of a common stock with an indefinite

In excel: = PV(rate, periods, payment, FV, type)

if 8% bond, $1000 par, 5 years = PV(.08, 5, 80, 1000, 0)

since payment #1 comes in one year, not today

[1] This chapter emphasizes models that determine value by discounting future cash flows at an appropriate discount rate. In Chapters 18 and 19, we will examine a different approach to valuation known as *no-arbitrage pricing*. In essence, no-arbitrage pricing makes use of the fact that, in equilibrium, two assets that offer identical future benefit streams must sell for the same price. Otherwise, investors can make a risk-free profit by engaging in *arbitrage*, simultaneously buying and selling identical assets at different prices.

rate = market rate, not contract rate

life span. In either case, this equation provides us with a vehicle for valuing almost any type of asset. Consider the example in the following Applying the Model.

APPLYING THE MODEL 4.1

On April 11, 2005, Microsoft Corp. and Gateway Inc. announced that they had entered into an agreement to resolve legal issues between the two companies and to work together going forward on marketing and developing Gateway personal computing products. The settlement resulted from the mid-1990s case of the *United States v. Microsoft* in which the Court ruled that Microsoft violated antitrust laws resulting in harm to Gateway's business. The 2005 settlement agreement provided for Microsoft to pay Gateway $150 million over four years in exchange for Gateway's complete release of all antitrust claims against Microsoft. The timing of Microsoft's payments to Gateway was not disclosed. But Microsoft did announce that as a result of the settlement with Gateway, it was taking a $123 million pretax charge in the quarter ended March 31, 2005. So how did Microsoft convert its $150 million settlement into a $123 million pretax charge? Suppose Microsoft paid the $150 million settlement in four end-of-year payments of $37.5 million, and suppose Microsoft's required return on low-risk investments was 8.5 percent. The present value of Microsoft's settlement cost was determined as follows:

$$P_0 = \frac{\$37.5 \text{ million}}{(1 + .085)^1} + \frac{\$37.5 \text{ million}}{(1 + .085)^2} + \frac{\$37.5 \text{ million}}{(1 + .085)^3} + \frac{\$37.5 \text{ million}}{(1 + .085)^4}$$

$$= \$123 \text{ million}$$

Microsoft immediately deducted the $123 million present value of its settlement with Gateway. Although $123 million is a sizable amount, it is relatively small in comparison to Microsoft's $37 billion in annual revenue and $270 billion market value at that time. Although we would expect the value of Microsoft to drop by $123 million upon the announcement of its settlement agreement with Gateway, this amount is too small to observe in the value of Microsoft.

With this simple framework in hand, we now turn to the problem of pricing bonds. Though bond-pricing techniques can be very complex, we will focus on "plain-vanilla" bonds, those that promise a fixed stream of cash payments over a finite time period. Among the largest issuers of such "fixed income" securities are national governments and large, multinational corporations.

Concept Review Questions

1. Why is it important for corporate managers to understand how to price bonds and stocks?

2. Holding constant an asset's future benefit stream, what happens to its price if the asset's risk increases?

3. Holding constant an asset's risk, what happens to its price if the asset's future benefit stream increases?

4. Keeping in mind Equation 4.1, discuss how one might determine the price per acre of farmland in a particular region.

4.2 BOND VALUATION

BOND VOCABULARY

know these terms

Bonds are debt instruments used by business and government to raise large sums of money, often from a diverse group of lenders. Though bonds come in many varieties, most bonds share certain basic characteristics. First, a bond promises to pay investors a fixed amount of interest, called the bond's __coupon__. Borrowers usually make coupon payments semiannually (every six months). Second, bonds typically have a limited life, or **maturity**. When the bond matures, the borrower repays investors a lump sum known as the bond's face value, or **par value**, often $1,000. Third, a bond's __coupon rate__ equals the bond's annual coupon payment divided by its par value. Fourth, a bond's **coupon yield** equals the coupon payment divided by the bond's current market price (which does not always equal its par value).[2] To illustrate, suppose that a firm issues a bond with a $1,000 par value and promises to pay investors $35 every six months over the life of the bond. The bond's *coupon* is $70 per year, and its *coupon rate* is 7 percent ($70 ÷ $1,000). If the current market value of this bond is $980, then its *coupon yield* is 7.14 percent ($70 ÷ $980).

- always an annual number

coupon / par

coupon / market value

Bonds can have a variety of additional features, such as a *call feature* that allows the issuer to redeem the bond at a predetermined price prior to maturity, or a *conversion feature* that grants bondholders the right to redeem their bonds for a predetermined number of shares of stock in the borrowing firm. Chapter 17 discusses these and other features in detail. For now, we focus our attention on pricing ordinary bonds. We'll begin with the basic bond valuation equation and then describe its application to risk-free and risky bonds.

if bond is trading at a discount, yield to maturity is more than contract yield since the new buyer gets a bonus when the bond matures (pays $961, gets $1000 at maturity)

THE BASIC EQUATION (ASSUMING ANNUAL INTEREST)

Because the cash flows from a bond are known and contractual, bonds are far easier to value than stocks, which do not have known contractual cash flows.

Initially, for convenience we will assume that bonds pay annual interest at a stated coupon rate, i, that M represents the bond's par or face value, that n is the number of years to the bond's maturity, and that r is the required return on the bond. As for any financial asset, the bond's price equals the present value of its future cash flows. The cash flows include two components: (1) the annual coupon, C, which equals the stated coupon rate, i, multiplied by M, the par value (that is, $C = i \times M$), received for each of the n years, and (2) the par value, M, received at maturity in n years. Equation 4.2 uses this notation to show that the bond's price is merely the sum of the present value of the interest cash flow stream (an annuity) plus the present value of its par value (a lump sum), typically $1,000.

$$\text{Price} = C \times \left[\frac{1}{(1+r)^1} + \frac{1}{(1+r)^2} + \cdots + \frac{1}{(1+r)^n} \right] + M \times \left[\frac{1}{(1+r)^n} \right] \quad \textbf{(Eq. 4.2)}$$

Present value of interest cash flows

Present value of par value

[2.] The *coupon yield* is but one of several important measures of a bond's return that goes by the term *yield*. Other common measures of a bond's return that use the word *yield* include *bond equivalent yield* and *yield to maturity*, both of which we discuss later in this section.

APPLYING THE MODEL 4.2

On January 1, 2007, Worldwide United had outstanding a $1,000 par value bond with a 9.125 percent coupon rate, which we will assume pays interest at the end of each calendar year. The bond matures at the end of 2017—in exactly 11 years. In 2007, bonds of similar risk had a required return of 8 percent. The annual coupon on this bond, C, is .09125 × $1,000 = $91.25. The bond's cash flows appear below the time line in Figure 4.1. Substituting these values into Equation 4.2, we get the following result:

$$\text{Price} = \$91.25 \times \left[\frac{1}{(1+.08)^1} + \frac{1}{(1+.08)^2} + \cdots + \frac{1}{(1+.08)^{11}} \right]$$

$$+ \ \$1,000 \times \left[\frac{1}{(1+.08)^{11}} \right]$$

$$= \$651.43 + \$428.88 = \$1,080.31$$

A financial calculator or spreadsheet could also be used to find this value. The Worldwide United bond sells at a *premium* of about $80 above its par value because the bond contractually pays 9.125 percent even though investors require only an 8 percent return at the time. As a result, investors will bid the bond price up to $1,080.31, at which point it will provide the required 8 percent return.

Figure 4.1
Time Line for Bond Valuation (Assuming Annual Interest) (Worldwide United 9⅛% Coupon, $1,000 Par Bond, Maturing at End of 2017; Required Return Assumed to Be 8%)

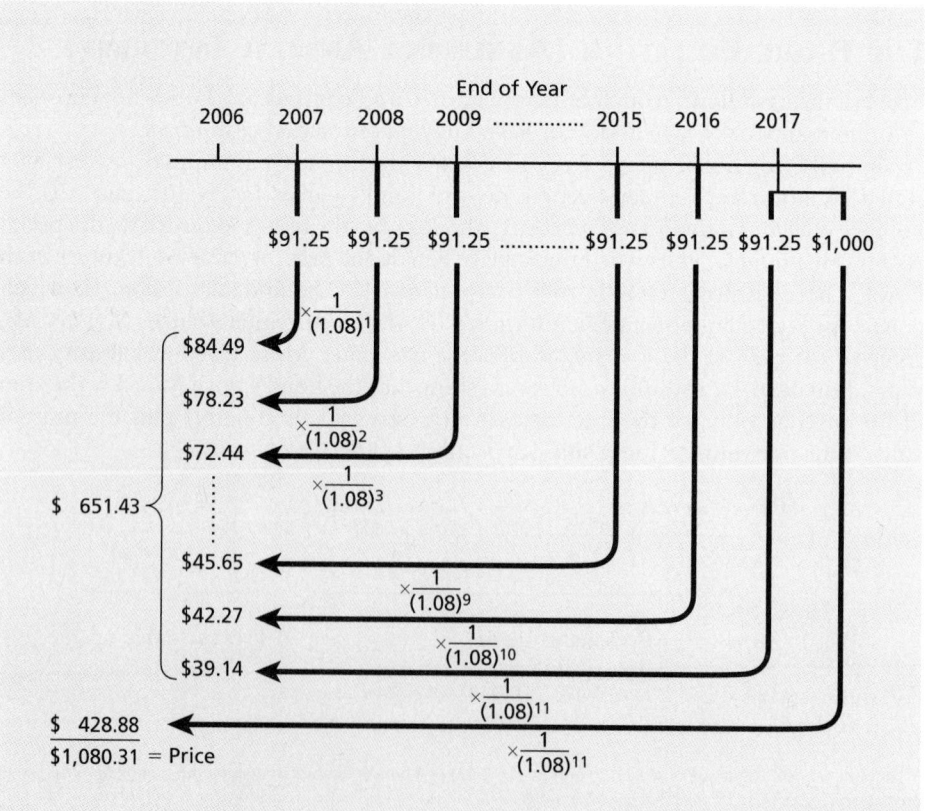

Again, we want to emphasize the fundamental lesson that the price of a bond equals the present value of its future cash flows. We now turn to a more in-depth development of the concepts underlying bond valuation, starting with risk-free bonds.

RISK-FREE BONDS

A **risk-free bond** is a bond that has no chance of default by its issuer. Although these bonds have no default risk, their prices do fluctuate as market conditions change. In practice, investors view only those bonds issued by the most creditworthy national governments as risk-free. The world's largest issuer of risk-free bonds is the U.S. Treasury. Treasury securities come in a wide range of maturities, ranging from just a few weeks to 30 years.[3] Most of these make semiannual coupon payments, but some short-term Treasury securities, called "discount" or "zero-coupon" bonds, do not make coupon payments at all. Instead, they sell at a discount relative to par value, as the next section illustrates.

Zero-Coupon Treasuries. Pure discount instruments, such as U.S. Treasury bills, promise investors a single fixed payment on a specified future date. They make no intermediate interest payments, and therefore are sometimes called **zero-coupon bonds.** How can bonds that pay no interest be attractive investments? That's where the word *discount* comes into play. Investors purchase Treasury bills at a discount from their par value. If held to maturity, Treasury bills offer a dollar return equal to the difference between the par value and the purchase price. For example, an investor might purchase a Treasury bill maturing in six months for $9,800. When the bill matures, the U.S. Treasury pays $10,000, the par value of the bill, and the investor earns a $200 return. The bill pays no coupon interest. Using Equation 4.2, we can obtain the percentage return on this investment as follows:

$$\$9,800 = \$10,000 \times \left[\frac{1}{(1 + r)^1} \right]$$

$$r = \left(\frac{\$10,000}{\$9,800} \right) - 1 = 1.0204 - 1 = 0.0204 = 2.04\%$$

Of course, 2.04 percent represents the rate of return for six months, so we could state the percentage return on an annual basis in either of two ways. By multiplying the 6-month rate, denoted r_{6mo}, times 2, we obtain the simple-interest annual rate, 4.08 percent:

$$r_{simple} = r_{6mo} \times 2$$
$$= 0.0204 \times 2 = 0.0408 = 4.08\%$$

This is a simple-interest rate because it ignores the impact of compounding. Alternatively, we could obtain a compound annual rate, r_{ann}, as follows:

$$r_{ann} = (1 + r_{6mo})^2 - 1$$
$$= (1 + 0.0204)^2 - 1 = 0.0412 = 4.12\%$$

This rate represents the return that an investor would earn at the end of one year if she invested for six months at a rate of 2.04 percent and then reinvested the proceeds

---

[3.] Some countries offer even longer maturity on their government bonds. In 2005, Japan issued 40-year bonds for the first time, and the U.K. and France became the first governments to issue 50-year bonds.

for another six months at the same rate. The rate slightly exceeds the simple-interest figure of 4.08 percent because this calculation takes into account the investor's opportunity to earn interest during the second half of the year on both the original principal and the interest from the first six months. To see how this works in practice, consider the following example from a Treasury bill auction.

The Treasury conducts periodic auctions of bills with maturities ranging from 4 to 26 weeks. The following quote obtained from the Treasury website (http://www .treasury.gov) illustrates bill pricing in a typical auction:

Term	Issue Date	Maturity Date	Discount Rate %	Investment Rate %	Price Per $100	CUSIP
182-DAY	4-21-2005	10-20-2005	3.040	3.130	98.463111	912795VW8

The first entry indicates that this particular bill matures in 182 days, or about six months. The second item gives the date of the auction in which the bill was sold, and following that appears the bill's maturity date. The fourth and fifth entries in the quote are measures of the bond's yield, which we will discuss shortly. The sixth item is the bond's price, and the final item in the quote is the bill's CUSIP,[4] essentially a tracking number that allows traders to communicate with each other about a specific security. Look at the next-to-last number in the quote, 98.463111; it represents the market price of the bill (as determined by the auction) per $100 of par value. If an investor submitted a successful bid to purchase bills having a par value of $10,000, the purchase price for this order would be $9,846.31. If the investor purchases bills and holds them to maturity, the dollar return on that investment will be $153.69, the difference between the $10,000 par value and the purchase price. The percentage return is calculated as follows:

$$\frac{(\$10{,}000 - \$9{,}846.31)}{\$9{,}846.31} = 0.01561 = 1.561\%$$

However, this is a return over just six months. We could annualize this using simple interest as follows:

$$0.01561 \times \left(\frac{365}{182}\right) = 0.03130 = 3.130\%$$

Notice that this number, 3.130 percent, appears in the bond quotation shown previously. Bond traders call it the **bond equivalent yield,** and it is a simple-interest measure of an investor's annual return from holding a Treasury bill.[5] We can substitute the second equation into the first and rearrange terms to arrive at a Treasury bill

---

[4.] CUSIP stands for Committee on Uniform Securities Identification Procedures. A CUSIP number identifies most securities, including: stocks of all registered U.S. and Canadian companies, and U.S. government and municipal bonds.

[5.] In this market, it is traditional to calculate one other measure of the bill's return, the **bank discount yield:**

$$\frac{(\$10{,}000 - \$9{,}846.31)}{\$10{,}000}\left(\frac{360}{182}\right) = .03040 = 3.040\%$$

Note that this number appears just before the bond equivalent yield in the price quote. For several reasons, this is a poor measure of an investor's return, but traders nonetheless use it to communicate with each other about current prices in the market. The important lesson here is not to memorize the differences between bond equivalent and bank discount yields, but to understand that the price of a Treasury bill is just the present value of the cash payment at maturity.

pricing formula that looks more like the generic present value pricing relationship given in Equation 4.1:

$$\frac{(\$10,000 - \$9,846.31)}{\$9,846.31} = 0.01561 = \frac{0.03130}{\left(\dfrac{365}{182}\right)}$$

$$\text{Price} = \frac{\$10,000}{\left[1 + 0.03130\left(\dfrac{182}{365}\right)\right]} = \$9,846.31$$

In other words, the price of the bond equals the $10,000 payment that it will make in six months, discounted using a 182-day interest rate. In this equation, the interest rate, 3.130 percent, is multiplied by the fraction of the year that will have elapsed at the bond's maturity date. This equation can be stated in a more general form:

$$\text{Price} = \frac{\text{Par}}{\left[1 + r\left(\dfrac{1}{2}\right)\right]} = \frac{\text{Par}}{\left(1 + \dfrac{r}{2}\right)}$$

where we have made the simplifying assumption that the bill matures in exactly one-half year (or that 2 is a sufficiently close approximation for $365 \div 182$). In this equation, r represents the market's required return on the bill, and we divide it by 2 because the bill matures in six months.[6] When conversing about current market conditions, Treasury bill traders will often refer to a bill's return rather than its price. It should be clear that if you know the bill's return, you can calculate its price, and vice versa. You can use the previous equation to price most pure discount bonds. Just discount the par value at an appropriate interest rate to obtain the price.

Coupon-Paying Treasuries. Valuing coupon-paying instruments, such as Treasury notes and bonds, requires only a slight modification to the discount bond–pricing equation. Treasury notes and bonds like bills are risk-free in that they receive backing by the full faith and credit of the U.S. government. However, unlike Treasury bills, notes and bonds make interest payments every six months, and they also have longer maturities than bills. It is a simple matter to modify the general bond-pricing equation, Equation 4.2, to fit the characteristics of coupon-paying notes or bonds:

$$\text{Price} = \frac{\dfrac{C}{2}}{\left(1 + \dfrac{r}{2}\right)^1} + \frac{\dfrac{C}{2}}{\left(1 + \dfrac{r}{2}\right)^2} + \frac{\dfrac{C}{2}}{\left(1 + \dfrac{r}{2}\right)^3} + \cdots + \frac{\dfrac{C}{2} + \$1,000}{\left(1 + \dfrac{r}{2}\right)^{2n}} \quad \textbf{(Eq. 4.3)}$$

In this equation, C refers to the annual coupon payment, so $C/2$ represents the semi-annual payment. Note that in the last period, the bond makes its final coupon payment and repays the par value or principal (in this case, $1,000). As before, r represents the bond's yield, which you can think of as the market's required rate of return

---

[6.] Here's a pop quiz. Does the value r in this equation represent the simple-interest or compound-interest annual return? Because the equation calculates the 6-month rate by simply dividing the annual rate by 2, r is a simple-interest rate.

on this bond.[7] The bond matures in n years, so there are $2n$ semiannual payments. Simply stated, the price (or value) of a bond is the sum of the present value of interest payments and the present value of the par value, both discounted at the market's required return.

APPLYING THE MODEL 4.3

Suppose that six months ago the Treasury issued the new 5-year, $1,000 par value note quoted below in a fashion similar to Treasury bills.

Security	Term	Type	Issue Date	Maturity Date	Interest Rate %	Yield %	Price Per $100	CUSIP
5-YEAR		NOTE	04-15-2005	04-15-2010	4.000	4.046	99.793649	912828DR8

The coupon rate is 4.0 percent. Assume that the bond just made its first interest payment, so the next one will be due in six months. Since the bond was first issued, market conditions have changed and investors now require a return of 5 percent per year. What is the price of the bond? Given its coupon rate, the bond pays $40 in interest per year, or $20 every six months.

$$\text{Price} = \frac{\$20}{\left(1 + \dfrac{.05}{2}\right)^1} + \frac{\$20}{\left(1 + \dfrac{.05}{2}\right)^2} + \frac{\$20}{\left(1 + \dfrac{.05}{2}\right)^3} + \cdots + \frac{\$1,020}{\left(1 + \dfrac{.05}{2}\right)^9}$$

$$= \$960.15$$

The bond has nine interest payments remaining (plus the principal repayment) and is worth $960.15.[8]

In the example above, the bond's price was below its $1,000 par value. We say that a bond sells at a **discount** when its price is less than par value.[9] The bond sells at a discount because its coupon rate, 4 percent, offers a return lower than that currently required by the market, 5 percent. If investors demand a 5 percent return, the only way they can get it from a bond that pays 4 percent interest is to purchase the bond at a discount. At a price of $960.15, the bond offers a coupon yield of 4.17 percent ($40 ÷ $960.15), still not up to the 5 percent required return. For investors who purchase this bond and hold it to maturity, the total return will reflect both the interest payments and a capital gain of $39.85 ($1,000 − $960.15) when the Treasury repays the $1,000 principal. Combined, the interest payments and capital gain generate a return of 5 percent. The same logic can work in reverse. Suppose that the market's required return on this bond was 3 percent rather than 5 percent. When the market requires only a 3 percent return, a bond that pays 4 percent interest would be quite attractive.

[7.] Notice once again that this equation calculates the present value of payments arriving every six months by taking the annual interest rate (r) and dividing by 2 to get a semiannual rate. Therefore, the value r in this equation represents a simple-interest rate, the convention for quoting rates in the bond market. Remember that whenever we calculate an annual interest rate by multiplying a semiannual rate times 2 (or calculate a semiannual rate by dividing an annual rate by 2), we are dealing with simple rather than compound interest.

[8.] You can easily use Excel to calculate this number. First, enter the bond's nine payments in cells A1 through A9 on a spreadsheet. Next, in any empty cell, type the formula = NPV(.025,A1:A9), and Excel will produce the price of the bond. In the formula, .025 reflects the semiannual interest rate.

[9.] Because this bond trades below par value, it sells at a discount. It is not, however, a pure discount bond like a Treasury bill.

Investors would purchase this bond, driving its price above par value. In that case, the bond would sell for a **premium.** Substituting 3 percent for 5 percent in the equation above, you can verify that the market price of the bond would be $1,041.80.

RISKY BONDS

How do you know what return the market "requires" for a particular bond? Your intuition probably tells you that the riskier the bond, the higher the rate of return the market will require, but putting that language into quantitative terms is a challenge. Chapters 5 and 6 explore the tradeoff between risk and return in some depth, but for now we will make use of a convenient shortcut. Because Treasury bonds provide a known contractual stream of cash flows, if you can observe the market price of a bond, you can infer what the market's required return must be. Suppose that a Treasury bond with par value of $1,000 matures in exactly 2.5 years and pays a 6 percent coupon. You look at the market and observe that the price of this bond is $988.63. Because this bond sells at a discount, you know that the market requires a return on the bond greater than 6 percent, the bond's coupon rate. But how much greater? Just use the bond-pricing equation (Equation 4.3) to solve for the discount rate that equates the present value of the bond's cash flows to its current price:

$$\frac{\$30}{\left(1+\dfrac{r}{2}\right)^1} + \frac{\$30}{\left(1+\dfrac{r}{2}\right)^2} + \frac{\$30}{\left(1+\dfrac{r}{2}\right)^3} + \frac{\$30}{\left(1+\dfrac{r}{2}\right)^4} + \frac{\$1,030}{\left(1+\dfrac{r}{2}\right)^5} = \$988.63$$

By using a financial calculator or spreadsheet program, or by trial and error, you can solve this equation to find $r/2 = 0.0325$, so $r = 0.065$ or 6.5 percent. In this equation, the value of r is called the bond's **yield to maturity (YTM).**[10] The yield to maturity of any bond is the discount rate that equates the present value of the bond's cash flows to its market price. For Treasury bonds, the yield to maturity measures the market's required return.

Valuing an ordinary corporate bond involves the same steps: write down the cash flows, determine an appropriate discount rate, and calculate the present value. The discount rate on a corporate bond should be higher than on a Treasury bond with the same maturity because corporate bonds carry **default risk,** the risk that the corporation may not make all scheduled payments. Bond traders often speak of the yield spread between Treasury bonds and corporate bonds. The **yield spread** is the difference in yield to maturity between two bonds or two classes of bonds with similar maturities. An example will demonstrate this.

APPLYING THE MODEL 4.4

Assume that a 1 percent yield spread exists between high-quality 10-year Treasury bonds and 10-year corporate bonds. If the yield to maturity on 10-year Treasury bonds is 7 percent, then the yield to maturity on a 10-year corporate bond would be 8 percent. If you want to determine the price of a 10-year corporate bond with a 9 percent coupon, substituting $C = \$90$, and $r = .08$ or 8 percent, and $n = 10$ into

---

[10.] A bond's yield to maturity is also called its **internal rate of return (IRR).** It can be calculated using a financial calculator or spreadsheet. In Excel, you can calculate a bond's *YTM* using the = IRR function. See Problem 4-11 for an illustration.

Handwritten margin notes:

— YTM = IRR (remember to put the cost as a negative # in period 1)

if there are multiple sign changes, you might have multiple IRRs (so then need to do a data table to show NPVs)

Equation 4.3, we get:

$$Price = \frac{\$45}{\left(1 + \frac{.08}{2}\right)^1} + \frac{\$45}{\left(1 + \frac{.08}{2}\right)^2} + \frac{\$45}{\left(1 + \frac{.08}{2}\right)^3} + \cdots + \frac{\$1,045}{\left(1 + \frac{.08}{2}\right)^{20}}$$

$$= \$1,067.95$$

The bond's price should therefore be $1,067.95.

Bonds may seem like safe investments: Investors who purchase Treasury bonds or high-quality corporate bonds can be fairly confident that promised cash payments will be made as scheduled. Even so, bond prices can be volatile and, for most bonds, volatility is as important as default risk in determining the risk of investing in bonds. Before discussing the relationship between bond prices and interest rates, we will consider the common bond issuers and bond ratings.

Bond Issuers.   A simple way to classify bonds is based upon the identity of the issuer. Large companies who need money to finance new investments and to fulfill other needs issue **corporate bonds.** Corporations issue bonds with maturities ranging from 1 to 100 years. When a company issues a debt instrument with a maturity of one to ten years, the instrument is usually called a *note* rather than a bond, but notes and bonds are essentially identical instruments. Most corporate bonds have a par value of $1,000 and pay interest semiannually. **Municipal bonds** are issued by local and state government entities. In the United States, federal law gives local and state governments a significant tax break by exempting interest received on municipal bonds from the bondholder's federal income tax. Obviously, this makes municipal bonds especially attractive to investors who face high marginal tax rates. The tax exemption on municipal bond interest allows state and local governments to raise money at lower interest rates than they would otherwise be able to do.

The largest single issuer of bonds is the U.S. government. The debt instruments issued by the government range in maturity from a few weeks to thirty years. **Treasury bills** are debt instruments that mature in less than a year. The maturities of **Treasury notes** range from one to ten years. Before 2001, the government also issued **Treasury bonds** with maturities of up to thirty years, but discontinued their issuance until February 2006, when it was resumed. The federal government issues bonds to raise money to cover budget deficits, and these securities are backed by the "full faith and credit" of the United States. That pledge means that investors generally regard Treasury bills, notes, and bonds as very safe investments.

Some federal government agencies issue their own bonds, called **agency bonds,** to finance operations. The government charters these agencies with the task of providing credit for certain sectors of the economy such as farming, real estate, and education. The Federal Home Loan Bank (FHLB), the Federal National Mortgage Association (FNMA or "Fannie Mae"), the Government National Mortgage Association (GNMA or "Ginnie Mae"), and the Federal Home Loan Mortgage Corporation (FHLMC or "Freddie Mac") are the major mortgage-related agencies that issue bonds. Agency debt is not necessarily backed by the full faith and credit of the Treasury, so investors recognize that agency debt carries a small amount of additional risk relative to Treasury securities.

Bond Ratings.   For information on the likelihood that a particular bond issue may default, investors turn to bond rating agencies such as Moody's, Standard & Poor's (S&P), and Fitch. These organizations provide an independent assessment of the risk

Table 4.1
Bond Ratings

Rating Description	Moody's	S&P and Fitch	
Highest quality	Aaa	AAA	Investment-grade
High quality	Aa1, Aa2, Aa3	AA+, AA, AA−	bonds
Upper medium	A1, A2, A3	A+, A, A−	
Medium	Baa1, Baa2, Baa3	BBB+, BBB, BBB−	
Noninvestment grade	Ba1	BB+	Junk bonds
Speculative	Ba2, Ba3	BB, BB−	
Highly speculative	B1, B2, B3	B+, B, B−	
Very risky, default	Caa1 or lower	CCC+ or lower	

of most publicly traded bond issues, and they assign a letter **bond rating** to each issue to indicate its degree of risk. Table 4.1 lists the major bond-rating categories provided by each of the agencies and the interpretation associated with each rating class. Bonds rated Baa3 or higher by Moody's, and BBB− or higher by S&P and Fitch fall into the investment-grade category. Bonds rated lower than that are called noninvestment grade or **junk bonds.** The term "junk bonds" has a pejorative connotation but simply means that these bonds are riskier than investment-grade bonds. For example, for bonds in the investment grade category, the probability of default is extremely low, perhaps as low as 1 percent. A recent study put the probability of a B-rated bond defaulting in its first year at almost 8 percent.[11]

Table 4.2 demonstrates the relationship between bond ratings and yield spreads for corporate bonds at different maturities at a given point in time.[12] The yield spreads

Table 4.2
The Relationship Between Bond Ratings and Spreads at Different Maturities at a Given Point in Time

Rating	1 yr	2 yr	3 yr	5 yr	7 yr	10 yr	30 yr
Aaa/AAA	10	12	23	29	46	58	78
Aa1/AA+	19	27	28	40	56	69	90
Aa2/AA	21	33	35	44	59	71	93
Aa3/AA−	22	36	37	49	63	75	101
A1/A+	44	49	53	61	76	90	113
A2/A	47	52	55	63	78	92	117
A3/A−	51	55	58	67	81	95	118
Baa1/BBB+	59	69	77	87	117	139	165
Baa2/BBB	62	77	5	92	124	147	172
Baa3/BBB−	69	82	87	97	129	154	177
Ba1/BB+	330	340	350	360	380	400	420
Ba2/BB	340	350	360	370	390	410	430
Ba3/BB−	350	360	370	380	400	420	440
B1/B+	470	480	490	520	560	600	650
B2/B	480	490	500	530	570	610	660
B3/B−	490	500	510	540	580	620	670
Caa/CCC	890	900	910	935	945	955	985

[11.] See Phoa in Fabozzi (2002).

[12.] We focus exclusively on corporate bonds in Table 4.2 because the yields on corporate and municipal bonds with the same rating will be quite different. As noted earlier, interest payments from municipal bonds are not subject to federal income tax. This means that investors will accept a lower yield on a municipal bond than they will accept on a corporate bond having the same rating.

are quoted in **basis points;** 100 basis points = 1.00%. The first entry in the top left corner of the table shows a corporate bond with the highest possible Aaa/AAA rating and a maturity of one year. It offered investors a yield to maturity that was just ten basis points higher than a one-year Treasury bill at the given point in time. Moving across the row, we see that yield spreads increase with time to maturity. As expected, yield spreads increase as you move down the rows. The bottom row shows that the lowest-rated bonds, those that are at or near the point of default, offer yields that are 9 to 10 percent higher than comparable maturity Treasury securities. To illustrate an extreme case, suppose that the yield to maturity on a ten-year Treasury bond equals 3 percent. The next-to-last entry in Table 4.2 shows that a ten-year corporate bond rated Caa/CCC must offer a yield that is 9.55 percent higher than the Treasury bond, or 12.55 percent. If that seems like an attractive return, remember the risk dimension. An investor who buys a large number of bonds rated Caa/CCC will almost certainly not earn an average yield of 12.55 percent, because some of these bonds will default. When default occurs, bondholders usually do not receive all the payments they were originally promised, so the yield they realize on their bonds falls short of the promised yield to maturity.[13]

The vast majority of corporate bonds do not wind up in default, so investors typically receive the cash flows they are promised when they buy bonds. However, this does not mean that bonds are risk-free, even if they do not default. The next section explores how market forces affect bond prices.

Bond Prices

Bond Price Quotations. The prices of bonds are quoted in the financial press. In each edition of *The Wall Street Journal,* quotations for the prior trading day's forty most active fixed-coupon corporate bonds are reported. Their format is demonstrated below for a few bonds traded on Wednesday April 20, 2005, and reported in *The Wall Street Journal* on Thursday, April 21, 2005.

COMPANY(TICKER)	COUPON	MATURITY	LAST PRICE	LAST YIELD	EST SPREAD	UST	EST $ VOL (000's)
SBC Communications Inc (SBC)	5.100	Sep 15, 2014	99.928	5.109	92	10	72,743
Weyerhaeuser (WY)	6.750	Mar 15, 2012	110.214	4.979	76	10	70,080
General Motors (GM)	7.200	Jan 15, 2011	85.459	10.654	682	5	63,637

The first column of the bond quotations lists the name and ticker symbol of the bond issuer. The second column shows the annual coupon rate, and the third column reports the maturity date. Corporate bond prices are quoted as a percent of par value. For example, the first row of the table indicates that the SBC Communications bond paying a coupon rate of 5.10 percent and maturing on September 15, 2014, recently sold for $999.28 (or 99.928 percent of par value). Given the price, coupon, and maturity date, the fifth column calculates the SBC bond's yield to maturity, which equals 5.109 percent.

[13.] According to The Salomon Center for the Study of Financial Institutions, the default rate a among junk bonds reached a record 12.8% in 2002. In a very rough sense, this means that one of eight junk bond issues in the market defaulted that year. The Center estimates that investors who held defaulted bonds recovered only 25% of par value. With the improving economy in 2003, the default rate fell to 4.6% and the recovery rate increased to 45%.

The estimated spread (noted "EST SPREAD") in the sixth column equals the difference in yield to maturities between the given bond and a Treasury bond at roughly the same maturity. By convention, these spreads are quoted in terms of *basis points*. Because corporate bonds are riskier than Treasury bonds, they offer higher yields, so the yield spread is always a positive number. The seventh column specifies what we mean by a "similar" bond. The column heading, UST, stands for U.S. Treasury, and the numbers in the column refer to the maturity of the Treasury security to which each corporate bond is compared to calculate the yield spread. Looking at those two columns, we see that the SBC Communications bond offers a yield that is 92 basis points (or 0.92 percentage points) above the yield on a Treasury bond maturing in ten years. The ten-year Treasury bond is a relevant comparison because the SBC Communications bond's maturity is that far off in the future at 2014. Notice that the yield spread on General Motors bonds, which mature in 2011, is reported relative to a five-year Treasury note.

As you might expect, bond spreads reflect a direct relationship with default risk. The greater the risk that the borrower may default on its debts, the higher the spread that bonds issued by the borrower must offer investors to compensate them for the risk they take. For investors, estimating the default risk of a particular bond issue is a crucial element in determining what the required return on the bond should be. Bond ratings are helpful in making such estimates.

Bond Price Behavior. The value of a bond in the marketplace changes constantly. One factor that can cause a bond's price to move is simply the passage of time. Whether a bond sells at a discount or a premium, its price will converge to par value (plus the final interest payment) as time elapses and the maturity date draws near. This is easy to understand if you imagine a bond that will mature in one day. The final cash flow of the bond is its par value plus the last coupon payment. If this final payment arrives just one day in the future, to determine the bond's price, you simply discount this payment for one day and see that the price and the final payment are virtually identical. In addition to the passage of time, forces in the economy can cause movements in a bond's price. Whenever the required return on a bond changes, the bond's price changes in the opposite direction. You can see this inverse relationship between price and required return in the bond-pricing equation. The higher the bond's required return, the lower its price, and vice versa. How much a bond's price responds to changes in required returns depends on several factors, but among the most important is the bond's maturity.

Figure 4.2 shows how the prices of two bonds change as their required returns change. To focus on the effects of changes in required returns on bond prices, assume that both bonds are free of default risk. Both pay a 6 percent coupon, but one matures in 2 years while the other matures in 10 years. As the figure shows, when the required return equals the coupon rate, 6 percent, both bonds trade at their $1,000 par value. However, as the required return increases, the bonds' prices fall. The rate of decline in the 10-year bond's price far exceeds that of the 2-year bond. Likewise, as the required return decreases, the prices of both bonds increase, but the 10-year bond's price increases much faster than that of the 2-year bond. The general point is that *the prices of long-term bonds display greater sensitivity to changes in interest rates than do the prices of short-term bonds.*[14]

[14.] In certain unusual circumstances, there can be exceptions to this rule. For example, the prices of short-term bonds that sell at a deep discount can be more sensitive to interest-rate movements than the prices of bonds with longer maturities that sell at a premium. A better measure of a bond's sensitivity to interest rate movements is its *duration*, a metric that considers both the timing and the magnitude of the cash payments that the bond makes during its life.

Figure 4.2 illustrates that the most important risk for bond investors to consider is usually **interest rate risk,** the risk that changes in market interest rates will cause fluctuations in a bond's price. Changes in the required returns on bonds can occur as a result of economy-wide forces, such as increases in inflation, or of firm-specific factors, such as a decline in the creditworthiness of the borrower. The experience of France Telecom illustrates what can happen to corporate bonds when business conditions deteriorate. In an attempt to refinance its massive short-term debt obligations, France Telecom conducted the largest (at the time) corporate bond offering in history in March 2001 by selling the equivalent of $16.4 billion worth of bonds to investors around the world. France Telecom simultaneously issued bonds in three different currencies: U.S. dollars, euros, and British pounds. Days after successfully floating its bonds, France Telecom announced that it would not be able to retire as much short-term debt as it had originally anticipated, thereby signaling to the market that its cash flows were weaker than expected. Prices and yields of France Telecom bonds responded accordingly. For example, the required return on France Telecom's 5-year dollar bonds, issued with a 7.2 percent coupon, rose to about 8.5 percent. The following equation shows that this increase in the required return was associated with a decline in price of $52.07, or 5.2 percent, from the original $1,000 par value:

$$\frac{\$36}{\left(1+\dfrac{.085}{2}\right)^1} + \frac{\$36}{\left(1+\dfrac{.085}{2}\right)^2} + \cdots + \frac{\$1,036}{\left(1+\dfrac{.085}{2}\right)^{10}} = \$947.93$$

Fortunately, the same effect can occur in reverse. Consider what might have happened if France Telecom's business had improved suddenly after the bond issue. Suppose that the bond market became convinced that France Telecom's brighter cash flow outlook lowered the risk of the 5-year bonds. If investors lowered their required

Figure 4.2
The Relationship between Bond Prices and Yields for Bonds with Differing Times to Maturity but the Same 6% Coupon Rate

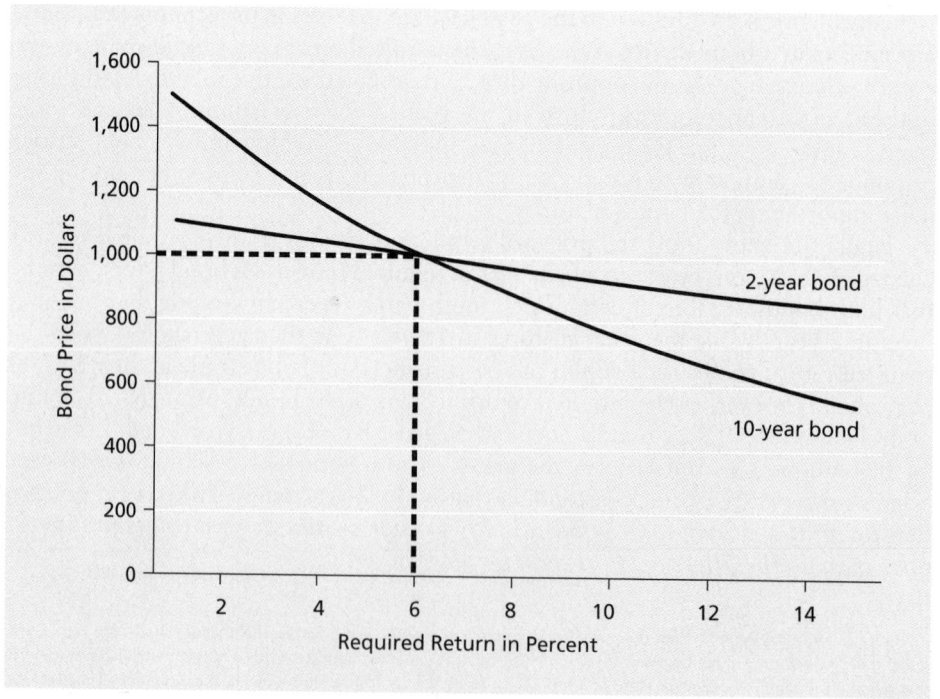

return on these bonds to 6.5 percent, the price of the 5-year bonds would have risen to $1,029.48.

APPLYING THE MODEL 4.5

On May 1, 2000, the U.S. Treasury issued a 30-year bond paying a coupon rate of 6.25 percent on a par value of $1,000. The auction price of this bond was $987.71, resulting in a yield to maturity of 6.34 percent. In the ensuing 60 months, the U.S. economy weakened and interest rates fell. By the time the bond made its tenth interest payment, its *YTM* had fallen to about 4.65 percent. What was the bond's price?

After making 10 coupon payments, this bond had 50 payments remaining, 2 payments per year for the next 25 years. Use Equation 4.2 to calculate the price of the bond:

$$\frac{\$31.25}{\left(1+\frac{.0465}{2}\right)^1} + \frac{\$31.25}{\left(1+\frac{.0465}{2}\right)^2} + \frac{\$31.25}{\left(1+\frac{.0465}{2}\right)^3} + \cdots + \frac{\$1,031.25}{\left(1+\frac{.0465}{2}\right)^{50}}$$

$$= \$1,235.05$$

Compared to its price when issued, the value of the bond had risen by nearly 25 percent in response to a decline in the required rate of return from 6.34 percent to 4.65 percent.

You might argue that this entire discussion is irrelevant if an investor holds a bond to maturity rather than sells it. If the bond is held to maturity, there is a good chance that the investor will receive all interest and principal payments as promised, so any price decrease (or increase) that occurs between the purchase date and the maturity date is just a "paper loss." Though the tax code may ignore investment gains and losses until investors realize them, financial economists argue that losses matter whether investors realize them by selling assets or whether the losses exist only on paper. For example, when the France Telecom bond's value falls from $1,000 to $947.93, an investor holding the bond experiences an opportunity loss. Because the bond's price has fallen, the investor no longer has the opportunity to invest $1,000 elsewhere.

Thus far, we have maintained a simplifying assumption in our valuation models. You can see that assumption embedded in Equations 4.1 and 4.2. Both equations assume that a single discount rate, *r*, can be applied to determine the present value of cash payments made at any and all future dates. In other words, the models assume that investors require the same rate of return on an investment that pays cash 1 year from now and on one that pays cash 10 years from now. In reality, required rates of return depend on the exact timing of cash payments, as the next section illustrates.

5. What is the difference between the terms *coupon, coupon rate,* and *yield to maturity* for a bond?

6. Who are the major issuers of bonds? What role do *bond ratings* play in evaluating bonds? What are *junk bonds*?

7. Why are bond prices and interest rates inversely related?

Concept Review Questions

4.3 ADVANCED BOND VALUATION— THE TERM STRUCTURE OF INTEREST RATES

A quick glance at actual prices and yields of bonds having different maturities reveals an important fact: yields vary with maturity. That is, if you examine the yield to maturity on a number of bonds that are similar (e.g., all Treasury bonds), except that they mature at different times, you will find that yields are not the same for short-term and long-term bonds. *The Wall Street Journal* and many other financial publications regularly display a graph that plots the relationship between *YTM* and maturity for a group of similar bonds. Finance professionals refer to this graph as the **yield curve,** and they call the relationship between yield to maturity and time to maturity the **term structure of interest rates.**

EVALUATING THE YIELD CURVE

Figure 4.3 shows how the yield curve for U.S. government bonds looked at four different dates. Usually, long-term bonds offer higher yields than short-term bonds, and the yield curve slopes up. That was the case in January 1983 and in July 1993. However, the level of the yield curve was much higher in 1983 than in 1993. Differences in expected inflation rates in those two years largely explain why the yield curve was so much higher in 1983. In the 24 months just prior to January 1983, the annual rate of U.S. inflation had averaged about 6 percent. Assume that investors expected inflation to remain roughly at that level in the near term. Investors who purchased short-term Treasury bills in January 1983 earned a return of about 7.5 percent, slightly higher than the expected inflation rate. In contrast, in the 24 months prior to July 1993, the annual inflation rate averaged just under 3 percent. In July 1993, T-bills offered a return of roughly 3.75 percent, again just slightly above the inflation rate at that time. The general lesson here is that the yields offered by bonds must be sufficient to offer investors a positive **real return.** The real return on an investment approximately equals the difference between its stated or **nominal return** and the inflation rate.[15]

The other two lines in Figure 4.3 illustrate that the shape of the yield curve can change over time. In February 1998, the yield curve was nearly flat, with yields on

Figure 4.3
Yield Curves for U.S.
Government Bonds

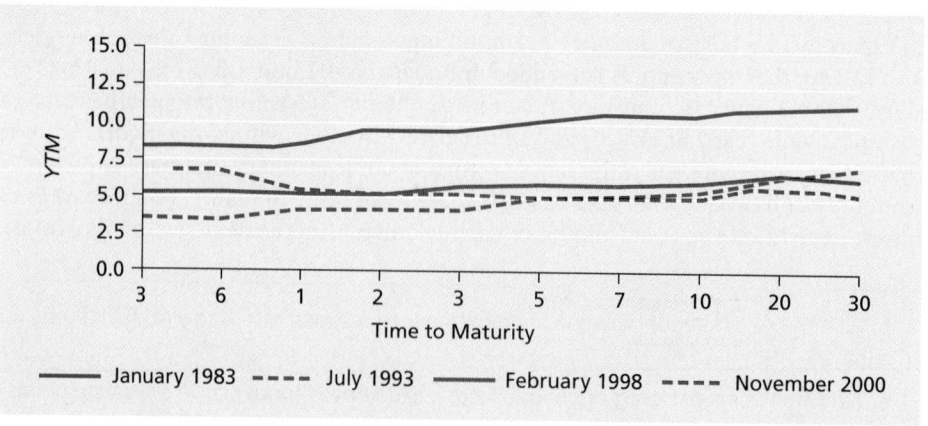

---

[15] Investors will be more concerned with the expected rate of inflation going forward than with the past inflation rate. We will discuss the relationship between expected inflation and returns in more depth in the next two chapters.

COMPARATIVE CORPORATE FINANCE

Is the Yield Curve a Good Economic Predictor?

Economists have known for many years that the slope of the yield curve—that is, the difference between yields on short-term and long-term Treasury securities—helps predict future economic growth in the United States. The same is true in many other countries, though the reliability of growth forecasts based on the yield curve varies internationally. The chart reports measures of the reliability of forecasts based on the yield curve in 11 different countries.

The forecasting models illustrated here are very simple, even naive. The models use an ordinary linear regression in which the dependent variable is the percentage change in economic activity, and the independent variable is the difference between short-term and long-term bond rates. The three measures of economic activity studied here are the percentage change in real gross domestic product (GDP), the percentage change in industrial production, and the change in the unemployment rate. The height of the bars indicates the R-square value from each regression in each country. From statistics, remember that the R-square value measures how well the independent variable (the slope of the yield curve) predicts the dependent variable (changes in economic activity). For a perfect forecasting model, the R-square value equals 1.0. If the forecasting model is completely useless, the R-square value equals 0.0.

The chart indicates that the yield curve is most useful in predicting future economic activity in the United States and Canada. The yield curve's ability to predict economic activity is weaker, but still significant, in most European countries—the exception is Switzerland. The predictive power of the yield curve is also quite weak in Australia and Japan.

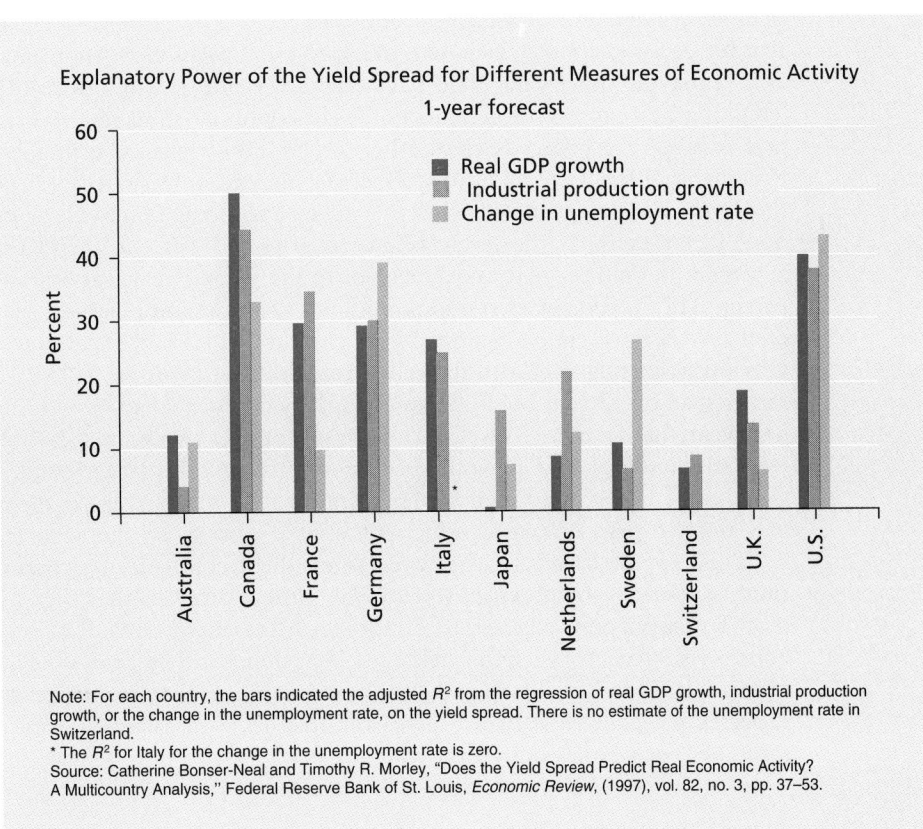

Explanatory Power of the Yield Spread for Different Measures of Economic Activity
1-year forecast

Note: For each country, the bars indicated the adjusted R^2 from the regression of real GDP growth, industrial production growth, or the change in the unemployment rate, on the yield spread. There is no estimate of the unemployment rate in Switzerland.
* The R^2 for Italy for the change in the unemployment rate is zero.
Source: Catherine Bonser-Neal and Timothy R. Morley, "Does the Yield Spread Predict Real Economic Activity? A Multicountry Analysis," Federal Reserve Bank of St. Louis, *Economic Review*, (1997), vol. 82, no. 3, pp. 37–53.

short-term and long-term bonds hovering around 5 percent. But by November 2000, the yield curve had inverted, with short-term yields lying slightly above long-term yields. Inverted yield curves typically occur prior to and during recessions.[16] In fact, Duke University economist Campbell Harvey (1993) argues that economic forecasts based on the slope of the yield curve perform as well as or better than many forecasts produced using complex statistical models. Research in this area shows that the yield curve works well as a predictor of economic activity, not only in the United States, but also in Canada, Germany, and other large industrialized economies.[17]

TERM STRUCTURE THEORIES

Economists have studied the yield curve intensely for several decades, trying to understand how it behaves and what it portends for the future. From this research, we know that economic growth forecasts that include the slope of the yield curve perform well relative to forecasts that ignore the yield curve. Can the yield curve also tell us something about the direction in which interest rates are headed? The answer is a highly qualified yes. To understand the logic underlying the hypothesis that the slope of the yield curve might predict interest rate movements, we first consider the expectations theory.

Expectations Theory. Russell wants to invest $1,000 for two years. He does not want to take much risk, so he plans to invest the money in U.S. Treasury securities. Consulting the Treasury website, Russell learns that 1-year Treasury bonds currently offer a 5 percent *YTM*, and 2-year bonds offer a 5.5 percent *YTM*. At first, he thinks that his decision about which investment to purchase is easy. He wants to invest for two years, and the 2-year bond pays a higher yield, so why not just buy that one? Thinking a bit more, Russell realizes that he could invest his money in a 1-year bond and reinvest the proceeds in another 1-year bond when the first bond matures. Whether that strategy will ultimately earn a higher return than that of simply buying the 2-year bond depends on what the yield on a 1-year bond will be one year from now. If, for example, the 1-year bond rate rises to 7 percent, then Russell will earn 5 percent in the first year and 7 percent in the second year, for a grand total of 12 percent (12.35 percent after compounding). Over the same period, the 2-year bond offers just 5.5 percent per year or 11 percent total (11.3 percent after compounding). Obviously, in this scenario, Russell earns more by investing in two 1-year bonds rather than one 2-year bond. But what if the yield on a 1-year bond is just 5 percent next year? In that case, Russell earns 10 percent over two years (or 10.25 percent after compounding), and he would be better off buying the 2-year bond. If next year's yield on the 1-year bond is about 6 percent, then he will earn approximately the same over the two years no matter which investment strategy he chooses.

This example illustrates the **expectations theory** of the term structure: in equilibrium, investors should expect to earn the same return whether they invest in long-term Treasury bonds or a series of short-term Treasury bonds. If the yield on 2-year bonds is 5.5 percent when the yield on 1-year bonds is 5 percent, then investors must expect next year's yield on a 1-year bond to be 6 percent. Suppose not. If they expected a higher yield than 6 percent, investors would be better off purchasing a series of 1-year bonds than they would be from buying the 2-year bond. Conversely,

---

[16]. One possible explanation for this phenomenon is that investors, faced with the prospect of a recession, anticipate that the weakening economy will lead to lower inflation, or perhaps deflation, in the long term. This may cause long-term interest rates to fall below short-term rates. Go to http://www.smartmoney.com/bonds/, and click the link for the "Living Yield Curve" to see how the yield curve has behaved in the United States since 1977.

[17]. See Bonser-Neal and Morley (1997).

if investors expected next year's bond rate to be less than 6 percent, they would flock to the 2-year bond. Equilibrium occurs when investors' expectations are such that the expected return on a 2-year bond equals the expected return on two 1-year bonds. In this example, equilibrium occurs when investors believe that next year's interest rate will be 6 percent.

Figure 4.4 illustrates this idea. The first part of the figure shows that the value of $1 invested in one 2-year bond will grow to $(1 + r)^2$. In this expression, r represents the current interest rate on a 2-year bond. Next, the figure shows that investors expect $1 invested in a sequence of two 1-year bonds to grow to $(1 + r_1)[1 + E(r_2)]$. Here, r_1 represents the current 1-year bond rate, and $E(r_2)$ represents the expected 1-year bond rate in the second year. Equilibrium occurs when the two strategies have identical expected returns, or when the expected 1-year interest rate is about 6 percent.[18]

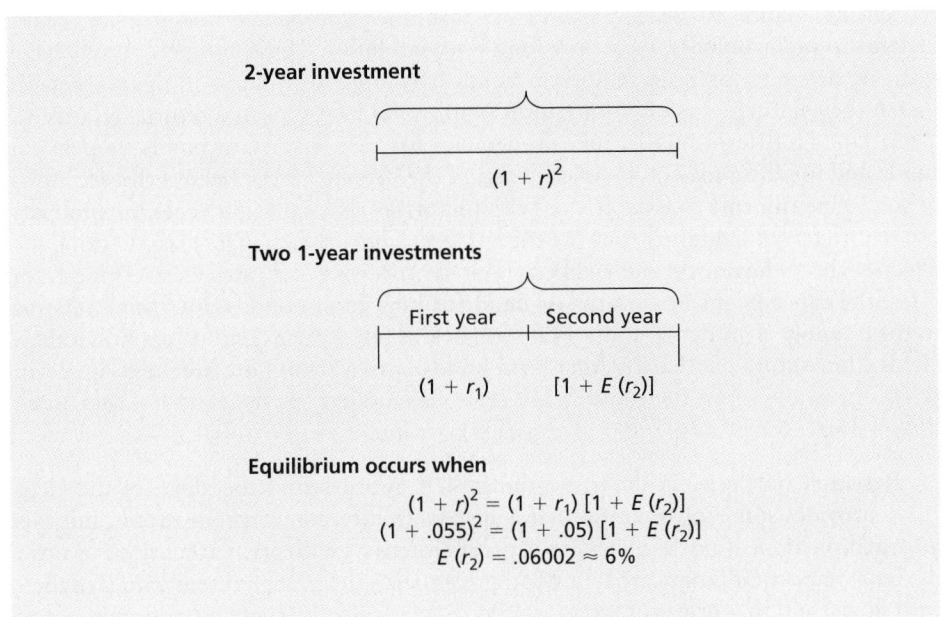

Figure 4.4
The Expectations Theory

The expectations theory says that when the yield curve is upward sloping—that is, when long-term bond yields exceed short-term bond yields—then investors must expect short-term yields to rise. According to the theory, only if investors expect short-term rates to rise will they be willing to forgo the higher current yield on a long-term instrument by purchasing a short-term bond. Conversely, when the yield curve inverts and short-term yields exceed long-term yields, investors must expect short-term rates to fall. Only then would they willingly accept the lower yield on long-term bonds.

Liquidity Preference Theory. Unfortunately, the slope of the yield curve does not always provide a reliable signal of future interest rate movements, perhaps because the expectations theory ignores several factors that may be important to investors and that may influence the shape of the yield curve. The first factor is that investors may have a preference for investing in short-term securities. As we have

---

[18.] When we solve for the expected interest rate in year 2 that equates the returns on two 1-year investments to the returns on one 2-year investment, we are solving for the *forward interest rate*. Under the expectations theory, forward interest rates provide unbiased forecasts of future spot interest rates. That is, forward interest rates predict where interest rates are headed in the future.

seen, for a given change in the required return, the prices of long-term bonds fluctuate more than the prices of short-term bonds, so this added risk might deter some investors from investing in long-term bonds. To attract investors, perhaps long-term bonds must offer a return that exceeds the expected return on a series of short-term bonds. Therefore, when the yield curve slopes up, we cannot be sure whether this is the result of investors expecting interest rates to rise in the future, or simply a reflection of compensation for risk. The **liquidity preference theory** of the term structure recognizes this problem and states that the slope of the yield curve is influenced not only by expected interest rate changes, but also by the liquidity premium that investors require on long-term bonds.[19]

Preferred Habitat Theory. A second factor clouds the interpretation of the slope of the yield curve as a signal of interest rate movements if certain investors always purchase bonds with a particular maturity. For instance, pension funds that promise retirement income to investors, and life insurance companies that provide death benefits to policyholders, have very long-term liabilities. These companies may have a strong desire to invest in long-term bonds (the longest available in the market) to match their liabilities, even if long-term bonds offer low expected returns relative to a series of short-term bonds. Indeed, demand for very long term bonds by pension funds and life insurance companies is one of the driving forces behind the decisions of some governments to issue bonds with maturities as long as 50 years. Economists use the **preferred habitat theory** (or the *market segmentation theory*) to describe the effect of this behavior on the yield curve. If short-term bond rates exceed long-term rates, the cause might be that the demand for long-term bonds is very high relative to their supply. This demand drives up long-term bond prices and drives down their yields. If investors purchasing long-term bonds have a strong preference to invest in those securities despite their low yields, then the fact that the yield curve slopes down does not necessarily imply that investors expect interest rates to fall.[20]

Research on the yield curve continues.[21] It appears that the slope of the yield curve provides some information that is helpful in forecasting interest rates, but this information alone is not sufficient to generate forecasts with great accuracy. For now, the most important points are that bond prices derive from the present values of their cash flows, and that prices of long-term bonds generally fluctuate more than those of short-term bonds in response to interest rate changes. We now turn our attention from pricing bonds to pricing stocks.

Concept Review Questions	**8.** What is the *yield curve*? What type of information does it provide? **9.** Briefly compare and contrast the three theories presented to explain yield-curve behavior. Which is generally accepted?

---

[19] Note that whether long-term or short-term bonds are riskier depends on the investment horizon. For example, if you want to invest money for one year, then buying a 2-year bond is risky because you cannot be sure what price you will obtain when you sell the bond in one year. On the other hand, if you want to invest for two years, then buying a 1-year bond is risky because you cannot be sure what interest rate you will earn when you buy a new 1-year bond to replace the first bond when it matures. Therefore, the theoretical possibility exists that short-term bonds might have to offer a premium over long-term bonds if most investors in the market have long-term investment horizons. However, the weight of the evidence suggests that long-term bonds offer a risk premium.

[20] Do you have a favorite place to go to enjoy a beer with your peers? Is the price of beer there the lowest price in town? If not, you are behaving according to the preferred habitat theory. You prefer to go to a particular establishment to socialize, even though you could buy the same beer at another location for less money. In the same way, some investors could prefer to invest in long-term bonds even though a series of short-term bonds might offer a higher expected return.

[21] Backus, Foresi, Mozumdar, and Wu (2001) summarize some of the existing work on using the term structure to forecast interest rates and present a new approach of their own.

4.4 STOCK VALUATION

In this section, we examine valuation models for two types of stock: preferred and common. Even though the characteristics of bonds and stocks seem quite different, the principles involved in valuing debt and equity are much the same. However, applying those principles to equity securities can be quite challenging. Therefore, we begin with preferred stock, a security that resembles debt as much as it does equity. Before getting into the valuation process, we will quickly review stock quotations, which report the market's valuation of shares each day.

STOCK PRICE QUOTATIONS

Summary statistics are reported daily on the activity of widely followed stocks. Regardless of the market on which a stock trades, its price quotation typically appears in a standardized format. To see how price quotations work and what they mean, consider the quotes that appear daily in *The Wall Street Journal*. As we'll see, the quotations provide not only current prices, but a great deal of additional information as well. A portion of the Nasdaq National Market stock quotations from *The Wall Street Journal* appears in Figure 4.5. Let's use the highlighted Starbucks quotations for purposes of illustration. These quotes were published on April 22, 2005, and are for trades that occurred the day before. A glance at the quotes shows that stocks, like most other securities, are priced in dollars and cents.

Looking at the Starbucks quotes, the first column (YTD % CHG) gives the stock's year-to-date change in price; note that Starbucks stock went down 25.6 percent since the first of the year. The two columns labeled "HI" and "LO" show the highest and lowest prices at which the stock sold during the past fifty-two weeks. You can see that Starbucks traded between $64.26 and $36.74 during the preceding fifty-two-week period. Listed to the right of the company's name is its stock symbol, SBUX. These ticker symbols are the abbreviations used on the market tapes seen in brokerage offices and on television, as well as on Internet sites such as Yahoo!, to identify specific securities. The figure listed right after the stock symbol is the annual cash dividend paid on each share of stock. This is followed by the dividend yield. Because Starbucks paid no cash dividend during the past year, its *dividend yield,* which equals

Figure 4.5
Stock Price Quotes
Source: The Wall Street Journal, April 22, 2005 Reprinted with permission. Copyright 2005 Dow Jones & Company, Inc. All Rights Reserved Worldwide.

YTD % CHG	52-WEEK HI	52-WEEK LO	STOCK (SYM)	DIV	YLD %	PE	VOL 100s	CLOSE	NET CHG
−19.0	27.12	13.60	StdMicsys SMSC		...	cc	1955	14.44	0.48
4.3	17.42	11.50	StdParkng STAN n		...	...	36	16	0.50
−5.3	53.69	38.44	StanlyFurn STLY	.48f	1.1	13	z9324	42.57	0.07
−11.2	22.59	15.83	Staples SPLS s	.17	.8	21	63632	19.95	1.31
−12.3	7.10	2.50	StarScnfc STSI		...	dd	5907	4.46	0.03
−25.6	64.26	36.74	Starbucks SBUX		...	45	30232	46.41	0.74
0.6	31.83	23.02	StatAutoFnl STFC	.18	.7	10	z50786	26	0.48
19.9	37.90	26.78	StateFnl SFSW	.68f	1.9	...	z15022	36.13	0.51
−21.3	46.40	20.77 +	SteelDyn STLD	.40	1.3	6	24782	29.82	0.68
−22.2	33.56	18.89	SteelTch STTX	.30f	1.4	5	3812	21.40	0.58
27.0	23.11	12.23	SteinMart SMRT		...	25	1160	21.66	0.44
6.7	37	16.75	SteinerLsre STNR		...	16	z74881	31.87	0.61
−16.1	9.25	6.05	Stellent STEL		...	dd	z46144	7.40	0.17
−33.7	12.67	6	Stereotaxis STXS n		...	...	z30189	6.52	0.26
−3.3	53.21	41.70	Stericycle SRCL		...	26	6447	44.42	0.30
−2.8	15	12.07	SterBcsh SBIB	.24f	1.7	25	5559	13.87	1.00
−11.3	41.25	28.57	StriFnlWA STSA s	stk	...	14	z75412	34.82	0.61
−11.1	30.50	22.58	StriFnlPA SLFI	.64	2.5	17	z35784	25.48	1.67
−9.1	20.60	15.59	StvMadden SHOO		...	20	z60556	17.15	0.07
−20.9	8.24	5.14 +	StewartEnt A STEI	.03e	.5	28	3991	5.53	0.05
32.3	41.04	11.28	StltNel ADS SNSA	2.00e	5.3	5	z27479	37.75	0.66
23.9	8.63	2.09	StltOffshr ADS SOSA		...	57	3884	8.03	0.15
4.5	12	5.90	Stratagene STGN n		...	...	z11166	8.10	−0.06

NASDAQ NATIONAL MARKET ISSUES

the ratio of the dividend divided by the closing stock price, is zero. The next entry is the P/E ratio, which is the current market price divided by the per-share earnings for the most recent twelve-month period. Note that Starbucks was trading at forty-five times its earnings.

The daily trading volume follows the P/E ratio. Here, the sales numbers are listed in round lots (of 100 shares), so a figure of 30,232 for Starbucks indicates that 3,023,200 shares of Starbucks stock traded that day. The next entry, labeled "CLOSE," shows the closing (final) price of $46.41 on April 21, 2005. Finally, as the last (NET CHG) column shows, Starbucks closed up 0.74. This means the stock closed seventy-four cents higher than it did the day before.

The same quotation system applies to stocks traded on the New York Stock Exchange (NYSE). However, some stocks that trade on the American Stock Exchange (AMEX) and the over-the-counter market (OTC) use more abbreviated quotes that list only the stock name, symbol, volume, closing price, and price change.

PREFERRED STOCK VALUATION

SMART PRACTICES VIDEO

Todd Richter, Managing Director, Head of Equity Healthcare Research, Bank of America Securities

"The concepts of value, the things that drive value, don't change."

See the entire interview at **SMARTFinance**

Neither a pure debt nor a pure equity instrument, preferred stock exhibits characteristics of both. Like bonds, preferred stocks usually pay investors a fixed cash flow stream over time. The fixed cash flow, the *preferred dividend*, is typically expressed as a percentage of par value, similar to a bond's coupon rate. However, if firms do not generate enough cash flow to meet preferred dividend payments, preferred shareholders, unlike bondholders, cannot force the firm into bankruptcy. In that sense, preferred stockholders are in a legal position similar to that of common shareholders, although preferred shares generally do not carry the right to vote. Most preferred stock is *cumulative*, which means that if a firm skips a preferred dividend payment, it cannot pay dividends to common shareholders until it makes up for all unpaid dividends to preferred shareholders. Finally, like equity, preferred stock typically has no fixed maturity date. For that reason, we treat preferred stock as a security with an infinite life in our valuation formulas.

In Chapter 3, you learned a shortcut for valuing a *perpetuity*—an annuity with an infinite life. To find today's value of a preferred stock, PS_0, we use Equation 3.10 for the present value of a perpetuity, dividing the preferred dividend, D_P, by the required rate of return on the preferred stock, r_P:

$$PS_0 = \frac{D_P}{r_P}$$

[handwritten annotations: So, if dividend = $8/year and interest rates are 8%, $PS_0 = \frac{\$8}{.08} = \$100$ — market's required return for that risk — price of stock]

APPLYING THE MODEL 4.6

Suppose that a particular preferred stock pays an annual dividend of $8. If the next dividend payment occurs in one year and the market's required return on this stock is 10 percent, then its price will be $80 ($8 ÷ 0.10). If you know the price of a preferred stock, you can easily determine its yield by dividing the dividend by the price.

As a source of capital for American industry, preferred stock has been in decline for at least six decades and now represents well under 5 percent of the net external financing for U.S. companies each year. This is at least partly due to tax factors. The

U.S. tax code treats preferred dividends more like dividends on common stock than interest on bonds. Firms cannot treat preferred dividends as deductible business expenses as they can treat interest payments on debt. Individuals, who receive preferred stock dividends from domestic corporations, are subject to the same 15 percent maximum tax rate that is levied on common stock dividends received. Because preferred shares offer a fixed dividend, the prospect of earning large capital gains (which are generally taxed at the same preferential rates as common and preferred dividends) on them is small relative to the potential for gains on common stock. Consequently, preferred stocks face a tax disadvantage relative to bonds at the corporate level, and a capital gain disadvantage relative to common stocks at the investor level.

Preferred stocks do enjoy one type of comparative tax advantage. In order to avoid taxing cash payments between corporate parents and subsidiaries, Congress has allowed corporations that receive preferred dividends to exclude a large fraction of those receipts from corporate tax. For this reason, corporations have become the principal holders of preferred stock in the United States. Additionally, businesses sometimes issue new preferred stock as part of merger and acquisition transactions, especially when the company being purchased has preferred stock outstanding. In these cases, the acquiring firm often issues its own preferred shares to replace those previously issued by the target company. Acquirers commonly issue *convertible preferred stock*, shares that the holder can convert into a prespecified number of shares of common stock, in exchange for the common stock of the target firm.

Preferred stock also plays a key role in one other fairly small, but extremely influential area of American finance—venture capital financing. Venture capital firms raise and invest billions of dollars each year in private firms, usually with high growth potential. Venture capitalists frequently structure their investments in these high-risk, high-return companies in the form of convertible preferred stock.[22]

THE BASIC COMMON STOCK VALUATION EQUATION

Consistent with Equation 4.1 and the value of bonds and preferred stock, the value of a share of common stock equals the present value of all future benefits that investors expect it to provide. Unlike bonds, which have contractual cash flows, common stocks have cash flows that are noncontractual and unspecified. What are the benefits expected from a share of common stock? When you buy a share of stock, you may expect to receive a periodic dividend payment from the firm, and you probably hope to sell the stock at a future date for more than its purchase price. But when you sell the stock, you are simply passing the rights to future benefits to the buyer. The buyer purchases the stock from you in the belief that the future benefits, dividends and capital gains, justify the purchase price. This logic extends to the next investor who buys the stock from the person who bought it from you, and so on ad infinitum. Simply put, the value of common stock equals the present value of all future dividends that investors expect the stock to distribute.[23]

The easiest way to understand this argument is as follows. Suppose that an investor buys a stock today for price P_0, receives a dividend equal to D_1 at the end of

---

[22.] Venture capital financing will be discussed more fully in Web Chapter 26, at http://smart.swlearning.com. For more information and statistics on the venture capital industry, visit the National Venture Capital Association's website at http://www.nvca.org.

[23.] Firms can distribute cash directly to shareholders in forms other than dividends. For instance, many firms regularly buy back their own shares. Also, when an acquiring firm buys a target, it may distribute cash to the target's shareholders. In this discussion, we assume for simplicity that cash payments always come in the form of dividends, but the logic of the argument does not change if we allow for other forms of cash payments.

one year, and immediately sells the stock for price P_1. The return on this investment is easy to calculate:

$$r = \frac{D_1 + P_1 - P_0}{P_0}$$

The numerator of this expression equals the dollar profit or loss, and dividing that by the purchase price converts the return into percentage form. Rearrange this equation to solve for the current stock price:

$$P_0 = \frac{D_1 + P_1}{(1 + r)} \qquad \text{(Eq. 4.4)}$$

This equation indicates that the value of a stock today equals the present value of cash that the investor receives in one year. But what determines P_1, the selling price at the end of the year? Use Equation 4.4 again, changing the time subscripts to reflect that the price next year will equal the present value of the dividend and selling price received two years from now:

$$P_1 = \frac{D_2 + P_2}{(1 + r)}$$

Now, take this expression for P_1 and substitute it back into Equation 4.4:

$$P_0 = \frac{D_1 + \frac{D_2 + P_2}{(1 + r)}}{(1 + r)} = \frac{D_1}{(1 + r)^1} + \frac{D_2 + P_2}{(1 + r)^2}$$

We have an expression that says that the price of a stock today equals the present value of the dividends it will pay over the next two years, plus the present value of the selling price in two years. Again we could ask, what determines the selling price in two years, P_2? By repeating the last two steps over and over, we can determine the price of a stock today, as shown in Equation 4.5:

$$P_0 = \frac{D_1}{(1 + r)^1} + \frac{D_2}{(1 + r)^2} + \frac{D_3}{(1 + r)^3} + \frac{D_4}{(1 + r)^4} + \frac{D_5}{(1 + r)^5} + \cdots \qquad \text{(Eq. 4.5)}$$

Comparing Equation 4.5 to the general valuation equation, Equation 4.1, we see that those equations are identical except that the cash flows, CF, in Equation 4.1 are replaced with the common stock dividends, D, in Equation 4.5.

The price today equals the present value of the entire dividend stream that the stock will pay in the future. To calculate this price, an analyst must have two inputs: the future dividend amounts and the appropriate discount rate. Neither input is easy to estimate. The discount rate, or the rate of return required by the market on this stock, depends on the stock's risk. We defer a full discussion of how to measure a stock's risk and how to translate that into a required rate of return until Chapters 5 and 6. Instead, we now focus on the problem of estimating dividends. In most cases, analysts can formulate reasonably accurate estimates of dividends one year in the future. The real trick is to determine how quickly dividends will grow over time. Our discussion of stock valuation centers on three possible scenarios for dividend growth: zero growth, constant growth, and variable growth. We follow the dividend models with the presentation of the free cash flow approach for enterprise valuation.

ZERO GROWTH

The simplest approach to dividend valuation, the **zero growth model,** assumes a constant dividend stream. If dividends do not grow, then we can write the following equation:

$$D_1 = D_2 = \cdots = D$$

Plugging the constant value D for each dividend payment into Equation 4.5, you can see that the valuation formula simply reduces to the equation for the present value of a perpetuity:

$$P_0 = \frac{D}{r}$$

In this special case, the formula for valuing common stock is identical to that for valuing preferred stock.

APPLYING THE MODEL 4.7

Ryder System, Inc. (ticker symbol R), a provider of transportation and supply chain management solutions, paid a dividend of $0.15 per quarter, or $0.60 per year, without interruption from March 1989 to November 2004. Perhaps after 15 years of receiving the same dividend, investors believe that Ryder will continue to pay this steady dividend indefinitely. What price would they be willing to pay for Ryder stock?

The answer depends on Ryder's required rate of return. If investors demand a 10 percent return on Ryder stock, then the stock should be worth $0.60 ÷ 0.10, or $6 (making the simplifying assumption that the dividend is paid once per year).[24] In fact, in the Spring of 2005, Ryder stock traded in the vicinity of $40 to $45 per share. This implies one of two things: either investors require a rate of return on Ryder stock that is much less than 10 percent, which is implausible, or investors expected dividends to grow even if they hadn't for a long time. That expectation was partially realized because the firm increased its dividend for the first time in 16 years to $0.16 per quarter in February 2005.

CONSTANT GROWTH

Of all the relatively simple stock valuation models that we consider in this chapter, the **constant growth model** probably sees the most use in practice. This model assumes that dividends will grow at a constant rate, g. If dividends grow at a constant

---

[24.] If you do not make this assumption, you can apply the same formula to quarterly dividends as long as you make an appropriate adjustment in the interest rate. For example, if investors expect a 10 percent effective annual rate of return on Ryder stock, then they expect a quarterly return of $(1.10)^{.25} - 1$, or 2.41 percent. Using this figure, you can recalculate the stock price by dividing $0.15, the quarterly dividend, by 0.0241 to obtain $6.22. Why is Ryder stock more valuable in this calculation? Because Ryder's dividends arrive more often than once a year, the present value of the dividend stream is greater.

rate forever, then we can calculate the value of that cash flow stream by using the formula for a growing perpetuity, given in Equation 3.11. Denoting next year's dividend as D_1, we can determine the value today of a stock that pays a dividend growing at a constant rate:[25]

[handwritten note in left margin: use PV in year 0 (or 1, 2, ...) and dividend rate in year +1]

$$P_0 = \frac{D_1}{r - g}$$

[handwritten: g = growth rate (need to be careful about this because % GDD + inflation is an upper bound)]

(Eq. 4.6)

The constant growth model in Equation 4.6 is commonly called the **Gordon growth model,** after Myron Gordon, who popularized this formula during the 1960s and 1970s.

APPLYING THE MODEL 4.8

Few public companies have achieved a longer streak of uninterrupted increases in dividends than Peoples Energy Corp. (ticker symbol PGL), a holding company that provides administrative support primarily to its regulated utility subsidiaries. Peoples Energy increased its dividend every year for 21 years, from 1983 to 2004. Over this period, the compound annual dividend growth rate was 3.7 percent. Suppose that in 2005 investors expected an annual dividend of $2.18. Though this dividend is paid quarterly, we assume that the entire dividend comes at the end of 2005 and is expected to continue to grow at 3.7 percent annually. What should be the price of Peoples Energy stock?

Suppose that investors require a 10 percent rate of return on Peoples Energy Corp. stock. Substituting into the constant growth model, Equation 4.6, we obtain the following value for Peoples stock at the end of 2004:

$$P_0 = \frac{\$2.18}{0.100 - 0.037} = \$34.60$$

In April 2005, Peoples Energy shares traded on the NYSE in the $40 to $45 range, so we have underestimated the price a bit. If we either decrease the required return by 1.00 percent to 9.00 percent or add just 1.00 percent to our estimate of dividend growth, increasing it to 4.7 percent per year, then the model generates a price of $41.13.

We do not want to oversell the accuracy of the constant growth model. We based our calculations on a reasonable set of assumptions, using the long-run growth rate in dividends for g and the long-run rate of return on Peoples Energy stock for r. By making small adjustments to the dividend, the required rate of return, or the growth rate, we could easily obtain an estimate for Peoples Energy stock that matches the current market price in April 2005. But we could also obtain a very different price with an equally reasonable set of assumptions. For instance, increasing the required rate of return from 10 percent to 10.5 percent and decreasing the dividend growth

SMART
CONCEPTS
See the concept
explained
step-by-step at
SMARTFinance

---

[25] To apply this equation, one must assume that $r > g$. Of course, some firms may grow very rapidly for a time, so that $g > r$ temporarily. We treat the case of firms that grow rapidly for a finite period later in the discussion. In the long run, it is reasonable to assume that r must eventually exceed g.

rate from 3.7 percent to 3.2 percent decreases the price to $29.86! Obviously, analysts want to estimate the inputs for Equation 4.6 as precisely as possible, but the amount of uncertainty inherent in estimating required rates of return and growth rates makes obtaining precise valuations very difficult.

Nevertheless, the constant growth model provides a useful way to frame stock-valuation problems, highlighting the important inputs and, in some cases, providing price estimates that seem fairly reasonable. But the model should not be applied blindly to all types of firms, especially not to those enjoying very rapid, albeit temporary, growth.

VARIABLE GROWTH

The zero and constant growth common stock valuation models just presented do not allow for any shift in expected growth rates. Many firms go through periods of relatively fast growth, followed by a period of more stable growth. Valuing the stock of such a firm requires a **variable growth model,** one in which the dividend growth rate can vary. Using our earlier notation and letting D_0 equal the last or most recent per share dividend paid, g_1 equal the initial (fast) growth rate of dividends, g_2 equal the subsequent (stable) growth rate of dividends, and N equal the number of years in the initial growth period, we can write the general equation for the variable growth model as follows:

$$P_0 = \underbrace{\frac{D_0(1 + g_1)^1}{(1 + r)^1} + \frac{D_0(1 + g_1)^2}{(1 + r)^2} + \cdots + \frac{D_0(1 + g_1)^N}{(1 + r)^N}}_{\substack{\text{Present value of} \\ \text{dividends during} \\ \text{initial growth period}}} + \underbrace{\left[\frac{1}{(1 + r)^N} \times \frac{D_{N+1}}{r - g_2}\right]}_{\substack{\text{Present value of price} \\ \text{of stock at end of} \\ \text{initial growth period}}} \quad \text{(Eq. 4.7)}$$

As noted by the labels, the first part of the equation calculates the present value of the dividends expected during the initial growth period, and the second part is the present value of the stock price calculated at the end of the initial growth period, which is found using the constant growth model. We can use an example to demonstrate its application:

APPLYING THE MODEL 4.9

A food company has developed a new fat-free ice cream, and as the popularity of the product increases, the firm (unlike its customers) will grow quite rapidly, perhaps 20 percent per year. Over time, as the market share of this new food increases, the firm's growth rate will reach a steady state. At that point, the firm may grow at the same rate as the overall economy, perhaps 5 percent per year. Assume that the market's required rate of return on this stock is 14 percent.

To value this firm's stock, you need to break the future stream of cash flows into two parts. The first consists of the period of rapid growth, and the second is the constant growth phase. Suppose that the firm's most recent (year 0) dividend was $2 per share. You anticipate that the firm will increase the dividend by 20 percent per year for the next three years, and after that the dividend will grow at 5 percent per year indefinitely. The expected dividend stream looks like this:

Fast Growth Phase ($g_1 = 20\%$)		Stable Growth Phase ($g_2 = 5\%$)	
Year 0	$2.00	Year 4	$3.63
Year 1	2.40	Year 5	3.81
Year 2	2.88	Year 6	4.00
Year 3	3.46	Year 7	4.20

The value of the dividends during the fast growth phase is calculated as follows:

$$PV \text{ of dividends in fast growth phase} = \frac{\$2.40}{(1.14)^1} + \frac{\$2.88}{(1.14)^2} + \frac{\$3.46}{(1.14)^3}$$

$$= \$2.11 + \$2.22 + \$2.33 = \$6.66$$

The stable growth phase begins with the dividend paid four years from now. The final term of Equation 4.7 is actually Equation 4.6, which indicates that the value of a constant growth stock at time t equals the dividend one year later, at time $t + 1$, divided by the difference between the required rate of return and the growth rate. Applying that formula here means valuing the stock at the end of year 3, just before the constant growth phase begins:

$$P_3 = \frac{D_4}{r - g_2} = \frac{\$3.63}{.14 - .05} = \$40.33$$

Don't forget that $40.33 is the price of the stock three years from now. Today's present value equals $40.33 \div (1.14)^3 = \$27.22$. This represents the value today of all dividends that occur in year 4 and beyond. Putting the two pieces together, we get the following:

Total value of stock, $P_0 = \$6.66 + \$27.22 = \$33.88$

This calculation is depicted on the time line in Figure 4.6. It can be more compactly shown in the following single algebraic expression:

$$P_0 = \frac{\$2.40}{(1.14)^1} + \frac{\$2.88}{(1.14)^2} + \frac{\$3.46 + \$40.33}{(1.14)^3} = \$33.88$$

The numerator of the last term contains both the final dividend payment of the fast growth phase, $3.46, and the present value *as of the end of year 3* of all future dividends, $40.33. The value of the firm's stock using the variable growth model is $33.88. This value can be calculated more efficiently by using a financial calculator or spreadsheet.

HOW TO ESTIMATE GROWTH

By now it should be apparent that a central component in many stock-pricing models is the growth rate. Unfortunately, analysts face a tremendous challenge in estimating a firm's growth rate, whether that growth rate refers to dividends, earnings, sales, or

Figure 4.6
Time Line for Variable
Growth Valuation

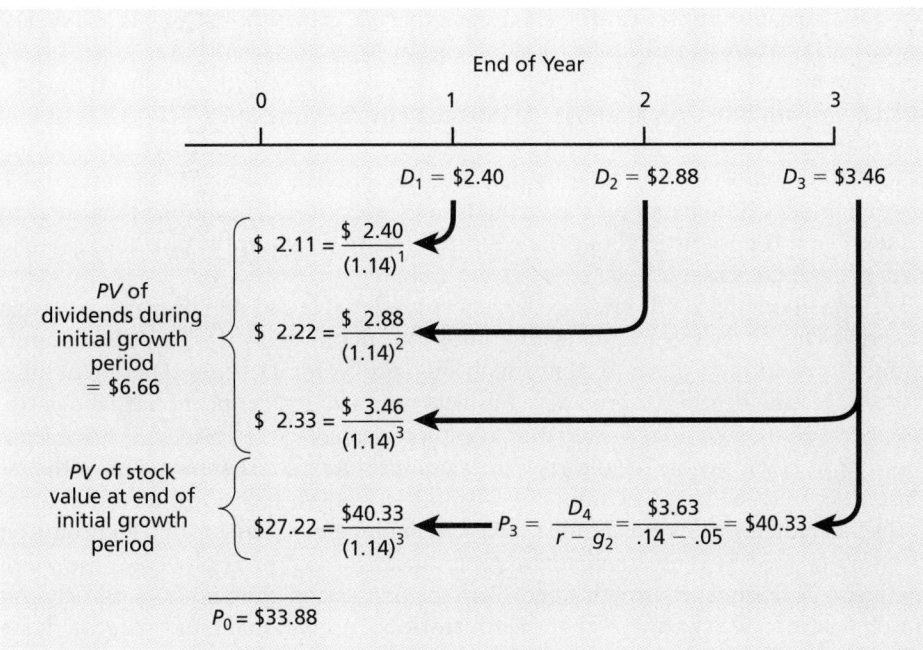

almost any other measure of financial performance. A firm's rate of growth depends on several factors, but among the most important are the size of the investments it makes in new and existing projects and the rate of return those investments earn.

A simple, but rather naive method for estimating how fast a firm will grow uses information from financial statements. This approach acknowledges the importance of new investments in driving future growth. First, calculate the magnitude of new investments that the firm can make by determining its *retention rate, rr,* the fraction of the firm's earnings that it retains. Second, calculate the firm's return on common equity, *ROE,* to estimate the rate of return that new investments will generate. The product of those two values is the firm's expected growth rate, *g.*

$$g = rr \times ROE \tag{Eq. 4.8}$$

APPLYING THE MODEL 4.10

Simon Manufacturing traditionally retains 75 percent of its earnings to finance new investments and pays out 25 percent as dividends. Last year, Simon's net income was $44.6 million and the book value of its equity was $297.33 million, resulting in a return on common equity of 15 percent. Substituting into Equation 4.8 and multiplying the retention rate by the return on common equity, we estimate Simon's expected growth rate:

$$g = 0.75 \times 0.15 = 0.1125$$

The resulting value is 11.25 percent.

An alternative approach to estimating expected growth rates makes use of historical data. Analysts track a firm's sales, earnings, and dividends over several years in an attempt to identify growth trends. But how well do growth rates from the past predict growth rates in the future? Unfortunately, the correlation between past and future growth rates for most firms is surprisingly low. Chan, Karceski, and Lakonishok (2003) report that future growth is almost completely unrelated to past growth —there is very little persistence in growth rates over time. They argue that analysts tend to be too optimistic about the expected future growth of firms that have had high growth rates in the past.

That expected growth rates are largely unpredictable should not come as a great surprise. One of the most fundamental ideas in economics is that competition limits the ability of a firm to generate abnormally high profits for a sustained period of time. When one firm identifies a profitable business opportunity, people notice, and entrepreneurs (or other companies) attempt to enter the same line of business. As more and more firms enter, profits (or the growth rate in profits) fall. At some point, if the industry becomes sufficiently competitive, profits will fall to such a low level that some firms will exit. As firms exit, profits for the remaining firms rise again. The constant pressure created by these competitive forces means it is rare to observe a firm with a consistent, long-term growth trend. Perhaps one reason companies like Microsoft and Intel are so well known is that their histories of exceptional long-run growth are so uncommon.

Although it may be extremely difficult to predict how rapidly firms will grow, there can be no doubt that stock prices reflect the value of firms' expected growth opportunities. Consider the consumer products firm Procter & Gamble (P&G). In the late spring of 2005, most analysts predicted that P&G would generate earnings of about $2.89 per share in fiscal 2006. Suppose that investors believed that P&G would stop reinvesting earnings to finance new investments and that P&G would simply distribute all its earnings to investors. If P&G could distribute $2.89 per share in perpetuity, and if the required return on P&G stock were 10 percent, then the price of P&G stock would be $28.90 ($2.89 ÷ 0.10). In fact, the price of P&G stock in late spring of 2005 fluctuated around $54. That price clearly implies that investors expect P&G to make new investments that will increase earnings and dividends over time.

We generalize this idea as follows. The price of any stock can be divided into two parts. The first part is the amount that investors would be willing to pay if a firm generated a constant annual earnings stream, E, in perpetuity and distributed it to investors. The second part represents the additional value associated with expected future growth opportunities, $PVGO$. Mathematically, this idea can be expressed as follows:

$$P_0 = \frac{E}{r} + PVGO$$

This equation indicates that the current stock price equals the present value of a perpetual earnings stream, plus the present value of growth opportunities, $PVGO$. For Procter & Gamble, the present value of growth opportunities in late spring of 2005 was about $25.10, the difference between the actual $54 stock price and $28.90, the present value of a constant earnings stream of $2.89 per share.

WHAT IF THERE ARE NO DIVIDENDS?

After seeing the different versions of the dividend growth models, students usually ask, "What about firms that don't pay dividends?" Though many large, well-established firms in the United States pay regular dividends, the majority of firms do not pay dividends at all. Of the more than 5,000 U.S. companies listed on the NYSE, AMEX, and Nasdaq, as many as 80 percent pay no cash dividends in a given year. Fama and French (2001) report that the percentage of U.S. firms paying cash dividends fell from 66.5 percent in 1978 to 20.8 percent in 1999. In part, this trend reflects a shift in the characteristics of U.S. public corporations. Specifically, the fraction of relatively young firms rose with the boom of the initial public offering (IPO) market in the 1990s, especially in the technology sector. Younger firms with excellent growth prospects are traditionally less likely to pay dividends than are more mature firms. However, even controlling for the changing characteristics of listed firms, Fama and French report that the propensity for a given type of firm to pay dividends has fallen over time.

Can we apply the stock-valuation models covered thus far to firms that pay no dividends? Yes and no. On the affirmative side, firms that do not currently pay dividends may begin paying them in the future. In that case, we simply modify the equations presented earlier to reflect that the firm pays its first dividend not in one year, but several years in the future. However, from an entirely practical standpoint, predicting when firms will begin paying dividends and what the dollar value of those far-off dividends will be is extremely difficult. Consider the problem of forecasting dividends for a company like Yahoo! Since its IPO in April 1996, Yahoo! has paid no cash dividends even though its revenues have increased from about $19 million to more than $4.8 billion. Although the company reported a net loss in 2001, it was profitable from 2002 to 2005, and it accumulated more than $2 billion in cash reserves. Is Yahoo! ready to start paying dividends, will it continue to reinvest income to finance growth, or will it be acquired by another firm? In all likelihood, investors will have to wait several years to receive Yahoo!'s first dividend, and there is no way to determine with any degree of precision when that will happen.

Perhaps firms that don't pay dividends will repurchase stock instead. In that event, we modify the valuation equations to focus on cash payments made to shareholders, whether the payments come in the form of dividends or share buybacks. However, Fama and French (2001) show that the firms that engage in share repurchases typically pay dividends. Repurchases apparently do not help us solve the valuation problem for no-dividend firms.

Analysts confronted with the problem of valuing firms that do not pay dividends have several alternative models at their disposal. Each of these models has strengths and weaknesses, and each should be applied with caution. Before discussing the details of those models, we want to comment on another question we hear frequently: What happens if a company never plans to pay a dividend, repurchase shares, or otherwise distribute cash to investors? Students point to a firm like Oracle that has been in business for many years and certainly has sufficient cash flow to pay dividends. Don't thousands of investors buy and sell Oracle shares every day with no expectation of ever receiving dividends? Our answer to this question is that for a stock to have value, there must be some expectation that the firm will distribute cash in some form to investors at some point in the future. That cash could come in the form of dividends or share repurchases. If the firm is acquired by another company for cash, the cash payment will come when the acquiring firm purchases the shares of the target. Investors must believe that they will receive cash at some point in the future. If you have a hard time believing this, we invite you to buy shares in the Smart, Megginson, & Gitman Corporation, a firm expected to generate an attractive revenue stream from selling its products and services. This firm promises never to distribute cash to shareholders in any form. If you buy shares, you will have to sell them to another investor later to realize any return on your investment. How much are you willing to pay for these shares? Why would you buy them?

VALUING THE ENTERPRISE— THE FREE CASH FLOW APPROACH

One way to deal with the valuation challenges presented by a firm that does not pay dividends is to value the firm as a whole rather than try to value only the firm's shares. The advantage of this procedure is that it requires no assumptions about when or in what form (i.e., dividends or share repurchases) the firm distributes cash to stockholders. Instead, when using the free cash flow approach, we begin by asking, what is the total *operating cash flow* (OCF) generated by a firm? Next, we subtract from the firm's operating cash flow the amount needed to fund new investments in both fixed assets and current assets. The difference is total **free cash flow** (**FCF**). Free cash flow represents the cash amount that a firm could distribute to investors after meeting all its other obligations. Note that we used the word *investors* in the previous sentence. Total free cash flow is the amount that the firm could distribute to *all types of investors,* including bondholders, preferred shareholders, and common stockholders. Once we have estimates of the *FCFs* that a firm will generate over time, then we can discount them at an appropriate rate to obtain an estimate of the total enterprise value.

But what do we mean by "an appropriate discount rate"? This is a subtle issue, discussed at greater length in Chapter 9. To understand the main idea, recall that *FCF* represents the total cash available for *all* investors. For investors in a given firm, debt is not as risky as preferred stock, and preferred stock is not as risky as common stock. This means that bondholders, preferred shareholders, and common stockholders each have a different required return in mind when they buy the firm's securities. Somehow we have to capture these varying required rates of return to come up with a single discount rate to apply to free cash flow, the aggregate amount available for all three types of investors. The solution to this problem is known as the **weighted average cost of capital** (**WACC**). The WACC is the after-tax weighted average required return on all types of securities issued by the firm, where the weights equal the percentage of each type of financing in the firm's overall capital structure. For example, suppose that a firm finances its operation with 50 percent debt and 50 percent common stock equity. Suppose a firm pays an after-tax return of 8 percent on its outstanding debt, and that investors require a 16 percent return on the firm's shares of common stock. The WACC for this firm would be calculated as:

$$WACC = (.50 \times 8\%) + (.50 \times 16\%) = 12\%$$

If we obtain forecasts of the *FCFs*, and if we discount those cash flows at a 12 percent rate, then the resulting present value is an estimate of the total value of the firm.

When analysts value free cash flows, they use some of the same types of models we have used to value dividend streams. We could assume that a firm's free cash flows will experience zero, constant, or variable growth, and in each instance the procedures and equations would be the same as those introduced earlier for dividends, except we would now substitute *FCF* for dividends.

Recall that our goal in using the free cash flow approach was to develop a method for valuing a firm's shares of common stock without making assumptions about its dividends. The free cash flow approach begins by estimating the total value of the firm. To find out what the firm's shares of common stock are worth, V_S, we subtract from the total enterprise value, V_F, the value of the firm's debt, V_D, and the value of the firm's preferred stock, V_P. Equation 4.9 depicts this relationship:

$$V_S = V_F - V_D - V_P$$

(Eq. 4.9)

We already know how to value bonds and preferred shares, so this step is relatively straightforward. Once we subtract the value of debt and preferred stock from the total enterprise value, the remainder equals the total value of the firm's shares of common stock. Simply divide this total by the number of shares outstanding to calculate the value per share, P_0.

APPLYING THE MODEL 4.11

Had a good cup of coffee lately? Probably the best-known purveyor of coffee is Starbucks Corp. (ticker symbol SBUX). Its stock traded in the $50–$60 range during the first calendar quarter of 2005. At the end of its 2004 fiscal year (September 30, 2004), Starbucks had debt with a market value of about $200 million, no preferred stock, and 399 million shares of common stock outstanding. Its fiscal year-2004 *free cash flow* (FCF), calculated using the techniques presented in Chapter 2, was about $233 million. Its revenues and operating profits grew at compound annual rates of about 27 percent and 38 percent, respectively, between fiscal years 2002 and 2004. Indeed, many consumers were buying Starbucks coffee during that period. At the same time the coffee market was growing, competition was beginning to heat up. We assume that because of this competition, Starbucks will experience about 25 percent annual growth in *FCF* from the end of 2004 through 2008, followed by 10 percent annual growth thereafter, due to competition and maturation of the market. We assume that Starbucks' *WACC* equals 12 percent.

The table below shows our forecasts for Starbucks' free cash flow, starting with the actual free cash flow in 2004 and going out to 2009, the beginning of the stable growth phase.

End of Fiscal Year	Growth Status	Growth Rate (%)	FCF Calculation	FCF
2004	Historic	—	Given	$233,000,000
2005	Fast	25	$233,000,000 \times (1.25)^1$	$291,250,000
2006	Fast	25	$233,000,000 \times (1.25)^2$	$364,062,500
2007	Fast	25	$233,000,000 \times (1.25)^3$	$455,078,125
2008	Fast	25	$233,000,000 \times (1.25)^4$	$568,847,656
2009	Stable	10	$568,847,656 \times (1.10)^1$	$625,732,422

Letting $D_t = FCF_t$ in Equation 4.7, and substituting $N = 4$, $r = .12$, and $g_2 = .10$, we can estimate Starbucks' enterprise value at the beginning of 2005, V_{F2005}:

$$V_{F2005} = \frac{\$291,250,000}{(1.12)^1} + \frac{\$364,062,500}{(1.12)^2} + \frac{\$455,078,125}{(1.12)^3} + \frac{\$568,847,656}{(1.12)^4}$$

$$+ \left[\frac{1}{(1.12)^4} \times \frac{\$625,732,422}{(.12 - .10)} \right]$$

$$= \$264,044,643 + \$290,228,396 + \$323,915,621 + \$361,512,969$$

$$+ \$19,883,210,000$$

$$= \$21,122,911,629$$

Substituting Starbucks' enterprise value, V_F, of $21,122,911,629, its debt value, V_D, of $200 million, and its preferred stock value, V_P, of $0 into Equation 4.9, we get its total common stock share value, V_S:

$$V_S = \$21,122,911,629 - \$200,000,000 - \$0 = \$20,922,911,629$$

Dividing the total share value by the 398,790,000 shares outstanding at the beginning of 2005, we get the per-share value of Starbucks' stock, P_{2005}.

$$P_{2005} = \frac{\$20,922,911,629}{398,790,000} = \$52.47$$

Our estimate of Starbucks' total common stock value at the beginning of calendar year 2005 of $20,922,911,629, or $52.47 per share, is within its actual trading range of $50–$60 per share during the first calendar quarter of 2005.[26]

The free cash flow approach offers an alternative to the dividend discount model that is especially useful when valuing shares that pay no dividends. As we'll see in the next section, security analysts have several alternative approaches at their disposal for estimating the value of shares, some of which do not rely on the discounted cash flow methods that we have studied thus far.

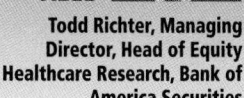

SMART PRACTICES VIDEO

Todd Richter, Managing Director, Head of Equity Healthcare Research, Bank of America Securities

"For each and every company that I analyze I try to build a sector model."

See the entire interview at **SMARTFinance**

Concept Review Questions

10. What preferred stock features resemble the characteristics of bonds more than common stock?

11. In the 1990s, many finance professionals interpreted the booming stock market as a sign that investors were requiring lower future returns on common stocks than they had in the past. Explain.

12. Using a dividend forecast of $2.18, a required return of 10%, and a growth rate of 3.7 percent, we obtained a price for Peoples Energy Corp. of $34.60. Holding all these assumptions fixed, what will the price of the stock be one year later? What price increase from the original value of $34.60 does your new estimate represent (in percentage terms)? Explain.

13. How can analysts use the *free cash flow* approach to resolve the valuation challenge presented by firms that do not pay dividends? Compare and contrast this model to the dividend valuation models.

4.5 OTHER APPROACHES TO COMMON STOCK VALUATION

Practitioners employ many different approaches to value common stock. The more popular approaches include the use of book value, liquidation value, and price multiples.

---

[26] Here's an interesting postscript for this example. At the time of this analysis, the Summary screen for Starbucks at the Yahoo! Finance site (http://finance.yahoo.com) showed a market capitalization of $18.92 billion (versus our estimate of about $20.92 billion) and a 1-year price estimate for the stock of $58.50 per share (versus our estimate of about $52.47 per share). All in all, it appears that our estimates are in the ballpark. Note that from the late April 2005 stock quotation in Figure 4.5, Starbucks' stock price had dropped to $46.41 by that time, probably as a result of the then generally poor stock market conditions.

Book Value

Book value refers to the value of a firm's equity shown on its balance sheet. Calculated using generally accepted accounting principles (GAAP), the book value of equity reflects the historical cost of the firm's assets, adjusted for depreciation, net of the firm's liabilities. Because of its backward-looking emphasis on historical cost figures, book value usually provides a conservative estimate of value. Book value does not incorporate information about a firm's potential to generate cash flows in the future and usually falls short of the market value of equity. An exception to this general rule occurs when firms experience financial distress. In some cases, such as when a firm's earnings prospects are very poor, the book value of equity may actually exceed its market value.

Liquidation Value

To calculate **liquidation value,** analysts estimate the amount of cash that would be left over if the firm's assets were sold and all liabilities paid. Liquidation value may be more or less than book value, depending on the marketability of the firm's assets and the depreciation charges that have been assessed against fixed assets. For example, an important asset on many corporate balance sheets is real estate. The value of raw land appears on the balance sheet at historical cost, but in many cases its market value is much higher. In that instance, liquidation value exceeds book value. In contrast, suppose that the largest assets on a firm's balance sheet are highly customized machine tools, purchased two years ago. If the firm depreciates these tools on a straight-line basis over five years, the value shown on the books would equal 60 percent of the purchase price. However, there may be little or no secondary market for tools that have been customized for the firm's manufacturing processes. If the firm goes bankrupt and the machine tools have to be liquidated, they may sell for much less than book value.

Price Multiples

The *price/earnings (P/E) ratio,* introduced in Chapter 2, reflects the amount investors are willing to pay for each dollar of earnings. The ratio simply equals the current stock price divided by annual earnings per share (*EPS*). The *EPS* used in the denominator of the P/E ratio may reflect either the earnings that analysts expect a firm to generate over the next year or earnings from the previous year.[27] An analyst using this method to value a stock might proceed as follows. First, the analyst attempts to forecast what the firm's *EPS* will be in the next year. Second, the analyst tries to calculate a "normal" P/E ratio for that firm or industry. Third, the analyst obtains an estimate of the stock price by simply multiplying the earnings forecast times the P/E ratio.

Though P/E ratios are widely quoted in the financial press, interpreting them can be very difficult. Stock analysts frequently tie a firm's P/E ratio to its growth prospects, using logic similar to the following. Suppose one firm has a P/E ratio of 50 while another has a P/E of 20. Why would investors willingly pay $50 per dollar of earnings for the first company and only $20 per dollar of earnings for the second? One possibility is that investors expect the first firm's earnings to grow more rapidly than those of the second firm.

[27.] Analysts refer to "leading" or "trailing" P/E ratios depending on whether the earnings number in the denominator is a forecast or a historical number.

To see this relationship more clearly, look again at Equation 4.6, which indicates that the price of a stock depends on three variables: the dividend next period, the required rate of return on stock, and the dividend growth rate. We can modify this formula by assuming that a firm pays out a constant percentage of its earnings as dividends. If we denote this payout percentage as d and next year's earnings per share as E_1, we can rewrite Equation 4.6 as follows:

$$P_0 = \frac{dE_1}{r - g}$$

where we replace the dividend next year in the numerator with the payout ratio times earnings next year. Now, divide both sides of this equation by E_1 to obtain the following:

$$\frac{P_0}{E_1} = \frac{d}{r - g}$$

On the left-hand side is the P/E ratio using next period's earnings. Notice that if the value of g increases, so does the P/E ratio. That provides some justification for the common notion that stocks with high P/E ratios have high growth potential. However, the equation illustrates that either an increase in the dividend payout or a decrease in the required rate of return will also increase the P/E ratio. Therefore, when comparing P/E ratios of different firms, one cannot conclude that the firm with the higher P/E ratio necessarily has better growth prospects. In addition, interpreting a P/E ratio is virtually impossible when the firm's earnings are negative or close to zero. For example, in April 2005, Genzyme Corp. (ticker symbol, GENZ), a global biotechnology company, had a P/E ratio of 163. Was Genzyme a company with exceptional growth prospects, which justified a very high P/E ratio? Not likely. A better explanation is that the firm's EPS at the time was just $0.37. Even though Genzyme stock traded in the $60–$61 range, dividing that price by $0.37 resulted in a high P/E.

Despite the difficulties associated with P/E ratios, analysts frequently use them to make rough assessments of value. For instance, an analyst might calculate the average P/E ratio in a particular industry and then compare that average to the P/E ratio for a specific firm. If a particular stock's P/E ratio falls substantially above (below) the industry average, the analyst might suspect that the stock is overvalued (undervalued). In the same way, analysts sometimes look at the aggregate P/E ratio for the entire stock market to make judgments about whether stocks generally are over- or undervalued. Historically the average P/E ratio has been in the 15–25 range.

When a private firm wants to convert to public ownership via an IPO, or when a private firm is the target in an acquisition, investment bankers examine P/E ratios of public firms with characteristics similar to those of the private company to estimate the value of the shares of the private company. For example, suppose that a firm that makes computer network security software wants to go public by selling 4 million shares in an IPO. The firm's projected earnings for the coming year are $1 million, or $0.25 per share. If investment bankers observe that the average P/E ratio for other networking software companies is 40, they would multiply that figure times the earnings per share to arrive at an estimate of $10 per share for the IPO. In the 1990s, many firms conducting IPOs were very young and had never generated any profit, making comparisons with P/E ratios of public firms impossible. As a result, analysts began to compare *price/sales (P/S) ratios* of similar public and private companies to determine the appropriate selling prices for shares of private firms.[28] Because profit margins vary from industry to industry and from firm to firm, P/S ratios are even more difficult to interpret than P/E ratios. At best, both P/E and P/S ratios serve only as a rough guide for pricing shares. Professional securities analysts generally examine P/E and P/S ratios in conjunction with other valuation models to determine a reasonable price for a particular stock.

---

14. Why is use of either book value or liquidation value inconsistent with the concept of a "going concern"?

15. Why is it dangerous to conclude that a firm with a high P/E ratio will probably grow faster than a firm with a lower P/E ratio?

Concept Review Questions

4.6 SUMMARY

- Conceptually, valuing either bonds or stock is quite straightforward: simply discount the stream of cash flows that will accrue to a security holder over that security's life, and the sum of the discounted cash flows is the security's current, or present, value.
- The appropriate discount rate to use to value a given bond or stock is based primarily on the risk of that security's cash flows. Payments on Treasury securities are discounted at a (default) risk-free rate; all other debt and equity securities are discounted at higher rates to reflect their higher risk.
- Bond issuers include corporations, municipalities, the U.S. government, and federal government agencies. Bond ratings help investors judge bond risk; low-rated, high-risk bonds are called junk bonds. Bond prices are quoted regularly in the financial press.
- Ordinary bonds make periodic fixed cash payments, called coupons, to investors. Bond prices move in the opposite direction of interest rates, and prices of long-term bonds are generally more sensitive to interest rate movements than are prices of short-term bonds.
- The term structure of interest rates is the relationship between time to maturity and yield to maturity on bonds having similar risk. A graphic representation of the term structure is called the yield curve. The slope of the yield curve is helpful in predicting future economic activity.
- Stock prices are regularly quoted in the financial press. Preferred stock has no maturity and pays a constant periodic dividend. Therefore, preferred shares can be valued using the formula for the present value of a perpetuity.
- Common stock is often very difficult to value, due to both the inherent difficulty of determining the "appropriate" risk-adjusted discount rate to use and the difficulty of estimating dividends (or other cash payments to shareholders) far into the future.
- Common stock valuation is much easier when dividends per share either are not growing or are growing at a constant rate. When dividends per share are ex-

---

[28.] Investment bankers use many different multiples to estimate the value of a firm. One variant of the P/E ratio uses *EBITDA*, rather than earnings, in the denominator. Bankers sometimes argue that *EBITDA*, earnings before interest, taxes, depreciation, and amortization, provides a clearer measure of a firm's earning power than does net income. Ever the skeptic, Warren Buffet wondered in one of his annual reports whether advocates of the *EBITDA* measure ignored depreciation because they thought the tooth fairy paid for capital expenditures.

pected to change their rate of growth one or more times in the future, stock valuation can become very complex.

- Discounting dividends to determine the stock price does not work very well for certain firms, particularly those that have no history of paying dividends. To value these firms, analysts may value free cash flows to determine the enterprise value, which can be reduced to total common stock share value by deducting the value of all debt and preferred stock from the total enterprise value.

- Other approaches to valuing common stock include book value and liquidation value, both of which consider historic accounting values rather than future cash flows. More forward-looking, but simpler approaches involve use of P/E or P/S multiples.

INTERNET RESOURCES

Note: *For updates to links, please go to the book's website at* http://smart.swcollege.com.

http://www.investinginbonds.com—Contains a wealth of information about markets for Treasury, corporate, and municipal bonds, including easy-to-read tutorials on bond basics, reading bond price quotations, and many other topics

http://www.bondmarkets.com—An extremely comprehensive site with extensive coverage of current events, policy issues, and research related to the bond markets; has an extensive list of links to other bond sites on the web

http://www.financenter.com—A consumer-oriented site offering various online financial calculators that allow you to calculate a bond's after-tax yield to maturity, the effect of interest rate movements on a bond's price, and many other figures

http://www.stockcharts.com/charts/YieldCurve.html—Offers a Java-animated yield curve juxtaposed to a plot of the S&P 500—an index of stock-price movements that includes 500 of the biggest and most important firms in the market; allows you to watch historical movements in stock and bond markets simultaneously

http://finance.yahoo.com—Can download historical price and dividend data for any firm by entering its ticker symbol

http://www.bondsonline.com—Provides an enormous amount of information on the bond markets

KEY TERMS

agency bonds	free cash flow (*FCF*)
bank discount yield	Gordon growth model
basis points	interest rate risk
bond equivalent yield	internal rate of return (*IRR*)
bond rating	junk bonds
book value	liquidation value
constant growth model	liquidity preference theory
corporate bonds	maturity
coupon	municipal bonds
coupon rate	nominal return
coupon yield	par value
default risk	preferred habitat theory
discount	premium
expectations theory	real return
forward interest rate	risk-free bond

term structure of interest rates   yield curve
Treasury bills   yield spread
Treasury bonds   yield to maturity (*YTM*)
Treasury notes   zero growth model
variable growth model   zero-coupon bonds
weighted average cost of capital (*WACC*)

QUESTIONS

4-1.   A firm issues a bond at par value. Shortly thereafter, interest rates fall. If you calculated the coupon rate, coupon yield, and yield to maturity for this bond after the decline in interest rates, which of the three values would be highest and which would be lowest? Explain.

4-2.   Twenty-five years ago, the U.S. government issued 30-year bonds with a coupon rate of about 8 percent. Five years ago, the U.S. government sold 10-year bonds with a coupon rate of about 5 percent. Suppose that the current coupon rate on newly issued 5-year Treasury bonds is 2.5 percent. For an investor seeking a low-risk investment maturing in five years, do the bonds issued 25 years ago with a much higher coupon rate provide a more attractive return than the new 5-year bonds? What about the 10-year bonds issued five years ago?

4-3.   What's a simple way to assess and compare the default risk of publicly traded bonds? Describe how a bond's interest rate risk is related to its maturity.

4-4.   Under the expectations theory, what does the slope of the yield curve reveal about the future path of interest rates? If the yield curve is typically upward sloping, what would this imply about the long-term path of interest rates if the expectations theory were true?

4-5.   As the market becomes too volatile, many investors start buying high quality bonds. What effect does this have on high quality bond prices and the associated yield to maturity?

4-6.   Visit a website that posts an up-to-date yield curve. What is the current yield on long-term Treasury bonds? Next, using the web or the financial section of a newspaper, find the current prices of several outstanding preferred stocks. Make sure that the preferred shares you choose pay a fixed dividend and are not convertible into common stock. For each preferred stock, divide the current market price into the annual dividend that the stock pays. Compare this figure to the yield on long-term Treasuries. What should you expect to find?

4-7.   Go to http://www.stockcharts.com/charts/YieldCurve.html, and click on the animated yield-curve graph. Answer the following questions:
   a. Is the yield curve typically upward sloping, downward sloping, or flat?
   b. Notice the behavior of the yield curve and the S&P 500 between July 28, 1998, and October, 19, 1998. In August 1998, Russia defaulted on billions of dollars of foreign debt. Then, in late September, came the news that at the behest of the Federal Reserve, 15 financial institutions would infuse $3.5 billion in new capital into the Long-Term Capital Management hedge fund, which had lost nearly $2 billion in the previous month. Comment on these events as they related to movements in the yield curve and the S&P 500 that you see in the animation.

4-8.   At http://www.nber.org/cycles.html, you can find the official beginning and ending dates for U.S. business cycles according to the National Bureau of Economic Research (NBER). For example, the NBER indicates that the U.S. economy was in recession from January 1980 to July 1980, from July 1981 to November 1982, and from July 1990 to March 1991. Next, go to http://www.smartmoney.com/onebond/index.cfm?

story=yieldcurve, and click on the animation of the Living Yield Curve. Pause the animation at November 1978. Then, click one frame at a time until May 1980. Pause again at November 1981, and click one frame at a time until August 1982. Let the animation play again until you reach March 1989. What association do you notice between the shape of the yield curve and the NBER's dates for recessions?

4-9. Go to http://www.smartmoney.com/onebond/index.cfm?story=yieldcurve, and click on the animation of the Living Yield Curve. Make a note of the overall level of the yield curve from about mid-1979 to mid-1982, and compare that to the level of the curve for most of the 1990s. What accounts for the differences in yield-curve levels in these two periods?

4-10. The value of common stocks cannot be tied to the present value of future dividends because most firms don't pay dividends. Comment on the validity, or lack thereof, of this statement.

4-11. A common fallacy in stock market investing is assuming that a good company makes a good investment. Suppose we define a "good company" as one that has experienced rapid growth in the recent past. Explain the reasons why shares of "good companies" may or may not turn out to be "good investments."

4-12. Why is the book value of equity typically less than the market value? Can you describe a scenario in which the liquidation value of equity would exceed its market value?

PROBLEMS

Valuation Fundamentals

4-1. A best-selling author decides to cash in on her latest novel by selling the rights to the book's royalties for the next four years to an investor. Starting in one month, the royalty stream will be $400,000, and that stream will decline at the rate of 5 percent per month for the next 11 months. Royalties in the second year will be $150,000 per month, followed by flat monthly royalties of $100,000 and $50,000 per month in the third and fourth years, respectively. If the investor requires a 0.5 percent return *per month* on this investment, what should he pay for the royalty stream?

Bond Valuation

4-2. A five-year bond pays interest annually. The par value is $1,000, and the coupon rate equals 7 percent. If the market's required return on the bond is 8 percent, what is the bond's market price?

4-3. A bond that matures in two years makes semiannual interest payments. The par value is $1,000, the coupon rate equals 4 percent, and the bond's market price is $1,019.27. What is the bond's yield to maturity?

4-4. A bond makes two $45 interest payments each year. Given that the bond's par value is $1,000 and its price is $1,050, calculate the bond's coupon rate and coupon yield.

4-5. A bond with a $1,000 par value makes semiannual interest payments. Its coupon rate is 8 percent, and its coupon yield is 6 percent. What is the bond's price?

4-6. Calculate the price of a 5-year, $1,000 par value bond that makes semiannual payments, has a coupon rate of 8 percent, and offers a yield to maturity of 7 percent.

4-7. Recalculate the price of the bond in the previous problem, assuming a *YTM* of 9 percent. What is the relationship between the prices you have calculated in these two problems and the bond's par value? Explain.

4-8. A bond pays a $100 annual coupon, and it matures in four years. If investors require a 10 percent return on this investment, what is the bond's price?

4-9.   A bond pays a $100 annual coupon in two $50 semiannual installments. The bond matures in four years. If investors also require an annual return of 10 percent on this bond, should its price be higher than, lower than, or identical to the price of the bond in the previous problem? Use Equation 4.3 and let r = 10%. What price do you obtain? Can you explain the apparent paradox?

4-10.   Two bonds offer a 5 percent coupon rate, paid annually, and sell at par ($1,000). One bond matures in two years and the other matures in ten years.

    a. What are the YTMs on each bond?
    b. If the YTM changes to 4 percent, what happens to the price of each bond?
    c. What happens if the YTM changes to 6 percent?

4-11.   A bond makes annual interest payments of $75. The bond matures in four years, has a par value of $1,000, and sells for $975.30. Calculate the *YTM* of this bond using a financial calculator or Excel as follows:

- Enter the price of the bond in cell A1, but enter the price as a *negative* number.
- Enter the four remaining payments that the bond makes in cells A2–A5.
- Enter the formula "=IRR(A1:A5, .05)" into any empty cell.
- The number .05 in the formula above simply represents a guess of what the *YTM* will turn out to be; Excel searches iteratively for the correct value, but you have to give Excel a starting value or guess to begin; it doesn't matter much whether the guess that you enter into the formula is a good one or not.
- The formula should calculate a *YTM* of 8.25 percent. (*Hint:* If you see only 8 percent when you enter the formula, be sure you use the "Format" command to force Excel to show you the additional numbers that occur after the decimal point.)

4-12.   A $1,000 par value bond offers a 6 percent coupon that it pays in two semiannual installments. The bond matures in five years. Its price is $1,019.50. What is its *YTM*?

4-13.   A $1,000 par value bond offers a 2 percent coupon that it pays semiannually. The bond matures in eight years, and its price is $919.25. What is its *YTM*?

4-14.   Two bonds make semiannual interest payments of $40. One bond matures in 2 years and the other matures in 10 years. Both bonds currently sell at par ($1,000), meaning that they offer a *YTM* of 8 percent. Calculate the price of each bond if the *YTM* drops to 6 percent, and then calculate the price of each bond if the *YTM* rises to 10 percent. Comment on the patterns that you observe.

4-15.   Suppose that a 5-year Treasury bond with a $1,000 par value offers a coupon rate of 6 percent, paid semiannually. If the *YTM* on the bond is 6.5 percent, what is the bond's price?

4-16.   What is the price of a 15-year $1,000 par value bond with a 7 percent coupon that pays interest semiannually assuming its yield to maturity is 8 percent? What would the price of the bond be if its *YTM* were 9 percent? Compute the percentage change in price: (new price − initial price) ÷ initial price. Repeat the exercise for a 10-year $1,000 bond with a 7 percent coupon paying interest semiannually using the same two yields. What do you notice about the percentage change in price for the 10-year bond when compared to the 15-year bond?

Advanced Bond Valuation—The Term Structure of Interest Rates

4-17.   A one-year Treasury security offers a 4 percent *yield to maturity* (YTM). A two-year Treasury security offers a 4.25 percent YTM. According to the *expectations hypothesis,* what is the expected interest rate on a one-year security next year?

4-18.   A one-year Treasury bill offers a 6 percent *yield to maturity*. The market's consensus forecast is that one-year T-bills will offer 6.25 percent next year. What is the current yield on a 2-year T-bill if the *expectations hypothesis* holds?

4-19.   Using the yield curve, a 3-year $1,000 bond with 5 percent annual coupons is priced in the following manner:

$$\frac{\$50}{(1 + 6\%)} + \frac{\$50}{(1 + 6.1\%)^2} + \frac{\$50}{(1 + 6.3\%)^3} + \frac{\$1,000}{(1 + 6.3\%)^3} = \$965.74$$

What is the *yield to maturity* for the bond (i.e. what single discount rate will produce the same bond price)? Given the manner in which the bond is priced, what is the expected one-year interest rate for next year?

Stock Valuation

4-20.   City Power & Light has preferred stock outstanding that pays an annual dividend of $8 per share. If investors demand a 10 percent return on this stock, what is the price?

4-21.   Suppose that a company's preferred shares sell for $33, and they pay an annual dividend of $4. What rate of return do investors require on these shares?

4-22.   Investors demand a 12 percent return on a particular preferred share that sells for $65. What is the annual dividend on this stock?

4-23.   Omega Healthcare Investors (ticker symbol, OHI) pays a dividend on its Series B preferred stock of $0.539 per quarter. If the price of Series B preferred stock is $25 per share, what quarterly rate of return does the market require on this stock, and what is the effective annual required return?

4-24.   Zenith Propulsion, Inc., is expected to pay a dividend next year of $2.45 per share. Investors think that Zenith will continue to increase its dividend by 5 percent each year for the foreseeable future.

    a. If the required rate of return on Zenith stock is 13 percent, what is Zenith's stock price?

    b. Investors expect Zenith to pay out 50 percent of its earnings as dividends. What is Zenith's price/earnings ratio (defined as current price divided by next year's earnings)?

    c. Maintaining all the other assumptions, recalculate Zenith's stock price and P/E ratio if investors expect dividends to grow at 8 percent per year rather than at 5 percent.

4-25.   The restaurant chain Applebee's International, Inc. (ticker symbol, APPB) announced an increase of their quarterly dividend from $0.05 to $0.06 per share in December 2004. This continued a long string of dividend increases. Applebee's was one of a few companies that had managed to increase its dividend at a double-digit clip for more than a decade. Suppose you want to use the dividend growth model to value Applebee's stock. You believe that dividends will keep growing at 10 percent per year indefinitely, and you think the market's required return on this stock is 11 percent. Let's assume that Applebee's pays dividends annually and that the next dividend is expected to be $0.23 per share. The dividend will arrive in exactly one year. What would you pay for Applebee's stock right now? Suppose you buy the stock today, hold it just long enough to receive the next dividend, and then sell it. What rate of return will you earn on that investment?

4-26.   One year from today, investors anticipate that Groningen Distilleries Inc. stock will pay a dividend of $3.25 per share. After that, investors believe that the dividend will grow at 20% per year for three years before settling down to a long-run growth rate of 4%. The required rate of return on Groningen stock is 15%. What is the current stock price?

4-27.   Yesterday, September 22, 2007, Wireless Logic Corp. (WLC) paid its annual dividend of $1.25 per share. Because WLC's financial prospects are particularly bright, investors believe that the company will increase its dividend by 20 percent per year for the next four years. After that, WLC will increase the dividend at a modest annual rate of 4 percent. Investors require a 16 percent return on WLC stock, and WLC always makes its dividend payment on September 22 of each year.

a. What is the price of WLC stock on September 23, 2007?

b. What is the price of WLC stock on September 23, 2008?

c. Calculate the percentage change in price of WLC stock from September 23, 2007, to September 23, 2008.

d. For an investor who purchased WLC stock on September 23, 2007, received a dividend on September 22, 2008, and sold the stock on September 23, 2008, what was the total rate of return on the investment? How much of this return came from the dividend, and how much came from the capital gain?

e. What is the price of WLC stock on September 23, 2011?

f. What is the price of WLC stock on September 23, 2012?

g. For an investor who purchased WLC stock on September 23, 2011, received a dividend on September 22, 2012, and sold the stock on September 23, 2012, what was the total rate of return on the investment? How much of this return came from the dividend, and how much came from the capital gain? Comment on the differences between your answers to this question and your answers to part (d).

4-28. Today's date is March 30, 2007. E-Pay, Inc., stock pays a dividend every year on March 29. The most recent dividend was $1.50 per share. You expect the company's dividends to increase at a rate of 25 percent per year through March 29, 2010. After that, dividends will increase at 5 percent per year. Investors require a 14 percent return on E-Pay stock. Calculate the price of the stock on the following dates: March 30, 2007; March 30, 2011; and September 30, 2008.

4-29. In the spring of 2005, analysts predicted that The Finish Line (ticker symbol, FINL), a specialty retailer offering athletic footwear and apparel, would generate earnings per share of $1.70 in the next 12 months. Finish Line stock was trading at about $19. Assuming that investors required a 10 percent return on Finish Line stock, calculate the present value of growth opportunities (*PVGO*) per share.

4-30. Roban Corporation is considering going public but is unsure of a fair offering price for the company. Before hiring an investment banker to assist in making the public offering, managers at Roban have decided to make their own estimate of the firm's common stock value. The firm's CFO has gathered data for performing the valuation using the free cash flow valuation model.

The firm's weighted average cost of capital is 12 percent, and it has $1,400,000 of debt at market value and $500,000 of preferred stock at its assumed market value. The estimated free cash flows over the next five years, 2008 through 2012, are given below. Beyond 2012 to infinity, the firm expects its free cash flow to grow by 4 percent annually.

Year (*t*)	Free cash flow (*FCF_t*)
2008	$250,000
2009	290,000
2010	320,000
2011	360,000
2012	400,000

a. Estimate the value of Roban Corporation's entire company by using the *free cash flow approach*.

b. Use your finding in part (a), along with the data provided above, to find Roban Corporation's common stock value.

c. If the firm plans to issue 220,000 shares of common stock, what is its estimated value per share?

4-31. Assume that you have an opportunity to buy the stock of Pedal Systems, Inc., an IPO being offered for $13 per share. Although you are very much interested in owning the company, you are concerned about whether it is fairly priced. In order to determine the value of the shares, you have decided to apply the free cash flow approach to the firm's financial data that you've developed from a variety of data sources. The following table summarizes the key values you have compiled.

Free Cash Flow		
Year (t)	FCF_t	Other Data
2008	$ 750,000	Growth rate of FCF, beyond 2008 to infinity = 3%
2009	850,000	Weighted average cost of capital = 9%
2010	1,000,000	Market value of all debt = $2,500,000
2011	1,150,000	Market value of preferred stock = $1,200,000
		Number of shares of common stock
		outstanding = 1,000,000

a. Use the *free cash flow approach* to estimate Pedal Systems' common stock value per share.

b. Judging on the basis of your finding in part (a) and the stock's offering price, should you buy the stock?

c. Upon further analysis, you find that the growth rate in FCF beyond 2011 will be 4 percent rather than 3 percent. What effect would this finding have on your responses in parts (a) and (b)?

Other Approaches to Common Stock Valuation

4-32. A firm follows a policy of paying out 50 percent of its earnings as dividends. Next year's earnings are expected to be $10 per share. The long-run growth rate of dividends for this firm is 5 percent, and investors require a 15 percent rate of return on the stock. What is the firm's P/E ratio?

4-33. Dauterive Barber Shops (DBS) specializes in providing quick and inexpensive haircuts for middle-aged men. The company retains about half of its earnings each year and pays the rest out as a dividend. Recently, the company paid a $3.25 dividend. Investors expect the company's dividends to grow modestly in the future, about 4 percent per year, and they require a 9 percent return on DBS shares. Based on next year's earnings forecast, what is DBS's price/earnings ratio? How would the price/earnings ratio change if investors believed that DBS's long-term growth rate was 6 percent rather than 4 percent? Retaining the original assumption of 4 percent growth, how would the price/earnings ratio change if investors became convinced that DBS was not very risky and were willing to accept a 7 percent return on their shares going forward?

THOMSON ONE BUSINESS SCHOOL EDITION

4-34. Look up the bond ratings in the 10-K reports of Best Buy (ticker symbol, BBY) and Radio Shack (ticker symbol, RSH). (*Hint:* You can access the 10-K reports under the Filings tab and clicking on the 10-K link in the Filings box.) Which company has the better ratings? Which company's bonds are considered "investment grade"? Is this what you would expect given the company's respective leverage and profitability ratios?

4-35. Using Equation 4.8, what is the growth rate for Coca Cola (ticker symbol, KO)? (*Hint:* The relevant data can be found on the Worldscope Income Statement Ratios Report.) Assuming that Coke will maintain this growth rate forever and has just paid a dividend, what rate of return do investors require on Coke? Use the latest available closing price as the current stock price. How does this required rate of return compare with the compound annual stock return over the last five years? Did Coke's return over this period adequately compensate shareholders?

4-36. Are shares of Berkshire Hathaway (ticker symbol, BRK) "A" shares currently under- or overpriced? Using Berkshire Hathaway's five-year average Price/Earnings Ratio–Close (this can be found on the Worldscope Income Statement Ratios Report), determine the price per share using the median *EPS* estimate for the next fiscal year end (which can be found on the Thomson Estimates Tearsheet). Is this estimate higher or lower than the latest closing price for Berkshire Hathaway?

MINI-CASE: BOND AND STOCK VALUATION

Laissez-Faire Recliners issued $10,000,000 of corporate bonds with a 30-year maturity five years ago. The bonds have a coupon rate of 10.125 percent, pay interest semiannually, and have a par value of $1,000 per bond. The bonds are currently trading at a price of $879.625 per bond. A 25-year Treasury bond with a 6.825 percent coupon rate (paid semiannually) and $1,000 par is currently selling for $975.42.

1. Determine the yield spread between the corporate bond and the Treasury bond. If you are considering investing in Laissez-Faire's bonds and you have an 11 percent required rate of return, would you purchase them, assuming you plan to hold them to maturity? Why or why not?

2. Alternatively, you are considering purchasing Laissez-Faire's preferred stock. Assume the preferred stock has a current market price of $42, a par value of $50 and a dividend of 10 percent of par. Would you be willing to buy the firm's preferred stock? Why or why not? You have a required rate of return of 12.5 percent for investments of this type.

3. Now assume that Laissez-Faire has EPS of $1.89; 750,000 common shares outstanding; and recently paid a dividend of $0.65 per share. Additionally, the firm generated a net income of $1,417,500 and has common stockholders' equity of $6,000,000 (book value). You believe the firm is in a constant state of growth and your required rate of return for investments of this risk level is 18 percent. The firm's common stock is currently trading for $45 per share. Based upon this information, would you be willing to purchase shares of common stock in the firm? Why or why not? Use both the present value of cash flows model and the free cash flow approach to determine your answer. The firm's current free cash flow is $109,237. Use the firm's weighted average cost of capital of 15.83 percent as the appropriate discount rate.

4. Would your decision to purchase shares of Laissez-Faire's common stock change if, rather than expecting the firm to experience a constant rate of growth, you expect the following variable growth pattern?

> Fast growth of 25 percent for years 1 through 6
> Moderate growth of 20 percent for years 7 through 10
> Stable growth of 15 percent for years 11 and beyond

Chapter 5

The Trade-off between Risk and Return

SMART**Finance**
Use the learning tools at www
.thomsonedu.com/finance/smartfinance

Some Helpful Investment TIPS

In June 2005, French utility Veolia announced its plan to become the first euro-market corporation to raise money by issuing *inflation-linked bonds*. Veolia's decision to issue €600 million of such bonds came as new issues of inflation-indexed debt surged in 2004–2005. Amid conflict in the Middle East, oil prices surpassed a record $60 per barrel in the summer of 2005, prompting corporations and governments from about three dozen countries to issue an unprecedented volume of securities that offered investors some inflation protection. Demand for these new offerings was strong, and the global inflation-linked bond market grew to roughly $600 billion in 2005.

As the name suggests, inflation-linked bonds make payments that rise with the overall inflation rate. The U.S. Treasury's inflation-indexed debt, called Treasury Inflation-Protected Securities (or TIPS), has a design typical of that seen in other countries. The Treasury issues TIPS with a fixed coupon rate, expressed as a percentage of par value; the par value moves up over time in lockstep with the Consumer Price Index (CPI). For example, suppose an investor buys a $1,000 par value inflation-linked bond with a coupon rate of 2 percent. With semiannual coupon payments, the investor expects two $10 payments per year. However, suppose that between the date of issue and the time the first coupon payment is due, the CPI increases 5 percent. The par value of the bond will move up by 5 percent (to $1,050), and the coupon payment will be based on this new principal. With a 2 percent coupon rate, the investor now expects semiannual coupon payments of $10.50; those payments will continue to rise with inflation. These inflation adjustments maintain the purchasing power of the bond's cash flows. In other words, the *real return* offered by this bond remains at 2 percent whether inflation is high or low.

These bonds obviously appeal to investors who worry about rising inflation. They also have a more subtle charm: Historically, periods of high inflation have meant low returns in the stock market. The stock market has turned in its best performance in years when inflation has been relatively low. By design, the cash flows paid by inflation-linked bonds are highest when the inflation rate is high, and the lowest when the inflation rate is low. In technical terms, this points to a low correlation between stocks and inflation-indexed bonds. Thus, these bonds offer substantial diversification benefits for investors who also own stocks. Investors witnessed this effect when the broad U.S. stock indexes lost value in 2000, 2001, and 2002. TIPS posted positive returns in each of those years and double-digit returns in 2000 and 2002.

Sources: Ivar Simensen, "Veolia Plans First 'Linker,'" The Financial Times Limited, June 2, 2005; And "Euro Credit Pipeline Robust, Covered Bonds Eyed," The Main Wire, June 8, 2005, http://www.veoliaenvironnement-finance.com/press_release/press080605VA .htm (accessed June 2005).

[handwritten note at top: different kinds of risk — some matter and some don't]

[handwritten note in right margin: If Smart asks what the expected return is for a game like flipping a coin over and over, the answer is ∞ — St. Petersburg paradox]

Perhaps the most important question in finance is, "What is it worth?" For an investor contemplating a stock purchase or a corporate manager weighing a proposal to build a new plant, placing a value on risky assets is fundamental to the decision-making process. The most common procedure for valuing a risky asset involves three basic steps: (1) determining the asset's expected cash flows, (2) choosing a discount rate that reflects the asset's risk, and (3) calculating the present value. Finance professionals apply these three steps, known as **discounted cash flow (DCF) analysis,** to value a wide range of real and financial assets. Chapter 3 introduced you to the rather mechanical third step of this process, converting a sequence of future cash flows into a single number reflecting an asset's present value. In this chapter and the next, we will emphasize the second step in DCF analysis—determining the appropriate discount rate.

Matching a discount rate to a specific asset requires answers to two critical questions. First, how risky is the asset, investment, or project? Second, how much return should the project offer, given its risk? This chapter offers an answer to the first question, showing how different ways of defining and measuring risk apply to individual assets, as compared to portfolios (collections of different assets). The central insight of this chapter is that some risks, especially those affecting many different securities at the same time, are more important than others. Investors need a means to quantify the risks that matter, and they can diversify their investment portfolios to eliminate all other sources of risk.

Building on this foundation, Chapter 6 provides a solution to the second problem: Determining the required return for an asset with a particular risk level. As we explain here, the capital asset pricing model (CAPM) proposes a specific way to measure this risk and to determine what compensation investors should expect in exchange.

The CAPM's most basic insight, and indeed that of all asset pricing models, is that a trade-off exists between risk and return: To achieve higher returns, investors generally have to accept greater risks. The notion that an unavoidable trade-off between the two exists is grounded in fact. In countries around the world, historical capital market data offer compelling evidence of a positive relationship between risk and return. It is to that evidence that we now turn.

5.1 RISK AND RETURN FUNDAMENTALS

AN HISTORICAL OVERVIEW OF RISK AND RETURN

During the past 30 years, the percentage of U.S. households that own common stock more than doubled to roughly 50 percent.[1] Although stock ownership levels vary internationally, they increased rapidly in most industrialized countries over the past three decades. This trend may seem counterintuitive given the uncertainty surrounding common stock returns, especially compared to safer investment alternatives such as bonds. What accounts for the increasing global popularity of stocks?

Figure 5.1 provides one answer to this question. The figure compares the long-run performance of alternative investments in several countries from 1900–2004. Each graph in the figure shows how the value of one local currency unit (e.g., one dollar, one pound, one Swiss franc) would have grown over time if it had been

---

[1.] The Investment Company Institute (ICI) reports that the percentage of U.S. households owning mutual funds, funds that pool contributions from many different investors to purchase financial assets, increased by a factor of 9 from 1980 to 2001. For this and other statistical data on the mutual fund industry in the United States, visit the ICI's website at http://www.ici.org.

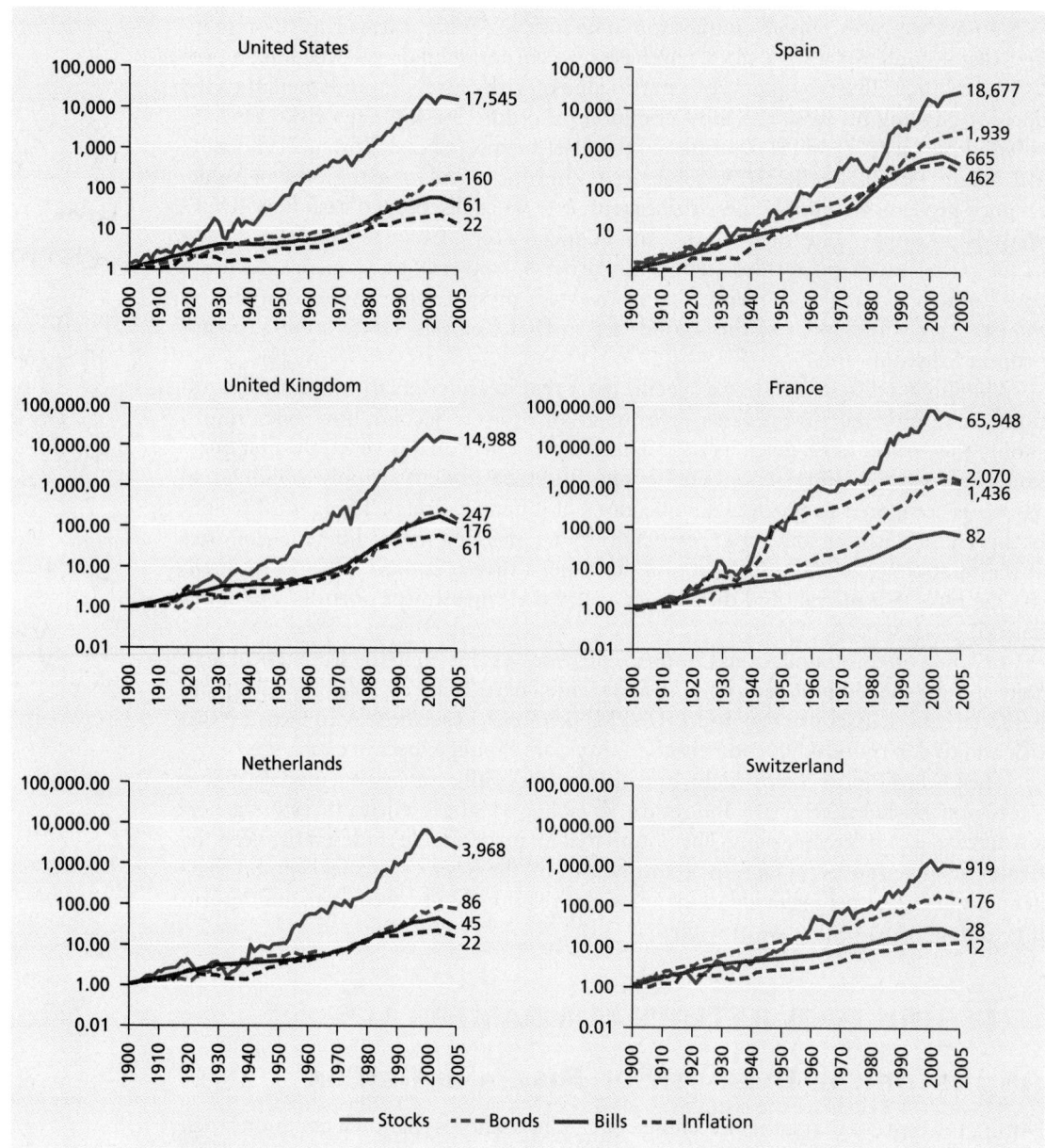

Figure 5.1
Value of Alternative Investments in Different Countries, 1990–2004
*Each graph shows how the value of one local currency unit would have grown from 1900 to 2004
if it had been invested in stocks, bonds, or bills. In most countries around the world, stocks earn
higher returns in the long run compared to bonds and bills.*
Source: Elroy Dimson, Paul Marsh, and Mike Staunton, *Triumph of the Optimists: 101 Years of Global Investment
Returns,* Princeton University Press. Additional updates provided by Dimson et al. Reprinted with permission.

invested in 1900 in one of three asset classes: common stocks, long-term government
bonds, or short-term government bills. In addition, the graphs plot the inflation rate
in each country over the last 105 years.

A quick glance at Figure 5.1 reveals an inescapable conclusion: In the United
States, the United Kingdom, France, the Netherlands, Switzerland, and Spain, common stocks outperformed the other asset classes. For example, $1 invested in U.S.

stocks at the start of 1900 would have been worth $17,545 by the end of 2004; $1 invested in government bonds or bills would have reached just $160 or $61 respectively. In the United Kingdom, a £1 investment in common stocks in 1900 grew to £14,988 in 2004, compared to £247 for bonds and £176 for bills. In Switzerland, investors earned more than five times as much by investing their francs in stocks rather than bonds (2004 accumulated value of SF919 vs. SF176). Though the performance of equities relative to bonds and bills varied by country, common stocks earned higher long-term returns than government bonds and bills in each country represented in Figure 5.1, and in many other countries not shown in the figure.

Figure 5.1 teaches a second important lesson about the relationship between investment returns and inflation. Looking at the U.S. graph, we see that prices rose by a factor of 22 since 1900. This means the purchasing power of $1 in 1900 was equivalent to the purchasing power of $22 in 2004. Why do we include an inflation plot in a graph focusing on investment returns? When people invest, they forgo the opportunity to spend their money today in exchange for the opportunity to consume more tomorrow. Economists refer to the increase in purchasing power that an investment provides as its **real return.** An asset that merely keeps pace with inflation offers a real return of zero and fails to deliver increased future consumption.

For example, suppose that a boy born on January 1, 1900, received one share of stock in Millennium Company from a generous relative and held it for a lifetime. Imagine that the price of this stock was $1 at the time. Over the next 105 years, the Millennium Company never paid a dividend. Its stock price reached $22 by January 1, 2005. What could our elderly investor purchase if he sold his stock on his 105th birthday? With the 22-fold rise in prices, one share of Millennium stock would buy no more or less than it did in 1900.[2]

With the definition of a real return in mind, look again at Figure 5.1. Notice that in every country except France, the lines for bond and bill returns generally lie above the line for inflation, but not by much. In the United States, individuals who invested only in bills over the past 105 years would have increased their purchasing power about 2.8 times ($61 ÷ $22 = 2.8), compared to a sevenfold purchasing-power increase for bond investors ($160 ÷ $22 = 7.3). Both U.S. bills and bonds provided a positive real return during the century. But the real returns on these instruments pale in comparison to the real return generated by common stocks. Investors who held U.S. stocks over the century would have increased their purchasing power almost 800 times ($17,545 ÷ $22 = 798). Even in France, the only country in Figure 5.1 where bond and bill returns trail the inflation rate, equities earn positive real returns. In light of this evidence, the rising tide of stock ownership is hardly surprising.

Table 5.1 looks at the data on U.S. and U.K. long-term returns from another perspective. The first column shows the average annual real return on each asset class; the second column gives the standard deviation of annual returns.[3] Recall from statistics that the standard deviation measures the dispersion of a random variable

---

[2] Comparisons of this type are a bit tricky. Suppose it cost $66 to visit a dentist in January 2005. That price is roughly equivalent to $3 in 1900. But if you invented a time travel device, would you be eager to have your dental work done in 1900, even if it only cost $3? The quality of goods and services improve over time, just as their prices increase, but it is difficult to adjust price indexes to capture quality enhancements. Bils and Klenow (2001) gather data on consumer spending on 66 different products and show how quality improvements affect inflation statistics.

[3] Table 5.1 also shows statistics for inflation. You can closely approximate the real return on an investment by subtracting the inflation rate from the nominal, or actual, return, which of course means that you can add the real return to the inflation rate to obtain the nominal return. For example, Table 5.1 shows that U.S. stocks earned an average annual real return of 8.6 percent, while inflation averaged 3.1 percent annually. The nominal average annual return on equities must therefore be roughly equal to the sum of these figures, 11.7 percent. A more precise definition of the real return is:

$$\text{real rate} = \left[\frac{(1 + \text{nominal rate})}{(1 + \text{inflation rate})} \right] - 1$$

Table 5.1
Real Returns on U.S. and U.K. Investments, 1900–2004
This table provides evidence of a positive relationship between risk and return. Stocks offer higher real returns on average compared to bonds and bills, but stock returns are much more volatile than are returns on bonds and bills.

Country/ Asset	Mean Return (%)	Standard Deviation (%)	Highest Year (%)	Lowest Year (%)
United States				
Stocks	8.6	20.2	56.8	−38.0
Bonds	2.4	9.9	35.1	−19.4
Bills	1.1	4.7	19.7	−15.1
Inflation	3.1	4.9	20.5	−10.6
United Kingdom				
Stocks	7.2	20	96.7	−57.1
Bonds	2.3	14.3	61.2	−34.1
Bills	1.2	6.5	42.4	−15.4
Inflation	4.2	6.8	24.9	−26.0

Source: Elroy Dimson, Paul Marsh, and Mike Staunton, *Triumph of the Optimists, 101 Years of Global Investment Returns* (Princeton, NJ: Princeton University Press, 2002). Additional updates provided by Dimson, et al. Reprinted with permission.

around its average. Thus, we can interpret it as a measure of the uncertainty associated with each asset class. The third and fourth columns list the highest and lowest single-year real returns for each investment.

A glance at the table reveals that higher returns on equity investments come at a price—higher volatility. In the United States, the average real return on equity was 8.6 percent; average real returns on bonds and bills were just 2.4 percent and 1.1 percent, respectively. However, the annual standard deviation of U.S. common stock returns was 20.2 percent. Furthermore, the spread between the best (+56.8 percent) and worst (−38.0 percent) years was an astounding 94.8 percent! By comparison, the standard deviations of bond and bill returns were much lower, just 9.9 percent and 4.7 percent. The story was much the same in the United Kingdom, with average real equity returns of 7.2 compared to 2.3 percent for bonds and 1.2 percent for bills. The standard deviation of U.K. equity returns was 20.0 percent, but just 14.3 percent for bonds and 6.5 percent for bills. The fundamental lesson here is that although equities earn higher average returns than bonds or bills, stocks fluctuate more. Conversely, markets offer very little reward (about 1 percent annually in real terms) to investors who opt for the relative safety of government bills.

Financial economists refer to the difference in equity returns and returns on safe investments as the **equity risk premium.** For example, simply by taking the difference in U.S. stock and bond returns from Table 5.1, we obtain an estimate of the U.S. equity risk premium of 6.2 percent (or a 7.5 percent premium on stocks versus bills). U.K. equities earned a premium of 4.9 percent over bonds and 6.0 percent over bills. As we will see in subsequent chapters, the equity risk premium plays an important role in many financial models. Investment banks, consulting firms, and large corporations need estimates of the risk premium to set acceptable rates of return on investment opportunities and to value whole companies. The data in Table 5.1 tell us what the equity risk premium has been historically, but that may or may not be a useful forward-looking estimate of the future risk premium.[4] Even so, analysts use

SMART IDEAS VIDEO

Elroy Dimson, London Business School
"The worldwide average equity premium has been somewhere in the 4 to 5 percent range."

See the entire interview at
SMARTFinance

[4.] One way to estimate the equity risk premium is to ask financial experts what they expect the premium to be in the future. Welch (1998, 2001) and Graham and Harvey (2003) report survey evidence on the equity risk premium that reveals that financial experts expect a risk premium (relative to bills) between four and seven percent. Fama and French (2002) develop an approach that relies on dividends and earnings to estimate the equity risk premium.

historical equity risk premium figures as a starting point for many different types of analysis.

APPLYING THE MODEL 5.1

Suppose that an investment banker wants to estimate the value of a firm that a client may acquire. The banker projects the firm's cash flows going forward and decides to discount them at a rate comparable to the expected return on the overall U.S. stock market.

How can the analyst make a long-term projection of U.S. equity returns? By consulting Table 5.1, the analyst sees that the premium on equities versus bonds averaged about 6.2 percent over the last 105 years. Suppose that at the time of this analysis, the yield on long-term Treasury bonds is 4.0 percent. Adding the 6.2 percent equity premium to this figure yields a 10.2 percent forecast for equity returns.[5] Using historical data is a common, but very rough approach for estimating the equity risk premium in the future. We discuss alternative methods in Chapter 9.

The term *equity risk premium* implies that stocks are riskier than bonds or bills. Certainly a comparison of the standard deviations of stock, bond, and bill returns in Tables 5.1 and 5.2 supports that conclusion. But the volatility of stocks relative to bond or bills depends on the time horizon over which we measure investment returns. The standard deviations in Tables 5.1 and 5.2 reflect year-to-year fluctuations in each asset's returns. However, it is possible to do these calculations using longer horizons. For example, we might measure the returns on stocks, bonds, and bills over two-year intervals and then calculate the standard deviation of two-year returns for each instrument. Repeating these calculations over various time horizons, we find an interesting pattern: Return volatilities fall as the investment horizon lengthens. Stocks do not necessarily exhibit greater volatility than bills and bonds at long horizons.

Figure 5.2 illustrates this phenomenon using a 200-year sample of U.S. investment returns.[6] Assuming a one-year investment horizon, the standard deviation of stocks is two times greater than the standard deviation of bonds. (The standard deviation is three times greater than that for government bills.) As the horizon increases, the standard deviation of all three investments declines, but it declines most rapidly for stocks. With a 20-year holding period, stocks, bonds, and bills have nearly identical standard deviations. At longer horizons, stocks actually have a lower standard deviation than either bonds or bills.

So are stocks riskier than bonds? In the short run, the answer is absolutely yes. In the long run, it is harder to say. Relative to the risk of investing in bonds or bills, the risk of buying stocks declines rapidly over long periods of time. However, we must temper that conclusion with an important observation: Even with 200 years of data to examine, we have fewer than seven independent (non-overlapping) 30-year periods from which to draw conclusions. The data indicate that stocks and bonds

---

[5.] This is an approximation. The exact formula is much like the one that links real returns to nominal returns and inflation:

$$\text{equity premium} = \left[\frac{(1 + \text{equity return})}{(1 + \text{bond return})} \right] - 1$$

Plugging in 0.062 for the equity premium and 0.040 for the bond return yields an equity return of 0.104 or 10.4 percent.
[6.] We thank Jeremy Siegel for granting permission to use this figure, which appears in the third edition of his book, *Stocks for the Long Run* (New York: McGraw-Hill, 2002).

COMPARATIVE CORPORATE FINANCE

The Equity Risk Premium in the U.S. and Europe (1900–2004)

Table 5.2 shows average annual real returns on common stocks, government bonds, and government bills from 1900 to 2004 for nine different countries. Several robust patterns emerge from the table. First, in every country, the average return is lowest for bills and highest for common stocks, with bond returns falling in between. Second, the same pattern holds for standard deviations across countries. Bills exhibit the least year-to-year volatility, while stocks show the most variability. If we accept volatility as a measure of risk, this pattern makes sense because we expect riskier investments to pay higher returns over time. In other words, *investors seeking higher returns must generally accept more risk.*

Notice that in real terms, bills are not really risk-free investments. Remember, the real return on an investment approximately equals the nominal return minus the inflation rate. In France and Italy, the average real return on bills falls below zero. Assuming that no one expects a negative return when investing, the negative average returns on bills suggest that investors in these two countries encountered higher-than-expected inflation over time. That risk helps explain the growing popular of inflation-indexed bonds, such as the TIPS offered by the U.S. Treasury. As explained in this chapter's Opening Focus, the coupon and principal payments on TIPS rise and fall with the inflation rate, so unexpected changes in inflation cannot cause the real returns of TIPS to turn negative.

By subtracting the average return on bills from the average equity return, we can estimate the equity risk premium in each country. The premium ranges from a high of 9.1 percent in Italy to a low of 5.0 percent in Switzerland. The 7.5 percent U.S. premium takes fifth place among these nations. Keep in mind that these figures represent the historical equity risk premium in each country, which may or may not be a good forecast of the future risk premium.

A careful reader may notice one troubling pattern in the table. Thus far, we have used the standard deviation of returns as a proxy for risk, a practice that seems to work well when comparing one asset class to another. In every country, the data show a positive link between the standard deviation of returns and the average return when we compare bills to bonds or bonds to stocks. Can we extend this logic to compare one country to another? In Table 5.2, the country with the most volatile stock market over the last century was Germany, but the average equity return in Germany ranked only third among the 9 nations in the table. Similarly, the nation with the least volatile stock market was Switzerland, but both France and Spain has lower average stock returns.

Perhaps the positive relationship between risk and returns that holds from one asset class to another does not hold across national boundaries. Another explanation, and one to which we will return later in this chapter, is that the standard deviation of returns may not be an appropriate proxy for risk.

Table 5.2
The Equity Risk Premium in the U.S. and Europe (1900–2004)

Country	Stocks Mean Return (%)	Stocks Standard Deviation (%)	Bonds Mean Return (%)	Bonds Standard Deviation (%)	Bills Mean Return (%)	Bills Standard Deviation (%)	Equity Risk Premium Stocks-Bonds	Equity Risk Premium Stocks-Bills
France	5.7	22.6	0.6	13.2	−2.5	9.8	5.1	8.2
Germany	8.2	32.3	0.6	15.7	0.2	10.4	7.6	8.0
Italy	6.4	29.2	−0.5	14.4	−2.7	11.8	6.9	9.1
Netherlands	7.0	21.3	1.7	9.6	0.8	5.1	5.3	6.2
Spain	5.8	21.9	2.1	12.0	0.5	6.0	3.7	5.3
Sweden	9.8	22.6	3.2	0.6	2.2	7.0	6.6	7.6
Switzerland	6.0	19.6	2.9	7.9	1.0	5.1	3.1	5.0
United Kingdom	7.2	20.0	2.3	4.3	1.2	6.5	4.9	6.0
United States	8.6	20.2	2.4	9.9	1.1	4.7	6.2	7.5

Source: Elroy Dimson, Paul Marsh, and Mike Staunton, *Triumph of the Optimists, 101 Years of Global Investment Returns* (Princeton, NJ: Princeton University Press, 2002).
Additional updates provided by Dimson et al. Reprinted with permission.

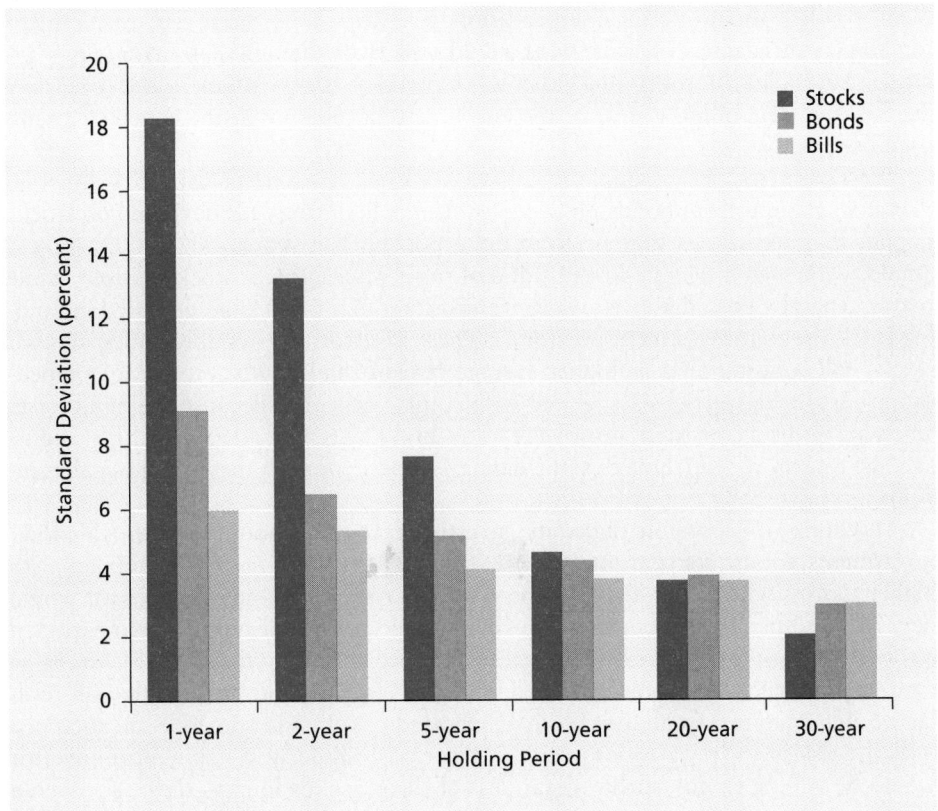

Figure 5.2
The Standard Deviation
of Stocks, Bonds,
and Bills for Different
Holding Periods
(1802–2001)
*Although stock returns
are much more volatile
than bond and bill
returns using an annual
investment horizon, at
longer horizons the
volatility of stock returns
relative to other invest-
ment alternatives falls
dramatically.*
Source: Siegel (2002).

have had a similar degree of risk for long holding periods. We are hesitant to conclude, though, that the next 200 years of data will reveal the same pattern.

RISK AVERSION

To understand why riskier investments offer a premium, it is necessary to make some
assumptions describing the preferences and behavior of investors. Most financial
models begin with the assumption that investors are **risk-averse.** Risk aversion does
not imply that investors always shun risk. Instead, risk aversion means that investors
require compensation for taking risk.

Here's a simple illustration that makes the point. Suppose a friend offers you the
following gamble. You roll a fair die. If the number six comes up, you win $6,000;
otherwise, you win nothing. Your friend offers to let you play this game for a $1,000
fee. Would you play? Assuming that the die is fair, the probability that you will roll
a six and win $6,000 is one-sixth, or 16.67 percent. Thus, we can calculate your ex-
pected payoff (or expected dollar return) from playing the game as follows:

$$\text{Expected payoff} = \text{expected winnings} - \text{fee} = (16.67\% \times \$6,000) - \$1,000$$

$$= \$0$$

Statisticians refer to a gamble like this one as a **fair bet,** meaning that it offers an expected payoff of zero. Risk-averse investors will not accept a fair bet because it exposes

them to risk without offering compensation in return. To persuade risk-averse investors to play this game, either the odds would have to be tilted in their favor (e.g., paying the $6,000 payoff for rolling either a five or a six), the payoff increased (e.g., paying $10,000 for rolling a six), or the entry fee reduced so that the expected payoff becomes positive.[7]

We can extend this example to capital markets. The data in Table 5.1 illustrate that stocks outperform bonds on average, but the high standard deviation on stocks implies that sometimes they perform quite poorly. The years 2000–2002, for example, witnessed a decline in the value of most international stock indexes, while bonds generally posted above-average returns. Yet many investors persisted in holding stocks in their investment portfolios. These investors presumably anticipate that stocks will continue to earn higher average returns than bonds, providing compensation for the higher risks associated with equity securities. Because the numbers in Table 5.1 show a consistent positive relationship between an asset's volatility and its average return, we conclude that the data are consistent with the hypothesis that investors are generally risk-averse.

Of course, it is possible that some investors care only about the returns on their investments, totally disregarding risk. **Risk-neutral** investors prefer investments with higher returns whether or not they entail greater risk. A risk-neutral investor would neither avoid nor accept our die-throwing gamble because it offers a zero expected return. But such an investor would accept the bet with only the slightest favorable modification, such as increasing the payoff from $6,000 to $6,001. Adding one dollar would generate a small, but positive expected payoff, and someone unconcerned with the risk of the proposition would roll the die. Similarly, a risk-neutral investor would be willing to buy stocks, regardless of their risk, as long as they offer even a tiny premium over other investments.

Finally, we can define an almost pathological **risk-seeking** investor. A risk-seeking individual *prefers* to take risk and will invest in a risky asset even when its expected return falls below that of a safer alternative. Risk-seeking investors may purchase investments with negative expected returns. A risk-seeking investor might accept the die-throwing bet even if the payoff from rolling a six was just $4,000, resulting in a negative expected payoff. Risk-seeking investors would jump at the opportunity to buy stocks even if they offered lower returns than bonds. Clearly, the evidence on stock and bond returns does not support the notion that most people exhibit risk-seeking behavior when they invest their savings. Even so, examples of risk-seeking behavior easily come to mind. Lottery tickets and Las Vegas casinos give investors the opportunity to make high-risk "investments" with negative average returns.[8]

The most plausible explanation for the relationship between risk and return observed in capital markets is that investors are risk-averse. High-risk investments must offer the prospect of high returns to attract investors. For a risk-averse investor, the ideal portfolio is the one that offers the most favorable trade-off between risk and return. The rest of this chapter deals with the search for that portfolio. That search begins with precise definitions of *risk* and *return.*

[7.] Risk aversion is closely related to the principle in economics known as diminishing marginal utility. Diminishing marginal utility means that the incremental increase in utility from having additional wealth gets smaller as wealth increases. As Arnold Schwarzenegger puts it, "Money doesn't make you happy. I now have $50 million, but I was just as happy when I had $48 million."

[8.] One could argue that the negative return on gambling reflects its consumption value. After all, where else besides Las Vegas can you take in Wayne Newton and Carrot Top on the same night?

1. If the *real return* on a risk-free investment is barely above zero, will a very cautious investor do almost as well to hide his or her money inside a mattress rather than buy a Treasury bill (T-bill)?

2. Is purchasing insurance an example of *risk-averse, risk-neutral,* or *risk-seeking* behavior? Explain.

**Concept
Review
Questions**

5.2 BASIC RISK AND RETURN STATISTICS

RETURN OF A SINGLE ASSET

The total gain or loss on an investment over a given period of time is called the investment's return. The **return** on an asset includes the change in its value (either a gain or loss) plus any cash distributions (such as dividends or interest payments). The mathematical expression for the return on an asset from time t to $t + 1$ is given by Equation 5.1:

$$R_{t+1} = \frac{(P_{t+1} - P_t + CF_{t+1})}{P_t} \qquad \text{(Eq. 5.1)}$$

where P_{t+1} represents the asset's price at time $t + 1$, P_t is the price at time t, and CF_{t+1} is the cash flow paid by the asset at time $t + 1$. The numerator represents the dollar return on this investment from time t to time $t + 1$. Dividing that return by the initial price of the asset, P_t, converts this dollar return into a fractional return. Multiplying this by 100 yields a percentage return. This equation measures returns after the fact, or *ex post*.

But uncertainty about asset returns forms the very fabric of portfolio theory. Thus, we need a measure of an asset's *ex ante*—its expected—return. Estimating expected returns is very difficult, and we defer a more detailed discussion of that process to the next chapter. However, as a starting point, suppose that the past tells us something useful about the future. By observing returns on an investment or a group of similar investments over time (as in Table 5.1), we may surmise that the average return earned in the past provides a reasonable guess about the average return going forward.

A technical issue arises when using average historical returns to estimate expected returns. To illustrate the problem, look at the returns earned by a stock from 2003 to 2006:

2006	+12.2%
2005	+20.2%
2004	−18.2%
2003	+23.9%

What was the average annual return on this stock over these years? The simplest way to answer this question is to calculate the **arithmetic average return** by adding up the annual returns and dividing the sum by the number of observations (in this case, 4). From 2003 to 2006, the arithmetic average return was 9.525 percent.

An alternative approach is to calculate the, **geometric average return.** The geometric average represents the *compound* annual return earned by an investor who

Handwritten margin notes:

historical returns and risks

	ave annual return	stdev
large stocks	13%	20.3%
small stocks	17.7%	33.9%
long-term corp bonds	6.1%	8.7%
long-term gov. bonds	5.6%	9.2%
U.S. treasury bills	3.8%	3.2%
inflation	3.2%	4.5%

U.S. treasury bills have a higher return since they include inflation

long-term gov. bonds have higher return than T-Bills b/c they include changing interest rates

Standard deviation does *not* help you predict returns within any single group of investments (large cap stocks)

arithmetic average is always (unless annual returns are all identical) larger than geometric average →

bought and held the stock for four years. We can calculate the geometric average of a series of annual returns over t years using Equation 5.2:

$$\text{Geometric average return} = [(1 + R_1)(1 + R_2)(1 + R_3)\cdots(1 + R_t)]^{1/t} - 1] \qquad \text{(Eq. 5.2)}$$

Applying this formula to our example yields a geometric average return of 0.081, or 8.1 percent.

Notice that the arithmetic average exceeds the geometric average by about 1.4 percent in this example. If returns vary through time, the geometric average will always fall below the arithmetic mean, and the difference between the two figures increases the greater the volatility in returns.

For example, let's compare the arithmetic and geometric average real returns, as well as the standard deviation of returns, for common stock investments in Australia and Japan.[9]

Country	Geometric Average (%)	Arithmetic Average (%)	Standard Deviation (%)
Australia	11.9	13.3	16.6
Japan	12.5	15.9	29.5

During the twentieth century, the arithmetic average nominal return on equities in Australia was 13.3 percent, 1.4 percentage points higher than the geometric average return of 11.9 percent. Over the same period, Japanese equities earned an arithmetic average annual return of 15.9 percent, while the geometric average was just 12.5 percent. The gap between the arithmetic average and the geometric average is more than twice as large in Japan as it is in Australia. The reason is that Japanese stocks were much more volatile than Australian stocks during the past century. The standard deviation of nominal returns in Japan was 29.5 percent, compared to just 16.6 percent in Australia.

In Tables 5.1 and 5.2, we examined the equity risk premium by comparing the average returns on stocks and bills over 100 years. The returns in those tables are arithmetic averages. We know stock returns display more volatility than bill returns do. So, the difference between the arithmetic and geometric average returns for stocks will be much higher than the same difference for bills (just as the difference is higher for Japan than for Australia). Therefore, we will obtain a much higher estimate of the equity risk premium if we take the difference in arithmetic averages between stocks and bills than if we use geometric returns.

But which number, the geometric or the arithmetic mean, serves as a better estimate of expected returns? Keep in mind that arithmetic and geometric means measure different things. The arithmetic mean is an estimate of the return one might expect, on average, in a single period. The geometric mean represents the average annual compound return one might expect after a series of repeated "draws" from a distribution of returns. Some economists look first at the time period involved: They recommend using the arithmetic mean when the holding period for the investment under consideration is very short; and recommend using the geometric mean when a long holding period applies. Beyond the time period, there are technical reasons that lead most financial economists to calculate the *arithmetic average* when using historical data to estimate expected returns. We will return to this issue in Chapter 6.

---

[9]. *Source:* Dimson, Marsh, and Staunton (2002).

Risk of a Single Asset

Definitions of risk involve a degree of subjectivity. To most people, the word "risk" connotes the possibility of a bad outcome, perhaps earning a negative return on an investment, or worse, losing the entire sum of money invested. However, most financial models do not define risk strictly in terms of unfavorable outcomes. There are several reasons for this, but the simplest explanation arises from the properties of historical returns. An examination of the year-to-year returns earned by different types of investments yields an interesting symmetry: Those assets that earn the highest returns in good times often earn the lowest returns in bad times. Even recent history teaches that lesson. The Nasdaq Composite Index, a U.S. stock index heavily weighted with high-tech companies (which tend to have higher-than-average risk) rose 82 percent in 1999; over the 31 months beginning in January 2000, the index declined by 68 percent. In contrast, the Standard & Poor's 500 Index (S&P 500), a collection of 500 large firms from a wide variety of industries, rose nearly 20 percent in 1999; over the next 31 months, it fell by 36 percent.

A **probability distribution** tells us what outcomes are possible and associates a probability with each outcome. Suppose we have been told that the returns offered by some investment follow a particular probability distribution. Unfortunately, the probability distribution for almost any real-world investment cannot be known with certainty. But by plotting a histogram showing the relative frequencies of different outcomes in the past, we can gain insight into the underlying, unknown distribution.

Figure 5.3 is a histogram of annual common stock returns in the United States from 1900 to 2000. You can see that stock returns tend to cluster near the middle of the histogram, with extremely good and bad years occurring infrequently. If you draw a smooth curve that just touches the top of each bar in the picture, you will generate a curve that is somewhat bell shaped. This looks like the familiar **normal distribution** curve.

The normal distribution has several properties that make it useful in financial modeling. First, the distribution is symmetric around its mean. This symmetry implies that the probability of an outcome in the far right tail (e.g., very high returns) matches the probability of an outcome in the far left tail (e.g., very low returns). The normal distribution's symmetry makes it easy to determine the probabilities of events that fall within certain ranges. For example, about 68 percent of the time a normally distributed random variable falls within one standard deviation of the mean; about

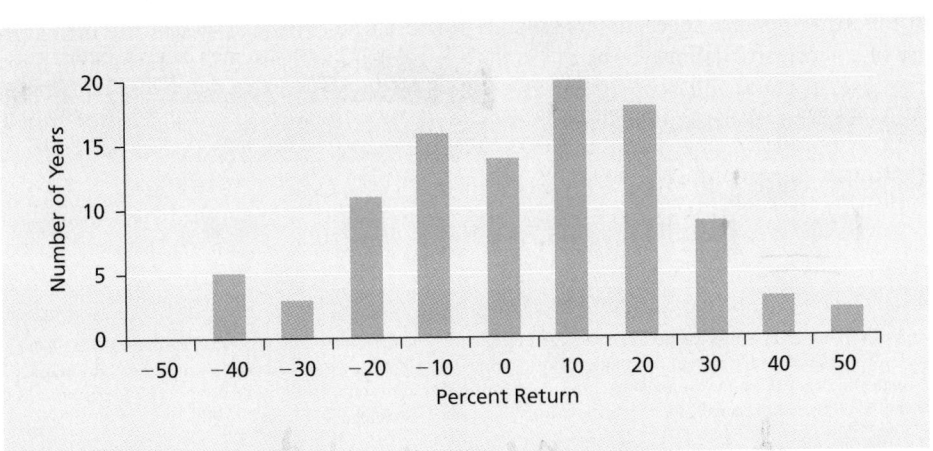

Figure 5.3
Histogram of Real Stock Returns in the United States (1900–2000)
Source: Dimson and Marsh (2002).

95 percent of the time it falls within two standard deviations of the mean. Second, just two characteristics—the mean and variance—fully describe the normal distribution. Therefore, if returns follow a normal distribution, then investors only need to estimate the mean and variance of the underlying distribution to understand the statistical properties of stock returns.

But does the normal distribution reasonably approximate returns on the assets available to investors in the real world? A glance at Figure 5.3 suggests that the approximation is a good one, though not perfect. One problem is that the histogram appears to be more "lumpy" than a normal curve. Even after 100 years of stock market history, there still may not be enough data to generate a perfectly smooth histogram.

Beyond that, histograms of stock returns often exhibit an elongated right tail, indicating that very high returns occur more frequently than very low returns. This "right skewness" appears most dramatically when returns are measured over horizons of a year or more. In part, the skewness results from the limited liability protection afforded corporations. The minimum possible return on a share of common stock is -100 percent because a stock's price cannot fall below zero. On the other hand, there is no upper limit on a stock's return, resulting in the long right tail in return histograms.[10]

If we were to compare the histogram in Figure 5.3 to the same type of diagram for bond returns, we would find that the likelihood of very low returns on stocks is greater than on bonds, but so is the likelihood of very high returns. If investments that offer a good chance of making a very high return also carry a substantial risk of very low returns, perhaps a reasonable way to define risk is to focus on the *dispersion* of returns. The most common measure of dispersion used as a proxy for risk in finance is the *variance,* or its square root, the *standard deviation.* A distribution's variance equals the expected value of squared deviations from the mean. Suppose we treat the return on an investment as a random variable denoted R, with a mean (expected value) of $E(R)$. Equation 5.3 gives the variance of returns for this investment, usually denoted by the Greek letter σ (sigma) squared, or σ^2:

$$\text{Variance} = \sigma^2 = E\{[R - E(R)]^2\} \qquad \text{(Eq. 5.3)}$$

where E stands for "expected value of."

If we knew all possible returns that an investment might earn, along with the probability attached to each outcome, then we could calculate the variance using these probabilities. Consider the following hypothetical example. Suppose that a firm is involved in product liability litigation, and a decision in the case is expected today. If the firm's defense succeeds, its stock will rise 15 percent. You assess the probability of a successful defense to be 0.55 (slightly better than even odds). If the firm loses the case, its stock will drop 10 percent. We can calculate today's expected return and variance for this stock as follows:[11]

$$\text{Expected return} = 0.55(15\%) + 0.45(-10\%) = 3.75\%$$

$$\text{Variance} = 0.55(15\% - 3.75\%)^2 + 0.45(-10\% - 3.75\%)^2 = 154.7\%^2$$

[10.] A distribution that allows for right skewness and more closely matches long-term historical return data is the lognormal distribution. Like the normal distribution, the lognormal distribution is fully described by its mean and variance.

[11.] In the variance calculation, we are using percentage figures for returns rather than decimals—that is, 15 percent rather than 0.15. If we used decimals, the expected return and variance would be 0.0375 and .01547.

Notice the peculiar units of measure in the variance calculation—percent squared! Rather than worry about how to interpret these admittedly odd units, simply take the square root to convert variance to standard deviation:

$$\text{Standard deviation} = \sigma = \sqrt{154.7\%^2} = 12.4\%$$

There may be special cases in which calculating the variance of returns for an investment using this probability-based approach makes sense. In most cases, it is not feasible to list either the full set of returns that an investment might earn or their associated probabilities. Instead, financial analysts often gather historical data and estimate the variance and standard deviation from these observations. In that case, we can use Equation 5.4 to calculate the variance:

$$\text{Variance} = \sigma^2 = \frac{\sum\limits_{i=1}^{N}(R_{it} - \overline{R}_i)^2}{N - 1} \qquad \text{(Eq. 5.4)}$$

where R_{it} represents the return on a particular investment i during period t, and $\overline{R}_i$ represents the asset's sample mean return over the sample's N periods (replacing the unobservable expected return, $E(R)$).[12] As usual, the formula for standard deviation is simply the square root of the variance.

APPLYING THE MODEL 5.2

To demonstrate, let's estimate the standard deviation for the Standard and Poor's 500 Stock Index (S&P 500) and for the pharmaceutical firm Merck, using 10 years of data (1995–2004). The table below shows that the S&P 500 earned an arithmetic average return of 13.8 percent compared to Merck's 13.4 percent average.

| Year | Annual Return (%) | |
	S&P 500	Merck
2004	10.7	−29.0
2003	28.2	−11.2
2002	−21.6	−1.2
2001	−12.1	−36.0
2000	−9.8	41.8
1999	20.4	−7.5
1998	28.7	41.3
1997	33.5	35.6
1996	21.8	24
1995	38.0	76.5
Average	**13.8**	**13.4**

[12.] If you have the historical returns loaded into an Excel spreadsheet, you can use the formula "=var()" to calculate variance, or "=stdev()" to calculate standard deviation.

Using Equation 5.4, we find the S&P 500's variance equals:

$$\sigma^2_{S\&P500} = \frac{(10.7\% - 13.8\%)^2 + (28.2\% - 13.8\%)^2 + (-21.6\% - 13.8\%)^2 + \cdots + (38.0\% - 13.8\%)^2}{10 - 1}$$

$$= 444.6\%^2$$

Taking the square root of this figure gives a standard deviation of 21.1 percent. For Merck, we find the variance equals:

$$\sigma^2_{Merck} = \frac{(-29.0\% - 13.4\%)^2 + (-11.2\% - 13.4\%)^2 + (-1.2\% - 13.4\%)^2 + \cdots + (76.5\% - 13.4\%)^2}{10 - 1}$$

$$= 1,296.1\%^2$$

Taking the square root once more, we obtain an estimate of Merck's standard deviation of 36.0 percent.

The preceding example illustrates more than how to calculate the variance or standard deviation from historical data. The S&P 500 and the Merck stock earned very similar average returns over this period. But notice that Merck's standard deviation was about 70 percent higher than the S&P 500's (36.0% ÷ 21.1% = 1.7). This raises two interesting questions. First, why are the returns on an individual stock so much more volatile than the returns on a portfolio of stocks (as represented by the stock index)? Second, if Merck stock exhibits more volatility than does the S&P 500, is Merck a riskier investment? If Merck is riskier, shouldn't its shareholders earn higher returns as a reward for bearing that risk? Section 5.3 addresses the first of these questions, and Section 5.4 answers the second.

Concept Review Questions

3. "Variance measures the dispersion of an investment's returns, both above and below the average. A measure of risk should focus only on the bad outcomes." Comment.

4. An investor purchases a share of stock for $20 on January 2, 2006, and sells it for $30 a year later. Is the rate of return on this investment 50 percent? What do you need to know to be sure?

5.3 RISK AND RETURN FOR PORTFOLIOS

PORTFOLIO RETURNS

So far, we have seen risk and return calculations only for single assets. The most valuable insights regarding the trade-off between risk and return come when we examine what happens when investors combine individual assets to form *portfolios*.

Consider a simple portfolio consisting of just two assets. Denote the fraction (or weight) invested in each asset with w_1 and w_2.[13] The expected return on this portfolio

[13.] At a broader level, you can think of w_1 and w_2 as representing the fraction of an investor's total wealth invested in two classes of assets. Note that the sum of w_1 and w_2 must be 1.0, but the individual weights can be either positive or negative. A negative value of w_1 means that the investor short sells the first asset. Short selling means borrowing the asset from someone else, selling it, and investing the proceeds in the second asset.

is a simple weighted average of the expected returns of the two assets, $E(R_1)$ and $E(R_2)$, in the portfolio:

$$E(R_p) = w_1 \, E(R_1) + w_2 \, E(R_2) \qquad \text{(Eq. 5.5)}$$

SMART
CONCEPTS
See the concept explained step-by-step at
SMARTFinance

Suppose the expected returns on assets 1 and 2 are 10 percent and 20 percent, respectively. If an investor creates a portfolio invested 30 percent in asset 1 and 70 percent in asset 2, the portfolio's expected return equals:

$$E(R_p) = 0.30(10\%) + 0.70(20\%) = 17\%$$

The equation for the portfolio's expected return is linear. This means the expected return on this portfolio increases at a constant rate as the proportion invested in asset 1 falls, and the proportion invested in asset 2 rises. The general expression for the expected return of a portfolio with N assets is a natural extension of the two-asset case:

$$E(R_p) = w_1 \, E(R_1) + w_2 \, E(R_2) \; w_3 \, E(R_3) + \cdots + w_N \, E(R_N) \qquad \text{(Eq. 5.6)}$$

When estimating expected returns using historical averages, replace the terms $E(R_i)$ in the equation with $\overline{R}_i$.

APPLYING THE MODEL 5.3

Suppose that you want to invest one-third of your money in corporate bonds, one-third in large-firm stocks, and one-third in small-company stocks. You think that the expected returns on the asset classes are 6.1 percent, 13.0 percent, and 17.7 percent, respectively. What is the expected return on your portfolio?

$$E(R_p) = \left(\frac{1}{3}\right)6.1\% + \left(\frac{1}{3}\right)13.0\% + \left(\frac{1}{3}\right)17.7\% = 12.3\%$$

PORTFOLIO VARIANCE—AN EXAMPLE

Determining the variance or standard deviation of a portfolio is a bit more complicated. First, look at Table 5.3. The table shows monthly returns on four stocks from 1999 to 2001. The first column of data lists returns for MeadWestvaco Corp. (Mead), a major producer and distributor of paper and wood products, including office and school supplies. The second column reports monthly returns on the stock of Boise Cascade, distributor of paper and building products and owner of more than 2 million acres of timberland in the United States.[14] The next two columns contain returns for Nike, the well-known designer and marketer of athletic footwear and apparel, and Arrow International, producer of disposable catheters and related products for critical and cardiac care. Underneath the series of monthly returns are each stock's average monthly return and standard deviation.

[14.] Boise Cascade recently sold its forest products assets to a private equity group and changed its name to OfficeMax.

Table 5.3
Monthly Returns and Descriptive Statistics for Individual Stocks and Portfolios, 1999–2001

Date	Mead Corp.	Boise Cascade	Nike Inc.	Arrow International	50% Mead 50% Boise	50% Nike 50% Arrow
January 99	−2.35%	−3.02%	12.17%	−10.76%	−2.68%	0.71%
February 99	6.89%	3.33%	17.45%	−12.08%	5.11%	2.68%
March 99	1.03%	4.31%	8.18%	−12.21%	2.67%	−2.02%
April 99	37.11%	24.81%	7.80%	4.35%	30.96%	6.07%
May 99	−11.01%	−1.55%	−2.01%	13.02%	−6.28%	5.51%
June 99	11.71%	8.58%	4.20%	1.97%	10.14%	3.08%
July 99	−1.80%	−9.62%	−17.95%	4.83%	−5.71%	−6.56%
August 99	−8.60%	−6.13%	−10.10%	7.12%	−7.37%	−1.49%
September 99	−7.87%	0.58%	21.91%	−11.85%	−3.64%	5.03%
October 99	4.73%	−2.06%	−1.54%	6.11%	1.33%	2.29%
November 99	−0.40%	−2.98%	−17.86%	10.57%	−1.69%	−3.64%
December 99	21.72%	17.40%	8.01%	−3.13%	19.56%	2.44%
January 00	−14.24%	−12.65%	−8.20%	9.70%	−13.45%	0.75%
February 00	−19.17%	−15.72%	−37.50%	24.35%	−17.45%	−6.57%
March 00	16.70%	17.06%	39.76%	−20.57%	16.88%	9.60%
April 00	−0.36%	−6.29%	9.62%	8.76%	−3.33%	9.19%
May 00	−11.00%	−10.56%	−1.29%	−3.12%	−10.78%	−2.21%
June 00	−18.05%	−10.64%	−6.86%	1.52%	−14.35%	−2.67%
July 00	0.50%	6.76%	9.89%	1.87%	3.63%	5.88%
August 00	6.33%	8.14%	−9.57%	4.57%	7.24%	−2.50%
September 00	−12.82%	−10.59%	1.57%	2.11%	−11.70%	1.84%
October 00	23.80%	8.00%	−0.31%	10.82%	15.90%	5.26%
November 00	−8.05%	0.65%	6.73%	−7.60%	−3.70%	−0.44%
December 00	18.68%	16.97%	31.22%	1.30%	17.82%	16.26%
January 01	−3.27%	−2.07%	−1.42%	−7.18%	−2.67%	−4.30%
February 01	−9.19%	−2.58%	−29.03%	4.74%	−5.89%	−12.14%
March 01	−8.40%	−1.65%	4.15%	3.25%	−5.02%	3.70%
April 01	12.40%	11.40%	3.11%	0.93%	11.90%	2.02%
May 01	3.44%	0.77%	−1.70%	−1.33%	2.11%	−1.51%
June 01	−6.41%	0.20%	2.46%	2.32%	−3.11%	2.39%
July 01	9.51%	2.93%	13.24%	−3.80%	6.22%	4.72%
August 01	12.42%	1.38%	5.15%	−0.18%	6.90%	2.49%
September 01	−16.73%	−19.21%	−6.14%	1.33%	−17.97%	−2.40%
October 01	−3.03%	−3.19%	5.45%	2.01%	−3.11%	3.73%
November 01	15.83%	12.18%	7.35%	−0.38%	14.01%	3.49%
December 01	−0.10%	6.62%	6.36%	5.55%	3.26%	5.95%
Average monthly return	1.11%	0.88%	2.06%	1.08%	0.99%	1.57%
Standard deviation	13.00%	9.88%	14.53%	8.42%	11.12%	5.21%

Notice that from 1999 to 2001, Nike stock earned the highest average monthly return, 2.06 percent, but also had the highest standard deviation, 14.53 percent per month. Boise Cascade stock produced the lowest returns, just 0.88 percent per month; it was also much less volatile than Nike stock, with a standard deviation of 9.88 percent. Mead Corp. shares offered the second-highest monthly return at 1.11 percent, with volatility second only to Nike's. Arrow International's average monthly return was 1.08 percent; it was the least volatile stock, with a standard deviation of 8.42 percent. Though there is not a one-for-one correspondence between stocks' average returns and standard deviations, this example offers some support for the notion that a trade-off exists between volatility and returns. However, you will soon see that a stock's standard deviation sometimes yields a misleading estimate of its risk.

The last two columns of Table 5.3 illustrate the monthly returns that an investor would have earned by forming portfolios of these stocks. One portfolio contains 50 percent of Mead stock and 50 percent of Boise Cascade; the other contains equal amounts of Nike and Arrow International stock. Because you know that average monthly returns on Mead and Boise were 1.11 percent and 0.88 percent, respectively, you might guess that the monthly return on the Mead-Boise portfolio would fall in between these two figures. Exactly right! The *return on a portfolio* is simply the weighted average of the returns of the stocks in the portfolio. Because this portfolio consists of equal amounts (50%) of each stock, its return is 0.99 percent, exactly halfway between Mead's return and Boise's. Similarly, the average monthly return on the Nike-Arrow portfolio is 1.57 percent, exactly the midpoint between the returns of Nike and Arrow.

Look closely at the standard deviation of these portfolios, starting with the combination of Mead and Boise Cascade. Mead's standard deviation is 13.00 percent, and Boise's is 9.88 percent. Your intuition might suggest that an equally weighted portfolio of these stocks would have a standard deviation halfway between Mead's and Boise's, or 11.44 percent. In fact, the portfolio's standard deviation is a little less, 11.12 percent. But note that the portfolio's volatility still falls between that of Mead and Boise, as you anticipated.

Now, turn to the Nike-Arrow portfolio. Recalling that the standard deviations for Nike and Arrow are 14.53 percent and 8.42 percent respectively, you conjecture that the standard deviation of a 50–50 portfolio should be about halfway between these two figures, 11.48 percent. Or perhaps, learning from the Mead-Boise example, you guess that the portfolio's standard deviation will be a bit less than the midpoint. In fact, the standard deviation is just 5.21 percent! *The portfolio exhibits less volatility than either of the stocks it contains.* More important, it achieves a substantial reduction in risk while still offering a return that exceeds the return on Arrow International. In other words, by choosing a portfolio containing both Nike and Arrow, instead of holding only Arrow stock, an investor simultaneously obtains higher returns and lower risk, the best of both worlds. How can this happen?

THE IMPORTANCE OF COVARIANCE

The risk reduction achieved in these portfolios occurs because fluctuations in one asset partially offset fluctuations in the other. This effect is especially dramatic in the Nike-Arrow portfolio because the best months for Nike stock were often the worst months for Arrow, and vice versa. Examine February and July 2001 for prominent examples of this phenomenon. In contrast, the best (worst) periods for Boise were typically periods in which Mead stock also performed well (poorly). September and November 2001 illustrate that tendency. In general, the risk of a portfolio will depend crucially on *whether the portfolio's components move together*, as in the Mead-Boise

the covariance of two random variables measures their average co-movement around their means

case, or *whether they tend to move in opposite directions,* as Nike and Arrow did from 1999 to 2001.

In the concept of **covariance**, statistics provides a way to measure the co-movements of two random variables. Continuing to use the symbols R_1 and R_2 to represent returns on two different assets, the covariance of returns between them, denoted by σ_{12}, is given by Equation 5.7:

$$\text{Covariance } (R_1, R_2) = \sigma_{12} = E\{[R_1 - E(R_1)][R_2 - E(R_2)]\} \qquad \text{(Eq. 5.7)}$$

To calculate the covariance directly from this equation, an analyst would have to know the probability distribution describing returns for assets 1 and 2. In virtually all practical applications, this probability distribution is unknown, so analysts estimate the covariance using historical data. Given a sample of N periods during which returns on the assets are observed, the formula for covariance becomes:[15]

$$\text{Covariance } (R_1, R_2) = \sigma_{12} = \frac{\left[\sum_{t=1}^{N}(R_{1t} - \overline{R}_1)(R_{2t} - \overline{R}_2)\right]}{N - 1} \qquad \text{(Eq. 5.8)}$$

Examine the numerator of this formula. Imagine that stocks 1 and 2 tend to *move together,* as did Mead and Boise Cascade in the previous example. When both stocks experience above-average returns, both terms in parentheses will be positive, yielding a positive product when multiplied together. Similarly, when both stocks realize below-average returns, both terms in parentheses will be negative, again resulting in a positive product when multiplied. Thus, two assets that tend to move together will have a *positive* covariance. (For example, the covariance between Mead and Boise is 0.0114.)

Conversely, suppose the two stocks move in *opposite directions,* as did Nike and Arrow International. When Nike earns above-average returns, Arrow's will be below average. The product in the numerator will be negative. Likewise, if Arrow's returns are atypically high, Nike's will be unusually low, again resulting in a negative product. Consequently, two assets that tend to move in opposite directions will have a *negative* covariance. (The covariance between Nike and Arrow is −0.0087.) When two assets move independently—that is, when one asset's return yields no information about the other asset—then the covariance will be zero.

Covariance figures can be difficult to interpret because they depend on the units of measurement. A covariance calculation for stock returns will yield very different numerical results depending on whether the stock returns are measured in percentages, decimals, or dollars. Does the 0.0114 covariance between Mead and Boise indicate a strong or weak tendency for these two stocks to move together? A standardized measure, one that does not depend on units of measure, would help answer this question.

---

[15] Perhaps you are wondering why we divide by $N - 1$ here and in the variance formula when there are N observations in the sample. The reason is that estimating variance or covariance first requires estimating a mean, and you lose one degree of freedom in doing so. If you had the full population of returns for an investment, rather than just a sample, you could divide by N. Excel gives you the option, when calculating variance or standard deviation, to use formulas that are appropriate for either a sample or a population. In virtually all practical applications, the sample formula is appropriate. An unfortunate quirk of Excel is that its only formula for calculating covariance, "=covar()", divides by N and is, strictly speaking, inaccurate for a sample. However, in a reasonably large sample, dividing by N or $N - 1$ makes little difference.

Fortunately, the correlation coefficient is such a measure. Denoted by the Greek letter ρ (rho), the correlation coefficient between two random variables is shown in Equation 5.9:

$$\text{Correlation coefficient} = \rho_{12} = \frac{\sigma_{12}}{\sigma_1\sigma_2} \qquad \text{(Eq. 5.9)}$$

The **correlation coefficient** standardizes the covariance measure. It divides the covariance measure by the product of the standard deviations of each asset. Looking back at the formula for covariance, you can see that, like variance, it is measured in "percent-squared" units. Notice that the denominator of the correlation coefficient equation multiplies two figures together that are each measured in percentage units. Therefore, both the numerator and denominator are in "percent-squared" units that cancel out each other. The correlation coefficient is a unit-free measure of the co-movement of two assets. It ranges between a maximum value of 1.0 and a minimum value of -1.0. If the correlation coefficient between two assets reaches 1.0, they exhibit *perfect positive correlation*. *Perfect negative correlation* occurs when the correlation coefficient between two assets is -1.0.

We now can apply this formula to compare the correlation between Mead and Boise Cascade to that of Nike and Arrow International:

$$\frac{\text{Mead}}{\text{Boise correlation}} = \frac{0.00114}{(0.13)(0.0988)} = 0.89$$

$$\frac{\text{Nike}}{\text{Arrow correlation}} = \frac{-0.0087}{(0.1453)(0.0842)} = -0.71$$

These figures indicate a fairly strong tendency for Mead and Boise returns to move together. This is not surprising given that they operated in some of the same industry segments during the 1999–2001 period. The figures also indicate a somewhat weaker tendency for Nike and Arrow to move in opposite directions. We would have predicted that Mead and Boise would display a high positive correlation, but the negative correlation between Arrow and Nike is unusual. Why would good times for Nike translate into bad times for Arrow, and vice versa? Perhaps when people are getting a lot of exercise, and spending plenty of money on Nike products, they are less likely to have heart attacks or other ailments that would make them customers of Arrow International!

Although that reasoning might appeal to someone with a dark sense of humor, we are skeptical. Common macroeconomic factors, such as changes in interest rates, inflation, and economic growth, should affect Nike and Arrow in similar ways, and those common factors tend to generate a positive correlation between most pairs of stocks. Statistics offers a simpler, and more likely, explanation for the negative correlation between Nike and Arrow. When we use a sample to estimate the value of some underlying parameter (like the correlation coefficient), it is always possible that by chance, we draw an unusual sample. Indeed, if we use monthly data on Nike and Arrow shares from January 2002 to June 2005, the correlation between Nike and Arrow rises to 0.21. Even at that level, the correlation between the two stocks is relatively weak, but the example illustrates the difficulties analysts face when they estimate the statistical properties of stock returns using historical data.[16]

[16.] Though our estimate of the correlation between Nike and Arrow changes a great deal when we use more recent data to do the estimation, that is not true for Mead and Boise. The correlation between these two stocks from 2002–2005 was 0.75, a relatively high figure and similar to the estimate we obtained using data from 1999–2001.

VARIANCE OF A TWO-ASSET PORTFOLIO

In Table 5.3, you saw the monthly returns on two equally weighted portfolios, calculated by taking a 50–50 weighted average of the individual stock returns in each month. The portfolio containing Nike and Arrow International stock exhibited very low volatility, and we now know the explanation for that phenomenon lies in the notion of covariance or correlation. In fact, the variance of any two-asset portfolio depends on three factors: the weight invested in each asset, w_i, the variance of each asset, σ_i^2, and the covariance between the two assets, σ_{ij}. Equation 5.10 provides the general formula for a two-asset portfolio's variance:

$$\text{Portfolio variance} = \sigma_p^2 = w_1^2\sigma_1^2 + w_2^2\sigma_2^2 + 2w_1w_2\sigma_{12} \qquad \text{(Eq. 5.10)}$$

Looking back at Equation 5.9, we can see that the covariance can be expressed as follows:

$$\sigma_{12} = \rho_{12}\sigma_1\sigma_2 \qquad \text{(Eq. 5.11)}$$

Plugging this new expression for covariance into Equation 5.10 results in Equation 5.12:

$$\text{Portfolio variance} = \sigma_p^2 = w_1^2\sigma_1^2 + w_2^2\sigma_2^2 + 2w_1w_2\rho_{12}\sigma_1\sigma_2 \qquad \text{(Eq. 5.12)}$$

Notice the importance of the correlation between assets 1 and 2 in this expression. When ρ_{12} is positive, the third term in the equation is positive, leading to a higher overall portfolio variance. Conversely, if ρ_{12} is negative, the third term serves to reduce the variance of the portfolio.

APPLYING THE MODEL 5.4

What is the standard deviation for a portfolio containing 40 percent Nike and 60 percent Arrow International stock? Using the figures from Table 5.3 and the correlation coefficient between Nike and Arrow of -0.71, you can calculate the portfolio standard deviation in two steps. First, calculate the variance:

$$\sigma^2 = (0.4)^2(0.1453)^2 + (0.6)^2(0.0842)^2$$
$$+ 2(0.4)(0.6)(-0.71)(0.1453)(0.0842)$$
$$= 0.00176$$

Then, take the square root to obtain the standard deviation, 0.0419, or 4.19 percent. Notice that this portfolio has an even lower standard deviation than the 50–50 portfolio in the table.

The equation for portfolio variance allows quick recomputations if the portfolio weights change. Figure 5.4 plots the monthly return and standard deviation for many different combinations of (a) Mead-Boise and (b) Nike-Arrow. Notice that portfolios of Mead-Boise trace out an upward-sloping arc. The figure shows that if you add Mead stock to a portfolio containing only Boise shares, the portfolio's average return and standard deviation increase. Intuitively, we might conclude that Mead is a riskier

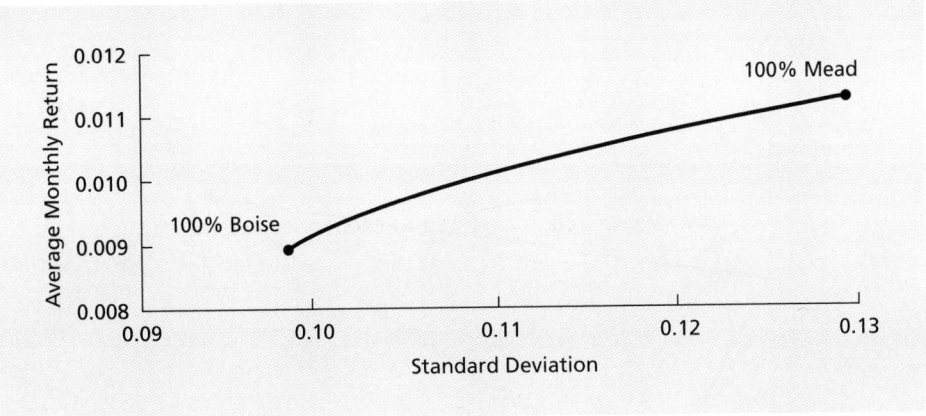

Figure 5.4(a)
Average Return and
Standard Deviation for
Portfolios of Mead and
Boise Cascade

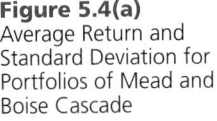

You get a curve
like this if the
correlations b/t the
two stocks is
weak (between
-.4 and
.4)

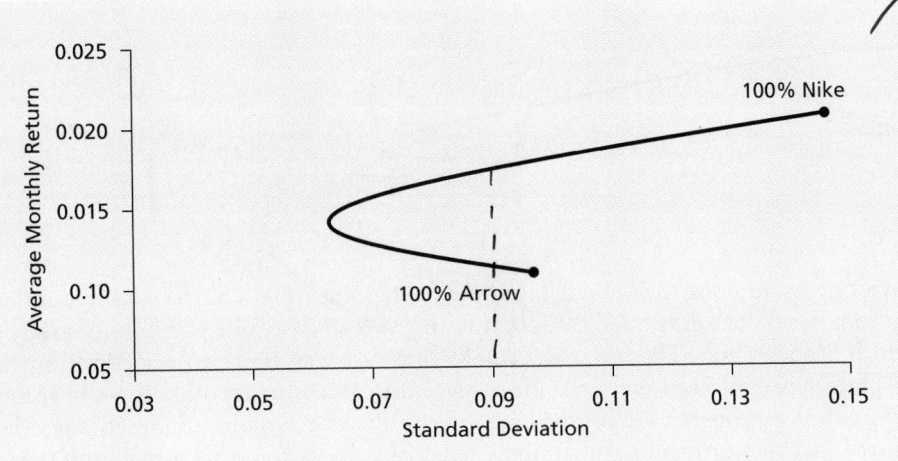

Figure 5.4(b)
Average Return and
Standard Deviation for
Portfolios of Nike and
Arrow International

investing where the
curve goes backwards
is inefficient b/c
at the same risk
point (.09) you can
have higher return
with the same
risk

stock than Boise because it has a higher standard deviation, and because adding Mead shares to Boise stock increases the volatility of the portfolio.

But that intuition is not always correct. Look at the backward-bending arc representing alternative portfolios of Nike and Arrow International. Adding some Nike shares to a portfolio invested 100 percent in Arrow stock results in an increase in the portfolio's average return (because Nike's average return is higher than Arrow's), but the portfolio's standard deviation falls, at least up to a point. Holding a portfolio of Nike and Arrow, rather than holding only Arrow stock, gives investors the best of both worlds—higher returns and less volatility. Indeed, this is the crux of diversification and the basis for the advice, "Don't keep all your eggs in one basket." But this example raises questions about using standard deviation as a measure of risk. If adding a few Nike shares to the portfolio makes the portfolio less volatile, can we really say that Nike is riskier than Arrow just because its standard deviation is higher?

The key lesson from Figure 5.4 is that the volatility of a two-asset portfolio depends on the correlation between the two assets. Figure 5.5 illustrates this point in a general setting with two assets, A and B. Note the change in the y-axis label. In this diagram, we presume that estimates of the expected returns on assets A and B are available (perhaps derived from historical average returns), enabling us to plot expected returns on portfolios. If these two investments are perfectly positively correlated ($\rho = +1.0$), then portfolios will lie along the straight line connecting A and B. If A and B are perfectly negatively correlated ($\rho = -1.0$), then portfolios of the two

Figure 5.5
Portfolio Performance
with Different
Values of ρ
*As the correlation
between the returns of
assets A and B falls, the
volatility of portfolios of
A and B declines.*

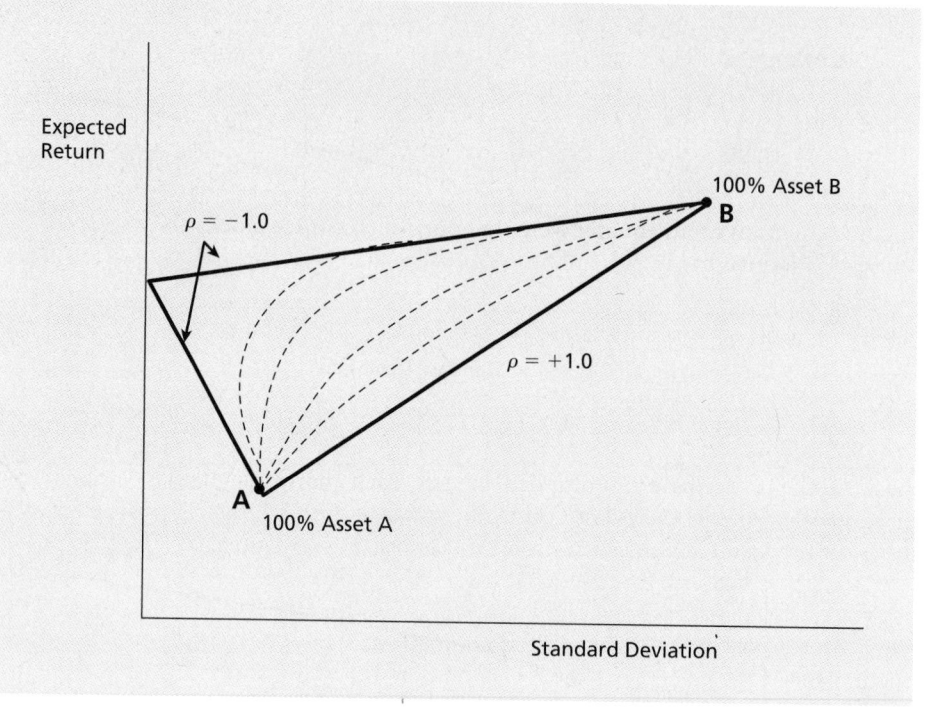

investments lie along the kinked line going from point A back to the y-axis, and then up to point B. The graph indicates that in this special case, one portfolio of assets A and B has zero risk. Though it is virtually impossible to find two real-world stocks displaying perfect negative correlation, investors can construct other types of securities with this property. As you will see later in the text, option-pricing theory relies on the fact that investors can combine two risky assets to create a portfolio that is risk-free. The dotted lines in Figure 5.5 illustrate intermediate cases in which the value of ρ falls between $+1.0$ and -1.0.

**Concept
Review
Questions**

5. "If two assets are negatively correlated, when one has a positive return, the other will have a negative return. A portfolio of these assets will not make any money." Is this correct?

6. If you pick two stocks at random, would you guess that their returns would be positively correlated, independent, or negatively correlated? Why?

7. Imagine that two stocks have the same average return (10%) and the same standard deviation (30%). Would the average return on a 50–50 portfolio of these two stocks be equal to, greater than, or less than 10 percent? Would the portfolio standard deviation be equal to, greater than, or less than 30 percent?

5.4 SYSTEMATIC AND UNSYSTEMATIC RISK

WHAT DRIVES PORTFOLIO RISK?

A simple modification extends the variance equation to a portfolio with more than two assets. Remember, the equation for portfolio variance consists of three elements: portfolio weights, variances of individual assets, and covariances (or correlations) of pairs of assets. We can express the variation equation for a portfolio with three stocks as shown in Equation 5.13:

$$\sigma_p^2 = w_1^2\sigma_1^2 + w_2^2\sigma_2^2 + w_3^2\sigma_3^2 + 2w_1w_2\sigma_{12} + 2w_1w_3\sigma_{13} + 2w_2w_3\sigma_{23} \qquad \text{(Eq. 5.13)}$$

important equation

You can see the importance of the covariance between assets in a portfolio by applying this equation to an equally weighted portfolio of three stocks. With one-third of the portfolio invested in each security, we calculate the portfolio variance as follows:

$$\text{Portfolio variance} = \sigma_p^2 = \frac{1}{9}\sigma_1^2 + \frac{1}{9}\sigma_2^2 + \frac{1}{9}\sigma_3^2 + 2\left(\frac{1}{3}\right)\left(\frac{1}{3}\right)\sigma_{12} + 2\left(\frac{1}{3}\right)\left(\frac{1}{3}\right)\sigma_{13}$$
$$+ 2\left(\frac{1}{3}\right)\left(\frac{1}{3}\right)\sigma_{23}$$

Because the σ^2 terms are multiplied by 1/9, each individual stock's variance contributes very little to the overall portfolio variance. Instead, the covariance terms receive more weight in the calculation. In a portfolio containing 10 assets, each individual stock's variance would be multiplied by 1/100, receiving just 1 percent of the weight in the overall variance calculation. In general, the larger the number of securities in a portfolio, the less the individual variance terms matter and the greater the impact of the covariance terms. The following example demonstrates this point mathematically.

Consider an equally weighted portfolio consisting of a large number of securities denoted by N. The variance formula for this portfolio will have N distinct variance terms $(\sigma_1, \sigma_2, \ldots, \sigma_N)$ and $N^2 - N$ [or $N(N - 1)$] covariance terms $(\sigma_{12}, \sigma_{13}, \ldots, \sigma_{1N}, \sigma_{21}, \sigma_{23}, \ldots, \sigma_{2N}, \ldots, \sigma_{N1}, \sigma_{N2}, \ldots, \sigma_{N,N-1})$. Figure 5.6 places all the terms in a matrix, called the *variance-covariance matrix*. Each element on the main diagonal of this matrix represents the contribution to portfolio risk from an individual as-

Variance-Covariance Matrix

Stock	1	2	3	...	N
1	$\left(\frac{1}{N}\right)^2\sigma_1^2$	$\left(\frac{1}{N}\right)^2\sigma_{12}$	$\left(\frac{1}{N}\right)^2\sigma_{13}$	...	$\left(\frac{1}{N}\right)^2\sigma_{1N}$
2	$\left(\frac{1}{N}\right)^2\sigma_{21}$	$\left(\frac{1}{N}\right)^2\sigma_2^2$	$\left(\frac{1}{N}\right)^2\sigma_{23}$	...	$\left(\frac{1}{N}\right)^2\sigma_{2N}$
3	$\left(\frac{1}{N}\right)^2\sigma_{31}$	$\left(\frac{1}{N}\right)^2\sigma_{32}$	$\left(\frac{1}{N}\right)^2\sigma_3^2$	...	$\left(\frac{1}{N}\right)^2\sigma_{3N}$
⋮	⋮	⋮	⋮	⋱	⋮
N	$\left(\frac{1}{N}\right)^2\sigma_{N1}$	$\left(\frac{1}{N}\right)^2\sigma_{N2}$	$\left(\frac{1}{N}\right)^2\sigma_{N3}$	...	$\left(\frac{1}{N}\right)^2\sigma_N^2$

Portfolio Variance Equation

$$\sigma_p^2 = N\left(\frac{1}{N}\right)^2\overline{\sigma^2} + N(N - 1)\left(\frac{1}{N}\right)^2\overline{\sigma_{ij}}$$

$$\sigma_p^2 = \frac{\overline{\sigma^2}}{N} + \left(\frac{N - 1}{N}\right)\overline{\sigma_{ij}}$$

Figure 5.6
The Variance-Covariance Matrix and Portfolio Variance Equation for an Equally Weighted Portfolio of N Stocks

set's variance. Because each of these terms is multiplied by $(1/N)^2$ and because N is a large number, the terms contribute very little to the portfolio variance. Each covariance term is also multiplied by $(1/N)^2$, but there are many more covariance terms, and collectively they largely determine the portfolio's variance.

A final illustration clarifies the main point. The matrix in Figure 5.6 contains N variance terms and $N(N-1)$ covariance terms. Each variance and covariance term is multiplied by $(1/N)^2$. Suppose that the average stock in this portfolio has a variance equal to $\overline{\sigma^2}$, and across any pair of stocks, say, stock i and stock j, the average covariance is $\overline{\sigma_{ij}}$. Then the portfolio variance equation can be written as shown at the bottom of Figure 5.6.

As the number of stocks in the portfolio, N, becomes very large, the term $N\left(\dfrac{1}{N}\right)^2\overline{\sigma^2}$ approaches zero. This means the average variance of individual stocks has no impact on portfolio variance. As N increases, the second term in the equation converges to $\overline{\sigma_{ij}}$, indicating that what really determines the risk of a large portfolio is the average covariance between all pairs of securities. A portfolio consisting of securities that are, on average, only weakly correlated with each other will have a lower variance than a portfolio that consists of highly correlated securities.

Figure 5.7 plots the relationship between the number of securities in a portfolio and the portfolio's variance given by this equation. For investors, the figure contains both good and bad news. The good news is that as the number of securities in the portfolio increases, the portfolio's variance declines. Given the proliferation of low-cost mutual funds available today, investors can construct portfolios containing hundreds of securities without having to pay substantial transactions costs. The bad news is that the marginal risk-reduction benefit of adding more securities to the portfolio declines as the number of securities in the portfolio rises. Not even a very well diversified portfolio can eliminate all risk.

Figure 5.7
The Effect of Diversification on Portfolio Variance
Adding more securities to a portfolio lowers the portfolio's volatility, but the incremental benefit of adding more securities declines as the number of securities rises.

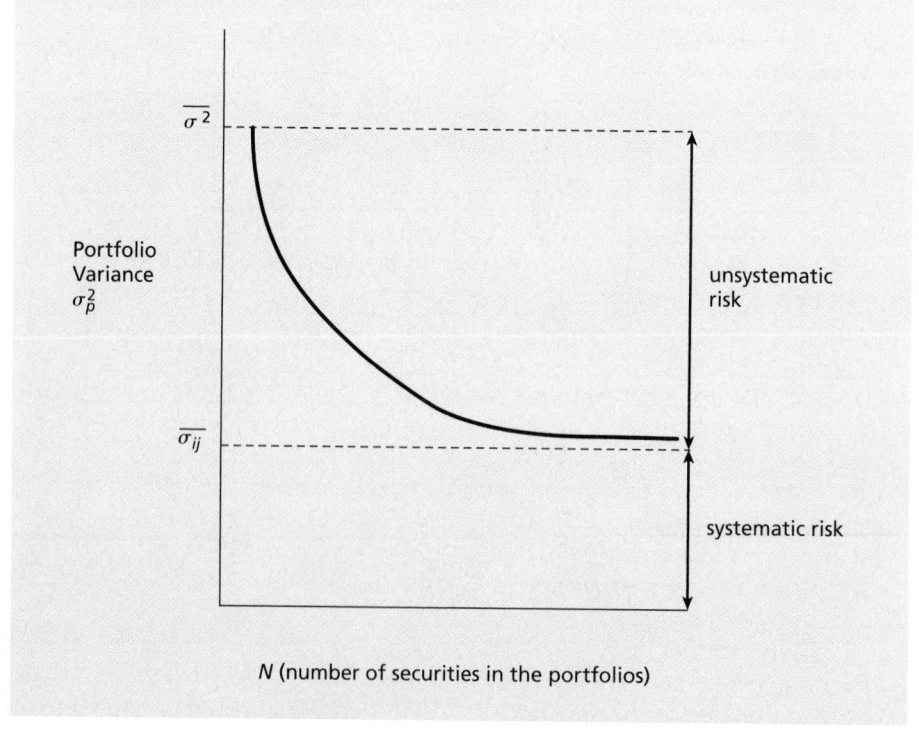

Because some risks systematically affect almost all securities, there is a limit to the risk reduction achievable by adding more securities to a portfolio. The term $\overline{\sigma_{ij}}$ represents this limit. No matter how diversified a portfolio becomes, its variance cannot fall below the average covariance of securities in the portfolio. Financial economists give this type of risk special names: undiversifiable risk, **systematic risk,** or sometimes, market risk. Similarly, the risk that diversification eliminates is called diversifiable risk, **unsystematic risk,** idiosyncratic risk, or unique risk.

In real-world terms, what exactly is systematic risk? This is a difficult question to answer, and we explore it in more depth in the next chapter. For now, we will just say that systematic risks are those that are common across all types of securities. Fluctuations in GDP, inflation, oil prices, or interest rates might fit into this category, and so might certain political factors. For example, the legal system governing investors and markets in a given country can influence systematic risk because that system determines the level of protection given to minority shareholders, creditors, and ordinary investors. In stock markets it is impossible, and perhaps even undesirable, to create a totally level playing field among different types of investors. However, when investors perceive that the legal system protects their interests, their willingness to trade and invest in securities increases, and the returns they require for bearing risk decline.

If investors can cheaply eliminate some risks through diversification, then we should not expect the market to pay them higher returns for the risks that they needlessly bear. The market should not reward investors who fail to diversify. Instead, investors can expect compensation only for bearing systematic risk. Refer back to the example on page 185 showing that the average return on Merck stock was about the same over 10 years as the average return on the S&P 500 even though Merck stock was much more volatile than the index. An undiversified investor who held only Merck stock had to bear twice as much volatility as an investor who owned the S&P 500, even though both investors earned the same reward. This is not to say that Merck was or is a bad investment. The point is that holding Merck—or any company in a single industry—*in isolation* is a poor investment strategy. Undiversified portfolios are generally suboptimal because they expose investors to unsystematic risk without offering higher returns.

MEASURING THE SYSTEMATIC RISK OF AN INDIVIDUAL SECURITY

The previous section demonstrated two important facts. First, the formula for portfolio variance shows that each security contributes to a portfolio's risk through two channels, the security's own variance, and its covariance with all other securities in the portfolio. In diversified portfolios, only the second channel matters. This implies that a stock's variance may be a poor measure of its risk. The variance of a stock captures its total volatility, some of which is idiosyncratic and some of which is systematic. Second, because diversification eliminates unsystematic risk, the market provides no reward for bearing it. As a consequence, though we still expect to see a positive relationship in the market between risk and return, we can no longer be confident that a positive relationship will exist between returns on individual assets and their variances. Again, a stock's variance captures both its systematic and unsystematic fluctuations, but only the systematic component should be correlated with returns.

We need a new measure for an individual asset's risk, one that captures only the systematic component of its volatility. Remember, the primary contribution to portfolio risk from a single asset comes from its covariance with all the other assets in the portfolio. Imagine that an investor holds a fully diversified portfolio, literally a port-

folio containing every asset available in the market. How would this investor determine the contribution of a single security to the portfolio's risk? One way to do that
would be to measure the covariance between a single asset and the portfolio. Recall,
though, the difficulties associated with interpreting covariance calculations. A standardized measure would be preferable, and finance theory gives us just such a measure
in the concept of beta:

$$\beta_i = \frac{\sigma_{im}}{\sigma_m^2} \qquad\qquad \textbf{(Eq. 5.14)}$$

The **beta** of a particular asset, β_i, equals the covariance of the asset's returns with the
returns on the overall portfolio divided by the portfolio's variance. As you will see in
the next chapter, the portfolio we refer to here is known as "the market portfolio," a
value-weighted portfolio of all available assets.[17] In a security's beta, we have a standardized measure of its covariance with all other assets, or a measure of its systematic
risk. If the market rewards only systematic risk, and if beta captures the systematic risk
of an individual asset, then we should observe a positive relationship between betas
and returns in the market.

   Notice that the formula for an asset's beta closely resembles that of the correlation coefficient:

$$\beta_i = \frac{\sigma_{im}}{(\sigma_m)(\sigma_m)}$$

$$\rho_i = \frac{\sigma_{im}}{(\sigma_i)(\sigma_m)}$$

The equations are identical except in one respect: The denominator of the correlation coefficient multiplies the standard deviations of the asset and the market; the denominator of the beta formula squares the standard deviation of the market. This
small adjustment to the denominator makes the interpretation of beta a little different
from that of the correlation coefficient. First, unlike ρ, beta has no maximum or minimum value. Second, beta indicates how much the individual asset's return moves, on
average, when the market moves by 1 percent. For example, if a stock has a beta of
1.5, when the market return increases by 1 percent, the stock return will increase by
1.5 percent, on average.

APPLYING THE MODEL 5.5

Now that we have a new measure of a stock's risk, how does it compare to the
measure we started with, standard deviation? Comparing the monthly returns on
each of the four stocks listed in Table 5.3 to returns on the overall stock market,
suppose you calculate the following statistics:

[17.] The term "value-weighted" means that the fraction invested in a particular security is equal to that security's total market value as a percentage of the market value of all securities. For example, if the total market value of all securities in the
market is $10 trillion, and the total market value of a certain company's stock equals $100 billion, then the fraction of
that stock in a value-weighted portfolio would be 0.01, or 1 percent.

Stock	Covariance with Market
Mead	0.0031
Boise	0.0026
Nike	0.0011
Arrow	0.0003

If the variance of market returns were 0.0028, then the betas of the stocks are as follows:

Mead   1.11   Boise   0.93   Nike   0.39   Arrow   −0.11

These figures contain several surprises. First, based on comparison of the standard deviations of each stock in Table 5.3, we concluded that Nike was the riskiest security. Comparing the betas, however, we find that Nike appears to be less risky than either Mead or Boise Cascade. Remember the dramatic risk reduction achieved in the Nike-Arrow portfolio. Apparently, much of the volatility of Nike and Arrow, at least over the 1999–2001 period, was unsystematic. That is, the volatility was uncorrelated with the broader market. Thus, Nike and Arrow contribute very little risk to a portfolio.

The second surprise is that Arrow's beta is negative, though just barely. This is surprising because over long periods of time, economic booms tend to lift returns on all types of stocks, and recessions tend to lower them. To find a security that usually blossoms when the market swoons (and vice versa) is something of an anomaly. Though it is theoretically possible for a stock to have a negative beta, Arrow's −0.11 beta probably results from drawing an unusual sample from the historical record.

The third surprise is the relationship between the betas and the returns of these four companies. If the market rewards investors only for bearing systematic risk, and if beta measures systematic risk, then we might expect to see a positive relationship between beta and returns. In this case, Nike delivered the highest return but had a relatively low beta. Nike's standard deviation was the highest of the group, so we might be tempted to conclude that market returns are more strongly correlated with total risk (standard deviation) than with systematic risk (beta). For a variety of reasons, such a conclusion would be premature at this point.

SMART CONCEPTS
See the concept explained step-by-step at
SMARTFinance

LIMITATIONS OF BETA

The example in Applying the Model 5.5 suggests two conclusions about beta: First, estimates of beta may not yield perfect measures of the systematic risk exposure of specific stocks. Second, at best an imprecise link exists between beta and returns. Nike stock had the highest returns, but Nike also had the next-to-smallest beta. If beta provides a good measure of systematic risk, and if a positive correlation exists between systematic risk and returns, then the Nike figures present something of an anomaly. Using data from more than three years to examine the link between beta and returns might make this anomaly vanish. And certainly it makes sense to examine more than four companies before drawing any firm conclusions about the relationship between beta and returns. Nevertheless, this simple example suggests that the search for a measure of the systematic risk of an individual stock may not end with beta.

Chapter 6 explores the relationship between beta and expected returns in greater depth. For now, the important point is that a stock's variance (or standard deviation) measures its total risk, but total risk contains both systematic and unsystematic components. Only the systematic part is priced in the market. Beta is one way to measure the systematic risk of an asset.

Concept Review Questions

8. Would you expect a portfolio consisting only of U.S. stocks to have a higher or lower variance than a portfolio consisting of stocks from the United States, Japan, the United Kingdom, France, and Germany?

9. Suppose you track the stock of an Internet company and notice it swinging wildly from month to month. You do some research on the Internet and find several sites reporting relatively low betas for this firm. Is this possible, or are the websites miscalculating?

10. Why should investors not use a stock's standard deviation as a way to measure the stock's risk?

5.5 SUMMARY

- Historically, in the United States and in most other countries, stocks have earned higher average returns than bonds, but stock returns have also been more volatile. However, the difference between the volatility of stock and bond returns depends on the investment horizon. The longer the horizon, the smaller the difference between the volatility of stock and bond returns.
- When individuals save and invest money, they want to increase their purchasing power over time, so the most relevant measure of an investment's return is its real return.
- Most investors are risk-averse, which means that they expect compensation for bearing risk.
- The return of an asset measures the amount by which it increases an investor's wealth over time. When calculating average returns from historical data, an analyst must decide whether to compute the arithmetic or geometric average. The geometric average will generally be lower than the arithmetic average.
- Risk can be defined in many ways, including the chance of a loss or the dispersion of returns around the average. Sophisticated financial models recognize that a better measure of risk captures an investment's contribution to the overall variability of a portfolio. This is the only type of risk that the market should reward; we call it systematic risk.
- The systematic risk of any asset depends on its covariance with other assets. One measure of systematic risk is beta, which equals the ratio of the covariance of an asset's returns with the overall market's return divided by the variance of the market's returns.

INTERNET RESOURCES

Note: *For updates to links, please go to the book's website at http://smart.swcollege.com.*

http://www.yahoo.com—One of the best websites for obtaining historical stock return data

Problem 5-16 gives step-by-step instructions on how to download this information into an Excel spreadsheet, but you must do the analysis. This site is also useful for selecting securities based on logical statements.

http://www.money.cnn.com/markets (CNN Money)—Useful for obtaining up-to-the-minute market-pricing data

http://www.nyse.com (The New York Stock Exchange)—Useful for obtaining up-to-the-minute market-pricing data and general market information

http://www.nasdaq.com (National Association of Securities Dealers Automated Quotation system)—Useful for obtaining up-to-the minute OTC market-pricing and other market information

http://www2.standardandpoors.com (Standard & Poor's)—For a fee, provides a wealth of data on U.S. and/or international assets

http://www.ibbotson.com (Ibbotson Associates)—For a fee, provides a wealth of historical data on various financial assets

KEY TERMS

arithmetic average return
beta
correlation coefficient
covariance
discounted cash flow (DCF) analysis
equity risk premium
fair bet
geometric average return
normal distribution

probability distribution
real return
return
risk-averse
risk-neutral
risk-seeking
systematic risk
unsystematic risk

QUESTIONS

5-1. When using discounted cash flow analysis to value an asset, explain why it is important to measure the risk of the asset and to associate an expected return with that risk measure.

5-2. When we examined historical investment return data from many different countries, what trade-off becomes apparent?

5-3. Why are investors more concerned with the real returns than the nominal returns on their investments?

5-4. You observe that the price of some financial asset falls, but you do not believe that the expected future cash flows from the investment have changed. After the price decline, what has happened to the asset's expected return?

5-5. What is meant by the term *risk premium*? Why must riskier assets offer a risk premium?

5-6. How does the long-run historical U.S. equity risk premium compare to the risk premium that financial experts say they expect when they respond to surveys? How does the historical equity risk premium in the United States compare to the equity risk premium in other countries?

5-7. What is the basis for the claim that, relative to other investments, stocks are not as risky in the long run as they are in the short run?

5-8. How does risk affect the decision-making process of risk-averse and risk-neutral individuals?

5-9. How do historical data on investment returns line up with the assumption that most investors are risk-averse?

5-10. An investor purchases a bond at par value. The bond pays a coupon rate of 8 percent. Assume that the firm pays interest just once per year. The investor holds the bond for one year and sells it just after it makes its first coupon payment. Will the investor's total return on this investment equal 8 percent? Why or why not?

5-11. Given a series of historical returns on some investment, what is the relationship between the arithmetic and geometric average returns obtained from this series? Why is this important when comparing average returns on alternative investments?

5-12. If two securities are considered "uncorrelated," does this mean the correlation coefficient is -1.0?

5-13. Can variance and standard deviation ever be negative? Can the two measures ever be zero?

5-14. Can the covariance ever be negative? Can the covariance ever have a different sign than the associated correlation coefficient?

5-15. Security A sells for $25.00 and has a guaranteed one-year return of 4% (i.e. a future price of $26.00). Security B has the potential to be $50.00 with a probability of 1% or $25.76 with a probability of 99% (i.e. an expected price of $26.00). Assuming investors are risk averse, should Security B sell for more than $25.00, less than $25.00, or exactly $25.00? Answer this question again assuming investors are risk neutral.

5-16. How does the variance of a portfolio compare to the weighted average of the variances of the securities in the portfolio? Upon what does this depend?

5-17. Suppose that returns on two stocks are perfectly negatively correlated. That is, the correlation coefficient is -1.0. Does this imply that whenever the price of one security goes up, the price of the other security goes down?

5-18. Under what circumstances can you construct a risk-free portfolio with only risky securities? What would be the required return on such a portfolio?

5-19. What is the basis for saying that the variance of an individual asset is not a good measure of that asset's risk?

5-20. Explain why covariance matters more than variance in determining the risk of a large portfolio.

5-21. Suppose that a portfolio consists of ten stocks. In the equation defining the variance of this portfolio:
   a. How many terms will be linked to the variance of the individual stocks in the portfolio?
   b. How many terms will be linked to the covariance between pairs of assets in the portfolio?

5-22. Describe two measures of the risk of an investment discussed in this chapter. How do these measures differ?

5-23. What comprises total risk, and how is it measured? Of the two components of total risk, which one can investors eliminate? What is the remaining risk, and how is it measured?

5-24. Explain why the curve in Figure 5.7 does not reach all the way down to the x-axis.

5-25. Why do we say that the only risk that the market rewards with higher expected returns is systematic risk?

5-26.   What is the logic behind the claim that a stock's beta provides a better measure of its systematic risk than its standard deviation does?

PROBLEMS

Risk and Return Fundamentals

5-1.   According to Figure 5.1, what would be the real value in 2004 of a £1 investment placed in British stocks in 1900?

5-2.   Suppose you know that the current yield-to-maturity on Swedish government bonds is 3 percent. Use this data and figures from Table 5.2 to formulate a long-term forecast of the return on Swedish stocks. Is this figure in nominal or real terms?

5-3.   Would a risk-averse person accept a gamble that offered a 50 percent chance of making $1,000 and a 50 percent chance of losing $1,000? Why or why not? Would a risk-seeking person accept the gamble?

5-4.   A particular gamble offers a 50 percent chance of winning $1,000 and a 50 percent chance of losing $900. Can you say for sure whether a risk-averse person would accept this gamble? Why or why not? What would a risk-neutral person do?

5-5.   Return to the dice-throwing example of a fair bet on page 179 of Section 5.1. If we think about the $1,000 entry fee as the price of playing the game, what is the expected percentage return on this investment? Calculate the expected percentage return on the game if the entry fee is $900. Repeat the calculation if the entry fee equals $800. What general relationship does this reveal between the price of an asset and its expected return (holding expected future cash flows constant)?

5-6.   A risk-averse investor owns a stock portfolio worth $1 million. The investor believes that over the next year, this portfolio will rise in value by 20 percent or fall by 10 percent, with each outcome being equally likely. An investment bank offers the investor the following proposition: One year from today, the bank will pay the investor $100,000 if his portfolio value has decreased, but if the portfolio value goes up the investor receives nothing. In return, the investor must pay the investment bank $50,000 today. Does the investor accept the deal?

Basic Risk and Return Statistics

5-7.   On January 3, 2006, you purchased 100 shares of stock for $45 per share. On January 3, 2007, you received a dividend of $2 per share, and then you immediately sold your shares at a price of $48 per share. What was your dollar return on this investment? What was your percentage return? Is your return from 2006–2007 different if you keep the shares rather than sell them?

5-8.   Figure 5.1 shows that £1 invested in U.K. government bonds at the beginning of 1900 would be worth £247 at the end of 2004, but over the same period prices in the United Kingdom rose by a factor of 61.

   a. What is the real value at the end of 2004 of a £1 investment in U.K. bonds made at the start of 1900?

   b. Table 5.1 reports that the average annual real return on U.K. bonds from 1900–2004 was 2.3 percent. (To be more precise, it was 2.3529 percent.) Starting with £1 in January 1900, what should an investment in bonds grow to by December 31, 2004? Why is this answer so different from the answer to part a?

5-9.   In a two-and-a-half year span during 2000–2002, the S&P 500 Index fell by about 45 percent. Suppose that the long-run arithmetic average return on this index is 12 percent per year in nominal terms. At that rate, how many years would it take the index to recover its losses? How would your answer change if you decided to use the geometric average return rather than the arithmetic average? Assume that the geometric average nominal return is 10 percent.

5-10. Calculate the expected return and standard deviation for an investment with the following probability distribution:

Return (%)	Probability (%)
−10	20
5	20
10	20
15	30
25	10

5-11. You are weighing the risk and return characteristics of a particular investment. You believe that the return of this investment can be characterized by the probability distribution that follows:

Return (%)	Probability (%)
−16	12.5
−8	12.5
0	12.5
4	12.5
8	12.5
12	12.5
16	12.5
32	12.5

a. Calculate the expected return and standard deviation for this investment.
b. Suppose that the returns listed in the first column are not points on a probability distribution. (In other words, ignore the probabilities in the second column.) Instead, imagine that they are the actual returns earned by this investment over the last eight years. Calculate the arithmetic average return and the standard deviation using this eight-year sample. Comment on any differences between your answers to this question and those in part (a).
c. Next, suppose we list 100 different possible outcomes for an investment's returns, each of which might occur with probability of 1 percent. We then ask you to calculate the expected return and standard deviation using that probability distribution. Conceptually, how would your answers change if we ask you to calculate the expected return and standard deviation using 100 years' worth of historical returns?

Risk and Return for Portfolios

5-12. Using the probability distribution below, determine the mean, variance, and standard deviation of all four securities:

Probability:	Security A:	Security B:	Security C:	Security D:
15%	8%	−1.88%	1.94%	3%
35%	5%	−4.28%	3.14%	3%
20%	−4%	−11.48%	6.74%	3%
30%	−6%	−13.08%	7.54%	3%

a. Compute the correlation coefficient between: Security A and Security B, Security A and Security C, and Security A and Security D
b. Which security is the risk-free security? Explain your answer using the statistical measures that have already been computed.

    c. Because Security B has all negative returns, can one simply assume it is perfectly negatively correlated with Security A?

    d. Should the correlation between the risk-free security and any risky security be zero?

5-13. Compute the correlation coefficient between the two securities below:

Probability:	Security A:	Security B:
20%	7%	9%
40%	5%	6%
30%	7%	4%
10%	15%	6%

If two securities are uncorrelated, one of the securities must be the risk-free security. How valid is this statement based on the calculation of the correlation coefficient in this instance?

5-14. Compute the mean, variance, and standard deviation for the three securities below:

Probability:	Security A:	Security B:	Security C:
15%	8%	6%	6.8%
35%	5%	3%	3.8%
20%	−4%	2%	−0.4%
30%	−6%	10%	3.6%

    a. Compute the covariance and correlation coefficient between Security A and Security B.

    b. Find the portfolio mean, variance, and standard deviation for a portfolio with 40% invested in Security A and 60% invested in Security B.

    c. Calculate the mean, variance, and standard deviation of returns for Security C. Compare your answer to part b. (*Hint:* Notice that in each row of the table, the return on Security C equals 40% times the return on Security A plus 60% times the return on Security B.)

5-15. Calculate the covariance and correlation coefficient for two assets with the following returns over the past year.

Month	Asset #1	Asset #2
Jan.	0.05	0.02
Feb.	0.10	0.06
Mar.	−0.02	−0.11
Apr.	0.01	0.09
May	0.07	0.08
June	−0.12	−0.06
July	0.03	0.04
Aug.	0.08	0.11
Sep.	−0.05	−0.01
Oct	−0.07	−0.04
Nov.	0.04	0.05
Dec.	0.00	0.01

SMART SOLUTIONS
See the problem and solution explained step-by-step at
SMARTFinance

5-16. Go to http://www.yahoo.com, and click the link labeled "Finance." The next screen asks you to enter a ticker symbol; type in "PMCS" (the ticker symbol for P.M.C. Sierra, a company that designs and develops high-speed broadband communications equipment), and hit "GO." After clicking the "GO" button, you will see very current information about this stock, as well as a number of additional links to explore.

    Start by clicking "Historical Prices." At the top of the next page, you are given several choices about the time period over which you want to collect data. In the "Start" boxes, enter "Dec, 31, 2001." In the "End" boxes, type in "Dec, 31, 2004." Also click "Monthly" to indicate that you want monthly data rather than daily or weekly. Next, click the link "Get Prices." You will then see a table containing 37 months of data for this company. The table gives you the price at the beginning (open) and end (close) of each month, as well as the high and low prices during the month. It also tells you how many shares were traded during the month. The final column contains the "Adjusted Close," a month-end price that reflects dividend payments, stock dividends, or stock splits.

You can calculate the monthly return just by calculating the percentage difference in adjusted closing prices. For example, the adjusted close in December 2001 was $21.26, and in January 2002 it was $23.87. Therefore, the percentage return during January 2002 was 12.3 percent [($23.87 − $21.26) / $21.26]. Click the link labeled "Download To Spreadsheet" below the table, and save the file when prompted. This should save the data in a comma-delimited file (with the .csv file extension), which you can open in Excel. Alternatively, you can download the file "Problem 5-16.xls" from the text's website.

a. Using the series of adjusted closing prices, calculate the return for P.M.C. Sierra stock in each month from January 2002 through December 2004.

b. Using the "=average()" function in Excel, calculate the average monthly return.

c. What is the geometric average monthly return?

d. Using the functions "=var()" and "=stdev()" in Excel, calculate the variance and standard deviation of monthly returns.

e. Repeat the steps outlined above to obtain monthly data from December 2001 to December 2004 for Broadcom, Inc., another producer of broadband semiconductor products (ticker symbol, BRCM). Calculate the monthly returns for Broadcom, and then calculate the average, variance, and standard deviation of Broadcom's returns.

f. Calculate the covariance and correlation coefficient between the returns on PMC Sierra and Broadcom. How would you characterize the correlation between these two stocks? Is that surprising or expected?

g. Imagine that you constructed a portfolio equally invested in PMC Sierra and Broadcom stock. Calculate the return that this portfolio would have earned each month during 2002–2004 using this equation:

$$\text{Portfolio monthly return} = 0.50(\text{PMC monthly return}) + 0.50(\text{Broadcom monthly return})$$

Now use Excel to calculate the average value of the monthly return series you just constructed. What is the average monthly portfolio return?

h. Calculate the portfolio's return using Equation 5.5 where $w_1 = w_2 = 0.50$. You will use your previous answers for the average returns on each stock (see parts b and e above) in place of the expected returns shown in Equation 5.5. Verify that your answer here is the same as in part g above.

i. Use the "=stdev" function in Excel to calculate the standard deviation of the monthly returns on the 50–50 portfolio. Next, calculate the portfolio's standard deviation using Equation 5.10 (or Equation 5.12). Do the two answers match?

j. Compare the standard deviations of PMC and Broadcom returns (from parts d and e above) to the standard deviation of the 50–50 portfolio's returns. How does the portfolio standard deviation compare to the standard deviations of the individual shares? How is that comparison tied to the correlation coefficient from part f?

5-17. Repeat the steps outlined above to download historical prices from December 2001 to December 2004 for C. R. Bard, maker of surgical and diagnostic medical devices (ticker symbol, BCR), and Glacier Water Services, a company that operates self-service vending machines that dispense drinking water to customers (ticker symbol, HOO). You can obtain the data from Yahoo or simply download the file "Problem 5-17.xls" from the text's website.

a. Calculate the average monthly return, variance, and standard deviation for each of the two stocks.
b. Calculate the covariance and correlation coefficient between C. R. Bard and Glacier Water Services. Are these two stocks strongly or weakly correlated over this period? Can you explain the correlation by arguing that when people drink more water they are healthier and are less likely to buy products from C. R. Bard, or is something else at work here?
c. Calculate the return that a portfolio invested equally in each company would have earned in each month during 2002–2004. Next, calculate the monthly average return on the portfolio and the standard deviation of the portfolio's returns.
d. How does the average portfolio return compared to the average returns on the individual stocks?
e. How does the portfolio standard deviation compare to the standard deviations of the individual stocks? How is this related to the correlation between the two stocks?

5-18.   You observe the following returns on two different stocks over the past several years:

Year	Stock 1 (%)	Stock 2 (%)
1998	5	3
1999	25	14
2000	−8	1
2001	13	9
2002	12	13
2003	1	−1
2004	−17	2
2005	−5	11
2006	46	20

a. Calculate the arithmetic average return for each stock over these nine years.
b. Calculate the geometric average return for each stock over the same period.
c. Compare your answers to parts (a) and (b), and explain the general points that these calculations illustrate.
d. For each stock, calculate the value of $1,000 invested at the beginning of 1998, assuming that you hold the stock until the end of 2008.
e. Calculate the standard deviation of returns for each stock, and then calculate the covariance and correlation coefficient between stock 1 and stock 2. (*Hint:* Be sure to use $N - 1$ in the denominator because you are using a sample of data.)
f. Using the historical arithmetic average return for each stock as an estimate of its expected return, calculate the expected return and standard deviation for a portfolio consisting of 35 percent stock 1 and 65 percent of stock 2.

5-19.   You are given the following data on two stocks:

	Stock 1	Stock 2
Expected return	10%	14%
Standard deviation	20%	40%
Correlation coefficient	0.50	

a. Calculate the expected return and standard deviation of the following portfolios, where w_1 represents the fraction invested in stock 1, and w_2 represents the fraction invested in stock 2. Plot these figures on a graph similar to Figure 5.5.

w_1	w_2	$E(R)$	σ
75%	25%		
50%	50%		
25%	75%		

b. Suppose an investor currently has $1,000 invested in stock 2 but would like to invest more. The investor borrows $250 worth of stock 1 from a broker, agreeing to return the shares in one year. Immediately after receiving these borrowed shares from the broker, the investor sells them in the market, and then uses the $250 proceeds to increase her investment in stock 2. This investment approach is called *short selling*. What are the new portfolio weights, w_1 and w_2, and what is the expected return and standard deviation of this portfolio? Add it to your graph from part a. Give an intuitive explanation of what the graph shows.

5-20. Asset 1 has an expected return of 10 percent and a standard deviation of 20 percent. Asset 2 has an expected return of 20 percent and a standard deviation of 50 percent. The correlation coefficient between the two assets is 0.0. Calculate the expected return and standard deviation for each of the following portfolios, and plot them on a graph:

Portfolio	% Invested in Asset 1	% Invested in Asset 2
A	100	0
B	75	25
C	50	50
D	25	75
E	0	100

Now, repeat the calculations above, changing just one assumption. Suppose the standard deviation of asset 1 equals zero. In other words, asset 1 pays a risk-free (because it never varies) return of 10 percent. How does the graph of the expected return and standard deviation for various portfolios change in this case?

5-21. Earlier this year you purchased the stock of a grocery store chain and added it to your portfolio. The purchase price was $40 per share. The end of the year is just a few days away, and your grocery stock currently sells for $22. If you sell the stock and realize the $18 per share loss, you can deduct the loss from income for tax purposes. But you feel that the stock is an important part of your overall portfolio, and you believe it may bounce back. You'd like to go ahead and realize the loss to capture the tax deduction, and then immediately repurchase the stock and put it back into your portfolio. Unfortunately, the tax authorities impose something called the "wash sale rule" which roughly states that if you repurchase the stock within 30 days of selling it, you lose the tax deduction. How can you use the concept of correlation to capture the tax loss without missing out on the potential benefits from owning the stock that might occur immediately after your sale?

5-22. Security X has a mean return of 8% and an associated standard deviation of 36%. Security Y has a mean return of 12% and an associated standard deviation of 46%.

a. Assuming a correlation coefficient of -1.0, what is the portfolio variance if 56.10% of the portfolio is invested in Security X and the rest is invested in Security Y?

b. Assuming a correlation coefficient of 1.0, what is the portfolio variance if 460% of the portfolio is invested in Security X and the rest is invested in Security Y (Note: the weight for Security Y is negative, indicating short selling)?

c. Does perfect correlation allow one to eliminate all portfolio risk, assuming short selling is permitted?

d. Based on your calculations, can all portfolio risk be eliminated if short selling is not permitted? If so, what must the correlation coefficient equal?

Systematic and Unsystematic Risk

5-23. You hold a portfolio consisting of N different stocks. The average variance of a stock in your portfolio is 0.16. (Remember, variance is measured in units of "percent squared"—the average standard deviation would be 0.4 or 40%.) The average covariance between a pair of stocks in your portfolio is 0.12.

    a. Calculate the variance and standard deviation of your portfolio if $N = 5$.

    b. Repeat these calculations assuming that $N = 10$ and $N = 100$. What lesson do these calculations illustrate?

5-24. Suppose that you form an equally weighted portfolio of 100 different stocks.

    a. In the equation defining the variance of this portfolio, how many terms appear representing the variance of individual stocks?

    b. What weight is associated with each variance term when calculating the portfolio's variance?

    c. How many terms are there in the portfolio variance equation representing the covariance or correlation between a pair of stocks?

5-25. Calculate the standard deviation of the following three-asset portfolio.

SMART SOLUTIONS
See the problem and solution explained step-by-step at
SMARTFinance

| | Asset | | |
Statistic	1	2	3
Standard deviation	30%	25%	10%
Correlation with 1	1.00	0.75	0.25
Correlation with 2	0.75	1.00	0.40
Correlation with 3	0.25	0.40	1.00
Portfolio weight	50%	30%	20%

5-26. You observe that the standard deviation of a particular stock is 40 percent per year; the standard deviation on a broad market index is 25 percent per year. If the correlation coefficient between the stock and the market index is 0.8, what is the stock's beta?

5-27. You observe that the standard deviation of a particular stock is 60 percent per year; the standard deviation on a broad market index is 25 percent per year. If the correlation coefficient between the stock and the market index is 0.8, what is the stock's beta? Holding the market's standard deviation and the correlation between the market and the stock fixed, how does an increase in a stock's standard deviation affect its beta? Repeat the problem assuming that the stock's standard deviation is just 15 percent.

THOMSON ONE BUSINESS SCHOOL EDITION

5-28. Calculate the arithmetic average and standard deviation of monthly returns for Apple Computer Inc. (ticker symbol, AAPL), Dell Computer Corp. (ticker symbol, DELL), and General Mills (ticker symbol, GIS) over the last 12 months. (*Hint:* You can obtain price data in ThomsonONE under Prices → Overviews → Datastream Market Data → Actual Value Price History Report.)

    Assume you have an equally weighted portfolio (equal amount of money invested in each security) of AAPL, DELL, and GIS. Calculate the arithmetic average and standard deviation of the monthly returns for the equally weighted portfolio.

    Assume you have a value-weighted portfolio (equal number of shares in each security) of AAPL, DELL, and GIS. Calculate the arithmetic average and standard deviation of the monthly returns for the value-weighted portfolio.

    How do the average returns and standard deviations of the three individual securities compare to the average returns and standard deviations of the portfolios? Is there a benefit to combining the securities into a portfolio? Does your answer change if you are comparing the average return and standard deviation for the equally weighted portfolio versus the value-weighted portfolio?

5-29.   Calculate the monthly geometric average over the last 12 months for Apple Computer Inc. (ticker symbol, AAPL), Dell Computer Corp. (ticker symbol, DELL), and General Mills (ticker symbol, GIS). How do the geometric averages compare to the arithmetic averages computed in 5-28 above? Which is the better "average" return—arithmetic or geometric?

5-30.   Using Equation 5.14, calculate the betas for Apple Computer Inc. (ticker symbol, AAPL), Dell Computer Corp. (ticker symbol, DELL), and General Mills (ticker symbol, GIS) using monthly returns for the last 12 months. Use the S&P 500 Composite as the market index (DSMnemonic, S&PCOMP). How would you expect these betas to change if you were to use the NASDAQ Composite (DSMnemonic, NASCOMP) or the DJIA (DSMnemonic, DJINDUS) as the market index?

MINI-CASE

The end-of-year stock prices for KFD Corporation for the past five years, and annual dividends per share, are as follows:

Year	Stock Price	Dividends
2006	$85.23	$0.22
2005	$79.14	$0.18
2004	$37.86	$0.14
2003	$45.99	$0.10
2002	$23.33	$0.10
2001	$14.67	—

During 2007 you have the following expectations for KFD's stock price:

Outlook	Probability	Stock Price
Good	45%	$93.42
Average	35%	$89.15
Bad	20%	$81.87

You think KFD will pay a dividend of $0.22 during 2007, regardless of the economic outlook.

1.   Calculate the annual returns for KFD Corporation's stock for the years 2002 through 2006. Determine the geometric and arithmetic means for the returns, as well as the variance and standard deviation of the arithmetic mean.

2.   Forecast the overall expected return and standard deviation for KFD's stock during 2007.

You are considering adding KFD stock to your current portfolio, which is now comprised of equal weights of Mellon Corporation and Insignia Enterprises. The expected returns and standard deviation of expected returns for Mellon and Insignia are:

	Mellon Corporation	Insignia Enterprises
Expected Return	23.14%	18.93%
Standard Deviation	26.56%	20.77%

The correlation coefficients between the three corporations are:

	Mellon Corporation	Insignia Enterprises	KFD Corporation
Mellon Corporation	1.0000		
Insignia Enterprises	0.5385	1.0000	
KFD Corporation	0.4233	0.3982	1.0000

3.   If you were to form a portfolio comprised of 30% Mellon Corporation, 60% Insignia Enterprises, and 10% KFD Corporation, determine the expected return, variance, and standard deviation of the portfolio.

4.   The correlation coefficient between KFD Corporation and the market is 0.2532, while the variance of the market is 0.04. Determine the beta for KFD Corporation.

Chapter 6

Risk and Return: The CAPM and Beyond

SMARTFinance
Use the learning tools at www
.thomsonedu.com/finance/smartfinance

212

OPENING FOCUS
CFOs Count on CAPM to Gauge Stockholders' Expectations

When companies raise money by selling stocks and bonds, how do they know what returns investors expect to earn on their money? The answer to that question is important because when firms make investments that earn disappointing returns, stock prices fall. Similarly, when firms deliver higher-than-expected returns to investors, stock prices rise. Therefore, investors' expected returns establish a kind of hurdle rate that firms must exceed when they build new plants, develop new products, or pursue almost any kind of significant investment opportunity.

When firms borrow money by issuing debt, assessing the lender's expected return is relatively straightforward. The interest rate the lender charges the firm provides a convenient and intuitive measure of the lender's required return. But how does a firm measure the return that stockholders expect when they buy the firm's common shares? With common stock, there is no obvious measure like the interest rate or yield to maturity on debt that executives can rely on to gauge stockholders' expectations. Firms might assess shareholder expectations by looking at the average returns investors earned on shares in the past, or they might simply ask stockholders what return they would like the company to deliver.

In a recent survey, Duke economists John Graham and Campbell Harvey asked 392 Chief Financial Officers (CFOs) how they determined what returns their stockholders expected. Fewer than 14 percent of the CFOs said that they relied on direct communication with investors to understand their expectations. Almost 40 percent of the executives said that they look at historical returns on their firms' shares to determine what stockholders would expect going forward. And an overwhelming majority (73 percent) of the CFOs said that they relied on the Capital Asset Pricing Model (CAPM) to measure investors' expectations. Developed in the 1960s, the CAPM has become the workhorse model in corporate finance for quantifying the tradeoff between risk and return that confronts both investors and corporate managers. To understand how the CAPM works and why its predictions have become controversial, read on.

Source: The Theory and Practice of Corporate Finance: Evidence from the Field, Journal of Financial Economics, 60, 2001, pp. 187–243.

C hapter 5 introduced the basic elements of portfolio theory, starting with a simple observation: Investments that historically have offered the highest average returns have also displayed the greatest volatility. The positive relationship between returns and volatility in the historical data makes sense in a world populated by risk-averse investors. If riskier investments did not offer the prospect of higher returns, they could not survive in the market. But as a measure of risk, total volatility (i.e., the variance or standard deviation of returns) has serious flaws. Investors can easily reduce volatility through diversification. Accordingly, investors can only expect a reward for bearing systematic risk, the volatility that cannot be diversified away. Asset pricing models attempt to quantify systematic risk and to determine the rate of return investors expect as compensation for bearing systematic risk. Remember, the price of a financial asset equals the present value of its future cash flows. If we know the return that the market requires on a given asset, then we know the rate at which the market discounts the asset's cash flows, a critical piece of information necessary to determine the asset's price.

For decades, beta stood alone as the most popular metric for an investment's systematic risk. *Beta,* as defined in Chapter 5, measures the sensitivity of an investment's returns to fluctuations in overall market returns. Investments with below-average levels of systematic risk have betas below 1.0, and those with above-average systematic risk have betas greater than 1.0. Put another way, high-beta investments increase the systematic risk exposure of a portfolio, while low-beta investments decrease it. If investors concern themselves only with systematic risk, and if beta measures that risk accurately, then we should anticipate a positive relationship between beta and returns. This is the crux of the *capital asset pricing model (CAPM)*.

This chapter traces the development of the CAPM, explaining its intellectual foundations as well as its practical impact. We explain how recent criticisms led to modifications of the original CAPM, as well as to entirely new approaches to asset pricing. We conclude with a discussion of the current state of the "CAPM controversy" and descriptions of the leading alternatives to the CAPM.

6.1 EFFICIENT RISKY PORTFOLIOS

THE EFFICIENT FRONTIER WITH TWO ASSETS

Are some portfolios better than others? For risk-averse investors, the answer is clearly yes. Recall the portfolios we examined containing different combinations of Nike and Arrow International shares in Figure 5.4(b). An investor holding a portfolio consisting entirely of Arrow shares could unambiguously improve the portfolio's performance by selling some Arrow shares and using the proceeds to buy Nike stock. By doing so, the investor increases the portfolio's return while simultaneously decreasing its standard deviation, at least up to a point. In this example, diversification achieves two goals at once—increasing portfolio returns and decreasing portfolio volatility.

Figure 6.1 illustrates this phenomenon for two generic stocks, A and B. Stock A has a lower expected return and a lower standard deviation than stock B. The curve connecting A and B, called the **feasible set,** plots the expected return and standard deviation for all possible portfolios of these two stocks. By glancing at the figure, we can conclude that the correlation between the returns for A and B falls below 1.0— otherwise, portfolios of A and B would lie on a straight, upward-sloping line connecting the two points. Likewise, because the arc connecting A and B does not bend

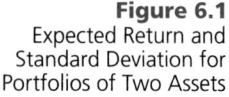

Figure 6.1
Expected Return and
Standard Deviation for
Portfolios of Two Assets

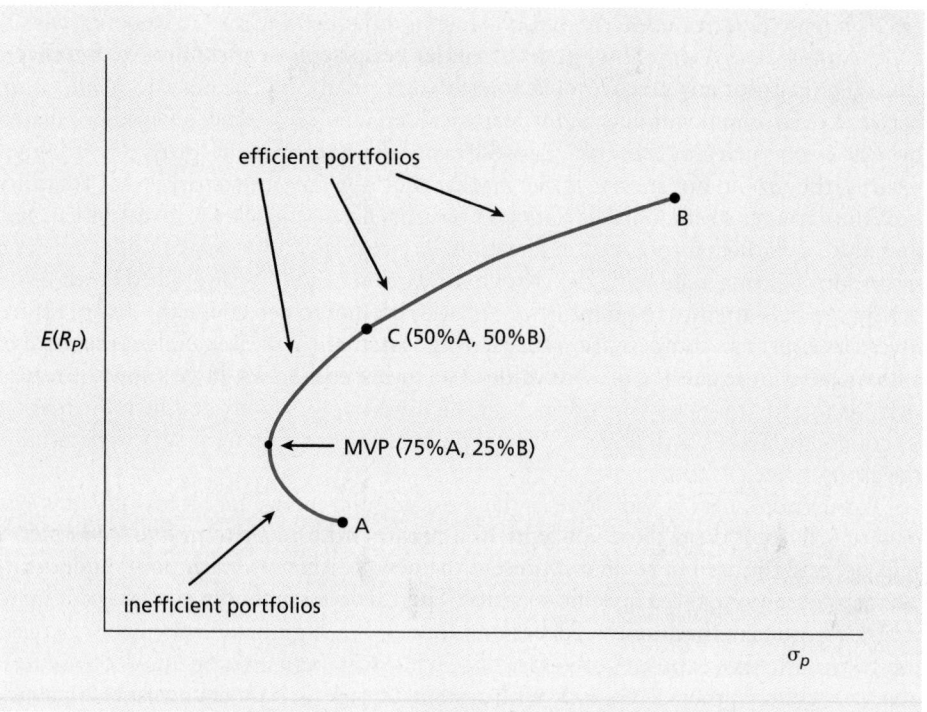

all the way back to the y-axis, the correlation between A and B exceeds -1.0. Figure 6.1 therefore illustrates an intermediate case, one that you might observe by picking any pair of stocks at random.

Because the arc initially bends backward toward the y-axis, an investor can construct a portfolio of A and B that has less volatility than either A or B. By trial and error (or by using calculus), you can find the combination of A and B shares that results in the portfolio marked MVP, the **minimum variance portfolio.** No other combination of assets A and B yields a portfolio with a lower standard deviation. For the sake of illustration, suppose that investing 75 percent in A and 25 percent in B results in the MVP. How can an investor use this information?

Examine the two segments of the arc separated by the point MVP. An investor allocating money between A and B should avoid buying shares in company A exclusively because another portfolio that offers a higher return for the same level of volatility exists on the arc. The same statement could be made for any portfolio lying on the upward-sloping portion of the arc, from A to MVP. At any point on this segment, another portfolio exists with the same standard deviation and a higher expected return. Therefore, all portfolios lying on the segment from A to MVP (i.e., all portfolios with less than 25 percent invested in B) are **inefficient portfolios.** We say that a portfolio is inefficient if it offers a lower expected return than another portfolio with the same standard deviation. Faced with the investment opportunities portrayed in Figure 6.1, an investor knows that 25 percent is the minimum rational investment in stock B. Any smaller investment in B results in an inefficient portfolio.

By the same token, all portfolios lying on the segment connecting MVP and B qualify as **efficient portfolios.** A portfolio is efficient if it offers the highest expected return among the group of portfolios with equal or less volatility. In other words, if you mark any point on the arc from MVP to B, you will notice that no other portfolio promises a higher expected return without adding more volatility. The terms *efficient set* and *efficient frontier* refer to all the points on the arc from MVP to B. Investors want to hold portfolios that lie on the efficient frontier because those portfolios maximize expected returns for any given level of volatility.

If the minimum rational investment in asset B is 25 percent, can we say that a portfolio containing 50 percent B would be even better? Not necessarily. The answer depends on the investor's tolerance for risk. A 50-50 portfolio plots on Figure 6.1 at point C. This portfolio provides a higher expected return than the MVP, but only at the cost of higher volatility. Some very risk-averse investors might decide that C's additional return is inadequate compensation for the extra risk, while other investors might take the opposite view. Portfolio theory says that no investor should choose an inefficient portfolio (lying between A and MVP), but choosing among efficient portfolios involves subjective assessments that vary from one investor to another.

THE EFFICIENT FRONTIER WITH MANY ASSETS

Figure 6.2 generalizes these concepts to a market with more than two investments. The arc and the area beneath it represent the new feasible set. Each point underneath the arc corresponds to a specific security. The feasible set simply consists of all possible portfolios of these assets. As before, the upward-sloping portion of the arc forming the northwest boundary of the feasible set is the efficient frontier. Inefficient portfolios in this figure include points such as D, E, and F. For each of these assets, a portfolio on the frontier exists offering a higher expected return for the same risk.

We must make two important points here. First, in describing the feasible set and efficient frontier in Figures 6.1 and 6.2, we have often used the terms "stock" or "share" to describe the individual investments available to investors. However, the important lessons of portfolio theory apply to the full universe of investment classes,

Figure 6.2
The Efficient Frontier
with Many Assets

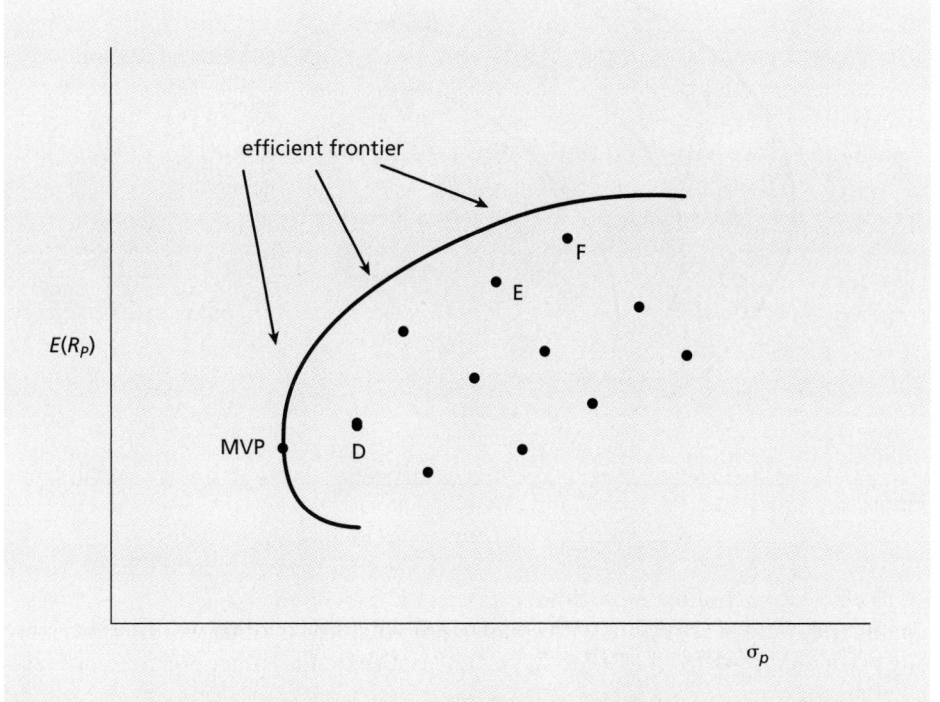

not just to common stocks. For example, the feasible set consists not only of portfolios that might be formed by purchasing shares in companies listed on the New York Stock Exchange, but also portfolios that include assets such as corporate and government bonds, real estate, and even exotic investments such as precious metals or art. Furthermore, there is no reason to restrict the feasible set to domestic investments. It also includes stocks and bonds that trade in foreign countries. Chapter 5 demonstrated that diversification reduces portfolio risk, and that lesson applies here. *The broader the range of investments included in the feasible set, the greater the risk reduction achievable through diversification.* Figure 6.3 illustrates the point by showing hypothetical efficient frontiers for different feasible sets encompassing an expanding array of investment choices.

A second important lesson to glean from this section relates to the concepts of systematic and unsystematic risk from Chapter 5. Examine point D in Figure 6.2. Because D lies beneath the efficient frontier, another asset or portfolio exists that dominates D, meaning that it offers a higher return for the same volatility. If that is the case, you might ask, how can asset D survive in the market if no one wants to own it? The answer is subtle. Although it would not be wise for an investor to hold asset D in isolation, it does not follow logically that investors will avoid D entirely. In fact, investors may need to hold some fraction of their wealth in D to construct a portfolio that lies on the efficient frontier. For example, suppose that asset D exhibits very low correlation with the other assets in the feasible set. Adding such an asset to a portfolio reduces the portfolio's level of systematic risk. In that case, investors will be willing to hold asset D as part of their portfolios even if it offers a relatively low return.[1]

Figure 6.3
The Effect of Expanding the Set of Investment Alternatives on the Efficient Frontier (EF)

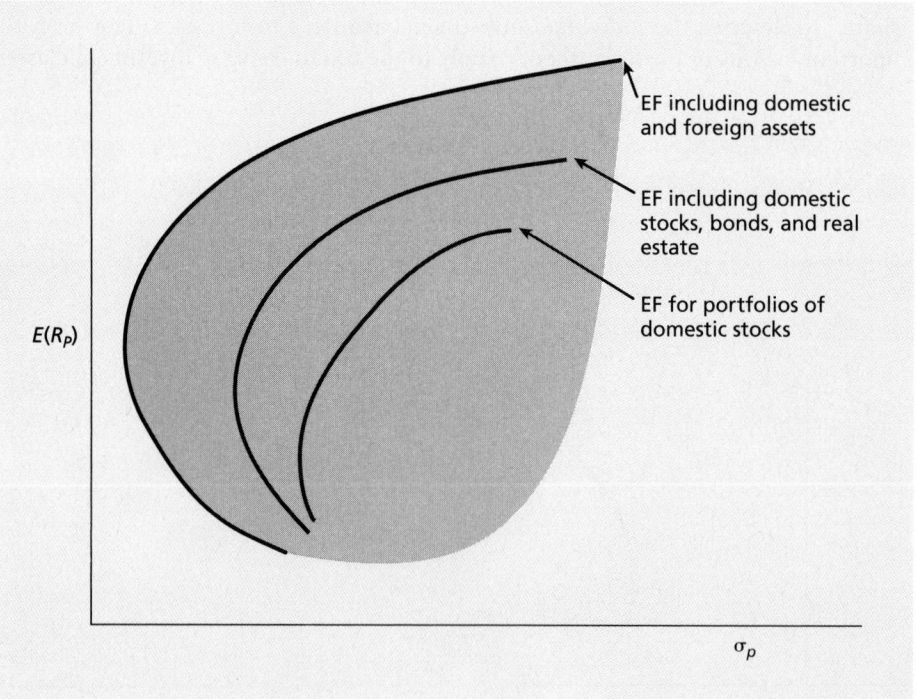

[1] In other words, the risk of a portfolio that contains asset D is less than it would be if asset D were removed. Insurance provides a more concrete example of this phenomenon. Because fire and casualty insurance companies price their policies to make a profit, the average purchaser of fire insurance loses money. As a consequence, purchasers of fire insurance can expect negative returns on their policies, on average. Is it irrational to buy fire insurance? Absolutely not. A fire

APPLYING THE MODEL 6.1

A few simple calculations illustrate the main points to take away from this section. Chapter 5 examined the risk-and return characteristics of two different portfolios, one containing shares of Mead Corp. and Boise Cascade, and the other made up of shares of Nike and Arrow International. Table 6.1 calculates the expected monthly return and standard deviation for 16 different portfolios consisting of various combinations of these four stocks.[2] Figure 6.4 plots the expected return and standard deviation for each portfolio. Notice how closely the shape of the set in this figure resembles those shown in Figures 6.2 and 6.3. You could trace the boundary of this set by drawing lines connecting portfolios 2 through 8 in the figure, and the upward-sloping portion of that boundary (including portfolios 3, 4, and 8) would roughly trace out the efficient frontier.

Take a moment to examine a few inefficient portfolios lying beneath the efficient frontier. Portfolio 9, for example, is clearly inferior to portfolios 3 and 4, both of which offer higher returns and lower standard deviations than portfolio 9. For the same reason, portfolio 5 dominates portfolios 11–12 and 14–16.

Portfolio 1, consisting entirely of Arrow International stock, falls well below the efficient frontier. Does this mean investors should stay away from Arrow stock? Not

Table 6.1
Expected Return (per month) and Standard Deviation for Various Portfolios

	Percentage Invested in Each Stock				Portfolio Characteristics	
Portfolio Number	Boise Cascade	Mead Corp.	Nike	Arrow International	Expected Return (per month)	Standard Deviation
1	0	0	0	100	1.08	8.42
2	50	0	0	50	0.98	5.34
3	25	0	25	50	1.28	4.37
4	0	0	50	50	1.57	5.12
5	0	25	50	25	1.58	8.14
6	10	10	70	10	1.75	10.99
7	5	5	85	5	1.91	12.70
8	0	0	100	0	2.06	14.53
9	0	50	0	50	1.09	6.95
10	25	25	25	25	1.28	7.31
11	20	20	40	20	1.44	8.17
12	50	0	50	0	1.47	10.93
13	0	50	50	0	1.59	11.88
14	100	0	0	0	0.88	9.88
15	50	50	0	0	0.99	11.12
16	0	100	0	0	1.11	13.00

Note: Portfolios 3 through 8 are efficient portfolios.

insurance policy pays off big at precisely the time that the value of an investor's home declines sharply (i.e., when the home is reduced to ashes). For most people, a home represents a significant fraction of total wealth. Because the correlation between the return on a home and the return on a fire insurance policy is negative, combining them in a portfolio makes sense. Fire insurance reduces overall portfolio risk, even though most individuals can expect to lose money on the fire insurance component of their portfolios.

2. The data for these calculations come from Table 5.4.

Figure 6.4
Expected Return (per month) and Standard Deviation for Various Portfolios

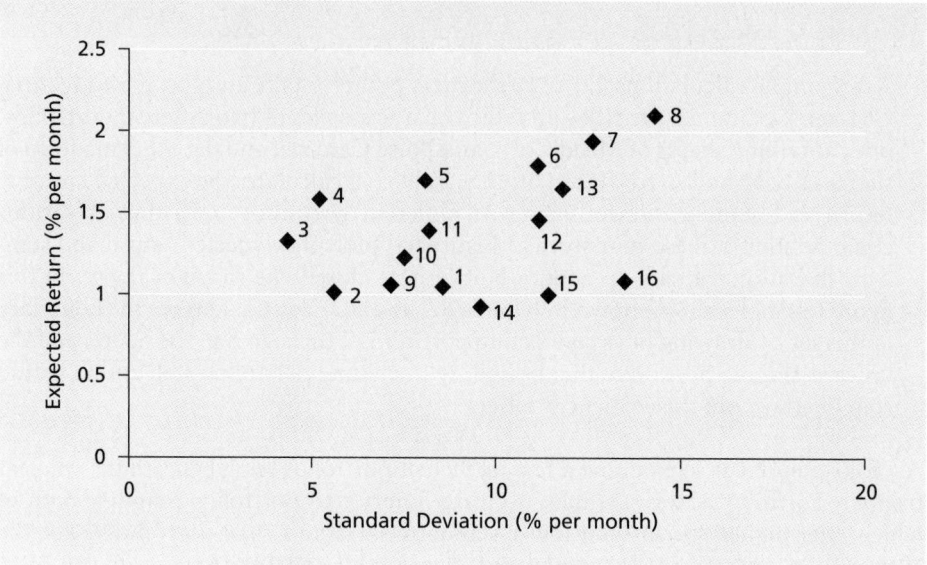

at all. Notice that portfolios 3 and 4, both of which lie on the efficient frontier, contain significant investments in Arrow. Arrow's returns are negatively correlated with returns on each of the other three stocks, so when investors mix Arrow shares with other stocks, the resulting portfolios benefit from diversification. Notice that the portfolios containing no Arrow shares fall below the frontier, again with the exception of portfolio 8.[3] By itself, Arrow International looks like a bad investment, offering relatively low returns and relatively high risk. But Arrow shines in a portfolio!

Concept Review Questions

1. Is the minimum variance portfolio always an efficient portfolio? Is an efficient portfolio always the minimum variance portfolio?

2. An efficient portfolio is one that maximizes expected return for any given level of risk. Is it equivalent to define an efficient portfolio as one that minimizes risk for any level of expected return?

3. What effect does expanding the types of assets included in the feasible set have on the efficient frontier?

4. Examine portfolio 10 in Table 6.1 and Figure 6.4. This portfolio contains equal investments in all four stocks. Why do you think it falls below the efficient frontier?

6.2 RISK-FREE BORROWING AND LENDING

PORTFOLIOS OF RISKY AND RISK-FREE ASSETS

By plotting the expected return and standard deviation for portfolios of two or more assets, we have seen that these portfolios define a set with a curved boundary. The lower the correlation between the assets in the portfolio, the more this boundary

---

[3.] Investors wanting to create a portfolio with the highest possible expected return have just one choice—invest everything in the stock with the highest expected return, Nike. However, that conclusion will change in the next section when we allow investors to borrow and lend when forming portfolios.

curves back toward the y-axis. Now we introduce a new possibility. What happens if investors can add a risk-free investment to their portfolios?

By definition, the expected return equals the actual return on a risk-free investment. That is, investors holding this asset get exactly the return they expected when they bought it. There is no uncertainty about what return the asset will generate. In reality, no investment is completely free of risk, but an investment such as a U.S. Treasury bill comes very close to that ideal. Keep in mind that when they buy U.S. T-bills, investors lend money to the government, albeit on a very short-term basis.

For now, assume that a truly risk-free investment exists. Denoting its return by R_f, we can write the following equations:

$$E(R_f) = R_f$$

$$\text{Var}(R_f) = \sigma_{Rf}^2 = 0$$

$$\text{Std. dev. } (R_f) = \sigma_{Rf} = 0$$

Imagine that an investor currently holds a diversified mutual fund of risky securities with an expected return equal to $E(R_{MF})$ and a variance of σ_{MF}^2. We can treat this mutual fund as a single asset. Now form a portfolio by investing w_{Rf} percent in the risk-free asset and w_{MF} percent in the mutual fund. You can derive the expected return and variance of this new, two-asset portfolio using the standard equations for any two-asset portfolio:

$$E(R_p) = w_{Rf}R_f + w_{MF}R_{MF}$$

$$\text{Var}(R_p) = \sigma_p^2 = (w_{Rf})^2\sigma_{Rf}^2 + (w_{MF})^2\sigma_{MF}^2 + 2(w_{Rf})(w_{MF})\text{Cov}(R_f, R_{MF})$$

Because the risk-free asset's return has no variance, $\sigma_{Rf}^2 = 0$. Likewise, if the risk-free return is constant, it cannot covary with any other asset, so $\text{Cov}(R_f, R_{MF}) = 0$. Therefore, the equation for the variance of a portfolio consisting of a risky asset and a risk-free asset reduces to the following:

$$\text{Var}(R_p) = \sigma_p^2 = (w_{MF})^2\sigma_{MF}^2$$

Taking the square root to obtain the standard deviation of this portfolio results in the following:

$$\sigma_p = w_{MF}\sigma_{MF}$$

The standard deviation of this two-asset portfolio increases linearly as the fraction invested in the risky asset increases. Geometrically, that means that portfolios of risky and risk-free assets lie along the straight line shown in Figure 6.5. Point A in the figure represents a portfolio invested 50 percent in the risk-free asset and 50 percent in the risky asset. But what about point B? How can investors form portfolios of risky and risk-free assets that lie above and to the right of the risky asset, MF?

The answer is that investors can borrow money and invest the proceeds in risky assets. Consider an individual who has $1,000 to invest. Assume that the risk-free asset pays 6 percent and the expected rate of return on the mutual fund she wants to buy is 12 percent, with a standard deviation of 30 percent. She could put all of her money in the risky asset and reach point MF in the figure, she could put all of it in the risk-free asset and reach point R_f, or she could buy some of both and reach an intermediate point

Figure 6.5
Portfolios of Risky and
Risk-Free Assets

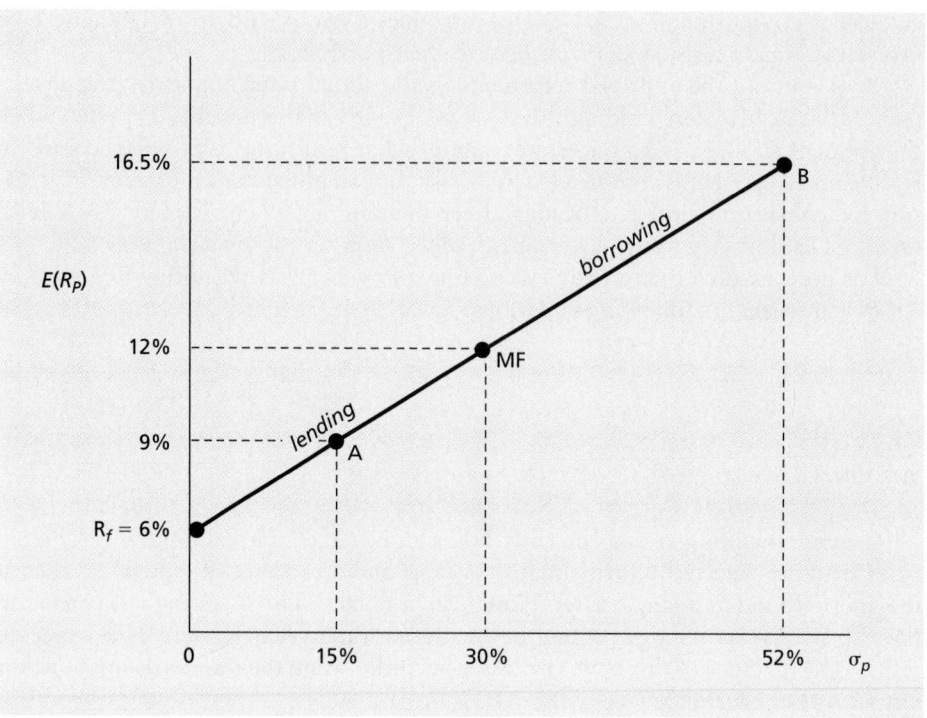

such as point A. But what if she can borrow money at 6 percent interest? By borrowing money and investing the proceeds in the risky asset, she can increase the fraction of her portfolio invested in *MF* to more than 100 percent. In other words, she invests all of her own money *plus* borrowed funds in the risky security. For instance, if she borrows $750 and invests it, she effectively invests 175 percent of her initial wealth in *MF*. The expected return on her portfolio is shown in the following equation:

$$E(R_p) = -0.75(6\%) + 1.75(12\%) = 16.5\%$$

The first term in this equation, $-0.75(6\%)$, reflects the fact that borrowing is just the opposite of lending. The investor borrows an amount equal to 75 percent of her initial wealth. The minus sign indicates that her return on these borrowed funds will be negative—she has to pay 6 percent interest on the amount she borrows. However, she reinvests the $750 (plus her own $1,000) in the mutual fund that has a higher expected return. Because the mutual fund's expected return exceeds the interest rate on her loan, she expects to magnify her rate of return relative to what she could earn using only her own money. In this case, her expected return is 16.5 percent.

Of course, the downside to all this is the risk that the *actual return* on the mutual fund may turn out to be less than expected. Suppose that the mutual fund earns a 0 percent return. At the end of the year, the total value of her portfolio will be just what it was at the beginning, $1,750. Of this total, however, $795 belongs to the lender ($750 principal and $45 interest). Our investor, who began the year with $1,000, now has just $955, a loss of 4.5 percent. The general pattern that this numerical example illustrates is that the return on a portfolio financed with borrowed money fluctuates more than the return on the portfolio's underlying assets, as demonstrated by the following calculations.

If the mutual fund's return is	her return is
18%	27%
12%	16.5%
6%	6%
0%	−4.5%
−6%	−15%

To see how volatile this portfolio is, just use the equation for standard deviation:

$$\sigma_p = w_{MF}\sigma_{MF} = 1.75(30\%) = 52.5\%$$

The lesson here is straightforward. *The greater the amount of money invested in the risky asset, the higher will be the expected return and volatility of the portfolio. The greater the investment in the risk-free asset, the lower will be the portfolio's volatility and return.*

FINDING THE OPTIMAL PORTFOLIO

The opportunity to borrow and lend at the risk-free rate fundamentally changes an investor's portfolio-selection problem. In a world with only risky assets, risk-averse investors search for portfolios that lie on the efficient frontier, then select from that set of portfolios the one that best matches their tolerance for risk. Though all investors can rule out many portfolios as inefficient (e.g., those underneath the frontier), there can be no agreement on which of the portfolios on the frontier is best. It is a matter of individual taste.

Figure 6.6 demonstrates how adding a risk-free asset alters the picture. The graph shows the familiar feasible set and efficient frontier. Point R_f on the vertical axis indicates the return available on the risk-free security. In this world, any investor can form a portfolio consisting of the risk-free asset and any other risky portfolio. For instance, the line marked L_1 represents all portfolios that an investor might create by combining the risk-free asset with risky portfolio X. Notice that some of these portfolios lie outside the old feasible set, meaning that the availability of a risk-free security opens up new investment opportunities.

The portfolios that lie along line L_1 are inferior to those on line L_2, formed by combining the risk-free asset with risky portfolio Y. For any portfolio on line L_1, a portfolio exists on line L_2 that has the same standard deviation and a higher expected return. But other portfolios exist that dominate those on line L_2. Only when investors reach line L_3, combining the risk-free asset with risky portfolio M, have they maximized the expected return on their portfolio for a given standard deviation. In other words, *line L_3 defines a new efficient frontier*. Risky portfolios X and Y, which lie along the old efficient frontier in a world without a risk-free asset, are no longer efficient. To reach this new efficient frontier, investors first search for the point of tangency on the line connecting the risk-free asset to the old efficient frontier. That is, investors endeavor to determine the composition of portfolio M. Next, investors allocate their wealth between portfolio M and the risk-free asset according to their risk preferences. This amounts to deciding where on the line they want their portfolios to lie. Investors who are very risk averse will invest heavily in the risk-free asset, thereby locating their portfolios near the *y*-axis. Investors who are less risk averse will

SMART IDEAS VIDEO

Andrew Karolyi, The Ohio State University
"Investors who seek to diversify internationally to reduce their global risk can leave money on the table if they ignore the unique industrial compositions of markets."

See the entire interview at
SMARTFinance

Figure 6.6
A New Efficient Frontier
*When individuals can
invest in both risky and
risk-free securities, a
new efficient frontier
emerges. The new
efficient frontier is
defined by a line that
starts at point R_f and is
tangent to the old
frontier.*

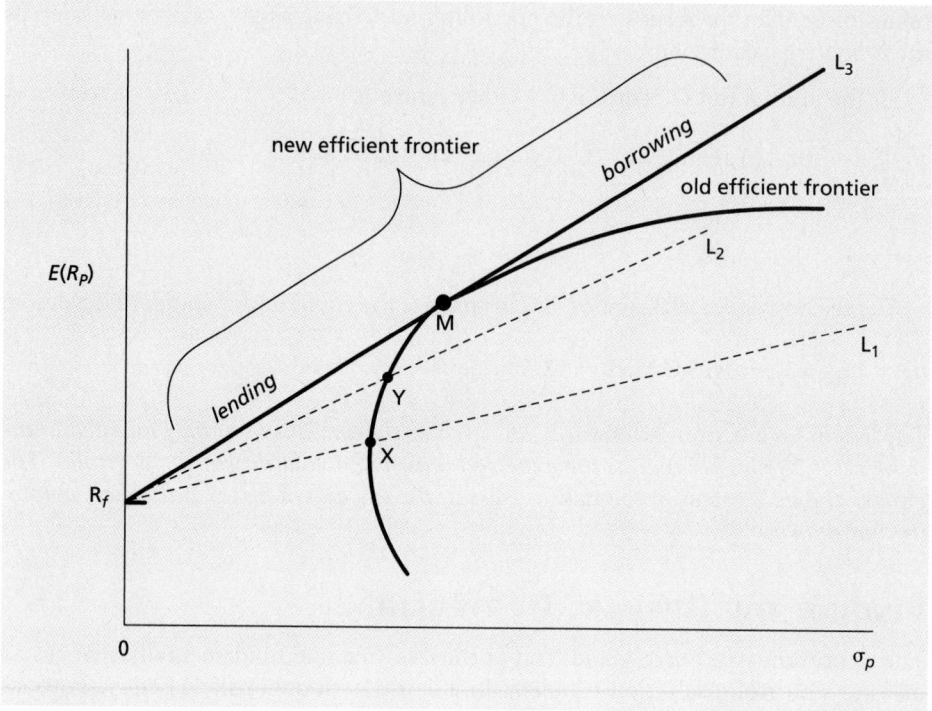

allocate more of their money to the risky asset, perhaps even borrowing money to structure a portfolio lying to the right of point M.[4]

APPLYING THE MODEL 6.1

Suppose that Rachel can borrow or lend at the risk-free rate of 3 percent. She needs to decide which of seven risky portfolios she should hold in combination with a position in the risk-free asset. Figure 6.7 plots the standard deviation and expected return of each portfolio. To determine which portfolio is best, she draws a line from the risk-free rate to each dot in the figure and chooses the line with the highest slope. As the figure indicates, the portfolio with a standard deviation of 19 percent and an expected return of 15 percent maximizes the slope. Investing money in any of the other portfolios is irrational. They offer lower returns for any level of risk than can be achieved by choosing a portfolio on this line.

To see this point more clearly, it is useful to derive the equation of the line in Figure 6.7. Two points in the figure, the first at coordinates [$\sigma_p = 0\%$, $E(R) = 3\%$] and the second at [$\sigma_p = 19\%$, $E(R) = 15\%$], determine this line. Its slope equals the difference in expected returns divided by the difference in standard deviations between the two points:

$$\text{Slope} = \frac{(15\% - 3\%)}{(19\% - 0\%)} = 0.632$$

[4.] Economists refer to this process of first finding portfolio M and then deciding how to allocate funds between M and the risk-free asset as the two-fund separation principle. When a risk-free asset exists, the optimal strategy for all investors is to invest some money in M and some in the risk-free security. The only thing that changes from one investor to another is how much to invest in each type of asset.

Figure 6.7
Finding the Optimal
Portfolio

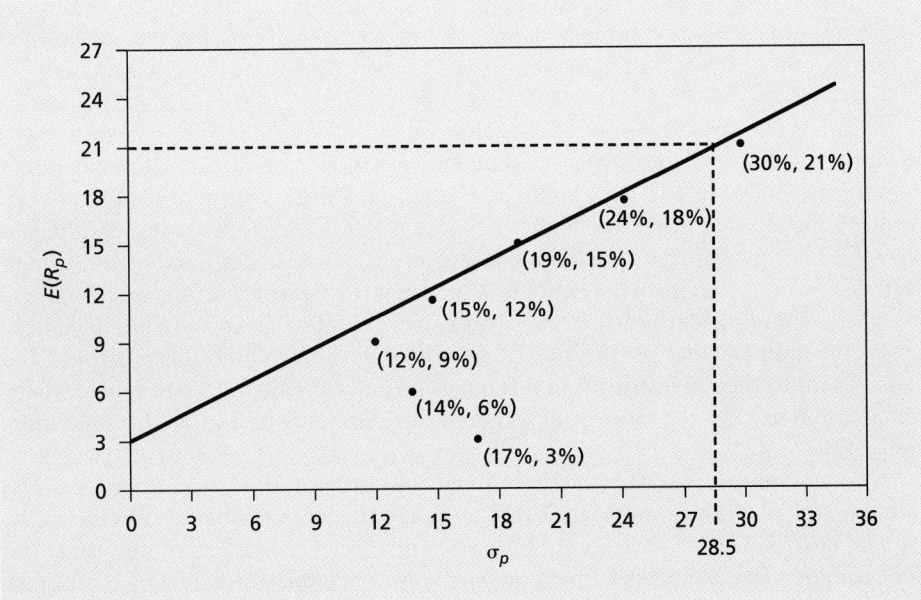

Because the intercept occurs at the risk-free rate, the equation of the line is as follows:

$$E(R_p) = 3\% + \left[\frac{(15\% - 3\%)}{(19\%)} \right] \sigma_p = 0.03 + 0.632\sigma_p$$

The terms $E(R_p)$ and σ_p in this equation refer to the expected return and standard deviation of a portfolio lying on the line. Every portfolio on this line reflects some mixture of the risk-free asset and the "optimal" risky portfolio. Investors can alter the mix of risky and risk-free assets according to their own tolerance for risk.

Suppose that Rachel, who has a very high tolerance for risk, reasons that she should hold the risky portfolio with the highest expected return (i.e., the one appearing in the top right portion of the figure). This portfolio offers a return of 21 percent, much higher than the "optimal" portfolio identified previously. Rachel might ask, "If I don't mind the fact that this portfolio has a standard deviation of 30 percent, why would I bother investing in something with a lower expected return?"

The answer is that another approach exists that allows Rachel to construct a portfolio with the same expected return, 21 percent, but with less risk. Start by determining how to create a portfolio of the risk-free asset and the "optimal" portfolio to achieve a 21 percent return. Let w represent the fraction invested in the risk-free asset, leaving $(1 - w)$ to be invested in the optimal portfolio:

$$E(R_p) = 21\% = w(3\%) + (1 - w)(15\%)$$

$$w = -0.5 = -50\%$$

Rachel should borrow an amount equal to 50 percent of her wealth, allowing her to invest 150 percent in the optimal portfolio. What will be the standard deviation of this new portfolio? It equals the standard deviation of the risky portfolio times the fraction invested in that portfolio:

$$\sigma_p = 1.5(19\%) = 28.5\%$$

Figure 6.7 highlights the advantage of this portfolio. By borrowing funds and investing them in the optimal risky portfolio, Rachel achieves her target expected return, but with a standard deviation of 28.5 percent rather than 30 percent.

Before going on, let us summarize what we know so far. Because all risky assets are not perfectly correlated, investors should diversify. Diversification allows investors to eliminate unsystematic risk. Some diversified portfolios will perform better than others in the sense of providing higher expected returns for the same standard deviation. We call these efficient portfolios. However, if investors can borrow and lend at the risk-free rate, then from the entire feasible set of risky portfolios, one portfolio will emerge that maximizes the return investors can expect for a given standard deviation. This is the **optimal risky portfolio.** All investors will want to hold this portfolio, and they will adjust their investments in this portfolio and the risk-free asset to achieve the combination of expected return and standard deviation that best suits their individual preferences.

How do you go about finding that optimal risky portfolio? We have good news and bad news for you. The good news is that although the mathematics of solving for the optimal portfolio gets a little complex, many software packages can do the computations for you. The bad news is that you have to provide the software with a set of inputs that in themselves present a challenge. Specifically, to determine the composition of the optimal portfolio, you need to know the expected return and standard deviation for every risky asset, as well as the covariance between every pair of assets. Even taking the simple approach of estimating these quantities using historical data involves a lot of number crunching.

As we will see later in this chapter, the *capital asset pricing model (CAPM)* tells us the composition of the optimal portfolio from a theoretical standpoint. Recognizing that everyone engages in the same search for an optimal portfolio, the CAPM makes certain assumptions about investors' information to derive its prediction for the composition of that portfolio. Those assumptions lead to a novel and practical way to assess the expected return of any risky asset by using beta to measure its sensitivity to the optimal portfolio.

Concept Review Questions

5. If the covariance between two risky assets is zero, portfolios of these two assets will lie along a backward-bending curve. The covariance between a risky and a risk-free asset is zero, yet portfolios of these two assets lie along a straight line. Explain.

6. Explain how investors can use leverage (i.e., borrowed money) to increase both the expected return and the risk of their portfolios.

7. How does an investor's portfolio-selection problem change when risk-free borrowing and lending is possible?

8. Explain the following statement: With risk-free borrowing and lending, there is only one optimal risky portfolio, but there are still many efficient portfolios.

6.3 EQUILIBRIUM AND THE MARKET PORTFOLIO

THE MARKET PORTFOLIO

The preceding analysis suggests that all investors should search for the composition of the optimal portfolio. That search begins when investors form estimates of the expected returns, standard deviations, and covariances for all risky assets in the economy. Think for a moment about how investors might arrive at these estimates. First, they might look at the historical record to see how asset prices moved in the past. To conduct this analysis, they will use one of the websites providing historical data on stock returns or purchase the data directly from a vendor, such as the Center for Research on Securities Prices. Second, they may examine other sources of public information, such as documents available from the Securities and Exchange Commission's EDGAR database (http://www.sec.gov/edgar.shtml). Third, they could listen to the opinions of analysts in the media or subscribe to one of the popular investment newsletter services. The point is, in their search for the optimal portfolio, investors will sift through more or less the same information sources to arrive at their estimates of expected returns, standard deviations, and covariances.

Recognizing that most investors have access to similar types of information, economists ask what happens if all investors reach the same conclusions from their analyses. That is, if all investors have access to the same information, perhaps their estimates of the inputs needed to solve for the optimal portfolio are identical. Although it is clearly true that differences of opinion exist from one investor to another, economists adopt the assumption of **homogeneous expectations** as a way to consider how the market will reach equilibrium.

If all investors agree on the risk-and-return characteristics of specific assets, then they will all agree on the shape of the efficient frontier. Given knowledge of the risk free rate, every investor will find the same point of tangency with the efficient frontier—that is, the same optimal portfolio. Because that portfolio allows investors to maximize expected return for any level of standard deviation, all investors want to hold it.

In economics, equilibrium occurs in a market when the market price equates the quantity demanded and supplied of a good. If all investors want to hold the same portfolio, then equilibrium requires that to be the portfolio supplied by the market. Economists refer to this portfolio, designated by point M in Figure 6.6, as the **market portfolio.** In theory, the market portfolio literally consists of every available asset, with each asset weighted by its market value relative to the total market value of all assets. In practice, no such portfolio exists, but we can approximate it with a value-weighted, diversified portfolio of many different assets, such as the Standard & Poor's 500 Stock Index.

THE CAPITAL MARKET LINE

Under the assumption of homogeneous expectations, portfolio M in Figure 6.6 receives a special designation, the market portfolio. Similarly, the line connecting point M to the risk-free rate, L_3, is referred to as the **capital market line (CML).** The *CML* quantifies the relationship between the expected return and standard deviation for portfolios consisting of the risk-free asset and the market portfolio, using Equation 6.1:

$$E(R_p) = R_f + \left\{ \frac{[E(R_m) - R_f]}{\sigma_m} \right\} \sigma_p \qquad \text{(Eq. 6.1)}$$

This equation indicates that the expected return on any portfolio, $E(R_p)$, equals the risk-free rate plus a premium that depends on the portfolio's risk, σ_p. The term in brackets measures the risk premium on the market portfolio relative to its standard deviation. Sometimes called the reward-to-risk ratio, or the **market price of risk,** this term is what investors try to maximize as they search for the optimal risky portfolio. Risk-averse investors want as much reward as they can obtain for a given level of risk.

The *CML* defines the efficient frontier when investors have homogeneous expectations and can borrow and lend at the risk-free rate. Investors should hold no portfolios other than those located on the *CML*. But what does this imply regarding the expected return and risk for individual assets? The capital asset pricing model, to which we now turn, answers this question.

9. Do investors want to maximize or minimize the market price of risk? Why?

10. Refer to the equation for the *CML*. Is it possible to construct a portfolio such that σ_p exceeds σ_m? How?

6.4 THE CAPITAL ASSET PRICING MODEL (CAPM)

THE SECURITY MARKET LINE

The basic CAPM was developed almost simultaneously during the mid-1960s by William Sharpe (1964), John Lintner, and Jan Mossin (1966), and was quickly embraced by academic researchers. Finance practitioners took somewhat longer to accept the model, but it was ultimately hailed as a simple and powerful tool to measure expected (or required) returns on risky assets. The reason for this enthusiasm is not hard to understand—for the first time, researchers and practitioners alike had a model that generated testable predictions about the risk-and-return characteristics of individual assets by specifying how they would covary with the market portfolio.

The formal development of the CAPM requires several assumptions about investors and markets. Rather than present a detailed list of these assumptions, we present the logic of the CAPM as it flows from the material we have covered so far.

1. Investors are risk averse and require higher returns on riskier investments.
2. Because investors can diversify, they care only about the systematic risk of any investment.
3. The market offers no reward for bearing unsystematic risk.
4. Some portfolios are better than others. Portfolios that maximize expected return for any level of risk are efficient portfolios.
5. If investors can borrow and lend at the risk-free rate, then there exists a single risky portfolio that dominates all others. Only portfolios consisting of the risk-free asset and the optimal risky portfolio are efficient.
6. If investors have homogeneous expectations, they will agree on the composition of the optimal portfolio and unanimously demand it. In equilibrium, the optimal portfolio will be the market portfolio.
7. The central insight of the CAPM is that if all investors hold the market portfolio, when they evaluate the risk of any specific asset, they will be concerned with the covariance of that asset with the overall market. The implication is that any measure of an asset's systematic risk exposure must capture how it covaries with the rest of the market. An asset's beta provides a quantitative measure of this risk, and therefore the CAPM predicts a positive, linear relationship between expected return and beta.

The **capital asset pricing model (CAPM)** indicates that the expected return on a specific asset, $E(R_i)$, equals the risk-free rate plus a premium that depends on the asset's beta, β_i, and the expected risk premium on the market portfolio, $E(R_m) - R_f$:

$$E(R_i) = R_f + \beta_i[E(R_m) - R_f] \tag{Eq. 6.2}$$

Recall that beta measures an asset's sensitivity to a broader portfolio, in this case the market portfolio. The higher the beta of a security, the greater the security's exposure to systematic risk and the higher the expected return it must offer investors. Though there are three variables on the right-hand side of the CAPM equation—R_f, β_i, and $E(R_m)$—only beta changes from one security to the next. For that reason, analysts classify the CAPM as a **single-factor model,** meaning that just one variable explains differences in returns across securities.

Figure 6.8 plots the CAPM equation on a diagram with the expected return on the y-axis and beta on the x-axis. The intercept of this line is R_f, and its slope is $E(R_m) - R_f$. According to the CAPM, the equilibrium expected returns of all securities must plot on this line, called the **security market line** (**SML**). An asset that offered an expected return above the line, like asset A, would be under-priced. Investors would snap up this stock, driving up its price and driving down its expected return down until it reached the line. Conversely, if an asset's expected return fell below the line, as depicted by point B, then it would be overpriced. Investors would divest their holdings of this asset, driving its price down and its expected return up.

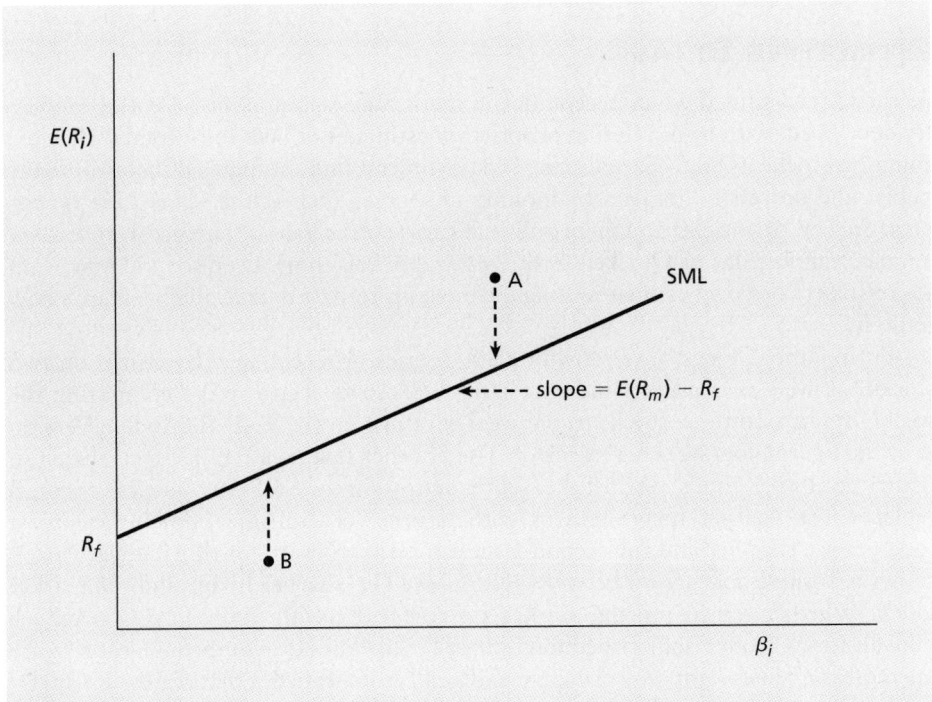

Figure 6.8
The Security Market Line
*In equilibrium, all assets
should be on the SML.*

APPLYING THE MODEL 6.2

Suppose that the risk-free rate is 5 percent and the expected return on the market portfolio is 13 percent. If a particular stock has a beta of 1.5, what is its expected return?

$$E(R) = 5\% + 1.5(13\% - 5\%) = 17\%$$

Because this stock has a relatively high beta, its expected return exceeds the expected return of the market portfolio. What if the stock had a beta of 1.0?

$$E(R) = 5\% + 1.0(13\% - 5\%) = 13\%$$

In this case, the stock displays average systematic risk, so its expected return equals the market portfolio's return. Finally, suppose that you could find a stock with a beta of 0.0:

$$E(R) = 5\% + 0.0(13\% - 5\%) = 5\%$$

SMART CONCEPTS
See the concept explained step-by-step at
SMARTFinance

Here the expected return equals the risk-free rate. Does that mean that this stock is identical to a Treasury bill? Not exactly. An investor who buys a Treasury bill and holds it to maturity earns a certain, nominal return. Not so with a zero beta stock. The realized return on the stock is not locked in like the return on a T-bill. However, if the stock has a zero beta, it has zero exposure to systematic risk, and its returns fluctuate independently of market returns. Because the stock carries no systematic risk, it can offer an equilibrium expected return equivalent to a risk-free government security.

ESTIMATING BETAS

As the CAPM gained wider acceptance in the business community, a cottage industry developed, with firms offering proprietary estimates of beta for virtually all listed common stocks in the U.S. markets. Today you can find estimates of betas in many public and university libraries by looking in sources such as the *Value Line Investment Survey,* or you can find them online at sites such as Yahoo! Finance (http://www.finance.yahoo.com) or Quicken (http://www.quicken.com). Even so, you may want to construct your own estimates using the most up-to-date data available. Here's how to do it.

From Yahoo! Finance we downloaded a series of recent weekly returns on two stocks, as well as a market index. Figure 6.9 shows scatter plots comparing the weekly returns on these stocks to the weekly return on the S&P 500 Index. Version A of the figure plots weekly returns on The Sharper Image, a retailer specializing in luxury consumer goods, against the weekly return on the S&P 500 Index. Version B replaces The Sharper Image returns with returns on ConAgra Foods, the largest food-service supplier and the second-largest food retailer in North America. Part A shows a positive correlation between returns on The Sharper Image and the market index. Whether returns on the market are correlated with returns on ConAgra is difficult to say from visual inspection of Part B. The lines drawn through each figure are regression lines estimated using Excel. Recall from statistics that regression analysis identifies a line through a series of data points that minimizes the sum of squared

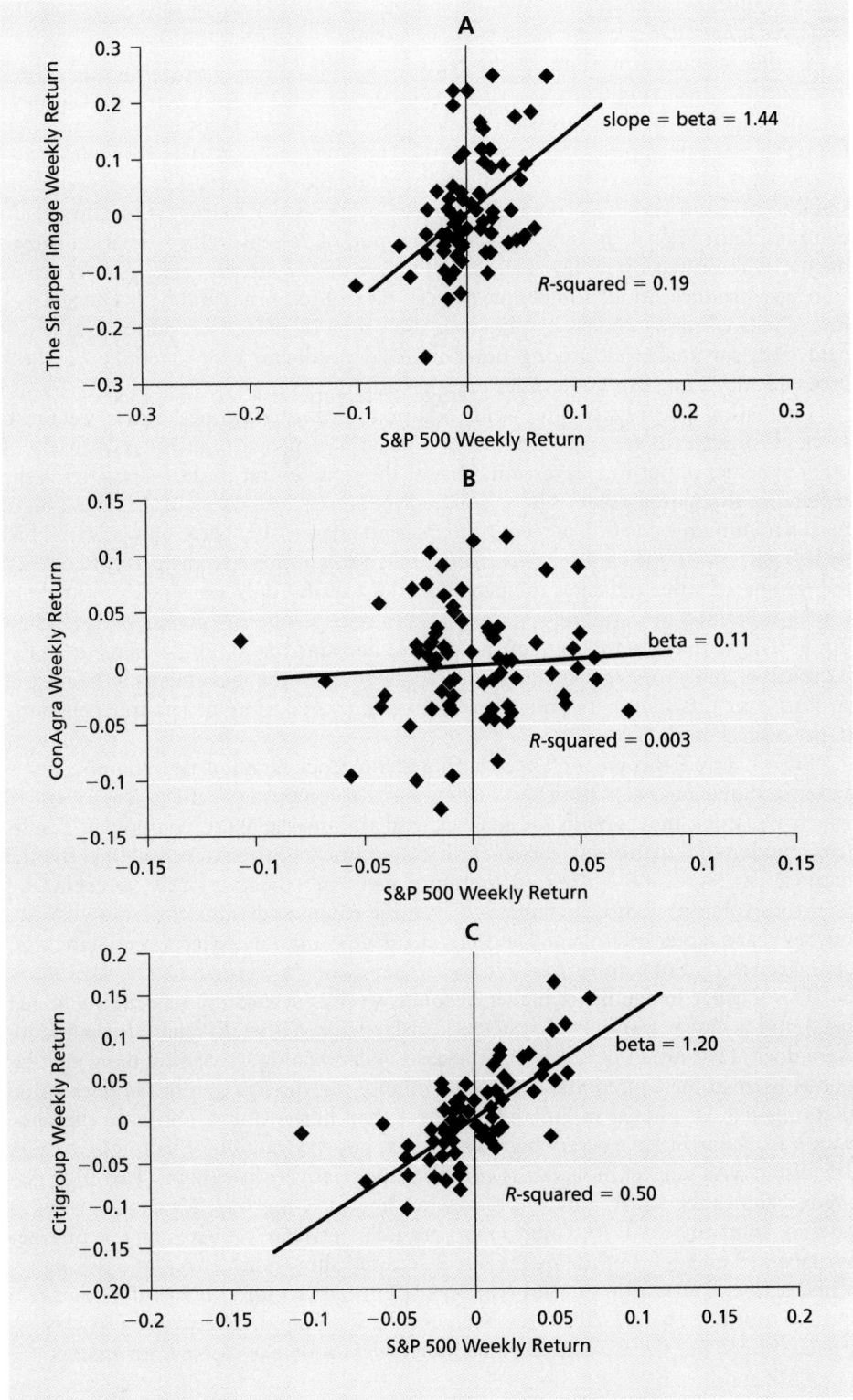

Figure 6.9
Scatterplots of Weekly
Returns for Sharper
Image, ConAgra, and
Citigroup, and the S&P
500 Index

errors or distances between the points and the line. The slope of the regression line indicates how much impact changes in one variable have on another.

In this instance, the slope of the regression lines indicates the extent to which movements in individual stocks are associated with movements in the overall market. In other words, the regression line's slope equals the stock's beta.[5] Notice that the regression line appears much steeper for The Sharper Image than for ConAgra — The Sharper Image has a higher beta. The general tendency is for The Sharper Image stock to perform very well (poorly) when the overall stock market is up (down). In contrast, returns on ConAgra stock display much less sensitivity to market movements, as indicated by its low beta of 0.11. But these patterns make perfect sense. ConAgra produces food, and people have to eat in good times and bad. The Sharper Image sells vibrating chairs, brushes that use ozone to reduce pet odors, and hand-held body-fat analyzers, among other unusual products. People indulge in these products much more in good times than in bad.

Estimating a regression line yields additional information besides the beta of a stock. Typically, the regression output produced by a program includes a variety of other statistics about the regression. One of the most useful of these statistics is the regression R-squared value. The R-squared measures "goodness of fit" and ranges from a minimum value of 0 percent (if there is no relationship between two variables) to 100 percent (if one variable is perfectly linked to another). In the present context, the R-squared value indicates the percentage of variability in the stock's return that can be explained by variability in the market's return. The R-squared values in Figure 6.9 show that fluctuations in the market account for about 19 percent of the movements in The Sharper Image and virtually none of the movements in ConAgra. At least over this sample period, ConAgra stock moved more or less independently of the overall market.

But what does this mean? The volatility of any stock contains two components — systematic and unsystematic risk. The systematic component reflects the extent to which the stock moves with the market, and the unsystematic component results from random fluctuations in the stock that are unrelated to (or unexplained by) the market. The regression R-squared, therefore, gives an indication of the percentage of an asset's volatility that is systematic. Given the R-squared values in Figure 6.9, we can say that a larger fraction of The Sharper Image's volatility reflects systematic risk, compared to that of ConAgra.

The Sharper Image has a higher absolute level of systematic risk (i.e., a higher beta) and a higher fraction of systematic risk (i.e., a higher R-squared) than ConAgra does. That need not always be the case. As an analogy, there are more cellular phone users in the United States than in Finland, but the fraction of the population that uses cellular phones in Finland is greater than in the United States. In the same way, a stock might have a very high (low) beta, but the fraction of its total volatility associated with market movements could still be relatively low (high). Part C of Figure 6.9 shows the scatterplot and regression line for Citigroup, a financial services holding company. At 1.20, Citigroup's beta falls between the betas of The Sharper Image and ConAgra, but the regression R-squared shows that systematic risk represents a larger proportion of total risk for Citigroup than for either of the other two firms. According to the CAPM, the beta, not the R-squared, determines a stock's expected return, but the R-squared value nonetheless provides useful information.

---

[5] Sometimes, analysts use net returns or excess returns rather than use actual returns to generate these plots. Thus, the y-axis would plot the actual return on a stock net of the risk-free rate, and the x-axis would show the net return on the market index.

To conclude this section, we mention some of the thorny issues encountered when estimating betas. To obtain the estimates in Figure 6.9, we used weekly data for each stock and for the market index, but we could have used data gathered at other frequencies as well (e.g., daily, monthly, or quarterly). The factors determining which type of data to use are somewhat subjective. For instance, from statistics we learn that larger samples often yield better estimates. But in the context of a financial market, collecting a larger sample may necessitate gathering data from more distant time periods. We collected 74 *weekly* observations spanning 1.5 years to form our beta estimates. Had we gathered the same number of *monthly* observations, our data would have covered more than 6 years. Over time, companies often change the mix of industries in which they compete by acquiring new businesses and divesting old ones. Consequently, data drawn from several years past may not reflect the current risks of a particular stock. Why not use 74 daily observations then? Illiquidity presents a problem when using daily data. Many stocks do not trade each and every day. On the average business day, slightly less than 2 percent of NYSE-listed stocks and about 10 percent of Nasdaq stocks do not trade at all. On days when no trading occurs, it is impossible to measure the return on the stock in the same way that it is hard for homeowners to know the value of their homes unless they sell them. Deciding which type of data to use when estimating a beta requires evaluating the trade-off between having the most up-to-date information about a stock (which argues for high frequency data) against having a large sample of returns (which argues for low frequency data). Practitioners using the CAPM in business and researchers testing the model both confront these trade-offs.

Concept Review Questions

11. Why does an underpriced asset lie above the security market line?

12. Running a regression with an individual asset's return as the dependent variable and the market's return as the independent variable yields two estimates of systematic risk: beta and *R*-squared. Explain how these relate to systematic risk and how they differ from each other.

13. You run regressions on two different stocks. One stock has a higher beta, and the other has a higher *R*-squared. Which stock would have a higher expected return according to the CAPM?

6.5 EMPIRICAL EVIDENCE ON THE CAPM

Since William Sharpe published his seminal paper on the CAPM, researchers have subjected the model to numerous empirical tests. Early on, most of these tests seemed to support the CAPM's main predictions. Over time, however, evidence mounted indicating that the CAPM had serious flaws. In this section, we briefly describe the most important findings from empirical tests of the CAPM, and in the sections that follow, we describe how asset pricing theory has evolved beyond the CAPM.

Testing the CAPM poses several challenges to researchers. First, the CAPM makes predictions about a variable that is inherently unobservable—the expected return on an asset. There is no database that measures the returns that investors expect when they trade securities. Researchers testing the CAPM must therefore invoke the assumption of **rational expectations,** which means that even if investors make mistakes when they form assessments about expected returns, their errors are not systematic.

In other words, if investors are not right all the time, they are at least correct on average. By assuming that investors have rational expectations, researchers can use realized historical returns as a proxy for expected returns.[6]

A second challenge arises because the CAPM is a one-period model. That is, the model describes the way investors form expectations one period ahead, but it does not address how those expectations might change from one period to the next. Similarly, the CAPM treats a security's beta as a constant, but researchers testing the model must contend with the possibility that betas can change over time as firms invest in new industries, alter their capital structures, or take other actions that can cause betas to change. Furthermore, the CAPM does not even specify what unit of time corresponds to "one period." The model offers researchers no guide about whether they should run their tests using daily, weekly, monthly, or even annual historical returns.

The third problem confronting empirical studies of the CAPM relates to the risk-free rate. Intuitively, we know that no investment is truly risk free like the investment contemplated in the CAPM, and the returns on the closest real-world proxies for the risk-free asset (e.g., Treasury securities) fluctuate over time rather than remain constant as the CAPM assumes. In addition, the CAPM is silent on whether researchers should use short-term Treasury bills or long-term Treasury bonds as a proxy for the risk-free rate.

The fourth—and perhaps the most difficult—problem that tests of the CAPM face involves the market portfolio. Recall that in the CAPM, the market portfolio is a value-weighted combination of every asset in the economy. The CAPM assumes that every asset in the economy is tradable, so investors who want to hold "the market" can easily do so. In practice, there is no index or other mechanism that allows investors to hold every asset in the economy in just the right proportion. Empirically, researchers have to use a proxy for the market portfolio, calculating individual security betas by calculating their covariance relative to this proxy. This implies that whether a test rejects or fails to reject the CAPM's predictions, researchers can never be certain whether their results truly reflect the model's strengths and weaknesses, or whether the results simply reflect the difficulties of measuring betas when the market portfolio is unobservable. And just as betas can fluctuate over time, so too can the expected risk premium on the market portfolio, further confounding empirical tests.

These difficulties notwithstanding, scholars have published dozens, perhaps hundreds of tests of the CAPM over the last four decades. To put these studies in context, we must first clarify which of the model's predictions one could test. First, the model shows that the relationship between betas and expected returns is linear, that the security market line (*SML*) should be a straight line rather than a curve. The model predicts that the slope of this line equals the expected risk premium on the market portfolio, and the line's intercept should equal the risk-free rate. Second, the CAPM asserts that no factor other than beta should be systematically related to expected returns. This means that if one were to run a regression with returns as the dependent variable and with a host of independent variables (including the stock's variance, its dividend yield, the company's historical growth rate, and so on), the only independent variable that should display a significant correlation with returns is beta.

[6.] Miller (1999) recounts the merciless ribbing that he and his corecipients (Harry Markowitz and William Sharpe) of the Nobel Prize in economics endured when they accepted their award in Stockholm. The physicists and chemists present at the awards ceremony were amused to hear Miller admit that the basic unit of their research, the expected return on an asset, could not be observed.

One of the earliest tests was conducted by Black, Jensen, and Scholes (1972). Their study found a positive relationship between beta and returns, just as the CAPM predicted. However, the difference in returns between high-beta and low-beta stocks was not as large as they expected. Put differently, the authors found that the *SML* was "too flat." A year later, Fama and MacBeth (1973) reported the disquieting result that the relationship between beta and returns was unstable. From one 5-year period to the next, betas seemed to fluctuate almost randomly, hardly comforting for practitioners using historical beta estimates to formulate investment strategies or to estimate the cost of capital for a corporation.

More than a decade later, more evidence of the CAPM's shortcomings emerged. Roll (1988) demonstrated that even with the benefit of hindsight, the CAPM could explain no more than 40 percent of the cross-sectional variation in stock returns. In Roll's "best-case scenario," more than half of the difference between stocks that earned high returns and those that earned low returns was still a mystery. In a series of later papers, Eugene Fama and Ken French (1992, 1996, 2002) argued that two other factors did a much better job explaining why some stocks earned higher returns than others. These factors were the size of the firm (as measured by its market capitalization) and the firm's book-to-market value ratio. Fama and French discovered that small firms earned consistently higher average returns than large firms, and similarly, firms with high book-to-market ratios earned higher returns than firms with low book-to- market ratios. Controlling for these two effects, Fama and French found almost no relationship between beta and returns. In other words, the *SML* was not just "too flat"; it was completely flat.[7]

Where does all of this leave us? From an academic point of view, the answer is uncertain. The empirical and theoretical shortcomings of the CAPM are by now well documented, and though the literature offers several alternative asset pricing models, none has emerged as the CAPM's clear heir apparent. As a matter of practice, however, the CAPM still reigns supreme in the corporate finance realm. Graham and Harvey (2001) show that corporations use the CAPM more than any other model to estimate the cost of equity capital. Likewise, professionals in the investment field do not neglect the CAPM. Most brokerage and investment advisory firms still offer estimates of betas as part of their service package. Whether that will be the case in another 10 or 20 years is anyone's guess. To prepare you for that uncertain future, we now briefly review two of the leading alternatives to the CAPM—arbitrage pricing theory (APT) and the Fama-French three-factor model (F-F).

---

14. What does it mean to say that early tests of the CAPM indicated that the *SML* was "too flat"?

15. Suppose that, on average, individuals become more risk averse during recessions and less risk averse during economic booms. How might this complicate tests of the CAPM?

Concept Review Questions

---

[7] Financial theorists made major improvements to the CAPM after it first appeared in 1964. Brennan (1970) developed a version of the CAPM that incorporated the possibility that investors might have to pay taxes on their returns. Mayers (1972) modified the model to allow for nontradable assets such as human capital. Merton (1973) extended the CAPM to a multiperiod setting, while Breeden (1979) refocused the CAPM on investors' consumption opportunities rather than wealth per se. Adler and Dumas (1983) added a global slant to the debate with their international asset pricing model. But critics of the CAPM were working on the theoretical dimension, too. Roll (1977) offered the best-known theoretical critique of the CAPM, arguing that the CAPM is not testable as long as the true market portfolio is unobservable.

6.6 ALTERNATIVES TO THE CAPM

ARBITRAGE PRICING THEORY

The earliest theory to receive widespread support as an alternative to the CAPM was the **arbitrage pricing theory (APT)**, developed in the mid-1970s by Stephen Ross (1976, 1977). Mathematically and intuitively more challenging than the CAPM, the APT begins with the notion that financial markets are frictionless. Investors can buy or sell short any of a large number of assets that trade in this market. **Short-selling** is a transaction in which an investor sells borrowed assets that must be returned to the lender of the assets at a later date. In the simplest case, short sales are made in an attempt to profit from an expected decline in a given asset's value.[8] The APT assumes that all investors know that returns on specific assets follow this simple relationship:

$$R = \alpha + \beta_1(\text{risk factor 1}) + \beta_2(\text{risk factor 2}) + \beta_3(\text{risk factor 3}) \cdots + \text{random error}$$

Unlike the CAPM, which is a single-factor model, the APT posits that asset returns are driven by a group of different factors. The APT specifies neither the identity nor the number of these factors (except for the restriction that the number of assets available must be much larger than the number of factors). The risk factors represent sources of systematic risk that cannot be diversified away. For example, unexpected fluctuations in oil prices, interest rates, inflation, exchange rates, or economic growth might be candidates for risk factors. Even fluctuations in the market portfolio could represent a significant risk factor, just as is the case in the CAPM. The APT leaves the identification of these factors as an empirical matter for researchers to sort out.

In the world of the APT, each asset can be affected by each risk factor. That is, each firm has its own set of "factor betas," just as each stock has its own beta in the CAPM. Also like the CAPM, each risk factor is associated with a risk premium. For example, if fluctuations in oil prices represent a source of systematic risk, then stocks that are sensitive to that factor will have to pay investors higher returns as compensation. This relationship can be summarized as follows:

$$R_i - R_f = \beta_{i1}(R_1 - R_f) + \beta_{i2}(R_2 - R_f) + \beta_{i3}(R_3 - R_f) + \cdots + \beta_{in}(R_n - R_f) \qquad \textbf{(Eq. 6.3)}$$

The left-hand side of this equation represents the risk premium on a particular asset. The betas reflect that particular asset's sensitivity to each of the factors, and the terms in parentheses stand for the risk premium associated with each factor.[9] You can see that if there is only one factor, the market factor, then this equation reduces to something that looks just like the CAPM.

Recall that the APT offers no guidance about what factors should be important, or even how many factors should be included in Equation 6.3. Empirical work on the APT suggests that between two and five factors are linked to stock returns, but

---

[8.] In Section 6.2, we discussed how lending and borrowing in combination with the optimal risky portfolio can be used to create a new efficient frontier. As an alternative to borrowing at the risk-free rate, an investor could sell the risk-free asset—assumed to be a 6 percent Treasury bill in the earlier example—short, and thereby effectively borrow risk-free money at a 6 percent T-bill rate. Therefore, short-selling a T-bill is equivalent to borrowing at the T-bill rate.

[9.] Technically, each term in parentheses represents the expected risk premium on a security with a beta equal to 1.0 for a particular factor and betas equal to 0.0 for all the other factors.

interpreting these factors can be tricky. If we observe, for example, that the difference between long-term and short-term bond yields is correlated with stock returns, we are left wondering why this is so. Is the correlation a sign of some deep, causal economic relationship, or is it a statistical fluke? Without additional theory, it is impossible to say, because the APT itself is silent on the question.

One avenue of empirical research that offers hope of yielding interpretable results is the **observable variables approach.** This involves estimating which macroeconomic variables significantly influence security prices. The foremost study adopting this approach is presented by Chen, Roll, and Ross (1986). They test whether unanticipated movements in various macroeconomic variables are risks that are priced in the stock market. They find that security prices are significantly related to (1) changes in industrial production; (2) the yield spread between long- and short-term interest rates (interpreted as a business-cycle proxy); (3) the yield spread between low- and high-grade bonds (interpreted as a proxy for overall business risk in the economy); and (4) changes in expected and unexpected inflation—though this is highly significant only during periods of pronounced inflation volatility. Perhaps most intriguing are the variables the authors find that are not significant. After they account for the macroeconomic factors, they find that the return on the overall stock market itself is not significant and there is no significant relationship between stock returns and aggregate consumption. Unfortunately, more recent tests using this approach have proven less successful.

THE FAMA-FRENCH (F-F) MODEL

We have already mentioned the criticisms leveled at the CAPM by Eugene Fama and Ken French in their series of papers beginning in the early 1990s. It is one thing to criticize a theoretical model, but it is another thing entirely to suggest an alternative. Fortunately, Fama and French did both. Fama and French (1992, 1996, 2002) sought to explain "the cross section of expected returns," or why some stocks earned higher average returns than others. They make two key points in attacking the CAPM and presenting their alternative. The first point is that two factors, the size of a firm and the ratio of the book value of its equity to its market value, are systematically related to returns. Looking back through the historical record, Fama and French found that small firms earned higher returns than large firms, even after holding beta constant, and firms with high book-to-market ratios (*value stocks*) outperformed firms with low book-to-market ratios (*glamour stocks*). The second point is that after controlling for firm size and market-to-book ratio, beta has little or no impact on returns. Why then did early tests of the CAPM indicate that high-beta stocks earned higher returns than low-beta stocks? Perhaps high-beta stocks tend to originate with small firms with high book-to-market ratios. Fama and French argue that if you look at a group of firms of similar size (and similar book-to-market ratio), within that group, high-beta stocks earn about the same returns as low-beta stocks.

The mathematical expression of the Fama-French (F-F) model looks very much like the APT with three factors:

SMART IDEAS VIDEO

Kenneth French, Dartmouth College

"The three-factor model is an application of the arbitrage pricing theory."

See the entire interview at **SMARTFinance**

$$R_i - R_f = \alpha + \beta_{i1}(R_m - R_f) + \beta_{i2}(R_{\text{small}} - R_{\text{big}}) + \beta_{i3}(R_{\text{high}} - R_{\text{low}}) \qquad \textbf{(Eq. 6.4)}$$

The risk premium on stock i equals a constant term, α, plus a risk premium that depends on the stock's sensitivity to each factor, and the risk premium associated with each factor. The term β_{i1} is the sensitivity of stock i to the market factor, and $(R_m - R_f)$ is the familiar risk premium on the market. β_{i2} is the stock's sensitivity to the size factor and $(R_{\text{small}} - R_{\text{big}})$ is the added expected return on small stocks compared to large stocks. Finally, β_{i3} represents the stock's sensitivity to the book-to market factor, with $(R_{\text{high}} - R_{\text{low}})$ representing the book-to-market risk premium. If the Fama-French model explains the cross section of expected returns, then the average value of α should be close to zero.

What really distinguishes the Fama-French approach from both the CAPM and the APT is that it is an entirely empirical attempt to model asset prices. Fama and French do not derive their pricing equation from a rigorous theoretical model as the other asset pricing models do; neither do they offer mathematical arguments for why these three factors (as opposed to some other set of factors) predict returns. Certainly, one can tell plausible stories to explain why small firms are riskier than large firms, or why firms with high book-to-market ratios are riskier than low book-to-market firms. For instance, a firm with very dim prospects, teetering on the edge of financial disaster, would probably have a very small market capitalization. That same firm might have a significant amount of equity "on the books" either from external financing raised in the past or from accumulated profits from earlier periods. In that case, the firm would not only be small, but would have a high book-to-market ratio. Such a firm would indeed be very risky and would be priced by the market to reflect a high expected return.[10]

But critics of Fama and French have their own stories. According to the three-factor model, a firm with a low book-to-market ratio is less risky and will offer lower returns than a firm with a high ratio. But what sorts of firms often have low book values and high market values (i.e., a low book-to-market ratio)? New firms, especially those in high-technology industries, often fit this description. In the late 1990s, stocks in the Internet sector had astronomical market values relative to their book values. Critics of Fama-French say that it is hard to conceive that investors viewed these as low-risk firms. Interestingly, some critics of the Fama-French model do not dispute the claim that a positive correlation exists between returns and book-to-market ratios, but they offer a different interpretation of that fact. Perhaps investors become too pessimistic about some firms, driving down their market values and pushing up their book-to-market ratios. Over time, investors learn that they underestimated these firms, and they drive prices back up. The reverse happens for low book-to-market firms, generating the positive correlation observed in the historical data.

Both the APT and Fama-French models share the view that other factors beyond the market factor affect asset returns. Some researchers have found that liquidity risk influences asset prices, with investors demanding higher returns on less liquid stocks (or stocks where the degree of liquidity is more uncertain). The Comparative Corporate Finance feature illustrates that one risk factor that may affect asset returns is the enforcement of insider trading regulations.

[10.] Students sometimes find it counterintuitive that a firm with poor prospects would be priced to offer a high return. It may help to think of junk bonds. When firms with outstanding debt get into financial trouble, their bonds may slip from investment grade to the junk category. As this happens, the price on the bonds declines, but the yield on the bond (interest paid divided by price) rises. An investor who buys such a bond earns a very high rate of return if the firm survives long enough to meet its debt obligations.

COMPARATIVE CORPORATE FINANCE

In a fascinating study, Bhattacharya and Daouk (2002) examined the existence and enforcement of insider trading regulations during the 20th century. The figure below plots the number of countries in the world, the number of countries with stock markets, the number of countries with restrictions on insider trading, and the number of countries with at least one enforcement action related to an insider trading violation. Though many countries officially prohibit insider trading, enforcement of insider trading regulations is spotty. Even in the United States, the first case involving federal insider trading laws occurred in 1961, 27 years after insider trading laws were passed.

What makes this study interesting is that Bhattcharya and Daouk try to measure the effect of the existence and enforcement of insider trading laws on expected equity returns. If a country's legal environment protects investors from insider trading, then perhaps they will perceive equity investing in that country to be less risky, resulting in a lower required return. It turns out that passing a law has no effect on equity returns, but enforcing a law lowers the required return on equity by as much as seven percent. In part, enforcement of insider trading laws appears to encourage more trading, which in turn makes a market more liquid. Improving liquidity also lowers the risk of investing in equities, adding an indirect channel by which law enforcement can systematically affect stock returns.

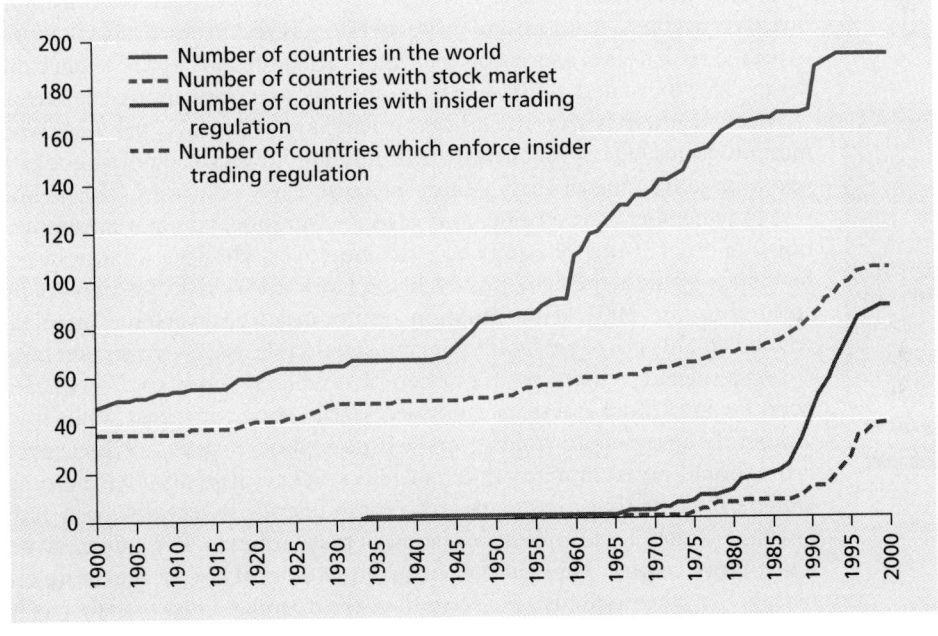

Concept Review Questions

16. Over time, firms with high book-to-market ratios earn higher returns than firms with low book-to-market ratios do. Offer two interpretations that might explain this pattern.

17. In what sense is it reasonable to say that the Fama-French model is really an application of arbitrage pricing theory?

6.7 THE CURRENT STATE OF ASSET PRICING THEORY

What is the state of asset pricing theory early in the twenty-first century? Theory provides us with several competing models to describe asset returns, but unfortunately, no clear leader among those models has emerged. Even so, there are several valuable conclusions that we can draw based on the material in this chapter and Chapter 5. First, investors demand compensation for taking risk because they are risk averse. This fact in itself is important to keep in mind as you think about market valuations. To see why, imagine that a cultural shift takes place, and investors generally become less risk averse. Why might this occur? Over time, more and more investors learn the basic facts presented in Table 5.1. In the United States, stocks have generally outperformed safer investments such as bonds by a wide margin, at least in the last 70+ years. Of course, there is no guarantee that the same pattern will emerge in the next 70 years, but presented with the historical evidence, many investors may become more comfortable with the idea of investing in stocks. Remember, the percentage of the population that owns stock has been increasing over time, in the United States and abroad. What is the implication of a decline in the population's aversion to risk? As risk aversion decreases, the compensation that a risky investment must offer to attract investors declines. As more and more investors invest in stocks, market prices rise and expected returns fall. Many commentators attribute part of the remarkable bull market in U.S. stocks in the 1990s to declining risk aversion among U.S. investors.

Second, there is widespread agreement that systematic risk drives returns. At a minimum, this tells us that investors should hold diversified portfolios rather than invest a large fraction of their wealth into just a few securities. This is important advice to remember as you begin your career. Over time, you may accumulate stock options or other forms of equity in your employer. Holding a large fraction of your financial wealth in the firm for which you work is very risky, as Enron employees discovered in late 2001. This situation results in an undiversified financial portfolio, which is highly correlated with your most valuable asset—your own human capital.

As a sidebar, we will point out here that when it comes to diversification, what is good for individual investors is not necessarily good for firms. While it is clearly advisable for investors to hold diversified portfolios, it does not logically follow that firms should invest in many different industries to diversify their holdings. An individual can diversify across many different industries at very low cost, perhaps by following a strategy as simple as investing in mutual funds. For a firm, diversification is much more costly. One way that firms often diversify is by acquiring existing businesses. But when one firm buys another, the acquirer must usually pay a significant premium over the target's market value to gain control. Furthermore, managers who are very successful at operating a firm in one line of business may be less successful in other industries. There may also be a kind of managerial capacity constraint that makes it difficult for firms to manage many different businesses at once. The bottom line is that because investors can diversify at low cost on their own, there is no reason for them to pay a premium for firms to diversity on their behalf. In fact, recent research in finance documents just the opposite, that investors tend to place lower values on diversified firms than on those that are more focused.[11]

SMART IDEAS VIDEO

Diane Denis, Purdue University
"At this point it's fairly well documented that diversified firms don't seem to do as well as undiversified firms."

See the entire interview at **SMARTFinance**

[11.] Servaes (1996) documents that diversified firms traded at a substantial discount during the 1960s, a finding corroborated in the 1980s by Lang and Stulz (1994). Lins and Servaes (1999) find that diversified firms in the United Kingdom and in Japan trade at 15 percent and 10 percent discounts, respectively, relative to undiversified firms. Rajan, Servaes,

Third, you can measure systematic risk in several different ways depending on the asset pricing model you choose. In the CAPM, beta captures the systematic risk of any investment. In the APT or the Fama-French three-factor model, each asset will have several betas capturing the asset's sensitivity to each of the factors. The CAPM and the APT provide a theoretical apparatus that explains why assets are priced in a particular way, while the Fama-French approach is purely empirical. On the other hand, the CAPM and the Fama-French model tell you what factors influence returns, but you have to guess which factors count in the APT (or rely on the lessons from past research). And while the CAPM presumes that just one systematic risk factor drives returns, the APT and the Fama-French model allow for several independent factors. In the end, each model has its advantages and disadvantages.

Fourth, despite its flaws, the CAPM is still widely used in practice in both corporate finance and investment-oriented professions. Understanding how to estimate and interpret expected returns using the CAPM is part of the required tool kit for business school graduates. Perhaps in time, finance theory will provide an indisputably superior model to the CAPM that will make its way into practice. Until then, we muddle through. As Richard Roll observed in his 1988 presidential address to the American Finance Association, "The immaturity of our science is illustrated by the conspicuous lack of predictive content about some of its most intensely interesting phenomena, particularly changes in asset prices." We still have far to go before we catch up with the predictive ability of the physical sciences, but at least we are closer than we were before Harry Markowitz explained portfolio theory to us in 1952.

SMART IDEAS VIDEO

William Sharpe, Stanford University, Co-founder, Financial Engines

"To the extent that there is a premium for bearing risk, it is a premium for bearing the risk of doing badly in bad times."

See the entire interview at **SMARTFinance**

---

18. Summarize the lessons of asset pricing theory that go beyond specific asset pricing models such as the CAPM, APT, and Fama-French.

Concept Review Question

6.8   SUMMARY

- Finance teaches that markets reward investors for bearing risk, but only systematic risk. Asset pricing models attempt to measure systematic risk and to quantify the trade-off between systematic risk and returns.
- Some portfolios are better than others. In general, risk-averse investors should only hold efficient portfolios, portfolios that maximize expected returns for any level of risk.
- If investors can borrow and lend at the risk-free rate, then a unique, efficient risky portfolio exists. Investors must first attempt to learn the composition of this portfolio. Then they can divide their wealth between the efficient risky portfolio and the risk-free asset according to their own risk preferences.
- Under certain conditions, the optimal risky portfolio is the market portfolio, a value-weighted combination of all the assets in the economy.
- The CAPM predicts a linear, positive relationship between expected returns and betas. The beta measures the systematic risk exposure of a particular asset. The graphical representation of the relationship between expected returns and beta is called the security market line.

---

and Zingales (2000) attribute the discount to inefficient allocation of resources across divisions of diversified firms. Comment and Jarrell (1995), Denis, Denis, and Sarin (1997), Lamont and Polk (2001), Whited (2001), and Bernardo and Chowdhry (2002) examine other elements of this diversification discount.

- Early empirical tests offered some support for the CAPM, but the weight of the evidence now suggests that the CAPM offers at best an incomplete explanation of why some assets earn higher average returns than others do.
- Two leading alternatives to the CAPM are the APT and the Fama-French three-factor model. Neither has completely supplanted the CAPM, especially in the corporate finance realm, where the CAPM sees widespread use.

INTERNET RESOURCES

Note: *For updates to links, please go to the book's website at http://smart.swcollege.com.*

http://www.yahoo.com—One of the best websites for obtaining historical stock return data

http://www.money.cnn.com /markets (CNN Money)—Useful for obtaining up-to-the-minute market-pricing data

http://www.nyse.com (The New York Stock Exchange)—Useful for obtaining up-to-the-minute market-pricing data and general market information

http://www.nasdaq.com (National Association of Securities Dealers Automated Quotation system)—Useful for obtaining up-to-the minute OTC market-pricing and other market information

http://www.londonstockexchange.com (The London Stock Exchange)—Useful in obtaining current London Stock Exchange market-pricing and other market information

http://www.marketguide.com /home.asp (Multex Investor)—For information on investing in specific securities

http://www.wallstreetcity.com (Wall Street City)—For information on investing in specific securities and programs for searching for securities meeting various criteria

http://www.standardandpoors.com (Standard & Poor's [publisher of COMPUSTAT])—For a fee, provides a wealth of data on U.S. and/or international assets

http://www.ibbotson.com (Ibbotson Associates)—For a fee, provides a wealth of historical data on various financial assets

http://www.datastream.com (Datastream and Thomson Financial)—For a fee, provides a wealth of data on various financial assets

http://www.bloomberg.com (Bloomberg)—For a fee, provides pricing, return, and many other types of data on various financial assets

KEY TERMS

arbitrage pricing theory (APT)
capital asset pricing model (CAPM)
capital market line (*CML*)
efficient frontier
efficient portfolios
efficient set
Fama-French (F-F) model
feasible set
homogeneous expectations
inefficient portfolios

market portfolio
market price of risk
minimum variance portfolio
observable variables approach
optimal risky portfolio
rational expectations
security market line (*SML*)
short-selling
single-factor model
two-fund separation principle

QUESTIONS

6-1.   Define the terms "feasible set" and "efficient set."

6-2.   Why is the efficient frontier generally a curved arc rather than a straight line?

6-3.   Suppose that you adopt the rule of investing only in portfolios that have the minimum level of risk possible at a given expected return. If you follow this rule, will you always hold an efficient portfolio? (Answer this question assuming that only risky assets are available—there is no risk-free asset.)

6-4.   Suppose that there are two risky assets. One offers a higher return than the other, but it also has a higher standard deviation. Will one of these assets always lie on the efficient frontier? Will one of them always be inefficient if held alone?

6-5.   Suppose that the rate of inflation is negatively correlated with the rate of return in the stock market. A few years ago, the U.S. Treasury began issuing inflation-indexed bonds, bonds that pay a variable interest rate that rises and falls with the inflation rate. Explain what effect this new security has had on the feasible set available to investors.

6-6.   Why is the relationship between expected return and standard deviation for portfolios of risky and risk-free assets linear?

6-7.   Suppose that you have a friend who likes to invest in technology stocks. "Sure, they're risky," he says, "but the technology sector can go up 50 percent in a year. You'll never achieve that kind of return with a diversified portfolio." How should you respond?

6-8.   In Japan, interest rates on short-term government bonds have been just over 0 percent in the last several years. If you could borrow and lend at a risk-free rate of 0 percent, would using borrowed money to finance part of your portfolio still increase the risk of your position?

6-9.   Refer to Figure 6.1. Suppose that a risk-free rate was available in this diagram, and that the risk-free rate was at a level such that the tangent line from Rf to the efficient frontier went through point C. From that level, if the risk-free interest rate rises, what happens to the composition of the optimal portfolio?

6-10.   How does the homogeneous expectations assumption lead to the conclusion in the CAPM that the optimal risky portfolio is the market portfolio?

6-11.   Consumers generally prefer low prices rather than high prices, yet we say that investors want to maximize the market price of risk (i.e., the slope of the CML). Explain this apparent paradox.

6-12.   According to the CAPM, is it possible in equilibrium for an asset with a variance greater than zero (i.e., an asset other than the risk-free asset) to have an expected return below the risk-free rate?

6-13.   Suppose that stock A has a higher variance than stock B. According to the CAPM, can stock A survive in the market if its expected return is lower than that for stock B?

6-14.   Suppose that a mutual fund has a beta equal to 0.75. Is it necessarily the case that the standard deviation of returns on the fund is less than the standard deviation of market returns?

6-15.   Suppose that investors generally become less risk averse. What effect would this have on stock prices and on expected returns?

6-16.   If an asset lies above the SML, is it underpriced or overpriced? Why?

6-17.   Is the expected return on a stock with a beta = 2.0 twice the expected return on a stock with a beta = 1.0?

6-18. Stock A has a beta of 1.5, and stock B has a beta of 1.0. Using concepts from portfolio theory and the CAPM, determine whether each of the following statements is true or false:

a. Stock A has a higher expected return than stock B.

b. The expected return on stock A is 50 percent higher than the expected return on the market portfolio.

c. In a regression with the individual stock's return as the dependent variable and the market's return as the independent variable, the R-squared value is higher for stock A than it is for stock B.

6-19. Do you want to short sell a security when it is increasing or decreasing in price?

6-20. What is the CAPM beta for the risk-free security and the market portfolio? Is the risk-free security uncorrelated with the market portfolio?

6-21. In a regression using an asset's returns as the dependent variable, y, and returns on a market index as the independent variable, x, interpret both the regression slope coefficient and the regression R^2 value.

6-22. Beta estimates may be obtained from data gathered at different frequencies (daily, weekly, monthly, etc.) Explain the trade-offs analysts confront when choosing the data's frequency.

6-23. What problems do researchers encounter when trying to test the validity of the CAPM?

6-24. What evidence supporting the CAPM have researchers found?

6-25. What data would you need to estimate the required return on equity for a particular company using the CAPM? What data would you need to do the same analysis using the Fama-French model?

6-26. Describe what each of the following pairs of asset pricing models has in common, and how they differ:

a. APT and CAPM

b. CAPM and F-F

c. F-F and APT

PROBLEMS

Some of the following problems require you to download monthly returns on several stocks from the Yahoo! website. Step-by-step instructions for gathering this data may be found in Problem 5-16 in Chapter 5.

Risk-Free Borrowing and Lending

6-1. Security X has an expected return of 8% with an associated standard deviation of 28%. Security Y has an expected return of 10% with an associated standard deviation of 36%. Assuming a covariance of -0.023732, find the portfolio's expected return and standard deviation for the following portfolio weight combinations:

Weight of X:	Weight of Y:
20%	80%
40%	60%
60%	40%
80%	20%

Which portfolio weight combination appears to be the minimum variance portfolio (MVP)? Aside from the MVP, which portfolio combinations are efficient?

6-2.   Security Y is a risk-free security with an expected return of 5%. Security Z has an expected return of 10% with an associated standard deviation of 28%. Find the expected portfolio return and standard deviation for the following portfolio weight combinations:

Weight of Y:	Weight of Z:
20%	80%
40%	60%
60%	40%
80%	20%

Does the slope of expected portfolio return versus portfolio risk (measured as standard deviation) change? Answer this question by comparing the slope between the first two portfolios and the last two portfolios. Is the risk-return trade-off simply a straight line in this instance?

6-3.   Refer to Table 6.1 and Figure 6.4. Suppose that you can borrow and lend at the risk-free rate of 0.5 percent per month. Under these circumstances, which risky portfolio is optimal to hold in combination with the risk-free asset?

6-4.   Repeat Problem 6-4 with a risk-free rate of 1.3 percent per month.

6-5.   The expected return on a particular stock is 15 percent, and its standard deviation is 38 percent. The risk-free return is 4 percent. Calculate the expected return and standard deviation on the following portfolios:

%Risky	%Risk-Free	$E(R)$	Standard Deviation
75	25	_____	_____
50	50	_____	_____
25	75	_____	_____
150	−50	_____	_____

6-6.   You have the following data on three different risky assets:

	Asset A	Asset B	Asset C
Expected return %	10	14	12
Standard deviation %	20	40	30

Correlation coefficient between A & B = 0.5; A & C = 0.1; B & C = −0.35.

a. Calculate the expected return and standard deviation for each of the following portfolios:

% in A	% in B	% in C	$E(R)$	Standard Deviation
100	0	0	_____	_____
0	100	0	_____	_____
0	0	100	_____	_____
50	50	0	_____	_____
50	0	50	_____	_____
0	50	50	_____	_____
10	40	50	_____	_____
30	30	40	_____	_____
40	20	40	_____	_____
50	40	10	_____	_____
0	75	25	_____	_____

b. Considered in isolation, which asset lies on the efficient frontier?

c. Which of the portfolios are efficient, and which are inefficient?

SMART
SOLUTIONS
See the problem and
solution explained
step-by-step at
SMARTFinance

6-7. If the market has an expected return of 13 percent and a standard deviation of 28 percent, and the risk-free rate is 5 percent, explain how you can construct a portfolio with an expected return of 20 percent. What will be the standard deviation of this portfolio?

6-8. Refer to the numbers given in Problem 6-7. Explain how you can create a portfolio with a standard deviation of 16 percent. What will be the expected return on this portfolio?

Equilibrium and the Market Portfolio

6-9. You must allocate your wealth between two securities. Security 1 offers an expected return of 10 percent and has a standard deviation of 30 percent. Security 2 offers an expected return of 15 percent and has a standard deviation of 50 percent. The correlation between the returns on these two securities is 0.25.

a. Calculate the expected return and standard deviation for each of the following portfolios, and plot them on a graph:

% Security 1	% Security 2	E(R)	Standard Deviation
100	0	_____	_____
80	20	_____	_____
60	40	_____	_____
40	60	_____	_____
20	80	_____	_____
0	100	_____	_____

b. Based on your calculations in part (a), which portfolios are efficient and which are inefficient?

c. Suppose that a risk-free investment is available that offers a 4 percent return. If you must divide your wealth between the risk-free asset and one of the risky portfolios in the table above, which risky portfolio would you choose?

d. Repeat your answer to part (c) assuming that the risk-free return is 8 percent rather than 4 percent. Can you provide an intuitive explanation for why the optimal risky portfolio changes?

e. Now suppose that you can short-sell (i.e., borrow to purchase) either security, investing the proceeds in the other. Calculate the expected return and standard deviation of the following portfolios and add them to your graph in part (a).

% Security 1	% Security 2	E(R)	Standard Deviation
140	40	_____	_____
120	20	_____	_____
−20	120	_____	_____
−40	140	_____	_____

6-10. In this problem, you will use several Excel features to map out a portfolio frontier. Assume there are two stocks available in the market with the following characteristics:

Stock	E(R)	Standard Deviation
1	12%	35%
2	18%	60%

Correlation coefficient = 0.15

Follow these instructions to create an Excel data table that will allow you to rapidly calculate the expected return and standard deviation for a large number of portfolios of these two assets. By plotting these figures, you can see the portfolio frontier.

a. Starting in cell A2 and going down to cell A5, type in the following numbers:

−.50;   −.49;   −.48;   −.47

You can see that the pattern is to decrease the number in increments of 0.01 as you move down the column. Highlight all four numbers and grab the lower corner of the highlighted rectangle. As you drag the corner down, Excel will recognize the pattern and fill out the rest of the column (or you can use a formula to accomplish this task). Stop when cells A2 through A202 are full, with numbers that begin with $-.50$ and increase until you reach the value 1.50 in cell A202. The numbers in this column represent the fraction of the portfolio invested in the first stock. Because this value ranges from $-.50$ to 1.50, this problem will allow short-selling (i.e., borrowing to purchase). That is, the investor can take a short position of up to 50 percent of his or her wealth, investing the proceeds in the other stock.

b. In cell B1, type an Excel formula that will calculate the standard deviation of a portfolio consisting of these two stocks. This formula will use a cell reference to A1 instructing Excel to look in column A for the portfolio weight to place in stock 1. Note that so far, cell A1 is empty. Type the following formula in cell B1:

$$= ((A1\text{^}2)*(0.35\text{^}2)*(0.60\text{^}2) + 2*A1*(1-A1)*0.35*0.60*0.15)\text{^}.5$$

c. In cell C1, type an Excel formula that will calculate the expected return of a portfolio consisting of these two stocks. Again, this formula will reference cell A1 to tell Excel where to find the percentage invested in stock 1. Type the following formula in cell C1:

$$= A1*0.12 + (1-A1)*0.18$$

d. Now, to create the data table, highlight the entire rectangle from cell A1 to cell C202. Once this is highlighted, select the "Data" menu and choose "Table." In the blank space that says "Column input cell," type "A1" and hit OK. Excel will automatically calculate the standard deviation (in column B) and the expected return (in column C) for every possible portfolio.

   1. What is the minimum variance portfolio?

   2. For an investor to create an efficient portfolio, what is the minimum rational investment in security 1?

   3. If an investor is willing to endure a portfolio standard deviation of 35 percent, how much can the investor increase the portfolio's expected return by diversifying rather than by holding security 1 alone?

e. Finally, click the chart wizard, and select "XY Scatter" as the type of graph you want to create. Tell Excel that the data series are in columns ranging from cells B2:C202. Add titles and headers if you like; then, produce the graph in a separate sheet.

6-11. The stock of Adams Teleped Corp. offers an expected return of 8 percent and has a standard deviation of 55 percent. Shares of Feldman Cosmetics, Inc., have an expected return of 13 percent and a standard deviation of 40 percent. The correlation coefficient between the two assets' returns is -0.2.

a. Plot each stock on a graph with standard deviation on the x-axis and expected return on the y-axis.

b. Calculate the expected return and standard deviation of the following portfolios, and add them to the graph from part (a):

% Adams	% Feldman	E(R)	Standard Deviation
100	0	_____	_____
80	20	_____	_____
60	40	_____	_____
50	50	_____	_____
40	60	_____	_____
20	80	_____	_____
0	100	_____	_____

c. Now suppose that the investor can short-sell (i.e., borrow to purchase) Adams shares and invest the proceeds in Feldman stock. Calculate and plot (on the same graph) the expected return and standard deviation of the following portfolios:

%Adams	% Feldman	E(R)	Standard Deviation
−10	110	_____	_____
−30	130	_____	_____
−50	150	_____	_____

d. Can the situation depicted in this problem persist in a general equilibrium setting? That is, can one stock survive in the market when another stock with a lower standard deviation offers a higher expected return?

The Capital Asset Pricing Model (CAPM)

6-12. The risk-free asset pays 5 percent, the market portfolio's expected return is 13 percent, and its standard deviation is 35 percent. What is the slope of the capital market line?

6-13. The expected return on a particular asset is 10 percent, and its beta is 1.5. The risk-free return is 2 percent, and the expected return on the market portfolio is 14 percent. Does this asset lie on, above, or below the security market line? Explain.

6-14. A particular stock has a beta of 1.2 and an expected return of 10.2 percent. The expected risk premium on the market portfolio is 6 percent. What is the expected return on the market portfolio?

6-15. If a stock has a beta of 1.5 and the standard deviation of the market is 30 percent, what is the covariance between the stock and the market?

6-16. Assume that the expected risk premium on the market portfolio is 8 percent and the risk-free rate is 5 percent. If an asset has an expected return of 15 percent, what is its CAPM beta?

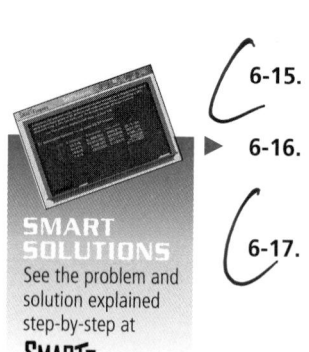

SMART
SOLUTIONS
See the problem and
solution explained
step-by-step at
SMARTFinance

6-17. Suppose a risk-free security pays a 6% return, and a market portfolio has an expected return of 10%. What is the expected return on a portfolio that has $6,000.00 invested in the risk-free security and $4,000.00 invested in the market portfolio? What is the CAPM beta of the portfolio? Does the CAPM beta correspond to the portfolio weight invested in the market portfolio?

6-18. Suppose the risk-free security pays a 5% return, and the market portfolio has an expected return of 12%. What is the expected return on a portfolio that has $2,000.00 borrowed at the risk-free rate and $12,000.00 invested in the market portfolio? What is the CAPM beta of the portfolio? If the CAPM beta is greater than one, does it mean that the associated portfolio on the Capital Market Line (CML) has leverage (i.e., does the portfolio contain borrowed funds)?

6-19. Security A, Security B, and Security C have expected returns of 12%, 18%, and 9%, respectively. Assuming a risk-free rate of 3% and a market premium of 6% (the market premium is equal to $[E(R_m) - R_f]$), what are the CAPM betas for the three securities? Assuming a portfolio is composed 20% of Security A, 45% of Security B, and 35% of security C, what is the portfolio's expected return and CAPM beta? Does the portfolio CAPM beta equal: 20%*(Beta of A) + 45%*(Beta of B) + 35%*(Beta of C) (perform this calculation as part of your answer)?

6-20. Compute the slope of the Security Market Line (SML) using two securities: the risk-free security and the market portfolio. Next, use two random securities, X and Y (assume X has a greater expected return than Y), to calculate the slope of the SML and demonstrate that it is the same as the previous calculation. (*Hint:* Substitute $R_f + \beta_x^*$ $[E(R_m) - R_f]$ for the expected return of X and $R_f + \beta_y^* [E(R_m) - R_f]$ for the expected return of Y.) Describe how the slope of the *SML* is related to the expected return on the market portfolio.

6-21. When considering a portfolio on the Capital Market Line (*CML*), it is a combination of the risk-free security and the market portfolio. The portfolio mean is $W_f^* R_f + W_m^* E(R_m)$, where $W_f + W_m = 100\%$ and represent the portfolio weights of the risk-free security and the market portfolio. Demonstrate how this equation for the portfolio mean is equivalent to $R_f + W_m^*[E(R_m) - R_f]$. (*Hint:* Substitute $(1 - W_m)$ for W_f.) What are the equations for the variance and standard deviation of a given portfolio on the *CML* relative to the market portfolio (let σ_m represent the standard deviation of the market portfolio)?

6-22. Let W_Q and W_S be the weight in the market portfolio for Portfolio Q and Portfolio S, which are both on the Capital Market Line (*CML*). Using $\{R_f + W_Q^*[E(R_m) - R_f]\}$ to represent the expected return on Portfolio Q, and $\{R_f + W_S^*[E(R_m) - R_f]\}$ to represent the expected return on Portfolio S, calculate the slope of the *CML* (assume Security S has the greater expected return). In what manner is the slope of the *CML* related to the market portfolio?

6-23. Security G has a beta of 1.2 and a standard deviation of 43%. Assuming a risk-free rate of 4% and an expected return on the market portfolio of 9%, what is the expected return of Security G? Suppose that the standard deviation of the market portfolio is 30%. It is possible to find a portfolio on the Capital Market Line (*CML*) that has the same expected return as Security G. To construct that portfolio, how much would you have to invest in the risk-free asset, and how much would you have to invest in the market portfolio? What is the standard deviation of the *CML* portfolio with an expected return identical to that of Security G? Compare the standard deviations of the *CML* portfolio and Security G. Why does Security G have a higher standard deviation?

Alternatives to the CAPM

6-24. Suppose that you believe three risk factors drive stock returns: unexpected changes in oil prices, unexpected shifts in GDP, and unexpected movement in the overall stock market. The risk premium for bearing oil-price risk is 4 percent, the risk premium for bearing GDP risk is 5 percent, and the risk premium for bearing market risk is 6 percent.

A particular firm's fortunes are very sensitive to oil prices, meaning that its "oil price beta" is 2.0. Its GDP beta is 0.5, and its market beta is 1.0. If the risk-free rate is 3 percent, what is the expected return on this stock?

6-25. The expected risk premium on small stocks relative to large stocks is 6 percent, and the expected risk premium on low book-to-market stocks relative to high book-to-market stocks is 4 percent. Assume that the expected risk premium on the overall stock market relative to the risk-free rate is 5 percent. A particular stock has a market beta of 0.8, a size beta of 0.2, and a book-to-market beta of 0.4. If the risk-free rate is 4 percent, what is the expected return on this stock according to the Fama-French model?

THOMSON ONE BUSINESS SCHOOL EDITION

6-26. Calculate the monthly returns for Toys "R" Us, Inc. (ticker symbol, TOY) and FedEx Corp. (ticker symbol, FDX) over the last 12 months. Using the S&P 500 Composite as the market index (DSMnemonic, S&PCOMP), calculate the betas of TOY and FDX by running a regression between the market returns and the individual security returns. (*Hint:* Using Excel will simplify this process.) How do your beta estimates compare to the reported betas on ThomsonONE? Based on your calculations and using Equation 6.2, have TOY and FDX performed as expected? Use the rate on the current 10-year Treasury note as the risk-free rate.

6-27. Using the weights below, calculate the arithmetic average and standard deviation of monthly returns for a portfolio of Toys "R" Us, Inc. (ticker symbol, TOY) and FedEx Corp. (ticker symbol, FDX) over the last 12 months.

Toys "R" Us Weight	FedEx Weight
0%	100%
10%	90%
20%	80%
30%	70%
40%	60%
50%	50%
60%	40%
70%	30%
80%	20%
90%	10%
100%	0%

Graph the monthly returns and standard deviations. Which of these portfolios are efficient? Which weight combination results in the minimum variance portfolio?

6-28. Using the weights below, the current 10-year Treasury note rate, and the return for a portfolio consisting of 50% Toys "R" Us, Inc. (ticker symbol, TOY) and 50% FedEx Corp. (ticker symbol, FDX), calculate the arithmetic average and standard deviation of monthly returns over the last 12 months.

Treasury Note Weight	Toys "R" Us/FedEx Portfolio Weight
0%	100%
10%	90%
20%	80%
30%	70%
40%	60%
50%	50%
60%	40%
70%	30%
80%	20%
90%	10%
100%	0%

Graph the monthly returns and standard deviations. Which of these portfolios is efficient? Which weight combination results in the minimum variance portfolio?

MINI-CASE

Andrea Corbridge is considering forming a portfolio comprised of Kalama Corp and Adelphia Technologies. The two corporations have a correlation of -0.1789. The expected return and standard deviation of the two corporations is:

	Kalama Corp	Adelphia Technologies
Expected Return	14.86%	23.11%
Standard Deviation	23.36%	31.89%

1.   Calculate the frontier for all possible investment combinations of Kalama Corp. and Adelphia Technologies (from 0% to 100%, in 1% increments). If the risk-free rate is 3%, determine the optimal risky portfolio.

2.   Andrea has $50,000 and wants to earn a 19% expected return on her investment. What is the optimal manner in which to structure her portfolio, both in dollar amounts and in weights relative to her $50,000, based on the above information?

3.   Andrea is also seriously considering buying some shares of Medford Barnett Corporation's stock (MBC). The stock prices and dividends for MBC and the Standard and Poor's 500 Index (S&P) for the past 24 months are provided below. She estimates that MBC will earn a 14% return during the next year, while she expects the market will earn a 12% return during the same time period. In addition, she expects the relationship exhibited between the S&P and MBC to stay the same as it has been in the past. Assuming Andrea would be pulling MBC into a fully diversified portfolio, is it a good decision?

Date	S&P	MBC
Oct-05	1,198.41	58.04
Sep-05	1,228.81	65.36
Aug-05	1,220.33	48.48
Jul-05	1,234.18	53.32
Jun-05	1,191.33	57.59
May-05	1,191.50	49.23
Apr-05	1,156.85	55.57
Mar-05	1,180.59	50.99
Feb-05	1,203.60	64.10
Jan-05	1,181.27	50.45
Dec-04	1,211.92	50.65
Nov-04	1,173.82	51.23
Oct-04	1,130.20	46.68
Sep-04	1,114.58	51.09
Aug-04	1,104.24	50.75
Jul-04	1,101.72	59.80
Jun-04	1,140.84	52.78
May-04	1,120.68	49.22
Apr-04	1,107.30	53.47
Mar-04	1,126.21	49.26
Feb-04	1,144.94	48.55
Jan-04	1,131.13	61.32
Dec-03	1,111.92	48.06
Nov-03	1,058.20	58.88
Oct-03	1,050.71	46.19

PART 3: Capital Budgeting

No decisions have a greater impact on the long-term success or failure of businesses than investment decisions. How companies decide to invest the money that shareholders and lenders entrust to them largely dictates whether they will thrive or whither over time. The process of analyzing and prioritizing investment opportunities is called capital budgeting. This section illustrates the analysis that financial managers perform to determine which investment opportunities firms ought to pursue, and which investments companies ought to avoid.

Chapter 7 describes several techniques that firms use to justify their investment choices. Although simple techniques such as payback analysis enjoy widespread use in practice, the best method for analyzing capital investment projects is the net present value (NPV) method. Chapter 7 explains the conceptual underpinnings of the NPV approach and highlights the strengths and weaknesses of other capital budgeting methods.

The first step in analyzing an investment opportunity is estimating the incremental cash inflows and outflows associated with the investment. Chapter 8 uses an extended case example to illustrate how to generate the cash flow numbers, which are an essential part of NPV analysis. In addition to listing the various types of cash flows commonly occurring in large investment projects, the chapter also explains how to deal with issues such as inflation or excess capacity when estimating project cash flows.

The second step in an NPV calculation is estimating a discount rate that is appropriate given the risk of the investment opportunity under consideration. Chapter 9 shows how the process of finding the right discount rate depends on the nature of the investment opportunity as well as the financial structure of the firm. In this chapter we introduce a key concept in finance called the weighted average cost of capital, or WACC. Almost all large companies calculate their WACC as part of their capital budgeting decision process.

Chapter 7

Capital Budgeting Process and Techniques

Why would a company spend around $500,000 to ship a 210-ton machine by air? Sounds ridiculous, but that's exactly what AU Optronics Corp. did in August of 2004. When the company ordered a 210-ton machine for their new flat-screen factory in Taiwan, they asked the manufacturer to rush its delivery from Germany. Rather than pay about $250,000 to have the machine shipped by sea, AU Optronics elected to pay twice that amount to have it shipped by air using the world's largest plane—the Soviet-built, six-engine Antonov 225.

AU estimated that by using air-shipment it would shorten its construction of the $2.3 billion factory by about 40 days, and that the time-savings could mean tens of millions of dollars in production. Ten similar factories were under construction at a total cost of about $20 billion for plant and equipment. At the time, consumers were grabbing up more flat-panel TVs, and the makers of flat screens—all located in Taiwan, South Korea, and Japan—were racing to finish new factories and make inroads into what was expected to become one of the largest and most lucrative markets.

AU Optronics, the third largest producer of flat screens after Samsung Electronics Co. and LG Philips LCD of South Korea, had about 12% of the market whereas both Samsung and LG Philips each controlled about 22% of the market. AU sold to contract manufacturers such as Acer and Compal, and original equipment manufacturers (OEMs) including Audiovox, Matsushita, and Sony.

Given a deadline of just seven months for constructing the 2.4 million square foot plant, general contractor Fu Tsu Construction Co. began construction even before the plant's architects were done; they were actually working on the first floor before the second-floor design was finalized. The rush to bring production online was driven by the time value of money. Clearly, the sooner AU received cash flow from flat-screen production, the quicker it could repay the investment required to build, equip, and begin operations in its new plant.

When managers, analysts, and investors evaluate the major investments that firms like AU Optronics undertake, they have several tools at their disposal to help them determine whether the investments will benefit or harm shareholders. Two of the most widely used investment evaluation techniques are the net present value and the internal rate of return methods. Read on to learn how to apply these techniques to the investment decision process.

Sources: Evan Ramstad, "Once a Footnote, Flat Screens Grow Into Huge Industry" The Wall Street Journal, (August 30, 2004), pp. A1, A8; www.biz.yahoo.com/ic/107/107576.html; Michelle Kessler, "Prices of Flat-Panel TVs, Monitors Could Drop More", USA Today, (June 27, 2004).

SMART**Finance**
Use the learning tools at www
.thomsonedu.com/finance/smartfinance

On a daily basis, firms make decisions that have financial consequences. Some decisions, such as extending credit to a customer or ordering inventory, have consequences that are short-lived. Moreover, managers can reverse these short-term actions with relative ease. In contrast, some decisions that managers face have a long-term impact on the firm and can be very difficult to unwind once started. Major investments in plant and equipment fit this description, but so might spending on advertising designed to build brand awareness and loyalty among consumers. The terms **capital investment** and **capital spending** refer to investments in these kinds of long-lived assets, and the term **capital budgeting** refers to the process of identifying which of these investment projects a firm should undertake.

The capital budgeting process involves three basic steps:

1. Identifying potential investments
2. Analyzing the set of investment opportunities, isolating those that will create shareholder value, and perhaps prioritizing them
3. Implementing and monitoring the investment projects selected in Step 2

The capital budgeting process begins with an idea and ends with implementation and monitoring. Ideas for investment projects can come from virtually anywhere within the firm. Marketing may propose that the firm spend money to reach a new class of customers. Operations may want to modernize equipment to realize production efficiencies. Engineering may seek resources to engage in research and development designed to improve existing products or create new ones. Information Systems may want to upgrade the firm's computer network to enable more efficient information-sharing across functional areas and physical locations. Each group will undoubtedly have a compelling story to justify spending money on its pet project. The firm will analyze each proposal considering its risk and return; some projects will be approved and others rejected.

Once a project gains approval, the attention of financial managers turns to implementation. Financial managers devote a significant portion of their time to Step 3, implementing and monitoring investments that the firm has decided to make. When firms undertake a capital investment, they almost always do so with a specific budget, outlining the financial objectives and constraints of that investment. Financial managers work to ensure that project managers adhere to budget guidelines, and they help track a project's success over time to determine if an investment's initial promises were realized.

Without understating the importance of Steps 1 and 3, our focus in this chapter is on the second step in the process, analyzing the merits of investment proposals. In practice, firms use many different techniques to justify their capital investments, ranging from simple to sophisticated. In this chapter, we describe several of these techniques, highlighting their strengths and weaknesses. In the end, the preferred technique for evaluating most capital investments is one called "net present value."

7.1 INTRODUCTION TO CAPITAL BUDGETING

WHAT DO MANAGERS REALLY WANT?

Firms use a variety of techniques to evaluate capital investments. Some techniques involve very simple calculations and are intuitively easy to grasp. Financial managers prefer (1) an easily applied technique that (2) focuses on cash flow, (3) accounts for the time value of money, (4) adjusts for differences in risk across projects, and

(5) when applied, leads to higher stock prices. Easy application accounts for the popularity of some simple capital budgeting methods such as the *accounting rate of return* and the *payback period* (both defined later).

More complex methods such as *net present value (NPV)*, *internal rate of return (IRR)*, or the *profitability index (PI)* generally lead to better decisions because they take into account important factors that the simpler methods ignore. Moreover, we will learn that the net present value approach provides a direct estimate of the increase or decrease in shareholder value resulting from a particular investment. Managers who seek to maximize shareholder value must understand not only how to use the more complex techniques but also the logic that explains why some methods are better than others. As challenging as that sounds, there is no reason to worry. We have already seen these tools at work in valuing bonds and stocks, and now we will apply the discounted cash flow apparatus to real assets such as plant and equipment.

A CAPITAL BUDGETING PROBLEM

We apply each of the decision-making techniques in this chapter to a single, simplified business problem currently facing Global Wireless Incorporated, a (fictitious) U.S.-based worldwide provider of wireless telephone services. At this time, wireless carriers are scrambling to attract and retain customers in this highly competitive market. According to customer surveys, the number one reason for selecting a given carrier (or for switching to a new one) is the quality of service. Customers who lose calls as they commute to work or travel from one business location to another are apt to switch if another carrier offers fewer service interruptions.

Against this backdrop, Global Wireless is contemplating a major expansion of its wireless network in two different regions. Figure 7.1 depicts the projected cash inflows

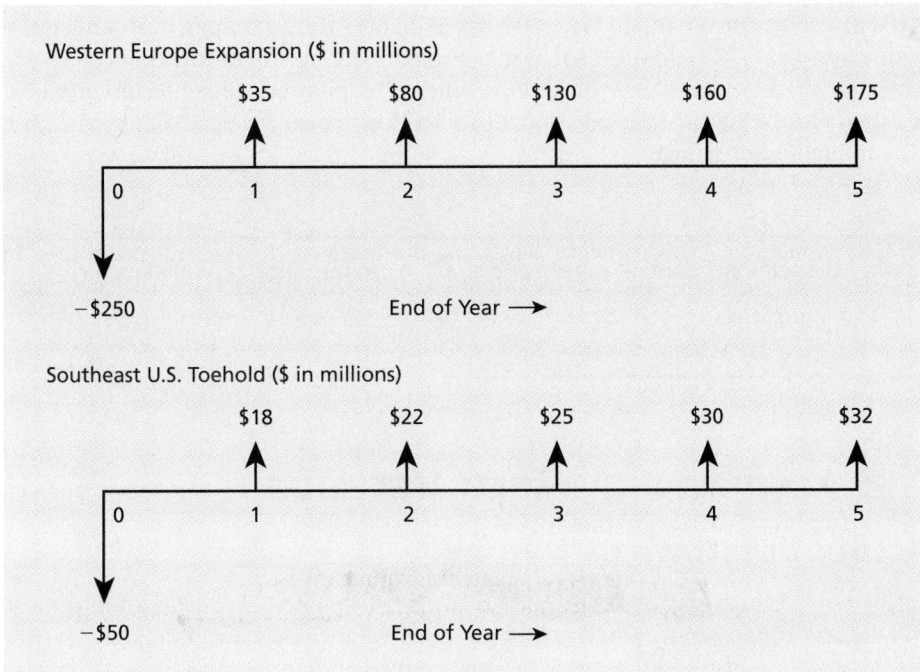

Figure 7.1
Global Wireless
Investment Proposals

and outflows of each project over the next five years. By investing $250 million, Global Wireless could add up to 100 new cell sites to its existing base in Western Europe, giving it the most comprehensive service area in that region. Company analysts project that this investment could generate year-end net after-tax cash inflows that could grow over the next five years, as outlined below:

Initial Outlay	−$250 million
Year 1 inflow	$ 35 million
Year 2 inflow	$ 80 million
Year 3 inflow	$130 million
Year 4 inflow	$160 million
Year 5 inflow	$175 million

Alternatively, Global Wireless could make a much smaller investment to establish a toehold in a new market in the southeast United States. For an initial investment of $50 million, Global Wireless believes it can create a southeast network, with its hub centered in Atlanta, Georgia. The projected end-of-year cash flows associated with this project are as follows:

Initial outlay	−$50 million
Year 1 inflow	$18 million
Year 2 inflow	$22 million
Year 3 inflow	$25 million
Year 4 inflow	$30 million
Year 5 inflow	$32 million

Which investment should Global Wireless make? If the company can undertake both investments, should it do so? If it can make only one investment, which one is better for shareholders? We will see how different capital budgeting techniques lead to different investment decisions, starting with the least-sophisticated approach, the accounting rate of return.

Concept Review Question	**1.** What characteristics does management desire in a capital budgeting technique? Why?

7.2   ACCOUNTING-BASED METHODS

ACCOUNTING RATE OF RETURN

For better or worse, managers in many firms focus as much on how a given project will influence reported earnings as on how it will affect cash flows. Managers justify this focus by pointing to the positive (or negative) stock-price response that occurs when their firms beat (or fail to meet) earnings forecasts made by Wall Street securities analysts. Managers may also pay more attention to the accounting-based earnings of a project than they pay to its cash flows because their compensation is based on meeting accounting-based performance measures such as earnings-per-share or return-on-total-assets targets. Consequently, many firms decide whether to invest in a given project based on the rate of return the investment will earn on an accounting basis.

Companies have many different ways of defining a *hurdle rate* for their investment in terms of accounting rates of return. Almost all these metrics involve two steps: (1) to identify the net income associated with the project in each year of its life, and (2) to measure the amount of invested capital, as shown on the balance sheet, devoted to the project in each year. Given these two figures, a firm may calculate an **accounting rate of return** by dividing net income by the book value of assets, either on a year-by-year basis or by taking an average over the project's life. Note that this measure is comparable to *return on total assets (ROA)*, also called *return on investment (ROI)*, introduced in Chapter 2, for measuring a firm's overall effectiveness in generating returns with its available assets. **Companies will usually establish some minimum accounting rate of return that projects must earn before they can be funded.** When more than one project exceeds the minimum standard, firms prioritize projects based on their accounting rates of return, and invest in projects with higher returns first.

APPLYING THE MODEL 7.1

Suppose that the practice at Global Wireless is to calculate a project's accounting rate of return by taking the project's average contribution to net income and dividing by its average book value. Global Wireless ranks projects based on this measure and accepts those that offer an accounting rate of return of at least 25 percent. So far, we have been given the cash flows from each of the two projects that Global Wireless is evaluating. Chapter 8 discusses in more depth the differences between cash flow and net income, but for now, we assume that we can determine each project's contribution to net income by subtracting depreciation from cash flow each year. We assume that the company depreciates fixed assets on a straight-line basis over five years. Therefore, the Western Europe project will have an annual depreciation charge of $50 million (one fifth of $250 million), and the southeast U.S. project will have an annual depreciation charge of $10 million (one fifth of $50 million). These assumptions yield the following net income figures for the next five years:

Year	Western Europe Project ($ in millions)	Southeast U.S. Project ($ in millions)
1	−15	8
2	30	12
3	80	15
4	110	20
5	125	22

The Western Europe project begins with a book value of $250 million and after five years of depreciation has a book value of $0. Therefore, the average book value of that project is $125 million [($250 − $0) ÷ 2]. The project's average net income equals $66 million [(−$15 + $30 + $80 + $110 + $125) ÷ 5], so its average accounting rate of return is an impressive 52.8 percent ($66 ÷ $125). The same steps applied to the southeast U.S. project yield an average book value of

$25 million [($50 − $0) ÷ 2], an average net income of $15.4 million [($8 + $12 + $15 + $20 + $22) ÷ 5], and an accounting rate of return of 61.6 percent ($15.4 ÷ $25). On the basis of this analysis, Global Wireless should be willing to invest in either project, but it would rank the southeast U.S. investment above the Western Europe expansion.

Pros and Cons of the Accounting Rate of Return. Because of their convenience, ease of calculation, and ease of interpretation, accounting-based measures are used by many firms to evaluate capital investments. However, these techniques have serious flaws. First, as the preceding Applying the Model demonstrates, the decision about what depreciation method to use has a large effect on both the numerator and the denominator of the accounting rate of return formula. Second, this method makes no adjustment for the time value of money or project risk. Third, investors should be more concerned with the market value than the book value of the assets that a firm holds. After five years, the book value of Global Wireless's investment (in either project) is zero, but the market value will almost certainly be positive and may be even greater than the initial amount invested. Fourth, as explained in Chapter 2, finance theory teaches that investors should focus on a company's ability to generate cash rather than on its net income. Fifth, the choice of the 25 percent accounting rate of return hurdle rate is essentially arbitrary. This rate is not based on rates available on similar investments in the market, but reflects a purely subjective judgment on the part of management.

Concept Review Questions

2. Why do managers focus on the effect that an investment will have on reported earnings rather than on the investment's cash flow consequences?

3. What factors determine whether the annual *accounting rate of return* on a given project will be high or low in the early years of the investment's life? In the latter years?

7.3 PAYBACK METHODS

THE PAYBACK DECISION RULE

The payback method is the simplest of all capital budgeting decision-making tools. It enjoys widespread use, particularly in small firms. The **payback period** is the amount of time it takes for a given project's cumulative net cash inflows to recoup the initial investment. **Firms using the payback approach define a maximum acceptable payback period and accept only those projects that have payback periods less than the maximum; all other projects are rejected.** If a firm decides that it wants to avoid any investment that does not "pay for itself" in three years or less, then the payback decision rule is to accept projects with a payback period of three years or less and reject all other investments. If several projects satisfy this condition, then firms may prioritize investments, based on which ones achieve payback more rapidly. The decision to use three years as the cutoff point is somewhat arbitrary, and there are no hard-and-fast guidelines that establish what the "optimal" payback period should be. Nevertheless, suppose that Global Wireless uses 3.00 years as its cutoff when doing payback analysis. What investment decision would it make?

APPLYING THE MODEL 7.2

The investment to expand the wireless network in Western Europe requires an initial outlay of $250 million. According to the firm's cash flow projections, this project will bring in just $245 million in its first three years ($35 million in year 1 + $80 million in year 2 + $130 million in year 3) and $405 million after four years ($245 million in the first 3 years + $160 million in year 4). So the firm will fully recover its $250 million initial outlay sometime during year 4. Because the firm only needs to recover $5 million ($250 million initial outlay − $245 million recovered in the first 3 years) in year 4, assuming cash flow occurs at a constant rate throughout the year, we can estimate the fraction of year 4 as 0.03, by dividing the $5 million that needs to be recovered in year 4 by the $160 million expected to be recovered in that year. *The payback period for Western Europe is therefore 3.03 years, so Global Wireless would reject the investment because this payback period is longer than the firm's maximum 3.00-year payback period.*

The toehold investment in the southeast U.S. project requires just $50 million. In its first two years, this investment generates $40 million in cash flow ($18 million in year 1 + $22 million in year 2). By the end of year 3, it produces a cumulative cash flow of $65 million ($40 million in the first 2 years + $25 million in year 3). Thus, the project earns back the initial $50 million at some point during year 3. It needs to recover $10 million ($50 million initial outlay − $40 million recovered in the first 2 years) in year 3. We can estimate the fraction of year 3 as 0.40, by dividing the $10 million that needs to be recovered in year 3 by the $25 million expected to be recovered that year. *The payback for the southeast U.S. project is therefore 2.40 years. Global Wireless would undertake the investment because this payback period is shorter than the firm's maximum 3.00-year payback period.*

PROS AND CONS OF THE PAYBACK METHOD

Arguments for the Payback Method. Simplicity is the main virtue of the payback approach. Once a firm estimates a project's cash flows, it is a simple matter of addition to determine when the cumulative net cash inflows equal the initial outlay. The intuitive appeal of the payback method is strong. It sounds reasonable to expect a good investment to pay for itself in a fairly short period of time. Indeed, time value of money principles suggest that, other things being equal, a project that brings in cash flow faster ought to be more valuable than one with more distant cash flows. Some managers say that establishing a short payback period is one way to account for a project's risk exposure. They argue that projects that take longer to pay off are intrinsically riskier than those that recoup the initial investment more quickly. This is partially attributable to the fact that forecast errors tend to increase with the length of the forecast horizon. The payback period is a very popular decision-making technique in highly uncertain situations. It is popular for international investments made in unstable economic/political environments and risky domestic investments such as oil drilling and new business ventures. In these situations, it is frequently used as the primary decision-making technique.

Another justification given for evaluating investment opportunities using the payback method is that some firms face financing constraints. Advocates of the payback rule argue that it makes sense for cash-strapped firms to use payback because that

SMART PRACTICES VIDEO

Daniel Carter, Chief Financial Officer of Charlotte Russe

"It's a metric that frankly most of our operators can truly appreciate."

See the entire interview at **SMARTFinance**

method indicates how quickly the firm can generate cash flow to repay debt or to pursue other investment opportunities. Career concerns may also lead managers to prefer the payback rule. Particularly in large companies, managers rotate quite often from one job to another. To obtain promotions and to enhance their reputations, managers want to make investments that enable them to point to success stories at each stage of their careers. A manager who expects to stay in a particular position in the firm for just two or three years may prefer to undertake investments that recover costs quickly rather than those that have payoffs far into the future. In that case, selecting projects based on how quickly they meet the payback requirement offers considerable appeal to someone trying to build a career.

Arguments Against the Payback Method. Despite these apparent virtues, the payback method suffers from several serious problems. First, the payback cutoff period is simply a judgemental choice with little or no connection to shareholder value maximization. How can we be sure that projects that pay back within 3.00 years will maximize shareholder wealth as opposed to those that pay back within two years or four years? Second, the way that the payback method accounts for the time value of money is crude in the extreme. The payback method assigns a 0 percent discount rate to cash flows that occur before the cutoff point. That is, if the payback period is three years, then cash flows that occur in years 1, 2, and 3 receive equal weight in the payback calculation. Beyond the cutoff point, the payback method implicitly assigns an infinite discount rate to all future cash flows, thereby ignoring them. In other words, cash flows in year 4 and beyond receive zero weight (or have zero present value) in today's decision to invest or not invest.[1] Third, using the payback period as a way to control for project risk is equally crude. Finance teaches that riskier investments should offer higher returns. If it is true, as managers sometimes argue, that riskier projects have longer payback periods, then the payback rule simply rejects all such investments even if they offer higher returns in the long run. Managers who naively follow the payback rule tend to underinvest in long-term projects that could offer substantial rewards for shareholders. Fourth, if career concerns lead managers to favor projects with very quick payoffs, then that is an *agency problem*. Agency problems should be resolved through a firm's governance mechanisms, not by adopting a suboptimal decision rule. Firms could reduce incentives for managers to focus on short-term successes by rewarding them for their efforts in meeting the short-term goals of long-term projects (e.g., staying on budget, meeting revenue forecasts), as well as for long-term results.

DISCOUNTED PAYBACK

The **discounted payback** rule is essentially the same as the payback rule except that in calculating the payback period, managers discount cash flows first. In other words, the discounted payback method calculates how long it takes for a project's discounted cash flows to recover the initial outlay. This represents a minor improvement over the simple payback method in that it does a better job of accounting for the time value of cash flows that occur within the payback cutoff period. As with the ordinary

---

[1] We know that the present value of a future cash flow becomes smaller and smaller as we discount at higher and higher interest rates. Discounting at an infinite interest rate results in a future cash flow having zero present value.

payback rule, discounted payback totally ignores cash flows that occur beyond the cutoff point.

APPLYING THE MODEL 7.3

Suppose that Global Wireless uses the discounted payback method, with a discount rate of 18 percent and a cutoff period of 3.00 years. The following schedules show the present values of each project's cash flows during the first three years. For example, $29.7 million is the present value of the $35 million that the Western Europe investment is expected to earn in its first year, $57.4 million is the present value of the $80 million that the project is expected to earn in its second year, and so on.

Present Value	Western Europe Project ($ in millions)	Southeast U.S. Project ($ in millions)
PV of year 1 inflow	29.7	15.2
PV of year 2 inflow	57.4	15.8
PV of year 3 inflow	79.1	15.2
Cumulative PV years 1–3	166.2	46.2

Recall that the initial outlay for the Western Europe expansion project is $250 million, whereas it is $50 million for the southeast U.S. toehold project. Because, after three years, neither project's cumulative present value of cash flows exceeds its initial outlay, it is clear that neither investment satisfies the condition that the discounted cash flows recoup the initial investment in 3.00 years or less. Therefore, Global Wireless would reject both projects.

PROS AND CONS OF DISCOUNTED PAYBACK

The discounted payback rule offers essentially the same set of advantages and disadvantages as does ordinary payback analysis. The primary advantage is its relative simplicity. Discounted payback does correct the payback rule's problem of implicitly applying a 0 percent discount rate to all cash flows that occur before the cutoff point. However, like the ordinary payback rule, the discounted payback approach ignores cash flows beyond the cutoff point, in essence applying an infinite discount rate to these cash flows. In the final analysis, even though it represents a marginal improvement over the simplest version of the payback rule, discounted payback analysis is likely to lead managers to underinvest in profitable projects with long-run payoffs.

By now you may have noticed some common themes in our discussion of the pros and cons of different approaches to capital budgeting. None of the methods discussed thus far factor all the cash flows of a project into the decision-making process. Each of these methods fails to properly account for the time value of money, and none of them deal adequately with differences in risk from one investment to another. In spite of these criticisms, both payback and discounted payback are widely used in practice due to their simplicity and broad intuitive appeal. Given the uncertain nature of forecast project cash flows, some analysts find these simple techniques effective in making good investment decisions. We now turn our attention to a method that solves all these difficulties and therefore enjoys widespread support from both academics and businesspeople.

4. What factors account for the popularity of the *payback method*? In what situations is it often used as the primary decision-making technique? Why?

5. What are the major flaws of the *payback period* and *discounted payback* approaches?

7.4 NET PRESENT VALUE

NET PRESENT VALUE CALCULATIONS

A project's **net present value (NPV)** equals the sum of its cash inflows and outflows, discounted at a rate consistent with the project's risk. Calculating an investment's *NPV* is relatively straightforward. First, write down the net cash flows that the investment will generate over its life. Second, discount these cash flows at an interest rate that reflects the risk inherent in the project. Third, add up the discounted cash flows to obtain the *NPV*, and invest in the project only when its *NPV* exceeds zero.[2]

$$NPV = CF_0 + \frac{CF_1}{(1+r)^1} + \frac{CF_2}{(1+r)^2} + \frac{CF_3}{(1+r)^3} + \cdots + \frac{CF_N}{(1+r)^N} \qquad \text{(Eq. 7.1)}$$

In this expression, CF_t represents net cash flow in year t, r is the discount rate, and N represents the life of the project. The cash flows in each year may be positive or negative, though we usually expect projects to generate cash outflows initially and cash inflows later on. For example, suppose that the initial cash flow, CF_0, is a negative number representing the outlay necessary to get the project started, and suppose that all subsequent cash flows are positive. In this case, the *NPV* can be defined as the *present value of future cash inflows minus the initial outlay*. The *NPV* decision rule says that firms should invest when the sum of the present values of future cash inflows exceeds the initial project outlay. That is, $NPV > \$0$, when the following occurs:

$$-CF_0 < \frac{CF_1}{(1+r)^1} + \frac{CF_2}{(1+r)^2} + \frac{CF_3}{(1+r)^3} + \cdots + \frac{CF_N}{(1+r)^N}$$

Simply stated, **the *NPV* decision rules are:**

$NPV > \$0$ invest
$NPV < \$0$ do not invest

---

[2] What about investments with $NPV = \$0$? A zero *NPV* represents a breakeven point. That is, when an investment's *NPV* is positive, a firm creates wealth for its shareholders. When the *NPV* is negative, the firm destroys wealth by undertaking the project. When the *NPV* is zero, although investing will increase the book value of the firm's assets, it neither creates nor destroys wealth. Therefore, in this case, shareholders are generally indifferent to whether the firm accepts or rejects the project.

Why does the *NPV* rule generally lead to good investment decisions?
Remember that the firm's goal in choosing investment projects is to maximize share-holder wealth. Conceptually, the discount rate, *r*, in the *NPV* equation represents an opportunity cost, the highest rate of return that investors can obtain in the market-place on an investment with risk equal to the risk of the specific project. When the *NPV* of a cash flow stream equals zero, that stream of cash flows provides a rate of return exactly equal to the shareholders' required return. Therefore, when a firm finds a project with a positive *NPV*, the project offers an expected return that exceeds the shareholders' requirements. A firm that consistently finds positive *NPV* investments expects to surpass the shareholders' requirements and enjoy a rising stock price. The *NPV*, in effect, represents the amount of additional value created by the investment. Clearly, the acceptance of positive *NPV* projects is consistent with the firm's value-creation goal. Conversely, if the firm makes an investment with a negative *NPV*, the in-vestment will destroy value and disappoint shareholders. A firm that regularly makes negative *NPV* investments expects to see its stock price lag as it persists in generating lower-than-required returns for stockholders.

We can develop an analogy, drawing on what we already know about valuing bonds, to drive home the point about the relationship between stock prices and the *NPV* rule. Suppose that at a given point in time, investors require a 5 percent return on five-year Treasury bonds. Of course, this means that if the U.S. Treasury issues five-year, $1,000 par value bonds paying an annual coupon of $50, the market price of these bonds will be $1,000, exactly equal to par value.[3]

$$\$1,000 = \frac{\$50}{1.05^1} + \frac{\$50}{1.05^2} + \cdots + \frac{\$1,050}{1.05^5}$$

Now apply *NPV* logic. If an investor purchases one of these bonds for $1,000, the *NPV* equals zero because the bond's cash flows precisely satisfy the investor's ex-pectation of a 5 percent return.

$$NPV = \$0 = -\$1,000 + \frac{\$50}{1.05^1} + \frac{\$50}{1.05^2} + \cdots + \frac{\$1,050}{1.05^5}$$

Next, imagine that in a fit of election-year largesse, the U.S. Congress decrees that the coupon payments on all government bonds will double, so this bond now pays $100 in interest per year. If the bond's price remains fixed at $1,000, this investment's *NPV* will suddenly switch from zero to positive:

$$NPV = \$216.47 = -\$1,000 + \frac{\$100}{1.05^1} + \frac{\$100}{1.05^2} + \cdots + \frac{\$1,100}{1.05^5}$$

Of course, the bond's price will not remain at $1,000. Investors will quickly rec-ognize that at a price of $1,000 and with a coupon of $100, the return offered by these bonds substantially exceeds the required rate of 5 percent. Investors will flock to buy the bonds, rapidly driving up bond values until prices reach the point at which buying bonds becomes a zero *NPV* investment once again.[4] In the new equilibrium,

---

[3.] Though Treasury bonds pay interest semiannually, we assume annual interest payments here to keep the example simple.
[4.] Recall that in Chapter 6, we said that an underpriced stock would lie above the security market line. The same thing is happening here. At a price of $1,000, the bond is underpriced if Congress raises the bond's coupon to $100. The price of the bond rises, and its expected return falls.

the bond's price will rise by $216.47, exactly the amount of the *NPV* that was created when Congress doubled the coupon payments:

$$NPV = \$0 = -\$1,216.47 + \frac{\$100}{1.05^1} + \frac{\$100}{1.05^2} + \cdots + \frac{\$1,100}{1.05^5}$$

NPV and Stock Price. The same forces drive up a firm's stock price when it makes a positive *NPV* investment, as shown in Figure 7.2. In the figure, we depict a firm that investors believe will pay an annual dividend of $4 in perpetuity. If investors require a 10 percent return on this firm's stock, the price will be $40.[5] What happens if the firm makes a new equally risky investment? If the return on this investment is greater than 10 percent, it will have a positive *NPV*. Investors will recognize that the firm has made an investment that exceeds their expectations, and investors will raise their forecast of future dividends, perhaps to $4.10 per year. At that level, the new stock price will be $41. The same thing happens in reverse if the firm makes an investment that earns a return below 10 percent. At that rate, the project has a negative *NPV*. Shareholders recognize that this investment's cash flows fall below their expectations, so they lower their estimates of future dividends to $3.90 per year. As a consequence, the stock price falls to $39.

Now apply this process to Global Wireless. Suppose its shareholders demand an 18 percent return on their shares. According to the principles we discussed in Chapter 4, the price of Global Wireless stock will reflect the value of all future cash distributions that investors expect from the company, discounted at a rate of 18 percent. But what if Global Wireless discovers it can make an investment that offers a return substantially above 18 percent? By definition, such an investment has a positive *NPV*, and by undertaking it, Global Wireless will increase the price of its stock as investors come to realize that the company is able to distribute higher-than-anticipated cash flows as a result of the investment opportunity. How far will the stock price rise?

Figure 7.2
The *NPV* Rule and Shareholder Wealth

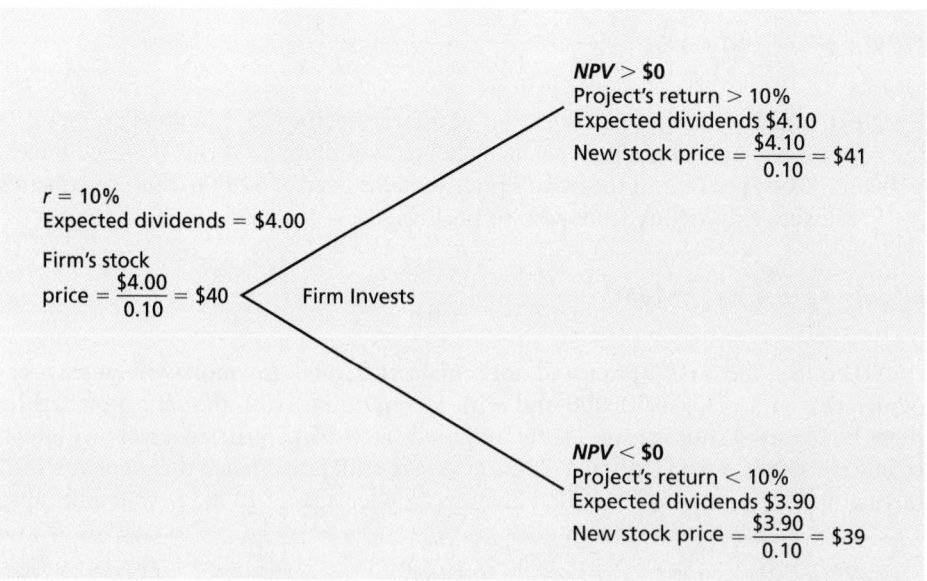

[5.] Remember that the price of a stock that pays a constant dividend in perpetuity equals the annual dividend divided by the required rate of return—in this case, $4 ÷ 0.10 = $40.

Simply divide the project's *NPV* (which represents the amount of wealth the project is expected to create) by the number of outstanding shares. The result is the amount by which Global Wireless's stock price should increase.

APPLYING THE MODEL 7.4

What are the *NPV*s of the investment opportunities now facing Global Wireless? Time lines depicting the *NPV* calculations for Global Wireless's projects appear in Figure 7.3. Discounting each project's cash flows at 18 percent yields the following results:[6]

$$NPV_{\text{Western Europe}} = -\$250 + \frac{\$35}{(1.18)^1} + \frac{\$80}{(1.18)^2} + \frac{\$130}{(1.18)^3} + \frac{\$160}{(1.18)^4} + \frac{\$175}{(1.18)^5} = \$75.3$$

$$NPV_{\text{Southeast U.S.}} = -\$50 + \frac{\$18}{(1.18)^1} + \frac{\$22}{(1.18)^2} + \frac{\$25}{(1.18)^3} + \frac{\$30}{(1.18)^4} + \frac{\$32}{(1.18)^5} = \$25.7$$

Both projects increase shareholder wealth, so both are worth undertaking. One could say that "both projects outrun the firm's 18 percent required return and are therefore acceptable." However, if the company can make only one investment, it should choose to expand its presence in Western Europe. That investment is expected to increase shareholder wealth by $75.3 million, whereas the southeast U.S. investment is expected to increase wealth by only about one third as much. If Global Wireless has 100 million shares of common stock outstanding, then accepting the Western Europe project should increase the stock price by about $0.75 ($75.3 million ÷ 100 million shares). Accepting the southeast U.S. investment should increase the stock price by almost $0.26 ($25.7 million ÷ 100 million shares).

PROS AND CONS OF *NPV*

The net-present-value method solves all the problems we have identified with the payback and discounted payback rules, as well as the problems associated with decision rules based on the accounting rate of return. First, the *NPV* rule focuses on cash flow, not accounting earnings. Second, when properly applied, the net-present-value method makes appropriate adjustments for the time value of money. Third, the decision rule to invest when *NPV*s are positive and to refrain from investing when *NPV*s are negative reflects the firm's need to compete for funds in the marketplace rather than an arbitrary judgment of management. Fourth, the *NPV* approach offers a relatively straightforward way to control for differences in risk among alternative investments. Cash flows on riskier investments should be discounted at higher rates. Fifth, the *NPV*

[6.] Of course, you can do this calculation with a financial calculator or in Excel using the "=*NPV*" function. Imagine that you have all the Western Europe project's cash flows in column A of a spreadsheet, with the initial outlay in row 1, the first year's inflow in row 2, and so on. In any blank cell, type the formula "=*NPV*(0.18,A2:A6) + A1." Excel will return the value $75.26, which represents the *NPV* of the project. Notice that the *NPV* function contains as its first argument the discount rate, and following that are the cash flows from year 1 to year 5 (contained in rows 2–6). By design, Excel's *NPV* function assumes that the first cash flow listed in the function (in this case, the cash flow in cell A2) occurs one year after the initial investment. We add the initial cash outflow, contained in cell A1, as a separate argument to get the total project *NPV*. Remember, the numerical value in cell A1 equals −$250, so by adding a negative number, we are subtracting the initial cash outflow from the present value of the cash inflows in years 1–5. Excel's *NPV* function assumes that the project's cash flows are equally spaced through time and occur at the end of each period.

Figure 7.3
NPV of Global Wireless's Projects at 18% ($millions)

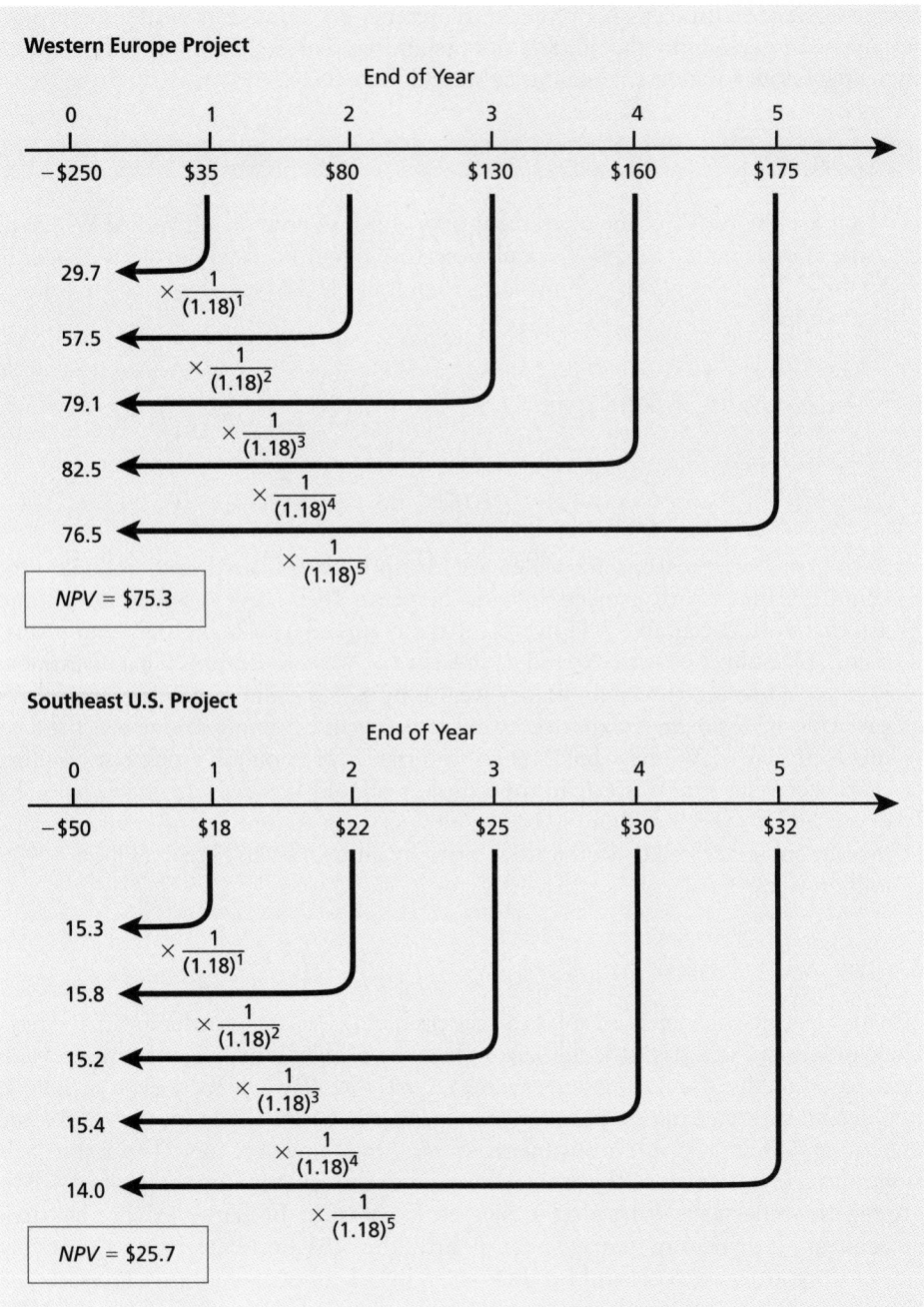

method incorporates all the cash flows that a project generates over its life, not just those that occur in the project's early years. Sixth, the *NPV* gives a direct estimate of the change in shareholder wealth resulting from a given investment.

Although we are enthusiastic supporters of the *NPV* approach, especially when compared with the other decision methods examined thus far, we must acknowledge that the *NPV* rule suffers from a few weaknesses. Relative to alternative capital budgeting tools, the *NPV* rule seems less intuitive to many users. When you hear that Global Wireless's southeast U.S. project has an *NPV* of $25.7 million, does that seem more or less intuitive than learning that it earns an accounting rate of return of 61.6 percent or that the investment pays back its initial cost in 2.4 years? Though the mathematics of an *NPV* calculation can hardly be called sophisticated, it is still easier to calculate a project's accounting rate of return or payback period than its *NPV*.

There is one other subtle drawback to the *NPV* rule, a drawback that results from the inability to incorporate the value of managerial flexibility when calculating a project's *NPV*. What we have in mind when we use the term "managerial flexibility" are options that managers can exploit after an investment has been made to increase its value. For example, if a firm makes an investment that turns out better than expected, managers have the option to expand that investment, making it even more valuable. Conversely, if a firm invests in a project that does not generate as much positive cash flow as anticipated, then managers have the option to scale back the investment and redeploy resources to more productive uses. The *NPV* method (like every other method studied in this chapter) does a poor job of capturing the value of managerial flexibility, or the value of options open to managers to improve the returns on investments after they have been made. To incorporate the value of these options into the analysis requires a highly sophisticated approach that relies on the principles of option pricing. We offer a brief introduction to valuing investments with option-like characteristics in Chapter 9, but defer an in-depth discussion of that technique until Chapter 19.

Whereas most large corporations apply the *NPV* method, perhaps in conjunction with other capital budgeting tools, to make major investment decisions, the *NPV* rule has a close cousin known as the *internal rate of return,* that is even more widely used. The internal rate of return uses essentially the same mathematics as *NPV* does for evaluating a project's merits. The output of internal rate of return analysis is a single, intuitively appealing number representing the return that an investment earns over its life. *In most cases, the internal rate of return yields investment recommendations that are in agreement with the* NPV *rule, although important differences between the two approaches arise when ranking alternative projects.*

---

6. What does it mean if a project has an *NPV* of $1 million?

7. Why might the discount rates used to calculate the *NPV*s of two competing projects differ at a given point in time?

Concept Review Questions

7.5 INTERNAL RATE OF RETURN

FINDING A PROJECT'S *IRR*

As methods used for evaluating investment projects, accounting rate of return, payback, and discounted payback suffer from common problems—the complete or partial failure to make adjustments for the time value of money and for risk. Alternative methods, such as *NPV*, correct these shortcomings. Perhaps the most popular and most intuitive of these alternatives is known as the **internal rate of return (IRR)** method. An investment's internal rate of return is analogous to a bond's *yield to maturity (YTM),* a concept we introduced in Chapter 4. Recall that the *YTM* of a bond is the discount rate that equates the present value of the bond's future cash flows to its market price. The *YTM* measures the compound annual return that an investor earns by purchasing a bond and holding it until maturity (provided that all payments are made as promised and that interest payments can be reinvested at the same rate). In a similar vein, the *IRR* of an investment project is the compound annual rate of return on the project, given its up-front costs and subsequent cash flows.

A project's *IRR* is the discount rate that causes the net present value of all project cash flows to equal zero:

$$NPV = CF_0 + \frac{CF_1}{(1+r)^1} + \frac{CF_2}{(1+r)^2} + \frac{CF_3}{(1+r)^3} + \cdots + \frac{CF_N}{(1+r)^N} = \$0 \quad \textbf{(Eq. 7.2)}$$

To find a project's *IRR*, we must begin by specifying the project's cash flows. Next, using a financial calculator, spreadsheet, or even trial and error, we find the discount rate that equates the present value of cash flows to zero. Once we have the *IRR* in hand, we compare it with a prespecified hurdle rate established by the firm. The hurdle rate represents the firm's minimum acceptable return for a given project, so **the *IRR* decision rule is to invest only if the project's *IRR* exceeds the hurdle rate; otherwise reject the project.**

But where does the hurdle rate come from? How do firms decide whether to require projects to exceed a 10 percent hurdle or a 20 percent hurdle? The answer to this question provides insight into another advantage of *IRR* over capital budgeting methods that focus on a project's accounting rate of return or payback period. A company should set the hurdle rate at a level that reflects market returns on investments that are just as risky as the project under consideration. For example, if the project at hand involves expanding a chain of fast-food restaurants, then the hurdle rate should reflect the returns that other fast-food businesses offer investors in the marketplace. Therefore, the *IRR* method, like the *NPV* method, establishes a hurdle rate or a decision criterion that is *market based,* unlike the accounting-based and payback approaches that establish arbitrary thresholds for investment approval. In fact, *for a given project, the hurdle rate used in* IRR *analysis should be the discount rate used in* NPV *analysis.*

Figure 7.4 is a **net present value (*NPV*) profile,** which plots a project's *NPV* (on the *y* axis) against various discount rates (on the *x* axis). The *NPV* profile illustrates

Figure 7.4
NPV Profile and
Shareholder Wealth

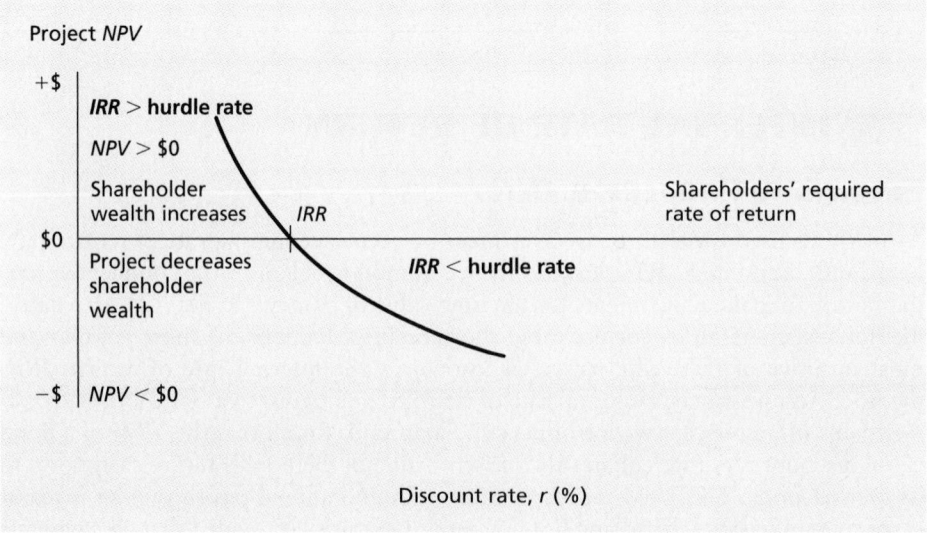

the relationship between a typical project's *NPV* and its *IRR*. By "typical," we mean a project with its initial cash outflow and subsequent cash inflows. In this case, the *NPV* declines as the discount rate used to calculate the *NPV* increases. Not all projects have this feature, as we will soon see. The line in Figure 7.4 plots the *NPV* of a project at various discount rates. When the discount rate is relatively low, the project has a positive *NPV*. When the discount rate is high, the project has a negative *NPV*. *At some discount rate, the* NPV *of the project will equal zero, and that rate is the project's* IRR.

APPLYING THE MODEL 7.5

Suppose that Global Wireless requires its analysts to calculate the *IRR* of all proposed investments, and the company agrees to undertake only those investments that offer an *IRR* exceeding 18 percent, a rate that Global Wireless believes to be an industry standard. Figure 7.5 presents a time line depicting the *IRR* calculation procedure for Global Wireless's two projects. To obtain the *IRR* for each project currently under consideration, just solve these two equations:

$$\$0 = -\$250 + \frac{\$35}{(1 + r_{WE})^1} + \frac{\$80}{(1 + r_{WE})^2} + \frac{\$130}{(1 + r_{WE})^3} + \frac{\$160}{(1 + r_{WE})^4} + \frac{\$175}{(1 + r_{WE})^5}$$

$$\$0 = -\$50 + \frac{\$18}{(1 + r_{SE})^1} + \frac{\$22}{(1 + r_{SE})^2} + \frac{\$25}{(1 + r_{SE})^3} + \frac{\$30}{(1 + r_{SE})^4} + \frac{\$32}{(1 + r_{SE})^5}$$

where r_{WE} is the *IRR* for the Western Europe project and r_{SE} is the *IRR* for the southeast U.S. project. Solving these equations yields the following:[7]

$r_{WE} = 27.8\%$

$r_{SE} = 36.7\%$

Because both investments exceed the hurdle rate of 18 percent, Global Wireless would like to undertake both projects. But what if it can invest in only one project or the other? Should the company invest in the southeast U.S. project because it offers a higher *IRR* than the alternative?

ADVANTAGES OF THE IRR METHOD

A number of advantages make the *IRR* one of the most widely used methods for evaluating capital investments. First, the *IRR* makes an appropriate adjustment for the time value of money. The value of a dollar received in the first year is greater than the value of a dollar received in the second year. Even cash flows that arrive several years

---

[7.] Of course, you can make this calculation using a financial calculator or *Excel*. Here's how to use Excel to solve for the *IRR*. Put the numbers for the Western Europe project in column A of a spreadsheet, and put the numbers for the southeast U.S. project in column B. In row 1, type in the cash outflow for each project, entering the values as negative numbers. In rows 2–6 of the spreadsheet, enter the cash inflows in each year. Then, in any empty cell, type "=*IRR*(A1:A6, 0.10)" to calculate the *IRR* of the Western Europe project. The cells A1:A6 contain the relevant cash flows, and the value "0.10" is just a starting value that Excel uses to begin searching for the *IRR*. Likewise, enter the formula "=*IRR*(B1:B6, 0.10)" in any empty cell to calculate the *IRR* of the southeast U.S. investment.

Figure 7.5
IRR of Global Wireless's
Projects ($millions)

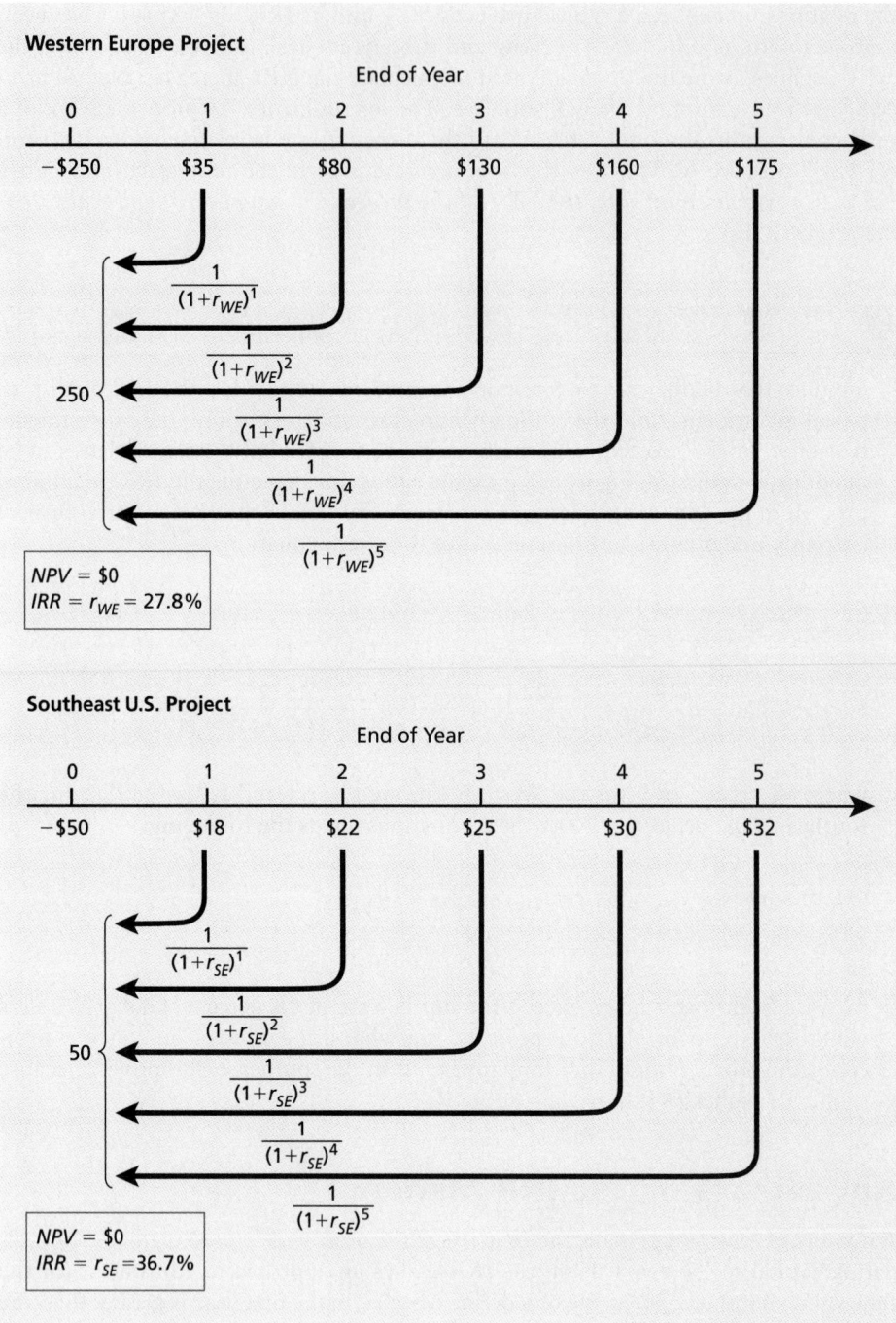

in the future receive some weight in the analysis (unlike payback, which totally ignores distant cash flows). Second, the hurdle rate itself can be based on market returns obtainable on similar investments. Because market rates vary based on the
risks of different instruments, firms can similarly choose different hurdle rates for
projects with different risks. This takes away some of the subjectivity that creeps into

other methods. Third, because the "answer" that comes out of an *IRR* analysis is a rate of return, its meaning is easy for both financial and nonfinancial managers to grasp intuitively. As we will see, however, the intuitive appeal of the *IRR* approach has its drawbacks, particularly when ranking investments with different *IRRs*. Fourth, the *IRR* technique focuses on cash flow rather than on accounting measures of income.

PROBLEMS WITH THE INTERNAL RATE OF RETURN

Though it represents a substantial improvement over the accounting rate of return or payback analysis, the *IRR* technique has some quirks and problems that in certain situations should concern analysts. Some of these problems arise from the mathematics of the *IRR* calculation, but other difficulties come into play only when companies must discriminate between **mutually exclusive projects.** If two projects offer *IRRs* in excess of the hurdle rate, but the firm can only invest in one, which project should it pursue? It turns out that the intuitive answer, to select the project with the highest *IRR,* sometimes leads to bad decisions.

We can identify two classes of problems that analysts encounter when evaluating investments using the *IRR* technique. The first class can be described as "mathematical problems," which are difficulties in interpreting the numbers that one obtains from solving an *IRR* equation. For example, consider a simple project with cash flows at three different points in time:

CF_0 CF_1 CF_2

0   1   2

years $\longrightarrow$

CF_0 is the immediate cash flow when the project begins, and CF_1 and CF_2 are cash flows that occur at the end of years 1 and 2, respectively. Note that conceptually the values of CF_0, CF_1, and CF_2 could be either positive or negative. Solving for this project's *IRR* means setting the net present value of all these cash flows equal to zero:

$$NPV = CF_0 + \frac{CF_1}{(1 + r)^1} + \frac{CF_2}{(1 + r)^2} = \$0$$

Notice that this equation involves terms such as $[1/(1 + r)]^1$ and $[1/(1 + r)]^2$. In other words, this is a quadratic equation in terms of $[1/(1 + r)]$. Solving a quadratic equation can result in a variety of possible outcomes, including (1) a unique solution, (2) multiple solutions, and (3) no real solution. The following examples illustrate some of the problems that may arise when interpreting solutions to an *IRR* equation.[8]

[8.] Another "problem" that we do not discuss due to its unnecessary focus on mathematical precision is commonly called the **reinvestment rate assumption.** It results from the fact that when using *IRR* there is an implicit assumption that in order to actually earn the calculated IRR on the project's full initial cash outlay, the firm must be able to reinvest its *intermediate cash inflows*—cash inflows received during the project's life—at a rate equal to the *IRR*. Although *NPV* suffers from similar criticism, most analysts much prefer its very conservative assumption that intermediate cash flows can be reinvested at the firm's cost of capital. Clearly, the more conservative reinvestment rate assumption of *NPV* has appeal, because it doesn't assume that other projects earning the *IRR* are available for reinvestment of intermediate cash flows. On this technical point, we likewise favor *NPV.*

Lending versus Borrowing. A firm establishes a hurdle rate of 20 percent for new investments. Consider two projects with cash flows occurring at just two dates—now and one year from now.

Project	Cash Flow Now	Cash Flow in One Year	IRR	NPV (20%)
1	−$100	+$150	50%	+$25
2	+100	−150	50	−25

The first project displays the familiar pattern of an initial cash outflow followed by a cash inflow. Most investment projects probably fit this profile. But the second project begins with a cash inflow followed by a cash outflow. What kinds of projects in the real world follow this pattern? Think of a firm that is cutting timber. The timber is cut and sold immediately at a profit, but when harvesting is complete, the company must replant the forest at considerable expense. Similarly, consider an optional warranty sold with a new car. The warranty seller receives payment up front but must pay claims later on.

Both projects have a 50 percent IRR, but are the two projects equally attractive? Are these projects equally desirable? It should be intuitive to you that project 1 is superior because it generates net cash inflows over time, while project 2 generates net cash outflows. Indeed, the NPVs bear this out, as project 1 generates a positive $25 NPV, whereas project 2 yields a negative $25 NPV.

The problem we are confronting here is known as the lending versus borrowing problem. We can think of project 1 as analogous to a loan. Cash flows out today in exchange for a larger amount of cash in one year. When we lend money, a higher interest rate, or a higher internal rate of return, is preferable, other things held constant. In contrast, project 2 is analogous to borrowing money. We receive cash up front but have to pay back a larger amount later. When borrowing money, a lower interest rate, or a lower IRR is preferred, other factors held constant. Therefore, we can modify the internal rate of return decision rule as follows:

1. When projects have initial cash outflows and subsequent cash inflows, invest when the project IRR exceeds the hurdle rate.
2. When projects have initial cash inflows and subsequent cash outflows, invest when the project IRR falls below the hurdle rate.

Figure 7.6 illustrates this situation. The NPV of project 1 falls as the discount rate rises, as we would normally expect. Therefore, if the IRR exceeds the hurdle rate, the project's NPV is positive; but if the IRR falls below the hurdle rate, the NPV is negative. Thus, following the usual rule of accepting projects when the IRR exceeds the hurdle rate makes sense. Notice that the NPV of project 2 actually rises as the discount rate rises. This counterintuitive relationship holds because the firm is essentially borrowing money in project 2. The higher the rate at which the firm discounts the amount it will have to repay, the lower the present value of that payment and the higher the NPV of the project. In this case, it makes sense to accept projects only when the IRR falls short of the firm's hurdle rate.

Multiple IRRs. A second difficulty with the IRR method can occur when a project's cash flows alternate between negative and positive values—that is, when the project generates an alternating series of net cash inflows and outflows. In that case, there may be more than one solution to the IRR equation. As an example, consider a project with the following stream of cash flows:

Figure 7.6
Lending versus
Borrowing

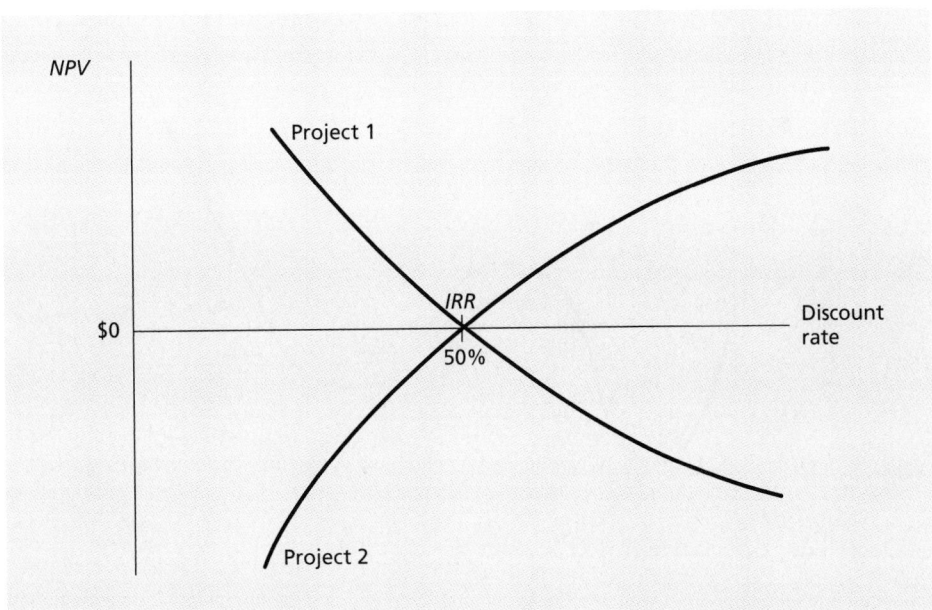

Year	CF ($ in millions)
0	+100
1	−460
2	+791
3	−602.6
4	+171.6

Admittedly, this project has a rather strange sequence of alternating net cash inflows and outflows, but it is not hard to think of real-world investments that generate cash flow streams that flip back and forth like this. For example, think about high-technology products. A new product costs money to develop. It generates plenty of cash for a year or two, but it quickly becomes obsolete. Obsolescence necessitates more spending to develop an upgraded version of the product, which then generates cash again. The cycle continues indefinitely.

Figure 7.7 presents the NPV profile for a project with the cash flow shown above at various discount rates. Notice that there are four points on the graph at which the project NPV equals zero. In other words, there are four IRRs for this project, including $IRR_1 = 0$ percent, $IRR_2 = 10$ percent, $IRR_3 = 20$ percent, and $IRR_4 = 30$ percent. How does one apply the IRR decision rule in a situation such as this? Suppose that the hurdle rate for this project is 15 percent. Two of the four IRRs on this project exceed the hurdle rate, and two fall below the hurdle rate. Should the firm invest or not? The only way to know for sure is to check the NPV. On the graph, we see that at a discount rate of 15 percent, the project's NPV is positive, so the firm should invest.

The general rule of thumb is that the maximum number of IRRs that a project can have equals the number of sign changes in the cash flow stream. Therefore, in the typical project with cash outflows up front and cash inflows later on, there is just one sign change, and there will be at most one IRR. In the previous example, there are four sign changes in the cash flow stream and four different IRRs. *In the event that you have to evaluate a project with more than one sign change in the cash flows, be-*

Figure 7.7
Multiple *IRR*s

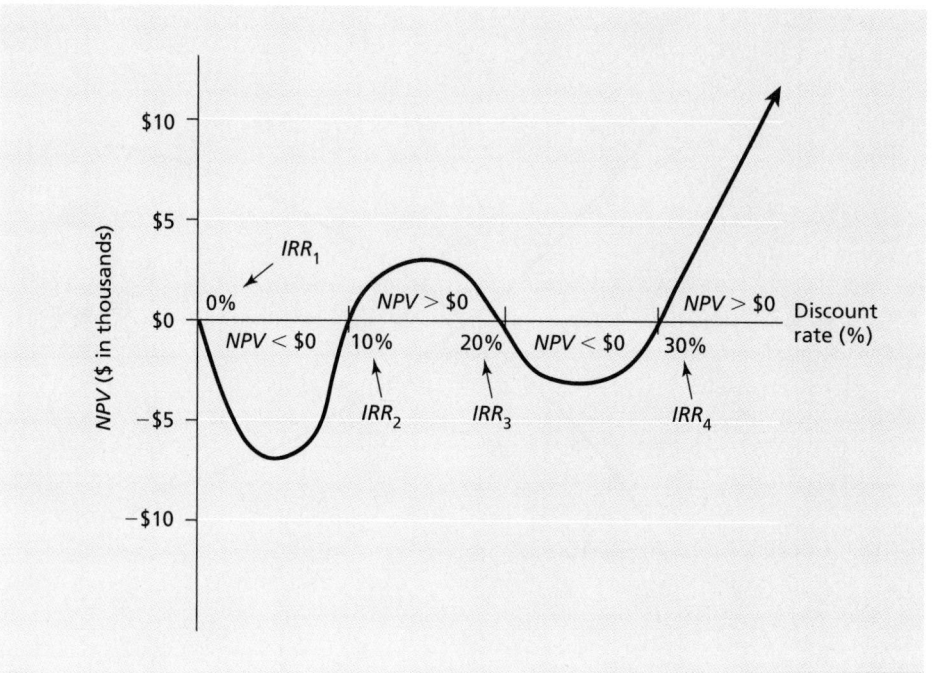

ware of the multiple IRR *problem.* In this situation, analyze the *NPV* profile because using the *IRR* may lead to an incorrect investment.

Using Modified Internal Rate of Return to Eliminate Multiple *IRR*s. One way to apply *IRR* and eliminate potential multiple *IRR*s is to begin with the last cash outflow (negative cash flow), discount it back one year at the firm's cost of capital, and add it to the earlier years' cash flow. Next, discount that sum back another year and add it to the earlier years' cash flow, repeating this process until the sum results in a cash inflow. This method eliminates all non-year-zero cash outflows, which should assure only one sign change in the modified cash flow stream, and therefore only one *IRR*, called the **modified internal rate of return (*MIRR*).** An example demonstrates this technique.

APPLYING THE MODEL 7.6

We can use the following cash flows to calculate the project's *MIRR*.

Year	CF ($)
0	+657
1	−601
2	−986
3	−52
4	+1,000

This project, which has two sign changes in its cash flow stream, has two different *IRR*s—one at 1.5% and another at 49.9%. Because its *NPV* at the firm's 15% cost of capital is about −$74, it is clear that the firm's *NPV* would be negative between its 1.5% and 49.9% *IRR*s. The project is clearly not acceptable.

We begin by discounting the year 3 cash outflow back one year and adding its present value to the year 2 cash flow, which results in a cash outflow of $1,031 at the end of year 2.

$$PV \text{ of Year 2 and Year 3 Cash Flow at End of Year 2} = -\$986 + \frac{-\$52}{(1.15)^1}$$

$$= -\$986 - \$45 = -\$1,031$$

Next, we discount the new year 2 cash outflow back one year and add its present value to the year 1 cash outflow, which results in a cash outflow of $1,498 at the end of year 1.

$$PV \text{ of Year 1 and New Year 2 Cash Flow at End of Year 1} = -\$601 + \frac{-\$1,031}{(1.15)^1}$$

$$= -\$601 - \$897 = -\$1,498$$

Finally, we discount the new year 1 cash outflow back one year and add its present value to the year 0 cash inflow, which results in a cash outflow of $646 at time 0:

$$PV \text{ of Year 0 and New Year 1 Cash Flow in Year 0} = \$657 + \frac{-\$1,498}{(1.15)^1} = -\$646$$

Substituting these combined year 0, 1, 2, and 3 cash flows into the original cash flow stream for the year 0 cash flow, the new cash flow stream is as follows:

Year	CF ($)
0	−646
1	0
2	0
3	0
4	1,000

Note that there is now only one sign change in the new cash flow stream. We can now solve for the *IRR*.

$$\$0 = -\$646 + \frac{\$0}{(1 + MIRR)^1} + \frac{\$0}{(1 + MIRR)^2} + \frac{\$0}{(1 + MIRR)^3} + \frac{\$1,000}{(1 + MIRR)^4}$$

Using a financial calculator or *Excel* to solve for the *MIRR*, we get:

$$MIRR = 11.54\%$$

Because the *MIRR* of 11.54% is less than the firm's 15% cost of capital, the project would not be acceptable. We noted earlier that at the 15% cost of capital the project would have a negative *NPV* and therefore would not be acceptable. So the *MIRR* and *NPV* result in the same "reject" decision.

No Real Solution. Occasionally, when you enter the cash flows from a particular investment into a calculator or a spreadsheet, you may receive an error message indicating that there is no solution to the problem. For some cash flow patterns, it is possible that there is no real discount rate that equates the project's *NPV* to zero.

In these cases, the only solution to the *IRR* equation involves imaginary numbers, hardly something that we can compare with a firm's hurdle rate.

APPLYING THE MODEL 7.7

When we first looked at the Global Wireless Western Europe expansion project, we examined cash flows over a 5-year project life. Let's modify the example a little. Suppose that the project life is six years rather than five, and in the sixth year the firm must incur a large negative cash flow (an outflow). The modified cash flow projections now look like this:

	Western Europe Project
Year	($ in millions)
0	−250
1	35
2	80
3	130
4	160
5	175
6	−355

When we attempt to calculate the *IRR* for this stream of cash flows, we find that *Excel* (or our financial calculator) returns an error code. The problem is that for this stream of cash flows, there is no real solution to the *IRR* equation. That is, there is no interest rate at which the present value of cash flows equals zero. If we cannot determine the *IRR* of this project, how can we determine whether the project meets the firm's hurdle rate of 18 percent? In this particular example, the magnitudes of the cash outflows at the beginning and end of the modified project are such that intuition suggests that Global Wireless should not invest. However, it is possible to generate scenarios in which no solution to the *IRR* equation exists, and the pattern of cash flows over time is sufficiently complex that it is difficult to decide whether to invest based on intuition.

The last three examples illustrate various problems that analysts may encounter when using the *IRR* decision rule. These problems are mathematical in nature in the sense that they involve difficulties in getting a solution to the *IRR* equation or in interpreting the solution that you obtain. Although we do not want to diminish the importance of watching out for these problems, we suspect that, in practice, they are of secondary importance. We mean that most investment projects you will evaluate using the *IRR* method will probably have a unique solution with little ambiguity about whether the project involves borrowing or lending (because most projects involve cash outflows up front followed by cash inflows). However, two additional problems may arise when analysts use the *IRR* method to prioritize projects or to choose between mutually exclusive projects.

IRR, NPV, AND MUTUALLY EXCLUSIVE PROJECTS

The Scale Problem. Suppose that a friend promises to pay you $2 tomorrow if you lend him $1 today. If you make the loan and your friend fulfills his end of the bargain, you will have made an investment with a 100 percent *IRR*.[9] Now consider a different case. Your friend asks you to lend him $100 today in exchange for $150

[9.] The *IRR* is 100 percent per day in this example, which is not a bad return if you annualize it.

tomorrow. The *IRR* on that investment is 50 percent, exactly half the *IRR* of the first example. Both of these loans offer very high rates of return. Assuming that you trust the friend to repay you in either case, which investment would you choose if you could choose only one? The first investment increases your wealth by $1, and the second increases your wealth by $50. Even though the rate of return is lower on the second investment, most people would prefer to lend the larger amount because of its substantially greater payoff.

The point of these examples is to illustrate the *scale problem* inherent in *IRR* analysis. When choosing between mutually exclusive investments, we cannot conclude that the one offering the highest *IRR* necessarily provides the greatest wealth-creation opportunity. When several alternative investments offer *IRRs* that exceed a firm's hurdle rate, choosing the investment that maximizes shareholder wealth involves more than picking the project with the highest *IRR*. For example, take another look at the investment opportunities faced by Global Wireless, opportunities that vary dramatically in scale.

APPLYING THE MODEL 7.8

Here again are the *NPV* and *IRR* figures for the two investment alternatives.

Project	IRR	NPV (18%)
Western Europe	27.8%	$75.3 million
Southeast U.S.	36.7	25.7 million

If we had to choose just one project, and we ranked them based on their *IRRs*, we would choose to invest in the southeast U.S. project. But we also have seen that the Western Europe project generates a much higher *NPV*, meaning that it creates more wealth for Global Wireless shareholders. The *NPV* criterion tells us to expand in Western Europe rather than in the southeast United States. Why the conflict? The scale of the Western Europe expansion is roughly five times that of the southeast U.S. project. Even though the southeast U.S. investment provides a higher rate of return, the opportunity to make the much larger Western Europe investment (an investment that also offers a return well above the firm's hurdle rate) is more attractive.

Fortunately for analysts who prefer to use the *IRR* method, there is a resolution to the scale problem. The solution involves calculating the *IRR* for a hypothetical project, a project with cash flows equal to the difference in cash flows between the large-scale (Western Europe) and small-scale (southeast U.S.) investments. Call this the incremental project. The logic of this approach is as follows: We already know that both investments have *IRRs* that exceed the hurdle rate, but due to limitations of money or managerial talent, we can invest in only one. But we can think of the Western Europe investment as consisting of two investments rolled into one. The Western Europe project equals the sum of the southeast U.S. project and the incremental project. If we examine the incremental project's *IRR* and find that it also exceeds our hurdle rate, then by accepting the Western Europe project, we are essentially making two investments, not just one. In accepting the Western Europe project, it is as if we are accepting one project with cash flows identical to those of the southeast U.S. investment and another with cash flows equal to those of the incremental project.[10]

[10.] The *incremental project cash flows* are found by subtracting the year-to-year cash flows of the small-scale project from those of the large-scale project. Here we subtract each years' cash flow of the southeast U.S. project from the comparable years' cash flow of the Western Europe project. Note that the cash flows of both projects are shown in Figure 7.1.

Year	Incremental *CF* [Western Europe − Southeast U.S.] ($ in millions)
0	−200
1	17
2	58
3	105
4	130
5	143

The *IRR* of this cash flow stream equals 25.8 percent. Because this exceeds the 18 percent hurdle rate, we conclude that we would like to accept the incremental project AND the southeast U.S. project, but of course, the only way to do both is to accept the Western Europe project!

The Timing Problem. Managers of public corporations often receive criticism for neglecting long-term investment opportunities for the sake of meeting short-term financial performance goals. We prefer to remain noncommittal on whether corporate managers, as a rule, put too much emphasis on short-term performance. However, we agree with the proposition that a naive reliance on the *IRR* method can lead to investment decisions that sometimes favor investments with short-term payoffs over those that offer returns over a longer horizon. The *Applying the Model* illustrates the problem we have in mind.

APPLYING THE MODEL 7.9

A company wants to evaluate two investment proposals. The first involves a major effort in new product development. The initial cost is $1 billion, and the company expects the project to generate relatively meager cash flows in the first four years, followed by a big payoff in year 5. The second investment is a significant marketing campaign to attract new customers. It too has an initial outlay of $1 billion, but it generates significant cash flows almost immediately and lower levels of cash in the later years. A financial analyst prepares cash flow projections and calculates each project's *IRR* and *NPV* as shown in the following table (the firm uses 10 percent as its hurdle rate):

Cash Flow	Product Development ($ in millions)	Marketing Campaign ($ in millions)
Initial Outlay	−1,000	−1,000
Year 1	0	450
Year 2	50	350
Year 3	100	300
Year 4	200	200
Year 5	1,500	100
Technique		
IRR	14.1%	15.9%
NPV (@10%)	$184.44	$122.44

The analyst observes that the first project generates a higher *NPV*, whereas the second offers a higher *IRR*. Bewildered, he wonders which project to recommend to senior management.

use NPV to → Compare long-term projects w/ short-term ones

Even though both projects require the same initial investment and both last for five years, the marketing campaign generates more cash flow in the early years than the product development proposal. Therefore, in a relative sense the payoff from product development occurs later than the payoff from marketing. We know from our discussion of interest-rate risk in Chapter 4 that when interest rates change, long-term bond prices move more than short-term bond prices. The same phenomenon is at work here. Figure 7.8 plots the *NPV* profiles for the two proposals on the same set of axes. Notice that the line plotting *NPVs* for the product development idea is much steeper than the other. In simple terms, this means the *NPV* of that investment is much more sensitive to the discount rate than is the *NPV* of the marketing campaign.

Each investment's *IRR* appears in Figure 7.8 where the *NPV* lines cross the *x*-axis. Figure 7.8 shows that both *IRRs* exceed the hurdle rate of 10 percent and that the marketing campaign has the higher *IRR*. The two lines intersect at a discount rate of 12.5 percent. At that discount rate, the *NPVs* of the projects are equal. At discount rates below 12.5 percent, product development, which has a longer-term payoff, has the higher *NPV*. At discount rates above 12.5 percent, the investment in the marketing campaign offers a larger *NPV*. Given that the required rate of return on investments for this particular firm is 10 percent, the firm should choose to spend the $1 billion on product development. However, if the firm bases its investment decision solely on achieving the highest *IRR,* it will choose the marketing campaign instead.

In summary, we can say that when the timing of cash flows is very different from one project to another, the project with the highest *IRR* may or may not have the highest *NPV*. As in the case of the scale problem, the timing problem can lead firms to reject investments they should accept. We want to emphasize that this problem (and the scale problem) occurs only when firms must choose between mutually exclusive projects. In the previous example, if the firm could invest in both projects, it should.

When firms must prioritize projects, leaving some acceptable projects on the table, there are two ways they can avoid falling into the timing trap. First, using *NPV* will lead to the correct decision when evaluating projects with very different cash

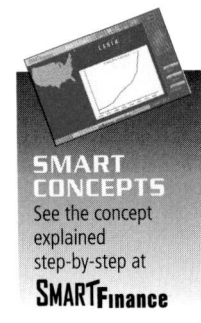

**SMART
CONCEPTS**
See the concept explained step-by-step at
SMARTFinance

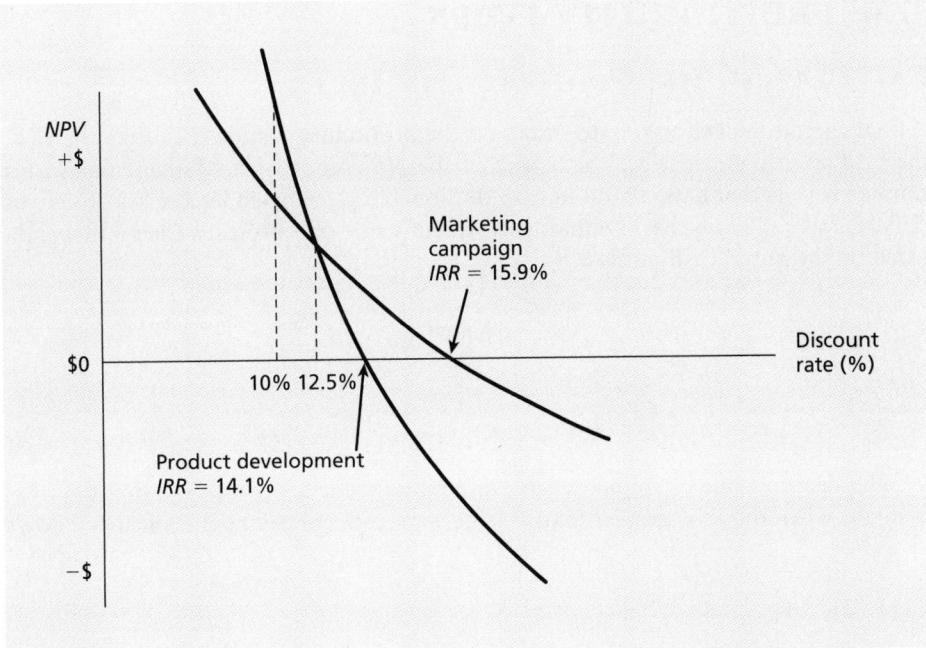

www.thomsonedu.com/finance/smartfinance

Figure 7.8
NPV Profiles Demonstrating the Timing Problem

flow patterns over time. Second, analysts can look at the incremental cash flows on the long-term project compared to those on the short-term project, the same technique we used to deal with the *IRR*'s scale problem. For example, calculating the incremental cash flows on the product development idea compared to the marketing campaign by subtracting the marketing campaign cash flows from those associated with product development, we obtain the following:

	[Product Development –
Cash Flow	Marketing Campaign] ($ in millions)
Year 0	0
Year 1	−450
Year 2	−300
Year 3	−200
Year 4	0
Year 5	1,400

The *IRR* of this incremental cash flow stream is 12.5 percent. Because the *IRR* on the incremental project exceeds the firm's hurdle rate (10 percent), it makes sense to invest in product development.

Concept Review Questions

8. Describe how the *IRR* and *NPV* approaches are related.

9. If the *IRR* for a given project exceeds a firm's hurdle rate, does that mean that the project necessarily has a positive *NPV*? Explain.

10. What causes multiple *IRR*s? How can the *modified internal rate of return (MIRR)* be used to eliminate multiple *IRR*s?

11. Describe the "scale problem" and the "timing problem" and explain the potential effects of these problems on the choice of mutually exclusive projects, using *IRR* versus *NPV*.

7.6 PROFITABILITY INDEX

CALCULATING THE PROFITABILITY INDEX

A final capital budgeting tool to discuss is the **profitability index (*PI*).** Like the *IRR*, the profitability index is a close cousin of the *NPV* approach. Mathematically, for simple projects that have an initial cash outflow (CF_0) followed by a series of inflows ($CF_1, CF_2, \ldots, CF_N$), the *PI* equals the present value of a project's cash inflows, divided by the initial cash outflow.[11]

$$PI = \frac{\dfrac{CF_1}{(1+r)^1} + \dfrac{CF_2}{(1+r)^2} + \cdots + \dfrac{CF_N}{(1+r)^N}}{CF_0}$$

(Eq. 7.3)

The decision rule to follow when evaluating investment projects using the *PI* is to invest when the *PI* is greater than 1.0 (i.e., when the present value of cash inflows

---

[11.] An alternate definition is $PI = \dfrac{NPV}{CF_0}$. Although this formula reduces the calculated *PI* by 1.00, it results in the same ordering of projects that results using Equation 7.3. Some analysts prefer the alternative definition due to its computational simplicity.

exceeds the initial cash outflow) and to refrain from investing when the *PI* is less than 1.0. Notice that if the *PI* is above 1.0, the *NPV* must be greater than zero. This means *the NPV and PI decision rules will always yield the same investment recommendation when we are simply trying to accept or reject a single project.*

APPLYING THE MODEL 7.10

To calculate the *PI* for each of Global Wireless's investment projects, calculate the present value of its cash inflows from years 1–5 and then divide by the initial cash outflow to obtain the following result:

Project	PV of CF (1–5) ($ in millions)	Initial Outlay ($ in millions)	PI
Western Europe	325.3	250	1.3
Southeast U.S.	75.7	50	1.5

Both projects have a *PI* greater than 1.0, so both are worthwhile. However, notice that if we rank projects based on the *PI*, the southeast U.S. project looks better.

Because the *NPV, IRR,* and *PI* methods are so closely related, they share many of the same advantages relative to accounting rate of return or payback analysis, and there is no need to reiterate those advantages here. However, it is worth pointing out that the *PI* and the *IRR* share an important flaw. Both suffer from the *scale problem* described earlier. Recall that our *NPV* calculations suggested that the Western Europe project created more value for shareholders than the southeast U.S. endeavor, whereas the *IRR* and *PI* comparisons suggest just the opposite project ranking. The reason that the *IRR* and *PI* analyses identify the southeast U.S. project as the superior investment is that they do not take into account the differences in scale between the two projects. For the southeast U.S. project, the *PI* indicates that project cash inflows exceed the initial cash outflow by 50 percent on a present-value basis. The present value of cash inflows for the Western Europe investment exceeds the initial cash outflow by just 30 percent. But the Western Europe project is much larger, and as our *NPV* figures reveal, it generates considerably more wealth for Global Wireless stockholders.

When we encountered the scale problem before, we found that it could be solved by looking at the *IRR* of an incremental project. In the same way, we can modify our analysis using the *PI* to solve its scale problem. First, calculate the incremental cash flows on the Western Europe investment relative to the southeast U.S. investment. Next, take the present value of these incremental cash flows in years 1–5. Finally, divide this present value by the incremental initial cash outflow. If the profitability index on the incremental project exceeds 1.0, then invest in the larger project.

[Western Europe − Southeast U.S.]

Year	Incremental CF ($ in millions)	PV (18%)
0	−200	−200.0
1	17	14.4
2	58	41.7
3	105	63.9
4	130	67.0
5	143	62.5

$$PI = \frac{\$14.4 + \$41.7 + \$63.9 + \$67.0 + \$62.5}{\$200.0} = \frac{\$249.5}{\$200.0} = 1.25$$

Because the *PI* of the incremental project equals 1.25, we should choose the large-scale project, the Western Europe expansion proposal.

THE PROFITABILITY INDEX AND CAPITAL RATIONING

At several points in this chapter, we have asked the following question: If a firm must choose between several investment opportunities, all of which are worth taking, how does the firm prioritize projects? We have seen that the *IRR* and *PI* methods sometimes rank projects differently than the *NPV* does, though it is often possible to reconcile differences in the recommendations of each method by examining incremental cash flows between projects.

There is a fundamental question that we have avoided until now. If the firm has many projects with positive *NPV*s (or investments with acceptable *IRR*s), why not accept all of them? One possibility is that the firm simply does not have enough money to finance all its attractive investment opportunities. But surely large, publicly traded firms could raise money by issuing new shares to investors and use the proceeds to undertake any and all appealing investments?

If you watch firms closely over a period of time, you will notice that most do not issue new shares very often. As Chapter 11 discusses more fully, firms seem to prefer to finance investments with internally generated cash flow and will only infrequently raise money in the external capital markets by issuing new equity. There are several possible reasons for this apparent reluctance to issue new equity. First, when firms announce their intention to raise new equity capital, they may send an unintended negative signal to the market. Perhaps investors will interpret the announcement as a sign that the firm's existing investments are not doing very well. Perhaps investors will see the decision to issue new shares as an indication that managers believe the firm's stock is overvalued. In either case, investors may react negatively to this announcement, causing the stock price to fall. Undoubtedly, managers will try to persuade investors that the funds being raised will be invested in profitable projects, but convincing investors that this is the true motive for the issue will be an uphill struggle.

A second reason why managers may avoid issuing new equity is that by doing so, they dilute their ownership stake in the firm (unless they participate in the offering by purchasing some of the new shares). A smaller ownership stake means that managers control a shrinking block of votes, raising the potential of a corporate takeover or other threat to their control of the firm.

In conversations with senior executives, we often hear a third reason why firms do not fund every investment project that looks promising. Behind each idea for a new investment is a person, someone who may have an emotional attachment to the idea or a career-building motivation for proposing it. Upper-level managers are wise to be a little skeptical of the cash flow forecasts they see on projects with favorable *NPV*s or *IRR*s. It is a given that every cash flow forecast will prove to be wrong, but if the forecasting process is unbiased, half the time forecasts will be too pessimistic, and half the time they will be too optimistic. Which half is likely to surface on the radar screen of a CFO or CEO in a large corporation? Rationing capital is one mechanism by which senior managers impose discipline on the capital budgeting process. By doing so, they hope to weed out some of the investment proposals with an optimistic bias built into the cash flow projections.

Whatever the motivation for their behavior, managers cannot always invest in every project that offers a positive *NPV*. In such an environment, **capital rationing** occurs. Given a set of attractive investment opportunities, managers must choose a combination of projects that maximizes shareholder wealth, subject to the constraint of limited funds. In this environment, ranking projects using the *PI* can be very useful. Once managers rank projects, they select the investment with the highest *PI*. If the total amount of capital available has not been fully exhausted, then managers invest in the project with the second-highest *PI*, and so on until no more capital remains to invest. By following this routine, managers will select a portfolio of projects that in aggregate generates a higher *NPV* than any other combination of projects.[12]

Table 7.1 illustrates this technique. A particular firm has five projects to choose from, all of which have positive *NPV*s and *IRR*s that exceed the firm's hurdle rate of 12 percent. Notice that the first project has the highest *IRR* and the highest *PI*, but project 5 has a larger *NPV*. This is again the familiar scale problem. Suppose that this firm can invest no more than $300 million this year. What portfolio of investments maximizes shareholder wealth?

Table 7.1
Capital Rationing and the Profitability Index

Year	Projects ($ in millions)				
	1	2	3	4	5
0	−70	−80	−100	−150	−200
1	30	30	40	50	90
2	40	35	50	55	80
3	50	55	60	60	80
4	55	60	65	90	110
NPV	$59.2	$52.0	$59.6	$38.4	$71.0
IRR	44%	36%	36%	23%	28%
PI	1.8	1.6	1.6	1.3	1.4

Notice that there are several combinations of projects that satisfy the constraint of investing no more than $300 million. If we begin by accepting the project with the highest *PI*, then continue to accept additional projects until we bump into the $300 million capital constraint, we will invest in projects 1, 2, and 3. With these three projects, we have invested just $250 million, but this does not leave us with enough capital to entertain either project 4 or 5. The total *NPV* obtainable from the first three projects is $170.8 million. No other combination of projects that satisfies the capital constraint yields a higher aggregate *NPV*. For example, investing in projects 3 and 5—thereby using up the full allotment of $300 million in capital—generates a total *NPV* of just $130.6 million. Likewise, investing in projects 1, 2, and 4, another combination that utilizes all $300 million in capital, generates an aggregate *NPV* of $149.6 million.

---

12. How are the *NPV, IRR,* and *PI* approaches related?

13. Why doesn't choosing the projects with the highest *PIs* (within the budget constraint) always lead to the best *capital rationing* decisions?

Concept Review Questions

[12.] We are simplifying a bit here. Sorting projects according to the *PI* and selecting from that list until capital runs out may not maximize shareholder wealth when capital is rationed not only at the beginning of an investment's life, but also in all subsequent periods. This method can also lead to suboptimal decisions when projects are interdependent—that is, when one investment is contingent on another. In these situations, more-complex decision tools, such as integer programming, may be required.

COMPARATIVE CORPORATE FINANCE

Capital Budgeting in Sweden, South Africa, and the United Kingdom

We have seen that managers of publicly traded U.S. firms use discounted cash flow techniques in capital budgeting far more today than in the past. But what of managers in other countries? Three recent academic studies present survey evidence of how frequently discounted cash flow techniques are used by managers of Swedish, South African, and British companies. The results are somewhat encouraging. Sandahl and Sjögren (2003) find that 64.8 percent of the 128 responding Swedish companies use either *NPV* (52.3 percent) or *IRR* (22.7 percent), or both, with larger firms more likely to use one of these methods than smaller companies. On the other hand, 78.1 percent of the responding companies use the payback period. This is by far the most commonly employed tool for companies that use only one capital budgeting decision rule, with 58.3 percent using payback versus 12.5 percent for both *NPV* and *IRR*.

In a survey of companies listed on the Industrial Sector of the Johannesburg Stock Exchange, Hall (2000) finds that two thirds of responding South African firms use discounted cash flow techniques to make capital budgeting decisions. Specifically, 32.3 percent of these

firms report that they believe that the *IRR* method is the best tool for evaluating capital investments, while 16.9 percent say that *NPV* is their preferred tool, and 16.9 percent rely on discounted payback. Moreover, the importance of these techniques in the investment decision process rises with the size of the firm. Among the smallest South African firms in the survey, just over 14 percent calculate the *NPV* or *IRR* of their investment projects, but 75 percent of the largest firms do. Finally, a study published in Lumby (1991) reports similar patterns among UK firms, with 54 percent using discounted cash flow techniques. The same positive relationship between a firm's size and its tendency to use discounted cash flow analysis that exists in South Africa also emerges in the United Kingdom.

Sources: Gert Sandahl and Stefan Sjögren, "Capital Budgeting Methods among Sweden's Largest Groups of Companies: The State of the Art and a Comparison with Earlier Studies," *International Journal of Production Economics* 84 (April 2003), pp. 51–69; J. H. Hall, "An Empirical Investigation of the Capital Budgeting Process," (2000), University of Pretoria working paper; and L. Lumby, *Investment Appraisal and Investment Decisions,* 4th ed. London: Chapman & Hall, 1991.

7.7 WHICH TECHNIQUES DO FIRMS ACTUALLY USE?

In a survey of 392 chief financial officers (CFOs), Graham and Harvey (2001) studied the capital budgeting methods that companies use to make real investment decisions. They asked CFOs to indicate how frequently they used several capital budgeting methods by ranking them on a scale ranging from 0 (never) to 4 (always). The techniques CFOs use most often are *NPV* (score, 3.08) and *IRR* (score 3.09), with roughly 75 percent of CFOs indicating that they always or almost always use these techniques. A 30-year-old study by Gitman and Forrester (1977) found that only 9.8 percent of large firms used *NPV* as a primary capital budgeting tool, so Graham and Harvey's results clearly illustrate that the popularity of the *NPV* approach has grown over time. Interestingly, the popularity of the *NPV* approach is correlated both with the size of the firm and the educational background of its CFO. Large, publicly traded firms run by CFOs with MBAs are much more likely to rely on the *NPV* method than are small, private firms headed by CFOs without MBAs.

Third on the list of most frequently used capital budgeting tools is the payback method. Small firms, in particular, use the payback approach almost as often as they use *NPV* and *IRR*. Older CFOs and those without MBA degrees also tend to make decisions based on payback analysis much more frequently than do other CFOs. Most CFOs reported that they rarely used accounting rate of return, discounted payback, or the profitability index when making investment decisions. The Comparative Corporate Finance insert above compares Graham and Harvey's results to similar studies conducted in Sweden, South Africa, and the United Kingdom. All these papers point to the preeminence of discounted cash flow analysis in making investment decisions around the world.

7.8 SUMMARY

- The capital budgeting process involves identifying, isolating, prioritizing, implementing, and monitoring long-term investment proposals that are consistent with the firm's strategic goals.
- Other things being equal, managers would prefer an easily applied capital budgeting technique that considers cash flow, recognizes the time value of money, fully accounts for expected risk and return, and when applied, leads to higher stock prices.
- Though simplicity is a virtue, the simplest approaches to capital budgeting do not always lead firms to make the best investment decisions.
- Capital budgeting techniques include the accounting rate of return, payback period, and discounted payback period, which are less-sophisticated techniques because they do not explicitly deal with the time value of money and are not tied to the firm's wealth-maximization goal. More-sophisticated techniques include net present value (NPV), internal rate of return (IRR), and profitability index (PI). These methods often give the same accept-reject decisions, but do not necessarily rank projects the same.
- Using the IRR approach can lead to poor investment decisions when projects have cash flows alternating between net inflows and outflows. The modified internal rate of return (MIRR) can be used to overcome one of the major problems resulting from alternating cash flow streams.
- Although the NPV and IRR techniques give the same accept or reject decisions, these techniques do not necessarily agree in ranking mutually exclusive projects. The IRR technique may provide suboptimal project rankings when different investments have very different scales or when the timing of cash flows varies dramatically from one project to another. Although the most straightforward and, theoretically, the best decision technique is NPV, the scale and timing problems of IRR can be eliminated by finding the IRR of the incremental project.
- The profitability index (PI) is a close cousin of the NPV approach, but it suffers from the same scale problem as the IRR approach. The PI approach is most useful in capital rationing situations.

INTERNET RESOURCES

Note: *For updates to links, please go to the book's website at http://smart.swlearning.com.*

http://www.teachmefinance.com/—A site that has definitions and examples of many finance concepts, including most of the capital budgeting tools discussed in this chapter

http://clinton3.nara.gov/pcscb/—Contains a report by the President's Commission to Study Capital Budgeting, a group created in 1997 to evaluate capital budgeting techniques used by other governments and the private sector

http://www.swlearning.com/finance/finance_news/fin_capital_budgeting.html/—A site maintained by Thomson/South Western that summarizes news events relating to capital budgeting and investment evaluation techniques

KEY TERMS

accounting rate of return	lending versus borrowing problem
capital budgeting	modified internal rate of return (*MIRR*)
capital investment	mutually exclusive projects
capital rationing	net present value (*NPV*)
capital spending	*NPV* profile
discounted payback	payback period
incremental project	profitability index (*PI*)
internal rate of return (*IRR*)	reinvestment rate assumption

QUESTIONS

7-1. In statistics, you learn about Type I and Type II errors. A Type I error occurs when a statistical test rejects a hypothesis when the hypothesis is actually true. A Type II error occurs when a test fails to reject a hypothesis that is actually false. We can apply this type of thinking to capital budgeting. A Type I error occurs when a firm rejects an investment project that would actually enhance shareholder wealth. A Type II error occurs when a firm accepts a value-decreasing investment, an investment it should have rejected.

   a. Describe the features of the payback rule that could lead to Type I errors.
   b. Describe the features of the payback rule that could lead to Type II errors.
   c. Which error do you think is more likely to occur when firms use payback analysis? Does your answer depend on the length of the maximum payback period? You can assume a "typical" project cash flow stream, meaning that most cash outflows occur in the early years of a project.

7-2. Holding the maximum payback period fixed, which method has a more severe bias against long-lived projects, payback or discounted payback?

7-3. In what way is the *NPV* consistent with the principle of shareholder wealth maximization? For a firm that uses the *NPV* rule to make investment decisions, what consequences result if the firm misestimates the shareholders' required returns and consistently applies a discount rate that is "too high"?

7-4. "Cash flow projections more than a few years out are not worth the paper they're written on. Therefore, using payback analysis, which ignores long-term cash flows, is more reasonable than making wild guesses as one has to do in the *NPV* approach." Respond to this comment.

7-5. "Smart analysts can massage the numbers in *NPV* analysis to make any project's *NPV* look positive. It is better to use a simpler approach like accounting rate of return or payback that gives analysts fewer degrees of freedom to manipulate the numbers." Respond to this comment.

7-6. A particular firm's shareholders demand a 15 percent return on their investment, given the firm's risk. However, this firm has historically generated returns in excess of shareholder expectations, with an average return on its portfolio of investments of 25 percent.

   a. Looking back, what kind of stock-price performance would you expect to see for this firm?
   b. A new investment opportunity arises, and the firm's financial analysts estimate that the project's return will be 18 percent. The CEO wants to reject the project because it would lower the firm's average return and therefore lower the firm's stock price. How do you respond?

7-7.   What are the potential faults in using the *IRR* as a capital budgeting technique? What role does use of the modified internal rate of return (*MIRR*) play in eliminating those faults?

7-8.   Suppose a project has a discounted payback period equal to the life of the project (assuming a 10% discount rate). What is the *NPV* of the project, and what is the *IRR*?

7-9.   Why is the *NPV* considered to be theoretically superior to all other capital budgeting techniques? Reconcile this result with the prevalence of the use of *IRR* in practice. How would you respond to your CFO if she instructed you to use the *IRR* technique to make capital budgeting decisions on projects with cash flow streams that alternate between inflows and outflows?

7-10.   Outline the differences between *NPV, IRR,* and *PI.* What are the advantages and disadvantages of each technique? Do they agree with regard to simple accept or reject decisions?

7-11.   Under what circumstances will the *NPV, IRR,* and *PI* techniques provide different capital budgeting decisions? Are these differing results found in analysis of independent or mutually exclusive projects? Why are the differences found in one type of project analysis and not the other?

7-12.   What is the only relevant decision for independent projects if an unlimited capital budget exists? How does your response change if the projects are mutually exclusive? How does your response change if the firm faces *capital rationing*?

7-13.   Project A costs $1,000.00 and has annual cash flows of $400.00, $600.00, and $300.00. Project B costs $1,500.00 and has annual cash flows of $500.00, $500.00, $500.00, and $10,000.00. Based on having the shortest payback period, which project is better? Is this really the best decision? If not, what is the problem with payback period criteria?

PROBLEMS

Accounting-Based Methods

7-1.   Kenneth Gould is the general manager at a small-town newspaper that is part of a national media chain. He is seeking approval from corporate headquarters (HQ) to spend $20,000 to buy some Macintosh computers and a laser printer to use in designing the layout of his daily paper. This equipment will be depreciated using the straight-line method over four years. These computers will replace outmoded equipment that will be kept on hand for emergency use.

HQ requires Kenneth to estimate the cash flows associated with the purchase of new equipment over a four-year horizon. The impact of the project on net income is derived by subtracting depreciation from cash flow each year. The project's average accounting rate of return equals the average contribution to net income divided by the average book value of the investment. HQ accepts any project that (1) has an average accounting rate of return that exceeds the cost of capital of 15 percent, and (2) returns the initial investment within four years (on a cash flow basis). The following are Kenneth's estimates of cash flows:

	Year 1	Year 2	Year 3	Year 4
Cost Savings	$7,500	$9,100	$9,100	$9,100

a. What is the average contribution to net income across all four years?
b. What is the average book value of the investment?

c. What is the average *accounting rate of return*?
d. What is the *payback period* of this investment?
e. Critique the company's method for evaluating investment proposals.

Payback Methods

7-2.   Suppose that a thirty-year U.S. Treasury bond offers a 4 percent coupon rate, paid semiannually. The market price of the bond is $1,000, equal to its par value.

a. What is the *payback period* for this bond?
b. With such a long payback period, is the bond a bad investment?
c. What is the *discounted payback period* for the bond, assuming its 4 percent coupon rate is the required return? What general principle does this example illustrate regarding a project's life, its discounted payback period, and its *NPV*?

7-3.   The cash flows associated with three different projects are as follows:

Cash Flows	Alpha ($ in millions)	Beta ($ in millions)	Gamma ($ in millions)
Initial Outflow	−1.5	−0.4	−7.5
Year 1	0.3	0.1	2.0
Year 2	0.5	0.2	3.0
Year 3	0.5	0.2	2.0
Year 4	0.4	0.1	1.5
Year 5	0.3	−0.2	5.5

a. Calculate the *payback period* of each investment.
b. Which investments does the firm accept if the cutoff payback period is three years? Four years?
c. If the firm invests by choosing projects with the shortest payback period, which project would it invest in?
d. If the firm uses *discounted payback* with a 15 percent discount rate and a four-year cutoff period, which projects will it accept?
e. One of these almost certainly should be rejected, but may be accepted if the firm uses payback analysis. Which one?
f. One of these projects almost certainly should be accepted (unless the firm's opportunity cost of capital is very high), but may be rejected if the firm uses payback analysis. Which one?

7-4.   Nader International is considering investing in two assets—A and B. The initial outlay, annual cash flows, and annual depreciation for each asset is shown in the table below for the assets' assumed five-year lives. As can be seen, Nader will use straight-line depreciation over each asset's five-year life. The firm requires a 12 percent return on each of those equally risky assets. Nader's maximum payback period is 2.5 years, its maximum discounted payback period is 3.25 years, and its minimum accounting rate of return is 30 percent.

Initial Outlay (CF_0)	Asset A $200,000		Asset B $180,000	
Year (t)	Cash Flow (CF_t)	Depreciation	Cash Flow (CF_t)	Depreciation
1	$ 70,000	$40,000	$80,000	$36,000
2	80,000	40,000	90,000	36,000
3	90,000	40,000	30,000	36,000
4	90,000	40,000	40,000	36,000
5	100,000	40,000	40,000	36,000

    a. Calculate the *accounting rate of return* from each asset, assess its acceptability, and indicate which asset is best, using the accounting rate of return.

    b. Calculate the *payback period* for each asset, assess its acceptability, and indicate which asset is best, using the payback period.

    c. Calculate the *discounted payback* for each asset, assess its acceptability, and indicate which asset is best, using the discounted payback.

    d. Compute and contrast your findings in parts (a), (b), and (c). Which asset would you recommend to Nader, assuming that they are mutually exclusive? Why?

Net Present Value

7-5. Calculate the *net present value* (*NPV*) for the following 20-year projects. Comment on the acceptability of each. Assume that the firm has an opportunity cost of 14 percent.

    a. Initial cash outlay is $15,000; cash inflows are $13,000 per year.

    b. Initial cash outlay is $32,000; cash inflows are $4,000 per year.

    c. Initial cash outlay is $50,000; cash inflows are $8,500 per year.

7-6. Michael's Bakery is evaluating a new electronic oven. The oven requires an initial cash outlay of $19,000 and will generate after-tax cash inflows of $4,000 per year for eight years. For each of the costs of capital listed, (1) calculate the *NPV*, (2) indicate whether to accept or reject the oven, and (3) explain your decision.

    a. The cost of capital is 10 percent

    b. The cost of capital is 12 percent.

    c. The cost of capital is 14 percent.

7-7. Using a 14 percent cost of capital, calculate the *NPV* for each of the projects shown in the following table and indicate whether or not each is acceptable.

Initial cash outflow (CF_0)	Project A	Project B	Project C	Project D	Project E
	$20,000	$600,000	$150,000	$760,000	$100,000
Year (t)			Cash Inflows (CF_t)		
1	$3,000	$120,000	$18,000	$185,000	$ 0
2	3,000	145,000	17,000	185,000	0
3	3,000	170,000	16,000	185,000	0
4	3,000	190,000	15,000	185,000	25,000
5	3,000	220,000	15,000	185,000	36,000
6	3,000	240,000	14,000	185,000	0
7	3,000		13,000	185,000	60,000
8	3,000		12,000	185,000	72,000
9	3,000		11,000		84,000
10	3,000		10,000		

7-8. Scotty Manufacturing is considering the replacement of one of its machine tools. Three alternative replacement tools—A, B, and C—are under consideration. The cash flows associated with each are shown in the following table. The firm's cost of capital is 15 percent.

Initial cash	A	B	C
outflow (CF_0)	$95,000	$50,000	$150,000
Year (t)		Cash Inflows (CF_t)	
1	$20,000	$10,000	$58,000
2	20,000	12,000	35,000
3	20,000	13,000	23,000
4	20,000	15,000	23,000
5	20,000	17,000	23,000
6	20,000	21,000	35,000
7	20,000	—	46,000
8	20,000	—	58,000

a. Calculate the *NPV* of each alternative.
b. Using *NPV*, evaluate the acceptability of each tool.
c. Rank the tools from best to worst, using *NPV*.

7-9. Erwin Enterprises has 10 million shares outstanding with a current market price of $10 per share. There is one investment available to Erwin, and its cash flows are provided below. Erwin has a cost of capital of 10 percent. Given this information, determine the impact on Erwin's stock price and firm value if capital markets fully reflect the value of undertaking the project.

Initial cash outflow = $10,000,000

Year	Cash Inflow
1	$3,000,000
2	4,000,000
3	5,000,000
4	6,000,000
5	9,800,000

(handwritten) $= NPV\ (0.1\ ,\ 3,000,000,\ 4000000,\ 5000000,\ 6000000,\ 9800000\ )\ -\ 10000000$

7-10. Project LMN has an initial cost of $10,000 and annual cash inflows of $2,825, $3,192, $3,607, and $4,076 in years 1–4. What is the *NPV* assuming a 12% discount rate? When the project was completed, none of the cash flows were reinvested. Sum up the cash flows and determine the annual return on the project based on the initial $10,000 investment. Why is the annual return on the project below the 12% discount rate? (*Hint:* Think about the reinvestment rate assumption.)

Internal Rate of Return

7-11. For each of the projects shown in the following table, calculate the *internal rate of return* (*IRR*).

Initial cash	Project A	Project B	Project C	Project D
outflow (CF_0)	$72,000	$440,000	$18,000	$215,000
Year (t)		Cash Inflows (CF_t)		
1	$16,000	$135,000	$7,000	$108,000
2	20,000	135,000	7,000	90,000
3	24,000	135,000	7,000	72,000
4	28,000	135,000	7,000	54,000
5	32,000	—	7,000	—

7-12. William Industries is attempting to choose the better of two mutually exclusive projects for expanding the firm's production capacity. The relevant cash flows for the projects are shown in the following table. The firm's cost of capital is 15 percent.

Initial cash outflow (CF_0)	Project A	Project B
	$550,000	$358,000
Year (t)	Cash Inflows (CF_t)	
1	$110,000	$154,000
2	132,000	132,000
3	165,000	105,000
4	209,000	77,000
5	275,000	55,000

a. Calculate the *IRR* for each of the projects.
b. Assess the acceptability of each project based on the *IRR*s found in part (a).
c. Which project is preferred, based on the *IRR*s found in part (a)?

7-13. A project costs $4,000 and has annual cash flows of $1,090, $1,188, $1,295, and $1,411 in years 1–4. The firm has a discount rate of 9%. Find the following for the project.

a. Payback period
b. Discounted payback period
c. *NPV*
d. *IRR*

7-14. Project Z has an initial cost of $6,000 and has annual cash inflows of $1,725, $1,984, $2,281, and $2,624 in years 1–4. Assuming a 15% discount rate, find the following for the project.

a. Discounted payback period
b. *NPV*
c. Profitability index
d. *IRR*

7-15. Contract Manufacturing, Inc., is considering two alternative investment proposals. The first proposal calls for a major renovation of the company's manufacturing facility. The second involves replacing just a few obsolete pieces of equipment in the facility. The company will choose one project or the other this year, but it will not do both. The cash flows associated with each project appear below, and the firm discounts project cash flows at 15 percent.

Year	Renovate	Replace
0	−$9,000,000	−$1,000,000
1	3,500,000	600,000
2	3,000,000	500,000
3	3,000,000	400,000
4	2,800,000	300,000
5	2,500,000	200,000

a. Rank these investments based on their *NPV*s.
b. Rank these investments based on their *IRR*s.
c. Why do these rankings yield mixed signals?
d. Calculate the *IRR* of the incremental project. Reconcile your answer to this question with those from parts (a) and (b).

7-16. Consider a project with the following cash flows and a firm with a 15 percent cost of capital.

End of Year	Cash Flow
0	−$20,000
1	50,000
2	−10,000

a. What are the two *IRR*s associated with this cash flow stream?
b. If the firm's cost of capital falls between the two *IRR* values calculated in part (a), should it accept or reject the project?
c. What is this project's *modified internal rate of return (MIRR)*? Is the project acceptable?

7-17. Jess Oil, an oil exploration company, is considering drilling a new well in an established field. Estimates indicate that a *cash outflow* of $480,000 will be incurred at time zero for drilling and preparing the well for production. The well is expected to generate *cash inflow* of about $1,560,000 in the first year, and a $120,000 *cash outflow* will result in the second year to shut down the well and clean up the site.

a. What are the two *IRR*s associated with the drilling decision?
b. Calculate the project's *NPV* at each of the following discount rates: 0%, 50%, 100%, 150%, 200%, and 250%, and use these points to draw the project's *NPV profile*.
c. Should the firm drill the proposed well if its cost of capital is 25 percent?
d. Calculate the project's *modified internal rate of return (MIRR)* and use it to assess the project's acceptability.
e. Compare and discuss your findings in parts (c) and (d).

7-18. A certain project has the following stream of cash flows:

Year	Cash Flow
0	$ 17,500
1	− 80,500
2	138,425
3	− 105,455
4	30,030

a. Fill in the following table:

Cost of Capital (%)	Project NPV
0	_____
5	_____
10	_____
15	_____
20	_____
25	_____
30	_____
35	_____
50	_____

b. Use the values developed in part (a) to draw an *NPV profile* for this project.
c. What is this project's *IRR*?
d. Describe the conditions under which the firm should accept this project.

Profitability Index

7-19. Evaluate the following three projects, using the profitability index. Assume a cost of capital of 15 percent.

	Project		
	Liquidate	Recondition	Replace
Initial cash outflow	−$100,000	−$500,000	−$1,000,000
Year 1 cash inflow	50,000	100,000	500,000
Year 2 cash inflow	60,000	200,000	500,000
Year 3 cash inflow	75,000	250,000	500,000

a. Rank these projects by their *PI*s.
b. If the projects are independent, which would you accept according to the *PI* criterion?
c. If these projects are mutually exclusive, which would you accept according to the *PI* criterion?
d. Apply the *NPV* criterion to the projects, rank them according to their *NPV*s, and indicate which you would accept if they are independent and mutually exclusive.
e. Compare and contrast your answer from part (c) with your answer to part (d) for the mutually exclusive case. Explain this result.

7-20. You have a $10 million capital budget and must make the decision about which investments your firm should accept for the coming year. Use the following information on three mutually exclusive projects to determine which investment your firm should accept. The firm's cost of capital is 12 percent.

	Project 1	Project 2	Project 3
Initial cash outflow	−$4,000,000	−$5,000,000	−$10,000,000
Year 1 cash inflow	1,000,000	2,000,000	4,000,000
Year 2 cash inflow	2,000,000	3,000,000	6,000,000
Year 3 cash inflow	3,000,000	3,000,000	5,000,000

a. Which project do you accept on the basis of *NPV*?
b. Which project do you accept on the basis of *PI*?
c. If these are the only investments available, which one do you select?
d. Now assume that another independent project is available to you. This new project has a cost of $5 million, with an *NPV* of $1.5 million. Given the availability of this new project, which of the mutually exclusive projects do you accept?
e. Is the *NPV* or *PI* the better technique in the situation described in part(d)? Why?

7-21. Project ABC has an initial cost of $1,000 and generates cash inflow of $2,000 at the end of year 1. Project QRS has an initial cost of $10,000 and has annual cash inflows of $4,400, $4,840, and $5,324 in years 1–3. Assuming a 10% discount rate, calculate the *NPV* and profitability index for both projects. Which project is better based on *NPV*? Which project is better based on the *profitability index*?

7-22. Project X has an initial cost of $3,300 and has annual cash inflows of $1,232, $1,380, $1,545, and $1,731 in years 1–4. Project Y has an initial cost of $5,000 and has annual cash inflows of $1,413, $1,596, $1,804, $2,038, and $2,303 in years 1–5. The discount rate is 12% for Project X and 13% for Project Y.

a. What is the *discounted payback* period for each project?
b. Which project is better based on a maximum discounted payback of 42 months?
c. Which project is better based on *NPV*?
d. Which project is better based on the *profitability index*?

Which Techniques Do Firms Actually Use?

7-23. Both Old Line Industries and High Tech, Inc., use the *IRR* to make investment decisions. Both firms are considering investing in a more efficient $4.5 million mail-order processor. This machine could generate after-tax savings of $2 million per year over the next three years for both firms. However, due to the risky nature of its business, High Tech has a much higher cost of capital (20%) than does Old Line (10%). Given this information, answer parts (a)–(c).

  a. Should Old Line invest in this processor?
  b. Should High Tech invest in this processor?
  c. Based on your answers in parts (a) and (b), what can you infer about the acceptability of projects across firms with different costs of capital?

7-24. Butler Products has prepared the following estimates for an investment it is considering. The initial cash outflow is $20,000, and the project is expected to yield cash inflows of $4,400 per year for seven years. The firm has a 10 percent cost of capital.

  a. Determine the *NPV* for the project.
  b. Determine the *IRR* for the project.
  c. Would you recommend that the firm accept or reject the project? Explain your answer.

7-25. Reynolds Enterprises is attempting to evaluate the feasibility of investing $85,000, CF_0, in a machine having a 5-year life. The firm has estimated the *cash inflows* associated with the proposal as shown below. The firm has a 12 percent cost of capital.

End of Year (t)	Cash Inflows (CF_t)
1	$18,000
2	22,500
3	27,000
4	31,500
5	36,000

  a. Calculate the *payback period* for the proposed investment.
  b. Calculate the *NPV* for the proposed investment.
  c. Calculate the *IRR* for the proposed investment.
  d. Evaluate the acceptability of the proposed investment using *NPV* and *IRR*. What recommendation would you make relative to implementation of the project? Why?

7-26. Sharpe Manufacturing is attempting to select the best of three mutually exclusive projects. The initial cash outflow and after-tax cash inflows associated with each project are shown in the following table.

Cash Flows	Project X	Project Y	Project Z
Initial cash outflow (CF_0)	$80,000	$130,000	$145,000
Cash inflows (CF_t), years $(t) = 1–5$	27,000	41,000	43,000

  a. Calculate the *payback period* for each project.
  b. Calculate the *NPV* of each project, assuming that the firm has a cost of capital equal to 13 percent.
  c. Calculate the *IRR* for each project.
  d. Summarize the preferences dictated by each measure, and indicate which project you would recommend. Explain why.

7-27. Wilkes, Inc., must invest in a pollution-control program in order to meet federal regulations to stay in business. There are two programs available to Wilkes: an all-at-once program that will be immediately funded and implemented, and a gradual program that will be phased in over the next three years. The immediate program costs $5 million, whereas the phase-in program will cost $1 million today and $2 million per year for the following three years. If the cost of capital for Wilkes is 15 percent, which pollution-control program should Wilkes select?

7-28. JK Products, Inc. is considering investing in either of two competing projects that will allow the firm to eliminate a production bottleneck and meet the growing demand for its products. The firm's engineering department narrowed the alternatives down to two—Status Quo (SQ) and High Tech (HT). Working with the accounting and finance personnel, the firm's CFO developed the following estimates of the cash flows for SQ and HT over the relevant six-year time horizon. The firm has an 11 percent required return and views these projects as equally risky.

	Project SQ	Project HT
Initial Outflow (CF_0)	$670,000	$940,000
Year (t)	Cash Inflows (CF_t)	
1	$250,000	$170,000
2	200,000	180,000
3	170,000	200,000
4	150,000	250,000
5	130,000	300,000
6	130,000	550,000

  a. Calculate the *net present value* (*NPV*) of each project, assess its acceptability and indicate which project is best, using *NPV*.
  b. Calculate the *internal rate of return (IRR)* of each project, assess its acceptability and indicate which project is best, using *IRR*.
  c. Calculate the *profitability index (PI)* of each project, assess its acceptability, and indicate which project is best, using *PI*.
  d. Draw the *NPV profile* for project SQ and HT on the same set of axes and use this diagram to explain why the *NPV* and the *IRR* show different preferences for these two mutually exclusive projects. Discuss this difference in terms of both the "scale problem" and the "timing problem."
  e. Which of the two mutually exclusive projects would you recommend that JK Products undertake? Why?

7-29. A consumer product firm finds that its brand of laundry detergent is losing market share, so it decides that it needs to "freshen" the product. One strategy is to maintain the current detergent formula but repackage the product. The other strategy involves a complete reformulation of the product in a way that will appeal to environmentally conscious consumers. The firm will pursue one strategy or the other but not both. Cash flows from each proposal appear below, and the firm discounts cash flows at 13 percent.

SMART
SOLUTIONS
See the problem and solution explained step-by-step at
SMARTFinance

Year	Repackage	Reformulate
0	−$3,000,000	−$25,000,000
1	2,000,000	10,000,000
2	1,250,000	9,000,000
3	500,000	7,000,000
4	250,000	4,000,000
5	250,000	3,500,000

   a. Rank these investments based on their *NPV*s.
   b. Rank these investments based on their *IRR*s.
   c. Rank these investments based on their *PI*s.
   d. Draw *NPV profiles* for the two projects on the same set of axes and discuss these profiles.
   e. Do these investment rankings yield mixed signals?
   f. Calculate the *IRR* of the incremental project. Reconcile your answer to this question with those from parts (a) and (b).

7-30. Lundblad Construction Co. recently acquired 10 acres of land and is weighing two options for developing the land. The first proposal is to build 10 single-family homes on the site. This project would generate a quick cash payoff as the homes are sold over the next two years. Specifically, Lundblad estimates that it would spend $2.5 million on construction costs immediately, and it would receive $1.6 million as cash inflows in each of the next two years.

   The second proposal is to build a strip shopping mall. This project calls for Lundblad to retain ownership of the property and to lease space for retail businesses that would serve the neighborhood. Construction costs for the strip mall are also about $2.5 million, and the company expects to receive $350,000 annually (for each of 50 years, starting one year from now) in net cash inflows from leasing the property. Lundblad's cost of capital is 10 percent.

   a. Rank these projects based on their *NPV*s.
   b. Rank these projects based on their *IRR*s.
   c. Rank these projects based on their *PI*s. Do these rankings agree with those based on *NPV* or *IRR*?
   d. Draw *NPV profiles* for these projects on the same set of axes. Use this graph to explain why, in this case, the *NPV* and *IRR* methods yield mixed signals.
   e. Which project should Lundblad choose? Calculate the *IRR* of the incremental project to verify your answer.
   f. Which project should Lundblad choose if its cost of capital is 13.5 percent? 16 percent? 20 percent?

THOMSON ONE BUSINESS SCHOOL EDITION

7-31. Locate the 10-K report (filed January 29, 2005) for Wilsons The Leather Experts, Inc. (ticker symbol, WLSN). Search the 10-K report for the term "internal rate of return." What rate of return does Wilsons expect to earn on its stores?

7-32. Locate the 10-K report (filed September 30, 2005) for Chordiant Software Inc. (ticker symbol, CHRD). Search the 10-K report for the term "net present value." What does Chordiant evaluate using net present value? What discount rate(s) does Chordiant use in calculating net present value?

MINI-CASE: CAPITAL BUDGETING PROCESS AND TECHNIQUES

Durango Cereal Company is considering adding a new kind of cereal to its product line—one geared toward children and the other toward adults. The company is currently at full capacity and will have to invest a large sum in machinery and production space. However, given the nature of cereal production, the investment in machinery will be more costly for the children's cereal (Poofy Puffs) than for the adult cereal (Filling Fiber). The expected cash flows for both cereals are:

Year	Poofy Puffs	Filling Fiber
0	−$24,890,000	−$13,500,000
1	12,950,000	7,230,000
2	10,923,000	8,100,000
3	8,231,000	8,629,000
4	7,242,000	5,238,900

Also, the expected net income figures for the two cereals are:

Year	Poofy Puffs	Filling Fiber
1	$6,727,500	$3,855,000
2	4,700,500	4,725,000
3	2,008,500	5,254,000
4	7,242,000	1,863,900

The average book value for the Poofy Puffs project is $12,445,000, while the average book value for Filling Fiber is $6,750,000. Management requires a minimum return of 15% in order for the project to be acceptable from an accounting rate of return perspective. The discount rate for projects of this level of risk is 10%. Management requires projects with this type of risk to have a minimum payback of 1.75 years.

Assuming the projects are independent and ignoring the issue of scale, what should Durango Cereal Company do? Include calculations for the payback method, the discounted payback method, accounting rate of return (using averages), net present value, internal rate of return, and profitability index in your analysis. Revisit the problem considering the scaling issue. Which project should the company consider, if any?

Chapter 8

Cash Flow and Capital Budgeting

France Telecom Enjoys Orange's Jus

In October 2003, debt-laden France Telecom S.A. announced a tender offer for the outstanding shares of mobile phone company, Orange, at a price of €9.5 per share. The deal was motivated in part by Orange's significant positive cash flow. Because Orange was profitable while France Telecom was not, combining the two firms resulted in a significant tax savings as the losses of one firm offset the profits of the other.

Documents filed with regulators by France Telecom's investment banker, Goldman Sachs International, revealed that a discounted cash flow valuation of Orange suggested an offer price for the tender offer between €8.0 and €11.8 per share. This valuation relied on France Telecom estimates of the cash flows that Orange would generate from 2003–2006. In estimating Orange's cash flows, France Telecom started with after-tax operating income and made additional adjustments for increases in fixed assets and working capital that Orange would have to make to generate the projected earnings. Of course, in deciding to purchase Orange's shares, France Telecom did not simply assume that Orange would stop generating cash flows in 2006. Instead, France Telecom analysts captured the value of Orange's cash flows in 2007 and beyond by estimating the target company's terminal value. To calculate this value, France Telecom assumed that after 2006, Orange would increase its cash flows by 2.5 percent per year in Western Europe and by 3.0 percent in Eastern Europe, in perpetuity. By selecting a discount rate that reflected the risks of Orange business and by applying the formula for a growing perpetuity presented in Chapter 3, France Telecom could arrive at a long-term discounted cash flow valuation of Orange.

Sources: France Telecom Bids for Orange Minority, by Liz Vaughan-Adams, 9-2-03, The Independent (London), p. 17.

France Telecom Squeezes Orange, Le Monde, 9-2-03

France Telecom's second bite at Orange is a sign of the times: The move to take back full ownership signifies how much the former state monopoly has regained control of its destiny, by Jo Johnson, The Financial Times, 9-2-03

Orange S.A. – Offer by France Telecom S.A., AFX News Limited, 10-29-03

T he France Telecom acquisition of Orange is an example of a very large scale capital budgeting problem. In an acquisition, the buyer must decide if the future cash flows obtained by purchasing the target firm justify the initial investment. In that respect, an acquisition resembles many other projects in which companies routinely invest. Chapter 7 described various capital budgeting techniques that analysts use when evaluating and ranking investment proposals. Each of the examples in Chapter 7 began with a sequence of cash flows, though we did not discuss the origins of those cash flow figures. This chapter describes procedures for determining a project's relevant cash flows, the inputs for the capital budgeting decision tools from Chapter 7. We begin with an overview of the kinds of cash flows that may appear in almost any type of investment. An extended capital budgeting example follows. Next, we demonstrate how to deal properly with the problem of inflation in capital budgeting problems. Then we discuss special problems and situations that frequently arise in the capital budgeting process. The chapter concludes with a brief discussion of the human element in capital budgeting.

8.1   TYPES OF CASH FLOWS

CASH FLOW VERSUS ACCOUNTING PROFIT

When accountants prepare financial statements for external reporting, they have a very different purpose in mind than financial analysts have when they evaluate the merits of an investment. Accountants want to produce financial statements that fairly and accurately represent the state of a business at a particular point in time, as well as over a period of time. Given this purpose, accountants measure the inflows and outflows of a business's operations on an accrual basis rather than on a cash basis. For example, accountants typically credit a firm for earning revenue once a sale is made, even though customers may not pay cash for their purchases for several weeks or months. Similarly, accountants typically will not record the full cost of an asset as an expense if they expect the asset to confer benefits to the firm over a long period of time. The best example of this approach is **depreciation.** If a firm spends $1 billion on an asset that it plans to use over 10 years, accountants may count only one-tenth of the purchase price, or $100 million, as a current-year depreciation expense.

For capital budgeting purposes, financial analysts focus on *incremental* cash inflows and outflows. In part, this emphasis simply recognizes that no matter what earnings a firm may show on an accrual basis, it cannot survive for long unless it generates cash to pay its bills. If a firm purchases an asset for $500 million, and if the purchase contract requires an immediate payment, then the firm must come up with $500 million in cash even if it plans to deduct only a portion of the purchase price each year as depreciation expense. The importance placed on cash flow in capital budgeting also reflects the time value of money. If a firm sells a product for $1,000, the value of that sale is greater if the customer pays immediately rather than 30 or 90 days in the future.

Much of this chapter focuses on which cash flows to include in calculating a project's *NPV,* but we should also mention an important category of cash flows that should be excluded—financing cash flows. When calculating a project's *NPV,* analysts should ignore the costs of raising the money to finance the project, whether those costs come in the form of interest expense from debt financing or dividend payments to equity investors. It may seem counterintuitive to ignore an item—such as interest expense—that appears on the income statement, but it is necessary to do so because financing costs are fully captured in the process of discounting a project's future cash flows to the present. In previous chapters we have seen that the present discounted value of a cash flow is less than its future value. When analysts discount a project's future cash flows, they are taking into account the opportunity that investors have to invest in other firms. Therefore, if an analyst deducted items flowing to investors, such as dividend and interest payments, the analyst would, in effect, double count the financing costs of the investment.

Analysts should measure all cash flows of a project on an after-tax basis. Remember, when deciding whether an investment is worth taking or not, we must determine whether the cash flows of the project are sufficient to meet or exceed shareholders' expectations. The firm can only distribute after-tax cash flows to investors, and thus, only after-tax cash flows are relevant in the decision process. The tax consequences associated with a particular investment can be very complex, in part because cash flows from a single investment may fall under several tax jurisdictions (local, state, national, international, etc.). An examination of all the nuances of the tax code is well beyond the scope of this book, but we will offer simplified illustrations of the principles involved in measuring after-tax cash flows. The most important of these principles is that financial managers should measure the after-tax cash flows of a given investment by using the firm's **marginal tax rate.** The marginal tax rate equals the percentage of taxes owed on an incremental dollar of income. Usually, a firm's marginal tax rate exceeds its average tax rate, which equals total taxes paid divided by total pretax income. Throughout this chapter, we will assume that the marginal tax rate equals 40 percent.

A second tax-related principle relevant for measuring cash flows is that analysts cannot entirely ignore noncash expenses such as depreciation when projecting cash flows, because noncash expenses reduce taxable income, and therefore they reduce cash tax payments. There are two ways to calculate cash flows that take this effect into account. First, we can add noncash expenses back to after-tax earnings. Second, we can ignore noncash expenses when calculating after-tax earnings, and then add back the tax savings created by noncash deductions.[1]

APPLYING THE MODEL 8.1

Let's take a look at two ways to treat noncash expenses to obtain cash flow numbers for a simple project. Suppose that today a firm spends $30,000 in cash to purchase a fixed asset that it plans to fully depreciate on a straight-line basis over three years.

Using this machine, the firm produces 10,000 units of some product each year. The product sells for $3 and costs $1 to make. The following is an income statement for a typical year of this project:

Sales	$30,000
Less: Cost of goods	10,000
Gross profit	$20,000
Less: Depreciation	10,000
Pretax income	$10,000
Less: Taxes (40%)	4,000
Net income	$ 6,000

---

[1] Deriving accurate cash flow numbers from real financial statements issued by real companies is considerably more complex than the following simple example might lead you to believe.

How much cash flow does this project generate in a typical year? There are two ways to arrive at the answer. First, take net income and add back depreciation, for which there was no cash outlay:

Cash flow = net income + depreciation

$$= \$6,000 + \$10,000 = \$16,000$$

Second, calculate after-tax net income ignoring depreciation expense, and then add back the tax savings generated by the depreciation deduction:

Sales	$30,000	
Less: Cost of goods	10,000	
Pretax income	$20,000	
Less: Taxes (40%)	8,000	
After-tax income	$12,000	
Plus: Depreciation tax savings	4,000	(40% × $10,000)
Total cash flow	$16,000	

DEPRECIATION

The largest noncash item for most investment projects is depreciation. Analysts must know the magnitude and timing of depreciation deductions for a given project because these deductions affect the amount of taxes the firm will pay. Treating depreciation properly is complicated by the fact that the law allows firms to use several different depreciation methods. For example, in the United States and the United Kingdom, firms can (and do) keep separate sets of books, one for tax purposes and one for financial reporting purposes, using different depreciation methods for each set. As a result, most U.S. and U.K. firms use accelerated depreciation methods for tax purposes and straight-line depreciation for financial reporting. In contrast, in nations such as Japan, Sweden, and Germany, the law requires that the income that firms report to the tax authorities be substantially the same as the income they report to investors. Naturally, firms in these countries want to enjoy the tax benefits of accelerated depreciation, so they depreciate assets using methods such as double-declining balance or sum-of-the-years' digits almost exclusively.[2] Because we are interested in the cash flow consequences of investments, and because depreciation only affects cash flow through taxes, we will consider only the depreciation method that a firm uses for tax purposes when determining project cash flows.

Table 8.1 illustrates the tax depreciation allowed in the United States on various classes of equipment. The Tax Reform Act of 1986 set forth a **modified accelerated cost recovery system (MACRS)**, which defined the allowable annual depreciation deductions for various classes of assets. Automobiles used for business purposes fall under the 3-year class, computer equipment is part of the 5-year class, and most manufacturing equipment is part of the 7-year class. A quick glance at the table reveals that U.S. tax laws allow firms to take larger depreciation deductions in the early years of an asset's life. The cash flow impact of this system is to accelerate the tax benefits associated with depreciation.[3]

[2.] The International Forum on Accountancy Development (IFAD) maintains a website where you can find a brief overview of accounting standards in 62 different countries, all benchmarked against international accounting standards (IAS). See Internet Resources in this chapter.

[3.] That is, the tax benefits accrue faster than would be the case under straight-line depreciation. An observant reader of Table 8.1 will notice that the law grants four years of depreciation deductions on the 3-year asset class, six years of deductions for assets in the 5-year class, and so on. There appears to be one "extra year" of depreciation for each asset class because the

Table 8.1
Tax Depreciation
Schedules by Asset Class

Year(s)	3-Year	5-Year	7-Year	10-Year	15-Year	20-Year
1	33.33	20.00	14.29	10.00	5.00	3.75
2	44.45	32.00	24.49	18.00	9.50	7.22
3	14.81	19.20	17.49	14.40	8.55	6.68
4	7.41	11.52	12.49	11.52	7.70	6.18
5		11.52	8.93	9.22	6.93	5.71
6		5.76	8.93	7.37	6.23	5.28
7			8.93	6.55	5.90	4.89
8			4.45	6.55	5.90	4.52
9				6.55	5.90	4.46
10				6.55	5.90	4.46
11				3.29	5.90	4.46
12					5.90	4.46
13					5.90	4.46
14					5.90	4.46
15					5.90	4.46
16					2.99	4.46
17–20						4.46
21						2.25

Notes: U.S. tax depreciation allowed for various MACRS asset classes. Figures represent the percentage of asset value depreciable in each year.

FIXED ASSET EXPENDITURES

Many capital budgeting decisions involve the acquisition of a fixed asset. The cost of this investment often appears as the initial cash outflow for a project (assuming that the firm pays the full purchase price in one cash payment). Additional factors that influence the cash consequences of fixed asset acquisitions include installation costs and proceeds from sales of existing fixed assets.

In many cases, the cost of installing new equipment can be a significant part of a project's initial outlay. Firms combine the asset's purchase price and its installation cost to arrive at the asset's depreciable tax basis. Though depreciation itself is not a cash outflow, we have seen that depreciation deductions affect future cash flows by lowering taxes. Depreciation deductions influence taxes through another channel when firms sell old fixed assets. Specifically, when a firm sells an old piece of equipment, there will be a tax consequence of the sale if the selling price exceeds or falls below the old equipment's book value. If the firm sells an asset for more than its book value, the firm must pay taxes on the difference. If a firm sells an asset for less than its book value, then it can treat the difference as a tax-deductible expense.

APPLYING THE MODEL 8.2

Electrocom Manufacturing purchased $100,000 worth of new computers three years ago. Because of the speed at which technology changes, it now must replace the computers with newer, faster ones. Because computers qualify as 5-year equip-

first year's deduction reflects an assumption that, on average, investments in fixed assets are in service for just one-half of the first year. The last half-year of depreciation deductions for an asset falling in the N-year class occurs in year $N + 1$. Special rules apply to real estate assets. In general, land is not depreciable. The law does allow depreciation deductions for structures, with the depreciable life of the structure depending on whether it is a commercial or residential property.

ment under MACRS depreciation rules, the company has depreciated 71.20 percent of the old machines' cost, leaving a book value of $28,800. Electrocom sells its old computers to another firm for $10,000. This allows Electrocom to report a loss on the sale of $18,800. Assuming that Electrocom's business is otherwise profitable, it can use this loss to shelter other sources of current income, resulting in a tax savings of $7,520, or 40 percent of $18,800.

WORKING CAPITAL EXPENDITURES

Consider a retail firm evaluating the opportunity to open a new store. Part of the cost of such an investment involves expenditures on fixed assets—shelving, cash registers, and merchandise displays—but stocking the store with inventory constitutes another important cost. A portion of this cost may be deferred if the firm can purchase inventory from suppliers on credit. By the same token, cash inflows from selling the inventory may be delayed if the firm sells to customers on credit.

Just as a firm must account for cash expenditures on fixed assets, it must also weigh the cash inflows and outflows associated with changes in net working capital. **Net working capital** equals the difference between current assets and current liabilities. Frequently, the term **working capital** is used to refer to what is more correctly known as "net working capital." An increase in net working capital represents a cash outflow. Notice that net working capital increases if current assets rise (e.g., if the firm buys more inventory) or if current liabilities fall (e.g., if the firm pays down accounts payable). Therefore, any increase in a current asset account or any decrease in a current liability account results in a cash outflow.[4] Similarly, a decrease in net working capital represents a cash inflow. Net working capital decreases when current assets fall (as when a firm sells inventory) or when current liabilities increase (as when the firm borrows from suppliers). A decrease in any current asset or an increase in any current liability results in a cash inflow.

APPLYING THE MODEL 8.3

Have you ever noticed the cottage industries that temporarily spring up around certain big events? Think about the booths that open in shopping malls near the end of each year and sell nothing but calendars. Suppose you are evaluating the opportunity to operate one of these booths from November to January. You begin by ordering (on credit) $15,000 worth of calendars. Your suppliers require a $5,000 payment on the first day of each month starting in December. You anticipate that you will sell 30 percent of your inventory in November, 60 percent in December, and 10 percent in January. You sell entirely on a cash basis. You also plan to keep $500 in the cash register until you close up shop on February 1. Your balance sheet at the beginning of each month looks like this:

[4.] Of course, one important current asset account is cash. It may seem counterintuitive to argue that if the balance in the cash account increases, this should be treated as a cash outflow. However, consider again the example of a new retail store. If the company opens a new store, a small amount of cash will have to be held in that store for transactions purposes. Holding fixed the amount of cash that the firm maintains in all of its other stores and in its corporate accounts, opening a new store requires a net increase in the firm's cash holdings. If the firm did not open the new store, then it could invest the cash that it would have held in reserve in the new store in a different project. Likewise, consider what happens if the company decides to close one of its stores. The cash kept in reserve at that location can be redeployed for another use, so reducing cash at that store represents a cash inflow to the firm as a whole. As we will see in Chapter 23, cash management tools have become so sophisticated today that few investments require significant changes in cash holdings. Changes in the other working capital items, such as inventory, receivables, and payables, typically have a much larger cash flow impact than changes in cash balances.

	Oct. 1	Nov. 1	Dec. 1	Jan. 1	Feb. 1
Cash	$0	$ 500	$ 500	$ 500	$ 0
Inventory	$0	15,000	10,500	1,500	0
Accounts payable	$0	15,000	10,000	5,000	0
Net working capital	$0	500	1,000	−3,000	0
Monthly net working capital change	NA	+500	+500	−4,000	+3,000

The cash flows associated with changes in net working capital are as follows:

$500 cash outflow from October to November
$500 cash outflow from November to December
$4,000 cash inflow from December to January
$3,000 cash outflow from January to February

Notice that at the start of November, purchases of inventory are entirely on credit, so the increase in inventory is exactly offset by an increase in accounts payable. The only working capital cash outflow occurs because you must raise $500 to put in the cash register. During November, sales reduce your inventory by $4,500 (inflow), but you have to pay suppliers $5,000 (outflow). You still have the same amount in the cash register as before, $500, so on net you have an outflow of $500, exactly equal to the increase in net working capital from the prior month. During the month of December, sales reduce your inventory by $9,000 (inflow), and you pay $5,000 to suppliers (outflow). That leaves you with cash inflow of $4,000, equal to the decrease in net working capital during the month. By February 1, sales reduce your inventory by the remaining $1,500 in calendars (inflow), you empty $500 from the cash register (inflow), and you pay the last $5,000 to suppliers (outflow). The net effect is a $3,000 cash outflow during January.[5]

TERMINAL VALUE

Some investments have a well-defined life span. The life span may be determined by the physical life of a piece of equipment, by the length of time until a patent expires, or by the period of time covered by a leasing or licensing agreement. Often, however, investments have an indefinite life. When France Telecom acquired Orange, it was undoubtedly the case that FT managers expected Orange's assets to continue to generate cash flow for a very long period of time.

When managers invest in an asset with a long life span, they typically do not construct cash flow forecasts more than 5 to 10 years into the future. One reason they give for this behavior is that forecasts more than 5 to 10 years in the future have so much error that the fine detail of an item-by-item cash flow projection is not very meaningful. Instead, managers project detailed cash flow estimates for 5 to 10 years, then calculate a project's terminal value as of some future date. The **terminal value** is a number intended to reflect the value of a project at a given future point in time, and there are a number of ways to estimate this value.

Perhaps the most common approach to calculate terminal value is to take the final year of cash flow projections and make an assumption that all future cash flows from

---

[5.] Notice that we are only looking at the working capital cash flows associated with this project. We have not considered any fixed asset investment up front. We are not considering the profits from selling calendars at a markup, nor the labor costs of operating the booth.

the project will grow at a constant rate. For example, in valuing a large acquisition, many firms project cash flows from the target company for 5 to 10 years in the future. After that, they assume that cash flows will grow at a rate equal to the growth rate in gross domestic product (GDP) for the economy.[6]

> ### APPLYING THE MODEL 8.4
>
> Suppose that analysts at France Telecom projected that their acquisition of Orange would generate the following stream of cash flows:
>
> | | |
> |---|---|
> | Year 1 | $0.50 billion |
> | Year 2 | 1.00 billion |
> | Year 3 | 1.75 billion |
> | Year 4 | 2.50 billion |
>
> In year 5 and beyond, analysts believed that cash flows would continue to grow at 2.75 percent per year. What is the terminal value of this investment? Recall that in Chapters 3 and 4 we learned that we can determine the present value of a stream of cash flows growing at a perpetual rate, g, by using the following formula:
>
> $$PV_t = \frac{CF_{t+1}}{(r - g)}$$
>
> We know that the cash flow in year 5 is 2.75 percent more than in year 4, or, $2.57 billion. Put that figure in the numerator of the equation. We also know that $g = 2.75$ percent. Suppose that France Telecom discounted the cash flows of this investment at 10 percent. Using the formula above, we can determine that the present value, *as of year 4,* of cash flows in years 5 and beyond equals the following:
>
> $$PV_5 = \frac{\$2.57}{(0.10 - 0.0275)} = \$35.45$$
>
> This means that the terminal value, the value of the project at the end of year 4, equals $35.45 billion. To determine the entire value of the project, just discount this figure along with all the other cash flows at 10 percent to obtain a total value of $28.5 billion:[7]

Notice in the preceding example that the terminal value was very large relative to all the other cash flows. If we discount the terminal value for five years at 10 percent, we find that $24.2 billion of the project's total $28.5 billion present value comes from the terminal value assumptions. Those proportions are not uncommon for long-lived investments, illustrating just how important estimates of terminal value can be in assessing an investment's merit. Analysts must think very carefully about

---

[6.] We should emphasize that when companies assume that an investment's cash flows will grow at some rate in perpetuity, the rate of growth in GDP, either in the local economy or the world economy, serves as a maximum potential long-run growth rate. Why? If an investment generates cash flows that grow forever at a rate that exceeds the growth of GDP, then eventually that one investment becomes the entire economy.

[7.] Notice that this is the gross present value, not the *NPV*, because we are not deducting any up-front cost for acquiring Orange.

the assumptions they make when calculating terminal value. For example, the growth rate used to calculate a project's terminal value does not always equal the long-run growth rate of the economy. A factory with fixed capacity might offer zero growth in cash flows, or growth that just keeps pace with inflation, once the firm hits the capacity constraint.

Several other methods enjoy widespread application in terminal value calculations. One method calculates terminal value by multiplying the final year's cash flow estimate by a market multiple such as a price-to-cash-flow ratio for publicly traded firms with characteristics similar to those of the investment. For example, the last specific cash flow estimate for the Orange acquisition was $2.57 billion in year 5. France Telecom might observe that the average price-to-cash-flow ratio for companies in this industry is 15. Multiplying $2.57 billion by 15 results in a terminal value estimate of $38.6 billion, quite close to the estimate obtained from the perpetual growth model. One hazard in using this approach is that market multiples fluctuate through time, which means when year 5 finally arrives, even if Orange generates $2.57 billion in cash flow as anticipated, the market may place a much lower value on that cash flow than it did when the acquisition originally took place.

Other approaches to this problem use an investment's book value or its expected liquidation value to estimate the terminal value figure. Using book value is most common when the investment involves physical plant and equipment with a limited useful life. In such a case, firms may plausibly assume that after a number of years of depreciation deductions, the asset's book value will be zero. Depending on whether the asset has fairly standard characteristics that would enable other firms to use it, its liquidation value may be positive, or it may be zero.[8] Some assets may even have negative terminal values if disposing of them entails substantial costs. Projects that involve the use of substances hazardous to the environment fit this description. When an investment has a fixed life span, part of the terminal value or terminal cash flow may also include recovery of working capital investments. When a retail store closes, for example, the firm realizes a cash inflow from liquidating inventory.

INCREMENTAL CASH FLOW

We have seen that many investment problems have similar types of cash flows that analysts must estimate: initial outlays on fixed assets, working capital outlays, operating cash flow, and terminal value. But in a broader sense, there is only one type of cash flow that matters in capital budgeting analysis—incremental cash flow. To rephrase the oath that witnesses take in television courtroom dramas, analysts must focus on "all incremental cash flow and nothing but incremental cash flow." Determining which cash flows for a given project are incremental and which are not can become complicated at times.

Consider, for example, the incremental cash flows associated with a student's decision to pursue an MBA degree. Many of the incremental outflows are fairly obvious, such as tuition and fees, the cost of textbooks, and possibly relocation expenses. What about expenditures on room and board? Whether a student decides to pursue an MBA or not, he or she still has to eat and have a place to sleep at night. Therefore, room and board expenditures are not incremental to the decision to go back to school.[9]

[8.] Asplund (2000) estimates that firms can expect to recover no more than 20–50 percent of the original purchase cost of a new machine once it has been installed. This is true even for assets with reasonably active secondary markets.

[9.] Of course, there may be a difference between money spent on housing and food depending on whether the person is a student or a working professional. The difference in spending would be an incremental cash flow, but it could be an incre-

The cash inflows associated with an investment in an MBA degree are more difficult to estimate. For most students, obtaining an MBA degree offers the opportunity to earn higher pay after graduation than they earned before returning to school. Furthermore, most students hope that their salary trajectory will be steeper after obtaining an MBA. Students expect their pay to increase at a faster rate than it would had they not obtained an MBA. The net cash flow equals the difference in salary a student would earn with an MBA versus the salary the student would earn without an MBA—after taxes, of course.

SMART PRACTICES VIDEO

**Paul Savastano,
Director of Information
Technology, Sprint Corp.**
"So the challenge becomes, how do you quantify the benefits when a big piece of the investment is going to be for things that people never see?"

See the entire interview at
SMARTFinance

APPLYING THE MODEL 8.5

Norman Paul makes $60,000 per year working as an engineer for an auto manufacturer, and he pays taxes at a flat rate of 35 percent. He expects salary increases each year of about 5 percent. Lately, Norm has been thinking about going back to school to earn an MBA. A few months ago he spent $1,000 to enroll in a Graduate Management Admission Test (GMAT) study course. He also spent $2,000 visiting various MBA programs in the United States. From his research on MBA programs, Norm has learned a great deal about the costs and benefits of the degree. At the beginning of each of the next two years, his out-of-pocket costs for tuition, fees, and textbooks will be $35,000. He expects to spend roughly the same amount on room and board in graduate school that he spends now. At the end of two years, he anticipates that he will receive a job offer with a salary of $90,000, and he expects that his pay will increase by 8 percent per year over his career (about the next 30 years). The schedule of incremental cash flows for the next few periods, excluding the salary Norm gives up if he goes back to school (more on that later), looks like this:

Year 0	− $35,000
Year 1	− 35,000
Year 2	+ 15,503

Notice that Norm's cash outflows do not include the money he has already spent on the GMAT review course and on visits to MBA programs. These are **sunk costs,** costs that have already been spent and are not recoverable if Norm decides to keep working rather than go back to school. The cash inflow figure for year 2 requires some explanation. Had Norm stayed at his current job for the next two years rather than go back to school, his pay would have increased to $66,150. Therefore, the difference between that figure and his $90,000 post-MBA salary represents a net cash inflow of $23,850. Assuming that Norm pays about 35 percent of his earnings in taxes, the after-tax inflow would be $15,503. In year 3, Norm expects to earn 8 percent more, or $97,200, compared to what he would have earned at his old job, $69,458. The after-tax cash inflow in year 3 equals $18,032. If you carry these steps out for 30 years, you will quickly see that the MBA has a substantial positive *NPV* at almost any reasonable discount rate.

Incremental cash flows show up in surprising forms. One type of incremental cash outflow that firms must be careful to measure when launching a new product is called **cannibalization.** This simply means that when a firm introduces a new prod-

---

mental inflow (if these costs are lower in graduate school) or an outflow (if the MBA program is located in a city with a high cost of living).

uct, some of the new product's sales may come at the expense of the firm's existing products. In the food products industry, sales of a low-fat version of a popular product may reduce sales of the original (presumably high-fat) version. Firms must be careful to consider the incremental cash outflows from existing product sales that are cannibalized by a newer product.[10]

OPPORTUNITY COSTS

We made a number of simplifying assumptions in the preceding Applying the Model example. For instance, we assumed that Norm received his pay in a lump sum each year and that he faced a flat tax rate. Actually, the incremental salary that Norm earns arrives monthly, and his higher earnings may be taxed at a higher rate. All these effects are easy to account for, although the calculations become a bit more tedious.

However, there is one major error in our analysis of Norm's investment problem. We ignored a significant opportunity cost. Undertaking one investment frequently means giving up an alternative. In capital budgeting, the **opportunity costs** of one investment are the cash flows on the alternative investment that the firm (or in this case, the individual) decides *not* to make. If Norm did not attend school, he would earn $60,000 ($39,000 after taxes) the first year and $63,000 ($40,950 after taxes) the second year. This is Norm's *opportunity cost* of getting an MBA, and it is just as important in the overall calculation as his out-of-pocket expenses for tuition and books. Though it is still true, given the assumptions of our example, that the *NPV* of an MBA is positive, the value of the degree falls substantially once we recognize opportunity costs. As every MBA student knows, opportunity costs are real, not just hypothetical numbers from a textbook. Directors of MBA programs all over the world know that MBA applications are countercyclical. That is, the number of students applying to MBA programs rises during economic downturns and falls during booms. The most plausible explanation of this phenomenon is that potential MBA students face higher opportunity costs when the economy is strong.

What kinds of opportunity costs do businesses encounter in capital budgeting problems? One interesting example arises when one company buys another by exchanging the target firm's shares for shares in the acquiring firm. For example, in July 2000, JDS Uniphase exchanged $41 billion worth of its stock to acquire the shares of SDL. Later, as the market for high-technology stocks dropped precipitously, JDS was forced to "write down" the value of its investment in SDL. As a result, JDS reported the largest ever fiscal-year loss, roughly $50 billion, during the summer of 2001. Some "experts" indicated that the cash flow consequence of this transaction was nil. Firms just traded pieces of paper, and no one paid or received cash. This ignores JDS's opportunity cost. Though it may be true that JDS could not have raised $41 billion in cash had it attempted to sell the same number of shares that it gave to SDL shareholders in the acquisition, JDS certainly could have raised a substantial amount of cash from a stock sale. The amount of cash that JDS gave up by issuing shares to pay for the acquisition, rather than selling them, is the opportunity cost of the acquisition.

Probably the most common type of opportunity cost encountered in capital budgeting problems involves the alternative use of an asset owned by a firm. Suppose that a company owns raw land that it purchased some years ago in anticipation of an expansion opportunity. Now the firm is ready to expand by building new facilities on the raw land. Even though the firm may have paid for the land many years ago, us-

---

[10.] On a capital budgeting exam problem, one of our students mentioned that a firm needed to be wary that its new product should not "cannibalize the existing sales force." Needless to say, that's not the kind of cannibalization that we have in mind, although should it occur, it would certainly represent an incremental cash outflow.

ing the land for expansion entails an incremental opportunity cost. The opportunity cost is the cash that could be raised if the firm sold the land or leased it for another purpose. That cost should be factored into the *NPV* calculation for the firm's expansion plans.

In the next section, we work through an extended example of a capital budgeting project, illustrating how to apply the principles from this section to calculate the project's cash flows each year. Before getting into the details, we want to remind you of the big picture. Cash flows are important because they are necessary to calculate a project's *NPV*, and estimating the *NPV* is important because it provides an estimate of the increase or decrease in shareholder value that will occur if the firm invests. McConnell and Muscarella (1985) demonstrate the connection between capital investment decisions and shareholder value by showing that stock prices rise on average when firms publicly announce significant new capital investment programs. This suggests that, on average, firms invest in positive *NPV* projects. The Comparative Corporate Finance feature offers evidence supporting this big picture by showing that what matters is not just the amount of investment that firms undertake, but how efficiently they invest.

SMART ETHICS VIDEO

Scott Lee, Texas A&M University
"We have found evidence that the market punishes firms that were involved in defense procurement fraud."

See the entire interview at **SMARTFinance**

Concept Review Questions

1. Why do we consider *changes* in net working capital associated with a project to be cash inflows or outflows?

2. For what kinds of investments would terminal value account for a substantial fraction of the total project *NPV*, and for what kinds of investments would terminal value be relatively unimportant?

3. A real estate development firm owns a fully leased 40-story office building. A tenant recently moved its offices out of 2 stories of the building, leaving the space temporarily vacant. If the real estate firm considers moving its own offices into this 40-story office building, what cost should it assign for the space? Is the cost of the vacant space zero because the firm paid for the building long ago, a cost that is sunk, or is there an incremental opportunity cost?

4. Suppose that an analyst makes a mistake and calculates the *NPV* of an investment project by discounting the project's contribution to net income each year rather than by discounting its cash flows. Would you expect the *NPV* based on net income to be higher or lower than the *NPV* calculated using cash flows?

8.2 CASH FLOWS FOR CLASSICALTUNES.COM

Classicaltunes.com is a (fictitious) profitable Internet-based music club selling classical-music CDs to its membership.[11] The company is considering a proposal to expand its music selection to include jazz recordings. Management believes that many lovers of classical music also enjoy jazz, and so the company has a built-in clientele for the new music offerings. If the company decides to undertake this project, it will begin selling jazz-music CDs next month when its new fiscal year begins. The company accepts projects with positive *NPV*s, and it uses a 10 percent discount rate to calculate *NPV*.

Up-front costs associated with the investment include $50,000 in computer equipment (which falls under the MACRS 5-year asset class) and $4,500 in inven-

---

[11.] Some might say that because Classicaltunes.com is a profitable Internet-based firm, it must be fictitious.

COMPARATIVE CORPORATE FINANCE

Is a High Investment Rate Good for a Nation's Economic Health?

Most people would accept as a given that a high investment rate, measured as capital investment spending as a percentage of GDP, is strongly correlated with rapid growth in industrial production and overall employment. As the table below illustrates, no such strong relationship exists for industrialized countries over the period 1980 to 2000. The industrialized country with the highest investment rate, Japan, indeed saw industrial production increase rapidly between 1980 and 1990, but industrial production barely rose in the following decade, and total employment declined by more than 2 percent between 1980 and 2000. Similarly, the large continental European economies of France, Germany, and Italy had about-average investment rates throughout the 1980–2000 period, but industrial production grew more slowly than the average for all industrial countries, and all three nations experienced large net employment *declines* over these two decades. Country-specific factors help explain the exceptional performance of two of the smaller countries in the table, Ireland and Norway. Ireland adopted an explicit open market strategy after 1980 and attracted large net inflows of foreign direct investment over the next two decades—with a spectacular payoff in industrial production plus a more muted, but still significant, increase in employment. Norway benefited from an investment boom resulting from exploration and development of massive North Sea petroleum deposits. However, by far the best-performing large economy was that of the United States. Despite having a below-average investment rate throughout this period, industrial production increased by 84 percent, and employment increased by 46 percent between 1980 and 2000. The moral is clear: How efficiently capital is invested is far more important to a nation's economic health than is the absolute level of investment.

Source: International Financial Statistics Yearbook 2001 (Washington, D.C.: International Monetary Fund).

Country	Capital Investment Spending (as a % of GDP)			Industrial Production Index (1995 = 100)			Total Employment (1995 = 100)		
	1980	1990	2000[a]	1980	1990	2000[a]	1980	1990	2000[a]
United States	23.5	18.0	21.4	69.7	86.5	128.5	77.2	93.4	112.4
Canada	19.7	20.7	20.5	71.8	88.8	119.5	114.1	112.6	120.6
Japan	32.4	32.8	25.9	71.4	105.3	106.4	92.9	101.7	90.9
France	25.0	23.4	20.5	89.6	100.4	115.5	132.6	113.6	97.2
Germany	25.1	24.6	22.6	86.8	103.2	113.5	103.3	100.0[b]	85.9[b]
Ireland	27.8	21.0	23.9	32.7	62.1	159.8	107.4	90.7	114.5
Italy	27.0	22.2	20.5	82.2	93.5	108.2	123.9	107.7	99.7
Spain	23.2	25.4	24.1	80.5	96.9	119.3	94.7	104.5	120.2
Norway	28.3	23.3	21.5	55.1	86.5	110.4	92.1	97.7	102.8
Sweden	21.3	21.3	17.9	74.5	87.8	115.5	133.3	124.7	99.1
Switzerland	28.5	28.3	21.5	79.7	97.0	121.1	122.6	119.4	94.7
United Kingdom	17.6	20.2	17.8	76.7	94.1	105.0	101.0	102.5	107.4
Industrial country average	23.5	22.6	22.0	75.0	95.2	115.4	95.6	102.4	102.4

[a] Or most recent year, usually 1999.

[b] Employment index for Germany: 1990 = 100 and data end in 1994.

tory ($2,500 of which is purchased on credit). For transactions purposes, the firm plans to increase its cash balance by $1,000 immediately. The firm does not expect to begin selling CDs until the new fiscal year begins, though it is entitled to take the first half-year of MACRS depreciation in the current fiscal year.[12] Currently, the

---

[12.] In most end-of-chapter problems we will make the simplifying assumption that the first available depreciation deduction comes one year after the initial investment.

average selling price of Classicaltunes.com's CDs is $13.50, and company executives believe that CD prices will increase over time at a 2 percent annual rate. Classical-tunes.com knows that some of its suppliers will sell CDs on credit. In addition to re-lying on this trade credit, the firm expects to finance this investment using cash flow generated from its existing classical-music business.

Like most new business ventures, this one will not be profitable immediately. Managers expect unit sales volume to increase rapidly in the first few years before reaching a long-run stable growth rate. As sales volume increases, the firm expects gross profit margins to widen slightly. The firm does allow credit sales to customers with excellent payment histories. Expanding sales volume will require increases in current assets, as well as additional spending on fixed assets. Classicaltunes.com pays taxes at a 40 percent rate.

Table 8.2 shows various projections for the jazz-music CD project. The top two lines list anticipated selling prices and unit volumes in each of the next six years. Un-derneath that appears a series of projected income statements for the next six years. Top-line revenue simply equals the product of expected selling price and unit volume each year. The figures for cost of goods sold and selling, general, and administrative expenses (SG&A) reflect management's belief that costs as a percentage of sales will fall slightly as volume increases. Depreciation expense each year is determined by spending on fixed assets and the MACRS schedule for 5-year equipment.

Beneath the income statement appears a series of balance sheets. Each shows the project's total asset requirements (including both current and fixed assets) as well as the financing available from suppliers in the form of accounts payable. As men-

Table 8.2
Projections for Classicaltunes.com's Jazz-Music CD Proposal

Year	0	1	2	3	4	5	6
Price per unit	$13.50	$13.77	$14.05	$14.33	$14.61	$14.91	$15.20
Units	0	4,000	10,000	16,000	22,000	24,000	25,000
Abbreviated Projected Income Statements							
Revenue	$ 0	$55,080	$140,454	$229,221	$321,482	$357,722	$380,080
− Cost of goods sold	0	41,861	105,341	169,623	234,682	259,349	273,657
Gross profit	$ 0	$13,219	$ 35,113	$ 59,598	$ 86,800	$ 98,373	$106,423
− SG&A expenses	0	8,262	19,664	29,799	35,363	35,772	38,008
− Depreciation	10,000	18,000	13,800	14,280	23,872	25,208	18,512
Pretax profit	−$10,000	−$13,043	$ 1,649	$ 15,519	$ 27,565	$ 37,393	$ 49,903
Abbreviated Projected Balance Sheets							
Cash	$ 1,000	$ 2,000	$ 2,500	$ 3,000	$ 3,200	$ 3,300	$ 3,500
Accounts receivable	0	4,590	11,705	19,102	26,790	29,810	31,673
Inventory	4,500	7,344	18,727	30,563	42,864	47,696	50,677
Current assets	$ 5,500	$13,934	$32,932	$52,665	$ 72,854	$ 80,806	$ 85,850
Gross P&E	$50,000	$60,000	$65,000	$90,000	$130,000	$145,000	$155,000
− Accumulated depreciation	10,000	28,000	41,800	56,080	79,952	105,160	123,672
Net P&E	$40,000	$32,000	$23,200	$33,920	$ 50,048	$ 39,840	$ 31,328
Total assets	$45,500	$45,934	$56,132	$86,585	$122,902	$120,646	$117,178
Accounts payable	$ 2,500	$ 4,320	$11,016	$17,978	$ 25,214	$ 28,057	$ 29,810

tioned previously, any additional financing the project requires will come from internally generated funds from the classical-music CD side of the business. To determine whether this is an investment opportunity worth taking, we will determine the project's cash flows through time and discount them at 10 percent to calculate the project's *NPV*. As part of this calculation, we will have to estimate the value of the endeavor beyond the sixth year. In other words, we will have to estimate the project's terminal value.

YEAR 0 CASH FLOW

The firm will have cash outlays of $50,000 for computer equipment immediately. MACRS rules allow the firm to take a depreciation deduction of 20 percent, or $10,000, in the first year. Because the company has no other expenses or revenues, the project's incremental pretax profit this year is −$10,000. However, the $10,000 loss does not represent a cash outflow because it derives entirely from a noncash depreciation expense. Assuming that this expense can be deducted from the firm's classical-music CD profits, the expense will save Classicaltunes.com $4,000 in taxes (40% × $10,000). The firm purchases $4,500 in inventory and sets up a cash account with an initial balance of $1,000. Accounts payable totaling $2,500 are used to finance a portion of these outlays, resulting in an initial working capital investment of $3,000 ($4,500 inventory + $1,000 cash − $2,500 accounts payable). Therefore, the net cash flow for year 0 is shown as follows:

Increase in gross fixed assets	−$50,000
Tax savings	4,000
Initial working capital investment	− 3,000
Net cash flow	−$49,000

YEAR 1 CASH FLOW

Notice in Table 8.2 that gross plant and equipment (P&E) increases by $10,000 in year 1. This means that Classicaltunes.com has purchased $10,000 in additional computer equipment or other fixed assets. Depreciation in the first full year of operation equals $18,000, the difference between accumulated depreciation in year 1 and year 0. That figure combines a depreciation charge of 32 percent of the initial $50,000 investment in fixed assets ($16,000) and a deduction of 20 percent of the current-year $10,000 investment in fixed assets ($2,000).

With sales volume increasing, the firm also makes additional investments in working capital. Cash balances increase by $1,000, receivables rise by $4,590, and inventories go up by $2,844. Partially offsetting the increase in current assets is an increase in accounts payable of $1,820. Therefore, net working capital increases by $6,614, a net cash outflow for the firm.

At a sales volume of 4,000 units in its first year of operation, the jazz-music CD business earns a pretax loss of $13,043. To convert this figure into cash flow, we must make two adjustments. First, if Classicaltunes.com can charge this loss against profits in its other operations, then the loss will generate tax savings of $5,217 (40% × $13,043). Second, we need to add depreciation expense back into the pretax loss because depreciation involves no cash outlay. Together these adjustments result in a net operating cash inflow of $10,174 (−$13,043 + $18,000 + $5,217).

Combining each source of cash flow, we can determine the net cash flow for the project's first full year:

Increase in gross fixed assets	−$10,000
Change in working capital	− 6,614
Operating cash inflow	10,174
Net cash flow	−$ 6,440

YEAR 2 CASH FLOW

We can simply repeat the steps we followed in year 1 to determine cash flow for year 2.

First, gross fixed assets increase by $5,000. Depreciation for year 2 is $13,800 (the difference between accumulated depreciation in year 2 and year 1). The depreciation in year 2 equals the sum of allowable depreciation on assets purchased up front (19.20% × $50,000), assets purchased in year 1 (32% × $10,000), and assets purchased in year 2 (20% × $5,000).

Sales continue to rise in year 2, requiring a large investment in working capital. Total current assets increase by $18,998, but accounts payable rises by $6,696. The net increase in working capital equals $12,302 and results in a cash outflow.

In year 2, the firm earns a small pretax profit of $1,649. After taxes of $660 are deducted, the net earnings amount to $989. Add to that figure the depreciation expense of $13,800 to arrive at operating cash inflow of $14,789. The following are the total net cash flows in year 2:

Increase in fixed assets	−$ 5,000
Change in working capital	− 12,302
Operating cash inflow	14,789
Net cash flow	−$ 2,513

Table 8.3 illustrates the annual net cash flows for the jazz-music CD project all the way through the sixth year. As you can see, project cash flows do not turn from negative to positive until the fifth year. If we take the *NPV* of the stream of cash flows shown in Table 8.3, it is clear that the project will not generate a positive *NPV*. However, just because the year-by-year cash flow projections end in year 6 does not mean that the project ends at that time. To complete our analysis, we must estimate the project's terminal value.

TERMINAL VALUE

We will produce two different terminal value estimates for this project. In the first, we assume that by year 6 the project has reached a steady state, meaning that cash flows will continue to grow at 2 percent per year indefinitely. In the second, we as-

Table 8.3
Annual Cash Flow Estimates for Classicaltunes.com

	Year 0	Year 1	Year 2	Year 3	Year 4	Year 5	Year 6
New fixed assets	−$50,000	−$10,000	−$ 5,000	−$25,000	−$40,000	−$15,000	−$10,000
Change in working capital	− 3,000*	− 6,614	− 12,302	− 12,771	− 12,953	− 5,109	− 3,291
Operating cash flow	4,000	10,174	14,789	23,591	40,411	47,644	48,454
Net cash flow	−$49,000	−$ 6,440	−$ 2,513	−$14,180	−$12,542	$27,535	$35,163

* Represents the initial working capital investment.

sume that the firm sells its investment at the end of year 6 and receives a cash payment equal to the project's book value.

In year 6, the project generates a net cash inflow of $35,163. Assuming that cash flows beyond the sixth year grow at 2 percent per year, and discounting those cash flows at 10 percent, we can determine the terminal value of the project *as of the end of year 6* as follows:

$$\text{Terminal Value} = \frac{\$35,866}{0.10 - 0.02} = \$448,325$$

Notice that the numerator of this expression is 2 percent greater than the cash flow in year 6. Remember, when valuing a stream of cash flows that grows at a perpetual rate, the *value today* equals *next year's cash flow* divided by the difference between the discount rate and the growth rate. Thus, to determine the terminal value in year 6, we must use the cash flow in year 7 in the numerator.

As a second approach, assume that the terminal value of the project simply equals the book value at the end of year 6. At that time, the firm owns fixed assets worth $31,328. If the firm liquidates its current assets and pays off outstanding trade credit, it will generate an additional $56,040 in cash. The terminal value equals the sum of these two items, $87,368. Notice that this value is just one-fifth of the value we obtained using the perpetual growth model. The magnitude of that difference should not surprise us too much. In general, a profitable, growing business will have a market value that exceeds its book value.

JAZZ-MUSIC CD PROJECT *NPV*

Putting all this together, we arrive at two different estimates of the project's *NPV*, depending on which estimate of terminal value we use. Assuming that this business will continue to increase profits forever, we arrive at the following *NPV*:

$$NPV = -\$49,000 - \frac{\$6,440}{1.1^1} - \frac{\$2,513}{1.1^2} - \frac{\$14,180}{1.1^3} - \frac{\$12,542}{1.1^4} + \frac{\$27,535}{1.1^5}$$
$$+ \frac{\$35,163 + \$448,325}{1.1^6} = \$213,862$$

However, if we assume that the terminal value is only equal to book value after six years, then we arrive at the following *NPV*:

$$NPV = -\$49,000 - \frac{\$6,440}{1.1^1} - \frac{\$2,513}{1.1^2} - \frac{\$14,180}{1.1^3} - \frac{\$12,542}{1.1^4} + \frac{\$27,535}{1.1^5}$$
$$+ \frac{\$35,163 + \$87,368}{1.1^6} = \$10,111$$

SMART PRACTICES VIDEO

David Nickel, Controller for Legal and Risk Management, Intel Corp.

"Capital budgeting is the key theme for deciding which programs get funded."

See the entire interview at **SMARTFinance**

In this example, the project yields a positive *NPV* no matter which terminal value estimate we choose, so investing will increase shareholder wealth. But in many real-world situations, especially those involving long-lived investments, the "go" or "no-go" decision will depend critically on terminal value assumptions. It is not at all uncommon for the perpetual growth approach to yield a positive *NPV* while the book value approach shows a negative *NPV*. In that case, managers have to think more deeply about the long-run value of their enterprise.

5. Embedded in the analysis of the jazz-music CD proposal is an assumption about how Classicaltunes.com's customers will behave when they are able to choose from a new set of CDs. What is that assumption?

6. What other ways might Classicaltunes.com estimate the terminal value of this project?

7. Suppose that Congress passes a new MACRS schedule that reclassifies computers as 3-year equipment rather than 5-year equipment. In general, what impact would this legislation have on the project's *NPV*?

8.3 CASH FLOWS, DISCOUNTING, AND INFLATION

At least since World War II, inflation has been a pervasive element of the macroeconomic environment in most countries. Inflation rates can vary dramatically across countries and across time for a given country. There are several ways to deal with inflation in capital budgeting analysis, but a simple way to characterize the proper treatment of inflation is as follows. If inflation is in the numerator, be sure that it is also in the denominator. If the numerator ignores inflation, so too must the denominator.

In Chapter 5, we commented on the difference between the nominal rate of return and the real rate of return on an investment. The *nominal return* reflects the actual dollar return, whereas the *real return* measures the increase in purchasing power gained by holding a certain investment. In general, when the inflation rate is high, so too will be the nominal rate of return offered by various investments, because investors will demand a return that not only keeps pace with inflation, but also offers a positive real return.

APPLYING THE MODEL 8.6

Imagine that a movie ticket today costs $10. If you have $1,000, you have the power to watch 100 movies. Now suppose that you put $1,000 into a mutual fund that earns a 23 percent nominal return over the next year. Suppose also that the inflation rate for that year was 6 percent. By the end of the year, each movie ticket costs $10.60. Your money has grown to $1,230, so you have enough to purchase 116 movie tickets. In other words, your purchasing power increased by 16 percent during the year, which represents your real return on the mutual fund.

Remember that we formalized the relationship between the nominal rate of return, the inflation rate, and the real rate through the following equation:[13]

$$(1 + \text{nominal rate}) = (1 + \text{inflation rate}) \times (1 + \text{real rate})$$

We can rearrange the terms to solve for the real interest rate:

$$\text{Real rate} = \frac{1 + \text{nominal rate}}{1 + \text{inflation rate}} - 1 \qquad \text{(Eq. 8.1)}$$

[13.] Students may be more familiar with the expression that shows the nominal rate approximately equals the real rate plus the inflation rate. If you multiply out the terms in Equation 8.1, you will see that the nominal rate equals the real rate, plus the inflation rate, plus the product of the real rate and the inflation rate. The quality of this approximation declines as either the real rate or the inflation rate increases. For instance, in our movie ticket example (Applying the Model 8.6), the real rate plus the inflation rate equals 22 percent, while the nominal rate equals 23 percent.

Plugging in the figures from our movie ticket example, we find that the real interest rate is just a little more than 16 percent:

$$\text{Real rate} = \frac{1 + .23}{1 + .06} - 1 = 0.1604 = 16.04\%$$

In most cases, when firms establish a discount rate for capital budgeting purposes, the discount rate reflects then-current market rates of return. As we have seen, embedded in market interest rates is an assumption about inflation, or more precisely, an estimate of expected inflation. Therefore, if we use a market interest rate in the denominator of an NPV calculation, we must be careful that the cash flow estimates in the numerator are **nominal cash flows**, which reflect the same inflation rate that the interest rate does. We refer to this as Inflation Rule 1.

Inflation Rule 1—When we discount cash flows at a nominal interest rate, embedded in the discount rate is an estimate of expected inflation. We must employ the same inflation assumption when forecasting project cash flows.

APPLYING THE MODEL 8.7

Refer again to Table 8.2. Notice that two factors cause the project's revenues to rise over time. The first factor is that the average price of a CD increases 2 percent each year. In this example, 2 percent is the underlying inflation rate, meaning that all prices rise, on average, 2 percent per year. The second factor causing revenues to rise is the increase in sales volume. Multiplying price times quantity gives us revenue in *nominal terms*—that is, the actual dollar revenue figure that the firm expects to generate each year. Because the cash flow projections for the project include a 2 percent inflation rate, the discount rate used to calculate the NPV should be the nominal rate.

As long as the 10 percent discount rate used by Classicaltunes.com reflects current market returns, the company is treating inflation properly. It is discounting nominal cash flows with a nominal discount rate.

Occasionally, an investment's cash flow projections may be stated in *real* terms. **Real cash flows** only reflect current prices and do not incorporate upward adjustments for expected inflation. When project cash flows are stated in real terms, the proper discount rate to use in calculating the NPV is the real rate.

APPLYING THE MODEL 8.8

An alternative way to construct Table 8.2 would be to use the current-year price of CDs, $13.50, all the way through the analysis. If we took that approach, being careful to use current-year labor costs, current-year prices for fixed assets, and so on, then we would be stating cash flows in real terms. For example, if we calculate revenues in all future years using today's CD price of $13.50, we find that real revenues are about 2 percent lower in year 1 than the figure shown in Table 8.2. In year 2, real revenues are about 4 percent less than the number given in Table 8.2. In general, to convert nominal cash flows into real cash flows, we "discount" the nominal figures by the rate of inflation. By doing so, we restate cash flows to reflect today's prices, not prices in the future that have risen due to inflation. With cash flows stated in real terms, the real rate is the appropriate discount rate to use. From Equation 8.1, we can calculate the real rate for Classicaltunes.com:

$$\text{Real rate} = \frac{1 + 0.10}{1 + 0.20} - 1 = 0.0784 = 7.84\%$$

Using a real rate to discount real cash flows should result in the same project *NPV* as using a nominal rate to discount nominal cash flows. To demonstrate this, we have restated all the project's cash flows in real terms in the following equations. For example, the net cash flow in year 1 of −$6,440 has been restated in real terms by deflating the nominal cash figure by the inflation rate:

$$-\frac{\$6,440}{1.02} = -\$6,314$$

Similarly, we restate the nominal cash flow in year 2 into real terms as follows:

$$-\frac{\$2,513}{1.02^2} = \$2,415$$

Converting cash flows in every year (except the cash flows that occur immediately) from nominal to real terms and then discounting at the real rate of 7.84 percent yields the following *NPV*:[14]

$$NPV = -\$49,000 - \frac{\$6,314}{1.0784^1} - \frac{\$2,415}{1.0784^2} - \frac{\$13,362}{1.0784^3} - \frac{\$11,587}{1.0784^4}$$

$$+ \frac{\$24,939}{1.0784^5} + \frac{\$31,224 + \$398,100}{1.0784^6} = \$213,862$$

When cash flow figures for a particular project ignore the effects of inflation (i.e., when cash flows are in real terms), it is necessary to discount those cash flows at a rate that also excludes the impact of inflation—the real rate. This leads to Inflation Rule 2.

> *Inflation Rule 2*—When project cash flows are stated in real rather than in nominal terms, the appropriate discount rate is the real rate.

Discounting real cash flows at a real interest rate should yield the same *NPV* as discounting nominal cash flows at a nominal rate. Errors occur when firms discount real cash flows using a nominal interest rate, or when firms discount nominal cash flows using a real discount rate. Figure 8.1 illustrates four possible scenarios in which

Figure 8.1
Capital Budgeting and Inflation

	Nominal Cash Flows	Real Cash Flows
Nominal Discount Rate	✓	*NPV* understated
Real Discount Rate	*NPV* overstated	✓

[14.] Notice that we are once again using the perpetual growth approach to estimate the project's terminal value. In addition, the equation shows a discount rate of 7.84 percent, but in reality we are using 7.8431 percent to get exactly the same *NPV* figure as we obtained before. Using 7.84 percent makes the *NPV* in this case look a little larger than it was before, but that is simply a rounding error.

firms can choose to project cash flows in nominal or in real terms and to discount those cash flows using a nominal or real discount rate. As long as both cash flows are either in real terms or in nominal terms, firms obtain the correct *NPV*. However, if firms project nominal cash flows that increase over time due to inflation, and discount those cash flows using a real rate, then they will overstate the project's *NPV*. This bias will lead firms to accept projects that they should, in fact, reject. Just the opposite happens when firms discount real cash flows, which are not adjusted upward for inflation, using a nominal discount rate. The resulting *NPV* understates the project's true contribution to shareholder value, and firms may be misled into rejecting projects they should accept.

Concept Review Questions

8. Look back at the cash flow projections for Classicaltunes.com's jazz-music CD project. Are the depreciation deductions stated in nominal or in real terms?

9. Can you think of a project for which it might be easier to project real cash flows than to project nominal cash flows?

8.4 SPECIAL PROBLEMS IN CAPITAL BUDGETING

Though our objective in writing this book was to give it the most real-world focus possible, real business situations are more complex and occur in more varieties than any textbook can reasonably convey. In this section, we examine common business decisions with special characteristics that make them a little more difficult to analyze than the examples we have covered thus far. We will see that while the analysis may require a little more thinking, the principles involved are the same ones discussed throughout this chapter and Chapter 7.

EQUIPMENT REPLACEMENT AND EQUIVALENT ANNUAL COST

Assume that a firm must purchase an electronic control device to monitor its assembly line. Two types of devices are available, and both meet the firm's minimum quality standards, but they differ in three dimensions. First, one device (A) costs less than the other (B). Second, the cheaper device (A) requires higher maintenance expenditures. Third, the less expensive device does not last as long as the more expensive one, so it will have to be replaced sooner. The sequence of expected *cash outflows* (we have omitted the negative signs for convenience, and for simplicity we are ignoring taxes and depreciation) for each device are as follows:

Device	0	1	2	3	4
			End of Year		
A	$12,000	$1,500	$1,500	$1,500	$ 0
B	$14,000	$1,200	$1,200	$1,200	1,200

Notice that the maintenance costs do not rise over time. This means either that the expected rate of inflation equals zero, in which case the nominal discount rate and the real discount rate are one and the same, or that we have ignored inflation in making the projections. In the latter case, we must be careful to discount cash flows at the real rate.[15] Suppose this firm uses a real discount rate of 7 percent. Following is the *NPV* of each stream of cash flows:

Device	NPV
A	$15,936
B	$18,065

Purchasing and operating device A seems to be much cheaper than B (remember that we are looking for a lower *NPV* because these are cash outflows). But this calculation ignores the fact that using device A will necessitate a large replacement expenditure in year 4, one year earlier than device B must be replaced. We need a way to capture the value of replacing device B less frequently than device A.

One way to do this is to look at both machines over a 12-year time horizon. Over the next 12 years, the firm will replace device A four times and device B three times. At the end of the twelfth year, both machines have to be replaced, and thus begins another 12-year cycle. Table 8.4 shows the streams of cash flows over the cycle. Notice that in years in which the firm must replace one of the devices, it must pay both the maintenance cost on the old device (to keep it running through the year) and the purchase price of the new device. Following is the present value (using a 7% discount rate) of cash flows over the entire 12-year period:

Device	NPV
A	$48,233
B	$42,360

Taking into account the greater longevity of device B, it is the better choice.

An alternative approach to this problem is called the **equivalent annual cost (EAC)** method. The EAC method begins by calculating the present value of cash

Table 8.4
Operating and Replacement Cash Flows for Two Devices

Year	Device A	Device B
0	$12,000	$14,000
1	1,500	1,200
2	1,500	1,200
3	13,500	1,200
4	1,500	15,200
5	1,500	1,200
6	13,500	1,200
7	1,500	1,200
8	1,500	15,200
9	13,500	1,200
10	1,500	1,200
11	1,500	1,200
12	1,500	1,200
NPV (7%)	$48,233	$42,360

Note: At the end of 12 years, the firm would have to replace equipment regardless of whether it chooses device A or B; thus, a new 12-year cycle begins.

[15.] Of course, we could restate the cash flows, building in an inflation assumption, then discount the cash flows at the nominal interest rate.

flows for each device over its lifetime. We have already seen that the *NPV* for operating device A for three years is $15,936, and the *NPV* for operating B for four years is $18,065. Next, the EAC method asks, what annual expenditure over the life of each machine would have the same present value? That is, the EAC solves each expression as follows:

$$\$15,936 = \frac{X}{1.07^1} + \frac{X}{1.07^2} + \frac{X}{1.07^3} \qquad X = \$6,072$$

$$\$18,065 = \frac{Y}{1.07^1} + \frac{Y}{1.07^2} + \frac{Y}{1.07^3} + \frac{Y}{1.07^4} \qquad Y = \$5,333$$

In the first equation, the variable *X* represents the annual cash flow from a 3-year annuity that has the same present value as the actual purchase and operating costs of device A. If the firm purchases A and keeps replacing it every three years for the indefinite future, the firm will incur a sequence of cash flows over time with the same present value as a perpetuity of $6,072. In other words, $6,072 is the equivalent annual cost of device A. Likewise, in the second equation, *Y* represents the annual cash flow from a 4-year annuity with the same present value as the purchase and operating costs of device B. If the firm buys B and replaces it every four years, then the firm will incur a sequence of cash flows having the same present value as a perpetuity of $5,333. The firm should choose the machine with the lower EAC, device B.

Our approaches for solving the problem of choosing between equipment with unequal lives both assume that the firm will continue to replace worn-out equipment with similar machines for a long period of time. That may not be a bad assumption in some cases, but many times new technology makes old equipment obsolete. For example, suppose the firm in our example believes that in three years a new electronic device will be available that is more reliable, less costly to operate, and longer lived. If this new device becomes available in three years, the firm will replace whatever device it is using at the time with the newer model. Furthermore, the superior attributes of the new model imply that the salvage value for the old devices will be zero. How should the firm proceed?

Knowing that it will replace the old device with an improved one in three years, the firm can simply discount cash flows for three years:

$$NPV_A = \$12,000 + \frac{\$1,500}{1.07^1} + \frac{\$1,500}{1.07^2} + \frac{\$1,500}{1.07^3} = \$15,936$$

$$NPV_B = \$14,000 + \frac{\$1,200}{1.07^1} + \frac{\$1,200}{1.07^2} + \frac{\$1,200}{1.07^3} = \$17,149$$

In this case, the best device to purchase is A rather than B. Remember that B's primary advantage was its longevity. In an environment in which technological developments make old machines obsolete, longevity is not much of an advantage.

EXCESS CAPACITY

Firms often operate at less than full capacity. In such situations, managers encourage alternative uses of the excess capacity because they view it as a free asset. Although it may be true that the marginal cost of using excess capacity is zero in the very short run, using excess capacity today may accelerate the need for more capacity in the future. When that is so, managers should charge the cost of accelerating new capacity development against the current proposal for using excess capacity.

Imagine a retail department store chain with a regional distribution center in the southeastern United States. At the moment, the distribution center is not fully utilized. Managers know that in two years, as new stores are built in the region, the firm will have to invest $2 million (cash outflow) to expand the distribution center's warehouse. A proposal surfaces to lease all the excess space in the warehouse for the next two years at a price that would generate cash inflow of $125,000 per year. If the firm accepts this proposal, it will have no excess capacity. In order to hold inventory for new stores coming on line in the next few months, the firm will have to begin expansion immediately. The incremental investment in this expansion is the difference between investing $2 million now versus investing $2 million two years from today. The incremental cash inflow is, of course, the $125,000 lease cash flows that are received today and one year from today. Should the firm accept this offer? Assuming a 10 percent discount rate, the *NPV* of the project is shown as follows:[16]

$$NPV = \$125,000 - \$2,000,000 + \frac{\$125,000}{1.1^1} + \frac{\$2,000,000}{1.1^2} = -\$108,471$$

Notice that we treat the $2 million investment in the second year as a cash inflow in this expression, because by building the warehouse today, the firm avoids having to spend the money two years later. Even so, the *NPV* of leasing excess capacity is negative. However, a clever analyst might propose a counteroffer derived from the follow equation:

$$NPV = X - \$2,000,000 + \frac{X}{1.1^1} + \frac{\$2,000,000}{1.1^2} = \$0$$

The value of *X* represents the amount of the lease cash inflow (one received today and the other received in one year) that would just make the firm indifferent to the proposal. Solving the equation, we see that if the lease cash inflows are $181,818, the project *NPV* equals zero. Therefore, if the firm can lease its capacity for a price above $181,818, it should do so.

Concept Review Questions

10. Under what circumstance is the use of the equivalent annual cost method to compare substitutable projects with different lives clearly more efficient computationally than the use of multiple investments over a common period, where both projects terminate in the same year?

11. In almost every example so far, firms must decide to invest in a project immediately or not at all. But suppose that a firm could invest in a project today or it could wait one year before investing. How could you use *NPV* analysis to decide whether to invest now or later?

12. Can you articulate circumstances under which the cost of excess capacity is zero? Think about why the cost of excess capacity normally is not zero.

8.5 THE HUMAN FACE OF CAPITAL BUDGETING

This chapter illustrates which cash flows analysts should discount and which cash flows they should ignore when valuing real investment projects. Though there are relatively simple rules of thumb that guide managers in this task, executing these rules well in practice is obviously a challenge. Deciding which costs are incremental and which are not, incorporating the myriad tax factors that influence cash flows, and

---

[16.] Again for simplicity we ignore depreciation here. A more complete analysis would take into account the changes in depreciation deductions that this decision would trigger.

measuring opportunity costs properly are all much more complex in practice than we or anyone else can convey in a textbook. The nuances of capital budgeting are best learned through practice.

There is another factor that makes real-world capital budgeting more complex than textbook examples—the human element. Neither the ideas for capital investments nor the financial analysis used to evaluate them occurs in a vacuum. Almost any investment proposal important enough to warrant a thorough financial analysis has a champion behind it, someone who believes that the project is a good idea, or at least that the project will advance the individual's own career. When companies allocate investment capital across projects or across divisions, they must recognize the potential for an optimistic bias to creep into the numbers. This bias can arise through intentional manipulation of the cash flows to make an investment look more attractive, or it may simply arise if the analyst calculating the *NPV* is also the cheerleader advocating the project in the first place.

One way that companies attempt to control for this bias is by putting responsibility for analyzing an investment proposal under an authority independent from the individual or group proposing the investment. For example, it is common in large firms for a particular group to have the responsibility of conducting the financial analysis required to value any potential acquisition targets. In this situation, financial analysts play a kind of gatekeeper role, protecting shareholders' interests by steering the firm away from large negative-*NPV* investments. Naturally, these independent analysts face intense pressure from the advocates of each project to portray the investment proposal in its best possible light. Consequently, financial experts need to know more than just which cash flows count in the *NPV* calculation. They also need to have a sense of what is reasonable when forecasting a project's profit margin and its growth potential. Analysts must also prepare to defend their assumptions, explaining why their (often more conservative) projections do not line up with those offered by the managers advocating a certain investment.

Many experienced managers will say that they have never seen an investment with a negative *NPV*. In saying this, they do not mean that all investments are good investments, but rather that all analysts know enough about *NPV* analysis to know how to make any investment look attractive. Small adjustments to cash flow projections and discount rates can often sway a project's *NPV* from negative to positive. In this environment, another skill comes into play in determining which project receives funding. We might refer to this skill as storytelling, as opposed to number crunching. Most good investments have a compelling story behind them, a reason, based on sound economic logic, that the investment's *NPV should be* positive. The best financial analysts can provide not only the numbers to highlight the value of a good investment, but also can explain why the investment makes sense, highlighting the competitive opportunity that makes one investment's *NPV* positive and another's negative. We will return to this storytelling element of capital budgeting in Chapter 9.

SMART IDEAS VIDEO

Raghu Rajan, University of Chicago

"Capital budgeting is not just about estimating cash flows and discount rates, but is also a lot about horse trading."

See the entire interview at **SMARTFinance**

Concept Review Question

13. What role does the human factor play in the capital budgeting decision process? Could it cause a negative-*NPV* project to be accepted?

8.6 SUMMARY

- Certain types of cash flow are common to many different kinds of investments. These include cash expenditures on fixed assets and working capital, operating cash flow, and terminal value estimates.

- The costs of financing an investment, such as interest paid to lenders and dividends paid to shareholders, should not be counted as part of a project's cash outflows. The discount rate captures the financing costs, so deducting interest expense and dividends from a project's cash flows would be double counting.
- To find working capital cash flow, calculate the change in net working capital from one period to the next. Increases in working capital represent cash outflows, while decreases in working capital represent cash inflows.
- To find operating cash flow, calculate after-tax net income and add back any non-cash expenses.
- To find terminal value, or terminal cash flow, employ one of several methods, such as the perpetual growth model or book value.
- Only the incremental costs associated with a project should be included in *NPV* analysis. The analyst should avoid including sunk costs.
- Opportunity costs should be included in cash flow projections.
- Discount nominal cash flows at a nominal rate, and real cash flows at a real rate. Failure to match the type of cash flow with the correct discount rate will either overstate or understate the value of a project.
- When evaluating alternative equipment purchases with unequal lives, determine the equivalent annual cost of each type of equipment and choose the one that is least expensive.
- When confronted with proposals to use excess capacity, think carefully about the true cost of that capacity. It is rarely zero.
- When analyzing capital budgeting projects, it is important to consider human factors and make sure that the project, in addition to having a positive *NPV*, makes sense.

INTERNET RESOURCES

Note: *For updates to links, please go to the book's website at http://smart.swlearning.com.*

http://www.ifad.net /content /ie/ie_f_gaap_frameset.htm—An excellent comparison of accounting standards for different countries

http://clinton3.nara.gov/pcscb/—An interesting report prepared in 1999 for President Clinton, outlining capital budgeting trends and practices in both the public and private sectors

http://www.quicken.com /taxes/investing/marginal /yahoo—Can be used for personal investment decisions by calculating your own marginal tax rate

http://www.secondarymarket.com—Site can be searched by registered users for used equipment in many different industrial sectors; can use market prices of used equipment to form estimates of salvage value or terminal value for a long-lived project

KEY TERMS

cannibalization
depreciation
equivalent annual cost (EAC) method
marginal tax rate
modified accelerated cost recovery system (MACRS)
net working capital

nominal cash flows
opportunity costs
real cash flows
sunk costs
terminal value
working capital

QUESTIONS

8-1. In capital budgeting analysis, why do we focus on cash flow rather than accounting profit?

8-2. Should the costs of evaluating a project be included as a portion of the project's cost?

8-3. Is the ability to use money allocated to a project for another purpose an example of a sunk cost?

8-4. Explain how depreciation creates a cash inflow even though there is no cash inflow or outflow associated with the depreciation deductions themselves.

8-5. In the technology industry, product prices and production costs typically fall over time. If you are putting together cash flow projections for a new high-tech product, explain how you would construct your forecasts if you wanted to state them in nominal terms. What if you want to state them in real terms?

8-6. Is a negative change in net working capital a problem (assuming profitability and sales are maintained)?

8-7. To finance a certain project, a company must borrow money at 10 percent interest. How should it treat interest payments when it analyzes the project's cash flows?

8-8. Answer questions a through d, which deal with the role of depreciation in capital budgeting analysis.

   a. Does depreciation affect cash flow in a positive or negative manner?
   b. From a net present value perspective, why is accelerated depreciation preferable?
   c. Is it acceptable to utilize one depreciation method for tax purposes and another for financial reporting purposes?
   d. Which method is relevant for determining project cash flows?

8-9. In what sense does an increase in accounts payable represent a cash inflow?

8-10. List several ways to estimate a project's terminal value.

8-11. What are the tax consequences of selling an investment asset for more than its book value? Does this have an effect on project cash flows that must be accounted for in relevant cash flows? What is the effect if the asset is sold for less than its book value?

8-12. Why must incremental after-tax cash flows rather than total cash flows be evaluated in project analysis?

8-13. Differentiate between sunk costs and opportunity costs. Which of these costs should be included in incremental cash flows, and which should be excluded?

8-14. Before entering graduate school, a student estimated the value of earning an MBA at $300,000. Based on that analysis, the student decided to go back to school. After completing the first year, the student ran the *NPV* calculations again. How would you expect the *NPV* to look after the student has completed one year of the program? Specifically, what portion of the analysis must be different than it was the year before?

8-15. Punxsutawney Taxidermy Inc. (PTI), operates a chain of taxidermy shops across the Midwest, with a handful of locations in the South. A rival firm, Heads Up Corp., has a few Midwestern locations, but most of its shops are located in the South. PTI and Heads Up decide to consolidate their operations by trading ownership of a few locations. PTI will acquire four Heads Up locations in the Midwest, and in exchange will relinquish control of its Southern locations. No cash changes hands up front. Does this mean that an analyst working for either company can evaluate the merits of this deal by assuming that the project has no initial cash outlay? Explain.

8-16. True or False: If a company's practice is to calculate project *NPVs* using nominal cash flows and a nominal discount rate, it must have a forecast for expected inflation. However, if the company discounts real cash flows at the real rate, developing an inflation forecast is unnecessary.

8-17. Explain why the *EAC method* helps firms evaluate alternative investments with unequal lives.

8-18. Why isn't excess capacity free?

PROBLEMS

Types of Cash Flows

8-1. Currently, a firm has $30 million in cash, $20 million in accounts receivable, $45 million inventory, and $10 million in taxes payable. The firm tends to not finance its inventory, making it necessary to keep a large amount of cash on hand. The firm is considering financing its inventory in the future. Analysis provides a projection of the future working capital accounts: $10 million in cash, $20 million in accounts receivable, $60 million in inventory, $40 million in accounts payable for the inventory, and $10 million in taxes payable.

   a. Calculate the present and future projected net working capital for the firm.
   b. Based on the change in net working capital, does the financing of inventory appear to be a potentially beneficial practice for the firm?
   c. If the firm decided to go with a *just-in-time* inventory process that reduced the current inventory to $5 million and the current cash account to $15 million (other accounts remaining the same), would this reduce the change in net working capital even further than the inventory financing scheme?

8-2. A project's annual (operating) cash flows for the next five years are: $1.2 million, $1.4 million, $1.7 million, $2 million, and $2.5 million. Assuming a discount rate of 15% and a terminal growth rate of 4%,

   a. What is the terminal value for assessing the cash flows after the fifth year?
   b. What is the total value of the cash flows of the firm?
   c. What proportion of the total cash flow value is dependent on the terminal value?

8-3. The terminal value of a project's cash flow is $51.5 million: $3.605 million ÷ (10% − 3%). What is the equivalent price-to-cash-flow ratio that would produce this same terminal value (Note: you will need to reduce the $3.605 million projected cash flow by one growth period)?

8-4. The final projected cash flow for a firm is $4.2 million and, using a price-to-cash-flow-ratio of 16.5, generates a terminal value of $69.3 million. Assuming a 14% discount rate, what terminal growth rate will produce the same terminal value? If a terminal growth rate of 4.2% is considered appropriate, is the terminal value of $69.3 million an over-estimation or an under-estimation? Using 4.2% as the terminal growth rate, what is the terminal value? Based on this number, what price-to-cash-flow ratio does it reflect?

8-5. A project costs $10 million dollars and is expected to have the following annual cash flows: $5.6 million, $6.272 million, and $7.025 million. What is the *NPV* of the project assuming a 12% discount rate? After two years, the project has realized cash flows totaling $15 million (much beyond projections); however, to realize a third year of cash flow from the project, another $6 million dollar investment must be made. Assume the third year projected cash flow is $6.6 million (down from the original $7.025 million) and the discount rate is still 12%. Should the firm continue the project (compute the *NPV* of the additional $6 million investment in making your decision)? Should the previous success of the project influence the analysis?

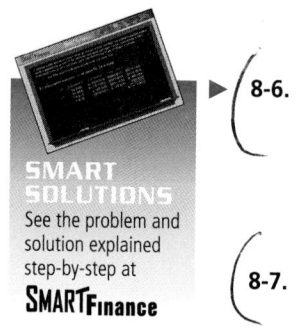

8-6. Calculate the present value of depreciation tax savings on a depreciable asset with a purchase price of $5 million and zero salvage value, assuming a 10 percent discount rate, a 34 percent tax rate, and the following type of depreciation:

a. The asset is depreciated over a 3-year life according to Table 8.1.

b. The asset is depreciated over a 7-year life according to Table 8.1.

c. The asset is depreciated over a 20-year life according to Table 8.1.

8-7. A certain piece of equipment costs $32 million plus an additional $2 million to install. This equipment qualifies under the 5-year MACRS category. For a firm that discounts cash flows at 12 percent and faces a tax rate of 34 percent, what is the present value of depreciation tax savings associated with this equipment? By how much would that number change if the firm could treat the $2 million installation cost as a deductible expense rather than include it as part of the depreciable cost of the asset?

8-8. The government is considering a proposal to allow even more-accelerated depreciation deductions than specified by MACRS.

a. For which type of company would this change be more valuable: a company facing a 10 percent tax rate or one facing a 30 percent tax rate?

b. If companies take larger depreciation deductions in the early years of an investment, what will the impact be on reported earnings? On cash flows? On project *NPV*s? How do you think the stock market might respond if the tax law changes to allow more-accelerated depreciation?

8-9. Taylor United is considering overhauling its equipment to meet increased demand for its product. The cost of equipment overhaul is $3.8 million plus $200,000 in installation costs. The firm will depreciate the equipment modifications under MACRS using a 5-year recovery period. Additional sales revenue from the overhaul should amount to $2.2 million per year, and additional operating expenses and other costs (excluding depreciation) will amount to 35 percent of the additional sales. The firm has an ordinary tax rate of 40 percent. Answer the following questions about Taylor United for each of the next six years.

a. What additional earnings before depreciation and taxes will result from the overhaul?

b. What additional earnings after taxes will result from the overhaul?

c. What incremental operating cash flows will result from the overhaul?

8-10. Wilbur Corporation is considering replacing a machine. The replacement will cut operating expenses by $24,000 per year for each of the five years the new machine is expected to last. Although the old machine has a zero book value, it has a remaining useful life of five years. The depreciable value of the new machine is $72,000. Wilbur will depreciate the machine under MACRS using a 5-year recovery period and is subject to a 40 percent tax rate on ordinary income. Estimate the incremental operating cash flows attributable to the replacement. Be sure to consider the depreciation in year 6.

8-11. Advanced Electronics Corporation is considering purchasing a new packaging machine to replace a fully depreciated packaging machine that will last five more years. The new machine is expected to have a 5-year life and depreciation charges of $4,000 in year 1; $6,400 in year 2; $3,800 in year 3; $2,400 in both year 4 and year 5; and $1,000 in year 6. The firm's estimates of revenues and expenses (excluding depreciation) for the new and old packaging machines are shown in the following table. Advanced Electronics is subject to a 40 percent tax rate on ordinary income.

	New Packaging Machine		Old Packaging Machine	
Year	Revenue	Expenses (excluding depreciation)	Revenue	Expenses (excluding depreciation)
1	$50,000	$40,000	$45,000	$35,000
2	$51,000	$40,000	$45,000	$35,000
3	$52,000	$40,000	$45,000	$35,000
4	$53,000	$40,000	$45,000	$35,000
5	$54,000	$40,000	$45,000	$35,000

a. Calculate the operating cash flows associated with each packaging machine. Be sure to consider the depreciation in year 6.

b. Calculate the incremental operating cash flows resulting from the proposed packaging machine replacement.

c. Depict on a time line the incremental cash flows found in part (b).

8-12. Premium Wines, a producer of medium-quality wines, has maintained stable sales and profits over the past eight years. Although the market for medium-quality wines has been growing by 4 percent per year, Premium Wines has been unsuccessful in sharing this growth. To increase its sales, the firm is considering an aggressive marketing campaign that centers on regularly running ads in major food and wine magazines and running TV commercials in large metropolitan areas. The campaign is expected to require an *annual* tax-deductible expenditure of $3 million over the next five years. Sales revenue, as noted in the following income statement for 2006, totaled $80 million. If the proposed marketing campaign is not initiated, sales are expected to remain at this level in each of the next five years, 2007–2011. With the marketing campaign, sales are expected to rise to the levels shown in the sales forecast table for each of the next five years; cost of goods sold is expected to remain at 75 percent of sales; general and administrative expense (exclusive of any marketing campaign outlays) is expected to remain at 15 percent of sales; and annual depreciation expense is expected to remain at $2 million. Assuming a 40 percent tax rate, find the relevant cash flows over the next five years associated with Premium Wines' proposed marketing campaign.

Premium Wines
Income Statement
for the year ended December 31, 2006

Sales revenue		$80,000,000
Less: Cost of goods sold (75%)		60,000,000
Gross profits		$20,000,000
Less: Operating expenses		
General and administrative expense (15%)	$12,000,000	
Depreciation expense	2,000,000	
Total operating expense		$14,000,000
Net profits before taxes		$ 6,000,000
Less: Taxes (rate = 40%)		2,400,000
Net profits after taxes		$ 3,600,000

Premium Wines
Sales Forecast

Year	Sales Revenue
2007	$82,000,000
2008	$84,000,000
2009	$86,000,000
2010	$90,000,000
2011	$94,000,000

8-13. Barans Manufacturing is developing the incremental cash flows associated with the proposed replacement of an existing stamping machine with a new, technologically advanced one. Given the following costs related to the proposed project, explain whether each would be treated as a *sunk cost* or an *opportunity cost* in developing the incremental cash flows associated with the proposed replacement decision.

a. Barans would be able to use the same dies and other tools, which had a book value of $40,000, on the new stamping machine that it used on the old one.

b. Barans would be able to link the new machine to its existing computer system in order to control its operations. The old stamping machine did not have a computer control system. The firm's excess computer capacity could be leased to another firm for an annual fee of $17,000.

c. Barans would have to obtain additional floor space to accommodate the larger new stamping machine. The space that would be used is currently being leased to another company for $10,000 per year.

d. Barans would use a small storage facility to store the increased output of the new stamping machine. The storage facility was built by Barans at a cost of $120,000 three years earlier. Because of its unique configuration and location, it is currently of no use to either Barans or any other firm.

e. Barans would retain an existing overhead crane, which it had planned to sell for its $180,000 market value. Although the crane was not needed with the old stamping machine, it would be used to position raw materials on the new stamping machine.

8-14. Blueberry Electronics is exploring the possibility of producing a new handheld device that will serve both as a basic PC with Internet access and as a cell phone. Which of the following items are relevant for the project's analysis?

a. Research and development funds that the company has spent working on a prototype of the new product.

b. The company's current-generation product has no cell phone capability. The new product would therefore make the old one obsolete in the eyes of many consumers.
    However, Blueberry expects that other companies will soon bring to market products combining cell phone and PC features, and these will also reduce sales on Blueberry's existing products.

c. Costs of ramping up production of the new device.

d. Increases in receivables and inventory that will occur as production increases.

Cash Flows for Classicaltunes.com

8-15. New York Pizza is considering replacing an existing oven with a new, more sophisticated oven. The old oven was purchased three years ago at a cost of $20,000, and this amount was being depreciated under MACRS using a 5-year recovery period. The oven has five years of usable life remaining. The new oven being considered costs $30,500, requires $1,500 in installation costs, and would be depreciated under MACRS using a 5-year recovery period. The old oven can currently be sold for $22,000 without incurring any removal or cleanup costs. The firm pays taxes at a rate of 40 percent on both ordinary income and capital gains. The revenues and expenses (excluding depreciation) associated with the new and the old ovens for the next five years are given in the following table.

	New Oven		Old Oven	
Year	Revenue	Expenses (excluding depreciation)	Revenue	Expenses (excluding depreciation)
1	$300,000	$288,000	$270,000	$264,000
2	$300,000	$288,000	$270,000	$264,000
3	$300,000	$288,000	$272,000	$264,000
4	$300,000	$288,000	$271,000	$264,000
5	$300,000	$288,000	$270,000	$264,000

a. Calculate the initial cash outflow associated with replacement of the old oven by the new one.

b. Determine the incremental cash flows associated with the proposed replacement. Be sure to consider the depreciation in year 6.

c. On a time line, depict the relevant cash flows found in parts (a) and (b) associated with the proposed replacement decision.

8-16. Speedy Auto Wash is contemplating the purchase of a new high-speed washer to replace the existing washer. The existing washer was purchased two years ago at an installed cost of $120,000; it was being depreciated under MACRS using a 5-year recovery period. The existing washer is expected to have a usable life of five more years. The new washer costs $210,000 and requires $10,000 in installation costs; it has a 5-year usable life and would be depreciated under MACRS using a 5-year recovery period. The existing washer can currently be sold for $140,000 without incurring any removal or cleanup costs. To support the increased business resulting from purchase of the new washer, accounts receivable would increase by $80,000, inventories by $60,000, and accounts payable by $116,000. At the end of five years, the existing washer is expected to have a market value of zero; the new washer would be sold to net $58,000 after removal and cleanup costs and before taxes. The firm pays taxes at a rate of 40 percent on both ordinary income and capital gains. The estimated *profits before depreciation and taxes* over the five years for both the new and the existing washer are shown in the following table.

	Profits before Depreciation and Taxes	
Year	New Washer	Existing Washer
1	$86,000	$52,000
2	$86,000	$48,000
3	$86,000	$44,000
4	$86,000	$40,000
5	$86,000	$36,000

a. Calculate the initial cash outflow associated with the replacement of the existing washer with the new one.

b. Determine the incremental cash flows associated with the proposed washer replacement. Be sure to consider the depreciation in year 6.

c. Determine the terminal cash flow expected at the end of year 5 from the proposed washer replacement.

d. On a time line, depict the relevant cash flows associated with the proposed washerreplacement decision.

8-17. TransPacific Shipping is considering replacing an existing ship with one of two newer, more efficient ones. The existing ship is three years old, cost $32 million, and is being depreciated under MACRS using a 5-year recovery period. Although the existing ship has only three years (years 4, 5, and 6) of depreciation remaining under MACRS, it has a remaining usable life of five years. Ship A, one of the two possible replacement ships, costs $40 million to purchase and $8 million to outfit for service. It has a 5-year usable life and will be depreciated under MACRS using a 5-year recovery period. Ship B costs $54 million to purchase and $6 million to outfit. It also has a 5-year usable life and will be depreciated under MACRS using a 5-year recovery period. Increased investments in net working capital will accompany the decision to acquire ship A or ship B. Purchase of ship A would result in a $4 million increase in net working capital; ship B would result in a $6 million increase in net working capital. The projected *profits before depreciation and taxes* with each alternative ship and the existing ship are given in the following table.

	Profits before Depreciation and Taxes		
Year	Ship A	Ship B	Existing Ship
1	$21,000,000	$22,000,000	$14,000,000
2	$21,000,000	$24,000,000	$14,000,000
3	$21,000,000	$26,000,000	$14,000,000
4	$21,000,000	$26,000,000	$14,000,000
5	$21,000,000	$26,000,000	$14,000,000

The existing ship can currently be sold for $18 million and will not incur any removal or cleanup costs. At the end of five years, the existing ship can be sold to net $1 million before taxes. Ships A and B can be sold to net $12 million and $20 million before taxes, respectively, at the end of the 5-year period. The firm is subject to a 40 percent tax rate on both ordinary income and capital gains.

a. Calculate the initial outlay associated with each alternative.
b. Calculate the operating cash flows associated with each alternative. Be sure to consider the depreciation in year 6.
c. Calculate the terminal cash flow at the end of year 5 associated with each alternative.
d. Depict on a time line the relevant cash flows associated with each alternative.

8-18. The management of Kimco is evaluating replacing their large mainframe computer with a modern network system that requires much less office space. The network would cost $500,000 (including installation costs) and would generate $125,000 per year in operating cash flows (accounting for taxes and depreciation) over the next five years due to efficiency gains. The mainframe has a remaining book value of $50,000 and would be immediately donated to a charity for the tax benefit. Kimco's discount rate is 10 percent and its tax rate is 40 percent. On the basis of *NPV*, should management install the network system?

8-19. Pointless Luxuries Inc. (PLI) produces unusual gifts targeted at wealthy consumers. The company is analyzing the possibility of introducing a new device designed to attach to the collar of a cat or dog. This device emits sonic waves that neutralize airplane engine noise, so that pets traveling with their owners will enjoy a more peaceful ride. PLI estimates that developing this product will require up-front capital expenditures of $10 million. These costs will be depreciated on a straight-line basis for five years. PLI believes that it can sell the product initially for $250. The selling price will increase to $260 in years 2 and 3 before falling to $245 and $240 in years 4 and 5, respectively. After five years the company will withdraw the product from the market and replace it with something else. Variable costs are $135 per unit. PLI forecasts sales volume of 20,000 units the first year, with subsequent increases of 25 percent (year 2), 20 percent (year 3), 20 percent (year 4), and 15 percent (year 5). Offering this product will force PLI to make additional investments in receivables and inventory. Projected end-of-year balances appear in the following table.

	Year 0	Year 1	Year 2	Year 3	Year 4	Year 5
Accounts receivable	$0	$200,000	$250,000	$300,000	$150,000	$0
Inventory	0	500,000	650,000	780,000	600,000	0

The firm faces a tax rate of 34 percent. Assume that cash flows arrive at the end of each year, except for the initial $10 million outlay.

a. Calculate the project's contribution to net income each year.

b. Calculate the project's cash flows each year.

c. Calculate two *NPV*s, one using a 10 percent discount rate and one using 15 percent.

d. A PLI financial analyst reasons as follows: "With the exception of the initial outlay, the cash flows from this project arrive in more or less a continuous stream rather than at the end of each year. Therefore, by discounting each year's cash flow for a full year, we are understating the true *NPV*. A better approximation is to move the discounting six months forward (e.g., discount year-1 cash flows for six months, year-2 cash flows for 1.5 years, and so on), as if all the cash flows arrive in the middle of each year rather than at the end." Recalculate the *NPV* (at 10% and 15%) maintaining this assumption. How much difference does it make?

8-20. TechGiant Inc. (TGI) is evaluating a proposal to acquire Fusion Chips, a young company with an interesting new chip technology. This technology, when integrated into existing TGI silicon wafers, will enable TGI to offer chips with new capabilities to companies with automated manufacturing systems. TGI analysts have projected income statements for Fusion five years into the future. These projections appear in the income statements that follow, along with estimates of Fusion's asset requirements and accounts payable balances each year. These statements are designed assuming that Fusion remains an independent, stand-alone company. If TGI acquires Fusion, analysts believe that the following changes will occur.

1. TGI's superior manufacturing capabilities will enable Fusion to increase its gross margin on its existing products to 45 percent.

2. TGI's massive sales force will enable Fusion to increase sales of its existing products by 10 percent above current projections (for example, if acquired, Fusion will sell $110 million, rather than $100 million, in 2007). This increase will occur as a consequence of regularly scheduled conversations between TGI salespeople and existing customers and will not require added marketing expenditures. Operating expenses as a percentage of sales will be the same each year as currently forecasted (ranges from 10% to 12%). The fixed asset increases currently projected through 2011 will be sufficient to sustain the 10 percent increase in sales volume each year.

3. TGI's more efficient receivables and inventory management systems will allow Fusion to increase its sales as previously described without making investments in receivables and inventory beyond those already reflected in the financial projection. TGI also enjoys a higher credit rating than Fusion, so after the acquisition, Fusion will obtain credit from suppliers on more favorable terms. Specifically, Fusion's accounts payable balance will be 30 percent higher each year than the level currently forecast.

4. TGI's current cash reserves are more than sufficient for the combined company, so Fusion's existing cash balances will be reduced to $0.

5. Immediately after the acquisition, TGI will invest $50 million in fixed assets to manufacture a new chip that integrates Fusion's technology into one of TGI's best-selling products. These assets will be depreciated on a straight-line basis for eight years. After five years, the new chip will be obsolete, and no additional sales will occur. The equipment will be sold at the end of year 5 for $1 million. Before depreciation and taxes, this new product will generate $20 million in (incremental) profits the first year, $30 million the second year, and $15 in each of the next three years. TGI will have to invest $3 million in net working capital up front, all of which it will recover at the end of the project's life.

6. Both companies face a tax rate of 34 percent.

Fusion Chips
Income Statements
($ in thousands for years ended December 31)

	2007	2008	2009	2010	2011
Sales	$100,000	$150,000	$200,000	$240,000	$270,000
− Cost of goods sold	60,000	90,000	120,000	144,000	162,000
Gross profit	$ 40,000	$ 60,000	$ 80,000	$ 96,000	$108,000
− Operating expenses	12,000	17,250	22,000	25,200	27,000
− Depreciation	12,000	18,000	24,000	28,800	32,400
Pretax income	$ 16,000	$ 24,750	$ 34,000	$ 42,000	$ 48,600
− Taxes	5,440	8,415	11,560	14,280	16,524
Net income	$ 10,560	$ 16,335	$ 22,440	$ 27,720	$ 32,076

Assets and Accounts Payable
($ in thousands on December 31)

	2006	2007	2008	2009	2010	2011
Cash	$ 400	$ 400	$ 525	$ 600	$ 600	$ 600
Accounts receivable	6,000	7,000	10,500	14,000	16,800	18,900
Inventory	10,000	12,500	18,750	25,000	30,000	33,750
Total current assets	$16,400	$ 19,900	$ 29,775	$ 39,600	$ 47,400	$ 53,250
Plant and equipment						
Gross	$80,000	$113,000	$166,500	$226,000	$283,200	$336,900
Net	50,000	71,000	106,500	142,000	170,400	191,700
Total assets	$66,400	$ 90,900	$136,275	$181,600	$217,800	$244,950
Accounts payable	$ 7,500	$ 13,500	$ 20,250	$ 27,000	$ 32,400	$ 36,450

Note: The 2004 figures represent the balances currently on Fusion's balance sheet.

a. Calculate the cash flows generated by Fusion as a stand-alone entity in each year from 2007 to 2011.

b. Assume that by 2011, Fusion reaches a "steady state," which means that its cash flows will grow by 5 percent per year in perpetuity. If Fusion discounts cash flows at 15 percent, what is the present value as of the end of 2011 of all cash flows that Fusion will generate from 2012 forward?

c. Calculate the present value as of 2006 of Fusion's cash flows from 2007 forward. What does this *NPV* represent?

d. Suppose that TGI acquires Fusion. Recalculate Fusion's cash flows from 2007 to 2011, making all the changes previously described in items 1–4 and 6.

e. Assume that after 2011 Fusion's cash flows will grow at a steady 5 percent per year. Calculate the present value of these cash flows as of 2011 if the discount rate is 15 percent.

f. Ignoring item 5 in the list of changes, what is the *PV* as of 2006 of Fusion's cash flows from 2007 forward? Use a discount rate of 15 percent.

g. Finally, calculate the *NPV* of TGI's investment to integrate its technology with Fusion's. Considering this in combination with your answer to part (f), what is the maximum price that TGI can pay for Fusion? Assume a discount rate of 15 percent.

8-21. A project generates the following sequence of cash flows over six years:

Year	Cash Flow ($ in millions)
0	−59.00
1	4.00
2	5.00
3	6.00
4	7.33
5	8.00
6	8.25

a. Calculate the *NPV* over the six years. The discount rate is 11 percent.

b. This project does not end after the sixth year, but instead will generate cash flows far into the future. Estimate the *terminal value*, assuming that cash flows after year 6 will continue at $8.25 million per year in perpetuity, and then recalculate the investment's *NPV*.

c. Calculate the *terminal value*, assuming that cash flows after the sixth year grow at 2 percent annually in perpetuity, and then recalculate the *NPV*.

d. Using market multiples, calculate the *terminal value* by estimating the project's market value at the end of year 6. Specifically, calculate the terminal value under the assumption that at the end of year 6, the project's market value will be 10 times greater than its most recent annual cash flow. Recalculate the *NPV*.

8-22. Sherry Bishop of Thayer Industries is considering investing in a capital project that costs $1.2 million and is expected to generate after-tax operating cash flows of $500,000 in the first year and decline by $100,000 per year until the final year of the project's life in five years. Assume that Thayer's nominal discount rate for this project is 12 percent and the annual inflation rate is 3 percent.

a. Calculate the project's *NPV*, assuming that cash flows given in the problem are in nominal terms. Would you accept this project?

b. Calculate the real values of future cash flows.

c. Recalculate the project's *NPV*, using the real cash flows and the appropriate real discount rate. Does your accept/reject decision change from your decision in part (a)?

8-23. A certain investment will require an immediate cash outflow of $4 million. At the end of each of the next four years, the investment will generate cash inflows of $1.25 million.

a. Assuming that these cash flows are in nominal terms and the nominal discount rate is 10.25 percent, calculate the project's *NPV*.

b. Now assume that the expected rate of inflation is 5 percent per year. Recalculate the project's cash flows in real terms, discount them at the real interest rate, and verify that you obtain the same *NPV*.

8-24. The engineers in the aircraft manufacturing division of a diversified conglomerate want the firm to fund a certain investment proposal. The investment will require an initial outlay of $75 million and will generate the following net cash inflows over five years:

Year	Cash Inflow ($ in millions)
1	10
2	20
3	20
4	30
5	40

SMART SOLUTIONS
See the problem and solution explained step-by-step at
SMARTFinance

This project will compete for funds with one proposed by the company's consumer products division. The alternative project requires an initial $55 million outlay and will generate the following net cash inflows over five years:

Year	Cash Inflow ($ in millions)
1	10
2	12
3	14
4	20
5	25

In the airline division, it is common practice to state all project cash flows in nominal terms, whereas in the consumer products division, all cash flows are stated in real terms. The expected rate of inflation is 5 percent, and the required real rate of return on investments in both divisions is 8 percent. Which project should the firm accept if it can accept only one?

Special Problems in Capital Budgeting

8-25. Semper Mortgage wishes to select the best of three possible computers, each expected to meet the firm's growing need for computational and storage capacity. The three computers—A, B, and C—are equally risky. The firm plans to use a 12 percent cost of capital to evaluate each of them. The initial outlay and annual cash flows over the life of each computer are shown in the following table.

Initial Outlay (CF_0)	Computer A	Computer B	Computer C
	$50,000	$35,000	$60,000
Year (t)		Cash Inflows (CF_t)	
1	$7,000	$ 5,500	$18,000
2	7,000	12,000	18,000
3	7,000	16,000	18,000
4	7,000	23,000	18,000
5	7,000	—	18,000
6	7,000	—	—

a. Calculate the *NPV* for each computer over its life. Rank the computers in descending order based on *NPV*.

b. Use the *equivalent annual cost (EAC)* approach to evaluate and rank the computers in descending order based on the EAC.

c. Compare and contrast your findings in parts (a) and (b). Which computer would you recommend that the firm acquire? Why?

8-26. Seattle Manufacturing is considering the purchase of one of three mutually exclusive projects for improving its assembly line. The firm plans to use a 14 percent cost of capital to evaluate these equal-risk projects. The initial outlay and annual cash flows over the life of each project are shown in the following table.

Initial Outlay (CF_0)	Project X	Project Y	Project Z
	$156,000	$104,000	$132,000
Year (t)		Cash Inflows (CF_t)	
1	$34,000	$56,000	$30,000
2	50,000	56,000	30,000
3	66,000	—	30,000
4	82,000	—	30,000
5	—	—	30,000
6	—	—	30,000
7	—	—	30,000
8	—	—	30,000

   a. Calculate the *NPV* for each project over its life. Rank the projects in descending order based on *NPV*.
   b. Use the *equivalent annual cost (EAC)* approach to evaluate and rank the projects in descending order based on the EAC.
   c. Compare and contrast your findings in parts (a) and (b). Which project would you recommend that the firm purchase? Why?

8-27. As part of a hotel renovation program, a company must choose between two grades of carpet to install. One grade costs $22 per square yard, and the other, $28. The costs of cleaning and maintaining the carpets are identical, but the less expensive carpet must be replaced after six years, whereas the more expensive one will last nine years before it must be replaced. Which grade should the company choose? The relevant discount rate is 13 percent.

8-28. Gail Dribble is a financial analyst at Hill Propane Distributors. Gail must provide a financial analysis of the decision to replace a truck used to deliver propane gas to residential customers. Given its age, the truck will require increasing maintenance expenditures if the company keeps it in service. Similarly, the market value of the truck declines as it ages. The current market value of the truck, as well as the market value and required maintenance expenditures for each of the next four years appears below.

Year	Market Value	Maintenance Cost
Current	$7,000	$ 0
1	5,500	2,500
2	3,700	3,600
3	0	4,500
4	0	7,500

The company can purchase a new truck for $40,000. The truck will last 15 years and will require end-of-year maintenance expenditures of $1,500. At the end of 15 years, the new truck's salvage value will be $3,500.

   a. Calculate the *equivalent annual cost (EAC)* of the new truck using a discount rate of 9 percent.
   b. Suppose the firm keeps the old truck one more year and sells it then rather than selling it now. What is the opportunity cost associated with this decision? What is the present value of the cost of this decision as of today? Restate this cost in terms of year-1 dollars.
   c. Based on your answers to (a) and (b), is it optimal for the company to replace the old truck immediately?
   d. Suppose the firm decides to keep the truck for another year. Next, Gail must analyze whether replacing the old truck after one year makes sense or whether the truck should stay in use another year. As of the end of year 1, what is the present value of the cost of using the truck and selling it at the end of year 2? Restate this answer in year-2 dollars. Should the firm replace the truck after two years?
   e. Suppose that the firm keeps the old truck in service for two years. Should it replace it rather than keep it in service for the third year?

8-29. A firm that manufactures and sells ball bearings currently has excess capacity. The firm expects that it will exhaust its excess capacity in three years, at which time it will spend $5 million to build new capacity. Suppose that this firm can accept additional manufacturing work as a subcontractor for another company. By doing so, the firm will receive net cash inflows of $250,000 immediately and in each of the next two years. However, the firm will also have to spend $5 million two years earlier than originally planned to bring new capacity online. Should the firm take on the subcontracting job? The discount rate is 12 percent. What is the minimum cash inflow

**SMART
SOLUTIONS**
See the problem and
solution explained
step-by-step at
SMARTFinance

that the firm would require (per year) to accept this job? For simplicity you may ignore depreciation.

8-30. Calculate Sara Lee Corporation's (ticker symbol, SLE) cash flow for the last four years, using the formula Cash flow = Net income + Depreciation. Do these figures match Sara Lee's net cash flow from operating activities? If not, list three specific reasons why they are different.

8-31. Using the most recent two years' data, does the change in accumulated depreciation equal the change in the property, plant, and equipment–net for General Electric (ticker symbol, GE)? If not, why might they be different? Using the average tax rate (income taxes divided by pretax income), what was the tax savings from depreciation for the most current year?

8-32. What has caused the change in net working capital over the last three years for Family Dollar Stores, Inc. (ticker symbol, FDO)?

MINI-CASE: CASH FLOWS AND CAPITAL BUDGETING

Kirk Tiberius is the financial manager for MicroDryer Enterprises, a company that manufactures microwave dryers. Using microwaves eliminates shrinkage of cotton and wool because clothing can be dried at a much lower surface temperature. The firm currently offers a full-size microwave dryer that is extremely energy efficient and dries clothes much faster than conventional dryers. However, it appears as though the American consumer is either uninterested in energy efficiency or unwilling to spend the initial cost to purchase the rather high-end full-size microwave dryer. Thus, MicroDryer Enterprises is considering expanding into a new product—a countertop microwave dryer that could be used in dorm rooms, apartments, hotels or RVs. Kirk's job is to determine the financial feasibility of this venture based on sales and cost estimates provided by the marketing division and others. Kirk has been provided with the following estimates:

- Expected annual unit sales at time 1 are 235,000 units (Sales are expected to increase at a rate of 15% a year *through* year 4 at which point sales will decrease at a rate of 20% a year through year 10.)
- No sales cannibalization is expected to occur.
- Expected sales price is $250 per unit in today's dollars.
- Expected development costs of the product (at time 0) are $50,000,000, which will be depreciated over 10 years using the straight-line method.
- Annual fixed costs of production are $1,000,000 in today's dollars.
- Variable costs of production are estimated to be $100 per unit in today's dollars.
- Variable costs, fixed costs of production, and the sales price will increase at the rate of inflation each year, which is expected to be 2.89% annually.
- The tax rate for MicroDryer Enterprises' is 34%.
- The inventory balance is 35% of revenues, accounts payable are 50% of inventory, and accounts receivable are 10% of revenue.

- The expected life of project is not known, so the company has decided that *cash flows* after the tenth year will increase at an annual rate of 3.5%.
- The firm's nominal discount rate is 11%.

Based on the above information, what recommendation should Kirk make concerning the countertop microwave dryer project? Use nominal values for your analysis.

Chapter 9

Cost of Capital and Project Risk

SMARTFinance
Use the learning tools at www
.thomsonedu.com/finance/smartfinance

Cendant Unwinds to Unlock Value

On October 24, 2005, the $20 billion conglomerate, Cendant, announced plans to break itself into four separate companies focusing on real estate, travel distribution, hospitality, and car rentals. Cendant spent 15 years acquiring and nurturing the components of its far-flung enterprises: diverse businesses such as real estate brokerages Century 21 and Coldwell Banker, hotel chains Days Inn, Howard Johnson, and Ramada Inn, car rental agencies Avis and Budget, and travel service providers like Orbitz, Why then would the company unwind the products of years of hard work to create four distinct companies?

Cendant's chairman and CEO, Henry Silverman, explained that, "Creating four strong and focused pure play companies is the best way to unlock the full value of Cendant's businesses. . . ." This view was consistent with an emerging body of academic research documenting a "diversification discount" for conglomerate firms. Researchers compared the prices of diversified, conglomerate firms to the prices of hypothetical "portfolio firms," each of which consisted of several independent, pure play firms (i.e., firms focused on a single line of business). Though the findings from these studies remain controversial, they indicate that diversified firms trade at a discount relative to portfolios of otherwise similar undiversified firms. Cendant's view was apparently in line with this research, because they believed that the market values of the four independent firms would exceed the prebreakup value of Cendant.

Whether diversified firms trade at a discount and why is unsettled, but one theory proposes that diversified firms struggle to make value-maximizing capital budgeting decisions. Finance theory argues that when firms invest in a wide variety of projects having varying degrees of risk, firms should assign higher discount rates to riskier projects when calculating net present values. However, a survey by Graham and Harvey (2001) finds that firms rarely follow that prescription, and instead discount cash flows from all projects at a single rate—the weighted average cost of capital. Applying the same discount rate to all projects, regardless of risk, tends to understate the values of less risky investments and overstate the values of more risky projects. Potentially, this could lead firms to reject some projects with positive *NPV*s and accept others with negative *NPV*s. That in turn could explain the diversification discount."

Sources: Cendant Corporation Board of Directors Announces Plan to Separate Cendant into Four Publicly Owned, Pure-Play Companies; Creation of Separate Publicly Traded Real Estate, Travel Distribution, Hospitality and Vehicle Rental Companies Intended to Maximize Value for Cendant Shareholders, PR Newswire, October 24, 2005.
Cendant Struggles to Merge Ebookers, Financial Times, October 26, 2005.
This Just Isn't Working Out, CNNMoney, November 1, 2005.
How 1+1+1+1 Can Equal Less than 4, New York Times, November 6, 2005.

T his chapter concludes our coverage of capital budgeting. Chapter 7 preached the virtues of *NPV* analysis, and Chapter 8 showed how to generate the cash flow estimates required to calculate a project's *NPV*. This chapter focuses on the risk dimension of project analysis. To calculate an *NPV*, an analyst must evaluate the risk of a project and decide what discount rate adequately reflects the opportunity costs of investors who are willing to invest in the project. In many cases, the best place to discover clues for solving this problem is the market for the firm's securities. The chapter begins with a discussion of how managers can look to the market to calculate a discount rate that properly reflects the risk of a firm's investment projects. Even when managers are confident that they have estimated project cash flows carefully and chosen a proper discount rate, they want to perform additional analysis to understand the sources of a project's risk. Such tools include break-even analysis, sensitivity analysis, simulation, and decision trees, all covered in the middle part of this chapter. The chapter concludes with two sections—one on real options and the other on strategy—that describe the sources of value in investment projects and illustrate how *NPV* analysis can sometimes understate the value of certain kinds of investments.

9.1 CHOOSING THE RIGHT DISCOUNT RATE

COST OF EQUITY

What discount rate should managers use to calculate a project's *NPV*? This is a very difficult question, undoubtedly the source of heated discussions when firms evaluate capital investment proposals. Conceptually, when a firm establishes a project's discount rate, the rate should reflect the opportunity costs of investors who can choose to invest either in the firm's project or in similar projects undertaken by other firms. This is a rather roundabout way of saying that a project's discount rate must be high enough to compensate investors for the project's risk. One implication of this statement is that if a firm undertakes many different kinds of investment projects, each of which may have a different degree of risk, managers err if they apply a single, firm-wide discount rate to each investment. In principle, the appropriate discount rate to use in *NPV* calculations can vary from one investment to another as long as risks vary across investments.

To simplify things a little at the start, we consider a firm that finances its operations using only equity and invests in only one industry. Because the firm has no debt, its investments must provide returns sufficient to satisfy just one type of investor—common stockholders. Because the firm invests in only one industry, we may assume that all its investments are *equally risky*. Therefore, when calculating the *NPV* of any project that this firm might make, its managers can use the required return on equity, often called the *cost of equity*, as the discount rate. If the firm uses the cost of equity as its discount rate, by definition, any project with a positive *NPV* will generate returns that exceed shareholders' required returns.

To quantify shareholders' expectations, managers must look to the market. Recall from Chapter 6 that according to the CAPM, the expected or required return on any security equals the risk-free rate plus the security's beta times the expected market risk premium:

$$E(R_i) = R_f + \beta_i[E(R_m) - R_f] \qquad \text{(Eq. 9.1)}$$

Managers can estimate the return that shareholders require if they know (1) their firm's stock beta, (2) the risk-free rate, and (3) the expected market risk premium. Graham and Harvey (2001) show that managers actually do use the CAPM to compute their firm's cost of equity this way.

APPLYING THE MODEL 9.1

Carbonlite Inc. manufactures bicycle frames that are both extremely strong and very light. Carbonlite, which finances its operations 100 percent with equity, is evaluating a proposal to build a new manufacturing facility that will enable the firm to double its frame output within three years. Because Carbonlite sells a luxury good, its fortunes are very sensitive to macroeconomic conditions, and its stock has a beta of 1.5. Carbonlite's financial managers observe that the current interest rate on risk-free government bonds is 5 percent, and they believe the expected return on the overall stock market will be about 11 percent per year in the future. Given this information, Carbonlite should calculate the NPV of the expansion proposal using a discount rate of 14 percent:

$$E(R) = 5\% + 1.5(11\% - 5\%) = 14\%$$

To reiterate, Carbonlite can use its cost of equity capital, 14 percent, to discount cash flows because we have assumed both that the company has no debt on its balance sheet and that undertaking any of Carbonlite's investment proposals will not alter the firm's risk. If either assumption is invalid, then the cost of equity is not the appropriate discount rate.

In the preceding example, Carbonlite's stock beta is 1.5 because sales of premium bicycle frames are highly correlated with the state of the economy. Therefore, Carbonlite's investment in new capacity is riskier than an investment in new capacity by a firm producing a product with sales that are relatively insensitive to economic conditions. For example, managers of a food-processing company might apply a lower discount rate to an expansion project than Carbonlite's managers would because the stock of a food processor would have a lower beta. The general lesson is that the same type of capital investment project (such as capacity expansion, equipment replacement, or new product development) may require different discount rates in different industries. The level of systematic risk varies from one industry to another, and so too should the discount rate used in capital budgeting analysis.

Several other factors affect betas, which in turn affect project discount rates. One of the most important factors is a firm's cost structure, specifically its mix of fixed and variable costs. In general, holding all other factors constant, the greater the importance of fixed costs in a firm's overall cost structure, the more volatile will be its cash flows and the higher will be its stock beta. **Operating leverage** measures the tendency of the volatility of operating cash flows to increase with fixed operating costs. Mathematically, the definition of operating leverage can be expressed as follows:

$$\text{Operating leverage} = \frac{\left(\dfrac{\Delta EBIT}{EBIT}\right)}{\left(\dfrac{\Delta \text{sales}}{\text{sales}}\right)}$$

(Eq. 9.2)

where *EBIT* means "earnings before interest and taxes" and the symbol Δ (delta) means "change in." Operating leverage equals the percentage change in earnings before interest and taxes divided by the percentage change in sales. When a small percentage increase (decrease) in sales leads to a large percentage increase (decrease) in *EBIT*, the firm has high operating leverage. The connection between operating leverage and the relative importance of fixed and variable costs is easy to see in the following example.

APPLYING THE MODEL 9.2

Carbonlite Inc. uses robotic technology to paint its finished bicycle frames, whereas its main competitor, Fiberspeed Corp., offers customized, hand-painted finishes to its customers. Robots represent a significant fixed cost for Carbonlite, but robots help keep variable costs low. Fiberspeed incurs very low fixed costs, but it has high variable costs due to the time required to paint frames by hand. Both firms sell their bike frames at an average price of $1,000 apiece. Last year each firm made a profit of $1 million on sales of 10,000 bicycle frames, as shown in Table 9.1. Suppose that next year both firms experience a 10 percent increase in sales volume to 11,000 frames, holding constant all the other figures. Carbonlite's fixed costs do not change, and its *EBIT* will increase by $600 ($1,000 price minus $400 variable costs) per additional frame sold. Carbonlite's *EBIT* will increase 60 percent from $1 million to $1.6 million, while Fiberspeed's *EBIT* will grow from $1 million to $1.3 million, an increase of just 30 percent. Because Carbonlite has higher fixed costs and lower variable costs, its profits increase more rapidly in response to a given increase in sales than Fiberspeed's profits do. In short, Carbonlite has more operating leverage. Figure 9.1 shows this graphically. The figure shows two lines, one tracing out the relationship between sales growth (from the base of 10,000 bicycles per year) and *EBIT* growth (from the $1 million *EBIT* base) for Carbonlite, and the other illustrating the same linkage for Fiberspeed.[1] Because of its higher operating leverage, Carbonlite has a much steeper line than Fiberspeed does. Even though Carbonlite and Fiberspeed compete in the same industry, they may use different discount rates in their capital budgeting analysis because operating leverage increases the risk of Carbonlite's cash flows relative to Fiberspeed's.

Table 9.1
Financial Data for Carbonlite Inc. and Fiberspeed Corp.

Item	Carbonlite	Fiberspeed
Fixed cost per year	$5 million	$2 million
Variable cost per bike frame	$400	$700
Sale price per bike frame	$1,000	$1,000
Contribution margin[a] per bike frame	$600	$300
Last year's sales volume	10,000 frames	10,000 frames
EBIT[b]	$1 million	$1 million

[a]*Contribution margin* is the sale price per unit minus the variable cost per unit. In this case: Carbonlite: $1,000 − $400 = $600 per bike Fiberspeed: $1,000 − $700 = $300 per bike
[b]*EBIT* equals sales volume times the contribution margin minus fixed costs. In this case: Carbonlite: (10,000 × $600) − $5,000,000 = $1,000,000 Fiberspeed: (10,000 × $300) − $2,000,000 = $1,000,000

[1] These comparisons are based on a reference point of 10,000 bikes per year sold for $1,000 per bike and *EBIT* of $1 million. All changes described and shown in Figure 9.1 assume these points of reference in each case. Clearly, the sensitivity of these values to change will vary depending on the point of reference utilized.

Figure 9.1
Operating Leverage
for Carbonlite and
Fiberspeed
The higher operating leverage
of Carbonlite is reflected in its
steeper slope, demonstrating
that its *EBIT* is more responsive to changes in sales than is
the *EBIT* of Fiberspeed.

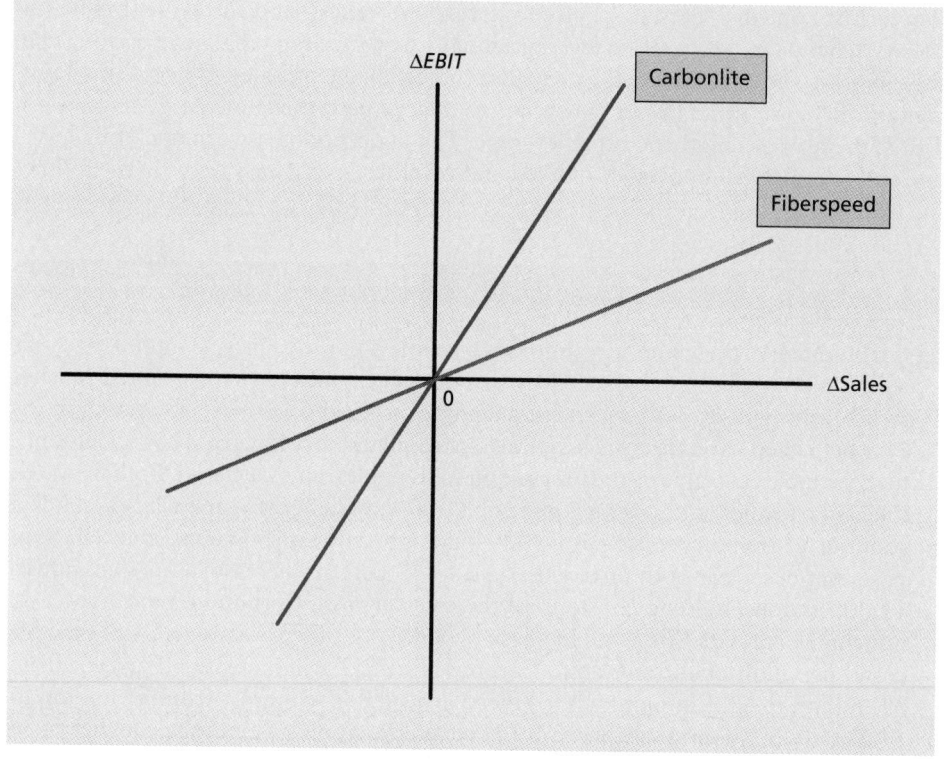

We have seen that Carbonlite's sales are very sensitive to the business cycle because the firm produces a luxury item. We have also observed that Carbonlite's profits
are quite sensitive to sales changes due to high operating leverage. Both of these factors contribute to Carbonlite's relatively high stock beta of 1.5 and its correspondingly high cost of equity of 14 percent. One other factor looms large in determining
whether firms have high or low stock betas. Remember that Carbonlite's financial
structure is 100 percent equity. In practice it is much more common to see both debt
and equity on the right-hand side of a firm's balance sheet. When firms finance their
operations with debt and equity, the presence of debt creates **financial leverage,** which
leads to a higher stock beta. The effect of financial leverage on stock betas is much
the same as the effect of operating leverage. When a firm borrows money, it creates
a fixed cost that it must repay whether sales are high or low.[2] As was the case with
operating leverage, an increase (decrease) in sales will lead to sharper increases (decreases) in earnings for a firm with financial leverage compared to a firm that has
only equity on its balance sheet.

Table 9.2 illustrates the effect of financial leverage on the volatility of a firm's cash
flows, and hence on its beta. The table compares two firms, A and B, which are identical in every respect except that Firm A finances its operations with 100 percent equity,
and Firm B uses 50 percent long-term debt with an interest rate of 8 percent and 50 percent equity. For simplicity, we assume that neither firm pays taxes. Firms A and B sell
identical products at the same price, they both have $100 million in assets, and they
face the same production costs. Suppose that over the next year both firms generate

---

[2.] Note that even if a firm enters a loan agreement with a variable interest rate, the cost of repaying the debt does not generally vary with sales. In that sense, even a loan with a variable interest rate creates a fixed expense with respect to sales.

Table 9.2
The Effect of Financial Leverage on Shareholder Returns

Account	Firm A	Firm B
Assets	$100 million	$100 million
Debt	$ 0	$ 50 million
Equity	$100 million	$ 50 million
When Return on Assets Equals 20 Percent		
EBIT	$20 million	$20 million
Less: Interest	0	$(.08 \times \$50$ million$) = 4$ million
Cash to equity	$20 million	$16 million .
ROE	$20 million/$100 million = 20%	$16 million/$50 million = 32%
When Return on Assets Equals 5 Percent		
EBIT	$5 million	$5 million
Less: Interest	0	$(.08 \times \$50$ million$) = 4$ million
Cash to equity	$5 million	$1 million
ROE	$5 million/$100 million = 5%	$1 million/$50 million = 2%

EBIT equal to 20 percent of total assets, or $20 million. Firm A pays no interest, so it can distribute all $20 million to its shareholders, a 20 percent return on their $100 million investment. Firm B pays 8 percent interest on $50 million for a total interest cost of $4 million. After paying interest, Firm B can distribute $16 million to shareholders, but that represents a 32 percent return on their investment of $50 million. Conversely, suppose the firm earns *EBIT* equal to just 5 percent of its assets, or $5 million. Firm A pays out all $5 million to its shareholders, a return of 5 percent. Firm B pays out $4 million in interest, leaving just $1 million for shareholders, a return of only 2 percent. Therefore, in periods when business is very good, shareholders of Firm B earn higher returns than shareholders of Firm A, and the opposite happens when business is bad.

The inclusion of debt as part of a firm's capital structure complicates discount-rate selection in two ways. First, debt creates financial leverage, which increases a firm's stock beta relative to the value it would obtain if the firm financed investments only with equity. Second, when a firm issues debt, it must satisfy two groups of investors rather than one. Cash flows generated from capital investment projects must be sufficient to meet the return requirements of both bondholders and stockholders. Therefore, a firm that issues debt cannot discount project cash flows using only its cost of equity capital. It must choose a discount rate that reflects the expectations of both investor groups. Fortunately, finance theory offers a way to find that discount rate.

WEIGHTED AVERAGE COST OF CAPITAL (WACC)

In Chapter 5, we learned that the expected return on a portfolio of two assets equaled the weighted average of the expected returns of each asset in the portfolio. We can apply that idea to the problem of selecting an appropriate discount rate for a firm that has both debt and equity in its capital structure. Imagine that Lox-in-a-Box Inc., a chain of kosher fast-food stores, has outstanding $100 million worth of common stock on which investors require a return of 15 percent. In addition, the firm has outstanding $50 million in bonds that offer a 9 percent return.[3] What rate of return must the firm earn on its investments to satisfy both groups of investors?

The answer lies in a concept known as the **weighted average cost of capital** (**WACC**). Let the letters D and E represent the *market value* of the firm's debt and equity securities, respectively, and let r_d and r_e represent the rate of return that investors require on bonds and shares. The *WACC* is the simple weighted average of the required rates of return on debt and equity, where the weights equal the percentage of each type of financing in the firm's overall capital structure.

$$WACC = \left(\frac{D}{D + E}\right)r_d + \left(\frac{E}{D + E}\right)r_e$$

As a practical matter, firms in many countries can deduct interest payments to bond-holders when they calculate taxable income. If a firm's interest payments are tax deductible, and if the corporate tax rate equals T_c, we have the following:

$$WACC = \left(\frac{D}{D + E}\right)(1 - T_c)r_d + \left(\frac{E}{D + E}\right)r_e \qquad \text{(Eq. 9.3)}$$

Plugging in the values from our example, and assuming that the firm must pay one-third of its cash flows to tax authorities, we find that the *WACC* for Lox-in-a-Box equals 12 percent:

$$WACC = \left(\frac{\$50}{\$50 + \$100}\right) \times 9\%(1 - 0.33) + \left(\frac{\$100}{\$50 + \$100}\right) \times 15\% = 12\%$$

How can Lox-in-a-Box managers be sure that a 12 percent return on its investments will satisfy the expectations of both bondholders and shareholders? Suppose the company is considering a new investment project that will cost $60. The firm's financial analysts expect this project to generate pretax cash flows of $10.8 per year in perpetuity. If the corporate tax rate is one-third, then the after-tax annual cash flow equals $10.8(1 − 0.33), or $7.2. A careful reader may wonder why, in calculating the after-tax cash flow, we ignored the tax deduction that Lox-in-a-Box will receive because it uses debt to finance part of this project. Recall that in earlier chapters we said that in doing capital budgeting analysis, we want to keep the investment decision separate from the financing decision. One implication of this statement is that when we estimate cash flows for an *NPV* analysis, we exclude interest expense. This may seem counterintuitive because interest payments to investors shelter some of a project's cash flows from taxes. Rather than adjust our cash flow numbers to capture this tax benefit, we will capture the value of interest tax shields by discounting cash flows at the *WACC*. By multiplying the required return on debt times one minus the corporate tax rate, we account for the value of debt's tax benefits by lowering the discount rate rather than raising our cash flow figures.

[3.] The return we have in mind here is the yield to maturity (*YTM*) on the firm's bonds. Unless the bonds sell at par, the coupon rate and the *YTM* will be different, but the *YTM* provides a better measure of the return that investors who purchase the firm's debt can expect. If the probability that the firm will default on its debt is nontrivial, then the *YTM* actually overstates the expected return on the firm's bonds. For now, we will keep things simple by assuming the likelihood of default is very low, so the *YTM* provides a close approximation to the expected return on debt.

Let's calculate the *NPV* of this project using the *WACC* as the discount rate.[4]

$$NPV = -60 + \frac{7.2}{0.12} = 0$$

A project with a zero NPV qualifies as "barely acceptable," meaning that it just manages to satisfy the demands of the firm's investors. We can check to be sure that the project meets both shareholders' and bondholders' expectations as follows.

Suppose Lox-in-a-Box sets up this project as a stand-alone firm financed two-thirds with equity ($40) and one-third with debt ($20). Because Lox-in-a-Box finances this new investment with $20 of debt paying 9 percent interest, they must pay debtholders $1.8 in interest each year, but the after-tax interest cost to the firm equals $1.2 ($20 × 0.09 × (1 − 0.33)). If the project's after-tax cash flows, ignoring interest, equal $7.2, then subtracting the $1.2 after-tax interest charge leaves $6 for shareholders. Equity investors contributed $40 to the project, so the $6 cash flow they receive in perpetuity represents a 15 percent return, exactly equal to the required return on equity.

To summarize, we calculated the project's *NPV* by discounting its after-tax cash flows (ignoring interest payments) at the 12 percent *WACC*. In other words, we calculated the project's cash flows as if the firm financed the project with all equity, but we discounted those cash flows using a rate that reflected both the mix of debt and equity financing and the tax benefit associated with debt. That produced a zero *NPV*, meaning that the project earned exactly the *WACC*. Next, we calculated the cash flowing from the project to debtholders and stockholders and found that both groups received exactly the returns they required. Hence, Lox-in-a-Box managers can be sure that a 12 percent return on its investments will satisfy the expectations of both bondholders and shareholders.

The *WACC* is a figure of critical importance to almost all firms. Firms that use the *WACC* to value real investments know that a higher *WACC* means investments have to pass a higher hurdle before they generate shareholder wealth. If an event beyond the firm's control increases the firm's *WACC*, both its existing assets and its prospective investment opportunities become less valuable. The Comparative Corporate Finance insert borrows from a PricewaterhouseCoopers consulting report to demonstrate the importance of the *WACC* to managers around the world.

Firms can modify the *WACC* formula to accommodate more than two sources of financing. For instance, suppose a firm raises money by issuing equity, *E*, long-term debt, *D*, and preferred stock, *P*. We will assume that dividends to common and preferred shareholders are not tax deductible, but interest payments are. Denoting the required return on each security with r_e, r_d, and r_p, we can determine the following *WACC* for this firm:

$$WACC = \left(\frac{E}{E + D + P}\right)r_e + \left(\frac{D}{E + D + P}\right)r_d(1 - T_c) + \left(\frac{P}{E + D + P}\right)r_p$$

APPLYING THE MODEL 9.3

The S. D. Williams Company has 1 million shares of common stock outstanding, which currently trade at a price of $50 per share. The company believes that its stockholders require a 15 percent return on their investment. The company also

---

[4.] Recall that the present value of a perpetuity equals the annual cash flow divided by the discount rate, so the second term in this equation is just the present value of the project's cash inflows, while the first term is the project's cost.

COMPARATIVE CORPORATE FINANCE

The Cost of Capital in India

In December 1999, PricewaterhouseCoopers (PwC) conducted a survey of leaders in the business and finacial communities in India to determine the forces that influenced the cost of capital in India. Some of the study's more interesting findings included the following: When asked to rank the importance of cost of capital and six other factors from most to least important in determining corporate value, managers of Indian firms ranked cost of capital first, ahead of other factors such as sales growth, working capital efficiency, and corporate taxes (see chart below).

- Firms in India used the CAPM more frequently than any other method to determine their cost of equity.
- The most common approach to estimate the CAPM beta was to use data from weekly stock returns over a period of three years.
- Almost all respondents reported using the yield on 10-year government bonds to proxy for the CAPM's

risk-free rate. In 1999, this rate was almost 11 percent, roughly twice as high as seen in Western industrialized economies at the time.

- Estimates of the cost of equity capital in India averaged about 20 percent.
- Inflation expectations in India provided a partial explanation for the high cost of capital in that country. In late 1999, Indian managers expected future inflation to be in the 5–7 percent range.
- During the 1990s, firms in India reduced their reliance on debt and increased their reliance on equity.
- In 1999, the average Indian firm's capital structure consisted of approximately 40 percent debt and 60 percent equity.
- The *WACC* for Indian companies falls in the 15–20 percent range, and the average *WACC* for U.S. firms falls in the 8–12 percent range.

Ranking of Important Value Drivers by Managers in Several Countries
(1 corresponds to the highest level of importance, 7 to the lowest level)

Factor	India	Hong Kong	U.K.	Australia
Profit margin	1	1	1	1
WACC	1	3	2	2
Sales growth	4	2	2	3
Fixed capital efficiency	1	4	4	4
Working capital efficiency	6	4	4	4
Corporate tax rate	7	7	6	7
Time period until positive returns	5	6	7	5

has $47.1 million (par value) in 5-year, fixed-rate notes with a coupon rate of 8 percent and a yield to maturity of 7 percent. Because the yield on these bonds is less than the coupon rate, they trade at a premium. The current market value of the 5-year notes is $49 million. Lastly, the company has 200,000 outstanding preferred shares, which pay an $8 annual dividend and currently trade for $80 per share. What is the company's *WACC* if the corporate tax rate is 35 percent?

Begin by calculating the market value of each security. S. D. Williams has $50 million in common stock, $49 million in long-term debt, and $16 million in preferred stock, for a total capitalization of $115 million. Next, determine the required rate of return on each type of security. The rates on common stock, long-term debt, and preferred stock are 15 percent, 7 percent, and 10 percent, respectively. Plug all these values into the *WACC* equation to obtain 9.8 percent:

$$WACC = \left(\frac{\$50}{\$115} \right)0.15 + \left(\frac{\$49}{\$115} \right)0.07(1 - 0.35) + \left(\frac{\$16}{\$115} \right)0.10 = 0.109 = 9.8\%$$

Now we have seen two approaches for determining the correct discount rate to apply to capital budgeting problems. A firm that uses all equity should discount project cash flows using the cost of equity, and a firm that uses both debt and equity should discount cash flows using the *WACC*. Both recommendations are subject to the important proviso that the firm makes investments in only one line of business—or stated differently, that the firm discounts cash flows using the *WACC* only when the project under consideration is very similar to the firm's existing assets. For example, if managers at Lox-in-a-Box believe the firm should vertically integrate by investing in a salmon-fishing fleet, they should not discount cash flows from that investment at the firm's *WACC*. The risks of salmon fishing hardly resemble those of running a fast-food chain, and it is the latter that are reflected in the firm's *WACC*. Evaluating investments that deviate significantly from a firm's existing investments requires a different approach. To understand that approach, we need to revisit the CAPM to see how it is related to the *WACC*.

Connecting the *WACC* to the **CAPM**

The CAPM states that the required return on any asset is directly linked to the asset's beta. By now we are used to thinking about betas of shares of common stock, but there is nothing about the CAPM that restricts its predictions to shares. When a firm issues bonds or preferred stock, the required returns on those securities should reflect their systematic risks (i.e., their betas) just as the required returns on the firm's common shares do. Because both preferred stock and bonds generally make fixed, predictable cash payments over time, measuring the rate of return that investors require on these securities is relatively easy, even without knowing their betas. For preferred stock, the dividend yield (dividend/price) provides a good measure of required returns, and for debt, the yield to maturity does the same. However, this does not rule out the possibility that we could estimate the beta of a share of preferred stock or of a bond. Calculating the beta of a preferred share or a bond is no different than calculating the beta of common stock—just estimate the covariance between returns on the security of interest and returns on the market, and divide by the variance of the market's returns.

Remember, though, that returns on preferred shares and bonds are generally not as sensitive to the market's up-and-down movements as are returns on common stocks. This implies that the beta on a firm's bonds, for example, will be low relative to the beta of its shares. A lower beta translates to a lower expected return, but that is exactly what we should expect. Bonds, because they are less risky than stocks, offer lower expected returns.

SMART PRACTICES VIDEO

Beth Acton, Vice President and Treasurer of Ford Motor Co. (former). Currently, Chief Financial Officer, Comerica

"For us it's a very critical calculation because we use it to assess product programs, to assess other capital investments, and to analyze acquisitions."

See the entire interview at **SMARTFinance**

APPLYING THE MODEL 9.4

Suppose an analyst gathers monthly returns on the bonds of a large corporation. Because interest rates and bond prices fluctuate from month to month, bond returns fluctuate too. The analyst calculates the covariance between returns on the bonds and returns on a diversified portfolio of securities, then divides by the variance of returns on the portfolio to obtain an estimate of the bond's beta. The number obtained is 0.1. Assuming that the risk-free rate of interest equals 5 percent and the expected return on the market portfolio equals 15 percent, the analyst estimates the required return on the bonds using the CAPM equation:

$$r_d = 5\% + 0.1 \times (15\% - 5\%) = 6\%$$

The number 0.1 equals the **debt beta.** Not surprisingly, the debt beta is very close to zero because the bond's returns are not highly correlated with the market portfolio.

Of course, there is another way to estimate the debt beta. Suppose the analyst observes that a firm's bonds offer a yield to maturity of 6 percent. Making the same assumptions as before about the risk-free rate (5%) and the expected return on the market (15%), the analyst could estimate the debt beta indirectly by solving this equation:

$$6\% = 5\% + \beta_d(15\% - 5\%) \qquad \beta_d = 0.1$$

The preceding example illustrates that applying the concept of beta to a bond, a share of preferred stock, or any other asset is no different from applying it to common stock. *Any asset that generates cash flows has a beta, and that beta establishes the required return on the asset through the CAPM.* This allows us to establish a link between the CAPM and the WACC as follows. Recall that the WACC represents the rate of return that a company must earn on its investments to satisfy both bondholders and stockholders:[5]

$$WACC = \left(\frac{D}{D + E}\right)r_d + \left(\frac{E}{D + E}\right)r_e$$

However, the CAPM establishes a direct link between required rates of return on debt and equity and the betas of these securities. This connection leads to the following relationship for the asset's beta, β_A:

$$\beta_A = \left(\frac{D}{D + E}\right)\beta_d + \left(\frac{E}{D + E}\right)\beta_e \qquad \text{(Eq. 9.4)}$$

Equation 9.4 states that the beta of a firm's assets equals the weighted average of the firm's debt and equity betas.[6] What is an asset beta? It is simply a measure of the systematic risk of a real asset, or the covariance of the cash flows generated by that asset divided by the variance of cash flows from the market portfolio. Suppose a company owns a factory that it uses to produce tires. The cash flows of this operation will vary due to changes in the business cycle and other factors. The factory's asset beta measures the systematic risk of the cash flow stream generated by the factory.

The asset beta on the left-hand side of Equation 9.4 represents a measure of the risk of a physical asset. The terms on the right-hand side illustrate how the risk of the asset is allocated between debt and equity investors. For instance, suppose a firm has manufacturing assets with a beta of 1.0. If the firm is financed entirely with equity, then we have the following:

$$\beta_A = 1.0 = \left(\frac{\$0}{\$0 + E}\right)\beta_d + \left(\frac{E}{\$0 + E}\right)\beta_E = \beta_E$$

When there are no bondholders, shareholders bear all the risk associated with the firm's assets, so the asset beta and the equity beta both equal 1.0. However, suppose that the same firm decides to raise 20 percent of its money by issuing relatively safe bonds with a beta of 0.1. The assets of this firm have not changed, so the asset beta

---

[5.] For simplicity, we will assume a zero corporate tax rate to begin this example.

[6.] Again, we are just applying a basic concept from portfolio theory. If an investor holds a portfolio of two securities, then the beta of the portfolio equals the weighted average of the betas of the securities in the portfolio. Hamada (1972) was the first to demonstrate how equity betas could be converted into asset betas, and vice versa.

still equals 1.0. The firm's bonds are substantially less risky than the firm's assets, and equity holders must therefore bear all the residual risk. Using the previous equation and substituting 0.1 for the debt beta and 0.2 and 0.8 for the fractions of debt and equity financing, respectively, we find the following:

$$\beta_A = 1.0 = (0.2)(0.1) + (0.8)\beta_E$$

$$\beta_E = \frac{1.0 - (0.2)(0.1)}{0.8} = 1.225$$

Compared to the all-equity firm, the firm with 20 percent debt has a much higher equity beta. That is exactly what we should have expected given our previous discussion of the effects of financial leverage on equity betas. There is a kind of "law of conservation of risk" at work here. The fundamental risk of a firm depends on the risk of the assets in which it chooses to invest. This is what the asset beta captures. The firm can allocate that risk between different types of investors any way it sees fit. If a firm chooses to offer investors a security such as a bond that has relatively low risk, it does not change the fact that the firm's underlying assets are still risky. If bondholders are not bearing this risk, then the task must fall to shareholders. The more promises a firm makes to provide investors with a "safe" return (i.e., the more debt it issues), the greater the uncertainty surrounding the returns that the firm will be able to provide to shareholders.

It is easy to see the effect of leverage on equity betas if we make the assumption that the debt beta equals zero. Given that assumption, rearranging terms in Equation 9.4 yields the following:

$$\beta_E = \beta_A \left(1 + \frac{D}{E} \right) \qquad \text{(Eq. 9.5)}$$

Once again, we can see in this equation that if the firm has zero debt, the asset beta equals the equity beta. For firms that use debt, the term $[1 + (D/E)]$ will be greater than 1.0, which in turn means that $\beta_E > \beta_A$. Holding the asset beta—the risk of the firm's assets—constant, the more money the firm raises by issuing debt, the greater its financial leverage, and the higher its equity beta.

After such a long digression on linkages between the WACC and the CAPM, it is worthwhile to stop and recall our original objective—to find the right discount rate for capital budgeting projects. When a new project is very similar to a firm's existing projects, managers should discount cash flows using the WACC. However, the WACC does not apply when a firm is considering a project outside its normal line of business or when a firm has many different lines of business under one corporate umbrella. In the latter case, the WACC represents the required rate of return on the firm's "average" investment, but some divisions of a company may be inherently riskier than others. Applying the WACC to all projects will tend to overstate the NPVs of projects that are more risky than average and understate the NPVs of projects that are less risky than average. Managers can solve this problem by focusing their attention on the asset betas of specific projects, sometimes called project betas.

ASSET BETAS AND PROJECT DISCOUNT RATES

General Electric Corp. (ticker symbol GE) is a diversified conglomerate with significant investments in industries as wide ranging as lighting, aircraft engine manufacturing, broadcasting, and financial services. Suppose that GE's WACC equals 13 percent.

When GE evaluates a proposal to replace existing equipment in its aircraft engine division, it should not necessarily calculate the *NPV* using a 13 percent discount rate, because engine manufacturing may be more or less risky than the average GE investment. The *WACC* tells GE that on average it must earn 13 percent across all its investments to keep its investors happy, but GE should discount its most risky investments at rates above 13 percent and its least risky investments at lower rates. Similarly, if GE decides to invest in a brand-new line of business, it should not use its *WACC* as the hurdle rate for that investment. Instead, for every investment that it makes, GE must assess the underlying risk of the investment and establish a discount rate appropriate for that risk level. To do this, GE should measure the asset betas of different investments.

As an example, suppose that GE decides to diversify into oil and gas production. How can GE managers determine an appropriate rate with which to discount cash flows from new investments in this industry? The answer is that GE's managers should look to the market. By looking at characteristics of existing oil and gas firms whose securities trade in the market, GE analysts can gain considerable insight into the risks and required returns in this industry.

As a starting point, GE managers should look for firms that compete in only one industry—oil and gas production. A firm that competes in a single line of business is called a **pure play,** so GE wants to find pure play firms in the oil and gas business. Two such firms are Berry Petroleum Co. (ticker symbol BRY) and Forest Oil Corp. (ticker symbol FST). Table 9.3 lists several characteristics of these two firms that should be of interest to analysts at GE. Note that even though both companies produce oil and gas, the equity beta of Forest Oil (0.90) is almost 40 percent higher than the equity beta of Berry Petroleum (0.65). If both of these firms operate in the same industry, why are their stock betas so different? One possibility is that the companies use different production technologies with different degrees of operating leverage. Another is that the companies make different financing decisions, with one firm using more debt than the other. Indeed, Table 9.3 shows that Forest obtains 39 percent of its financing from debt and Berry borrows just 14 percent of the money it needs to do business. Even if the underlying risks of the two firms are identical—that is, even if their asset betas are equal—Forest's greater use of financial leverage will result in a higher stock beta. Besides, GE is not interested in the risk of Berry Petroleum and Forest Oil shares, because the investment GE plans to make is not a purchase of oil and gas stocks. Rather, GE plans to invest in assets required to produce oil and gas, so GE managers need to know the asset beta for this industry.

We will make two assumptions to simplify this example. First, we will assume that the debt of both companies has very little risk, so their debt betas equal zero.

Table 9.3
Data for Berry Petroleum and Forest Oil[a] Berry Petroleum Forest Oil

	Berry Petroleum	Forest Oil
Stock beta	0.65	0.90
Debt (*D*) proportion	0.14	0.39
Equity (*E*) proportion	0.86	0.61
D/E ratio	0.16	0.64
Asset beta[b]	0.56	0.55

[a]Data taken from Value Line Investment Survey, March 2002.
[b]Using Equation 9.4 and assuming debt beta = 0.00

Second, we will ignore taxes for now. Given the information in the table, we can use Equation 9.4 to calculate the asset betas, β_A, for each firm:

For Berry Petroleum: $\beta_A = (0.14)(0) + (0.86)(0.65) = 0.56$

For Forest Oil: $\beta_A = (0.39)(0) + (0.61)(0.90) = 0.55$

The calculations show that despite the rather large differences in equity betas between the two companies, Berry and Forest have nearly identical asset betas. That should not be too surprising because they make very similar investments with similar risks and rewards. The differences in the equity betas apparently are driven by differences in leverage between the two firms. The asset beta calculations for these firms take away the effects of leverage to reveal striking similarities in the firms' underlying risks. When we remove the effects of leverage on an equity beta in this way, we are calculating a figure that analysts sometimes refer to as an **unlevered equity beta.** Therefore, *when a firm uses no leverage, its equity beta equals its asset beta,* so an unlevered beta simply tells us how risky the equity of a company might be if it used no leverage at all.[7]

An analyst at GE might calculate asset betas for many other firms in this industry, starting with each firm's equity beta and unlevering it if necessary. Next, the analyst might take an average across all those firms to arrive at a final asset beta estimate. This is a measure of the risk of the assets in which GE plans to invest. The next step is to incorporate GE's own capital structure into the analysis by "relevering" the asset beta. In other words, once GE estimates the oil and gas asset beta, it must adjust this beta upward if GE's capital structure contains both debt and equity. With this "relevered beta" in hand, the analyst calculates the appropriate project discount rate using the CAPM.

APPLYING THE MODEL 9.5

To determine the appropriate discount rate for a proposed investment in oil and gas production, a financial manager at GE calculates asset betas for several pure-play firms in the industry and averages them to arrive at an industry asset beta of 0.55. Next, the analyst recognizes that GE's capital structure consists of 20 percent debt and 80 percent equity (implying a debt/equity ratio of 0.25) and determines the following relevered project beta:

$$\beta_{GE} = \beta_A \times \left(1 + \frac{D}{E}\right) = 0.55(1 + 0.25) = 0.69$$

Suppose that the risk-free rate of interest equals 6 percent and the expected risk premium on the market equals 7 percent. By plugging these figures, as well as the relevered project beta, into the CAPM equation, the analyst obtains the rate of return that a GE shareholder would require on this oil and gas investment—10.83 percent:

$$E(R) = 6\% + 0.69(7\%) = 10.83\%$$

[7] In mid-1996, Conrail was the target of takeover bids from two rivals, Norfolk Southern and CSX. For an extended illustration of how the investment bank Lazard Frères & Co. used the concepts of levered and unlevered betas to calculate the WACC in its valuation of Conrail, see Thompson (2000).

There is still one more step necessary to find the right discount rate for GE's investment in this industry. The analyst should calculate a project *WACC* (sometimes called a *divisional WACC* in reference to the firm's oil and gas division) using Equation 9.3. For instance, suppose equity makes up 80 percent of GE's financing, and debt accounts for the remaining 20 percent. Suppose also that investors expect a return of 6.5 percent on GE's bonds (just over the risk-free rate). The project *WACC* equals

$$WACC_{project} = 10.83\%(80\%) + 6.5\%(20\%) = 9.96\%$$

We do not want to overstate the precision of this process. Calculating the discount rate requires several steps, each of which involves estimating an uncertain number. If the GE analyst arrives at a figure of 9.96 percent for the oil and gas discount rate, as shown in the preceding Applying the Model example, the report might show that the appropriate discount rate should be "between 9 and 11 percent." There is certainly room to argue around this figure, but notice that it is less than the *WACC* of 13 percent we assumed for GE.

Summarizing the main lessons of this section, we offer the following rules about finding the right discount rate for an investment project:

1. When an all-equity firm invests in an asset similar to its existing assets, the cost of equity is the appropriate discount rate to use in *NPV* calculations.
2. When a firm with both debt and equity invests in an asset similar to its existing assets, the *WACC* is the appropriate discount rate to use in *NPV* calculations.
3. In conglomerates, the *WACC* reflects the return that the firm must earn on average across all its assets to satisfy investors, but using the *WACC* to discount cash flows of a particular investment leads to mistakes. The reason for this is that a particular investment may be more or less risky than the firm's average investment, requiring a higher or lower discount rate than the *WACC*.
4. When a firm invests in an asset that is different from its existing assets, it should look for pure-play firms to find the right discount rate. Firms can calculate an industry asset beta by unlevering the betas of pure play firms. Then it must relever the industry asset beta based on the acquiring firm's existing capital structure. Given the relevered industry asset beta, firms can determine an appropriate discount rate using the CAPM.[8]

Nothing in the real world is as simple as it is portrayed in textbooks. One important item that we have neglected thus far in our discussion of asset betas is the effect of taxes on project discount rates. The opportunity to deduct interest payments reduces the after-tax cost of debt and changes the relationship between asset betas and equity betas this way:

$$\beta_E = \beta_A\left[1 + (1 - T_c)\frac{D}{E}\right] \qquad \text{(Eq. 9.6)}$$

Fortunately, the four main lessons listed previously do not change when we add taxes to the picture. Only the calculations change. When a firm is making an "ordinary" investment, it can use Equation 9.3 to determine its after-tax *WACC* to serve as the discount rate in *NPV* calculations. Alternatively, when a firm makes an invest-

SMART ETHICS VIDEO

Robert Bruner, University of Virginia

"We discovered a remarkable degree of convergence among the best practitioners."

See the entire interview at **SMARTFinance**

---

[8] Though this advice is theoretically sound, Graham and Harvey (2001) document the curious fact that most real managers use the firm's own discount rate for all capital budgeting projects, even for those that are in industries different from the firm's core business.

ment in a new line of business, it can use Equation 9.6 to calculate asset betas for pure play firms to arrive at an industry asset beta. As before, once analysts have an industry beta in hand, they simply relever it if necessary to reflect their own firm's capital structure; then they plug the beta into the CAPM to find the right discount rate for the investment.

A NOTE ON THE EQUITY RISK PREMIUM

When managers use the CAPM to determine the discount rate for an investment project, they must know three things: (1) the project or asset beta, (2) the risk-free rate, and (3) the expected risk premium on the market portfolio. In Chapter 6 we demonstrated how to use regression analysis to estimate the beta of a share of stock, and in this chapter we have shown how to use the betas of the firm's securities to estimate its asset beta. Measuring the risk-free rate is a straightforward exercise that involves nothing more complex than obtaining current market rates on government bills or bonds. Now we briefly turn our attention to measuring the expected risk premium on the market portfolio.

Recall that in the CAPM, the market portfolio is a value-weighted combination of all assets in the economy. At present, we are unaware of any market index that attempts to incorporate every type of asset. When using the CAPM, most practitioners and academics use the returns on a broad-based stock index as a proxy for the true market portfolio. Accordingly, rather than try to estimate the expected risk premium on the market portfolio, analysts usually focus on the expected equity risk premium, the difference in expected returns between a portfolio of common stocks and a risk free asset such as a Treasury bond.

Chapter 5 demonstrated that in the United States and many other countries, average returns on stocks exceed average returns on government bonds over long time periods. During the twentieth century, the average real return on stocks outpaced the average real return on U.S. Treasury bills by 7.7 percent per year. But in the CAPM, what matters is not the actual equity risk premium from the past, but the expected equity risk premium looking forward. Though many analysts trust the historical evidence and simply plug in a figure close to 8 percent for the term $E(R_m - R_f)$, a naive reliance on long-run historical averages may not be the best approach for estimating the expected risk premium. Getting an unbiased estimate is important because an error in the risk premium translates directly into an error in a project's discount rate, and hence its *NPV*.

One variable that analysts can use for a forward-looking estimate of the risk premium is the market's aggregate earnings yield (*E/P*), or the reciprocal of the price-to-earnings ratios. For example, to calculate the earnings yield for the S&P 500, add up the earnings of all 500 companies and divide by the aggregate market value of these firms. Corporate earnings fluctuate with the business cycle, so analysts usually try to smooth out, or normalize, these temporary effects before using the earnings yield to estimate the risk premium. In the United States, the long-run average value of the earnings yield is about 7 percent, not far from the average real return on stocks. It should not be surprising that the earnings yield is closely related to the real return on stocks. After all, stocks represent a claim on the earnings of firms. In recent years, the normalized earnings yield on U.S. stocks fluctuated between 4 and 5 percent. To many experts, this figure signals lower future returns on stocks than the historical record might suggest.

A second forward-looking method for estimating the equity risk premium makes use of the dividend growth model from Chapter 4. Recall that the dividend growth model calculates the present value of a perpetual dividend stream that grows at a constant rate, g:

$$P_0 = \frac{D_1}{r - g}$$

Rearranging this equation a little shows that the required return on the stock equals the sum of the dividend yield and the dividend growth rate:

$$r = \frac{D_1}{P_0} + g$$

To use this model to estimate the equity risk premium, we must think of the equation in aggregate, macroeconomic terms. In other words, r represents the (real) required return on the stock market rather than the required return on a specific stock. The ratio D_1/P_0 represents the aggregate dividend yield, and g represents the (real) growth rate of aggregate dividends. Fama and French (2002) show that from 1872 to 1950, the expected equity risk premium derived from this model almost exactly matched the actual risk premium measured using average historical returns (a little more than 4 percent), but from 1950 to 2000, the average real return on equities was much higher than the dividend growth model predicted. Fama and French conclude that fundamental indicators such as growth rates in dividends and earnings all point to an expected equity risk premium below the long-run historical average premium.[9]

Perhaps the most direct forward-looking approach is simply to gather forecasts of the equity premium made by experts. Yale economist Ivo Welch did just that by surveying finance and economics professors in 1998 and again in 2001. Welch (2001) reports that the average equity premium forecast declined considerably from 1998 to 2001, a period in which U.S. stocks earned low average returns. In 2001, the average forecast of the 1-year equity premium was 3.4 percent, in contrast to 5.8 percent in the 1998 survey. When Welch asked professors in 2001 for a forecast of the arithmetic average equity premium over the next 30 years, their average prediction was 5.5 percent, in contrast to 7.1 percent in the 1998 survey.[10]

All three forward-looking indicators—the earnings yield, the dividend growth model, and the consensus of academic experts—point toward a future equity risk premium that is lower than the average historical premium.

Concept Review Questions

1. Why is using the cost of equity to discount project cash flows inappropriate when a firm uses both debt and equity in its capital structure?

2. Two firms in the same industry have very different equity betas. Offer two reasons why this can occur.

3. For a firm considering expansion of its existing line of business, why is the *WACC* rather than the cost of equity the preferred discount rate if the firm has both debt and equity in its capital structure?

[9.] Ritter (2001) argues that the expected equity risk premium could be as low as 1 percent due to two factors. First, Ritter concurs with Fama and French that real equity returns in the future are likely to be lower than they have been in the past. Second, he observes that the real return on inflation-indexed bonds in the United States has risen. A decline in real equity returns coupled with an increase in real, risk-free returns squeezes the equity risk premium from both ends.

[10.] Graham and Harvey (2002) surveyed chief financial officers and obtained average estimates of the equity risk premium ranging from 3.0 to 4.7 percent.

**Concept
Review
Questions**

4. The cost of debt, r_d, is generally less than the cost of equity, r_e, because debt is a less risky security. A naive application of the *WACC* formula might suggest that a firm could lower its cost of capital (thereby raising the *NPV* of its current and future investments) by using more debt and less equity in its capital structure. Give one reason why using more debt might not lower a firm's *WACC* even if $r_d < r_e$.

5. Explain the difference between a levered and an unlevered equity beta.

9.2 A CLOSER LOOK AT RISK    Skip

Thus far, the only consideration we have given to risk when doing capital budgeting analysis is selecting the right discount rate. But it would be simplistic to say that, given a set of project cash flows, once an analyst has discounted those cash flows using a risk-adjusted discount rate to determine the *NPV*, the analyst's work is done. Managers generally want to know more about a project than just its *NPV*. They want to know the sources of uncertainty in the project as well as the quantitative importance of each source. Managers need this information to decide whether a project requires additional analysis, such as market research or product testing. Managers also want to identify a project's key value drivers so they can closely monitor these factors after an investment is made. In this section, we explore several techniques that give managers deeper insights into the uncertainty structure of capital investments.

BREAK-EVEN ANALYSIS

When firms make investments, they do so with the objective of making a profit. But another objective that sometimes enters the decision process is avoiding losses. Managers often want to know what is required for a project to break even. **Break-even analysis** can be couched in many different ways. For instance, when a firm introduces a new product, it may want to know the level of sales at which incremental net income turns from negative to positive. Evaluating a new product launch over several years, managers might ask what growth rate in sales the firm must achieve to reach a project *NPV* of zero. When considering a decision to replace old production equipment, a firm might calculate the level of production volume needed to generate cost savings equal to the cost of the new equipment.

> **APPLYING THE MODEL 9.6**
>
> Take another look at Table 9.1, which shows price and cost information for Carbonlite Inc. and Fiberspeed Corp. How many bicycle frames must each firm sell to achieve a break-even point with *EBIT* equal to zero? We can obtain the answer by dividing fixed costs by the contribution margin, sale price per unit minus variable cost per unit:
>
> Carbonlite break-even point = $5,000,000 ÷ ($1,000 − $400) = 8,333 frames
>
> Fiberspeed break-even point = $2,000,000 ÷ ($1,000 − $700) = 6,667 frames
>
> Figure 9.2 illustrates the break-even point for each firm. Despite its $600 contribution margin, Carbonlite's high fixed costs result in a break-even point at higher sales volume than Fiberspeed's break-even point. This should not surprise us, as we already know that Carbonlite's production process results in higher operating leverage than Fiberspeed's.

Figure 9.2(a)
Break-Even Point
for Carbonlite

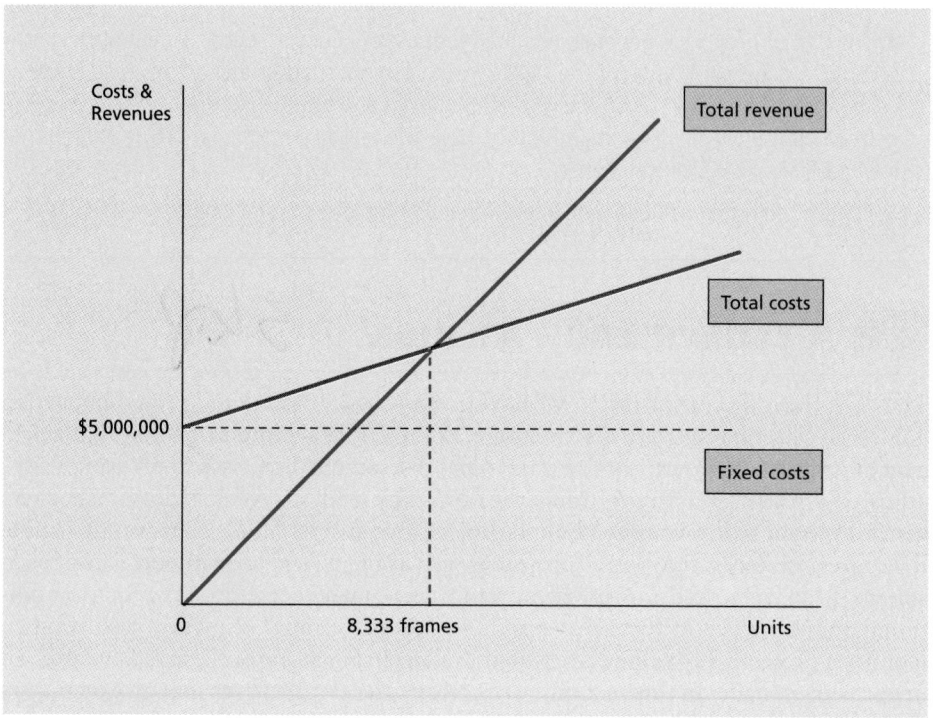

Figure 9.2(b)
Break-Even Point
for Fiberspeed

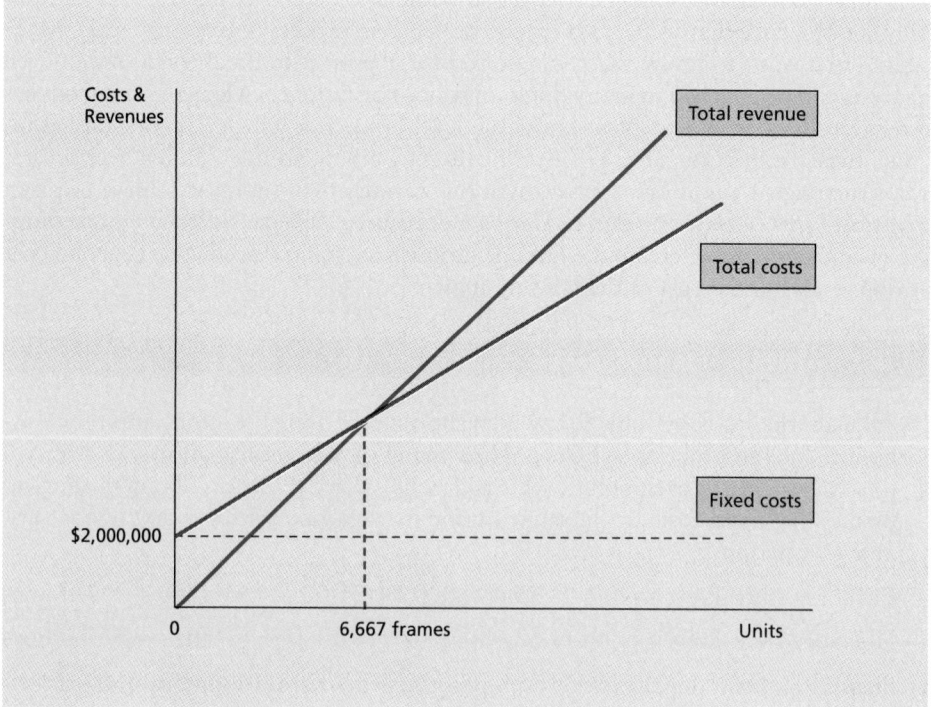

The popularity of break-even analysis among practitioners arises in part because it gives managers very clear targets. From break-even calculations, managers can derive specific targets for different functional areas in the firm (for example, produce at least 10,000 units, gain at least a 5 percent market share, hold variable costs to no more than 65 percent of the selling price). As always, we encourage managers to use breakeven analysis in the context of net present values rather than earnings. A project that reaches the break-even point in terms of net income may destroy shareholder value because it does not recover the firm's cost of capital.

SENSITIVITY ANALYSIS

Most capital budgeting problems require analysts to make many different assumptions before arriving at a final *NPV*. For instance, forecasting project cash flows may require assumptions about the selling price of output, costs of raw materials, market share, and many other unknown quantities. In **sensitivity analysis,** managers have a tool that allows them to explore the importance of each individual assumption, holding all other assumptions fixed, on the project's *NPV*. To conduct a sensitivity analysis, firms establish a "base-case" set of assumptions for a particular project and calculate the *NPV* based on those assumptions. Next, managers allow one variable to change while holding all others fixed, and they recalculate the *NPV* based on that change. By repeating this process for all the uncertain variables in an *NPV* calculation, managers can see how sensitive the *NPV* is to changes in baseline assumptions.

Imagine that Greene Transportation Incorporated (GTI) has developed a new skateboard equipped with a gyroscope for improved balance. GTI's estimates indicate that this project has a positive *NPV* of $236,000 under the following base-case assumptions:

1. The project's life is five years.
2. The project requires an up-front investment of $7 million.
3. GTI will depreciate the initial investment on a straight-line basis for five years.
4. One year from now, the skateboard industry will sell 500,000 units.
5. Total industry unit volume will increase by 5 percent per year.
6. GTI expects to capture 5 percent of the market in the first year.
7. GTI expects to increase its market share by one percentage point each year after year 1.
8. The selling price will be $200 in year 1.
9. The selling price will decline by 10 percent per year after year 1.
10. All production costs are variable and will equal 60 percent of the selling price.
11. GTI's tax rate is 30 percent.
12. The appropriate discount rate is 14 percent.

Under the base-case assumptions, the project has a small (relative to the $7 million investment), positive *NPV*, but GTI managers may want to explore how sensitive the *NPV* is to changes in the assumptions. Analysts often begin a sensitivity analysis by developing both pessimistic and optimistic forecasts for each of the model's important assumptions. These forecasts may be based on subjective judgments about the range of possible outcomes, or on historical data drawn from the firm's past investments. For example, a firm with historical data available on output prices might set the pessimistic and optimistic forecasts at one standard deviation below and above their expected price.

Table 9.4 shows pessimistic and optimistic forecasts for several of the *NPV* model's key assumptions. Next to each assumption is the project *NPV* that results

Table 9.4
Sensitivity Analysis of the Gyroscope Skateboard Project (dollar values in thousands except price)

NPV	Pessimistic	Assumption	Optimistic	NPV
−$558	$8,000	Initial investment	$6,000	$1,030
−$343	450,000 units	Market size in year 1	550,000 units	$815
−$73	2% per year	Growth in market size	8% per year	$563
−$1,512	3%	Initial market share	7%	$1,984
−$1,189	0%	Growth in market share	2% per year	$1,661
−$488	$175	Initial selling price	$225	$960
−$54	62% of sales	Variable costs	58% of sales	$526
−$873	−20% per year	Annual price change	0% per year	$1,612
−$115	16%	Discount rate	12%	$617

from changing one and only one assumption from the base-case scenario. For example, if GTI can sell its product for $225 rather than $200 per unit the first year, the project *NPV* increases to $960,000. If, however, the selling price is less than expected, say $175 per unit, the project *NPV* declines to −$488,000. A glance at Table 9.4 reveals that small deviations in market-share assumptions generate very large *NPV* changes, whereas changes in market-size figures have less impact on *NPV*s.

SCENARIO ANALYSIS AND MONTE CARLO SIMULATION

Scenario analysis is just a more complex variation on sensitivity analysis. Rather than adjust one assumption up or down, analysts conduct scenario analysis by calculating the project *NPV* when a whole set of assumptions changes in a particular way. For example, if consumer interest in GTI's new skateboard is low, the project may achieve a lower market share and a lower selling price than originally anticipated. If production volume falls short of expectations, cost as a percentage of sales may also be higher than expected.

Developing realistic scenarios requires a great deal of thinking about how an *NPV* model's assumptions are related to each other. Analysts must ask questions such as, if the market doesn't grow as fast as we expect, which other of our assumptions will also probably be wrong? As with sensitivity analysis, firms often construct a base-case scenario along with more optimistic and pessimistic ones. For instance, consider a worst-case scenario for GTI's new skateboard. Suppose that Murphy's Law kicks in and every pessimistic assumption from Table 9.4 becomes reality. In that case, the project *NPV* is a disastrous negative $4.9 million. On the other hand, if all the optimistic assumptions turn out to be correct, then the *NPV* rises to a positive $11.7 million. Neither of these outcomes is particularly surprising. If everything goes wrong, the company should expect an extremely negative *NPV*, and it should expect just the opposite if the project does better than predicted in every possible way. These scenarios are still useful in that they illustrate the range of possible *NPV*s.

An even more sophisticated variation on this theme is Monte Carlo simulation. In a **Monte Carlo simulation,** analysts specify a range or a distribution of potential outcomes for each of the model's assumptions. For example, a simulation might specify that GTI's skateboard price is a random variable drawn from a normal distribution with a mean of $200 and a standard deviation of $30. Similarly, the analyst could dictate that the skateboard might achieve an initial market share anywhere between 1 percent and 10 percent, with each outcome being equally likely (i.e., a

uniform distribution). It is even possible to specify the degree of correlation between key variables. The model could be structured in such a way that when the demand for skateboards is unusually high, the likelihood of obtaining a high price increases.

Analysts enter all the assumptions about distributions of possible outcomes into a spreadsheet. Next, a simulation software package begins to take random "draws" from these distributions, calculating the project's cash flows (and perhaps its *NPV*) over and over again, perhaps thousands or tens of thousands of times. After completing these calculations, the software package produces a large amount of statistical output, including the distribution of project cash flows (and *NPV*s) as well as sensitivity figures for each of the model's assumptions.

The use of Monte Carlo simulation has grown dramatically in the last decade because of steep declines in the costs of computer power and simulation software.[11] Unfortunately, misuse of simulation analysis has grown as well.

Perhaps the most common misuse involves the calculation and misinterpretation of a distribution of project *NPV*s using the cost of capital. If managers use a computer to generate a distribution of *NPV*s, they should discount cash flows using the risk-free rate. Why not use the cost of capital? Remember that the purpose of discounting cash flows at the cost of capital is to take into account the uncertainty of expected project cash flows. When a simulation package calculates an *NPV*, the cash flows in the numerator represent just one outcome drawn from a large distribution of possible outcomes, not the expected value. Therefore, plotting an entire distribution of *NPV*s and looking at the mean and variance of that distribution is, in a sense, double counting risk. A better approach is to calculate *NPV*s using the risk-free rate. A distribution of *NPV*s generated by discounting at the risk-free rate is free of any prior risk adjustment, so the volatility of that distribution to some degree measures the risk of the project.

However, interpreting a distribution of *NPV*s calculated using the risk-free rate has its own problems. For example, if analysts look at the variance of such a distribution to draw inferences about risk, they ignore the opportunities of shareholders to eliminate some of the risk through diversification.[12] Moreover, the simulated distribution of one project's *NPV*s can be artificially reduced by joining one project with another and rerunning the simulation. If an examination of *NPV* distributions is part of a firm's project approval process, then employees will soon learn to propose joint projects that have less volatility than stand-alone investments.

The bottom line is that Monte Carlo simulation is a powerful, effective tool when used properly. Using simulation to explore the distribution of a project's cash flows, and the major sources of uncertainty driving that distribution, is very sensible, but be wary of distributions of *NPV*s produced by a simulation program.

DECISION TREES

Most important investment decisions involve much more complexity than simply forecasting cash flows, discounting at the appropriate rate, and investing if the *NPV* exceeds zero. In the real world, managers face a sequence of future decisions that

SMART PRACTICES VIDEO

Pam Roberts, Executive Director of Corporate Services, Cummins Inc.

"We recognize that we can't predict each parameter with great accuracy."

See the entire interview at **SMARTFinance**

[11.] Just a few of the companies that we know have used Monte Carlo simulation include Merck, Intel, Procter & Gamble, General Motors, Pfizer, Owens-Corning, and Cummins Engine. For an account of how Merck uses simulations, see Nichols (1994).

[12.] Note that calculating a single *NPV* using the *WACC* or another appropriate discount rate does not suffer from this problem because the discount rate selected depends on the project's beta, a measure of its systematic risk.

influence an investment's value. These decisions might include whether to expand or abandon a project, whether to alter a marketing program, when to upgrade manufacturing equipment, and, most important, how to respond to the actions of competitors. A **decision tree** is a visual representation of the choices that managers face over time with regard to a particular investment. Sketching out a decision tree is somewhat like thinking several moves ahead in a game of chess. The value of decision trees is that they force analysts to think through a series of "if-then" statements that describe how they will react as the future unfolds.

Imagine that Trinkle Foods Limited of Canada has invented a new salt substitute, branded Odessa, which it plans to sell in consumer snack foods such as potato chips and crackers. The company is trying to decide whether to spend 5 million Canadian dollars (C$) to test-market in Vancouver, British Columbia, a new line of potato chips flavored with Odessa. Depending on the outcome of that test, Trinkle may spend an additional C$50 million one year later to launch a full line of snack foods across Canada. If consumer acceptance in Vancouver is high, the company predicts that its full product line will generate net cash inflows of C$12 million per year for 10 years.[13] If consumers in Vancouver respond less favorably, Trinkle expects cash inflows from a nationwide launch to be just C$2 million per year for 10 years. Trinkle's cost of capital equals 15 percent.

Figure 9.3 shows the decision tree for this problem. Initially, the firm can choose to spend the C$5 million on test-marketing or not. If Trinkle goes ahead with the market test, it estimates the probability of high and low consumer acceptance to be 50 percent. After the company sees the test results, it will decide whether to invest C$50 million for a major product launch.

The proper way to work through a decision tree is to begin at the end and work backward to the initial decision. Suppose that one year from now Trinkle learns that

Figure 9.3
Decision Tree for Odessa
Investment

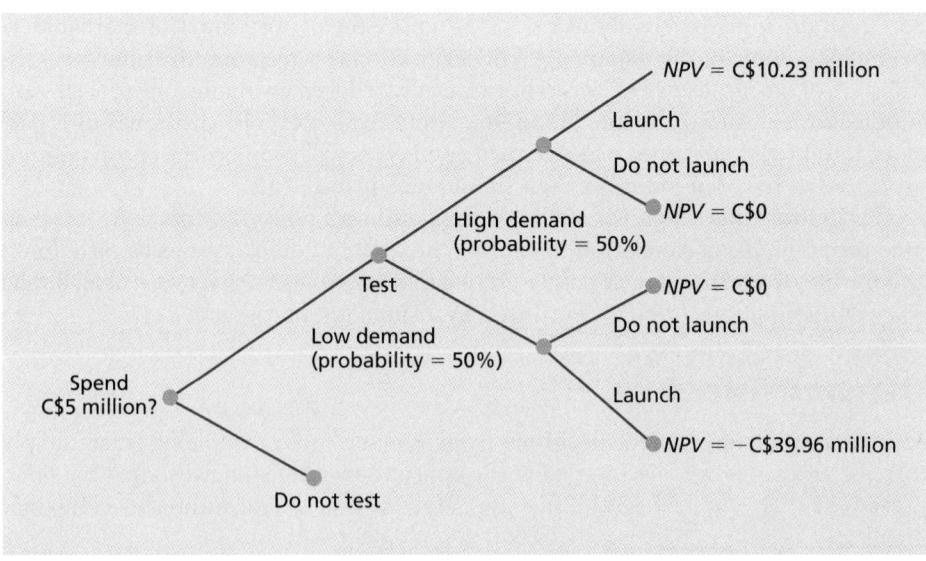

<hr />

13. Note that the test begins immediately, the C$50 million investment starts one year later, and the stream of C$12 million annual cash inflows begins one year after that.

the Vancouver market test was successful. At that point, the *NPV* (in millions of Canadian dollars) of launching the product can be determined as follows:

$$NPV = -C\$50 + \frac{C\$12}{1.15^1} + \frac{C\$12}{1.15^2} + \frac{C\$12}{1.15^3} + \cdots + \frac{C\$12}{1.15^{10}} = C\$10.23$$

Clearly, Trinkle will invest if it winds up in this part of the decision tree, but what if initial test results are unfavorable and it launches the product? In that situation, the following *NPV* (in millions of Canadian dollars) results:

$$NPV = -C\$50 + \frac{C\$2}{1.15^1} + \frac{C\$2}{1.15^2} + \frac{C\$2}{1.15^3} + \cdots + \frac{C\$2}{1.15^{10}} = -C\$39.96$$

The best decision to make if the initial test does not go well is to walk away. After the test has been done, its cost is a sunk cost. Therefore, as of time 1, the *NPV* of doing nothing is zero.

Now we have a set of simple "if-then" decision rules that come from the decision tree. If initial test results indicate high consumer acceptance of Odessa, Trinkle should go ahead with the full product launch to capture a positive *NPV* of C\$10.23 million. On the other hand, if initial results show that consumers do not particularly like foods flavored with Odessa, Trinkle should not invest the additional C\$50 million.

Finally, with this information in hand, we can evaluate today's decision about whether or not to spend the C\$5 million on testing. Recall that we calculated the *NPV*s in terms of year-1 dollars—that is, as of the date of the decision whether or not to launch the product nationwide. In terms of today's Canadian dollars (in millions), the expected *NPV* of conducting the market test is determined as follows:

$$NPV = -C\$5 + 0.5\left(\frac{C\$10.23}{1.15}\right) + 0.5\left(\frac{C\$0}{1.15}\right) = -C\$0.55$$

Spending the money for market testing does not appear to be worthwhile. However, there is a very subtle flaw in our analysis. Can you spot it? At the present time, when Trinkle must decide whether or not to invest in test-marketing, it does not know what the results of the test will be. One year later, when the firm chooses whether or not to invest C\$50 million for a major product launch, it knows a great deal more. If Odessa is a big success in Vancouver, the risk that it will flop elsewhere in Canada may be very low. If so, does it make sense to use a discount rate of 15 percent when calculating the *NPV* of the product launch decision? Even a one-point reduction in the discount rate from 15 percent to 14 percent would be sufficient to change Trinkle's decision about test-marketing.

Though decision trees are useful tools for sharpening strategic thinking, the previous example illustrates their most serious flaw. The risk of many investments changes as you move from one point in the decision tree to another. Worse, analysts have no obvious way to make adjustments to the discount rate to reflect these risk changes. That makes it very difficult to know whether the final *NPV* obtained from a decision tree is the correct one.

Another practical difficulty in using decision trees is determining the probabilities for each branch of the tree. Unless firms have a great deal of experience making similar "bets" over and over again, estimating these probabilities is more an art than a science. How does Trinkle Foods know that the probability of a successful Vancouver market test equals 50 percent? Why not 80 percent or 10 percent? The only way to form even remotely reliable estimates of these probabilities is to rely on experience—your experience or the experience of others. For example, large pharmaceutical companies have enough experience investing in potential drug compounds to make reasonable estimates of the odds that any particular drug will ever make it to market.

<table>
<tr>
<td>

Concept Review Questions

</td>
<td>

6. Why would a project that reaches the break-even point in terms of net income potentially be bad for shareholders?

7. Which variable do you think would be more valuable to examine in a project sensitivity analysis—the growth rate of sales or the allowable depreciation deductions each year? Explain.

8. You work for an airline that is considering a proposal to offer a new, nonstop flight between Atlanta and Tokyo. Senior management asks a team of analysts to run a Monte Carlo simulation of the project. Your job is to advise the group on what assumptions they should put in the simulation regarding the distribution of the ticket price your airline will be able to charge. How would you go about this task?

9. Why might the discount rate vary as you move through a decision tree?

</td>
</tr>
</table>

9.3 REAL OPTIONS

WHY *NPV* DOESN'T ALWAYS GIVE THE RIGHT ANSWER

Only a few decades ago, the net present value method was essentially absent from the world of corporate practice. Today it has become the standard tool for evaluating capital investments, especially in very large firms. Even so, *NPV* can systematically overstate or understate the value of certain types of investments. These systematic errors occur because the *NPV* method is essentially static. That is, *NPV* calculations do not take into account actions by managers to increase the value of an investment once it has been made. When managers can react to changes in the environment in ways that alter an investment's value, we say that the investment has an embedded **real option.** A real option is the right, but not the obligation, to take a future action that changes an investment's value. We will present an in-depth analysis of how option-pricing techniques can be used to improve capital budgeting processes in Chapters 18 and 19, so only an overview can be presented here. Hopefully, this will be enough to convince you that identifying and valuing—even if only conceptually—the real options embedded in most capital investment projects can help managers make better investment decisions.[14]

A simple example shows where *NPV* can go wrong. Suppose you are bidding on the rights to extract oil from a proven site over the next year. You expect extraction costs from this field to run about $50 per barrel. Currently, oil sells for $45 per barrel. You know that oil prices fluctuate over time, but you do not possess any unique ability to predict where the price of oil is headed next. Accordingly, you assume that the

---

[14.] Brennan and Schwartz (1985) wrote the pathbreaking paper showing how option-pricing concepts can be used to describe embedded real options. They apply option-pricing theory to the operation of a mine and describe optimal decision rules regarding when to open a closed mine or shut down a mine that is currently operating. Seventeen years later, Moel and Tufano (2002) showed that managers do indeed seem to make decisions about opening and closing mines in the manner predicted by Brennan and Schwartz.

price of oil follows a random walk, a term that means prices wander aimlessly, with no connection to past price changes and no tendency to return to a mean value over time. So your best estimate of the future price of oil is just today's price. How much would you bid?

An *NPV* analysis would tell you not to bid at all. If your best forecast of the future price of oil is $45 per barrel, then you cannot make money when extraction costs are $50 per barrel. The expected *NPV* of this investment is negative no matter how much oil you can pump out of the ground.

A real options approach to the problem yields a different answer. If you own the rights to extract oil, you are not obligated to do so without regard to the price of your output. You reason that you will pump oil only when the market price is high enough to justify incurring the extraction costs. Predicting exactly when the price of oil will be high enough to make pumping profitable is impossible, but historical price fluctuations persuade you that the price of oil will be higher than extraction costs at least some of the time. Therefore, extraction rights at this site are worth more than zero.[15]

The oil-extraction problem is analogous to the test-marketing problem in the previous section. In both cases, managers have an option to choose to spend additional resources at a future date. These options add to a project's value in a way that *NPV* analysis, because of its static approach to decision making, cannot capture. In general, we can say that the value of a project equals the sum of two components—the part captured by *NPV* and the remaining value of real options.

Project value = *NPV* ± option value

The *NPV* may either understate or overstate a project's value, depending on whether the proposed investment creates or destroys future options for the firm. In the oil drilling example, buying extraction rights creates an option, the option to pump or not to pump oil in the future, and the *NPV* understates the investment's value. It is easy to imagine projects that eliminate options rather than create them. For instance, if the firm signs a long-term contract to supply a refinery with a certain quantity of crude oil each month, then it loses flexibility in the extraction decision.

Like Monte Carlo simulation, real options analysis is growing in popularity in many industries. We defer a full-blown discussion of the real options approach to capital budgeting to a later chapter. Instead, we now turn to a description of common types of real options encountered in capital budgeting decisions.

TYPES OF REAL OPTIONS

Expansion Options. What do companies do when one of their investments becomes a huge success? They look for new markets in which to expand that investment. For instance, DVD technology has gained enormous popularity so that now consumers can rent DVDs in video stores, grocery stores, and many other places where they were previously unavailable. The same is true for DVD players. The number of retail outlets selling DVD players has expanded dramatically. It is even possible in many major airports to rent a DVD player and a movie to watch during your flight.

Naturally, companies invest in expansion only for their most successful investments. As mentioned in the decision-tree problem, the risk of expanding an already successful project is much less than the risk when the project first begins. An *NPV*

---

[15] To determine exactly how much these rights are worth, we have to use techniques covered in later chapters.

calculation misses both of these attributes—the opportunity to expand or not depending on initial success, and the change in risk that occurs when the initial outcome is favorable.

Abandonment Options. Just as firms have the right to invest additional resources to expand projects that enjoy early success, they also may withdraw resources from projects that fail to live up to short-run expectations. In an extreme case, a firm may decide to withdraw its entire commitment to a particular project and exercise its *option to abandon.*

In legal systems that provide limited liability to corporations, shareholders have the ultimate abandonment option. A firm may borrow money to finance its operations, but if it cannot generate cash flow sufficient to pay back its debts, shareholders can declare bankruptcy and turn over the company's assets to lenders and walk away. Though declaring bankruptcy is not what shareholders hope for when they invest, it offers shareholders considerable protection against personal liability for a firm's debts. Put another way, investors who buy shares are willing to pay a little more because of the option to abandon (in this case, the *default option*) than they would be willing to pay without that option.

Share value = *NPV* + value of default option

Consider the same situation from the perspective of lenders. When they commit funds to a corporation, lenders know that the borrower may default and their ability to recover their losses does not extend to shareholders' personal assets. We could even say that when an investor buys a bond from a corporation, the investor is simultaneously selling an option to the firm—the option to default. Notice that this option to default is essentially absent in U.S. Treasury securities. Suppose that a Treasury bond and a corporate bond offer the same interest payments to investors. Which one would sell at a higher price?

Corporate bond value = Treasury bond value − value of firm's default option

Abandonment options crop up in expected places, and it is important for managers to recognize whether a given investment has an attached abandonment option or grants another party the right to abandon. Consider refundable and nonrefundable airline tickets. With a refundable ticket, the traveler has the right to abandon travel plans without incurring a penalty. Such a ticket is more valuable than one that requires a traveler to pay a penalty if plans change.

Follow-on Investment Options. A follow-on investment option is similar to an expansion option. It entitles a firm to make additional investments should earlier investments prove to be successful. The difference between this and the expansion option is that the subsequent investments are more complex than a simple expansion of the earlier ones.

Hollywood offers an excellent example of follow-on options. Did you know that the rights to movie sequels are sometimes bought and sold before the original movie is completed? By purchasing the right to produce a sequel, a studio obtains the opportunity to make an additional investment should the first film become a commercial success.

Flexibility Options. The final types of options that have recently come to prominence in capital budgeting analyses are collectively known as flexibility options. Three examples illustrate the nature of flexibility options. First, Kulatilaka (1993) describes how the ability to use multiple production inputs creates option value. An example of this *input flexibility* is a boiler that can switch between oil or gas as a fuel source, enabling managers to switch from one type of fuel to another as prices change. Second, Trigeorgis and Mason (1987), Triantis and Hodder (1990), and Baldwin and Clark (1992) demonstrate the value of a flexible production technology capable of producing (and switching between) a variety of outputs using the same basic plant and equipment. This type of *output/operating flexibility* creates value when output prices are volatile.

Finally, McLaughlin and Taggart (1992) and Kogut and Kulatilaka (1994) document the option value of maintaining excess production capacity that managers can utilize quickly to meet peaks in demand. Though costly to purchase and maintain, this *capacity flexibility* can be quite valuable in capital-intensive industries subject to wide swings in demand and long lead times for building new capacity. Kogut and Kulatilaka's paper is especially important because it studies the profit opportunities a multinational company can employ if it has the excess capacity needed to move production around the world in response to real exchange rate movements.

THE SURPRISING LINK BETWEEN RISK AND REAL OPTION VALUES

Up to now, every valuation problem covered in this text satisfies the following statement: Holding other factors constant, an increase in an asset's risk decreases its price. If two bonds offer the same coupon, but investors perceive one to be riskier than the other, the safer bond will sell at a higher price. If two investment projects have identical cash flows, but one is riskier, analysts will discount the cash flows of the riskier project at a higher rate, resulting in a lower *NPV*.

A surprising fact is that this relationship does not hold for options. For an explanation, we go back to the oil-extraction problem. The current price of oil is $45 per barrel, and extraction costs at a particular site are $50. The expected future price of oil is the same as the current price, so an *NPV* calculation would say that this investment is worthless.

Consider two different scenarios regarding the future price of oil. In the low-risk scenario, the price of oil in the future will be $49 or $41, each with probability of one-half. This means that the expected price of oil is still $45. However, both an *NPV* and an options analysis would conclude that bidding on the rights to this site is not a good idea because the price of oil will never be above the extraction cost.

Next, think about the high-risk scenario. The price of oil may be $60 or $30 with equal probability, so again we have an expected price of $45. If the price turns out to be $30, extracting the oil clearly does not make sense. But if the price turns out to be $60, extracting oil generates a profit of $10 per barrel. Therefore, a real options analysis would say that bidding at least a little for the right to extract the oil is a sensible decision.

Why does more risk lead to higher option values? Notice in the two previous scenarios that the payoff from extracting oil equals zero whether the price of oil falls to $41 or all the way to $30. At either price, an oil producer would simply decline to incur extraction costs. A huge decline in the price of oil is no more costly than a small decline. On the other hand, the payoffs on the upside increase, the higher the price of oil goes. In other words, options are characterized by asymmetric payoffs. When the price of oil is extremely volatile, the potential benefits if prices rise are quite large. At the same time, if oil prices fall precipitously, there is no additional cost relative to a slight decline in prices. In either case, the payoff is zero.

SMART PRACTICES VIDEO

Andy Bryant, Executive Vice President of Finance and Enterprise Systems, Chief Financial Officer, Intel Corp.

"Option theory was always used to show why we should do something. I never saw an analysis that said why we should not do something."

See the entire interview at **SMARTFinance**

10. Give a real-world example of an expansion option and an abandonment option.

11. We know that riskier firms must pay higher interest rates when they borrow money. Explain this using the language of real options.

9.4 STRATEGY AND CAPITAL BUDGETING

COMPETITION AND *NPV*

Finance textbooks tend to focus on the mechanics of project evaluation—how to calculate an *NPV* or *IRR,* how to estimate cash flows, how to select the right discount rate, and so on. This emphasis on technique is not entirely misplaced. Knowing how to apply quantitative discipline to the project selection process is very important. Nevertheless, experienced managers rarely make major investment decisions solely on the basis of *NPV* calculations. The best managers have a well-honed intuition that tells them why a particular project would or would not be a good investment. Their business acumen helps them to recognize projects that will create shareholder value, even if the *NPV* numbers from financial analysts are negative, and to avoid investments that will destroy value, even when the *NPV* calculations are positive.[16]

No textbook can adequately substitute for the invaluable experience of making many investment decisions over several years, watching some of them succeed and some of them fail. However, there are certain common characteristics shared by projects that enhance shareholder value, and in this section we give you some guidance on how to identify these characteristics.

Recall some of the most basic lessons from microeconomics about a perfectly competitive market. In such a market, there are many buyers and sellers trading a homogeneous product or service. Because every agent in the market is small relative to the market as a whole, everyone behaves as a price taker. Competition and the lack of entry or exit barriers for sellers ensures that the product's market price equals the marginal cost of producing it, and no firm earns pure economic profit.[17] In a market with zero economic profits, the *NPV* of any investment equals zero because every project earns just enough to recover the cost of capital: no more and no less.

Therefore, if we want to form an intuitive judgment about whether or not an investment proposal should have a positive *NPV* (before actually calculating the *NPV*), we have to identify ways in which the project deviates from the perfectly competitive ideal. For instance, if the proposal calls for production of a new good, is there something about this good that clearly differentiates it from similar goods already in the market? If the new product is genuinely unique, will the firm producing this good be able to erect some kind of entry barrier that will prevent other firms from producing

---

[16.] One of the authors of this textbook had a humbling (but also awe-inspiring) lesson in the intuitive powers of good managers. On a consulting assignment for a Fortune 100 corporation, the author was asked to evaluate the assumptions of a firm's *NPV* calculations for a major acquisition. After gathering thousands of data points and running a week or two of simulations, the author was prepared to present his work to the chief financial officer (CFO). "From my work, I can tell you what the probability is that this acquisition will ever be profitable for your company," claimed the intrepid author. "But I already know that," the CFO responded. In a fit of hubris, the author challenged, "OK, tell me what you think that probability is." After hearing the CFO's response, the author had to admit that after several weeks of work, he had arrived at exactly the same probability estimate that the CFO had reached intuitively.

[17.] Remember that the notion of "economic profit" is very different from accounting profit. If a firm makes a zero economic profit, it earns just enough to pay competitive prices for the labor and capital that it employs to produce a good or service.

their own nearly identical versions of the product, thereby competing away any pure economic profits?

Competitive advantages of this sort can come in many forms. One firm may have superior engineering or R&D talent that generates a continuous stream of innovative products. Another may excel at low-cost manufacturing processes. Still another may create a sustainable competitive advantage through its unique marketing programs. The main point is that if any project is to have a positive NPV, advocates of that project ought to be able to articulate the project's competitive advantage even before "running the numbers." No matter how positive the project's NPV appears to be on paper, if no one can explain its main competitive advantage in the market, the firm should probably think twice about investing. Similarly, when an investment proposal has a compelling story explaining its competitive edge but the NPV numbers come out negative, it may be worth sending the financial analysts back to their desks to take a second look at their assumptions.[18]

SMART ETHICS VIDEO

Jon Olson, Vice President of Finance, Intel Corp. (former). Currently, Chief Financial Officer, Xilinx Corp.

"Our job at the company is to test the limits, not just create financial analysis that ratifies peoples' intuition."

See the entire interview at **SMARTFinance**

STRATEGIC THINKING AND REAL OPTIONS

We conclude this chapter with a return to the topic of real options. The technical aspects of calculating the real option value of a given project (which we cover later in this book) can be quite complex. Real options techniques are still relatively new and are used extensively by only a handful of firms in a few industries. Though we expect an increasing number of firms to include real options analysis as part of their standard capital budgeting approach, we claim that just thinking about a project from a real options perspective can be valuable, even if coming up with a dollar value for a real option proves to be elusive.

Investments generally have real option value as long as they are not "all-or nothing" bets. Almost all investments fit this description. Managers usually have opportunities subsequent to the initial investment to make decisions that can increase or decrease the value of the investment. These decisions can create (or perhaps destroy) an investment's option value. To maximize an investment's option value, or at least to recognize that value, managers should try to describe up front, before the firm commits to an investment, all the subsequent decisions they will make as events unfold. In other words, managers must articulate their strategy for a given investment. This strategy will consist of a series of statements like these:

- If sales in the first year exceed our expectations, then we will commit another $50 million to ramp up production.
- If consumers enjoy sending and receiving e-mail on their cell phones, then we will be prepared to invest additional resources so that our cell phones will be capable of performing other tasks on the Internet.
- If our MP3 player cannot hold as many songs as the leading model, the unit must weigh at least one ounce less than the market leader, or we will not commit the resources necessary to manufacture it.

This series of "if-then" statements is necessary to value a real option, but it also has intangible value in that it forces managers to think through their strategic options before they invest. Identifying a real option is tantamount to identifying future

---

[18.] We want to emphasize here that we still believe the numbers are extremely important. Our point is that the numbers and the intuition should line up. When they are in conflict, managers need to think hard about whether the NPV model is in error or whether the project lacks a true competitive advantage. These conflicts can also result from human factors as explained in Chapter 8, Section 8.5.

points at which it may be possible for managers to create and sustain competitive advantages.

12. Why must manager intuition be part of the investment decision process regardless of a project's *NPV* or *IRR*? Why is it helpful to think about real options when making an investment decision?

9.5 SUMMARY

- All-equity firms can discount their "standard" investment projects at the cost of equity. Managers can estimate the cost of equity using the CAPM.
- The cost of equity is influenced by a firm's operating leverage as well as its financial leverage.
- Firms with both debt and equity in their capital structures can discount their "standard" investments using the weighted average cost of capital, or *WACC*.
- The *WACC* equals the weighted average of the cost of each source of financing used by a firm, with the weights equal to the proportion of the market value of each source of financing.
- The *WACC* and the CAPM are connected in that the cost of debt and equity (and any other financing source) are driven by the betas of the firm's debt and equity.
- When a firm wants to make an "unusual" investment—an investment outside its normal line of business—it should try to estimate the asset beta for this industry using pure play firms.
- To estimate the asset beta for a different industry, analysts first must unlever the equity beta of the pure play firm that uses debt. Then the analyst must relever the industry asset's beta based on his firm's existing capital structure.
- A variety of tools exist to assist managers in understanding the sources of uncertainty of a project's cash flows. These include break-even analysis, sensitivity analysis, scenario analysis, Monte Carlo simulation, and decision trees.
- The value of many investments includes not just the *NPV*, but also the investment's option value. As a static analytical tool, *NPV* misses the value of management's ability to alter an investment's value in response to environmental changes that may occur after an investment is made.
- Types of real options include the option to expand, the option to abandon, the option to make follow-on investments, and flexibility options.
- An investment's option value, unlike its *NPV*, increases as risk increases.
- For an investment to have a positive *NPV*, it should have a competitive advantage, something that distinguishes it from the economic ideal of perfect competition.
- Valuing an investment's option value requires strategic thinking. Articulating the strategy may be as important as calculating the option value.

INTERNET RESOURCES

Note: *For updates to links, please go to the book's website at http://smart.swlearning.com.*

http://www.quicken.com—Contains information relevant to calculating the *WACC*, including equity betas, total market value of equity, and debt/equity ratios http://valuation.ibbotson.com—A fee-based site with cost-of-capital estimates for more than 300 industries

http://www.stern.nyu.edu /_adamodar—Website of NYU professor Aswath Damodaran; contains downloadable data sets with levered and unlevered industry betas as well as industry- level estimates of the cost of capital

KEY TERMS

asset beta
break-even analysis
contribution margin
debt beta
decision tree
financial leverage
Monte Carlo simulation
operating leverage

pure play
random walk
real option
scenario analysis
sensitivity analysis
unlevered equity beta
weighted average cost of capital (*WACC*)

QUESTIONS

9-1.   Why is it important for the project not to alter the firm's risk profile in order to use the firm's beta for the project's discount rate?

9-2.   Does the tax rate affect a firm's operating leverage?

9-3.   Explain when firms should discount projects using the cost of equity. When should they use the *WACC* instead? When should they use neither?

9-4.   If a firm takes actions that increase its operating leverage, we might expect to see an increase in its equity beta. Why?

9-5.   Suppose two computer manufacturers produce and sell very similar machines. One company sells its computers through nationwide electronics chain stores, and the other sell via its own network of stores. Which of these sales/distribution strategies results in higher operating leverage?

9-6.   Why do you think it is important to use the market values of debt and equity rather than book values to calculate a firm's *WACC*?

9-7.   Assuming that there are no corporate income taxes, what is the connection between a firm's *WACC* and its asset beta?

9-8.   What is the relationship between the size of a firm's debt beta and the total amount of debt the firm borrows?

9-9.   Suppose that two firms have identical asset betas but very different equity betas. Why might this be so?

9-10.   Many high-tech companies use the following compensation strategy to attract key talent: They offer a relatively low base salary (low relative to what employees with a given level of experience and training might earn in another industry), but they augment this below-market salary with large incentive-pay packages including cash bonuses and stock options. Presumably, there is a trade-off at work in the labor market such that high-tech firms could attract the same employees by offering a higher base and lower incentive pay. Which of these two strategies would lead to a higher stock beta, assuming other factors are held constant?

9-11. What is the relationship between the equity risk premium and the aggregate value of the stock market? If the equity risk premium declined suddenly (holding all other factors constant), what would happen to the value of the stock market?

9-12. In what sense could one argue that if managers make decisions using break-even analysis, they are not maximizing shareholder wealth? How can break-even analysis be modified to solve this problem?

9-13. Explain the differences between *sensitivity analysis* and *scenario analysis*. Offer an argument for the proposition that scenario analysis offers a more realistic picture of a project's risk than sensitivity analysis does.

9-14. In Chapter 8, we discussed how one might calculate the *NPV* of earning an MBA. Suppose you are asked to do a sensitivity analysis on the MBA decision. Which of the following factors do you think would have the greatest impact on the degree's *NPV*?

   a. The ranking of the school you choose to attend
   b. Your choice of a major
   c. Your GPA
   d. The state of the job market when you graduate

9-15. Suppose that you wanted to model the value of an MBA degree with decision trees. What would such a decision tree look like?

9-16. If you decide to invest in an MBA, what is your abandonment option? Your follow on investment option?

9-17. Your company is selling the mineral rights to several hundred acres of land it owns that are believed to contain silver deposits. The current price of silver is $5 per ounce, but of course, future prices are uncertain. Would you expect the mineral rights to sell for more or less if investors believe that silver prices will be more volatile in the future than they have been in the past? Explain.

9-18. Why might an oil company lease land with reserves that will cost $55.00 a barrel to extract when the current price of oil is $52.50 a barrel (assume the price of oil is fairly volatile)?

PROBLEMS

Choosing the Right Discount Rate

9-1. Puritan Motors has a capital structure consisting almost entirely of equity.

   a. If the beta of Puritan stock equals 1.6, the risk-free rate equals 6 percent, and the expected return on the market portfolio equals 11 percent, what is the cost of equity?

   b. Suppose that a 1 percent increase in expected inflation causes a 1 percent increase in the risk-free rate. Holding all other factors constant, what will this do to the firm's cost of equity? Is it reasonable to hold all other factors constant? What other part of the calculation of the cost of equity is likely to change if expected inflation rises?

9-2. Download historical stock-price data for the pharmaceutical industry giant, Merck (ticker symbol MRK). Be sure to check the box indicating that you want monthly data, and use September 1, 1996, as your start date and September 1, 2005, as your end date.

Retrieve data from Yahoo! and download it into an Excel spreadsheet (the file downloads in comma delimited format with a .csv file extension, but once you have the data, save it as an Excel file with the familiar .xls file extension). Repeat this process using exactly the same settings (e.g., monthly data using the same starting and ending dates) and the ticker symbol SPY, which stands for Standard & Poor's Depository Receipts (SPDRs), commonly called *Spiders*. Returns on SPDRs will closely approximate returns on the S&P 500 index, our proxy for the market portfolio in this problem.

a. Calculate the monthly return on Merck by dividing the adjusted closing price in any particular month by the adjusted closing price the previous month and subtracting 1. This should yield 71 monthly returns for Merck (you can calculate returns in only 71 of the 72 months because of the need to have the previous month's price to calculate the current month's return).

b. Calculate the monthly return on the S&P 500 Index the same way. Paste the returns on the S&P and the returns on Merck into a single spreadsheet (use the "Paste-Special-Values" sequence in Excel).

c. You will run a regression in Excel using the returns on Merck as the dependent, or *Y* variable, and returns on the S&P 500 as the independent, or *X* variable. There are two ways to do this. You can use the data analysis function under the tools menu (you may have to first click "Add ins" under the tools menu and then check the box labeled "Analysis ToolPak"). Click "Tools—Data Analysis Regression" to set up the regression. Type in the cell range containing Merck returns for the input *Y* range, and type in the cell range containing the S&P returns for the input *X* range.

(The other way to estimate a regression in Excel is to use the "_linest function." We refer the reader to Excel's help feature for more information on that function.)

The figure to the right of the label "*X* Variable 1" is the slope of the regression line, and it represents Merck's equity beta. Does it surprise you that Merck would have an equity beta less than 1.0? What economic rationale can you give for this finding?

d. Suppose the risk-free rate is 5 percent and the expected return on the market is 10 percent. What is Merck's cost of equity? Assuming Merck's capital structure is virtually 100 percent equity, what is its *WACC*?

e. Now go back and repeat the steps necessary to download monthly data for General Electric (ticker symbol, GE). Calculate monthly returns on GE stock as before, pair them up with monthly returns on the S&P 500 Index, and using regression analysis, estimate GE's beta. Given that GE is a highly diversified conglomerate, what would you expect GE's beta to be before estimating it? Does your estimate confirm your intuition?

Operating and Financial Leverage

9-3. In its 2001 annual report, The Coca-Cola Company reported sales of $20.09 billion for fiscal year 2001, and $19.89 billion for fiscal year 2000. The company also reported operating income (roughly equivalent to *EBIT*) of $5.35 billion and $3.69 billion in 2001 and 2000, respectively. Meanwhile, arch-rival PepsiCo, Inc. reported sales of $26.94 billion in 2001, and $25.48 billion in 2000. PepsiCo's operating profit was $4.03 billion in 2001 and $3.82 billion in 2000. Based on these figures, which company had higher operating leverage?

9-4. Suppose a firm's EBIT increases by 12% after sales change from $2.3 million to $2.507 million. What is the firm's operating leverage? If the firm's sales increase to $2.7577 million with EBIT increasing by only 11%, what is the new operating leverage for the firm?

SMART SOLUTIONS
See the problem and solution explained step-by-step at

SMARTFinance

9-5. A firm has no debt and a tax rate of 40%. If the net income changes from $2.5 million to $2.75 million based on a net profit margin of 10% (see Chapter 2), what is the firm's operating leverage? Suppose the net profit margin goes down to 9% when the net income increases to $2.75 million. What is the new operating leverage?

9-6. Firm QTP has fixed costs of $5.2 million with variable costs of $295.00 per unit. If each unit sells for $450.00, what is QTP's breakeven point? Currently, QTP sells 32,000 units per year, but QTP believes 60,000 units per year can be sold if the selling price is lowered to $385 per unit. What is the operating leverage for QTP and what is its new breakeven point?

9-7. Firm ARN has assets worth $6.9 million. Two million dollars is financed with debt that costs 10% a year in interest. If ARN's contribution margin is $175.00 per unit, how many units must be sold to cover the interest payments? If ARN sells 2,500 units this year, how much return on a pretax basis (i.e., return based on earnings prior to taxes) do shareholders earn? How much pretax return would the shareholders receive if ARN had no debt?

9-8. Firms A and B have the same asset base of $65 million. Firm A has $20 million of debt that costs 8% annually in interest. Firm B has $10 million in debt that costs 7% interest annually. Determine the shareholder pretax return (i.e., return based on earnings prior to taxes) for both firms based on EBIT values of $0.5 million, $1.0 million, $1.6 million, $3.2 million, and $6.8 million. If Firm C has assets identical to Firms A and B, but has no debt, at what EBIT levels do Firm C's shareholders have an advantage over Firm A's and B's shareholders, based on pretax return?

Choosing the Right Discount Rate

9-9. A firm has an equity multiplier of 2.0 (see Chapter 2). The firm's debt pays 12% interest annually and common shareholders demand an 18% return. Assuming a 34% tax rate, what is the weighted average cost of capital ($WACC$) for the firm? Suppose 5% of the firm is funded with preferred stock with a return of 15%. The preferred stock and the common stock still maintain an equity multiplier of 2.0. What is the $WACC$ of the firm when considering the preferred stock as well?

9-10. A firm has a debt-to-equity ratio of 1.0. Assuming the firm's debt pays 11% interest annually, the equity has a 19% annual return, and the tax rate is 40%, what is the firm's weighted average cost of capital ($WACC$)?

9-11. A firm has an asset base of $5.3 million, of which $2.5 million was purchased with bonds. If $0.2 million is paid in interest annually and the shareholders expect a 16% annual return, what is the weighted average cost of capital ($WACC$) assuming no corporate taxes? What is the $WACC$ if corporate taxes are 45%?

9-12. The risk-free rate equals 5 percent, and the expected risk premium on the market portfolio equals 6 percent. A particular company has bonds outstanding that offer investors a yield to maturity of 6.5 percent. What is the debt beta?

9-13. The risk-free rate equals 5 percent, and the expected risk premium on the market portfolio equals 6 percent. A particular company has bonds outstanding that offer investors a yield to maturity of 6.5 percent. The company also has common stock outstanding (with market value equal to its bonds outstanding) with an expected return of 15 percent. What is the firm's $WACC$? What is the beta of the firm's assets? You may assume there are no taxes.

9-14. A firm's assets have a beta of 1.0. Assuming that the debt beta equals 0.0 and that there are no taxes, calculate the firm's equity beta under the following assumptions:

a. The firm's capital structure is 100 percent equity.
b. The capital structure is 20 percent debt and 80 percent equity.

   c. The capital structure is 40 percent debt and 60 percent equity.
   d. The capital structure is 60 percent debt and 40 percent equity.
   e. The capital structure is 80 percent debt and 20 percent equity.

Do you believe that the assumption of a zero debt beta is equally valid for each of these capital structures? Why or why not?

9-15. A diversified firm with investments in many industries is considering investing in the fast-food industry. By looking at data on publicly traded fast-food companies, an analyst discovers the following information for McDonald's Corporation and Wendy's International Inc.

- The expected return on the market portfolio is 10 percent.
- The debt beta for McDonald's and Wendy's is zero.
- The corporate tax rate is 34 percent.
- The equity betas are 0.8 for Wendy's and 1.0 for McDonald's.
- Wendy's has a debt-to-equity ratio of 0.15, and McDonald's has a ratio of 0.25.
- The risk-free rate is 5 percent.

Calculate the asset beta for McDonald's and Wendy's, and illustrate how these could be used to calculate the discount rate for an investment in the fast-food business.

9-16. The market portfolio has an expected return of 9%, and the risk-free rate is 3%. A firm's debt pays interest of 6%, and its equity has an expected return of 12%. Assuming a debt ratio of 60% and a tax rate of 42%, what is the firm's weighted average cost of capital ($WACC$)? What is the beta for the $WACC$? Does the beta for the $WACC$ equal: $[D/(E + D)]*(1 - T_C)*$(debt beta) $+ [E/(E + D)]*$(equity beta)? Does the answer to the previous question change if corporate taxes are set to zero?

9-17. The market portfolio has a risk premium of 8%, and the risk-free rate is 4%. Assuming a firm's debt pays 6% interest, what is the debt beta? The firm also has stock with an expected return of 14%. What is the equity beta? Assuming the firm has equal amounts of debt and equity and the tax rate is 34%, what is the firm's weighted average cost of capital ($WACC$)? Demonstrate numerically that the beta for the WACC is equivalent to: $[D/(E + D)]*(1 - T_C)*$(debt beta) $+ [E/(E + D)]*$(equity beta) $- \{[D/(E + D)]*$(risk-free rate)$*T_C \div$ (market premium)$\}$.

9-18. Firm BNT's stock currently sells for $14.17, with a current dividend of $0.65. Assuming BNT's return on equity (ROE) is 12%, and the retention ratio is 75% (see Chapter 4 to determine how this information is used to calculate a growth rate), what is the discount rate implied from this stock price?

9-19. Firm ASF expects to distribute a dividend of $0.77 (up from $0.70). The current price of ASF stock is $15.40. What is the implied discount rate based on the stock price? Assuming an expected market return of 18% and a risk-free rate of 3%, what is the beta associated with the implied discount rate? Assuming the firm has no debt and a 42% tax rate, what is the firm's equity beta (use Equation 9.6)?

9-20. A particular firm has an asset beta of 1.50 with a debt ratio of 60% and a tax rate of 30%. What is the equity beta for this firm (use Equation 9.6)? Based on this equity beta, what is the asset beta for a different firm with a debt ratio of 50% and a tax rate of 40% (use equation 9.6)?

9-21. The equity beta for a particular industry is 0.75 based on an expected market premium of 6% and a risk-free rate of 4%. Calculate the discount rates for the following three firms based on their debt ratio and tax rates (use Equation 9.6).

Firm A: 75% debt ratio and 35% tax rate
Firm B: 20% debt ratio and 38% tax rate
Firm C: 80% debt ratio and 45% tax rate

Recalculate the discount rates for the firms based on Equation 9.5.

9-22. A firm is to be analyzed using an equity beta for an industry that is comparable to the firm. The firm is funded half with debt and the appropriate tax rate is 30%. The equity beta for the industry is 1.10 based on a risk-free rate of 3% and a market premium of 5%. What is the appropriate discount rate for the firm under analysis? Later you find there has been a mistake and the equity beta for the industry is actually the asset beta for the industry. Based on a debt-to-equity ratio of 1.0 and a tax rate of 30%, what is the correct equity beta for the industry? What is the discount rate for the firm under analysis using the corrected equity beta?

A Closer Look at Risk

9-23. Alliance Pneumatic Manufacturing, a specialty machine-tool producer, has fixed costs of $200 million per year. Across all the firm's products, the average contribution margin equals $1,200. What is Alliance's break-even point in terms of units sold?

9-24. Turn to the figures in Table 9.4. Determine which of the following has the greater impact on the NPV of the gyroscope skateboard project—an increase in the selling price of 10 percent (compared to the base case), or an increase in the size of the market of 10 percent in year 1.

9-25. T. Nixon Enterprises (TNXN) sells its product for $3.99 per unit. The product costs $1.42 per unit to produce, not including any fixed costs. Assuming fixed costs of $4 million, what is the breakeven point? If TNXN projects sales of 1.5 million units at the current price, will TNXN be profitable? TNXN is considering lowering the unit price to $3.49, which would boost projected sales to 2.2 million units. Based on the breakeven point, is this a better option?

9-26. E. Craft Industries (ECR) is considering entry into a new market in which it believes it can sell 500,000 units of its product. Depending on where ECR chooses to manufacture the product, the fixed costs and the contribution margin will vary. Determine the profitability (i.e., units*contribution margin – fixed costs) of each manufacturing facility:

Facility X: $4.67 contribution margin with fixed costs of $2 million
Facility Y: $3.95 contribution margin with fixed cost of $1.7 million
Facility Z: $2.25 contribution margin with fixed costs of $1.2 million

Which facility should be used for manufacturing the product?

9-27. A project has a cost of $1.1 million and next year will generate either $2 million or $100,000.00 with equal probability. Assuming a 5% discount rate, what is the NPV of the project based on the expected cash flows next year (Hint: calculate the mean of the future cash flows)? If the firm could pay $50,000.00 today for an exclusive right to manufacture the product, this would allow the firm to make the $1.1 million investment under conditions of generating $2 million in cash flow, and not manufacture the product under the $100,000.00 cash flow scenario. Assess the NPV of this exclusive right to manufacture (a type of abandonment option allowing the firm to *not* manufacture under poor conditions) by calculating the profit under both cash flow scenarios:

a. $2 million less $1.1 million for the $2 million scenario
b. Zero for the $100,000.00 cash flow scenario (Note: there is an assumption that the firm can manufacture the product immediately and that manufacturing costs do not increase, which may not be realistic).
c. Should the firm pay $50,000.00 for the exclusive right to manufacture?

9-28. Calculate the operating leverage and financial leverage for Toys "R" Us, Inc. (ticker symbol, TOY) and FedEx Corp. (ticker symbol, FDX) for the last three years. Higher operating leverage and higher financial leverage lead to higher betas. Is this statement consistent with the betas calculated (in the ThomsonONE problem) in Chapter 6?

9-29. Using the equity beta reported on ThomsonONE, calculate, using Equation 9.5, the asset beta for International Paper Company (ticker symbol, IP) for the last three years. How has the asset beta changed over this time period?

MINI-CASE: COST OF CAPITAL AND PROJECT RISK

Cascade Water Company (CWC) currently has 30,000,000 shares of common stock outstanding, trading at a price of $42 per share. CWC also has 500,000 bonds outstanding that are currently trading at $923.38 per bond. CWC has no preferred stock outstanding and has an equity beta of 2.639. The risk-free rate is 3.5%, and the market is expected to return 12.52%.

CWC is considering adding a 'healthy' bottled water geared toward children to its product mix. The initial outlay for the project is expected to be $3,000,000, which will be depreciated using the straight-line method to a zero salvage value, and sales are expected to be 1,250,000 units per year at a price of $1.25 per unit. Variable costs are estimated to be $0.24 per unit, and fixed costs of the project are estimated at $200,000 per year. The project is expected to have a three-year life and a terminal value (excluding the operating cash flows in year three) of $500,000. CWC operates in a 34% marginal tax rate. For the purposes of this project, working capital effects will be ignored. Bottled water with a focus toward children is expected to have different risk characteristics from the firm's current products. As such, CWC has decided to use the 'pure play' approach to evaluate this project. After researching the market, CWC managed to find two 'pure-play' firms. The specifics for those two firms are:

Firm	Equity Beta	D/E	Tax Rate
Fruity Water	1.72	0.43	34%
Ladybug Drinks	1.84	0.35	36%

1. Determine the current weighted average cost of capital for CWC.

2. Determine the appropriate discount rate for the healthy bottled water project.

3. Should the firm undertake the healthy bottled water project? As part of your analysis, include a sensitivity analysis for sales price, variable costs, fixed costs, and unit sales at ±10%, 20%, and 30% from the base case. Also perform a scenario analysis assuming: the best case is to sell 2,500,000 units at a price of $1.24 each, with variable costs of production of $0.22 per unit; and the worst case scenario of selling only 950,000 units at a price of $1.32 per unit, with variable costs of production of $0.27 per unit.

PART 4: Capital Structure and Dividend Policy

The previous chapters provided a framework for deciding how a firm should invest its money. Next we examine the opposite side of that question: Can managers rely on valuation signals generated by the market to decide which investments to fund and which sources of capital to tap? How should managers finance the investments they undertake? Should managers pay for new investments by using cash the firm generates internally or should external sources of funds be tapped? Is it better to finance with equity or with debt? If the firm's investments are successful, should the company reward its shareholders by paying a dividend or should it repurchase shares instead? To answer these questions, managers should weigh the benefits and costs of alternative actions.

Chapter 10 asks whether financial markets are informationally efficient—do investors respond rationally to corporate information releases and do they accurately value corporate securities? These are vital questions for managers, because investment and financing actions will only increase firm value if markets are efficient. Recently, a new way of viewing how managers make decisions and how investors respond to news about these decisions has emerged. Chapter 10 presents the key managerial implications of this new worldview, known as behavioral finance, which asserts that markets are not always efficient and investors are not always fully rational.

Chapter 11 describes some of the trade-offs firms face when they choose between internal or external financing, or between debt and equity. The chapter explains how firms acquire the funds needed to finance investments. The difference between investment needs and internal financing is a firm's financial deficit, and corporations fund this financial deficit in different ways in different countries. American managers rely more on internal funding and external debt, while managers from other countries rely relatively more on loans from banks for their external funding needs.

In Chapters 12, 13, and 14, we explore whether managers can increase the value of a firm by financing its operations with an optimal mix of debt and equity. Chapter 12 first surveys actual capital structure practices and patterns observed around the world, and then presents modern finance's core theoretical model of capital structure choice. We then examine how including corporate and personal taxation changes the theory's prediction that capital structure choices cannot affect firm value. Chapter 13 shows how accounting for agency costs and bankruptcy costs can lead to a unique leverage level that maximizes firm value. Finally, Chapter 14 ties together capital budgeting and capital structure choices, and shows how managers can increase firm value by financing capital investment with the right mix of funds.

Chapter 15 examines the related question of how managers can affect the value of a firm through dividend policy. In Chapter 5, we presented a model that claimed that the value of any stock should equal the present value of all dividends the stock will pay through time (or more broadly, the value of all cash payments that the stock will make). The surprising message of this chapter is that—although dividends are clearly important—dividend policy may or may not affect the value of a firm.

377

Investors Applaud a CEO's Dismissal—By Purchasing the Wrong Stock!

The *efficient market hypothesis,* a focus of this chapter, predicts that financial markets rapidly and fully incorporate new information into asset prices. The stock market reaction to the news that Hewlett-Packard Company's board of directors had accepted CEO Carly Fiorina's "resignation" the morning of February 9, 2005, offered both support for and evidence contradicting market efficiency. The market's overall reaction to news of her departure was very positive: Investors bid up the stock price by 10 percent during the day—on trading volume twelve times higher than normal. Given that Ms. Fiorina's reign as CEO had been tumultuous, this rapid and enthusiastic response fully supported market efficiency.

That day, another stock also reacted positively to news of Ms. Fiorina's departure: In early morning trading, shares of the stock with NYSE ticker symbol HP surged by almost 3 percent. Once it became clear to uninformed investors that HP referred to the firm Helmerich and Payne Inc., rather than Hewlett-Packard (ticker symbol HPQ), the company's stock price dropped back below the previous day's close. The quick increase in the HP stock price contradicted market efficiency: Several investors had applauded the dismissal of an unloved CEO by purchasing shares of the wrong company's stock!

n this chapter, we turn our attention from product markets to purely financial ones and ask, "Can financing activities create value for a company in the same way that investment activities can?" Our study of capital budgeting implied that product markets are less than perfectly competitive, and observing real industries supports this conclusion. Many products are manufactured by relatively few companies, and firms invest in research and development only because they believe that R&D will give them sole access to new investment opportunities. Positive-*NPV* investment opportunities derive from these market imperfections.

Do financial markets offer financial managers the same positive-*NPV* investment opportunities as imperfectly competitive product markets? We will argue in this chapter that they usually do not, for several reasons. First, financial assets are much more similar to each other than are real assets. By comparing the prices of similar financial assets, investors can identify and exploit pricing discrepancies, ensuring that similar assets offer similar expected returns. Second, the sheer size and transparency of modern financial markets should make them more competitive than markets for goods and services. Prices of financial asset are set in large, competitive markets, governed by rules designed to maximize efficient trading.

An excellent example of the competitiveness of financial markets is the foreign exchange market. It is perhaps the closest thing to a perfectly competitive market in the world today. The trading volume in this market is over $1.9 trillion *per day*, with literally thousands of traders dealing in the largest currencies. The size, sophistication, and low trading costs of this market ensure that currencies will be perfect substitutes for each other. This means that if traders can exchange 1 U.S. dollar ($) for 2 Swiss francs (SF) or for 100 Japanese yen (¥), then SF1 must also be worth ¥50. If any deviation from this pricing relationship occurs, traders will observe and act on the deviation instantly. No comparable process ensures that the relative pricing of American, Swiss, and Japanese scientific instruments will be the same in all markets worldwide.

A third distinction between financial and real asset markets is that far more analysts study and report on financial assets. Perhaps several hundred business and professional reporters will comment on the technical merits of the products offered by large companies such as IBM, Shell Oil, or Toyota Motors. In contrast, thousands of financial analysts routinely evaluate the these companies' debt and equity securities. The rapid growth of electronic media has also hugely increased the volume of financial information available to investors. As the cost of accessing financial information has fallen, the demand for it has risen accordingly.

In summary, financial markets are larger and more efficient than product markets. Does this imply that there is no gain to be made from creative financing strategies? Not necessarily, but it does imply that there will be fewer opportunities to profit from clever financing strategies than from smart capital investment spending, and that the former will be generally less profitable. It also implies that those financial value-creating opportunities that do exist will involve searching out areas of financial markets that are less than perfectly competitive.

Concept Review Questions

1. Suppose that traders can exchange 1 U.S. dollar ($) for 2 Swiss francs (SF) or for 100 Japanese yen (¥). Explain how competition in financial markets ensures that SF1 will be worth ¥50. Then, describe a comparable process for a manufactured product, such as a machine tool. Which process seems more realistic?

2. Describe how the Internet might push the market for airline tickets closer to the theoretical ideal of perfect competition. How might the Internet have the same impact on the stock market?

10.1 WHAT IS AN EFFICIENT FINANCIAL MARKET?

DEFINITIONS OF EFFICIENCY

So far, we have couched our discussion of financial markets in terms of how competitive they are compared to product markets. Although this is obviously important, analysts and researchers are actually more interested in the informational efficiency of financial markets. **Informational efficiency** refers to the tendency for prices in a market to rapidly and fully incorporate new, relevant information. The concept of informational efficiency is somewhat different from more familiar economic notions of efficiency. **Allocative efficiency** means that markets channel resources to their most productive uses; **operational efficiency** determines whether markets produce outputs at the lowest possible cost. These are vital measures of the economic utility of markets. But for financial markets, informational efficiency is more important because it is more basic. Informationally-efficient capital markets incorporate all relevant information into financial asset prices, which in turn helps ensure that economically promising investments receive funding.[1]

The concept of informationally efficient capital markets is one of the most influential contributions that financial economics has made to modern economic thought. The **efficient markets hypothesis (EMH)**, as formally presented by Eugene Fama in 1970, has revolutionized financial thought, practice, and regulation.[2] The EMH asserts that financial asset prices fully reflect all available information. What do we mean by the phrase "all available information"? The answer to that question varies and defines three distinct versions of the efficient markets hypothesis, which we will discuss below.

The rest of Section 10.1 and all of Section 10.2 examine how the efficient markets hypothesis has affected modern financial practice. Section 10.2 discusses empirical tests of the EMH, and Section 10.3 presents the contrary evidence marshaled by researchers. In recent years, many of these scholars have advanced an alternative to market efficiency known as behavioral finance.

Behavioral finance asserts that because traders in financial markets are human beings, they are subject to all the foibles and fads that bedevil human judgment in other spheres of life. Moreover, behaviorists claim that human errors do not simply "cancel out" in markets. Instead, these errors cause prices to deviate far from "fundamental value" in ways that market competition does not eliminate, at least not immediately.

Here we present only a brief overview of the evidence for and against the EMH. The references in the text and footnotes will guide interested readers to academic sources and survey articles describing how the EMH has altered financial thought. It is a fascinating story.

[1.] Although these three forms of efficiency usually go hand in hand, a financial market *can* be operationally efficient without being informationally efficient, and vice versa. For example, a nation's banking system may extend credit to borrowers at a very low cost in terms of labor and overhead expense, yet still price the loans too high or too low based on the borrower's creditworthiness. The distinction between the informational and allocative efficiency of a financial market is less clear-cut. Even though a market must be informationally efficient to allocate capital to its most profitable use, the converse does not necessarily apply. The securities of a monopolist can be priced quite rationally in a financial market, offering investors only a normal return on their investments, even if the monopolist is earning very large economic profits.

[2.] This model's soul mate in economic thought, the *rational expectations hypothesis,* has transformed the way people view macroeconomic policymaking. Indeed, the worldwide adoption of market-oriented economic policies in the past 25 years is based on an intellectual acceptance of the idea that markets efficiently process information and then allocate resources to their best use (or at least, markets allocate capital more efficiently than do government bureaucrats).

THE THREE FORMS OF MARKET EFFICIENCY

The EMH presents three increasingly stringent definitions of efficiency, based on what information market prices reflect. As we discuss below, these are weak-form, semistrong-form, and strong-form efficiency.

Weak-Form Efficiency. In markets characterized by **weak-form efficiency**, asset prices incorporate all information from the historical record. In other words, prices in a weak-form efficient market incorporate all information about price trends or repeating patterns that occurred in the past. This proposition implies that trading strategies based on analyses of historical pricing trends or relationships cannot consistently yield market-beating returns.

Prices in a weak-form efficient market will be unpredictable and will change only in response to the arrival of new information. In technical terms, this means that prices follow a random walk.[3] As mentioned in the previous chapter, this deliciously descriptive phrase means that prices wander aimlessly, with no connection to past price changes and no tendency to return to a mean value over time.[4] Equation 10.1 expresses this idea mathematically: the expected price of an asset next period, $E(P_t)$, is equal to today's price, P_0, plus a random error, e_t, which has an expected value of zero.

$$E(P_t) = P_0 + e_t \qquad \textbf{(Eq. 10.1)}$$

A modified version of the random walk model recognizes that stock prices do not move entirely at random. Rather, prices move randomly around a long-term trend, since part of a stock's long-term expected return will come from price appreciation. For stock that pays no dividends, we can express this "random walk with drift" mathematically as follows:

$$E(\Delta P_t) = E(R) + e_t \qquad \textbf{(Eq. 10.1a)}$$

where $E(\Delta P_t)$ is the expected price change next period, $E(R)$ is the expected return, and e_t is again a random-error term.

Semistrong-Form Efficiency. The second form of market efficiency is **semistrong-form efficiency**. This version of the EMH asserts that asset prices incorporate *all publicly available information*. The key point about this form of efficiency is that it requires only that prices reflect information that can be gleaned from *public* sources (e.g., newspapers, press releases, computer databases).

There is both a "stock" and a "flow" aspect to the information-processing capabilities of semistrong-form efficient markets: First, the *level* of asset prices should correctly reflect all pertinent historical, current, and predictable future information that

---

[3.] Malkiel, Burton G., *A Random Walk Down Wall Street,* 8th Edition, W.W. Norton, © 2003.

[4.] The CFO of a sporting goods company once told us that his company's stock always performed exceptionally well during the Summer Olympics because the games caused an increase in demand for his firm's products. Without a doubt, seasonal demand patterns exist for many kinds of products, but this is hardly a surprise to financial markets. Even though this firm's stock might have performed well during previous Olympic years, imagine what would happen if investors expected the pattern to repeat over time. Investors would buy the shares in the spring, before the Summer Olympics began. Buying pressure in the spring would cause the stock price to increase several weeks or months before the summer. Seeing this, investors might purchase shares even farther ahead of the next Olympics, and eventually the seasonal pattern would simply disappear. See Ritter (1996) for an amusing account of this dynamic in futures markets.

investors can obtain from public sources. Second, asset prices should *change* fully and instantaneously in response to the arrival of relevant new information.

Strong-Form Efficiency. In markets characterized by **strong-form efficiency**, asset prices reflect *all* information, public and private. This extreme form of market efficiency implies that important company-specific information will be fully incorporated in asset prices with the very first trade after the information is generated. For example, a firm's stock price should increase immediately after the board of directors votes for a dividend increase and before the firm publicly announces the increase.

In strong-form efficient markets, most insider trading would be unprofitable, and there would be no benefit to ferreting out information on publicly traded companies. Any data morsel so obtained would already be reflected in stock and bond prices. Like semistrong-form efficiency, strong-form efficiency also implies that there is both a stock and flow aspect to a market's information-processing abilities.

Table 10.1 describes the three forms of market efficiency and summarizes the key implications of each form.

DOES EMPIRICAL EVIDENCE SUPPORT MARKET EFFICIENCY?

Ultimately, whether financial markets are informationally efficient is an empirical question. For more than a quarter of a century, the efficient market hypothesis enjoyed overwhelming support among financial economists. However, in recent years a large body of empirical evidence challenging the EMH has caused many former "true believers" to take a fresh look at the efficiency question. Adding to this disquiet, there have been several dramatic recent examples of markets surging for an extended period, then collapsing suddenly, the so-called **bubble phenomenon.**

Table 10.1
Forms of Informational Market Efficiency

Form of Efficiency	Definition	Example
Weak form	Financial asset (stock) prices incorporate *all historical information* into current prices; future stock prices cannot be predicted based on an analysis of past stock prices.	Nothing of value is to be gained by analyzing past stock price changes, since this doesn't help you predict future price changes—renders "technical analysis" useless.
Semistrong form	Stock prices incorporate *all publicly available information* (historical and current); there will not be a delayed response to information disclosures.	The relevant information in an SEC filing will be incorporated into a stock price as soon as the filing is made public.
Strong form	Stock prices incorporate *all information*—private as well as public; prices will react as soon as new information is generated, rather than as soon as it is publicly disclosed.	Stock prices will react to a dividend increase as soon as the firm's board of directors votes—and before the board announces its decision publicly.

Figure 10.1
Rational Market
Valuation or Price
Bubble? Nasdaq and
Internet Stock Prices,
January 1998 to January
2001
Source: "The Party's Over:
A Survey of Corporate
Finance," *The Economist*
(January 27, 2001), p.14,
fig. 6.

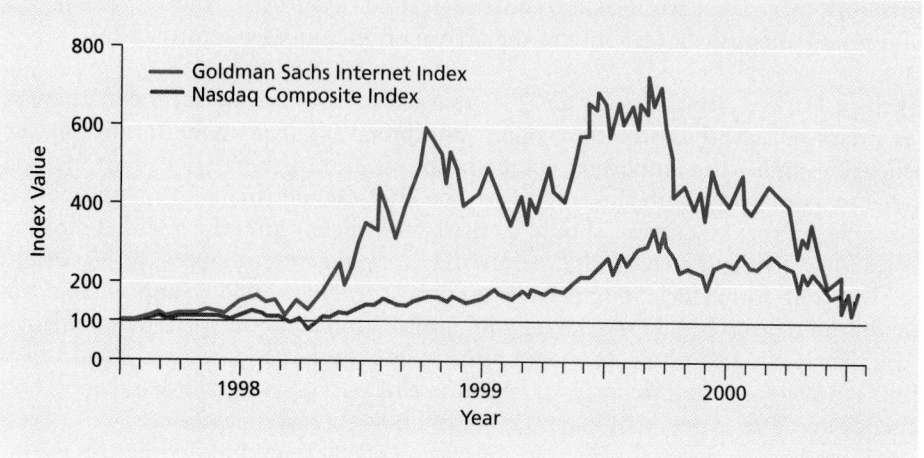

Figure 10.1 details the most recent "boom-and-bust" cycle, the rise in U.S. technology stock prices from January 1998 to January 2001, and their ruinous decline thereafter. The Nasdaq Composite Index tripled over the three-year period leading up to March 2000, while the Goldman Sachs Internet Index increased by *600 percent*. Because there was no comparable rise and fall in "dot.com" company earnings during this period, many have concluded that this (and other) recent market collapses were the result of exploding *price bubbles*. Subscribers to behavioral finance argue that bubbles occur when investors irrationally bid prices to unsustainable levels, and that when investors finally realize their errors, prices fall dramatically (and often suddenly). If bubbles do in fact occur, they would constitute direct evidence against market efficiency.

Not surprisingly, the debate between behaviorists and those who believe strongly in market efficiency has triggered a surge in research. In this chapter, we present a very brief synthesis of more than 30 years of research on market efficiency, breaking our discussion into two main sections. Section 10.2 adopts an updated version of the classification scheme used by Eugene Fama when he surveyed the existing literature in 1991. Though we discuss some of the classic empirical tests Fama describes, we focus on papers published since 1991. Section 10.3 then summarizes the evidence supporting the behavioral finance critique of market efficiency. We present our own assessment of the validity of the market efficiency hypothesis, and what market efficiency means for corporate financing, in Section 10.4.

**Concept
Review
Questions**

3. Describe the differences between *allocative* efficiency, *operational* efficiency, and *informational* efficiency.

4. Many people criticize the efficient markets hypothesis as unrealistic but do not then describe what the absence of efficiency would imply. Give a specific example of how a semi-strong-form *inefficient* market would react to new information. Does this seem realistic?

5. There is frequently an upward drift in the stock price of a firm that will eventually become the target of a takeover attempt prior to the announcement of the bid itself. What do you think causes this drift, and is this phenomenon consistent with market efficiency?

10.2 EMPIRICAL EVIDENCE ON MARKET EFFICIENCY

Instead of relying on the three "forms" of market efficiency, Fama (1991) classified empirical tests of market efficiency into three categories: (1) tests for return predictability, (2) event studies (or tests for rapid price adjustment), and (3) tests for private information. We look at those three categories in this section.

TESTS FOR RETURN PREDICTABILITY

Much of the research on market efficiency has examined the validity of the weak-form efficiency prediction that past price changes do not predict future changes, or that prices follow a random walk. Research papers studying this aspect of market efficiency are called *tests for return predictability.*

We further classify these tests into four categories:

1. *Tests of simple trading rules* examine whether an investor can construct a consistently profitable trading strategy based on observed trends in very recent stock returns.[5]
2. *Tests of the effectiveness of technical analysis* examine whether it is profitable to buy or sell stocks based on historical pricing "patterns" identified by stock analysts.
3. *Tests for return predictability* study whether there is an exploitable tendency for stock-price changes to continue from one period to the next or, conversely, to reverse direction each period.
4. *Tests of the performance of newly issued shares* examine whether firms issuing shares to the public underperform stock market indexes over the next several years.

We will examine the evidence associated with each of these tests.

Simple Trading Rule Tests. Prior to the 1950s, most experts believed that perceptive investors could identify stock-price patterns that could be exploited. It therefore came as quite a surprise when Maurice Kendall (1953) documented that stock-price changes were essentially uncorrelated with each other. Thus, simply knowing that a stock price fell yesterday does not tell you anything useful about what it will do today or tomorrow. Kendall's finding also implies that daily stock returns are unpredictable.

Subsequent studies supported Kendall's conclusion and found that stock prices seemed to follow a random walk. This meant that a strategy of buying recent winners and selling recent losers would not be profitable. Fama and Blume (1966) tested a number of more sophisticated filter rules, such as "buy a stock after it has increased by x percent, and don't sell it until it has decreased by y percent." They found that none of these strategies generated significant profits, particularly after accounting for trading costs.

Another way to test whether stock prices follow a random walk is to measure whether returns are serially correlated (i.e., correlated from one period to the next). *Positive serial correlation* means there is a consistent tendency for positive (negative) stock returns in one period to be followed by positive (negative) returns in another.

[5.] To be more precise about what we mean by the term "profitable" here, market efficiency tests usually ask whether a given trading strategy earns higher returns than some benchmark. The benchmark is the "normal" or "expected" return from investing in securities of a given risk level.

Negative serial correlation means that positive returns in one period tend to be followed by negative returns in the next. Academic studies find little evidence of serial correlation.

If trading strategies based on filter tests and serial correlation do not yield consistent profits, what about other mechanical trading strategies? In the early 1980s, researchers discovered several "anomalies" that seemed to offer investors the opportunity to earn large profits. These included the *day-of-the-week effect* (Gibbons and Hess 1981), the *small-firm effect* (Banz 1981), and the *January effect* (Keim 1983). Gibbons and Hess documented significantly negative abnormal returns for stocks on Mondays. Banz found significantly positive excess returns on very small (low market-capitalization) stocks. Keim pointed out that small stocks earned particularly high returns relative to large stocks in the first few trading days of January. In each case, it seemed that investors could exploit the anomaly through a relatively simple trading strategy. For example, if returns are on average lower on Mondays than during the rest of the week, wouldn't it pay an investor (or a mutual fund) to short-sell stocks on Friday afternoons and repurchase them at a lower price on Tuesday mornings?

Further research examining the profitability of such trading strategies typically shows that they do not yield excess profits (such as corporate profits from the war on Iraq, or profits such as those experienced by the oil companies in the third quarter of 2005).[6] There are several reasons for this: First, strategies designed to exploit pricing anomalies generally involve a great deal of trading. Strategies that require a great deal of trading naturally generate high transactions costs that eat away most or all of the gross profits from implementing the strategy. Second, some anomalies seem to disappear once they have been identified. Fama (1991) documented that the January effect diminished after Keim's 1983 discovery. Several other anomalies have suffered a similar fate.

Financial economists wishing to test market efficiency must confront a basic dilemma that was first identified by Roll (1977): the **joint-hypothesis problem.** It is almost unavoidable that tests of the EMH are joint tests of market efficiency and of the particular asset pricing model used to conduct the test. When an anomaly appears, it may be the result of market inefficiency or of a deficient asset pricing model. For example, Ritter and Chopra (1989) found that the size of the January effect was very sensitive to the choice of stock index used in the test.

The current standard in market efficiency research is to use several different asset pricing models to test the robustness of potential anomalies. For most anomalies, reasonable changes in the asset pricing model used to form the benchmark "expected returns" result in the abnormal returns shrinking or vanishing entirely.

Tests for the Effectiveness of Technical Analysis. The term **technical analysis** describes an investing approach in which analysts search for profitable trading strategies based on recurring patterns in stock prices. Historically, analysts pored over stock charts to identify most of these patterns, and they described them with graphical phrases such as "head and shoulders" or "double tops." Not surprisingly, the investment community began to refer to practitioners of technical analysis as **chartists.** Today, technical analysis involves sophisticated statistical and mathematical tools, as well as computing-intensive tools. Even so, the goal of technical analysis has not changed—to find ways to identify and profit from recurring patterns in prices.

[6.] An important exception to this assertion is the study by Lakonishok and Smidt (1988). They find that several seasonal anomalies yield statistically significant, though quite small, trading profits.

Academic finance has long ridiculed technical analysis because it violates even the weak form of market efficiency. Most empirical research contradicts the usefulness of technical analysis and supports weak-form market efficiency. However, a recent study by Lo, Mamaysky, and Wang (2000) restored a small measure of respectability to chartists. Rather than test whether technical trading rules yield excess profits to investors, these researchers asked whether any of the standard pricing patterns can be identified *statistically* (rather than visually). Applying their methodology to a large sample of U.S. stock returns from 1962 to 1996, they find that several technical patterns are in fact observed much more frequently than chance would predict. Figure 10.2 shows the four most frequently observed patterns. "Double tops" and "double bottoms" occur almost four times more frequently than chance alone would suggest; "head and shoulders" and "inverse head and shoulders" show up three times more often than they should.

Though intriguing, these results do not necessarily amount to a clear violation of market efficiency. Lo, Mamaysky, and Wang themselves acknowledge that identifying recurring patterns does not mean that trading on these patterns would be profitable. In fact, the results presented by previous researchers explicitly show that technical

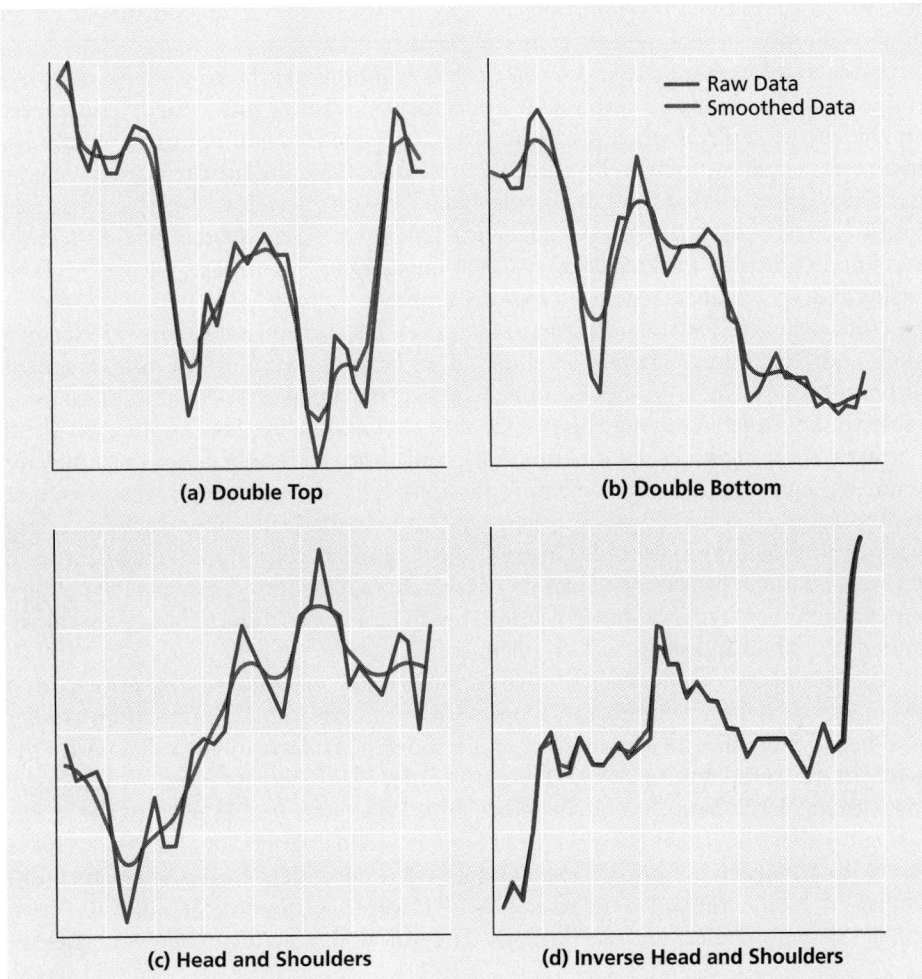

Figure 10.2
The Most Common Technical Analysis Patterns Observed in Stock Prices

These graphs visually describe the four most common patterns in U.S. stock prices over the period 1982 to 1996. The graphs express stock price on the vertical (y) axis and trading days on the horizontal (x) axis.

Source: Andrew W. Lo, Harry Mamaysky, and Jiang Wang, "Foundations of Technical Analysis: Computational Algorithms, Statistical Inference, and Empirical Implementation," *Journal of Finance* 55 (August 2000), pp. 1705–1765.

trading rules *do not* generate excess profits when applied out of sample or when realistic transactions costs are accounted for. Market efficiency survives another round.

Tests for Stock Market Underreaction and Overreaction. One of the key predictions of the efficient markets hypothesis is that stock prices should react rapidly and *fully* to new information. Several researchers have tested this proposition by examining the completeness of the market's reaction to specific corporate news announcements. Two types of seemingly anomalous patterns have emerged.

One group of studies finds evidence that prices underreact to announcements such as dividend initiations and omissions (Michaely, Thaler, and Womack 1995). This means that stock prices typically react positively to a dividend initiation announcement, and then a positive, ongoing reaction continues over the next several months. This gives rise to a pattern known as stock-price *momentum*: positive initial returns are followed by more positive returns in the intermediate term. Momentum studies examine whether stocks that perform very well or very poorly in one period (day, month, year, multiyear period) continue to do so in subsequent periods.

The opposite of **underreaction** to corporate news announcements or prior period returns is **overreaction**. Several studies have examined whether a positive (negative) average reaction to a corporate announcement such as listing of a firm's stock on a new exchange is generally followed by negative (positive) returns on that stock in subsequent months (e.g., see Dharan and Ikenberry 1995).

Evidence of underreaction or overreaction would refute the efficient markets hypothesis because it would imply that a mechanical trading rule would yield excess profits. For example, if stock prices underreact to dividend initiations or omissions, an investor could exploit this by purchasing all stocks that initiate dividend payments and short-selling all that omit dividends. If such a strategy yielded positive abnormal returns, semistrong-form market efficiency would be violated because the strategy uses publicly available information to "beat the market." Therefore, we need to look further at tests for underreaction or overreaction.

Underreaction Tests. Underreaction tests fall into several categories. First, some studies have examined whether stock prices underreact to important but infrequent corporate events. These studies examine whether that an investor could follow a profitable trading rule of buying the stocks of firms announcing stock splits, dividend increases, share repurchases, and spin-offs, and short-selling the stocks of firms announcing equity issues and dividend omissions. The second type of underreaction studies examines whether stock prices tend to systematically underreact to certain types of routine information disclosures, particularly earnings announcements and recommendations by security analysts. Researchers have found some evidence supporting both these types of underreaction, but in most cases these studies have shown limited economic and statistical significance.

The third type of underreaction studies examines whether buying prior-period "winners" or selling prior-period "losers" is profitable. These momentum studies have been by far the most numerous and important underreaction tests, partly because the measured returns have been on the order of 6-8 percent per year. Jegadeesh and Titman (1993) find that buying stocks that have increased in price in the recent past and selling those that have performed poorly yields significant abnormal returns over 3- to 12-month holding periods. Others also find evidence supporting the profitability of momentum trading strategies.[7] However, Lesmond, Schill, and Zhou (2004), strongly challenge these findings. They show that because such strategies re-

---

[7.] See Chan, Jegadeesh, and Lakonishok (1996), Moskowitz and Grinblatt (1999), Badrinath and Wahal (2002), Lewellen (2002), George and Hwang (2004), Mikhail, Walther, and Willis (2004), and Sapp and Tiwari (2004).

quire frequent trading in high-cost stocks, momentum profits disappear after accounting for realistic trading costs.

Overreaction Tests. One of the most important early tests of market overreaction was a study by DeBondt and Thaler (1985). Their results indicate that portfolios of prior extreme "losers" dramatically outperform prior extreme "winners," even though the latter are more risky. This effect is dubbed the *value stock phenomenon,* because stocks in the "loser" portfolio trade at low prices relative to earnings, dividends, and other measures of fundamental value. DeBondt and Thaler's principal results appear in Figure 10.3; nearly 3 years after portfolio formation, the prior-period losing stocks earned 25 percent more than the winners. Studies by Jegadeesh (1990) and Jegadeesh and Titman (1993) also test trading strategies based on stock-price overreaction, and find seemingly massive profit opportunities.

Though the profitable trading opportunities offered by an overreaction investing strategy appear impressive, many people (ourselves included) remain unconvinced. Skeptics make three key points: First, studies by McQueen (1992) and Jones (1993) show that the price reversals documented by DeBondt and Thaler were much larger during the Depression and World War II than in any other period. Ball, Kothari, and Shanken (1995) find that the DeBondt and Thaler results were distorted by some very large percentage gains (up to 3,500%) on some very low-priced stocks.

Second, the potential profits identified by the overreaction studies are simply too large to be credible. If real, such simple trading strategies should have been adopted by at least a few mutual fund managers, and thus would have left a discernible trace in the empirical literature. But no evidence of this exists.[8] Most telling, Fama (1998) points out that the empirical evidence documents a roughly equal number of examples of stock-price overreactions as underreactions. This is what you would expect to find by chance if a great many talented researchers pored over the same database (the historical record of U.S. stock prices) searching for anomalies.

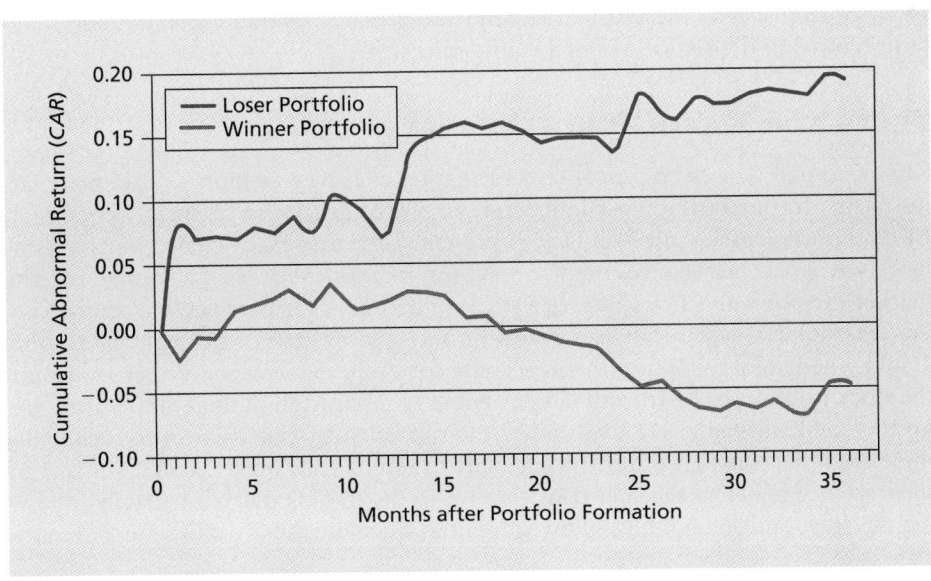

Figure 10.3
Potential Returns from Pursuing an "Overreaction" Strategy

This figure documents the average 3-year (36-month) return achievable from purchasing a portfolio of extreme "losers" (the 35 stocks with the worst 3-year return prior to portfolio formation) and extreme "winners" (the 35 stocks with the best 3-year return) over the period January 1933 to December 1980.
Source: Werner F. M. DeBondt and Richard Thaler, "Does the Stock Market Overreact?," *Journal of Finance* 40 (July 1985), pp. 793–805.

[8.] Later in this subsection, we survey the literature on mutual fund investment performance, but there is little evidence that managers of these funds can consistently beat the market. In fact, a well-known academic, Richard Roll (1994), argues from personal experience as a multi-billion-dollar mutual fund manager that real trading strategies based on overreaction and other anomalies do not yield excess returns.

Tests of Long-Run Returns to Firms Issuing Common Stock. As early as 1975, academic researchers began to document the strange result that initial public offerings were, on average, significantly underpriced. Ibbotson (1975) found that an investor who purchased the typical IPO at the offering price and sold the stock at the end of the first day's trading earned an *initial return* that averaged around 15 percent. Not a bad return for a one-day investment!

Sixteen years later, Ritter (1991) documented an equally baffling long-term return anomaly. He showed that investors who purchased shares in newly public companies *after* the IPO earned significantly negative abnormal returns over the next several years. In fact, such an investment strategy left investors with 44 percent less wealth than they would have had by simply buying the market portfolio. Such a large negative excess return would directly contradict weak-form efficiency. It raises the question, "Why do investors keep buying shares in IPOs when the average return is so bad?" This anomaly became even more puzzling when Loughran and Ritter (1995, 2000) and Spiess and Affleck-Graves (1995) also documented negative average long-run returns following seasoned equity offerings. These were similar in magnitude to the negative IPO returns, and they raised the same perplexing question about why investors continue to buy newly issued stock.

Several researchers have cast doubt on the validity and/or interpretation of the findings of negative long-run returns to firms issuing common stock. Brav and Gompers (1997) find that only the smallest IPOs not backed by venture capital firms underperform; venture capital–backed firms and larger IPOs do not underperform. Furthermore, Brav, Geczy, and Gompers (2000) find that small firms generally are the ones who underperform the market. Finally, Gompers and Lerner (2003) show that there was no evidence of poor long-term performance for IPO stocks in the period before the formation of Nasdaq in 1972.

It is unclear both whether a separate new-issue effect exists and whether this constitutes a de facto violation of market efficiency. This is one of the most important challenges to the EMH, and it is likely to remain hotly debated for years to come. Chapter 18 discusses more fully the empirical research examining initial and long-term returns to IPOs and seasoned equity offerings.

TESTS FOR RAPID PRICE ADJUSTMENT

Fama's second type of empirical tests of market efficiency examines rapid price adjustments. In one of the most influential empirical articles in financial economics, Fama, Fisher, Jensen, and Roll (1969) presented the first **event study**, which examined how stock markets respond to new information releases. They analyzed the market's response to stock splits. In a stock split, firms distribute new shares to existing shareholders, which causes a decline in the stock price. For example, in a 2-for-1 split, shareholders receive one new share for every existing share they own, and the stock price drops by roughly 50 percent. The innovation of this study was to line up the companies in *event time* rather than in calendar time. For every company, these researchers assigned day 0 to the date the stock split was executed, day −1 to the trading day before the split date, day +1 to the trading day immediately following the split, and so on.[9] This allowed them to calculate the average return for each

---

[9.] Fama, Fisher, Jensen, and Roll (FFJR) actually used monthly, rather than daily, stock return data because only monthly data were available in the late-1960s. However, because we are discussing FFJR as the paradigm of event studies, and because most post-1980 event studies have employed daily data, we will use the term "event-day" even in our discussion of FFJR's results. Brown and Warner (1985) and MacKinlay (1997) describe and assess event-study methodologies.

event-day simply by summing up all the sample returns from, for example, day −1 to day +5, and then dividing by the number of observations.

The study results, which appear in Figure 10.4, show that firms that choose to split their stock do so after an extended period in which their stock earns above-market returns. After the split, however, the stock earns returns roughly equal to those of the overall market. This suggests that markets are efficient: investors who buy shares after split announcements do not earn above-market returns.

The event study soon became one of the key tools empirical researchers use to study how the stock market reacts to many different corporate events, such as security issues or merger announcements. Such studies have dramatically advanced our understanding of how stockholders view dividend payments, security issues, takeover bids, and myriad other internal and external financial events. With some important exceptions, event studies tend to support market efficiency, revealing that stock prices respond quickly and completely to news announcements. A recent study by Chordia, Roll, and Subrahmanyam (2005) shows that between 5 and 30 minutes of trading is required to achieve convergence to market efficiency among NYSE stocks.

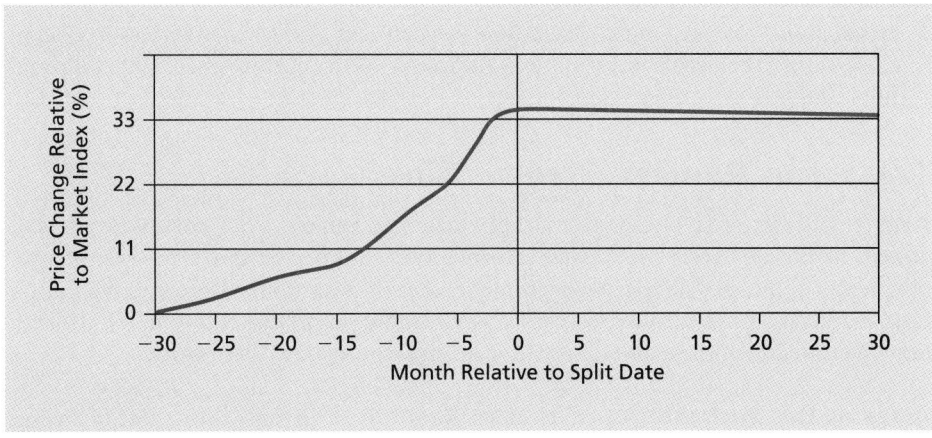

Figure 10.4
The First Event Study—Stock Splits

This figure describes the average stock price response to the "event" of a stock split where a company distributes, say, two shares to investors for every one share they already own (a 2-for-1 stock split). The stock prices are lined up in "event time," where the month of the stock split is defined as 0. Because all of the information in the stock split is incorporated into stock prices by the event date, there is on average no tendency for prices to change after the split.

Source: Eugene F. Fama, Lawrence Fisher, Michael C. Jensen, and Richard Roll, "The Adjustment of Stock Prices to New Information," *International Economic Review* 10 (February 1969), pp. 1–21, as presented in Ray Ball, "The Theory of Stock Market Efficiency: Accomplishments and Limitations," *Journal of Applied Corporate Finance* 8 (Spring 1995), pp. 4–17.

APPLYING THE MODEL 10.1

The employment report released by the U.S. Department of Labor at 8:30 A.M. on the first Friday of every month is perhaps the most intently watched of all the economic statistics released by the federal government. A report showing rapid employment growth and declining unemployment often indicates that the Federal Reserve Board will feel pressure to tighten monetary policy and raise interest rates. Conversely, a weak job report typically signals a slowing economy, declining interest rates, and a less-restrictive monetary policy. The connection between the employment report and Federal Reserve actions, combined with the influence of interest rates on economic activity and asset prices, means that bond and stock prices often react dramatically to surprises contained in the Labor Department's report.

Imagine then the Labor Department's embarrassment when the October 1998 employment report was inadvertently posted on an internal working section of the department's Internet site on Thursday morning, November 5, rather than on Friday, November 6. Almost instantly, a financial analyst at a large brokerage firm noted the statistic, contacted a Labor Department spokesperson for verification, and then disseminated the number to the brokerage firm's customers and the business news media. Within minutes of its discovery, the number had been broadcast worldwide, and its impact on interest rates and financial asset prices had been felt in full. (The report showed a smaller than expected monthly rise in employment.)

During the rest of Thursday, the Labor Department struggled to disclose all the supplementary data that typically accompanies the headline employment numbers. (It also tried to determine how such a breach of security could have occurred.) The lesson for financial markets, however, was clear: Significant information will immediately affect financial markets, even if the information is unexpectedly released at the "wrong" time. The Labor Department also learned its lesson, and no comparable premature information disclosure has occurred since 1998 (through July 2005).

TESTS FOR PRIVATE INFORMATION

In place of tests of strong-form market efficiency, Fama's 1991 survey article suggested the phrase "tests for private information." Implied in this is an examination of whether someone, such as a corporate insider or a particularly perceptive mutual fund manager, could earn excess returns by trading on private (nonpublic) information. We categorize these tests into three groups and review them below.

Tests of the Profitability of Insider Trading. The most direct test of strong-form market efficiency is whether corporate insiders can earn abnormal profits when they trade in their own firms' securities. As you surely suspect, studies document that insiders *do* earn excess returns on these trades—a finding contrary to strong-form market efficiency.

The studies differ, however, on the critical issue of whether outside investors can earn excess profits by mimicking insider trades after they are publicly disclosed. Jaffe (1974) reports that outsiders can profit from mimicking insiders' trades, a finding that constitutes a rejection of semistrong-form efficiency. However, Seyhun (1986) argues that investors cannot learn about and trade on insider trades as quickly as Jaffee assumes they can. Using actual information-release dates, Seyhun shows that outside investors cannot profit by mimicking the announced trades of corporate insiders. In a subsequent study, Seyhun and Bradley (1997) also show that insiders frequently sell shares of their firms' stock prior to filing for bankruptcy protection and make significant abnormal profits on these transactions.

These three studies thus represent a rejection of strong-form market efficiency, though Seyhun's work does support semistrong-form efficiency. Intriguing, related efficiency questions are whether and how quickly market prices incorporate private information through the act of trading. In her study of traders convicted of illegal trading on nonpublic information, Meulbroek (1992) documents that the abnormal return surrounding insider trades averages 3 percent per day. Combining all cases of known insider trading prior to takeover bids, she finds that almost half the pretakeover run-up in the target firm's stock price occurs on days when insiders illegally trade. This clearly shows that markets incorporate some nonpublic information into stock prices.[10] Finally, Easley, Hvidkjaer, and O'Hara (2002) show that stocks with higher probabilities of information-based trading have higher required rates of return.

Tests of Mutual Fund Investment Performance. In our experience, students approach the notion of market efficiency with a great deal of skepticism. Surely, they think, smart investors can beat the market if they work hard enough. Research on the performance of professionally managed mutual funds offers perhaps the most compelling evidence that outguessing the market is extremely difficult.

More than 30 years ago, Sharpe (1966) and Jensen (1968) reported negative net returns for the majority of mutual fund managers. Net returns in this context equal gross returns minus fund operating costs. Jensen's model for assessing mutual fund performance has been used by many subsequent researchers:

$$R_{pt} - R_{ft} = \alpha_p + \beta_p(R_{mt} - R_{ft}) + u_{pt} \qquad \textbf{(Eq. 10.2)}$$

where $R_{pt} - R_{ft}$ = the excess return, above the risk free rate R_{ft}, on a managed portfolio,

β_p = the beta of the portfolio during period t,

$R_{mt} - R_{ft}$ = the excess return on the market portfolio during period t,

α_p = the regression alpha or intercept term, and

u_{pt} = an error term

In this framework, the product of a fund's beta times the risk premium on the market, $\beta_p(R_{mt} - R_{ft})$, measures the fund's expected risk premium. Superior investment performance would be returns that reflect more than just compensation for risk. Therefore, testing for superior performance reduces to a test of whether the intercept term, α_p, is significantly greater than zero. To this day, even casual discussions of a mutual fund's performance will often be couched as, "What is the fund's alpha?" Jensen found that the funds in his sample had negative alphas, meaning that they did not even match the market return. Because Sharpe documented a similar result, the received wisdom within the finance profession (at least within academia) was that mutual fund managers, on average, could not beat the stock market on a risk-adjusted basis.[11]

Following publication of the Sharpe and Jensen studies, a veritable cottage industry emerged to assess the investment performance of mutual fund managers. Most of these studies separate managerial investment performance into two components: **selectivity** (stock-picking ability) and **timing** (the ability to time market turns—getting in before upturns and getting out before crashes). Several important studies claim to document superior mutual fund performance, at least before fund expenses

---

[10.] Though it is not a test of market efficiency, the survey of insider trading laws and enforcement around the world provided in Bhattacharya and Daouk (2001) shows that insider trading is a severe problem in almost every market outside the United States and a few other advanced industrial countries. Insider trading is so severe in Mexico, in fact, that Bhattacharya, Daouk, Jorgenson, and Kehr (2000) find that stock prices do not react *at all* to company-specific news announcements. All the information content of the announcement had been embedded in stock prices due to insider trading beforehand. Using data from 100 countries, Buhman, Piotroski, and Smith (2005) also show that insider trading has high social and economic costs because it crowds out private information acquisition.

[11.] We add the modifier "on a risk-adjusted basis" because if a fund beats the market simply by investing in very risky stocks, the higher return does not reflect superior stock-selection ability by the manager. Instead, the higher return merely compensates investors for the extra risk they take when investing in the fund.

are deducted to calculate a net return to fund investors.[12] Naturally, some mutual fund managers will beat the market over a given period of time, even if the average fund manager does not.

An important question for researchers and investors alike is whether the performance of a fund persists over time, or whether fund performance, like stock prices, fluctuates randomly. Hendricks, Patel, and Zeckhauser (1993) find that the relative performance of no-load, growth-oriented mutual funds persists in the near term, with the strongest evidence being found for a one-year evaluation horizon. They also present provocative findings that an investor who pursues an investment strategy of buying the funds managed by "hot hands" and avoiding funds managed by "icy hands" (the evil twin of hot hands) will earn risk-adjusted abnormal returns as high as 6 percent per year. Goetzmann and Ibbotson (1994) and Carpenter and Lynch (1999) also present evidence that successful mutual fund managers tend to earn above-average returns in subsequent periods.

Carhart (1997) disputes these results. He finds, as do Pástor and Stambaugh (2002), that individual fund managers who follow a momentum strategy do not earn excess returns. Defenders of market efficiency have also attacked the studies finding superior (or at least break-even) mutual fund performance. In perhaps the best such retort, Malkiel (1995), whose books have popularized the notion that stock prices follow a random walk, points out two critical biases in most of the tests showing superior performance. The first and most serious is the *survivorship bias*. This involves examining the returns of mutual funds over some period and comparing the returns on the funds still in existence at the end of the period to those of the S&P 500 or some other index. By definition, such a strategy involves examining only *surviving, successful* funds and ignores funds with seemingly equal promise at the beginning of the period that earned sub-par returns and were closed down (or merged). As Table 10.2 clearly shows, this survivorship bias dramatically overstates the returns earned by mutual

Table 10.2
Differences in Rates of Return of Surviving and Nonsurviving Mutual Funds

Year	Total Funds in Existence		Total Number of Funds Surviving until 1992		Funds That Did Not Survive until 1992			T-test for Difference between Means of Surviving and Nonsurviving Funds
	Mean Return	Number	Mean Return	Number	Mean Return	Number	Mortality Rate	
1982	25.03	331	26.03	272	20.42	59	17.8	3.09
1983	20.23	353	21.66	296	12.80	57	16.1	7.15
1984	−2.08	395	−1.25	331	−6.39	64	16.2	3.67
1985	27.17	431	28.10	371	21.42	60	13.9	5.77
1986	13.39	511	14.39	425	8.45	86	16.8	6.29
1987	0.47	581	0.92	489	−1.91	92	15.8	3.04
1988	14.44	686	15.48	586	8.35	100	14.6	7.54
1989	23.99	720	24.91	639	16.73	81	11.3	7.57
1990	−6.27	724	−6.00	685	−11.07	39	5.4	4.07

Source: Burton G. Malkiel, "Return from Investing in Equity Mutual Funds 1971 to 1991," *Journal of Finance* 50 (June 1995), pp. 549–572.

[12.] Bjerring, Lakonishok, and Vermaelen (1983); Cumby and Modes (1987); Ippolito (1989); Edelen (1999); and Wermers (2000).

fund managers. For example, funds that were closed between 1982 and 1992 earned lower returns than those that survived. Therefore, if researchers begin their analysis by looking only at the funds that survived (which is clearly something that an investor choosing a fund in 1982 could not do), they overstate the average fund's performance.

The second bias Malkiel documents is the tendency of mutual fund management companies to privately launch a large number of "incubator" funds (say, 10 funds), and then after a few years to publicly launch those two or three of the funds that have been the most successful. The mutual fund shuts down the seven or eight poorly performing funds; their returns are not included in the "stellar" fund averages.

Once these two biases are accounted for, Malkiel finds that mutual funds underperform the S&P 500, even before deducting transaction costs and load fees. Their net return (after fees and expenses) is far worse.[13] Bogle (2005) reports similarly poor performance for mutual fund managers (2.7 percent per year lower average returns than the S&P 500 Index) over the more recent 1983–2003 period.

Like many other MBA students, your first reaction to this litany of academic studies favoring market efficiency is probably disbelief. What about Peter Lynch, Warren Buffet, George Soros, or the other investment gurus whose performances have become part of Wall Street lore?[14] Or, for that matter, if mutual fund managers actually subtract value from the portfolios they manage, why have they been so successful over the past decade that today there are over twice as many mutual funds as there are stocks listed on the New York Stock Exchange? Although it is indeed difficult to deny that a few individuals and funds have long-term performance that seems inexplicably high, this is actually what you would expect as a result of the survivorship bias discussed earlier.

To see this, consider the following exercise: At the beginning of a 10-year period (say, the year 2007), survey all 8,000 currently active mutual fund managers, and ask each to pick a basket of stocks that he or she expects to outperform the S&P index over the coming year. Market efficiency predicts that by chance, roughly half of the managers will pick a portfolio that outperforms the S&P in 2007, and half will pick one that underperforms. Those that outperform the index in 2007 are asked to try again in 2008, and so on as long as they continue to beat the market. By the end of the decade, the original 8,000 managers will be whittled down to a mere eight. Put differently, eight of 8,000 managers can be expected to outperform the market 10 years in a row merely by chance, but these 8 will be the ones who are lionized as investment gurus.[15]

Tests of Pension Fund and Hedge Fund Investment Performance. Somewhat surprisingly, the investment performance of pension funds (professionally managed funds that invest employee pensions) has attracted far less attention than has

---

[13.] Several other studies also find that mutual fund managers have average investment performance records that are dominated by the S&P 500 Index. See, for example, Grinblatt and Titman (1989), and Elton, Gruber, Das, and Hlavka (1993).

[14.] Actually, the investment advice of even recognized gurus is less valuable than commonly imagined. Desai and Jain (1995) show this dramatically in their study of the returns an investor would have earned if he or she had followed the buy recommendations made by the most widely respected money managers each year, as published in *Barron's*, over the period 1968 to 1991. These recommendations earn significant abnormal returns of 1.91 percent between the time they are made and the date they are published (a period of about 14 days), but the abnormal returns are essentially zero for one- to three-year postpublication holding periods. Remember, these managers are believed to be the best of the best. A more general study by Graham and Harvey (1996) examining the value of a sample of 237 investment newsletter strategies over the period 1980–1992 reaches a similar conclusion.

[15.] Greene and Smart (1999) documented this pattern in a *Wall Street Journal* stock-picking contest in which 100 professional investors picked stocks that they expected to beat the market over a six-month period. After six months, those contestants who beat the market were invited to try again. Market efficiency predicts that 50 analysts would beat the market in the first round, 25 would do so in the second round, and so on. In fact, 53 analysts succeeded in the first round and 27 did in the second. The pros' success rate is statistically indistinguishable from the outcome predicted by the efficient markets hypothesis.

COMPARATIVE CORPORATE FINANCE

International Market Efficiency and Headaches for International Mutual Fund Managers

In this chapter's Opening Focus, we saw how the U.S. stock market reacted quickly to a premature employment report from the Department of Commerce. It should not surprise you that the U.S. stock market is not the only one that responds to these announcements. Becker, Finnerty, and Friedman (1995) studied the reaction of the U.K. equity market to U.S. news announcements and found that the U.K. market moved quickly in response to news from across the Atlantic Ocean. The U.S. government typically releases key macroeconomic statistics at 8:30 A.M. Eastern Standard Time (EST), which corresponds to 1:30 P.M. Greenwich Mean Time (GMT). Although the government intentionally releases this information before the U.S. stock markets open, analysts can measure the impact of the news by comparing the market's opening level on the day of an important announcement to its close the previous day (the *overnight return*). Measuring the impact of these announcements on U.K. stocks is easier because the London Stock Exchange is active at that time.

The first row of the table below shows the correlation between the overnight return on the S&P 500 and the return on the Financial Times Stock Exchange 100 Index (FTSE) from 1:30 to 2:00 P.M. GMT on days with and without macroeconomic news announcements. Not surprising, these returns are highly correlated (0.63) on announcement days and are relatively uncorrelated (0.056) on other days. The second row calcu-

lates the variance of FTSE returns from 1:30 to 2:00 on announcement and nonannouncement days. Notice that in the half hour around U.S. news announcements, the variance of the FTSE index is more than five times higher than it is during the same half hour on days with no news. However, the difference in volatility on days with and without announcements vanishes just one-half hour later (third row), suggesting that the FTSE response to U.S. news is indeed very rapid.

The linkages that exist when stock markets around the world are efficient create headaches for mutual fund managers. A standard practice in the mutual fund industry is to calculate the price at which investors can buy or sell fund shares (the net asset value, or *NAV*), using market closing prices. Mutual fund managers who invest in overseas markets must contend with the fact that markets around the world open and close at different times, and this creates a "stale price" problem that smart investors can exploit to earn arbitrage profits. Consider, for example, the case of a U.S. mutual fund that invests in Japanese stocks. The Japanese market closes each day at 1:00 A.M. EST, several hours before the U.S. market opens. During the U.S. trading day, news develops that will influence stock prices in Japan when trading resumes. If the news is good, investors can purchase shares in the Japanese mutual fund at prices that reflect the previous day's close. Or, if the news is bad, investors can sell shares in the fund, putting their

that of mutual funds, even though pension funds control more assets. Brinson, Hood, and Beebower (1986) demonstrate that investment policy (the percentage allocation of funds to different asset classes) is far more important than investment strategy in explaining the variation in pension fund returns. They also document that active management yields an average total return 1.10 percent per year *less* than that achievable with a passive strategy of buying the market index. On the other hand, Coggin, Fabozzi, and Rahman (1993) find that the best pension fund managers produce risk-adjusted excess returns 6 percent higher than those achieved by less-able fund managers.

One of the most interesting types of professionally managed investment funds to reach prominence in recent years is the *hedge fund*. Hedge funds differ from U.S. mutual funds in their organizational structure (most are partnerships instead of corporations), in their generally higher appetites for risk taking, in their extensive use of performance-based compensation, and in their being largely unregulated. In the first major empirical study of hedge funds, Ackermann, McEnally, and Ravenscraft (1999) test whether their sample of 906 hedge funds outperforms mutual funds over the period 1988 to 1995. They show that hedge funds consistently outperform mutual funds, but not standard market indexes.

Impact of U.S. Macroeconomic News Announcements on FTSE Index

Statistic	Days without Announcements	Days with Announcements
Correlation between U.S. overnight return and FTSE 1:30–2:00 P.M. GMT return	0.056	0.630
Variance of FTSE returns from 1:30 to 2:00 P.M. GMT	0.264	1.445
Variance of FTSE returns from 2:00 to 2:30 P.M. GMT	0.510	0.475

money into a safe investment, such as a money market fund, until the next good news arrives.

The events of October 28 and 29, 1997, illustrate the problem fund managers face. On October 28, stock markets around the world fell precipitously, especially in Asia. At the end of the trading day in Asia, U.S. fund managers calculated the *NAVs* of their funds using the closing prices in Japan, Hong Kong, and so on. A few hours after the Asian markets closed, the U.S. market rallied, rising more than 10 percent in the morning, and closing up about 4.5 percent for the day. This signaled to investors that Asian markets would likely reopen higher, and investors in droves took the opportunity to buy shares of Asian-focused mutual funds at the now-stale *NAVs*. As expected, Asian markets followed the U.S. rally on October 29, and some investors earned re-

turns of 8–9 percent on a single day. Goetzmann, Ivkovic, and Rouwenhorst (2001) estimate that this type of arbitrage beats a buy-and-hold strategy by roughly 20 percent per year, while Greene and Hodges (2002) show that the trades of arbitrageurs dilute returns for passive investors in international mutual funds by as much as 1 percent per year.

Sources: Kent G. Becker, Joseph E. Finnerty, and Joseph Friedman, "Economic News and Equity Market Linkages between the U.S. and U.K.," *Journal of Banking and Finance* 19 (1995), pp. 1191–1210; William N. Goetzmann, Zoran Ivkovic, and K. Geert Rouwenhorst, "Day Trading International Mutual Funds: Evidence and Policy Solutions," *Journal of Financial and Quantitative Analysis* 36 (September 2001), pp. 287–309; Jason T. Greene and Charles W. Hodges, "The Dilution Impact of Daily Fund Flows on Open-end Mutual Funds," *Journal of Financial Economics* 65 (July 2002), pp. 131–158.

In summary, there is no unambiguous answer to the question of whether professionally managed funds are able to achieve investment returns comparable to that from a naive buy-and-hold investment strategy. Even this lack of conclusive evidence, however, amounts to damning fund managers with faint praise: There is no evidence that they can achieve significantly positive *net* returns (after deducting fees and expenses) for fund shareholders.

Tests of the Stock-Picking Abilities of Security Analysts. Do security analysts and investment newsletter writers demonstrate superior stock-picking abilities? Many students have heard that the *Value Line Investment Survey* has a reputation for selecting stocks that subsequently outperform the market portfolio, and there is some empirical evidence to support this belief (Stickel 1985). The question for market efficiency is whether this is a common phenomenon: Can security analysts make recommendations that consistently beat the markets?

There is some evidence that they can. For example, Womack (1996) documents that brokerage recommendations do embody valuable information for which a brokerage firm should be compensated. Asquith, Mikhail, and Au (2005) also show that equity analysts' forecasts provide valuable information. Additionally, Barber, Lehavy,

McNichols, and Trueman (2001; hereafter BLMT) show that investors who followed the consensus advice of the 4,340 analysts (and 361,620 individual recommendations) in the *Zacks Recommendation Database* from 1985 to 1996 earned excess profits of more than 4 percent per year. The specific strategy in the BLMT study is to buy a stock when analysts move it into a more favorable recommendation category and to short-sell a stock when it moves into a less-favorable category. Figure 10.5 shows the annual returns on buying and selling stocks that move among the Zacks five recommendation categories, along with the average annual return on the market portfolio.

On its face, the BLMT study seems to provide striking evidence in favor of security analysts' stock-selection ability, and in contradiction to market efficiency. The catch is that very high portfolio turnover, of up to *400 percent* per year, is required to achieve these returns. Trading costs make this strategy far less profitable. Using a comprehensive and bias-free database covering analysts' recommendations from 1980 to 1996, Metrick (1999) finds no significant evidence of stock-picking ability.

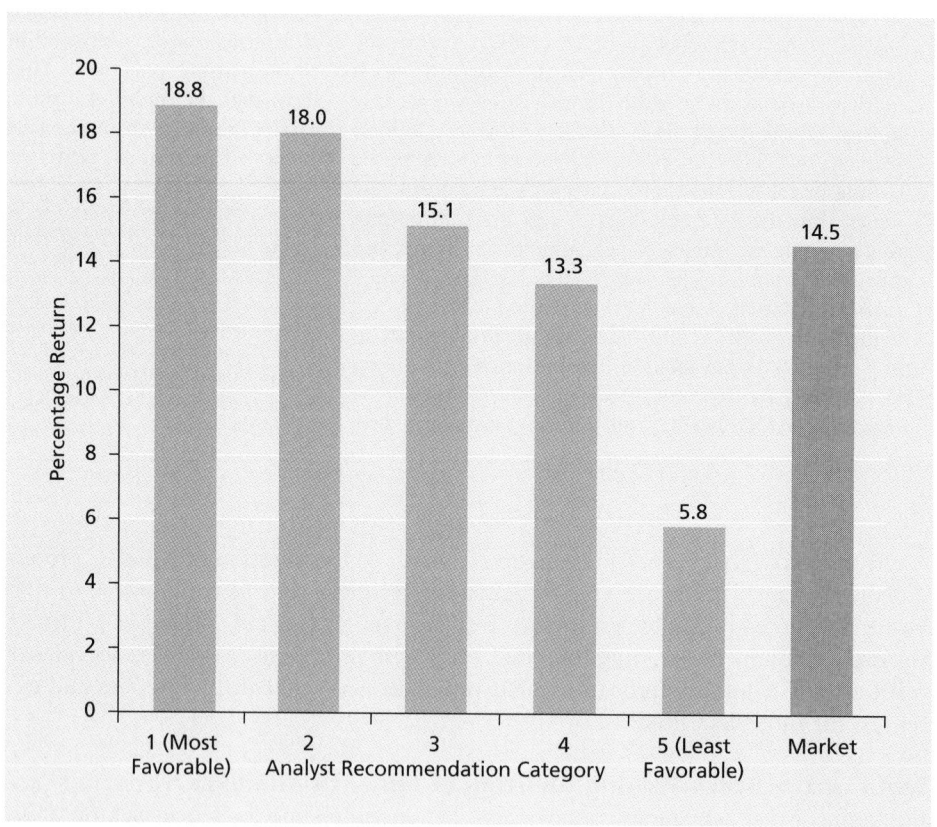

Figure 10.5

Can Security Analysts Beat the Market? Returns Earned by Portfolios Formed on the Basis of Consensus Analyst Recommendations, 1986–1996

This figure describes annualized geometric mean percentage returns an investor could earn by forming portfolios based on changes in the consensus of analyst recommendations of individual stocks from 1986 to 1996. The consensus forecast is generated using Zacks' Recommendation Database, which details the recommendations made by analysts at top-tier brokerage firms. The specific trading strategy detailed in the figure involves buying a stock that is moved into a more favorable category and short-selling a stock that is moved to a less favorable category.

Source: Brad Barber, Reuven Lehavy, Maureen McNichols, and Brett Trueman, "Can Investors Profit from the Prophets? Security Analyst Recommendations and Stock Returns," *Journal of Finance* 56 (April 2001), pp. 531–563.

Additionally, Metrick finds no evidence of abnormal short-run performance persistence, or hot hands, among the analysts studied.[16]

An interesting question, also related to analysts' stock-picking ability, is whether they herd together by following each others' recommendations. Obviously, few analysts would admit to such behavior. Nonetheless, there is substantial theoretical and empirical evidence that herding behavior is very common among newsletter writers, as shown most recently by Clement and Tse (2005).

On balance, there seems to be little empirical evidence to suggest that the advice offered by security analysts allows investors to consistently beat the market portfolio of stocks. Together with the other empirical evidence surveyed in this section, the EMH appears undamaged. Before reaching this conclusion, however, we must weigh the evidence marshaled against market efficiency by the followers of behavioral finance.

Concept Review Questions

6. What are the strongest pieces of evidence in support of the EMH? Against it?

7. The "Super Bowl Predictor" suggests that the stock market will rise during a year when a former-NFL professional football team wins the Super Bowl, and will fall when a former-AFL team wins. This predictor has correctly forecast the stock market's actual performance roughly 80 percent of the time since the first Super Bowl in 1967, far better than most human forecasters. What do you think explains this superior predictive performance? Is this predictor consistent with market efficiency?

8. Describe how you would construct an event study to test the stock market reaction to CEO resignations, and to examine whether the market reaction is different for voluntary versus involuntary resignations.

9. Several academic researchers have suggested that legalizing insider trading would improve market efficiency by more rapidly incorporating private information into market prices. What do you think would be the costs and benefits of such a legal change?

10.3 THE BEHAVIORAL FINANCE CRITIQUE OF MARKET EFFICIENCY

The EMH has long held sway among financial professionals (especially academics), both because it provided a logical, internally consistent theoretical model of how markets work and because empirical evidence weighed in its favor. However, the past 15 years have seen the rise of a group of respected economists who reject the EMH as a model of investor behavior and security market performance. Because these economists draw many of their insights from the findings of psychological research, they have become known as *behaviorists;* their collective research is called *behavioral finance.* In Barberis and Thaler (2003), two of the leading behaviorists present an excellent survey of this research.

The behavioral finance attack on market efficiency has occurred on several levels. First, behaviorists interpret the empirical evidence surveyed in Section 10.2 much

SMART CONCEPTS
See the concept explained step-by-step at
SMARTFinance

[16.] In a September 2002 working paper, BLMT update their study of the performance of analysts' recommendations and find that "the years 2000–2001 were disasters." Stocks that analysts ranked as least favorable outperformed stocks ranked most favorable by more than 20 percentage points per year. Even so, for the entire 1986–2001 period, stocks that analysts ranked in the highest category outperformed those in the lowest category by a little less than 12 percent per year.

differently than do believers in market efficiency, who for brevity we will refer to as "true believers" throughout this discussion.[17] Behaviorists make a persuasive case that financial markets in general, and stock markets in particular, are simply too volatile for prices to be based on rational valuations. Behaviorists also believe that investors are emotional creatures who process financial information in systematically biased ways. They suggest that this cognitive process in fact causes investors to overreact to some types of financial information and underreact to others. Additionally, behaviorists point out that the process of arbitrage is both difficult and costly, a point verified empirically by Mitchell, Pulvino, and Stafford (2002). **Arbitrage** is the process of buying something at a low price in one market and simultaneously selling it in another market at a higher price to generate an immediate, risk-free profit. Opportunities for such maneuvers supposedly will ensure that assets are valued correctly relative to each other.

We examine the behavioral finance critique of market efficiency in the next three subsections. The first surveys the empirical evidence that behaviorists have stressed in their critique of the EMH. The second briefly describes the theoretical underpinnings of behavioral finance and discusses the biases that are believed to color investor behavior. In the final subsection, we present our own assessment of the relative merits of behavioral finance and market efficiency.

BUBBLES, FADS, AND CASCADES: THE EMPIRICAL EVIDENCE ON BEHAVIORAL FINANCE

Few objective observers would disagree with the proposition that financial asset prices tend to be highly volatile. Behaviorists go a step further and claim that financial markets are *irrationally* volatile. As such, they are prone to recurring bubbles, fads, and information cascades. The terms *bubbles* and *fads* are easily understood. An **information cascade** occurs when a piece of "information" rapidly travels through a large group of market participants, influencing trading behavior and being accepted as correct—whether it is or not. All three of these phenomena, if they in fact exist, are inconsistent with market efficiency.

SMART IDEAS VIDEO

Robert Shiller, Yale University
"When the P/E ratio is high it's typically justified by an argument that earnings will go up in the future."

See the entire interview at
SMARTFinance

One of the most respected behavioral economists, Robert Shiller, makes the case in his best-selling book *Irrational Exuberance* that stock prices are not determined rationally. His book hit the stores in March 2000, just as the Nasdaq market's nearly 75 percent swoon commenced. Figure 10.6, from Schiller's book, shows the relationship between U.S. stock prices and earnings from 1871 to 2000, as well as the price/earnings ratio of the S&P Composite Index over the same period. Shiller argues that the enormous rise in valuations between 1990 and 2000 was both unprecedented in scale and unexplained by any comparable increase in corporate sales and profits.

THEORETICAL UNDERPINNINGS OF BEHAVIORAL FINANCE

It is one thing to marshal empirical evidence against the EMH, as the behaviorists have done, and something else entirely to develop a full-blown theoretical model to replace such evidence. Although there is not yet a fully developed model of behavioral finance, behaviorists have explained how markets might be less than fully efficient.

[17.] To someone trying to objectively weigh the merits of the EMH and behavioral finance, this tendency to interpret the same empirical evidence in fundamentally different ways is disconcerting. The best example of this can be seen by comparing the studies cited in Appendix A of Daniel, Hirshleifer, and Subrahmanyam (1998) with the virtually identical list of papers cited in Table 1 of Fama (1998). Since these are arguably the best academic papers, respectively, supporting and refuting behavioral finance, it is easy to see why a professional consensus has to date been very hard to reach. More recent empirical research supporting behavioral finance includes Hirshleifer and Shumway (2003) and Coval and Shumway (2005).

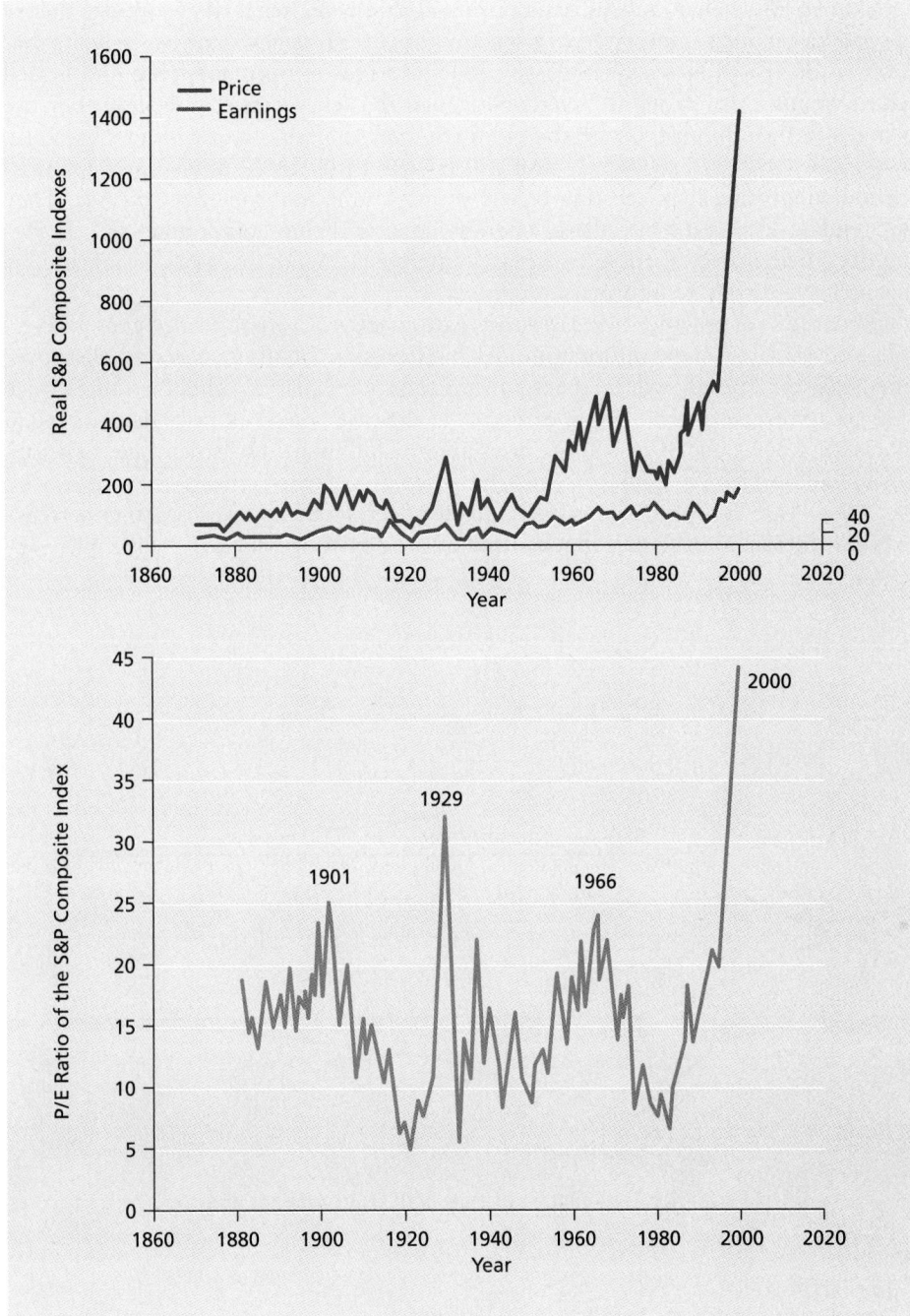

Figure 10.6
Is This Rational Pricing?
Stock Prices versus
Earnings and Price-
Earnings Ratios For U.S.
Stocks, 1871–2000

*Real (inflation-corrected)
S&P Composite Stock
Price Index, monthly,
January 1871 through
January 2000 (upper
series), and real S&P
Composite earnings
(lower series), January
1871 to September
1999.*
Source: Author's calculations
using data from S&P Statisti-
cal Service; U.S. Bureau of
Labor Statistics; Cowles and
Associates, *Common Stock
Indexes;* and Warren and
Pearson, *Gold and Prices.*

*Price-earnings ratio,
monthly, January 1881
to January 2000.
Numerator: real
(inflation-corrected) S&P
Composite Stock Price
Index. Denominator:
moving average over
preceding ten years of
real S&P Composite
earnings. Years of peaks
are indicated.*
Source: Robert J. Shiller,
Irrational Exuberance
(Broadway Books; New
York, 2000), p. 6, fig. 1.1;
p. 8, fig. 1.2.

One track of this development of theory has sought to explain how biases in human cognition can cause individual investors to misprice financial assets. The thrust
of this research has been to explain investor under- and overreaction to specific information announcements. The second track of theoretical research seeks to explain
how these irrational *individual* valuations can affect overall *market* valuations. In
other words, even if individual investors make bad valuation decisions, why don't
other more rational investors or arbitrageurs act swiftly to correct any observed mispricing of assets?

Daniel, Hirshleifer, and Subrahmanyam (1998; hereafter DHS) propose a theory of securities market under- and overreaction to corporate news announcements that is based on two well-documented psychological biases: **overconfidence** and **biased self-attribution.** Investors are overconfident in the sense that they believe they are better informed about the true state of a company's affairs than is in fact the case. Investors with biased self-attribution will interpret the arrival of new private information supporting their existing beliefs as important confirmatory evidence. They will tend to disregard contradictory new evidence as being "random noise." As Figure 10.7 demonstrates, these two biases interact to make investors systematically misinterpret corporate information releases.

Regardless of whether news is positive or negative, overconfidence causes investors to overreact to new information. As the true state of affairs becomes clear over time, investors' beliefs will fall back toward rational valuation, and this causes price changes to reverse over time. For example, in the case of a stock price that has fallen on negative news, the price will rise after initially falling below "true value." The opposite will occur for a stock price that has risen above true value.

The self-attribution bias has the opposite effect: It causes investors to underreact to public information signals that contradict their existing beliefs. For example, sup-

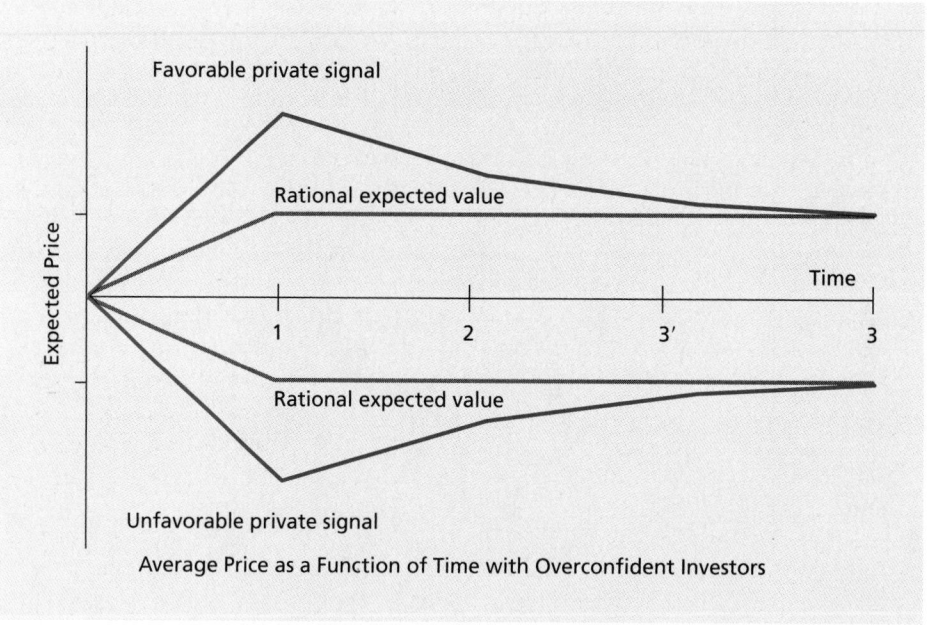

Figure 10.7
A Theoretical Explanation of Overreaction and Underreaction

This figure shows how stock prices can theoretically overreact to some corporate announcements and underreact to others. When firms announce good news, stock prices should react to the Rational Expected Values on the top part of this figure. But because investors are overconfident, in the sense that they believe they have more accurate private information about a firm's real value than is in fact the case, they drive stock prices above their rational values immediately after receiving the information signal (the good news). Over time, investors realize their mistake, which means that stock prices will drift back to their rational values in later periods. This series of price changes induces overraction in stock prices, with a subsequent reversal as time passes. The bottom part of this figure shows the pattern that would result from a negative initial price signal.

Source: Kent Daniel, David Hirshleifer, and Avindhar Subrahmanyam, "Investor Psychology and Under and Overreactions," *Journal of Finance* 53 (December 1998), pp. 1839–1882.

pose that an investor who expects a stock to perform poorly receives information contradicting this belief. At first, the investor discounts the value of this information ("I know better than they do"). Over time, as more good news emerges, the investor's opinion gradually changes from negative to positive. If many investors behave this way, stock prices will respond gradually to new information, rising slowly in response to good news and falling slowly after bad news. In other words, the self-attribution bias leads to "continuation" or momentum in stock prices, just the opposite effect of overconfidence.[18]

ASSESSING BEHAVIORAL FINANCE AND MARKET EFFICIENCY

An unbiased observer must come away from a reading of the behavioral literature more than a little impressed. In particular, behaviorists present persuasive evidence that price bubbles occur, and somewhat less-compelling evidence that the U.S. stock market was grossly overvalued near the turn of the century. On balance, however, we believe that investors and managers are wise to take the efficient markets hypothesis very seriously. Even though the quantity of evidence challenging the EMH has grown in recent years, stock prices and prices of other financial assets are still largely unpredictable.

In addition, even if we accept the notion that there is some degree of predictability in stock prices, the finance profession is far from understanding *why* this is so. The theory behind the efficient markets hypothesis is logically consistent and has stood the test of time very well. Behavioral finance provides an admittedly puzzling set of empirical facts, with a collection of fairly loosely knit stories that might explain the data. Perhaps the puzzles of behavioral finance will be solved by the development of a new asset pricing model or some other theory. Until behaviorists offer a consistent, testable alternative to the efficient market model, we will remain skeptical of irrationality as the cause of anomalies in financial markets.

Finally, proponents of any important pricing anomaly must explain how it has remained stable in the face of the explosive growth in the size, sophistication, liquidity, and technical efficiency of financial markets during the past two decades. When billions of dollars are committed to arbitraging bond-pricing errors as small as a few basis points, it seems inconceivable that deviations from fundamental valuation as gross as those implied by the behavioral finance literature could long endure.

On the other hand, this chapter offers a tribute to the intellectual impact behavioral finance research has had and is likely to continue having on our profession. Behavioral finance has provided by far the strongest challenge to the EMH in the last three decades and has won many converts in academia and business. An unscientific poll of our colleagues suggests that the consensus in favor of the EMH is not as strong as it was a decade ago, though we believe that the majority of financial economists (in academia at least) lean toward the efficient markets view.

[18.] For a humorous (but very informative) assessment of how behavioral finance notions are likely to influence economic thought over the next two decades, see Thaler (2000). Among his predictions: *Homo Economicus* will begin losing IQ points (will become less than perfectly informed) and will become a slower learner.

Additionally, Barber and Odean (2002) present striking evidence of overconfidence in their study of online investors. These (mostly young and male) investors generally had been very successful, telephone-based traders prior to going online, but once they began trading over the Internet, their trading increased dramatically and their performance began to trail the overall market by 3 percent annually. Barber and Odean (2000) show that, without regard to whether investors trade online or over the phone, the most active traders earn the lowest net returns. They argue that these investors trade too much because they are overconfident in their ability to pick winning stocks.

Concept Review Questions

10. Evaluate your driving skill as better than average, average, or worse than average. Take a poll of friends and relatives, asking the same question. What percentage of people put themselves into each group, and what does this say about the tendency of people to be overconfident? By definition, can the majority of drivers be better than average?

11. Gather a group of friends and try this experiment. Invite each person to write down a number between 0 and 100 without showing the number to anyone else. You, as the moderator of the experiment, will collect the pieces of paper and calculate the average of these numbers. Next, you will divide the average number by 2. The person who wrote down a number closest to this final value wins a $10 prize. If there is a tie, the proceeds should be equally divided among the winners. If everyone is rational, what number should everyone write down? If some people do not behave rationally (because they do not think carefully enough about the rules of the game), how does that change the strategy of a rational player?

10.4 WHAT DOES MARKET EFFICIENCY IMPLY FOR CORPORATE FINANCING?

We have surveyed the academic research on market efficiency and reached a highly nuanced conclusion: that modern financial markets tend to be informationally efficient most of the time. What specifically does this imply for the practice of financial management?

Perhaps the simplest way to summarize efficiency's lesson for practicing managers is to paraphrase Lincoln's dictum about citizens in a democracy: "You can't fool all the people (investors) all of the time." Therefore, you as a manager might as well assume that you are facing informed, active market participants who will not be fooled by financial gimmicks or "creative accounting." As we describe in this section, this assumption has specific implications for managerial practices with regard to accounting choices, financing choices, and selection of a corporate strategy for communicating with investors.

HOW DO MARKETS PROCESS ACCOUNTING AND OTHER INFORMATION RELEASES?

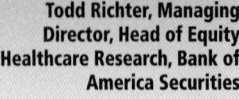

SMART PRACTICES VIDEO

Todd Richter, Managing Director, Head of Equity Healthcare Research, Bank of America Securities

"I don't necessarily believe that markets are efficient. I believe that markets tend toward efficiency."

See the entire interview at **SMARTFinance**

Financial managers tend to devote a great deal of energy and attention to selecting different accounting policies, such as whether to use last-in, first-out (LIFO) or first in, first-out (FIFO) inventory accounting techniques in financial statement reporting. The logic of market efficiency, buttressed by substantial empirical evidence, suggests this managerial obsession is misplaced, for two reasons. First, unless an accounting change affects cash flows, investors will not be concerned with its impact on a company's income statement or balance sheet. Second, if the accounting change merely involves the release, in a new form, of previously disclosed information, managers can assume that investors will already have calculated the new information on their own.

A striking example of the ambiguous role of accounting information involves the disclosure of the largest net loss ever reported by a U.S. corporation. In March 2002, AOL Time Warner announced a record loss of $54 billion resulting from a write-off of goodwill. Analysts had known for some time that (1) AOL had grossly overpaid for many of the companies it had acquired, and (2) that a large write-off of these excessive acquisition payments was in the works. Thus, the actual stock-price response to the announcement of the specific amount was negligible.

This *irrelevance thesis* can be overdone, of course. Financial statements do convey vital information. Also, changes in reporting requirements that affect a firm's cash flows or its ability to borrow can dramatically impact share valuation. In addition, when corporate earnings announcements convey new information about current business conditions and/or future earnings prospects, the stock-price reaction can be very dramatic.

How Do Markets Respond to Corporate Financing Announcements?

Yet another common but unproductive managerial fixation, according to the EMH, is the attempt by managers to "time" security issues. Several academic studies, which we survey in later chapters, show that managers on average announce new seasoned equity issues *after* a period in which their firm's stock prices have experienced unusually large increases in value. Another widely noted tendency is an unwillingness to issue new equity at a time when stock prices are believed to be "too low." Both of these behavioral tendencies imply that managers believe they know better than the market what the value of their stock "should" be. To the extent that managers have inside information about the firm's prospects that has not yet been disclosed, this might be true. In the more common case where managers think they are more perceptive than investors and can predict when stock prices will naturally adjust, the EMH suggests that they are simply delusional.

Because investors know that managers *may* have superior information about their firm's prospects, there is a clear danger that investors will interpret all managerial actions as being based on inside information, even when managers are not better informed. For example, the announcement of an equity issue conveys to investors that management thinks the firm's current stock price is too high. Likewise, announcement of a debt issue or share repurchase program conveys management's belief that the stock price is too low. In fact, investors may interpret an announcement of *any* financing event as a signal that the firm will experience a cash flow shortfall of some kind.

Investors are not all-knowing, but their interpretations are, on balance, surprisingly accurate. Studies by Hansen and Crutchley (1990) and others have shown that firms that raise cash through security issues do experience earnings shortfalls in subsequent quarters, and the larger the earnings decline, the more capital must be raised. Additionally, investors differentiate between announcements of the type of security offers: Investors usually react negatively to public security offers, but they view privately placed security issues much more favorably. In other words, investors react to all aspects of new financing announcements as though the terms and type of security selected convey useful information.

How Can Managers Devise a Corporate "Communications" Policy?

Can managers minimize the likelihood that investors will misinterpret their intentions or react to essentially meaningless events? Put differently, how can a manager devise a value-maximizing communication strategy that will credibly (and accurately) convey both positive and negative information to investors and other stakeholders, and also interpret the signals conveyed by these same parties?

We suggest that managers develop a communications strategy with the following four principles in mind: (1) Assume that your words and actions have consequences. (2) Assume that loose lips sink corporate ships. (3) Consider honesty to be the best policy. (4) Listen to your stock price.

Assume That Your Words and Actions Have Consequences. As our discussion of financing events makes clear, market participants will react to actions that managers take or to statements they make, so be careful what you do and say. You should try to predict how investors will interpret any particular news announcement and be ready to respond if the actual reaction is other than what you expected.

This is true for both good and bad news. Needlessly withholding good news (i.e., a dividend increase) can lead to the impression that you were sitting on this information until you and other insiders had the opportunity to profit by trading on it.[19] The same is true for bad news. For instance, if you learn that quarterly earnings are less than the market was expecting, your wisest strategy will usually be to disclose this news immediately, along with an unbiased assessment of whether you believe the earnings decline is likely to be temporary or permanent.

Assume That Loose Lips Sink Corporate Ships. The opposite sin is to discuss publicly information that should be kept private, or to prematurely disclose sensitive information. For example, it is almost always unwise (and sometimes illegal) to publicly discuss ongoing merger negotiations, planned security offerings, actual or potential corporate litigation, or personnel issues of almost any kind.[20]

Most corporate managers have also learned not to comment on analysts' earnings forecasts (except in the most innocuous manner), as this is usually a no-win situation for the executive involved. If the manager confirms an analyst's forecast of unexpectedly high earnings, and earnings actually end up less than predicted, the manager will anger investors who purchased stock on the expectation of higher profits. On the other hand, a manager who acts conservatively and supports a forecast of lower earnings risks alienating investors who sold their stock based on the executive's statements, only to be surprised by higher-than-predicted earnings.

Consider Honesty to Be the Best Policy. Although this mandate sounds naive, it is actually a core prediction of the efficient markets hypothesis. Investors will rationally form beliefs concerning the trustworthiness of corporate managers based on their observed behavior. Managers who convey good and bad information honestly and do not try to fool the market with accounting gimmicks or other misleading strategies will be believed, while managers with reputations for deception will be viewed skeptically.

The same is true regarding a manager's reputation for maximizing shareholder wealth. Investors will tend to support managers with a history of acting in the shareholders' best interests and will oppose managers who put their own interests ahead of those of the shareholders. In other words, though stock *prices* lack memories, stock market *investors* have long memories regarding managerial performance and honesty.

Listen to Your Stock Price. Most of our discussion thus far has dealt with how managers should convey information to investors. Market efficiency also implies that

---

[19.] Since, as we have shown, there are many studies documenting the pervasiveness of insider trading, such a suspicion is not necessarily a sign of paranoia. In any case, even paranoids (investors) have enemies (unscrupulous managers).

[20.] One important exception to this general rule involves the announcement of layoffs. Here, it is almost always best to make *all* the bad news public as soon as legally permissible, both for the sake of those who will be asked to leave and for those who will be asked to stay.

managers should listen to what the markets *are telling them* in return. Managers should view financial markets as vast information processors that generate unbiased assessments of corporate performance. Markets convey essentially two types of information to managers: (1) reactions to specific corporate announcements, and (2) movements in the firm's stock price relative to the overall market over extended time periods. Both can be very informative to the alert manager.

Consider first the stock-price reaction to a specific corporate announcement. For example, assume you announce that your firm is planning to acquire another company at a price per share that is 40 percent higher than the target's closing stock price yesterday. If your firm's stock price rises in response to this announcement, you should feel reassured that the market believes the takeover is a wise step and that you negotiated a fair price for the acquisition. If, on the other hand, your firm's stock price falls on the acquisition announcement, you should realize either that the market believes the acquisition is unwise or that your firm is paying too much, or both. Even though this decline is typically what happens to bidding-firm share prices, particularly in mergers paid for with bidding-firm stock, managers often refuse to accept the market's assessment that they acted foolishly. Alas, the weight of empirical evidence supports investors rather than bidding-firm managers.

An equally common conflict between managers and investors occurs when executives articulate a business strategy that seems brilliant to them, yet the firm's stock price languishes. The natural tendency is for managers to bemoan the idiocy of investors. It would usually be better for the managers to rethink their strategy's objectives and/or implementation. Unfortunately, examples of unwise corporate strategies pursued with heedless passion abound. Of course, the converse is also true. Managers who pursue an unconventional or unpopular strategy can draw comfort if investors bid up their firms' stock values, even if their colleagues and competitors view the strategy with befuddlement. In either case, a wise manager should not ignore what the market says about strategic moves.

---

12. Why do you think the average stock-price response to private security placements is significantly positive, while the average response to almost all public security issues is significantly negative?

13. What should a manager do when he or she firmly believes that a particular corporate strategy is wise, even though the stock market has clearly indicated disapproval of this strategy?

Concept Review Questions

10.5 SUMMARY

- In comparison to product markets, financial markets tend to be much more competitive and efficient because the assets traded tend to be very similar.
- Efficiency can be defined several ways. An allocatively efficient market ensures that capital is invested very productively. An operationally efficient market is one where outputs are produced at the lowest possible input cost. Financial economists are most concerned with the informational efficiency of financial markets, which refers to how quickly and fully asset prices incorporate relevant new information.
- In weak-form efficient markets, prices reflect all information available in the record of historical prices. Semistrong-form efficient markets reflect all publicly

available information, whether historic or current. In strong-form efficient markets, prices reflect all information—private as well as public.

- The efficient markets hypothesis has been extensively tested, and empirical research has generally found that the major Western stock and bond markets are weak-form and semistrong-form efficient, but not strong-form efficient. In particular, the efficacy of crude forms of "technical analysis" is easily rejected. However, the evidence against more-sophisticated trading rules is less overwhelming, and people with access to "inside" (nonpublic) information can earn excess profits by trading on this knowledge.

- Most empirical studies find that asset prices respond fully and nearly instantaneously to the release of relevant new information. On the other hand, it is much more difficult to test whether prices always are "accurate" in the sense that they rationally reflect fundamental value at all times.

- Research in behavioral finance argues that market participants make systematic errors in valuing assets due to cognitive problems such as overconfidence and self-attribution bias. If these cognitive biases are widespread, they can cause prices of financial assets to deviate from fundamental value for long periods of time.

- Market-efficiency research offers several lessons for practicing financial managers. It suggests that managers should not try to "fool" markets by manipulating earnings numbers or through other accounting gimmicks, as investors will usually see through these games.

- Managers should be very careful in making public utterances. If a public statement is required, however, it is imperative that managers speak truthfully. Managers also should interpret changes in stock price following release of corporate information as an unbiased market assessment of that information.

INTERNET RESOURCES

Note: *For updates to links, please go to the book's website at* http://smart.swcollege.com.

http://www.dfaus.com/philosophy/markets/—Dimensional Fund Advisors, a professional money management company with roughly $35 billion under management, has an investment philosophy firmly rooted in the philosophy of efficient markets. The website explains how this philosophy shapes the company's investment strategies and offers an interesting piece by Eugene Fama on the impact of behavioral finance.

http://www.vanguard.com/bogle_site/sp20011021.html—John C. Bogle founded Vanguard, the giant mutual fund company, and introduced the first indexed mutual fund for individual investors in 1975. Index funds represent a "passive" approach to investing in which a fund does not try to select winners and losers, but rather holds a broad basket of stocks to mimic the returns on an index like the S&P 500. At this site you can read one of Bogle's speeches offering his evidence on the superiority of indexing over an "active" approach to selecting stocks.

KEY TERMS

allocative efficiency	biased self-attribution
arbitrage	chartists
behavioral finance	efficient markets hypothesis (EMH)

event study

hedge fund

informational efficiency

joint-hypothesis problem

overconfidence

overreaction

random walk

selectivity

semistrong-form efficiency

strong-form efficiency

technical analysis

timing

underreaction

weak-form efficiency

QUESTIONS

10-1. In what way does *informational efficiency* impact corporate finance and investment decisions? In an efficient market, can a corporate manager enhance shareholder value through changes in financial reporting that have no impact on a company's cash flows?

10-2. Distinguish between *allocational, operational,* and *informational* efficiency. Does the existence of one of these efficiencies imply that the other two exist? Explain.

10-3. List and describe the three forms of informational efficiency. What is the implication for technical analysis under each of these forms?

10-4. What is a *random walk,* and how does it relate to weak-form efficiency?

10-5. If stock returns follow a random walk with drift, does this mean that investing in stocks is akin to gambling?

10-6. Explain why market efficiency implies that "the stock of an exceptionally well-run company will not necessarily be an exceptionally good investment."

10-7. What types of information are reflected in asset prices under the assumption of semistrong-form efficiency? How is this different from strong-form efficiency?

10-8. Comment on the profitability of trading on inside information in capital markets that are strong-form efficient. What about the profitability of trading on public information?

10-9. Over the long term, stocks of high-tech companies tend to earn higher returns than stocks of public utilities. Does this trend violate market efficiency?

10-10. Distinguish between the types of empirical tests of market efficiency. How does each type actually test market efficiency?

10-11. One investor follows a strategy of buying a stock whenever it hits a 52-week low and holding it for a year before selling it. Another investor follows a strategy of buying a stock whenever it hits a 52-week high and holding it for a year before selling it. Suppose that the first investor's portfolio outperforms the second investor's portfolio over time. Is this inconsistent with efficient markets? Why or why not?

10-12. What is an asset-pricing anomaly? Discuss the "January effect," and explain why it represents an anomaly. In particular, explain why it is difficult to argue that this anomaly is merely a manifestation of the *joint-hypothesis problem.*

10-13. Explain why the efficient markets hypothesis says that analysts should not be able to predict future stock returns based on recurring patterns observed in past stock returns.

10-14. Discuss the difference between *overreaction* and *underreaction* to information events. Which of the two is related to a *momentum strategy?* How is a momentum strategy applied to investing?

10-15. What is an *event study* designed to test?

10-16.   Do empirical studies support or reject the notion that corporate insiders earn abnormal profits on their trades? What about outside investors who mimic their trades? What forms of market efficiency, if any, are supported by these studies?

10-17.   In terms of mutual fund performance assessment, what is the meaning of the term "alpha"? Historically, have actively managed mutual funds exhibited positive or negative alphas, on average? What do these results imply about market efficiency?

10-18.   What other empirical results have been documented regarding the relationship between active mutual fund performance and market efficiency? What conclusion does Burton Malkiel draw about the performance of actively managed mutual funds?

10-19.   Suppose that you study the performance of 50 equity mutual funds over the past 10 years. Does the efficient markets hypothesis predict that none of these 50 funds will have a positive alpha? What predictions about alpha does the efficient markets hypothesis offer?

10-20.   Have security analysts generally been able to offer valuable stock-picking advice? If they could, why would this pose a challenge to the efficient markets hypothesis?

10-21.   What is an asset *price bubble*? Do you think the rapid rise, and even more rapid subsequent fall, in Nasdaq stock market prices between 1998 and 2000 is evidence of a pricing bubble? Why or why not?

10-22.   What is *behavioral finance*? Describe the two key cognitive biases that investors are prone to, according to behaviorists. How might these biases explain stock market over- and underreaction?

10-23.   Describe how Robert Shiller concluded that U.S. capital markets are too volatile to be rational. Do you agree with this assessment? Why or why not?

10-24.   What empirical evidence do defenders of market efficiency offer to counter the behavioral finance challenge?

10-25.   Briefly describe the four principles of external communications strategy that a corporate manager should consider.

10-26.   Why should a corporate manager "listen to the stock price"? If capital markets are efficient and if a company's stock price lags behind those of its peer group, what message should the manager infer?

10-27.   If a price moves in the following pattern: up, down, up, down, up, down, etc., is it an example of negative serial correlation or positive serial correlation?

10-28.   A friend insists that he routinely beats the market when picking stocks. Looking in the newspaper, you are able to find that your friend does consistently pick stocks that go up in value slightly, based on closing prices. How may transaction costs affect your friend's performance in the stock market?

10-29.   If a stock is incorrectly priced by $0.05 and it costs $0.25 to exploit the opportunity, is the market inefficient?

PROBLEMS

What Is an Efficient Financial Market?

10-1.   The stock of Ultrasound Communications Company (UCC) is listed for trading on the Euronext-Paris stock exchange. For the past several weeks, UCC's stock price has remained around €35.00 per share. Assume that a competitor, Broadband Telephony Company (BTC), announces that it wishes to acquire UCC in an all-cash tender offer for €60.00 per share. BTC also announces that it is willing to pay this price for all UCC's shares tendered to it under the offer, and BTC says that UCC's managers support the takeover attempt. If the tender offer is successful, a merger will be effected in three months' time, and UCC will cease to exist as a separate company. Thus, its stock will be delisted from the exchange.

a. What price do you think UCC's stock will sell for immediately after this announcement?

b. Draw a figure illustrating the likely evolution of UCC's stock price over the next three months.

c. Suppose that rather than offering cash, BTC offers to exchange four of its own shares (which recently traded for €15.00 each) for each outstanding share of UCC. However, after this announcement, BTC shares drop to €12.00. Answer parts (a) and (b) again under this new scenario.

10-2.   You want to measure the cumulative abnormal return (CAR) on a particular stock over a period of time. Assume that the stock has a beta of 1.0, so its expected return equals the market's expected return. Each day, you calculate the return on the stock and subtract the return on the market that day to get the daily abnormal return. As time passes, you simply add these daily abnormal returns together to get the CAR.

a. Fill in the missing values in the following table.

Day	Stock Return (%)	Market Return (%)	Daily Abnormal Return	CAR
1	2.0	1.8	_____	_____
2	−0.35	0.1	_____	_____
3	0.25	−0.15	_____	_____
4	0.65	0.75	_____	_____
5	0.53	0.49	_____	_____

b. Next, suppose that you gather a sample of stocks that just reported higher earnings per share figures than most analysts had anticipated. You calculate the CAR for each company over the 30 days preceding the earnings announcement. You continue to follow these firms for the next 30 days, keeping track of the $CARs$ each day. The following three figures plot the average CAR across all stocks in your sample for the 30 days prior to and the 30 days after the earnings announcement. One of these graphs is inconsistent with the notion that markets are efficient. Identify that graph, and explain why it violates market efficiency. Also explain why the other two graphs do not necessarily violate market efficiency.

10-3.   Stock XYZ has a current price of $70.00 and you own 100 shares. The stock splits 2-for-1 (i.e., 100 shares becomes 200 shares) and has a closing price the next day of $37.50. Calculate the value of your stock holdings pre-split and post-split. Given your findings, is the market inefficient, assuming that XYZ also announces just after the stock split that it has been found innocent of wrong-doing in a multibillion dollar lawsuit?

10-4.   A friend has a trading system in which he buys Stock QLM in the morning and then sells the stock in the afternoon before the exchange closes. Comparing the opening price and closing price, the evidence over the last five days seems to support your friend's strategy given that there has been no news about the company released over the last five days.

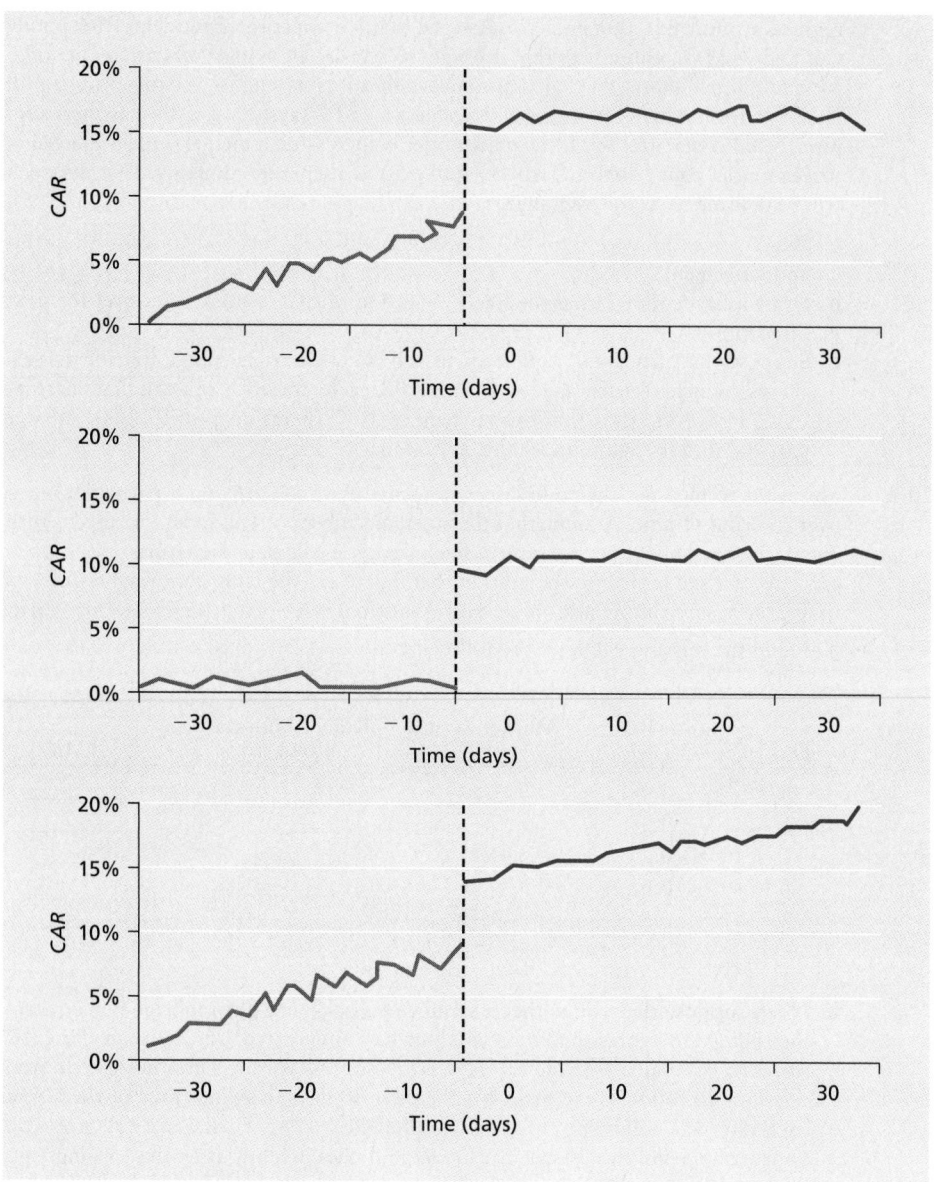

Day	Opening Price	Closing Price
1	$32.00	$32.15
2	$32.10	$32.15
3	$32.15	$32.20
4	$32.15	$32.25
5	$32.20	$32.25

"Stress test" your friend's trading strategy by buying 100 shares at the opening price and then selling the shares at the closing price. After calculating the profit, convert it to average daily profit and determine if the trading costs of $10.00 a day make the strategy viable. How many shares (on average) would you need to trade each day to cover daily overhead of $300.00 (transaction costs plus the value of your time)?

10-5. A professional trader (Trader G) views the price of Stock ABC as either being $25.00 or $45.00 next year with equal probability. Trader Q views the price to be $25.00 with 60% probability and $45.00 with 40% probability next year. Determine the expected (mean) future price for both traders (see Chapter 5), and discount the price by 15% to determine the appropriate price for today. At a spot price of $29.50, who will be willing to buy/sell the stock? Assuming both traders have access to the same public information for determining their price projections, is the market inefficient based on their trading behavior?

10-6. Advisors Inc. will tell 50% of its clients to buy Stock ZZZ and the rest of its clients to short (or sell) Stock ZZZ. Next year, it will do the same with the clients who received the correct advice last year. How many clients must Advisors Inc. start with to receive at least 100 testimonials about the benefit of their advising (assuming only investors who receive the correct advice over the two-year period are willing to give testimonials)? Does Advisors Inc. provide any information beyond what is already publicly available? Does the existence of Advisors Inc. affect the efficiency of the market?

Empirical Evidence on Market Efficiency

10-7. You have been asked to assess the performance, relative to that of the overall stock market, of several mutual fund managers over the past year. During the past year, the risk-free interest rate was 3.0 percent ($R_f = 0.03$) and the return on the S&P 500 Index was 10 percent ($R_m = 0.10$). The following table details each mutual fund's portfolio beta, measured return over the past year, and the management fee charged by each manager.

Fund	Portfolio Beta	Return (%)	Management Fee (%)
Aggressive Growth	1.60	14.5	1.25
Conservative Income	0.90	11.0	0.75
Contrarian	0.40	5.6	1.00

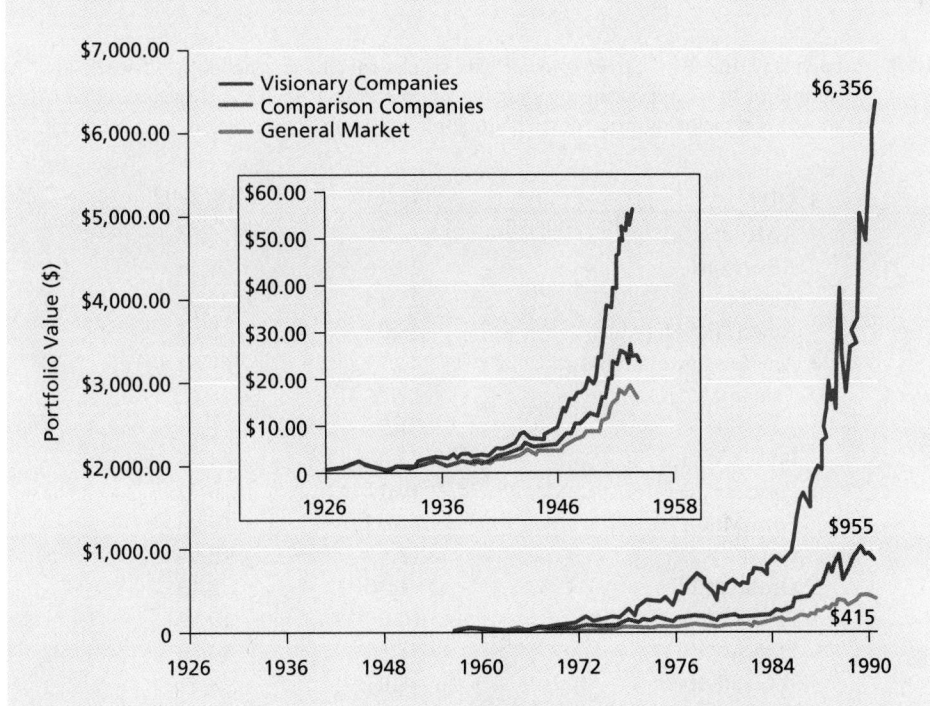

Source: James C. Collins and Jerry I. Porras, *Built to Last: Successful Habits of Visionary Companies* (New York: HarperCollins, 1994).

a. Compute Jensen's *alpha* for each fund, both before accounting for the fund manager's fee and on a net basis.

b. Discuss whether each fund manager created value (outperformed the market index) for investors.

10-8. In the 1994 business best-seller, *Built to Last,* James Collins and Jerry Porras described lessons that all corporate managers should learn by studying a set of "Visionary Companies." In the book's first chapter, the authors plotted a graph showing that, over the long term, a $1 investment in a portfolio of visionary firms substantially outperformed a $1 investment in either a portfolio of comparison firms from the same industries or the broad market index. We reproduce that graph at the bottom of page 413, as well as an updated graph here showing the performance of visionary and comparison companies during the 1990s. What the lessons about market efficiency can you glean from these diagrams?

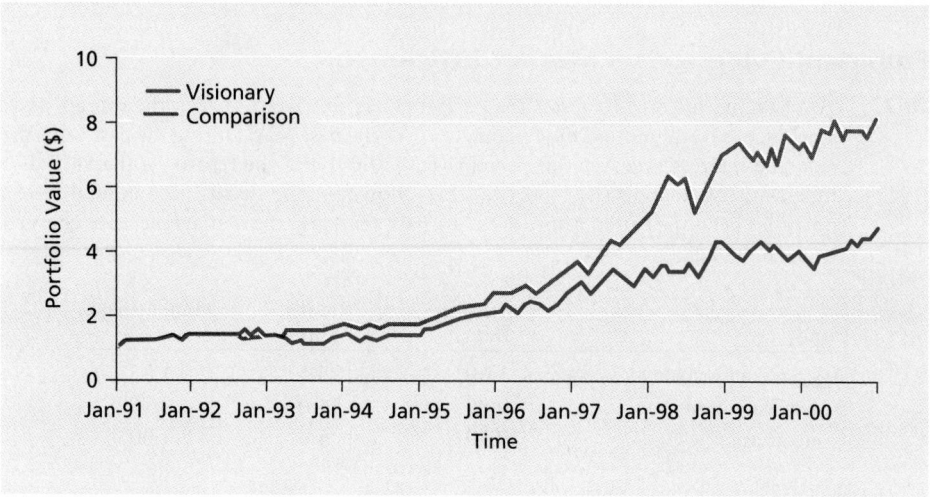

10-9. Each day, the *Wall Street Journal* lists stocks that have reached a 52-week low. A sample of firms appearing on that list on September 4, 2002, appears below. Also shown is the closing price of each stock nine trading days later on September 18.

Firm	9/4/2002	9/18/2002
AAR	$ 6.11	$ 5.05
Albertsons	24.96	25.38
Alcoa	23.14	20.93
American Safety Ins.	8.05	8.05
Ameron International	46.79	47.61
Ashland	27.76	28.62
ATS	1.88	2.05
Boise Cascade	25.85	24.55
Footstar	10.11	10.42
Ford Motor	11.05	10.26
Goodyear	12.87	10.94
Grubb & Ellis	1.30	2.13
Heico	10.09	10.83
Hitachi	51.35	54.13
JLG Industries	8.61	8.71

Firm	9/4/2002	9/18/2002
Longview Fibre	6.15	7.20
Manulife Financial	22.29	21.62
National Semiconductor	15.18	11.93
Oakley	9.70	10.62
Oakwood Homes	1.60	1.70
PCW	1.60	1.44
Sothebys	9.40	7.43
SPS Technologies	27.50	28.03
Stillwater Mining	7.31	6.43
TECO Energy	15.84	15.31
Teradyne	12.19	11.05
Three-Five Systems	5.29	5.20
U.S. Steel	13.13	12.04
ValuCity	1.99	1.90
Vishay Intertechnology	13.37	10.31

a. What fraction of these stocks increased after hitting their 52-week lows, and what fraction continued to decline? Is this consistent with what we would expect if prices follow a random walk?

b. Assuming no dividend payments, calculate the percentage return on each stock from September 4 to September 18. Next, calculate the return on an equally weighted portfolio of these stocks by simply calculating the average return across all firms. Does this return seem consistent with market efficiency? Why or why not?

c. Over the same period, the return on the Nasdaq Composite Index was −1.27 percent. Does this change your answer to part (b)?

10-10. As a simple test of whether stock prices move randomly, go to Yahoo! (http://www .yahoo.com) and download a few weeks of daily returns for a particular stock. Yahoo! gives you the stock's high, low, and closing prices each day. If stock prices display momentum, then we might expect the closing price to be equal to either the high or the low price for the day. Why? Compare the closing price each day to the day's high price, the day's low price, and the midpoint of the high and low prices. What does this tell you about the tendency of stock prices to move randomly?

SMART SOLUTIONS
See the problem and solution explained step-by-step at
SMARTFinance

10-11. The Super Bowl indicator predicts that the stock market will decline in a year following a Super Bowl victory by a team from the old American Football League (AFL) and that the market will otherwise rise. The table below indicates the signal that this indicator gave to investors in each year from 1967 to 2004, as well as the returns on the Dow Jones Industrial Average (DJIA) in the 12 months after each Super Bowl. Note that there is no prediction for 2003, since the Tampa Bay Buccaneers—an expansion team that had never been part of either the AFL or NFL—won that year.

Year	Super Bowl Indicator	Subsequent DJIA (%)	Year	Super Bowl Indicator	Subsequent DJIA (%)
2004	sell	3.1	1996	buy	25.4
2003	NA	–	1995	buy	36.8
2002	sell	−16.8	1994	buy	4.7
2001	sell	−3.7	1993	buy	13.7
2000	buy	3.6	1992	buy	3.2
1999	sell	8.8	1991	buy	13.4
1998	sell	8.9	1990	buy	9.7
1997	buy	24.3	1989	buy	16.3

Year	Super Bowl Indicator	Subsequent DJIA (%)	Year	Super Bowl Indicator	Subsequent DJIA (%)
1988	buy	9.0	1977	sell	−20.7
1987	buy	−6.9	1976	sell	−3.7
1986	buy	30.1	1975	sell	131.6
1985	buy	33.1	1974	sell	−14.1
1984	sell	11.2	1973	sell	−9.9
1983	buy	3.8	1972	buy	2.9
1982	buy	34.9	1971	sell	5.6
1981	sell	−15.4	1970	sell	13.0
1980	sell	12.9	1969	sell	−14.1
1979	sell	6.7	1968	buy	7.7
1978	buy	9.0	1967	buy	0.1

a. Calculate the compound annual percentage return on the DJIA over this period.

b. Suppose that you have followed the Super Bowl indicator every year since 1967. Specifically, when the indicator directed you to buy stocks, you held a portfolio that earned a return comparable to that of the DJIA. In years when the indicator suggested that you should sell stocks, you put your money in Treasury bills earning 4 percent. Also assume that you invest in T-bills during 2003, when the indicator does not yield a signal. Calculate the compound annual rate of return on this strategy.

c. The New England Patriots, an AFC team, won the Super Bowl in 2005. How did U.S. stocks fare in that year?

d. Is this phenomenon inconsistent with market efficiency? Would you advise investors to follow this indicator going forward?

10-12. KPN NV, is a telecommunications company in the Netherlands. The following table lists the monthly closing price, the monthly return, and the previous month's return from August 2001 to June 2005. Calculate the correlation coefficient between each month's return and the previous month's return. Are your findings consistent with market efficiency?

Date	Price	Return	Previous Month's Return
1-Jun-05	8.1	0.011236	−0.04301
2-May-05	8.01	−0.04301	−0.029
1-Apr-05	8.37	−0.029	−0.06911
1-Mar-05	8.62	−0.06911	0.001081
1-Feb-05	9.26	0.001081	0.007625
3-Jan-05	9.25	0.007625	0.102041
1-Dec-04	9.18	0.102041	0.084635
1-Nov-04	8.33	0.084635	0.07113
1-Oct-04	7.68	0.07113	−0.02977
1-Sep-04	7.17	−0.02977	0.051209
2-Aug-04	7.39	0.051209	−0.03699
1-Jul-04	7.03	−0.03699	0.051873
1-Jun-04	7.3	0.051873	0.023599
3-May-04	6.94	0.023599	−0.05307
1-Apr-04	6.78	−0.05307	−0.01105
1-Mar-04	7.16	−0.01105	−0.03979
2-Feb-04	7.24	−0.03979	0.077143

Date	Price	Return	Previous Month's Return
2-Jan-04	7.54	0.077143	−0.02235
1-Dec-03	7	−0.02235	0.045255
3-Nov-03	7.16	0.045255	0.005874
1-Oct-03	6.85	0.005874	0.086124
2-Sep-03	6.81	0.086124	0.009662
1-Aug-03	6.27	0.009662	−0.04167
1-Jul-03	6.21	−0.04167	0.017268
2-Jun-03	6.48	0.017268	0.039152
1-May-03	6.37	0.039152	0.038983
1-Apr-03	6.13	0.038983	−0.0264
3-Mar-03	5.9	−0.0264	−0.04416
3-Feb-03	6.06	−0.04416	0.087479
2-Jan-03	6.34	0.087479	−0.03156
2-Dec-02	5.83	−0.03156	0.069272
1-Nov-02	6.02	0.069272	0.223913
1-Oct-02	5.63	0.223913	−0.07631
3-Sep-02	4.6	−0.07631	0.191388
1-Aug-02	4.98	0.191388	0
1-Jul-02	4.18	0	0.082902
3-Jun-02	4.18	0.082902	−0.06311
1-May-02	3.86	−0.06311	−0.10435
1-Apr-02	4.12	−0.10435	0.067285
1-Mar-02	4.6	0.067285	−0.01147
1-Feb-02	4.31	−0.01147	−0.05217
2-Jan-02	4.36	−0.05217	0.108434
3-Dec-01	4.6	0.108434	0.182336
1-Nov-01	4.15	0.182336	0.432653
1-Oct-01	3.51	0.432653	−0.08922
4-Sep-01	2.45	−0.08922	−0.39002
1-Aug-01	2.69	−0.39002	−0.14202

10-13. Fund TZY has an alpha of 2% when compared to Index ZZZ. The return on Index ZZZ is 12% with a beta of 0.8 associated with the stock (the risk-free rate is 2%). A different index, Index XXX, has a return of 14% with an associated beta for the fund of 0.9. What is the alpha for Fund TZY using Index XXX? Another index, Index VVV, has a return of 15% with an associated beta for the fund of 0.70. What is the alpha for the fund using Index VVV? Which index makes the fund manager look best?

The Behavioral Finance Critique of Market Efficiency

10-14. In September 2001, the month of the terrorist attacks on New York and Washington, D.C., the American Stock Exchange Airline Index declined 47 percent. However, from the end of September to the end of March the next year, the index rose 55 percent.

a. How might behavioral finance explain this pattern of returns?

b. From September 30, 2001, through September 19, 2002, the return on the airline index was negative 44 percent. Does this seem consistent with your answer to part (a)? From a behavioral point of view, does it appear that investors over- or underreacted to the events of September 11, 2001?

10-15. You have a $30,000.00 portfolio that consists of equal investments in stocks A, B and C, each with a current price of $25.00. After one year, Stock A is worth $40.00, Stock B is worth $30.00, and Stock C is worth $12.50. You wish to rebalance your portfolio to equal investments in each stock. How much do you buy/sell of the shares of each stock to rebalance the portfolio? A common behavioral hypothesis is that investors sell winners too soon and hold losers too long. Are your rebalancing actions consistent with this hypothesis?

THOMSON ONE BUSINESS SCHOOL EDITION

10-16. Retrieve the daily closing price for Tivo (ticker symbol, TIVO) for the last year and calculate the daily returns. Find the three largest one-day percent changes in price (either positive or negative). Search for news for the day prior to each return. Is the news positive or negative? Does the stock price reaction to the news make sense? Do positive (negative) returns follow positive (negative) news? Are the results consistent with the market efficiency? How are they consistent or not consistent?

10-17. Using the price data from question 10-16, can you identify any over- or underreactions for Tivo? Be sure to justify your answer.

MINI-CASE: MARKET EFFICIENCY AND BEHAVIORAL FINANCE

The closing prices for Yahoo! are provided below:

Date	Price	Date	Price	Date	Price
Dec-05	40.35	Jan-05	35.21	Feb-04	22.17
Nov-05	40.23	Dec-04	37.68	Jan-04	23.49
Oct-05	36.97	Nov-04	37.62	Dec-03	22.51
Sep-05	33.84	Oct-04	36.19	Nov-03	21.50
Aug-05	33.32	Sep-04	33.91	Oct-03	21.85
Jul-05	33.34	Aug-04	28.51	Sep-03	17.69
Jun-05	34.65	Jul-04	30.80	Aug-03	16.69
May-05	37.20	Jun-04	36.40	Jul-03	15.56
Apr-05	34.50	May-04	30.66	Jun-03	16.35
Mar-05	33.90	Apr-04	25.26		
Feb-05	32.27	Mar-04	24.24		

1. Determine the monthly rate of return from July 2003 to December 2005, and find the correlation coefficient between each month's return and the previous month. What does your finding suggest about the weak form of the efficient markets hypothesis as it applies to Yahoo!?

2. Below you will find the monthly closing net asset value for several mutual funds, as well as the monthly risk-free rate and the monthly closing values for the Standard & Poor's Index. Using Jensen's alpha, determine which of the mutual funds, if any, outperformed the market on a risk-adjusted basis.

	Net Asset Value—Close			S&P500 Index	Monthly Risk-Free Rate
Date	ABCAX	DEKVX	JFKZX		
Nov-05	21.80	48.91	16.70	1249.48	0.34%
Oct-05	20.85	47.63	15.83	1207.01	0.33%
Sep-05	21.00	48.36	16.25	1228.81	0.30%
Aug-05	20.40	46.89	16.58	1220.33	0.30%
Jul-05	20.27	46.33	17.09	1234.18	0.28%
Jun-05	19.67	44.25	16.16	1191.33	0.26%
May-05	19.41	43.28	15.85	1191.50	0.25%
Apr-05	18.70	41.21	14.92	1156.85	0.25%
Mar-05	19.60	41.58	15.45	1180.59	0.25%
Feb-05	19.81	42.21	15.78	1203.60	0.23%
Jan-05	18.71	41.59	15.62	1181.27	0.21%
Dec-04	19.16	44.80	16.35	1211.92	0.20%
Nov-04	19.00	42.27	15.76	1173.82	0.19%
Oct-04	17.87	39.59	14.97	1130.20	0.17%
Sep-04	17.25	39.67	14.31	1114.58	0.15%
Aug-04	16.22	38.00	13.54	1104.24	0.14%
Jul-04	16.55	36.97	13.74	1101.72	0.14%
Jun-04	17.92	39.54	14.92	1140.84	0.13%
May-04	17.42	39.42	14.60	1120.68	0.11%
Apr-04	16.88	38.11	14.36	1107.30	0.09%
Mar-04	17.24	38.16	14.98	1126.21	0.08%
Feb-04	16.85	37.96	14.61	1144.94	0.08%
Jan-04	16.74	36.98	14.02	1131.13	0.08%
Dec-03	16.50	36.16	13.24	1111.92	0.08%
Nov-03	15.98	34.08	13.28	1058.20	0.08%
Oct-03	15.77	33.88	12.95	1050.71	0.08%
Sep-03	8.52	32.79	11.98	995.97	0.08%
Aug-03	8.71	33.05	12.25	1008.01	0.09%
Jul-03	8.54	32.76	11.65	990.31	0.08%
Jun-03	8.36	32.40	10.73	974.50	0.08%
May-03	8.30	31.79	10.28	963.59	0.09%

Chapter 11

An Overview of Long-Term Financing

SMARTFinance
Use the learning tools at www
.thomsonedu.com/finance/smartfinance

420

OPENING FOCUS

So You Think the U.S. Has a Stock Market–Based Corporate Finance System?

Most people would accept as a given that the United States economy relies on our nation's stock markets. The New York Stock Exchange and Nasdaq markets are the largest (and some would say the most efficient) in the world, and U.S. investors, managers, and government policymakers all pay close attention to stock prices. In a crucial sense, however, it is incorrect to say that the United States has a stock market–based financial system: Very few established U.S. companies raise capital by selling new stock in any given year. In fact, Figure 11.1 makes clear that U.S. firms, on net, retire more equity than they issue in many years. Although the stock market serves as a forum in which companies raise capital initially (and stockholders trade ownership interests), companies tend to look elsewhere for subsequent financing. The number of companies looking for additional financing far outnumbers the number seeking initial financing, and the amounts of initial financing are dwarfed by the amounts of other long-term financing.

Three reasons explain why the net-equity statistics frequently turn negative. First, corporate acquisitions paid for with cash—which often total as much as $1 trillion per year—remove the stock of the acquired company from the market. Second, U.S. corporations repurchase over $100 billion worth of their own shares each year, which also removes stock from the market. Third, only a small fraction of large U.S. corporations sell new common stock in a given year. In fact, many of them have not sold new stock for several decades.

Why then is the United States considered a stock market–based economy if equity issues are only a small source of new capital? The answers are surprising and revealing. First, the stock market is an extremely important source of funding for one key group of firms, entrepreneurial growth companies. Each year, these firms raise between $25 and $60 billion in new equity capital through initial public offerings (IPOs). This initial capital influx enables them to grow rapidly.

Second, and more important, U.S. stock markets play a central role in the U.S. system of "corporate governance." This term refers to the system of laws, institutions, and practices that determine how a public company is run, and in whose interest. One of the key governance roles assigned to stock markets is to serve as arenas for corporate-control contests. These contests involve both individual and institutional investors; the end game for such contests usually results in mergers and acquisitions.

So, the next time someone asks you if the United States has a corporate financial system based on stock markets, you can answer with a ringing "Yes, but . . . ."

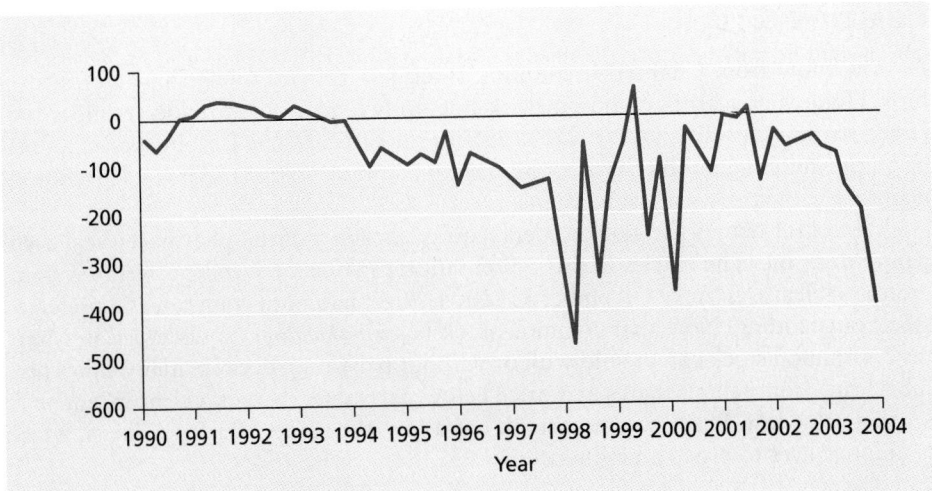

Figure 11.1
Net Equity Issues of the U.S. Corporate Sector, 1990–2004 ($ billion)
Source: 1990–2000 data, "The Party's Over: A Survey of Corporate Finance," *The Economist* (January 27, 2001), p. 11. 2001–2004 data updated by author using U.S. Department of Commerce data.

*L*ong-term financing provides companies with the funds they need to operate and grow. By obtaining financing for the long term (typically considered to be x to y years), companies establish a financing structure for the firm and lock in funding costs that, if all goes well, enable them to succeed. This chapter introduces the primary instruments that companies around the world use for long-term financing, and it examines key patterns observed in corporate financial systems. The basic instruments of long-term financing, which are similar worldwide, are common stock, preferred stock, and long-term debt. As the chapter will show, corporations the world over display common tendencies, particularly the near universal reliance on internally generated cash flow (retained earnings) as the dominant source of new financing.

We begin this chapter with a brief survey of the principal instruments used in corporate finance. We then describe the critical choices companies make regarding their use of internal versus external financing, and their reliance on capital markets versus financial intermediaries for external funding. Next we examine the expanding role of securities markets, key providers of long-term financing, in the global economy. The final section examines the key role that corporate governance plays in modern finance. The effectiveness of a country's corporate governance system influences both national productivity and the financial performance of individual companies.

11.1   THE BASIC INSTRUMENTS OF LONG-TERM FINANCING

Companies have two main sources of corporate long-term financing: debt and equity. **Equity capital** represents an ownership interest, in the form of either common or preferred stock. **Debt capital** is a borrowing—a legally enforceable claim with cash flows that either are fixed or vary according to a predetermined formula. These basic financial instruments exist in most countries, and the rights and responsibilities of the holders of these instruments are very similar worldwide. This section examines these basic instruments of long-term financing.

COMMON STOCK

As you know from Chapter 4, common stock is a general ownership interest in a firm. Holders of a firm's common stock line up behind its debt holders and its preferred stockholders (if any) for claims against the firm's assets. Despite its lack of priority, the investing public has great interest in common stock, and it is a key component of a company's long-term financing.

Table 11.1 details the stockholders' equity accounts of the pharmaceutical company Pfizer, Inc. The entries in this presentation provide an excellent overview common stock features. As of December 31, 2004, Pfizer had both common and preferred stock outstanding. Note that common stock has a *par value*. As discussed in Chapter 2, common stock can be sold with or without par value. Because many states prohibit firms from selling shares at a price below par value, there is a clear incentive to set this value low. Pfizer common stock has a low par value, $0.05 per share, which is unlikely ever to prove a binding constraint.[1]

Table 11.1
Stockholders' Equity Accounts for Pfizer December 31, 2004 and 2003 (dollar values in millions)

	2004	2003
Preferred stock, no par value		
Shares authorized: 27,000,000		
Shares issues: (2004: 4,791; 2003: 5,445)	$ 193	$ 219
Common stock, par value $0.05 per share		
Shares authorized: 12,000,000,000		
Shares issued: (2004: 8,754,000,000; 2003: 8,702,000,000)	$ 438	$ 435
Additional paid-in	67,098	66,396
Employee benefits trust	(1,229)	(1,898)
Treasury stock, at cost		
(2004: 1,281,000,000; 2003: 1,073,000,000)	(35,992)	(29,352)
Retained earnings	35,492	29,382
Accumulated other comprehensive income	2,278	195
Total shareholders' equity	**$68,278**	**$65,377**

Source: 2004 Pfizer Annual Report (posted at *www.pfizer.com*).

At the end of 2004, Pfizer had 12,000,000,000 **shares authorized**, meaning that the firm's stockholders have given Pfizer's board of directors the right to sell up to this number of common shares without further stockholder approval. At that time, there were 8,754,000,000 **shares issued** and outstanding (compared with 8,702,000,000 at year-end 2003). The total par value of these shares was $438 million ($0.205/share × 8,754,000,000 shares). Pfizer also listed $67,098 million of **additional paid-in capital**, or capital in excess of par value. This means that the company actually received $67,536 million ($438 million par value + $67,098 million capital in excess of par) from selling stock during its history, or an average of $7.71 per share.

An amount that does not appear *per se* in the stockholders' equity section, but that is of some interest to investors, is a company's **market capitalization**. This represents the value of shares owned by stockholders and is calculated as market price

---

[1.] Outside the United States par values are often higher because it is common practice for firms to quote dividend payments and other cash distributions as a percentage of par value.

per share times the number of common shares outstanding. Since Pfizer's stock price was $26.50 per share at the end of December 2004, Pfizer's market capitalization on that date was $232.0 billion ($26.50/share $\times$ 8,754,000,000 shares outstanding).

In addition to the shares that were outstanding at the end of 2004, Pfizer has been aggressively repurchasing its shares in the open market for several years. The company repurchased 208 million shares worth $6.66 billion in 2004 and 407 million shares worth an astounding $13.04 billion in 2003. The company holds the stock repurchased during these two years as **treasury stock.** The value of Pfizer's treasury stock was $35,992 million on December 31, 2004.

Finally, Pfizer's accounts show that the firm had *retained earnings* of $35,492 million at year-end 2004. This represents the cumulative amount of profits that the firm has reinvested over the years. Don't be fooled by the $35.5 billion balance of this account. Retained earnings do not represent a pool of cash that the firm can use when a need for cash arises. Retained earnings simply reflect earnings that Pfizer reinvested in previous years.

Common Stockholders as Residual Claimants Shareholders of common stock receive periodic cash distributions from the company in the form of cash dividends. However, firms cannot pay dividends on common stock until they first pay what they owe to creditors and preferred shareholders. Because shareholders hold the right to receive only the cash flow that remains after all other claims against the firm have been satisfied, they are sometimes called **residual claimants.** Obviously, holding the most junior claim on a firm's assets and cash flows is very risky. For this reason, common stockholders generally expect to earn a higher, though more variable, return on their investment than do creditors or preferred shareholders.

Stockholder Voting Rights As residual claimants, stockholders have several important rights, the most important of which is the right to vote at any shareholders' meeting.[2] Most U.S. corporations have a single class of common stock outstanding, and every shareholder has the same rights and responsibilities. Most U.S. corporations also have a **majority voting system,** which allows each shareholder to cast one vote per share for each open position on the board of directors. It stands to reason that the owners (or owner) of 50.1 percent of the firm's stock can decide every contested issue and can elect the people they want to become directors. In practice, an investor or group of investors can control most corporate elections, even if they own less than 50.1 percent of the outstanding shares, because many investors do not bother to vote.

A number of states, including California, Illinois, and Michigan, require corporations to use a **cumulative voting system** to elect directors, unless shareholders explicitly vote for a majority system. Other states permit cumulative voting if the corporation's charter allows it. This system gives to each share of common stock a number of votes equal to the total number of directors to be elected. The votes can be given to *any* director(s) the stockholder desires. Minority shareholders have a better chance of electing at least some directors under a cumulative voting system because they can concentrate all their votes on just one contested board seat.

U.S. companies will occasionally have two or more outstanding classes of stock, usually with differential voting rights. In these cases, corporate insiders will generally

---

[2.] U.S. public corporations must hold a general shareholders' meeting at least once per year. Additionally, special shareholders' meetings may be held to allow stockholders to vote on especially important questions, such as approving corporate mergers, divestitures, or major asset sales.

concentrate their holdings in the superior voting-share class, and ordinary investors will hold relatively more of the inferior voting-share class. This dual-class capital structure is much more common in many other countries than it is in the United States, at least partly because both the New York Stock Exchange and the SEC have actively discouraged U.S. companies from adopting such a structure.[3]

Proxies and Proxy Contests Because most shareholders who own small amounts of stock do not attend the annual meeting to vote, they may sign a **proxy statement** giving their votes to another party. The firm's incumbent managers generally receive most of the stockholders' proxies, partly because managers can solicit them at company expense. Occasionally, when the firm's stock ownership is widely dispersed, outsiders may attempt to gain control by waging a **proxy fight.** This involves soliciting enough votes to challenge, and hopefully unseat, existing directors. In their study of 97 proxy contests, Ikenberry and Lakonishok (1993) found that firms targeted for the proxy fights generally experienced poor financial performance leading up to the proxy battle. More recently, Mulherin and Poulsen (1998) studied the effects of 270 proxy contests and reported that these clashes usually caused share prices to increase, especially when the targeted firm was ultimately acquired by another company.

A significant fraction of stockholders routinely fail to vote. In some cases, brokers and banks that hold shares in "street name" on behalf of their clients are allowed to vote, and they almost always side with management. Bethel and Gillan (2002) showed that when managers submit a proposal for a shareholder vote that they believe will be close, they can craft the proposal in a way that maximizes the votes cast by brokers and banks. Therefore, managers have a limited ability to manipulate the proxy process to obtain outcomes favorable to their own interests.

Rights to Dividends and Other Distributions A firm's board of directors decides whether to pay dividends. Most U.S. corporations that pay dividends pay them quarterly; the common practice in other developed countries is to pay dividends semiannually or annually.

Firms usually pay dividends in cash, but they may also make dividend payments using stock or (on rare occasions) merchandise. Common stockholders have no guarantee that the firm will pay dividends, but shareholders come to expect certain payments based on the company's historical dividend payouts. We examine the dividend decision and its impact on firm valuation in detail in Chapter 16.

Just as shareholders have no guarantee they will receive dividends, they have no assurance they will receive any cash settlement if the firm is liquidated. Due to limited liability, however, shareholders cannot lose more than they invest in the firm. Moreover, the common stockholder can receive unlimited returns through dividends and through share price appreciation. In other words, although nothing is guaranteed, the *possible* rewards for providing equity capital can be considerable.

[3.] For most of its modern history, the NYSE automatically delisted any firm that adopted a dual-class capital structure and also refused to list any company with such a capitalization. The exchange was forced to back off this policy in 1986, when General Motors adopted a two-class structure as part of its acquisitions of Hughes and EDS. Two years later, however, the SEC issued a ruling prohibiting publicly traded companies from adopting a dual-class structure, though the ruling did allow firms going public with such a structure to retain it. Academic papers have examined dual-class capitalizations in the United States (Lease, McConnell, and Mikkelson 1983; DeAngelo and DeAngelo 1985); Israel (Levy 1983); Canada (Jog and Riding 1986); Italy (Zingales 1994); the United Kingdom (Megginson 1990); and Sweden (Bergstrom and Rydqvist 1990). Nenova (2003) presents a multi-country analysis of dual-class firms.

PREFERRED STOCK

Preferred stock investors hold claims that are in most respects senior to those held by common stockholders. The firm promises preferred stockholders a fixed periodic return, stated either as a percentage or as a dollar amount. To use the example of Pfizer presented in Table 11.1, the firm had a single class of preferred stock at the end of 2004. Of the 27 million preferred shares authorized, only 4,791 shares were outstanding.

The amount of preferred stock issued by U.S. companies has been steadily declining. In fact, the total value of nonconvertible preferred stock issued publicly by U.S. firms during 2004, $26.9 billion, represented less than 0.8 percent of the total value of all securities issued. Only four of the 30 companies in the Dow Jones Industrial Average index have any preferred stock outstanding, and even in these cases preferred stock is a miniscule fraction of the firms' total capital.

Is preferred stock going the way of the VHS tape? No. Although it is uncommon for industrial firms to issue preferred stock, public utilities, acquiring firms in merger transactions, and firms that wish to attract corporate rather than individual investors still issue preferred stock. As we will discuss in Chapter 17, venture capitalists also typically structure their investments in entrepreneurial growth companies as convertible preferred stock. The convertibility feature enables holders to opt to convert the preferred shares into a fixed number of common shares.

Historically, state agencies have controlled the rates that public utilities in the United States can charge for their services. Some elements of this highly regulated rate-setting process give utilities the incentive to issue a hybrid security. Because it counts as equity capital, that hybrid increases the firm's credit rating and its debt capacity yet does not carry as high a required rate of return as common stock does. Thus many utilities raise capital by issuing preferred stock.

Firms sometimes issue preferred stock in connection with mergers and acquisitions to capture certain tax advantages that arise when one company buys another's assets. A large fraction of the dividends that corporations holding preferred shares receive are tax-deductible, so corporations rather than individuals own much of the preferred stock issued in the United States.

Like common stockholders, preferred investors hold claims with no fixed maturity date and a lower priority than lenders' claims if the firm is liquidated. In most other ways, though, the rights of preferred stockholders resemble those of creditors. For example, preferred shareholders, like lenders, receive contractually-specified cash payments that do not vary with the profits of the firm (except when profits are so low that the firm defaults). Preferred shareholders also hold a claim that is senior to that of common stockholders, just as lenders do. However, unlike lenders, who can force a firm into bankruptcy if it fails to make scheduled interest and principal payments, preferred stockholders cannot force the firm into bankruptcy if it skips a preferred dividend payment. Finally, because of their preferred status to a claim on company assets, preferred shareholders typically do not have voting rights as do common stockholders.

LONG-TERM DEBT

We now come to the third of the three instruments of long-term financing, long-term debt. Because we provide in-depth coverage of long-term debt in Chapter 19, we present only the briefest sketch of its key features here, beginning with the various methods of classifying debt.

Classifying Long-Term Debt The simplest classification of debt instruments is based on their maturities. **Short-term debt** matures in one year or less, and **long-term debt** matures in more than one year. In this section, we focus on long-term debt.

We can classify long-term debt instruments in various ways: (1) seniority, (2) secured, (3) type of interest rate (fixed or floating), (4) convertibility/callability, and (5) tradability. In this section, we look at each of those types of debt.

Seniority. As stated earlier, debt is always a senior claim to equity, meaning that companies must make interest payments before they can pay any dividends. In the event of corporate bankruptcy, all debt claims must be paid in full before anything can be distributed to equity investors. However, there can be differences in seniority status among a firm's debt claims. **Subordinated debt** securities are junior claims to senior debt. Holders of subordinated debt are entitled to receive interest or principal payments only if the firm has paid senior debt claims in full. Naturally, subordinated debt offers a higher interest rate than senior debt as compensation for its greater default risk.

Security. Still another means of classifying debt is whether the debt is secured or unsecured. Most corporate borrowing from banks and other financial intermediaries is **secured** debt, meaning that the loan is backed by assets that creditors can seize in the event of default. Such pledged assets are termed **collateral** for the loan. A loan secured by real property is usually called a **mortgage**, while loans extended for the purchase of transportation equipment are often structured as **equipment trust receipts**.

Perhaps surprisingly, most of the publicly traded bonds issued by U.S. corporations are backed only by the general faith and credit of the borrowing company. Such bonds are called **debentures**. In many other developed countries, virtually all company borrowing is secured, and the corporate bond market is typically quite small.

Fixed or Floating Rate. We may also classify debt instruments based on whether they pay fixed-rate or floating-rate interest. Most publicly traded corporate bonds promise **fixed-coupon** interest payments. That is, they promise an unchanging series of interest payments (usually semiannual) over the life of the bond. A corporation that issues a 10-year, 8 percent coupon rate debenture with a $1,000 principal value promises to make 20 equal semiannual coupon payments of $40 each ($80 per year) for 10 years, at the end of which time the firm will repay the $1,000 principal to the investor.

Although U.S. debentures typically have fixed-coupon interest rates, most bank loans are **floating-rate instruments.** The interest rate charged on these loan periodically changes to reflect changes in market interest rates. For example, the interest rates on most large **syndicated bank loans** (loans that are funded by a large number of commercial banks, called a *syndicate*) fluctuate with a market rate known as **LIBOR**, the London interbank offered rate. The syndicated loan market is the world's largest single corporate financing market, with over $2 trillion in credits arranged most years ($2.65 trillion during 2004).

APPLYING THE MODEL 11.1

On March 21, 2005, Allied Waste Industries, Inc. (NYSE: AW) announced that it had completed the refinancing and refunding of a syndicated loan agreement worth $3.425 billion. The new credit facility includes a $1.35 billion term loan, a

$1.575 billion revolving credit facility, and a $500 million line of credit (LOC) facility. The syndicate that arranged the loan had priced both the term loan and LOC facility at LIBOR plus 200 basis points (2.0 percentage points), and the revolving credit facility at LIBOR plus 300 basis points. The three facilities had maturities ranging between 2010 and 2012. In addition, all three had financial covenants mandating that Allied Waste maintain strong interest coverage and total leverage ratios.

Convertibility/Callability. We can further classify corporate bonds by noting whether they are convertible or callable. Most bonds issued by U.S. corporations are **callable,** meaning that the issuing corporation has the right to force investors to sell the bonds back to the company at the firm's discretion. This right becomes valuable for corporations when market interest rates decline: It allows the firm to refinance its long-term, fixed-rate borrowing at a lower interest rate.

Obviously, what is good for the issuing corporation is bad for the investor, so callable bonds have to offer higher interest rates than similar noncallable debt. Furthermore, most bonds are protected from being called for several years after they are issued, and corporations usually must pay a call premium (frequently set at one year's additional interest) to call bonds after the protection period ends.

Some corporate bonds grant investors the right to exchange their bonds for shares of stock rather than cash. Called **convertibles,** these bonds offer investors the seniority (relative to equity) of a debt instrument and the potential for much higher returns if the underlying stock rises in value. Convertible bonds usually grant investors the right to exchange one bond for a fixed number of shares. Because the number of shares per bond is fixed, the value of the conversion option rises as the price of the underlying stock does. Because the option to convert bonds into shares is valuable, convertible bonds pay lower interest rates than otherwise similar nonconvertible bonds.

Companies can sell convertible bonds that are repaid in shares of another company that the issuing firm happens to own, as the following Applying the Model shows.

SMART IDEAS VIDEO

David Mauer, Southern Methodist University
"What is the short-term market price reaction to call events?"

See the entire interview at **SMARTFinance**

APPLYING THE MODEL 11.2

March 2005 saw an unusually large volume (over $3.5 billion) of convertible debt being sold to international investors. The Dutch banking and insurance group Fortis sold $700 million worth of bonds that will be redeemed in shares of Assurant, a U.S. insurance company that Fortis once owned. Similarly, JPMorgan sold €1,600 million of bonds that will be repaid in shares of the German insurer Allianz, and Switzerland's UBS sold €700 million of bonds that will be converted into shares of DaimlerChrysler. In all three cases, the issuing company received the bond proceeds, even though bond repayment will be made in another company's shares.

Tradability. Finally, we can distinguish those debt instruments that can be traded among investors, called **securities,** from those that are essentially loan products offered by financial intermediaries. In our previous discussions, we have used the terms "loan," "bond," and "debt instrument" more or less interchangeably. However, the terms and conditions imposed upon a company borrowing from a financial intermediary in the form of loans or lines of credit are often quite different from those that would be imposed if the same company sold (issued) debt securities directly to investors using the public capital markets.

As will be discussed in greater detail in Chapter 17, a bank generally imposes what are called restrictive covenants, restrictions placed on a firm by its lenders to keep the firm from defaulting on its obligations. **Loan covenants** are placed on a borrower in an attempt to protect the bank's investment. **Positive covenants** specify what borrowers *must* do, such as provide audited financial statements and maintain minimum debt coverage ratios. **Negative covenants** specify what the borrowing firm *must not* do, such as sell assets without the bank's approval or borrow additional senior debt. Additionally, banks are usually willing and able to monitor a borrower's operating and financial performance over the life of the loan and can intervene when a problem emerges.[4]

Borrowing Choices Large corporations have a variety of choices to meet their borrowing needs. As an example, Table 11.2 demonstrates the short- and long-term debt accounts for Pfizer at the end of 2004. Pfizer has several borrowing patterns typical of most large U.S. companies:

1. The book value of Pfizer's short-term debt of $11,016 million is *comparable in amount* to its long-term debt of $7,279 million.
2. A large fraction of the short-term borrowing takes the form of **commercial paper**. This is a type of short-term instrument that is sold directly to corporate and individual investors and is usually held to maturity. Commercial paper is almost always supported by a standby borrowing arrangement with a commercial bank.[5]
3. The company has numerous publicly traded debentures outstanding with varying maturities, interest rates, and even currencies.
4. The notes to Pfizer's balance sheet (not shown in Table 11.2) show that the company has substantial unused borrowing capacity that it could draw on very quickly. Pfizer has several different borrowing programs in place that are not being tapped to the full, including various bank loan arrangements and note-issuance facilities. As one of the world's best-known and most respected corporations, Pfizer has virtually unlimited access to capital markets around the world.

This section has described the major types of financial instruments that companies use to raise long-term financing. The number of variations on each of these types is truly astonishing. Finnerty and Emery (2002) identify 80 distinct securities that have been introduced in the United States since 1970. Each is designed to fill a specific gap in the market. For example, **catastrophe bonds** distribute interest and principal payments based on whether the issuer, an insurance company, experiences losses of a certain magnitude from a natural disaster, such as a hurricane or an earth-

---

[4.] Public security issues also contain positive and negative covenants, but since there are usually a large number of small investors for any single bond issue, these covenants are very difficult to monitor and enforce. Although an agent (trustee) is appointed to represent the investors' interests, it remains true that less corporate monitoring will generally be undertaken with publicly issued debt than with intermediated borrowing.

[5.] According to U.S. Federal Reserve Board statistics, U.S. companies had over $1.43 *trillion* worth of commercial paper outstanding at the end of March 2005, of which some $133 billion was issued by nonfinancial corporations such as Pfizer. The remaining $1.30 trillion was issued by financial institutions. In order to be exempt from registration as a publicly issued "security," commercial paper must have an original maturity of 270 days or less; most issues have much shorter maturities.

Table 11.2
Short and Long-Term
Debt of Pfizer
December 31, 2004
and 2003 (dollar values
in millions)

Short-term debt[a]		2004	2003
Commercial paper		$ 9,109	$7,781
Short-term loans		1,000	300
Long-term debt: Current maturities		907	726
Total		$11,016	$8,807

Long-term debt		2004	2003
U.S. Dollars	**Maturities**	**Amount**	**Amount**
Senior unsecured notes:			
LIBOR-based floating-rate[b]	January 2006	$ 1,000	—
5.625%	February 2006	771	804
6.60%	December 2028	749	736
4.50%	February 2014	742	—
2.50%	March 2007	686	—
5.625%	April 2009	644	656
6.50%	December 2018	528	521
3.30%	March 2009	294	296
4.65%	March 2018	294	290
6.00%	January 2008	266	275
5.75%	December 2005	—	615
Unsecured notes: Commercial paper-based floating-rate	March 2005	—	200
Other: Debentures, notes, borrowings and mortgages		719	803
Japanese yen (0.80%)	March 2008	586	559
Total long-term debt		$ 7,279	$5,755

[a]The weighted-average interest rate for short-term borrowings at December 31 was 2.5% in 2004 and 1.7% in 2003.

[b]The LIBOR-based floating-rate notes bear interest of 1.8% at December 31, 2004.

Source: 2004 Pfizer, Inc. Annual Report (posted at *www.pfizer.com*).

quake. Insurance companies sell these bonds to redistribute some of the risk of their product portfolios. Delta Air Lines recently used another financial product innovation, called exchangeable notes, to try to avoid a bankruptcy filing, as described in Applying the Model 11.3.

APPLYING THE MODEL 11.3

In September 2004, Delta Air Lines asked holders of its unsecured short-, medium-, and long-term debt—with an aggregate par value (face value) of $2.6 billion— to exchange their securities for $680 million of bonds backed by aircraft and flight-training equipment. Delta indicated that it would make the offering only if sufficient numbers of each class of bondholders tendered their securities, and if Delta successfully negotiated wage concessions from its pilots' union. Delta justified launching this exchangeable note, with its punitive exchange ratio, as a way to show its employees that the company's suppliers and investors were also suffering because of Delta's financial problems.

Two months later, having achieved a wage deal with its pilots, Delta announced that a sufficient number its short-term creditors had tendered their bonds; the company issued $257 million of new collateralized bonds in exchange. However, not enough intermediate- and long-term bondholders tendered their bonds, so Delta returned the original those securities and canceled that part of the exchangeable note issue.

Concept Review Questions

1. What relationship would you expect between the interest rate offered on a callable bond and the call premium?

2. Most large Japanese corporations hold their annual shareholders' meeting on the same day and require voting in person. What does this practice say about the importance and clout of individual shareholders in Japanese corporate finance?

11.2 THE BASIC CHOICES IN LONG-TERM FINANCING

Companies the world over face the same basic financing problem: how to fund those projects and activities the firm needs to undertake to grow and prosper. This section examines the choices firms face in selecting among financing alternatives, particularly the choices regarding internal versus external financing.

THE NEED TO FUND A FINANCIAL DEFICIT

Corporations everywhere are net dissavers, which is a way in economics of saying they demand more financial capital than they supply in the form of retained profits. Corporations must close this **financial deficit** by borrowing or by issuing new equity securities. Every major firm confronts four critical financing decisions on an ongoing basis:

1. How much capital must the company raise each year?
2. How much of this must the company raise externally rather than through retained profits?
3. How much of the external funding should the company raise through borrowing from a bank or another financial intermediary, and how much capital should it raise selling securities directly to investors?
4. What proportion of the external funding should be structured as common stock, preferred stock, or long-term debt?

The answer to the first question depends on the capital budgeting process of a particular firm, as discussed in Chapters 8–10. A company must raise enough capital to fund all its positive-*NPV* investment projects and to cover its working capital needs. The true financing decision begins with question 2, the choice between internal versus external finance.

THE CHOICE BETWEEN INTERNAL VERSUS EXTERNAL FINANCING

At first glance, the internal/external choice seems to be a decision that firms can make mechanically. A company's managers might approximate external funding needs by subtracting cash dividend payments from the firm's **cash flow from operations** (net income plus depreciation and other noncash charges). The difference between this internally generated funding and the firm's total financing needs would equal the external financing requirement. The decision is not that simple, however, because management may wish to build up or reduce working capital stocks over time and because dividend policy is not fixed, except in the very short term.

Nonetheless, it is basically true that the total amount of net external financing a firm requires each year is a residual amount, calculated as the difference between the firm's total capital needs and its cash flow from operations (net of dividend payments). Not surprising, the residual nature of external funding needs implies that this figure will vary highly from year to year for individual companies. External funding is also a highly variable figure for the U.S. corporate sector as a whole, and the same is true for most other developed economies.

External funding needs tend to peak at the ends of economic expansions and bottom out during recessions. Intuitively, this makes sense because firms invest little during recessions and much during expansions. Also, internal cash flow is the dominant source of corporate funding in the United States. U.S. businesses regularly finance two-thirds to three-quarters of all their capital spending needs internally.

Over time, other countries are also moving in the same direction. Whereas European corporations relied quite heavily on external funding as recently as the 1970s, the corporate sectors of Western European nations now meet the majority of their total funding needs internally. Japanese corporations still meet up to half of their total financing needs externally, primarily through bank borrowing, but this still implies far lower dependence on external funding than was the case prior to the 1980s.

OTHER FINANCING CHOICES

Once a company has determined how much capital it needs to raise externally, it must then confront the next two financing decisions: whether to raise money through financial intermediaries or through the sale of securities, and how to allocate between debt and equity the money required. We will defer discussion of this third decision —the proportion of equity and debt financing—until Chapters 12 and 13, where we examine the firm's capital structure decision.

The remainder of this chapter will describe the firm's choice between intermediated and capital market financing and the need for effective corporate governance. We begin by examining the role intermediaries play in the corporate finance systems of the United States and other countries. We then detail the rapidly growing role of capital markets in funding corporate activities around the world. Finally, we describe what corporate governance means and discuss why it has assumed such prominence in corporate finance the world over.

COMPARATIVE CORPORATE FINANCE

What Do Private Pension Funds and Capital Markets Have in Common?

While not obvious at first glance, there is in fact a strong link between the pension system covering most of a nation's citizens size of that nation's capital markets. Countries that rely primarily on a privately financed, or "funded" pension system tend to also have large capital markets, partly because most of the annual pension fund contributions are invested in the nation's stock and bond markets. The United States and Britain have the world's largest pension fund investments at year-end 2002—$5,934 billion and $1,049 billion (2001), respectively—while the Netherlands and Switzerland have the largest private pension fund investments expressed as a percentage of GDP, with 106 percent (2001) and 125 percent, respectively. These four countries also have capital markets that are among the world's largest and most efficient. Most other developed countries, especially the large continental European nations, rely al-

most exclusively on state-run, "pay as you go" (unfunded) pension systems, and have much smaller capital markets. In an unfunded pension system, a younger generation of employed workers supports an older generation of retirees. These unfunded systems are coming under severe strain, for two reasons. First, declining birth rates in all of these countries are causing the average age of the population to rise rapidly, thus reducing the ratio of employed workers to retirees. Second, most of these countries offer very generous payments to pensioners, which can only be supported by equally high taxes on workers. Most countries with pay as you go systems are attempting to switch to a funded system—or at least increase the role of private financing in pensions—but the chart above makes clear how difficult this transition will be.

What Do Private Pension Funds and Capital Markets Have in Common?
Sources: The Economist for France (2000 pension fund assets as % of GDP); OECD for all other countries (2001 or 2002 pension fund investment as % of GDP and stock market capitalization)

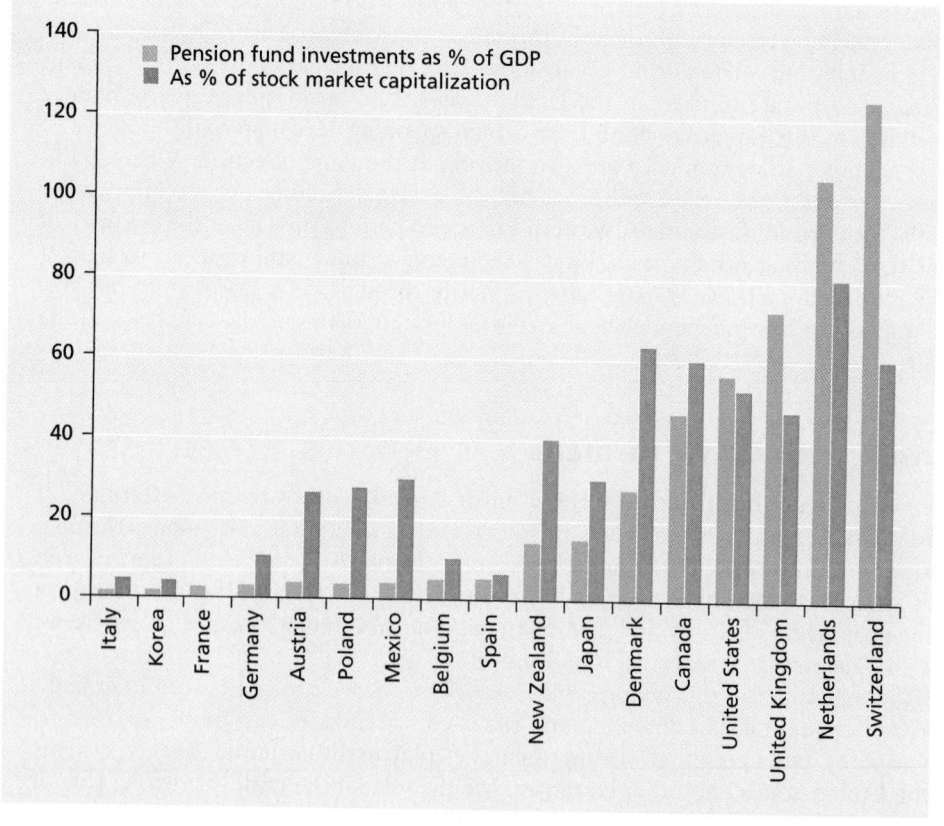

3. Why do you think corporations maintain a fixed dividend payment and thus make net external financing the "residual" financial choice, rather than the other way around? In other words, why don't firms make dividends the residual?

4. Why do you think that corporations around the world rely so heavily on internally generated funds for investment capital? Why do you think firms sometimes simultaneously increase dividends and sell securities?

11.3 THE ROLE OF FINANCIAL INTERMEDIARIES IN FUNDING CORPORATE INVESTMENT

Should a corporation care whether it raises capital by selling securities to investors in public capital markets or by dealing more directly with a financial intermediary such as a commercial bank? Because money is a commodity, a bank's money and an investor's money should seemingly be perfect substitutes. In reality, however, a corporation's choice between intermediated and security-market financing significantly influences its post-financing ownership structure, financial flexibility, and repayment burden. On a broader scale, whether a country emphasizes intermediary or capital market–based financing also influences the key features of the corporate finance system that nation develops. Before analyzing this issue, however, we should formally define what a financial intermediary is and briefly describe what services it provides.

What Is a Financial Intermediary, and What Does It Do?

A **financial intermediary** (FI) is an institution that raises capital by issuing liabilities against itself—for example, in the form of demand or savings deposits. The intermediary then pools the funds raised and uses them to make loans to borrowers or, where allowed, to make equity investments in nonfinancial firms. Borrowers repay the intermediary and have no direct contact with the individual savers who actually funded the loans. In other words, both borrowers and savers deal directly with the intermediary. Because of their role between borrowers and savers, intermediaries specialize in credit analysis and collection, and they offer financial products tailored to the specific needs of both groups.

Intermediaries provide many financial services to corporations, but the most important is **information intermediation**. In financial markets, investors have great difficulty assessing the true creditworthiness of borrowers prior to lending them money and in monitoring how borrowers subsequently use these funds. Faced with these information problems, investors will either choose not to lend at all or will do so only at high interest rates. A commercial bank or other FI can overcome these problems by becoming a **corporate insider,** trusted with confidential information about the borrowing firm's operations and interacting with corporate managers on an ongoing basis. If successful, the bank will be able to first assess and then meet the firm's evolving financial needs.[6]

[6.] Petersen and Rajan (1994) document the value of banking relationships, particularly to small firms. Other academic researchers present similar findings.

THE ROLE OF FINANCIAL INTERMEDIARIES IN U.S. CORPORATE FINANCE

Americans have long distrusted concentrated private economic power, and this has dramatically influenced U.S. financial regulation. In response to public opinion, policymakers discouraged the growth of large intermediaries (especially commercial banks), in part by imposing on them severe geographical restrictions. Existing geographical restrictions were codified into national law when Congress passed the **McFadden Act** in 1927, which prohibited interstate banking. After numerous failed attempts to repeal the McFadden Act over the years, in July 2004 Congress finally approved a bill allowing full interstate branch banking. This act prompted an acceleration of the trend toward consolidation of the banking industry. The number of independent U.S. banks declined by about a third between October 1992 and December 2003, primarily through mergers.

The second pivotal law affecting American FIs was the **Glass-Steagall Act,** which was passed in 1933 in response to perceived banking abuses during the Great Depression. This legislation mandated the separation of investment and commercial banking: It prohibited commercial banks from underwriting corporate security issues, providing security brokerage services to their customers, or even owning voting equity securities on their own account. Banking's corporate financing role was thus effectively restricted to making commercial loans and providing closely related services, such as leasing. As with the McFadden Act, there were repeated attempts to repeal Glass-Steagall, and these finally succeeded when Congress passed the **Gramm-Leach-Bliley Act** in November 1999.

Nonbank FIs also play important roles in U.S. corporate finance, both as creditors and as equity investors. Insurance companies, for example, provide much of the long-term financing for large real estate development and factory construction. They also directly own roughly 5 percent of all publicly traded corporate equity. Also, specialized finance companies such as General Electric Credit Corporation and General Motors Acceptance Corporation have carved out very successful niches as secured lenders for major equipment purchases. Finally, public and private pension funds have emerged in recent years as by far the single most important class of equity investor in the United States, and these institutions have assumed the role of activist monitors of corporate managers.

Perhaps the most interesting U.S. nonbank financial intermediaries are the institutional venture capital firms, which we examine in depth in Chapter 17. These companies have enjoyed remarkable success over the years in identifying, financing, and nurturing to maturity many of today's best-known high-technology companies—including Intel, Microsoft, Dell, Amgen, Cisco Systems, Sun Microsystems, and more recently, Yahoo, Amazon.com, eBay, and Google.

THE CORPORATE FINANCE ROLE OF NON-U.S. FINANCIAL INTERMEDIARIES

In markets outside the United States, commercial banks typically play much larger roles in corporate finance. In most countries, a relative handful of very large banks service most large firms, and the size and competence of these banks give them tremendous influence over corporate financial and operating policies. This power is further strengthened by the ability of most non-U.S. banks to underwrite corporate security issues and to make direct equity investments in commercial firms. Whereas the

United States, Britain, and a few other nations have promoted the development of a security market–based corporate finance system, most other advanced countries have chosen to emphasize intermediated systems.

In many countries, financial intermediaries also play extremely important corporate governance roles, distinct from their activities in granting credit and monitoring loan repayment. Commercial banks, in particular, frequently help set client firms' operating and financial policies by serving on corporate boards and monitoring the performance of senior managers. In countries such as Germany, where banks can both directly own large equity stakes and vote the shares they hold in trust for individual customers, financial intermediaries wield tremendous economic power.

In countries with a long state-ownership tradition, state-owned banks are usually the chosen vehicle for exercising financial control. For political and historical reasons, however, the United States has chosen to effectively prohibit commercial banks from exercising any significant corporate governance role, and has discouraged other intermediaries (insurance companies, pension funds, mutual funds) from actively monitoring corporate managers.

Concept Review Questions

5. What factors might lead to better information intermediation by a financial intermediary as compared to a public financial market?

6. How do you think a bank's incentives change if it is allowed to hold the equity securities of firms in addition to offering them loans?

7. Compare the intermediation services performed by a small community bank and a large corporate pension fund. What do they have in common, and what are their major differences?

11.4   THE EXPANDING ROLE OF SECURITIES MARKETS IN THE GLOBAL ECONOMY

There have been significant differences between countries regarding how heavily firms rely on capital markets rather than financial intermediaries for funding. For example, the corporate financial systems of industrialized countries with legal systems based on English common law—such as Canada, the United States, Britain, and Australia—have large, highly liquid stock and bond markets. Other industrialized countries, particularly those in continental Europe with legal systems based on German or French civil law, have had much smaller capital markets and rely primarily on commercial banks for corporate financing.

No trend in modern finance is as clear or as transforming as the worldwide shift toward corporate reliance on securities markets rather than intermediaries for external financing. We begin this section by documenting this global trend toward market-based financing and then look specifically at security issuance in U.S. capital markets. We conclude by describing security-issue patterns in other advanced countries.

OVERVIEW OF SECURITIES ISSUES WORLDWIDE

Table 11.3 presents summary information from the *Investment Dealers' Digest* on primary security issues, both worldwide and for the United States alone, for the years 1990–2004. **Primary issues** are those in which a company makes a first public offer-

Table 11.3
Worldwide Securities Issues, 1990–2004

Type of Security Issue	2004	2003	2002	2001	2000	1995	1990
Worldwide offerings	$5,693	$5,362	$4,257	$4,075	$3,268	$1,066	$504
[debt & equity]	(20,067)	(20,146)	(18,006)	(16,748)	(14,659)	(9,305)	(7,574)
Global debt (2000–04)	5,188	4,973	3,938	3,610	2,624	385	184
International debt (1990–99)	(16,445)	(17,474)	(15,811)	(14,033)	(10,827)	(2,548)	(1,376)
High-grade corp debt (2001–04)	1,922	1,758	1,337	—	946	280	172
Eurobonds (1990–2000)	(6,194)	(6,207)	(5,506)	(3,858)	(1,840)	(1,213)	
Yankee bonds (2000–04)	124	96	59	36	47	45	13
Foreign bonds (1990–99)	(489)	(460)	(212)	(84)	(112)	(237)	(81)
International common stock	277	145	135	148	335	21	7
[excluding U.S.][a]	(2,395)	(1,412)	(1,481)	(1,659)	(2,662)	(242)	(132)
U.S. Issuers worldwide[b]	3,399	3,417	2,859	2,880	1,958	700	313
[debt & equity]	(11,510)	(12,401)	(10,646)	(12,269)	(15,686)	(6,807)	(6,141)
All debt[c]	3,204	3,228	2,695	2,618	1,726	—	—
	(10,479)	(11,521)	(9,964)	(11,271)	(7,824)	—	—
Straight corporate debt[d]	1,227	1,259	1,017	1,209	744	417	109
	(4,015)	(4,294)	(3,867)	(4,423)	(2,986)	(4,562)	(1,016)
High-yield corporate debt	141	135	59	76	43	28	1
	(544)	(496)	(261)	(261)	(196)	(153)	(7)
Collateralized securities[e]	1,557	1,451	1,261	935	488	155	175
	(2643)	(2,391)	(2,029)	(1,623)	(1,201)	(709)	(4,542)
Convertible debt and	47	97	60	103	56	9	5
preferred stock	(104)	(284)	(137)	(210)	(161)	(57)	(43)
Common stock[f]	147	91	104	126	223	82	14
	(832)	(596)	(545)	(559)	(955)	(1,159)	(362)
Initial public offerings[f]	50	16	27	37	60	30	5
	(194)	(91)	(97)	(106)	(386)	(572)	(174)

Notes: This table details the total value, in billions of U.S. dollars, and number (in parentheses) of securities issues worldwide (including the United States) for selected years in the period 1990–2004. The data are taken from early-January issues of the *Investment Dealers' Digest*.
[a]Capital-raising private-sector offers; does not include privatization issues.
[b]From 1998, all figures include Rule 144A offers on U.S. markets.
[c]Includes mortgage-backed securities (MBS), asset-backed securities (ABS) and municipal bonds.
[d]Years 1999–2004 are long-term straight debt only. Before 1999, figures are for investment grade debt.
[e]Asset-backed securities plus mortgage-backed securities.
[f]Excludes closed-end fund. Data for 1990-2000 are not comparable to 2001 due to definition change.

ing of the security; such issues actually raise capital for firms. Primary issues are different from **secondary offerings,** in which an investor sells his or her holdings of existing securities. Secondary offerings raise no additional capital for the firm.

The total value of primary issues around the world in 2004 was a record $5.693 trillion. Worldwide security offerings were $1.066 trillion in 1995 and less than $400 billion as recently as 1988. The 14-fold increase in the value of security market financing between 1988 and 2004 was not matched by a remotely comparable increase in world trade, investment, or economic activity. Instead, this increase reflects the trend toward the "securitization" of corporate finance. **Securitization** involves the repackaging of loans and other traditional bank-based credit products into securities that can be sold to public investors. The entries in Table 11.3 show just some of the many securities available.

Security Issues by U.S. Corporations Besides securitization, another major trend that appears in these data is the relatively steady fraction of worldwide security offerings accounted for by U.S. issuers. U.S. issues represented 59.8 percent ($3.399 trillion of $5.693 trillion) of the worldwide total value of security offerings in 2004, and U.S. issuers have sold between 59 percent and 74 percent of the global total every year since 1990.

Looking more closely at the statistics for the United States alone, we can identify several other trends that are transforming U.S. finance. First, companies issue far more debt than equity each year. During 2004, U.S. issuers raised $3.204 trillion through debt offerings versus $147 billion of common stock and a mere $26.9 billion of nonconvertible preferred stock (not listed in Table 11.3). Debt therefore represented *over 94 percent* of the total capital raised by U.S. companies through public security issues in 2004. The common stock issued in 2004 represented a mere 4.3 percent of the capital-raising total. Even though this fraction was unusually small, equity issues always account for a very small share of the total amount of capital raised through public security issues in the United States.[7] Add in the roughly $1.5 trillion in syndicated bank loans that U.S, companies arrange each year, and it becomes clear that firms needing to raise capital externally greatly prefer to issue debt rather than common or preferred stock.

Second, **initial public offerings** (IPOs), excluding closed-end investment funds, accounted for over one-third ($50 billion of the $147 billion total) of common stock issued by companies in 2004. Initial public offerings involve the first public sale of stock to outside investors. Chapter 18 discusses them in depth. Companies must register IPOs, as well as subsequent **seasoned** issues, with the SEC, and virtually all companies choose to list their stock on one of the organized exchanges so that investors can easily buy or sell the stock. America's IPO market is easily the world's largest and most liquid source of equity capital for small, rapidly growing firms, and most observers consider it a key national asset.

Security Issues for Non-U.S. Firms Table 11.3 also reveals a number of patterns in the international security-issuance data. First, international corporate issuers show the same preference for issuing debt rather than equity that U.S. companies have: Debt securities accounted for over 86 percent of the capital raised by non-U.S. firms during 2004.

Certain securities, most notably Eurobonds, can be sold to international investors that cannot be offered in the United States. A **Eurobond** issue is a single-currency bond sold in several countries simultaneously. A dollar-denominated bond issued by a U.S. corporation and sold to European investors is an example of a Eurobond. In contrast, a **foreign bond** is an issue sold by a nonresident corporation in a single foreign country, and denominated in the host country's currency. A Swiss franc–denominated bond sold in Switzerland by a Japanese corporate issuer is an example of a foreign bond. Table 11.3 shows that in 2004, as in most years, **Yankee bonds** sold by foreign corporations to U.S. investors were the single largest category of for-

SMART ETHICS VIDEO

Kent Womack, Dartmouth College
"It's very easy for analysts to have conflict of interest problems."

See the entire interview at
SMARTFinance

[7.] Remember that these are all gross issue amounts; once the value of stock removed from public markets through mergers and stock repurchases is accounted for, net equity issues are often negative.

eign bond issue; Swiss (Heidi bonds) and Japanese (Samurai) foreign bonds were the next largest.

A second pattern observable in the international finance data is that **international common stock** issues raised $277 billion in 2004. These are equity issues that are sold in more than one country by nonresident corporations.[8] The 2004 amount was somewhat less than 2000's $335 billion record, but up dramatically from the $21 billion total in 1995. This total has grown steadily over the years, and now exceeds the U.S. domestic equity issuance volume, though roughly half of the international total is usually **Yankee common stock** issued by foreign firms in the U.S. market.

To summarize, the growth in international security issues has kept pace with that in the United States, though this growth has probably affected non-U.S. economies more because it began from a much smaller base. This is particularly true for the countries of continental Europe. Over the past decade these countries have become very acquainted with a phenomenon long associated with U.S. financial markets: large numbers of mergers and acquisitions.

THE WORLDWIDE SURGE IN MERGERS AND ACQUISITIONS

In the last decade, the value of mergers and acquisitions (M&A) has surged worldwide. Figure 11.2 details the total value of mergers and acquisitions around the world from 1990 to 2004. The global value of M&A hovered around $500 billion from 1990 to 1993. By 1998, it had increased sevenfold to $2.5 trillion, and reached more than $3.4 trillion in 2000 before dropping sharply during 2001–03. The global value of M&A then rebounded to $1.95 trillion in 2004. No comparable period in financial history saw as dramatic an increase in takeover activity as did 1992–2000, and 2000's record $3.46 trillion in announced takeover deals equaled almost 10 percent of world GDP.

The fraction of each year's mergers and acquisitions total accounted for by U.S. versus European transactions fluctuated between 40 percent and 65 percent over the decade. Deals done by non-U.S. companies outpaced those of U.S. acquirers in the early 1990s, and transactions by U.S. firms predominated later. Acquisitions that had U.S. targets had a total value of $1.12 trillion in 2004 (versus $1.8 trillion in 2000), whereas deals involving European targets had a total value of $349.2 billion (versus $1.0 trillion in 2000). M&A activity outside Europe and the United States represents less than 10 percent of the worldwide total most years.

What accounts for this amazing increase in takeover activity in Europe and the United States? Although the root industrial and economic causes of takeover waves are still poorly understood, two things are clear. First, takeover waves tend to occur during periods of rising stock market valuations. As our discussions earlier in this book showed, stock market valuations in Europe and America surged during the 1990s. Second, mergers and acquisitions appear to be an unavoidable side-effect of increasing reliance on capital markets for financing. This is true even though relatively little new common stock is issued each year. As the size and efficiency of public capital markets increase, the demand for firm-specific information disclosure also

---

[8.] Note that the international common stock figure does not include proceeds from *privatization issues,* which are typically not capital-raising events because the government is merely selling off existing shares. Total privatization proceeds (including asset sales) reached a record $180 billion in 2000, with two-thirds of this total being raised in Europe. This activity fell dramatically during 2001–2003, but then rebounded somewhat to $96 billion in 2004.

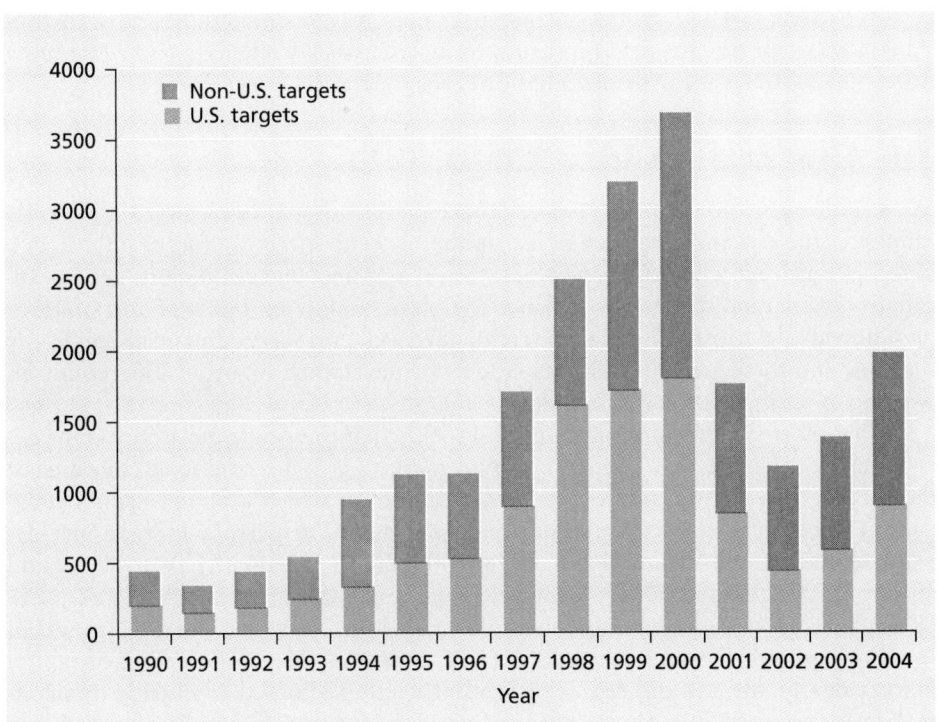

Figure 11.2
Global Mergers and Acquisitions, 1991–2004 ($ billions)

increases. These factors work to promote the growth of all capital markets, equity as well as debt.

In order for a nation's capital markets to grow, however, an effective system of corporate governance must be in place. Academic research now clearly documents that effective corporate governance promotes both individual company performance and national economic achievement. We conclude this chapter by briefly discussing what this research implies for practicing financial managers.

---

8. What patterns are observed in U.S. security issues each year? How do these patterns compare to those in international security issues?

9. Why do you think that mergers and acquisitions have grown rapidly during the past decade? If stock market valuations do not grow as rapidly over the next 10 years, what impact will this have on the total value of M&A's?

Concept Review Questions

11.5 LAW AND FINANCE: THE IMPORTANCE OF CORPORATE GOVERNANCE

As mentioned in the Opening Focus, a nation's **corporate governance** system is the set of laws, regulations, institutions, and practices that determine how a public company will be governed and how control of a company can be contested. A nation's system of corporate governance encompasses both private- and public-sector institutions. Important private-sector institutions include stock exchanges and accounting firms; the public sector provides a nation's legal and regulatory systems.

THE LAW AND FINANCE MODEL

Most students are not surprised to learn that a nation's regulatory regime significantly influences the size and efficiency of its capital markets. After all, history influences a citizenry's attitude toward business enterprise, and financial regulations arise naturally in democratic societies to balance the often conflicting rights of corporations and individuals. Most industrial countries have well-established financial regulatory systems, and these are often used as models by developing and transition countries wishing to set up a regulatory regime.

What most students *are* surprised to learn is that the single most important determinant of the size of a country's capital markets is something much more basic than its regulatory framework: the legal tradition on which a nation's commercial code is based. In an important recent stream of academic papers, La Porta, López-de-Silanes, Shleifer, and Vishny (1997, 1998, 2000, 2002; hereafter LLSV), Shleifer and Vishny (1997), Levine (1997), Demirgüç-Kunt and Maksimovic (1998), and many others have developed what has come to be called the **"Law and Finance" model** of economic growth. This model states that the most important determinant of capital market development is the degree of legal protection afforded to outside (noncontrolling) investors. This determining factor in turn depends largely on whether a country's legal system is based on English common law or another legal tradition.

Countries that were once part of the British Commonwealth—such as Australia, Canada, India, New Zealand, the United States, and Britain itself—afford great protection to external creditors and minority shareholders, who are thus willing to invest their capital in public companies. Managers always have an incentive to expropriate investors' wealth, but the legal protections offered by *English common law* temper these incentives and give investors legal recourse if they are wronged. Over time, countries with common-law systems have evolved large stock and bond markets. Markets in these countries are characterized by **atomistic** ownership structures —that is, by large numbers of individual investors and low levels of ownership concentration in most public firms. In other words, capital markets have grown large because investors are willing to accept small ownership and creditor positions in public companies.

The other three major Western legal traditions, or families, are *German law, Scandinavian law,* and *French civil law.* LLSV (1998) describe the key rules within each legal family that pertain to the rights and duties of investors. They conclude that French civil law offers by far the weakest legal protections to outside investors; German law and Scandinavian law fall between the civil and common-law systems. Table 11.4, derived from LLSV (1997), details the impact of a nation's legal family on the size of its capital markets, on its economic growth rate, and on the incentive for a citizen to become an entrepreneur. This last variable is represented by the number of domestic firms per 1 million people. The last three columns of Table 11.4 present summary measures of a nation's tradition of law and order, as well as the effectiveness of the legal system in protecting the rights of outside investors.

The results presented in Table 11.4 are striking: English common-law countries have much larger public equity and debt markets than do countries with other legal systems. Common-law countries also demonstrate much higher entrepreneurial tendencies, with an average of 35.45 domestic firms per million citizens in these

Table 11.4
Law and Finance—An English Common Law System Promotes Capital Market Growth

Country (1)	External Capitalization/ GDP (2)	Debt/ GDP (3)	GDP Growth Rate (4)	Domestic Firms/ Population (5)	Rule of Law (6)	Antidirector Rights (7)	Creditor Rights (8)
Australia	0.49	0.76	3.06%	63.55	10.00	4	1
Canada	0.39	0.72	3.36	40.86	10.00	4	1
Israel	0.25	0.66	4.39	127.60	4.82	3	1
United Kingdom	1.00	1.13	2.27	35.68	8.57	4	4
United States	0.58	0.81	2.74	30.11	10.00	5	1
English origin average	**0.60**	**0.68**	**4.30%**	**35.45**	**6.46**	**3.39**	**3.11**
Belgium	0.17	0.38	2.46%	15.59	10.00	0	2
France	0.23	0.96	2.54	8.05	8.98	2	0
Greece	0.07	0.23	2.46	21.60	6.18	1	1
Italy	0.06	0.55	2.82	3.91	8.33	0	2
Spain	0.17	0.75	3.27	9.71	7.80	2	2
French origin average	**0.21**	**0.45**	**3.18%**	**10.00**	**6.05**	**1.76**	**1.58**
Austria	0.06	0.79	2.74%	13.87	10.00	2	3
Germany	0.13	1.12	2.60	5.14	9.23	1	3
Japan	0.62	1.22	4.13	17.78	8.98	3	2
Korea	0.44	0.74	9.52	15.88	5.35	2	3
Switzerland	0.62	—	1.18	33.85	10.00	1	1
German origin average	**0.46**	**0.97**	**5.29%**	**16.79**	**8.68**	**2.00**	**2.33**
Denmark	0.21	0.34	2.09%	50.40	10.00	3	3
Finland	0.25	0.75	2.40	13.00	10.00	2	1
Norway	0.22	0.64	3.43	33.00	10.00	3	2
Sweden	0.51	0.55	1.79	12.66	10.00	2	2
Scandinavian origin average	**0.30**	**0.57**	**2.42%**	**27.26**	**10.00**	**2.50**	**2.00**
Sample average (44 countries)	**0.44**	**0.59**	**3.79%**	**21.59**	**6.85**	**2.44**	**2.30**

Source: Rafael LaPorta, Florencio Lopez-de-Silanes, Andrei Shleifer, and Robert Vishny, "Legal Determinants of External Finance," *Journal of Finance* 52 (July 1997), pp. 1131–1150.
Notes: This table details the relationship between the type of legal system on which a country's commercial code is based and the size of that nation's capital markets for selected countries in 1994. Column 2 of this table is the ratio of the stock market capitalization held by minority (noncontrolling) shareholders to GDP, and column 3 provides a similar measure for private sector debt (bank loans and bonds). Column 4 presents the country's average annual GDP growth rate over 1970–1993, and column 5 is the ratio of the number of domestic firms in a country to its population, in millions. Columns 6–8 present summary measures of the law and order traditions in a country (column 6) and of how well its legal code protects the rights of shareholders (column 7) and creditors (column 8). In all three cases, the higher the rating the better the legal protection accorded investors. Countries with English common law systems, presented first in this table, provide the best legal protections for investors, and thus have the largest stock and bond markets. French civil law countries provide the poorest legal protection for outside investors, and thus tend to have very small capital markets. German and Scandinavian legal systems fall between these two extremes.

countries versus 27.26 and 16.79 firms per million people, respectively, in countries with a tradition of Scandinavian law and German law, and only 10.00 in countries with civil law traditions. It is not clear whether entrepreneurs are able to start companies more easily in common-law countries than in others because the laws are more encouraging or because the entrepreneurs are better able to attract external financing, or both. The empirical evidence surveyed in Levine (1997) shows that capital market development and economic growth are indeed positively related.

Applying the Law and Finance Model to Corporate Control What does the Law and Finance research imply for financial managers in different countries? A lot more than might seem obvious. A key implication of this research is that corporate ownership is likely to be much less concentrated in common-law countries than in other advanced economies, and the evidence supports this prediction. Figure 11.3 presents the median size of the largest voting block of shares in a random sample of 250 publicly traded industrial companies from nine European countries and the United States. In Italy, Germany, Austria, and Belgium, a single investor or a single block of shareholders controls a majority of the voting stock in the typical public company. In the Netherlands and Spain, the largest voting block controls 43 and 33 percent of the voting shares, respectively. Although France's 20 percent median voting block seems small by comparison, this figure is only for the companies that make up the CAC 40 Index (40 of the nation's largest public companies). The median voting blocks for the common-law countries Britain and the United States are much lower.

Who belongs to the voting blocks shown in Figure 11.3? Overwhelmingly, these are members of a firm's founding family, and the reason they must retain such concentrated ownership long after the founder's death relates directly to the legal system in place. Founding families in Britain and America tend to divest their concentrated ownership stakes in favor of other investments once the founding generation passes away. In civil-law and German-law countries, families must retain concentrated ownership either to ensure they retain managerial control of the firm or to protect them-

Figure 11.3
Ownership Structure and Corporate Governance in Continental Europe
This figure details the median size of the largest voting block of shares in several European countries, as well as the United States, in 1999. In Italy, the country with the most concentrated ownership structures, a single block of shares controls 54 percent of the voting stock in the typical publicly listed industrial company. Majority block-holdings are also the norm in Germany, Austria, and Belgium, and concentrated ownership is also prevalent in the Netherlands, Spain, and France. On the other hand, the largest single shareholder owns less than 5 percent of the voting stock in the typical American and Japanese (not listed) listed industrial company.

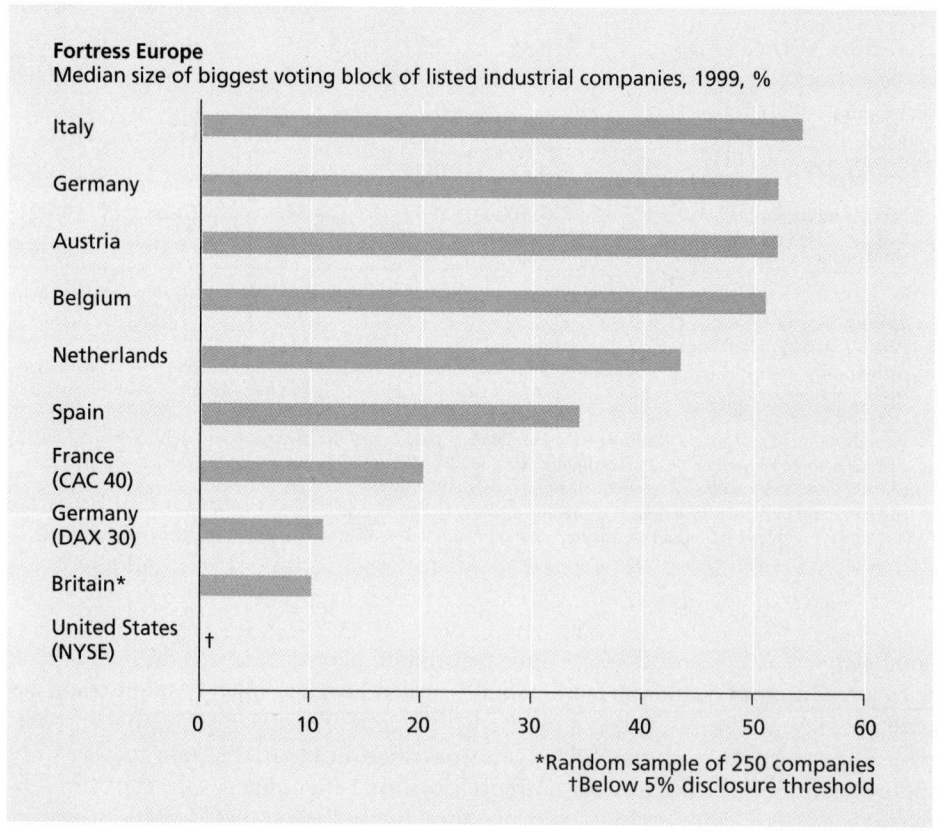

Fortress Europe
Median size of biggest voting block of listed industrial companies, 1999, %

*Random sample of 250 companies
†Below 5% disclosure threshold

Source: "Lean, Mean and European: A Survey of European Business," The *Economist* (April 29, 2001), p. 12.

selves from expropriation by incumbent managers, or both. There is thus a clear cost to continental European families in terms of less-than-optimal wealth diversification. There is also an economic-efficiency loss to civil-law and German-law countries, because the need to preserve concentrated ownership discourages companies from making new public security issues, particularly stock offerings, which in turn lowers the rate at which companies can grow.

The good news is that ownership structures have become much less concentrated in continental Europe since the mid-1990s, and this is likely to continue apace with capital market growth. The practicing financial manager must, however, still understand how the corporate governance system of the nation he or she is operating in affects the firm's ability to raise external capital—and on what terms.

Concept Review Questions

10. What impact do you think a nation's regulatory framework has on its corporate governance system? What does this imply for the newly democratic counties in Central and Eastern Europe?

11. Why should a nation's legal tradition have such a strong influence on the size of its capital markets? Why do you think the effect is similar for stockholders and bondholders?

11.6 SUMMARY

- The three basic instruments of long-term financing are much the same in all market economies: common stock, preferred stock, and long-term debt. The way these instruments are used and the degree to which corporations rely on capital markets rather than financial intermediaries for funding differs between countries.

- In almost all market economies, internally generated funds (primarily retained earnings) are the dominant source of funding for corporate investment. External financing is used only when needed, and then debt is almost always preferred to equity financing. The difference between a firm's total funding needs and its internally generated cash flow is referred to as its financial deficit.

- Financial intermediaries are institutions that raise funds by selling claims on themselves (often in the form of demand deposits, or checking accounts), then use those funds to purchase the debt and equity claims of corporate borrowers. Intermediaries thus break, or *intermediate*, the direct link between final savers and borrowers that exists when companies sell securities directly to investors.

- Though financial intermediaries are essential to the smooth running of the U.S. economy, FIs play a relatively small direct role in financing U.S. corporations. This is especially true of large, multinational firms. Intermediaries remain very important in the corporate financial systems of most other nations, however.

- The total volume of security issues has surged 14-fold since 1988, reaching $5.69 trillion worldwide in 2004, but U.S. corporate issuers routinely account for two-thirds of the worldwide total.

- Recent academic research shows that an effective system of corporate governance significantly impacts the financial performance of individual companies and entire economies. The legal tradition upon which a country's commercial code is based is especially important; countries with legal systems based on English common law tend to have larger stock and bond markets than do countries with other legal systems.

INTERNET RESOURCES

Note: *For updates to links, please go to the book's website at http://smart.swcollege.com.*

http://marketrac.nyse.com/mt/index.html—A portion of the NYSE site offering an exceptional virtual tour of the exchange floor, showing which stocks trade at each "post" and numerous up-to-date trading statistics for each stock

http://www.sec.gov/edgar.shtml—The U.S. Securities and Exchange Commission' EDGAR database, where all registration statements and other required filings by companies with securities that are publicly traded on U.S capital markets are available for downloading

http://www.federalreserve.gov/releases—The U.S. Federal Reserve Board's main website where economic, financial, and banking data are disclosed

KEY TERMS

additional paid-in capital
atomistic
callable
cash flow from operations
catastrophe bonds
collateral
commercial paper
convertibles
corporate governance
corporate insider
cumulative voting system
debenture
debt capital
equipment trust receipts
equity capital
Eurobond
financial deficit
financial intermediary
fixed-coupon
floating-rate instruments
foreign bond
Glass-Steagall Act
Gramm-Leach-Bliley Act
information intermediation
initial public offerings

international common stock
"Law and Finance" model
loan covenants
long-term debt
majority voting system
market capitalization
McFadden Act
mortgage
negative covenant
positive covenant
proxy fight
proxy statement
residual claimants
secondary offerings
secured debt
securities
securitization
shares authorized
shares issued
short-term debt
subordinated debt
syndicated bank loans
treasury stock
Yankee bond
Yankee common stock

QUESTIONS

11-1. What role does par value play in the pricing and sale of common stock by the issuing corporation? Why do most firms assign relatively low par values to their shares?

11-2. How can you find the initial proceeds per share received by an issuer of common stock if you know the number of shares issued, the par value per share, and the total additional paid-in capital?

11-3. Assuming you know the number of authorized shares, the number of issued shares, and the amount of treasury stock held by the corporation, how can you find the number of outstanding shares? How does a firm typically end up with treasury stock?

11-4. Why are common stockholders known as residual claimants? What does this imply about the risk and required return on common stock relative to other security classes?

11-5. Distinguish between majority and cumulative voting structures. Which is more advantageous to minority shareholders?

11-6. What is a proxy fight? Why does the existing management have an advantage in a proxy fight?

11-7. Why is preferred stock often referred to as a hybrid of common stock and debt? Why do U.S. corporations generally prefer to receive preferred stock dividends rather than debt interest payments from other corporations as a source of investment income?

11-8. Discuss the basic rights and features of preferred stock. Include in your discussion the topics of seniority of claims relative to other securities, voting rights, callability, and convertibility.

11-9. Why do subordinated debts pay higher interest rates than senior debts? Is most corporate debt from banks and other intermediaries unsecured or secured?

11-10. List and describe the various types of secured debt that constitute corporate borrowing. What mechanisms can be attached to debentures in order to reduce their default risk?

11-11. How are the interest rates typically set on debentures? On loans obtained by both U.S. and non-U.S. corporations? What market rate is typically used to price syndicated bank loans?

11-12. Why are corporate bonds issued by most U.S. companies callable? Does the inclusion of this feature by the corporation have a cost? Is there a cost to the company of issuing convertible rather than straight bonds?

11-13. How are restrictive covenants used to protect debt holders' investments? Why is the monitoring of these covenants different for intermediated and for public debt?

11-14. What are the key features and costs of commercial paper?

11-15. How should a corporation estimate the amount of financing that must be raised externally during a given year? Once that amount is known, what other decision must be made?

11-16. What is the dominant source of capital funding in the United States? Given this result and the fact that most corporations are net dissavers, what decisions must most managers face in order to address this financial deficit?

11-17. Define the term "financial intermediary." What role do financial intermediaries play in U.S. corporate finance? How does this compare to the role of non-U.S. financial intermediaries?

11-18. Discuss the U.S. banking system regulations that have had a major impact on the development of the U.S. financial system. In what ways has the U.S. system been affected (positively and negatively) by these regulations?

11-19. Differentiate between a U.S. commercial bank and the merchant banks found in other developed countries. How have these differences affected the securities markets in the United States versus those in other developed countries?

11-20. What are the general trends regarding public security issuance by U.S. corporations? Specifically, which security type is most often sold to the public? What is the split between initial and seasoned equity offerings?

11-21. Distinguish between a Eurobond, a foreign bond, and a Yankee bond. Which of these three represents the greatest volume of security issuance?

11-22. How does the corporate governance function of financial intermediaries differ between the United States and most other countries?

11-23. How would you describe the recent levels of M&A activity in the United States and elsewhere? What accounts for this change in activity?

11-24. List and briefly discuss the roles played by the key institutions and legal/regulatory systems that make up a nation's system of corporate governance. Apart from legal tradition, which influence do you think is the most important?

11-25. Why does a nation's legal tradition have such a large impact on the size of its capital markets? Do you think that a nation can really change its legal tradition, even if doing so would promote capital market development?

11-26. How does the concentration of corporate ownership differ between common-law and other countries? Why? What implication do these differences have on the corporate financial manager's ability to raise funds?

11-27. When a firm supplies the capital for a project internally, it is not uncommon to state that the firm is "funding the project from retained earnings." Are retained earnings a true source of funding?

11-28. Firm A is trying to acquire the majority of shares of Firm B. Firm B realizes Firm A's intentions and begins acquiring its own shares on the market as well. To keep the numbers simple, assume that there are 101 shares available and both Firm A and Firm B own 55 shares each. The extra shares have been supplied by investors who are short selling Firm B's stock. What are the implications for the short sellers? (*Hint:* Can the short sellers actually purchase stock to cover their position?) (Note: Short selling allows an investor to borrow a share of stock and then sell it on the market with the understanding that at some point in the future, the share is to be purchased in the market and returned to the original owner.)

11-29. Despite having net income in excess of the cumulative amount of dividends to be paid, why might a firm still need to borrow money to pay the dividends? (*Hint:* Does net income equate to cash?)

PROBLEMS

The Basic Instruments of Long-Term Financing

11-1. How many shares are needed to elect two directors out of a slate of seven if a firm has 10 million shares outstanding and uses cumulative voting in its election?

11-2. Schrell Corporation has 1,700,000 shares of voting common stock outstanding. Recent board actions and their dismal outcomes have raised the ire of many shareholders.

A major group of dissident shareholders that controls 600,000 shares of the common stock wishes to change the composition of the firm's seven-member board to improve the quality of the firm's governance. Management effectively controls the other 1,100,000 shares, many through proxies granted them by shareholders. Management's slate of directors for the upcoming election includes all of the existing directors.

The dissident shareholders want to obtain as much representation as possible in the upcoming election of all seven directors.

a. If the firm has a *majority voting system,* how many directors can the dissident group of shareholders elect?

b. If the firm has a *cumulative voting system,* how many directors can the dissident shareholders elect?

c. If the dissident shareholders decide to wage a *proxy fight* to obtain additional votes, how many additional votes would they need to gain voting control of the board (i.e., control four of seven votes) under majority voting? Under cumulative voting?

11-3. The equity section of the balance sheet for Lopez Digital Entertainment follows:

Common stock, $0.50 par	545,000
Paid-in capital surplus	229,000
Retained earnings	649,000

a. How many shares has the company issued?

b. What is the book value per share?

c. Suppose that Lopez Digital has made only one offering of common stock. At what price did it sell shares to the market?

11-4. Go to the website for Gateway, Inc. (http://www.gateway.com), one of the major direct marketers of personal computers and related products and services. Click successively on "About Us," "Investor Relations," and "Annual Reports," and then on the most recent "Complete Report" and find within it the "Consolidated Balance Sheets." Use the statement to answer the following questions.

a. How much preferred stock did Gateway have outstanding at the statement date?

b. How many shares of common stock was Gateway authorized to issue? What is its par value?

c. How many shares of common stock has Gateway issued? How much did the firm raise from the initial sale of its common stock?

d. How many shares of common stock did Gateway hold in its treasury at the statement date?

e. How many shares of common stock did Gateway have outstanding at the statement date?

f. How much retained earnings did Gateway have at the statement date? By how much did this value change from the previous year? What does this change represent?

11-5. Firm XYZ currently has 11,500,000 shares outstanding and a current stock price of $42.50. In one week, the firm is expected to split its shares 2-for-1 (i.e., each current share will be worth two new shares). It is not uncommon for market participants to consider a stock split to be a signal of "good news." Consequently, the new shares are anticipated to sell for $22.00 each.

a. Determine the market capitalization of the firm under its current price.

b. Determine the market capitalization under the anticipated price after the stock split.

c. Is there a change in the market capitalization that indicates the market is anticipating "good news" about the company?

11-6. A firm has a stock account of $4,000,000.00 (at $0.25 par) reported on its balance sheet. Yesterday the firm's stock had a closing price of $22.25. Today, the firm paid a $0.35 dividend and the closing price is $22.00.

   a. Determine the firm's market capitalization at the end of the day yesterday.

   b. Determine the firm's market capitalization at the end of the day today.

   c. Did the firm's shares lose value or gain value between yesterday and today? Calculate the amount of the loss or gain as part of your answer.

11-7. A firm's preferred stock pays a dividend of $1.40. Assuming there is a 35% personal income tax and a 45% corporate tax structure, what is the after-tax value of the preferred dividend to the personal investor and the corporate investor? Reevaluate the corporate investor's after-tax dividend assuming that 90% of the dividend value is exempt from taxes. Given this latter structure, do preferred dividends favor personal or corporate investors? Explain.

11-8. A firm's balance sheet reports $2,000,000.00 in stock ($1.00 par) and an account reporting "excess paid above par" of $32,460,000.00. What is the average price of each share of stock reported in the balance sheet?

The Basic Choices in Long-Term Financing

11-9. Meltzer Electronics estimates that its total financing needs for the coming year will be $34.5 million. The firm's required financing payments on its debt and equity financing during the coming fiscal year will total $12.9 million. The firm's financial manager estimates that operating cash flows for the coming year will total $33.7 million and that the following changes will occur in the accounts noted.

Account	Forecast Change
Gross fixed assets	$8.9 million
Change in current assets	+2.3 million
Change in accounts payable	+1.3 million
Change in accrued liabilities	+0.8 million

   a. Use Equation 2.3 and the data provided to estimate Meltzer's *free cash flow* in the coming year.

   b. How much of the free cash flow will the firm have available as a source of new internal financing in the coming year?

   c. How much external financing will Meltzer need during the coming year to meet its total forecast financing need?

11-10. Last year Guaraldi Instruments Inc. conducted an IPO, issuing 2 million common shares with a par value of $0.25 to investors at a price of $15 per share. During its first year of operation, Guaraldi earned net income of $0.07 per share and paid a dividend of $0.005 per share. At the end of the year, the company's stock was selling for $20 per share. Construct the equity account for Guaraldi at the end of its first year in business, and calculate the firm's market capitalization.

THOMSON ONE BUSINESS SCHOOL EDITION

11-11. Determine the sources of long-term financing for Google Inc. (ticker symbol, GOOG) and Yahoo! Inc. (ticker symbol, YHOO) for the last three years. What percentage of each firm's permanent financing is long-term debt and what percentage is equity? What are the components of each firm's equity (preferred versus common stock)? What percentage of new equity has been raised internally versus externally for both firms? What are some similarities and differences between the sources of long-term financing for Google and Yahoo!?

KajunKorp currently has 1,500,000 shares of common stock outstanding with a $0.75 par value. The firm issued all 1,500,000 shares via an initial public offering at $11.26 per share. The firm's total common equity balance is $28,649,000 and the firm has no Treasury Stock. Determine the following balances:

Common stock, $0.75 par: _____

Additional paid-in capital: _____

Retained earnings: _____

Also, KajunKorp estimates that it will need $12,000,000 in additional financing to support new projects in the upcoming year. The firm's current debt ratio is 30% and it wishes to maintain that percentage. KajunKorp expects to generate *EBIT* of $6,429,000 and it currently has $10,000,000 in outstanding long-term debt with a coupon rate of 7%. Any new debt issued will have the same coupon rate. KajunKorp's tax rate is 35% and the firm currently pays a dividend of $0.10 per share; however, they would like to increase the dividend to $0.11 per share. Determine how much the firm expects to generate in retained earnings during the upcoming year and how many new shares (if any) of common stock KajunKorp will need to issue at the current stock price of $11.26 to finance the equity portion of the additional financing.

Chapter 12

Capital Structure: Theory and Taxes

SMART**Finance**
Use the learning tools at www
.thomsonedu.com/finance/smartfinance

Each spring, *Fortune* magazine publishes a list of the most admired public companies in the United States, and a comparable listing of international firms. Dell topped the U.S. list in 2005, followed by General Electric, Starbucks, Wal-Mart, Southwest Airlines, FedEx, Berkshire Hathaway, Microsoft, Johnson & Johnson, and Procter & Gamble. Eight of these companies made the 2004 top ten, and most have been enshrined on the list for several years.

What characteristics do these ten companies have in common that enable them to prosper and impress, year after year? All ten companies have achieved stellar sales growth, at least over the past decade, all are profitable, and as a group, they have turned in long-term increases in stock price that outperforms the S&P 500 index. Seven of the ten companies pay dividends. All but one, Berkshire Hathaway, have price-to-earnings ratios over 20. (Among them, the average P/E ratio is 27.4.) This list includes the world's largest company in terms of sales, Wal-Mart, as well as the second most valuable firm, GE (market capitalization of $380 billion).

However, the accompanying table illustrates that these companies take very different approaches when it comes to financing their operations with debt or equity. The purpose of this chapter is to help you understand why some firms use a great deal of debt, while other firms use very little. For some people, the low-debt strategies of firms such as Microsoft and Starbucks are intuitively appealing. The relatively conservative financing strategy these firms employ follows William Shakespeare's advice, "Neither a borrower nor a lender be." On the other hand, readers with a basic understanding of the U.S. tax code will see a benefit to GE's high-debt strategy. The tax law treats interest payments as a tax-deductible business expense, but the same treatment does not apply to dividends. Therefore, by using more debt, GE shelters more of its cash flow from taxation.

	Debt-to-Equity Ratio, % (book value)	Debt-to-Equity Ratio, % (market value)
Wal-Mart	46	9
Berkshire Hathaway	12	8
Southwest Airlines	31	15
General Electric	193	56
Dell	8	1
Microsoft	0	0
Johnson & Johnson	8	1
Starbucks	0	0
FedEx	35	10
IBM	50	10

That all of these firms prosper even though they adopt very different strategies with regard to debt raises an interesting question: Does using debt or avoiding it influence how firms perform?

Almost 50 years ago, Franco Modigliani and Merton Miller reached a controversial and counterintuitive answer to this question. In work that eventually earned them Nobel Prizes, they demonstrated that, under certain conditions, a firm could not increase or decrease its value simply by borrowing more or less money. In this chapter and the next, we examine whether this conclusion holds in the real world, where the "perfect markets" conditions in Modigliani and Miller's work do not apply.

Source: "America's Most Admired Companies," Fortune (March 7, 2005), and author's calculations.

Why do some firms have high debt, while other companies issue little or none? This chapter and the next describe the key influences on managers' decisions to finance with debt or equity. We begin by illustrating a basic trade-off that firms confront in their debt versus equity choices. We then describe several capital structure patterns that occur worldwide, facts that a capital structure theory should explain. We then provide an overview of four prominent capital structure models. After that, we present the classic Modigliani and Miller (M&M) theory which offers the revolutionary conclusion that capital structure decisions may be *irrelevant*. Next, we explain how the tax code might affect managers' decisions regarding debt, and we review several tax-based capital structure theories. The chapter concludes with a checklist that managers can use in making financing decisions.

12.1 WHAT IS FINANCIAL LEVERAGE AND WHAT ARE ITS EFFECTS?

When firms borrow money, we say that they use *financial leverage*. Similarly, we say that a firm with debt on its balance sheet is a *levered firm*, and a firm that finances its operations entirely with equity is an *unlevered firm*. In Britain, they refer to debt as *gearing*. These terms imply that debt magnifies a firm's financial performance in some way. That effect can be either positive or negative, depending on the returns a firm earns on the money it borrows. A simple example illustrates this principle. Consider the decision facing Susan Smith, chief financial officer of High-Tech Manufacturing Corporation (HTMC), a publicly traded company with no debt. Analysts expect HTMC to generate a $1,000,000 net cash flow each year for the foreseeable future. Given HTMC's risk, shareholders require a 10 percent return on their investment. Using the present value formula for a perpetuity, we find the company's value equals $10,000,000 ($1,000,000 ÷ 0.10). HTMC has 200,000 common shares outstanding worth $50 each.

A shareholder suggests to Ms. Smith that HTMC should issue $5,000,000 in long-term debt, at an interest rate of 6 percent, and use the proceeds to repurchase half the company's common stock. This **recapitalization** would be a dramatic shift in the firm's financing mix. It would change HTMC's capital structure, but it would not change the company's total value as long as the 100,000 shares remaining after the transaction still sell for $50. HTMC's capital structure would change from 100 percent equity to 50 percent debt and 50 percent equity. In other words, this strategy would convert HTMC's debt-to-equity ratio from 0 to 1.0. Table 12.1 summarizes HTMC's current and proposed capital structures.

HTMC's shareholder suggests this strategy will increase earnings per share available to common stockholders. Though initially skeptical, Ms. Smith decides to analyze the proposal. She agrees with analysts that HTMC's earnings before interest and

Table 12.1
The Current and
Proposed Capital
Structures for High-Tech
Manufacturing
Corporation

	Current	Proposed
Assets	$10,000,000	$10,000,000
Equity	$10,000,000	$ 5,000,000
Debt	$ 0	$ 5,000,000
Debt-to-equity ratio	0	1.0
Shares outstanding	200,000	100,000
Share price	$ 50.00	$ 50.00
Interest rate on debt	—	6.0%

taxes (*EBIT*) will probably be $1,000,000 next year, assuming the economy continues to grow at a normal rate.[1] Other outcomes are possible, however. If the economy booms, *EBIT* will reach $1,500,000. If a recession occurs, *EBIT* will fall to $500,000. How do shareholders fare under the current and proposed capital structures if *EBIT* equals $1,000,000 as expected? With 200,000 shares and no debt, earnings per share (*EPS*) equals $5. If HTMC pays out all earnings as a dividend, then shareholders receive $5 on their $50 investment, a 10 percent return. Alternatively, with 100,000 shares and $5 million in debt, HTMC must pay $300,000 in interest, leaving $700,000 for shareholders. However, with half as many shares outstanding, $700,000 in *EBIT* translates into *EPS* of $7, or a 14 percent return for shareholders. The first two columns in Table 12.2 summarize these calculations.

So far, the recapitalization plan looks rather attractive. But what happens if a recession or a boom occurs? Table 12.2 shows the payoffs to HTMC's investors under those economic scenarios. The middle columns show that if the economy booms and High-Tech's *EBIT* reaches $1,500,000, shareholders earn more under the new capital structure than the old (*EPS* of $12 versus $7.50, or a return equal to 24 percent versus 15 percent). If a recession hits, HTMC shareholders fare worse under the new capital structure than they would have under the old one. In the recession scenario, a 50–50 mix of debt and equity generates *EPS* of $2 (a return of 4 percent), whereas under the all-equity capital structure, shareholders receive earnings of $2.50 per share (a 5 percent return).

Figure 12.1 illustrates how High-Tech's capital structure affects the relationship between *EBIT* and *EPS*. In good economic times, the company enjoys higher *EPS* with the 50–50 capital structure than with 100 percent equity. However, in a recession, HTMC's shareholders earn more under the old capital structure. Now you see how the terms leverage and gearing apply to the decision to borrow money: Relative to the all-equity capital structure, borrowing money makes shareholders better off when times are good and the firm's earnings are high, but shareholders fare worse in bad economic times. Leverage magnifies both the good outcomes and the bad ones.

The lines in Figure 12.1 cross when *EBIT* equals $600,000. When *EBIT* exceeds $600,000, HTMC's shareholders earn more with the 50–50 mix than with the current all-equity structure. For any *EBIT* below $600,000, the reverse is true—shareholders earn higher *EPS* with all-equity financing than they would if HTMC borrows money.

---

[1] You may wonder why we focus on EBIT here rather than on cash flow. For now, assume there are no taxes, so there is no difference between *EBIT* and net income for an unlevered company like HTMC. We relax this no-tax assumption in Section 13.5. Furthermore, we assume that HTMC invests in capital expenditures each year at a rate equal to its depreciation charge. With these assumptions, we can approximate cash flow with EBIT.

Table 12.2
Expected Cash Flows to Stockholders and Bondholders under the Current and Proposed Capital Structure for High-Tech Manufacturing Corporation for Three Equally Likely Economic Outcomes

	Normal		Boom		Recession	
EBIT	$1,000,000		$1,500,000		$500,000	
	All-Equity Financing	50% Debt, 50% Equity	All-Equity Financing	50% Debt, 50% Equity	All-Equity Financing	50% Debt, 50% Equity
Less: Interest paid (6.0%)	$ 0	($300,000)	$ 0	($ 300,000)	$ 0	($300,000)
Net income	$1,000,000	$700,000	$1,500,000	$1,200,000	$500,000	$200,000
Shares outstanding	200,000	100,000	200,000	100,000	200,000	100,000
Earnings per share	$ 5.00	$ 7.00	$ 7.50	$ 12.00	$ 2.50	$ 2.00
% Return on shares (P_0 = $50.00/share)	10.0%	14.0%	15.0%	24.00%	5.0%	4.0%

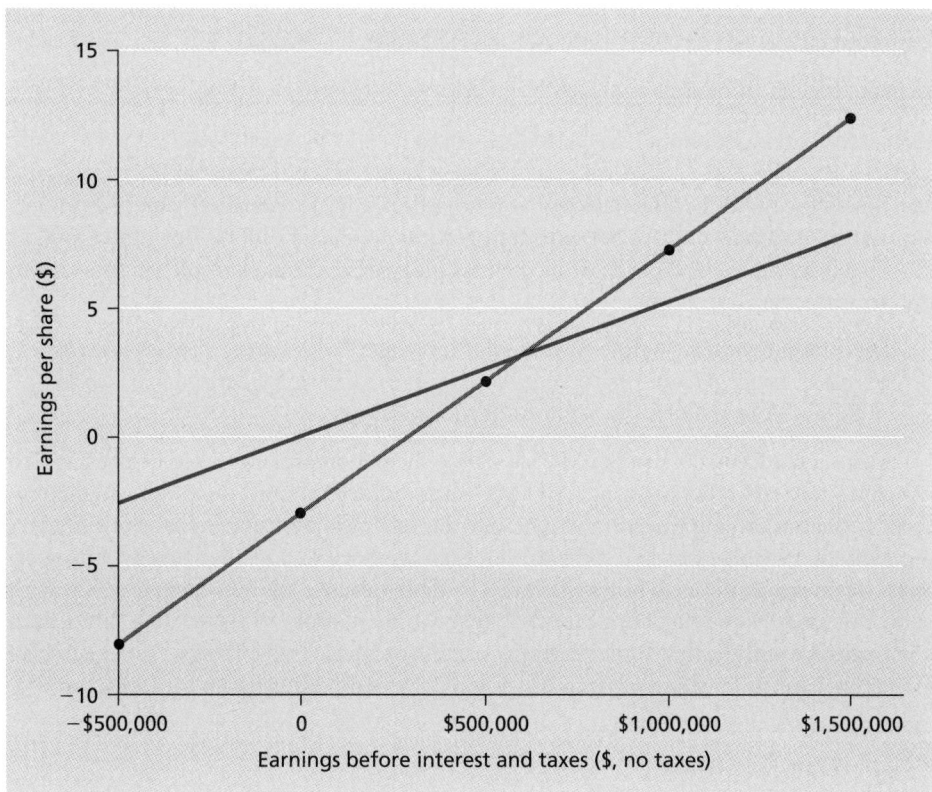

Figure 12.1
Using Debt to Increase Expected Earnings per Share for High-Tech Manufacturing Corporation (HTMC)

For the proposed recapitalization, the *break-even level of operating profits*—the level of *EBIT* yielding the same return on investment for both capital structures—occurs when *EBIT* equals $600,000. It is no accident that $600,000 defines the breakeven point here. Notice that if HTMC earns $600,000 on assets of $10 million, then its return on assets equals 6 percent, the same rate that it pays on borrowed funds. If the firm can earn more on its assets than it pays on its debt, then *EPS* goes up, relative to the all-equity case. If *EBIT* falls short of $600,000, the firm earns less on its investments than it pays in interest, and *EPS* goes down, relative to the all-equity case.

The slopes of the lines in the figure indicate that debt magnifies the effect on *EPS* of any change in *EBIT*. Starting from the breakeven point, if *EBIT* increases by 25 percent (from $600,000 to $750,000), then *EPS* increases by 50 percent (from $3.00 to $4.50) under the 50=−50 capital structure. However, *EPS* increases by only 25 percent (from $3.00 to $3.75) under an all-equity capital structure. On the other hand, if *EBIT* declines by 25 percent (from $600,000 to $450,000), the decline in *EPS* will be far greater under the proposed capital structure (−50 percent) than under the existing all-equity structure (−25 percent).

What should Ms. Smith do? Suppose she believes that each of the three economic scenarios is equally likely. Based on that view, we can calculate the expected values of HTMC's earnings before interest and taxes, as well as the expected payoffs to shareholders under each capital structure:

Expected $EBIT = (\frac{1}{3})\$1,000,000 + (\frac{1}{3})\$1,500,000 + (\frac{1}{3})\$500,000 = \$1,000,000$

Expected EPS (no debt) $= (\frac{1}{3})\$5.00 + (\frac{1}{3})\$7.50 + (\frac{1}{3})\$2.50 = \$5$

Expected EPS (with debt) $= (\frac{1}{3})\$7.00 + (\frac{1}{3})\$12.00 + (\frac{1}{3})\$2.00 = \$7$

Expected ROE (no debt) $= (\frac{1}{3})10\% + (\frac{1}{3})15\% + (\frac{1}{3})5\% = 10\%$

Expected ROE (with debt) $= (\frac{1}{3})14\% + (\frac{1}{3})24\% + (\frac{1}{3})4\% = 14\%$

Ms. Smith faces a difficult decision. Switching the capital structure from all equity to half equity and half debt raises expected returns to shareholders. But it also makes those returns more variable than in the all equity case. This example leads us to an important general principle:

> The **fundamental principle of financial leverage:** *Substituting debt for equity increases expected returns to shareholders—measured by earnings per share or ROE—and the risk (dispersion) of those returns.*

Although adding debt to HTMC's balance sheet increases expected returns, it also increases risk. As a consequence, HTMC shareholders should demand a higher return. If the underlying question is whether the recapitalization benefits shareholders (i.e., whether it increases HTMC's value), then we have to consider two offsetting effects. On average, the cash flows that HTMC distributes to shareholders increase with debt, but so does the discount rate that shareholders apply to those cash flows. In a few pages we will see that under certain conditions, these two effects offset exactly, so managers cannot increase or decrease a firm's value by altering its capital structure.

Concept Review Questions	**1.** What is a recapitalization? **2.** What tradeoffs do managers face when they consider changing a firm's capital structure?

12.2 WORLDWIDE CAPITAL STRUCTURE PATTERNS

Now that we have studied the general effects of leverage, we will take a step back and survey capital structures used by companies around the world. Research and observation establish a set of key facts that a capital structure theory should explain. Some of these facts seem intuitive, but others are more surprising. In general, capital structure research documents the following patterns.

1. Firms in the same industry often have similar capital structures regardless of their home country. Worldwide, firms in certain industries have high debt-to-equity (leverage) ratios, whereas firms in other industries employ little or no debt. Utilities, transportation companies, and many capital-intensive manufacturing firms tend to have high leverage ratios. Firms in the service, mining, and high-technology industries generally have low debt. These patterns suggest that an industry's operating environment and asset mix influence the leverage choices of firms in that industry.[2]

Table 12.3 illustrates these industry patterns using data of large U.S. firms. The table lists book value and market value leverage ratios for each firm. A glance at the table reveals that leverage ratios vary across industries. For example, the high-tech firms (listed first) use almost no debt; utilities and auto makers borrow much more. The final column shows the market value of equity divided by its book value. These *market-to-book ratios* vary a great deal from one firm to another, but you can see that they tend to decrease as you move down the table. Firms with high market-to-book ratios use less debt than firms with low market-to-book ratios.

2. Capital structures vary across countries. Table 12.4 shows three leverage measures for seven developed countries ("the G-7") and for 10 developing countries. Do firms in some countries rely more heavily on debt? The answer depends on what leverage ratios we use—whether we examine *total debt* or *long-term debt* and whether we measure debt relative to assets using book values or market values. Some observations:

- Looking at the *book value of total debt,* we see that firms in Japan, Italy, France, Germany, and South Korea use more debt than firms in the United Kingdom, Canada, Brazil, Mexico, and many other countries.
- If we focus only on *long-term debt,* the rankings change, especially for German firms.
- On a *market-value basis,* German companies use less long-term debt than firms in any other developed economy.

Even though the leverage rankings change depending on what leverage ratio we use, Table 12.4 does show that, on average, firms in developing countries borrow less than do firms in developed countries.[3]

Why leverage ratios vary so much across countries is an unsolved puzzle. In part, leverage differences may reflect variation in the industrial composition of national economies. Also, historical, institutional, and even cultural factors all probably play a part, as does a nation's reliance on capital markets versus banks for corporate financing.[4]

3. Leverage ratios vary inversely with financial distress costs. Both across industries and across countries, the larger the costs of bankruptcy and financial distress,

SMART IDEAS VIDEO

Mitchell Petersen, Northwestern University
"When firms structure their business, they need to think about trading off operating and financial leverage."

See the entire interview at
SMARTFinance

---

[2] The classic article documenting these relationships is by Bradley, Jarrell, and Kim (1984). More recent articles documenting similar relationships include those by Long and Malitz (1985), Titman and Wessels (1988), Smith and Watts (1992), Alderson and Betker (1995), Hovakimian, Opler, and Titman (2001), and Campello (2003).

[3] For book value data, see Rutterford (1988), Sekely and Collins (1988), Frankel [Japan] (1991), Rajan and Zingales [G7 countries] (1995), and Booth, Aivazian, Demirgüç-Kunt, and Maksimovic [10 developing countries] (2001). Market value leverage ratios are presented in Rajan and Zingales (1995), Shin and Park [Korea] (1999), Booth et al. (2001), and de Miguel and Pindado [Spain] (2001). Graham and Harvey (2001) survey U.S. corporate managers regarding their leverage choices, and Bancel and Mittoo (2004) do the same for European managers.

[4] The importance of a nation's reliance on capital markets versus financial intermediaries for external corporate financing was first discussed by Mayer (1990), and evidence of its importance in Japanese capital structure decisions is presented in Anderson and Makhija (1999).

Table 12.3
Debt Ratios for Selected U.S. Corporations in 2002

Company	Industry	Debt to Total Assets		Long-Term Debt to Total Capital[b]		Market to Book Ratio[c]
		Book Values	Market Values[a]	Book Values	Market Values	
Microsoft	Computer software	0	0	0	0	5.54
Cisco Systems	Computer systems	0	0	0	0	3.94
Intel	Semiconductors	0.03	0.01	0.03	0.01	4.03
Dell Computer	Computer hardware	0.04	0.01	0.10	0.01	14.87
IBM	Computer hardware	0.27	0.16	0.40	0.11	5.54
Exxon Mobil	Integrated petroleum	0.07	0.04	0.09	0.03	3.72
Chevron Texaco	Integrated petroleum	0.25	0.16	0.21	0.08	2.71
Johnson & Johnson	Pharmaceuticals	0.08	0.02	0.08	0.01	7.32
Merck	Pharmaceuticals	0.23	0.08	0.30	0.04	7.18
Eli Lilly	Pharmaceuticals	0.32	0.06	0.31	0.03	8.54
AOL Time Warner	Entertainment, media	0.11	0.29	0.13	0.29	0.74
Walt Disney	Entertainment, media	0.21	0.27	0.28	0.25	1.92
Coca Cola	Consumer products	0.12	0.04	0.10	0.02	12.85
Procter & Gamble	Consumer products	0.45	0.12	0.49	0.07	10.13
Duke Energy	Electricity trading	0.29	0.46	0.49	0.39	1.73
United Technologies	Aerospace	0.18	0.12	0.34	0.11	3.76
Boeing	Aerospace	0.25	0.27	0.50	0.24	3.65
Lockheed Martin	Aerospace	0.28	0.20	0.53	0.19	4.33
Alcoa	Aluminum production	0.24	0.21	0.38	0.20	2.58
Wal Mart	Retailing	0.27	0.08	0.35	0.06	7.01
Kroger	Retailing	0.46	0.36	0.71	0.34	4.49
Southwest Airlines	Airline	0.15	0.12	0.25	0.12	3.13
AMR	Airline	0.35	0.78	0.65	0.73	0.60
Delta Air Lines	Airline	0.36	0.77	0.69	0.75	0.82
SBC Communications	Telecommunications	0.26	0.20	0.35	0.14	3.53
BellSouth	Telecommunications	0.39	0.23	0.45	0.17	3.18
Verizon Commun	Telecommunications	0.36	0.36	0.58	0.26	3.63
American Elec Power	Electric Utility	0.31	0.54	0.54	0.36	1.62
Southern Company	Electric Utility	0.35	0.37	0.51	0.30	2.32
General Electric	Conglomerate	0.40	0.44	0.59	0.17	5.38
Georgia Pacific	Forest products	0.49	0.69	0.68	0.55	1.19
General Motors	Auto manufacturing	0.51	0.84	0.89	0.83	4.12
Ford Motor	Auto manufacturing	0.60	0.84	0.96	0.84	4.24
Caterpillar	Construction equip	0.53	0.50	0.67	0.35	2.52

Notes: This table presents book value and market value leverage ratios for 33 of the most valuable publicly-traded U.S. corporations in June 2002. Companies are listed by industry, beginning with the industry with the lowest leverage (computer software) and ranging through the highest leverage (automobile manufacturing).

[a]Total liabilities (book value) divided by the market value of equity plus the book value of debt.

[b]Long-term debt (book value) divided by the sum of the market value of equity plus the book value of long-term debt.

[c]Per share price of company stock divided by the per share book value of shareholders' common equity.

Source: Data taken from each company's financial information on *cnnfn.com* on June 12, 2002.

Table 12.4
Leverage Ratios for Publicly Traded Firms in G7 and Selected Developing Countries

Country	Number of Firms	Total Debt to Total Assets (book value, %)	Long-term Debt to Total Capital (book value, %)	Long-term Debt to Total Capital (market value, %)
United Kingdom	608	0.54	0.28	0.35
Canada	318	0.56	0.39	0.35
United States	2,580	0.58	0.37	0.28
Japan	514	0.69	0.53	0.29
Italy	118	0.70	0.47	0.46
France	225	0.71	0.48	0.41
Germany	191	0.73	0.38	0.23
Brazil	49	0.30	0.10	N/A
Mexico	99	0.35	0.14	N/A
Zimbabwe	48	0.42	0.13	0.26
Malaysia	96	0.42	0.13	0.07
Jordan	38	0.47	0.12	0.19
Thailand	64	0.49	N/A	N/A
Turkey	45	0.59	0.24	0.11
Pakistan	96	0.66	0.26	0.19
India	99	0.67	0.34	0.35
South Korea	93	0.73	0.49	0.64

Book and market value leverage measures for nonfinancial companies from the G7 group of industrialized countries and 10 developing countries. The G7 results are from Rajan and Zingales (1995) and are based on data for 1991 reported in the *Global Vantage* database. The developing-country results are from Booth et al. (2001) and are based on data for varying periods from 1980 to 1991, depending upon the country, as reported by the World Bank.
Sources: Raghuram G. Rajan and Luigi Zingales, "What Do We Know About Capital Structure? Some Evidence from International Data," *Journal of Finance* 50 (December 1995), pp. 1421–1460; and Laurence Booth, Varouj Aivazian, Asli Demirguc-Kunt, and Vojislav Maksimovic, "Capital Structures in Developing Countries," *Journal of Finance* 56 (February 2001), pp. 87–130.

the less debt firms use. For example, firms whose principal assets consist mostly of intangibles (e.g., brands, intellectual property) stand to lose more if they experience financial distress than do firms with hard assets that they can pledge as collateral or sell to satisfy lenders. Therefore, firms with high-value intangible assets use less debt than firms that invest in more tangible assets. Similarly, firms in countries with legal systems that provide the greatest protections to creditors tend to borrow less than firms in countries that afford creditors less protection.[5]

4. **Corporate and personal taxes influence capital structures, but taxes alone cannot explain differences in leverage across firms, industries, or countries.** In the United States and many other countries, corporations can treat interest paid on borrowed funds as a deductible business expense. In contrast, dividends paid to shareholders are not deductible. Naturally, this tax difference influences firms' financing decisions. Similarly, investors may face different tax rates on interest income, dividends, and capital gains, so personal taxes as well as corporate taxes can influence capital structure choices. In addition, individual investors' tax situations can influence capital structure choices. If firms make a capital structure choice that is undesirable to individual investors, investors may sell (or not buy) the stock, and the stock price could fall.

[5.] For example, see Titman (1984), Maksimovic and Titman (1991), Pulvino (1999), Rajan and Zingales (1995), Desai, Foley, and Hines (2004), as well as articles cited in footnote 3.

Even so differences in tax rates across time and across countries cannot explain all the differences in leverage choices. For example, U.S. corporations apparently used no less debt prior to the income tax's introduction in 1913 than they did afterwards. During World War II, tax rates peaked in the United States while corporate debt ratios reached their lowest point in modern history. Figure 12.2 shows that, on a book value basis, equity's (debt's) share in U.S. firms' capital structures declined (rose) steadily during much of the twentieth century.[6] Figure 12.3 indicates that the market value share of equity (debt) fell (rose) from 1951 to 1974, but the trend subsequently reversed. These gradual leverage changes seem at odds with the sudden tax law changes (and hence, sudden changes in debt's tax advantage) that occurred over the last 50 years.

On the other hand, research shows that higher corporate income tax rates prompt firms to use more debt. Similarly, tax cuts that lower the personal tax burden on dividends and capital gains relative to interest income lead firms to borrow less.[7]

5. Markets interpret leverage-increasing events as "good news" and leverage-decreasing events as "bad news." A surprising empirical regularity is that the stock market generally responds favorably when firms increase leverage. Almost all studies show that stock prices rise when a company announces leverage-increasing events, such as debt-for-equity exchange offers, debt-financed share repurchase programs,

Figure 12.2
Book Value Leverage Measures for U.S. Non-financial Corporations, 1951–1996
This figure plots the average book value of long-term debt (LTD) to total capitalization (TC), short-term debt to total capital, and preferred stock to total capital ratios for U.S. non-financial firms over the period 1951–1996.
Source: Eugene F. Fama and Kenneth R. French, "The Corporate Cost of Capital and the Return on Corporate Investment," *Journal of Finance* 54 (December 1999), pp. 1939–1967, Figure 2.

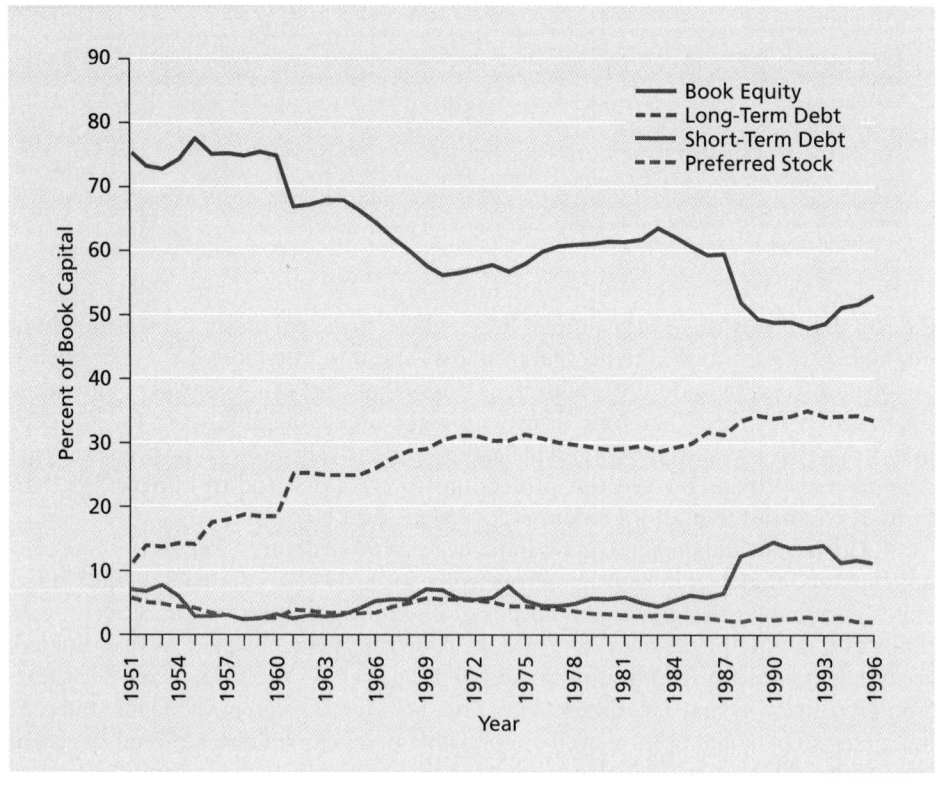

[6.] For historical information on U.S. capital structure measures, see Taggart (1985), Bernanke and Campbell (1988), Barclay, Smith, and Watts (1995), Fama and French (1999), Baker and Wurgler (2002), and Frank and Goyal (2003).
[7.] Evidence regarding the impact of taxes on corporate financing decisions is presented in Mackie-Mason (1990), Wedig, Hassan, and Morrisey (1996), Graham (1996, 2000), Fama and French (1998), Calegari (2000), Graham and Harvey (2001), and Desai, Foley, and Hines (2004). Fung and Theobald (1984), Hamada and Scholes (1985), and Ang and Megginson (1990) study how taxes impact national average debt ratios.

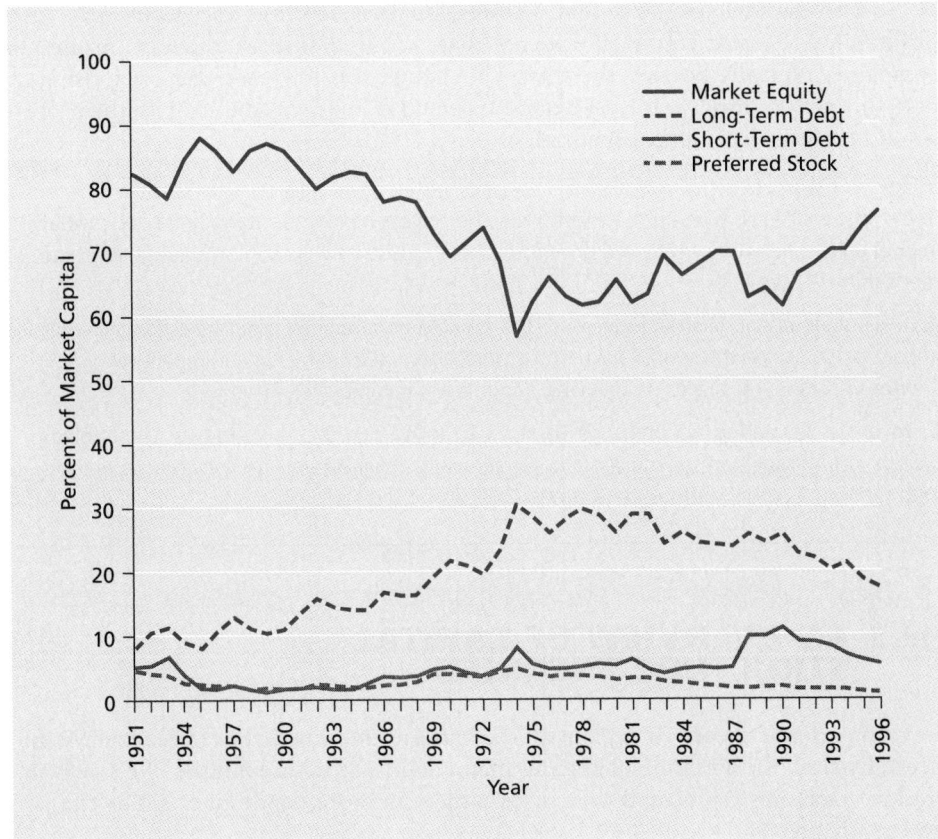

Figure 12.3
Market Value Leverage
Measures for U.S.
Corporations,
1951–1996
*This figure plots the
average market value of
long-term debt (LTD) to
total capitalization (TC),
short-term debt to total
capital, and preferred
stock to total capital
ratios for U.S. non-
financial firms over the
period 1951–1996.*
Source: Eugene F. Fama and
Kenneth R. French, "The
Corporate Cost of Capital
and the Return on Corporate
Investment," *Journal of
Finance* 54 (December 1999),
pp. 1939–1967, Figure 1.

and debt-financed cash tender offers to acquire another company.[8] On the other hand, leverage-decreasing events, such as equity-for-debt exchange offers, new stock offerings, and acquisitions financed with the acquirer's shares, almost always lower stock prices.[9]

6. **Corporations strive to maintain target capital structures.** Research suggests that corporations like to operate within **target leverage zones** and will issue new equity (debt) when debt ratios get too high (low). Accumulating profits or losses, or unforeseen events, will spark deviations from target ratios. Forced departures from target debt ratios occur frequently, particularly for U.S. corporations that issue new debt to finance (or defend against) takeovers. The first priority of companies after completing these transactions is to pay down the debt to a more comfortable level.[10]

[8.] The first major paper documenting this phenomenon is Masulis (1980). Subsequent related articles include Dann (1981), Mikkelson and Partch (1986), Travlos (1987), Billett, King and Mauer (2004), Eckbo (1986), James (1987), and Lummer and McConnell (1989).

[9.] See Dann and Mikkelson (1984), Asquith and Mullins (1986), Linn and Pinegar (1988), Shah (1994), Loughran and Ritter (1995), and Spiess and Affleck-Graves (1995). Hansen and Crutchley (1990) offer an explanation for these patterns, by showing that firms tend to issue new stock before significant earnings declines, suggesting these issues are at least partly made to cover a cash flow shortfall resulting from lower-than-expected earnings.

[10.] The most dramatic example of this phenomenon has occurred in leveraged buyouts, as the debt levels of newly private companies are often extremely high. See Muscarella and Vetsuypens (1990). Fischer, Heinkel, and Zechner (1989), Hovakimian, Opler, and Titman (2001), Korajczyk and Levy (2003), Hovakimian, Hovakimian, and Tehranian (2004), and Liu (2004) show that firms have target leverage ratios that they return to gradually. These more recent findings challenge earlier research—by Marsh (1982) for British firms, and by Asquith and Mullins (1986) and Korajczyk, Lucas, and Mc-Donald (1991) for U.S. companies—showing that companies issue equity after large stock price runups and essentially refuse to issue new equity after share prices drop.

7. There is some evidence that, within industries, leverage varies inversely with profitability. There is empirical evidence that, within industries, the most profitable companies typically borrow the least.[11] Although this may not seem surprising at first, this pattern raises some deep questions, and is in direct conflict with the proposition that firms have target debt ratios.

<table>
<tr><td>

**Concept
Review
Questions**

</td><td>

3. In most countries, firms in high-tech industries invest heavily in intangible assets. What impact do you think the continued growth of these industries will have on average leverage ratios in the future?

4. If the government decided to increase the tax rate on retained corporate earnings, what impact do you think this would have on corporate leverage? Why? What impact would increases in personal tax rates on dividend and interest income likely have?

5. Leverage-decreasing actions such as stock-financed takeover bids reduce shareholder wealth, on average, yet these events occur regularly. How do you reconcile these actions with running a corporation in the shareholders' best interests?

</td></tr>
</table>

12.3 AN OVERVIEW OF CAPITAL STRUCTURE THEORIES

Devising a single theory to explain all the patterns described above is extremely difficult. Even so, the literature offers four major capital structure models. We briefly introduce each one below, and then discuss them in more depth later in this chapter and in Chapter 13.

THE AGENCY COST/TAX-SHIELD TRADE-OFF MODEL

The first of the four capital structure models is the **agency cost/tax-shield trade-off model,** or simply the **trade-off model.** As its name suggests, the model predicts that managers choose the capital structure that strikes a balance between debt's tax advantages and its agency costs.

Because firms can deduct interest payments from taxable income, more debt leads to lower taxes. However, agency costs of debt rise as borrowing increases. In particular, high leverage increases the probability that the firm will encounter financial distress and incur its associated costs. For example, consider the costs an airline might face if the public believed that the firm was almost bankrupt. Fearing that the airline might cut maintenance expenses, some customers would choose another carrier. Pilots, mechanics, and flight attendants would defect to other airlines.

The trade-off model suggests that firms weigh the tax savings of debt against the expected costs of financial distress when choosing their capital structures.

THE PECKING-ORDER MODEL

The **pecking-order model** is the strongest challenger to the trade-off model.[12] The pecking-order model consists of two assumptions: first, that managers are better informed about their own firms' prospects than are outside investors (an *asymmetric*

[11.] See Myers (1993), Fama and French (1998), Shyam-Sunder and Myers (1999), Graham (1996, 2000), Fama and French (2002), and Baker and Wurgler (2002) for evidence on leverage's link with profitability.

[12.] See Myers (1984, 1993), Myers and Majluf (1984), and Shyam-Sunder and Myers (1999).

information assumption), and second, that managers act in the best interests of *existing* shareholders. Under these conditions, a firm will sometimes forgo positive-NPV projects if accepting them forces the firm to issue undervalued equity to *new* investors. This in turn provides a rationale for firms to value **financial slack,** such as large cash and marketable security holdings or unused debt capacity. Financial slack permits firms to undertake projects that they might decline if they had to issue new equity to invest.

This model explains three patterns that we see in the data. First, the most profitable firms generate financial slack internally and therefore have little need to issue new equity or debt. Second, in the pecking-order model, a firm issues equity when it cannot generate enough cash internally or when managers think their equity is overpriced. Either case is bad news for shareholders, so markets should react negatively to new equity issues, which is what happens on average. Third, the pecking-order model explains why firms hold vast cash and marketable securities reserves.

THE SIGNALING MODEL

A third capital structure theory is the **signaling model.** As in the pecking-order model, the signaling model assumes that managers know more about a firm's prospects than investors do and that in the absence of any compelling evidence to the contrary, investors assign an "average" valuation to each firm. If managers feel that investors undervalue the firm, the only way to convince investors of the firm's true value is to *send a signal* that a less-valuable firm cannot mimic.

One such signal is to issue debt. Issuing debt raises the odds of financial distress and its associated costs. According to the signaling model, investors know this, so they interpret a firm's decision to borrow money as a credible signal that managers believe that high future cash flows will prevent financial distress. Lower-quality firms will not mimic this signal because of the higher financial distress risk. Investors respond to the signal by bidding up the share prices of debt-issuing firms.

THE MARKET-TIMING MODEL

Baker and Wurgler (2002) offer one of the newest and most intuitively appealing theories—the **market-timing model**—to explain the debt-equity choice. They argue that firms *time the market* by issuing equity when share values are high and by issuing debt when share prices are low. As a consequence, a firm's capital structure simply reflects the cumulative effects of its managers' past market-timing activities. Baker and Wurgler find evidence that firms with high leverage are those that raised capital when their stock prices were low, whereas firms with low leverage are those that raised capital when their share prices were high. Baker and Wurgler cite several studies that support their theory, the most important of which is Graham and Harvey's (2001) CFO survey, in which executives report that the level of stock prices influences their decisions to issue equity.

**SMART
PRACTICES
VIDEO**

**Keith Woodward,
Vice President of Finance,
General Mills**
"In General Mills we have lots of discussions about what is the optimal capital structure."

See the entire interview at
SMARTFinance

**Concept
Review
Questions**

6. Table 12.3 shows that debt ratios vary from one industry to another. How might the trade-off model explain this? Specifically, given that interest expense is deductible in all industries, if high-tech firms use less debt than automobile manufacturers, then the *trade-off model* indicates that the expected costs of financial distress must be greater for high-tech firms. Why might this be so?

7. Stock prices respond favorably to leverage-increasing events and unfavorably to leverage-decreasing events. Furthermore, research indicates that firms issuing equity exhibit below-average long-run stock performance. Explain how these two facts relate to the *market-timing model.*

12.4 THE MODIGLIANI & MILLER PROPOSITIONS

We now turn our attention to the **Modigliani and Miller** (hereafter, M&M) **argument** that capital structure decisions cannot affect firm value. The M&M argument is an important one to understand, even though most financial economists today reject the notion that capital structure choices do not matter.

M&M's work is important for in modern finance for two reasons: First, by understanding why leverage choices have no value impact in "perfect markets," managers who operate in imperfect markets can see more clearly how market imperfections might lead them to choose one capital structure over another. Second, M&M's argument rests on the principle of *no arbitrage,* a principle that drives many important concepts in finance, from the determination of exchange rates to option pricing. Seeing how this principle applies to the capital structure decision will clarify its use in other areas throughout the book.

ASSUMPTIONS OF THE M&M CAPITAL STRUCTURE MODEL

Modigliani and Miller begin by making several assumptions about capital markets and about firms. These assumptions simplify their analysis and focus it entirely on the valuation effects of debt. The M&M assumptions are as follows:

1. Capital markets are *frictionless,* meaning that neither firms nor investors pay taxes or transactions costs.
2. Investors can borrow and lend at the same rate that corporations can.
3. Firms are identical in every respect except for capital structure.

Using these assumptions, M&M put forth two propositions, detailed below. In the following examples, we will examine the capital structure decisions of two firms with identical business risk and expected operating cash flows. Of course, it is impossible to find two identical firms in the real world, but to grasp the M&M intuition, think of firms operating in the same industry.

PROPOSITION I

Proposition I asserts that in perfect markets, a firm's total market value equals the value of its assets and is independent of the firm's capital structure. The value of the assets, in turn, equals the present value of the cash flows generated by the assets. Because the proposition leads to the conclusion that the firm's capital structure does not matter, it is popularly known as the "irrelevance proposition."

We can develop a simple, mathematical expression of this idea as follows. Assume that investors expect a company to generate a constant cash flow stream each year for the foreseeable future. For convenience, let's designate this cash flow with the symbol *NOI* (net operating profit). The firm may have outstanding debt with market value equal to D, and equity with a market value equal to E. By definition, the total value of the firm's outstanding securities is V, where $V = E + D$. That expression simply says that a firm's value equals the combined value of all the securities the firm issues.[13] Finally, the cash flows generated by the firm's assets are risky, so investors discount them at the rate r. M&M's Proposition I, then, claims the following:

$$V = (E + D) = \frac{NOI}{r} \qquad \text{(Eq. 12.1)}$$

In terms of the firm's capital structure, Equation 12.1 means that *the firm's market value equals the present value of the cash flows it generates regardless of the capital structure it chooses.* The market value of any firm is independent of its capital structure and is given by capitalizing its expected net operating income at the rate r.

M&M proved their proposition using an arbitrage argument. **Arbitrage** means simultaneously buying and selling identical assets at different prices to earn a risk-free profit. In well-functioning markets, arbitrage opportunities arise infrequently and as traders exploit them, vanish soon after they appear. The "no-arbitrage principle," upon which M&M's argument rests, simply states that in equilibrium, market prices must adjust to a point at which no arbitrage opportunities remain. M&M demonstrate that if a levered firm's value differs from that of an identical unlevered firm, an arbitrage opportunity exists. Because arbitrage opportunities can't last very long, the values of the two firms must be identical in equilibrium. This is easiest to show with an example.

APPLYING THE MODEL 12.1

Consider two equally risky firms, UnleverCo and LeverCo. Each expects the same operating profit, $100,000 per year. Furthermore, assume that the required return on both firms' assets, r, is 10 percent, implying a total firm value of $1 million ($100,000 operating profit ÷ 0.10 required return). UnleverCo has no debt outstanding. Instead, it has 20,000 common shares, worth $50 each.[14] Note that because UnleverCo has no debt, the required return on its shares equals the required return on its assets, 10 percent. We denote the required return on unlevered shares as r_u.

LeverCo, on the other hand, began life as an all-equity firm, but recently issued debt and used the proceeds to retire shares. Assume it issued $500,000 worth of debt at 6 percent interest, and it used the debt proceeds to repurchase half of its outstanding equity. This means LeverCo purchased 10,000 shares at $50 each.[15] It therefore has 10,000 shares remaining that should also be worth $50 each, for a total of $500,000.

---

13. Note that we are not talking about just the value of the firm's equity here. When we use the term, value of the firm, we mean the market value of the firm's assets, not just the value of the residual claim that shareholders own.

14. You can derive the $50 stock price in two ways. First, divide total value firm value, $1 million, by the shares outstanding, 20,000, to obtain the $50 share price. Second, divide expected operating income, $100,000, by the number of shares to get $5 earnings per share. Remember that the required return on these shares is 10 percent, so the market price per share must be $50.

15. To keep this analysis clearly focused on pure capital structure changes, it is vital to assume that the firm uses any money raised by issuing debt to retire outstanding equity. This keeps the total value of the firm's assets constant, and allows one to examine financial changes in isolation.

But what return can LeverCo's shareholders expect on their levered shares? Recall that LeverCo will earn $100,000 in operating profits, from which it must pay $30,000 in interest on its debt (0.06 × $500,000). This leaves $70,000 for the firm's 10,000 shareholders, or $7 per share. If LeverCo's shares sell for $50, investors must expect a 14 percent return ($7 ÷ $50). We will refer to the required return on levered equity as r_l. Table 12.5 summarizes the two firms' financial characteristics.

Proving Proposition I Using Homemade Leverage Now let's see how an investor could profit if the market value of LeverCo exceeds that of UnleverCo. Let us assume that investors will pay a premium for the shares of levered firms. If the price of LeverCo's shares exceeds $50, then the company's investors must be willing to accept a return below 14 percent. Let's say that LeverCo's shareholders expect a 12.5 percent return. This implies that LeverCo's equity is worth $560,000 ($70,000 net income ÷ 0.125 required return), or $56 per share. Combining the value of LeverCo's debt and equity, we obtain a total firm value equal to $1,060,000. UnleverCo's market value remains $1 million. Table 12.6 summarizes these new conditions.

How can investors profit in this situation? Suppose an investor currently owns 1 percent of LeverCo's outstanding stock (100 shares worth $5,600) and expects to

Table 12.5
Financial Characteristics
of UnleverCo and
LeverCo

	UnleverCo	LeverCo
Net operating income (NOI)	$ 100,000	$ 100,000
Less: Interest paid (0.06 × D)	0	30,000
Net income [$NOI - (0.06 × D)$]	$ 100,000	$ 70,000
Required return on assets (r)	0.10	0.10
Total firm value (NOI / r)	$1,000,000	$1,000,000
Required return on equity (r_u or r_l)	0.10	0.14
Shares outstanding	20,000	10,000
Market value of equity (E)	$1,000,000	$ 500,000
Interest rate on debt (r_d)	0	0.06
Market value of debt (D)	0	$ 500,000

Table 12.6
Disequilibrium Values for
UnleverCo and LeverCo

	UnleverCo	LeverCo
Net operating income (NOI)	$ 100,000	$ 100,000
Less: Interest paid (0.06 × D)	0	30,000
Net income [$NOI - (0.06 × D)$]	$ 100,000	$ 70,000
Total firm value (NOI / r)	$1,000,000	$1,060,000
Required return on equity (r_u or r_l)	0.10	0.125
Shares outstanding	20,000	10,000
Market value of equity (E)	$1,000,000	$ 560,000
Interest rate on debt (r_d)	0	0.06
Market value of debt (D)	0	$ 500,000

earn a 12.5 percent return on that investment, or $700. The investor could earn an arbitrage profit from the following transactions:

1. Sell all 100 LeverCo shares for $5,600.
2. Borrow $5,000, an amount equivalent to 1 percent of LeverCo's debt, promising to pay 6 percent interest, or $300 per year.
3. Use $10,000 of the proceeds from steps 1 and 2 to purchase 1 percent (200 shares) of UnleverCo's stock. The investor will have $600 in cash left over.

What has our investor accomplished with this series of transactions? Initially, the investor held 1 percent of the stock of a company with a capital structure containing equal proportions of debt and equity. In other words, the investor held a small levered equity position. Simply selling LeverCo shares and buying stock in UnleverCo could not be called arbitrage, because differences in leverage between the two firms means that LeverCo's shares are riskier than UnleverCo's stock. Remember, arbitrage means buying and selling *identical assets*. Therefore, to make the new investment in UnleverCo stock just as risky as the original investment in LeverCo shares, the investor must create **homemade leverage**. Investors can create homemade leverage by borrowing on their own. Having added risk through the personal borrowing, the investor can then buy stock in an unlevered firm.

What return can the investor expect on the new portfolio? Because the expected payoff on each UnleverCo share equals $5, the investor's 200-share portfolio generates $1,000 in cash flow each year. However, the investor owes $300 in interest on personal borrowings, so the net cash flow from the portfolio will be $700 annually. This is exactly the expected annual cash flow from the prior holdings of 100 LeverCo shares. Now we can see that the original portfolio is identical to the new one. *Given that LeverCo finances its operations with 50 percent equity and 50 percent debt, holding 1 percent of LeverCo's stock is equivalent to holding 1 percent of UnleverCo's stock and financing half of that investment with personal debt.*

In what sense is this an arbitrage opportunity? Recall that after selling LeverCo shares, borrowing money, and buying UnleverCo stock, the investor had $600 in cash left over. That $600 represents the investor's arbitrage profit. The risk and expected return of the new portfolio exactly match the old one, but the new portfolio cost $600 less. Such an arbitrage opportunity will not last very long. As investors sell LeverCo shares to buy UnleverCo stock, the share prices will change until the market reaches a new equilibrium in which the total market values of the two firms are identical—just as Proposition I says they should be.

What if the price on LeverCo's shares was originally *too low?* In this case, arbitrage would proceed in the opposite direction. An investor would sell UnleverCo shares and then purchase 1 percent of *both* the equity and the debt of LeverCo. Purchasing LeverCo's debt and its equity makes the new portfolio just as risky as an investment in UnleverCo shares. However, after completing this transaction, the investor will have cash remaining because LeverCo's shares are undervalued.

The key point is that under the assumption of the M&M model, the profit-maximizing activities of investors will ensure that Proposition I holds. Whether a company uses leverage or not will have no impact on its total market value.

Proposition II and the *WACC*

M&M established in Proposition I that a firm's debt-to-equity ratio is not related to its market value. In a second proposition, they also dispelled a common misperception about the debt/equity choice. Refer back to the description of UnleverCo in

Table 12.5. The table indicates that UnleverCo's shareholders expect a 10 percent return, but UnleverCo could issue debt at a cost of 6 percent. Wouldn't it be wise for UnleverCo's managers to raise money from the cheapest source, and isn't that source debt?

M&M's second important insight is that even though debt is less costly for firms to issue than equity, issuing debt causes the required return on the remaining equity to rise. Based on the core finance principle that investors expect compensation for risk, shareholders of levered firms demand higher returns than do shareholders in all-equity companies. Table 12.5 demonstrates this clearly: Even though LeverCo and UnleverCo are essentially identical businesses, LeverCo's shareholders expect a 14 percent return on their investment, considerably higher than the 10 percent return required by UnleverCo stockholders. Therefore, when managers are tempted to issue debt because it seems less costly than equity, they do well to remember that adding debt raises the cost of equity.

We can formalize all of this mathematically as follows: Remember that the required return on the firm's assets is r, the interest rate on its debt is r_d, and the market values of its debt and equity are D and E, respectively. M&M's **Proposition II** says that the expected return on a levered firm's equity, r_l, rises with the debt-to-equity ratio:

$$r_l = r + (r - r_d)\left(\frac{D}{E}\right) \qquad \text{(Eq. 12.2)}$$

Observe what Equation 12.2 says about a firm with no debt at all. In that case, the equation implies that the return on equity equals the return on assets, a relationship that we mentioned earlier. As debt increases, however, the return on equity rises as well. When a firm replaces debt for equity, it is true that it is replacing a high cost source of finance with a low cost one. But there is no net benefit from doing this because the increase in the required return on the firm's remaining equity *exactly offsets* the savings from replacing some of the old equity with debt.

This should not be a surprise; it ties right back to Proposition I. If a firm could lower its total financing costs by substituting debt for equity, then that would increase the firm's value. Proposition I rules this out, so substituting debt for equity (or vice versa) should have no net impact on the firm's financing costs.

With a little rearranging, we can write Equation 12.2 this way:

$$r = r_l\left(\frac{E}{D+E}\right) + r_d\left(\frac{D}{D+E}\right)$$

Does this look familiar? It should. It's the expression for a firm's weighted average cost of capital (*WACC*), a concept we introduced in Chapter 9 Recall that the *WACC* is the discount rate that the firm uses to value its investments in real assets. It is also the return that a firm must earn to satisfy shareholders and lenders. When Proposition II holds, the *WACC* is independent of capital structure, and the term r is a constant. But if the *WACC* is unrelated to leverage, so is the value of the firm, because the *WACC* is the rate we use to discount the firm's cash flows to obtain its market value. Hence the connection between Propositions I and II.

If you examine Equation 12.2, you may wonder how we can claim that the *WACC* remains constant even as the debt-to-equity mix changes. Mathematically, it seems that any adjustment to the terms on the right-hand side of the *WACC* equation must result in a change on the left-hand side. Thus, changes in capital structure should affect the *WACC*. But M&M Proposition II implies that *changes in leverage cause an offsetting change in the required return on equity.* That offsetting change would leave the return on assets—the *WACC*—unchanged. We can see this by calculating the *WACC* for our two hypothetical firms.

$$WACC_{\text{UnleverCo}} = 0.10\left(\frac{\$1,000,000}{\$0 + \$1,000,000}\right) + 0.06\left(\frac{\$0}{\$0 + \$1,000,000}\right) = 0.10$$

$$WACC_{\text{LeverCo}} = 0.14\left(\frac{\$500,000}{\$500,000 + \$500,000}\right) + 0.06\left(\frac{\$500,000}{\$500,000 + \$500,000}\right) = 0.10$$

Both firms have a 10 percent *WACC*, even though their capital structures vary a great deal. LeverCo finances half its operations with 6 percent debt, which is considerably less expensive than its 10 percent cost of equity. However, because it uses so much debt, LeverCo's shareholders require a 14 percent return, much higher than the return UnleverCo promises its shareholders. *On balance, then, there is no advantage to using all equity or a mix of equity and debt.* Figure 12.4 illustrates M&M's Proposition II: It shows that the rising cost of equity, which accompanies a higher debt-to-equity ratio, leaves a firm's *WACC* unchanged.

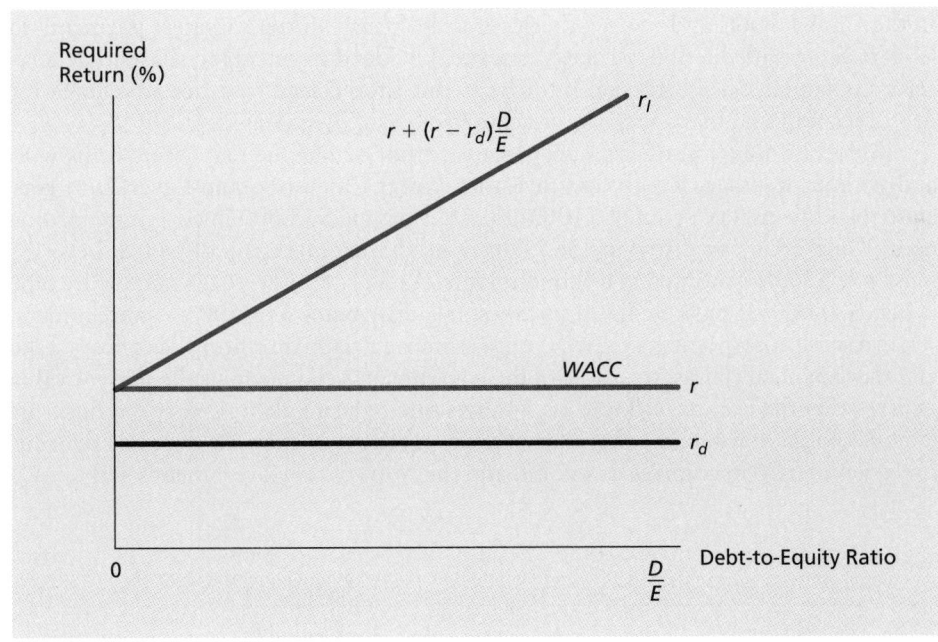

Figure 12.4
M&M Proposition II Illustrated—The Cost of Equity, Cost of Debt, and Weighted Average Cost of Capital (*WACC*) for a Firm in a World without Taxes

Where: $r + (r - r_d)\dfrac{D}{E}$ = cost of equity

r_d = cost of debt

$WACC = r$ = weighted average cost of capital

D = market value of debt outstanding

E = market value of stock outstanding

8. Explain how *Propositions I and II* are different, as well as what they have in common.

9. What is the difference between levered and unlevered equity? Suppose a shareholder of an unlevered firm, like Intel Corp., wanted the company to include more debt in its capital structure. What could the investor do on his or her own that would have the same effect as the company borrowing more?

10. M&M used an analogy of trying to create value by separating whole milk into skim milk and cream to demonstrate the futility of repackaging a firm's cash flows into debt and equity streams. How does this analogy relate to Proposition I? Can separating whole milk into cream and skim components create value? Why or why not?

12.5 M&M AND TAXES

M&M derived their famous propositions by starting with the assumption that firms operate in frictionless markets (markets without taxes or transactions costs). In this section, we look at what happens when we introduce an important source of friction, taxes, into the M&M framework.

THE M&M MODEL WITH CORPORATE TAXES

In the United States and many other countries, firms can treat interest payments to lenders as a tax-deductible business expense. Dividend payments to shareholders receive no similar tax advantage. Intuitively, this should lead to a tax advantage for debt, meaning that managers can increase firm value by issuing debt.

Table 12.7 illustrates how a 35 percent corporate income tax affects firms with and without leverage. Recall that investors expect UnleverCo and LeverCo to generate the same pretax profit of $100,000. After paying $35,000 in corporate income taxes, UnleverCo can distribute $65,000 to its shareholders as a dividend. LeverCo must pay $30,000 in interest to bondholders. As a result, LeverCo's taxable income is just $70,000. It pays $24,500 in taxes and distributes $45,500 to shareholders.

In a sense, a corporate tax gives the government a claim on a firm's cash flows. Like all other financial claims, the value of the government's claim equals the present value of taxes that the firm pays. Table 12.7 shows that by using debt, LeverCo reduces its tax bill and thereby reduces the value of the government's claim. By avoiding debt entirely, UnleverCo maximizes its tax bill and the value of the government's stake.

Table 12.7
Income Statements for UnleverCo and LeverCo with Corporate Income Taxes

	UnleverCo	LeverCo
Net operating income (NOI)	$100,000	$100,000
Less: Interest paid to bondholders ($0.06 \times D$)	0	30,000
Taxable income [$NOI - (0.06 \times D)$]	$100,000	$ 70,000
Less: Tax at 35% ($T_c = 0.35$)	35,000	24,500
Net income (NI)	$ 65,000	$ 45,500
Total income to private investors (interest on bonds + net income)	$ 65,000	$ 75,500
Value of tax shield each period ($T_c \times .06 \times D = 0.35 \times$ interest)	$　　 0	$ 10,500

We can now compute the value of UnleverCo (V_U), using the basic M&M valuation formula used before, modified to discount after-tax net income. Taxes don't change the risk of the firm, so we can assume that investors still require a 10 percent return on the firm's assets. Denoting the corporate tax rate as T_c, we have the following:

$$V_u = \frac{[NOI(1 - T_c)]}{r} = \frac{\$65,000}{0.10} = \$650,000 \qquad \text{(Eq. 12.3)}$$

In the no-tax world, UnleverCo's market value was $1,000,000. Thus, we can conclude that the 35 percent corporate profits tax causes the company's value to drop by $350,000. This represents a wealth transfer from UnleverCo's shareholders to the government.

Figure 12.5 illustrates the impact of taxes on firm value. Panel A represents the situation in the original no-tax case: There, the size of the pie (i.e., the value of the firm) does not depend on how you divide the pie between debt and equity claims. With a corporate income tax, though, a firm's capital structure influences its value: debt determines how much of the pie goes to the government. The more the firm borrows, the smaller is the government's claim, and therefore the larger are the claims held by private investors. Panel B of Figure 12.5 illustrates this point. At the limit, the government's slice (its tax claim) disappears when the firm finances its operations entirely through debt and pays all its earnings in tax-deductible interest.

DETERMINING THE PRESENT VALUE OF DEBT TAX SHIELDS

Equation 12.3 reveals that corporate taxes reduce an unlevered firm's value (compared to its value with no taxes). By issuing debt, a firm can shield some of its cash flows from taxation and hence increase its value. Can we quantify the benefit of this tax shield?

If we assume that the firm always renews its debt when it matures, the interest deduction becomes a perpetuity equal to the tax rate times the interest paid. To find the perpetuity's present value, we discount the tax shield at r_d, the interest rate on the firm's debt.[16] With these assumptions, we can compute the present value of the interest tax shields as follows:

$$PV \text{ interest tax shields} = \frac{(T_c \times r_d \times D)}{r_d} = T_c \times D = 0.35(\$500,000) \qquad \text{(Eq. 12.4)}$$
$$= \$175,000$$

In other words, the benefit of debt equals the tax rate times the face value of debt outstanding. Therefore, the value of LeverCo, V_L, equals the value of UnleverCo *plus* the value of the interest tax shields:

$$V_L = V_U + PV \text{ tax shield} = V_U + T_c D = \$650,000 + \$175,000 \qquad \text{(Eq. 12.5)}$$
$$= \$825,000$$

[16.] We use r_d as the discount rate here because the interest tax shield only materializes when the firm makes its debt payments. So the risk of the interest tax deduction is similar to the risk of the firm's debt.

Figure 12.5
The Impact of Taxes
on Proposition I

Panel A
With no taxes, the size of the pie, or the value of the firm, does not depend on the mix of debt and equity that the firm chooses. Proposition I holds, and capital structure is irrelevant.

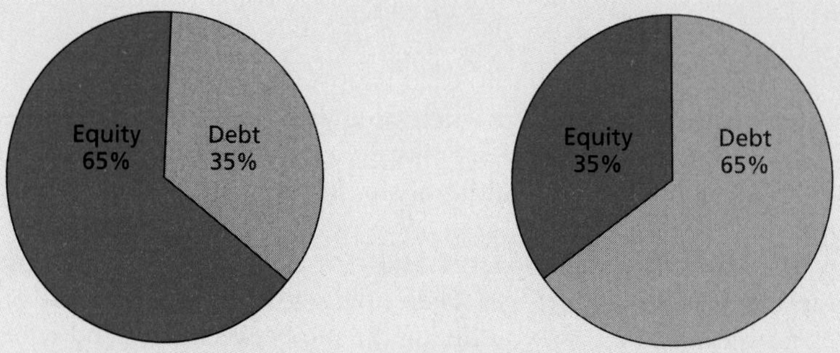

Equity 65% Debt 35%

Equity 35% Debt 65%

Panel B
With a corporate income tax, a portion of the firm's cash flows goes to the government, diminishing the value of claims held by private investors. The government's slide of the pie shrinks the more debt a firm uses because the government does not tax interest payments. A company could shelter nearly all of its cash flows by financing its operations almost entirely with debt. Therefore, capital structure matters because firm value rises with debt.

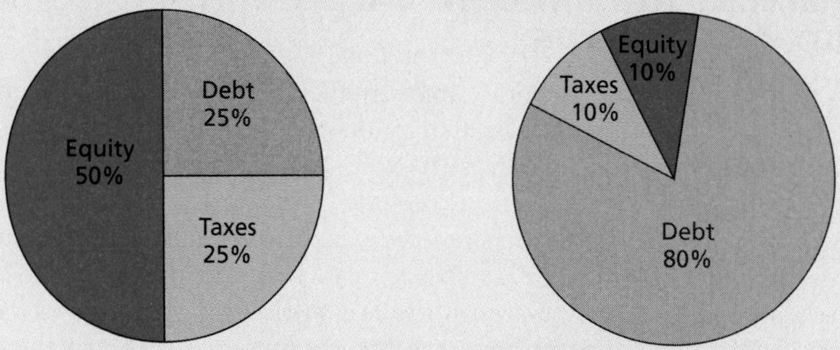

Equity 50% Debt 25% Taxes 25%

Equity 10% Taxes 10% Debt 80%

SMART CONCEPTS
See the concept explained step-by-step at
SMARTFinance

What a deal! In essence, the government has given LeverCo's managers a $175,000 subsidy to employ debt financing rather than equity.

But why should the firm's management stop there? If a 50–50 capital structure increases total firm value by $175,000 (compared to the all-equity case), then the *optimal* leverage ratio for any firm is embarrassingly obvious: 100 percent debt! More than anything else, this implication of M&M's early work created skepticism about their conclusions. How could the theory be correct if it predicted that firms should be so highly levered?

THE M&M MODEL WITH CORPORATE AND PERSONAL TAXES

After M&M published their findings, finance researchers and practitioners faced a quandary. Their best theoretical models said managers either should not worry about the capital structure decision or should borrow as much as possible to minimize taxes. Then Miller (1977) offered an explanation for the puzzle. Debt levels had averaged between 30 percent and 40 percent of total capital for several decades (except during the Depression), in spite of the fact that corporate tax rates had varied from zero to over 50 percent during the same period. Miller pointed out that legislators had almost invariably changed corporate and personal tax rates at the same time and in the same direction.[17] Furthermore, in many periods the tax rate that investors faced on interest income from corporate bonds exceeded the tax rate they faced on dividends and capital gains from stock. Miller argued that debt's tax advantage over equity *at the corporate level* might be partially or fully offset by a tax *disadvantage at the individual level.*

Synthesizing differences in corporate income tax rates as well as personal tax rates on interest, dividends, and capital gain, Miller produced the following formula to calculate the gains from using leverage, G_L:

$$G_L = \left\{ 1 - \left[\frac{(1 - T_c)(1 - T_{ps})}{(1 - T_{pd})} \right] \right\} D \qquad \text{(Eq. 12.6)}$$

where T_c = tax rate on corporate profits, as before

T_{ps} = personal tax rate on income from stock (dividends and capital gains)

T_{pd} = personal tax rate on income from debt (interest income)

D = market value of a firm's outstanding debt

Equation 12.6 helps resolve the seeming conflict between leverage and taxes. It says that the capital structure decision can increase, decrease, or have no affect on firm value depending on parameters of the tax code. For example, when there are no taxes at all ($T_c = T_{ps} = T_{pd} = 0$), G_L equals zero, and the original M&M propositions hold. If the government taxes corporations but not individuals ($T_c = 0.35$; $T_{ps} = T_{pd} = 0$), then G_L equals T_cD, and an all-debt capital structure emerges as the optimal choice. However, with a high personal tax burden on interest income relative to equity income, the gains from leverage can turn negative.

To see how the gains from leverage can be negative, consider an extreme case with a zero tax rate on income from stocks ($T_{ps} = 0$). This is not as wild as it might sound, as U.S. investors pay capital gains taxes *only upon realization,* and taxes on some equity investments can be skipped entirely with careful estate planning. Combine this assumption with a 35 percent corporate income tax and a 40 percent personal tax rate on interest income, and debt's tax advantage turns into a disadvantage:

$$G_L = \left\{ 1 - \left[\frac{(1 - 0.35)(1 - 0.0)}{(1 - 0.4)} \right] \right\} D = (-0.083)D$$

With this set of tax rates, the "gain" from leverage is actually negative!

In some cases, the effects of corporate and personal taxes may exactly offset each other. If the personal tax on equity income is 7.7 percent, the gain from leverage is zero and capital structure is again irrelevant.

---

[17] For a listing of U.S. corporate and personal tax rates during the twentieth century, see Table 1.6 of Taggart (1985). As do others, Beatty (1995) provides empirical evidence that the stock market values financial policies (i.e., employee stock ownership plans) that minimize corporate tax payments.

APPLYING THE MODEL 12.2

To illustrate how personal and corporate taxes interact to determine the net gains from leverage, consider a situation in which the corporate tax rate is 35 percent, the personal tax rate on interest income is 40 percent, and the personal tax rate on dividends is 15 percent. Suppose that a firm finances its operations entirely with equity. In a particular year, this firm earns net operating income of $1 million, or $650,000 after corporate taxes, and it pays out this profit as a dividend. Given the dividend tax rate of 15 percent, shareholders experience an after-tax gain of $552,500 ($0.85 \times \$650,000$).

Now imagine that this firm had financed its operations entirely with debt rather than equity. The entire $1 million operating profit flows to bondholders and escapes corporate taxes entirely. However, bondholders receiving the interest owe $400,000 in personal taxes, netting $600,000 after taxes. Under these conditions, the all-debt capital structure still produces higher returns for investors, but personal taxes on interest lower debt's tax advantage compared to the case when governments tax only corporate income.

By changing the corporate and personal tax rates, legislators change the relative merits of debt and equity financing. For instance, lowering the corporate tax rate from 35 percent to 29 percent in this example erases the tax advantage of debt.

Naturally, the importance of interactions between personal and corporate tax rates in determining the relative merits of debt and equity is not limited to firms in the United States. As the *Comparative Corporate Finance* insert on the next page shows, countries the world over must choose capital structures keeping in mind the influence of corporate and personal taxes. Increasingly, the personal tax element matters most.

BOND MARKET EQUILIBRIUM WITH CORPORATE AND PERSONAL TAXES

Miller's (1977) gain-from-leverage model has an interesting implication regarding the equilibrium level of interest rates in a market economy. Consider what happens immediately after a government first introduces corporate income taxes into a previously untaxed economy. Whereas firms had been indifferent to whether they issued debt or equity, now income destined for shareholders has become worth only $(1 - T_c)(NOI)$, and interest paid to bondholders escapes corporate taxation entirely.

This change means that firms have an incentive to borrow, and as more and more firms increase their borrowing, interest rates will rise. Equilibrium occurs when the higher interest rates completely offset the tax advantages of the interest deduction. This occurs when pretax, nominal interest rates rise from r_d to $r_d/(1 - T_c)$. At that point, individual firms are again indifferent to whether they issue debt or equity, but the equilibrium level of debt in the economy is far higher than in the no-tax case.

You have probably noticed that we have not said anything yet about personal taxes due on interest income received by investors. Wouldn't taxable investors also demand a higher interest rate to compensate them for taxes due? The answer is yes, but it is not that simple. Miller explains that interest rates do not rise immediately for two reasons: (1) Some investors, such as endowments and pension funds, do not have to pay taxes on interest income. (2) Investors who do not enjoy this tax-exempt status can buy municipal bonds which pay interest that is tax free. Municipal bonds pay an interest rate of r_0, which is equal to the after-tax return on similar-risk corporate bonds, or $(1 - T_{pd})r_d$.

COMPARATIVE CORPORATE FINANCE

Is the State Withering Away? No, Based on Government Spending Levels

Given the spread of market-based economic policies around the world, plus the large number of privatizations, is the economic role of the government in developed nations declining? The nearby figure seems to support that idea. Government spending as a percentage of nominal GDP declined between 1993 and 2004 for all the countries in this figure except Japan and Switzerland.

However, this is a very recent trend. In the prior decades, government spending rose steadily in all countries. Between 1965 and 1993, government spending as a percent of GDP increased by 23 percentage points for Italy, 21 points for Canada, 11 points for France, 10 points for Japan, 11 points for Britain, 7 points for the United States, and 4 points for Germany.

To meet demands for increased spending, taxes have also increased significantly since the 1960s. Almost without exception, however, Western democratic governments have *decreased* tax rates for corporations even as they increased effective personal income tax rates. The reason for favoring corporate over individual taxpayers is simple: Corporations are mobile and will often move their operations to countries with more favorable tax regimes, but few individuals have that option.

Source: Fiscal Balances and Public Indebtedness, Organization for Economic Cooperation and Development, (December 22, 2004), downloaded from http://www.oecd.org.

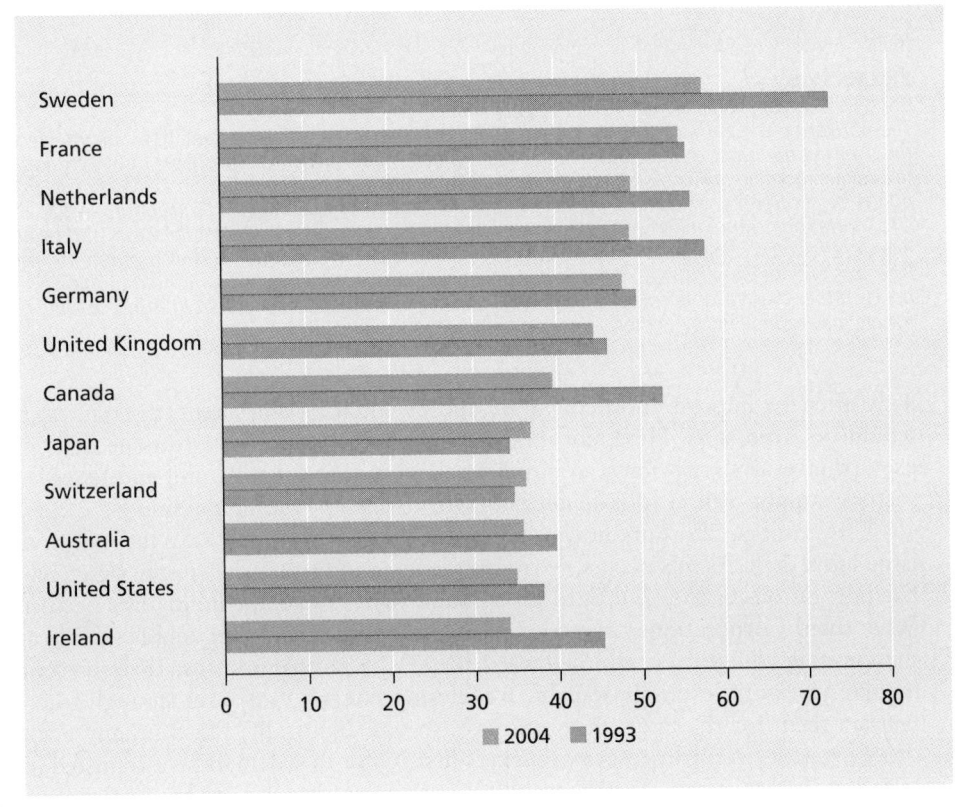

Government Spending (All Levels) as Percent of Nominal GDP, 2004 versus 1993

Figure 12.6 illustrates the relationship between the total amount of corporate bonds outstanding (D) and the interest rate. The horizontal line labeled $r_s(D)$ is the supply curve for corporate bonds. As we previously argued, corporations have an incentive to issue debt as long as equilibrium interest rates are less than or equal to this interest rate. The upward-sloping line $r_d(D)$ is the demand curve for debt. Immedi-

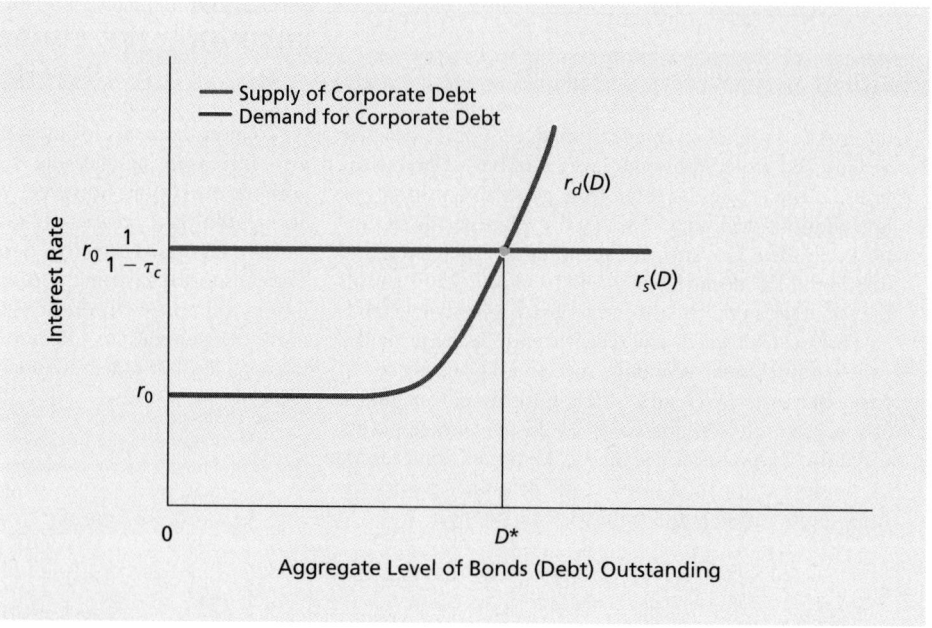

Figure 12.6
Bond Market Equilibrium in the Miller (1977) Model
The horizontal line in this figure represents the supply curve of corporate debt. This line intersects the y-axis at the point at which the interest rate on corporate debt exactly offsets debt's corporate tax advantage. The upward-sloping line represents the demand curve for debt, and indicates that bonds must offer higher rates to attract investors from higher tax brackets. Equilibrium occurs at D*. At that point, the only investors holding corporate bonds are tax-exempt investors and taxable investors facing a personal tax rate on interest income less than or equal to the corporate tax rate. Investors with personal tax rates above the corporate tax rate would choose to hold municipal bonds rather than taxable corporate bonds. D* is the aggregate level of debt in the economy, but for any particular company, there is no net advantage to using debt or equity.

ately after the imposition of corporate and personal income taxes, the interest rate would be at point r_0. Here, corporations have a huge incentive to issue debt, tax-exempt investors are willing to buy debt (lend money) at this rate, and taxable investors shun taxable corporate debt in favor of tax-free municipal bonds.

This is not equilibrium, however, because corporations still have the incentive to issue more debt. As this occurs, we move farther and farther out (to the right) on the flat portion of curve $r_d(D)$, until all demand for tax-exempt bonds has been met. What then? Corporations can no longer issue debt at rate r_0, but debt is still cheaper than issuing equity [r_d is still below $r_0/(1 - T_c)$]. Companies must therefore entice taxable investors to purchase debt, by offering interest rates high enough to compensate them for the taxes they will have to pay. Naturally, the company attracts those investors in the lowest tax brackets first. Once that demand is exhausted, corporations will raise rates further to entice investors in the next tax bracket, and so on until the marginal interest rate paid has been **grossed up** (increased to provide a given after-tax yield) to equal $r_0/(1 - T_c)$. At this point, represented as D^*, corporations are again indifferent to whether they issue debt or equity, and capital market equilibrium is reestablished.

To phrase this differently, the first corporations to issue bonds after passage of the Income Tax Amendment to the U.S. Constitution in 1913 were able to issue debt at unusually low rates [between r_0 and $r_0/(1 - T_c)$]. But from that time forward, Miller argued, equilibrium interest rates fully reflected investor tax rates, and capital structure has been irrelevant, from a tax standpoint, ever since.

Although few people suggest that the Miller model perfectly describes reality, the model is both intuitively appealing and supported by some (but not all) empirical research. For example, U.S. tax-exempt municipal bonds have generally offered nominal yields that equal 65–80 percent of the yield on corporate bonds of comparable risk and maturity. This suggests that the marginal bond investor's personal tax rate has fluctuated between 20 percent and 35 percent. Further empirical support comes from research using data from countries such as Great Britain, Australia, Italy, and France, which have *imputation* or split-rate tax systems. These systems seek to partially offset the tax incentive for debt by giving investors a tax credit for corporate taxes paid on dividends received. Figure 12.7 presents corporate and personal tax rates for several OECD countries.

Academic research suggests that tax changes that penalize equity income (i.e., increasing taxes on dividends and capital gains) lead to higher aggregate debt ratios. The reverse is true for changes that reduce effective tax rates on equity income. Keep in mind that firms can exploit debt's tax advantage only when they have profits to shelter with interest deductions. Research in the 1980s suggested that firms that can use other ways of sheltering income from tax, called *nondebt tax shields,* may not need to borrow money to shelter income.

OTHER TAX-BASED MODELS OF CAPITAL STRUCTURE

Following Miller, several authors developed tax-based extensions of the basic capital structure models. The most important of these, by DeAngelo and Masulis (1980), incorporates **nondebt tax shields (NDTS)** as substitutes for debt in corporate financial structures. Their NDTS hypothesis states that companies with large amounts of depreciation, investment tax credits, R&D expenditures, and other nondebt tax shields should employ less debt financing than otherwise equivalent companies with fewer such shields. Plausible as this hypothesis is, however, later research found just the reverse.[18] Leverage seemed to be directly, not inversely, related to the availability of NDTS.

Researchers interpreted this finding as evidence that assets that generated such tax shields could also be used as collateral for additional debt. The implication is that firms rich in tangible assets are able to use higher levels of (secured) debt. This **secured-debt hypothesis** has been supported both theoretically and empirically.

More recent research has been able to measure the separate effects of NDTS and assets that can be collateralized, and provides support for both the nondebt tax shields and the secured-debt hypotheses.[19]

Concept Review Questions

11. Holding other factors constant, how do you think corporate capital structures might change if the corporate income tax were abolished?

12. Over time, institutional investors, especially pension funds, which are effectively untaxed on their investment income, have held an increasing percentage of common stock. What do you think this trend implies for corporate leverage?

13. In 1964, Britain adopted a corporation taxation system with separate company-level taxation of corporate operating income and personal taxation of distributed profits (dividends). After 1964, debt levels increased in Britain. Offer an explanation of this phenomenon.

[18.] See Bradley, Jarrell, and Kim (1984) and Titman and Wessels (1988).
[19.] A selection of good papers in this literature includes Scott (1977), MacKie-Mason (1990), Hovakimian, Opler, and Titman (2001), Desai, Foley, and Hines (2004), Graham (1996, 2000), Fama and French (1998), and Kahle and Shastri (2005).

Figure 12.7
Corporate and Personal
Income Tax Rates
in Selected OECD
Countries
*Source: OECD Tax
Database,*Organization for
Economic Cooperation and
Development (January 2005),
downloaded from http://
www.oecd.org.

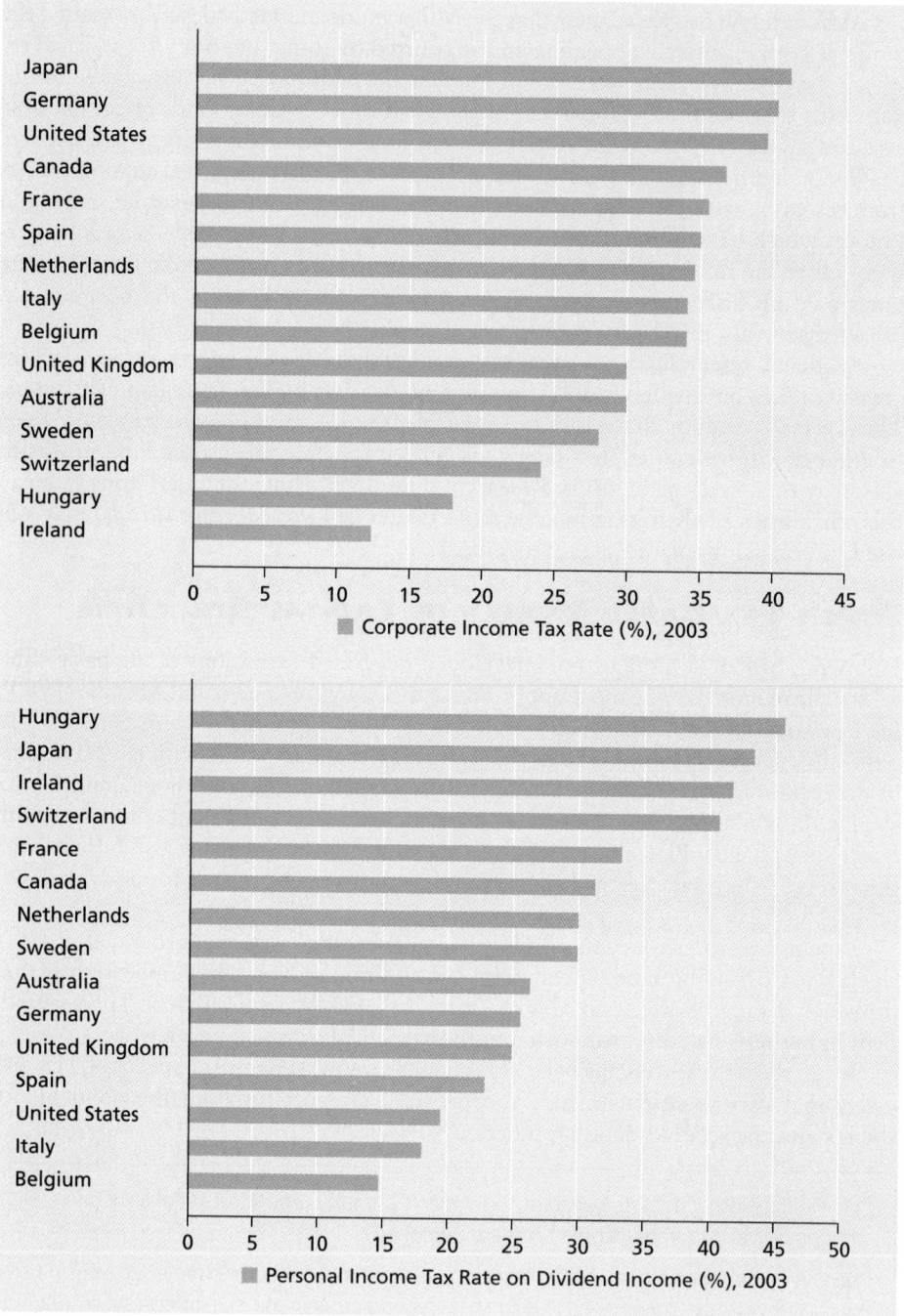

12.6 A CHECKLIST OF HOW TAXES SHOULD AFFECT CAPITAL STRUCTURE

Although the impact of taxes on corporate leverage is often complex, we can at least summarize three theoretical predictions that empirical research supports. Other things equal, and assuming that interest is a tax-deductible expense for corporations but that dividend payments are not, the following relationships should hold:

1. **The higher the corporate income tax rate, T_c, the higher will be the equilibrium leverage level economy-wide.** An increase in T_c should cause debt ratios to increase for most firms.
2. **The higher the personal tax rate on equity-related investment income (dividends and capital gains), T_{ps}, the higher will be the equilibrium leverage level.** An increase in T_{ps} should cause debt ratios to increase.
3. **The higher the personal tax rate on interest income, T_{pd}, the lower will be the equilibrium leverage level.** An increase in T_{pd} should cause debt ratios to fall.

These relationships have proven quite robust over time and across tax regimes. The challenge for corporate financial managers is to make financing decisions that maximize the value of the firm for any given taxation regime.

12.7 SUMMARY

- Financial leverage refers to debt financing that increases expected earnings per share and the volatility of earnings per share.
- Corporate debt ratios measure the ratio of a firm's long-term debt to its equity capital. Leverage ratios measure either book value or market value. Ratios based on market values tend to indicate less leverage than book value measures do.
- Several regularities occur in capital structure patterns around the world. In general, industries rich in fixed assets and/or with assets that retain their value in bankruptcy tend to have high leverage; industries rich in intangible assets tend to have low leverage. Firms in R&D–intensive industries usually have especially low debt ratios.
- Though firms in the same industries tend to exhibit similar debt levels across countries, there are also significant differences in average leverage levels between countries. In those countries where bankruptcy laws favor creditors, especially Britain and Germany, market-value leverage levels tend to be lower than in nations where debtors enjoy greater bankruptcy protection.
- Modigliani and Miller (M&M) (1958) showed that capital structure is irrelevant in a world of frictionless capital markets. This means that the leverage choice does not affect a firm's value.
- In a world with only company-level taxation of operating profits and tax-deductible interest payments, the optimal corporate strategy is to use the maximum possible leverage. This minimizes the government's claim on profits and maximizes income flowing to private investors.
- When governments impose taxes both at the corporate and personal levels, debt's tax advantage usually appears to be lower than when there is a corporate income tax only; in some cases, higher personal taxes on interest income may lead to a net tax disadvantage for debt.

INTERNET RESOURCES

Note: *For updates to links, please go to the book's website at http://smart.swcollege.com.*

http://www.quicken.com; http://www.yahoo.com; http://www.sec.gov—Three sites from which you can download leverage figures for specific companies and compare them to figures for firms in the same industry as well as firms in other industries

http://www.taxsites.com/international.html—A site providing country-specific tax information for dozens of countries, as well as links to a wide variety of tax-related sites

KEY TERMS

agency cost/tax-shield trade-off model
arbitrage
financial leverage
financial slack
fundamental principle of financial leverage
grossed up
homemade leverage
market-timing model
Modigliani & Miller (M&M) argument
municipal bonds

nondebt tax shield hypothesis
pecking-order model
Proposition I
Proposition II
recapitalization
secured-debt hypothesis
signaling model
target leverage zones
trade-off model

QUESTIONS

12-1.   Why is the use of long-term debt financing referred to as using *financial leverage?*

12-2.   What is the fundamental principle of financial leverage?

12-3.   What industrial and national capital structure patterns are exhibited globally? What factors seem to be driving these patterns?

12-4.   What is a target debt ratio? What does having a target debt ratio imply that companies will do over time to adjust their actual leverage levels? Do U.S. corporations behave as though they have target debt ratios?

12-5.   How influential are corporate and personal taxes on capital structure? Historically, have changes in U.S. tax rates greatly affected debt ratios?

12-6.   How do stock prices generally react to announcements of firms' changes in leverage?

12-7.   Briefly describe each of the four major models of capital structure choice. Which of these models are based on an assumption of asymmetric information between managers and outside investors?

12-8.   According to the *pecking-order hypothesis,* what is the purpose of maintaining financial slack? How does this relate to the assumption in this hypothesis of asymmetric information?

12-9.   How does the *signaling model* of financial structure differ from the pecking-order model with respect to the assumption of asymmetric information?

12-10. What are the *market-timing model*'s key predictions about corporate debt levels? What assumptions about managerial behavioral motivate this model?

12-11. What is the basic conclusion of the original Modigliani and Miller *Proposition I?* What argument do M&M offer as a defense of this conclusion? How is *homemade leverage* used within this argument?

12-12. Following from the conclusion of Proposition I, what is the crux of M&M *Proposition II?* What is the natural relationship between the required returns on debt and equity that results from Proposition II?

12-13. In what way did M&M change their conclusion regarding capital structure choice with the additional assumption of corporate taxes? In this context, what explains the difference in value between levered and unlevered firms?

12-14. By introducing personal taxes into the model for capital structure choice, how did Miller alter the previous M&M conclusion that 100 percent debt is optimal? What happens to the gains from leverage if personal tax rates on interest income are significantly higher than those on stock-related income?

12-15. What does the Miller (1977) model imply about the equilibrium level of interest rates? In your answer, address the concept of interest rates that are *grossed up*.

12-16. List and describe the three predictions made by academic researchers regarding the impact of taxes on corporate leverage. Have these predictions been supported empirically?

PROBLEMS

What Is Financial Leverage and What Are Its Effects?

12-1. As Chief Financial Officer of Magnificent Electronics Corporation (MEC), you are considering a recapitalization plan that would convert MEC from its current all-equity capital structure to one including substantial financial leverage. MEC now has 500,000 shares of common stock outstanding, which are selling for $60 each. You expect the firm's *EBIT* to be $2,400,000 per year, for the foreseeable future.

The recapitalization proposal is to issue $15,000,000 worth of long-term debt, at an interest rate of 6.0 percent, and use the proceeds to repurchase 250,000 shares of common stock worth $15,000,000. Assuming there are no market frictions such as corporate or personal income taxes, calculate the expected return on equity for MEC shareholders, under both the current all-equity capital structure and under the recapitalization plan.

12-2. All-Star Production Corporation (APC) is considering a recapitalization plan that would convert APC from its current all-equity capital structure to one including some financial leverage. APC now has 10,000,000 shares of common stock outstanding, which are selling for $40 each. You expect the firm's *EBIT* to be $50,000,000 per year, for the foreseeable future.

The recapitalization proposal is to issue $100,000,000 worth of long-term debt, at an interest rate of 6.50 percent, and use the proceeds to repurchase as many shares as possible, at a price of $40 per share. Assume there are no market frictions such as corporate or personal income taxes. Calculate the expected return on equity for APC shareholders, under both the current all-equity capital structure and under the recapitalization plan.

a. Calculate the number of shares outstanding, the per share price, and the debt-to-equity ratio for APC if it adopts the proposed recapitalization.

b. Calculate the earnings per share (*EPS*) and the return on equity for APC shareholders, under both the current all-equity capitalization and the proposed mixed debt/equity capital structure.

c. Calculate the breakeven level of *EBIT*, where earnings per share for APC stockholders are the same, under the current and proposed capital structures.

d. At what level of *EBIT* will APC shareholders earn zero *EPS*, under the current and the proposed capital structures?

12-3. As Chief Financial Officer of Uptown Service Corporation (USC), you are considering a recapitalization plan that would convert USC from its current all-equity capital structure to one including substantial financial leverage. USC now has 150,000 shares of common stock outstanding, which are selling for $80 each.

The recapitalization proposal is to issue $6,000,000 worth of long-term debt, at an interest rate of 7.0 percent, and use the proceeds to repurchase 75,000 shares of common stock worth $6,000,000. USC's earnings in the next year will depend on the state of the economy. If there is normal growth, *EBIT* will be $1,200,000. *EBIT* will be $600,000 if there is a recession, and *EBIT* will be $1,800,000 if there is an economic boom. You believe that each economic outcome is equally likely. Assume there are no market frictions such as corporate or personal income taxes.

a. If the proposed recapitalization is adopted, calculate the number of shares outstanding, the per-share price, and the debt-to-equity ratio for USC.

b. Calculate the earnings per share (*EPS*) and the return on equity for USC shareholders, under all three economic outcomes (recession, normal growth, and boom), for both the current all-equity capitalization and the proposed mixed debt/equity capital structure.

c. Calculate the breakeven level of *EBIT*, where earnings per share for USC stockholders are the same, under the current and proposed capital structures.

d. At what level of *EBIT* will USC shareholders earn zero *EPS*, under the current and the proposed capital structures?

12-4. Firm QRS is an all-equity firm and has 500,000 shares outstanding selling for $40 a share. Currently, the firm has an *EBIT* of $5 million with a 40% tax rate and a 40% dividend payout ratio. Calculate QRS' earnings per share (*EPS*) and dividend per share (multiply *EPS* by dividend payout ratio).

QRS is considering a $10 million debt issue with a coupon rate of 8%. Calculate how this affects the debt-to-equity ratio, the *EPS*, and the dividend per share, assuming the *EBIT* increases to $8 million due to the expansion. Next, calculate the *EPS* and dividend per share, assuming the expansion is financed with a stock issue instead.

12-5. Firm BOB has a debt-to-equity ratio of 1.0 and desires to maintain the ratio should there be any expansion/retraction of the firm. Currently, the stock sells for $25 and there are 300,000 shares outstanding. The existing debt has an annual coupon of $120 per $1,000 bond. Given a current *EBIT* of $1,650,000 and a tax rate of 40%, what are BOB's earnings per share (*EPS*)?

A $5 million expansion of BOB will require a stock and bond issue (assume bonds sell at $1,000 par). How many shares of stock and how many bonds will be required to finance the expansion? What level will the *EBIT* need to be to maintain BOB's current *EPS*?

12-6. VD's shareholders believe that if its current level of debt ($2.5 million) was replaced by equity, the earnings per share will increase. Assuming the debt has a 10% interest rate, the tax rate is 45%, there are 400,000 shares outstanding selling for $25 a share, and the current *EPS* is $1.85, calculate the *EPS* with no debt. Are the shareholders correct that an all equity firm would increase the *EPS*?

12-7. The shareholders of firm NBY have determined that if all of the $1 million debt were retired and replaced with stock, their earnings per share would increase from $0.91 to $0.933. Currently, the *EBIT* is $4 million, the tax rate is 30%, and the interest on the debt is 10%. The shareholders calculate the current net income to be $2.73 million, which, distributed over 3 million shares ($10 share price), is $0.91. The shareholders then calculate the net income to be $2.8 million without the debt, which, distributed over 3 million shares, is $0.93. Redo the shareholders' calculation and verify where the calculations are in error. What did the shareholders do wrong in their calculation and do the corrected calculations indicate an increase in *EPS* by eliminating debt?

12-8. Investor Q believes that leverage within firm ZZZ would improve the return on ZZZ's stock. Q currently earns a 14% after-tax return on a $5,000 investment in ZZZ's stock. If Q borrows $2,500 at an after-tax rate of 4.5% and invests all of it in ZZZ stock, what is Q's debt-to-equity ratio? What is Q's after-tax return on the portfolio of debt and ZZZ stock (see Chapter 5)?

12-9. Investor R has $5,000 of debt costing a pretax interest rate of 8%. Investor R also has $10,000 worth of LAN stock that has a pretax return of 15%. Assuming that

R can deduct the debt interest prior to taxes and must pay tax on the stock return, what is R's after-tax return based on a 40% tax rate? If R sells $5,000.0 of the LAN stock to retire the debt, what is the after-tax return on R's new unlevered portfolio? Should R have unlevered the portfolio, assuming no possibility of financial distress within LAN?

12-10. A firm's *EBIT* is $2.5 million with a 42% tax rate. Calculate how much the government extracts from the firm through taxation. If $10 million worth of debt with 10% interest exists, what is the new amount of taxes paid? Of the interest paid to the debt holders, what is the new amount of taxes paid? Of the interest paid to the debt holders, what proportion of the interest would have been lost to taxes had the debt holders not existed?

Worldwide Capital Structure Patterns

12-11. Go to Yahoo! and download recent balance sheets for Microsoft, Merck, Archer Daniels Midland, and General Mills (ticker symbols MSFT, MRK, ADM, and GIS, respectively). Calculate several debt ratios for each company and comment on the differences that you observe in the use of leverage. What factors do you think account for these differences?

The Modigliani & Miller Propositions

12-12. An unlevered company operates in perfect markets and has net operating income of $250,000. Assume that the required return on assets for firms in this industry is 12.5 percent, and that the firm issues $1 million worth of debt with a required return of 5 percent and uses the proceeds to repurchase outstanding stock.
   a. What is the market value and required return of this firm's stock before the repurchase transaction?
   b. What is the market value and required return of this firm's remaining stock after the repurchase transaction?

12-13. Assume that capital markets are perfect. A firm finances its operations with $50 million in stock with a required return of 15 percent and $40 million in bonds with a required return of 9 percent. Assuming that the firm could issue $10 million in additional bonds at 9 percent, using the proceeds to retire $10 million worth of equity, what would happen to the firm's *WACC?* What would happen to the required return on the company's stock?

12-14. A firm operates in perfect capital markets. The required return on its outstanding debt is 6 percent, the required return on its shares is 14 percent, and its *WACC* is 10 percent. What is the firm's debt-to-equity ratio?

12-15. Assume that two firms, U and L, are identical in all respects except one: Firm U is debt-free, whereas Firm L has a capital structure that is 50 percent debt and 50 percent equity by market value. Further suppose that the assumptions of the Modigliani & Miller capital structure irrelevance proposition hold (no taxes or transactions costs, no bankruptcy costs, etc.) and that each firm will have net operating income of $800,000.

SMART SOLUTIONS
See the problem and solution explained step-by-step at
SMARTFinance

If the required return on assets, *r,* for these firms is 12.5 percent and risk-free debt yields 5 percent, calculate the following values for both Firm U and Firm L: (1) total firm value, (2) market value of debt and equity, and (3) required return on equity.

Then, recompute these values, assuming that the market mistakenly assigns Firm L's equity a required return of 15 percent, and *describe* the arbitrage operation that will force Firm L's valuation back into equilibrium.

12-16. Hearthstone Corp. and The Shaky Image Co. are companies that compete in the luxury consumer goods market. The two companies are virtually identical, except that Hearthstone is financed entirely with equity and The Shaky Image uses equal amounts of debt and equity. Suppose that each firm has assets with a total market value of $100 million. Hearthstone has 4 million shares of stock outstanding worth $25 each. Shaky has 2 million shares outstanding, and it also has publicly traded debt with a market value of $50 million. Both companies operate in a world with perfect capital markets (no taxes, etc.). The WACC for each firm is 12 percent. The cost of debt is 8 percent.

a. What is the price of Shaky stock?

b. What is the cost of equity for Hearthstone? For Shaky?

c. Suppose that you want to buy 1 percent of the outstanding Shaky shares, but you do not like the fact that Shaky uses leverage. Assuming that you can borrow and lend at 8 percent, show how you can trade on your own account to unwind the effects of Shaky's leverage.

d. Suppose that you want to buy 1 percent of the outstanding Hearthstone shares, but you wish that the firm's managers were not so conservative, refraining entirely from issuing debt. Demonstrate how you can trade on your own account to create an investment in Hearthstone that is equivalent in terms of risk and return to buying 1 percent of Shaky's shares.

12-17. An unlevered company operates in perfect markets and has net operating income (EBIT) of $2,000,000. Assume that the required return on assets for firms in this industry is 8 percent. The firm issues $10 million worth of debt, with a required return of 6.5 percent, and uses the proceeds to repurchase outstanding stock. There are no corporate or personal taxes.

a. What is the market value and required return of this firm's stock before the repurchase transaction, according to M&M Proposition I?

b. What is the market value and required return of this firm's remaining stock after the repurchase transaction, according to M&M Proposition II?

12-18. In the mid-1980s, Michael Milken and his firm, Drexel Burnham Lambert, popularized the term "junk bonds"—bonds with low credit ratings. Many of Drexel's clients issued junk bonds to the public to raise money to conduct a leveraged buyout (LBO) of a target firm. After the LBO, the target firm would have an extremely high debt-to-equity ratio, with only a small portion of equity financing remaining. Many politicians and members of the financial press worried that the increase in junk bonds would bring about an increase in the risk of the U.S. economy because so many large firms had become highly leveraged. Merton Miller disagreed. See if you can follow his argument by assessing whether each of the statements below is true or false:

a. The junk bonds issued by acquiring firms were riskier than investment-grade bonds.

b. The remaining equity in highly leveraged firms was more risky than it had been before the LBO.

c. After an LBO, the target firm's capital structure would consist of very risky junk bonds and very risky equity. Therefore, the risk of the firm would increase after the LBO.

d. The junk bonds issued to conduct the LBO were less risky than the equity they replaced.

12-19. Currently, a firm has a debt-to-equity ratio of 0.0 and a return on its shares of 15%. Assuming the firm can issue debt at a cost of 10%, what is the return on the equity at the following debt-to-equity ratios: 0.5, 1.0, and 1.5? (*Hint:* WACC does not change under any of these scenarios.)

M&M and Taxes

12-20. Herculio Mining has net operating income of $5 million. It has $50 million of debt outstanding, with a required rate of return of 6 percent. The required rate of return on the industry is 12 percent, and the corporate tax rate is 40 percent. Assume there are corporate taxes but no personal taxes.

a. Determine the present value of the interest tax shield of Herculio Mining, as well as the total value of the firm.

b. Determine the gain from leverage if personal taxes of 20 percent on stock income and 30 percent on debt income exist.

12-21. An all-equity firm is subject to a 30 percent tax rate. Its total market value is initially $3,500,000. There are 175,000 shares outstanding. The firm announces a program to issue $1 million worth of bonds at 10 percent interest and to use the proceeds to buy back common stock. Assume that there is no change in costs of financial distress and that the debt is perpetual.

a. What is the value of the tax shield that the firm acquires through the bond issue?

b. According to Modigliani & Miller, what is the likely increase in market value per share of the firm after the announcement, assuming efficient markets?

c. How many shares will the company be able to repurchase?

12-22. Intel Corp. uses almost no debt and had a total market capitalization of about $179 billion in April 2004. Assume that Intel faces a 35 percent tax rate on corporate earnings. Ignore all elements of the decision, except the corporate tax savings.

a. By how much could Intel managers increase the value of the firm by issuing $50 billion in bonds (which would be rolled over in perpetuity) and simultaneously repurchasing $50 billion in stock? Why do you think that Intel has not taken advantage of this opportunity?

b. Suppose the personal tax rate on equity income, faced by Intel shareholders, is 10 percent, and the personal tax rate on interest income is 40 percent. Recalculate the gains to Intel from replacing $50 billion of equity with debt.

12-23. SoonerCo has $15 million of common stock outstanding, net operating income of $2.5 million per year, and $15 million of debt outstanding with a required return (interest rate) of 8 percent. The required rate of return on assets in this industry is 12.5 percent, and the corporate tax rate is 35 percent. Within the M&M framework of corporate taxes but no personal taxes, determine the present value of the interest tax shield of SoonerCo, as well as the total value of the firm. Finally, determine the gain from leverage if personal tax rates exist in the form of 15 percent on stock income and 25 percent on debt income.

12-24. Westside Manufacturing has *EBIT* of $10 million. It has $60 million of debt outstanding, with a required rate of return of 6.5 percent. The required rate of return on the industry is 10 percent. The corporate tax rate is 30 percent. Assume there are corporate taxes but no personal taxes.

a. Determine the present value of the interest tax shield of Westside Manufacturing, as well as the total value of the firm.

b. Determine the gain from leverage, if personal taxes of 10 percent on stock income and 35 percent on debt income exist.

A Checklist of How Taxes Should Affect Capital Structure

12-25. How does the value of an unlevered firm change if it takes on debt in a perfect capital market? Abercrombie & Fitch (ticker: ANF) is an all-equity firm. Using the latest year's net operating income (*EBIT*) and its weighted average cost of capital (*WACC*), calculate the value of ANF. If the company decides to change its debt-to-equity ratio to 0.5, by issuing debt and by using the proceeds to repurchase stock, what will ANF's value be after the change in capital structure? Assume that its cost of debt is one-quarter of its cost of equity and that markets are perfect. What happens to its cost of equity after the new debt is issued? What is likely to happen to ANF's equity beta after debt is issued?

12-26. How does the value of an unlevered firm change if it takes on debt in the presence of corporate taxes? Repeat the analysis for ANF from the previous problem, after relaxing only the "no corporate tax" assumption of perfect capital markets. Use the average tax rate (income taxes divided by pretax income from the income statement) for the latest available year.

a. What is the value of ANF after it issues debt? What is the benefit of issuing debt when there are corporate taxes?

b. How will the beta for a levered ANF, in the presence of corporate taxes, compare to that of an all-equity ANF and that of a levered ANF, in perfect capital markets?

c. When capital markets are perfect, except for corporate taxes, what is the optimal level of debt the company should issue? In reality, do we observe firms that maintain this optimal level of debt? Why or why not?

THOMSON ONE BUSINESS SCHOOL EDITION

12-27. Estimate the gain from leverage for Maxwell Technology (ticker symbol, MXWL) for the last five years. Estimate the tax rate as income taxes/pretax income. Are the changes in the gain from leverage mainly due to changes in the estimated tax rate or to the amount of long-term debt? Repeat the analysis for American Technology Ceramic (ticker symbol, AMK). As a percentage of assets, which firm has the greater gain from leverage? What is driving the difference in the gain from leverage for the two firms?

MINI-CASE: CAPITAL STRUCTURE: THEORY AND TAXES

DataCore Inc. currently has an all-equity capital structure. However, the firm is considering recapitalizing by structuring the firm with 25% debt and 75% equity by issuing an appropriate amount of debt and repurchasing an equal amount of common stock, and expects that the debt will have a 5% coupon rate. The firm expects the following scenarios over the next year for earnings before interest and taxes (*EBIT*):

Outlook	Probability	*EBIT*
Good	35%	$800,000
Average	40%	$525,000
Poor	25%	$ 75,000

The firm currently has 200,000 shares of common stock outstanding at $43 per share. The firm is in a 0% tax bracket.

1. Determine the expected earnings before interest and taxes (*EBIT*), net income (*NI*), and earnings per share (*EPS*) if the firm maintains its current unlevered capital structure versus if it recapitalizes at 25% debt and uses that money to repurchase common stock.

2. Following the assumptions behind M&M's Proposition I, calculate the stockholders' required rate of return of the firm in an unlevered versus a levered state. Calculate the value of the levered firm, separating it into debt and equity. Also, calculate the weighted average cost of capital (*WACC*) for the firm in a levered versus an unlevered state.

3. Assuming the firm is in a 35% corporate tax bracket, determine the value of the unlevered firm versus the value of the levered firm.

OPENING FOCUS

France Telecom Launches a $15 Billion Rights Offering to Reduce Its Leverage

By early 2003, France Telecom (FT) had become the world's most heavily indebted company, with total borrowings of over $70 billion. Since being partially privatized by the French government six years before, FT had been on a nonstop $100 billion spending spree: acquiring controlling stakes in telecom companies being privatized in the emerging economies of Eastern Europe; paying top prices for third generation cellular phone licenses; purchasing the mobile phone provider Orange; and generally acting as though the 1990s technology boom would never end. And so, when the technology boom turned to bust after March 2000, FT quickly fell into severe financial distress.

As FT's losses mounted during 2001 and 2002, the company's managers and the French state—still FT's majority shareholder—realized that the only chance to save the company was to raise a large chunk of new equity, even though this would obviously have to be done under distressed terms. Accordingly, FT launched a €15 billion ($15.8 billion) rights offering in March 2003. New shares were priced at €14.50 each, a substantial discount to the previous day's closing price of €20.00, but the offering was successful and significantly reduced FT's debt ratio.

Shortly after FT's record rights offering, the global telecommunications industry's fortunes took a decided turn for the better. Over the next two years, FT's strong profits, reduced capital spending, and excellent stock performance further reduced leverage levels. The firm's debt rating was raised from BBB to A by Fitch Ratings Services in June 2004, and in early 2005 by Standard & Poors. By June 2005, FT had cut its total borrowing by a remarkable €28 billion, and the company had announced plans to more than double its annual dividend to €1.00 per share. Perhaps most significantly, France Telecom even returned to the acquisitions trail in late 2005, with its €8.9 billion ($10.7 billion) purchase of Amena, Spain's third-largest mobile phone operator. This acquisition was financed primarily with a new issue of stock, priced at €22.63 per share, and was approved by both firms' shareholders—including the French government, which by then had reduced its FT stake to a mere 33 percent.

Source: Financial Times *(http://www.ft.com), various issues.*

SMARTFinance
Use the learning tools at www
.thomsonedu.com/finance/smartfinance

485

At the start of this chapter, we are like readers who are halfway through a mystery novel. We know the mystery to be solved: how corporate leverage impacts firm value. We also know that it is a complicated case: Capital structure is irrelevant in perfect markets, but firms act as though leverage matters. We have cleared some suspects of the crime: Corporate and personal taxes influence debt levels, but they neither cause nor prevent corporate leverage. Other suspects—bankruptcy costs, the agency costs of debt and equity, and a firm's asset characteristics—remain to be interrogated. Our job in this chapter is to question the remaining suspects and interpret the evidence to solve the leverage mystery.

Under the assumptions of the M&M theory, capital structure is irrelevant. Corporate income taxes, viewed in isolation, give firms a strong incentive to use leverage, but things are much less clear-cut when personal income taxes enter the analysis. If taxes do not explain why firms pay attention to capital structure, then what does?

To see how capital structure *can* be relevant, we simply need to turn the M&M assumptions around. If leverage does matter, markets must be imperfect in some way. Market imperfections that could influence capital structures include financial distress costs, or costs tied to negotiating and enforcing contracts between managers and stockholders. Perhaps a connection exists between leverage and firms' investment opportunities, or perhaps firms borrow money in part to send a credible signal to the market about their ability to generate cash in the future. This chapter will consider each of these possibilities, beginning with bankruptcy and financial distress.

13.1   COSTS OF BANKRUPTCY AND FINANCIAL DISTRESS

It seems obvious that the threat of bankruptcy might make some firms use debt sparingly. Companies that cannot service their debts and managers who run those companies face bleak prospects.[1] As Table 13.1 shows, over 35,000 businesses (and over 1 million individuals) file for bankruptcy protection in the United States each year. Experience shows that a bankrupt company's security-holders, even supposedly protected senior bondholders, can lose their entire investment in a firm. Surely, then, differing costs of bankruptcy and financial distress between industries can cause firms in one industry to employ less debt than do comparable firms in other industries, right?

Before reaching this conclusion, we need a precise definition of the term *bankruptcy costs*. In the first place, bankruptcy costs are distinct from the decline in firm value that leads to financial distress. Poor management, unfavorable movements in input and output prices, and recessions can push a firm into bankruptcy, but they are not examples of bankruptcy costs. Instead, **bankruptcy costs** refer to direct and indirect costs of the bankruptcy process itself.

In the United States, a firm becomes bankrupt when it comes under the supervision of the federal government's bankruptcy courts and ceases to operate as an independent legal entity. The court can then choose to liquidate the firm and distribute money to the firm's creditors to satisfy their claims. Or, the court can choose to reorganize the firm's operations and finances, thereby allowing it to emerge from bank-

---

[1.] Altman (1984) is the first study to clearly show that bankruptcy is costly for firms. Later, Gilson (1989) and Gilson and Vetsuypens (1993) also document that bankruptcy can be similarly painful for individual managers.

Table 13.1
Bankruptcy Petitions Filed and Pending in the United States, by Type and Chapter

Item	1992	1996	2000	2001	2002	2003
Total Filed	971,517	1,178,555	1,253,444	1,492,129	1,577,651	1,660,245
Business[a]	70,643	53,549	35,472	40,099	38,540	35,037
Chapter 7[b]	38,125	30,659	20,335	23,482	22,321	20,631
Chapter 11[c]	19,436	10,738	9,197	10,641	10,286	8,474
Nonbusiness[d]	900,874	1,125,006	1,217,972	1,452,030	1,539,111	1,625,208
Chapter 7[b]	643,538	770,741	838,885	1,031,493	1,087,602	1,156,274
Chapter 13[e]	254,18	344,092	378,400	419,750	450,516	467,999

Notes: This table covers only bankruptcy cases filed under the Bankruptcy Reform Act of 1978. Bankruptcy is defined as the legal recognition that a company or individual is insolvent and must restructure or liquidate. Petitions "filed" means the commencement of a proceeding through the presentation of a petition to the clerk of the court. "Pending" is a proceeding in which the administration has not been completed.
[a]Business bankruptcies include those filed under chapters 7, 11, 12, or 13.
[b]Chapter 7: liquidation of nonexempt assets of businesses or individuals.
[c]Chapter 11: individual or business reorganization.
[d]Nonbusiness bankruptcies include those filed under chapters 7, 11, or 13.
[e]Chapter 13: adjustment of debts of an individual with regular income.
Source: United States Bankruptcy Court Statistics (http://www.uscourts.gov/bnkrpctystats/bankruptcystats.htm).

ruptcy as a new company. In theory, the firm's original shareholders lose their entire investment in either case, and ownership of firm's remaining assets will pass to bond-holders and other creditors. These investors then become the firm's new stockholders. The process of reorganizing a firm and negotiating terms with the firm's managers, shareholders, and creditors consumes resources. The resources thus consumed are the bankruptcy costs.

THE IMPORTANCE OF BANKRUPTCY COSTS

Contrary to popular misconception, bankruptcy is not a "cremation" (Haugen and Senbet 1978). Rather, it is a legal process that reorganizes financial claims and transfers corporate ownership. Even if a firm is liquidated, its assets will not disappear but will instead be employed by a new owner. Thus, bankruptcy is the *result* of economic failure, not the cause. Think about what a bankruptcy filing actually means for a firm's shareholders: It means they are exercising their **option to default** on the company's debt. As noted earlier, limited liability is a key benefit of the corporate form of organization. Absent this feature, shareholders would have to pay off the firm's creditors out of their own pockets instead of simply handing creditors the company's assets in bankruptcy court.

Therefore, unless the *process* of bankruptcy imposes costs on a company that a similarly distressed, but nonbankrupt firm would not have to bear, the mere possibility of falling into bankruptcy cannot influence capital structure decision making. Similarly, a firm cannot consider financial leverage itself as something to avoid unless debt financing somehow makes financial distress more painful for a levered company than it would be for an all-equity company. The following example shows that the mere prospect of bankruptcy does not imply that capital structure decisions will influence firm value. Capital structure affects firm value only if the bankruptcy process is costly.

APPLYING THE MODEL 13.1

Both Low-Debt Parking Company and High-Debt Parking Company have one-year contracts to manage identical parking lots for the resort town of Falling Rivers. The value of these contracts depends on local economic conditions next year. If the economy booms, Falling Rivers will attract many visitors. However, if a recession occurs, the number of visitors will fall drastically. The probability that the good economic conditions will continue is the same as the probability of a recession, 50 percent. If the economic boom continues, each company will earn a management fee (net of the costs of operating the lots) of $900,000. If a recession occurs, each will net just $200,000.

Each company financed its purchase of the parking-management contract from the City of Falling Rivers in part with borrowed money, which must be repaid with interest when the parking contracts expire in one year. At maturity, Low-Debt will owe $106,000 in principal and interest; High-Debt will owe $270,000. If there is a recession, High-Debt will be unable to pay its creditors in full and will file for bankruptcy. If there are no costs of bankruptcy, High-Debt's stockholders will lose their investment, and the firm's creditors will receive the $200,000 cash flow.

Assume that High-Debt's stockholders require a return of 11.54 percent and its bondholders expect a return of 8 percent. Both stockholders and bondholders of Low-Debt are willing to accept slightly lower returns because the firm uses leverage more sparingly. Low-Debt's stockholders require an 11 percent return, and its bondholders require 6 percent. The following table details the payoffs to security-holders of both firms under the additional assumption that neither firm pays taxes.

Item	Low-Debt Parking Company		High-Debt Parking Company	
	Expansion (probability = 0.5)	Recession (probability = 0.5)	Expansion (probability = 0.5)	Recession (probability = 0.5)
Cash flow at contract expiration	$900,000	$200,000	$900,000	$200,000
Debt-service payment (interest and principal)	106,000	106,000	270,000	200,000
Distributions to stockholders	794,000	94,000	630,000	0

To value the equity, E, and debt, D, of these two firms, we first compute the expected value of the payoffs to each investor group and then find the present value of the payoffs using the required returns to discount cash flows. The value, V, of the firm is then the sum of equity and debt values, $V = E + D$.

$$E_{\text{Low-Debt}} = [(0.5 \times \$794,000) + (0.5 \times \$94,000)] \div 1.11$$

$$= \$444,000 \div 1.11 = \$400,000$$

$$D_{\text{Low-Debt}} = [(0.5 \times \$106,000) + (0.5 \times \$106,000)] \div 1.06$$

$$= \$106,000 \div 1.06 = \$100,000$$

$$V_{\text{Low-Debt}} = \$400,000 + \$100,000 = \$500,000$$

$$E_{\text{High-Debt}} = [(0.5 \times \$630,000) + (0.5 \times \$0)] \div 1.1154$$

$$= \$315,000 \div 1.1154 = \$282,407\,^2$$

$$D_{\text{High-Debt}} = [(0.5 \times \$270,000) + (0.5 \times \$200,000)] \div 1.08$$

$$= \$235,000 \div 1.08 = \$217,593$$

$$V_{\text{High-Debt}} = \$282,407 + \$217,593 = \$500,000$$

Because both firms have the same total market value, we can conclude that costless bankruptcy will not affect a firm's market value. Therefore, the fact that High-Debt's financing strategy makes bankruptcy more likely *does not affect the value of the firm, and capital structure is irrelevant.*

It is worth noting that High-Debt's bondholders have a *promised* return of more than 24 percent [$(270,000 - 217,593) \div 217,593$] but an *expected* return of only 8 percent, so the possibility of partial default is priced into the bonds today.

In fact, however, bankruptcy *is* a costly process, and those costs can influence a firm's leverage choices. Consider three ways that bankruptcy costs can influence a firm's mix of debt and equity:

1. If the process of bankruptcy entails *deadweightcosts*—such as cash payments to lawyers, accountants, or advisers—then firms have an incentive to minimize leverage to reduce the likelihood of bankruptcy.
2. Bankruptcy costs are important if encountering financial distress reduces demand for a firm's products or increases its costs of production.
3. Bankruptcy costs matter if financial distress gives the firm's managers, operating as the shareholders' agents, perverse incentives to take operating or financial actions that reduce overall firm value.

As you might imagine, empirical research shows these costs do arise and do significantly impact observed leverage ratios. Again, let's look at an example.

APPLYING THE MODEL 13.2

To demonstrate our point, we use the same assumptions made previously for Low-Debt Parking Company and High-Debt Parking Company, with one change: We

---

[2.] We are actually using a discount rate of 11.541 percent here. You can double-check that given the percentages of debt and equity used by each firm, and given the required return on each firm's debt and equity, the weighted average cost of capital for managing parking lots is 10 percent. Does it surprise you that High-Debt's WACC is the same as Low-Debt's?

now assume that if there is a recession and High-Debt is forced to file for bankruptcy, the process will be contentious and costly. Instead of receiving the full $200,000 terminal cash flow as in the costless bankruptcy case, High-Debt's creditors will receive only $120,000. In other words, the conflicts between High-Debt's stockholders and bondholders (and their lawyers) consume $80,000 of value.

When we recompute the stock and bond values for each firm, it becomes clear that if the process of bankruptcy involves real costs, they reduce the current value of a highly levered firm. For High-Debt Parking Company, costly bankruptcy reduces overall firm value by $37,037 ($500,000 − $462,963).

$$E_{\text{Low-Debt}} = [(0.5 \times \$794,000) + (0.5 \times \$94,000)] \div 1.11$$

$$= \$444,000 \div 1.11 = \$400,000$$

$$D_{\text{Low-Debt}} = [(0.5 \times \$106,000) + (0.5 \times \$106,000)] \div 1.06$$

$$= \$106,000 \div 1.06 = \$100,000$$

$$V_{\text{Low-Debt}} = \$400,000 + \$100,000 = \$500,000$$

$$E_{\text{High-Debt}} = [(0.5 \times \$630,000) + (0.5 \times \$0)] \div 1.1154$$

$$= \$315,000 \div 1.1154 = \$282,407$$

$$D_{\text{High-Debt}} = [(0.5 \times \$270,000) + (0.5 \times \$120,000)] \div 1.08$$

$$= \$195,000 \div 1.08 = \$180,556$$

$$V_{\text{High-Debt}} = \$282,407 + \$180,556 = \$462,963$$

ASSET CHARACTERISTICS AND BANKRUPTCY COSTS

SMART IDEAS VIDEO

Robert Bruner, University of Virginia

"The case of Revco illustrates the principle of too much or too little debt."

See the entire interview at **SMARTFinance**

Clearly, some firms should weather financial distress better than others. For example, if you only once purchase a commodity item (i.e., raw flour) or only once use a service (i.e., printing a set of business cards), you care little whether the company providing the commodity or service remains in business after your transaction. On the other hand, if you plan to purchase a large new computer system or a commercial airplane, the long-term viability of the supplier becomes very important. Therefore, producers of complex products or services tend to use less debt than do firms producing nondurable goods or basic services. It is important for producers of durable goods to assure customers that their firms will be able to provide ongoing service, warranty and repair work, and product improvements.[3] Based on this logic, it is not surprising that Table 12.3 showed that companies such as Intel, IBM, United Technologies, and Boeing use leverage very sparingly.

A firm's asset mix also influences its leverage decisions. Companies whose assets are mostly tangible and have well-established secondary markets should be less fearful of financial distress than companies whose assets are mostly intangible. Therefore, trucking companies, airlines, construction firms, pipeline companies, and railroads can all employ relatively more debt than can companies with few, if any,

---

[3.] This point is made most clearly in Titman (1984) and Maksimovic and Titman (1991).

tangible assets, such as pharmaceutical manufacturers, food distributors (what is the collateral value of week-old tomatoes?), or pure service companies. Once again, Table 12.3 verifies this logic: Delta Air Lines and AMR have much higher leverage ratios than do Merck and Eli Lilly.

Financial distress can be particularly damaging to firms that produce research and development—intensive goods and services, for two reasons. First, most of the production expenses are sunk costs, which can be recovered only with a long period of profitable sales. Second, "cutting-edge" goods require ongoing R&D spending to ensure market acceptance. A bankrupt firm cannot make these investments. Further, intangible assets such as patents and trademarks are extremely valuable, but are unlikely to pass through bankruptcy intact. Microsoft, Intel, and Cisco Systems are classic examples of companies that invest massive sums in R&D, and Table 12.3 shows that all three firms are essentially debt free!

Financial distress can also increase production costs for many companies. Suppliers may not extend credit to a very risky company, and the firm may be unable to attract business partners for joint ventures or other risk-sharing projects. Most important of all, a risky firm will have difficulty attracting and retaining talented employees.[4] Any firm that depends on the creativity, loyalty, and stability of its workforce is thus highly vulnerable to financial distress and will employ less debt than other firms.

**SMART
IDEAS
VIDEO**

**Sheridan Titman,
University of Texas at Austin**
"It seems to be the case that the product-market strategies of firms to a large extent dictate how firms are financed."

**See the entire interview at
SMARTFinance**

The Asset Substitution Problem One major problem with financial distress is that it provides otherwise trustworthy managers with reprehensible, but rational, incentives to play a variety of "games," mostly at bondholders' expense. Two such games—asset substitution and underinvestment—are especially damaging. Both games begin when managers realize the firm will probably not fulfill its obligations to creditors.

Asset substitution is the promise to invest in a safe asset to obtain an interest rate reflecting the risk, and then substituting a riskier asset promising a higher expected return. To illustrate, assume a firm has $10 million in bonds outstanding that mature in 30 days. These bonds were issued years ago when the firm was prospering. The company's operations are currently unprofitable, but the firm's managers believe the firm can be profitable again once the economy picks up. Despite its problems, the firm still has $8 million in cash on hand that it can invest in one of two projects or simply hold in reserve to partially repay the bonds in 30 days.

The first investment is a low-risk project requiring an $8 million investment that will pay off $8.15 million in 30 days with virtual certainty. This is a monthly return of 1.88 percent, or annual return of almost 25 percent. In other words, it is a positive-*NPV* project that will increase firm value, but it does not earn a return high enough to fully repay the maturing bonds.

The second investment, given the code name Project Vegas, is basically a gamble. It also requires $8 million and offers a 40 percent chance of a $12 million payoff and a 60 percent chance of a $4 million payoff. Because its expected value is only $7.2 million, Vegas is a negative-*NPV* project. The firm's managers would reject it

---

[4.] One of this book's authors experienced these problems personally while working for a large petroleum refiner in financial distress. Suppliers refused to deliver merchandise on credit, shippers refused to deliver refined products unless they were paid in advance, and it became extremely hard to replace departing employees (of which there were many). The most dramatic examples of the company's financial problems were the cash discounts the firm offered its customers for prompt payment. The annual interest rates implied by these discounts often exceeded 50 percent.

if the firm did not have debt outstanding. However, if Vegas succeeds, its $12 million payoff will allow the company to fully pay off the bonds and pocket a $2 million profit.

Consider the incentives that managers face. Clearly, bondholders would want the managers either to select the low-risk project or retain the firm's cash in reserve. But this is certainly not in the interests of the firm's shareholders. Because they will lose control of the firm if it cannot fully repay the maturing bonds, shareholders want managers to accept Project Vegas. They are effectively "playing with the bondholders' money." If successful, the project will yield enough for shareholders to pay off the creditors and retain ownership. If Project Vegas is unsuccessful, the shareholders will default and hand the firm over to bondholders, the same outcome as if the firm played it safe. Shareholders have everything to gain and nothing to lose from this strategy of substituting a riskier asset for a safer one, and their agent (the manager) controls the firm's investment policy until default actually occurs. As we will see, bondholders can use restrictive covenants that offer some protection, but these only partially solve the problem.

The Underinvestment Problem The second game set up by financial distress is **underinvestment.** Like asset substitution, this game arises when a firm's managers realize default is likely. Assume that a firm on the verge of declaring bankruptcy gains access to a very profitable, but short-lived, investment opportunity. Let's say that a supplier offers to sell its inventory to the company at a dramatically discounted price, provided that the firm pays for the inventory immediately with cash. The inventory will cost $9 million today, but taking advantage of the offer will allow the firm to accumulate the $10 million cash needed to pay off the maturing bond issue in just 30 days. However, because the firm has only $8 million in cash on hand today, shareholders—through stock issuance or dividend reduction—must contribute the additional $1 million needed to strike a deal. Accepting this project maximizes overall firm value. The shareholders rationally forgo the project because they must invest the additional $1 million, but all the benefits accrue to the bondholders.[5]

All-equity firms are not vulnerable to either of these two games. In such firms, managers always choose the project that maximizes firm value in the first example, and always contribute cash for positive-*NPV* projects in the second example. Because these financial distress costs arise due to conflicts of interest between groups of security-holders, they are considered *agency costs*, which we discuss in more depth later in the chapter.

DIRECT AND INDIRECT COSTS OF BANKRUPTCY

If bankruptcy is sufficiently costly, firms will limit financial leverage to minimize the possibility of going bankrupt. To demonstrate, we must distinguish between the direct and indirect costs of bankruptcy.

Direct costs of bankruptcy are out-of-pocket cash expenses directly related to bankruptcy filing and administration. Document printing and filing expenses, as well as professional fees paid to lawyers, accountants, investment bankers, and court personnel are all direct bankruptcy costs. These can run to several million dollars per

---

[5.] Myers (1977) describes theoretically the incentive problem associated with leverage. Lang, Ofek, and Stulz (1996) document debt's role in limiting growth by firms with poor investment opportunities.

Other things equal, firms that invest large sums of money in research and development (R&D) typically employ relatively little debt. Casual observation suggests that R&D spending is an extremely important source of innovation and growth for many U.S. corporations, as well as for the United States as a nation. In fact, U.S. corporations, governments, and universities spent some $277.1 billion on R&D in 2002, or about 2.82 percent of GDP.

The chart below puts that level of spending into international perspective, by showing the R&D spending to GDP ratio for the 30 nations that are members of the Organisation of Economic Cooperation and Develop-

ment (OECD). These countries collectively spent $638.4 billion on R&D, or about 2.3 percent of overall GDP. Though the U.S. ranks first in total R&D spending, it ranks only sixth among industrialized economies in the fraction of GDP spent on R&D. Not surprisingly, developing and transition economies invest relatively less in R&D than do developed countries.

Source: OECD Countries Spend More on Research and Development, Face New Challenges (December 23, 2004), Organisation of Economic Cooperation and Development, downloaded from http://www.oecd.org/document/2/0,2340,en_2649_37417_34100162_1_1_1_37417,00.html.

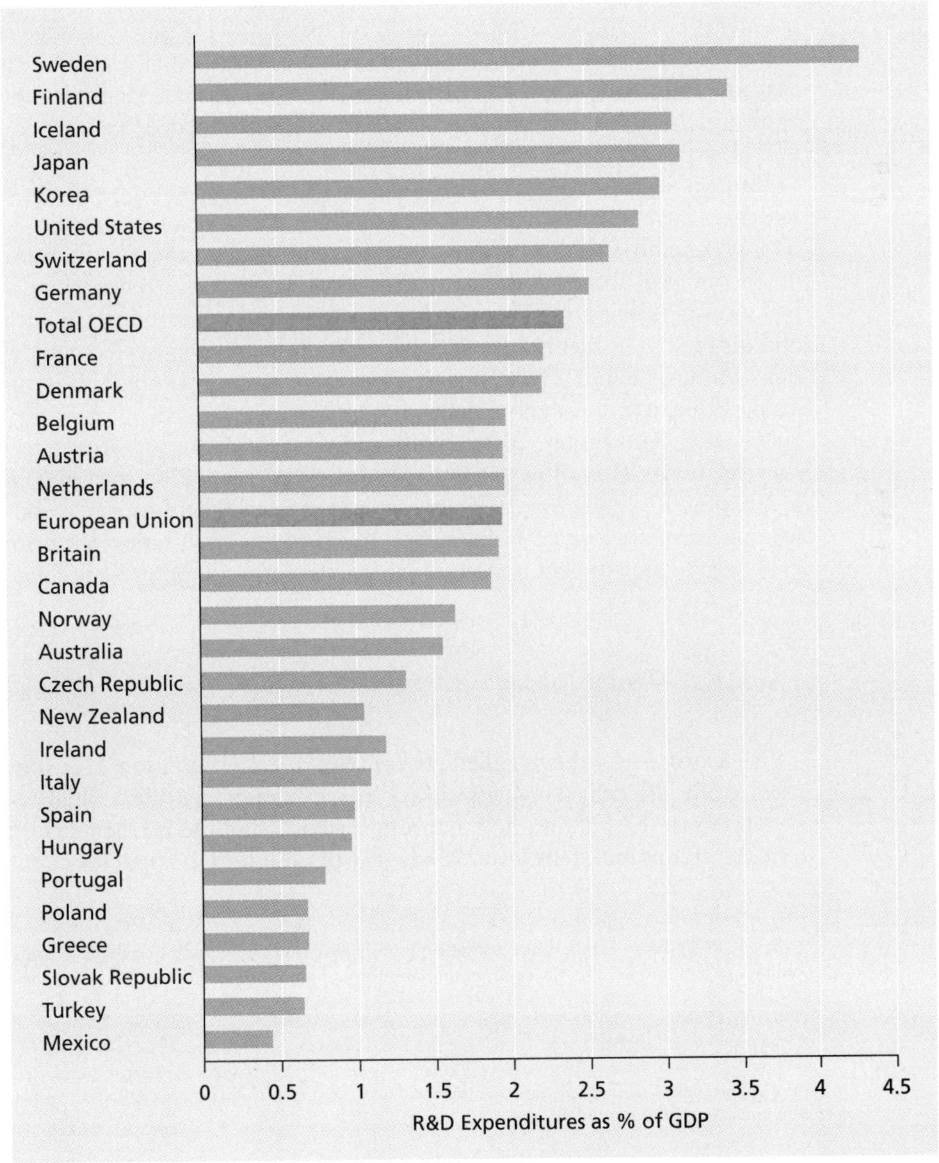

R&D Expenditures as % of GDP

Sweden	
Finland	
Iceland	
Japan	
Korea	
United States	
Switzerland	
Germany	
Total OECD	
France	
Denmark	
Belgium	
Austria	
Netherlands	
European Union	
Britain	
Canada	
Norway	
Australia	
Czech Republic	
New Zealand	
Ireland	
Italy	
Spain	
Hungary	
Portugal	
Poland	
Greece	
Slovak Republic	
Turkey	
Mexico	

month for complex cases. However, empirical research shows that—relative to the prebankruptcy market value of large firms—direct costs are too small to provide an effective deterrent to the use of debt.[6] In addition, when firms consider using debt, only the *expected* bankruptcy costs are important. In other words, if the direct costs for a firm are $10 million, and the probability of bankruptcy is 10 percent, then the expected bankruptcy costs are just $1 million.

Indirect costs of bankruptcy are expenses that result from bankruptcy but are not cash expenses spent on the process itself. These costs include the diversion of management's time, lost sales during and after bankruptcy, constrained capital investment and R&D spending, and the loss of key employees. Although indirect bankruptcy costs are difficult to measure, research shows they are significant.[7]

Recent studies present four key findings relating to indirect bankruptcy costs. First, firms entering bankruptcy have lower sales in the years after filing than an extrapolation of prebankruptcy sales growth rates predicts. This implies that customers shy away from firms in distress. Second, managers lose their jobs much more frequently than do managers of nonbankrupt firms, and the pay of managers who retain their jobs falls dramatically. Third, U.S. courts deviate from the absolute priority rules that are supposed to govern wealth distributions among security-holders. Fourth, bankruptcy reduces a firm's debt less than is usually needed, leaving many firms vulnerable to reentering bankruptcy later.

Studies show that firms facing higher expected bankruptcy risk use less debt. Researchers have documented three key findings about this relationship. First, companies with highly variable earnings use less debt than do those with more stable profits. Second, the observed leverage ratios across industries are systematically related to that industry's investment opportunities. Capital-intensive industries with few growth options tend to be highly levered, whereas high-tech industries with many growth options use little debt.[8] Third, if a firm's assets can pass through bankruptcy without losing value, it will use more debt.

Clearly, bankruptcy costs significantly influence capital structure decisions in complex ways. This allows us to expand the basic valuation formula, first presented in Chapter 12 (Equation 12.5), to include expected bankruptcy costs. Specifically, we can express a levered firm's value, V_L, in terms of an unlevered firm's value, V_U, the present value of debt and nondebt tax shields, and the present value of expected bankruptcy costs:

$$V_L = V_U + PV \text{ tax shields} - PV \text{ bankruptcy costs} \qquad \text{(Eq. 13.1)}$$

We can see why this is called the *trade-off model:* Equation 13.1 states that managers trade off debt's benefits (lower taxes) against its costs (higher bankruptcy costs). Figure 13.1 shows how bankruptcy costs and the tax benefits interact to determine an optimal debt level. Managers of all-equity companies can increase firm

---

[6] Warner (1977) shows that the direct costs of bankruptcy are of essentially trivial magnitude for large firms.

[7] Altman (1984) provides the best direct *empirical* evidence to date that the indirect costs of financial distress are large enough to discourage excessive use of financial leverage. Lang and Stulz (1992), Opler and Titman (1994), Phillips (1995), and Pulvino (1998) show that high leverage can weaken a firm's industrial competitiveness.

[8] One of the most interesting recent studies of this kind is by Goyal, Lehn, and Racic (2002). They argue that defense contractors enjoyed tremendous growth opportunities in the early 1980s under the Reagan administration, but many of these opportunities vanished a decade later with the end of the Cold War. The authors find that defense firms used less debt in the 1980s and more in the 1990s.

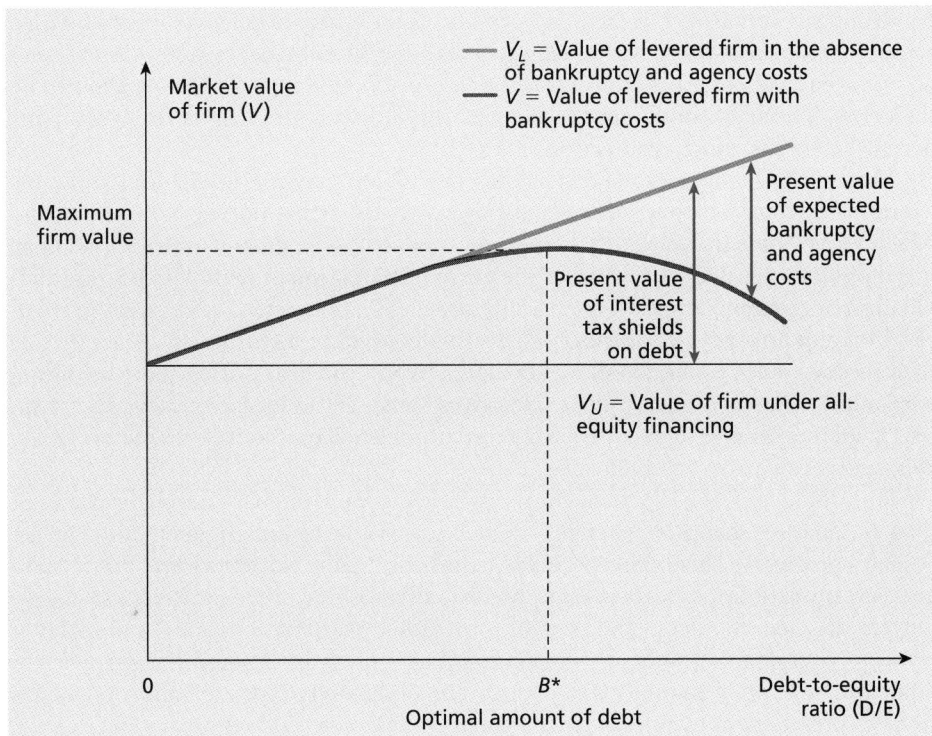

Figure 13.1
The Agency Cost/Tax Shield Trade-Off Model of Corporate Leverage
This model describes the optimal level of debt for a given firm as a trade-off between the tax benefits of corporate borrowing and the increasing agency and bankruptcy costs that come from additional borrowing.
Source: Stewart C. Myers, "The Capital Structure Puzzle," *Journal of Finance* 39 (July 1984), pp. 575–592.

value by replacing equity with debt, thus shielding more cash flow from taxes. Without bankruptcy costs, managers would maximize value by maximizing debt, a situation represented by the blue line in Figure 13.1. The red line shows how bankruptcy costs alter this conclusion. As a firm borrows more, it increases both the probability that it will go bankrupt and its expected bankruptcy costs. Beyond some point, the incremental expected bankruptcy costs offset debt's incremental tax advantage. The red line in Figure 13.1 peaks when managers find the mix of debt and equity that maximizes firm value.

INTERNATIONAL DIFFERENCES IN BANKRUPTCY COSTS

Although Chapter 28 (available on the text website) discusses U.S. and international bankruptcy procedures, we mention a few important details here. The bankruptcy codes of all advanced economies share many features, but differences in these codes help explain why firms tend to use more debt in some countries than in others.[9]

In the United States, there are two types of business bankruptcy filings. In a **Chapter 7** filing, the court liquidates the firm's assets and pays investors according to the priority of their claims (i.e., debt before equity, secured before unsecured debt, and so on). A **Chapter 11** filing is a petition to reorganize the firm's liabilities to allow the company to emerge again as an independent business. Managers sometimes file for

---

[9.] The discussion in this section draws heavily on the material presented in Table VII of Rajan and Zingales (1995). More in-depth coverage of European bankruptcy procedures, as well as an analysis of the implications of the laws' varying terms on corporate financial incentives, is provided in Kaiser (1996) and Strömberg (2000).

bankruptcy voluntarily, but creditors can also force a firm into bankruptcy provided certain conditions hold. Once a judge accepts a bankruptcy petition, the court issues an order barring creditors from further prosecution of claims, except as allowed by the court. The bankruptcy judge becomes the ultimate authority over a company once it enters the court's protection.

Most OECD countries make a similar distinction between liquidation and reorganization. However, they differ regarding creditors' rights during bankruptcy and which party holds the initiative as the process unfolds. In most countries, the judge may appoint a **trustee** who replaces the current management team and oversees liquidation or reorganization. Countries differ greatly in how often courts appoint trustees. In many European countries, judges usually appoint a trustee. In contrast, U.S. bankruptcy courts generally allow managers to run the firm during reorganization, particularly after a voluntary filing. This gives managers an incentive to file for Chapter 11 voluntarily and then to propose reorganization plans quickly, without ongoing collection pressure from creditors.

Philosophically, the U.S. bankruptcy code leans toward rehabilitating firms rather than liquidating them, an objective that explains the seemingly lax treatment accorded borrowers. This bias can be disastrous for creditors if the courts allow managers to operate firms in their own interests or those of other parties such as employees and shareholders. The laws of most other Western countries tend to favor creditors over debtors, so courts intervene sooner and order delinquent borrowers to liquidate more often than do U.S. courts. The philosophy of these bankruptcy laws seeks to preserve asset values. This presumably makes creditors more willing to lend, but it also discourages managers from using excessive debt, especially in countries where bankruptcy laws most strongly favor creditors over debtors.

Concept Review Questions

1. As late as the nineteenth century, people who could not (or would not) pay their debts were sent to debtors' prison. What do you think was the primary rationale for these laws, and what effect do you think this had on personal borrowing?

2. Revisit the example of the High-Debt and Low-Debt parking companies. The required returns on equity and debt are higher for High-Debt than for Low-Debt. How can the cost of capital for both firms be 10 percent?

3. Suppose someone borrows from a bank to buy a new car. A few months later, the borrower realizes he will have to default on this loan in a few months, after which the bank will repossess the car. What kind of underinvestment problem might occur here?

4. Suppose a commercial bank suffers loan losses so severe that it approaches insolvency. What kinds of asset-substitution problems might arise? How might bank regulators act to prevent these problems?

13.2 AGENCY COSTS AND CAPITAL STRUCTURE

In 1976, Michael Jensen and William Meckling presented an **agency cost theory of financial structure.** Few papers in the history of finance have had a comparable impact on how we view issues of corporate control, capital structure, or financial contracting. Jensen and Meckling observe that when an entrepreneur owns all of a company's stock, no separation between corporate ownership and control exists. In plain

English, this means that the entrepreneur bears all the costs, and reaps all the benefits, of her actions. Once the entrepreneur sells stock to outsiders, she bears only a fraction of the cost of any actions she takes that reduce firm value. This gives the entrepreneur a clear incentive to, in Jensen and Meckling's tactful phrasing, "consume perquisites." By selling a stake in her company, the entrepreneur lowers the cost of perquisite ("perk") consumption.

> ### APPLYING THE MODEL 13.3
>
> The founder of a software company in San Jose, California, must travel to Tokyo to close a sale. The airfare for a first-class seat on Northwest Airlines is \$4,333; a seat in coach costs just \$703. Assuming there is no additional value to the firm if the entrepreneur buys a first-class ticket, flying in first class lowers the value of the firm by \$3,630 (\$4,333 − \$703).
>
> If the entrepreneur owns all of his firm's shares, then he bears the full cost of this value reduction. On the other hand, if he owns half of his firm's shares and outside investors own the rest, the cost borne by the entrepreneur is just \$1,815. In general, if the entrepreneur sells a fraction, α, of the firm's shares to outside investors, he bears just $(1 - \alpha)$ of the cost of any perquisites he consumes. The higher the value of α, the lower a manager's cost of consuming perquisites.

This illustrates a nice deal for the entrepreneur, right? No, not in an efficient market. Informed investors expect the entrepreneur's performance to change after they buy shares, so they will pay only a price that fully reflects the entrepreneur's perk consumption. In other words, shareholders charge the entrepreneur in advance for the perks he will consume after the equity sale. Once again, the entrepreneur bears the full costs of his actions. Society also suffers because these agency costs of (outside) equity reduce the market value of corporate assets.

We are therefore at an impasse: Selling stock to outside investors creates agency costs of equity that the entrepreneur bears, but which also harm society and discourage additional entrepreneurship. On the other hand, selling external equity is vital for entrepreneurs and for society as a whole. Doing so allows firms to pursue growth opportunities that would exhaust an entrepreneur's personal wealth. Selling stock also permits entrepreneurs to diversify their portfolios). Given the importance of external equity, a logical next question is, "Is there any way to overcome the agency costs of outside equity?"

USING DEBT TO OVERCOME THE AGENCY COSTS OF OUTSIDE EQUITY

Jensen and Meckling (1976) point out that using debt helps overcome the *agency costs of outside equity*. It does so in two ways: First, using debt means a firm can sell less external equity and still finance its operations. If agency costs of outside equity rise more than proportionally as α increases, then minimizing outside equity sales will reduce the deadweight agency costs. The second, and more important, benefit of using debt is that it reduces managerial perquisite consumption. The need to make regular debt-service payments effectively disciplines managers. The cost of excessive perk consumption might well include the entrepreneur losing the company. In Jensen and Meckling's words, external debt serves as a **bonding mechanism:** Managers use the debt to convey their good intentions to outside shareholders, who will pay a higher price for the firm's shares.

You may think this is all esoteric theory, but consider for a minute just how important the agency costs of equity are for a large public company. Officers and directors of most Fortune 500 companies collectively own less than 5 percent of their company's shares, yet they reap major financial and nonfinancial benefits from controlling a large, prestigious firm. The typical Fortune 500 CEO makes over $8.1 *million* per year in salary, bonuses, and stock options, and some directors receive fees and services worth as much as $100,000 per year for attending fewer than a dozen meetings (Lavelle 2004).

Consider what shareholders can do to discipline management if they become dissatisfied with a firm's performance: They can vote against management at the annual shareholders' meeting or sell their shares. But even an institutional investor, with millions of dollars invested in a company, owns only a small fraction of a large company's outstanding shares, so voting against management or selling shares gets little notice. Investors can try to sue management, but proving malfeasance is difficult. The legal doctrine of the **Business Judgment Rule** gives directors broad discretion to use their business judgment and protects boards of directors from shareholder second-guessing in all but obvious cases of abuse. Finally, an active takeover market offers investors some protection from entrenched managers, but it has proven to be an uncertain and costly disciplining mechanism.

Our point is not to berate inept or greedy managers, but to show that agency costs for managers and stockholders are real and difficult to reduce. In two ways, debt offers a means of controlling agency costs. First, it subjects managers to direct monitoring by public capital markets.[10] If lenders doubt management's competence, they will charge a high interest rate, or they will insist on restrictive debt covenants to constrain management's freedom of action, or both. Second, debt limits management's ability to destroy value through incompetence or perquisite consumption. If management fails to operate the firm well enough to cover its debt-service payments, lenders can force the firm into bankruptcy, take control of the firm, and dismiss the offending managers. By issuing debt, managers risk being replaced, which reduces the agency costs of the manager/stockholder relationship.

AGENCY COSTS OF OUTSIDE DEBT

If debt is such an effective disciplining device, why don't firms use "maximum debt" financing? The answer is that there are also *agency costs of debt*. To see this, remember that bondholders begin taking on an increasing fraction of the firm's business and operating risk as firms use more debt. But shareholders and managers still control the firm's investment and operating decisions. This gives managers incentives to transfer wealth from bondholders to themselves and other shareholders. For example, managers might sell bonds and then pay a huge dividend to shareholders, leaving bondholders with an empty corporate shell.[11]

Shareholders might also exploit bondholders by making an asset substitution—borrowing money to finance a "safe" investment, and then investing the money borrowed in a risky project. Lenders who believe that firms will use their money prudently will accept a low interest rate. Therefore, if managers and stockholders can

---

[10.] The logic of using capital market financing requirements as a means of disciplining management is expressed most clearly in Easterbrook (1984).

[11.] Kalay (1982) describes how bondholders protect themselves from firms paying excessive dividends, and Bernando and Talley (1996) examine the perverse investment incentives that outstanding debt can engender for corporate managers who are acting in their shareholders' interest.

find enough naive bondholders, they can borrow at a "safe" interest rate and then make high-risk, high-return investments. If these investments succeed, shareholders can fully repay bondholders and pocket any excess project returns. If the project fails, shareholders simply default and bondholders take whatever remains. This "bait and switch" game can be devastating for bondholders.

As you might imagine, experienced bond investors rarely fall for this ploy, and they take steps to prevent managers from playing these games. Smart investors look for very detailed covenants in bond contracts. These covenants constrain borrowers' actions and limit their ability to expropriate bondholder wealth. Unfortunately, they make bond agreements costly to negotiate and enforce, and they may also prevent managers from making value-increasing investments. For example, if a bond covenant limits a firm's ability to issue additional debt of equal or greater seniority (one of the most common covenants), managers might pass up value-increasing investments if financing them would require the firm to issue new debt. Other covenants restrict dividend payments, even for profitable firms.

In any case, the agency costs of debt are real, and they become more important as a firm's leverage ratio increases. Consequently, firms must weigh the benefits of leverage in reducing the agency costs of outside equity against the agency costs of increased debt.

THE AGENCY COST/TAX SHIELD TRADE-OFF MODEL OF CORPORATE LEVERAGE

Jensen and Meckling's (1976) model predicts that, starting from an all-equity position, managers will substitute bonds for stock in order to reduce the agency costs of equity. As this process continues, however, the agency costs of debt begin to rise. The firm's optimal (value-maximizing) debt-to-equity ratio occurs at the point where the agency cost of an additional dollar of debt issued exactly equals the agency cost of the dollar of equity retired.

We are now ready to tie together all the threads of the modern agency cost/tax shield trade-off capital structure theory. The **trade-off model** expresses a levered firm's value in terms an unlevered firm's value, adjusted for the present values of tax shields, bankruptcy costs, and the agency costs of debt and equity, as shown in Equation 13.2.

$$V_L = V_U + PV \text{ tax shields} - PV \text{ bankruptcy costs} + PV \text{ agency}$$
$$\text{costs of outside equity} - PV \text{ agency costs of outside debt} \qquad \textbf{(Eq. 13.2)}$$

This model provides intuition about how firms establish their capital structures. Unfortunately, the individual components of the model are difficult to estimate. This means that although the trade-off model in Equation 13.2 offers sound theoretical advice, implementing the model's recommendations poses a challenge to managers. For example, what do we need to know to calculate the optimal capital structure for Microsoft? Debt's tax-shield value is relatively easy to obtain. Looking at historical bankruptcy cases, we might derive estimates of the direct and indirect costs of bankruptcy for Microsoft, and we might even estimate the probability of bankruptcy given a certain degree of leverage. Harder questions to answer are, how much value would Microsoft create by reducing the agency costs of equity by issuing bonds, and at what debt level would the agency costs of debt outweigh these benefits?

Empirical research in finance offers support for the trade-off model, modified to include agency costs of debt and equity, but the model is not sufficiently developed to offer precise recommendations for the optimal capital structures of individual firms. At least not yet.

13.3 THE PECKING-ORDER HYPOTHESIS

Although the trade-off model is the "mainstream" capital structure theory today, there are three empirical regularities that it has difficulty explaining:

1. Some studies find that the most profitable firms in an industry have the lowest debt ratios (though the most recent empirical studies do not find this result). A negative relationship between leverage and profitability violates a fundamental prediction of the trade-off model—that firms with high profits will use more debt to shelter income from taxation.
2. Leverage-increasing events, such as stock repurchases and debt-for-equity exchange offers, almost always increase stock prices, while leverage-decreasing events reduce stock prices. Such a finding goes against the trade-off model because it seems to imply that firms systematically use too little leverage.
3. Firms issue debt securities frequently, but seasoned equity issues (equity issues from firms that already have stock) are rare. In fact, few large U.S. companies issue new stock as often as once per decade, and non-U.S. firms are even less inclined to sell new equity. Announcements of new seasoned equity issues are invariably greeted with a large decline in the firm's stock price—often equal to one-third or more of the value of the new offering.

How can we account for these perplexing facts? One answer was put forward by Stewart Myers in 1984, when he proposed the pecking-order theory. We looked at this theory briefly in Chapter 12 and will look at it more closely here.

ASSUMPTIONS UNDERLYING THE PECKING-ORDER THEORY

The pecking-order theory squares with the three empirical patterns, noted above, that the trade-off theory has trouble explaining. The theory also is based on four other observations Myers noted about corporate financial behavior. First, dividend policy is "sticky." Managers tend to maintain a stable dividend payment, and they neither increase nor decrease dividends in response to temporary fluctuations in profits.[12] Second, firms prefer internal financing (retained earnings and depreciation) to external financing of any sort, debt or equity. Third, if a firm must obtain external financing, it will issue the safest security first. Finally, as a firm requires more external financing, it will work down the "pecking order" of securities, beginning with safe debt, then progressing through risky debt, convertible securities, preferred stock, and finally, common stock as a last resort.

Myers provides additional justification for the pecking order, based on asymmetric information, in a paper with Nicholas Majluf. Myers and Majluf (1984) make two plausible assumptions about managers. First, they assume a firm's managers know more about the company's current earnings and investment opportunities than do outside investors—asymmetric information. Second, they assume managers act in *existing* shareholders' interests—pecking order theory.

Why are these two assumptions crucial? The asymmetric information assumption implies that managers who develop or discover a marvelous new positive-*NPV* investment opportunity cannot convey that information to the market because outside investors don't believe the managers' statements. After all, every management team has an incentive to announce wondrous new projects, and investors cannot immediately verify these claims. Skeptical investors will buy new equity issues only at a large discount from what the stock price would be without informational asymmetries. Corporate managers understand these problems, and in certain cases they will reject positive-*NPV* investments to avoid selling equity to new investors at a discount, which would thereby transfer wealth from old to new shareholders.

What a dilemma! Investors cannot trust managers, so investors place a low value on common stocks. Managers forgo valuable projects because they cannot credibly convey their private information to existing shareholders. Endemic information problems in financial markets do not have easy solutions.

What, then, must managers do? According to Myers and Majluf, corporations retain sufficient *financial slack* to fund positive-*NPV* projects internally. Financial slack includes a firm's cash and marketable securities holdings, as well as unused debt capacity. Firms with sufficient financial slack finesse the information problem because they never have to issue equity to finance investment projects. In addition, the optimal investment rule is once again in force, because managers can accept all positive-*NPV* projects without harming existing shareholders. This theory also explains why highly profitable firms might retain earnings. (Intel is a classic example.) These firms are building both financial slack and financial flexibility.

The pecking-order theory also explains stock market reactions to leverage-increasing and leverage-decreasing events. Firms with valuable investment opportunities find a way to finance their projects internally, or use the least risky securities possible if they have to obtain financing externally. Therefore, only managers who consider the firm's shares to be overvalued will issue equity. Investors understand these incentives, and also realize that managers are better informed about a firm's prospects than they are. Investors thus always greet the announcement of a new equity issue as bad news, as a sign that management considers the firm's shares to be overvalued.[13]

[12.] This is one of the most constant phenomena in all of finance. In fact, corporate managers are as intent on maintaining stable nominal dividend payments today as they were when Lintner (1956) first documented this behavior in the 1950s.
[13.] This works in reverse, too. The CFO of a Fortune 500 company with billions in cash reserves told us that his company wanted to distribute some of the cash to investors, but management did not want to force investors to pay taxes on high dividend payments, and they were reluctant to repurchase shares because they thought the firm's stock was overvalued.

LIMITATIONS OF THE PECKING ORDER

Unfortunately, the pecking order cannot explain all capital structure regularities. It fails to explain how taxes, bankruptcy costs, security-issuance costs, and investment opportunities influence debt ratios. Furthermore, the theory ignores significant agency problems that arise when too much financial slack makes managers immune to market discipline. Finally, the most recent empirical studies do not find a negative relationship between leverage and profitability—which is one of the key underpinnings of the pecking-order theory.[14]

Frank and Goyal (2003) perform one of the cleanest tests of the pecking-order theory by studying whether net debt issues mirror the financial deficits of most firms. This would result if firms issued bonds first when they needed to raise external capital to fund a financial deficit, as the pecking order predicts. Instead, Frank and Goyal find that net *equity* issues almost perfectly follow the financial deficit; net debt issues are essentially uncorrelated with the financial deficit. Figure 13.2 shows their main result. This pattern directly contradicts the pecking order theory.

Concept Review Questions

8. Other than the pecking-order theory, what explanation might there be for the most profitable firms having the lowest leverage?

9. Do you think that allowing firms to make a rights issue—sell stock only to their existing shareholders, perhaps at a below-market price—would negate the informational asymmetry problem described by Myers and Majluf?

13.4 SIGNALING AND MARKET-TIMING MODELS

Beginning in the late 1970s, Ross (1977) and others developed a capital structure **signaling model** based on information asymmetries between managers and outside shareholders. These models assume that managers with favorable inside information have an incentive to convey this information to outside investors in order to increase the firm's stock price. Managers cannot simply announce this good news because shareholders will be properly skeptical about such statements.

HOW SIGNALING WITH CAPITAL STRUCTURE CAN CONVEY INFORMATION

As discussed briefly in Chapter 12, one solution to this problem of information asymmetry is for managers of high-value firms (firms with good news to convey) to *signal* this information to investors. They do so by taking some action, or adopting some financial policy, that is prohibitively costly for less valuable firms to mimic.

For example, suppose that managers have inside information that their firm's investments will generate spectacular cash flows in the future. To credibly convey the good news, the firm's managers can adopt a heavily leveraged capital structure. This commits the firm to paying out large sums to bondholders. In equilibrium, firms signal good news by issuing debt. Because investors know that only firms with good

---

[14.] Frank and Goyal (2003), Hovakimian, Hovakimian, and Tehranian (2004), and Liu (2004).

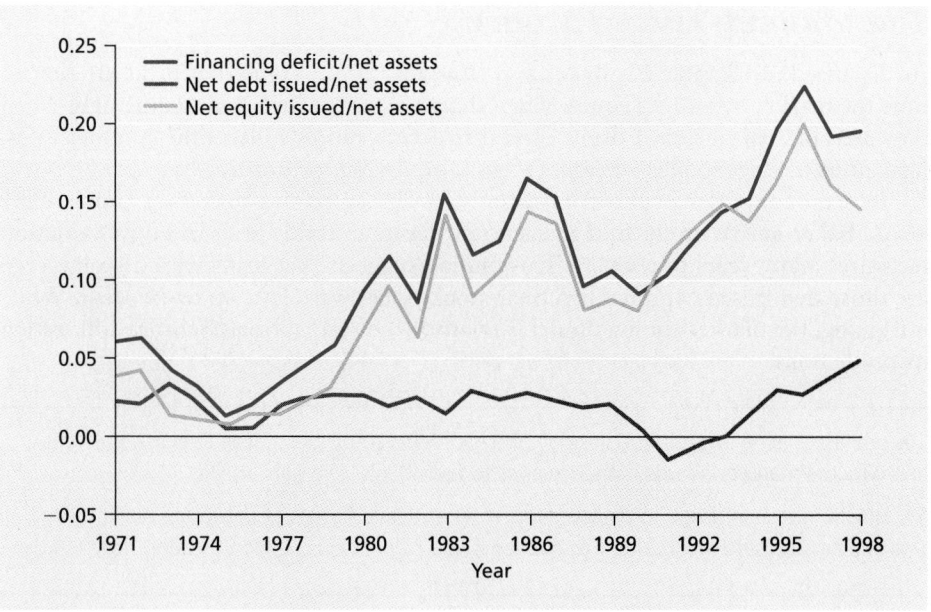

Figure 13.2
The Relationship between Average Financial Deficit, Net Equity Issues, and Net Debt Issues for U.S.
Public Corporations, 1971–1998
*The figure plots annual averages of the ratios of financing deficit to net assets, net debt issued
to net assets, and net equity issued to net assets for the period between 1971 and 1998. The
sample comprises U.S. firms on the Compustat files. Financial firms and regulated utilities are
excluded. The financing deficit is calculated as cash dividends plus investments plus change in
working capital minus internal cash flow. Net debt issued is long-term debt issuance minus long-
term debt redemption. Net equity issued is the issue of stock minus the repurchase of stock. The
variables are constructed using data from Compustat funds-flow statements.*
Source: Murray Z. Frank and Vidhan K. Goyal, "Testing the Pecking Order Theory of Capital Structure," *Journal of
Financial Economics* 67 (February 2003), pp. 217–248, Figure 1.

prospects can afford to take on debt, they recognize a debt issuance as good news,
and they bid up the firm's shares.

Empirical Evidence on Signaling Models Even though signaling models have
intuitive appeal, they enjoy little empirical support. As we have seen, leverage ratios
are, if anything, *negatively* related to profitability in almost every industry. Signaling
models predict a *positive* relationship.

The signaling model also predicts that companies rich in growth opportunities
and other intangible assets should employ more debt than mature firms rich in tangible assets. Why? Because growth companies have more-severe information asymmetry problems, and thus have a greater need to signal. As we know, asset-rich companies use far more debt than do growth companies.

Even in those research studies that present a best-case scenario for signaling theory, the bottom line is discouraging. Barclay, Smith, and Watts (1995) examine
signaling models empirically and find they receive support that is statistically significant, but economically trivial. "High-quality" firms employ more leverage than
"low-quality" ones, after controlling for other factors, but the differences in leverage
are minor.

THE MARKET-TIMING MODEL

As discussed in Chapter 12, Baker and Wurgler (2002) argue that firms attempt to time the market by issuing equity when share values are high and issuing debt when they are not. This means a firm's capital structure simply reflects the cumulative effects of its managers' past attempts to issue equity opportunistically.

By examining the financial histories of U.S. companies that went public after 1972, Baker and Wurgler find that current leverage ratios are related to valuation measures many years previously. This finding suggests that firms with high leverage are those that raised capital when their stock prices were low, and vice versa. While intriguing, the **market-timing model** is relatively new and researchers are still testing its predictions.

Concept Review Questions	**10.** Use a *signaling argument* to explain why students return to school to pursue an MBA and why the market rewards higher salaries to individuals who earn MBAs.
	11. How might cash dividend payments serve as effective signals of corporate profitability? This will be discussed in Chapter 16, but see if you can reason the idea through now.

13.5 DEVELOPING A CHECKLIST FOR CAPITAL STRUCTURE DECISION MAKING

Having surveyed the theoretical models of corporate leverage and assessed the empirical support for each, we can summarize what we know about capital structure decision making. Table 13.2 summarizes the results of over 30 empirical studies regarding the relationship between corporate leverage and several operating, ownership, and macroeconomic variables. The table describes the link between leverage and other factors in a similar (though more concrete) fashion. The independent (explanatory) variables listed in the table fall into three categories: (1) firm- or industry-specific operating and financial variables, (2) ownership structure variables, and (3) macroeconomic and country variables. We assess the findings relating to these categories in the remainder of this chapter.

LEVERAGE AND FIRM- AND INDUSTRY-SPECIFIC OPERATING AND FINANCIAL VARIABLES

Profitability The first section of Table 13.2 summarizes the relationship between financial leverage and firm- or industry-level characteristics. The table's first line shows that many researchers have found that the more profitable a firm or industry is, the lower its leverage will tend to be. However, the most recent research finds no such negative relation between firm/industry profitability and leverage, so we label this relationship as unclear.

Market-to-Book Ratio Empirical studies document a clear negative relationship between leverage and the market-to-book (MTB) ratio. Economists interpret the market-to-book ratio as a measure of a firm's growth options—options that often depend on intangible rather than tangible fixed assets. The meaning of the negative relationship between leverage and the MTB ratio, then, is that growth companies use little or no debt. Other proxies for growth options, such as advertising or research

Table 13.2
A Checklist for Capital Structure Decision Making

Variable	Description	Documented Relationship between Variable and Leverage
Profitability	Level of corporate profits	Unclear
Market-to-book (MTB) ratio	Market value of firm divided by book value of assets; proxy for growth options	Negative
Earnings volatility	The variability of corporate earnings over time	Negative
Nondebt tax shields	Presence and amount of noninterest tax shields	Negative
Effective tax rate	Effective marginal corporate income tax rate actually faced (not statutory rate)	Positive
Regulation	Is the firm operating in a regulated industry?	Positive
Size	Firm size, measured by assets or sales	Positive
Asset tangibility	Tangible assets as fraction of total assets (similar, but opposite to MTB)	Positive
Growth rate	Rate of growth in firm sales or assets	Ambiguous: Positive and Negative
Insider share ownership	Percentage of firm stock owned by officers and directors	Ambiguous: Positive and Negative
Managerial entrenchment	Is the management team able to deter internal or external challenges to their tenure?	Negative
Creditor power in bankruptcy	Do nation's bankruptcy laws support rights of creditors over corporate debtors?	Negative
Corporate income tax rate	Statutory rate of tax on corporate profits	Positive
Personal tax rate, equity	Statutory personal tax rate on equity income	Negative
State ownership	Is firm a state-owned enterprise?	Positive

Notes: This table summarizes the empirically documented relationship between leverage and several operating, financial, ownership structure, tax, and country-specific variables.

and development expenditures as a percentage of sales, also tend to vary inversely with leverage.

Earnings Volatility The negative relationship between leverage and earnings volatility verifies the importance of bankruptcy costs in capital structure decision making. The more volatile a firm's cash flows, the greater the likelihood that earnings will fail to cover debt-service payments, and the more likely the firm will default on its debts. Firms in industries such as mining and petroleum exploration, which often experience wildly fluctuating sales and profits, tend to issue less debt than do firms with less-volatile revenue streams and fewer fixed-cost production technologies.

Nondebt Tax Shields The negative relationship between leverage and the presence and amount of nondebt tax shields (NDTS) confirms the prediction made by De-Angelo and Masulis (1980). Firms with unused depreciation allowances, tax loss carryforwards, investment tax credits, and other tax credits or deductions have less incentive to shelter corporate profits from income taxes by paying interest on borrowed funds. Although earlier, cross-sectional capital structure studies found a positive relationship between NDTS and leverage, more recent studies that examine the relationship between marginal security issuance decisions and the presence of NDTS strongly support the DeAngelo and Masulis thesis.

Effective Tax Rate The next variable in Table 13.2, the effective marginal tax rate, measures the tax rate charged on the next dollar of pretax corporate income. It is in many ways the inverse of NDTS. Firms with unused NDTS face a low (perhaps even zero) marginal tax rate. The greater a firm's marginal tax rate, the stronger is its incentive to find ways to shelter income from taxes. Recent empirical studies convincingly show that firms facing high marginal tax rates use more debt than other firms.

Regulation Although relatively few empirical studies examine the relationship between leverage and industry regulation, the work that does exist suggests that firms in regulated industries are highly leveraged. Industries such as banking, electric power generation, transportation, and telecommunications have historically been stringently regulated. Firms in these industries have higher debt ratios than do unregulated firms. One explanation for this is that regulation tends to reduce competition and business risk in an industry. Thus, there is less variability in the earnings streams of regulated firms and less danger of the firm encountering financial distress. Additionally, investors believe that regulation involves at least a partial guarantee that the government will not allow regulated firms to go bankrupt. This implicit insurance makes it feasible for regulated firms to use more leverage.

Recent years have witnessed an ideological sea change in many Western countries, in favor of deregulating many industries. This change offers researchers a golden opportunity to test capital structure theories. As countries simultaneously deregulate industries and open them to competition, we should observe significant reductions in leverage ratios of the surviving firms.[15]

Size Although capital structure theories make few predictions about the relationship between leverage and firm size, empirical studies show that large firms borrow more than small firms. This could be because large, more-established firms have better access to debt capital markets than do small firms. Perhaps large companies control a more diversified pool of assets, resulting in less-variable revenue and earnings streams compared to those of small firms. Or perhaps large firms have fewer growth opportunities to pursue.

Asset Tangibility *Asset tangibility* measures tangible assets as a fraction of total assets. The positive relationship between asset tangibility and leverage shows that tangible-asset-rich firms use more debt than do firms that rely more on patents, copyrights, and other intangible assets.

Growth Rate The empirical evidence on the relationship between leverage and the firm's growth rate is mixed. Two early studies find that rapidly growing firms use more debt than slow growing firms. Also, Frank and Goyal (2003) find that sales growth and increased debt use are positively correlated. Other studies find the opposite result. The results presented in Lang, Ofek, and Stulz (1996) are especially persuasive; they find that only firms with poor investment opportunities find growth to be hampered by leverage. For firms with better investment opportunities and fewer agency problems between managers and shareholders, the growth/leverage relationship is insignificantly positive. Fama and French (2002) also show that small high-

---

15. The evidence on U.S. telecommunications industry deregulation in Barclay, Smith, and Watts (1995) supports this prediction.

growth firms tend to issue large amounts of new equity. Given these conflicting findings, we label the relationship as ambiguous.

LEVERAGE AND OWNERSHIP STRUCTURE VARIABLES

Empirical studies have historically focused on the relationship between leverage and firm- or industry-specific operating or financial variables. Several studies examine how a firm's ownership structure influences its capital structure. Two ownership variables have received special attention: officer and director (insider) ownership, and the degree to which a firm's current management team is entrenched.

Insider Share-Ownership Unfortunately, the empirical results regarding the leverage/insider ownership relationship remain ambiguous. Berger, Ofek, and Yermack (1997) examine the importance of managerial entrenchment incentives on corporate leverage. This work documents a significant positive relationship, but two other studies find that managerial ownership and debt levels are inversely related.

In a sense, this ambiguity is not surprising, because there are two potentially offsetting effects of insider shareholdings. On one hand, a manager/owner with a large holding of stock in the firm has much to fear from excessive corporate leverage: both his human and financial capital will be put at risk if the firm encounters financial distress. On the other hand, a manager wishing to protect her tenure in office could do so by substituting debt for equity in her company's capital structure, because this maximizes the voting power of her own stockholdings. At present, empirical research has not determined which of these two effects dominates.

Managerial Entrenchment The evidence on the relationship between leverage and managerial entrenchment is much more clear-cut, thanks again to Berger, Ofek, and Yermack (1997). These researchers show that entrenched management teams prefer to employ little debt, even when this policy is harmful to the firm's shareholders. Intriguingly, they find that when an unexpected event, such as a takeover attempt, reduces the perceived entrenchment of a management team, those managers respond in a value-maximizing way by increasing debt. By this response, they commit themselves to pay out more cash flow to investors in the future. To summarize, entrenched managers opt for the easy life of a low-debt capital structure, while management teams subject to effective monitoring/disciplining by shareholders employ more leverage.

LEVERAGE AND MACROECONOMIC AND COUNTRY-SPECIFIC VARIABLES

A significant body of research compares capital structure policies in different countries. We briefly summarize the key lessons this literature offers concerning how a nation's bankruptcy laws, tax policies, and attitudes toward state ownership affect the capital structure decisions made by managers in that country. The key findings of these studies are surprisingly clear-cut.

Creditor Power in Bankruptcy In probably the single most influential international capital structure study yet published, Rajan and Zingales (1995) document that one important determinant of a country's average corporate leverage level is the relative power of creditors in bankruptcy court. They show that the two Group of Seven (G7) countries with bankruptcy laws most favorable to creditors, Germany and Great Britain, also have the lowest average market-value corporate debt levels.

Apparently, when managers know that creditors will have great power over them in the event of financial distress, they are much less likely to borrow excessively. Conversely, managers in countries like the United States, where the bankruptcy laws tend to favor debtors over creditors, are more willing to adopt a highly leveraged capital structure.

Corporate and Personal Income Tax Rates Given the prominent roles taxes play in capital structure theory, surprisingly few studies attempt to estimate the impact of tax rates and rate changes on leverage decisions. A recent study by Desai, Foley, and Hines (2004) clearly shows that high corporate income tax rates encourage multinational companies to finance their foreign subsidiaries with debt rather than equity.

Estimating the impact of a tax change is possible when a country switches from one system of taxing corporate and personal income to a new one. Although this seems a highly unlikely event to most people, Great Britain changed taxation systems no less than four (arguably, six) times between 1947 and 1973. Two of the studies underlying Table 13.2 examine one or more of these British tax changes. As expected, increases in the corporate income tax rate are associated with increases in average corporate leverage, and vice versa. The same relationship holds for increases in the personal tax rate on equity income (dividends and capital gains).

State Ownership The final country-specific variable, whether a company is wholly or partly state-owned, may seem alien to most U.S. readers of this text, but is surely well known to international readers. Most state-owned enterprises are heavily indebted, partly because they cannot raise equity capital from private investors. Several empirical studies of privatization's impact on the operating and financial policies of divested firms indicate that privatization reduces leverage.[16] We therefore conclude that state-owned enterprises tend to use more debt than do otherwise comparable privately owned firms.

The observant reader will notice that most of the relationships summarized in Table 13.2 support the trade-off model over its competitors. We should not, however, overstate our ability to explain the actual steps that corporate managers take in setting their firms' leverage levels. Graham and Harvey's (2001) survey of corporate financial practices shows a clear connection between finance theory and practice in the area of capital budgeting, but finds little evidence that managers establish capital structures in ways that resemble the models we discuss here. That may change in time. After all, the widespread use of *NPV* analysis in capital budgeting did not occur immediately after the technique was first recommended, and most financial theories have been adopted by industry only gradually.

[16.] Megginson, Nash, and van Randenborgh (1994) and D'Souza and Megginson (1999) examine privatizations mainly in developed countries; Boubakri and Cosset (1998) examine sales in developing countries. All three studies find that leverage declines after privatization.

13.6 SUMMARY

- In addition to corporate and personal income taxation, several characteristics of a firm's asset structure, operating environment, investment opportunities, and ownership structure significantly influence the level of debt that firm will choose to have.
- Firms with many tangible assets—such as buildings, transportation equipment, and general-purpose machine tools—rely heavily on debt. These assets can pass through bankruptcy with their values relatively intact. In contrast, firms that rely more on intangible assets—such as brand names and research and development spending—use little debt.
- Creditors know that corporate managers, who operate their firms in the interests of shareholders, have incentives to expropriate creditor wealth by playing a series of "games" with the firm's investment policy. Asset substitution is one such game. It involves promising to invest in a safe asset to obtain an interest rate reflecting this risk, and then substituting a riskier asset promising a higher expected return. Creditors protect themselves from these games in several ways, especially by inserting restrictive covenants into loan agreements.
- There are several important agency costs inherent in the relationship between corporate managers and outside investors and creditors. In some cases, using financial leverage can help overcome these agency problems; in others, using leverage worsens the problems. The modern trade-off *model* of corporate leverage predicts that a firm's optimal debt level is set by trading off the tax benefits of increasing leverage against the increasingly severe agency costs of heavy debt usage.
- Three competing theories have been put forth to explain observed corporate leverage levels. The pecking-order theory predicts that managers will operate their firms in such a way as to minimize the need to secure outside financing—for example, by retaining profits to build up financial slack. These same managers will use the safest source of funding, usually senior debt, when they must secure outside financing. The signaling theory predicts that managers will select their firms' leverage levels to signal that the firm is strong enough to employ high debt and still fund its profitable investment opportunities. The market-timing model predicts that firms attempt to time the market by issuing equity when share values are high and issuing debt when share prices are low. A firm's capital structure thus reflects only the cumulative effects of its managers' past attempts to issue equity opportunistically.
- Most empirical research supports the trade-off theory of corporate leverage over the pecking-order, signaling, or market-timing models.

INTERNET RESOURCES

Note: *For updates to links, please go to the book's website at* http://smartfinance .swlearning.com.

http://www.quicken.com; http://www.yahoo.com; http://www.sec.gov—Three sites from which you can download leverage figures for specific companies and compare them to figures for firms in the same industry as well as firms in other industries

http://www.bondsonline.com—A site that offers a wealth of information regarding bonds

http://www.standardandpoors.com—A site with information on bond ratings and the latest changes to ratings on outstanding bonds

KEY TERMS

agency cost theory of financial structure

asset substitution

bankruptcy costs

bonding mechanism

Business Judgment Rule

Chapter 7

Chapter 11

direct costs of bankruptcy

financial slack

indirect costs of bankruptcy

market-timing model

option to default

pecking-order theory

signaling model

trade-off model

trustee

underinvestment

QUESTIONS

13-1. Empirically, how do bankruptcy costs and agency costs influence capital structure decisions? What are the general relationships between these factors and leverage?

13-2. Why do a firm's stockholders hold a valuable "default option" (option to default)? Why might this option induce stockholders to employ high debt?

13-3. All else equal, which firm would face higher costs of financial distress: a software development firm or a hotel chain? Why would financial distress costs affect these firms so differently?

13-4. Describe how managers of firms that have debt outstanding and face financial distress might jeopardize the investments of creditors with the "games" of asset substitution and underinvestment.

13-5. Differentiate between direct and indirect costs of bankruptcy. Which of the two is generally more significant?

13-6. What empirical results have been documented regarding indirect bankruptcy costs? What have other empirical studies shown regarding the relationship between the risk of bankruptcy and levels of leverage?

13-7. What are some of the differences in U.S bankruptcy laws and those in place internationally? What incentives do these differences provide for U.S. managers and for their peers in most other countries?

13-8. What does it mean to use external debt as a bonding mechanism for managers? In what way does this bonding mechanism reduce the agency costs of external equity? How can restrictive covenants in bonds be both an agency cost of debt and a way to prevent agency costs of debt?

13-9. What are the trade-offs in the agency cost/tax shield trade-off model? How is the firm's optimal capital structure determined under the assumptions of this model? Does empirical evidence support this model?

13-10. What is the main premise underlying the pecking-order theory? What is the "pecking order" of sources of financing? Why is dividend policy so important to this theory? How does the concept of financial slack relate to this theory?

13-11. What type of information is conveyed in a signaling model of capital structure? According to this model, how should leverage affect the market value of firms? Does empirical evidence support this model?

13-12. Outline the empirically defined relationships between leverage and firm- or industry-specific operating and financial variables. In general, which of the models of capital structure are supported by these results?

13-13. What capital structure choices might managers seeking to entrench themselves choose? How does this decision relate to the bonding mechanism?

13-14. A CFO says that her firm chooses a capital structure that allows it to maintain a credit rating of AA. She reasons that a credit rating of AAA would be too conservative, but anything less than AA would be too risky. What capital structure model does this firm appear to follow?

PROBLEMS

Costs of Bankruptcy and Financial Distress

13-1. Firm TYH is composed entirely of equity and is valued at $1.5 million. Firm YPL has $400,000 worth of debt costing 9% that becomes due next year with interest. Both firms compete in the same market and next year's expected cash flows for both firms are $300,000 with 50% probability and $3.15 million with 50% probability. What is the expected cash flow of both firms, ignoring taxes and bankruptcy costs? What is the expected equity return for TYH? How much debt is due at the end of the year for YPL? What is the discounted value of YPL's debt? What is the expected return on YPL's equity, assuming YPL is valued comparably to TYH?

13-2. Firm TDC has $700,000 worth of debt due at the end of the year (includes interest). TDC's expected cash flows (ignoring taxes) for next year are: $1.2 million (30% probability), $2.8 million (50% probability), and $1.8 million (20% probability). Assuming the equity has an expected return of 25% and the firm is valued at $1.772 million, what is the expected return on the firm's debt? Will bankruptcy costs affect the value of the firm? What is the expected return on equity if TDC had no debt?

13-3. Firm NDC has debt of $1.2 million due at the end of the year (principal and interest). NDC's expected cash flows (ignoring taxes) are $1 million with 40% probability and $2 million with 60% probability. Assuming the equity has an expected return of 25% and the firm is valued at $1.4 million, what is the expected return on the firm's debt? How much does the firm's value decrease if bankruptcy costs are $0.5 million? What is the expected return on equity if NDC had no debt?

13-4. If firms in a certain industry are expected to have a weighted average cost of capital (WACC; see Chapter 9) of 17%, calculate the cost of debt (ignoring taxes) based on the cost of equity provided for the firms below. Assume the firms under consideration are worth $4 million.

Firm A: $2 million of equity with a 24% expected return
Firm B: $2.5 million of equity with a 22% expected return
Firm C: $3 million of equity with a 20% expected return

13-5. If firms in a certain industry are expected to have a weighted average cost of capital (WACC; see Chapter 9) of 20%, calculate the cost of equity based on the cost of debt (ignoring taxes) provided for the firms below. Assume the firms under consideration are worth $10 million.

Firm A: $4 million of debt with a 10% expected return
Firm B: $6 million of debt with a 14% expected return
Firm C: $7 million of debt with a 15% expected return

If bankruptcy costs are $1.2 million with only a 10% chance of bankruptcy occurring, how much value is lost for each firm due to bankruptcy costs?

13-6. Using the data presented in Table 13.1, compute the following ratios for the years provided in the table:

  a. Business versus nonbusiness bankruptcy filings
  b. Voluntary versus nonvoluntary bankruptcy filings
  c. Liquidations (Chapter 7 of the Bankruptcy Code) versus reorganizations (Chapter 11) as a percentage of business filings

13-7. Using the ratios computed in Problem 13-1, discuss whether the following statements are true or false:

  a. There is a trend toward more business bankruptcy filings and fewer nonbusiness bankruptcy filings over time.
  b. Reorganization filings represent a fairly constant percentage of total filings over time.

13-8. You are the manager of a financially distressed corporation, with $1.5 million in debt outstanding that will mature in three months. Your firm currently has $1 million cash on hand. Assume that you are offered the opportunity to invest in either of the following two projects:

  Project 1: The opportunity to invest $1 million in risk-free Treasury bills, with a 4 percent annual interest rate (a quarterly interest rate of 1 percent = 4% per year ÷ 4 quarters per year)

  Project 2: A high-risk gamble, which will pay off $1.6 million in two months if it is successful (probability = 0.4), but will pay only $400,000 if it is unsuccessful (probability = 0.6).

  a. Compute the expected payoff for each project. If you were operating the firm in the shareholders' best interests, which one you would adopt, and why?
  b. Which project would you accept if the firm was unlevered? Why?
  c. Which project would you accept if the company was organized as a partnership rather than a corporation? Why?

13-9. You are the manager of a financially distressed corporation with $10 million in debt outstanding, which will mature in one month. Your firm currently has $7 million cash on hand. Assume that you are offered the opportunity to invest in either of the following two projects:

  Project 1: The opportunity to invest $7 million in risk-free Treasury bills, with a 4 percent annual interest rate (or a 0.333% per month interest rate)

  Project 2: A high-risk gamble that will pay off $12 million in one month if it is successful (probability = 0.25), but will pay only $4,000,000 if it is unsuccessful (probability = 0.75).

  a. Compute the expected payoff for each project. Which one you would adopt if you were operating the firm in the shareholders' best interests? Why?
  b. Which project would you accept if the firm was unlevered? Why?
  c. Which project would you accept if the company was organized as a partnership rather than a corporation? Why?

13-10. A firm has the choice of investing in one of two projects. Both projects last one year. Project 1 requires an investment of $11,000; it yields $11,000 with a probability of 0.5 and $13,000 with a probability of 0.5. Project 2 also requires an investment of $11,000; it yields $5,000 with a probability of 0.5 and $20,000 with a probability of 0.5. The firm is capable of raising $10,000 of the investment required through a bond issue carrying an annual interest rate of 10 percent.

  a. Assuming the investors are concerned only about expected returns, which project would stockholders prefer? Why?
  b. Which project would bondholders prefer? Why?

13-11. An all-equity firm has 100,000 shares outstanding worth $10 each. The firm is considering a project requiring an investment of $400,000 that has an *NPV* of $50,000. The company is also considering financing this project with a new issue of equity.

    a. What is the price at which the firm needs to issue the new shares so that the existing shareholders are indifferent to whether or not the firm takes on the project with this equity financing?

    b. What is the price at which the firm needs to issue the new shares so that the existing shareholders capture the full benefit associated with the new project?

13-12. You are the manager of a financially distressed corporation that has $5 million in loans coming due in 30 days. Your firm has $4 million cash on hand. Suppose that a long-time supplier of materials to your firm is planning to exit the business but has offered to sell your company a large supply of material at the bargain price of $4.5 million—but only if payment is made immediately in cash. If you choose not to acquire this material, the supplier will offer it to a competitor, and your firm will have to acquire the materials at market prices totaling $5 million over the next few months.

    a. Assuming that you are operating the firm in shareholders' best interests, would you accept the project? Why or why not?

    b. Would you accept this project if the firm were unlevered? Why or why not?

    c. Would you accept the project if the company were organized as a partnership? Why or why not?

13-13. Run-and-Hide Detective Company currently has no debt and expects to earn $5 million in *EBIT* each year, for the foreseeable future. The required return on assets for detective companies of this type is 10 percent, and the corporate tax rate is 35 percent. There are no taxes on dividends or interest at the personal level. Run-and-Hide calculates that there is a 5 percent chance that the firm will fall into bankruptcy in any given year. If bankruptcy does occur, it will impose direct and indirect costs totaling $8 million. If necessary, use the industry required return for discounting bankruptcy costs.

    a. Compute the present value of bankruptcy costs for Run-and-Hide.

    b. Compute the overall value of the firm.

    c. Recalculate the value of the company, assuming the firm's shareholders face a 15 percent personal tax rate on equity income.

Agency Costs and Capital Structure

13-14. Magnum Enterprises has net operating income of $5 million. There is $50 million of debt outstanding, with a required rate of return of 6 percent. The required rate of return on the industry is 12 percent. The corporate tax rate is 40 percent; there are corporate taxes, but no personal taxes. Compute the value of Magnum, assuming that the present value of bankruptcy costs is $10 million.

13-15. Slash and Burn Construction Company currently has no debt and expects to earn $10 million in net operating income each year for the foreseeable future. The required return on assets for construction companies of this type is 12.5 percent, and the corporate tax rate is 40 percent. There are no taxes on dividends or interest at the personal level. Slash and Burn calculates that there is a 10 percent chance the firm will fall into bankruptcy in any given year, and if bankruptcy does occur, it will impose direct and indirect costs totaling $12 million. Assume that if bankruptcy occurs, the firm will reorganize and continue operations indefinitely, with a constant 10 percent probability of reentering bankruptcy. If necessary, use the industry required return for discounting bankruptcy costs.

    a. Compute the present value of bankruptcy costs for Slash and Burn.

    b. Compute the overall value of the firm.

13-16. Using the data from Problem 13-10, calculate the value of Slash and Burn Construction Company, assuming that the firm's shareholders face a 25 percent personal tax rate on equity income.

13-17. Assume that the managers of Slash and Burn Construction Company, described in Problem 13-10, are weighing two capital structure alteration proposals, as follows.

Proposal 1: Borrow $20 million at an interest rate of 6 percent and use the proceeds to repurchase an equal amount of outstanding stock. With this level of debt, the likelihood that Slash and Burn will fall into bankruptcy in any given year increases to 15 percent, and if bankruptcy occurs, it will impose direct and indirect costs totaling $12 million.

Proposal 2: Borrow $30 million at an interest rate of 8 percent and use the proceeds to repurchase an equal amount of outstanding stock. With this level of debt, the likelihood of Slash and Burn falling into bankruptcy in any given year rises to 25 percent, and the associated direct and indirect costs of bankruptcy, if it occurs, increase to $20 million.

For each proposal, calculate both the present value of the interest tax shields and the overall value of the firm, assuming there are no personal taxes on debt or equity income.

Developing a Checklist for Capital Structure Decision Making

13-18. Go to the home page for Ford Motor Company (http://www.ford.com), and search for its most recent annual report to shareholders. Within this report, find management's discussion and analysis of financial condition and results of operations. Find management's discussion about liquidity and capital resources about halfway through the report. Use that information to answer the following questions.

a. How large a cash position does Ford hold? How large is this cash position relative to Ford's overall capital structure (also found in the annual report)?

b. Does Ford's cash position indicate a preference for or against financial slack by Ford's management?

13-19. View the balance sheet information summarized for Sears Holding Corporation (ticker symbol, SHLD) from January of 2005:

Assets		Liabilities and Equity	
Cash	$3,435	Current liabilities	$2,086
Short-term investments	$ 0	Long-term liabilities	$2,096
Other current assets	$4,106	Total liabilities	$4,182
Net fixed assets	$1,110	Total equity	$4,469
Total assets	$8,651	Total liabilities and equity	$8,651

All numbers in millions.

a. What is Sears' current ratio (see Chapter 2)?

b. What portion of Sears' liabilities can be paid off immediately with cash?

c. What is Sears' debt ratio (see Chapter 2)?

d. Can Sears pay off its long-term debt now? Does this allow Sears financial slack?

13-20. View the balance sheet information summarized for Gateway Inc. (ticker symbol, GTW) from December of 2004:

Assets		Liabilities and Equity	
Cash	$ 382.972	Current liabilities	$1,122.652
Short-term investments	$ 260.537	Long-term liabilities	$ 404.098
Other current assets	$ 756.108	Total liabilities	$1,526.750
Net fixed assets	$ 372.170	Total equity	$ 245.037
Total assets	$1,771.787	Total liabilities and equity	$1,771.787

All numbers in millions.

a. What is the ratio of Gateway's cash and short-term investments relative to its long-term liabilities?

b. Considering the ratio above and Gateway's current ratio (see Chapter 2), does Gateway have significant financial slack?

c. What is Gateway's debt ratio (see Chapter 2)?

13-21. View the balance sheet information summarized for Microsoft Corporation (MSFT) from June of 2005:

Assets		Liabilities and Equity	
Cash	$ 4,851	Current liabilities	$16,877
Short-term investments	$32,900	Long-term liabilities	$ 5,823
Other current assets	$10,986	Total liabilities	$22,700
Net fixed assets	$22,078	Total equity	$48,115
Total assets	$70,815	Total liabilities and equity	$70,815

All numbers in millions.

a. Can Microsoft pay off all of its liabilities with its cash position and short-term investments? Is this an indication of significant financial slack?

b. What is Microsoft's current ratio (see Chapter 2)?

c. Describe the signal Microsoft may be sending by having debt in its balance sheet?

THOMSON ONE BUSINESS SCHOOL EDITION

13-22. In 2002, United Airlines (ticker symbol, UAUA) filed for Chapter 11 bankruptcy. In 2006, United emerged from bankruptcy. What was the change in the book value of equity from before to after the bankruptcy? What was the change in the market value of equity from before to after the bankruptcy? What other costs would be relevant when calculating the total cost of United's bankruptcy?

MINI-CASE: NONTAX DETERMINANTS OF CORPORATE LEVERAGE

MarCher Industries is considering undertaking a new project with a one-year life.

	High-Risk Project	Low-Risk Project
Cash flow (boom)	$1,500,000	$1,000,000
Cash flow (bust)	$ 400,000	$ 500,000

The firm currently has no debt, but it is considering borrowing $870,000 on a short-term basis to help finance the purchase of the project. The firm will owe $900,000, including principal and interest in one year. There is a 60% chance a boom will occur and only a 40% chance a bust will occur.

1. Calculate the expected value of the high- and low-risk project to MarCher Industries' stockholders if the firm remains unlevered. Which project would the stockholders prefer?

2. Calculate the expected value of the high- and low-risk project to MarCher's stockholders and bondholders, assuming the firm does borrow money to partially finance the purchase of the project. Which project would the bondholders prefer? Which project would the stockholders prefer?

3. Explain why a conflict exists between the bondholders and stockholders.

Chapter 14

The Link between Capital Structure and Capital Budgeting

OPENING FOCUS

In December 2005, two Japanese companies, Mitsubishi Corp. and Idemitsu Kosan Co. Ltd., announced an agreement to combine their assets in the liquefied petroleum gas (LPG) industry to create a new company, Astomos Energy Corp. With projected revenues of about ¥400 billion, Astomos would capture a 20 percent share of the Japanese LPG market, importing almost 3 million tons per year. Those figures would make Astomos Japan's largest primary LPG distributor.

In Japan, the world's largest importer of LPG, roughly 50 million households rely on LPG for their day-to-day energy needs. Mitsubishi and Idemitsu believed that by combining their LPG businesses, they would realize cost-saving synergies, enhancing the new company's competitive position in the industry. But in any business combination such as this, how to determine the ownership stakes in the new enterprise frequently becomes a source of contention between the partners. In this transaction, Mitsubishi retained KPMG FAS to value its LPG assets as well as those held by Idemitsu. Complicating this valuation exercise were differences in the capital structures employed by Mitsubishi and Idemitsu. Relying on a method known as adjusted present value, which captures valuation differences arising from financing decisions, KPMG suggested an ownership split of 51 percent for Mitsubishi and 49 percent for Idemitsu.

Sources: (1) "Mitsubishi Corp.–LPG Business Integration," Company News Feed, *12-20-05. (2) "Idemitsu Kosan, Mitsubishi to merge LPG operations in April 2006,"* Japan Economic Newswire, *3-15-05, (3) "Mitsubishi, Idemitsu to Merge LPG Units in April,"* Jiji Press Ticker, *12-16-05, (4) Company Press Release*

SMARTFinance
Use the learning tools at www
.thomsonedu.com/finance/smartfinance

516

14.1 M&M, CAPITAL BUDGETING, AND THE *WACC*

In this chapter, we will pull together many of the ideas from the text's first 13 chapters to address a critical question—how do financing choices affect capital investment decisions? In a world of perfect capital markets, Modigliani and Miller proved that a firm's value does not depend on its capital structure. By the same token, Proposition I implies that a capital investment project's value will not depend on how the firm finances the project, as long as markets are perfect. But in the last two chapters we've seen how financing decisions can affect firm value when we consider market imperfections such as taxes. If market imperfections lead to violations of Proposition I, meaning that firm value does depend on capital structure, then by extension, the mix of debt and equity that a firm uses to finance an investment project can affect the project's value.

In Chapter 8, we finessed this issue by arguing that analysts should exclude from their capital budgeting spreadsheets any cash flows associated with a project's financing. As an example, we said that if a firm pays for a project's initial outlay by borrowing money, analysts should not deduct interest expenses from the project's cash flows. We argued that by choosing the proper project discount rate, analysts effectively account for financing costs in the denominator of their *NPV* calculations rather than in the numerator. But what does the phrase "the proper project discount rate" mean precisely?

Chapter 9 offered one answer to this question by introducing the weighted average cost of capital, or *WACC*. Recall that to calculate the *WACC*, a firm must determine the after-tax required return on its debt, and the required return on its equity. Next, the firm multiplies these rates by the percentage of equity and debt in its capital structure, basing those percentages on market values, not book values. For convenience, we repeat the basic *WACC* equation here:

$$WACC = \left[\frac{D}{(D + E)}\right](1 - T_c)r_d + \left[\frac{E}{(D + E)}\right]r_e \qquad \text{(Eq. 14.1)}$$

The *WACC* method captures the effects of financing choices on a project's value through the discount rate. Because firms can deduct interest payments when they calculate taxable income, the tax code essentially subsidizes corporate debt. The after-tax cost of debt is less than the pretax cost as long as the corporate tax rate, T_c, is positive. In other words, the *WACC* approach accounts for the interaction between the investment and financing decisions by lowering the project discount rate for debt-financed investments. A lower discount rate leads to a higher project value. This line of argument extends to the value of the entire firm. Chapter 12 illustrated how the introduction of corporate taxes caused M&M's Proposition I to break down. With an available tax deduction for interest payments, firms increase firm value (or equivalently, lower the cost of capital) by using more debt.

Because the *WACC* accounts for the valuation effects of debt by adjusting the discount rate, when analysts discount a project's cash flows using the *WACC*, the cash flows that they discount should ignore financing costs such as interest expense. That is, the cash flows to be discounted should be unlevered cash flows. But there are two other approaches analysts can use to calculate project values when firms use both debt and equity. The first approach, called the **adjusted present value (*APV*)** method, calculates an investment's value as if it were financed only with equity, then adds back the present value of any financing side effects. The second approach, known as the **flow-to-equity (FTE)** method, uses the firm's cost of equity to discount levered project cash flows. Under certain conditions, these methods yield the same estimate of an investment project's value, an estimate that also agrees with that obtained by using the *WACC* approach. However, each of these approaches has its own advantages and disadvantages, and the valuations that they generate need not be identical in all circumstances.

To see how the *WACC*, *APV*, and *FTE* methods work, let's revisit an earlier example. In Chapter 9 we examined a fast-food company, Lox-in-a-Box, that had a market value of $150 million. Lox-in-a-Box outstanding equity has a market value of $100 million, so its bonds are worth $50 million. Given the firm's current capital structure (which we will assume is the long-run target capital structure), stockholders require a return of 15 percent, and bondholders expect a 9 percent return on their investment.

Financial managers at Lox-in-a-Box are valuing an investment opportunity that requires an initial outlay of $60 million. To maintain their target capital structure, the company will finance this investment with $40 million in equity and $20 million in debt.[1] They expect the investment will generate a perpetual pretax cash flow stream of $10.8 million per year, starting next year. If the company faces a corporate tax rate of 33 percent (one-third), then the after-tax annual cash flow, ignoring the interest tax shield, is $7.2 million. To calculate the *NPV* of this project, discount the unlevered cash flow of $7.2 million using the firm's *WACC*:

$$WACC = \left(\frac{\$50}{\$50 + \$100} \right)\left(1 - \frac{1}{3} \right)0.09 + \left(\frac{\$100}{\$50 + \$100} \right)0.15 = 0.12$$

$$NPV = -\$60 + \frac{\$7.2}{0.12} = 0$$

The zero *NPV* implies that this project offers a minimally acceptable return for Lox-in-a-Box. Let us now reevaluate the project using the *APV* method.

Concept Review Questions

1. What information is required to estimate a firm's *WACC*? How difficult is it to obtain this information?

2. In the Lox-in-a-Box example, does $7.2 million represent the cash flow that goes to stockholders each year? If not, is the stockholder's cash flow higher or lower than $7.2 million?

14.2 THE ADJUSTED PRESENT VALUE METHOD

The *APV* approach begins by calculating the project's unlevered cash flows, just as the *WACC* does. However, the *APV* method discounts these cash flows using the discount rate that applies if the firm is financed only with equity. Next, analysts using

---

[1.] The company's current debt-to-equity ratio is 100 over 50 or 2.0. If the company uses $40 million in equity and $20 million in debt to finance the project, the debt-to-equity ratio will remain at 2.0.

the *APV* technique have to add (or subtract) the present values of any financing side effects that arise because the firm uses leverage. The result is the adjusted present value of the investment project:

$$APV = NPV \text{ (unlevered)} + NPV \text{ of financing effects} \qquad \text{(Eq. 14.2)}$$

In Chapters 12 and 13 we learned that debt financing can have many different side effects, including tax savings, increases in expected bankruptcy costs, and agency costs. We could also include in this list the money paid to investment bankers when firms finance projects by issuing new securities, or special subsidies that may be available, for example, when a government grants a below-market loan to company making an investment that policy makers want to encourage. Of these side effects, the easiest to quantify are the tax savings, and in all likelihood they are larger than the other side effects, except perhaps for firms in or near financial distress. A glance back at Equation 13.2 from the previous chapter suggests that the present value of bankruptcy costs and agency costs may have offsetting effects. We will assume, as most practitioners do, that the only material financial side effect that we must measure in an *APV* analysis is the tax effect.

APPLYING THE MODEL 14.1

Returning to the Lox-in-a-Box project, we have already determined that the unlevered, after-tax annual cash flow is $7.2 million. The *APV* method requires that we discount this cash flow at the rate that would apply if Lox-in-a-Box were an all equity firm. To arrive at this rate, use M&M Proposition II from Chapter 12, making an adjustment for the tax deductibility of interest.

Proposition II expresses the required return on levered equity, r_l, as a function of the required return on the firm's assets, r, the required return on debt, r_d, and the debt-to-equity ratio. Repeating Equation 12.2 we have:

$$r_l = r + (r - r_d)\frac{D}{E}$$

Notice that if the firm employs no debt, then $r_l = r$ and we can interpret r as the required return on an unlevered firm. Now, to incorporate the tax effect, we modify this equation as follows:

$$r_l = r + (r - r_d)\frac{D}{E}(1 - T_c) \qquad \text{(Eq. 14.3)}$$

Plugging in known values for Lox-in-a-Box, we have

$$0.15 = r + (r - 0.09)\frac{1}{2}(1 - 0.33)$$

It takes just a little rearranging to determine that the unlevered cost of capital in this equation is 13.5 percent. In other words, 13.5 percent is the return that investors would require from Lox-in-a-Box if the firm used no debt. Use that fact along with the $7.2 million unlevered project cash flow to determine what the *NPV* of the project would be without debt financing:

$$NPV \text{ (unlevered)} = -\$60 + \frac{\$7.2}{0.135} = -\$6.67$$

This suggests that the project is not worthwhile, but we have not yet taken into account the debt tax shields that will arise because the firm uses $20 million in debt financing to undertake the project. The size of the annual tax shield depends on the tax rate, the cost of debt, and the amount of debt used to finance the project:

$$\text{Annual tax shield} = T_c \times r_d \times D = 0.33 \times 0.09 \times 20 = 0.60$$

Lox-in-a-Box will pay lower taxes in perpetuity, by $0.60 million per year, due to its decision to finance part of this project with debt. Assuming that the interest tax shields are just as risky as the firm's debt, we can take the present value of the tax savings by discounting them at 9 percent:

$$PV \text{ of tax savings} = \frac{0.60}{0.09} = 6.67$$

Finally, we have everything we need to calculate the project's value using the *APV* method. The project's *APV* equals the unlevered *NPV* (−$6.67 million) plus the present value of tax shields ($6.67 million). In other words, the project *APV* equals zero. As we found when valuing the project using the *WACC* approach, the *APV* valuation suggests that the project is barely acceptable.

Given the assumptions we've made thus far, we obtain the same project value whether we follow the *WACC* or the *APV* approach. In that case, why do we need two methods? The answer to that question follows shortly, but first we want to examine a third method for valuing investment projects, the flow-to-equity approach.

Concept Review Questions

3. How is the *APV* method different from the *WACC*?

4. Compare the *WACC* for Lox-in-a-Box to the cost of unlevered equity that we calculated as part of the *APV* analysis. Why are the two rates different?

14.3 THE FLOW-TO-EQUITY METHOD

The *FTE* method differs from the *WACC* and *APV* approaches by focusing exclusively on cash flows that flow to shareholders. Whereas the *WACC* and *APV* project cash flow calculations ignore interest expense, an *FTE* analysis deducts interest costs and taxes from project cash flows. We will refer to this type of cash flow calculation as **levered cash flow**. In essence, an *FTE* analysis captures the effects of financing in the numerator (i.e., the cash flows) rather than in the denominator.

What cash flow does the proposed investment generate for Lox-in-a-Box shareholders? Start with pretax cash flow of $10.8 million. Next, deduct annual interest expense, which amounts to $1.8 million ($20 million in debt at 9 percent). That leaves pretax cash flow of $9 million. With a corporate tax rate of 33 percent, shareholders are left with $6 million per year in perpetuity.

Because the $6 million annual cash flow we've just calculated flows directly to shareholders, it is appropriate to discount that cash flow at the cost of equity. Take care here. The cost of equity we require to complete the *FTE* analysis is not the unlevered cost of equity that we calculated for the *APV* calculation (13.5 percent), nor is it Lox-in-Box's *WACC* (12 percent). Instead, we need the rate of return that Lox-in-a-Box shareholders demand, given that the firm maintains a debt-to-equity ratio of 2.0. But that's just the 15 percent cost of equity we were given at the very beginning. Therefore, the present value of the cash flows that shareholders can claim is $40 million:

$$PV \text{ of cash flows flowing to equity} = \frac{6}{0.15} = \$40 \text{ million}$$

Does that mean that the project creates $40 million in value for Lox-in-a-Box shareholders? Not quite. Recall that to finance the project, the company planned to use $20 million in debt and $40 million in equity. Therefore, the project's *NPV* is zero. The value of the project's cash flows flowing to equity investors exactly matches the initial outlay that stockholders have to fund.

Table 14.1 summarizes the three methods. The *WACC* begins with unlevered project cash flows, discounts them at the *WACC*, and then subtracts the initial outlay to obtain an *NPV*. Notice that when estimating a project's value using this method, the cash flow calculations essentially assume that the project is financed entirely with equity. The benefit of debt financing comes through in the denominator, not the numerator. The *APV* method also starts with unlevered project cash flows, but these cash flows are discounted using the unlevered cost of equity. The present value of financing side effects are calculated separately an added back to the "unlevered *NPV*." As with the *WACC* approach, the *APV* method subtracts the initial outlay to arrive at a final estimate of a project's worth. Finally, the *FTE* method estimates a project's value by focusing only on cash flows flowing to equity, discounting those using a levered cost of equity, and then subtracting the part of the initial outlay that equity holders must bear.

If the three methods lead to the same answers, why is it necessary to cover all three approaches? As we have noted earlier in the text, most firms value investment projects by discounting cash flows at the *WACC*. This is fine as long as two assumptions hold. First, the business risk of the project under consideration should be similar to the business risk of the firm's existing assets. The *WACC* applies a firm's current costs of equity and debt to arrive at a project discount rate, but those costs reflect the risks of the investments that the firm has already undertaken. Second, the *WACC*

Table 14.1
A Comparison of *WACC*, *APV*, and *FTE*

Method	Cash Flow	Discount Rate	Plus	Minus
WACC	Unlevered	*WACC*		Initial outlay
APV	Unlevered	Unlevered cost of equity	Financing side effects	Initial outlay
FTE	Levered	Levered cost of equity		Part of initial outlay paid for by shareholders

assumes that the investment project does not materially alter the firm's long-run target debt-to-equity ratio. When a company plans to invest in a project with a risk profile that differs markedly from that of its existing assets, or when a new project substantially alters the firm's capital structure, then analysts have to make adjustments to the *WACC* calculations. We illustrated how to do this in Chapter 9.

As with the *WACC*, the *FTE* method assumes that a firm maintains a target debt-to-equity ratio over time. Recall that the *FTE* calculation discounts a project's levered cash flows using the levered cost of equity. If an investment project causes a firm's leverage to change over time, then the cost of equity will vary too. Much of the research surveyed in Chapters 12 and 13 suggests that managers of most firms tend to act as if they have long-run target debt ratios in mind, even if they "correct" deviations from those targets slowly over time. If that is correct, then the *WACC* and *FTE* methods are probably appropriate for most capital budgeting decisions.

Finally, the *APV* approach makes a very different assumption about the firm's capital structure. Recall that the *APV* technique calculates the present value of financing side effects as a separate item. For example, to calculate the present value of interest tax shields, what analysts need to know is not the mix of debt and equity, but the amount of debt borrowed to fund the project. So *APV* is the preferred method when analysts do not expect the firm to adjust its debt and equity positions to maintain a constant target ratio. Perhaps the most common example of this situation is a leveraged buyout, or LBO. In a leveraged buyout, a group of investors (or a firm) borrows a large sum to acquire an existing business. Initially, the firm may have a capital structure consisting of 90 percent debt or more. In this situation, there is no expectation that the firm will maintain leverage at such a high level in the long run. Instead, in the early years after the buyout, most of the firm's cash flows go towards paying down the debt. In deciding how much to bid for the target company (and also how much to borrow to pay for the acquisition), LBO investors should use the *APV* method to capture the time-varying tax benefits of leverage.

In addition to differences between *APV* and the other two approaches regarding assumptions about the permanence, or lack thereof, of a firm's capital structure, the *APV* method allows for a broader range of financial side effects. For example, the *WACC* equation accounts for only one financial side effect, the tax deductibility of interest. On the other hand, we can include a wide range of financing effects in *APV* calculations, such as the flotation costs of selling debt or equity securities to investors. Therefore, when the side effects of debt are numerous and extend beyond the basic tax advantage that we've discussed here, *APV* may be the better approach.

Concept Review Questions

5. In a *FTE* calculation, is the numerator the same or different compared to the *WACC* calculation? What about the denominator?

6. What assumption is typically maintained in both *WACC* and *FTE* calculations?

14.4 A CHECKLIST FOR THE INTERACTIONS BETWEEN INVESTMENT AND FINANCING DECISIONS

How should practicing financial managers evaluate capital investment decisions, whether those decisions are on a small scale, such as replacing old equipment, or on a large scale, such as acquiring an entire firm. We can summarize this chapter's key recommendations for capital investment analysis as follows.

1. Under certain conditions, all three methods (*WACC, FTE,* and *APV*) generate estimates of an investment's value that agree. In this case, choose the method that is easiest to apply given the available data.
2. When the firm plans to maintain a constant target debt-to-equity ratio in the long run, use the *WACC* or *FTE* methods.
3. When the firm's debt-to-equity ratio varies over a project's life, but the amount of debt outstanding at any given time is known, use the *APV* method.
4. When financing side effects, beyond the interest tax shield, are an important part of the investment project under consideration, use the *APV* method.

14.5 SUMMARY

- When the M&M perfect markets assumptions hold, then the basic capital budgeting methods covered in the early chapters of this book work well. In that case, investment and financing decisions are completely separable.
- The most obvious violation of the perfect markets assumption is the corporate income tax. Because interest payments are generally tax deductible, that tends to increase the value of debt-financed projects relative to projects financed entirely with equity.
- The *WACC* method captures the value of interest tax shields by adjusting the project discount rate downward.
- The *APV* method estimates a project's value by separating the value of the project itself and the value of financing side effects, such as the interest tax shield.
- The *FTE* approach focuses exclusively on the cash flows flowing to equity investors. A project's value is the present value of these "levered" cash flows, discounted at a levered cost of equity.
- In most cases, the *FTE* and *WACC* methods lead to value-maximizing investment decisions. The *APV* approach is preferred in certain special cases, such as LBOs.

INTERNET RESOURCES

www.ssrn.com—The site of the Social Science Research Network. Here you can download a number of papers comparing the different approaches to investment valuation covered in this chapter.

KEY TERMS

adjusted present value
flow to equity
weighted average cost of capital

QUESTIONS

14-1. Why do violations of the M&M perfect markets assumptions require revisions to our capital budgeting analysis?

14-2. Which method would you use to evaluate an investment project that involved modernizing a firm's existing plant? The project will not affect the firm's target debt-to-equity ratio.

14-3. If you assume that investment projects are financed entirely with equity, will you tend to over value or under value these projects?

14-4. List three potential financing side effects that the *APV* approach can account for.

14-5. Which is higher, the discount rate used in the *FTE* approach or the *WACC*?

14-6. In calculating a firm's cost of debt, why is the yield-to-maturity preferable to the coupon rate on the firm's outstanding bonds?

14-7. Suppose you are calculating the *WACC* for a firm with outstanding junk bonds. You use the yield to maturity on these bonds as the cost of debt in the *WACC* formula. Is this correct?

14-8. A foreign government offers your company a below-market interest rate to finance a favored investment in their country. How do you incorporate this factor in your investment analysis?

PROBLEMS

M&M, Capital Budgeting, and the *WACC*

14-1. A firm has 1,000,000 shares of stock outstanding, and each share is currently worth $20. The shares have a beta of 1.2. The firm also has 10-year bonds outstanding with a par value of $10,000,000, a coupon rate of 6 percent, and a yield-to-maturity of 7 percent. The yield on the bonds is currently 2 percentage points above the risk-free rate and 4 percentage points below the expected return on the overall market. What is the firm's *WACC* if the corporate tax rate is 35 percent?

14-2. A project has unlevered cash flow of $4 million per year in perpetuity. Suppose the project (and the firm) is financed entirely with equity having a required return of 15 percent. What is the project's *NPV* if the initial outlay is $20 million?

14-3. A project has unlevered cash flow of $4 million per year in perpetuity. Suppose the firm considering this project finances its operations with an equal mix of debt and equity. The required return on debt is 5 percent, and the required return on equity is 15 percent. The marginal corporate tax rate is 30 percent. What is the project's *NPV* if the initial outlay is $20 million?

14-4. When computing the *NPV* based on the *WACC*, Project X has an *NPV* of $1.3 million. When the *NPV* is calculated using the unlevered cost of capital, the *NPV* becomes −$0.5 million. Based on these two calculations, what is the value of the debt tax shields available within Project X? (*Hint:* Think of how *APV* is calculated.)

14-5. Firm GTO is considering a project that will produce annual cash flows of $1.8 million for the next 22 years. The firm has a debt-to-equity ratio of 1.5 with debt having a yield of 8% APR and the cost of equity being 18% APR. Assuming a 38% tax rate, what is the WACC for GTO? Assuming the project is to be funded in the same manner as GTO's existing capital structure, what is the NPV of the project based on a cost of $10 million? If the tax rate is reduced to 32%, what is the NPV of the project (remember to adjust the cash flows and the WACC)?

The Adjusted Present Value Method

14-6. Find a formula for the unlevered cost of equity r based on Equation 14.3.

14-7. Firm SMG's stock currently sells for $13.75 based on a recent dividend of $0.45 and a dividend growth rate of 10% (see Chapter 4). The firm has a debt ratio of 50% and a tax rate of 40%. Assuming the debt has a 6% yield, what is the unlevered cost of equity? What is the WACC?

14-8. The NPV of a project based on the cost of equity is −$5.85 million. To complete the APV analysis, the debt shield must be calculated based on a tax rate of 30%. The firm can choose to issue $10 million of 7% debt over a 20-year period or the firm can issue $15 million of 6% debt over 15 years (assume all debt is issued at par). Which debt issue will provide the better APV and will the project be acceptable?

14-9. A project is expected to produce cash flows of $5 million annually for the next 18 years. The tax rate is currently 35% and the unlevered cost of equity is 16%. The project will cost $22 million, of which, $15 million dollars will be raised using 10-year bonds with 8% coupons (sold at par). What is the APV for the project? Suppose the local government provides a tax incentive that lowers the tax rate to 30%. What is the APV now?

14-10. Project Z is expected to produce annual cash flows of $4 million for the next 30 years. Assuming a tax rate of 40% and an unlevered cost of equity of 14%, determine the APV based on a cost of $18 million and no debt financing. Suppose there is a tax incentive to initiate the project in a particular locality that lowers the tax rate to 32.5%. What is the APV with this tax incentive included?

14-11. The nation's largest chicken-wing producer, Consolidated Eggleston Inc. (CEI), plans to expand its capacity by building more chicken coups. The expansion project will require an initial outlay of $10 million and will generate an unlevered cash flow of $1 million in perpetuity. CEI uses twice as much equity as debt to finance its operations. Its pretax cost of debt is 6 percent, and its cost of equity is 10 percent. The marginal corporate tax rate is 30 percent. Calculate the value of this investment opportunity using the APV method.

14-12. The popular fashion design company, Oogle, has $200 million of debt outstanding and $100 million of equity. Investors require a 7 percent return on Oogle's bonds and 14 percent on its stock. Oogle's marginal corporate tax rate is 40 percent. An analyst at the company is using the APV method to value one of Oogle's new investment opportunities. As a first step, the analyst wants to calculate what this opportunity would be worth were it financed entirely with equity. The analyst reasons that he should use a 14 percent discount rate at this stage of the analysis. Do you agree? If so, why, and if not, what rate would you recommend?

The Flow-to-Equity Method

14-13. If an unlevered cash flow is $1.5 million based on a 40% tax rate, what is the levered cash flow if the interest on debt is $1 million annually?

14-14. Suppose a firm is funded 20% with debt (yield of 9% APR) and has a 32% tax rate. What is the (levered) cost of equity assuming the unlevered cost of equity is 14%? What is the firm's WACC?

14-15. A firm is funded with 40% debt (9% annual yield) and has a tax rate of 40%. What is the (levered) cost of equity if the *WACC* is 12.06%?

14-16. Quicksand Construction Inc. is examining a potential investment opportunity that will require the company to spend $40 million up front. The company will finance this project with $30 million in equity with a required return of 12 percent and $10 million in debt offering a yield of 6 percent. The project will generate a perpetual cash flow, before interest and taxes, of $2.8 million annually. Value the project using the *FTE* method. The tax rate is 30 percent.

14-17. An investment project requires an initial outlay of $75 million. A certain firm plans to undertake this investment, financing the up-front cost with $50 million in equity and $25 million in debt. The firm's cost of equity is 16 percent, and its after-tax cost of debt is 4 percent. The corporate tax rate is 50 percent. If the investment generates a perpetual cash flow of $5 million annually, after interest and taxes, what is the investment worth according to the *FTE* method?

14-18. Project ZTZ is expected to produce annual cash flows of $6.2 million for the next 30 years. Assuming a tax rate of 40%, $1.4 million in annual interest payments, and a (levered) cost of equity of 17%, determine the *NPV* using the FTE method based on a cost of $15 million. What does the *NPV* become if the tax rate is 35%?

THOMSON ONE BUSINESS SCHOOL EDITION

14-19. Conduct an Advanced Search using the WtdAvgCostofCapital variable. (*Hint:* Click on Search for Companies and then click the Advanced Search button.) Search for firms that are in the top 10% for the WtdAvgCostofCapital. Select two of these firms. Next, conduct a second search for firms that are in the bottom 10% for the WtdAvgCostofCapital. Select two firms from this group. Comment on why the WtdAvgCostofCapital is so different for the firms in the two different groups. Would these WtdAvgCostofCapital estimates differ if the firms were considering projects that were significantly less risky than the average project for the firm? What adjustments might be made to the WtdAvgCostofCapital estimate to account for the difference in risk?

MINI-CASE: THE LINK BETWEEN CAPITAL STRUCTURE AND CAPITAL BUDGETING

Fiera Corporation is evaluating a new project that costs $45,000. The project will be financed using 60% equity and 40% debt, thus maintaining the firm's current debt-to-equity ratio. The firm's stockholders have a required rate of return of 18.36% while bondholders expect a 10.68% rate of return. The project is expected to generate annual cash flows of $13,000 before taxes for the next two decades. Fiera Corporation is in the 36% tax bracket.

1. Determine the weighted average cost of capital of the firm.

2. Calculate the traditional net present value of the project. Should the project be undertaken?

3. Using Modigliani and Miller's Proposition II, determine the required return on unlevered equity.

4.   Determine whether or not the project should be undertaken using the adjusted present value method.

5.   Calculate whether or not the project should be undertaken using the flow-to-equity method.

Chapter 15

Dividend Policy

SMARTFinance
Use the learning tools at www
.thomsonedu.com/finance/smartfinance

528

OPENING FOCUS

Microsoft Pays the World's Largest Dividend

On July 20, 2004, Microsoft Corporation announced plans to pay a special dividend of $3.00 per share, or $32.6 billion in total, in what would be the largest single cash distribution from a corporation to its investors. In the same announcement, Microsoft doubled its annual dividend to $0.32 per share and promised to repurchase stock worth $30 billion over the next four years. Even for a company famous for doing things on a grand scale, announcing plans to pay out nearly $70 billion in cash was breathtaking, and the stock price surged 5 percent.

In its first 28 years, Microsoft never paid a cash dividend to its shareholders, preferring instead to reinvest all profits, to finance growth. By the late 1990s, Microsoft faced more limited growth opportunities, although its long profitable history left the company with a cash hoard approaching $50 billion. Facing investor pressure to disgorge some of its cash, Microsoft initiated an annual $0.08-per-share dividend in 2003 and then doubled it a few months later.

Not surprisingly, Microsoft's shareholders approved the $32.6 billion special dividend payment in November 2004. Microsoft then announced that it would pay these dividends on December 13, 2004, to shareholders of record—those whose names were on the company's books—on November 17, 2004. Any investor who purchased Microsoft stock before the ex-dividend day (Monday, November 15) would receive the dividends; anyone purchasing the stock on or after this day would not. Reflecting this fact, Microsoft's stock dropped by $2.56 per share on the ex-dividend day.

Microsoft's recent dividend history neatly reflects the issues corporate managers face in setting dividend policies. Should we distribute cash to shareholders? How much should we pay? Should we distribute cash as a regular dividend, as a special dividend, or as a share repurchase? Microsoft's announcement was unique because it committed the firm to making cash distribution of all three types. That is dividend policy with style.

Sources: Multiple articles from Financial Times, *July–December, 2004.*

A firm's *dividend policy* refers to the choices its managers make about distributing cash to shareholders. These choices include whether to pay shareholders a regular (recurring) cash dividend, how large the cash dividend should be, and how frequently it should be paid. The **dividend payout ratio**, calculated by dividing the cash dividend per share by its earnings per share, indicates the percentage of each dollar earned that firms distribute to the owners. The **dividend yield,** which equals a stock's dividend divided by its price, measures the rate of return represented by the dividend payment. In setting dividend policy, managers also decide whether to include special (nonrecurring) dividends or share repurchases as part of their overall strategy for distributing cash to investors. After initiating dividends, managers subsequently decide whether to increase, decrease, or maintain the current dividend payment, weighing how investors will react to dividend policy changes.

Dividends are both pervasive and perplexing. They are pervasive in that companies have been paying regular dividends for more than three centuries.[1] Dividends are perplexing (especially to financial economists) because it is not obvious why investors sometimes clamor for dividends when they could obtain cash by selling a few shares instead. This is particularly true for the institutional investors that dominate stock ownership and trading worldwide.

As we move through this chapter, we want to keep in mind three broad trends that reflect the dividend decisions of thousands of U.S. corporate managers. First, there has been a massive increase since the mid-1980s in the number of firms implementing **share repurchase programs** and in the total value of these programs. Companies announcing share repurchase programs state they will buy back some of their own shares, usually through open-market purchases. Share repurchases give managers an alternative method to distribute cash to shareholders. In fact, the annual value of share repurchases in the United States sometimes exceeds that of dividends, and investors clearly welcome repurchase announcements.[2]

The second important dividend trend, documented by Fama and French (2001) and Julio and Ikenberry (2004), is the decline in the fraction of U.S. companies paying dividends. The two graphs of Figure 15.1 come from Fama and French's study. The top graph shows that the percentage of dividend payers fell from about 80 percent to 20 percent during the last half century; the bottom graph reveals that this trend is particularly strong among the young, high-growth companies listed on Nasdaq. Fama and French also find that dividend-paying firms distributed a lower fraction of their earnings in 1999 than they did before. In other words, companies had a lower *propensity* to pay dividends in 1999 than they had in years past.

Until recently, it appeared that the decline in dividend payments reflected a long-term secular trend, pointing to the eventual eclipse of dividends in American corporate life. However, recent research by Julio and Ikenberry (2004) and others documents a clear rebound in the number of companies paying dividends and provides somewhat less clear-cut evidence of an increase in average dividend payout ratios. Figure 15.2, from Julio and Ikenberry, shows that the proportion of U.S. industrial firms paying dividends increased to 21 percent in early 2004, after bottoming out at 16 percent in 2000. They find several factors influenced this rebound, including a

---

[1.] Dewing (1953, p. 93) notes that an act of Parliament in 1697 formalized the restriction that dividends could only be paid out of a company's profits, not its capital, clearly indicating that dividends were important even then. A similar provision appeared in the Massachusetts Land Bank's charter, granted in 1739.

[2.] Numerous studies document significant, positive abnormal returns to shareholders at the announcement of repurchase programs. The first two of these are by Dann (1981) and Vermaelen (1981). Subsequent articles examining share repurchases include those by Ikenberry, Lakonishok, and Vermaelen (1995), Guay and Harford (2000), Lie (2000), and Jagannathan, Stephens, and Weisbach (2000), Maxwell and Stephens (2003), and Grullon and Michaely (2004).

Figure 15.1
The Fraction of Publicly
Traded U.S. Firms Paying
Cash Dividends,
1926–1999
*This figure details the
percentage of all publicly
traded firms in the
United States that paid
regular cash dividends
over the period 1926–
1999. The top graph
shows this for all
publicly traded firms,
whereas the bottom
graph breaks this out by
exchange, from 1962
(AMEX) and 1972
(Nasdaq) onward.*
Source: Eugene F. Fama
and Kenneth R. French,
"Disappearing Dividends:
Changing Firm Characteristics or Lower Propensity
to Pay?" *Journal of Applied
Corporate Finance* 14
(Spring 2001), pp. 67–79.

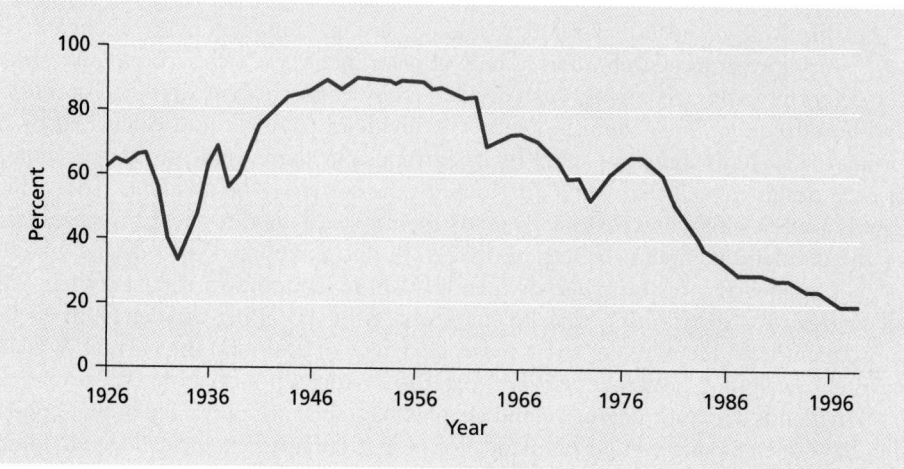

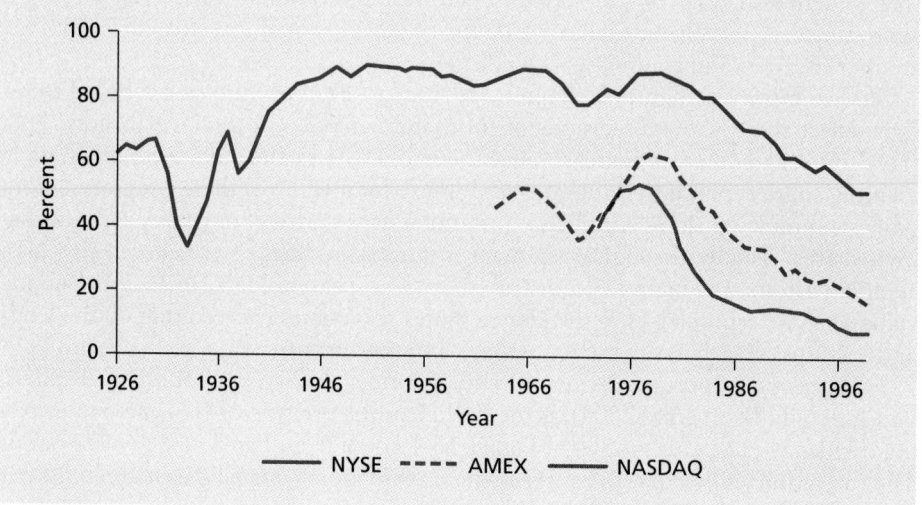

Figure 15.2
Proportion of Dividend
Payers among All U.S.
Industrial Firms,
1984–2004
*This figure plots the
percentage of all
individual firms paying
dividends from 1984
through the first quarter
2004. Each quarter, a
firm is designated as a
dividend payer if it paid
a positive dividend in
that quarter.*
Source: Figure 1 in Brandon
Julio and David L. Ikenberry,
"Reappearing Dividends,"
*Applied Corporate
Finance* 16 no. 4 2004,
pp. 89–100.

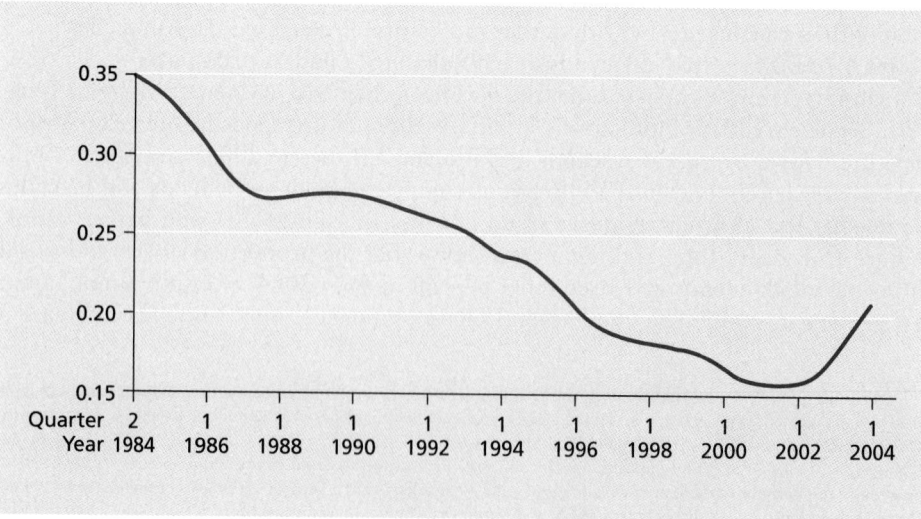

"maturity effect," where companies that went public during the 1990s initiated dividends after their growth rates slowed. They also find some evidence that the Jobs and Growth Tax Relief Reconciliation Act of 2003 (hereafter, the Tax Relief Act of 2003), which significantly reduced tax rates on dividend income for individual investors, led many companies to initiate or increase dividends.[3]

The third key trend is the increasing concentration of corporate profits and dividends among a few large companies. DeAngelo, DeAngelo, and Skinner (2004) show that while total real dividends grew more than 22 percent from 1978 to 2000, this $7.1 billion increase came from just 100 big firms. The share of aggregative dividends paid by these firms rose from 67.3 percent in 1978 to 81.8 percent in 2000, a trend that aggregate profit figures mirror. In other words, a mere 100 companies earn most of the profits and pay most of the dividends in the United States. These facts explain why dividend payments as a percent of GDP increased steadily, even as the fraction of companies paying dividends declined.

Our objective in this chapter is to answer two basic questions. First, does dividend policy matter? Can managers change a firm's value simply by changing its dividend payments? Second, if dividends do matter, what factors determine a firm's optimal payout policy? We begin by providing a brief overview of dividend fundamentals, defining key terms, and discussing issues corporate managers everywhere face in setting dividend policies. Section 15.2 outlines dividend payment patterns around the world, patterns that a modern dividend theory should explain. Section 15.3 establishes a classic result—dividend policy has no impact on firm value in perfect, frictionless markets. But when market imperfections such as taxes exist, some dividend policies may be better than others. Section 15.4 shows how market imperfections affect dividend policy decisions. Finally, Section 15.5 reviews predictions from dividend theories and provides a checklist that managers can consult when making dividend decisions.

15.1 DIVIDEND FUNDAMENTALS

CASH DIVIDEND PAYMENT PROCEDURES

In the United States, as in most countries, shareholders have no legal right to receive dividends. Instead, a firm's board of directors decides what dividends the firm will pay.

Most U.S. firms that pay dividends do so once every quarter, whereas corporations in other industrialized countries generally pay dividends annually or semiannually. Firms adjust the size of their dividends periodically, but not necessarily every quarter. For example, among the roughly 1,300 U.S. firms that paid dividends continuously from 1999 to 2003, just over 36 percent changed their dividend once a year, on average. About 14 percent of these firms maintained a constant dividend during this five-year span, and about 23 percent changed their dividend more frequently than once a year. Only five of the 1,300 firms changed their dividend every quarter.[4] These figures suggest that firms maintain a constant dividend until significant increases or decreases in earnings justify changing it.

---

[3] Blouin, Raedy, and Shackleford (2004) also find that the 2003 tax change led to increased dividend payments.
[4] Author's calculations using data from the Center for Research on Securities Prices (CRSP), excluding closed-end mutual funds, real estate investment trusts (REITs), and other investment companies.

Relevant Dates. When firms declare dividends, they also establish certain dates that determine which shareholders receive the dividends. *Shareholders of record,* all persons whose names appear as stockholders on the **date of record,** are entitled to the dividend. However, because it takes time to make bookkeeping entries after stocks trade, investors who buy stock on the *record date* will miss the dividend payment. To receive the dividend, an investor must own the stock before the **ex-dividend date,** usually two business days prior to the date of record. Firms distribute dividends on the **payment date,** which usually comes a few weeks after the record date. Figure 15.3 shows a timeline illustrating these events.

Figure 15.3
A Timeline Illustrating
Important Dates in the
Dividend Process

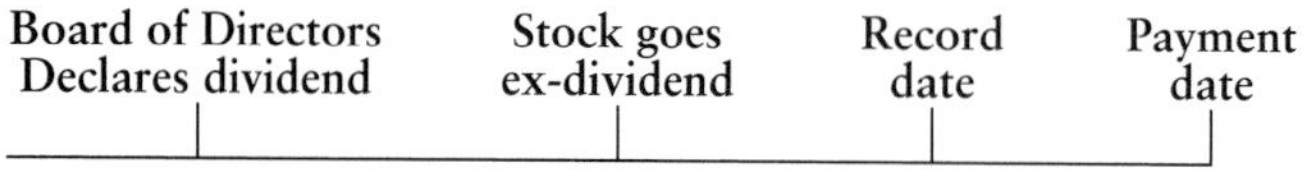

Board of Directors Declares dividend	Stock goes ex-dividend	Record date	Payment date

When a stock goes ex-dividend, its price should drop by the amount of the dividend. To see why, consider that an investor who buys a stock just prior to the ex-dividend date will receive the dividend a few days later, whereas an investor who buys on the ex-dividend date misses this payment. Therefore, investors who buy on the ex-dividend date will pay less for the stock. For example, suppose a stock that pays a $1 dividend sells for $51 just before going ex-dividend. Once the ex-dividend date passes, the price should drop to $50, in the absence of any other news affecting the stock.

APPLYING THE MODEL 15.1

On January 2, 2006, RPM International Inc. of Medina, Ohio, announced that its board of directors declared a regular quarterly cash dividend of $0.16 per share, payable on January 31, 2006, to shareholders of record as of January 13, 2006. Since RPM is a New York Stock Exchange-listed firm, the ex-dividend day is set three business days before the record date, or on January 11, 2006. Thus anyone who buys RPM stock on or before January 10 will receive this dividend payment, while an investor buying the stock on or after January 11 will not.

Research shows that in the United States and many other countries, the ex-dividend price drop tends to be less than the dividend payment. Later we will explore a tax-based explanation for this pattern.

EXTERNAL FACTORS AFFECTING DIVIDEND POLICY

Most U.S. states prohibit corporations from paying out as dividends any portion of their "legal capital," which the law defines as the par value of common stock. Some states define legal capital to include the common stock's par value and any additional paid-in capital. States establish these *capital-impairment restrictions* to provide a sufficient equity base to protect creditors' claims. The example presented for the Alpha Corporation in Table 15.1 clarifies the varying definitions of capital. An earnings requirement limiting dividends to the sum of a firm's present and past earnings is sometimes imposed. In other words, Alpha cannot pay more in dividends than the sum of its most recent and historic retained earnings. However, *laws do not prohibit a firm from paying more in dividends than its current earnings.*

If a firm has overdue liabilities or is legally insolvent, most states prohibit cash dividend payments. In addition, the Internal Revenue Service prohibits firms from ac-

Alpha Corporation's Stockholders' Equity	
Common stock at par	$100,000
Paid-in capital, in surplus of par	200,000
Retained earnings	140,000
Total stockholders' equity	$440,000

Table 15.1
Calculating the Maximum
Amount a Firm Can Pay
in Cash Dividends

Note: This table presents the stockholders' equity account of the Alpha Corporation. In states where a firm's legal capital is defined as the par value of its common stock, the firm could pay out a maximum of $340,000 ($200,000 + $140,000) in cash dividends without impairing its capital. In states where a firm's capital includes all paid-in capital, the firm could pay out only $140,000 in cash dividends.

cumulating earnings to reduce the owners' taxes. A firm's owners must pay income taxes on dividends when they are received, but the owners pay no tax on capital gains until they sell the stock. A firm may retain a large portion of earnings to delay the payment of taxes by its owners. If the IRS can determine that a firm has accumulated excess earnings to allow owners to delay paying ordinary income taxes, it may levy an **excess earnings accumulation tax** on any retained earnings above a specified amount. This rarely occurs in practice, however.

Restrictive provisions in loan agreements sometimes constrain dividends. Generally, these provisions forbid dividends until the firm achieves an earnings threshold, or they may impose a cap on dividends.[5] These constraints help protect creditors from losses due to insolvency. If a firm violates one of these contractual restrictions, creditors generally have the right to demand immediate repayment of their loans.

TYPES OF DIVIDEND POLICIES

One can imagine several ways that a firm might establish its dividend policy. The following sections describe three potential dividend policies, but bear in mind that one of these predominates in every major economy. A particular firm's cash dividend policy may incorporate elements of each policy type.

Constant Payout Ratio Policy. A company following a **constant payout ratio policy** promises to pay a set fraction of its earnings to shareholders each period. This policy implies that dividends fluctuate in lockstep with earnings. Apparently, managers find this consequence unappealing, because very few companies follow a constant payout policy.

Constant Nominal Payment Policy. With a **constant nominal payment policy,** the firm pays the same dividend each period. Companies following this policy may increase dividends once a *permanent* increase in earnings occurs, but they almost never cut dividends unless a true crisis arises.[6]

[5.] Specific bond covenant constraints on dividend payment policy are discussed in depth in Smith and Warner (1979) and Kalay (1982).
[6.] The Fall 2001 issue of the *Journal of Portfolio Management* described a unique variant of a constant dividend payment strategy. The Smith Company is a private investment company whose primary objective is to provide a constant stream of real dividend payments to approximately 100 members of the Smith family. In other words, the company aims to pay out an inflation-adjusted dividend stream with constant purchasing power over time. DeAngelo and DeAngelo (1990) and DeAngelo, DeAngelo, and Skinner (2000) document the extreme reluctance of ordinary corporate mangers to reduce dividend payments by showing that losses play a key role in dividend cuts and omissions.

A firm that pays a steady dividend may build its policy around a **target payout ratio.** Under this policy, the firm attempts to pay out a certain percentage of earnings. Rather than let dividends fluctuate, however, it pays a stated dollar dividend and slowly adjusts it toward the target payout, as proven earnings increases occur. This is known as a *partial-adjustment strategy,* and it implies that at any given time, firms may be in a transition between two dividend payment levels.

Low-Regular-and-Extra Policy. Some firms establish a **low-regular-and-extra policy** that pays a low regular dividend, supplemented by an additional cash payment at irregular intervals. When earnings are high, a firm can make a large, one-time payment designated as an **extra dividend** or a **special dividend.** A firm uses the "special" designation to communicate to shareholders that the earnings supporting the dividend are temporarily above normal and will not sustain a high dividend forever.[7] For example, interest rates on residential mortgages declined to a 35-year low during 2003. As a result, many homeowners refinanced their loans, and the refinancing boom caused a sharp increase in fees earned by mortgage lenders. Managers of these financial institutions knew that the earnings surge couldn't last forever, so they used special dividends to distribute the temporary increase in profits to investors.

OTHER FORMS OF DIVIDENDS

Managers can pay dividends without actually distributing cash by declaring a stock dividend or a stock split. Managers can also distribute cash to shareholders without paying dividends simply by repurchasing shares. We include these transactions in our discussion of dividend policy because they represent an alternative to the cash dividend payments discussed previously.

Stock Dividends. A firm can give its shareholders additional shares of stock rather than cash. Such a distribution is called a **stock dividend.** For example, if a firm declares a 20 percent stock dividend, it will issue 20 new shares for every 100 shares that an investor owns.[8] However, a 20 percent stock dividend does not make shareholders 20 percent wealthier. If a firm pays a 20 percent stock dividend and nothing else about the firm changes, then the number of outstanding shares increases by 20 percent, and the stock price drops by 20 percent. The stock dividend neither increases nor decreases the value of investors' shareholdings.

Stock Splits. Stock splits, like stock dividends, have mostly cosmetic effects. When a firm executes a **stock split,** its share price declines because the number of outstanding shares increases. In a 2-for-1 split, the firm doubles the number of shares outstanding but the stock price falls to half its previous level. Managers who implement stock splits generally say they are trying to reduce the per-share price of the firm's stock back within a "standard" trading range that individual investors desire. They believe that by keeping the stock price low enough to appeal to retail investors, they can achieve a higher overall firm value.

[7.] Evidence that investors are quite savvy about interpreting the information in these dividends is presented in Brickley (1983), Lie (2000), and DeAngelo, DeAngelo, and Skinner (2000).

[8.] Though hardly rare in the United States, stock dividends are more common in Britain, where they are called "scrip dividends." These are discussed at length in Lasfer (1997) and Ang, Blackwell, and Megginson (1991). Crawford, Franz, and Lobo (2005) examine stock dividend announcements in the United States from 1967 to 1996 and verify results from earlier studies showing that the share prices of firms announcing these dividends increase by a statistically significant 3.41 percent. As was also true with earlier studies, Crawford et al. cannot fully explain why investors react so positively to this noncash distribution of additional shares.

Intuition suggests that stock splits should not create value for shareholders. After all, if someone offers to give you two $5 bills in exchange for one $10 bill, you are no better off. A stock split should also have no effect on the firm's capital structure because it changes the number rather than the value of outstanding shares. In spite of this logic, research stretching from Grinblatt, Masulis, and Titman (1984) to Crawford, Franz, and Lobo (2005) documents that stock splits do increase the market value of a firm's equity by about 2.5 percent. On the other hand, Byun and Rozeff (2003) find that the stocks of companies that split their shares do not outperform the market over the long term.

Though most stock splits increase the number of shares outstanding, firms sometimes conduct **reverse stock splits,** replacing a certain number of outstanding shares with just one new share. For example, in a 1-for-2 split, one new share replaces two old shares. A firm may initiate a reverse stock split when its stock sells at a very low price, possibly to prevent the exchange where the stock trades from delisting of the stock.

Share Repurchases. U.S. firms have dramatically increased share repurchases since 1982 [see Grullon and Ikenberry (2000)]. An SEC ruling that year clarified when companies could and could not repurchase their shares, without fear of being charged with insider trading or price manipulation. Figure 15.4 illustrates the dramatic growth in repurchases between 1972 and 2001. A variety of motivations influence firms' share repurchases. Firms may buy back shares that they intend to use to acquire another company. Firms with employee stock option plans may repurchase shares to offset the dilution that occurs when employees exercise their right to buy new shares. Some managers may repurchase shares simply to reduce the number of outstanding shares and thereby raise earnings per share. Depending on how the tax code treats dividends and capital gains, share repurchases may offer firms a way to minimize the taxes that shareholders pay when they receive cash distributions. Finally, managers may choose to buy back shares when they think the market undervalues the firm's stock.

Prior to the passage of the Jobs and Growth Tax Relief Reconciliation Act of 2003, there was a substantial tax advantage to distributing cash to shareholders via share repurchases rather than dividends. Dividends were taxable as ordinary income

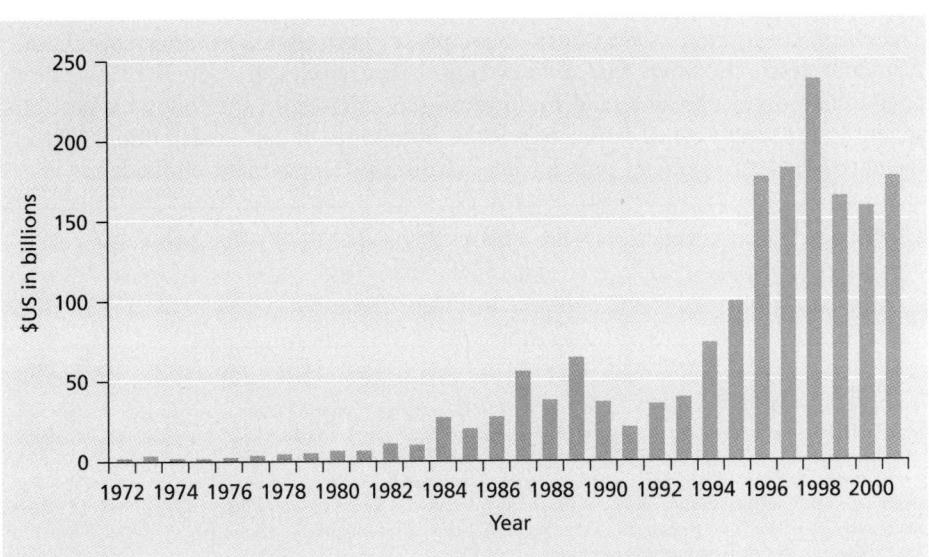

Figure 15.4
Market Value of Share Repurchases by U.S. Corporations, 1972–2001
Source: Table B-90, Economic Report of the President (2002) and Thomson Financial Securities Data, as reported in Table 1 of J. Fed Weston and Juan A. Siu (2003) "Changing Motives for Share Repurchases," *Finance* Paper 3 (2003), Anderson Graduate School of Management, UCLA.

when received. In contrast, the only taxpayers with an immediate tax liability result-ing from a share repurchase were those who sold their shares back to the firm. For these investors, only the difference between the selling price and the original purchase price was taxable, and the applicable tax rate was the capital gains rate, not the rate on ordinary income.

To see the tax advantages, consider a firm that is weighing the choice of distrib-uting $2 million as a cash dividend or repurchasing an equal amount of stock. If the firm pays a cash dividend, the shareholders pay ordinary income taxes on the entire $2 million (under the old tax law). However, if the firm buys back $2 million worth of its shares, the total tax bite is lower, because only the shareholders who chose to sell pay taxes, only the capital gain portion of the proceeds from the stock sale is tax-able, and the tax rate on capital gains is less than that on dividends. Investors who do not sell shares could defer paying taxes on their gains indefinitely.

The Jobs and Growth Tax Relief Reconciliation Act of 2003 reduced the tax ad-vantage for share repurchases. Dividends are now taxed at either 5 or 15 percent—the same rates that apply to capital gains income. Although too little time has elapsed since the passage of this act to tell what effect it will have on share repurchases and dividends, it seems clear that the tax incentive for American corporations to favor repurchases over dividends has weakened. The tax benefits have not been eliminated entirely. Repurchase programs still give investors the option to participate or not, so investors can still defer capital gains taxes indefinitely.

Companies use different methods to repurchase shares. In the most common ap-proach, an *open-market share repurchase,* firms buy back their shares in the open market. In a *tender offer,* or *self-tender,* firms offer to buy back a certain number of shares at a premium above the current market price. The market reaction to self-tender announcements is generally quite positive. In a Dutch auction repurchase, firms ask investors to submit prices at which they are willing to sell their shares. If the firm wants to buy back 2 million shares, it reviews the offers submitted by share-holders and determines the lowest price at which shareholders will tender 2 million shares. In a Dutch auction, all investors receive the same price when they sell back their shares, even if they expressed a willingness to sell at a lower price in their orig-inal offer.

The phenomenal growth in repurchases in the United States complicates our dis-cussion in this chapter, because it blurs exactly what we mean by "dividend payout." Repurchases today equal between one-third and one-half the total value of dividends. Therefore, corporate payout policy encompasses both dividends and repurchases.[9] Academic research shows that dividends and repurchases are complements: Firms paying high dividends also tend to do more repurchases. In the following sections, we adopt the term *payout policy* to refer to both types of cash distributions. We use the narrower term *dividend policy* when we discuss the payment of dividends.

Concept Review Questions	**1.** What policies and payments comprise a firm's "dividend policy"? Why is determining divi-dend policy more difficult today than in decades past?

[9.] Michaely and Allen (2002) point out that an even broader definition of "payout" encompasses cash payments for shares acquired by bidding firms in mergers and acquisitions. Because the acquired firm disappears as a separate entity after the merger, cash payments by the acquirer to the target's stockholders are effectively the same as a liquidating cash dividend. In recent years, cash payments in mergers have exceeded the combined value of share repurchases and ordinary dividends, which means that the total cash payout from the corporate sector significantly exceeds the total net profits of U.S. com-panies every year. This "excess payout" must be financed with new security issues (roughly one-third equity, two-thirds debt) and net borrowing from financial institutions.

2. What do you think the typical stock market reaction is to the announcement that a firm will increase its dividend payment? Why?

3. Assume you are the sole owner of a profitable, private U.S. corporation. What do you think would be the most tax-efficient method of receiving ownership income (via salary, perks, retained earnings, or dividends)?

4. Well-diversified investors are willing to tolerate great volatility in the prices of stocks they own. Why do you think they might value a constant dividend payment, even though the underlying corporate profits on which dividends are ultimately based are highly variable?

15.2 PATTERNS OBSERVED IN PAYOUT POLICIES WORLDWIDE

By observing worldwide dividend payment and share repurchase patterns we can clarify what a robust theory of payout policy should explain. The following stylized facts reveal remarkable similarities in the dividend policies observed around the world, but there are equally fascinating differences as well.

PAYOUT PATTERNS OBSERVED

1. Payout policies show distinct national patterns. Table 15.2 shows that companies that are headquartered in countries with legal systems based on English common law generally have higher dividend payout ratios than do companies that are headquartered in countries with civil law systems. British, Australian, Singaporean, and South African firms have especially high payout ratios, whereas U.S. firms are nearer the global average.[10] French and Italian firms tend to have lower payouts than do other Western companies. Companies that are headquartered in developing countries typically have very low dividend payouts, if they pay dividends at all. Many factors influence these patterns, but the nation's legal system seems especially important. Common law countries that rely heavily on capital markets for financing tend to see higher dividend payments than do continental European and other countries, which rely more on financial intermediaries.[11] Countries with a strong socialist tradition or those with a long history of state involvement in the economy tend to discourage dividend payments to private investors.[12]

2. Payout policies show pronounced industry patterns, and these are the same worldwide. Large, profitable firms in mature industries tend to pay out much larger frac-

---

[10] Having the United States fall in the mid-range of national payout policies actually represents a major break with the past. American companies have historically ranked near the top of the dividend payout league, but this has changed since the early 1990s, for three reasons. First, as noted earlier, share repurchases have grown dramatically in recent years. Including these with dividends once again makes the United States a high-payout country. Second, as discussed in Fama and French (2001), a far lower fraction of publicly traded U.S. firms pay dividends today than in the past—and those that do pay dividends pay out less than in previous years. Third, European and Japanese companies have significantly increased their payout ratios since the early 1990s. America would also be classified as a high-payout country if payout is measured in a macro-economic sense, as total dividends divided by total corporate profits, rather than by measuring the average payout of the population of listed companies, due to the concentration of earnings and dividends documented by DeAngelo, DeAngelo, and Skinner (2004).

[11] LaPorta, Lopez-de-Silanes, Shleifer, and Vishny (2000) document the importance of common law codes versus civil law codes in explaining differences in dividend payout. Dewenter and Warther (1998) compare U.S. and Japanese corporate dividend payment patterns.

[12] Several studies document that state-owned enterprises that are privatized significantly increase (or initiate) dividend payouts after divestment. These are summarized in D'Souza and Megginson (1999).

Table 15.2
Dividend Payout
Measures for OECD and
Selected Developing
Countries

Country	Number of Firms	Dividends to Cash Flow (%)	Dividends to Earnings (%)	Dividends to Sales (%)
Belgium	33	11.77%	39.38%	1.09%
Denmark	75	6.55	17.27	0.71
Finland	39	8.08	21.27	0.77
France	246	9.46	23.55	0.63
Germany	146	12.70	42.86	0.83
Italy	58	9.74	21.83	0.92
Japan	149	13.03	52.88	0.72
Netherlands	96	11.29	30.02	0.74
Norway	50	10.74	23.91	0.98
Spain	33	15.77	30.45	1.04
Sweden	81	5.59	18.33	0.78
Switzerland	70	10.38	25.30	0.98
Civil Law Median	**33**	**9.74%**	**25.11%**	**0.83%**
Australia	103	22.83%	42.82%	2.22%
Canada	236	8.00	19.78	0.78
Hong Kong	40	35.43	45.93	7.51
Malaysia	41	15.29	37.93	3.12
Singapore	27	22.28	41.04	2.14
South Africa	90	16.16	35.62	1.90
United Kingdom	799	16.67	36.91	1.89
United States	1,588	11.38	22.11	0.95
Common Law Median	**40**	**18.28%**	**37.42%**	**2.02%**
Sample Median	**39**	**11.77%**	**30.02%**	**0.98%**

Source: Rafael LaPorta, Florencio Lopez-de-Silanes, Andrei Shleifer, and Robert W. Vishny, "Agency Problems and Dividend Policies around the World," *Journal of Finance* 55 (February 2000), pp. 1–33.
Note: This table classifies countries by legal origin (civil law versus common law) and presents three measures of average dividend payout for the firms from each country.

tions of their earnings than do firms in younger, more rapidly growing industries. Utility and transportation companies have very high dividend payouts in almost every country, while high-technology firms have low payouts. The most important influences on payout decisions appear to be industry growth rate, capital investment needs, profitability, earnings variability, and asset characteristics (the mix between tangible and intangible assets).[13] Table 15.3 lists average dividend payout ratios for several U.S. industries.

3. Asset-rich, regulated, and slow-growing companies tend to have high dividend payout ratios. Companies in which tangible assets make up a large fraction of total value tend to have higher dividend payouts, whereas companies in which intangible assets are more important tend to have low payouts. Furthermore, regulated companies (particularly utilities) pay out more of their earnings than do unregulated companies. The relationship between dividend payout and growth rate is equally clear. Rapidly growing firms hoard cash and pay low dividends. As these companies ma-

---

[13.] Four recent empirical studies document these relationships. See Smith and Watts (1992), Gaver and Gaver (1993), Barclay, Smith, and Watts (1995), and Fama and French (2002).

Table 15.3
Dividend Payout Ratios
for Selected U.S.
Industries

Industry	Simple Average Payout Ratio (%)	Weighted Average Payout Ratio (%)
Biotechnology	0	0
Airlines	0	0
Computer software	0	0
Semiconductors	8.3[a]	14.1[a]
Computer hardware	14.3	19.9
Transportation: Commercial	21.0	22.6
Insurance: Property and casualty	22.3	18.5
Pharmaceuticals	24.3	23.1
Aerospace and defense	29.3[a]	35.7[a]
Natural gas distribution	35.3[a]	36.1[a]
Foods and nonalcoholic beverages	36.5	37.2
Autos and auto parts	40.7[a]	40.2[a]
Electric utilities	41.4	44.5
Banking	41.7[a]	33.7[a]
Household nondurables	43.0	44.2
Alcoholic beverages and tobacco	49.5	47.6
Paper and forest products	49.5[a]	62.8[a]
Telecommunications: Wireless	51.0[a]	49.8[a]
Oil and gas production and marketing	52.0	52.5
Metals: Industrial	57.0	77.1
Telecommunications: Wireline	63.0	68.37
Basic chemicals	73.7	74.1

Source: Standard and Poors Corporation, *Industry Reports*, various issues (July–December 2003).

Notes: This table describes the average dividend payout ratios for the four largest companies in selected American industries (based on sales), using data presented in Standard and Poors' *Industry Reports*, from July to December 2003. The simple average ratio gives equal weight to all four firms in an industry, whereas the weighted average weights firms by their most recent annual sales.

[a]Average based on three firms instead of four, due to extremely high payout ratios (over 125%) resulting from very low (or negative) levels of earnings for one firm.

ture, dividend payouts typically increase. Table 15.4 reports payout ratios and dividend yields for the 35 most valuable U.S. companies in 2004. Rapidly growing and/or high-technology companies, such as Cisco and Dell, pay no dividends; slower-growing, less-high-technology firms, such as Coca-Cola, JP Morgan Chase, and SBC Communications, pay out more than half their net profits and have relatively high dividend yields.

4. Firms maintain constant nominal dividend payments per share for significant periods of time. Put another way, companies tend to "smooth" dividends, which show far less variability than do the corporate profits on which they are based.[14] In the terminology introduced in Section 15.1, firms follow a policy of constant nominal dividend payments (regular dividends), with partial adjustments made as earnings change. Managers do not increase per-share dividends until they believe that "permanent" earnings have increased enough to support a higher dividend. Even then, managers increase dividend payments gradually to reach a new equilibrium payment.

[14.] The tendencies of firms to smooth dividends and make partial adjustments were first described by Lintner (1956) and Fama and Babiak (1968). More recently, Garrett and Priestley (2000) examined dividend smoothing empirically.

Table 15.4   Dividend Ratios for Selected U.S. Corporations in 2004

Company	Industry	Payout Ratio (%)	Dividend Yield (%)	Annual Dividend per Share ($)	Market-to-Book Ratio[a]
Cisco Systems	Computer systems	0	0	0	5.19
Intel	Semiconductors	14%	1.33%	$0.32	3.75
Dell Computer	Computer hardware	0	0	0	15.21
IBM	Computer hardware	15	0.74	0.72	5.09
HP	Computer hardware	28	1.50	0.28	1.59
Microsoft	Computer software	43	1.17	0.32	3.91
Berkshire Hathaway	Insurance, conglomerate	0	0	0	1.61
Home Depot	Retailing	15	0.81	0.34	3.81
Wal-Mart	Retailing	23	0.99	0.52	4.67
Time Warner	Entertainment, media	0	0	0	1.56
Viacom	Entertainment, media	82	0.78	0.28	0.96
UPS	Transportation	40	1.30	1.12	5.95
Exxon Mobil	Integrated petroleum	30	2.17	1.08	3.25
ChevronTexaco	Integrated petroleum	31	3.07	1.60	2.69
American Intl Group	Financial	6	0.46	0.30	2.18
American Express	Financial	18	0.87	0.48	4.21
Fannie Mae	Financial	27	2.95	2.08	3.27
Wells Fargo	Financial	48	3.11	1.92	2.86
Bank of America	Financial	49	3.93	1.80	2.62
Citigroup	Financial	51	3.48	1.60	2.34
J. P. Morgan Chase	Financial	70	3.60	1.36	1.72
PepsiCo	Consumer products	39	1.82	0.92	6.38
3M	Consumer products	40	1.83	1.44	7.08
Procter & Gamble	Consumer products	41	1.85	1.00	7.03
Coca-Cola	Consumer products	53	2.49	1.00	6.24
Altria Group	Consumer products	58	5.06	2.92	4.55
Amgen	Pharmaceuticals	0	0	0	3.60
Johnson & Johnson	Pharmaceuticals	37	1.89	1.14	5.86
Merck	Pharmaceuticals	56	5.45	1.52	3.58
Pfizer	Pharmaceuticals	57	2.50	0.68	3.04
Eli Lilly	Pharmaceuticals	60	2.65	1.42	5.87
General Electric	Conglomerate	52	2.27	0.80	4.30
Comcast	Telecommunications, cable	0	0	0	1.58
SBC Communications	Telecommunications	80	4.92	1.25	2.16
Verizon Communications	Telecommunications	128	3.72	1.54	3.32

Sources: Dividend data for each company's from http://money.cnn.com (December 7, 2004).

Notes: This table presents the annual dividend payment, as well as dividend yield and payout ratios, for the 35 most valuable publicly traded U.S. corporations in May 2004, as reported in "The Business Week Global 1000," *Business Week* (July 26, 2004). Companies are listed from the industry with the lowest leverage (semiconductors) to the industry with the highest leverage (telecommunications).

[a]Per-share price of company stock, divided by the per-share book value of shareholders' common equity.

Likewise, corporate managers try to maintain constant per-share dividends, even when earnings fall. Facing a persistent earnings decline, managers will then reduce dividends, and they will make the full downward adjustment in one large cut.[15]

[15.] The extreme reluctance of managers to reduce or eliminate dividends is documented in DeAngelo and DeAngelo (1990) and DeAngelo, DeAngelo, and Skinner (1992).

5. **Whereas the number (and fraction) of publicly traded companies that pay dividends has been declining since roughly the 1970s, the aggregate payout ratio of the U.S corporate sector has been increasing.** Figure 15.5 shows how the fraction of net income distributed by U.S. corporations varied from 1972 to 2001. Whether we look at dividends alone or include repurchases in the analysis, American corporations have increased their payout ratios since the 1970s. Because large firms account for a large fraction of aggregate dividend payments, total dividend payments can rise even while the percentage of firms paying dividends falls, precisely the pattern observed in recent years.

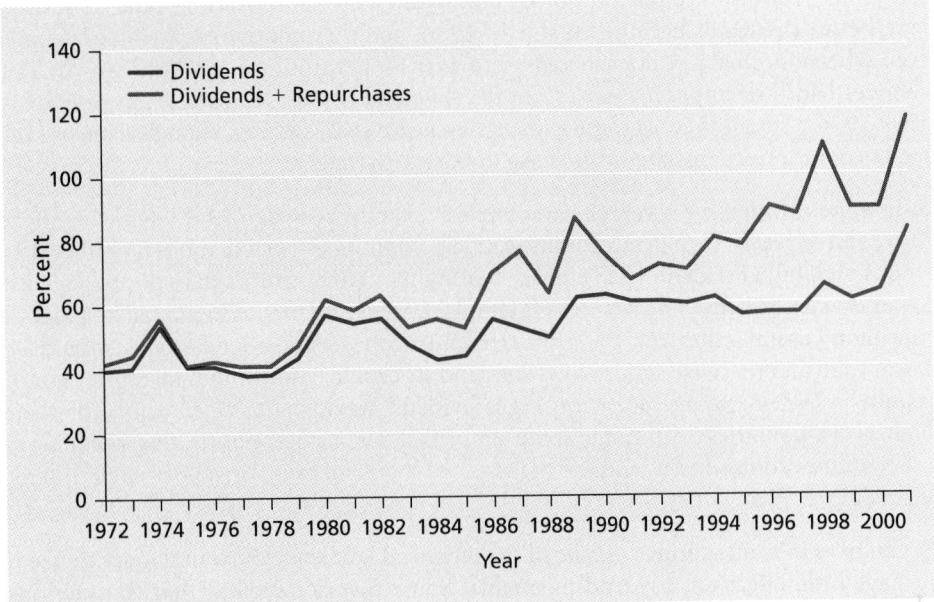

Figure 15.5
Aggregate Payout Ratio (Dividends and Share Repurchases) for the U.S. Corporate Sector, 1972–2001
Source: Table B-90, Economic Report of the President (2002) and Thomson Financial Securities Data, as reported in Table 2 of J. Fed Weston and Juan A. Siu (2003) "Changing Motives for Share Repurchases," *Finance* Paper 3 (2003), Anderson Graduate School of Management, UCLA.

6. **Investors react positively to dividend (and share repurchase) initiations and increases but react negatively to dividend decreases or eliminations.** When a company announces either its first regular cash dividend payment (an initiation) or an increase in its existing per-share dividend, that company's stock price typically increases by 1 to 3 percent. A similar response occurs when firms announce share repurchase programs.[16] Investors apparently interpret dividend increases as a sign that earnings will remain high. On the other hand, the markets punish firms that cut dividends, often shaving 25 percent or more from the company's stock price. Because of the market's severe reaction, managers cut dividends only in dire circumstances.

> **APPLYING THE MODEL 15.2**
>
> On February 18, 2003, the NorthWestern Corporation announced that it was suspending its common stock dividend to free up $48 million to help pay down its $2.2 billion debt burden. NorthWestern thus became the 11th publicly traded

---

[16.] Dividend initiations were first studied in Asquith and Mullins (1983), while Aharony and Swary (1980) present the first large-sample study of the wealth effects of announcements of dividend increases and decreases. Ghosh and Woolridge (1988) and Healy and Palepu (1988) were the first to examine dividend omissions. The magnitude of the price response to share repurchase announcements is much larger when firms engage in a tender offer for their own shares, paying a premium price for a limited time to repurchase a limited number of shares. In most cases, firms repurchase shares in the open market, and these announcements yield significantly positive stock returns.

electric utility to cut its dividend as a result of the industry-wide credit crunch that followed Enron Corporation's collapse in late 2001. The firm also announced plans to sell off noncore assets to raise cash. Following the news of the dividend cut, NorthWestern's shares fell by 7 percent.

7. Taxes influence payout policies, but taxes neither cause nor prevent companies from initiating dividend payments or share repurchases. It seems obvious that levying personal income taxes on dividends should reduce the demand for dividends and thus prompt companies to retain more of their profits. In the extreme, very high tax rates should cause firms to stop paying dividends entirely. Plausible as these arguments may be, they are not supported empirically. U.S. corporations paid dividends long before dividends became taxable in 1936, and they continued paying dividends even when marginal tax rates increased to over 90 percent during World War II. Tax changes had little apparent impact on the dividend payout ratios of U.S. companies after 1936, though there is some evidence that the 2003 tax law change is encouraging corporations to initiate or increase dividend payments.[17]

8. In spite of intensive research, it is unclear exactly how dividend payments affect the required return on a firm's common stock. Some asset-pricing models predict that stocks with high dividend yields must offer higher pretax returns than do stocks with lower dividend yields. The intuition is simple; because dividends are taxed at a higher rate than capital gains are, the after-tax return on high-dividend stocks should be lower than on otherwise similar low-dividend stocks. In equilibrium, investors should require a higher pretax return on high-dividend stocks as compensation for their higher tax liabilities. Although some empirical research supports this prediction, other studies contradict it, and the net effect of dividend taxes on equity valuation remains unresolved.

9. Changes in transactions costs or in the technical efficiency of capital markets seem to have little effect on dividend payments. Some theories suggest that transactions costs should cause investors to value dividends, since these put cash in investors' hands without requiring them to pay brokerage commissions or other transactions costs. This logic suggests investors should demand more dividends if transactions costs rise and fewer dividends if trading costs fall. However, a simple observation contradicts this notion. Transactions cost have declined dramatically since the 1970s, especially in the United States, yet dividend payout ratios have either remained the same or increased.

10. Ownership matters. One of the most enduring patterns worldwide is that private and closely held companies rarely pay dividends, but publicly traded companies tend to pay out large fractions of their earnings each year.[18] In almost every country and every industry, firms with tight ownership structures, composed of a few controlling shareholders, tend to have very low dividend payouts. Widely held companies with diffuse ownership tend to have higher payouts.

[17.] Studies that find little or no relationship between taxes and dividends include Poterba (1987), Eades, Hess, and Kim (1984, 1994), Barclay (1987), and Christie and Nanda (1994). However, more recent studies find that tax policy can affect firms' decisions to pay dividends and the valuation consequences of those decisions. Among these studies are Cannavan, Finn, and Gray (2004), Y-T Lee, Liu, Roll, and Subrahmanyam (2004), Graham, Michaely, and Roberts (2003), Julio and Ikenberry (2004), and Blouin, Raedy, and Shackleford (2004).

[18.] This relationship is documented in Walker and Petty (1978) and in Dwyer and Lynn (1989). Lipson, Macquieira, and Megginson (1998) examine why managers of newly public companies take the essentially irreversible step of initiating regular cash dividend payments.

INTRODUCTION TO THE AGENCY COST MODEL OF DIVIDENDS

It is hard to imagine a single theoretical model explaining all the dividend patterns just described. Nonetheless, several theoretical models have been developed, and each has garnered some empirical support. We concentrate on one of these, the **agency cost/contracting model** of dividends (or simply, the agency cost model). We also briefly introduce the agency cost model's two principal competitors, the signaling model and the new catering theory of dividends.

The agency cost model assumes that firms begin paying to overcome the agency problems resulting from a separation of corporate ownership and control. In privately held companies with tight ownership structures, there is little separation between ownership and control. Because agency problems in these firms are minimal, dividends are unnecessary. Even after a company goes public, it rarely begins paying dividends immediately, because ownership remains concentrated for several years after an IPO. Eventually, ownership becomes widely dispersed, as firms raise new equity capital and as the original owners diversify their holdings. With dispersed ownership, few investors have the incentive or the ability to monitor corporate managers, so agency problems become especially severe in large, mature firms that generate substantial free cash flow. Managers naturally face temptation to spend this cash, even when good investment opportunities are scarce. Investors understand these temptations and will pay a low price for manager-controlled firms that hoard cash. On the other hand, shareholders pay higher prices for companies with more responsive managers who commit to pay out free cash flow by initiating dividend payments. This model thus explains why dividend initiations or increases increase stock prices. Other aspects of the model help explain cross-sectional variations in dividend payments, based on industry growth rates, firm size, or asset characteristics.

APPLYING THE MODEL 15.3

The agency cost model predicts that dividend-paying firms are older and larger than nonpaying companies. It also predicts that dividend payers have fewer growth opportunities. The data for U.S. firms confirm these predictions. If we compare U.S. firms that pay dividends with firms that do not, we find that the average market value of dividend payers is more than seven times larger than that of nonpayers, and payers grow much more slowly. The average age of dividend payers is more than twice the average age of nonpayers.

	Dividend Payers	Nonpayers
Market cap ($ in millions)	$8,998	$1,222
Sales growth (%)	3.2%	5.1%
Firm age (years)	27.4	11.9

Note: Figures determined by author's calculations and Compustat. Dividend payers are firms that paid dividends in 1999, and nonpayers are those that did not. Market capitalization is as of 1999. Sales growth is the compound annual growth rate in sales, from 1999 to 2002, for the median firm in each group. Firm age is calculated based on the number of years of data available.

Grullon, Michaely, and Swaminathan (2002) show that firms that increase dividends become less profitable and less risky, whereas the opposite happens to firms that cut dividends. Similarly, dividend-increasing firms cut back on capital spending after raising payouts, whereas dividend-decreasing firms increase capital expenditures. These results are broadly consistent with the agency cost model. When a firm has many profitable investment opportunities on hand, it reinvests more cash and distributes less to investors. When a firm's investment opportunities dim, it pays higher dividends, rather than reinvesting its cash in negative-NPV projects.

The **signaling model** of dividends assumes that managers use dividends to convey positive information to poorly informed shareholders.[19] Cash dividends are costly, both to the paying firms, because this reduces the amount of money the firm can invest, and to shareholders receiving the dividends, because they must pay taxes on the dividends received. This means that only the "best" (most profitable) firms can bear the costs of paying dividends. Weaker firms cannot mimic the dividend payments of strong firms, so dividends help investors solve an asymmetric information problem —distinguishing between high-quality and low-quality firms. Like the agency cost model, the signaling model predicts that stock prices should rise (fall) in response to dividend increases (cuts). However, the signaling model also predicts that firms with high-growth opportunities will pay higher dividends, contrary to the empirical evidence.

The **catering theory** of dividends, proposed by Baker and Wurgler (2004a), predicts that corporate managers cater to investor preferences by paying dividends when investors assign a premium to dividend-paying stocks and by not paying when investors assign a discount to dividend payers. In other words, corporations respond more or less passively to investor preferences regarding whether profits should be distributed as dividends or retained inside the firm. The empirical evidence in Baker and Wurgler (2004b) suggests that the catering theory explains observed U.S. dividend payments over 1963–2000 better than alternative models, so this theory may have merit. Nonetheless, it does not adequately describe why dividends are paid in the first place, nor does it explain what causes investors to change their preferences over time.

Nearly all the theoretical and empirical work that has broadened our understanding of dividend policy since the 1960s owes an intellectual debt to the early work of Miller and Modigliani (1961). Much like their work on capital structure, Miller and Modigliani's research on dividends reached the surprising (at the time) conclusion that a manager could not influence a firm's value by changing its dividend policy. Miller and Modigliani proved that dividend policy is irrelevant when markets are perfect. Therefore, modern research on dividends usually begins by studying how a particular market imperfection might reverse the irrelevance conclusion and lead to an optimal dividend policy. The next section reviews Miller and Modigliani's conclusions regarding dividend policy.

Concept Review Questions

5. How do average dividend payout ratios for companies headquartered in English common law countries compare with those of companies headquartered in civil law countries? What explains this difference?

6. If high-dividend stocks offer a higher expected (and required) return than low-dividend stocks, due to the higher personal taxes levied on the former, why don't corporations simply reduce dividend payments and thus lower their cost of capital?

[19.] The first major dividend signaling paper was by Bhattacharya (1979). Important subsequent signaling models were developed in Miller and Rock (1985), John and Williams (1985), Ambarish, John, and Williams (1987), John and Lang (1991), and Noe and Rebello (1996).

15.3 DIVIDEND IRRELEVANCE IN A WORLD WITH PERFECT CAPITAL MARKETS

In a world of frictionless capital markets, payout policy cannot affect the market value of the firm. Value derives solely from the profitability of the firm's assets and the competence of its management team. Even without perfect markets, we must show how dividend policy *will* matter if frictions such as taxes, transactions costs, information asymmetries, and other market imperfections exist.

The notion that dividends are irrelevant appears to be a contradiction. After all, we argued in Chapter 4 that a stock's value equals the present value of its future dividend payments. How then do we arrive at a dividend-irrelevance result? As with capital structure, the answer emerges that a firm's value derives solely from its current and expected future operating profits. As long as the firm accepts all positive-*NPV* investment projects and has *costless* access to capital markets, it can pay any level of dividends it desires. But if a firm pays out its earnings as a dividend, it must issue new shares to raise the cash required to finance its ongoing investments. So a company can retain all its profits and finance its investments with internally generated cash flow, or it can pay out all its earnings as dividends and raise the cash needed for investment by selling new shares. As usual, this principle is best explained with an example.

Consider two firms, Retention and Payout, which are the same size today (January 1, 2007), are in the same industry, and have access to the same investment opportunities. Suppose both companies have assets worth $20 million that will generate a net cash inflow of $2 million by December 31, 2007. Each firm thus earns a 10 percent return on investment. Furthermore, assume investors require a return, r, of 10 percent per year and that at the end of this year each company will have the opportunity to invest $2 million in a positive-*NPV* project. Each company currently has 1 million shares outstanding, implying a share price of $20 ($P_{\text{Jan07}} = \$20$). Payout's managers want to pay out the firm's earnings as dividends and finance the $2 million investment by issuing new shares. Retention's managers prefer to retain the firm's earnings to fund the $2 million investment program. If each management team pursues its preferred strategy, will the two firms still have identical values next year?

Yes. To see how, we first examine Retention's strategy. Retention's managers finance the $2 million investment project by retaining $2 million in profits. Retention's market value on December 31, 2007, equals the $20 million beginning value, plus the $2 million ($2 per share) in reinvested earnings, plus the investment's net present value. For simplicity, assume that the project's *NPV* is positive but small enough to be ignored. Retention's year-end 2007 value is $22 million ($20 million + $2 million), or $22 per share ($P_{\text{Dec07}} = \$22$), because the firm did not have to issue any new shares to finance its investments. Plugging these data into our basic valuation equation from Chapter 4 verifies that Retention's shareholders indeed earn their required 10 percent return on investment:

$$r = \frac{D_{2007} + P_{Dec07} - P_{Jan07}}{P_{Jan07}} = \frac{\$0 + \$22 - \$20}{\$20} = 10\%$$

We can extend this example indefinitely into the future. In each period, Retention commits to reinvesting all its annual profits (10% return on assets), and shareholders earn an acceptable return because their share values increase 10 percent each year. Retention never issues new shares, so the number of outstanding shares remains fixed at 1 million.

So far, so good. But what about firm Payout? This company's managers decide to pay a $2 million dividend at the end of the year, so they must raise the $2 million needed for investment by selling new shares. But how many shares must they sell? To answer that, we must deduce what the price of Payout's shares will be on December 31, 2007. After it distributes the dividend, Payout will have assets worth $20 million, exactly what it started with on January 1. With 1 million shares outstanding, the share price will still be $20, so Payout must issue 100,000 new shares to raise the $2 million it needs to undertake its investment project. After the company issues new shares and invests the proceeds, Payout's total market value will equal $22 million ($20 per share × 1.1 million shares outstanding). Payout's market value of $22 million on December 31, 2007, matches Retention's value. We can verify that Payout's original shareholders earn the same 10 percent return earned by Retention's investors:

$$r = \frac{D_{2007} + P_{Dec07} - P_{Jan07}}{P_{Jan07}} = \frac{\$2 + \$20 - \$20}{\$20} = 10\%$$

Once again, we can repeat this process indefinitely. Each year, Payout distributes all of its net cash flow as a dividend, issuing new shares to finance new investments.

We have shown that the market values of Retention and Payout are equal on December 31, 2007, even though they follow radically different dividend policies. Retention has 1 million shares outstanding worth $22 each, while Payout has 1.1 million shares outstanding worth $20 each. Because both companies have a total value of $22 million, we can say that dividend policy is irrelevant to valuing a firm, at least when markets are frictionless. But what if Retention's investors prefer the company pay out earnings rather than reinvest them, or what if Payout's shareholders prefer that the company reinvest earnings rather than issue new shares? We reinforce dividend policy irrelevance by demonstrating in the following example that investors can "unwind" firms' dividend policy decisions. In the end, what is true for the firm as a whole is true for each investor: Dividend policy is irrelevant.

APPLYING THE MODEL 15.4

Consider two investors, Burt and Ernie. On January 1, 2007, Burt owns an 11 percent stake (110,000 shares) in Retention, whereas Ernie holds an 11 percent stake (also 110,000 shares) in Payout. By the end of 2007, Burt has received no dividend, but he still owns 11 percent of Retention's outstanding shares, which are now worth $22 each. Ernie, however, receives a $220,000 dividend during 2007, but because Payout issues 100,000 shares to finance its investment opportunity, the shares Ernie owns now represent only a 10 percent stake in Payout (110,000 ÷ 1,100,000).

If either Burt or Ernie is unhappy with the dividend policy of the firm in which he has invested, he can "unwind" that policy. For example, suppose Burt wishes to receive a dividend. At the end of 2007, Burt can sell 10,000 of his shares for $22 each, generating a cash inflow of $220,000, exactly equal to the dividend that Ernie receives on his investment. By selling some of his shares, Burt creates *home-made dividends*. By the end of the year, Burt owns just 10 percent of Retention's equity, but that's exactly equal to the ownership stake that Ernie holds in Payout.

Conversely, suppose that Ernie prefers that Payout did not pay dividends. The solution to Ernie's problem is simple. When he receives the $220,000 dividend, he simply reinvests the money by purchasing 11,000 new Payout shares. That would bring his total ownership to 121,000, or 11 percent, of Payout's shares (121,000 ÷ 1,100,000). In other words, Ernie's position is just like Burt's.

This may seem complex, but the essential points of these examples are simple. Investors don't care whether the firm (1) retains earnings to fund positive-*NPV* investments or (2) pays dividends and sells new shares to finance investments. In either case, cash flows from the firm's investments, not dividend decisions, determine shareholders' returns.

---

9. Imagine a firm that has an "intermediate" dividend policy compared to Payout and Retention. This firm pays out half its earnings to shareholders and finances new investment partially through new share issues and partially through retained profits. Describe how dissatisfied shareholders in this firm could "unwind" the dividend policy if they preferred either higher or lower dividends.

10. Managers of slow-growing, but profitable, firms (e.g., tobacco companies) *should* pay out these high earnings as dividends. What can they choose to do instead?

11. How do Miller and Modigliani (M&M) arrive at their conclusion that dividend policy is irrelevant in a world of frictionless capital markets? Why is the assumption of fixed investment policy crucial to this conclusion?

12. Around the world, utilities generally have the highest dividend payouts of any industry, yet they also tend to have massive investment programs to finance through external funding. How do you reconcile high payouts and large-scale security issuance?

Concept Review Questions

15.4 REAL-WORLD INFLUENCES ON DIVIDEND POLICY

Few of us ever trade in frictionless capital markets, so our next task is to examine whether dividend policy remains irrelevant when we account for realistic factors such as taxes, trading costs, and information differences between managers and investors. Our final goal is to determine whether a given firm has an "optimal" (value-maximizing) dividend policy and, if so, how managers should set that policy. As we proceed, you may notice a puzzling fact. Almost all the real-world issues we discuss —such as taxes, transactions costs, and uncertainty about a firm's investment opportunities—argue *against* paying dividends, yet both U.S. and non-U.S. companies pay out over half their annual earnings most years. We show that accounting for agency costs between managers and investors does a better job of explaining dividend policies than do arguments based on taxes or market frictions. In other words, dividends do not exist to overcome changing technical problems with markets and tax regimes; *dividends exist to overcome unchanging human problems with trust, communication, and commitment.*

PERSONAL INCOME TAXES

When the personal tax rate on dividends exceeds the tax rate on capital gains, we have a clear-cut prediction: Firms should not pay dividends. Instead, profitable companies should retain their earnings, and shareholders should realize returns by selling stock after it appreciates. Any distribution from the firm should be through a share repurchase program. This offers investors the choice of either receiving cash in a tax-favored form (as a capital gain) or foregoing the cash altogether by not selling shares and thus seeing their share values increase as their fractional ownership increases.

What if government imposes a large capital gains tax? Will that reestablish dividend-policy irrelevance? (Before reading on, see if you can reason through to an answer.) Apparently, imposing a capital gains tax at a rate equal to the dividend tax rate should make investors once more indifferent between receiving taxable dividends and receiving taxable capital gains. But this will happen only if the tax on stock appreciation is levied every period, regardless of whether investors sell their shares; such a levy is called a **wealth tax.** Although never used in the United States, such a tax has been tried in Norway and some other Western European countries. Most countries dictate that investors pay capital gains taxes only when they *realize* their gains by selling shares. Furthermore, in the United States and other countries, investors can avoid capital gains taxes by bequeathing stock to heirs. So investors generally have a tax preference for capital gains over dividends, even if the nominal tax rates for both types of income are the same.[20]

National governments that levy income taxes on corporate profits, and then tax these profits again at the personal level when firms pay dividends, have a **corporate tax system.** This creates the infamous double taxation of dividends. The U.S government has long used the corporate tax system, and while the Tax Relief Act of 2003 reduced the overall tax bite on corporate income, it did not eliminate double taxation. Many other industrialized countries, including Australia [described in Cannavan, Finn and Gray (2004)], employ an **imputation tax system.** This gives individual investors an "imputed" tax credit along with the dividends they receive from companies. The investors can then claim the corporate income tax paid by the firm as a credit against their personal tax liability. Since this system effectively eliminates double taxation, researchers can test whether personal taxes influence dividends by comparing payouts in countries with corporate tax systems and those with imputation tax systems. Unfortunately, the evidence is mixed; high-payout countries like Britain and Australia employ imputation system, but so do the low-payout countries France and Germany.

What else have researchers found regarding the effect of taxes on dividends? Researchers have employed two principal techniques to study tax effects. The first

---

[20.] Bell and Jenkinson (2002) describe an interesting example in Britain where just the opposite was true—an important class of investors had a tax preference for dividends over retained earnings. Prior to a tax law change in 1997, British pension funds and other tax-exempt investors could effectively receive a refund of personal income taxes withheld by the paying corporation on net dividends paid to stockholders. After the law was changed, the authors document a significant decline in the valuation of dividend income among those (high-yield) shares that should be most attractive to tax-exempt investors.

method tests whether investors demand a higher pretax return on high-dividend-paying stocks than they do on stocks paying a low dividend. We might expect such a differential if investors pay a higher effective tax rate on dividends than on capital gains. Studies using this approach show mixed results. Proponents of a tax-effect model also have great difficulty explaining why corporate managers would ever pay dividends if doing so resulted in a higher pretax required return. Managers could increase the firm's stock price and thus lower its cost of capital simply by cutting dividends.

The second way to test for tax effects is called an **ex-dividend-day study,** because it examines whether (and how) differing capital gains and dividend income tax rates impact the average change in a firm's stock price on its ex-dividend day. Consider the problem facing a taxable investor who holds a stock that has increased in value and who wants to sell it near an ex-dividend date. She can sell the stock before the ex-dividend date at the higher *cum-dividend* (with dividend) price—and take her return as a capital gain—or she can wait until the stock goes *ex-dividend,* sell the stock at a lower price, and receive the dividend. If personal tax rates on capital gains and dividend income are the same, and if our investor expects the stock price to fall by the full amount of the dividend payment, she is indifferent between selling before or after the ex-dividend day. Her expected after-tax return is the same either way. However, if capital gains are taxed at lower rates than are dividends, she prefers to sell shares before they go ex-dividend, since she earns a higher after-tax return than she does by receiving a dividend. The only circumstance where this investor is indifferent between taking the dividend and taking the capital gain is if she expects the stock price to fall on the ex-dividend day by less than the dividend payment. In that case, the higher pretax return from receiving the dividend offsets its tax disadvantage. The empirical observation that stock prices typically fall by less than the dividend (on average, by about 60–70 cents on the dollar) on the ex-dividend day has often been interpreted as evidence of a tax effect in dividend valuation.[21]

APPLYING THE MODEL 15.5

Three months ago, you purchased a share of stock for $20. Today that share sells for $22, a gain of 10 percent. The stock will pay a $2 dividend in a few days, and the ex-dividend date is tomorrow. Suppose you want to sell the stock, and you face a 33 percent tax rate on dividend income and a 20 percent tax rate on capital gains. If you sell today, you earn an after-tax profit of $1.60 ($2 capital gain minus $0.40 in taxes). That represents an 8 percent return on your original $20 investment. If you sell tomorrow, your after-tax return depends on how far the price drops when the stock goes ex-dividend. If the price drops by the full $2, then you earn no capital gain, and your after-tax profit equals $1.34 ($2 dividend minus $0.66 in taxes), or 6.7 percent. Clearly, in this scenario your after-tax return is higher if you sell the stock before it goes ex-dividend. However, suppose you expect the stock price to drop by just $1 on the ex-dividend day. In that case, if you wait to sell the stock, you receive a $1 capital gain (worth $0.80 after taxes) and a $2 dividend (worth $1.34 after taxes), for an after-tax return of $2.14, or 10.7 percent. In that case, it pays to wait for the dividend. Only when you expect the

[21] Modern ex-dividend studies trace their roots to Elton and Gruber (1970). Subsequent papers include those by Eades, Hess, and Kim (1984, 1994), Bell and Jenkinson (2002), Graham, Michaely, and Roberts (2003), and Jakob and Ma (2004).

stock to fall by $1.675 on the ex-dividend date would you be indifferent about selling now or waiting until the stock goes ex-dividend.

Although many ex-dividend-day studies show plausible results, it is unclear whether the price changes truly reflect differential tax effects, since transactions costs must be very high for a pure tax effect to occur. Tax-free traders have an incentive to buy stocks just before they go ex-dividend if they expect the price to decline by less than the dividend. For example, suppose the stock described earlier will soon pay a $2 dividend and that traders expect the price to drop by $1.67 on the ex-dividend date. Though a taxable investor is indifferent between selling the stock immediately or waiting to sell after it goes ex-dividend, a tax-free investor is not indifferent. This investor can buy the stock at $22, receive the $2 dividend, and then sell the stock immediately afterward for $20.33, generating a one-day profit of $0.33. If the transactions costs for this strategy do not exceed $0.33 per share, then tax-free investors can engage in profitable "dividend arbitrage." Dividend arbitrage will continue until the ex-dividend-day price drops by the full dividend (less the transactions costs of the arbitrage). Because the per-share cost of a round-trip trade can be as low as a few pennies today, the actions of tax-free investors should increase the ex-dividend-day price decline to almost the entire dividend.

Perhaps we may soon be able to determine, once and for all, if the ex-dividend-day price effect is indeed a tax effect. Since the Jobs and Growth Tax Relief Reconciliation Act of 2003 made the federal tax rate on dividends equal to the investor's marginal capital gains tax rate, there is now little tax reason to forego dividends. If taxes were driving the effect historically, the average ex-dividend-day stock-price drop should move closer to the dividend amount. If the average ex-dividend-day price drop remains below the dividend, this will suggest that differential personal tax rates are not the key influence on ex-dividend-day price changes.

On balance, incorporating personal taxes into our model does not help us understand why firms pay dividends. However, tax effects may account for some of the patterns we observe, such as the rise in share repurchase programs in the United States and other industrialized countries.

TRADING AND OTHER TRANSACTIONS COSTS

If personal taxes cannot explain dividends, what about transactions costs of issuing and trading stocks? Large trading costs affect payout incentives in two potentially offsetting ways. First, if investors find it costly to sell just a few shares to generate cash (i.e., to create homemade dividends), they might pay a premium for stocks that regularly pay dividends. This argument predicts that dividend payments will be highest in undeveloped markets with very high transactions costs. In reality, dividend payments are highest in developed countries with liquid, low-cost stock markets but are low or nonexistent in most developing countries. A transactions-cost argument also cannot explain why dividend payments in the United States have remained fairly high, even as transactions costs in U.S. markets have declined dramatically.

A corporation paying dividends may need to replace some of that cash by issuing shares, so the transactions cost of issuing new equity could discourage firms from paying dividends. Miller and Modigliani's dividend irrelevance assumes that companies can fund new investments either by retaining profits or by issuing new shares. As long as share issues are costless, investors are indifferent between receiving their returns as capital gains (on non-dividend-paying shares) or as dividends. If issuing securities entails large costs, however, all parties prefer a full-retention strategy. No corporation should ever both pay dividends and raise funds for investment by issuing new stock. Because many large corporations do just that, transactions costs alone obviously do not explain observed dividend policy.[22]

THE RESIDUAL THEORY OF DIVIDENDS

The previous discussion suggests another possible explanation of observed dividend payments. Might they simply be a *residual,* the cash left over after corporations have funded all their positive-*NPV* investments? This would help explain why firms in rapidly growing industries retain almost all their profits, whereas firms in mature, slow-growing industries tend to have very high dividend payouts. It would also explain the "life-cycle" pattern of dividend payments for individual firms, where young, fast-growing companies rarely pay dividends. But those same companies typically change to a high-payout strategy once they mature and their growth rate slows.

The **residual theory** of dividends probably has some merit, but it suffers from one massive empirical problem. Dividend payments do not vary as much as they would if firms viewed them as residuals from cash flow. In fact, dividend payments fluctuate less than almost any cash flow stream coming in or out of a firm. All available evidence suggests that corporate managers smooth dividends, and they hesitate to change established payout levels. Clearly, the residual theory is not the sole explanation of observed dividend payments.

PAYING DIVIDENDS AS A MEANS OF COMMUNICATING INFORMATION

Firms might pay dividends to convey information to investors. Can managers, who understand the firm's true financial condition better than do shareholders, convey this information to shareholders through their choice of dividend policy? Managers have a natural inclination to make positive public statements about their firms' prospects; but by committing to distribute cash through dividend payments, managers gain credibility in the markets. Investors know that weak firms, those without the ability to generate high positive cash flows in the future, are reluctant to make long-term commitments to distribute cash via dividends. Therefore, managers of high-quality firms can use dividends to help investors distinguish good firms from bad ones. Viewed this way, every aspect of a firm's dividend policy might convey significant new information.

What Type of Information Is Being Communicated? Perhaps a dividend conveys management's confidence that the firm is now profitable enough to fund its investment projects and pay out cash. Because investors and managers know that cutting or eliminating dividend payments, once that begins, results in a very negative market reaction, dividend initiations might signal management's assessment of the firm's long-term ability to generate cash.

The same logic applies to dividend increases. Because everyone understands the negative consequences of dividend cuts, management's willingness to increase dividend payments implies confidence that profits will remain high enough to support the new dividend level. Dividend increases suggest a *permanent* increase in a firm's profitability.[23] Unfortunately, this logic applies even more strongly to dividend de-

---

[22.] Interestingly, at least one academic researcher, Easterbrook (1984), suggests that corporations pay dividends precisely *because* this forces them into the capital market for financing (rather than relying solely on internal financing), where investors have the incentive and the ability to monitor and discipline corporate management.

[23.] Papers by B-S Lee (1995) and Koch and Sun (2004) discuss the relative importance of temporary versus permanent earnings changes in explaining dividend changes.

creases. Investors view dividend cuts as very bad news. Managers reduce dividend payments only when they have no choice, such as when there is a cash flow crisis. Therefore, it is no surprise that the market reaction is often severe when managers do cut dividends.

APPLYING THE MODEL 15.6

The period following the September 11, 2001, terrorist attacks on the World Trade Center and the Pentagon was extremely difficult for the world's airlines, including British Airways (BAY). In early October 2001, in response to severe financial pressures, British Airways suspended its December dividend payment. The company also announced that its full-year dividend for fiscal year 2002 was in serious jeopardy. This dividend suspension was very traumatic for BAY because the company had taken great pride in paying a dividend every six months since its privatization in 1987. Over the years, its dividend payment had increased steadily and stood at 17.8 pence per share for fiscal year 2001. In line with industry norms, this payment represented over 57 percent of BAY's net profits for 2001. But with massive financial losses looming and job cuts of 7,000 employees already announced, BAY's managers felt there was no alternative but to eliminate dividend payments. The firm was clearly fighting for financial survival.

There is much empirical support for the informational role of dividend payments, beginning with Lintner's (1956) article documenting that corporate managers approach dividend decisions with great care and adjust dividends very slowly. Fama and Babiak (1968) show that managers have target payout ratios in mind and that dividend payments track the course of corporate profits over time. However, Fama and Babiak also show that managers employ a partial adjustment strategy in adjusting dividend payments to changes in corporate profits, so higher dividends follow higher profits only after several quarters.

However, recent empirical studies contradict the idea that dividend increases imply that managers believe earnings will be higher in the future. DeAngelo, DeAngelo, and Skinner (1996) study the dividend decisions of firms that experience an earnings decline after a long period of growth. For these firms, dividends provide no clue about future earnings, for two reasons. First, managers tend to be overly optimistic about their firms' prospects, so they increase dividends even when the future is not as bright as the past. Second, managers adjust dividends in such small increments that changes in dividends do not really signal a major commitment to distribute additional cash. These small changes in dividends undermine the credibility of the signal. Benartzi, Michaely, and Thaler (1997) find that managers do not even try to forecast future earnings when they change dividend levels. Instead, firms alter dividends in response to *past* changes in earnings. There is essentially no correlation between a dividend change one year and earnings changes in subsequent years. The authors answer the question asked in their paper's title, "Do Changes in Dividends Signal the Future or the Past?" by concluding that dividends reflect what *has* happened rather than what *will* happen.[24]

[24.] Koch and Sun (2004) also show that the most important informational role dividends play is to verify the size and persistence of recent changes in reported company profits.

DIVIDEND PAYMENTS AS SOLUTIONS TO AGENCY PROBLEMS

In our opinion, the agency cost/contracting model, which emphasizes conflicts arising from the separation of ownership and control of large firms, best explains why corporations pay dividends. When firms are small and growing rapidly, they not only have tight ownership structures but also tend to have many profitable investment opportunities. Because these companies can profitably use all their internally generated cash flow, they have no reason to pay dividends. If their early investments succeed, these firms eventually generate lots of cash, even as new positive-*NPV* investments become increasingly scarce. Jensen (1986) defines free cash flow as any cash flow in excess of that needed to fund all positive-*NPV* projects. Managers of firms with free cash flow *should* begin to pay dividends to ensure that they will not invest the free cash flow in negative-*NPV* projects. However, managers may prefer to retain cash and spend it, because running a larger (though not necessarily more valuable) company offers increased status. Jensen asserts that if managers have proper incentives, they will pay out free cash flow rather than invest it unwisely.

The agency cost/contracting model makes three key predictions. First, it says that investors will interpret dividend-initiation announcements as good news, causing stock prices to rise. Second, firms (and industries) that generate the most free cash flow should also pay the highest dividends. Third, firms will design compensation contracts in a way that gives managers incentives to pursue a value-maximizing dividend policy. The empirical patterns described in Section 15.2 are all consistent with these predictions.

---

13. In what way can managers use dividends to convey pertinent information about their firms? Why would a manager choose to convey information this way? Does empirical evidence support or refute dividends' informational role?

14. Why is it difficult for a firm with weaker cash flows to mimic a dividend increase undertaken by a firm with stronger cash flows?

15. According to the residual theory, how does a firm set its dividend? With which dividend policy is this theory most compatible? Does it appear to be empirically validated?

16. Why should we expect a firm's stock price to decline by approximately the amount of the dividend payment on the ex-dividend date? Why do U.S. stock prices generally fall by less than the amount of the dividend payment?

Concept Review Questions

15.5 A CHECKLIST FOR DIVIDEND PAYMENTS

The agency cost model explains dividends as an attempt by managers to minimize the agency costs resulting from the separation of ownership and control. The severity of these agency problems relates to a firm's *investment opportunity set* and its *ownership structure*. A firm's investment opportunity set encompasses the industry in which it operates, the company's size, the capital intensity of its production process, the free cash flow generated, and its access to positive-*NPV* investment opportunities. Ownership structure refers to the number of shareholders, the size of each investor's holdings, and the presence or absence of active investors willing and able to monitor corporate managers. Transactions costs and taxes influence dividend pol-

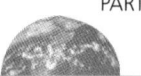

COMPARATIVE CORPORATE FINANCE

Dividend Policies of the 25 Most Valuable Non-U.S. Public Companies

Company Name	Country	Industry	Market Value, May 31, 2004 ($US Billions)	Dividend Payout Ratio (%)	Dividend Yield (%)	P/E Ratio
BP	*Britain*	*Petroleum*	*$193*	*61%*	*3.2%*	*19*
Royal Dutch Shell	Netherlands/UK	Petroleum	175	64	4.2	15
HSBC Holdings	Britain	Banking	161	53	4.1	13
Vodafone Group	Britain	Telecommunications	159	24	1.6	15
Toyota Motor	Japan	Automobiles	131	12	1.1	11
Novartis	Switzerland	Pharmaceuticals	126	43	1.8	24
GlaxoSmithKline	Britain	Pharmaceuticals	124	52	3.7	14
Total	*France*	*Petroleum*	*123*	*64*	*4.6*	*14*
Nestle	Switzerland	Food and beverages	105	46	2.2	21
Roche Holdings	Switzerland	Pharmaceuticals	96	48	1.3	37
Royal Bank of Scotland Group	Britain	Banking	94	31	3.1	10
NTT DoCoMo	*Japan*	*Telecommunications*	*92*	*8*	*0.5*	*15*
UBS	Switzerland	Banking	85	41	2.9	14
ENI	*Italy*	*Petroleum*	*82*	*59*	*4.5*	*13*
Nippon Telegraph & Telephone	*Japan*	*Telecommunications*	*79*	*12*	*0.9*	*13*
AstraZeneca	Britain	Pharmaceuticals	78	46	1.7	27
Telefonica	*Spain*	*Telecommunications*	*72*	*58*	*3.4*	*17*
Samsung	Korea	Electronics	71	17	1.1	15
Gazprom	*Russia*	*Natural gas*	*71*	*5*	*0.3*	*15*
Deutsche Telekom	Germany	Telecommunications	71	0	0	172
Nokia	Finland	Mobile phone manufacture	67	39	2.6	15
Unilever	Netherlands/UK	Consumer products	65	44	3.3	13
Aventis	*France*	*Pharmaceuticals*	*64*	*44*	*1.9*	*23*
Siemens	Germany	Engineering	63	30	1.9	16
France Telecom	*France*	*Telecommunications*	*59*	*21*	*1.9*	*11*

Note: As this table shows, the dividend policies of the world's most valuable companies are becoming increasingly similar, regardless of the country in which they are headquartered. Privatized companies, which are indicated with *italics*, have led the way in promoting high dividend payments by publicly traded, non-U.S. firms, especially since these are usually some of the largest and most valuable companies in most national markets. *Source:* "The Business Week Global 1000," *Business Week* (July 26, 2004).

icy, as do a country's legal system and the relative importance of capital markets and financial intermediaries in funding business investment.

DEVELOPING A CHECKLIST FOR DIVIDEND POLICY

This section summarizes what managers need to know about dividends. The following lists provide the predictions of the agency cost model about the relationship between corporate-level variables and dividends. The second column shows how an increase in each variable should affect dividend payments.

Firm-Level Variable	Effect of Increase on Dividend Payout
Asset growth rate	Reduce
Positive-*NPV* investment opportunities	Reduce
Capital intensity of the production process	Increase
Free cash flow generated	Increase
Number of individual shareholders	Increase
Relative "tightness" of ownership coalition	Reduce
Size of largest block holder	Reduce

In addition to firm-level variables, macroeconomic and national financial variables influence dividend payments. The following list details the agency cost/contracting model's predictions concerning these variables. Again, the second column shows the effect on dividend payout of an increase in each macroeconomic variable in the first column.

Macroeconomic Variable	Effect of Increase on Dividend Payout
Transactions costs of security issuance	Increase
Personal tax rates on dividend income	Reduce
Personal tax rates on capital gains income	Increase
Importance of institutional investors	Reduce
Corporate governance power of institutional investors	Reduce
Capital market, relative to intermediated (bank) financing	Increase

15.6 SUMMARY

- Public companies regularly pay out large fractions of their profits as dividends. These payments change slowly and do not fluctuate as much as earnings do. United States firms usually pay dividends quarterly, but annual and semiannual dividends are common elsewhere.
- Among developed countries, dividend payout ratios tend to be highest in British Commonwealth countries, whereas payouts are much smaller in most of continental Europe. The payout ratio for the U.S. corporate sector is very high, even though relatively few companies now pay cash dividends, because payments are concentrated among a few extremely large and profitable firm. However, some industries, such as utilities and transportation, have high dividend payouts in all countries. Others, such as high technology and health science industries, have low dividend payouts in all countries.
- Corporations repurchase shares partly because paying dividends triggers higher taxes for shareholders than does buying back stock. In recent years, repurchases by U.S. corporations have exceeded $100 billion per year, and dividend payments have been around $250 billion annually.
- Stock splits and stock dividends reduce stock prices. In a 2-for-1 split, for example, investors receive one new share for every existing share they own, and the stock price falls by roughly half.
- Without market imperfections, dividend policy is irrelevant and cannot affect a firm's value. The fact that many firms pay dividends is puzzling because most market imperfections (such as taxes) argue against paying dividends.

- Managers can use dividends to credibly convey inside information to investors, although research shows that dividends convey information about the company's past rather than its future. Specifically, dividends verify managers' beliefs about recently announced earnings changes.

- The agency cost/contracting model assumes that dividend payments reduce agency conflicts between corporate managers and external investors by committing the firm to pay out free cash flow. Dividend payments prevent managers from consuming these cash flows as perquisites or wasting them on unwise capital investments. Most of the empirical evidence supports this model.

- In addition to ownership considerations, several other aspects of a firm's operating and regulatory environment influence dividend payouts. Other things being equal, closely held corporations, which operate in a high-growth industry where large ongoing capital investments are needed to compete, have lower dividend payouts than do widely held firms in slow-growing or highly regulated industries.

INTERNET RESOURCES

Note: *For updates to links, please go to the book's website at http://smart.swcollege.com.*

http://www.tenpercentdividends.com—Describes how to identify and to invest in companies with high dividend yields

http://www.ex-dividend.com—Lists recent stock splits and dividend changes; includes record dates, ex-dividend dates, and payment dates

http://www.dripcentral.com—Describes what a dividend reinvestment plan (DRIP) is and how it works; lists the companies that offer these plans, which allow shareholders to automatically use the cash they receive in dividends to purchase additional shares of company stock

http://www.ishares.com/fund_info/detail.jhtml?symbol=DVY—The iShares Dow Jones Select Dividend Index Fund (NYSE ticker symbol DVY) is a basket of 100 of the highest dividend-yielding securities in the Dow Jones U.S. Total Market Index.

KEY TERMS

agency cost/contracting model	dividend yield	residual theory
catering theory	ex-dividend	reverse stock splits
constant nominal payment policy	ex-dividend-day study	share repurchase programs
constant payout ratio policy	excess earnings accumulation tax	signaling model
corporate tax system	extra dividend	special dividend
date of record	imputation tax system	stock dividend
dividend payout ratio	low-regular-and-extra policy	stock split
	payment date	target payout ratio
		wealth tax

QUESTIONS

15-1. What is a firm's dividend yield? How does this compare to that firm's dividend payout ratio?

15-2. What fraction of U.S. public companies pays regular dividends today? How has this changed over the past 50 years? What has happened to the average cash dividend payout ratio of U.S. corporations over time? What explains this trend? How would your answer change if share repurchases were included in calculating U.S. dividend payout ratios?

15-3.   How does the fraction of Nasdaq-listed companies that pay regular dividends compare to the fraction of NYSE-listed firms that regularly pay dividends? What accounts for this difference?

15-4.   What has happened to the total volume of share repurchases announced by U.S. public companies since 1982? Why did that year mark such an important milestone in the history of share repurchase programs in the United States?

15-5.   What do record date, ex-dividend date, and payment date mean with regard to dividends? Why would you expect the price of a stock to drop by the amount of the dividend on the ex-dividend date? What rationale has been offered for why this does not actually occur?

15-6.   Compare and contrast the constant payout ratio policy and the constant nominal payment policy. Which policy do most public companies actually follow? Why?

15-7.   What is a low-regular-and-extra policy? Why do firms pursuing this policy explicitly label some cash dividend payments as "extra"?

15-8.   What is a stock dividend? How does this differ from a stock split?

15-9.   What factors have contributed to the growth in share repurchase programs by American public companies over the past 15 years? What is the expected impact on share repurchase programs of the passage of the Jobs and Growth Tax Relief Reconciliation Act of 2003?

15-10. How do the industrial patterns observed for dividend payouts compare to the patterns observed for capital structures? For example, are industries characterized by high dividend payouts also characterized by high leverage?

15-11. What does it mean to say that corporate managers "smooth" cash dividend payments? Why do managers do this?

15-12. What is the average stock market reaction to: (a) a dividend initiation; (b) a dividend increase; (c) a dividend termination; and (d) a dividend decrease [cut]? Are these reactions logically consistent?

15-13. Around the world, utilities generally have the highest dividend payouts of any industry, yet they also tend to have massive investment programs to finance through external funding. How do you reconcile high payouts and large-scale security issuance?

15-14. What are the key assumptions and predictions of the agency cost/contracting model? Are these predictions supported by empirical research findings?

15-15. What are the key assumptions and predictions of the signaling model? Are these predictions supported by empirical research findings?

15-16. Why do firms with more-diverse shareholder bases typically pay higher dividends than private firms or public firms with more concentrated ownership structures? How are fixed dividends used as a bonding (commitment) mechanism by managers of firms with dispersed ownership structures and large amounts of free cash flow?

15-17. What is the expected relationship between dividend payout levels and the growth rate and availability of positive-*NPV* projects under the agency cost model? What about the expected relationship between dividend payout and the diffusion of firm shareholders? Free cash flow? Consider a firm such as Microsoft awash in free cash flow, positive-*NPV* projects available, and a relatively diffuse shareholder base in an industry with increasing competition. Does either the agency model or signaling model adequately predict the dividend policy of Microsoft? Which does the better job?

15-18. If a firm notices potentially profitable future opportunities, then, according to signaling theory, should the firm (a) cut dividends to retain money for project investment, (b) leave dividends at the current level and raise capital for funding new projects, or (c) increase the dividend and raise capital for funding new projects?

15-19. Investor A owns $1,000 worth of stock that does not pay a dividend. Investor B owns $1,000 of an equivalent stock that, after paying a dividend, becomes an investment in stock and cash: $900 in stock and $100 in dividend income. If the capital gains tax is lower than the tax on dividends, which investor has the better position: Investor A selling 10% of the stock to make an equivalent homemade dividend, or Investor B?

PROBLEMS

Dividend Fundamentals

15-1. Beta Corporation has the following shareholders' equity accounts

Common stock at par	$ 5,000,000
Paid-in capital in excess of par	$ 2,000,000
Retained earnings	$25,000,000
Total stockholders' equity	$32,000,000

   a. What is the maximum amount that Beta Corporation can pay in dividends without impairing its legal capital if it is headquartered in a U.S. state where capital is defined as the par value of common stock?

   b. What is the maximum amount that Beta Corporation can pay in dividends without impairing its legal capital if it is headquartered in a U.S. state where capital is defined as the par value of common stock plus paid-in capital in excess of par?

15-2. What are alternative ways in which investors can receive a cash return from their investment in the equity of a company? From a tax standpoint, which of these would be preferred, assuming that investors pay a 35% tax rate on dividends and a 15% tax rate on capital gains? What if investors faced the same 15 percent tax on income and capital gains? What are the pros and cons of paying out dividends?

15-3. Delta Corporation earned $2.50 per share during fiscal year 2006 and paid dividends of $1.00 per share. During the fiscal year that just ended on December 31, 2007, Delta earned $3.00 per share, and the firm's managers expect to earn this amount per share during fiscal years 2008 and 2009 as well.

   a. What was Delta's payout ratio for fiscal year 2006?

   b. If Delta's managers wish to follow a constant nominal dividend policy, what dividend per share will they declare for fiscal year 2007?

   c. If Delta's managers wish to follow a constant payout ratio dividend policy, what dividend per share will they declare for fiscal year 2008?

   d. If Delta's managers wish to follow a partial-adjustment strategy, with a target payout ratio equal to FY 2006's, how might they change dividend payments during 2007, 2008, and 2009?

15-4. General Manufacturing Company (GMC) follows a policy of paying out 50 percent of its net income as dividends to its shareholders each year. The company plans to do so again this year, during which GMC earned $100 million in net profits after tax. The company has 40 million shares outstanding and pays dividends annually.

   a. What is the company's nominal dividend payment per share each year?

   b. Assuming that GMC's stock price is $54 per share immediately before its ex-dividend date, what is the expected price of GMC stock on the ex-dividend date if there are no personal taxes on dividend income received?

15-5. General Manufacturing Company (GMC) follows a policy of paying out 50 percent of its net income as dividends to its shareholders each year. The company plans to do so again this year, during which GMC earned $100 million in net profits after tax. The company has 40 million shares outstanding and pays dividends annually. Assume that an investor purchased GMC stock a year ago at $45. The investor, who faces a personal tax rate of 15 percent on both dividend income and on capital gains, plans to sell the stock very soon. Transactions costs are negligible.

   a. Calculate the after-tax return this investor will earn if she sells GMC stock at the current $54 stock price prior to the ex-dividend date.

   b. Calculate the after-tax return the investor will earn if she sells GMC stock on the ex-dividend date, assuming that the price of GUC stock falls by the dividend amount on the ex-dividend date.

15-6. General Manufacturing Company (GMC) pays out 50 percent of its net income as dividends to its shareholders once each quarter. The company plans to do so again this year, during which GMC earned $100 million in net profits after tax. If the company has 40 million shares outstanding and pays dividends quarterly, what is the company's nominal dividend payment per share each quarter?

15-7. Twilight Company's stock is selling for $60.25 per share, and the firm's managers have just announced a $1.50-per-share dividend payment.

   a. What should happen to Twilight Company's stock price on the ex-dividend date, assuming that investors do not have to pay taxes on dividends or capital gains and do not incur any transactions costs in trading shares?

   b. What should happen to Twilight Company's stock price on the ex-dividend date, assuming that it follows the historical performance of U.S. stock prices on ex-dividend days?

   c. If the historical "ex-dividend-day price effect" observed in U.S. stock markets was indeed a tax effect, what should happen to Twilight Company's stock price on the ex-dividend date, given the tax changes embodied in the Jobs and Growth Tax Relief Reconciliation Act of 2003?

15-8. Global Financial Corporation (GFC) has 10 million shares outstanding, each of which is currently worth $80 per share. The firm's managers are considering a plan to split the company's stock two-for-one, but are concerned with the impact this split announcement will have on the firm's stock price.

   a. If GFC's managers announce a two-for-one stock split, what exactly will the company do and what will GFC's stock price likely be after the split?

   b. How many total shares of GFC stock will be outstanding after the stock split?

   c. If GFC's managers believe the "ideal" stock price for the firm's shares is $20 per share, what should they do? How many shares would be outstanding after this action?

   d. Why do you think GFC's managers are considering a stock split?

15-9. Maggie Fiduciary is a shareholder in the Superior Service Company (SSC). The current price of SSC's stock is $33 per share, and there are 1 million shares outstanding. Maggie owns 10,000 shares, or 1 percent of the stock, which she purchased one year ago for $30 per share. Assume that SSC makes a surprise announcement that it plans to repurchase 100,000 shares of its own stock at a price of $35 per share. In response to this announcement, SSC's stock price increases $1 per share, from $33 to $34, but this price is expected to fall back to $33.50 per share after the repurchase is completed. Assume that Maggie faces marginal personal tax rates of 15 percent on both dividend income and capital gains.

   a. Calculate Maggie's (realized) after-tax return from her investment in SSC shares, assuming that she chooses to participate in the repurchase program and all of the shares she tenders are purchased at $35 per share.

   b. How many shares will Maggie be able to sell if all SSC's shareholders tender their shares to the firm as part of this repurchase program and the company purchases shares on a pro rata basis?

   c. What fraction of SSC's total common equity will Maggie own after the repurchase program is completed if she chooses not to tender her shares?

15-10. The net income for a firm is currently $1,000,000 and is projected to grow annually for the next four years as follows: $1,200,000, $1,300,000, $1,500,000, and $1,700,000. Assuming the dividend payout ratio is 20% and there are 1,000,000 shares outstanding, what is the current dividend per share? Further assuming that the firm does not change its nominal dividend, what is the dividend payout ratio for the next four years? (*Note:* All figures are in thousands.)

15-11. A firm's shares currently sell for $32.48, with 5 million shares outstanding. The firm is considering a 20% stock dividend in which 100 shares become 120 shares. After the stock dividend, at what price will the shareholders' value be unchanged? (*Hint:* Consider shareholder value to be the market capitalization, which equals the number of shares outstanding multiplied by the stock price.) If the stock price became $27.50 after the stock dividend, do the shareholders benefit?

15-12. A firm's shares currently sell for $3.50 with 4 million shares outstanding. The firm is going to reverse split its stock by combining two shares into one share. If the price after reverse split is $6.52, do shareholders gain or lose value from the reverse split? How much value is gained or lost? (*Hint:* Consider shareholder value to be the market capitalization, which equals the number of shares outstanding multiplied by the stock price.)

15-13. Firm QRS decides that it will use a Dutch auction for the repurchase of 2 million shares. Investors have submitted bids on the price and quantity they are willing to sell shares to the firm, using the following schedule:

Price	Shares
$24.45	100,000
$24.50	200,000
$24.60	600,000
$24.75	1,100,000
$24.95	2,000,000
$25.15	2,500,000
$25.50	5,000,000

Determine the lowest price at which the firm is able to purchase 2 million shares. (*Note:* If the firm is willing to purchase shares for $25.50, then it will also purchase all shares at the lesser prices for $25.50 . . . the goal is to find the lowest price at which the firm can purchase the 2 million shares.) Given the purchase price of the shares, how much extra money do the shareholders realize at the lower share prices?

15-14. Investor A recognizes $100 in dividend income that is taxed at a rate of 20%. Investor B also wants to recognize the same after-tax revenue as Investor A, but Investor B owns stock that does not pay dividends. If Investor B's stock sells for $12 a share (originally purchased for $7 a share) and the capital gains tax is 40%, how many shares must Investor B sell?

Patterns Observed in Payout Policies Worldwide

15-15. Go to the home page of Cisco Systems, Inc. (http://www.cisco.com), and link to its financial reports page. Download the most recent annual report, and observe the capital investment and dividend policies of Cisco Systems. Now do the same for ChevronTexaco (http://www.chevrontexaco.com). Which of the two firms appears to have the higher-growth, positive-*NPV* investment opportunities? Which pays the higher relative dividend? Do these results support the agency cost model? The signaling model?

15-16. Go to the home page of ExxonMobil Corporation (http://www.cisco.com), and link to its financial reports page. Now do the same for Royal Dutch Petroleum Company (http://www.shell.com), BP plc (www.bp.com), and Total Group (http://www.total.com/ho/en). Compare the dividend and capital investment policies of these four major international oil companies. How do the dividend-payment policies of the three European-based companies differ from that of the U.S.-based company in terms of payout percentages, absolute amount, and payment frequency? Why do you think that BP's accounts are denominated in dollars, even though the group is headquartered in London?

15-17. Go to the home page for Dogs of the Dow (http://www.dogsofthedow.com), look at the year-to-date figures, and observe the dividend yields of the 30 stocks of the Dow Jones Industrial Average. Which industries contain the higher-dividend-yielding stocks, and which contain the lower-yielding stocks? Are there differences in the growth prospects between the high- and low-yielding stocks? Is this what you expected? Explain.

15-18. A publicly traded firm announces an increase in its dividend, with no other material information accompanying the announcement. What inside information is this announcement likely to convey, and what is the expected stock-price impact due to the market's assimilation of this information?

15-19. Stately Building Company's shares are selling for $75 each, and its dividend yield is 2.0 percent. What is the amount of Stately's dividend per share?

15-20. The stock of Up-and-Away Inc. is selling for $80 per share, and is currently paying a quarterly dividend of $0.25 per share. What is the dividend yield on Up-and-Away stock?

15-21. Well-Bred Service Company earned $50 million during 2005 and paid $20 million in dividends to the holders of its 40 million shares. If the current market price of Well-Bred's stock is $31.25, calculate the following: (a) the company's dividend payout ratio; (b) the nominal dividend per share, assuming Well-Bred pays dividends annually; (c) the nominal dividend per share, assuming Well-Bred pays dividends in four equal quarterly payments; and (d) the current dividend yield on Well-Bred stock.

Payout Policy Irrelevance in a World with Perfect Capital Markets

15-22. It is January 1, 2007, and Boomer Equipment Company (BEC) currently has assets of $250 million and expects to earn a return of 10 percent during 2007. There are 20 million shares of BEC stock outstanding. The firm has an opportunity to invest in a positive-*NPV* (minimal) project that will cost $25 million over the course of 2007, and it is trying to determine if it should finance this investment by retaining profits over the course of the year or whether it should pay the profits earned as dividends and issue new shares to finance the investments. Show that the decision is irrelevant in a world of frictionless markets.

15-23. Swelter Manufacturing Company (SMC) currently has assets of $200 million and a required return of 10 percent on its 10 million shares outstanding. The firm has an opportunity to invest in positive-NPV (minimal) projects that will cost $20 million and is trying to determine if it should withhold this amount from dividends payable to finance the investments or if it should pay out the dividends and issue new shares to finance the investments. Show that the decision is irrelevant in a world of frictionless markets. What happens to the dividend-irrelevance result if a personal income tax of 15 percent is introduced into the model?

15-24. Assume that it is now January 1, 2007, and you are examining two unlevered firms that operate in the same industry, have identical assets worth $80 million that yield a net profit of 12.5 percent per year, and have 10 million shares outstanding. Further assume that during 2007 and all subsequent years each firm has the opportunity to invest an amount equal to its net income in (slightly) positive-*NPV* investment projects. The Beta Company wishes to finance its capital spending through retained earnings. The Gamma Company wishes to pay out 100 percent of its annual earnings as dividends and to finance its investments with a new share offering each year. There are no taxes or transactions costs to issuing securities.

  a. Calculate the overall and per-share market value of the Beta Company at the end of 2007 and each of the two following years (2008 and 2009). What return on investment will this firm's shareholders earn?

  b. Describe the specific steps that the Gamma Company must take today (1/1/2007) and at the end of each of the next three years (year-end 2007, 2008, and 2009) if it is to pay out all of its net income as dividends and still grow its assets at the same rate as that of the Beta Company.

c. Calculate the number and per-share price of shares the Gamma Company must sell today and at the end of 2007, 2008, and 2009 if it is to pay out all its net income as dividends and still grow its assets at the same rate as that of the Beta Company.

d. Assuming that you currently own 100,000 shares (1 percent) of Gamma Company stock, compute the fraction of the company's total outstanding equity that you will own three years from now if you do not participate in any of the share offerings the firm will make during this holding period.

15-25. Investors anticipate that Sweetwater Manufacturing Inc.'s next dividend, due in one year, will be $4 per share. Investors also expect earnings to grow at 5 percent in perpetuity, and they require a return of 10 percent on their shares. Use the Gordon growth model (see Equation 4.6) to calculate Sweetwater's stock price today.

15-26. Super-Thrift Pharmaceuticals Company traditionally pays an annual dividend equal to 50 percent of its earnings. Earnings this year are $30 million. The company has 15 million shares outstanding. Investors expect earnings to grow at a 5 percent annual rate in perpetuity, and they require a return of 12 percent on their shares.

a. What is Super-Thrift's current dividend per share? What is it expected to be next year?

b. Use the Gordon growth model (see Equation 4.6) to calculate Super-Thrift's stock price today.

15-27. Casual Construction Corporation (CCC) earned $60 million during 2006 and expects to earn $63 million during 2007, in line with the firm's long-term earnings growth rate. There are 20 million CCC shares outstanding, and the firm has a policy of paying out 40 percent of its earnings as dividends. Investors require a 10 percent return on CCC shares.

a. What is CCC's current dividend per share? What is it expected to be next year?

b. Use the Gordon growth model (see Equation 4.6) to calculate CCC's stock price today.

Real-World Influences on Dividend Policy

15-28. Universal Windmill Company (UWC) has assets worth $50 million. Investors require a return of 10 percent on UWC's 2 million shares outstanding. The firm can invest in projects that will cost $5 million. Managers want to know if the firm should withhold this money from dividends or if it should pay dividends and issue new shares to finance the new investments. Show that the decision is irrelevant in frictionless markets. What happens if investors pay a 15 percent tax on dividends but they owe no tax on capital gains?

15-29. Sam Sharp purchased 100 shares of Electric Lighting Inc. (ELI) one year ago for $60 per share, and he also received dividends of $5 per share since then. Now that ELI's stock price has increased to $64.50, Sam has decided to sell his holdings. What is Sam's gross (pretax) and after-tax return on this investment, assuming that he faces a 15 percent tax rate on dividends and capital gains?

THOMSON ONE BUSINESS SCHOOL EDITION

15-30. Using the data found in the Worldscope Income Statement Ratios Report, calculate the dividend payout ratio for the last five years for Ford (ticker symbol, F), General Motors (ticker symbol, GM), DaimlerChrysler (ticker symbol, DCX), Toyota (ticker symbol, TM), and Honda Motor Company Limited (ticker symbol, HMC). How do the payout ratios change over time? How do the dividends per share change over time? Do the payout ratios and dividends per share change in the same direction? How do the earnings per share change over time? Do the dividends per share and earnings per share change in the same direction?

MINI-CASE: DIVIDEND POLICY

Yevaud Enterprises has the following historical prices. Each price is on the closing day of the month. The prices in the months with splits are the prices after the split has occurred.

Date	Closing Price	Stock Split	Date	Closing Price	Stock Split
Dec–05	$ 79.94	2 for 1	Dec–04	111.63	
Nov–05	124.38		Nov–04	83.75	
Oct–05	100.06		Oct–04	110.88	
Sep–05	125.13		Sep–04	99.75	2 for 1
Aug–05	118.75		Aug–04	88.13	
Jul–05	172.06		Jul–04	91.75	
Jun–05	172.19		Jun–04	85.53	
May–05	128.13		May–04	77.00	
Apr–05	116.94	3 for 1	Apr–04	59.00	
Mar–05	321.25		Mar–04	60.25	
Feb–05	192.00		Feb–04	49.50	
Jan–05	126.44		Jan–04	61.00	

1. If you had purchased the stock for $61 on the last day of January 2004, what rate of return would you have earned had you sold it the last day of December 2005, after adjusting for the stock splits.

   Yevaud Enterprises has $37 million in assets and expects to generate a return on assets of 12.6%. The stockholders require a 12.6% return on their investment as well. Yevaud can either:

   A. invest the entire cash flow generated this year in a new project with a positive NPV (albeit close to zero), or
   B. pay out the entire amount out as dividends and raise the cash for the positive-NPV project by issuing new shares.

   The new project will cost $4,662,000 in one year. Yevaud currently has 10,000,000 outstanding shares of common stock.

2. Calculate the value of the firm's stock and the stockholders' rate of return if Yevaud uses Alternative A to finance the purchase of the project.

3. How many shares of stock will Yevaud have to issue to finance the purchase of the new project in one year? Calculate the value of the firm's stock and the stockholders' rate of return if Yevaud uses Alternative B to finance the purchase of the project.

4. Will Yevaud's choice as to how to raise the money for the project impact the firm's stock price in one year?

5. Assume you currently own 50,000 shares of stock in Yevaud Enterprises and Yevaud pursued Alternative A. How could you, as a stockholder, generate cash flows equal to what they could have been had Yevaud pursued Alternative B? Would this change your percentage ownership of Yevaud's total stock outstanding?

PART 5: Long-Term Financing

This section addresses issues of long-term financing. Chapter 16 describes the investment banking industry and examines how these banks assist corporations to issue equity securities directly to investors. We describe the key laws governing public sale of equity securities in the United States, examine the procedures used by firms issuing common and preferred stock, and discuss how the market values of initial public offerings (IPOs) and seasoned equity offerings (SEOs) are determined. Though we focus on U.S. investment banking practices, we also discuss international IPO and SEO practices.

Chapter 17 examines long-term debt and leasing. It may seem odd to put debt and leasing together, but if you think about it, a lease can be a long-term obligation just like the obligation that firms undertake when they borrow money by issuing bonds. We describe how bonds are rated as to default likelihood and discuss how managers decide whether to refund an outstanding bond issue after market interest rates fall. We also present the special terminology that applies to different types of lease contracts and show how managers should decide whether to borrow money and buy an operating asset or to finance the asset acquisition with a lease.

Google Inc. has always considered itself a special type of company. From its founding in September 1998 by two Stanford computer science doctoral students, Sergey Brin and Larry Page, Google quickly rose to dominate the nascent Internet search business, all the while developing a loyal base of corporate advertisers and individual web surfers. It was thus no surprise that Google's managers would try to change the rules of initial public offerings (IPOs) when in spring 2004 they announced that Google would "go public" later that year. Since the *Financial Times* had labeled Google's planned offering "the most widely anticipated stock market listing in more than a decade," and since investment banks were lining up to underwrite the company's IPO, Google's managers figured they had the market power to change Wall Street's time honored —and, in Google's mind, unethical—securities issuance practices.

Specifically, Google's managers insisted that the company's shares be priced and allocated by an open auction process rather than by the traditional method of book-building, where investment banks privately assess what favored institutional investors are willing to pay. In another break with tradition, Google insisted that no fewer than 31 investment banks be included in the "syndicate," or group of investment banks charged with actually selling shares to investors. This prevented larger investment banks from taking their traditional leading role in allocating shares to initial buyers— a role that gives them great power to favor certain investors with "hot IPOs" expected to shoot up in price after the offering. Only the two lead underwriters, Morgan Stanley and Credit Suisse First Boston (CSFB) were accorded any pride of place in the syndicate, and they had to accept a much reduced underwriting fee to win the lead roles.

The "Dutch auction" process Google adopted allowed anyone with a brokerage account at one of the 31 syndicate-member banks (later reduced to 30 after Merrill Lynch withdrew) to submit a bid for shares before the offering's "effective date," when trading begins. There was separate bidding process for individual and institutional investors, and many banks allowed investors to bid using the Internet. All orders were accumulated in a central electronic order book, and revealed investor demand was used to set the offer price and allocate shares. In addition to wresting pricing power away from the underwriting banks, Google hoped the auction process would price the firm's shares closer to their expected postissue market value. As Google's IPO worked its way through the regulatory process, investment banks griped anonymously about the deal's structure, but few were willing to openly challenge Google and risk their place in what promised to be a historic share issue. The company posted an indicated price range of $108–$135 per share and confidently predicted that the offering would raise $2.7 billion.

As the final offering date approached, however, Google's confidence evaporated, as did the critics' quietude. A series of small

SMART**Finance**
Use the learning tools at www
.thomsonedu.com/finance/smartfinance

567

but highly publicized mistakes by Google managers, including discussing the offering in a *Playboy* interview and failing to disclose details of shares previously awarded to employees as incentive compensation, coupled with a slide in Internet stock prices, opened up the company and its revolutionary auction process to determined criticism. The worst blow of all came two days before the offering's effective date of August 19, 2004, when slack demand from individuals forced Google to cut the offering price to $85 per share, cut back the number of shares to be sold, and allocate over three-quarters of these shares to institutional customers of the largest investment banks. It looked like Google's experiment in investor democracy was headed for disaster.

In the end, the contest ended in a draw. Google's shares proved extremely popular, jumping in price by 18 percent the first day of trading and an additional 4 percent the second day. Unfortunately for Google, the major underwriters' institutional customers captured all this initial return, and the banks effectively reasserted their gatekeeper role in IPOs. Google's shares continued to rise over subsequent months, rising above $430 per share by December 2005, but no other IPO issuing firm has tried to adopt an auction process.

Sources: Google Inc.'s final share offering prospectus, plus multiple articles downloaded from the Financial Times *website (www.ft.com).*

Although corporations around the world rely on internal financing for most of their funding, companies also raise large amounts of capital externally each year. This chapter describes how companies obtain equity financing and also shows how investment banks help firms acquire external capital. Chapter 17 examines how firms acquire external debt and lease financing.

Once corporate managers have decided to raise external capital and to raise equity rather than debt, they must decide whether to enlist an **investment bank** to help sell the firm's securities. Almost all issuing firms do employ investment bankers. Either issuing firm managers can negotiate privately with individual banks regarding the terms of the equity sale, or they can solicit competitive bids for the business. Firms can issue shares to a small group of sophisticated investors in a private placement, they can issue new shares to existing shareholders through a rights offering, or they can engage in a much broader public share offering, reaching domestic as well as international investors.

We begin by examining investment banks and the services they offer to equity issuers. Next, we describe the legal rules governing public security sales in the United States, paying special attention to the disclosure requirements imposed on firms raising equity capital. We then examine equity sales conducted by two types of firms: companies issuing equity for the first time in an initial public offering (IPO), and existing public companies conducting seasoned equity offerings (SEOs). As you might imagine, the dynamics of the process are quite different in IPOs and SEOs. Finally, we conclude the chapter with sections covering private placements and international equity issues.

16.1 INVESTMENT BANKING

AN OVERVIEW OF THE GLOBAL INVESTMENT BANKING INDUSTRY

Investment banks (IBs) play an important role in helping firms raise long-term debt and equity financing in the world's capital markets. During the past 20 years, and especially since 1990, the global investment banking industry has grown dramatically in scale and in the variety of services it provides to corporations. Furthermore, the 1999 passage of the Gramm-Leech-Bliley Act has allowed commercial banks to provide investment banking services in the United States. They were formerly excluded from this business by the Glass-Steagall Act of 1933. Table 16.1 presents a **league table,** ranking the world's 15 largest investment banks by the total value of securities underwritten worldwide during 2004.

Several interesting patterns emerge from the table. First, investment banks headquartered in the United States dominate the top ranks of global IB firms.[1] The five banks with the highest market share—Citigroup, Morgan Stanley, JP Morgan Chase, Merrill Lynch, and Lehman Brothers—are all U.S. based, as are Goldman Sachs (9) and Banc of America Securities (10). Several European banks have broken into the top tier of the global industry in recent years, often by purchasing one or more U.S. banks. Swiss banks such as Credit Suisse First Boston (CSFB) and Union Bank of Switzerland (UBS) have been especially successful in this regard.

Second, Table 16.1 points out the sheer scale of the global securities issuance business. The top 15 firms arranged security issues worth $4.39 *trillion* during calendar year 2004, while the industry total was a record $5.69 trillion. For perspective, total "world GDP" in 2004 was about $40 trillion. Table 16.1 also reveals a

Firm Rank 2004 (2003 in parentheses)	Proceeds ($ millions)	Market Share (%)	Number of Issues Underwritten	Disclosed Fees ($ millions)
1. Citigroup (1)	$ 534,612	9.4%	1,893	$ 1,736
2. Morgan Stanley (2)	413,554	7.3	1,334	1,392
3. JP Morgan Chase (3)	385,798	6.8	1,492	1,086
4. Merrill Lynch (4)	374,477	6.6	1,565	1,188
5. Lehman Brothers (5)	369,628	6.5	1,292	754
6. Credit Suisse First Boston (6)	362,442	6.4	1,359	895
7. Deutsche Bank (7)	334,835	5.9	1,299	527
8. UBS (9)	299,592	5.3	1,175	813
9. Goldman Sachs (8)	285,869	5.0	855	1,160
10. Banc of America Securities (10)	203,735	3.6	780	363
11. Barclays Capital (13)	188,142	3.3	652	292
12. Bear Stearns (11)	183,642	3.2	523	191
13. Royal Bank of Scotland (12)	182,981	3.2	504	90
14. HSBC Holdings (15)	138,852	2.4	555	190
15. ABN Amro (14)	129,016	2.3	606	331
Industry Total	**$5,693,164**	**100.0%**	**20,067**	**$15,893**

Table 16.1
Securities Underwriting League Table for 2004, Based on Total Value of Securities Underwritten Worldwide

Source: Investment Dealers' Digest (January 10, 2005), p. 50.
Note: This table presents the global investment banking league table for the year 2004, based on the total value of securities sold. Full credit for each offering is credited to the lead underwriter (book-runner).

---

[1] This American preeminence is at least partly a result of the U.S. investment banking industry's being deregulated much earlier than Europe's. In particular, the SEC forced U.S. investment banks to end fixed stock-trading commissions in May 1975, which prompted both a competitive free-for-all and rapid growth in share trading volume and securities issuance. In contrast, British capital markets were not significantly deregulated until the "Big Bang" reforms were implemented in 1986, and continental European (and Japanese) markets were opened fully only during the 1990s.

high degree of concentration in the industry, with the top eight banks lead managing over half of the total value of securities issued worldwide.

Third, Table 16.1 shows a high degree of persistence in the industry rankings. The highest-ranked firms in 2004 generally occupied the top rankings in 2003 and in most previous years. In 2004, seven banks underwrote over $300 billion worth of new securities, and these firms are perennial members of investment banking's prestigious bulge bracket. **Bulge bracket** firms generally occupy the lead or co-lead manager's position in large new security offerings, meaning that they take primary responsibility for the new offering (even though other banks participate as part of a syndicate) and, as a result, earn higher fees. You can readily identify the lead investment bank in a security offering by looking at the offering *prospectus,* the legal document that describes the terms of the offering. The lead bank's name appears on the front page, usually in larger, bolder print than the names of other participating banks.

Tables 16.2 and 16.3 present 2004 league tables for, respectively, merger and acquisition advising and arranging syndicated loans. The same banks dominate advising for the $1.95 trillion in global mergers and acquisitions as in securities issuance, but the order in Table 16.2 is significantly different. As in most years, Goldman Sachs was the leading M&A advisor, followed by J.P. Morgan Chase and Citigroup. Table 16.3 shows that banks specialize in different areas. The three leading arrangers of syndicated loans (JP Morgan Chase, Citigroup, and Banc of America) hold similar rankings in Tables 16.1 and 16.2, but the next 12 league table ranks go to international groups centered around a large commercial bank. Perhaps unsurprisingly, European banks such as Barclays Capital, Deutsche Bank, and BNP Paribas arrange large volumes of syndicated loans for clients, as do large Japanese banks such as Mizuho Financial Group and Sumitomo Mitsui Banking. In contrast, pure investment banks, such as Morgan Stanley, Goldman Sachs, and Merrill Lynch, are stronger

Table 16.2
Merger and Acquisition (M&A) Advising League Table for 2004, Based on Total Value of M&A Transactions Worldwide

Firm Rank 2004 (2003 in parentheses)	Value of Transactions ($ millions)	Number of Deals (announced targets)
1. Goldman Sachs (1)	$ 577,019	337
2. JP Morgan Chase (4)	511,772	397
3. Citigroup (3)	484,928	378
4. Morgan Stanley (2)	382,102	300
5. Merrill Lynch (5)	368,059	222
6. Lehman Brothers (9)	308,365	176
7. Deutsche Bank (10)	247,435	219
8. Rothschild (12)	232,124	269
9. Lazard (6)	229,658	207
10. UBS (7)	219,313	289
11. Credit Suisse First Boston (8)	200,977	271
12. ABN Amro (16)	150,728	160
13. BNP Paribas (13)	101,561	96
14. Banc of America Securities (11)	72,874	109
15. Evercore Partners (105)	59,528	16
Industry Total	**$1,951,496**	**30,599**

Source: Investment Dealers' Digest (January 17, 2005), p. 27.
Note: This table presents the worldwide M&A advising league table for the year 2004, based on the total value of all announced M&A targets. Full credit for each offering is credited to the lead underwriter (book-runner).

Table 16.3
Syndicated Loans
League Table for 2004,
Based on Total Value
of Syndicated Loans
Arranged Worldwide

Firm Rank 2004 (2003 in parentheses)	Proceeds ($ millions)	Market Share (%)	Number of Loans Arranged
1. JP Morgan Chase (1)	$ 499,871	18.9%	1,153
2. Citigroup (2)	334,469	12.6	768
3. Banc of America Securities (3)	289,431	10.9	1,114
4. Barclays Capital (5)	119,878	4.5	337
5. Deutsche Bank (4)	105,107	4.0	261
6. BNP Paribas (8)	88,729	3.4	377
7. Wachovia (14)	81,847	3.1	407
8. Royal Bank of Scotland (11)	71,742	2.7	279
9. Mizuho Financial Group (6)	66,071	2.5	636
10. ABN Amro (9)	59,755	2.3	298
11. Sumitomo Mitsui Banking (10)	52,680	2.0	546
12. HSBC Holdings (15)	52,657	2.0	289
13. Credit Suisse First Boston (6)	52,007	2.0	165
14. Calyon (15)	49,891	1.9	188
15. Société Générale (16)	48,361	1.8	209
Industry Total	$2,650,036	100.0%	7,170

Source: *Investment Dealers' Digest* (January 10, 2005), p. 50.
Note: This table presents the global investment banking league table for the year 2004, based on the total value of securities sold. Full credit for each offering is credited to the lead underwriter (book-runner).

in securities underwriting and M&A advisory work. In part, this pattern derives from the historical separation of U.S. commercial and investment banking activities. Though this degree of separation began to erode as early as 1987, the Gramm-Leach-Bliley Act removed the remaining competitive barriers.

KEY INVESTMENT BANKING ACTIVITIES

Investment banks provide a broad range of services to corporations. The three principal lines of business are *corporate finance, trading,* and *asset management.* Of the three business lines, corporate finance enjoys the highest visibility; it includes security underwriting and M&A advisory work (R. C. Smith, 2001). Corporate finance tends to be the most profitable line of business, especially for more prestigious banks, such as Goldman Sachs and Morgan Stanley, which can charge the highest underwriting and advisory fees. However, corporate finance generates less than one-fourth of the typical IB's revenues.

Investment banks earn revenue from trading debt and equity securities in two important ways. First, they act as dealers, facilitating trade between unrelated parties and earning fees in return. Second, they hold inventories of securities and can make or lose money as inventory values fluctuate. Trading revenues, on average, account for about one-quarter of large banks' revenues. Finally, asset management encompasses several different activities, including managing money for individuals with high net worth, operating and advising mutual funds, and managing pension funds. Revenues from asset management exceed those from the other primary investment banking services.

THE INVESTMENT BANKER'S ROLE IN EQUITY ISSUES

We now turn to the services investment banks provide to issuing companies. The focus is on U.S. practices, but Prowse (1996) and Ljungqvist, Jenkinson, and Wilhelm (2003) document an increasing tendency for security issues around the world to conform to U.S. standards. We also focus on common stock offerings, though the procedures for selling bonds—described in Livingston and Miller (2000) and Song (2004)—and preferred stocks are similar. Investment banks play several different roles throughout the securities offering process, and this section describes the evolution of these roles over the course of an issue. We also describe how issuers compensate IBs for the services they provide.

Though firms can issue stock without the assistance of investment bankers, in practice almost all firms hire IBs to help issue equity. Firms can choose an investment banker in one of two ways. The most common approach is a **negotiated offer,** where the issuing firm negotiates the terms of the offer directly with one investment bank. Alternatively, in a **competitively bid offer** the firm announces the terms of its intended equity sale, and investment banks bid for the business. Though intuition suggests that competitive bidding should be cheaper, the empirical evidence is mixed.[2] One clear sign that competitive offers are not better and cheaper is that the vast majority of equity sales are negotiated. If the costs of negotiated deals were truly higher, why would so many firms choose that approach?

Firms issuing securities often hire more than one investment bank. In these cases, one of the banks is usually named the **lead underwriter,** or *book-runner,* while the other leading banks are called **co-managers.** Chen and Ritter (2000) argue that firms often prefer to issue securities with several co-managers because doing so increases the number of stock analysts that will follow the firm after the offering. Firms believe that a higher analyst following leads to greater liquidity and higher stock values. Cliff and Denis (2004) verify the importance of attracting top-rated-analyst coverage by showing that issuing firms willingly allow their IPO share price to be set low enough to attract excess demand and high post-issue trading volume, since this will indirectly compensate the underwriters' star analysts.

Investment bankers sell equity under two types of contracts. In a **best-efforts offering,** the investment bank merely promises to give its best effort to sell the firm's securities at the agreed-upon price but makes no guarantee about the ultimate success of the offering. If there is insufficient demand, the firm withdraws the issue from the market. Best-efforts offerings are most commonly used for small, high-risk companies, and the IB receives a commission based on the number of shares sold.

In contrast, in a **firm-commitment offering** the investment bank agrees to underwrite the issue, meaning that the bank guarantees (**underwrites**) the offering price. The IB actually purchases the shares from the firm and resells them to investors. This

---

[2] Bhagat (1986), Bhagat and Frost (1986), and Hansen and Khanna (1994) examine the choice between competitive and negotiated offerings and find lower costs in negotiated deals. However, competitive offers may appear to be less costly only because the types of firms that use them are different from the types of firms that use negotiated offers. Logue and Tiniç (1999) examine multiple offers by the same firm, AT&T, and find no cost differences in the two offer types. Two other recent studies examine other aspects of the design of underwriting syndicates and the relationship between IBs and issuing firms. Narayanan, Rangan, and Rangan (2004) document that the reentry of commercial banks into the securities underwriting business allows lead underwriters to lower issuance costs for firms selling seasoned equity, by including in the underwriting syndicate commercial banks that have an existing lending relationship with the issuing firm. Fernando, Gatchev, and Spindt (2005) develop and empirically verify a model demonstrating how issuing firms and IB underwriters associate by mutual choice. Though it seems obvious that firms and IBs should choose each other, previous theoretical models had in fact posited a unidirectional choice.

arrangement requires the investment bank to bear the risk of inadequate demand for the issuer's shares, but banks mitigate this risk in two ways. First, the lead under-writer forms an **underwriting syndicate** consisting of many investment banks. These banks collectively purchase the firm's shares and market them, thus spreading the risk across the syndicate. Second, underwriters go to great lengths to determine the demand for a new issue before it comes to market, and they generally set the issue's *offer price* and take possession of the securities no more than a day or two before the issue date. These steps help ensure that the investment bank faces only a small risk of being unable to sell the shares that it underwrites.

In firm-commitment offerings, investment banks receive compensation for their services via the **underwriting spread,** the difference between the price at which the banks purchase shares from firms (the **net price**) and the price at which they sell the shares to institutional and individual investors (the **offer price**). In some offerings, the underwriters receive additional compensation in the form of warrants that grant the right to buy shares of the issuing company at a fixed price. Underwriting fees are substantial, especially for firms issuing equity for the first time. Chen and Ritter (2000) report that most U.S. initial public offerings have underwriting spreads of ex-actly 7 percent, though lower spreads are common in very large IPOs. For example, if a firm conducting an IPO wants to sell shares worth $100 million, it will receive $93 million, and the underwriter earns the gross spread of $7 million.

APPLYING THE MODEL 16.1

The underwriting discount for Google's IPO in August 2004, described in this chapter's Opening Focus, was $2.3839 per share, deducted from the $85.00 per share offering price. This gives an underwriting spread of only 2.80 percent, which is a reflection of both the unusual size of Google's IPO ($2.7 billion) and Google's bargaining power over the underwriters.

Underwriting spreads vary considerably depending on the type of security being issued. As Table 16.4 indicates, banks charge higher spreads on equity issues than on debt issues. They also charge higher spreads for **unseasoned equity offerings** (i.e., IPOs) than they do for **seasoned equity offerings** (SEOs), which are equity issues by firms that already have common stock outstanding. In general, the riskier the secu-rity being offered, the higher the spread charged by the underwriter. Notice that spreads on non-investment-grade ("junk") bonds exceed those on investment-grade bonds. Securities that have both debt- and equity-like features, such as convertible bonds and preferred stock, have spreads higher than those of ordinary debt but lower than those of common stock.

Figure 16.1 reveals two additional factors that influence equity underwriting spreads: (1) The percentage spread falls as the issuing firm's risk decreases and as the firm's size increases; and (2) holding issuing firm size and risk constant, spreads de-cline as the offer size increases, but only up to a point. It is not surprising that spreads decline as the offer size increases because many underwriting costs—organizing and managing the syndicate, soliciting interest from investors, assuring regulatory com-pliance—are largely fixed. However, Figure 16.1 shows that beyond some point, in-creasing the size of an offer does increase the issuing firm's cost.

Ljungqvist, Jenkinson, and Wilhelm (2003) show that the spreads on interna-tional IPOs are significantly lower than on U.S. initial offers. In part, this reflects dif-ferences in underwriting practices across countries. U.S. underwriters typically use a

Table 16.4
Underwriting Spreads for Different Types of Securities, 2004 Versus 2003

Security Type	2004		2003	
	Gross Spread ($ millions)	Average Fee (%)	Gross Spread ($ millions)	Average Fee (%)
Debt				
Long-term straight debt	$ 2,393	0.386%	$3,476	0.490%
Long-term high grade	1,685	0.515	2,011	0.508
Long-term high yield	371	1.887	304	1.781
Asset-backed	385	0.294	350	0.221
Equity	$ 5,756	3.694%	$4,600	4.341%
Initial public offerings	2,544	5.272	892	6.172
Seasoned offerings	2,781	3.122	2,461	3.870
Preferred Stock				
Nonconvertible	$ 524	2.324%	$ 649	2.870%
Convertible Debt and Preferred	$ 432	2.334%	$ 834	2.413
Industry Total	$8,970.5	0.819%	$8,614	0.718%

Source: "Corporate Edition: Underwriting Fees," *Investment Dealers' Digest* (January 17, 2005), pp. 36–37. This table presents total underwriting spreads and average underwriting fees charged by U.S. investment banking firms in 2004 and 2003.

Figure 16.1
Predicted Underwriter Spreads for Seasoned Common Stock Offerings
Source: Figure 3 in Oya Altinkiliç and Robert S. Hansen, "Are There Economies of Scale in Underwriting Fees? Evidence of Rising External Financing Costs," *Review of Financial Studies* 13 (Spring 2000), pp. 191–218.

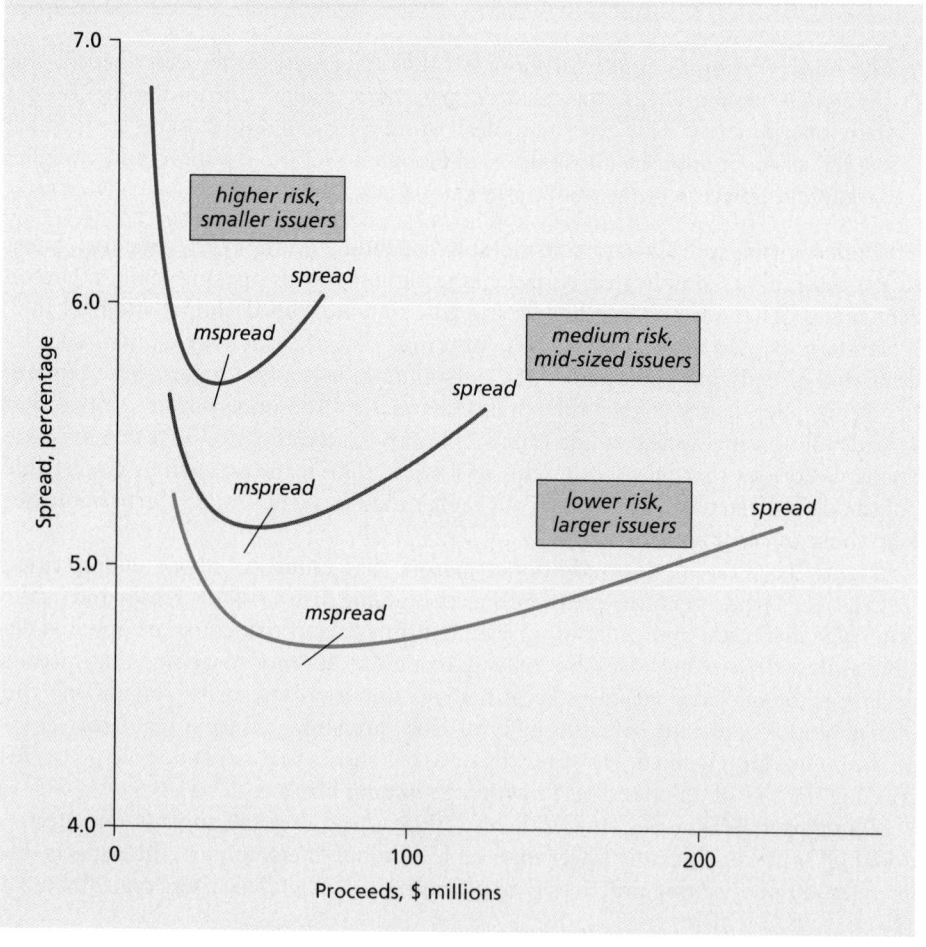

process known as **book building** to assess demand for a company's shares and to set the offer price, in which underwriters ask prospective investors to reveal information about their demand for the offering.[3] Through conversations with investors, the underwriter tries to measure the demand curve for a given issue, and the investment bank sets the offer price after gathering all the information it can from investors. In international markets, book building is becoming increasingly common, but a method called a **fixed-price offer** also survives. In fixed-price offers, underwriters set the final offer price for a new issue weeks in advance. This imposes more risk on the underwriter, which must either charge higher spreads or price the shares far below the expected postoffer price to willingly take on this additional risk. Table 16.5, which is drawn from Ljungqvist, Jenkinson, and Wilhelm (2003), lists underwriting spreads on international IPOs. This table shows that underwriters charge significantly *lower* spreads on fixed-price offerings, but the authors find that book-built offerings are less underpriced.

Services Provided before the Offering. Precisely how do investment banks earn their fees? Investment banks provide many services, from performing the analytical work required to price a new security offering, to assisting the firm with regulatory compliance, marketing the new issues, and developing an orderly market for the firm's securities once they begin trading. The chronology of a typical equity offering provides a useful framework for describing these services.

Early in the process of preparing for an equity offering, an investment bank will help the firm file the necessary regulatory documents, starting with the *registration statement*. This provides detailed information about the securities being offered and the issuing firm. Though document preparation may sound like a trivial undertaking, in fact it is one of the most time-consuming (and expensive) parts of the capital-raising process, especially for IPOs.

While it is preparing the necessary legal documents, the investment bank must also begin estimating the value of the securities the firm intends to sell. This task is much simpler for debt than for equity, and, of course, it is easier to value seasoned equity offerings than to value IPOs. Investment banks use a variety of methods to value IPO shares, including discounted cash flow models and market "comparables." In the latter case, an investment bank compares the firm issuing equity to similar publicly traded firms, often estimating the value of the new stock issue by applying a price-to-earnings or price-to-sales multiple to the issuing firm's current or projected financial results.

However, one key lesson from the IPO market over the past few years is that pricing new equity issues is not a science. Several weeks before the scheduled offering, the firm and its bankers take a whirlwind tour of major U.S. and international cities to assess investor demand for the offering. Affectionately called the **road show,** this

---

[3.] Benveniste and Spindt (1989) explain how investment bankers provide investors with an incentive to reveal their demand for a firm's shares. When demand for a new issue is particularly strong, investment bankers do not fully adjust the offer price upward to a market-clearing level. This implies that investors who want to buy shares will be rationed, but it also implies that investors who revealed their interest in the stock will be rewarded when trading begins because they will receive shares that immediately increase in value. This information-revelation model is recently tested in Cornelli and Goldreich (2001, 2003), Aggarwal, Prabhala, and Puri (2002), and Jenkinson and Jones (2004), with mixed results. Both Cornelli and Goldreich studies and the Aggarwal et al. study support the idea that book building is informative and that that informative bidders are rewarded with better share allocations, while Jenkinson and Jones find little evidence that bids are informative or that large bidders are rewarded with preferential share allocations. Finally, Sherman and Titman (2003) model the trade-off a lead underwriter faces when increasing the size of the underwriting syndicate. They find that increasing the size of the syndicate by inviting in more investors increases pricing accuracy—by incorporating more information—but at the cost of greater underpricing.

Table 16.5
Gross Spreads on International IPOs: Book-Buildings Versus Fixed-Price Offers

Country	Book-Buildings		Fixed-Price Offerings		*t*-Test of Difference in Means
	Number of Observations	Gross Spread (mean %)	Number of Observations	Gross Spread (mean %)	
Europe	**645**	**4.43%**	370	2.19%	−22.53***
France	64	4.49			
Germany	164	4.70	10	4.09	−1.56
Italy	53	4.37	2	3.50	−1.15
Netherlands	60	4.46	2	3.55	−0.84
Sweden	25	4.46	2	2.93	−1.69
United Kingdom	83	4.42	333	2.01	−12.76***
Rest of Western Europe	161	4.17	19	3.66	−1.32
Eastern Europe	35	4.18	2	5.13	0.83
Asia Pacific	**214**	**4.10%**	225	2.21%	−14.41***
China	60	3.80	27	3.30	−1.40
Hong Kong	42	4.09	79	2.50	−6.34***
Japan	39	5.38			
Malaysia	2	3.00	40	1.47	−4.22***
Singapore	5	5.07	50	1.51	−9.58***
Rest of Asia/Pacific	66	3.57	29	2.65	−3.11*
North and South America	**103**	**5.17%**	1	5.00%	
Canada	32	6.34	1	5.00	
Mexico	24	4.75			
Rest of N/S America	47	4.58			
Africa and Middle East	**64**	**6.37%**	13	2.19%	−6.07***
Israel	42	7.44	3	5.17	−2.05*
South Africa	3	4.67	10	1.30	−5.01***
Rest of Africa & Middle East	19	4.27			
Total Sample	**1,025**	**4.55%**	610	2.20%	−28.88***

Source: Alexander P. Ljungqvist, Tim Jenkinson, and William J. Wilhelm, Jr., "Global Integration in Primary Equity Markets: The Role of U.S. Banks and U.S. Investors," *Review of Financial Studies* 16 (Spring 2003), 63–99.
Notes: This table examines the difference in underwriter spreads for 1,635 non-U.S. initial public stock offerings executed via U.S.-style book-building techniques versus those executed through traditional fixed-price underwritings.
***, **, * indicates statistical significance at the 1, 5, and 10% levels, respectively.

grueling process usually lasts one to three weeks, and it gives managers the opportunity to pitch their business plan to institutional investors. The investment banker's goal in this process is to build a book of orders for shares that is greater (often many times greater) than the amount of stock the firm intends to sell. The expressions of interest by investors during the road show are not legally binding purchase agreements, and the investment bank typically does not commit to an offer price at this point but gives investors a range of prices at which they expect to sell the offer. Given the tentative nature of the demand expressed on the road show, the banker seeks to **oversubscribe** the offering to minimize the bank's underwriting risk. Naturally, one way to create excess demand for an offering is to set a low offer price. As we will see, the vast majority of IPOs in the United States and other countries are **underpriced**, meaning that IPO shares typically begin trading at a price higher than the offer price. When firms conduct seasoned equity offerings, they also tend to sell shares at a slight discount to the market price of the outstanding shares, though underpricing is not as severe in SEOs as in IPOs. As the road show progresses, investment bankers can and do adjust the offer price upward, but they almost always leave money on the table—set the offer price below the expected post-issue selling price—in part to reward the investors who reveal their demand for the share issue. Hanley (1993) shows that investment banks only partially adjust the offer price upward in response to favorable demand signals from investors.

Investment bankers perform additional services designed to ensure that the firm's securities will be attractive to investors. One such service is "cleaning up the balance sheet," essentially consolidating different classes of stock and other forms of financing that are common in firms issuing equity for the first time. In addition, bankers negotiate **lockup agreements** with the client's managers and directors, in which these corporate insiders promise not to sell their personal stock holdings for several months (usually 18 or 24) after the offering. Bankers require these agreements because insiders typically have private information about the firm's prospects at the time of the equity offering. Insiders are motivated to communicate this information to potential investors so the firm's shares will not be undervalued, but this is difficult to do because such information cannot be directly verified. Insiders thus face the problem of how to credibly signal what they know. One believable signal is for insiders to retain shares in the firm after the offering, but this will only be credible if lockup agreements prevent insiders from selling in the aftermarket soon after trading begins.[4]

Services Provided during and after the Offering. The lead underwriter conducts the stock offering and ensures that participating investors receive their shares, plus a copy of the **final prospectus,** on the offer date. The lead underwriter exercises some discretion over the distribution of shares among syndicate members and the **selling group,** investment banks that assist in selling shares but are not formal members of the syndicate. In oversubscribed offerings, the lead underwriter may exercise a **Green Shoe option** (or **overallotment option**), essentially an option to sell up to an additional 15 percent more shares than originally planned.

Once a firm's securities begin trading, the underwriter may engage in **price stabilization.** This means that, if a new issue begins to falter in the market, the investment bank may buy shares on its own account, supporting the market price at or slightly above the offer price. The possibility of having to stabilize market prices gives underwriters an additional incentive to underprice new issues at the outset.

After a share offering is successfully sold, the lead underwriter often serves as the principal **market maker** for trading in the firm's stock. This means the bank will continuously quotes bid and ask prices for the new shares, thus "making a market" in the new issue. Corwin, Harris, and Lipson (2004) examine the development of after-market liquidity for IPOs and show that trading volumes are typically (and temporarily) very high immediately after the IPO. The lead underwriter also typically assigns one or more research analysts to cover the issuing firm; the research reports these analysts write (which naturally tend to be flattering) help generate additional

---

[4.] Three recent studies examine the importance of IPO lockup agreements. Aggarwal, Krigman, and Womack (2002) develop and validate a model where managers strategically underprice IPOs to maximize personal wealth from selling shares at the lockup expiration. Ofek and Richardson (2003), in their exploration of the rise and fall of internet stock prices during the "bubble" period, link the bursting of this bubble to the large number of lockup expirations during the spring and summer of 2000. Finally, Ang and Brau (2003) examine the relationship between insider share shares (secondary sales) and IPO lockup agreements and show that insiders will agree to longer lockup periods in exchange for being allowed to sell more secondary shares in an IPO.

interest in trading the firm's securities. In fact, some firms choose their investment bankers in large measure based on the reputation of the analyst that will cover the stock once it goes public. Loughran and Ritter (2004) suggest the importance of attracting postoffer research with their "analyst lust hypothesis" explanation for why managers are willing to accept high of IPO underpricing. Table 16.6 summarizes the chronology of an investment bank's activities through the IPO process.

We conclude this section by highlighting the important conflicts of interest faced by investment bankers. On the one hand, issuing firms want to obtain the highest possible price for their shares, but they also want favorable coverage from their in-

Table 16.6
Key Steps in the Initial Public Offering Process

Major Steps and Main Events	Role of the Underwriter (U/W) in the Main Events
1. Initial step	
Select book-running manager and co-manager	Book-running manager's role includes forming the syndicate and being in charge of the entire process.
Letter of intent	Letter specifies gross spread, Green Shoe (overallotment) option, and protects U/W from unexpected expenses. Doesn't guarantee price or number of shares to be issued.
2. Registration process	
Registration statement and due diligence	After conducting due diligence, U/W files necessary registration statement with SEC.
Red herring	Once the registration statement is filed with the SEC, it is transformed into a preliminary prospectus (red herring).
3. Marketing	
Distribute prospectus; road show	The red herring is sent to salespeople and institutional investors around the country. Concurrently, company and underwriter conduct a road show and the IB builds a book based on expressed demand—but not legally binding.
4. Pricing and allocation	
Pricing; allocation	Once registration statement has SEC approval, U/W files an acceleration request, asking SEC to accelerate date issue becomes effective. Firm and U/W meet the day before the offer to determine price, number of shares, and allocation of shares.
5. Aftermarket activities	
Stabilization; overallotment option	Lead U/W supports the stock price by purchasing shares if price declines. Support can only occur at or below offer price and can continue for only a relatively short period. If stock price goes up, U/W uses overallotment option to cover short position. If price goes down, U/W covers overallotment by buying stock in open market.
Research coverage	Final stage of IPO process begins 25 calendar days after IPO, when the "quiet period" ends. Only after this can U/W and other syndicate members comment on the value of the firm and provide earnings estimates.

Source: Katrina Ellis, Roni Michaely, and Maureen O'Hara, "When the Underwriter Is the Market Maker: An Examination of Trading in the IPO Aftermarket," *Journal of Finance* 55 (June 2000), pp. 1039–1074.

vestment banks' analysts. Investors, on the other hand, want to purchase securities at the lowest price possible, but they also value dispassionate, unbiased advice from analysts. (Unfortunately, whether they ever receive such advice is questionable). Investment bankers must therefore walk a thin line, in terms of both ethics and economics, in pleasing their constituents. Firms issuing securities are wise to remember this. Investment bankers deal with investors, especially institutional investors, on a repeated basis. They must approach this group each time a new offering comes to the market. In contrast, over the life of a firm, there is just one IPO and perhaps a few SEOs.[5]

---

1. What are the principal lines of business for top-tier investment banks? How do the business strategies of IBs that are affiliated with large commercial banks differ from those of unaffiliated IBs?

2. What are the major sources of revenue for investment banks?

3. What does the term *bulge bracket* mean? What recent regulatory change may create upheaval in the bulge bracket?

4. What services does an investment bank provide before an IPO? After?

Concept Review Questions

16.2 LEGAL RULES GOVERNING PUBLIC SECURITY SALES IN THE UNITED STATES

Security issues in the United States are regulated at both the state and federal levels. The most important federal law governing the sale of new securities is the **Securities Act of 1933** and its amendments. The basis for federal regulation of the sale of securities is the concept of **full disclosure,** which means that issuers must reveal all relevant information concerning the company selling the securities and the securities themselves to potential investors. The other major federal law governing securities issues is the **Securities and Exchange Commission Act of 1934.** This act and its amendments established the U.S. Securities and Exchange Commission (SEC) and laid out specific procedures for both the public sale of securities and the governance of public companies.[6]

Given the emphasis U.S. securities law places on disclosure, it is not surprising that investment banks are required to perform **due diligence** examinations of potential security issuers. This means that IBs must search out and disclose all relevant information about an issuer before selling securities to the public. Investors can sue underwriters if they do not perform adequate due diligence, and, of course, the underwriter's reputation suffers as well. Because investors understand that the most prestigious investment bankers have the most to lose from inadequate due diligence, the mere fact that these firms are willing to underwrite an issue provides valuable **certification** that the issuing company is in fact disclosing all material information.

The principal disclosure document for all public security offerings is the **registration statement.** Firms must file this highly detailed document with the SEC before

---

[5.] A CEO of a company that conducted an IPO during the 1990s told us, "You have two friends in an IPO: your lawyer and your accountant." Notice that the investment banker didn't make the list.

[6.] Much of the discussion in this section is based on the legal sections of Ritter (1998) and the updated information from his website (http://bear.cba.ufl.edu/ritter/ipodata.htm). Official information can also be accessed from the SEC's website at http://www.sec.gov.

they can solicit investors. A final revised version must be approved by the commission before an offering can become **effective,** meaning before any shares can actually be sold to public investors. There are two basic parts to the registration statement: Part I, the **prospectus,** is distributed to all prospective investors; Part II, **supplemental disclosures,** is filed only with the SEC, although investors can obtain a copy from the commission.[7]

It is not completely accurate to talk about "the" prospectus, because an issuing firm may file a half-dozen or more amended prospectuses with the SEC during the registration period preceding an offer. The first, or **preliminary prospectus,** serves as the principal marketing tool during the period from initial filing with the SEC to the time when the firm responds to the commission's initial findings. The preliminary prospectus is often called a **red herring,** because it has a standard legal disclaimer printed across its cover in red stating that the securities described therein are not (yet) being offered for sale. The red herring lists a range of prices rather than a single price at which the securities may be offered. Usually, the final offer price is set the day before (or even the day of) the offering, and a final prospectus is then distributed with shares sold in the offering.

As the underwriting syndicate responds to SEC feedback, additional prospectuses are printed, until the commission allows the offer to become effective—that is, to proceed to public sale. At that time, a final prospectus is printed that includes the definitive offering price and number of shares being sold. This prospectus is then distributed to initial purchasers of the stock. The actual sale of securities cannot occur until each investor receives a final prospectus. Figure 16.2 presents the title page from the final prospectus of Google's IPO in August 2004. Morgan Stanley and Credit Suisse First Boston were the co-lead underwriters for this offering. An additional eight IBs were included in the title page's bulge bracket, including Goldman Sachs, Citigroup, and Lehman Brothers.

MATERIAL COVERED IN AN OFFERING PROSPECTUS

The format of the prospectus is both highly standardized and remarkably informative to an experienced observer. The title page presents details about the number of shares being offered and about the underwriting agreement (participants and terms) governing the offering. The next several pages of the prospectus present a thumbnail description of the company and its products, a table detailing the offering and listing how the proceeds will be used, a financial summary of operating results for the past few years, and a simplified balance sheet.

The main part of the prospectus begins with a more detailed portrait of the company as it currently operates and of its recent history and then proceeds to a detailed discussion of specific "risk factors" that make the offering especially risky. If a firm's fortunes rest on unproven technology, on key suppliers or customers, or on the talents of key personnel, the firm must disclose these risks. The firm must also disclose whether insiders will control a majority of the votes after the offering.[8] It is often said, only partly in jest, that no investor who actually reads a prospectus ever willingly buys the stock.

[7.] You can download the prospectus from current and past offerings (going back to the mid-1990s) on the SEC's *EDGAR* website (http://www.sec.gov/edgar.shtml).

[8.] The risk-factors section often makes for interesting reading. A recent prospectus for a chain of funeral homes listed a decline in the U.S. death rate as an important risk factor. A ski resort's prospectus mentioned that "the success or failure of a new business depends greatly on the ability of its management," and (nearby) "the management has no previous experience in owning and operating a ski resort or any of its amenity services."

Prospectus
August 18, 2004

19,605,052 Shares

Class A Common Stock

Google Inc. is offering 14,142,135 shares of Class A common stock and the selling stockholders are offering 5,462,917 shares of Class A common stock. We will not receive any proceeds from the sale of shares by the selling stockholders. This is our initial public offering and no public market currently exists for our shares. The initial public offering price is $85.00 per share.

Following this offering, we will have two classes of authorized common stock, Class A common stock and Class B common stock. The rights of the holders of Class A common stock and Class B common stock are identical, except with respect to voting and conversion. Each share of Class A common stock is entitled to one vote per share. Each share of Class B common stock is entitled to ten votes per share and is convertible at any time into one share of Class A common stock.

Our Class A common stock will be quoted on The Nasdaq National Market under the symbol "GOOG."

Investing in our Class A common stock involves risks. See "Risk Factors" beginning on page 4.

Price $85.00 A Share

	Price to Public	Underwriting Discounts and Commissions	Proceeds to Google	Proceeds to Selling Stockholders
Per Share	$ 85.00	$ 2.3839	$ 82.6161	$ 82.6161
Total	$1,666,429,420	$46,736,483	$1,168,368,039	$451,324,897

The selling stockholders have granted the underwriters the right to purchase up to an additional 2,940,757 shares to cover over-allotments.

The price to the public and allocation of shares were determined by an auction process. The minimum size for a bid in the auction was five shares of our Class A common stock. The method for submitting bids and a more detailed description of this auction process are included in "Auction Process" beginning on page 34. As part of this auction process, we attempted to assess the market demand for our Class A common stock and to set the size and price to the public of this offering to meet that demand. As a result, buyers should not expect to be able to sell their shares for a profit shortly after our Class A common stock begins trading. We determined the method for allocating shares to bidders who submitted successful bids following the closing of the auction.

The Securities and Exchange Commission and state securities regulators have not approved or disapproved of these securities, or determined if this prospectus is truthful or complete. Any representation to the contrary is a criminal offense.

It is expected that the shares will be delivered to purchasers on or about August 24, 2004.

Morgan Stanley	**Credit Suisse First Boston**
Goldman, Sachs & Co.	**Citigroup**
Lehman Brothers	**Allen & Company LLC**
JPMorgan	**UBS Investment Bank**
WR Hambrecht+Co	**Thomas Weisel Partners LLC**

Figure 16.2
Title Page from Google's IPO Prospectus
Reprinted by permission of Google Inc.

Deeper in the prospectus, investors find more detailed information about the issuer's financial condition, its business strategies, and the experience of its management team. The prospectus also reveals key information about how the firm will be governed after the offer. For instance, the prospectus lists the members of the board of directors and any business relationships they have with the corporation. The prospectus discloses the shares (and options) owned by corporate officers and directors, both before and after the offer, and describes the compensation packages of the firm's top managers. If the purpose of the offering is to allow an existing shareholder to sell some of her stock, the issue is a **secondary offering** and raises no capital for the firm. If the shares offered for sale are all newly issued, which increases the number of outstanding shares and raise new capital for the firm, the issue is a **primary offering.** If some of the shares come from existing shareholders and some are new, the issue is a **mixed offering.** Google's IPO was a mixed offering. Ang and Brau (2003) find that 32 percent of all underwritten IPOs between 1980 and 1997 included at least some secondary shares, and these account for an average 27 percent of total proceeds.

The final section of an offering prospectus consists of various appendixes. One of the first of these presents the **cold comfort letter** provided by the firm's auditors, almost invariably one of the major accounting firms. This "letter" is actually a simple statement that the company's financial statements were prepared according to generally accepted accounting principles and accurately reflect all relevant information. Depending on the complexity of a company's business, the cold comfort letter may then be followed by from one to several dozen other appendixes that provide additional details about a firm's operations and/or financial structure. The entire IPO prospectus typically runs 80 to 160 pages in length.

Securities can be exempt from registration under certain conditions. Securities with a maturity of less than 270 days are exempt, as are intrastate security offerings and securities issued or guaranteed by a bank.[9] In addition, the sale of unregistered securities is allowed in private placements. These are discussed in depth in Section 16.5.

SHELF REGISTRATION (RULE 415)

As an alternative to filing a lengthy registration statement and awaiting SEC approval, firms with more than $150 million in outstanding common stock can use a procedure known as **shelf registration** (**Rule 415**) for the issue. This procedure, described in Blackwell, Marr, and Spivey (1990), allows a qualifying company to file a *master registration statement,* which is a single document summarizing planned financing covering a 2-year period. Once the SEC approves the issue, it is placed "on the shelf," and the company can sell the new securities to investors out of inventory (off the shelf) as needed any time over the next 2 years. This has proven to be immensely popular with issuing corporations, which previously had to incur the costs (including costs of delay) of filing separate SEC registrations for each new security issue. In addition to saving time and money, shelf registration allows firms to issue securities in response to changing market conditions.

Shelf registration is especially popular with large firms that frequently need access to the capital markets for funding. Although in principle shelf registration allows firms to reduce their reliance on investment bankers, the investment banker continues to be the key link between the firm and the capital markets. Interestingly, academic research documents that underwriting expenses are lower for shelf registrations than for traditional security issues and that firms rarely use shelf registration when they issue equity, whereas debt shelf registrations are quite common. This research result, first documented by Denis (1991), means that firms enjoy a greater benefit from having investment bankers "certify" the value of equity securities but that certification is less valuable for bonds.

[9.] This exemption is why commercial paper (discussed in Chapter 17) invariably has an original maturity of less than 270 days. As it happens, most commercial paper is of much shorter maturity, but the fact that this most important source of short-term financing for top-tier U.S. corporations is specifically designed to be an unregulated financial instrument reveals both the importance of security laws and the lengths businesses will go to escape such regulation.

ONGOING REGULATORY REQUIREMENTS FOR A PUBLICLY TRADED FIRM

Once a company successfully completes an IPO and lists its shares for trading on an exchange, it becomes subject to all the costs and reporting requirements of a public company. These include cash expenses such as exchange-listing fees and the cost of mailing proxies, annual reports, and other documents to shareholders. Additionally, public companies must hold general shareholders' meetings at least once each year and must obtain shareholder approval for important decisions, such as approving a merger, authorizing additional shares of stock, and approving new stock option plans. By far the most costly regulatory constraints on public companies are the disclosure requirements for the firm, its officers and directors, and its principal shareholders. In essence, the company must report any material change in its operations, ownership, or financing. Once a firm "goes public," life becomes very public indeed.

Concept Review Questions

5. What is the guiding principle behind most of the important U.S. securities legislation? What role does the security registration play in implementing this philosophy?

6. What is a *red herring*?

7. What is *shelf registration?* Why do you think this has proven to be so popular with issuing firms, and why is it employed so frequently for debt offerings and so infrequently for equity issues?

16.3 THE U.S. MARKET FOR INITIAL PUBLIC OFFERINGS

Given its role in providing capital market access for entrepreneurial growth companies, the U.S. initial public offering market is widely considered a vital economic and financial asset. Indeed, a welcoming IPO market has long been a key building block of America's success in high-technology industries. It is thus not surprising that all the U.S. stock markets compete fiercely for IPO listings. The competition is particularly intense between the two largest, the New York Stock Exchange (NYSE) and the Nasdaq electronic market. Although the number of IPOs (usually a few hundred per year) and the total capital raised ($30 billion to $75 billion) each year since the mid-1990s may seem trivial in an $11 trillion economy, IPOs generally represent 30–40 percent of all new common equity raised by U.S. corporations each year. In other words, IPOs raise almost half as much external equity capital each year as do established giants such as IBM, Exxon, and General Motors.

PATTERNS OBSERVED IN THE U.S. IPO MARKET

To the uninitiated, a quick survey of the U.S. IPO market reveals some decidedly odd patterns.[10] For example, it is one of the most highly cyclical securities markets imaginable. As Table 16.7 makes clear, aggregate IPO volume shows a very distinct

---

[10.] The reader interested in quickly developing a working knowledge of the workings of the U.S. IPO market should read Loughran and Ritter (2004). These authors are leading IPO researchers, and this paper efficiently summarizes key pricing and trading patterns for unseasoned issues. Other recent papers examining overall IPO patterns include Lowry (2003), Benveniste, Ljungqvist, Wilhelm, and Yu (2003), Bruner, Chaplinsky, and Ramchand (2004), and Lowry and Schwert (2004).

Table 16.7
Number of Offerings,
First-Day Returns, and
Gross Proceeds of U.S.
Initial Public Offerings,
1975–2004

Year	Number of Offerings	Average First-Day Returns (%)	Gross Proceeds ($ millions)
1975	12	−1.5%	$ 262
1976	26	1.9	214
1977	15	3.6	127
1978	20	11.2	209
1979	39	8.5	312
1980	78	15.2%	$ 962
1981	202	6.4	2,386
1982	83	10.6	1,081
1983	523	8.8	12,047
1984	227	2.6	3,012
1985	215	6.2	5,488
1986	464	6.0	16,195
1987	322	5.5	12,160
1988	121	5.6	4,053
1989	113	7.8	5,212
1990	104	10.8%	4,080
1991	273	12.1	12,280
1992	385	10.2	20,970
1993	483	12.8	28,160
1994	387	9.8	16,240
1995	432	21.5	24,460
1996	621	16.7	40,60
1997	432	13.9	28,970
1998	267	22.3	32,200
1999	457	71.7	62,690
2000	346	56.1%	60,540
2001	76	14.4	33,970
2002	67	8.9	22,110
2003	62	12.1	9,580
2004	182	12.0	32,650
1975–1979	112	5.7%	$ 1,124
1980–1989	2,348	6.8	62,596
1990–2004	4,574	23.3%	$429,600

Source: Jay R. Ritter, "Some Factoids about the 2004 IPO Market," downloaded from his website (http://bear .cba.ufl.edu/ritter/ipodata.htm). Gross proceeds data are from Securities Data Corporation and exclude over-allotment options but include international tranches, if any.
Note: This table presents summary details about IPOs with an offering price of at least $5 per share sold on U.S stock markets between 1975 and 2004. This table excludes American Depositary Receipts (ADRs), best-efforts offers, unit offers, Regulation A offerings, real estate investment trusts (REITs), partnerships, and closed-end funds. Average first-day returns are computed as the equally weighted average percentage return from the offering price to the first closing market price.

pattern of boom and bust. The IPO market boomed throughout most of the 1990s, but it entered truly frothy territory during the "Internet bubble years" of 1999 and 2000.[11] In 1999, for example, the market saw 491 transactions take place (almost

---

[11.] Demers and Lewellen (2003), Ljungqvist, Jenkinson, and Wilhelm (2003), and Loughran and Ritter (2004) all examine IPO pricing during the bubble years. Though the latter two papers both document changing firm and market characteristics—such as a heavier weighting of young Internet companies, lower insider share ownership, and increasing use

two per business day), and these raised more than $65 billion. The torrid pace continued during the first part of 2000. But when prices of U.S. stocks tumbled, a chill fell over the market. The number of transactions in 2001 was barely one-sixth of 1999's peak, and only a few dozen companies attempted to go public during 2002. Though this most recent cycle was among the most dramatic in history, the general pattern was by no means unprecedented, following boom-and-bust cycles from the 1960s, 1970s, and 1980s.

Another interesting pattern observed in the IPO market is the tendency for firms going public in a certain industry to "cluster" in time. It is common to see bursts of IPO activity in fairly narrow industry sectors, such as energy, biotechnology, communications, and, in the late 1990s, Internet-related companies. Indeed, the last half of the 1990s saw an incredible boom in both the number of Internet companies going public and the valuations assigned to them by the market. Companies such as Netscape, Yahoo!, Amazon.com, and eBay were able to raise hundreds of millions of dollars in equity despite their relatively short operating histories and nonexistent profits. Investors were so eager to purchase shares in these firms that their stock prices often doubled the first day they began trading.

APPLYING THE MODEL 16.2

The short-term stock price increases for Internet-related IPOs had financial experts scratching their heads in 1999, none more so than the December 9, 1999, debut of VA Linux. The company went public with an offer price of $30 per share; after one trading day, the stock closed at almost $240 per share. For investors who bought shares at the offer price and sold them as soon as possible, the one-day return was an astronomical *700 percent*. Investors who held on for the long term did not fare as well. After the IPO, the stock closed above $240 only once; by March 2005, the company, by then renamed VA Software, saw its stock trading at just $1.65 per share.

As recently as the early 1980s, investment banks targeted initial offerings almost exclusively at individual investors, more particularly at retail customers of the brokerage firms involved in the underwriting syndicate. Since the mid-1980s, however, institutional investors have grown in importance, and now they generally receive 50 to 75 percent of the shares offered in the typical IPOs and up to 90 percent or more of the "hot" issues.[12]

A final pattern emerging in the U.S. IPO market is its increasingly international flavor. The largest and most visible of the international IPOs are associated with privatizations of formerly state-owned enterprises. However, both established interna-

---

of directed share ownership ("friends and family") programs—during the bubble years, they reach differing conclusions regarding the relative importance of each factor. Ljungqvist, Jenkinson, and Wilhelm (2003) conclude that it was the issuing firms—and their managers' incentives—that were different during the bubble, whereas Loughran and Ritter (2004) find that this period's extreme underpricing resulted from issuing firm managers' desire to attract research coverage from analysts at the top investment banks.

[12.] Academic analyses of the strategic share-allocation decisions made by investment bankers can be found in Hanley and Wilhelm (1995), Booth and Chua (1996), Ljungqvist and Wilhelm (2002), Aggarwal, Prabhala, and Puri (2002), and Aggarwal (2003). Hanley and Wilhelm, Ljungqvist and Wilhelm, and Aggarwal all find that underwriters typically allocate almost two-thirds of all shares on offer to institutional investors. Ljungqvist and Wilhelm conclude that "discretionary" IPO allocations favoring institutional investors actually work in the best interests of issuing firms. Aggarwal, Prabhala, and Puri document a positive relationship between an IPO's first-day return and the fraction of IPO shares allocated to institutional investors. In other words, institutions receive greater allocations in the "hot" IPOs, those with strong pre-market demand.

COMPARATIVE CORPORATE FINANCE

The Widely Varying Importance of Stock Market Finance in Developed Countries

Country	Equity Issues by Domestic Companies		Total Value of Stock Offerings ($ million)	Gross Domestic Product ($ million)	Value of Stock and Bond Offerings as % GDP
	By Already Listed Companies ($ million)	By Newly Listed Companies ($ million)			
United States: NYSE	$54,197	$27,362	$93,212	$11,664,600	0.799%
Nasdaq	6,365	5,288			
Japan	33,940	39	33,979	4,300,900	0.790
Germany	0	0	0	2,687,100	0
United Kingdom	22,624	7,591	30,215	2,115,000	1.430
Italy	3,021	11,356	14,377	1,671,100	0.860
China	1,735	6,095	7,830	1,412,300	0.744
Canada	9,439	8,465	17,904	977,000	1.833
Spain	5,371	12,439	17,810	972,300	1.832
Korea	0	612	612	663,200	0.092
Mexico	691	42	733	660,400	0.111
Australia	16,824	6,013	22,837	639,000	3.574
Austria	1,078	1,701	2,779	660,400	0.421
India	5,192	5,338	10,530	607,900	1.732
Turkey	497	12	509	295,000	0.173
Norway	52	834	886	250,700	0.353
Hong Kong, SAR	19,855	7,598	27,453	156,700	17.523
Chile	0	2,573	2,573	72,100	3.569

Sources: Stock and bond issuance data, World Federation of Exchanges (formerly International Federation of Stock Exchanges) website [www .fibv.com]. GDP data: Organization of Economic Cooperation and Development website (www.oecd.org and International Financial Statistics Yearbook 2004 (International Monetary Fund, Washington, DC).

Note: This table details the total value of new equity security issues on selected national stock markets for the year 2003. It lists the total value (in $US million [$ million]) of seasoned and unseasoned (IPOs) offerings and the relative importance of this total stock market funding as a percent of year 2003 GDP (expressed in U.S. dollars). The countries are ranked by year 2003 GDP, though the table does not include countries whose stock exchanges are not members of the World Federation of Exchanges, nor does it include France, the Netherlands, Belgium, or Portugal since these exchanges are all part of Euronext and individual national issuance totals are not listed separately. There are striking differences in the relative importance of capital market finance, even between countries with roughly similar levels of national income.

tional companies and non-U.S. entrepreneurial firms are also choosing to make initial stock offerings to U.S. investors, either publicly via a straight IPO or to institutional investors through a **Rule 144A offering.** This special type of offer, which was first approved in April 1990, allows issuing companies to waive some disclosure requirements by selling stock only to sophisticated institutional investors, who may then trade the shares among themselves.

ADVANTAGES AND DISADVANTAGES OF AN IPO

The decision to convert from private to public ownership is not an easy one. The benefits of having publicly traded shares are numerous, but so too are the costs. This section describes the costs and benefits of IPOs for U.S. firms. Interestingly, as we discuss more fully in Section 16.6, Pagano, Panetta, and Zingales (1998) show that the motivations for going public are significantly different for continental European business owners than for their U.S. counterparts.

Benefits of Going Public. Chapter 2 of the accounting firm KPMG Peat Marwick's publication *Going Public: What the CEO Needs to Know* (1998) suggests the following advantages of an IPO to an entrepreneur.

1. **New capital for the company.** An initial public offering gives the typical private firm access to a larger pool of equity capital than is available from any other source. Whereas venture capitalists can provide perhaps $10 million to $40 million in funding throughout a company's life as a private firm, an IPO allows that same company to raise many times that amount in one offering. Loughran and Ritter (2004) find that the typical U.S. IPO during 1990–2004 raised an average of $93.9 million. An infusion of common equity not only permits the firm to pursue profitable investment opportunities, but also improves the firm's overall financial condition and provides additional borrowing capacity. Furthermore, if the firm's stock performs well, the company will be able to raise additional equity capital in the future.

2. **Publicly traded stock for use in acquisitions.** Unless a firm has publicly traded stock, the only way it can acquire another company is to pay in cash. After going public, a firm has the option of exchanging its own stock for that of the target firm. Not only does this minimize cash outflow for the acquiring firm, but such a payment method may be free from capital gains tax for the target firm's owners. This tax benefit may reduce the price that an acquirer must pay for a target company.

3. **Listed stock for use as a compensation vehicle.** Having publicly traded stock allows the company to attract, retain, and provide incentives for talented managers by offering them stock options and other stock-based compensation. Going public also offers liquidity to managers who were awarded options while the firm was private.

4. **Personal wealth and liquidity.** Entrepreneurship almost always violates finance's basic dictum about diversification: real entrepreneurs generally have most of both their financial wealth and human capital tied up in their companies. Going public allows entrepreneurs to reallocate cash from their businesses and diversify their portfolios. Entrepreneurial families also frequently execute IPOs during times of transition when, for example, the company founder wishes to retire and provide a method of allocating family assets among those heirs who do and do not wish to remain active in the business.

In addition to these benefits, the act of going public generally results in a blaze of media attention, which often helps promote the company's products and services. Being a public company also increases a firm's overall prestige. However, the often-massive costs must be weighed against all the obvious benefits of an IPO.

Drawbacks to Going Public. KPMG Peat Marwick's listing also includes the drawbacks of an IPO for a firm's managers.

1. **The financial costs of an IPO.** Few entrepreneurs are truly prepared for just how costly the process of going public can be in terms of out-of-pocket cash expenses and opportunity costs. Total cash expenses of an IPO, such as printing, accounting, and legal services, frequently approach $1 million, and most of these must be paid even if the offering is postponed or canceled. Additionally, the combined costs associated with the underwriter's discount (usually 7 percent) and initial

underpricing of the firm's stock (roughly 15 percent on average) represents a very large transfer of wealth from current owners to the underwriters and to the new stockholders.[13]

2. **The managerial costs of an IPO.** As costly as an IPO is financially, many entrepreneurs find the unremitting claims made on their time during the IPO planning and execution process to be even more burdensome. Rarely, if ever, can CEOs and other top managers delegate these duties, which grow increasingly intense as the offering date approaches. There are also severe restrictions on what an executive can say or do during the immediate preoffering period. Because the IPO process can take many months to complete, the managerial distraction costs of going public are very high. Top executives must also take time to meet with important potential stockholders before completing the IPO and forever thereafter.

3. **Stock-price emphasis.** Owners/managers of private companies frequently operate their firms in ways that balance competing personal and financial interests. This includes seeking profits but frequently also includes employing family members in high positions and other private benefits. Once a company goes public, however, external pressures build to maximize the firm's stock price. Furthermore, as managerial shareholdings fall, managers become vulnerable to losing their jobs either through takeover or through dismissal by the board of directors.[14]

4. **Life in a fishbowl.** Public shareholders have the right to a great deal of information about a firm's internal affairs, and releasing this information to stockholders also implies releasing it to competitors and potential acquirers as well. Managers must disclose, especially in the IPO prospectus, how and in what markets they intend to compete, information that is obviously valuable to competitors. Additionally, managers who are also significant stockholders are subject to binding disclosure requirements and face serious constraints on their ability to buy or sell company stock.

In spite of these drawbacks, we have seen that several hundred management teams each year decide that the benefits of going public outweigh the costs and begin the process of planning for an IPO. In addition to these "standard" IPOs, four "special" types of IPOs warrant special attention.

SPECIALIZED INITIAL PUBLIC OFFERINGS: ECOs, SPIN-OFFS, REVERSE LBOs, AND TRACKING STOCKS

The four special types of IPOs are equity carve-outs (ECOs), spin-offs, reverse LBOs, and tracking stocks. An *equity carve-out* occurs when a parent company sells shares of a subsidiary corporation to the public through an initial public offering. The parent company may sell some of the subsidiary shares that it already owns, or the subsidiary may issue new shares. In any event, the parent company almost always retains a controlling stake in the newly public company.[15]

[13.] The financial costs of an IPO are documented in Ritter (1988) and Lee, Lochhead, Ritter, and Zhao (1996). Intriguingly, Chen and Ritter (2000) show that the spreads received by underwriters on most midsize IPOs are *exactly* 7 percent, though Altinkiliç and Hansen (2000), Yeoman (2001), and Hansen (2001) contend that this is not necessarily a sign of insufficient competition among underwriters. Schenone (2004) shows that issuing firms with a preexisting lending relationship with a prospective underwriting investment bank can reduce underwriting spreads by an average of 17 percent.

[14.] Field and Karpoff (2002) show that managers anticipate their exposure to takeover threat. In their sample of more than 1,000 IPOs, at least 53 percent go public with some form of antitakeover defense in place.

[15.] Equity carve-outs are examined empirically in Schipper and Smith (1986), Nanda (1991), Slovin, Sushka, and Ferraro (1995), Michaely and Shaw (1995), and, most recently, Vijh (1999). These studies generally find that announcements of carve-outs are viewed as good news by investors (the parent stock experiences a positive abnormal return) and that the long-term returns to buyers of carve-outs are better than those for buyers of other types of common stock offerings. Vijh

A **spin-off** occurs when a public parent company "spins off" a subsidiary to the parent's shareholders by distributing shares on a pro rata basis. Thus, after the spin-off, there will be two public companies rather than one. Conceptually, the stock price of the parent should drop by approximately the amount that the market values the shares of the newly public spin-off, though Hite and Owers (1983), Miles and Rosenfeld (1983), and Schipper and Smith (1983) all document significantly positive price reactions for the stock of divesting parent companies at the time of spin-off announcements, perhaps indicating that the market expects that the two independent companies will be managed more effectively than they would have been had they remained together.

APPLYING THE MODEL 16.3

Lamont and Thaler (2002) describe one of the most puzzling spin-offs ever. In March 2000, 3Com Corp. sold a 5 percent stake in its subsidiary, Palm Inc., via an equity carve-out. 3Com also announced its intention to spin off the remaining 95 percent of Palm to existing 3Com shareholders, who would receive 1.5 shares of Palm for each share of 3Com they owned. This gave investors two ways to purchase Palm shares. For example, an investor who wanted to buy 150 Palm shares could buy them directly in the carve-out IPO, or the investor could purchase 100 shares of 3Com and wait to receive 150 Palm shares after the spin-off. Of course, in the latter strategy, the investor would ultimately own 150 shares of Palm and 100 shares of 3Com.

What was puzzling about this spin-off was the behavior of 3Com and Palm shares after the carve-out. Conceptually, the stand-alone value of 3Com shares cannot be negative. Therefore, the price of 3Com shares prior to the spin-off should have been *at least* 1.5 times the price of Palm shares in the carve-out (because anyone who owned 1 share of 3Com would ultimately receive an additional 1.5 shares of Palm). In fact, after a single trading day, Palm shares sold for almost 1.2 times more than 3Com shares were worth! In this case, and a few other high-tech spin-offs, it seems that only irrational exuberance can explain the market's response.

In a **reverse LBO** (or **second IPO**), a formerly public company that has previously gone private through a leveraged buyout goes public again. Reverse LBOs are easier to price than traditional IPOs because information exists about how the market valued the company when it was publicly traded. Muscarella and Vetsuypens (1989) and DeGeorge and Zeckhauser (1993, 1996) study reverse LBOs and find that the LBO partners earn very high returns on these transactions. One reason for this is obvious: Only the most successful LBOs can subsequently go public again.

The final type of specialized equity offering, **tracking stocks,** is a very recent innovation. These are equity claims based on (and designed to mirror, or *track*) the earnings of wholly owned subsidiaries of diversified firms. They are hybrid securities, because the tracking stock "firm" is not separated from the parent company in any way, but instead remains integrated with the parent legally and operationally. In contrast, both carve-outs and spin-offs result in legally separate firms. AT&T conducted the largest common stock offering in U.S. history when it issued $10.6 billion in

---

reports (Table 2) that the mean (median) offering value as a percentage of subsidiary value was 38.2 (32.2) percent for 628 carve-outs during the 1981–1995 period. The average percentage ownership of the subsidiary by the parent after the carve-out was 58.6 (62.5) percent.

AT&T Wireless tracking stock in April 2000. As has been true for most other tracking stock offerings, AT&T's stock rose significantly when it announced the Wireless offering. Unfortunately, both parent and tracking stock performed abysmally during the months after the issue, and in July 2001, AT&T Wireless became an independent company; it was acquired by Cingular Wireless in October 2004.

THE INVESTMENT PERFORMANCE OF INITIAL PUBLIC OFFERINGS

Are IPOs good investments? The answer seems to depend on the investment horizon of the investor and whether or not the investor can purchase IPO shares at the offer price. If an investor can buy shares at the offer price and **flip** them, selling them on the first trading day, then the returns on IPOs are substantial.[16] If, instead, the investor buys shares in the secondary market and holds them for the long term, the returns are much less rewarding.

Positive Initial Returns for IPO Investors (Underpricing). Year in and year out, in virtually every country around the world, the very short-term returns on IPOs are surprisingly high. In the United States, the share price in the typical IPO closes roughly 15 percent above the offer price after just one day of trading. Researchers refer to this pattern as **IPO underpricing,** meaning that the offer price in the prospectus is consistently lower than what the market is willing to bear.[17] To capture this **initial return,** an investor must be fortunate enough to receive an allocation of shares from the investment banker and to sell those shares at the first opportunity. Investors who buy IPO shares when open-market trading begins receive much smaller returns, and take on much greater risks, than do investors who participate in the initial offering.

APPLYING THE MODEL 16.4

On February 19, 2002, shares of the pioneer in Internet payment methods, Paypal Inc. (ticker symbol, PYPL), began trading for the first time. According to the IPO prospectus, Paypal offered its shares for $13.00 to participating investors. At the close of the first day, Paypal shares were worth $18.20, for a one-day return of 40 percent. However, for investors who could not buy shares from the syndicate and instead bought shares once trading began, the first-day results were not as good. Paypal shares opened the first day of trading at $19.29 before falling 5.7 percent by the day's end. Paypal was acquired by e-Bay in October 2002 at twice the price that e-Bay had offered one year earlier to then-privately held Paypal's owners.

---

[16] Not surprising, underwriters tend to discourage flipping because it raises the odds that they will have to help stabilize the price once trading begins. Siconolfi and McGeehan (1998) describe how investment banks try to identify and punish flippers. Krigman, Shaw, and Womack (1999) offer a different assessment of the economic value of flippers. They find that flipping is both a rational response to perceived pricing errors (caused primarily by issuing firms' unwillingness to lower share offering prices in the face of weak demand) and accurately predicts future returns on newly issued shares. Finally, Aggarwal (2003) shows that flippers account for only an average 19 percent of immediate post-IPO trading volume (and only 15 percent of shares offered) and that hot IPOs are flipped more than cold offerings. She also shows that explicit penalty bids are used in only 13 percent of offerings and are small in size but have an important deterrent effect.

[17] The academic literature on IPO underpricing is far too voluminous to cite in depth. Instead, we encourage the interested reader to see the references in the survey and empirical articles by Ibbotson, Sindelar, and Ritter (1994), Loughran, Ritter, and Rydqvist (1994), Lee, Lochhead, Ritter, and Zhao (1996), Bruner, Chaplinsky, and Ramchand (2004), and Loughran and Ritter (2004).

Average one-day returns on IPOs of 15 percent present quite a puzzle to financial economists, who in studying these returns have uncovered the following patterns.

1. **Large IPOs tend to be less underpriced than smaller offerings.** The smaller the offering, the more it is underpriced, and best-efforts offers are more underpriced than firm-commitment issues.

2. **Initial returns are higher in "hot-issue markets" than in more normal times.** Anyone wishing to make a case that financial markets are prone to irrational exuberance will quickly seize on initial offerings, for the IPO market does appear especially prone to fads. Partly because of the IPO market's relatively small scale, a small change in investor appetite for new issues can have a profound impact on the reception accorded individual offerings. As Ljungqvist, Jenkinson, and Wilhelm (2003) show, this was most true during the "Internet bubble" of 1999, when average IPO initial returns hit 69 percent and Internet IPOs were underpriced on average by a stunning 89 percent. During 1999 and the first three quarters of 2000, nearly 200 firms conducting IPOs saw their stock price increase by 100 percent or more on the first trading day. However, the IPO market cooled by the fall of 2000; from October of that year through the end of 2002, only one IPO doubled in price in its debut.

3. **The mean initial return is much higher than the median.** Although the "headline" underpricing figures are quite dramatic, only 60 to 70 percent of all IPOs are substantially underpriced, and the median IPO's initial return is roughly half the average value. The average, in turn, is inflated by a relative handful of extraordinarily popular offerings with initial returns of 50 percent or more.

4. **The mean return overstates the actual profits earned by most investors.** Rock (1986) argues that IPO investors, especially those who are less sophisticated than the institutions that are the investment banks' best clients, face a classic problem of the **winner's curse.** When an IPO is extremely "hot," both sophisticated and unsophisticated investors will demand shares, and the issue will be heavily oversubscribed. In these deals, investors will be rationed (with rationing most severe for "ordinary" investors), receiving only a fraction of the shares they would like. On the other hand, when an IPO is "cold" and the syndicate has difficulty selling the issue to more sophisticated clients, ordinary investors will receive all the shares they requested. Unfortunately, the short-term returns for these IPOs will be below average. Because they receive small allocations in hot deals and large allocations in cold deals, the unsophisticated players in this market will earn much lower returns than a glance at the average one-day return for all IPOs might suggest.

5. **It is unclear whether venture capital backing or the use of a prestigious underwriter increases or decreases IPO underpricing.** At least during the years prior to 1990, venture capital–backed IPOs were, on average, less underpriced than non-venture-backed offers, and issues brought to market by more prestigious underwriters yielded lower first-day returns than those handled by lesser-known investment bankers. Stated differently, existing owners of venture-backed firms were able to capture more of the postoffer value of their company than could owners of other companies executing IPOs, and the same was true of firms taken public by prestigious underwriters. It is unclear whether this is still true today. Beatty and Welch (1996) show that underwriter prestige and initial return are positively correlated after 1990, though exactly why this has occurred remains a puzzle.

SMART ETHICS VIDEO

Jay Ritter, University of Florida
"Every single country in the world has IPOs underpriced on average."

See the entire interview at
SMARTFinance

The empirical regularities detailed earlier make clear just how expensive going public tends to be for most companies. Significant underpricing means that money is "left on the table" by the owners of a company executing an IPO, since the high initial returns are captured by the original share purchasers rather than by the issuing company. Why IPOs are underpriced is something of a mystery. Presumably, the firms issuing stock would prefer to receive a higher price (with less underpricing) for their shares, and they could choose investment banks with a track record of less underpricing. Competition among investment banks on this dimension might reduce underpricing to an economically insignificant level, on average.

Finance theory offers several possible explanations for the underpricing phenomenon. First, given the problem of the winner's curse, firms may have to underprice shares, on average, to keep relatively unsophisticated players in the market. If the average IPO were not underpriced, then unsophisticated investors would receive large allocations of the IPOs with negative returns and small allocations of those with positive returns, and they would eventually drop out of the market. Second, firms could underprice their IPOs in an attempt to achieve higher stock valuations later, when they conduct seasoned offerings. For example, a firm with excellent future prospects might be willing to leave money on the table initially (something a less healthy firm could not afford to do) to convince investors of just how bright its future looks. If investors recognize and respond to this signal, then the long-term value of the firm's shares will be higher, and it can recoup the initial underpricing costs in future equity offerings.

Third, a firm might be willing to underprice its shares to generate excess demand for the offering. With excess demand, the firm (or its investment bank) could spread the shares across many different investors, with no single investor holding a large block. A dispersed ownership structure could benefit the firm if it leads to a more liquid market for the shares and hence a lower cost of capital. Managers might selfishly prefer more ownership dispersion because investors who own just a few shares are less likely than those owning large blocks to threaten managers if the firm's stock performs poorly. In the extreme, managers can create a dual-class equity structure before going public and concentrate their ownership in the share class with greater voting rights [Smart and Zutter (2003)]. Fourth, firms may underprice to give investors an incentive to reveal useful information they have about the true value of the firm's stock.

Whatever the case, underpricing is a pervasive phenomenon. However, the long-run performance of IPOs presents a different puzzle.

Long-Term IPO Returns. Early research on the long-run performance of IPOs was not encouraging for investors. Loughran and Ritter (1995) show that investors who buy IPO shares at the end of the first month of trading and then hold these shares for five years thereafter fare much worse than they would have by purchasing the shares of comparable, size-matched firms. On average, investors' net returns are over 40 percent below what they would have earned after five years on alternative equity investments.

Because these findings challenge the notions that investors are rational and financial markets efficient, they are quite controversial. More recent research casts doubt on this long-run underperformance for IPO shares. Studies by Brav and Gompers (2000), Fama (1998), Brav, Geczy, and Gompers (1997), Eckbo, Masulis, and Norli (2000), Gompers and Lerner (2003), and Eckbo and Norli (2005) conclude that most IPOs do not yield significant long-run underperformance, provided that IPO returns are compared to an appropriate benchmark. In particular, Eckbo, Masulis, and Norli (2000) make a compelling case that much of the observed underperformance can be explained by leverage effects and risk reductions resulting from the IPO itself.

**SMART
ETHICS
VIDEO**

Jay Ritter, University of Florida
"By the middle of 2001, 97% of Internet companies were trading below the offer price."

See the entire interview at
SMARTFinance

They show that a company's raising new equity capital in an IPO reduces the firm's leverage and its financial risk, so investors will accept a lower required return subsequent to the offering. Schultz (2003) provides theoretical evidence against long-term IPO underperformance by demonstrating that managers can be expected to issue stock after share prices increase, even when these managers have no forecasting or timing ability. He also shows that underperformance disappears when calendar-time returns (which weight all months equally) are used to compute abnormal performance rather than event-time returns—which weight active IPO-issuance months more heavily than cold months. On balance, we conclude that IPOs tend to earn normal long-term returns.

8. What patterns have been observed in the types of firms going public in the United States? Why do you think that certain industries become popular with investors at different times?

9. What are the principal benefits of going public? What are the key drawbacks?

10. Distinguish between an *equity carve-out* and a *spin-off*. How might a spin-off create value for shareholders?

11. What does the term *underpricing* refer to? If the average IPO is underpriced by about 15 percent, how might an unsophisticated investor who regularly invests in IPOs earn an average return less than 15 percent?

12. How does underpricing add to the cost of going public?

Concept Review Questions

16.4 SEASONED EQUITY OFFERINGS IN THE UNITED STATES

Seasoned equity offerings (SEOs) are surprisingly rare for both U.S. and non-U.S. companies. In fact, the typical large U.S. company will not sell new common stock even as frequently as once per decade, though when an SEO is launched, it tends to be much larger than the typical IPO. Seasoned common stock issues must generally follow the same regulatory and underwriting procedures as unseasoned offerings. Besides its larger average size, a seasoned offering differs from an unseasoned offering principally because seasoned securities have an observable market value when the offering is priced—which obviously makes pricing much easier. Corwin (2003) finds that, during the 1980s and 1990s, U.S. SEOs are priced an average 2.2 percent below their closing day market prices, with the discount increasing substantially over time. He also finds that underpricing is positively related to offer size, especially for shares with relatively inelastic demand, which is consistent with the offering's exerting temporary downward price pressure on the market.[18] However, ease of pricing does not mean that investors welcome new equity offering announcements, as we now discuss.

[18.] Altinkiliç and Hansen (2003) document similar levels of SEO underpricing, while Loderer, Sheehan, and Kadlec (1991) show that SEOs during the 1970s and 1980s were priced very near their current market price.

STOCK PRICE REACTIONS TO SEASONED EQUITY ISSUE ANNOUNCEMENTS

One reason corporations issue seasoned equity only rarely is that stock prices usually fall when firms announce plans to conduct SEOs. On average, the price decline is about 3 percent.[19] In the United States, the average dollar value of this price decline is equal to almost one-third of the dollar value of the issue itself. Clearly, the announcement of seasoned equity issues conveys negative information to investors, though precisely what information is transmitted is not always clear. The message may be that management, which is presumably better informed about a company's true prospects than are outside investors, believes the firm's current stock price is too high. Alternatively, the message may be that the firm's earnings will be lower than expected in the future and management is issuing stock to make up for this internal cash flow shortfall.

There is some evidence that SEOs are bad news for shareholders not only at the time they are announced, but also over longer holding periods of one to five years. Negative long-run returns following seasoned equity offerings are also documented in Loughran and Ritter (1995), Spiess and Affleck-Graves (1995), and Jegadeesh (2000). As is the case with long-run IPO returns, however, whether or not long-run returns following SEOs are unusually low depends somewhat on the comparison benchmark. Gibson, Safieddine, and Sonti (2004) offer an intriguing twist to the debate regarding the long-run return to SEOs with their finding that SEO issuers experiencing the greatest increase in institutional investor ownership around the offer date outperform their benchmarks in the year following the offer. This suggests that institutional investors are able to identify above-average SEO firms at the time of the offering and increase their holdings in these potential stars.

Most equity sales in the United States fall under the category of **general cash offerings**. However, there is a special type of seasoned equity offering that allows the firm's existing owners to buy new shares at a bargain price or to sell that right to other investors. These rights offerings are relatively scarce in the United States but are growing in importance internationally.

RIGHTS OFFERINGS

One of the basic tenets of English common law, and thus of U.S. commercial laws derived from it, is that shareholders have first claim on anything of value distributed by a corporation. These **preemptive rights** give common stockholders the right to maintain their proportionate ownership in the corporation by purchasing shares whenever the firm sells new equity.[20] **Rights offerings** are stock issues sold exclusively to a firm's existing shareholders. Because this strategy keeps all the gains and losses on share issues "within the family," firms usually price rights offerings well below the current market price in order to ensure that the offering sells out and the firm raises the funds needed. The laws of most American states grant shareholders the preemptive right to participate in new issues, unless this right is removed by shareholder consent. However, the vast majority of publicly traded U.S. companies have removed

---

[19.] Myers and Majluf (1984) provide a theoretical explanation for this negative market response to seasoned equity issue announcements based on informational asymmetry between managers and investors: Investors interpret SEO announcements as a sign that managers believe that the firm's shares are overvalued.

[20.] Bhagat (1983) documents that the removal of preemptive rights from corporate charters decreases shareholder wealth. In spite of this, the vast majority of publicly traded companies have removed preemptive rights.

preemptive rights from their corporate charter, so rights offerings by large American companies are quite rare today.[21] Rights offerings are still quite common in other countries, however.

APPLYING THE MODEL 16.5

After a decade of extremely rapid growth in capital spending, many telecommunications companies found themselves teetering on the brink of bankruptcy by the summer of 2001. In order to avert financial meltdown, two of the largest European telecoms—British Telecom (BT) and The Netherlands' KPN—took the highly unusual step of launching immense rights offerings of common stock. BT raised £5.9 billion ($8.5 billion) in June 2001, and KPN issued €5 billion ($4.5 billion) six months later, briefly making these the two largest rights offerings in history. BT sold its shares, which were selling for 435 pence each at the time of the rights issue, for 300 pence each, while KPN priced its new shares at a smaller (but still significant) 4.5 percent discount to their market price of €5.11 each. In March 2003, France Telecom eclipsed both of these issues with its own €15 billion ($15.8 billion) rights offering. FT shares were sold for €14.50 each, a 28 percent discount from their market price at the time.

---

13. What happens to a firm's stock price when the firm announces plans for a seasoned equity offering? What are the long-term returns to investors following an SEO?

14. Why do you think that rights offerings have largely disappeared in the United States?

Concept Review Questions

16.5 PRIVATE PLACEMENTS IN THE UNITED STATES

As noted earlier, a **private placement** involves the sale of securities in a transaction that is exempt from the registration requirements imposed by federal securities law. A private placement occurs when an investment banker arranges for the direct sale of a new security issue to an individual, several individuals, an institutional investor, or a group of institutions. The investment banker is then paid a commission for acting as an intermediary in the transaction. To qualify for a private-placement exemption, the sale of the securities must be restricted to a small group of **accredited investors,** who are individuals or institutions that meet certain income and wealth requirements. The rationale for the private-placement exemption is that accredited investors are financially sophisticated agents who do not need the protection afforded by the registration process. Typical accredited institutional investors include insurance companies, pension funds, mutual funds, and venture capitalists.

[21.] The phenomenon of declining U.S. rights offerings is examined in C. W. Smith (1977) and Hansen and Pinkerton (1982). The most likely explanation, discussed in Hansen (1988), is that firms announcing rights issues suffer larger price drops than do firms announcing underwritten offers, thereby negating the benefits of lower underwriting fees. Khorana, Wahal, and Zenner (2002) examine rights offerings by closed-end mutual funds, and their findings suggest that managers execute these offerings primarily to enrich themselves at shareholders' expense.

TRADITIONAL PRIVATE PLACEMENTS VERSUS RULE 144A ISSUES

The private-placement exemption is a **transactional exemption,** which means that the securities must be registered before they can be resold or the subsequent sale must also qualify as a private placement. **Rule 144A,** adopted in 1990, provides a private placement exemption for institutions with assets exceeding $100 million (known as **qualified institutional buyers**) and allows them to freely trade privately placed securities among themselves. The principal reasons for instituting Rule 144A were to increase liquidity and reduce issuing costs in the private-placement market. Another reason was to attract large foreign issuers who were unable or unwilling to conform to U.S. registration requirements for public offerings.

Private placements have several advantages over public offerings. They are less costly in terms of time and money than registering with the SEC, and the issuers do not have to reveal confidential information. Also, because there typically are far fewer investors, the terms of a private placement are easier to renegotiate, if necessary. The disadvantage of private placements is that the securities have no readily available market price, they are less liquid, and there is a smaller group of potential investors than in the public market.[22] There are about 2,500 private placements in the United States each year, and these usually raise $400 to $500 billion in total. Over 90 percent of these are debt offerings, with an average value of around $250 million, and Rule 144A issues represent three-fourths of total issues.

Concept Review Questions

15. What is a *qualified institutional buyer?* How does this differ from an *accredited investor?*

16. What are the relative advantages and disadvantages of private placements compared to those of public offerings of stock and bond issues?

16.6 INTERNATIONAL COMMON STOCK OFFERINGS

The international market for equity offerings can be broken down into two parts: each nation's market for domestic stock offerings and the international, or cross-border, market for equity offerings. We briefly look at each in turn, beginning with a survey of national markets.

NON-U.S. INITIAL PUBLIC OFFERINGS

Any nation with a well-functioning stock market must have some mechanism for taking private firms public, and the total number of IPOs outside the United States each year usually exceeds the American total by a wide margin. However, far less money

---

[22.] Two recent empirical studies examine U.S. private placements (PPs). Hertzel, Lemmon, Linck, and Smith (2002) examine PP pricing as well as the initial and long-run return to stockholders of companies executing private placements. They find that PPs are sold at an average discount of 16.5 percent from the market price of traded shares and that the announcement period return is a significantly positive 2.4 percent. Measured returns become negative over the long term, however, with average 3-year abnormal returns between −23.8 and −45.2 percent, depending on the benchmark used for comparison. Wu (2004) documents that PPs largely fail to improve the performance of issuing firms. She finds that PP investors do not engage in more monitoring of managers than do public offering investors, and she concludes that PPs mostly serve to entrench managers.

is raised in aggregate by private-sector issuers on non-U.S. markets, because these international IPOs are, on average, very much smaller than those on the Nasdaq or NYSE. Yet many of the same investment anomalies documented in the United States are also observed internationally. First, non-U.S. private-sector IPOs also demonstrate significant first-day returns that are often much higher than for U.S. IPOs. Figure 16.3 summarizes IPO underpricing studies from 38 different countries; all show significant underpricing, and 20 of these countries have mean initial returns greater than the U.S. average.

A second empirical regularity common to both U.S. and international IPOs is that unseasoned international offers also may yield negative long-term returns. However, studies of non-U.S. long-run returns are subject to all the methodological problems bedeviling U.S. studies (perhaps even more), so it is unclear whether international IPOs truly underperform or not. Third, popular non-U.S. issues also tend to be heavily oversubscribed, and the allocation rules mandated by national law or exchange regulations largely determine who captures the IPO initial returns. Fourth, hot-issue markets are as prevalent internationally as in the United States. Finally, taxation issues (particularly capital gains tax rules) significantly impact how issues are priced and/or which investors the offers target.

International IPO markets do, however, differ in important ways from U.S. markets. For example, many governments impose politically inspired mandates on firms wishing to go public, requiring them to allocate minimum fractions of the issue to

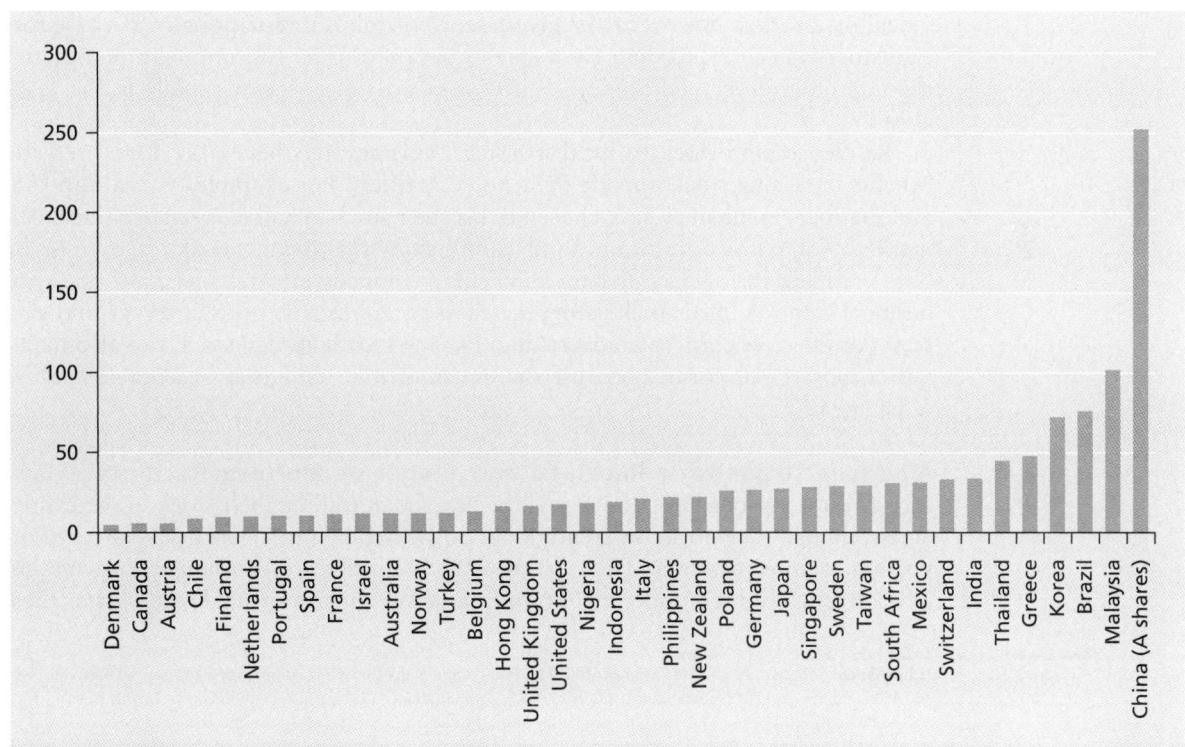

Figure 16.3
Average First-Day Returns on IPOs for 38 Countries
Source: Studies cited in Tim Loughran, Jay R. Ritter, and Kristian Rydqvist, "Initial Public Offerings: International Insights," *Pacific-Basin Finance Journal* 2 (June 1994), pp. 165–1999, updated June 25, 2003, downloaded from Jay Ritter's website (http://bear.cba.ufl.edu/ritter/ipodata.htm).

their employees or to other targeted groups. Furthermore, the net effect of pricing restrictions in many countries is to ensure that IPOs are severely underpriced; this is especially common in countries where shares must be priced on a par value basis and/or where minimum dividend payouts are mandated. Some governments (including ones as advanced as Japan's) routinely prohibit firms from making IPOs during periods when market conditions are "unsettled" and/or require explicit permission to be obtained before an IPO can be launched. Many countries require that initial offering prices be set far in advance of the issue, which usually means that offerings that actually proceed tend to be highly underpriced. Finally, Pagano, Panetta, and Zingales (1998) show that non-U.S. entrepreneurs often have different motivations for taking firms public than do owner/managers of U.S. private companies. Whereas many U.S. companies go public to acquire the equity capital needed to finance rapid growth, continental European entrepreneurs (specifically, Italian) go public mainly to rebalance their firms' capital structures and to achieve personal liquidity. On a more balanced note, most other countries place fewer restrictions on preoffer marketing and dissemination of information than do U.S. regulators.

INTERNATIONAL COMMON STOCK ISSUES

Although the international market for common stock is not, and probably never will be, as large as the international market for debt securities, cross-border trading and issuance of common stock have increased dramatically since 1990. Much of this increase can be accounted for by a growing desire on the part of institutional and individual investors to diversify their investment portfolios internationally. Because foreign stocks currently account for a small fraction of U.S. institutional holdings and those in other developed economies, this total will surely grow rapidly in the years ahead.

Besides issuing stock to local investors, corporations have also discovered the benefits of issuing stock outside their home markets. For example, several top U.S. multinational companies have chosen to list their stock in half a dozen or more stock markets. Chaplinsky and Ramchand (2000) show that issuing stock internationally both broadens the ownership base and helps a company integrate itself into the local business scene. A local stock listing increases local business press coverage and also serves as effective corporate advertising. Having locally traded stock can also facilitate corporate acquisitions because shares can then be used as an acceptable method of payment.[23]

American Depositary Receipts and Global Depositary Receipts. Many foreign corporations have discovered the benefits of trading their stock in the United States, though they do so differently than do U.S. companies. The disclosure and reporting requirements mandated by the U.S. Securities and Exchange Commission have historically discouraged all but the largest foreign firms from directly listing their

[23.] Intriguingly, Pagano, Röell, and Zechner (2002) find that while many European companies listed abroad between 1986 and 1997, mainly on U.S. exchanges, the number of U.S. companies cross-listing in Europe declined. Bruner, Chaplinsky, and Ramchand (2004) find that foreign companies going public on U.S. markets experience roughly the same total issuance costs as domestic IPOs. The higher risk of foreign IPOs due to asymmetric information and home-country risk is offset by their larger average size and greater tangible asset holdings. Siegel (2005) studies whether companies from countries with weak corporate governance standards can bond themselves by "renting" U.S. securities laws by issuing debt or equity securities on U.S. capital markets. He finds some evidence that bonding can be effective, but that this is no panacea in most cases. On the other hand, Doidge, Karolyi, and Stulz (2004) show that foreign companies with shares cross-listed in the U.S. have significantly higher values than do otherwise-similar non-cross-listed firms from the same country, largely because a U.S. listing offers corporate governance benefits.

shares on the New York or American Stock Exchanges. For example, in mid-1993, Daimler Benz announced that it would become the first large German company to seek such a listing. Most foreign companies instead tap the U.S. market through **American Depositary Receipts (ADRs)**. These dollar-denominated claims issued by U.S. banks represent ownership of shares of a foreign company's stock held on deposit by the U.S. bank in the issuing firm's home country.[24]

ADRs have proven to be very popular with U.S. investors, at least partly because they allow investors to diversify internationally. However, because the shares are covered by American securities laws and pay dividends in dollars (dividends on the underlying shares are converted from the local currency into dollars before being paid out), U.S investors are able to diversify at very low cost. Since an ADR can be converted into ownership of the underlying shares, arbitrage ensures rational dollar valuation of this claim against foreign-currency-denominated stock.[25] Figure 16.4 details the rapid growth in market value and trading volume of ADRs on the three major U.S. stock exchanges over the period 1990–2004.

ADRs can be either sponsored or unsponsored. A **sponsored ADR** is one for which the issuing (foreign) company absorbs the legal and financial costs of creating

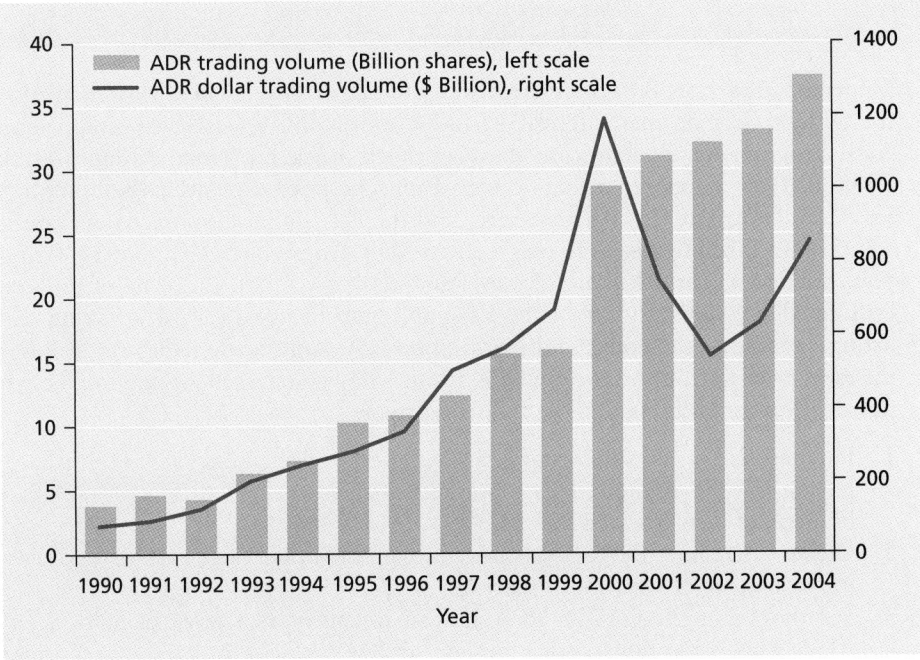

Figure 16.4
Trading Volume in Public American Depositary Receipt (ADR) Issues, 1990–2004
Sources: The Bank of New York, "Depositary Receipt Market Review 2004" and "Depositary Receipts (ADRs and GDRs) 2000 Year-End Market Review," downloaded from company's website (http://adrbny.com).

---

24. ADRs have been the subject of a significant amount of academic research. Both Jayaraman, Shastri, and Tandon (1993) and Miller (1999) present evidence that listings of ADRs are associated with positive abnormal returns on the underlying shares in their home markets. Muscarella and Vetsuypens (1996) use a sample of "solo splits," or splits of ADR stocks that are not accompanied by splits of the stock in the home-country market, to differentiate between two theoretical explanations for the widely noted increase in share prices around stock splits. They interpret their findings as supportive of the liquidity explanation (splits lower stock prices and thus increase demand for shares by individual investors) over the signaling explanation of the effects of stock-split announcements. Blass and Yafeh (2001) find that Israeli firms that choose a New York listing over a listing in the home market (Tel Aviv) are younger, more high-tech, and of generally higher quality than their stay-at-home counterparts. Finally, both Errunza and Miller (2000) and Lins, Strickland, and Zenner (2005) show that ADRs lower the cost of capital for issuing firms—especially those headquartered in developing countries.
25. Given the success of ADRs, many large international equity issues use this form even for share **tranches** (portions of the issue) that are destined for sale outside the United States. Large international issues that use this form are often called **Global Depositary Receipts (GDRs)** to emphasize their multinational characteristics.

and trading the security. In this case, the company will pay a U.S. depositary bank to create an ADR issue. An **unsponsored ADR** is one in which the issuing firm is not involved with the issue at all and may even oppose it. Historically, unsponsored ADRs resulted from U.S. investor demand for shares of particular foreign companies. Since 1983, however, the SEC has required that all new ADR programs be sponsored, so relatively few unsponsored ADRs still exist. There are also four different levels of ADR programs, corresponding to different levels of required disclosure and tradability. As described in Karolyi (1998) and Miller (1999), the least costly—in terms of both required disclosure and out-of-pocket expenses—are Level I and Rule 144A offerings, but the shares offered cannot subsequently be traded on one of the major stock exchanges or Nasdaq. Home-country accounting standards are also allowed for these two types of ADR programs. In contrast, Level II and III programs require the use of GAAP and are significantly costlier to arrange, but these shares can be listed for trading on public markets. At the end of 2004, a record 1,858 sponsored ADRs from 73 countries were available to U.S. investors. Of these, 498 were listed for public trading. Nokia was by far the most actively traded ADR; over 3.13 billion Nokia ADRs, worth $49.8 billion, traded hands during 2004 alone.

APPLYING THE MODEL 16.6

To demonstrate how ADRs are created, assume that Bayerische Motoren Werke, the famous German manufacturer of BMW automobiles, wishes to establish an ADR program for its shares on the New York Stock Exchange. In late March 2005, BMW's shares are trading on the Deutsche Börse (formerly the Frankfurt Stock Exchange) at €34.45 per share, and the U.S. dollar/euro exchange rate is $1.3316/€. If BMW wishes to establish an ADR program worth about $100 million, the firm might ask Bank of New York (ticker symbol, BK), one of the two leading ADR issuers, to handle the issue and offer to pay all of BK's issuing and listing expenses—including underwriting fees. Assume further that BK believes the ideal price to trade on the NYSE is about $90 per share. BK would implement this ADR program by taking the following steps.

1. Purchase 2.2 million shares of BMW on the Deutsche Börse at €34.45/share, paying €75.79 million. This represents an investment worth $100,921,964 by Bank of New York (€75,790,000 × $1.3316/€).
2. Create 1.1 million ADRs for listing on the NYSE, with each ADR representing ownership of two BMW shares.
3. Sell the 1.1 million ADRs to American investors at a price of $91.75 per ADR. This is the dollar price implied by BMW's price in euros, the current $/€ exchange rate, and the fact that each ADR is worth two BMW shares (€34.45/share × 2 shares /ADR × $1.3316/€ = $91.75/ADR).

The total proceeds of this offering are $100,921,964, which is exactly equal to the amount BK paid for the shares originally. Holders of these ADRs have a security that is denominated in dollars but that perfectly reflects both BMW's share price in euros and fluctuations in the dollar/euro exchange rate.

To demonstrate how ADRs reflect changes in BMW's stock price, assume that BMW's shares increase by €1.00 per share (to €35.45 each) in early-morning trading in Germany. We can compute that the ADRs should rise by $2.66 each (€1.00/share × 2 shares/ADR × $1.3316/€) to $94.41 per share when they begin trading in New York later that day. To demonstrate how ADRs reflect exchange rate movements, assume that BMW's price remains unchanged at €42 per share but that the euro appreciates from \$1.3316/€ to \$1.3509/€ immediately before trading begins in New York. The ADRs should begin trading at \$94.41 per share (€34.45/share × 2 shares/ADR × \$1.3509/€) when the NYSE opens. In other words, either an increase in BMW's stock price from €34.45 to €35.45 per share (holding exchange rates constant) or an appreciation of the euro from \$1.3316/€ to \$1.3509/€ (holding BMW's stock price unchanged) can cause the price of each BMW ADR to rise by \$2.66, from \$91.75 to \$94.41 per ADR.

There have been numerous high-profile ADR offerings in recent years. For example, Deutsche Bank established an American Depositary Receipt program on the New York Stock Exchange on October 1, 2001. Citibank sponsored the company's ADRs, each of which represents five ordinary shares and trades under the symbol TSM. Another example is Braskem, SA, a major Brazilian exporter of petrochemical products, which raised \$281.5 million with a new ADR program on the NYSE on September 22, 2004. Each of the company's ADRs, which were sponsored by Bank of New York, trades under the symbol BAK and represents *1,000* ordinary shares.

SHARE ISSUE PRIVATIZATIONS

Anyone who examines international share offerings is soon struck by the size and importance of share issue privatizations in non-U.S. stock markets. A government executing a **share issue privatization (SIP)** will sell all or part of its ownership in a state-owned enterprise to private investors via a public share offering. The words *public* and *private* can become confusing in this context; an SIP involves the sale of shares in a state-owned company to *private* investors via a *public* capital market share offering. Since Britain's Thatcher government first popularized privatizations in the early 1980s, there have been almost 900 privatizing share offerings by over 100 national governments. These SIPs have raised over \$850 billion.[26]

For our purposes, the most important aspect of privatization programs is the transforming role they have played in developing many national stock markets in general and IPO markets in particular. Share issue privatizations are particularly important for market development because of their size and the way their shares are allocated to potential investors. As Table 16.8 makes clear, SIPs tend to be vastly larger than their private-sector counterparts; in fact, the 10 largest (and 27 of the 29 largest) share offerings in world history have all been privatizations. Almost without exception, SIPs have been the largest share offerings in a country's history, and the first several large privatization IPOs generally yield a dramatic increase in the national stock market's trading volume and liquidity. In addition to size, SIPs differ from private-sector share issues in being almost exclusively secondary offerings. In other words, the proceeds from SIPs go to the government rather than to the firm being privatized. The sole major exception to this rule to date has occurred in China; almost all Chinese SIPs have been primary offerings.

The importance of SIPs in creating new shareholders derives from the way these issues are generally priced and allocated. Governments almost always set offer prices

---

[26.] An even more frequently used method of privatization is an asset sale, where a government sells a state-owned firm directly to a private company or to a group of private investors. Asset sales have raised an additional \$450 billion since the early 1990s, so the cumulative value of proceeds from privatizations now exceeds \$1.25 *trillion.* The material in this discussion is drawn primarily from Megginson, Nash, Netter, and Schwartz (2000), Boutchkova and Megginson (2000), Jones, Megginson, Nash, and Netter (1999), and Bortolotti, DeJong, Nicodano, and Schindele (2005). Additionally, Subrahmanyam and Titman (1999) present a theoretical explanation for the role share offerings (SIPs, as well as private-sector offerings) can play in developing a nation's capital markets.

Table 16.8
Details of the World's Largest Share Offerings

Date	Company	Country	Amount ($ million)	IPO/SEO
Nov 87	Nippon Telegraph & Telephone	Japan	$40,260	SEO
Oct 88	Nippon Telegraph & Telephone	Japan	22,400	SEO
Nov 99	ENEL	Italy	18,900	IPO
Oct 98	NTT DoCoMo	Japan	18,000	IPO
Mar 03	France Telecom	France	15,800	SEO[a]
Oct 97	Telecom Italia	Italy	15,500	SEO
Feb 87	Nippon Telegraph & Telephone	Japan	15,097	IPO
Nov 99	Nippon Telegraph & Telephone	Japan	15,000	SEO
Jun 00	Deutsche Telekom	Germany	14,760	SEO
Nov 96	Deutsche Telekom	Germany	13,300	IPO
Oct 87	British Petroleum	United Kingdom	12,430	SEO
Apr 00	*ATT Wireless (tracking stock)*	*United States*	*10,600*	*IPO*
Nov 98	France Telecom	France	10,500	SEO
Nov 97	Telstra	Australia	10,530	IPO
Oct 99	Telstra	Australia	10,400	SEO
Jun 99	Deutsche Telekom	Germany	10,200	SEO
Dec 90	Regional Electricity Companies[b]	United Kingdom	9,995	IPO
Dec 91	British Telecom	United Kingdom	9,927	SEO
Oct 04	ENEL	Italy	9,600	SEO
Jun 00	Telia	Sweden	8,800	IPO
Dec 89	U.K. Water Authorities[b]	United Kingdom	8,679	IPO
Feb 01	NTT DoCoMo	Japan	8,200	SEO
Dec 86	British Gas	United Kingdom	8,012	IPO
Jun 98	Endesa	Spain	8,000	SEO
Jul 97	ENI	Italy	7,800	SEO
Apr 00	*Oracle Japan*	*Japan*	*7,500*	*IPO*
Jul 93	British Telecom	U.K.	7,360	SEO
Oct 93	Japan Railroad East	Japan	7,312	IPO
Dec 98	Nippon Telegraph & Telephone	Japan	7,300	SEO
Oct 97	France Telecom	France	7,080	IPO

Source: Table 12 of William L. Megginson and Jeffry M. Netter, "From State to Market: A Survey of Empirical Studies on Privatization," *Journal of Economic Literature* 39 (2001), pp. 321–389. Updated by author.

Note: Offers are reported in nominal amounts (not inflation-adjusted) and are translated into millions of US dollars (US$ million) using the contemporaneous exchange rate. **Private-sector offerings** are presented in boldface, italicized type, while share issue privatizations (SIPs) are presented in normal typeface. Amounts reported for SIP offers are as described in the *Financial Times* at the time of the issue. Private-sector offering amounts are from the *Securities Data Corporation* file or *Financial Times*.

[a]Rights offering, in which the French government participated proportionately, so not a SIP in the traditional sense. Though a share offering by a state-owned firm, government ownership did not decline.

[b]Indicates a group offering of multiple companies that trade separately after the IPO.

well below their expected open-market value (they deliberately underprice), thereby ensuring great excess demand for shares in the offering. The issuing governments then allocate shares in a way that ensures maximum political benefit. Invariably, governments favor employees and other small domestic investors (who typically have never purchased common stock before) with relatively large share allocations, whereas domestic institutions and foreign investors are allocated far less than they desire. The net result of this strategy is to guarantee that most of the short-term capital gains of privatization IPOs are captured by the many citizen/investors (who vote) rather than by institutional and foreign investors (who do not). Furthermore, the long-run excess returns to investors who purchase privatizing share issues are significantly positive. All these features help promote popular support for privatization and other economic reform measures the government might wish to enact. In all, privatization share offerings have done as much to promote the development of international stock markets since the mid-1990s as any other single factor.

---

1. In what ways are non-U.S. (private-sector) initial public offerings similar to U.S. IPOs, and in what ways are they different?

2. What are *American Depositary Receipts (ADRs),* and how are these created? Why do you think ADRs have proven so popular with U.S. investors?

3. In what key ways do *share issue privatizations (SIPs)* differ from private-sector share offerings? Why do you think governments deliberately underprice SIPs?

Concept Review Questions

16.7 SUMMARY

- Companies wishing to raise capital externally must make a series of decisions, beginning with whether to issue debt or equity and whether to employ an investment bank to assist with the securities sale. This chapter focuses on common stock offerings, but the decisions and issuing procedures are very similar for preferred stock and debt securities.

- Firms wishing to raise new common stock equity must decide whether to sell stock to public investors, through a general cash offering, or to rely on sales to existing stockholders in a rights offering. Rights issues are now fairly rare in the United States, though they remain common in other developed countries.

- Common stock can be sold through private placements to accredited investors, or it can be sold to the public if the securities are registered with the SEC. A company's first public offering of common stock is known as its initial public offering, or IPO. The average IPO in the United States is underpriced by about 15 percent, and this has held true for several decades. International IPOs are also underpriced. It is unclear whether or not IPOs are poor long-term investments.

- Subsequent offerings of common stock are known as seasoned equity offerings, or SEOs. The announcement of a seasoned equity issue tends to decrease a company's stock price, and there is evidence that firms issuing seasoned equity underperform over the long term.

- Investment banks assist companies in selling new securities by underwriting security offerings. Underwriting a security offering involves three tasks: (1) managing the offering, which includes advising the company about the type and amount of securities to sell, (2) underwriting the offering by purchasing the securities from the issuer at a fixed price to shift the price risk from the issuer to the investment bank, and (3) selling the securities to investors.

- The largest share offerings in world history have all been share issue privatizations, or SIPs. Governments have raised over $850 billion since 1981 through these share offerings, and they have transformed stock market capitalization, trading volume, and the number of citizens owning shares in many countries.

INTERNET RESOURCES

Note: *For updates to links, please go to the book's website at* http://smart.swcollege.com.

http://www.ipohome.com—Site operated by Renaissance Capital, offers up-to-date information on three types of new equity financing: venture capital, IPOs, and seasoned equity offerings; has a calendar of upcoming financing events

http://marketrac.nyse.com/mt/index.html—A portion of the NYSE site offering an exceptional virtual tour of the exchange floor, showing which stocks trade at each "post" and numerous up-to-date trading statistics for each stock

http://www.sec.gov/edgar.shtml—The U.S. Securities and Exchange Commission's EDGAR database, where all registration statements and other required filings by companies with securities that are publicly traded on U.S capital markets are available for downloading

http://www.investorhome.com/ipo.htm—A site full of links to other sites with IPO data, research articles, and other information

http://adrbny.com—The Bank of New York's ADR website, provides detailed information about ADR listing and trading patterns. This site also makes available the bank's semiannual ADR *Market Summary* report.

KEY TERMS

accredited investors
American Depositary Receipts (ADRs)
best-efforts offering
book building
bulge bracket
certification
cold comfort letter
co-managers
competitively bid offer
due diligence
effective
final prospectus
firm-commitment offering
fixed-price offer
flip
full disclosure
general cash offerings
Global Depositary Receipts (GDRs)
Green Shoe option
initial return
investment bank
IPO underpricing
lead underwriter
league table
lockup agreements
market maker
mixed offering
negotiated offer
net price
offer price

overallotment option
oversubscribe
preemptive rights
preliminary prospectus
price stabilization
private placement
prospectus
qualified institutional buyers
red herring
registration statement
reverse LBO
rights offerings
road show
Rule 144A
Rule 144A offering
Rule 415
seasoned equity offerings (SEOs)
second IPO
secondary offering
Securities Act of 1933
Securities and Exchange Commission Act of 1934
selling group
share issue privatization (SIP)
shelf registration
spin-off
sponsored ADR
supplemental disclosures
tracking stocks
transactional exemption

underpriced

underwrite

underwriting spread

underwriting syndicate

unseasoned equity offerings

unsponsored ADR

winner's curse

QUESTIONS

16-1. What preferences do you think common stock shareholders would have regarding a company's source of equity financing?

16-2. Rights offerings are seldom used in the United States to raise equity capital, but they are often used in Europe. How might you explain that fact?

16-3. What do you think are the most important costs and benefits of becoming a publicly traded firm? If you were asked to advise an entrepreneur whether to take his or her firm public, what are the key questions you would ask before making your recommendation?

16-4. If you were an investment banker, how would you determine the offering price of an IPO?

16-5. Are the significantly positive short-run and significantly negative long-run returns earned by IPO shareholders compatible with market efficiency? If not, why not?

16-6. Why do investment banks require *lockup agreements* when they underwrite security offerings? As a potential investor, what would you think if all the shares in an equity offering were being sold by the company's management and none were new shares being sold by the company itself?

16-7. List and briefly describe the key services investment banks provide to firms issuing securities before, during, and after the offering.

16-8. What are *American Depositary Receipts (ADRs)*, and why have they proven so popular with U.S. investors?

16-9. How would you explain the fact that the underwriting spread on IPOs averages about 7 percent of the offering price, whereas the underwriting spread on a seasoned offering of common stock averages less than 5 percent?

16-10. Discuss the various issues that must be considered in selecting an investment banker for an IPO. Which type of placement is usually preferred by the issuing firm?

16-11. In terms of IPO investing, what does it mean to *flip* a stock? According to the empirical results regarding short- and long-term returns following equity offerings, is flipping a wise investment strategy?

16-12. What materials are presented in an IPO prospectus? In general, what result is documented regarding sales of shares by insiders and venture capitalists?

16-13. How do you explain the highly politicized nature of *share issue privatization (SIP)* pricing and share allocation policies? Are governments maximizing offering proceeds, or are they pursuing primarily political and economic objectives?

PROBLEMS

Investment Banking

16-1. West Coast Manufacturing Company (WCMC) is executing an initial public offering with the following characteristics. The company will sell 10 million shares at an offer price of $25 per share, the underwriter will charge a 7 percent underwriting fee, and the shares are expected to sell for $32 per share by the end of the first day's trading. Assuming this IPO is executed as expected, answer the following.

a. Calculate the initial return earned by investors allocated shares in the IPO.

b. How much will WCMC receive from this offering?

c. What is the total cost (underwriting fee and underpricing) of this issue to WCMC?

16-2. Continuing from Problem 16-1, assume that you purchase shares in the West Coast Manufacturing Company at the postoffering market price of $32 per share and hold the shares for one year. You then sell your WCMC shares for $35 per share. WCMC does not pay dividends, and you are not subject to capital gains taxation. During this year, the return on the overall stock market was 11 percent. What net return did you earn on your WCMC share investment? Assess this return in light of the overall market return.

16-3. Norman Internet Service Company (NISC) is interested in selling common stock to raise capital for capacity expansion. The firm has consulted First Tulsa Company, a large underwriting firm, which believes that the stock can be sold for $50 per share. The underwriter's investigation found that its administrative costs will be 2.5 percent of the sale price and its selling costs will be 2.0 percent of the sale price. If the underwriter requires a profit equal to 1 percent of the sale price, how much will the spread have to be in dollars to cover the underwriter's costs and profit?

16-4. LaJolla Securities Inc. specializes in the underwriting of small companies. The terms of a recent offering were as follows:

Number of shares	2 million
Offering price	$25 per share
Net proceeds	$45 million

LaJolla Securities' expenses associated with the offering were $500,000. Determine LaJolla Securities' profit on the offering if the secondary market price of the shares immediately after the offering began were as follows:

a. $23 per share

b. $25 per share

c. $28 per share

The U.S. Market for Initial Public Offerings

16-5. Go to http://www.ipohome.com and find (under IPO Marketwatch, then Pricings) information about firms that went public in the first few weeks of 2006. Write down the ticker symbols and offer prices for the firms you select; then go to Yahoo! and download daily price quotes since the IPO date. For each firm, calculate the following:

a. The percentage return measured from the offer price to the closing price the first day

b. The percentage return measured from the opening price to the closing price the first day

16-6. Four companies conducted IPOs last month: Hot.Com, Biotech Pipe Dreams Corp., Sleepy Tyme Inc., and Bricks N Mortar International. All four companies went public at an offer price of $10 per share. The first-day performance of each stock (measured as the percentage difference between the IPO offer price and the first-day closing price) was as follows:

Company	First-Day Return
Hot.Com	45%
Biotech Pipe Dreams	30%
Sleepy Tyme	5%
Bricks N Mortar	0%

a. If you submitted a bid through your broker for 100 shares of each company, if your orders were filled completely, and if you cashed out of each deal after one day, what was your average return on these investments?

b. Next, suppose that your orders were not all filled completely because of excess demand for "hot" IPOs. Specifically, after ordering 100 shares of each company, you were able to buy only 10 shares of Hot.Com, 20 shares of Biotech Pipe Dreams, 50 shares of Sleepy Tyme, and 100 shares of Bricks N Mortar. Recalculate your average return taking into account that your orders were only partially filled.

Seasoned Equity Offerings in the United States

16-7.   The Bloomington Company needs to raise $20 million of new equity capital. Its common stock is currently selling for $42 per share. The investment bankers require an underwriting spread of 7 percent of the offering price, and the company's legal, accounting, and printing expenses associated with the seasoned offering are estimated to be $450,000. How many new shares must the company sell to net $20 million?

16-8.   SMG Corporation sold 20 million shares of common stock in a seasoned offering. The market price of the company's shares immediately before the offering was $14.75. The shares were offered to the public at $14.50, and the underwriting spread was 4 percent. The company's expenses associated with the offering were $7.5 million. How much new cash did the company receive?

16-9.   After a banner year of rising profits and positive stock returns, the managers of Raptor Pharmaceuticals Corporation (RPC) have decided to launch a seasoned equity offering to raise new equity capital. RPC currently has 10 million shares outstanding, and yesterday's closing market price was $75.00 per RPC share. The company plans to sell 1 million newly issued shares in its seasoned offering. The investment banking firm Robbum and Blindum (R&B) has agreed to underwrite the new stock issue for a 2.5 percent discount from the offering price, which RPC and R&B have agreed should be $0.75 per share lower than RPC's closing price the day before the offering is sold.

    a. What is likely to happen to RPC's stock price when the plan for this seasoned offering is publicly announced?

    b. Assuming that RPC's stock price closes at $72.75 per share the day before the seasoned offering is launched, what net proceeds will RPC receive from this offering?

    c. Calculate the return earned by RPC's *existing* stockholders on their shares from the time before the seasoned offering was announced through the time it was actually sold for $72.75 per share.

    d. Calculate the total cost of the seasoned equity offering to RPC's existing stockholders as a percentage of the offering proceeds.

International Common Stock Offerings

16-10.   Assume that the Rome Electricity Company (REC) wishes to create a sponsored ADR program worth $300 million to trade its shares on the New York Stock Exchange. Assume that REC is currently selling on the Borsa Italiana (the Italian Stock Exchange, in Milan) for €30.00 per share and that the current dollar/euro exchange rate is $1.2500/€. American Bank and Trust (ABT) is handling the ADR issue for REC and has advised REC that the ideal trading price for utility company shares on the NYSE is about $75 per share (or per ADR).

    a. Describe the precise steps ABT must take to create an ADR issue meeting REC's preferences.

    b. Assume that REC's stock price rises from €30.00 to €33.00 per share. If the exchange rate does not also change, what will happen to REC's ADR price?

    c. If the euro appreciates from $1.2500/€ to $1.2900/€ but the price of REC's shares remains unchanged in euros, what will happen to REC's ADR price?

16-11.   Assume that Nippon Computer Manufacturing Company (NCM) wishes to create a sponsored ADR program worth $250 million to trade its shares on Nasdaq. Assume that NCM is currently selling on the Tokyo Stock Exchange for ¥1,550 per share and that the current dollar/yen exchange rate is $0.008089/¥, or, equivalently, ¥123.62/$. Metropolis Bank and Trust (MBT) is handling the ADR issue for NCM and has advised NCM that the ideal trading price for high-technology shares on the Nasdaq is about $20 per share (or per ADR).

   a. Describe the precise steps MBT must take to create an ADR issue meeting NCM's preferences.
   b. Assume that NCM's stock price rises from ¥1,550 to ¥1650 per share. If the exchange rate does not also change, what will happen to NCM's ADR price?
   c. If the yen depreciates from $0.008089/¥ to $0.008050/¥ but the price of NCM's shares remains unchanged in yen, what will happen to NCM's ADR price?

16-12. Assume that Zurich Semiconductor Company (ZSC) wishes to create a sponsored ADR program worth $75 million to trade its shares on the NASDAQ stock market. Assume that ZSC is currently selling on the SWX Swiss Exchange for SF25.00 per share and that the current dollar/Swiss franc exchange rate is $0.8264/SF. American Bank and Trust (ABT) is handling the ADR issue for ZSC and has advised the company that the ideal trading price for high-technology shares on the NASDAQ is about $60 per share (or per ADR).

   a. Describe the precise steps ABT must take to create an ADR issue meeting ZSC's preferences.
   b. Assume that ZSC's stock price declines from SF25.00 to SF22.50 per share. If the exchange rate does not also change, what will happen to ZSC's ADR price?
   c. If the Swiss franc depreciates from $0.8264/SF to $0.7850/SF but the price of ZSC's shares remains unchanged in Swiss francs, how will ZSC's ADR price change?

THOMSON ONE BUSINESS SCHOOL EDITION

16-13. Read the prospectus filed on February 15, 2006, by Morgan Hotels Group (ticker symbol, MHGC). (*Hint:* You can access the prospectus under the Filings tab and look for PROSP under Filing Type.) What type of securities did Morgan Hotels offer to the public for sale? What was the total dollar amount of funds raised by Morgan Hotels? If you had purchased this security at its offering price, what would be your total return to date?

16-14. On September 16, 2005, Google, Inc. (ticker symbol, GOOG) filed a prospectus for a seasoned equity offering. Read this prospectus and determine how many shares Google proposed to sell in the secondary offering. What was the proposed secondary offering price relative to the market price of Google at the time of the offering? How much did the secondary offering cost Google in underwriting discounts and commissions?

MINI-CASE: INVESTMENT BANKING & PUBLIC SALE OF EQUITY SECURITIES

PC Unlimited wishes to go public by issuing 20 million shares of common stock at an offer price of $14.63 each. Skrail Underwriters, Inc. will charge a 6.5% underwriting fee.

1.   How much will PC Unlimited raise in cash, assuming all the shares sell?

2. If PC Unlimited wishes to raise $250 million in cash, what proportion of its initial offering must be sold?

3. Assume you purchased shares at the IPO price and you sold them after one year for $36.42 each. Calculate your after-tax return, assuming you fall into a 15% tax bracket for capital gains.

Chapter 17

Long-Term Debt and Leasing

SMARTFinance
Use the learning tools at www
.thomsonedu.com/finance/smartfinance

610

From the sublime (or at least solvent) to the ridiculous in one year! In May 2001, WorldCom Group, then America's second-largest long-distance phone company, successfully floated the largest bond offering in U.S. history. The $11.9 billion, multicurrency, long-term debt issue carried an investment-grade bond rating (A by one rating agency, BBB by two others) and was underwritten by two of the world's most prestigious investment banks, Salomon Smith Barney and JP Morgan Chase. In spite of well-known difficulties facing all telecom firms in 2001, investors welcomed WorldCom's bond issue, which was three times oversubscribed. In fact, World-Com originally planned to issue only $8 billion and raised the offering size in response to investor demand.

By the summer of 2002, WorldCom's financial and operating problems deepened to the point that bonds issued at par 12 months before sold for 71 cents on the dollar. The firm's bond ratings fell to junk bond levels, and the company's founder and CEO resigned. Nonetheless, in May 2002, WorldCom appeared fundamentally solvent, and many financial analysts still rated the firm's securities as a "buy." One month later, however, WorldCom made the stunning announcement that it improperly recorded almost $4 billion in operating expenses as capital expenditures, meaning that the company had charged only a fraction of the total against earnings. After revising their earnings figures sharply downward, WorldCom fired its longtime chief financial officer and blamed him, along with the company's auditors, for perpetrating the accounting fraud.

The impact of WorldCom's admission was immediate. The company's stock price fell so low (to less than $0.15 per share, from a 1999 high of over $65 per share) that the Nasdaq began delisting proceedings. However, stock prices are supposed to fall sharply when a company encounters financial distress, so this was no real surprise. Much more shocking was the impact on WorldCom's bondholders, who, after all, had purchased investment-grade securities barely one year before. The market value of the bonds issued in May 2001 fell from 71 cents on the dollar to 14 cents almost immediately. These values fell even further in July 2002, when WorldCom defaulted on $4.25 billion in maturing loans, and by the end of July the company was headed for Chapter 11 bankruptcy. For the company's bondholders, however, the lesson to be drawn from WorldCom's swift collapse was all too clear: Bond ratings are helpful tools for evaluating most corporate debt offerings by corporations, but a favourable bond rating does not guarantee long-term (or even short-term) financial strength.

On April 14, 2003, WorldCom filed a Plan of Reorganization with the U.S. Bankruptcy Court and announced a brand name change to MCI. MCI formally emerged from U.S. Chapter 11 protection on April 20, 2004, and by mid-2005 MCI was in the process of being acquired by Verizon Communications. At year-end

2005 the FCC had approved the deal that had yet to clear Washington State authorities, but was expected to close in February 2006.

Sources: "Bond Sale Sets U.S. Record," Reuters (May 10, 2001); Dena Aubin, "WorldCom Bondholders Propose Debt-Equity Swap," Reuters (July 6, 2002); Vincent Boland and Jenny Wiggins, "WorldCom Bondholders Face Bitter Battle for Cash," Financial Times (July 6, 2002); MCI's company website (http//www.mci.com); MCI press releases of April 14, 2003, April 20, 2004, and May 2, 2005, and "Verizon One State Away from MCI Deal," Pittsburgh Business Times, December 15, 2005.

Corporations and governments around the world issue long-term debt in order to finance capital investments or to fund current operations. As we saw in Chapter 11, the vast majority of external capital that is raised by companies each year is debt rather than equity, and most debt is long-term.[1] This chapter focuses on two external sources of capital for business: long-term debt and leasing. We examine the key features, costs, advantages, and disadvantages of each of these funding sources, beginning with long-term debt.

17.1 CHARACTERISTICS OF LONG-TERM DEBT FINANCING

Long-term debt is the dominant form of long-term, external financing in all developed economies. On the balance sheet, accountants classify debt as long-term if it matures in more than one year. Firms obtain long-term debt by negotiating with a financial institution for a term loan or through selling bonds. We discuss each of these in the following sections, as well as *syndicated lending,* which has emerged as one of the most important sources of debt financing for companies located in the 30 member countries of the Organization for Economic Cooperation and Development (OECD)—and especially in the United States. This section first analyzes the choice between public and private debt offerings and then discusses long-term debt covenants and costs.

THE CHOICE BETWEEN PUBLIC AND PRIVATE DEBT ISSUES

Once a firm's managers decide to employ long-term debt financing, they face a series of practical choices regarding how best to structure the debt. The first, and arguably the most important, decision managers must make is whether to issue debt publicly or privately. In the United States, public long-term debt offerings involve selling securities (bonds and notes) directly to investors, almost always with the help of investment bankers. Firms must register these offerings with the SEC, and most long-term corporate bond offerings take the form of unsecured debentures, as discussed in Section 17.3. Furthermore, the vast majority of U.S. public debt offerings are **fixed-rate offerings,** meaning they have a coupon interest rate that remains constant throughout the issue's life.

Private debt issues take one of two principal forms. **Loans** are private debt agreements arranged between corporate borrowers and financial institutions, especially

---

[1] By definition, governments can only issue debt, since few investors would wish to purchase "government equity," even if such a financial creature existed. Although government debt issuance is an extremely important and interesting topic, we henceforth focus exclusively on corporate debt issuance.

commercial banks, whereas **private placements** are unregistered security offerings sold directly to *accredited investors*. The best-known and most common form of loan is a *term loan* arranged between a borrower and a single bank. However, the total value of large-denomination, *syndicated* loans arranged for a single borrower but funded by multiple banks exceeds that of single-lender term loans by a wide margin. The overwhelming majority of both term loans and syndicated loans extended to corporate borrowers are **floating-rate issues,** where the loan is priced at a fixed spread above a base interest rate, usually **LIBOR,** the London Interbank Offered Rate, or the U.S. bank **prime lending rate.** The interest rate paid by issuers of floating-rate debt thus adjusts up and down over time as the base interest rate changes.

Numerous academic researchers have analyzed the factors that influence a firm's choice between issuing debt publicly or privately.[2] Relative costs are obviously important, and higher fixed costs for public issues lead to the straightforward prediction that firms will issue larger offerings publicly and smaller ones privately. However, factors other than simple differences in interest rates also influence the public versus private issue decision. In particular, the value of ongoing creditor monitoring of the borrower seems to be very important, as are the borrower's investment opportunities. In general, private borrowing is preferable for firms where growth options represent more of the firm's value than do tangible assets and for companies with nontransparent production processes, because in these firms creditor monitoring helps to ensure that the firm uses borrowed funds properly.

LOAN COVENANTS

Long-term debt agreements, whether resulting from a term loan or a bond issue, normally include certain *loan covenants*. These are contractual clauses that place specific operating and financial constraints on the borrower. As noted in Chapter 11, there are two types of covenants: *Positive covenants* require the borrower to take a specific action, and *negative covenants* prohibit certain actions. Debt covenants do not normally place a burden on a financially sound business and typically remain in force for the life of the debt agreement.[3]

Covenants allow the lender to monitor and control the borrower's activities to protect itself against the agency problem created by the relationship between owners and lenders. Without these provisions, the borrower could take advantage of the lender by investing in riskier projects without compensating lenders with a higher interest rate on their loans.

Positive Covenants. As noted, positive covenants specify things that a borrower "must do." Some of the most common positive covenants include the following.

1. The borrower is required to maintain satisfactory accounting records in accordance with generally accepted accounting principles (GAAP).
2. The borrower is required periodically to supply audited financial statements that the lender uses to monitor the firm and enforce the debt agreement.
3. The borrower is required to pay taxes and other liabilities when due.

---

[2] Key early theoretical papers in this literature include those by Diamond (1991) and Rajan (1992). The choice between public and private debt in the United States is examined empirically in Houston and James (1996), Carey (1998), and Krishnaswami, Spindt, and Subramaniam (1999). Anderson and Makhija (1999) perform a similar analysis for Japan.
[3] Debt covenants have been extensively examined in the finance literature beginning with what remains a classic analysis by Smith and Warner (1979). Subsequent papers include those by Press and Weintrop (1990) and El-Gazzar and Pastena (1990).

4. The borrower is required to maintain all facilities in good working order, thereby behaving as a going concern.

5. The borrower is required to maintain a minimum level of *net working capital.* Net working capital below the minimum is considered indicative of inadequate liquidity, a common precursor to default.

6. The borrower is required to maintain life insurance policies on certain "key employees" without whom the firm's future would be in doubt. These policies provide the financial resources to hire qualified people quickly in the event that a key person dies or is disabled.

7. The borrower is often considered to be in default on all debts if it is in default on any debt to any lender. This is known as a **cross-default covenant.**

8. Occasionally, a covenant specifically requires the borrower to spend the borrowed funds on a proven financial need.

Negative Covenants. Negative covenants specify what a borrower "must not do." Common negative covenants include the following.

1. Borrowers may not sell accounts receivable to generate cash because doing so could cause a long-run cash shortage if the borrower uses the proceeds to meet current obligations.

2. Long-term lenders commonly impose fixed asset restrictions on the borrower. These constrain the firm with respect to the liquidation, acquisition, and encumbrance of fixed assets because any of these actions could damage the firm's ability to repay its debt.

3. Many debt agreements prohibit borrowing additional long-term debt or require that additional borrowing be subordinated to the original loan. **Subordination** means that all subsequent or more junior creditors agree to wait until all claims of the senior debt are satisfied in full before having their own claims satisfied.

4. Borrowers are prohibited from entering into certain types of leases in order to limit their additional fixed-payment obligations.

5. Occasionally, the lender prohibits business combinations by requiring the borrower to agree not to consolidate, merge, or combine in any way with another firm because such an action could significantly change the borrower's business and financial risk.

6. To prevent liquidation of assets through large salary payments, the lender may prohibit or limit salary increases for specified employees.

7. A relatively common provision prohibits the firm's annual cash dividend payments from exceeding 50 to 70 percent of its net earnings or a specified dollar amount.

In the process of negotiating the terms of long-term debt, the borrower and lender must agree to an acceptable set of covenants. If the borrower violates a covenant, the lender may demand immediate repayment, waive the violation and continue the loan, or waive the violation but alter the terms of the original debt agreement.

Cost of Long-Term Debt

In addition to specifying positive and negative covenants, the long-term debt agreement specifies the interest rate, the timing of interest payments, and the size of principal repayment. The major factors affecting the cost, or interest rate, of long-term debt are loan maturity, loan size, borrower risk, and the basic cost of money.

Loan Maturity. Generally, long-term loans have higher interest rates than short-term loans. Recall from Chapter 4 that the yield curve, which plots the relationship between yield to maturity and time to maturity for bonds having similar risk, typically slopes upward. Factors that can cause an upward-sloping yield curve include (1) the general expectation of higher future inflation or interest rates; (2) lender preferences for shorter-term, more liquid loans; and (3) greater demand for long-term rather than short-term loans relative to the supply of such loans. In a more practical sense, the longer the term, the greater the default risk associated with the loan. To compensate for all these factors, the lender typically charges a higher interest rate on long-term loans.[4]

Loan Size. The size of the loan usually affects the interest cost of borrowing in an inverse manner due to economies of scale. Loan administration costs per dollar borrowed are likely to decrease with increasing loan size. However, the risk to the lender increases, because larger loans result in less diversification. The size of the loan sought by each borrower must therefore be evaluated to determine the net administrative cost and risk trade-off.

Borrower Risk. As noted in Chapters 9 and 13, the higher the firm's operating leverage, the greater the risk (volatility) of its operating cash flows. Also, the higher the borrower's *debt ratio* or the lower its *times interest earned ratio,* the greater the risk (volatility) of the shareholders' cash flows. The lender's main concern is with the borrower's ability to fully repay the loan as prescribed in the debt agreement. A lender uses an overall assessment of the borrower's operating and financing risk, along with information on past payment patterns, when setting the interest rate on a loan.

Basic Cost of Money. The cost of money is the basis for determining the actual interest rate charged. Generally, the rate on U.S. Treasury securities with equivalent maturities is used as the basic (lowest-risk) cost of money. To determine the actual interest rate to be charged, the lender will add premiums for borrower risk and other factors to this basic cost of money for the given maturity. Alternatively, some lenders determine a prospective borrower's risk class and find the rates charged on loans with similar maturities and terms to firms in the same risk class. Instead of having to determine a risk premium, the lender can use the risk premium prevailing in the marketplace for similar loans.

Concept Review Questions

1. What factors should a manager consider when deciding on the amount and type of long-term debt to be used to finance a business?

2. What factors should a manager consider when negotiating the loan covenants in a long-term debt agreement?

3. How can managers estimate their firms' cost of long-term debt prior to meeting with a lender?

[4] The debt maturity structure choice for publicly traded U.S. firms is analyzed empirically in Barclay and Smith (1995a, 1995b) and Guedes and Opler (1996); Scherr and Hulburt (2001) examine the debt maturity structure of small U.S. firms. International differences in average corporate debt maturity are described and examined empirically in Demirgüç-Kunt and Maksimovic (1999).

17.2 TERM LOANS

A **term loan** is made by a financial institution to a business and has an initial maturity of more than 1 year, generally 5 to 12 years. Term loans are often made to finance permanent working capital needs, to pay for machinery and equipment, or to liquidate other loans.

Term loans are essentially private placements of debt. However, firms typically negotiate term loans directly with the lender rather than use an investment banker as an intermediary. An advantage of term loans over publicly traded debt is their flexibility. The securities (bonds or notes) in any given public debt issue are usually purchased by many different investors, so it is almost impossible to alter the terms of the borrowing agreement, even if new business conditions make such changes desirable. With a term loan, the borrower can negotiate with a single lender for modifications to the borrowing agreement.[5]

CHARACTERISTICS OF TERM LOAN AGREEMENTS

The actual term loan agreement is a formal contract ranging from a few to a few hundred pages. The following items commonly appear in the document: the amount and maturity of the loan, payment dates, interest rate, positive and negative covenants, collateral (if any), purpose of the loan, action to be taken in the event the agreement is violated, and stock purchase warrants. Of these, only payment dates, collateral requirements, and stock purchase warrants require further discussion.

Payment Dates. Term loan agreements usually specify monthly, quarterly, semi-annual, or annual loan payments. Generally, these equal payments fully repay the interest and principal over the life of the loan. Occasionally, a term loan agreement will require periodic interest payments over the life of the loan followed by a large lump-sum payment at maturity. This so-called **balloon payment** represents the entire loan principal if the periodic payments represent only interest.

Collateral Requirements. Term lending arrangements may be unsecured or secured. Secured loans have specific assets pledged as **collateral**. The collateral often takes the form of an asset such as machinery and equipment, plant, inventory, pledges of accounts receivable, and pledges of securities. Unsecured loans are obtained without pledging specific assets as collateral. Whether lenders require collateral depends on the lender's evaluation of the borrower's financial condition.[6]

[5.] Companies typically arrange loans with commercial banks as part of a larger, ongoing banking relationship. Large companies often have dozens of these bilateral relationships, but a critical decision for smaller firms is whether to maintain one large banking relationship or several smaller bilateral relationships in order to minimize the risk of not being able to arrange financing during an emergency. Petersen and Rajan (1994) examine this decision for U.S. companies and conclude that fewer, larger relationships are generally preferable to numerous, smaller ones. The primary benefit of a banking relationship for companies comes in the form of larger amounts that they can borrow rather than in cheaper loan rates. Interestingly, Detragiache, Garella, and Guiso (2000) find that Italian companies must pursue exactly the opposite strategy and maintain multiple bilateral banking relationships in order to ensure funding when needed. Finally, Ongena and Smith (2001) show that Norwegian companies frequently terminate their banking relationships as they mature, demonstrating that these firms do not become "locked into" bilateral relationships.

[6.] The use of collateral as backing for a loan has been analyzed theoretically by Stulz and Johnson (1985) and Igawa and Kanatas (1990) and has been examined empirically by Booth (1992). This study supports earlier findings that collateral is associated with higher, rather than lower, interest rates (spreads over a base rate) on secured loans. This implies that collateral allows riskier borrowers to receive credit that would not be granted to them through unsecured lending.

Term lending is often referred to as asset-backed lending, though term lenders in reality are primarily cash flow lenders. They hope and expect to be repaid out of cash flow but require collateral both as an alternative source of repayment and as "ransom" to decrease the incentive of borrowing firms to default (because a defaulting borrower would lose the use of valuable corporate assets). Most pledged assets are secured by a **lien,** which is a legal contract specifying under what conditions the lender can take title to the asset if the loan is not repaid and prohibiting the borrowing firm from selling or disposing of the asset without the lender's consent. The liens serve two purposes: They establish clearly the lender's right to seize and liquidate collateral if the borrower defaults, and they serve notice to subsequent lenders of a prior claim on the asset(s). Some of the more technical aspects of loan default are presented in Chapter 25.

Not all assets make acceptable collateral, of course. For an asset to be useful as collateral, it should (1) be nonperishable, (2) be relatively homogeneous in quality, (3) have a high value relative to its bulk, and (4) have a well-established secondary market where seized assets can be turned into cash without a severe price penalty.

Stock Purchase Warrants. The corporate borrower often gives the lender certain financial benefits, usually **stock purchase warrants,** in addition to the payment of interest and repayment of principal. Stock purchase warrants are instruments that give their holder the right to purchase a certain number of shares of the firm's common stock at a specified price over a certain period. These are designed to entice institutional lenders to make long-term loans, possibly under relatively favorable terms. Warrants are also frequently used as "sweeteners" for corporate bond issues. We discuss the valuation of stock purchase warrants in detail in Chapter 19.

TERM LENDERS

Students are often surprised to learn about the wide array of sources for term loans. The primary lenders making term loans to businesses are commercial banks, insurance companies, pension funds, regional development companies, the U.S. federal government's Small Business Administration, small business investment companies, commercial finance companies, and equipment manufacturers' financing subsidiaries.

Concept Review Questions

4. Suppose that a specialty retail firm takes out a term loan from a bank. Which do you think the bank would prefer to receive as collateral, a claim on the firm's inventory or its receivables?

5. A problem with collateral is that its value is positively correlated with the borrower's ability to repay. Explain.

17.3 CORPORATE BONDS

A *corporate bond* is a debt instrument indicating that a corporation has borrowed a certain amount of money from institutions or individuals and promises to repay it in the future under clearly defined terms. Firms issue bonds with maturities of 10–30 years (debt securities with an original maturity of 1–10 years are called *notes*) and with a par, or face, value of $1,000. The coupon interest rate on a bond represents the percentage of the bond's par value that the firm will pay to investors each year. In the United States, firms typically pay interest semiannually in two equal coupon payments. Bondholders receive the par value back when the bonds mature.

POPULAR TYPES OF BONDS

Bonds can be classified in a variety of ways. Here we break them into traditional bonds, the basic types that have been around for years, and new, innovative bonds. Table 17.1 summarizes the traditional types of bonds issued by corporations in terms of their key characteristics and priority of lender's claim in the event of default. Note that the first three types, **debentures, subordinated debentures,** and **income bonds,**

Table 17.1
Features of Conventional Bonds

Bond Type	Characteristics	Priority of Lender's Claim
Debentures	Unsecured bonds that only creditworthy firms can issue. Most convertible bonds are debentures.	Claims are the same as those of any general creditor. May have other unsecured bonds subordinate to them.
Subordinated debentures	Claims are not satisfied until those of the creditors holding certain (senior) debts have been fully satisfied.	Claim is that of a general creditor but not as good as a senior debt claim.
Income bonds	Payment of interest is required only when earnings are available from which to make such payment. Commonly issued in reorganization of a failed or failing firm.	Claim is that of a general creditor. Not in default when interest payments are missed, because they are contingent only on earnings being available.
Mortgage bonds	Secured by real estate or buildings. Can be *open-end* (additional bonds issued against collateral), *limited open-end* (a specified amount of additional bonds can be issued against collateral), or *closed-end*; may contain an *after-acquired clause* (property subsequently acquired becomes part of mortgage collateral).	Claim is on proceeds from sale of mortgaged assets; if not fully satisfied, the lender becomes a general creditor. The *first mortgage* claim must be satisfied before distribution of proceeds to *second mortgage* holders. A number of mortgages can be issued against the same collateral.
Collateral trust bonds	Secured by stock and/or bonds that are owned by the issuer. Collateral value is generally 25 to 35 percent higher than bond value.	Claim is on proceeds from stock and/or bond collateral; if not fully satisfied, the lender becomes a general creditor.
Equipment trust certificates	Used to finance transportation equipment—airplanes, trucks, boats, and railroad cars. A trustee buys such an asset with funds raised through the sale of trust certificates and then leases it to the firm, which, after making the final scheduled lease payment, receives title to the asset. A type of leasing.	Claim is on proceeds from the sale of the asset; if proceeds do not satisfy outstanding debt, trust certificate lenders become general creditors.

are unsecured; but the last three, **mortgage bonds, collateral trust bonds,** and **equipment trust certificates,** are secured. As noted, the majority of U.S. corporate bonds are debentures, where the debt is backed by the faith and credit of the issuing corporation itself rather than by specific pledged collateral.[7]

In recent years, corporations have developed a profusion of new debt instruments designed to attract a unique clientele of bond investors, who presumably would be willing to pay a higher price for a given special feature. A detailed discussion of these new offerings is beyond the scope of an overview chapter, but Table 17.2 surveys the characteristics of a few of these innovative bonds.

Table 17.2
Features of Innovative Bonds

Bond Type	Characteristics[a]
Zero (or low) coupon bonds	Issued with no (zero) or a very low coupon (stated interest) rate and sold at a large discount from par. A significant portion (or all) of the investor's return therefore comes from gain in value (i.e., par value minus purchase price). Generally callable at par value. Because the issuer can annually deduct the current year's interest accrual without having to actually pay the interest until the bond matures (or is called), its cash flow each year is increased by the amount of the tax shield provided by the interest deduction.
Junk bonds	Debt rated Ba or lower by Moody's or BB or lower by Standard & Poor's. During the 1980s, commonly used by rapidly growing firms to obtain growth capital, most often as a way to finance mergers and takeovers of other firms. High-risk bonds with high yields —typically yielding at least 3 percentage points more than high-quality corporate debt.
Floating-rate bonds	Stated interest rate is adjusted periodically within stated limits in response to changes in specified money or capital market rates. Popular when future inflation and interest rates are uncertain. Tend to sell at close to par as a result of the automatic adjustment to changing market conditions. Some issues provide for annual redemption at par at the option of the bondholder.
Extendible notes	Debt instruments with short maturities, typically 1–5 years, that can be redeemed or renewed for a similar period at the option of the holders. Similar to a floating-rate bond. An issue might be a series of 3-year renewable notes over a period of 15 years; every 3 years, the notes could be extended for another 3 years, at a new rate that is competitive with market interest rates prevailing at the time of renewal.
Putable bonds	Bonds that can be redeemed at par (typically, $1,000) at the option of their holder either at specified dates, such as 3–5 years after the date of issue and every 1 to 5 years thereafter, or when and if the firm takes specified actions such as being acquired, acquiring another company, or issuing a large amount of additional debt. In return for the right to "put the bond" at specified times or actions by the firm, the bond's yield is lower than that of a nonputable bond.

[a]The claims of lenders (i.e., bondholders) against issuers of each of these types of bonds vary, depending on their other features. Each of these bonds can be unsecured or secured.

[7.] Although not a direct source of financing for individual corporations, the market for mortgage-backed securities (MBS) has been growing much faster and now represents a market worth more than a half-trillion dollars per year in the United States alone. MBS offerings are created by pooling large numbers of home mortgage loans and then selling securities backed by these mortgages directly to investors. This market has revolutionized home mortgage lending in the United States because it allows financial institutions to economize on the use of their capital by originating mortgage loans and then selling them to MBS specialists.

LEGAL ASPECTS OF CORPORATE BONDS

When they issue bonds, corporations raise hundreds of millions of dollars from many unrelated investors. The dispersion in the investor base creates a need for special legal arrangements to protect lenders.

Bond Indenture. A bond **indenture** is a complex and lengthy legal document stating the conditions under which a bond has been issued. It specifies both the rights of the bondholders and the duties of the issuing corporation. In addition to specifying the interest and principal payment dates and containing various positive and negative covenants, the indenture frequently contains *sinking fund requirements* and provisions with respect to a security interest (if the bond is secured).

Sinking Fund Requirements. We have already described the positive and negative covenants for long-term debt and for bond issues in Section 17.1. However, an additional positive covenant often included in a bond indenture is a **sinking fund** requirement. Its objective is to provide for the systematic retirement of bonds prior to their maturity.[8] To carry out this requirement, the corporation makes semiannual or annual payments to a trustee, who uses these funds to retire bonds by purchasing them in the marketplace. This process is simplified by inclusion of a limited call feature, which permits the issuer to repurchase a fraction of outstanding bonds each year at a stated price. The trustee will exercise this limited call option only when sufficient bonds cannot be purchased in the marketplace or when the market price of the bond is above the call price.

Although U.S. corporations (and non-U.S. companies that can issue bonds in U.S. markets) have the opportunity to issue longer-maturity bonds than those of their international competitors, the actual average maturity of the typical U.S. bond issue is far less than its stated maturity would imply. The reasons for this are the ability of companies to call (and then refinance) bonds and the pervasiveness of mandated sinking funds in long-term U.S. debt security issues. Sinking funds work in such a way that the typical bond issue with, say, $100 million principal amount and a 15-year maturity will probably have only a few million dollars worth of bonds still outstanding when the last bonds are redeemed a decade and a half after issuance. Depending on the terms of the sinking fund, the actual average maturity of this issue (the weighted average years outstanding) will probably be less than 10 years, rather than the 15 years advertised.

Because sinking funds force the corporation to redeem part of each issue early, they reduce the risk of default on an individual issue, for two reasons. First, sinking funds increase the likelihood that investors will become aware of any financial difficulties an issuing firm encounters (by the firm's missing a sinking fund payment) early rather than late. This will trigger the demand for effective corrective action, up to and including the removal of the issuing firm's incumbent management team. Second, because at maturity only a fraction of a given bond issue will remain outstanding, the issuing firm's managers will have less incentive to default on the issue and attempt to expropriate bondholder wealth by filing for bankruptcy protection.

Security Interest. The bond indenture is similar to a loan agreement, in that any collateral pledged against the bond is specifically identified in the document. Usually, the

SMART IDEAS VIDEO

Annette Poulsen, University of Georgia

"There is a tradeoff between flexibility for the corporation and protection for the bondholder."

See the entire interview at
SMARTFinance

[8.] Dunn and Spatt (1984) examine sinking funds theoretically; Dyl and Joehnk (1979), Ho and Singer (1984), Mitchell (1991), and Wu (1993) examine sinking funds empirically.

title to the collateral is attached to the indenture, and the disposition of the collateral in various circumstances is specifically described. The protection of bond collateral is crucial to increasing the safety, and thus to enhancing the marketability, of a bond issue.

Trustee. A **trustee** is a third party to a bond indenture and can be an individual, a corporation, or, most often, a commercial bank trust department. The trustee, whose services are paid for by the issuer, acts as a "watchdog" on behalf of the bondholders, making sure that the issuer does not default on its contractual responsibilities. The trustee is empowered to take specified actions on behalf of bondholders if the borrower violates any indenture terms.

Methods of Issuing Corporate Bonds

Public issues of corporate bonds in the United States are sold using the general cash offering procedures described in Chapter 16. Corporate issues sold to public investors must be registered with the Securities and Exchange Commission, and large offerings are generally underwritten by an investment banking syndicate. However, there is a tremendous variation in actual offering procedures, and this heterogeneity has increased over time as new debt securities have been developed. In particular, two recent financial and regulatory innovations have transformed U.S. bond-issuance patterns. First, the introduction of *shelf registration* in the early 1980s allowed corporations to register large blocks of debt securities and then sell them in discrete pieces over the subsequent two years as market conditions warranted. As discussed in Chapter 16, shelf registration can be used for both debt and equity offerings, but relatively few issuers use this technique for selling stock. In contrast, most companies that can use shelf registration for debt offerings do so.

The second major innovation occurred in 1990, when the SEC created a new private-placement market by implementing *Rule 144A,* which was described in Chapter 16. This allowed qualified institutional investors (those with assets exceeding $100 million) to trade nonregistered securities among themselves, and corporate issuers soon found this was a welcoming market for new equity and, especially, debt issues. Because Rule 144A issues offer investors much greater liquidity than do traditional private placements and yet are less costly than traditional public offerings, U.S. and international corporations now sell a total of between $400 billion and $500 billion in securities each year using this rule.

General Features of a Bond Issue

Three features commonly observed in a U.S. bond issue are (1) a call feature, (2) a conversion feature, and (3) stock purchase warrants. Each of these features grants an option, either to the issuer or the investor, that has a significant impact on a bond's value.

Call Feature. The call feature is included in most corporate bond issues and gives the issuer the opportunity to repurchase bonds prior to maturity. The call price is the stated price at which bonds may be repurchased. Sometimes the call privilege is exercisable only during a certain period. Typically, the call price exceeds the par value of a bond by an amount equal to one year's interest. For example, a $1,000 bond with a 10 percent coupon interest rate would be callable for around $1,100 [$1,000 + (10% × $1,000)]. The amount by which the call price exceeds the bond's par value is commonly referred to as the *call premium*. This premium compensates bondholders for having the bond called away from them and is the cost to the issuer of calling the bonds.[9]

The call feature is generally advantageous to the issuer because it enables the issuer to retire outstanding debt prior to maturity. Thus, when interest rates fall, an issuer can call an outstanding bond and reissue a new bond at a lower interest rate. When interest rates rise, the call privilege will not be exercised, except possibly to meet sinking fund requirements. Of course, to issue a callable bond, the firm must pay a higher interest rate than that on noncallable bonds of equal risk to compensate bondholders for the risk of having the bonds called away.

Conversion Feature. The conversion feature of **convertible bonds** allows bondholders to change each bond into a stated number of shares of common stock. Bondholders will convert their bonds only when the market price of the stock is greater than the conversion price, hence providing a profit for the bondholder. We discuss the valuation of convertible bonds in detail in Chapter 19.

Stock Purchase Warrants. Like term loans, bonds occasionally have warrants attached as "sweeteners" to make them more attractive to prospective buyers. As we noted earlier, a *stock purchase warrant* gives its holder the right to purchase a certain number of shares of common stock at a specified price over a certain period of time. We also discuss the valuation of stock purchase warrants in depth in Chapter 19.

HIGH-YIELD BONDS

As discussed in Chapter 4, the risk of publicly traded bond issues is assessed by independent agencies such as Moody's and Standard & Poor's (S&P). Both agencies have 10 major *bond ratings* derived by using financial ratio and cash flow analyses. Bonds rated Baa or higher by Moody's (BBB by S&P) are known as **investment-grade bonds**. Bonds rated below investment-grade are known as **high-yield bonds** or **junk bonds**. As the pejorative name suggests, junk bonds carry a much higher default risk than do investment-grade bonds, but they also offer higher yields. Prior to the late 1970s, such issues were quite rare. Historically, most of the sub-investment-grade bonds trading in the market were **fallen angels**, bonds that received investment-grade ratings when they were first issued but later fell to junk status. During the late 1970s, however, Michael Milken and the investment bank he worked for, Drexel Burnham Lambert, began arranging new junk bond issues for companies such as Turner Broadcasting and MCI. Milken and Drexel also helped corporate raiders issue junk bonds to finance their hostile takeover bids.

When junk bond default rates rose sharply during the 1990–1991 recession, many commentators wrote off high-yield debt as a viable financing tool. As Figure 17.1 shows, however, the junk bond market not only survived but prospered between 1992 and 1998. Beginning in 1999 the default rates again began to rise. Junk bond investors recognize that they are assuming much of the issuing firm's business risk when they purchase high-yield debt, but they are willing to do so in return for promised yields that approach the returns earned by stockholders.

Of course, a higher *promised* yield may or may not result in a higher *realized* return, because the higher yield reflects a higher expected likelihood that the borrower

---

[9.] For recent examples of the academic literature on the callability of corporate bonds, see Thatcher (1985), Vu (1986), Mitchell (1991), Crabbe and Helwege (1994), and Sarkar (2001).

Figure 17.1
Par Value Amounts
Outstanding and Default
Rates for High-Yield
Bonds (Junk Bonds),
1971–2002.
Source: Edward I. Altman
and Gaurav Bana, "Report
on Defaults and Returns on
High Yield Bonds: The Year
2002 in Review and Market
Outlook." NYU Salomon
Center, February 2003,
Figure 1.

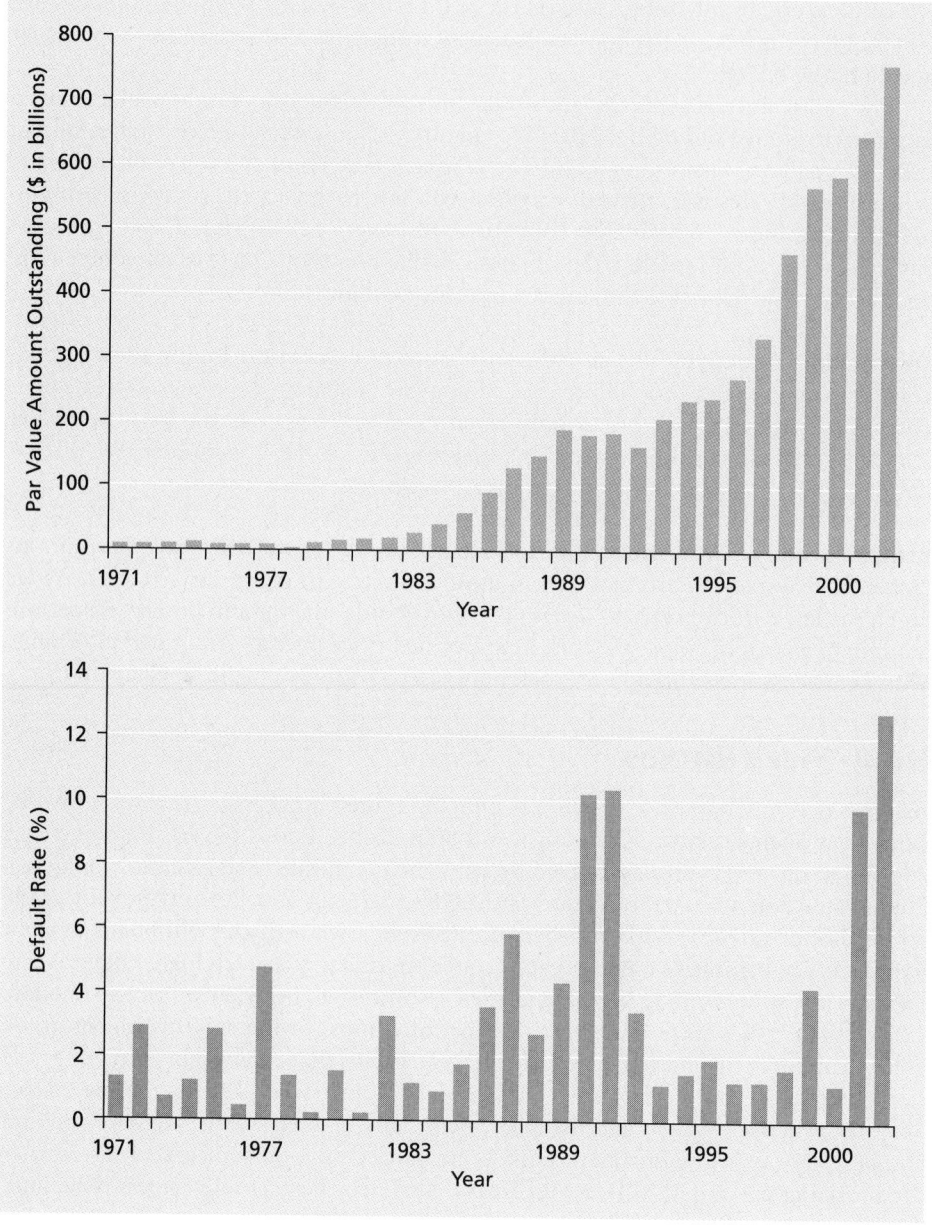

will default (in whole or in part) on the bond sometime during its life. For example, as the U.S. economy sagged in 2002, the default rate on junk bonds reached 12.8 percent, and the loss rate reached 10.2 percent. In other words, almost 1 in 8 junk bonds was in some form of default during the year, and this caused a reduction of 10.2 percent in the returns junk bond investors earned (relative to what they would have earned in the absence of defaults).

After a bond is rated, the rating is not changed unless the likelihood of the company's defaulting on the bond issue changes. Perhaps surprising, bond issuers themselves pay the ratings companies to issue ratings on newly issued bonds. The reason for this apparently masochistic behavior is that bonds are essentially unmarketable without a rating. Additionally, having the issuing firm pay for ratings allows the firm

COMPARATIVE CORPORATE FINANCE

Islamic Finance: How Do You Sell Bonds When You Cannot Charge Interest?

The past two decades have seen a handful of Muslim countries modify their commercial banking laws to make them consistent with the principle of *Syariah*, or the prohibition on the charging of interest on loans. Several other countries have allowed banks to operate under the *Syariah* principle, which is similar to the Catholic church's injunction against usury (charging interest) during the Middle Ages in Europe. Needless to say, bankers have found this restriction on a core source of revenue to be a serious challenge, but many have been able to comply with the religious intent of the laws by structuring loans as investment partnerships—where the bank's return comes in the form of a share of profits—or by structuring loan payments as fees or dividends rather than interest.

While Islamic banking has, perhaps unsurprisingly, made few inroads in global markets, it has been relatively successful within the borders of at least some of the countries that have adopted it. But how do you attract international investors to an Islamic bond issue when the same *Syariah*-based restriction on payment of interest applies? As it happens, several governments and one major international development bank have executed successful Islamic finance bond offerings since July 2002. That month, the Malaysian government raised $600 million with the world's first Global Islamic Bond offering targeted primarily at investors in West Asia and the Middle East. The bond issue carried an investment-grade rating, and investors were promised a return (comparable to dividend payments) equal to 0.95 percentage points above LIBOR, funded by rentals from Malaysian government properties.

The second Islamic bond offering was even more intriguing, since the issuer was the government of Iran, and this was its first international capital marker offering since the fundamentalist regime came to power in 1979. The €500 million issue was assigned a B+ bond rating by Fitch and was priced at 425 basis points over the reference rate for interest rate swaps of similar risk. Perhaps most surprisingly, the issue was targeted at European investors and sold out very quickly.

The year 2003 saw two even more important Islamic bond offerings. First, the Islamic Development Bank (IDB) executed a $400 million offering, targeted at European investors, while Qatar sold a $700 million offering in October. The Qatari issue was the largest-ever bond offering that met *Syariah* requirements. Intriguingly, non-Muslim investors purchased 7 percent of the IDB issue, according to Saad Ashraf, the head of Citigroup's Global Islamic Finance Group, which managed the sale.

By mid-2005, the worldwide value of the Islamic finance market was estimated between $200 and $250 billion and was growing at a rate of 15 percent per year, according to a study released by the Kuala Lumpur Stock Exchange. Moreoever, this study suggested there is over $1.3 trillion worth of untapped Islamic funds worldwide. Give this potential, it is not surprising that virtually every major international investment bank has established an Islamic Finance unit, and that several highly successful Islamic finance mutual funds have sprung up to cater to this wealthy and pious investor clientele.

Sources: Ishun P. Ahmad, "Islamic Bond Investors in for the Long Term," *The New Straits Times Press* [Malaysia] (July 13, 2002); Arkady Ostrovsky and Bayan Rhaman, "Capital Markets: Iran Pays More to Raise €500m," *Financial Times* (July 15, 2002); "Islamic Bond Market Expands with Record Sale by Qatar: Didn't Exist 15 Months ago," *Financial Post* [Cananda] (October 1, 2003); Mark Warner, "Tapping into the Potential of the East," *Lloyds List* (April 16, 2004), and Farhan Bokhari, "Once-closed Arab World Opens Up," *Financial Times* (October 7, 2005), all downloaded from the *Financial Times* website at http://www.ft.com.

to communicate sensitive information privately to the ratings agency. This information can then be usefully reflected in market data without being disclosed to competitors (Kliger and Sarig 2000). Empirical research has shown that bond ratings and, especially, ratings changes convey economically relevant information to investors (Dichev and Piotroski 2001).

INTERNATIONAL CORPORATE BOND FINANCING

Companies can sell bonds internationally by tapping the *Eurobond* or *foreign bond* markets. Both of these provide established, creditworthy borrowers the opportunity to obtain large amounts of long-term debt financing quickly and efficiently, in their choice of currency and with flexible repayment terms. The following sections briefly describe these markets.

Eurobonds. A **Eurobond** is a bond issued by an international borrower and sold to investors in countries with currencies other than the currency in which the bond is denominated. A dollar-denominated bond issued by a U.S. corporation and sold to Western European investors is an example of a Eurobond. The Eurobond market first developed in the early 1960s, when several European and U.S. borrowers discovered that many European investors wanted to hold dollar-denominated, **bearer bonds.** Investors wanted bearer bonds because they would both shelter investment income from taxation—because coupon interest payments were made to the bearer of the bond and names were not reported to tax authorities—and provide protection against exchange rate risk.

Until the mid-1980s, "blue-chip" U.S. corporations were the largest single class of Eurobond issuers, and many of these companies were able to borrow in this market at interest rates below those the U.S. government paid on Treasury bonds (Kim and Stulz 1988). As the market matured, issuers were able to choose the currency in which they borrowed, and European and Japanese borrowers rose to prominence. In more recent years, the Eurobond market has become much more balanced in terms of the mix of borrowers, total issue volume, and currency of denomination. Most Eurobond issues today are, in fact, executed as part of a complicated financial engineering transaction known as a *currency swap,* wherein companies headquartered in different countries issue bonds in their home-country currencies and then exchange principal and interest payments with each other. Swaps are described in depth in Web Chapter 27 on "Risk Management and Financial Engineering."

Foreign Bonds. In contrast to a Eurobond, which is issued by an international borrower in a single currency (frequently dollars) in a variety of countries, a **foreign bond** is a bond issued in a host country's financial market, in the host country's currency, by a foreign borrower. A Swiss franc–denominated bond issued in Switzerland by a U.S. company is an example of a foreign bond. Other examples are a dollar-denominated bond issued in the United States by a German company and a yen-denominated bond issued by an American company in Japan. Many of these issues have colorful names. For example, the two bonds just mentioned would be called Yankee bonds and Samurai bonds, respectively. Similar issues in Britain would be called Bulldog bonds, and issues in Switzerland and the Netherlands would be referred to as Heidi and Rembrandt bonds, respectively. The three largest foreign bond markets are Japan, Switzerland, and the United States.

BOND-REFUNDING OPTIONS

A firm that wishes to avoid a large single repayment of principal in the future or to refund a bond prior to maturity has two options. Both require foresight and careful analysis on the part of the issuer.

Serial Issues. The borrower can issue **serial bonds,** a certain proportion of which matures each year. When firms issue serial bonds, they attach different interest rates to bonds maturing at different times. Although serial bonds cannot necessarily be retired at the option of the issuer, they do permit the issuer to systematically retire the debt.

Refunding Bonds by Exercising a Call. If interest rates drop following the issuance of a bond, the issuer may wish to refund (refinance) the debt with new bonds at the lower interest rate. If a call feature has been included in the issue, the issuer can easily retire it. In an accounting sense, bond refunding will increase earnings per share by lowering interest expense. Of course, the desirability of refunding a bond through exercise of a call is not necessarily obvious, and assessing its long-term consequences requires the use of present value techniques. This bond-refunding decision is another application of the capital budgeting techniques we described in Chapters 7 and 8.

Here the firm must find the net present value (NPV) of the bond-refunding cash flows. The initial investment is the incremental after-tax cash outflows associated with calling the old bonds and issuing new bonds, and the annual cash flow savings are the after-tax cash savings that are expected from the reduced debt payments on the new lower-interest bond. These cash flows are the same each year. The resulting cash flow pattern surrounding this decision is "typical": an outflow followed by a series of inflows. The bond-refunding decision can be made using the following three-step procedure.

Step 1. **Find the initial investment** by estimating the incremental after-tax cash outflow required at time 0 to call the old bond and issue a new bond in its place. Any overlapping interest resulting from the need to pay interest on both the old and new bonds is treated as part of the initial investment.

Step 2. **Find the annual cash flow savings,** which is the difference between the annual after-tax debt payments with the old and new bonds. This cash flow stream will be an annuity, with a life equal to the maturity of the old bond.

Step 3. Use the after-tax cost of the new debt (as the discount rate) to **find the net present value (NPV)** by subtracting the initial investment from the present value of the annual cash flow savings. The annual cash flow savings is a certain cash flow stream that represents the difference between two contractual debt-service streams, the old bond and the new bond. Therefore, the decision is virtually risk-free because it does not increase the firm's financial risk (i.e., degree of indebtedness or ability to service debt). Therefore, *the after-tax cost of debt is used as the discount rate* because it represents the firm's lowest cost of financing. If the resulting NPV is positive, the proposed refunding is recommended; otherwise, it should be rejected.

Application of these bond-refunding decision procedures can be illustrated in the upcoming Applying the Model. However, a few tax-related points must be clarified first.

Call Premiums. The amount by which the call price exceeds the par value of the bond is the **call premium.** It is paid by the issuer to the bondholder to buy back outstanding bonds prior to maturity. The call premium is treated as a tax-deductible expense in the year of the call.

Bond Discounts and Premiums. When bonds are sold at a discount or at a premium, the firm is required to amortize (write off) the discount or premium in equal portions over the life of the bond. The amortized discount is treated as a tax-deductible expenditure, whereas the amortized premium is treated as taxable income. If a bond is retired prior to maturity, any unamortized portion of a discount or premium is deducted from or added to pretax income at that time.

Flotation or Issuance Costs. Any costs incurred in the process of issuing a bond must be amortized over the life of the bond. The annual write-off is therefore a tax-deductible expenditure. If a bond is retired prior to maturity, any unamortized portion of this cost is deducted from pretax income at that time.

APPLYING THE MODEL 17.1

The Davis Corporation, a manufacturer of industrial piping, is contemplating calling $50 million of 30-year, $1,000 par value bonds (50,000 bonds) issued five years ago with a coupon interest rate of 9 percent. The bonds have a call price of $1,090 and initially netted proceeds of $48.5 million due to a discount of $30 per bond (50,000 bonds × $970 net per bond). The initial floatation cost was $400,000. The company intends to sell $50 million of 25-year, $1,000 par value bonds with a 7 percent (coupon) interest rate to raise funds for retiring the old bonds. The floatation costs on the new issue are estimated to be $450,000. The firm is currently in the 30 percent tax bracket and estimates its after-tax cost of debt to be 4.9 percent [$0.07 \times (1 - 0.30)$]. Because the new bonds must first be sold and their proceeds then used to retire the old bonds, the firm expects a two-month period of overlapping interest during which interest must be paid on both the old and the new bonds.

Step 1. Find the initial investment. Finding the initial investment requires a number of calculations.

a. *Call premium.* The call premium per bond is $90 ($1,090 call price − $1,000 par value). Because the total call premium is deductible in the year of the call, its after-tax cost is calculated as follows:

Before tax ($90 × 50,000 bonds)	$4,500,000
Less: Taxes (0.30 × $4,500,000)	1,350,000
After-tax cost of call premium	$3,150,000

b. *Floatation cost of new bond.* This cost was given as $450,000.
c. *Overlapping interest.*[10] The after-tax cost of the overlapping interest on the old bond is treated as part of the initial investment and calculated as follows:

Before tax (0.09 × 2 ÷ 12 × $50,000,000)	$750,000
Less: Taxes (0.30 × $750,000)	225,000
After-tax cost of overlapping interest	$525,000

d. *Unamortized discount on old bond.* The firm was amortizing the $1,500,000 discount ($50,000,000 par value − $48,500,000 net proceeds from sale) on the old bond over 30 years. Because only 5 of the 30 years' amortization of the discount has been applied, the firm can deduct the remaining 25 years of unamortized discount as a lump sum, thereby reducing taxes by $375,000 (25 ÷ 30 × $1,500,000 × 0.30).
e. *Unamortized floatation cost of old bond.* The firm was amortizing the $400,000 initial floatation cost on the old bond over 30 years. Because only 5 of the 30 years' amortization of this cost has been applied, the firm can deduct the remaining 25 years of unamortized floatation cost as a lump sum, thereby reducing taxes by $100,000 (25 ÷ 30 × $400,000 × 0.30).

---

10. Technically, the after-tax amount of overlapping interest could be reduced by the after-tax interest earnings from investment of the average proceeds available from the sale of the new bonds during the interest overlap period. For clarity, any interest earned on the proceeds from sale of the new bonds during the overlap period is ignored.

Table 17.3
Finding the Initial
Investment for the Davis
Corporation's Bond-
Refunding Decision

a. **Call premium**
   Before tax [($1,090 − $1,000) × 50,000 bonds] $4,500,000
   Less: Taxes (0.30 × $4,500,000)   (1,350,000)
      After-tax cost of call premium $3,150,000
b. **Floatation cost of new bond**   450,000
c. **Overlapping interest**
   Before tax (0.09 × 2 ÷ 12 × $50,000,000) $ 750,000
   Less: Taxes (0.30 × $750,000)   (225,000)
      After-tax cost of overlapping interest   525,000
d. **Tax savings from unamortized discount on old bond**
   [25 ÷ 30 × ($50,000,000 − $48,500,000) × 0.30]   (375,000)
e. **Tax savings from unamortized floatation cost of
   old bond**
   (25 ÷ 30 × $400,000 × 0.30)   (100,000)
      Initial investment $3,650,000

Summarizing these calculations in Table 17.3, we find the initial investment to be $3,650,000. This means that the Davis Corporation must pay out $3,650,000 now to implement the proposed bond refunding.

Step 2. Find the annual cash flow savings. To find the annual cash flow savings requires a number of calculations.

a. *Interest cost of old bond.* The after-tax annual interest of the old bond is calculated as follows:

Before tax (0.09 × $50,000,000) $4,500,000
Less: Taxes (0.30 × $4,500,000)   1,350,000
After-tax interest cost $3,150,000

b. *Amoritization of discount on old bond.* The firm was amortizing the $1,500,000 discount ($50,000,000 par value − $48,500,000 net proceeds from sale) on the old bond over 30 years, resulting in an annual write-off of $50,000 ($1,500,000 ÷ 30). Because it is a tax-deductible noncash charge, the amoritzation of this discount results in an annual tax savings of $15,000 (0.30 × $50,000).

c. *Amortization of floatation cost on old bond.* The firm was amortizing the $400,000 floatation cost on the old bond over 30 years, resulting in an annual write-off of $13,333 ($400,000 ÷ 30). Because it is a tax-deductible noncash charge, the amortization of the floatation cost results in an annual tax savings of $4,000 (0.30 × $13,333).

d. *Interest cost of new bond.* The after-tax annual interest cost of the new bond is calculated as follows:

Before tax (0.07 × $50,000,000) $3,500,000
Less: Taxes (0.30 × $3,500,000)   1,050,000
After-tax interest cost $2,450,000

e. *Amortization of floatation cost on the new bond.* The firm will amortize the $450,000 floatation cost on the new bond over 25 years, resulting in an annual write-off of $18,000 ($450,000 ÷ 25). Because it is a tax-deductible noncash charge, the amortization of the floatation cost results in an annual tax-savings of $5,400 (0.30 × $18,000).

Table 17.4 summarizes these calculations. Combining the first three values [(a), (b), and (c)] yields the annual after-tax debt payment for the old bond of $3,131,000. When the values for the new bond [(d) and (e)] are combined, the annual after-tax debt payment for the new bond is $2,444,600.

Subtracting the new bond's annual after-tax debt payment from that of the old bond, we find that implementation of the proposed bond refunding will result in an annual cash flow savings of $686,400 ($3,131,000 − $2,444,600).

Step 3. Find the net present value (*NPV*). Table 17.5 shows the calculations for determining the *NPV* of the proposed bond refunding. The present value of the annual cash flow savings of $686,400 at the 4.9 percent after-tax cost of debt over the 25 years is computed (using Equation 3.7) to be $9,771,792. Subtracting the initial investment of $3,650,000 from the present value of the annual cash flow

Table 17.4
Finding the Annual Cash Flow Savings for the Davis Corporation's Bond-Refunding Decision

Old Bond		
a. Interest cost		
Before tax (0.09 × $50,000,000)	$4,500,000	
Less: Taxes (0.30 × $4,500,000)	(1,350,000)	
After-tax interest cost		$3,150,000
b. Tax savings from amortization of discount		
[($1,500,000[a] ÷ 30) × 0.30]		(15,000)
c. Tax savings from amortization of flotation cost		
[($400,000 ÷ 30) × 0.30]		(4,000)
(1) Annual after-tax debt payment		$3,131,000
New Bond		
d. Interest cost		
Before tax (0.07 × $50,000,000)	$3,500,000	
Less: Taxes (0.30 × $3,500,000)	(1,050,000)	
After tax interest cost		$2,450,000
e. Tax savings from amortization of floatation cost		
[($450,000 ÷ 25) × 0.30]		(5,400)
(2) Annual after-tax debt payment		$2,444,600
Annual cash flow savings [(1) − (2)]		$ 686,400

[a]$50,000,000 par value − $48,500,000 net proceeds from sale.

Table 17.5
Finding the Net Present Value of the Davis Corporation's Bond-Refunding Decision

Present value of annual cash flow[a]

$$\$686,400 \times \frac{1}{r}\left[1 - \frac{1}{(1+r)^n}\right] = \$686,400 \times \frac{1}{0.049}\left[1 - \frac{1}{(1.049)^{25}}\right]$$

$686,400 × 14.236 =	$9,771,792
Less: Initial investment (from Table 17.3)	(3,650,000)
Net present value (*NPV*) of refunding	$6,121,792

Decision: The proposed refunding is recommended because the *NPV* of refunding of $6,121,792 is greater than $0.

[a]Annual cash flow savings from Table 17.4 multiplied by the present value factor of a 25-year, 4.9 percent annuity (Equation 3.7).

savings results in a net present value of $6,121,792. Because a positive *NPV* results, the proposed bond refunding is recommended.

**Concept
Review
Questions**

6. What factors should a manager consider when choosing between a term loan and a bond issue for raising long-term debt?

7. What factors might influence the choice between a bond issue with a *sinking fund* requirement and a *serial bond* issue?

8. What factors, other than the current interest rate at which new debt could be sold, should a manager consider when deciding to refund a bond issue?

17.4 SYNDICATED LOANS

A **syndicated loan** is a large-denomination credit arranged by a group (a *syndicate*) of commercial banks for a single borrower. Although syndicated lending has been a fixture of U.S. and international finance since the early 1970s, syndicated loans have increased dramatically in size, volume, and importance since the early 1990s. During the 1970s and early 1980s, many syndicated loans were arranged for governments in developing countries. These *petrodollar loans* were funded with the (dollar-denominated) trade surpluses that oil-exporting countries built up following the surge in oil prices in 1974–1975 and 1980–1982. Oil producers deposited their surpluses in global banks, which then "recycled" these funds into petrodollar loans. The "Third World debt crisis" of the early 1980s occurred after developing-country debt loads hit critical levels and the borrowing countries defaulted on some of their interest and principal payments.

The majority of syndicated loans were arranged for Western corporate borrowers even during the 1970s and 1980s, and since that time the market has become overwhelmingly corporate. Today, over $2 trillion worth of syndicated loans are arranged annually, roughly two-thirds of which go to corporate borrowers. The syndicated loan market appeals to borrowers who need to arrange very large loans quickly. Loans for top-tier corporate borrowers are floating-rate credits with very narrow spreads (10–75 basis points) over LIBOR. Typically, lenders structure these loans as lines of credit that borrowers can draw down as needed over four to six years. After that time, the loans generally convert to term credits that firms must repay on a set schedule. One increasingly important use of syndicated lending is as funding for debt-financed acquisitions by U.S. corporate borrowers, where the ability to borrow large sums quickly and (relatively) discreetly is especially valuable. Table 17.6 provides details of syndicated loans arranged between January 1980 and April 2000, as well as for five loan groupings. *Project finance loans* are limited or nonrecourse lending to stand-alone companies, and they are typically arranged to finance large infrastructure projects.[11] *Corporate control loans* are arranged to finance corporate acquisitions or leveraged buyouts, and *general corporate-purpose loans* are raised without a specific fund use being designated. *Capital structure loans* are booked for repayment of maturing lines of credit or for recapitalizations, share repurchases, debtor-in-possession financing, standby commercial paper support, or other unspecified purposes. *Fixed asset–based loans* are intended for mortgage lending or funding purchases of aircraft, property, or shipping.

[11.] A *stand-alone company* is a company created solely to own and operate the project being financed.

Table 17.6

Characteristics of All Syndicated Loans and Various Loan Categories, 1980–2000

Variable of Interest	All Syndi-cated Loans	Project Finance Loans	Corporate Control Loans	General Corporate-Purpose Loans	Capital Structure Loans	Fixed Asset–Based Loans
Number of loans	90,783	4,956	10,795	39,653	25,313	4,680
Total volume, $US in millions	$13,298,457	$634,422	$2,292,431	$4,275,803	$5,289,793	$410,175
Loan size, $US in millions: average	$146	$128	$212	$108	$209	$88
Loan size, $US in millions: median	$50	$52	$59	$39	$65	$50
Average maturity, years	4.8 years	8.6 years	5.1 years	4.5 years	3.9 years	8.1 years
Loans with fixed price (%)	5.9%	13.9%	2.7%	4.9%	3.9%	6.2%
Loans priced vs. LIBOR (%)	69.5%	38.8%	84.6%	66.2%	70.8%	72.5%
Loans to U.S. borrowers (%)	55.8%	13.9%	68.8%	50.3%	74.0%	20.4%
Average spread over LIBOR, basis points (bp)	134 bp	130 bp	195 bp	113 bp	135 bp	86 bp
Average number of syndicate banks	10.7	14.5	11.9	9.4	11.5	9.6
Average country risk score	90.0	74.6	95.4	87.3	94.1	82.7

Source: Data are from the CapitalDATA Loanware database, as employed in Stefanie Kleimeier and William L. Megginson, "Are Project Finance Loans Different from Other Syndicated Credits?" *Journal of Applied Corporate Finance* 13 (Spring 2000), pp. 75–87.

SPECIALIZED SYNDICATED LENDING

Though syndicated loans are used for virtually all types of corporate finance, there are two uses that stand out as so distinct and important that they merit special discussion: Eurocurrency lending and project finance.

Eurocurrency Lending. The **Eurocurrency loan market** consists of a large number of international banks that stand ready to make floating-rate, hard-currency loans (typically, U.S. dollar–denominated) to international corporate and government borrowers. For example, a British bank that accepts a dollar-denominated deposit in London is creating a *Eurodollar deposit,* and if it then relends the deposit to another bank or corporate borrower, it is making a *Eurodollar loan.* These loans are usually structured as lines of credit on which borrowers can draw. Most large loans (over $500 million) are syndicated, thereby providing a measure of diversification to the lenders.[12] Eurocurrency syndicated loans sometimes exceed $10 billion in size, and loans of $1 billion or more are quite common. Furthermore, in total size, the Eurocurrency market dwarfs all other international corporate financial markets.

Project Finance. **Project finance (PF) loans** are typically arranged for infrastructure projects—such as toll roads, bridges, power plants, seaports, tunnels, and airports—that require large sums to construct but that, once built, generate significant amounts of free cash flow for many years.[13] Although project finance lending almost always involves the use of syndicated loans, these differ from other types of syndicated credits in two vital ways. First, PF loans are extended to **stand-alone companies,** sometimes called vehicle companies, created for the sole purpose of constructing and operating a single project. For example, Esty (1999) shows that the PF loans booked to develop a large oil field in Venezuela were extended to the company, Petrozuata, rather than to either or both of the venture's operating partners—the Venezuelan national oil company, PDVSA, or the American oil company, Conoco. Second, PF loans are almost always limited or nonrecourse credits, backed only by the assets and cash flows of the project, so the sponsors of the project do not guarantee payment of the loan. As described in Kleimeier and Megginson (2000), project finance loans have been employed in many famous recent projects, such as the Eurotunnel under the English Channel, Euro Disneyland in France, the new Athens International Airport, and the Seoul–Pusan High-Speed Rail Project in Korea.

---

9. What aspect of syndicated lending is most attractive to the lenders?

10. Why are syndicated loans especially useful for financing takeovers?

11. How do *project finance (PF) loans* differ from other types of syndicated loans?

Concept Review Questions

17.5 LEASING

Leasing, like long-term debt, requires the firm to make a series of periodic, tax-deductible payments that may be fixed or variable. You can think of a lease as being

---

[12.] Altman and Suggitt (2000) study the default rates in the syndicated loan market, and Megginson, Poulsen, and Sinkey (1995) examine stock market responses to bank announcements that they are participating in syndicated loans to sovereign or corporate borrowers. Some trends in syndicated lending are described in Jones, Lang, and Nigro (2000).

[13.] The early history of PF lending is described in Kensinger and Martin (1988). Brealey, Cooper, and Habib (1996) discuss how PF lending helps mitigate the agency problems that arise between borrower and lender in standard credit relationships. Finally, Esty (2002) analyzes how PF loans are structured and priced to ensure an adequate return to lenders.

comparable to secured long-term debt, because in both cases there is an underlying asset tied to the firm's financial obligation. The **lessee** uses the underlying asset and makes regular payments to the **lessor,** who retains ownership of the asset. Leasing can take a number of forms. Here we discuss the basic types of leases, lease arrangements, the lease contract, the lease-versus-purchase decision, the effects of leasing on future financing, and the advantages and disadvantages of leasing.

BASIC TYPES OF LEASES

The two basic types of leases available to a business are *operating leases* and *financial leases*. Accountants also use the term *capital leases* to refer to financial leases.

Operating Leases. An **operating lease** is typically a contractual arrangement whereby the lessee agrees to make periodic payments to the lessor, often for five years or less, to obtain an asset's services. The lessee generally receives an option to cancel the lease by paying a cancellation fee. Assets that are leased under operating leases have useful lives that are longer than the lease's term, although, as with most assets, the economic usefulness of the assets declines over time. Computer systems are prime examples of assets whose relative efficiency diminishes with new technological developments. The operating lease is a common arrangement for obtaining such systems as well as for other relatively short-lived assets, such as automobiles. When an operating lease expires, the lessee returns the asset to the lessor, who may lease it again or sell it. In some instances, the lease contract will give the lessee the opportunity to purchase the asset. In operating leases, the underlying asset usually has significant market value when the lease ends, and the lessor's original cost generally exceeds the total value of the lessee's payments.

Financial or Capital Leases. A **financial** (or **capital**) **lease** is longer term than an operating lease. Financial leases are noncancelable and therefore obligate the lessee to make payments over a predefined period. Even if the lessee no longer needs the asset, payments must continue until the lease expires. Financial leases are commonly used for leasing land, buildings, and large pieces of equipment. The noncancelable feature of the financial lease makes it quite similar to certain types of long-term debt. As is the case with debt, failure to make the contractual lease payments can result in bankruptcy for the lessee.

Another distinguishing characteristic of the financial lease is that the total payments over the lease period are greater than the lessor's initial cost. In other words, the lessor earns a return by receiving more than the asset's purchase price. Technically, under Financial Accounting Standards Board (FASB) Standard No. 13, "Accounting for Leases," a financial (or capital) lease is defined as having one of the following elements.

1. The lease transfers ownership of the property to the lessee by the end of the lease term.
2. The lease contains an option to purchase the property at a "bargain price." Such an option must be exercisable at a "fair market value" for the lease to be classified as an operating lease.
3. The lease term is equal to 75 percent or more of the estimated economic life of the property (exceptions exist for property leased toward the end of its usable economic life).
4. At the beginning of the lease, the present value of the lease payments is equal to 90 percent or more of the fair market value of the leased property.

The emphasis in this chapter is on financial leases because they result in inescapable long-term financial commitments by the firm.

LEASE ARRANGEMENTS

Lessors use three primary techniques for obtaining assets for leasing. The method selected depends largely on the desires of the prospective lessee. A **direct lease** results when a lessor acquires the assets that are leased to a given lessee. In other words, the lessee did not previously own the assets that it is leasing. In a **sale-leaseback arrangement,** one firm sells an asset to another for cash and then leases the asset from its new owner. You can see the resemblance of this arrangement to a collateralized loan. In such a loan, the lender gives the firm cash up front in exchange for a stream of future payments. If the borrower defaults on those payments, the lender keeps the collateral. In a sale-leaseback, the firm receives cash immediately (giving up ownership of the asset) and effectively repays this loan by leasing back the underlying asset. Sale-leaseback arrangements are therefore attractive to firms that need cash for operations. Leasing arrangements that include one or more third-party lenders are **leveraged leases.** Unlike in direct and sale-leaseback arrangements, the lessor in a leveraged lease acts as an equity participant, supplying only about 20 percent of the cost of the asset, and a lender supplies the balance. In recent years, leveraged leases have become especially popular in structuring leases of very expensive assets.[14]

A lease agreement usually specifies whether or not the lessee is responsible for maintenance of the leased assets. Both operating and financial leases generally include **maintenance clauses** specifying who is to maintain the assets and make insurance and tax payments. Under operating leases these costs are typically the lessor's responsibility, whereas under financial leases the lessee is typically responsible for these costs. The lessee often has the option to renew a lease at its expiration. **Renewal options** are especially common in operating leases because their term is generally shorter than the useful life of the leased assets. **Purchase options** allowing the lessee to purchase the leased asset at maturity occur in both operating and financial leases.[15]

The lessor can be one of a number of parties. In operating lease arrangements, the lessor is quite likely to be the manufacturer's leasing subsidiary or an independent leasing company. Financial leases are frequently handled by independent leasing companies or by the leasing subsidiaries of large financial institutions, such as commercial banks and life insurance companies. Life insurance companies are especially active in real estate leasing. Pension funds, like commercial banks, have also been increasing their leasing activities.

THE LEASE CONTRACT

The key items in a lease contract generally include a description of the leased assets, the term or duration of the lease, provisions for its cancellation, lease payment amounts and dates, provisions for maintenance and associated costs, renewal options, purchase options, and other provisions specified in the lease negotiation process. Furthermore, lease contracts spell out the consequences of the violation of any lease provision by either the lessee or the lessor.

[14.] For a discussion of why manufacturers may prefer to lease rather than sell their products, see Smith and Wakeman (1985) and Waldman (1997).
[15.] For a discussion on determining the appropriate lease rate for a lease that contains various options, see Grenadier (1995).

THE LEASE-VERSUS-PURCHASE DECISION

The **lease-versus-purchase** (or **lease-versus-buy**) **decision** is one that commonly confronts firms contemplating the acquisition of new fixed assets. The alternatives available are to (1) lease the assets, (2) borrow funds to purchase the assets, or (3) purchase the assets using available liquid resources. Similar financial analysis applies to alternatives 2 and 3. Even if the firm has the liquid resources with which to purchase the assets, the use of these funds is viewed as equivalent to borrowing. Therefore, here we need to compare only the leasing and purchasing alternatives.

The lease-versus-purchase decision involves application of the capital budgeting methods we presented in Chapters 7 and 8. We first determine the relevant cash flows and then apply present value techniques. Although the approach we demonstrate here analyzes and compares the present values of the cash flows for the lease and the purchase, an alternative approach would calculate the net present value of the incremental cash flows. The following steps are involved in the analysis.

Step 1. Find the after-tax cash flow for each year under the lease alternative. This step generally involves a simple tax adjustment of the annual lease payments. In addition, the cost of exercising a purchase option in the final year of the lease term may be included.[16]

Step 2. Find the after-tax cash flows for each year under the purchase alternative. This step involves adjusting the sum of the scheduled loan-payment and maintenance-cost outlay for the tax shields resulting from the tax deductions attributable to maintenance, depreciation, and interest.

Step 3. Calculate the present value of the cash flows associated with the lease (from Step 1) and purchase (from Step 2) alternatives using the after-tax cost of debt as the discount rate. Although some controversy surrounds the appropriate discount rate, *we use the after-tax cost of debt to evaluate the lease-versus-purchase decision* because the decision itself involves the choice between two financing alternatives having very low risk. If we were evaluating whether a given machine should be acquired, we would use the appropriate risk-adjusted discount rate or cost of capital; but in this type of analysis, we are attempting to determine only the better financing technique, leasing or borrowing.

Step 4. Choose the alternative with the lower present value of cash outflows from Step 3. This will be the least costly financing alternative.

The application of each of these steps is demonstrated in the following example.

APPLYING THE MODEL 17.2

The Portland Company, a small lumber mill, would like to acquire a new machine tool costing $24,000. The firm is in the 40 percent tax bracket and can either lease or purchase the machine.

Lease. The firm obtains a 5-year lease requiring annual *beginning*-of-year lease payments of $6,000.[17] The lessor will pay all maintenance costs, and the firm will

[16] Including the cost of exercising a purchase option in the lease-alternative cash flows ensures that under both the lease and purchase alternatives, the firm owns the asset at the end of the relevant time horizon. The alternative would be to include the cash flows from the sale of the asset in the purchase-alternative cash flows at the end of the lease term. These approaches guarantee avoidance of unequal project lives, which we discussed in Chapter 8. They also make any subsequent cash flows irrelevant because they would either be identical or nonexistent, respectively, under each alternative.
[17] Lease payments are generally made at the *beginning of the lease period* (in this case, a year), and we make that assumption here.

pay insurance and other costs. The firm exercises its option to purchase the machine for $4,000 at termination of the lease—at the end of year 4 (beginning of year 5).

Purchase. The firm finances the purchase of the machine with a 9 percent, 5-year loan requiring end-of-year installment payments of $6,170.[18] The machine will be depreciated under MACRS using a 5-year recovery period. The firm pays $1,500 per year for a service contract that covers all maintenance costs and also pays insurance and other costs. The firm plans to keep the machine and use it beyond its 5-year recovery period.

Using these data, we can apply the steps presented in the introduction to this model.

Step 1. The annual after-tax cash outflow from the lease payments can be found by multiplying the before-tax payment of $6,000 by 1 minus the tax rate, T_C, of 40 percent.

$$\text{Annual after-tax cash outflow from lease} = \$6,000 \times (1 - T_C)$$

$$= \$6,000 \times (1 - 0.40) = \$3,600$$

Therefore, the lease alternative results in annual cash outflows over the 5-year lease of $3,600, paid at the beginning of each year. In the final year, the $4,000 cost of the purchase option would be added to the $3,600 lease outflow to get a total cash outflow at the end of year 4 (beginning of year 5) of $7,600 ($3,600 + $4,000).

Step 2. The after-tax cash outflow from the purchase alternative is a bit more difficult to find. First, the interest component of each annual loan payment must be determined, because the Internal Revenue Service allows the deduction from income of interest only, not principal, for tax purposes.[19] Table 17.7 presents the calculations required to split the loan payments into their interest and principal components. Columns 3 and 4 show the annual interest and principal paid in each of the five years. Column 1 lists the annual loan payment.

Next, we find the annual depreciation write-off resulting from the $24,000 machine. Using the applicable MACRS 5-year asset class depreciation percentages from Table 8.1 (on page 302) of 20 percent in year 1, 32 percent in year 2, 19.2 percent in year 3, and 11.52 percent in years 4 and 5 results in the annual depreciation for years 1 through 5 given in column 3 of Table 17.8.[20]

Table 17.8 presents all the calculations required to determine the cash outflows associated with borrowing to purchase the new machine.[21] Column 7 of the

---

[18.] The annual loan payment on the 9 percent, 5-year loan of $24,000 is calculated by using the loan amortization technique that we described in Chapter 3.

[19.] When the rate of interest on the loan used to finance the purchase just equals the cost of debt, the present value of the after-tax loan payments (annual loan payments − interest tax shields) discounted at the after-tax cost of debt would just equal the initial loan principal. In such a case, it is unnecessary to amortize the loan to determine the payment amount and the amounts of interest when finding the after-tax cash outflows. The loan payments and interest payments (columns 1 and 4 in Table 17.8) could be ignored, and in their place the initial loan principal ($24,000) would be shown as an outflow occurring at time 0. To allow for a loan interest rate that is different from the firm's cost of debt and to facilitate understanding, here we isolate the loan payments and interest payments rather than use this computationally more efficient approach.

[20.] The year-6 depreciation is ignored because we are considering the cash flows solely over a 5-year time horizon. Similarly, depreciation on the leased asset when purchased at the end of the lease for $4,000 is ignored. The tax benefits resulting from this depreciation would make the lease alternative even more attractive. Clearly, the analysis would become more precise and more complex if we chose to look beyond the 5-year time horizon, though the basic conclusions would remain unchanged.

[21.] Although other cash outflows, such as insurance and operating expenses, may be relevant here, they would be the same under the lease and purchase alternatives and therefore would cancel out in the final analysis.

Table 17.7
Determining the Interest and Principal Components of the Portland Company Loan Payments

End of Year	Loan Payments (1)	Beginning-of-Year Principal (2)	Payments		End-of-Year Principal [(2) − (4)] (5)
			Interest [0.09 × (2)] (3)	Principal [(1) − (3)] (4)	
1	$6,170	$24,000	$2,160	$4,010	$19,990
2	6,170	19,990	1,799	4,371	15,619
3	6,170	15,619	1,406	4,764	10,855
4	6,170	10,855	977	5,193	5,662
5	6,170	5,662	510	5,660	—[a]

[a]The values in this table have been rounded to the nearest dollar, which results in a slight difference ($2) between the beginning-of-year-5 principal (in column 2) and the year-5 principal payment (in column 4).

Table 17.8
After-Tax Cash Outflows Associated with Purchasing for the Portland Company

End of Year	Loan Payments (1)	Maintenance Costs (2)	Depreciation (3)	Interest[a] (4)	Total Deductions [(2) + (3) + (4)] (5)	Tax Shields [0.40 × (5)] (6)	After-Tax Cash Outflows [(1) + (2) − (6)] (7)
1	$6,170	$1,500	$4,800	$2,160	$ 8,460	$3,384	$4,286
2	6,170	1,500	7,680	1,799	10,979	4,392	3,278
3	6,170	1,500	4,608	1,406	7,514	3,006	4,664
4	6,170	1,500	2,765	977	5,242	2,097	5,573
5	6,170	1,500	2,765	510	4,775	1,910	5,760

[a]From Table 17.7, column 3.

table presents the after-tax cash outflows associated with the purchase alternative. A few points should be clarified with respect to the calculations in Table 17.8. The major cash outflows are the total loan payment for each year given in column 1 and the annual maintenance cost, which is a tax-deductible expense, in column 2. The sum of these two outflows is reduced by the tax savings from writing off the maintenance, depreciation, and interest expenses associated with the new machine and its financing, respectively. The resulting cash outflows are the after-tax cash outflows associated with the purchase alternative.

Step 3. The present values of the cash outflows associated with the lease (from Step 1) and purchase (from Step 2) alternatives are calculated in Table 17.9 using the firm's 5.4 percent after-tax cost of debt [9.0% × (1 − 0.40)]. Applying the appropriate present value interest factors given in columns 2 and 5 to the after-tax cash outflows in columns 1 and 4 results in the present values of lease and purchase cash outflows given in columns 3 and 6, respectively. Column 3 presents the sum of the present values of the cash outflows for the leasing alternative, and column 6 gives the sum for the purchasing alternative.

Step 4. Because the present value of cash outflows for leasing ($19,490) is lower than that for purchasing ($19,943), the leasing alternative is preferable. Leasing results in an incremental savings of $453 ($19,943 − $19,490) and is therefore the less costly alternative.

The techniques described here for comparing lease and purchase alternatives may be applied in different ways. The approach illustrated by using the Portland Com-

Table 17.9
A Comparison of the Cash Outflows Associated with Leasing versus Purchasing for the Portland Company

| End of Year | Leasing | | | Purchasing | | |
	After-Tax Cash Outflows (1)	Present Value Factors (2)	Present Value of Outflows [(1) × (2)] (3)	After-Tax Cash Outflows[a] (4)	Present Value Factors (5)	Present Value of Outflows [(4) × (5)] (6)
0	$3,600	1.000	$ 3,600	$ 0	1.000	$ 0
1	3,600	0.949	3,416	4,286	0.949	4,066
2	3,600	0.900	3,241	3,278	0.900	2,951
3	3,600	0.854	3,075	4,664	0.854	3,983
4	7,600[b]	0.810	6,158	5,573	0.810	4,514
5	0	0.769	0	5,760	0.769	4,429
		PV of cash outflows	$19,490		PV of cash outflows	$19,943

[a]From column 7 of Table 17.8.
[b]After-tax lease payment outflow of $3,600 plus the $4,000 cost of exercising the purchase option.

pany's data is one of the most straightforward. It is important to recognize that the lower cost of one alternative over the other results from factors such as the differing tax brackets of the lessor and the lessee, different tax treatments for leases versus purchases, and differing risks and borrowing costs for the lessor and the lessee. Therefore, when making a lease-versus-purchase decision, the firm will find that inexpensive borrowing opportunities, high required lessor returns, and a low risk of obsolescence increase the attractiveness of purchasing.[22] Subjective factors must also be included in the decision-making process. Like most financial decisions, the lease-versus-purchase decision requires a certain degree of judgment and/or intuition.

EFFECTS OF LEASING ON FUTURE FINANCING

Because leasing is considered a type of debt financing, it affects a firm's future financing ability. Lease payments are shown as a tax-deductible expense on the firm's income statement. Anyone analyzing the income statement would probably recognize that assets are being leased, although the actual details of the amounts and terms of the leases might be unclear. The following sections discuss the lease disclosure requirements established by the Financial Accounting Standards Board (FASB) and the effect of leases on financial ratios.

Lease Disclosure Requirements. Standard No. 13 of the FASB, "Accounting for Leases," requires explicit disclosure of financial (capital) lease obligations on the firm's balance sheet. Such a lease must be shown as a *capitalized lease,* meaning that the present value of all its payments is included as an asset and corresponding liability on the firm's balance sheet. An operating lease, on the other hand, need not be

---

[22.] Smith and Wakeman (1985), Krishnan and Moyer (1994), Barclay and Smith (1995b), Grenadier (1995, 1996), and Waldman (1997) examine the lease-versus-purchase decision using U.S. data. Lasfer and Levis (1998) perform a similar analysis using British data, while Beattie, Goodacre, and Thomson (2000) examine the choice between operating and financial leases in Britain. To date, no clear-cut patterns are observed, though firm size, tax status, the relative importance of growth options to firm value, and the likelihood of bankruptcy all seem to play a role. As do most subsequent researchers, Schallheim, Johnson, Lease, and McConnell (1987) find that lease rates are significantly higher than otherwise-comparable lending rates, so firms clearly choose leasing for reasons other than lower cost alone.

capitalized, but its basic features must be disclosed in a footnote to the financial statements. Standard No. 13, of course, establishes detailed guidelines to be used in capitalizing leases to reflect them as an asset and corresponding liability on the balance sheet. Subsequent standards have further refined lease capitalization and disclosure procedures. The following Applying the Model provides an example.

APPLYING THE MODEL 17.3

Altmont Company, a manufacturer of printing equipment, is leasing an asset under a 10-year lease requiring annual beginning-of-year payments of $15,000. The lease can be capitalized merely by calculating the present value of the lease payments over the life of the lease. However, the rate at which the payments should be discounted is difficult to determine.[23] If 10 percent is used, the present, or capitalized, value of the lease is found by multiplying the annual lease payment by the present value factor of a 10-year, 10 percent annuity due (Equation 3.8). This value of $101,385 ($15,000 × 6.759) would be shown as an asset and corresponding liability on the firm's balance sheet, which should result in an accurate reflection of the firm's true financial position.

Leasing and Financial Ratios. Because the consequences of missing a financial lease payment are the same as those of missing an interest or principal payment on debt, a financial analyst must view the lease as a long-term financial commitment of the lessee. With FASB Standard No. 13, the inclusion of each financial (capital) lease as an asset and corresponding liability (i.e., long-term debt) provides for a balance sheet that more accurately reflects the firm's financial status. It thereby permits various types of financial ratio analyses to be performed directly on the statement by any interested party.

ADVANTAGES AND DISADVANTAGES OF LEASING

Leasing has a number of commonly cited advantages and disadvantages that should be considered when making a lease-versus-purchase decision. Although not all these advantages and disadvantages hold in every case, several of them may apply in any given situation.

Commonly Cited Advantages.
1. Leasing allows the lessee, in effect, to depreciate land, which is prohibited if the land were purchased. Because the lessee who leases land is permitted to deduct the total lease payment as an expense for tax purposes, the effect is the same as if the firm had purchased the land and then depreciated it.
2. The use of sale-leaseback arrangements may permit the firm to increase its liquidity by converting an asset into cash, which can then be used as working capital. A firm short of working capital or in a liquidity bind can sell an owned asset to a lessor and lease the asset back for a specified number of years.
3. Leasing provides 100 percent financing. Most loan agreements for the purchase of fixed assets require the borrower to pay a portion of the purchase price as a

---

[23.] The Financial Accounting Standards Board in Standard No. 13 established certain guidelines for the appropriate discount rate to use when capitalizing leases. Most commonly, the rate that the lessee would have incurred to borrow the funds to buy the asset with a secured loan under terms similar to the lease repayment schedule would be used. This simply represents the before-tax cost of a secured loan.

down payment. Therefore, the borrower is able to borrow (at most) only 90–95 percent of the purchase price of the asset.

4. When a firm becomes bankrupt or is reorganized, the maximum claim of lessors against the corporation is three years of lease payments, and the lessor, of course, reclaims the asset. If debt is used to purchase an asset, the creditors have a claim that is equal to the total outstanding loan balance.

5. In a lease arrangement, the firm may avoid the cost of obsolescence if the lessor fails to accurately anticipate the obsolescence of assets and sets the lease payment too low. This is especially true in the case of operating leases, which generally have relatively short lives.

6. A lessee avoids many of the negative covenants that are usually included as part of a long-term loan. Requirements with respect to the sale of accounts receivable, subsequent borrowing, business combinations, and so on are not generally found in a lease agreement.

7. In the case of low-cost assets that are infrequently acquired, leasing, especially through operating leases, may provide the firm with needed financing flexibility. That is, the firm does not have to arrange other financing for these assets and can obtain them somewhat conveniently through a lease.

Commonly Cited Disadvantages.

1. A lease does not have a stated interest cost. In many leases, the return to the lessor is quite high, so the firm might be better off borrowing to purchase the asset.

2. At the end of the term of the lease agreement, the lessor realizes the salvage value, if any, of an asset. If the lessee had purchased the asset, it could have claimed the asset's salvage value. Of course, in a competitive market, if the lessor expects a higher salvage value, then the lease payments would be lower.

3. Under a lease, the lessee is generally prohibited from making improvements on the leased property or asset without the approval of the lessor. If the property were owned outright, this difficulty would not arise. Of course, lessors generally encourage leasehold improvements when they are expected to enhance the asset's salvage value.

4. If a lessee leases an asset that subsequently becomes obsolete, it still must make lease payments over the remaining term of the lease. This is true even if the asset is unusable.

> **12.** Why is it considered important whether a lease is classified as an *operating lease* or as a *financial* (or *capital*) *lease*?
>
> **13.** What factors should be considered when deciding between leasing an asset and borrowing funds to purchase the asset?

Concept Review Questions

17.6 SUMMARY

- Long-term debt and leasing are important sources of capital for businesses. Long-term debt can take the form of term loans or bonds. The characteristics of each can be tailored to meet the needs of both the borrower and the lender.

- The conditions of a term loan are specified in the loan agreement. This agreement specifies the rights and responsibilities of both creditor and borrower, and the agreement typically lists several positive and negative covenants that the borrower must not violate.
- The conditions of a bond issue are specified in the bond indenture and are enforced by a trustee. These legal agreements are highly detailed and not easily modified, because bonds are held by many individual investors. In contrast, privately arranged loan terms can be modified rather easily, because the borrower can negotiate directly with one creditor or a relatively small number of creditors.
- Frequently when interest rates drop, bond issuers make refunding decisions, which involve finding the *NPV* associated with calling outstanding bonds and issuing new, lower-interest-coupon bonds to replace the refunded bonds.
- Syndicated loans are large credits arranged by a syndicate of commercial banks for a single borrower. These have been increasing in importance in recent years because very large loans can be arranged quickly and inexpensively and can have very flexible borrowing terms.
- Leasing serves as an alternative to borrowing funds to purchase an asset. Operating leases need not be shown on a firm's balance sheet, whereas financial lease obligations must be shown. Firms often make lease-versus-purchase decisions, which involve choosing the alternative with the lower present value of cash outflows.
- Leasing affects a firm's future financing ability. Capital leases must be capitalized and shown as an asset and corresponding liability on the firm's balance sheet, whereas operating leases must only be described in a footnote to the firm's financial statements. Financial analysts view leases as long-term financial commitments. A variety of advantages and disadvantages of leasing are commonly cited.

INTERNET RESOURCES

Note: *For updates to links, please go to the book's website at http://smart.swcollege.com.*

http://www.bondsonline.com — Offers a wealth of information on the bond market

http://www.investinginbonds.com — A site with statistics on the Treasury, municipal, and corporate bond markets

KEY TERMS

balloon payment	financial lease	lessor
bearer bonds	fixed-rate offerings	leveraged leases
call premium	floating-rate issues	LIBOR
capital lease	foreign bond	lien
collateral	high-yield bonds	loans
collateral trust bonds	income bonds	maintenance clauses
convertible bonds	indenture	mortgage bonds
cross-default covenant	investment-grade bonds	mortgage-backed securities
debentures	junk bonds	(MBS)
direct lease	lease-versus-buy decision	operating lease
equipment trust certificates	lease-versus-purchase	prime rate
Eurobond	decision	private placements
Eurocurrency loan market	leasing	project finance (PF) loans
fallen angels	lessee	purchase options

refund	sinking fund	subordination
renewal options	stand-alone companies	syndicated loan
sale-leaseback arrangement	stock purchase warrants	term loan
serial bonds	subordinated debentures	trustee

QUESTIONS

17-1.   Comment on the following proposition: Using floating-rate debt eliminates interest rate risk (the risk that interest payment amounts will change in the future) for both the borrower and the lender.

17-2.   What purpose do *covenants* serve in a debt agreement? What factors should a manager consider when negotiating covenants?

17-3.   What is a *debenture*? Why do you think that this is the most common form of corporate bond in the United States but is much less commonly used elsewhere?

17-4.   How do *sinking funds* reduce default risk?

17-5.   What is a *trustee*? Why do bondholders insist that a trustee be included in all public bond offerings? Why are these less necessary in private debt placements?

17-6.   What impact has adoption of *Rule 144A* had on debt-issuance patterns in the United States?

17-7.   Why are most corporate bonds callable? Who benefits from this feature, and what is the cost of adopting a call provision in a public bond issue?

17-8.   Why do corporations have their debt rated? Compare the role played by rating agencies and a company's outside auditors.

17-9.   What does *investment grade* mean in the context of corporate bond issues? How do these bonds differ from *junk bonds*, and why have the latter proven so popular with investors?

17-10.   What is a *Eurobond*? Why did these bonds come into existence? Why do Eurobond investors like the fact that these are typically "bearer bonds"? What risk does an investor run from holding bearer bonds rather than registered bonds?

17-11.   Explain how uncertainty concerning future interest rates would affect the decision to refund a bond issue.

17-12.   What is a *syndicated loan*? What is a *project finance loan*? What role does a *stand-alone company* play in the typical project finance deal?

17-13.   What elements must be included in a lease in order for it to be considered a financial (capital) lease?

17-14.   How would the availability of floating-rate debt rather than fixed-rate debt affect the lease-versus-buy decision?

17-15.   What are the key advantages of leasing as compared to borrowing to acquire an asset? What are the key disadvantages of leasing?

PROBLEMS

Corporate Bonds

17-1.   The initial proceeds per bond, the size of the issue, the initial maturity of the bond, and the years remaining to maturity are shown in the following table for a number of bonds. In each case, the firm is in the 40 percent tax bracket, and the bond has a $1,000 par value.

Bond	Proceeds per Bond	Size of Issue	Initial Maturity of Bond	Years Remaining to Maturity
A	$ 985	10,000 bonds	20 years	15 years
B	1,025	20,000	25	16
C	1,000	22,500	12	9
D	960	5,000	25	15
E	1,035	10,000	30	16

a. Indicate whether each bond was sold at a discount, at a premium, or at its par value.
b. Determine the total discount or premium for each issue.
c. Determine the annual amount of discount or premium amortized for each bond.
d. Calculate the unamortized discount or premium for each bond.
e. Determine the after-tax cash flow associated with the retirement now of each of these bonds, using the values developed in part (d).

17-2. For each of the callable bond issues in the following table, calculate the after-tax cost of calling the issue. Each bond has a $1,000 par value, and the various issue sizes and call prices are shown in the following table. The firm is in the 40 percent tax bracket.

Bond	Size of Issue	Call Price
A	12,000 bonds	$1,050
B	20,000	1,030
C	30,000	1,015
D	50,000	1,050
E	100,000	1,045
F	500,000	1,060

17-3. The flotation cost, the initial maturity, and the number of years remaining to maturity are shown in the following table for a number of bonds. The firm is in the 40 percent tax bracket.

Bond	Flotation Cost	Initial Maturity of Bond	Years Remaining to Maturity
A	$250,000	30 years	22 years
B	500,000	15	5
C	125,000	20	10
D	750,000	10	1
E	650,000	15	6

a. Calculate the annual amortization of the flotation cost for each bond.
b. Determine the tax savings, if any, expected to result from the unamortized flotation cost if the bond were called today.

17-4. The initial proceeds per bond, the size of the issue, the initial maturity of the bond, and the years remaining to maturity are shown in the following table for a number of bonds. In each case, the firm is in the 35 percent tax bracket and the bond has a $1,000 par value.

Bond	Proceeds per Bond	Size of Issue	Initial Maturity of Bond	Years Remaining to Maturity
A	$ 975	50,000 bonds	10 years	5 years
B	1,020	25,000	20	15
C	1,000	100,000	25	12

    a. Indicate whether each bond was sold at a discount, at a premium, or at its par value.

    b. Determine the total discount or premium for each issue.

    c. Determine the annual amount of discount or premium amortized for each bond.

    d. Calculate the unamortized discount or premium for each bond.

    e. Determine the after-tax cash flow associated with the retirement now of each of these bonds, using the values developed in part (d).

17-5. The principal, coupon interest rate, and interest overlap period are shown in the following table for a number of bonds.

Bond	Principal	Coupon Interest Rate	Interest Overlap Period
A	$ 15,000,000	6.5%	2 months
B	20,000,000	7.0	3
C	15,000,000	6.0	4
D	100,000,000	8.0	6

    a. Calculate the dollar amount of interest that must be paid for each bond during the interest overlap period.

    b. Calculate the after-tax cost of overlapping interest for each bond if the firm is in the 40 percent tax bracket.

17-6. The principal, coupon interest rate, and interest overlap period are shown in the following table for a number of bonds.

Bond	Principal	Coupon Interest Rate	Interest Overlap Period
A	$ 5,000,000	8.0%	3 months
B	40,000,000	7.0	2
C	50,000,000	6.5	3
D	100,000,000	9.0	6
E	20,000,000	5.5	1

    a. Calculate the dollar amount of interest that must be paid for each bond during the interest overlap period.

    b. Calculate the after-tax cost of overlapping interest for each bond if the firm is in the 40 percent tax bracket.

17-7. Schooner Company is contemplating offering a new $50 million bond issue to replace an outstanding $50 million bond issue. The firm wishes to take advantage of the decline in interest rates that has occurred since the initial bond issuance. The old and new bonds are described in what follows. The firm is in the 40 percent tax bracket.

    Old bonds. The outstanding bonds have a $1,000 par value and a 9 percent coupon interest rate. They were issued five years ago with a 20-year maturity. They were initially sold for their par value of $1,000, and the firm incurred $350,000 in flotation costs. They are callable at $1,090.

    New bonds. The new bonds would have a $1,000 par value, a 7 percent coupon interest rate, and a 15-year maturity. They could be sold at their par value. The flotation cost of the new bonds would be $500,000. The firm does not expect to have any overlapping interest.

    a. Calculate the tax savings that are expected from the unamortized portion or the old bonds' flotation cost.

    b. Calculate the annual tax savings from the flotation cost of the new bonds, assuming the 15-year amortization.

    c. Calculate the after-tax cost of the call premium that is required to retire the old bonds.

d. Determine the initial investment that is required to call the old bonds and issue the new bonds.

e. Calculate the annual cash flow savings, if any, that are expected from the proposed bond-refunding decision.

f. If the firm has a 4.2 percent after-tax cost of debt, find the net present value (*NPV*) of the bond-refunding decision. Would you recommend the proposed refunding? Explain your answer.

17-8. High-Gearing Incorporated is considering offering a new $40 million bond issue to replace an outstanding $40 million bond issue. The firm wishes to do this to take advantage of the decline in interest rates that has occurred since the original issue. The two bond issues are described in what follows. The firm is in the 40 percent tax bracket.

    Old bonds. The outstanding bonds have a $1,000 par value and a 10 percent coupon interest rate. They were issued five years ago with a 25-year maturity. They were initially sold at a $25 per bond discount, and a $200,000 flotation cost was incurred. They are callable at $1,100.

    New bonds. The new bonds would have a 20-year maturity, a par value of $1,000, and a 7.5 percent coupon interest rate. It is expected that these bonds can be sold at par for a flotation cost of $250,000. The firm expects a 3-month period of overlapping interest while it retires the old bonds.

a. Calculate the initial investment that is required to call the old bonds and issue the new bonds.

b. Calculate the annual cash flow savings, if any, expected from the proposed bond-refunding decision.

c. If the firm uses its after-tax cost of debt of 4.5 percent to evaluate low-risk decisions, find the net present value (*NPV*) of the bond-refunding decision. Would you recommend the proposed refunding? Explain your answer.

17-9. Well-Sprung Corporation is considering offering a new $100 million bond issue to replace an outstanding $100 million bond issue. The firm wishes to take advantage of the decline in interest rates that has occurred since the original issue. The two bond issues are described in what follows. The firm is in the 30 percent tax bracket.

    Old bonds. The outstanding bonds have a $1,000 par value and an 8.5 percent coupon interest rate. They were issued 5 years ago with a 20-year maturity. They were initially sold at a $30 per bond discount, and a $750,000 floatation cost was incurred. They are callable at $1,085.

    New bonds. The new bonds would have a 15-year maturity, a par value of $1,000, and a 7.0 percent coupon interest rate. It is expected that these bonds can be sold at par for a floatation cost of $600,000. The firm expects a 3-month period of overlapping interest while it retires the old bonds.

a. Calculate the initial investment that is required to call the old bonds and issue the new bonds.

b. Calculate the annual cash flow savings, if any, expected from the proposed bond-refunding decision.

c. If the firm uses its after-tax cost of debt of 4.9 percent of evaluate low-risk decisions, find the net present value (*NPV*) of the bond-refunding decision. Would you recommend the proposed refunding? Explain your answer.

17-10. Web Tools Company is considering using the proceeds from a new $50 million bond issue to call and retire its outstanding $50 million bond issue. The details of both bond issues are outlined in what follows. The firm is in the 40 percent tax bracket.

    Old bonds. The firm's old issue has a coupon interest rate of 10 percent, was issued four years ago, and had a 20-year maturity. The bonds sold at a $10 discount from their $1,000 par value, flotation costs were $420,000, and their call price is $1,100.

    New bonds. The new bonds are expected to sell at par ($1,000), have a 16-year maturity, and have flotation costs of $520,000. The firm will have a 2-month period of overlapping interest while it retires the old bonds.

   a. What is the initial investment that is required to call the old bonds and issue the new bonds?

   b. What are the annual cash flow savings, if any, from the proposed bond-refunding decision if (1) the new bonds have an 8 percent coupon interest rate and (2) the new bonds have a 9 percent coupon interest rate?

   c. Construct a table showing the net present value (*NPV*) of refunding under the two circumstances given in part (b) when (1) the firm has an after-tax cost of debt of 4.8 percent [0.08 × (1 − 0.40)] and (2) the firm has an after-tax cost of debt of 5.4 percent [0.09 × (1 − 0.40)].

   d. Discuss the set(s) of circumstances (described in part [c]) when refunding would be favorable and when it would not.

   e. If the four circumstances summarized in part (d) were equally probable (each had 0.25 probability), would you recommend refunding? Explain your answer.

Leasing

17-11. For each of the loan amounts, interest rates, loan terms, and annual payments shown in the following table, calculate the annual interest paid each year over the term of the loan, assuming that the payments are made at the *end of each year*.

Loan	Amount	Interest Rate	Term	Annual Payment
A	$ 20,000	8%	4 years	$ 6,038
B	35,500	7	6	7,448
C	152,500	9	5	39,207
D	250,000	7.5	10	36,421
E	575,500	6	15	59,204

17-12. Shredding Pines Company wishes to purchase an asset that costs $750,000. The full amount needed to finance the asset can be borrowed at 9 percent interest. The terms of the loan require equal end-of-year payments for the next eight years. Determine the total annual loan payment, and break it into the amount of interest and the amount of principal paid for each year.

17-13. Given the lease payments and terms shown in the following table, determine the yearly after-tax cash outflows for each firm, assuming that lease payments are made at the *beginning of each year* and that the firm is in the 40 percent tax bracket. Assume that no purchase option exists.

Firm	Annual Lease Payment	Term of Lease
A	$ 250,000	5 years
B	160,000	12
C	500,000	8
D	1,000,000	20
E	25,000	6

17-14. GMS Corporation is attempting to determine whether to lease or purchase research equipment. The firm is in the 40 percent tax bracket, and its after-tax cost of debt is currently 6 percent. The terms of the lease and the purchase are as follows:

   Lease. Annual beginning-of-year lease payments of $93,500 are required over the 3-year life of the lease. The lessor will pay all maintenance costs; the lessee will pay insurance and other costs. The lessee will exercise its option to purchase the asset for $25,000 paid along with the final lease payment.

   Purchase. The $250,000 cost of the research equipment can be financed entirely with a 10 percent loan requiring annual end-of-year payments of $100,529 for three years. The firm in this case will depreciate the equipment under MACRS using a 3-year recovery period. (See Table 8.1 on page 302 for applicable MACRS percentages.) The firm will pay $9,500 per year for a service contract that covers all maintenance costs; the firm will pay insurance and other costs. The firm plans to keep the equipment and use it beyond its 3-year recovery period.

a. Calculate the after-tax cash outflows associated with each alternative.

b. Calculate the present value of each cash outflow stream using the after-tax cost of debt.

c. Which alternative, lease or purchase, would you recommend? Why?

17-15. Strident Corporation is attempting to determine whether to lease or purchase a new telephone system. The firm is in the 40 percent tax bracket, and its after-tax cost of debt is currently 4.5 percent. The terms of the lease and the purchase are as follows:

    Lease. Annual beginning-of-year lease payments of $22,000 are required over the 5-year life of the lease. The lessor will pay all maintenance costs; the lessee will pay insurance and other costs. The lessee will exercise its option to purchase the asset for $30,000 paid along with the final lease payment.

    Purchase. The $100,000 cost of the telephone system can be financed entirely with a 7.5 percent loan requiring annual end-of-year payments of $24,716 for 5 years. The firm in this case will depreciate the equipment under MACRS using a 5-year recovery period. (See Table 8.1 on page 302 for applicable MACRS percentages.) The firm will pay $3,500 per year for a service contract that covers all maintenance costs; the firm will pay insurance and other costs. The firm plans to keep the equipment and use it beyond its 5-year recovery period.

a. Calculate the after-tax cash outflows associated with each alternative.

b. Calculate the present value of each cash outflow stream using the after-tax cost of debt.

c. Which alternative, lease or purchase, would you recommend? Why?

17-16. Eastern Trucking Company needs to expand its facilities. To do so, the firm must acquire a machine costing $80,000. The machine can be leased or purchased. The firm is in the 40 percent tax bracket, and its after-tax cost of debt is 5.4 percent. The terms of the lease and purchase plans are as follows:

    Lease. The leasing arrangement requires beginning-of-year payments of $16,900 over five years. The lessor will pay all maintenance costs; the lessee will pay insurance and other costs. The lessee will exercise its option to purchase the asset for $20,000 paid along with the final lease payment.

    Purchase. If the firm purchases the machine, its cost of $80,000 will be financed with a 5-year, 9 percent loan requiring equal end-of-year payments of $20,567. The machine will be depreciated under MACRS using a 5-year recovery period. (See Table 8.1 on page 302 for applicable MACRS percentages.) The firm will pay $2,000 per year for a service contract that covers all maintenance costs; the firm will pay insurance and other costs. The firm plans to keep the equipment and use it beyond its 5-year recovery period.

a. Determine the after-tax cash outflows of Eastern Trucking under each alternative.

b. Find the present value of the after-tax cash outflows for each alternative using the after-tax cost of debt.

c. Which alternative, lease or purchase, would you recommend? Why?

17-17. Given the lease payments, terms remaining until the leases expire, and discount rates shown in the following table, calculate the capitalized value of each lease, assuming that lease payments are made annually at the beginning of each year.

Lease	Lease Payment	Remaining Term	Discount Rate
A	$ 40,000	12 years	10%
B	120,000	8	12
C	9,000	18	14
D	16,000	3	9
E	47,000	20	11

17-18.   Read the prospectus filed on March 15, 2006, by Walt Disney Company (ticker symbol, DIS). (*Hint:* You can access the prospectus under the Filings tab and look for PROSP under Filing Type.) What type of debt did Disney offer to the public for sale? What dollar amount of debt did Disney propose to sell? What percentage of the sales price did Disney net (after discounts and commissions)? What did Disney state they would use the funds for? Was the debt secured or unsecured?

MINI-CASES: LONG-TERM DEBT & LEASING

Nientindoe Corporation (NC) issued $100 million of 7.375% coupon bonds 10 years ago. Each bond has a par value of $1,000, and they are callable at 104% of par value. Flotation costs were ½ of 1%, and the bonds were initially sold at par. However, interest rates are currently 6.175% for 20-year bonds, and Nientindoe Corporation is considering issuing 20-year bonds and retiring the old bond issue. Because the new bonds would have to be issued to generate sufficient cash to pay off the old bonds, a 1.5-month period would exist when both the old and the new issue would be outstanding. Nientindoe Corporation is in a 35% tax bracket. Flotation costs on the new issue would be ¼ of 1%, and the new bonds will be sold at par.

1.   Determine the initial investment if NC issues new bonds to retire the old bonds. Assume that NC will have to issue enough bonds to cover both the principal and the call premium associated with retiring the old issue.

2.   Determine the annual cash flow savings if NC refunds the old bond issue.

3.   Calculate the net present value of the bond refunding. Should NC refund the old issue?

Barclay Polymers needs to acquire a new extruding machine, with a purchase price of $600,000. However, the firm could lease the extruder from Primal Leasing Corporation for a five-year period and make annual payments of $115,000 at the beginning of the year. If the extruder is leased, Primal Leasing Corporation would pay all maintenance costs and Barclay would have the opportunity to purchase the asset for $130,000 at the beginning of year 5. If the extruder is purchased by Barclay, it will be financed with a five-year loan at an annual rate of 8.75%. Barclay would use the MACRS depreciation method over a five-year recovery period, would purchase a service contract for $8,000 a year, and would keep the extruder after its recovery period. If the firm pursues the purchase alternative, it would purchase a maintenance contract for an expected cost of $3,000 annually. The firm is in a 35% tax bracket.

1.   Calculate the annual after-tax cash outflow for the leasing alternative.

2.   Determine the annual interest and principal payments for the purchase alternative.

3.   Determine the annual depreciation deduction for the purchase alternative.

4.   Calculate the net present value of both the leasing and the purchase alternatives. Which method should Barclay Polymers use to obtain the extruder?

PART 6: Options, Derivatives, and International Financial Management

No area of finance has witnessed more innovation and more explosive growth than the field of derivative securities. Derivatives are financial assets whose values depend on, or derive from, the values of other assets. For example, if your employer grants you the option to buy shares of stock in the company at a fixed price, the value of that option depends on the company's stock price. Derivative securities markets have grown dramatically in the last two decades, in part because these securities help corporations hedge their exposures to different types of risk.

Chapter 18 provides an introduction to options, one of the three main types of derivative instruments. The chapter describes the basic features of put and call options, and it demonstrates how investors can use options and portfolios of options to construct innovative trading strategies. The chapter concludes with a discussion of a method for pricing options called the binomial option pricing model.

Chapter 19 extends the analysis of the previous chapter by exploring how many different types of assets have option-like characteristics. The chapter begins with an overview of the Nobel Prize–winning Black and Scholes option pricing model, highlighting the connections between this model and the binomial model from Chapter 18. Next, we show how many different types of securities, such as convertible bonds, have option-like features, suggesting that knowledge of option price techniques is required to value these instruments. The chapter's final section explores how even certain real investment opportunities, such as drilling for oil or expanding a fast-food franchise, can have option-like traits. For these investments, an option-pricing valuation framework may lead to better decisions than the traditional *NPV* approach.

One of the drivers of explosive growth in derivatives markets is the worldwide expansion of international trade. In Chapter 20 we look at the particular challenges faced by multinational corporations. Our focus here is primarily on the risks that arise when firms do business across national boundaries and in multiple currencies. The chapter begins with a discussion of exchange rates and foreign exchange markets. Then we explore the forces that cause currency values to rise and fall over time and the instruments and strategies that firms can employ to deal with currency related risk.

long-call
short-call

long-put

short-put

Long-bond
$\textcircled{s}$ prize

short-bond
$\textcircled{s}$ negative prize

Fiat Accompli

The year 2005 was one that managers at General Motors would probably like to forget. In May, the rating agency Standard and Poors downgraded GM's credit rating to "junk" status in response to continuing financial problems at the automaker. Coming at a time when GM shares were trading near a 12-year low, the downgrade affected roughly $300 billion in outstanding GM debt. Fitch Ratings and Moody's issued their own downgrade announcements for GM later that summer. To recover its investment-grade credit rating, GM would have to convince rating agencies and investors that it could turn around its slumping financial performance.

Perhaps the last thing that GM needed was to invest billions in the purchase of another ailing auto manufacturer, but that is precisely what managers at the Italian car maker Fiat were trying to force GM to do. Years earlier, as part of a transaction in which GM purchased a small stake in Fiat, GM granted Fiat a put option. The holder of a put option has the right to sell shares of stock at a predetermined price to the put option seller, so in this case Fiat had the right to sell GM all of the shares in Fiat that GM did not already own at a price negotiated when auto shares were trading much higher. Credit rating agencies and stock analysts repeatedly mentioned Fiat's outstanding put option as one of the reasons for their negative outlook for GM securities.

Though GM steadfastly maintained that Fiat had violated the terms of their original agreement and hence had no right to force GM to buy Fiat shares, the two firms ultimately settled the issue when GM agreed to pay Fiat €1.55 billion to "acquire an interest in key strategic assets" and to terminate the put option.

Sources: "GM to pay Fiat 1.55 bln eur to end alliance, acquire Fiat diesel assets," AFX .COM, 2-13-05 (this story reported in dozens of media outlets); "Moody's cuts GM rating, reviews Ford," AFX.COM, 4-5-05 (again, reported in dozens of stories from different sources.)

A bit of folk wisdom says, "Always keep your options open." This implies that choices have value and that having the right to do something is better than being obligated to do it. This chapter shows how to apply that intuition to financial instruments called options. In their most basic forms, **options** allow investors to buy or sell an asset at a fixed price during a given period of time. As the Opening Focus illustrates, having the right (but not the obligation) to buy or sell shares at a fixed price can be extremely valuable, provided the price of the underlying stock moves in the right direction.

Many commentators see options merely as a form of legalized gambling for the rich. We strongly disagree with that perspective. Options exist because they provide real economic benefits that come in many different forms.

First, options do provide incentives for managers to take actions that increase their firms' stock prices, thereby increasing the wealth of shareholders.[1] Abuses may occur when firms award excessive option grants or renegotiate the terms of options agreements after a period of poor stock performance. We see these abuses as a corporate governance problem, not a problem with options per se.

Second, a wide variety of options exist that grant holders the right to buy and sell many different types of assets, not just shares of stock in a single company.[2] Sometimes, trading the option is more cost effective than trading the underlying asset. For example, trading a stock index option, which grants the right to buy or sell a portfolio of stocks such as the S&P 500, enables investors to avoid paying all the transactions costs that would result from trading 500 individual stocks.

Third, firms use options to reduce their exposure to certain types of risk. Firms regularly buy and sell options to shelter their cash flows from movements in exchange rates, interest rates, and commodity prices. In that function, options resemble insurance much more than they resemble gambling.

Fourth, options facilitate the creation of innovative trading strategies. For instance, suppose that an investor is following a pharmaceutical company that has a genetically engineered cancer drug in clinical trials. The company has invested vast resources in this project, so much so that its future depends on the outcome of these trials. If the tests are successful, the company's stock will skyrocket. If not, the firm may go bankrupt. An investor with choices limited to buying or selling the company's stock must decide whether the clinical trials will succeed or fail. As we will see, an investor who can buy and sell options can construct a trading strategy to profit from a large movement in the firm's stock price, regardless of whether that movement is up or down.

The growth in options trading, and trading in other exotic financial instruments such as futures contracts, offers some evidence of our claim that options provide real economic benefits to society. As the Comparative Corporate Finance insert explains, the growth in options markets has been a worldwide phenomenon for over 25 years. In many of the world's largest economies, trading in stock options exceeds the trading volume in the underlying stocks themselves.

One might ask why a chapter on options belongs in a corporate finance textbook. We offer three answers. First, employees of large and small corporations regularly receive options as part of their compensation. It is valuable for both the employees and

---

[1.] For a skeptic's view of this claim, see Lee (2002). Even those who believe that options provide managers with proper incentives disagree on how companies should report the cost of their employee stock option plans in financial statements. Stiglitz (2002) and Malkiel and Baumol (2002) offer contrasting views on this subject.

[2.] Though this chapter focuses primarily on options to buy and sell shares of stocks, investors can trade options that grant the right to buy or sell currencies, commodities, fixed-income securities, and many other types of assets at fixed prices.

the employers to understand the value of this component of pay packages. Second, firms often raise capital by issuing securities with embedded options. For example, firms can issue debt that is convertible into shares of common stock at a lower interest rate than ordinary, nonconvertible debt. To evaluate whether the interest savings is worth giving bondholders the opportunity to convert their bonds into shares requires an understanding of option pricing. Third, many capital budgeting projects have option-like characteristics. As we discussed in Chapters 7–9, the net present value method can generate incorrect accept/reject decisions for projects with downstream options. The best way to develop the ability to recognize which real investment projects have embedded options and which ones do not is to become an expert on ordinary financial options.

We begin this chapter with a brief description of the most common types of stock options and their essential characteristics. Next, we turn our attention to options payoffs, illustrating how options can be used to construct portfolios and unique trading strategies and gaining insight into how prices of different kinds of options are linked together in the market. The rest of the chapter examines qualitative factors that influence option values and introduces a simple yet powerful tool for calculating the prices of many different kinds of options.

SMART IDEAS VIDEO

Myron Scholes, Stanford University, and Chairman of Oak Hill Platinum Partners
"Options markets have grown dramatically over the last 30 years."

See the entire interview at SMARTFinance

18.1 OPTIONS VOCABULARY

An option is one of the three main types of **derivative securities,** a class of financial instruments that derive their values from other assets.[3] An option fits this description because its value depends on the price of the underlying stock that the option holder can buy or sell at a fixed price. The asset from which a derivative security obtains its value is called the **underlying asset.** A **call option** grants the right to purchase a share of stock (or some other asset) at a fixed price on or before a certain date. Clearly, a call option increases in value as the underlying stock price increases. The price at which a call option allows an investor to purchase the underlying share is called the **strike price** or the **exercise price.** Call options grant investors the right to purchase a share for a fairly short time period, usually just a few months.[4] The point at which this right expires is called the option's **expiration date.** An **American call option** gives holders the right to purchase stock at a fixed price on or before its expiration date, whereas a **European call option** grants that right only on the expiration date. If we compare the prices of two options that are identical in every respect except that one is American and one is European, the price of the American option should be at least as high as the European option because of the American option's greater flexibility.

A **put option** grants the right to sell a share of stock at a fixed price on or before a certain date. The right to sell stock at a fixed price becomes more and more valuable as the price of the underlying stock decreases. Thus, we have the most basic distinction between put and call options—put values rise as the underlying stock price goes down, and call prices increase as the underlying stock price goes up. Just like

---

[3.] The other main types of derivatives are futures contracts (and their close cousins, forward contracts) and swaps. A *futures contract* is an agreement between two parties to trade an asset at a fixed price on a specific future date. Unlike an option, a futures contract obligates both parties to fulfill their end of the bargain. A *swap* is an agreement between two parties to exchange streams of cash flows over time. For instance, a currency swap might involve one company's paying British pounds to another in exchange for Japanese yen. We discuss other types of derivatives in more detail in our web chapter on risk management and financial engineering.

[4.] Employee stock options, which typically give workers the right to buy stock at a fixed price for up to 10 years, are an important exception to this rule. Some publicly traded options have long expiration dates too, such as the Long-term Equity AnticiPation Securities (LEAPS) introduced by the American Stock Exchange in 1990.

COMPARATIVE CORPORATE FINANCE

International Derivatives Trading

Since options began trading in the United States in 1973, the growth in options (and other derivatives) trading has been remarkable, and not only in the United States. In 1978, call options on just 10 stocks began trading on the London Traded Options Market, and that same year the European Options Exchange opened in Amsterdam. Today, equity-linked derivatives such as stock options, stock index options, and index futures contracts trade in roughly 30 countries, including most of the largest economies of North America, Europe, and Asia. Even Brazil, which formed its Bolsa de Mercadorias & Futuros exchange in 1985, now ranks among the world's top-10 equity derivative markets in terms of annual trading volume. Other nations with derivative mar-

kets ranking in the top 10 include the United States, the United Kingdom, Germany, and France.

In many of these markets, trading in equity derivatives exceeds the volume of trading in the underlying stocks. The accompanying figure shows the volume of trading in equity options and equity futures contracts, each relative to trading in stocks, in 13 countries. Using the combined trading volume of options and futures contracts, we see that trading in derivatives is greater than trading in the underlying shares in every country except Canada and Sweden.

Source: Jack C. Francis, William W. Toy, and J. Gregg Whittaker (eds.), *Handbook of Equity Derivatives,* rev. ed. (New York: John Wiley & Sons, 2000).

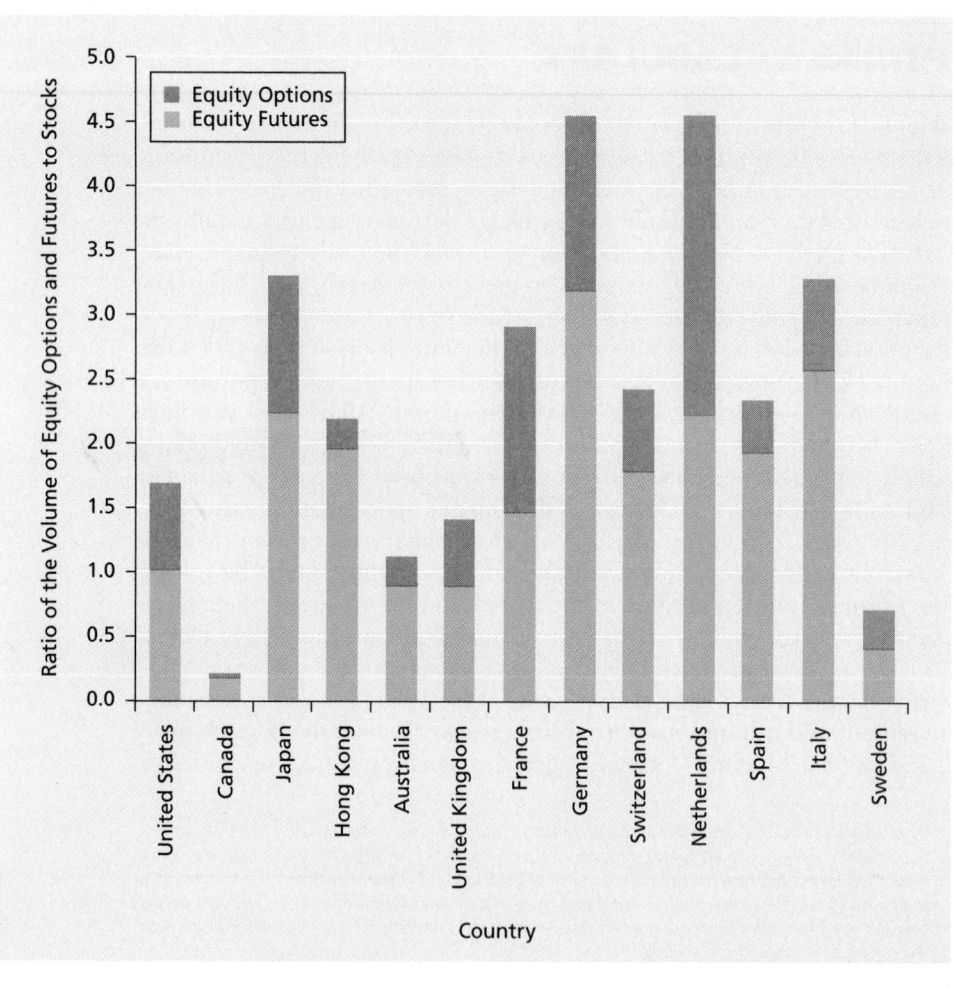

call options, puts specify an exercise price at which investors can sell the underlying stock, and they also specify an expiration date at which the right to sell vanishes. Also, put options come in American and European varieties, just as call options do.

The most distinctive feature of options, both puts and calls, can be deduced from the term *option*. Investors who own calls and puts have the right to buy or sell shares, but they are not obligated to do so. This feature creates an asymmetry in option pay-offs, and that asymmetry is central to understanding how to use options effectively and how to price them, as we will soon see.

An important feature distinguishing calls and puts from other securities, such as stocks and bonds, is that options are not necessarily issued by firms.[5] Rather, an option is a contract between two parties, neither of whom has to have any connection to the company whose stock serves as the underlying asset for the contract. For example, suppose that Tony and Oscar, neither of whom works for General Electric, decide to enter into an options contract. Tony agrees to pay Oscar $5 for the right to purchase one share of General Electric stock for $50 at any time during the next month. As the option buyer, Tony has a **long position** in a call option. He can decide at any point whether he wants to exercise the option or not. If he chooses to **exercise** his option, he will pay Oscar $50, and Oscar will deliver one share of GE stock to Tony. Naturally, Tony will choose to exercise the option only if GE stock is worth more than $50. If GE stock is worth less than $50, Tony will let the option expire worthless and will lose his $5 investment.

On the other side of this transaction, Oscar, as the seller of the option, has a **short position** in a call option.[6] If Tony decides to exercise his option, Oscar's *obligation* is to follow through on his promise to deliver one share of GE for $50. If Oscar does not already own a share of GE stock, he can buy one in the market. Why would Oscar agree to this arrangement? Because he receives the **option premium,** the $5 payment Tony made at the beginning of their agreement. If GE's stock rises above $50, Oscar will lose part or all of the option premium because he must sell Tony an asset for less than it is worth. On the other hand, if GE's stock price does not rise above $50, then Tony will not attempt to buy the asset, and Oscar can keep the $5 option premium.

Option trades do not usually occur in face-to-face transactions between two parties. Instead, options trade either on an exchange, such as the Chicago Board Options Exchange (CBOE) in the United States, or in the **over-the-counter market.** Exchanges list options on a limited number of stocks, with a limited set of exercise prices and expiration dates. By limiting the number and variety of listed options, the exchange expects greater liquidity in the options contracts that are available for trading. Furthermore, an options exchange may serve as a guarantor, fulfilling the terms of an options contract if one party defaults. In contrast, over-the-counter (OTC) options come in a seemingly infinite variety. They are less liquid than exchange-traded options, and traders of OTC options face **counterparty risk,** the risk that the counterparty on a specific trade will default on its obligation.

Most investors who trade options never exercise them. An investor who holds an option and wants to convert that holding into cash can do so in several ways. First, one investor can simply sell the option to another investor, as long as there is some time remaining before expiration. Second, an investor can receive a **cash settlement**

[5.] This is not to say that firms cannot issue options if they want to. Firms do issue options to employees, and they may also sell options as part of their risk-management activities.

[6.] We may also say that Oscar **writes an option** when he sells the option to Tony.

for the option. To understand how cash settlement works, go back to Tony's call option to buy GE stock for $50. Suppose that the price of GE is $60 per share when the option expires. Rather than have Tony pay Oscar $50 in exchange for one share of GE, Oscar might agree to pay Tony $10, the difference between the market price of GE and the option's strike price. Settling in cash eliminates the need for Oscar to buy a share of GE to give to Tony and the need for Tony to sell that share if he wants to convert his profit into cash. Avoiding these unnecessary trades saves transactions costs.

Table 18.1 shows a set of Intel Corp. (ticker symbol, INTC) option-price quotations taken from the Chicago Board Options Exchange website on December 17, 2005.[7] The first column indicates that the options being quoted are on Intel common stock. The closing price of Intel on the day that these option prices were obtained was $26.38. The second column illustrates the range of expiration dates available for Intel options. The prices illustrated in the table are for options expiring either in January, April, or July. The third column shows the range of option strike prices available, from $25.00 to $32.50. The fourth and fifth columns give the most recent trading price for calls and puts.[8] For instance, an investor who wanted to buy a call option on Intel stock, with a strike price of $27.50 and an expiration date in April, would pay $1.10. For an April put with the same strike price, an investor would pay $1.90.

Table 18.1
Prices of Options on Intel Stock

Company	Expiration	Strike	Call	Put	
Intel	January	25.00	1.75	0.25	Out-of-the-money puts
26.38	April	25.00	2.40	0.75	In-the-money calls
26.38	July	25.00	2.95	1.10	
26.38	January	27.50	0.30	1.35	
26.38	April	27.50	1.10	1.90	
26.38	July	27.50	1.60	2.25	
26.38	January	30.00	0.10	3.60	In-the-money puts
26.38	April	30.00	0.40	3.80	Out-of-the-money calls
26.38	July	30.00	0.75	4.00	
26.38	January	32.50	0.05	6.10	
26.38	April	32.50	0.15	6.20	
26.38	July	32.50	0.90	6.30	

Note: Option quotes retrieved from www.cboe.com on December 17, 2005.

Options traders say that a call option is **in the money** if the option's strike price is less than the current stock price. For puts, an option is in the money if the strike price exceeds the stock price. Using these definitions, we can say that the call options in the upper three rows of Table 18.1 and the put options in remaining rows are in the money. Similarly, options traders say that a call option is **out of the money** when the

---

[7] This table shows only a handful of the options contracts available on Intel stock. We have also chosen to exclude from the table the daily trading volume figures that are usually contained in option-price quotations.

[8] Two minor institutional details are worth mentioning here. At the CBOE, options expire on the third Saturday of the month. Second, an options contract grants the right to buy or sell 100 shares of the underlying stock, even though the price quotes in the table are on a "per-share" or "per-option" basis. That is, the $1.10 price for a call option expiring in April with a $27.50 strike means that for $110 an investor can purchase the right to buy 100 shares of Intel at $27.50 per share. All the examples in this chapter are constructed as if an investor can trade one option to buy or sell one share. We make that assumption just to keep the numbers simple, but it does not affect any of the main lessons of the chapter.

strike price exceeds the current stock price, and puts are out of the money when the strike price falls short of the stock price. Finally, an option is **at the money** when the stock price and the strike price are equal.

Examine the April call option with a strike price of $25.00. If an investor who owned this option exercised it, he or she could buy Intel stock for $25.00 and resell it at the market price of $26.38, a difference of $1.38. But the current price of this option is $2.40, about $1 more than the value the investor would obtain by exercising it. In this example, $1.38 is the option's **intrinsic value.**[9] You can think of intrinsic value as measuring the profit an investor makes from exercising the option (ignoring transactions costs as well as the option premium). If an option is out of the money, its intrinsic value is zero. The difference between an option's intrinsic value and its market price, $1.02 for the April call, is the option's **time value.** At the expiration date, the time value equals zero.

Suppose that you purchase the April call with a $25 strike price for $2.40. Suppose also that on the option's expiration date, the price of Intel stock has increased from its current level, $26.38, to $30. That's an increase of 13.7 percent. What would the option be worth at that time? Because the option holder could buy Intel stock at $25 and then immediately resell it for $30, the option should be worth about $5. If the option sells for $5, that's an increase of 108 percent from the $2.40 purchase price! Similarly, if Intel's stock price is just $24.99 when the option expires, then the option will be worthless. If you purchased the call for $2.40, your return on that investment would be -100 percent, even though Intel's stock fell just $1.39, or -5.3 percent, from the date of your purchase.

This example illustrates what may be the most important fact to know about options: *When the price of a stock moves, the dollar change in the stock is generally more than the dollar change in the option price, but the percentage change in the option price is much greater than the percentage change in the stock price.* We have heard students argue that buying a call option is less risky than buying the underlying share because the maximum dollar loss that an investor can experience is much less on the option. That's true only if we compare the $26.38 investment required to buy one share of Intel to the $2.40 required to buy one April Intel call. It is accurate to say that the call investor can lose at most $2.40 while an investor in Intel stock might lose $26.38. But there are two problems with this comparison. First, the likelihood that Intel will go bankrupt and its stock will fall to $0 between December and April is negligible. The likelihood that Intel's stock might dip below $25, resulting in a $0 value for the call option, is much greater. Second, it is better to compare an equal dollar investment in Intel stock and Intel calls rather than compare one stock to one call. An investment of $26.38 would purchase almost 11 Intel call options. Which position do you think is riskier—one share of stock or 11 call options?

Concept Review Questions

1. Explain the difference between the stock price, the *exercise price,* and the *option premium.* Which of these are market prices determined by the forces of supply and demand?

2. Explain the difference between a *long position* and a *short position.* With respect to call options, what is the maximum gain and loss possible for an investor who holds the long position? What is the maximum gain and loss for the investor on the short side of the transaction?

[9.] For put options, the intrinsic value equals either $X - S$ or $0, whichever is greater. For example, the intrinsic value of each of the three put options with a strike price of $32.50 is $6.12 ($32.50 − $26.38).

3. Suppose that an investor holds a call option on Nestlé stock. If the investor decides to exercise the option, what will happen to the total shares of common stock outstanding for Nestle?

4. Which of the following would increase the value of a put option: an increase in the stock price, an increase in the strike price, or a lengthening of the expiration period?

18.2 OPTION PAYOFF DIAGRAMS

So far, our discussion of options has been mostly descriptive. Now we turn to the problem of determining an option's market price. Valuing an option is an extraordinarily difficult problem, so difficult in fact that the economists who solved the problem won a Nobel Prize for their efforts. In earlier chapters where we studied the pricing of bonds and stocks, we began by describing their cash flows. We will do the same here, focusing initially on the relatively simple problem of outlining cash flows of options on the expiration date. Eventually, that will help us understand the intuition behind complex option-pricing models.

CALL OPTION PAYOFFS

We define an option's **payoff** as the price an investor would be willing to pay for the option the instant before it expires.[10] An option's payoff is distinct from its price, or premium, because the payoff refers only to the price of the option at a particular instant in time, the expiration date. **Payoff diagrams** are graphs that illustrate an option's payoff as a function of the underlying stock price. They are extremely useful tools for understanding how options behave and how they can be combined to form portfolios with fascinating properties.

Suppose that an investor purchases a call option with a strike price of $75 and an expiration date three months in the future. To acquire this option, the investor pays a premium of $8. When the option expires, what will it be worth? If the underlying stock price is less than $75 on the expiration date, the option will be worthless. No investor would pay anything for the right to buy this stock for $75 when the investor could easily buy it for less in the market. What if the stock price equals $76 on the expiration date? In that case, owning the right to buy the stock at $75 is worth $1, the difference between the stock's market price and the option's exercise price. Ignoring transactions costs, an investor who owns the option can buy the stock for $75 and immediately sell it in the market for $76, earning a $1 payoff. In general, the payoff of this option will equal the greater of (1) $0 if the stock price is less than $75 at expiration or (2) the difference between the stock price and $75 if the stock price is more than $75 at expiration. The blue line in Panel A of Figure 18.1 shows a payoff diagram for the call option buyer, or the long position. This picture is a classic in finance known as the **hockey-stick diagram**. It shows that the option will at worst be worth $0 and that at best the option's value is unlimited. The black line in the figure represents the investor's **net payoff**. The net-payoff line appears $8 lower than the solid line, reflecting the $8 premium the investor paid to acquire the option. On

---

[10.] Alternatively, we could define the payoff as the value an investor would receive, ignoring transactions costs, if he or she exercised the option when it expired. If it did not make sense to exercise the option when it expired, the payoff would be zero.

Figure 18.1
Payoff of Call Option
at Expiration

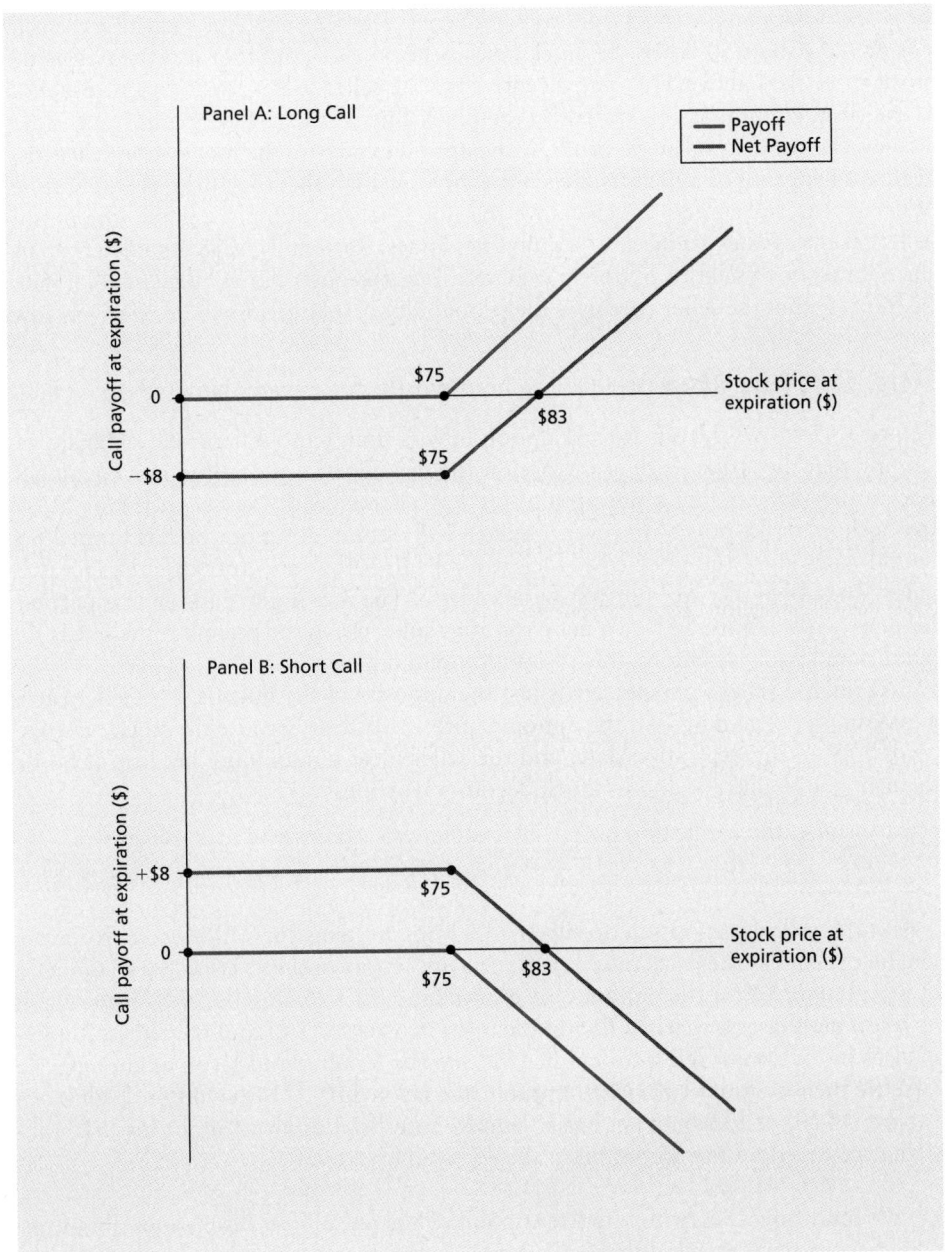

long = buy
short = sell

a net basis, the holder of the call option makes a profit when the price of the stock exceeds $83.[11]

Panel B of Figure 18.1 shows the payoffs from the seller's perspective, or the short position. Options are a zero-sum game, meaning that profits on the long position

---

[11.] Notice that when the stock price is above $75 but below $83, it still makes sense for the investor to exercise the option, or to sell it, because it reduces the investor's losses. For example, if the stock price at expiration equals $80, the option payoff is $5, reducing the net loss to −$3. The careful reader will notice that we seem to be making a major error by comparing the $8 premium paid up front to the payoff received three months later. At this point, ignoring the time value of money in the graphs is relatively harmless, but rest assured that we will take that into account later when we determine the price of an option.

represent losses on the short side, and vice versa. The blue line illustrates that the seller's payoff equals $0 when the stock price is below $75 and that it decreases as the stock price rises above $75. The incentive for the seller to engage in this transaction is the $8 premium, as illustrated by the black line. If the option expires out of the money, the seller earns an $8 profit. If the option expires in the money, the seller may realize a net profit or a net loss, depending on how high the stock price is at that time. Whereas the call option buyer enjoys the potential for unlimited gains, the option seller faces exposure to the risk of unlimited losses. Rationally, if $8 is sufficient to induce someone to sell this option and thereby face the potential of huge losses, it must be the case that the seller perceives the probability of a large loss to be relatively low.

PUT OPTION PAYOFFS

Figure 18.2 shows payoffs for put option buyers (long) and sellers (short), again assuming that the strike price of the option is $75 and the option premium equals $8. For an investor holding a put option, the payoff rises as the stock price falls below the option's strike price. However, unlike a call option, a put option has limited potential gains since the price of a stock cannot fall below zero (because the law provides limited liability for a firm's shareholders). The maximum gain on this particular put equals $75 (or $67 on a net basis after subtracting the premium), whereas the maximum loss is, as before, the $8 option premium.

Again, the seller's perspective is just the opposite of the buyer's. The seller earns a maximum net gain of $8 if the option expires worthless because the stock price exceeds $75 on the expiration date, and the seller faces a maximum net loss of $67 if the firm goes bankrupt and its stock becomes worthless.

APPLYING THE MODEL 18.1

Jennifer sells a put option on Electro-Lighting Systems Inc. (ELS) stock to Jason. The option's strike price is $65, and it expires in one month. Jason pays Jennifer a premium of $5 for the option. One month later, ELS stock sells for $45 per share. Jason purchases a share of ELS in the open market for $45 and immediately exercises his option to sell it to Jennifer for $65 (or Jennifer and Jason might agree to settle their contract by having Jennifer pay Jason $20). The payoff on Jason's option is $20, or $15 on a net basis. Jennifer loses $20 on the deal, or just $15 taking into account the $5 premium she received up front.

We must now clarify an important point. Thus far, all our discussions about options payoffs have assumed that each option buyer or seller had what traders refer to as a **naked option position**. A naked call option, for example, occurs when an investor buys or sells an option on a stock without already owning the underlying stock.

Similarly, when a trader buys or sells a put option without owning the underlying stock, the trader creates a naked put option. Buying or selling naked options is an act of pure speculation. Investors who buy naked calls believe that the stock price will rise. Investors who sell naked calls believe the opposite. Similarly, buyers of naked puts expect the stock price to fall, and sellers take the opposite view.

But many options trades do not involve this kind of speculation. Investors who own a particular stock may purchase a put option on that stock, not because they expect the stock price to decline, but because they want protection in the event that it does. Executives who own shares of their companies' stock may sell call options, not on speculation that the price will not rise, but because they are willing to give up po-

Figure 18.2
Payoff of a Put Option
at Expiration

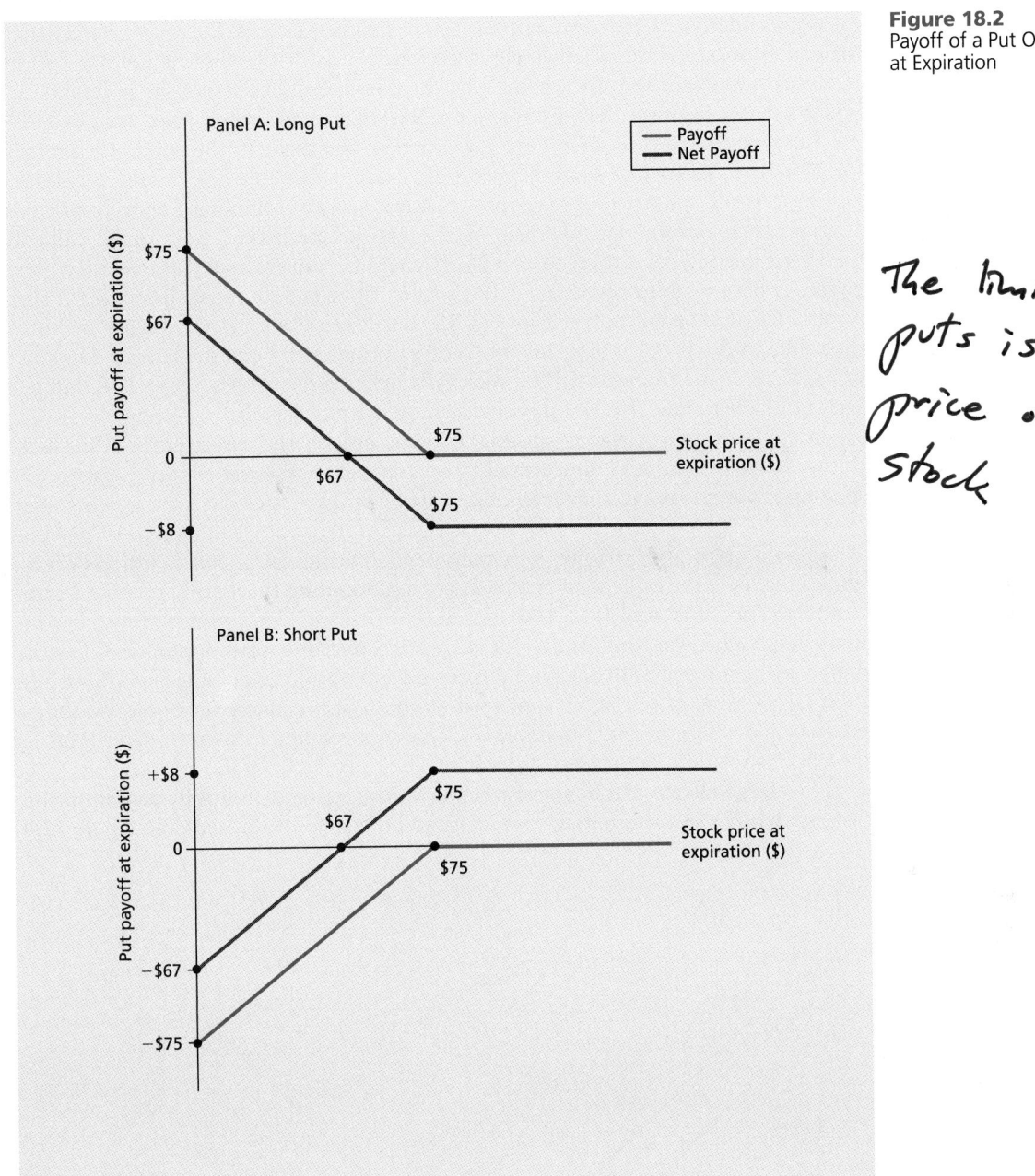

The limit on puts is the price of the stock

tential profits on their shares in exchange for current income. To understand this proposition, we need to examine payoff diagrams for portfolios of options and other securities.

PAYOFFS FOR PORTFOLIOS OF OPTIONS AND OTHER SECURITIES

Experienced options traders know that by combining different types of options, they can construct a wide range of portfolios with unusual payoff structures. Think about what happens if an investor simultaneously buys a call option and a put option on the same underlying stock and with the same exercise price. We have seen before that the call option pays off handsomely if the stock price rises, whereas the put option is most profitable if the stock price falls. By combining both into one portfolio, an investor has a position that can make money whether the stock price rises or falls.

Suppose that Cybil cannot decide whether she expects the stock of Internet Phones Corp. (IPC) to rise or fall from its current value of $30. Cybil decides to purchase a call option and a put option on IPC stock, both having a strike price of $30 and an expiration date of April 20. She pays premiums of $4.50 for the call and $3.50 for the put, for a total cost of $8. Figure 18.3 illustrates Cybil's position. The payoff of her portfolio equals $0 if IPC's stock price is $30 on April 20; and if that occurs, Cybil experiences a net loss of $8. But if the stock price is higher or lower than $30 on April 20, at least one of Cybil's options will be in the money. On a net basis, Cybil makes a profit if IPC stock falls below $22 or rises above $38, but she does not have to take a view on which outcome is more likely.

In this example, Cybil is speculating, but not on the direction of IPC stock. Rather, Cybil's gamble is on the *volatility* of IPC shares. If the shares move a great deal, either up or down, she makes a net profit. If the shares have not moved much by April 20, she experiences a net loss. Options traders refer to this type of position as a **long straddle**, a portfolio consisting of long positions in calls and puts on the same stock with the same strike price and expiration date. Naturally, creating a **short straddle** is possible, too. If Cybil believed that IPC stock would not move far from its current value, she could simultaneously sell a put and a call option on IPC stock with a strike price of $30. She would receive $8 in option premiums from this trade; if IPC stock were priced at $30 on April 20, both of the options she sold would expire worthless. On the other hand, if IPC stock moved up or down from $30, one of the options would be exercised, reducing Cybil's profits from the options sale.

Now let's look at what happens when investors form portfolios by combining options with other securities, such as stocks and bonds. To begin, examine Figure 18.4,

Figure 18.3
Payoff of a Long Straddle
By purchasing a call and a put having the same strike price, an investor can profit from a significant change in the underlying stock price in any direction.

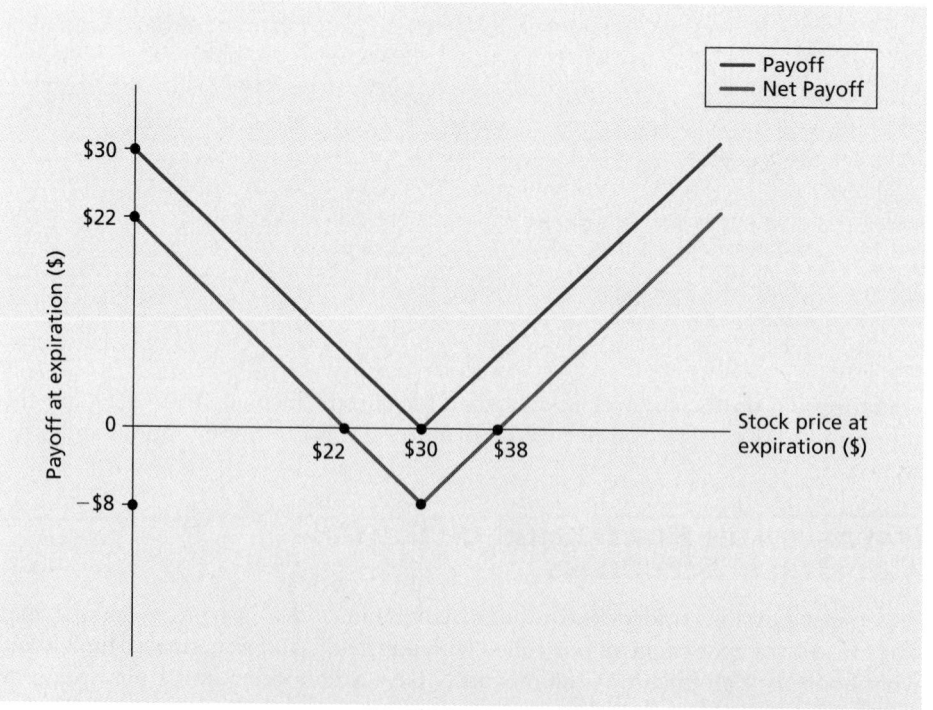

Figure 18.4
Payoff Diagrams for
Stocks and Bonds

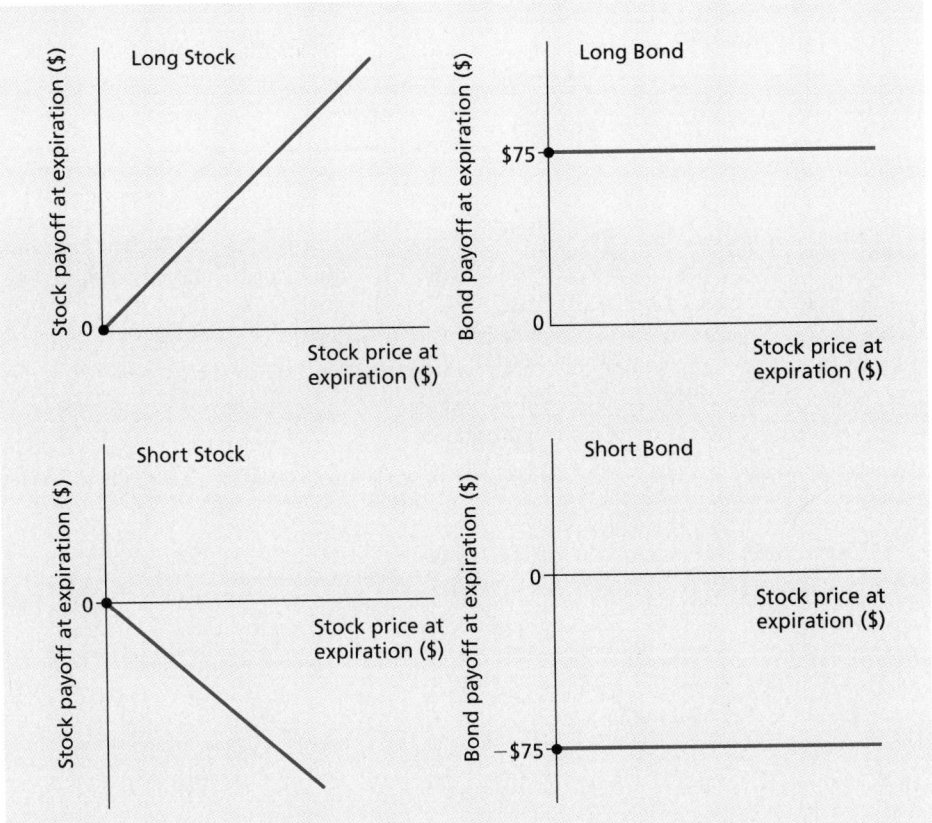

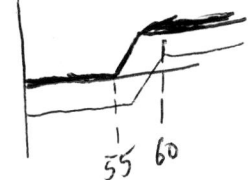

which displays payoff diagrams for a long position in common stocks and bonds.[12] Remember, a payoff diagram shows the total value of a security (in this case, one share of common stock or one bond) on a specific future date on the y-axis, and the value of a share of stock on that same date on the x-axis. In Figure 18.4, the payoff diagram from holding a share of stock is simply a 45-degree line emanating from the origin because both axes of the graph are plotting the same thing—the value of the stock on a future date.[13]

The payoff diagram for the bond requires a little more explanation. The type of bond we have in mind in this example is very special. It is a risk-free, zero-coupon bond with a face value of $75. The bond matures at precisely the same time as the put and call options expire. The payoff for an investor who purchases this bond is simply $75, no matter what the price of the stock underlying the put and call options turns out to be. Thus, the diagram shows a horizontal line at $75 for the long bond's payoff.[14] Again the payoff from shorting the bond is the opposite of the long-bond payoff diagram.

---

[12] In Figure 18.4, we do not plot the net payoff, meaning that the diagram ignores the initial cost of buying stocks or bonds, or the revenue obtained from shorting them.

[13] Figure 18.4 also shows the payoff diagram for a short position in stock, and, as always, it is just the opposite of the long payoff diagram. When investors *short-sell* a stock, they borrow the share from another investor, promising to return the share at a future date. Short-selling therefore creates a liability. The magnitude of that liability is just the price of the stock that the short-seller must return on a future date.

[14] Is it really possible to buy a risk-free bond with a face value of $75? Perhaps not, but an investor could buy 75 Treasury bills, each with a face value of $1,000, resulting in a risk-free bond portfolio with a face value of $75,000. The assumption that investors can buy risk-free bonds with any face value is just a simplification to keep the numbers in our examples manageable.

Figure 18.5
Payoff Diagram for
Covered Call Strategy

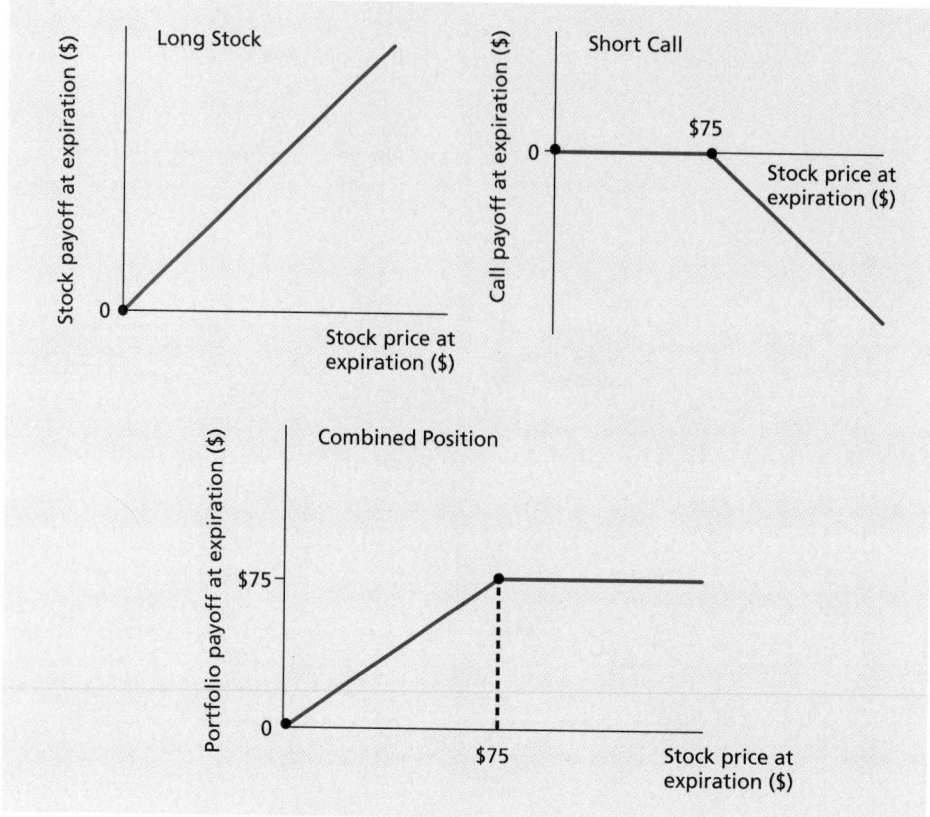

Figure 18.5 illustrates **writing covered calls,** a common trading strategy that mixes stock and call options. In this strategy, an investor who owns a share of stock sells a call option on that stock. By selling the call, the investor receives the option premium immediately. However, the trade-off is that if the stock price rises, the holder of the call option will exercise the right to purchase it at the strike price, and the investor will lose the opportunity to benefit from the appreciation in the stock. For example, suppose that Michael owns a share of IBM stock. Michael sells a call option on his share to Kathryn for $6. The option has a strike price of $75. As long as the stock price does not rise above $75, Michael will keep the $6 option premium and will retain ownership of his IBM share. If the price rises above $75, however, Kathryn will call the share away from Michael. He will get $75 in cash from Kathryn, but he will not benefit from appreciation beyond that point.

Consider a portfolio consisting of one share of stock and one put option on that share with a strike price of $75. If, on the option's expiration date, the stock price equals $75, the put option will be worthless. Therefore, the portfolio's total value will be $75. Notice that the total value of this portfolio cannot drop below $75, even if the stock price does. Imagine that the stock price falls to $50. At that point, the put option's payoff is $25, leaving the combined portfolio value at $75. Simply stated, the put option provides a kind of portfolio insurance, for it guarantees that the share of stock can be sold for at least that amount. However, if the price of the stock rises, the portfolio value will rise right along with it. Though the put option will be worthless, any increase in the stock price beyond $75 increases the portfolio's value as well, as shown in Figure 18.6. This strategy is known as a **protective put.**

Next, evaluate the payoffs of a portfolio consisting of one risk-free, zero-coupon bond with a face value of $75 and one call option with an exercise price of $75. As

Figure 18.6
Payoff of a Put Option
and a Share of Stock—
a Protective Put

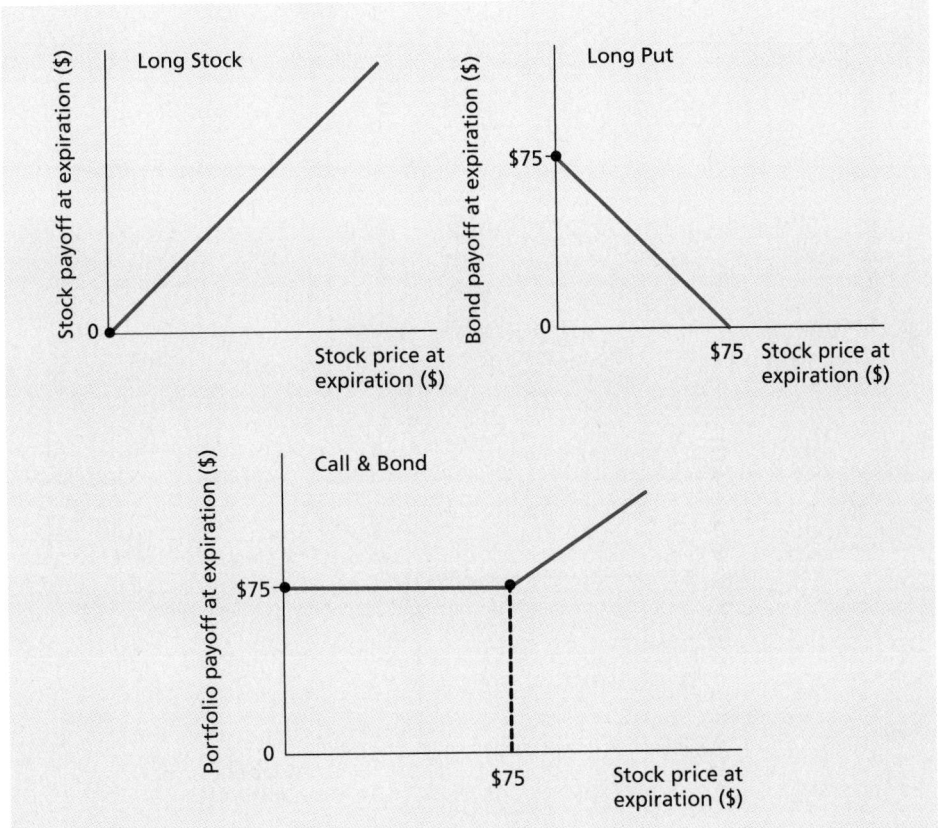

Figure 18.7 shows, the bond guarantees that an investor holding this portfolio will have a payoff of at least $75. The payoff can be more if the stock price increases above $75, causing the call value to increase.

A careful look at Figures 18.6 and 18.7 reveals a surprising fact. The payoffs of the portfolio containing one share of stock and one put option are exactly the same as the payoffs of the portfolio containing one bond and one call option. Both portfolios offer a minimum return of $75, with considerable upside potential should the underlying stock price increase. If both of these portfolios offer investors the same cash flows when the options expire, then both portfolios must have the same value today.[15] This **put-call parity** is one of the most fundamental results in option-pricing theory. Put-call parity holds only under a rather restrictive set of assumptions, but it nevertheless has many important practical applications.

PUT-CALL PARITY

Using Put-Call Parity to Find Arbitrage Opportunities. Figures 18.6 and 18.7 illustrate that a portfolio of a stock and a put option offers exactly the same future cash flows as a portfolio of a bond and a call option. To be absolutely certain that the cash flows of these portfolios will be identical at the options' expiration date, the following conditions must be met:

1. The call and put options must be on the same underlying stock.
2. The call and put options must have the same exercise price.

[15.] In other words, the prices of puts and calls on the same underlying stock are not entirely independent of one another.

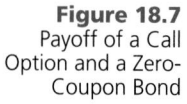

Figure 18.7
Payoff of a Call
Option and a Zero-
Coupon Bond

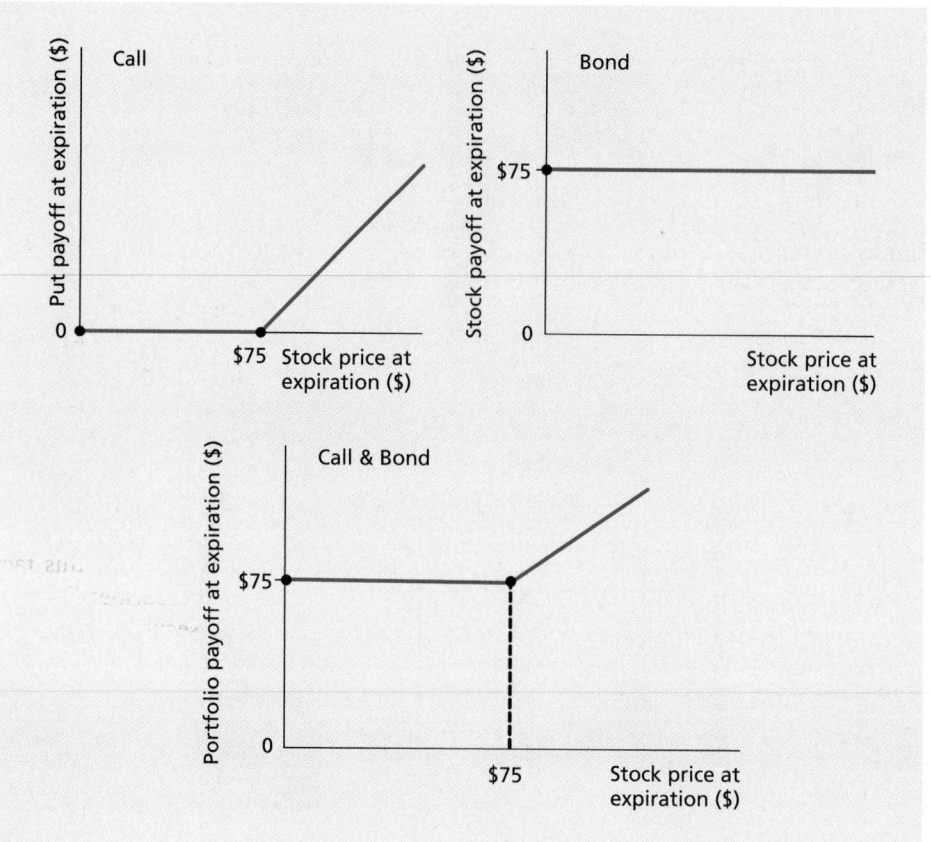

3. The call and put options must share the same expiration date.
4. The underlying stock must not pay a dividend during the life of the options.
5. The call and put options must be European options.
6. The bond must be a risk-free, zero-coupon bond with a face value equal to the strike price of the options and with a maturity date identical to the options' expiration date.

The only points on this list not already mentioned are 4 and 5. For put-call parity to hold, both the call and put options must be European options. Recall that American options can be exercised at any time up to and including the expiration date. In the two portfolios considered in Figures 18.6 and 18.7, if either the call or the put is exercised early, there will be a discrepancy on the expiration date between the portfolios' cash flows. If the cash flows do not match exactly, then put-call parity will not hold. Similarly, if the underlying stock pays a dividend, the portfolio consisting of the stock plus the put option will receive the dividend, but the portfolio containing the call option and the bond will not. Therefore, the cash flows of the two portfolios will not match exactly, and parity will not hold.

If all these conditions are met, we can make the following strong claim. The price of one share of stock plus the price of one put option on that stock with a strike price of X must equal the sum of the prices of a call option on the stock (also having a strike price of X) and a risk-free bond with a face value of X. The following is a simple algebraic expression of this idea:

$$S + P = B + C$$
$$S + P = PV(X) + C$$

(Eq. 18.1)

In these equations, S stands for the current stock price; P and C represent the current premiums on the put and call options, respectively; and B equals the current price of the risk-free, zero-coupon bond. In the second equation, we substitute $PV(X)$ for B simply to indicate that if the bond's face value is $\$X$, then the price of that bond will be the present value of $\$X$, discounted at the risk-free rate.

If you blinked, you may have missed the significant intellectual leap we just took. Up to now, all our discussions about options have focused on their payoffs. Remember, we defined an option's payoff as the price someone would pay for it just before it expired. Determining the market value of an option just before it expires is rather trivial, but in Equation 18.1 we are talking about option prices at *any moment in time*, not just on the expiration date. Because the portfolios on the right- and left-hand sides of Equation 18.1 offer investors identical future cash flows, they must have identical market values on the expiration date, one day before expiration, one week before expiration, and at any other moment in time. One implication of this fact is that investors who know the market prices of any three of the securities listed in Equation 18.1 can determine what the market price of the fourth security must be to prevent arbitrage opportunities.

APPLYING THE MODEL 18.2

Mototronics Inc. stock currently sells for $28 per share. Put and call options on Mototronics shares are available with a strike price of $30 and an expiration date of one year. The price of the Mototronics call option is $6, and the risk-free rate of interest is 5 percent. What is the appropriate price for the Mototronics put option? Using Equation 18.1 and plugging in the values we know, we can derive a price for the put option:

$$S + P = PV(X) + C$$

$$\$28 + P = \frac{\$30}{1.05^1} + \$6$$

$$P = \$6.57$$

How can we be sure that $6.57 is the right price for the put option? Because at any other price, investors would have an arbitrage opportunity, a chance to earn unlimited profits without taking any risk. To see how this would work, suppose that the actual market price of the Mototronics put option is $7 rather than $6.57. At that price, the put option is overvalued, so smart investors will sell it. But doing nothing more than selling the put option is not arbitrage. Arbitrage means simultaneously buying and selling identical assets at different prices to earn a risk-free profit. Therefore, if the first step in the arbitrage is to sell the put for $7, then traders must also buy an identical asset at a lower price. What kind of asset is identical to a put option? Rearranging the put-call parity equation just a little holds the answer:

$$S + P = PV(X) + C$$
$$P = PV(X) + C - S$$

By now, we are aware that put-call parity says that a portfolio containing a share of stock and a put is identical to one containing a bond and a call option. The second equation just shown makes a similar claim. It says that a put option offers cash flows that are identical to those produced by a portfolio containing a bond, a call option, and a short position in the underlying stock.[16] In options lingo, we say that traders can create a **synthetic put option** by purchasing a bond and a call option while simultaneously short-selling the stock.

To exploit the arbitrage opportunity, investors will sell the actual put option for $7. Next, to offset the risk of the first trade, arbitrageurs will purchase a bond and a call option and will short-sell the stock. The immediate consequences of these trades are outlined as follows:

Cash Inflows		**Cash Outflows**	
Sell put	+$7	Buy bond	$\dfrac{-\$30}{1.05^1} = -\$28.57$
Sell stock	+$28	Buy call	−$6

Net cash flow = $28 + $7 − $28.57 − $6 = +$0.43

Traders following this strategy pocket $0.43 each time they execute this sequence of trades. Notice that this value equals the difference between the put option's theoretically correct price, $6.57, and its actual price of $7. What remains to be shown is that the profits from this strategy are truly risk-free. Figure 18.8 and Table 18.2 show just that. First, look at the figure. The upper part of the figure shows the payoff from taking a short position in the put option. The lower part shows that by combining a long bond, a long call, and a short stock, an investor creates a portfolio with a payoff identical to a that of a long put option. The short put at the top of the figure and the synthetic long put at the bottom cancel each other out, resulting in a risk-free portfolio.

In the first column of Table 18.2, we list a range of prices that Mototronics stock might reach in one year, when these options are expiring. In the next four columns, we list the values of each of the individual positions that arbitrageurs create by following our strategy, given the stock price in the first column. Take a look at the first row of the table, where we consider what happens if the value of Mototronics stock in one year is $10. The first trade in our arbitrage strategy was to sell a put option with a $30 exercise price. If Mototronics stock is worth $10, then the investor to whom the put option was sold will exercise it, resulting in a loss to the arbitrageur of $20. The second part of the arbitrage strategy was buying a risk-free bond with a face value of $30. Clearly, the value of this holding will be $30 in one year. The third part of the trade was buying a call option with an exercise price of $30. With Mototronics stock at $10, this call will be worthless. The final part of the trade was to short-sell Mototronics stock. At the end of the year, an arbitrageur must return that share to its owner, and doing so will cost the trader $10, the current market price of the stock. Adding all this together, we have the following:

Put option	−$20
Bond	+$30
Call option	$ 0
Short stock	−$10
Total value	$ 0

[16.] In put-call parity math, a negative sign means "sell" rather than "buy." Therefore, the terms on the right side of the equation, $PV(X) + C − S$, mean "buy a bond, buy a call, and sell (or sell short) the stock."

Figure 18.8
Put-Call Parity Arbitrage

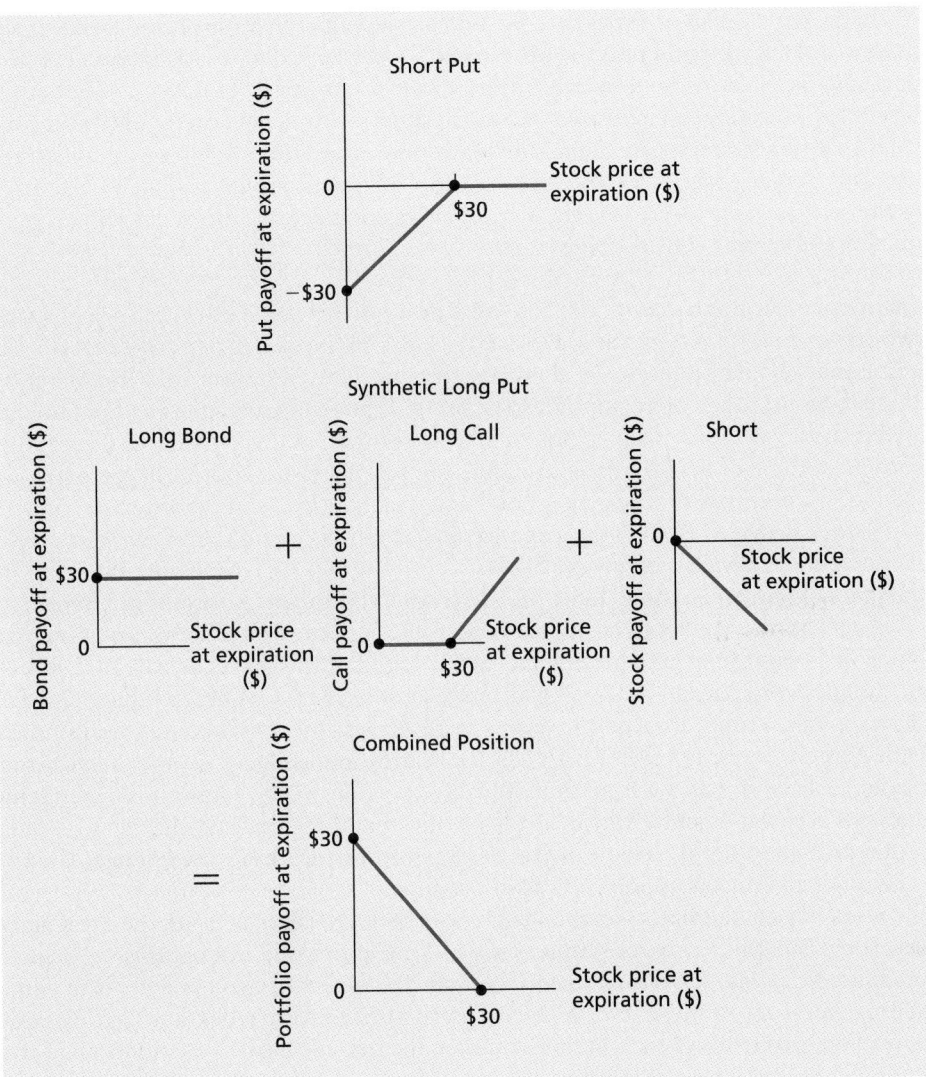

Table 18.2
Using Arbitrage to Exploit a Mispriced Put

	Value of Synthetic Put (all values in $)				
If Mototronics Stock Price Is ($)	Value of (short) Actual Put Is	Value of Long Bond Is	Value of Long Call Is	Value of Short Stock Is	Total Portfolio Value ($)
10	−20	30	0	−10	−20 + 30 + 0 − 10 = 0
15	−15	30	0	−15	−15 + 30 + 0 − 15 = 0
20	−10	30	0	−20	−10 + 30 + 0 − 20 = 0
25	−5	30	0	−25	−5 + 30 + 0 − 25 = 0
30	0	30	0	−30	0 + 30 + 0 − 30 = 0
35	0	30	5	−35	0 + 30 + 5 − 35 = 0
40	0	30	10	−40	0 + 30 + 10 − 40 = 0

No matter what value Mototronics stock takes, the value of the actual put that the arbitrageur sold is precisely offset by the value of the synthetic put that the arbitrageur purchased. The arbitrage portfolio consists of short positions in the put option and the stock, and long positions in the bond and the call. The put and call options have an exercise price of $30, and $30 is the bond's face value.

In the last column of Table 18.2, we add up the values of these positions and show that no matter what the price of Mototronics stock turns out to be in one year, the portfolio of securities held by arbitrageurs will be worthless. Holding a portfolio of worthless securities may not seem like much of an investment strategy, until you consider that this strategy generated a net cash inflow up front. Arbitrageurs could repeat this strategy over and over again, reaping unlimited profits as long as the prices of the securities they were trading did not change. Of course, the prices will change, quickly eliminating the arbitrage profit.

Corporate Finance Applications of Put-Call Parity. Put-call parity gives us two types of useful information. First, it tells us how the prices of puts, calls, stocks, and bonds should be interrelated. When the prices of these securities become misaligned, an arbitrage opportunity exists. Second, put-call parity tells us how to create synthetic positions. That is, put-call parity shows that it is possible to use combinations of three of the securities to mimic the payoffs of the fourth. In the previous section, we observed that buying a bond and a call option while shorting the underlying stock provided exactly the same payoffs as buying a put option. We can derive the synthetic equivalent of any particular security simply by rearranging the terms in the put-call parity equation. Table 18.3 lists several synthetic positions of interest.

Applications of put-call parity are numerous. Suppose Serex Corporation owns a block of shares of the firm Meggit Inc. Serex acquired the shares as part of a strategic alliance with Meggit that will end in six months. Serex wants to liquidate these shares to raise money for a new investment. However, due to its ongoing relationship with Meggit, Serex is reluctant to sell the shares immediately, even though Serex managers believe that the firm's investment opportunity may vanish if the company does not act on it quickly. Managers also worry that if the price of Meggit stock falls in the next six months, selling the stock at that time may not raise enough capital, even if the investment opportunity is still available.

Serex has an alternative to an outright sale of its Meggit shares on the open market. Serex can sell the shares synthetically as long as put and call options on Meggit stock are available. A synthetic sale accomplishes the firm's two main goals of eliminating exposure to the risk of a decline in the price of the stock and getting cash immediately to reinvest elsewhere. Rearrange the put-call parity equation to find the synthetic equivalent of selling stock:

$$S + P = PV(X) + C$$
$$-S = P - PV(X) - C$$

Rather than selling the stock $(-S)$, Serex can purchase put options (P), take out a loan $(-PV(X))$, and sell call options $(-C)$. By purchasing put options on Meggit

Table 18.3
Using Put-Call Parity to Create Synthetic Positions

$S + P = PV(X) + C$	
Actual Position	**Equivalent Synthetic Position**
Long stock (S)	Long bond, long call, short put: $PV(X) + C - P$
Short stock $(-S)$	Short bond, short call, long put: $P - PV(X) - C$
Long call (C)	Long stock, long put, short bond: $S + P - PV(X)$
Long bond $PV(X)$	Long stock, long put, short call: $S + P - C$
Short Put $(-P)$	Long stock, short bond, short call: $S - PV(X) - C$

shares, Serex obtains protection against the risk of a decline in the stock price (remember the protective put). By borrowing money, Serex obtains cash today to reinvest elsewhere. By selling call options, Serex earns premium income that partially offsets the cost of the puts, but the company also gives up any stock price appreciation (remember the covered call strategy).

Let's put some numbers in this example. Suppose the current market price of Meggit stock is $80. At-the-money call and put options sell for $10.33 and $8, respectively. The risk-free rate of interest is 6 percent per year, or just 3 percent per six months. By selling its shares synthetically, Serex will generate an immediate cash inflow of $80 per share:

$$\text{Buy put } -\$8 \qquad \text{Borrow}PV(\$80) = \frac{\$80}{1.30^1} = \$77.67 \qquad \text{Sell call } +\$10.33$$

Of course this is precisely the same cash inflow Serex would receive from selling one Meggit share. Six months later, if Meggit's stock price has risen above $80, the Meggit shares that Serex owns will be called away at a price of $80. If the stock price has fallen below $80, the put option will enable Serex to sell the shares for $80. Either way, Serex will part with its shares in return for $80 in cash, with which Serex will repay its loan.

This strategy may be attractive whenever a company wants to divest its holdings of another firm. The motivation to sell synthetically may come from the tax code (i.e., the tax liability of a synthetic sell might be lower than the liability of selling the shares immediately) or from some other barrier, such as illiquidity of the stock or a minimum required holding period. Individual and institutional investors can also use this strategy to sell investments synthetically.

SMART ETHICS VIDEO

John Eck, President of Broadcast and Network Operations, NBC

"That allowed us to create some doubt around the transaction and allowed us not to have to book the gain up front but to book it as the cash came in."

See the entire interview at **SMARTFinance**

Concept Review Questions

5. What would happen if an investor combined the *protective put* and *covered call* strategies by simultaneously buying a put option with a strike price of $50 and selling a call option with a strike price of $50? You can assume that the investor already owns the underlying stock.

6. Is selling a call the same as buying a put? Explain why or why not.

7. A major corporation is involved in high-profile antitrust litigation with the government. The firm's stock price is somewhat depressed due to the uncertainty of this case. If the company wins, investors expect its stock price to shoot up. If it loses, the stock price will decline even more than it already has. If investors expect a resolution to the case in the near future, what effect do you think it will have on put and call options on the company's stock? (*Hint:* Think about the *long-straddle* investment strategy.)

8. Take another look at the six conditions that must be met for put-call parity to hold. Can you explain why each one of them is necessary?

18.3 QUALITATIVE ANALYSIS OF OPTION PRICING

FACTORS THAT INFLUENCE OPTION VALUES

Before getting into the rather complex quantitative aspects of pricing options, let's see if we can develop some intuition that will help us understand the factors that influence option prices. We begin by taking a closer look at some of the December 17,

2005, price quotations for Intel stock options in Table 18.1. Begin by focusing only on the prices of call and put options that have an exercise price of $27.50. Here are the figures from the table:

Intel	Expiration	Strike	Call	Put
$26.38	January	$27.50	$0.30	$1.35
$26.38	April	$27.50	$1.10	$1.90
$26.38	July	$27.50	$1.60	$2.25

You should notice a striking pattern here. The prices of both calls and puts rise the longer the time before expiration. To understand why, think about the call option that expires in January. Currently, this option is out of the money because it grants the right to purchase Intel stock for $27.50, but investors can buy Intel in the open market at $26.38. Buying the January call option requires an investment of just $0.30. The option is inexpensive because there is relatively little chance that in the month remaining before the option expires, Intel's stock price will increase enough to make exercising the option worthwhile. No investor would exercise this option until Intel stock reached at least $27.51, representing an increase of more than 4 percent from its current price. Investors are not willing to pay more than $0.30 for this option because they doubt that Intel stock will rise that much in one month.

However, the price of the July call option with a strike price of $27.50 is more than five times greater than the price of the January call. The July option expires in about seven months, so investors must think that the odds of a 4 percent increase (or more) in Intel stock over that time period are much higher than the odds of seeing the same move by the third Saturday of January. The same pattern holds for puts. The July put option sells for $0.90 more than the January put option because investors recognize that the chance of a significant drop in Intel stock by January is much lower than the chance of a large decrease over the next seven months. We can generalize all this as follows: *Holding other factors constant, call and put option prices increase as the time to expiration increases.*[17]

Next, let's examine the prices of all the Intel calls and puts that expire in April. Here are the figures from Table 18.1:

Intel	Expiration	Strike	Call	Put
$26.38	April	$25.00	$2.40	$0.75
$26.38	April	$27.50	$1.10	$1.90
$26.38	April	$30.00	$0.40	$3.80
$26.38	April	$32.50	$0.15	$6.20

Once again, a clear pattern emerges. The prices of call options fall as the strike price increases, and the prices of put options rise as the strike price increases. This relationship is quite intuitive. A call option grants the right to buy stock at a fixed price. That right is more valuable the cheaper the price at which the option holder can buy the

---

[17.] There are a few exceptions to this rule. Flip back the calendar to November 2001, and imagine that you own a European put option on Enron stock. Enron's stock trades for pennies a share. If the strike price of your put option is $20, then you can make a profit of almost $20 by exercising your option, if you can exercise it immediately. But what if the option's expiration date is several months away? The potential for further declines in Enron stock, given that it already sells for just a few cents, is negligible, but there is some chance that Enron stock might recover. In this case, you would rather have the right to exercise your option right away, so you would pay more for a European option that expires immediately than you would pay for one that expires a few months in the future.

stock.[18] Conversely, put options grant the right to sell shares at a fixed price. That right is more valuable the higher the price at which investors can sell.

We can see a similar relationship by looking at what happened to the prices of April Intel options on the next trading day, Monday, December 19, 2005, a day on which Intel stock fell slightly from $26.38 to $25.78:

Intel	Expiration	Strike	Call	Put
$25.78	April	$25.00	$1.95	$0.90
$25.78	April	$27.50	$0.80	$2.25
$25.78	April	$30.00	$0.25	$4.30
$25.78	April	$32.50	$0.10	$6.70

Comparing these prices to those of the previous trading day, we see that the prices of all four call options fell with the decline of Intel shares, and all put values increased. Combining the lessons of the last few paragraphs, we can say that *call prices decrease and put prices increase when the difference between the underlying stock price and the exercise price* $(S - X)$ *decreases.*

Finally, to isolate the most important, and the most subtle, influence on option prices, take a look at a new set of option prices in Table 18.4. The table shows call and put prices for food giant, Kraft (KFT) and chip manufacturer Advanced Micro Devices (AMD). The first column shows the stock prices of Kraft ($28.42) and AMD ($30.02). Because AMD stock is trading $1.60 higher than Kraft stock is, we might expect AMD call options to be worth more than Kraft calls with the same strike price and expiration date. Table 18.4 confirms that prediction. The January 2007 AMD call options are worth more than Kraft calls expiring at the same time.

By the same logic, with AMD stock trading above Kraft, we might predict that Kraft put options would be worth more than similar AMD options. But the prices in Table 18.4 show just the opposite pattern. For example, the AMD put expiring in January 2007 with a $30 strike price sells for $1.40 that the identical Kraft option.

Company	Expiration	Strike	Call	Put
KFT	January 07	25.00	6.20	1.00
28.42	January 07	30.00	1.70	3.10
28.42	January 07	35.00	0.30	6.60
AMD	January 07	25.00	8.70	2.30
30.02	January 07	30.00	5.73	4.50
30.02	January 07	35.00	3.80	7.30

Note: Option prices retrieved from www.cboe.com on December 23, 2005.

Table 18.4
Option Prices for Kraft and Advanced Micro Devices

[18.] After a period of very poor stock performance, firms sometimes *reprice* employee stock options. Repricing typically means that the firm reduces the strike prices of outstanding options earned by employees when the stock price was much higher. Critics argue that if firms simply reset option strike prices after poor performance, then options do little to give managers proper incentives. Carter and Lynch (2001) offer evidence that repricing is necessary to realign the incentives of managers and to retain employees in a highly competitive labor market. Chauvin and Shenoy (2001) suggest another way that managers can lower the strike prices of their options. Managers can selectively disclose bad news just before they receive option grants. Because most firms set the strike price of employee stock options equal to the current market price of the company's stock, executives who release negative information just prior to receiving option grants effectively lower the strike prices of those grants. Chauvin and Shenoy find that in a sample of 783 stock option grants to CEOs, stock returns were unusually low in the 10 days before chief executives received their option packages.

That seems strange because the AMD put is roughly at the money, but the Kraft put is already in the money. Why are both types of AMD options more valuable?

Figure 18.9 contains a clue to the answer. The graph displays the daily percentage price change in AMD and Kraft shares during 2005. A quick glance at the figure shows that AMD stock was more volatile than Kraft stock over this period. Almost all the daily price changes in Kraft stock fell inside the ±3 percent band. In contrast, AMD's shares experienced a percentage change of 3 percent or more roughly once every three weeks during this period.

Why should AMD's higher volatility lead to higher call and put option prices? The answer lies in the asymmetry of option payoffs. When a call option expires, its payoff will be zero for a wide range of stock prices. Whether the stock price falls below the option's strike price by $1, $10, or $100, the payoff will be zero. On the other hand, as the stock price rises above the strike price, the option's payoff increases. A similar relationship holds for puts. The value of a put at expiration will be zero if the stock price is greater than the strike price, and whether the stock price is just above the strike price or far above it does not change the payoff. However, the put option will have a larger payoff the lower the stock price falls, once it falls below the strike price. The bottom line is that *call and put option prices increase as the volatility of the underlying stock increases.*

Figure 18.9
Daily Percent Price Changes for AMD and Kraft Shares

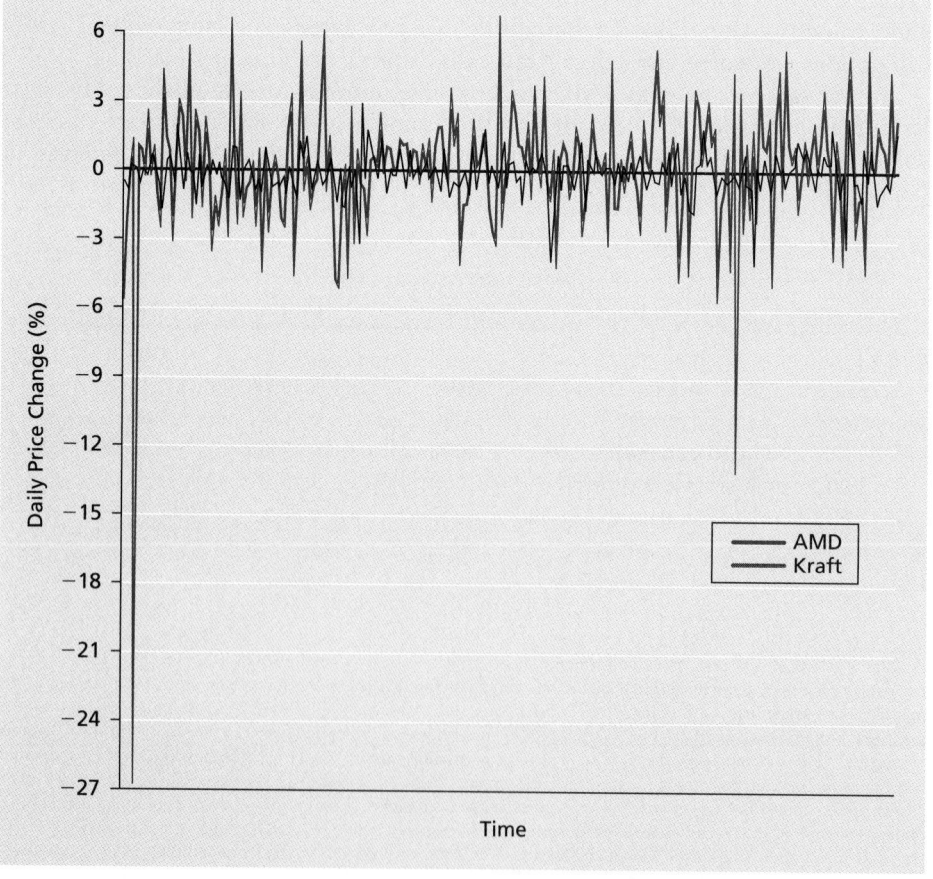

APPLYING THE MODEL 18.3

Suppose that you are tracking two stocks, one of which exhibits much more volatility than the other. Call the more volatile stock Extreme Inc. and the less volatile one Steady Corp. At present, shares of both companies sell for about $40. At-the-money call and put options are available on both stocks with an expiration date in three months. Based on the historical volatility of each stock, you estimate a range of prices that you think the shares might attain by the time the options expire. Next to each possible stock price, you write down the option payoff that will occur if the stock actually reaches that price on the expiration date (the strike price is $40 for both options).

The following table gives the numbers:

Stock	Potential Prices	Call Payoff	Put Payoff
Extreme Inc.	$15	$ 0	$25
	$25	0	15
	$35	0	5
	$45	5	0
	$55	15	0
	$65	25	0
Steady Corp.	$30	$ 0	$10
	$34	0	6
	$38	0	2
	$42	2	0
	$46	6	0
	$50	10	0

The payoffs of calls and puts for both companies are zero exactly half the time. But when the payoffs are not zero, they are much larger for Extreme Inc. than they are for Steady Corp., which makes options on Extreme Inc. shares much more valuable than options on Steady Corp. stock.

Summing up, we now know that option prices increase as time to expiration increases and as the risk of the underlying asset increases. Call option prices decrease the smaller the difference between the stock price and the strike price $(S - X)$, whereas put prices increase as this difference decreases. We are now ready to tie all this together and calculate market price of calls and puts. We conclude this chapter by studying a simple but powerful tool for valuing options, the binomial option-pricing model. In Chapter 19, we will learn about an even more complex approach, one that earned its authors Nobel Prize recognition, known as the Black and Scholes option-pricing model.

Concept Review Questions

9. Throughout most of this book, we have shown that if an asset's risk increases, its price declines. Why is the opposite true for options?

10. Call options increase in value when stock prices rise, and put options increase in value when stock prices fall. How can the same movement in an underlying variable (e.g., an increase in time before expiration or an increase in volatility) cause both call and put prices to rise at the same time?

18.4 CALCULATING OPTION PRICES

THE BINOMIAL OPTION-PRICING MODEL

Earlier in this chapter, we studied an important relationship linking the prices of puts, calls, shares, and risk-free bonds. Put-call parity establishes a direct link between the prices of these assets, a link that must hold to prevent arbitrage opportunities. We saw in Section 18.2 that if an option's price gets too high, an arbitrageur can exploit the situation by selling the overpriced option and purchasing an identical synthetic option. A similar logic drives the **binomial option-pricing model.** The binomial model recognizes that investors can combine options (either calls or puts) with shares of the underlying asset to construct a portfolio with a risk-free payoff.[19] Any asset with a risk-free payoff is relatively easy to value—just discount its future cash flows at the risk-free rate. But if we can value a portfolio containing options and shares, then we can also calculate the value of the options simply by subtracting the value of the shares from the value of the portfolio.

We will work through an example that proceeds in three distinct steps showing how to price an option using the binomial method. First, we must find a portfolio of stock and options that generates a risk-free payoff in the future. Second, given that the portfolio offers a risk-free cash payment, we can calculate the present value of that portfolio by discounting its cash flow at the risk-free rate. Third, given the portfolio's present value, we can determine how much of the portfolio's value comes from the stock and how much comes from the option. By subtracting the value of the underlying shares from the value of the portfolio, we obtain the option's market price.

Create a Risk-Free Portfolio. Assume that the shares of Financial Engineers Ltd. currently sell for $55. We want to determine the price of a call option on Financial Engineers stock with an exercise price of $55 and an expiration date in one year. Assume the risk-free rate is 4 percent.

The binomial model begins with an assumption about the volatility of the underlying stock. Specifically, the model assumes that by the time the option expires, the stock will have increased or decreased to a particular dollar value. In this problem, we will assume that one year from now, Financial Engineers' stock price will have risen to $70 or it will have fallen to $40. Figure 18.10 provides a simple diagram of this assumption.[20]

The call option we want to price has a strike price of $55. Therefore, if the underlying stock reaches $70 in one year, the call option will be worth $15. However, if Financial Engineers stock falls to $40, the call option will be worthless.

Here is the crux of the first step. We want to find some combination of Financial Engineers stock and the call option that yields the same payoff whether the stock goes up or down over the next year. In other words, we want to create a risk-free combination of shares and calls. To begin, suppose we purchase one share of stock and h call options. At the moment, we do not know the value of h, but we can solve for it. Because our portfolio objective is to generate the same cash payment one year from

---

[19] The seminal work on the binomial model is by Cox, Ross, and Rubenstein (1979).

[20] How can we possibly know that the price of Financial Engineers stock will be either $70 or $40? Of course, we cannot know that. Almost any price is possible one year in the future. Very soon we will illustrate that this assumption, which seems completely ridiculous now, isn't really necessary in a more complex version of the binomial model. But let's understand the simple version first.

Figure 18.10
Binomial Option Pricing

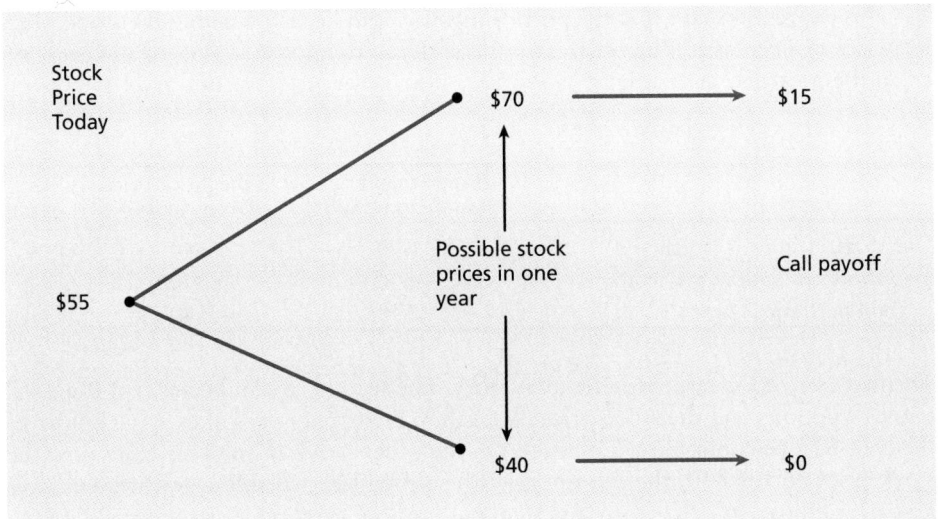

now whether our share of stock rises or falls, we can write down the portfolio's pay-offs in each possible scenario and then choose h so that the payoffs are equal:

	Cash Flows One Year from Today	
	If the Stock Price Goes Up to $70	If the Stock Price Drops to $40
One share of stock is worth	$70	$40
h call options are worth	$15h	$0h
Total portfolio is worth	$70 + $15h	$40 + $0h

A portfolio containing one share of stock and h call options will have the same cash value in one year if we choose the value of h that solves this equation:

$$\$70 + 15h = \$40 + \$0h$$
$$h = -2$$

The value of h represents the number of call options in our risk-free portfolio. Because h equals -2, to create a risk-free portfolio we must *sell two call options* and combine that position with our single share of stock. Why do we sell options to achieve this objective? Remember that the value of a call option rises as the stock price rises. If we own a share of stock and a call option (or several call options) on that stock, the assets in our portfolio will be positively correlated, rising and falling at the same time. Recall from Chapter 5 that the only circumstance in which it is possible to combine two risky assets into a risk-free portfolio occurs when the correlation between the two assets is negative (in fact, -1.0). Therefore, if we buy a share, we must sell call options to create a negative correlation between the assets in our portfolio.

What happens to our portfolio if, in fact, we buy one share and sell two calls? You can see the answer in two ways. First, just plug the value -2 back into the equation we used to solve for h: $40 = $40

This expression says that the portfolio payoff will be $40 whether the stock price increases or decreases. The other way to see this is to lay out the payoffs of each asset in the portfolio in a table.

	Cash Flows One Year from Today	
	If the Stock Price Goes Up to $70	If the Stock Price Drops to $40
One share of stock is worth	$70	$40
Two short call options are worth	−$30	$ 0
Total portfolio is worth	$40	$40

The first row of the table is self-explanatory. The second row indicates that if we sell two call options and the stock price equals $70 next year, we will owe the holder of the calls $15 per option, or $30 total. On the other hand, if one year from now the stock price equals $40, the call options we sold will be worthless and we will have no cash outflow. In either case, the total cash inflow from the portfolio will be $40.

Because this portfolio pays $40 in one year no matter what happens, we call it a perfectly hedged portfolio. The value of h is called the **hedge ratio** because it tells us what combination of stocks and calls results in a perfectly hedged position.[21]

Calculating the Present Value of the Portfolio. Because the portfolio consisting of one share of stock and two short call options pays $40 for certain next year, we can say that the portfolio is a type of synthetic, risk-free bond. The second step requires us to calculate the present value of the portfolio. Because we already know that the risk-free rate equals 4 percent, we can determine the present value of the portfolio:

$$PV = \frac{\$40}{1.04^1} = \$38.46$$

It is crucial at this step to understand the following point. Buying one share of stock and selling two calls yields the same future payoff as buying a risk-free, zero-coupon bond with a face value of $40. Because both of these investments offer $40 at the end of one year with certainty, they should both sell for the same price today. This insight allows us to determine the option's price in the next step.

Determine the Price of the Call Option. If a risk-free bond paying $40 in one year costs $38.46 today, then the net cost of buying one share of Financial Engineers stock and selling two call options must also be $38.46. Why? Because both investment strategies are risk-free and offer the same future cash flows, they must both sell for the same price. Therefore, to determine the price of the option, all we need to do is write down an expression for the cost of our hedged portfolio and set that expression equal to $38.46.

From the information given in the problem, purchasing one share of stock costs $55. Partially offsetting this cost will be the revenue from selling two call options. De-

---

[21.] The *hedge ratio* can be defined either as the ratio of calls to shares in a perfectly hedged portfolio (the definition we use here) or as the ratio of shares to calls. In this example, the hedge ratio equals either −2:1 (using our definition) or −1:2 (using the alternative definition). Either way, the hedge ratio defines the mix of options and shares that results in a hedged portfolio.

noting the price of the call option with the letter C, we can calculate the total cost of the portfolio as follows:

Total Portfolio cost = $55 − 2C = $38.46

Solving for C, *we obtain a call value of $8.27.*

   At this point, it is worth reviewing what we have accomplished. We began with an assumption about the future movements of the underlying stock. Next, given the type of option we want to value and its characteristics, we calculated the payoffs of the option for each of the two possible future stock prices. Given those payoffs, we discovered that by buying one share and selling two calls, we could generate a certain payoff of $40 in one year. The present value of that payoff is $38.46, so the net cost of buying the share and selling the calls must also equal $38.46. This implies that we received revenue of $16.54 from selling two calls, or $8.27 each. The following Applying the Model repeats the process to value an identical put option on the same underlying stock.

SMART CONCEPTS
See the concept explained step-by-step at
SMARTFinance

APPLYING THE MODEL 18.4

We begin this problem with the same set of assumptions for Financial Engineers given earlier. Financial Engineers stock sells for $55 but may increase to $70 or decrease to $40 in one year. The risk-free rate equals 4 percent. We want to use the binomial model to calculate the value of a 1-year put option with a strike price of $55. We begin by finding the composition of a perfectly hedged portfolio. As before, begin by writing down the payoffs of a portfolio containing one share of stock and h put options:

	Cash Flows One Year from Today	
	If the Stock Price Goes Up to $70	If the Stock Price Drops to $40
One share of stock is worth	$70	$40
h put options are worth	$0h	$15h
Total portfolio is worth	$70 + $0h	$40 + $15h

Notice that the put option pays $15 when the stock price drops, and it pays nothing when the stock price rises. Set the payoffs in each scenario equal to each other and solve for h:

$$\$70 + 0h = \$40 + \$15h$$

$$h = 2$$

To create a perfectly hedged portfolio, we must buy one share of stock and two put options. Notice that in this problem, we are buying options rather than selling them. Put values increase when stock values decrease, so it is possible to form a risk-free portfolio containing long positions in both stock and puts because they are negatively correlated.[22] By plugging the value of $h = 2$ back into the equation,

---

[22.] If the stock underlying a put option has a positive beta, then the put option itself will have a negative beta. In Chapter 6, we learned that the capital asset pricing model predicts that any asset with a negative beta will have an expected return below the risk-free rate. Coval and Shumway (2001) verify that this prediction holds for put options. They estimate that at-the-money put options on the S&P 500 Index earn weekly average returns of −7.7 to −9.5 percent per week. However, the news for the CAPM is only half good. Although put returns fall below the risk-free rate, as the CAPM predicts, put returns are much too negative to be entirely consistent with the CAPM.

we see that an investor who buys one share of stock and two put options essentially creates a synthetic bond with a face value of $70:

$$\$70 + \$0(2) = \$40 + \$15(2)$$
$$\$70 = \$70$$

Given a risk-free rate of 4 percent, the present value today of $70 is $67.31. It would cost $67.31 to buy a 1-year, risk-free bond paying $70, so it must also cost $67.31 to buy the synthetic version of that bond, one share and two puts. Given that the current share price is $55, and letting P stand for the price of the put, we find that the put option is worth $6.15 (rounding to the nearest penny):

$$\text{Cost of 1 share} + 2 \text{ puts} = \$67.31 = \$55 + 2P$$
$$\$12.31 = 2P$$
$$\$6.15 = P$$

Take a moment to look over the two examples of pricing options using the binomial approach. Make a list of the data needed to price these options:

1. The current price of the underlying stock
2. The amount of time remaining before the option expires
3. The strike price of the option
4. The risk-free rate
5. The possible values of the underlying stock in the future

On this list, the only unknown is the fifth item. You can easily find the other four necessary values simply by looking at current market data.

At this point, we pause to ask one of our all-time favorite exam questions. Look back at Figure 18.10. What assumption are we making there about the probabilities of an up and a down move in Financial Engineers stock? Most people see that the figure shows two possible outcomes and guess that the probabilities must be 50–50. This is not true; at no point in our discussion of the binomial model did we make any assumption about the probabilities of up and down movements in the stock. We don't have to know what those probabilities are to value the option, which is convenient because estimating them could be very difficult.

Why are the probabilities of no concern to us? The first answer is that the market sets the current price of the stock at a level that reflects the odds of future up and down moves. In other words, the probabilities are embedded in the stock price, even though no one can see them directly.

The second answer is that the binomial model prices an option through the principle of "no arbitrage." Because it is always possible to combine a share of stock with options (either calls or puts) into a risk-free portfolio, the binomial model says that the value of that portfolio must be the same as the value of a risk-free bond—otherwise, an arbitrage opportunity would exist because identical assets would be selling at different prices. Because the portfolio containing stock and options offers a risk-free payoff, the probabilities of up and down moves in the stock price do not enter the calculations. An investor holding the hedged portfolio does not need to worry about movements in the stock because they do not affect the portfolio's payoffs.

Almost all students object to the binomial model's assumption that the price of a stock can take just two values in the future. Fair enough. It is certainly true that one year from today, the price of Financial Engineers stock might be $70, $40, or almost any other value. However, it turns out that more complex versions of the binomial do not require analysts to specify just two final prices for the stock. The binomial model can accommodate a wide range of final prices. To see how this works, consider a slight modification to our original problem.

Rather than presume that Financial Engineers stock will rise or fall by $15 over a year's time, suppose that it may rise or fall by $7.50 every six months. That's still a big assumption. But if we make it, we find that the list of potential prices of Financial Engineers stock one year from today has grown from two values to three. Figure 18.11 proves this claim. After one year, the price of the stock might be $40, $55, or $70. Now let's modify the assumption one more time. Suppose that the price of stock can move up or down $3.75 every three months. Figure 18.11 shows that in this case, the number of possible stock prices one year in the future grows to five.

Given a tree with many branches like the last one in Figure 18.11, we can solve for the value of a call or put option following the same steps we used to value options

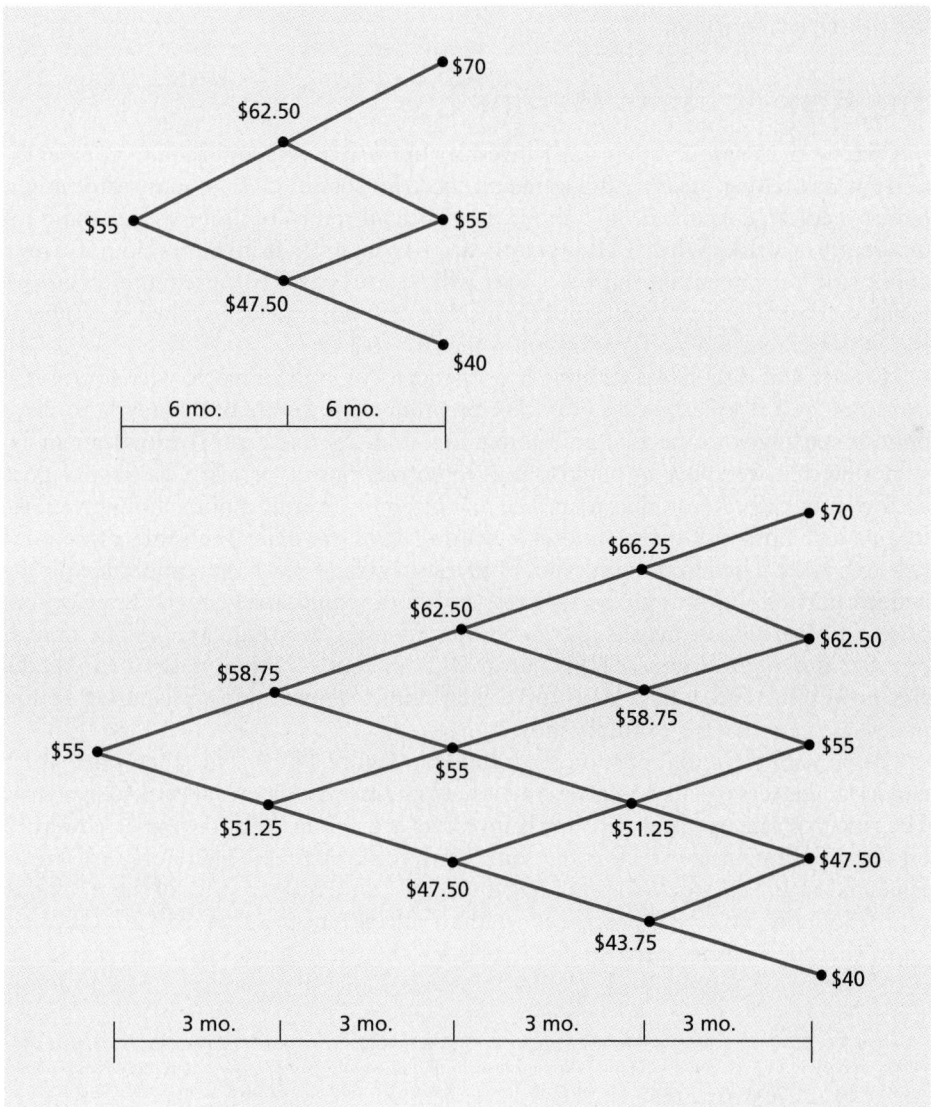

Figure 18.11
Multistage Binomial Trees

with a simple two-step tree. Now imagine a much larger tree, one in which the stock moves up or down every few minutes or even every few seconds. Each change in the stock price is very small, perhaps a penny or two. But as the tree unfolds and time passes, the number of branches rapidly expands, as does the number of possible values of the stock at the option's expiration date. Looking at the tree's terminal nodes, we see that when the option expires in a year, the price of Financial Engineers stock can take any one of hundreds, or even thousands, of different values, so the complaint about the model's artificial assumption of just two possible stock prices no longer applies. Though extremely tedious, solving for the call value involves working all the way through the tree, applying the same steps over and over again.[23]

The binomial model is an incredibly powerful, flexible tool that analysts can use to price all sorts of options, from ordinary calls and puts to complex real options embedded in capital investment projects. The genius of the model is in its recognition of the opportunity to use stock and options to mimic the payoffs of risk-free bonds, the easiest of all securities to price. The binomial model has a close cousin that also makes use of the ability to construct risk-free portfolios using stock and options—the risk-neutral method.

THE RISK-NEUTRAL METHOD

In Chapter 5, we argued that most investors are risk averse and require compensation for risk taking. Just briefly, we mentioned the possibility that an investor might be risk neutral, concerned only about the expected return of an investment and indifferent to its risk. What if all investors are risk neutral? If investors do not worry about risk, then in equilibrium, no asset will have to pay a risk premium to survive in the market. The expected return on a share of common stock will be the same as the expected return on a Treasury bill—the risk-free rate.

Clearly, this discussion is purely hypothetical. We live in a world with risk-averse investors, and risky assets do offer risk premiums. However, it is possible to price options starting with the assumption that investors are risk neutral. How can an assumption that we know to be false lead to correct option prices? The answer goes back to arbitrage. Recall that we priced an option by creating a portfolio with a risk-free payoff. Both risk-averse and risk-neutral investors place the same value on a risk-free asset. Therefore, both types of investors would place the same value on the hedged portfolio of options and shares, and both would arrive at the same option price. In other words, because we price options using arbitrage arguments, we can proceed *as if* all investors are risk neutral. Making that assumption we can apply the **risk-neutral method,** which leads to an even simpler approach to calculating option prices, as the following example shows.

Begin with the initial conditions outlined in Figure 18.10. The stock price of Financial Engineers equals $55 now, and it may increase to $70 or fall to $40 in a year. The risk-free rate equals 4 percent. If investors are risk neutral, the expected return on Financial Engineers stock is the same as the risk-free rate. Therefore, as long as Financial Engineers stock does not pay dividends, the expected price of the stock one year from now must be 4 percent more than the current price, or $57.20. Once we know that the expected price in one year is $57.20, we can infer what the probabili-

---

[23.] Fortunately, Black and Scholes (1973) and Merton (1973) developed a much more elegant model to solve for option values when the stock price can move in small increments moment by moment. We will study the Black and Scholes model in Chapter 19. For interested students, the final problem in Chapter 18 offers an animated solution for a multistage binomial tree.

ties of an up and a down move must be. Let the probability of an up move in the stock be p and the probability of a down move be $1 - p$. We can solve for the probabilities using this expression:[24]

$$\$70p + (1 - p)\$40 = \$57.20$$
$$p = 0.5733$$
$$1 - p = 0.4267$$

If the probabilities of up and down moves are 57.33 percent and 42.67 percent, respectively, then the expected stock price is $57.20, resulting in an expected 1-year return of 4 percent. Now let's use those probabilities to calculate the value of the call option. As before, if the stock price reaches $70, then the call with a $55 strike price will be worth $15. The call will be worth nothing if the stock price ends up at $40. To value the call, just calculate the option's expected cash flow in one year, and discount that at the risk-free rate:

$$\text{Expected cash flow} = p(\$15) + (1 - p)(\$0) = 0.5733(\$15) + \$0 = \$8.60$$

$$\text{Call value} = \frac{\$8.60}{1.04} = \$8.27$$

Notice that $8.27 is precisely the same call value we obtained using the binomial model, which made no assumption about investors' attitudes toward risk. The binomial model works because it is based on the principle that markets do not allow arbitrage opportunities to exist, at least not for long. Therefore, if a combination of stock and options is risk-free, then that combination must sell for the same price as a risk-free bond. If an asset promises a risk-free payoff, risk-averse and risk-neutral investors agree on how it should be valued because neither group requires a risk premium on the asset. Thus, if the binomial model works by creating a risk-free portfolio, it does no harm to assume that investors are risk neutral from the start. Whether investors are risk averse or risk neutral, the binomial model's calculations are the same. That opens the door for us to assume investors are risk neutral, and that assumption gives us a new way to value options.

APPLYING THE MODEL 18.5

Assuming investors are risk neutral, let's value the Financial Engineers put option with a strike of $55. If the stock increases to $70, the put is worthless. If the stock falls to $40, the put option pays $15. We already know the probabilities of up and down moves from our risk-neutral valuation of the call option, so we will use

---

[24.] The trick here is to choose the probabilities of up and down moves so that the expected future price is $r\%$ higher than the current price, where r is the risk-free rate. There is a shortcut formula for calculating the probability (p) of an up move in the underlying asset:

$$p = \frac{r^* - d}{u - d}$$

where r^* is 1 plus the risk-free rate, u is 1 plus the percentage increase in the stock price when it goes up, and d is 1 plus the percentage decrease in the stock price when it goes down. For instance, in the Financial Engineers problem, the stock may either increase or decrease by $15, which is equal to 27.3 percent of the current market price. Therefore, $r^* = 1.04$, $u = 1.273$, $d = 0.727$, and $p = 0.5733$.

those probabilities to calculate the expected cash flow from the put. Once we have the expected cash flow, we can discount it at 4 percent to obtain the current market price of the put:

$$\text{Expected cash flow} = p(\$0) + (1 - p)\$15 = \$0 + 0.4267(\$15) + \$0 = \$6.40$$

$$\text{Call value} = \frac{\$6.40}{1.04} = \$6.15$$

As expected, the put value obtained from risk-neutral valuation matches exactly the price calculated using the binomial model.

Concept Review Questions

11. To value options using the *binomial options-pricing method,* is it necessary to know the expected return on the stock? Why or why not?

12. There is an old saying that nature abhors a vacuum. The financial equivalent is that "markets abhor arbitrage opportunities." Explain the central role this principle plays in the binomial model.

13. Part of the *risk-neutral method* involves calculating the probability of an up or a down move in the underlying stock. Do you think these probabilities correspond to real-world probabilities of up and down moves? Explain.

18.5 SUMMARY

- Options are contracts that grant the buyer the right to buy or sell stock at a fixed price.
- Call options grant the right to purchase shares; put options grant the right to sell shares.
- Options provide a real economic benefit to society and are not simply a form of legalized gambling.
- American options allow investors to exercise their options before the options expire, but European options do not.
- Payoff diagrams show the value of options or portfolios of options on the expiration date. Payoff diagrams are extremely useful in understanding how different options trading strategies work.
- Put-call parity establishes a link between the market prices of calls, puts, shares, and bonds, provided certain conditions hold.
- Put-call parity can be used to calculate the fair value of an option (provided the other prices are known) or to find ways to form synthetic securities.
- Call option prices decrease and put option prices increase as the difference between the underlying stock price and the exercise price decreases.
- Calls and puts both increase in value (usually) when there is more time left before expiration.
- An increase in the volatility of the underlying asset increases the values of calls and puts.
- The binomial option-pricing model and the risk-neutral method permit us to calculate option prices with a minimal set of assumptions.

INTERNET RESOURCES

Note: *For updates to links, please go to the book's website at* http://smart.swcollege.com.

http://www.cboe.com—Offers price quotes for many options and provides several tutorials explaining the characteristics of options and how they are traded

KEY TERMS

American call option
at the money
binomial option-pricing model
call option
cash settlement
counterparty risk
derivative securities
European call option
exercise price
exercise the option
expiration date
hedge ratio
hockey-stick diagram
in the money
intrinsic value
long position
long straddle
naked option position
net payoff

options
option premium
out of the money
over-the-counter market
payoff
payoff diagrams
protective put
put option
put-call parity
risk-neutral method
short position
short straddle
strike price
synthetic put option
time value
underlying asset
writes an option
writing covered calls

QUESTIONS

18-1.   Explain why an option is a *derivative security*.

18-2.   Is buying an option more or less risky than buying the underlying stock?

18-3.   What is the difference between an option's price and its payoff?

18-4.   List five factors that influence the prices of calls and puts.

18-5.   What are the economic benefits that options provide?

18-6.   What is the primary advantage of settling options contracts in cash?

18-7.   Suppose that you want to invest in a particular company. What are the pros and cons of buying the company's shares as compared to buying their options?

18-8.   Suppose that you want to make an investment that will be profitable if a company's stock price falls. Contrast the approach of short-selling the company's stock versus buying put options on the stock.

18-9.   Is buying a call the same as selling a put? Explain why or why not.

18-10.   Suppose that you own an American call option on Pfizer stock. Pfizer stock has gone up in value considerably since you bought the option, so your investment has been profitable. There is still one month to go before the option expires, but you decide to go ahead and take your profits in cash. Describe two ways that you could accomplish this goal. Which one is likely to leave you with the higher cash payoff?

18-11. Explain why *put-call parity* does not hold for American options.

18-12. Look at the Intel call option prices in Table 18.1. For a given expiration date, call prices increase as the strike price decreases. The strike prices decrease in increments of $2.50. Do the call option prices increase in constant increments? That is, does the call price increase by the same amount as the strike price drops from $32.50 to $30 and so on? Explain.

18-13. Explain the difference between the *binomial option-pricing model* and the *risk-neutral method* of option pricing.

PROBLEMS

Option Payoff Diagrams

[handwritten margin note: solution shows it increases @ $40, but really @ $50]

18-1. Draw payoff diagrams for each of the following portfolios (X = strike price):

  a. Buy a call with X = $50, and sell a call with X = $60.

  b. Buy a bond with a face value of $10, short a put with X = $60, and buy a put with X = $50.

  c. Buy a share of stock, buy a put option with X = $50, sell a call with X = $60, and short a bond (i.e., borrow) with a face value of $50.

  d. What principle do these diagrams illustrate?

18-2. Draw a payoff diagram for the following portfolio (X = strike price): Buy two call options, one with X = $20 and one with X = $30, and sell two call options, both with X = $25.

18-3. Suppose that you buy one AMD call option with X = $25 and one with X = $35. You also sell two AMD calls with X = $30. Using the prices from Table 18.4, determine the net cost of the option portfolio, and draw a new payoff diagram showing the net payoffs at expiration. Over what range of prices would you make money, and over what range would you lose money? What is your maximum possible loss and gain?

18-4. Draw a payoff diagram for each of the following portfolios (X = strike price):

  a. Buy a bond with a face value of $80, buy a call with X = $80, and sell a put with X = $80.

  b. Buy a share of stock, buy a put with X = $80, and sell a call with X = $80.

  c. Buy a share of stock, buy a put with X = $80, and sell a bond with a face value of $80.

18-5. Look at the option prices in Table 18.1. For each row of the table, perform the following calculation: (stock price + put price − call price). According to put-call parity, a portfolio containing a share of stock, a put, and a short call has the same payoff as what security? When you perform this calculation for each row of Table 18.1, do your results seem to indicate that the put-call parity holds, at least approximately, or not? Explain. As background information, the annual rate of interest on short-term U.S. Treasury bills was about 4 percent at the time the quotes in the table were obtained from the CBOE website.

18-6. Referring to Problem 18-5, if some of the prices in Table 18.1 fail to satisfy put-call parity, provide an explanation for this apparent violation of the "no arbitrage" principle. Put differently, even if prices in the table do not satisfy parity, is it possible that there is still no arbitrage opportunity to exploit?

18-7. Imagine that a stock sells for $33. A call option with a strike price, X, of $35 and an expiration date in six months sells for $4.50. The annual risk-free rate is 5 percent. Calculate the price of a put option that expires in six months and has a strike price of $35.

18-8. Refer to Problem 18-7. Suppose that the put option described actually sells for $5. Explain in detail how an arbitrageur could exploit this mispricing to earn a risk-free profit.

18-9. Monitoring option prices in the United Kingdom, you notice that call and put prices on the stock of the British exotic-pet importer Python Inc. seem to be out of alignment. Specifically, the price of Python stock is £55, and the price of 3-month call and put options on Python stock with exercise prices of £60 are £5.75 and £7.25, respectively. The U.K. risk-free rate of interest is 8 percent (or 2 percent per three months). How can we exploit this arbitrage opportunity?

18-10. Suppose that an American call option is in the money, so the stock price, S, is greater than the strike price, X. Demonstrate that the market price of this call (C) cannot be less than the difference between the stock price and the exercise price. That is, explain why this must be true: $C > S - X$. (*Hint:* Consider what would happen if $C < S - X$.)

Calculating Option Prices

18-11. A call option expires in three months and has a strike price $X = $40. The underlying stock is worth $42 today. In three months, the stock may increase by $7 or decrease by $6. The risk-free rate is 2 percent per year. Use the binomial option-pricing model to value the call option.

18-12. A certain stock sells for $42 today, but in three months it may be worth $49 or $36. Value a 3-month put option with a strike price $X = $40. The risk-free rate is 2 percent per year.

18-13. Given the call and put prices you calculated in Problems 18-11 and 18-12, check to see if put-call parity holds.

18-14. A put option has a strike price of $90. The underlying stock sells for $88, but in four months it could increase to $95 or decrease to $82. The risk-free rate is 3 percent, and the put expires in four months. Use the risk-neutral method to value the put.

18-15. A stock sells for $88 now, but in four months its price may rise by $7 or fall by $6. The risk-free rate is 3 percent. Use the risk-neutral method to calculate the value of a 4-month call with a strike price $X = $90. After you have determined the call price, use your answer from problem 18-15 to check to see if put-call parity holds.

18-16. This problem requires you to use the binomial model to price a complex call option with a variable strike price. Suppose that the current price of a particular stock is $80. The stock pays no dividends and has a beta of 1.2. The strike price of a 6-month call option is $78, but the strike price is not fixed. Specifically, the strike price is indexed to the S&P 500, meaning that if the S&P 500 changes by x percent, then the option's strike price will move in the same direction by x percent. Suppose you believe that the S&P 500 will either rise 20 percent or fall 10 percent in the next six months. If the risk-free rate is 4 percent, what is the value of the call option? (*Hint:* Use the stock's beta to determine the future values of the stock, which will depend on how the S&P 500 behaves.)

18-17. Explain the following paradox. A put option is a highly volatile security. If the underlying stock has a positive beta, then a put option on that stock will have a negative beta and an expected return below the risk-free rate. How can an equilibrium exist in which a highly risky security such as a put option offers an expected return below that of a much safer security such as a Treasury bill?

18-18. A stock currently trades for $84. In the next three months it may rise or fall by $5. Similarly, in the three months after that the stock price could increase or decrease by $5. Calculate the price of a 6-month put option with a strike price of $87.50, assuming that the risk-free rate of interest is 1 percent per quarter (roughly 4 percent per year).

18-19. A stock currently trades for $84. In the next three months it may rise or fall by $5. Similarly, in the three months after that the stock price could increase or decrease by $5. Calculate the price of a 6-month call option with a strike price of $87.50, assuming that the risk-free rate of interest is 1 percent per quarter (roughly 4 percent per year).

MINI-CASE: OPTIONS BASICS

Microsoft's common stock is currently trading for $27.02 per share. The values of several call options, which expire in February 2006 and April 2006, are as follows:

Symbol	Call Price	Strike Price
February 2006		
MQFBD	7.10	20.00
MSQBX	4.60	22.50
MSQBJ	2.15	25.00
MSQBY	0.40	27.50
MSQBK	0.05	30.00
April 2006		
MQFDD	7.20	20.00
MSQDX	4.80	22.50
MSQDJ	2.45	25.00
MSQDY	0.75	27.50
MSQDK	0.15	30.00

1. Which call options are in the money? Which call options are out of the money?

2. Calculate the intrinsic value and time value for each of the call options.

3. Construct a diagram showing the payoff and net payoff for the MSQBJ option from the perspective of a long position and again from a short position.

4. Using the concept of put-call parity, determine the price of a put option on Microsoft's stock with a strike price of $27.50 that expires in February 2006. The appropriate risk-free rate of interest is 2.06 percent. Assume that Microsoft will not pay a dividend and that the options are European options.

5. Assume that in one year Microsoft's stock will have either increased in value to $33 or have fallen to $21.80. Calculate the hedge ratio and the value of a call option with a strike price of $25 and one year to expiration. The appropriate risk-free rate of interest is 2.75 percent.

6.   Assume that one week has passed and Microsoft's stock has risen in value to $28.72. The value of the MSQBJ call option is now $3.80. Calculate the value of a long position in Microsoft's stock versus a long position in the MSQBJ call option, assuming you bought them one week ago and sold them today.

Chapter 19

Black and Scholes and Beyond

The Value of Amazon's Real Options

When most investors think about Internet stocks, they probably envision the huge number of once-valuable enterprises that disappeared during the U.S. stock market swoon from 2000 to 2002. But the Internet spawned a few businesses that enjoyed tremendous success, such as Yahoo!, Google, eBay, and Amazon.com. By the beginning of 2006, Google was a stock market darling, trading above $300 per share. With a wide variety of new product offerings in 2005, such as Google Maps and Google Earth, the search engine company seemed poised to become a dominant player, not only in the search engine business, but in many other business segments as well. Meanwhile, shares of eBay and Amazon.com were down 42 percent and 25 percent, respectively, in just the first half of 2005.

To Legg Mason analyst Scott Devitt, Amazon.com looked like a bargain. In July 2005, Devitt projected that Amazon shares could rise as much as 23 percent over the coming 12 months, largely due to the value of the company's real options. Like a financial option, a real option confers the right, but not the obligation, to do something. Real options come in many forms, but one of the most common is the option to expand an existing, successful line of business into a new area. Devitt pointed out that Amazon's A9 search engine, Alexa toolbar and traffic-measuring device, and digital audio and video products all represented internally nurtured businesses that might take off in the near future. Having the option to expand any of these activities could allow Amazon to compete outside its core business, and Devitt believed that Amazon.com's share price ignored the value of these real options.

Sources: "Amazon.com's innovation gets noticed: Analyst sets $42 US target," by Bambi Francisco, National Post's Financial Post & FP Investing (Canada), July 6, 2005; "Amazon shares gain pre-market on Legg Mason upgrade," AFX.com, July 5, 2005; The boom is back: US dotcom share prices are soaring again. What is different this time around? asks Heather Connon, The Observer, July 17, 2005.

SMARTFinance
Use the learning tools at www
.thomsonedu.com/finance/smartfinance

690

From the simple call and put stock options traded on major exchanges, to opportunities to expand successful business concepts, options are everywhere. This chapter continues our discussion of options, starting with the famous option-pricing formula developed by Black and Scholes. Next, we expand our focus to include option-like securities such as convertible bonds and warrants, before completing our coverage of options with an in-depth analysis of real options—capital investments with characteristics that resemble options.

In 1973, Myron Scholes and Fisher Black published what might fairly be called a trillion-dollar research paper. Their research produced, for the first time, a formula that traders could use to calculate the value of call options, a path-breaking discovery that had eluded researchers for decades. Black and Scholes did not have to wait long to see if their formula would have an impact in financial markets. That same year, options began trading in the United States on the newly formed Chicago Board Options Exchange (CBOE). Traders on the floor of the exchange used handheld calculators with the Black and Scholes formula programmed in. From that beginning, trading in options exploded over the next three decades, hence the trillion-dollar moniker given to the original research paper.[1] As this chapter's Comparative Corporate Finance feature indicates, the explosive growth in options trading has not been limited to the United States.

This chapter begins with an introduction to the Black and Scholes model. This model has much in common with the binomial model we studied in the previous chapter, and it is easier to use. Next we will discuss how many securities issued by corporations often contain embedded options. Understanding the pros and cons of these securities, either from the buyer's or the seller's perspective, requires some facility with option-pricing concepts. Finally, we will return once more to the topic of real options to see how analysts use the binomial and Black and Scholes models in a capital budgeting environment.

19.1 THE BLACK AND SCHOLES MODEL

CALCULATING BLACK AND SCHOLES OPTIONS VALUES

When you first encounter it, the **Black and Scholes option-pricing equation** looks rather intimidating. As a matter of fact, the editor at the prestigious academic journal where Black and Scholes published their prize-winning formula originally rejected their paper because he felt it was too technical and not of interest to a wide audience. Although the derivation of the formula requires advanced mathematics, the intuition behind the equation is fairly straightforward. In fact, the logic of the Black and Scholes model mirrors that of the binomial model.

Black and Scholes began by asking a question: If investors can buy and sell stock as well as stock options, does a combination of options and shares exist that provides a risk-free payoff? That should sound familiar, because the binomial model takes the same approach to determine an option's value. However, Black and Scholes' method for valuing options does not mimic the binomial structure exactly.

---

[1] Myron Scholes won the Nobel Prize in economics in 1997 for this achievement, an honor he shared with Robert Merton, another researcher who made seminal contributions to options research. Fisher Black undoubtedly would have been a corecipient of the award, but he died in 1995.

COMPARATIVE CORPORATE FINANCE

The Global Value of Options Trading

Few scholars can claim that their research helped to develop a multi-trillion-dollar global industry, but such a claim by Myron Scholes, Fisher Black, and Robert Merton would hardly be an exaggeration. Call and put options on common shares began trading on the Chicago Board Options Exchange in 1973, and since that time the volume of options trading, the variety of options available for trading, and the number of exchanges where traders can buy and sell options have grown dramatically. The accompanying chart shows how options markets have blossomed in North America, Europe, Asia, and the rest of the world since 1986. The figures in the graph reflect the notional amount of stock-index options, currency options, and interest rate options in each region since 1986. In North America, where the largest and most active markets are located, the outstanding value of exchange-traded options contracts was almost $25 trillion in 2005. Collectively, European markets were about half that size, with $12.4 trillion outstanding in 2005 (note that the vertical axis is plotted on a logarithmic scale). Despite rapid growth from the mid-1980s through the mid-1990s, options markets in Asia and elsewhere in the world haven't expanded much since 1996. In contrast, since 1990, markets in Europe and North American have enjoyed almost unlimited growth at more than 30 percent per year.

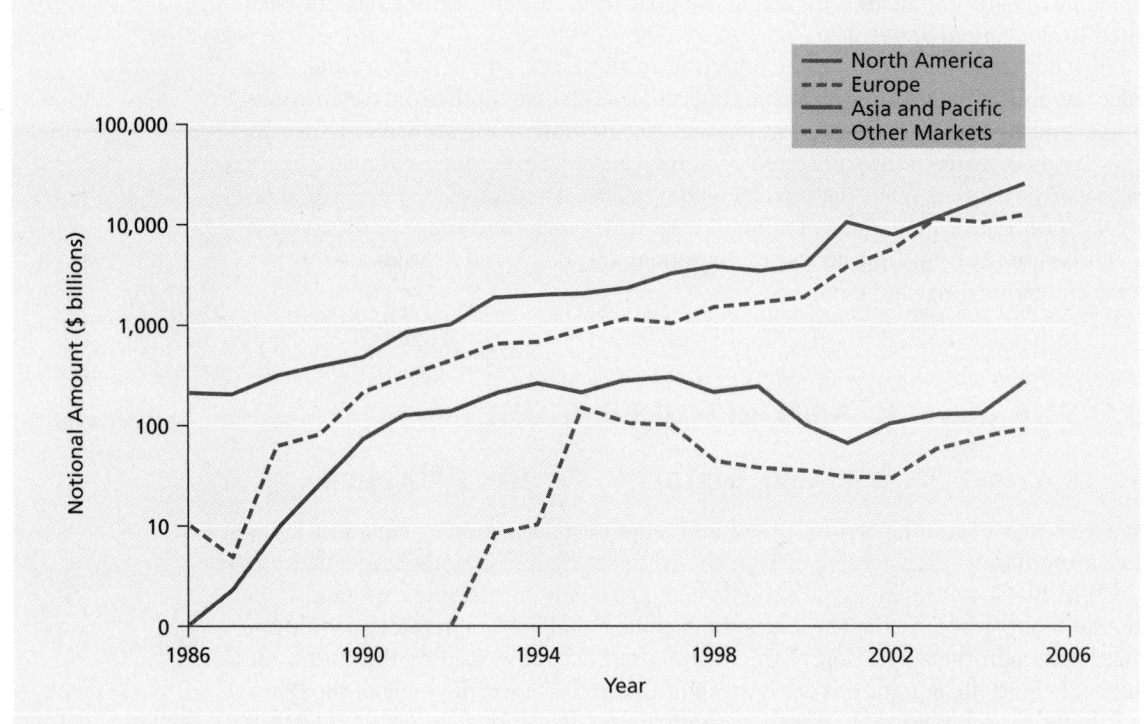

Global Value of Exchange Traded Options (includes stock index options, currency options, and interest rate options)
Source: Bank for International Settlements

First, recall from Chapter 18 that the binomial model assumes that over a given time period, the stock price will move up or down by a known amount. In Figure 18.11, we showed that by shortening the length of the period during which the stock price moves, we increase the number of different prices that the stock might reach by the option's expiration date. The Black and Scholes model takes this approach to its logical extreme. It presumes that stock prices can move at every moment. If we were to illustrate this assumption by drawing a binomial tree like those in Figure 18.11, the tree would have an infinite number of branches, and on the option's expiration date the stock price could take on almost any value.

Second, Black and Scholes did not assume that they knew precisely what the up and down movements in the stock would be at every instant. They recognized that these movements were essentially random and, therefore, unpredictable. Instead, they assumed that the volatility, or standard deviation, of a stock's movements was known. As we will see, practitioners using the Black and Scholes model struggle to find a reliable way to estimate the volatility of the stock underlying an option.

With these assumptions in place, Black and Scholes calculated the price of a European call option (on a non-dividend-paying stock) with the following equations:

$$C = SN(d_1) - Xe^{-rt}N(d_2)$$

$$d_1 = \frac{\ln\left(\dfrac{S}{X}\right) + \left(r + \dfrac{\sigma^2}{2}\right)t}{\sigma\sqrt{t}}$$

(Eq. 19.1)

options delta

$$d_2 = d_1 - \sigma\sqrt{t}$$

(Eq. 19.2)

Let's dissect this carefully. Most of the terms in the equation we have seen before:

use normsdist function to find $N(d_1)$ and $N(d_2)$

S = current market price of underlying stock

X = strike price of option

t = amount of time before option expires (in years)

r = annual risk-free interest rate

σ = annual standard deviation of underlying stock's returns

e = 2.718 (approximately)

$N(X)$ = probability of drawing a value less than or equal to X from the **standard normal distribution.**

Does this list of variables look familiar? It should, because it is nearly identical to the list of inputs required to use the binomial model. The stock price, S, the strike price, X, the time until expiration, t, and the risk-free rate, r, are all variables that the binomial model uses to price options. The new item that the Black and Scholes model requires is the standard deviation of the underlying asset's returns, σ. We illustrate a conventional method for estimating this value in an appendix following this chapter, but for now assume that you have an estimate of volatility from historical data.

What about the term Xe^{-rt}? Recall from our discussion of continuous compounding in Chapter 3 that the term e^{-rt} reflects the present value of $1 discounted at r percent for t years. Therefore, Xe^{-rt} simply equals the present value of the option's strike price.[2] With this in mind, look again at Equation 19.1. The first term

---

[2.] Remember, this expression can be written in two ways:

$$Xe^{-rt} = \frac{X}{e^{rt}}$$

Assuming the continuously compounded risk-free rate of interest equals r and the amount of time before expiration equals t, this is simply the present value of the strike price. See Table A6 in Appendix A for present value factors with continuous discounting.

equals the stock price multiplied by a quantity labeled $N(d_1)$. The second term is the present value of the strike price multiplied by a quantity labeled $N(d_2)$. Therefore, we can say that the call option value equals the "adjusted" stock price minus the present value of the "adjusted" strike price, where $N(d_1)$ and $N(d_2)$ represent some kind of adjustment factors. In Chapter 18, we saw that call option values increase as the difference between the stock price and the strike price, $S - X$, increases. The same relationship holds here, although we must now factor in the terms $N(d_1)$ and $N(d_2)$.

In the Black and Scholes equation, d_1 and d_2 are simply numerical values (calculated using Equation 19.2) that depend on the model's inputs: the stock price, the strike price, the interest rate, the time to expiration, and volatility. The expressions $N(d_1)$ and $N(d_2)$ convert the numerical values of d_1 and d_2 into probabilities using the standard normal distribution.[3] Figure 19.1 shows that the value $N(d_1)$ equals the area under the standard normal curve to the left of value d_1. For example, if we calculate the value of d_1 and find that it equals 0, then $N(d_1)$ equals 0.5 because half of the area under the curve falls to the left of zero. The higher the value of d_1, the closer $N(d_1)$ gets to 1.0; and the lower the value of d_1, the closer $N(d_1)$ gets to zero. The same relationship holds between d_2 and $N(d_2)$. Given a particular value of d_1 (or d_2), to calculate $N(d_1)$, you need a table showing the cumulative standard normal probabilities, or you can plug d_1 into the Excel function "=normsdist(d_1)."

A common intuitive interpretation of $N(d_1)$ and $N(d_2)$ is that they represent the risk-adjusted probabilities that the call will expire in the money. Therefore, the following is a verbal description of Equation 19.1: *The call option price equals the stock price minus the present value of the exercise price, adjusted for the probability that when the option expires, the stock price will exceed the strike price (i.e., the probability that the option expires in the money).*

Figure 19.1
Standard Normal Distribution
The expression $N(d_1)$ equals the probability of drawing a particular value, d_1, or a lower value from the standard normal distribution. In the figure, $N(d_1)$ is represented by the shaded portion under the bell curve. Because the normal distribution is symmetric about the mean, we can write $N(d_1) = 1 - N(-d_1)$. Appendix B provides a table of probabilities for the standard normal distribution.

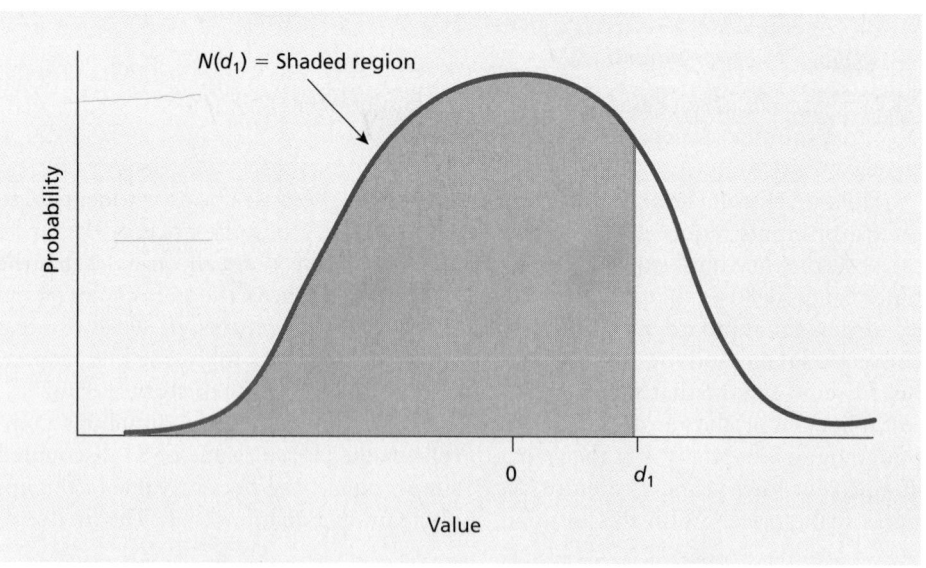

APPLYING THE MODEL 19.1

The stock of Cloverdale Food Processors currently sells for $40. A European call option on Cloverdale stock has an expiration date six months in the future and a strike price of $38. The estimate of the annual standard deviation of Cloverdale stock is 45 percent, and the risk-free rate is 6 percent. What is the call worth?

$$d_1 = \frac{\ln\left(\frac{40}{38}\right) + \left(0.06 + \frac{0.45^2}{2}\right)\frac{1}{2}}{0.45\sqrt{\frac{1}{2}}} = \frac{0.0513 + 0.0806}{0.3182} = 0.4146$$

$$d_2 = d_1 - \sigma\sqrt{t} = 0.4146 - 0.45\sqrt{\frac{1}{2}} = 0.0964$$

$$N(0.4146) = 0.6608 \qquad N(0.0964) = 0.5384$$

$$C = 40(0.6608) - 38(2.718^{-(0.06)(0.5)})(0.5384) = \$6.58$$

In Figure 19.2, the solid blue line shows how the call option's value changes as the stock price changes. The dashed line shows the standard call payoff diagram. When the stock price is far below the strike price, the values $N(d_1)$ and $N(d_2)$ will approach zero and so will the call price. As the stock price approaches the exercise price, the odds that the option will expire in the money increase, so the call price rises. Finally, when the stock price exceeds the strike price by a large amount, we can

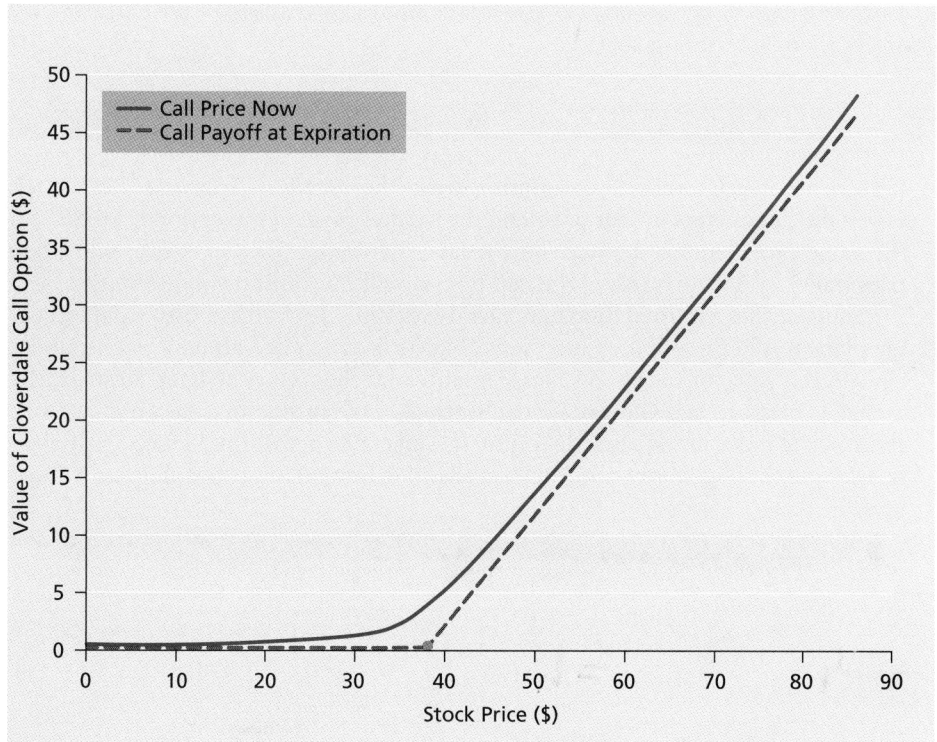

Figure 19.2
Black and Scholes Call Values for Cloverdale
The figure shows the Black and Scholes call price at different stock prices assuming the following:

the call's strike price is $38 ($x = 38$)

the option expires in 6 months ($t = \frac{1}{2}$)

the risk-free rate is 6% ($r = .06$)

the standard deviation of the stock is 45% ($\sigma = 0.45$)

$C = SN(d_1) - Xe^{-rt}N(d_2)$

be nearly certain that the option will expire in the money. In that case, $N(d_1)$ and $N(d_2)$ will be close to 1.0, and the call price will (almost) equal the stock price minus the present value of the strike price. Throughout the range of possible stock prices, the solid line is at least as high as the dotted line, and usually it is higher. This means that the option's market price is at least equal to its intrinsic value, and usually it exceeds intrinsic value. However, at the expiration date, the two lines would lie on top of each other.

Take another look at Figure 19.2, this time focusing on the slope of the solid line. That slope measures how much the call price changes as the underlying stock price changes. Options traders refer to this as the **option's delta,** and mathematically the delta equals the value $N(d_1)$ from the Black and Scholes equation. When a call option is far out of the money, the solid line in Figure 19.2 is almost flat and the option's delta is close to zero. This means that stock price movements have very little impact on the option's market value, which is not surprising because the odds are high that the option will expire worthless. Conversely, when the option is deep in the money, the slope of the solid line is almost 1.0 and so is the delta. The call's market price moves almost dollar for dollar with changes in the stock price. This makes sense too, because a deep-in-the-money option will almost certainly be exercised. That means the call option holder of will almost certainly own the stock eventually, so the option's value should fluctuate in line with the underlying stock.

We can use the concept of an option's delta to make another connection between the Black and Scholes and binomial models. In Chapter 18, we introduced the binomial model's three-step process to value options. The first step was to find a portfolio of stock and options with a risk-free payoff. We denoted the ratio of the number of options to the number of shares in this perfectly hedged portfolio with the symbol h, and we labeled that number the **hedge ratio.** In Black and Scholes' parlance, the ratio $1 \div N(d_1)$ is equivalent to the hedge ratio from the binomial model. This ratio tells options traders approximately how many options they need to offset the fluctuations of a single common share.

SMART CONCEPTS
See the concept explained step-by-step at
SMARTFinance

APPLYING THE MODEL 19.2

Let's revisit the Cloverdale call option from the previous Applying the Model. Given the parameters in that problem, the market price of the option is $6.58 and the value $N(d_1)$ equals 0.6608. This means that if the price of Cloverdale stock rises (falls) by $1, the price of the call option will rise (fall) by about $0.66.

Suppose that a mutual fund manager owns 100,000 shares of Cloverdale stock. He plans to sell these shares in a week, but he is concerned about a potential decline in the value of the shares between now and then. As a hedging strategy, the manager plans to sell Cloverdale call options. He reasons that because call and share prices move in the same direction, he can create a position that is nearly risk-free by purchasing shares and selling calls. But how many Cloverdale calls must he sell?

By taking the reciprocal of $N(d_1)$, the manager discerns that he needs to sell roughly 1.513 calls for each share in his portfolio, or 151,300 total, to construct the hedged position:

$$\frac{1}{N(d_1)} = \frac{1}{0.6608} = 1.513 = h$$

Now suppose that a week passes and Cloverdale's stock price has fallen from $40 to $38. This means the manager's stock portfolio has declined by $200,000

($2 per share x 100,000 shares). However, what has happened to the value of the options the manager sold? Use the Black and Scholes equation to calculate the option's price, except this time use $38 for the stock price and 0.48 years for the time until expiration (one week less than six months). The new call value is $5.20, so the call price dropped $1.38 during the week. Because the fund manager took a short position in call options, the decline in the call price represents a profit of $1.38 per call, or $208,794. That is, the fund manager received $6.58 per call when he sold them, and now a week later he can buy calls at the lower price to close out his position. Notice that the $208,794 net gain on the option trades almost perfectly offsets the $200,000 decline on the manager's Cloverdale stock. In other words, the manager created a hedged portfolio.

The Black and Scholes model was originally conceived to price a European call option on an underlying stock that paid no dividends. Applying the model when the underlying stock pays dividends requires a small adjustment. Holding all else constant, when a firm pays a dividend, the stock price will fall. This effect is largely neutral to shareholders, who experience a decline in their shares but also receive the dividend, but it clearly harms investors holding call options, who are not entitled to receive dividends. If investors expect a firm to pay a dividend during the life of a call, they will pay a lower price for the call than if they did not expect any dividends. A simple way to account for this in Equation 19.1 is to reduce the current stock price, S, by the present value of expected dividend payments. That adjustment makes sense because the current price of the stock overstates, by the amount of the dividend, the value of the underlying claim that option investors have the right to purchase.[4]

With a slight modification to Equation 19.1, we can use the Black and Scholes model to value puts rather than calls. To derive a Black and Scholes equation for a put option, we will use put-call parity. Remember, put-call parity establishes an equilibrium relationship between the price of a call option, C, a put option, P, the underlying stock, S, and a risk-free bond, $PV(X)$. Put-call parity states the following:

$$S + P = PV(X) + C$$

To put this expression in a form like the Black and Scholes model, replace the term $PV(X)$ with Xe^{-rt}, move the symbol for the stock price to the right-hand side, and replace the symbol for the call price with Equation 19.1. After these steps, we have the following:

$$P = Xe^{-rt} + [SN(d_1) - Xe^{-rt} N(d_2)] - S$$

With a little algebraic manipulation, we obtain the following put option formula:

$$P = Xe^{-rt}[1 - N(d_2)] - S[1 - N(d_1)] \qquad \text{(Eq. 19.3)}$$

Black + Scholes model for a put

where d_1 and d_2 have the same definitions as in Equation 19.2. Notice how the terms in this equation have reversed compared to their placement in Equation 19.1. Intuitively, we understand that the terms in the equation switch positions because the

---

[4.] Option investors have the right to buy a claim on all the firm's future cash flows, except for the dividend that will be paid before the option expires. Fenn and Liang (2001) find a negative correlation between a firm's dividend payout and the quantity of stock options held by the firm's managers, and a positive correlation between managerial option holdings and the firm's share repurchase activity. It seems that managers are well aware that paying dividends decreases option values, whereas repurchasing shares, if it increases the stock price, increases option values.

circumstances in which a put option is in the money are precisely opposite those that dictate when a call option is in the money. For the same reason, the probabilities $N(d_1)$ and $N(d_2)$ from Equation 19.1 switch in Equation 19.3 to $1 - N(d_1)$ and $1 - N(d_2)$.

The solid blue line in Figure 19.3 illustrates how put prices change as the underlying stock price changes. The shape of this line is, in many respects, the mirror image of the line in Figure 19.2 for calls. As the stock price falls, the put value increases; as the stock price rises, the put value approaches zero.[5] Unlike a call option, a put option does not always sell for more than its intrinsic value. When the stock price is low, the put value falls below intrinsic value (the dashed line). The interpretation of this phenomenon is as follows. When the stock price is very low, the option holder is almost certain to exercise the option, receiving the strike price in cash. However, because this is a European option, the investor must wait to exercise the option until it expires. The amount by which the option's price falls below its intrinsic value represents the time value of money the investor loses by having to wait until expiration to exercise the option.

One of the most interesting aspects of the Black and Scholes equation is what it does not contain—the expected return on the underlying stock. In other words, it is not necessary to know what return investors expect on the underlying stock to determine an option's price. This, too, has a parallel in the binomial model. Remember

Figure 19.3
Black and Scholes
Put Values
*The figure shows the
Black and Scholes put
price at different stock
prices assuming the
following:*

the call's strike price
is $38 ($x = 38$)

the option expires in
6 months ($t = \frac{1}{2}$)

the risk-free rate is 6%
($r = .06$)

the standard deviation
of the stock is 45%
($\sigma = 0.45$)

$P = Xe^{-rt} \times$
$[1 - N(d_2) - S(1 - N(d_1))]$

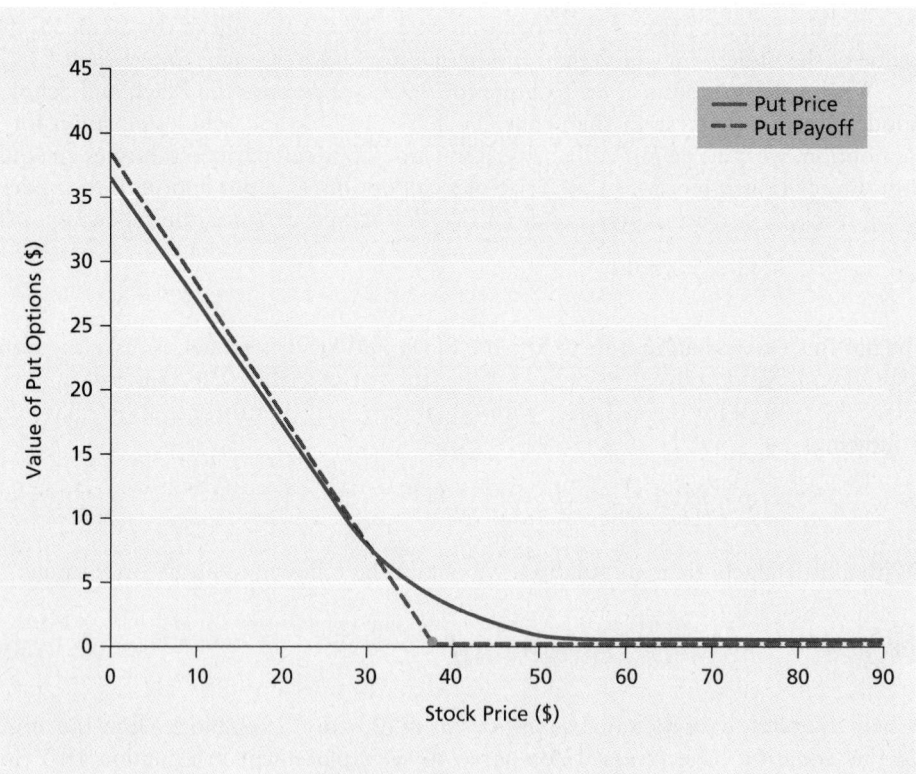

5. As in Figure 19.2, when the stock price is very low, $N(d_1)$ and $N(d_2)$ are close to zero. Consequently, the terms $1 - N(d_1)$ and $1 - N(d_2)$ in the put pricing equation become very close to 1.0, and the put value approaches the present value of the strike price minus the stock price. At high stock prices, $N(d_1)$ and $N(d_2)$ get close to 1.0, so $1 - N(d_1)$ and $1 - N(d_2)$ approach zero, as does the put value.

that the binomial model begins with an assumption about up and down movements in the underlying stock, but the model does not make any assumption about the probabilities of those up and down movements. The binomial and Black and Scholes models both depend on the notion that traders can combine options and shares to create a risk-free portfolio, so the future direction of the underlying asset does not enter the pricing mechanics.

VOLATILITY

The Black and Scholes model requires five inputs, four of which can be readily observed in the market. Only the underlying stock's volatility remains uncertain. For companies whose stocks have traded in the public markets for a long time, plenty of historical data exist that analysts can use to estimate volatility, an exercise illustrated in the appendix to this chapter. Even so, what is relevant for option pricing is the volatility of the underlying asset over the life of the option. Estimates of volatility obtained from historical data, even fairly recent data, may or may not be good predictors of the future.

In Chapter 6, we discussed issues that analysts face when they use historical data to estimate a stock's variance or its covariance with other stocks, and those same issues apply here. When the stock of interest trades frequently in a liquid market, analysts can gather a reasonably large sample using daily data. Daily data offer the advantage of being the most recent information available. However, when trading in a stock is thin, daily data can generate misleading signals about a security's true volatility; in that case, using weekly or monthly data to estimate volatility may be preferable.[6]

Pricing an option using Black and Scholes requires an estimate of the underlying stock's volatility. However, if traders can observe the market price of an option directly, they can "invert" the Black and Scholes equation to calculate the volatility implied by the option's market price. The value of σ obtained in this manner is called an option's **implied volatility.**

APPLYING THE MODEL 19.3

In the previous chapter, we saw that the market price of an April Intel call option with $X = \$25.00$ was $2.40. Suppose that at the time the option was trading at that price, it had four months (approximately one-third of a year) remaining before expiration. The risk-free rate at that time was 3.5 percent and the price of Intel stock was $26.38. Given these values, we can use a computer to find the value of σ that would generate a Black and Scholes call value of $2.40. In this case, the implied volatility of the April Intel call is 24 percent.[7]

Of course, traders cannot use an option's implied volatility to calculate its price because they have to know the price to calculate implied volatility. In other words, traders can use the Black and Scholes equation, along with an estimate of the stock's

---

[6] Estimating volatility is a thorny issue that has occupied researchers both in academia and in the research departments of investment banks. For a few seminal works in this field, see Cox and Ross (1976), Engle (1982), Bollerslev (1986), and Hull and White (1987).

[7] Intel stock usually pays a dividend in February, but in 2005 the dividend amount was just $0.08, small enough to have a negligible impact on these calculations.

volatility, to estimate the price of an option; or, if traders know the price of the option, they can use Black and Scholes to find the volatility implied by that price.

Of what practical value is an option's implied volatility if you must first know the option's price to calculate its implied volatility? One application is to use implied volatilities to test the accuracy of the Black and Scholes model. For example, suppose that several call options with different strike prices but the same expiration date trade on the same underlying stock. If we can observe the market prices of these options, then we can determine each option's implied volatility. The Black and Scholes model predicts that the implied volatilities will be identical because all the options share the same underlying asset. If a systematic pattern between an option's strike price and its implied volatility exists, then the Black and Scholes model does not price options correctly at all strike prices.

Early tests of Black and Scholes found that options with the same underlying stock indeed had different implied volatilities, which varied with the exercise price.[8] In particular, the implied volatilities of out-of-the-money options seemed much higher than the implied volatilities of at-the-money options. Further tests found that the option prices generated by Black and Scholes were close to actual market prices for at-the-money options, but pricing errors were more substantial for out-of-the-money options.

The existence of a relationship between an option's implied volatility and its strike price affects option-trading practices in several ways. Some traders adopt speculative strategies to try to exploit differences in implied volatility for a single underlying asset. For example, we know that the value of a call option rises with the volatility of the underlying stock. Therefore, one might argue that when two options on the same underlying stock have very different implied volatilities, the option with high implied volatility is overpriced and the option with low implied volatility is underpriced. Traders who hold this belief can take a short position in the first option and a long position in the second to try to profit from any pricing discrepancies. A slightly more sophisticated version of this technique begins by estimating the volatility of an underlying stock by taking a weighted average of the implied volatilities of several options on that stock. The weights might be a function of how close the stock's market price is to the option's strike price, or they might depend on the volume of trading at each strike price. The implied volatilities of some options will naturally be above the weighted average, and others will fall below the average. Traders take speculative long positions in the options with below-average implied volatilities and short positions in those with above-average implied volatilities.

Why have we invested so much time on valuing ordinary call and put options, given that only a small fraction of business school students become professional options traders? The answer is that options are everywhere, embedded in other corporate securities as well as in capital investment projects. The methods used to price call and put options have much wider applications than it may at first appear.

SMART PRACTICES VIDEO

Myron Scholes, Stanford University, and Chairman of Oak Hill Platinum Partners
"Implied volatility is measured by inverting the Black-Scholes model."

See the entire interview at
SMARTFinance

Concept Review Questions

1. What do the Black and Scholes and binomial models have in common? What are their main differences?

2. Examine Figure 19.2. When the stock price is very high, the two lines in the figure are virtually parallel. Why?

[8.] See Black (1975), MacBeth and Merville (1979), and Emanuel and MacBeth (1982). Researchers found that plotting implied volatility on the *y*-axis and the strike price on the *x*-axis resulted in a slightly U-shaped pattern dubbed the *volatility smile*.

**Concept
Review
Questions**

3. Look again at Figure 19.2, especially at the portion where the stock price is high. At a given stock price (for example, $70 in the figure), what is the approximate vertical distance between these two lines? In other words, when the call option is deep in the money, what is the difference between the call option's price and its intrinsic value?

4. Using your answer to the previous question as a guide, what happens to the market price of a call option if the risk-free rate increases?

5. Given that options are very risky securities, why do we use the risk-free rate in the Black and Scholes equation?

19.2 OPTIONS EMBEDDED IN OTHER SECURITIES

PLAIN-VANILLA STOCKS AND BONDS

Casual observers of financial markets sometimes argue that bonds are boring compared to the more exotic world of options. After all, what's exciting about an investment that pays a fixed cash flow at regular intervals for a fixed amount of time? In fact, corporate bonds do have something in common with options. When a firm borrows money, it has the option to default on its loans if cash flow is insufficient to repay the debt. The default option explains why corporate bonds must offer higher yields than government bonds.

Suppose that a company has $250 million in equity financing and $250 million in 3-year, zero-coupon bonds with a current market value of $200 million. The company plans to invest $450 million in cash in an asset of some kind, and it hopes that the asset's future cash flows will be sufficient to offer attractive returns to both stockholders and bondholders. However, both bondholders and stockholders know that if the cash flows are not sufficient even to pay bondholders their $250 million at maturity, the firm can walk away from its debts, leaving bondholders to claim whatever cash they can by selling off the firm's remaining assets.

Figure 19.4 shows that the position occupied by bondholders in this example is identical to that of investors holding a combination of risk-free bonds and a short put option. The lower graph in the figure shows a payoff diagram for the firm's bondholders. The underlying asset in this graph is not the value of common stock, as we have grown used to, but the value of the firm's total assets in three years, when the bonds mature. When the value of assets is high, bondholders receive the $250 million they were promised and no more. When the value of assets is low, bondholders receive less than $250 million. How much less depends on the value of the remaining assets.

The upper portion of the figure shows the payoffs from a hypothetical portfolio containing a long position in risk-free government bonds with a face value of $250 million and a short position in put options with a strike price of $250 million. As before, the underlying asset for the put option is not the firm's stock, but the firm's assets. Because bondholders are, in effect, selling this put option to the firm, if the firm's assets turn out to be worth less than $250 million, the firm will give the assets to the bondholders for $250 million in cash.[9] The net cash flow to bondholders will equal

---

[9]. When firms go bankrupt, bondholders do not usually pay out cash in exchange for the firm's assets. They do something equivalent, however. A bankrupt firm can hand over its assets to lenders, and in exchange the shareholders of the firm can walk away from their debts. In other words, receiving a cash payment of $250 million is equivalent, in economic terms, to having an outstanding debt of $250 million canceled.

Figure 19.4
Options Embedded in
Ordinary Corporate
Bonds
*Corporate bond inves-
tors hold a position that
is equivalent to a port-
folio of risk-free debt
and a short put option.
If the firm's assets are
not sufficient to repay
its debt at maturity, then
the firm puts its assets
to the bondholders.*

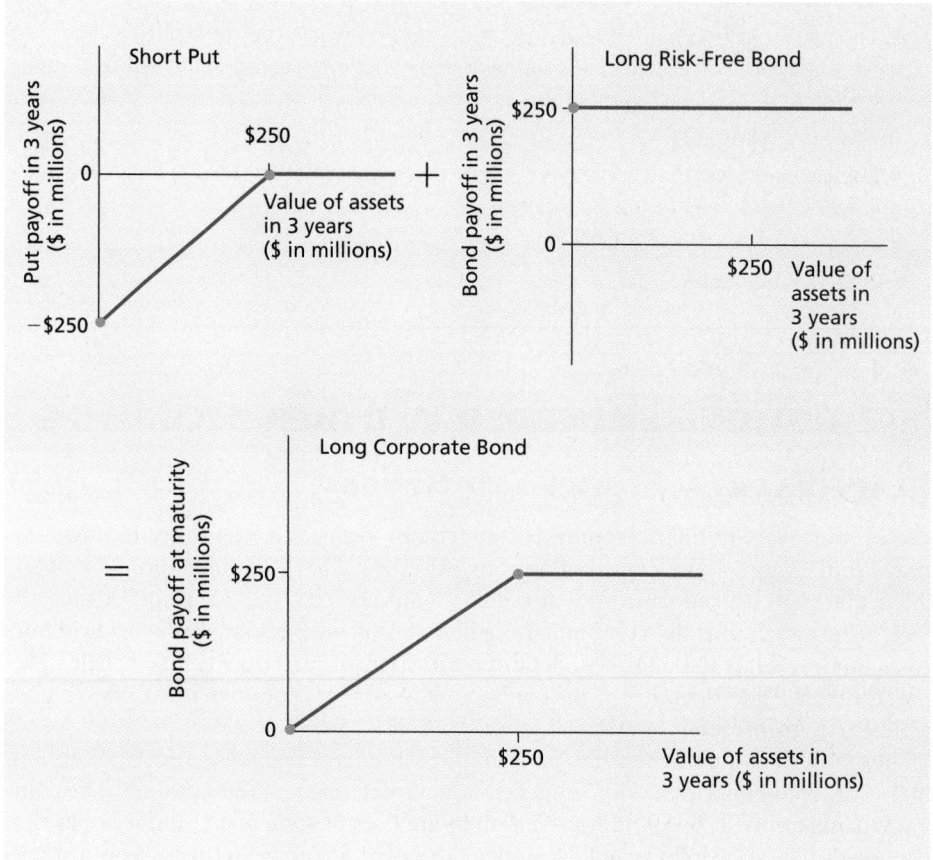

the $250 million they earn on risk-free bonds, minus any losses they incur on the put option.

In principle, it is possible to quantify the value of the put option that bondholders in effect sell to shareholders. To do so requires an estimate of the volatility of the firm's assets. Depending on what assets the firm invests in, such an estimate may or may not be difficult to obtain. However, there is another way to place a value on the put option. If holding a risky corporate bond is identical to holding a risk-free bond and selling a put option, then we can calculate the put value by simply comparing the market value of the firm's debt to the market value of identical bonds that are risk free. The difference in prices must equal the put value:

$$\text{Value of risky debt} = \text{value of risk-free debt} - \text{put value} \qquad \text{(Eq. 19.4)}$$

APPLYING THE MODEL 19.4

The market value of this firm's outstanding bonds is $200 million, implying that they offer investors a yield to maturity of 7.72 percent. If the yield to maturity on 3-year government bonds is just 6 percent, the $250 million face value of zero-coupon government bonds would sell today for $250 million/$1.06^3$, or $210 million. The $10 million difference equals the value of the put option on the firm's assets—that is, the default option.

Now, let's consider all this from the perspective of shareholders. When the firm borrows $250 million, shareholders know that if the firm cannot repay the loan, they will receive nothing. However, if cash flows are more than sufficient to pay bondholders $250 million, then shareholders receive any excess cash. Figure 19.5 shows a payoff diagram for shareholders. As always, the underlying asset is the value of the firm's assets in three years. Do you recognize this picture? From the shareholders' point of view, they own a claim that is equivalent to a long call option on the underlying assets with a strike price of $250 million.

Figure 19.5 contains some unsettling news for bondholders. Suppose that the objective of this firm's management is to maximize the wealth of shareholders. If holding a share of stock in this company is like holding a call option, then maximizing the share price should be analogous to maximizing the value of a call option. What actions might managers take to maximize the call value? We have seen that a critical factor in determining option values is the volatility of the underlying asset. Managers could increase share prices by increasing the volatility of the firm's assets. Once the firm has outstanding debt, its stock behaves like a call option, so making riskier investments benefits shareholders at the expense of bondholders.

If it seems far-fetched that managers would intentionally take more risk to increase share values, we offer two pieces of evidence that we will hope will persuade you that managers recognize this opportunity. The first piece of evidence is somewhat indirect. When companies enter loan contracts with banks and other lenders, the companies must often agree to abide by a set of loan covenants designed to protect lenders by, among other things, restricting the uses to which firms can apply borrowed funds. If lenders did not worry that firms might borrow to make risky investments (actually, to make riskier investments than they disclosed when they borrowed the money), then there would be no reason for lenders to insist on covenants of this type.

The second piece of evidence is much more direct. In an interesting study, Berger, Ofek, and Yermack (1997) examined the connection between firms' compensation plans and their capital structures. They reasoned as follows. Suppose that a firm

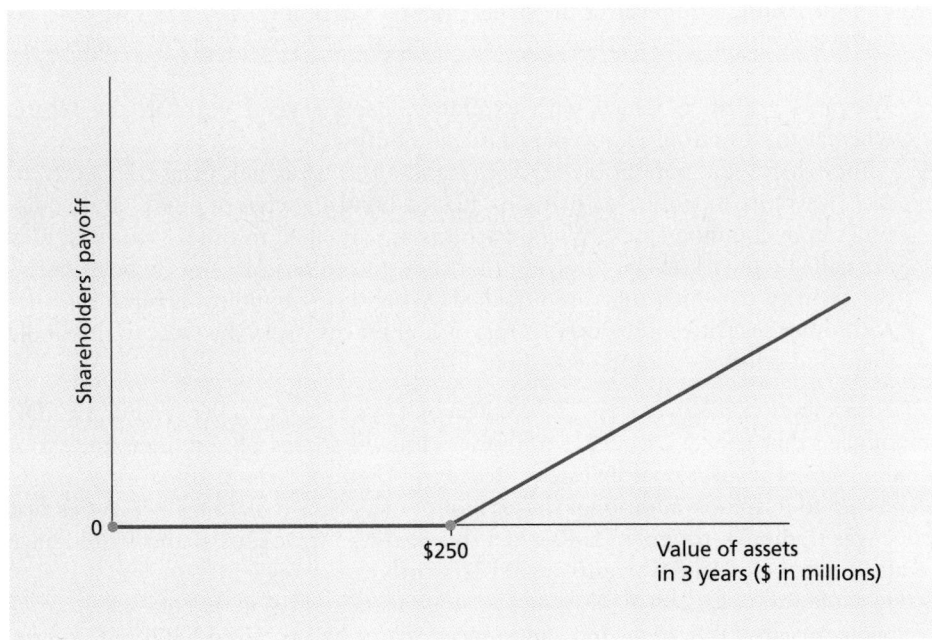

Figure 19.5
Options Embedded in the Stock of a Levered Firm
The shareholders of a levered firm hold a call option. If the firm's assets are worth more than the value of its debts, then shareholders keep the surplus. If not, shareholders receive nothing when the firm defaults.

chooses to emphasize stock options in the compensation package it offers managers. Managers know that the value of these options depends on several factors, one of which is the volatility of the underlying stock. Therefore, managers who receive a great deal of pay in the form of stock options have the incentive not only to increase the price of the stock, but also to increase its volatility. One way to increase the volatility of equity is to use more debt in the capital structure. Berger, Ofek, and Yermack found a positive correlation between the number of stock options held by a firm's CEO and the firm's debt-to-assets ratio. Though a correlation between option compensation and leverage does not prove that managers increase leverage after receiving stock options, it is at least consistent with that hypothesis. In a similar vein, Rajgopal and Shevlin (2002) find that managers of oil and gas firms with employee stock options take greater exploration risks and engage in less hedging than managers without stock options.

Even plain-vanilla investments such as stocks and corporate bonds have option-like characteristics. Recognizing these characteristics provides unique insights into the forces that influence stock and bond prices as well as relationships between borrowers and lenders and between managers and shareholders. Now we turn our attention to other types of corporate securities that have more transparent option features.

WARRANTS

Warrants are securities issued by firms that grant the right to buy shares of stock at a fixed price for a given period of time. Warrants bear a close resemblance to call options, and the same five factors that influence call option values will also affect warrant prices (stock price, risk-free rate, strike price, expiration date, and volatility). However, there are some important differences between warrants and calls.

1. Warrants are issued by firms, whereas call options are contracts between investors who are not necessarily connected to the firm whose stock serves as the underlying asset.
2. When investors exercise warrants, the number of outstanding shares increases and the issuing firm receives the strike price as a cash inflow. When investors exercise call options, no change in outstanding shares occurs and the firm receives no cash.
3. Warrants are often issued with expiration dates several years in the future, whereas most options expire in just a few months.
4. Although call and put options trade as stand-alone securities, firms frequently attach warrants to public or privately placed bonds, preferred stock, and sometimes even common stock. When warrants are attached to other securities, they are called **equity kickers,** implying that they give additional upside potential to the security to which they are attached. When firms bundle warrants together with other securities, they may or may not grant investors the right to unbundle them and sell the warrants separately.

For example, on November 7, 2005, Beacon Power Corp. (ticker symbol, BCON) announced that it had issued 9.9 million additional shares of common stock to a small group of institutional investors. Beacon also granted these investors warrants to buy up to 3 million additional shares at a price of $2.21. Because Beacon's stock price was trading at roughly $1.80 when this deal was struck, its shares would have to appreciate before the warrants would be worth exercising.

Just a few days earlier, on November 3, the tiny Canadian maker of "smart card" payment devices, QI Systems Inc., announced that it had received $206,666 in proceeds from the exercise of warrants that it issued as part of an equity sale two years earlier. These warrants gave investors the right to buy QI Systems shares for $0.20 each. With the firms' shares trading around $0.30 in November 2005, exercising the warrants allowed investors to buy shares at a below-market price.

In each case, the firm receives capital from warrants, once when they are issued and again if they are exercised. This stands in sharp contrast to the buying, selling, and exercising of call options, which occurs without having any direct cash flow impact on the underlying firms. Nevertheless, the Black and Scholes model can be used to value warrants, provided an adjustment is made to account for the dilution that occurs when firms issue new shares to warrant holders. A simple example will illustrate how to adjust for dilution.

Assume that a small firm has 1,000 shares outstanding worth $10 each. The firm has no debt, so the value of its assets equals the value of its equity, $10,000. Two years ago, when the firm's stock price was just $8, the firm issued 100 shares of common stock to a private investor. Each share had an attached warrant granting the right to purchase one share of stock for $9 for two years. The warrants are about to expire, and the investor intends to exercise them.

What would the investor's payoff be if he held ordinary call options (sold to him by another private investor) rather than warrants? Because the price of the stock is $10 and the strike price is $9, the investor would earn a profit of $1 per share, or $100 on the calls. If calls were exercised, the firm would still have 100 shares outstanding worth $10 each. From the firm's point of view, the call exercise would generate neither a cash inflow nor a cash outflow.

In contrast, if the investor exercises his warrants, two changes take place. First, the firm receives cash equal to the strike price ($9) times the number of warrants exercised (100), or a total inflow of $900. This raises the total value of the firm's assets to $10,900. Simultaneously, the firm's outstanding shares increase from 1,000 to 1,100, so the new price per share can be calculated as follows:

$$\text{New price per share} = \frac{\$10,900}{1,100} = \$9.91$$

The investor's payoff on the warrants is just $0.91, compared to $1.00 on a comparable call option. Fortunately, it's easy to use the Black and Scholes model to value a call option with characteristics similar to those of a warrant and then multiply the call value times an adjustment factor for dilution. If N_1 represents the number of "old shares" outstanding and N_2 represents the number of new shares issued as a result of the warrants being exercised, then the price of the warrants equals the price of an identical call option, $C, multiplied by the following dilution factor, $N_1/(N_1 + N_2)$:

(Eq. 19.5)

$$\text{Warrant value} = \$C\left(\frac{N_1}{N_1 + N_2}\right)$$

APPLYING THE MODEL 19.5

UQM Technologies recently sold 1,160,095 common shares to investors. For every five shares of common stock that an investor purchased, the investor received one warrant to buy an additional UQM share for $5.73. After this offering, UQM had 18,829,848 shares of common stock outstanding. We will use the Black and Scholes formula and the adjustment factor in Equation 19.5 to value UQM's warrants. To value the warrants, we must know the price of UQM stock, the expiration date of the warrants, the strike price, and the risk-free rate. We must also have an estimate of UQM's volatility. Here are the relevant figures: stock price = $4.40; strike price = $5.73; risk-free rate = 2 percent; expiration = two years; standard deviation = 77 percent.[10]

$$d_1 = \frac{\ln\left(\dfrac{4.40}{5.73}\right) + \left(0.02 + \dfrac{0.77^2}{2}\right)2}{0.77\sqrt{2}} = \frac{(-0.264) + (0.633)}{1.089} = 0.339$$

$$d_2 = d_1 - \sigma\sqrt{t} = 0.339 - 1.089 = -0.750$$

$$N(0.339) = 0.633 \qquad N(-0.750) = 0.226$$

$$C = 4.40(0.633) - 5.73(2.718^{-(.02)(2)})(0.226) = \$1.54$$

$$\text{Warrant} = \frac{18,829,848}{18,829,848 + 232,019}(1.54) = \$1.52$$

The warrants in this transaction acted as a "sweetener" because for each share that an investor purchased, that investor received one-fifth of a warrant, worth about $0.30.

CONVERTIBLES

A convertible bond grants investors the right to receive payment in the shares of an underlying stock rather than in cash. Usually, the stock that investors have the right to "purchase" in exchange for their bonds is the stock of the firm that issued the bonds. In some cases, however, a firm that owns a large amount of common stock in a different firm will use those shares as the underlying asset for a convertible bond issue. In either case, a **convertible bond** is essentially an ordinary corporate bond with an attached call option or warrant.

In February 2002, the biotech giant, Amgen Inc., announced a sale of 30-year, zero-coupon bonds that would generate proceeds for the company of approximately $2.5 billion. Amgen's bonds offered investors a yield to maturity of just 1.125 percent, well below the yields on long-term government bonds at the time. How could a biotech firm borrow money at a lower rate than the government? Investors were willing to buy Amgen's bonds despite the low yield because the bonds were convertible into Amgen common stock. Specifically, each Amgen bond having a face value of $1,000 could be converted into 8.8601 shares of Amgen common stock.

Convertible bonds offer investors the security of a bond and the upside potential of common stock. If Amgen's shares increase in value, the bondholders will redeem their bonds for Amgen shares rather than cash. To see how far Amgen's shares would

---

[10.] We estimated the 77 percent figure for standard deviation based on daily trading data over the preceding three months. See the appendix at the end of the chapter for the calculation.

have to rise before bondholders would want to convert, we must first calculate the market price of Amgen's bonds:

$$\text{Price} = \frac{\$1,000}{(1.01125)^{30}} = \$714.90$$

The **conversion ratio** defines how many Amgen shares bondholders will receive if they convert. In this case, the conversion ratio is 8.8601; so if bondholders chose to convert immediately, they would effectively be paying a **conversion price** or Amgen calculated as follows:

$$\text{Conversion price} = \frac{\$714.90}{8.8601} = \$80.69$$

At the time Amgen issued these bonds, its stock was selling for approximately $57 per share. Holding the price of the bond constant, Amgen's shares would have to rise more than 41 percent before bondholders would want to convert their bonds into Amgen's shares. This 41 percent figure equals the bond's **conversion premium.** At present, it does not make sense for holders of Amgen's convertible bonds to trade them for shares of stock. Nevertheless, we can still ask what value bondholders will receive if they do convert. If Amgen stock sells for $57 and each bond can be exchanged for 8.8601 shares, the conversion value of one bond equals $505.03 (8.8601 × $57). **Conversion value** is important because it helps define a lower bound on the market value of a convertible bond. For example, suppose that interest rates jump suddenly and the yield on Amgen's bonds goes from 1.125 percent to 2.5 percent. Ignoring the opportunity to convert the bonds, the price would drop as follows:

$$\text{Price} = \frac{\$1,000}{(1.025)^{30}} = \$476.74$$

However, the price of Amgen's bonds cannot dip this low if Amgen's stock remains at $57. If it did drop, investors could exploit an arbitrage opportunity by purchasing one bond for $476.74 and immediately converting it into 8.8601 shares of stock worth $505.03.

In general, we can say that the price of a convertible bond will be, at a minimum, the higher of (1) the value of an identical bond without conversion rights or (2) the conversion value. Figure 19.6 demonstrates this pattern for a generic convertible bond with a par value of $1,000 and a conversion ratio of 20. The horizontal line represents the present value of the convertible bond's scheduled interest and principal payments, which, for convenience, we assume to be $1,000. The upward-sloping line shows the bond's conversion value at different stock prices, and the curve shows the convertible bond's price. When the stock price is very low, the odds that the bonds will ever be worth converting into shares are low, so the convertible bond sells at a price comparable to that of an ordinary bond. As the share price rises, the value of the conversion option increases.

Most convertible bonds have another feature that complicates matters slightly. When firms issue convertibles, they almost always retain the right to call back the bonds. When firms call their outstanding bonds, bondholders can choose, within 30 days of the call, to receive either the call price in cash or a quantity of shares equal

Figure 19.6
The Value of a
Convertible Bond
*The convertible bond
must sell for at least
its value as a straight
bond or its conversion
value, whichever is
greater. If the bond's
value is $1,000 and the
conversion ratio is 20,
then the conversion
price equals $50. For
each $1 increase in the
stock price beyond $50,
the bond's conversion
value rises by $20.*

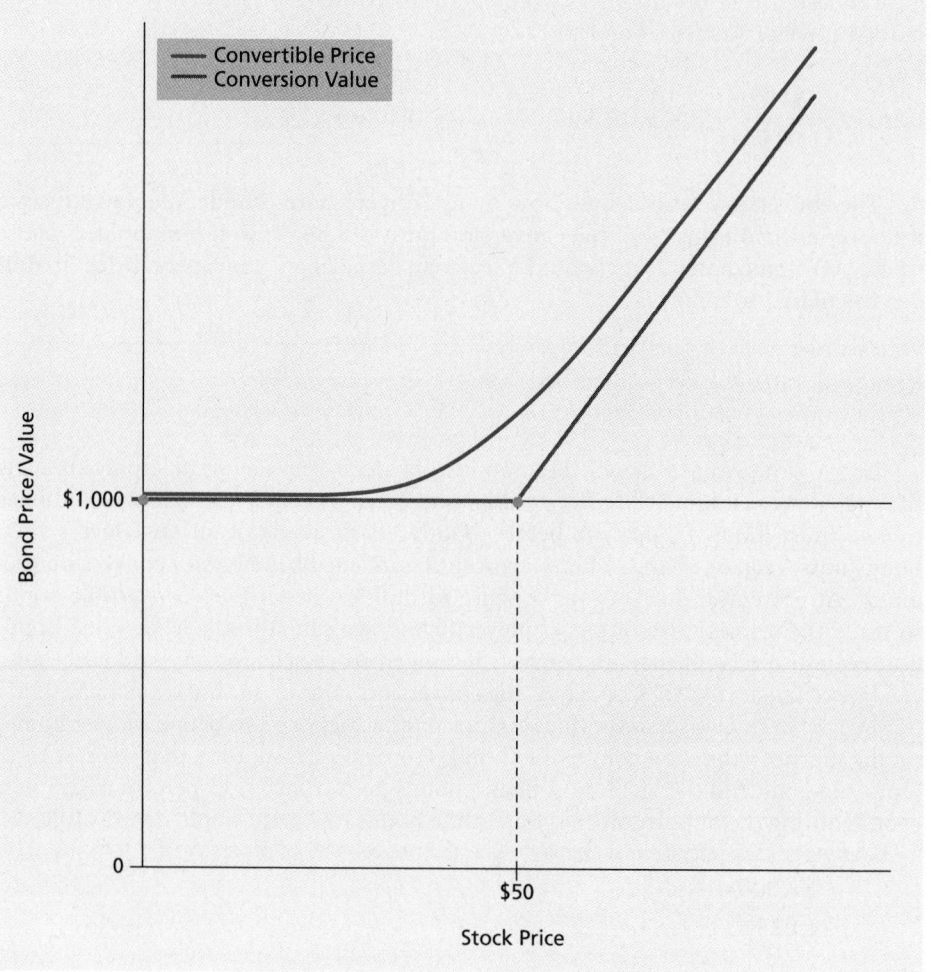

to the conversion ratio. Effectively, the call option that firms retain allows them to shorten the conversion option held by bondholders. If a firm calls its bonds, investors will choose cash if the call price exceeds conversion value, and they will choose shares if the opposite is true.

Under what circumstances should a firm call its convertible bonds? If managers are acting in the interests of shareholders, they will never call bonds that are worth less than the call price. Doing so would transfer wealth from shareholders to bondholders. Similarly, if the price of a bond rises above the call price, because the underlying stock has increased in value, then firms should call the bonds. If the firm does not call the bonds and the stock price continues to increase, then when investors ultimately choose to convert their bonds into shares, the firm will be selling stock at a bargain. Again, the result is a transfer of wealth from shareholders to bondholders. Therefore, the optimal policy is to call the bonds when their market value equals the call price.[11]

[11.] Actually, this would be the optimal call policy if firms could force investors to choose cash or shares immediately upon receiving the call. However, because investors have 30 days to decide whether they want cash or shares, the optimal time

Convertible securities come in many flavors, and each flavor usually has its own colorful acronym. For example, LYONs (liquid-yield option notes) are zero-coupon bonds, convertible into the shares of the issuing firm, which are both callable by the issuer and putable by the investors. When a bond is putable, investors have the right to force the issuer to redeem their bonds in cash. DECS (debt exchangeable for common shares) are convertibles that automatically convert to shares at a future date. The conversion ratio of DECS can be variable, such that bondholders must endure the downside risk of the underlying stock, but they do not necessarily enjoy all the upside potential. LYONs, DECS, and other exotic convertibles usually offer investors an interest rate higher than the dividend yield on the underlying stock.[12] Recently, several Internet companies issued a new type of convertible bond named *death spiral* convertibles, as described in Hillion and Vermaelen (2002). These convertible bonds promise lenders a fixed dollar amount of shares, which in turn implies a variable conversion ratio. If the underlying share price falls, the only way to pay lenders a fixed dollar amount of shares is to convert their bonds into more shares. However, as with warrants, convertible bonds create dilution. The name *death spiral* comes from the possibility that as a firm's share price declines and it issues more shares to convertible bondholders, the subsequent dilution will force share prices even lower.

The lesson from this section is that many types of securities issued by corporations have embedded options, and understanding the characteristics of these options is central to pricing the securities with which they are bundled. But an even broader application of option-pricing theory has developed since the mid-1980s, one that is gaining ground in the corporate world: real options—applying the theoretical apparatus developed for financial options to real investment projects with option-like qualities.

Concept Review Questions

6. Using option-pricing logic, explain why debt covenants often restrict firms from taking out additional loans without the initial lender's consent.

7. Firms wanting to save on borrowing costs should always issue convertible bonds because investors will buy them even though they offer lower yields than ordinary bonds. Comment on this statement.

8. After issuing warrants, what actions might a firm take that would be to the detriment of warrant holders?

19.3 OPTIONS EMBEDDED IN CAPITAL INVESTMENTS—REAL OPTIONS

In Chapters 7 and 9, we learned that the *NPV* rule does not always lead to value-maximizing decisions when firms are considering major investment proposals. The reason is that the *NPV* approach fails to capture the value of managerial flexibility

---

to call may be when the market value of the bonds exceeds the call price slightly. The reason is that if the firm calls the bonds precisely when the market price hits the call price, the stock price might fall during the 30-day decision period. A decline in the stock price would lower the conversion value, and the firm would be forced to redeem the bonds for cash. Allowing the conversion value of the bonds to rise a little beyond the strike price gives the firm a little "slack." See Asquith (1995).

[12.] For a discussion of LYONs, see McConnell and Schwartz (1992).

as the passing of time resolves uncertainty surrounding a particular investment. Managers usually have the option to abandon or to expand an initial investment, and that flexibility often adds to a project's value above and beyond its *NPV*. Smart managers understand this intuitively; but in recent years, tools have emerged that help quantify and refine this intuition.

In this section, we show how to calculate the option value of two capital investment projects. In the first example, which involves oil extraction, we will use the Black and Scholes model to show that oil-drilling rights have value even when it is not economic to drill right away. In the second example, we will use the binomial model to quantify the value to McDonald's Corporation of a pilot investment in a new type of storefront, McTreat Spot.

THE OPTION VALUE OF DRILLING RIGHTS

Let's return to a problem we studied briefly in Chapter 9. A company has the opportunity to bid for drilling rights for one year on a tract of land. The cost of extracting the oil is $50 per barrel, and the current (and expected future) price of oil is $45 per barrel. Because drilling has a negative contribution margin, an *NPV* calculation says that the drilling rights have negative value.

Adding a little more structure to this problem, suppose that the annual standard deviation of the price of oil is 30 percent. Given this volatility, a firm contemplating a bid for the drilling rights can expect that at some point the price of oil may rise to a level that makes drilling profitable. But without knowing when or how high the price of oil may rise, how can the firm quantify the value of the opportunity to drill only when oil prices are sufficiently high?

The right to drill oil is like a call option. By paying the exercise price of $50, the firm has the right to receive one barrel of oil. The option lasts for one year, until drilling rights expire. Adding the assumption that the risk-free rate equals 4 percent, we can value this option using the Black and Scholes model:

$$d_1 = \frac{\ln\left(\frac{45}{50}\right) + \left(0.04 + \frac{0.30^2}{2}\right)1}{0.30\sqrt{1}} = -0.0679$$

$$d_2 = d_1 - \sigma\sqrt{t} = -0.3679$$

$$N(-0.0679) = 0.4729 \qquad N(-0.3679) = 0.3565$$

$$C = 45(0.4729) - 50(2.718^{-(.04)(1)})(0.3565) = \$4.16$$

The value of drilling rights equals $4.16 per barrel, so the firm can determine its bid by multiplying this value times the number of barrels expected in the field. If there are fixed costs of drilling above and beyond the $50 extraction costs, bidding makes sense only if the total option value exceeds the fixed costs.

Without question, this problem represents an oversimplification of a real-world drilling-rights problem. For example, the Black and Scholes calculation assumes that the option exercise occurs on a single date one year in the future. In reality, a firm can decide to pump oil at any time during the year, and it can stop pumping once it has started if the price of oil falls. Modeling this flexibility requires a complex binomial tree, one in which the price of oil moves a little bit each week over the option's life. A complete binomial tree like this will show many different paths that oil prices might take. At each point on each path, the firm must decide whether to begin pumping oil or, if they are already pumping at that point in the tree, whether to stop. Because the binomial valuation approach recognizes that managers have a higher degree of flexibility than contemplated in the Black and Scholes calculation, we expect that a binomial analysis would lead to an option above our current estimate of $4.16 per barrel. Even so, the Black and Scholes model offers a "first cut" at estimating the option value of drilling rights, and it leads the firm to a different conclusion than it would reach from *NPV* analysis alone.

MINI-CASE: REAL OPTIONS AT MCDONALD'S— MCTREAT SPOT [13]

McDonald's Corporation is constantly looking for ways to grow its U.S. business by leveraging its various hamburger-chain strengths (brand management, inventory and cost control, location development, etc.) into new non-hamburger-store formats. One concept currently under consideration (June 2006) is the McTreat Spot.

The idea behind McTreat Spot is to provide potential customers with convenient places to satisfy their sweet tooth. The current vision of a McTreat Spot is a small kiosk located in high-traffic/high-volume locations like airport concourses and shopping malls, offering ice cream and frozen yogurt products such as sundaes and milkshakes.

There are many uncertainties involved with this new concept. First of all, the company is unsure whether these very small storefronts in high-rent areas can achieve sufficient sales to cover costs and provide a return on capital. Perhaps more important, it is unclear whether customers would like to purchase McDonald's dessert products outside of McDonald's existing stores when faced with specialty-store alternatives (TCBY, Ben & Jerry's, etc.). Finally, as is true in all of McDonald's businesses, there is uncertainty about the overall economy; McDonald's management believes that the McTreat Spot enterprise value will be sensitive to the overall state of the economy.

Faced with this uncertainty, McDonald's Corporation has decided to test the new store format in selected shopping malls, the Minneapolis Airport, the Circus-Circus Casino in Las Vegas, and even a few Blockbuster Video outlets. Such testing is extraordinarily expensive because each storefront must be uniquely designed and scale economies are not exploitable. In fact, the test stores have negative *NPV*s on their own (i.e., they use more cash than they generate). But the management at McDonald's knows that they have "strategic" value. The question is this: How much is McDonald's willing to spend in the name of "strategy"? In other words, what is the investment value of the McTreat Spot test stores?

Of course, McDonald's does not disclose detailed financial information on individual projects such as this, but we can construct hypothetical values to illustrate how a financial analyst at McDonald's might approach the problem. First, let's consider what would happen if McDonald's were to launch the new concept without testing. Management feels that the potential market is perhaps 1,000 store-

---

[13.] We thank Richard Shockley for providing this example. Although this example is based on a real project being considered by McDonald's, the numbers in this case are purely hypothetical and are intended only to illustrate how a real options analysis might be applied to the McTreat Spot investment proposal. See Horowitz (2001) and Shockley (2001).

fronts, and each would cost $750,000 to outfit and get going. This investment is ir-reversible; if McDonald's decides to take the big gamble, it would cost $750 million (1,000 × $750,000) up front. Rollout would take two years; at the end of that roll-out period, the value of the business would be readily apparent: Either it would be a hit, in which case the *PV* of the free cash flows from operations would be $1.5 bil-lion, or it would be a bust, in which case the *PV* of the free cash flows from op-erations would be only $500 million. Management is somewhat sanguine about the project and feels it will be a "hit" with probability 0.40 and a bust with probabil-ity 0.60. To an analyst evaluating this problem in June 2006, the problem would look like this:

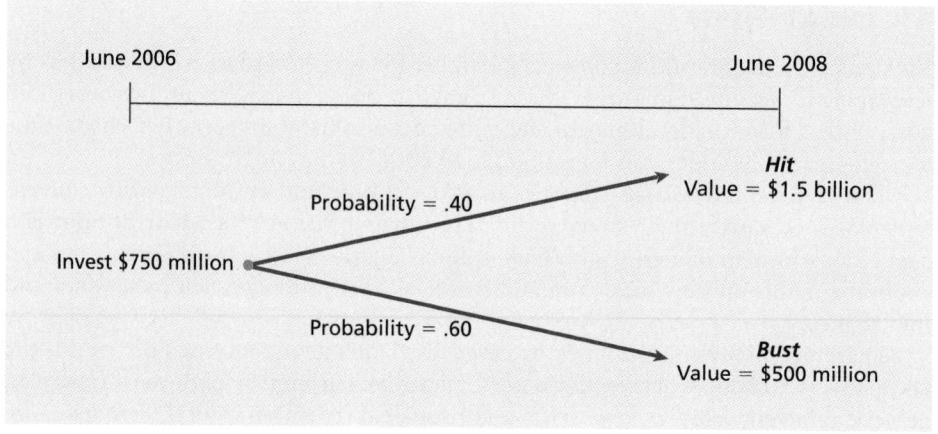

Suppose that McDonald's management assigned a 13 percent discount rate to this project. At that rate, the *NPV* of an immediate rollout of McTreat Spot is nega-tive in June 2006:

$$NPV = \frac{.4(\$1.5 \text{ billion}) + .6(\$500 \text{ million})}{(1.13)^2} - \$750 \text{ million}$$

$$= \frac{\$900 \text{ million}}{1.277} - \$750 \text{ million}$$

$$= \$704.8 \text{ million} - \$750 \text{ million} = -\$45.2 \text{ million}$$

In other words, immediate rollout is a value-destroying activity for McDonald's shareholders. The present value of cash inflows from entering this business is only $704.8 million, whereas the cost of entering the business is $750 million.

Even though the 2006 *NPV* of the McTreat Spot concept was negative and the *NPV* of any test stores would surely be negative, McDonald's management intuitively understood that the test-store program was very valuable. The reason is that the test stores generate information in addition to cash flow: By doing the testing program for two years, McDonald's can learn the value of a 1,000-store chain *before* invest-ing $750 million. If the test stores indicate that McTreat Spot is a hit, the firm will spend the capital and take the positive-*NPV* business. On the other hand, if the test stores indicate that McTreat Spot is a bust, management will walk away only having spent the cost of the testing program. So the test-store program gives a very different picture:

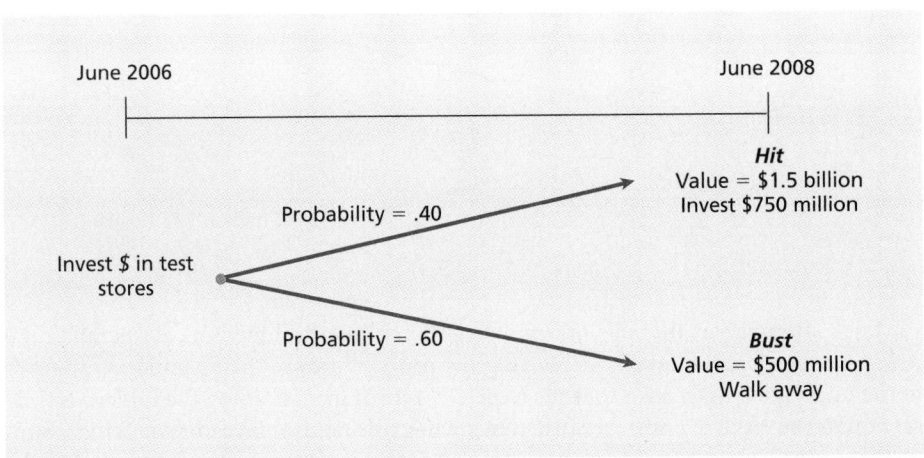

Investing in test stores allows McDonald's to capture the positive *NPV* in the "up" branch of the tree and to walk away without making an additional investment in the "down" branch. This is just like a call option that an investor chooses to exercise if the stock price goes up or to throw away if the stock price goes down. This option, like an ordinary call option, has an underlying asset that determines its value, and it has a strike price that must be paid to acquire the underlying asset. The underlying asset here is the value of the cash inflows from a 1,000-kiosk McTreat chain, and the strike price is the $750 million needed to build all those kiosks. If McDonald's learns that the value of the business is greater than the $750 million cost, the company will exercise its call option by building 1,000 kiosks at a cost of $750 million. That will allow the firm to take the *NPV* of $750 million ($1.5 billion–$750 million) as the payoff in 2008. If McDonald's learns that the value of the business is less than $750 million, it will let the option die unexercised, and the payoff in 2008 will be zero.

Because the test stores create the real option on a 1,000-store chain, we can determine the value of the test-store program itself, which is simply equal to the value of the option it creates plus the *NPV* of its own cash flows. In other words, we can now answer this very difficult question: What is the most McDonald's should spend on the test stores? As long as the option value created by the test stores exceeds their cost (their negative *NPV*), then the test stores actually create value for McDonald's shareholders.

McDonald's can value the option created by the test stores using the binomial model. The key issue is to understand the June 2006 value of the underlying asset. The underlying asset is always what you would get if you exercised the option; in this case, exercise of the option results in McDonald's receiving a 1,000-store McTreat Spot chain. The beginning value of the underlying asset is always the value of what you get if you exercise immediately; in this case, it is the June 2006 estimated value of the McTreat Spot chain (which we have determined to be $704.8 million). Our binomial option problem looks like this:

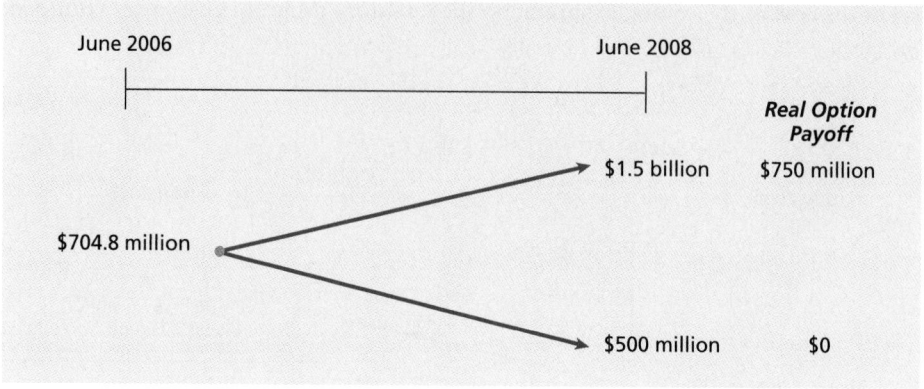

Let's attempt to value this option using the risk-neutral method. Remember, the risk-neutral approach involves choosing the probabilities of the up and down moves in the underlying asset such that the expected return from holding the underlying asset equals the risk-free rate (because that's what risk-neutral investors demand). Suppose that the risk-free rate in this problem is 5 percent. At that rate, the value of the underlying asset would grow in two years to the following:

$$\$704.8(1.05)^2 = \$777.0$$

Next, let p represent the probability of an up move and $1 - p$ represent the probability of a down move. Setting the expected payoff on the underlying asset equal to the risk-free rate, we determine the following ($ in millions):

$$\$1,500p + \$500(1 - p) = \$777$$
$$1 - p = 0.723$$

Now, use those probabilities to calculate the expected cash flow in 2008 from the call option. In the up state, the call pays $750, and in the down state, it pays nothing, so the expected cash flow is calculated as follows:

$$\text{Expected cash flow from call option} = \$750p + \$0(1 - p)$$
$$= \$750(0.277) = \$207.8$$

Finally, discount this cash flow for two years at 5 percent to obtain the current price of the call option:

$$\text{Call value today} = \frac{\$207.8}{1.05^2} = \$188.4$$

In other words, the most McDonald's should be willing to spend on the test stores (given our assumptions) is $188.4 million. As long as the testing program costs less than this (in capital investment as well as negative free cash flow), then testing creates value for the shareholders.

Consider the errors McDonald's might make if it attempts to value this project using decision trees with management's estimate of the up and down probabilities of

40 percent and 60 percent, respectively. In the initial decision tree where we calculated the expected *NPV*, ignoring the option to walk away if McTreat Spot was not a hit, McDonald's found a negative *NPV* of −$45.2 million. Focusing on that number alone would be a mistake because it ignores McTreat Spot's option value. What if McDonald's recognized the option value but priced it using the second decision tree, again with the 40 percent and 60 percent probabilities? Discounting the expected cash flows from that decision tree at 13 percent, the expected *NPV* is calculated as follows:

$$\frac{.4(\$750 \text{ million}) + .6(\$0)}{(1.13)^2} = \$235 \text{ million}$$

That's right—applying management's probabilities to the decision tree of call option payoffs would overvalue the test-store investment by $47.1 million, an error of 25 percent! Why does a decision tree give such an incorrect answer? Because decision trees are not risk adjusted. As discussed previously, the test-store program creates a call option on a full-blown store. One of the things we have learned is that call options are much riskier than the underlying asset on which they are written. Therefore, if the underlying asset here, a fully built McTreat Spot chain, has a risk-adjusted required rate of return of 13 percent, the required rate of return for the *option* on the McTreat Spot chain must be higher. How much higher? We cannot know that without doing the option valuation. But now that we know the correct option value, we can "infer" the proper discount rate by applying management's probabilities of future outcomes and solving for the discount rate that provides the option value:

$$\frac{.4(\$750) + .6(0)}{(1 + r^2)} = \$188.4 \quad r = 26.2\%$$

In summary, an expected *NPV* calculation undervalues the McTreat project because it ignores the project's option value. However, a decision-tree approach to valuing that option using the 40 percent and 60 percent probabilities overvalues the option. This is a common pattern. *NPV* calculations often understate the value of an investment, but pricing corporate growth options using decision trees leads to overvaluation errors. Analysts must always value real options with the appropriate technology—that is, an option-pricing model such as the binomial or the Black and Scholes.

SMART IDEAS VIDEO

Anjan Thakor, University of Michigan
"Banks seem to be moving in the opposite direction from the rest of corporate America, where firms have refocused more."

See the entire interview at
SMARTFinance

Concept Review Questions

9. In the oil-drilling example, how should a firm change its bid if it believes the volatility of oil prices will increase? How would the firm change its bid if it valued the drilling rights using *NPV* analysis rather than taking an options perspective on the investment?

10. In the McTreat problem, management believes that the probability of a "hit" is 40 percent. What impact does this belief have on the option valuation of the investment?

19.4 SUMMARY

- Analysts can use the Black and Scholes formula to value a European call on a stock that pays no dividends.

- The Black and Scholes formula requires five inputs: the stock price, the strike price, the risk-free rate, the time to expiration, and the underlying asset's volatility.
- Of the five inputs to the model, only volatility is an unknown that analysts must estimate.
- If analysts can observe the market price of an option, they can use the Black and Scholes equation to solve for the underlying asset's implied volatility.
- When a firm borrows money, both its debt and equity have option-like characteristics.
- Warrants are similar to call options, though pricing warrants requires an adjustment to the Black and Scholes model to account for dilution.
- Convertible securities combine the characteristics of ordinary bonds with call options.
- Capital investments with option-like characteristics may be valued using either the binomial or the Black and Scholes model; which valuation approach is appropriate depends on the characteristics of the investment.

INTERNET RESOURCES

Note: *For updates to links, please go to the book's website at http://smart.swcollege.com.*

http://www.cboe.com—Offers price quotes for many options and provides several tutorials explaining the characteristics of options and how they are traded

http://www.real-options.com—A site with an extensive real options reading list, plus links to news clips and conferences dealing with real options

KEY TERMS

Black and Scholes option-pricing equation
conversion premium
conversion price
conversion ratio
conversion value
convertible bond
equity kickers

forward rate
hedge ratio
implied volatility
option's delta
standard normal distribution
warrants

QUESTIONS

19-1. Project A has a guaranteed payoff of $200 million, which will exactly compensate the debtholders of the firm. Project B has a 50 percent probability of a $400 million payoff and a 50 percent probability of a zero payoff. Which project do the debtholders prefer and which project do the shareholders prefer?

19-2. In what sense can the terms $N(d_1)$ and $N(d_2)$ in the Black and Scholes model be interpreted as probabilities that a call option will expire in the money?

19-3. How are the values $N(d_1)$ and $N(-d_1)$ related?

19-4. What happens to the value of a call option when the risk-free rate increases, holding everything else constant?

19-5. You observe that the value of a particular put option has increased significantly over the last few days. However, neither the risk-free rate nor the price of the underlying stock has changed. What is the most likely explanation for the change in the value of the put?

19-6. In Section 19.2, we learned that buyers of a corporate bond hold an instrument that is equivalent to a risk-free bond and a short put with the firm's total assets serving as the underlying asset. But the holder of a corporate bond can also be said to hold the following portfolio: (a) The bondholder owns the assets of the firm (the same way that you might say that the bank owns your car until you have paid it off) and (b) the bondholder sold a call option on the firm's underlying assets. Explain how (a) + (b) is equivalent to a corporate bond.

19-7. In Section 19.2, we learned that a shareholder of a levered firm essentially owns a call option on the firm's assets. But we can also view the shareholder's position as the following portfolio: (a) The shareholder owns the firm's assets, (b) the shareholder is short a risk-free bond, and (c) the shareholder owns a put option on the firm's assets with a strike price equal to the risk-free bond's face value. Explain how (a) + (b) + (c) is equivalent to a share of stock in a levered firm.

19-8. In terms of pricing, what are the most important differences between warrants and call options?

19-9. Is the conversion ratio of the Amgen bonds mentioned in Section 19.2 constant through time? What about the conversion price?

19-10. What elements of the oil-drilling problem do not fit the Black and Scholes model very well?

19-11. Why is it inappropriate to calculate the expected *NPV* of the McTreat project and use that to base the go or no-go decision?

PROBLEMS

The Black and Scholes Model

19-1. Price a six-month call option with a strike price of $40.00, assuming an annual volatility (i.e., standard deviation of return) of 30 percent, a risk-free rate of 5 percent APR, and a current spot price of $41.25. Price the associated put using put-call parity (see Chapter 18). Reprice both options after changing the risk-free rate to 6 percent APR.

19-2. Price a three-month call option with a strike price of $20.00, assuming an annual volatility (i.e., standard deviation of return) of 20 percent, a risk-free rate of 5 percent APR, and a current spot price of $19.85. Price the associated put using put-call parity (see Chapter 18). Reprice both options after changing the maturity to one year.

19-3. Suppose a one-year call option sells for $6.78. The current underlying stock price is $24.02, and the strike price is $25.00. Assuming a risk-free rate of 4 percent APR, what is the price of the associated put option? (*Hint:* Use put-call parity from Chapter 18.)

19-4. Use the Black and Scholes model to value a call option with the following characteristics: The strike price is $55, the underlying stock's price is $65, the risk-free rate is 4 percent, the time to expiration is six months, and the standard deviation of the underlying asset is 35 percent. What is the value of $N(d_1)$?

19-5. Recalculate the value of the option in the previous problem assuming that the underlying stock sells for $66. By how much does the call price change? Compare this to the value of $N(d_1)$ in the previous problem.

19-6. The following table shows daily closing prices for the common stock of NVIDIA Corp. (ticker symbol NVDA) and for call options on NVIDIA shares during the last week of June 2002. For each pair of consecutive days, calculate the ratio of the dollar change in the price of the option divided by the dollar change in the price of the stock. Next, calculate the ratio of the percentage change in the option price divided by the percentage change in the stock price. What general patterns emerge from these calculations?

Date	Stock	Option
June 28	$17.18	$2.00
June 27	$17.08	$1.95
June 26	$20.07	$3.55
June 25	$21.17	$4.25
June 24	$23.08	$5.55

19-7. A particular stock sells for $40 and has a standard deviation of 35 percent. Value a call option on this stock that has three months left before expiration and an exercise price of $55. The risk-free rate is 4 percent.

19-8. Recalculate the value of the call in the previous problem assuming that the stock price is $41. How much did the call value increase? Compare this to the value of $N(d_1)$ in the previous problem.

19-9. Use the Black and Scholes model to value a put option with a strike price of $35 and an expiration date in four months. The underlying stock sells for $40 and has a standard deviation of 55 percent, and the risk-free rate is 6 percent.

19-10. Suppose that the current market price of a stock is $63. The standard deviation of the stock's returns is 35 percent per year, and the risk-free rate is 4 percent. Calculate the value of a 1-year call option with a strike price of $40. What is the value of $N(d_1)$?

19-11. Recalculate the price of the option in Problem 19-7 using the binomial model under the assumption that in one year's time the stock price will move up or down by one standard deviation, or 35 percent (up to $85.05 or down to $40.95). What is the value of the hedge ratio, h, in this problem? Draw a connection between this value and the value of $N(d_1)$ in the previous problem.

19-12. Repeat the calculations in Problems 19-7 and 19-8 assuming that the call's strike price is $80 rather than $40. Once again, compare the values of $N(d_1)$ and h. Comment on what you find.

SMART SOLUTIONS
See the problem and solution explained step-by-step at
SMARTFinance

19-13. A money manager holds 10,000 shares of stock in a particular company and expects to sell them in one week. She is concerned about the possibility that the stock price might fall before she sells, so she decides to buy 10,000 put options. The current market price of the stock is $70, which is also the strike price of the puts. The standard deviation of the underlying stock is 45 percent, and the risk-free rate is 3 percent. The put options expire in four months. One week from today, the manager plans to unwind her position by selling both the shares and the puts at the prevailing market price.

    a. What is the aggregate value of the manager's current holdings in this company's stock?

b. What will she have to pay for 10,000 puts? After purchasing the puts, what is the total market value of her holdings in both stock and puts?

c. One week later when it is time for her to sell, what will be the market value of her holdings if the stock price has risen to $75? What if the stock price has fallen to $65?

d. Repeat parts (b) and (c) assuming that the manager bought 20,000 puts rather than 10,000. Comment on how the purchase of twice as many puts affects your answers.

19-14. Using the following table, price one-year call options using different annual volatilities. The strike price is $30.00, with an underlying spot price of $30.00 and a risk-free rate of 3 percent APR.

Volatility	$N(d_1)$	$N(d_2)$	Call Price
20%	0.5987	0.5199	
25%	0.5968	0.4980	
30%	0.5987	0.4801	

19-15. Using the following table, price one-year put options using different annual volatilities. The strike price is $35.00, with an underlying spot price of $32.50 and a risk-free rate of 3 percent APR.

Volatility	$N(d_1)$	$N(d_2)$	Put Price
20%	0.4520	0.3743	
25%	0.4795	0.3815	
30%	0.5012	0.3832	

19-16. A six-month call option with a strike price of $25.00 is selling for $3.50. Assuming the underlying stock price is also $25.00 and the risk-free rate is 6 percent APR, use the following table to determine the volatility (i.e., standard deviation of the return) implied using the option price. (*Hint:* Price the option using the table to determine which volatility generates a price of $3.50.)

Volatility	$N(d_1)$	$N(d_2)$
40%	0.5799	0.4859
45%	0.6000	0.4742
50%	0.6032	0.4634

19-17. A three-month put option with a strike price of $25.00 is selling for $4.87. Assuming the underlying spot price is 20.00 and the risk-free rate is 4 percent APR, use the following table to determine the volatility (i.e., standard deviation of the return) implied using the option price. (*Hint:* Convert the put option into a call option using put-call parity [Chapter 18], and then price the call option using the table to determine which volatility generates the correct price.)

Volatility	$N(d_1)$	$N(d_2)$
30%	0.0892	0.0673
35%	0.1291	0.0959
40%	0.1671	0.1291

19-18. There are currently 10 million shares outstanding for Firm TKO. Some time ago, TKO issued warrants for one million more shares that will come due in six months.

Assuming the associated call option is worth $6.98, what is the value of the warrant (see Equation 19.5)?

19-19. A call option at its maturity is about to be exercised today with a strike price of $50.00. Given a spot price of $55.00, what is the value of a set of warrants that will also expire today, assuming the warrants will double the number of shares outstanding?

Options Embedded in Other Securities

19-20. Company A owns a large block of shares of Company B. Company A issues bonds that at maturity will be converted into shares of Company B (conversion is mandatory). The number of Company B shares that bondholders will receive at maturity is determined by the following schedule:

Price of Company B (P)	Number of Shares Given to Bondholders
$P < 50$	1 share
$50 \leq P \leq 60$	$\dfrac{1}{P}$ shares
$60 < P$	$\dfrac{5}{6}$ shares

Draw a payoff diagram showing on the y-axis the dollar value of what bondholders receive and on the x-axis the stock price of Company B. Then describe how the bonds consist of a portfolio of ordinary bonds and options on Company B's stock.

19-21. Meg and Sons Incorporated has 2 million shares of common stock outstanding, which sell for $40 per share. The company plans to issue $10 million face value in 5-year notes. Each $1,000 par value bond has 20 attached warrants, granting investors the right to purchase Meg and Sons stock for $55 in five years. If the risk-free rate is 5 percent and the standard deviation of Meg and Sons shares is 30 percent, what is the value of the warrants?

19-22. Look again at the Amgen convertible bonds in Section 19.2.
   a. If the yield to maturity does not change, what will be the price of the bonds one year after they are issued?
   b. What will be the conversion price at that time? The conversion premium?

19-23. A company issues 5-year convertible bonds that pay a 6 percent coupon rate and sell at par value, $1,000. The conversion ratio of the bonds is 15.
   a. What is the conversion price?
   b. If the current stock price for this company is $60, what is the conversion value of the bonds?
   c. What is the conversion premium?

Options Embedded in Capital Investments—Real Options

19-24. Recalculate the value of drilling rights from Section 19.3 assuming that the standard deviation of the price of oil is 40 percent rather than 30 percent. Comment on how your conclusion changes when you value this investment using option-pricing logic rather than *NPV*.

▶ **19-25.** Value the McTreat Spot option described in Section 19.3 using the binomial method rather than the risk-neutral approach. Verify that either approach results in the same option value.

MINI-CASE: BLACK AND SCHOLES AND BEYOND

A call option on Amazon.com, Inc. is currently trading at $3.20. The option has a strike price of $42.50 while Amazon's stock is trading at $45.22. The annual risk-free rate is 4.50 percent and the option has 21 days until expiration. You estimate the standard deviation of Amazon's stock to be 42 percent.

1. Based on the above information, is the call option correctly valued, overvalued, or undervalued? What is the implied volatility of the call option? (*Hint:* Use the "goal seek" feature in Excel to determine the implied volatility.)

2. If a put option with the same strike price is trading for $1.30, is it currently over-, under-, or correctly valued?

3. You own 5,000 shares of Amazon.com, Inc.'s common stock, which you plan to sell in two weeks. You are worried the stock will decline over the next two weeks, so you decide to hedge against a decline in the stock price by selling call options on the stock. How many of the call options must you sell to perfectly hedge your stock position? (*Hint:* Use the hedge ratio from the implied volatility calculation.)

4. Assume two weeks have passed and the value of Amazon's stock has dropped to $43.58. Calculate the value of the call option at this point using the implied volatility calculated earlier. Ignoring commissions, calculate the net profit/loss on your overall position in both Amazon's common stock and call options on Amazon's stock.

5. Amazon.com, Inc. recently sold an additional 30 million shares. Before the new issue, the firm had 415 million shares of common stock outstanding. Attached to the new shares were warrants allowing the stockholder the right to purchase one additional share of Amazon.com's stock for $85 for every seven shares of common stock purchased. The warrants expire in two years. Again, Amazon's stock is trading at $45.22 and the annual risk-free rate is 4.50 percent. Use an estimated standard deviation on Amazon's stock of 35 percent. Determine the value of each warrant.

APPENDIX 19A ESTIMATING VOLATILITY FOR THE BLACK AND SCHOLES MODEL

In this appendix, we illustrate how to calculate the standard deviation for a Black and Scholes option valuation. We will use stock-price data for UQM Technologies, which warrants we priced earlier. The first task is to gather historical trading data for UQM stock. There is no hard-and-fast rule about how much data to gather or about the frequency with which returns should be measured. As is the case with estimating any parameter with market data, such as a beta, analysts face trade-offs between sample size, data relevance, and the accuracy with which returns can be measured at different frequencies. For instance, if we want our sample to consist of 60 observations, we could choose the last 60 days, weeks, or months. Daily returns probably do a better job of portraying the current state of the company and the market, but daily returns may be subject to measurement problems if the stock does not trade frequently. Weekly or monthly returns solve the measurement problem, but they require us to look so far back to gather 60 observations that some data points may no longer reflect the company's current situation. For example, if a company changed its capital structure significantly in the recent past, the stock's current volatility could be quite different from the volatility observed just a few months back.

From Yahoo! we downloaded daily closing prices for UQM stock from January 10 to April 12, 2002, the date that it issued its warrants. The closing prices and corresponding dates appear in columns 1 and 2 of Table 19A.1. Next, we calculate the *price relative* on each day, defined as that day's price divided by the price one day earlier:

$$\text{Price relative} = \frac{P_t}{P_{t-1}} = 1 + r_{\text{daily}}$$

Notice that this ratio equals 1 plus the daily return on the stock. To convert this into a continuously compounded return (recall that Black and Scholes assumes continuous compounding), we take the natural logarithm of the price relative. These figures appear in the fourth column of the table. Using this sequence of daily returns, we calculate the standard deviation in the usual way. Finally, to convert our standard deviation from a daily to an annual basis, we multiply it times the square root of the number of trading days in one year, roughly 250.[14] This yields an estimate of annual volatility that we can plug directly into the Black and Scholes equation.

[14.] The reason we convert the standard deviation to an annual basis by multiplying by the square root of the number of trading days in a year can be better understood by looking at the conversion for variance. If there are 250 trading days in a year, then the daily variance times 250 equals the annual variance. Take the square root of both sides to get the appropriate conversion factor for standard deviation.

Table 19A.1
Calculating the Standard Deviation of Returns for UQM Stock

Date (2002)	Closing Price ($)	Price Relative	$\ln(P_t/P_{t-1})$
Apr 12	4.46	1.021	0.020
Apr 11	4.37	1.002	0.002
Apr 10	4.36	1.000	0.000
Apr 9	4.36	1.038	0.037
Apr 8	4.20	0.977	−0.024
Apr 5	4.30	0.998	−0.002
Apr 4	4.31	1.009	0.009
Apr 3	4.27	0.938	−0.064
Apr 2	4.55	1.046	0.045
Apr 1	4.35	0.946	−0.056
Mar 28	4.60	1.000	0.000
Mar 27	4.60	1.022	0.022
Mar 26	4.50	0.978	−0.022
Mar 25	4.60	0.979	−0.022
Mar 22	4.70	1.011	0.011
Mar 21	4.65	0.979	−0.021
Mar 20	4.75	1.011	0.011
Mar 19	4.70	1.033	0.032
Mar 18	4.55	1.000	0.000
Mar 15	4.55	1.007	0.007
Mar 14	4.52	0.976	−0.024
Mar 13	4.63	0.953	−0.048
Mar 12	4.86	0.970	−0.030
Mar 11	5.01	0.936	−0.066
Mar 8	5.35	1.338	0.291
Mar 7	4.00	1.036	0.036
Mar 6	3.86	0.977	−0.023
Mar 5	3.95	0.985	−0.015
Mar 4	4.01	0.990	−0.010
Mar 1	4.05	1.013	0.012
Feb 28	4.00	1.026	0.025
Feb 27	3.90	0.963	−0.038
Feb 26	4.05	1.000	0.000
Feb 25	4.05	1.015	0.015
Feb 22	3.99	0.973	−0.027
Feb 21	4.10	0.976	−0.024
Feb 20	4.20	1.000	0.000
Feb 19	4.20	0.966	−0.035
Feb 15	4.35	1.002	0.002
Feb 14	4.34	1.021	0.021
Feb 13	4.25	0.984	−0.016
Feb 12	4.32	0.995	−0.005
Feb 11	4.34	1.046	0.045
Feb 8	4.15	0.988	−0.012
Feb 7	4.20	0.988	−0.012
Feb 6	4.25	1.000	0.000

(continued)

Table 19A.1
(Continued)

Date (2002)	Closing Price ($)	Price Relative	$\ln(P_t/P_{t-1})$
Feb 5	4.25	0.955	−0.046
Feb 4	4.45	0.991	−0.009
Feb 1	4.49	0.945	−0.056
Jan 31	4.75	0.990	−0.010
Jan 30	4.80	1.011	0.010
Jan 29	4.75	1.080	0.077
Jan 28	4.40	1.023	0.023
Jan 25	4.30	0.966	−0.034
Jan 24	4.45	1.011	0.011
Jan 23	4.40	1.011	0.011
Jan 22	4.35	0.967	−0.034
Jan 18	4.50	0.978	−0.022
Jan 17	4.60	0.968	−0.032
Jan 16	4.75	1.000	0.000
Jan 15	4.75	0.990	−0.010
Jan 14	4.80	0.896	−0.110
Jan 11	5.36	0.989	−0.011
Jan 10	5.42	NA	NA

0.048 Standard deviation of daily returns (column 4)
0.766 Annualized standard deviation (daily times $\sqrt{250}$)

Almost as soon as the waters began to recede in the aftermath of Hurricane Katrina, a flood of money from global capital markets began to pour into the Gulf Coast region. In one case, Mooring Financial Corp. (MFC), a private investment firm with holdings in commercial loans, property tax liens, and other specialized investments, sought to purchase rights to an in-default loan backed by tugboats. In the chaos following Katrina, MFC could not determine how badly the tugboats had been damaged by the storm or even whether their owner had maintained insurance on his boats. Given the uncertainty surrounding the collateral, Mooring bid roughly 50 cents on the dollar to buy the loan. Mooring's bid failed because another buyer offered a higher price and was willing to accept the risk at a lower return.

Mooring's experience was a microcosm of a global phenomenon. Since 2000, assets held by pension funds, mutual funds, and insurance companies around the world grew by almost 33 percent to reach $46 trillion by mid-2005. With huge sums to deploy, investors the world over scoured the landscape for attractive investment opportunities, bidding up prices and driving down returns, a situation described by incoming U.S. Federal Reserve Chair Ben Bernanke as a global savings glut. Bernanke speculated that high savings, especially outside the United States, would sustain a prolonged period of low interest rates around the world, despite relatively robust economic growth. The surge in capital affected returns on a wide array of investments, from assets as safe as government bonds to risky investments such as hedge funds. A report by Van Hedge Fund Advisors predicted that hedge fund industry assets would grow fourfold from 2005 to 2009.

In this chapter, we consider the special challenges that arise when firms do business across national boundaries and in different currencies. A central theme of the chapter is that the value of a nation's currency is linked not only to interest rates in the domestic economy, but also to interest rates abroad. With the ability to move vast amounts of capital from country to country nearly instantaneously, global investors have a profound effect on currency markets as they seek out the most profitable investment opportunities. For their part, multinational companies strive to manage the risks that fluctuating currency values have on their business.

Sources: "Huge Flood of Capital to Invest Spurs World-Wide Risk Taking," Greg Ip and Mark Whitehouse, Wall Street Journal, 11-3-05; Hedge Fund Demand and Capacity, 2005–2015; Is Worldwide Hedge Fund Demand Outstripping Capacity?, Business Wire, 8-25-05; On Rebalancing the World Economy, Global News Wire—Asia Africa Intelligence Wire, 10-05-05.

SMARTFinance
Use the learning tools at www
thomsonedu.com/finance/smartfinance

725

Walk down the aisle of a grocery store, visit a shopping mall, go hunting for a new automobile, or check the outstanding balance of your credit card. In each of these activities, chances are that you will be dealing with products and services provided by **multinational corporations (MNCs)**, businesses that operate in many countries around the world. In recent decades, international trade in goods and services has expanded dramatically, and so too have the size and scope of MNCs. Although all the financial principles covered in this text thus far apply to MNCs, companies operating across national borders also face unique challenges. Primary among them is coping with exchange rate risk. An **exchange rate** is simply the price of one currency in terms of another, and for the past 35 years the exchange rates of major currencies have fluctuated daily. These movements create uncertainty for firms that earn revenue and pay operating costs in more than one currency. Currency movements also add to the competitive pressures faced by wholly domestic companies that face competition from foreign firms.

This chapter focuses on the problems and opportunities firms face as a result of globalization, with special emphasis on currency-related issues. First, we explain the rudimentary features of currency markets, including how and why currencies trade and the rules governments impose on trading in their currencies. Second, we describe equilibrium factors that drive currency values—at least for those countries that allow their currency value to float—constantly responding to market forces. Third, we discuss the special risks faced by MNCs and the strategies they employ to manage those risks. We conclude by illustrating some of the long-term and short-term financial decisions confronting MNCs.

20.1 EXCHANGE RATE FUNDAMENTALS

We begin our coverage of exchange rate fundamentals by describing the "rules of the game" as dictated by national governments.

FIXED VERSUS FLOATING EXCHANGE RATES

Since the mid-1970s, the major currencies of the world have had a floating exchange rate relationship with respect to the U.S. dollar and to one another. A **floating exchange rate** means that forces of supply and demand continually move currency values up and down. The opposite of a floating exchange rate regime is a fixed exchange rate system. Under a **fixed exchange rate** system, governments fix (or *peg*) their currency's value, usually in terms of another currency, such as the U.S. dollar. Once a government pegs its currency at a particular value, it must stand ready to pursue economic and financial policies necessary to maintain that value.[1] For example, if demand for the currency increases, the government must stand ready to sell it so that the increase in demand does not cause the currency to appreciate. Conversely, if demand for the currency falls, then the government must be ready to buy its own currency, thereby supporting the exchange rate. In many countries with fixed exchange

---

[1.] The fixed exchange rate system that collapsed in 1973, called the *Bretton Woods system*, was based on the U.S. dollar and had governed international finance since the late 1940s. Under this system, countries established fixed exchange rates (par values) for their currencies versus the dollar, which often did not change for two decades or more.

rates, governments impose restrictions on the free flow of currencies into and out of the country. Even so, maintaining a currency peg can be quite difficult. For example, in response to mounting economic problems, the government of Argentina allowed the peso, which had been linked to the U.S. dollar, to float freely for the first time in a decade on January 11, 2002. After one day, the peso lost more than 40 percent of its value relative to the dollar.

In addition to using purely fixed and purely floating exchange rate systems, countries—usually those that are developing—employ several intermediate or hybrid models. A **managed floating rate system** is a hybrid in which a nation's government loosely "fixes" the value of the national currency in relation to that of another currency but does not expend the effort and resources that would be required to maintain a completely fixed exchange rate. Other countries simply choose to use another nation's currency as their own, and a handful of nations have adopted a *currency board arrangement*. In such an arrangement, the national currency continues to circulate, but every unit of the currency is fully backed by government holdings of another currency—usually the U.S. dollar.

The International Monetary Fund, in its *International Financial Statistics Yearbook 2001*, details the exchange rate systems in place for 186 countries as of March 31, 2001. Forty-seven countries had independently floating exchange rates (including most of the Organization for Economic Cooperation and Development [OECD] countries), 44 had conventional fixed exchange rates, 33 had managed floats, 39 used another currency as their country's legal tender (including the 12 European countries using the euro), 8 maintained currency boards (including Hong Kong), and 15 maintained some other type of hybrid system.

In terms of trading volume, the major currencies in international finance today are (in no particular order) the British pound sterling (£), the Swiss franc (SF), the Japanese yen (¥), the Canadian dollar (C$), the U.S. dollar (US$, or simply $), and the euro (€). The **euro** was adopted for financial transactions by 11 continental European countries in January 1999, and in early 2002 this became the only currency circulating in these countries—as well as in Greece, which qualified for membership in the European Monetary Union (EMU) in 2001.

EXCHANGE RATE QUOTES

Figure 20.1 shows exchange rate values quoted in the *Wall Street Journal* on November 16, 2005. Note that the figure states each exchange rate in two ways. The first two columns report the "US$ Equivalent" value of a given currency. The numbers in these columns show the dollar cost of one unit of foreign currency. In row 1, for example, we see that on Tuesday, November 15, one Argentine peso cost $0.3388 in U.S. dollars. One day earlier, one peso cost $0.3371. Because the value of one peso in terms of U.S. currency rose slightly from Monday to Tuesday, we say that the peso **appreciated** against the dollar.

The third and fourth columns of Figure 20.1 present the same information in a slightly different way. These columns show the value of each foreign currency relative to one U.S. dollar. Again, in row 1 we see that on Monday, November 14, it cost 2.9665 pesos to purchase one U.S. dollar, but on the next day one dollar was worth a little less, 2.9516 pesos. Because the value of one dollar in terms of pesos fell from Monday to Tuesday, we say that the dollar **depreciated** against the peso. Of course, the exchange rate quotes in the first two columns reveal exactly the same information

Figure 20.1
Exchange Rates Versus
the U.S. Dollar,
November 15, 2005
Source: Wall Street Journal,
November 16, 2005, p. C12.
Copyright 2005 Dow Jones
& Company, Inc. All Rights
Reserved Worldwide.

Exchange Rates

The New York foreign exchange mid-range rates below apply to trading among banks in amounts of $1 million and more, as quoted at 4 p.m. Eastern time by Reuters and other sources. Retail transactions provide fewer units of foreign currency per dollar.

Country	U.S. $ EQUIVALENT Tue.	Mon.	CURRENCY PER U.S. $ Tue.	Mon.
Argentina (Peso)-y	.2732	.2762	3.6600	3.6200
Australia (Dollar)	.5385	.5468	1.8570	1.8287
Bahrain (Dinar)	2.6525	2.6525	.3770	.3770
Brazil (Real)	.3429	.3444	2.9160	2.9040
Britain (Pound)	1.5587	1.5784	.6416	.6336
1-month forward	1.5558	1.5754	.6428	.6348
3-months forward	1.5503	1.5700	.6450	.6369
6-months forward	1.5414	1.5614	.6488	.6405
Canada (Dollar)	.6307	.6393	1.5855	1.5642
1-month forward	.6302	.6388	1.5868	1.5654
3-months forward	.6291	.6377	1.5896	1.5681
6-months forward	.6275	.6361	1.5937	1.5721
Chile (Peso)	.001433	.001443	698.05	692.85
China (Renminbi)	.1208	.1208	8.2770	8.2770
Colombia (Peso)	.0003913	.0003975	2555.50	2516.00
Czech. Rep. (Koruna)				
Commercial rate	.03265	.03318	30.627	30.136
Denmark (Krone)	.1327	.1355	7.5330	7.3783
Ecuador (US Dollar)	1.0000	1.0000	1.0000	1.0000
Hong Kong (Dollar)	.1282	.1282	7.8000	7.8000
Hungary (Forint)	.004035	.004119	247.81	242.80
India (Rupee)	.02055	.02054	48.670	48.680
Indonesia (Rupiah)	.0001111	.0001134	9005	8818
Israel (Shekel)	.2138	.2156	4.6780	4.6380
Japan (Yen)	.008497	.008598	117.69	116.31
1-month forward	.008511	.008612	117.50	116.12
3-months forward	.008536	.008637	117.14	115.78
6-months forward	.008576	.008678	116.61	115.23
Jordan (Dinar)	1.4184	1.4184	.7050	.7050

Country	U.S. $ EQUIVALENT Tue.	Mon.	CURRENCY PER U.S. $ Tue.	Mon.
Kuwait (Dinar)	3.3212	3.3300	.3011	.3003
Lebanon (Pound)	.0006610	.0006610	1512.88	1512.88
Malaysia (Ringgit)-b	.2632	.2632	3.8000	3.8000
Malta (Lira)	2.3855	2.4166	.4192	.4138
Mexico (Peso)				
Floating rate	.1036	.1036	9.6505	9.6485
New Zealand (Dollar)	.4733	.4793	2.1128	2.0864
Norway (Krone)	.1304	.1333	7.6697	7.5044
Pakistan (Rupee)	.01677	.01677	59.645	59.625
Peru (new Sol)	.2832	.2839	3.5310	3.5225
Philippines (Peso)	.01981	.01985	50.475	50.375
Poland (Zloty)	.2430	.2464	4.1150	4.0590
Russia (Ruble)-a	.03172	.01370	31.530	31.550
Saudi Arabia (Riyal)	.2666	.2666	3.7505	3.7505
Singapore (Dollar)	.5726	.5769	1.7465	1.7335
Slovak Rep. (Koruna)	.02213	.02248	45.186	44.482
South Africa (Rand)	.0990	.1001	10.1035	9.9895
South Korea (Won)	.0008598	.0008654	1163.10	1155.60
Sweden (Krona)	.1041	.1061	9.6030	9.4265
Switzerland (Franc)	.6788	.6921	1.4731	1.4449
1-month forward	.6793	.6926	1.4721	1.4439
3-months forward	.6801	.6934	1.4703	1.4421
6-months forward	.6815	.6949	1.4673	1.4391
Taiwan (Dollar)	.03022	.03046	33.090	32.830
Thailand (Baht)	.02442	.02472	40.945	40.445
Turkey (Lira)	.00000060	.00000060	1677500	1677500
United Arab (Dirham)	.2723	.2723	3.6728	3.6728
Uruguay (Peso)				
Financial	.03774	.04167	26.500	24.000
Venezuela (Bolivar)	.000758	.000763	1318.50	1310.50
SDR	1.3425	1.3454	.7449	.7433
Euro	.9866	1.0078	1.0136	.9923

Special Drawing Rights (SDR) are based on exchange rates for the U.S., British, and Japanese currencies. Source: International Monetary Fund.

a-Russian Central Bank rate. b-Government rate. y-Floating rate.

as the quotes in the second two columns. Each of these methods of quoting exchange rates is simply the reciprocal of the other:

$$\frac{\text{dollars}}{\text{pesos}} = \frac{1}{\frac{\text{pesos}}{\text{dollars}}} \qquad \$0.3388/\text{Ps} = \frac{1}{\text{Ps}2.9516/\$}$$

In Figure 20.1, we can also see that some currencies do not float freely against the dollar, because the exchange rates did not move at all from Monday to Tuesday. These currencies include the Hong Kong dollar, the Kuwaiti dinar, and the Saudi Arabian riyal.

In expressing "exchange rates," one's location matters. A **direct quotation** is a quote that gives the home currency price of a unit of foreign currency, while an **indirect quotation** gives the foreign currency price of one unit of the home currency. For a trader based in the United States, therefore, a direct quotation is $0.3388/Ps and an indirect quotation is Ps2.9516/$. A trader based in Mexico expresses a direct peso/dollar exchange rate quotation as Ps2.9516/$, while $0.3388/Ps is an indirect quotation.

We can also distinguish between two types of exchange rates. The exchange rate that applies to currency trades that occur immediately is called the <u>spot exchange rate</u>. However, in many currencies it is possible to enter a contract today to trade foreign currency at a fixed price at some future date. The price at which that future trade will take place is called the <u>**forward exchange rate.**</u> For example, a U.S. trader wishing to exchange dollars for British pounds could do so on November 15 at the spot exchange rate of $1.7360/£ (or, equivalently, £0.5760/$). Alternatively, the trader could enter into an agreement to trade dollars for pounds one month later at the forward rate of

$1.7354/£ (or, equivalently, £0.5762/$). If the trader chose to transact through a forward contract, no cash would change hands until the date specified by the contract. Though the figure only quotes forward contracts at maturities of one, three, and six months, a much richer set of forward contracts is available in the foreign exchange market.

Just as we compared movements in the spot exchange rate from Monday to Tuesday, we can also examine differences in the spot exchange rate for current transactions and the forward rate for future transactions. For example, look at the rate quotes for Japanese yen. On the spot market, one yen costs $0.008415, but the exchange rate for trades that will take place 180 days (6 months) later is $0.008606/¥. The yen's cost on the forward market is slightly higher than it is on the spot market. Whenever one currency buys more of another on the forward market than it does on the spot market, traders say that the first currency trades at a **forward premium**. The forward premium is usually expressed as a percentage relative to the spot rate, so for the yen we can calculate the 180-day forward premium as follows:

$$\frac{F - S}{S} = \frac{\$0.008606/¥ - \$0.008415/¥}{\$0.008415/¥} = 0.0227 \quad \text{or} \quad 2.27\%$$

where F is the symbol for the forward rate and S stands for the spot rate, both quoted in terms of $/¥. Recognizing that the yen's 2.27 percent forward premium refers to a 6-month contract, we could restate the premium in annual terms by multiplying the premium times 2, which would yield an annualized forward premium of 4.54 percent.

If the yen trades at a forward premium relative to the dollar, then the dollar must trade at a **forward discount** relative to the yen, meaning that one dollar buys fewer yen on the forward market than it does on the spot market. Using the same equation, we focus on currency units in terms of ¥/$:

$$\frac{F - S}{S} = \frac{¥116.20/\$ - ¥118.84/\$}{¥118.84/\$} = -0.0222 \quad \text{or} \quad -2.22\%$$

The dollar trades at a −2.22 percent forward discount for a 6-month contract, or about −4.44 percent per year. In other words, the forward discount on the dollar is opposite in sign and similar in magnitude to the forward premium on the yen, though the discount is always smaller in absolute value than the premium. In general, to calculate the annualized forward premium or discount on a currency, based on a forward contract to be executed in N days, use the following equation:

$$\frac{F - S}{S} \times \frac{360}{N} \qquad\qquad \text{(Eq. 20.1)}$$

APPLYING THE MODEL 20.1

Using the exchange rate quotes in Figure 20.1, we can calculate the annualized forward discount (or premium) on the Swiss franc (SF) relative to the dollar ($). We will calculate this based on the rate for a 3-month forward contract. The spot rate equals $0.7598/SF, and the 3-month (or 90-day) forward rate equals $0.7663/SF.

Notice that the franc buys more dollars on the forward market than it does on the spot market, so it trades at a forward premium. We can determine the annualized premium as follows, given that we are using a 90-day contract:

$$\frac{\$0.7663/SF - \$0.7598/SF}{\$0.7598/SF} \times \frac{360}{90} = 0.0342 \quad \text{or} \quad 3.42\%$$

The forward discount or premium gives traders information about more than just the price of exchanging currencies at different points in time. The forward premium is tightly linked to differences in interest rates on short-term, low-risk bonds across countries, a relationship that we explore in depth in the next section.

One last lesson remains to be gleaned from Figure 20.1. In its daily exchange rate table, the *Wall Street Journal* quotes the value of the world's major currencies relative to the U.S. dollar. But what if someone wants to know the exchange rate between British pounds and Canadian dollars? In fact, all the information needed to calculate this exchange rate appears in the figure. We simply need to calculate a **cross exchange rate** by dividing the dollar exchange rate for one currency by the dollar exchange rate for the other currency. For example, using Tuesday's spot rates from the figure, we can determine the £/C$ exchange rate:

$$\frac{\$1.7360/£}{\$0.8388/C\$} = C\$2.0969/£$$

How can we be sure that one pound buys 2.0696 Canadian dollars simply by taking this ratio? The answer is that if the value of the pound, relative to the Canadian dollar, were different from this number, then currency traders could engage in **triangular arbitrage,** trading currencies simultaneously in different markets to earn a risk-free profit. Because currency markets operate virtually 24 hours per day, and because currency trades take place with lightning speed and with very low transactions costs, arbitrage maintains actual currency values in different markets relatively close to this theoretical ideal.

APPLYING THE MODEL 20.2

Suppose that on November 15, 2005, a trader learns that the exchange rate being offered by a bank in London is C$2.1000/£ rather than C$2.0696/£ as calculated previously. What is the arbitrage opportunity? First, note that the figure C$2.1000/£ is "too high" relative to the theoretically correct rate. This means that in London, one pound costs too much in terms of Canadian dollars; the pound is overvalued, and the Canadian dollar is undervalued. Therefore, a U.S. trader could make a profit by executing the following steps.

1. Convert U.S. dollars to British pounds in New York at the prevailing spot rate. Assume that the trader starts with $1 million, which will convert to £576,000.
2. Simultaneously, the trader sells £576,000 in London (because pounds are overvalued there) at the exchange rate of C$2.1000/£. The trader will then have C$1,209,600.
3. Convert the Canadian dollars back into U.S. currency in New York. Given the spot rate of $0.8388/C$, the trader will receive $1,014,612 in exchange for C$1,209,600.

After making these trades, all of which can occur in the blink of an eye, the trader winds up $14,612 richer, all without taking risk. As long as the exchange rates do not change, the trader can keep making a profit over and over again.

The preceding example shows that a trader can repeatedly make a profit if the exchange rates do not change. But exchange rates will change, of course, and they will change in a way that brings the market back into equilibrium. Figure 20.2 illustrates what happens as arbitrage takes place. As traders in New York sell U.S. currency in exchange for pounds, the pound appreciates against the U.S. dollar, and the exchange rate will rise from $1.7360/£ to some new, higher level. Likewise, as traders in London sell pounds in exchange for Canadian dollars, the pound will depreciate against the Canadian currency and the exchange rate will fall below C$2.1000/£. Finally, as traders reap their profits in New York by selling Canadian and buying U.S. currency, the exchange rate between Canadian and U.S. dollars will rise from C$0.8388/$. Though we cannot say exactly how much each of these exchange rates will move, we can say that collectively they will move enough to reach a new equilibrium in which the cross exchange rate in New York and the exchange rate quoted in London will be virtually identical.

With this basic understanding of foreign exchange rates in place, let us now turn to some important institutional features of the foreign exchange market.

THE FOREIGN EXCHANGE MARKET

The **foreign exchange (forex) market** is not actually a physical exchange, but a global telecommunications market. In fact, it is the world's largest financial market, with total volume of almost $2 trillion *per day*. The forex market operates continuously during the business week, with trading beginning each business day in Tokyo. As the

Figure 20.2
Triangular Arbitrage and Foreign Exchange Market Equilibrium

Exchange Rates Available in New York	U.S. $ Equivalent
British £	1.7360
Canadian $	0.8388

Exchange Rate Available in London	£1 = C$2.1000

Market Is Not in Equilibrium Because $\dfrac{1.7360}{0.8388} < 2.1000$

Effects of Arbitragers' Trades

1. Selling US$ and buying £ in New York puts upward pressure on the pound in that market . . . . . . 1.7360 ↑
2. Selling £ and buying C$ in London puts downward pressure on the pound in London . . . . . . 2.1000 ↓
3. Selling C$ and buying US$ in New York puts downward pressure on the C$ in that market . . . . . . 0.8388 ↓
4. The left-hand side of the equation above gets bigger, while the right-hand side gets smaller, until a new equilibrium is reached

$$\frac{1.7360\,\uparrow}{0.8388\,\downarrow} < 2.1000\,\downarrow \longrightarrow \text{New equilibrium}$$

day evolves, trading moves westward as major dealing centers in Singapore, Bahrain (Persian Gulf), continental Europe, London, and finally North America (particularly New York and Toronto) come online. Dealers in all these markets quote buy and sell prices (bid/ask) for currencies versus the U.S. dollar and, to a limited degree, other currencies as well. Prices for all the floating currencies are set by global supply and demand. Trading in fixed-rate currencies is more constrained and regulated and frequently involves a national government (or a state-owned bank) as counterparty on one side of the trade.

The players in the forex market are numerous, as are their motivations for participating in the market. We can break participants in this market into six distinct (but not mutually exclusive) groups: (1) exporters and importers, (2) investors, (3) hedgers, (4) speculators, (5) dealers, and at times, (6) governments.

Importers and Exporters. Businesses that export goods to or import goods from a foreign country need to enter the foreign exchange market to pay bills denominated in foreign currency or to convert foreign currency revenues back into the domestic currency. Along with all the other players in the market, exporters and importers influence currency values. For instance, if Europeans develop a taste for California wines, then European importers will exchange euros (or perhaps pounds, kroner, francs, etc.) for dollars to purchase wine. Other factors held constant, these trades will tend to put upward pressure on the value of the dollar and downward pressure on European currencies.

Investors. Investors also trade foreign currency when they seek to buy and sell financial assets in foreign countries. In the fall of 2005, political turmoil in continental Europe—including an indecisive German national election and prolonged rioting in France—led some investors to pull out of their European investments and seek investment opportunities elsewhere. Those who did had to sell euros and buy the currency of the country in which they wanted to invest, putting downward pressure on the euro relative to other currencies. In general, the pressures exerted on currencies by investors are much larger than those exerted by exporters and importers because investors account for a larger fraction of currency trading volume. For example, the total value of goods and services traded internationally each year is about $10 trillion, whereas the aggregate value of currency trading is 50 times that, some $500 trillion annually.

Hedgers. Hedgers influence currency values when they take positions to offset the risks of their existing exposures to certain currencies. In contrast, speculators take positions not to reduce risk but to increase it. Speculators sell a currency if they expect it to depreciate and buy if they expect it to appreciate. Some speculators, such as George Soros, have become famous for the enormous profits (or losses) they have earned by taking large positions in certain currencies. When external pressures force a country with a pegged currency to devalue its currency, speculators often take the blame.

Whether they deserve blame for causing, accelerating, or exacerbating currency crises or not, speculators can play a useful economic role by taking the opposite side of a transaction from that of hedgers. Speculators help make the foreign currency market more liquid and more efficient.

Dealers. As in all financial markets, dealers play a crucial role in the foreign exchange business. Most foreign currency trades go through large, international banks in the leading financial centers around the globe: London, New York, Tokyo, and so on. These banks, the dealers, provide a means for buyers and sellers to come together, and as their reward they earn a small fee—the bid-ask spread—on each round-trip buy-and-sell transaction they facilitate.

Government. Finally, governments intervene in financial markets to put upward or downward pressure on currencies as circumstances dictate. Governments that attempt to maintain a fixed exchange rate with the rest of the world generally must intervene more frequently than those that intervene only in times of crisis. Currency movements create winners and losers not only across national boundaries, but within a given country. For example, a rise in the value of the U.S. dollar makes U.S. exports more expensive and foreign imports cheaper. Remember, an exchange rate is simply a price—the price of trading one currency for another. Though the financial press dramatizes changes in exchange rates by attaching an adjective such as *strong* or *weak* to a given currency, this practice is rather odd when you recognize that they are just talking about a price. For instance, if the price of apples rises and the price of bananas falls, we do not refer to apples as being strong and bananas as being weak. If the price of apples is high, that is good for apple producers and bad for apple consumers. In the same way, a rise in the value of a particular currency benefits some and harms others. Therefore, at least for the major, free-floating currencies, governments are reluctant to intervene because doing so does not unambiguously improve welfare across the board.

Even when governments want to intervene in currency markets, doing so is complicated by the fact that currency values are not set in a vacuum but are linked to other economic variables, such as interest rates and inflation. In the next section, we discuss four parity relationships that illustrate the linkages that should hold in equilibrium between exchange rates and other macroeconomic variables.

Concept Review Questions

1. Explain how a rise in the euro might affect a French company exporting wine to the United States, and compare that to the impact on a German firm importing semiconductors from the United States.

2. Holding all other factors constant, how might an increase in interest rates in Britain affect the value of the pound?

3. If someone says, "The exchange rate between dollars and pounds increased today," can you say for sure which currency appreciated and which depreciated? Why or why not?

4. Define spot and forward exchange rates. If a trader expects to buy a foreign currency in one month, can you explain why the trader might prefer to enter into a forward contract today rather than wait a month and transact at the spot rate prevailing then?

20.2 THE PARITY CONDITIONS IN INTERNATIONAL FINANCE

In this section, we discuss the major forces that influence the values of all the world's free-floating currencies. Theory suggests that when markets are in equilibrium, spot and forward exchange rates, interest rates, and inflation rates should be linked across countries. Market imperfections, such as trade barriers and transactions costs, may prevent these parity conditions from holding precisely at all times, but they are still powerful determinants of exchange rate values in the long run.

FORWARD–SPOT PARITY

If the spot rate governs foreign exchange transactions in the present and the forward rate equals the price of trading currencies at some point in the future, intuition suggests that the forward rate might be useful in predicting how the spot rate will change over time. For example, suppose that a British firm intends to import U.S. wheat, for which it must pay $1.80 million in one month. The pound currently trades at a forward premium, and the prevailing spot and forward exchange rates are as follows:

Spot = $1.75/£   1-month forward = $1.80/£

The U.K. firm faces a choice. Either it can lock in the forward rate today, guaranteeing that it will pay £1 million for its wheat ($1.8 million ÷ $1.80/£), or it can wait a month and transact at the spot rate prevailing then. Let us suppose that the U.K. firm in this example is risk neutral. This assumption implies that the firm does not care about exchange rate risk, and it will decide to enter the forward contract only if it believes that trading at the forward rate will be less expensive than trading at the spot rate in 30 days.

This results in a simple decision rule for the U.K. importer. First, it must form a forecast of what the spot exchange rate will be in one month. Let's call that the expected spot rate and denote it with the symbol $E(S)$. We can now determine the U.K. firm's decision rule:

1. Enter the forward contract today if $E(S) < $1.80/£$.
2. Wait and buy dollars at the spot rate if $E(S) > $1.80/£$.

For example, assume the firm's forecast is that the spot rate will not change from its current level of $1.75/£. Given this forecast, the expected cost of purchasing $1.80 million in 30 days is £1,028,571 ($1.8 million/$1.75/£); and given that the firm will need only £1 million if it locks in the forward rate, it does not pay to wait. Conversely, assume that the U.K. firm believes that over the next 30 days, the pound will appreciate to $1.85/£. In that case, the expected cost of paying for the wheat is just £972,973, and the firm should wait. Only if the firm's forecast of the expected spot rate is $1.80/£, equal to the current forward rate, will it be indifferent to whether it locks in the forward contract now or waits 30 days to transact at that day's spot rate.

If we look at this problem from the perspective of a U.S. firm that must pay in pounds in 30 days to import some good from the United Kingdom, we get just the opposite decision rule. For the (risk-neutral) U.S. firm, entering a forward contract to buy pounds makes sense if the expected spot rate in 30 days is greater than the current forward rate [$E(S) > $1.80/£$]. Clearly, appreciation in the pound increases the cost of importing from Britain, so if a U.S. firm expects the pound to appreciate above the current forward rate, it will lock in a forward contract immediately. On the other hand, if the U.S. firm expects the spot rate to be less than $1.80/£ in 30 days, it will choose to wait rather than lock in at the forward rate.

Now we broaden the example to include all U.S. and U.K. firms who face a future need to buy foreign currency, and we maintain the assumption of risk neutrality. Ideally, U.S. firms who need to buy pounds to import British goods could trade with U.K. firms who must sell pounds and buy dollars to import U.S. goods. However, there is a problem, because the circumstances under which firms in each country prefer to trade in the spot market rather than the forward market are mirror images of each other:

1. If $E(S) > F$, the U.K. firms do not want the forward contract, but U.S. firms do.
2. If $E(S) < F$, the U.K. firms want the forward contract, but U.S. firms do not.

[handwritten margin notes:]

does forward-spot parity really work?

Regression evidence:

$Spot_{(t+1)} = a + b \, Fwd_{(t)}$

If parity holds, $a = 0$ and $b = 1$

most studies reject both of these conditions

R-squared (predictability) very low

Short-run FX movements are almost random

Equilibrium will occur in this market only when the forecast of the spot rate is equal to the current forward rate. In that case, U.S. and U.K. firms are indifferent to whether they transact in the spot or the forward market. This yields our first parity condition, known as **forward–spot parity.** It says that the forward rate should be an unbiased predictor of where the spot rate is headed:

$$E(S) = F \qquad\qquad \text{(Eq. 20.2)}$$

It would certainly be convenient for currency traders if the forward exchange rate provided a reliable forecast of future spot rates. Unfortunately, most studies suggest that this is not the case. Some researchers have found that, on average, the spot rate moves in the opposite direction than that predicted by the forward rate. Other studies find that whereas the direction of spot rate movements is consistent with the direction predicted by forward rates, the magnitudes are too small. That is, when a currency trades at a forward premium, suggesting the currency will appreciate on the spot market, the currency does appreciate, but not by as much as the forward rate predicted. Finally, virtually all studies of exchange rate movements find a great deal of "noise," or randomness, in spot rate movements. Even if spot rates tend to move in the direction predicted by forward rates, they do not do so with a high degree of reliability.

If forward rates do not accurately predict movements in currency values over time, perhaps something else does. Economists have long observed a correlation between currency movements and inflation rate differentials across countries. To illustrate, the following table reports the cumulative inflation that occurred in the United States, Japan, Germany, and France from 1984 to 1996. In addition, the table shows the difference between U.S. inflation and that which occurred in the other countries, as well as the cumulative change in the values of the yen, the German mark, and the French franc against the dollar over the same period:

	Comparative Figures for 1984–1996		
Country	% Cumulative Inflation	% U.S. Inflation—Foreign	% Change against the $
U.S.	51	NA	NA
Japan	17	+34	+46
Germany	52	−1	−4.5
France	100	−49	−50

Notice the remarkable correspondence between the numbers in the second and third columns. Japan's was the only currency that appreciated against the dollar from 1984 to 1996, and it was the only country on the list with less inflation than the United States. German and U.S. inflation was about equal, and the dollar–mark exchange rate was about the same in 1996 as it was in 1984. French inflation was roughly 50 percentage points higher than U.S. inflation, about equal to the decline in the franc.

These figures suggest that differences in inflation do a good job of explaining currency movements, at least over a long period of time. The second parity relationship reveals why.

PURCHASING POWER PARITY

One of the simplest ideas in economics is **the law of one price.** This means that identical goods trading in different markets should sell at the same price, absent any barriers to trade. The law of one price has a natural application in international finance.

Suppose that a DVD of a hit movie retails in the United States for $20 and that the identical DVD can be purchased in Tokyo for ¥2,000. Does the law of one price hold? It depends on the exchange rate. If the spot rate of exchange equals ¥100/$, then the answer is yes. A U.S. consumer can spend $20 to purchase the DVD in the United States or can convert $20 to ¥2,000 and purchase the item in Tokyo. We can generalize this example as follows. Suppose the price of an item in domestic currency is P_{dom} and the price of the identical item in foreign currency is P_{for}. If the spot exchange rate quoted in foreign currency per domestic is $S^{for/dom}$, then the law of one price holds if the following is true:

$$\frac{P_{for}}{P_{dom}} = S^{for/dom}$$

(Eq. 20.3)

Naturally, the law of one price extends to any pair of countries, not just the United States and Japan. When Equation 20.3 does not hold, traders may engage in arbitrage to exploit price discrepancies across national boundaries.

APPLYING THE MODEL 20.3

Suppose that a pair of Maui Jim sunglasses sells for $200 in the United States and for €160 in Italy. The exchange rate between dollars and euros is €0.85/$. Does the law of one price hold? Apparently not, because the following is true:

$$\frac{160}{200} < 0.85$$

How can arbitrageurs exploit this violation of the law of one price? The previous equation reveals that the price of sunglasses in Italy is too low, or the price in the United States is too high, relative to the current exchange rate. Therefore, suppose that a trader buys sunglasses in Italy for €160 and ships them to the United States. After selling them for $200, the trader can convert back to euros, receiving €170 (C$200 × €0.85/$). The arbitrage profit is €10. As long as the transaction costs of making these trades are less than €10, and as long as there are no other barriers to trade, then the process will continue until the market reaches equilibrium.

Now we will add a new wrinkle to the law of one price. Suppose that prices in different countries satisfy Equation 20.3, not just at one moment in time, but all the time. We do not necessarily expect this to be the case for every type of good sold in two countries. But if price discrepancies for similar goods become too large, the forces of arbitrage should push them back in line. Of course, the prices of goods and services change every day due to inflation (or deflation), and there is no reason to expect the inflation rate in one country to be the same as in another. If different countries are subject to different inflation pressures, how can the law of one price hold on an ongoing basis? The answer is that the exchange rate adjusts to maintain equilibrium.

APPLYING THE MODEL 20.4

Suppose that the forces of arbitrage have changed the prices of Maui Jim sunglasses in the United States and in Italy so that the law of one price now holds.

Specifically, the U.S. price is $195, and the Italian price is €165.75. If the exchange rate is still €0.85/$, then the law of one price holds because the following is true:

$$\frac{€165.75}{\$195} = €0.85/\$$$

Now suppose that the expected rate of inflation in Italy over the next year is 4 percent but that no inflation is expected in the United States. One year from today, Maui Jim sunglasses will still sell for $195 in the United States, but with 4 percent inflation the price in Italy will rise to €172.38 (€165.75 × 1.04). If these forecasts are correct, then in a year the exchange rate must rise to €0.8840/$ for the law of one price to hold:

$$\frac{€172.38}{\$195} = €0.8840/\$$$

Remember, this exchange rate is expressed in euros per dollar, so an increase from €0.85/$ to €0.8840/$ represents appreciation of the dollar and depreciation of the euro.

Purchasing power parity is an extension of the law of one price. **Purchasing power parity** says that if the law of one price holds at all times, then differences in expected inflation between two countries are associated with expected changes in currency values. Mathematically, we can express this idea as follows:

$$\frac{E(S^{\text{for/dom}})}{S^{\text{for/dom}}} = \frac{[1 + E(i_{\text{for}})]}{[1 + E(i_{\text{dom}})]} \qquad \textbf{(Eq. 20.4)}$$

where, as before, the expected spot rate is $E(S)$, the current spot rate is S, the expected rate of inflation in the foreign country is $E(i_{\text{for}})$, and the expected rate of inflation in the domestic country is $E(i_{\text{dom}})$. Notice that the left-hand side of this equation exceeds 1.0 if traders expect the domestic currency to appreciate and is less than 1.0 if traders expect the foreign currency to appreciate. Likewise, the right-hand side of the equation exceeds 1.0 when expected inflation is higher abroad than it is at home, and the ratio falls below 1.0 when the opposite is true. Therefore, the equation produces the already familiar prediction that if inflation is higher in one country than another, then the currency of the country with higher inflation will depreciate. The equation also offers the helpful information that traders who want to forecast currency movements should invest resources in forecasting inflation rates.

How accurately does purchasing power parity predict exchange rate movements? As we have already seen, over the long term there is a very high correlation between currency values and inflation rates. Countries with high inflation see their currencies depreciate over time, whereas the opposite happens for countries with lower inflation. This is no accident. If we did not observe this correlation in the data, it would be a signal of gross violations of the law of one price and a sign that arbitrage was not working to bring prices back into line.

But purchasing power parity does not fare as well in the short run. Violations of the law of one price do occur frequently, and many studies suggest that they persist from three to four years on average. Again, arbitrage, or in this case limits to arbitrage, explain why. When goods prices in different countries are out of equilibrium, arbitrageurs must trade the goods, moving them across national borders, to earn a profit. This process cannot occur without investments in time and money, and for certain goods trade may be impossible due to legal restrictions or the physical impediments to transporting goods. Accordingly, there is no reason to expect goods to flow from one market to the other instantaneously at any moment when the law of one price does not hold. Only if price discrepancies across markets are large enough and persistent enough will arbitrageurs find it profitable to trade. Hence, purchasing power parity does a good job of explaining long-run movements in currencies but not day-to-day, or even year-to-year, fluctuations.

INTEREST RATE PARITY

Although it is both time-consuming and expensive to move goods across borders, the same cannot generally be said about purely financial transactions. Large institutional investors can buy and sell currencies very rapidly and at low cost, and they can buy and sell financial assets denominated in different currencies just as quickly. **Interest rate parity** applies the law of one price to financial assets, specifically to risk-free assets denominated in different currencies. Interest rate parity means that risk-free investments should offer the same return (after converting currencies) everywhere.

To illustrate, assume that a U.S. institution has $10 million that it wants to invest for 180 days in a risk-free government bill. The current annual interest rate on 180-day U.S. Treasury bills is 4 percent per year (2% for six months), so if the institution chooses this investment, it will have $10.2 million six months later:

$$\$10,000,000\left(1 + \frac{R_{US}}{2}\right) = \$10,200,000$$

Alternatively, the institution might choose to convert its $10 million into another currency and invest abroad. However, even if it invests in a risk-free government bill issued by a foreign government, the institution must enter into a forward contract to convert back into dollars when the investment matures. Otherwise, the return on the foreign investment is not risk-free and will depend on changes in currency values over the next six months.

For example, suppose the annual interest rate on a 6-month Swiss government bill is 0.55 percent per year (0.275% for six months). Suppose also that the spot and 6-month forward exchange rates are SF1.3161/$ and SF1.2938/$, respectively, as given in Figure 20.1. The U.S. institution converts $10 million into SF13,161,000 at the spot rate. It invests the Swiss francs for six months at the Swiss interest rate and enters into a forward contract to convert those francs back into dollars when the Swiss bill matures. At the end of six months, the institution has the following:[2]

$$\$10,000,000(S^{SF/\$})\left(1 + \frac{R_{Swiss}}{2}\right)\left(\frac{1}{F^{SF/\$}}\right) = \$10,200,110$$

Given the prevailing interest rates on short-term, risk-free U.S. and Swiss bonds, and given current spot and forward exchange rates between dollars and Swiss francs, investors are fairly indifferent to whether they invest in the United States or

---

[2.] Notice that in this equation we divide by the forward rate to convert Swiss Francs back into dollars. Also, the $110 difference between the payoffs on the U.S. and Swiss investment strategies results from the fact that we only quoted the Swiss interest rate to two decimals. Using a 6-month Swiss rate of 0.2739 percent (corresponding to an annual Swiss rate of 0.5478 percent) brings the two payoffs within $2 of each other.

Switzerland. In other words, with respect to short-term, risk-free financial assets, the law of one price holds—and this relationship is called *interest rate parity*. As usual, we can express interest rate parity in mathematical terms. Letting R_{for} and R_{dom} represent the risk-free rates on foreign and domestic government debt, respectively, we obtain the following equation:[3]

$$\frac{F^{for/dom}}{S^{for/dom}} = \frac{(1 + R^{for})}{(1 + R^{dom})} \qquad \text{(Eq. 20.5)}$$

What is the intuitive interpretation of this expression? Observe that if the left-hand side of the equation is greater than 1.0, the domestic currency trades at a forward premium. If domestic investors send money abroad, when they convert back to domestic currency they will realize an exchange loss because the foreign currency buys less domestic currency than it did at the spot rate. Domestic investors know this, so they require an incentive in the form of a higher foreign interest rate before they will send money abroad. To maintain equilibrium, the right-hand side must also be greater than 1.0, which means that the foreign interest rate must exceed the domestic rate. The bottom line is that when a nation's currency trades at a forward premium (discount), risk-free interest rates in that country should be lower (higher) than they are abroad.[4]

As is the case with purchasing power parity, deviations from interest rate parity create arbitrage opportunities. However, these arbitrage opportunities involve buying and selling financial assets rather than physical commodities. As we know, trade in securities can occur rapidly and much less expensively than trade in goods, so the forces of arbitrage are more powerful in maintaining interest rate parity.

APPLYING THE MODEL 20.5

Suppose that the 6-month, risk-free rate in the United States is 4 percent per year (2 percent for 6 months) and in Canada is 3.2 percent per year (1.60 percent for 6 months). The spot exchange rate is C$1.1922/$, and the 180-day forward rate is C$1.1862/$. Interest rate parity does not hold, as shown in the following equation:

$$\frac{C\$1.1862/\$}{C\$1.1922/\$} < \frac{1 + \dfrac{0.032}{2}}{1 + \dfrac{0.04}{2}}$$

Because the right-hand side of this equation is "too large" relative to parity, the interest rate in Canada is "too high" or the rate in the U.S. is "too low." The

---

[3.] Be careful to match the term of the forward rate to the term of the interest rate in this expression. For example, if you are comparing interest rates on 180-day government bills, you must use a 180-day forward rate. You can see this by going back to the example of the institution with $10 million to invest. If you set the equation representing the institution's U.S. return equal to the equation representing its Swiss return, the following equation results:

$$\frac{F^{SF/\$}}{S^{SF/\$}} = \frac{1 + \dfrac{R_{Swiss}}{2}}{\left(1 + \dfrac{R_{US}}{2}\right)}$$

[4.] If interest rates in one country are higher than in another, does that mean that the high-rate country's currencies will depreciate? Though that prediction has obvious intuitive appeal, the opposite seems to occur, on average. See Fama (1984) and Backus, Foresi, and Telmer (2001).

arbitrage opportunity is as follows: An investor borrows money (say $1 million) at 4 percent in the United States, converts the proceeds into Canadian dollars, and then invests them at 3.20 percent. Six months later, the investor converts the Canadian dollars back into U.S. currency to repay the loan. Anything left over is pure arbitrage profit.

Borrow $1 million in the U.S. at 4 percent for six months → must repay $1,020,000
    $1 million → converted at spot rate → C$1,192,200
    C$1,192,200 invested for six months at 3.20 percent →
      (C$1,192,200) (1.016) → C$1,211,275
    C$1,211,275 converted to US$ at the forward rate → $1,021,105
    $1,020,000 needed to repay U.S. loan → leaves $1,105 arbitrage profit

The effect of all of these transactions, repeated again and again, is to push exchange rates and interest rates back toward parity. As investors borrow in the United States, the U.S. interest rate will rise from 4 percent to a higher level. Similarly, as investors purchase Canadian government bonds, the bond prices will rise and the risk-free rate in Canada will fall. When investors sell U.S. dollars to buy Canadian dollars on the spot market, the C$/$ spot rate will fall (the U.S. dollar will depreciate), and just the opposite happens on the forward market as investors sell Canadian dollars to buy U.S. dollars. In terms of the interest rate parity equation, we can see how these forces drive markets to equilibrium:

$$\text{This ratio is increasing} \leftarrow \frac{\text{C\$1.1862/\$}\uparrow}{\text{C\$1.1922/\$}\downarrow} < \frac{1 + \dfrac{0.032\downarrow}{2}}{1 + \dfrac{0.04\uparrow}{2}} \rightarrow \text{This ratio is decreasing}$$

New equilibrium occurs when an inequality becomes an equality.

The process illustrated in the preceding example is known as **covered interest arbitrage** because traders attempt to earn arbitrage profits arising from differences in interest rates across countries, and they "cover" their currency exposures with forward contracts. Implicit in this example was the assumption that investors could borrow and lend at the risk-free rate in each country. Not all investors can do this, but large, creditworthy institutions can get very close to this ideal. Moreover, they can execute the trades described in the example at very high speed and at low cost. In the real world, deviations from interest rate parity are small and transitory.

REAL INTEREST RATE PARITY (THE FISHER EFFECT)

If nominal rates of return on risk-free investments are equalized around the world, after adjusting for currency translation, perhaps real rates of return are also equalized. **Real interest rate parity** means that investors should earn the same real rate of return on risk-free investments no matter the country in which they choose to invest.[5] Recall from Chapter 5 that the real rate of interest is defined as follows:

$$1 + r_{\text{real}} = \frac{(1 + R)}{[1 + E(i)]}$$

[5.] Real interest rate parity is sometimes called the *Fisher effect*, after the economist who first recognized the relationship between nominal and real interest rates and the inflation rate.

where r_{real} is the real rate of interest, R is the nominal rate, and $E(i)$ is the expected inflation rate. If market forces equalize real rates across national borders, then we can write the following equation:

$$\frac{(1 + R_{for})}{(1 + R_{dom})} = \frac{[1 + E(i_{for})]}{[1 + E(i_{dom})]} \qquad \text{(Eq. 20.6)}$$

This equation says that if real rates are the same in the domestic and the foreign country, then the ratio of (1 plus) nominal interest rates in the two countries must equal the ratio of (1 plus) expected inflation rates. If expected inflation is higher in one country than in another, then the country with higher inflation must offer higher interest rates to give investors the same real return.

APPLYING THE MODEL 20.6

Suppose that expected inflation in the United States equals zero and expected inflation in Italy is 4 percent. If the 1-year, risk-free rate in the United States is 3 percent, what would the 1-year, risk-free rate have to be in Italy to maintain real interest rate parity?

$R_{Italy} = 7.12\%$

As with purchasing power parity, real interest rate parity need not hold at all times, because when deviations from parity occur, limits to arbitrage prevent market forces from quickly reaching a new equilibrium. In this case, the limits to arbitrage include the scarcity of risk-free investments that offer fixed real, rather than nominal, returns. In the United States and a few other countries, governments issue bonds with payouts tied to the inflation rate. These bonds offer investors a way to lock in a fixed real rate. In the long run, we expect that real interest rate parity will hold, at least approximately, but that will not necessarily be the case in the short run.

We conclude this section with a quick review of the four parity relationships, highlighting how they are linked together. If we combine Equations 20.2, 20.4, 20.5, and 20.6, we have the following relationships:[6]

$$\frac{E(S)}{S} = \frac{F}{S} = \frac{(1 + R_{for})}{(1 + R_{dom})} = \frac{[1 + E(i_{for})]}{[1 + E(i_{dom})]} = \frac{E(S)}{S} \qquad \text{(Eq. 20.7)}$$

The first equality simply restates the forward–spot parity relationship. The second equality is the expression for interest rate parity, and the third and fourth equalities define real interest rate parity and purchasing power parity, respectively. Here we see for the first time that if markets are in equilibrium, spot and forward exchange rates, nominal interest rates, and expected inflation rates are all linked internationally. If we want to understand why currency values change, Equation 20.7 gives us a number of clues. The equation also illustrates how difficult it can be for countries to manage their exchange rates. Attempts to push the exchange rate in a particular

---

[6.] Notice that we have divided both sides of Equation 20.2 by the spot rate here. This does no harm to the equality, and it allows us to highlight the connections between forward–spot parity and the other parity relationships.

direction invariably lead to changes in other macroeconomic variables that policy-makers may not desire.[7]

THE ASSET MARKET MODEL OF EXCHANGE RATES

The four parity conditions provide important insights into the factors that set relative currency values, but they provide an incomplete picture of what will cause exchange rates to change over time and of how this change will occur. Clearly, all the parity conditions suggest that rising inflation will cause a nation's nominal interest rate to rise and its currency to depreciate. But will this depreciation occur in the spot or the forward market, and will it occur immediately or over time? Moreover, how can we explain the observed tendency of currency traders to react to economic news not covered by the parity conditions—in particular, to news about relative economic growth prospects in two countries?

Before proceeding, we should make a distinction between nominal and real exchange rate changes. Changes in the *nominal exchange rate* are those that exactly mirror changes in relative inflation rates between two countries, whereas changes in the *real exchange rate* measure changes in the purchasing power of a currency. For example, if inflation is 2 percent higher in Europe than in the United States, purchasing power parity predicts that the nominal value of the euro (the dollar) will fall (rise) by about 2 percent, leaving the real exchange rate unchanged. If, in fact, the dollar rises by 3 percent against the euro, then the real value of the dollar has increased.

A model that offers additional insights into the causes of currency movements is the **asset market model of exchange rates.** This model makes a distinction between the demand for a currency as a means of payment (transactions demand) and the demand for currency as a financial asset (as a store of value). It predicts that currency values will be set by investors, who demand a currency in order to invest in that country, rather than by traders, who demand a currency in order to pay for exports or imports.

The asset market model is both flexible and powerful, for it can explain the effect that changes in investor expectations can have on relative currency values. For example, assume that investors receive news suggesting that America's economic growth rate over the next several quarters will be higher than expected. In the absence of comparable new information regarding Europe's growth prospects, international investors will increase their demand for dollars on the foreign exchange market either to make direct investments in U.S. businesses or to make portfolio investments in U.S. capital markets. Other things equal, this increased demand for dollars (or, equivalently, the increased supply of euros), in the face of stable demand for euros, will cause the dollar to appreciate and the €/$ exchange rate to rise. Reputation effects also play a role in the asset market model of exchange rates. If a government establishes a reputation for pursuing sound economic policies, that nation's currency will tend to appreciate as investors come to trust the currency as a store of value.

[7.] In October 1997, market pressure was building for a devaluation of the Hong Kong dollar. Hong Kong's currency board reacted by purchasing vast amounts of Hong Kong currency. One consequence of their activity was that overnight interest rates in Hong Kong briefly reached 280 percent. See Gerlach (2002) for details. A year later, a similar spike occurred in Russian interest rates as the government unsuccessfully attempted to support the ruble.

**Concept
Review
Questions**

5. Explain the logic behind each of the four parity relationships.

6. Explain the role of arbitrage in maintaining the parity relationships.

7. In what sense is interest rate parity an application of the law of one price?

8. An investor who notices that interest rates are much lower in Japan than in the United States borrows in Japan and invests the proceeds in the United States. This is called *uncovered interest arbitrage,* but is it really arbitrage? Why or why not?

20.3 MANAGING FINANCIAL, ECONOMIC, AND POLITICAL RISK

Any firm that might experience an adverse change in the value of any of its cash flows as a result of exchange rate movements faces exposure to *exchange rate risk*. Almost every firm is exposed to exchange rate risk to some degree, even if it operates strictly in one country and has cash flows in only one currency. Such a firm will face exchange rate risk if (1) it produces a good or service that competes with imports in the home market, or (2) it uses as a production input an imported product or service.

Nonetheless, some types of companies face greater exchange rate risk than do others. MNCs obviously face this risk in all aspects of their business, but they also have many opportunities to minimize that risk by, for example, moving production facilities to the countries where their products are sold so that costs and revenues can be in the same currency. The greatest exchange rate exposure occurs when a firm's costs and revenues are largely denominated in different currencies.

As usual, it is easiest to describe the importance of exchange rate risk to an exporter with an example. Assume that the Boeing Co. has just sold an airplane to a Japanese buyer, with the following details: First, Boeing must price the airplane in terms of yen so that it receives payment worth $1 million to cover its U.S. dollar costs and generate an acceptable profit. Second, suppose Boeing agrees to receive payment for the aircraft in yen. Third, assume that the current yen/dollar exchange rate is ¥100.00/$. Therefore, Boeing negotiates a price of ¥100 million for the airplane, but the company is primarily concerned with the dollars it will collect when payment is made in yen and then converted into dollars on the foreign exchange market.

If Boeing negotiates the terms of this sale at the same time that it receives payment, it does not face any foreign exchange risk. The company will simply exchange ¥100 million for $1 million on the spot market. In reality, Boeing will probably negotiate payment terms months before it expects payment from the Japanese customer. This simple fact creates exchange rate risk, because between the dates when Boeing sets the price in yen for the plane and when it receives payment, the exchange rate can move. Because the contract is denominated in yen, Boeing bears this exchange rate risk. But the risk would not be eliminated by denominating the sales contract in dollars—the risk would simply be shifted to the Japanese buyer.

Suppose that after Boeing agrees to a price, it must wait six months for payment. In that time, the exchange rate changes to ¥110.00/$, meaning that the dollar has appreciated, and the yen has depreciated. Boeing will still receive the same ¥100 million, but now the amount is worth just $909,091. Appreciation in the dollar results in Boeing realizing an *exchange rate loss* of $90,909. If the yen appreciates, say, to ¥90.00/$, Boeing will receive $1,111,111 and will realize an *exchange rate gain* of $111,111.

This exchange rate risk, known as **transactions exposure,** cannot be eliminated, but it can be **hedged** (transferred to a third party) by using financial contracts. Boeing has many hedging options to choose from, including hedging (1) in the forward or futures market, (2) in the currency options market, (3) via swaps, and (4) via money market instruments. Because specific hedging strategies are described in depth in the risk management chapter, we will not describe each strategy here. We will demonstrate the use of forward contracts in the following discussion, and we briefly describe other strategies in Table 20.1.

Assume that instead of remaining unhedged, Boeing books the airplane's sale and immediately afterward asks Citibank for a price quote for yen, with delivery to be made in six months. Citibank quotes Boeing a forward price of ¥99/$, which Boeing accepts. Boeing thus *sells yen forward* today, committing itself to deliver ¥100 million and receive $1,010,101 from Citibank exactly six months from now. Once this

Table 20.1   Exchange Rate Risk Management and Hedging Tools

Tool	Description	Impact on Risk Exposure
Borrowing and lending	Borrow money in currency in which payment is to be received and lend in home country currency. Pay off borrowing when payment is made.	Eliminates exchange rate risk as long as there is no risk of default on underlying account receivable.
Forward contract	If foreign currency payment is to be received, sell currency forward, locking in a home country price for foreign currency. If foreign currency payment must be made, buy currency forward.	Forwards eliminate risk, but also eliminate opportunity to profit from favorable changes in currency value. No intermediate cash flows, so can be risky unless counterparty well known.
Futures contract	Used similarly to a forward contract, but involves standardized, exchange-traded financial instrument. Often used for hedging smaller obligations, due to relatively small denomination.	Futures also eliminate both risk and profit opportunity, because futures are an obligation to make or take delivery. Less default risk because exchange traded and marked to market each day.
Options contract	Call options are rights (not obligations) to sell a standard amount of currency at a fixed price; puts are rights to sell. If a forward contract payment is to be received, buy a put option to sell forward contract; if payment is to be made, buy a call option.	Options uniquely hedge risk of adverse exchange rate movements, but preserve potential to profit from favorable exchange rate changes. Downside: very expensive, because premium must be paid for both calls and puts whether exercised or not.
Interest rate swap	Allows the trading of one interest rate stream (e.g., on a fixed-rate U.S. dollar instrument) for another (e.g., on a floating-rate U.S. dollar instrument).	Permits firms to change the interest rate structure of their assets/liabilities and achieves cost savings due to broader market access.
Currency swap	Two parties exchange principal amounts of two different currencies initially; they pay each other's interest payments, then reverse principal amounts at a pre-agreed exchange rate at maturity; more complex than interest rate swaps.	All the features of interest rate swaps, plus it allows firms to change the currency structure of their assets/liabilities.

forward contract is executed, Boeing is no longer exposed to exchange rate risk. The risk has not disappeared; it has simply been transferred from Boeing to Citibank. But why would Citibank be willing to assume this risk?

International banks—and, increasingly, other types of financial institutions—are uniquely positioned to bear exchange rate risk because they can create what amounts to a **natural hedge,** or offsetting risk exposure, as a normal course of their business. This means they are able to easily arrange mirror-image positions with other customers. To see this, consider what type of foreign exchange contract Toyota Motors might demand from Citibank. The exchange rate risk problem for Toyota (one of Japan's biggest exporters) is the opposite of Boeing's: Toyota exports many automobiles from Japan and sells them in the United States. The company receives U.S. dollars as payment, but its costs are in yen, so it would need to *sell dollars forward* (locking in a yen price) in order to cover its costs and make an acceptable profit. Citibank is thus naturally able to buy dollars forward (sell yen) from Toyota and simultaneously sell dollars forward (buy yen) to Boeing and thus net out the exchange rate exposure on its own books. This is, of course, a simplified example, because Citibank may not have a perfectly offsetting exposure for Boeing's needs, but in that case it would simply execute its own forward contract with another bank—perhaps with Toyota's main bank.

We have discussed how to measure exchange rate risk as it applies to specific transactions and have briefly discussed one method of dealing with it using a forward market hedge. However, transactions exposure is but one of many types of exchange rate risk.

TRANSLATION AND ECONOMIC RISK

For MNCs, there are additional complexities involved with operating internationally if they have affiliates or subsidiaries on the ground in a foreign country. One such complication arises when MNCs translate costs and revenues denominated in foreign currencies to report on their financial statements, which, of course, are denominated in the home currency. This type of risk is called *translation exposure* or **accounting exposure.** In other words, foreign exchange rate fluctuations affect individual accounts in the financial statements. A related, and generally more important, risk element is **economic exposure,** which is the overall impact of foreign exchange rate fluctuations on the firm's value.[8] A firm faces economic exposure when exchange rate changes affect its cash flows, even those cash flows not specifically tied to transactions in other currencies. For example, a rise in the value of the dollar against the euro makes European wines less expensive to U.S. consumers, and it makes U.S. wine more expensive for European consumers. A winery operating in the United States, even one that does not sell directly to foreign customers, may realize a decline in cash flows due to competition from suddenly less expensive European vintners.

What can managers do about these risks? Hedging economic exposure is more difficult than hedging transactions exposure, in part because measuring the exposure is more difficult. For instance, a U.S. winery concerned about the declining prices of foreign wines could engage in currency trades that would result in a profit if the dollar appreciates against the euro. In theory, the profits could offset the decline in earnings that occurs when European wines become less expensive. But exactly how large

---

[8.] See Pringle and Connolly (1993) or Harris, Nahum, and Shibano (1996) for excellent discussions on these types of exposures and the way firms manage them.

will these losses be for a given change in the exchange rate? Increasingly, MNCs manage their economic exposures both by using sophisticated currency derivatives and by matching costs and revenues in a given currency. For instance, a foreign company exporting to Japan might issue yen-denominated bonds, so-called Samurai bonds, to create a yen-based liability that would partially or fully offset the exposure resulting from yen-based receivables. However, it is important to emphasize that unless the cash inflows and outflows match exactly, some residual yen exposure will remain.

POLITICAL RISK

Another important risk facing MNCs is **political risk,** which refers to actions taken by a government that have a negative impact on the value of foreign companies operating in that country. These negative impacts may include raising taxes on a firm's activities or erecting barriers that prevent a firm from repatriating profits back to the home country. In its most extreme form, political risk can mean confiscation of a corporation's assets by a foreign government.

Political risk has two basic dimensions: *macro* and *micro*. **Macro political risk** means that *all* foreign firms in the country will be subject to political risk because of political change, revolution, or the adoption of new policies by a host government. Thus, no individual country or firm is treated differently. An example of macro political risk occurred when communist regimes came to power in China in 1949 and Cuba in 1959–1960. More recently, the near collapse of Indonesia's currency in late 1997 and early 1998, plus the attendant political and economic turmoil elsewhere in Asia, highlights the real and present danger that macro political risk can pose to MNCs and international investors alike.[9] **Micro political risk,** on the other hand, refers to a foreign government's targeting punitive action against an individual firm, a specific industry, or companies from a particular foreign country. Examples include the nationalization by a majority of the oil-exporting countries of the assets of the international oil companies in their territories during the 1970s.

Although political risk can take place in any country—even in the United States—the political instability of many developing countries generally makes the positions of multinational companies most vulnerable in those countries. At the same time, some of the countries in this group have the most promising markets for the goods and services being offered by MNCs. The main question, therefore, is how to engage in operations and foreign investment in such countries and still avoid or minimize the potential political risk.

There are both positive and negative approaches that MNCs may be able to adopt to cope with political risk. Negative approaches include taking a trade dispute with a host country to the World Trade Organization (described later) or threatening to withhold additional investments from a country unless the MNC's demands are met. Firms may also negotiate agreements with host governments that build in costs the host government must bear if it breaches the terms of the original agreement. Positive approaches for MNCs include working proactively to develop environmental and labor standards in a country and generally attempting to become perceived as a domestic company by the host country's citizenry.

[9.] Twice each year, *Euromoney* magazine publishes a country risk rating index that assigns a number between 0 (extremely risky) and 100 (essentially risk-free) to the world's largest developed and developing countries. In the March 2002 index, Luxembourg was the least risky country (with an index value of 99.27), followed by Switzerland (97.41), the United States (95.92), and Norway (95.42). North Korea and Afghanistan were ranked lowest (184 and 185), with index values of 6.30 and 2.04, respectively.

EUROPEAN MONETARY UNION AND THE RISE OF REGIONAL TRADING BLOCS

As a result of the Maastricht Treaty of 1991, 11 of the 15 European Union (EU) nations adopted a single currency, the euro, as a continent-wide medium of exchange beginning January 2, 1999. In early 2002, the national currencies of the then 12 countries participating in monetary union disappeared and were completely replaced by the euro. Two years later, in May 2004, the European Union admitted ten new members from Eastern Europe and the Mediterranean region, and in summer 2005 began negotiating with Turkey on its possible entry into the EU. Whatever its final shape, the new community of Europe will offer both challenges and opportunities to a variety of players, including multinational firms. MNCs, especially those based in the United States, will face heightened levels of competition when operating inside the EU.

Another major trading bloc that arose during the 1990s is the Mercosur Group of countries in South America. Beginning in 1991, the nations of Brazil, Argentina, Paraguay, and Uruguay began removing tariffs and other barriers to intraregional trade. The second stage of Mercosur's development began at the end of 1994 and involved the development of a customs union to impose a common tariff on external trade while enforcing uniform and lower tariffs on intragroup trade. To date, Mercosur has been even more successful than its founders had imagined, though the long-term importance of Mercosur will likely depend on whether the U.S. Congress overcomes its reluctance to extend the North American Free Trade Agreement (NAFTA) throughout Central and South America. In any case, the Mercosur countries represent well over half of total South American GDP and thus will loom large in the plans of any MNC wishing to access the growth markets of this region.

Although it may seem that the world is splitting into a handful of trading blocs, this is less dangerous than it may appear because many international treaties are in force that guarantee relatively open access to at least the largest economies. The most important such treaty is the **General Agreement on Tariffs and Trade (GATT)**, which celebrated its fiftieth anniversary in May 1998. The current agreement extends free trading rules to broad areas of economic activity—such as agriculture, financial services, and intellectual property rights—that had not previously been covered by international treaty and that were thus effectively off-limits to foreign competition. The 1994 revised GATT treaty also established a new international body, the **World Trade Organization (WTO)**, to police world trading practices and to mediate disputes between member countries. The WTO began operating in January 1995, and one extremely important nation, the People's Republic of China, became a member in 2002. By November 2005, the WTO had commenced negotiations with Saudi Arabia and Russia regarding their ultimate entry into the global trading fraternity.

THE LONG-TERM SUCCESS OF WORLD TRADE AND FOREIGN DIRECT INVESTMENT

Although world trade has recently become a controversial topic, we believe any hostility is misplaced. Trade is by definition a voluntary exchange between two parties (nations, corporations), and several developing countries have achieved dramatic increases in living standards in a generation by adopting open-market policies and promoting exports. Trade has been one of the great economic success stories of the past half-century, especially since the collapse of the Bretton Woods fixed exchange rate system in 1973. The total value of merchandise trade increased at a compound annual growth rate of 8.1 percent over the 1973–2004 period, rising from about

$750 billion per year to $6.4 trillion in 2000 and then to more than $9.15 trillion over the next four years. Trade in commercial services has grown almost as rapidly, reaching $2.13 trillion in 2004. Even after accounting for inflation, this implies that trade among nations has grown much faster than have the underlying economies of the principal trading nations themselves. And, in contrast to the lopsided pattern of direct investment flows, the growth in trade has benefited developing countries far more (proportionally) than it has the developed countries. Developing countries accounted for a minuscule fraction of total exports in 1973, but developing-country exports now account for over 40 percent of the world's total. It will probably surprise no one that almost all this growth has been achieved by the export-oriented economies of eastern Asia.

Figure 20.3 describes the worldwide growth in merchandise and service exports over 1994–2004, while Figure 20.4 shows the trend in merchandise exports for the five leading exporting countries over this same period. Either Germany or the United States is always the top merchandise exporting nation, but the most dramatic pattern revealed by Figure 20.4 is the phenomenal rise of China. Chinese merchandise exports almost quintupled between 1994 and 2004, rising from $120 billion to $593 billion, and probably by now placing China ahead of Japan as the world's third largest goods exporter.

Foreign direct investment (FDI) is the transfer by a multinational firm of financial, managerial, and technical assets from its home country to a host country. The equity participation on the part of an MNC can be 100 percent (resulting in a wholly owned foreign subsidiary) or less (usually involving a joint-venture project with foreign participants). In contrast to passive, return-oriented portfolio investments undertaken by individuals and companies (e.g., internationally diversified mutual funds), FDI involves equity participation, managerial control, and day-to-day operational activities on the part of MNCs. Therefore, FDI projects will be subject not only to business, financial, inflation, and exchange rate risks (as would foreign portfolio investments), but also to the additional element of political risk.

Figure 20.3
Worldwide Merchandise and Service Exports, US$ Billions, 1994–2004
Source: World Trade Organization (http://www.wto.org).

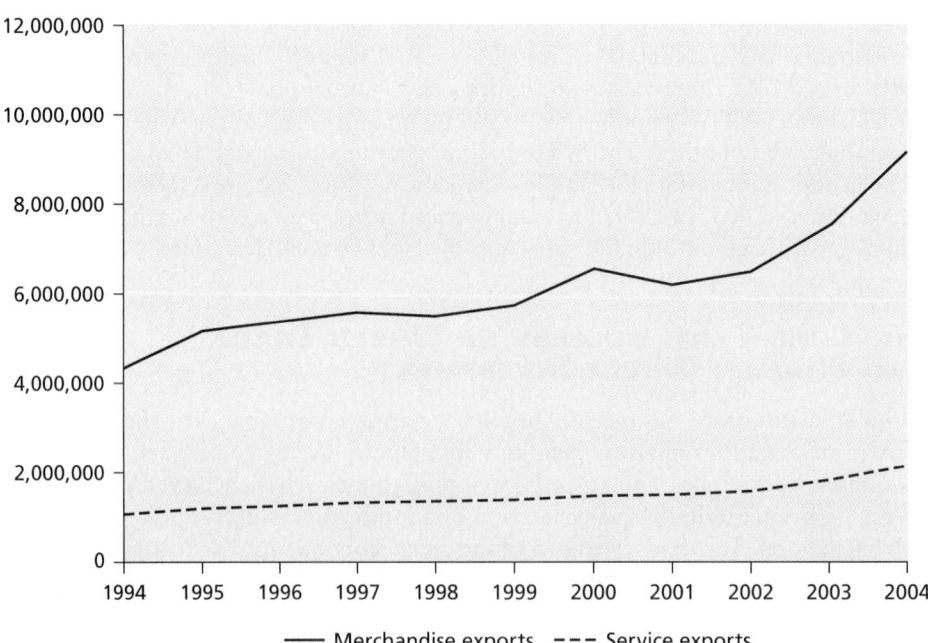

Merchandise exports   --- Service exports

The dramatic growth in the total value of foreign direct investment worldwide over the period 1990–2004 is detailed graphically in Figure 20.5. The total value of FDI inflows dropped to less than $180 billion during the recession year of 1991, before surging to almost $1.4 trillion in 2000. The United States is the largest recipient of FDI inflows every year, though the actual flows change significantly from year to year. The United States received $314.0 billion FDI in 2000 but only $95.9 billion in 2004. American firms and investors are also the largest foreign investors each year, with the outflow totals for 2000 ($142.6 billion) and 2004 ($229.3 billion) almost

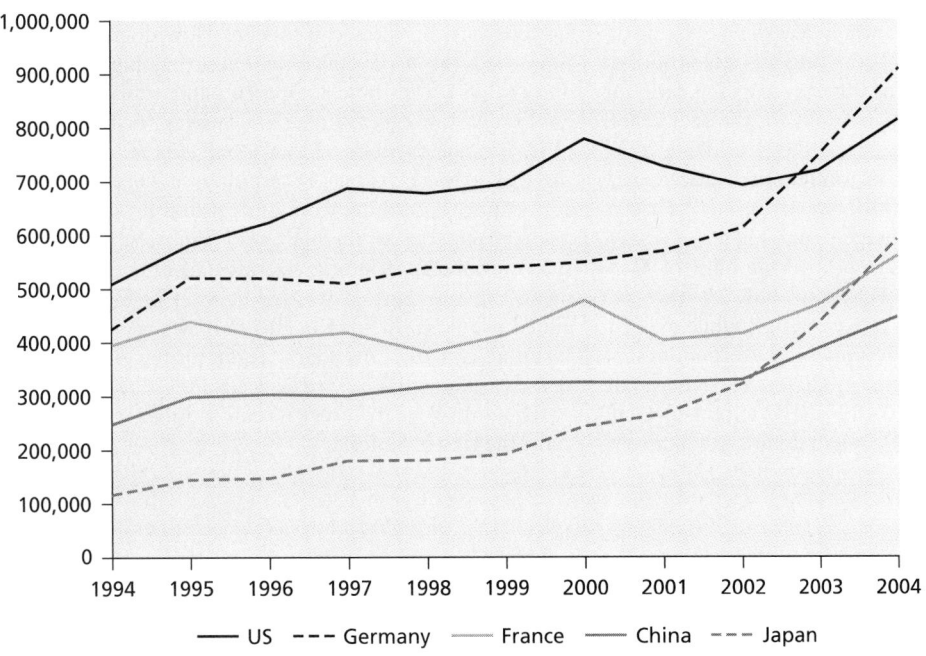

Figure 20.4
Merchandise Exports for Leading Exporting Countries, US$ Billions, 1994–2004
Source: World Trade Organization (http://www.wto.org).

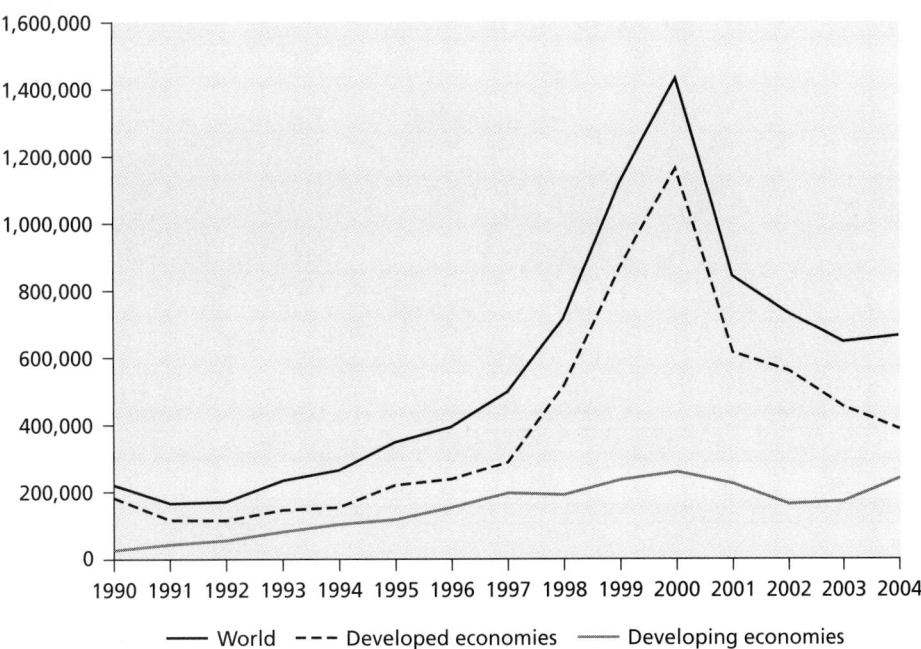

Figure 20.5
Foreign Direct Investment Inflows, 1990–2004 (US$ Billions)
Source: United Nations Conference on Trade and Development (http://www.unctad.org).

COMPARATIVE CORPORATE FINANCE

What Is Japan's Export-to-GDP Ratio?

Although the *globalization of business* has become so widespread that the phrase has now entered popular culture, the actual importance of international trade nonetheless varies dramatically among countries. One key measure of the importance of trade to an economy is a nation's export-to-GDP ratio, or the total value of the nation's exports of goods and services during a year divided by the total value of goods and services produced the same year. The following table presents this ratio for several important exporting nations for the year 2004. Although the United States is the world's leading exporter in absolute terms, its total export-to-GDP ratio is a low 9.7 percent (the U.S. import-to-GDP ratio is usually about three percentage points higher). Canada (37.2%) and the large European economies of Germany, France, Spain, the U.K., and Italy all have export ratios in the 24 to 38 percent range, while exports represent much larger fractions of the economies of Korea (43.3%), greater China (53.8%), the Netherlands (74.7%), and Belgium (101.8%). The export-to-GDP ratios for Hong Kong and Singapore are, respectively,

196.3 and 203.2 percent. But how important are exports to Japan's economy?

Most students (and professors) are astonished to learn that Japan's export-to-GDP ratio is only 14.3 percent, not much larger than America's. In other words, like the United States, Japan is overwhelmingly a domestic economy. But how can this be? How does a nation renowned for producing and exporting high-quality automobiles, electronic equipment, and industrial gear have such a low export ratio? The answer lies in the very narrow range of products that Japan exports. Whereas the United States, Canada, and many European countries export everything from agricultural products and primary minerals to the highest of high-tech manufactured products, including aircraft and military equipment, Japan exports a relative handful of high-value-added products. In spite of this narrow specialization, Japan perennially runs a large trade surplus—meaning that the value of its exports exceeds the value of its imports—with virtually every nation it trades with, especially the United States.

Country	Merchandise Exports, 2004 (US$ billion)	Service Exports, 2004 (US$ billion)	Total Exports, 2004 (US$ billion)	Total Exports-to-GDP Ratio, 2004 (%)
United States	$ 819	$ 318	$ 1,137	9.74
Germany	912	134	1,046	38.5
China; PRC and Hong Kong	859	116	975	53.8
China; PRC only	593	62	655	39.7
Japan	566	95	661	14.3
France	449	109	558	27.9
United Kingdom	347	172	519	24.2
Netherlands	358	73	431	74.7
Italy	349	82	431	25.8
Canada	317	47	364	37.2
Belgium	307	49	356	101.8
Korea	254	40	294	43.3
Spain	179	84	263	26.5
Singapore	180	37	217	203.2
World	$9,153	$2,127	$11,280	27.6

Sources: GDP values, World Bank Group (http://www.worldbank.org); trade data, World Trade Organization (http://www.wto.org).

mirror images of the inflow totals. The United Kingdom and China almost always rank second and third, with inflows of $78.4 billion and $60.6 billion, respectively, in 2004. The vast majority of all FDI is invested in developed rather than developing countries each year. It is clear that developed nations invest mostly in each other (and China), and most investors are investing in an attempt to better serve other Western consumer markets.

9. Distinguish between transactions, translation, and economic exposure.

10. Describe how a domestic firm might use a forward contract to hedge an economic exposure. Why does uncertainty about the magnitude of the exposure make this difficult?

11. Consider a U.S. firm that has for many years exported to European countries. How does the creation of the euro simplify or complicate the management of transactions exposure for this firm?

Concept Review Questions

20.4 LONG-TERM INVESTMENT DECISIONS

In Chapters 7 through 9, we emphasized the importance of sound capital budgeting practices for the long-term survival of a corporation. The same lessons covered in those chapters apply to multinational corporations. Whether investing at home or abroad, MNCs should evaluate investments based on their incremental cash flows and should discount those cash flows at a rate that is appropriate given the risk of the investment. However, when a company makes investments denominated in many different currencies, this process becomes a bit more complicated. First, in what currency should the firm express a foreign project's cash flows? Second, how does one calculate the cost of capital for an MNC or for a given project?

CAPITAL BUDGETING

Suppose that a U.S. firm is weighing an investment that will generate cash flows in euros. The company's financial analysts have estimated the project's cash flows in euros as follows:

Initial Cost	Year 1	Year 2	Year 3
−€2 million	€900,000	€850,000	€800,000

To calculate the project's *NPV*, the U.S. firm can take either of two approaches. First, it can discount euro-denominated cash flows using a euro-based cost of capital. Having done this, the firm can then convert the resulting *NPV* back to dollars at the spot rate. For example, assume that the risk-free rate in Europe is 5 percent and that the firm estimates the cost of capital (expressed as a euro rate) for this project to be 10 percent (in other words, there is a 5% risk premium associated with the investment). The *NPV*, rounded to the nearest thousand euros, equals €122,000:

$$NPV = -2,000,000 + \frac{900,000}{1.1^1} + \frac{850,000}{1.1^2} + \frac{800,000}{1.1^3} = 122,000$$

Assume that the current spot rate equals $1.15/€. Multiplying this times the *NPV* yields a dollar-based *NPV* of $140,000 (rounded to the nearest thousand dollars).

In this example, we did not make specific year-by-year forecasts of the future spot rates. Doing so is unnecessary because the firm can choose to hedge its currency exposure through a forward contract. Hedging the currency exposure allows the firm to separate the decision to accept or reject the project from projections of where the dollar-to-euro exchange rate might be headed. Of course the firm may have a view on the exchange rate question. But even so, it is wise first to consider the merits of the investment on its own. For instance, suppose that this project has a negative NPV, but managers believe that the euro will appreciate over the life of the project, increasing the project's appeal in dollar terms. Given that belief, there is no need for the firm to undertake the project. Instead, it could purchase euros directly, invest them in safe financial assets in Europe, and convert them back to dollars several years later. If the firm wants to speculate on currency movements, it need not invest in physical assets to accomplish that objective.

A second approach for evaluating the investment project is to calculate the NPV in dollar terms, assuming the firm hedges the project's cash flows using forward contracts. To begin this calculation, we must know the risk-free rate in the United States. If the rate is 4 percent, and recognizing that interest rate parity must hold, we can use Equation 20.5 to calculate the 1-year forward rate:

$$\frac{F^{\$/euro}}{S^{\$/euro}} = \frac{(1 + R_{US})}{(1 + R_{euro})} \qquad \frac{F}{1.15} = \frac{1.04}{1.05} \qquad F = \$1.1390/€$$

Similarly, we can calculate the 2-year and 3-year forward rates as follows:

$$\frac{F^{\$/euro}}{S^{\$/euro}} = \frac{(1 + R_{US})^2}{(1 + R_{euro})^2} \qquad \frac{F}{1.15} = \frac{(1.04)^2}{(1.05)^2} \qquad F = \$1.1282/€$$

$$\frac{F^{\$/euro}}{S^{\$/euro}} = \frac{(1 + R_{US})^3}{(1 + R_{euro})^3} \qquad \frac{F}{1.15} = \frac{(1.04)^3}{(1.05)^3} \qquad F = \$1.1175/€$$

Next, multiply each period's cash flow in euros times the matching spot or forward exchange rate to obtain a sequence of cash flows in dollars (rounded to the nearest thousand dollars):

Currency	Initial Investment	Year 1	Year 2	Year 3
€	2,000,000 × 1.15	900,000 × 1.1390	850,000 × 1.1282	800,000 × 1.1175
$	2,300,000	1,025,000	959,000	894,000

All that remains is to discount this project's cash flows at an appropriate risk-adjusted U.S. interest rate. But how do we determine that rate? Recall that the European discount rate used to calculate the euro-denominated NPV was 10 percent, 5 percent above the European risk-free rate. Intuitively, we might expect the comparable U.S. rate to be 9 percent, representing a 5 percent risk premium over the current risk-free rate in the United States. That intuition is roughly correct. To be precise, use the following formula to solve for the project's required return in U.S. dollar terms:

$$(1 + R) = (1 + 0.10)\frac{(1 + 0.04)}{(1 + 0.05)} \qquad R = 8.95\%$$

This equation takes the project's required return in euro terms, 10 percent, and rescales it to dollar terms by multiplying by the ratio of risk-free interest rates in each country. We can verify that discounting the dollar-denominated cash flows using this rate results in the same *NPV* (again, rounding to the nearest thousand dollars) that we obtained by discounting the cash flows in euros and converting to dollars at the spot rate:

$$NPV = \$140,000$$

These calculations demonstrate that a company does not have to "take a view" on currency movements when it invests abroad. Whether the company hedges a project's cash flows using forward contracts or whether it calculates a project's *NPV* in local currency before converting to the home currency at the spot exchange rate, future exchange rate movements need not cloud the capital budgeting decision.

COST OF CAPITAL

In the preceding example, we assumed that the project's cost of capital in Europe was 10 percent, which translated into a dollar-based discount rate of 8.95 percent. But where did the 10 percent come from? We return to the lessons of Chapter 9, namely that the discount rate should reflect the project's risk. One way to assess that risk is to calculate a beta for the investment. However, calculating the beta for an international project raises some questions for which finance as yet has no definitive answer.

For example, suppose that shareholders of the U.S. firm investing in Europe hold mostly U.S. stocks in their portfolios. Perhaps the costs of diversifying internationally are prohibitively expensive for many investors. In that case, when a firm diversifies internationally, it creates value for its shareholders. This stands in sharp contrast to when a firm diversifies domestically. Because U.S. investors can diversify their domestic investments at very low cost, they will not realize any benefit if a firm diversifies on their behalf.

If a firm's shareholders cannot diversify internationally, then when the firm invests abroad, it should calculate a project's beta by measuring the covariance of similar European investments with the U.S. market, not the European market. The reason is that from the perspective of U.S. investors, the project's systematic risk depends on its covariance with the other assets that U.S. investors already own. A U.S. firm planning to build an electronics manufacturing facility in Germany might compare the returns of existing German electronics firms with returns on a U.S. stock index to estimate a project beta.[10]

In contrast, if the firm's shareholders do hold internationally diversified portfolios, the firm should calculate the project's beta by comparing the covariance of its returns (or returns on similar investments) with returns on a worldwide stock index. This generates the project's "global beta." To estimate the project's required return, the firm should apply the CAPM, multiplying the global market risk premium times the project's beta, and adding the risk-free rate. In all likelihood, because a globally diversified portfolio is less volatile than a portfolio containing only domestic securities, the risk premium on the global market will be less than the domestic risk premium.

[10.] Of course, the U.S. firm would have to worry about the effects of leverage, unlevering the equity betas of German firms with debt on their balance sheets.

> ### APPLYING THE MODEL 20.7
>
> A Japanese auto manufacturer decides to build a plant to make cars for the North American market. The firm estimates two project betas. The first calculation takes returns on U.S. auto stocks and calculates their betas relative to those on the Nikkei stock index. Based on these calculations, the Japanese firm decides to apply a beta of 1.1 to the investment. The risk-free rate of interest in Japan is 2 percent, and the market risk premium on the Nikkei index is 8 percent, so the project's required return is calculated as follows:
>
> $$R_{project} = 2\% + 1.1(8\%) = 10.8\%$$
>
> The second calculation takes the returns on U.S. auto manufacturers and determines their betas relative to those on a world stock index. It turns out that U.S. auto stocks are more highly correlated with the world market than they are with the Nikkei. Combined with the fact that the variance of the world market portfolio is lower than the variance of the Nikkei, this calculation leads to a higher estimate of the project beta, say 1.3. However, offsetting this effect is the fact that the risk premium on the world market portfolio is just 5 percent. Therefore, the second estimate of the project's required return is calculated as follows:
>
> $$R_{project} = 2\% + 1.3(5\%) = 8.5\%$$

Concept Review Questions

12. Why does discounting the cash flows of a foreign investment using the foreign cost of capital and then converting that into the home currency at the spot rate yield the same *NPV* as converting the project's cash flows to domestic currency at the forward rate and then discounting them at the domestic cost of capital?

13. What factors determine whether a project's beta will be higher or lower when calculated against a domestic stock index versus a world stock index?

14. Why is it not surprising to find that the risk premium on the world market portfolio is lower than the domestic risk premium?

20.5 SHORT-TERM FINANCIAL DECISIONS

Though the focus in international finance is rightly on long-term investments and economic exposure, managers must also actively measure and manage short-term financial exposures. We have already demonstrated and discussed transactions exposure in the context of exchange rate risk. We now conclude by looking at several other issues related to short-term financial decision making in an international context.

CASH MANAGEMENT

In its international cash management, a multinational firm can respond to exchange rate risks by protecting (hedging) its undesirable cash and marketable securities exposures or by making certain adjustments in its operations. Whereas the former approach is more applicable in responding to *accounting exposures*, the latter is better suited against *economic exposures*. Each of these two approaches is examined here.

Hedging Strategies. Hedging strategies are techniques used to offset or protect against risk, and they are most applicable to transactions exposure. In international cash management, these strategies include actions such as borrowing or lending in different currencies; undertaking contracts in the forward, futures, and/or options markets; and also swapping assets/liabilities with other parties. We refer the reader to Section 20.3 and the risk management chapter for detailed examples.

Adjustments in Operations. In responding to exchange rate fluctuations, MNCs can give some protection to international cash flows through appropriate adjustments in assets and liabilities. Two routes are available to a multinational company to respond to economic exposure. The first centers on the operating relationships that a subsidiary of an MNC maintains with *other* firms. Depending on management's expectation of a local currency's position, adjustments in operations would involve the reduction of liabilities if the currency is appreciating, or the reduction of financial assets if the currency is depreciating. For example, if a U.S.-based MNC with a subsidiary in Mexico expects the Mexican currency to *appreciate* in value relative to the U.S. dollar, local customers' accounts receivable would be *increased* and accounts payable would be reduced, if at all possible. If the Mexican currency was instead expected to *depreciate*, the local customers' accounts receivables would be *reduced* and accounts payables would be increased.

The second route focuses on the operating relationship a subsidiary has with its parent or with other subsidiaries within the same MNC. In dealing with exchange rate risks, a subsidiary can rely on *intra-MNC accounts*. Specifically, undesirable exchange rate exposures can be corrected to the extent that the subsidiary can take the following steps:

1. In appreciation-prone countries, intra-MNC accounts receivable are collected as soon as possible, and payment of intra-MNC accounts payable is delayed as long as possible.
2. In depreciation-prone countries, intra-MNC accounts receivable are collected as late as possible, and intra-MNC accounts payable are paid as soon as possible.

This technique is known as **leading and lagging,** or simply as "leads and lags." The following example illustrates its potential effectiveness.

APPLYING THE MODEL 20.8

Assume that a U.S.-based parent company, American Computer Corporation (ACC), buys parts from and sells parts to its wholly owned Mexican subsidiary, Tijuana Computer Company (TCC). Assume further that ACC has accounts payable of $10 million that it is scheduled to pay TCC in 30 days and in turn has accounts receivable of (Mexican peso) MP106.5 million due from TCC within 30 days. Because today's exchange rate is MP10.65/$, the accounts receivable are also worth $10 million. Therefore, parent and subsidiary owe each other equal amounts (though in different currencies), and both are payable in 30 days. But because TCC is a wholly owned subsidiary of ACC, the parent has complete discretion over the timing of these payments.

If ACC believes the Mexican peso will depreciate from MP10.65/US$ to, say, MP12.00/US$ during the next 30 days, the combined companies can profit by collecting the weak-currency (MP) debt immediately but delaying payment of the strong-currency (US$) debt for the full 30 days allowed. If parent and subsidiary do this and the peso depreciates as predicted, the net result is that the MP106.5 million payment from TCC to ACC is made immediately and is safely converted into

more upside potential with currency options than forward contracts, but they cost more

Forward contracts are cheap but just remove volatility

Swaps are strings of forward contracts (use if you have interest payments to make along the way)

Spot hedge gives you your home currency today, forward hedge gives it in the future

if $ is at forward discount, interest rate SHOULD be higher in the U.S.

$10 million at today's exchange rate, whereas the delayed $10 million payment from ACC to TCC will be worth MP120 million (MP12.00/$ × $10,000,000). Thus, the Mexican subsidiary will experience a foreign exchange trading profit of MP13.5 million (MP120,000,000 − MP106,500,000), whereas the U.S. parent receives the full amount ($10 million) due from TCC and therefore is unharmed. Of course, if the dollar is expected to depreciate against the peso, these steps would be reversed.

The example demonstrates that the manipulation of an MNC's consolidated intracompany accounts by one subsidiary generally benefits one subsidiary (or the parent) while leaving the other subsidiary (or the parent) unharmed. The exact degree and direction of the actual manipulations, however, may depend on the tax status of each country. The MNC obviously would want to have the exchange rate losses in the country with the higher tax rate. Finally, changes in intra-MNC accounts can also be subject to restrictions and regulations put forward by the respective host countries of the various subsidiaries.

CREDIT AND INVENTORY MANAGEMENT

Multinational firms based in different countries compete for the same global export markets. Therefore, it is essential that they offer attractive credit terms to potential customers. Increasingly, however, the maturity and saturation of developed markets are forcing MNCs to maintain and increase revenues by exporting and selling a higher percentage of their output to developing countries. Given the risks associated with the latter group of buyers, as partly evidenced by the greater volatility of many developing nations' currencies, the MNC must employ a variety of tools to protect such revenues. In addition to the use of hedging and various asset and liability adjustments (described earlier), MNCs should seek the backing of their respective governments in both identifying target markets and extending credit. Multinationals based in a number of western European nations and those based in Japan currently benefit from extensive involvement of government agencies that provide them with the needed service and financial support suggested here. For U.S.-based MNCs, the international positions of government agencies such as the Export-Import Bank of the United States currently do not provide a comparable level of support.

In terms of inventory management, MNCs must consider a number of factors related to both economics and politics. In the former category, in addition to maintaining the appropriate level of inventory in various locations around the world, a multinational firm is compelled to deal with exchange rate fluctuations, tariffs, nontariff barriers, integration schemes such as the EU, and other rules and regulations. Politically, inventories can be subjected to wars, expropriations, blockages, and other forms of government intervention.

Concept Review Questions

15. Assume that a U.S. multinational company has wholly owned subsidiaries in both Britain and Switzerland that trade with each other and the parent regularly. Further assume that the British pound is expected to appreciate versus the dollar and the Swiss franc. How could you profit from this using the technique of "leads and lags"?

16. Assume that your firm has sold a computer to a British company, with delivery and payment (in British pounds) to occur in 30 days. You will receive a fixed payment of £2,000, and the current exchange rate is $1.40/£. What risk do you run by remaining unhedged, and how could you hedge that risk using a forward contract?

20.6 SUMMARY

- Large, globally active firms known as multinational corporations (MNCs) dominate international investment and trade today. MNCs tend to be the most dynamic and successful firms in their industry, and most modern international financial and accounting techniques have been designed to meet their special financial needs.
- Any company that exports a significant amount of goods and services is exposed to exchange rate risk, or the chance that a change in the home currency's value relative to the currency in the customer's market can impose financial losses on the exporter. Importers can face similar risks, though this is less common because sales are usually denominated in the customer's currency. A variety of hedging techniques have been developed to handle this risk—the most commonly used is hedging with a forward contract.
- The total volume of foreign direct investment (FDI) surged during the 1990s and shows no sign of permanently slackening. FDI implies that the investor will exercise operating control of the asset being purchased, which is usually a business firm, a factory, or a significant piece of real estate. Portfolio investment, which is much more passive in nature, has also increased dramatically in recent years. The recent economic troubles in Asia, Latin America, and Russia have slowed FDI and portfolio investment only slightly, because most of this occurs between developed economies.
- MNCs must pay particularly careful attention to their management of cash, accounts receivable, and other short-term assets, given the potential danger of loss from exchange rate fluctuations. However, MNCs can also use a variety of techniques not only to survive but even to profit from these fluctuations.

INTERNET RESOURCES

Note: *For updates to links, please go to the book's website at http://smart.swlearning.com.*

http://www.economist.com/markets/currency/map.cfm—The *Economist* magazine's website; offers a worldwide currency map showing data for each country, including currency name and exchange rate vis-à-vis any other currency, population, capital, and land area; map uses color codes to highlight which nations' currencies have appreciated or depreciated (vis-à-vis any other currency) over the past day, week, month, or year

http://www.bis.org—Bank for International Settlements website; offers interesting publications and data on the international banking industry as well as on derivatives

http://www.oanda.com—A site with enormous coverage of the foreign exchange markets

http://news.ft.com/markets—*Financial Times* website; offers a wealth of data on worldwide financial markets

http://www.securities.com—Internet Securities, Inc. website; specializes in providing data and news on emerging markets

http://www.euribor.org—Provides information on the Euribor (Euro Interbank Offered Rate), a rate on loans between prime banks within the European Monetary Union, analogous to LIBOR

http://www.x-rates.com—Allows you to create charts or historical data tables for virtually any of the world's currencies

http://www.world-exchanges.org—Provides data on 52 futures and stock exchanges around the world

KEY TERMS

accounting exposure
appreciated
asset market model of exchange rates
covered interest arbitrage
cross exchange rate
depreciated
direct quotation
economic exposure
euro
exchange rate
fixed exchange rate
floating exchange rate
foreign direct investment (FDI)
foreign exchange (forex) market
forward discount
forward exchange rate
forward premium
forward rate
forward–spot parity

General Agreement on Tariffs and
    Trade (GATT)
hedged
hedging strategies
indirect quotation
interest rate parity
law of one price
macro political risk
managed floating rate system
micro political risk
multinational corporations (MNCs)
natural hedge
political risk
purchasing power parity
real interest rate parity
spot exchange rate
transaction exposure
triangular arbitrage
World Trade Organization (WTO)

QUESTIONS

20-1. Define a multinational corporation (MNC). What factors must the manager of an MNC consider that a manager of a purely domestic firm is not forced to face?

20-2. Who are the major players in foreign currency markets, and what are their motivations for trading?

20-3. If an exchange rate is quoted in terms of euros per pound, in what direction would it move if the euro appreciated against the pound?

20-4. Explain how triangular arbitrage ensures that currency values are essentially the same in different markets around the world at any given moment.

20-5. In what sense is it a misnomer to refer to a currency as weak or strong? Who benefits and who loses if the yen appreciates against the pound?

20-6. What does a spot exchange rate have in common with a forward rate, and how are they different?

20-7. What does it mean to say that a currency trades at a forward premium?

20-8. Explain how the law of one price establishes a relationship between changes in currency values and inflation rates.

20-9. We developed the notion of forward–spot parity by assuming risk-neutral traders. Suppose that managers who make decisions about whether to hedge or not are risk averse. How might this alter the forward–spot parity logic?

20-10. Why does purchasing power parity appear to hold in the long run but not in the short run?

20-11. In terms of risk, is a U.S. investor indifferent about whether to buy a U.S. government bond or a U.K. government bond? Why or why not?

20-12.   If the euro trades at a forward premium against the yen, explain why interest rates in Japan would have to be higher than they are in Europe.

20-13.   Suppose that the U.S. Federal Reserve suddenly decides to raise interest rates. Trace out the potential impact that this action might have on (1) interest rates abroad, (2) the spot value of the dollar, and (3) the forward value of the dollar.

20-14.   Interest rates on risk-free bonds in the United States are about 4 percent, whereas interest rates on Swiss government bonds are 6 percent. Can we conclude that investors around the world will flock to buy Swiss bonds? Why or why not?

20-15.   A Japanese investor decides to purchase shares in a company that trades on the London Stock Exchange. The investor's plan is to hold the shares for one year and then to sell them at year's end and convert the proceeds into yen. During the year, the pound appreciates against the yen. Does this enhance or diminish the investor's return on the stock?

20-16.   Suppose that the dollar trades at a forward discount relative to the yen. A U.S. firm must pay a Japanese supplier ¥10 million in three months. A manager in the U.S. firm reasons that because the dollar buys fewer yen on the forward market than it does on the spot market, the firm should not enter a forward hedge to eliminate its exchange rate exposure. Comment on this opinion.

20-17.   How is hedging exchange rate exposure using options different from hedging using forward contracts? What does this suggest about the costs of hedging with options rather than forwards?

20-18.   What are some strategies for minimizing political risk in a developing country?

PROBLEMS

Exchange Rate Fundamentals

20-1.   A "direct quote" is when an exchange rate is expressed as the cost in domestic currency for one unit of foreign currency. The following quotes are "indirect quotes" (i.e., one unit of domestic currency is valued in terms of the foreign currency):

2 £/$
1.2 €/$
1.25 C$/$

Find the corresponding direct quotes and determine which currency is the domestic currency unit. Is an indirect quote for the domestic currency the same as a direct quote for the foreign currency?

20-2.   Suppose we expect the British pound to appreciate relative to the euro over the next year (i.e., current spot of 0.75 £/€ and a future spot of 0.70 £/1 €). What are the appreciation rate of the pound and the depreciation rate of the euro? If the future spot rate occurs in six months, then what are the annualized appreciation/depreciation rates?

20-3.   Consider the following three exchange rates:

$1.25/£
0.95 £/€
0.8421 €/$

Convert $1,000.00 into pounds, then into euros, and then back to dollars (round to the nearest dollar). Is there an ability to make profits using triangular arbitrage with these exchange rates? If the first exchange rate changed to $1.20/£ and the second exchange rate remained constant, what would the third exchange rate (euro to dollar) need to be to prevent arbitrage? Next, change the second exchange rate change to 0.925 £/€. What would the third exchange rate need to be to prevent arbitrage?

20-4. On November 11, 2005, the U.S. dollar-British pound (£) exchange rate was $1.7423/£ (£0.5740/$). On November 18, 2005, the exchange rate was $1.7150/£ (£0.5831/$). Which currency appreciated and which depreciated? Calculate both the percentage appreciation of the currency that rose in value and the percentage depreciation of the currency that declined in value.

20-5. Using the data presented in Figure 20.1, calculate the spot exchange rate between Canadian dollars and British pounds (in pounds per dollar).

20-6. Using the data presented in Figure 20.1, specify whether the following currencies appreciated or depreciated (against the dollar) from Monday to Tuesday: the yen, the Swiss franc, and the Polish zloty. (Focus only on spot rates.)

20-7. Go to http://www.economist.com. Under the "Markets & Data" section, activate the foreign exchange map. On the menu at the far left, choose the U.S. dollar as the base currency.

   a. Click on the "1-month" selection to show the appreciation or depreciation of the world's currencies relative to the dollar. Does it appear that the dollar is appreciating or depreciating against most of the world's currencies, or is the answer mixed?

   b. Next, choose the "1-year" option, and identify two or three countries whose currencies have depreciated the most against the U.S. dollar and two or three whose currencies have appreciated the most. Search the web to try to find out what the most recent inflation figures from those countries are. What lesson does this reveal?

20-8. On November 15, 2005, the *Wall Street Journal* reported the following spot and forward rates for the Japanese yen (¥):

Spot: $0.008415/¥ (¥118.84/$)
1-month: $0.008446/¥ (¥118.40/$)
3-month: $0.008508/¥ (¥117.54/$)

Supply the forward yen premium or discount (specify which it is) for both the 1-month and 3-month quotes as an annual percentage rate.

20-9. Using the data presented in Figure 20.1, specify whether the U.S. dollar traded at a forward premium or discount relative to the Canadian dollar, the Japanese yen, and the Swiss franc. Use the 3-month forward rates to determine the answer.

20-10. Using the data presented in Figure 20.1, determine the forward premium or discount on the Canadian dollar relative to the British pound, the Japanese yen, and the Swiss franc. Use the 6-month forward rates to determine the answer, and express your answer as an annual rate.

20-11. Assume that you are quoted the following series of exchange rates for the U.S. dollar ($), the Canadian dollar (C$), and the British pound (£):

$0.6000/C$ C$1.6667/$
$1.2500/£   £0.8000/$
C$2.5000/£   £0.4000/C$

If you have $1 million in cash, how can you take profitable advantage of this series of exchange rates? Show the series of trades that would yield an arbitrage profit, and calculate how much profit you would make.

The Parity Conditions in International Finance

20-12. Use the data presented in Figure 20.1 to answer this problem. A particular commodity sells for $5,000 in the United States and ¥600,000 in Japan.

    a. Does the law of one price hold? If not, explain how to profit through arbitrage.

    b. Taking the commodity prices in the United States and Japan as given, at what exchange rate (in terms of yen per dollar) would the law of one price hold?

20-13. If the expected rate of inflation in the United States is 2 percent, the 1-year risk-free interest rate is 4 percent, and the 1-year risk-free rate in Britain is 4.5 percent, what is the expected inflation rate in Britain?

20-14. Go to http://www.economist.com. Under the "Markets & Data" section, find the link for the "Big Mac index." After exploring this part of the site, explain why the Big Mac index might foreshadow changes in exchange rates. What features of the Big Mac would suggest that Big Macs may not satisfy the law of one price?

20-15. Refer to Problem 20-9. If it costs ¥15,000 to transport the commodity from the United States to Japan, is there still an arbitrage opportunity? At what exchange rate (in yen per dollar) would buying the commodity in the United States and shipping it to sell in Japan become profitable?

20-16. Refer to Problem 20-12. Given shipping costs of ¥15,000, at what exchange rate would it be profitable to buy the commodity in Japan and ship it to the United States to sell? Comment on the general lesson from the last few questions.

20-17. Assume that the annual interest rate on a 6-month U.S. Treasury bill is 5 percent, and use the data presented in Figure 20.1 to answer the following.

    a. Calculate the annual interest rate on 6-month bills in Canada and Japan.

    b. Suppose that the annual interest rate on a 6-month bill in Japan is 0.5 percent. Illustrate how to exploit this through covered interest arbitrage.

    c. Suppose the annual interest rate on a 3-month U.K. government bond is 4 percent. What is the annual interest rate on a 3-month government bond in Switzerland?

    d. Suppose the actual Swiss interest rate is 0.5 percent. Illustrate how to conduct covered interest arbitrage to exploit this situation.

20-18. Shortly after it was introduced, the euro traded just below parity with the dollar, meaning that one dollar purchased more than one euro. This implies

    a. that U.S. inflation was lower than European inflation

    b. that U.S. interest rates were lower than European rates

    c. that the law of one price does not hold

    d. none of the above

20-19. Assume the following information is known about the current spot exchange rate between the U.S. dollar and the British pound (£), inflation rates in Britain and the United States, and the real rate of interest—which is assumed to be the same in both countries:

Current spot rate, $S = \$1.4500/£$ ($£0.6897/\$$)
U.S. inflation rate, $i_{US} = 1.5$ percent per year (0.015)
British inflation rate, $i_{UK} = 2.0$ percent per year (0.020)
Real rate of interest, $R = 2.5$ percent per year (0.025)

Based on these data, use the parity conditions of international finance to compute the following:

    a. Expected spot rate next year

    b. U.S. risk-free rate (on a 1-year bond)

c. British risk-free rate (on a 1-year bond)

d. 1-year forward rate

Finally, show how you can make an arbitrage profit if you are offered the chance to sell or buy pounds forward (for delivery one year from now) at the current spot rate of $1.4500/£ (£0.6897/$). Assuming that you can borrow $1 million, or £689,700, at the risk-free interest rate, what would your profit be on this arbitrage transaction?

20-20.   The current exchange rate between the United States and Canada is $0.92/C$. A particular item in the United States sells for $23.95 and for 25.75 C$ in Canada. Shipping costs between the United States and Canada are $300.00 (or 326.09 C$) per 1,000 units. In which country is the item selling for less money, and can the price discrepancy be exploited after considering shipping costs?

20-21.   Suppose the spot exchange rate between the United States and the United Kingdom is $0.89/£ and the spot rate one year in the future is expected to be $0.90/£. If the expected annual inflation in the United States is 4 percent, what is the expected annual inflation in the United Kingdom? If the future spot rate occurs in six months, then what is the annualized forward premium?

20-22.   If the expected annual inflation in a foreign country is 7 percent and the expected annual domestic inflation is 3.2 percent, what is the domestic risk-free rate assuming the foreign risk-free rate is 12 percent APR? If the current exchange rate is 0.75 units of domestic currency per one unit of foreign currency, what is the expected exchange rate six months in the future and twelve months in the future? Does it matter if the six-month rate is set based on inflation or on the risk-free rate?

20-23.   The annual forward premium between the U.S. dollar and the euro is 4.3 percent APR, with the U.S. dollar appreciating in value. If the United States is expected to have −1.0 percent inflation throughout the year, what inflation rate can be expected relative to the euro? If the annual risk-free rate for the United States is 5.4 percent APR, what is the annual risk-free rate in Europe?

Managing Financial and Political Risk

20-24.   Suppose that the spot exchange rate follows a random walk, which means that the best forecast of the spot rate at some future date is simply its current value. Now suppose that a U.S. firm owes €1 million to a Spanish supplier. If the U.S. firm is risk neutral, describe the circumstances under which the firm will or will not enter into a forward contract to hedge its exposure.

20-25.   Classic City Exporters (CCE) recently sold a large shipment of sporting equipment to a Swiss company that intends to sell it in Zurich. The sale was denominated in Swiss francs (SF) and was worth SF500,000. Delivery of the sporting goods and payment by the Swiss buyer are due to occur in six months. The current spot exchange rate is $0.7598/SF (SF1.3161/$), and the 6-month forward rate is $0.7729/SF (SF1.2938/$). What risk would CCE run if it remained unhedged, and how could it hedge that risk with a forward contract? Assuming that the actual exchange rate in six months is $0.7000/SF (SF1.4286/$), compute the profit or loss—and state which it is—that CCE would experience if it remains unhedged versus hedging in the forward market.

20-26.   A British firm will receive $1 million from a U.S. customer in three months. The firm is considering two strategies to eliminate its foreign exchange exposure. The first strategy is to pledge the $1 million as collateral for a 3-month loan from a U.S. bank at

4 percent interest. The U.K. firm will then convert the proceeds of the loan to pounds at the spot rate. When the loan is due, the firm will pay the $1 million balance due by handing its U.S. receivable over to the bank. This strategy allows the U.K. firm to "monetize" its receivable immediately. The spot exchange rate is 0.6550 pounds per dollar.

The second strategy is to enter a forward contract at an exchange rate of 0.6450 pounds per dollar. This ensures that the U.K. firm will receive £645,000 in three months. If the firm wanted to monetize this payment immediately, it could take out a 3-month loan from a U.K. bank at 8 percent, pledging the proceeds of the forward contract as collateral. Which of these strategies should the firm follow?

Long-Term Investment Decisions

20-27. The cost of capital in a particular foreign country is 15 percent APR. Domestic inflation is expected to be 2.7 percent APR, and inflation in the foreign country is expected to be 7 percent APR. What is the cost of capital relative to the domestic country? (*Hint:* Look at the relationships established in Equation 20.7.)

20-28. A foreign firm is evaluating a project in the United States using cost of capital based on the U.S. dollar of 15 percent APR. The current exchange rate is $0.85/1 unit of foreign currency with a 1-year forward rate of $0.82/1 unit of foreign currency. What is the domestic cost of capital for the foreign firm? (*Hint:* Look at the relationships established in Equation 20.7.)

20-29. A German company manufactures a specialized piece of manufacturing equipment and leases it to a U.K. enterprise. The lease calls for five end-of-year payments of £1 million. The German firm spent €3.5 million to produce the equipment, which is expected to have no salvage value after five years. The current spot rate is €1.5/£. The risk-free interest rate in Germany is 3 percent, and in the United Kingdom it is 5 percent. The German firm reasons that the appropriate (German) discount rate for this investment is 7 percent. Calculate the *NPV* of this investment in two ways.

   a. First, convert all cash flows to pounds, and discount at an appropriate (U.K.) cost of capital. Convert the resulting *NPV* to euros at the spot rate.

   b. Second, calculate forward rates for each year, convert the pound-denominated cash flows into euros using those rates, and discount at the German cost of capital. Verify that the *NPV* obtained from this approach matches (except perhaps for small rounding errors) that obtained in part (a).

Short-Term Financial Decisions

20-30. A Canadian firm owes ¥3 million to its Japanese subsidiary. The subsidiary in turn owes the Canadian firm C$45,000. Both payments are due in 30 days, but managers believe that the yen will appreciate against the Canadian dollar over the next 30 days. Specifically, they expect the spot exchange rate to change from ¥70/C$ to ¥60/C$.

   a. If the firm can accelerate one of these payments to the present, which one should it accelerate?

   b. What will be the exchange rate gain from accelerating the payment compared to making the payment in 30 days if rates change as expected?

20-31. A U.S. firm must borrow $1 million to meet operating needs for one year. A U.S. bank offers a 1-year loan at 5 percent interest. A U.K. bank is willing to lend (in pounds) for one year at 7 percent, and a Canadian bank offers a loan at 6 percent (denominated in

Canadian dollars). In all cases, the U.S. firm will repay the loan in a lump sum at the end of the year. If it borrows from a foreign lender, the firm will hedge its currency exposure with a forward contract. The current spot and 1-year forward exchange rates are as follows:

| Country | Foreign Currency per US$ | |
	Spot	1-Year Forward
Canada	1.1922	1.1802
United Kingdom	0.5760	0.5772

Which loan should the firm accept?

THOMSON ONE BUSINESS SCHOOL EDITION

20-32.   In 2005, Fedex Corporation (ticker symbol, FDX) was one of the top ten most-profitable companies in the world, and McDonald's Corporation (ticker symbol, MCD) was one of the world's largest employers. What geographic regions of the world generate the greatest percentage of revenue for each firm? How would a change in exchange rates impact the reported financial results of these firms? (*Hint:* Under the Financials tab, go to More, then WorldScope Reports and Charts, then Geographic Segment Review.) How are the stock returns for both firms impacted by changes in exchange rates? (*Hint:* Under the Prices tab, go to Overviews, then Thomson Market Data, then Stock Performance Overview and click the $ to change the currency used to calculate the returns.) Which of the major currencies yielded the greatest return for each firm over the last five years?

MINI-CASE: INTERNATIONAL FINANCIAL MANAGEMENT

Frog Enterprises recently purchased 50,000 flat-panel monitors from Tokyo Technologies for 2,000 yen each. The invoice, payable in yen, is due in 30 days. The spot rate is 118.15 yen per U.S. dollar, and the 30-day forward rate is 117.757 yen per U.S. dollar.

1.   If Frog Enterprises were to buy the yen today, how much would it cost in U.S. dollars?

2.   If Frog Enterprises were to engage in the forward contract, how much would it cost in U.S. dollars?

3.   Calculate the indirect quote for the spot rate (i.e., how many U.S. dollars will one yen purchase?) and the indirect forward rate.

4.   Calculate the annualized forward premium and discount for the yen and the U.S. dollar.

5.   Assuming the invoice is due today and the spot rate for one Canadian dollar is US$ = C$1.14, would it make sense for Frog Enterprises to buy Canadian dollars and convert them to yen to pay the invoice? Justify your argument numerically.

6.   Regarding the previous question, what would the cross exchange rate between the Canadian dollar and the yen have to be in order to make the arbitrage opportunity disappear?

7.   Suppose Frog Enterprises could have purchased identical monitors from another company located in England. How much should each monitor cost in British pounds for the purchasing power parity theory to hold, if the spot rate is 0.5634 British pounds per U.S. dollar?

PART 7: Short-Term Financing Decisions

In addition to making recommendations regarding important episodic financial decisions such as capital budgeting, capital structure, dividends, and long-term financing, financial managers in large corporations spend significant time dealing with more routine short-term financing decisions. One important activity is their intimate involvement in both strategic (long-term) and operational (short-term) financial planning. The financial manager must work with other managers to convert the firm's goals into a set of financial plans. In addition, the financial manager must oversee the day-to-day management of the firm's current accounts in order to ensure adequate liquidity. This activity involves managing both current assets such as cash, inventory, and accounts receivable, and current liabilities such as accounts payable and short-term debt. This part includes three chapters that address the financial manager's role in the firm's short-term financing activities.

Chapter 21 describes the strategic and operational financial planning processes. Financial planning methods vary widely, but almost all firms' financial plans have certain characteristics in common. Most firms develop strategic plans that look ahead two to five years or more. They also have very detailed operating plans that they use to project inflows and outflows of cash, as well as earnings, over the next year or two. Financial plans help firms identify problems before they arise, and they help managers line up financing before cash shortfalls become critical.

Chapter 22 takes a closer look at how cash moves through a firm and the popular procedures for managing inventory and accounts receivable. The *cash conversion cycle* illustrates how managers can track the length of time that it takes a firm to recover cash from selling its goods. Clearly, the amount of time a firm can delay paying its vendors, the amount of time a firm's goods spend in inventory, and how long the firm must wait before its customers pay for their orders, play central roles in determining how quickly a firm recovers its cash. As with other financial decisions, when managers determine how much to invest in items such as inventories and receivables, they must consider the costs and benefits of those investments.

Chapter 23 examines the factors that firms consider when they decide how much cash to hold. Part of the decision revolves around the firm's cash collection procedures and the timing of its cash disbursements, which somewhat depend on the terms under which the firm's suppliers grant it credit. In addition, the financial manager must use short-term investing and borrowing in order to maintain the desired cash position (liquidity).

General Motors Corp. (GM) is no ordinary company. Its annual sales of more than $190 billion dwarf the sales of most companies. Its annual payroll of $8.7 billion directly or indirectly supports nearly 900,000 jobs, from car salespeople to office-supply vendors. As testimony to its economic force, GM's 54-day shutdown in 1998, due to labor problems, cost the firm $2 billion and $9 per share in valuation. Also, the U.S. economic growth rate that quarter dropped a full percentage point. At the time, the often-cited adage, "What's bad for General Motors is bad for America" seemed to ring true.

Today GM is in a difficult position. In the first quarter of 2005, it lost $1.1 billion largely because it is saddled with "legacy costs" of $1,600 per vehicle. Most of that cost is attributable to retiree health and pension benefits. At the Berkshire Hathaway annual meeting on April 30, 2005, investing icon (and contract-bridge devotee) Warren Buffet told shareholders that GM has "an extremely difficult hand to play." In May 2005, the three major bond-rating agencies lowered GM's rating to junk-bond status. Clearly, GM has many challenges to address. GM CEO Rick Wagoner, Jr.'s immediate "to do" list includes the following items for turning the company around: negotiate with unions for relief from the $5.6 billion in annual health-care costs, negotiate with suppliers to reduce costs, accelerate delivery of new sport-utility vehicles and pickups, and close at least a couple auto plants to reduce overcapacity.

Although GM will likely plan much restructuring, the company is making its single-biggest research bet on developing a hydrogen-powered car. Its goal is to develop a hydrogen-fuel-cell vehicle by 2010 that would compete on cost with traditional vehicles. GM has a thousand people in government, university, and private labs in 14 countries working to achieve this goal; it has spent $1 billion on the effort since 1996. However, many analysts doubt that success in this program can happen soon enough to make a difference to GM.

The challenges GM faces illustrate the importance of corporate financial planning. In its efforts to grow, GM did not accurately anticipate the strength of competition, rising health-care costs, rising raw material costs, and the need for greater operating efficiency. As a result, in early 2005, the company's market share dropped 2 percentage points to 25.6 percent, which hovered around GM's breakeven level of cash flow. Though better financial plans could not have prevented the current situation, they may have helped GM develop contingencies that would have allowed the company to more quickly adapt to these challenges and avoid many of its current problems.

Sources: "Buffet Gives Detroit a Thumbs Down," Business Week (May 16, 2005), p. 10; Jonathan Fahey, "Hydrogen Gas," Forbes (April 25, 2005), pp. 78–83; Richard J. Newman, "Upping the Ante at GM," Business Week (May 16, 2005), pp. 42–44; and David Welch and Dan Beucke, "Why GM's Plan Won't Work," Business Week (May 9, 2005), pp. 85–94.

SMART Finance

Use the learning tools at www thomsonedu.com/finance/smartfinance

n our experience, almost everyone working in a large corporation encounters two areas of corporate finance on a regular basis. The first is justification of spending plans, or capital budgeting. Chapters 7 through 9 covered the elements of capital budgeting analysis that business professionals in any discipline should know. The second part of corporate finance that touches almost all functional groups in a firm is financial planning. Financial planning encompasses a wide array of activities: setting long-run strategic goals, preparing quarterly and annual budgets, and managing day-to-day fluctuations in cash balances. No one with corporate work experience is completely unfamiliar with budgeting processes.

In this chapter, we discuss various elements of a firm's financial planning processes. The chapter emphasizes both long-term and short-term financial planning. In Chapters 22 and 23 we consider the operational aspects of short-term financial decisions. The three chapters in Part 7 demonstrate how firms' financial plans must balance the interests and objectives of different business units and functional areas. For example, in setting long-run strategic and financial goals, a firm must prioritize its desires to increase sales and market share; to change or maintain its exposure to financial risk; to achieve production efficiencies; to attract and retain capable employees; and to distribute cash to shareholders. In almost every instance, making incremental progress on one of these objectives means an incremental sacrifice on one or more of the other goals.

Financial planning, particularly long-term planning, is more art than science—the connection between most financial planning models and the objective of shareholder wealth maximization is tenuous at best.[1] (For example, the Comparative Corporate Finance on page 771 provides data that confirm the difficulty of making accurate macroeconomic forecasts.) At one level, the advice we would give to a firm constructing a long-term plan is trivial: "Do whatever is necessary to invest in all positive-NPV projects." In practice, a variety of factors make following that advice a major challenge. CFOs usually tell us that they have many more acceptable projects than they can possibly undertake. Limits on capital, production capacity, human resources, and many other inputs make the planning process more complex than simply accepting all projects that look promising. In this chapter, we concede that the theoretical underpinnings of planning models are weak, and therefore we focus as much as possible on practice. We describe how firms *actually* build long-term and short-term financial plans rather than argue about how they *should* plan.

SMART PRACTICES VIDEO

Jackie Sturm, Director of Finance for Technology and Manufacturing, Intel Corp.

"Once the product line business plan is completed, we move into our annual planning process, which is more of a tactical exercise."

See the entire interview at SMARTFinance

21.1 OVERVIEW OF THE PLANNING PROCESS

A long-term financial plan begins with strategy. Typically, the senior management team analyzes the markets in which the firm competes. Managers try to identify ways to protect and increase the firm's competitive advantage in those markets. For example, a firm that competes by achieving the lowest production cost in an industry might seek to determine whether it should make additional investments in manufacturing facilities to achieve even greater production efficiencies. Of course, being the low-cost producer is difficult if the firm's fixed assets are chronically underutilized.

---

[1] In the early 1980s a number of models such as economic value added (EVA®) and shareholder value added (SVA) were developed for tying financial decisions and plans to shareholder value. Those widely used models will be discussed briefly later in this chapter.

COMPARATIVE CORPORATE FINANCE

Public versus Private Forecasts

In corporate finance, many planning processes begin with a sales forecast. One of the key pieces of information that firms use to develop their forecasts is an overall assessment of how the macroeconomy will perform. Managers, especially, worry about the prospect of an economic recession. Thus, many firms track economic forecasts produced both by governmental bodies and by private economic-research firms.

Some have argued that forecasts produced by private entities should be more accurate than those produced in public institutions. Forecasts generated in the public sector might be influenced by political factors, but private-sector predictions should be unbiased. A recent study produced at the International Monetary Fund (IMF) tests that claim by comparing the ability of private- and public-sector forecasts to predict recessions in 63 different countries. The study tabulates a "consensus forecast" by collecting numerous private-sector forecasts and averaging them. The study then compares the consensus to a variety of forecasts published by organizations such as the IMF, the World Bank, and other public institutions. Two important conclusions emerge from this research.

First, private sector forecasts perform no better or worse than forecasts produced by the IMF and other similar agencies. Second, and more troubling for managers putting together their financial planning models, both public- and private-sector forecasts are much too optimistic, especially leading up to recessions. Pooling together the data from all countries in the study, there were 60 recessions that economic forecasters might have predicted. Forecasters managed to predict just two of these episodes as early as April the year before they occurred; only 20 of the recessions were predicted as late as April of the year in which the recession actually started. As the accompanying table shows, virtually all of the forecasts, including those that were calling for a recession, were too optimistic and predicted a growth rate higher than what the economy ultimately produced. For example, in April of the year prior to a recession, the average forecast predicted that the economy would grow 5.76 percent faster than it actually did grow the following year.

The good news, if you can call it that, is that the bias toward optimism in these forecasts was smaller for forecasts that were looking less than one year ahead. Knowing that professional forecasters can foresee a recession only when one is imminent is of little comfort to managers who must build long-range plans around their sales forecasts.

Performance of Forecasts Prior to 60 Recessions in 63 Countries

	Year Prior to Recession		Year Recession Began	
	April	October	April	October
Number of recessions predicted	2	3	20	47
Number of optimistic forecasts	60	60	59	50
Average forecast error—all countries	5.76%	4.87%	2.91%	0.89%
For industrial countries	3.77%	3.15%	1.84%	0.81%
For developing countries	10.31%	8.62%	4.89%	1.05%

Source: Prakash Loungani, "How Accurate Are Private Sector Forecasts? Cross-Country Evidence from Consensus Forecasts of Output Growth," *International Journal of Forecasting*, Vol. 17, No. 3 (July–Sept 2001), pp. 419–432.

This type of firm, therefore, will try to forecast market demand and develop contingency plans for the possibility that the expected demand does not materialize. If a firm's competitive advantage derives from the value of its brand, it might begin by assessing whether new or expanded marketing programs might increase the value of the brand relative to its competitors.

SUCCESSFUL LONG-TERM PLANNING

Long-term planning requires more than paying close attention to a firm's existing markets. Even more important is the ability to identify and prioritize *new* market opportunities. Successful long-term planning means asking and answering questions such as the following:

1. In what emerging markets might we have a sustainable competitive advantage?
2. How can we leverage our competitive strengths across existing markets in which we currently do not compete?
3. What threats to our current business exist, and how can we meet those threats?
4. Where in the world should we produce? Where should we sell?
5. Can we deploy resources more efficiently by exiting certain markets and using those resources elsewhere?

As the firm's senior managers develop answers to these questions, they construct a **strategic plan.** This is a multiyear action plan for the major investments and competitive initiatives that they believe will drive the future success of the enterprise.

THE ROLE OF FINANCE IN LONG-TERM PLANNING

Finance plays several roles in long-term planning. First, financial managers draw on a broad set of skills to assess the likelihood that a given strategic objective can be achieved. With respect to a major new investment proposal, their first questions should be, "Does this investment make sense?" and "Is there good reason to expect this proposal to generate wealth for our shareholders?"

Second, the finance function assesses the feasibility of a strategic action plan, given a firm's existing and prospective sources of funding. Though some corporate giants, such as Microsoft and Intel, hold such vast amounts of cash that they are nearly unconstrained in their ability to make large, new investments, for most companies financial constraints are more limiting. Given a broad set of strategic objectives, financial managers must determine whether the firm's ability to generate cash internally, plus its ability to raise cash externally, will be sufficient to fund new spending initiatives. Financial analysts generally treat expected dividend payments as a factor that limits a firm's ability to make new investments. Similarly, if fulfilling strategic objectives will require a significant increase in leverage, it is finance's role to communicate that trade-off to the top management team. We will see in the next section that financial managers have several tools that enable them to highlight the trade-offs firms face when setting growth targets.

Third, finance clearly plays an important control function as firms implement their strategic plans. Financial analysts prepare and update cash budgets to make sure that firms do not unknowingly slip into a liquidity crisis. At an even more detailed level, analysts monitor individual items in the cash budget, such as changes in inventories and receivables (our focus in Chapter 22) and changes in payables (our focus in Chapter 23). Here, too, financial managers must evaluate trade-offs.

Fourth, a major contribution of finance to the strategic planning process involves risk management. When a firm's strategy calls for making new investments in overseas markets (either producing or selling abroad), the firm faces a new set of risk exposures. The finance function manages these exposures so that the firm takes those risks that it believes it has a comparative advantage in taking and hedges risks for which it has no advantage. Similarly, more than in any other functional area, the job of finance is to identify problems that could develop in the future if the firm's strategic plans unfold in unexpected ways. Developing "problem scenarios" and options for dealing with them is an important part of finance's risk-management responsibility.

In this chapter, we focus primarily on the second and third roles just described. The next section discusses the financial tools that help managers determine the trade-offs they face when setting growth objectives for the future.

Concept Review Questions

1. A company decides to compete by making a major investment to modernize production facilities. Describe two ways in which meeting this objective might force a firm to sacrifice other objectives.

2. Firm A competes in a market in which the demand for its product and its selling price are highly unpredictable. Firm B competes in a market in which these factors are much more stable. Which firm probably creates and monitors cash budgets more frequently?

21.2 PLANNING FOR GROWTH

SUSTAINABLE GROWTH

Most firms strive to grow over time, and most firms view rapid growth as preferable to slow growth. Of course, rapid growth is not wealth-maximizing for all firms at all times; at times it is even detrimental to shareholders. Here, though, we put aside the question of whether growth is desirable. Assuming that firms seek growth, they can focus on one or a number of possible growth targets.

Popular Growth Targets. Three of the more popular growth targets are the accounting return on investment (*ROI*), economic value added (EVA®), and growth in sales or assets. All of these targets tend to rely on accounting data and are typically measured on an annual basis. *ROI* and EVA® are described as follows.

Return on Investment. The **accounting return on investment** (*ROI*) is merely the firm's earnings available for common stockholders divided by its total assets. (In Chapter 2 we referred to this measure by its alternate name, *return on total assets, ROA*.) Return on investment measures the firm's overall effectiveness in using its assets to generate returns to common stockholders.

Firms that use this metric as a growth target attempt to maintain *ROI* above some minimum *hurdle rate* and to grow it over time. These firms often set hurdle rates for minimum *ROI* at the firm's cost of capital. They assume if the *ROI* is greater than the cost of capital, then shareholder value will be created. The problem with this approach is that it compares the *accounting-based ROI* to an *economic-based* measure of the return demanded by suppliers of capital. Although use of this method has practical appeal, its theoretical roots are shallow at best.

Economic Value Added. Developed (and copyrighted) by consultants Stern, Stewart & Co. in 1982, this measure has been adopted by many major companies, including Coca-Cola and Siemens. **Economic value added (EVA®)** is the difference between net operating profits after taxes (*NOPAT*) and the cost of funds.[2] The cost

---

[2.] A similar model developed at about the same time by Alfred Rappaport results in *shareholder value added (SVA)*, a metric which although less widely cited than EVA®, is believed to be theoretically superior to it. For detailed development of EVA®, see G. Bennett Stewart, *The Quest for Value* (New York: HarperBusiness, 1999). For detailed development of SVA, see Alfred Rappaport, *Creating Shareholder Value* (New York: The Free Press, 1998). For a summary of EVA®, see Shaun Tully, "The Real Key to Creating Wealth," *Fortune* (September 20, 1993), pp. 38–49.

of funds is found by multiplying the firm's cost of capital by its investment. Analysts can apply EVA® to individual investments or to the entire firm, but its use in financial planning tends to focus on the entire firm.

Firms that employ EVA® in the planning process typically build the EVA® model into their spreadsheets and evaluate various scenarios by calculating their EVA®s. By comparing all positive EVA®s, the firm can implement the set of plans with the highest EVA®, which should create the most value for shareholders. Although widely examined in the financial literature,[3] EVA®'s degree of positive correlation with actual share valuations remains unclear. Most agree that the measure is conceptually valid, but like *ROI*, EVA® suffers from a disconnect between accrual-based accounting values (*NOPAT* and investment) and economic value (cost of capital and share price). This disconnect, coupled with its increased computational complexity, tends to result in greater planning focus on growth rates.

Defining Growth. Firms frequently set planning goals in terms of *target growth rates,* typically annual growth in sales or assets. For the moment, we lay aside the question of whether growth creates or destroys shareholder value. We instead focus on target growth rates in light of their intuitive, computational, and practical appeal. Our goal is to demonstrate a simple model that highlights the trade-offs that firms must weigh when they choose to grow. These trade-offs depend on several factors: how rapidly the firm plans to grow; how profitable its existing business is; how much of its earnings it retains and how much it pays out to shareholders; how efficiently it manages its assets; and how much financial leverage it is willing to bear.

First, let us define what we mean by "growth." A firm's growth can be measured by increases in its market value, its asset base, the number of people it employs, or any number of other metrics. For now, let us imagine that a firm establishes a growth target in terms of *sales*. That is, when we say that a firm plans to grow next year by 10 percent, we mean that it hopes to achieve a 10 percent increase in sales. *Our experience suggests that most firms define and measure growth targets in terms of sales,* so we will adopt that convention as well.

With sales growth in mind, think about what growth means for a firm in terms of its balance sheet. An increase in sales probably requires additional investments in assets. Certainly, we would anticipate that increased sales volume would require additional investments in current assets, such as inventories and receivables. Over time, increases in sales will also require new investments in fixed assets, such as production capacity and office space. As a shortcut, let us assume that a firm's total asset turnover ratio, the ratio of sales (S) divided by total assets (A), remains constant through time. In other words, any increase in sales will be matched by a comparable percentage increase in assets. Because the balance sheet equation must hold, increases in liabilities and shareholders' equity must equal the increase in assets. In what forms do we expect increases in liabilities and shareholders' equity to occur?

In previous chapters, we learned that most companies issue new common shares very infrequently, so we will rule that out as a potential source of new financing. As with inventories and receivables, accounts payable should increase (higher sales volume means higher purchases). We might also expect to see higher accruals and higher short-term liabilities of other types. Similarly, if a firm's business is profitable,

---

[3.] For some critical analysis of EVA®, see Ray D. Dillion and James E. Owers, "EVA® as a Financial Metric: Attributes, Utilization, and Relationship to NPV," *Financial Practice and Education* (Spring/Summer 1997), pp. 32–40; John D. Martin, J. William Petty, and Steven P. Rich, "A Survey of EVA® and Other Residual Income Models of Firm Performance," *Journal of Financial Literature* (Winter 2005), pp. 1–20; and John M. Griffith, "The True Value of EVA®," *Journal of Applied Finance* (Fall/Winter 2004), pp. 25–29.

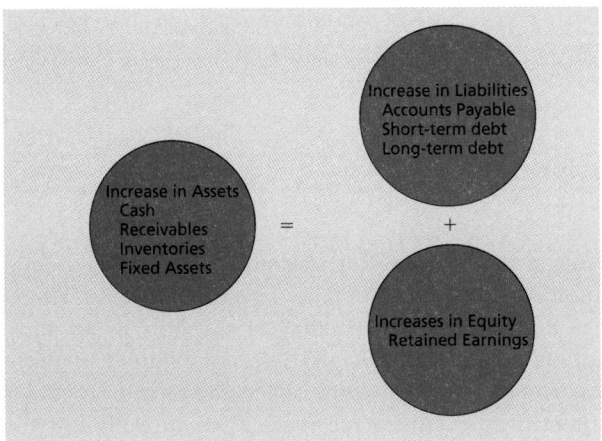

Figure 21.1
Sustainable Growth Equality
As a firm grows, it must invest in new assets to support increased sales volume. The investments in new assets must be financed with some combination of increased liabilities and increased equity.

its equity account will increase, even if it does not issue any new stock, by the amount of earnings it retains. Figure 21.1 illustrates that the growth in assets must equal growth in these liability and equity accounts over time.

Developing the Sustainable Growth Model. The **sustainable growth model**,[4] starts with a balance sheet identity. It then adds a few assumptions, and derives an expression that determines how rapidly a firm can grow while maintaining a balance between its outflows (increases in assets) and inflows (increases in liabilities and equity) of funds. Specifically, the sustainable growth model assumes the following:

1. The firm has only common stock (E) and will issue no new shares of its common stock next year.
2. The firm's total asset turnover ratio, S/A, remains constant.
3. The firm pays out a constant fraction, d, of its earnings as dividends.
4. The firm maintains a constant assets-to-equity ratio, A/E.
5. The firm's net profit margin, m, is constant.

Consider a firm that wants to increase sales next period by g percent. If total assets in the current period equal A and if the asset turnover ratio remains constant, then assets must increase in the next period by gA. This represents the change in the left-hand side of the firm's balance sheet next period. That change must be met with an equal change on the right-hand side.

Given sales this period of S, a net profit margin (in this case, defined as net income ÷ sales) equal to m, and a dividend payout ratio of d, we can determine the firm's retained earnings next period:

$$S(m)(1 + g)(1 - d)$$

The product of S and m yields net profits in the current year. Multiplying this product times $(1 + g)$ results in next year's profits; multiplying this result times $(1 - d)$ gives next year's retained earnings. This is the amount by which the equity component of the balance sheet will grow. Next, observe that the ratio of assets to equity (total assets

---

[4.] The sustainable growth model was developed by Higgins (1981).

to common stock equity) equals 1 plus the ratio of total liabilities, L, to shareholders' equity:

$$A = E + L$$

$$\frac{A}{E} = \frac{E + L}{E} = 1 + \frac{L}{E}$$

The assumption that the firm maintains a constant assets-to-equity ratio is equivalent to an assumption that the ratio of liabilities to equity remains constant. Therefore, for each dollar of earnings that the company retains, it can borrow an additional L/E dollars to keep the mix of debt and equity constant. For example, if a firm finances half of its assets with debt and half with equity, then the ratio L/E equals 1.0. If the firm retains \$1 million in earnings in a given year, it can afford to borrow an additional \$1 million to maintain the desired mix of debt and equity. The increase in liabilities next year simply equals the product of next year's retained earnings and the ratio of liabilities to equity:

$$[S(m)(1 + g)(1 - d)](L/E)$$

Finally, if the increases in assets must match the increase in the sum of liabilities and equity, we can write the following:

$$gA = S(m)(1 + g)(1 - d) + [S(m)(1 + g)(1 - d)](L/E)$$

↑assets   ↑ret. earnings   ↑liabilities

$$= [S(m)(1 + g)(1 - d)](1 + L/E)$$

↑(equity + liabilities)

The insight of the sustainable growth model is that there will be some rate of growth, g^*, that keeps the outflows and inflows of funds in balance. This is the *sustainable growth rate*, calculated from the preceding equation and represented as follows:

$$g^* = \frac{m(1 - d)\dfrac{A}{E}}{\dfrac{A}{S} - m(1 - d)\dfrac{A}{E}} \qquad \text{(Eq. 21.1)}$$

Notice how each of the key variables in Equation 21.1 affects the sustainable growth rate:

- If a firm's profit margin (m) increases, the numerator rises and the denominator falls, so g^* increases. Therefore, generating a higher quantity of profits per dollar of sales provides fuel for a higher growth rate.
- Similarly, an increase in the ratio of assets-to-equity—which can occur only if the firm is willing to accept higher financial leverage—also increases the sustainable growth rate. Firms willing to borrow more can grow more rapidly.
- If a firm can increase its total asset turnover ratio (S/A), then the ratio of A/S falls and the sustainable growth rate rises. Firms that manage assets more efficiently and generate higher sales volume per dollar of assets can achieve more rapid growth.

- Finally, a reduction in dividend payouts (d) also tends to increase g^*. When firms retain more earnings, they can finance faster growth.

APPLYING THE MODEL 21.1

In 2003, Yahoo! Inc. reported the following financial data:

Sales	$1,625.1 million
Net income	$ 237.9 million
Total assets	$5,931.7 million
Total equity	$4,363.5 million
Dividends	$0

From these figures, we can determine that Yahoo!'s net profit margin was 14.64 percent, its assets-to-equity ratio was 1.36, its total asset turnover ratio was 0.27 (which implies assets-to-sales ratio of 3.70), and its dividend payout ratio was 0.0. Plugging these values into Equation 21.1 yields a sustainable growth rate of a little under 5.7 percent. For Yahoo! this meant that the company could increase sales by 5.7 percent without issuing new shares of common stock and without changing total asset turnover, dividend policy, profit margins, or leverage.

Interpreting the Sustainable Growth Model. It is just as important to understand what the sustainable growth model *does not* say as it is to grasp what it does say. From the previous calculation, should we assume that Yahoo! managers should set as their firm's growth target an increase in sales of 5.7 percent, equal to the sustainable growth rate? Not at all. Yahoo! managers should decide what rate of growth maximizes shareholder wealth, and then they should use the sustainable growth model as a planning device to help them prepare for the consequences of their growth plans. Suppose that Yahoo! decides it is best for its shareholders if the firm grows more rapidly than 5.7 percent. To do so, Yahoo! must alter one or more of the baseline assumptions of the model. It could try to find ways to raise its profit margin, to increase its asset turnover, or to increase leverage. Yahoo! does not pay dividends, so it cannot use a dividend cut to increase growth.

APPLYING THE MODEL 21.2

In fact, from 2003 to 2004, Yahoo!'s sales increased by roughly 120 percent, almost 21 times the sustainable rate. The sustainable growth model would suggest that to finance this rapid growth, Yahoo! must have achieved some combination of higher profit margins, faster asset turnover, and increased financial leverage. Indeed, by the end of 2004, Yahoo!'s net profit margin had increased by over 60 percent (from 14.64 percent to 23.49 percent) and its total asset turnover ratio had increased by 44 percent (from 0.27 to 0.39). These two large increases provided the fuel for rapid growth, even though Yahoo!'s assets-to-equity ratio fell roughly 5 percentage points (from 1.36 to 1.29) in 2004.

The sustainable growth model gives managers a shorthand projection that ties together growth objectives and financing needs. It provides hints about the levers that managers must pull to achieve growth above the sustainable rate. It also identifies some of the financial benefits of growing more slowly than the sustainable rate. A firm that expects to grow at a rate below g^* can plan to reduce leverage or asset turnover, or it can increase dividends. Again, we emphasize that the model does not say anything about how fast the firm *should* grow.

The sustainable growth model also highlights tensions that can develop as firms pursue multiple objectives simultaneously. We have seen that one way to finance faster growth is to increase leverage, so the goals of increasing sales while maintaining the current degree of leverage may be difficult to achieve simultaneously. For the firm to achieve faster sales growth, the marketing function may indicate that the firm should offer a wider array of products. Doing so may result in lower inventory turns and reduced total asset turnover. If the firm is unwilling to increase leverage, and if expanding the product line means reducing asset turnover, then meeting the sales target will depend on improving profit margins or cutting dividend payouts. Compensation issues may further compound the competing objectives: For example, the compensation of the vice president of marketing may be tied to generating additional sales volume, whereas the CFO's compensation may depend on maintaining the firm's credit rating.

The primary advantage of the sustainable growth model is its simplicity. However, the financial planning process generally involves more complex projections. These projections are usually embodied in a set of pro forma income statements and balance sheets that firms use to provide a benchmark against which to judge future performance.

Pro Forma Financial Statements

Periodically, firms produce **pro forma financial statements,** which are forecasts of what they expect their income statement and balance sheet to look like a year or two ahead. Occasionally, firms use these statements to communicate their plans to outside investors (such as at the time of an IPO or earnings announcement). Most of the time, managers construct pro forma financial statements for internal planning and control purposes. By making projections of sales volume, profits, fixed asset requirements, working capital needs, and sources of financing, the firm can establish goals to which compensation may be tied. It also can predict liquidity problems with enough lead time to have additional financing sources available when needed.

The Sales Forecast. The process of creating pro forma financial statements varies from firm to firm, but there are some common elements. Most pro forma statements begin with a *sales forecast*. The sales forecast may be derived through either a "top-down" or "bottom-up" approach.

Top-down sales forecasts rely heavily on macroeconomic and industry forecasts. Some firms use complex statistical models or subscribe to forecasts produced by econometric-modeling firms. In the top-down approach, senior managers establish a firmwide objective for increased sales. Next, individual divisions or business units receive targets that collectively aggregate to achieve the firm's overall growth target. Division heads pass down sales targets to product line managers and other smaller-scale units. The sales targets will vary across units within the division, but they must add up to achieve the divisional goal.

Firms that use a **bottom-up sales forecast** begin by talking with customers. Sales personnel try to assess demand in the coming year on a customer-by-customer basis. Managers add up these figures across sales territories, product lines, and divisions to arrive at the overall sales forecast for the company. Bottom-up forecasting approaches generally do not rely on mathematical and statistical models.

Not surprisingly, many firms use a blend of these two approaches. For example, a firm may generate a set of assumptions regarding the macroeconomic environment to which all divisions must adhere. It then can generate forecasts from the customer level and aggregate them to an overall forecast for the firm, consistent with the macro assumptions. Some firms produce two sets of forecasts, one that uses a statistical approach and another that relies on customer feedback. Senior managers then compare the two forecasts to see how far apart they are before setting a final sales objective.

Constructing Pro Forma Statements. Starting with the sales forecast, financial analysts construct pro forma income statements and balance sheets using a mix of facts and assumptions. For example, if a firm's strategic plan calls for major investments in fixed assets, the analyst will incorporate those projections in the forecast of total fixed asset requirements, as well as in the forecast of depreciation expense. In the absence of any specific knowledge of capital spending plans, an analyst may assume that total fixed assets will remain at a fixed percentage relative to sales or total assets; that assumption in turn would drive the depreciation line item on the income statement.

Similarly, an analyst can make projections for line items that vary with sales volume. For example, by assuming a constant gross profit margin, the analyst can estimate cost of goods sold, directly from the sales forecast. When firms construct pro forma statements by assuming that all items grow in proportion to sales and by extending that percentage to all income statement and balance sheet accounts, they are using the **percentage-of-sales method.** This is a convenient way to construct pro forma statements, and it is usually a good starting point when making financial projections. However, on the balance sheet, items such as receivables, inventory, and payables typically increase with sales, though not always in a linear fashion. For example, a company with $100 billion in sales may not need 100 times as much inventory as a firm with $1 billion in sales.

In constructing pro forma statements, analysts usually leave one line item on the balance sheet as a **plug figure.** They adjust this account after making all their other projections, in order to balance the balance sheet. For example, the analyst may make projections for all asset, liability, and equity accounts except for the cash balance. When the projections are complete, the analyst simply adjusts the cash account to make the balance sheet balance. Alternatively, the analyst might leave a short-term liability account open to serve as the plug figure. The analyst could, for example, use the line item representing the amount borrowed on a bank line of credit to bring the right-hand and left-hand sides of the balance sheet into equality.

APPLYING THE MODEL 21.3

Table 21.1 shows the 2007 balance sheet and income statement for Zinsmeister Shoe Corporation. We will use this historical information plus some assumptions to generate pro forma financial statements for 2008. We make the following assumptions:

1. Zinsmeister plans to increase sales by 30 percent in 2008.
2. The company's gross profit margin will remain at 35 percent.
3. Operating expenses will equal 10 percent of sales as they did in 2007.
4. Zinsmeister pays 10 percent interest on both its long-term debt and its credit line.

Table 21.1
Financial Statements of Zinsmeister Shoe Corporation for 2007 ($ in thousands)

Zinsmeister Shoe Corporation
Balance Sheet as of December 31, 2007

Assets		Liabilities and Equity	
Cash	$ 10,000	Accounts payable	$ 19,500
Accounts receivable	21,250	Credit line	5,000
Inventory	25,000	Current long-term debt	5,000
Current assets	$ 56,250	Current liabilities	$ 29,500
Gross fixed assets	$ 80,000	Long-term debt	$ 20,000
Less: Accumulated depreciation	20,000	Common stock	$ 20,200
Net fixed assets	$ 60,000	Retained earnings	$ 46,550
Total assets	$116,250	Total liabilities and equity	$116,250

Zinsmeister Shoe Corporation
Income Statement for the Year Ended December 31, 2007

Sales	$250,000
Less: Cost of goods sold	162,500
Gross profit	$ 87,500
Less: Operating expenses	25,000
Less: Interest expense	3,000
Less: Depreciation	10,000
Pretax income	$ 49,500
Less: Taxes	17,325
Net income	$ 32,175

5. Zinsmeister will invest an additional $20 million in fixed assets in 2008, which will increase depreciation expense from $10 million to $15 million in 2008.
6. The company faces a 35 percent tax rate.
7. The company plans to increase cash holdings by $1 million next year.
8. Accounts receivable equal 8.5 percent of sales.
9. Inventories equal 10 percent of sales.
10. Accounts payable equal 12 percent of cost of goods sold.
11. The company will repay an additional $5 million in long-term debt in 2008.
12. The company will pay out 50 percent of its net income as a cash dividend.
13. The company plans to use its credit line as the *plug figure*.

From this set of assumptions and the data in Table 21.1, we can construct the pro forma statements for 2008 shown in Table 21.2. First, Zinsmeister's sales increase to $325 million. Cost of goods sold and operating expenses increase 30 percent over the prior year (hitting the percentage-of-sales assumptions above). Interest expense is a tricky item. To begin, assume that Zinsmeister will maintain a $5 million balance on its credit line and will retire the current portion of long-term debt. This means that its total outstanding debt will be $25 million. At 10 percent, interest expense should equal $2.5 million. (As we will see, that assumption may change as we continue to build the statements.)

Putting these figures together in the pro forma income statement, we see that Zinsmeister earns a net profit of just over $41 million, half of which it pays out to shareholders.

Table 21.2
Pro Forma Financial
Statements for
Zinsmeister Shoe
Corporation for 2008
($ in thousands)

Zinsmeister Shoe Corporation
Pro Forma Balance Sheet as of December 31, 2008

Assets		Liabilities and Equity	
Cash	$ 11,000	Accounts payable	$ 25,350
Accounts receivable	27,625	Credit line	3,306
Inventory	32,500	Current long-term debt	5,000
Current assets	$ 71,125	Current liabilities	$ 33,656
Gross fixed assets	$100,000	Long-term debt	$ 15,000
Less: Accumulated depreciation	35,000	Common stock	$ 20,200
Net fixed assets	$ 65,000	Retained earnings	$ 67,269
Total assets	$136,125	Total liabilities and equity	$136,125

Zinsmeister Shoe Corporation
Pro Forma Income Statement for the Year Ended December 31, 2008

Sales	$325,000
Less: Cost of goods sold	211,250
Gross profit	$113,750
Less: Operating expenses	32,500
Less: Interest expense	2,500
Less: Depreciation	15,000
Pretax income	$ 63,750
Less: Taxes	22,312
Net income	$ 41,438
Dividends	$ 20,719

Next, we build the pro forma balance sheet. Cash is given at $11 million ($10 million in 2007 plus a $1 million increase). Accounts receivable and inventory increase with sales as stated, so current assets increase to $71.125 million. With the additional investment in fixed assets of $20 million, less 2008's depreciation expense, net fixed assets grow to $65 million. Total assets equal $136.125 million.

On the liabilities/equity side, accounts payable increases with sales, the current portion of long-term debt remains at $5 million, total long-term debt declines by $5 million, and common stock does not change. The retained earnings figure for 2008 equals the 2007 figure plus half of 2008's net income. Zinsmeister uses its credit line as the *plug figure*. That is, given all the assumptions so far, the credit line will decline from $5 million to $3.306 million because that is the figure necessary to keep assets in balance with liabilities and equity.

However, because the credit line declines, our estimate of interest expense in the income statement is too high. Recall that we predicted interest expense of $2.5 million based on a 10 percent interest rate on total outstanding debt of $25 million. The pro forma balance sheet now shows long-term and short-term debt of just $23.306 million, so interest expense falls to $2.33 million. A decline in interest expense leads to an increase in profits and retained earnings. Higher retained earnings means that the firm can reduce the line of credit even more, and the cycle repeats. To find the amount of borrowing on the credit line and the corresponding interest expense that reconciles the balance sheet with the income statement, an analyst would need to use an iterative approach, such as *Excel*'s Solver function.

The bottom line for Zinsmeister is that its pro forma outlook is quite good. If the company achieves its sales growth target and keeps expenses and current asset and current liability accounts in line with historical norms, it can simultaneously invest $20 million in new fixed assets and reduce its outstanding interest-bearing debt.

In one sense, that conclusion is hardly surprising. If we take the 2007 data for Zinsmeister and plug it into Equation 21.1, we find that the company's sustainable growth rate is 31.8 percent. Therefore, the firm's target growth rate of 30 percent should leave it with some "financial slack." Going through the added steps to build pro forma statements provides the firm with much more information than the sustainable growth rate does. With the figures in Tables 21.1 and 21.2 programmed into a spreadsheet, analysts could easily study the effects of changes in any of the assumptions on Zinsmeister's ability to pay down debt, or perhaps identify a need to increase the credit line balance.

A Shorthand Approach for Estimating External Funds Required. We can use the notation defined earlier to present another shorthand approach for estimating the amount of **external funds required (*EFR*)**—the external financing that a firm will require. Equation 21.2 states that *EFR* is a function of three factors. The first term in the equation, $(A \div S)\Delta S$, indicates the additional investment in assets required for a firm if it plans to maintain its total asset turnover ratio and increase the dollar volume of sales by ΔS. The second term measures the inflow of funds available to finance this growth. The inflow represented by this second term assumes that the relationship between a firm's sales and its spontaneous liabilities (in this case, accounts payable) remains constant. The third term captures the additional financing inflows that the firm creates internally through retained earnings.

$$EFR = \frac{A}{S}\Delta S - \frac{AP}{S}\Delta S - mS(1 + g)(1 - d)$$ (Eq. 21.2)

If we apply this shorthand calculation to Zinsmeister, we can determine its external funds required (in thousands of dollars):

$$EFR = \frac{\$116,250}{\$250,000}(\$75,000) - \frac{\$19,500}{\$250,000}(\$75,000)$$

$$-\left(\frac{\$32,175}{\$250,000}\right)\$250,000(1 + 0.30)(1 - 0.50) = \$8,111$$

Under the assumptions of this model, Zinsmeister will require additional external funding of $8.1 million. In the pro forma projections in Table 21.2, Zinsmeister's total external financing actually declines by $6.7 million.[5] Why the discrepancy? Closer examination of the pro forma statements reveals that several of the assumptions in Equation 21.2 do not hold in a more complete analysis. For instance, from 2007 to 2008, Zinsmeister's ratio of assets to sales is not constant, as the equation assumes; instead, the ratio declines from 0.465 to 0.419. Zinsmeister is increasing sales more rapidly than assets, so its funding needs are actually less than Equation 21.2 assumes. When we build projections on an account-by-account basis, the apparent need for external funding predicted by Equation 21.2 turns into a financial surplus.

[5] The figure in Table 21.2 includes a $5 million reduction in long-term debt and a $1.7 million reduction in the line of credit. The figure in this equation is still imprecise because the interest expense and outstanding debt figures in Table 21.2 are not fully reconciled.

Some Concluding Remarks. This discussion has presented two important points. First, shorthand approaches such as the sustainable growth model or the equation for determining external funds required help managers predict whether they should expect a scarcity or a surplus of financial resources, given the firm's growth objectives. Second, firms can construct a more complete picture of their funding requirements by building pro forma income statements and balance sheets. Managers can use any of these models to avoid unpleasant financial surprises a year or two ahead.

Besides planning for growth that will occur over a period of years, companies also construct financial plans with shorter time horizons. These plans generally focus on temporary cash surpluses or deficits due to seasonal fluctuations in transactions volume. The next section examines this dimension of financial planning.

---

3. Describe and evaluate the use of *return on investment (ROI)* and *economic value added (EVA®)* as growth targets in financial planning. Why do firms often use annual growth in sales or assets as a target growth rate?

4. Explain the difference between a firm's *sustainable growth rate* and its optimal growth rate. In what circumstances is a firm's optimal growth rate likely to exceed its sustainable growth rate? Under what conditions would you expect the opposite to be true?

5. Current asset accounts, especially cash and inventory, usually increase at a rate slightly less than the growth rate in sales. Why? What is the implication of that fact for the *sustainable growth model?*

Concept Review Questions

21.3 PLANNING AND CONTROL

SHORT-TERM FINANCING STRATEGIES

In the previous section, we observed that most firms establish growth as one of their long-term objectives. Therefore, it is not unusual to observe a distinct upward trend in any company's historical sales volume. However, in a single year many firms experience sharp quarter-to-quarter sales changes due to seasonal factors. Construction-related businesses generate much higher volume in the summer than they do in the winter. In contrast, toy companies experience peak volume in the winter.

Because sales volume tends to fluctuate around a long-term upward trend, we expect to observe the same pattern when we examine a firm's total assets over time. As sales volume grows, so does the firm's need for current and fixed assets. During the year, a firm's investment in current assets will tend to rise and fall with sales. This seasonal pattern creates temporary cash surpluses and deficits that the firm must manage. In the remainder of this section, we use relevant data for Hershey Foods to demonstrate alternative financing strategies.

Hershey Foods' Quarterly Sales and Total Current Assets. Panel A of Figure 21.2 plots quarterly sales figures for Hershey Foods from 1992 through the fourth quarter of 2004. Hershey's fiscal year matches the calendar year, so its quarterly income statements report sales for quarters ending in March, June, September, and December each year. For Hershey, sales usually peak in the third or fourth quarter of each year. Sales troughs typically occur in the second quarter. Panel A of Figure 21.2 also reveals a gradual upward trend in Hershey sales, from 1992 to 1999. That growth trend leveled off from 2000 to 2004 with the U.S. economic recession.

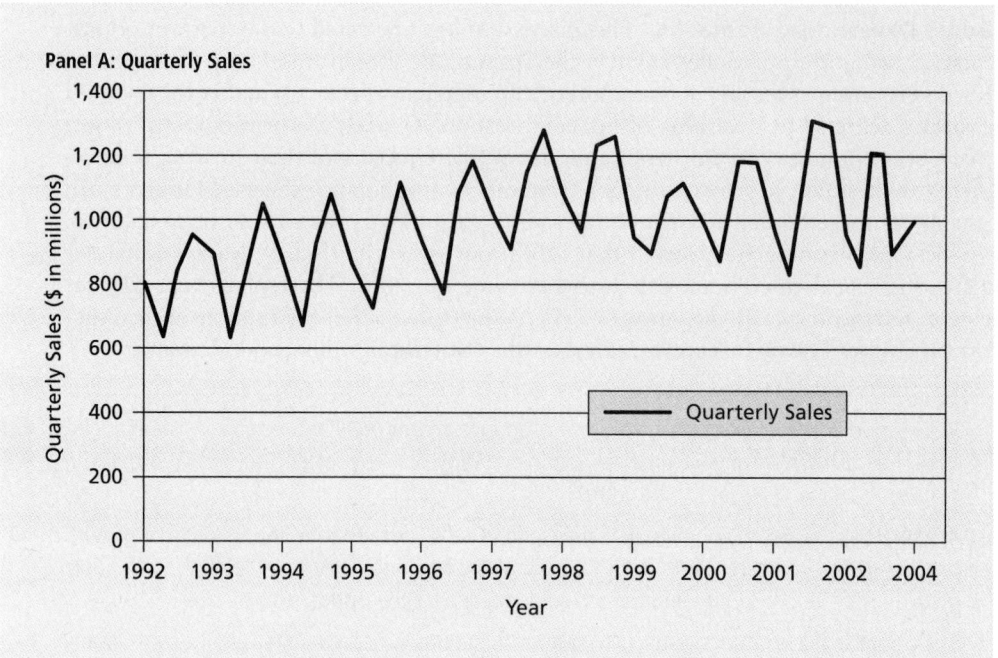

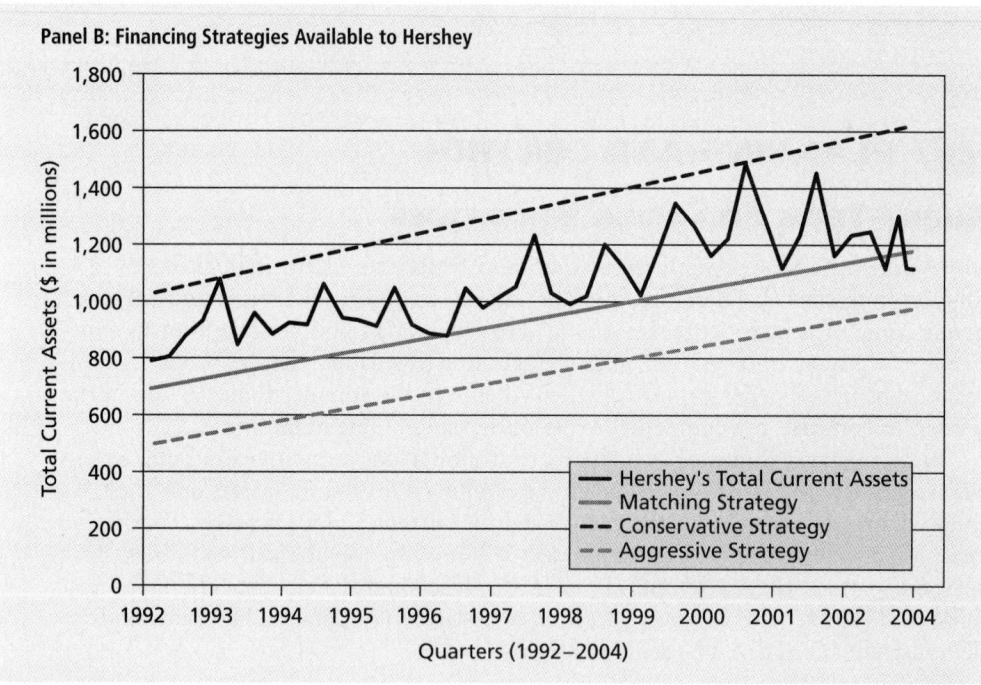

Figure 21.2
Quarterly Sales and Total Current Assets for Hershey Foods (1992 through the fourth quarter of 2004)
Panel A shows the seasonal pattern in Hershey's sales, and Panel B shows a similar pattern for total current assets. Panel B assumes that Hershey finances all of its fixed assets and a portion of its current assets with long-term financing; the straight lines in this panel represent the amount of total current assets covered by Hershey's long-term financing. The black dashed line is a conservative strategy: *Hershey has sufficient long-term financing to pay for both the permanent upward trend and the seasonal fluctuations in total current assets. The gray dashed line represents an* aggressive strategy, *in which Hershey does not secure enough long-term financing to cover the permanent component of the growth in total current assets. The gray solid line is a* matching strategy, *a middle-of-the-road approach in which Hershey finances permanent assets (fixed assets plus the permanent component of total current assets) with long-term financing, and finances temporary or seasonal total current asset requirements with short-term debt.*

Panel B of Figure 21.2 plots Hershey's quarterly total current assets over the same period. You can see that the patterns closely match those in Panel A. Hershey's total current assets show the same seasonal pattern (with a lag of one quarter) and the same upward trend that the company's sales follow. Hershey builds current assets, mostly inventory and receivables, during the third and fourth quarters of each year, and it draws down these items during the first and second quarters.

Because Hershey's total current assets fluctuate around a long-term upward trend, we can think of the company's current assets as containing both a temporary and a permanent component. The temporary component reflects the differences between the seasonal peaks and troughs of Hershey's business. The permanent component represents the sizeable investment in current assets that Hershey maintains, even during the quarters when business is slow.

Hershey's fixed assets (not shown in the figure) do not exhibit the seasonal pattern that sales and current assets do. However, its fixed assets do follow the long-term upward trend, essentially following the long-term growth in Hershey's sales.

Alternative Financing Strategies. What financing strategies might Hershey employ to fund both the long-term trend and the seasonal fluctuations in its total current assets? First, Hershey might adopt a **conservative strategy** one in which the firm makes sure it has enough long-term financing to cover its permanent and seasonal investments in current assets. For example, Hershey might issue long-term bonds to generate enough cash to cover all its cash needs for several years. This strategy is represented graphically by the black dashed line in Panel B of Figure 21.2. Using such a strategy, Hershey has a cash surplus for much of the year, drawing down that surplus only when total current assets reach their peak during the third and fourth quarters each year. Hershey will invest its excess cash balances in marketable securities. We describe this strategy as conservative because it minimizes the risk that Hershey will experience a liquidity crisis during peak quarters. However, keep in mind that large investments in cash and marketable securities are not likely to make Hershey shareholders rich.[6] Furthermore, because the term structure of interest rates (the *yield curve*) is typically upward-sloping, Hershey will generally pay higher interest rates on its long-term debt than it would pay if it were willing to borrow on a short-term basis.

The second strategy that Hershey might adopt is much more aggressive. In this **aggressive strategy,** Hershey relies heavily on short-term borrowing, not only to meet the seasonal peaks each year but also to finance a portion of the long-term growth in total current assets. In Panel B of Figure 21.2, the gray dashed line represents the aggressive strategy. The difference between that line and the one representing Hershey's total current assets indicates how much short-term debt Hershey has outstanding at any moment in time. During peak quarters, Hershey increases its short-term borrowings. But even during the first and second quarters, when business is relatively slow, Hershey continues to finance at least part of its operations with short-term debt. Thus, Hershey uses short-term financing to fund a portion of its long-term, or permanent, growth in total current assets. With this strategy, Hershey takes advantage of short-term interest rates, which are usually lower than long-term rates. However, if short-term rates rise, Hershey will face increased interest expense. Hershey also

---

[6.] Companies sometimes argue that a large cash reserve is a strategic asset because it enables the firm to make acquisitions quickly as opportunities arise. We agree that, in principle, a cash reserve could have strategic value, but it also enables managers to make value-reducing investments without facing the discipline of raising money in the capital markets. As you will see in Chapter 24, the research evidence suggests that managers of acquiring firms generally do not create wealth for their shareholders.

faces a significant *refinancing risk* in this strategy. That is, if Hershey's financial condition weakens, it may not be able to roll over short-term debt as it had in the past.

A third strategy is the **matching strategy.** Firms that follow the matching strategy finance the permanent component of total current assets with long-term financing, and they finance the temporary or seasonal portion of total current assets with short-term debt. The matching strategy is represented by the gray solid line in Panel B of Figure 21.2. In the figure, notice that Hershey will increase short-term borrowing during peak periods. It will repay those loans as it draws down its investment in total current assets during slow periods.

The matching strategy is a middle-of-the-road approach. If Hershey finances its short-term assets with short-term debt, then it will have smaller cash surpluses than under the conservative approach, but its borrowing costs will be lower, on average. (It substitutes less costly short-term debt for long-term debt.) Hershey's interest costs will be higher under the matching approach than in the aggressive strategy, but it will face less exposure to refinancing risk, and its interest costs will not fluctuate as much from quarter to quarter.

Regardless of which strategy Hershey decides to pursue, the company will pay very careful attention to short-term inflows and outflows of cash. Doing so will allow the company to invest unanticipated cash surpluses and cover unexpected deficits. The primary tool for managing cash flow on a short-term basis is the cash budget.

THE CASH BUDGET

Managers use the tools described in the section on planning for growth (Section 21.2) to make financial projections over horizons of a year or more. They also need to monitor the firm's financial performance over shorter horizons. Because it takes cash to operate on a day-to-day basis, firms monitor their cash inflows and outflows very closely, and the primary tool they use is the cash budget.

A **cash budget** is a statement of the firm's planned inflows and outflows of cash. Firms use the cash budget to ensure they will have enough cash available to meet short-term financial obligations. Any surplus cash resources can be invested quickly and efficiently. Typically, the cash budget spans a one-year period, with more frequent breakdowns provided as components of the budget. The CFO of Finish Line Inc., a specialty retailer, once described his company to us as a "cash and inventory business." What he meant was that running a successful retail enterprise requires very close attention to managing cash flows and inventory. A company like Finish Line needs to know its exact cash position at the end of every business day. For other firms, monitoring cash positions on a weekly or monthly basis may be sufficient. Besides the volume of cash transactions, other factors that determine the frequency with which firms construct cash budgets include the volatility of prices and volume and the importance of seasonal fluctuations.

Running out of cash is an ever-present threat at small and medium-size companies. Especially vulnerable are those companies that are growing rapidly. Even in large corporations, though, astonishing changes in cash reserves can occur over just a few years. For example, in December 1999, Boeing Co. reported cash and marketable security holdings in excess of $4.4 billion. Just two years later, that figure had fallen to $0.6 billion. Over the same two years, cash holdings at Phillip Morris, United Parcel Service, and Sears Roebuck fell $4.7 billion, $4.6 billion, and $2.8 billion, respectively. With the possibility of such dramatic swings in cash holdings, even large firms must monitor their cash positions closely.

As was the case with pro forma financial statements, the key input required to build a cash budget is the firm's sales forecast. On the basis of the forecast, the financial

manager estimates the monthly cash inflows from cash sales, receivable collections, and other sources. Naturally, a complete cash budget also contains estimates of cash outflows; some of these vary directly with sales and some do not. Cash outlays include purchases of raw materials, labor and other production expenses, selling expenses, and fixed-asset investments. A cash budget usually presents projected inflows (cash receipts) first. Next come the projected outflows (cash disbursements). Finally, the cash budget shows whether the firm expects a net cash inflow or outflow for the period. Depending on the firm's cash balance at the start of the period, the cash budget will either reveal a need for additional financing or demonstrate that the firm will have surplus cash to invest in short-term marketable securities.

Cash Receipts. **Cash receipts** include all the firm's cash inflows in a given period. The most common components of cash receipts are cash sales, collections of accounts receivable, and other cash receipts. The firm estimates collections of accounts receivable using the payment patterns of its customers.[7]

APPLYING THE MODEL 21.4

Consider the cash receipts projections of Farrell Industries, a candy manufacturer, which is developing a cash budget for October, November, and December. Farrell's sales in August and September were $300,000 and $600,000, respectively. The firm forecasts sales of $1,200,000, $900,000, and $600,000 for October, November, and December, respectively. Typically, 90 percent of Farrell's sales are on credit, and 10 percent are cash sales. Farrell collects about 60 percent of each month's sales in the next month; it has to wait two months to collect the remaining 30 percent of sales. Bad debts for Farrell have been negligible. In December, the firm expects to receive a $90,000 dividend from stock it holds in a subsidiary.

Table 21.3 presents the schedule of projected cash receipts. The first row shows total sales in each month. Remember, the figures for October–December are projections. The second row lists cash sales in each month, which, by assumption, equal 10 percent of total monthly sales. The third and fourth rows report the expected cash inflows from collecting receivables from the previous two months' sales. The next line reports cash receipts not related to sales, and the final line shows total cash receipts each month.

For example, consider the month of November. Projected sales are $900,000, which implies that expected cash sales equal $90,000 (0.10 × $900,000). During November, Farrell expects to collect receivables equal to 60 percent of October's

	August	September	October	November	December
Forecast sales	$300	$600	$1,200	$900	$ 600
Cash sales (10%)	$ 30	$ 60	$ 120	$ 90	$ 60
Collection of accounts receivable					
Previous month (60%)		180	360	720	540
Two months prior (30%)			90	180	360
Other cash receipts					90
Total cash receipts			$ 570	$990	$1,050

Table 21.3
Schedule of Projected Cash Receipts for Farrell Industries ($ in thousands)

[7.] We discuss payment patterns more fully in Chapter 22.

$1,200,000 sales, or $720,000. Farrell also expects to collect the 30 percent of September $600,000 sales still on the books as receivables, or $180,000. The firm expects no other cash flows in November, so total cash receipts equal $990,000 ($90,000 + $720,000 + $180,000).

Cash Disbursements. **Cash disbursements** include all outlays of cash by the firm in the period. The most common cash disbursements are cash purchases, fixed-asset outlays, payments of accounts payable, wages, interest payments, taxes, and rent and lease payments. Cash disbursements may also include items such as dividends and share repurchases. It is important to remember that depreciation and other noncash expenses are *not* included in the cash budget. They are not outlays of cash, but merely represent a scheduled write-off of an earlier cash outflow. (Depreciation does have a cash outflow *effect* through its impact on tax payments.)

APPLYING THE MODEL 21.5

Farrell Industries has gathered the following data needed for the preparation of a cash disbursements schedule for October, November, and December:

> *Purchases:* The firm's purchases average 70 percent of sales. Of this amount, Farrell pays 20 percent in cash, 60 percent in the month following the purchase, and the remaining 20 percent two months following the purchase. Thus, October purchases are $840,000 (0.70 × $1,200,000). Of that amount, Farrell pays $168,000 (0.20 × $840,000) in cash, and puts $504,000 (0.60 × $840,000) on account to pay in November, and $168,000 (0.20 × $840,000) on account to pay in December.
>
> *Rent payments:* Farrell will pay rent of $20,000 each month.
>
> *Wages and salaries:* The firm's wages and salaries equal 10 percent of monthly sales plus $30,000. Thus, October's wages and salaries will be $150,000 [(0.10 × $1,200,000) + $30,000]. The figures for November and December are calculated in the same manner.
>
> *Tax payments:* Farrell must pay taxes of $75,000 in December.
>
> *Fixed asset outlays:* The firm will purchase new machinery costing $390,000 and pay for it in November.
>
> *Interest payments:* An interest payment of $30,000 is due in December.
>
> *Cash dividend payments:* Farrell will pay cash dividends of $60,000 in October.
>
> *Principal payments:* A $60,000 principal payment is due in December.

Table 21.4 presents the firm's schedule of projected cash disbursements, based on the preceding data.

Net Cash Flow, Ending Cash, Financing Needs, and Excess Cash. We can calculate the firm's net cash flow by subtracting its cash disbursements from its cash receipts for each period. By adding the beginning cash balance to the firm's net cash flow, we determine the ending cash balance for each period.

Like most companies, Farrell does not want its cash balance to dip below some minimum level at any time. Therefore, by subtracting the desired minimum cash balance from the ending cash balance, we arrive at one of two results: the required total financing or the excess cash balance. If the ending cash balance is less than the

	August	September	October	November	December
Purchases (70% of sales)	$210	$420	$840	$ 630	$420
Cash purchases (20%)	$ 42	$ 84	$168	$ 126	$ 84
Payments of accounts payable					
Previous month (60%)		126	252	504	378
Two months prior (20%)			42	84	168
Rent payments			20	20	20
Wages and salaries			150	120	90
Tax payments					75
Fixed asset outlays				390	
Interest payments					30
Cash dividend payments			60		
Principal payments					60
Total cash disbursements			$692	$1,244	$905

Table 21.4
Schedule of Projected
Cash Disbursements
for Farrell Industries
($ in thousands)

desired minimum cash balance, then the firm has a short-term financing need. The firm meets this need with short-term borrowing, typically notes payable. If the ending cash balance exceeds the desired minimum cash balance, then the firm has an excess cash balance that it can invest in short-term marketable securities.

APPLYING THE MODEL 21.6

Table 21.5 presents the cash budget for Farrell Industries based on the cash receipt and disbursement schedules developed in earlier examples and the following additional information: (1) Farrell's cash balance at the end of September is $200,000. (2) Notes payable and marketable securities are $0 at the end of September. (3) The desired minimum cash balance is $50,000.

	October	November	December
Total cash receipts[a]	$570	$ 990	$1,050
Less: Total cash disbursements[b]	692	1,244	905
Net cash flow	−$122	−$ 254	$ 145
Add: Beginning cash	200	78	− 176
Ending cash balance	$ 78	−$ 176	−$ 31
Less: Minimum cash balance	50	50	50
Required total financing (notes payable)[c]		$ 226	$ 81
Excess cash balance (marketable securities)[d]	$ 28		

Table 21.5
Cash Budget for
Farrell Industries
($ in thousands)

[a]From Table 21.3.
[b]From Table 21.4.
[c]Values are placed on this line when the ending cash balance is *less than* the desired minimum cash balance. These amounts are typically financed short-term, and therefore are represented by notes payable.
[d]Values are placed on this line when the ending cash balance is *greater than* the desired minimum cash balance. These amounts are typically invested in short-term vehicles and therefore are represented by marketable securities.

For Farrell to maintain its desired minimum ending cash balance of $50,000, it will have notes payable (short-term borrowing) balances of $226,000 in November and $81,000 in December. In October, the firm will have excess cash of $28,000, which it can invest in marketable securities. The required total financing figures in the cash budget refer to *how much the firm will owe at the end of each month,* but the figures do not represent the monthly change in borrowing. For Farrell, the monthly financial activities are as follows:

October: Farrell invests $28,000 of excess cash.

November: The firm liquidates $28,000 of excess cash and borrows $226,000. Net cash flow of −$254,000 uses all the available cash reserves ($50,000 minimum cash balance from October + $28,000 excess cash), leaving an ending cash balance of −$176,000. To cover that negative balance and the desired minimum cash balance, Farrell must borrow $226,000 ($176,000 + $50,000).

December: Net cash flows of $145,000 reduced Farrell's end-of-month borrowing needs to $81,000, which is a reduction from November's borrowing needs of $226,000. Thus, Farrell repays $145,000 of the amount borrowed.

The cash budget provides the firm with figures indicating whether a cash shortage (financing need) or a cash surplus (short-term investment opportunity) is expected in each of the months covered by the forecast. In our example, Farrell Industries can expect a cash surplus of $28,000 in October, followed by cash shortages of $226,000 in November and $81,000 in December. Each of these values is based on the internal constraint of a minimum cash balance of $50,000.

Because the firm expects to borrow as much as $226,000 during the three-month period, the financial manager should establish a line of credit to ensure the availability of the necessary funds. The maximum amount of borrowing available on the line of credit should exceed the $226,000 forecast, to allow for errors in the forecast.

Dealing with Uncertainty in the Cash Budget. Because the cash budget provides only month-end totals, it does not ensure that the firm has sufficient credit to cover intra-month financing needs. For example, what if a firm's disbursements occur before its receipts during a particular month? In that case, its intra-month borrowing needs will exceed the monthly totals shown in its cash budget. To ensure sufficient credit, the firm may forecast its expected receipts and disbursements on a *daily* basis and use these estimates, along with its cash budget, to arrange adequate credit to cover its maximum expected cash deficit.

The monthly cash surpluses and deficits predicted in the budget are affected by virtually all facets of a firm's operations. For example, changes in receivables collection, in payment patterns, and in inventory turnover can have a dramatic impact on financing needs. Any action that slows collections from customers or accelerates payments to suppliers will increase monthly financial deficits (or reduce surpluses). In that sense, almost any functional area in the firm can affect, or be affected by, the cash budget.

APPLYING THE MODEL 21.7

Consider the effect on Farrell Industries of a change in customer payment patterns. In the original example, Farrell's collection pattern on accounts receivable and its resulting cash position were as follows:

1. 10 percent cash sales, resulting in a $28,000 cash surplus in October
2. 60 percent collected one month after sale, resulting in $226,000 total borrowing in November
3. 30 percent collected two months after sale, resulting in $81,000 total borrowing in December

   Now assume that Farrell Industries has a slowdown in its collection pattern, perhaps due to the effects of an economic recession. The new pattern is:

1. 5 percent cash sales
2. 40 percent collected one month after sale
3. 50 percent collected two months after sale
4. 5 percent uncollectible

This collection pattern changes Farrell's cash receipts to (1) $450,000 in October, (2) $825,000 in November, and (3) $1,080,000 in December. If Farrell's cash disbursements remain unchanged, the cash budget will show the following:

1. $92,000 total borrowing in October
2. $511,000 total borrowing in November
3. $336,000 total borrowing in December

Comparing these values to the initial collection pattern, it is clear that Farrell's short-term financing requirements have increased.

   The preceding example demonstrates two important points: First, changes in a firm's collection or payment pattern alter the timing and magnitude of its financing needs. Second, a slowdown in collections increases the firm's short-term financing needs and, conversely, a speedup in collections decreases the firm's financing needs. With regard to payment patterns, a speedup in payments would likely increase the firm's financing needs, whereas a slowdown in payments would reduce financing needs. The next two chapters focus on the management of current accounts such as inventory, receivables, cash, and payables. By managing these items carefully, firms can increase the profitability of their enterprises and lower the need for external financing.

   In this chapter, we have emphasized the importance of financial planning and illustrated a few of the most widely used tools of the trade. We end with a word of caution: When firms construct financial plans, they clearly hope to meet the plans' goals. But the value of planning is not just in attaining established goals. Rather, its importance derives from the thinking it forces managers to do, not only about what they expect to occur in the future, but what they will do if their expectations are not realized.

---

6. Suppose that a firm follows the *matching strategy*. Does this imply that the firm's current assets will equal its current liabilities?

7. Why do firms prepare *cash budgets*? How do (a) collection patterns and (b) payment patterns affect the cash budget?

8. What can be done to deal with uncertainty in the cash budgeting process? Why might an intra-month view of the firm's cash flows cause a well-prepared cash budget to fail?

Concept Review Questions

21.4 SUMMARY

- Strategic (long-term) financial plans guide firms in preparing operating (short-term) financial plans. For most firms, strategic plans are driven by competitive forces that are not always explicitly financial in nature. However, strategic plans have important financial consequences.

- The finance function partners with other functional units in developing the firm's strategic plan. Once the firm establishes the plan, finance personnel ensure that the plan is feasible given the firm's financial resources. Finance personnel also play a crucial role in monitoring progress and in managing risks associated with financial plans.

- Most firms strive to grow over time. Popular growth targets include: (1) achieving accounting return on investment (*ROI*) in excess of the cost of capital; (2) undertaking only actions that result in positive economic value added (EVA®); and (3) realizing a target growth rate in sales or assets. Target growth rates are widely used due to their intuitive, computational, and practical appeal.

- The sustainable growth model is a tool that is used to determine the feasibility of a target growth rate under certain conditions. When the growth rate that maximizes shareholder value does not match the sustainable rate, the firm must make adjustments to the model's assumptions—such as altering leverage or dividend policy—to achieve the desired growth rate.

- Pro forma financial statements are projected, or forecast, financial statements typically based on the historical financial relationships within the firm. Preparation of these statements begins with a sales forecast that can be developed by using a top-down or a bottom-up approach, or a blend of these two approaches. The key inputs to pro forma statements are a mix of facts and assumptions.

- Firms can prepare pro forma financial statements using the percentage-of-sales method, which assumes that all items grow in proportion to sales. Certain balance sheet accounts, such as receivables, inventory, and payables, do not typically increase in a linear fashion. As a result, analysts typically use one line item on the balance sheet as a plug figure that can be used to make sure the pro forma balance sheet balances.

- Analysts also can estimate directly the amount of external financing required to fund a firm's anticipated growth by using the equation for external funds required *(EFR)*. This approach, like the preparation of pro forma statements, helps managers determine if they can expect a scarcity or surplus of financial resources, given the firm's growth objectives.

- During the year, a firm's investment in current assets tends to rise and fall with sales. This seasonal pattern creates temporary cash surpluses and deficits that the firm must manage. Three basic financing strategies—conservative, aggressive, and matching—can be used to fund both the long-term trend and seasonal fluctuations in a business. The conservative strategy is the least risky and least profitable, the aggressive strategy is the most risky and most profitable, and the matching strategy falls between the two in terms of risk and profits.

- A cash budget forecasts the short-term cash inflows and outflows of a firm. For a firm with significant seasonal variations, the financial manager typically prepares the cash budget month by month. This allows the firm to determine peak short-term financing needs and peak short-term investment opportunities, typically over a one-year period.

- The financial manager must also consider intra-month cash flows to ensure that sufficient credit is available. Changes in collection and payment periods, which change the cash conversion cycle, can significantly affect the magnitude and timing of the firm's cash flows and the resulting financing reflected in its cash budget.

INTERNET RESOURCES

Note: *For updates to links, please go to the book's website at http://smart.swcollege.com.*

    http://www.sba.gov (Small Business Administration)—Provides useful resources for managing small businesses

    http://www.toolkit.cch.com—Provides a number of interesting resources, including a cash budgeting spreadsheet template

    http://www.cfo.com/magazine—Website for *CFO Magazine*, a publication devoted to issues facing corporate CFOs, including corporate planning

    http://www.acg.org—Website of the Association for Corporate Growth

    http://www.gtnews.com—An excellent site for news regarding cash and treasury management functions

KEY TERMS

aggressive strategy	matching strategy
bottom-up sales forecast	percentage-of-sales method
cash budget	plug figure
cash disbursements	pro forma financial statements
cash receipts	return on investment (*ROI*)
conservative strategy	strategic plan
economic value added (EVA®)	sustainable growth model
external funds required (*EFR*)	top-down sales forecast

QUESTIONS

21-1. How do you convert return on investment (*ROI*) into return on equity (*ROE*)? (*Hint:* See Chapter 2.)

21-2. Is the assets-to-equity ratio equal to the equity multiplier? (*Hint:* See Chapter 2.)

21-3. In what manner does increasing *A* in Equation 21.1 affect the sustainable growth rate? What effect does decreasing *A* have on the sustainable growth rate?

21-4. There is an expression that it is best to operate a business using "other people's money." Given that other people's money is in the form of accounts payable, how does accounts payable affect the external funds required (*EFR*) and is the expression correct based on *EFR*?

21-5. What is the financial planning process? What is a *strategic plan*? Describe the roles that financial managers play with regard to strategic planning.

21-6. Briefly describe the following popular growth targets: (1) accounting *return on investment (ROI)*, (2) *economic value added (EVA®)*, and (3) *target growth rate* of sales or assets. Which is most widely used, and why?

21-7. What does the word "sustainable" mean in *sustainable growth model*? In what ways can the sustainable growth model highlight conflicts between a firm's competing objectives?

21-8. With reference to Equation 21.1, explain how each of the variables influences the firm's sustainable growth rate. If high leverage allows a firm to increase its sustainable growth rate, does that mean higher leverage is necessarily good for the firm?

21-9. A firm chooses to grow at a rate above its sustainable rate. What changes might we expect to see on the firm's financial statements in the next year? What changes would result from growing at a rate below the firm's sustainable rate?

21-10. What is the logic of the *percentage-of-sales method* for calculating *pro forma financial statements*? On a year-to-year basis, which balance sheet and income statement items do you think will fluctuate most closely with sales, and which items are not likely to vary as directly with sales volume?

21-11. Describe the differences between the *top-down sales forecast* and the *bottom-up sales forecast* methods. Describe advantages and disadvantages of each. Do you think one approach is likely to be more accurate than the other?

21-12. Why does it make sense to let the firm's cash balance or a short-term liability account serve as the *plug figure* in pro forma projections? Why not use gross fixed assets as the plug figure?

21-13. Why might pro forma statements and the equation for *external funds required (EFR)* yield different projections for a firm's financing needs?

21-14. What is the difference between the *conservative strategy,* the *aggressive strategy,* and the *matching strategy* for funding the long-term trend and seasonal fluctuations in a firm's total current assets? Which strategy is most risky? Which is least profitable?

21-15. How is a *cash budget* different from a set of pro forma financial statements? Why do you think that firms typically create cash budgets at higher frequencies than they create pro forma financial statements?

21-16. Explain how slower inventory turnovers, slower receivables collections, or faster payments to suppliers would influence the numbers produced by a cash budget.

PROBLEMS

Planning for Growth

21-1. Using an equation, demonstrate how the assets-to-equity ratio is related to the debt ratio (from Chapter 2). Next, *g* defined as the growth rate within the stock pricing equation in Chapter 4 is equal to the return on equity (*ROE*) multiplied by the retention ratio. Notice in Equation 21.1 that *ROE* equals [*S*(*m*)/*E*] and the retention ratio equals (1 − *d*). Simplify Equation 21.1 in terms of *g*, where *g* = *ROE* * retention ratio (i.e., the growth rate from Chapter 4).

21-2. Net operating profit after taxes (*NOPAT*) equals (revenues − cost of goods sold − operating expenses − depreciation) * (1 − tax rate) and is a component of economic value added (EVA®), which equals *NOPAT* less the cost of funds. A project's revenues, operating expenses, cost of goods sold, depreciation, and tax rate are: $1 million, $150,000, $550,000, $100,000, and 43 percent, respectively. What is the *NOPAT* for the project? The firm's cost of capital is 16 percent and the investment for the project is $715,000. What is the EVA® for the project for this period? If depreciation can be accelerated to be $150,000, how much will the EVA® change? By keeping depreciation at $100,000 and reducing operating expenses to $125,000, how much will the EVA® change?

21-3. The firm, R.H. Nicholson, has a return on equity (*ROE*) of 25 percent based on sales of $6 million, with a $6 million asset base. R.H. Nicholson has a debt-to-equity ratio of 1.0 and never pays dividends. What is R.H. Nicholson's sustainable growth rate? The firm is willing to sacrifice some sustainable growth by paying a dividend, but the firm will not allow for a sustainable growth rate below 25 percent. What is the largest dividend (based on the dividend payout ratio) that the firm can pay? What is the equivalent retention ratio, assuming the dividend is paid?

21-4. Firm PQZ has a net profit margin of 10 percent, a total asset turnover of 1.5, and an equity multiplier of 1.0 (i.e., there is no debt). Assuming PQZ pays out 35 percent of its net income as dividends, what is the firm's sustainable growth based on Equation 21.1? Assuming a sales level of $4.4 million (up 10% from the previous year while maintaining the same total asset turnover) and a cost of funds of $375,000, what is the economic value added (EVA®)? Assuming there is no accounts payable because the firm is all equity, what external funds required (*EFR*) was necessary for the 10 percent increase in sales?

21-5. Firm QTP currently has sales of $10 million with an asset base of $25 million. QTP has no accounts payable, a net profit margin of 10 percent, and a dividend payout ratio of 60 percent. If QTP decides to grow sales by 20 percent, how much external funds required (*EFR*) are necessary? Assuming QTP now has accounts payable of $0.5 million, what is the *EFR*? In addition to having these accounts payable, QTP decides to cut its dividend, making the dividend payout ratio equal to 45 percent. What then is the associated *EFR*? Based on the signaling model of dividends (see Chapter 15), should QTP increase or decrease the dividend to indicate its new plan of sales expansion?

21-6. Firm MBK is projecting next year's sales revenue to be $4.424 million (a 12% increase). Current assets, fixed assets, and current liabilities are expected to be proportionate to sales in the same manner as they are currently: 20%, 125%, and 16%, respectively. The accumulated depreciation is currently $2,037,500 and is expected to be $2.53 million next year. What is MBK's current and expected total asset turnover? What is MBK's current and expected current ratio? Will the future current ratio change if the sales increase by only 10 percent (demonstrate your answer numerically)? Does the change on the total asset turnover ratio violate an assumption within the sustainable growth rate model?

21-7. Eisner Amusement Parks reported the following data in its most recent annual report:

Sales	$42.5 million
Net income	$ 3.8 million
Dividends	$ 1.1 million
Assets	$50.0 million

Eisner is financed 100 percent with equity. What is the company's *sustainable growth rate*? Suppose that Eisner issued bonds to the public and used the proceeds to repurchase half of its outstanding shares. This recapitalization would create additional interest expenses of $2 million. Assuming that the company faces a 35 percent tax rate, what impact would this restructuring have on its sustainable growth rate?

21-8. Use this key financial data from the most recent annual report of Rancho, Inc. to answer the questions that follow.

Sales	$12.7 million
Net income	$ 1.3 million
Total assets	$ 7.6 million
Total equity	$ 5.2 million
Dividends	$ 0.3 million

The firm's CFO wishes to use these data to estimate the firm's sustainable growth rate.

a. Use the data provided to calculate Rancho's net profit margin, assets-to-equity ratio, total asset turnover ratio, and its dividend payout ratio.
b. Use your findings in part (a) to find Rancho's *sustainable growth rate*.
c. Interpret the sustainable growth rate calculated in part (b). Does this rate of growth ensure shareholder wealth maximization? Explain.
d. If the firm's Board feels that it is best for its shareholders if the firm grows more slowly, what alterations in each of the baseline assumptions would be necessary to achieve this objective?

21-9. Review the abbreviated financial statements, below, for the last two years for Norne Energy Corp. All values are expressed in British pounds (£) in billions.

Norne Energy Corp.
Balance Sheet

	2007	2006
Current assets	£2.7	£2.5
Fixed assets	3.5	3.4
Total assets	£6.2	£5.9
Current liabilities	£1.9	£1.8
Long-term debt	2.1	2.2
Shareholders' equity	2.2	1.9
Total liabilities and equity	£6.2	£5.9

Norne Energy Corp.
Income Statement

	2007	2006
Sales	£7.5	£7.1
Net income	0.5	0.4
Dividends	0.2	0.1

a. What was Norne's *sustainable growth rate* at the end of 2006?
b. How rapidly did Norne actually grow in 2007?
c. What changes in Norne's financial condition from 2006 to 2007 can you trace to the difference between the actual and sustainable growth rates?

21-10. The 2008 sales forecast for Clearwater Development Co. is $150 million. Interest expense will not change in the coming year. Use Clearwater's 2007 income statement ($ in thousands), presented below, to answer the questions that follow.

Clearwater Development Co.
Income Statement

Sales	$125,000
Less: Cost of goods sold	80,000
Gross profit	$ 45,000
Less: Operating expenses	30,000
Less: Interest	10,000
Pretax profit	$ 5,000
Less: Taxes (35%)	1,750
Net income	$ 3,250

a. Use the *percentage-of-sales method* to construct a pro forma income statement for 2008.

b. You learn that 25 percent of the cost of goods sold and operating expense figures for 2007 are fixed costs that will not change in 2008. Reconstruct the pro forma income statement.

c. Compare and contrast the statement prepared in parts (a) and (b). Which statement will likely provide the better estimate of 2008 income? Explain.

21-11. Hill Propane Distributors wants to construct a pro forma balance sheet for 2008. Build the statement using the following data and assumptions:

1. Projected sales for 2008 are $35 million.
2. Hill's gross profit margin is 35 percent.
3. Operating expenses average 10 percent of sales.
4. Depreciation expense last year was $5 million.
5. Hill faces a tax rate of 35 percent.
6. Hill distributes 20 percent of its net income to shareholders as a dividend.
7. Hill wants to maintain a minimum cash balance of $3 million.
8. Accounts receivable equal 8.5 percent of sales.
9. Inventory averages 10 percent of cost of goods sold.
10. Last year's balance sheet lists net fixed assets of $30 million. All of these assets are depreciated on a straight-line basis, and none of them will be fully depreciated for at least three years.
11. Hill plans to invest an additional $1 million in fixed assets that it will depreciate over a five-year life on a straight-line basis.
12. In 2007, Hill reported common stock and retained earnings of $20 million.
13. Accounts payable averages 9 percent of sales.

Will Hill Propane's cash balance at the end of 2008 exceed its minimum requirement of $3 million?

21-12. Planet Inc. wishes to construct a pro forma income statement and a pro forma balance sheet for the coming year using the following data.

1. Sales are forecast to grow by 5 percent from $809.5 million last year to $850 million in the coming year.
2. Cost of goods sold is expected to represent 72 percent of forecast sales.
3. Operating expenses are expected to represent 11 percent of forecast sales.
4. Depreciation expense on the firm's existing net fixed assets, which currently total $275 million, is expected to remain at $55 million per year for at least four more years.
5. Planet's marginal tax rate is expected to remain at 40 percent.
6. Planet is expected to continue its policy of paying out 10 percent of net income as dividends.

7. Planet's net profit margin last year was 5.2 percent.
8. Planet wishes to maintain a minimum cash balance of $8 million in the coming year.
9. The firm's accounts receivable are expected to equal about 15 percent of sales.
10. The firm's inventory has historically averaged about 12 percent of cost of goods sold.
11. Planet is planning to invest an additional $35 million in fixed assets that will be depreciated on a straight-line basis over a seven-year life.
12. The firm's accounts payable, which totaled $63.5 million at the end of last year, is expected to equal about 11 percent of cost of goods sold in the coming year.
13. Planet plans to maintain its notes payable of $42 million, requiring annual interest of 5 percent, which totals $2.1 million.
14. The firm has $80 million of long-term debt that matures as a lump-sum due and payable in full in five years. Annual interest of $4.8 million must be paid on this debt.
15. Planet has no preferred stock outstanding, and its retained earnings and common stock currently total $250 million.
16. Planet's total assets at the end of last year were $435 million.

   a. Use the preceding data to prepare Planet's pro forma income statement for the coming year.
   b. Use the data provided and your findings in part (a) to prepare Planet's pro forma balance sheet for the coming year. Use notes payable as the balancing figure and ignore any change in annual interest expense caused by the change in notes payable.
   c. Explain the amount of notes payable used as the balancing figure in part (b). Indicate the resulting amount of the *plug figure* needed to create the balancing figure. Will Planet be able to fund its planned growth internally? Explain.
   d. Use Equation 21.2 along with Planet's relevant data to determine its *external funds required (EFR)*. Compare this value with the plug figure you found in part (c), and explain in general terms why differences between these two values might result.

21-13. Review the following 2007 balance sheet and income statement for T. F. Baker Cosmetics Inc. The numerical values are in thousands of dollars.

T. F. Baker Cosmetics Inc.
Balance Sheet

Cash	$ 5,000	Accounts payable	$10,000
Accounts receivable	12,500	Short-term bank loan	15,000
Inventory	10,000	Long-term debt	10,000
Current assets	$27,500	Common stock	15,000
Gross fixed assets	$65,000	Retained earnings	12,500
Less: Accumulated		Total liabilities and equity	$62,500
depreciation	30,000		
Net fixed assets	$35,000		
Total assets	$62,500		

T. F. Baker Cosmetics Inc.
Income Statement

Sales	$150,000
Less: Cost of goods sold	120,000
Gross profit	$ 30,000
Less: Operating expenses	15,000
Less: Depreciation	5,000
Less: Interest expense	2,000
Pretax profit	$ 8,000
Less: Taxes (35%)	2,800
Net income	$ 5,200

At a recent board meeting, the firm set the following objectives for 2008:

1. The firm would increase liquidity. For competitive reasons, the firm expects accounts receivable and inventory balances to continue their historical relationships with sales and cost of goods sold, respectively, but the board felt that the company should double its cash holdings.
2. The firm would accelerate payments to suppliers. This would have two effects: First, by paying more rapidly, the firm would be able to take advantage of early payment discounts, which would increase its gross margin from 20 percent to 22 percent. Second, by paying earlier, the firm's accounts payable balance, which historically averaged about one twelfth of cost of goods sold, would decline to 4 percent of cost of goods sold.
3. The firm would expand its warehouse, which would require an investment in fixed assets of $10 million. This would increase projected depreciation expense from $5 million in 2007 to $7 million in 2008.
4. The firm would issue no new common stock during the year, and it would initiate a dividend. Dividend payments in 2008 would total $1.2 million.
5. Operating expenses would remain at 10 percent of sales.
6. The firm did not expect to retire any long-term debt, and it was willing to borrow up to the limit of its current credit line with the bank, $20 million. The interest rate on its outstanding debts would average 8 percent.
7. The firm set a sales target for 2008 of $200 million.

Develop a set of pro forma financial statements to determine whether or not T. F. Baker Cosmetics can achieve all these goals simultaneously.

Planning and Control

21-14. A firm has actual sales of $50,000 in January and $70,000 in February. It expects sales of $90,000 in March and $110,000 in both April and May. Assuming that sales are the only source of cash inflow, and that 60 percent of these are for cash and the rest are collected evenly over the following two months, what are the firm's expected cash receipts for March, April, and May?

21-15. Bachrach Fertilizer Corp. had sales of $2 million in March and $2.2 million in April. Expected sales for the next three months are $2.4 million, $2.5 million, and $2.7 million. Bachrach has a cash balance of $200,000 on May 1 and does not want its balance to dip below that level. Prepare a *cash budget* for May, June, and July given the following information:

1. Of total sales, 30 percent are for cash, 50 percent are collected in the month after the sale, and 20 percent are collected two months after the sale.
2. Bachrach has cash receipts from other sources of $100,000 per month.

SMART SOLUTIONS
See the problem and solution explained step-by-step at
SMARTFinance

3. The firm expects to purchase items for $2 million in each of the next three months. All purchases are paid for in cash.

4. Bachrach has fixed cash expenses of $150,000 per month and variable cash expenses equal to 5 percent of the previous month's sales.

5. Bachrach will pay a cash dividend of $300,000 in June.

6. The company must make a $250,000 loan payment in June.

7. Bachrach plans to acquire fixed assets worth $500,000 in July.

8. Bachrach must make a tax payment of $225,000 in June.

21-16. Sportif, Inc.'s financial analyst has compiled sales and total cash disbursement estimates for the coming months of January through May. Historically, 60 percent of sales are for cash with the remaining 40 percent collected in the following month. The ending cash balance in January is $1,000. The firm's minimum cash balance is $1,000. The analyst plans to use this data to prepare a cash budget for the months of February through May.

Sportif, Inc.

Month	Sales	Total Cash Disbursements
January	$ 5,000	$6,000
February	6,000	8,000
March	10,000	8,000
April	10,000	6,000
May	10,000	5,000

a. Use the data provided to prepare Sportif's *cash budget* for the four months February through May.

b. How much total financing will Sportif need to meet its financial requirements for the period February to May?

c. If Sportif prepared a pro forma balance sheet dated at the end of May from the information presented, how much would the firm have in accounts receivable?

21-17. The actual sales and purchases for White Inc. for September and October 2007, along with its forecast sales and purchases for the November 2007 through April 2008, follow.

Year	Month	Sales	Purchases
2007	September	$310,000	$220,000
2007	October	350,000	250,000
2007	November	270,000	240,000
2007	December	260,000	200,000
2008	January	240,000	180,000
2008	February	280,000	210,000
2008	March	300,000	200,000
2008	April	350,000	190,000

The firm makes 30 percent of all sales for cash and collects 35 percent of its sales in each of the two months following the sale. Other cash inflows are expected to be $22,000 in September and April, $25,000 in January and March, and $37,000 in February. The firm pays cash for 20 percent of its purchases. It pays for 40 percent of its purchases in the following month and for 40 percent of its purchases two months later.

Wages and salaries amount to 15 percent of the preceding month's sales. The firm must pay lease expenses of $30,000 per month. Interest payments of $20,000 are due in January and April. A principal payment of $50,000 is also due in April. The firm expects to pay a cash dividend of $30,000 in January and April. Taxes of $120,000 are due in April. The firm also intends to make a $55,000 cash purchase of fixed assets in December.

   a. Assuming that the firm has a cash balance of $42,000 at the beginning of November and its desired minimum cash balance is $25,000, prepare a *cash budget* for November through April.

   b. If the firm is requesting a line of credit, how large should the line be? Explain your answer.

21-18. Berlin Inc. expects sales of $300,000 during each of the next three months. It will make monthly purchases of $180,000 during this time. Wages and salaries are $30,000 per month plus 5 percent of monthly sales. The firm expects to make a tax payment of $60,000 in the first month and a $45,000 purchase of fixed assets in the second month. It expects to receive $24,000 in cash from the sale of an asset in the third month. All sales and purchases are for cash. Beginning cash and the minimum cash balance equal zero.

   a. Construct a *cash budget* for the next three months.

   b. Berlin is unsure of the level of sales, but all other figures are certain. If the most pessimistic sales figure is $240,000 per month and the most optimistic is $360,000 per month, what are the monthly minimum and maximum ending cash balances that the firm can expect for each month?

   c. Discuss how the financial manager can use the data in parts (a) and (b).

THOMSON ONE BUSINESS SCHOOL EDITION

21-19. Using Equation 21.2, calculate the estimated amount of external funds required for Avon Products (ticker symbol, AVP) for each of the last four years. Do the estimates of the external funds required equal the actual external funds raised by Avon?

21-20. Calculate the sustainable growth rate for Estée Lauder Companies (ticker symbol, EL) for each of the last four years. Compare the sustainable growth rates to the actual growth rates. How and why do they differ?

21-21. Using the percentage of sales method, construct a pro forma balance sheet and income statement for Estée Lauder Companies and Avon Products. Assume sales will increase by the sustainable growth rate of the last fiscal year. What plug figure is needed to make the forecasted balance sheet to balance?

MINI-CASE: PRO FORMA STATEMENTS AND THE CASH BUDGET

Gobusi Technologies has the following financial statements dated December 31, 2007:

Gobusi Technologies
Balance Sheet
December 31, 2007

Assets		Liabilities and Equity	
Current assets		Current liabilities	
Cash	$ 50,000	Accounts payable	$ 62,000
Accounts receivable	75,000	Credit line	10,000
Inventory	89,000	Current long-term debt	5,000
Total current assets	$ 214,000	Total current liabilities	$ 77,000
Gross fixed assets	$1,500,000	Long-term debt	$ 185,000
Less: Accumulated depreciation	400,000	Common stock	$ 700,000
Net fixed assets	$1,100,000	Retained earnings	$ 352,000
Total assets	$1,314,000	Total liabilities and equity	$1,314,000

Gobusi Technologies
Income Statement
For the year ending December 31, 2007

Sales	$5,867,000
Less: Cost of goods sold	2,726,000
Gross profit	$3,141,000
Less: Operating expenses	2,617,000
Less: Interest expense	17,575
Less: Depreciation	100,000
Pretax income	$ 406,425
Less: Taxes	138,185
Net income[a]	$ 268,240

[a]Gobusi has a dividend payout ratio of 25%.

Gobusi has the following expectations for 2008:

- The expected rate of growth in sales is 20%.
- Gobusi expects to lower its cost of goods sold to 42% of sales.
- Operating expenses will remain the same proportion of sales as they were in 2007.
- Gobusi's rate of interest on both short-term and long-term debt is 8%. The firm will retire the current portion of its long-term debt and will keep its credit line at the bank if necessary.
- The firm is operating at full capacity with respect to its fixed assets. Therefore, any increase in sales will result in a corresponding increase in fixed assets. Depreciation will be 10% of this increase plus an additional $100,000 depreciation on its existing fixed assets.
- Gobusi is in a 34% tax bracket and expects to maintain its 25% dividend payout ratio.
- The firm expects all other current assets and current liabilities (except the firm's credit line) to remain at 2007 proportions relative to sales. Use the firm's credit line as a plug figure. If excess funds exist, assume the firm will retire long-term debt.

1.   Determine the firm's *sustainable growth rate*.

2.   Prepare a pro forma balance sheet and income statement for 2008, determine the firm's external financing required, and discuss problems with this method.

3.   Prepare a schedule of projected cash receipts, a schedule of projected cash disbursements, and an overall *cash budget* for the firm for the first quarter of 2008 based upon the following information:

- The firm's sales during November and December of 2007 were $489,230 and $562,800, respectively. Sales during the first four months of 2008 are expected to be:

January	$515,580
February	$497,410
March	$512,890
April	$526,700

- Historically, 85% of the firm's sales are on credit, with about 50% of each month's sales collected one month after the sale and the remainder collected two months after the sale.
- Inventory purchases are typically 25% of sales and are generally paid 20% with cash and the remainder become accounts payable. Of the accounts payable, 60% are paid one month after the purchase and the remainder is paid two months after the purchase. Inventory is typically purchased one month prior to sale.
- Rent payments of $120,000 are due each month.
- Wages are 10% of sales and are paid in the month incurred, while salaries total $98,000 per month.
- Factory overhead is $15,000 a month.
- Taxes of $64,000 must be paid in March.
- The firm plans a fixed-asset expenditure of $300,000 in February.
- Interest payments of $8,000 are due in March.
- Cash dividend payments of $32,894 are due in March.
- As of December 31, 2007, the firm has $50,000 in cash. This is also the firm's target minimum monthly ending cash balance.

4.   Based on the cash budget in question 3, how much short-term financing does Gobusi need during the first quarter of 2008?

Chapter 22

Cash Conversion, Inventory, and Receivables Management*

Contents are listed below.

SMARTFinance
Use the learning tools at www
.thomsonedu.com/finance/smartfinance

Effective Short-Term Financial Management at Dell

Dell Inc. is one of the personal computer industry's biggest success stories. Founded in the mid-1980s by 19-year-old Michael Dell, the company has become a leader in the manufacturing and distribution of personal computers, now a commodity business. Dell's competitive advantage comes from building computers faster than its competitors and from consuming fewer resources in the process. Dell's business model emphasizes minimizing short-term investment, maintaining tight cost controls, generating high sales turnover, and owning few fixed assets.

Dell uses a direct-marketing approach. Taking orders directly from customers allows Dell to build its PCs to demand rather than to an inexact sales forecast. As a result, customers get what they want. Dell strives to deliver PCs quickly, often in a few days, with all of the customer's software preloaded. Dell is not saddled with unwanted inventory, and it does not have to pay distribution fees to intermediaries such as retailers.

Dell uses a just-in-time production process that requires the company to hold just over four days of inventory. In contrast, its main competitors, Hewlett-Packard and IBM, hold about 43 and 20 days of inventory, respectively. A network links suppliers to Dell's worldwide manufacturing facilities and provides hourly feedback on inventory levels. This is a huge edge in an industry where the prices of chips, drives, and other computer parts typically decline by 1 percent per week. By taking advantage of the latest prices in components, Dell lowers its production costs. Thus, Dell has the enviable choice of either taking a higher profit or undercutting its rivals' prices. Dell's inventory turnover, on average, is five times faster than the industry average, and its total asset turnover is typically a little less than twice the industry norm.

Besides keeping only about four days of inventories, Dell collects its receivables in about 33 days and pushes its payables out about 128 days. This means that Dell typically receives payment on the sale of a PC long before it pays suppliers for the component parts, giving the company another significant financial advantage. One sign of this advantage is Dell's high level of liquidity. Dell's cash and marketable securities are three times larger than the industry average. Thus, Dell's short-term financial management efforts allow the company to respond rapidly to changes in the business environment. Industry competitors typically are cash-squeezed and have to be more aggressive in reducing costs and staffing or deferring technology enhancements in order to respond to changes in the business environment.

Sources: Andrew Parks, "How Dell Keeps from Stumbling," Business Week (May 14, 2001), pp. 38B–38D; and Peter Burrows, "Dell, the Conqueror," Business Week (September 24, 2001), pp. 92–102. Data for Dell and its competitors updated to 2004 by the authors.

---

*Professor Dubos J. Masson, CCM, CertCM, of Pepperdine University and the Resource Alliance, assisted in preparation of a large part of this chapter. The authors very much appreciate D.J.'s important contribution.

I n order to grow and prosper, a firm must manage both its operating assets and its short-term financing. **Operating assets** include cash, marketable securities, accounts receivable, and inventories, all of which the firm needs to support its day-to-day operations. The firm's **short-term financing** consists of accounts payable, commercial paper, and various types of short-term loans used to finance seasonal fluctuations. The firm should efficiently manage and control investments in operating assets because they consume the firm's scarce cash resources. As we saw in Chapter 21, the firm uses short-term financing to finance seasonal fluctuations and to provide adequate liquidity to achieve its growth objectives and meet its financial obligations. The overall objective for managing current assets and liabilities is to be as efficient as possible, minimizing unnecessary operating assets and maximizing the use of inexpensive short-term financing.

What evidence can we cite suggesting that firms spend time and effort trying to economize on their investments in current (operating) assets while taking advantage of relatively inexpensive current liabilities (short-term financing)? Table 22.1 reports the median investment in current assets and current liabilities for a sample of 200 large U.S. companies in existence from 1981 to 2004. In 1981, current assets accounted for 36.6 percent of total assets for the median firm in this group. By 2004 that figure had dropped to just 27.9 percent. Over the same period, the importance of current liabilities in financing these firms decreased from 23.1 percent in 1981 to 21.5 percent in 2004.

Table 22.1 also shows the aggregate investment in current assets and current liabilities for all U.S. manufacturing firms, expressed as a percentage of the aggregate assets of these firms. In 1981, current assets accounted for 32.2 percent of aggregate corporate assets; current liabilities made up 22.6 percent of the financing for those assets. By 2004, those figures had changed to 24.5 percent and 17.9 percent, respectively. Put another way, the aggregate *current ratio* of U.S. manufacturing firm declined from 1.42 in 1981 to 1.37 in 2004. These figures illustrate both the importance of and the changes in short-term financial management by U.S. firms.

A variety of forces prompted firms to find efficiencies in short-term financial management between the years shown in Table 22.1. For example, high inflation in the early 1980s gave firms a tremendous incentive to reduce their investments in non-interest-bearing operating assets. Perhaps even more important, developments in information technology allowed firms to become much more efficient in managing cash, inventories, and payables, monitoring receivables, and establishing short-term loans. With better access to information and the ability to move and dispatch funds electronically, firms today can operate with lower levels of operating-asset investment.[1]

This chapter focuses on the cash conversion cycle and the efficient management of two key operating assets—inventory and accounts receivable. We begin with the cash conversion cycle and the actions that can be used to manage it. Next, we describe the cost trade-offs in short-term financial management. Then we briefly consider the key concerns of the financial manager with regard to inventory, and review some popular inventory management techniques. We next discuss effective accounts receivable management and review two important aspects of it—credit standards and credit terms. Finally, we briefly discuss some other receivables management activities.

SMART PRACTICES VIDEO

Vern LoForti, Chief Financial Officer, Overland Storage Inc.

"Working capital management is extremely important because it results in good cash flow."

See the entire interview at SMARTFinance

SMART PRACTICES VIDEO

Jackie Sturm, Director of Finance for Technology and Manufacturing, Intel Corp.

"Inventory loses value every day you hold it."

See the entire interview at SMARTFinance

---

[1] A popular professional certification in the field of treasury and financial management is the Certified Treasury Professional (CTP) credential offered by the Association for Financial Professionals (http://www.afponline.org). More than 15,000 CTPs have passed an exam reflecting the required expertise in the field of treasury and financial management, and they participate in ongoing professional education to maintain the CTP credential.

Table 22.1
Current Assets and
Current Liabilities as a
Percentage of Total
Assets for U.S.
Companies, 1981 and
2004

For a Sample of 200 Large Firms (median)

Year	Current Assets	Current Liabilities
1981	36.6%	23.1%
2004	27.9%	21.5%

For the Aggregate Manufacturing Corporate Sector

Year	Current Assets	Current Liabilities	Current Ratio
1981	32.2%	22.6%	1.42
2004	24.5%	17.9%	1.37

Source: Compustat and authors' calculations.

22.1 THE CASH CONVERSION CYCLE

OPERATING CYCLE

A central concept in short-term financial management is the notion of the operating cycle. A firm's **operating cycle (OC)** measures the time that elapses from the firm's receipt of raw materials to its collection of cash from the sale of finished products. As you might expect, operating cycles vary widely by industry. For instance, a bakery—which uses fresh ingredients, keeps finished goods in inventory for only a day or two, and generally sells its products for cash—will have a very short operating cycle. In contrast, semiconductor manufacturers take several months to convert raw materials into finished products, which are sold on credit. The operating cycle for such a firm may extend to six months or longer.

The operating cycle influences a company's need for internal or external financing. In general, the longer a firm's operating cycle, the greater its need for financing. For example, a bakery might pay its suppliers and its employees using the revenues generated each week. The semiconductor manufacturer probably cannot persuade suppliers and employees to wait the months it takes to earn cash from chip sales. Therefore, the semiconductor firm has a greater need for financing day-to-day operations.

The operating cycle encompasses two major short-term asset categories, inventory and accounts receivable. To measure the operating cycle, we use two ratios covered in Chapter 2. First, calculate the *average age of inventory (AAI)* and the *average collection period (ACP)*. Next, take the sum of these two items to determine the length of the operating cycle.

Table 22.2 presents the actual operating cycles for some well-known computer manufacturers and a number of other firms. Lines 1 through 5 present data for fiscal-year 2004, and lines 6 through 8 calculate the time periods (in days) for *AAI, ACP,* and *average payment period (APP)*, respectively. Using the *AAI* and *ACP* calculated in lines 6 and 7, the table shows, in line 9, the *OCs* for each firm. Note that among the five computer manufacturers—IBM, Dell, Gateway, Apple, and Hewlett-Packard—the make-to-order firm, Dell, has the shortest operating cycle, closely followed by Apple and Gateway. IBM and Hewlett-Packard's operating cycles of 135 and 142 days, respectively, are far longer than the 37- to 56-day range of operating cycles for Dell, Apple, and Gateway, probably as a result of their diversified computer businesses. The final four columns show the operating cycles for four noncomputer firms. Clearly, the

Table 22.2

Operating Cycles (OC) and Cash Conversion Cycles (CCC) for Selected Companies, Fiscal Year 2004

Data ($ in billions)	Computer Manufacturers					Other Companies			
	IBM (IBM)	DELL (DELL)[a]	Gateway (GTW)	Apple (AAPL)	Hewlett-Packard (HPQ)	Albertsons (ABS)[a]	Polo Ralph Lauren (RL)	GM (GM)	McDonald's (MCD)
(1) Sales	96.293	49.205	3.650	8.279	79.905	39.897	2.650	193.517	19.065
(2) Cost of sales	60.261	40.190	3.343	6.020	60.150	28.711	1.326	159.951	8.579
(3) A/P	25.524	14.136	0.960	2.680	20.911	2.250	0.501	28.830	2.658
(4) A/R	30.365	4.414	0.342	1.005	21.754	0.675	0.463	21.236	0.746
(5) Inventory	3.316	0.459	0.196	0.101	7.071	3.162	0.364	12.247	0.148
Time Periods (in days)									
(6) AAI $\{[5] \div [(2) \div 365]\}$	20.08	4.17	21.40	6.12	42.91	40.20	100.20	27.95	6.30
(7) ACP $\{[4] \div [(1) \div 365]\}$	115.10	32.74	34.20	44.31	99.37	6.18	63.77	40.05	14.28
(8) APP $\{[3] \div [(2) \div 365]\}$[b]	154.60	128.38	104.82	162.49	126.89	28.60	137.91	65.79	113.09
Cycles (in days)									
(9) OC [(6) + (7)]	135.18	36.91	55.60	50.43	142.28	46.38	163.97	68.00	20.58
(10) CCC [(9) − (8)]	−19.42	−91.47	−49.22	−112.06	15.39	17.78	26.06	2.21	−92.51

[a]FY ending January 2005.

[b]Note that because "annual purchases" cannot be found in published financial statements, this value is calculated using "cost of sales" (line 2), which is an approach external analysts commonly use. Because annual purchases are likely to be smaller than the cost of sales, these APPs may be understated.

operating cycle varies greatly across industries as well as across different types of companies within a given industry.

CASH CONVERSION CYCLE

The elapsed time between the points at which a firm pays for raw materials and at which it receives payment for finished goods is called the **cash conversion cycle (CCC)**. The difference between the operating cycle and the cash conversion cycle is simply the amount of time that suppliers are willing to extend credit. Most firms obtain a significant amount of their financing through trade credit, represented by accounts payable. By taking advantage of trade credit, a firm reduces the amount of financing it needs from other sources to make it through the operating cycle.

To calculate the cash conversion cycle, start with the operating cycle and then subtract the *average payment period* (APP) on accounts payable. The formula for the cash conversion cycle follows:

$$CCC = OC - APP = AAI + ACP - APP \qquad \text{(Eq. 22.1)}$$

As Equation 22.1 shows, the cash conversion cycle has three main components: (1) average age of the inventory, (2) average collection period, and (3) average payment period. It also shows that if a firm changes any of these time periods, it changes the amount of time its resources are tied up in day-to-day operations.

Again referring to Table 22.2, we can see that the cash conversion cycle for each firm is calculated in line 10, by subtracting the average payment periods in line 8 from the operating cycles calculated in line 9. Reviewing the *CCC* for the computer manufacturers, we see that IBM, Dell, Gateway, and Apple have negative CCCs. This result means that these firms receive cash inflows ahead of having to make the cash outflows needed to generate those inflows. This very desirable *CCC* is in effect a pay-up-front-and-we'll-manufacture-and-ship-the-product-to-you-later type of business. The other top computer manufacturer, Hewlett-Packard, has a positive but relatively short *CCC*, reflecting very effective current account management. It is interesting to note that one of the other firms, McDonald's, also has a negative *CCC*. Looking at the time periods for its *AAI, ACP,* and *APP* in lines 6 through 8, respectively, we can see that its vendors are effectively financing McDonald's operations: Its high *APP* more than covers the time delays in inventory and accounts receivable. Albertsons, Polo Ralph Lauren, and GM have positive *CCCs*, primarily due to their somewhat lengthy inventory periods. The cash conversion cycles in Table 22.2 demonstrate both inter- and intra-industry differences in the amount of time firms have their money tied up.

APPLYING THE MODEL 22.1

Reese Industries has annual sales of $5 billion, a cost of goods sold of 70 percent of sales, and purchases that are 60 percent of cost of goods sold. Reese has an *AAI* of 70 days, *ACP* of 45 days, and *APP* of 40 days. Also, the 45-day *ACP* can be broken into 37 days until the customer places the payment in the mail and an additional 8 days before the funds are available to the firm in a spendable form. Thus, Reese's operating cycle is 115 days (70 + 45), and its cash conversion cycle is 75 days (70 + 45 − 40). Figure 22.1 presents Reese's operating and cash conversion cycles on a time line.

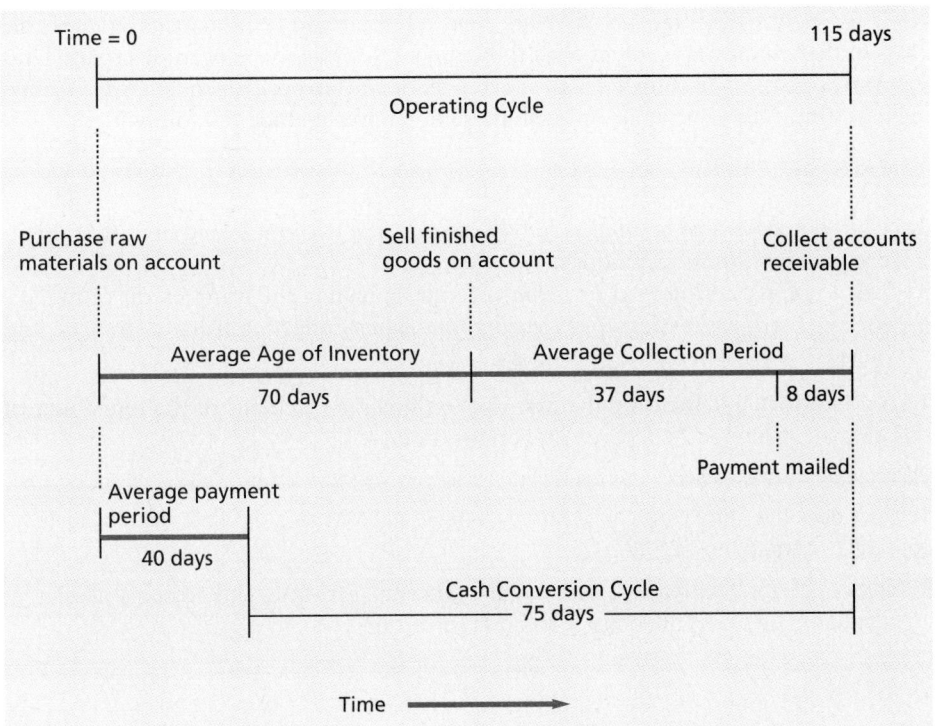

Figure 22.1
Time Line for the Operating and Cash Conversion Cycles for Reese Industries

Reese has invested the following resources in its cash conversion cycle:

Inventory = ($5 billion × 0.70) × (70/365) = $671.2 million

+ Accounts receivable = ($5 billion) × (45/365) = $616.4 million

− Accounts payable = ($5 billion × 0.70 × 0.60) × (40/365)

= $230.1 million

= Resources invested = $1,057.5 million

If Reese could reduce from 8 days to 3 days the amount of time it takes to receive, process, and collect payments after they are mailed by its customers, it would reduce its average collection period to 40 days (37 + 3). This would shorten the cash conversion time line by 5 days (8 − 3) and thus reduce the amount of resources Reese has invested in operations. For Reese, a 5-day reduction in the average collection period would reduce the resources invested in the cash conversion cycle by $68.5 million [$5 billion × (5 ÷ 365)].

SHORTENING THE CASH CONVERSION CYCLE

In order *to maximize shareholder value, the financial manager should manage the firm's short-term activities in a way that shortens the cash conversion cycle.* This will enable the firm to operate with minimum cash investment. The firm can find alternative uses for any cash that it is not using to fund the cash conversion cycle: It can disburse it to more productive long-term investments, use it to pay down expensive long-term financing, or distribute it to owners as dividends.

A positive cash conversion cycle means that trade credit does not provide enough financing to cover the firm's entire operating cycle. In that case, the firm must seek other forms of financing, such as bank lines of credit and term loans. However, the costs of these financing sources tend to be higher than the costs of trade credit. Thus the firm benefits by finding ways to shorten its operating cycle or to lengthen its payment period. Actions that accomplish these objectives include the following:

1. *Turn over inventory as quickly as possible* without stockouts that result in lost sales.
2. *Collect accounts receivable as quickly as possible* without losing sales from high-pressure collection techniques.
3. *Pay accounts as slowly as possible* without damaging the firm's credit rating.
4. *Reduce mail, processing, and clearing time* when collecting from customers, and increase them when paying vendors.

Techniques for implementing the first two actions are the focus of the remainder of this chapter. Chapter 23 focuses on actions 3 and 4.

22.2 COST TRADE-OFFS IN SHORT-TERM FINANCIAL MANAGEMENT

When attempting to manage the firm's short-term accounts so as to minimize cash while adequately funding the firm's operations, the financial manager must focus on competing costs. Decisions with regard to the optimum levels of both operating assets and short-term financing involve cost trade-offs. For convenience, we will view the current-account decision strategies as revenue neutral and therefore examine their cost trade-offs solely with the *goal of minimizing total cost.*

The optimum levels of the key operating assets—cash and marketable securities, accounts receivable, and inventory—involve trade-offs between the cost of holding the operating asset and the cost of maintaining too little of the asset. Figure 22.2 depicts the cost trade-offs and optimum level of a given operating asset. Cost 1 is the holding cost, which increases with larger operating asset account balances. Cost 2 is the cost of holding too little of the operating asset, which decreases with larger operating asset account balances. The *total cost* is the sum of cost 1 and cost 2 associated with a given account balance for the operating asset. As noted, the optimum balance occurs at the point where total cost is minimized.

The table at the bottom of Figure 22.2 provides more detail on the specific costs for each operating asset. For example, consider cash and marketable securities. As the balance of these accounts *increases,* the opportunity costs (cost 1) of the funds held in the firm rise. At the same time, the illiquidity and solvency costs (cost 2) fall; the higher the cash and marketable securities balance, the greater the firm's liquidity and the lower its likelihood of becoming insolvent. The optimum balance of cash and marketable securities is therefore the one that minimizes the total of these two competing costs. We can evaluate the cost trade-offs for accounts receivable and inventory in similar fashion, using the cost descriptions given in the table and relating them to the two cost functions in the figure. Clearly, in all cases a *decrease* in the operating asset account balance would have the opposite effect.

Figure 22.2
Trade-off of Short-Term
Financial Costs

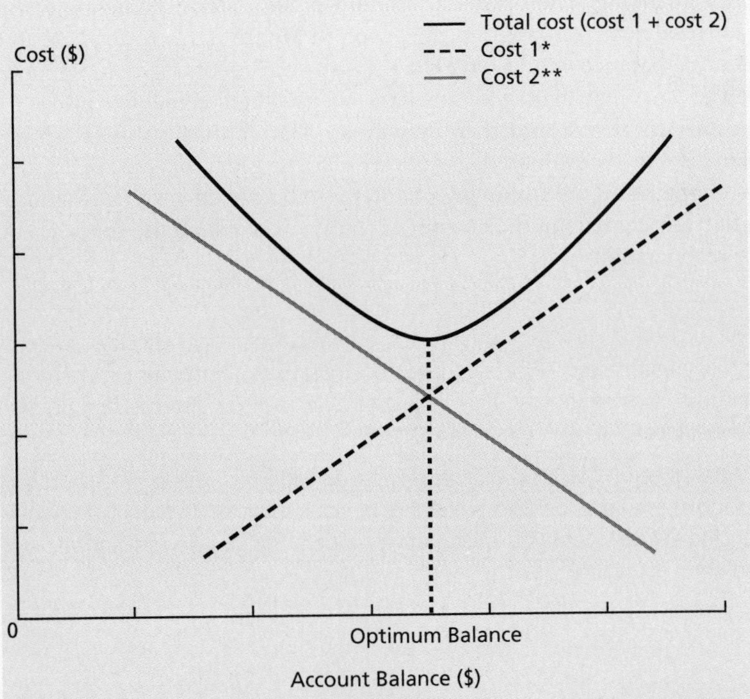

SMART
CONCEPTS
See the concept
explained
step-by-step at
SMARTFinance

Effect of an Increase in Account Balance

	*Cost 1	**Cost 2
Operating Assets		
Cash and marketable securities	Opportunity cost of funds	Illiquidity and solvency costs
Accounts receivable	Cost of investment in accounts receivable and bad debts	Opportunity cost of lost sales due to overly restrictive credit policy and/or terms
Inventory	Carrying cost of inventory, including financing, warehousing, obsolescence costs, etc.	Order and setup costs associated with replenishment and production of finished goods
Short-Term Financing		
Accounts payable, accruals, and notes payable	Cost of reduced liquidity caused by increasing current liabilities	Financing costs resulting from the use of less expensive short-term financing rather than more expensive long-term debt and equity financing

The optimum level of *short-term financing* (accounts payable, accruals, and notes payable) involves the same type of cost trade-offs as demonstrated in Figure 22.2 for operating assets. As noted in the bottom portion of the accompanying table, as the short-term financing balance *increases*, the firm faces an increasing cost of reduced liquidity (cost 1). At the same time, the firm's financing costs (cost 2) decline;

short-term financing costs are lower than the alternative of using long-term debt and equity financing. The optimum amount of short-term financing is that which minimizes total cost, as shown in the graph in Figure 22.2. A *decrease* in the short-term financing balance would have the opposite effects on the competing costs.

The financial manager's primary focus when managing current accounts is to minimize total cost and thereby increase shareholder value. Each of these account balances can be evaluated quantitatively using decision models. The remainder of this chapter and the following chapter emphasize effective techniques and strategies for actively managing the current accounts over which the financial manager has direct responsibility.

Concept Review Questions

3. What general cost trade-offs must the financial manager consider when managing the firm's operating assets? How do these costs behave as a firm considers reducing its accounts receivable by offering more restrictive credit terms? How can the firm determine the optimum balance?

4. What general cost trade-offs are associated with the firm's level of short-term financing? How do these costs behave when a firm substitutes short-term financing for long-term financing? How would you quantitatively model this decision to find the optimal level of short-term financing?

22.3 INVENTORY MANAGEMENT

Inventory is an important current asset: For the typical U.S. manufacturer, inventory represents between 10 percent and 20 percent of total assets—a sizable investment. It is made up of the firm's stock of raw materials, work in process, and finished goods. Although inventory management is the responsibility of operations managers, given its large investment, it is also a major concern of the financial manager.

The firm's goal should be to move inventory quickly in order to minimize its investment. At the same time, it must be careful to maintain adequate inventory to meet demand and to minimize stockouts that can result in lost sales. The financial manager attempts to maintain optimal inventory levels that reconcile these conflicting objectives. Also, because obsolescence can severely reduce the value of inventories, the firm needs to carefully control inventory to avoid potential major losses in asset values.

Here we consider the aspects of inventory that concern the financial manager —the amount invested in inventory, and several popular techniques for controlling inventory.[2]

INVESTING IN INVENTORY

A firm must evaluate its investment in inventory in terms of associated revenues and costs. Simply stated, additional investment must be justified by additional returns. From a financial point of view, constraining inventory levels improves returns by releasing funds that the firm can use in more profitable investments. However, from

---

[2.] For detailed discussions of these and other inventory-management techniques, see Thomas E. Vollman, William Lee Berry, David Clay Whybark, and R. Robert Jacobs, *Manufacturing Planning and Control for Supply Chain Management,* 5th Edition (Burr Ridge, IL: McGraw-Hill Irwin, 2005).

production and marketing perspectives, expanding inventories provides for uninterrupted production runs, good product selection, and prompt delivery schedules. The firm needs to balance the conflicting preferences of finance, production, and marketing managers in order to effectively manage inventory.

The financial manager should consider several specific factors in evaluating an inventory system. On the asset side of the balance sheet, inventories represent an important short-term investment. The smaller the level of inventory needed to support the firm's sales, the faster the total asset turnover, and the higher the returns on total assets. (Note: This is consistent with the DuPont system discussed in Chapter 2.) More rapid inventory turnover also reduces the potential for obsolescence and resulting price concessions. On the liability side, smaller inventories reduce the firm's short-term financing requirements and thereby lower financing costs and improve profits. The following example illustrates the key financial trade-off associated with inventory investment.

APPLYING THE MODEL 22.2

Kerry Manufacturing is contemplating larger production runs to reduce the high setup costs associated with a major product. The firm estimates the total annual savings in setup costs to be $120,000. It currently turns this product's inventory six times a year; with the proposed larger production runs, its inventory turnover is expected to drop to five. If the firm's cost of goods sold of $30.0 million for this product is unaffected by this proposal, and assuming the firm's required return on similar-risk investments is 15 percent, the analysis would be as follows.

Analysis:

Average investment in inventory = cost of goods sold ÷ inventory turnover

Proposed system	= $30.0 million ÷ 5 =	$6.0 million
Less: Present system	= 30.0 million ÷ 6 =	5.0 million
Increased inventory investment		$1.0 million
× required return		× 0.15
Annual cost of increased inventory investment		$ 150,000
Less: Annual savings in setup costs		120,000
Net loss from proposed plan		$ 30,000

Decision:

Don't do it; an annual loss of $30,000 would result from the proposed plan.

TECHNIQUES FOR CONTROLLING INVENTORY

Although inventory control is an operations/production management task, the financial manager serves as a "watchdog" over this activity. This oversight is important given the firm's typically sizable investment in inventory. Firms commonly use a variety of techniques, discussed below, to control inventory. Although these techniques are typically used by operations and production managers, a good financial manager should understand them.

ABC System. A firm using the **ABC system** segregates its inventory into three groups, A, B, and C. The A items are the most costly inventory items. The B group consists of the items accounting for the next largest investment. The C group typically consists of a large number of items accounting for a small dollar investment.

Separating its inventory into A, B, and C groups allows the firm to determine the level and types of inventory control procedures needed. Control of the A items should be most intensive due to the high dollar investments involved; the B and C items would be subject to correspondingly less sophisticated procedures.

Basic Economic Order Quantity (EOQ) Model. A popular tool for determining the optimal order quantity for an inventory item is the **economic order quantity (EOQ) model.** This model could be used to control the firm's big-ticket inventory items such as those included in the A group of an ABC system. The EOQ model considers operating and financial costs and determines the order quantity that minimizes overall inventory costs. Using the following notation, the EOQ for a given inventory item is given in Equation 22.2.

S = inventory usage per period (typically one year)

O = order cost per order

C = carrying cost per unit per period

Q = order quantity in units

$$EOQ = \sqrt{\frac{2SO}{C}}$$

(Eq. 22.2)

APPLYING THE MODEL 22.3

Garrison Industries currently uses 16,000 units of an expensive inventory item each year. The firm estimates order cost to be $500 per order and carrying cost for this item to be $100 per unit per year. Garrison wishes to estimate the optimal quantity in which to order this item. By substituting S = 16,000, O = $500, and C = $100 into Equation 22.2, we calculate the EOQ for this item as:

$$EOQ = \sqrt{\frac{2 \times 16{,}000 \times \$500}{\$100}} = \sqrt{160{,}000} = 400 \text{ units}$$

If Garrison Industries orders this item in quantities of 400 units, it will minimize its total inventory cost for this item.

Reorder Points and Safety Stock. The simple EOQ model just presented assumes that inventory is instantaneously replenished precisely at the time the inventory is exhausted. This model implies perfect certainty with regard to the rate of usage and the timing of receipt from suppliers. Assuming a constant rate of usage, a firm can easily estimate a *reorder point* as follows:

Reorder point = lead time in days × daily usage

For example, if Garrison Industries uses about 44 units per day (16,000 units per year ÷ 365 days), and it typically takes the firm 4 days to place and receive an order, the firm should place an order when its inventory falls to 176 units (4 days × 44 units).

To allow for faster-than-anticipated rates of usage and delayed deliveries, many firms maintain *safety stocks* of inventory. Management determines the size of these

**SMART
PRACTICES
VIDEO**

**Vern LoForti, Chief Financial
Officer, Overland Storage Inc.**

"You have to have a high level of confidence in those suppliers who are holding that inventory at their warehouse."

**See the entire interview at
SMARTFinance**

stocks by analyzing the probabilities of both increased usage rates and delivery delays. For example, Garrison Industries estimates that a safety stock equal to 2 percent of its annual usage of the given item will adequately protect against stockouts due to faster-than-anticipated usage and order fulfillment delays. Given that estimate, Garrison will maintain a safety stock of 320 units (0.02 × 16,000 units). A variety of more sophisticated models are available for setting both reorder points and safety stocks.

Material Requirements Planning. Many manufacturing firms use computerized systems to control the flow of resources, particularly inventory, within the production process. **Material requirements planning (MRP)** is one such system. MRP uses a master schedule to ensure that the materials, labor, and equipment needed for production are at the right places in the right amounts at the right times. The schedule is based on forecasts of the demand for the company's products. The schedule says exactly what will be manufactured during the next few weeks or months and when the work will take place.

Sophisticated computer programs coordinate all the elements of MRP. The computer determines material requirements by comparing production needs to the materials the company already has in inventory. The programs place orders so that items will be on hand when they are needed for production. MRP helps ensure a smooth flow of finished products.

Manufacturing resource planning II (MRPII) expands on MRP. Using a complex computer system, it integrates data from many departments, including finance, marketing, accounting, engineering, and manufacturing. MRPII can generate a production plan for the firm, as well as management reports, forecasts, and financial statements. It allows the firm to track and manage key inventory items (typically A items) on a real-time basis. The system lets managers assess the impact of production plans on profitability. If one department's plans change, the system transmits the effects of those changes throughout the company.

Just-in-Time System. An important and widely adopted inventory management technique, imported from Japan, is the **just-in-time (JIT) system.** JIT is based on the belief that materials should arrive exactly when they are needed for production, rather than being stored on-site. Relying closely on computerized systems such as MRP and MRPII, manufacturers determine what parts will be needed and when, and then order them from suppliers so they arrive "just in time."

Under the JIT system, inventory products are "pulled" through the production process in response to customer demand. JIT requires close teamwork among vendors and purchasing and production personnel; any delay in deliveries of supplies could bring production to a halt. Clearly, unexpected events, such as 9/11, can cause problems for firms using a JIT system. In spite of such risks, a properly employed JIT system can significantly reduce inventory levels and carrying costs, thereby freeing funds for more productive uses.

Concept Review Questions

5. How might the financial manager's view of inventory differ from that of managers in production and marketing? What is the relationship between inventory turnover and inventory investment? Explain.

6. What is the *ABC system*? What role does the *EOQ model* play in controlling inventory?

7. From the financial manager's perspective, describe the role of reorder points, safety stock, MRP, MRPII, and a *just-in-time system* in managing a firm's inventory.

22.4 ACCOUNTS RECEIVABLE STANDARDS AND TERMS

Accounts receivable (A/R) result from a company selling its products or services on credit and are represented in the cash conversion cycle by the *average collection period (ACP)*. This period is the average length of time from a sale on credit until the payment becomes usable funds for the firm. The average collection period has two parts. The first, and generally the longer, is the credit period. It is measured as the time from the sale (or customer invoicing) until customers place their payments in the mail. The second is the time from when the customers place payments in the mail to when the firm has spendable funds in its bank account. The first part of the average collection period involves managing the credit available to the firm's customers. The second part involves receiving, processing, and collecting payments. This section discusses customer credit; Chapter 23 discusses receiving, processing, and collecting payments.

As with all current accounts, receivables management requires managers to balance competing interests. On the one hand, managers (generally the cash or treasury managers) prefer to receive cash payments sooner rather than later. That preference leads toward strict credit terms and strict enforcement of those terms. On the other hand, firms can use credit terms as a marketing tool to attract new customers (or to keep current customers from defecting to another firm). This objective argues for easier credit terms and more flexible enforcement.

It is also important to understand that in many firms the credit policy is generally not under the control of the financial (cash or treasury) managers, but under the sales or customer-service functions. For many companies, in order to be competitive, credit terms are a very necessary part of determining the ultimate sales price for their products and services.

EFFECTIVE ACCOUNTS RECEIVABLE MANAGEMENT

Effectively managing the credit and accounts receivable process involves cooperation among sales, customer-service, finance, and accounting staffs. The key areas of concern involve:

1. Setting and communicating the company's general credit and collections policies.
2. Determining who is granted credit and how much credit is extended to each customer.
3. Managing the billing and collection process in a timely and accurate manner.
4. Applying payments and updating the accounts receivable ledger.
5. Monitoring accounts receivable on both an individual and aggregate basis.
6. Following up on overdue accounts and initiating collection procedures, if required.

In the typical company, the credit and accounts receivable departments handle most of these tasks. The cash management or treasury area will usually be responsible for managing the actual receipt of payments. The cash manager usually also will have to collect and organize the remittance data that is sent along with the payments so that the A/R department will be able to determine what invoices have been paid. We will cover this *cash application* process in greater detail later in the chapter.

The first decision a company must make is whether it will offer trade credit at all. There are many reasons for offering credit, including increasing or facilitating sales, meeting terms offered by competitors, attracting new customers, or providing general convenience. In a typical business-to-business environment, a company may have to offer trade credit just to generate sales. This is especially the case for a large company selling to smaller companies, where the smaller company literally needs the credit period to sell merchandise so it can pay its supplier. The small company would not usually have access to other types of credit, so if the supplier did not offer credit, there would be no sale.

As mentioned earlier, many companies see trade credit and credit terms as simply an extension of the sales price. They may use credit terms to motivate customers or to compete with other suppliers. In many cases, industry practices dictate whether firms offer credit and what the terms are. The Comparative Corporate Finance on page 818 compares the level of trade credit in the United States to that in other major countries throughout the world. In today's financial environment, there are also many opportunities for companies to outsource part or all of the credit and accounts receivable process. Various outsourcing alternatives are use of credit cards, third-party financing, and **factoring,** which involves the outright sale of receivables to a third-party *factor* at a discount.

Once a company has decided to offer trade credit, it must then do the following:

1. Determine its credit standards: Who is offered credit and how much?
2. Set its credit terms: How long do customers have to pay, and are any discounts offered for early payment?
3. Develop its collection policy: How should delinquent accounts be handled?
4. Monitor its accounts receivable on both an individual and aggregate basis: What is the status of each customer and the overall quality of its receivables?

In addition, the firm must have effective cash-application procedures in place.

CREDIT STANDARDS

The first, and most important, aspect of accounts receivable management is setting credit standards. This process involves applying techniques for determining which customers should receive credit and how much credit should be granted. Much of the focus is on making sure that a company does not accept substandard customers (i.e., potential defaulters on trade credit). However, a firm must take care not to set the standards so high that potential good customers will be rejected. A company's accounts receivable default rates should generally be in line with those of other companies in the same industry if it wants to remain competitive.

Granting Credit to Customers. In analyzing credit requests and determining the level of credit to be offered, the company can gather information from both internal and external sources. The usual internal sources of credit information are the credit application and agreement and, if available, the company's own records of the applicant's payment history. External sources typically include financial statements, trade references, banks or other creditors, and credit-reporting agencies. Each of these sources involves the internal costs of analyzing the data; some sources, such as credit-reporting agencies, also have explicit external costs (a charge for obtaining the data).

The company must also take into account the variable costs of the products it would be selling on credit. For example, a company selling a product with a low variable cost (i.e., magazine subscriptions) will often grant credit to almost anyone without a credit check. It doesn't have much to lose if payment isn't made, but on the other hand, potential profits are great. Companies selling products with high variable costs (i.e., heavy-equipment manufacturers) will typically do extensive credit checks before granting credit and shipping merchandise.

The amount of the credit limit is also an important factor. To reduce some of the credit-decision costs, a company may routinely grant small levels of credit to new customers, allowing the credit limit to rise as the customer proves to be a good credit risk.

COMPARATIVE CORPORATE FINANCE

Trade Credit Practices around the World

Trade credit is perhaps the single most important source of short-term external financing for U.S. businesses. The use of trade credit varies widely across countries. The accompanying chart shows the ratio of accounts payable to sales and of accounts receivable to sales for the median firm in 26 countries. Accounts payable is a measure of the trade credit that a firm receives from its suppliers; accounts receivable captures the trade credit that a firm grants to its customers.

As important as trade credit is in the United States, it appears to be a much more important source of financing in other countries. Italian firms use (and grant) more trade credit than firms in any other country. Heavy trade credit usage is common among the Mediterranean countries of Europe. In northern Europe (e.g., Finland and Germany), firms use trade credit at a rate similar to that in the United States.

The use of trade credit varies across countries for many reasons. Probably the most important factor is whether a country has well-developed markets for external capital, including a thriving banking sector. When sources of external funds are few, firms may rely more heavily on trade credit as a means of financing operations. Another factor that helps to explain cross-country differences in trade credit is firm size. Large firms have access to broader capital sources than small firms do, so in a country where firms are relatively small (e.g., Italy), trade credit may be more important.

Source: Data from Worldscope; calculations by Inessa Love.

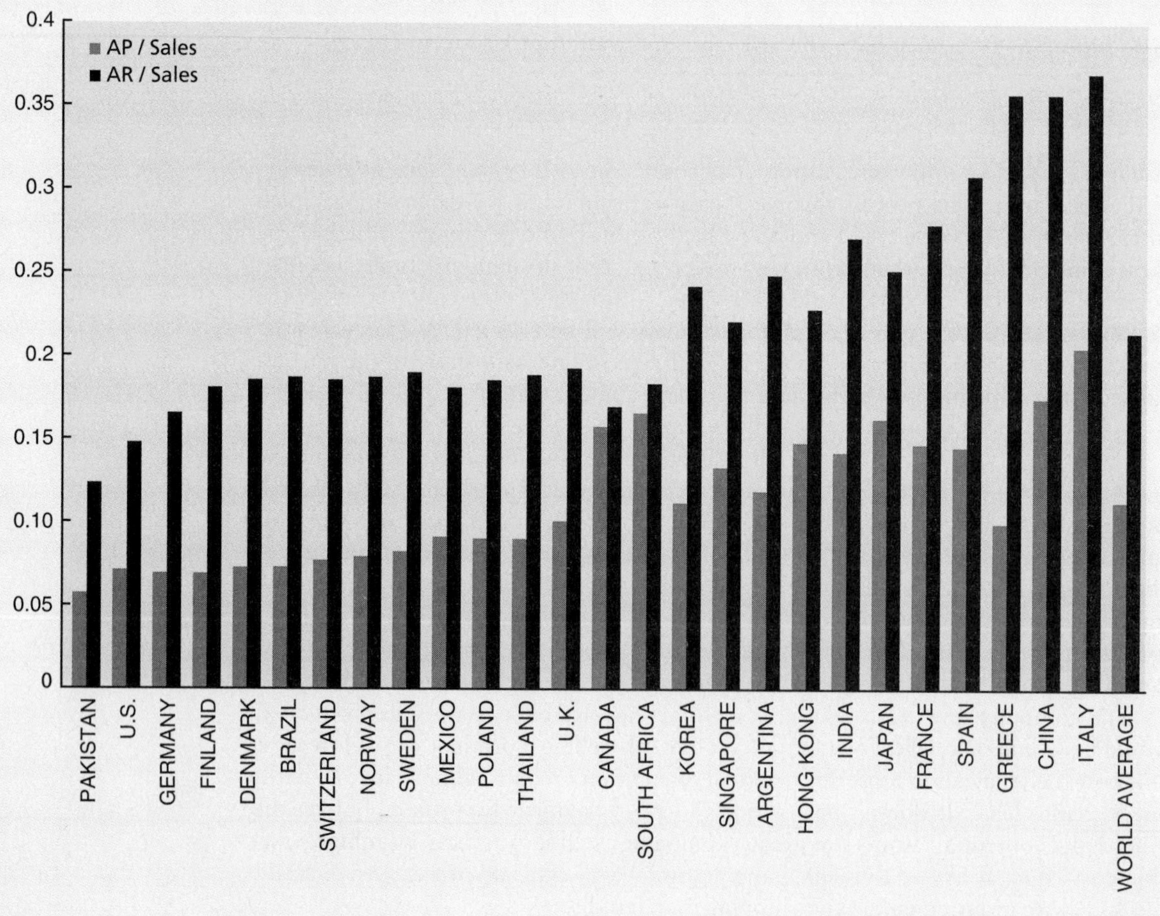

[Bar chart: "AP / Sales" and "AR / Sales" ratios by country. Countries shown left to right: Pakistan, U.S., Germany, Finland, Denmark, Brazil, Switzerland, Norway, Sweden, Mexico, Poland, Thailand, U.K., Canada, South Africa, Korea, Singapore, Argentina, Hong Kong, India, Japan, France, Spain, Greece, China, Italy, World Average. Vertical axis from 0 to 0.4.]

Two popular approaches to the credit-granting process are (1) the five C's of credit and (2) credit scoring.

Five C's of Credit. The **five C's of credit** provide a framework for performing in-depth credit analysis, but do not provide a specific accept-or-reject decision. This credit-selection method is typically used for high-dollar credit requests. Although applying the five C's does not speed up collection of accounts, it does lower the probability of default. The five C's are defined as follows:

1. *Character* refers to the applicant's record of meeting past obligations. The lender would consider the applicant's payment history, as well as any pending or resolved legal judgments against the applicant. The question addressed here is whether this applicant will pay its account, if able, within the specified credit terms.
2. *Capacity* is the applicant's ability to repay the requested credit. The lender typically assesses the applicant's capacity by using financial statement analysis focused on cash flows available to service debt obligations.
3. *Capital* refers to the financial strength of the applicant as reflected by its capital structure. The lender frequently analyzes the applicant's debt relative to equity and its profitability ratios to assess its capital. The analysis of capital determines whether the applicant has sufficient equity to survive a business downturn.
4. *Collateral* is the assets the applicant has available for securing the credit. In general, the more valuable and more marketable the assets are, the more credit lenders will extend. However, trade credit is rarely a secured loan. Therefore, collateral is not the primary consideration in deciding to grant credit. Rather, it strengthens the creditworthiness of a customer who appears to have sufficient cash flows to meet its obligation.
5. *Conditions* refer to current general and industry-specific economic conditions. It also considers any unique conditions surrounding a specific transaction. For example, a firm that has excess inventory of a given item may be willing to accept a lower price or extend more attractive credit terms in order to sell the item.

Credit Scoring. Credit scoring is commonly used with high-volume–low-dollar credit requests. **Credit scoring** applies statistically derived weights for key financial and credit characteristics to predict whether a credit applicant with specific scores for each characteristic will pay the requested credit in a timely fashion.[3] Analysts determine the derived weights using *discriminant analysis*. The specific scores for the applicant are assigned either subjectively by an analyst or by a computer using an expert system. The weighted-average score is the sum of the products of the applicant's score and the associated predetermined weight for each characteristic, and the resulting score determines whether to accept or reject the credit applicant. That is, the procedure results in a score that measures the applicant's overall credit strength, and the company uses that score to make the accept-or-reject decision for granting credit. Credit scoring is most commonly used by large credit card operations, such as those of banks, oil companies, and department stores.

APPLYING THE MODEL 22.4

WEG Oil, a major oil company, uses credit scoring to make its consumer credit decisions. Each applicant fills out a credit application. WEG Oil inputs data from the application into an expert system, and a computer generates the applicant's

---

[3.] See Srinivasan, Kim, and Eisenbeis (1987) for a discussion of various analytical methods of credit scoring.

final credit score, creates a letter indicating whether the application was approved, and if approved, issues the credit card.

Table 22.3 demonstrates the scoring of a consumer credit application, and Table 22.4 describes WEG's predetermined credit standards. Because the applicant in Table 22.3 has a credit score of 83.25, it will be extended WEG's standard credit terms (see Table 22.4).

The purpose of credit scoring is to make a relatively informed credit decision, recognizing that the cost of a single bad scoring decision is small. However, if bad debts from scoring decisions increase, then the company must reevaluate the scoring system. As with the five C's of credit, credit scoring does not speed up the collection of accounts. Instead, scoring allows the firm to quickly and inexpensively identify those customers that are likely to pay their accounts within the stated credit terms. The other advantage to credit scoring is that it is a quantitative approach; it can generally be verified as statistically valid for compliance with fair-credit regulations.

Changing Credit Standards. The vast majority of sales by U.S. corporations are made on credit. Thus, as a practical matter, it is important to understand how establishing and changing credit standards affect sales, costs, and overall cash flows for a given company. As we discussed earlier, it is essential that firms accurately assess the creditworthiness of individual customers who buy on credit. This does not mean that a firm should extend credit *only* to those customers who are certain to repay their debts. Following such an excessively conservative strategy will cost the company many profitable sales, especially if industry practice is to be more generous in extending credit. Instead, the firm should accept a degree of default risk in order to increase

Table 22.3
Consumer Credit Application Credit Score by WEG Oil

Financial and Credit Characteristics	Score (0 to 100) (1)	Predetermined Weight (2)	Weighted Score [(1) × (2)] (3)
Credit references	80	0.15	12.00
Home ownership	100	0.15	15.00
Income range	75	0.25	18.75
Payment history	80	0.25	20.00
Years at address	90	0.10	9.00
Years on job	85	0.10	8.50
	Totals	1.00	Credit score 83.25

Note: Column (1): Scores assigned by analyst or computer based on information supplied on credit application. Scores range from 0 (lowest) to 100 (highest). Column (2): Weights based on the company's analysis of the relative importance of each characteristic in predicting whether or not a customer will pay its account in a timely fashion. The weights must add up to 1.00.

Table 22.4
WEG Oil's Credit Standards

Credit Score	Action
Higher than 75	Extend standard credit terms
65 to 75	Extend limited credit; if account is properly maintained, convert to standard credit terms after one year
Lower than 65	Reject application

sales, but not so much that the additional profit from sales is overwhelmed by additional accounts receivable investment and bad debts. The decision to change credit terms usually rests with the sales or customer-service departments. The financial manager is, however, typically responsible for estimating the cash flow and financial impact of a proposed change in credit standards.

Fortunately, measuring the overall financial impact of changes in credit standards is fairly straightforward. Any change will likely yield both benefits and costs; the decision to change standards will depend on whether the benefits exceed the costs. We can describe the general impact of changes in credit standards as follows:

- *Relaxing credit standards* will generally yield increased unit sales and additional profits. (The additional profit from relaxed credit standards assumes that each unit is sold at a positive contribution margin. The **contribution margin** is a product's price per unit minus variable costs per unit, and is thus a direct measure of gross profit per unit sold.) Relaxing credit standards will also yield higher costs from additional investment in accounts receivable and additional bad debt expense.
- *Tightening credit standards* will generally yield reduced investment in accounts receivable and lower bad debt expense at the cost of lower sales and profits.

It is easiest to demonstrate how to calculate the net effect of changing credit standards using an example.

APPLYING THE MODEL 22.5

Yeoman Manufacturing Company (YMC) produces and sells a CD organizer to music stores nationwide. YMC charges $20/unit and all of its sales are on credit, with customers selected for credit on the basis of a scoring process. With its existing credit standards, YMC expects to sell 120,000 units (*un*) over the coming year, yielding total sales of $2,400,000 (120,000 units × $20/unit). Variable costs are $12/unit, and YMC has fixed costs of $240,000 per year.

YMC is contemplating a relaxation of its credit standards and expects the following effects: a 5 percent increase in sales to 126,000 units; an increase in the average collection period from 30 days (the current level) to 45 days; and an increase in bad debt expense from 1 percent (the current level) to 2 percent of sales. YMC plans to keep the product's sale price unchanged at $20/unit, which implies that total sales will increase to $2,520,000 (126,000 units × $20/unit). If the firm's required return on investments of equal risk is 12 percent, should YMC relax its credit standards?

To make this decision, YMC's managers must calculate: (1) how much profits will increase from the additional sales that relaxed credit standards are expected to generate, (2) the cost of the marginal investment in accounts receivable, (3) the cost of marginal bad debts, and (4) whether the financial benefits exceed the costs.

1. **Marginal profit contribution from sales.** We are assuming that a 5 percent increase in sales volume will not cause YMC's fixed costs to increase. Thus, we need account only for changes in revenues and variable costs. Specifically, we can compute the marginal increase in profits as the increased unit sales volume times the contribution margin per unit sold, as in Equation 22.3:

$$\text{Marginal profit from increased sales} = \Delta\text{Sales} \times CM$$
$$= \Delta\text{Sales} \times (\text{Price} - VC)$$

(Eq. 22.3)

where ΔSales = change in unit sales resulting from the change in credit policies

CM = contribution margin

Price = price per unit

VC = variable cost per unit

With the assumptions just detailed for YMC, we can use Equation 22.3 to determine that relaxing credit standards as suggested will yield a marginal profit of $48,000:

Marginal profit from increased sales = 6,000 un × ($20/$un$ − $12/$un$)

= 6,000 un × ($8/$un$) = $48,000

2. **Cost of the marginal investment in accounts receivable.** To determine the cost of the marginal investment in accounts receivable, we must calculate the cost of financing the current level of accounts receivable and compare it to the expected cost under the new credit standards. This is more complicated than it sounds: We must first calculate how much YMC currently has invested in accounts receivable, based on its current annual sales, variable costs, and accounts receivable turnover. We then repeat this process for the level of sales expected to result from a change in credit standards. Equations 22.4, 22.5, and 22.6 present the steps required. *Note that we use variable costs in calculating investment in accounts receivable because this is the firm's actual cash expense incurred (and tied up in receivables).*

$$\frac{\text{Average investment in}}{\text{accounts receivable } (AIAR)} = \frac{\text{total variable cost of annual sales}}{\text{turnover of accounts receivable}} \qquad \textbf{(Eq. 22.4)}$$

$$\frac{\text{Total variable cost of}}{\text{annual sales } (TVC)} = \text{annual unit sales} \times \text{variable cost/unit} \qquad \textbf{(Eq. 22.5)}$$

$$\frac{\text{Turnover of accounts}}{\text{receivable } (TOAR)} = \frac{365}{\text{average collection period } (ACP)} \qquad \textbf{(Eq. 22.6)}$$

We can use these equations to compute the **average investment in accounts receivable** (*AIAR*) for the current, $AIAR_{\text{current}}$, and proposed, $AIAR_{\text{proposed}}$, credit standards. First, we compute the **total variable cost (*TVC*) of annual sales** under the current credit standards, TVC_{current}, and the proposed plan, TVC_{proposed}, using Equation 22.5:

TVC_{current} = 120,000 un × $12/$un$ = $1,440,000

TVC_{proposed} = 126,000 un × $12/$un$ = $1,512,000

Next, we note that the average collection period under the current plan, ACP_{current}, which is 30 days, is expected to rise to 45 days under the proposed plan, ACP_{proposed}. This allows us to use Equation 22.6 to compute the **turnover of accounts receivable (*TOAR*)** under the current, $TOAR_{\text{current}}$, and proposed, $TOAR_{\text{proposed}}$, credit terms:

$$TOAR_{current} = \frac{365}{ACP_{current}} = \frac{365}{30 \text{ days}} = 12.2 \text{ times/year}$$

$$TOAR_{proposed} = \frac{365}{ACP_{proposed}} = \frac{365}{45 \text{ days}} = 8.1 \text{ times/year}$$

These turnover measures suggest that if YMC relaxes its credit standards, the turnover of its accounts receivable will slow down from 12.2 times per year to 8.1 times per year. Clearly, this slowing is attributable to the generally slower paying of the additional credit customers generated by the relaxed credit standards.

We now have all the inputs required to use Equation 22.4 to compute the $AIAR_{current}$ and $AIAR_{proposed}$:

$$AIAR_{current} = \frac{TVC_{current}}{TOAR_{current}} = \frac{\$1,440,000}{12.2} = \$118,033$$

$$AIAR_{proposed} = \frac{TVC_{proposed}}{TOAR_{proposed}} = \frac{\$1,512,000}{8.1} = \$186,667$$

With these measures, we can now determine the **cost of the marginal investment in accounts receivable.** This amount is the marginal investment in accounts receivable required to support the proposed change in credit policy multiplied by the required return on investment, r_a, as shown in Equation 22.7:

$$
\begin{aligned}
\text{Cost of marginal investment in accounts receivable} &= \text{additional investment} \times \text{required return} \\
&= (AIAR_{proposed} - AIAR_{current}) \times r_a \\
&= (\$186,667 - \$118,033) \times 0.12 = \$68,634 \times 0.12 = \$8,236
\end{aligned}
$$

(Eq. 22.7)

This value of $8,236 is a cost of adopting the relaxed credit standards; it represents the opportunity cost of investing an additional $68,634 in accounts receivable rather than investing these funds in another earning asset.

3. **Cost of marginal bad debts.** YMC expects that relaxing its credit standards will increase its bad debt expense by 1 percent, from 1 percent to 2 percent of sales. We can calculate the cost of this by subtracting the current level of bad debt expense from the expected level of bad debt expense under the proposed new credit standards. Equation 22.8 shows the calculations required to determine bad debt expense, and Equation 22.9 demonstrates the calculation of the cost of marginal bad debts if YMC relaxes its credit standards:

$$
\begin{aligned}
\text{Bad debt expense } (BDE) &= \text{annual sales (Sales)} \\
&\quad \times \text{bad debt expense rate } (\%BDE) \\
BDE_{proposed} &= (Sales_{proposed}) \times (\%BDE_{proposed}) \\
&= \$2,520,000 \times 0.02 = \$50,400 \\
BDE_{current} &= (Sales_{current}) \times (\%BDE_{current}) \\
&= \$2,400,000 \times 0.01 = \$24,000
\end{aligned}
$$

(Eq. 22.8)

$$\text{Cost of marginal bad debts} = BDE_{\text{proposed}} - BDE_{\text{current}} \qquad \textbf{(Eq. 22.9)}$$
$$= \$50{,}400 - \$24{,}000 = \$26{,}400$$

4. **Net profit for the credit decision.** Now that we have calculated the individual financial benefits and costs of changing YMC's credit standards, we can use Equation 22.10 to compute the overall net profit for the credit decision:

$$\begin{matrix}\text{Net profit for the} \\ \text{credit decision}\end{matrix} = \begin{matrix}\text{Marginal profit} \\ \text{from increased} \\ \text{sales}\end{matrix} - \begin{matrix}\text{Cost of marginal} \\ \text{investment in} \\ \text{accounts receivable}\end{matrix} - \begin{matrix}\text{Cost of marginal} \\ \text{bad debts}\end{matrix}$$

$$= \$48{,}000 - \$8{,}236 - \$26{,}400 = \underline{\$13{,}364} \qquad \textbf{(Eq. 22.10)}$$

Because relaxing YMC's credit standards is expected to yield $13,364 in increased profit, the firm should implement the proposed change. The marginal profit from additional sales will more than offset the total cost of the marginal investment in accounts receivable and marginal bad debts.

CREDIT TERMS

Credit terms are the terms of sale for customers. Terms of *net 30* mean the customer has 30 days from the beginning of the credit period (typically *end of month [EOM]* or *date of invoice*) to pay the full invoice amount. Some firms offer cash discounts with terms, such as *2/10 net 30*. These terms mean the customer can take a 2 percent *cash discount* from the invoice amount if the payment is made within the 10-day *cash discount period*, or the customer can pay the full amount of the invoice within the 30-day *credit period*.

The nature of a firm's business influences its regular credit terms.[4] For example, a firm selling perishable items will have very short credit terms because its items have little long-term collateral value. These firms will typically offer short terms, where the buyer has 7 to 10 days to make payment. A firm in a seasonal business may tailor its terms to fit the industry cycles with terms known as *seasonal dating*. Most managers want their company's regular credit terms to be consistent with its industry's standards. If the company's terms are more restrictive than those of its competitors, it will lose business. If its terms are less restrictive than those of its competitors, it will attract customers with poor financial histories that probably are unable to pay under the standard industry term.

A popular method used to lower a firm's investment in accounts receivable is to include a **cash discount** in the credit terms. The cash discount provides a cash incentive for customers to pay sooner. By speeding collections, the discount will decrease the firm's investment in accounts receivable—which is the objective. But the discount will also decrease the per-unit profit because the customer pays less than the full invoice amount. Additionally, initiating a cash discount should reduce bad debts

[4.] See Ng, Smith, and Smith (1999) for a discussion of the determinants of credit terms. Smith (1987) analyzes trade credit based on information asymmetry. Peterson and Rajan (1997) also discuss theories concerning trade credit. Adams, Wyatt, and Kim (1992) conduct a contingent claims analysis of trade credit, and Scherr (1996) examines optimal trade credit limits. For a thorough discussion of accounts receivable policy, see Dyl (1977) and Gitman and Sachdeva (1981).

because customers will pay sooner, and should increase sales volume because the customers taking the cash discount pay a lower price for the product. Firms that consider offering a cash discount must perform a cost-benefit analysis to determine if the discount is profitable enough.

APPLYING THE MODEL 22.6

Masson Industries has an average collection period of 45 days—37 days until the customers place their payments in the mail and a further 8 days to receive, process, and collect payments. Masson is contemplating a change in its credit terms from *net 30* to *2/10 net 30*. The change should reduce the average collection period to 26 days.

Masson currently sells 1,200 units of its product for $2,500 per unit. Its variable cost per unit is $2,000. It estimates that 70 percent of its customers will take the 2 percent discount, and that offering the discount will increase sales by 50 units per year, but will not alter its bad debt percentage for this product. Masson's opportunity cost of funds invested in accounts receivable is 13.5 percent per year. Should Masson offer the proposed cash discount? The cost-benefit analysis, presented in Table 22.5, shows that the *net cost* of the cash discount is $2,846. Thus, *Masson should not implement the proposed cash discount.*

8. Why do a firm's regular credit terms typically conform to its industry's standards? On what basis other than credit terms should the firm compete?

9. How are the *five C's of credit* used to perform in-depth credit analysis? Why is this framework typically used only on high-dollar credit requests?

Concept Review Questions

Table 22.5
Analysis of Offering a Cash Discount at Masson Industries

Marginal profit from increased sales		
[50 units × ($2,500 − $2,000)]		$25,000
Current investment in accounts receivable		
($2,000[a] × 1,200 units) × (45/365)	$295,890	
New investment in accounts receivable		
($2,000[a] × 1,250 units) × (26/365)[b]	178,082	
Reduction in accounts receivable investment	$117,808	
Cost savings from reduced investment		
in accounts receivable (.135 × $117,808)[c]		15,904
Cost of cash discount (0.02 × $2,500 × 1,250 × 0.70)		43,750
Net profit (cost) from proposed cash discount		$(2,846)

[a]In analyzing the investment in accounts receivable, we use the $2,000 variable cost of the product sold instead of its $2,500 sales price, because the variable cost represents the firm's actual cash expense incurred and tied up in receivables.
[b]The new investment in accounts receivable is tied up for 26 days instead of the 45 days under the original terms. The 26 days is calculated as [(0.70 × 10 days + 0.30 × 37 days) + 8 days] = 26.1 days, which is rounded to 26 days.
[c]Masson's opportunity cost of funds is 13.5% per year.

Concept Review Questions

10. How is *credit scoring* used in the credit-selection process? In what types of situations is it most useful?

11. What are the key variables to consider when evaluating the benefits and costs of *changing credit standards*? How do these variables differ when evaluating the benefits and costs of *changing credit terms*?

12. Why do we include only the variable cost of sales when estimating the average investment in accounts receivable? Why do we apply an opportunity cost to this investment to estimate its cost?

13. What are the key elements of a firm's *credit terms*? What is a key determinant of the credit terms offered by a firm?

22.5 COLLECTING, MONITORING, AND APPLYING CASH TO RECEIVABLES

SMART PRACTICES VIDEO

Jon Olson, Vice President of Finance, Intel Corp. (former). Currently, Chief Financial Officer, Xilinx Corp.

"Because cash is king, we want to make sure that we have a high quality collections organization."

See the entire interview at
SMARTFinance

In addition to establishing the firm's accounts receivable standards and terms, the financial manager's responsibilities include collecting and monitoring receivables. The collection and monitoring process is an ongoing activity that is also the responsibility of finance personnel. Here we consider collection policy, credit monitoring, and cash application.

COLLECTION POLICY

A company must determine what its **collection policy** will be and how it will implement that policy. As with credit standards and terms, the approach to collections may be a function of the industry and the competitive environment. For many delinquent accounts, a reminder, form letter, telephone call, or personal visit may initiate customer payment. At a minimum, the company should generally suspend further sales to the customer until the delinquent account is brought current.

If these actions fail to generate customer payment, it may be necessary to negotiate with the customer for past-due amounts and report the customer to credit bureaus. It is possible that the company sold the goods with a lien attached, obtained a pledge of collateral against the account, or had other corporate or personal guarantees from the customer. In these cases, the company should utilize these options for obtaining payment. Generally as a last resort, the account can be turned over to a collection agency or referred to an attorney for direct legal action. Obviously, a cost-benefit analysis should be made at each stage to compare the cost of further collection actions against the cost of simply writing off the account as a bad debt.

CREDIT MONITORING

Credit monitoring involves ongoing review of a firm's accounts receivable to determine if customers are paying according to the stated credit terms. If customers are not paying on time, credit monitoring will alert the firm to the problem. Companies must monitor credit on both an individual and an aggregate basis. Individual monitoring is necessary to determine if each customer is paying in a timely manner and to assess if the customer is within its credit limits.

Credit monitoring on an aggregate basis indicates the overall quality of the company's accounts receivable. Slow payments are costly to a firm because they increase the average collection period and thus the firm's investment in accounts receivable. If a company is also using its accounts receivable as collateral for a loan, the lending institution will generally exclude any past-due accounts from those used as backup for the credit line. Changes in accounts receivable over time could diminish the company's overall liquidity and increase the need for additional financing. Analysis of accounts receivable payment patterns can also be essential for forecasting future cash receipts in the cash budget.

The three most frequently cited techniques for monitoring the overall quality of accounts receivable are (1) the average collection period, (2) aging of accounts receivable, and (3) payment-pattern monitoring.

Average Collection Period. The *average collection period* (ACP), also known as *days' sales outstanding* (DSO), is the second component of the cash conversion cycle. As noted in Chapter 2, it represents the average number of days credit sales are outstanding. The average collection period has two components: (1) the time from sale until the customer places the payment in the mail, and (2) the time to receive, process, and collect the payment once it has been mailed by the customer. Equation 22.11 gives the formula for determining the average collection period:

$$\text{Average collection period} = \frac{\text{accounts receivable}}{\text{average sales per day}} \qquad \textbf{(Eq. 22.11)}$$

Assuming that receipt, processing, and collection time is constant, the average collection period tells the firm, on average, the number of days it takes its customers to pay their accounts. In applying this formula, analysts must be consistent in the use of the sales period and must adjust for known seasonal fluctuations.

APPLYING THE MODEL 22.7

P. Scofield Enterprises has an accounts receivable balance of $1.2 million. Sales during the past 90 days were $3.6 million, for an average daily sales figure of $40,000. Dividing $1.2 million by $40,000 yields Scofield's average collection period, 30 days.

However, a diligent analyst at Scofield notices that sales have been increasing recently, with average daily sales over the last 30 days of $45,000 per day. Using this figure in the denominator of Equation 22.11 results in an average collection period of 26.7 days.

The average collection period allows the firm to determine whether there is a general problem with its accounts receivable. However, the *ACP* can also send misleading signals when daily sales fluctuate. In the example in Applying the Model 22.7, suppose that Scofield's credit terms are net 25. Using the most recent month to calculate average daily sales results in an average collection period of 26.7 days, which is right on target given Scofield's credit terms. However, using average daily sales over the past three months yields the higher 30-day collection period. Therefore, when using this ratio to assess the performance of the collections department, analysts must be aware of the impact of sales fluctuations on their calculations.

If a firm believes it has a collections problem, a first step in analyzing the problem is to *age the accounts receivable.* By doing so, the firm can determine if the problem exists in its accounts receivable in general or is attributable to a few specific accounts or to a given time period.

Aging of Accounts Receivable. The **aging of accounts receivable** requires the firm to break down its accounts receivable into groups based on the time of origin. Aging results in a schedule indicating the portions of the total accounts receivable balance that have been outstanding for specified periods of time. The breakdown is typically made on a month-by-month basis, going back three or four months.

The purpose of aging accounts receivable is to allow the firm to pinpoint problems. For example, if a firm with terms of net 30 has an average collection period (minus receipt, processing, and collection time) of 50 days, the firm will want to age its accounts receivable. If the majority of accounts are two months old, then the firm has a general problem and should review its accounts receivable operations. If the aging shows that the firm collects most accounts in about 35 days and a few accounts are significantly past due, then the firm should analyze and pursue collection of those specific past-due accounts. If the firm has an abnormally high percentage of outstanding accounts initiated in a given month, it may be attributable to a specific event during that time period, such as hiring a new credit manager or selling a substandard product whose quality is being disputed by one customer withholding payment.

Table 22.6 provides an example of an *aging schedule*. If the stated credit terms for the company in this example were net 60 days, then the aging schedule would tell us that 80 percent of the company's receivables are current and 20 percent are past due.

Payment-Pattern Monitoring. The average collection period and the aging of accounts receivable are excellent monitoring techniques when sales are relatively constant. However, for cyclical or growing firms, both techniques provide potentially misleading results. For example, the average collection period divides the accounts receivable balance by the average daily sales. If the accounts receivable balance is measured during a cyclical firm's high sales period, then the average collection period is distorted by the cyclical sales peak. Use of the firm's customer payment pattern avoids the problems of cyclical or growing sales when monitoring accounts receivable.

The **payment pattern** is the normal timing in which a firm's customers pay their accounts, expressed as the percentage of monthly sales collected in each month following the sale. Every firm has a pattern in which its credit sales are paid. If the payment pattern changes, the firm should review its credit policies.

One approach to determining this pattern is to analyze a company's sales and resulting collections on a monthly basis. That is, for each month's sales, the company computes the amount collected in the month of sale and each of the following months. By tracking these patterns over a period of time, the company can determine the

Table 22.6
Sample Aging Schedule for Accounts Receivable

Age of Accounts	Accounts Receivable	Percentage of Accounts Receivable
0–30 days	$1,200,000	50%
31–60 days	720,000	30
61–90 days	336,000	14
91+ days	144,000	6
Total accounts receivable	$2,400,000	100%

average pattern of its collections using either a spreadsheet or regression analysis. For most companies, these patterns tend to be fairly stable over time, even as sales volumes might be fluctuating.

APPLYING THE MODEL 22.8

To demonstrate the payment pattern, consider DJM Manufacturing, which has determined that it collects, on average, 10 percent of credit sales in the month of sale, 60 percent in the month following the sale, and the remaining 30 percent in the second month following the sale. Thus, if sales for the month of January were $200,000, the company would expect to collect $20,000 in January, $120,000 in February, and the remaining $60,000 in March. Table 22.7 shows an example of this approach, which can be extended to develop the cash receipts portion of the cash budget.

CASH APPLICATION

Cash application is the process through which a customer's payment is posted to its account and the outstanding invoices are cleared as paid. In most business-to-business environments, the typical application method is known as *open item*. In this approach, the company records each customer invoice in the A/R journal, and it "matches" received payments to the invoices in order to clear them. This task is complicated by the usual practice of paying multiple invoices with a single check. Ideally, the remittance information accompanying the check should clearly indicate any adjustments, discounts, or allowances taken related to each invoice in that remittance. Unfortunately, the remittance information is sometimes no more than barely legible copies of the invoices with handwritten notes on the adjustments stapled to the check. One of the critical tasks of the accounts receivable department, therefore, is to figure out what has been paid for so the outstanding invoices can be closed out.

Some companies are able to use an alternative approach called *balance forward*. In this system, the company applies customer payments to outstanding balances and simply carries forward any unpaid amounts to the next billing period. Examples are utilities and credit card companies, where the only remittance information needed is

Table 22.7
Forecasted Collections for DJM Manufacturing Using Payment-Pattern Monitoring

	Forecasted Collections for DJM Manufacturing				
Sales Forecast	**January**	**February**	**March**	**April**	**May**
January: $200,000	$20,000	$120,000	$ 60,000		
February: 150,000		15,000	90,000	$ 45,000	
March: 300,000			30,000	180,000	$ 90,000
April: 400,000				40,000	240,000
May: 250,000					25,000
Total projected collections for cash budget			$180,000	$265,000	$355,000

Note: This table is created using the assumption that the company collects 10 percent of each month's sales in the month of sale, 60 percent in the month following sale, and the remaining 30 percent in the second month following sale. The first column provides forecasted sales for each month; the remaining columns total up the actual cash flows for each month. In an actual application, the remaining collections from the prior year's last quarter would be included to complete the projected cash flows in January and February.

the customer's account number, the amount of payment, and the date received. These systems also generally utilize a scannable remittance document, which allows for automated capture of payment and account information. Automated processing reduces the costs of the cash application process.

<table>
<tr>
<td>

**Concept
Review
Questions**

</td>
<td>

14. What is a *collection policy*? What is the typical sequence of actions taken by a firm when attempting to collect an overdue account?

15. Why should a firm actively monitor the accounts receivable of its credit customers? How does each of the following credit monitoring techniques work: (a) average collection period, (b) aging of accounts receivable, and (c) payment-pattern monitoring?

</td>
</tr>
</table>

22.6 SUMMARY

- The cash conversion cycle has three main components: (1) the average age of inventory (AAI), (2) the average collection period (ACP), and (3) the average payment period (APP). The operating cycle (OC) is the sum of the AAI and ACP. The cash conversion cycle (CCC) is $OC - APP$. The length of the cash conversion cycle determines the amount of resources the firm must invest in its operations.

- The financial manager's focus in managing the firm's short-term activities is to shorten the cash conversion cycle. The basic strategies are to turn inventory quickly; collect accounts receivable quickly; pay accounts slowly; and manage mail, processing, and clearing time efficiently.

- When managing the firm's short-term accounts, the financial manager must focus on competing costs. These cost trade-offs apply to managing cash and marketable securities; accounts receivable; inventory; and accounts payable, accruals, and notes payable. The goal is to balance the cost trade-offs in a way that minimizes the total cost of each of these accounts.

- The large inventory investment made by most firms makes inventory a major concern of the financial manager, who must make sure that the amount of money tied up in inventory—raw materials, work in process, and finished goods—is justified by the returns generated from such investment.

- Operations/production managers use a number of techniques to control inventory. Included are the ABC system, the basic economic order quantity (EOQ) model, reorder points and safety stock, material requirements planning, and the just-in-time (JIT) system. Financial managers tend to serve a "watchdog" role over these activities.

- The objective for managing accounts receivable is to balance the competing interests of financial managers, who prefer to receive cash payments sooner, and those of sales personnel, who wish to use liberal credit terms to attract new customers. The key aspects of accounts receivable management include credit standards, credit terms, collection policy, credit monitoring, and cash application.

- To analyze credit applicants, the firm can gather information from both internal and external sources. Two popular approaches to granting credit to customers are the five C's of credit and, for high-volume–low-dollar requests, credit scoring, which is used to make relatively informed credit decisions quickly and inexpensively.

- Companies should perform a cost-benefit analysis of credit standards, credit terms, and other accounts receivable changes to make sure such policies are profitable. Key variables involved in such an analysis include the marginal profit contribution from sales, the cost of the marginal investment in accounts receivable, and the cost of marginal bad debts.

- The firm's collection policy involves a planned sequence of actions aimed at collecting delinquent accounts—typically, reminders, form letters, telephone calls, or personal visits. If these actions are ineffective, the firm sends negative reports to credit bureaus, and may turn over the account to a collection agency or an attorney for collection.

- The three most popular techniques for credit monitoring are the average collection period, aging of accounts receivable, and payment-pattern monitoring. Firms typically make cash application of customer payments using either the open-item method or the balance-forward method.

INTERNET RESOURCES

Note: *For updates to links, please go to the book's website at http://smart.swcollege.com.*

http://www.bankone.com—A large Chicago-based bank—the sixth-largest U.S. bank—that offers numerous commercial banking services, including cash management and lending.

http://www.dunandbradstreet.com—A site that sells mercantile credit reports on thousands of companies; opening a D&B account is required for full access.

KEY TERMS

ABC system
aging of accounts receivable
average investment in accounts
    receivable (*AIAR*)
cash application
cash conversion cycle (*CCC*)
cash discount
collection policy
contribution margin
cost of marginal investment in
    accounts receivable
credit monitoring
credit scoring
credit terms

economic order quantity (EOQ) model
factoring
five C's of credit
just-in-time (JIT) system
manufacturing resource planning II
    (MRPII)
material requirements planning (MRP)
operating assets
operating cycle (*OC*)
payment pattern
short-term financing
total variable cost of annual sales (*TVC*)
turnover of accounts receivable (*TOAR*)

QUESTIONS

22-1.   The owner of a hot dog cart purchases inventory with credit every morning and sells all of the inventory by 2 o'clock in the afternoon. The hot dogs and drinks are sold only for cash. Will the owner have a negative cash conversion cycle?

22-2. How is the cash conversion cycle (CCC) affected if the operating cycle (OC) increases by 10 days and the average payment period also increases by 10 days?

22-3. A firm has the option to write a check to a supplier (which will take 4 days to be received and cashed) or to use a direct-deposit facility that withdraws the money immediately. Based on the concept of float and the cash conversion cycle, which method of payment should the firm use?

22-4. A furniture store makes an offer that if a purchase over $1,000 is paid in full by 12 months, there is no interest charge (i.e., a 12-month same-as-cash promotion). If the average age of inventory (AAI) is 60 days and the average collection period (ACP) is 420 days, how can this financing offer benefit the furniture store?

22-5. If the cash conversion cycle increases (assume the income statement does not change substantially), what implications are there for net working capital from Chapter 2 (cash + accounts receivable + inventory − accounts payable − accruals)?

22-6. Is the average age of the inventory affected by a decrease in the inventory turnover ratio (see Chapter 2)?

22-7. Why would a firm wish to minimize its *cash conversion cycle* (CCC) even though each of its components is important to the operation of the business? What key actions should the firm pursue to achieve this objective?

22-8. What impact would aggressive action aimed at minimizing a firm's cash conversion cycle (CCC) have on the following financial ratios: inventory turnover, average collection period, and average payment period? What are the key constraints on aggressive pursuit of these strategies with regard to inventory, accounts receivable, and accounts payable?

22-9. What are some of the key cost trade-offs that the financial manager must focus on when attempting to manage short-term accounts in a manner that minimizes cash? Prepare a graph describing the general nature of these cost trade-offs and the optimal level of total cost.

22-10. Assume that the financial manager is considering stretching the firm's accounts payable by paying its vendors at a later date. What key cost trade-offs would be involved when making this stretching decision? How would you quantitatively model this decision?

22-11. What is the financial manager's primary goal with regard to inventory management? How does this goal compare with the inventory goals of production and marketing?

22-12. What trade-off confronts the financial manager with regard to inventory turnover, inventory cost, and stockouts? In what way is inventory viewed as an investment? Why is it important for the financial manager to understand the inventory control techniques used by operations/production managers?

22-13. What role does the *ABC system* play in inventory control? What group of inventory items does the *EOQ model* focus on controlling? Describe the objective and cost trade-off addressed by the EOQ model.

22-14. Why would a firm extend credit to its customers given that such an action would lengthen its cash conversion cycle? What key cost trade-offs would be involved in this decision? What typically dictates the actual credit terms the firm extends to its customers?

22-15. Why is using the *five C's of credit* appropriate for evaluating high-dollar credit requests but not high-volume–low-dollar requests, such as department store credit cards?

22-16. What is *credit scoring*? In what types of situations is it most useful? If you were developing a credit-scoring model, what factors might be most useful in predicting whether or not a credit customer would pay in a timely manner?

22-17. What are the key variables to consider when evaluating potential changes in a firm's credit standards? Why are only variable costs of sales included when estimating the firm's *average investment in accounts receivable*?

22-18. If you sell an item to a customer for $20, your cost of that item sale is $16, and the customer defaults and does not pay, how much have you actually lost? When quantifying the analysis of potential accounts receivable policy changes, why are the costs of any bad debts recognized at the sale price rather than the cost of the sale?

22-19. If a firm contemplates an increase in the cash discount it offers its credit customers for early payment, what key variables need to be considered when quantitatively analyzing this decision? How do the variables used in this analysis differ from those considered when analyzing a potential change in the firm's credit standards?

22-20. What is *credit monitoring*? How can each of the following techniques be used to monitor accounts receivable? What are their attributes?
   a. Average collection period
   b. Aging of accounts receivable
   c. Payment-pattern monitoring

PROBLEMS

The Cash Conversion Cycle

22-1. A manager is deciding between two systems to manage the cash conversion cycle (CCC). System A will make the CCC only 60 days, and the cash emerges with a 10 percent return each rotation through the cycle. System B allows for more customer credit and slows the CCC to 90 days. However, the cash that emerges through each rotation of the cycle has a 13 percent return. Which system is better? Defend your answer numerically. (*Hint:* Figure out the amount of annual compounding each system generates.)

22-2. Firm Q currently has sales of $5 million (assume the cost of goods sold is $4 million, or a 20% margin) and an inventory turnover of 5.0 (i.e., the firm tends to sell out its inventory five times throughout the year; see Chapter 2). Through a new promotion, sales are expected to increase by 10 percent while maintaining the same average inventory. How does this affect the average age of the inventory (*AAI*), the operating cycle (*OC*), and the cash conversion cycle (*CCC*)? Support your answers with calculations. If the sales promotion offers customers credit (i.e., increases the accounts receivable), how would this affect your previous answer?

22-3. A firm using a LIFO system for inventory reduces the inventory account (as it is sold) by the amount associated with the cost of the most recent inventory. A FIFO system for inventory reduces the inventory account (as it is sold) with the amount associated with the cost of the oldest inventory. Suppose there are ten units of inventory. The five oldest units have a book value of $12,000 each, and the five newest units have a book value of $14,000 each. In this period, six units are sold. What is the average age of inventory (*AAI*) based on the cost of goods sold for the period, the closing inventory figure, and a 365-day year under a FIFO system and under a LIFO system? Re-calculate the *AAI* under FIFO and LIFO based on an average inventory figure (average inventory = [starting inventory + ending inventory] ÷ 2). How does the convention of LIFO and FIFO affect the operating cycle (*OC*)? Should investors expect a firm's *OC* to increase after announcing a switch from FIFO to LIFO (assuming no other changes in the firm's environment)?

22-4. A firm's average age of inventory is 40 days (assume a 365-day year), and its inventory capacity averages 20,000 units. Assuming it takes 5 days to ship the inventory to the firm when ordered, what is the reorder point quantity? Is it better to have 5,000-unit capacity trucks (shipping costs of $500 each) deliver the inventory, or smaller 2,000-unit capacity trucks (shipping costs of $270) deliver the inventory? If a system can be implemented to speed up the ordering/shipping to 3 days instead of 5 days, would you still use the same truck(s)? Provide numerical support for your decision.

22-5. A firm currently has an average payment period (*APP*) of 60 days. The average age of inventory (*AAI*) is 70 days with an assOCiated cost of goods sold of $340,000. The supplier has offered to decrease the price of the inventory by 5 percent if the firm pays its bills much earlier. The effect on the *APP* would be to reduce it to 45 days. How much will the *AAI* be reduced, and will the change offset the reduction in *APP* to maintain the firm's cash conversion cycle (*CCC*)? If the *CCC* does not reduce due to the supplier's offer, are there any benefits to the firm in terms of profitability?

22-6. Canadian Products is concerned about managing its operating assets and liabilities efficiently. Inventories have an average age of 110 days, and accounts receivable have an average age of 50 days. Accounts payable are paid approximately 40 days after they arise. The firm has annual sales of $36 million, its cost of goods sold represents 75 percent of sales, and its purchases represent 70 percent of cost of goods sold. Assume a 365-day year.

a. Calculate the firm's operating cycle (*OC*).
b. Calculate the firm's cash conversion cycle (*CCC*).
c. Calculate the amount of total resources Canadian Products has invested in its *CCC*.
d. Discuss how management might be able to reduce the amount of total resources invested in the *CCC*.

22-7. The cash conversion cycle is an important tool for the financial manager in managing day-to-day operations of the firm. As an investor, knowing how the firm manages its *CCC* would provide useful insights about management's effectiveness in managing the firm's resource investment in the *CCC*. Access Microsoft's annual statement at http://www.microsoft.com, and calculate Microsoft's *CCC*. Discuss any difficulties you had in obtaining adequately detailed data from Microsoft's website for use in calculating its *CCC*. Evaluate Microsoft's *CCC* in light of your calculations.

SMART
SOLUTIONS
See the problem and
solution explained
step-by-step at
SMARTFinance

22-8. A firm is weighing five plans that affect several current accounts. Given the five plans and their probable effects on inventory, receivables, and payables, as shown in the following table, which plan would you favor? Explain.

	Change		
Plan	Average Age of Inventory (days)	Average Collection Period (days)	Average Payment Period (days)
A	+35	+20	+10
B	+20	−15	+10
C	−10	+5	0
D	−20	+15	+5
E	+15	−15	+20

22-9. King Manufacturing turns its inventory 9.1 times each year, has an average payment period of 35 days, and has an average collection period of 60 days. The firm's annual sales are $72 million, its cost of goods sold represents 50 percent of sales, and its purchases represent 80 percent of cost of goods sold. Assume a 365-day year.

a. Calculate the firm's operating cycle (*OC*) and cash conversion cycle (*CCC*).
b. Calculate the firm's total resources invested in its *CCC*.
c. Assuming the firm pays 14 percent to finance its resource investment in its *CCC*, how much would it save annually by reducing its *CCC* by 20 days if this reduc-

tion were achieved by shortening the average age of inventory by 10 days, shortening the average collection period by five days, and lengthening the average payment period by five days?

   d. If the 20-day reduction in the firm's CCC could be achieved by a 20-day change in only one of the three components of the CCC, which one would you recommend? Explain.

22-10. Bradbury Corporation turns its inventory five times each year, has an average payment period of 25 days, and has an average collection period of 32 days. The firm's annual sales are $3.6 billion, its cost of goods sold represents 80 percent of sales, and its purchases represent 50 percent of cost of goods sold. Assume a 365-day year.

   a. Calculate the firm's operating cycle (OC) and cash conversion cycle (CCC).
   b. Calculate the total resources invested in the firm's CCC.
   c. Assuming that the firm pays 18 percent to finance its resource investment, how much would it increase its annual profits by reducing its CCC by 12 days if this reduction were solely the result of extending its average payment period by 12 days?
   d. If the 12-day reduction in the firm's CCC in part (c) could have alternatively been achieved by shortening either the average age of inventory or the average collection period by 12 days, would you have recommended one of those actions rather than the 12-day extension of the average payment period specified in part (c)? Which change would you recommend? Explain.

22-11. Aztec Products wishes to evaluate its cash conversion cycle (CCC). One of the firm's financial analysts has discovered that on average the firm holds items in inventory for 65 days, pays its suppliers 35 days after purchase, and collects its receivables after 55 days. The firm's annual sales (all on credit) are about $2.1 billion, its cost of goods sold represent about 67 percent of sales, and purchases represent about 40 percent of cost of goods sold. Assume a 365-day year.

   a. What are Aztec Products' operating cycle (OC) and cash conversion cycle (CCC)?
   b. How many dollars of resources does Aztec have invested in (1) inventory, (2) accounts receivable, (3) accounts payable, and (4) the total CCC?
   c. If Aztec could shorten its cash conversion cycle by reducing its inventory holding period by five days, what effect would that have on its total resource investment found in part (b)?
   d. If Aztec could shorten its CCC by five days, would it be best to reduce the inventory holding period, reduce the receivable collection period, or extend the accounts payable period? Why?

22-12. Go to http://finance.yahoo.com, and input the ticker symbols noted in parentheses following each of the company names listed below. Under the Financials heading in the left-hand column, click on "Income Statement" and then "Balance Sheet" to obtain the most recent income statement and balance sheet for each firm. Use the appropriate financial statement data for each firm to respond to the following instructions and questions.

Anheuser-Busch Companies, Inc. (BUD)
Coca-Cola Company (KO)
Molson Coors Company (TAP)
PepsiCo, Inc. (PEP)

   a. Use the formulas given in the chapter to calculate the following time periods (in days) for each of the firms:
      (1) Average age of inventory (AAI)
      (2) Average collection period (ACP)
      (3) Average payment period (APP)
   b. Use the time periods calculated in part (a) to calculate each firm's operating cycle (OC) and cash conversion cycle (CCC).
   c. Compare, contrast, and evaluate the OC and CCC calculated in part (b) for each of the following combinations:

(1) The two soft drink companies (KO and PEP)

(2) The two beer companies (BUD and TAP)

How would you describe the differences found for each pair of firms?

d. Compare and contrast the OC and CCC for the two soft drink companies to those of the two beer companies. Explain any differences you observe.

Cost Trade-offs in Short-Term Financial Management

22-13.   Geet Industries wants to install a just-in-time (JIT) inventory system in order to significantly reduce its in-process inventories. The annual cost of the system is gauged to be $95,000. The financial manager estimates that with this system, the firm's average inventory investment will decline by 40 percent from its current level of $2.05 million. All other costs are expected to be unaffected by this system. The firm can earn 14 percent per year on equal-risk investments.

a. What is the annual cost savings expected to result from installation of the proposed JIT system?

b. Should the firm install the system?

22-14.   Sheth & Sons Inc. is considering changing its pay period for its salaried management from every two weeks to monthly. The firm's CFO, Ken Smart, believes that such action will free up cash that can be used elsewhere in the business, which currently faces a cash crunch. In order to avoid a strong negative response from the salaried managers, the firm will simultaneously announce a new health plan that will lower managers' cost contributions without cutting benefits.

Ken's analysis indicates that the salaried managers' bimonthly payroll is $1.8 million and is expected to remain at that level for the foreseeable future. With the bimonthly system, there were 2.2 pay periods in a month. Because the managers will be paid monthly, the monthly payroll will be about $4.0 million (2.2 x $1.8 million). The annual cost to the firm of the new health plan will be $180,000. Ken believes that because managers' salaries accrue at a constant rate over the pay period, the average salaries over the period can be estimated by dividing the total amount by 2. The firm believes that it can earn 15 percent annually on any funds made available through the accrual of the managers' salaries.

a. How much additional financing will Sheth & Sons obtain as a result of switching the pay period for managers' salaries from every two weeks to monthly?

b. Should the firm implement the proposed change in pay periods?

22-15.   Firm CFT is trying to determine the optimal amount of a particular inventory item to carry in its warehouse. CFT tends to sell 1,000 units a year, with each unit costing $1,200 and an additional carrying cost of $300. How many units should CFT optimally hold in its inventory? The supplier will only ship 100 units at a given time. Consequently, CFT wants to manage its carrying cost to accommodate this constraint. What carrying cost would make 100 units the optimal quantity? CFT finds that it can only reduce carrying cost to $260. What per unit cost would make 100 units the optimal amount to hold in inventory? Would it make sense for CFT to negotiate with its supplier for this price?

Inventory Management

22-16.   Calculate the average investment in inventory for each of the following situations. Assume a 365-day year.

a. A firm's annual sales were $18 million, its gross profit margin was 32 percent, and its average age of inventory is 45 days.

b. A firm's annual sales were $325 million, its cost of goods sold was 80 percent of sales, and it turns its inventory 10 times per year.

c. A firm's annual cost of goods sold total $120 million, and it turns its inventory about every 70 days.

22-17. GEP Manufacturing is mulling over a plan to rent a proprietary inventory-control system at an annual cost of $4.5 million. The firm predicts its sales will remain relatively stable at $585 million and its gross profit margin will continue to be 28 percent. It expects that as a result of the new inventory-control system its average age of inventory (*AAI*) will drop from its current level of 83 days to about 46 days. The firm's required return on similar-risk investments is 12 percent. Assume a 365-day year.

    a. Calculate GEP's average inventory investment both currently and assuming it rents the inventory-control system.

    b. Use your findings in part (a) to determine the annual savings expected to result from the proposed inventory-control system.

    c. Based on your finding in part (b), would you recommend that GEP rent the inventory control system? Explain your recommendation.

22-18. Iverson Industries uses 80,000 units of an "A" item of raw material inventory each year. The firm maintains level production throughout the year given the steady demand for its finished products. The raw material order cost is $225 per order, and carrying costs are estimated to be $10.50 per unit per year. The firm wishes to maintain a safety stock of 10 days of inventory; it takes 5 days for the firm to receive an order once it is placed. Assume a 365-day year.

    a. Calculate the economic order quantity (EOQ) for Iverson's raw material.

    b. How large a *safety stock* (in units) of inventory should the firm maintain?

    c. What is Iverson's *reorder point* for this item of inventory? (*Hint:* Be sure to include the safety stock.)

22-19. Litespeed Products buys 200,000 motors per year from a supplier that can fulfill orders within two days of receiving them. Litespeed transmits its orders to this supplier electronically so the lead time to receive orders is two days. Litespeed's order cost is about $295 per order and its carrying cost is about $37 per motor per year. The firm maintains a safety stock of motors equal to six days of usage. Assume a 365-day year.

    a. What is Litespeed's economic order quantity (EOQ) for the motors?

    b. What is its *total cost* at the EOQ?

    c. How large a *safety stock* (in units) of motors should Litespeed maintain?

    d. What is Litespeed's *reorder point* for motors? (*Hint:* Be sure to include the safety stock.)

    e. If Litespeed has an opportunity to reduce either its order cost or its carrying cost by 10 percent, which would result in the lowest total cost at the associated new EOQ?

    f. How much total cost savings will result from the lowest-cost strategy found in part (e) relative to the total cost found in part (b)?

22-20. Vargas Enterprises wishes to determine the economic order quantity (EOQ) for a critical and expensive inventory item that it uses in large amounts at a relatively constant rate throughout the year. The firm uses 450,000 units of the item annually and has order costs of $375 per order; its carrying costs associated with this item are $28 per unit per year. The firm plans to hold safety stock of the item equal to five days of usage, and it estimates that it takes 12 days to receive an order of the item once placed. Assume a 365-day year.

    a. Calculate the firm's EOQ for the item of inventory described above.

    b. What is the firm's *total cost* based upon the EOQ calculated in part (a)?

    c. How many units of *safety stock* should Vargas hold?

    d. What is the firm's *reorder point* for the item of inventory being evaluated? (*Hint:* Be sure to include the safety stock.)

Accounts Receivable Standards and Terms

22-21. International Oil Company (IOC) uses credit scoring to evaluate gasoline credit card applications. The following table presents the financial and credit characteristics and weights (indicating the relative importance of each characteristic) used in the credit decision. The firm's credit standards are to accept all applicants with credit scores of 80 or higher, to extend limited credit on a probationary basis to applicants with scores higher than 70 and lower than 80, and to reject all applicants with scores below 70.

Financial and Credit Characteristics	Predetermined Weight
Credit references	0.25
Education	0.10
Home ownership	0.10
Income range	0.15
Payment history	0.30
Years on job	0.10

The firm needs to process three applications scored recently by one of its credit analysts. The scores for each of the applicants are summarized in the following table.

Financial and Credit Characteristics	Applicant's scores (0 to1000)		
	X	Y	Z
Credit references	60	90	80
Education	75	80	80
Home ownership	100	90	60
Income range	70	70	80
Payment history	60	85	70
Years on job	50	60	90

a. Use the data presented to find the credit score for each of the applicants.

b. Recommend the action that the firm should take for each of the three applicants.

SMART SOLUTIONS
See the problem and solution explained step-by-step at
SMART**Finance**

22-22. Barans Company currently has an average collection period of 55 days and annual sales of $1 billion. Assume a 365-day year.

a. What is the firm's average accounts receivable balance?

b. If the variable cost of each product is 65 percent of sales, what is the *average investment in accounts receivable*?

c. If the equal-risk opportunity cost of the investment in accounts receivable is 12 percent, what is the total annual cost of the resources invested in accounts receivable?

22-23. Melton Electronics currently has an average collection period of 35 days and annual sales of $72 million. Assume a 365-day year.

a. What is the firm's average accounts receivable balance?

b. If the variable cost of each product is 70 percent of sales, what is the firm's *average investment in accounts receivable*?

c. If the equal-risk opportunity cost of the investment in accounts receivable is 16 percent, what is the total annual cost of the resources invested in accounts receivable?

d. If the firm can shorten the average collection period to 30 days by offering a cash discount of 1 percent for early payment, and 60 percent of the customers take this discount, should the firm offer this discount, assuming its cost of bad debts will rise by $150,000 per year?

22-24. Davis Manufacturing Industries (DMI) produces and sells 20,000 units of a machine tool each year. All sales are on credit, and DMI charges all customers $500 per unit. Variable costs are $350 per unit, and incurs $2 million in fixed costs each year.

DMI's top managers are evaluating a proposal from the firm's CFO that the firm relax its credit standards to increase its sales and profits. The CFO believes this change will increase unit sales by 4 percent. Currently, DMI's average collection period is 40 days, and the CFO expects this to increase to 60 days under the new policy. Bad debt expense is also expected to increase from 1 percent to 2.5 percent of annual sales. The firm's board of directors has set a required return of 15 percent on investments with this level of risk. Assume a 365-day year.

   a. What is DMI's *contribution margin*? By how much will profits from increased sales change if DMI adopts the new credit standards?
   b. What is DMI's *average investment in accounts receivable* under the current credit standards? What would it be under the proposed credit standards? What is the cost of this additional investment?
   c. What is DMI's cost of marginal bad debts resulting from the relaxation of its credit standards?
   d. What is DMI's net profit/loss from adopting the new credit standards? Should DMI relax its credit standards?

22-25. Jeans Manufacturing thinks that it can reduce its high credit costs by tightening its credit standards. However, the firm believes that as a result of the planned tightening, its annual sales will drop from $38 million to $36 million. On the positive side, the firm expects its average collection period to fall from 58 to 45 days and its bad debts to drop from 2.5 percent to 1 percent of sales. The firm's variable cost per unit is 70 percent of its sale price, and its required return on investment is 15 percent. Assume a 365-day year. Evaluate the proposed tightening of credit standards, and make a recommendation to the management of Jeans Manufacturing.

22-26. Belton Company is considering relaxing its credit standards to boost its currently sagging sales. It expects its proposed relaxation will increase sales by 20 percent from the current annual level of $10 million. Managers expect the firm's average collection period to increase from 35 days to 50 days, and bad debts to increase from 2 percent of sales to 7 percent of sales by relaxing the firm's credit standards as proposed. The firm's variable costs equal 60 percent of sales, and its fixed costs total $2.5 million per year. Belton's opportunity cost is 16 percent. Assume a 365-day year.

   a. What is Belton's *contribution margin*?
   b. Calculate Belton's *marginal profit contribution from sales*.
   c. What is Belton's *cost of the marginal investment in accounts receivable*?
   d. What is Belton's *cost of marginal bad debts*?
   e. Use your findings in parts (b), (c), and (d) to determine the net profit (cost) of Belton's proposed relaxation of credit standards. Should it relax its credit standards?

22-27. Webb Inc. currently makes all sales on credit and offers no cash discounts. The firm is considering a 2 percent cash discount for payments within 10 days. The firm's current average collection period is 65 days, sales are 400,000 units, selling price is $50 per unit, and variable cost per unit is $40. The firm expects that the changes in credit terms will result in an increase in sales to 410,000 units, that 75 percent of the sales will take the discount, and that the average collection period will fall to 45 days. Bad debts are expected to drop from 1.0 to 0.9 percent of sales. If Webb's required rate of return on equal-risk investments is 25 percent, assuming a 365-day year, should the firm offer the proposed discount?

22-28. Microboard, Inc., a major computer chip manufacturer, is contemplating lengthening its credit period from net 30 days to net 50 days. Presently, its average collection period is 40 days; the firm's CFO believes that with the proposed new credit period, the average collection period will be 65 days. The firm's sales are $900 million, but the CFO believes that with the new credit terms sales will increase to $980 million. At the current $900 million sales level, the firm's total variable costs are $630 million. The firm's CFO estimates that with the proposed new credit terms, bad debt expenses will increase from the current level of 1.5 percent of sales to 2.0 percent of sales. The CFO also estimates that due to the increased sales volume and accompanying receivables, the firm will have to add additional facilities and personnel to its credit and collections department. The annual cost of the expanded credit operations resulting from the proposed new credit period is estimated to be $10 million. The firm's required return on similar-risk investments is 18 percent. Assume a 365-day year and evaluate the economics of Microboard's proposed credit-period lengthening, and make a recommendation to the firm's management.

Collecting, Monitoring, and Applying Cash to Receivables

22-29. United Worldwide's accounts receivable totaled $1.75 million on August 31, 2007. The table below shows a breakdown of these outstanding accounts on the basis of the month of the initial credit sale. The firm extends net 30, EOM credit terms to its credit customers.

Month of Credit Sale	Accounts Receivable
August 2007	$ 640,000
July 2007	500,000
June 2007	164,000
May 2007	390,000
April 2007 or before	56,000
Total (August 31, 2007)	$1,750,000

a. Prepare an *aging schedule* for United Worldwide's August 31, 2007, accounts receivable balance.
b. Using your findings in part (a), evaluate the firm's credit and collection activities.
c. What are some probable causes of the situation discussed in part (b)?

22-30. Big Air Board Company, a global manufacturer and distributor of surfboards and snowboards, is in a seasonal business. Although surfboard sales are only mildly seasonal, the snowboard sales are very seasonal, driven by peak demand in the first and fourth calendar quarters of each year. The following table gives the firm's monthly sales for the immediate past quarter (October through December 2007) and its forecast monthly sales for the coming year (calendar-year 2008).

Month	Sales ($ in millions)
Historic	
October 2007	$3.7
November 2007	3.9
December 2007	4.3
Forecast	
January 2008	$3.8
February 2008	2.6
March 2008	2.2
April 2008	1.6
May 2008	1.8
June 2008	1.9
July 2008	2.0
August 2008	2.2
September 2008	2.4
October 2008	4.1
November 2008	4.6
December 2008	5.1

The firm extends 2/10 net 30, EOM credit terms to all customers. It collects 98 percent of its receivables; it typically writes off the other 2 percent as bad debts. Big Air

Board's historic collection pattern, which is expected to continue through 2008, is 5 percent collected in the month of the sale, 65 percent collected in the first month following the sale, and 28 percent collected in the second month following the sale. Using the data given, calculate the payment pattern of Big Air Board's accounts receivable, and comment on the firm's monthly collections during calendar-year 2008.

THOMSON ONE BUSINESS SCHOOL EDITION

22-31. Compute the average age of inventory, average collection period, and average payment period for 7-Eleven, Inc. (ticker symbol, SE), Caterpillar, Inc. (ticker symbol, CAT), Kohl's Corporation (ticker symbol, KSS), and Wal-Mart Stores, Inc. (ticker symbol, WMT) for the last four years. Also calculate the operating cycle and the cash conversion cycle for each of the firms for the same time period. Why are there differences in each of the measures across the different firms? For each firm, comment on how the cash conversion cycle and each of its components have changed over the last four years. Can you conclude that one firm's cash conversion cycle is "better" simply because it has a lower value?

MINI-CASE: CASH CONVERSION, INVENTORY AND RECEIVABLES MANAGEMENT

Bracelet Blanks, Inc. (BB) generated $43,803,000 in sales (all on credit) during 2007. Cost of goods sold was 57% of that total. Accounts receivable totaled $3,240,222, inventory totaled $842,020, and accounts payable totaled $1,826,070.

1.   Calculate BB's current cash conversion cycle.

2.   BB currently uses 3,000 ingots of aluminum each year to manufacture bracelet blanks. The order cost including shipping is $5,000 per order, and carrying costs are $75 per unit per year. Determine the economic order quantity (EOQ), the amount of safety stock, and the reorder point for aluminum ingots assuming there is a one-week lead time and the firm would like a safety stock of 3 percent.

3.   Also, in an attempt to boost sales, the firm is considering relaxing its credit standards by extending more credit to small firms. BB charges $1.50 per unit. Variable costs are $0.5126 per unit and fixed costs are $10,000,000 per year. The relaxation of credit standards is expected to result in a 3.8% increase in sales (the firm has sufficient excess capacity to handle the increase), and an increase in the average collection period of 3 days. They also expect bad debts to rise from the current level of 0% to 0.5% of sales. Assuming BB requires a 13% return on investments of this type, should the firm relax its credit standards?

4.   Additionally, BB currently offers its credit customers terms of net 30. However, it is considering changing the terms to 2/10 net 30 in an attempt to reduce the amount of time it takes to collect its accounts receivables. The firm believes this change alone will decrease the average collection period by 5 days. BB also expects 63% of its customers will elect to pay within the discount period and that the increased attractiveness of the terms will increase sales by 1% a year. It is not expected that bad debts will change from the current level of 0% as result of this change in terms. BB's opportunity cost of funds invested in accounts receivable is 10%. Should the firm offer the cash discount? Evaluate this scenario separately from the one described in question 3.

Chapter 23

Liquidity Management*

SMARTFinance

Use the learning tools at www
.thomsonedu.com/finance/smartfinance

OPENING FOCUS

The Electronic Payment Revolution?

Many believe that moving money by wire was the original form of e-business; its roots can be traced back nearly 100 years. Yet, today many aspects of cash management involve the same manual process used 45 years ago. During the 1960s, a firm was considered efficient if it could process an order in 4 to 7 days, have the product delivered in 14 to 21 days, get the invoice within a week, and pay within 45 to 60 days. Today, a firm is considered "old school" if its customers can't order today, have it shipped to their door tomorrow, get the invoice that same day, but still pay in 45 to 60 days!

To address this issue in today's e-everything world, some firms are embracing e-invoicing when making business-to-business transactions. The clunky technical term for this process, which involves sending bills and payments electronically, is *electronic invoice presentment and payment,* or simply EIPP. Big-name enterprise software developers such as PeopleSoft, Oracle, and SAP offer sophisticated packages that tie payments to procurement and make it easier for firms to use EIPP.

However, firms lack an incentive to speed their payments to vendors, so it's not surprising that the adoption of EIPP has been slow. Clearly, paying faster is contrary to the firm's goal of shortening the cash conversion cycle (*CCC*) and thereby reducing its resource investment. Xign Corp., a leader in on-demand order-to-pay business software, is pushing a strategy for increasing the adoption of EIPP: The buyer agrees to pay quickly in exchange for an attractive early-pay discount from the vendor. Xign believes a cash discount of around 2 percent for payments made within 10 days adequately reduces the buyer's cost enough to compensate it for the earnings lost by paying sooner than would otherwise have been the case. In addition, by making the transaction and payment electronically, the buyer and seller will reduce their manual labor costs.

As testimony to EIPP, Bill Dvorak, CFO of Cimco Communications, an Oakbrook Terrace, Illinois, telecommunications service firm, puts the cost of receiving, auditing, processing, and paying a paper invoice at $100 or more. As part of its services, the firm now mails clients a printed summary of charges but relies on EIPP to do most of the work, keeping overhead low. Cimco says it also fields fewer customer service calls about bills now that customers can get a full range of details using the Internet to look into the EIPP system.

Some major companies, such as Dell Inc., Wells Fargo & Co., Office Depot Inc., and Pacific Care Health Systems, have adopted EIPP. Yet, to date, its universal adoption has been relatively slow. A key issue is that each company that adopts it must convince its customers to sign on. Beth Robertson, a senior research analyst at

---

* Professor Dubos J. Masson, CCM, CertCM, of Pepperdine University and the Resource Alliance, assisted in preparation of a large part of this chapter. The authors very much appreciate D.J.'s important contribution.

research and advisory firm TowerGroup, suggests the growth in EIPP will be gradual. She predicts a quadrupling of the number of invoices sent electronically between 2003 and 2007 from 30 million to about 130 million. She suggests that broad technical standards need to be established and security issues resolved before there will be widespread adoption of EIPP.

Sources: Julie Sturgeon, "Electronic Payments," CFO (Winter 2003), pp. 52–53; Doug Roberts, "Giving Cash Management a Technology Boost," Financial Executive (December 2003), pp. 62–63.

C hapter 22 described the operating and cash conversion cycles and then focused on management of the two key components of the operating cycle—inventory and accounts receivable. Here we shift focus to liquidity—both cash and accounts payable. Clearly, cash is the lifeblood of the firm. Thus it is the primary focus of the financial manager, who must conserve it by gathering cash receipts and making cash disbursements in a cost-effective manner. Additionally, the financial manager conserves cash by using efficient mechanisms to transfer cash within and between the firm's operating units. As noted in Chapter 22, short-term financing decisions should result from an analysis of cost trade-offs with the goal of minimizing total cost.

Accounts payable are also an important component of the cash conversion cycle. The firm must manage them in a way that lengthens the payment period and still preserves the firm's credit reputation. This strategy will help shorten the cash conversion cycle and reduce the firm's resource investment. The financial manager also will use other strategies and tools to slow down disbursements.

Of course, all of these cash management strategies are based on the firm's ability to maintain adequate liquidity to preserve the firm's solvency. Specifically, the firm must be able to earn a positive return on idle excess cash balances and also to obtain low-cost financing for meeting unexpected needs and seasonal cash shortages. This important activity, which includes managing cash and accounts payable, is commonly called **liquidity management.**

This chapter emphasizes the key procedures for managing cash, payables, and liquidity. We begin with a discussion that focuses on float in the cash collection-payment system, and the principles of managing the firm's cash position. Next, we consider cash collection, placing emphasis on the types of collection systems, lockbox systems, cash concentration, and various funds transfer mechanisms. Then we review some key aspects of accounts payable and disbursements, including cash discounts, disbursement products and methods, and new developments. Finally, we consider the firm's use of short-term investing and borrowing to maintain adequate liquidity.

23.1 CASH MANAGEMENT

Many companies employ financial specialists known as **cash managers.** One of their primary roles is to manage the cash flow time line related to collection, concentration, and disbursement of the company's funds. Their job typically starts when a customer (the payer) initiates payment to the company (the payee) in any format (cash, check, or electronic). Because most business-to-business payments are still generated by sending a check in the mail, the collections process usually involves trying to reduce mail, processing, and check-collection delays.

The cash manager is also responsible for concentrating cash from remote collection points into a central account, and for initiating payments from the company to its suppliers. The final stage of this process usually involves reconciling the company's various bank accounts and managing all the banking relationships. Managing the cash flow time line is a vital role, because any delay in timing affects the flow of cash. Delays on either the collection or disbursement side of the cash flow process are generally referred to as *float*.

FLOAT

Float refers to funds that have been sent by the payer but are not yet usable by the payee. Float is important in the cash conversion cycle; it increases both the firm's average collection period and its average payment period. The primary role of the cash manager on the collections side is to *minimize collection float* wherever possible. On the payments side, trying to *maximize disbursement float* is a common practice that raises an important ethical question: Is it ethical to intentionally pay a supplier late, beyond the term within which a firm agreed to pay? This topic will be discussed in greater detail later in this chapter.

We can view float from either the receiving party's (payee's) perspective or the paying party's (payer's) perspective. The following list points out that both mail and processing float are generally the same from both perspectives. The four components of float are defined as follows:

1. **Mail float** is the time delay between when payment is placed in the mail and when payment is received. This float component can range from one day to as much as five days or more, depending on location and other factors.
2. **Processing float** is the time between receipt of the payment and its deposit into the firm's account. In a mail-based system, this involves opening the envelope, separating the check from the remittance advice, preparing the check for deposit, and actually depositing the check at the payee's bank. This float component can range from less than one day to three or more days, depending on any processing delays the company may have.
3. **Availability float** is the time between deposit of the check and availability of the funds to the firm's bank account. Although this may be related to the actual clearing time of the check, it is ultimately a function of the availability schedule offered by the deposit bank. For most business checks, this ranges from same day up to three business days, depending on the bank on which the check is drawn.
4. **Clearing float** is the time between deposit of the check and presentation of the check back to the bank on which it is drawn. This component of float depends on the time required for a check to clear the banking system and to have funds debited from the payer's account. In today's clearing system for business checks, availability float and clearing float are generally the same, but there are some exceptions when checks are drawn on small, geographically remote banks.

In addition to managing the collection, concentration, and disbursement of funds, the cash manager is also responsible for the following:

- *Financial relationships:* Managing relationships with banks and other providers of cash management services
- *Cash flow forecasting:* Determining future cash flows to predict surpluses or deficits (see Chapter 21)
- *Investing and borrowing:* Managing the investment of short-term surpluses or borrowing for short-term deficits

- *Information management:* Developing and maintaining information systems to gather and analyze cash management data

The cash manager typically resides in the firm's treasury area along with such functions as external financing and risk management. In smaller companies, accounting or clerical staff may perform the cash management function. The following sections describe the specific cash management tasks related to collection, concentration, and disbursement of funds.

CASH-POSITION MANAGEMENT

On a daily basis, the primary cash management tasks related to the collection, concentration, and disbursement of funds are generally referred to as **cash-position management**. Each day the cash manager determines the amount of funds to be collected, moves balances to the appropriate accounts, and funds the projected disbursements. With proper forecasting of future cash flows, he or she can manage the cash position with some degree of accuracy many weeks into the future. Most of the cash management products and services offered by banks and other financial institutions are associated with some part of this process.

At the end of the day, the cash manager must determine (1) whether the company will have a surplus or a deficit of funds in each checking account and (2) how to manage the difference. If the company has a *surplus* of funds, then the cash manager may place the money in some type of short-term investment, such as an interest-bearing bank account or a portfolio of marketable securities. If the firm has a deficit at the end of the day, then the cash manager must arrange either to transfer funds from investment accounts or to draw on a short-term credit agreement with the firm's bank.

Many companies, especially smaller ones, do not actively engage in cash-position management, but rather set a **target cash balance** for their checking accounts. The primary approach to determining target cash balances is based on transactions requirements or a minimum balance set by the bank. The transactions requirement is determined simply by how much cash a firm needs to fund its day-to-day operations. Firms with a high volume of daily inflows and outflows will find that some balances remain in non-interest-bearing checking accounts, regardless of the firm's forecasting ability. Many banks also require a specified minimum balance in customer checking accounts. For smaller companies and banks, this minimum balance is designed to provide adequate compensation to the bank for the services it provides. For larger companies, most banks perform *account analysis,* which compares the value of the balances a firm leaves on deposit to the value of the services it receives from the bank.

A **bank account analysis statement** is a report (usually monthly) to a bank's commercial customers that specifies all services provided, including items processed and any charges assessed. It is basically a detailed invoice that lists all checks cleared, account charges, lockbox charges, electronic transactions, and so on. The statement also lists all balances held by the firm at the bank and includes a computation of the credit earned by the firm on those balances. Although, under current federal regulations, a bank is not allowed to pay actual interest on corporate checking account balances, it can offer an *earnings credit* on these balances that offsets service charges. In the account analysis, most companies will receive some credit for the transaction balances they leave in the account, and the credit typically will only partially offset the service fees. The balance of fees owed the bank will then be deducted as a service charge for the month in question.

1. What is *float*? What are its four components? What is the difference between *availability float* and *clearing float*?

2. What activities are involved in *cash-position management*? How does the cash manager monitor and take actions with regard to the end-of-day checking account balances?

3. How do smaller firms that do not engage in cash-position management typically set their *target cash balance*? What is typically detailed in a *bank account analysis statement*?

23.2 COLLECTIONS

The primary objective of the collections process is to quickly and efficiently collect funds from customers and others. This process includes gathering and disseminating information related to the collections. In some cases, the information may be as important as the money itself. One key requirement is to make sure the accounts receivable department has the remittance information needed to properly post receipts and update customer files. A secondary requirement is to provide audit trails for the company's internal and external auditors.

As discussed earlier, a major delay in the collections process results from *collection float,* which is a function of the mail, processing, and availability float. The primary goal of collections is to reduce each of these float components as much as possible. Collection float is typically measured in *dollar-days*—the number of dollars in the collection process multiplied by the number of days of float. For example, $10 million of checks with an average of five days of float would represent $50 million dollar-days of float.

It is important to understand the various payment practices in the U.S. business environment. In the United States, most business-to-business payments are still made via a check in the mail. But retail establishments must handle cash, debit, and credit cards in addition to checks. The U.S. business environment is also characterized by a large number of financial institutions (approximately 20,000, according to recent FDIC statistics) and a lack of true nationwide branch banking.

The Comparative Corporate Finance on page 843 provides insight into the cost to those working abroad of sending money back to Latin American countries. Clearly, funds transfers of this type can be costly, although these costs are declining.

Speeding up collections reduces the firm's *average collection period,* which, in turn, reduces the investment the firm must make in its cash conversion cycle. In our example of the *cash conversion cycle* in Chapter 22 (Applying the Model 22.1), Reese Industries had annual sales of $5 billion and eight days of total collection float (mail, processing, and availability time). If Reese can reduce its collection float time by three days (to five days), it reduces its investment in the cash conversion cycle by $41.1 million [$5 billion × (3 days/365 days)]. Companies can implement a number of popular collection systems and techniques to speed up collections.

TYPES OF COLLECTION SYSTEMS

The nature of a firm's business primarily determines its collection system. Many high-volume retail establishments, such as fast-food restaurants or convenience stores, still receive the bulk of their payments in cash. Other types of retail operations, such as department and variety stores, now collect most of their payments by check, debit card, or credit card.

COMPARATIVE CORPORATE FINANCE

Please Send Money

Over the past two decades, U.S. corporations in the United States and other countries have dramatically reduced their cash holdings. The decision to reduce cash holdings results from an analysis of the associated costs and benefits of holding a specified cash balance. The primary cost of holding a large cash balance is the opportunity cost of the funds. Corporations earn very low returns on cash balances and short-term marketable securities, and stockholders expect firms to invest all of their assets, including cash, to maximize shareholder wealth. On the other hand, maintaining a large cash balance gives the firm flexibility to meet fluctuating daily operating needs. When cash needs are uncertain, a firm may decide that the benefit of having a cash buffer is worth the cost of holding a cash balance that earns a low return. As financial institutions developed innovative cash management tools and new technology enabled firms to maintain almost up-to-the-minute monitoring of their cash position, the benefits of a large cash buffer declined, and so did cash balances of large companies.

The same trend at work in the corporate finance world is also having its impact in the personal finance realm. The accompanying chart shows how changes in the cost of handling cash have affected people working abroad who send money back to their home country. Since 1999, technological innovation and competition among banks changed the cost of remitting money to one's home country from more than 15 percent to less than 8 percent. In no part of the world is this effect more pronounced than in Latin America, which received more than $38 billion in remittances in 2003. Within the region, the cost of sending money home varies widely, from about $12 per $200 payment in Ecuador and Peru, to almost $25 in Cuba. If the cost of sending money home continues to decline, we should expect to see increases in remittances, especially in those countries that achieve the greatest cost reductions.

Source: Richard Lapper, "Latin Americas Tops League for Remittances," *Financial Times* (March 26, 2004), p. 2.

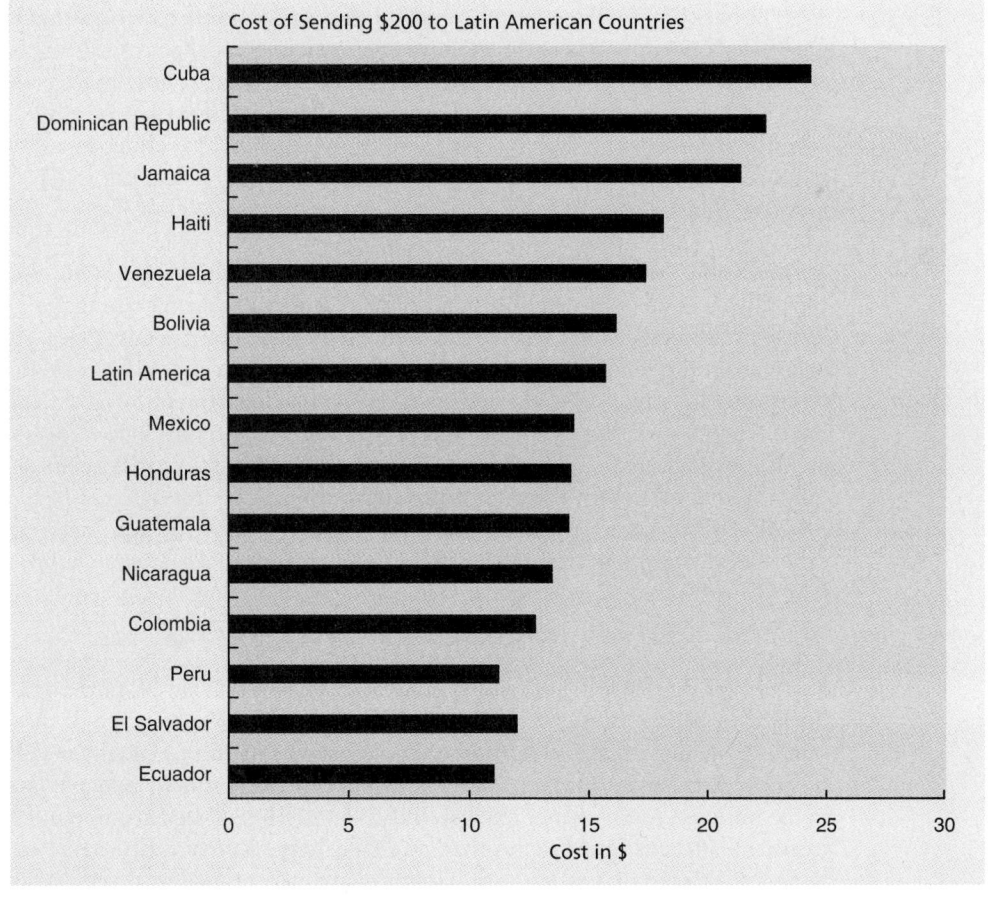

Some types of time-critical transactions, such as real estate closings or high-dollar payments, may be received via wire transfers with same-day value. Other forms of high-volume-low-dollar receipts, especially those of a recurring nature (utility payments, insurance premiums, etc.), may come through the *automated clearinghouse (ACH) system*, which generally offers next-day settlement with fairly low transaction costs. The important thing to understand is that the collection system a company uses is usually a function of both the type of business and the customary methods of payment for that type of business.

Field-Banking System. In a **field-banking system**, companies make most collections either over the counter (as at a retail store) or at a collection office (often used by utilities). These systems are characterized by many collection points ("in the field," as opposed to a centralized location). Each of these collection points may have a depository account at a local bank.

The main collection problem in this type of system involves transferring the funds from the local (often small) banks to the main account at the company's primary bank. Given the lack of an effective nationwide branch banking system, many large national retailers find they must maintain hundreds or even thousands of bank relationships as part of their collections system. Typically, the collections in a field-banking system are local checks, cash, debit cards, and credit cards. Although the debit card and credit card processing is usually highly automated and efficient, the checks and cash must be processed and deposited at the local deposit bank. The funds must then be concentrated into the company's main account before the money can be used.

The backbone of this type of system is information management—that is, the company needs to know where the money is before it can use the funds. Most large retailers utilize *point-of-sale (POS) information systems* that enable them to know on a daily basis how much money has been collected, in what formats (cash, check, debit card, or credit card) it was received, and how much of it was deposited at the local bank. The task of moving this money into a concentration account is discussed in the section on cash concentration.

Mail-Based Collection System. In a **mail-based collection system**, the company typically has one or more collection points that process the incoming mail payments. These processing centers receive the mail payments, open the envelopes, separate the check from the remittance information, prepare the check for deposit, and send the remittance information to the accounts receivable department for application of payment. Companies that utilize standardized, scannable remittance information, such as utilities and credit-card processors, can often process the payments they receive quickly and efficiently using automated equipment. Although many high-volume processors can justify the cost of the equipment needed for automated processing, other companies may find that using a *lockbox* (discussed later) is more cost effective. However, recent developments in payment processing equipment have made automated processing available to smaller companies at reasonable prices.

Electronic Systems. Electronic collection systems are developing rapidly as both businesses and consumers begin to understand their benefits. One of the key developments in this area is **electronic invoice presentment and payment (EIPP)** in the business-to-business market, and **electronic bill presentment and payment (EBPP)** in the business-to-consumer market. In EIPP and EBPP systems, companies send electronic bills to customers, who then can pay them electronically. Most of these systems are Internet-based and are gaining some acceptance in the marketplace. The most successful of the consumer systems offer a consolidator-type service, where customers can go to one site to view and pay all their bills rather than visiting individual billing sites. Electronic payment systems are only slowly gaining acceptance in the business-to-business environment.

Some of the primary advantages of using a system such as the EIPP for business-to-business payments are (1) reduced float to the receiving party, (2) lower cost of receivables processing for the receiver and of payment initiation and reconciliation costs for the payer, and (3) better forecasting for both parties. Though there may be a need for negotiation of payment dates and possible discounts for changed payment timing, companies that have implemented electronic payments report significant overall savings as a result.

LOCKBOX SYSTEMS

A **lockbox system** is a popular technique for speeding up collections because it affects all the components of float. It works like this: Instead of mailing payments to the company, customers mail payments to a post office box, which the firm's bank empties regularly. The bank processes each payment and deposits the payments into the firm's account. The bank sends (or transmits electronically) deposit slips and enclosures to the firm so the firm can properly credit its customers' accounts.

Lockboxes are typically dispersed geographically to match the locations of the firm's customers. As a result, lockboxes reduce mail time. They reduce clearing time because the payer's bank is often close to the payee's depository bank. They also reduce processing time to nearly zero because the bank deposits payments before the firm processes them.

Although a lockbox system reduces collection float, it does so with a cost. Therefore, a firm must perform a cost-benefit analysis to determine if it should implement a lockbox system. Equation 23.1 presents a simple formula for the cost-benefit analysis of a lockbox system:

$$\text{Net benefit (cost)} = (FVR \times r_a) - LC \qquad \text{(Eq. 23.1)}$$

where FVR = float value reduction in dollars

r_a = cost of capital

LC = annual operating cost of the lockbox system

If the return on the float reduction exceeds the cost of the lockbox system, the firm should implement the lockbox system.

APPLYING THE MODEL 23.1

To demonstrate, consider Reese industries, which has $5 billion in annual sales and eight days of customer collection float in its cash conversion cycle. Reese wants to determine if it should implement a lockbox system that reduces customer collection float to five days. The reduction in float value from this decrease in customer float is $41.1 million [$5 billion × (3 days/365 days)]. Reese has a cost of capital of 13.5 percent per year. Thus, the value to Reese of reducing customer float by three days is $5.55 million (0.135 × $41.1 million). If the annual cost of the lockbox system is less than $5.55 million, Reese should implement the system.

Large firms whose customers are geographically dispersed commonly use lockbox systems. Smaller firms also may find a lockbox system advantageous. The benefit to small firms often comes primarily from transferring the processing of payments to a bank.

Lockboxes are typically classified as either retail or wholesale. A *retail lockbox* uses standardized, scannable remittance documents in order to highly automate the processing of incoming payments. These systems are characterized by very high volumes of low-dollar payments, and the key issue is processing the payments at a minimum cost per dollar collected. Given the low-dollar amounts of the payments, availability float is generally not a big issue.

Wholesale lockboxes, on the other hand, primarily process high-dollar payments with nonstandard remittance information. The key issues in this type of system are (1) reducing the availability float related to the large checks and (2) quickly forwarding the remittance information to the accounts receivable department for application of payment. The current practice for wholesale lockboxes is to make extensive use of imaging technology to quickly and accurately relay copies of the remittance information back to the A/R department.

CASH CONCENTRATION

SMART PRACTICES VIDEO

**Daniel Carter,
Chief Financial Officer
of Charlotte Russe**

"Each of our stores makes deposits into a local account, which are concentrated back into our corporate account."

See the entire interview at
SMARTFinance

With a lockbox system, the firm has deposits in each lockbox bank. **Cash concentration** is the process of bringing the lockbox and other deposits together into one bank, commonly called the *concentration bank*.

Cash concentration has three main advantages. First, it creates a large pool of funds for use in making short-term cash investments. Because there is a fixed-cost component in the transaction cost associated with making marketable security investments, investing a single pool of funds reduces the firm's transaction costs. The larger investment pool also allows the firm to choose from a larger variety of marketable securities. Second, concentrating the firm's cash in one account improves the tracking and internal control of the firm's cash. Third, having one concentration bank allows the firm to implement payment strategies that preserve its invested balances for as long as possible.[1]

The configuration of a company's cash concentration system is generally a function of the collection system. That is, a company with a *field-banking system* will need a way to move money quickly and efficiently from many small deposit banks into its concentration account. A company with several collection centers or lockboxes will typically use wire transfers to quickly move large balances from a limited number of collection points into its concentration account. The type of disbursement system (discussed in a later section) is also an important consideration, because the firm must fund these accounts either by internal transfer or wire transfer.

FUNDS TRANSFER MECHANISMS

There are three commonly used mechanisms for transferring cash from the depository banks to the concentration bank. These mechanisms are: (1) depository transfer checks, (2) automated clearinghouse debit transfers, and (3) wire transfers.

[1.] In the process of transferring deposits between banks, it is possible that balances may exist at two banks simultaneously. These dual balances are created by "slippage" in the clearing system. *Clearing system slippage* is often cited as an advantage of cash concentration. However, rarely can a firm concentrating its cash take advantage of the slippage, so we therefore ignore slippage in our discussions.

Depository Transfer Checks. A depository transfer check (DTC) is an unsigned check drawn on one of the firm's bank accounts and deposited in another of the firm's bank accounts. For cash concentration, a firm would draw a DTC on each deposit bank account and deposit it in the concentration bank account. Once the DTC clears the bank on which it is drawn, the actual transfer of funds is completed. Most firms provide deposit information by telephone to the concentration bank, which then prepares and deposits into its account the DTC drawn on the collecting bank account. Because these paper-based items are subject to normal check-clearing delays, today most companies utilize faster, electronic methods than DTCs to concentrate funds.

Automated Clearinghouse Debit Transfers. The second mechanism is an **automated clearinghouse (ACH) debit transfer**, which is a preauthorized electronic withdrawal from the payer's account. This transfer is generally known in the cash-management trade as an **electronic depository transfer (EDT)**. An ACH can be thought of as an electronic DTC; it is generally slightly cheaper to use than a paper-based DTC.

The automated clearinghouse (ACH), a computerized clearing facility, makes a paperless transfer of funds between the payer and payee banks. An ACH settles accounts among participating banks; individual accounts are settled by respective bank balance adjustments. ACH transfers of this type generally clear in one day, offering significant advantages over the paper-based DTC.

For cash concentration, the concentration bank initiates an ACH debit and sends it to each deposit bank. Funds then move from the deposit bank into the concentration bank. These transfers can be automatically created from deposit information and can then be centrally initiated from the company's headquarters through its concentration bank. A large nationwide retailer can easily concentrate deposits from many small deposit banks into its concentration account by using the daily deposit information gathered from its stores' point-of-sale (POS) systems.

Wire Transfers. The third funds transfer mechanism is a **wire transfer**. In the United States, the primary wire transfer system, known as *Fedwire,* is run by the Federal Reserve System and is available to all depository institutions. A Fedwire transfer is an electronic communication that removes funds from the payer's bank and deposits the funds in the payee's bank on a same-day basis via bookkeeping entries in the financial institution's Federal Reserve account.

Wire transfers can eliminate mail float and clearing float and may reduce processing float as well. For cash concentration, the firm moves funds using a wire transfer from each deposit account to its concentration account. Wire transfers are a substitute for DTC and ACH debit transfers, but they are generally much more expensive, with both the sending and receiving banks charging significant fees for the transaction. Wire transfers are usually used only for high-dollar transfers, where the investment value of the funds outweighs the cost of the transfer.

Selecting the Best Transfer Mechanism. The firm must balance the benefits and costs of concentrating cash to determine the type and timing of transfers from its lockbox accounts to its concentration account. The transfer mechanism it selects should be the one that is most profitable (i.e., profit per period equals earnings on the increased funds' availability minus the cost of the transfer system). In general practice, most companies use wire transfers for large transfers of funds from lockbox deposits, and they use EDTs for high-volume, low-dollar transfers from small deposit banks.

APPLYING THE MODEL 23.2

To demonstrate alternative transfer methods, consider DJM Manufacturing, which needs to transfer $120,000 from its deposit account to its concentration account. It has two choices: an EDT with a total cost of $1, or a wire transfer with a total cost of $15. Because this would be a midweek transfer, the funds would be accelerated by one day using a wire transfer. (*Note:* A Friday transfer would represent three days of funds' acceleration.) The firm's opportunity cost for these funds is 7 percent.

In this example, the value of moving the funds via wire transfer is the one day of interest that could be earned if the funds arrived in the concentration account today rather than tomorrow. DJM calculates this amount to be $23.01 (0.07/365 × $120,000). Because the differential cost of wire transfer versus an EDT is $14 ($15 − $1), the company should use a wire transfer in this case because it would result in a net benefit of $9.01 ($23.01 − $14.00).

We could also determine the *minimum transfer amount* for which a wire transfer would be beneficial given the opportunity cost and transfer fees. We take the differential cost of a wire transfer ($14.00) and divide by the daily interest rate (0.07/365). In this case, it would be $73,000 [$14.00 ÷ (0.07/365)]. If DJM were transferring funds on a Friday and thus could earn three days of interest, the minimum transfer amount would be one third of the standard amount, or $24,333 ($73,000 ÷ 3).

Concept Review Questions

4. What is the firm's objective with regard to *collection float*? What are the common types of collection systems?

5. What are the benefits of using a *lockbox system*? How does it work? How can the firm assess the economics of a lockbox system?

6. Why do firms employ *cash concentration* techniques? What are some of the popular transfer mechanisms firms use to move funds from depository banks to their concentration banks?

7. How can the cash manager model the benefits and costs of various funds transfer mechanisms to assess their economics? How can he or she use this analysis to determine the *minimum transfer amount*?

23.3 ACCOUNTS PAYABLE AND DISBURSEMENTS

OVERVIEW OF THE ACCOUNTS PAYABLE PROCESS

The final component of the cash conversion cycle is the *average payment period (APP)*, which has two parts: (1) the time from the purchase of raw materials until the firm places the payment in the mail, and (2) payment float time (disbursement float). The payment float is the time it takes after the firm places its payment in the mail until the supplier has withdrawn funds from the firm's account. Section 23.1 discussed issues related to payment float time. In this section, we discuss the management of the time that elapses between the purchase of raw materials and mailing the payment to the supplier. This activity is called **accounts payable management.**

Purpose of the Accounts Payable Function. The primary purpose of the accounts payable (A/P) function is to examine all incoming invoices and determine the proper amount to be paid. As part of this process, the cash manager matches the invoice to both the purchase order and receiving information. The goal is to ensure that the goods/services were ordered by an authorized person and that they were actually received. As a result of this review, the accounts payable clerk may make adjustments to the invoiced amount for price or quantity differences.

Once payment has been authorized (sometimes referred to as "vouchering"), the cash manager is often responsible for the actual payment itself, either managing the preparation and mailing of checks or initiating the electronic transfer of funds. Companies usually pay multiple invoices with a single check. A company has the right to make full use of any credit period offered, but intentionally delaying payments or increasing disbursement float is considered an unethical cash-management practice.

Types of Payment Systems. The other issue involved with managing disbursements is the choice of a centralized or decentralized payables and payments system. In a *centralized system,* all invoices go to a central accounts payable department, which authorizes payment and initiates checks or other forms of payment. Centralized systems offer many advantages, including easier concentration of funds, improved access to cash position information, better control, and reduced transaction and administrative costs. There are, however, several problems with centralized payables, such as slow payment times (which could damage relationships with vendors or cause missed opportunities for cash discounts) and the need to coordinate between central payables and field offices/managers to resolve any disputes.

Some companies utilize a more *decentralized system* for payables and disbursements, wherein payments are authorized and, in some cases, initiated at the local level. Although this approach generally helps to improve relationships with vendors and enhance local management autonomy, it makes it harder to concentrate funds and obtain daily cash position information. It increases the chance of unauthorized disbursements.

CASH DISCOUNTS

In Chapter 22, we discussed *cash discounts* that suppliers offer to encourage customers to pay before the end of the credit period. Accounts payable with cash discounts have stated credit terms, such as *2/10 net 30*. This means the purchaser can take a *2 percent discount* from the invoice amount if the payment is made within *10 days* of the beginning of the credit period; otherwise, it must pay the full amount within *30 days* of the beginning of the credit period. The credit period begins at a specific date set by the supplier, typically either the end of the month in which the purchase is made (noted as *EOM*) or on the *date of the invoice.* Taking the discount is at the discretion of the purchaser.

When a firm is extended credit terms that include a cash discount, it has two options: (1) pay the full invoice amount at the end of the credit period, or (2) pay the invoice amount less the cash discount at the end of the cash discount period. In either case, the firm purchases the same goods. Thus, the difference between the payment amount without and with the cash discount is, in effect, the interest payment made by the firm to its supplier.

A firm in need of short-term funds must therefore compare the interest rate charged by its supplier to the best rate charged by providers of short-term financing (typically banks) and choose the lowest-cost option. This comparison is important: If the firm

takes the cash discount, it will shorten its average payment period and thus increase the amount of resources it has invested in operating assets, which will require additional negotiated short-term financing.

To calculate the relevant cost, we assume the firm will always render payment on the *final day of the specified payment period* (the credit period or cash discount period). Equation 23.2 presents the formula for calculating the interest rate, $r_{discount}$, associated with *not taking the cash discount and paying at the end of the credit period* when cash discount terms are offered:

$$r_{discount} = \frac{d}{(1-d)} \times \frac{365}{(CP - DP)} \qquad \text{(Eq. 23.2)}$$

where d = percent discount (in decimal form)

$\quad CP$ = credit period

$\quad DP$ = cash discount period

APPLYING THE MODEL 23.3

Assume that a supplier to Masson Industries has changed its terms from *net 30* to *2/10 net 30*. Masson has a line of credit with a bank, and the current interest rate on the line of credit is 6.75 percent per year. Should Masson take the cash discount or continue to use 30 days of credit from its supplier? The interest rate from the supplier is calculated using Equation 23.2:

$$r_{discount} = \frac{0.02}{(1 - 0.02)} \times \frac{365}{(30 - 10)} = 0.372 = 37.2\% \text{ per year}$$

Thus, the supplier is charging those customers not taking the cash discount an annualized rate of 37.2 percent, whereas the bank charges 6.75 percent. Masson should take the cash discount and obtain needed short-term financing by drawing on its bank line of credit.

DISBURSEMENT PRODUCTS AND METHODS

Zero-Balance Accounts. Zero-balance accounts (ZBAs) are disbursement accounts that always have an end-of-day balance of zero. The purpose is to eliminate nonearning cash balances in corporate checking accounts. A ZBA is often used as a disbursement account under a cash concentration system.

A ZBA works as follows: Once all of a given day's checks are presented to the firm's ZBA for payment, the bank notifies the firm of the total amount to be drawn, and the firm transfers funds into the account to cover the amount of that day's checks. This leaves an end-of-day balance in the ZBA of $0 (zero dollars). The firm keeps all operating cash in an interest-earning account, thereby eliminating idle cash balances. Thus, a firm that uses a ZBA in conjunction with a cash concentration system would need two accounts. The firm would concentrate its cash from the lockboxes into an interest-earning account and write checks against its ZBA. In many cases, the funding of the ZBA is made automatically and only involves an accounting entry on the part of the bank.

A ZBA allows the firm to *maximize earnings on its cash balances by capturing the full float time on each check it issues*. The firm accomplishes this by keeping all of its cash in an interest-earning account instead of leaving nonearning balances in its checking account to later cover the checks the firm has written.

Banks offer a variety of products similar to ZBAs. Another common product that achieves the same goal as a ZBA is a *sweep account,* in which the bank "sweeps" account surpluses into the appropriate interest-earning vehicle and liquidates similar vehicles in order to cover account shortages when they occur. Many banks also offer *multitiered ZBAs* that segregate operating units in multidivisional companies, or different types of payments (payrolls, dividends, accounts payable). This type of account allows the cash manager to better control balances and funding of the master account and associated ZBAs, thus reducing excess balances and transfers.

Controlled Disbursement. Controlled disbursement is a bank service that provides early notification of checks that will be presented against a company's account on a given day. For most large cash management banks, the Federal Reserve Bank makes two presentments of checks to be cleared each day. A bank that offers controlled-disbursement accounts would get advance electronic notification from the Fed several hours prior to the actual presentment of the items. This allows the bank to let its controlled-disbursement customers know as early in the day as possible what will be presented to their accounts. This, in turn, allows customers to determine their cash position and make any necessary investment/borrowing decisions in the morning, before the checks are presented for payment. Controlled-disbursement accounts are often set up as ZBAs to allow for automatic funding through a company's concentration account.

Positive Pay. Positive pay is a bank service used to combat the most common types of check fraud. Given the availability of inexpensive computers, scanners, and printers, it is very easy to create excellent copies of corporate checks or change payees or amounts. The risk to a company issuing checks is that the bank might pay fraudulent items, and the fraud would not be revealed until the account is reconciled. In using a positive-pay service, when the checks are issued, the company transmits to the bank a check-issued file, designating the check number and amount of each item. The bank matches the presented checks against this file and rejects any items that do not match. It is important to note that several courts have ruled that positive pay is a "commercially reasonable" measure to prevent check fraud. This means that a company that does not use this service when available may find itself liable for fraudulent items accepted by its bank.

DEVELOPMENTS IN ACCOUNTS PAYABLE AND DISBURSEMENTS

Integrated Accounts Payable. Integrated accounts payable, also known as *comprehensive accounts payable,* provides a company with outsourcing of its accounts payable or disbursement operations. The outsourcing may be as minor as contracting with a bank to issue checks and perform reconciliations, or as major as outsourcing the entire payables function.

One of the most typical approaches to A/P outsourcing is to send a bank (or other financial service provider) a data file containing a listing of all payments to be made. The bank will maintain a vendor file for the company and send each vendor payment (in the preferred format) in accordance with the company's remittance advice.

Purchasing/Procurement Cards. Many companies are implementing **purchasing** (or **procurement**) **card programs** as a means of reducing the cost of low-dollar indirect purchases. Though companies have been using credit cards for travel and related expenses for many years, they have only recently begun using them to make routine purchases of supplies, equipment, or services. The firm issues purchasing cards to designated employees and limits both dollar amounts and vendors where the cards can be used.

Companies that have implemented such programs report significant cost savings from streamlining the purchasing process for low-cost items. The other advantage is that the firm can pay the issuer of the purchasing card in a single, large payment that consolidates many small purchases.

Imaging Services. Many disbursement services offered by banks and other vendors incorporate **imaging services** as part of the package. This technology allows both sides of the check, as well as remittance information, to be converted into digital images. The images can then be transmitted via the Internet or easily stored for future reference. Imaging services are especially useful when incorporated with positive pay services.

Fraud Prevention in Disbursements. In recent years, disbursement fraud, especially related to check payments, has increased significantly. Crooks can easily create fraudulent checks using inexpensive scanners, computers, and laser printers. As a result, fraud prevention and control have become even more important in the accounts payable and disbursement functions. Some of the common fraud prevention measures include the following:

- Written policies and procedures for creating and disbursing checks.
- Separating the various parts of check-issuance duties: approval, signing, and reconciliation.
- Using safety features on checks (microprinting, watermarks, tamper resistance, etc.).
- Setting maximum dollar limits and/or requiring multiple signatures on checks.
- Using positive-pay services.
- Increasing the use of electronic payment methods.

Concept Review Questions

8. What is the primary purpose of the accounts payable function? Describe the procedures used to manage accounts payable. What are the key differences between *centralized* and *decentralized* payables and payment systems?

9. When is it advantageous for a company to pay early and take an offered cash discount? Under what circumstance should the firm always take any offered cash discounts?

10. What is the difference between a *ZBA* and a *controlled disbursement* account? Are they direct substitutes?

11. What are some of the recent developments in the accounts payable and disbursements area? What role does new technology play in fraud prevention in disbursements?

23.4 SHORT-TERM INVESTING AND BORROWING

After determining the company's cash position, the cash manager will generally have either surplus funds to invest or deficit funds that create a need for short-term borrowing. Clearly, the goal is to earn relatively safe returns on short-term surpluses, and to borrow at reasonable cost to meet short-term deficits. This section reviews some of the key options available to the financial manager for investing short-term surpluses and borrowing to meet short-term deficits.

SHORT-TERM INVESTING

Making sure that the company has access to liquid assets when and where they are needed is one of the critical tasks for the cash manager. The primary form of liquidity will generally be a company's checking or demand deposit accounts at its banks. These accounts usually do not earn interest, and so the company should not hold excess balances in these accounts. To earn some type of short-term return, a company will hold some "near-cash" assets in the form of short-term investments, often labeled *marketable securities*. These investments may be either a source of reserve liquidity or a place to maintain temporary surplus funds.[2]

Because the short-term investments are essentially a substitute for cash, *providing liquidity* and *preserving principal* should be the primary concerns. Earning a competitive return is also a consideration; however, the cash manager should take care not to place the underlying principal at risk. Remember that the primary purpose of short-term investments is to maintain a pool of liquid assets as a substitute for cash, *not to generate profits* for the company. To this end, it is important that a company establish policies and guidelines for the management of short-term investments. These guidelines should clearly specify the purpose of the investment portfolio and provide recommendations and/or restrictions on acceptable investments and the amount of diversification.

Money Market Mutual Funds. Many large companies will manage their own portfolios of short-term investments, but most companies (especially small ones) use money market mutual funds as an alternative. **Money market mutual funds** are professionally managed portfolios that invest in the same types of short-term instruments in which cash managers invest. They may, in fact, offer even more flexibility and stability than a self-managed fund. Using these types of funds makes sense, especially when the costs of running and managing a short-term portfolio are considered.

In most cases, these funds set their *net asset value (NAV)* at a fixed $1 per share in order to preserve the principal value of the fund. As the value of the fund increases, the fund pays investors in additional shares rather than allowing the share price to increase. Commercial money market mutual funds are available from independent companies, as well as from most large banks.

Money Market Financial Instruments. Short-term financial instruments are primarily fixed-income securities issued in registered form (rather than bearer form). (Such financial instruments are often incorrectly called "marketable securities.") Many of these securities are also issued in *discount form*, meaning the investor pays less than face value for the security at the time of purchase and receives the face value at maturity. Table 23.1 lists the common securities used for money market investments.

U.S. Treasuries. *U.S. Treasury bills (T-bills)* are the benchmark of money market financial instruments. The U.S. government issues these short-term securities to finance its activities, and they appeal to a wide range of investors, both domestic and foreign. T-bills are backed by the "full faith and credit" of the U.S. government—making them essentially free of default risk—and they have a very active secondary market.

---

[2] *Temporary surplus funds* may result from ongoing operations, seasonal performance, sales of large assets, or proceeds from a large securities issue.

Table 23.1 Money Market Financial Instruments

U.S. Treasuries	Interest Basis	Maturity
Treasury bills (T-bills)	Discount	A few days to 26 weeks
Treasury notes (T-notes)	Interest-bearing	1–10 years
Treasury bonds (T-bonds)	Interest-bearing	10–30 years

Federal Agency Issues	Underlying Assets	Backing
Government National Mortgage Association (Ginnie Mae)	Home mortgages	Full faith and credit
Department of Veterans Affairs (Vinnie Mac)	VA home loans	Full faith and credit
Federal National Mortgage Association (Fannie Mae)	Home mortgages	GSE[a]—Implied federal backing
Federal Home Loan Mortgage Corporation	Home mortgages	GSE[a]—Implied federal backing
SLM Holding Corporation (Sallie Mae)	Student loans	Quasi-GSE[a]—Implied federal backing
Federal Farm Credit Banks Funding Corporation	Agricultural loans	GSE[a]—Implied federal backing
Farm Credit System Insurance Corporation	Insurer of Farm Credit Banks	GSE[a]—Implied federal backing
Central Bank for Cooperatives (CoBank)	Loans to agricultural cooperatives	GSE[a]—Implied federal backing
Federal Agricultural Mortgage Corporation (Farmer Mac)	Agricultural loans, rural real estate, and home mortgages	GSE[a]—Implied federal backing

Bank Financial Instruments	Special Features
Certificates of deposit— CDs (domestic)	Interest-bearing deposits at financial institutions in the U.S.; may be fixed rate or floating rate with maturities from 7 days to several years
Overnight sweep accounts	Interest-bearing accounts used for investing end-of-day surplus funds
Yankee CDs	Dollar-denominated CDs issued by U.S. branches of foreign banks
Eurodollar CDs	Dollar-denominated CDs issued by banks outside the U.S.
Eurodollar time deposits	Nonnegotiable, fixed-rate time deposits issued by banks outside the U.S., with maturities ranging from overnight to several years
Banker's acceptances	Negotiable short-term instruments used for trade finance
Bank notes	Unsecured or subordinated debt of the bank (not insured)

Corporate Obligations	Special Features
Commercial paper	Unsecured promissory notes issued by corporations; maturities from 1 to 270 days; usually sold on a discount basis and backed by a credit guarantee from a bank
Adjustable-rate preferred stock	Tax advantaged for corporate holders due to dividend exclusion rule; dividend rate adjusts to maintain stable pricing

Other Short-Term Investments	Special Features
Money market mutual funds	Available directly from funds or through banks
Asset-backed securities	Debt obligations issued by companies that are secured by assets such as receivables, credit card obligations, consumer finance loans, major retailers, and automobile companies
International money market investments	Short-term bills or notes issued by foreign governments, foreign commercial paper, or other types of interest-bearing deposits in foreign currencies
Repurchase agreements (repos)	A collateralized transaction between a securities dealer or bank and an investor; generally backed by Treasuries or agency securities

[a]GSE is a government-sponsored enterprise.

The government issues T-bills in weekly auctions on a discount basis with maturities of less than one year (usually 13 or 26 weeks). T-bills are available in minimum denominations of $1,000, but are generally traded in round lots of $1 million. Other Treasury instruments such as *Treasury notes* (*T-notes*) and *Treasury bonds* (*T-bonds*) are initially issued as long-term securities, but may be suitable for a short-term portfolio as they approach maturity.

All treasury securities are registered and issued in *book entry form* (a computer entry at the Federal Reserve Bank rather than a paper certification) and are exempt from state income taxes.

Federal agency issues. These instruments have some degree of federal government backing and are issued by either federal agencies or private, shareholder-owned companies known as *government-sponsored enterprises* (*GSEs*). Most of the agencies are securitized investments backed by home mortgages, student loans, or agricultural lending. Two of the agencies (Ginnie Mae and Vinnie Mac) are backed by the "full faith and credit" of the U.S. government. The rest are backed by the implied intervention of the government in the event of a crisis.

Bank financial instruments. U.S. and foreign banks issue short-term *certificates of deposit (CDs)* as well as *time deposits* and *banker's acceptances*. Many banks also offer money market mutual funds and sweep accounts in which their customers can invest short-term cash.

Corporate obligations. The primary corporate obligation in the short-term market is **commercial paper.** Highly-rated corporations typically issue this investment, which is structured as an unsecured promissory note with a maturity of less than 270 days. The short maturity allows for issuance without SEC registration, and commercial paper is usually sold to other corporations rather than the general public. Most issues are also backed by credit guarantees from a financial institution and sold on a discount basis, similar to T-bills.

The other corporate obligation used for short-term investments is **adjustable- rate preferred stock.** These stocks take advantage of the exclusion of dividends (of 70 percent or more) on stock in one corporation held by another corporation. In order to make this investment suitable for short-term holdings, the dividend rate paid on the stock is adjusted according to some rate index. This will stabilize the price, even if interest rates change during the 45-day holding period required to qualify for the dividend exclusion.

Yield Calculations for Discount Instruments (T-Bills or Commercial Paper).[3] The yield for short-term *discount investments* such as T-bills and commercial paper is typically calculated using algebraic approximations rather than more precise present value methods. In the case of a **discount investment**, the investor pays less than face value at the time of purchase, and then receives the face value of the investment at its maturity date. There are generally no interim interest or coupon payments during the course of holding such an investment.

Determining the yield of T-bills or commercial paper generally involves a two-step process. In most cases, the rate on the investment is expressed as the discount rate, which is used to compute the "dollar discount" and selling price for the instrument. For example, a one-year, $100,000 T-bill[4] sold at a 5 percent discount would

---

[3.] The calculations demonstrated in this section are the same ones we introduced in our discussion of bond valuation in Section 4.2 of Chapter 4. For convenience as well as custom, we present these formulas a bit differently here.

[4.] Although the U.S. government no longer issues T-bills in one-year maturities, we use a one-year T-bill here for computational convenience and clarity.

sell for $95,000 [$100,000 × (1 – 0.05)]. The investor would pay $95,000 today and receive $100,000 in one year at the maturity date. The yield on this investment would be approximately 5.26 percent ($5,000/$95,000). Though the calculations for a shorter-term investment are slightly more complicated, they follow the same basic approach. **Money market yield** (*MMY*) for discount instruments is calculated on a 360-day basis but must be converted to **bond equivalent yield** (*BEY*) to compare discount instruments to interest-bearing investments, such as bank CDs. The following example illustrates yield calculations.

APPLYING THE MODEL 23.4

We can use two steps to determine the yield on a 91-day, $1 million T-bill that is selling at a discount of 3.75 percent. Note that the convention in the discount market is to use 360 days when calculating the purchase price and money market yield.

Step 1: Calculate the dollar discount and purchase price.

Dollar discount = (face value × discount rate) × (days to maturity/360)

$$= (\$1,000,000 \times 0.0375) \times (91/360) = \$9,479.17$$

Purchase price = face value − dollar discount

$$= (\$1,000 − \$9,479.17) = \$990,520.83$$

Step 2: Calculate *MMY* and *BEY*.

Money market yield (*MMY*) = (dollar discount/purchase price)
$$\times (360/\text{days to maturity})$$

$$= (\$9,479.17/\$990,520.83)$$
$$\times (360/91) = \underline{\underline{3.786\%}}$$

Bond equivalent yield (*BEY*) = money market yield × (365/360)

$$= 3.786\% \times (365/360) = \underline{\underline{3.839\%}}$$

SHORT-TERM BORROWING

For many companies, two primary sources of liquidity that provide needed funds are short-term lines of credit and commercial paper programs. This is especially the case for companies in seasonal businesses in which large amounts of operating capital may be needed for only a few months of the year. The role of the cash manager in establishing short-term borrowing is to ensure that the company has credit facilities sufficient to meet short-term cash requirements. Obviously, these arrangements should provide maximum flexibility at a minimum cost.

Most short-term borrowing is done on a variable-rate basis, with rates quoted in terms of a base rate plus a spread. The spread is essentially an adjustment for the relative riskiness and overall creditworthiness of the borrower. The base rate and the spread are referred to as the **all-in-rate**.

Typical base rates include the *prime rate* and *LIBOR (London Interbank Offered Rate)*. The **prime rate** is the rate of interest the largest U.S. banks charge their best business borrowers for short-term loans. **LIBOR** is the rate that the most creditworthy international banks that deal in Eurodollars charge on interbank loans.

For bank lines of credit, lending agreements may require *commitment fees* (fees paid for the bank's agreement to make money available) and/or *compensating balance requirements* (minimum deposit balances that must be maintained by the borrower at the lending bank). These agreements may also be set up on a multiyear, revolving basis and may use current assets such as receivables or inventory as collateral. In any type of bank lending, most of the terms and conditions result from negotiations between the borrower and the bank.

The **effective borrowing rate (*EBR*)** on a bank line of credit is generally determined as the total amount of interest and fees paid, divided by the average usable loan amount. The bank then adjusts this rate for the actual number of days the loan is outstanding. A demonstration of this calculation follows.

APPLYING THE MODEL 23.5

We can determine the *effective borrowing rate, EBR,* on a one-year line of credit with the following characteristics:

CL = total credit line, $500,000
AL = average loan outstanding, $200,000
CF = commitment fee, 0.35 percent (35 basis points) on the *unused portion* of the line
IR = interest rate, 2.5 percent over LIBOR (LIBOR is assumed to be 5.75 percent), which equals 8.25 percent
No compensating balances required
Year basis, 365 days

$$EBR = \frac{(IR \times AL) + [CF \times (CL - AL)]}{AL} \times \frac{365}{\text{days loan is outstanding}}$$

$$= \frac{(0.0825 \times \$200,000) + [0.0035 \times (\$500,000 - \$200,000)]}{\$200,000} \times \frac{365}{365}$$

$$= \frac{(\$16,500) + (\$1,050)}{\$200,000} \times \frac{365}{365} = \frac{\$17,550}{\$200,000} \times 1 = \underline{\underline{8.775\%}}$$

The effective borrowing rate of 8.775 percent is about 50 basis points (0.50 percent) above the 8.25 percent interest rate as a result of the commitment fee paid on the unused portion of the line.

---

12. Why are *providing liquidity* and *preserving principal* the primary concerns in choosing short-term investments? What guidelines should a company include in its short-term investment policy?

13. What securities are considered the benchmark for money market financial instruments, and why? What are some of the popular non-U.S.-Treasury money market instruments?

14. What are the key base rates used in variable rate short-term borrowing? How do they factor into the *all-in-rate*? What other charges might be applicable to short-term borrowing? How do they affect the *effective borrowing rate (EBR)*?

Concept Review Questions

23.5 SUMMARY

- The cash manager's job is to manage the cash flow time line related to collection, concentration, and disbursement of the company's funds. Mail float and processing float are viewed the same from the perspectives of both the receiving party and the paying party. The third float component is availability float (to the receiving party) and clearing float (to the paying party). The receiving party's goal is to minimize collection float, whereas the paying party's goal is to maximize disbursement float.

- Cash managers are also responsible for financial relationships, cash flow forecasting, investing and borrowing, and information management. In large firms, they must manage the firm's cash position. In small firms, they set target cash balances based on transactions requirements and minimum balances set by their bank.

- In managing collections, the cash manager attempts to reduce collection float using various collection systems, such as field-banking systems, mail-based systems, and electronic systems. Large firms whose customers are geographically dispersed commonly use lockbox systems, although small firms can also benefit from them.

- Firms use cash concentration to bring lockbox and other deposits together into one bank, often a concentration bank. Firms often use depository transfer checks, automated clearinghouse (ACH) debit transfers—also known as electronic depository transfer (EDT), and wire transfers to transfer funds from the depository bank to the concentration bank.

- The objective for managing the firm's accounts payable is to pay accounts as slowly as possible without damaging the firm's credit rating. If a supplier offers a cash discount, a firm in need of short-term funds must determine the interest rate associated with not taking the discount and paying at the end of the credit period, and then compare it with its lowest-cost, short-term borrowing alternative. If it can borrow elsewhere at a lower cost, the firm should take the discount; otherwise, it should not take it.

- Financial managers use popular disbursement products and methods such as zero-balance accounts (ZBAs), controlled disbursement, and positive pay. Some of the key developments in accounts payable and disbursements are integrated accounts payable, use of purchasing/procurement cards, imaging services, and a number of fraud-prevention measures.

- The cash manager will hold near-cash assets in the form of short-term investments to earn a return on temporary excess cash balances. Companies should establish investment policies and guidelines for management of short-term investments.

- Small companies are likely to invest their short-term surpluses in money market mutual funds. Larger firms will invest in any of a variety of short-term, fixed-income securities, including U.S Treasuries, federal agency issues, bank financial instruments, and corporate obligations, such as commercial paper and adjustable-rate preferred stock. The yield on discount investments, such as T-bills and commercial paper, is typically approximated by calculating the money market yield (MMY) and converting it into a bond equivalent yield (BEY).

- Short-term borrowing can be obtained through the issuance of commercial paper, primarily by large firms, and through lines of credit. Most short-term borrowing is done at a rate quoted at a base rate—the prime rate or LIBOR—plus a spread reflecting the borrower's relative riskiness. The effective borrowing rate (EBR) captures both the interest costs and other fees associated with a short-term loan.

INTERNET RESOURCES

Note: *For updates to links, please go to the book's website at* http://smart.swcollege.com.

http://www.csfb.com (Credit Suisse First Boston)—Part of the Credit Suisse global banking corporation, which offers numerous cash management, investment, and lending services to its corporate customers

http://www.phoenixhecht.com—A site that contains a variety of cash and treasury management resources, including links to various areas such as payment systems, cash and treasury management, and electronic commerce

http://www.wellsfargo.com—The fifth-largest U.S. bank, which offers numerous commercial banking services, including business lending and leasing, cash management and treasury, and institutional investments

KEY TERMS

accounts payable management
adjustable-rate preferred stock
all-in rate
automated clearinghouse (ACH) debit transfer
availability float
bank account analysis statement
bond equivalent yield (*BEY*)
cash concentration
cash manager
cash-position management
clearing float
commercial paper
controlled disbursement
depository transfer check (DTC)
discount investment
effective borrowing rate (*EBR*)
electronic bill presentment and payment (EBPP)
electronic depository transfer (EDT)
electronic invoice presentment and payment (EIPP)

field-banking system
float
imaging services
integrated accounts payable
LIBOR
liquidity management
lockbox system
mail float
mail-based collection system
money market mutual funds
money market yield (*MMY*)
positive pay
prime rate
processing float
procurement card programs
purchasing card programs
target cash balance
wire transfer
zero-balance accounts (ZBAs)

QUESTIONS

23-1.   What is *float*? What are its four basic components? Which of these components is the same from both a collection and a payment perspective? What is the difference between *availability float* and *clearing float,* and from which perspective—collection or payment—is each relevant?

23-2.   What is *cash-position management*? What types of firms set a *target cash balance*? Why? What is a bank's purpose in requiring the firm to maintain a minimum balance in its checking account? How does this relate to a *bank account analysis statement*?

23-3.   What is the firm's goal with regard to cash collections? Describe each of the following types of collection systems:

a. Field-banking system
b. Mail-based collection system
c. Electronic system

23-4. What is a *lockbox system*? How does it work? Briefly describe the economics involved in performing a cost-benefit analysis of such a system.

23-5. Does a lockbox system favor riskier firms (i.e., higher cost of capital) or safer firms (i.e., lower cost of capital), assuming both types of firms benefit from equivalent float value reduction (*FVR*) and an equivalent cost for a lockbox system?

23-6. Briefly describe each of the following funds transfer mechanisms:

   a. Depository transfer check (DTC)
   b. Automated clearinghouse (ACH) debit transfer
   c. Wire transfer

   Why are wire transfers typically used only for high-dollar transfers?

23-7. What is the goal with regard to managing accounts payable as it relates to the *cash conversion cycle*? Briefly describe the process involved in managing the accounts payable function.

23-8. How can a firm in need of short-term financing decide whether or not to take a *cash discount* offered by its supplier? How would this decision change in the event the firm has no alternative source of short-term financing? How would it change for a firm that needs no additional short-term financing?

23-9. Briefly describe each of the following disbursement products/methods:

   a. Zero-balance accounts (ZBAs)
   b. Controlled disbursement
   c. Positive pay

   How does a ZBA relate to the firm's *target cash balance*?

23-10. Briefly describe each of the following developments in accounts payable and disbursements:

   a. Integrated accounts payable
   b. Purchasing/procurement cards
   c. Imaging services
   d. Fraud prevention in disbursements

23-11. What is the firm's goal in short-term investing? How does it use *money market mutual funds*? Describe some of the popular money market financial instruments in each of the following groups:

   a. U.S. Treasuries
   b. Federal agency issues
   c. Bank financial instruments
   d. Corporate obligations

23-12. How is interest paid on a *discount investment*? What is the *money market yield (MMY)*? How can the *MMY* be converted into a *bond equivalent yield (BEY)*?

23-13. How are the rates on short-term borrowing typically set? What role does either the *prime rate* or *LIBOR* play in this process? What is the *effective borrowing rate (EBR)*? How does the *EBR* differ from the stated *all-in-rate*?

PROBLEMS

SMART SOLUTIONS
See the problem and solution explained step-by-step at
SMARTFinance

Cash Management

▶ **23-1.** Nickolas Industries has daily cash receipts of $350,000. A recent analysis of the firm's collections indicated that customers' payments are in the mail an average of two days. Once received, the payments are processed in 1.5 days. After the payments are deposited, the receipts clear the banking system, on average, in 2.5 days. Assume a 365-day year.

   a. How much *collection float* (in days) does the firm have?
   b. If the firm's opportunity cost is 11 percent, would it be economically advisable for the firm to pay an annual fee of $84,000 for a lockbox system that reduces collection float by 2.5 days? Explain why or why not.

23-2. Gale Supply estimates that its customers' payments are in the mail for three days, and once received, they are processed in two days. After the payments are deposited in the firm's bank, the bank makes the funds available to the firm in 2.5 days. The firm estimates its total annual collections from credit customers, received at a constant rate, to be $87 million. Its annual opportunity cost of funds is 9.5 percent. Assume a 365-day year.

   a. How many days of *collection float* does Gale Supply have?
   b. What is the current annual dollar cost of Gale Supply's collection float?
   c. If the installation of an *electronic invoice presentment and payment (EIPP) system* would result in a four-day reduction in Gale's collection float, how much could the firm earn annually on this float reduction?
   d. Based on your findings in part (c), should Gale install the EIPP system if the system's annual cost is $85,000? Explain your recommendation.

23-3. NorthAm Trucking is a long-haul trucking company that serves customers all across the continental United States and in parts of Canada and Mexico. At present, staff at corporate headquarters in Bloomington, Indiana, handles all billing activities, from preparation to collection. The firm's bank, Hoosier National, records and deposits payments once a day. You have been hired to recommend ways to reduce collection float and thereby generate cost savings.

   a. Suggest and explain at least three specific ways that NorthAm could reduce its *collection float*.
   b. Assume your preferred recommendation will cut the collection float by four days. NorthAm bills $108 million per year. If collections are evenly distributed throughout a 365-day year and the firm's cost of short-term financing is 8 percent, what savings could the company achieve by implementing the suggestion?
   c. If the cost of implementing your recommendation is $100,000 per year, based on your finding in part (b), should NorthAm implement it?

Collections

23-4. A particular lockbox system costs $1.25 million annually. Based on a cost of capital of 18 percent, what is the minimum float value reduction (*FVR*) that provides a net benefit of zero? What is the *FVR* if the cost of capital is reduced to 15 percent? Assuming an *FVR* of $8.9 million, what cost of capital provides a net benefit of zero?

23-5. Firm A has annual revenues of $1.6 billion and can reduce its float by four days using a lockbox system. Due to A's significant risk, A has a high cost of capital of 22 percent. Firm B has annual revenues of $850 million and can reduce its float by three days using a similar lockbox system. Firm B is less risky than Firm A, as is revealed by B's cost of capital of 10 percent. Assuming the lockbox system costs $2 million, which firm benefits more from using the system? If the two firms merge, making it necessary to have only one lockbox system for the combined firm, how much is the net benefit of having the lockbox system under this circumstance?

23-6. Qtime Products believes that use of a lockbox system can shorten its accounts receivable collection period by four days. The firm's annual sales, all on credit, are $65 million, billed on a continuous basis. The firm can earn 9 percent on its short-term investments. The cost of the lockbox system is $57,500 per year. Assume a 365-day year.

    a. What amount of cash will be made available for other uses under the lockbox system?

    b. What net benefit (or cost) will the firm receive if it adopts the lockbox system? Should it adopt the proposed lockbox system?

23-7.   Quick Burger Inc., a national chain of hamburger restaurants, has accumulated a $27,000 balance in one of its regional collection accounts. It wishes to make an efficient, cost-effective transfer of $25,000 of this balance to its corporate concentration account, thus leaving a $2,000 minimum balance in the regional collection account. It has the following options:

Option 1: DTC at a cost of $1 and requiring four days to clear.
Option 2: EDT at a cost of $2.50 and requiring one day to clear.
Option 3: Wire transfer at a cost of $12 and clearing the same day (zero days to clear).

    a. If Quick Burger can earn 6 percent on its short-term investments, assuming a 365-day year, which of the options would you recommend to minimize the transfer cost?

    b. Compare Options 2 and 3, and determine the minimum amount the company would have to transfer in order for the wire transfer (Option 3) to be more cost-effective than the EDT (Option 2).

23-8.   Firm NBG is trying to determine under what circumstances a wire transfer is beneficial. The cost of a wire transfer is $20. If the transfer speeded up the deposit by three days, assuming an annual cost of capital of 12.34 percent, what is the minimum amount that would need to be transferred? If the wire transfer can only speed up deposits by one day, what is the minimum amount that would need to be transferred? NBG's analysis finds that its average daily cash inflows are $38,950 and that the inflows are reasonably steady throughout the week. Should NBG use wire transfers Monday through Thursday when the firm would gain one additional day in deposits? Should NBG use wire transfers on Fridays when the firm would gain three additional days in deposits? How do the answers to the last two questions change during the height of NBG's selling season in which daily average inflow increases to $89,456?

23-9.   Firm OPL has average daily cash inflows (Monday through Saturday) of $15,890, $13,267, $20.654, $24,956, $37,923, and $42,516, respectively. A wire transfer deposits money into a concentration account faster by one day if executed Monday through Thursday, and by three days if executed on a Friday. Assuming the additional cost of a wire transfer is $15.62 and OPL has a cost of capital of 16 percent annually, on which days should wire transfers be considered? (*Note:* Saturday inflows should be combined with Monday inflows because banks close too early on Saturday to recognize the cash inflow.)

Accounts Payable and Disbursements

23-10.   Assume a firm receives the following credit terms from six suppliers. Also assume a 365-day year.

Supplier 1:	2/10 net 50
Supplier 2:	1/10 net 30
Supplier 3:	2/10 net 150
Supplier 4:	3/10 net 60
Supplier 5:	1/10 net 45
Supplier 6:	1/20 net 80

    a. Determine the interest rate associated with not taking the cash discount and paying at the end of the credit period for each of the six suppliers' credit terms.

    b. In part (a), you calculated the interest rate associated with not taking the discount for each supplier's credit terms. Now you must decide whether to take the cash discount by paying within the discount period. To pay early, you will need to borrow from your firm's line of credit at the local bank. The interest rate on the line of credit is the prime rate plus 2.5 percent. You can get the most recent prime rate from the

Federal Reserve at http://www.federalreserve.gov/releases/h15/data.htm. For each supplier's terms, use the current prime rate to determine whether the firm should borrow from the bank or borrow from the supplier.

23-11. Access Enterprises is considering four possible suppliers of an important raw material used in its production process, all offering different credit terms. The products offered by each supplier are virtually identical. The following table shows the credit terms offered by these suppliers. Assume a 365-day year.

Supplier	Credit Terms
A	1/10 net 40
B	2/20 net 90
C	1/20 net 60
D	3/10 net 75

a. Calculate the interest rate associated with not taking the discount from each supplier.

b. If the firm needs short-term funds, which are currently available from its commercial bank at 11 percent, and if each of the suppliers is viewed *separately*, which, if any, of the suppliers' cash discounts should the firm not take? Explain why.

c. What impact, if any, would the fact that the firm could stretch its accounts payable (net period only) by 20 days from supplier A have on your answer in part (b) relative to this supplier?

23-12. Derson Manufacturing wishes to evaluate the credit terms offered by its four biggest suppliers of raw materials. The prime rate is 7.0 percent, and Derson can borrow short-term funds at a spread of 2.5 percent above the prime rate. Assume a 365-day year and that the firm always pays it suppliers on the last day allowed by their stated credit terms. The terms offered by each supplier are as follows:

Supplier 1:	2/10 net 40
Supplier 2:	1/15 net 60
Supplier 3:	3/10 net 70
Supplier 4:	1/10 net 50

a. Calculate the interest rate associated with not taking the discount from each supplier.

b. Assuming the firm needs short-term financing and considering each supplier separately, indicate whether the firm should take the discount from each supplier.

c. If the firm did not need any short-term financing, when should it pay each of the suppliers?

d. If the firm could not obtain a loan from banks and other financial institutions and needed short-term financing, when should it pay each of the suppliers?

e. What impact, if any, would the fact that Derson could stretch its accounts payable (net period only) from Supplier 1 to day 90 without damaging its credit rating have on your recommendation in part (b) with regard to Supplier 1? Explain your answer.

23-13. Union Company is examining its operating cash management. One of the options the firm is considering is a *zero-balance account (ZBA)*. The firm's bank is offering a ZBA with monthly charges of $1,500, and the bank estimates that the firm can expect to earn 8 percent on its short-term investments. Determine the minimum average cash balance that would make this ZBA a benefit to the firm. Assume a 365-day year.

Short-Term Investing and Borrowing

23-14. Treasury bills (face value of $10,000) with maturities of 30 days, 90 days, and 180 days sell at the following annualized discounts: 4.25%, 4.35%, and 4.92%, respectively. What are the respective money market yields for these T-bills? What are the respective bond equivalent yields for these T-bills?

SMART
SOLUTIONS
See the problem and
solution explained
step-by-step at
SMARTFinance

23-15. Suppose short-term discounts on Treasury bills are "flat" and set at 3.90% APR for all maturities. Examining 30-day, 180-day, and 360-day T-bills, determine if the money market yields and bond equivalent yields are also "flat."

23-16. Sager Inc. just purchased a 91-day, $1 million T-bill that was selling at a discount of 3.25 percent.

  a. Calculate the dollar discount and purchase price on this T-bill.
  b. Find the *money market yield (MMY)* on this T-bill.
  c. Find the *bond equivalent yield (BEY)* on this T-bill.
  d. Rework parts (a), (b), and (c) assuming the T-bill was selling at a 3.0 percent discount. What effect does this drop of 25 basis points in the T-bill discount have on its *BEY*?

23-17. Rosa Inc. has arranged a one-year, $2 million credit line with its lead bank. The bank set the interest rate at the prime rate plus a spread of 1.50 percent. The prime rate is expected to remain stable at 5.25 percent during the coming year. In addition, the bank requires Rosa to pay a 0.50 percent commitment fee on the average unused portion of the line. Assume a 365-day year.

  a. Calculate the *effective borrowing rate (EBR)* on Rosa's line of credit during the coming year assuming an average loan balance outstanding during the year is $1.8 million.
  b. Calculate Rosa's *EBR* on the line of credit during the coming year assuming the average loan balance outstanding during the year is $0.8 million.
  c. Compare and contrast the *EBR*s calculated for Rosa Inc. in parts (a) and (b). Explain the causes of the differences in *EBR*s.

23-18. Matthews Manufacturing is negotiating a one-year credit line with its bank, Worldwide Bank. The amount of the credit line is $6.5 million with an interest rate set at 1.5 percent above the prime rate. The bank will charge a commitment fee of 0.50 percent (50 basis points) on the unused portion of the line. No compensating balances are required, and the loan is made on a 365-day basis.

  a. If the prime rate is assumed constant at 4.25 percent during the term of the loan and Matthews' average loan outstanding during the year is $5.0 million, calculate the firm's *effective borrowing rate (EBR)*.
  b. What effect would an increase in the prime rate to 4.75 percent for the entire year have on Matthews' *EBR* calculated in part (a)?
  c. What effect would a decrease in Matthews' average loan outstanding during the year to $4.0 million have on the *EBR* calculated in part (a)?
  d. Using your findings in parts (a), (b), and (c), compare, contrast, and discuss the effects of interest rate changes versus changes in the average loan outstanding on Matthews' effective borrowing rates.

23-19. Firm MGST is reviewing its one-year line of credit, currently set at 9.15% APR. The credit line is for $1 million, but the firm only tends to use half of it throughout the year. The commitment fee is 42 basis points. Calculate MGST's effective borrowing rate *(EBR)*. MGST is considering lowering the credit line to $0.7 million. The commitment fee increases to 55 basis points, but the interest rate lowers to 9.00% APR. Should MGST lower the credit line based on *EBR*?

23-20. Firm JJBT is considering two types of one-year credit lines. Plan A has a fixed rate of 8.25% APR with a commitment fee of 30 basis points. Plan B has a floating rate set 3 percent above the prime rate (currently 4.75%), with a commitment fee of 45 basis points. JJBT tends to average $450,000 in loans throughout the year, but would like the line of credit to be $750,000. Calculate the effective borrowing rate *(EBR)* for both plans under current conditions. Next, determine the prime rate that sets both plans to the same *EBR*. Assuming you believe the prime rate will not increase to more than 5.10% over the next year, which credit line would you choose and why? Determine if your answer would change based on a credit line of $500,000 rather than $750,000.

23-21. Using the Statement of Cash Flows, analyze the short-term borrowing of Dell (ticker symbol, Dell), Wal-Mart (ticker symbol, WMT), Ford (ticker symbol, F), and Monster Worldwide (ticker symbol, MNST). Which firms have increased and which have decreased their reliance on short-term borrowing relative to total assets? Can you explain why some of these firms might rely more or less on short-term borrowing relative to assets?

23-22. Using the common-size balance sheets, analyze the cash and short-term investments of Dell (ticker symbol, Dell), Wal-Mart (ticker symbol, WMT), Ford (ticker symbol, F), and Monster Worldwide (ticker symbol, MNST). Which firms have increased and which firms have decreased their cash and short-term investments relative to total assets? Can you explain why some of these firms might need more or less cash relative to assets?

MINI-CASE: LIQUIDITY MANAGEMENT

Foah's Designs sells precious metal jewelry throughout the western half of the United States. It is based in Yakima, Washington and currently all customers mail their payments to the Yakima office. The average amount of float is 6.5 days. The firm is considering implementing a lockbox system in Los Angeles. Total annual sales that are expected to be routed to the Los Angeles lockbox are $68,000,000, with an average check amount of $1,300. The lockbox system would be administered by California State Bank, which will charge a $0.25 fee per check and an annual fixed charge of $10,000. Foah's Designs has a cost of capital of 12% per year, and the lockbox is expected to reduce float to 4 days. However, there is some chance that the lockbox will only reduce float to 5 days.

The firm must also decide between using EDT or wire transfers when transferring funds between California State Bank and their local bank, Yakima State Bank. Using the wire transfer method would cost $20 per transfer while the EDT method would cost only $1.50 per transfer. However, the wire transfer method would result in the funds arriving at Yakima State Bank one day sooner.

Foah's Designs is also faced with a decision concerning its accounts payable. Foah's purchases its inventory from Jewelry Findings, Inc. on credit. Jewelry Findings' terms of trade are 3/15 net 45 and Foah's Designs normally pays after exactly 45 days. However, it has been considering accessing a line of credit from Yakima State Bank to pay its accounts payable after exactly 15 days instead. The commitment fee on the unused portion of the credit line is 0.3%, and the interest rate on the loan from Yakima State Bank is 8.9%. There are no compensating balance requirements. Use a 365-day year.

1. Should Foah's Designs implement the lockbox system?

2. If Foah's Designs plans to transfer money on a weekly basis (every Tuesday) from California State Bank to Yakima State Bank, which transfer method should it use, assuming it could earn 0.5% on its funds in Yakima State Bank over and above what it earns from California State Bank?

3. Assuming Foah's Designs has a line of credit of $2,000,000 and its accounts payable average $1,417,000, determine whether the firm should continuing paying Jewelry Findings, Inc. after 45 days or if it should begin accessing the line of credit from Yakima State Bank.

PART 8: Special Topics

In this section we take a look at two special topics. Chapter 24 covers one of the most exciting areas of finance—mergers, acquisitions, and corporate governance. Historically, mergers have come in waves, with a huge volume of merger transactions occurring in some years, and very few mergers in others. And the same statement can be made looking across countries rather than across time. In the United States, mergers and acquisitions are simply part of the economic landscape. Managers know that engaging in a merger is one strategic choice open to them, and they also know if they do not make choices that increase shareholder wealth, they themselves may become the target of a takeover attempt. In this chapter, we study some of the motivations for mergers and the tactics that firms use to buy other firms or to defend against unwanted bids.

We conclude this text by discussing the future of finance in Chapter 25. Naturally, this will be a highly speculative undertaking, but we try to predict how the theory and practice of corporate finance will change over the four-decade working career of most of this book's readers. Several mega-trends can be observed in the business world today, such as the economic rise of the BRIC countries (Brazil, Russia, India, and China) and the financial challenge of providing adequate pensions to industrialized nations' citizens at affordable cost. Other forces likely to influence the evolution of financial practice can be identified from the academic literature. These include incorporating option pricing more fully into corporate capital budgeting processes, understanding why investors are reluctant to invest outside of their home countries, developing financial instruments that allow firms and individuals to hedge the most important life and business risks (such as an individual's home value or a firm's base profits), and identifying once and for all exactly which systematic risk factor is actually priced in corporate securities' markets.

State-Controlled Chinese Oil Company Bids against Chevron for Union Oil of California

Takeover contests are frequently dramatic events, but few ever generate as much passion and controversy as the long battle between Chevron Corporation and the China National Overseas Oil Company (CNOOC) for control of Union Oil of California (Unocal). This saga began as many corporate control contests do, with a report (in the January 6, 2005, issue of the *Financial Times*—FT) that CNOOC's managers were considering making a bid for Unocal, which then had a market value of about $11 billion, plus $4.6 billion in net debt outstanding. CNOOC's motivation was clear: The Chinese economy's breakneck growth was fueling rapidly rising demand for petroleum products, and CNOOC hoped to acquire Unocal to gain control over the U.S. firm's Asian oil and gas reserves. FT reported that the Chinese firm was contemplating making a $13 billion offer for Unocal, which would be by far the largest overseas acquisition ever attempted by a mainland Chinese company.

The FT report had enormous impact, both on CNOOC and on Unocal. News of CNOOC's interest put Unocal "in play," causing most of the major international oil companies to weigh their own possible bids for the firm. Ironically, CNOOC's nonexecutive directors, peeved at having been kept out of the decision-making loop, voted against allowing CNOOC to formally make a bid in January. This was a decision the directors would come to regret and reconsider five months later.

After much media speculation—and after extensive negotiations with Unocal's managers—Chevron Corporation (which was called ChevronTexaco at the time) announced a $16 billion cash and share bid for Unocal on April 4, 2005. Even though this combination between two of the largest U.S. oil companies would certainly face regulatory scrutiny on antitrust grounds, Unocal managers supported the proposed merger. It soon emerged that Unocal agreed to pay Chevron a $500 million breakup fee in the event the deal was to be canceled, and Chevron agreed to pay Unocal executives benefits worth $108.7 million in the event the deal was to be completed. Both agreements are fairly common in American takeover deals. The two companies then set out to win regulatory approval for their merger so that the proposal could be submitted to a shareholder vote by August. The two American agencies responsible for approving large mergers, the Federal Trade Commission and the Securities and Exchange Commission, quickly approved the proposed deal, without significant conditions.

Frustrated at seeing its prize slipping away, CNOOC reentered the fray by launching its own $18.5 billion all-cash offer of $67 per share for Unocal on June 22, 2005. Stock market investors responded enthusiastically to CNOOC's bid, bidding up both its shares and those of Unocal—which had fallen by 7 percent during the month since Chevron's bid was announced. Unocal managers responded cautiously, reiterating their preference for completing the deal with Chevron but also expressing interest in talking further with CNOOC. In fact, had shareholders been the only parties besides regulators with a say in the outcome of this takeover battle (as is usually the case), CNOOC might well have prevailed. However, the prospect of a state-controlled Chinese company acquiring a major American oil producer hit a political nerve. In response, the U.S. Congress held hearings on CNOOC's bid; in late July Congress passed an amendment to an energy bill requiring three government agencies (the State, Defense, and Energy Departments) all to report on the proposed acquisition's national security implications before CNOOC's offer would be allowed to become effective. The energy bill's passage in early August, coupled with a decision by Chevron to raise its bid for Unocal to $64 per Unocal share ($17.3 billion total), sealed the fate of CNOOC's bid. The Chinese company formally withdrew its offer on August 2, and Unocal's shareholders voted in favor of accepting Chevron's sweetened offer eight days later.

Source: Financial Times, *various issues.*

Corporations have emerged as the modern world's single most powerful and productive economic organizations. As corporate power has grown, so has interest in ensuring that these institutions operate in a socially constructive manner that benefits both the firm's private owners and society at large. Corporate governance is the term describing the set of laws, practices, and institutions that determine how— and in whose interests—corporations headquartered in a particular country are operated. This chapter will describe corporate governance practices in the United States and in other important countries. We begin by examining how corporate control is exercised over American corporations.

As its name implies, **corporate control** refers to the monitoring, supervision, and direction of a corporation or other business organization. The most common change in corporate control results from the combination of two or more business entities into a single organization, as happens in a merger or acquisition. A change in corporate control also occurs with the consolidation of voting power within a small group of investors, as found in going-private transactions such as leveraged buyouts (LBOs) and management buyouts (MBOs). Transfer of ownership of a business unit with a divestiture and the creation of a new corporation through a spin-off are other ways to bring about such a change.

The forces effecting changes in corporate control and the resulting impact on the business community present some of the most interesting and hotly contested debates in the field of finance. For example, the corporate control contest for RJR Nabisco captivated corporate America in the fall of 1988, spawned a book and a movie about the takeover, and remains a source of debate for academics and politicians over the social benefit of corporate control activities. We address the causes and consequences of changes in corporate control in this chapter as well as provide real-world examples of the merger/acquisition process and the technical aspects a corporate manager must consider before making decisions regarding corporate control changes.

24.1 OVERVIEW OF CORPORATE CONTROL ACTIVITIES

You probably understand what the terms *mergers and acquisitions* and *M&As* mean in general. However, the terminology of corporate control is far more expansive than these generic terms indicate. For instance, the popular press often uses the term *takeover* to conjure up images of an unwelcome bidder commandeering control of a corporation through the techniques of high finance and the means of great sums of money. A **takeover,** however, simply refers to any transaction in which the control of one entity is taken over by another. Thus, a friendly merger negotiated between the boards of directors and shareholders of two independent corporations is a takeover, as is a successful entrepreneur selling out her enterprise to a corporation. The terminology of corporate control can be easily misconstrued and must be clearly defined to prevent such ambiguities. In the following discussion, we will define the many terms and concepts encountered in the corporate control arena.

CORPORATE CONTROL TRANSACTIONS

Changes in corporate control occur through several mechanisms, most notably via acquisitions. An **acquisition** is the purchase of additional resources by a business enterprise. These resources may come from the purchase of new assets, the purchase of some of the assets of another company, or the purchase of another whole business entity, which is known as a merger. **Merger** is itself a general term applied to a transaction in which two or more business organizations combine into a single entity. Often, however, the term *merger* is reserved for a transaction in which one corporation takes over another upon the approval of both companies' boards of directors and shareholders after a friendly and mutually agreeable set of terms and conditions and a price are negotiated. Payment is in the form of an exchange of common stock. In actuality, there are many different types of mergers, and they (as well as other corporate control activities) can be differentiated according to several criteria. We define mergers by the mode of target integration used by the acquiring firm, by the level of business concentration created by the merger, and by other transaction characteristics for which mergers are commonly known.

There are a number of ways to integrate the assets and resources of an acquired firm into the acquiring company (the acquirer). The following discussion describes the various forms of resource integration that may be used to combine the resources of an acquirer and target.

Statutory Merger. A **statutory merger** is a form of target integration in which the acquirer can absorb the target's resources directly, with no remaining trace of the target as a separate entity. Many intrastate bank mergers are of this form.

Subsidiary Merger. Conversely, an acquirer may wish to maintain the identity of the target as either a separate subsidiary or division. A **subsidiary merger** is often the integration vehicle when there is brand value in the name of the target, such as the January 2005 acquisition of Molson by Adolph Coors, to form Molson Coors Brewing. Sometimes, separate "tracking" or "target" shares are issued in the subsidiary's name. Sometimes, these shares are issued as new common shares in exchange for the target's common shares, as occurred when General Motors issued new Class E and Class H shares to acquire, respectively, Electronic Data Systems and Hughes Electronics during the 1980s. Alternatively, a new class of preferred stock may be issued by the bidding firm to replace the common shares of the target as well.

Consolidation. **Consolidation** is another integrative form used to effect a merger of two publicly traded companies. Under this form, both the acquirer and target disappear as separate corporations and combine to form an entirely new corporation with new common stock. This form of integration is common in mergers of equals, where the market values of the acquirer and target are similar. Many of these new corporations adopt a name that is merely a hybrid of the former names, such as the 2001 consolidation of Chevron and Texaco to become ChevronTexaco. But some managers of newly created companies want a "fresh start" with a company name. Perhaps the most important recent example of this occurred in 2000, when the Amsterdam Stock Exchange, the Paris Bourse, and the Brussels Stock Exchange merged to form Euronext.

LBOs, MBOs, and Dual-Class Recapitalizations

Changes in corporate control also occur when voting power is concentrated in the hands of one individual or a small group. Going-private transactions are one way to achieve this concentration of control. Just as they sound, **going-private transactions** transform public corporations into private companies through issuance of large amounts of debt used to buy all (or at least a voting majority) of the outstanding shares of the corporation. The acquiring party may be a leveraged-buyout (LBO) firm, such as Kohlberg, Kravis, and Roberts (KKR), which specializes in such deals; the current managers of the corporation (known as a **management buyout,** or **MBO**); or even the employees of the corporation itself through an **employee stock ownership plan (ESOP)**. A prime example of both an LBO and an MBO attempt is the 1988 corporate control contest for RJR Nabisco. H. Ross Johnson, the CEO of RJR Nabisco, led a management team that attempted to take the company private but was outbid by KKR in a $29 billion LBO.[1] An LBO that sells shares to the public again in a second initial public offering is known as a **reverse LBO.**

A **dual-class recapitalization** may also concentrate control. Under this form of organizational restructuring, the parties wishing to concentrate control (usually management) buy all the shares of a newly issued Class B stock, which carries "super" voting rights (100 votes per share, for example). Traditional Class A shareholders generally receive some form of compensation, such as higher dividends, for the dilution of their voting power. Dual-class companies are uncommon in the United States, but, as described in Nenova (2003), these are very common in other countries. The higher stock price typically assigned to the share class with superior voting rights, often called the *voting premium,* has been used as a measure for the private benefits of control in a publicly traded firm.[2]

Tender Offers, Acquisitions, and Proxy Fights

An acquirer can also attain control of a public corporation through a nonnegotiated purchase of the corporation's shares in the open market or through the voting control of other stockholders' shares via proxy. Theoretically, an acquirer can gain control simply through open-market purchases of a target firm's shares, though regulation severely restricts this form of "creeping acquisition" in most developed countries. Generally, an acquirer must explicitly bid for control through a tender offer for shares. A **tender offer** is a structured purchase of the target's shares in which the acquirer announces a public offer to buy a minimum number of shares at a specific price. Inter-

---

[1.] For an insightful and entertaining look at this deal, as well as the LBO/MBO process, see Burroughs and Helyar, (1993).

[2.] Dyck and Zingales (2004) define private benefits of control as "the proportion of a firm's value that does not accrue to all shareholders on a per-share basis, but is instead captured by inside shareholders." They find considerable variation in control premiums—higher prices paid for purchases of controlling versus noncontrolling share stakes—among the 39 countries they study. Twelve countries (including the English common law countries of Australia, Britain, Canada, South Africa, and the United States) had control premiums of 2 percent or less, but 10 had premiums of more than 25 percent, with Brazil's 65 percent premium being the highest.

ested stockholders may then "tender" their shares at the offer price. If at least the minimum number of shares is tendered, then the acquirer buys those shares at the offer price. The acquirer has the option of buying the shares tendered at the offer price or canceling the offer altogether if the minimum number of shares is not tendered.[3] A two-tiered offer results when the acquirer offers to buy a certain number of shares at one price and then more shares at another price. These offers are especially popular in situations where the acquirer wishes to purchase 100 percent of the shares outstanding as quickly as possible and offers to buy 51 percent at a higher price and the remaining 49 percent at a lower price in an attempt to provide an incentive for shareholders to tender their shares early in order to receive the higher price. A **tender-merger** is a merger that occurs after an acquirer secures enough voting control of the target's shares through a tender offer to effect a merger. Figure 24.1 presents the total number (Panel A) and value (Panel B) of mergers and acquisitions in the United States between January 1962 and July 2005.

Tender offers are often associated with hostile takeovers, but these are the highly publicized minority cases. In fact, Bhagat, Dong, Hirshleifer, and Noah (2005) find that target management resisted only 221 of the 1,018 attempted tender offers (21.7 percent) for publicly traded U.S. companies from 1962 through 2001. If mergers are included with tender offers, the fraction of all acquisitions that are hostile is truly small. Andrade, Mitchell, and Stafford (2001) find that only 8.3 percent of the 4,256 completed takeovers of U.S. companies between 1973 and 1998 were hostile at any point—and the hostile bidder was ultimately successful in over half of these cases. They also show that hostile takeovers peaked during the 1980s, when 14.3 percent were hostile at some point, but this fraction dropped to only 4.0 percent during the 1990s. Hostile takeovers are even rarer in other countries than in the United States. Rossi and Volpin (2004) show only 1.01 percent of the 45,686 mergers and acquisitions announced between January 1, 1990, and December 31, 1999 (and completed by December 31, 2002), were opposed by target firms, and America's 6.44 percent hostile fraction was the highest of the 49 countries studied.

Yet open-market purchases, tender offers, and proxy fights may all be used in combination to launch a "surprise attack" on an unwitting (and often unwilling) target. In the United States, individuals or corporations may own up to 5 percent of any corporation's stock before facing the requirement of filing a Schedule 13-d form with the Securities and Exchange Commission (SEC) identifying themselves as a significant stockholder in the company. Thus, an interested potential acquirer could accumulate a substantial number of shares (known as a *foothold*) without the knowledge of the target's management and then follow a number of acquisition strategies. Target firms employ defensive measures, such as **antitakeover amendments** to their corporate charters (also known as **shark repellents**), **poison pills,** the pursuit of **white knights** ("friendly" acquirers who will top the price of an unwelcome bidder), MBOs, stock buybacks, and payment of greenmail (see Footnote 5), among other defensive tactics.[4] Comment and Schwert (1995) show that 87 percent of U.S.-listed firms had some type of takeover defense in place by the early 1990s. Table 24.1 describes the most important antitakeover defenses.[5]

[3.] The U.S. tender offer process is strictly regulated by the Williams Act, an amendment to the Securities and Exchange Act. See the discussion of the Williams Act in Section 24.5 for more details on the regulation of tender offers.

[4.] *Poison pills* are takeover defenses that can be triggered unilaterally by the target firm's board and effectively make a hostile takeover prohibitively expensive to the potential acquirer. These are typically adopted *without* shareholder approval.

[5.] One notorious practice that was fairly common during the 1980s was for a corporate "raider" to accumulate a large block of share and then threaten the target with a hostile tender offer and/or proxy fight in order to force the board of directors to repurchase the raider's shares at a premium price. This became known as **greenmail**, and it is now outlawed in many states and taxed heavily by the Internal Revenue Service.

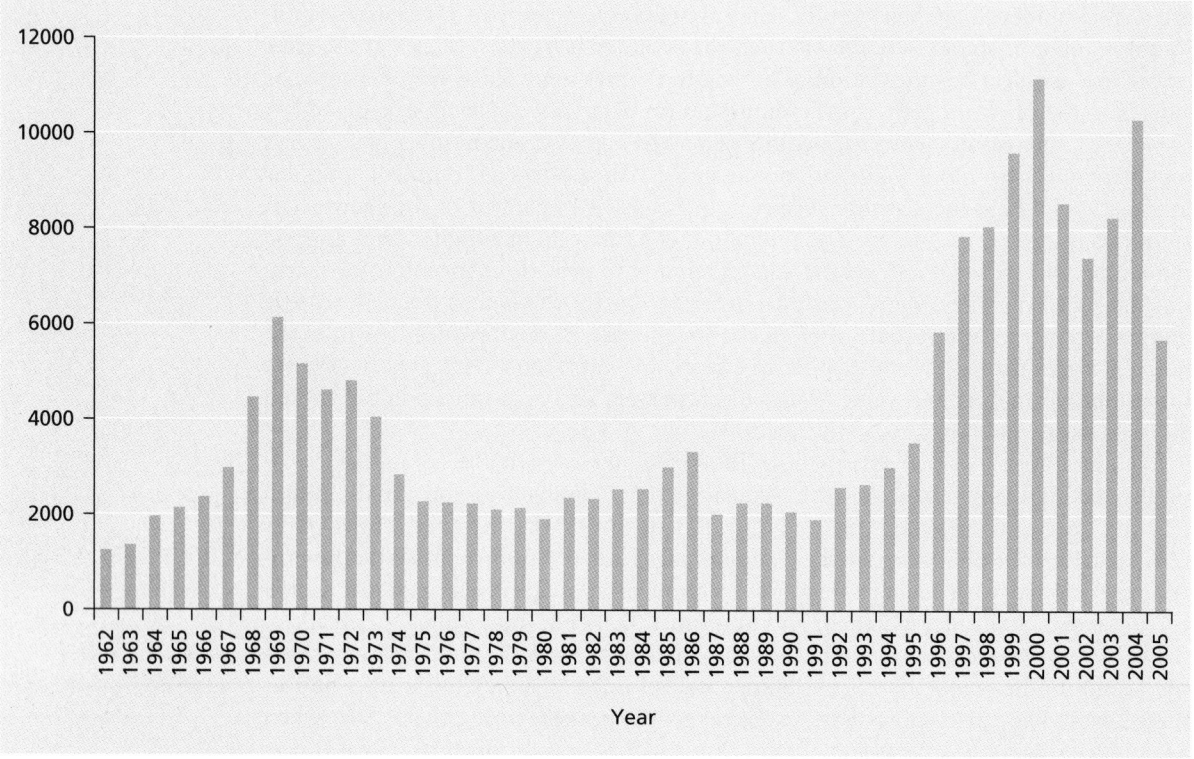

Figure 24.1
Panel A: Merger and Acquisition Activity in the United States, Number of Deals, 1962–2005
Panel B: Merger and Acquisition Activity in the United States, Total Value of Deals ($ Billion), 1968–2005
Source: Mergerstat (downloaded from www .mergerstat.com).

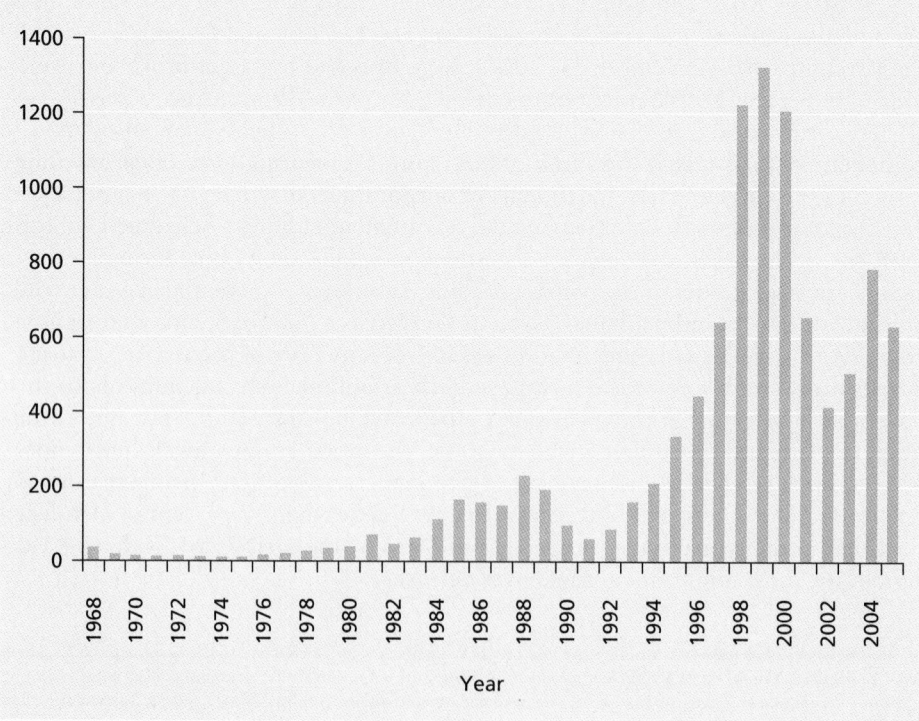

Table 24.1
Commonly Used
Antitakeover Measures

Measure	Antitakeover Effect
Fair price amendments	Corporate charter amendments mandating that a "fair price," usually defined as the highest price paid to any shareholder, be paid to all of the target firm's shareholders in the event of a takeover
Golden parachutes	Large termination arrangements made for executives that are activated after a takeover
Greenmail	The payment of a premium price for the shares held by a potential hostile acquirer but not paid to all stockholders
Just-say-no defense	Refusal to entertain a takeover offer on the grounds that no consideration offered is sufficient to relinquish control
Pac-Man defense	The initiation of a takeover attempt for the hostile acquirer itself
Poison pills	Dilution of the value of shares acquired by a hostile bidder through the offer of additional shares to all other existing shareholders at a discounted price
Poison puts	Deterrent to hostile takeovers through put options attached to bonds that allow the holders to sell their bonds back to the company at a prespecified price in the event of a takeover
Recapitalization	A change in capital structure designed to make the target less attractive.
Staggered director elections	Corporate charter amendments designed to make it more difficult for an hostile acquirer to replace the board of directors with persons sympathetic to a takeover
Standstill agreements	Negotiated contracts that prevent a substantial shareholder from acquiring more shares for a defined period of time
Supermajority approvals	Corporate charter amendments that require the approval of large majorities (67% or 80%) for a takeover to occur
White knight defense	The pursuit of a friendly acquirer to take over the company instead of a hostile acquirer
White squire defense	The sale of a substantial number of shares to an entity that is sympathetic to current management but has no intention of acquiring the firm

DIVESTITURES AND SPIN-OFFS

Sometimes, managers prefer to transfer control of certain assets and resources through divestitures, spin-offs, split-offs, equity carve-outs, split-ups, or bust-ups. A **divestiture** occurs when the assets and/or resources of a subsidiary or division are sold to another organization. The sale by Vivendi of its Universal Studios to General Electric in early 2004 is an important example of a divestiture.

In a **spin-off,** a parent company creates a new company with its own shares by spinning off a division or subsidiary. Existing shareholders receive a pro rata distribution of shares in the new company. This happened when PepsiCo spun off its restaurant operations (Pizza Hut, Taco Bell, and KFC) in 1997 as a new company named Tricon Global Restaurants (with the catchy ticker symbol YUM). A **split-off** is similar to a spin-off, in that a parent company creates a newly independent company from a subsidiary, but ownership of the company is transferred to only certain existing shareholders in exchange for their shares in the parent. *Equity carve-outs* (described more fully in Chapter 16) bring a cash infusion to the parent through the sale of a partial interest in a subsidiary through a public offering to new stockholders. Split-ups and bust-ups are the ultimate transfers of corporate control. As it sounds, the **split-up** of a corporation is the split-up and sale of all its subsidiaries so that it ceases to exist (except possibly as a holding company with no assets). A **bust-up** is the takeover of a company that is subsequently split up.

Concept Review Questions	**1.** Why are acquired resources integrated into a company in so many different forms? What transaction-specific circumstances might lead to a preference of one integrative form over another?
	2. How does a tender offer differ from a proxy fight? Why might these two corporate control actions be considered different ways to achieve the same objective?

24.2 HORIZONTAL, VERTICAL, AND CONGLOMERATE MERGERS

Mergers may also be classified by the relatedness of the business activities of the merging firms. There are several different classification schemes utilized for the business relatedness of the acquiring and acquired firms, but the most commonly applied scheme is the abbreviated classification offered by the Federal Trade Commission (FTC). In the following paragraphs, we define these FTC classifications as well as others that are used and introduce their importance to our eventual discussion of antitrust laws.

HORIZONTAL MERGERS

In a strict sense, the FTC defines a **horizontal merger** as a combination of competitors within the same geographic market; the commission defines a **market extension merger** as a combination of firms that produce the same product in different geographic markets. As interstate commerce and technology have rendered geographic market classification less meaningful over time, the common interpretation of a horizontal merger has loosened to become a merger between companies that produce identical or closely related products in any geographic market. For example, a merger between two electric companies, one in Oregon and the other in Oklahoma, would have once been considered a market extension merger but would now be classified as horizontal.

The classification of mergers is important with regard to the regulatory authority of the FTC and the Department of Justice (DOJ), especially in the case of horizontal mergers. The FTC and DOJ have broad regulatory powers that can be used to prevent any merger that is deemed to be anticompetitive in nature, and the combinations that have the greatest potential to be anticompetitive are horizontal mergers.

APPLYING THE MODEL 24.1

The failed 1997 merger attempt of Staples and Office Depot illustrates the legal perils facing companies wishing to execute horizontal mergers. Both companies were discount office supply retailers with some overlapping geographic markets and only one major competitor (OfficeMax). FTC and DOJ regulators opposed the merger on the grounds that it would be anticompetitive. Staples and Office Depot countered with an offer to sell all the Office Depot stores sharing the same market as a Staples store and an OfficeMax, making the merger more of a traditional market extension merger than a "strict" horizontal merger. The companies also sought to have their market more broadly defined as general discount retail (such as Target and Wal-Mart) so that the impact of the merger would not appear so anticompetitive. The regulators prevailed, however, and the companies had to abandon their proposed merger. Government regulators fared much less well in 2004, when they challenged Oracle's proposed acquisition of PeopleSoft in federal court on antitrust grounds. Oracle successfully litigated the case and consummated the PeopleSoft acquisition in early 2005.

Horizontal mergers also have the greatest potential for wealth creation. Firms with similar businesses and assets have the ability to benefit from economies of scale and scope from combining their resources. These mergers also have the greatest *possibility* of realizing cost savings through the reduction or elimination of overlapping resources. **Market power** is another obvious benefit that might arise from a horizontal merger. Increased market power results when competition is too weak (or nonexistent) to prevent the merged company from raising prices in a market at will. Of course, this is exactly the kind of anticompetitiveness that the regulators in the Staples–Office Depot merger sought to prevent. Perhaps surprisingly, recent research by Fee and Thomas (2004), Shahrur (2005), and Bittlingmayer and Hazlett (2000) finds little evidence that horizontal mergers create abusive market power or that government antitrust enforcement is unambiguously beneficial.[6]

VERTICAL MERGERS

A **vertical merger** occurs when companies with current or potential buyer-seller relationships combine to create a more integrated company. These mergers are easiest to think of in terms of steps in the production process. Consider the process of producing and selling finished petroleum products. Petroleum exploration and production is followed by transportation, refining, and end-use sales. If a company in the drilling business acquires a company that refines crude oil, then the driller is moving forward in the production process by purchasing the potential buyer of its crude oil. This type of vertical merger is a **forward integration.** Had a refiner and distributor acquired a driller, then the merger would be a **backward integration,** as exemplified by the 1984 merger between Texaco and Getty Oil. Texaco needed Getty's drilling operations and reserves to complement its own refineries and distribution and marketing outlets in order to be a fully integrated oil company.

There are several obvious potential benefits to vertical integration via merger. One advantage to a vertical merger is that product quality and procurement can be ensured from earlier stages of the production process with backward integration. For instance, a manufacturer of precision surgical devices might wish to ensure the high-quality standards required of an input such as a laser beam by acquiring the company that manufactures the laser beam. Or a manufacturer with great sensitivity to

---

[6.] Bittlingmayer and Hazlett present an intriguing analysis of the impact of federal antitrust enforcement actions against Microsoft on the market values of Microsoft's *competitors*. They find these actions reduce competitors' market values, by an average of more than $1 billion for each of the 29 events studied between 1991 and 1997. They conclude (p. 329) that "financial markets reveal compelling evidence against the joint hypothesis that (a) Microsoft conduct is anticompetitive and (b) antitrust policy enforcement produces net efficiency gains."

inventory conversion cycles could more efficiently monitor an orderly inventory flow by acquiring a supplier of raw materials. Another advantage to backward integration is the reduction of input prices. The "middleman" and associated price markup are eliminated.

Forward integration may also offer benefits. Whereas backward integration emphasizes inputs, forward integration focuses on output quality and distribution. Provision of an outlet for a product is an advantage to forward integration. One reason for Disney's merger with Capital Cities/ABC was to gain access to a television network as an outlet for Disney's television entertainment production.[7] Vertical integration can also be used as a marketing tool. Many retail stores and automobile manufacturers have acquired financing subsidiaries to make it easier for a customer to obtain credit to purchase their products (e.g., Ford Motor Credit).

However, there are also disadvantages to vertical mergers. The major disadvantage is the entry into a new line of business. Acquiring managers are likely to have some knowledge of the target firm's business because it is part of the same production process, but similarities do not always imply compatibility. A manager of an automobile manufacturer might find that what works well for manufacturing cars does not work well for renting them, even though both businesses revolve around automobiles (as Chrysler found out with its Thrifty Rent-a-Car unit). Managers might also find that the cost savings from "eliminating the middleman" are not as great as expected. Eliminating the markup might reduce costs for the acquirer, but it also means that the acquired subsidiary is no longer producing profits for the parent company. The acquirer might overlook or underestimate this factor when attempting to value a target. Finally, vertical mergers may also be subject to antitrust regulation, albeit with a smaller probability than with horizontal mergers.

CONGLOMERATE MERGERS

The remaining two types of FTC-defined mergers are diversifying in nature. **Product extension mergers,** or related diversification mergers, are combinations of companies with similar but not exact lines of business. **Pure conglomerate mergers,** or unrelated diversification mergers, occur between companies in completely different lines of business.

Product extension mergers, like market extension mergers, are something of a hybrid classification, in this case a cross between vertical and purely conglomerate mergers. These mergers are not vertical because they are not between firms in different stages of the production process, but their business operations are still related. The merger between the New York Stock Exchange and Archipelago Holdings, completed in late 2005, is a fascinating example of a product extension merger, in that the world's largest and most successful stock exchange merged with a much smaller electronic trading company—and yet offered Archipelago shareholders no less than 30 percent of the combined entity.[8] Managers tend to pursue these types of mergers when searching for a higher-growth business that is not entirely new to them.

Pure conglomerate mergers marry two companies that operate in totally unrelated businesses. Although popular in the 1960s, these mergers have significantly de-

---

[7.] Interestingly, this forward integration strategy proved largely unsuccessful for Disney, as ABC experienced an extended ratings swoon almost immediately after Disney acquired the network. The failure of this strategy was one reason why Disney appeared vulnerable to a hostile takeover attempt launched by Comcast Corporation in early 2004. The takeover attempt eventually fizzled, though Disney was forced to adopt significant changes to its corporate governance rules.

[8.] In part, the NYSE pursued this merger as a backhand way of becoming a publicly traded company, since Archipelago was listed but the NYSE itself was not. Since most of the NYSE's most important competitors are publicly traded, this method of "going public" was very attractive both because of its immediacy and because it finessed internal divisions among the Exchange's members.

clined in frequency since the 1980s. Andrade, Mitchell, and Stafford (2001) show a steady increase in the fraction of mergers between firms in the same industry, rising from 29.9 percent during 1970 to 1973 to 47.8 percent during 1990 to 1998. Based on the principles of portfolio diversification, the purpose of conglomerate mergers is to put together two companies that operate in businesses so different that if some systematic or idiosyncratic event has an adverse effect on one business, then the other business will be minimally (or even positively) impacted. Merging these two firms is expected to make earnings and cash flows less volatile. The 1984 merger of automaker General Motors and computer/business service consulting firm Electronic Data Systems is a prime example of a pure conglomerate merger. The empirical evidence on conglomerate mergers, surveyed in depth in Section 24.4, generally shows these yield disappointing results.

OTHER CONCENTRATION CLASSIFICATIONS

The abbreviated (horizontal/vertical/conglomerate) and full (abbreviated plus market and product extension) FTC merger classifications are not always satisfactory for determining the degree of business concentration created by a merger. Compare the following two hypothetical mergers for an illustration of a possible shortcoming of the FTC classification. The first merger pairs two software companies that operate in no other lines of business. The second merger occurs between the companies in Table 24.2. The acquirer in this merger derives 50 percent of its revenue from chemicals, 30 percent from crude oil refining, and 20 percent from coal-mining operations. Chemicals are also the primary line of business for the target at 40 percent of revenues, followed by 30 percent from retail drugs and 30 percent from plastics. Because the acquirer and target are in the same primary line of business in both mergers, both are classified as horizontal mergers under the abbreviated FTC scheme. But do both mergers have the same level of business concentration? Obviously not—the first merger clearly has more concentration than the second. The need for a finer definition of business concentration in such cases gave rise to the creation of alternative measures, such as degree of overlapping business and change in corporate focus (defined later).

Healey, Palepu, and Ruback (1992, henceforth HPR) introduced the concept of classifying mergers according to the degree of overlapping business operations between the acquirer and target. Reviewing the lines of business of the acquirer and

Table 24.2
Level of Business Concentration Resulting from Merger—Example of Various Classifications

Line of Business	Acquirer			Target			Combined		
	Revenues	%	$\%^2$	Revenues	%	$\%^2$	Revenues	%	$\%^2$
Chemicals	$ 500,000,000	50.0	.2500	$200,000,000	40.0	.1600	$ 700,000,000	46.7	.2180
Oil refining	300,000,000	30.0	.0900	0	0.0	.0000	300,000,000	20.0	.0400
Coal mining	200,000,000	20.0	.0400	0	0.0	.0000	200,000,000	13.3	.0178
Retail drugs	0	0.0	.0000	150,000,000	30.0	.0900	150,000,000	10.0	.0100
Plastics	0	0.0	.0000	150,000,000	30.0	.0900	150,000,000	10.0	.0100
Total	$1,000,000,000	100.0	.3800	$500,000,000	100.0	.3400	$1,500,000,000	100.0	.2958

Note: Abbreviated FTC classification: horizontal
   Business overlap classification: medium overlap
   Change in focus classification: focus-decreasing

target, HPR categorized mergers as having high, medium, and low levels of overlapping business. These categories loosely correspond to (respectively) horizontal, vertical, and conglomerate classifications, but more flexibility exists for assessing the concentration of more complex cases, such as our merger in Table 24.2. Although considered a horizontal merger under traditional classification, this merger would fall under medium overlap in the HPR categorization rather than high overlap. You can easily see how the flexibility of the HPR classification allows for a truer account of a merger's business concentration.

An even more finely tuned measure of business concentration revolves around the concept of **corporate focus.** A focused firm concentrates its efforts on its core (primary) business, the opposite end of the spectrum from a diversified firm. A measure known as the **Herfindahl Index (HI)** demonstrates the relationship between corporate focus and shareholder wealth. The HI is computed as the sum of the squared percentages, in this case the proportion of revenues derived from each line of business. Thus, the HI exaggerates the difference between focused and diversified firms. A completely focused firm has an HI of 1.00, compared with the diversified acquiring firm in our example, which has an HI of 0.38 ($0.5^2 + 0.3^2 + 0.2^2$). A merger (or divestiture) increases focus if the HI of the merged firm is greater than that of the acquiring firm prior to the merger, preserves focus if the HI does not change, and decreases focus if the HI declines. In our hypothetical mergers, the first merger between the software companies preserves corporate focus, whereas the second merger between the diversified companies decreases corporate focus, as the HI declines from 0.380 to 0.296.

Concept Review Questions

4. What is the purpose of classifying mergers by degree of business concentration? Why do you think these classifications have changed over time?

5. As conglomerate mergers and corporate diversification have proven to be failures in general, why would any manager pursue these objectives? Can you think of any cases where corporate diversification has worked successfully? What distinguishes these cases from the norm?

6. What is a Herfindahl Index, and what is it meant to measure?

24.3 MERGER AND ACQUISITION TRANSACTION CHARACTERISTICS

Corporate control events can be categorized according to certain defining characteristics of the transactions, including the method of payment used to finance a transaction, the attitude or response of target management to a takeover attempt, and the accounting treatment used when the firms combine.

METHOD OF PAYMENT

Just like any other type of investment, a merger must be financed with capital components—including debt, retained earnings, and newly issued common stock. These components comprise the consideration offered in a transaction and sum to the transaction value, the dollar value of all forms of payment offered to the target for control of the company. Cash on hand from retained earnings and/or generated from an issue of debt is used in financing a cash-only deal, where the target's share-holders receive only cash for their shares in a public company or the target's owner(s) receives cash for the private enterprise.[9] More rarely, the target receives a new issue of debt in exchange for control in a debt-only transaction.

Bidders almost always offer target firm shareholders a price for their shares that is significantly higher than the target's current market price. The merger premium is the difference between premerger market value and acquisition value. For example, in August 2005, Adidas offered to pay Reebok International stockholders $59 in cash for each share tendered; this price was 34 percent higher than Reebok's closing stock price the day before the offer was announced. Andrade, Mitchell, and Stafford (2001) document an average 37.9 percent premium for completed U.S. mergers between 1973 and 1998, while Rossi and Volpin (2004) document a mean 44.3 percent premium for U.S. mergers initiated during the 1990s. These authors also document positive merger premiums for 48 of the 49 countries they examine (the sole exception being Japan), ranging, respectively, from 10.5 and 11.0 percent for Brazil and Switzerland to 120.2 and 122.5 percent for Israel and Indonesia. The British, Dutch, Danish, and South Korean average premiums are all within one or two percentage points of America's.

The bidding firm's stock is the only mode of payment in a stock-swap merger, or **pure stock exchange merger.** The general stock-swap merger involves the issuance of new shares of common stock in exchange for the target's common stock, but payment may come in the form of either preferred stock or subsidiary tracking shares. The number of shares of the surviving firm's common stock that target shareholders receive is determined by the exchange ratio. The surviving firm is either the acquiring firm or the new firm created in a consolidation. For instance, an acquirer with a current stock price of $20 that sets an exchange ratio of 0.75 for a target with a current stock price of $12 and 100 million shares outstanding will issue 75 million new shares in exchange for the target's shares. The transaction value of this merger would be $1.5 billion ($20 × 75 million).[10] An individual who owns 100 shares ($1,200) of the target stock would receive acquirer stock worth $1,500 ($20 × 75 shares), a 25 percent control premium.

Mergers may also be financed with a combination of cash and securities, in transactions known as **mixed offerings.** Andrade, Mitchell, and Stafford (2001) report that 35.4 percent of U.S. mergers during 1973 to 1998 were all-cash offerings, 45.6 percent were all-stock offerings, and the remaining 19 percent were mixed offerings. For example, in January 2005, SBC Communications offered AT&T shareholders a combination of SBC stock worth $18.41 per share plus $1.30 in cash. Likewise, as discussed in the Opening Focus, Chevron's offer for Unocal was $27.60 in cash plus 0.618 Chevron share for each Unocal share, worth about $63 total per share. For political reasons, this bid topped CNOOC's $67 per-share all-cash offer for Unocal. Sometimes, target shareholders are also offered a choice for the medium of exchange. For example, target shareholders could be offered the choice of either $30 cash or

---

[9.] Intriguingly, Harford (1999) shows that cash-rich acquiring firms make poor bidders. These firms launch more takeover attempts, these attempts are value-destroying in the short term, and they underperform other acquirers that also pay with cash. Bharadwaj and Shivdasani (2003) show that banks extend financing in 70 percent of their sample of cash tender offers between 1990 and 1996 and finance the entire tender offer in half of these takeovers. Bank-financed acquisitions are associated with large and significantly positive acquirer announcement returns. Finally, Faccio and Masulis (2005) examine the determinants of the cash versus stock method of payment in European acquisitions of public and private companies during 1997–2000. They find that tax, corporate governance and control, and debt financing considerations all play a role in this choice—and that the choice will be different in different national markets.

[10.] This is under the assumption that the acquirer's stock price remains the same—a very optimistic assumption, as we will later see. In most stock-swap mergers, an acceptable range of stock prices and exchange ratios is negotiated from the outset.

1.25 shares of the surviving company's shares for each share that they hold. This way, the shareholders can decide whether the exchange ratio is sufficient for them to remain shareholders in the surviving company or whether they should "take the money and run" with the cash offer.

ACCOUNTING TREATMENT

Prior to June 30, 2001, two financial accounting procedures existed for recording a merger in the United States: the pooling-of-interests and purchase methods. However, with implementation of Financial Accounting Standards Board (FASB) Statement 141 and the near-concurrent (December 31, 2001) Statement 142, there now exists one standard method of accounting for mergers. Under these new standards, target liabilities remain unchanged, but target assets are "written up" to reflect current market values, and the equity of the target is revised upward to incorporate the purchase price paid. These revised values are then carried over to the surviving firm's financial statements. The intangible asset *goodwill* is created if the restated values of the target lead to a situation in which its assets are less than its liabilities and equity. This **goodwill** reflects the premium that an acquiring firm is willing to pay in excess of net asset market value in order to capture synergies from the merger—goodwill becomes an intangible asset on the acquiring firm's balance sheet. Going forward, the value of this intangible asset must be evaluated to determine if it has been "impaired" due to a decline in fair value relative to carrying value. If the value of goodwill is impaired, then the amount of the impairment is "written down" from the goodwill account on the balance sheet and charged off against earnings. Otherwise, it remains unchanged on the balance sheet indefinitely. Many large write-downs were taken soon after FASB 142 went into effect at the beginning of 2002. JDS Uniphase, AOL Time Warner, and Nortel Networks all took multi-billion-dollar write-downs in 2002 for acquisitions completed in prior years, while the newly renamed MCI Inc. took a $75 billion write-down in early 2004 for acquisitions completed by the company when it was named WorldCom. See Applying the Model 24.2 for a mathematical example of accounting for mergers.

APPLYING THE MODEL 24.2

Assume that a target firm has 5 million shares outstanding priced at $10 per share. The acquiring firm offers a 20 percent takeover premium ($12 per share), for a transaction value of equity of $60 million. The acquiring firm wants the R&D capabilities of the target firm and is willing to pay a premium to obtain those capabilities and leverage R&D synergies. The market value of the target's fixed assets is $65 million. Along with the $10 million in current assets, the target has a market value of assets of $75 million. Deducting the $5 million in current liabilities and $25 million in long-term liabilities, the target firm has a net asset value of $45 million. Thus, the acquiring firm is willing to pay $15 million ($60 million less $45 million) for intangible assets in the form of R&D.

Current assets	$10,000,000
Restated fixed assets	65,000,000
Less: Liabilities	30,000,000
Net asset value	$45,000,000
Purchase price paid	60,000,000
Less: Net asset value	45,000,000
Goodwill	$15,000,000

Further assume that the target firm is treated as a separate reporting subsidiary after the merger. Going forward, the firm must value its intangible assets (goodwill) to determine if the value of $15 million on the balance sheet (shown in the following table) represents a fair value. As long as the firm can demonstrate that the goodwill is fairly valued, then it will remain unaffected on the balance sheet. However, if the value is "impaired," then the value loss must be reported, deducted from the balance sheet, and taken as a write-off against earnings. For example, if two years later the R&D of the subsidiary does not turn out as synergistic as hoped for, then the fair market value and net asset value of the subsidiary will be estimated. If the fair market value is estimated at $70 million and the net asset value at $60 million, then the value of goodwill is only $10 million—a $5 million impairment. This $5 million will be deducted from the balance sheet and taken as an intangible asset write-down on the income statement.

	Acquirer ($ millions)	Target ($ millions)	Merged ($ millions) Subsidiary	Merged ($ millions) Consolidated
Assets				
Current	$ 50	$10	$10	$ 60
Fixed	350	$50	$65	$415
Goodwill	0	0	15	15
Total assets	$400	$60	$90	$490
Liabilities				
Current	$ 50	$ 5	$ 5	$ 55
Long-term	250	25	25	275
Total	$300	$30	$30	$330
Owner's equity	100	30	60	160
Total liabilities and equity	$400	$60	$90	$490

SHAREHOLDER WEALTH EFFECTS AND TRANSACTION CHARACTERISTICS

How do the shareholders of companies involved in mergers and acquisitions generally fare? The consensus result obtained in merger studies is that the common stockholders of target firms in successful takeovers experience large and significant wealth gains. Acquirer returns are much smaller and not as generalized, and we discuss the theories offered to explain the cross-sectional differences in acquirers' returns. We also explore the wealth effects of various transaction characteristics.

RETURNS TO TARGET AND BIDDING FIRM SHAREHOLDERS

Target Returns. As previously noted, target-firm stockholders almost always experience substantial wealth gains due to the premium offered for giving up control of their company.[11] An early survey article, Jensen and Ruback (1983), finds that, on average, U.S. target-firm common stockholders receive takeover premiums of 29.1 percent in successful tender offers and 15.9 percent in successful mergers. More recently, Bhagat, Dong, Hirshleifer, and Noah (2005) find that the average announcement-

---

[11.] The rare case where a target shareholder receives a negative takeover premium is known as a *takeunder*.

period abnormal return for target-firm shareholders in 1,018 attempted tender offers from 1962 to 2001 is 30.01 percent using a five-day event window and 24.47 percent using an event window beginning 90 days before the announcement and ending one day afterwards. Andrade, Mitchell, and Stafford (2001) find that the announcement-period abnormal return for target-firm shareholders in 4,256 completed tender offers and mergers during 1979 to 1998 is 16.0 percent using a three-day event window [−1 day, +1 day] and 23.8 percent using a window stretching from 20 days before the offer through the merger completion. These authors also show that target returns in all completed M&A deals have remained essentially constant over time, while Bhagat, Dong, Hirshleifer, and Noah find that target abnormal returns in tender offers have risen steadily over time. Target returns are also higher when there are multiple bidders and when managerial resistance leads to a higher offer, but takeover premiums are lost when resistance is too great and prevents a takeover.

Acquirer Returns. Results concerning the common stock returns of U.S. acquiring firms are far less conclusive than those for target shareholders, and they are very different depending on whether one examines average percentage returns or overall dollar returns to bidder shareholder. Bhagat, Dong, Hirshleifer, and Noah (2005) find that the average announcement-period abnormal return for the shareholders of firms launching successful tender offers is very close to zero for their entire 1962 to 2001 study periods, with these average returns fluctuating between positive and negative over time. Andrade, Mitchell, and Stafford (2001) document average announcement-period excess returns for successful acquiring-firm shareholders of −0.7 percent using a short event window and −3.8 percent using their event period stretching through merger completion.

Moeller, Schlingemann, and Stulz (2004, 2005, henceforth MSS) examine acquirer returns by calculating both average percentage return and overall dollar returns to bidding-firm shareholders. They find strong evidence of a size effect, where relatively small bidding firms earn positive returns, but larger bidders fare much worse. In MSS (2004), they document that the equally weighted abnormal announcement-period return to bidders in 12,023 acquisitions over 1980 to 2001 is 1.1 percent, but acquiring-firm shareholders lose $25.2 million on average upon announcement. In MSS (2005), they show that these negative dollar returns are concentrated in the frenzied 1998 to 2001 merger period and more particularly result from 87 "large loss" bidders that each lost at least $1 billion in market value in a single transaction. Figure 24.2 presents the aggregate dollar return for the acquiring firms in MSS (2005), clearly showing the massively negative returns for 1998 to 2001, when acquirers lost $240 billion in total. During this period, the large-loss bidders shed an incredible $397 billion of market value. If these 87 deals are excluded, total acquiring-firm returns for 1998 to 2001 are $157 billion.

Combined Returns. An important early study by Bradley, Desai, and Kim (1988, henceforth BDK) computed the capitalization-weighted announcement-period returns to combined bidder and target-firm shareholders and presented these as a measure of the total synergistic gains expected to be realized from the merger. They find that the weighted-average return of acquirers and targets consistently ranged between 7 percent and 8 percent over the period 1962 to 1984, reflecting a constant anticipated synergistic gain from the combination of the two firms. But the protective provisions of the 1968 Williams Act seem to have caused a transfer of this consistent gain from acquirer to target-firm shareholders, because acquirer returns were significantly positive prior to the Williams Act and have become slightly negative since.

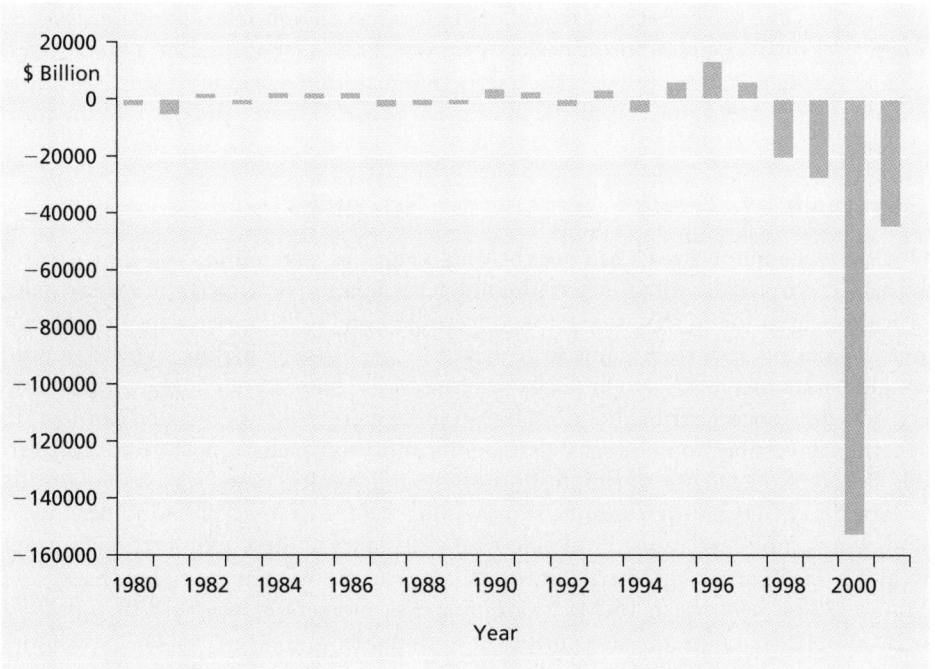

Figure 24.2
Yearly Aggregate Dollar Return of U.S. Acquiring-Firms Shareholders, 1980–2001 ($ Billions)
Source: Figure 1 in Sara B. Moeller, Frederik P. Schlingemann, and René M. Stulz, "Wealth Destruction on a Massive Scale? A Study of Acquiring-Firm Returns in the Recent Merger Wave," *Journal of Finance* 60 (April 2005), pp. 757–782.

In recent years, several research teams have used the BDK approach to measure total synergistic gains for combined bidder and target-firm shareholders. Andrade, Mitchell, and Stafford (2001) document combined returns of about 2 percent for merging-firm stockholders using both short and long event windows, while Bhagat, Dong, Hirshleifer, and Noah (2005) find somewhat higher combined returns of around 5 percent in their sample of tender offers.

Mode of Payment. The mode of payment used to finance an acquisition explains much of the cross-sectional variance in acquirers' returns. Travlos (1987) and Loughran and Vijh (1997) find higher returns in cash transactions than in stock transactions and that the higher returns observed by both acquirers and targets in tender offers relative to negotiated mergers are attributable to the fact that most tender offers are financed by cash, whereas most negotiated mergers are equity financed. Announcement-period target returns are 13 percentage points greater for cash deals, acquirer returns in cash-financed deals are near zero, and those in stock-financed deals are significantly negative. Long-term results are even more startling: Common stockholders in cash tender offers outperform those in stock-swap mergers by 123 percent through the fifth postacquisition year.

Researchers have proposed several theories to explain the differential returns between cash and stock offers. The most prominent of these theories revolves around the signaling model first described in Chapter 13. In the context of this model, the mode of payment offered by acquiring firms signals inside information to the capital markets. Managers will finance acquisitions with the cheapest source of capital available. Financing an acquisition with equity signals to the market that managers believe equity is a (relatively) cheap source of capital because they think the acquirer's stock price is overvalued. Receiving this signal, the capital markets will make a downward revision of the value of the acquirer's equity. Other theories concerning the differential returns due to financing method include the tax and preemptive bidding hypotheses. The *tax hypothesis* postulates that target shareholders must be awarded a capital gains tax premium in cash offers, which is not required in a stock offer. The *preemptive bidding hypothesis* asserts that acquirers wishing to ward off other potential bidders for a target offer a substantial initial takeover premium in the form of cash.

RETURNS TO OTHER SECURITY HOLDERS

Obviously, common stocks are not the only securities affected in corporate control activities. Corporate control events also impact bonds and preferred stocks. Early empirical research found that some nonconvertible bondholders experience significant wealth gains but that these gains were driven by the bonds of acquiring firms in non-conglomerate mergers.[12] No financial synergies were realized in conglomerate mergers, and the nonconvertible bondholders in these mergers neither gained nor lost. In general, convertible bond returns were significantly higher than those of nonconvertible bonds. No evidence of significant bondholder wealth losses was systematically observed in LBOs, though specific transactions yielded dramatic bondholder losses. Both convertible and nonconvertible preferred stockholders exhibited significant wealth gains in nonconglomerate mergers. A more recent study by Billett, King, and Mauer (2004, henceforth BKM), examining 254 mergers between 1979 and 1997 with complete data for all the securities of both bidder and target, shows many more significant wealth changes for bondholders in mergers. They find clear evidence supporting the coinsurance effect predicted by several theorists. This asserts that merging two firms with less than perfectly correlated cash flow streams will benefit the financially riskier firm's bondholders, because the merged cash flows reduce the chance that this firm will default on its debt during a period of operating losses. The bondholders' gain is a wealth transfer from the merging firms' shareholders—especially the financially healthier firm's shareholders—since cash flows that they would have received in the weaker firm's loss period are instead diverted to pay the bondholders' claims. BKM find that below-investment-grade target bonds earn significantly positive announcement-period returns, while acquiring-firm bondholders earn negative returns. Since BKM's other findings also support the coinsurance theory, their study suggests corporate managers pursue mergers at least partly to reduce financial risk, benefiting themselves and other fixed claimants, such as bondholders, but harming shareholders.

INTERNATIONAL MERGERS AND ACQUISITIONS

During most recent years, roughly two-thirds of the world's mergers and acquisitions involved non-U.S. bidders and targets, and these mergers represented half or more of overall M&A value. Table 24.3 describes the geographic distribution of announced M&A deals during 2004 and 2003, while Figure 24.3 presents the industrial distribution of global M&A for the same years. The Americas—primarily Canada and the United States—accounted for around 34 percent of the total number of announced deals worldwide during 2004 and 2003, but these represented 48.3 and 45.9 percent of the total value of announced deals during 2004 and 2003, respectively. Europe is the next most active M&A region, accounting, respectively, for 30.8 and 34.7 percent of the total number and 35.1 and 36.6 of the total value of announced deals in 2004 and 2003. The United Kingdom was easily Europe's most active single market both years, wracking up higher total numbers and values than the next two national

---

12. See Wansley, Lane, and Yang (1983), Dennis and McConnell (1986), Lehn and Poulsen (1989), Asquith and Wizman (1990), Macquieira, Megginson, and Nail (1998), and, more recently, Megginson, Morgan, and Nail (2004).

Table 24.3
Geographic Distribution of Worldwide Announced Mergers and Acquisitions, 2004 versus 2003

Region/Country	2004		2003	
	Value ($US billions)	Number of Deals	Value ($US billions)	Number of Deals
AMERICAS	$ 942	10,457	$ 634	9,488
United States	834	8,313	570	7,702
Canada	60	1,045	35	1,135
AFRICA/MIDDLE EAST	22	457	24	452
EUROPE	684	9,379	505	9,954
France	126	993	57	774
Germany	59	1,175	55	1,200
United Kingdom	255	2,494	128	2,714
ASIA-PACIFIC	291	10,133	215	8,758
Australia	93	1,787	42	1,635
Japan	109	2,090	76	1,790
WORLDWIDE	**$1,949**	**30,426**	**$1,380**	**28,652**

Source: Mergers and Acquisitions Report, Thomson Financial (www.thomson.com/league).

Figure 24.3
Industrial Distribution of Worldwide Announced Mergers and Acquisitions, Value in $ Millions, 2004 versus 2003
Source: Mergers and Acquisitions Report, Thomson Financial (www.thomson.com/league).

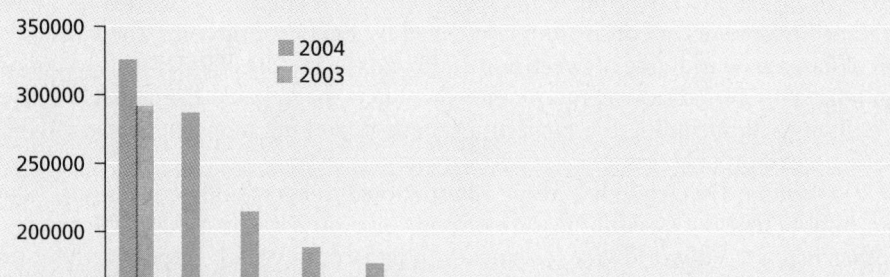

markets (Germany and France) combined. Outside of Europe and North America, the only truly active national M&A markets are Australia and Japan. Australia has a particularly vibrant M&A market, given that its 6 percent share of global deal count and its 3 to 5 percent share of overall deal value are only slightly lower than Japan's shares of deal count and value—despite the fact that Australia's economy is only one-eighth as large as Japan's. The four large English common law countries of

Britain, Canada, Australia, and the United States alone account for over 45 percent of the number and up to 66 percent (during 2004) of the total value of announced mergers and acquisitions worldwide, which is what the "Law and Finance" theory of comparative financial development that we discuss in Section 24.6 would predict.

Figure 24.3 shows that mergers and acquisitions occur in the same key industries year after year. During 2004, the financial sector accounted for 16.7 percent of the total $1.95 trillion value of announced M&A deals worldwide, followed by energy and power (15.0 percent), telecommunications (10.8 percent), health care (9.8 percent), real estate (9.0 percent), materials (6.7 percent), and media and entertainment (6.2 percent). Though the market share percentages were somewhat different, these industries held the same relative positions during 2003. Most of these industries are consolidating very rapidly, in response to either profound technological changes or shifting industry cost structures leading to increasing economies of scale. As examples, consider the telecommunications and financial industries. Between February 2004 and February 2005, no fewer than four huge telecom mergers were announced —Cingular Wireless' $41 billion acquisition of AT&T Wireless in February 2004, Sprint's $71 billion merger with Nextel in December 2004, SBC's $16 billion bid for AT&T in January 2005, and Verizon's announced merger with MCI in February 2005. Shortly thereafter, the Israeli, Czech, and Pakistani governments all executed sales of large stakes in their state-owned telecoms to international buyers, and the Italian electric utility Enel sold Wind, its mobile phone subsidiary, for $12 billion to Weather Investments, a consortium controlled by Egypt's Orascom. The consolidation of banking worldwide between late 2003 and the middle of 2005 was even more dramatic. This period saw mergers create three new mega-banks, with assets of over $1 trillion each, including the birth of a Japanese banking monster named MUFG, with $1.7 trillion of assets.

It is very hard to generalize about international mergers and acquisitions, other than to note that the essential feature of one company's acquisition of the assets of another is observed worldwide. Countries differ not only with respect to how frequently takeover attempts are launched, but also how often these are friendly versus hostile bids, how often these are cross-border deals (involving a bidder and a target firm in different countries), the average control premium offered, and the likelihood that payment will be made strictly in cash. Table 24.4 presents global average values for these variables—plus national average values for a selected group of 14 countries —derived from a study by Rossi and Volpin (2004) of 45,686 mergers in 49 countries completed between 1990 and 2002. Hostile takeovers rarely occur, except in the United States, Norway, Canada, and Britain, while all-cash bids account for the majority of offers outside of Japan, Canada, and America. Over 40 percent of all M&As are cross-border deals, and this is very common except in Japan and the United States. Perhaps surprisingly, the average non-U.S. "takeover" deal involves acquisition of less than one-fourth of the outstanding stock of the target company—though this will be sufficient to transfer effective control in many cases.

Concept Review Questions	**7.** What are the two most important methods of paying for corporate acquisitions?
	8. What is *goodwill* in the context of merger accounting? What must an acquiring company do if the value of an acquired company is revealed to have declined after a merger?
	9. Who wins and who loses in corporate takeovers? Why do acquiring firm shareholders generally lose in stock-swap mergers but either benefit or at least break even in acquisitions paid for with cash?

Table 24.4
Descriptive Data on
International Mergers
and Acquisitions,
1990–2002

Country	Volume (%)	Hostile Takeover (%)	Cross-Border Ratio (%)	Premium (mean)	All-Cash Bid (%)	No. of Observations
Australia	34	0.65	27	129.5	60	212
Canada	30	4.60	23	132.9	36	157
France	56	1.68	34	133.4	88	112
Germany	36	0.30	26	116.7	77	13
Hong Kong	34	0.41	39	129.8	93	46
India	2	0.02	56	178.6	67	9
Italy	56	3.04	36	127.7	88	26
Japan	6	0	13	99.0	36	73
Norway	61	5.86	37	136.0	76	37
Singapore	34	0.40	31	152.9	85	39
Sweden	62	3.74	35	141.7	71	45
Switzerland	38	1.43	44	111.0	89	9
United Kingdom	54	4.39	23	145.8	64	614
United States	66	6.44	9	144.3	37	2,443
World Average	**24**	**1.01**	**43**	**141.6**	**48**	**4,007**

Source: Derived from Tables 1 and 2 in Stefano Rossi and Paolo F. Volpin, "Cross-Country Determinants of Mergers and Acquisitions," *Journal of Financial Economics* 74 (November 2004), pp. 277–304.

Note: This table presents descriptive data on international mergers and acquisitions in 49 countries announced between January 1, 1990, and December 31, 1999, and completed by December 31, 2002. *Volume* is the percentage of the stock of traded companies targeted in a completed deal. *Cross-border ratio* is the number of cross-border deals as a percentage of all completed deals. *Premium* is the bid price as a percentage of the closing price of the target four weeks before the announcement. *All-cash bid* is a dummy variable that equals 1 if the acquisition is paid entirely in cash and zero otherwise.

24.4 RATIONALE AND MOTIVES FOR MERGERS AND ACQUISITIONS

As we have seen, the primary objective of any corporation's management team should be the maximization of shareholder wealth. Management should undertake a potential merger or acquisition, like any other investment, as long as its net present value is positive and enhances shareholder value. Mergers may be value enhancing in several ways. However, we know that corporate managers do not always act as proper agents for their shareholders, and agency problems arise when managers engage in non-value-maximizing behavior. In this section, we examine both the value-maximizing and non-value-maximizing motives that lead managers to pursue mergers and acquisitions.

VALUE-MAXIMIZING MOTIVES

Mergers create value when managers seek goals such as increasing operating profit, realizing gains from restructuring poorly managed firms, and creating greater barriers to entry in their industry. These and other value-enhancing objectives can be achieved through mergers and acquisitions that garner access to new geographic markets, increase market power, capitalize on economies of scale, or create value through the sale of underperforming target resources. Mergers can also increase efficiency if they remove inefficient management and transfer control of the firm to more capable managers.[13]

Expansion. Geographic expansion (both domestic and international) may enhance shareholder wealth if the market entered is subject to little or no competition. Managers considering expansion must first evaluate two mutually exclusive alternatives: internal versus external expansion. Internal expansion into a new market, also known as **greenfield entry,** involves acquiring and organizing all resources required for each stage of the investment. These stages encompass contracting with an engineering firm to build a new plant, hiring new employees to staff the plant, implementing training programs for the new staff, establishing distribution outlets, and so on.

External expansion is the acquisition of a firm with resources already in place. Acquirers pay a control premium to the owners of the acquired firm for relinquishing control, but the payment of this premium ensures that many of the potential problems of greenfield entry are avoided. For instance, external expansion avoids construction delays in the building of a new plant or the inability to adequately staff a new facility. Usually, external expansion is the better option in situations where rapid expansion is desired or when great uncertainty exists about the success of any stage of greenfield entry. International expansion is another good reason to choose external expansion over internal expansion. The business operations, political climate, and social mores differ so greatly between some countries that an acquisition is often the only viable alternative for international expansion.[14] The May 2004 merger between KLM and Air France maintained the separate identities of both airline subsidiaries, at least partly to finesse political sensitivities in the Netherlands and France, respectively.

SYNERGY, MARKET POWER, AND STRATEGIC MERGERS

A **strategic merger** is one that seeks to create a more efficient merged company than the two premerger companies operating independently. This efficiency-enhancing effect is known as **synergy.** Michael Eisner, CEO of Disney at the time, provided the best definition of synergy with his perception of the value created by his company's 1995 merger with Capital Cities/ABC: "1 + 1 = 4." There are three types of merger-related synergies—*operational, managerial,* and *financial.* Revealingly, the synergies expected to result from the Disney-Capital Cities/ABC combination proved elusive, and this disappointing result is observed in almost half of all mergers.

Synergies. The main sources of **operational synergy** are economies of scale, economies of scope, and resource complementarities. **Economies of scale** result when relative operating costs are reduced because of an increase in size that allows for the reduction or elimination of overlapping resources. For example, the reason given for the elimination of 12,000 positions in the 1995 merger of Chemical Bank and Chase Manhattan Bank was the cost savings generated from the elimination of overlapping jobs. Similar reasons were given for eliminating 7,000 jobs following the 2004 Cingular Wireless acquisition of AT&T Wireless. **Economies of scope** are other value-creating benefits of increased size. The ability for a merged firm to launch a na-

---

[13] Kini, Kracaw, and Mian (2004) examine the disciplinary role of corporate takeovers using a sample of 279 successful acquisitions of U.S. companies between 1979 and 1998. Their evidence is consistent with the takeover market's serving as a "court of last resort" or as an external source of discipline when internal control mechanisms are weak or ineffective.

[14] Joint ventures and strategic alliances also allow access to foreign markets through existing resources, but these are partnering relationships in which profits must be shared.

tional advertising campaign that would not have been feasible for either of the pre-merger firms is such a benefit. **Resource complementarities** exist when a firm with a particular operating expertise merges with a firm with another operating strength to create a company that has expertise in multiple areas. A good example of such a complementarity is the merger of two pharmaceutical companies, the first a specialist in researching and developing new drugs and the second a master marketer of drug products. The KLM/Air France merger was also driven by a search for resource complementarities—specifically, the desire to combine the two carriers' extensive global route networks to better serve international business customers. Operating synergies are most likely to be achieved in horizontal mergers and least likely to be realized in conglomerate mergers. However, resource complementarities are just as likely to be realized in vertical mergers as in horizontal mergers, because vertical combinations pair companies that specialize in different areas.

Managerial synergies, like operational synergies, cause two firms to have greater value when combined than when they are independent. Managerial synergies, however, result in efficiency gains from the combination of management teams. Similar to resource complementarities, managerial synergies arise when management teams with different strengths are paired. Consider a merger between two retailing firms with differing managerial expertise. The first retailer has a management team that emphasizes revenue growth and excels in recognizing customer trends. The second retailer has a technically oriented management team that excels in cost containment and has perfected inventory control with its superior information systems. A merger between these two firms should benefit from managerial synergies with a joint emphasis on and expertise in revenue growth and cost containment, assuming the two management teams can mesh together smoothly.

Financial synergies occur when a merger results in less volatile cash flows, lower default risk, and a lower cost of capital. Because financial synergies are largely the anticipated result of conglomerate mergers, we defer this discussion to the section on the diversification motive for mergers.

Market Power. Other, more controversial motives support increasing firm size through mergers and acquisitions. As we have seen, horizontal mergers have the potential to create more efficient companies through size-related operational synergies. Horizontal mergers may also profit from size in another fashion: increased market power. Because horizontal mergers are those that take place between competitors, the number of competitors in an industry will necessarily decline. Presumably, price competition will also decline if the merger creates a dominant firm that has the power to control prices in a market.

Consider the Staples–Office Depot merger attempt previously mentioned. The two largest competitors in an industry with only three true competitors attempted to merge. The regulatory authorities denied this merger on the grounds that the merged company would have the power to control prices in the office supplies market, with only one, much smaller, competitor to provide price competition. Regulatory authorities must balance the corporate benefit of increased efficiency against the consumer cost of increased market power when making decisions on allowing a merger to take place—especially a horizontal merger.

Other Strategic Rationales. Other strategic reasons also motivate managers to pursue mergers. As we mentioned earlier, in vertical mergers, product quality can sometimes be more closely monitored. Another strategic motive is defensive consolidation in a mature or declining industry. As consumer demand declines in an industry, competitors may seek each other out for a merger in order to survive the permanent industry downturn. Not only does the merged firm stand to benefit from economies of scale and scope, but it will also benefit from the reduction of competition. Of course, this does introduce the market power issue for regulators. But recent history has seen regulators adopt a more permissive attitude toward defensive consolidation—for example, the consolidation in the U.S. defense industry in the post–Cold War period. It is literally inconceivable that American regulators would have approved the 1997 acquisition by Boeing of McDonnell-Douglas, its sole remaining U.S.-based competitor producing commercial aircraft, during the 1970s or 1980s.

CASH FLOW GENERATION AND FINANCIAL MERGERS

Financial mergers are motivated by the prospect of uncovering hidden value in a target through a major restructuring or the generation of free cash flow from merger-related tax advantages. Many of the hostile deals of the 1980s were junk-bond-financed financial mergers aimed at either "busting up" undervalued firms by selling off the assets of the acquired firm for a value greater than the acquisition price or restructuring the acquired firm to increase its corporate focus. A typical financial merger involves a focused acquirer that acquires a diversified firm with some business operations in the acquirer's line of business. The acquirer then sells the noncore businesses and uses the cash flow to pay down the cost of the acquisition.

Tax considerations may also motivate managers to pursue a particular target for a merger. The asymmetrical nature of the U.S. tax code provides an incentive to merge in certain circumstances. Although taxes must always be paid on positive income, negative income (net losses) creates only tax-loss carrybacks and carryforwards that offset taxes paid (on past income) or due on future income; the government does not pay negative taxes (cash payments) to firms suffering net losses. **Tax-loss carryforwards** can be charged against future income for up to 15 years. Acquiring a target that has accumulated tax-loss carryforwards could shelter taxable income and redistribute that cash flow to other uses.

As junk bond financing of acquisitions has declined since the 1980s, so has the occurrence of financial mergers. This merger motive was further minimized by a change in the tax code in 1986 that limited the extent to which tax-loss carryforwards could be used after a merger. Financial mergers still occur, but their importance in the market for corporate control has declined significantly.

NON-VALUE-MAXIMIZING MOTIVES

Unfortunately, not all mergers are motivated for the purpose of maximizing shareholder wealth. Although the motives of managers may not be intentionally value reducing, most revolve around agency problems between managers and shareholders. We discuss these improper motives next.

Agency Problems. Managers will sometimes disguise their attempts to derive personal benefits from creating and managing larger corporations as the need to expand through mergers and acquisitions. Academic research confirms the importance of this motive with findings that merger activity is positively related to growth in sales and assets but not related to increased profits or stock prices. Considering these findings, Mueller (1969) offered the **managerialism theory of mergers**. According to this theory, poorly monitored managers will pursue mergers to maximize their corporation's asset size because managerial compensation is usually based on firm size, regardless of whether or not these mergers create value for stockholders.

Roll (1986) offers a somewhat different rationale with his **hubris hypothesis of corporate takeovers.** Roll contends that some managers overestimate their own managerial capabilities and pursue takeovers with the belief that they can better manage their takeover target than the target's current management team can. Acquiring managers then overbid for the target and fail to realize the gains expected from the merger in the postmerger period, thereby diminishing shareholder wealth. Thus, the intent of the managers is not contrary to the best interests of shareholders (the managers think they will create value), but the result is still value decreasing.

Shleifer and Vishny (2003) present a model of M&A based on stock market misvaluation of the combining firms and of the potential synergies that can be reaped from merging these companies. They assume that investors periodically overvalue some firms, whose managers are then tempted to use their company's stock as currency to acquire other firms that the market has undervalued. In contrast to Roll's hubris hypothesis, Shleifer and Vishny's model assumes that acquiring firm managers are perfectly rational and act in the best interest of their own shareholders, but the stock market is frequently (and dramatically) irrational in assigning stock values. Their model explains several empirical patterns, including when stock is likely to be used instead of cash as payment, why takeovers seem to occur in industry waves, and why the short- and long-term return to acquiring firm shareholders is frequently negative.

The most recent and perhaps most persuasive explanation of why bidding-firm managers might pursue value-destroying mergers is Jensen's (2005) model of the agency cost of **overvalued equity.** He predicts that when a company's stock becomes significantly overvalued, this sets in motion a set of organizational forces that inevitably push managers to take actions that destroy part or all of the firm's core value. A manager's stock is overvalued when she realizes that she cannot, except by pure luck, produce the performance required to justify this stock price. Once this manager has accepted all positive-*NPV* investment projects, she will inevitably be enticed to pursue ever larger, negative-*NPV* projects, such as nonsynergistic mergers. This theory seems to explain, all too well, the massive losses suffered by acquiring-firm shareholders in the mega-mergers of the period 1998 to 2001 documented by Moeller, Schlingemann, and Stulz (2004, 2005).

Diversification. As recently as the late 1960s, diversification was actually considered a value-maximizing motive for merger. Over time, however, the capital markets have learned of the failure of corporate diversification strategies, especially those emphasizing unrelated diversification. Given these empirical discoveries, we must now consider that diversification is a non-value-enhancing motive for merger.

As previously discussed, corporate diversification and conglomerate mergers were an experiment in portfolio theory applied to corporations. The basic premise of corporate diversification is that the combination of two businesses with less than perfectly correlated cash flows will create a merged firm with less volatile cash flows and inherently lower business risk, where bad outcomes in one business can be offset by good outcomes in another business. Diversification supporters contend that these less volatile cash flows make debt service less risky, lowering default risk and the required return on debt. As described by Lewellen (1971), financial synergy is created by this **coinsurance of debt,** because the debt of each combining firm is now insured with cash flows from two businesses. Other proponents of unrelated diversification cite the existence of internal capital markets as another reason to pursue conglomerate mergers. **Internal capital markets** are created when the high cash flows (*cash cow*) businesses of a conglomerate generate enough cash flow to fund the "rising star" businesses. Since this financing is accomplished internally, underwriting costs are avoided and riskier business ventures can be financed with "cheaper" capital generated from more mature and less risky businesses.

Additional research on corporate diversification generated theories describing the flaws in the diversification motive for merger. Realizing that conglomerate mergers are not likely to benefit from any synergies other than financial, Galai and Masulis (1976) and Shastri (1990) showed that the net effect of conglomerate mergers is zero wealth creation and that any wealth gains experienced by bondholders due to financial synergies are merely redistributed from stockholders. Subsequent empirical research by Berger and Ofek (1995), Comment and Jarrell (1995), Lamont and Polk (2002), and Ahn and Denis (2004) generally verified that corporate diversification reduced firm value. Although Schoar (2002) and Graham, Lemmon, and Wolf (2002) do not find a diversification discount and Villalonga (2004) actually documents a diversification premium, the consensus among financial analysts is that corporate diversification does not of itself create wealth and that managers should not execute mergers in search of financial synergies. Further, internal capital markets fell into disrepute when it became obvious that managerial control over free cash flow created its own, often severe, agency problems. In particular, capital attained and invested without having to pass a market test is often wasted.

Concept Review Questions	**10.** What characteristics surrounding a merger would lead you to conclude that it is motivated by value-maximizing managers rather than non-value-maximizing managers? What actions could directors or stockholders take to prevent non-value-maximizing mergers?
	11. If you wanted to expand your operations into a foreign country with nebulous laws and an unstable political climate, would you favor internal or external expansion? Why?
	12. What does Jensen's agency cost of overvalued equity model predict about the valuation effect of mergers, particularly those paid for with bidding-firm stock? Why do you think that managers might be tempted to pursue size-increasing mergers even when these do not maximize value?

24.5 HISTORY AND REGULATION OF MERGERS AND ACQUISITIONS

Merger activity in the United States has been defined more by waves of concentrated intensity than by continuous activity over time. These waves tend to be positively related to high growth rates in the overall economy and are also related to "industry shocks," or industrywide events such as deregulation that affect the corporate control activities of whole industries and lead to these merger waves. In this section, we identify the key merger waves in U.S. history and discuss the factors that led to their occurrence as well as the corporate control regulation that has evolved over time.

THE HISTORY OF MERGER WAVES

The United States has witnessed five major merger waves in its history, most of which have been similar in nature. They begin with a robust stock market, and the types of mergers occurring in each wave reflect the current regulatory environment. Activity is generally concentrated in industries undergoing changes (shocks), and the merger waves tend to end with large declines in the stock market. The following discussion presents an overview of these waves.

The first major merger wave began in 1897 and was largely the result of a growing emphasis on a truly national economy rather than a grouping of regional economies. Merger activity peaked in 1899 in this wave and ended with the stock market crash of 1904. Another merger wave began shortly after World War I, with a zeal for consolidation equal to that of the first wave. Like the first wave, the second wave ended with a stock market decline, the infamous 1929 crash. Conglomerate mergers set the tone for the third merger wave, in the 1960s. Corporations became portfolios of business units; the diversification across different industries was supposed to reduce the risk of the corporation and the volatility of its cash flows in the same manner as portfolio diversification. The push for conglomeration was so great during this wave that approximately 70 percent of the mergers that took place in the 1960s were either pure conglomerate or product extension mergers. This wave ended with the stock market decline of 1969.

The most interesting and dramatic merger wave occurred in the 1980s. Initiated by the more lax regulatory emphasis of the Reagan administration, the fourth merger wave saw a shift back to corporate specialization and witnessed such occurrences as junk bond financing, hostile takeovers, corporate raiders, greenmail, LBOs, MBOs, and poison pills. Many antitakeover measures were adopted in the 1980s to prevent such hostile takeover attempts. This merger wave differs from previous ones in that it did not end with a major stock market decline, but rather petered out as the 1980s bull market ended.

Friendly stock-swap mergers became the transaction method of choice in the fifth and latest wave of mergers, which began in 1993 and ended with the sharp drop in takeovers during 2001. Following the trend of corporate specialization from the fourth wave, the vast majority of mergers in this wave occurred between companies in the same industry. Federal regulators remained relatively open to horizontal mergers as merger activity in other countries also led to larger (and supposedly more efficient) foreign competitors. Merger activity in this wave surpassed that in all the others, reaching $3.4 trillion in aggregate transaction value in the peak year of 2000. Of this aggregate value, slightly less than $1.8 trillion was generated from deals completed in the United States and about $1.6 trillion from deals outside the United States. The total value of mergers worldwide fell by more than half over the next two years, before rebounding sharply during 2004 and the first two quarters of 2005. Table 24.5 details the 15 largest corporate mergers of all time.

REGULATION OF CORPORATE CONTROL ACTIVITIES

The legal environment affecting mergers evolved from a state of virtually no regulation during the first merger wave to what is currently a relatively complex nexus of interrelated legal issues, including antitrust enforcement, tender offer regulation, and laws regarding the actions of managers and directors and even actions of state and international regulators. This section addresses these legal issues and their ramifications for the decision to merge.

Antitrust Regulation. Antitrust legislation is intended to prevent an anticompetitive business environment. Obviously, mergers—especially horizontal mergers—often represent the most expedient manner to create corporate giants with the power to control prices in their markets. For this reason, antitrust enforcement encompasses the prevention of mergers that are deemed to have anticompetitive effects. Antitrust

Acquirer	Target	Transaction Value ($ billions)	Year
Vodafone AirTouch PLC (UK)	Mannesmann AG (Germany)	$202.8	2000
America Online Inc. (US)	Time Warner Inc. (US)	164.7	2001
Pfizer Inc. (US)	Warner-Lambert Co. (US)	89.2	2000
Royal Dutch Petroleum (Netherlands)	Shell Trading and Transport (UK)	80.1	2005
Exxon Corp. (US)	Mobil Corp. (US)	78.9	1999
Glaxo Wellcome PLC (UK)	SmithKline Beecham (UK)	76.0	2000
Travelers Group Inc. (US)	Citicorp (US)	72.6	1998
Sprint (US)	Nextel Communications (US)	71.0	2004
Sanofi (France)	Aventis (France)	65.7	2004
SBC Communications Inc. (US)	Ameritech Corp. (US)	62.6	1999
NationsBank Corp. (US)	BankAmerica Corp. (US)	61.6	1998
Vodafone Group PLC (UK)	AirTouch Communications (US)	60.3	1999
JP Morgan (US)	Bank One (US)	58.8	2004
Pfizer (US)	Pharmacia (US/Europe)	58.0	2003
British Petroleum (UK)	American Oil Company (US)	48.2	1999

Source: Mergers & Acquisitions (SDC Publishing), Mergers and Acquisitions Report (Thomson Financial), and *Financial Times* (from www.ft.com).

regulation began with the loophole-ridden Sherman Antitrust Act of 1890, was reinforced by the Clayton Act of 1914, and then was further strengthened by the Celler-Kefauver Act of 1950. The level of antitrust enforcement, administered in part by the Department of Justice (DOJ), tends to be related to the philosophy of the governing executive administration. Following passage of the Celler-Kefauver Act, antitrust laws were relatively strictly enforced, until the Reagan administration took office and relaxed antitrust enforcement. Aside from a few noted cases, antitrust enforcement has remained more lax since the 1980s.[15] The following sections outline the major aspects of various antitrust laws as well as the guidelines established by the regulatory agencies for determining the anticompetitive potential of a merger.

Antitrust Laws. The Sherman Antitrust Act initiated antitrust regulation in 1890 and has been amended and modified many times since. The last major federal antitrust legislation was enacted in 1976, but the interpretation of antitrust laws is a dynamic process in which regulatory agencies maintain an ongoing dialogue on the application of the laws.

Determination of Anticompetitiveness. Much like the business concentration classifications of the Federal Trade Commission (FTC), the measures and determinants of anticompetitiveness have evolved over time. The DOJ established the first set of merger guidelines for determining anticompetitiveness in 1968 and modified them in 1982, 1984, and 1992. The following guidelines are those currently utilized by the DOJ and FTC.

The 1982 guidelines introduced the use of the Herfindahl-Hirschman Index (HHI), a variant of the Herfindahl Index defined earlier, to determine market con-

---

[15.] Such exceptions include the DOJ's refusal to allow Microsoft and Intuit to merge in 1994 and its continued pursuit of Microsoft for anticompetitive business practices.

centration in the same manner that we used the index to measure business concentration earlier in the chapter. The DOJ determines the anticompetitive effect of a merger by evaluating that merger's impact on the HHI of the industry involved. The HHI is calculated as the sum of the squares of each company's percentage of sales within a market (industry). This HHI is then used to establish a range of concentration levels within a market or industry:

HHI > 1,800	Highly concentrated
HHI = 1,000–1,800	Moderately concentrated
HHI < 1,000	Not concentrated

Mergers resulting in an HHI measure in the highly concentrated category are the most likely to be challenged. Consider the example in Table 24.6. The premerger HHI of this industry is 1,450 (moderately concentrated). A merger between Company 7 and Company 8 would reduce the number of competitors in the industry, but the marginal impact of a merger between the two smallest players in the industry would increase the HHI to only 1,500 and would likely not face a challenge. However, a merger between the two largest firms in the industry would result in an HHI of 2,050—moving this industry from moderately to highly concentrated and likely prompting a challenge by the DOJ or FTC.

Realizing the efficiency-enhancing benefits of economies of scale and scope, which come only from increased size, the regulatory authorities developed an alternative measure to determine the anticompetitiveness of a merger. This alternative, an elasticity measure, offers an advantage over the strict use of the HHI: The elasticity measure does not necessarily deem a merger to be anticompetitive because of fewer competitors in a highly concentrated industry. Instead, an elasticity measure determines if a merged firm will have the market power to control prices in its market. The DOJ uses a "5 percent rule" to measure elasticity: If a 5 percent increase in price results in a greater than 5 percent decline in demand in a market, then that market is elastic. Elastic markets are less likely to be adversely impacted by a merger and also less likely to be strictly governed by the HHI measure.

Table 24.6
Determination of Anticompetitiveness—an Illustration of the Use of the Herfindahl-Hirschman Index (HHI)

Premerger Concentration			Postmerger Concentration					
Firm	Market Share (%)	Market Share Squared	Firm	Market Share (%)	Market Share Squared	Firm	Market Share (%)	Market Share Squared
1	20	0.0400	1	20	0.0400	1 + 2	35	0.1225
2	15	0.0225	2	15	0.0225	3	15	0.0225
3	15	0.0225	3	15	0.0225	4	15	0.0225
4	15	0.0225	4	15	0.0225	5	15	0.0225
5	15	0.0225	5	15	0.0225	6	10	0.0100
6	10	0.0100	6	10	0.0100	7	5	0.0025
7	5	0.0025	7 + 8	10	0.0100	8	5	0.0025
8	5	0.0025						
Sum		0.1450			0.1500			0.2050
HHI		1,450			1,500			2,050
Concentration	Moderate			Moderate			High	

APPLYING THE MODEL 24.3

The failed 1997 merger attempt of Staples and Office Depot exemplifies the role of regulatory agencies in preventing what are deemed to be anticompetitive combinations. On September 4, 1996, Staples and Office Depot announced their intent to merge in a $3.4 billion deal. At the time, Office Depot and Staples were the largest and second-largest office supply superstores, respectively. Of the $14.0 billion in sales in this market, Office Depot had a market share of $6.6 billion, followed by Staples with $4.1 billion, and the only other major competitor, Office-Max, with sales of $3.3 billion.

As permitted under the Hart-Scott-Rodino Act, the Federal Trade Commission (FTC) reviewed the proposed merger for anticompetitive effects and requested more information from the companies at the end of the initial review period. At the end of the second review, the FTC concluded that the proposed merger would have an anticompetitive impact if allowed to be consummated and rejected the merger proposal. One of the key points cited by the FTC in its rejection was the market power that the merged firm would be able to wield in those markets where no stores other than Staples or Office Depot existed (the 5 percent rule). In order to remedy this obstacle, Staples and Office Depot proposed to sell 63 stores to Office-Max in the geographic market where both Staples and Office Depot were located. The FTC again rejected the merger and threatened to sue the companies in federal court if they attempted to pursue their merger. The FTC further threatened that if it could not prevent the merger under the Hart-Scott-Rodino Act through its federal lawsuit, it would continue to pursue the merged firm for antitrust violations.

The managers of both companies continued to fight for their merger, despite the FTC's threats. When presenting their argument to the federal judge assigned to the case, lawyers for the companies presented the companies' willingness to sell off stores in order to satisfy the FTC and enhance competition and also contended that the FTC had improperly defined their industry when determining the Herfindahl-Hirschman Index. The FTC had limited their industry classification to office supply superstores with three competitors and an HHI of 3,634 (already highly concentrated), which would increase to 6,394 after the merger. Lawyers for the companies, however, stated that the appropriate industry classification should be discount retailers and should include such retailers as Wal-Mart and Kmart in addition to office supply stores. The judge in the case disagreed with the companies' lawyers and sided with the FTC in barring the merger from taking place. The managers of Staples and Office Depot announced their intentions to abandon their merger plans shortly thereafter.

Although merger guidelines have evolved over time and now seem to be less hostile toward horizontal combinations, the DOJ and FTC remain active enforcers of antitrust laws.

Other Antitrust Considerations. Managers contemplating a merger now face antitrust scrutiny from sources other than U.S. federal regulators. Globalization and proactive state regulators have created more recent obstacles to merger approval. Individual states have become more active participants in the oversight of anticompetitive business practices since the 1990s. State attorneys general from 14 states joined the antitrust lawsuit first lodged against Microsoft by the Justice Department in 1994. Even after the federal government abandoned its case against Microsoft in 2001 in an effort to settle the case out of court, many of the states refused to abandon their status as plaintiffs against Microsoft. Although only California has expressed an open willingness to file suit in opposition to a merger on the grounds of anticompetitiveness, the vigilance of the plaintiff states in the antitrust case against Microsoft indicates that state regulators could become an impediment to future mergers.

The Williams Act. During the conglomerate merger wave of the 1960s, hostile tender offers became an increasingly frequent and controversial means to facilitate takeovers. The controversy over these tender offers revolved around target shareholders' inability to evaluate the terms of the tender offers in the often-short periods of time for which they were open and around the abuses of higher takeover premiums being offered to select shareholders. In response to this controversy, the Williams Act passed in 1967 and was enacted in 1968 as an amendment to the Securities and Exchange Commission Act of 1934. Section 13 of the Williams Act introduced ownership disclosure requirements, and Section 14 created rules for the tender offer process.

Ownership Disclosure Requirements. Section 13-d of the Williams Act now requires public disclosure of ownership levels beyond 5 percent.[16] This section of the act mandates that any individual, group of individuals acting in concert, or firm must file a Schedule 13-d form within 10 days of acquiring a 5 percent or greater stake in a publicly traded company. This disclosure sends a warning signal to the managers and stockholders of a corporation that a potential acquirer might be lurking about and provides background information on that potential acquirer. Stockholders or managers of the corporation may sue for damages if any material misrepresentation (such as initiating a later takeover attempt when the stated purpose of ownership is for investment purposes) is made on the form.[17]

Tender Offer Regulation. Prior to the passage of the Williams Act, tender offers were largely unregulated open calls to the shareholders of public companies to tender (sell) their shares at offered prices. Section 14 changed this free-form nature of the tender offer market to a much more restrictive and structured process. Any party initiating a tender offer must file a Schedule 14-d-1 form (a tender offer statement). Managers of tender offer targets are then required to file a Schedule 14-d-9 form, which contains their recommendation to shareholders on whether to accept, reject, or refrain from supplying an opinion on the offer. Section 14 also provides structural rules and restrictions on the tender offer process. These rules include a minimum tender offer period of 20 days, the right of target shareholders to withdraw shares already tendered at any time during the tender offer period, and the requirement that the acquirer accept all shares tendered and that all tendered shares will receive the same price.

Other Legal Issues Concerning Corporate Control. Federal securities laws also regulate the actions of managers in corporate control events. The high-profile insider-trading scandals of the 1980s generated a keen interest in these laws, while the 2001 Enron and WorldCom scandals prompted Congress to pass the Sarbanes-Oxley Act of 2002. While this act primarily targeted accounting practices, it also mandated significant changes in how, and how much, information companies must report to investors. Individual states have also become more interested in promoting corporate control legislation after witnessing business practices that were perceived as detrimental to the welfare of the electorate. In recent years, many states have developed antitakeover and antitrust laws designed to regulate takeovers of corporations located in

---

[16.] The threshold was originally 10 percent but was dropped to 5 percent in 1970.

[17.] It is also illegal to "park" shares, which means engaging another individual to buy shares for you in order to avoid disclosure requirements.

their states. We describe the major elements of these other federal and state corporate control laws in the following sections.

Laws Affecting Corporate Insiders. A variety of federal securities laws govern the actions of corporate managers and other individuals considered to be corporate insiders during corporate control events. The majority of these laws attempt to prevent informed trading on material nonpublic information (inside information), such as an upcoming takeover attempt known only to the insiders of the acquiring firm. Rule 10-b-5 dictated by the Securities and Exchange Commission outlaws material misrepresentation of information used in the sale or purchase of a security. Trading on inside information about a pending merger is such a material misrepresentation because material information (news of the merger) is being withheld. Also, SEC Rule 14-e-3 specifically forbids trading on inside information in tender offers. The Insider Trading Sanctions Act of 1984 strengthened both SEC rules with triple damage awards. Managers are also restricted from issuing misleading information regarding merger negotiations and may be sued if they deny the existence of merger negotiations that are actually taking place. Finally, Section 16 of the Securities and Exchange Act establishes a monitoring facility for the trading of corporate insiders.

State Laws. Individual states have increasingly regulated corporate control activities over the years. Some states have adopted various antitakeover and anti-bust-up provisions and formed antitrust agencies that restrict corporate control activities in their states beyond the level of federal regulations.

Antitakeover and anti-bust-up provisions include voting initiatives, such as supermajority voting, which requires that large majorities (usually 67 percent) approve a takeover, and control share provisions that require the approval of target shareholders before a potential acquirer may even buy a substantial number of shares in the target firm. Fair price provisions and cash-out statutes are also popular measures that further restrict tender offers. **Fair price provisions** ensure that all target shareholders receive the same offer price in any tender offers initiated by the same acquirer, limiting the ability of acquirers to buy minority shares cheaply with a two-tiered offer. **Cash-out statutes** are "all-or-none" rules that disallow a partial tender offer/acquisition of a company and the ability to control that company with less than 100 percent ownership. Business combination rules prevent the bust-up or other major restructuring of a company that is taken over. These provisions are often used in conjunction with each other, and individual state laws must be reviewed when considering a takeover to determine if these provisions are present and, if so, what impact their presence will have on the value of the takeover. The formation of state-level antitrust regulatory boards is an even more recent trend in state corporate control regulation. California has filed antitrust lawsuits and merger injunctions. Other states are following California's lead and have become more active antitrust monitors as well.

INTERNATIONAL REGULATION OF MERGERS AND ACQUISITIONS

International regulatory authorities, especially in Europe, have become a force to be reckoned with for those companies attempting large-scale mergers. The European Commission (EC) first signaled its more stringent antitrust regulatory authority in 1999, when it vetoed the proposed merger of U.S. communications giants WorldCom and Sprint. The EC expressed concerns about the pricing power that the combined firm could have if the second- and third-largest U.S. communications firms (behind industry leader AT&T) merged to become the first- or second-largest

COMPARATIVE CORPORATE FINANCE

Searching for Effective Corporate Governance and Value-Enhancing Mergers

Enron, WorldCom, Global Crossing, Royal Ahold, Qwest Communications, Parmalat, Tyco——These are but a few of the high-profile corporate bankruptcies or near failures that have destroyed shareholder wealth and shaken investor confidence since the great 1990s bull market ended in March 2000. Underlying the much-publicized accounting scandals and extraordinary executive compensation paid out in the American corporate failures is the ultimate factor that led to their demise—ineffective corporate governance. Stockholders, bondholders, employees, journalists, and politicians (of course) are all demanding to know where the boards of directors were who were supposed to be monitoring the managers. Reforms to restore confidence in corporate America are being demanded, and proposed reforms are being sought from both domestic and international sources.

One domestic reform had already taken place before the spate of corporate failures began. Beginning in 2001, the Financial Accounting Standards Board (FASB) enacted Standards 141 and 142 to more accurately reflect merger and acquisition accounting and the goodwill account created in these transactions. The Sarbanes-Oxley Act of 2002 mandated even more detailed information disclosure and required executives to personally certify the accuracy of financial statements. However, these new standards were promulgated too late to prevent the old tricks from being used in merger and acquisition accounting in the 1990s. Before the new standards were enacted, firms could manipulate merger and acquisition accounting rules to overstate their true financial performance. When the merger wave waned and the firms could no longer use their overvalued stock to fund acquisitions, the firms' true financial performance was revealed.

International proposals for corporate governance reform have been under consideration for several years. In 1999, the Organization for Economic Cooperation and Development (OECD) first published what became a very influential list of recommended corporate governance guidelines and practices.[1] Governance structures in the United Kingdom and continental Europe are being discussed as possible alternatives to the typical governance structure in place in publicly traded U.S. corporations. In particular, two major British committees issued guidelines for more effective corporate governance during the 1990s. The three basic recommendations of the Cadbury Committee on the Financial Aspects of Corporate Governance (1992) and the Hempel Committee (1998) were that a corporation's chairman of the board and chief executive officer (CEO) always be separate persons, that the board of directors should have a majority of independent directors, and that no corporate insiders should serve on the board's audit committee. The similarity of capital markets in Britain and America appears to make these guidelines implementable as listing policies for either the New York Stock Exchange or NASDAQ.

In many continental European corporations (especially in Germany), management responsibilities are split between two mutually exclusive groups: a management board and a supervisory board consisting of representatives from the government, financial institutions, labor unions, and other interested parties. Corporate mangers do not serve on the supervisory board, which is charged with overseeing the management team. However, the continental governance system is much less consistent with the U.S. model than is the British system. First, hostile takeovers are virtually unheard of in continental Europe, whereas these are commonly used as a disciplining device in Great Britain and the United States. Second, unlike U.S. corporations, financial institutions (and often the government) have substantial ownership stakes in European corporations. On the other hand, the complete separation of a supervisory board and managers offers an appealing alternative for those seeking to reform U.S. corporate governance.

As the search continues for effective corporate governance structures in the Unites States and abroad, it has become clear that no country or system has perfected a corporate governance structure. Concurrent with the spectacular U.S. corporate failures that occurred during the spring and summer of 2002 were the precipitous declines in shareholder value and CEO ousters witnessed at French conglomerate Vivendi and German telecom giant Deutsche Telekom. In both cases the firms could not recover from acquisitions that destroyed firm value. Especially disconcerting was the saga of Sir Christopher Gent, CEO of British telecom firm Vodafone. These were followed by major scandals at Parmalat in 2003 and Royal Dutch Shell in 2004. Parmalat's entire executive team ended up in an Italian jail, while Shell's CEO was fired and the company's complex shareholding structure modified in 2005. And the search for effective corporate governance goes on.

[1.] An updated listing of these guidelines was published in 2004 and in available for downloading at http://www.oecd.org/dataoecd/32/18/315577724.pdf.

communications firm in many European markets. The managers of both WorldCom and Sprint abandoned their effort to merge after the EC's decision. EC competition commissioner Mario Monti created an international stir in 2001 when he denied the petition to merge filed by General Electric and Honeywell, although the merger had already been approved by U.S. antitrust authorities. Monti's stern defense of his position and denial of the petition on appeal sends a clear message that firms with international operations that are considering a merger must account for antitrust authorities outside the United States, even if the merger is between U.S. firms. Monti caused an even bigger stir when in early 2004 his commission sued Microsoft in an attempt to force the company to uncouple application packages from its operating system (Windows). The commission maintained that this tie gave Microsoft monopoly power. The EC won this court case in 2005, and, though Microsoft plans to appeal, this judgment has the potential to seriously undermine Microsoft's global competitive position.

Concept Review Questions

13. Which industries do you anticipate will experience industry shocks that will spur merger activity in the near future?

14. How does the dynamic interpretation of antitrust laws affect managers' acquisition strategies? What impact does the involvement of individual states have on the acquisition decision?

15. Do you believe that increasing global competition will further heighten merger activity?

24.6 CORPORATE GOVERNANCE

Every sovereign nation has a system of corporate governance, though very few countries are content with their system as it currently functions. As noted at the beginning of this chapter, a nation's corporate governance system can be defined as the set of laws, institutions, practices, and regulations that determine how limited-liability companies will be run—and in whose interest. This section begins by briefly describing why corporate governance has emerged as the single most important influence on the size and efficiency of a nation's capital markets. We then describe why efficient capital markets are so important: They promote rapid economic growth. Finally, we discuss the role that privatization programs have played in promoting capital markets and corporate governance practices around the world.

LAW AND FINANCE: CAPITAL MARKETS AND NATIONAL LEGAL SYSTEMS

Andrei Shleifer and Robert Vishny can be credited with popularizing interest in corporate governance. The research they initiated, together and with other colleagues, has examined how a country's legal system—especially whether the system is based on English common law—influences the size, efficiency, and productivity of that nation's capital markets. Using a sample of 49 countries, La Porta, Lopez-de-Silanes, Shleifer, and Vishny (1997, hereafter LLSV) show that countries with poorer investor protection—measured by both the character of legal rules and the quality of law enforcement—have smaller and less liquid capital markets. This is true for both debt and equity markets, suggesting that stock and bond markets are complements rather than supplements, and both require the proper legal infrastructure to reach maturity.

LLSV (1997) also show that French civil law countries offer much poorer investor protection than do common law countries, and LLSV (1998) describe why this is so. They examine the investor protection characteristics of the world's four basic legal systems (English common law, French civil law, and German and Scandinavian law) and find that the common law countries offer by far the greatest protection to noncontrolling investors. This study also documents (and provides a rationale for) the fact that ownership concentration is highest in countries offering poor investor protection, which is consistent with the idea that small, diversified shareholders are unlikely to be important in countries that fail to protect outside investors. Because legal systems play such a key explanatory role in explaining cross-country patterns of financial sector development and ownership structures, LLSV's 1998 study and all their subsequent work has been called the law and finance model of economic development.

In a specific investigation of the ownership structures of the largest publicly traded companies in the world's developed economies, La Porta, Lopez-de-Silanes, and Shleifer (1999) show that dispersed ownership structures are common only in the United States, Japan, and Britain. Effective family control over even the largest companies, often exercised through pyramidal share ownership structures, is the norm everywhere else. This finding is verified for Western Europe by Faccio and Lang (2002), who analyze the ultimate ownership and control of 5,232 corporations in 13 countries. LLSV (2000) also find that dividend policies in different nations are related to the agency costs of different ownership structures. Empirical studies by LLSV and others support their proposition that a nation's legal system influences the optimal ownership structures of publicly listed companies and that ownership structure "matters." LLSV (1999) find that the size of a nation's government is related to its efficiency, honesty (the legal system again), and the demographic makeup of its citizenry. LLSV (2002) document that countries offering the greatest legal protection for investors also assign the highest valuation to publicly traded shares. The clear implication of this finding is that individual investors are more willing to entrust their savings to capital market investments when they are confident that their wealth will not be expropriated by insiders.

Many other researchers have used the law and finance theoretical framework to explain cross-country differences in financial sector development. Demirgüç-Kunt and Maksimovic (1998) show that in countries whose legal systems score high on an efficiency index, a greater proportion of firms use long-term external financing. Since their measure of efficiency is different from LLSV's, the results are not a direct test of the LLSV hypothesis that common law countries offer better investor protection than civil law countries (especially since France receives higher efficiency scores than Britain). Nonetheless, Demirgüç-Kunt and Maksimovic document that an active stock market and large banking sector are associated with externally financed firm growth and that companies in countries with weak financial sectors are unable to fund maximum achievable growth.

EFFICIENT CAPITAL MARKETS PROMOTE RAPID ECONOMIC GROWTH

There is now little doubt that an efficient financial sector fosters rapid economic development. Rajan and Zingales (1998) provide evidence supporting the positive influence of financial development on economic growth by means of reducing the cost of external financing to firms. They find that financial development is especially important for the process of creating new firms in an economy, while Beck, Demirgüç-Kunt and Maksimovic (2005) show that financial impediments hinder the growth of smaller firms the most. Levine and Zervos (1998) also provide evidence suggesting that banking efficiency is critically important to the development of an economy and that banking services are different from those provided by stock markets. In fact, an entire stream of research has now emerged documenting the critical importance of an efficient financial system to sustainable economic growth.[18] The basic themes that emerge from this research are that an efficient financial system is vital and that it is very difficult to construct such a system from scratch or in place of existing (typically less effective) systems, due to the determined opposition from entrenched parties.

Rajan and Zingales (2003) actually describe the amount of national financial development as a function of the degree of interest group opposition to open markets. Whereas financial development benefits society as a whole, entrenched players such as monopolist producers and owners of financial institutions have strong incentives to stunt development of markets they cannot control. Rajan and Zingales also show that financial development does not increase monotonically over time. In fact, many countries had more developed financial markets in 1913 than they did in 1980. Figure 24.4 presents average values for three measures of financial sector development —bank deposits to GDP, equity issues to gross fixed capital formation, and stock market capitalization to GDP—for 39 mostly Western countries at roughly decade-long intervals from 1913 to 1999. All three measures were higher in 1913 than in 1980, and the 1929 peaks of deposits to GDP and equity issues to gross capital formation had still not been reached again by 1999. Only stock market capitalization relative to GDP is higher today than before the Great Depression.

Research findings demonstrating the utility and efficacy of financial markets are very important because for many years a debate has raged within academic finance regarding whether a capital market–based system of corporate finance is inherently better or worse than a bank-based system. During the late 1980s and early 1990s, when Japan and Germany appeared to be outperforming major capital market–

Figure 24.4
The Evolution of Financial Development in 39 Countries over Time, 1913–1999
Source: Table 1 in Raghuram G. Rajan and Luigi Zingales, "The Great Reversals: The Politics of Financial Development in the Twentieth Century," *Journal of Financial Economics* 69 (July 2003), pp. 5–50.

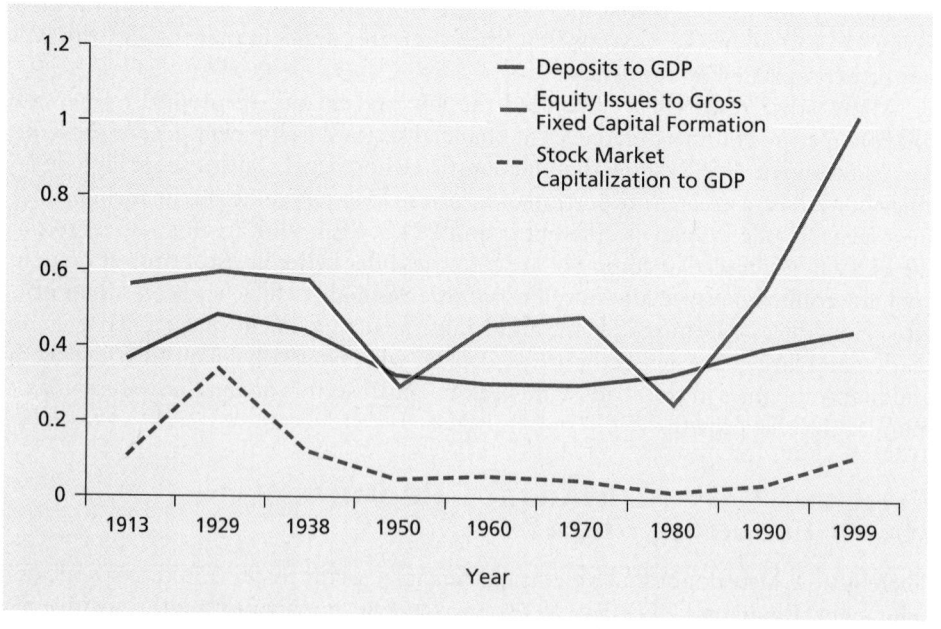

[18.] Important recent papers in this literature are Carlin and Mayer (2003), Beck, Demirgüç-Kunt, and Levine (2003), and, most recently, Claessens and Laeven (2005).

oriented countries such as Britain and the United States, the academic literature often favored bank-based systems. More recently, however, the weight of opinion has swung strongly in favor of the idea that capital markets have decisive comparative advantages over banks and other financial intermediaries as optimal monitors and financiers of a nation's corporate life. This reassessment has been driven in part by the observation, discussed earlier, that capital markets have been prospering relative to banks for many years now. Additionally, the repetitive nature and massive costs of banking crises in developing and developed countries alike has convinced many observers that banks are inherently fragile institutions whose role in corporate finance should be minimized as much and as quickly as possible.

While experience and observation have driven much of the reassessment of the optimal role of capital markets in corporate finance, academic research has also been important, since it now strongly favors capital markets over banks. The single most important paper in the stream of research documenting that capital markets are essential for good corporate governance is the influential survey article by Levine (1997). Additional papers by Levine and Zervos (1998), Rajan and Zingales (1998), and Demirgüç-Kunt and Maksimovic (1998) all provide direct or indirect support for the capital market optimality hypothesis. Other empirical studies of the impact of financial development on economic growth have documented that the size of the financial system (banks and capital markets) is not as important for growth as is the system's efficiency.

PRIVATIZATION'S IMPACT ON STOCK AND BOND MARKET DEVELOPMENT

We conclude this section by describing the impact that privatization programs—particularly those emphasizing share issue privatizations (SIPs)—have had on the development of stock and bond markets outside of the United States. A careful examination of the historical evolution of non-U.S. stock markets since 1980 suggests that large SIPs have indeed played a key expansive role almost everywhere, especially because they are generally among the largest and most valuable firms in national markets. It is clear that national governments have been among the biggest winners from privatization programs, since these have dramatically increased government revenues, which is clearly one reason the policy has spread so rapidly. The cumulative amount raised by privatizing governments since 1977 now exceeds $1.25 trillion. As an added benefit, these revenues have come to governments without their having to raise taxes or cut other public services.

While it is very difficult to establish a direct cause-and-effect relationship between SIP programs and stock market development, indirect evidence suggests that the impact has been very significant. At the end of 1983, the total market capitalization of the handful of British, Chilean, and Singaporean firms that had been privatized by then was far less than $50 billion. By the end of May 2000, the 152 privatized firms listed in either the *Business Week* "Global 1000" ranking of the most valuable companies in developed-nation stock markets or in the *Business Week* "Top 200 Emerging Market Companies" ranking had a total market capitalization of $3.31 trillion. This was equal to approximately 13 percent of the combined market capitalization of the firms on the two lists but was equal to over 27 percent of the non-U.S. total. This is because American firms accounted for 484 of the Global 1000 firms—and $13.1 trillion of the $23.9 trillion Global 1000 total capitalization in May 2000.

The total valuation of privatized companies fell sharply during 2001 and 2002, declining to $2.83 trillion by May 2002. However, the valuations of nonprivatized companies declined even more, to $17.74 trillion. By May 2004, the total valuation of the 152 privatized firms on the *Business Week* "Global 1000" list (there was no 2004 Emerging Markets list) hit a record value of $3.18 trillion, while the value of the 848 nonprivatized companies on the 2004 list, $17.9 trillion, was still below the May 2000 level. The privatized companies thus represented 15 percent of the total market value of all firms on the Global 1000 list and 31 percent of the non-U.S. market value. Therefore, between 2000 and 2004, the privatized companies significantly increased their proportional share of global stock market value from 13 percent to 15 percent and raised their share of the non-U.S. total valuation even more, from 27 percent to 31 percent. This implies that investors who purchased privatization share offerings have fared much better since March 2000 than have investors in other type of companies.

It is almost certainly the case that privatized firms have had an even greater impact on the development of non-U.S. stock markets than these aggregate numbers suggest, because they are generally among the largest firms in these markets. Using data from the 2004 Business Week Global 1000 list, Table 24.7 details which of the three most valuable companies in a nation's stock market are privatized firms. Privatized companies have the highest market values in four of the five largest non-U.S

Table 24.7
How Many of the Most Valuable Companies in Different National Stock Markets Are Privatized Firms in July 2005?

Country	Most Valuable	Second Most Valuable	Third Most Valuable
Australia		x	x
Austria		x	x
Brazil	x	x	
Britain	x		
China	x	x	x
Czech Republic	x	x	x
Finland		x	x
France	x	x	x
Germany	x		
Greece	x		x
Hungary	x		
India	x		
Israel		x	x
Italy	x	x	x
Japan		x	x
Korea			x
Malaysia		x	x
Mexico	x		x
Norway	x	x	x
Poland	x	x	x
Portugal	x	x	x
Russia	x	x	x
Singapore	x		
South Africa		x	
Spain	x		x
Taiwan		x	

Source: "The Business Week Global 1000," *Business Week* (July 26, 2004), downloaded from www.businessweek.com.

markets—Britain, France, Germany, and Italy—as well as in the four largest emerging markets—China, India, Mexico, and Brazil. They are the second most valuable firms in Australia, Finland, Israel, Japan, Malaysia, the Netherlands, South Africa, and Taiwan. Privatized companies occupy the three (or more) top slots in the developed countries France, Italy, and Norway and in the emerging markets China, the Czech Republic, Hungary, Poland, and Russia. In most of these national markets, privatized companies also dominate stock trading volume and are owned by more individual investors than all nonprivatized firms combined. It is no exaggeration to assert that the primary initial experience with stock market ownership for most of the world's investors has been purchasing stock in a privatized company.

---

16. What does the term *corporate governance* mean?

17. Would you expect corporate ownership to be more widely dispersed among a nation's investors in a country with a common law system of corporate law or a civil law system? Why?

18. How important are privatized firms for most non-U.S. stock markets?

Concept Review Questions

24.7 SUMMARY

- Mergers and acquisitions are major corporate finance events that, when executed efficiently and with the proper motives, can help managers realize their ultimate goal of maximizing shareholder wealth. Merging firms may be integrated in a number of ways, and the circumstances surrounding the merger determine the means of integration. Transactions may be hostile or friendly; may be financed by cash, stock, debt, or some combination of the three; and may increase, preserve, or decrease the acquirer's level of business concentration.

- Research on corporate control is bountiful. Major empirical findings include the following: Target shareholders almost always win but acquirers' returns are mixed. The combined value of merging firms also increases, especially in nonconglomerate combinations. The highest announcement-period returns are found in mergers between well-managed acquirers and poorly managed targets. Long-term performance is highest for focus-increasing deals financed with cash and lowest for diversifying mergers financed with stock.

- Managers have either value-maximizing or non-value-maximizing motives for pursuing mergers. Value-maximizing motives include expansion into new markets, capturing size economies and other synergies, establishing market power, and generating free cash flow to make better investments. Agency problems result in such non-value-maximizing motives as empire building, entrenchment, hubris, and diversification.

- Merger activity occurs in waves spurred by industrywide events such as deregulation. Domestically, we have witnessed five major merger waves: a turn-of-the-twentieth-century wave of horizontal mergers, a 1920s wave of vertical mergers, the 1960s wave of conglomerate mergers, the 1980s wave that deconstructed many of the 1960s conglomerates, and a recent wave of deregulation-based mergers and consolidations made in preparation for an increasingly global economy. Antitrust enforcement at the time affects activity in each of these waves.

- Corporate control activities are regulated by federal, and, increasingly, state and international authorities. Federal antitrust legislation has been developed over the course of the century, but its enforcement ebbs and flows with the executive administration in office. The Williams Act established disclosure requirements for ownership in public corporations as well as regulation of tender offers. Federal securities laws also prohibit corporate insiders from trading on the nonpublic information of a pending takeover.

- Corporate governance refers to the set of laws, institutions, practices, and regulations that determine how limited-liability companies will be run—and in whose interest. The law and finance model of economic development asserts that countries with English common law systems of corporate law will have larger and more efficient capital markets than will countries with civil law commercial codes, because common law offers greater legal protections to individual investors. Ownership of corporate equity will be more widely dispersed in common law countries for the same reason. Research now conclusively shows that having large, efficient financial markets allows a country to achieve more rapid economic growth and that share issue privatization programs have contributed to stock market development around the world.

INTERNET RESOURCES

Note: *For updates to links, please go to the book's website at http://megginson.swcollege.com.*

http://www.sec.gov/about/laws.shtml—"The Laws That Govern the Securities Industry" section of the U.S. Securities and Exchange Commission's website; provides a brief overview of the six key laws that the SEC enforces, including those relating to tender offers and M&A regulations

http://europa.eu.int/pol/comp/index_en.htm—The "Competition" section of the European Union's official website; describes the key legislation setting up this commission, provides an overview of its enforcement philosophy, and describes key ongoing cases

http://www.oecd.org/dataoecd/32/18/31557724.pdf—The OECD's Principles of Corporate Governance 2004

KEY TERMS

acquisition
agency cost of overvalued equity
antitakeover amendments
backward integration
bust-up
cash-out statutes
coinsurance of debt
conglomerate mergers
consolidation
corporate control
corporate focus
divestiture
dual-class recapitalization
economies of scale
economies of scope

employee stock ownership plan (ESOP)
fair price provisions
financial synergies
forward integration
going-private transactions
goodwill
greenfield entry
greenmail
Herfindahl Index (HI)
horizontal merger
hubris hypothesis of corporate takeovers
internal capital markets
management buyout (MBO)
managerial synergies
managerialism theory of mergers

market extension merger
market power
merger
mixed offerings
operational synergy
overvalued equity
poison pills
product extension mergers
pure conglomerate mergers
pure stock exchange merger
resource complementarities
reverse LBO
shark repellents

spin-off
split-off
split-up
statutory merger
strategic merger
subsidiary merger
synergy
takeover
tax-loss carryforwards
tender offer
tender-merger
vertical merger
white knights

QUESTIONS

24-1. What is meant by a change in corporate control? List and describe the various ways in which a change of corporate control may occur.

24-2. What is a tender offer, and how can it be used as a mechanism to orchestrate a merger?

24-3. Differentiate between the different levels of business concentration created by mergers. Explain how the changing business environment has caused an evolution in the classification of concentration from the original FTC classification to the abbreviated FTC classification and now to the measures of overlap and focus.

24-4. Elaborate on the significance of the mode of payment for the stockholders of the target firm and their continued interest in the surviving firm. Specifically, which form of payment retains the stockholders of the target firm as stockholders in the surviving firm? Which payment form receives preferential tax treatment?

24-5. What is the signaling theory of mergers? What is the relationship between signaling and the mode of payment used in acquisitions? Is there a relationship between the mode of payment used in acquisitions and the level of insider shareholdings of acquiring firms?

24-6. Empirically, what are the wealth effects of corporate control activities? Who wins and who loses in corporate control contests? What explanations or theories are offered for the differences in returns of acquiring firms' common stocks? Why are higher takeover premiums paid in cash transactions than in stock transactions? How do other security holders fare in takeovers?

24-7. Relate the industry shock theory of mergers to the history of merger waves. What were the motivating factors for increased merger activity during each of the five major merger waves?

24-8. Under what conditions would external expansion be preferable to internal expansion? What is the ultimate decision criterion for determining the acceptability of any expansion strategy?

24-9. Delineate the value-maximizing motives for mergers. How are these motives interrelated?

24-10. Define the three types of synergy that may result from mergers. What are the sources of these synergies?

24-11. Explain how agency problems may lead to non-value-maximizing motives for mergers. Discuss the various academic theories offered as the rationale for these agency problem-induced motives.

24-12. Describe the relationship between conglomerate mergers and portfolio theory. What is the desired result of merging two unrelated businesses? Has the empirical evidence proven corporate diversification to be successful?

24-13. List the federal laws regulating antitrust and anticompetitive mergers. What are the actions governed by each law? How do the regulatory agencies determine anticompetitiveness?

24-14. What is the purpose of the Williams Act? What are the specific provisions of the act?

24-15. What are the restrictions faced by corporate insiders during corporate control events?

24-16. How have individual states become more active monitors of takeover activity?

24-17. What is the law and finance model of economic development, and what are its key predictions? Have these predictions been verified by empirical testis?

24-18. Respond to the following statement: "Countries with large and efficient financial systems will generally achieve higher rates of economic growth than will countries with smaller, inefficient financial sectors."

24-19. How have share issue privatization (SIP) programs promoted the development of non-U.S. stock markets over the past quarter-century?

PROBLEMS

Overview of Corporate Control Activities

24-1. A firm has four divisions—food, cookware, retail, and credit services—that generate revenues of $1.5 million, $3.8 million, $5.7 million, and $3.1 million, respectively. Compute the Herfindahl Index (HI) for the firm. The firm is considering the purchase of a rival retailer, which would increase the retail division's revenues by another $3.2 million. The firm is also considering selling its credit services division. Assuming these two actions occur, what will the HI become? What is the HI if the sale of the credit division does not occur, but the rival is acquired?

24-2. HHG Consultants has been asked to analyze Carol & Carroll Co. (C&C), which has one retail division. C&C is concerned that it is not focused on its core mission of sales despite only having one division. Each store is divided into departments: casual clothing (CC), formal clothing (FC), outerwear (OW), shoes (S), and specialty items (SI). C&C's initial impression is that all of the departments contribute equally towards sales. However, upon examination of the sales of each department, the actual breakdown of sales is much different: $5.2 billion (CC), $2.7 billion (FC), $3.75 billion (OW), $4.5 billion (S), and $1.7 billion (SI). Compute a Herfindahl Index (HI) based on the departments having equal sales and based on the actual sales. Your conclusion of the firm becoming "unfocused" will be based on the actual HI being lower than the equivalent sales HI scenario. What does your analysis find with regard to the focus of C&C's retailing division?

24-3. Firm X has three divisions that generate revenues of $1.3 billion, $2.5 billion, and $5.2 billion. Firm Y is a competitor with three associated divisions that generate $2 billion each. Using a Herfindahl Index (HI) to measure focus, determine if both Firm X and Firm Y shareholders would see a merger as focus increasing or focus decreasing.

24-4. Shareholders of the firm Up-4-Grabs (U4G) have been offered $36.00 per share in cash for each of their U4G shares currently selling for $29.53. What is the control premium being offered in this cash deal? U4G is also considering a stock swap offer from another firm, BuyNow Inc. (BYN). BYN will issue one share for every two shares of U4G. At what price will BYN shares be equivalent to the control premium available in the cash offer? When news leaks out about the merger, BYN shares increase to $77.00 and U4G shares increase to $35.24. What control premium does BYN offer now?

24-5. HBABB Corp. has purchased all of the 10 million shares of BOBCO stock for $43.75 a share. BOBCO's net asset value is $350 million. How much goodwill does HBABB need to consider on its balance sheet. Suppose part of the deal requires HBABB to pay $30 million of BOBCO's debt. Refigure the net asset value (i.e., reduce the debt by $30 million) and recalculate the goodwill. One of your accountants tells you that the net asset value should not be changed and the $30 million used for BOBCO's debt is added to the purchase price. Refigure the goodwill calculation and determine if there really is a difference. If there is a difference, which calculation is correct?

24-6. Mega Service Corporation (MSC) is offering to exchange 2.5 shares of its own stock for each share of target firm Norman Corporation stock as consideration for a proposed merger. There are 10 million Norman Corp shares outstanding, and its stock price was $60 before the merger offer. MSC's preoffer stock price was $30. What is the control premium percentage offered? Now suppose that when the merger is consummated eight months later, MSC's stock price drops to $25. At that point, what is the control premium percentage and total transaction value?

24-7. Bulldog Industries is offering, as consideration for merger, target Blazerco 1.5 shares of their stock for each share of Blazerco. There are 1 million shares of Blazerco outstanding, and its stock price was $50 before the merger offer. Bulldog's preoffer stock price was $40. What is the control premium percentage offered? Now suppose that when the merger is consummated six months later, Bulldog's stock price drops to $30. At that point, what is the control premium percentage and total transaction value?

24-8. You are the director of capital acquisitions for Crimson Software Company. One of the projects you are considering is the acquisition of Geekware, a private software company that produces software for finance professors. Dave Vanzandt, the owner of Geekware, is amenable to the idea of selling his enterprise to Crimson, but he has certain conditions that must be met before selling. The primary condition set forth is a nonnegotiable, all-cash purchase price of $20 million. Your project analysis team estimates that the purchase of Geekware will generate the following marginal cash flow:

Year	Cash Flow
1	$1,000,000
2	3,000,000
3	5,000,000
4	7,500,000
5	7,500,000

Of the $20 million in cash needed for the purchase, $5 million is available from retained earnings, with a required return of 12 percent, and the remaining $15 million will come from a new debt issue yielding 8 percent. Crimson's tax rate is 40 percent. Should you recommend acquiring Geekware to your CEO?

24-9. You are the director of capital acquisitions for Morningside Hotel Company. One of the projects you are deliberating is the acquisition of Monroe Hospitality, a company that owns and operates a chain of bed-and-breakfast inns. Susan Sharp, Monroe's owner, is willing to sell her company to Morningside only if she is offered an all-cash purchase price of $5 million. Your project analysis team estimates that the purchase of Monroe Hospitality will generate the following after-tax marginal cash flow:

Year	Cash Flow
1	$1,000,000
2	1,500,000
3	2,000,000
4	2,500,000
5	3,000,000

If you decide to go ahead with this acquisition, it will be funded with Morningside's standard mix of debt and equity, at the firm's weighted average (after-tax) cost of capital of 9 percent. Morningside's tax rate is 30 percent. Should you recommend acquiring Monroe Hospitality to your CEO?

24-10. Firm A plans to acquire Firm B. The acquisition would result in incremental cash flows for Firm A of $10 million in each of the first five years. Firm A expects to divest Firm B at the end of the fifth year for $100 million. The β for Firm A is 1.1, which is expected to remain unchanged after the acquisition. The risk-free rate, R_f, is 7 percent, and the expected market rate of return, R_m, is 15 percent. Firm A is financed by 80 percent equity and 20 percent debt, and this leverage will also remain unchanged after the acquisition. Firm A pays interest of 10 percent on its debt, which will also remain unchanged after the acquisition.

   a. Disregarding taxes, what is the maximum price that Firm A should pay for firm B?

   b. Firm A has a stock price of $30 per share and 10 million shares outstanding. If Firm B shareholders are to be paid the maximum price determined in part (a) via a new stock issue, how many new shares will be issued, and what will be the post-merger stock price?

24-11. Charger Incorporated and Sparks Electrical Company are competitors in the business of electrical components distribution. Sparks is the smaller firm and has garnered the attention of the management of Charger, for Sparks has taken away market share from the larger firm by increasing its sales force over the past few years. Charger is considering a takeover offer for Sparks and has asked you to serve on the acquisition valuation team that will turn into the due diligence team if an offer is made and accepted. Given the following information and assumptions:

   a. Make your recommendation about whether or not the acquisition should be pursued.

   b. Assume Sparks has accepted the takeover offer from Charger, and now the new subsidiary must be consolidated within Charger's financial statements. Taking Sparks' most recent balance sheet and a restated market value of assets of $295.6 million, calculate the goodwill that must be booked for this transaction.

Sparks Electrical Company Condensed
Balance Sheet Previous Year ($ in millions)

	2006
Current assets	$ 12.2
Fixed assets	442.5
Total assets	$454.7
Current liabilities	$ 10.1
Long-term debt	150.0
Total liabilities	$160.1
Shareholders' equity	$294.6
Total liabilities and equity	$454.7

Sparks Electrical Company
Condensed Income Statement
Previous Five Years
($ in millions)

	2006	2005	2004	2003	2002
Revenues	$1,626.5	$1,614.1	$1,485.2	$1,380.5	$1,373.4
Less: Cost of goods sold	1,488.1	1,490.9	1,359.5	1,271.4	1,268.0
Gross profit	$ 138.4	$ 123.2	$ 125.7	$ 109.1	$ 105.4
Selling, general, & administrative expenses (SG&A)	$ 41.1	$ 36.8	$ 41.2	$ 35	$ 36.1
Noncash expense (depreciation & amortization)	7.3	6.7	7.1	6.6	6.4
Less: Operating expense	$ 48.4	$ 43.5	$ 48.3	$ 41.6	$ 42.5
Operating profit (*EBIT*)	$ 90.0	$ 79.7	$ 77.4	$ 67.5	$ 62.9
Less: Interest expense	11.5	12.0	12.0	12.0	12.0
Earnings before taxes (*EBT*)	$ 78.5	$ 67.7	$ 65.4	$ 55.5	$ 50.9
Less: Taxes paid	24.3	20.8	19.9	16.8	15.3
Net income	$ 54.2	$ 46.9	$ 45.5	$ 38.7	$ 35.6

Assumptions:

- Sparks would become a wholly owned subsidiary of Charger.
- Revenues will continue to grow at 4.3 percent for the next five years and will level off at 4 percent thereafter.
- Cost of goods sold will represent 95 percent of revenue going forward.
- Sales force layoffs will reduce SG&A expenses to $22 million next year, with a 2 percent growth rate going forward.
- These layoffs and other restructuring charges are expected to result in expensed restructuring charges of $30 million, $15 million, and $5 million, respectively, over the next three years.
- Noncash expenses are expected to remain around $7 million going forward.
- Interest expenses are expected to remain around $11.5 million going forward.
- A tax rate of 31 percent is assumed going forward.
- Charger's cost of equity is 12 percent.
- Sparks' current market capitalization is $315.7 million.
- Charger will offer Sparks a takeover premium of 20 percent over current market capitalization.

24-12. Referring to Problem 24-6, assume it is now two years after the acquisition of Sparks, and you must perform a goodwill-impairment test of the subsidiary. Growth expectations have been lowered to 3 percent going forward. Using the following five-year projection of cash flows and a 12 percent cost of equity, estimate the value of the subsidiary beyond year 5, the current value of the subsidiary, the current value of goodwill, and any goodwill impairment. Total assets (excluding intangibles) are now $612.5 million, and total liabilities are $175.0 million.

	Cash Flow Projection for Next Five Years				
	2009	2010	2011	2012	2013
Revenues	$1,815.2	$1,869.7	$1,925.7	$1,983.5	$2,043.0
Less: Cost of goods sold @95% of revenue	1,724.4	1,776.2	1,829.5	1,884.3	1,940.9
Gross profit	$ 90.8	$ 93.5	$ 96.2	$ 99.2	$ 102.1
SG&A expense @2% growth rate going forward	$ 23.0	$ 23.5	$ 23.9	$ 24.4	$ 24.9
Noncash expense (depreciation & amortization)	7.0	7.0	7.0	7.0	7.0
Less: Operating expense	$ 30.0	$ 30.5	$ 30.9	$ 31.4	$ 31.9
Operating profit (*EBIT*)	$ 60.8	$ 63.0	$ 65.3	$ 67.8	$ 70.2
Less: Interest expense	11.5	11.5	11.5	11.5	11.5
Less: Restructuring charges	5.0	0.0	0.0	0.0	0.0
Earnings before taxes (*EBT*)	$ 44.3	$ 51.5	$ 53.8	$ 56.3	$ 58.7
Less: Taxes paid	13.7	16.0	16.7	17.4	18.2
Net income	$ 30.6	$ 35.5	$ 37.1	$ 38.9	$ 40.5
Free cash flow	$ 54.1	$ 54.0	$ 55.6	$ 57.4	$ 59.0

24-13. Firms AFD, TYU, CHG, and LAN are competitors within an industry. Their respective sales figures are $2.8 billion, $3.9 billion, $4.8 billion, and $2.1 billion. What is the Herfindahl-Hirschman Index (HHI) for the industry, and is the industry considered highly concentrated, moderately concentrated, or not concentrated? Assuming two more firms are added to the industry figures, QBC ($3.6 billion in sales) and RTY ($2.7 billion in sales), does the concentration level of the industry change (recompute HHI to determine this)? If the three smallest firms merged (AFD, LAN, and RTY), would the FTC be concerned, and if so, why? [*Note:* The HHI is measured in units of (%)^2. For example, 50% $\times$ 50% = 2,500 (%)^2. To make the conversion mathematically, multiply the answer by 10,000, using the same example: 50% $\times$ 50% $\times$ 10,000 = 2,500.]

24-14. A given market was initially segmented evenly among 20 firms (Phase 1). Five years later, the market was still segmented evenly among competing firms, but there were now only ten firms (Phase 2). Eventually six firms emerged with equal portions of the market (Phase 3), but a move toward deregulation of the industry has prompted two of the firms to merge. Determine the Herfindahl-Hirschman Index (HHI) for the three phases documented. Next, determine if the merger will make the industry be considered "highly concentrated." In a preemptive move (fearing the FTC), the merged firms agree to sell off portions of the market to the other four firms to make the market equally divided between all five firms. How does this affect the HHI and is the merger viable under these circumstances? [*Note:* The HHI is measured in units of (%)^2. For example, 50% $\times$ 50% = 2,500 (%)^2. To make the conversion mathematically, multiply the answer by 10,000, using the same example: 50% $\times$ 50% $\times$ 10,000 = 2,500.]

THOMSON ONE BUSINESS SCHOOL EDITION

24-15. On November 18, 2005, SBC Communications, Inc. completed its acquisition of AT&T Corporation. The combined company was named AT&T Inc. (ticker symbol, T). Examine the 8-K report filed on November 18, 2005 (19 pages). How many shares of AT&T Inc. were exchanged for each share of AT&T Corporation? What was the total number of shares issued to the "old" AT&T shareholders? At the time of the merger, what percentage of the "new" AT&T was owned by "old" AT&T shareholders? Did "old" AT&T shareholders receive any additional compensation? What was the estimated value of the merger, based on the closing stock price on November 17, 2005?

MINI-CASE: MERGERS, CORPORATE CONTROL, AND GOVERNANCE

Jackson Enterprises (JE) is offering a 25 percent takeover premium to Michael Studios, Inc. (MSI) for the firm's 2 million outstanding shares, which are currently trading for a prebid price of $20 per share.

The balance sheet for MSI is:

Assets		Liabilities	
Current	$15,000,000	Current	$ 7,500,000
Fixed	$45,000,000	Long-term	$25,000,000
Total	$60,000,000	Total	$32,500,000
		Owner's equity	$27,500,000
		Total liabilities and equity	$60,000,000

The market value of MSI's fixed assets is $60,000,000.

The sales (in millions) for the industry by company are:

	Sales
ABC	$89
CWC	66
DEF	35
JE	45
KOJ	42
MSI	18
SEE	76

1.   Determine the amount Jackson Enterprises is willing to pay in terms of goodwill.

2. If JE's shares are currently trading at $62.43, how many shares should JE offer for every share of MSI?

3. Assuming that MSI will be treated as a separate reporting subsidiary following the merger, develop the balance sheet for the subsidiary.

4. Calculate the Herfindahl-Hirschman Index for the industry pre- and postmerger.

WorldCom Emerges from Bankruptcy with a New Name, New Management, and a New Capital Structure—and Is Soon Acquired

It had been the largest bankruptcy in U.S. history, but was now coming to an end. On April 20, 2004, MCI Inc. emerged from Chapter 11 bankruptcy with an announcement that it had begun distributing securities and cash to its creditors according to a court-approved reorganization plan. MCI's chief executive officer, Michael Capellas, heralded a new beginning for his company, which had filed for bankruptcy court protection 21 months earlier—when the company was called WorldCom—after disclosing an $11 billion accounting fraud. At the time of its Chapter 11 filing, WorldCom had assets totaling nearly $104 billion and debts of $32 billion.

WorldCom shocked the business world when the company announced in June 2002 that it had fraudulently overstated $3.9 billion of expenses as capital expenditures, which had allowed it to book higher profits during the telecom boom years of 1998 to 2001. WorldCom Chief Financial Officer Scott Sullivan was fired the day the accounting fraud was disclosed, and his exit followed that of founder and long-time CEO Bernie Ebbers, who had been forced out in April 2002. Over the next two years, more than $7 billion in additional accounting errors and frauds were uncovered, bringing the total misstatements to $11 billion, and in a March 2004 restatement of its 2001 and 2002 financial results the company wrote off over $74 billion in previously booked profits and goodwill. After pleading guilty to several crimes, Sullivan testified against Ebbers in his 2005 federal trial, which resulted in Ebbers' being sentenced to 25 years in prison on July 13, 2005.

WorldCom's trip through Chapter 11 bankruptcy, while painful, was also remarkably successful. With the bankruptcy court's blessing, creditors installed Capellas (formerly CEO of Compaq Computer) as CEO in November 2002. He submitted a reorganization plan five months later that called for almost all of the company's debt to be converted into equity, and over 90 percent of WorldCom's creditors voted to approve this plan. Soon thereafter, Capellas also announced that the company would change its name from the tainted WorldCom to that of its principal consumer brand, MCI Inc. Therefore, when MCI finally emerged from Chapter 11 in April 2004, the company had a new name, a new management team, and an entirely new capital structure that in some ways gave it a competitive advantage over its more heavily indebted telecom competitors.

Remarkably, within months of emerging from Chapter 11, MCI became the target of a frenzied takeover battle between Verizon Communications and Qwest Communications. Qwest initiated the contest with a $6.5 billion offer—later raised to $8 billion—in February 2005, but Verizon ultimately triumphed with an $8.45 billion bid. MCI's lucky shareholders approved the Verizon acquisition in October 2005.

Source: Financial Times, multiple issues.

A fundamental concept in economics is that competition drives markets toward a state of long-term equilibrium in which surviving companies produce at minimum average cost. This transition process eliminates firms using obsolete technologies, inefficient firms, and firms producing goods and services that are in excess supply. Consumers benefit because, in the long run, products are manufactured and sold at the lowest possible price. The mechanism through which inefficient firms leave the market is frequently bankruptcy, the legal procedure applied to businesses that fail.

In this chapter, we will examine first how and why firms fail. We then look at U.S. bankruptcy law and the ways that a business that has failed can resolve its difficulties, either voluntarily or involuntarily, through bankruptcy.

25.1 BUSINESS FAILURE FUNDAMENTALS

A **business failure** is an unfortunate circumstance. Although the majority of firms that fail do so within the first year or two of life, other firms grow, mature, and fail much later. The failure of a business can be viewed in a number of ways and can result from one or more causes.

TYPES OF BUSINESS FAILURE

A firm can fail because its returns are negative or low. A firm that consistently reports operating losses will probably experience a decline in market value. If the firm fails to earn a return that is greater than its cost of capital, it can be viewed as having experienced **economic failure.** Several old-line American industries—particularly automobile manufacturing and airlines—have been experiencing economic failure for years. Negative or low returns, unless remedied, are likely to result eventually in a more serious type of failure. This happened in late 2005, when Delphi, North America's largest auto parts maker, and both Delta and Northwest Airlines filed for bankruptcy within weeks of each other (Delta and Northwest actually filed on the same day, September 14).

A second type of failure, **technical insolvency,** occurs when a firm is unable to pay its liabilities as they come due. When a firm is technically insolvent, its assets are still greater than its liabilities, but it is confronted with a **liquidity crisis.** If some of its assets can be converted into cash within a reasonable period, the company may be able to escape complete failure. For example, in February 2001, Amazon.com, the online retailer, had to deny that it was facing a liquidity crisis. "The company has never been in better shape," chief executive Jeff Bezos was quoted as saying. The company indeed survived and prospered, but at least one Amazon supplier said that it had limited the amount of business it did with Amazon. Limiting business with a retailer is a typical first step for a creditor trying to protect itself from loss. Other techniques include shortening the terms under which a creditor will extend credit or even asking for cash in advance.

If a company cannot convert its assets into cash quickly enough, the result is the third and most serious type of failure, **insolvency bankruptcy.** Insolvency occurs when a firm's liabilities exceed the fair market value of its assets. Because the firm's assets equal the sum of its liabilities and stockholders' equity, the only way a firm that has more liabilities than assets can balance its balance sheet is to have a negative stockholders' equity. This means that the claims of creditors cannot be satisfied unless the firm's assets can be liquidated for more than their book value.

Although an insolvent firm is often said to be "bankrupt," **bankruptcy** technically occurs only when a company enters bankruptcy court and effectively surrenders control of the firm to a bankruptcy judge.[1] The failing firm may file for bankruptcy protection itself, or it may be forced into bankruptcy court (under certain conditions, discussed later in this chapter) by its creditors. We should also reiterate the point made initially in Chapter 13—that the ability to file for bankruptcy protection is a major benefit for the firm's shareholders, because this vital aspect of limited liability protects them from having to personally repay corporate debts. Additionally, as Haugen and Senbet (1978) pointed out a generation ago, bankruptcy *results* from a firm's falling into financial distress and is not the cause of the distress.[2]

Table 25.1 shows the largest bankruptcies in U.S. history through December 14, 2005. The largest U.S. bankruptcy was that of WorldCom in July 2002, as discussed in this chapter's Opening Focus. WorldCom followed very closely on the heels of Enron's massive bankruptcy in December 2001, the second largest in American history, and was followed only five months later by Conseco's bankruptcy, the third largest in U.S. history. In other words, the three largest bankruptcies in American financial history occurred within 12 months of each other and involved over $228 billion worth of prebankruptcy assets. Before Enron, the largest U.S. bankruptcies were

Company	Bankruptcy Date	Total Assets, Prebankruptcy
WorldCom	July 21, 2002	$103,914,000,000
Enron Corp.	December 2, 2001	$ 63,392,000,000
Conseco	December 18, 2002	$ 61,392,000,000
Texaco, Inc.	April 12, 1987	$ 35,892,000,000
Financial Corp. of America	September 9, 1988	$ 33,864,000,000
Refco Inc.	October 5, 2005	$ 33,333,172,000
Global Crossing Ltd.	January 28, 2002	$ 30,185,000,000
Pacific Gas and Electric Co.	April 6, 2001	$ 21,470,000,000
UAL Corporation	December 9, 2002	$ 25,197,000,000
Delta Air Lines, Inc.	September 14, 2005	$ 21,801,000,000
Adelphia Communications	June 25, 2002	$ 21,499,000,000
MCorp	March 31, 1989	$ 20,228,000,000
Mirant Corporation	July 14, 2003	$ 19,415,000,000
Delphi Corporation	October 8, 2005	$ 16,593,000,000
First Executive Corp.	May 13, 1991	$ 15,193,000,000

Source: Bankruptcy.com, December 14, 2005 (http://www.bankruptcydata.com).

Table 25.1
Largest Bankruptcies in U.S. History as of December 14, 2005

---

[1] According to Ingram (2005), the term *bankruptcy* comes from the Latin *banca rotta* ("broken bench"). When vendors in ancient Rome lost all their capital, the legal authorities would break their trading benches in half so they could no longer do business.

[2] Several researchers attempt to differentiate between and measure the economic costs of financial distress and the specific costs associated with the bankruptcy process itself. The out-of-pocket direct costs of bankruptcy, first measured by Warner (1977) and later verified by Lubben (2000), are surprisingly low—amounting to no more than a few percent of the pre–distress market values of public firms. Initial estimates of the indirect costs of bankruptcy (lost sales due to reputation declines, diversion of managerial time and effort, etc.), presented in Altman (1984), appeared to be significantly higher, but more recent studies by Andrade and Kaplan (1998) and Maksimovic and Phillips (1998) suggest that the separate cost of bankruptcy itself is small compared to the costs of encountering financial distress.

those of Texaco in 1987 and Financial Corporation of America in September 1988. In December 2003, a massive scandal involving forged documents and fictitious cash accounts in the Cayman Islands forced the Italian milk company Parmalat into bankruptcy and landed key company executives in an Italian jail. Although Parmalat's accounts are still being unwound, it appears that this may well become the single largest bankruptcy in world financial history. Clearly, the early years of the 21st century have been interesting times for bankruptcy courts around the world.

MAJOR CAUSES OF BUSINESS FAILURE

The primary cause of business failure is financial distress (as briefly discussed in Chapter 13). This, in turn, is often the result of mismanagement, which accounts for more than 50 percent of all business failures. Numerous specific managerial faults can cause the firm to fail. Overexpansion, poor financial controls, an ineffective sales force, and high production costs can all singly or in combination cause the firm's ultimate failure. For example, poor financial controls include bad capital budgeting decisions based on unrealistic sales and cost forecasts, failure to identify all relevant cash flows, failure to assess risk properly, inadequate financial evaluation of the firm's strategic plans prior to making financial commitments, inconsistent or inadequate cash flow planning, and failure to control receivables and inventories. Because all major corporate decisions are eventually measured in terms of dollars, the financial manager usually plays a key role in avoiding or causing a business failure. One of the financial manager's key duties must therefore be to monitor the firm's financial pulse.

Economic activity can contribute to the failure of a firm, especially during economic downturns. The success of some firms runs countercyclical to economic activity, and other firms are unaffected by economic activity. For example, the sale of sewing machines is likely to increase during a recession because people are more willing to make their own clothes and less willing to pay for the labor of others. The sale of boats and other luxury items may decline during a recession, whereas sales of staple items such as food and electricity are likely to be unaffected. In terms of beta, the measure of nondiversifiable risk, a stock with a negative beta would be associated with a firm whose behavior is generally countercyclical to economic activity.

However, the fortunes of most firms are positively tied to the business cycle, so business bankruptcy filings always spike upward during economic contractions. If the economy goes into a recession, sales may decrease abruptly, leaving the firm with high fixed costs and insufficient revenues to cover them. In addition, rapid rises in interest rates just prior to a recession can further contribute to cash flow problems and make it more difficult for the firm to obtain and maintain needed financing. If the recession is prolonged, the likelihood of survival decreases even further. A number of major business failures occurring during 2001 and 2002, such as those of the FINOVA Group and Reliance Group Holdings, resulted from overexpansion and the recessionary economy. On the other hand, the bankruptcy of Pacific Gas and Electric in 2001 was a direct result of policies enacted during a flawed deregulation of California's electricity market during the mid-1990s. Several other extremely large bankruptcies occurred during the 2001 to 2002 period, including those of Adelphia, Global Crossing, Qwest Communications, and, of course, WorldCom, Enron, and Conseco. On the other hand, three of the 15 largest bankruptcies in U.S. financial history (those of Refco Inc., Delta Air Lines, and Delphi Corporation) occurred during 2005, an otherwise extremely prosperous year.

A final cause of business failure is corporate maturity. Firms, like individuals, do not have infinite lives. Like a product, a firm may go through the stages of birth, growth, maturity, and eventual decline. The firm's management should attempt to prolong the growth stage through research, the development of new products, and mergers. Once the firm has matured and has begun to decline, it should seek to be acquired by another firm or liquidate before it fails. Effective management planning should help the firm postpone decline and ultimate failure.

APPLYING THE MODEL 25.1

Polaroid is an example of a company that has failed because of corporate maturity. Beginning in the early 1990s, digital photography brought warnings of the demise of instant photography. Before long, computer chips would capture and store images and instant, self-developing film would disappear. That prediction came true most recently in the form of Polaroid's insolvency. The company, which dominated the instant photography business for years, filed for Chapter 11 bankruptcy protection (discussed later) on October 12, 2001. The stock price had fallen from nearly $50 per share in 1998 to 28 cents on October 11. Polaroid, it turns out, was unable to change with the times.

The company's troubles date back to the late 1980s when it went deeply into debt to fight off a hostile takeover bid. That was followed by a string of strategic errors, including its failure to anticipate how much digital photography would cut into its instant film business. The company's latest generation of instant cameras has fallen flat because digital cameras for consumers are just as instant and much more versatile. Although the company tried to reorganize its debts and continue operating, this failed and the firm's remaining assets were purchased by an investment group associated with Bank One of Ohio in an auction conducted by the bankruptcy court in July 2002. As often occurs in bankruptcies, Polaroid's shareholders (including employees) were effectively wiped out by the failed reorganization, and litigation by unsecured creditors against the investment group that acquired the renamed Primary PDC, Inc., was not settled until April 2004. Polaroid's unfunded pension liabilities were taken over by the federal government.

Sometimes the cause of a business failure is difficult to anticipate and can happen quite suddenly in response to an economic or political event. For example, ANC Rental Corp., the owner of the Alamo and National car rental chains, filed for Chapter 11 bankruptcy protection on November 13, 2001, as the downturn in the travel sector worsened the company's troubles. ANC claims to have been the hardest-hit car rental company after the September 11 terrorist attacks, mainly because most of its rental offices were at airports. "The drastic decline in travel after September 11 has taken a tremendous toll on our business, and our current capital and expense structure cannot absorb the shortfall," CEO Michael Egan was quoted as saying. ANC, which listed assets of nearly $6.5 billion, estimated it had more than 1,000 creditors at the time of its filing.

As it happens, ANC's trip through Chapter 11 bankruptcy was quite successful. The company was sold by auction to a private investment group in June 2003 and exited the bankruptcy court's protection shortly thereafter. Renamed Vanguard Car Rental, the company announced plans in early 2004 to expand its operations in an effort to double its share of the car rental market, back to the 4.5 percent level achieved in mid-2001. By early 2005, Vanguard was making news for purchasing over 200,000 model-year 2004 vehicles from General Motors in order to rebuild its rental fleet and for announcing aggressive expansion plans in Europe.

1. Are the occurrence of operating losses, technical insolvency, and bankruptcy independent, or are they likely to be related?

2. Why do the managers of a business allow its condition to deteriorate to the point where bankruptcy occurs? Why don't the shareholders intervene?

3. Explain how business failures help the economy overall.

25.2 VOLUNTARY SETTLEMENTS

When a firm becomes technically insolvent or bankrupt, it may arrange a **voluntary settlement,** or **workout,** with its creditors, which enables it to bypass many of the costs involved in legal bankruptcy proceedings. The debtor firm usually initiates the settlement, because such an arrangement may enable it to continue to exist or to be liquidated in a manner that gives the owners the greatest chance of recovering part of their investment. The debtor, possibly with the aid of a key creditor, arranges a meeting between itself and all its creditors. At the meeting, a committee of creditors is selected to investigate and analyze the debtor's situation and recommend a plan of action. The committee discusses its recommendations with both the debtor and the creditors and draws up a plan for sustaining or liquidating the firm.

VOLUNTARY REORGANIZATION

Generally, the rationale for sustaining a firm is that it is reasonable to believe that the firm's recovery is feasible. By sustaining the firm, the creditor can continue to receive business from it. A number of strategies are commonly used to implement a **voluntary reorganization.** An **extension** is an arrangement wherein the firm's creditors are promised payment in full, although not immediately. Usually, when creditors grant an extension, they require the firm to make cash payments for purchases until all past debts have been paid.

A second arrangement, called a **composition,** is a pro rata cash settlement of creditor claims. Instead of receiving full payment for their claims, as in the case of an extension, creditors receive only a partial payment. A uniform percentage of each dollar owed is paid in satisfaction of each creditor's claim.

A third arrangement is **creditor control.** In this case, the creditor committee may decide that the only circumstance in which maintaining the firm is feasible will be replacement of the operating management. The committee may then take control of the firm and operate it until all claims have been settled. Sometimes, a plan involving some combination of extension, composition, and creditor control will result. An example of this would be a settlement whereby the debtor agrees to pay a total of 75 cents on the dollar in three annual installments of 25 cents on the dollar. The creditors also agree to sell additional merchandise to the firm on 30-day terms, if a new management team that is acceptable to them replaces the existing managers.[3]

VOLUNTARY LIQUIDATION

After the credit committee has investigated the situation of the firm, made recommendations, and held talks with the creditors and the debtor, the only acceptable course of action may be liquidation of the firm. **Liquidation** involves winding up the

---

[3.] For evidence that transaction costs discourage debt reductions by financially distressed firms when they restructure their debt out of court, see Gilson (1997).

firm's operations, selling off its assets, and distributing the proceeds to creditors. Liquidation can be carried out in one of two ways, privately or through the legal procedures provided by bankruptcy law. If the debtor firm is willing to accept liquidation, legal procedures may not be required. Generally, avoiding litigation enables the creditors to obtain quicker and higher settlements. However, all the creditors must agree to a private liquidation for it to be feasible.

The objective of the voluntary liquidation process is to recover as much per dollar owed as possible. Under voluntary liquidation, common stockholders, who are the firm's true owners, cannot receive any funds until the claims of all other parties have been satisfied. A common procedure is to have a meeting of the creditors at which they make an **assignment** by passing the power to liquidate the firm's assets to an adjustment bureau, a trade association, or a third party that is designated the *assignee*. The assignee's job is to liquidate the assets, obtaining the best price possible. The assignee is sometimes referred to as **trustee,** because it is entrusted with the title to the company's assets and the responsibility to liquidate them efficiently. Once the trustee has liquidated the assets, it distributes the recovered funds to the creditors and owners (if any funds remain for the owners). The final action in a private liquidation is for the creditors to sign a release attesting to the satisfactory settlement of their claims. If a voluntary settlement for a failed firm cannot be agreed upon, the creditors can force the firm into bankruptcy. Because of bankruptcy proceedings, the firm may be either reorganized or liquidated.

An alternative to liquidation of the firm is for it to be acquired. Merger with a financially sound company may allow the firm suffering from financial distress to return to profitability and continue as a going concern.

---

4. If you were a supplier and creditor to a company that had undergone a voluntary reorganization, would you continue to do business with the company?

5. If you were a creditor of a company that was undergoing a voluntary reorganization, what would be the advantages and disadvantages from your perspective of handling it as an extension, composition, or creditor control?

6. Why would a firm's shareholders agree to a voluntary liquidation if the business had a negative net worth and they could expect to receive nothing?

Concept Review Questions

25.3 BANKRUPTCY LAW IN THE UNITED STATES

As already stated, bankruptcy in the legal sense occurs when a firm cannot pay its bills or when its liabilities exceed the fair market value of its assets and the firm is forced into bankruptcy court. In either of these situations, a firm may be declared legally bankrupt. However, creditors generally attempt to avoid forcing a firm into bankruptcy if it appears to have opportunities for future success.

The governing bankruptcy legislation in the United States today is the **Bankruptcy Reform Act of 1978,** which significantly modified earlier bankruptcy legislation. This law contains eight odd-numbered chapters (1 through 15) and one even-numbered chapter (12). Several of these chapters would apply in the instance of failure; the two key ones are Chapters 7 and 11. We briefly discuss international differences in bankruptcy laws in Chapter 13 (of this book, not of the bankruptcy code).

Chapter 7 of the Bankruptcy Reform Act of 1978 details the procedures to be followed when liquidating a failed firm. This chapter typically comes into play once it has been determined that a fair, equitable, and feasible basis for the reorganization of a failed firm does not exist (although a firm may of its own accord choose not to reorganize and may instead go directly into liquidation). Chapter 7 includes the rules, known as **absolute priority rules (APR)**, that determine the order in which creditor claims are to be paid. As described in detail in Section 25.5, the APR specify which claimants are to be paid first, and in full, before any payments can be made to more junior claimants.

Chapter 11 outlines the procedures for reorganizing a failed or failing firm, whether its petition is filed voluntarily or involuntarily. If a workable plan for reorganization cannot be developed, the firm will be liquidated under Chapter 7. Table 25.2 shows how the total number of U.S. corporate bankruptcies was divided between Chapter 7 and Chapter 11 filings for the period from 1980 to June 30, 2005. The table shows that in 2004 there were a total of 1,618,987 bankruptcy filings in the United States, down slightly from 2003's record 1,661,996 filings. The 2004 filings consisted of 29,679 business failures and 1,584,170 nonbusiness (mostly personal)

Table 25.2
Business and Nonbusiness Bankruptcy Cases Filed in U.S. Bankruptcy Courts, by Chapter of the Bankruptcy Code, 1980–2005

Fiscal Year[a]	Total Filings	Business Filings		Nonbusiness Filings	
		Chapter 7	Chapter 11	Total	Chapter 7
1980	298,492	30,402	5,333	259,160	194,491
1981	362,233	34,356	7,795	315,250	230,139
1982	373,853	41,863	14,696	310,330	219,930
1983	362,051	39,573	17,608	297,835	203,096
1984	346,500	38,649	17,396	283,618	196,541
1985	383,510	41,838	19,864	314,378	216,090
1986	507,557	48,976	21,110	429,334	307,972
1987	568,430	49,471	18,333	482,300	353,087
1988	604,759	39,803	16,025	538,636	391,428
1989	656,980	27,228	15,703	595,511	427,147
1990	749,981	36,687	17,789	685,429	484,671
1991	918,988	38,705	20,394	848,812	599,799
1992	977,478	38,467	20,070	905,753	646,399
1993	897,231	35,807	17,068	832,374	585,264
1994	837,797	30,781	13,379	783,372	541,190
1995	883,457	28,800	11,168	832,415	569,450
1996	1,111,964	30,289	11,358	1,058,444	731,363
1997	1,367,364	31,862	10,092	1,313,112	926,183
1998	1,436,964	29,229	7,884	1,389,839	996,905
1999	1,354,376	23,499	8,238	1,315,751	935,792
2000	1,262,102	20,687	9,135	1,226,037	850,118
2001	1,437,354	22,800	9,787	1,398,860	991,337
2002	1,547,669	22,574	10,702	1,508,578	1,061,762
2003	1,661,996	21,008	9,185	1,625,813	1,156,284
2004	1,618,987	20,243	9,436	1,584,170	1,133,622
2005[b]	1,653,533	21,848	5,931	1,619,431	1,200,195

Source: United States Bankruptcy Courts (http://www.uscourts.gov/bnkrpctystats/statistics.htm).
Notes: Chapter 7 is "straight bankruptcy"—liquidation; Chapter 11 is reorganization.
[a]The fiscal year end runs through September 30.
[b]Annualized, based on first three quarters of FY 2005 (October 1, 2004, through June 30, 2005).

COMPARATIVE CORPORATE FINANCE

Companies Can Declare Bankruptcy—Why Not Countries?

On January 6, 2002, Argentina abandoned the decade-old parity between its currency and the U.S. dollar by devaluing the peso. "We are bankrupt," admitted Economy Minister Jorge Remes Lenicov when he announced the devaluation. The government also confirmed that Argentina cannot continue to service its $155 billion of foreign-currency debt, and it declared a moratorium on payments. Because of the default, the price of Argentine bonds fell to about 25 percent of their par value.

Argentina's creditors braced themselves for a long fight for their money. The Argentine bondholders formed a committee in November 2001 to communicate some of the large investors' views to the Argentine government. The committee included investment banks that began to pay out on credit-default swaps, derivative securities that guarantee payment should a borrower default. The default swaps total almost $4 billion, and the investment banks now own the bonds returned to them under the terms of the swaps.

The questions for bondholders are how vigorously they should react and how quickly they should call their lawyers. The announcement of a default means that bondholders can now "accelerate" their claims by demanding immediate payment of all principal and interest from the debtor. However, acceleration is unlikely to result in prompt payment because, as the bondholders realize, Argentina has serious problems. Most creditors figure that they will receive more money by negotiation than by confrontation.

While the moratorium gave Argentina room to maneuver, it was clear by spring 2004 that no quick turn-around was in sight. After an extremely severe economic contraction during 2002 and 2003, the Argentine economy began to grow again, but not at a fast enough pace to service their existing debt, much less to begin actual repayment. The Argentine government has also consistently refused to make net payments to creditors (pay more in interest and principal than it receives in new loans). However, if Argentina ignores its creditors, then difficulties might arise with even the simplest trade

finance transactions. In the worst case, creditors could seize Argentine assets abroad, such as ships and aircraft. Also, many of the bond covenants do not contain so-called collective action clauses; therefore, each bond-holder is free to litigate individually, a frightening scenario, except for the lawyers.

The question remains: What should Argentina do? Whereas companies can declare bankruptcy and seek protection from their creditors, countries have no such option. They are faced with the bleak choice between bailouts and chaotic defaults. However, that could change. The International Monetary Fund (IMF) has suggested that a country whose debts are "truly unsustainable" should have a mechanism for restructuring them, in the same way that companies can file for bankruptcy protection and reorganize their obligations.

The idea is that a country in financial distress would get temporary legal protection when it stopped making payments on its debt. In return, it would have to promise to negotiate with its creditors in good faith. Lenders would get an incentive to provide new "working capital" by giving new debt seniority over old. Also, small creditors would have to go along with the reorganization plan if enough creditors agreed.

Sovereign bankruptcy is appealing because it might eliminate the need for IMF bailouts while avoiding the legal quagmire of unilateral default. Both creditors and debtors would benefit from clear rules about the procedure for debt restructuring, if the rules balanced the rights of debtors and creditors. Since Argentina has become the single largest, and by far the most trouble-some, borrower from the IMF, this institution is particularly keen to develop alternative workout procedures for heavily indebted countries.

Previous proposals on sovereign bankruptcy have failed, in part, because the details are difficult to work out. Who, for instance, will act as the impartial judge? Also, how do you force a debtor country to negotiate in good faith? After all, countries cannot be threatened with liquidation or a forcible change in "management."

bankruptcies. Keep in mind that the total population of the United States was about 280 million in 2004, so roughly 1 percent of all American adults filed for bankruptcy in that year alone! It is also likely that personal bankruptcies during calendar year 2005 will have hit another record, since there was a huge surge in filings during early September of that year. This was prompted by a desire to file before the more stringent terms of the Bankruptcy Abuse Prevention and Consumer Protection Act of 2005 came into effect. While this law did not fundamentally change bankruptcy procedures and will likely have minimal effect on business filings, it did make personal bankruptcy significantly more punitive.

When a company files either to reorganize or liquidate in bankruptcy, a collective legal procedure begins by which all claims against the company are resolved. When a firm declares bankruptcy, individual creditors are prevented (stayed) from beginning or continuing with lawsuits against the debtor. Thus, bankruptcy law is substituted for the commercial and tax laws that normally govern firms.

Without a collective procedure, individual creditors would engage in a costly and unproductive race to be first to sue the company for repayment of their own claims. Creditors that sued first would be paid in full until the firm's resources were exhausted, after which other creditors would receive nothing. Both the creditors' duplicative expenses and the costs of the lawsuits themselves would consume assets. Bankruptcy eliminates the benefit of being the first to sue because all claims against the firm are settled simultaneously, and all creditors having the same type of claim receive the same settlement. Although there is still an incentive for creditors to attempt to sue the firm first, the incentive is diminished because a large number of suits will cause the firm to enter bankruptcy voluntarily.[4]

Concept Review Questions	**7.** Why is it necessary to have bankruptcy laws? Why is normal contracting under commercial law insufficient?
	8. How does society benefit by allowing firms to declare bankruptcy?
	9. Why is it important that bankruptcy law eliminate the incentive for creditors to be the first to sue for repayment of claims?

25.4 REORGANIZATION IN BANKRUPTCY

A company's managers typically make the initial decision to attempt to reorganize their firm under the protection of Chapter 11 of the bankruptcy laws. The **reorganization** process in bankruptcy is designed to allow businesses that are in temporary financial distress but that are worth saving to continue operating while the claims of creditors are settled using a collective procedure.[5] A disadvantage of this procedure is that the managers of the company and not an outside party make the decision to file under Chapter 11. Thus, managers have an incentive to choose the bankruptcy procedure that is best for themselves and for equity holders and not the firm's creditors. This sometimes results in the reorganization of firms that are not worth saving because of a lack of economic efficiency. Thus, a problem with reorganization is that even though it may allow some efficient firms to continue operating that would otherwise be liquidated, it is also likely to allow some economically inefficient firms to be saved.[6]

[4.] There has long been a debate regarding whether Chapter 11 is economically and socially optimal, particularly given that bankruptcy procedures in other developed countries tend to emphasize liquidation over reorganization and to more strongly favor creditor claims over those of stockholders and employees. This literature is summarized in Bris, Schwartz, and Welch (2005). Interestingly, several countries have recently revised their bankruptcy laws to more closely resemble Chapter 11 reorganization, suggesting that for all its flaws, Chapter 11's presumption of the possibility of financial resurrection is economically attractive.

[5.] Eberhart, Altman, and Aggarwal (1999) describe the stock return performance of firms emerging from Chapter 11. Alderson and Betker (1995) examine the postbankruptcy cash flows of firms emerging from Chapter 11.

[6.] See Thorburn (2000) and Strömberg (2000) for descriptions of an alternative procedure used in Sweden in which bankrupt firms are auctioned as going concerns.

REORGANIZATION PROCEDURES

The procedures for initiation and execution of corporate reorganization under Chapter 11 entail five separate steps: filing, appointment, development and approval of a reorganization plan, acceptance of the plan, and payment of expenses.

Filing. A firm must file a reorganization petition under Chapter 11 in a federal bankruptcy court. There are two basic types of bankruptcy reorganization petitions: voluntary and involuntary. Any firm that is not a municipal or financial institution can voluntarily file a petition for reorganization on its own behalf. Firms sometimes file a voluntary petition to obtain temporary legal protection from creditors or from prolonged litigation. Once they have straightened out their legal or financial affairs, prior to further reorganization or liquidation actions, they will have the petition dismissed. Although such actions are not the intent of the bankruptcy laws, difficulty in enforcing the law has allowed this abuse to occur.

An outside party, usually a creditor, initiates **involuntary reorganization.** An involuntary petition against a firm can be filed if one of three conditions is met:

1. The firm has past-due debts of $5,000 or more.
2. Three or more creditors can prove that they have aggregate unpaid claims of $5,000 against the firm. If the firm has fewer than 12 creditors, any creditor that is owed more than $5,000 can file the petition.
3. The firm is **insolvent,** which means that (a) it is not paying its debts as they come due, (b) within the immediately preceding 120 days a custodian (a third party) was appointed or took possession of the debtor's property, or (c) the fair market value of the firm's assets is less than the stated value of its liabilities.

If the debtor challenges an involuntary petition, a hearing must be held to determine whether the firm is insolvent. If it is, the court enters an "Order for Relief" that formally initiates the process.

Appointment. Upon the filing of a reorganization petition, the filing firm becomes the **debtor in possession (DIP)** of the assets, and its existing management usually remains in control. However, one or more creditors' committees are appointed to represent the interests of creditors.

If the creditors object to the filing firm's being the debtor in possession, they can petition the bankruptcy court to appoint a trustee to replace management. However, the incompetence of the existing management, which is strongly suggested by the fact that the firm is in bankruptcy, is not considered a sufficient reason for replacing management. To replace existing management, the creditors usually must present evidence that the management is making preferential transfers to favored creditors or stealing the company's assets.

Because reorganization activities are largely in the hands of the DIP, it is useful to understand the DIP's responsibilities. The DIP's first responsibility is the valuation of the firm to determine whether reorganization is appropriate. To do this, the DIP must estimate both the liquidation value of the business and its value as a going concern.[7] If the DIP finds that its value as a going concern is less than its liquidation value, it will recommend liquidation. If the opposite is true, the DIP will recommend reorganization. If the DIP recommends reorganization of the firm, a plan of reorganization must be drawn up.

[7.] Perhaps not surprisingly, determining a newly bankrupt firm's value is both difficult and contentious, since the key players have directly conflicting incentives. As described in Gilson, Hotchkiss, and Ruback (2000), senior creditors have incentives to calculate a low firm value, while junior creditors and stockholders will prefer a higher valuation in hopes of receiving something of value when the firm is reorganized or liquidated.

Perhaps surprisingly, many companies are able to arrange DIP financing from commercial banks and other lenders immediately after filing for reorganization. They are able to do this because the bankruptcy judge grants these loans super-priority status, and the economic justification for allowing this type of financing is that the firm must have ongoing access to business credit to continue operating while it tries to reorganize.[8] Delphi arranged this type of funding soon after filing for Chapter 11 in October 2005, when a group of lenders led by Citigroup (a leading DIP financier) and JP Morgan Chase committed up to $2 billion in secured DIP financing.

REORGANIZATION PLAN

After reviewing its situation, the debtor in possession submits a plan of reorganization to the court and files the plan and a disclosure statement summarizing the plan. A hearing is held to determine whether the plan is fair, equitable, and feasible and whether the disclosure statement contains adequate information. The court's approval or disapproval is based on its evaluation of the plan in light of these standards. A plan is considered fair and equitable if it maintains the priorities of the contractual claims of the creditors, preferred stockholders, and common stockholders. The court must also find the reorganization plan *feasible,* meaning that it must be workable. The reorganized corporation must have sufficient working capital, sufficient funds to cover fixed charges, sufficient credit prospects, and sufficient ability to retire or refund debts as proposed by the plan.

The key portion of the reorganization plan generally concerns the firm's capital structure. Because most firms' financial difficulties result from high fixed charges, the company's capital structure is generally recapitalized, or altered, to reduce these charges. Under **recapitalization,** debts are generally exchanged for equity or the maturities of existing debts are extended. The DIP, when recapitalizing the firm, places a great deal of emphasis on building a mix of debt and equity that will allow the firm to meet its debts and provide a reasonable level of earnings for its owners.

Once the optimal capital structure has been determined, the DIP must establish a plan for exchanging outstanding obligations for new securities. The guiding principle is to observe priorities. Senior claims are those with higher legal priority that must be satisfied in full before paying junior claims (those with lower legal priority). To comply with this principle, senior suppliers of capital must receive a claim on new capital equal to their previous claim. The common stockholders are the last to receive any new securities, and it is not unusual for them to receive nothing. Security holders do not necessarily have to receive the same type of security they held before; often they receive a combination of securities. Once the debtor in possession has determined the new capital structure and distribution of capital, it will submit the reorganization plan and disclosure statement to the court as described.

The DIP is in a strong bargaining position in negotiations over the reorganization plan. During the first four months after the bankruptcy filing—plus any extensions, which are often granted—managers have the exclusive right to propose a plan. Then an extra two months are allowed for voting on management's plan. Only then, and only if no further extensions have been granted, can creditors propose reorganization plans.

[8.] Dahiya, John, Puri, and Ramirez (2003) find that 30 percent of all firms filing for Chapter 11 bankruptcy protection between 1988 and 1997 received some form of DIP financing. These authors also find that firms receiving DIP financing emerge from bankruptcy significantly more rapidly than firms that do not.

Acceptance of the Reorganization Plan. Once approved by the bankruptcy court, the plan and the disclosure statement are given to the firm's creditors and shareholders for their acceptance. Under the Bankruptcy Reform Act, creditors and owners are separated into groups with similar types of claims. Intense bargaining and litigation often occur concerning the construction of the classes of creditors in a reorganization. Creditors that are in substantially the same position are placed in the same class to ensure that they receive the same treatment under the reorganization plan. Creditors in different positions are placed in different classes. However, managers sometimes wish to prevent a particular creditor from defeating a reorganization plan. They accomplish this by arguing that the creditor should be part of a larger class in which the creditor's opposition to the plan will be outvoted.

There are two procedures for instituting a reorganization plan: the unanimous consent procedure and the cramdown procedure. Under the **unanimous consent procedure (UCP)**, creditors and equity classes must consent unanimously to the reorganization plan, although not all members of each class are required to consent. The UCP assumes that the company's assets will be worth more if it reorganizes and continues operations than if it liquidates. This difference in value, which under the absolute priority rule (APR) of Chapter 7 would belong entirely to the creditors with senior claims, must be divided up among all the creditors and equity classes by means of a negotiating process, with all classes sharing the difference in value.

A company must be solvent to use the UCP. That is, the value of creditors' claims must be less than the value of the company as a going concern. This implies that the firm's existing equity has some value. If the existing equity is worthless, then the company is considered insolvent, and the UCP cannot be used because equity holders cannot consent to a reorganization plan that eliminates their interest. To make a firm appear solvent, reorganization plans sometimes use inflated valuations of the firm's assets to make them appear to be worth more than the liabilities under the proposed plan.

Reorganization plans using the UCP must be approved by all classes of creditors and by equity as a class. Each class of unsecured creditors must vote for the plan by a two-thirds margin, weighing claims by value, and also by a simple majority, weighing all claims equally. Each secured creditor is a class, and each must vote for the plan if its claims are impaired. (If its claims are not impaired, a secured creditor's consent to the plan is not needed.) Because equity holders must vote for the plan by a two-thirds margin, reorganization plans under the UCP yield a different division of the company's value than would occur under the APR of a Chapter 7 liquidation. Under the UCP, every class, even the equity holders, must receive some value. Under the APR, the equity holders and junior creditors often receive nothing.

Managers can also threaten to transfer the firm's bankruptcy filing from Chapter 11 to Chapter 7 if the creditors do not agree to a plan, a threat that is often effective in prodding unsecured creditors to accept the plan, for they anticipate receiving little or nothing if liquidation occurs. Managers also run the firm during the negotiating process, so secured creditors often fear that the value of their lien assets will decline. Finally, even after their exclusive period for proposing a reorganization plan ends, managers remain in a strong bargaining position. Individual creditors typically are unrepresented except in the largest cases, and severe free-rider problems arise when creditors attempt to form groups and raise funds to take an active part in bargaining.

The **cramdown procedure** is used when a reorganization plan fails to meet the standard for approval by all classes under the UCP or when the firm is clearly insolvent and the existing equity has no value. In a cramdown, if at least one class of creditors has voted for a reorganization plan, the bankruptcy court can approve the plan without the consent of the other classes, as long as each dissenting class is treated fairly and equitably. The fair and equitable standard closely reflects the APR by requiring either that all unsecured creditors receive full payment of their claims over the period of the plan or that all junior classes receive nothing. The cramdown procedure also requires that secured creditors retain their prebankruptcy liens on assets and that they receive periodic cash payments equal to the value of their claims. Cramdowns typically involve higher transaction costs than UCP reorganization plans because the bankruptcy judge often requires asset valuations by outside experts and more court hearings usually occur before the plan is approved.

When no reorganization plan is adopted under either the UCP or cramdown, managers sometimes voluntarily sell the firm as a going concern. In that case, the proceeds of the sale are paid to creditors according to the APR. This liquidating reorganization is similar to a Chapter 7 liquidation, except that the firm is sold as a going concern and is not shut down. Finally, if no progress is being made toward completion of a Chapter 11 reorganization, some creditor usually petitions the bankruptcy judge to order a shift of the firm's bankruptcy filing to a Chapter 7 liquidation.

Payment of Expenses. After the reorganization plan has been approved or disapproved, all parties to the proceedings whose services were beneficial or contributed to the approval or disapproval of the plan file a statement of expenses. If the court finds these claims acceptable, the debtor must pay these expenses within a reasonable period.

APPLYING THE MODEL 25.2

Campbell Technologies, a telecommunications equipment manufacturer, has filed Chapter 11 bankruptcy and is seeking to reorganize because it cannot service its debt. The company's current capital structure is as follows:

Debentures (unsecured debt)	$4,000,000
Subordinated debentures	2,000,000
Common stock (100,000 shares)	2,000,000
Total	$8,000,000

The company's book-value leverage is high, with a debt/equity ratio of 3.0 ($6,000,000/$2,000,000). It has been determined that Campbell Technologies is worth $5 million as a going concern. The company can be reorganized as follows:

Debentures (unsecured debt)	$2,000,000
Subordinated debentures	1,000,000
Common stock (200,000 shares)	2,000,000
Total	$5,000,000

The face value of the debt is cut in half, but the debt holders receive 100,000 shares, or half of the company's equity. The debt/equity ratio of Campbell Technologies is now a more reasonable 1.5 ($3,000,000/$2,000,000), and the company's operating profits should be more than sufficient to service the reduced debt burden.

SUBSIDIES TO FIRMS THAT REORGANIZE

Reorganization is viewed as a means of providing breathing space to viable firms that are in temporary financial distress in order to save jobs and avoid disruption to local communities. In contrast, liquidation is viewed as the process of winding up the operation of firms that are not viable. Therefore, in order to make reorganization attractive to managers and equity holders, Congress has provided a number of subsidies to firms in reorganization. These subsidies come either from the government or from creditors. They give firms in reorganization advantages relative to firms that continue operating outside of bankruptcy and firms that liquidate. The six major subsidies are as follows.

1. When reorganizing firms settle liabilities for less than their face value, the amount of debt forgiveness is deducted as a loss by the creditor but is not immediately treated as taxable income to the reorganizing firm. The debt forgiveness amount becomes taxable when the reorganized firm becomes profitable by reducing either its tax loss carryforward or its depreciation allowances.

2. Firms reorganizing under Chapter 11 have the right to terminate underfunded pension plans, and the U.S. government's Pension Benefit Guaranty Corporation (PBGC) picks up the uncovered pension costs. Unfortunately for American taxpayers, the PBGC has been forced to absorb huge liabilities recently, and its deficit hit $23.3 billion during 2004. This was before including a record $6.6 billion of unfunded liabilities from UAL in April 2005, and perhaps twice that much from the pending Chapter 11 reorganizations of Delphi, Delta, and Northwest.

3. Firms that reorganize retain most of their accrued tax loss carryforwards, which would be lost if they liquidated. These loss carryforwards shelter the firm from paying taxes on corporate profits for a period in the future, if its operations start to be profitable. They also make reorganized firms attractive merger partners for profitable firms, because the profitable firm can use the tax loss carryforward immediately. This subsidy makes reorganization more attractive than liquidation for a failing firm but has no effect on the choice between reorganization and remaining out of bankruptcy.

4. When firms file for bankruptcy, their obligation to pay interest to prebankruptcy creditors, both secured and unsecured, ceases. They do not have to start paying interest again until a reorganization plan is approved, and the unpaid interest does not become a claim against the firm. This subsidy clearly gives managers of failing firms an incentive to file for bankruptcy earlier and to delay proposing a reorganization plan.

5. Firms in reorganization can reject any of their contracts that are not substantially completed. Thus, they can get out of any unprofitable contracts. Although firms are still liable for damages to other parties to rejected contracts, such damage claims are unsecured and likely to receive a low payoff rate. Thus, the cost to the firm of shedding unprofitable contracts is small.

6. Firms in reorganization can reject their collective bargaining labor agreements. Since 1984, however, this step has required the approval of the bankruptcy judge. This has particularly benefited unionized firms in industries that have a mixture of unionized and nonunionized establishments by enabling them to cut all wages to nonunionized levels. A prominent example is Continental Airlines, which, following airline deregulation, filed to reorganize in bankruptcy in 1983. Continental was allowed to cut wages by 50 percent and cut its workforce by 65 percent.

APPLYING THE MODEL 25.3

Although companies are no longer able to unilaterally revoke collective bargaining agreements after they file for bankruptcy protection, the supervising judges allow companies this flexibility frequently enough that the companies are often able to win concessions from their unionized employees by *threatening* to file for bankruptcy. American Airlines used this tactic very successfully in April 2003, when it secured some $1.8 billion in annual cost savings from its eight principal unions by credibly threatening to file for Chapter 11 protection if the wage cuts were not approved. In the previous eight months, no less than three major North American airlines had in fact filed for bankruptcy protection. The second largest U.S. carrier, UAL Corporation, filed for Chapter 11 in December 2002 and number 7, US Airways, had filed in August—though US Airways emerged from Chapter 7 a mere seven months later, only to reenter during 2004. Air Canada filed for protection from creditors, in the Canadian bankruptcy courts, in early April 2003. This tactic was again used, successfully, several times during late 2005. Delphi, Delta, and Northwest all coerced their unions into agreeing to dramatic labor cost cuts—by threatening to ask the bankruptcy court judge to impose even more drastic cuts unilaterally if the unions balked.

PREPACKAGED BANKRUPTCIES

Sometimes companies prepare a reorganization plan that is negotiated and voted on by creditors and stockholders before the company actually files for Chapter 11 bankruptcy. This process, known as a **prepackaged bankruptcy,** shortens and simplifies the process, saving the company money and frequently generating more for the creditors because there is less spent in legal and related fees, less disruption to the company's business, and less damage to its goodwill [see Tashijian, Lease, and McConnell (1996)].

For example, Regal Cinemas, the largest U.S. movie theater chain, simultaneously filed a voluntary petition for Chapter 11 bankruptcy protection and a prepackaged plan of reorganization on October 12, 2001. The reorganization plan gave effective control of the operation of 3,831 movie screens to Denver billionaire Philip Anschutz, who has used the theater industry's misfortunes to gain control of two other chains, United Artists and Edwards. The reorganization plan gives Regal's senior debt holders 100 percent of the reorganized company's stock. As it turns out, Anschutz owns the majority of the senior debt, having bought it for pennies on the dollar from Regal's bankers earlier in the year. Regal Cinemas emerged from bankruptcy in January 2002, an astonishingly short three months after filing!

Concept Review Questions

10. Under what circumstances would it make sense for a company to reorganize rather than liquidate?

11. Why is the existing management generally allowed to remain in control when a company files for bankruptcy?

12. Why is a cramdown procedure sometimes necessary when a company reorganizes?

25.5 LIQUIDATION IN BANKRUPTCY

The liquidation of a bankrupt firm usually occurs once the courts have determined that reorganization is not feasible. The managers or creditors of the bankrupt firm must normally file a petition for reorganization. If no petition is filed, if a petition is filed and denied, or if the reorganization plan is denied, the firm must be liquidated. Three important aspects of liquidation in bankruptcy are the procedures, the priority of claims, and the final accounting.

PROCEDURES

When a firm is adjudged bankrupt, the judge may appoint a trustee to perform the many routine duties required in administering the bankruptcy. The trustee takes charge of the property of the bankrupt firm and protects the interest of its creditors. Between 20 and 40 days after the firm has been adjudged bankrupt, the creditors must hold a meeting. The bankruptcy court clerk presides over this meeting, during which the creditors are made aware of the prospects for the liquidation.[9] The trustee is then given the responsibility of liquidating the firm, keeping records, examining creditors' claims, disbursing money, furnishing information as required, and making final reports on the liquidation. In essence, the trustee is responsible for the liquidation of the firm. Occasionally, the court will call subsequent creditor meetings, but only a final meeting for closing the bankruptcy is required.[10]

PRIORITY OF CLAIMS

The trustee has the responsibility to liquidate all the firm's assets and to distribute the proceeds to the holders of provable claims. The courts have established certain procedures for determining the provability of claims, known as the absolute priority rules. The priority of claims, which is specified in Chapter 7 of the Bankruptcy Reform Act, must be maintained by the trustee when distributing the funds from liquidation. It is important to recognize that if in a liquidation any **secured creditors** have specific assets pledged as collateral, they receive the proceeds from the sale of those assets. If these proceeds are inadequate to meet their claim, the secured creditors become **unsecured** (or **general**) **creditors** for the unrecovered amount because specific collateral no longer exists. These and all other unsecured creditors will divide up, on a pro rata basis, any funds remaining after all prior claims have been satisfied. If the proceeds from the sale of secured assets are in excess of the claims against them, the excess funds become available to meet claims of unsecured creditors.[11]

The complete order of priority of claims is as follows.

1. The expenses of administering the bankruptcy proceedings.
2. Any unpaid interim expenses incurred in the ordinary course of business between filing the bankruptcy petition and the entry of an Order of Relief in an involuntary proceeding. (This step is not applicable in a voluntary bankruptcy.)

[9.] See Pulvino (1999) for a description of the effects of bankruptcy court protection on sales of assets.

[10.] For a discussion on the size of liquidation costs, see Alderson and Betker (1995).

[11.] Despite the seemingly hard-and-fast rules governing the distribution of liquidation proceeds, Weiss (1990), Eberhart, Moore, and Roenfeldt (1990), and Frank and Torous (1994) all report that violations of absolute priority rules by bankruptcy courts are quite common, partly because shareholders have significant bargaining power (perhaps holdup power would be a better description) during bankruptcy negotiations.

3. Wages of not more than $2,000 per worker that have been earned by workers in the 90-day period immediately preceding the commencement of bankruptcy proceedings.

4. Unpaid employee benefit plan contributions that were to be paid in the 180-day period preceding the filing of bankruptcy or the termination of business, whichever occurred first. For any employee, the sum of this claim plus eligible unpaid wages cannot exceed $2,000.

5. Claims of farmers or fishermen in a grain-storage or fish-storage facility, not to exceed $2,000 for each producer.

6. Unsecured customer deposits, not to exceed $900 each, resulting from purchasing or leasing a good or service from the failed firm.

7. Taxes legally due and owed by the bankrupt firm to the federal government, state government, or any other governmental subdivision.

8. Claims of secured creditors, who receive the proceeds from the sale of collateral held, regardless of the priorities described earlier. If the proceeds from the liquidation of the collateral are insufficient to satisfy the secured creditors' claims, the secured creditors become unsecured creditors for the unpaid amount.

9. Claims of unsecured creditors. The claims of unsecured, or general, creditors and unsatisfied portions of secured creditors' claims are treated equally.

10. Preferred stockholders, who receive an amount up to the par, or stated, value of their preferred stock.

11. Common stockholders, who receive any remaining funds, which are distributed on an equal per-share basis. If different classes of common stock are outstanding, priorities may exist.

In spite of the priorities listed in items 1 through 7, secured creditors have first claim on proceeds from the sale of their collateral. The claims of unsecured creditors, including the unpaid claims of secured creditors, are satisfied next, and, finally, the claims of preferred and common stockholders. Also, some unsecured creditors' claims may be subordinated to those of other unsecured creditors. In the event of liquidation, the subordinated creditors do not receive any cash until the claims to which they are subordinated are paid in full. The following Applying the Model gives a simple example of the application of these priorities by the trustee in bankruptcy liquidation proceedings.

APPLYING THE MODEL 25.4

Table 25.3 presents the balance sheet of Oxford Company, a manufacturer of computer drives. The trustee has liquidated the firm's assets, obtaining the largest amounts possible. He obtained $2.1 million for the firm's current assets and $1.8 million for the firm's fixed assets. The total proceeds from the liquidation, therefore, were $3.9 million. It is clear that the firm is legally insolvent because its liabilities of $5.5 million exceed the $3.9 million market value of its assets.

The next step is to distribute the proceeds to the various creditors. The only liability that is not shown on the balance sheet is $500,000 in expenses for administering the bankruptcy proceedings and satisfying unpaid bills incurred between the time of filing the bankruptcy petition and the entry of an Order of Relief. Table 25.4 shows the distribution of the $3.9 million among the firm's creditors and

Table 25.3
Balance Sheet for
Oxford Company

Assets		Liabilities and Stockholders' Equity	
Cash	$ 100,000	Accounts payable	$ 200,000
Accounts receivable	1,200,000	Notes payable—bank	1,500,000
Inventories	3,150,000	Accrued wages[a]	100,000
Total current assets	$4,450,000	Unpaid employee benefits[b]	110,000
Land	$2,000,000	Unsecured customer deposits[c]	90,000
Net plant	1,500,000	Taxes payable	300,000
Net equipment	1,100,000	Total current liabilities	$2,300,000
Total fixed assets	$4,600,000	First mortgage[d]	$1,400,000
Total	$9,050,000	Second mortgage[d]	800,000
		Subordinated debentures[e]	1,000,000
		Total long-term debt	$3,200,000
		Preferred stock (7,000 shares)	$ 700,000
		Common stock (20,000 shares)	$ 200,000
		Paid-in capital in excess of par	300,000
		Retained earnings	$2,350,000
		Total common stockholders' equity	$2,850,000
		Total	$9,050,000

[a]Represents wages of $2,000 or less per employee earned within 90 days of filing bankruptcy for the firm's employees.
[b]These unpaid employee benefits were due in the 180-day period preceding the firm's bankruptcy filing, which occurred simultaneously with the termination of its business.
[c]Unsecured customer deposits not exceeding $900 each.
[d]The first and second mortgages are on the firm's total fixed assets.
[e]The debentures are subordinated to the bank's note payable.

Table 25.4
Distribution of the
Liquidation Proceeds of
Oxford Company

Proceeds from liquidation	$3,900,000
Expenses of administering bankruptcy and paying bills	$ 500,000
Wages owed workers	100,000
Unpaid employee benefits	110,000
Unsecured customer deposits	90,000
Taxes owed governments	300,000
Funds available for creditors	$2,800,000
First mortgage, paid from $2 million proceeds of fixed asset	$1,400,000
Second mortgage, partially paid from the remaining assets	400,000
Funds available for unsecured creditors	$1,000,000

illustrates that once all prior claims on the proceeds to liquidation have been satisfied, the unsecured creditors get the remaining funds. Table 25.5 gives the pro rata distribution of the $1 million among the unsecured creditors. The disposition of funds in the Oxford Company liquidation should be clear from Tables 25.4 and 25.5. Because the claims of the unsecured creditors have not been fully satisfied, the preferred and common shareholders receive nothing.

Table 25.5
Pro Rata Distribution of
Funds among the
Unsecured Creditors of
Oxford Company

Unsecured Creditors' Claims	Amount	Settlement at 32%[a]	After Subordination
Unpaid balance on second mortgage	$ 400,000[b]	$ 129,032	$ 129,032
Accounts payable	200,000	64,516	64,516
Notes payable—bank	1,500,000	483,871	806,452
Subordinated debentures	1,000,000	322,581	0
Totals	$3,100,000	$1,000,000	$1,000,000

[a]The 32% rate is calculated by dividing the $1 million available for the unsecured creditors by the $3.1 million owed the unsecured creditors. Each is entitled to a pro rata share.
[b]This figure represents the difference between the $800,000 second mortgage and the $400,000 payment on the second mortgage from the proceeds from the sale of the collateral remaining after satisfying the first mortgage.

FINAL ACCOUNTING

The trustee, after liquidating the bankrupt firm's assets and distributing proceeds to satisfy all provable claims in the appropriate order of priority, makes a final accounting to the bankruptcy court and creditors. Once the court approves the final accounting, the liquidation is complete.

Concept Review Questions

13. What is the purpose of having the absolute priority rule? Why shouldn't the bankruptcy judge be given more discretion?

14. What is the significance of subordinating a claim if a firm is liquidated?

15. Why is the payment of the expenses of administering the bankruptcy proceeding given the highest priority?

25.6 PREDICTING BANKRUPTCY

Predicting bankruptcy with some degree of accuracy is possible using Altman's Z score, named after Professor Ed Altman of New York University. The **Z score** is the product of a quantitative model that uses a blend of traditional financial ratios and a statistical technique known as multiple discriminant analysis. The Z score has been found to be about 90 percent accurate in forecasting bankruptcy one year in the future and about 80 percent accurate in forecasting it two years in the future. The model is as follows:

$$Z = 1.2 * X_1 + 1.4 * X_2 + 3.3 * X_3 + 0.6 * X_4 + 1.0 * X_5$$

where X_1 = working capital ÷ total assets

X_2 = retained earnings ÷ total assets

X_3 = earnings before interest and taxes ÷ total assets

X_4 = market value of equity ÷ book value of total liabilities

X_5 = sales ÷ total assets

The following are guidelines for classifying businesses: Z score less than 1.8, high probability of failure; Z score between 1.81 and 2.99, unsure; and Z score above 3.0, failure unlikely.

Table 25.6
Balance Sheet for
Poff Industries

Assets		Liabilities and Stockholders' Equity	
Cash	$ 100,000	Accounts payable	$ 2,000,000
Accounts receivable	1,000,000	Notes payable—bank	1,500,000
Inventories	3,000,000	Total current liabilities	$ 3,500,000
Total current assets	$ 4,100,000	Mortgage	$ 2,000,000
Land	$ 2,000,000	Debentures	3,000,000
Net plant	2,500,000	Total long-term debt	$ 5,000,000
Net equipment	3,000,000	Common stock	
Total fixed assets	$ 7,500,000	(1,000,000 shares)	1,000,000
Total	$11,600,000	Paid-in capital in excess	
		of par	1,000,000
		Retained earnings	1,100,000
		Total stockholders' equity	$ 3,100,000
		Total	$11,600,000

Table 25.7
Income Statement
for Poff Industries

Sales	$5,000,000
Less: Cost of goods sold	3,000,000
Less: Selling and administrative expenses	1,000,000
Earnings before interest and taxes	$1,000,000
Less: Interest	$ 500,000
Earnings before taxes	$ 500,000
Less: Taxes (40%)	$ 200,000
Net Income	$ 300,000

APPLYING THE MODEL 25.5

Table 25.6 presents the balance sheet, and Table 25.7 presents the income statement for Poff Industries, a manufacturer of computer power supplies. The company's stock price currently is $3.50 per share.

The company's Z score can be calculated as follows:

$$1.157 = 1.2*(0.052) + 1.4*(0.095) + 3.3*(0.086) + 0.6*(0.418)$$
$$+ 1.0*(0.431)$$

The Z score of 1.157 indicates that the probability that Poff Industries will fail is quite high.

---

16. Why is predicting bankruptcy a useful ability?

17. How are the five factors that determine a Z score related to the financial health of a business?

**Concept
Review
Questions**

25.7 SUMMARY

- A business can fail in two ways. When it cannot pay its liabilities when they come due, the firm is technically insolvent due to a liquidity crisis. When its liabilities exceed the fair market value of its assets, the firm is insolvent. Bankruptcy occurs once a company comes under the authority of a bankruptcy court, which then exercises ultimate control over the firm.

- Mismanagement is the primary cause of business failure. Managerial faults include overexpansion, poor financial actions, an ineffective sales force, and high production costs. Other causes are economic downturns and corporate maturity.

- The financial distress a pending business failure places on a company and its management can have a profound effect on how the firm behaves and how its suppliers and customers perceive it. When a firm is in financial distress, suppliers are reluctant to extend credit and customers are concerned about service and warranties.

- Companies facing financial distress can voluntarily reorganize or liquidate. By acting voluntarily, firms reduce the legal and administrative expenses associated with a formal bankruptcy filing.

- The Bankruptcy Reform Act of 1978 specifies in Chapter 7 how firms are liquidated and in Chapter 11 how firms are reorganized.

- Firms can reorganize under Chapter 11 by means of the unanimous consent procedure or the cramdown procedure. In a reorganization, the terms of the debt can be relaxed by extending the payment term or lowering the interest rate. Also, debt can be exchanged for equity in the firm, thus reducing the amount of cash flow required to service the debt.

- Firms are liquidated under Chapter 7 by means of the absolute priority rule, which ranks the order for paying creditors from the proceeds of the liquidation of the firm's assets.

- The likelihood of bankruptcy can be predicted with a fair degree of accuracy (at least in the short term) using Altman's Z score.

KEY TERMS

absolute priority rules (APR)
assignment
bankruptcy
Bankruptcy Reform Act of 1978
business failure
Chapter 7
Chapter 11
composition
cramdown procedure
creditor control
debtor in possession (DIP)
economic failure
extension
general creditors
insolvency bankruptcy
insolvent

involuntary reorganization
liquidation
liquidity crisis
prepackaged bankruptcy
recapitalization
reorganization
secured creditors
technical insolvency
trustee
unanimous consent procedure (UCP)
unsecured creditors
voluntary reorganization
voluntary settlement
workout
Z score

INTERNET RESOURCES

Note: *For updates to links, please go to the book's website at* http://smart.swcollege.com.

http://www.bankruptcydata.com/—Searchable website providing data and information on bankruptcies in the United States. Though most of the data are fee-based, a significant amount can be obtained for free.

http://www.uscourts.gov/bankruptcycourts.html—The main website for the United States Bankruptcy Courts, offering access to both data and information about bankruptcy filings.

QUESTIONS

25-1. Discuss why it makes sense to offer subsidies to firms that reorganize rather than liquidate.

25-2. Explain why the option to delay entering bankruptcy has value for corporate managers.

25-3. Why do creditors usually accept a plan for financial rehabilitation rather than demand liquidation of a business?

25-4. A certain number of bankruptcies are good for the economy. Discuss why you agree or disagree with this statement.

25-5. A business should always be liquidated when the liquidation value exceeds the business's value as a going concern. Discuss why you agree or disagree with this statement.

25-6. What are the advantages and disadvantages of a voluntary workout to resolve financial distress? What are the advantages and disadvantages of declaring bankruptcy to resolve financial distress?

25-7. A business can be liquidated for $700,000, or it can be reorganized. Reorganization would require an investment of $400,000. If the company is reorganized, earnings are projected to be $150,000 per year, and the company would trade at a price/earnings ratio of 8.0 times. Should the company be liquidated or reorganized?

25-8. Explain why the priorities for liquidation are determined as they are. Do you agree with the order?

25-9. What is the difference between economic failure and financial distress? Which situation is likely to lead to liquidation, and which is likely to result in reorganization?

25-10. Who would use Altman's Z score to predict bankruptcy? Why would the ability to predict bankruptcy be useful to them?

25-11. What is the purpose of a prepackaged bankruptcy? Would a prepackaged bankruptcy be more likely to be used for a liquidation or a reorganization?

25-12. Why would some creditors be willing to subordinate their claims to the claims of other creditors?

PROBLEMS

Voluntary Settlements

25-1. For a firm with outstanding debt of $2.4 million, classify each of the following voluntary settlements as an extension, a composition, or a combination of the two.

    a. Paying all creditors 40 cents on the dollar in exchange for complete discharge of the debt

    b. Paying all creditors in full in three periodic installments

    c. Paying a group of creditors with claims of $1 million in full over two years and immediately paying the remaining creditors 75 cents on the dollar.

25-2. For a firm with outstanding debt of $125,000, classify each of the following voluntary settlements as an extension, a composition, or a combination of the two.

    a. Paying a group of creditors in full in four periodic installments and paying the remaining creditors in full immediately

    b. Paying a group of creditors 80 cents on the dollar immediately and paying the remaining creditors 70 cents on the dollar in two periodic installments

    c. Paying all creditors in full in 270 days.

25-3. For a firm with outstanding debt of $200 million, classify each of the following voluntary settlements as an extension, a composition, or a combination of the two.

    a. Paying a group of creditors in full in three periodic installments and paying the remaining creditors 70 cents on the dollar immediately

    b. Paying a group of creditors 60 cents on the dollar immediately and paying the remaining creditors 80 cents on the dollar in five periodic installments

    c. Paying all creditors 25 cents on the dollar.

25-4. For a firm with outstanding debt of $50 million, classify each of the following voluntary settlements as an extension, a composition, or a combination of the two.

    a. Paying a group of creditors in full in six periodic installments and paying the remaining creditors 75 cents on the dollar immediately

    b. Paying a group of creditors 50 cents on the dollar immediately and paying the remaining creditors 70 cents on the dollar in five periodic installments

    c. Paying all creditors 30 cents on the dollar.

25-5. Go to http://www.bankruptcydata.com, and find what were the largest public company bankruptcies during the previous year. Compare the list of the largest bankruptcies in U.S. history presented in Table 25.1 with the current list at http://www.bankruptcydata.com. Have any bankruptcies that occurred after 2006 made the list?

25-6. Jacobi Supply Company recently ran into financial difficulties that have resulted in the initiation of voluntary settlement procedures. The firm currently has $250,000 in outstanding debts and approximately $100,000 in marketable short-term assets. Indicate, for each of the following plans, whether the plan is an extension, a composition, or a combination of the two. Also indicate the cash payments and timing of the payments required of the firm under each plan.

    a. Each creditor will be paid 40 cents on the dollar immediately, and the debts will be considered fully satisfied.

    b. Each creditor will be paid 40 cents on the dollar in two quarterly installments of 20 cents and 20 cents. The first installment is to be paid in 90 days.

    c. Each creditor will be paid the full amount of its claims in three installments of 50 cents, 25 cents, and 25 cents on the dollar. The installments will be made in 60-day intervals, beginning in 60 days.

25-7. Heriot Manufacturing Company recently ran into certain financial difficulties that have resulted in the initiation of voluntary settlement procedures. The firm currently has $2 million in outstanding debts and approximately $1.2 million in marketable short-term assets. Indicate, for each of the following plans, whether the plan is an extension, a composition, or a combination of the two. Also indicate the cash payments and timing of the payments required of the firm under each plan.

a. Each creditor will be paid 60 cents on the dollar immediately, and the debts will be considered fully satisfied.

b. Each creditor will be paid 80 cents on the dollar in two quarterly installments of 50 cents and 30 cents. The first installment is to be paid in 90 days.

c. A group of creditors with claims of $600,000 will be immediately paid in full; the rest will be paid 85 cents on the dollar, payable in 90 days.

Liquidation in Bankruptcy

25-8. A firm has $450,000 in funds to distribute to its unsecured creditors. Three possible sets of unsecured creditor claims are presented. Calculate the settlement, if any, to be received by each creditor in each case shown in the following table.

Unsecured Creditors' Claims	Case I	Case II	Case III
Unpaid balance of second mortgage	$300,000	$200,000	$ 500,000
Accounts payable	200,000	100,000	300,000
Notes payable—bank	300,000	100,000	500,000
Unsecured bonds	100,000	200,000	500,000
Total	$900,000	$600,000	$1,800,000

25-9. A firm has $5 million in funds to distribute to its unsecured creditors. Three possible sets of unsecured creditor claims are presented. Calculate the settlement, if any, to be received by each creditor in each case shown in the following table.

Unsecured Creditors' Claims	Case I	Case II	Case III
Unpaid balance of second mortgage	$1,000,000	$2,000,000	$3,000,000
Accounts payable	2,000,000	1,000,000	3,000,000
Notes payable—bank	3,000,000	2,000,000	1,000,000
Unsecured bonds	1,000,000	3,000,000	2,000,000
Total	$7,000,000	$8,000,000	$9,000,000

25-10. A firm has $8 million in funds to distribute to its unsecured creditors. Three possible sets of unsecured creditor claims are presented. Calculate the settlement, if any, to be received by each creditor in each case shown in the following table.

Unsecured Creditors' Claims	Case I	Case II	Case III
Unpaid balance of second mortgage	$ 2,000,000	$ 2,500,000	$ 5,000,000
Accounts payable	2,500,000	3,000,000	4,000,000
Notes payable—bank	3,500,000	3,500,000	1,500,000
Unsecured bonds	4,000,000	5,000,000	5,500,000
Total	$12,000,000	$14,000,000	$16,000,000

25-11. Keck Business Forms recently failed and will be liquidated by a court-appointed trustee, who will charge $300,000 for her services. The preliquidation balance sheet follows. Assume that the trustee liquidates the assets for $4.8 million, with $2.6 million coming from the sale of current assets and $2.2 million coming from fixed assets. Also assume that the unsecured bonds are subordinate to the notes payable. Prepare a table indicating the amount to be distributed to each claimant. Do the firm's owners receive any funds?

Keck Business Forms
Balance Sheet
as of December 31, 2007

Assets		Liabilities and Stockholder's Equity	
Cash	$ 100,000	Accounts payable	$1,200,000
Marketable securities	50,000	Notes payable—bank	1,100,000
Accounts receivable	1,100,000	Accrued wages[a]	300,000
Inventories	2,400,000	Unpaid employee benefits[b]	200,000
Prepaid expenses	400,000	Unsecured customer deposits[c]	250,000
Total current assets	$4,050,000	Taxes payable	100,000
		Total current liabilities	$3,150,000
Land	$1,000,000	First mortgage[d]	$1,500,000
Net plant	2,100,000	Second mortgage[d]	1,000,000
Net equipment	2,300,000	Unsecured bonds	2,000,000
Total fixed assets	$5,400,000	Total long-term debt	$4,500,000
Total	$9,450,000	Preferred stock (5,000 shares)	$ 500,000
		Common stock (10,000 shares)	1,000,000
		Retained earnings	300,000
		Total stockholders' equity	$1,800,000
		Total	$9,450,000

[a]Represents wages of $2,000 or less per employee earned within 90 days of filing bankruptcy for 400 of the firm's employees.
[b]Unpaid employee benefits that were due in the 180-day period preceding the firm's bankruptcy filing, which occurred simultaneously with the termination of its business.
[c]Unsecured customer deposits not exceeding $900 each.
[d]First and second mortgages on the firm's total fixed assets.

25-12. Oxygen Filtration Systems recently failed and will be liquidated by a court-appointed trustee, who will charge $500,000 for his services. The preliquidation balance sheet follows. Assume that the trustee liquidates the assets for $10.2 million, with $5.8 million coming from the sale of current assets and $4.4 million coming from fixed assets. Also assume that the unsecured bonds are subordinate to the notes payable. Prepare a table indicating the amount to be distributed to each claimant. Do the firm's owners receive any funds?

Oxygen Filtration Systems
Balance Sheet
as of December 31, 2007

Assets		Liabilities and Stockholder's Equity	
Cash	$ 600,000	Accounts payable	$ 2,500,000
Marketable securities	750,000	Notes payable—bank	4,000,000
Accounts receivable	1,750,000	Accrued wages[a]	750,000
Inventories	2,25,000	Unpaid employee benefits[b]	500,000
Prepaid expenses	900,000	Unsecured customer deposits[c]	500,000
		Taxes payable	1,000,000
Total current assets	$ 6,250,000	Total current liabilities	$ 9,250,000

(*continued on next page*)

Oxygen Filtration Systems
Balance Sheet
as of December 31, 2007
(continued)

Assets		Liabilities and Stockholder's Equity	
Land	$ 3,000,000	First mortgage[d]	$ 3,000,000
Net plant	5,000,000	Second mortgage[d]	2,000,000
Net equipment	6,250,000	Unsecured bonds	3,500,000
Total fixed assets	$14,250,000	Total long-term debt	$ 8,500,000
Total	$20,500,000	Preferred stock (10,000 shares)	$ 500,000
		Common stock (20,000 shares)	2,000,000
		Retained earnings	250,000
		Total stockholders' equity	$ 2,750,000
		Total	$20,500,000

[a]Represents wages of $2,000 or less per employee earned within 90 days of filing bankruptcy for 400 of the firm's employees.
[b]Unpaid employee benefits that were due in the 180-day period preceding the firm's bankruptcy filing, which occurred simultaneously with the termination of its business.
[c]Unsecured customer deposits not exceeding $900 each.
[d]First and second mortgages on the firm's total fixed assets.

Predicting Bankruptcy

25-13. Sosbee Foods has a working capital/total assets ratio of 0.2, a retained earnings/total assets ratio of 0.1, an earnings before interest and taxes/total assets ratio of 0.25, a market value of equity/book value of total liabilities ratio of 0.6, and a sales/total assets ratio of 0.8. Calculate and interpret the company's Z score.

25-14. Express Trailers has a working capital/total assets ratio of 0.3, a retained earnings/total assets ratio of 0.15, an earnings before interest and taxes/total assets ratio of 0.20, a market value of equity/book value of total liabilities ratio of 0.5, and a sales/total assets ratio of 0.75. Calculate and interpret the company's Z score.

SMART SOLUTIONS
See the problem and solution explained step-by-step at
SMARTFinance

25-15. The following balance sheet and income statement are for Weber Industries. The firm's stock currently is priced at $6.00 per share. Calculate and interpret the company's Z score.

Weber Industries
Balance Sheet
as of December 31, 2007

Assets		Liabilities and Stockholders' Equity	
Cash	$ 400,000	Accounts payable	$ 5,000,000
Accounts receivable	3,000,000	Notes payable—bank	1,000,000
Inventories	4,000,000	Total current liabilities	$ 6,000,000
Total current assets	$ 7,400,000	Mortgage	$ 4,000,000
Land	$ 1,000,000	Debentures	6,000,000
Net plant	5,000,000	Total long-term debt	$10,000,000
Net equipment	8,000,000	Preferred stock (100,000 shares)	$ 1,000,000
Total fixed assets	$14,000,000	Common stock (500,000 shares)	1,000,000
Total	$21,400,000	Paid-in capital in excess of par	2,000,000
		Retained earnings	1,400,000
		Total stockholders' equity	$ 5,400,000
		Total	$21,400,000

Weber Industries
Income Statement
for the Year Ending December 31, 2007

Sales:	$6,000,000
Less: Cost of goods sold	3,500,000
Less: Selling and administrative	1,000,000
Earnings before interest and taxes	$1,500,000
Less: Interest	1,100,000
Earnings before taxes	400,000
Less: Taxes (30%)	120,000
Net Income	$ 280,000

25-16. Compute the Z score for 3M with the following information:

3M Financial Information (year-end 2004)	
Current assets	$ 8,720,000.00
Current liabilities	$ 6,071,000.00
Retained earnings	$15,649,000.00
Total assets	$20,708,000.00
Total liabilities	$10,330,000.00
Shares outstanding	772,422,684
Share price	$ 70.00
Sales	$20,011,000.00
EBIT	$ 4,578,000.00

All values in thousands except share price and shares outstanding.

What proportion (measured as a percentage) is the Z score composed of $0.60*X_4$? Is 3M likely to go bankrupt in the near future based on the Z score?

25-17. Compute the Z score for Ford Motor Company with the following information:

Ford Financial Information (year-end 2004)	
Current assets	$ 49,414,000.00
Current liabilities	$ 52,676,000.00
Retained earnings	$ 11,175,000.00
Total assets	$292,654,000.00
Total liabilities	$276,609,000.00
Shares outstanding	1,747,000,000
Share price	$ 7.97
Sales	$171,652,000.00
EBIT	$ 11,924,000.00

All values in thousands except share price and shares outstanding.

What proportion (measured as a percentage) is the Z score composed of $0.60*X_4$? Is Ford likely to go bankrupt in the near future?

25-18. Compute the Z score for General Motors Corporation with the following information:

GM Financial Information (year-end 2004)

Current assets	$ 91,213,000.00
Current liabilities	$106,557,000.00
Retained earnings	$ 15,768,000.00
Total assets	$479,603,000.00
Total liabilities	$451,877,000.00
Shares outstanding	564,721,304
Share price	$ 20.95
Sales	$193,517,000.00
EBIT	$ 13,172,000.00

All values in thousands except share price and shares outstanding.

At what share price would GM have a Z score equal to 3.00?

25-19. Compute the Z score for Wal-Mart with the following information:

Wal-Mart Financial Information (year-end 2004)

Current assets	$ 38,491,000.00
Current liabilities	$ 42,888,000.00
Retained earnings	$ 43,854,000.00
Total assets	$120,223,000.00
Total liabilities	$ 70,827,000.00
Shares outstanding	4,233,002,095
Share price	$ 42.35
Sales	$287,989,000.00
EBIT	$ 17,292,000.00

All values in thousands except share price and shares outstanding.

What proportion (measured as a percentage) is the Z score composed of $0.60*X_4$?
What proportion (measured as a percentage) is the Z score composed of $1.00*X_5$?

THOMSON ONE BUSINESS SCHOOL EDITION

25-20. In February 2005, Winn-Dixie Stores (ticker symbol, WNDXQ) filed for bankruptcy protection. Calculate Altman's Z score for Winn-Dixie for the years 2001–2004. Was there deterioration in Altman's Z score over this time period? Did Altman's Z score correctly predict Winn-Dixie's bankruptcy? If so, how many years in advance of the bankruptcy?

25-21. Calculate Altman's Z score for Great Atlantic & Pacific Company (ticker symbol, GAP) for the years 2001–2004. What is the trend in Altman's Z score over this time period? How do the Z scores for Great Atlantic & Pacific compare to Winn-Dixie's?

MINI-CASE: BANKRUPTCY AND FINANCIAL DISTRESS

Flanan Photography Studios, Inc. (FPS) is preparing for a court-ordered bankruptcy and has the following preliquidation financial statements:

Flanan Photography Studios, Inc.
Balance Sheet
As of December 31, 2006

Assets		Liabilities and Stockholders' Equity	
Cash	$ 800,000	Accounts payable	$ 2,600,000
Marketable securities	$ 24,000	Notes payable	$ 2,200,000
Accounts receivable	$ 3,500,000	Accrued wages	$ 700,000
Inventories	$ 4,000,000	Unpaid employee benefits	$ 385,000
Prepaid expenses	$ 1,000,000	Taxes payable	$ 250,000
Total current assets	$ 9,324,000	Total current liabilities	$ 6,135,000
		First mortgage	$ 8,500,000
Land	$10,000,000	Second mortgage	$27,000,000
Net plant	$28,000,000	Unsecured bonds	$28,000,000
Net equipment	$32,000,000	Total long-term debt	$63,500,000
Total fixed assets	$70,000,000	Preferred stock (15,000 shares)	$ 1,500,000
Total	$79,324,000	Common stock (1,500,000 shares)	$ 7,500,000
		Retained earnings	$ 689,000
		Total stockholders' equity	$ 9,689,000
		Total	$79,324,000

Flanan Photography Studios, Inc.
Income Statement
For the year ending December 31, 2006

Sales	$14,420,000
Cost of goods sold	$ 7,210,000
Selling and administrative expenses	$ 787,000
Earnings before interest and taxes	$ 6,423,000
Interest expense	$ 5,715,000
Earnings before taxes	$ 708,000
Taxes (30%)	$ 283,200
Net income	$ 424,800

TruValue Trustees Services (TTS) has been appointed to oversee the sale and disbursement of funds from the liquidation and will charge $450,000 for the service. TTS can obtain $7,250,000 from the sale of FPS's current assets and $49,850,000 from the sale of fixed assets. Accrued wages represent wages of $2,000 or less per employee, and the wages were earned within 90 days of filing bankruptcy. Unpaid employee benefits represent an amount that was due within the 180-day period preceding the bankruptcy filing. The first and second mortgages are upon the firm's total fixed assets. The firm's stock is currently trading for $3.25 per share.

1.   Calculate the amount to be received by each claimant.

2.   Calculate and interpret the firm's Z score.

Table A1

Future Value Factors for One Dollar Compounded at r Percent for n Periods

$$FVF_{r\%,n} = (1 + r)^n$$

Period	1%	2%	3%	4%	5%	6%	7%	8%	9%	10%	11%	12%	13%	14%	15%	16%
1	1.010	1.020	1.030	1.040	1.050	1.060	1.070	1.080	1.090	1.100	1.110	1.120	1.130	1.140	1.150	1.160
2	1.020	1.040	1.061	1.082	1.103	1.124	1.145	1.166	1.188	1.210	1.232	1.254	1.277	1.300	1.323	1.346
3	1.030	1.061	1.093	1.125	1.158	1.191	1.225	1.260	1.295	1.331	1.368	1.405	1.443	1.482	1.521	1.561
4	1.041	1.082	1.126	1.170	1.216	1.262	1.311	1.360	1.412	1.464	1.518	1.574	1.630	1.689	1.749	1.811
5	1.051	1.104	1.159	1.217	1.276	1.338	1.403	1.469	1.539	1.611	1.685	1.762	1.842	1.925	2.011	2.100
6	1.062	1.126	1.194	1.265	1.340	1.419	1.501	1.587	1.677	1.772	1.870	1.974	2.082	2.195	2.313	2.436
7	1.072	1.149	1.230	1.316	1.407	1.504	1.606	1.714	1.828	1.949	2.076	2.211	2.353	2.502	2.660	2.826
8	1.083	1.172	1.267	1.369	1.477	1.594	1.718	1.851	1.993	2.144	2.305	2.476	2.658	2.853	3.059	3.278
9	1.094	1.195	1.305	1.423	1.551	1.689	1.838	1.999	2.172	2.358	2.558	2.773	3.004	3.252	3.518	3.803
10	1.105	1.219	1.344	1.480	1.629	1.791	1.967	2.159	2.367	2.594	2.839	3.106	3.395	3.707	4.046	4.411
11	1.116	1.243	1.384	1.539	1.710	1.898	2.105	2.332	2.580	2.853	3.152	3.479	3.836	4.226	4.652	5.117
12	1.127	1.268	1.426	1.601	1.796	2.012	2.252	2.518	2.813	3.138	3.498	3.896	4.335	4.818	5.350	5.936
13	1.138	1.294	1.469	1.665	1.886	2.133	2.410	2.720	3.066	3.452	3.883	4.363	4.898	5.492	6.153	6.886
14	1.149	1.319	1.513	1.732	1.980	2.261	2.579	2.937	3.342	3.797	4.310	4.887	5.535	6.261	7.076	7.988
15	1.161	1.346	1.558	1.801	2.079	2.397	2.759	3.172	3.642	4.177	4.785	5.474	6.254	7.138	8.137	9.266
16	1.173	1.373	1.605	1.873	2.183	2.540	2.952	3.426	3.970	4.595	5.311	6.130	7.067	8.137	9.358	10.748
17	1.184	1.400	1.653	1.948	2.292	2.693	3.159	3.700	4.328	5.054	5.895	6.866	7.986	9.276	10.761	12.468
18	1.196	1.428	1.702	2.026	2.407	2.854	3.380	3.996	4.717	5.560	6.544	7.690	9.024	10.575	12.375	14.463
19	1.208	1.457	1.754	2.107	2.527	3.026	3.617	4.316	5.142	6.116	7.263	8.613	10.197	12.056	14.232	16.777
20	1.220	1.486	1.806	2.191	2.653	3.207	3.870	4.661	5.604	6.727	8.062	9.646	11.523	13.743	16.367	19.461
21	1.232	1.516	1.860	2.279	2.786	3.400	4.141	5.034	6.109	7.400	8.949	10.804	13.021	15.668	18.822	22.574
22	1.245	1.546	1.916	2.370	2.925	3.604	4.430	5.437	6.659	8.140	9.934	12.100	14.714	17.861	21.645	26.186
23	1.257	1.577	1.974	2.465	3.072	3.820	4.741	5.871	7.258	8.954	11.026	13.552	16.627	20.362	24.891	30.376
24	1.270	1.608	2.033	2.563	3.225	4.049	5.072	6.341	7.911	9.850	12.239	15.179	18.788	23.212	28.625	35.236
25	1.282	1.641	2.094	2.666	3.386	4.292	5.427	6.848	8.623	10.835	13.585	17.000	21.231	26.462	32.919	40.874
30	1.348	1.811	2.427	3.243	4.322	5.743	7.612	10.063	13.268	17.449	22.892	29.960	39.116	50.950	66.212	85.850
35	1.417	2.000	2.814	3.946	5.516	7.686	10.677	14.785	20.414	28.102	38.575	52.800	72.069	98.100	133.176	180.314
40	1.489	2.208	3.262	4.801	7.040	10.286	14.974	21.725	31.409	45.259	65.001	93.051	132.782	188.884	267.864	378.721
45	1.565	2.438	3.782	5.841	8.985	13.765	21.002	31.920	48.327	72.890	109.530	163.988	244.641	363.679	538.769	795.444
50	645	2.692	4.384	7.107	11.467	18.420	29.457	46.902	74.358	117.391	184.565	289.002	450.736	700.233	1083.657	1670.704

Table A1 (continued)

Period	17%	18%	19%	20%	21%	22%	23%	24%	25%	30%	35%	40%	45%	50%
1	1.170	1.180	1.190	1.200	1.210	1.220	1.230	1.240	1.250	1.300	1.350	1.400	1.450	1.500
2	1.369	1.392	1.416	1.440	1.464	1.488	1.513	1.538	1.563	1.690	1.823	1.960	2.103	2.250
3	1.602	1.643	1.685	1.728	1.772	1.816	1.861	1.907	1.953	2.197	2.460	2.744	3.049	3.375
4	1.874	1.939	2.005	2.074	2.144	2.215	2.289	2.364	2.441	2.856	3.322	3.842	4.421	5.063
5	2.192	2.288	2.386	2.488	2.594	2.703	2.815	2.932	3.052	3.713	4.484	5.378	6.410	7.594
6	2.565	2.700	2.840	2.986	3.138	3.297	3.463	3.635	3.815	4.827	6.053	7.530	9.294	11.391
7	3.001	3.185	3.379	3.583	3.797	4.023	4.259	4.508	4.768	6.275	8.172	10.541	13.476	17.086
8	3.511	3.759	4.021	4.300	4.595	4.908	5.239	5.590	5.960	8.157	11.032	14.758	19.541	25.629
9	4.108	4.435	4.785	5.160	5.560	5.987	6.444	6.931	7.451	10.604	14.894	20.661	28.334	38.443
10	4.807	5.234	5.695	6.192	6.727	7.305	7.926	8.594	9.313	13.786	20.107	28.925	41.085	57.665
11	5.624	6.176	6.777	7.430	8.140	8.912	9.749	10.657	11.642	17.922	27.144	40.496	59.573	86.498
12	6.580	7.288	8.064	8.916	9.850	10.872	11.991	13.215	14.552	23.298	36.644	56.694	86.381	129.746
13	7.699	8.599	9.596	10.699	11.918	13.264	14.749	16.386	18.190	30.288	49.470	79.371	125.252	194.620
14	9.007	10.147	11.420	12.839	14.421	16.182	18.141	20.319	22.737	39.374	66.784	111.120	181.615	291.929
15	10.539	11.974	13.590	15.407	17.449	19.742	22.314	25.196	28.422	51.186	90.158	155.568	263.342	437.894
16	12.330	14.129	16.172	18.488	21.114	24.086	27.446	31.243	35.527	66.542	121.714	217.795	381.846	656.841
17	14.426	16.672	19.244	22.186	25.548	29.384	33.759	38.741	44.409	86.504	164.314	304.913	553.676	985.261
18	16.879	19.673	22.901	26.623	30.913	35.849	41.523	48.039	55.511	112.455	221.824	426.879	802.831	1477.892
19	19.748	23.214	27.252	31.948	37.404	43.736	51.074	59.568	69.389	146.192	299.462	597.630	1164.105	2216.838
20	23.106	27.393	32.429	38.338	45.259	53.358	62.821	73.864	86.736	190.050	404.274	836.683	1687.952	3325.257
21	27.034	32.324	38.591	46.005	54.764	65.096	77.269	91.592	108.420	247.065	545.769	1171.356	2447.530	4987.885
22	31.629	38.142	45.923	55.206	66.264	79.418	95.041	113.574	135.525	321.184	736.789	1639.898	3548.919	7481.828
23	37.006	45.008	54.649	66.247	80.180	96.889	116.901	140.831	169.407	417.539	994.665	2295.857	5145.932	11222.741
24	43.297	53.109	65.032	79.497	97.017	118.205	143.788	174.631	211.758	542.801	1342.797	3214.200	7461.602	16834.112
25	50.658	62.669	77.388	95.396	117.391	144.210	176.859	216.542	264.698	705.641	1812.776	4499.880	10819.322	25251.168
30	111.065	143.371	184.675	237.376	304.482	389.758	497.913	634.820	807.794	2619.996	8128.550	24201.432	69348.978	191751.059
35	243.503	327.997	440.701	590.668	789.747	1053.402	1401.777	1861.054	2465.190	9727.860	36448.688	130161.112	444508.508	*
40	533.869	750.378	1051.668	1469.772	2048.400	2847.038	3946.430	5455.913	7523.164	36118.865	163437.135	700037.697	*	*
45	1170.479	1716.684	2509.651	3657.262	5313.023	7694.712	11110.408	15994.690	22958.874	134106.817	732857.577	*	*	*
50	2566.215	3927.357	5988.914	9100.438	13780.612	20796.561	31279.195	46890.435	70064.923	497929.223	*	*	*	*

*Not shown because of space limitations.

Table A2
Present Value Factors for One Dollar Discounted at r Percent for n Periods

$$PVF_{r\%,n} = 1/(1 + r)^n$$

Period	1%	2%	3%	4%	5%	6%	7%	8%	9%	10%	11%	12%	13%	14%	15%	16%
1	0.990	0.980	0.971		0.952	0.943	0.935	0.926	0.917	0.909	0.901	0.893	0.885	0.877	0.870	0.862
2	0.980	0.961	0.943		0.907	0.890	0.873	0.857	0.842	0.826	0.812	0.797	0.783	0.769	0.756	0.743
3	0.971	0.942	0.915		0.864	0.840	0.816	0.794	0.772	0.751	0.731	0.712	0.693	0.675	0.658	0.641
4	0.961	0.924	0.888		0.823	0.792	0.763	0.735	0.708	0.683	0.659	0.636	0.613	0.592	0.572	0.552
5	0.951	0.906	0.863		0.784	0.747	0.713	0.681	0.650	0.621	0.593	0.567	0.543	0.519	0.497	0.476
6	0.942	0.888	0.837		0.746	0.705	0.666	0.630	0.596	0.564	0.535	0.507	0.480	0.456	0.432	0.410
7	0.933	0.871	0.813	0.760	0.711	0.665	0.623	0.583	0.547	0.513	0.482	0.452	0.425	0.400	0.376	0.354
8	0.923	0.853	0.789	0.731	0.677	0.627	0.582	0.540	0.502	0.467	0.434	0.404	0.376	0.351	0.327	0.305
9	0.914	0.837	0.766	0.703	0.645	0.592	0.544	0.500	0.460	0.424	0.391	0.361	0.333	0.308	0.284	0.263
10	0.905	0.820	0.744	0.676	0.614	0.558	0.508	0.463	0.422	0.386	0.352	0.322	0.295	0.270	0.247	0.227
11	0.896	0.804	0.722	0.650	0.585	0.527	0.475	0.429	0.388	0.350	0.317	0.287	0.261	0.237	0.215	0.195
12	0.887	0.788	0.701	0.625	0.557	0.497	0.444	0.397	0.356	0.319	0.286	0.257	0.231	0.208	0.187	0.168
13	0.879	0.773	0.681	0.601	0.530	0.469	0.415	0.368	0.326	0.290	0.258	0.229	0.204	0.182	0.163	0.145
14	0.870	0.758	0.661	0.577	0.505	0.442	0.388	0.340	0.299	0.263	0.232	0.205	0.181	0.160	0.141	0.125
15	0.861	0.743	0.642	0.555	0.481	0.417	0.362	0.315	0.275	0.239	0.209	0.183	0.160	0.140	0.123	0.108
16	0.853	0.728	0.623	0.534	0.458	0.394	0.339	0.292	0.252	0.218	0.188	0.163	0.141	0.123	0.107	0.093
17	0.844	0.714	0.605	0.513	0.436	0.371	0.317	0.270	0.231	0.198	0.170	0.146	0.125	0.108	0.093	0.080
18	0.836	0.700	0.587	0.494	0.416	0.350	0.296	0.250	0.212	0.180	0.153	0.130	0.111	0.095	0.081	0.069
19	0.828	0.686	0.570	0.475	0.396	0.331	0.277	0.232	0.194	0.164	0.138	0.116	0.098	0.083	0.070	0.060
20	0.820	0.673	0.554	0.456	0.377	0.312	0.258	0.215	0.178	0.149	0.124	0.104	0.087	0.073	0.061	0.051
21	0.811	0.660	0.538	0.439	0.359	0.294	0.242	0.199	0.164	0.135	0.112	0.093	0.077	0.064	0.053	0.044
22	0.803	0.647	0.522	0.422	0.342	0.278	0.226	0.184	0.150	0.123	0.101	0.083	0.068	0.056	0.046	0.038
23	0.795	0.634	0.507	0.406	0.326	0.262	0.211	0.170	0.138	0.112	0.091	0.074	0.060	0.049	0.040	0.033
24	0.788	0.622	0.492	0.390	0.310	0.247	0.197	0.158	0.126	0.102	0.082	0.066	0.053	0.043	0.035	0.028
25	0.780	0.610	0.478	0.375	0.295	0.233	0.184	0.146	0.116	0.092	0.074	0.059	0.047	0.038	0.030	0.024
30	0.742	0.552	0.412	0.308	0.231	0.174	0.131	0.099	0.075	0.057	0.044	0.033	0.026	0.020	0.015	0.012
35	0.706	0.500	0.355	0.253	0.181	0.130	0.094	0.068	0.049	0.036	0.026	0.019	0.014	0.010	0.008	0.006
40	0.672	0.453	0.307	0.208	0.142	0.097	0.067	0.046	0.032	0.022	0.015	0.011	0.008	0.005	0.004	0.003
45	0.639	0.410	0.264	0.171	0.111	0.073	0.048	0.031	0.021	0.014	0.009	0.006	0.004	0.003	0.002	0.001
50	0.608	0.372	0.228	0.141	0.087	0.054	0.034	0.021	0.013	0.009	0.005	0.003	0.002	0.001	0.001	0.001

Table A2 (continued)

Period	17%	18%	19%	20%	21%	22%	23%	24%	25%	30%	35%	40%	45%	50%
1	0.855	0.847	0.840	0.833	0.826	0.820	0.813	0.806	0.800	0.769	0.741	0.714	0.690	0.667
2	0.731	0.718	0.706	0.694	0.683	0.672	0.661	0.650	0.640	0.592	0.549	0.510	0.476	0.444
3	0.624	0.609	0.593	0.579	0.564	0.551	0.537	0.524	0.512	0.455	0.406	0.364	0.328	0.296
4	0.534	0.516	0.499	0.482	0.467	0.451	0.437	0.423	0.410	0.350	0.301	0.260	0.226	0.198
5	0.456	0.437	0.419	0.402	0.386	0.370	0.355	0.341	0.328	0.269	0.223	0.186	0.156	0.132
6	0.390	0.370	0.352	0.335	0.319	0.303	0.289	0.275	0.262	0.207	0.165	0.133	0.108	0.088
7	0.333	0.314	0.296	0.279	0.263	0.249	0.235	0.222	0.210	0.159	0.122	0.095	0.074	0.059
8	0.285	0.266	0.249	0.233	0.218	0.204	0.191	0.179	0.168	0.123	0.091	0.068	0.051	0.039
9	0.243	0.225	0.209	0.194	0.180	0.167	0.155	0.144	0.134	0.094	0.067	0.048	0.035	0.026
10	0.208	0.191	0.176	0.162	0.149	0.137	0.126	0.116	0.107	0.073	0.050	0.035	0.024	0.017
11	0.178	0.162	0.148	0.135	0.123	0.112	0.103	0.094	0.086	0.056	0.037	0.025	0.017	0.012
12	0.152	0.137	0.124	0.112	0.102	0.092	0.083	0.076	0.069	0.043	0.027	0.018	0.012	0.008
13	0.130	0.116	0.104	0.093	0.084	0.075	0.068	0.061	0.055	0.033	0.020	0.013	0.008	0.005
14	0.111	0.099	0.088	0.078	0.069	0.062	0.055	0.049	0.044	0.025	0.015	0.009	0.006	0.003
15	0.095	0.084	0.074	0.065	0.057	0.051	0.045	0.040	0.035	0.020	0.011	0.006	0.004	0.002
16	0.081	0.071	0.062	0.054	0.047	0.042	0.036	0.032	0.028	0.015	0.008	0.005	0.003	0.002
17	0.069	0.060	0.052	0.045	0.039	0.034	0.030	0.026	0.023	0.012	0.006	0.003	0.002	0.002
18	0.059	0.051	0.044	0.038	0.032	0.028	0.024	0.021	0.018	0.009	0.005	0.002	0.001	0.001
19	0.051	0.043	0.037	0.031	0.027	0.023	0.020	0.017	0.014	0.007	0.003	0.002	0.001	0.001
20	0.043	0.037	0.031	0.026	0.022	0.019	0.016	0.014	0.012	0.005	0.002	0.001	0.001	*
21	0.037	0.031	0.026	0.022	0.018	0.015	0.013	0.011	0.009	0.004	0.002	0.001	*	*
22	0.032	0.026	0.022	0.018	0.015	0.013	0.011	0.009	0.007	0.003	0.001	0.001	*	*
23	0.027	0.022	0.018	0.015	0.012	0.010	0.009	0.007	0.006	0.002	*	*	*	*
24	0.023	0.019	0.015	0.013	0.010	0.008	0.007	0.006	0.005	0.002	0.001	*	*	*
25	0.020	0.016	0.013	0.010	0.009	0.007	0.006	0.005	0.004	0.001	0.001	*	*	*
30	0.009	0.007	0.005	0.004	0.003	0.003	0.002	0.002	0.001	*	*	*	*	*
35	0.004	0.003	0.002	0.002	0.001	0.001	0.001	0.001	*	*	*	*	*	*
40	0.002	0.001	0.001	0.001	*	*	*	*	*	*	*	*	*	*
45	0.001	0.001	*	*	*	*	*	*	*	*	*	*	*	*
50	*	*	*	*	*	*	*	*	*	*	*	*	*	*

* PVF is zero to three decimal places.

Table A3
Future Value Factors for a One-Dollar Ordinary Annuity Compounded at r Percent for n Periods

$$FVFA_{r\%,n} = PMT \times \frac{(1+r)^n - 1}{r}$$

Period	1%	2%	3%	4%	5%	6%	7%	8%	9%	10%	11%	12%	13%	14%	15%	16%
1	1.000	1.000	1.000	1.000	1.000	1.000	1.000	1.000	1.000	1.000	1.000	1.000	1.000	1.000	1.000	1.000
2	2.010	2.020	2.030	2.040	2.050	2.060	2.070	2.080	2.090	2.100	2.110	2.120	2.130	2.140	2.150	2.160
3	3.030	3.060	3.091	3.122	3.153	3.184	3.215	3.246	3.278	3.310	3.342	3.374	3.407	3.440	3.473	3.506
4	4.060	4.122	4.184	4.246	4.310	4.375	4.440	4.506	4.573	4.641	4.710	4.779	4.850	4.921	4.993	5.066
5	5.101	5.204	5.309	5.416	5.526	5.637	5.751	5.867	5.985	6.105	6.228	6.353	6.480	6.610	6.742	6.877
6	6.152	6.308	6.468	6.633	6.802	6.975	7.153	7.336	7.523	7.716	7.913	8.115	8.323	8.536	8.754	8.977
7	7.214	7.434	7.662	7.898	8.142	8.394	8.654	8.923	9.200	9.487	9.783	10.089	10.405	10.730	11.067	11.414
8	8.286	8.583	8.892	9.214	9.549	9.897	10.260	10.637	11.028	11.436	11.859	12.300	12.757	13.233	13.727	14.240
9	9.369	9.755	10.159	10.583	11.027	11.491	11.978	12.488	13.021	13.579	14.164	14.776	15.416	16.085	16.786	17.519
10	10.462	10.950	11.464	12.006	12.578	13.181	13.816	14.487	15.193	15.937	16.722	17.549	18.420	19.337	20.304	21.321
11	11.567	12.169	12.808	13.486	14.207	14.972	15.784	16.645	17.560	18.531	19.561	20.655	21.814	23.045	24.349	25.733
12	12.683	13.412	14.192	15.026	15.917	16.870	17.888	18.977	20.141	21.384	22.713	24.133	25.650	27.271	29.002	30.850
13	13.809	14.680	15.618	16.627	17.713	18.882	20.141	21.495	22.953	24.523	26.212	28.029	29.985	32.089	34.352	36.786
14	14.947	15.974	17.086	18.292	19.599	21.015	22.550	24.215	26.019	27.975	30.095	32.393	34.883	37.581	40.505	43.672
15	16.097	17.293	18.599	20.024	21.579	23.276	25.129	27.152	29.361	31.772	34.405	37.280	40.417	43.842	47.580	51.660
16	17.258	18.639	20.157	21.825	23.657	25.673	27.888	30.324	33.003	35.950	39.190	42.753	46.672	50.980	55.717	60.925
17	18.430	20.012	21.762	23.698	25.840	28.213	30.840	33.750	36.974	40.545	44.501	48.884	53.739	59.118	65.075	71.673
18	19.615	21.412	23.414	25.645	28.132	30.906	33.999	37.450	41.301	45.599	50.396	55.750	61.725	68.394	75.836	84.141
19	20.811	22.841	25.117	27.671	30.539	33.760	37.379	41.446	46.018	51.159	56.939	63.440	70.749	78.969	88.212	98.603
20	22.019	24.297	26.870	29.778	33.066	36.786	40.995	45.762	51.160	57.275	64.203	72.052	80.947	91.025	102.444	115.380
21	23.239	25.783	28.676	31.969	35.719	39.993	44.865	50.423	56.765	64.002	72.265	81.699	92.470	104.768	118.810	134.841
22	24.472	27.299	30.537	34.248	38.505	43.392	49.006	55.457	62.873	71.403	81.214	92.503	105.491	120.436	137.632	157.415
23	25.716	28.845	32.453	36.618	41.430	46.996	53.436	60.893	69.532	79.543	91.148	104.603	120.205	138.297	159.276	183.601
24	26.973	30.422	34.426	39.083	44.502	50.816	58.177	66.765	76.790	88.497	102.174	118.155	136.831	158.659	184.168	213.978
25	28.243	32.030	36.459	41.646	47.727	54.865	63.249	73.106	84.701	98.347	114.413	133.334	155.620	181.871	212.793	249.214
30	34.785	40.568	47.575	56.085	66.439	79.058	94.461	113.283	136.308	164.494	199.021	241.333	293.199	356.787	434.745	530.312
35	41.660	49.994	60.462	73.652	90.320	111.435	138.237	172.317	215.711	271.024	341.590	431.663	546.681	693.573	881.170	1120.713
40	48.886	60.402	75.401	95.026	120.800	154.762	199.635	259.057	337.882	442.593	581.826	767.091	1013.704	1342.025	1779.090	2360.757
45	56.481	71.893	92.720	121.029	159.700	212.744	285.749	386.506	525.859	718.905	986.639	1358.230	1874.165	2590.565	3585.128	4965.274
50	64.463	84.579	112.797	152.667	209.348	290.336	406.529	573.770	815.084	1163.909	1668.771	2400.018	3459.507	4994.521	7217.716	10435.649

Table A3 (continued)

Period	17%	18%	19%	20%	21%	22%	23%	24%	25%	30%	35%	40%	45%	50%
1	1.000	1.000	1.000	1.000	1.000	1.000	1.000	1.000	1.000	1.000	1.000	1.000	1.000	1.000
2	2.170	2.180	2.190	2.200	2.210	2.220	2.230	2.240	2.250	2.300	2.350	2.400	2.450	2.500
3	3.539	3.572	3.606	3.640	3.674	3.708	3.743	3.778	3.813	3.990	4.173	4.360	4.553	4.750
4	5.141	5.215	5.291	5.368	5.446	5.524	5.604	5.684	5.766	6.187	6.633	7.104	7.601	8.125
5	7.014	7.154	7.297	7.442	7.589	7.740	7.893	8.048	8.207	9.043	9.954	10.946	12.022	13.188
6	9.207	9.442	9.683	9.930	10.183	10.442	10.708	10.980	11.259	12.756	14.438	16.324	18.431	20.781
7	11.772	12.142	12.523	12.916	13.321	13.740	14.171	14.615	15.073	17.583	20.492	23.853	27.725	32.172
8	14.773	15.327	15.902	16.499	17.119	17.762	18.430	19.123	19.842	23.858	28.664	34.395	41.202	49.258
9	18.285	19.086	19.923	20.799	21.714	22.670	23.669	24.712	25.802	32.015	39.696	49.153	60.743	74.887
10	22.393	23.521	24.709	25.959	27.274	28.657	30.113	31.643	33.253	42.619	54.590	69.814	89.077	113.330
11	27.200	28.755	30.404	32.150	34.001	35.962	38.039	40.238	42.566	56.405	74.697	98.739	130.162	170.995
12	32.824	34.931	37.180	39.581	42.142	44.874	47.788	50.895	54.208	74.327	101.841	139.235	189.735	257.493
13	39.404	42.219	45.244	48.497	51.991	55.746	59.779	64.110	68.760	97.625	138.485	195.929	276.115	387.239
14	47.103	50.818	54.841	59.196	63.909	69.010	74.528	80.496	86.949	127.91	187.954	275.300	401.367	581.859
15	56.110	60.965	66.261	72.035	78.330	85.192	92.669	100.815	109.687	167.286	254.738	386.420	582.982	873.788
16	66.649	72.939	79.850	87.442	95.780	104.935	114.983	126.011	138.109	218.472	344.897	541.988	846.324	1311.682
17	78.979	87.068	96.022	105.931	116.894	129.020	142.430	157.253	173.636	285.014	466.611	759.784	1228.170	1968.523
18	93.406	103.740	115.266	128.117	142.441	158.405	176.188	195.994	218.045	371.518	630.925	1064.697	1781.846	2953.784
19	110.285	123.414	138.166	154.740	173.354	194.254	217.712	244.033	273.556	483.973	852.748	1491.576	2584.677	4431.676
20	130.033	146.628	165.418	186.688	210.758	237.989	268.785	303.601	342.945	630.165	1152.210	2089.206	3748.782	6648.513
21	153.139	174.021	197.847	225.026	256.018	291.347	331.606	377.465	429.681	820.215	1556.484	2925.889	5436.734	9973.770
22	180.172	206.345	236.438	271.031	310.781	356.443	408.875	469.056	538.101	1067.280	2102.253	4097.245	7884.264	14961.655
23	211.801	244.487	282.362	326.237	377.045	435.861	503.917	582.630	673.626	1388.464	2839.042	5737.142	11433.182	22443.483
24	248.808	289.494	337.010	392.484	457.225	532.750	620.817	723.461	843.033	1806.003	3833.706	8032.999	16579.115	33666.224
25	292.105	342.603	402.042	471.981	554.242	650.955	764.605	898.092	1054.79	2348.803	5176.504	11247.199	24040.716	50500.337
30	647.439	790.948	966.712	1181.882	1445.151	1767.081	2160.491	2640.916	3227.174	8729.985	23221.570	60501.081	154106.618	383500.118
35	1426.491	1816.652	2314.214	2948.341	3755.938	4783.645	6090.334	7750.225	9856.761	32422.868	104136.251	325400.279	987794.463	*
40	3134.522	4163.213	5529.829	7343.858	9749.525	12936.535	17154.046	22728.803	30088.655	120392.883	466960.385	*	*	*
45	6879.291	9531.577	13203.424	18281.310	25295.346	34971.419	48301.775	66640.376	91831.496	447019.389	*	*	*	*
50	15089.502	21813.094	31515.336	45497.191	65617.202	94525.279	135992.154	195372.644	280255.693	*	*	*	*	*

*Not shown because of space limitations.

Table A4
Present Value Factors for a One-Dollar Ordinary Annuity Discounted at r Percent for n Periods

$$PVFA_{r\%,n} = \frac{PMT}{r} \times \left[1 - \frac{1}{(1+r)^n}\right]$$

Period	1%	2%	3%	4%	5%	6%	7%	8%	9%	10%	11%	12%	13%	14%	15%	16%
1	0.990	0.980	0.971	0.962	0.952	0.943	0.935	0.926	0.917	0.909	0.901	0.893	0.885	0.877	0.870	0.862
2	0.980	0.961	0.943	0.925	0.907	0.890	0.873	0.857	0.842	0.826	0.812	0.797	0.783	0.769	0.756	1.605
3	0.971	0.942	0.915	0.889	0.864	0.840	0.816	0.794	0.772	0.751	0.731	0.712	0.693	0.675	0.658	2.246
4	0.961	0.924	0.888	0.855	0.823	0.792	0.763	0.735	0.708	0.683	0.659	0.636	0.613	0.592	0.572	2.798
5	0.951	0.906	0.863	0.822	0.784	0.747	0.713	0.681	0.650	0.621	0.593	0.567	0.543	0.519	0.497	3.274
6	0.942	0.888	0.837	0.790	0.746	0.705	0.666	0.630	0.596	0.564	0.535	0.507	0.480	0.456	0.432	3.685
7	0.933	0.871	0.813	0.760	0.711	0.665	0.623	0.583	0.547	0.513	0.482	0.452	0.425	0.400	0.376	4.039
8	0.923	0.853	0.789	0.731	0.677	0.627	0.582	0.540	0.502	0.467	0.434	0.404	0.376	0.351	0.327	4.344
9	0.914	0.837	0.766	0.703	0.645	0.592	0.544	0.500	0.460	0.424	0.391	0.361	0.333	0.308	0.284	4.607
10	0.905	0.820	0.744	0.676	0.614	0.558	0.508	0.463	0.422	0.386	0.352	0.322	0.295	0.270	0.247	4.833
11	0.896	0.804	0.722	0.650	0.585	0.527	0.475	0.429	0.388	0.350	0.317	0.287	0.261	0.237	0.215	5.029
12	0.887	0.788	0.701	0.625	0.557	0.497	0.444	0.397	0.356	0.319	0.286	0.257	0.231	0.208	0.187	5.197
13	0.879	0.773	0.681	0.601	0.530	0.469	0.415	0.368	0.326	0.290	0.258	0.229	0.204	0.182	0.163	5.342
14	0.870	0.758	0.661	0.577	0.505	0.442	0.388	0.340	0.299	0.263	0.232	0.205	0.181	0.160	0.141	5.468
15	0.861	0.743	0.642	0.555	0.481	0.417	0.362	0.315	0.275	0.239	0.209	0.183	0.160	0.140	0.123	5.575
16	0.853	0.728	0.623	0.534	0.458	0.394	0.339	0.292	0.252	0.218	0.188	0.163	0.141	0.123	0.107	5.668
17	0.844	0.714	0.605	0.513	0.436	0.371	0.317	0.270	0.231	0.198	0.170	0.146	0.125	0.108	0.093	5.749
18	0.836	0.700	0.587	0.494	0.416	0.350	0.296	0.250	0.212	0.180	0.153	0.130	0.111	0.095	0.081	5.818
19	0.828	0.686	0.570	0.475	0.396	0.331	0.277	0.232	0.194	0.164	0.138	0.116	0.098	0.083	0.070	5.877
20	0.820	0.673	0.554	0.456	0.377	0.312	0.258	0.215	0.178	0.149	0.124	0.104	0.087	0.073	0.061	5.929
21	0.811	0.660	0.538	0.439	0.359	0.294	0.242	0.199	0.164	0.135	0.112	0.093	0.077	0.064	0.053	5.973
22	0.803	0.647	0.522	0.422	0.342	0.278	0.226	0.184	0.150	0.123	0.101	0.083	0.068	0.056	0.046	6.011
23	0.795	0.634	0.507	0.406	0.326	0.262	0.211	0.170	0.138	0.112	0.091	0.074	0.060	0.049	0.040	6.044
24	0.788	0.622	0.492	0.390	0.310	0.247	0.197	0.158	0.126	0.102	0.082	0.066	0.053	0.043	0.035	6.073
25	0.780	0.610	0.478	0.375	0.295	0.233	0.184	0.146	0.116	0.092	0.074	0.059	0.047	0.038	0.030	6.097
30	0.742	0.552	0.412	0.308	0.231	0.174	0.131	0.099	0.075	0.057	0.044	0.033	0.026	0.020	0.015	6.177
35	0.706	0.500	0.355	0.253	0.181	0.130	0.094	0.068	0.049	0.036	0.026	0.019	0.014	0.010	0.008	6.215
40	0.672	0.453	0.307	0.208	0.142	0.097	0.067	0.046	0.032	0.022	0.015	0.011	0.008	0.005	0.004	6.233
45	0.639	0.410	0.264	0.171	0.111	0.073	0.048	0.031	0.021	0.014	0.009	0.006	0.004	0.003	0.002	6.242
50	0.608	0.372	0.228	0.141	0.087	0.054	0.034	0.021	0.013	0.009	0.005	0.003	0.002	0.001	0.001	6.246

Table A4 (continued)

Period	17%	18%	19%	20%	21%	22%	23%	24%	25%	30%	35%	40%	45%	50%
1	0.855	0.847	0.840	0.833	0.826	0.820	0.813	0.806	0.800	0.769	0.741	0.714	0.690	0.667
2	1.585	1.566	1.547	1.528	1.509	1.492	1.474	1.457	1.440	1.361	1.289	1.224	1.165	1.111
3	2.210	2.174	2.140	2.106	2.074	2.042	2.011	1.981	1.952	1.816	1.696	1.589	1.493	1.407
4	2.743	2.690	2.639	2.589	2.540	2.494	2.448	2.404	2.362	2.166	1.997	1.849	1.720	1.605
5	3.199	3.127	3.058	2.991	2.926	2.864	2.803	2.745	2.689	2.436	2.220	2.035	1.876	1.737
6	3.589	3.498	3.410	3.326	3.245	3.167	3.092	3.020	2.951	2.643	2.385	2.168	1.983	1.824
7	3.922	3.812	3.706	3.605	3.508	3.416	3.327	3.242	3.161	2.802	2.508	2.263	2.057	1.883
8	4.207	4.078	3.954	3.837	3.726	3.619	3.518	3.421	3.329	2.925	2.598	2.331	2.109	1.922
9	4.451	4.303	4.163	4.031	3.905	3.786	3.673	3.566	3.463	3.019	2.665	2.379	2.144	1.948
10	4.659	4.494	4.339	4.192	4.054	3.923	3.799	3.682	3.571	3.092	2.715	2.414	2.168	1.965
11	4.836	4.656	4.486	4.327	4.177	4.035	3.902	3.776	3.656	3.147	2.752	2.438	2.185	1.977
12	4.988	4.793	4.611	4.439	4.278	4.127	3.985	3.851	3.725	3.190	2.779	2.456	2.196	1.985
13	5.118	4.910	4.715	4.533	4.362	4.203	4.053	3.912	3.780	3.223	2.799	2.469	2.204	1.990
14	5.229	5.008	4.802	4.611	4.432	4.265	4.108	3.962	3.824	3.249	2.814	2.478	2.210	1.993
15	5.324	5.092	4.876	4.675	4.489	4.315	4.153	4.001	3.859	3.268	2.825	2.484	2.214	1.995
16	5.405	5.162	4.938	4.730	4.536	4.357	4.189	4.033	3.887	3.283	2.834	2.489	2.216	1.997
17	5.475	5.222	4.990	4.775	4.576	4.391	4.219	4.059	3.910	3.295	2.840	2.492	2.218	1.998
18	5.534	5.273	5.033	4.812	4.608	4.419	4.243	4.080	3.928	3.304	2.844	2.494	2.219	1.999
19	5.584	5.316	5.070	4.843	4.635	4.442	4.263	4.097	3.942	3.311	2.848	2.496	2.220	1.999
20	5.628	5.353	5.101	4.870	4.657	4.460	4.279	4.110	3.954	3.316	2.850	2.497	2.221	1.999
21	5.665	5.384	5.127	4.891	4.675	4.476	4.292	4.121	3.963	3.320	2.852	2.498	2.221	2.000
22	5.696	5.410	5.149	4.909	4.690	4.488	4.302	4.130	3.970	3.323	2.853	2.498	2.222	2.000
23	5.723	5.432	5.167	4.925	4.703	4.499	4.311	4.137	3.976	3.325	2.854	2.499	2.222	2.000
24	5.746	5.451	5.182	4.937	4.713	4.507	4.318	4.143	3.981	3.327	2.855	2.499	2.222	2.000
25	5.766	5.467	5.195	4.948	4.721	4.514	4.323	4.147	3.985	3.329	2.856	2.499	2.222	2.000
30	5.829	5.517	5.235	4.979	4.746	4.534	4.339	4.160	3.995	3.332	2.857	2.500	2.222	2.000
35	5.858	5.539	5.251	4.992	4.756	4.541	4.345	4.164	3.998	3.333	2.857	2.500	2.222	2.000
40	5.871	5.548	5.258	4.997	4.760	4.544	4.347	4.166	3.999	3.333	2.857	2.500	2.222	2.000
45	5.877	5.552	5.261	4.999	4.761	4.545	4.347	4.166	4.000	3.333	2.857	2.500	2.222	2.000
50	5.880	5.554	5.262	4.999	4.762	4.545	4.348	4.167	4.000	3.333	2.857	2.500	2.222	2.000

Table A5
Future Value Factor for One Dollar Compounded Continuously at *r* Percent for *n* Periods

$$FVF_{r\%,n} = e^{rn}$$

Period	1%	2%	3%	4%	5%	6%	7%	8%	9%	10%	11%	12%	13%	14%	15%	16%
1	0.990	0.980	0.971	0.962	0.952	0.943	0.935	0.926	0.917	0.909	0.901	0.893	0.885	0.877	0.870	1.174
2	1.970	1.942	1.913	1.886	1.859	1.833	1.808	1.783	1.759	1.736	1.713	1.690	1.668	1.647	1.626	1.377
3	2.941	2.884	2.829	2.775	2.723	2.673	2.624	2.577	2.531	2.487	2.444	2.402	2.361	2.322	2.283	1.616
4	3.902	3.808	3.717	3.630	3.546	3.465	3.387	3.312	3.240	3.170	3.102	3.037	2.974	2.914	2.855	1.896
5	4.853	4.713	4.580	4.452	4.329	4.212	4.100	3.993	3.890	3.791	3.696	3.605	3.517	3.433	3.352	2.226
6	5.795	5.601	5.417	5.242	5.076	4.917	4.767	4.623	4.486	4.355	4.231	4.111	3.998	3.889	3.784	2.612
7	6.728	6.472	6.230	6.002	5.786	5.582	5.389	5.206	5.033	4.868	4.712	4.564	4.423	4.288	4.160	3.065
8	7.652	7.325	7.020	6.733	6.463	6.210	5.971	5.747	5.535	5.335	5.146	4.968	4.799	4.639	4.487	3.597
9	8.566	8.162	7.786	7.435	7.108	6.802	6.515	6.247	5.995	5.759	5.537	5.328	5.132	4.946	4.772	4.221
10	9.471	8.983	8.530	8.111	7.722	7.360	7.024	6.710	6.418	6.145	5.889	5.650	5.426	5.216	5.019	4.953
11	10.368	9.787	9.253	8.760	8.306	7.887	7.499	7.139	6.805	6.495	6.207	5.938	5.687	5.453	5.234	5.812
12	11.255	10.575	9.954	9.385	8.863	8.384	7.943	7.536	7.161	6.814	6.492	6.194	5.918	5.660	5.421	6.821
13	12.134	11.348	10.635	9.986	9.394	8.853	8.358	7.904	7.487	7.103	6.750	6.424	6.122	5.842	5.583	8.004
14	13.004	12.106	11.296	10.563	9.899	9.295	8.745	8.244	7.786	7.367	6.982	6.628	6.302	6.002	5.724	9.393
15	13.865	12.849	11.938	11.118	10.380	9.712	9.108	8.559	8.061	7.606	7.191	6.811	6.462	6.142	5.847	11.023
16	14.718	13.578	12.561	11.652	10.838	10.106	9.447	8.851	8.313	7.824	7.379	6.974	6.604	6.265	5.954	12.936
17	15.562	14.292	13.166	12.166	11.274	10.477	9.763	9.122	8.544	8.022	7.549	7.120	6.729	6.373	6.047	15.180
18	16.398	14.992	13.754	12.659	11.690	10.828	10.059	9.372	8.756	8.201	7.702	7.250	6.840	6.467	6.128	17.814
19	17.226	15.678	14.324	13.134	12.085	11.158	10.336	9.604	8.950	8.365	7.839	7.366	6.938	6.550	6.198	20.905
20	18.046	16.351	14.877	13.590	12.462	11.470	10.594	9.818	9.129	8.514	7.963	7.469	7.025	6.623	6.259	24.533
21	18.857	17.011	15.415	14.029	12.821	11.764	10.836	10.017	9.292	8.649	8.075	7.562	7.102	6.687	6.312	28.789
22	19.660	17.658	15.937	14.451	13.163	12.042	11.061	10.201	9.442	8.772	8.176	7.645	7.170	6.743	6.359	33.784
23	20.456	18.292	16.444	14.857	13.489	12.303	11.272	10.371	9.580	8.883	8.266	7.718	7.230	6.792	6.399	39.646
24	21.243	18.914	16.936	15.247	13.799	12.550	11.469	10.529	9.707	8.985	8.348	7.784	7.283	6.835	6.434	46.525
25	22.023	19.523	17.413	15.622	14.094	12.783	11.654	10.675	9.823	9.077	8.422	7.843	7.330	6.873	6.464	54.598
30	25.808	22.396	19.600	17.292	15.372	13.765	12.409	11.258	10.274	9.427	8.694	8.055	7.496	7.003	6.566	121.510
35	29.409	24.999	21.487	18.665	16.374	14.498	12.948	11.655	10.567	9.644	8.855	8.176	7.586	7.070	6.617	270.426
40	32.835	27.355	23.115	19.793	17.159	15.046	13.332	11.925	10.757	9.779	8.951	8.244	7.634	7.105	6.642	601.845
45	36.095	29.490	24.519	20.720	17.774	15.456	13.606	12.108	10.881	9.863	9.008	8.283	7.661	7.123	6.654	1339.431
50	39.196	31.424	25.730	21.482	18.256	15.762	13.801	12.233	10.962	9.915	9.042	8.304	7.675	7.133	6.661	2980.958

Table A5 (continued)

Period	17%	18%	19%	20%	21%	22%	23%	24%	25%	30%	35%	40%	45%	50%
1	1.185	1.197	1.209	1.221	1.234	1.246	1.259	1.271	1.284	1.405	1.419	1.492	1.568	1.649
2	1.405	1.433	1.462	1.492	1.522	1.553	1.584	1.616	1.649	1.822	2.014	2.226	2.460	2.718
3	1.665	1.716	1.768	1.822	1.878	1.935	1.994	2.054	2.117	2.460	2.858	3.320	3.857	4.482
4	1.974	2.054	2.138	2.226	2.316	2.411	2.509	2.612	2.718	3.320	4.055	4.953	6.050	7.389
5	2.340	2.460	2.586	2.718	2.858	3.004	3.158	3.320	3.490	4.482	5.755	7.389	9.488	12.182
6	2.773	2.945	3.127	3.320	3.525	3.743	3.975	4.221	4.482	6.050	8.166	11.023	14.880	20.086
7	3.287	3.525	3.781	4.055	4.349	4.665	5.003	5.366	5.755	8.166	11.588	16.445	23.336	33.115
8	3.896	4.221	4.572	4.953	5.366	5.812	6.297	6.821	7.389	11.023	16.445	24.533	36.598	54.598
9	4.618	5.053	5.529	6.050	6.619	7.243	7.925	8.671	9.488	14.880	23.336	36.598	57.397	90.017
10	5.474	6.050	6.686	7.389	8.166	9.025	9.974	11.023	12.182	20.086	33.115	54.598	90.017	148.413
11	6.488	7.243	8.085	9.025	10.074	11.246	12.554	14.013	15.643	27.113	46.993	81.451	141.175	244.692
12	7.691	8.671	9.777	11.023	12.429	14.013	15.800	17.814	20.086	36.598	66.686	121.510	221.406	403.429
13	9.116	10.381	11.822	13.464	15.333	17.462	19.886	22.646	25.790	49.402	94.632	181.272	347.234	665.142
14	10.805	12.429	14.296	16.445	18.916	21.758	25.028	28.789	33.115	66.686	134.290	270.426	544.572	1096.633
15	12.807	14.880	17.288	20.086	23.336	27.113	31.500	36.598	42.521	90.017	190.566	403.429	854.059	1808.042
16	15.180	17.814	20.905	24.533	28.789	33.784	39.646	46.525	54.598	121.510	270.426	601.845	1339.431	2980.958
17	17.993	21.328	25.280	29.964	35.517	42.098	49.899	59.145	70.105	164.022	383.753	897.847	2100.646	4914.769
18	21.328	25.534	30.569	36.598	43.816	52.457	62.803	75.189	90.017	221.406	544.572	1339.431	3294.468	8103.084
19	25.280	30.569	36.966	44.701	54.055	65.366	79.044	95.583	115.584	298.867	772.784	1998.196	5166.754	13359.727
20	29.964	36.598	44.701	54.598	66.686	81.451	99.484	121.510	148.413	403.429	1096.633	2980.958	8103.084	22026.466
21	35.517	43.816	54.055	66.686	82.269	101.494	125.211	154.470	190.566	544.572	1556.197	4447.067	12708.165	36315.503
22	42.098	52.457	65.366	81.451	101.494	126.469	157.591	196.370	244.692	735.095	2208.348	6634.244	19930.370	59874.142
23	49.899	62.803	79.044	99.484	125.211	157.591	198.343	249.635	314.191	992.275	3133.795	9897.129	31257.043	98715.771
24	59.145	75.189	95.583	121.510	154.470	196.370	249.635	317.348	403.429	1339.431	4447.067	14764.782	49020.801	162754.791
25	70.105	90.017	115.584	148.413	190.566	244.692	314.191	403.429	518.013	1808.042	6310.688	22026.466	76879.920	268337.287
30	164.022	221.406	298.867	403.429	544.572	735.095	992.275	1339.431	1808.042	8103.084	36315.503	162754.791	729416.370	
35	383.753	544.572	772.784	1096.633	1556.197	2208.348	3133.795	4447.067	6310.688	36315.503	208981.289	*	*	*
40	897.847	1339.431	1998.196	2980.958	4447.067	6634.244	9897.129	14764.782	22026.466	162754.791	*	*	*	*
45	2100.646	3294.468	5166.754	8103.084	12708.165	19930.370	31257.043	49020.801	76879.920	729416.370	*	*	*	*
50	4914.769	8103.084	13359.727	22026.466	36315.503	59874.142	98715.771	162754.791	268337.287	*	*	*	*	*

* Not shown because of space limitations.

Table A6
Present Value Factor — Dollar Discounted Continuously at r Percent for n Periods

$$PVF_{r\%,n} = e^{-rn}$$

Period	1%	2%	3%	4%	5%	6%	7%	8%	9%	10%	11%	12%	13%	14%	15%	16%
1	0.990	0.980	0.970	0.961	0.951	0.942	0.932	0.923	0.914	0.905	0.896	0.887	0.878	0.869	0.861	0.852
2	0.980	0.961	0.942	0.923	0.905	0.887	0.869	0.852	0.835	0.819	0.803	0.787	0.771	0.756	0.741	0.726
3	0.970	0.942	0.914	0.887	0.861	0.835	0.811	0.787	0.763	0.741	0.719	0.698	0.677	0.657	0.638	0.619
4	0.961	0.923	0.887	0.852	0.819	0.787	0.756	0.726	0.698	0.670	0.644	0.619	0.595	0.571	0.549	0.527
5	0.951	0.905	0.861	0.819	0.779	0.741	0.705	0.670	0.638	0.607	0.577	0.549	0.522	0.497	0.472	0.449
6	0.942	0.887	0.835	0.787	0.741	0.698	0.657	0.619	0.583	0.549	0.517	0.487	0.458	0.432	0.407	0.383
7	0.932	0.869	0.811	0.756	0.705	0.657	0.613	0.571	0.533	0.497	0.463	0.432	0.403	0.375	0.350	0.326
8	0.923	0.852	0.787	0.726	0.670	0.619	0.571	0.527	0.487	0.449	0.415	0.383	0.353	0.326	0.301	0.278
9	0.914	0.835	0.763	0.698	0.638	0.583	0.533	0.487	0.445	0.407	0.372	0.340	0.310	0.284	0.259	0.237
10	0.905	0.819	0.741	0.670	0.607	0.549	0.497	0.449	0.407	0.368	0.333	0.301	0.273	0.247	0.223	0.202
11	0.896	0.803	0.719	0.644	0.577	0.517	0.463	0.415	0.372	0.333	0.298	0.267	0.239	0.214	0.192	0.172
12	0.887	0.787	0.698	0.619	0.549	0.487	0.432	0.383	0.340	0.301	0.267	0.237	0.210	0.186	0.165	0.147
13	0.878	0.771	0.677	0.595	0.522	0.458	0.403	0.353	0.310	0.273	0.239	0.210	0.185	0.162	0.142	0.125
14	0.869	0.756	0.657	0.571	0.497	0.432	0.375	0.326	0.284	0.247	0.214	0.186	0.162	0.141	0.122	0.106
15	0.861	0.741	0.638	0.549	0.472	0.407	0.350	0.301	0.259	0.223	0.192	0.165	0.142	0.122	0.105	0.091
16	0.852	0.726	0.619	0.527	0.449	0.383	0.326	0.278	0.237	0.202	0.172	0.147	0.125	0.106	0.091	0.077
17	0.844	0.712	0.600	0.507	0.427	0.361	0.304	0.257	0.217	0.183	0.154	0.130	0.110	0.093	0.078	0.066
18	0.835	0.698	0.583	0.487	0.407	0.340	0.284	0.237	0.198	0.165	0.138	0.115	0.096	0.080	0.067	0.056
19	0.827	0.684	0.566	0.468	0.387	0.320	0.264	0.219	0.181	0.150	0.124	0.102	0.085	0.070	0.058	0.048
20	0.819	0.670	0.549	0.449	0.368	0.301	0.247	0.202	0.165	0.135	0.111	0.091	0.074	0.061	0.050	0.041
21	0.811	0.657	0.533	0.432	0.350	0.284	0.230	0.186	0.151	0.122	0.099	0.080	0.065	0.053	0.043	0.035
22	0.803	0.644	0.517	0.415	0.333	0.267	0.214	0.172	0.138	0.111	0.089	0.071	0.057	0.046	0.037	0.030
23	0.795	0.631	0.502	0.399	0.317	0.252	0.200	0.159	0.126	0.100	0.080	0.063	0.050	0.040	0.032	0.025
24	0.787	0.619	0.487	0.383	0.301	0.237	0.186	0.147	0.115	0.091	0.071	0.056	0.044	0.035	0.027	0.021
25	0.779	0.607	0.472	0.368	0.287	0.223	0.174	0.135	0.105	0.082	0.064	0.050	0.039	0.030	0.024	0.018
30	0.741	0.549	0.407	0.301	0.223	0.165	0.122	0.091	0.067	0.050	0.037	0.027	0.020	0.015	0.011	0.008
35	0.705	0.497	0.350	0.247	0.174	0.122	0.086	0.061	0.043	0.030	0.021	0.015	0.011	0.007	0.005	0.004
40	0.670	0.449	0.301	0.202	0.135	0.091	0.061	0.041	0.027	0.018	0.012	0.008	0.006	0.004	0.002	0.002
45	0.638	0.407	0.259	0.165	0.105	0.067	0.043	0.027	0.017	0.011	0.007	0.005	0.003	0.002	0.001	0.001
50	0.607	0.368	0.223	0.135	0.082	0.050	0.030	0.018	0.011	0.007	0.004	0.002	0.002	0.001	0.001	*

*Discount factor is zero to three decimal places.

Table A6 (continued)

Period	17%	18%	19%	20%	21%	22%	23%	24%	25%	30%	35%	40%	45%	50%
1	0.844	0.835	0.827	0.819	0.811	0.803	0.795	0.787	0.779	0.741	0.705	0.670	0.638	0.607
2	0.712	0.698	0.684	0.670	0.657	0.644	0.631	0.619	0.607	0.549	0.497	0.449	0.407	0.368
3	0.600	0.583	0.566	0.549	0.533	0.517	0.502	0.487	0.472	0.407	0.350	0.301	0.259	0.223
4	0.507	0.487	0.468	0.449	0.432	0.415	0.399	0.383	0.368	0.301	0.247	0.202	0.165	0.135
5	0.427	0.407	0.387	0.368	0.350	0.333	0.317	0.301	0.287	0.223	0.174	0.135	0.105	0.082
6	0.361	0.340	0.320	0.301	0.284	0.267	0.252	0.237	0.223	0.165	0.122	0.091	0.067	0.050
7	0.304	0.284	0.264	0.247	0.230	0.214	0.200	0.186	0.174	0.122	0.086	0.061	0.043	0.030
8	0.257	0.237	0.219	0.202	0.186	0.172	0.159	0.147	0.135	0.091	0.061	0.041	0.027	0.018
9	0.217	0.198	0.181	0.165	0.151	0.138	0.126	0.115	0.105	0.067	0.043	0.027	0.017	0.011
10	0.183	0.165	0.150	0.135	0.122	0.111	0.100	0.091	0.082	0.050	0.030	0.018	0.011	0.007
11	0.154	0.138	0.124	0.111	0.099	0.089	0.080	0.071	0.064	0.037	0.021	0.012	0.007	0.004
12	0.130	0.115	0.102	0.091	0.080	0.071	0.063	0.056	0.050	0.027	0.015	0.008	0.005	0.002
13	0.110	0.096	0.085	0.074	0.065	0.057	0.050	0.044	0.039	0.020	0.011	0.006	0.003	0.002
14	0.093	0.080	0.070	0.061	0.053	0.046	0.040	0.035	0.030	0.015	0.007	0.004	0.002	0.001
15	0.078	0.067	0.058	0.050	0.043	0.037	0.032	0.027	0.024	0.011	0.005	0.002	0.001	0.001
16	0.066	0.056	0.048	0.041	0.035	0.030	0.025	0.021	0.018	0.008	0.004	0.002	0.001	*
17	0.056	0.047	0.040	0.033	0.028	0.024	0.020	0.017	0.014	0.006	0.003	0.001	*	*
18	0.047	0.039	0.033	0.027	0.023	0.019	0.016	0.013	0.011	0.005	0.002	0.001	*	*
19	0.040	0.033	0.027	0.022	0.018	0.015	0.013	0.010	0.009	0.003	0.001	0.001	*	*
20	0.033	0.027	0.022	0.018	0.015	0.012	0.010	0.008	0.007	0.002	0.001	*	*	*
21	0.028	0.023	0.018	0.015	0.012	0.010	0.008	0.006	0.005	0.002	0.001	*	*	*
22	0.024	0.019	0.015	0.012	0.010	0.008	0.006	0.005	0.004	0.001	*	*	*	*
23	0.020	0.016	0.013	0.010	0.008	0.006	0.005	0.004	0.003	0.001	*	*	*	*
24	0.017	0.013	0.010	0.008	0.006	0.005	0.004	0.003	0.002	0.001	*	*	*	*
25	0.014	0.011	0.009	0.007	0.005	0.004	0.003	0.002	0.002	0.001	*	*	*	*
30	0.006	0.005	0.003	0.002	0.002	0.001	0.001	0.001	0.001	*	*	*	*	*
35	0.003	0.002	0.001	0.001	0.001	*	*	*	*	*	*	*	*	*
40	0.001	0.001	0.001	*	*	*	*	*	*	*	*	*	*	*
45	*	*	*	*	*	*	*	*	*	*	*	*	*	*
50	*	*	*	*	*	*	*	*	*	*	*	*	*	*

*Discount factor is zero to three decimal places.

Appendix B
Cumulative Probability, $N(d)$, of Drawing a Value Less than or Equal to d from the Standard Normal Distribution

d	0	0.01	0.02	0.03	0.04	0.05	0.06	0.07	0.08	0.09
0	0.5000	0.5040	0.5080	0.5120	0.5160	0.5199	0.5239	0.5279	0.5319	0.5359
0.1	0.5398	0.5438	0.5478	0.5517	0.5557	0.5596	0.5636	0.5675	0.5714	0.5753
0.2	0.5793	0.5832	0.5871	0.5910	0.5948	0.5987	0.6026	0.6064	0.6103	0.6141
0.3	0.6179	0.6217	0.6255	0.6293	0.6331	0.6368	0.6406	0.6443	0.6480	0.6517
0.4	0.6554	0.6591	0.6628	0.6664	0.6700	0.6736	0.6772	0.6808	0.6844	0.6879
0.5	0.6915	0.6950	0.6985	0.7019	0.7054	0.7088	0.7123	0.7157	0.7190	0.7224
0.6	0.7257	0.7291	0.7324	0.7357	0.7389	0.7422	0.7454	0.7486	0.7517	0.7549
0.7	0.7580	0.7611	0.7642	0.7673	0.7704	0.7734	0.7764	0.7794	0.7823	0.7852
0.8	0.7881	0.7910	0.7939	0.7967	0.7995	0.8023	0.8051	0.8078	0.8106	0.8133
0.9	0.8159	0.8186	0.8212	0.8238	0.8264	0.8289	0.8315	0.8340	0.8365	0.8389
1	0.8413	0.8438	0.8461	0.8485	0.8508	0.8531	0.8554	0.8577	0.8599	0.8621
1.1	0.8643	0.8665	0.8686	0.8708	0.8729	0.8749	0.8770	0.8790	0.8810	0.8830
1.2	0.8849	0.8869	0.8888	0.8907	0.8925	0.8944	0.8962	0.8980	0.8997	0.9015
1.3	0.9032	0.9049	0.9066	0.9082	0.9099	0.9115	0.9131	0.9147	0.9162	0.9177
1.4	0.9192	0.9207	0.9222	0.9236	0.9251	0.9265	0.9279	0.9292	0.9306	0.9319
1.5	0.9332	0.9345	0.9357	0.9370	0.9382	0.9394	0.9406	0.9418	0.9429	0.9441
1.6	0.9452	0.9463	0.9474	0.9484	0.9495	0.9505	0.9515	0.9525	0.9535	0.9545
1.7	0.9554	0.9564	0.9573	0.9582	0.9591	0.9599	0.9608	0.9616	0.9625	0.9633
1.8	0.9641	0.9649	0.9656	0.9664	0.9671	0.9678	0.9686	0.9693	0.9699	0.9706
1.9	0.9713	0.9719	0.9726	0.9732	0.9738	0.9744	0.9750	0.9756	0.9761	0.9767
2	0.9772	0.9778	0.9783	0.9788	0.9793	0.9798	0.9803	0.9808	0.9812	0.9817
2.1	0.9821	0.9826	0.9830	0.9834	0.9838	0.9842	0.9846	0.9850	0.9854	0.9857
2.2	0.9861	0.9864	0.9868	0.9871	0.9875	0.9878	0.9881	0.9884	0.9887	0.9890
2.3	0.9893	0.9896	0.9898	0.9901	0.9904	0.9906	0.9909	0.9911	0.9913	0.9916
2.4	0.9918	0.9920	0.9922	0.9925	0.9927	0.9929	0.9931	0.9932	0.9934	0.9936
2.5	0.9938	0.9940	0.9941	0.9943	0.9945	0.9946	0.9948	0.9949	0.9951	0.9952

Example: Let $d = 1.15$. There is an 87.49% chance of drawing a value less than or equal to d from the standard normal distribution.

APPENDIX C: Key Formulas

Free Cash Flow

A firm's free cash flow (FCF) is derived from operating cash flow (OCF) and changes in asset and liability accounts as:

$$FCF = OCF - \Delta FA - (\Delta CA - \Delta A/P - \Delta \text{accruals})$$ (Eq. 2.4)

Present Value of an Ordinary Annuity

The present value of an n-year ordinary annuity of $1 per year is:

$$PV = \frac{PMT}{r} \times \left[1 - \frac{1}{(1+r)^n} \right]$$ (Eq. 3.7)

Present Value of a Perpetuity

The present value of a perpetual stream of $1 annual payments is:

$$PV = PMT \times \frac{1}{r} = \frac{PMT}{r}$$ (Eq. 3.10)

Present Value of a Growing Perpetuity

The present value of a perpetual stream of payments, which grows at an annual rate g, is:

$$PV = \frac{CF_1}{r - g} \qquad r > g$$ (Eq. 3.11)

Effective Annual Interest Rate

The effective annual interest rate (EAR) can be derived from the stated rate r (given m compounding periods) as:

$$EAR = \left(1 + \frac{r}{m} \right)^m - 1$$ (Eq. 3.14)

Expected Return on a Portfolio

If the expected returns for individual assets in a portfolio are known, the expected return of an n-asset portfolio (with individual asset weights w_i) can be found as:

$$E(R_p) = w_1 E(R_1) + w_2 E(R_2) + w_3 E(R_3) + \cdots + w_N E(R_N)$$ (Eq. 5.6)

Measures of Risk

Variance of Returns of a Single Asset

The variance of returns on a single asset i can be derived from a historical return series on N periods as:

$$\text{Variance} = \sigma^2 = \frac{\sum_{t=1}^{N}(R_{it} - \overline{R}_i)^2}{N - 1} \qquad \text{(Eq. 5.4)}$$

Covariance of Returns between Two Assets

The covariance between the returns on two assets, 1 and 2, is calculated using historical return series over N periods as:

$$\text{Covariance} (R_1, R_2) = \sigma_{12} = \frac{\sum_{t=1}^{N}(R_{1t} - \overline{R}_1)(R_{2t} - \overline{R}_2)}{N - 1} \qquad \text{(Eq. 5.8)}$$

Correlation Coefficient

The correlation coefficient is a normalized measure of co-movement between two assets, and is derived from the covariance (σ_{12}) as:

$$\text{Correlation coefficient} = \rho_{12} = \frac{\sigma_{12}}{\sigma_1 \sigma_2} \qquad \text{(Eq. 5.9)}$$

Variance of a Portfolio of Two Stocks

When two stocks are combined into a portfolio, the variance of the portfolio's return is usually less than a weighted average of the individual variances, and is computed as:

$$\text{Portfolio variance} = \sigma_p^2 = w_1^2 \sigma_1^2 + w_2^2 \sigma_2^2 + 2w_1 w_2 \rho_{12} \sigma_1 \sigma_2 \qquad \text{(Eq. 5.12)}$$

Beta

A stock's beta is a measure of the degree of co-movement between that stock's return and the overall market's return:

$$\beta_i = \frac{\sigma_{im}}{\sigma_m^2} \qquad \text{(Eq. 5.14)}$$

The Capital Market Line

The CML plots the trade-off between an asset or portfolio's risk and return in terms of expected return and standard deviation of return:

$$E(R_p) = R_f + \left\{ \frac{[E(R_m) - R_f]}{\sigma_m} \right\} \sigma_p \qquad \text{(Eq. 6.1)}$$

The Capital Asset Pricing Model

The CAPM yields a unique expected return for an asset or portfolio as a linear function of that asset's beta (β_i) and the risk-free rate R_f:

$$E(R_i) = R_f + \beta_i [E(R_m) - R_f] \qquad \text{(Eq. 6.2)}$$

Arbitrage Pricing Theory

The APT formula computes an asset's return as a function of two or more systematic return factors (R_j) and the sensitivity (β_{ij}) of that asset's return to each factor:

$$R_i - R_f = \beta_{i1}(R_1 - R_f) + \beta_{i2}(R_2 - R_f) + \beta_{i3}(R_3 - R_f) + \cdots + \beta_{in}(R_n - R_f)$$

(Eq. 6.3)

The Fama-French Model

The Fama-French asset-pricing model generates expected returns as a function of an asset's sensitivity to a market factor ($R_m - R_f$), a size factor ($R_{small} - R_{big}$), and a book-to-market ($R_{high} - R_{low}$) factor:

$$R_i - R_f = \alpha + \beta_{i1}(R_m - R_f) + \beta_{i2}(R_{small} - R_{big}) + \beta_{i3}(R_{high} - R_{low})$$

(Eq. 6.4)

Net Present Value

Finance's basic valuation model computes the NPV of a project or an asset, usually by subtracting the sum of a series of discounted cash inflows $\dfrac{CF_i}{(1 + r)^i}$ from a single cash outflow (CF_0):

$$NPV = CF_0 + \frac{CF_1}{(1 + r)^1} + \frac{CF_2}{(1 + r)^2} + \frac{CF_3}{(1 + r)^3} + \cdots + \frac{CF_N}{(1 + r)^N}$$

(Eq. 7.1)

The Weighted Average Cost of Capital [with taxes]

Incorporating corporate taxes allows calculation of a firm's $WACC$ when it must pay taxes at rate T_c on its income:

$$WACC = \left(\frac{D}{D + E}\right)(1 - T_c)r_d + \left(\frac{E}{D + E}\right)r_e$$

(Eq. 9.3)

Asset Beta [without taxes]

Asset betas are derived from equity betas as:

$$\beta_A = \left(\frac{D}{D + E}\right)\beta_d + \left(\frac{E}{D + E}\right)\beta_e$$

(Eq. 9.4)

Equity Beta [with taxes]

When a firm must pay corporate income taxes, the relationship between asset and equity betas is given by:

$$\beta_E = \beta_A\left[1 + (1 - T_c)\frac{D}{E}\right]$$

(Eq. 9.6)

M&M Proposition I

Modigliani and Miller's famous Proposition I says that a firm's value (V) is determined by discounting its stream of expected net operating income, and is independent of capital structure:

$$V = (E + D) = \frac{NOI}{r}$$

(Eq. 12.1)

M&M Proposition II

Proposition II determines the rate at which the expected return on a levered firm's equity (r_l) must increase as debt is substituted for equity in its capital structure:

$$r_l = r + (r - r_d)\left(\frac{D}{E}\right)$$ (Eq. 12.2)

Value of a Levered Firm [including only corporate taxes]

In the presence of corporate income taxes, the value of a levered firm is equal to the value of an otherwise equivalent unlevered firm plus the value of the interest tax shields on its debt:

$$V_L = V_U + PV \text{ tax shield} = V_U + T_cD = \$650,000 + \$175,000$$

$$= \$825,000$$ (Eq. 12.5)

Gain from Leverage

In the presence of both corporate and personal taxes, the gain from leverage for a firm is a function of the effective tax rates on corporate profits (T_c), equity income received by investors (T_{ps}), and interest income received by investors (T_{pd}):

$$G_L = \left\{1 - \left[\frac{(1 - T_c)(1 - T_{ps})}{(1 - T_{pd})}\right]\right\}D$$ (Eq. 12.6)

Put-Call Parity

The put-call parity formula shows the relationship that must hold between the values of the stock price (S), the put (P), the call (C), and the present value of the common exercise ($\$X$) price of the put and call options in order to prevent arbitrage:

$$S + P = B + C$$

$$S + P = PV(X) + C$$ (Eq. 18.1)

The Black-Scholes Option Pricing Model

The value of a call option, C, is given as:

$$C = SN(d_1) - Xe^{-rt}N(d_2)$$

$$d_1 = \frac{\ln\left(\frac{S}{X}\right) + \left(r + \frac{\sigma^2}{2}\right)t}{\sigma\sqrt{t}}$$ (Eq. 19.1)

$$d_2 = d_1 - \sigma\sqrt{t}$$ (Eq. 19.2)

S = current market price of underlying stock
X = strike price of option
t = amount of time before option expires (in years)
r = annual risk-free interest rate
σ = annual standard deviation of underlying stock's returns
e = 2.718 (approximately)
$N(X)$ = probability of drawing a value less than or equal to X from the standard normal distribution

The Forward Premium or Discount [exchange rates]

The annualized forward discount or premium of a currency is:

$$\frac{F - S}{S} \times \frac{360}{N}$$

(Eq. 20.1)

The Parity Conditions of International Finance

Forward–Spot Parity

In equilibrium, the forward rate (F) observed for a currency should be equal to the expected future spot exchange rate, $E(S)$, for that currency:

$$E(S) = F$$

(Eq. 20.2)

Purchasing Power Parity

PPP expresses a currency's expected future spot exchange rate [$E(S^{for/dom})$], relative to today's spot rate ($S^{for/dom}$), as a function of the relative expected inflation rates in the foreign, $E(i_{for})$, and domestic, $E(i_{dom})$, markets:

$$\frac{E(S^{for/dom})}{S^{for/dom}} = \frac{[1 + E(i_{for})]}{[1 + E(i_{dom})]}$$

(Eq. 20.4)

Interest Rate Parity

IRP expresses a currency's forward exchange rate ($F^{for/dom}$), relative to today's spot rate ($S^{for/dom}$), as a function of the relative interest rates in the foreign (R_{for}) and domestic (R_{dom}) markets:

$$\frac{F^{for/dom}}{S^{for/dom}} = \frac{(1 + R_{for})}{(1 + R_{dom})}$$

(Eq. 20.5)

Real Interest Parity

The real interest parity relationship expresses interest rate parity in real rather than nominal terms:

$$\frac{(1 + R_{for})}{(1 + R_{dom})} = \frac{[1 + E(i_{for})]}{[1 + E(i_{dom})]}$$

(Eq. 20.6)

Forward Price of an Asset

Given a risk-free rate of interest R_f, the forward price (F) of an asset or commodity to be delivered n periods in the future can be derived from the current spot price (S_0) as:

$$F = S_0(1 + R_f)^n$$

(Eq. 27.1)

BIBLIOGRAPHY

Ackermann, Carl, Richard McEnally, and David Ravenscraft. 1999. "The Performance of Hedge Funds: Risk, Return, and Incentives." *Journal of Finance* 54 (June), pp. 833–874.

Ackert, Lucy F., and Brian F. Smith. 1993. "Stock Price Volatility, Ordinary Dividends, and Cash Flows to Shareholders." *Journal of Finance* 48 (September), pp. 1147–1160.

Adams, Paul D., Steve B. Wyatt, and Yong H. Kim. 1992. "A Contingent Claims Analysis of Trade Credit." *Financial Management* 21, pp. 95–103.

Adler, Michael, and Bernard Dumas. 1983. "International Portfolio Choice and Corporation Finance: A Synthesis." *Journal of Finance* 38 (July), pp. 925–984.

Admati, Anat R., and Paul Pfleiderer. 1994. "Robust Financial Contracting and the Role of Venture Capitalists." *Journal of Finance* 49 (June), pp. 371–402.

Aggarwal, Reena. 2003. "Allocation of Initial Public Offerings and Flipping Activity." *Journal of Financial Economics* 68 (April), pp. 111–135.

Aggarwal, Reena, Laurie Krigman, and Kent Womack. 2002. "Strategic IPO Underpricing, Information Momentum, and Lockup Expiration Selling." *Journal of Financial Economics* 66 (October), pp. 105–137.

Aggarwal, Reena, Nagpurnanand R. Prabhala, and Manju Puri. 2002. "Institutional Allocation in Initial Public Offerings: Empirical Evidence." *Journal of Finance* 57 (June), pp. 1421–1442.

Agrawal, Anup, Jeffrey F. Jaffe, and Gershon N. Mandelker. 1992. "The Post-Merger Performance of Acquiring Firms: A Reexamination of an Anomaly." *Journal of Finance* 47 (September), pp. 1605–1622.

Aharony, Joseph, and Itzhak Swary. 1980. "Quarterly Dividend and Earnings Announcements and Stockholders' Returns: An Empirical Analysis." *Journal of Finance* 35 (March), pp. 1–12.

Ahn, Seoungpil, and David J. Denis. 2004. "Internal Capital Markets and Investment Policy: Evidence from Corporate Spinoffs." *Journal of Financial Economics* 71 (March), pp. 489–516.

Akerlof, George. 1970. "The Market for 'Lemons,' Qualitative Uncertainty and the Market Mechanism." *Quarterly Journal of Economics* 84 (August), pp. 488–500.

Alderson, Michael J., and Brian L. Betker. 1995. "Liquidation Costs and Capital Structure." *Journal of Financial Economics* 39 (September), pp. 45–69.

Altinkiliç, Oya, and Robert S. Hansen. 2000. "Are There Economies of Scale in Underwriting Fees? Evidence of Rising External Financing Costs." *Review of Financial Studies* 13 (Spring), pp. 191–218.

———. 2003. "Another Equity Issue Riddle: Why Is the Bear So Often There?" Working paper, University of Pittsburgh (August).

Altman, Edward. 1984. "A Further Empirical Investigation of the Bankruptcy Cost Question." *Journal of Finance* 39 (September), pp. 1067–1089.

———. 2000. "Revisiting the High Yield Market: Mature but Never Dull." *Journal of Applied Corporate Finance* 13 (Spring), pp. 64–74.

Altman, Edward I., and Heather J. Suggitt. 2000. "Default Rates in the Syndicated Bank Loan Market: A Mortality Analysis." *Journal of Banking and Finance* 24, pp. 229–253.

Ambarish, Ramasastry, Kose John, and Joseph Williams. 1987. "Efficient Signalling with Dividends and Investments." *Journal of Finance* 42 (June), pp. 321–343.

Amihud, Yakov, and Baruch Lev. 1981. "Risk Reduction as a Managerial Motive for Conglomerate Mergers." *Bell Journal of Economics* 12 (Autumn), pp. 605–617.

Amihud, Yakov, Baruch Lev, and Nikolaos Travlos. 1990. "Corporate Control and the Choice of Investment Financing: The Case of Corporate Acquisitions." *Journal of Finance* 45 (June), pp. 603–616.

Anderson, Christopher W., and Anil K. Makhija. 1999. "Deregulation, Disintermediation and Agency Costs of Debt: Evidence from Japan." *Journal of Financial Economics* 51 (February), pp. 309–339.

Andrade, Gregor, and Steven N. Kaplan. 1998. "How Costly Is Financial (Not Economic) Distress? Evidence from Highly Leveraged Transactions That Became Distressed." *Journal of Finance* 53 (October), pp. 1443–1493.

Andrade, Gregor, Mark Mitchell, and Erik Stafford. 2001. "New Evidence and Perspectives on Merger." *Journal of Economic Perspectives* 15 (Spring), pp. 103–120.

Ang, James S. 1993. "On Financial Ethics." *Financial Management* 22 (Autumn), pp. 32–59.

Ang, James S., David W. Blackwell, and William L. Megginson. 1991. "The Effect of Taxes on the Relative Valuation of Dividends and Capital Gains: Evidence from Dual-Class British Investment Trusts." *Journal of Finance* 46 (March), pp. 383–399.

Ang, James S., and James C. Brau. 2003. "Concealing and Confounding Adverse Signals: Insider Wealth-Maximizing Behavior in the IPO Process." *Journal of Financial Economics* 67 (January), pp. 149–172.

Ang, James, and William L. Megginson. 1990. "A Test of the before-Tax versus after-Tax Equilibrium Models of Corporate Debt." *Research in Finance* 8, pp. 97–118.

Arundale, Keith. 2001. "European Private Equity and Venture Capita—Current State of the Market and Prospects for the Industry." Working paper, PricewaterhouseCoopers UK.

Asquith, Paul. 1983. "Merger Bids, Uncertainty and Stockholder Returns." *Journal of Financial Economics* 11 (April), pp. 51–83.

———. 1995. "Convertible Bonds Are Not Called Late." *Journal of Finance* 50 (September), pp. 1275–1289.

Asquith, Paul, Robert Bruner, and David Mullins. 1983. "The Gains for Bidding

Firms from Merger." *Journal of Financial Economics* 11 (April), pp. 121–139.

Asquith, Paul, and David Mullins, Jr. 1983. "The Impact of Initiating Dividend Payments on Shareholders' Wealth." *Journal of Business* 56 (January), pp. 77–96.

———. 1986. "Equity Issues and Stock Price Dilution." *Journal of Financial Economics* 15 (January/February), pp. 61–89.

Asquith, Paul, and Thierry Wizman. 1990. "Event Risk, Covenants, and Bondholder Returns in Leveraged Buyouts." *Journal of Financial Economics* 27 (September), pp. 195–213.

Aylward, Anthony. 1998. "Trends in Venture Capital Finance in Developing Countries." IFC discussion paper no. 36, World Bank (Washington, D.C.).

Backus, David, Silverio Foresi, Abon Mozumdar, and Liuren Wu. 2001. "Predictable Changes in Yields and Forward Rates." *Journal of Financial Economics* 59 (March), pp. 281–311.

Backus, David K., Silverio Foresi, and Chris I. Telmer. 2001. "Affine Term Structure Models and the Forward Premium Anomaly." *Journal of Finance* 56 (February), pp. 279–304.

Baker, H. Kent, Gail E. Farrelly, and Richard B. Edelman. 1985. "A Survey of Management Views on Dividend Policy." *Financial Management* 14 (Autumn), pp. 78–84.

Baker, Malcolm, and Paul A. Gompers. 2001. "The Determinants of Board Structure at the Initial Public Offering." Working paper, Harvard Business School.

Baker, Malcolm, and Jeffrey Wurgler. 2002. "Market Timing and Capital Structure." *Journal of Finance* 57 (February), pp. 1–32.

———. 2004a. "A Catering Theory of Dividends." *Journal of Finance* 59 (June), pp. 1125–1165.

———. 2004b. "Appearing and Disappearing Dividends: The Link to Catering Incentives" *Journal of Financial Economics* 73 (August), pp. 271–288.

Baldwin, Carliss, and Kim B. Clark. 1992. "Capabilities and Capital Investment: New Perspectives on Capital Budgeting." *Journal of Applied Corporate Finance* 15 (Summer), pp. 67–82.

Ball, Ray. 1995. "The Theory of Market Efficiency: Accomplishments and Limitations." *Journal of Applied Corporate Finance* 8 (Spring), pp. 4–17.

Ball, Ray, and Philip Brown. 1968. "An Empirical Investigation of Accounting Income Numbers." *Journal of Accounting Research* 6 (Autumn), pp. 159–178.

Ball, Ray, S. P. Kothari, and Jay Shanken. 1995. "Problems in Measuring Portfolio Performance: An Application to Contrarian Investment Strategies." *Journal of Financial Economics* 38, pp. 79–107.

Banz, Rolf W. 1981. "The Relationship between Return and Market Value of Common Stocks." *Journal of Financial Economics* 9 (March), pp. 3–18.

Barber, Brad, Reuven Lehavy, Maureen McNichols, and Brett Trueman. 2001. "Can Investors Profit from the Prophets? Security Analyst Recommendations and Stock Returns." *Journal of Finance* 56 (April), pp. 531–563.

———. 2002. "Prophets and Losses: Reassessing the Returns to Analysts' Stock Recommendations." Working paper (September).

Barber, Brad M., and Terrance Odean. 2000. "Trading Is Hazardous to Your Wealth." *Journal of Finance* 55 (April), pp. 773–806.

———. "Online Investors: Do the Slow Die First?" *Review of Financial Studies* 15 (Special), pp. 455–487.

Barclay, Michael J. 1987. "Dividends, Taxes, and Common Stock Prices before the Income Tax." *Journal of Financial Economics* 19 (September), pp. 31–44.

Barclay, Michael J., and Clifford W. Smith, Jr. 1995a. "The Maturity Structure of Corporate Debt." *Journal of Finance* 50 (June), pp. 609–631.

———. 1995b. "The Priority Structure of Corporate Liabilities." *Journal of Finance* 50 (July), pp. 899–917.

Barclay, Michael J., Clifford W. Smith, Jr., and Ross L. Watts. 1995. "The Determinants of Corporate Leverage and Dividend Policies." *Journal of Applied Corporate Finance* 17 (Winter), pp. 4–19.

Bascha, Andreas, and Uwe Walz. 2001. "Convertible Securities and Optimal Exit Decisions in Venture Capital." *Journal of Corporate Finance* 7 (September), pp. 285–306.

Baytas, Ahmet, and Nusret Cakici. 1999. "Do Markets Overreact: International Evidence." *Journal of Banking and Finance* 23, pp. 1121–1144.

Beatty, Anne. 1995. "The Cash Flow and Informational Effects of Employee Stock Ownership Plans." *Journal of Financial Economics* 38 (June), pp. 211–240.

Beatty, Randolph P., and Ivo Welch. 1996. "Issuer Expenses and Legal Liability in Initial Public Offerings." *Journal of Law and Economics* 39 (December), pp. 545–602.

Beck, Thorsten, Asli Demirgüç-Kunt, and Ross Levine. 2003. "Law, Endowments and Finance." *Journal of Financial Economics* 70 (November), pp. 137–181.

Beck, Thorsten, Asli Demirgüç-Kunt, and Vojislav Maksimovic. 2005. "Financial and Legal Constraints to Growth: Does

Firm Size Matter?" *Journal of Finance* 60 (February), pp. 137–177.

Becker, Kent G., Joseph E. Finnerty, and Joseph Friedman. 1995. "Economic News and Equity Market Linkages between the U.S. and U.K." *Journal of Banking and Finance* 19, pp. 1191–1210.

Bell, Leonie, and Tim Jenkinson. 2002. "New Evidence of the Impact of Dividend Taxation on the Identity of the Marginal Investor." *Journal of Finance* 57 (June), pp. 1321–1346.

Benartzi, Shlomo, Roni Michaely, and Richard Thaler. 1997. "Do Changes in Dividends Signal the Future or the Past?" *Journal of Finance* 52 (July), pp. 1007–1035.

Benoit, Bertrand. 2001. "Neuer Markt Starts to Feel Squeeze." *Financial Times* (July 11), p. 19.

Benveniste, Lawrence M., Alexander Ljungqvist, William J. Wilhelm, Jr., and Xiaoyun Yu. 2003. "Evidence of Information Spillovers in the Production of Investment Banking Services." *Journal of Finance* 58 (April), pp. 577–608.

Benveniste, Lawrence M., and Paul A. Spindt. 1989. "How Investment Bankers Determine the Offer Price and Allocation for New Issues." *Journal of Financial Economics* 24 (October), pp. 343–361.

Berger, Philip, and Eli Ofek. 1995. "Diversification's Effect on Firm Value." *Journal of Financial Economics* 37 (January), pp. 39–65.

———. 1996. "Bustup Takeovers of Value-Destroying Diversified Firms." *Journal of Finance* 51 (September), pp. 1175–2000.

Berger, Philip G., Eli Ofek, and David L. Yermack. 1997. "Managerial Entrenchment and Capital Structure Decisions." *Journal of Finance* 54 (September), pp. 1411–1438.

Berglöf, Erik. 1994. "A Control Theory of Venture Capital Finance." *Journal of Law, Economics and Organization* 10, pp. 447–471.

Berglöf, Erik, and Enrico Perotti. 1994. "The Governance Structure of the Japanese Keiretsu." *Journal of Financial Economics* 36 (October), pp. 259–284.

Bergstrom, C., and K. Rydqvist. 1990. "The Determinants of Corporate Ownership: An Empirical Study of Swedish Data." *Journal of Banking and Finance* 14, pp. 237–254.

Bernanke, Ben S., and John Y. Campbell. 1988. "Is There a Corporate Debt Crisis?" *Brookings Papers on Economic Activity* 1, pp. 83–125.

Bernard, Victor L., and Jacob K. Thomas. 1990. "Evidence That Stock Prices Do Not Fully Reflect the Implications of

Current Earnings for Future Earnings." *Journal of Accounting and Economics* 12 (December), pp. 305–341.

Bernard, Victor, Jacob K. Thomas, and Jeffery S. Abarbanell. 1993. "How Sophisticated Is the Market in Interpreting Earnings News?" *Journal of Applied Corporate Finance* 6 (Summer), pp. 54–63.

Bernardo, Antonio E., and Bhagwan Chowdhry. 2002. "Resources, Real Options, and Corporate Strategy." *Journal of Financial Economics* 63 (February), pp. 211–234.

Bernardo, Antonio E., and Eric L. Talley. 1996. "Investment Policy and Exit-Exchange Offers within Financially Distressed Firms." *Journal of Finance* 51 (July), pp. 871–888.

Bernstein, Peter L. 1999. "Why the Efficient Market Offers Hope to Active Management." *Journal of Applied Corporate Finance* 12 (Summer), pp. 129–136.

Bethel, Jennifer E., and Stuart L. Gillan. 2002. "The Impact of the Institutional and Regulatory Environment on Shareholder Voting." *Financial Management* 31 (Winter).

Bhagat, Sanjai. 1983. "The Effect of Preemptive Right Amendments on Shareholder Wealth." *Journal of Financial Economics* 12 (November), pp. 289–310.

———. 1986. "The Effect of Management's Choice between Negotiated and Competitive Equity Offerings on Shareholder Wealth." *Journal of Financial and Quantitative Analysis* 21 (June), pp. 181–196.

Bhagat, Sanjai, Ming Dong, David Hirshleifer, and Robert Noah. 2005. "Do Tender Offers Create Value? New Methods and Evidence." *Journal of Financial Economics* 76 (April), pp. 3–60.

Bhagat, Sanjai, and Peter Frost. 1986. "Issuing Costs to Existing Shareholders in Competitive and Negotiated Underwritten Public Utility Offerings." *Journal of Financial Economics* 15 (January/February), pp. 223–259.

Bhagat, Sanjai, Andrei Shleifer, and Robert Vishny. 1990. "Hostile Takeovers in the 1980s: The Return to Corporate Specialization." *Brookings Papers on Economic Activity,* pp. 1–72.

Bharadwaj, Anu, and Anil Shivdasani. 2003. "Valuation Effects of Bank Financing in Acquisitions." *Journal of Financial Economics* 67 (January), pp. 113–148.

Bhattacharya, Sudipto. 1979. "Imperfect Information, Dividend Policy, and 'the Bird in the Hand' Fallacy." *Bell Journal of Economics* 10 (Spring), pp. 259–270.

Bhattacharya, Utpal, and Hazem Daouk. 2002. "The World Price of Insider Trading." *Journal of Finance* 57, pp. 75–108.

Bhattacharya, Utpal, Hazem Daouk, Brian Jorgenson, and Carl-Heinrich Kehr. 2000. "When Is an Event Not an Event: The Curious Case of an Emerging Market." *Journal of Financial Economics* 55, pp. 69–101.

Bhide, Amar. 1992. "Bootstrap Finance: The Art of Start-Ups." *Harvard Business Review* (November/December), pp. 109–117.

———. 1993. "The Hidden Costs of Stock Market Liquidity." *Journal of Financial Economics* 34 (August), pp. 31–51.

Bianchi, Alessandra. 1992. "Why You Won't Sell Your Business." *Inc.* (August), pp. 58–63.

Bicksler, James, and Andrew H. Chen. 1986. "An Economic Analysis of Interest Rate Swaps." *Journal of Finance* 41 (July), pp. 645–655.

Billett, Matthew T., Tao-Hsien Dolly King, and David C. Mauer. 2004. "Bondholder Wealth Effects in Mergers and Acquisitions: New Evidence from the 1980s and 1990s." *Journal of Finance* 59 (February), pp. 107–135.

Birnbaum, Jeffrey H. 1999. "Uncle Sam, Venture Capitalist." *Fortune* (May 24), p. 66.

Bittlingmayer, George, and Thomas W. Hazlett. 2000. "DOS Kapital: Has Antitrust Action against Microsoft Created Value in the Computer Industry?" *Journal of Financial Economics* 55, pp. 329–359.

Bjerring, James H., Josef Lakonishok, and Theo Vermaelen. 1983. "Stock Prices and Financial Analysts' Recommendations." *Journal of Finance* 38 (March), pp. 187–204.

Black, Bernard. 1992. "Institutional Investors and Corporate Governance: The Case for Institutional Voice." *Journal of Applied Corporate Finance* 5 (Fall), pp. 19–32.

Black, Bernard S., and Ronald J. Gilson. 1998. "Venture Capital and the Structure of Capital Markets: Banks versus Capital Markets." *Journal of Financial Economics* 47 (March), pp. 243–277.

Black, Fischer. 1975. "Fact and Fantasy in the Use of Options." *Financial Analysts Journal* 31 (July/August), pp. 36–41, 61–72.

Black, Fischer, Michael C. Jensen, and Myron Scholes. 1972. "The Capital Asset Pricing Model: Some Empirical Tests." In *Studies in the Theory of Capital Markets,* edited by Michael C. Jensen (New York: Praeger).

Black, Fischer, and Myron S. Scholes. 1973. "The Pricing of Options and Corporate Liabilities." *Journal of Political Economy* 81 (May/June), pp. 637–654.

Blackwell, David W., M. Wayne Marr, and Michael F. Spivey. 1990. "Shelf Regis-

tration and the Reduced Due Diligence Argument: Implications of the Underwriter Certification and the Implicit Insurance Hypothesis." *Journal of Financial and Quantitative Analysis* 25 (June), pp. 245–259.

Blass, Asher, and Yishay Yafeh. 2001. "Vagabond Shoes Longing to Stray: Why Foreign Firms List in the United States." *Journal of Banking and Finance* 25 (March), pp. 555–572.

Blouin, Jennifer L., Jana Smith Raedy, and Douglas A. Shackleford. 2004. "Did Dividends Increase Immediately after the 2003 Reduction in Tax Rates?" NBER working paper W10301, National Bureau of Economic Research (February).

Bollerslev, Tim. 1986. "Generalized Conditional Autoregressive Heteroscedasticity." *Journal of Econometrics* 31 (April), pp. 307–327.

Bonser-Neal, Catherine, and Timothy Morley. 1997. "Does the Yield Spread Predict Real Economic Activity: A Multi-Country Analysis." Federal Reserve Bank of Kansas City *Economic Review* (Third Quarter), pp. 37–53.

Booth, James R. 1992. "Contract Costs, Bank Loans, and the Cross-Monitoring Hypothesis." *Journal of Financial Economics* 31 (February), pp. 25–41.

Booth, James R., and Lena Chua. 1996. "Ownership Dispersion, Costly Information, and IPO Underpricing." *Journal of Financial Economics* 41, pp. 291–310.

Booth, James R., Richard L. Smith, and Richard W. Stolz. 1984. "Use of Interest Rate Futures by Financial Institutions." *Journal of Bank Research* 15, pp. 15–20.

Booth, Laurence, Varouj Aivazian, Asli Demirgüç-Kunt, and Vojislav Maksimovic. 2001. "Capital Structures in Developing Countries." *Journal of Finance* 56 (February), pp. 87–130.

Bortolotti, Bernardo, Frank DeJong, Giovanna Nicodano, and Ibolya Schindele. 2005. "Privatization and Stock Market Liquidity." FEEM working paper, Fondazione Eni Enrico Mattei, Milan (March).

Boubakri, Narjess, and Jean-Claude Cosset. 1998. "The Financial and Operating Performance of Newly Privatized Firms: Evidence from Developing Countries." *Journal of Finance* 53 (June), pp. 1081–1110.

Boutchkova, Maria K., and William L. Megginson. 2000. "Privatization and the Rise of Global Capital Markets." *Financial Management* 29 (Winter), pp. 31–76.

Boyd, John H., and Mark Gertler. 1994. "Are Banks Dead? Or Are the Reports

Greatly Exaggerated?" Federal Reserve Bank of Minneapolis *Quarterly Review* (Summer), pp. 2–23.

Bradley, Daniel J., Bradford D. Jordan, Ha-Chin Yi, and Ivan C. Roten. 2001. "Venture Capital and IPO Lockup Expiration: An Empirical Analysis." *Journal of Financial Research* 24 (Winter), pp. 465–492.

Bradley, Michael, Anand Desai, and E. Han Kim. 1988. "Synergistic Gains from Corporate Acquisitions and Their Division between the Stockholders of Target and Acquiring Firms." *Journal of Financial Economics* 21 (May), pp. 3–40.

Bradley, Michael, Gregg Jarrell, and E. Han Kim. 1984. "On the Existence of an Optimal Capital Structure: Theory and Evidence." *Journal of Finance* 39 (May), pp. 857–878.

Brav, Alon, Christopher Geczy, and Paul A. Gompers. 2000. "Is the Abnormal Return following Equity Issuances Anomalous?" *Journal of Financial Economics* 56, pp. 209–249.

Brav, Alon, and Paul A. Gompers. 1997. "Myth or Reality? The Long-Run Underperformance of Initial Public Offerings: Evidence from Venture and Non-Venture Capital–Backed Companies." *Journal of Finance* 52 (December), pp. 1791–1821.

Brav, Alon, and J. B. Heaton. 2002. "Competing Theories of Financial Anomalies." *Review of Financial Studies* 15 (Special), pp. 575–606.

Brealey, Richard A., Ian A. Cooper, and Michel A. Habib. 1996. "Using Project Finance to Fund Infrastructure Investments." *Journal of Applied Corporate Finance* 9 (Fall), pp. 25–38.

Breeden, Douglas T. 1979. "An Intertemporal Asset Pricing Model with Stochastic Consumption and Investment Opportunities." *Journal of Financial Economics* 7, pp. 265–296.

Brennan, Michael J. 1970. "Taxes, Market Valuation and Corporate Financial Policy." *National Tax Journal* 23 (December), pp. 417–427.

Brennan, Michael J., and Eduardo S. Schwartz. 1985. "Evaluating Natural Resource Investments." *Journal of Business* 58 (April), pp. 135–157.

Brewer, Elijah, III, and Hesna Genay. 1994. "Small Business Investment Companies: Financial Characteristics and Investments." Working paper, Series no. 94-10, Federal Reserve Bank of Chicago.

Brickley, James A. 1983. "Shareholder Wealth, Information Signalling and the Specially Designated Dividend: An Empirical Study." *Journal of Financial Economics* 12 (August), pp. 187–209.

Brinson, Gary P., L. Randolph Hood, and Gilbert L. Beebower. 1986. "Determinants of Portfolio Performance." *Financial Analysts Journal* 50 (July/August), pp. 39–44.

Bris, Arturo, Alan Schwartz, and Ivo Welch. 2005. "Who Should Pay for Bankruptcy Costs?" *Journal of Legal Studies* 34 (June), pp. 296–341.

Brock, William, Josef Lakonishok, and Blake LeBaron. 1992. "Simple Technical Trading Rules and the Stochastic Properties of Stock Returns." *Journal of Finance* 47 (December), pp. 1731–1764.

Brown, Stephen J., and Jerold B. Warner. 1980. "Measuring Security Price Performance." *Journal of Financial Economics* 8 (September), pp. 205–258.

———. 1985. "Using Daily Stock Returns in the Case of Event Studies." *Journal of Financial Economics* 14 (March), pp. 205–258.

Bruner, Robert F. 2002. "Does M&A Pay? A Survey of Evidence for the Decision-Maker." *Journal of Applied Finance* 12 (Spring/Summer), pp. 48–68.

Bruner, Robert, Susan Chaplinsky, and Latha Ramchand. 2004. "US-Bound IPOs: Issue Costs and Selective Entry." *Financial Management* 33 (Autumn), pp. 39–60.

Burroughs, Bryan, and John Helyar. 1993. *Barbarians at the Gate: The Fall of RJR Nabisco* (New York: HarperCollins).

Byun, Jinho, and Michael S. Rozeff. 2003. "Long-Run Performance after Stock Splits: 1927 to 1996." *Journal of Finance* 58 (June), pp. 1063–1085.

Calegari, Michael J. 2000. "The Effect of Tax Accounting Rules on Capital Structure and Discretionary Accruals." *Journal of Accounting and Economics* 30 (August), pp. 1–31.

Campbell, John Y., and John Ammer. 1993. "What Moves the Stock and Bond Markets? A Variance Decomposition for Long-Term Asset Returns." *Journal of Finance* 48 (March), pp. 3–37.

Campbell, Katharine. 2001a. "Stock Market Volatility Fails to Put Off Investors." *Financial Times* (June 14), p. 6.

———. 2001b. "Informal Financing Totals $196bn a Year." *Financial Times* (November 15), p. 31.

Cannavan, Damien, Frank Finn, and Stephen Gray. 2004. "The Value of Dividend Imputation Tax Credits in Australia" *Journal of Financial Economics* 73 (July), pp. 167–197.

Carey, Mark. 1998. "Credit Risk in Private Debt Portfolios." *Journal of Finance* 52 (August), pp. 1363–1387.

Carhart, Mark M. 1997. "On Persistence in

Mutual Fund Performance." *Journal of Finance* 52 (March), pp. 57–82.

Carlin, Wendy, and Colin Mayer. 2003. "Finance, Investment, and Growth." *Journal of Financial Economics* 69 (July), pp. 191–226.

Carpenter, Jennifer N., and Anthony W. Lynch. 1999. "Survivorship Bias and Attrition Effects in Measures of Performance Persistence." *Journal of Financial Economics* 54 (December), pp. 337–374.

Carter, Mary E., and Luann J. Lynch. 2001. "An Examination of Executive Stock Option Repricing." *Journal of Financial Economics* 61 (August), pp. 207–225.

Carter, Richard B., and Howard E. Van Auken. 1990. "Personal Equity Investment and Small Business Financial Difficulties." *Entrepreneurship Theory and Practice* (Winter), pp. 51–60.

Chambers, Donald R., and Nelson J. Lacey. 1996. "Corporate Ethics and Shareholder Wealth Maximization." *Financial Practice and Education* 6 (Spring/Summer), pp. 93–96.

Chan, Louis K. C., Narasimhan Jegadeesh, and Josef Lakonishok. 1996. "Momentum Strategies." *Journal of Finance* 51 (December), pp. 1681–1713.

Chan, Louis K. D., Jason Karceski, and Josef Lakonishok. 2003. "The Level of Persistence of Growth Rates." *Journal of Finance* (forthcoming).

Chang, Eric C., Joseph W. Cheng, and Ajay Khorana. 2000. "An Examination of Herd Behavior in Equity Markets: An International Perspective." *Journal of Banking and Finance* 24, pp. 1651–1679.

Chaplinsky, Susan, and Latha Ramchand. 2000. "The Impact of Global Equity Offerings." *Journal of Finance* 55 (December), pp. 2767–2789.

Chauvin, Keith W., and Catherine Shenoy. 2001. "Stock Price Decreases Prior to Executive Stock Option Grants." *Journal of Corporate Finance: Contracting, Governance, and Organization* 7 (March), pp. 53–76.

Chen, Hsuan-Chi, and Jay Ritter. 2000. "The Seven Percent Solution." *Journal of Finance* 55 (June), pp. 1105–1131.

Chen, N., R. Roll, and S. A. Ross. 1986. "Economic Forces and the Stock Market: Testing the APT and Alternative Asset Pricing Theories." *Journal of Business* 59 (July), pp. 383–403.

Chidambaran, N. K., Chitru S. Fernando, and Paul A. Spindt. 2001. "Credit Enhancement through Financial Engineering: Freeport McMoRan's Gold-Denominated Depository Share." *Journal of Financial Economics* 60 (May), pp. 487–528.

Chowdhry, Bhagwan, and Ann Sherman. 1996. "International Differences in Oversubscription and Underpricing of IPO." *Journal of Corporate Finance* 2, pp. 359–381.

Christie, William G., and Vikram Nanda. 1994. "Free Cash Flow, Shareholder Value, and the Undistributed Profits Tax of 1936 and 1937." *Journal of Finance* 49 (December), pp. 1727–1754.

Christopher, Alistair. 2001. "VC and the Law: Potential Legal Hurdles Involved in Funding the Next Big Thing." *Venture Capital Journal* (February), pp. 43–45.

Claessens, Stijn, and Luc Laeven. 2003. "Financial Development, Property Rights, and Growth." *Journal of Finance* 58 (December), pp. 2401–2437.

Cliff, Michel, and David Denis. 2004. "Do Initial Public Offering Firms Purchase Analyst Coverage with Underpricing?" *Journal of Finance* 59 (December), pp. 2871–2901.

Coggin, T. Daniel, Frank J. Fabozzi, and Shafiqur Rahman. 1993. "The Investment Performance of U.S. Equity Pension Fund Managers: An Empirical Investigation." *Journal of Finance* 48 (July), pp. 1039–1055.

Cole, Jonathan E., and Albert L. Sokol. 1997. "Structuring Venture Capital Investments." In *Pratt's Guide to Venture Capital Sources*, edited by Stanley E. Pratt (New York: Securities Data Publishing).

Comment, Robert, and Gregg Jarrell. 1995. "Corporate Focus and Stock Returns." *Journal of Financial Economics* 37 (January), pp. 67–87.

Comment, Robert, and William Schwert. 1995. "Poison or Placebo? Evidence on the Deterrence and Wealth Effects of Modern Antitakeover Measures." *Journal of Financial Economics* 39, pp. 3–43.

Conrad, Jennifer, and Gautam Kaul. 1988. "Time Variation in Expected Returns." *Journal of Business* 61 (October), pp. 409–425.

———. 1989. "Mean Reversion in Short-Horizon Expected Returns." *Review of Financial Studies* 2, pp. 225–240.

———. 1993. "Long-Term Market Overreaction or Biases in Computed Returns." *Journal of Finance* 48 (March), pp. 39–64.

Cornell, Bradford, and Alan C. Shapiro. 1987. "Corporate Stakeholders and Corporate Finance." *Financial Management* 16 (Spring), pp. 5–14.

Cornelli, Francesca, and David Goldreich. 2001. "Bookbuilding and Strategic Allocation." *Journal of Finance* 56 (December), pp. 2337–2370.

———. 2003. "Bookbuilding: How Informative Is the Order Book?" *Journal of Finance* 58 (August), pp. 1415–1443.

Corwin, Shane A. 2003. "The Determinants of Underpricing for Seasoned Equity Offers." *Journal of Finance* 58 (October), pp. 2249–2279.

Corwin, Shane, Jeffrey H. Harris, and Marc L. Lipson. 2004. "The Development of Secondary Market Liquidity for NYSE-Listed IPOs." *Journal of Finance* 58 (October), pp. 2339–2373.

Cox, Don R., and David R. Peterson. 1994. "Stock Returns following Large One-Day Declines: Evidence on Short-Term Reversals and Longer-Term Performance." *Journal of Finance* 49 (March), pp. 255–267.

Cox, John C., Jonathon E. Ingersoll, Jr., and Stephen A. Ross. 1981. "The Relation between Forward and Futures Prices." *Journal of Financial Economics* 9 (December), pp. 321–346.

Cox, John C., and Stephen A. Ross. 1976. "The Valuation of Options for Alternative Stochastic Processes." *Journal of Financial Economics* 3 (January/March), pp. 145–166.

Cox, John C., Stephen A. Ross, and Mark Rubinstein. 1979. "Option Pricing: A Simplified Approach." *Journal of Financial Economics* 7 (September), pp. 229–263.

Crabbe, Leland E., and Jean Helwege. 1994. "Alternative Tests of Agency Theories of Callable Corporate Bonds." *Financial Management* 23 (Winter), pp. 3–20.

Crawford, Dean, Diana R. Franz, and Gerald J. Lobo. 2005. "Signaling Managerial Optimism through Stock Dividends and Stock Splits: A Reexamination of the Retained Earnings Hypothesis." *Journal of Financial and Quantitative Analysis* (forthcoming).

Cumby, Robert E., and David M. Modest. 1987. "Testing for Market Timing Ability: A Framework for Market Forecast Evaluation." *Journal of Financial Economics* 19 (September), pp. 169–189.

Cusatis, Patrick J., James A. Miles, and J. Randall Woolridge. 1993. "Restructuring through Spinoffs: The Stock Market Evidence." *Journal of Financial Economics* 33, pp. 293–311.

Dahiya, Sandeep, Kose John, Manju Puri, and Gabriel Ramirez. 2003. "Debtor-in-Possession Financing and Bankruptcy Resolution: Empirical Evidence." *Journal of Financial Economics* 69 (July), pp. 259–280.

Daniel, Kent, David Hirshleifer, and Avindhar Subrahmanyam. 1998. "Investor Psychology and Under- and Overreac-

tions." *Journal of Finance* 53 (December), pp. 1839–1882.

Dann, Larry. 1981. "Common Stock Repurchases: An Analysis of Returns to Bondholders and Stockholders." *Journal of Financial Economics* 9 (June), pp. 113–138.

Dann, Larry, and Wayne Mikkelson. 1984. "Convertible Debt Issuance, Capital Structure Change and Financing Related Information: Some New Evidence." *Journal of Financial Economics* 13 (June), pp. 157–186.

DeAngelo, Harry, and Linda DeAngelo. 1985. "Managerial Ownership of Voting Rights: A Study of Public Corporations with Dual Classes of Common Stock." *Journal of Financial Economics* 14 (March), pp. 33–69.

———. 1990. "Dividend Policy and Financial Distress: An Empirical Investigation of Troubled NYSE Firms." *Journal of Finance* 45 (December), pp. 1415–1431.

DeAngelo, Harry, Linda DeAngelo, and Douglas J. Skinner. 1992. "Dividends and Losses." *Journal of Finance* 47 (December), pp. 1837–1863.

———. 1996. "Reversal of Fortune: Dividend Signaling and the Disappearance of Sustained Earnings Growth." *Journal of Financial Economics* 40 (March), pp. 341–371.

———. 2000. "Special Dividends and Evolution of Dividend Signalling." *Journal of Financial Economics* 57 (September), pp. 309–354.

———. 2004. "Are Dividends Disappearing? Dividend Concentration and the Consolidation of Earnings." *Journal of Financial Economics* 72 (June), pp. 425–456.

DeAngelo, Harry, and Ronald W. Masulis. 1980. "Optimal Capital Structure under Corporate and Personal Taxation." *Journal of Financial Economics* 8 (March), pp. 3–30.

DeBondt, Werner, and Richard Thaler. 1985. "Does the Stock Market Overreact?" *Journal of Finance* 40 (July), pp. 793–805.

DeGeorge, Francois, and Richard Zeckhauser. 1993. "The Reverse LBO Decision and Firm Performance." *Journal of Finance* 48 (September), pp. 1323–1348.

———. 1996. "The Financial Performance of Reverse Leveraged Buyouts." *Journal of Financial Economics* 42 (November), pp. 293–332.

DeLong, Bradford, Andrei Shleifer, Lawrence H. Summers, and Robert J. Waldmann. 1990. "Noise Trader Risk in Financial Markets." *Journal of Political Economy* 98 (August), pp. 703–738.

DeMarzo, Peter M., and Darrell Duffie. 1995. "Corporate Incentives for Hedging and Hedge Accounting." *Review of Financial Studies* 8, pp. 743–771.

Demers, Elizabeth, and Katherina Lewellen. 2003. "The Marketing Role of IPOs: Evidence from Internet Stocks." *Journal of Financial Economics* 68 (June), pp. 413–437.

De Miguel, Alberto, and Julio Pindado. 2001. "Determinants of Capital Structure: New Evidence from Spanish Panel Data." *Journal of Corporate Finance* 7 (March), pp. 77–99.

Demirgüç-Kunt, Asli, and Vojislav Maksimovic. 1998. "Law, Finance, and Firm Growth." *Journal of Finance* 53 (December), pp. 2107–2139.

———. 1999. "Institutions, Financial Markets, and Firm Debt Maturity." *Journal of Financial Economics* 54 (December), pp. 295–336.

Denis, David J. 1991. "Shelf Registration and the Market for Seasoned Equity Offerings." *Journal of Business* 64 (April), pp. 189–212.

Denis, David J., Diane K. Denis, and Atulya Sarin. 1997. "Agency Problems, Equity Ownership, and Corporate Diversification." *Journal of Finance* 52 (March), pp. 135–160.

Dennis, Debra, and John McConnell. 1986. "Corporate Mergers and Security Returns." *Journal of Financial Economics* 16 (June), pp. 143–187.

Desai, Hemang, and Prem C. Jain. 1995. "An Analysis of the Recommendations of the 'Superstar' Money Managers at *Barron's* Annual Roundtable." *Journal of Finance* 50 (September), pp. 1257–1273.

———. 1997. "Long-Run Common Stock Returns following Stock Splits and Reverse Splits." *Journal of Business* 70 (July), pp. 409–433.

Detragiache, Enrica, Paolo Garella, and Luigi Guiso. 2000. "Multiple versus Single Banking Relationships: Theory and Evidence." *Journal of Finance* 55 (June), pp. 1133–1161.

Dewenter, Kathryn, and Vincent Warther. 1998. "Dividends, Asymmetric Information and Agency Conflicts: Evidence from a Comparison of the Dividend Policies of Japanese and US Firms." *Journal of Finance* 53 (June), pp. 879–904.

Dewing, Arthur Stone. 1953. *The Financial Policy of Corporations* (New York: The Ronald Press Company).

Dharan, Bala G., and David L. Ikenberry. 1995. "The Long-Run Negative Drift of Post-Listing Stock Returns." *Journal of Finance* 50 (December), pp. 1547–1574.

Dhillon, Upinder, and Herb Johnson. 1991. "Changes in the Standard & Poor's List." *Journal of Business* 64 (January), pp. 75–85.

Diamond, Douglas W. 1991. "Monitoring and Reputation: The Choice between Bank Loans and Directly Placed Debt." *Journal of Political Economy* 99, pp. 689–721.

Dichev, Ilia D., and Joseph D. Piotroski. 2001. "The Long-Run Stock Returns following Bond Ratings Changes." *Journal of Finance* 56 (February), pp. 173–203.

Dimson, Elroy, Paul R. Marsh, and Mike Staunton. 2002. *Triumph of the Optimists: 101 Years of Global Investments* (Princeton, NJ: Princeton University Press).

Doidge, Craig, G. Andrew Karolyi, and René M. Stulz. 2004. "Why Are Foreign Firms Listed in the U.S. Worth More?" *Journal of Financial Economics* 71 (February), pp. 205–238.

Dolde, Walter. 1993. "The Trajectory of Corporate Financial Risk Management." *Journal of Applied Corporate Finance* 6 (Fall), pp. 33–41.

D'Souza, Juliet, and William L. Megginson. 1999. "The Financial and Operating Performance of Newly Privatized Firms in the 1990s." *Journal of Finance* 54 (August), pp. 1397–1438.

Dunn, Kenneth B., and Chester S. Spatt. 1984. "A Strategic Analysis of Sinking Fund Bonds." *Journal of Financial Economics* 13 (September), pp. 399–424.

Dwyer, Hubert J., and Richard Lynn. 1989. "Small Capitalization Companies: What Does Financial Analysis Tell Us about Them?" *Financial Review* 24, pp. 397–414.

Dyck, Alexander, and Luigi Zingales. 2004. "Control Premiums and the Effectiveness of Corporate Governance Systems." *Journal of Applied Finance* 16 (Spring/Summer), pp. 51–72.

Dyl, Edward A., and Michael D. Joehnek. 1979. "Sinking Funds and the Cost of Corporate Debt." *Journal of Finance* 34 (September), pp. 887–893.

Eades, Kenneth, Patrick Hess, and E. Han Kim. 1984. "On Interpreting Security Returns during the Ex-dividend Day Period." *Journal of Financial Economics* 13 (March), pp. 3–34.

———. 1994. "Time Series Variation in Dividend Pricing." *Journal of Finance* 49 (December), pp. 1617–1638.

Easterbrook, Frank H. 1984. "Two Agency-Cost Explanations of Dividends." *American Economic Review* 74 (September), pp. 650–659.

Easterbrook, Frank H., and Daniel R. Fischel. 1983. "Voting in Corporate Law." *Journal of Law and Economics* 26 (June), pp. 395–427.

Eberhart, Allan, Edward I. Altman, and Reena Aggarwal. 1999. "The Equity Performance of Firms Emerging from Bankruptcy." *Journal of Finance* 54 (October), pp. 1855–1868.

Eberhart, Allan, William Moore, and Rodney Roenfeldt. 1990. "Security Pricing and Deviations from the Absolute Priority Rule in Bankruptcy Proceedings." *Journal of Finance* 45 (December), pp. 1457–1969.

Eckbo, B. Espen. 1983. "Horizontal Mergers, Collusion, and Stockholder Wealth." *Journal of Financial Economics* 11 (April), pp. 241–273.

———. 1986. "Valuation Effects of Corporate Debt Offerings." *Journal of Financial Economics* 15 (January/February), pp. 119–151.

Eckbo, B. Espen, Ronald W. Masulis, and Øyvind Norli. 2000. "Seasoned Public Offerings: Resolution of the 'New Issues Puzzle.'" *Journal of Financial Economics* 56 (May), pp. 251–291.

Eckbo, B. Espen, and Øyvind Norli. 2005. "Liquidity Risk, Leverage and Long-Run IPO Returns." *Journal of Corporate Finance* 11 (March), pp. 251–291.

Economist, The. 1996. "Remapping South America: A Survey of Mercosur" (October 12).

Edelen, Roger M. 1999. "Investor Flows and the Assessed Performance of Open-End Mutual Funds." *Journal of Financial Economics* 53 (September), pp. 439–466.

Ederington, Louis H., and Jae Ha Lee. 1993. "How Markets Process Information: News Releases and Volatility." *Journal of Finance* 48 (September), pp. 1161–1191.

El-Gazzar, Samir, and Victor Pastena. 1990. "Negotiated Accounting Rules in Private Financial Contracts." *Journal of Accounting and Economics* 12 (March), pp. 381–396.

Ellert, James. 1976. "Mergers, Antitrust Law Enforcement, and Stockholder Returns." *Journal of Finance* 31 (May), pp. 715–732.

Ellis, Katrina, Roni Michaely, and Maureen O'Hara. 2000. "When the Underwriter Is the Market Maker: An Examination of Trading in the IPO Aftermarket." *Journal of Finance* 55 (June), pp. 1039–1074.

Elton, Edwin J., and Martin J. Gruber. 1970. "Marginal Stockholder Tax Rates and the Clientele Effect." *Review of Economics and Statistics* 52 (February), pp. 68–74.

Elton, Edwin J., Martin J. Gruber, Sanjiv Das, and Matthew Hlavka. 1993. "Efficiency with Costly Information: A Reinterpretation of Evidence from Managed Portfolios." *Review of Financial Studies* 6, pp. 1–22.

Emanuel, David C., and James D. MacBeth. 1982. "Further Results on the Constant Elasticity of Variance Call Option Pricing Model." *Journal of Financial and Quantitative Analysis* 17 (November), pp. 533–554.

Engle, Robert F. 1982. "Autoregressive Conditional Heteroscedasticity with Estimates of the Variance of United Kingdom Inflation." *Econometrica* 50 (July), pp. 987–1007.

Errunza, Vihang R., and Darius P. Miller. 2000. "Market Segmentation and the Cost of Capital in International Equity Markets." *Journal of Financial and Quantitative Analysis* 35 (December), pp. 577–600.

Esty, Benjamin C. 1999. "Petrozuata: A Case Study of the Effective Use of Project Finance." *Journal of Applied Corporate Finance* 12 (Fall), pp. 26–42.

———. 2002. "Returns on Project Financed Investments: Theory and Implications." Harvard Business School teaching note 9-202-102 (February).

Faccio, Mara, and Larry H. P. Lang. 2002. "The Ultimate Ownership of Western European Corporations." *Journal of Financial Economics* 65 (September), pp. 365–395.

Faccio, Mara, and Ronald W. Masulis. 2005. "The Choice of Payment Method in European Mergers and Acquisitions." *Journal of Finance* 60 (June), pp. 1345–1388.

Fama, Eugene F. 1965. "The Behavior of Stock Market Prices." *Journal of Business* 38 (January), pp. 34–105.

———. 1970. "Efficient Capital Markets: A Review of Theory and Empirical Work." *Journal of Finance* 25 (May), pp. 383–417.

———. 1980. "Agency Problems and the Theory of the Firm." *Journal of Political Economy* 88 (April), pp. 288–307.

———. 1984. "Forward and Spot Exchange Rates." *Journal of Monetary Economics* 14 (November), pp. 319–338.

———. 1991. "Efficient Capital Markets: II." *Journal of Finance* 46 (December), pp. 1575–1617.

———. 1998. "Market Efficiency, Long-Term Returns, and Behavioral Finance." *Journal of Financial Economics* 49, pp. 283–306.

Fama, Eugene F., and Harvey Babiak. 1968. "Dividend Policy: An Empirical Analysis." *Journal of the American Statistical Association* 63 (December), pp. 1132–1161.

Fama, Eugene F., and Marshall E. Blume. 1966. "Filter Rules and Stock-Market Trading." *Journal of Business* 39 (January), pp. 226–241.

Fama, Eugene F., Lawrence Fisher, Michael C. Jensen, and Richard Roll. 1969. "The Adjustment of Stock Prices to New Information." *International Economic Review* 10 (February), pp. 1–21.

Fama, Eugene F., and Kenneth R. French. 1992. "The Cross-Section of Expected Returns." *Journal of Finance* 47 (June), pp. 427–465.

———. 1996. "Multifactor Explanations of Asset Pricing Anomalies." *Journal of Finance* 51 (March), pp. 55–84.

———. 1998. "Taxes, Financing Decisions, and Firm Value." *Journal of Finance* 53 (June), pp. 819–843.

———. 1999. "The Corporate Cost of Capital and the Return on Corporate Investment." *Journal of Finance* 54 (December), pp. 1939–1967.

———. 2001. "Disappearing Dividends: Changing Firm Characteristics or Lower Propensity to Pay?" *Journal of Financial Economics* 60 (April), pp. 3–43.

———. 2002a. "The Equity Premium." *Journal of Finance* 57 (April), pp. 637–659.

———. 2002b. "Testing Trade-off and Pecking Order Predictions about Dividends and Debt." *Review of Financial Studies* 15 (Spring), pp. 1–33.

Fama, Eugene F., and Michael C. Jensen. 1985. "Organizational Forms and Investment Decisions." *Journal of Financial Economics* 14, pp. 101–118.

Fama, Eugene F., and James D. MacBeth. 1973. "Risk, Return, and Equilibrium: Empirical Tests." *Journal of Political Economy* 81 (May–June), pp. 607–636.

Fama, Eugene F., and Merton H. Miller. 1972. *The Theory of Finance* (New York: Holt, Rinehart & Winston).

Fee, C. Edward, and Shawn Thomas. 2004. "Sources of Gains in Horizontal Mergers: Evidence from Customer, Supplier, and Rival Firms." *Journal of Financial Economics* 74 (December), pp. 423–460.

Fellers, Charles R. 2001a. "Making an Exit: VCs Examine Their Options." *Venture Capital Journal* (May), pp. 40–42.

———. 2001b. "With Companies Faltering, VCs Look at Redemption Exit." *Venture Capital Journal* (June), pp. 34–38.

Fenn, George W., and Nellie Liang. 2001. "Corporate Payout Policy and Managerial Stock Incentives." *Journal of Financial Economics* 60 (April), pp. 45–72.

Fernando, Chitru S., Vlaimir A. Gatchev, and Paul A. Spindt. 2005. "Wanna Dance? How Firms and Underwriters Choose Each Other." *Journal of Finance* 60, pp. 2437–2469.

Field, Laura Casares, and Jonathan Karpoff.

2002. "Takeover Defenses at IPO Firms." *Journal of Finance* 57, pp. 1857–1889.

Fineberg, Seth. 1997. "Canada's Labor Funds Adapt to Tighter Regs." *Venture Capital Journal* (March), pp. 28–30.

Finnerty, John D., and Douglas R. Emery. 2002. "Corporate Securities Innovation: An Update." *Journal of Applied Finance* 12 (Spring/Summer), pp. 21–47.

Fischer, Edwin O., Robert Heinkel, and Josef Zechner. 1989. "Dynamic Capital Structure Choice: Theory and Tests." *Journal of Finance* 44 (March), pp. 19–40.

Fisher, Irving G. 1965. *The Theory of Interest* (1930; reprint, New York: Augustus M. Kelly).

Foerster, Stephen R., and G. Andrew Karolyi. 2000. "The Long-Run Performance of Global Equity Offerings." *Journal of Financial and Quantitative Analysis* 35 (December), pp. 499–528.

Frankel, Jeffrey A. 1991. "The Japanese Cost of Finance: A Survey." *Financial Management* 20 (Spring), pp. 95–127.

Freear, John. 1994. "The Private Investor Market for Venture Capital." *The Financier* 1 (May), pp. 7–15.

Freear, John, Jeffrey E. Sohl, and William E. Wetzel, Jr. 2000. "The Informal Venture Capital Market: Milestones Passed and the Road Ahead." In *Entrepreneurship 2000,* edited by Donald L. Sexton and Raymond W. Smilor (Chicago: Upstart Publishing Company).

French, Kenneth R. 1989. "Pricing Financial Futures Contracts: An Introduction." *Journal of Applied Corporate Finance* 1 (Winter), pp. 59–66.

Fung, William K. H., and Michael F. Theobald. 1984. "Dividends and Debt under Alternative Tax Systems." *Journal of Financial and Quantitative Analysis* 19 (March), pp. 59–72.

Galai, Dan, and Ron Masulis. 1976. "The Option Pricing Model and the Risk Factor of Stock." *Journal of Financial Economics* 3 (January), pp. 53–81.

Garrett, Ian, and Richard Priestley. 2000. "Dividend Behavior and Dividend Signaling." *Journal of Financial and Quantitative Analysis* 35 (June), pp. 173–189.

Gaughan, Patrick. 1996. *Mergers, Acquisitions, and Corporate Restructurings* (New York: John Wiley & Sons).

Gaver, Jennifer J., and Kenneth M. Gaver. 1993. "Additional Evidence on the Association between the Opportunity Set and Corporate Financing, Dividend, and Compensation Policies." *Journal of Accounting and Economics* 16 (January/April/July), pp. 125–160.

Geczy, Christopher, Bernadette A. Minton, and Catherine Schrand. 1997. "Why

Firms Use Currency Derivatives." *Journal of Finance* 52 (September), pp. 1323–1354.

Gerlach, Stefan. 2002. "Hong Kong's Currency Board: Modelling the Discretion on the Strong Side." Working paper, Hong Kong Institute for Monetary Research.

Ghosh, Chimnoy, and J. Randall Woolridge. 1988. "An Analysis of Shareholder Reaction to Dividend Cuts and Omissions." *Journal of Financial Research* 11 (Winter), pp. 281–294.

Gibbons, Michael R., and Patrick Hess. 1981. "Day of the Week Effects and Asset Returns." *Journal of Business* 54 (October), pp. 579–596.

Gibson, Scott, Assem Safieddine, and Ramana Sonti. 2004. "Smart Investments by Smart Money: Evidence from Seasoned Equity Offerings." *Journal of Financial Economics* 72 (June), pp. 581–604.

Gilson, Stuart C. 1989. "Management Turnover and Financial Distress." *Journal of Financial Economics* 25 (December), pp. 241–262.

———. 1997. "Transactions Costs and Capital Structure Choice: Evidence from Financially Distressed Firms." *Journal of Finance* 52 (March), pp. 161–196.

Gilson, Stuart C., Edith S. Hotchkiss, and Richard S. Ruback. 2000. "Valuation of Bankrupt Firms." *Review of Financial Studies* 13 (Spring), 43–74.

Gilson, Stuart C., and Michael R. Vetsuypens. 1993. "CEO Compensation in Financially Distressed Firms: An Empirical Analysis." *Journal of Finance* 48 (June), pp. 425–458.

Goetzmann, William N., and Roger G. Ibbotson. 1994. "Do Winners Repeat?" *Journal of Portfolio Management* 20 (Winter), pp. 9–18.

Goetzmann, William N., Zoran Ivkovic, and K. Geert Rouwenhorst. 2001. "Day Trading International Mutual Funds: Evidence and Policy Solutions." *Journal of Financial and Quantitative Analysis* 36 (September), pp. 287–309.

Golder, Stanley C. 1997. "Structuring the Financing." In *Pratt's Guide to Venture Capital Sources,* edited by Stanley E. Pratt (New York: Securities Data Publishing).

Gompers, Paul A. 1995. "Optimal Investment, Monitoring, and the Staging of Venture Capital." *Journal of Finance* 50 (December), pp. 1461–1489.

———. 1996. "Grandstanding in the Venture Capital Industry." *Journal of Financial Economics* 42 (September), pp. 133–156.

Gompers, Paul A., and Josh Lerner. 1997. "Ownership and Control in Entrepre-

neurial Firms: An Examination of Convertible Securities in Venture Capital Investments." Working paper, Harvard Business School.

———. 1998a. "What Drives Venture Capital Fundraising?" *Brookings Papers on Economic Activity—Microeconomics,* pp. 149–192.

———. 1998b. "Venture Capital Distributions: Short-Run and Long-Run Reactions." *Journal of Finance* 53 (December), pp. 2161–2183.

———. 2000a. "Money Chasing Deals? The Impact of Fund Inflows on Private Equity Valuations." *Journal of Financial Economics* 55 (February), pp. 281–325.

———. 2000b. "The Really Long-Run Performance of Initial Public Offerings: The Pre-NASDAQ Evidence." Working paper, Harvard Business School (September).

———. 2001. "The Venture Capital Revolution." *Journal of Economic Perspectives* 15 (Spring), pp. 145–168.

———. 2003. "The Really Long-Run Performance of Initial Public Offerings: The Pre-NASDAQ Evidence." *Journal of Finance* 58 (August), pp. 1355–1392.

Gorman, Michael, and William A. Sahlman. 1989. "What Do Venture Capitalists Do?" *Journal of Business Venturing* 4, pp. 231–248.

Goyal, Vidhan K., Kenneth Lehn, and Stanko Racic. 2002. "Growth Opportunities and Corporate Debt Policy: The Case of the U.S. Defense Industry." *Journal of Financial Economics* 64 (April), pp. 35–59.

Graham, John R. 1996. "Debt and the Marginal Tax Rate." *Journal of Financial Economics* 41 (May), pp. 41–73.

———. 1999. "Herding among Investment Newsletters: Theory and Evidence." *Journal of Finance* 54 (February), pp. 237–268.

———. 2000. "How Big Are the Tax Benefits of Debt?" *Journal of Finance* 55 (October), pp. 1901–1941.

Graham, John R., and Campbell R. Harvey. 1996. "Market Timing Ability and Volatility Implied in Investment Newsletters' Asset Allocation Recommendations." *Journal of Financial Economics* 42 (November), pp. 397–421.

———. 2001. "The Theory and Practice of Corporate Finance: Evidence from the Field." *Journal of Financial Economics* 60, pp. 187–243.

———. 2002. "Expectations of Equity Risk Premia from a Corporate Finance Perspective." Working paper, Duke University.

Graham, John R., Michael L. Lemmon, and Jack G. Wolf. 2002. "Does Corporate

Diversification Destroy Value?" *Journal of Finance* 57 (April), pp. 695–720.

Graham, John R., Roni Michaely, and Michael R. Roberts. 2003. "Do Price Discreteness and Transactions Costs Affect Stock Returns? Comparing Ex-dividend Pricing before and after Decimalization." *Journal of Finance* 58 (December), pp. 2611–2635.

Greene, Jason T., and Charles W. Hodges. 2002. "The Dilution Impact of Daily Fund Flows on Open-End Mutual Funds." *Journal of Financial Economics* 65 (July), pp. 131–158.

Greene, Jason, and Scott Smart. 1999. "Liquidity Provision and Noise Trading: Evidence from the Investment Dartboard Column." *Journal of Finance* 54 (October), pp. 1885–1899.

Grenadier, Steven R. 1995. "Valuing Lease Contracts: A Real Options Approach." *Journal of Financial Economics* 38 (July), pp. 297–331.

———. 1996. "Leasing and Credit Risk." *Journal of Financial Economics* 42 (November), pp. 333–364.

Grinblatt, Mark S., Ronald W. Masulis, and Sheridan Titman. 1984. "The Valuation of Stock Splits and Stock Dividends." *Journal of Financial Economics* 13 (December), pp. 461–490.

Grinblatt, Mark, and Sheridan Titman. 1989. "Mutual Fund Performance: An Analysis of Quarterly Portfolio Holdings." *Journal of Business* 62 (July), pp. 393–416.

Grossman, Sanford J., and Robert J. Shiller. 1981. "The Determinants of the Variability of Stock Market Prices." *American Economic Review* 71 (May), pp. 222–227.

Gruber, Martin J. 1996. "Another Puzzle: The Growth in Actively Managed Mutual Funds." *Journal of Finance* 51 (July), pp. 783–810.

Grullon, Gustavo, and David L. Ikenberry. 2000. "What Do We Know about Stock Repurchases?" *Journal of Applied Corporate Finance* 13 (Spring), pp. 31–49.

Grullon, Gustavo, and Roni Michaely. 2004. "The Information Content of Share Repurchases Programs." *Journal of Finance* 59 (April), pp. 651–680.

Grullon, Gustavo, Roni Michaely, and Bhaskaran Swaminathan. 2002. "Are Dividend Changes a Sign of Firm Maturity?" *Journal of Business* 75 (July), pp. 387–424.

Grundfest, Joseph A. 1990. "Subordination of American Capital." *Journal of Financial Economics* 27 (September), pp. 89–114.

Guay, Wayne, and Jarrad Harford. 2000. "The Cash-Flow Permanence and Information Content of Dividend Increases versus Repurchases." *Journal of Financial Economics* 57 (September), pp. 385–415.

Guedes, Jose, and Tim Opler. 1996. "The Determinants of the Maturity of Corporate Debt Issues." *Journal of Finance* 51 (December), pp. 1809–1833.

Gupta, Udayan. 2001. "Truth in Numbers?" *Venture Capital Journal* (May), p. 35.

Hamada, Robert S. 1972. "The Effect of the Firm's Capital Structure on the Systematic Risk of Common Stocks." *Journal of Finance* 27 (May), pp. 435–452.

Hamada, Robert S., and Myron S. Scholes. 1985. "Taxes and Corporate Financial Management." In *Recent Advances in Corporate Finance*, edited by Edward I. Altman and Marti Subrahmanyan (Homewood, Ill.: Richard D. Irwin).

Hamao, Yasushi, Frank Packer, and Jay Ritter. 2000. "Institutional Affiliation and the Role of Venture Capital: Evidence from Initial Public Offerings in Japan." *Pacific Basin Finance Journal* 8, pp. 529–558.

Hanley, Kathleen W. 1993. "The Underpricing of Initial Public Offerings and the Partial Adjustment Phenomenon." *Journal of Financial Economics* 34 (October), pp. 231–250.

Hanley, Kathleen W., and William J. Wilhelm, Jr. 1995. "Evidence on the Strategic Allocation of Initial Public Offerings." *Journal of Financial Economics* 37 (February), pp. 239–257.

Hansen, Robert S. 1988. "The Demise of the Rights Issue." *Review of Financial Studies* 1, pp. 289–309.

———. 2001. "Do Investment Banks Compete in IPOs? The Advent of the '7% Plus Contract.'" *Journal of Financial Economics* 59 (March), p. 313.

Hansen, Robert S., and Claire Crutchley. 1990. "Corporate Earnings and Financings: An Empirical Analysis." *Journal of Business* 63 (July), pp. 347–371.

Hansen, Robert S., and Naveen Khanna. 1994. "Why Negotiation with a Single Syndicate May Be Preferred to Making Syndicates Compete: The Problem of Trapped Bidders." *Journal of Business* 67 (July), pp. 423–457.

Hansen, Robert S., and John M. Pinkerton. 1982. "Direct Equity Financing: A Resolution of a Paradox." *Journal of Finance* 37 (June), pp. 651–665.

Harford, Jarrad. 1999. "Corporate Cash Reserves and Acquisitions." *Journal of Finance* 54 (December), pp. 1969–1997.

Harris, Lawrence, and Eitan Gurel. 1984. "Price and Volume Effects Associated with Changes in the S&P 500 List: New Evidence for the Existence of Price Pressures." *Journal of Finance* 41 (September), pp. 815–830.

Harris, Milton, and Artur Raviv. 1991. "The Theory of Capital Structure." *Journal of Finance* 46 (March), pp. 297–355.

Harris, Trevor S., Nahum Melumad, and Toshi Shibano. 1996. "An Argument against Hedging by Matching the Currencies of Costs and Revenues." *Journal of Applied Corporate Finance* 9 (Fall), pp. 90–97.

Harvey, Campbell. 1993. "The Term Structure Forecasts Economic Growth." *Financial Analysts Journal* (May/June), pp. 6–8.

Hasbrouk, Joel. 1985. "The Characteristics of Takeover Targets." *Journal of Banking and Finance* 9 (September), pp. 351–362.

Haugen, Robert A., and Lemma W. Senbet. 1978. "The Insignificance of Bankruptcy Costs in the Theory of Optimal Capital Structure." *Journal of Finance* 33 (May), pp. 383–393.

Haushalter, G. David. 2000. "Financing Policy, Basis Risk, and Corporate Hedging: Evidence from Oil and Gas Producers." *Journal of Finance* 55 (February), pp. 107–152.

Healy, Paul M., and Krishna Palepu. 1988. "Earnings Information Conveyed by Dividend Initiations and Omissions." *Journal of Financial Economics* 21 (September), pp. 149–175.

Healy, Paul, Krishna Palepu, and Richard Ruback. 1992. "Does Corporate Performance Improve after Mergers?" *Journal of Financial Economics* 31 (April), pp. 135–176.

Heath, David C., and Robert A. Jarrow. 1988. "Ex-dividend Stock Price Behavior and Arbitrage Opportunities." *Journal of Business* 61 (January), pp. 95–108.

Heaton, John, and Robert Korajczyk. 2002. "Introduction to Review of Financial Studies Conference on Market Frictions and Behavioral Finance." *Review of Financial Studies* 15 (Special), pp. 353–361.

Hellmann, Thomas. 1998. "The Allocation of Control Rights in Venture Capital Contracts." *Rand Journal of Economics* (Spring), pp. 57–76.

———. 2002. "A Theory of Strategic Venture Investing." *Journal of Financial Economics* 64 (May), pp. 285–314.

Hellmann, Thomas, and Manju Puri. 2002. "Venture Capital and the Professionalization of Start-up Firms: Empirical Evidence." *Journal of Finance* 57 (February), pp. 169–197.

Hendricks, Darryll, Jayendu Patel, and Richard Zeckhauser. 1993. "Hot Hands in Mutual Funds: Short-Run Persistence of Relative Performance, 1974–1988." *Journal of Finance* 48 (March), pp. 93–130.

Hentzler, Herbert A. 1992. "The New Era of Eurocapitalism." *Harvard Business Review* (July/August), pp. 57–68.

Hertzel, Michael, Michael L. Lemmon, James S. Linck, and Richard L. Smith. 2000. "Long-Run Performance following Private Placements of Equity." *Journal of Finance* 57 (December), pp. 2595–2617.

Higgins, Robert C. 1981. "Sustainable Growth under Inflation." *Financial Management* 10, pp. 36–40.

Higgins, Robert, and Lawrence Schall. 1975. "Corporate Bankruptcy and Conglomerate Merger." *Journal of Finance* 30 (March), pp. 93–113.

Hillion, Pierre, and Theo Vermaelen. 2002. "Death Spiral Convertibles." Working paper, INSEAD (Fontainebleau, France).

Hines, James R., Jr. 1996. "Dividends and Profits: Some Unsubtle Foreign Influences." *Journal of Finance* 51 (June), pp. 661–689.

Hirshleifer, Jack. 1958. "On the Theory of Optimal Investment Decision." *Journal of Political Economy* 66 (August), pp. 329–352.

Hite, Gailen L., and James E. Owers. 1983. "Security Price Reactions around Corporate Spinoff Announcements." *Journal of Financial Economics* 12, pp. 409–436.

Ho, Thomas, and Donald F. Singer. 1984. "The Value of Corporate Debt with a Sinking Fund Provision." *Journal of Business* 57 (September), pp. 315–336.

Hoffman, Harold M., and James Blakey. 1987. "You Can Negotiate with Venture Capitalists." *Harvard Business Review* (March/April), pp. 16–24.

Horowitz, Bruce. 2001. "Disney Orders McDonald's Burger Joint for New Park." *USA Today* (January 15).

Houston, Joel, and Christopher James. 1996. "Bank Information Monopolies and the Mix of Private and Public Debt Claims." *Journal of Finance* 51 (December), pp. 1863–1889.

Hovakimian, Armen, Tim Opler, and Sheridan Titman. 2001. "The Debt-Equity Choice." *Journal of Financial and Quantitative Analysis* 36 (March), pp. 1–24.

Huang, Yen-Sheng, and Ralph Walkling. 1987. "Target Abnormal Returns Associated with Acquisition Announcements: Payment, Acquisition Form, and Managerial Resistance." *Journal of Financial Economics* 19 (December), pp. 329–349.

Hull, John C., and Alan D. White. 1987. "The Pricing of Options on Assets with Stochastic Volatilities." *Journal of Finance* 42 (June), pp. 281–300.

Ibbotson, Roger G. 1975. "Price Performance of Common Stock New Issues." *Journal of Financial Economics* 2 (September), pp. 235–272.

Ibbotson, Roger G., Jody L. Sindelar, and Jay R. Ritter. 1994. "The Market's Problems with the Pricing of Initial Public Offerings." *Journal of Applied Corporate Finance* 7 (Spring), pp. 66–74.

Igawa, Kazuhiro, and George Kanatas. 1990. "Asymmetric Information, Collateral, and Moral Hazard." *Journal of Financial and Quantitative Analysis* 25 (December), pp. 469–490.

Ikenberry, David, and Josef Lakonishok. 1993. "Corporate Governance through the Proxy Contest: Evidence and Implications." *Journal of Business* 66 (July), pp. 405–435.

Ikenberry, David, Josef Lakonishok, and Theo Vermaelen. 1995. "Market Underreaction to Open Market Stock Repurchases." *Journal of Financial Economics* 39 (October), pp. 181–208.

Ikenberry, David L., Graeme Rankine, and Earl K. Stice. 1996. "What Do Stock Splits Really Signal?" *Journal of Financial and Quantitative Analysis* 31 (September), pp. 357–375.

Ingram, Matt. 2005. "Bankruptcy and Financial Distress: A Literature Review." Working paper, University of Oklahoma (June).

Investment Dealers' Digest. 1997. "Kiss and Tell" (October 27), p. 19.

Ippolito, Richard A. 1989. "Efficiency with Costly Information: A Study of Mutual Fund Performance, 1965–1984." *Quarterly Journal of Economics* 104 (February), pp. 1–23.

Jaffe, Jeffrey F. 1974. "Special Information and Insider Trading." *Journal of Business* 47, pp. 410–428.

Jagannathan, Murali, Clifford P. Stephens, and Michael S. Weisbach. 2000. "Financial Flexibility and the Choice between Dividends and Stock Repurchases." *Journal of Financial Economics* 57 (September), pp. 355–384.

Jakob, Keith, and Tongshu Ma. 2004. "Tick Size, NYSE Rule 118, and Ex-dividend Day Stock Price Behavior." *Journal of Financial Economics* 72 (June), pp. 605–625.

James, Christopher. 1987. "Some Evidence on the Uniqueness of Bank Loans." *Journal of Financial Economics* 19 (December), pp. 217–235.

Jarrell, Gregg, James Brickley, and Jeffry Netter. 1988. "The Market for Corporate Control: The Empirical Evidence since 1980." *Journal of Economic Perspectives* 2 (Winter), pp. 49–68.

Jarrell, Gregg A., and Annette Poulsen. 1989a. "Stock Trading before the Announcement of Tender Offers: Insider Trading or Market Anticipation?" *Journal of Law, Economics, and Organization* 5, pp. 225–248.

———. 1989b. "Returns to Acquiring Firms in Tender Offers: Evidence from Three Decades." *Financial Management* 18 (Autumn), pp. 12–19.

Jayaraman, Narasimhan, Kuldeep Shastri, and Kishore Tandon. 1993. "The Impact of International Cross Listings on Risk and Returns: The Evidence of American Depository Receipts." *Journal of Banking and Finance* 17, pp. 91–103.

Jegadeesh, Narasimhan. 1990. "Evidence of the Predictable Behavior of Security Returns." *Journal of Finance* 45 (July), pp. 881–898.

———. 2000. "Long-Term Performance of Seasoned Equity Offerings: Benchmark Errors and Biases in Expectations." *Financial Management* 29 (Autumn), pp. 5–30.

Jegadeesh, Narasimhan, and Sheridan Titman. 1993. "Returns to Buying Winners and Selling Losers: Implications for Stock Market Efficiency." *Journal of Finance* 48 (March), pp. 65–91.

Jeng, L. A., and P. C. Wells. 2000. "The Determinants of Venture Capital Funding: Evidence across Countries." *Journal of Corporate Finance* 6 (September), pp. 241–289.

Jennings, Robert, and Michael Mazzeo. 1993. "Competing Bids, Target Management Resistance, and the Structure of Takeover Bids." *Review of Financial Studies* 6 (Winter), pp. 883–909.

Jensen, Michael C. 1968. "The Performance of Mutual Funds in the Period 1945–1964." *Journal of Finance* 23 (May), pp. 389–416.

———. 1986. "Agency Costs of Free Cash Flow, Corporate Finance and Takeovers." *American Economic Review* 76 (May), pp. 323–329.

———. 1993. "Presidential Address: The Modern Industrial Revolution, Exit, and the Failure of Internal Control Systems." *Journal of Finance* 48 (July), pp. 831–880.

———. 2005. "Agency Costs of Overvalued Equity." *Financial Management* 34 (Spring), pp. 5–19.

Jensen, Michael C., and George A. Benington. 1970. "Random Walks and Technical Theories: Some Additional Evidence." *Journal of Finance* 25 (May), pp. 156–169.

Jensen, Michael C., and William H. Meckling. 1976. "Theory of the Firm: Managerial Behavior, Agency Costs, and

Ownership Structure." *Journal of Financial Economics* 3 (October), pp. 305–360.

Jensen, Michael, and Richard Ruback. 1983. "The Market for Corporate Control: The Scientific Evidence." *Journal of Financial Economics* 11 (April), pp. 5–50.

Jog, Vijay M., and Allan L. Riding. 1986. "Price Effects of Dual-Class Shares." *Financial Analysts Journal* 42 (January/February), pp. 58–67.

John, Kose, and Eli Ofek. 1995. "Asset Sales and Increase in Focus." *Journal of Financial Economics* 37 (January), pp. 105–126.

John, Kose, and Larry H. P. Lang. 1991. "Insider Trading around Dividend Announcements: Theory and Evidence." *Journal of Finance* 40 (September), pp. 1361–1389.

John, Kose, and Joseph Williams. 1985. "Dividends, Dilution and Taxes: A Signalling Equilibrium." *Journal of Finance* 40 (September), pp. 1053–1070.

Jones, Jonathan, William W. Lang, and Peter Nigro. 2000. "Recent Trends in Bank Loan Syndications: Evidence for 1995 to 1999." Working paper no. 2000-10, Office of the Comptroller of the Currency.

Jones, Steven L. 1993. "Another Look at Time-Varying Risk and Return in a Long-Horizon Contrarian Strategy." *Journal of Financial Economics* 33, pp. 119–144.

Jones, Steven L., William L. Megginson, Robert C. Nash, and Jeffry M. Netter. 1999. "Share Issue Privatizations as Financial Means to Political and Economic Ends." *Journal of Financial Economics* 53 (August), pp. 217–253.

Julio, Brandon, and David L. Ikenberry. 2004. "Reappearing Dividends." *Journal of Applied Corporate Finance* 16 (Fall), pp. 89–100.

Kaiser, Kevin M. J. 1996. "European Bankruptcy Laws: Implications for Corporations Facing Financial Distress." *Financial Management* 25 (Autumn), pp. 67–85.

Kalay, Avner. 1982. "Stockholder-Bondholder Conflict and Dividend Constraints." *Journal of Financial Economics* 10 (July), pp. 211–233.

Kalay, Avner, and Marti G. Subrahmanyan. 1984. "The Ex-dividend Day Behavior of Option Prices." *Journal of Business* 57 (January), pp. 113–128.

Kaplan, Steven N., and Bernadette A. Minton. 1994. "Appointments of Outsiders to Japanese Boards: Determinants and Implications for Managers." *Journal of Financial Economics* 36 (October), pp. 225–258.

Kaplan, Steven, and Per Strömberg. 2000. "How Do Venture Capitalists Choose Investments?" Working paper, University of Chicago.

———. 2001. "Financial Contracting Theory Meets the Real World: An Empirical Analysis of Venture Capital Contracts." Working paper, University of Chicago.

Kaplan, Steven, and Michael Weisbach. 1992. "The Success of Acquisitions: Evidence from Divestitures." *Journal of Finance* 47 (March), pp. 107–138.

Karolyi, G. Andrew. 1998. "Sourcing Equity Internationally with Depositary Receipt Offerings: Two Exceptions That Prove the Rule." *Journal of Applied Corporate Finance* 10 (Winter), pp. 90–101.

Katz, David J. 1990. "Solving the Dilemma of Pricing Secondaries." *Venture Capital Journal* (October), pp. 21–33.

Keim, Donald B. 1983. "Size-Related Anomalies and Stock Return Seasonality: Further Empirical Evidence." *Journal of Financial Economics* 12 (June), pp. 13–32.

Kendall, Maurice G. 1953. "The Analysis of Economic Time Series." *Journal of the Royal Statistical Society,* Series A, 96, pp. 11–25.

Kensinger, John, and John D. Martin. 1988. "Project Finance: Raising Money the Old-Fashioned Way." *Journal of Applied Corporate Finance* 1 (Spring), pp. 69–81.

Kester, W. Carl. 1992. "Governance, Contracting, and Investment Horizons: A Look at Japan and Germany." *Journal of Applied Corporate Finance* 5 (Summer), pp. 83–98.

Khorana, Ajay, Sunil Wahal, and Marc Zenner. 2002. "Agency Conflicts in Closed-End Funds: The Case of Rights Offerings." *Journal of Financial and Quantitative Analysis* 37 (June), pp. 177–200.

Kim, Yong Cheol, and René M. Stulz. 1988. "The Eurobond Market and Corporate Financial Policy: A Test of the Clientele Hypothesis." *Journal of Financial Economics* 22, pp. 189–206.

Kini, Omesh, William Kracaw, and Shehzad Mian. 2004. "The Nature of Discipline by Corporate Takeovers." *Journal of Finance* 59 (August), pp. 1511–1552.

Kinn, Bruce A., and Arnold M. Zaff. 1997. "The Benefits of a Revitalized SBIC Program." In *Pratt's Guide to Venture Capital Sources,* edited by Stanley E. Pratt (New York: Securities Data Publishing), pp. 105–107.

Kleidon, Allan W. 1986. "Variance Bounds Tests and Stock Price Valuation Models." *Journal of Political Economy* 94 (October), pp. 953–1001.

Kleimeier, Stefanie, and William L. Megginson. 2000. "Are Project Finance Loans Different from Other Syndicated Credits?" *Journal of Applied Corporate Finance* 12 (Winter), pp. 75–87.

Kliger, Doron, and Oded Sarig. 2000. "The Information Value of Bond Ratings." *Journal of Finance* 55 (December), pp. 2879–2902.

Koch, Adam S., and Amy X. Sun. 2004. "Dividend Changes and the Persistence of Past Earnings Changes." *Journal of Finance* 59 (October), pp. 2093–2116.

Kogut, Bruce, and Nalin Kulatilaka. 1994. "Operating Flexibility, Global Manufacturing and the Option Value of a Multinational Network." *Management Science* 40 (January), pp. 123–139.

Korajczyk, Robert A., Deborah J. Lucas, and Robert L. McDonald. 1991. "The Effect of Information Releases on the Pricing and Timing of Equity Issues." *Review of Financial Studies* 4, pp. 685–708.

Kothari, S. P., and Jay Shanken. 1992. "Stock Return Variation and Expected Dividends: A Time Series Analysis." *Journal of Financial Economics* 31 (April), pp. 177–210.

———. 1993. "Fundamentals Largely Explain Stock Price Volatility." *Journal of Applied Corporate Finance* 6 (Summer), pp. 81–87.

KPMG Peat Marwick. 1998. *Going Public: What the CEO Needs to Know* (KPMG International).

Krigman, Laurie, Wayne H. Shaw, and Kent L. Womack. 1999. "The Persistence of IPO Mispricing and the Predictive Power of Flipping." *Journal of Finance* 54 (June), pp. 1015–1044.

Krishnan, V. Sivarama, and R. Charles Moyer. 1994. "Bankruptcy Costs and the Financial Leasing Decision." *Financial Management* 23 (Summer), pp. 31–42.

Krishnaswami, Sudha, Paul A. Spindt, and Venkat Subramaniam. 1999. "Information Asymmetry, Monitoring, and the Placement Structure of Corporate Debt." *Journal of Financial Economics* 51, pp. 407–434.

Kulatilaka, Nalin. 1993. "The Value of Flexibility: The Case of a Dual-Use Industrial Steam Boiler." *Financial Management* 22 (Autumn), pp. 271–280.

Lakonishok, Josef, and Seymour Smidt. 1988. "Are Seasonal Anomalies Real? A Ninety-Year Perspective." *Review of Financial Studies* 1 (Winter), pp. 403–425.

Lakonishok, Josef, and Theo Vermaelen. 1983. "Tax Reform and Ex-dividend Day Behavior." *Journal of Finance* 38 (September), pp. 1157–1175.

———. 1986. "Tax-Induced Trading around Ex-dividend Days." *Journal of Financial Economics* 16 (July), pp. 287–319.

———. 1990. "Anomalous Price Behavior around Repurchase Tender Offers." *Journal of Finance* 45 (June), pp. 455–477.

Lamont, Owen A., and Christopher Polk. 2001. "The Diversification Discount: Cash Flows versus Returns." *Journal of Finance* 56 (October), pp. 1693–1721.

Lamont, Owen A., and Christopher Polk. 2002. "Does Diversification Destroy Value? Evidence from the Industry Shocks." *Journal of Financial Economics* 63 (January), pp. 51–77.

Lamont, Owen, and Richard H. Thaler. 2002. "Can the Market Add and Subtract? Mispricing in Tech Stock Carve-Outs." Working paper, University of Chicago.

Lang, Larry, Eli Ofek, and René M. Stulz. 1996. "Leverage, Investment, and Firm Growth." *Journal of Financial Economics* 40 (January), pp. 3–29.

Lang, Larry H. P., and René M. Stulz. 1992. "Contagion and Competitive Intra-industry Effects of Bankruptcy Announcements." *Journal of Financial Economics* 32 (August), pp. 45–60.

———. 1994. "Tobin's q, Corporate Diversification, and Firm Performance." *Journal of Political Economy* 102 (December), pp. 1248–1280.

Lang, Larry, René Stulz, and Ralph Walkling. 1989. "Managerial Performance, Tobin's q and the Gains from Successful Tender Offers." *Journal of Financial Economics* 24 (September), pp. 137–154.

———. 1991. "A Test of the Free Cash Flow Hypothesis: The Case of Bidder Returns." *Journal of Financial Economics* 29 (October), pp. 315–335.

La Porta, Rafael, Florencio López-de-Silanes, and Andrei Shleifer. 1999. "Corporate Ownership around the World." *Journal of Finance* 54 (April), pp. 471–517.

La Porta, Rafael, Florencio López-de-Silanes, and Andrei Shleifer. 2000. "Government Ownership of Banks." NBER working paper 7620, National Bureau of Economic Research (Cambridge, Mass.).

La Porta, Rafael, Florencio López-de-Silanes, Andrei Shleifer, and Robert W. Vishny. 1997. "Legal Determinants of External Finance." *Journal of Finance* 52 (July), pp. 1131–1150.

———. 1998. "Law and Finance." *Journal of Political Economy* 106, pp. 1113–1150.

———. 1999. "The Quality of Government." *Journal of Law, Economics, and Organization* 15, pp. 222–279.

———. 2000. "Agency Problems and Dividend Policies around the World." *Journal of Finance* 55 (February), pp. 1–33.

———. 2002. "Investor Protection and Corporate Valuation." *Journal of Finance* 57 (June), pp. 1147–1170.

Lasfer, M. Ameziane. 1997. "On the Motivation for Paying Scrip Dividends." *Financial Management* 26 (Spring), pp. 62–80.

Lasfer, M. Ameziane, and Mario Levis. 1998. "The Determinants of the Leasing Decision of Small and Large Companies." *European Financial Management* (June), pp. 159–184.

Lavelle, Louis. 2001. "Special Report: Executive Pay." *Business Week* (April 16), pp. 75–80.

———. 2002. "Executive Pay: Special Report." *Business Week* (April 15), pp. 80–100.

Lease, Ronald C., John J. McConnell, and Wayne H. Mikkelson. 1983. "The Market Value of Control in Publicly-Traded Corporations." *Journal of Financial Economics* 11 (April), pp. 439–471.

Lee, Bong-Soo. 1995. "The Response of Stock Prices to Permanent and Temporary Shocks to Dividends." *Journal of Financial and Quantitative Analysis* 30 (March), pp. 1–22.

———. 1996. "Time-Series Implications of Aggregate Dividend Behavior." *Review of Financial Studies* 9 (Summer), pp. 589–618.

Lee, Chun I., Kimberly C. Gleason, and Ike Mathur. 2000. "Efficiency Tests in the French Derivatives Market." *Journal of Banking and Finance* 24, pp. 787–807.

Lee, Dwight R., and James A. Verbrugge. 1996. "The Efficient Market Thrives on Criticism." *Journal of Applied Corporate Finance* 9 (Spring), pp. 35–40.

Lee, Inmoo, Scott Lochhead, Jay Ritter, and Quanshui Zhao. 1996. "The Costs of Raising Capital." *Journal of Financial Research* 19 (Spring), pp. 59–74.

Lee, Susan. 2002. "The Ugly Option." *Wall Street Journal* (April 10).

Lee, Yi-Tsung, Yu-Jane Liu, Richard Roll, and Avanidhar Subrahmanyam. 2004. "Taxes and Dividend Clientele: Evidence from Trading and Ownership Structure." Working paper, University of California at Los Angeles (February).

Lehn, Kenneth, and Annette Poulsen. 1989. "Free Cash Flow and Shareholder Gains in Going Private Transactions." *Journal of Finance* 44 (July), pp. 771–787.

Leland, Hayne E., and David H. Pyle. 1977. "Informational Asymmetries, Financial Structure, and Financial Intermediation." *Journal of Finance* 32, pp. 371–387.

Lerner, Josh. 1994. "Venture Capitalists and the Decision to Go Public." *Journal of Financial Economics* 35 (June), pp. 293–316.

———. 1995. "Venture Capitalists and the Oversight of Private Firms." *Journal of Finance* 50 (March), pp. 301–318.

———. 1998. "Angel Financing and Public Policy: An Overview." *Journal of Banking and Finance* 22 (August), pp. 773–783.

———. 1999. "The Government as Venture Capitalist: The Long-Run Effects of the SBIR Program." *Journal of Business* 72 (July), pp. 285–318.

———. 2000. *Venture Capital and Private Equity: A Casebook* (New York: John Wiley & Sons).

LeRoy, Christian V., and Stephen F. LeRoy. 1991. "Econometric Aspects of the Variance-Bounds Tests: A Survey." *Review of Financial Studies* 4, pp. 753–791.

Levine, Ross. 1997. "Financial Development and Economic Growth: Views and Agenda." *Journal of Economic Literature* 35, pp. 688–726.

Levine, Ross, and Sara Zervos. 1998. "Stock Markets, Banks, and Economic Growth." *American Economic Review* 88, pp. 537–558.

Levy, Haim. 1983. "Economic Evaluation of Voting Power of Common Stock." *Journal of Finance* 38 (March), pp. 79–93.

Levy, Haim, and Marshall Sarnat. 1970. "Diversification, Portfolio Analysis, and the Uneasy Case for Conglomerate Mergers." *Journal of Finance* 25 (September), pp. 795–802.

Lewellen, Jonathan. 2002. "Momentum and Autocorrelation in Stock Returns." *Review of Financial Studies* 15 (Special), pp. 533–563.

Lewellen, Wilbur. 1971. "A Pure Financial Rationale for the Conglomerate Merger." *Journal of Finance* 26 (May), pp. 531–537.

Lewellen, Wilbur, Claudio Loderer, and Ahron Rosenfeld. 1985. "Merger Decisions and Executive Stock Ownership in Acquiring Firms." *Journal of Accounting and Economics* 7 (April), pp. 209–231.

Lie, Erik. 2000. "Excess Funds and Agency Problems: An Empirical Study of Incremental Cash Distributions." *Review of Financial Studies* 13 (Spring), pp. 219–248.

Linn, Scott C., and J. Michael Pinegar. 1988. "The Effect of Issuing Preferred Stock on Common and Preferred Stockholder Wealth." *Journal of Financial Economics* 22 (October), pp. 155–184.

Lins, Karl, and Henri Servaes. 1999. "International Evidence on the Value of Corporate Diversification." *Journal of Finance* 54 (December), pp. 2215–2239.

Lins, Karl V., Deon Strickland, and Marc Zenner. 2005. "Do Non-U.S. Firms Issue Equity on U.S. Exchanges to Relax Capital Constraints?" *Journal of Financial and Quantitative Analysis* 40, pp. 109–133.

Lintner, John. 1956. "Distribution of Incomes of Corporations among Dividends, Retained Earnings, and Taxes." *American Economic Review* 46 (May), pp. 97–113.

Lipson, Marc L., Carlos P. Macquieira, and William L. Megginson. 1998. "Dividend Initiations and Earnings Surprises." *Financial Management* 27 (Autumn), pp. 36–45.

Livingston, Miles, and Robert E. Miller. 2000. "Investment Banking Reputation and the Underwriting of Nonconvertible Debt." *Financial Management* 29 (Summer), pp. 21–34.

Ljungqvist, Alexander, Tim Jenkinson, and William J. Wilhelm, Jr. 2002. "Global Integration in Primary Equity Markets: The Role of U.S. Banks and U.S. Investors." *Review of Financial Studies* 16 (Spring), pp. 630–699.

Ljungqvist, Alexander P., and William J. Wilhelm, Jr. 2001. "IPO Pricing in the Dot-Com Bubble: Complacency or Incentives?" Working paper, New York University.

———. 2002. "IPO Allocations: Discriminatory or Discretionary?" *Journal of Financial Economics* 65 (August), p. 167.

Lo, Andrew W., and A. Craig MacKinlay. 1988. "Stock Market Prices Do Not Follow Random Walks: Evidence from a Simple Specification Test." *Review of Financial Studies* 1 (Spring), pp. 41–66.

———. 1990. "When Are Contrarian Profits due to Stock Market Overreaction?" *Review of Financial Studies* 3, pp. 175–205.

Lo, Andrew W., Harry Mamaysky, and Jiang Wang. 2000. "Foundations of Technical Analysis: Computational Algorithms, Statistical Inference, and Empirical Implementation." *Journal of Finance* 55 (August), pp. 1705–1765.

Loderer, Claudio F., Dennis P. Sheehan, and Gregory B. Kadlec. 1991. "The Pricing of Equity Offerings." *Journal of Financial Economics* 29, pp. 35–57.

Logue, Dennis E., and Seha M. Tiniç. 1999. "Optimal Choice of Contracting Methods: Negotiated versus Competitive Underwriting Revisited." *Journal of Financial Economics* 51 (March), pp. 451–471.

Long, Michael, and Ileen Malitz. 1985. "The Investment-Financing Nexus: Some Empirical Evidence." *Midland Corporate Finance Journal* 3 (Spring), pp. 53–59.

Loughran, Tim, and Jay R. Ritter. 1995. "The New Issues Puzzle." *Journal of Finance* 50 (March), pp. 23–51.

———. 2000. "Uniformly Least Powerful Tests of Market Efficiency." *Journal of Financial Economics* 55, pp. 361–389.

———. 2004. "Why Has IPO Underpricing Changed over Time?" *Financial Management* 33 (Autumn), pp. 5–37.

Loughran, Tim, Jay R. Ritter, and Kristian Rydqvist. 1994. "Initial Public Offerings: International Insights." *Pacific Basin Finance Journal* 2, pp. 165–199.

Loughran, Tim, and Anand Vijh. 1997. "Do Long-Term Shareholders Benefit from Corporate Acquisitions?" *Journal of Finance* 52 (December), pp. 1765–1790.

Lowry, Michelle. 2003. "Why Does IPO Volume Fluctuate So Much?" *Journal of Financial Economics* 67 (January), pp. 3–40.

Lowry, Michelle, and G. William Schwert. 2002. "IPO Market Cycles: Bubbles or Sequential Learning?" *Journal of Finance* 57 (June), pp. 1171–1200.

Lubben, Stephen. 2000. "The Direct Costs of Corporate Reorganization: An Empirical Examination of Professional Fees in Large Chapter 11 Cases." *American Bankruptcy Law Journal* 74 (Fall), pp. 509–552.

Lummer, Scott C., and John J. McConnell. 1989. "Further Evidence on the Bank Lending Process and the Capital Market Responses to Bank Loan Agreements." *Journal of Financial Economics* 25 (November), pp. 99–122.

Lynch, Anthony W., and Richard R. Mendenhall. 1997. "New Evidence on Stock Price Effects Associated with Changes in the S&P 500 Index." *Journal of Business* 70 (July), pp. 351–383.

MacBeth, James D., and Larry J. Merville. 1979. "An Empirical Examination of the Black-Scholes Call Option Pricing Model." *Journal of Finance* 34 (December), pp. 1173–1186.

MacKie-Mason, Jeffrey K. 1990. "Do Taxes Affect Corporate Financing Decisions?" *Journal of Finance* 45 (December), pp. 1471–1493.

Macquieira, Carlos, William Megginson, and Lance Nail. 1998. "Wealth Creation versus Wealth Redistributions in Pure Stock-for-Stock Mergers." *Journal of Financial Economics* 48 (April), pp. 3–25.

Maksimovic, Vojislav, and Gordon Phillips. 1998. "Asset Efficiency and Reallocation Decisions of Bankrupt Firms." *Journal of Finance* 53 (October), pp. 1495–1532.

Maksimovic, Vojislav, and Sheridan Titman. 1991. "Financial Policy and Reputation for Product Quality." *Review of Financial Studies* 4, pp. 175–200.

Malkiel, Burton G. 1995. "Returns from Investing in Equity Mutual Funds 1971 to 1991." *Journal of Finance* 50 (June), pp. 549–572.

Malkiel, Burton G., and William J. Baumol. 2002. "Stock Options Keep the Economy Afloat." *Wall Street Journal* (April 4), p. A18.

Manne, H. G. 1965. "Mergers and the Market for Corporate Control." *Journal of Political Economy* 73, pp. 110–120.

Markowitz, Harry. 1952. "Portfolio Selection." *Journal of Finance* 7 (March), pp. 77–91.

Marsh, Paul. 1982. "The Choice between Equity and Debt: An Empirical Study." *Journal of Finance* 37 (March), pp. 121–144.

Masulis, Ronald W. 1980. "The Effect of Capital Structure Change on Security Prices: A Study of Exchange Offers." *Journal of Financial Economics* 8 (June), pp. 139–177.

Maxwell, William F., and Clifford P. Stephens. 2003. "The Wealth Effects of Repurchases on Bondholders." *Journal of Finance* 58 (April), pp. 895–919.

Mayer, Colin. 1990. "Financial Systems, Corporate Finance, and Economic Development." In *Asymmetric Information, Corporate Finance and Investment,* edited by R. Glenn Hubbard (Chicago: University of Chicago Press).

Mayers, David. 1972. "Non-Marketable Assets and the Determination of Capital Market Equilibrium under Uncertainty." In *Studies in the Theory of Capital Markets,* edited by Michael Jensen (New York: Praeger).

Mayers, David, and Clifford Smith. 1982. "On the Corporate Demand for Insurance." *Journal of Business* 55 (April), pp. 281–296.

McConnell, John J., and Chris J. Muscarella. 1985. "Corporate Capital Expenditure Decisions and the Market Value of the Firm." *Journal of Financial Economics* 14 (September), pp. 399–422.

McConnell, John J., and Eduardo S. Schwartz. 1992. "The Origins of LYONs: A Case Study in Financial Innovation." *Journal of Applied Corporate Finance* 4 (Winter), pp. 82–89.

McLaughlin, Robyn, and Robert A. Taggart, Jr. 1992. "The Opportunity Cost of Excess Capacity." *Financial Management* 21 (Summer), pp. 12–23.

McQueen, Grant. 1992. "Long-Horizon Mean-Reverting Stock Prices Revisited."

Journal of Financial and Quantitative Analysis 27 (March), pp. 1–18.

Megginson, William L. 1990. "Restricted Voting Stock, Acquisition Premiums and the Market Value of Corporate Control." *Financial Review* 25 (May), pp. 175–198.

Megginson, William L., Angela Morgan, and Lance Nail. 2004. "The Determinants of Positive Long-Term Performance in Strategic Mergers: Corporate Focus and Cash." *Journal of Banking and Finance* 28 (March), pp. 523–552.

Megginson, William L., Robert C. Nash, Jeffry Netter, and Adam Schwartz. 2000. "The Long-Term Return to Investors in Share Issue Privatizations." *Financial Management* 29 (Spring), pp. 67–77.

Megginson, William L., Robert C. Nash, and Matthias van Randenborgh. 1994. "The Financial and Operating Performance of Newly-Privatized Firms: An International Empirical Analysis." *Journal of Finance* 49 (June), pp. 403–452.

———. 1996. "The Record on Privatization." *Journal of Applied Corporate Finance* 9 (Spring), pp. 403–452.

Megginson, William L., and Jeffry M. Netter. 2001. "From State to Market: A Survey of Empirical Studies on Privatization." *Journal of Economic Literature* 39 (June), pp. 321–389.

Megginson, William L., Annette B. Poulsen, and Joseph F. Sinkey, Jr. 1995. "Syndicated Loan Announcements and the Market Value of the Banking Firm." *Journal of Money, Credit, and Banking* 27 (May), pp. 457–475.

Megginson, William L., and Kathleen A. Weiss. 1991. "Venture Capital Certification in Initial Public Offerings." *Journal of Finance* 46 (July), pp. 879–903.

Mello, Antonio S., and John E. Parsons. 1999. "Strategic Hedging." *Journal of Applied Corporate Finance* 12 (Fall), pp. 43–54.

Menyah, Kojo, Krishna Paudyal, and Charles G. Inyangete. 1995. "Subscriber Return, Underpricing, and Long-Term Performance of U.K. Privatization Initial Public Offers." *Journal of Economics and Business* 47, pp. 473–495.

Merton, Robert C. 1973a. "An Intertemporal Capital Asset Pricing Model." *Econometrica* 41 (September), pp. 867–887.

———. 1973b. "Theory of Rational Option Pricing." *Bell Journal of Economics* 4 (Spring), pp. 141–183.

Metrick, Andrew. 1999. "Performance Evaluation with Transactions Data: The Stock Selection of Investment Newsletters." *Journal of Finance* 54 (October), pp. 1743–1775.

Meulbroek, Lisa K. 1992. "An Empirical Analysis of Illegal Insider Trading." *Journal of Finance* 47 (December), pp. 1661–1699.

Mian, Shehzad. 2001. "On the Choice and Replacement of Chief Financial Officers." *Journal of Financial Economics* 60, pp. 143–175.

Michaely, Roni, and Franklin Allen. 2002. "Payout Policy." In *Handbook of Economics,* edited by George Constantinides et al. (Amsterdam: North-Holland, forthcoming).

Michaely, Roni, and Wayne H. Shaw. 1995. "The Choice of Going Public: Spin-Offs and Carve-Outs." *Financial Management* 24 (Autumn), pp. 5–21.

Michaely, Roni, Richard H. Thaler, and Kent L. Womack. 1995. "Price Reactions to Dividend Initiations and Omissions: Overreaction or Drift?" *Journal of Finance* 50 (June), pp. 573–608.

Mikkelson, Wayne H., and M. Megan Partch. 1986. "Valuation Effects of Security Offerings and the Issuance Process." *Journal of Financial Economics* 15 (January/February), pp. 31–60.

Miles, James A., and James D. Rosenfeld. 1983. "The Effect of Voluntary Spin-Off Announcements on Shareholder Wealth." *Journal of Finance* (December), pp. 1597–1606.

Miller, Darius P. 1999. "The Market Reaction to International Cross-Listings: Evidence from Depositary Receipts." *Journal of Financial Economics* 51 (January), pp. 103–123.

Miller, Merton H. 1977. "Debt and Taxes." *Journal of Finance* 32 (May), pp. 261–276.

———. 1999. "The History of Finance: An Eyewitness Account." *Journal of Portfolio Management* (Summer), pp. 95–101. Reprint of a speech made to the German Finance Association on September 25, 1998.

Miller, Merton H., and Franco Modigliani. 1961. "Dividend Policy, Growth, and the Valuation of Shares." *Journal of Business* 34 (October), pp. 411–433.

Miller, Merton H., and Kevin Rock. 1985. "Dividend Policy under Asymmetric Information." *Journal of Finance* 40 (September), pp. 1021–1051.

Mitchell, Karlyn. 1991. "The Call, Sinking Fund, and Term to Maturity Features of Corporate Bonds: An Empirical Investigation." *Journal of Financial and Quantitative Analysis* 26 (June), pp. 201–222.

Mitchell, Mark, and Harold Mulherin. 1996. "The Impact of Industry Shocks on Takeover and Restructuring Activity." *Journal of Financial Economics* 41 (June), p. 93.

Mitchell, Mark, and Erik Stafford. 2000. "Managerial Decisions and Long-Term Stock Price Performance." *Journal of Business* 73 (July), pp. 287–320.

Modigliani, Franco, and Merton Miller. 1958. "The Cost of Capital, Corporation Finance, and the Theory of Investment." *American Economic Review* 48 (June), pp. 261–297.

———. 1963. "Corporate Income Taxes and the Cost of Capital." *American Economic Review* 53 (June), pp. 433–443.

Moehrle, Stephen, and Jennifer Reynolds-Moehrle. 2001. "Say Good-Bye to Pooling and Goodwill Amortization." *Journal of Accountancy* 192 (September), pp. 11–20.

Moel, Alberto, and Peter Tufano. 2002. "When Are Real Options Exercised? An Empirical Study of Mine Closings." *Review of Financial Studies* 15 (Spring), pp. 35–64.

Moeller, Sara B., Frederik P. Schlingemann, and René M. Stulz. 2004. "Firm Size and the Gains from Acquisitions." *Journal of Financial Economics* 73 (August), pp. 201–228.

———. 2005. "Wealth Destruction on a Massive Scale? A Study of Acquiring-Firm Returns in the Recent Merger Wave." *Journal of Finance* 60 (April), pp. 757–782.

Moore, James, Jay Culver, and Bonnie Masterman. 2000. "Risk Management for Middle Market Companies." *Journal of Applied Corporate Finance* 12 (Winter), pp. 112–119.

Morck, Randall, Andrei Shleifer, and Robert Vishny. 1988. "Management Ownership and Market Valuation: An Empirical Analysis." *Journal of Financial Economics* 20 (January), pp. 293–315.

———. 1990. "Do Managerial Objectives Drive Bad Acquisitions?" *Journal of Finance* 45 (March), pp. 31–48.

Morris, Jane Koloski. 1988. "The Pricing of a Venture Capital Investment." In *Pratt's Guide to Venture Capital Sources,* edited by Stanley E. Pratt (New York: Securities Data Publishing), pp. 55–61.

Moskowitz, Tobias J., and Mark Grinblatt. 1999. "Do Industries Explain Momentum?" *Journal of Finance* 54 (August), pp. 1249–1290.

Mossin, Jan. 1966. "Equilibrium in a Capital Asset Market." *Econometrica* 24 (October), pp. 768–783.

Mueller, Dennis. 1969. "A Theory of Conglomerate Mergers." *Quarterly Journal of Economics* 83, pp. 643–659.

Mulherin, J. Harold, and Annette Poulsen. 1998. "Proxy Contests and Corporate Change: Implications for Shareholder Wealth." *Journal of Financial Economics* 47 (March), pp. 279–313.

Murphy, Kevin. 1985. "Corporate Performance and Managerial Remuneration: An Empirical Analysis." *Journal of Accounting and Economics* 7 (April), pp. 11–42.

Muscarella, Chris J., and Michael R. Vetsuypens. 1989. "The Underpricing of 'Second' Initial Public Offerings." *Journal of Financial Research* (Fall), pp. 183–192.

———. 1990. "Efficiency and Organizational Structure: A Study of Reverse LBOs." *Journal of Finance* 45 (December), pp. 1389–1413.

———. 1996. "Stock Splits: Signaling or Liquidity? The Case of ADR 'Solo-Splits.'" *Journal of Financial Economics* 42 (September), pp. 3–26.

Myers, Stewart C. 1977. "The Determinants of Corporate Borrowing." *Journal of Financial Economics* 5 (November), pp. 147–176.

———. 1984. "The Capital Structure Puzzle." *Journal of Finance* 39 (July), pp. 575–592.

———. 1993. "Still Searching for an Optimal Capital Structure." *Journal of Applied Corporate Finance* 6 (Spring), pp. 4–14.

Myers, Stewart C., and Nicholas S. Majluf. 1984. "Corporate Financing and Investment Decisions When Firms Have Information the Investors Do Not Have." *Journal of Financial Economics* 13, pp. 187–221.

Nance, Deana R., Clifford W. Smith, Jr., and Charles W. Smithson. 1993. "On the Determinants of Corporate Hedging." *Journal of Finance* 48 (March), pp. 267–284.

Nanda, Vikram. 1991. "On the Good News in Equity Carve-Outs." *Journal of Finance* 46 (December), pp. 1717–1737.

Narayanan, Rajesh P., Kasturi P. Rangan, and Nanda K. Rangan. 2004. "The Role of Syndicate Structure in Bank Underwriting." *Journal of Financial Economics* 72 (June), pp. 555–580.

Nathan, Kevin, and Terrence O'Keefe. 1989. "The Rise in Takeover Premiums: An Exploratory Study." *Journal of Financial Economics* 23 (June), pp. 101–119.

Nenova, Tatiana. 2003. "The Value of Corporate Voting Rights and Control: A Cross-Country Analysis." *Journal of Financial Economics* 68 (June), pp. 325–351.

Ng, Chee K., Janet Kiholm Smith, and Richard L. Smith. 1999. "Evidence on the Determinants of Credit Terms Used in Interfirm Trade." *Journal of Finance* 54 (June), pp. 1109–1129.

Nichols, N. A. 1994. "Scientific Management at Merck: An Interview with Judy Lewent." *Harvard Business Review* 72 (January/February), p. 91.

Noe, Thomas H., and Michael J. Rebello. 1996. "Asymmetric Information, Managerial Opportunism, Financing, and Payout Policies." *Journal of Finance* 51 (June), pp. 637–660.

Ofek, Eli, and Matthew Richardson. 2003. "DotCom Mania: The Rise and Fall of Internet Stock Prices." *Journal of Finance* 58 (June), pp. 1113–1138.

Ojah, Kalu, and David Karemera. 1999. "Random Walks and Market Efficiency Tests of Latin American Emerging Equity Markets: A Revisit." *Financial Review* 34 (May), pp. 57–72.

Ongena, Steven, and David C. Smith. 2001. "The Duration of Bank Relationships." *Journal of Financial Economics* 21, pp. 449–475.

Opler, Tim C., and Sheridan Titman. 1994. "Financial Distress and Corporate Performance." *Journal of Finance* 49 (July), pp. 1015–1040.

Packer, Frank. 1996. "Venture Capital, Bank Shareholding, and IPO Underpricing in Japan." In *Empirical Issues in Raising Equity Capital,* edited by Mario Levis (Amsterdam: North-Holland), pp. 191–214.

Pagano, Marco, Fabio Panetta, and Luigi Zingales. 1998. "Why Do Companies Go Public? An Empirical Analysis." *Journal of Finance* 53 (February), pp. 27–64.

Pagano, Marco, Ailsa A. Röell, and Josef Zechner. 2002. "The Geography of Equity Listing: Why Do Companies List Abroad?" *Journal of Finance* 57 (December), pp. 2651–2694.

Pástor, Lubos, and Robert F. Stambaugh. 2002. "Mutual Fund Performance and Seemingly Unrelated Assets." *Journal of Financial Economics* 63, pp. 315–349.

Petersen, Mitchell A., and Raghuram G. Rajan. 1994. "The Benefits of Lending Relationships: Evidence from Small Business Data." *Journal of Finance* 49 (March), pp. 3–37.

Phillips, Gordon M. 1995. "Increased Debt and Industry Product Markets: An Empirical Analysis." *Journal of Financial Economics* 37 (February), pp. 189–238.

Poterba, James. 1987. "Tax Policy and Corporate Savings." *Brookings Papers on Economic Activity* 2 (December), pp. 455–515.

Pound, John, and Richard Zeckhauser. 1990. "Clearly Heard on the Street: The Effects of Takeover Rumors on Stock Prices." *Journal of Business* 63 (July), pp. 291–308.

Pratt, Stanley E. 1997. "The Organized Venture Capital Community." In *Pratt's Guide to Venture Capital Sources,* edited by Stanley E. Pratt (New York: Securities Data Publishing), pp. 75–80.

Press, Eric G., and Joseph B. Weintrop. 1990. "Accounting-Based Constraints in Public and Private Debt Agreements: Their Association with Leverage and Impact on Accounting Choice." *Journal of Accounting and Economics* 12 (January), pp. 65–95.

Pringle, John J. 1991. "Managing Foreign Exchange Exposure." *Journal of Applied Corporate Finance* 3 (Winter), pp. 73–82.

Pringle, John J., and Robert A. Connolly. 1993. "The Nature and Causes of Foreign Currency Exposure." *Journal of Applied Corporate Finance* 6 (Fall), pp. 61–72.

Prowse, Michael. 1992. "Is America in Decline?" *Harvard Business Review* (July/August), pp. 34–45.

Prowse, Stephen D. 1990. "Institutional Investment Patterns and Corporate Financial Behavior in the United States and Japan." *Journal of Financial Economics* 27, pp. 43–66.

———. 1996. "Corporate Finance in International Perspective: Legal and Regulatory Influences on Financial System Development." Federal Reserve Bank of Dallas *Economic Review* (Third Quarter), pp. 2–15.

Pulvino, Todd C. 1999. "The Effects of Bankruptcy Court Protection on Asset Sales." *Journal of Financial Economics* 52 (May), pp. 151–186.

Rajan, Raghuram G. 1992. "Insiders and Outsiders: The Choice between Informed and Arm's Length Debt." *Journal of Finance* 49, pp. 1367–1400.

Rajan, Raghuram, Henri Servaes, and Luigi Zingales. 2000. "The Cost of Diversity: The Diversification Discount and Inefficient Investment." *Journal of Finance* 55 (February), pp. 35–80.

Rajan, Raghuram G., and Luigi Zingales. 1995. "What Do We Know about Capital Structure? Some Evidence from International Data." *Journal of Finance* 50 (December), pp. 1421–1460.

———. 1998. "Financial Dependence and Growth." *American Economic Review* 88, pp. 559–586.

———. 2003. "The Great Reversals: The Politics of Financial Development in the Twentieth Century." *Journal of Financial Economics* 69 (July), pp. 5–50.

Rajgopal, Shivaram, and Terry J. Shevlin. 2002. "Empirical Evidence on the Relation between Stock Option Compensation and Risk Taking." *Journal of Accounting and Economics* 33 (June), pp. 145–171.

Ravenscraft, David, and F. M. Scherer. 1987. *Mergers, Sell-Offs, and Economic Efficiency* (Washington, D.C.: Brookings Institution).

Rawls, S. Waite, III, and Charles W. Smithson. 1989. "The Evolution of Risk Management Products." *Journal of Applied Corporate Finance* 1 (Winter), pp. 18–26.

Richardson, Matthew, and Tom Smith. 1994. "A Unified Approach to Testing for Serial Correlation in Stock Returns." *Journal of Business* 67 (July), pp. 371–399.

Riley, John. 1979. "Informational Equilibrium." *Econometrica* 47 (March), pp. 331–359.

Ritter, Jay R. 1984. "Signaling and the Valuation of Unseasoned New Issues: A Comment." *Journal of Finance* 39, pp. 1231–1237.

———. 1987. "The Costs of Going Public." *Journal of Financial Economics* 19 (December), pp. 269–281.

———. 1991. "The Long-Run Performance of Initial Public Offerings." *Journal of Finance* 46 (March), pp. 3–27.

———. 1996. "How I Helped Make Fischer Black Wealthier." *Financial Management* 24 (Winter), pp. 104–107.

———. 1998. "Initial Public Offerings." In *Handbook of Modern Finance,* edited by Dennis Logue and James Seward (Boston: Warren Gorham & Lamont).

———. 2001. "The Biggest Mistakes That We Teach." Working paper, University of Florida.

Ritter, Jay, and Navin Chopra. 1989. "Portfolio Rebalancing and the Turn-of-the-Year Effect." *Journal of Finance* 44 (March), pp. 149–166.

Roberts, Harry V. 1959. "Stock Market 'Patterns' and Financial Analysis: Methodological Suggestions." *Journal of Finance* 14 (March), pp. 1–10.

Rock, Kevin. 1986. "Why New Issues Are Underpriced." *Journal of Financial Economics* 15 (January/February), pp. 187–212.

Roe, Mark J. 1990. "Political and Legal Restraints on Ownership and Control of Public Companies." *Journal of Financial Economics* 27 (September), pp. 7–41.

———. 1997. "The Political Roots of American Corporate Finance." *Journal of Applied Corporate Finance* 9 (Winter), pp. 8–22.

Roll, Richard. 1977. "A Critique of the Asset Pricing Theory's Tests, Part I: On Past and Potential Testability of the Theory." *Journal of Financial Economics* 4, pp. 129–176.

———. 1986. "The Hubris Hypothesis of Corporate Takeovers." *Journal of Business* 59 (April), pp. 197–217.

———. 1994. "What Every CEO Should Know about Scientific Progress in Economics: What Is Known and What Remains to Be Resolved." *Financial Management* 23 (Summer), pp. 69–75.

Ross, Stephen A. 1976. "The Arbitrage Theory of Capital Asset Pricing." *Journal of Economic Theory* (December), pp. 341–360.

———. 1977a. "The Determination of Financial Structure: The Incentive-Signaling Approach." *Bell Journal of Economics* 8 (Spring), pp. 23–40.

———. 1977b. "Risk, Return, and Arbitrage." In *Risk and Return in Finance I,* edited by Irwin Friend and James L. Bicksler (Cambridge, Mass.: Ballinger), pp. 189–218.

Rossi, Stefano, and Paolo F. Volpin. 2004. "Cross-Country Determinants of Mergers and Acquisitions." *Journal of Financial Economics* 74 (November), pp. 277–304.

Rutterford, Janette. 1988. "An International Perspective on the Capital Structure Puzzle." In *New Developments in International Finance,* edited by Joel M. Stern and Donald H. Chew, Jr. (New York: Basil Blackwell).

Sahlman, William A. 1988. "Aspects of Financial Contracting in Venture Capital." *Journal of Applied Corporate Finance* 1 (Summer), pp. 23–36.

———. 1990. "The Structure and Governance of Venture Capital Organizations." *Journal of Financial Economics* 27 (September), pp. 473–524.

Samant, Ajay. 1996. "An Empirical Study of Interest Rate Swap Usage by Nonfinancial Corporate Business." *Journal of Financial Services Research* 10 (March), pp. 43–57.

Sarkar, Sudipto. 2001. "Probability of Call and Likelihood of the Call Feature in a Corporate Bond." *Journal of Banking and Finance* 25 (March), pp. 505–533.

Schallheim, James S., Ramon E. Johnson, Ronald C. Lease, and John J. McCon-

nell. 1987. "The Determinants of Yields on Financial Leasing Contracts." *Journal of Financial Economics* 19, pp. 45–68.

Schenone, Carola. 2004. "The Effect of Banking Relationships on the Firm's IPO Underpricing." *Journal of Finance* 59 (December), pp. 3–27.

Scherr, Frederick C., and Heather M. Hulburt. 2001. "The Maturity Structure of Small Firms." *Financial Management* 30 (Spring), pp. 85–111.

Schilit, W. Keith, and John T. Willig, eds. 1996a. "The Globalization of Venture Capital." In *Fitzroy Dearborn International Directory of Venture Capital Funds,* 2nd ed. (Chicago: Fitzroy Dearborn Publishers), pp. 79–80.

———. 1996b. "Structuring the Venture Capital Deal." In *Fitzroy Dearborn International Directory of Venture Capital Funds,* 2nd ed. (Chicago: Fitzroy Dearborn Publishers), pp. 71–77.

Schipper, Katherine, and Abbie Smith. 1983. "Effects of Recontracting on Shareholder Wealth: The Case of Voluntary Spin-Offs." *Journal of Financial Economics* 12, pp. 437–468.

———. 1986. "A Comparison of Equity Carve-Outs and Seasoned Equity Offerings: Share Price Effects and Corporate Restructuring." *Journal of Financial Economics* 15 (January/February), pp. 153–186.

Schoar, Antoinette. 2002. "Effects of Corporate Diversification on Productivity." *Journal of Finance* 57 (December), pp. 2379–2403.

Schultz, Paul. 2003. "Pseudo Market Timing and the Long-Run Underperformance of IPOs." *Journal of Finance* 58 (April), pp. 483–517.

Schwert, G. William. 1996. "Markup Pricing in Mergers and Acquisitions." *Journal of Financial Economics* 41 (June), pp. 153–192.

Scott, James H., Jr. 1977. "Bankruptcy, Secured Debt, and Optimal Capital Structure." *Journal of Finance* 32 (March), pp. 1–19.

Sekely, William S., and J. Markham Collins. 1988. "Cultural Influences on International Capital Structure." *Journal of International Business Studies* (Spring), pp. 87–100.

Servaes, Henri. 1991. "Tobin's q and the Gains from Takeovers." *Journal of Finance* 46 (March), pp. 409–420.

———. 1996. "The Value of Diversification during the Conglomerate Merger Wave." *Journal of Finance* 51 (September), pp. 1201–1225.

Seyhun, H. Nejat. 1986. "Insiders' Profits, Cost of Trading, and Market Efficiency."

Journal of Financial Economics 16 (June), pp. 189–212.

Seyhun, H. Nejat, and Michael Bradley. 1997. "Corporate Bankruptcy and Insider Trading." *Journal of Business* 70 (April), pp. 189–216.

Shah, Kshitij. 1994. "The Nature of Information Conveyed by Pure Capital Structure Changes." *Journal of Financial Economics* 36 (August), pp. 89–126.

Shahrur, Husan. 2005. "Industry Structure and Horizontal Takeovers: Analysis of Wealth Effects on Rivals, Suppliers, and Corporate Customers." *Journal of Financial Economics* 76 (April), pp. 61–98.

Sharpe, William F. 1964. "Capital Asset Prices: A Theory of Market Equilibrium under Conditions of Risk." *Journal of Finance* 19 (September), pp. 425–442.

———. 1966. "Mutual Fund Performance." *Journal of Business* 39 (January), pp. 119–138.

Shastri, Kuldeep. 1990. "The Differential Effects of Mergers on Corporate Security Values." *Research in Finance* 8, pp. 179–201.

Shefrin, Hersh. 2002. "Behavioral Corporate Finance." *Journal of Applied Corporate Finance* 14 (Fall), pp. 113–124.

Sherman, Ann, and Sheridan Titman. 2003. "Building the IPO Order Book: Underpricing and Participation Limits with Costly Information." *Journal of Financial Economics* 65 (July), pp. 3–29.

Shiller, Robert J. 1979. "The Volatility of Long-Term Interest Rates and Expectations Models of the Term Structure." *Journal of Political Economy* 87 (December), pp. 1190–1219.

———. 1981. "Do Stock Prices Move Too Much to Be Justified by Subsequent Changes in Dividends?" *American Economic Review* 71 (June), pp. 421–436.

———. 2000. *Irrational Exuberance* (Princeton, NJ: Princeton University Press).

Shin, Hyun-Han, and Young S. Park. 1999. "Financing Constraints and Internal Capital Markets: Evidence from Korean 'Chaebols.'" *Journal of Corporate Finance* 5 (June), pp. 169–191.

Shleifer, Andrei, and Lawrence Summers. 1988. "Breach of Trust in Hostile Takeovers." In *Corporate Takeovers: Causes and Consequences* (Chicago: University of Chicago Press).

———. 1990. "The Noise Trader Approach to Finance." *Journal of Economic Perspectives* 4 (Spring), pp. 19–33.

Shleifer, Andrei, and Robert Vishny. 1989. "Management Entrenchment." *Journal of Financial Economics* 25 (November), pp. 123–139.

———. 1997a. "The Limits to Arbitrage."

Journal of Finance 52 (March), pp. 35–55.

———. 1997b. "A Survey of Corporate Governance." *Journal of Finance* 52 (June), pp. 736–783.

———. 2003. "Stock Market Driven Acquisitions." *Journal of Financial Economics* 70 (December), pp. 295–311.

Shockley, Richard L., Jr. 2001. "McTreat Spots: Creating Options at McDonalds." Teaching case, Indiana University.

Shyam-Sunder, Lakshmi, and Stewart C. Myers. 1999. "Testing the Static Trade-off against Pecking Order Models of Capital Structure." *Journal of Financial Economics* 51 (February), pp. 219–244.

Siconolfi, Michael, and Patrick McGeehan. 1998. "Wall Street Boosts Penalty on IPO 'Flips.'" *Wall Street Journal* (July 31), p. C1.

Siegel, Jordan. 2005. "Can Foreign Firms Bond Themselves Effectively by Renting U.S. Securities Laws?" *Journal of Financial Economics* 75 (February), pp. 319–359.

Slovin, Myron B., Marie E. Sushka, and Steven R. Ferraro. 1995. "A Comparison of the Information Conveyed by Equity Carve-Outs, Spin-Offs, and Asset Sell-Offs." *Journal of Financial Economics* 37 (January), pp. 89–104.

Smart, Scott B., and Chad J. Zutter. 2003. "Control as a Motivation for Underpricing: A Comparison of Dual and Single-Class IPOs." *Journal of Financial Economics* 69, pp. 85–110.

Smith, Clifford W., Jr. 1977. "Alternative Methods of Raising Capital: Rights versus Underwritten Offerings." *Journal of Financial Economics* 5 (December), pp. 273–307.

———. 1992. "Economics and Ethics: The Case of Salomon Brothers." *Journal of Applied Corporate Finance* 5 (Summer), pp. 23–28.

Smith, Clifford W., Jr., Charles W. Smithson, and D. Sykes Wilford. 1989. "Managing Financial Risk." *Journal of Applied Corporate Finance* 1 (Winter), pp. 27–48.

Smith, Clifford W., Jr., and L. McDonald Wakeman. 1985. "Determinants of Corporate Leasing Policy." *Journal of Finance* 40 (July), pp. 895–908.

Smith, Clifford W., Jr., and Jerold B. Warner. 1979. "On Financial Contracting: An Analysis of Bond Covenants." *Journal of Financial Economics* 7 (June), pp. 117–161.

Smith, Clifford W., Jr., and Ross L. Watts. 1992. "The Investment Opportunity Set and Corporate Financing, Dividend, and Compensation Policies." *Journal of Financial Economics* 32 (December), pp. 263–292.

Smith, Roy C. 2001. "Strategic Directions in Investment Banking—A Retrospective Analysis." *Journal of Applied Corporate Finance* 14 (Spring), pp. 111–123.

Song, Wei-Ling. 2004. "Competition and Coalition among Underwriters: The Decision to Join a Syndicate." *Journal of Finance* 59 (October), pp. 2421–2444.

Sorensen, Eric H., and Thierry F. Bollier. 1994. "Pricing Swap Default Risk." *Financial Analysts Journal* 50, pp. 23–33.

Spence, Michael. 1973. "Job Market Signalling." *Quarterly Journal of Economics* 87 (August), pp. 355–374.

Spiess, D. Katherine, and John Affleck-Graves. 1995. "Underperformance in Long-Run Stock Returns following Seasoned Equity Offerings." *Journal of Financial Economics* 38 (July), pp. 243–267.

Stancill, James McNeill. 1987. "How Much Money Does Your New Venture Need?" *Harvard Business Review* (May/June), pp. 122–139.

Stickel, Scott. 1985. "The Effect of Value Line Investment Survey Rank Changes on Common Stock Prices." *Journal of Financial Economics* 14 (March), pp. 121–143.

Stiglitz, Joseph E. 2002. "Accounting for Options." *Wall Street Journal* (May 3).

Stillman, Robert. 1983. "Examining Antitrust Policy towards Mergers." *Journal of Financial Economics* 11 (April), pp. 225–240.

Strömberg, Per. 2000. "Conflicts of Interest and Market Illiquidity in Bankruptcy Auctions: Theory and Tests." *Journal of Finance* 55 (December), pp. 2641–2692.

Stulz, René M. 1988. "Managerial Control of Voting Rights: Financing Policies and the Market for Corporate Control." *Journal of Financial Economics* 20 (January), pp. 25–54.

———. 1990. "Managerial Discretion and Optimal Financing Policies." *Journal of Financial Economics* 26 (July), pp. 1–25.

———. 1996. "Rethinking Risk Management." *Journal of Applied Corporate Finance* 9 (Fall), pp. 8–24.

Stulz, René M., and Herb Johnson. 1985. "An Analysis of Secured Debt." *Journal of Financial Economics* 14 (December), pp. 501–521.

Subrahmanyam, Avanidhar, and Sheridan Titman. 1999. "The Going-Public Decision and the Development of Financial Markets." *Journal of Finance* 54 (June), pp. 1045–1082.

Sullivan, Ryan, Allan Timmerman, and Halbert White. 1999. "Data-Snooping, Technical Trading Rule Performance,

and the Bootstrap." *Journal of Finance* 54 (October), pp. 1647–1691.

Taggart, Robert A., Jr. 1985. "Secular Patterns in the Financing of U.S. Corporations." In *Corporate Capital Structures in the United States,* edited by Benjamin M. Friedman (Chicago: University of Chicago Press).

Targett, Simon. 2001. "Institutional Investment: Should Do More." *Financial Times* (June 14), European Private Equity Survey, p. 5.

Testa, Richard J. 1988. "The Legal Process of Venture Capital Investment." In *Pratt's Guide to Venture Capital Sources,* edited by Stanley E. Pratt (New York: Securities Data Publishing), pp. 66–77.

Thaler, Richard H. 2000. "From Homo Economicus to Homo Sapiens." *Journal of Economic Perspectives* 14 (Winter), pp. 133–141.

Thatcher, Janet S. 1985. "The Choice of Call Provisions Terms: Evidence of the Existence of Agency Costs of Debt." *Journal of Finance* 40 (June), pp. 549–561.

Thompson, Samuel C. 2000. "Demystifying the Use of Beta in Determining the Cost of Capital and an Illustration of Its Use in Lazard's Valuation of Conrail." *Journal of Corporation Law* 25, pp. 241–306.

Thorburn, Karin S. 2000. "Bankruptcy Auctions: Costs, Debt Recovery and Firm Survival." *Journal of Financial Economics* 58 (December), pp. 337–368.

Titman, Sheridan. 1984. "The Effect of Capital Structure on a Firm's Liquidation Decision." *Journal of Financial Economics* 13 (March), pp. 137–151.

———. 1992. "Interest Rate Swaps and Corporate Financing Choices." *Journal of Finance* 47 (September), pp. 1503–1516.

Titman, Sheridan, and Roberto Wessels. 1988. "The Determinants of Capital Structure Choice." *Journal of Finance* 43 (March), pp. 1–19.

Travlos, Nickolas G. 1987. "Corporate Takeover Bids, Methods of Payment, and Bidding Firms' Stock Returns." *Journal of Finance* 42 (September), pp. 943–963.

Triantis, Alexander J., and James E. Hodder. 1990. "Valuing Flexibility as a Complex Option." *Journal of Finance* 45 (June), pp. 549–565.

Trigeorgis, Lenos, and Scott P. Mason. 1987. "Valuing Managerial Flexibility." *Midland Corporate Finance Journal* 5 (Spring), pp. 14–21.

Tufano, Peter. 1996. "Who Manages Risk? An Empirical Examination of Risk Management Practices in the Gold Mining

Industry." *Journal of Finance* 51 (September), pp. 1097–1137.

Tyebjee, Tyzoon T., and Albert V. Bruno. 1984. "A Model of Venture Capitalist Investment Activity." *Management Science* 30 (September), pp. 1051–1066.

Vermaelen, Theo. 1981. "Common Stock Repurchases and Market Signalling." *Journal of Financial Economics* 9 (June), pp. 139–183.

Vijh, Anand M. 1999. "Long-Term Returns from Equity Carve-Outs." *Journal of Financial Economics* 51 (February), pp. 273–308.

Villalonga, Belén. 2004. "Diversification Discount or Premium? New Evidence from the Business Information Tracking Series." *Journal of Finance* 59 (April), pp. 479–506.

Vu, Joseph D. 1986. "An Examination of the Corporate Call Behavior of Nonconvertible Bonds." *Journal of Financial Economics* 16 (June), pp. 235–265.

Waldman, Michael. 1997. "Eliminating the Market for Secondhand Goods: An Alternative Explanation for Leasing." *Journal of Law and Economics* 40 (April), pp. 61–92.

Walker, Ernest W., and J. William Petty II. 1978. "Financial Differences between Large and Small Firms." *Financial Management* 7 (Winter), pp. 61–68.

Wansley, James, William Lane, and Ho Yang. 1983. "Abnormal Returns to Acquired Firms by Type of Acquisition and Method of Payment." *Financial Management* 12 (Autumn), pp. 16–22.

Warner, Jerold B. 1977. "Bankruptcy Costs: Some Evidence." *Journal of Finance* 32 (May), pp. 337–347.

Warren, Carl S., James M. Reeve, and Philip E. Fess. 2002. *Corporate Financial Accounting*, 7th ed. (Cincinnati, OH: Thomson South-Western).

Wassener, Bettina. 2002. "Tarnished Image in Need of Restoration." *Financial Times* Special Survey of Germany (June 12), p. 2.

Wedig, Gerard J., Mahmud Hassan, and Michael A. Morrisey. 1996. "Tax Exempt Debt and the Capital Structure of Nonprofit Organizations: An Application to Hospitals." *Journal of Finance* 51 (September), pp. 1247–1283.

Wei, Zhang, and Jiang Yanfu. 2002. "The Relationship between Venture Capitalists' Experience and Their Involvement in the VC-Backed Companies." Working paper, Tsinghua University (Beijing, China).

Welch, Ivo. 2000. "Herding among Security Analysts." *Journal of Financial Economics* 58, pp. 369–396.

———. 2001. "The Equity Premium Consensus Forecast Revisited." Working paper, Yale University.

Wermers, Russ. 2000. "Mutual Fund Performance: An Empirical Decomposition into Stock-Picking Talent, Style, Transactions Costs, and Expenses." *Journal of Finance* 55 (August), pp. 1655–1703.

Weston, Fred J., and Juan A. Siu. 2003. "Changing Motives for Share Repurchases." *Finance* (December 19), Paper 3-03.

Whited, Toni M. 2001. "Is It Inefficient Investment That Causes the Diversification Discount?" *Journal of Finance* 56 (October), pp. 1667–1691.

Williams, Frances. 2001. "Global Foreign Investment Flows 'Set to All by 40%.'" *Financial Times* (September 9), p. 9.

Williams, Joseph. 1988. "Efficient Signalling with Dividends, Investment, and Stock Repurchases." *Journal of Finance* 43 (July), pp. 737–747.

Womack, Kent L. 1996. "Do Brokerage Analysts' Recommendations Have Investment Value?" *Journal of Finance* 51 (March), pp. 137–166.

Wong, Andrew. 2001. "Angel Finance: The Other Venture Capital." Working paper, University of Chicago.

Wu, Chunchi. 1993. "Information Asymmetry and the Sinking Fund Provision." *Journal of Financial and Quantitative Analysis* 28 (September), pp. 399–416.

Wu, Yi Lin. 2004. "The Choice of Equity-Selling Mechanisms." *Journal of Financial Economics* 74 (October), pp. 93–119.

Yeoman, John C. 2001. "The Optimal Spread and Offering Price for Underwritten Securities." *Journal of Financial Economics* 62 (October), pp. 169–198.

Zingales, Luigi. 1994. "The Value of the Voting Right: A Study of the Milan Stock Exchange Experience." *Review of Financial Studies* 7, pp. 125–148.

Further Reading

Aggarwal, Reena, and Pat Conroy. 2000. "Price Discovery in Initial Public Offerings and the Role of the Lead Underwriter." *Journal of Finance* 55 (December), pp. 2903–2922.

Alderson, Michael J., and Brian L. Betker. 1999. "Assessing Post-Bankruptcy Performance: An Analysis of Reorganized Firms' Cash Flows." *Financial Management* 28 (Summer), pp. 68–82.

Allen, David S., Robert E. Lamy, and G. Rodney Thompson. 1990. "The Shelf Registration of Debt and Self Selection Bias." *Journal of Finance* 45 (March), pp. 275–287.

Altman, Edward I., and Pablo Arman. 2002. "Default and Returns on High Yield Bonds: Analysis through 2001." *Journal of Applied Finance* 12, pp. 98–112.

Ang, James S., Rebel A. Cole, and James Wuh Lin. 2000. "Agency Costs and Ownership Structure." *Journal of Finance* 55 (February), pp. 81–106.

Anstaett, Kurt W., Dennis P. McCrary, and Stephen T. Monahan, Jr. 1988. "Practical Debt Policy Considerations for Growth Companies: A Case Study Approach." *Journal of Applied Corporate Finance* 1 (Summer), pp. 71–78.

Asquith, Paul, and David W. Mullins, Jr. 1986. "Equity Issues and Offering Dilution." *Journal of Financial Economics* 15 (January/February), pp. 61–89.

Bagwell, Laurie Simon. 1991. "Share Repurchase and Takeover Deterrence." *Rand Journal of Economics* 22, pp. 72–88.

Baks, Klaas P., Andrew Metrick, and Jessica Wachter. 2001. "Should Investors Avoid All Actively Managed Mutual Funds? A Study in Bayesian Performance Evaluation." *Journal of Finance* 56 (February), pp. 45–85.

Ball, Ray, and S. P. Kothari. 1989. "Nonstationary Expected Returns: Implications for Tests of Market Efficiency and Serial Correlation in Returns." *Journal of Financial Economics* 25 (November), pp. 51–74.

Barber, Brad M., and John D. Lyon. 1997. "Detecting Long-Run Abnormal Stock Returns: The Empirical Power and Specification of Test Statistics." *Journal of Financial Economics* 43, pp. 341–372.

Barberis, Nicholas. 2000. "Investing for the Long Run When Returns Are Predictable." *Journal of Finance* 55 (February), pp. 225–264.

Barclay, Michael J., and Clifford W. Smith, Jr. 1988. "Corporate Payout Policy: Cash Dividends versus Open Market Repurchases." *Journal of Financial Economics* 22 (October), pp. 61–82.

———. 1999. "The Capital Structure Puzzle: Another Look at the Evidence." *Journal of Applied Corporate Finance* 12 (Spring), pp. 8–20.

Barnish, Keith, Steve Miller, and Michael Rushmore. 1997. "The New Leveraged Loan Syndication Market." *Journal of*

Applied Corporate Finance 10 (Spring), pp. 79–88.

Baron, David P. 1982. "A Model of the Demand for Investment Banking Advising and Distributions Services for New Issues." *Journal of Finance* 37 (September), pp. 955–976.

Baron, David P., and Bengt Holmstrom. 1980. "The Investment Banking Contract for New Issues under Asymmetric Information: Delegation and Incentive Problems." *Journal of Finance* 35 (December), pp. 1115–1138.

Barry, Christopher, Chris Muscarella, John Peavy, and Michael Vetsuypens. 1990. "The Role of Venture Capital in the Creation of Public Companies: Evidence from the Going Public Process." *Journal of Financial Economics* 27, pp. 447–471.

Barry, Christopher B., Chris J. Muscarella, and Michael R. Vetsuypens. 1991. "Underwriter Warrants, Underwriter Compensation, and the Costs of Going Public." *Journal of Financial Economics* 29, pp. 113–135.

Benveniste, Lawrence M., Walid Y. Busaba, and William J. Wilhelm, Jr. 1996. "Price Stabilization as a Bonding Mechanism in New Equity Issues." *Journal of Financial Economics* 42 (October), pp. 223–255.

Berens, James L., and Charles J. Cuny. 1995. "The Capital Structure Puzzle Revisited." *Review of Financial Studies* 8 (Winter), pp. 1185–1208.

Berger, Allen, and Gregory Udell. 1995. "Relationship Lending and Lines of Credit in Small Firm Finance. *Journal of Business* 68 (July), pp. 351–381.

Betker, Brian L. 1995. "Management's Incentives, Equity's Bargaining Power, and Deviations from Absolute Priority in Chapter 11 Bankruptcies." *Journal of Business* 68 (April), pp. 161–183.

Black, Bernard. 1992. "Agents Watching Agents." *UCLA Law Review* 39, pp. 811–893.

Black, Fischer. 1972. "Capital Market Equilibrium with Restricted Borrowing." *Journal of Business* 64 (July), pp. 444–455.

Blackwell, David W., and David S. Kidwell. 1988. "An Investigation of Cost Differences between Public Sales and Private Placements of Debt." *Journal of Financial Economics* 22 (December), pp. 253–278.

Blackwell, David W., M. Wayne Marr, and Michael F. Spivey. 1990. "Shelf Registration and the Reduced Due Diligence Argument: Implications of the Underwriter Certification and the Implicit Insurance Hypothesis." *Journal of Finan-*

cial and Quantitative Analysis 25 (June), pp. 245–259.

Blackwell, David, and Drew Winters. 1997. "Banking Relationships and the Effect of Monitoring on Loan Pricing." *Journal of Financial Research* 20 (Summer), pp. 275–289.

Blake, David, and Allan Timmerman. 1998. "Mutual Fund Performance: Evidence from the UK." *European Economic Review* 2, pp. 57–77.

Bohren, Øyvind, B. Espen Eckbo, and Dag Michalsen. 1997. "Why Underwrite Rights Offerings? Some New Evidence." *Journal of Financial Economics* 46, pp. 223–261.

Booth, James R., and Richard L. Smith, Jr. 1986. "Capital Raising, Underwriting and the Certification Hypothesis." *Journal of Financial Economics* 15 (January/February), pp. 261–281.

Bower, Nancy L. 1989. "Firm Value and the Choice of Offering Method in Initial Public Offerings." *Journal of Finance* 44 (July), pp. 647–662.

Brophy, David J., and Mark W. Guthner. 1988. "Publicly Traded Venture Capital Funds: Implications for Institutional 'Fund of Funds' Investors." *Journal of Business Venturing* 3 (Summer), pp. 187–206.

Brous, Peter A., Vinay Datar, and Omesh Kini. 2001. "Is the Market Optimistic about the Future Earnings of Seasoned Equity Offering Firms?" *Journal of Financial and Quantitative Analysis* 36 (June), pp. 141–168.

Carter, Richard B., Frederick H. Dark, and Ajai K. Singh. 1998. "Underwriter Reputation, Initial Returns, and the Long-Run Performance of IPO Stocks." *Journal of Finance* 53, pp. 285–311.

Chan, Louis K. C., Narasimhan Jegadeesh, and Josef Lakonishok. 1995. "Evaluating the Performance of Value versus Glamour Stocks: The Impact of Selection Bias." *Journal of Financial Economics* 38 (July), pp. 269–296.

Chemmanur, Thomas J., and Paolo Fulghieri. 1994. "Reputation, Renegotiation, and the Choice between Bank Loans and Publicly Traded Debt." *Review of Financial Studies* 7 (Fall), pp. 475–506.

Chirinko, Robert S., and Anua R. Singha. 2000. "Testing Static Trade-off against Pecking Order Models of Capital Structure: A Critical Comment." *Journal of Financial Economics* 58, pp. 417–425.

Cleary, Sean. 1999. "The Relationship between Firm Investment and Financial Status." *Journal of Finance* 54 (April), pp. 673–692.

Cornell, Bradford, and Alan C. Shapiro. 1988. "Financing Corporate Growth." *Journal of Applied Corporate Finance* 1 (Summer), pp. 6–22.

Cornell, Bradford, and Erik R. Sirri. 1992. "The Reaction of Investors and Stock Prices to Insider Trading." *Journal of Finance* 47 (July), pp. 1031–1060.

Corwin, Shane A., and Jeffrey H. Harris. 2001. "The Initial Listing Decisions of Firms That Go Public." *Financial Management* 30 (Spring), pp. 35–55.

Daniel, Kent, and Sheridan Titman. 1997. "Evidence on the Characteristics of Cross Sectional Variation in Stock Returns." *Journal of Finance* 52 (March), pp. 1–33.

Davidson, Wallace N., III, and Dipa Dutia. 1991. "Debt, Liquidity, and Profitability in Small Firms." *Entrepreneurship Theory and Practice* (Fall), pp. 53–64.

Dechow, Patricia M., and Richard G. Sloan. 1997. "Returns to Contrarian Investment Strategies: Tests of Naive Expectations Hypotheses." *Journal of Financial Economics* 43 (January), pp. 3–27.

DeLong, Bradford, Andrei Shleifer, Lawrence H. Summers, and Robert J. Waldmann. 1990. "Positive Feedback Investment Strategies and Destabilizing Rational Speculation." *Journal of Finance* 45 (June), pp. 379–395.

Diamond, Douglas. 1989. "Reputation Acquisition in Debt Markets." *Journal of Political Economy* 97, pp. 828–862.

Downes, David H., and Robert Heinkel. 1982. "Signaling and the Valuation of Unseasoned New Issues." *Journal of Finance* 37, pp. 1–10.

D'Souza, Julia, and John Jacob. 2000. "Why Firms Issue Targeted Stock." *Journal of Financial Economics* 56 (June), pp. 459–483.

Dunbar, Craig G. 2000. "Factors Affecting Investment Bank Initial Public Offering Market Share." *Journal of Financial Economics* 55, pp. 3–41.

Dyl, Edward A. 1977. "Another Look at the Evaluation of Investment in Accounts Receivable." *Financial Management* 6 (4), pp. 67–70.

Eberhart, Allan C., William T. Moore, and Reena Aggarwal. 1999. "The Equity Performance of Firms Emerging from Bankruptcy." *Journal of Finance* 54 (October), pp. 1855–1868.

Eberhart, Allan C., William T. Moore, and Rodney L. Roenfeldt. 1990. "Security Pricing and Deviations from the Absolute Priority Rule in Bankruptcy Proceedings." *Journal of Finance* 45 (December), pp. 1457–1469.

Fama, Eugene F., and Kenneth R. French. 1988. "Permanent and Temporary Components of Stock Prices." *Journal of Political Economy* 96 (April), pp. 246–273.

———. 1989. "Business Conditions and Expected Returns on Stocks and Bonds." *Journal of Financial Economics* 25 (November), pp. 23–49.

———. 1992. "The Cross-Section of Expected Stock Returns." *Journal of Finance* 47 (June), pp. 427–465.

———. 1995. "Size and Book-to-Market Factors in Earnings and Returns." *Journal of Finance* 50 (March), pp. 131–155.

———. 1996. "Multifactor Explanations of Asset Pricing Anomalies." *Journal of Finance* 51 (March), pp. 55–84.

———. 1997. "Industry Costs of Equity." *Journal of Financial Economics* 43 (February), pp. 153–193.

Fenn, George W. 2000. "Speed of Issuance and the Adequacy of Disclosure in the 144A High-Yield Debt Market." *Journal of Financial Economics* 56 (June), pp. 383–405.

Field, Laura Casares, and Gordon Hanka. 2001. "The Expiration of IPO Share Lock-Ups." *Journal of Finance* 56 (April), pp. 471–500.

Fraser, Jill Andresky. 1998. "How to Finance Anything." *Inc.* (February), pp. 34–42.

Froot, Kenneth A., David S. Scharfstein, and Jeremy C. Stein. 1993. "Risk Management: Coordinating Corporate Investment and Financing Policies." *Journal of Finance* 48 (December), pp. 1629–1658.

Gande, Amar, Manju Puri, and Anthony Saunders. 1999. "Bank Entry, Competition and the Market for Corporate Securities Underwriting." *Journal of Financial Economics* 54, pp. 165–195.

Garvey, Gerald T., and Gordon Hanka. 1999. "Capital Structure and Corporate Control: The Effect of Antitakeover Statutes on Firm Leverage." *Journal of Finance* 54 (April), pp. 519–546.

Gilson, Stuart C., Edith S. Hotchkiss, and Richard S. Ruback. 2000. "Valuation of Bankrupt Firms." *Review of Financial Studies* 13 (Spring), pp. 43–74.

Gitman, Lawrence J., and Kanwal S. Sachdeva. 1981. "Accounts Receivable Decisions in a Capital Budgeting Framework." *Financial Management* 10, pp. 45–49.

Gompers, Paul, and Josh Lerner. 1996. "The Use of Covenants: An Empirical Analysis of Venture Partnership Agreements." *Journal of Law and Economics* 39 (October), pp. 463–498.

———. 1999. "An Analysis of Compensation in the U.S. Venture Capital Partnership." *Journal of Financial Economics* 51 (January), pp. 3–44.

Graham, John R. 2001. "Estimating the Tax Benefits of Debt." *Journal of Applied Corporate Finance* 14 (Spring), pp. 42–54.

Graham, John R., and Clifford W. Smith, Jr. 1999. "Tax Incentives to Hedge." *Journal of Finance* 54 (December), pp. 2241–2262.

Gul, Ferdinand A. 1999. "Growth Opportunities, Capital Structure and Dividend Policies in Japan." *Journal of Corporate Finance* 5 (June), pp. 141–168.

Habib, Michel A., and Alexander P. Ljungqvist. 2001. "Underpricing and Entrepreneurial Wealth Losses in IPOs: Theory and Evidence." *Review of Financial Studies* 14 (Summer), pp. 433–458.

Hampson, Philip, John Parsons, and Charles Blitzer. 1991. "A Case Study in the Design of an Optimal Sharing Rule for a Petroleum Exploration Venture." *Journal of Financial Economics* 30 (November), pp. 45–67.

Hanley, Kathleen W., A. Arun Kumar, and Paul J. Seguin. 1993. "Price Stabilization in the Market for New Issues." *Journal of Financial Economics* 34 (October), pp. 177–197.

Hardymon, G. Felda, Mark J. DeNino, and Malcolm S. Salter. 1983. "When Corporate Venture Capital Doesn't Work." *Harvard Business Review* (May/June), pp. 114–120.

Hellmann, Thomas, and Manju Puri. 2000. "The Interaction between Product Market and Financing Strategy: The Role of Venture Capital." *Review of Financial Studies* 13 (Winter), pp. 959–984.

Hertzel, Michael, and Richard L. Smith. 1993. "Market Discounts and Shareholder Gains for Placing Equity Privately." *Journal of Finance* 48 (June), pp. 459–485.

Higgins, Robert C. 1977. "How Much Growth Can a Firm Afford?" *Financial Management* 6, pp. 7–16.

Hirschey, Mark, Vernon J. Richardson, and Susan Scholz. 2000. "Stock-Price Effects of Internet Buy-Sell Recommendations: *The Motley Fool* Case." *Financial Review* 35 (May), pp. 147–174.

Hirshleifer, David, Avanidhar Subrahmanyam, and Sheridan Titman. 1994. "Security Analysis and Trading Patterns When Some Investors Receive Information before Others." *Journal of Finance* 49 (December), pp. 1665–1698.

Huemer, Jason. 1992. "Public Venture Capital: Huge Market Goes Largely Untapped." *Venture Capital Journal* (February), pp. 38–44.

Hughes, Patricia J. 1986. "Signalling by Direct Disclosure under Asymmetric Information." *Journal of Accounting and Economics* 8 (June), pp. 119–142.

Indro, Daniel C., Robert T. Leach, and Wayne Y. Lee. 1999. "Sources of Gains to Shareholders from Bankruptcy Resolution." *Journal of Banking and Finance* 23 (January), pp. 21–47.

Ingersoll, Jonathan E., Jr., and Stephen A. Ross. 1992. "Waiting to Invest: Investment and Uncertainty." *Journal of Business* 65 (March), pp. 1–29.

Jain, Bharat A., and Omesh Kini. 1994. "The Post-Issue Operating Performance of IPO Firms." *Journal of Finance* 49 (December), pp. 1699–1726.

Jensen, Michael C. 1978. "Some Anomalous Evidence regarding Market Efficiency." *Journal of Financial Economics* 6 (June/September), pp. 95–101.

Johnson, Greg. 2000. "Yankee Bonds and Cross-Border Private Placements: An Update." *Journal of Applied Corporate Finance* 13 (Fall), pp. 80–91.

Kaplan, Steven, and Per Strömberg. 2001. "Venture Capitalists as Principals: Contracting, Screening, and Monitoring." *American Economic Review* 91 (May), pp. 426–430.

Kaplan, Steven N., and Luigi Zingales. 1997. "Do Financing Constraints Explain Why Investment Is Correlated with Cash Flow?" *Quarterly Journal of Economics* 112, pp. 169–215.

Khorana, Ajay. 1996. "Top Management Turnover: An Empirical Investigation of Mutual Fund Managers." *Journal of Financial Economics* 40 (March), pp. 403–427.

Koch, Paul D., and Catherine Shenoy. 1999. "The Information Content of Dividend and Capital Structure Policies." *Financial Management* 28 (Winter), pp. 16–35.

Kothari, S. P., and Jerold B. Warner. 1997. "Measuring Long-Horizon Security Price Performance." *Journal of Financial Economics* 43, pp. 301–340.

Krigman, Laurie, Wayne H. Shaw, and Kent L. Womack. 2001. "Why Do Firms Switch Underwriters?" *Journal of Finan-*

cial Economics 60 (May/June), pp. 245–284.

Lamont, Owen. 1997. "Cash Flow and Investment: Evidence from Internal Capital Markets." *Journal of Finance* (February), pp. 83–109.

Lee, Cheng-Few, and Shafiqur Rahman. 1990. "Market Timing, Selectivity, and Mutual Fund Performance: An Empirical Analysis." *Journal of Business* 63 (April), pp. 261–278.

Lee, Peggy M., and Sunil Wahal. 2002. "Venture Capital, Certification and IPOs." Working paper, Emory University.

Lerner, Josh. 1994. "The Syndication of Venture Capital Investments." *Financial Management* 23 (Autumn), pp. 16–27.

Lorie, James H., and Leonard J. Savage. 1955. "Three Problems in Rationing Capital." *Journal of Business* 28 (October), pp. 229–239.

Majd, Saman, and Robert S. Pindyck. 1987. "Time to Build, Option Value and Investment Decisions." *Journal of Financial Economics* 18 (March), pp. 7–28.

Mandelker, Gershon, and Artur Raviv. 1977. "Investment Banking: An Economic Analysis of Optimal Underwriting Contracts." *Journal of Finance* 32 (June), pp. 683–694.

Martin, John D., and J. William Petty. 1983. "An Analysis of the Performance of Publicly Traded Venture Capital Companies." *Journal of Financial and Quantitative Analysis* 18 (September), pp. 401–410.

Masson, Dubos J., ed. 2001. *Essentials of Cash Management,* 7th ed. (Bethesda, Md.: Association for Financial Professionals).

Masulis, Ronald W., and Ashok N. Korwar. 1986. "Seasoned Equity Offerings: An Empirical Investigation." *Journal of Financial Economics* 15 (January/February), pp. 91–118.

Miffre, Joëlle. 2001. "Efficiency in the Pricing of the FTSE 100 Futures Contract." *European Financial Management* 7, pp. 9–22.

Mikkelson, Wayne H., M. Megan Partch, and Kshitij Shah. 1997. "Ownership and Operating Performance of Companies That Go Public." *Journal of Financial Economics* 44, pp. 281–307.

Mukherjee, Tarun K. 1991. "A Survey of Corporate Leasing Analysis." *Financial Management* 20 (Autumn), pp. 96–107.

Obstfeld, Maurice, and Kenneth Rogoff. 2001. "The Six Major Puzzles in International Macroeconomics: Is There a Common Cause?" In *NBER Macroeconomics Annual 2000,* edited by Ben Bernanke and Kenneth Rogoff (Cambridge, Mass.: MIT Press), pp. 339–390.

Parrino, Robert, and Michael Weisbach. 1999. "Measuring Investment Distortions Arising from Stockholder-Bondholder Conflicts." *Journal of Financial Economics* 53 (July), pp. 3–42.

Petersen, Mitchell A., and Raghuram G. Rajan. 1994. "The Benefits of Lending Relationships: Evidence from Small Business Data." *Journal of Finance* 49 (March), pp. 3–37.

Pettit, Richard, and Ronald Singer. 1985. "Small Business Finance: A Research Agenda." *Financial Management* 14 (Spring), pp. 47–60.

Peyer, Urs, and Anil Shivdasani. 2001. "Leverage and Internal Capital Markets: Evidence from Leveraged Recapitalizations." *Journal of Financial Economics* 59 (March), pp. 477–515.

Pratt, Stanley E. 1988. "The Organized Venture Capital Community." In *Pratt's Guide to Venture Capital Sources,* edited by Stanley E. Pratt (New York: Securities Data Publishing), pp. 55–61.

Puri, Manju. 1999. "Commercial Banks as Underwriters: Implications for the Going Public Process." *Journal of Financial Economics* 54, pp. 133–163.

Rajan, Raghuram, and Mitchell Petersen. 1997. "Trade Credit: Some Theories and Evidence." *Review of Financial Studies* 10, pp. 661–692.

Rau, P. Raghavendra. 2000. "Investment Bank Market Share, Contingent Fee Payments, and the Performance of Acquiring Firms." *Journal of Financial Economics* 56 (May), pp. 293–324.

Ravid, S. Abraham, and Stefan Sundgren. 1998. "The Comparative Efficiency of Small-Firm Bankruptcies: A Study of the US and Finnish Bankruptcy Codes." *Financial Management* 27 (Winter), pp. 28–40.

Reese, William A., Jr. 1998. "Capital Gains Taxation and Stock Market Activity: Evidence from IPOs." *Journal of Finance* 53 (October), pp. 1799–1819.

Rodriguez, Ricardo. 1988. "The Wealth Maximization Ordering Quantity: An Extension." *Financial Review* 23 (May), pp. 227–232.

Rubinstein, Mark E. 1973. "A Mean-Variance Synthesis of Corporate Financial Policy." *Journal of Finance* 28 (March), pp. 167–181.

Safieddine, Assem, and Sheridan Titman. 1999. "Leverage and Corporate Performance: Evidence from Unsuccessful Takeovers." *Journal of Finance* 54 (April), pp. 547–580.

Samuelson, Paul A. 1965. "Proof That Properly Anticipated Prices Fluctuate Randomly." *Industrial Management Review* 6 (Spring), pp. 41–49.

Scherr, Frederick C. 1996. "Optimal Trade Credit Limits." *Financial Management* 25, pp. 71–85.

Schultz, Paul H., and Mir A. Zaman. 1994. "Aftermarket Support and the Underpricing of Initial Public Offerings." *Journal of Financial Economics* 35 (April), pp. 199–219.

Shapiro, Alan C., and Sheridan Titman. 1986. "An Integrated Approach to Corporate Risk Management." In *The Revolution in Corporate Finance,* edited by Joel Stern and Donald Chew (Oxford, U.K.: Basil Blackwell).

Sherman, Ann Geunther. 1992. "The Pricing of Best Efforts New Issues." *Journal of Finance* 47 (June), pp. 781–795.

Sirri, Erik R., and Peter Tufano. 1998. "Costly Search and Mutual Fund Flows." *Journal of Finance* 53 (October), pp. 1589–1622.

Slovin, Myron B., Marie E. Sushka, and K. W. L. Lai. 2000. "Alternative Flotation Methods, Adverse Selection, and Ownership Structure: Evidence from Seasoned Equity Issuance in the U.K." *Journal of Financial Economics* 57 (August), pp. 157–190.

Smith, Clifford W., Jr., and René M. Stulz. 1985. "The Determinants of Firms' Hedging Policies." *Journal of Financial and Quantitative Analysis* 20 (December), pp. 391–405.

Smith, Janet Kiholm. 1987. "Trade Credit and Informational Asymmetry." *Journal of Finance* 42 (September), pp. 863–872.

Sneddon, Gregory B., and Jay K. Turner. 1997. "Non-traditional Financing Sources." In *Pratt's Guide to Venture Capital Sources,* edited by Stanley E. Pratt (New York: Venture Economics), pp. 91–96.

Srinivasan, Venkat, Yong H. Kim, and R. A. Eisenbeis.1987. "Credit Granting: A Comparative Analysis of Classification Procedures." *Journal of Finance* 42 (July), pp. 665–681.

Stulz, René M. 1984. "Optimal Hedging Policies." *Journal of Financial and Quantitative Analysis* 19 (June), pp. 127–140.

Vuolteenaho, Tuomo. 2002. "What Drives Firm-Level Stock Returns?"

Journal of Finance 57 (April), pp. 233–264.

Wakita, Shigeru. 2001. "Efficiency of the Dojima Rice Future Market in Tokugawa-Period Japan." *Journal of Banking and Finance* 25 (March), pp. 535–554.

Weiss, Lawrence A. 1990. "Bankruptcy Resolution: Direct Costs and Violations of Absolute Priority of Claims." *Journal of Financial Economics* 27 (October), pp. 285–314.

Welch, Ivo. 1991. "An Empirical Examination of Models of Contract Choice in Initial Public Offerings." *Journal of Financial and Quantitative Analysis* 26 (December), pp. 497–518.

Whited, Toni M. 1992. "Debt, Liquidity Constraints and Corporate Investment: Evidence from Panel Data." *Journal of Finance* 47 (September), pp. 1425–1460.

Zingales, Luigi. 1998. "Survival of the Fittest or the Fattest? Exit and Financing in the Trucking Industry." *Journal of Finance* 53 (June), pp. 905–938.

GLOSSARY

ABC system An inventory control system that segregates inventory into three groups—A, B, and C. The A items require the largest dollar investment and the most intensive control, the B items require the next largest investment and less intensive control, and the C items require the smallest investment and the least intensive control.

absolute priority rules Rules contained in Chapter 7 of the Bankruptcy Reform Act of 1978 that specify the procedure by which secured creditors are paid first, then unsecured creditors, then preferred shareholders, and finally common stockholders.

accounting exposure Occurs when MNCs translate costs and revenues denominated in foreign currencies to report on their financial statements, which, of course, are denominated in the home currency. This type of risk arises because foreign exchange rate fluctuations affect individual accounts in the financial statements.

accounting rate of return Calculation of a hurdle rate by dividing net income by the book value of assets, either on a year-by-year basis or by taking an average over the project's life.

accounts payable management A short-term financing activity that involves managing the time that elapses between the purchase of raw materials and mailing the payment to the supplier.

accredited investors Individuals or institutions that meet certain income and wealth requirements.

accrual-based approach Revenues are recorded at the point of sale and costs when they are incurred, not necessarily when a firm receives or pays out cash.

acquisition The purchase of additional resources by a business enterprise.

activity ratio A measure of the speed with which various accounts are converted into sales or cash.

additional paid-in capital Capital in excess of par value.

adjustable-rate preferred stock A corporate obligation used for short-term investments. These stocks take advantage of the dividend exclusion (of 70 percent or more) for stock in one corporation held by another corporation. In order to make this investment suitable for short-term holdings, the dividend rate paid on the stock is adjusted according to some rate index. This will stabilize the price, even if interest rates change during the 45-day holding period required to qualify for the dividend exclusion.

adjusted present value A method for valuing investment projects or firms that discounts unlevered cash flows at the cost of equity and then adds the present value of any financing side effects, such as the tax shield associated with debt financing.

agency bonds Bonds issued by federal government agencies. Agency bonds are not explicitly backed by the full faith and credit of the U.S. government. Agencies issue bonds to promote the formation of credit in certain sectors of the economy such as real estate, education, and farming.

agency cost of overvalued equity Michael Jensen's model of the agency cost of overvalued equity predicts that when a company's stock becomes significantly overvalued, this sets in motion a set of organizational forces that inevitably push managers to take actions that destroy part or all of the firm's core value. A manager's stock is overvalued when she realizes that she cannot, except by pure luck, produce the performance required to justify this stock price.

agency cost/tax-shield trade-off model Theoretical model that predicts managers choose the mix of debt and equity that strikes a balance between the tax advantages of debt and the agency costs of using leverage.

agency cost theory of financial structure Michael Jensen and William Meckling (1976) observe that when an entrepreneur owns 100 percent of the stock of a company, there is no separation between corporate ownership and control; the entrepreneur bears all the costs, and reaps all the benefits, of her or his actions.

agency cost/contracting model A theoretical model that explains empirical regularities in dividend payment and share repurchase patterns.

agency costs The costs that arise due to conflicts of interest between shareholders and managers.

agency problems The conflict between the goals of a firm's owners and managers.

aggressive strategy When a company relies heavily on short-term borrowing, not only to meet the seasonal peaks each year but also to finance a portion of the long-term growth in sales and assets.

aging of accounts receivable A schedule that indicates the portions of the total accounts receivable balance that have been outstanding for specified periods of time.

all-in rate The base rate and the spread.

allocative efficiency Markets channeling resources to their most productive uses.

American call option Gives holders the right to purchase stock at a fixed price on or before the expiration date.

American Depositary Receipts (ADRs) Dollar-denominated claims, issued by U.S. banks, that represent ownership of shares of a foreign company's stock held on deposit by the U.S. bank in the issuing firm's home country.

angel capitalists Wealthy individuals who make private equity investments on an ad hoc basis.

annual percentage rate (*APR*) The stated annual rate calculated by multiplying the periodic rate by the number of periods in one year.

annual percentage yield (*APY*) The annual rate of interest actually earned reflecting the impact of compounding frequency.

annuity A stream of equal periodic (frequently annual) cash flows over a stated period of time.

annuity due An annuity for which the payments occur at the beginning of each period.

antitakeover amendments Adding defensive measures to corporate charters to avoid a hostile takeover.

appreciated The condition of a currency that has increased in value compared to another currency.

arbitrage The process of buying something in one market at a low price and simultaneously selling it in another market at a higher price to generate an immediate, risk-free profit.

arbitrage pricing theory (APT) Begins with the notion that financial markets are frictionless, so that investors can buy or sell short any of a large number of assets that trade in this market.

arithmetic average return The average annual return over a period of years.

asset beta A measure of the systematic risk of a real asset based on the covariance of the cash flows generated by that asset divided by the variance of cash flows from the market portfolio.

asset market model of exchange rates This model makes a distinction between the demand for a currency as a means of payment (transactions demand) and the demand for currency as a financial asset (as a store of value).

asset substitution An investment that will increase firm value but does not earn a return high enough to fully redeem the maturing bonds.

assets-to-equity (A/E) ratio A measurement of the proportion of total assets financed by a firm's equity.

assignment An agreement of the creditors by which they pass the power to liquidate the firm's assets to an adjustment bureau, a trade association, or a third party.

at the money Occurs when an option's stock price and strike price are equal.

atomistic Descriptive of capital markets grown large because of investors willing to accept small ownership and creditor positions in public companies.

automated clearinghouse (ACH) debit transfer A preauthorized electronic withdrawal from the payer's account.

availability float The time between deposit of a check and availability of the funds to a firm.

average age of inventory A measure of inventory turnover, calculated by dividing the turnover figure into 365, the number of days in a year.

average collection period The average length of time from a sale on credit until the payment becomes usable funds for a firm. Also called the *average age of accounts receivable*.

average investment in accounts receivable (*AIAR*) An estimate of the actual amount of cash tied up in accounts receivable at any time during the year.

average payment period Calculated by dividing the firm's accounts payable balance by its average daily purchases. Also called the *average payment period*.

Backward integration A merger in which the acquired company provides an earlier step in the production process.

balloon payment A term loan agreement that requires periodic interest payments over the life of the loan followed by a large lump-sum payment at maturity.

bank account analysis statement A regular report (usually monthly) provided to a bank's commercial customers that specifies all services provided, including items processed and any charges assessed.

bank discount yield A poor measure of a bond's return that is frequently used by bond traders to communicate with each other about current prices in the market.

bankruptcy Occurs only when a company enters bankruptcy court and effectively surrenders control of the firm to a bankruptcy judge.

bankruptcy costs The direct and indirect costs of the bankruptcy process.

Bankruptcy Reform Act of 1978 The governing bankruptcy legislation in the United States today.

basis points Yield spreads on bonds are normally quoted in terms of basis points. One basis point equals one one-hundredth of one percent, that is .01 percent. Simply put, 100 basis points = 1.00%.

basis risk The possibility of unanticipated changes in the difference between the futures price and the spot price.

bearer bonds Bonds that both shelter investment income from taxation and provide protection against exchange rate risk.

behavioral finance Asserts that because traders in financial markets are human beings, they are subject to all the foibles and fads that bedevil human judgment in other spheres of life.

best-efforts offering In a best-efforts offering, the investment bank merely promises to give its best effort to sell the firm's securities at the agreed-upon price, but makes no guarantee about the ultimate success of the offering. If there is insufficient demand, the firm withdraws the issue from the market. Best-efforts offerings are most commonly used for small, high-risk companies, and the investment bank receives a commission based on the number of shares sold.

beta A standardized measure of the risk of an individual asset, one that captures only the systematic component of its volatility.

biased self-attribution Investors with this trait will interpret the arrival of new private information supporting their existing beliefs as important confirmatory evidence, but will tend to disregard contradictory new evidence as being random noise.

binomial option-pricing model This model recognizes that investors can combine options (either calls or puts) with shares of the underlying asset to construct a portfolio with a risk-free payoff.

Black and Scholes option-pricing equation A stochastic differential equation relating the time to expiration and the strike price of an option, the current price and the volatility of its underlying stock, and the risk-free interest rate.

board of directors Elected by shareholders to be responsible for hiring and firing managers and setting overall corporate policies.

bond equivalent yield The percentage return on zero-coupon bonds calculated as the difference between the par value and the purchase price.

bond ratings Grades assigned based on degree of risk.

bonding mechanism Shareholders are willing to pay a higher price for a firm's shares, because taking on debt validates a manager's willingness to risk losing control of her firm if she fails to perform effectively.

bonds Debt with original maturities of more than seven years.

book building A process in which underwriters ask prospective investors to reveal information about their demand for the offering. Through conversations with investors, the underwriter tries to measure the demand curve for a given issue, and the investment bank sets the offer price after gathering all the information it can from investors.

book value The value of a firm's equity as shown on its balance sheet.

bottom-up sales forecast This kind of sales forecast relies on the assessment by sales personnel of demand in the coming year on a customer-by-customer basis.

break-even analysis A calculation that shows conditions under which a project's profits and losses, or cash inflows and outflows, balance out.

bulge bracket Consists of firms that generally occupy the lead or co-lead manager's position in large, new security offerings, meaning that they take primary responsibility for the new offering (even though other banks participate as part of a syndicate), and as a result they earn higher fees.

business failure The unfortunate circumstance of a firm's inability to stay in business.

Business Judgment Rule A legal doctrine giving directors broad legal discretion to use their business judgment and protecting boards of directors from shareholder second-guessing in all but obvious cases of abuse.

bust-up The takeover of a company that is subsequently split up.

Call option Grants the right to purchase a share of stock (or some other asset) at a fixed price on or before a certain date.

call premium The amount by which the call price exceeds the par value of a bond. Paid by corporations to call bonds after a protection period ends.

callable Bonds that the issuing corporation has the right to force investors to sell back to the firm at the firm's discretion.

cancellation option Option to deny or delay additional funding for a venture fund.

cannibalization Loss of sales of an existing product when a new product is introduced.

capital asset pricing model (CAPM) States that the expected return on a specific asset equals the risk-free rate plus a premium that depends on the asset's beta and the expected risk premium on the market portfolio.

capital budgeting The process of identifying which long-lived investment projects a firm should undertake.

capital budgeting function Selecting the best projects in which to invest the resources of the firm, based on each project's perceived risk and expected return.

capital investment Investments in long-lived assets such as plant, equipment, and advertising.

capital lease A noncancelable contractual arrangement whereby the lessee agrees to make periodic payments to the lessor, typically for more than five years, to obtain an asset's services.

capital market line (CML) Under the assumption of homogeneous expectations, the line connecting the market portfolio to the risk-free rate, which quantifies the relationship between the expected return and standard deviation for portfolios consisting of the risk-free asset and the market portfolio.

capital rationing Choosing a combination of projects that maximizes shareholder wealth, given a set of attractive investment opportunities and subject to the constraint of limited funds.

capital spending Investments in long-lived assets such as plant, equipment, and advertising.

capital structure decision Distributing the financial claims on the firm between debt and equity securities in order to maximize the market value of a firm.

capitalizing Predicting what the firm's cash flows will be over time and then determining the present value of that stream today.

cash application The process through which a customer's payment is posted to its account and the outstanding invoices are cleared as paid.

cash budget A statement of a firm's planned inflows and outflows of cash.

cash concentration The process of bringing the lockbox and other deposits together into one bank, often called the *concentration bank*.

cash conversion cycle (CCC) The elapsed time between the points at which a firm pays for raw materials and at which it receives payment for finished goods.

cash disbursements These include all outlays of cash by a firm in a given period.

cash discount A method of lowering investment in accounts receivable by rewarding prompt payment.

cash flow approach Used by financial professionals to focus attention on current and prospective inflows and outflows of cash.

cash flow from operations Cash inflows and outflows directly related to the production and sale of a firm's products or services. Calculated as net income plus depreciation and other noncash charges.

cash manager A specialist responsible for managing a firm's cash flow time line related to collection, concentration, and disbursement of the company's funds.

cash position management The collection, concentration, and disbursement of funds for the company.

cash receipts These include all of a firm's cash inflows in a given period.

cash settlement Investor sale of an option for cash eliminates the need for the seller to buy shares to give to the buyer, together with the need for the buyer to sell shares if he wants to convert his profit into cash.

cash-out statutes Antitrust "all-or-none" rules that disallow a partial tender offer/acquisition of a company and the ability to control that company with less than 100 percent ownership.

catastrophe bonds Bonds that distribute interest and principal payments that vary according to whether or not the issuer, an insurance company, experiences losses of a certain magnitude from a natural disaster, such as a hurricane or an earthquake. Insurance companies sell these bonds to redistribute some of the risk of their product portfolios. For investors, catastrophe bonds offer unique diversification benefits because the occurrence of natural disasters is not highly correlated with other sources of financial risk (e.g., interest rate movements, currency movements, business cycles).

catering theory Predicts that corporate managers cater to investor preferences by paying dividends when investors assign a premium to dividend-paying stocks, and by not paying when investors assign a discount to dividend payers. In other words, corporations respond more or less passively to investor preferences regarding whether profits should be distributed as dividends or retained inside the firm.

certification Assurance that the issuing company is in fact disclosing all material information.

Chapter 11 Section of the Bankruptcy Reform Act of 1978 that outlines the procedures for reorganizing a failed or failing firm, whether its petition is filed voluntarily or involuntarily.

Chapter 7 Section of the Bankruptcy Reform Act of 1978 that details the procedures to be followed when liquidating a failed firm.

chartists Practitioners of technical analysis.

chief executive officer (CEO) Hired by the board of directors to be responsible for managing day-to-day operations and carrying out the policies established by the board.

clearing float The time between deposit of the check and presentation of the check back to the bank on which it is drawn.

closing futures price The price used to settle all contracts at the end of each day's trading.

coinsurance of debt The debt of each combining firm in a merger is insured with cash flows from two businesses.

cold comfort letter A simple statement that a company's financial statements were prepared according to generally accepted accounting principles and accurately reflect all relevant information.

collateral The specific assets pledged to secure a loan.

collateral trust bonds A secured type of bond.

collection policy The procedures used by a company to collect overdue or delinquent accounts receivable. The approach used is often a function of the industry and the competitive environment.

collective action problem When an individual stockholder expends time and resources monitoring managers, bearing the costs of monitoring management while the benefit of his or her activities accrues to all shareholders.

co-managers Banks other than the lead underwriter when a firm enlists the services of more than one investment bank.

commercial paper The primary corporate obligation in the short-term market. Typically structured as an unsecured promissory note with a maturity of less than 270 days and sold to other corporations and individual investors. Most issues are also backed by credit guarantees from a financial institution, are sold on a discount basis, and are held to maturity.

common stock Stockholder's equity.

common-size income statement An income statement in which all entries are expressed as a percentage of sales.

competitively bid offer The less common approach firms can take in choosing an investment banker: The firm announces the terms of its intended equity sale, and investment banks bid for the business.

composition A pro rata cash settlement of creditor claims.

compound interest Interest earned both on the principal amount and on the interest earned in previous periods.

conglomerate mergers Pure conglomerate mergers, or unrelated diversification mergers, occur between companies in completely different lines of business.

conservative strategy When a company makes sure that it has enough long-term financing to cover its permanent investments in fixed and current assets as well as the additional investments in current assets that it makes during the third and fourth quarters each year.

consolidation A merger in which both the acquirer and target disappear as separate corporations, combining to form an entirely new corporation with new common stock.

constant growth model Assumes that dividends will grow at a constant rate forever, when calculating the value of a cash flow stream by using the formula for a growing perpetuity.

constant nominal payment policy Based on the payment of a fixed-dollar dividend in each period.

constant payout ratio policy Used by a firm to establish that a certain percentage of earnings is paid to owners in each dividend period.

continuous compounding Interest compounds at literally every moment as time passes.

contribution margin The sale price per unit minus variable cost per unit.

controlled disbursement A bank service that provides early notification of checks that will be presented against a company's account on a given day.

conversion premium Price to which shares would have to rise before bondholders would want to convert their bonds into shares.

conversion price The market price of a convertible bond divided by its conversion ratio. The conversion price shows the price that a bondholder effectively pays for common stock if the bondholder exercises the conversion option.

conversion ratio Defines how many shares bondholders will receive if they convert.

conversion value The value bondholders receive if they do convert. Conversion value is important because it helps define a lower bound on the market value of a convertible bond.

convertible Corporate bonds that grant an investor the right to exchange the bonds for shares of stock rather than cash.

convertible bond The investor is granted the right to receive payment in shares of an underlying stock rather than in cash.

corporate bonds Bonds with maturities ranging from 1 to 100 years issued by corporations.

corporate charter The legal document created at the corporation's inception to govern its operations.

corporate control The monitoring, supervision, and direction of a corporation or other business organization.

corporate finance The science of managing money in a business environment.

corporate focus A focused firm concentrates its efforts on its core (primary) business; the opposite end of the spectrum from a diversified firm.

corporate governance The system that encompasses a nation's body of commercial law, including the institutions, regulations, and practices that influence how, and in whose interest, managers run companies.

corporate governance function Developing an ownership and corporate governance structure for the company, which ensures that the managers act ethically and in the interests of the firm's stakeholders, particularly its stockholders.

corporate insider A commercial bank or other financial institution trusted with confidential information concerning a borrowing firm's operations and opportunities.

corporate tax system A system where governments levy income taxes on profits earned by corporations and then tax these profits again at the personal level when they are paid out as dividends.

corporate venture capital funds Subsidiaries or stand-alone firms established by nonfinancial corporations eager to gain access to emerging technologies by making early-stage investments in high-tech firms.

corporation In U.S. law, a separate legal entity with many of the economic rights and responsibilities enjoyed by individuals.

correlation coefficient A unit-free measure of the co-movement of two assets that standardizes the covariance measure by dividing it by the product of the standard deviations of each asset.

cost of marginal investment in accounts receivable The marginal investment in accounts receivable required to support a proposed change in credit standards multiplied by the required return on investment.

counterparty risk The risk that the counterparty on specific trade will default on its obligation.

coupon A fixed amount of interest that a bond promises to pay investors.

coupon rate The rate derived by dividing the bond's annual coupon payment by its par value.

coupon yield The amount obtained by dividing the bond's coupon by its current market price (which does not always equal its par value).

covariance A statistical concept that provides a way of measuring the co-movements of two random variables.

coverage ratio A debt ratio that focuses more on income statement measures of a firm's ability to generate sufficient cash flow to make scheduled interest and principal payments.

covered interest arbitrage Occurs when traders attempt to earn arbitrage profits arising from differences in interest rates across countries and "cover" their currency exposures with forward contracts.

cramdown procedure Used when a reorganization plan fails to meet the standard for approval by all classes, but at least one class of creditors has voted for a reorganization plan; or when the firm is clearly insolvent and the existing equity has no value.

credit monitoring The ongoing review of a firm's accounts receivable to determine if customers are paying according to the stated credit terms.

credit scoring Applies statistically derived weights for key financial and credit characteristics to predict whether or not a credit applicant with specific scores for each characteristic will pay the requested credit in a timely fashion.

credit terms The terms of sale for customers.

creditor control The creditor committee takes control of the firm and operates it until all claims have been settled.

cross exchange rate Calculated by dividing the dollar exchange rate for one currency by the dollar exchange rate for another currency.

cross-default covenant In which the borrower is often considered to be in default on all debts if it is in default on any debt.

cross-hedging The underlying securities in a futures contract and the assets being hedged have different characteristics.

cumulative voting system System that gives to each share of common stock a number of votes equal to the total number of directors to be elected.

currency forward contract Exchange of one currency for another at a fixed date in the future.

currency swap A swap contract in which two parties exchange payment obligations denominated in different currencies.

current ratio A measure of a firm's ability to meet its short-term obligations, defined as current assets divided by current liabilities.

Date of record The date on which the names of all persons who own shares in a company are recorded as stockholders and thus eligible to receive a dividend.

debentures Unsecured bonds backed only by the general faith and credit of the borrowing company.

debt Borrowed money.

debt beta A measure of the systematic risk of a real debt based on the covariance between return on debt and returns on a diversified portfolio of securities.

debt capital Capital provided by the firm's creditors.

debt ratio A measurement of the proportion of total assets financed by a firm's creditors.

debt-to-equity ratio A measurement calculated by dividing long-term debt by stockholders' equity.

debtor in possession (DIP) The firm filing a reorganization petition.

decision tree A visual representation of the choices that managers face over time with regard to a particular investment.

default risk The risk that the corporation selling a bond may not make all scheduled payments.

deferred taxes Reflect the discrepancy between the taxes that firms actually pay and the tax liabilities they report on their public financial statements.

depository transfer check (DTC) A method for transferring cash from the depository banks to the concentration bank. An unsigned check is drawn on one of the firm's bank accounts and deposited in another of the firm's bank accounts.

depreciated The condition of a currency that has decreased in value compared to a different currency.

depreciation A noncash expense that effectively spreads the cost of an asset over several accounting periods.

derivative securities A class of financial instruments that derive their values from other assets.

direct costs of bankruptcy Out-of-pocket cash expenses directly related to bankruptcy filing and administration.

direct lease A lessor acquires the assets that are leased to a given lessee.

direct quotation An exchange rate quote expressed in terms of home currency/foreign currency.

discount The difference between a bond's par value and the purchase price when the price is less than par value.

discount investment An investment vehicle for which the investor pays less than face value at the time of purchase and then receives the face value of the investment at its maturity date.

discounted cash flow (DCF) analysis A process of valuing a financial or nonfinancial asset by calculating the asset's cash flows and discounting them at an appropriate rate.

discounted payback The amount of time it takes for a project's discounted cash flows to recover the initial investment.

discounting Describes the process of calculating present values.

divestiture Assets and/or resources of a subsidiary or division are sold to another organization.

dividend payout ratio The percentage of current earnings available for common stockholders paid out as dividends. Calculated by dividing the firm's cash dividend per share by its earnings per share.

dividend per share (DPS) The portion of the earnings per share paid to stockholders.

dividend yield Computed by dividing a firm's annual dividend per share by its stock price.

double taxation problem Taxation of corporate income at both the company and the personal levels—the single greatest disadvantage of the corporate form.

dual-class recapitalization Organizational restructuring in which the parties wishing to concentrate control (usually management) buy all the shares of a newly issued Class B stock, which carries "super" voting rights (100 votes per share, for example).

due diligence Examination of potential security issuers in which investment banks are legally required to search out and disclose all relevant information about an issuer before selling securities to the public.

DuPont system An analysis that uses both income and balance sheet information to break the *ROA* and *ROE* ratios into component pieces.

Earnings available for common stockholders Net income net of preferred stock dividends.

earnings per share (EPS) Earnings available for common stockholders divided by the number of shares of common stock outstanding.

economic exposure The overall impact of foreign exchange rate fluctuations on the firm's value. Also, the risk that a change in prices will negatively impact the value of all cash flows of a firm.

economic failure A firm fails to earn a return that is greater than its cost of capital.

economic order quantity (EOQ) model A common tool used to estimate the optimal order quantity for big-ticket items of inventory. It considers operating and financial costs and determines the order quantity that minimizes overall inventory costs.

economic value added (EVA®) A copyrighted measure calculated as the difference between a firm's net operating profits after taxes (*NOPAT*) and its cost of funds. Often used by firms as a growth target.

economies of scale Relative operating costs are reduced for merged companies because of an increase in size that allows for the reduction or elimination of overlapping resources.

economies of scope Value-creating benefits of increased size for merged companies.

effective Status of an offering before any shares can actually be sold to public investors.

effective annual rate (EAR) The annual rate of interest actually paid or earned, reflecting the impact of compounding frequency.

effective borrowing rate (EBR) Generally determined as the total amount of interest and fees paid, divided by the average usable loan amount.

efficient frontier Portfolios that maximize expected returns for any given level of volatility.

efficient markets hypothesis (EMH) Asserts that financial asset prices fully reflect all available information (as formally presented by Eugene Fama in 1970).

efficient portfolio A portfolio that offers the highest expected return among the group of portfolios with equal or less volatility.

efficient set A set of portfolios, determined graphically, that offer the highest available expected returns without adding volatility.

electronic bill presentment and payment (EBPP) Customers are sent bills in an electronic format and can then pay them via electronic means.

electronic depository transfer (EDT) The term used in the cash management trade for a preauthorized electronic withdrawal from the payer's account.

electronic invoice presentment and payment (EIPP) A system in business-to-business transactions under which business customers are sent bills in an electronic format and then can pay them via electronic means.

employee stock ownership plan (ESOP) The transformation of a public corporation into a private company by the employees of the corporation itself.

entrepreneurial finance Study involving investment in and financing of entrepreneurial growth companies.

entrepreneurial growth companies (ECGs) Companies typically funded by venture capitalists.

equilibrium interest rate The rate that "clears the market," equating total savings and investment within an economy.

equipment trust certificates A secured type of bond.

equipment trust receipts Loans extended for the purchase of transportation equipment.

equity An ownership interest usually in the form of common or preferred stock.

equity capital Capital provided by the firm's owners. This includes common and preferred stock.

equity claimant Owner of a corporation's equity securities.

equity kickers Warrants that are attached to other securities.

equity multiplier A measurement of the proportion of total assets financed by a firm's equity.

equity risk premium The difference (historical or forward looking) between the returns on a portfolio of common stocks and a risk-free asset such as a Treasury bond or bill.

equivalent annual cost (EAC) method Calculates the present value of cash flows for each device over its lifetime.

ethics Standards of conduct in business dealings.

euro Currency adopted as a continent-wide medium of exchange by 12 of the 15 European Union (EU) nations as a result of the Maastricht Treaty of 1991.

Eurobond A bond issued by an international borrower and sold to investors in countries with currencies other than that in which the bond is denominated.

Eurocurrency loan market A large number of international banks that stand ready to make floating-rate, hard-currency loans to international corporate and government borrowers.

European call option Gives holders the right to purchase stock at a fixed price only on the expiration date.

event study Examination of how stock markets respond to new information releases.

ex-dividend A purchaser of a stock does not receive the current dividend.

ex-dividend-day study Examines whether (and how) differing capital gains and dividend income tax rates impact the average change in a firm's stock price on its ex-dividend day. Prior to this day, an investor who buys the stock receives the next dividend payment; after it goes ex-dividend, the former owner receives the dividend. By testing whether the average price change on the ex-dividend day is less than the amount of the dividend payments, researchers study whether personal taxes affect stock valuation.

excess earnings accumulation tax A tax levied by the IRS on a firm that has accumulated sufficient excess earnings to allow owners to delay paying ordinary income taxes.

exchange rate The price of one currency in terms of another.

executive compensation Incentives offered to a manager to encourage him or her to act in the best interests of the owners.

exercise price The price at which an option holder can buy or sell a stock on or before the option's expiration date.

exercise the option Purchase of stock in a call option.

expectations theory In equilibrium, investors should expect to earn the same return whether they invest in long-term Treasury bonds or a series of short-term Treasury bonds.

expiration date The date on which the right to purchase an option expires.

extension An arrangement wherein a firm's creditors are promised payment in full, although not immediately.

external funds required (EFR) The expectation of a scarcity or a surplus of financial resources, given the firm's growth objectives.

extra dividend The additional dividend that a firm pays if earnings are higher than normal in a given period.

Factoring The outright sale of receivables to a third party at a discount.

fair bet A gamble that offers an expected payoff of zero.

fair price provisions Antitrust rules that ensure that all target shareholders receive the same offer price in any tender offers initiated by the same acquirer, limiting the ability of acquirers to buy minority shares cheaply with a two-tiered offer.

fallen angels Bonds that received investment-grade ratings when first issued but later fell to junk status.

Fama-French (F-F) model A mathematical expression similar to the arbitrage pricing theory.

feasible set A set of points, determined graphically, representing the expected return and standard deviation for all possible portfolios of two stocks.

field-banking system System characterized by many collection points, each of which may have a depository account at a local bank.

final prospectus The part of a firm's security issue registration statement that must be distributed to all prospective investors. The registration statement is the principal disclosure document for all public security offerings. Firms must file this highly detailed document with the SEC before they can solicit investors. A final revised version must be approved by the commission before an offering can become effective, meaning before any shares can actually be sold to public investors.

financial deficit More financial capital for investment and investor payments than is retained in profits by a corporation.

financial engineering The process of using the principles of financial economics to design and price financial instruments.

financial intermediary An institution that raises capital by issuing liabilities against itself. Also, a commercial bank or other entity that lends to corporations.

financial lease A noncancelable contractual arrangement whereby the lessee agrees to make periodic payments to the lessor, typically for more than five years, to obtain an asset's services.

financial leverage Using debt to magnify both the risk and expected return on a firm's investments. Also, the result of the presence of debt when firms finance their operations with debt and equity, leading to a higher stock beta.

financial management function Managing the firm's internal cash flows and its mix of debt and equity financing, both to maximize the value of the debt and equity claims on the firm and to ensure that the company can pay off its obligations when they come due.

financial slack Large cash and marketable security holdings or unused debt capacity.

financial synergies A merger results in less-volatile cash flows, lower default risk, and a lower cost of capital.

financial venture capital funds Subsidiaries of financial institutions, particularly commercial banks.

financing flows Result from debt and equity financing transactions.

financing function Raising capital to support a company's operations and investment programs.

firm-commitment offering A type of offering in which the investment bankers actually purchase the shares from a firm and resell them to investors.

five C's of credit A framework for performing in-depth credit analysis without providing a specific accept or reject decision.

fixed asset turnover A measurement of the efficiency with which a firm uses its fixed assets, calculated by dividing sales by the number of dollars of fixed asset investment.

fixed exchange rate Occurs when governments fix (or *peg*) their currency's value, usually in terms of another currency such as the U.S. dollar. The opposite of a floating exchange rate.

fixed-coupon Debt instruments that pay interest at a coupon interest rate that is fixed for the life of the security and does not change when market rates change.

fixed-for-floating currency swap A combination of a currency swap and an interest rate swap.

fixed-for-floating interest rate swap Typically one party will make fixed-rate payments to another party in exchange for floating-rate payments.

fixed-price offer An offer in which the underwriters set the final offer price for a new issue weeks in advance.

fixed-rate offerings Offerings that have a coupon interest rate that remains constant throughout the issue's life.

flip To buy shares at the offer price and sell them on the first trading day.

float Funds that have been sent by the payer but are not yet usable by the payee.

floating exchange rate Occurs when forces of supply and demand continuously move currency values up and down.

floating-rate instruments Loan interest rates that periodically change to reflect changes in market interest rates.

floating-rate issues Debt issues with an interest (coupon) rate that periodically changes.

flow to equity A method for valuing investment projects or companies in which levered cash flows are discounted at the cost of equity.

foreign bond A bond issued in a host country's financial market, in the host country's currency, by a nonresident corporation.

foreign direct investment (FDI) The transfer by a multinational firm of financial, managerial, and technical assets from its home country to a host country.

foreign exchange (forex) market The financial market where investors and other participants trade one currency for another.

forward discount What a currency trades at when it buys less of another currency on the forward market than it does on the spot market.

forward exchange rate The price at which a future foreign currency trade will take place.

forward integration A merger in which the acquired company provides a later step in the production process.

forward interest rate The interest rate expected in a future year. It can be estimated mathematically by evaluating the difference in the returns between similar-risk bonds that differ in maturity by that one future year.

forward premium What a currency trades at when it buys more of another currency on the forward market than it does on the spot market.

forward price In a forward contract, the price agreed upon by two parties today, at which the purchaser will buy a specified amount of an asset from the seller at a fixed date sometime in the future and which has zero net present value.

forward rate In a currency forward contract, the forward price.

forward rate agreement (FRA) A forward contract in which the underlying asset is not an asset at all but an interest rate.

forward–spot parity Holds that the forward rate should be an unbiased predictor of where the spot rate is headed.

free cash flow (FCF) The net amount of cash flow remaining after the firm has met all operating needs and paid for investments, both long-term (fixed) and short-term (current). Represents the cash amount that a firm could distribute to investors after meeting all its other obligations.

full disclosure Requires issuers to reveal all relevant information concerning the company selling the securities and the securities themselves to potential investors.

fundamental principle of financial leverage The concept that substituting long-term debt for equity in a firm's capital structure increases both the level of expected returns to shareholders—measured by earnings per share or *ROE*—and the risk (dispersion) of those expected returns.

fungibility The ability to close out a position by taking an offsetting position.

future value Calculation of what the value of an investment made today will be worth at a specific future date.

futures contract Involves two parties agreeing today on a price at which the purchaser will buy a given amount of a commodity or financial instrument from the seller at a fixed date sometime in the future.

General Agreement on Tariffs and Trade (GATT) An international treaty that facilitates free trade by overseeing taxes on traded goods and working out trade disagreements.

general cash offerings Most equity sales in the United States fall under this category.

general creditors Creditors who have no specific assets pledged as collateral or the proceeds from the sale of whose pledged assets are inadequate to cover the debt.

general partners One or more participants in a limited partnership who operate the business and have unlimited personal liability.

geometric average return The compound annual return over a period of years.

Glass-Steagall Act Congressional act of 1933 mandating the separation of investment and commercial banking.

Global Depositary Receipts (GDRs) These are claims issued by international banks representing ownership of shares of a foreign company's stock held on deposit by the bank in the issuing firm's home country. Many large international equity issues use this format for share tranches (portions of the issue) that are destined for sale outside of the issuer's home country and the United States.

going-private transaction The transformation of a public corporation into a private company through issuance of large amounts of debt used to buy all (or at least a voting majority) of the outstanding shares of the corporation.

goodwill An intangible asset created if the restated values of the target in a merger lead to a situation in which its assets are less than its liabilities and equity.

Gordon growth model The constant growth valuation model named after Myron Gordon, who popularized this formula during the 1960s and 1970s. It views cash flows as an annuity with an infinite life, promising to pay a growing amount at the end of each year.

Gramm-Leach-Bliley Act Congressional act of 1999 that repealed the Glass-Steagall Act.

Green Shoe option An option to sell up to 15 percent more shares than originally planned. Also called an *overallotment option*.

greenfield entry Internal expansion into a new market.

greenmail Payment made to an acquirer who threatens the target with a hostile tender offer and/or proxy fight in order to gain initial or greater access to the board of directors. Greenmail occurs when the potential acquirer sells his or her shares to the target firm at a premium price that is not offered to other investors.

gross profit margin A measurement of the percentage of each sales dollar remaining after a firm has paid for its goods.

grossed up Increased to provide a given after-tax yield.

growing perpetuity An annuity with an infinite life, promising to pay a growing amount at the end of each year.

Hedge To transfer to a third party.

hedge fund A professionally managed investment fund.

hedge ratio The combination of stocks and options that results in a perfectly hedged portfolio. Also, the ratio of the number of options to the number of shares in a perfectly hedged portfolio.

hedged A hedged position or portfolio is one from which all risk has been removed. Typically, traders create a hedged position

by combining assets with returns that are negatively correlated so that their fluctuations offset.

hedging strategies Techniques used to offset or protect against risk.

Herfindahl Index (HI) A measure popularized by Comment and Jarrell (1995) to demonstrate the relationship between corporate focus and shareholder wealth.

high-yield bonds Bonds rated below investment grade (also known as *junk bonds*).

hockey-stick diagram A payoff diagram for the call option buyer showing the long position over a range of stock prices.

homemade leverage Borrowing on personal account.

homogeneous expectations The assumption that all investors have access to the same information and that their estimates of the inputs needed to solve for the optimal portfolio are identical.

horizontal merger A combination of competitors within the same geographic market.

hostile takeover The acquisition of one firm by another through an open-market bid for a majority of the target's shares if the target firm's senior managers do not support (or, more likely, actively resist) the acquisition.

hubris hypothesis of corporate takeovers Richard Roll (1986) contends that some managers overestimate their own managerial capabilities and pursue takeovers with the belief that they can better manage their takeover target than the target's current management team can.

Imaging services Disbursement services offered by banks and other vendors to allow both sides of the check, as well as remittance information, to be converted into digital images. The images can then be transmitted via the Internet or easily stored for future reference. Imaging services are especially useful when incorporated with positive pay services.

implied volatility The value of σ obtained by "inverting" the Black and Scholes equation to calculate the level of volatility implied by the option's market price.

imputation tax system This gives individual investors an "imputed" tax credit along with the cash dividends they receive from companies. The investors can then claim the corporate income tax paid by the firm as a credit against their personal tax liability. This system effectively eliminates double taxation of dividends.

in the money Occurs when a call option's strike price is less than the current stock price.

income bonds An unsecured type of bond.

incremental project A hypothetical project with cash flows equal to the difference in cash flows between large-scale and small-scale investments.

indenture A legal document stating the conditions under which a bond has been issued.

indirect costs of bankruptcy Expenses or economic losses that result from bankruptcy but are not cash outflows spent on the process itself.

indirect quotation A way of quoting a currency price that gives the foreign currency price of one unit of the home currency.

inefficient portfolio A portfolio that offers a lower expected return than another portfolio with the same standard deviation.

information intermediation Financial service provided to corporations by intermediaries to help assess borrowers and monitor subsequent use of funds borrowed.

informational efficiency The tendency (or lack thereof) for prices in a market to rapidly and fully incorporate new, relevant information.

initial margin The minimum dollar amount required of an investor when taking a position in a futures contract.

initial public offering (IPO) A corporation offers its shares for sale to the public for the first time; the first public sale of company stock to outside investors.

initial return The gain when an allocation of shares from an investment banker is sold at the first opportunity because the offer price is consistently lower that what the market is willing to bear.

insolvency bankruptcy A firm's liabilities exceed the fair market value of its assets.

insolvent A firm is *insolvent* when (a) it is not paying its debts as they come due; (b) within the immediately preceding 120 days a custodian (a third party) was appointed or took possession of the debtor's property; or (c) the fair market value of its assets is less than the stated value of its liabilities.

institutional venture capital funds Formal business entities with full-time professionals dedicated to seeking out and funding promising ventures.

integrated accounts payable Provides a company with outsourcing of its accounts payable or disbursement operations. The outsourcing may be as minor as contracting with a bank to issue checks and perform reconciliations or as major as outsourcing the entire payables function.

interest differential In an interest rate swap, only the differential is exchanged.

interest rate cap A call option on interest rates.

interest rate collar A strategy involving the purchase of an interest rate cap and the simultaneous sale of an interest rate floor, using the proceeds from selling the floor to purchase the cap.

interest rate floor A put option on interest rates.

interest rate parity Asserts that risk-free investments should offer the same return (after converting currencies) everywhere.

interest rate risk The risk that changes in market interest rates will cause fluctuations in a bond's price. Also, the risk of suffering losses as a result of unanticipated changes in market interest rates.

interest rate swap A swap contract in which two parties exchange payment obligations involving different interest payment schedules.

internal capital markets Created when the high-cash-flow businesses of a conglomerate generate enough cash to fund the riskier business ventures internally.

internal rate of return (IRR) The compound annual return on a project, given its up-front costs and subsequent cash flows.

international common stock Equity issues sold in more than one country by nonresident corporations.

intrinsic value A measure of the profit an investor makes from exercising an option (ignoring transactions costs as well as the option premium).

inventory turnover A measure of how quickly a firm sells its goods.

investment bank A bank that helps firms acquire external capital.

investment flows Cash flows associated with the purchase or sale of both fixed assets and business equity.

investment-grade bonds Bonds rated Baa or higher by Moody's (BBB by S&P).

involuntary reorganization A reorganization initiated by an outside party, usually a creditor.

IPO underpricing Occurs when the offer price in the prospectus is consistently lower than what the market is willing to bear.

Joint and several liability Each partner is personally liable for all the debts of the partnership.

joint-hypothesis problem When an anomaly appears, while using an asset pricing model to form judgments about the risks and expected returns of two portfolios, it may be the result of market inefficiency or of a deficient model (or both).

junk bonds Bonds rated below investment grade (also known as *high-yield bonds*).

just-in-time (JIT) system An inventory management technique used to make sure that materials arrive exactly when they are needed for production rather than being stored on site. To work effectively it requires close teamwork among vendors and purchasing and production personnel.

L"Law and Finance" model This model states that the most important determinant of capital market development is the degree of legal protection afforded to outside (noncontrolling) investors, which, in turn, depends largely on whether a country's legal system is based on English common law or another legal tradition. Countries with English common law commercial codes tend to have larger debt and equity markets than do civil law countries.

law of one price The idea that identical goods trading in different markets should sell at the same price, absent any barriers to trade.

lead underwriter The investment bank that manages a firm's underwritten security offering and forms an underwriting syndicate consisting of many investment banks. These banks collectively purchase the firm's shares and market them, thus spreading the risk across the syndicate.

leads and lags Adjustments in the collection and payment of intra-MNC accounts in order to correct for the appreciation and depreciation of currency.

league table A tabular ranking of the world's 15 largest investment banks by the total value of securities underwritten, or for a particular type of debt or equity security.

lease Comparable to secured long-term debt; a contractual arrangement providing for a series of periodic, tax-deductible payments in return for use of the underlying asset.

lease-versus-buy decision *See* **lease-versus-purchase decision.**

lease-versus-purchase decision The alternatives available are to (1) lease the assets, (2) borrow funds to purchase the assets, or (3) purchase the assets using available liquid resources. Even if the firm has the liquid resources with which to purchase the assets, the use of these funds is viewed as equivalent to borrowing.

leasing Acquiring use of an asset by renting rather than purchasing it.

lending versus borrowing problem Choice is offered between cash paid out today in exchange for a larger amount of cash in one year, or cash received today with payback of a larger amount later.

lessee The user of the underlying asset who makes regular payments to the lessor.

lessor The owner of the asset who receives regular payments for its use by the lessee.

leveraged leases The lessor acts as an equity participant, supplying only about 20 percent of the cost of the asset, and a lender supplies the balance.

LIBOR The London Interbank Offered Rate.

lien A legal contract specifying under what conditions a lender can take title to an asset if a loan is not repaid, and prohibiting the borrowing firm from selling or disposing of the asset without the lender's consent.

lifetime high prices The highest settlement prices recorded for a contract since its inception.

lifetime low prices The lowest settlement prices recorded for a contract since its inception.

limited liability company (LLC) A form of business organization that combines the tax advantages of a partnership with the limited liability protection of a corporation.

limited partners One or more totally passive participants in a limited partnership, who do not take any active role in the operation of the business and who do not face personal liability for the debts of the business.

limited partnership Most of the participants in the partnership (the limited partners) have the limited liability of corporate shareholders, but their share of the profits from the business is taxed as partnership income.

liquidation Winding up a firm's operations, selling off its assets, and distributing the proceeds to creditors.

liquidation value The amount of cash that would be left over if a firm sold all its assets and used the proceeds to pay off all of its liabilities.

liquidity A measure of a firm's ability to satisfy its short-term obligations as they come due.

liquidity crisis A firm is unable to pay its liabilities as they come due because assets cannot be converted into cash within a reasonable period of time.

liquidity management The process of managing a firm's cash and accounts payable in order to earn a positive return on excess cash balances and obtain low-cost financing for meeting unexpected needs and seasonal cash shortages.

liquidity preference theory States that the slope of the yield curve is influenced not only by expected interest rate changes, but also by the liquidity premium that investors require on long-term bonds.

liquidity ratios Measure a firm's ability to satisfy its short-term obligations *as they come due.*

loan amortization A borrower makes equal periodic payments over time to fully repay a loan.

loan amortization schedule Used to determine loan amortization payments and the allocation of each payment to interest and principal.

loan covenant Specifications imposed by a bank on a borrower in an attempt to protect the bank's investment.

loans Private debt agreements arranged between corporate borrowers and financial institutions, especially commercial banks.

lockbox system A technique for speeding up collections that is popular because it affects all three components of float. Instead of mailing payments to the company, customers mail payments to a post office box, which is emptied regularly by the firm's bank.

lockup agreement An agreement that bankers negotiate with a client's managers and directors, stipulating that these corporate insiders will not sell their personal stock holdings immediately after the offering.

long position Taking a long position in a security is equivalent to buying the security. In a *forward* or *futures contract,* the long position is obligated to pay the forward or futures price of the asset when the contract expires.

long straddle A portfolio consisting of long positions in calls and puts on the same stock with the same strike price and expiration date.

long-term debt Debt that matures more than one year in the future.

low-regular-and-extra policy Policy of a firm paying a low regular dividend supplemented by an additional cash dividend when earnings warrant it.

Macro political risk Risk that applies to *all* foreign firms in a country because of political change, revolution, or the adoption of new policies by the host government.

mail float The time delay between when payment is placed in the mail and when payment is received.

mail-based collection system Processing centers receive the mail payments, open the envelopes, separate the check from the remittance information, prepare the check for deposit, and send the remittance information to the accounts receivable department for application of payment.

maintenance clauses Specifying who is to maintain the assets and make insurance and tax payments.

maintenance margin Margin level required to maintain an open position.

majority voting system System that allows each shareholder to cast one vote per share for each open position on the board of directors.

managed floating-rate system A hybrid system in which a nation's government loosely "fixes" the value of the national currency in relation to that of another currency, but does not expend the effort and resources that would be required to maintain a completely fixed exchange rate regime.

management buyout (MBO) The transformation of a public corporation into a private company by the current managers of the corporation.

managerial synergies Efficiency gains from combining the management teams of merged companies.

managerialism theory of mergers Poorly monitored managers will pursue mergers to maximize their corporation's asset size because managerial compensation is usually based on firm size, regardless of whether or not these mergers create value for stockholders.

manufacturing resource planning II (MRPII) Expands on MRP by using a complex computerized system to integrate data from many departments and generate a production plan for the firm along with management reports, forecasts, and financial statements.

margin account The account into which the investor must deposit the initial margin.

marginal tax rate The percentage of taxes owed on an incremental dollar of income.

market capitalization The value of the shares of a company's stock that are owned by the stockholders: the total number of shares issued multiplied by the current price per share.

market extension merger A combination of firms that produce the same product in different geographic markets.

market maker A lead underwriter that continuously quotes bid and ask prices for new securities after a share offering is successfully sold.

market portfolio The portfolio that all investors want to hold as required for equilibrium, which in theory consists of every available asset with each asset weighted by its market value relative to the total market value of all assets.

market power A benefit that might arise from a horizontal merger when competition is too weak (or nonexistent) to prevent the merged company from raising prices in a market at will.

market price of risk Maximized by investors as they search for the optimal risky portfolio.

market/book (M/B) ratio A measurement that relates the market value of a firm's shares to their book value.

market timing model Model that predicts firms attempt to time the market by issuing equity when share values are high and by issuing debt when share prices are low. As a consequence, a firm's capital structure simply reflects the cumulative effects of its managers' past attempts to issue equity opportunistically.

marking-to-market Daily cash settlement of all futures contracts.

matching strategy When a company finances permanent assets (fixed assets plus the permanent component of current assets) with long-term funding sources and finances its temporary or seasonal asset requirements with short-term debt.

material requirements planning (MRP) A computerized system used to control the flow of resources, particularly inventory, within the production-sale process. Uses a master schedule to ensure that the materials, labor, and equipment needed for production are at the right places in the right amounts at the right times.

maturity The limited life of a bond.

McFadden Act Congressional act of 1927 that prohibited interstate banking.

merger A transaction in which two or more business organizations combine into a single entity.

micro political risk Refers to a foreign government's targeting punitive action against an individual firm, a specific industry, or companies from a particular foreign country.

minimum variance portfolio A portfolio of A and B that has less volatility than either A or B.

mixed offering An offering in which some of the shares come from existing shareholders and some are new. Also, a merger financed with a combination of cash and securities.

mixed stream A series of unequal payments reflecting no particular pattern.

modified accelerated cost recovery system (MACRS) Set forth in the Tax Reform Act of 1986 to define the allowable annual depreciation deductions for various classes of assets.

modified internal rate of return (MIRR) A capital budgeting technique used to eliminate all non-year-zero cash outflows to assure only one sign change in a cash flow stream and therefore only one *internal rate of return (IRR)*. It is commonly applied to projects with alternating positive and negative cash flows in order to eliminate multiple *IRRs*.

Modigliani & Miller (M&M) argument The original theoretical model showing that capital structure is irrelevant—it cannot affect overall firm value—in a world with frictionless capital markets and no taxes. M&M assert that the market value of any firm is independent of its capital structure and is given by capitalizing its expected net operating income at a single rate *r*.

money market The market for debt instruments maturing in one year or less.

money market mutual funds Used by many small companies and some large companies to manage their portfolio.

money market yield (MMY) The yield for short-term discount instruments such as T-bills and commercial paper is typically calculated using algebraic approximations rather than more precise present value methods.

Monte Carlo simulation A sophisticated analysis that provides for calculating the net present value when provided a range or distribution of potential outcomes for each set of assumptions.

mortgage A loan secured by real property.

mortgage bonds A secured type of bond.

mortgage-backed securities (MBS) Debt securities that pass through to investors the principal and interest payments that homeowners make on their mortgages.

multinational corporations (MNCs) Businesses that operate in many countries around the world.

municipal bonds Issued by U.S. state and local governments. Interest on these bonds is exempt from federal income tax.

mutually exclusive projects When several investments exceed the hurdle rate but only a subset of them can be undertaken at any given time.

Naked option position Results when an investor buys or sells an option on a stock without already owning the underlying stock.

natural hedge Offsetting risk exposure.

negative covenants Restrictions a borrower must accept in order to secure a loan.

negotiated offer The most common approach that firms take in choosing an investment banker: The issuing firm negotiates the terms of the offer directly with one investment bank.

net operating profits after taxes (NOPAT) A firm's earnings before interest and after taxes. Mathematically, earnings before interest and taxes (*EBIT*) $\times$ (1 − tax rate [*T*]).

net payoff The share price less the amount paid to acquire the call option.

net present value (NPV) The present value of a sequence of cash inflows and outflows. Also, a method for valuing capital investments.

net price The price at which banks purchase shares from firms.

net profit margin A measurement of the percentage of each sales dollar remaining after all costs and expenses, including interest, taxes, and preferred stock dividends, have been deducted.

net working capital The difference between a firm's current assets and its current liabilities. Often used as a measure of liquidity.

nominal cash flows Amounts that reflect an assumed inflation rate.

nominal return The stated return.

noncash charges Expenses that appear on the income statement but do not involve an actual outlay of cash.

non-debt tax shield hypothesis States that companies with large amounts of depreciation, investment tax credits, R&D expenditures, and other nondebt tax shields should employ less debt financing than otherwise equivalent companies with fewer such shields.

normal distribution The probability of investment outcomes forms a roughly bell-shaped curve that is symmetric about its mean, which makes it easy to determine the probabilities of events that fall within certain ranges and allows full description by just two characteristics, the mean and the variance.

notes Longer-term debt instruments with original maturities of less than seven years.

notional principal The hypothetical principal amount.

NPV profile A plot of a project's *NPV* (on the *y* axis) against various discount rates (on the *x* axis). It is used to illustrate the relationship between the *NPV* and the *IRR* for the typical project. Also called the *net present value profile*.

Observable variables approach An avenue of empirical research that offers hope of yielding interpretable results by estimating which macroeconomic variables significantly influence security prices.

offer price The price at which banks sell a firm's shares to institutional and individual investors.

open interest The number of contracts that are currently outstanding.

opening futures price Price on the first trade of the day.

operating assets Cash, marketable securities, accounts receivable, and inventories that are necessary for the day-to-day operation of a firm.

operating cash flow (*OCF*) The amount of cash flow generated by a firm from its operations. Mathematically, net operating profits after taxes (*NOPAT*), which equals $EBIT \times (1 - T)$, plus depreciation.

operating cycle (*OC*) Measurement of the time that elapses from the firm's receipt of raw materials to begin production to its collection of cash from the sale of the finished product.

operating flows Cash inflows and outflows directly related to the production and sale of a firm's products or services.

operating lease A contractual arrangement whereby the lessee agrees to make periodic payments to the lessor, often for five years or less, to obtain an asset's services. The lessee generally receives an option to cancel, and the asset has a useful life longer than the lease.

operating leverage Measures the tendency of the volatility of operating cash flows to increase with fixed operating costs.

operating profit margin A measurement of the percentage of each sales dollar remaining after deducting all costs and expenses other than interest and taxes.

operational synergy Economies of scale, economies of scope, and resource complementarities.

opportunity costs Lost cash flows on an alternative investment that the firm or individual decides not to make.

optimal risky portfolio The portfolio that maximizes the return that investors can expect for a given standard deviation.

option Allows an investor to buy or sell an asset at a fixed price during a given period of time.

option premium The purchase price of the option to buy is kept by the seller if the buyer decides not to make the purchase.

option to default A limited liability feature that allows a bankrupt firm to hand creditors the company's assets in bankruptcy court.

option's delta The slope measures how much the call price changes as the underlying stock price changes.

ordinary annuity An annuity for which the payments occur at the end of each period.

out of the money Occurs when a call option's strike price exceeds the current stock price.

overallotment option In oversubscribed common stock offerings, the lead underwriter may exercise a Green Shoe option (or overallotment option), essentially an option to sell up to an additional 15 percent more shares than originally planned.

overconfidence Investors exhibit this trait when they believe they are better informed about the true state of a company's affairs than is in fact the case.

overreaction The opposite of *underreaction* to corporate news announcements or prior period returns.

oversubscribe When the investment banker builds a book of orders for stock that is greater (often many times greater) than the amount of stock the firm intends to sell. These orders are not legally binding, and typically the offer price is given as a range of prices at which they expect to sell the offer.

overvalued equity A manager's stock is overvalued when she realizes that she cannot, except by pure luck, produce the performance required to justify this stock price.

over-the-counter market There are a seemingly infinite variety. They are less liquid than exchange-traded options.

ownership rights agreements Specify both the distribution of a firm's ownership and the allocation of board seats and voting rights to the participating venture capitalists investing in that company. Special voting rights often given to VCs include the right to veto major corporate actions and to remove the management team if the firm fails to meet performance goals.

Paid-in-capital The number of shares outstanding times the original selling price of the shares, net of the par value.

par value The face value of a bond, which the borrower repays at maturity. Also, an arbitrary value assigned to common stock on a firm's balance sheet.

participation rights These give venture capitalists the option to participate in any private stock sale the firm's managers arrange for themselves.

partnership A proprietorship with two or more owners who have joined together their skills and personal wealth.

payback period The amount of time it takes for a given project's cumulative net cash inflows to recoup the initial investment.

payment date The actual date on which a firm mails the dividend payment to the holders of record.

payment pattern The normal timing in which a firm's customers pay their accounts, expressed as the percentage of monthly sales collected in each month following the sale.

payoff The price an investor would be willing to pay for an option the instant before it expires.

payoff diagrams Graphs that illustrate an option's payoff as a function of the underlying stock price.

pecking-order hypothesis A hypothesis developed by Stewart Myers and his coauthors, which assumes that managers are better informed about the investment opportunities faced by their firms than are outside investors (an asymmetric information assumption), and that managers act in the best interests of existing shareholders.

percentage-of-sales method Constructing pro forma statements by assuming that all items grow in proportion to sales.

perpetuity An annuity with an infinite life, promising to pay the same amount at the end of every year forever.

plug figure A line item left on the balance sheet of a pro forma statement. After all other projections are made, this figure can be adjusted so that the balance sheet balances.

poison pills Defensive measures taken to avoid a hostile takeover.

political risk The actions taken by a government that have a negative impact on the value of foreign companies operating in that country.

positive covenant Requirements a borrower must meet to secure a loan.

positive pay A bank service used to combat the most common types of check fraud. A company transmits a check-issued file, designating the check number and amount of each item, to the bank when the checks are issued. The bank matches the presented checks against this file and rejects any items that do not match.

preemptive rights These hold that shareholders have first claim on anything of value distributed by a corporation.

preferred habitat theory The effect on the yield curve caused by a desire to invest to match liabilities, despite lower expected returns.

preferred stock Stockholder's equity.

preliminary prospectus The registration statement is the principal disclosure document for all public security offerings. There are two basic parts to the registration statement: Part I, the prospectus, is distributed to all prospective investors; an issuing firm may file a half dozen or more amended prospectuses with the SEC during the registration period preceding an offer. The first, or preliminary prospectus, serves as the principal marketing tool during the period from initial filing with the SEC to the time when the firm responds to the commission's initial findings. The preliminary prospectus is often called a red herring, because it has a standard legal disclaimer printed across its cover in red stating that the securities described herein are not (yet) being offered for sale. The red herring lists a range of prices rather than a single price at which the securities may be offered.

premium The difference between a bond's par value and the purchase price when the price is greater than par value.

prepackaged bankruptcy Companies prepare a reorganization plan that is negotiated and voted on by creditors and stockholders before the company actually files for Chapter 11 bankruptcy.

present value Calculation of the value today of a cash flow to be received at a specific date in the future.

president Hired by the board of directors to be responsible for managing day-to-day operations and carrying out the policies established by the board.

price stabilization Purchase of shares by an investment bank when a new issue begins to falter in the market, keeping the market price at or slightly above the offer price for an indefinite period.

price/earnings (P/E) ratio A measurement of a firm's long-term growth prospects by determining the amount investors are willing to pay for each dollar of a firm's earnings.

primary issues Debt and equity security issues that actually raise capital for firms and are thus distinct from secondary offerings, where an investor sells his or her holdings of existing securities.

primary market transaction Sale of securities to investors by a corporation to raise capital for the firm.

primary offering An offering in which the shares offered for sale are newly issued shares, which increases the number of outstanding shares and raises new capital for the firm.

prime rate The rate of interest charged by the largest U.S. banks on short-term loans to business borrowers with good credit ratings.

principal The amount of money on which interest is paid.

private placements Unregistered security offerings sold directly to accredited investors.

privatization When a state sells off all or part of its holdings in SOEs to private companies or to individual private investors.

pro forma financial statement A forecast of what a firm expects its balance sheet and income statement to look like a year or two ahead.

probability distribution A distribution that tells us what investment outcomes are possible and associates a probability with each outcome.

processing float The time that elapses between the receipt of payment by a firm and its deposit into the firm's account.

product extension merger A diversification merger that combines companies with similar but not identical lines of business.

profitability index (PI) A capital budgeting tool, defined as the ratio of the present value of a project's cash flows, excluding the initial cash outflow (the initial investment), divided by the initial cash outflow.

project finance (PF) loans Loans usually arranged for infrastructure projects such as toll roads, bridges, and power plants.

Proposition I The famous "irrelevance proposition," which imagines that a company is operating in a world of frictionless capital markets, and in a world where there is uncertainty about corporate revenues and earnings.

Proposition II Asserts that the expected return on a levered firm's equity is a linear function of that firm's debt-to-equity ratio.

prospectus The first part of a registration statement; it is distributed to all prospective investors.

protective put By granting the right to sell a share of stock at a

fixed price on or before a certain date, a put option provides a kind of portfolio insurance, guaranteeing that the share of stock can be sold for at least that amount.

proxy fight A ploy used by outsiders to attempt to gain control of a firm by soliciting a sufficient number of votes to unseat existing directors.

proxy statement Used by shareholders not attending an annual meeting to give their votes to another party.

public company A corporation whose shares of stock can be freely traded among investors without obtaining the permission of other investors and whose shares are listed for trading in a public security market.

purchase options The lessee may have the option to purchase the leased asset when the lease expires.

purchasing (or procurement) card programs Implemented by companies as a means of reducing the cost of low-dollar indirect purchases.

purchasing power parity An extension of the law of one price. It maintains that if the law of one price holds at all times, then differences in expected inflation between two countries are associated with expected changes in currency values.

pure conglomerate mergers An unrelated diversification merger that occurs between companies in completely different lines of business.

pure play A firm that competes in a single line of business.

pure stock exchange merger A merger in which stock is the only mode of payment.

put option Grants the right to sell a share of stock at a fixed price on or before a certain date.

put-call parity Results when the payoffs of a portfolio containing one share of stock and one put option are exactly the same as the payoffs of a portfolio containing one bond and one call option.

Qualified institutional buyers Institutions with assets exceeding $100 million.

quarterly compounding Interest involves four compounding periods within the year and is paid four times a year.

quick (acid-test) ratio Similar to the current ratio except that it excludes inventory, which is usually the least-liquid current asset.

Random walk A description of the movement of the price of a financial asset over time. When prices follow a *random walk*, future and past prices are statistically unrelated, and the best forecast of the future price is simply the current price.

ratchet provisions Protect the venture capital group's ownership rights in the event that the firm sells new equity under duress. Generally, these provisions ensure that the venture capital group's share values are adjusted so that entrepreneurs bear the penalty of selling low-priced new stock. For example, if the venture fund purchased shares initially for $1 each, and the start-up later sells new stock at $0.50 per share, a "full ratchet" provision mandates that the venture group receives one new share for each old share, thereby protecting the value of the VC's initial stake (a "partial ratchet" only partially protects the venture group).

ratio analysis Calculating and interpreting financial ratios to assess a firm's performance and status.

rational expectations The assumption that even if investors make mistakes when forming assessments concerning expected returns, their errors are not systematic.

real cash flows Amounts that reflect current prices only and do not incorporate upward adjustments for expected inflation.

real interest rate parity Asserts that investors should earn the same real rate of return on risk-free investments no matter the country in which they choose to invest.

real option The right, but not the obligation, to take a future action that changes an investment's value.

real return Approximately, the difference between an investment's stated or nominal return and the inflation rate.

recapitalization Alteration of a company's capital structure to reduce high fixed charges.

red herring Nickname often given to the preliminary prospectus because of the standard legal disclaimer printed across its cover in red, stating that the securities described herein are not (yet) being offered for sale.

redemption option Option for venture capitalists to sell a company back to its entrepreneur or founders.

refund To refinance a debt with new bonds at a lower interest rate.

registration statement The principal disclosure document for all public security offerings.

renewal options In an operating lease, the lessee often has the option to renew a lease at its expiration.

reorganization The process in bankruptcy designed to allow businesses that are in temporary financial distress but are worth saving to continue operating while the claims of creditors are settled using a collective procedure.

residual claimants Investors who have the right to receive cash flows only after all other claimants have been satisfied. Common stockholders are typically the residual claimants of corporations.

residual theory Predicts that cash dividend payments are simply a residual, the cash left over after corporations have funded all their positive-*NPV* investments.

resource complementarities A firm with a particular operating expertise merges with a firm with another operating strength to create a company that has expertise in multiple areas.

retained earnings The cumulative total of the earnings that a firm has reinvested since its inception.

return The total gain or loss on an investment over a given period of time.

return on common equity (*ROE*) A measurement that captures the return earned on the common stockholders' (owners') investment in a firm.

return on investment (*ROI*) A firm's earnings available for common stockholders divided by its total assets. Alternatively called *return on total assets (ROA)*.

return on total assets (*ROA*) A measurement of the overall effectiveness of management in generating returns to common stockholders with its available assets.

reverse LBO A formerly public company that has previously gone private through a leveraged buyout and then goes public again. Also called *second IPO*.

reverse stock split Occurs when a firm replaces a certain number of outstanding shares with just one new share.

rights offerings A special type of seasoned equity offering that allows the firm's existing owners to buy new shares at a bargain price or to sell that right to other investors.

risk management The process of identifying firm-specific risk exposures and managing those exposures by means of insurance products. Also includes identifying, measuring, and managing all types of risk exposures.

risk-averse A description of the preferences of investors who must be compensated to bear risk or will pay to shed risk.

risk-management function Managing the firm's exposures to all types of risk, both insurable and uninsurable, in order to

maintain the optimum risk-return trade-off and thereby maximize shareholder value.

risk-neutral Investors who care only about the returns on their investments, totally disregarding risk.

risk-neutral method A simpler approach to calculating option prices by using arbitrage arguments, in which the assumption is made that investors are risk neutral.

risk-seeking Investors who prefer to take risk and hence will be willing to invest in a risky asset even when its expected return falls below that of a safer alternative.

road show A tour of major U.S. and international cities taken by a firm and its bankers several weeks before a scheduled offering. The tour's goal is to solicit demand for the offering from investors.

Rule 415 This procedure allows a qualifying company to file a master registration statement, which is a single document summarizing planned financing covering a two-year period. Once the SEC approves the issue, it is placed "on the shelf," and the company can sell the new securities to investors out of inventory (off the shelf) as needed any time over the next two years.

Rule of 72 States that the approximate amount of time (n) required to double an initial deposit at an interest rate (r) is approximately $72/r$.

Rule 144A Provides a private-placement exemption for qualified institutional buyers and allows them to freely trade privately placed securities among themselves.

Rule 144A offering A special type of offer, first approved in April 1990, that allows issuing companies to waive some disclosure requirements by selling stock only to sophisticated institutional investors, who may then trade the shares among themselves.

S corporation An ordinary corporation in which the stockholders have elected to allow shareholders to be taxed as partners while still retaining their limited-liability status as corporate stockholders.

sale-leaseback arrangement One firm sells an asset to another for cash, then leases the asset from its new owner.

Sarbanes-Oxley Act of 2002 Legislation passed in the wake of corporate scandals at Enron and other firms that makes sweeping changes affecting the governance and control of public companies.

scenario analysis A more complex variation on sensitivity analysis that provides for calculating the net present value when a whole set of assumptions changes in a particular way.

seasoned equity offering (SEO) An equity issue by a firm that already has common stock outstanding.

second IPO In a reverse LBO (or second IPO), a formerly public company that has previously gone private through a leveraged buyout goes public again. Reverse LBOs are easier to price than traditional IPOs because information exists about how the market valued the company when it was publicly traded.

secondary market transactions Trades between investors that generate no new cash flow for the firm.

secondary offering An offering whose purpose is to allow an existing shareholder to sell a large block of stock to new investors. This kind of offering raises no new capital for the firm.

secured creditors Creditors who have specific assets pledged as collateral and who receive the proceeds from the sale of those assets.

secured debt A loan backed by collateral.

secured-debt hypothesis Asserts that assets generating tax shields could also be used as collateral for additional debt, so firms rich in tangible assets were able to use higher levels of secured debt.

Securities Act of 1933 The most important federal law governing the sale of new securities.

Securities and Exchange Commission Act of 1934 This act, and its amendments, established the U.S. Securities and Exchange Commission (SEC) and laid out specific procedures for both the public sale of securities and the governance of public companies.

securitization The repackaging of loans and other traditional bank-based credit products into securities that can be sold to public investors.

security market line (SML) The line plotted for the equilibrium expected returns of all securities.

selectivity Stock-picking ability; one of two components of managerial investment performance.

selling group Consists of investment banks that may assist in selling shares but are not formal members of the underwriting syndicate.

semiannual compounding Interest involves two compounding periods within the year and is paid twice a year.

semistrong-form efficiency This version of the EMH asserts that asset prices incorporate all publicly available information.

sensitivity analysis A tool that allows exploration of the importance of individual assumptions concerning a project's net present value by determining the impact of changing one variable while holding all others fixed.

separation of investment and financing The principle that corporations worry only about satisfying the impersonal demands of the financial market, not the personal preferences of investors.

serial bonds Bonds of which a certain proportion mature each year.

settlement date The future date on which the buyer pays the seller and the seller delivers the asset to the buyer.

settlement price The closing price of a futures contract at the end of a trading day. This is used to settle all contracts, in a process called "marking to market."

share issue privatization (SIP) A government executing one of these will sell all or part of its ownership in a state-owned enterprise to private investors via a public share offering.

share repurchase program A company announcing this kind of program states that it will buy some of its own shares over a period of time.

shareholder Owner of common and preferred stock of a corporation.

shares authorized The shares of a company's stock that are authorized by the stockholders to be sold by the board of directors without further stockholder approval.

shares issued The shares of a company's stock that are owned by the stockholders.

shark repellents Antitakeover measures added to corporate charters.

shelf registration A procedure that allows a qualifying company to file a "master registration statement," a single document summarizing planned financing over a two-year period.

short position Taking a *short position* is equivalent to selling the asset. In a forward or futures contract, the short position is obligated to sell the asset to the buyer at the forward or futures price.

short straddle A portfolio consisting of short positions in calls and puts on the same stock with the same strike price and expiration date.

short-selling A transaction in which an investor sells borrowed assets that must be returned to the lender of the assets at a later date.

short-term debt Debt that matures in one year or less.

short-term financing Accounts payable, bank loans, commercial paper, international loans, and secured short-term loans that are used by a firm to finance seasonal fluctuations in current asset investments and provide adequate liquidity to achieve its growth objectives and meet its obligations in a timely manner.

signaling model A capital structure theory that assumes that managers know more about a firm's prospects than investors do.

simple interest Interest paid only on the initial principal of an investment, not on the interest that accrues in earlier periods.

single-factor model Just one variable explains differences in returns across securities.

sinking fund An additional positive covenant included in a bond indenture, the objective of which is to provide for the systematic retirement of bonds prior to their maturity.

small business investment companies (SBICs) Federally chartered corporations established as a result of the Small Business Administration Act of 1958.

sole proprietorship A business with a single owner.

special dividend The additional dividend that a firm pays if earnings are higher than normal in a given period.

speculating Choosing not to hedge a risk exposure, or choosing to overhedge.

spin-off A parent company creates a new company with its own shares to form a division or subsidiary, and existing shareholders receive a pro rata distribution of shares in the new company.

split-off A parent company creates a new, independent company with its own shares, and ownership of the company is transferred to certain existing shareholders only, in exchange for their shares in the parent.

split-up The division and sale of all of a company's subsidiaries, so that it ceases to exist (except possibly as a holding company with no assets).

sponsored ADR An ADR for which the issuing (foreign) company absorbs the legal and financial costs of creating and trading the security.

spot exchange rate The exchange rate that applies to currency trades that occur immediately.

spot price A cash market transaction in which the buyer and seller conduct their transaction today.

spot rates Rates that call for immediate delivery.

staged financing Used by venture capitalists to minimize risk exposure.

stakeholders Customers, employees, suppliers, and creditors of a firm.

stand-alone companies Companies created for the sole purpose of constructing and operating a single project.

standard normal distribution A normal distribution with a mean of 0 and a standard deviation of 1.

stated annual rate The contractual annual rate charged by a lender or promised by a borrower.

state-owned enterprises (SOEs) Companies owned and operated by the government that conduct business activities in areas outside what many would consider purely governmental affairs.

statutory merger A target integration in which the acquirer can absorb the target's resources directly with no remaining trace of the target as a separate entity.

stock dividend The payment to existing owners of a dividend in the form of stock.

stock option plans Provide incentives for portfolio company managers in virtually all venture capital deals. As part of these plans, the firm sets aside a large pool of stock to compensate current managers for superior performance and to attract talented new managers as the company grows.

stock options Outright grants of stock to top managers or, more commonly, giving them the right to purchase stock at a fixed price.

stock purchase warrants Instruments that give their holder the right to purchase a certain number of shares of a firm's common stock at a specified price over a certain period.

stock split When a firm executes a stock split, its share price declines because the number of outstanding shares increases. For example, in a 2-for-1 split, the firm doubles the number of shares outstanding. Managers who implement stock splits generally say they are trying to reduce the per-share price of the firm's stock back within a "standard" trading range that individual investors desire.

strategic merger Seeks to create a more efficient merged company than the two premerger companies operating independently.

strategic plan A multiyear action plan for the major investments and competitive initiatives that a firm's senior managers believe will drive the future success of the enterprise.

strike price The price at which a call option allows an investor to purchase the underlying share. Also called the *exercise price*.

strong-form efficiency In markets characterized by this kind of efficiency, asset prices reflect all information, public and private.

subordinated debenture An unsecured type of bond.

subordinated debt Debt claims that are junior to other claims and therefore are entitled to receive interest or principal payments only if the senior debt claims have been paid in full.

subordination Agreement by all subsequent or more-junior creditors to wait until all claims of the senior debt are satisfied in full before having their own claims satisfied.

subsidiary merger A merger in which the acquirer maintains the identity of the target as a separate subsidiary or division.

sunk costs Costs that have already been spent and are not recoverable.

supplemental disclosures The second part to a registration statement. It is filed only with the SEC.

sustainable growth model Derives an expression that determines how rapidly a firm can grow while maintaining a balance between its sources (increases in assets) and uses (increases in liabilities and equity) of funds.

swap contract Agreement between two parties to exchange payment obligations on two underlying financial liabilities that are equal in principal amount but differ in payment patterns.

syndicated loan A large loan arranged by a group (a *syndicate*) of commercial banks for a single borrower.

synergy An efficiency-enhancing effect resulting from a strategic merger.

synthetic put option Traders can create this by purchasing a bond and a call option while simultaneously short-selling the stock.

systematic risk The proportion of risk that cannot be eliminated through diversification.

Tailing the hedge Purchasing enough futures contracts to hedge risk exposure, but not so many as to cause overhedging.

takeover Any transaction in which the control of one entity is taken over by another.

target cash balance A cash total is set for checking accounts to avoid engaging active cash position management.

target payout ratio Under this policy, the firm attempts to pay out a certain percentage of earnings, but rather than let dividends fluctuate, it pays a stated dollar dividend and adjusts it toward the target payout slowly as proven earnings increases occur.

target leverage zones An operating range of debt ratio within which corporations seem to prefer to operate.

tax-loss carryforwards Negative income (net losses) can be used to offset taxes due on future income.

technical analysis An investing approach in which analysts search for profitable trading strategies based on recurring patterns in stock prices.

technical insolvency A firm is unable to pay its liabilities as they come due, although its assets are still greater than its liabilities.

tender offer The structured purchase of a target's shares in which the acquirer announces a public offer to buy a minimum number of shares at a specific price.

tender-merger A merger that occurs after an acquirer secures enough voting control of the target's shares through a tender offer to effect a merger.

term loan A loan made by a financial institution to a business, with an initial maturity of more than 1 year, generally 5 to 12 years.

term structure of interest rates The relationship between yield to maturity and time to maturity.

terminal value A number intended to reflect the value of a project at a given future point in time.

time line A graphical presentation of values over time.

time value The difference between an option's intrinsic value and its market price.

time value of money The principle of finance that a dollar received today is more valuable than a dollar (euro, pound, franc, or yen) received in the future.

times interest earned ratio Earnings before interest and taxes divided by interest expense; it measures a firm's ability to make contractual interest payments.

timing The ability to time market turns—getting in before upturns and getting out before crashes. One of two components of managerial investment performance.

top-down sales forecast This kind of sales forecast relies heavily on macroeconomic and industry forecasts.

total asset turnover A measurement of the efficiency with which a firm uses all its assets to generate sales; calculated by dividing the dollars of sales a firm generates by the dollars of asset investment.

total variable cost of annual sales (*TVC*) Calculated by multiplying the annual sales in units by the variable cost per unit and used to estimate the average investment in accounts receivable under a stated policy.

tracking stocks Equity claims based on (and designed to mirror, or *track*) the earnings of wholly owned subsidiaries of diversified firms.

trade-off model A model of capital structure in which managers choose the mix of debt and equity that strikes a balance between the tax advantages of debt and the various costs of using leverage.

transactions exposure The risk that a change in prices will negatively affect the value of a specific transaction or series of transactions.

transactional exemption Requires that securities be registered before they can be resold, or that the subsequent sale must also qualify as a private placement.

Treasury bills Debt instruments issued by the federal government that mature in less than one year.

Treasury bonds Debt instruments issued by the federal government with maturities ranging from 10 to 30 years.

Treasury notes Debt instruments issued by the federal government with maturities ranging from 1 to 10 years.

treasury stock Common shares that a firm currently holds in reserve.

triangular arbitrage Trading currencies simultaneously in different markets to earn a risk-free profit.

trustee In bankruptcy, someone appointed by a judge to replace a firm's current management team and to oversee liquidation or reorganization.

turnover of accounts receivable (*TOAR*) Three-hundred-sixty-five divided by the *average collection period (ACP)*. Used to calculate the *average investment in accounts receivable (AIAR)* when evaluating accounts receivable policies.

two-fund separation principle The principle that says that investors should divide their wealth between two types of investments—a risk-free asset and a portfolio of risky assets.

Unanimous consent procedure (UCP) A reorganization plan instituted by consent of all creditors and equity classes.

underinvestment A situation of financial distress in which default is likely, yet a very profitable but short-lived investment opportunity exists.

underlying asset The asset from which a derivative security obtains its value.

underpriced Refers to the typical situation in which an IPO offering price is lower than its price at the end of the first day's trading.

underreaction When stock prices on average react positively to a dividend initiation, for example, but then an additional positive reaction continues over the next several months.

underwrite The investment banker purchases shares from a firm and resells them to investors.

underwriting spread The difference between the net price and the offer price.

underwriting syndicate Consists of many investment banks that collectively purchase the firm's shares and market them, thereby spreading the risk exposure across the syndicate.

unlevered equity beta The figure calculated by removing the effects of leverage on an equity beta.

unseasoned equity offering An IPO.

unsecured creditors Creditors who have no specific assets pledged as collateral, or the proceeds from the sale of whose pledged assets are inadequate to cover the debt.

unsponsored ADR An ADR in which the issuing firm is not involved with the issue at all and may even oppose it.

unsystematic risk The proportion of risk that can be eliminated through diversification.

Variable growth model Assumes that the growth rate dividend will vary during different periods of time, when calculating the value of a firm's stock.

venture capital A professionally managed pool of money raised for the sole purpose of making actively managed direct equity investments in rapidly growing private companies.

venture capital limited partnerships Funds established by professional venture capital firms.

venture capitalists Professional investors who specialize in high-risk/high-return investments in rapidly growing entrepreneurial businesses.

vertical merger Companies with current or potential buyer-seller relationships combine to create a more integrated company.

voluntary reorganization A strategy that sustains a firm so that the creditor can continue to receive business from it.

voluntary settlement A firm that becomes technically insolvent or bankrupt may make an arrangement with its creditors that enables it to bypass many of the costs involved in legal bankruptcy proceedings.

Warrants Securities issued by firms that grant the right to buy shares of stock at a fixed price for a given period of time.

weak-form efficiency In markets characterized by this kind of efficiency, asset prices incorporate all information from the historical price record.

wealth tax A capital gains tax at a rate equal to the dividend tax rate. This tax will make investors indifferent to whether they receive taxable dividends or taxable capital gains; but this will happen only if the tax on stock appreciation is levied every period, regardless of whether the shares are sold or not.

weighted average cost of capital (*WACC*) The after-tax weighted-average required return on all types of securities issued by a firm, in which the weights equal the percentage of each type of financing in a firm's overall capital structure.

white knights "Friendly" acquirers who will top the price of an unwelcome bidder to avoid a hostile takeover.

winner's curse Because they receive small allocations in hot deals and large allocations in cold deals, the unsophisticated players in this market will earn much lower returns.

wire transfer In the United States, the primary wire transfer system, known as *Fedwire*, is run by the Federal Reserve and is available to all depository institutions.

working capital Refers to what is more correctly known as *net working capital*.

workout A firm that becomes technically insolvent or bankrupt may make an arrangement with its creditors that enables it to bypass many of the costs involved in legal bankruptcy proceedings.

World Trade Organization (WTO) An international body that polices world trading practices and mediates disputes between member countries.

writing an option Selling an option.

writing covered calls A common trading strategy that mixes stock and call options. In this strategy, an investor who owns a share of stock sells a call option on that stock.

Yankee bonds Bonds sold by foreign corporations to U.S. investors.

Yankee common stock Stock issued by foreign firms in the U.S. market.

yield curve A graph that plots the relationship between yield to maturity and maturity for a group of similar bonds.

yield spread The difference in yield to maturity between two bonds or two classes of bonds with similar maturities.

yield to maturity (*YTM*) The discount rate that equates the present value of the bond's cash flows to its market price.

Z score The product of a quantitative model for forecasting bankruptcy that uses a blend of traditional financial ratios and a statistical technique known as *multiple discriminant analysis*. The Z score has been found to be about 90 percent accurate in forecasting bankruptcy one year in the future and about 80 percent accurate in forecasting it two years in the future.

zero growth model The simplest approach to dividend valuation that assumes a constant dividend stream.

zero-balance accounts (ZBAs) Disbursement accounts that always have an end-of-day balance of zero. The purpose is to eliminate nonearning cash balances in corporate checking accounts.

zero-coupon bonds Pure discount instruments, such as U.S. Treasury bills, that promise investors a single fixed payment on a specified future date.

NAME INDEX

COMPANY INDEX

SUBJECT INDEX

Overview

Contents

CHAPTER 4
Gross Income—Exclusions   4-1

CHAPTER 5
Property Transactions—Capital Gains and Losses   5-1

CHAPTER 6
Deductions and Losses   6-1

CHAPTER 7
Itemized Deductions   7-1

CHAPTER 8
Losses and Bad Debts   8-1

CHAPTER 9
Employee Expenses and Deferred Compensation 9-1

**CHAPTER 12
Property Transactions—Nontaxable
Exchanges   12-1**

**CHAPTER 13
Property Transactions—Section
1231 and Recapture   13-1**

CHAPTER 14
Special Tax Computation Methods, Payment of Tax, and Tax Credits   14-1

CHAPTER 15
Partnerships and S Corporations   15-1

CHAPTER 16
Corporations   16-1

CHAPTER 17
Tax Considerations for Investors   17-1

APPENDICES

Preface

OBJECTIVES AND USE

These text materials are principally designed for use in a first course in federal taxation for undergraduate accounting and business students. A companion volume, entitled *Prentice Hall's Federal Taxation, 1995: Corporations, Partnerships, Estates, and Trusts,* is published for use in the second course in federal taxation. The *Individuals* text may also be used as a one-term survey course for undergraduate or graduate students.

We are especially pleased to again offer the *Prentice Hall's Federal Taxation, 1995: Comprehensive Volume.* The comprehensive text is designed for either a one- or two-term course for undergraduates or graduate students. Its content contains selected chapters and sections from the original two volumes.

A primary objective has been to provide a readable format without sacrificing a high level of technical content. This objective has been accomplished by including separate sections in each chapter for tax planning considerations and tax compliance and procedural considerations, rather than including these materials in the main body of the text. We have also attempted to provide a more readable format by including minor exceptions in footnotes at the bottom of many pages. The text materials also include numerous examples to illustrate the concepts and technical rules that are discussed in the text.

UNIQUE FEATURES

For the 1995 Edition we have continued to include the following teaching and student learning aids in the text:

- Chapter learning objectives highlighted and keyed to the text.

- Problem materials identified and ordered by topic to facilitate student problem solving and to assist in the preparation of course syllabi.

- Expanded coverage of C corporations, S corporations, and partnerships. Instructors who use the text for a one-term survey course should appreciate this feature. Otherwise, Chapters 15 and 16 serve as a lead-in to the second course in federal taxation.

- A capstone chapter entitled Tax Considerations for Investors is intended to build upon the technical content coverage in previous chapters. Here, the economic considerations and tax planning issues related to investor and business decisions are discussed in depth.

- Tax research, sources of tax law, tax history, and tax policy topics are combined into one introductory chapter which has been expanded. Tax policy considerations are also covered in the other chapters to illustrate the rationale for tax provisions and changes in the tax law.

- Several of the chapters include completed tax forms based upon comprehensive examples that are presented in the body of the text.

- The appendices include a glossary of tax terms that are highlighted by bold type cross references in the text material. A full complement of indices by subjects, code sections, regulations, government promulgations, and court cases is provided along with blank tax forms, tax tables, and rate schedules.

- The text materials have been updated to reflect legislative, judicial, and administrative changes in the Federal tax law.

- Each chapter includes discussion questions, problems, comprehensive and tax form/return preparation problems, case study problems, and tax research problems. A number of the problems, questions, and case studies include ethical issues. The following designations indicate which problems can be solved by computer:

  o- denotes problems that can be solved using Lotus 1-2-3 Template Software.

   denotes problems that can be solved using TurboTax®. Students may purchase TurboTax with our Tax Practice Problems for Individuals.

- Tax rate schedules for individuals, corporations, estates and trusts and the unified transfer tax system are provided on the inside front and back covers. Also included is information about the amount of the standard deduction, personal, dependency and special exemptions, and unified transfer tax credit.

This year we are again offering a unique instructional tool that the students should find invaluable. Seven different kinds of marginal notes are provided to enrich the students' learning experience. These include:

- **Key Points**—emphasize those areas where students require repetition and reinforcement.

- **Typical Misconceptions**—identify those concepts that students are likely to misunderstand, and help them to correct their thinking before they take a wrong approach.

- **Real World Examples**—provide facts and anecdotes about actual companies and real-life strategies.

- **Additional Comments**—supporting comments which elaborate on the materials presented in the text.

- **Self-Study Questions**—questions for the student to think about. Each question is accompanied by a full solution. The student will obtain a reliable indicator of their understanding of the text material.

- **Historical Notes**—offer more comprehensive understanding of the concepts by examining them in their historical context.

- **Ethical Points**—focus on ethical questions that confront the tax practitioner.

 These are designated with an ethics icon.

Turn to virtually any page in the text and you will notice one or more of these annotations. We are confident that students will find this material a valuable aid in their course preparation.

Another key feature for students is the topic review. Each chapter contains several topic reviews. A topic review is presented when a major area of topical coverage has been completed. This topic review permits students to organize their thoughts about the concepts presented about a topic before proceeding on to the next topic. Many of these topic reviews are in chart or tabular form.

More emphasis is being placed on oral and written communication by the various accounting professional organizations (e.g., American Institute of CPAs and Accounting Education Change Commission). Each chapter in this volume contains one or more case study problems. Each case study problem incorporates facts likely to be encountered in a tax practice situation. The student is required to consider a number of alternatives and present a written or oral solution to the problem. Most often this solution is presented in the form of a memorandum.

All examples and problems have been written to incorporate the current year (1994) and actual individual and entity names. They have also been updated to reflect recent legislative, judicial, and administrative changes in the tax law.

SUPPLEMENTAL MATERIALS

The text includes a full complement of supplementary and ancillary materials. Adopters are encouraged to use these materials to enhance their teaching effectiveness and the students' learning experience. The following aids are available for instructor and student use:

Instruction Aids

- **Prentice Hall Course Manager, free upon adoption**—This three-ring binder of the textbook allows the professor complete flexibility in course customization.

- **Instructor's Guide**—The perfect companion to the Prentice Hall Course Manager, this specially crafted Instructor's Guide includes: a sample syllabus for semester- and quarter-length courses, instructor outlines, and solutions to the tax return/tax form, case study problems, and tax research problems. Instructor outlines are available in ASCII computer files to enable faculty members to make their own modifications to the master outlines prior to using them in class without having to retype the entire outline. Also, there is a cross reference table which cross references problems in the 1994 and the 1995 Editions as well as indicates the nature of the change (if any) to the problems from the 1994 Edition.

- **Test Bank**—Carefully reviewed by the text authors, this bank of test questions now includes fully worked-out solutions to many of the more complex problems.

- **Solutions Manual**—Prepared by the authors and thoroughly reviewed by the editors and a pool of graduate tax students, this volume includes solutions to the discussion questions, problems, comprehensive problems, and case study problems. The solutions to the tax form/return preparation problems, case studies, and the tax research problems are included in the *Instructor's Guide*.

- **Solutions to Prentice Hall's Tax Practice Problems for Individuals, Corporations and Partnerships, 1995 Edition**—Contains completed forms to solve the Tax Practice Problems for both volumes.

- **Transparencies to Prentice Hall's Federal Taxation Series, 1995, Edition**—Approximately 100 transparencies to enrich the teaching experience.

- **Prentice Hall Test Manager**—Unmatched by other computerized testing software, Prentice Hall Test Manager is a state-of-the-art classroom management system designed to take the tedium out of running classes.

- **New York Times Supplement**—*The New York Times* and Prentice Hall are sponsoring "Themes of the Times," a program designed to enhance student access to current information of relevance in the classroom.

  Through this program, the presentation of Taxation in the text is supplemented by a collection of both time-sensitive and historical articles from one of the world's most distinguished newspapers, *The New York Times*. These articles demonstrate the vital, ongoing connection between what is learned in the classroom and what is happening in the world around us.

- **Tax Return Problems Update**—Because even annual revisions become outdated when the new tax rates and deductions go into effect, we prepare an updated tax return/form problem solution set keyed into the PRENTICE HALL'S FEDERAL TAXATION series so that professors will have solutions tied into the most current tax forms.

- **Supplemental Tax Law Update**—Whenever major tax legislation is passed, we immediately provide an updating supplement. In addition, a mid-year supplement is provided when the inflation-adjusted numbers are available for the new tax year.

- **Registered Adopter Service**—Every year instructors have to worry about ordering new editions of their tax books and supplements. Every year tax instructors have to keep up-to-date on the changes in the tax law. Now Prentice Hall has a service to help in both of these cases. It's our Registered Adopter Service. By returning the registration card provided in the Instructor's Edition of *Prentice Hall's Federal Taxation: Individuals* you can add your name to the list of adopters who receive regular tax law updates and order forms for new books and supplements.

Student Aids

Our foremost goal has been to provide students with a perspective that stresses readability, accuracy, and familiarity with technical aids to tax practice. The following student aids are currently available:

- **Study Guide**—This study guide is designed to give students a better understanding of the laws and concepts presented in the textbook through use of extensive cross-referencing to tables and figures in the textbook.

- **Prentice Hall's Tax Practice Problems with TurboTax: Individuals, 1995 Edition**—This practice set gives the student hands-on experience preparing tax returns either manually or with a computer. The complete package includes three comprehensive tax return problems, IRS forms, IRS instructions, and documentation for the TurboTax software program. The tax practice problems are also available without TurboTax.

- **Income Tax Applications Using Lotus 1-2-3**—This practical book/disk package integrates income tax concepts with a student tutorial on how to use the electronic spreadsheet, giving students the opportunity to simultaneously learn about numerous tax concepts and issues as they learn Lotus 1-2-3.

- **Tax Tips for Graduates**—This booklet includes several hints designed to help the recent graduate pay the lowest possible tax.

ACKNOWLEDGMENTS

Our policy is to provide annual editions and to prepare timely updated supplements when major tax revisions occur. We are most appreciative of the suggestions made by outside reviewers for the 1995 Edition because these extensive review procedures have been valuable to the authors and editors during the revision process.

We wish to acknowledge the following reviewers, whose contributions over the past several years have helped shape the 1995 Edition:

Becky Andrews	Roane State Community College
Alan Attaway	University of Louisville
Robert Barker	California State University—Northridge
Susan Bates	Boise State University
Martin Batross	Franklin University
Cynthia E. Bolt	The Citadel
Faye Bradwick	Indiana University of Pennsylvania
George Britton	Florida Southern College
Sharen Brougham	Metropolitan State College
M. Robert Carver Jr.	Southern Illinois University at Edwardsville
Arthur Cassill	University of North Carolina at Greensboro
Caroline Craig	Illinois State University
Anthony P. Curatola	Drexel University
David Davidson	California State University—Long Beach

Shirley Dennis-Escoffier	University of Miami (Fla.)
M. Peter Dillaway	New Mexico State University
Paul Erickson	Baylor University
Carl Farinacci	Clarion University
Ramon Fernandez	University of St. Thomas (Texas)
George Frankel	San Francisco State University
Daniel Fulks	University of Kentucky
John Gardner	University of Wisconsin at LaCrosse
Vance Grange	Utah State University
Melvin Greenball	Ohio State University
Merrily Hoffman	San Jacinto College
Michael Holland	Valdosta State University
Frederick Jacobs	University of Minnesota
Patricia Janes	San Jose State University
Linda Johnson	Northern Illinois University
William Jordan	Florida State University
Kermit Keeling	Loyola College-Maryland
Ernest Larkins	Georgia State University
Brian Levinson	SUNY at Binghamton
Roland Lipka	Temple University
Gary L. Maydew	Iowa State University
Thomas McCain	Washington University
Joseph McCauley	Monroe Community College
Edward Milam	Mississippi State University
Kevin Misiewicz	University of Notre Dame
Karen H. Molloy	University of Illinois
Matthew Monippallil	Eastern Illinois University
Michael O'Dell	Arizona State University
Kenneth Orbach	Florida Atlantic University
Edmund Outslay	Michigan State University
Nelson Pion	University of Massachusetts
Steven M. Platau	The University of Tampa
Janis Reeder	University of Delaware
W. Peter Salzarulo	Miami University (Ohio)
Ragnor Seglund	California State University—Sacramento
Kathleen Sinning	Western Michigan University
Jerrold Stern	Indiana University
Paul Streer	University of Georgia
Caroline Strobel	University of South Carolina
Anne Townsend	University of Texas at Dallas
James Trebby	Marquette University
Joanne Turner	Rochester Institute of Technology
Robert Wyndelts	Arizona State University

We are also grateful to the the various graduate assistants, doctoral students, and colleagues who have reviewed the text and supplementary materials and checked solutions in order to maintain a high level of technical accuracy. In particular, we would like to acknowledge the following colleagues who assisted in the preparation of supplemental materials for this text:

Mary Drummond
   (Supplements Coordinator) University of Florida
John M. Beehler   University of Texas at Arlington
Arthur D. Cassill   University of North Carolina at Greensboro
John J. Connors   University of Wisconsin-Milwaukee
L. Howard Godfrey   University of North Carolina at Charlotte
Craig J. Langstraat   Memphis State University
Bobbie Martindale
Ken Milani   University of Notre Dame
Cherie J. O'Neil   University of South Florida
W. Peter Salzarulo   Miami University (Ohio)

Lawrence C. Phillips
John L. Kramer

1

An Introduction to Taxation

Key Point

In many situations, the use of the tax laws to influence human behavior is deliberate. As will be seen later in this chapter, the tax laws are often used to achieve social and economic objectives.

The federal tax system has a substantial effect upon investor, business, and personal decisions. Thus, it may alter the allocation of resources within the U.S. economy. The following examples illustrate the impact of the tax law upon various segments of our society:

- A business decision about whether to invest in a new plant or equipment may depend, in part, upon the existence of favorable tax provisions.

- An employee may decide to accept a new job because the prospective employer offers favorable tax-free fringe benefits or an attractive deferred compensation plan.

- An individual may decide to buy a principal residence rather than rent comparable property because of the availability of tax deductions for mortgage interest and real estate taxes.

- The terms of a property settlement agreement pursuant to a divorce decree may be structured to take into account the tax laws governing alimony and property settlements.

The purpose of this text is to provide an introduction to the federal income taxation of individuals. However, before discussing the specifics of the U.S. federal income tax law, it is helpful to have a broad conceptual understanding of the taxation process. Thus, this chapter provides an overview of the following topics:

- Historical developments of the federal tax system

- Objectives of the tax law

- Types of taxes levied and structural considerations

- Tax law sources and the legislative process

- Internal Revenue Service (IRS) collection, examination, and appeals processes

- The nature of tax practice including computer applications

- Tax research methods

HISTORY OF TAXATION IN THE UNITED STATES

Early Periods

The federal income tax is the dominant form of taxation in the United States. In addition, most states and some cities and counties also impose an income tax. Both corporations and individuals are subject to such taxes.

Prior to 1913 (the date of enactment of the modern-day federal income tax), the federal government relied predominantly upon customs duties and excise taxes to finance its operations. The first federal income tax on individuals was enacted in 1861 to finance the Civil War and was repealed after the war. The federal income tax was reinstated in 1894. However, that tax was challenged in the courts because the U.S. Constitution required that an income tax be apportioned among the states in proportion to their populations. This type of tax system, which would be both impractical and difficult to administer, would mean that different tax rates would apply to individual taxpayers depending upon their states of residence. In 1895, the Supreme Court ruled that the tax was in violation of the U.S. Constitution.[1]

Therefore, it was necessary to amend the U.S. Constitution to permit the passage of a federal income tax law. This was accomplished by the Sixteenth Amendment, which was ratified in 1913.

Historical Note

The reinstatement of the income tax in 1894 was the subject of heated political controversy. In general, the representatives in Congress from the agricultural South and West favored the income tax in lieu of customs duties. Representatives from the industrial eastern states were against the income tax and favored the protective tariff legislation.

Revenue Acts from 1913 to the Current Period

Historical Note

The Revenue Act of 1913 contained sixteen pages.

The Revenue Act of 1913 imposed a flat 1% tax (with no exemptions) upon a corporation's net income. The rate varied from 1% to 7% for individuals depending upon the individual's income level. However, very few individuals paid federal income taxes because a $3,000 personal exemption ($4,000 for married individuals) was permitted as an offset to taxable income. These amounts were greater than the incomes of most individuals in 1913.

Various amendments to the original law were passed between 1913 and 1939. For example, a deduction for dependency exemptions was provided in 1917. In 1939, the separate revenue acts were codified into the Internal Revenue Code of 1939. A similar codification was accomplished in 1954. The 1954 codification, which was known as the Internal Revenue Code of 1954, included the elimination of many "deadwood" provisions, a rearrangement and clarification of numerous code sections, and the addition of major tax law changes. Whenever changes to the Internal Revenue Code (IRC) are made, the old language is deleted and the new language added. Thus, the statutes are organized as a single document, and a tax advisor does not have to read through the applicable parts of all previous tax bills to find the most current law. In 1986, massive changes were made to the tax law, and the basic tax law was redesignated as the Internal Revenue Code of 1986.

The federal income tax became a "mass tax" on individuals during the early 1940s. This change was deemed necessary to finance the revenue needs of the federal government during World War II. In 1939, less than 6% of the U.S. population was

Historical Note

Before 1939, the tax laws were contained in the current revenue act, a reenactment of a prior revenue act plus amendments. In 1939 a permanent tax code was established, and it was revised in 1954 and 1986.

---

[1] *Pollock v. Farmers' Loan & Trust Co.*, 3 AFTR 2602, (USSC, 1895). Note, however, that a federal income tax on corporations that was enacted in 1901 was held to be constitutional because it was treated as an excise tax. See *Flint v. Stone Tracy Co.*, 3 AFTR 2834, (USSC, 1911).

subject to the federal income tax, whereas by 1945 74% of the population was taxed.[2] To accommodate the broadened tax base and to avoid significant tax collection problems, Congress enacted pay-as-you-go withholding in 1943.

Revenue Sources

As mentioned earlier, the largest source of federal revenues is individual income taxes. Other major revenue sources include social security (FICA) taxes and corporate income taxes (see Table 1-1). Note that the relative percentage contribution from social security taxes have increased somewhat due to increases in the contribution rates and ceiling amounts.

Typical Misconception

It is frequently assumed that the tax revenue from corporation income taxes is the largest source of tax revenue. However, the revenue generated from this tax represents less than 10% of total federal revenues.

TABLE 1-1   *Breakdown of Federal Revenues*

	1982	1987	1992
Individual income taxes	48%	46%	44%
Social insurance taxes and contribution	33	35	38
Corporation income taxes	8	10	9
Other	11	9	9
Total	100%	100%	100%

Source: Council of Economic Advisors, *Economic Indicators* (Washington DC: U.S. Government Printing Office, 1993) p. 33.

TYPES OF TAX RATE STRUCTURES

The Structure of Individual Income Tax Rates

OBJECTIVE 2
Differentiate between the three types of tax rate structures

Tax rates may be either progressive, proportional, or regressive. Income taxes are generally **progressive taxes** (i.e., the rate of tax increases as the taxpayer's taxable income increases). The federal income tax rates for individuals in 1993 and later years are 15%, 28%, 31%, 36%, and 39.6%.[3] In 1994, the 28% rate begins when taxable income exceeds $38,000 for married individuals filing a joint return. For single individuals, the 28% rate begins when taxable income exceeds $22,750. The 31% rate begins when taxable income exceeds $91,850 for married individuals filing jointly and $55,100 for single individuals.

Example 1-1 ■   Alice, who is single, has $10,000 taxable income and pays $1,500 in federal income taxes because a 15% tax rate is applied to taxable income up to $22,750. Allen, who is also single, has taxable income of $30,000. A 15% rate applies to Allen's taxable income up to $22,750, and a 28% rate applies to taxable income in excess of this amount. Thus, Allen's total tax is $5,442 ([0.15 × $22,750] + [0.28 × $7,250]). If Allen's taxable income is $56,000, a 31% rate applies to $900 of his taxable income ($56,000 − $55,100) because the 31% rate applies to taxable income in excess of $55,100 for a single individual. Thus, the tax rates are progressive because the rate of tax increases as a taxpayer's taxable income increases. ■

In 1993 and 1994 the 36% rate begins when taxable income exceeds $140,000 for married individuals filing a joint return. For single individuals, the 36% rate begins when taxable income exceeds $115,000. A 39.6% marginal tax rate applies to taxable

---

[2] Richard Goode, *The Individual Income Tax* (Washington, D.C.: The Brookings Institution, 1964), pp. 2–4.

[3] For 1991 and 1992 the rates were 15%, 28%, and 31%. (See the inside front cover, Appendix A and Chapter 2 for a discussion of the current tax computation, tax rate schedules, and tax tables.)

income in excess of $250,000 for both single individuals and married individuals filing a joint return.

Example 1-2 ■ Assume the same facts as in Example 1-1 except that Alice has taxable income of $120,000. Of Alice's taxable income, $5,000 ($120,000 − $115,000) is subject to the 36% rate. Also assume that Allen has taxable income of $260,000. Of Allen's taxable income, $135,000 ($250,000 − $115,000) is subject to the 36% rate and $10,000 ($260,000 − $250,000) is subject to a marginal rate of 39.6%. ■

A **proportional tax** rate, sometimes referred to as a **flat tax,** is one where the rate of tax is the same for all taxpayers, regardless of their income levels. This type of tax rate is generally used for real estate taxes, state and local sales taxes, personal property taxes, customs duties, and excise taxes.

Example 1-3 ■ Assume the same facts as in Example 1-1, except that a 15% tax rate applies to all amounts of taxable income. Based on the assumed tax rate structure, Alice's federal income tax is $1,500 on $10,000 of taxable income, and Allen's tax is $4,500 on $30,000 of taxable income and $8,400 on $56,000 of taxable income. The tax rate is proportional because the 15% rate applies to both taxpayers without regard to their income level. ■

A **regressive tax** rate decreases with an increase in the tax base (e.g., income). Regressive taxes are not often found in the United States. The social security (FICA) tax is regressive because a fixed rate of tax of 7.65% for both the employer and employee is levied up to a ceiling amount of $60,600 (in 1994). The employer and employee's FICA tax rate is only 1.45% for wages earned in excess of the ceiling amount.

The Structure of Corporate Tax Rates

The federal corporate income tax reflects a stair-step pattern of progression that tends to benefit small corporations. The corporate rates are as follows:[4]

Taxable Income	Tax
First $50,000	15% of taxable income
Over $50,000 but not over $75,000	$7,500 + 25% of taxable income over $50,000
Over $75,000 but not over $100,000	$13,750 + 34% of taxable income over $75,000
Over $100,000 but not over $335,000	$22,250 + 39% of taxable income over $100,000
Over $335,000	34% of taxable income
Over $10,000,000 but not over $15,000,000	$3,400,000 + 35% of taxable income over $10,000,000
Over $15,000,000 but not over $18,333,333	$5,150,000 + 38% over $15,000,000
Over $18,333,333	35% of taxable income

Self-Study Question

Assume a tax system with a tax of $1,000 on taxable income of $10,000 and a $1,500 tax on taxable income of $20,000. Is the tax rate system progressive, proportional, or regressive?

Answer

The tax system would be regressive. Even though the amount of tax has increased, the rate of taxation has decreased from 10% on the first $10,000 of taxable income to 5% on the second $10,000 of taxable income.

[4] For corporations with taxable income over $100,000, the lower rates of tax on the first $75,000 of income are gradually phased out by applying a 5 percentage point surtax on taxable income from $100,000 to $335,000 so that benefits of the favorable rates are eliminated once a corporation's taxable income reaches $335,000. Once taxable income exceeds $335,000 the tax equals 34% times taxable income. A 35% tax rate applies to taxable income from $10 million to $15 million. For corporations with taxable income in excess of $15 million, a 3 percentage point surcharge applies to taxable income from $15 million to $18,333,333 to eliminate the lower 34% rate which applies to the first $10 million of taxable income.

Marginal, Average, and Effective Tax Rates

A taxpayer's **marginal tax rate** is the tax rate that is applied to an incremental amount of taxable income that is added to the tax base. The marginal tax rate concept is useful for planning because it measures the tax effect of a proposed transaction.

Example 1-4 ■ Vania, who is single, is considering the purchase of a personal residence that will provide a $20,000 tax deduction for interest expense and real estate taxes. Vania's taxable income would be reduced from $80,000 to $60,000 if she purchases the residence. Since a 31% tax rate applies to taxable income from $60,000 to $80,000, Vania's marginal tax rate is 31%. Thus, Vania's tax savings from purchasing the personal residence would be $6,200 (0.31 × $20,000). ■

The **average tax rate** is computed by dividing the total tax liability by the amount of taxable income. This is different from a taxpayer's **effective tax rate,** which is the total tax liability divided by total economic income. **Total economic income** includes exclusions and deductions from the tax base (e.g., tax-exempt bond interest).

Example 1-5 ■ Amelia, who is single, has $25,000 of taxable income and her economic income is $35,000 in 1994. The difference is attributable to $10,000 of tax-exempt bond interest. Based upon tax rates applicable to a single taxpayer, Amelia's total tax is $4,042 ([0.15 × $22,750] + [0.28 × $2,250]). Her average tax rate is 16.17% ($4,042 ÷ $25,000). Amelia's effective tax rate is 11.55% ($4,042 ÷ $35,000). ■

Additional Comment

In the determination of tax rates, one should consider the incidence of taxation which involves the issue of who really bears the burden of the tax. If a city raises the real property tax but landlords simply raise rents to pass on the higher taxes to their tenants, the tax burden is shifted. The concept has important implications in determining any kind of average or effective tax rate.

The Income Tax Formula

Federal income taxes are imposed on individuals, corporations, estates, and trusts. Although the formulas themselves appear here, the details regarding the tax formulas for individuals and corporations are discussed in Chapter 2.

The major difference between the formula for an individual taxpayer (Table 1-2) and a corporate taxpayer (Table 1-3) is the fact that there is only one category of deductions for a corporation. There are no itemized deductions, standard deductions, or personal and dependency exemptions for a corporation.

TYPES OF TAXES

State Income and Franchise Taxes

OBJECTIVE 3

Describe the various types of taxes

Only seven states do not impose an individual income tax.[5] In most instances, state income tax rates are progressive and are based upon an individual's federal adjusted gross income (AGI), with minor adjustments.[6] (For example, interest income on federal government obligations is generally not subject to state income taxes.) Some states also allow a deduction for federal income taxes in the computation of taxable income for state income tax purposes.

Almost all states having a state income tax require the withholding of state income taxes and have established mandatory estimated tax payment procedures. The due

---

[5] These states are Alaska, Florida, Nevada, South Dakota, Texas, Washington, and Wyoming. New Hampshire has an income tax that is levied only on dividend and interest income and Tennessee's income tax applies only to income from stocks and bonds.

[6] See Chapter 2 for a discussion of the AGI computation.

TABLE 1-2 **Tax Formula for Individuals**

Income from whatever source derived	$xxx,xxx
Minus: Exclusions (e.g., tax-exempt bond interest)	(x,xxx)
Gross income	$ xx,xxx
Minus: Deductions *for* adjusted gross income (e.g., alimony payments)	(xx,xxx)
Adjusted gross income (AGI)	$ xx,xxx
Minus: Deductions *from* adjusted gross income. Larger of: itemized deductions or standard deduction	(xx,xxx)
Personal and dependency exemptions	(x,xxx)
Taxable income (tax base)	$ xx,xxx
Times: Tax rates (from tax table or rate schedule)	× .xx
Gross tax	$ xx,xxx
Minus: Credits and prepayments	(x,xxx)
Net tax payable or refund due	$ x,xxx

Additional Comment

State income tax rates for individuals have increased significantly in the past 20 years. Thirty-three states now have marginal tax rates of 6% or higher.

date for filing state income tax returns generally coincides with the due date for the federal income tax returns (e.g., the fifteenth day of the fourth month following the close of the tax year for individuals).

Most states impose a corporate income tax, although in some instances the tax is referred to as a **franchise tax.** Franchise taxes are usually based upon a weighted-average formula consisting of net worth, income, and sales.

Wealth Transfer Taxes

The Tax Reform Act of 1976 created a unified transfer tax system that imposes a single tax upon transfers of property taking place during an individual's lifetime and at death. (See the inside back cover of the text for the transfer tax rate schedules.) Formerly, the gift and estate tax laws were separate and distinct. The federal estate tax was initially enacted in 1916. The original gift tax law dates back to 1932. The gift tax was originally imposed to prevent widespread avoidance of the estate tax (e.g., taxpayers would otherwise make tax-free gifts of property prior to their death). Both the gift and estate taxes are wealth transfer taxes levied on the transfer of property and are based upon the fair market value (FMV) of the transferred property on the date of the transfer.

TABLE 1-3 **Tax Formula for Corporations**

Income from whatever source derived	$xxx,xxx
Minus: Exclusions (e.g., tax-exempt bond interest)	(x,xxx)
Gross income	$ xx,xxx
Minus: Deductions (e.g., business expenses)	(xx,xxx)
Taxable income (tax base)	$ x,xxx
Times Tax rates	× .xx
Gross tax	$ x,xxx
Minus: Credits and prepayments	(x,xxx)
Net tax payable or refund due	$ x,xxx

Key Point

The $10,000 annual exclusion is an important tax-planning tool for wealthy parents who want to transfer assets to their children and thereby minimize their gift and estate taxes. A husband and wife who have three children could transfer $60,000 to their children each year without incurring any gift tax.

The Federal Gift Tax. The **gift tax** is imposed upon the donor for transfers that are not supported by full and adequate consideration. To arrive at the amount of taxable gifts for the current year, a $10,000 annual exclusion is allowed per donee.[7] In addition, an unlimited marital deduction is allowed for transfers between spouses.[8] The formula for computing the gift tax is as follows:

FMV of all gifts made in the current year			$x,xxx
Minus:	Annual donee exclusions ($10,000 per donee)	$xx	
	Marital deduction for gifts to spouse	xx	
	Charitable contribution deduction	xx	(xxx)
Plus:	Taxable gifts for all prior years		xxx
Cumulative taxable gifts (tax base)			$x,xxx
Times:	Unified transfer tax rates		× .xx
Tentative tax on gift tax base			$ xxx
Minus:	Unified transfer taxes paid in prior years		(xx)
	Unified credit not claimed in prior periods		(xx)
Unified transfer tax (gift tax) due in the current year			$ xx

Additional Comment

The gift tax was enacted to make the estate tax more effective. Without a gift tax, estate taxes could be easily avoided by large gifts made before death.

Note that the gift tax is cumulative over the taxpayer's lifetime (i.e., the tax calculation for the current year includes the taxable gifts made in prior years). The detailed tax rules relating to the gift tax are covered in Chapter 12 of *Prentice Hall's Federal Taxation: Corporations, Partnerships, Estates, and Trusts* and in Chapter 23 of the *Comprehensive* volume. The following general concepts and rules for the federal gift tax are presented as background material for other chapters of this text dealing with individual taxpayers:

- Gifts between spouses are tax-exempt due to the operation of an unlimited marital deduction.

- The primary liability for payment of the gift tax is imposed upon the donor. The donee is contingently liable for payment of the gift tax in the event of nonpayment by the donor.

- The donor is permitted a $10,000 annual exclusion for gifts of a present interest to each donee.[9]

- Charitable contributions are effectively exempted from the gift tax because an unlimited deduction is allowed.

- The tax basis of the property to the donee is generally the donor's cost. It is the lesser of the donor's cost or the property's FMV on the date of the gift if the property is sold by the donee at a loss. (See Chapter 5 for a discussion of the gift tax basis rules.)

- A unified tax credit equivalent to a $600,000 deduction is available to offset any gift tax that would otherwise be due on gifts made to someone other than a spouse or a charity that are in excess of the $10,000 annual exclusion.[10]

---

[7] Sec. 2503(b).
[8] Sec. 2523(a).
[9] A gift of a present interest is an interest that is already in existence and the donee is currently entitled to receive the income from the property. For example, a gift of a future interest comes into being at some future date (e.g., property is transferred by gift to a trust in which the donee is not entitled to the income from the property until the donor dies).
[10] The $600,000 exemption is in the form of a $192,800 tax credit for 1987 and later years.

Example 1-6 ■ Antonio makes the following gifts in the current year:

- $25,000 cash gift to his wife
- $15,000 contribution to the United Way
- Gift of a personal automobile valued at $25,000 to his adult son
- Gift of a personal computer valued at $4,000 to a friend

The $25,000 gift to one's spouse is not taxed because of a $10,000 annual exclusion and a $15,000 tax exemption for transfers to spouses (i.e., the marital deduction). The $15,000 contribution to the United Way is also not taxed because of the $10,000 annual exclusion and the $5,000 deduction that is provided for charitable contributions. The $25,000 gift that Antonio made to his son is reduced by the $10,000 annual exclusion to each donee leaving a $15,000 taxable gift.[11] The $4,000 gift to the friend is exempt because of the annual exclusion of up to $10,000 in gifts to a donee in a tax year. Total taxable gifts for the current year that are subject to the unified transfer tax equal $15,000. ■

Typical Misconception

It is sometimes thought that the federal estate tax raises significant amounts of revenue when in fact it has not been a significant revenue producer since World War II.

The Federal Estate Tax. The **federal estate tax** is part of the unified transfer tax system that is based upon the total property transfers an individual makes during his lifetime and at death.

Example 1-7 ■ Amy dies during the current year. The formula for computing the estate tax upon Amy's estate is as follows:

Gross estate (FMV of all property owned by the decedent at the date of death)	$xxx,xxx
Minus: Deductions for funeral and administration expenses, debts of the decedent, charitable contributions, and the marital deduction for property transferred to a spouse	(x,xxx)
Taxable estate	$ x,xxx
Plus: Taxable gifts made after 1976	xx
Tax base	$ x,xxx
Times: Unified transfer tax rate(s)	× .xx
Tentative tax on estate tax base	$ xxx
Minus: Tax credits (e.g., the unified tax credit of $192,800)	(xx)
Gift taxes paid after 1976	(xx)
Unified transfer tax (estate tax) due	$ xx

■

Additional Comment

The unified transfer tax rate schedule contains rates that range from 18% to 55%.

The estate tax rules are discussed in depth in Chapter 13 of *Prentice Hall's Federal Taxation: Corporations, Partnerships, Estates, and Trusts* and in Chapter 24 of the *Comprehensive* volume. The following general rules are provided as background material for subsequent chapters of this text dealing with individual taxpayers:

- The decedent's property is valued at its FMV on the date of death unless the alternate valuation date (6 months after the date of death) is elected. The alternative valuation date may be elected only if the aggregate value of the gross

---

[11] This example assumes that the automobile is a gift rather than an obligation of support under state law and also assumes that Antonio's spouse does not join with Antonio in electing to treat the gift to the son as having been made by both spouses (a gift-splitting election). In such event, donee exclusions of $20,000 (2 × $10,000) would be available resulting in a taxable gift of only $5,000.

estate decreases during the 6-month period following the date of death and the election results in a lower estate tax liability.

- The basis of the property received by the estate and by the decedent's heirs is the property's FMV on the date of death (or the alternate valuation date if it is elected).

- Property that is transferred to the decedent's spouse is exempt from the estate tax due to the operation of the estate tax marital deduction provision.

Example 1-8 ■

Barry died in the current year, leaving a $1,000,000 gross estate. One-half of the property is transferred to his wife; taxable gifts made after 1976 were $150,000; and administrative and funeral expenses, and debts of the decedent amount to $200,000. The estate tax due is computed as follows:

Gross estate		$1,000,000
Minus:	Marital deduction	(500,000)
	Funeral and administrative expenses, and decedent's debts	(200,000)
Taxable estate		$ 300,000
Plus:	Taxable gifts made after 1976	150,000
Tax base		$ 450,000
Tentative tax on estate tax base		$ 138,800[a]
Minus:	Tax credits (unified tax credit)	(192,800)
Unified transfer tax due		$ —0—

■

[a] $70,800 + (0.34 × $200,000)

Even though the unified tax credit exceeds the gross estate tax amount, the estate is unable to obtain a refund of the excess amount because the estate tax is not a refundable credit.

Because of the generous credit and deduction provisions (e.g., the unified tax credit and the unlimited marital deduction), few estates must pay estate taxes. For example, an individual might leave $1 million of the property in his estate to his spouse and $600,000 to his children. No estate tax would be owed because a $1 million marital deduction is allowed and the unified tax credit of $192,800 is equivalent to a $600,000 tax exemption.

Other Types of Taxes

Additional Comment

Proposals to decrease reliance on the federal income tax have focused on a value added tax and selective energy taxes. A value added tax is a sales tax levied at each stage of production on the "value added."

Although the primary focus of this text is upon the federal income tax, some mention should be made of the following other types of taxes levied by federal, state, and local governments.

- Property taxes are based upon the value of a taxpayer's property, which may include both real estate and personal property. Real estate taxes are a major source of revenue for local governments. However, it is not uncommon for state and local governments to levy a personal property tax on intangibles such as securities and tangible personal property (e.g., the value of a personal automobile).

- Federal excise taxes and **customs duties** on imported goods have declined in relative importance over the years but remain significant sources of revenue. Federal excise taxes are imposed upon alcohol, tobacco, gasoline, telephone usage, production of oil and gas, and many other types of goods. Many state and local governments impose similar excise taxes upon goods and services.

Additional Comment

Anheuser-Busch Company ran a television commercial in 1990 during the deliberations on the Revenue Reconciliation Act of 1990 that asked viewers to call a toll-free telephone number to register their criticism of an increase in the excise tax on beer. The commercial asked viewers to "can the beer tax."

- Sales taxes are a major source of revenue for state and local governments. Sales taxes are imposed upon retail sales of tangible personal property (e.g., clothing, automobiles, and so on). Some states also impose a sales tax upon personal services (e.g., accounting and legal fees). Certain items are frequently exempt from the sales tax levy (e.g., food items or medicines), and the rates vary widely between individual state and local governments. Sales taxes are not deductible for federal income tax purposes unless incurred to produce income. (See Chapter 7 for a discussion of sales taxes.)

- **Employment taxes** include social security **(FICA)** and federal and state unemployment compensation taxes. If an individual is classified as an employee, a FICA tax is imposed on the employee at a 7.65% rate (for 1994) on wages up to $60,600 (in 1994) with an equal amount of tax imposed on the employer. The 1.45% hospital insurance (HI) portion of the FICA tax continues to apply to both the employee and employer. For wages received after 1993 the HI portion is not subject to a ceiling amount.[12] If an individual is self-employed, a self-employment tax is imposed at a 15.3% rate on the individual's self-employment income with a ceiling on the tax base of $60,600 (in 1994).[13] Self-employed individuals are also subject to the additional hospital insurance premium for self-employment income at a 2.9% rate and no ceiling is applied to amounts received after 1993.

- Employers are required to pay federal and state unemployment taxes to fund the payment of unemployment benefits to former employees. The federal rate is 6.2% on the first $7,000 of wages for each employee in 1994.[14] However, a credit is granted for up to 5.4% of wages for taxes paid to the state government so that the actual amount that is paid to the federal government may be as low as 0.8%.[15] The amount of tax that is paid to the state depends upon the employer's prior experience with respect to the frequency and amount of unemployment claims.

The types of taxes and structural considerations that were previously discussed are summarized in Topic Review 1-1.

CRITERIA FOR A TAX STRUCTURE

OBJECTIVE 4

Discuss what constitutes a "good" tax structure and the objectives of the federal income tax law

Establishing criteria for a "good" tax structure was first attempted in 1776 by economist Adam Smith.[16] Smith's four "canons of taxation"—equity, certainty, convenience, and economy—are still used today when tax policy issues are discussed.

Equity

Additional Comment

The Revenue Reconciliation Act of 1993 followed through on President Clinton's campaign promise to increase taxes on high-income taxpayers to correct perceived inequities resulting from the lowering of the top tax rates in the Tax Reform Act of 1986.

The tax law should be horizontally equitable (i.e., similarly situated taxpayers should be treated equally). A parallel notion (vertical equity) is that the incidence of taxation should be borne by those who have the "ability to pay" the tax, based upon income levels or wealth. The progressive tax rate structure is founded on this premise. Fairness or equity is, however, an elusive term that is extremely difficult to measure. For example, a tax credit for taxpayers who purchase business equipment may be

---

[12] The HI portion was subject to a ceiling of $135,000 in 1993.

[13] Self-employed individuals receive an income tax deduction equal to 50% of taxes paid on their self-employment income and this deduction is also allowed to compute the amount of self-employment income (see Secs. 164(f) and 1402(a)(12) and Chapter 14).

[14] Sec. 3301.

[15] Sec. 3302.

[16] Adam Smith, *The Wealth of Nations* (New York: Random House, Modern Library, 1937), pp. 777-79.

TOPIC REVIEW 1-1

Types of Taxes and Tax Structure

Type of Tax	Tax Structure	Tax Base
Individuals:		
Federal income tax	Progressive	Gross income from all sources unless specifically excluded by law reduced by deductions and exemptions
State income tax	Progressive	Generally based on AGI for federal income tax purposes with adjustments
Federal gift tax	Progressive	FMV of all taxable gifts made during the tax year
Federal estate tax	Progressive	FMV of property owned at death plus taxable gifts made after 1976
Corporations:		
Federal corporate income tax	Progressive	Gross income from all sources unless specifically excluded by law reduced by deductions
State corporate income tax	Proportional or progressive	Federal corporate taxable income with adjustments
State franchise tax	Proportional	Usually based on a weighted-average formula consisting of net worth, income, and sales
Other Types of Taxes:		
Property taxes	Proportional	FMV of personal and/or real property
Excise taxes	Proportional	Customs and duties on imported and domestic goods from alcohol to telephone usage
Sales taxes	Proportional	Retail sales of tangible personal property or personal services
FICA and self-employment taxes	Regressive	Based on wages or self-employment income
Unemployment taxes	Regressive	Usually first $7,000 of an employee's wages

viewed as either a proper investment incentive or as an unnecessary loophole. The federal tax law includes various measures to ensure that taxpayers are treated fairly. For example, a foreign tax credit is available to minimize the double taxation that would otherwise occur when U.S. taxpayers earn income in a foreign country that is taxed by both the United States and the country in which it is earned. (See the glossary at the end of this volume for a definition of tax credits and Chapter 14 for a discussion of the foreign tax credit.) Another example is the use of carryback and carryover rules for certain losses that are not deductible in any one year. For example, net operating losses may be carried back for 3 years and forward for 15 years and used to offset taxable income for any of the carryback or carryover years. (See Chapter 8 for a discussion of the net operating loss rules.)

Key Point

Using retroactive dates for changes in the tax law does not help to accomplish the objective of "certainty." For example, the effective date of the increase in the top tax rate was made retroactive to January 1, 1993 in tax legislation signed by President Clinton on August 19, 1993. This retroactive tax increase was unpopular with high-income taxpayers.

Certainty

A certain tax is one that assures the government a stable source of operating revenues and provides taxpayers with some degree of certainty concerning the amount of their annual tax liability. A tax that is simple to understand and administer provides certainty for taxpayers. For several years, our income tax laws have been criticized as being overly complex and difficult to administer. Consider the following remarks of a noted tax authority at a conference on federal income tax simplification, which was jointly sponsored by the American Bar Association and the American Law Institute:

> Tax advisers—at least some tax advisers—are saying that the income tax system is not working. They are saying that they don't know what the law provides, that the IRS does not know what the law provides, that taxpayers are not abiding by the law they don't know.[17]

This uncertainty in the tax law causes frequent disputes between taxpayers and the IRS and has resulted in extensive litigation.

The federal tax system has made some attempts to provide certainty for taxpayers. For example, the IRS issues advance rulings to taxpayers. This provides some assurance concerning the tax consequences of a proposed transaction for the taxpayer who requests the ruling. The taxpayer may rely on the ruling if the transaction is completed in accordance with the terms of the ruling request. For example, if a merger of two corporations is being considered, the transaction can be structured so that the shareholders and the corporations do not recognize gain or loss. If a favorable ruling is received, and the transaction is completed as planned, the IRS cannot later assert that the merger does not qualify for tax-free treatment.

Convenience

Additional Comment

For tax year 1991, 49.5% of all individual tax returns were prepared by paid tax-return preparers. And, for that same year, the IRS received 34,950,000 telephone inquiries.

A tax law should be easily assessed, collected, and administered. Taxpayers should not be overly burdened with the maintenance of records and compliance considerations (i.e., preparation of their tax returns, payment of their taxes, and so on). One of the reasons that the sales tax is such a popular form of tax for state and local governments is that it is convenient to pay and collect from the vendor. The consumer need not complete a tax return or keep detailed records.

Economy

An efficient tax structure should require only minimal compliance and administrative costs. The IRS collection costs are fairly minimal relative to the total collections of revenues from the federal income tax, amounting to less than 0.5% of revenues. Estimates of taxpayer compliance costs are less certain. One indicator of total compliance costs for taxpayers is the demand for tax professionals. Tax practice has been and continues to be one of the fastest growing areas in public accounting firms. Most large corporations also maintain sizable tax departments that engage in tax research, compliance, and planning activities. In addition, many commercial tax return preparer services are available to assist taxpayers who have relatively uncomplicated tax returns.

A more difficult question is whether the tax structure is economical in terms of taxpayer compliance. The issues of tax avoidance and tax evasion are becoming increasingly more important. A Treasury Department study estimate of taxpayer

---

[17] Sidney L. Roberts, "The Viewpoint of the Tax Adviser: An Overview of Simplification," *Tax Adviser*, January, 1979, p. 32.

compliance indicates surprisingly low compliance rates for some types of income.[18] For example, the voluntary reporting percentage for small business corporation income was only 65.4%.

OBJECTIVES OF THE FEDERAL INCOME TAX LAW

The primary objective of the federal income tax law is to raise revenues for government operations. In recent years, the federal government has broadened its use of the tax laws to accomplish various economic and social policy objectives.

Economic Objectives

The federal income tax law is used as a fiscal policy tool to stimulate private investment, reduce unemployment, and mitigate the effects of inflation on the economy. Consider the following example: Tax credits for businesses operating in distressed urban and rural areas (empowerment zones) were enacted in 1993 to provide economic revitalization of such areas.

The tax brackets, personal and dependency exemptions, and standard deduction amounts are adjusted for inflation by an indexation procedure using the consumer price index. These inflation adjustments provide relief for individual taxpayers who would otherwise be subject to increased taxes due to the effects of inflation. (See Chapter 2 for a discussion of the tax computation for individuals.)

Encouragement of Certain Activities and Industries

Additional Comment

Among the provisions in the tax law that are designed to enhance the level of health care are the deductibility of medical expenses, deductibility of charitable contributions to hospitals, and exclusion of fringe benefits provided by employers for medical insurance premiums and medical care.

The federal income tax law also attempts to stimulate and encourage certain activities, specialized industries, and small businesses. One such example is the encouragement of research activities by permitting an immediate write-off of expenses and a special tax credit for increasing research and experimental costs. Special incentives are also provided to the oil and gas industry through percentage depletion allowances and an election to deduct intangible drilling costs.

Certain favorable tax provisions are provided for small businesses, including reduced corporate tax rates of 15% on the first $50,000 of taxable income and 25% for the next $25,000 of taxable income. Favorable ordinary loss (instead of capital loss) deductions are granted to individual investors who sell their small business corporation stock at a loss provided that certain requirements are met.[19] In addition, noncorporate investors may exclude up to 50% of the gain realized from the disposition of qualified small business stock issued after August 10, 1993 if the stock is held for more than five years.[20]

Social Objectives

The tax law attempts to encourage or discourage certain socially desirable or undersirable activities. For example:

---

[18] U.S., Department of the Treasury, Internal Revenue Service Research Division, *Income Tax Compliance Research: Supporting Appendices to Publication 7285* [Publication 1415] (Washington DC: U.S. Government Printing Office, July, 1988).

[19] Sec. 1244.

[20] Sec. 1202.

- Special tax-favored pension and profit-sharing plans have been created for employees and self-employed individuals to supplement the social security retirement system.
- Charitable contributions are deductible to encourage individuals to contribute to charitable organizations.
- The claiming of a deduction for illegal bribes, fines, and penalties has been prohibited to discourage activities that are contrary to public policy.

Example 1-9 ■   Able Corporation establishes a qualified pension plan for its employees whereby it makes all of the annual contributions to the plan. Able's contributions to the pension trust are currently deductible and not includible in the employee's gross income until the pension payments are distributed during their retirement years. Earnings on the contributed funds are also nontaxable until such amounts are distributed to the employees. ■

Example 1-10 ■   Anita contributes $10,000 annually to her church, which is a qualified charitable organization. Anita's marginal tax rate is 28%. Her after-tax cost of contributing to the church is only $7,200 ($10,000 − [0.28 × $10,000]). ■

Example 1-11 ■   Ace Trucking Company incurs $10,000 in fines imposed by local and state governments for overloading its trucks during the current tax year. None of the fines are deductible because the activity is contrary to public policy. ■

The tax law objectives previously discussed are highlighted in Topic Review 1-2.

TAX LAW SOURCES

OBJECTIVE 5

Identify the various tax law sources and understand their implications for tax practice

Tax information for tax practitioners is obtained from legislative, administrative, and judicial sources.

Since Congress is not capable of anticipating every type of transaction in which taxpayers might engage, most tax statutes (i.e., tax legislation) contain very general language. Even if Congress could do so, it would not be feasible for the Internal Revenue Code (discussed below) to contain details addressing the tax consequences of all such transactions.

The general language contained in the Code makes both administrative and judicial interpretations necessary. Thus, the term *tax law,* as used by most tax advisors, encompasses administrative and judicial interpretations in addition to the statutes. Administrative interpretations include, for example, Treasury Regulations, revenue rulings, and revenue procedures. These are discussed in detail later in the chapter. Judicial interpretations consist of court decisions. The committee reports issued by Congressional committees (i.e., the House Ways and Means and Senate Finance Committees as well as any joint conference committees) involved in the legislative process are also a source of tax law. Such reports are helpful sources for determining Congressional intent prior to the issuance of Treasury Regulations.

Additional Comment

Televised broadcasts of the House Ways and Means Committee and the Senate Finance Committee can be seen on C-Span.

Example 1-12 ■   In 1984 Congress enacted Sec. 7872 of the Internal Revenue Code concerning the tax treatment of below-market interest rate loans. One subset of such rules applies to "gift loans," defined in Sec. 7872(f)(3) as "any below-market loan where the foregoing of interest is in the nature of a gift." The Conference Report elaborates on the transactions classified as gift loans as follows: "In general, there is a gift if

TOPIC REVIEW 1-2

Objectives of the Tax Law	
Objective	*Example*
Stimulate investment and reduce unemployment	Provide a tax credit for the purchase of business equipment
Prevent taxpayers from paying a higher percentage of their income in personal income taxes due to inflation (bracket creep)	Index the tax rates, standard deduction, and personal and dependency exemptions for inflation
Encourage research activities which will in turn strengthen the competitiveness of U.S. companies	Allow research expenditures to be written off in the year incurred and offer a tax credit for increasing research and experimental costs
Encourage venture capital for small businesses	Reduce corporate income tax rates on the first $75,000 of taxable income. Allow businesses to immediately expense $17,500 of certain depreciable business assets acquired each year.
Encourage social objectives	Provide a tax deduction for charitable contributions; provide favorable tax treatment for contributions to qualified pension plans.
Stimulate the economy	Provide tax credits for the acquisition of plant and equipment

Additional Comment

A knowledge of the tax law sources could be considered one of the most important topics in this book. It is similar to the old Chinese proverb which states that if you give a person a fish you have fed him for one day, but if you teach a person how to fish you have fed him for the rest of his life. By analogy, if a person has a knowledge of the tax law sources, he or she should be able to locate the answers to tax questions throughout their career.

Additional Comment

The Internal Revenue Code is sometimes difficult to read. The first sentence in Sec. 341(e) contains approximately 440 words. Not all code provisions are that technical or difficult to understand.

property (including foregone interest) is transferred for less than full and adequate consideration under circumstances where the transfer is a gift for gift tax purposes. A sale, exchange, or other transfer made in the ordinary course of business . . . generally is considered as made for full and adequate consideration. A loan between unrelated persons can qualify as a gift loan."[21] This definition can be quite important to a tax advisor because it may be many months until the Treasury issues regulations that elaborate on an issue (e.g., proposed regulations were issued on the Sec. 7872(f)(3) definition 10 months after the statute was enacted). Until such regulations were issued, this definition may have been the only "authoritative" interpretation of the "gift loans" term that was available. ∎

Internal Revenue Code

The current **Internal Revenue Code,** known as the Internal Revenue Code of 1986 or the Code, constitutes Title 26 of the federal statutes. It serves as the highest legislative authority for tax research, planning, and compliance activities.

The Code contains provisions addressing income taxes, estate and gift taxes, employment taxes, alcohol and tobacco taxes, and other excise taxes. For purposes of organization, Title 26 is further divided into subtitles, chapters, subchapters, parts, subparts, sections, subsections, paragraphs, subparagraphs, and clauses. Sections are the most frequently cited organizational category. For example, tax advisors often

---

[21] H. Rept. No. 98-861, 98th Cong., 2d Sess., p. 1,018 (1984).

refer to "Sec. 351 transactions," "Sec. 306 stock,"and "Sec. 1231 gains and losses." The Code contains several thousand sections and subsections, each providing general rules and exceptions regarding the tax consequences of a particular transaction. For example, Sec. 1033 permits taxpayers to elect to postpone the recognition of a gain arising from an involuntary conversion. One must be familiar with the Code's organizational scheme in order to read it correctly. The language of the Code is replete with cross-referencing to titles, paragraphs, subparagraphs, and so on. Figure 1-1 illustrates the overall organizational scheme of the Code.

Additional Comment

To cite a Code section it is not necessary to also provide the subtitle, chapter, subchapter, part, and subpart since the section numbers run consecutively from the beginning to the end of the Code.

Example 1-13 ■

Section 7701, a definitional section, begins by stating, "When used in this title . . . " and then lists a series of definitions. Thus, a definition in Sec. 7701 controls for all of Title 26—for purposes of the income tax, estate and gift tax, excise tax, and so on. ■

Example 1-14 ■

Section 302(b)(3) allows taxpayers whose stock holdings are completely terminated in a stock redemption (i.e., a corporation's purchase of its stock from one of its shareholders) to receive capital gain treatment on the excess of the redemption proceeds over the stock's basis instead of ordinary income treatment on the entire proceeds. Section 302(c)(2)(A) states, "In the case of a distribution described in subsection (b)(3), section 318(a)(1) shall not apply if . . .." Further, Sec. 302(c)(2)(C)(i) indicates "Subparagraph (A) shall not apply to a distribution to any entity unless . . .." Thus, in determining whether a taxpayer will receive capital gain treatment for a stock redemption transaction, a tax advisor must be able to locate and interpret the various sections, subsections, paragraphs, subparagraphs, and clauses. ■

Treasury Regulations

Treasury Regulations are the principal administrative source of the federal tax law. They reflect the Secretary of the Treasury's interpretation of the Code. The Regulations often give extensive examples providing invaluable assistance in under-

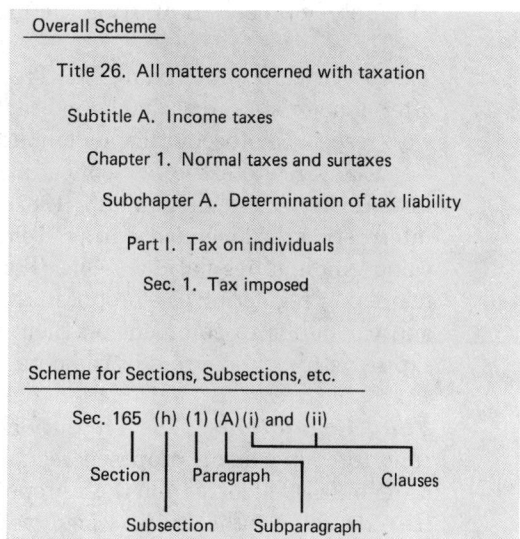

FIGURE 1-1 Organizational Scheme of the Internal Revenue Code.

Additional Comment

Legislative regulations have become more common in recent years as Congress has attempted to shift the complexity inherent in many of the new tax provisions to the Treasury Department.

standing the statutory language. The Regulations, which may be either legislative or interpretative, are issued in proposed, temporary, and final form. Each of these categories is discussed here.

Whenever the statute contains language such as, "The Secretary shall prescribe such regulations as he may deem necessary" or "under regulations prescribed by the Secretary," the regulations interpreting such statutes are **legislative regulations.** In effect, these regulations function as the details of the tax law. Perhaps the consolidated tax return regulations are the most dramatic example of legislative regulations. In Sec. 1502, Congress delegated to the Treasury the responsibility of writing regulations that would enable the tax liability of a group of affiliated corporations filing consolidated returns to be determined. As a requirement of electing the privilege of filing a consolidated tax return, corporations must consent to follow the consolidated return regulations. By consenting to follow the regulations, a taxpayer generally gives up the chance to argue that provisions in the regulations should be overturned by the courts.

Legislative regulations have a higher degree of authority than "interpretative regulations." **Interpretative regulations** primarily serve to broadly interpret the provisions of the Internal Revenue Code as drafted by Congress.

Additional Comment

Section 385, which deals with whether an interest in a corporation should be treated as debt or equity, was added to the Code in the Tax Reform Act of 1969. Final regulations were issued in 1980, but the effective date was delayed until the Regulations were subsequently withdrawn in 1983. No subsequent regulations under Sec. 385 have been issued.

Because of the frequency of statutory changes, the Treasury Department is not always able to update the regulations in a timely manner. Consequently, tax advisors should consult the introductory note when referring to a regulation in order to determine when the regulation was adopted. If the regulation was adopted prior to the most recent statutory revision of this section, the regulation should be applied with the understanding that it does not reflect the most recent version of the statute.

Proposed Regulations. Regulations are generally first issued to the public in so-called proposed form. That is, they provide guidance concerning the Treasury's interpretation of the statute, but they do not have authoritative weight. The public is given the opportunity to comment on them and suggest changes. The persons most likely to issue comments are tax accountants and tax attorneys. Thus, if the proposed regulations take a fairly protaxpayer approach, one can be sure that tax advisors will not attack them as being too lenient. Therefore, the final regulations will likely take the same approach as the proposed regulations. On the other hand, if Treasury receives considerable criticism about proposed regulations, it will likely adopt a more moderate approach in drafting the final regulations.

Key Point

Temporary regulations have the force and effect of final regulations. However, they cannot be temporary for more than a three-year period.

Temporary Regulations. The Treasury often issues temporary regulations soon after a major statutory change in order to give taxpayers and their advisors guidance with respect to procedural and computational matters. For example, in 1980 Congress essentially rewrote the law concerning the qualification for and the tax results of installment sales. In January 1981, the Treasury issued temporary regulations interpreting the amended statute. Temporary regulations have the same authoritative value as final regulations. The Treasury Department is required to issue any temporary regulation as a proposed regulation as well as to allow government agencies and the public to comment on them in the same manner.[22] Temporary regulations expire within three years of the date of issuance.

Final Regulations. The Treasury drafts final regulations after the public has had time to comment on proposed regulations. Most of the time, the final regulations differ at least slightly from their proposed version. For the most part, final regulations have the same authoritative weight as the Internal Revenue Code unless they are held

---

[22] Sec. 7805(e).

to be invalid by the courts. Final regulations generally take effect retroactive to the effective date of the statutory language that they interpret.

Administrative Interpretations

The National Office of the IRS issues several types of pronouncements including revenue rulings, revenue procedures, technical advice memoranda, and information releases. These pronouncements, which reflect administrative interpretations of the law by the IRS, do not have the same level of scope and authority as Treasury Regulations. Some of these interpretations are discussed below.

Revenue Rulings. Revenue rulings indicate the IRS's view of the tax consequences of a particular transaction. Several hundred such rulings are issued each year. They cover topics of interest to the general public. For example, a revenue ruling might indicate whether certain expenditures constitute support for purposes of claiming a dependency exemption for another individual. Since revenue rulings simply represent the viewpoint of the IRS, taxpayers do not have to follow them if they have sufficient authority for different treatment. However, the IRS presumes that its view is correct. Thus, examining agents will uphold that position.

Revenue Procedures. Revenue procedures are issued to assist taxpayers in complying with procedural issues that deal with tax return preparation and compliance issues.

For example, revenue procedures have been issued on topics such as the reporting of tip income and the requirements for reproducing paper substitutes for informational returns such as Form 1099.

Example 1-15 ■   Acme Corporation desires to change its accounting method for inventories. The approval of the IRS is required to change its accounting method. In Rev. Proc. 92-20, the IRS provides specific guidelines depending upon the type of change and terms and conditions upon which a change request will be granted, which must be followed by Acme if the approval is to be granted.[23]   ■

Additional Comment

The IRS will not issue letter rulings on certain questions. For example, no letter rulings will be issued if the problem is of an inherently factual nature. The IRS each year publishes a revenue procedure listing all no-ruling areas.

Additional Comment

A taxpayer who requests a private letter ruling is charged a fee for this service by the IRS. The normal fee is currently $300.

Letter Rulings. A more specialized form of IRS pronouncement originates from a taxpayer's request and is referred to as a **letter ruling** or **private letter ruling.** Letter rulings are initiated by taxpayers who write and ask the IRS to explain the tax consequences of a contemplated transaction. The IRS provides its explanation in the form of a letter ruling; that is, a personal response to the taxpayer requesting an answer. These rulings describe how the IRS will treat a proposed transaction, or a transaction that has been completed in a tax year that has not yet ended, upon a subsequent audit of the taxpayer. A letter ruling is binding upon the IRS only with respect to the person requesting the ruling provided that the taxpayer completes the transaction as proposed in the ruling. Nevertheless, letter rulings can furnish significant information to other taxpayers and to tax advisors because they lend insight into the IRS's opinion about the tax consequences of particular transactions. Certain letter rulings are deemed to be of general interest to taxpayers and are, therefore, eventually published by the IRS in the form of a revenue ruling.

Originally the public did not have access to letter rulings issued to other taxpayers. As a result of Code Sec. 6110, enacted in 1976, letter rulings (with any confidential

---

[23] 1992-1 C.B. 685.

information deleted) are available to the general public. The major tax publishers publish letter rulings in a letter rulings service. Commerce Clearing House's service is entitled *IRS Letter Rulings.*

Example 1-16 ■   Acorn Corporation is planning to acquire the Adobe Corporation in a business combination. For tax purposes, it is desirable to structure the transaction so that it meets the statutory and judicial requirements for a tax-free reorganization. Both corporations and their shareholders are concerned that the IRS might subsequently attempt to deny tax-free status because of the complex nature of the transaction. Therefore, Acorn Corporation requests a letter ruling from the National Office of the IRS that the proposed acquisition qualifies as a tax-free reorganization. If a favorable ruling is obtained and the parties complete the transaction as stated in the ruling request, the tax consequences may not be attacked by the IRS during a subsequent audit of the tax return.   ■

Technical Advice Memoranda. When a taxpayer's return is being audited with respect to a complicated technical matter, the taxpayer may request that the matter be referred to the IRS's National Office in Washington, D.C., for technical advice concerning the appropriate tax treatment. The "answer" from the National Office, in the form of a **technical advice memorandum,** is made available to the public as a letter ruling. Technical advice memos are easily identifiable because they generally begin with language such as, "In response to a request for technical advice . . . ."

Information Releases. If the IRS thinks that most of the general public will be interested in a particular interpretation, it may issue an **information release.** Information releases are written in lay terms and are dispatched to thousands of newspapers throughout the United States for publication therein. The IRS may, for example, write an information release to announce the amount of the standard mileage rate applicable to taxpayers who deduct the standard allowance per mile instead of deducting their actual automobile expenses for business travel.

Citation of Administrative Interpretations

Treasury Regulations. Treasury Regulations may be identified with the particular section of the Internal Revenue Code to which they relate through the use of a prefix numbering system. These citations are relatively easy to understand. One or more numbers appear before a decimal place, and several numbers follow the decimal place. The numbers preceding the decimal place indicate the general subject matter of the regulation. Numbers that frequently appear before the decimal place and their general subject matter are as follows:

Number	General Subject Matter
1	Income tax
20	Estate tax
25	Gift tax
301	Administrative and procedural matters
601	Procedural rules

The number appearing immediately to the right of the decimal place refers to the Code section being interpreted. The number following the Code section number

Additional Comment

When there has been a change in the tax law but no temporary or final regulations have yet been issued, the committee reports of the House Ways and Means Committee, the Senate Finance Committee, and the Joint [House-Senate] Conference Committee frequently provide a valuable source of authority.

indicates the number of the regulation, such as the fifth regulation. There is no relationship between this number and the subsection of the Code being interpreted. An example of a citation to a final regulation follows.

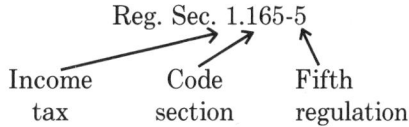

Reg. Sec. 1.165-5

Income tax → Code section → Fifth regulation

Citations to proposed or temporary regulations are in the same format. They are referenced as Prop. Reg. Sec. or Temp. Reg. Sec. According to its caption, the topic of Reg. Sec. 1.165-5 is worthless securities, a topic addressed in subsection (g) of Code Sec. 165. Sec. 165 itself refers to losses.

Revenue Rulings and Revenue Procedures. **Revenue rulings** and **revenue procedures** initially appear in the weekly Internal Revenue Bulletin (cited as I.R.B.). Both revenue rulings and revenue procedures are subsequently published by the IRS in the *Cumulative Bulletin,* a bound publication by the U.S. Government Printing Office. The following is an example of a revenue ruling citation: Rev. Rul. 82-204, 1982-2 C.B. 192. This citation refers to the 204th ruling issued by the IRS in 1982, which appears on page 192 in Volume 2 of the *Cumulative Bulletin* for the year 1982. The citation of a revenue procedure is similar to a ruling except that the words Rev. Proc. are used to designate the type of document (e.g., Rev. Proc. 77-28, 1977-2 C.B. 537 refers to the 28th revenue procedure issued by the IRS in 1977, which appears on page 537 in Volume 2 of the *Cumulative Bulletin* for the year 1977).

Judicial Interpretations of the Law

In many instances the tax law is uncertain regarding its application to a particular taxpayer's situation. So-called grey areas emerge, and this uncertainty needs to be resolved by administrative settlement procedures with the IRS or by the courts. A taxpayer may appeal a proposed deficiency assessment by entering into negotiations with the Appeals Office of the IRS. The Appeals Office is authorized to settle so-called grey areas through negotiation and compromise based on the "hazards of litigation" (i.e., the probability of winning or losing the issue in court). If a taxpayer is unable to administratively resolve a difference with the IRS, the dispute may be litigated in the courts. The role of the courts is to interpret the tax law.

Court decisions serve as the weight of authority for taxpayers who are deciding whether to pursue a particular course of action. The process of conducting tax research for a client usually involves an investigation and analysis of prior court cases involving similar facts and issues.

Judicial Doctrines. The courts have developed judicial doctrines that are applied to the tax law. Judicial doctrines generally evolve from Supreme Court cases and are not formally incorporated into the Internal Revenue Code. Certain precedent-setting cases have led to changes in the Code, however.

Judicial doctrines are extremely important because their concepts are used by the courts, Congress, and the Treasury Department in drafting new laws and regulations. Some examples of judicial doctrines include the following:

- *Substance over form.* Courts weigh more heavily the economic substance of a transaction than its legal form (i.e., a loan from a father to his son may be treated

Typical Misconception

It is easy to think that a large percentage of taxpayers having disputes with the IRS take their cases to Court. In fact, due to the cost of hiring an attorney and the time involved, most taxpayers resolve their disputes administratively with the IRS.

as a gift, even if the transfer is evidenced by a written promise to pay [a legal note], if no bona fide debtor-creditor relationship exists).

- *Tax benefit rule.* The recovery of an amount (e.g., insurance proceeds) in a subsequent year that produced a tax benefit (e.g., a loss deduction) in a prior year is taxable to the recipient.

- *Constructive receipt.* A taxpayer who uses the cash method of accounting cannot turn his back on the receipt of income if the funds are unequivocally made available in the earlier year (e.g., an employee cannot avoid being taxed upon a year-end bonus during the current year by not collecting his bonus check from the employer until the following year).

Federal Court System for Tax Cases. The judicial system applicable to federal tax law cases is depicted in Figure 1-2.

TRIAL COURT PROCEDURES. A dispute is initially considered by a trial court (i.e., the Tax Court, a district court, or the U.S. Court of Federal Claims). If the Tax Court is selected, a taxpayer may have the case decided under the *small cases procedure* if the amount in question for a particular year is $10,000 or less.[24] If the taxpayer decides to select a federal district court or the U.S. Court of Federal Claims, it is necessary to pay the tax deficiency immediately and then sue for a refund. However, if the Tax Court is selected, the payment of the deficiency plus interest is deferred until the litigation is completed. Other factors may also dictate the choice of an appropriate tax forum for litigating a tax dispute. For example, the Tax Court may have decided favorably on a similar issue in a prior case and may be more likely to decide favorably relative to the taxpayer's situation.

Example 1-17 ■   Angela is audited by the IRS and receives a tax deficiency assessment of $20,000 based upon several disputed items. Angela is unable to compromise or settle the case in an administrative appeal with the Appellate Division of the IRS. Tax research conducted by Angela's accountant indicates that there is a high probability of winning the case in the Tax Court because the Tax Court has held for another taxpayer in a prior case involving similar facts and issues. Angela has cash-flow problems and does not want to pay the deficiency assessment prior to the litigation, which could extend over a period of more than a year. Angela probably should take the case to the Tax Court rather than pay the deficiency and file a refund suit in a federal district court or the U.S. Court of Federal Claims.   ■

If the taxpayer loses in the Tax Court, he must pay the deficiency plus any interest and penalties. A taxpayer who thinks that a jury trial would be especially favorable should litigate in a federal district court, the only place where a jury trial regarding matters of fact (but not law) is possible.

TAX COURT POLICIES AND PROCEDURES. Regardless of the taxpayer's state of residence, all Tax Court cases end up in the same court. There are 19 Tax Court judges, including one chief judge. The President, with the consent of the Senate, appoints the judges for 15 years and may reappoint them for an additional term. The judges periodically travel to various major cities to hear cases. At present, the Tax Court hears cases in approximately 100 cities. In most instances only one judge hears a particular case.

The Tax Court issues both regular and memorandum (memo) decisions. The chief judge decides whether each opinion is to be published as a memo or a regular decision. Generally, the first time the Tax Court decides a particular legal issue its decision

---

[24] Sec. 7463(a). The $10,000 limitation on the amount in dispute includes penalties but excludes interest.

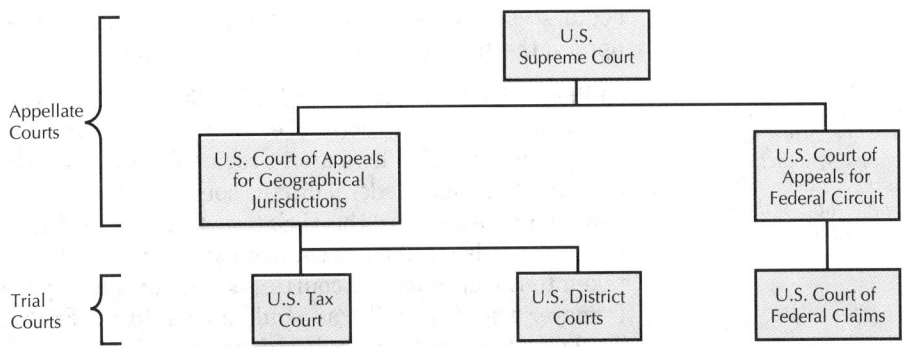

FIGURE 1-2 Federal Court System.

appears as a **regular decision. Memorandum decisions** usually deal with some factual variation on a matter for which the interpretation of the law was decided in an earlier case. Regular and memo decisions have the same precedential value.

At times the chief judge determines that a particular decision deals with a very important matter that the entire Tax Court should have a chance to consider. In such a situation the words "reviewed by the court" will appear at the end of the majority decision. If there are any concurring or dissenting opinions, they will appear after the opinion of the majority.

Other language sometimes appearing at the end of a Tax Court decision is "Entered under Rule 155." These words signify that the court has reached a decision concerning the appropriate tax treatment of an issue but it has left the computation of the exact amount of the deficiency to the two litigating parties.

Additional Comment

On average, opinions in small tax cases that are tried are filed within five months, compared to 14 months in other Tax Court cases.

SMALL CASE PROCEDURES. The Tax Court has a special policy concerning small tax cases. Taxpayers have the option of having their cases heard under the **small case procedures** if the amount of taxes and penalties in question for a particular year does not exceed $10,000. Such procedures are less formal than the regular Tax Court procedures, and taxpayers may appear without an attorney.[25] The cases are heard by special commissioners instead of by one of the 19 Tax Court judges. A disadvantage of the small case procedure for the losing party is that the decision cannot be appealed. The opinions for the small tax cases are not published and have no precedential value.

ACQUIESCENCE POLICY. Years ago the IRS adopted the policy of announcing whether it agreed or disagreed with some regular Tax Court cases decided in favor of the taxpayer. This policy is known as its **acquiescence policy.** If the IRS wants to announce that it agrees with a Tax Court decision, it acquiesces to the decision. If it wishes to go on record as disagreeing with a case, it issues a nonacquiescence to such case. The IRS does not, however, make a formal statement, an acquiescence or nonacquiescence, to every regular decision decided in favor of a taxpayer.

The IRS's decision to acquiesce or nonacquiesce has important implications for taxpayers. For example, suppose the IRS has nonacquiesced to a particular decision and another taxpayer in similar circumstances files a return that adopts the Tax Court's position. If the taxpayer's return is audited and the examining agent discovers that the taxpayer's return was prepared on the basis of the Tax Court's holding rather than the nonacquiescence statement, the agent must argue that the taxpayer owes more tax. Because an acquiescence or nonacquiescence statement is binding on the agent, about the only way the taxpayer can prevail is by litigation. If the IRS

---

[25] A taxpayer may represent himself in regular Tax Court proceedings also, even though he is not an attorney.

acquiesces to a decision, however, the implication is that the IRS will no longer oppose the taxpayer's position on this issue.

APPEALS COURT PROCEDURES. Either the taxpayer or the IRS may appeal a decision from the trial court (i.e., Tax Court, a federal district court, or the U.S. Court of Federal Claims). There are 11 regional courts of appeals, the circuit for the District of Columbia, and a federal circuit court of appeal. The federal circuit court of appeal hears all appeals from the U.S. Court of Federal Claims regardless of the taxpayer's place of residence. An appeal from the Tax Court or a federal district court must be taken to the appropriate court of appeal in the taxpayer's area of jurisdiction (e.g., a taxpayer who lives in Texas would appeal to the Fifth Circuit Court of Appeals). See Table 1-4 for jurisdictional locations. A trial court must abide by the precedents set by the court of appeals of the same jurisdiction. However, one court of appeals is not required to follow the decisions of another court of appeals. This frequently results in a conflict in the circuit courts in cases involving similar issues.

Additional Comment
The major function of the appellate courts is to determine whether a wrong decision has been reached by misapplication of the law to the facts of the case.

Example 1-18 ■ Arnie, who lives in Texas, loses his case in a federal district court and is considering whether to appeal to the Fifth Circuit Court of Appeals. The Fifth Circuit has not ruled on the issue, but the Seventh Circuit has ruled favorably for another taxpayer on the disputed issue. Arnie may have lost his case, in part, in the federal district court because the Seventh Circuit is not in the same jurisdiction as the district court and, therefore, the district court is not required to follow the finding of the Seventh Circuit. The Fifth Circuit is also not required to follow the decision of the Seventh Circuit. Even so, Arnie may decide to appeal the case to the Fifth Circuit because of the favorable existing weight of authority. ■

TABLE 1-4 *Jurisdiction of U.S. Circuit Court of Appeals*

First	Second	Third	Fourth
Maine	Connecticut	Delaware	Maryland
Massachusetts	New York	New Jersey	North Carolina
New Hampshire	Vermont	Pennsylvania	South Carolina
Rhode Island		Virgin Islands	Virginia
Puerto Rico			West Virginia

Fifth	Sixth	Seventh	Eighth
Louisiana	Kentucky	Illinois	Arkansas
Mississippi	Michigan	Indiana	Iowa
Texas	Ohio	Wisconsin	Minnesota
	Tennessee		Missouri
			Nebraska
			North Dakota
			South Dakota

Ninth	Tenth	Eleventh	District of Columbia Circuit
Alaska	Colorado	Alabama	District of Columbia
Arizona	Kansas	Florida	
California	New Mexico	Georgia	
Hawaii	Oklahoma		
Idaho	Utah		
Montana	Wyoming		
Nevada			
Oregon			
Washington			
Guam			
Northern Mariana Islands			

Example 1-19 ∎

Key Point
Both the Tax Court and the U.S. Court of Federal Claims are national courts, which means that they have nationwide jurisdiction. Each U.S. district court has limited geographical jurisdiction extending only to cases arising in a particular state or portion of the state.

Jose lives in Virginia and sues in the Tax Court. Virginia is in the jurisdiction of the Fourth Circuit Court of Appeals, which has already decided an issue involving similar facts and legal issues as are involved in the taxpayer's suit. The Tax Court must follow the precedent of the Fourth Circuit Court of Appeals and decide for the taxpayer even if it feels that the decision of the Fourth Circuit is incorrect.[26] ∎

APPEAL TO THE SUPREME COURT. The final appeal is to the U.S. Supreme Court. The Supreme Court will generally agree to hear a tax case (i.e., grant a **writ of certiorari**) only if there is a conflict in the circuit courts involving the same issue. Only a small number of tax cases are decided by the Supreme Court. A finding of the Supreme Court, however, has the force and effect of law and must be followed by the IRS, taxpayers, and the courts.

Citations of Judicial Interpretations

Regular decisions of the Tax Court are published by the U.S. Government Printing Office in a bound volume known as the *Tax Court of the United States Reports.* Soon after a decision is made public, it is also published by Research Institute of America and Commerce Clearing House in their loose-leaf reporters of Tax Court decisions. An official citation to a Tax Court decision is as follows:

J. Simpson Dean, 35 T.C. 1083 (1961).

The information in the citation indicates that this case appears on page 1083 in Volume 35 of the official *Tax Court of the United States Reports* and that the case was decided in 1961.

Tax Court memorandum decisions are not published by the U.S. Government Printing Office. The decisions are available in bound form from Research Institute of America as *RIA T.C. Memorandum Decisions* and from Commerce Clearing House as *CCH Tax Court Memorandum Decisions.* In addition, soon after an opinion is completed, it is published in loose-leaf form by the two publishers. Following are Research Institute of America and Commerce Clearing House citations to a Tax Court memo decision.

Edith G. McKinney, 1981 PH T.C. Memo ¶ 81,181, 41 TCM 1272.

Additional Comment
Most tax practitioners will not acquire the Federal Supplement, Federal Reporter, *or one of the Supreme Court reporters. All of these reporter services include the non-tax cases as well as the tax cases. Most tax professionals are interested only in the tax cases and subscribe to RIA's* American Federal Tax Reports *or to CCH's* U.S. Tax Cases.

McKinney is reproduced in Prentice Hall's (now Research Institute of America's)[27] 1981 *PH T.C. Memorandum Decisions* at paragraph 81,181 and on page 1272 of Volume 41 of Commerce Clearing House's *Tax Court Memorandum Decisions.* The 181 in the Research Institute of America's citation denotes that the case is the Tax Court's 181st memorandum decision of 1981. A more recent citation continues the same basic format to refer to Research Institute of America's (RIA) memorandum decisions.

---

[26] *Jack E. Golsen,* 54 T.C. 742 (1970). Where the facts or legal issues are not substantially the same, the Tax Court is not obligated to follow the *Golsen* rule.

[27] For a number of years the Prentice Hall Information Services Division published its *Federal Taxes 2nd* tax service and a number of related publications such as the *PH T.C. Memorandum Decisions.* Changes in ownership occurred, and in late 1991 Thomson Professional Publishing added the former Prentice Hall tax materials to the product line of its Research Institute of America tax publishing division. Some products like the *PH T.C. Memorandum Decisions* still have the Prentice Hall name on the spine of older editions.

Paul F. Belloff, 1992 RIA T.C. Memo ¶ 92,346, 63 TCM 3150.

Additional Comment

Each state in the United States has at least one district court and the more populous states have more than one district court.

District court decisions are officially reported in the *Federal Supplement* published by West Publishing Company. Some decisions are not officially reported. They are referred to as **unreported decisions.** Decisions by U.S. district courts on the topic of taxation are also published by Research Institute of America and Commerce Clearing House in secondary reporters that include only tax-related cases. The Research Institute of America's reporter is called *American Federal Tax Reports* (AFTR), and the Commerce Clearing House reporter is known as *U.S. Tax Cases* (USTC). Even though a case is not officially reported, it may nevertheless be published in the AFTR and USTC. An example of a citation to a U.S. district court decision is as follows:

Margie J. Thompson v. U.S., 429 F. Supp. 13, 39 AFTR 2d 77-1485, 77-1 USTC ¶ 9343 (D.C. Pa., 1977).

In the example above, the F. Supp. citation is referred to as the **primary cite.** The case appears on page 13 of Volume 429 of the *Federal Supplement.* **Secondary cites** are to Volume 39 of the second series of the AFTR, page 77-1485 (meaning page 1485 in a volume containing 1977 cases), and to Volume 1 of the 1977 USTC at paragraph 9343. The parenthetical information denotes that the case was decided by a district court in Pennsylvania in 1977. Because some judicial decisions have greater values as precedent (i.e., a Supreme Court decision versus a Tax Court decision), it is useful to the reader to know which court decided the case.

U.S. Claims Court decisions were reported officially in the *Claims Court Reporter,* a reporter published by West Publishing Company from 1982 to 1992. An example of a citation for a U.S. Claims Court decision appears below.

Benjamin Raphan v. U.S., 3 Cl. Ct. 457, 52 AFTR 2d 83-5987, 83-2 USTC ¶ 9613 (1983).

The *Raphan* case appears in Volume 3 of the *Claims Court Reporter* at page 457. Secondary cites are to Volume 52 of the second series of the AFTR, page 83-5987, and to Volume 2 of the 1983 USTC at paragraph 9613.

Effective with the 1992 name change, decisions of the U.S. Court of Federal Claims are now reported in the *Federal Claims Reporter.* An example of the citation appears on the next page.

Additional Comment

When a court case is being cited in an article or other publication, the author typically provides the primary cite and the secondary cites because the various readers will have access to different reporter services.

Jeffrey G. Sharp v. U.S., 27 Fed. Cl. 52, 70 AFTR 2d 92-6040, 92-2 USTC ¶ 50,561 (1992).

The *Sharp* case appears in Volume 27 of the *Federal Claims Reporter* at page 52, on page 6040 of the 70th volume of the AFTR, second series, and at paragraph 50,561 of Volume 2 of the 1992 USTC reporter. Note that even though the name of the reporter published by West Publishing Co. has changed, the volume numbers continue as if there had been no name change.

Circuit courts of appeals decisions—regardless of the topic (e.g., civil rights, securities law, taxation, and so on)—are reported officially in the *Federal Reporter, Second Series* (cited as F.2d) published by West Publishing Company. The *Federal Reporter, Second Series* is the primary citation. In addition, tax decisions of the circuit courts appear in the AFTR and the USTC. Below is an example of a citation to a decision by a circuit court.

Horace B. Rickey, Jr. v. U.S., 592 F.2d 1251, 43 AFTR 2d 79-1023, 79-1 USTC ¶ 9323 (5th Cir., 1979).

The *Rickey* case appears on page 1251 of Volume 592 of the *Federal Reporter, Second Series.* It is also reported at Volume 43, of the second series of the AFTR, page 79-1023, and Volume 1, paragraph 9323 of the 1979 USTC. Parenthetical information indicates that the Fifth Circuit decided the case in 1979.

All Supreme Court decisions, regardless of the subject matter, are published in the *United States Supreme Court Reports* (abbreviated U.S.) by the U.S. Government Printing Office, the *Supreme Court Reporter* (abbreviated S.Ct.) by West Publishing Company, and the *United States Reports, Lawyers' Edition* (abbreviated L.Ed.) of Lawyer's Co-Operative Publishing Company. In addition, the AFTR and USTC reporters contain Supreme Court decisions concerned with taxation. An example of a citation to a Supreme Court case appears below.

U.S. v. Maclin P. Davis, 397 U.S. 301, 25 AFTR 2d 70-827, 70-1 USTC ¶ 9289 (USSC, 1970).

According to the primary cite, this case appears at Volume 397, page 301, of the *United States Supreme Court Reports.* It is also reported at Volume 25, page 70-827, of the AFTR, second series, and at Volume 1, paragraph 9289 of the 1970 USTC.

Tax law sources and their weight of authority are summarized in Topic Review 1-3.

Tax Treaties

The United States has reached treaty agreements with numerous foreign countries. These treaties address tax and other matters. As a result, a tax advisor addressing the U.S. tax results of a U.S. corporation's business operations in another country, for example, Sweden, should determine whether there is a treaty between Sweden and the United States, and, if there is, the applicable provisions of the treaty.

Tax Periodicals

Writings of experts in tax periodicals can lend informative assistance in interpreting the tax law. For example, such writings can be especially helpful if they address a recently enacted statutory provision and it is too early for there to be any regulations, cases, or rulings on point.

Tax experts also frequently write articles in which they discuss the judicial authorities—often conflicting ones—with respect to a particular issue. The experts who most frequently write articles concerning technical tax matters are attorneys, accountants, and professors. Some periodicals that are devoted to providing in-depth discussions of tax matters are listed below.

— *The Journal of Taxation*

— *The Tax Adviser*

— *Taxation for Accountants*

— *Taxes—the Tax Magazine*

Key Point

Tax articles can be used to help find answers to tax questions. In such an instance, the statutory, administrative, or judicial authority used in the tax article should be cited as the authority and not the author of the article. The Courts and the IRS will place little, if any, reliance on mere editorial opinion.

TOPIC REVIEW 1-3

Tax Law Sources		
Source	Key Points	Weight of Authority
Internal Revenue Code	Contains provisions governing income, estate and gift, employment, alcohol, tobacco, and excise taxes.	Serves as the highest legislative authority for tax research, planning, and compliance activities.
Treasury Regulations	Represents the Secretary of the Treasury's interpretation of the tax code. Regulations may be initially issued in proposed, temporary, and final form and are interpretative or legislative.	Legislative regulations have a higher degree of authority than interpretative regulations. Proposed regulations do not have authoritative weight.
Administrative Interpretations	The IRS issues Revenue Rulings (letter rulings or published rulings), Revenue Procedures, Information Releases, and Technical Advice Memoranda.	These pronouncements reflect the IRS's interpretation of the law and do not have the same level of scope and authority as Treasury Regulations.
Judicial Doctrines	Judicial doctrines are concepts that have evolved from Supreme Court cases which are used by the courts to decide tax issues. Examples include—substance over form; tax benefit rule; constructive receipt.	Judicial doctrines that evolve from Supreme Court cases have substantial weight of authority because a finding of the Supreme Court has the force and effect of law.
Judicial Interpretations	Tax cases are initially considered by a trial court (i.e., the Tax Court, a Federal district court, or the U.S. Court of Federal Claims). Either the taxpayer or the IRS may appeal to an appeals court. A final appeal is to the U.S. Supreme Court.	A trial court must abide by the precedents set by the court of appeals of the same jurisdiction. An appeals court is not required to follow the decisions of another court of appeals. A Supreme Court decision must be followed by the IRS, taxpayers, and the lower courts.

— *Tax Law Review*

— *The Journal of Corporate Taxation*

— *The Journal of Partnership Taxation*

— *The Journal of Real Estate Taxation*

— *The Review of Taxation of Individuals*

— *Estate Planning*

— *Tax Notes*

The first five journals listed above contain articles dealing with a variety of topical areas. As the names of the next five suggest, these publications deal with specialized areas. All of these publications (other than *Tax Notes* which is published weekly) are monthly or quarterly publications. Daily tax reports, such as the *Daily Tax Reporter* published by the Bureau of National Affairs, are sometimes used by tax professionals where more timely updates on tax matters are needed than can be provided by monthly and quarterly publications.

Published articles and tax services (discussed below) are examples of secondary sources of authority. The Code and administrative and judicial interpretations are primary sources of authority. Your research efforts should always involve citing primary authorities.

ENACTMENT OF A TAX LAW

OBJECTIVE 6
Describe the legislative process for the enactment of the tax law

Under the U.S. Constitution, the House of Representatives is responsible for initiating new tax legislation. However, tax bills may also originate in the Senate as riders to nontax legislative proposals. Often, major tax proposals are initiated by the President and accompanied by a Treasury Department study or proposal, and then introduced into Congress by one or more representatives from the President's political party.

Steps in the Legislative Process

The specific steps in the legislative process are outlined in Table 1-5. These steps typically include

Additional Comment

In 1994 the chairman of the House Ways and Means Committee was Dan Rostenkowski and the chairman of the Senate Finance Committee was Daniel Patrick Moynihan.

- A tax bill is introduced in the House of Representatives and is referred to the House Ways and Means Committee.

- The proposal is considered by the House Ways and Means Committee, and public hearings are held. Testimony may be given by members of professional groups such as the American Institute of CPAs and the American Bar Association and from various special-interest groups.

- The tax bill is voted on by the House Ways and Means Committee and, if approved, is forwarded to the House of Representatives for a vote. Amendments to the bill from individual members of the House of Representatives are generally not allowed.

- If passed by the House, the bill is forwarded to the Senate for consideration by the Senate Finance Committee, and public hearings are held.

- The tax bill that is approved by the Senate Finance Committee may be substantially different from the House of Representatives' version.

Additional Comment

The corridors near Congress's tax-writing rooms are referred to as "Gucci Gulch," so named for the designer clothing worn by many of the lobbyists that congregate there when a tax bill is being considered.

- The Senate Finance Committee reports the Senate bill to the Senate for consideration. The Senate generally permits amendments (e.g., new provisions) to be offered on the Senate floor.

- If approved by the Senate, both the Senate and House bills are sent to a Joint Conference Committee consisting of an equal number of members from the Senate and the House of Representatives.

- The Senate and House bills are reconciled in the Joint Conference Committee. This process of reconciliation generally involves substantial compromise if the provisions of both bills are dissimilar. A final bill is then resubmitted to the House and Senate for approval.

Historical Note

The only practicing CPA ever elected to the U.S. Congress is Joe Dio Guardi. He was elected in 1984 from Winchester County, New York.

- If the Joint Conference Committee bill is approved by the House and Senate, it is sent to the President for approval or veto.

- A presidential veto may be overturned if a two-thirds majority vote is obtained in both the House and Senate.

TABLE 1-5 **Steps in the Legislative Process**

1. Treasury studies prepared on needed tax reform
2. President makes proposals to Congress
3. House Ways and Means Committee prepares House bill
4. Approval of House bill by the House of Representatives
5. Senate Finance Committee prepares Senate bill
6. Approval of Senate bill by the Senate
7. Compromise bill approved by a Joint Conference Committee
8. Approval of Joint Conference Committee bill by both the House and Senate
9. Approval or veto of legislation by the President
10. New tax law and amendments incorporated into the Code

- Committee reports are prepared by the staffs of the House Ways and Means Committee, the Senate Finance Committee, and the Joint Conference Committee as the bill progresses through Congress. These reports are helpful to explain the new law before the Treasury Department drafts regulations on the tax law changes.

ADMINISTRATION OF THE TAX LAW AND TAX PRACTICE ISSUES

Organization of the Internal Revenue Service

OBJECTIVE 7

Describe the administrative procedures under the tax law

Additional Comment

In a recent survey of members of the American Institute of CPAs, it was found that more than half of the 1,036 members who responded had an unfavorable opinion of the IRS, unchanged from a survey of three years ago. However, the accountants gave the IRS good marks for courtesy and a willingness to solve problems.

The **IRS** is the branch of the Treasury Department that is responsible for administering the federal tax law. It is organized on a national, regional, district, and service center basis. The responsibilities and functions of the various administrative branches include the following:

- The Commissioner of Internal Revenue is the chief officer of the IRS. This person is appointed by the President. This individual is supported by the Chief Counsel's office, which is responsible for preparing the government's case for the litigation of tax disputes.

- The National Office includes a deputy commissioner, a series of assistants to the commissioner, a chief inspector, and a chief counsel. A significant responsibility of the National Office is to process ruling requests and to prepare revenue procedures that assist taxpayers with compliance matters.

- Regional commissioners in the seven IRS regions are responsible for the settlement of administrative appeals for disputed tax deficiencies.

- District directors supervise the performance of IRS audits and collection of delinquent taxes.

- Ten service centers perform tax return processing work. They also select tax returns for audit.

Enforcement Procedures

All tax returns are initially checked for mathematical accuracy and items that are clearly erroneous. The Form W-2 amounts (e.g., wages, and so on) and Form 1099

Additional Comment
Individuals may call 800-366-4484 to report misconduct of IRS employees.

information return amounts (e.g., relating to dividend and interest payments, and so on) are checked against the amounts reported on the tax return. If differences are noted, the IRS Center merely sends the taxpayer a bill for the corrected amount of tax and a statement of the differences. In some instances the difference is due to classification error by the IRS, and the additional assessment can be resolved by written correspondence with the IRS. A refund check may be sent to the taxpayer if an overpayment of tax has been made.

Example 1-20 ■

Bart is an author of books and properly reports royalties on Schedule C (Profit or Loss from Business). The IRS computer matching of the Form 1099 information returns from the publishing companies incorrectly assumes that the royalties should be reported on Schedule E (Supplemental Income and Loss). If the IRS sends the taxpayer a statement of the difference and a corrected tax bill, this matter (including the abatement of added tax, interest, and penalties) should be resolved by correspondence with the IRS. ■

Selection of Returns for Audit

The U.S. tax system is based upon self-assessment and voluntary compliance, although a certain amount of enforcement is needed to ensure that taxpayers are in compliance. For example, the IRS conducts a complete (i.e., line-by-line) audit of a small number of taxpayers. The returns used in this audit are selected based on a stratified random sample known as the **Taxpayer Compliance Measurement Program (TCMP)**. This program is intended to test the extent to which taxpayers are in compliance with the law.

Additional Comment
A special task force has recommended that the percentage of returns which are audited be increased to 2.5%. Many individuals feel that the probability of being audited is so low as to be disregarded.

The IRS uses a **Discriminant Function System (DIF)** to select other individual returns for audit. This system is intended to identify tax returns that are most likely to contain errors, which result in the collection of significant amounts of additional tax revenues. In the aggregate, less than 1% of individuals are audited on an annual basis. Some examples of situations where individuals are more likely to be audited include the following:

- Investments and trade, or business expenses that produce significant tax losses
- Itemized deductions in excess of an average amount for the person's income level
- Filing of a refund claim by a taxpayer who has been previously audited, where substantial tax deficiencies have been assessed
- Individuals who are self-employed with substantial business income or income from a profession (e.g., a medical doctor)

Ethical Point
A CPA should not recommend a position to a client that exploits the IRS audit selection process.

Audit Procedures. Audits of most individuals are handled through an **office audit procedure** in an office of the IRS. In most cases, an individual is asked to substantiate a particular deduction, credit, or income item (e.g., charitable contributions that appear to be excessive). The office audit procedure does not involve a complete audit of all items on the return.

Example 1-21 ■

Brad obtains a divorce during the current year and reports a $30,000 deduction for alimony. The IRS may conduct an office audit to ascertain whether the amount is properly deductible as alimony and does not represent a disguised property settlement to Brad's ex-wife. Brad may be asked to submit verification (e.g., a property settlement agreement between the spouses that designates the payments as alimony). ■

A **field audit procedure** is frequently used for corporations and individuals who are engaged in a trade or business. A field audit is generally broader in scope than the office audit (e.g., several items on the tax return may be reviewed). A field audit is generally conducted at the taxpayer's place of business or the office of his tax advisor.

Most large corporations are subject to annual audits. The year under audit may be several years prior to the current year because the corporation will frequently waive the statute of limitations pending the resolution of disputed issues.

Statute of Limitations

Some taxpayers feel a sense of relief after they have received a refund for an overpayment of tax. However, an audit is possible even after a refund has been processed by the IRS.

As a rule of thumb, the IRS will not audit an individual's return after 2 years have passed from the date the return is filed. A statute of limitations prevents the IRS from assessing additional tax after 3 years from the later of the date the tax return is filed or its due date.[28] However, a 6-year statute of limitations applies if the taxpayer omits items of gross income that in total exceed 25% of the gross income reported on the return.[29] The statute of limitations remains open indefinitely if a fraudulent return is filed or if no return is filed.[30]

Betty, a calendar-year taxpayer, is audited by the IRS in February 1994 for the year 1991. During the course of the audit, a deficiency is proposed for 1991 because Betty failed to substantiate certain travel and entertainment expense deductions. During the course of the audit, it is discovered that Betty failed to file a tax return for 1989, and in 1990 an item of gross income amounting to $26,000 was not reported. Gross income reported on the 1990 return was $72,000. Assuming Betty's 1991 return was filed on or prior to its due date, the IRS may assess a deficiency for 1991 because the 3-year statute of limitations will not expire until April 15, 1995. A deficiency may also be assessed for the 1990 return because a 6-year statute of limitations applies since the omission is more than 25% of the gross income reported on the return. A deficiency may also be assessed for 1989 because there is no statute of limitations for fraud.   ■

Interest

Interest accrues on both assessments of additional tax due and on refunds that the taxpayer receives from the government.[31] No interest is paid on a tax refund if the amount is refunded by the IRS within 45 days prescribed for filing the return (e.g., April 15) determined without regard for extensions.[32] If a return is filed

---

[28] Secs. 6501(a) and (b)(1). Similar rules apply to claims for a refund filed by the taxpayer. Section 6511(a) requires that a refund claim must be filed within 3 years from the date the return was filed or within 2 years from the date the tax was paid, whichever is later.

[29] Sec. 6501(e).

[30] Sec. 6501(c).

[31] Sec. 6621(a). The rate is adjusted four times a year by the Treasury Department based upon the current interest rate for short-term federal obligations. The interest rate that individual taxpayers must pay to the IRS on underpayments of tax is the federal short-term rate plus three percentage points. The interest rate that is paid to taxpayers on overpayments of tax is the federal short-term rate plus two percentage points. The penalty assessed may be very small in some instances even though the taxpayer owes a large tax bill for the year because penalties are imposed upon the net tax due.

[32] Sec. 6611(e). This same 45-day rule has been extended to refunds of taxes other than income taxes (i.e., employment, excise, and estate and gift taxes) for returns filed on or after January 1, 1994 and for amended returns, claims for refunds, and IRS initiated adjustments for returns and refund claims filed on or after January 1, 1995.

after the filing date, no interest is allowed if the refund is not made within 45 days from the date the return was filed.

Example 1-23 ■

Beverly, a calendar-year taxpayer, files her 1993 tax return on February 1, 1994, and requests a $500 refund. No interest accrues on the refund amount if the IRS sends the refund check to Beverly within 45 days following the due date (e.g., April 15, 1994).

■

Penalties

Various nondeductible penalties are imposed upon the net tax due for failure to comply, including

- A penalty of 5% per month (or fraction thereof) subject to a maximum of 25% for failure to file a tax return[33]
- A penalty of 0.5% per month (or fraction thereof) up to a maximum of 25% for failure to pay the tax that is due[34]
- A negligence penalty of 20% of the underpayment attributable to negligence or disregard of rules and regulations.[35]
- A 75% penalty for fraud[36]
- A penalty based upon the current interest rate for underpayment of estimated taxes[37]

Administrative Appeal Procedures

If an IRS agent issues a deficiency assessment to the taxpayer, an appeal may be made to the IRS Appeals Division. Some disputes involve a grey area (e.g., a situation where some courts have held for the IRS while other courts have held for the taxpayer on facts that are similar to the disputed issue). In such a case, the taxpayer may be able to negotiate a compromise settlement (e.g., a percentage of the disputed tax amount plus interest and penalties) with the Appeals Division based on the "hazards of litigation" (i.e., the probability of winning or losing the case if it is litigated).

STATEMENTS ON RESPONSIBILITIES IN TAX PRACTICE

OBJECTIVE 8
Recognize the standards to which tax advisors should adhere

The standards set by professional organizations are not legally enforceable, although they have a great deal of moral clout. The most comprehensive guidelines for CPAs in tax practice were set forth by the Tax Division of the American Institute of Certified Public Accountants (AICPA) in their advisory ***Statements on Responsibilities in Tax Practice* (SRTP).**[38] The Tax Division articulated the following objectives for the SRTPs:

---

[33] Sec. 6651(a)(1). The percentages are increased to 15% per month (or fraction thereof) up to a maximum of 75% if the penalty is for fraudulent failure to file under Sec. 6651(f).

[34] Sec. 6651(a)(2). The penalty is increased to 1% per month after the IRS notifies the taxpayer that it will levy upon the taxpayer's assets.

[35] Sec. 6662.

[36] Sec. 6663.

[37] Sec. 6654.

[38] AICPA, *Statements on Responsibilities in Tax Practice, 1991 Revision,* Introduction, ¶ .03.

- To recommend appropriate standards of responsibilities . . . and to promote their uniform application by CPAs

- To encourage the development of increased understanding of the responsibilities of CPAs by the Treasury Department and Internal Revenue Service . . .

- To foster increased public understanding of, compliance with, and confidence in our tax system through awareness of the recommended standards of responsibilities of CPAs . . . [39]

Some of the more important guidelines contained in the SRTP are highlighted below. Statement No. 4 discusses the use of estimates in the following manner:

- A CPA may prepare tax returns involving the use of the taxpayer's estimates if it is impracticable to obtain exact data, and the estimated amounts are reasonable under the facts and circumstances known to the CPA. When the taxpayer's estimates are used, they should be presented in such a manner as to avoid the implication of greater accuracy than exists.

Keep in mind, however, that with respect to certain expenses, no deduction is available unless the taxpayer has the proper documentation.[40] Thus, a CPA cannot use estimates for such amounts.

Statement No. 6 contains guidelines concerning what CPAs should do when they have knowledge of errors made by clients or prior return preparers. The recommendations are as follows:

- The CPA should inform the client promptly upon becoming aware of an error in a previously filed return or upon becoming aware of a client's failure to file a required return. The CPA should recommend the measures to be taken. Such recommendation may be given orally. The CPA is not obligated to inform the Internal Revenue Service, and the CPA may not do so without the client's permission, except where required by law.

In Statement No. 7, the CPA's responsibilities in an administrative proceeding (e.g., an audit) are described.

- When the CPA is representing a client in an administrative proceeding with respect to a return which contains an error of which the CPA is aware, the CPA should inform the client promptly upon becoming aware of the error. The CPA should recommend the measures to be taken. Such recommendation may be given orally. The CPA is neither obligated to inform the Internal Revenue Service nor may the CPA do so without the client's permission, except where required by law.

- The CPA should request the client's agreement to disclose the error to the Internal Revenue Service.

Statement No. 8 makes the following comments about the form—oral or written—of the advice given by CPAs.

- Although oral advice may serve a client's needs appropriately in routine matters or in well-defined areas, written communications are recommended in important, unusual, or complicated transactions.

---

[39] Ibid.
[40] Section 274(d) precludes deductions for certain expenditures (e.g., travel expenses including meals and lodging) unless the taxpayer can substantiate them by "adequate records or sufficient" corroborating evidence.

With respect to the procedural aspects of return preparation, Statement No. 3 furnishes the guidance shown below.

- In preparing or signing a return, the CPA may in good faith rely without verification upon information furnished by the client or by third parties. Yet, the CPA should not ignore the implications of information furnished and should make reasonable inquiries if the information furnished appears to be incorrect, incomplete, or inconsistent either on its face or on the basis of other facts known to the CPA. In this connection, the CPA should refer to the client's returns for prior years whenever feasible.

- Where the Internal Revenue Code or income tax regulations impose a condition with respect to deductibility or other tax treatment of an item (such as taxpayer maintenance of books and records or substantiating documentation to support the reported deduction or tax treatment), the CPA should make appropriate inquiries to determine to his or her satisfaction whether such condition has been met.

- The individual CPA who is required to sign the return should consider information actually known to that CPA from the tax return of another client when preparing a tax return if the information is relevant to that tax return, its consideration is necessary to properly prepare that tax return, and use of such information does not violate any law or rule relating to confidentiality.

Statement No. 1 provides standards with which a CPA should comply in taking positions on a tax return or in recommending such positions. The following guidance is given.

- A CPA should not recommend to a client that a position be taken with respect to the tax treatment of any item on a return unless the CPA has a good faith belief that the position has a realistic possibility of being sustained administratively or judicially on its merits if challenged.

- A CPA should not prepare or sign a return as an income tax return preparer if the CPA knows that the return takes a position that the CPA could not recommend under the standard expressed [above].

- Notwithstanding [the above], a CPA may recommend a position that the CPA concludes is not frivolous as long as the position is adequately disclosed on the return or claim for refund.

- In recommending certain tax return positions and in signing a return on which a tax return position is taken, a CPA should, where relevant, advise the client as to the potential penalty consequences of the recommended tax return position and the opportunity, if any, to avoid such penalties through disclosure.

Statement No. 1 elaborates on the "good faith" belief requirement as follows:

- The standards suggested herein require that a CPA in good faith believe that the position is warranted in existing law or can be supported by a good faith argument for an extension, modification, or reversal of existing law. For example, the CPA may reach such a conclusion on the basis of well-reasoned articles, treatises, IRS General Counsel Memoranda, a General Explanation of a Revenue Act prepared by the staff of the Joint Committee on Taxation, and Internal Revenue Service written determinations (for example, private letter rulings), whether or not such sources are treated as "authority" under Sec. 6661.

COMPONENTS OF A TAX PRACTICE

OBJECTIVE 9

Describe the components of a tax practice and understand basic tax research procedures and computer applications

Tax practice is a rapidly growing field that provides substantial opportunities for tax specialists in public accounting, law, and industry. The tasks performed by a tax professional may range from the preparation of a simple Form 1040 for an individual to the conduct of tax research and planning for highly complex business situations. Tax practice consists of the following activities:

- Tax compliance and procedure (i.e., tax return preparation and representation of a client in administrative proceedings before the IRS)
- Tax research
- Tax planning

Tax Compliance and Procedure

Typical Misconception

Frequently some individuals have the opinion that a tax practitioner should serve in the capacity of a neutral, unbiased expert. They tend to forget that tax practitioners are being paid to represent their clients' interests. A tax practitioner may sometimes recommend a position that is defensible, but where the weight of authority is on the side of the IRS.

Preparation of tax returns is a significant component of tax practice. Tax practitioners frequently prepare federal, state, and local tax returns for individuals, corporations, estates, trusts, and so on. In larger corporations, the tax return preparation (i.e., compliance) function is usually performed by a company's internal tax department staff. In such a case, a CPA or other tax practitioner may assist the client with the tax research and planning aspects of their tax practice, and may even review their return before it is filed.

Tax procedure consists of assisting the client in negotiations with the IRS. If a client is audited, the practitioner acts as the client's representative in discussions with the IRS agent. If a tax deficiency is assessed, the practitioner assists the client if an administrative appeal is contemplated with the IRS's Appellate Division. In most instances, an attorney is retained if litigation is being considered.

Tax Research

Tax research is the search for the best possible defensibly correct solution to a problem involving either a completed transaction (e.g., a sale of property) or a proposed transaction (e.g., a proposed merger of two corporations). Research involves each of the following steps:

- Determine the facts
- Identify the problem
- Identify and analyze the tax law sources (i.e., code provisions, Treasury Regulations, administrative rulings, and court cases)
- Evaluate nontax (e.g., business) implications
- Problem solving
- Communicate the findings to the client

Tax research may be conducted in connection with tax return preparation, tax planning, or procedural activities. A discussion of how to do tax research is presented in greater depth under the heading "Tax Research Procedures" in this chapter.

Tax Planning

A noted but out-of-print text on tax research and planning has delineated the following tax planning principles:

- Keep sufficient records.
- Forecast the effect of future events.

- Support the plan with a sound business purpose.
- Base the plan on sound legal authorities.
- Do not carry a good plan too far.
- Make the plan flexible.
- Integrate the tax plan with other factors in decision making.
- Conduct research to learn whether a similar plan has previously proved unsuccessful (e.g., a court case involving similar facts may have upheld the IRS's position).
- Consider the "maximum" risk exposure of the client (e.g., if the plan is subsequently challenged by the IRS and the tax treatment is disallowed, what is the economic impact upon the taxpayer?).
- Consider the effect of timing (e.g., whether it is more beneficial to take a deduction in one year versus another).
- Shape the plan to the client's needs and desires.[41]

Because of the importance of planning in tax practice, subsequent chapters in this text include a separate section on tax planning to discuss issues that are related to the topical coverage. These tax planning principles should be kept in mind when attempting to use the tax planning recommendations.

TAX RESEARCH PROCEDURES

Tax research is a process involving several steps: (1) determine the facts, (2) identify the problem, (3) determine the best possible solution, and (4) make recommendations to the client. The process includes data gathering, identifying tax issues, and locating and evaluating tax law sources. Figure 1-3 illustrates the steps in the process. Tax research may also be used in the determination of tax policy. For example, policy-oriented research would determine the extent, if any, to which charitable organizations would be affected if contributions were no longer deductible. This type of tax research is usually conducted by economists to assess the effect of actions by the government. Client-oriented tax research either involves an investigation of a tax problem that is based upon a **closed-fact situation** (i.e., transactions or events that have already occurred) or an **open-fact situation** (i.e., the planning of a future course of action where the facts and events are still controllable). In a closed-fact situation, the research is primarily concerned with applying the law to the facts as they exist to determine how a particular item should be reported on a tax return. Unfortunately, in such situations, the tax consequences can be costly because the facts cannot be restructured to obtain more favorable tax results. In an open-fact situation, the principal focus is upon tax planning, which usually involves a choice of alternative courses of action.

In a closed-fact situation, the facts are often self-evident. However, if one is researching the tax consequences in an open-fact context, a number of the facts have not yet occurred, and the tax advisor's task is to determine which facts are likely to result in a particular tax outcome. This goal is accomplished by reviewing the authorities, especially court cases, and denoting which facts accompanied a favorable

---

[41] Fred W. Norwood, et al., *Federal Taxation: Research, Planning, and Procedures*, 2nd ed. (Englewood Cliffs, NJ: Prentice Hall, 1979), pp. 215-216.

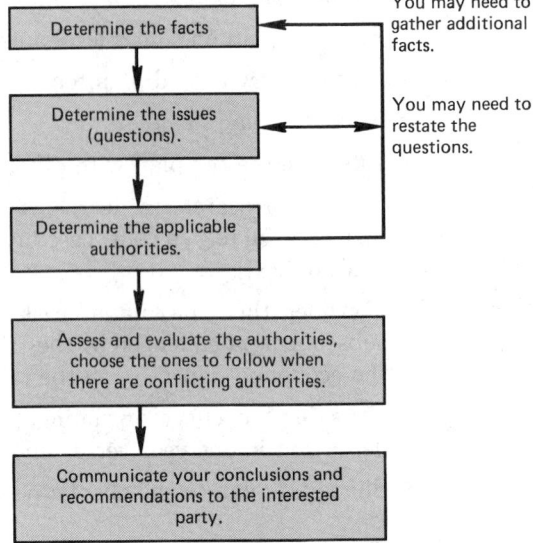

Key Point

The information in Figure 1-3 suggests that the first three steps in the tax research process are somewhat circuitous. In other words, after you have determined the issues or located the applicable authorities, you may realize that you have to go back and collect more facts.

FIGURE 1-3 Steps in the Tax Research Process

outcome and which produced an unfavorable result. For example, if a client hopes to achieve ordinary loss treatment from the anticipated sale of several plots of land in the same year, the advisor might compare and contrast the facts that were present in cases dealing with this type of situation. The advisor should consider cases both won and lost by taxpayers.

Often tax research deals with a grey area; that is, an issue for which no clear-cut, unequivocally correct solution exists. In such a situation, it is best to pursue the issue through a specifically tailored set of detailed questions. For example, in researching whether the taxpayer may deduct a loss as an ordinary loss instead of a capital loss, the tax advisor may need to investigate whether the presence of any investment motive precludes classifying a loss as ordinary.

Example 1-24 ■   Bob advises Bonnie, his tax advisor, that on November 4, 1994, he sold land held as an investment for $500,000 cash. His investment in the land was $50,000. On November 9, 1994, Bob reinvested the sales proceeds in another plot of investment land costing $500,000. This is a closed-fact situation in that Bob merely wants to know what amount of gain (if any) he must recognize.   ■

Example 1-25 ■   Candice seeks advice from Buddy, her tax advisor, about how to minimize her estate taxes. Candice is a widow with three children and five grandchildren and has property valued at $10 million. This is an open-fact situation. Buddy could advise Candice to leave all but a few hundred thousand dollars of her property to a charitable organization so that her estate would owe zero estate taxes. Although this recommendation would minimize Candice's estate taxes, Candice would likely reject it. Candice probably wants her children and grandchildren to receive the majority of her assets. Thus, reducing estate taxes to zero is inconsistent with her other objectives.   ■

Key Point

*Clients should be educated to consult their tax advisor **before** entering into any transaction that may have important tax consequences. After the transaction is completed, it is no longer possible to structure the facts to obtain the most favorable tax consequences.*

Gathering the Facts

Before an attempt is made to identify tax issues to be resolved, it is necessary to gather all pertinent facts and eliminate any extraneous information. In most situations, a client suggests a proposed course of action or asks a question concerning tax consequences arising from an already completed transaction without supplying a complete set of facts.

Example 1-26 ■   Ajax Corporation presents these facts: (1) its principal manufacturing facility was totally destroyed by fire a few days ago; and (2) the company has insurance on the building and its contents and carries business interruption insurance to cover any profits lost due to the plant shutdown during the replacement period. Ajax Corporation is concerned with (1) the tax consequences of both the fire and the replacement of the building and (2) the fire's impact upon the company's future course of action. These initial facts do not give the tax practitioner enough information to formulate a viable research plan.

    Additional questions or issues need to be raised at this point. Will the insurance proceeds be used to reinvest in a new building? What gain or loss is realized upon the destruction and reinvestment of the insurance proceeds in the plant? How much of this realized gain or loss must be recognized for tax purposes? Are the business interruption insurance benefits taxable? Will the fire have an impact upon the company's future business plans and activities? ■

Importance of the Facts to the Tax Results

At times, the statute is difficult to interpret, and a dilemma arises concerning the tax results. For example, one of the requirements a taxpayer must meet to claim a personal exemption for another person is to provide more than half of such person's support.[42] Neither the Code nor the Regulations define support. Consequently, if a taxpayer purchased a used automobile costing $5,000 for an elderly parent whose only source of income was $4,800 of social security, a question would arise with respect to whether the expenditure for the car constitutes support. The tax advisor would need to consult court cases and revenue rulings in order to find an interpretation of the word "support."

    In other situations, the statutory language may be quite clear, but there might be a question as to whether the taxpayer's transaction falls within the realm of the facts necessary to obtain the favorable tax consequences. The following discussion of two actual cases focuses on the importance of facts in determining the tax results. In each case the taxpayer was arguing about the proper amount of the deductible salary expense for payments made to the shareholder's spouse.

Facts of Case Where Taxpayer Won. Excerpts of the *Summit Publishing Company, Inc.* case appear below.[43] The Tax Court concluded that the corporation was entitled to a deduction for a portion of the purported salary payments to the shareholder's spouse. In the case, the taxpayer is referred to as the "petitioner" and the government as the "respondent."

FINDINGS OF FACT

At all times pertinent to this case, petitioner, Summit Publishing Company, Inc. (Summit) was a Texas corporation with its primary place of business in San Antonio, Texas. During the taxable years ended October 31, 1982, and October 31, 1983, Summit paid corporate officer and employee Marcia J. Mogavero (Mrs. Mogavero) compensation in the amounts of $72,780 and $183,910, respectively. These amounts were deducted in

Additional Comment

The Summit Publishing Company and the J.B.S. Enterprises, Inc. cases are used to illustrate how slightly different facts can result in very different tax consequences. The two cases must be carefully read to identify the subtle differences.

---

[42] Sec. 152(a).

[43] 1990 PH T.C. Memo ¶ 90,288, 59 TCM 833. In this and all other Tax Court cases, the *petitioner* is the person who originates the case—the taxpayer—and the government is the *respondent*. For an excellent discussion of how critical facts are for the outcome, see Ray M. Sommerfeld, et al., *Tax Research Techniques,* 4th. Ed., Rev. (New York: AICPA, 1990).

arriving at Summit's taxable income for the years in issue. Respondent determined that reasonable compensation for Mrs. Mogavero for the taxable years ended October 31, 1982 and 1983, was $41,050 and $50,083, respectively, and disallowed the difference between the amount claimed and determined.

Summit was incorporated during 1977 by Alfred G. Mogavero, Sr. (Mr. Mogavero) who, at all pertinent times, was Summit's sole shareholder and president. Mr. and Mrs. Mogavero were married around the time of petitioner's incorporation and continued to be married throughout the end of the taxable years in issue.

Summit's business activity involved the publishing of an in-flight magazine for Southwest Airlines (Southwest). Summit also did a limited amount of typesetting, production, layout, and art work for other companies. . . . Kenneth E. Lively (Lively) worked for Mr. Mogavero nearly from the beginning and his expertise related to the editing-publishing or creative side of the business activity. Mr. Mogavero's expertise related to sales and management.

During 1977, . . . Mrs. Mogavero began to work at Summit. Prior to that time she had no job experience, no formal education beyond high school, or any special skills, other than typing. Initially, Mrs. Mogavero performed routine clerical tasks. In time, and during the years in issue, she performed in the role of an office manager. Lively and Mr. Mogavero were principally responsible for publishing and sales . . .

Mrs. Mogavero supervised the clerical and support personnel, oversaw accounts receivable and payable, and reviewed the credit worthiness of advertisers. Although Summit had an accountant, Mrs. Mogavero did some of the bookkeeping and assisted in the compilation of certain of the financial information necessary for top management. She also assisted in the approval and location or layout of advertisements . . .

During the years in issue, Summit generally employed between 16 and 25 employees. . . .

Mr. Mogavero, as owner-operator of Summit, decided to increase Mrs. Mogavero's salary because the business was doing well . . . [Between the taxable years ended October 31, 1978 through October 31, 1983 the firm's gross profit rose from $484,680 to $3,409,438. Mr. Mogavero's compensation was $52,900 and $927,530 for the taxable years ended October 31, 1978 and October 31, 1983, respectively. Mrs. Mogavero's compensation increased from $16,715 for the fiscal year ended October 31, 1978 to $183,910 for the fiscal year ended October 31, 1983.]

During the taxable years ended October 31, 1982 and 1983, Summit paid cash dividends to its sole shareholder in the amounts of $232,690 and $382,359, respectively.

OPINION

. . . Many factors are relevant in determining whether compensation is reasonable, and no single factor is decisive; the totality of the facts and circumstances must be weighed. . . .The parties in this case have focused on about six of the factors enumerated in Foos v. Commissioner, TC Memo 1981-61 [Para. 81,061 PH Memo TC]. In Foos v. Commissioner, supra, the following factors were referenced:

1. Employee's qualifications and training.
2. Nature, extent, and scope of his duties.
3. Responsibilities and hours involved.
4. Size and complexity of business.
5. Results of the employee's efforts.
6. Prevailing rates for comparable employees in comparable business.
7. Scarcity of other qualified employees.
8. Ratio of compensation to gross and net income (before salaries and Federal income tax) of the business.
9. Salary policy of the employer to its other employees.
10. Amount of compensation paid to the employee in prior years.
11. Employee's responsibility for employer's inception and/or success. . . .
14. Correlation between the stockholder-employees' compensation and his stockholdings.
15. Corporate dividend history. . . .

Employee's Qualifications and Training

Respondent argues that Mrs. Mogavero's educational background and training were insufficient to justify the level of compensation claimed by Summit. Petitioner agrees that Mrs. Mogavero "had limited qualifications" when she began working for Summit in 1977, but that she acquired "extensive on-the-job training" qualifying her for the position held.

We agree with petitioner's analysis on this point. . . . [I]t is likely that actual experience is more significant than academic achievement in the operation and success of a particular business, especially one which is relatively small and unique requiring the personal service of the particular employee. Moreover, when measuring the value of education as opposed to actual experience, greater weight should usually be afforded to actual and successful experience in a particular position or discipline.

Nature, Extent, and Scope of Employee's Work

Petitioner contends that Mrs. Mogavero should be characterized as second-in-command of Summit. Respondent counters that Mrs. Mogavero was relegated to the more menial tasks and the major contributions that resulted in Summit's success were made by Mr. Mogavero and Lively. Respondent also argues that Mrs. Mogavero's position (second-in-command) with Summit is "primarily a function of her marriage to [Mr. Mogavero]."

To the extent that the subject employee has an ownership interest or is related to the owner, we should carefully scrutinize the question of the reasonableness of compensation. . . . In so doing we find that Mrs. Mogavero did not receive, relative to her experience, a large beginning salary when she began working at Summit at a time when all agree that her experience and skill levels were not great. . . .

Mrs. Mogavero was responsible for the day to day administrative and financial operations of Summit. In addition to playing a significant role in the business relationship with Southwest, she was also primarily responsible for matters which had a direct effect on Summit's success. . . .

Most importantly, Mrs. Mogavero acted on Mr. Mogavero's behalf while he was away on the business of Summit. . . .

In summary, we have found that Mrs. Mogavero's importance and contribution to the success and operation of Summit is somewhere between Lively's and Mr. Mogavero's.

Summit's Salary Scale and Policy

Here, respondent points to the wide disparity between owner, family members and other nonowner, nonfamily employees. . . .

During the 2 years in issue, total officers' compensation increased 15 and 74 percent and total employees' compensation increased 41 and 28 percent. . . . [W]e find that petitioner appears to have had a relatively generous policy regarding the increases of officer and employee compensation. We also note that, in a relative sense, it may be appropriate to give larger raises to the officers, as opposed to other employees, if the officers' efforts were more instrumental to the success of the business. . . .

Compensation in Prior Years
Size and Complexity of the Business

Regarding this aspect, respondent argues that Mrs. Mogavero's "salary increased from $16,715.53 per year to $183,910.00 per year over a period of only five years." Respondent cites several cases for the proposition that increases in salary should be a result of increases in responsibility. . . . Petitioner agrees that Mrs. Mogavero's salary was low and her experience was limited when she started with petitioner. Petitioner, however, argues that Mrs. Mogavero's salary increased in accord with their increased responsibilities in subsequent years.

. . . Considering that Summit's business was so successful, the number of employees supervised increased, inflationary indexing may have played a role, and Mrs. Mogavero played a significant role in some areas of the business which helped that business success, we believe that respondent has not determined sufficient compensation to Mrs. Mogavero for the years before the Court.

Prevailing Rates of Compensation in the Industry

. . . Accordingly, neither petitioner nor respondent has established, by expert testimony, or otherwise, the prevailing rates of compensation in this industry. We are herein limited to considering whether Mrs. Mogavero's salary is reasonable based upon the facts in the record.

Comparison of Salaries Paid with Summit's Gross and Net Income

. . . Petitioner argues that Mrs. Mogavero's salary was 2.71 and 15.34 percent of gross income and 7.55 and 13.42 percent of net income for the taxable years in issue. For the same 2 years Summit paid dividends to Mr. Mogavero (its sole shareholder) in the amounts of $232,690 and $382,359, which represented 24.14 and 27.89 percent of net income in those same 2 taxable years.

The relatively sizable dividends paid by petitioner (in addition to a relatively large salary to its president and sole shareholder) substantially diminish respondent's argument that there was a motive of tax avoidance in this case.

Summary

Our view of the record in this case results in our conclusion that Mrs. Mogavero's responsibilities and contribution to the success of Summit fell somewhere between those of Lively and Mr. Mogavero. . . . Additionally, Mrs. Mogavero did have certain responsibilities that directly contributed to the success of the business. . . .

[The court decided that a reasonable salary for Mrs. Mogavero for the taxable years ended October 31, 1982 and October 31, 1983 was $70,000 and $85,000, respectively (compared with $72,780 and $183,910 deducted on Summit's tax return).]

Facts of Case Where Taxpayer Lost. *J.B.S. Enterprises, Inc.* lost its case dealing with payments made to the sole shareholder's former wife.[44] The Tax Court held that the payments could not be characterized as salary.

FINDINGS OF FACT

Petitioner was a Texas corporation with its principal place of business in Fort Worth, Texas. . . . Petitioner owned three bars and restaurants in Fort Worth during the years at issue. Among the three bars was the Blues Bar, which opened for business during 1982. James B. Schusler, Mary Schusler's ex-husband, is petitioner's president and sole stockholder. James . . . and Mary . . . were separated during the years at issue. During this period Mary had only two sources of income, part-time secretarial work . . . and payments from petitioner. She had two minor children to support, as well as a child in college and a grown child. . . . Mary received the payments [in question] from petitioner, at James' direction. . . .

Schedule E (Compensation of Officers) of petitioner's Federal income tax returns (Form 1120) for the years at issue reported that Mary devoted "0%" of her time to business. Nevertheless, the return for the fiscal year ending April 30, 1986, reported that petitioner paid Mary compensation of $26,600 during the year, and claimed a business expense deduction for that amount. . . .

On its Federal income tax return for the year ending April 30, 1987, petitioner stated that it paid Mary a salary of $35,910 and claimed a business expense deduction in that amount. . . .

[The IRS agent disallowed the deduction for the payments to Mary. In its initial petition to the Tax Court the petitioner stated that an error was made in showing that the payments were made to Mary and that such payments should have been shown as made to James. Several months later, however, the petitioner amended its petition to the court and stated that Mary was Vice President and did in fact perform valuable services for the Corporation. It stated, further, that the amounts Mary received were reasonable in light of the services Mary performed and her experience and expertise.]

---

[44] 1991 T.C. Memo ¶ 91,254, 61 TCM 2829.

OPINION

. . . As a preliminary matter, we note that we attach little weight to the testimony of James, Mary, and Sue Ratcliff [the tax advisor]. The testimony, and documents which they signed under oath are replete with inconsistencies.

. . . The statements made to Gerald Yentes [the IRS agent] and the [first] protest letter . . . indicate that Mary performed no services for petitioner. The only explanation petitioner offered for the inconsistency in its current position is Sue Ratcliff's testimony that she thought it would be advantageous, with respect to taxes, to initially declare that Mary performed no services. It is clear to us that petitioner's position in the instant case has been motivated throughout by tax considerations. Because of inconsistencies in testimony and sworn documents, we do not accept petitioner's recantation of its original position. . . .

While petitioner did introduce documents showing that Mary reviewed petitioner's monthly profit and loss statement, given her marital status, her dependence on petitioner for support, and comments made to Revenue Agent Gerald Yentes, we conclude her review of the statements was for her own benefit, rather than for petitioner's. Petitioner introduced no other relevant documentary evidence. We find that petitioner has failed to carry its burden of proof, and that respondent has established that the payments at issue were a personal expense intended to provide support for Mary and her children.

Comparison of the Facts of the Two Cases. Table 1-6 provides a summary comparison of the two cases.

Both taxpayers were corporations that claimed a salary deduction for payments they made to the spouse or former spouse of the sole shareholder. In *Summit* the IRS contended that only a portion of the amount claimed as a salary expense was nondeductible whereas in the *JBS* case the IRS argued that none of the purported salary payments should be deductible. In *Summit* the spouse performed extensive, valuable services for the firm. In *JBS,* however, the former spouse appears to have performed no services for the corporation. In *Summit* the corporation's gross profit and net income increased substantially between the date the firm was founded and the years for which the salary deduction was in question. The court record for *JBS* does not discuss the firm's profitability. In *Summit* because rather large dividends were paid to the sole shareholder, it did not appear that the strategy for the payments to the shareholder's spouse was to have dividends masquerade as salary. In *JBS* the taxpayer did not present any documentation to prove that the ex-wife of the sole shareholder actually performed services for JBS. Moreover, some of the testimony presented indicated that positions were being taken on the tax return to achieve that lowest tax liability for the corporation.

The court allowed expense deductions in *Summit* for a portion of the payments that the IRS argued constituted unreasonable compensation. The court was im-

TABLE 1-6   *Summary Comparison of Facts in Summit and JBS*

Situation	Decision	
	Summit	JBS
Type of taxpayer	Corporation	Corporation
Person to whom "salary" was paid	Spouse of sole shareholder	Former spouse of sole shareholder
Dividend history of corporation	Substantial dividends had been paid	Not disclosed
Profit history of corporation	Substantial increase over the years	Not disclosed
Services performed by recipient of salary	Extensive, valuable services	None

pressed with how valuable the shareholder's spouse's services were to the firm; it also noted that dividends had been paid to the shareholder. The *JBS* case is a primer in how not to structure a transaction. The sole shareholder seemed to be attempting to disguise support payments made to his former wife as salary expense. The recipient, however, performed no services for which she should receive compensation.

Statement of Tax Issues

Deciding upon the particular issues that need to be researched is one of the most challenging aspects of the research process. At times, the client may raise an explicit question, such as "May I deduct the costs of a winter trip to Florida recommended by my physician?" Often, however, the tax advisor must read the pertinent documents and other papers submitted by the taxpayer to formulate the issues for which an investigation is appropriate. Thus, the tax advisor must have a fairly extensive knowledge of tax law in order to be able to determine which issues need to be researched. The following example assumes that all of the tax authorities are in agreement.

Key Point

Many tax practioners consider the statement of the tax issues step to be the most creative step in the tax research process. Sometimes younger tax practioners do an excellent job on this step since they are not preconditioned to consider only the normal alternatives.

Example 1-27 ■

Bryce calls tax advisor Carol and states that (1) he incurred a loss on renting his beach cottage in the current year and (2) he wonders if he may deduct the loss. He also states that he, his wife, and their minor child occupied the cottage only 8 days in the current year.

Assume that this is the first time that Carol has worked with the Sec. 280A vacation home rules. Upon reading Sec. 280A, Carol learns that a loss is *not* deductible if Bryce uses the cottage as a residence for personal purposes for longer than the greater of (1) 14 days or (2) 10% of the number of days the unit is rented at a fair rental value. She also learns that the property is *deemed* to be used by the taxpayer for personal purposes on any days on which it is used by any member of the family (as defined in Sec. 267(c)(4)). The Sec. 267(c)(4) definition of family members includes brothers, sisters, spouse, ancestors, or lineal descendants (i.e., children and grandchildren).

Bryce's 8-day use is not enough days to make the rental property loss nondeductible. However, Carol must inquire about the number of days, if any, Bryce's brothers, sisters, or parents used the property. (She already has information about use by Bryce, his spouse, and his lineal descendants.) In addition, Carol must find out how many days the cottage was rented to other persons at a fair rental value. Upon obtaining these additional facts, Carol can proceed to determine how to calculate deductible expenses. Carol then reaches her conclusion concerning the deductible loss, if any, and communicates it to Bryce. Assume that other rules contained in the Internal Revenue Code restricting a taxpayer's ability to deduct losses from real estate activities will not pose a problem for Bryce. (See Chapter 8 for a discussion of the passive loss rules.) ■

A tax problem frequently involves the interplay of several tax issues that need to be resolved before a solution is found to the problem. In addition, a business problem usually has tax and nontax implications (e.g., the tax consequences may be only one of many factors underlying a business decision). Tax issues should be viewed as highly tentative, because new issues may be identified during the conduct of the research that may alter the nature of the tax research process or the tax research conclusion.

Example 1-28 ■

The following tentative list of issues was drawn from discussions with the chief financial officer of Ajax Corporation regarding the involuntary conversion of the building that occurred in Example 1-26:

- Does the fire constitute an involuntary conversion where the taxpayer may elect to postpone the recognition of gain under Sec. 1033?

- If a gain or loss is realized, how should it be computed?

- What is the amount of recognized gain or loss?

- What is the character (e.g., capital or ordinary) of the gain or loss?

- What is the effect of the depreciation recapture rules under Secs. 291, 1245, and 1250? For example, since the building was subject to depreciation, a portion of the gain may be recharacterized as ordinary income based upon the amount of depreciation taken in prior years.

- If a gain is realized, can it be deferred under Sec. 1033 by reinvesting the insurance proceeds in acquiring replacement property?

- What type of replacement property can be acquired to permit the gain to be deferred?

- What is the basis of the replacement property if the deferral of gain is elected under Sec. 1033? ∎

Locating and Evaluating Tax Law Sources: Using Tax Reporter Services

Additional Comment

Tax reporter services are an indispensable aid in carrying on a tax practice. The annual subscription cost for the United States Tax Reporter *or the* Standard Federal Tax Reporter *is approximately $1,700.*

The most important tax law source is the Internal Revenue Code. A review of the appropriate Code sections should be conducted during the initial research phase. Other tax law sources include Treasury Regulations, IRS revenue rulings, court cases, and so on. The topical (or subject) index of a tax reporter service is the most convenient way to locate these specific tax law source materials. The most widely used tax services are the *United States Tax Reporter*, the tax service published by Research Institute of America (RIA), and Commerce Clearing House's (CCH) *Standard Federal Tax Reporter*. The subject index refers the reader to paragraph references in one or more of the tax volumes of the service. Both RIA and CCH have a separate index volume. If the relevant Code sections are known, the researcher can bypass the index volume and refer directly to the compilation materials, because both RIA and CCH organize the materials by Code section number.

Example 1-29 ∎ To locate tax law sources for the Ajax Corporation tax problem discussed in Examples 1-26 and 1-28, an initial reference to the Index (Volume) of CCH's *Standard Federal Tax Reporter* for the topic *Involuntary Conversions* refers the reader to paragraph 31,540. Paragraph 31,540 is the initial entry into the CCH tax service for material relating to Code Sec. 1033, Involuntary Conversions. This section is located in Volume 10, which includes paragraph references from 28,621 to 32,145. The tax services contain the following source materials:

- The relevant section in the Internal Revenue Code and related proposed, temporary, and final Treasury Regulations.

- Partial reprints of Congressional committee reports.

- Digests of court cases, rulings, and so on.

- Publishers' editorial comments that help to explain the law and its application.

- A citator, which informs the researcher of the location of a judicial decision, whether a case has been reversed on appeal to another court, and whether the IRS has acquiesced to a favorable Tax Court decision for the taxpayer. For example, the IRS may lose a case in the Tax Court and subsequently agree (or acquiesce) with the Tax Court and the taxpayer's position on a disputed issue. The citator also lists the names of other cases and IRS promulgations on point.

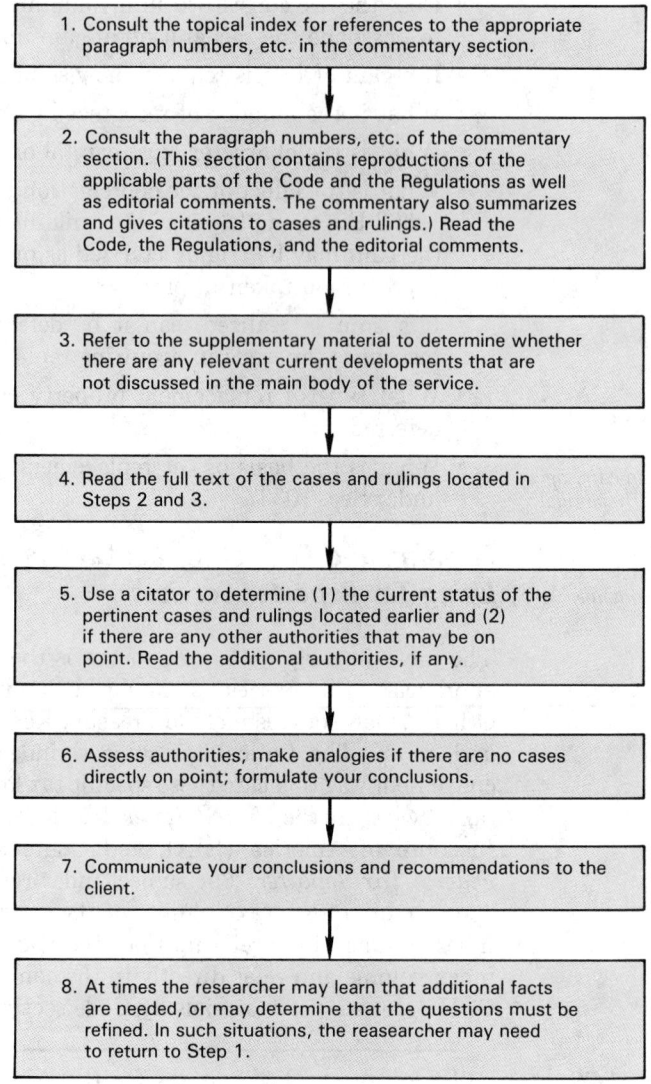

FIGURE 1-4 Use of Tax Services to Research a Tax Question

- A current matters volume that lists any recent changes (e.g., new judicial decisions or government promulgations, and so on) affecting the research process.
- A glossary of key terms (e.g., Index Volume in CCH's *Standard Federal Tax Reporter*). ■

If a court case or ruling is significant to the findings, the investigator should not rely exclusively upon the abbreviated digest of the case or ruling in the tax service or upon the publisher's editorial comments. The case or ruling should be reviewed in its entirety.

Arriving at a Solution and Recommendations

The solution to a tax problem begins with a resolution of the tax issues. However, after the tax issues have been resolved, nontax factors may need to be considered before a final solution is reached. In tax planning or open-fact tax research situations, it may be desirable to recommend alternative solutions depending upon the course of action selected by the taxpayer. The resolution of the tax issues facing the Ajax

Corporation in Examples 1-26, 1-28, and 1-29 indicates that if a gain is realized from the involuntary conversion, it can be deferred if (1) a timely election is made under Sec. 1033 and (2) the insurance proceeds are reinvested within a fixed time period in property of similar functional use. Insurance proceeds related to the business interruption are taxable under Sec. 61. The solutions and recommendations depend, in part, upon the corporation's business plans. For example, the ultimate decision depends upon whether it is desirable to replace the property with property of the same functional use.

Most research culminates with the preparation of an internal memo for the tax workpapers and a written report to the client. The memo should include (1) a statement of the facts and issues, (2) a discussion of the pertinent tax law sources (e.g., cases and rulings on point), (3) a statement of the results of the research, and (4) the logic for the recommended course of action. The written report to the client may be more abbreviated but should include documentation for the recommendations and may include a statement of the pertinent facts to make sure that all of the assumed conditions are correct. Most accounting firms require conclusions to be communicated to their clients in writing. Members or employees of such firms can answer questions orally, but their oral conclusions must be followed up with a written communication. As previously discussed in the discussion of the *Statements on Responsibilities in Tax Practice* published by the AICPA, although oral advice may serve a client's needs appropriately in routine matters or in well-defined areas, written communications are recommended in important, unusual, or complicated transactions. In the judgment of the CPA, oral advice may be followed by a written confirmation to the client. A written record will limit misunderstandings and provide a basis for future discussions, reference, planning, and implementation of suggestions.[45]

COMPUTER APPLICATIONS IN TAX PRACTICE

Tax Return Preparation

The use of computers in tax practice has experienced rapid growth in recent years. Many tax practitioners have used external data processing companies such as Computax and Fast-Tax to prepare tax returns for their clients. Tax practitioners fill out input sheets, which are sent to the data processing service organization for preparation of the return. These services are relatively expensive, however, and consequently accounting firms are increasingly using internally generated tax return software applications using microcomputers. With the increased use and decreased cost of microcomputers, the trend toward internally generated tax return preparation is expected to accelerate. As in-house tax return preparation software becomes more popular, it is anticipated that external data processing companies will offer better service at increasingly competitive prices. Computerized tax return preparation software applications are available for use with these course materials.

Tax Planning Applications

For several years many tax practitioners used computer terminal time-sharing systems to make the time-consuming complex tax calculations needed for tax

---

[45] AICPA, *Statement on Responsibilities in Tax Practice*, 1991 Revision, ¶ .05 and .06.

planning. For example, specialized computer programs were available to calculate the income and estate tax effects that would result from a proposed change in the client's tax situation. Many firms are now using software applications on microcomputers to accomplish similar tasks. For example, software applications are used to project depreciation and other tax consequences arising from a proposed acquisition of business assets, to determine whether a corporation has an accumulated earnings tax problem, and to make basis adjustments for real estate partnerships.

Tax Research Applications

Computerized information-retrieval systems are being used in tax research. The oldest of these data bases is LEXIS, which was developed by Mead Data Central. ACCESS, which is offered by Commerce Clearing House, also has widespread use. The database for these computerized systems contains in full text the same tax law sources (e.g., cases, rulings, committee reports, regulations, and commentary and analysis) that are included in a manual tax service as discussed previously. The system is entered by using a keyword or phrase or by entering a Code section number or case name. Researchers need to be imaginative in thinking of search requests; a computerized system will not locate an authority unless it contains the exact wording the researcher specifies, even though it contains synonymous terms.

Example 1-30 ■   A researcher is interested in whether a certain expenditure for clothing is deductible under Sec. 162 as a uniform expense. The researcher might instruct the computer to retrieve all cases containing the words "uniform" and "Sec. 162" in close proximity to each other. This search will turn up only cases containing those words. Cases using the words "work clothing" will not be retrieved. A more comprehensive search will take place if the researcher instructs the computerized system to look for either "uniform" or "work clothing" within close proximity to "Sec. 162." ■

Computerized systems can be especially valuable as a backup to the research one has conducted through the tax services. After researchers have located some authorities through the tax services, they can use ACCESS or LEXIS to determine whether there are additional authorities on point. Both systems are updated for new developments on a very timely basis.

Four tax services—Bender's *Federal Tax Service,* RIA's *Federal Tax Coordinator 2d,* CCH's *Standard Federal Tax Reporter,* and BNA's *Tax Management Portfolios* are available not only as a looseleaf tax service but also on compact disc, known as CD-ROM (compact disc read-only memory). The materials are organized the same as in the loose-leaf services. The compact discs are updated monthly. Information is retrieved from the compact discs by typing key words into the computer. For example, one may locate the index on the disk, consult the index and then refer to the portion of the disk that discusses the tax consequences of a related issue. The compact discs, of course, allow pages and pages of information to be stored in practically no space and avoid the need to file new pages. Extensive material is available on the CCH "ACCESS": CD-ROM. For example, the CD-ROM product includes the following: *Standard Federal Tax Reports, State Tax Reports,* Letter Rulings and IRS Positions, Revenue Rulings and Revenue Procedures, IRS Publications, Tax Forms and Instructions, and court cases dating back to 1913. The Matthew Bender compact discs include proceedings of a number of tax institutes. RIA anticipates adding court cases to its discs.

PROBLEM MATERIALS

DISCUSSION QUESTIONS

1-1. Why did the Supreme Court hold the income tax to be unconstitutional in 1895?

1-2. Why was pay-as-you-go withholding needed in 1943?

1-3. Congressman Patrick indicates that he is opposed to new tax legislative proposals that call for a proportional tax rate which are currently being considered by Congress because the new taxing structure would not be in accord with our traditional practice of taxing those who have the ability to pay the tax. Discuss the position of the congressman, giving consideration to (a) tax rate structures (e.g., progressive, proportional, and regressive) and (b) the concept of equity.

1-4. Carmen indicates that her average tax rate is 18% and her marginal tax rate is 28% for the current year. She is considering whether to make a charitable contribution to her church prior to the end of the tax year. Which tax rate is of greater significance in measuring the tax effect for her decision? Explain.

1-5. Discuss the principal differences between the tax formula for individuals and corporations.

1-6. Why are the gift and estate taxes both referred to as wealth transfer taxes? What is the tax base for computing each of these taxes?

1-7. Cathy, who is single, makes two gifts of $15,000 each to her two children.
   a. Is Cathy or her children primarily liable for the gift tax on the two gifts?
   b. If Cathy has never made a taxable gift in prior years, is a gift tax due on the two gifts?

1-8. Carlos inherits 100 shares of Allied Corporation stock from his father. The stock cost $8,000 and has a $10,000 FMV on the date of his father's death. The alternate valuation date was not elected. What is Carlos's tax basis for the Allied stock when it is received from the estate?

1-9. Why are most estates not subject to the federal estate tax?

1-10. Indicate which of the following taxes are generally progressive, proportional, or regressive:
   a. State income taxes
   b. Federal estate tax
   c. Corporate state franchise tax
   d. Property taxes

1-11. Carolyn operates a small business as a sole proprietor (unincorporated). Carolyn is considering operating the business as a corporation because of nontax advantages (e.g., limited liability and ability to raise outside capital). From the standpoint of paying social security taxes, would the total social security taxes increase or decrease if the business is incorporated? Why?

1-12. Chris is the president of a profitable closely held corporation that is considering a sale of the business to a large publicly traded corporation. Chris informs you that the acquiring corporation will obtain an advance letter ruling from the IRS that the proposed acquisition will qualify as a tax-free reorganization. Chris is concerned about the possible gain on which he might have to pay tax if the acquisition is later found to be taxable. What assurance is there that the transaction will be tax-free if an advance ruling is obtained?

1-13. Assume the same facts as in Problem 1-12, except that the parties involved do not plan to obtain an advance ruling due to the cost and time delays involved. Instead, they intend to rely upon a published ruling of the IRS involving similar facts.
   a. Should the taxpayers rely upon the published ruling? Explain.
   b. Does a ruling have the same amount of authority as the Treasury Regulations?

1-14. How does the carryback and carryover of net operating losses mitigate the effects of our progressive tax rate structure?

1-15. Why is the sales tax considered to be a convenient tax?

1-16. What are the four characteristics of a "good" tax structure?

1-17. The primary objective of the federal income tax law is to raise revenue. What are its secondary objectives?

1-18. If the objectives of the federal tax system are multifaceted and include raising revenues, providing investment incentives, encouraging certain industries, and meeting desired social objectives, is it possible to achieve a simplified tax system? Explain.

1-19. You are assigned to research a tax problem that has been affected by a recent change in the Internal Revenue Code. The intent of the recent tax law change is uncertain, and the Treasury Department has not issued regulations. What tax law source might be helpful to determine the Congressional intent for the recent tax law change?

1-20. Why is it important to be familiar with the organizational scheme of the Internal Revenue Code? What is the most frequently cited organizational category?

1-21. What is the difference between a legislative regulation and an interpretative regulation?

1-22. Distinguish among proposed, temporary, and final regulations.

1-23. List an advantage and a disadvantage of using the Tax Court's small case procedures.

1-24. Explain whether the following decisions have the same precedential value:
  a. Tax Court regular decisions
  b. Tax Court memorandum decisions
  c. Decisions issued under the Tax Court's small case procedures section.

1-25. Your tax accountant indicates that he doesn't know the exact answer to your problem because it is a grey area. What does a grey area in the tax law refer to?

1-26. Why is it important for a tax practitioner to consider judicial decisions involving similar facts and issues before deciding upon a particular course of action for his client?

1-27. What considerations are involved in the choice of a particular tax forum for litigating a tax issue?

1-28. How is it possible for the Fifth Circuit Court of Appeals to decide in favor of the taxpayer and the Fourth Circuit Court of Appeals to decide in favor of the IRS in two separate cases involving similar or identical facts and issues?

1-29. Under what circumstances is it more likely that the Supreme Court will hear a tax case?

1-30. Consult the *Levin Metals Corporation* case (92 T.C. 307).
  a. In which year was the case decided?
  b. What was the issue?
  c. Who won the case?
  d. Was the case reviewed?
  e. Is there an appellate decision?
  f. Has the case been cited in other cases?

1-31. Is the IRS required to abide by (i.e., acquiesce to) decisions rendered by each of the following courts:
  a. The Fifth Circuit Court of Appeals
  b. The federal district court for Southeastern Michigan
  c. The Tax Court
  d. The Supreme Court

1-32. What is a primary cite?

1-33. What is the role of the Joint Conference Committee in the passage of tax legislation?

1-34. Of what importance are Congressional committee reports to tax practitioners?

1-35. What is the primary service function provided by the National Office of the IRS?

1-36. What types of taxpayers are more likely to be audited by the IRS?

1-37. Anya is concerned that she will be audited by the IRS.

a. Under what circumstances is it possible that the IRS will review each line item on her tax return?

b. Is it likely that all items on Anya's return will be audited?

1-38. Should the IRS settle or compromise a case based upon the "hazards of litigation"? Why?

1-39. If a taxpayer receives a tax refund from the IRS, does this mean that the IRS feels that the return is correct and will not be subject to audit?

1-40. What is the statute of limitations for transactions involving:
a. Fraud (e.g., failure to file a tax return)
b. Disallowance of tax deduction items
c. The omission of rental income equal to 30% of the taxpayer's gross income

1-41. How is the interest rate paid on tax deficiencies and refunds determined by the Treasury Department?

1-42. When should a CPA sign a tax return as a preparer for purposes of the tax return preparer provisions of the Code? Can a CPA be penalized for failure to follow the *Statements on Responsibilities in Tax Practice* (SRTP)?

1-43. According to the SRTP, what standard should be met for a CPA to take a position on a tax return?

1-44. In reference to tax research, what is meant by "the best possible defensibly" correct solution?

1-45. Why is it important for a tax advisor to have an extensive knowledge of the tax law?

1-46. Explain how a microcomputer is useful to assist a tax practitioner in tax planning activities and in making complex tax calculations.

1-47. What is the principal difference between a closed-fact tax research problem and an open-fact tax research problem?

1-48. Why is a citator helpful in the conduct of tax research?

1-49. How do nontax factors influence the choice of the most desirable tax solution to a business problem involving "controllable facts"?

PROBLEMS

1-50. Jill and George are married and file a joint return. They expect to have $350,000 of taxable income in the next taxable year and are considering whether to purchase a personal residence that would provide additional tax deductions of $80,000 for mortgage interest and real estate taxes.
a. What is their marginal tax rate for purposes of making this decision? (Ignore the effects of a phase-out of personal exemptions and itemized deductions (see Chapters 2 and 7 respectively).
b. What is the tax savings if the residence is acquired?

1-51. *Gift Tax.* Chuck, a married taxpayer, makes the following gifts during the current year: $20,000 to his church; $30,000 to his daughter; and $25,000 to his wife.
a. What is the amount of Chuck's taxable gifts for the current year (assuming that he does not elect to split the gifts with his spouse).
b. How would your answer to Part a change if a gift-splitting election is made?

1-52. *Estate Tax.* Clay dies in the current year and has a gross estate valued at $800,000. Six months after the date of death, the gross assets are valued at $900,000. The estate incurs funeral and administration expenses of $125,000. It also has debts amounting to $75,000, and Clay bequeaths $350,000 of the property to his wife. During his life Clay made no taxable gifts.
a. What is the amount of Clay's taxable estate?
b. What is the tax base for computing Clay's estate tax?
c. What is the amount of estate tax that is owed if the tentative estate tax (before credits) is $70,800?

1-53. *Using the Cumulative Bulletin.* Refer to the 1990-1 Cumulative Bulletin.
   a. For the time period covered by the bulletin, to which cases did the IRS issue a nonacquiescence?
   b. What is the topical area of Rev. Rul. 90-10?
   c. Does this bulletin contain any revenue ruling that interprets Sec. 162? If so, list it.

1-54. *Tax Law Sources and Authority.* In researching a tax question you find that the Tax Court has held for the taxpayer in one case and a federal district court in California has held for the IRS in another case involving similar facts and issues. In the first case, an appeal was made by the IRS to the Fifth Circuit Court of Appeals and the court upheld the Tax Court decision and held for the taxpayer. The IRS has an outstanding published revenue ruling against you and has not acquiesced to the Tax Court decision. Your facts and issues are similar to these two cases. What weight is given to the various authorities, and what advice would you give to the taxpayer?

1-55. *IRS Audits.* Which of the following individuals is likely to be audited:
   a. Connie has a $20,000 net loss from her unincorporated business (a cattle ranch). She also received a $200,000 salary as an executive of a corporation.
   b. Craig has AGI of $20,000 from wages and uses the standard deduction.
   c. Dale fails to report $120 of dividends from a stock investment. His taxable income is $40,000, and he has no other unusually large itemized deductions or business expenses. A Form 1099 is reported to the IRS.

1-56. *Statute of Limitations.* In April 1994, Dan is audited by the IRS for the year 1992. During the course of the audit, the agency discovers that Dan's deductions for business travel and entertainment are unsubstantiated and a $600 deficiency assessment is proposed for 1992. The agent also discovers that Dan failed to report $40,000 of gross business income on his 1990 return. Gross income of $60,000 was reported in 1990. The agency also discovers that Dan failed to file a tax return in 1989.

   Will the statute of limitations prevent the IRS from issuing a deficiency assessment for 1992, 1990, or 1989? Explain.

1-57. *Using a Tax Service.* Use the topical index of the *United States Tax Reporter* tax service to locate authorities dealing with the deductibility of the cost of a facelift.
   a. At which paragraph(s) does the *United States Tax Reporter* service give a synopsis of these authorities and citations to them?
   b. List the authorities.
   c. Have there been any recent non-statutory developments concerning the tax consequences of facelifts? ("Recent" means authorities appearing in the cross-reference section.)
   d. May a taxpayer deduct the cost of a facelift paid for in the current year? Explain.

1-58. *Using a Tax Service.* Refer to Reg. Sec. 1.302-1 in the *United States Tax Reporter* service. Does the regulation interpret today's version of the Code? Explain.

1-59. *Using a Tax Service.* Use the topical index of the *Standard Federal Tax Reporter* to locate authorities dealing with whether termite damage qualifies for a casualty loss deduction.
   a. At which paragraph(s) does the *Standard Federal Tax Reporter* service give a synopsis of these authorities and citations to them?
   b. List the authorities.
   c. Have there been any recent developments concerning the tax consequences of termite damage? ("Recent" means new authorities appearing in Volume 13 of the reporter.)

CASE STUDY PROBLEM

1-60. John Gemstone, a wealthy client, has recently been audited by the IRS. The agent has questioned the following deduction items on Mr. Gemstone's tax return for the year under review:

   • A $10,000 loss deduction on the rental of his beach cottage.
   • A $20,000 charitable contribution deduction for the donation of a painting to a local art museum. The agent has questioned whether the painting is overvalued.
   • A $15,000 loss deduction from the operation of a cattle breeding ranch. The agent is concerned that the ranch is not a legitimate business (i.e., is a hobby).

Your supervisor has requested that you represent Mr. Gemstone in his discussions with the IRS.

a. What additional questions should you ask Mr. Gemstone in an attempt to substantiate the deductibility of the above items?

b. What tax research procedures might be applied to "build the best possible case" for your client?

CASE STUDY PROBLEM—ETHICAL ISSUES

1-61. Elaine Gold, a partner at the CPA firm of Gold & Johnson, is preparing Mr. Clark's 1994 return. In reviewing the client files, she notices that one of her staff accountants had made a significant error on last year's return regarding the medical expense deduction. Mr. Clark has been a client since she started her practice ten years ago and Elaine knows he will be very upset about the $5,000 overstatement in deductions and possibly want to find a new accountant. Elaine comes to you, a friend and fellow CPA, to ask your advice on whether or not to notify Mr. Clark and/or the IRS of the mistake. What advice should you give Elaine about the proper course of action to be taken as a CPA in such a case? Explain whether or not she must notify the client or any relevant authorities and how she should communicate (orally and/or in writing) any recommendations concerning the issue.

RESEARCH PROBLEMS

1-62. Read the following two cases and explain why the Supreme Court reached different conclusions for cases involving similar facts and issues:

- *CIR v. Court Holding Co.,* 33 AFTR 593, 45-1 USTC ¶ 9215 (USSC, 1945).
- *U.S. v. Cumberland Public Service Co.,* 38 AFTR 978, 50-1 USTC ¶ 9129 (USSC, 1950).

1-63. Your client has a tax problem, and your research reveals the following tax law sources:

- *U.S. v. Cumberland Public Service Co.,* 38 AFTR 978, 50-1 USTC ¶ 9129 (USSC, 1950).
- *Gino A. Speca v. CIR,* 47 AFTR 2d 81-468, 80-2 USTC ¶ 9692 (7th Cir., 1980).
- *Ruddick Corp. v. U.S.,* 47 AFTR 2d 81-846, 81-1 USTC ¶ 9221 (Ct. Cl., 1981).
- *Inter-County Title Co. v. U.S.,* 36 AFTR 2d 75-6395, 75-2 USTC ¶ 9845 (D.C. Cal., 1975).
- *Gavin S. Millar,* 1975 PH T.C. Memo ¶ 75,113, 34 TCM 554.
- *Henry D. Duarte,* 44 T.C. 193 (1965).
- Sec. 461(g).
- Reg. Sec. 1.465-1(T).
- Rev. Rul. 74-144, 1974-1 C.B. 105.
- Rev. Proc. 77-28, 1977-2 C.B. 537.

Give a brief description of each of the citations listed above.

2 *Determination of Tax*

LEARNING OBJECTIVES

After studying this chapter, you should be able to

1. Use the tax formula to compute an individual's taxable income
2. Determine the amount allowable for the standard deduction
3. Determine the amount and the correct number of personal and dependency exemptions
4. Determine the filing status of individuals
5. Explain the tax formula for corporations
6. Explain the basic concepts of property transactions

Additional Comment

"There is one difference between a tax collector and a taxidermist—the taxidermist leaves the hide." This is a quote from Mortimer Caplan, former Director of the Bureau of Internal Revenue, Time, Feb. 1, 1963.

Each year, over 100 million individuals and married couples file forms called tax returns, on which they compute their federal income tax. The income tax is imposed "on the taxable income of every individual."[1] The amount of tax actually owed by an individual taxpayer is determined by applying an extraordinarily complex set of rules that together comprise the income tax law. To understand the income tax, it is necessary to study the basic formula upon which the income tax computation is based. Therefore, this chapter introduces the income tax formula and begins the development of its components. Because the income tax formula constitutes the basis of the income tax, most of the remainder of this book is an expansion of the formula. For that reason, it is essential that the reader understand the formula presented here before proceeding to subsequent chapters.

FORMULA FOR INDIVIDUAL INCOME TAX

OBJECTIVE 1

Use the tax formula to compute an individual's taxable income

Additional Comment

The IRS estimates that the average taxpayer will spend 3 hours and 37 minutes to complete Form 1040.

Basic Formula

Most individuals compute their income tax by using the formula illustrated in Table 2-1. The formula itself appears rather simple. That is because the complexity of the income tax comes from the intricate rules that must be applied in order to arrive at the amounts that enter into the formula rather than from the basic formula.

The tax formula is incorporated into the income tax form. The tax formula illustrated in Table 2-1 can be compared with Form 1040, which is reproduced in Figure 2-1. There are some minor differences between the formula found in the tax law and the tax form itself. For example, taxpayers are generally not required to report exclusions (nontaxable income) on their tax returns. One exception does require taxpayers to disclose tax-exempt interest income. Also, Form 1040 is used to collect other taxes such as the alternative minimum tax. Hence, a line is provided for that tax on Form 1040. The main reason for differences between the formula and the form is clerical convenience. That is, there is no reason to require taxpayers to disclose income if the income is not subject to tax, and it is convenient to collect other taxes on the same tax form.

[1] Sec. 1.

Additional Comment

In the Revenue Reconciliation Act of 1993 there was a provision that increased the amount of the checkoff for the Presidential Election Campaign Fund from $1 to $3. The amount was increased because too few individuals were using the checkoff and a shortfall in the fund was projected for the 1996 election cycle. The checkoff can be found on Form 1040 below the address section.

TABLE 2-1   *Tax Formula for Individuals*

Income from whatever source derived	$ xxx,xxx
Minus: Exclusions	(xxx)
Gross income	$ xx,xxx
Minus: Deductions for adjusted gross income	(xxx)
Adjusted gross income	$ x,xxx
Minus: Deductions from adjusted gross income:	
Greater of itemized deductions or the standard deduction	(xx)
Personal and dependency exemptions	(xx)
Taxable income	$ x,xxx
Times: Tax rates (from tax table or schedule)	× .xx
Gross tax	$ xx
Minus: Credits and prepayments	(x)
Net tax payable or refund due	$ xx

Examination of the formula reveals terms such as gross income, exclusions, adjusted gross income, exemptions, gross tax, and credits. These terms and others that comprise the formula are defined below.

Definitions

Income. The term **income** includes both taxable and nontaxable income. Although the term is not specifically defined in the tax law, it does include income from any source.[2] Its meaning is close to that of the term **revenue.** It does not, however, include a "return of capital." Thus, in the case of the sale of property, only the gain, not the entire sales proceeds, is viewed as income. This view extends to the sale of inventory, where the gross profit is viewed as income, as opposed to the sale price. Also, where a receipt is offset by a debt, such as in the case of borrowed funds, there is no income.

Typical Misconception

It is not difficult to confuse an exclusion with a deduction. An exclusion is a source of income that can be omitted from the tax base, whereas a deduction is an expense that can be subtracted in arriving at taxable income. Both have the effect of reducing taxable income.

Exclusion. Not all income is taxable. An **exclusion** is any item of income that the tax law says is not taxable. Congress, over the years, has specifically exempted certain types of income from taxation for various social, economic, and political reasons. Chapter 4 discusses specific exclusions and the reasons for their existence. Table 2-2 contains a sample of the items that are excludable from gross income.

Gross Income. **Gross income** is income reduced by exclusions. In other words, it is income from taxable sources. As noted earlier, gross income is the only income that is actually reported on the return (i.e., excluded income need not be disclosed). Section 61(a) contains a partial list of items of gross income. The items listed in Sec. 61(a) are shown in Table 2-3. Note, however, that Sec. 61(a) states that unless otherwise provided, "gross income means all income from whatever source derived, including (but not limited to) the" listed items of income. Thus, the fact that an item is omitted from the list does not necessarily mean that the item is excluded. For example, illegal income, although omitted from the list, is taxable.[3]

Deductions for Adjusted Gross Income. In general, deductions are expenses that are specifically allowed by the tax law. Of course, not all expenses are deductible. On

---

[2] Sec. 61(a).
[3] *U.S. v. Manley S. Sullivan,* 6 AFTR 6753, 1 USTC ¶ 236 (USSC, 1927).

Form **1040**

Department of the Treasury—Internal Revenue Service

U.S. Individual Income Tax Return (B) 1993

IRS Use Only—Do not write or staple in this space.

For the year Jan. 1–Dec. 31, 1993, or other tax year beginning _____ , 1993, ending _____ , 19 ___ | OMB No. 1545-0074

Label

(See instructions on page 12.)

Use the IRS label. Otherwise, please print or type.

Your first name and initial: *Larry S.*   Last name: *Lane*

Your social security number: 123 45 6789

If a joint return, spouse's first name and initial: *Jane V.*   Last name: *Lane*

Spouse's social security number: 987 65 4321

Home address (number and street). If you have a P.O. box, see page 12.: *116 E. Edwards*   Apt. no.:

City, town or post office, state, and ZIP code. If you have a foreign address, see page 12.: *Lubbock, TEXAS 79409*

For Privacy Act and Paperwork Reduction Act Notice, see page 4.

Presidential Election Campaign

(See page 12.)

	Yes	No	Note: Checking "Yes" will not change your tax or reduce your refund.
Do you want $3 to go to this fund?		X	
If a joint return, does your spouse want $3 to go to this fund?		X	

Filing Status

(See page 12.)

Check only one box.

- 1 ☐ Single
- 2 ☒ Married filing joint return (even if only one had income)
- 3 ☐ Married filing separate return. Enter spouse's social security no. above and full name here. ▶ _____
- 4 ☐ Head of household (with qualifying person). (See page 13.) If the qualifying person is a child but not your dependent, enter this child's name here. ▶ _____
- 5 ☐ Qualifying widow(er) with dependent child (year spouse died ▶ 19 ___). (See page 13.)

Exemptions

(See page 13.)

- 6a ☒ **Yourself.** If your parent (or someone else) can claim you as a dependent on his or her tax return, **do not** check box 6a. But be sure to check the box on line 33b on page 2
- b ☒ **Spouse**

No. of boxes checked on 6a and 6b	2

c **Dependents:**

(1) Name (first, initial, and last name)	(2) Check if under age 1	(3) If age 1 or older, dependent's social security number	(4) Dependent's relationship to you	(5) No. of months lived in your home in 1993
BETTY		725 25 7774	*Daughter*	*12*

If more than six dependents, see page 14.

No. of your children on 6c who:
- lived with you: 1
- didn't live with you due to divorce or separation (see page 15)
- Dependents on 6c not entered above

- d If your child didn't live with you but is claimed as your dependent under a pre-1985 agreement, check here ▶ ☐
- e Total number of exemptions claimed

Add numbers entered on lines above ▶	3

Income

Attach Copy B of your Forms W-2, W-2G, and 1099-R here.

If you did not get a W-2, see page 10.

If you are attaching a check or money order, put it on top of any Forms W-2, W-2G, or 1099-R.

7	Wages, salaries, tips, etc. Attach Form(s) W-2	7	*70,000*
8a	**Taxable** interest income (see page 16). Attach Schedule B if over $400	8a	*1,000*
b	**Tax-exempt** interest (see page 17). DON'T include on line 8a 8b	*500*	
9	Dividend income. Attach Schedule B if over $400	9	
10	Taxable refunds, credits, or offsets of state and local income taxes (see page 17)	10	
11	Alimony received	11	
12	Business income or (loss). Attach Schedule C or C-EZ	12	
13	Capital gain or (loss). Attach Schedule D	13	
14	Capital gain distributions not reported on line 13 (see page 17)	14	
15	Other gains or (losses). Attach Form 4797	15	
16a	Total IRA distributions 16a _____ b Taxable amount (see page 18)	16b	
17a	Total pensions and annuities 17a _____ b Taxable amount (see page 18)	17b	
18	Rental real estate, royalties, partnerships, S corporations, trusts, etc. Attach Schedule E	18	
19	Farm income or (loss). Attach Schedule F	19	
20	Unemployment compensation (see page 19)	20	
21a	Social security benefits 21a _____ b Taxable amount (see page 19)	21b	
22	Other income. List type and amount—see page 20	22	
23	Add the amounts in the far right column for lines 7 through 22. This is your **total income** ▶	23	*71,000*

Adjustments to Income

(See page 20.)

24a	Your IRA deduction (see page 20)	24a	
b	Spouse's IRA deduction (see page 20)	24b	*2,000*
25	One-half of self-employment tax (see page 21)	25	
26	Self-employed health insurance deduction (see page 22)	26	
27	Keogh retirement plan and self-employed SEP deduction	27	
28	Penalty on early withdrawal of savings	28	
29	Alimony paid. Recipient's SSN ▶ _____	29	
30	Add lines 24a through 29. These are your **total adjustments** ▶	30	*2,000*

Adjusted Gross Income

31	Subtract line 30 from line 23. This is your **adjusted gross income.** If this amount is less than $23,050 and a child lived with you, see page EIC-1 to find out if you can claim the "Earned Income Credit" on line 56 ▶	31	*69,000*

Cat. No. 12598V   Form **1040** (1993)

FIGURE 2-1   Form 1040

Tax Computation	32	Amount from line 31 (adjusted gross income)		32	69,000

(See page 23.)

33a Check if: ☐ **You** were 65 or older, ☐ Blind; ☐ **Spouse** was 65 or older, ☐ Blind.
Add the number of boxes checked above and enter the total here . . . ▶ 33a ☐

b If your parent (or someone else) can claim you as a dependent, check here . ▶ 33b ☐

c If you are married filing separately and your spouse itemizes deductions or you are a dual-status alien, see page 24 and check here . . . . . . ▶ 33c ☐

34 Enter the **larger** of your:
  Itemized deductions from Schedule A, line 26, **OR**
  Standard deduction shown below for your filing status. **But if you checked any box on line 33a or b,** go to page 24 to find your standard deduction. If you checked **box 33c,** your standard deduction is zero.
  ● Single—$3,700   ● Head of household—$5,450
  ● Married filing jointly or Qualifying widow(er)—$6,200
  ● Married filing separately—$3,100

34	7,300

35 Subtract line 34 from line 32 . . . . | 35 | 61,700

36 If line 32 is $81,350 or less, multiply $2,350 by the total number of exemptions claimed on line 6e. If line 32 is over $81,350, see the worksheet on page 25 for the amount to enter . | 36 | 7,050

If you want the IRS to figure your tax, see page 24.

37 **Taxable income.** Subtract line 36 from line 35. If line 36 is more than line 35, enter -0- . | 37 | 54,650

38 Tax. Check if from **a** ☒ Tax Table, **b** ☐ Tax Rate Schedules, **c** ☐ Schedule D Tax Worksheet, or **d** ☐ Form 8615 (see page 25). Amount from Form(s) 8814 ▶ **e** _____ | 38 | 10,512

39 Additional taxes (see page 25). Check if from **a** ☐ Form 4970 **b** ☐ Form 4972 . . | 39 |

40 Add lines 38 and 39 . . . . ▶ | 40 | 10,512

Credits

(See page 25.)

41	Credit for child and dependent care expenses. Attach Form 2441	41	
42	Credit for the elderly or the disabled. Attach Schedule R . .	42	
43	Foreign tax credit. Attach Form 1116	43	
44	Other credits (see page 26). Check if from **a** ☐ Form 3800 **b** ☐ Form 8396 **c** ☐ Form 8801 **d** ☐ Form (specify) _____	44	

45 Add lines 41 through 44 . . . . | 45 |

46 Subtract line 45 from line 40. If line 45 is more than line 40, enter -0- . . . . . . ▶ | 46 | 10,512

Other Taxes

47 Self-employment tax. Attach Schedule SE. Also, see line 25 . . . . | 47 |

48 Alternative minimum tax. Attach Form 6251 . . . . | 48 |

49 Recapture taxes (see page 26). Check if from **a** ☐ Form 4255 **b** ☐ Form 8611 **c** ☐ Form 8828 | 49 |

50 Social security and Medicare tax on tip income not reported to employer. Attach Form 4137 . | 50 |

51 Tax on qualified retirement plans, including IRAs. If required, attach Form 5329 . . . | 51 |

52 Advance earned income credit payments from Form W-2 . . . . | 52 |

53 Add lines 46 through 52. This is your **total tax** . . . . ▶ | 53 | 10,512

Payments

Attach Forms W-2, W-2G, and 1099-R on the front.

54	Federal income tax withheld. If any is from Form(s) 1099, check ▶ ☐	54	11,000
55	1993 estimated tax payments and amount applied from 1992 return .	55	
56	**Earned income credit.** Attach Schedule EIC	56	
57	Amount paid with Form 4868 (extension request)	57	
58a	Excess social security, Medicare, and RRTA tax withheld (see page 28) .	58a	
b	Deferral of additional 1993 taxes. Attach Form 8841	58b	
59	Other payments (see page 28). Check if from **a** ☐ Form 2439 **b** ☐ Form 4136	59	

60 Add lines 54 through 59. These are your **total payments** . . . . ▶ | 60 | 11,000

Refund or Amount You Owe

61 If line 60 is more than line 53, subtract line 53 from line 60. This is the amount you **OVERPAID** . ▶ | 61 | 488

62 Amount of line 61 you want **REFUNDED TO YOU** . . . . ▶ | 62 | 488

63 Amount of line 61 you want **APPLIED TO YOUR 1994 ESTIMATED TAX** ▶ | 63 |

64 If line 53 is more than line 60, subtract line 60 from line 53. This is the **AMOUNT YOU OWE.** For details on how to pay, including what to write on your payment, see page 29 . . | 64 |

65 Estimated tax penalty (see page 29). Also include on line 64 | 65 |

Sign Here

Keep a copy of this return for your records.

Under penalties of perjury, I declare that I have examined this return and accompanying schedules and statements, and to the best of my knowledge and belief, they are true, correct, and complete. Declaration of preparer (other than taxpayer) is based on all information of which preparer has any knowledge.

Your signature	Date	Your occupation
Larry S. Lane	4/15/94	*Attorney*
Spouse's signature. If a joint return, BOTH must sign.	Date	Spouse's occupation
Jane S. Lane	4/15/94	*Student*

Paid Preparer's Use Only

Preparer's signature ▶	Date	Check if self-employed ☐	Preparer's social security no.
Firm's name (or yours if self-employed) and address ▶		E.I. No.	
		ZIP code	

FIGURE 2-1 Form 1040 (Continued)

TABLE 2-2   Major Exclusions

Gifts and inheritances
Life insurance proceeds
Welfare and certain other transfer payments
Certain scholarships and fellowships
Certain payments for injury and sickness
   Personal injury settlements
   Workmen's compensation
   Medical expense reimbursements
Certain employee fringe benefits
   Health plan premiums
   Group term life insurance premiums
   Meals and lodging
   Employee discounts
   Employee death benefits
   Disability payments
   Dependent care
   Educational assistance (expires on December 31, 1994)
Certain foreign-earned income
Interest on state and local government bonds
Certain interest of Series EE bonds
Improvements by lessee to lessor's property
Child support payments
Property settlements

the other hand, there are a few instances where deductions are permitted even if there is no specific corresponding expense. For example, taxpayers are entitled to a limited deduction for funds deposited to an individual retirement account (IRA), percentage depletion, and a standard deduction.

There are two categories of deductions for individual taxpayers: deductions *for* adjusted gross income and deductions *from* adjusted gross income. In general, **deductions for adjusted gross income** are business expenses like those on an income statement prepared for financial accounting purposes, such as compensation paid to employees, repairs to business property, and depreciation. For the most part, **deductions from adjusted gross income** are personal expenses that Congress has chosen to allow. This classification scheme is not always followed. For example, alimony, which would not appear on an income statement, is a deduction *for* adjusted

TABLE 2-3   Gross Income Items Listed in Sec. 61(a)

Compensation for services, including fees, commissions, and similar items
Gross income derived from business
Gains derived from dealings in property
Interest
Rents
Royalties
Dividends
Alimony and separate maintenance payments
Annuities
Income from life insurance and endowment contracts
Pension
Income from the discharge of indebtedness
Distributive share of partnership income
Income in respect of a decedent
Income from an interest in an estate or trust

gross income. Table 2-4 contains a partial list of deductions *for* adjusted gross income that is taken from Sec. 62.

Additional Comment

In 1991, AGI reported on the 114.9 million individual income tax returns was almost $3.5 trillion, an increase of 1.9% from 1990.

Adjusted Gross Income. **Adjusted gross income (AGI)** is a measure of income that falls between gross income and taxable income. It is important because it is the measure of income that is used in numerous other tax computations. For example, AGI is used to establish floors for the medical deduction and casualty loss deduction and to establish a ceiling for the charitable contribution deduction.

Deductions from Adjusted Gross Income. Section 62 lists deductions *for* AGI (see Table 2-4). Thus, any deduction not listed in Sec. 62 is a deduction *from* AGI. The two categories of deductions *from* adjusted gross income are (1) itemized or standard deductions and (2) personal and dependency exemptions.[4]

Additional Comment

In 1991, approximately 28% of taxpayers itemized their deductions while 72% took the standard deduction.

Itemized Deductions and the Standard Deduction. In general, taxpayers cannot deduct personal expenses.[5] Congress, however, has chosen to allow taxpayers to deduct specified personal expenses such as charitable contributions and medical expenses. In addition, taxpayers are allowed to itemize expenses related to the production or collection of income; the management of property held for the production of income; and the determination, collection, or refund of any tax.[6]

Taxpayers generally have a choice of claiming either itemized deductions or the standard deduction. The amount of the standard deduction varies depending on the taxpayer's filing status, age, and vision. As a practical matter, for most taxpayers the standard deduction is greater than the total itemized deductions. Taxpayers with small amounts of deductible expenses do not itemize and, in fact, do not have to keep records of medical expenses and other itemized deductions. The relationship between itemized deductions and the standard deduction is discussed later in this chapter.

Historical Note

In 1986, when parents were required merely to list the names of their children to claim them as a dependent, 77 million children were claimed. In 1987, when taxpayers were required to list children's Social Security numbers to prove that the exemptions were valid, the number of children claimed as dependents decreased to 70 million.

Personal and Dependency Exemptions. A **personal exemption** is a deduction equal to $2,350 in 1993 and $2,450 in 1994. The amount of an exemption is adjusted annually for increases in the cost of living. An additional exemption is allowed for each individual who is a dependent.

TABLE 2-4 Deductions for Adjusted Gross Income Listed in Sec. 62

Trade and business deductions
Reimbursed employee expenses and certain expenses of performing artists
Losses from the sale or exchange of property
Deductions attributable to rents and royalties
Certain deductions of life tenants and income beneficiaries of property
Contributions to retirement plans (Keoghs and IRAs)
Certain portion of lump-sum distributions from pension plans
Penalties forfeited because of premature withdrawal of funds
   from time savings accounts
One-half of self-employment taxes paid
Alimony
Reforestation expenses
Moving expenses
Certain required repayments of supplemental unemployment compensation
Jury duty pay remitted to an individual's employer

[4] Sec. 63.
[5] Sec. 262.
[6] Sec. 212.

Taxable Income. **Taxable income** is adjusted gross income reduced by deductions *from* AGI. It is the amount of income that is taxed.

Tax Rates and Gross Tax. Tax rates are the percentage rates, set by Congress, at which income is taxed. There are five individual income tax rates of 15%, 28%, 31%, 36%, and 39.6%. Many taxpayers compute their tax by actually multiplying the percentage rates found in the tax rate schedules times taxable income. Most taxpayers, however, simply look in the tax table to find their gross tax. These two alternatives are discussed in more detail later in this chapter. The **gross tax** is the amount of tax determined by this process.

Credits and Prepayments. **Tax credits,** which include prepayments, are amounts that can be subtracted from the gross tax to arrive at the net tax due or refund due. Prepayments are amounts paid to the government during the year through means such as withholding from wages. These amounts are often called **refundable tax credits.** **Nonrefundable tax credits** are allowances, such as the dependent care credit, that have been created by Congress for various social, economic, and political reasons. Nonrefundable tax credits can be subtracted from the tax but will not be paid to the taxpayer in situations where the credits exceed the tax. This is logical because no amount has been paid to the government in advance. A partial list of refundable and nonrefundable tax credits can be found in Table 2-5.

Tax Formula Illustrated

The following examples illustrate the tax formula and Form 1040.

Historical Note

As recently as 1986, the highest marginal tax rate was 50%, and as recently as 1981 it was 70%.

Self-Study Question

If a taxpayer is in the 28% marginal tax bracket, would he or she prefer $100 of tax credits or $300 of tax deductions.

Answer

The taxpayer would prefer the $100 of tax credits. The $300 of deductions will result in a tax savings of $84 ($300 × .28), while the $100 of credits would result in a tax savings of $100.

TABLE 2-5 *Partial List of Tax Credits*

Refundable (prepayments)

    Withholding from wages and back-up withholding
    Excess social security taxes paid
    Nonhighway-use gasoline tax
    Earned income credit
    Regulated investment company credit
    Estimated payments
    Overpayment of prior year's tax
    Payments made with extension request

Nonrefundable

    Credit for the elderly and disabled
    Foreign tax credit
    Child and dependent care credit
    Targeted jobs credit[a]
    Business energy credit
    Qualified electric vehicle credit
    Research and experimentation credit[b]
    Low-income housing credit[a]
    Building rehabilitation credit
    Qualified mortgage bond and mortgage credit[a]
    Orphan drug credit[a]
    Enhanced oil recovery credit

[a]These credits are scheduled to expire on December 31, 1994.
[b]This credit is scheduled to expire on June 30, 1995.

Example 2-1 ■   The following facts relate to Larry S. and Jane V. Lane for 1993.

Salary	$70,000
Interest Income:	
Taxable	1,000
Exempt	500
Individual Retirement Account contribution (IRA)	2,000
Itemized deductions	7,300
Personal and dependency exemptions (3 × $2,350)	7,050
Withholding from salary	11,000

Their tax will be computed as follows:

Income:		
	Salary	$70,000
	Taxable interest	1,000
	Exempt interest	500
	Total	$71,500
Minus:	Exclusion:	
	Exempt interest	(500)
Gross income		$71,000
Minus:	Deductions for AGI:	
	IRA contribution	(2,000)
Adjusted gross income		$69,000
Minus:	Deductions from AGI:	
	Itemized deductions	(7,300)
	Personal and dependency exemptions	(7,050)
Taxable income		$54,650
Gross tax (tax table)		$10,512
Minus:	Credits and prepayments	
	(e.g., Federal income tax withheld)	(11,000)
Tax due (refund)		($488)

■

   This tax is also computed on Form 1040 (see Figure 2-1). Note that certain additional information such as the taxpayers' address and social security numbers is included on the return.

DEDUCTIONS FROM ADJUSTED GROSS INCOME

Itemized Deductions

As noted on page 2-7, **itemized deductions** are claimed only if the total of such expenses exceeds the standard deduction. Here, consideration is given to which expenses may be itemized and to the relationship between itemized deductions and the standard deduction.

Additional Comment

The phase-out of itemized deductions for high-income taxpayers effectively raises their marginal tax rate by 0.93% which could be considered as a hidden tax rate.

Deductible Items. Congress has chosen to allow taxpayers to itemize specified personal expenses. These specified expenses include medical expenses,[7] taxes,[8] investment and residential interest,[9] charitable contributions,[10] casualty and theft losses,[11] and employee expenses.[12] In addition, taxpayers are allowed to itemize expenses related to the production or collection of income, the management of property held for the production of income, and the determination, collection, or refund of any tax.[13] A partial list of itemized deductions is found in Table 2-6.

Itemized Deduction Floors. There are four adjusted gross income floors associated with itemized deductions. Three of the floors apply to specific categories of itemized deductions while the remaining floor applies to total itemized deductions. Only medical expenses in excess of 7.5% of adjusted gross income are deductible. Casualty losses in excess of 10% of AGI and miscellaneous deductions in excess of 2% of AGI are deductible. In 1994, taxpayers must reduce total itemized deductions by the lesser of 3% of AGI over $111,800 ($55,900 for married persons filing separate returns) or 80% of the itemized deductions that are otherwise allowable.[14] In 1993, the reduction amount was $108,450 ($54,225 for married individuals filing a separate return).

Example 2-2 ■

In 1994, John and Jane file a joint tax return and report AGI of $150,000. Their itemized deductions include $14,000 of medical expenses and home mortgage interest of $10,000. The AGI floor reduces the medical expense deduction to $2,750 ($14,000 − [0.075 × $150,000]). The remaining $10,000 of itemized deductions are further reduced to $8,854 ($10,000 − 0.03 × [$150,000 − $111,800]) as a result of the overall floor for itemized deductions.   ■

Standard Deduction

OBJECTIVE 2
Determine the amount allowable for the standard deduction

Itemized deductions are claimed only if the total amount of such deductions exceeds the standard deduction. The **standard deduction** is a floor set by Congress. It varies depending on the taxpayer's filing status, age, and vision.

Key Point

The dollar amount of the standard deduction generally increases each year because it is indexed to the rate of inflation.

Filing Status	Standard Deduction	
	1993	*1994*
Single individual other than heads of households	$3,700	$3,800
Married couples filing joint returns and surviving spouses	6,200	6,350
Married persons filing separate returns	3,100	3,175
Heads of households	5,450	5,600

The differences between the 1993 and 1994 amounts represent an adjustment for the increase in the cost of living.

---

[7] Sec. 213.
[8] Sec. 164.
[9] Sec. 163.
[10] Sec. 170.
[11] Sec. 165(c)(3).
[12] Sec. 67.
[13] Sec. 212.

[14] The reduction in the itemized deductions can not exceed 80% of the total itemized deductions other than medical expenses, investment interest expenses, casualty losses, and wagering losses. (See Chapter 7 for a discussion of the 80% overall limitation.)

TABLE 2-6 *Partial List of Itemized Deductions*

Medical expenses (in excess of 7.5% of adjusted gross income)
Certain taxes
    State, local, and foreign income and real property taxes
    State and local personal property taxes
Residential interest and investment interest (limited)
Charitable contributions (limited)
Casualty and theft losses (in excess of 10% of adjusted gross income)
Miscellaneous deductions (in excess of 2% of adjusted gross income)
    Employee expenses (e.g., professional and union dues, professional publications, travel,
        transportation, education, job hunting, office-in-home, special clothing, and 50% of
        entertainment expenses)
    Expenses for producing investment income (e.g., accounting and legal fees, safe deposit
        rental, fees paid to an IRA custodian)
    Tax advice and tax return preparation and related costs
Other miscellaneous deductions
    Federal estate tax attributable to income in respect of a decedent
    Gambling losses to the extent of winnings
    Amortization of bond premium
    Amounts restored under claim of right

Historical Note

Before 1989 the additional standard deductions for the elderly and for the blind were treated as additional personal exemptions, and all taxpayers were entitled to the additional personal exemptions, regardless of income. Now these additional standard deductions will not be of benefit to those higher-income taxpayers who itemize their deductions. The change has the effect of providing more benefits to lower income taxpayers.

In 1994, a married taxpayer's standard deduction is increased by $750 if he is elderly or blind ($1,500 if the taxpayer is elderly and blind) or has a spouse who is elderly or blind (for a maximum possible addition of $3,000). If an unmarried taxpayer is elderly or blind, his standard deduction is increased by $950 ($1,900 if the taxpayer is elderly and blind). Thus, in 1994, a single taxpayer age 65 is entitled to a $4,750 standard deduction.

- The increase in the standard deduction for elderly taxpayers is available if the taxpayer turns 65 during the tax year. It is interesting that, a taxpayer is considered to be age 65 on the day before his or her sixty-fifth birthday. The adjustment is allowed on the final return of a deceased taxpayer only if he or she reached age 65 prior to death.

- The Code defines blindness as corrected vision in the better eye of no better than 20/200 or a field of no greater than 20 degrees. Vision is determined as of the last day of the tax year or, in the case of a deceased taxpayer, as of the date of death.

The purpose of the standard deduction is to simplify the computation. As previously noted, for most taxpayers the standard deduction is greater than total itemized deductions. Those taxpayers do not itemize and, in fact, do not even have to keep records of medical expenses and other itemized deductions.

Who actually itemizes and who does not? Home mortgage interest and property taxes are deductible. Therefore, homeowners who pay home mortgage interest and property taxes often itemize because those expenses alone usually exceed the standard deduction. Also, higher-income taxpayers are more likely to itemize than lower-income taxpayers simply because they incur more expenses that can be itemized. This is true even though the AGI floors (previously discussed) affect higher income taxpayers more than lower income taxpayers.

Example 2-3 ■   In 1994, Joan is a single homeowner who incurs property taxes of $3,000 and mortgage interest of $2,000. Joan's adjusted gross income is $30,000. Her taxable income is computed as follows:

Adjusted gross income		$30,000
Minus: Itemized deductions:		
Property taxes	$3,000	
Mortgage interest	2,000	(5,000)
Minus: Personal exemption		(2,450)
Taxable income		$22,550

Example 2-4 ■   Assume the same facts as in Example 2-3 except that Joan is not a homeowner. Assume Joan's only deduction is for state and local taxes of $500. Her taxable income is computed as follows:

Adjusted gross income	$30,000
Minus: Standard deduction	(3,800)
Minus: Personal exemption	(2,450)
Taxable income	$23,750

Loss of the Standard Deduction. Congress has decided that a few taxpayers should not be permitted to use the standard deduction. The standard deduction is unavailable to three categories of taxpayers who would otherwise receive an unintended tax benefit. These categories are as follows:[15]

- An individual filing a return for a period less than 12 months because of a change in accounting period.
- A married taxpayer filing a separate return in instances where the other spouse itemizes.
- Nonresident aliens.

To illustrate why Congress does not permit certain taxpayers to claim the standard deduction, consider what could happen if a married couple files separate returns but only one spouse itemizes. On a separate return in 1994 when the standard deduction is $3,175, one spouse could claim all itemized deductions while the other uses the standard deduction.

Example 2-5 ■   Clay and Joy, a married couple, have incomes of $15,000 and $14,000, respectively. Their itemized deductions total $4,500. They would claim a $6,350 standard deduction on a joint return. If Clay filed a separate return and claimed all of the deductions, his itemized deductions of $4,500 would be greater than the standard deduction. If Joy could claim the standard deduction on her return, their total deductions would equal $7,675 ($4,500 + $3,175). The law, however, requires that they both itemize or that they both use the standard deduction. ■

It should be noted that an individual who is the dependent of another may not be able to claim the full amount of the standard deduction (see later discussion).

Personal Exemptions

OBJECTIVE 3

Determine the amount and the correct number of personal and dependency exemptions

In general, taxpayers cannot deduct personal expenses except for certain itemized deductions that are specifically authorized under the tax law. Congress has recognized the need to protect a small amount of income from tax in order to allow the taxpayer

[15] Sec. 63(c)(6).

Additional Comment

A taxpayer would prefer that his or her child be born on December 31 rather than on January 1 of the following year since the taxpayer would be entitled to a full additional personal exemption deduction in the earlier year.

to meet personal expenses. Thus, almost every individual taxpayer is allowed a personal exemption of $2,350 in 1993 and $2,450 in 1994. Because there are two taxpayers on a joint return filed by a married couple, there are two personal exemptions. In addition, if a married person files a separate return, the taxpayer can claim a personal exemption for his or her spouse if the spouse has no gross income during the year and the spouse is not the dependent of another taxpayer.[16]

Under current law there is only one exemption for each person. Therefore, if an individual can be claimed as a dependent by another person, that individual is not entitled to a personal exemption on his or her own return. Despite the loss of the personal exemption, most dependents owe no tax. The limitation on gross income that must be met by most dependents means they have very little income and, therefore, are able to use the standard deduction to offset any income they may have. A son or daughter who is either under 19 or a full-time student and under age 24 is, however, exempt from the gross income limitation. As a result, a dependent son or daughter may owe a tax on a small amount of income.

Example 2-6 ■

In 1994, Jim, a 20-year-old college student, received more than half his support from his parents and qualified as their dependent. Jim earned $5,000 from a summer job. Had he been self-supporting, Jim would owe no tax because the standard deduction and personal exemption would be larger than his income ($3,800 + $2,450 is greater than $5,000). Because he is a dependent, Jim must pay a tax of $180 (0.15 × [$5,000 − $3,800]). ■

Dependency Exemptions

Additional Comment

One should forsake any preconceived notions as to what constitutes a dependent before examining the dependency tests.

Key Point

For someone to be claimed as a dependent, all five dependency tests must be satisfied.

In addition to claiming one personal exemption, an individual may claim an exemption for each dependent. An individual qualifies as a dependent only if the individual meets all five of the following tests:[17]

- Support—the taxpayer must provide over 50% of the dependent's support.
- Gross income—the dependent's gross income must be less than the amount of the exemption. A taxpayer's children who are either full-time students and under age 24 or under the age of 19 are exempt from this requirement.
- Joint return—in general, a married dependent cannot file a joint return.
- Relationship—dependents must either be related to the taxpayer or reside with the taxpayer.
- Citizenship—dependents must either be U.S. citizens, residents, or nationals or reside in Canada or Mexico.

The full exemption is available for dependents who are born or die during the year. No exemption is available for unborn or stillborn children. Dependents, age one and older, must have a social security number and that number must be reported on the taxpayer's return.

Support Test. The taxpayer normally must provide over one-half of the dependent's financial support during the year. Support includes amounts spent by the taxpayer, the dependent, and other individuals. Welfare[18] and social security benefits[19] spent on support count even if they are excluded from gross income.

---

[16] Sec. 151(b).
[17] Sec. 152.
[18] Rev. Rul. 71-468, 1971-2 C.B. 115.
[19] Rev. Ruls. 57-344, 1957-2 C.B. 112, and 58-419, 1958-2 C.B. 57.

Example 2-7 ■ Tarer provided $3,000 of support for his mother, Mary. Tarer's sister provided $1,000. Mary spent $4,500 of her savings for her own support. Since Mary provided over half of her own support, she cannot be claimed as a dependent. ■

Example 2-8 ■ George's father received social security benefits of $6,600, of which $1,800 was deposited into a savings account. He spent the remaining $4,800 on food, clothing, and lodging. George spent $5,600 to support his father. George meets the support test because the amount saved is not counted in the support test. ■

Typical Misconception

There is a tendency to define "support" too narrowly. The following items have been counted as "support": recreation, Christmas presents, motion picture shows, church contributions, singing and dancing lessons, wedding apparel and accessories, etc.

Support includes amounts spent for food, clothing, shelter, medical and dental care, education, and the like.[20] Support is not limited to these items.[21] Support does not include the value of services rendered by the taxpayer to the dependent.[22] A scholarship received by a son or daughter[23] is not counted as support in deciding whether a parent provided over one half of the child's support.[24] Also, the IRS and the courts have excluded various other expenses from support.[25]

Generally, the amount of support is equal to the cost of the item, but in the case of support provided in a noncash form, such as lodging, the amount of support is equal to the fair market value or fair rental value. The cost of an item such as a television or an automobile is included in support if the item actually constitutes support.[26]

Example 2-9 ■ Vicki's mother lives with her. Vicki purchases clothing for her mother costing $800, and provides her with a room that Vicki estimates she could rent for $2,800. Vicki spent $2,500 for groceries she shared with her mother and $1,200 for utilities. In addition, Vicki purchased a television for $750 that she placed in the living room. Vicki and her mother both used the television. The support for Vicki's mother would include the $800 she spent on her clothing; the $2,800 rental value of her room; and a portion, perhaps one-half, of the $2,500 spent on groceries. Whether a portion of the utilities could be included in support would depend on whether the rental rate for the room included utilities. The fact that the mother used the television set probably would not be sufficient to cause its cost to be viewed as support. On the other hand, if the television set was a gift to the mother, was placed in her room, and was used exclusively by her, the cost would probably qualify as support. ■

If a taxpayer contributes a lump sum for the support of two or more individuals, the amount is allocated between the individuals on a pro rata basis unless there is proof to the contrary.[27]

---

[20] Reg. Sec. 1.152-1(a)(2)(i).

[21] Examples of other items that have been held to be support include church contributions (Rev. Rul. 58-67, 1958-1 C.B. 62), telephone (*William K. Price, III,* 1961 PH T.C. Memo ¶ 61,173, 20 TCM 886), medical insurance premiums (*James Edward Parker,* 1959 PH T.C. Memo ¶ 52,182, 18 TCM 800), child care (*Marvin D. Tucker,* 1957 PH T.C. Memo ¶ 57,118, 16 TCM 488), toys (*Loren S. Brumber,* 1952 PH T.C. Memo ¶ 52,087, 11 TCM 289), and vacations (*George R. Melat,* 1953 PH T.C. Memo ¶ 53,141, 12 TCM 443).

[22] *Frank Markarian v. CIR.,* 16 AFTR 2d 5785, 65-2 USTC ¶ 9699 (7th Cir., 1965).

[23] Including adopted children, stepchildren, and foster children (if the foster children live with the taxpayer for the entire year).

[24] Sec. 152(d).

[25] Examples of items that have been excluded are funeral expenses (Rev. Rul. 65-307, 1965-2 C.B. 40), taxes (Rev. Rul. 58-67, 1958-1 C.B. 62), a rifle, lawn mower, and boat insurance (*Harriet C. Flower v. U.S.,* 52 AFTR 1383, 57-1 USTC ¶ 9655 (D.C. Pa., 1957)), and life insurance premiums (*John F. Miller,* 1959 PH T.C. Memo ¶ 59,155, 18 TCM 673).

[26] Rev. Rul. 77-282, 1977-2 C.B. 52.

[27] Rev. Rul. 64-222, 1964-2 C.B. 47.

Example 2-10 ■

Jaime pays rent of $6,000 for an apartment occupied by his sisters Alice, Beth, and Cindy. Alice spends $3,000 toward her own support, Beth spends $1,000, and Cindy spends $1,000. Jaime is assumed to have provided $2,000 of support for each sister. Thus, assuming the other 4 tests are met, Jaime can claim exemptions for Beth and Cindy, but not for Alice. ■

As stated, a taxpayer normally must provide over one-half of a dependent's support. There are two exceptions:

- A multiple support declaration permits one member of a group of taxpayers who collectively provide over 50% of an individual's support to claim a dependency exemption.
- Special rules determine which parent will receive dependency exemptions for children in the case of a divorce.

Often several persons will contribute to the support of a dependent. Under normal rules no one would be able to claim a dependency exemption unless one member of the group provided over one-half of the total support. When no member of the group provides over one-half of the support, eligible members of the group may decide to allow one group member to claim the exemption. Each eligible member (other than the taxpayer receiving the exemption) must complete a Multiple Support Declaration (Form 2120) that states he or she will not claim a dependency exemption under these rules. An individual must contribute more than 10% of the dependent's support and meet all requirements for claiming a dependency exemption except the support requirement.[28]

Example 2-11 ■

John T. Abel, who resides alone, spent $400 for his own support. His daughter contributed $2,000, his son contributed $2,800, and a friend contributed $2,800. Thus, total support was $8,000. Either the son or daughter can claim a dependency exemption if the other completes Form 2120. The friend cannot claim a dependency exemption because the friend is not related and Abel does not live with the friend. For this reason the friend need not complete Form 2120. A completed Form 2120 is illustrated in Figure 2-2. ■

As noted, special rules determine which parent will receive dependency exemptions for children in the case of a divorce or separation.[29] These rules are intended to avoid disputes over who provided more than one-half of a child's support. Generally, the parent who has custody of a child for the greater part of the year is entitled to the dependency exemption even if he or she did not provide over one-half of the child's support.[30]

The noncustodial parent may claim the dependency exemption only if the custodial parent agrees in writing. The signed statement must be attached to the noncustodial parent's return each year in which the exemption is claimed. Form 8332 may be used for this purpose (see Appendix B). In the case of a divorce or separation, the custodial spouse would probably be reluctant to relinquish the dependency exemption for a child. A noncustodial parent might be able to negotiate the exemption in exchange for increased child support payments. The rule discussed above is applicable to divorces

[28] Sec. 152(c).

[29] Including adopted children, stepchildren, and foster children (if the foster children live with the taxpayer for the entire year).

[30] This assumes that together the parents provided over one-half of the support, that no multiple support agreement is in effect, that together the parents had custody of the child for over one-half of the year and that the parents were divorced, separated, or lived apart for the last half of the year (Sec. 152[e]).

Form **2120** (Rev. May 1991) Department of the Treasury Internal Revenue Service	**Multiple Support Declaration** ▶ Attach to Form 1040 or Form 1040A.	OMB No. 1545-0071 Expires 5-31-94 Attachment Sequence No. **50**

Name of taxpayer claiming person as a dependent   Gabe I. Abel   Social security number   123 45 6789

During the calendar year 19 __94__ , I paid over 10% of the support of

John T. Able
(Name of person)

I could have claimed this person as a dependent except that I did not pay over 50% of his or her support. I understand that this person is being claimed as a dependent on the income tax return of

Gabe I. Able
(Name)

111 W. Baker St. Lawrenceville, N.J. 08649
(Address)

I agree not to claim this person as a dependent on my Federal income tax return for any tax year that began in this calendar year.

Mable B. Able   222 11 0001
(Your signature)   (Your social security number)

4/15/95   402 N. Lable Lane Lawrenceville, N.J. 08649
(Date)   (Address)

1

FIGURE 2-2   Form 2120

and separations taking place after 1984 and to earlier divorces and separations if the parties agree to come under current law. In cases covered by prior law, the noncustodial parent is entitled to the dependency exemption if he or she provided at least $600 for the child's support and if the pre-1985 agreement provides that he or she is to receive the exemption.

Example 2-12 ■

In the current year, Hal and Pam obtain a divorce under the terms of which Pam receives custody of their son. Hal is ordered to pay $900 per year of child support. In absence of a written agreement to the contrary. Pam will receive the dependency exemption for the child.   ■

Example 2-13 ■

Assume the same facts as in Example 2-12 except that Pam negotiates child support payments of $1,200 per year and agrees in writing to allow Hal to claim the dependency exemption for the child. The written agreement will enable Hal to claim the dependency exemption for the child.   ■

Example 2-14 ■

In 1982, Andy and Beth obtained a divorce under the terms of which Beth received custody of their daughter. Andy pays $1,200 per year of child support under the divorce agreement, which has been in effect since 1982. The divorce decree specifies that Andy is to receive the dependency exemption. Andy is entitled to the exemption without having to obtain a new written agreement.   ■

Gross Income Test. Generally, a dependent's gross income must be less than the amount of the dependency exemption. The statutory definition of gross income is used in applying this limitation. Therefore, nontaxable scholarships, tax-exempt bond interest, and nontaxable social security benefits are not considered; but salary, taxable interest, and rent are considered in deciding whether the person meets the limitation.

A very important exception to this requirement exempts from the gross income limitation the taxpayer's children who are either under age 19 or, in the case of full-time students, under age 24.[31] A child is considered to be a student if he is in

---

[31] Including adopted children, stepchildren, and foster children (if the foster children live with the taxpayer for the entire year).

full-time attendance at a qualified educational institution during at least five months of the year. To be full time, a student must carry the number of hours or courses which the educational institution requires a student to take in order to be considered full time. Note, however, that this is only an exception to the gross income test. Therefore, a self-supporting student cannot be claimed as a dependent by his or her parents. Such a student fails the support test.

Joint Return Test. Generally, a taxpayer loses the dependency exemption if a married dependent files a joint return. However, a taxpayer is entitled to the exemption if the dependent files a joint return solely to claim a refund of tax withheld (i.e., there is no tax on the joint return and there would have been no tax on two separate returns).[32] It is important for married dependents to weigh the taxes that would be saved by the family from an exemption against the taxes that would be saved by filing a joint return. Depending on the circumstances, either alternative may be more beneficial.

Relationship Test. In order to be claimed as a dependent, a person must be related to the taxpayer or reside with the taxpayer for the entire tax year.[33] Immediate family relationships include those based on blood, adoption, and marriage, while extended family relationships include only those based on blood and adoption.

Immediate Family Relationships include:

- Parent (including adoptive parent, stepparent, mother-in-law, and father-in-law)
- Sibling (including adoptive sibling, stepbrother, stepsister, brother-in-law, sister-in-law, half brother, and half sister)
- Child (including adoptive child, stepchild, son-in-law, daughter-in-law, and foster children [who live with the taxpayer for the entire year])

Extended Family Relationships include:

- Grandparents and their ancestors
- Grandchildren and their descendants
- Aunts and uncles
- Nephews and nieces

Example 2-15 ■   Jesse supports three persons: Tina, a small child who lives with him; his cousin, Judy; and his mother Vicki. Jesse can claim two dependency exemptions: one for Tina, who lives with Jesse (a person who lives with the taxpayer need not be related) and one for his mother. Jesse cannot claim a dependency exemption for Judy (cousins are not listed as relatives). ■

On a joint return it is necessary only that a dependent be related to one spouse.[34] Once established, an immediate family relationship is not terminated by death or divorce.[35]

---

[32] Rev. Ruls. 54-567, 1954-2 C.B. 108, and 65-34, 1965-1 C.B. 86. The theory is that the taxpayer is filing a claim for refund and not actually filing a tax return.

[33] The relationship between the taxpayer and the dependent cannot violate a local law (Sec. 152[b] [5]). The exemption has been disallowed where the relationship constituted "cohabitation" and was illegal in the state (*Cassius L. Peacock, III*, 1978 PH T.C. Memo ¶ 78,030, 37 TCM 177).

[34] Reg. Sec. 1.152-2(d).

[35] Ibid.

Example 2-16 ■

Self-Study Question

Beth's mother, who is a U.S. citizen, has moved to France to spend her declining years. She has retained her U.S. citizenship, but she is now a resident of France. Is it possible for Beth to claim her mother as a dependent?

Answer

Yes, the mother need only be a U.S. citizen.

Additional Comment

The phase-out of personal and dependency exemptions for high-income taxpayers effectively raises the 36% marginal rate by 0.7% for each exemption.

Ken and Lisa support Lisa's mother and claim her as a dependent on a joint return. Following Lisa's death, Ken continues to support Lisa's mother. Lisa's mother continues to be Ken's mother-in-law and can be claimed as a dependent by Ken. On the other hand, if Ken and Lisa had been supporting Lisa's niece, Ken would not be entitled to a dependency exemption. Although she would continue to be Ken's niece, she is not his niece by blood and cannot be claimed as a dependent unless she resides with Ken.
■

Citizenship Test. A dependent must be either a U.S. citizen,[36] national,[37] resident,[38] or a resident of Canada or Mexico. The citizenship or residence test need only be met for part of the year.

Phase-Out of Personal and Dependency Exemptions. Both personal and dependency exemptions are phased out for high income taxpayers. Exemptions are phased out at a rate of 2% for each $2,500 ($1,250 for married persons filing separate returns) or fraction thereof, of adjusted gross income above thresholds shown below. Thus, more than $122,500 ($61,250 on separate returns) of adjusted gross income in excess of the threshold results in the phase-out of the entire amount of the taxpayer's personal and dependency exemptions.[39]

	Phase-out Begins	Phase-out Ends (More Than)
Single	$111,800	$234,300
Joint return	167,700	290,200
Head of household	139,750	262,750
Married, filing separately	83,850	145,100

Example 2-17 ■

In 1994 Lee, a single taxpayer with no dependents, reports AGI of $121,800. The usual amount of the personal exemption of $2,450 is reduced by 8% to $2,254. ([$10,000 ÷ $2,500 = 4] [4 × 2% = 8%])
■

Note that the phase-out begins when the taxpayer's adjusted gross income *exceeds* the threshold. Thus, a single taxpayer with AGI of $111,800 is entitled to the full amount of his personal and dependency exemptions, while a single taxpayer with AGI of $111,801 is entitled to only 98% of his personal and dependency exemptions.

The rules for deducting personal and dependency exemptions are summarized in Topic Review 2-1.

DETERMINING THE AMOUNT OF TAX

Once taxable income has been computed, the next step is to determine the gross tax. Most individuals determine the amount of gross tax by looking in the tax table

---

[36] U.S. citizens living in foreign countries can claim dependency exemptions for adopted children even if the children are not U.S. citizens.

[37] A U.S. national is an individual born in an outlying possession such as American Samoa.

[38] A resident is a person who is not a U.S. citizen and who is legally residing in the United States with intent to stay here permanently (see Sec. 7701(b)).

[39] Sec. 151(d). The thresholds are adjusted for inflation. In 1993, the phase-out began at $108,450 for single taxpayers; $162,700 for a joint return; $135,600 for a head of household; and $81,350 for a married individual filing a separate return.

(Appendix A). This allows the taxpayer to arrive at the gross tax without the need for multiplication and, therefore, simplifies the computation and reduces the number of errors. Individuals are required to use the tax table unless taxable income exceeds the maximum income in the table (currently $100,000), or if the taxpayer files a short period return on account of a change in the annual accounting period.

Those taxpayers who cannot use the tax table instead use the tax rate schedule (Appendix A). Those taxpayers using the tax rate schedule must actually compute the tax.

Example 2-18 ■   Liz is single and has taxable income of $48,210 in 1993. Liz's tax is determined by reference to the tax table for single taxpayers (Appendix A). (At the time of this writing, the 1993 tax table was the most recent available.) The tax from the table is $10,630. ■

Example 2-19 ■   Jack and Pam are married, file a joint tax return, and have taxable income of $104,850 in 1994. They will use the tax rate schedule to compute their tax. The tax is computed as follows:

Tax on $38,000 at 0.15	$ 5,700.00
Tax on next $53,850 at 0.28	15,078.00
Tax on remaining $13,000 at 0.31	4,030.00
Gross tax	$24,808.00

■

OBJECTIVE 4
Determine the filing status of individuals

Additional Comment

Former President George Bush retreated from his "No new taxes—read my lips" campaign promise in 1990 and agreed to an increase in taxes. Some feel that this played a role in his failure to win reelection.

Key Point

The highest tax rates are those for married filing separately, and the lowest are those for married filing jointly.

There are five tax brackets applicable to individual taxpayers, 15%, 28%, 31%, 36%, and 39.6%. These rates are progressive in that as a taxpayer's income increases the taxpayer moves into the higher tax brackets. The income level at which the higher tax brackets begin depends on the taxpayer's filing status. There are four schedules and tables and five different filing statuses. This is because married couples filing jointly and certain surviving spouses use the same schedule or table. The five filing statuses are:

• Joint

• Surviving spouse

• Head-of-household

• Single

• Married filing separately

Prior to 1948, one rate schedule was used by all taxpayers. If a husband and wife both had income, each filed a return. This led to inequity because the laws in various states allocated income between spouses differently.

In general, community property law allocates community income equally between a husband and wife.[40] In other states, income belongs to the spouse who produces the income. With a progressive tax system, placing income on one return instead of two can result in a much greater tax. For this reason, couples residing in noncommunity property states often paid more tax than their counterparts who resided in community property states. In 1948, Congress developed the joint-rate schedule to rectify this problem.[41] Unmarried taxpayers who headed families felt they should also receive tax relief because they shared their incomes with their families. So, in 1957 Congress

---

[40] The community property states are Arizona, California, Idaho, Louisiana, Nevada, New Mexico, Texas, Wisconsin, and Washington. What is considered to be community income varies between these states. For a more detailed discussion, see Chapter 3.

[41] Several states had either adopted or had begun to adopt community property laws in order to reduce the federal taxes paid by their residents. After the joint rate schedule was created, those states without a tradition of community property law returned to common law.

TOPIC REVIEW 2-1

Personal and Dependency Exemptions

Exemptions in General
1. One exemption is available for each taxpayer (except when the taxpayer is the dependent of another) and for each dependent.
2. The amount of each exemption, which is adjusted annually for inflation, is $2,350 in 1993 and $2,450 in 1994.
3. Exemptions are phased out for high income taxpayers. For example, on a joint return the phase-out begins when the couple's adjusted gross income exceeds $167,700 and is completed when AGI exceeds $290,200.

Dependency Exemptions
1. One exemption is allowed for each dependent. As noted above the exemptions are phased out for higher income taxpayers.
2. Five conditions must be met for each dependency exemption. The dependent (1) must be supported by the taxpayer, (2) must meet a gross income test, (3) generally must not file a joint return, (4) must be related to the taxpayer (or live with the taxpayer), and (5) must meet a citizenship or residence test.

Self-Study Question

If Congress were to adopt a truly proportional tax system, would it be necessary to have the four different tax rate schedules?

Answer

No, if there was a proportional tax system, there would be no need for different rate schedules since all taxable income would be taxed at the same rate.

created a rate schedule for heads-of-households. In 1971, single taxpayers requested and received their own rate schedule. Here we shall consider who is covered by each filing status.

Joint Return

A *joint return* can be filed by a man and woman if

- They are legally married as of the last day of the tax year.[42] Whether a couple is married depends on the laws of the state of residence.[43] Couples in the process of a divorce are still considered married prior to the date the divorce becomes final. A couple need not be living together in order to file a joint return. A joint return can be filed if one spouse dies during the year so long as the survivor does not remarry before the year end. The executor of the estate must agree to the filing of a joint return.

- They have the same tax year end (except in the case of death).[44]

- Both the husband and wife are U.S. citizens or residents.[45] An exception allows a joint return if the nonresident alien spouse agrees to report all of his income on the return.[46]

Key Point

The surviving-spouse provision entitles the taxpayer to the lower joint return tax rate schedule and to the higher joint return standard deduction.

Surviving Spouse

A widow or widower can file a joint return for the year his or her spouse dies if the widow or widower does not remarry. For either of the two years subsequent to the year of death, the widow or widower can file as a surviving spouse only if he or she meets

---

[42] Sec. 6013.

[43] Thus, common law marriages recognized by the state of residence are covered. On the other hand, an annulled marriage is viewed as never having been valid. Thus, such a couple cannot file a joint return.

[44] Sec. 6013(a)(2).

[45] Sec. 6013(a)(1).

[46] Nonresident aliens are taxed only on income earned in the United States. If a joint return is filed by a U.S. citizen and his or her foreign spouse, they would receive the benefit of the low rate schedule, even though only the U.S. citizen reported income on the return. Thus, to file a joint return, the couple must agree to report both incomes (Sec. 6013[g]).

specific conditions. The **surviving spouse** (sometimes referred to as a qualifying widow or widower) must[47]

- Have not remarried as of the year end in which surviving spouse status is claimed.
- Be a U.S. citizen or resident.
- Have qualified to file a joint return in the year of death.
- Have at least one dependent child[48] living at home during the entire year and the taxpayer must pay over half of the expenses of the home.

In the year of death, a joint return can be filed. On the joint return the income of the deceased spouse (earned prior to death) and the survivor are both reported. Personal exemptions are allowed for both spouses. In the two years following death, surviving spouse status can be claimed only if the conditions outlined above are met. Only the surviving spouse's income is reported, and, of course, no personal exemption is available for the deceased spouse. What the two situations have in common is that they both involve the use of the same tax rate schedule or tax table.

Example 2-20 ■ Connie's husband dies in 1994. Connie can file a joint return with Clay, even though he died before the year end. Alternatively, Connie can file as a married individual filing a separate return. In 1995, however, Connie must file as a single taxpayer if she has no dependent who would qualify her as a surviving spouse or a head-of-household. ■

Head-of-Household

A second rate schedule or tax table is available to a head-of-household. The head-of-household rates are significantly higher than those applicable to married taxpayers filing jointly and surviving spouses, but lower than those applicable to other single taxpayers. To claim head-of-household status, a taxpayer must[49]

- Be unmarried as of the last day of the tax year. Exceptions apply to individuals married to nonresident aliens[50] and to abandoned spouses.[51] An individual cannot claim head-of-household status in the year his or her spouse died. Such individuals must file a joint return or a separate return.
- Not be a surviving spouse.
- Be a U.S. citizen or resident.
- Pay over half of the costs of maintaining a household in which a dependent relative lives for more than half of the tax year. The dependency exemption cannot be based on a multiple support agreement. There are two special rules. First, a taxpayer with a dependent parent qualifies even if the parent does not live with the taxpayer. Second, if an unmarried descendant lives with the taxpayer,[52] that descendant need not be the taxpayer's dependent.

The second exception deserves note as it often comes into play in cases of divorced parents. As noted earlier in the chapter, a written agreement can give the dependency

Self-Study Question

Beth's 23-year-old son earns $150,000 playing for a professional baseball team. The unmarried son does not qualify as a dependent, but he does reside in Beth's home. Does Beth qualify for head-of-household status?

Answer

Yes, if an unmarried child lives with the taxpayer, the child need not be a dependent.

---

[47] Sec. 2(a).

[48] Includes an adopted child, a stepchild, or a foster child. Most often individuals are widowed late in life after children are grown. As a result, most survivors cannot claim surviving spouse status.

[49] Sec. 2(b).

[50] Specifically, this refers to an individual married to a nonresident alien if he or she meets the remaining head-of-household requirements.

[51] Abandoned spouse rules are discussed under a separate heading later in this chapter.

[52] Includes adopted child, stepchild, and a descendant of a natural or an adopted child.

exemption to the noncustodial parent. The rule here may allow the custodial parent to still claim head-of-household status.

Example 2-21 ■

> Brad and Ellen divorce. Ellen receives custody of their child, and Brad is ordered by the court to pay child support of $2,400 per year. Ellen agrees in writing to allow Brad to claim the dependency exemption for the child. If Ellen maintains the home in which she and her child live, she can claim head-of-household status even though the child is Brad's dependent. ■

As noted, the taxpayer must pay over half of the costs of maintaining the household. These expenses include property taxes, mortgage interest, rent, utility charges, upkeep and repairs, property insurance, and food consumed on the premises. Such costs do not include clothing, education, medical treatment, vacations, life insurance, transportation, or the value of services provided by the taxpayer.[53]

Single Taxpayer

An unmarried individual who does not qualify as a surviving spouse or a head-of-household must file as a single taxpayer. The tax rates are higher than those that apply to other unmarried taxpayers.

Example 2-22 ■

Additional Comment

In 1991 approximately 30 married couples filed joint returns for every married couple that filed separately.

> Becky, a single taxpayer with no dependents, files her first tax return. She will file as a single taxpayer. ■

Married Filing a Separate Return

Married individuals who choose to file separate returns use the separate rate schedule. The rates on this schedule are higher than other individual rate schedules. Also, some married couples, such as couples with different tax years, cannot file a joint return and must file separately. The implications of joint returns versus separate returns are discussed later in this chapter.

Example 2-23 ■

Key Point

Several disadvantages are associated with the filing of separate returns by married individuals. For example, a taxpayer may lose all or part of the benefits of the deduction for individual retirement accounts, the child care credit, and the earned income credit. These topics will be studied in more detail later in this textbook.

> On December 31, Rose marries Joe. Since they were married before the year ended, they may elect to file jointly. Alternatively, they may file separate returns with each using the rate schedule applicable to separate returns. ■

The filing requirements for individuals are summarized in Topic Review 2-2.

Abandoned Spouse

Which rate schedule a taxpayer uses can have a great impact on the amount of tax. Without any special rule, an abandoned spouse would be required to file using the rate schedules for married persons filing separately. Congress has provided relief for taxpayers in this situation if they can meet certain conditions. A married individual can claim head-of-household status if[54]

- The taxpayer lived apart from his spouse for the last 6 months of the year.
- The taxpayer pays over half of the cost of maintaining a household in which the taxpayer and a dependent son or daughter live for over half of the year.[55]

[53] Reg. Sec. 1.2-2(d).
[54] Sec. 2(c).
[55] Includes adopted child, stepchild, and foster child.

TOPIC REVIEW 2-2

Filing Status and Requirements					
Filing Status	Must Maintain Household	Must Have Dependent	Marital Status	Must Be Citizen	Tax Rates
Joint	No requirement	No	Married	Yes	Lowest rates, but two incomes are included
Surviving spouse	Yes	Yes, son or daughter	Widowed in prior or second prior year	Yes	Uses same schedule as married couple filing joint return
Head of household	Yes	Generally, yes	Generally, single	Yes	Intermediate tax rates
Single	No requirement	No	Single	No	Highest tax rates for unmarried taxpayers
Separate	No requirement	No	Married	No	Highest tax rates

• The taxpayer is a U.S. citizen or resident.

The requirement that the taxpayer has a dependent child is met if a taxpayer who is otherwise qualified to claim the child as a dependent signs an agreement that allows the child's noncustodial parent to claim the dependency exemption for the child.[56]

Example 2-24 ■   Late in the year, Bob and Gail decide to separate. Gail supports their children after the separation and pays the costs of maintaining their home. Gail cannot claim abandoned spouse status, because Bob lived with her for over one-half of the year. If she had obtained a divorce before the end of the year, she could have filed as a head-of-household. In the absence of a divorce, Gail can file a separate return, or if they both agree, Bob and Gail may file a joint return. ■

Example 2-25 ■   Assume the same facts as in Example 2-24 except that Gail continues to support her children and pay household expenses during the next year. She can file as a head-of-household even if she has not obtained a divorce. ■

Key Point

When one thinks of a person who would qualify as an abandoned spouse, one thinks of a person in dire financial condition. If no relief was granted, this person would be required to use the married filing separately tax rate schedule, which contains the highest rates.

Dependents with Unearned Income

In the past, taxpayer's in high tax brackets were able to reduce their tax liability by shifting income to children and other dependents. Under prior law there was no tax due if the income was less than the dependent's personal exemption and standard deduction. Even if the shifted income was greater than these amounts, there was a tax savings if the dependent was in a low tax bracket. Under current law three rules apply that minimize the advantages of shifting income to dependents. These rules are:

---

[56] Sec. 152(e).

- Dependents do not receive a personal exemption on their own returns.

- A dependent's standard deduction is reduced to the greater of the dependent's earned income (such as salary) or $600 (also $600 in 1993).

- The tax on the net unearned income (such as dividends and interest) of a child under age 14 is figured by reference to the parents' tax rate if it is higher than the child's.

Key Point

Children under age 14 will not have their unearned income taxed at their parents' tax rate until their unearned income exceeds $1,200.

Under this last rule, the first $600 of unearned income can be offset by the standard deduction, the second $600 of unearned income is taxed at the child's own tax rate, but any remaining unearned income is taxed at the parents' tax rate.

Example 2-26 ■ In 1994, Tim is a self-supporting 18-year-old who received $2,000 of dividends and $900 from a part-time summer job. He is entitled to the full standard deduction and a personal exemption. Because these deductions exceed his income, Tim owes no tax. ■

Example 2-27 ■ Assume the same facts as in Example 2-26 except that Tim is a dependent of his parents, and they are in the 28% tax bracket. Because Tim is a dependent, he is not entitled to a personal exemption. Tim's standard deduction is limited to the greater of $600 or earned income (but not more than $3,800). Since his earned income is $900, the standard deduction is also $900. Therefore, Tim's taxable income is $2,000 ($2,900 AGI − $900 standard deduction). Because Tim is over age 13, his regular tax rate (15%) is used. The tax is $300 (0.15 × $2,000). ■

Example 2-28 ■ Assume the same facts as in Example 2-27 except that Tim is age 13. His standard deduction is still $900, and his taxable income is also $2,000. The first $600 of Tim's unearned income is offset by the standard deduction, the second $600 is taxed at Tim's own rate of 15%, and the remaining $800 of unearned income is taxed at his parents' 28% rate. The remaining $300 of Tim's standard deduction reduces earned income to $600 which is taxed at Tim's rate of 15%.

	Amount −	Standard Deduction =	Taxable ×	Tax Rate =	Tax
Unearned income					
First $600	$600	$600	$ 0	0%	$ 0
Second $600	600		600	15	90
Remainder taxed at the parents' rate	800		800	28	224
Earned income	900	300	600	15	90
Total	$2,900	$900	$2,000		$404

■

In figuring the tax where the parents file separate returns, the tax rate of the parent with the greater taxable income is used. If the parents are divorced, the parent with custody is the relevant parent.

Parents of a child under age 14 may elect to include the child's dividend and interest income on their own return.[57] This rule eliminates the need to file a tax return for the child. To be eligible for the election, the child's gross income must come solely from dividends and interest, and such income must not exceed $5,000. Further, there

---

[57] Sec. 1(g)(7).

can be no withholding or estimated payment using the child's social security number.[58]

CORPORATE TAX FORMULA AND RATES

OBJECTIVE 5

Explain the tax formula for corporations

The corporate tax formula and rates are discussed here to provide basic information needed for subsequent chapters. A more comprehensive discussion of corporate tax provisions is included in Chapter 16. Corporations are divided into two groups. **C corporations,** also called **regular corporations,** are treated as separate entities for tax purposes. Individuals are taxed on dividends they receive from C corporations but are not taxed on the corporation's undistributed income. The second group, **S corporations,** generally are not treated as separate entities for tax purposes. Thus, each S corporation shareholder is required to report a pro rata share of the S corporation's income on his tax return even if the income is not distributed. The shareholders must elect to be covered by the S corporation rules. Corporations must also meet a series of conditions, such as having 35 or fewer shareholders, before they can elect S corporation status. The detailed rules for S corporations are covered later in this volume.

The tax formula for C corporations is presented in Table 2-7. The major difference between the formula for an individual taxpayer and a corporate taxpayer is the fact that there is only one category of deductions for corporations. Personal expenses do not come into consideration. Therefore, there are no itemized deductions, standard deductions, or personal exemptions. The tax rates applicable to C corporations are as follows:[59]

Additional Comment

In 1990 there were 3.7 million corporation tax returns filed, of which 1,575,000 returns were from S corporations.

Key Point

The tax formula for C corporations differs from the tax formula for individuals in several important respects. The corporate tax formula does not contain an Adjusted Gross Income figure, personal and dependency exemptions, or the standard deduction.

TABLE 2-7 Tax Formula for C Corporations

Income from whatever source derived	$xxx,xxx
Minus: Exclusions	(xxx)
Gross income	$ xx,xxx
Minus: Deductions	(xxx)
Taxable income	$ x,xxx
Times: Tax rates	× .xx
Gross tax	$ xx
Minus: Credits and prepayments	(x)
Net tax payable or refund due	$ xx

Taxable Income	Tax
First $50,000	15% of taxable income
Over $50,000, but not over $75,000	$7,500 + 25% of taxable income over $50,000

[58] Parents use Form 8814, Parents' Election to Report Child's Interest and Dividends. Because of a drafting error in the law, the amounts used in the computation are not adjusted for inflation in the same manner as applies to children who report income on their own returns. If the child's income from dividends and interest is between $500 and $1,000, the child's tax is 15% of the income over $500. If the income is over $1,000, the tax is computed by multiplying the parents' tax rate times the child's income over $1,000 and adding $75. For example, if the child's dividend income is $2,000 and the parents' tax bracket is 28%, the tax is $355 (0.28 × [$2,000 − $1,000] + $75).

[59] Income of certain personal service corporations is taxed at a flat rate of 35%.

Taxable Income	Tax
Over $75,000, but not over $100,000	$13,750 + 34% of taxable income over $75,000
Over $100,000, but not over $335,000	$22,250 + 39% of taxable income over $100,000
Over $335,000, but not over $10,000,000	$113,900 + 34% of taxable income over $335,000
Over $10,000,000, but not over $15,000,000	$3,400,000 + 35% of taxable income over $10,000,000
Over $15,000,000, but not over $18,333,333	$5,150,000 + 38% of taxable income over $15,000,000
Over $18,333,333	$6,416,667 + 35% of taxable income over $18,333,333

In one sense, there is no formula to compute an S corporation's taxable income because the corporation normally does not pay a tax. S corporations do file returns. A residual income total, known as ordinary income, is computed on the return. Special items, such as capital gains and losses and charitable contributions, are kept separate from the ordinary income amount. This is because every item that would receive special treatment on a shareholder's return is passed through to the shareholder with its status intact. Each shareholder reports his or her share of the ordinary income and his or her share of each special item. Losses pass through and can be deducted by shareholders up to their respective bases in the corporation's stock. This assumes that the shareholder meets the material participation requirement discussed in Chapter 8.

TREATMENT OF CAPITAL GAINS AND LOSSES

OBJECTIVE 6

Explain the basic concepts of property transactions

Historical Note

Net capital gains reported on individual income tax returns dropped from nearly $300 billion in 1986 to about $133 billion in 1987. The latter amount was more in line with 1984 and 1985. The large amount reported in 1986 was due to the fact that a 60% long-term capital gain deduction was available to individuals in 1986, but was repealed as of December 31, 1986. Many taxpayers sold capital assets to take advantage of the lower effective rates that existed in 1986.

Capital gains and losses have been accorded special tax treatment since 1922. Today, however, the primary advantage accorded such gains is that they are not subject to the highest tax rates for individuals (i.e., 31%, 36%, or 39.6%). This preferential treatment is available only to long-term capital gains (discussed below). As a result, individual taxpayers who are in the 31% tax bracket or higher who realize long-term capital gains pay a 28% tax on such gains. Other types of income (e.g., salaries and wages, dividends, interest, and net short-term capital gains) are subject to the regular tax rates. Net long-term capital gains realized by individuals who are in the 15% and 28% tax brackets are taxed at the same rates as their other income.

On the other hand, individuals who suffer net capital losses can deduct only up to $3,000 of the losses from other income. The special rules that apply to property transactions are discussed in detail in Chapters 5, 12, and 13. Nevertheless, a brief introduction to the treatment of gains and losses from the sale or exchange of property is appropriate at this point.

Definition of Capital Assets

A purpose of the rules applicable to capital gains and losses is to distinguish capital appreciation from those gains attributable to ordinary business transactions and speculation. A **capital gain** or **loss** is the gain or loss from the sale or exchange of a capital asset. Unfortunately, the Code merely defines what does not constitute a capital asset. In other words, **capital assets** are assets other than those listed in Sec. 1221. A detailed discussion of the definition is found in Chapter 5. Here we simply note the major categories of properties included on the list and that are thereby excluded from capital asset status. The major categories are: inventory, trade receivables, certain properties created by the efforts of the taxpayer (such as works of art), depreciable business property and business land, and certain government publications. As was noted, a purpose of the rules applicable to capital gains and losses is to distinguish capital appreciation from gains derived from ordinary business operations. Thus, the profit from the sale of inventory and trade receivables is viewed as business profit as opposed to capital appreciation. Similarly, a gain realized by an artist on the sale of one of his or her own works is ordinary income from personal services where a capital gain or loss results if an investor in art sells a painting that was held as an investment.

Depreciable business property and business land are also excluded from capital asset status. These properties are given their own special status and referred to as **Sec. 1231 assets.** The various **Sec. 1231 gains and losses** realized by a taxpayer are netted. If the result is a net gain, that net gain is normally treated as a long-term capital gain. If the result is a net loss, the loss is treated as an ordinary loss. This process is complicated by the fact that other rules can come into play.[60] Under certain circumstances, these rules require taxpayers to report some ordinary income, instead of Sec. 1231 gains.

The major categories of gains are summarized as follows:

Capital gains	Gains attributable to the sale or exchange of appreciated investments (such as stocks and bonds), personal use property (such as a coin collection or personal residence), and certain business property (such as goodwill or a patent).
Sec. 1231 gains	Certain gains attributable to the sale or exchange of depreciable business property and business realty.
Ordinary gains	Gains attributable to the sale or exchange of inventory, trade receivables, certain property created by the taxpayer (such as a painting or musical composition), and certain government publications. May include a portion of the gain attributable to depreciable business property.

Netting Process

As noted, one purpose of the capital gains rules is to distinguish between gains attributable to capital appreciation and gains attributable to speculation. In an effort to do this, the tax laws divide capital gains and losses into long-term capital gains and losses (LTCG and LTCL) and short-term capital gains and losses (STCG and STCL). **Long-term capital gains** and **losses** are those gains and losses attributable to the sale or exchange of a capital asset held for over one year. **Short-term capital gains** and **losses** are those gains and losses attributable to the sale or exchange of a capital asset held for one year or less.

Tax Treatment of Net Gains and Losses

Taxpayers add together LTCGs and LTCLs. STCGs and STCLs are also netted. This leaves two amounts, either a net LTCG or LTCL and a net STCG or STCL. What happens at this point depends on the relative size of the two amounts and whether they are gains or losses. For now, it is perhaps essential only that you understand the following facts:

- Individuals are taxed on the excess of net capital gain over net capital loss. A net STCG (in excess of any net LTCL) is taxed at the same rates as any other

---

[60] See, for example, Secs. 1245 and 1250.

income. A net LTCG (in excess of any net STCL) is not subject to the 31%, 36%, or 39.6% tax brackets (i.e., the maximum tax rate for the net capital gain portion of taxable income of individuals is 28%).

• Individuals with net capital losses may deduct no more than $3,000 of such losses in any year. A net capital loss in excess of $3,000 can be carried over and offset against future capital gains or, subject to the $3,000 limitation, deducted from other income.

TAX PLANNING CONSIDERATIONS

Shifting Income Between Family Members

Because of the progressive tax system, families can often reduce their taxes by **shifting income** to family members who are in lower tax brackets.

Example 2-29 ■   Mary, who is in the 36% tax bracket, shifted $5,000 of income to her 22-year-old son, Steve, who suffered a business loss. In absence of the shift, 36% of the income would have gone for taxes. There is no tax on Steve's return because the income is offset by his loss. ■

Example 2-30 ■   Farouk, who is in the 36% tax bracket, shifted $2,000 of income to his 18-year-old daughter, Dana, who is in the 15% tax bracket. The tax savings from the shift is $420 [0.36 × $2,000] − [0.15 × $2,000]. ■

Additional Comment

All 50 states have enacted laws that simplify the procedures for making gifts to minors. This type of law, which in most states is called the "Uniform Gifts to Minors Act," is especially important when making gifts of securities.

As noted earlier in this chapter, the net unearned income of children under the age of 14 is taxed at their parents' tax rate. Hence, a shifting of income to young children is often an ineffective method of minimizing tax.

Shifting income must be distinguished from assigning income. Earned income is taxed to the person who produces it. Income from property is taxed to the person who owns the property. Ordering income to be paid to another is an assignment of income that does not change who is taxed on the income. Normally, in the case of income from property, ownership of the property must be transferred in order to shift the income.

Example 2-31 ■   John owns stock in Valley Corporation. John orders the corporation to pay this year's dividends to his daughter. John will be taxed on the income even though he has assigned it to another. ■

Example 2-32 ■   Kay owns stock in Valley Corporation. Kay gives the stock to her 17-year-old son. Future dividends on Valley stock will be taxed to the son instead of to Kay. ■

Individuals are often unwilling to give property away completely. As a result, personal preference may limit the amount of tax planning that is possible.

Splitting Income

Splitting income consists of creating additional taxable entities, especially corporations, in order to reduce an individual's effective tax rate.

Example 2-33 ■

Tom is a taxpayer in the 36% tax bracket who is involved in a variety of businesses. One business has been producing $20,000 of income per year for several years. Tom incorporates the business. The first $50,000 of a corporation's income is taxed at a 15% rate. Thus, the tax on the income is reduced by $4,200 ([0.36 × $20,000] − [0.15 × $20,000]). ■

Key Point

The ability to maximize itemized deductions by the timing of expenditures is somewhat limited. The two most significant items that would lend themselves to such a strategy would be property taxes and charitable contributions. Prepaid interest is not deductible until accrued.

The creation of a new entity to split income is not always desirable because a corporation's income will be taxed to the shareholder as a dividend if it is distributed. In addition, if income is allowed to accumulate in a corporation indefinitely, it may be subject to the accumulated earnings tax.[61]

Maximizing Itemized Deductions

Timing expenditures properly can often increase deductions. In general, cash-basis taxpayers deduct expenses in the year paid. If itemized deductions are less than the standard deduction, the taxpayer will receive no tax benefit from the deductions. A taxpayer in that situation could defer some payments or accelerate others to maximize expenses in one year, thereby creating a sufficient amount of deductions in that year.

Example 2-34 ■

Jean's property taxes are due on January 1 of each year. Jean is a single, cash-basis, calendar-year taxpayer. Itemized deductions other than property taxes total $2,000 in each year. Jean pays the 1994 property taxes of $1,200 on January 1, 1994, and the 1995 property taxes of $1,200 on December 31, 1994. In the absence of "doubling up," Jean would not have been able to itemize in either year. The itemized deductions of $3,200 ($2,000 + $1,200) would be less than the standard deduction of $3,800. By doubling up, Jean has itemized deductions of $4,400 ($2,000 + $1,200 + $1,200) in 1994. ■

Medical expenses are deductible only to the extent they exceed 7.5% of a taxpayer's AGI. In situations where medical expenses are just under 7.5% of AGI, taxpayers may be able to create a deduction by doubling up.

Example 2-35 ■

Troy's AGI is $20,000. So far in 1994, Troy's medical expenses have totaled $1,300. Troy has received a bill from his dentist for $500 which is due January 15, 1995. By paying the bill in 1994, Troy will have a deduction for medical expenses of $300 ($1,300 + $500 − [0.075 × $20,000]). This assumes that Troy's other itemized deductions exceed the standard deduction.[62] ■

Filing Joint or Separate Returns

Factors to Be Considered. In general, married couples may file either joint or separate returns. As noted earlier, if one spouse has significantly more than half of their combined income, filing separately will increase the couple's total income tax. Because of the potential tax saving from a joint return and because it is simpler to prepare one return instead of two, most married couples file jointly.

It should be noted that the joint return is not always preferred. Separate returns may result in increased deductions. Since only one spouse's income is reported on a

Additional Comment

In some states in the U.S., a married couple will be able to lower their total state income taxes by filing separately. If they file separately for state tax purposes, they must also file separately for federal income tax purposes. In many cases where the spouses have approximately equal incomes, the slightly higher federal income tax will be more than offset by the tax savings on the state income tax returns.

---

[61] Amounts accumulated in a corporation in excess of $250,000 may be subject to this tax. However, amounts accumulated for business purposes are exempt.

[62] For a discussion of restrictions on the deductibility of prepaid medical expenses see Chapter 7.

separate return, medical expenses are more likely to exceed the 7.5% of adjusted gross income floor if one spouse incurs most of the medical expenses. Similarly, casualty losses involving personal-use assets, which are allowable only to the extent they exceed 10% of AGI, may be deductible on separate returns.

Probably the most significant impact of the joint return is the joint income tax liability. Both the husband and wife are liable for taxes owed on a joint return. This could be a major problem in situations if a couple separates or divorces after filing a return.

Example 2-36 ■

Jim and Pat file a joint return. They are both informed as to the relevant information pertaining to the return. The next year they separate, and Jim moves out of town without leaving a forwarding address. The IRS audits their joint return and disallows $400 of charitable contributions deducted on the original return. Pat may be held responsible for the additional taxes owed. The IRS does not have to attempt to locate Jim in order to collect the tax. In this instance, it would make little difference who made the error on the return. ■

Ethical Point

Because innocent spouse rules are strict, it may sometimes be safer to file a separate return than run the risk of being held responsible for the acts of another.

Innocent Spouse Provision. Generally, each spouse is liable for the entire tax and any penalties imposed when they file a joint return.[63] This is true even if all of the income was earned by one spouse. This rule could prove unfair in some instances, especially where one spouse concealed information from the other. For that reason, the Code contains an **innocent spouse** provision. An innocent spouse is relieved of the liability for tax on unreported income if[64]

- The amount is attributable to grossly erroneous items of the other spouse.

- There is a substantial understatement of tax attributable to the item.

- The innocent spouse did not know and had no reason to know that there was such an understatement of tax.

- Under the circumstances, it would be inequitable to hold the innocent spouse liable for the understatement.

Example 2-37 ■

Dan and Joy file a joint return. Dan traveled much of the time and Joy had little information as to his whereabouts or income. Joy worked and her own salary was the sole source of her support. Their return was audited by the IRS. The audit disclosed that Dan had not reported income from a job he had held for several months during the year. The salary represented a substantial portion of the combined gross income that should have been reported on the return. In this situation, Joy may be able to avail herself of the innocent spouse provision in order to avoid being held liable for the tax on the unreported income. ■

Electing to Change to a Joint Return. In general, a husband and wife who file separate returns for a given year may elect to change to a joint return by filing an amended joint return.[65] This change is permitted after the due date but must be within three years of the due date including extensions.[66] Taxpayers may not change from a joint return to separate returns after the due date.[67]

---

[63] Sec. 6013(d)(3).
[64] Sec. 6013(e).
[65] Sec. 6013(b).
[66] Sec. 6013(b)(2)(B).
[67] Reg. Sec. 1.6013-1(a). However, a couple who filed a joint return whose marriage is later annulled must file amended returns as singles (Rev. Rul. 76-255, 1976-2 C.B. 40).

COMPLIANCE AND PROCEDURAL CONSIDERATIONS

Who Must File

Whether or not an individual must file a tax return is based on the amount of the individual's gross income.[68] The fact that the individual owes no tax does not mean that a return need not be filed. The gross income filing levels are[69]

Additional Comment

The IRS is encouraging nonfilers (i.e., both individuals and businesses who should have filed previous tax returns but did not) to come forward. The IRS estimates that there were 6 million nonfilers in 1990 alone.

	1994	*1993*
Single	$ 6,250	$ 6,050
Single (65 or over)	7,200	6,950
Married, filing jointly	11,250	10,900
Married, filing jointly (one spouse 65 or over)	12,000	11,600
Married, filing jointly (both 65 or over)	12,750	12,300
Surviving spouse	8,800	8,550
Surviving spouse (65 or over)	9,750	9,450
Married, filing separately	2,450	2,350
Married, living separately from spouse at year end	2,450	2,350
Head of household	8,050	7,800
Head of household (65 or over)	9,000	8,700

There are three situations where taxpayers must file even if the gross income is less than the amounts shown above:

Additional Comment

The IRS is required to impound tax refunds to help other agencies collect overdue student loans, child support, etc. However, the IRS found that people whose refunds were offset in 1985 and 1986 were far more likely than others to file no returns in the next two years or to file returns without paying all they owed.

- Taxpayers who receive advance payments of the earned income credit (see Chapter 14) must file regardless of their income levels.

- Taxpayers with net self-employment income of $400 or more must file regardless of their total gross income.

- Taxpayers who can be claimed as a dependent by another must file if they have either (1) unearned income over $600 or (2) total gross income in excess of the standard deduction.

In general, taxpayers must file if their gross income equals or exceeds the total of the standard deduction (including the additional standard deduction due to age but not blindness) and personal exemption. The blindness allowance and dependency exemptions are not considered. If the disallowance of the standard deduction rules apply, the standard deduction is ignored in determining whether taxpayers must file.

Example 2-38 ■ In 1994, Carol is a single, self-supporting taxpayer with no dependents. Carol must file if her gross income is $6,250 or greater ($3,800 + $2,450). ■

---

[68] Gross income has its usual meaning except that the gain excluded from the sale of a personal residence and excluded foreign earned income are included (Sec. 6012[c]).

[69] Sec. 6012(a)(1).

Due Dates for Filing Return

An individual taxpayer must file on or before the fifteenth day of the fourth month following the close of his or her tax year.[70] For calendar-year taxpayers, this is April 15. If the due date falls on a Saturday, Sunday, or a legal holiday, the due date is the next day that is not a Saturday, Sunday, or holiday.[71]

An automatic four-month extension of time to file is given to taxpayers who file Form 4868 by the due date for the return. This is an extension to file the return and not an extension of the time to pay the tax. The taxpayer must estimate the amount of tax due and pay it with Form 4868.[72]

Use of Forms 1040, 1040EZ, and 1040A

The primary individual tax return is Form 1040. Complicated returns often involve many additional forms and schedules. Two shorter forms are available to taxpayers with less complicated tax returns. Form 1040EZ is available to single taxpayers and married individuals who file a joint return. Such taxpayers must have taxable income of less than $50,000 and claim no dependents. To use Form 1040EZ, the taxpayer's income must consist of salary and wages plus no more than $400 of taxable interest income. No deductions (other than the standard deduction) or credits (other than withholding from salary and wages) can be taken on the return.

Form 1040A is available to taxpayers who have somewhat more involved returns. Form 1040A can be used by taxpayers claiming any number of exemptions or any filing status (other than surviving spouse). Salary, wages, dividends, interest, pension and annuity income, and unemployment compensation can be reported on Form 1040A. Taxpayers may deduct IRA contributions. Taxpayers may also claim credits for withholding, child care, and earned income.

Systems for Reporting Income

There is a significant and expanding relationship between computers, tax returns, the taxpayer identification system, and information returns. The IRS keeps records based on taxpayer identification numbers. Individual taxpayers report information based on social security numbers, while employer identification numbers (EIN) are used by corporations, other taxpayers, and tax-exempt entities. Individuals who employ others have both a social security number and an employer identification number.

Employers, banks, stockbrokers, savings and loans, and so on, report payments they make to others along with the payee's identification number. Today, the IRS computers match much of the reported information with tax returns, using the taxpayer identification number as the cross-reference. The need for accurate information returns is obvious. Some major information returns are listed below:

Basic Form	Type of Payment	Required if Amount Equals or Exceeds
1099-R	Pensions and annuities	$600
W-2	Salary, wages, etc.	600
1099-DIV	Dividends	10
1099-INT	Interest	600[73]
1099-B	Sale of security	All
1099-G	Unemployment compensation, tax refunds, etc.	10
1099-MISC	Rent, royalties, etc.	600
1099-R	Total lump-sum distributions from retirement plans	600[74]

[70] Sec. 6072(a).
[71] Sec. 7503.
[72] Reg. Sec. 1.6081-4(a)(1)-(5).
[73] For banks and corporations the amount is $10.
[74] Except that all IRA distributions must be reported.

This information-reporting system makes it more difficult for taxpayers to avoid IRS detection if they omit income from their returns.

PROBLEM MATERIALS

DISCUSSION QUESTIONS

2-1. What are the components of the formula for computing an individual taxpayer's taxable income?

2-2. Explain the distinction between income and gross income.

2-3. Explain the distinction between an exclusion and a deduction.

2-4. a. Explain the distinction between a deduction and a credit.
b. Which is worth more, a $10 deduction or a $10 credit?
c. Explain the difference between refundable and nonrefundable credits.

2-5. List the five conditions that must be met in order to claim a dependency exemption. Briefly explain each one.

2-6. a. Briefly explain the concept of support.
b. If a taxpayer provides 50% or less of another person's support, is it possible for the taxpayer to claim a dependency exemption? Explain.
c. Does support include the value of an automobile? Explain.

2-7. What are the two types of deductions *from* adjusted gross income?

2-8. Under what circumstances must a taxpayer use a rate schedule instead of a tax table?

2-9. a. What determines who must file a tax return?
b. Is an individual required to file a tax return if he owes no tax?

2-10. What conditions must be met by a taxpayer who wishes to claim head-of-household status?

2-11. What conditions must be met by a taxpayer who wishes to file as a surviving spouse?

2-12. What is the normal due date for the return of a calendar-year individual taxpayer? What happens to the due date if it falls on a Saturday, Sunday, or holiday?

2-13. Why are there five filing statuses but only four rate schedules?

2-14. Explain the meaning of the term *relative* as it is used in connection with the dependency exemption.

2-15. Can tax-exempt income qualify as support? Explain.

2-16. Can a scholarship qualify as support?

2-17. Explain the purpose of the multiple support agreement.

2-18. Summarize the rules that explain which parent receives the dependency exemption for children in cases of divorce.

2-19. What conditions must be met by a married couple before they can file a joint return?

2-20. Explain what is meant by the phrase "maintain a household."

2-21. Under what circumstances, if any, can a married person file as a head-of-household?

2-22. a. Explain the principal difference in the tax treatment of an S corporation and a C corporation.
b. Why would a C corporation be used if an S corporation is generally exempt from tax?

2-23. a. What assets are excluded from capital asset status?
    b. Are capital gains given favorable tax treatment?
    c. What is the significance of an asset being classified as a capital asset?

2-24. What is "Sec. 1231 property"?

2-25. Is there any tax advantage for an individual who has held an appreciated capital asset for 11 months to delay the sale of the asset? Explain.

2-26. a. Explain the difference between income splitting and income shifting.
    b. Why are taxpayers interested in shifting income from one tax return to another within the same family or economic unit?
    c. Is there a relationship between the kiddie tax and taxpayers who attempted to shift income?

2-27. a. Who is liable for additional taxes on a joint return?
    b. Why is this so important?

2-28. What conditions must be met in order to take advantage of the innocent spouse provision?

2-29. Can couples change from joint returns to separate returns? Separate to joint?

PROBLEMS

2-30. *Computation of Tax.* The following information relates to two married couples:

	Lanes	Waynes
Salary (earned by one spouse)	$20,000	$108,000
Taxable interest income	1,000	5,000
IRA contribution	2,000	0
Itemized deductions	8,000	7,000
Exemptions	4,900	4,900
Withholding	900	22,000

Compute the 1994 tax due or refund due for each couple. Assume that the itemized deductions have been reduced by the applicable floors.

2-31. *Dependency Exemptions.* Anna, age 65, who lives with her unmarried son, Mario, received $7,000, which was used for her support during the year. The sources of support were as follows:

Social Security benefits	$1,500
Mario	2,600
Caroline, an unrelated friend	800
Doug, Anna's son	500
Elaine, Anna's sister	1,600
Total	$7,000

a. Who might be able to claim Anna as a dependent?
b. What must be done before Mario can claim the exemption?
c. Can anyone claim head-of-household status based on Anna's dependency exemption? Explain.
d. Can Mario claim an old age allowance for his mother? Explain.

2-32. *Computation of Taxable Income.* The following information for 1994 relates to Tom, a single taxpayer, aged 18:

Salary	$1,800
Interest income	1,600
Itemized deductions	600

a. Compute Tom's taxable income assuming he is self-supporting.
b. Compute Tom's taxable income assuming he is a dependent of his parents.

2-33. *Joint Versus Separate Returns.* Carl and Carol have salaries of $14,000 and $22,000, respectively. Their itemized deductions total $5,000. They are married and both are under age 65.

    a. Compute their taxable income assuming they file jointly.

    b. Compute their taxable income assuming they file separate returns and that Carol claims all of the itemized deductions.

2-34. *Joint Versus Separate Returns.* Hal attended school much of 1994, during which time he was supported by his parents. Hal married Ruth in December 1994. Hal graduated and commenced work in 1995. Ruth worked during 1994 and earned $18,000. Hal's only income was $800 of interest. Hal's parents are in the 28% tax bracket. Thus, claiming Hal as a dependent would save them $686 (0.28 × $2,450) of taxes.

    a. Compute Hal and Ruth's gross tax if they file a joint return.

    b. Compute Ruth's gross tax if she files a separate return in order to allow Hal's parents to claim him as a dependent.

    c. Which alternative would be better for the family? In other words, will filing a joint return save Hal and Ruth more than $686?

2-35. *Dependency Exemption—Divorced Parents.* Joe and Joan divorce during the current year. Joan receives custody of their three children. Joe agrees to pay $1,000 of child support for each child.

    a. Assuming there is no written agreement, who will receive the dependency exemption for the children? Explain.

    b. Would it make any difference if Joe could prove that he provided over one-half of the support for each child?

2-36. *Filing Status and Dependency Exemptions.* For the following taxpayers, indicate which tax form should be used, the applicable filing status, and the number of personal and dependency exemptions available.

    a. Arnie is a single college student who earned $5,000 working part time. He had $200 of interest income and received $1,000 of support from his parents.

    b. Buddy is a single college student who earned $5,000 working part time. He had $600 of interest income and received $1,000 of support from his parents.

    c. Cindy is divorced and received $6,000 of alimony from her former husband and earned $12,000 working as a secretary. She also received $1,800 of child support for her son. According to a written agreement, her former husband is entitled to receive the dependency exemption.

    d. Debbie is a widow, age 68, who receives a pension of $8,000, nontaxable social security benefits of $8,000, and interest of $4,000. She has no dependents.

    e. Edith is married, but her husband left her two years ago, and she has not seen him since. Edith supported herself and her daughter, aged 6. She paid all household expenses. Her income of $16,000 consisted of a salary of $15,200 and interest of $800.

2-37. *Marriage and Taxes.* Bill and Mary plan to marry in December, 1994. Bill's salary is $32,000 and he owns his own residence. His itemized deductions total $9,000. Mary's salary is $36,000. Her itemized deductions total only $1,600 as she does not own her own residence. For purposes of this problem, assume 1995 tax rates, exemptions, and standard deductions are the same as 1994.

    a. What will their tax be if they marry before year end and file a joint return?

    b. What will their combined taxes be for the year if they delay the marriage until 1995?

    c. What factors contribute to the difference in taxes?

2-38. *Dependency Exemptions.* How many dependency exemptions are the following taxpayers entitled to, assuming the persons involved are U.S. citizens?

    a. Andrew supports his cousin Mary, who does not live with him. Mary has no income and is single.

    b. Bob and his wife are filing a joint return. Bob provided over one-half of his father's support. The father received social security benefits of $6,000 and taxable interest income of $800. The father is single and does not live with them.

    c. Clay provides 60% of his single daughter's support. She earned $2,600 while attending school during the year as a full-time student. She is 22 years old.

    d. Dave provided 30% of his mother's support, and she provided 55% of her own support. Dave's brother provided the remainder. The brother agreed to sign a multiple support agreement.

2-39. *Filing Requirement.* Which of the following taxpayers must file a 1994 return?

    a. Amy, age 19 and single, has $7,050 of wages, $300 of interest, and $350 of self-employment income.

    b. Betty, age 67 and single, has a taxable pension of $4,100, and social security benefits of $6,200.

    c. Chris, age 15 and single, is a dependent of his parents. Chris has earned income of $1,600 and interest of $400.

    d. Dawn, age 15 and single, is a dependent of her parents. She has earned income of $400 and interest of $1,600.

    e. Doug, age 25, and his wife are separated. He earned $3,000 while attending school during the year.

2-40. *Head-of-Household.* In the following situations, indicate if the taxpayer qualifies as a head-of-household.

    a. Allen is divorced from his wife. He maintains a household for himself and his dependent mother.

    b. Beth is divorced from her husband. She maintains a home for herself and supports an elderly aunt who lives in a retirement home.

    c. Cindy was widowed last year. She maintains a household for herself and her dependent daughter, who lived with her during the year.

    d. Dick is not divorced, but lived apart from his wife for the entire year. He maintains a household for himself and his dependent daughter. He does not receive any financial support from his wife.

2-41. *Computation of Taxable Income.* Jim and Pat are married and file jointly. In 1994, Jim earned a salary of $46,000. Pat is self-employed. Her gross business income was $49,000, and her business expenses totaled $24,000. Each contributed $2,000 to a deductible IRA. Their itemized deductions total $8,000. Compute parts a, b, and c without regard to self-employment tax.

    a. Compute their gross income.

    b. Compute their adjusted gross income.

    c. Compute their taxable income assuming they have a dependent daughter.

2-42. *Itemized or Standard Deduction.* Jan, a single taxpayer, has adjusted gross income of $250,000, home mortgage interest of $4,000, and charitable contributions of $3,000. Should she itemize her deductions or claim the standard deduction?

2-43. *Kiddie Tax.* Debbie is 16 years of age and a dependent of her parents. She earns $3,700 working part time and receives $1,600 interest on savings. She saves both the salary and interest. What is her taxable income? How would the answer be different if Debbie were 13 years of age?

2-44. *Personal and Dependency Exemptions.* Determine the number of personal and dependency exemptions in each of the following situations. Assume any condition for a dependency exemption not mentioned is met.

    a. Allen supports his older sister, who lives in her own apartment.

    b. Bob supports his aunt and her husband, who live in their own apartment.

    c. Charles and his two brothers support their mother. They agree to allow Charles to claim the exemption.

    d. Dan provides $2,800 of support for his sister, and she spent $2,600 of taxable interest income for her own support.

2-45. *Computation of Tax.* Compute the tax on $60,000 of taxable income assuming the taxpayer is the following:
- **a.** S corporation
- **b.** C corporation
- **c.** Married couple filing a joint return
- **d.** Single taxpayer

2-46. *Capital Gains and Losses.* Vicki has a long-term capital gain of $4,000 and a short-term capital loss of $15,000. Vicki has other income of $42,000. How much of the short-term capital loss can be deducted in the current year?

2-47. *Timing of Deductions.* Virginia is a cash-basis, calendar-year taxpayer. Her salary is $20,000, and she is single. She plans to purchase a residence in 1995. She anticipates her property taxes and interest will total $7,000. Each year, Virginia contributes approximately $1,000 to charity. Her other itemized deductions total approximately $1,000. For purposes of this problem, assume 1995 tax rates, exemptions, and standard deductions are the same as 1994.
- **a.** What will her gross tax be in 1994 and 1995 if she contributes $1,000 to charity in each year?
- **b.** What will her gross tax be in 1994 and 1995 if she contributes $2,000 to charity in 1994 but makes no contribution in 1995?
- **c.** What will her gross tax be in 1994 and 1995 if she makes no contribution in 1994 but contributes $2,000 in 1995?
- **d.** Alternative c results in a lower tax than either a or b. Why?

2-48. *Tax Forms and Filing Status.* Which tax form is used by the following individuals?
- **a.** Anita is single, age 68, and has a salary of $22,000 and interest of $300.
- **b.** Betty owns an apartment complex which produced rental income of $36,000. Expenses totaled $38,500.
- **c.** Clay's wife died last year. He qualifies as a surviving spouse. His salary is $24,000.
- **d.** Donna is a head-of-household. Her salary is $17,000 and she has $200 of interest income.

2-49. *Computation of Tax.* Jose is a single taxpayer with a dependent daughter. His salary is $44,000. Jose realized a long-term capital loss on the sale of stock of $45,000. He contributed $2,000 to a deductible IRA. His itemized deductions total $7,000.
- **a.** Compute Jose's adjusted gross income.
- **b.** Compute Jose's taxable income.
- **c.** Compute Jose's gross tax.

2-50. *Kiddie Tax.* Ralph and Tina (husband and wife) transferred taxable bonds worth $20,000 to Pam, their 12-year old daughter. Pam received $1,800 of interest on the bonds in the current year. Ralph and Tina have a combined taxable income of $51,000.
- **a.** Compute Ralph and Tina's gross tax.
- **b.** Compute Pam's taxable income and gross tax.
- **c.** What would be Pam's tax if she were age 16?

2-51. *Progressive or Proportional Tax.* Assume Gail is a wealthy widow whose husband died last year. Her dependent daughter lives with her for the entire year. Gail has dividend and interest income totaling $370,000 and she pays property taxes and home mortgage interest totaling $20,000.
- **a.** What filing status applies to Gail?
- **b.** Compute her taxable income and gross tax.
- **c.** Assume that Gail does not have a daughter. What is Gail's filing status?
- **d.** Compute Gail's taxable income and gross tax assuming she does not have a daughter.

TAX FORM/RETURN PREPARATION PROBLEMS

TurboTax **2-52.** Aida Petosa (Soc. Sec. No. 123-45-6789) is the 12 year old daughter of Alfredo Petosa (Soc. Sec. No. 987-65-4321). Her only income is $2,800 of interest on savings. Alfredo qualifies as a head of household, and his taxable income is $32,000. Compute her tax using Form 8615.

2-53. Wally B. Rains, age 32, is a single taxpayer who resides at 400 Golden Shore Drive, Long Beach, California 90802. His social security number is 987-65-4321. He does not wish to take advantage of the presidential election campaign check-off. Other relevant information includes:

Wages	$14,000
Interest income	260
Withholding	1,300

Complete Wally's Form 1040EZ.

2-54. James S. (Soc. Sec. No. 123-45-6789) and Lulu B. Watson (Soc. Sec. No. 987-65-4321) reside at 999 E. North Street, Richmond, Virginia 23174. They have one dependent child, Waldo, age 4, (Soc. Sec. No. 123-45-4321) and they are both under 65 years. They do not wish to take advantage of the presidential election campaign check-off. Other relevant information includes:

James's salary as a mechanic	$19,000
Lulu's salary as a teacher	24,000
Interest (First National Bank)	1,100
Withholding	4,500

Complete their Form 1040A.

TurboTax **2-55.** John R. Lane (Soc. Sec. No. 123-44-6666) lives at 1010 Ipsen Street, Yorba Linda, California 90102. John, a single taxpayer, age 66, provided 100% of his cousin's support. The cousin lives in Arizona. He wishes to take advantage of the presidential election campaign check-off. John is an accountant. Other relevant information includes:

Salary	$20,000
Taxable pension	30,000
Interest income	300
IRA deduction	2,000
Itemized deductions (from Schedule A)	6,000
Withholding	9,000

Assume that the supplemental Schedule A has already been completed. Complete Form 1040.

CASE STUDY PROBLEMS

2-56. Bala and Ann purchased as investments three identical parcels of land over a several year period. Two years ago they gave one parcel to their daughter, Kim, who is now age 12. They have an offer from an investor who is interested in acquiring all three parcels. The buyer is only able to purchase two of the parcels now, but wants to purchase the third parcel two or three years from now when he expects to have available funds to acquire the property. Because they paid different prices for the parcels, the sales will result in different amounts of gains and losses. The sale of one parcel owned by Bala and Ann will result in a $20,000 gain while the sale of the other parcel will result in a $28,000 loss. The sale of the parcel owned by Kim will result in a $19,000 gain. Kim has no other income and does not expect any significant income for several years. Bala and Ann, however, are in the 31% tax bracket. They do not have any other capital gains this year. Which two properties would you recommend that they sell this year? Why?

CASE STUDY PROBLEM—ETHICAL ISSUES

2-57. Larry and Sue separated at the end of the year. Larry has asked Sue to sign a joint income tax return for the year because he feels that the tax will be lower on a joint return. Larry and Sue both work. Sue received a salary of $25,000 while Larry's salary was $20,000. Larry works as a waiter at a local restaurant and received tips. The restaurant asked Larry to indicate the amount of tips he received so that they could report the information to the IRS. Larry reported to the employer that the tips amounted to $3,000, but Sue believes that the amount was more like $6,000 to $10,000. They do not have enough expenses to itemize. Sue has asked you what are the advantages and risks of filing a joint return.

TAX RESEARCH PROBLEMS

2-58. Ed has supported his stepdaughter, her husband, and their child since his wife's death three years ago. Ed promised his late wife that he would support her daughter from a former marriage and her daughter's husband until they both finished college. They live in another state, and meet gross income filing requirements. Is Ed entitled to dependency exemptions for the three individuals?

A partial list of research sources is

- Sec. 152.
- Reg. Sec. 1.152-2.
- *Desio Barbetti,* 9 T.C. 1097 (1947).

2-59. Bob and Sue were expecting a baby in January, but Sue was rushed to the hospital in December. She delivered the baby but it died the first night. Are Bob and Sue entitled to a dependency exemption for the baby?

A partial list of research sources is

- Rev. Rul. 73-156, 1973-1 C.B. 58.

2-60. Larry has severe vision problems and, in the past, he has claimed the additional standard deduction available to blind taxpayers. This year Larry's doctor prescribed a new type of contact lens that greatly improved his vision. Naturally, Larry was elated, but unfortunately new problems developed. He suffered severe pain, infection, and ulcers from wearing the new lens. The doctor recommended that he remove the lens and after several weeks his eyes healed. The doctor told him that he could wear the contacts again, but only for brief time periods. Otherwise the problems would reoccur. Can Larry claim the additional standard deduction available to blind taxpayers?

A partial list of research sources is

- *Emanuel Hollman,* 38 T.C. 251 (1963).

3

Gross Income—Inclusions

LEARNING OBJECTIVES

After studying this chapter, you should be able to

1. Explain the difference between the economic, accounting, and tax concepts of income
2. Explain the principles used to determine who is taxed on a particular item of income
3. Determine when a particular item of income is taxable under both the cash and accrual methods of reporting
4. Apply the rules of Sec. 61(a) to determine whether items such as compensation, dividends, alimony, and pensions are taxable

Computation of an individual's income tax liability begins with the determination of income. Although the meaning of the term *income* has long been debated by economists, accountants, tax specialists, and politicians, there is no universally accepted operational definition.

The Sixteenth Amendment to the Constitution gave Congress the power to tax "income from whatever source derived." To assure the constitutionality of the income tax, this phrase is incorporated in Sec. 61(a), where **gross income** is defined as follows, "Except as otherwise provided . . . gross income means all income from whatever source derived."

This chapter examines the concept of income for the purpose of determining what items of income are taxable. Chapter 4 considers those items of income that are not taxable. As noted in Chapter 2, many provisions in the tax law are created by a process of political compromise. Thus, there is no single explanation of why certain items are taxable and others are not. For this reason, determining whether a particular item of income is taxable often proves difficult.

ECONOMIC AND ACCOUNTING CONCEPTS OF INCOME

OBJECTIVE 1

Explain the difference between economic, accounting, and tax concepts of income

Economic Concept

In economics, income is defined as the amount that an individual could consume during a period and remain as well off at the end of the period as he was at the beginning of the period. To the economist, income includes both the wealth that flows to the individual and changes in the value of the individual's store of wealth.

Example 3-1 ■ Alice earned a salary of $40,000. She consumed $30,000 of food, clothing, housing, medical care, and other goods and services. Assets owned by Alice were worth $100,000 at the beginning of the year. Her assets, including $10,000 of salary that was saved, were worth $115,000 at the end of the year. Her liabilities did not change during the year. Alice's economic income is $45,000 ($30,000 + [$115,000 − $100,000]). ■

Under the economist's definition, unrealized gains, as well as gifts and inheritances, are income. Further, the economist adjusts for inflation in measuring income. There is no income to the extent that an increase in the measured value of property is caused by a decrease in the value of the measuring unit. In other words, inflation does not cause an individual to be better off.

Accounting Concept

In accounting, income is measured by a transaction approach. Accountants usually measure income when it is *realized* in a transaction. Values measured by transactions are relatively objective. Accountants recognize (i.e., report) income, gains, and losses that have been realized as a result of a completed transaction. The accountant believes that the economic concept of income is too subjective to be used as a basis for financial reporting. The accountant has traditionally employed historical costs in measuring income instead of using unconfirmed estimates of changes in market value. In accounting, the meaning of the term *realization* is critical to the income measurement process. Realization occurs when most of the uncertainty surrounding the receipt of income has been eliminated.

Example 3-2 ■	Assume the same facts as in Example 3-1. The amount consumed by Alice, the increase in the value of the property owned by her, and inflation are all ignored by the accountant in measuring her income. Only when she sells or otherwise disposes of the assets that have increased in value will the accountant recognize the gain. Thus, Alice's accounting income is $40,000. ■

TAX CONCEPT OF INCOME

Key Point

Section 446(a) states that taxable income shall be computed under the method of accounting on the basis which the taxpayer regularly computes his income in keeping his books. This provision would seem to require that tax accounting rules would conform to financial accounting rules. However, as will be seen later in this and other chapters, there are many differences.

The income tax law is much closer to the accountant's concept of income than the economist's. The reasons for this generally relate to matters of administrative convenience and the wherewithal-to-pay concept.

Administrative Convenience

The economic concept of income is considered to be too subjective to be used as a basis for determining income taxes. The need for objectivity is evident. If taxpayers were required to report increases in value as income, some individuals would feel compelled to understate values in order to reduce their tax liabilities. The IRS and even the most honest taxpayer would often disagree over values, and, as a result, the tax system would be practically impossible to administer. The disputes over valuation issues would be constant, and the courts would be burdened with added litigation. This is evidenced by the few situations where valuations are required in the determination of tax. For example, in certain instances taxpayers who contribute property to charity may deduct the value of the property. The courts are continuously having to resolve disputes between taxpayers and the IRS over the value of such contributions. Recently, penalties were added to the law for persons who substantially overvalue contributions. Further, in the case of certain large contributions of property, taxpayers are required to attach to their returns appraisals of the contributed property.

In some instances objectivity is achieved at the price of equity. For example, a taxpayer who owns land that has substantially declined in value generally cannot recognize the decline in value until it is realized through a disposition of the land. Similarly, an increase in value, no matter how large, is not taxed until there is a sale or exchange of the property. A taxpayer with a modest salary may feel that it is unfair that he is taxed on the salary while another person is not taxed on unrealized gains amounting to millions of dollars. But, as noted above, it would be practically impossible to administer an income tax law that was based on values.

Wherewithal-to-Pay

The wherewithal-to-pay concept suggests that a tax should be collected when the taxpayer can most easily pay it. A taxpayer who owns property that has increased in value does not necessarily have the cash needed to pay the tax. Taxing the gain when it is realized often means that the tax becomes due at the same time as the taxpayer collects the sales price. Wherewithal-to-pay is often at its greatest when income is realized. The wherewithal-to-pay concept is the rationale for the enactment of certain provisions of the tax law. For example, a taxpayer collects the proceeds from an installment sale transaction after the sale takes place. The tax law allows the taxpayer to report the sale on an installment basis under which the gain is reported as the sales proceeds are collected. This results in the tax becoming due when the taxpayer has the wherewithal to pay. The installment sale method cannot be used to report losses, as the wherewithal-to-pay concept is not an issue with losses.

The wherewithal-to-pay concept is also used to justify certain differences between tax law and financial accounting principles. In financial accounting, income is not reported in advance of the time it is earned, even if it is collected before it is earned. In general, prepaid income is taxed as it is collected rather than when it is earned for both cash and accrual-basis taxpayers. At that time the taxpayer has the cash available to pay the tax. It might prove more difficult to collect the tax if the government waited until the income was earned because the money might have been spent by then.

Gross Income Defined

Key Point
Congress has not adopted any particular concept or theory of income for tax purposes. Except as specifically limited by statute, the definition of income is broad and general.

Section 61(a) provides the following general definition and listing of income items:

General Definition.—Except as otherwise provided in this subtitle, gross income means all income from whatever source derived, including (but not limited to) the following items:

1. Compensation for services, including fees, commissions, fringe benefits, and similar items
2. Gross income derived from business
3. Gains derived from dealings in property
4. Interest
5. Rents
6. Royalties

Self-Study Question

Why should taxpayers who are using the cash method of accounting be required to include in gross income the value of property or services?

Answer

If taxpayers were not required to include the value of property or services in gross income, many taxpayers would arrange their financial affairs so that they would receive property or services instead of cash.

7. Dividends
8. Alimony and separate maintenance payments
9. Annuities
10. Income from life insurance and endowment contracts
11. Pensions
12. Income from discharge of indebtedness
13. Distributive share of partnership gross income
14. Income in respect of a decedent
15. Income from an interest in an estate or trust

This definition is not all inclusive. It does not indicate whether specific items of income such as insurance settlements, gambling winnings, or illegal income are taxable. One point is apparent: the phrase "except as otherwise provided" means that income is presumed to be taxable unless there is a specific exclusion in the income tax law. The IRS does not have to prove that an item of income is taxable. Rather, the taxpayer must prove that the item of income is excluded. Thus, gambling winnings and illegal income are taxable simply because there are no specific provisions in the tax law excluding the amounts from taxation.

Form of Receipt. Gross income is not limited to amounts received in the form of cash. According to Reg. Sec. 1.61-1(a), income may be "realized in any form, whether in money, property, or services." The important question is whether the taxpayer receives economic benefit.

Example 3-3 ■ King Corporation transfers 1,000 shares of its stock to its president. There are no restrictions on the stock, and it is part of the president's compensation. The president must include the value of the stock in gross income. ■

Example 3-4 ■ Ali, an attorney, performs certain legal services for Paul, a painter, in exchange for Paul's promise to paint Ali's residence. Each realizes income equal to the value of services received when the services are performed. ■

Example 3-5 ■ USA Corporation distributes an unneeded automobile to Vicki, a shareholder, in lieu of a cash dividend. Vicki must report the value of the automobile as dividend income. ■

Example 3-6 ■ Len has fallen behind on loan payments due Judy. Judy obtains a court order requiring Len's employer to pay part of Len's wages to her. Len will be taxed on the full wages even though a portion goes directly to Judy. Any interest Judy receives is includible in her gross income while principal payments are not taxable. ■

Example 3-7 ■ Wayne borrowed $3,000 from his employer. The employer awarded year-end bonuses to other employees but told Wayne that the debt was being forgiven in lieu of a bonus. Wayne must include the $3,000 in income. ■

Indirect Economic Benefit. As indicated earlier, the issue often is whether the taxpayer received economic benefit. In general, if a taxpayer benefits from an item, it is taxable. Frequently, employees incidentally benefit from an employer's expenditures. For example,

- Security guards patrol an employer's plant, protecting both the employer's property and the employees.

- An employer requires employees to undergo an annual checkup, the cost of which is paid by the employer.

- An employer provides uniforms and protective clothing worn by employees while on the job.

- A shipping company provides sleeping accommodations to sailors while ships are at sea.

- A company requires certain employees to wear shoes manufactured by the company and provide regular reports on the quality of the shoes.

It is now well established that taxpayers may exclude such indirect benefits from gross income. This rule holds that an expenditure is excludible if it is made in order to serve the business needs of the employer and any benefit to the employee is secondary and incidental.

This rule has developed over time. In a 1919 ruling, it was held that lodging furnished seamen aboard ship was not taxable.[1] This was followed by a 1925 court decision that held that an Army officer could exclude the value of quarters provided by the Army.[2] In 1951, the Tax Court concluded that employees need not report income if personal wants and needs of employees are satisfied secondarily and incidentally.[3] In 1960, an appeals court also required that an expenditure must serve a business purpose other than compensating an employee if a benefit is to be excluded from the employee's gross income.[4]

Recently, Congress has established rules dealing with situations where expenditures are made primarily to benefit employees. These rules permit employees to exclude certain benefits (such as employee discounts) from gross income. These rules are discussed in Chapters 4 and 9.

TO WHOM IS INCOME TAXABLE?

OBJECTIVE 2
Explain the principles used to determine who is taxed on a particular item of income

Once it is established whether income is taxable, it may be necessary to determine to whom it is taxable. Although such determinations are usually easy, it is not true that income is necessarily taxed to the person who receives it. If this were true, a family might reduce or eliminate its income tax by having income paid to children and other members who are in low tax brackets or have no tax liability.

Assignment of Income

In 1930, the Supreme Court held in the landmark case *Lucas v. Earl* that an individual is taxed on the earnings from his personal services.[5] Specifically, the Supreme Court held that a husband was taxed on the earnings from his law practice, even though he had signed a legally enforceable agreement with his wife that the earnings would be shared equally. An agreement to assign income one has or will earn does not permit a

---

[1] O.D. 265, 1 C.B. 71 (1919).
[2] *Clifford Jones v. U.S.,* 5 AFTR 5297, 1 USTC ¶ 129 (Ct. Cls., 1925). Section 119, discussed in Chapter 4, now provides specific requirements that must be satisfied before lodging may be excluded.
[3] *Gunnar Van Rosen,* 17 T.C. 834 (1951).
[4] *George D. Patterson v. Thomas,* 7 AFTR 2d 862, 61-1 USTC ¶ 9310 (5th Cir., 1961).
[5] 8 AFTR 10287, 2 USTC ¶ 496 (USSC, 1930).

Key Point

The law makes a clear distinction between a mere anticipatory assignment of income and an assignment of income-producing property. The income is taxable to the assignor in the former case, but where there is a bona fide gift of property the income is taxable to the assignee.

person to avoid being taxed on the income. The Court returned to a previously developed analogy which likens income to a fruit and capital to a tree.[6] Accordingly, the fruit (income) could not be attributed to a tree other than the one on which it grew.

In 1940, the Supreme Court extended the assignment of income doctrine to income from property in *Helvering v. Horst*.[7] In this case, the taxpayer detached interest coupons from bonds and gave the coupons to his son. The son collected the interest and reported it on his own return. The Supreme Court held that the taxpayer is taxed on the interest income because he owned the bonds. This leads to a basic rule that the income from property is taxed to the owner of the property. To transfer the income from property, the taxpayer must normally transfer ownership of the property itself.[8]

Although married couples may file joint returns today, this privilege did not become available until 1948. Assignment of income is an issue today when other individuals such as parents and children are involved, and it can still be an issue with married couples if they file separate returns.

Allocating Income Between Married Persons

Additional Comment

The community property states are generally located in the western or southwestern part of the U.S. Generally these states were settled by immigrants from France or Spain, and their state laws reflect this fact. The common law is derived from the English common law.

How income is allocated between a husband and wife depends on the state of residence. Eight states[9] utilize a community property system, whereas 42 states follow common law. Generally, the only **joint income** in a common law state is income from jointly owned property.[10] Income from an individual's labor or separate property belongs to the individual.

In community property states, income may be either separate or community. **Community income** is considered to belong equally to the spouses. In all community property states, the income from the personal efforts of either spouse is considered to belong equally to the spouses. Further, income from community property is considered to be community income. Thus, if a wife's salary is used to purchase stock, subsequent dividends are community income.

Couples can have separate property even in community property states. **Separate property** consists of all property owned before marriage and gifts and inheritances acquired after marriage. Whether income from separate property is community or separate depends on the state. In Idaho, Louisiana, and Texas, income from separate property is community income. In Arizona, California, Nevada, New Mexico, and Washington, such income is separate income.

Example 3-8 ■   A husband and wife file separate returns. The husband's salary is $40,000 and the wife's salary is $48,000. The wife received $1,000 of dividends on stock she had inherited from her parents. Interest of $1,200 was received on bonds that were purchased from the husband's salary. They received $2,600 in rent from farm land

---

[6] The analogy had been used some ten years earlier in *Eisner v. Myrtle H. Macomber*, 3 AFTR 3020, 1 USTC ¶ 32 (USSC, 1920). The court originally used the analogy in efforts to distinguish income from capital.

[7] 24 AFTR 1058, 40-2 USTC ¶ 9787 (USSC, 1940).

[8] A series of rather specific rules allocates income between the former and current owner when income-producing property is transferred. For example, in the case of bonds transferred by gift, the IRS has ruled that interest must be allocated based on the number of days the bonds were held by each owner during the interest period (Rev. Rul. 72-312, 1972-1 C.B. 22). A similar allocation must be made if bonds are sold (Rev. Rul. 72-224, 1972-1 C.B. 30).

[9] The states are Arizona, California, Idaho, Louisiana, Nevada, New Mexico, Texas, and Washington. Wisconsin's marital property law, while not providing for community property, is basically the same as community property.

[10] Historically, tenancy by the entirety, a form of joint ownership between spouses, allocated all income to the husband. Today, the laws of many states allocate income from property held in tenancy by the entirety equally between the spouses.

Historical Note

The community property laws led to the adoption of joint returns for married taxpayers in 1948. Married taxpayers residing in the community property states were able to split their income between them on separate tax returns. For example, a husband in California who earned $100,000 was able to report $50,000 on his return and his wife was able to report $50,000 on her return. With a progressive tax rate schedule, this resulted in tax savings that were unavailable to taxpayers in common law states. The joint return makes income splitting available to all taxpayers.

that they purchased jointly. The income would be allocated, depending on the state of residence, as follows:

California (A Community Property State)	Husband	Wife
Salary	$44,000	$44,000
Dividends		1,000
Interest	600	600
Rent	1,300	1,300
Total	$45,900	$46,900

Texas (A Community Property State)	Husband	Wife
Salary	$44,000	$44,000
Dividends	500	500
Interest	600	600
Rent	1,300	1,300
Total	$46,400	$46,400

Pennsylvania (A Common Law State)	Husband	Wife
Salary	$40,000	$48,000
Dividends		1,000
Interest	1,200	
Rent	1,300	1,300
Total	$42,500	$50,300

These rules are important if couples file separate returns. The community income rules can prove to be a problem if one spouse conceals income from the other. Normally, each spouse is expected to report one-half of all community income. This is inequitable if one spouse is not even aware that the community income had been earned. Special rules excuse an innocent spouse who fails to report community income on a separate return, provided that the spouse had no knowledge, nor reason to know, of the item and, as a result, the inclusion of the community income would be inequitable.[11] A corresponding provision permits the IRS to include the entire amount in the income of the other spouse.[12]

Income of Minor Children

As noted earlier, whether a husband or wife is taxed on income is determined by local law. Is the parent or the child taxed on a child's earnings? Compensation for the personal services of a child is taxable to the child regardless of state law and regardless of whether the income is in fact received by the child.[13] As noted in Chapter 2, the unearned income in excess of $1,200 of a child under age 14 is taxed at the parents' tax rate if it is higher than the child's rate. Alternatively, the parents may elect to include the child's unearned income on their return. In the case of spouses, who has a legal right to income determines who is taxed on it. In the case of children, however, who earned the income determines who is taxed on it.

[11] Sec. 66(b).
[12] Sec. 66(c).
[13] Sec. 73 and Reg. Sec. 1.73-1.

Allocating Other Joint Income

State law determines who is taxed on income from jointly owned property. In most states, joint tenants and tenants in common divide income equally.[14] Furthermore, if the property is sold, the sales price is typically allocated in equal amounts to the tenants.

Example 3-9 ■   William and Mario, who are brothers, inherited a fourplex from their mother. As joint tenants, each son is taxed on one-half of the rental income. If they sold the property, each would be taxed on one-half of any gain or loss. ■

Special rules are used to allocate income earned by partnerships, S corporations, estates, and trusts. In general, though, the income from a partnership is allocated among the partners as dictated by the partnership agreement as long as the agreement is bona fide. Complicated rules are used to allocate the income of an estate or trust.[15] The income from an S corporation is allocated between shareholders on the basis of the number of shares owned.

WHEN IS INCOME TAXABLE?

OBJECTIVE 3
Determine when a particular item of income is taxable under both the cash and accrual methods of reporting

Key Point

Neither the code nor the regulations define the terms "accounting" and "accounting method."

Additional Comment

Taxpayers who are engaged in more than one trade or business may use a different method of accounting for each separate trade or business.

The year in which income is taxed depends upon the taxpayer's accounting method. The three primary overall accounting methods are the **cash receipts and disbursements method,** the **accrual method,** and the **hybrid method.** A taxpayer's accounting method must clearly reflect income. The IRS has the power to determine what accounting method must be used by a taxpayer if, in the opinion of the IRS, the method being used does not clearly reflect income.[16] Thus, the Regulations require taxpayers to use the accrual method for determining purchases and sales when a taxpayer maintains an inventory.[17] In other words, income would not be clearly reflected if beginning and ending inventories were ignored.

Section 448 requires C corporations (and partnerships with corporate partners), tax shelters, and certain trusts to use the accrual method of accounting. Farming businesses, qualified personal service corporations, and entities with average gross receipts under $5 million are exempt from the requirement.

Once an accounting method has been adopted, it cannot be changed without permission of the IRS.[18]

Cash Method

The **cash receipts and disbursements method** of accounting is used by most individual taxpayers and most noncorporate businesses that do not have invento-

---

[14] Who paid for the property is usually irrelevant. In many states, tenants in common and joint tenants may agree to something other than an equal sharing of income. One significant exception is joint bank accounts. Interest income is typically allocated in proportion to amounts deposited to an account by each individual.

[15] In *Helvering v. George B. Clifford, Jr.,* 23 AFTR 1077, 40-1 USTC ¶ 9265 (USSC, 1940), the Supreme Court concluded that a taxpayer could not assign income by granting to another a short-term interest in a trust. Current law denies taxpayers the opportunity to shift income in most instances where the property in a trust reverts to the grantor.

[16] Sec. 446(b).

[17] Reg. Sec. 1.446-1(c)(2)(i).

[18] Sec. 446(e).

Additional Comment

The use of the cash receipts and disbursements method of accounting gives the taxpayer some control over the timing of the recognition of income and deductions. It also has the advantage of simplicity.

ries.[19] (See Chapter 11 for a more complete discussion of who is permitted to use the cash method.) Under this method, income is reported in the year the taxpayer actually or constructively receives the income rather than in the year the income is earned. The income can be received by the taxpayer or the taxpayer's agent and be in the form of cash, other property, or services.[20] In the case of property or services, the amount included in the income is the value of the property or services. An accounts receivable or other unsupported promise to pay is considered to have no value, and, as a result, no income is recognized until the receivable is collected. Topic Review 3-1 summarizes when various types of income are reported.

The fact that prepaid income is often taxed when received rather than when earned, often results in a mismatching of income and expenses.

Example 3-10 ■

In December of the current year, Troy rents an apartment and collects the first and last months' rent from the tenant. Troy must report two months' rent in the current year. The actual expenses associated with the last month's rental are not incurred until the last month. Thus, Troy reports two months' income this year, but deducts only one month's expenses. ■

Reporting prepaid income can have harsh results because there are no related deductions. If the income is taxed before the expenses are incurred, the taxpayer may not have enough cash to pay the expenses when they are incurred.[21] This burden is mitigated, in part, by Treasury Regulations and Revenue procedures discussed in this chapter (e.g., the treatment of prepaid income on page 3-12).

Additional Comment

There is no recognized doctrine of constructive payment.

Real World Example

Paul Hornung, a former football player with the Green Bay Packers, was awarded an automobile in 1961 for being the outstanding player in the NFL championship game, but he did not actually receive it until 1962. He attempted to invoke the constructive receipt doctrine and report the income in 1961. The court held that he could not claim constructive receipt because the car was not set aside in the year of the award. Paul V. Hornung, 47 T.C. 428 (1967).

Constructive Receipt. As noted, a cash-basis taxpayer must report income in the year that it is actually or constructively received.[22] This rule works to prevent taxpayers from deferring income that is otherwise available by "turning their backs" on it. A taxpayer cannot defer income recognition by refusing to accept payment.

Examples of constructive receipt where taxpayers are required to report taxable income even though no cash is actually received include

- A check received after banking hours[23]
- Interest credited to a bank savings account[24]
- Bond interest coupons which have matured but which have not been redeemed[25]
- Salary available to an employee who does not accept payment[26]

An amount is not considered to be constructively received if

- It is subject to substantial limitations or restrictions.
- The payor does not have the funds necessary to make payment.
- The amount is unavailable to the taxpayer.

Example 3-11 ■

Beth owns an ordinary life insurance policy with a cash surrender value. She need not report any income as the cash surrender value increases because the require-

---

[19] For example, accountants, lawyers, barbers, laundries, and insurance agents.
[20] An agent can be an employee, relative, or other person authorized to receive the income.
[21] This mismatching of income and expenses affects both cash and accrual basis taxpayers.
[22] Reg. Sec. 1.451-2(a).
[23] *Charles F. Kahler*, 18 T.C. 31 (1952).
[24] Reg. Sec. 1.451-2(b).
[25] Ibid.
[26] *James J. Cooney*, 18 T.C. 883 (1952).

TOPIC REVIEW 3-1

When Income Is Taxable		
Item	Cash Basis	Accrual Basis
Compensation	Year actually or constructively received.	Year earned or year received if prepaid.
Interest	Year actually or constructively received.	Year accrued or year received if prepaid.
Discount on Series E or EE Bonds	Choice of reporting interest as it accrues or at maturity.	Year accrued.
Dividends	Year actually or constructively received.	Year actually or constructively received.
Rent	Year actually or constructively received (does not apply to a deposit).	Year accrued or year received if prepaid (year accrued if services are associated, e.g., in a hotel or motel) (does not apply to a deposit).
Services (maintenance contracts, dance lessons, etc.)	Year actually or constructively received.	Year accrued or year received if prepaid except that a taxpayer may report the income as it accrues if all the services are to be performed by the end of the next tax year.
Sale of goods	In general, cash basis cannot be used to report sale of goods if inventories are an income-producing factor.	Year of sale or year cash is received if prepaid except may elect to report in year of sale if (1) goods are not on hand, (2) amount received is less than cost of item, and (3) same accounting method is used for financial accounting.
Subscriptions (newspapers, magazines, etc.)	Year actually or constructively received.	Year earned or year cash is received, if prepaid, except may elect to report income as newspaper, etc., is published.
Memberships (automobile clubs, etc.)	Year actually or constructively received.	Year earned or year received if prepaid (certain nonstock corporations may elect to report prepaid amounts over the membership period, if the period covers three years or less).
Sale of property (other than stock)	Year actually or constructively received.	Year transaction is completed (for example, the close of escrow in case of sale of real estate).
Sale of stock	Year transaction is executed.	Year transaction is executed.

ment that she cancel the policy in order to collect the cash surrender value constitutes a substantial restriction. ∎

Example 3-12 ∎   Cathy has received a paycheck from her employer but has been told to hold the check until the employer has sufficient funds to cover the payroll. Cathy need not report the amount of the check as income until funds are deposited to the employer's account. ∎

Example 3-13 ∎   On December 2, 1994, Dan sold land for $100,000 payable on February 2, 1995. During the negotiations, the buyer offered to pay cash. Since the parties did not agree to a cash transaction, there was no constructive receipt in 1994. Under the terms of the sale, funds were not available at the time of sale. Thus, Dan is permitted to defer the recognition of income under the contract since the contract is made before the income is earned. ∎

Exceptions. There are exceptions to the basic rule that cash-basis taxpayers report income when it is actually or constructively received.

- The interest on Series E and Series EE U.S. savings bonds need not be reported until the final maturity date, which varies but may be as long as 40 years after the date of issue, and can be deferred even longer if the bonds are exchanged within one year of the final maturity date for Series HH U.S. savings bonds.[27] Many taxpayers purchase bonds with a maturity date that falls after retirement when the taxpayer expects to be in a lower tax bracket.

- Crop insurance proceeds may be reported in the year following receipt if the crop would have ordinarily been sold in the following year. This helps farmers avoid reporting the income from two crops in one year.

- Taxpayers who are forced to sell livestock on account of drought may defer the recognition of income for one year if the sale would have taken place in a subsequent tax year had the drought not occurred and if the area is designated as eligible for federal assistance because of the drought. This also helps avoid a bunching of income into one year.

Accrual Method

Real World Example

The Ninth Circuit Court of Appeals has held that "markers" which customers gave to a gambling casino to evidence their indebtedness to the casino required accrual even though the receivables were legally unenforceable under state law. The court found that there need only be a "reasonable expectancy" that payment would be made. Flamingo Resort, Inc. v. U.S., 50 AFTR 2d 82-502, 82-1 USTC ¶ 9136 (9th Cir., 1982).

Taxpayers using the accrual method of accounting report income in the year it is earned. Income is considered to have been earned when all the events have occurred which fix the right to receive the income and when the amount of income can be determined with reasonable accuracy.[28] In the case of a sale of property, income normally accrues when title passes to the buyer.[29] Income from services accrues as the services are performed.

Prepaid Income. Prepaid income is generally taxable in the year of receipt. For example, if a lender receives January interest in the preceding December, it is taxable in the year received whether the lender uses the cash or accrual method. This is, of course, unlike financial accounting where the interest would be reported as it accrues.

Two exceptions to the general rule are worth noting. Accrual-basis taxpayers may defer recognizing income in the case of certain advance payments for *goods* and in the case of certain advance payments for *services* to be rendered. A taxpayer is permitted to defer advance payments for goods if:

Key Point

The prepaid income doctrine has diminished in importance over time. Until mid-1970 the IRS would attempt to tax all payments for future services.

- The goods are not on hand as of the last day of the tax year.
- The amount received is less than the taxpayer's cost of the goods.
- The taxpayer's method of accounting for the sale is the same for tax and financial accounting purposes.[30]

These conditions are often met in situations where sellers require deposits for special orders. Also, the conditions may be met in certain situations where the seller receives an order for an item that is out of stock.

Under Rev. Proc. 71-21, a taxpayer may defer advance payments for services if the payments are for services to be performed prior to the end of the tax year following the year of receipt.[31] The rule is not available if a payment covers a time period that

---

[27] The interest on the Series HH bonds is taxable as received.

[28] Reg. Sec. 1.451-1(a).

[29] Regulation Sec. 1.446-1(c)(1)(ii), however, does permit taxpayers the right to accrue income from the sale of inventory when the goods are shipped, when the product is delivered or accepted, or when title passes, as long as the method is consistently used.

[30] Reg. Sec. 1.451-5.

[31] 1971-2 C.B. 549.

extends beyond the end of the tax year following the year of receipt. The rule can be applied to a variety of services such as dance lessons, maintenance contracts (but not warranties included in the sales price of a product), and rent (if services are associated with the rent as is the case with a hotel or motel).

Example 3-14 ■ Bear Corporation, an accrual-basis taxpayer that uses the calendar year as its tax year, sells dance lessons under contracts ranging from 3 months to 2 years. Which contracts are covered by Rev. Proc. 71-21 varies depending on the month of sale. For example, contracts sold in the month of July that are for a term of longer than 18 months are not covered by the rule, and all income must be reported for these contracts in the year of the sale. Assume Bear Corporation sold 3 contracts in July 1994: one for 3 months costing $90, one for 1 year costing $300, and one for 2 years costing $500. Income would be recognized as follows:

Length of Contract	1994	1995
3 months	$ 90	
12 months	150	$150
24 months	500	

■

Hybrid Method

The **hybrid method** of accounting is really a combination of the cash and accrual methods. Under the hybrid method, some items of income or expense are reported under the cash basis and some are reported under the accrual method. Because this could create an opportunity for abuse, taxpayers who wish to use the method must obtain approval from the IRS.[32] The method is most often encountered in small businesses that are required to use the accrual method of accounting for purchases and sales of goods. Such businesses often prefer to use the cash method of reporting for other items because the cash method is simpler and may provide greater flexibility for tax planning. A taxpayer using an accrual method of accounting with respect to purchases and sales may use the cash method in computing all other items of income and expenses.[33]

ITEMS OF GROSS INCOME—SEC. 61(a)

Section 61(a), quoted earlier in this chapter, states that gross income includes, but is not limited to, 15 specifically listed types of income. These items are discussed here.

Compensation

Compensation is payment for personal services. It includes salaries, wages, fees, commissions, tips, bonuses, and specialized forms of compensation such as director's fees, jury fees, and marriage fees received by clergymen. What the compensation is called, how it is computed, the form and frequency of payment, and whether the

[32] Reg. Sec. 1.446-1(c)(2)(ii).
[33] Reg. Sec. 1.446-1(c)(1)(iv).

compensation is subject to withholding is of little significance. Similarly, the fact that the services are part-time, one-time, seasonal, or temporary is immaterial.

There are exclusions, however, for a variety of employer-provided fringe benefits such as group term life insurance premiums, health and accident insurance premiums, employee discounts, contributions to retirement plans, and free parking. These exclusions are discussed in greater detail later in this volume. In addition, there is a limited exclusion applicable to foreign-earned income. This exclusion is discussed in Chapter 4.

Business Income

Self-Study Question

A retailing company had sales of $1,000,000. It had the following costs: Cost of Goods Sold, $400,000; Salaries, $200,000 and Rent and Other Expenses, $100,000. What is the company's gross income?

Answer

The gross income is $600,000. The sales figure is reduced by the cost of goods sold.

The term *gross income* usually refers to the total amount received from a particular source. In the case of businesses that provide services (for example, accounting and law), the gross business income is the total amount received. In the case of manufacturing, merchandising, and mining, however, the gross income refers to total sales less the cost of goods sold.[34]

The cost of goods sold is, in effect, treated as a return of capital. Chapter 4 discusses a tax concept established long ago that a return of capital is not income and, therefore, cannot be subject to the income tax. Chapter 10 discusses the methods available for valuing inventory.

Gains from Dealings in Property

Gains realized from property transactions are included in gross income unless a nonrecognition rule applies. As is true with business inventories, taxpayers may deduct the cost of property in order to arrive at the gain from a property transaction.[35] The tax law contains over 30 nonrecognition rules which allow taxpayers to postpone the recognition of gains and losses from certain types of property transactions. In a few instances, these rules allow taxpayers to permanently exclude gains from gross income.[36]

Losses are not offset against gains in computing gross income. Rather, most losses are deductions *for* adjusted gross income. Further, net capital losses for individuals are subject to provisions that limit the amount that can be deducted from other income to $3,000 per year.[37] Losses from the sale or disposition of an asset held for personal use are not deductible.

Interest

Typical Misconception

It is sometimes mistakenly assumed that interest paid on federal obligations, such as Treasury bonds, notes, and bills, will also qualify for tax exemption.

Interest is compensation for the use of money. Taxable interest includes interest on bank deposits, corporate bonds, mortgages, life insurance policies, tax refunds, U.S. government obligations,[38] and foreign government obligations.[39] Nontaxable interest is discussed below.

Tax-Exempt Interest. Since the inception of the federal income tax in 1913, interest on obligations of states, territories, and U.S. possessions and their political

Historical Note

At one time the doctrine of intergovernmental immunity resulted in the exclusion of income earned by governors, mayors, and even college professors employed by state universities.

---

[34] Reg. Sec. 1.61-3(a).

[35] Note that business income and gains from dealings in property are overlapping terms. The gross profit from the sale of inventory is actually both business income and a gain from a property transaction. Typically, however, the phrase "gains from dealings in property" may be assumed to mean "gains from dealings in property other than inventory," so as to avoid confusion.

[36] For example, Sec. 121 allows taxpayers who are at least 55 years of age to exclude a limited amount of gain from a sale of a personal residence.

[37] See Chapters 5, 12, and 13 for detailed coverage of property transactions.

[38] The interest on many federal obligations issued before March 1, 1942, is tax exempt.

[39] Reg. Sec. 1.61-7.

Additional Comment

Many tax advisers consider the exclusion of interest on municipal bonds to be one of the few remaining tax shelters. As a result municipal bond funds have flourished in recent years.

subdivisions has been tax exempt.[40] Bonds issued by school districts, port authorities, toll road commissions, counties and fire districts have been held to be tax exempt. As noted above, this exclusion does not extend to interest paid on U.S. government obligations or foreign government obligations. Nor does the exclusion exempt from taxation gains from the sale of state or local government bonds.

There has always been some uncertainty as to whether the federal government could tax interest on state and local government obligations. The basic question is whether taxing these obligations would violate the doctrine of intergovernmental immunity in that the tax would reduce the ability of state and local governments to finance their operations because taxable bonds usually pay a higher rate of interest than tax-exempt bonds. The belief that taxing state and local government interest is unconstitutional is no longer widely held. There have been efforts to tax interest on state and local bonds. The only changes have been to limit the use of bonds for private activities, federally insured loans, and arbitrage. These limitations are:

Additional Comment

The doctrine of intergovernmental immunity also results in most states exempting from taxation income received from U.S. obligations.

- Bonds issued for certain private activities (e.g., sports facilities, convention facilities, and industrial park sites) generally are not tax exempt even if issued by a state or local government.

- The amount of debt that can be issued in a given year by a state for certain qualified activities is subject to a statutory limit equal to the greater of $150,000,000 or $50 per resident.[41] Bonds covered include those issued to fund student loans, the construction of exempt facilities (such as airports), qualified redevelopment, and qualified mortgages.

- If bonds are guaranteed by the federal government, they are taxable even if they are issued by a state or local government.[42]

- If a state or local government issues bonds for the purpose of using the proceeds to buy high interest investments, then the bonds issued by the state and local government are taxable. Such bonds are called arbitrage bonds.[43]

In addition, Sec. 501(c)(3) organizations may issue up to $150,000,000 of tax-exempt bonds. Such organizations include private universities, hospitals, churches, and similar nonprofit organizations.

Key Point

The exclusion is available only to an individual who purchased the bond after reaching age 24. The exclusion is not available to an individual who was the owner of a bond that was purchased by another individual, other than a spouse. Therefore, the exclusion is not allowable if bonds are purchased by a parent and put in the name of a child.

Series EE Savings Bond Exclusion. Taxpayers may purchase and eventually redeem Series EE bonds tax-free if they use the proceeds to pay certain college expenses for themselves, a spouse, or dependents.[44]

To qualify for the exclusion:

- The bonds must be purchased after 1989 by an individual who is age 24 or older at the time of the purchase.

- The bonds must be purchased by the owner and cannot be a gift to the owner.

- The receipts from the bond redemption must be used for tuition and fees, which are first reduced by tax exempt scholarships, veterans benefits, and other similar amounts[45]

- Married couples living together must file a joint return in order to obtain the exclusion.

---

[40] Sec. 103(a)(1).
[41] Sec. 146(d).
[42] Sec. 149(b).
[43] Sec. 148.
[44] Sec. 135(c).
[45] The exclusion is not permitted for amounts paid for sports, games, or hobbies unless they are part of a degree program (Sec. 135(c)(2)(B)).

Self-Study Question

Young parents, whose annual income is currently $45,000, begin a regular program of purchasing Series EE Savings Bonds for their 8-year-old daughter's college education. Is there any risk that when the bonds are redeemed the interest income will not be excludable?

Answer

Yes, the parents' income may increase over the years to such an extent that the interest exclusion will not be available.

The full amount of interest is excluded only if the combined amount of principal and interest received during the year does not exceed the net qualified educational expenses (tuition and fees reduced by exempt scholarships, etc.), and the taxpayer's 1994 modified adjusted gross income is not over $41,200 ($61,850 for married individuals filing a joint return). The exclusion is not available for married taxpayers filing jointly whose 1994 modified AGI is more than $91,850, or for single taxpayers whose modified AGI is in excess of $56,200.[46]

If the net qualified education expenses are less than the total principal and interest, a portion of the interest is excluded based on the ratio of the qualified educational expenses to the total principal and interest. The tentative exclusion is equal to:

$$\text{Series EE Interest} \times \frac{\text{Net Qualified Educational Expenses}}{\text{Series EE Interest} + \text{Principal}}$$

Example 3-15 ■

Additional Comment

A child born today will require about $100,000 for a four-year college education. If interest rates are around 6%, one would have to save about $245 a month until the child entered school to be able to pay this amount.

In 1994, Lois redeems Series EE bonds and receives $6,000, consisting of $1,875 of interest and $4,125 of principal. Further assume the net qualifying expenses total $4,800. Lois's educational expenses equal 80% of the total amount received ($4,800 ÷ $6,000). Thus, her exclusion is limited to $1,500 (0.80 × $1,875). ■

As noted, the amount of the exclusion is further reduced if modified adjusted gross income exceeds a $41,200 threshold ($61,850 for married individuals filing a joint return). These adjusted gross income thresholds are adjusted for inflation each year. Modified adjusted gross income includes the interest from education savings bonds and certain otherwise excludable foreign income.[47] The reduction is computed as follows:

$$\begin{array}{l}\text{Otherwise} \\ \text{Excludable} \times \dfrac{\text{Excess modified AGI}}{\$15,000\ (\$30,000\ \text{for joint filers})} \\ \text{Amount}\end{array}$$

Example 3-16 ■

Assume the same facts as in Example 3-15. Further assume that Lois is single and has other adjusted gross income of $44,325. Lois's otherwise available exclusion of $1,500 is reduced by $500 to $1,000. This reduction is computed by dividing the excess modified AGI of $5,000 ($44,325 + $1,875 − $41,200) by $15,000 and multiplying the result by $1,500. ■

Rents and Royalties

Amounts received as rents or royalties are included in gross income. As noted earlier, prepaid rent is taxable when received. Security deposits, however, which are refundable to tenants upon the expiration of a lease are not included in gross income. The deposit is included in gross income only if it is not refunded upon the expiration of the lease.

Example 3-17 ■

In December 1994, Buddy rents an apartment to Gary. Buddy receives the first and last months' rent plus a security deposit of $500. Buddy must include in 1994 gross income both the first and last months' rent. Assume that Gary moves out of the apartment in 1996 and Buddy keeps $300 of the security deposit to cover repairs

---

[46] Each of these amounts is adjusted annually for inflation. A drafting error in the Revenue Reconciliation Act of 1993 resulted in these amounts being reduced in 1994 compared to 1993.

[47] Specifically, modified adjusted gross income includes amounts that qualify for the foreign earned income exclusion (Sec. 911), the exclusion for possession's income (Sec. 931), and the exclusion for income from Puerto Rico (Sec. 933). The limitation is determined after taking the partial exclusion for social security benefits and railroad retirement (Sec. 86), claiming the allowable deduction for retirement contributions (Sec. 219), and applying the passive loss limitation (Sec. 469).

costing $200 and five days' unpaid rent, which amounts to $100. In 1996, Buddy would include the $300 in gross income and could deduct $200 for repairs. ■

Amounts received by a lessor to cancel, amend, or modify a lease are also taxable. **Royalties** are proceeds paid to an owner by others who do business under some right belonging to the owner. Royalties from copyrights, patents, oil, gas, and mineral rights are all taxable as ordinary income.

Improvements by Lessees. Improvements made by a lessee that increase the value of leased property are included in the lessor's income only if the improvements are made in lieu of paying rent or if rent is reduced because of the improvements. In such situations, the lessor must include the fair market value (FMV) of the improvement in gross income when it is made to the property.[48]

Example 3-18 ■   Rita rents an apartment to Anna. The apartment would normally rent for $500 per month, but Rita agrees to accept $200 per month for the first year if Anna builds a block wall around the property. It is estimated by Rita that she would have to pay someone $3,000 to build the wall. Rita is accepting reduced rent and must report gross income of $3,000 when the wall is added to the property. The $3,000 could be added to Rita's basis in the property and should qualify as a depreciable asset. ■

Improvements not made in lieu of rent are not income to the lessor. No adjustment is made to the lessor's basis in the property and, therefore, no depreciation is allowable. Gain or loss is recognized only when the property is disposed of.[49] Whether the improvements are in lieu of rent depends upon the intent of the parties. This determination is based on the facts of the particular situation. The rental rate, the terms of the rental agreement, and whether the improvements have an estimated useful life exceeding the term of the lease may all be indications of intent.

Dividends

Historical Note

Before 1987, individual taxpayers were permitted to exclude the first $100 of dividend income. This exclusion was designed to help ameliorate the double taxation of corporate profits.

Distributions to shareholders are taxable as dividends only to the extent they are made from either the corporation's current earnings and profits (a concept similar, although not identical, to current year's net income for financial accounting purposes) or accumulated earnings and profits (a concept similar, although not identical, to beginning of the year retained earnings).[50] Earnings and profits are discussed in greater depth in Chapter 4 of the *Prentice Hall's Federal Taxation: Corporations, Partnerships, Estates & Trusts* text and Chapter 17 of the Comprehensive volume. Distributions in excess of current and accumulated earnings and profits are treated as a nontaxable recovery of capital. Such distributions reduce the shareholder's basis in the stock. Distributions in excess of the basis of the stock are classified as capital gains.

Example 3-19 ■   Liz is the sole shareholder in Atlantic Corporation. The basis of her stock is $250,000. Atlantic distributes $40,000 to Liz in 1994. Accumulated earnings and profits at the beginning of 1994 equal $25,000, and current earnings and profits equal $10,000. Liz will report $35,000 of taxable dividend income and a nontaxable

---

[48] Reg. Sec. 1.109-1.
[49] Reg. Sec. 1.1019-1.
[50] Sec. 316(a). The federal income tax became effective on March 1, 1913. Thus, income accumulated prior to that date can still be distributed on a tax-exempt basis.

return of capital equal to $5,000. Liz must reduce her basis in the stock by $5,000. ■

Stock Dividends. A **stock dividend** is a distribution by a corporation to its shareholders of the corporation's own stock. In 1920, the Supreme Court held that simple stock dividends could not be taxed because they were not income.[51] More precisely, income had not been realized because there was no real change in the taxpayer's interest or the risks faced by the taxpayer. Over the years, however, the exclusion for stock dividends has been narrowed. If a shareholder has the option of receiving either cash or stock, the shareholder is taxed even if he opts to receive stock. The option to receive cash constitutes constructive receipt of the cash. Today, many other features of a stock dividend may cause it to be taxed. For example, a distribution which involves preferred stock being distributed to some common shareholders and common stock to others is taxable.[52] The recipient of a taxable stock dividend includes the value of the stock received in gross income, and that amount becomes the basis of the shares received.

A nontaxable stock dividend has no effect on a shareholder's income in the year received. The basis of the old shares is allocated between the old shares and the new shares. Furthermore, the holding period for the new shares starts on the same date as the holding period of the old.

Example 3-20 ■

In 1994, Carol purchased 100 shares of Mesa Corporation stock for $1,100 (or $11 per share). In 1996, Carol receives 10 shares of Mesa stock as a nontaxable stock dividend. After the dividend, Carol owns 110 shares of stock with a basis of $1,100 (or $10 per share). All of the stock is assumed to have been acquired in 1994. ■

Real World Example

In the well-publicized 1989 trial of Leona Helmsley, the billionaire hotel queen, it was disclosed that she had billed her companies for millions of dollars in personal items. The items ranged from a $12.99 girdle to a $1 million limestone-and-marble pool enclosure at her estate. She was sentenced to four years in prison and fined $7.1 million. The amounts paid to her by her companies represented constructive dividends.

Capital Gain Dividends. A **capital gain dividend** is a distribution by a regulated investment company (commonly referred to as a *mutual fund*) of capital gains realized from the sale of investments in the fund. Such dividends also include any undistributed capital gains allocated to shareholders by such companies.[53] Capital gain dividends are long-term regardless of how long the shareholder has owned the stock of the regulated investment company.

Constructive Dividends. In many corporations the same individuals are both shareholders and employees. A corporation may not deduct dividends paid to shareholders but is permitted to deduct reasonable compensation. Questions are frequently raised as to whether amounts identified as compensation are really disguised dividends. If an amount called compensation is unreasonable, it will be disallowed.[54] Often the reasonableness of compensation is determined by comparing the compensation paid to the employee-shareholders with amounts paid to others performing similar services.

Example 3-21 ■

Carmen owns 100% of the stock in Florida Corporation and receives a $400,000 salary for serving as president. The corporation reports no taxable income and pays no dividends. Presidents of similar companies received salaries ranging from $75,000 to $160,000. The IRS would likely disallow a portion of Carmen's salary as unreasonable. ■

[51] *Eisner v. Myrtle H. Macomber*, 3 AFTR 3020, 1 USTC ¶ 32 (USSC, 1920).
[52] Reg. Sec. 1.305-4.
[53] Sec. 852(b).
[54] Sec. 162(a)(1).

A variety of transactions may actually be viewed as constructive dividends. It is not necessary that the dividend be formally declared or that distributions be in proportion to stock holdings. **Constructive dividends** are often distributions that are intended to result in a deduction to the corporation and taxable income (such as compensation) to the shareholder.[55] Other constructive dividends are intended to produce a nonreportable benefit to the shareholder,[56] or even result in a deduction to the corporation without income to the shareholder.[57]

Alimony and Separate Maintenance Payments

The tax implications of alimony payments and property settlements associated with a divorce or separation may be critical.

<table>
<tr>
<td>

Example 3-22 ■

Additional Comment

The IRS has found that not all taxpayers report alimony payments as income. As a result, the IRS now generally matches deductions for alimony payments by one former spouse with the alimony income reported by the other.

</td>
<td>

Helen earned $500,000, and as a result of her divorce, she was required to pay William $250,000. If the payment were viewed as a property settlement, Helen could not deduct any the of $250,000 payment and William would not be required to include the payment in his income. However, if the $250,000 were viewed as alimony, Helen could deduct the full amount in computing her adjusted gross income. William would report the $250,000 as alimony income. ■

</td>
</tr>
</table>

A **property settlement** is a division of property. In general, each spouse is entitled to the property brought into the marriage and a share of the property accumulated during marriage.[58] A division of property does not result in any income to either spouse,[59] nor does either spouse receive a tax deduction. The basis of property received by either spouse as a result of the divorce or separation remains unchanged.

<table>
<tr>
<td>

Example 3-23 ■

</td>
<td>

As a result of a divorce Dawn receives stock that had been purchased by her and her former husband during their marriage. They had purchased the stock for $12,000. At the time of the divorce, the stock was worth $14,000. Neither Dawn nor her former husband report income from the transfer of the stock. If Dawn subsequently sold the stock for $15,000, she would report a $3,000 gain. ■

</td>
</tr>
<tr>
<td>

Additional Comment

Child-support payments are not deductible as alimony.

</td>
<td>

The tax law has rather specific rules that distinguish property settlements from alimony. The rules, which were originally enacted in 1942,[60] were significantly revised

</td>
</tr>
</table>

[55] Other examples include excessive royalties (*Peterson & Pegau Baking Co.,* 2 B.T.A. 637 [1925]) and rent (*Limericks, Inc. v. CIR,* 36 AFTR 649, 48-1 USTC ¶ 9146 [5th Cir., 1948]).

[56] Examples include bargain sales of corporate assets to shareholders (*J. E. Timberlake v. CIR,* 30 AFTR 583, 42-2 USTC ¶ 9822 [4th Cir., 1942]), redemptions of a shareholder's stock (Sec. 302), and loans to shareholders that are actually dividends (*George Blood Enterprises, Inc.,* 1976 PH T.C. Memo ¶ 76,102, 35 TCM 436).

[57] Examples include paying an employee's personal expenses (*The Lang Chevrolet Co.,* 1967 PH T.C. Memo ¶ 67,212, 26 TCM 1054) and purchasing assets for an employee's use (*Joseph Morgenstern,* 1955 PH T.C. Memo ¶ 55,086, 14 TCM 282).

[58] How the property accumulated during marriage is divided may be determined by an agreement of the parties, or if they are unable to agree, on a basis of state law.

[59] Prior to 1985, a transfer of appreciated property to a former spouse in satisfaction of marital rights was treated as a taxable event resulting in the transferor having to recognize gain. See *U.S. v. Thomas Crawley Davis,* 9 AFTR 2d 1625, 62-2 USTC ¶ 9509 (USSC, 1962).

[60] Prior to 1942, alimony was not deductible (*Gould v. Gould,* 3 AFTR 2958, 1 USTC ¶ 13 [USSC, 1917]).

Ethical Point

Tax consultants who choose to advise divorcing couples may face an ethical dilemma because advice that benefits one spouse may be detrimental to the other and because of the need to maintain confidential client relationships.

in 1984 and in 1986. The revised rules apply to agreements reached after 1984 and earlier agreements if the parties so elect in writing.

In order to be treated as alimony, payments must:

- Be made in cash.

- Be made pursuant to a divorce, separation, or a written agreement between the spouses.

- Terminate at the death of the payee.

- Not be designated as being other than alimony (e.g., child support).

- Be made between persons who are living in separate households.

The rules are summarized in Topic Review 3-2. Certain aspects of these rules will be discussed further. One such rule is the recapture provision found in the current law. The **recapture provision** has been established in order to prevent a large property settlement that might take place after a divorce from being treated as alimony so as to produce a deduction for the payor.

Recapture occurs if payments decrease sharply in either the second or third year. Specifically, the amount of second year alimony recaptured is equal to the

TOPIC REVIEW 3-2

Tax Rules for Alimony
Treatment of recipient
The recipient of alimony must include the amounts received in gross income. Property settlements and child support payments are not taxable.
Treatment of payor
The payor of alimony may deduct amounts paid *for* adjusted gross income. Property settlements and child support payments are not deductible.
Applicable to
Payments must be pursuant to a divorce, separation, or a written agreement between spouses.
Requirements
Spouses must be living in separate households. Payments must be in the form of cash paid to (or for the benefit of) a spouse or former spouse. Payments must terminate at the death of the payee. Payments may not be designated as being other than alimony (such as child support or a property settlement).
Recapture
If the amount of payments declines in the second or third year, a portion of the early payments may have to be recaptured as income by the payor. The payee may deduct the same recaptured amount.
Dates
Current rules apply to agreements reached after 1984. Current rules also apply to earlier agreements if both parties agree in writing. Different rules apply to other earlier agreements.

Additional Comment

If any amount specified in the divorce instrument will be reduced due to the happening of a contingency relating to a child or reduced at a time which can clearly be associated with such contingency, then the amount of the reduction is treated as child support.

second year alimony reduced by the total of $15,000 and the third year alimony. The amount of first year alimony recaptured is equal to the first year alimony reduced by the total of $15,000 and the average alimony paid in the second year (reduced by the recapture for that year) and the third year. Both first and second year amounts are recaptured by requiring the payor to report the excess as income (and allowing the payee to deduct the same amount) in the third year. Recapture is not required if payments cease because of either the death of either spouse or remarriage of the recipient.

Example 3-24 ∎
> As a result of their divorce, Hal is ordered to pay to Rose $100,000 alimony in 1994 and $20,000 per year thereafter until her death or remarriage. Hal must recapture the amount of the decrease in excess of $15,000 or $65,000 ($100,000 − $20,000 − $15,000). The $65,000 of alimony in 1994 must be reported by Hal as income during 1996. Also, Rose may deduct the $65,000 *for* AGI in 1996. ∎

Example 3-25 ∎
> As a result of their separation, Mary agrees to pay Tom $20,000 per year. The payments are to cease if Tom remarries. In the year after the agreement is reached, Tom remarries and Mary discontinues the payments. No recapture is required because the payments are contingent upon the remarriage of the recipient and the payments have been discontinued because of the occurrence of this contingency. ∎

Pensions and Annuities

Additional Comment

The three largest sources of nonwage income in 1991, in rank order, were taxable interest, income from pensions and annuities, and business and professional income.

An **annuity** is a series of regular payments that will continue for a fixed period of time or will continue until the death of the recipient. Elderly taxpayers occasionally purchase annuities from insurance companies to provide a source of funds during retirement years. The insurance company may agree to make payments to the insured for the remainder of the insured's life. The retired individual is assured of a steady flow of funds for life. The price paid for the annuity represents its cost. The insured taxpayer is permitted to recover this cost tax free.

Pensions are usually paid in the form of an annuity. In the case of a pension, an employer and/or the employee contribute funds to a plan during the years of employment. When the employee retires, the amounts contributed and income accumulated thereon become available to the retired employee. Often the retired employee has the option of receiving a lump-sum payment[61] or an annuity. The annuity rules for pensions are similar to the rules applicable to other types of annuities. Employees can recover their costs tax free. The employee's cost is the amount contributed (usually through withholding) by the employee to the plan. It does not include employer contributions.[62]

Individuals receiving an annuity are permitted to exclude their cost, but are taxed on the remaining portion of the annuity. The following steps can be followed to determine the nontaxable portion of the annuity:

Additional Comment

The expected multiples (life expectancies) as shown in Table 3-1 are calculated by professional actuaries. It is sometimes said that an actuary is a person who failed the personality test to become an accountant.

- Determine the **expected return multiple.** This is the number of years that the annuity is expected to continue. This may be a stated term, say 10 years, or it may be for the remainder of the taxpayer's life. In this situation, the expected

---

[61] Lump-sum distributions are subject to a special five-year forward averaging computation (see Chapter 14).
[62] The employee has not previously included the employer's contribution in income. The employee was, of course, taxed on the salary from which his or her own contribution was withheld.

return multiple (life expectancy) is determined by referring to a table (see Table 3-1) developed by the IRS.

- Determine the **expected return.** This is computed by multiplying the amount of the annual payment by the expected return multiple.
- Determine the **exclusion ratio.** This is computed by dividing the investment in the contract (its cost) by the expected return (from above).
- Determine the **current year's exclusion.** This is computed by multiplying the exclusion ratio (from above) times the amount received during the year.

Example 3-26 ■

David, a 65-year-old male, purchases an annuity for $30,000. Under the terms of the annuity, David is to receive $300 per month ($3,600 per year) for the rest of his life.

- The expected return multiple is 20.0. The multiple is obtained by reference to Table 3-1 (Part B).
- The expected return is $72,000 (20.0 × $3,600).
- The exclusion ratio is 0.417 ($30,000 ÷ $72,000).
- The exclusion is $1,500 (0.417 × $3,600). ■

The computation can be abbreviated. The annual exclusion can be determined by dividing the cost of the annuity by the expected return multiple.

Example 3-27 ■

Assume the same facts as in Example 3-26. David can determine his $1,500 annual exclusion by dividing the cost by his expected return multiple ($1,500 = $30,000 ÷ 20.0). ■

This computation assumes that payments are received throughout the year. This shortcut method would not work if payments were received for only part of the year. Thus, if payments start during the year (or end during the year), the longer method should be used.

After the entire cost of an annuity has been recovered, the full amount of all future payments is taxable. On the other hand, if an individual dies before recovering the entire cost, then the remaining unrecovered cost can be deducted as an itemized deduction on that individual's final return.

Advance Payments. Many pensions contain provisions that allow taxpayers to withdraw amounts prior to the normal starting date. Under current law, an amount withdrawn from a pension prior to the starting date is considered to be in part a recovery of the employee's contributions and part a recovery of the employer's contributions.[63] After all contributions have been withdrawn, additional withdrawals are fully taxable. In addition to being subject to the regular income tax, any amount withdrawn may also be subject to a 10% nondeductible penalty. The penalty is not applicable to a taxpayer who is age 59½ or older; to a disabled or deceased taxpayer; to a retired employee who is receiving an annuity based on his or her life expectancy; to a taxpayer who has reached the age of 55 and has taken early retirement; to a taxpayer who uses the distribution to pay medical expenses to the extent deductible under Sec. 213; or to an alternate payee pursuant to a qualified domestic relations order.[64]

[63] Sec. 72(e).
[64] Sec. 72(t)(2).

TABLE 3-1   Ordinary Life Annuities—One Life—Expected Return Multiple

Age	Multiple	Age	Multiple	Age	Multiple
5	76.6	42	40.6	79	10.0
6	75.6	43	39.6	80	9.5
7	74.7	44	38.7	81	8.9
8	73.7	45	37.7	82	8.4
9	72.7	46	36.8	83	7.9
10	71.7	47	35.9	84	7.4
11	70.7	48	34.9	85	6.9
12	69.7	49	34.0	86	6.5
13	68.8	50	33.1	87	6.1
14	67.8	51	32.2	88	5.7
15	66.8	52	31.3	89	5.3
16	65.8	53	30.4	90	5.0
17	64.8	54	29.5	91	4.7
18	63.9	55	28.6	92	4.4
19	62.9	56	27.7	93	4.1
20	61.9	57	26.8	94	3.9
21	60.9	58	25.9	95	3.7
22	59.9	59	25.0	96	3.4
23	59.0	60	24.2	97	3.2
24	58.0	61	23.3	98	3.0
25	57.0	62	22.5	99	2.8
26	56.0	63	21.6	100	2.7
27	55.1	64	20.8	101	2.5
28	54.1	65	20.0	102	2.3
29	53.1	66	19.2	103	2.1
30	52.2	67	18.4	104	1.9
31	51.2	68	17.6	105	1.8
32	50.2	69	16.8	106	1.6
33	49.3	70	16.0	107	1.4
34	48.3	71	15.3	108	1.3
35	47.3	72	14.6	109	1.1
36	46.4	73	13.9	110	1.0
37	45.4	74	13.2	111	.9
38	44.4	75	12.5	112	.8
39	43.5	76	11.9	113	.7
40	42.5	77	11.2	114	.6
41	41.5	78	10.6	115	.5

Source: Reg. Sec. 1.72-9 Table V

Note: This table should be used if any or all investments were made on or after July 1, 1986. If all investments were made before July 1, 1986 use Reg. Sec. 1.72-9 Table I (not shown).

Example 3-28 ■   Dick, age 45 and in good health, withdrew $2,000 from a pension plan during the current year. No exception exempts Dick from the 10% penalty. Dick had contributed $40,000 to the plan, and his employer had contributed $60,000. Dick must include $1,200 (0.60 × $2,000) in income. Since no exception applies, Dick must also pay an additional penalty of $120 (0.10 × $1,200). The penalty is not deductible by Dick. ■

Non-employee annuities are subject to different rules found in Sec. 72(e)(2) and (3). Distributions from non-employee annuities received prior to the starting date are taxable to the extent the cash surrender value of the annuity exceeds the taxpayer's investment in the annuity contract.

Income from Life Insurance and Endowment Contracts

The face amount of life insurance received because of the death of the insured is not taxable. If the proceeds are left with the insurance company and as a result earn interest, the interest payments are taxable. (See Chapter 4 for a detailed discussion of life insurance and endowment contracts.)

Income from Discharge of Indebtedness

In general, the forgiveness of debt is a taxable event. The person who owed the money must report the amount forgiven as income unless one of several exceptions found in the tax law applies. These exceptions are discussed in Chapter 4.

Income Passed Through to Taxpayer

In many instances, income is "passed through" one entity and is taxed to another. Section 61 specifically lists three such instances: (1) the distributive share of a partnership's income, (2) income in respect of a decedent, and (3) income from an interest in an estate or trust. Though not mentioned in Sec. 61, similar treatment is accorded S corporation income. In each case, one entity produces the income, but it is the person who will eventually benefit from the income who is taxed. The rules can be summarized as follows:

Key Point

The pass through of income by a partnership can create a situation known as "phantom income." In this situation a partner is required to report income on his or her individual tax return, but the partner may not have received a cash distribution from the partnership.

- Each partner reports his or her share of the partnership's income. Each partner deducts his or her share of the partnership's expenses. The income and deductions are reported by the partners whether or not any amount is actually distributed by the partnership during the year. The income belongs to the partner even if it is not distributed currently.

- Income in respect of a decedent is income earned by an individual prior to death that is paid to another after the death. For example, salary earned by a husband who uses the cash method of accounting prior to his death in an automobile accident may be paid to his widow after the accident. The recipient, in this case the widow, is taxed on the income if it has not been taxed to the decedent prior to his death.

- Estates and trusts are taxed on the income they accumulate.[65] Distributions to beneficiaries are deductible by estates and trusts. Such distributions are taxable to the beneficiaries. Thus, dividends received by a trust and distributed to the beneficiary of the trust are deductible by the trust and are taxable to the beneficiary.

- S corporations are taxed much like partnerships. Each shareholder in the corporation is taxed on his or her share of the corporation's income whether or not the income is actually distributed.

OTHER ITEMS OF GROSS INCOME

The preceding discussions considered items of gross income specifically listed in Sec. 61(a). The fact that an item of income is listed in Sec. 61(a) does not cause it to be

---

[65] Note the distinction between income in respect of a decedent and the income of an estate. Income in respect of a decedent is the income earned prior to death that was never taxed to the decedent. An example would be interest that was accrued but unpaid at death. Income of an estate is income earned after death that is paid to the estate. An example would be interest that accrues after the decedent's death.

taxable. Rather, the fact that it is not specifically excluded causes an item of income to be taxable. Some items of gross income not mentioned in Sec. 61(a) are discussed below.

Prizes, Awards, Gambling Winnings, and Treasure Finds

In general, prizes, awards, gambling winnings, and treasure finds are taxable.[66] Winnings in contests, competitions, and quiz shows as well as awards from an employer to an employee in recognition of some achievement in connection with his or her employment are taxable.[67] The value of the goods or services received is included in gross income. Total gambling winnings must be included in gross income.[68] This includes proceeds from lotteries, raffles, sweepstakes, and the like. Gambling losses (up to the amount of the current year's winnings) are allowable as an itemized deduction.[69] The Regulations state that a treasure find constitutes gross income to the extent of its value in the year in which it is reduced to undisputed possession.[70]

Example 3-29 ∎ Several years ago, Colleen purchased a used piano at an auction for $15. In the current year, she finds $4,500 of currency hidden in the piano. Colleen must report the $4,500 as income in the current year.[71] ∎

Illegal Income

Income from illegal activities is taxable.[72] Some people are surprised that this is part of the tax law, but it is this fact that serves as the basis for many criminal convictions. Al Capone was convicted of income tax evasion, not bootlegging or other crimes. It is reasonable to assume that few criminals report their illegal income. It is not necessary to prove that an individual had illegal income, merely that the individual had income.

Individuals have used varied defenses against this rule. One taxpayer was successful in convincing the Supreme Court that he should not be taxed on embezzlement gains because he had an unconditional obligation to repay the amount embezzled,[73] but the Supreme Court reversed this position in a later case.[74] The court concluded that although there is an obligation to repay, there is no "consensual recognition" (intent) to repay. In addition to embezzlement of funds, the courts have held that a kidnapper's ransom was taxable,[75] along with profits from bookmaking,[76] card playing,[77] forgery,[78] stealing,[79] bank robbery,[80] sale of narcotics,[81] illegal sale of liquor,[82] and bribes.[83]

---

[66] Exclusions for scholarships and fellowships and a limited exclusion for prizes awarded for scientific, charitable, or similar meritorious achievements are discussed in Chapter 4.
[67] Sec. 74 and Reg. Sec. 1.74-1.
[68] *U.S. v. Manley S. Sullivan*, 6 AFTR 6753, 1 USTC ¶ 236 (USSC, 1927).
[69] Sec. 165(d).
[70] Reg. Sec. 1.61-14(a).
[71] *Ermenegildo Cesarini v. U.S.*, 26 AFTR 2d 5107, 70-2 USTC ¶ 9509 (6th Cir., 1970).
[72] Reg. 1.61-14(a).
[73] *CIR v. Laird Wilcox*, 34 AFTR 811, 46-1 USTC ¶ 9188 (USSC, 1946).
[74] *Eugene C. James v. U.S.*, 7 AFTR 2d 1361, 61-1 USTC ¶ 9449 (USSC, 1961).
[75] *Murray Humphreys v. CIR*, 28 AFTR 1030, 42-1 USTC ¶ 9237 (7th Cir., 1942).
[76] *James P. McKenna*, 1 B.T.A. 326 (1925).
[77] *L. Weiner*, 10 B.T.A. 905 (1928).
[78] *Cass Sunstein*, 1966 PH T.C. Memo ¶ 66,043, 25 TCM 247.
[79] *Mathias Schira v. CIR*, 50 AFTR 1404, 57-1 USTC ¶ 9413 (6th Cir., 1957).
[80] *Gary Ayers*, 1978 PH T.C. Memo ¶ 78,341, 37 TCM 1415.
[81] *Antonino Farina v. McMahon*, 2 AFTR 2d 5918, 58-2 USTC ¶ 9938 (D.C. N.Y., 1958).
[82] *U.S. v. Manley S. Sullivan*, 6 AFTR 6753, 1 USTC ¶ 236 (USSC, 1927).
[83] *U.S. v. Patrick Commerford*, 12 AFTR 364, 1933 CCH ¶ 9255 (2nd Cir., 1933).

Unemployment Compensation

For many years, unemployment compensation was excluded from gross income. In 1978, Congress first taxed unemployment compensation because these benefits are a substitute for taxable wages. Initially, unemployment compensation was taxable if adjusted gross income exceeded certain base amounts. However, beginning in 1987, all unemployment compensation became taxable. This is true for both government-financed programs and employer-financed benefits.

Social Security Benefits

Social security benefits were excluded from gross income until 1984. Between 1984 and 1993, up to 50% of social security benefits were taxable. Beginning in 1994, up to 85% of social security benefits may be taxable. Under Sec. 86, the portion of social security benefits that are taxable depends on the taxpayer's provisional income and filing status. Provisional income is computed using the following formula.

Adjusted gross income (excluding social security benefits)		$xx,xxx
Plus:	Tax-exempt interest	x,xxx
	Excluded foreign income	x,xxx
	50% of social security benefits	x,xxx
Provisional income		$xx,xxx

Married filing separately. In the case of a married person filing separately, taxable social security benefits are equal to the lesser of:

- 85% of social security benefits, or
- 85% of provisional income.

Married filing jointly. For married couples filing jointly, the computation of the taxable portion of social security benefits is as below:

If provisional income is $32,000 or less, no social security benefits are taxable.

If provisional income is over $32,000 (but not over $44,000) taxable social security benefits equal the lesser of:

- 50% of the social security benefits or
- 50% of the excess of provisional income over $32,000.

If provisional income is over $44,000, taxable social security benefits are equal to the lesser of:

- 85% of the social security benefits, or
- the lesser of (1) $6,000 or (2) 50% of social security benefits, plus 85% of provisional income over $44,000.

Single taxpayers. For single taxpayers, the computation of the taxable portion of social security benefits is as below:

If provisional income is $25,000 or less, no social security benefits are taxable.

If provisional income is over $25,000 (but not over $34,000), taxable social security benefits are equal to the lesser of:

- 50% of the social security benefits, or
- 50% of the excess of provisional income over $25,000.

If provisional income is over $34,000, taxable social security benefits are equal to the lesser of:

- 85% of the social security benefits, or
- the lesser of (1) $4,500 or (2) 50% of social security benefits, plus 85% of provisional income over $34,000.

Example 3-30 ■

Real World Example

The requirement that tax-exempt income be included in determining the taxable portion of social security benefits has been challenged on the basis that such provision is unconstitutional. However, the court held that this provision placed only an indirect burden on the governmental unit that issued the tax-exempt bonds, which was not protected by the intergovernmental immunity doctrine. H.J. Goldin v. Baker, 59 AFTR 2d 87-444, 87-1 USTC ¶ 9128, (2nd Cir., 1987).

Holly is a single taxpayer with a taxable pension of $22,000, tax exempt interest of $10,000, and social security benefits of $8,000. Her provisional income is $36,000 determined as follows:

Adjusted gross income		$22,000
Plus:	Tax-exempt interest	10,000
	50% of social security benefits	4,000
	Provisional income	$36,000

The taxable social security benefits are equal to $5,700 which is the lesser of $6,800 (0.85 × $8,000) or $5,700 (the lesser of $4,500 or $4,000*, plus $1,700**).
*50% of the social security benefits
**($36,000 provisional income − $34,000 threshold) × 0.85 ■

The result of the computation is to exclude from gross income the social security benefits received by lower income individuals, but to tax a portion (up to 85%) of the benefits received by taxpayers with higher incomes.

The term **social security benefits** refers to basic monthly retirement and disability benefits paid under social security and also to tier-one railroad retirement benefits. It does not include supplementary Medicare benefits that cover the cost of doctors' services and other medical benefits.

Insurance Proceeds and Court Awards

Additional Comment

For a 65-year-old taxpayer who retired in 1993, the maximum monthly individual social security benefit was $1,128.

In general, insurance proceeds and court awards are taxable. Two exceptions are accident and health insurance benefits and the face amount of life insurance. (See Chapter 4 for a discussion of these benefits.)

Insurance proceeds or court awards received because of the destruction of property are included in gross income only to the extent the proceeds exceed the adjusted basis of the property. Involuntary conversion provisions permit taxpayers to avoid being taxed if they reinvest the proceeds in a qualified replacement property.[84] If the proceeds are less than the property's adjusted basis, they reduce the amount of any deductible loss. Proceeds of insurance guarding against loss of profits because of a casualty are taxable.[85] Similarly, if a taxpayer had to sue a customer to collect income owed to the taxpayer, the amount collected is taxable just as it would have been had the taxpayer collected the income without going to court.

Example 3-31 ■

Gulf Corporation's factory was destroyed by fire. Gulf Corporation collected insurance of $400,000, which equaled its basis in the building and $250,000 for the profits lost during the time the company was rebuilding its factory. The $400,000 is not taxable because it constitutes a recovery of the basis of the factory. The $250,000 is taxable because it represents lost income. Recall that the income would have been taxable had it been earned by the company from regular operations. ■

[84] The involuntary conversion provisions are discussed in Chapter 12.
[85] *Oppenheim's Inc. v. Kavanagh,* 39 AFTR 468, 50-1 USTC ¶ 9249 (D.C.-Mich., 1950).

Real World Example
During World War II citizens of Japanese ancestry were forcibly relocated and interned. Under the Civil Liberties Act of 1988 amounts were paid to these citizens in restitution. These payments were excludable since they were treated as damages for human suffering.

Although there are few exclusions designed specifically for insurance proceeds or court awards, such amounts may be covered by other, more general exclusions. For example, Sec. 104(a)(2) excludes "damages received (whether by suit or agreement) on account of personal injury or sickness." Thus, amounts collected because of personal injury suffered in an automobile accident are excluded.[86]

In addition to compensatory damages, individuals often seek punitive damages, an amount awarded to punish the defendant for intentional infliction of harm or negligence. In general, punitive damages are taxable only if compensatory damages are taxable. Thus, punitive damages awarded in a claim for loss of income are taxable.[87]

Example 3-32 ■ Gold Corporation brought suit against a competitor for patent infringement. Gold Corporation recovered $600,000 representing the profits it lost because of the acts of its competitor and punitive damages of $1,200,000. The $600,000 is taxable because it replaces taxable income. The $1,200,000 is taxable because it represents punitive damages. ■

An exception applies to punitive damages awarded in connection with personal injury cases. Such damages are excluded only in cases involving sickness and physical injury. Thus, punitive damages awarded in a case based on sex discrimination are taxable without regard to whether the compensatory damages are taxable.[88]

Recovery of Previously Deducted Amounts

On occasion, a taxpayer may deduct an amount in one year but recover the amount in a subsequent year. In general, the amount recovered must be included in the gross income in the year it is recovered. Cash-basis taxpayers encounter this situation more often than accrual-basis taxpayers because their expenses are generally deductible in the year they are paid. If the amount was overpaid, the taxpayer, of course, can anticipate a refund.

Example 3-33 ■ During 1994, Cindy's employer withheld $1,000 from her wages for state income taxes. She claimed the $1,000 as an itemized deduction on her 1994 federal income tax return. Her itemized deductions totaled $12,000. Her 1994 state income tax was only $800. As a result, Cindy received a $200 refund from the state in 1995. Because Cindy deducted the full $1,000 in 1994, she must report the $200 refund as income on her 1995 federal income tax return. ■

Any recovery of a previously deducted amount may lead to income recognition. Recovery, however, is often associated with expenses such as state income taxes or bad debts deducted in one year but recovered in a later year, medical expenses deducted in one year but reimbursed by insurance in a later year, casualty losses deducted in one year but reimbursed by court award or insurance in a later year, and deductions for amounts paid by check where the payee never cashed the check. Several related rules should be noted:

- If the refund or other recovery occurs in the same year, the refund or recovery reduces the deduction and is not reported as income.

---

[86] See Chapter 4 for a detailed discussion of this provision.
[87] *Glenshaw Glass Co. v. CIR*, 47 AFTR 162, 55-1 USTC ¶ 9308 (USSC, 1955).
[88] Sec. 104(a), effective for awards received after July 10, 1989.

- Interest on the amount refunded is taxable and is not subject to the tax benefit rule (discussed below).

- The character of the income reported in the year of repayment is dependent on the type of deduction previously reported. For instance, if the taxpayer deducted a short-term capital loss in one year, the subsequent recovery would be a short-term capital gain.[89]

Tax Benefit Rule. As noted above, a taxpayer who recovers an amount deducted in a previous year must report as gross income the amount recovered. The amount recovered need not be included in income, however, if the taxpayer received no tax benefit. There is a tax benefit only if the deduction reduced the tax for the year.[90]

Example 3-34 ■ In 1994, Jack's employer withheld $1,200 from his wages for state income tax. Jack claimed the $1,200 as an itemized deduction on his 1994 federal income tax return. Because of a variety of losses incurred by Jack, he reported a negative taxable income of $32,000 during 1994. The state refunded the $1,200 during 1995. Jack will not have to report the $1,200 as gross income on his federal return. He would have owed no federal income tax in 1994 even without the deduction for state income taxes. Therefore, Jack received no tax benefit from the deduction. ■

Tax benefit may be absent in other situations. For example, a taxpayer's total itemized deductions may have been less than the standard deduction, or the expense may have been less than the applicable floor. To illustrate, medical expenses can be deducted only to the extent they exceed a floor equal to 7.5% of adjusted gross income. If a taxpayer does not deduct medical expenses because they are less than the floor, the taxpayer does not have to report a subsequent reimbursement of the expense as income. If only a portion of an expense produces a tax benefit, only that portion has to be reported as income.

Example 3-35 ■ In 1994, Chris, an unmarried individual, had $1,000 withheld from her wages for state income tax. Her itemized deductions consisted of state income taxes of $1,250 and charitable contributions of $2,700. Her itemized deductions exceed the standard deduction by $150 ($1,250 + $2,700 − $3,800). If Chris received a state income tax refund of $200 in 1995 she must report only $150 as gross income in 1995. She benefited only from $150 of the deduction and so that is all she has to report as income. ■

Real World Example

An attorney collected fees from clients of his employer. Since the attorney and his employer were engaged in a dispute over ownership of the money, he deposited the disputed amount in a so-called trust account. The attorney was taxable on the amounts in the year received since he had control over the funds under the claim of right doctrine. Edward J. Costello, Jr., 1985 PH T.C. Memo ¶ 85,571, 50 TCM 1463.

Claim of Right

Sometimes taxpayers receive disputed amounts. For example, a contractor may receive payment on a job when the quality of the work is being questioned by the customer; a salesperson may receive commissions when there is a question as to whether the sales are final; or a litigant may receive a court award even though the case is on appeal. Under the claim of right doctrine, the recipient of a disputed amount must include the amount received in gross income as long as the use of the funds is unrestricted.

Example 3-36 ■ Jane wins a court case against a customer requiring the customer to pay her $10,000. The customer is unhappy with the result of the case and indicates that he

---

[89] *F. Donald Arrowsmith Exr. v. CIR,* 42 AFTR 649, 52-2 USTC ¶ 9527 (USSC, 1952).
[90] Sec. 111.

plans to appeal, but pays the $10,000 to avoid interest on the amount in the event he loses the appeal. Jane must include the $10,000 in gross income even though she will have to repay the amount in the event she loses the appeal. ■

Example 3-37 ■

Assume the same facts as in Example 3-36 except that the $10,000 is placed in escrow by the court awaiting the outcome of the appeal. Jane does not have to report the amount as she does not have use of the funds. ■

Of course, taxpayers may be required to repay the disputed amount in a subsequent year. Such taxpayers may deduct the previously reported amount in the year of repayment. The taxes saved from such a deduction, however, may be considerably less than the original tax. If the repayment is over $3,000, taxpayers have the option of reducing the current tax by the tax paid in the prior year or years on the repaid amount.[91]

Example 3-38 ■

Assume the same facts as in Example 3-36 except that after reporting the disputed $10,000 Jane loses the appeal and must repay the $10,000 to her customer. If Jane was in the 28% tax bracket when she reported the disputed amount, she would have paid a $2,800 (0.28 × $10,000) tax on the disputed amount. If she were in the 15% bracket when she made the repayment she would recover only $1,500 by deducting the $10,000. As the amount exceeds $3,000, Jane has the option of determining her current year's tax by deducting from the tax she would otherwise pay the original $2,800 tax paid in the earlier year. This amount is deductible in lieu of receiving a deduction of $1,500 (0.15 × $10,000) by using the current tax rate. ■

TAX PLANNING CONSIDERATIONS

Shifting Income

Key Point

The advantage of shifting income to children has been increased since the revision of the tax rate schedules in 1993. The highest and lowest marginal tax rates in 1992 were 31% and 15%, respectively. In 1993, the highest and lowest marginal rates are 39.6% and 15%, respectively.

A family can reduce its taxes by shifting income from family members who are in high tax brackets (say, parents) to family members who are in low tax brackets (say, children). Assignment of income rules prevent this from being done by merely redirecting the payment. A father cannot avoid a tax on his salary by ordering his employer to pay the salary to his daughter. Nevertheless, income can be shifted. For example, children may own stock in the family business. Dividends on the stock are taxed to the children. In the case of a child under age 14, the parents' (as opposed to the child's) tax rate, however, is applicable to unearned income. Series EE bonds may prove useful because the interest is deferred until the bond is redeemed or matures. The maturity date, of course, may be after the child reaches age 14. A child may work for the family business and be paid a reasonable salary. Such income is taxed at the child's tax rate, even if the child is under 14 years old and can be offset by the child's own standard deduction.

Shifting of income is constrained by several factors. As noted, the assignment of income doctrine limits transfers. Reasonableness limitations constrain compensation and other payments. Further, outright gifts of property are subject to gift taxes. Also, individuals are reluctant to transfer wealth to children for a variety of personal reasons. Yet, the tax saving potential of shifting income is often so great as to prompt many well-to-do families to use available shifting techniques.

---

[91] Sec. 1341.

Alimony

Whether payments made in connection with a divorce or separation are classified as alimony is of major tax significance. Such classification results in a deduction for the payor and income to the payee. Alimony is actually one way to shift income.

Example 3-39 ■ Tony, who has a 36% marginal tax rate, makes payments of $40,000 to his former wife. If deductible as alimony, Tony will save $14,400 (0.36 × $40,000) a year in federal income taxes. The amount of tax that the former wife must pay will depend on how much other income she has and whether she has deductions that will reduce the tax. Her tax might be even higher than her former husband's or as little as zero. ■

Two things are clear. One is that both parties should understand the implication of having amounts treated as alimony so as to avoid subsequent disputes. Second, the designation of the payments as alimony may be beneficial to both parties. The payor will, of course, benefit from a tax deduction. The payee may benefit because the fact that the payor can deduct alimony may mean that the payor will agree (and can afford) to make larger payments.

Real World Example

A dance studio using the accrual method was required to include in taxable income all advance payments for lessons in the form of cash and negotiable notes, plus contract installments due but remaining unpaid at year end. Mark E. Schlude v. CIR, 11 AFTR 2d 751, 63-1 USTC ¶ 9284 (USSC, 1963).

Prepaid Income

As explained earlier in this chapter, prepaid income is generally taxable when received. This accelerated recognition of income may be a significant disadvantage to the taxpayer if the related expenses are incurred in a later tax year. Thus, tax planning for prepaid amounts is essential.

Example 3-40 ■ Phil rents units in his apartment complex and requires tenants to pay the first and last months' rent before they move in. ■

Example 3-41 ■ Rita rents units in her apartment complex and requires tenants to pay the first month's rent and a refundable deposit (which equals one month's rent). ■

Historical Note

In 1954 Congress passed Sec. 452 allowing deferral of certain prepaid income, but in 1955 Congress retroactively repealed this section.

Although the full amount received by Phil in Example 3-40 is taxable when it is received, only one-half of the amount received by Rita in Example 3-41 is taxable when it is received. Rita is required to refund the deposit, assuming the tenant vacates leaving the property in good condition and having paid all rent. Therefore, the deposit is not taxable.

Taxpayers receiving advance payments in connection with services may be able to meet the requirements of Rev. Proc. 71-21 (discussed earlier in the chapter); while taxpayers receiving advance payments associated with the sale of merchandise may be able to meet the requirements of Reg. Sec. 1.451-5 (also discussed in this chapter). As noted, special rules exist for subscription income, membership fees, crop insurance proceeds, and drought sales of livestock, all of which allow taxpayers to defer recognizing income.

Taxable, Tax-Exempt, or Tax-Deferred Bonds

Which should a taxpayer choose: taxable bonds, tax-exempt bonds, or tax-deferred bonds? The answer depends on the relative interest rates and the taxpayer's current and future tax brackets. Taxable bonds yield the higher return, but the interest is taxable, of course. Tax-exempt bonds yield a lower return. Tax-deferred bonds generally yield a return somewhere close to that of taxable bonds. Interest on U.S. Series EE savings bonds is tax exempt if it is used for educational purposes and if other requirements of Sec. 135 are met (see the discussion earlier in this chapter). If these conditions are not met, the tax is deferred until the bonds are redeemed. The taxpayer may be in a lower bracket when the tax is eventually paid, and in the meantime, the interest that will eventually go to pay taxes is earning additional income.

The decision between taxable and exempt bonds is a rather easy one if the risk of the investments is assumed to be approximately equal. A taxpayer should invest in exempt bonds instead of taxable bonds if the interest on the exempt bonds is greater than the interest on the taxable bonds multiplied by 1 minus the taxpayer's marginal tax bracket (expressed as a decimal). Stated in a formula, this means invest in tax-exempt bonds if

$$\text{Return on the tax-exempt bonds} > \text{Return on the taxable bonds} \times (1 - \text{marginal tax bracket})$$

Example 3-42 ■

Self-Study Question

The highest marginal tax rate is currently 39.6%, but it was 31% in 1992. Assume that interest rates on taxable bonds have remained constant at 10% since 1992. Considering only the effect of the tax rates, is the rate of interest on tax-exempt bonds likely to have fallen, risen, or remained the same?

Answer

Everything else being equal, one would expect the spread between taxable and nontaxable to have widened. A taxpayer having a marginal tax rate of 31% would be indifferent between a taxable bond yielding 10% and a tax-exempt bond yielding 6.9%. However, if the marginal tax rate is 39.6%, the yield on the tax-exempt bond would have to decline to 6.04% for the taxpayer to remain indifferent.

Robert's marginal tax bracket is 28% and he is trying to decide between tax-exempt bonds, which pay 6% interest, and taxable bonds paying 8% interest. Robert should invest in the exempt bonds because 6% is greater than 5.76% $(0.08 \times [1 - 0.28])$. ■

Comparison of taxable bonds or exempt bonds to tax-deferred bonds is more complicated. As noted, the advantages of the tax-deferred bonds are twofold. First, the taxpayer may be in a lower tax bracket when the tax is paid (e.g., taxpayers who plan to redeem the bonds after retirement). Second, the amount that will eventually go to pay the tax earns income until the tax must be paid. Although the computation is not covered here, it is noted that taxpayers who anticipate that they will be in lower tax brackets and who plan to leave funds invested for several years may benefit from Series EE U.S. savings bonds compared with taxable bonds.

Reporting Savings Bond Interest

It may be desirable to purchase Series EE bonds in the name of a child despite the fact that such interest is subject to the kiddie tax (see Chapter 2). This is because there is no income tax as long as the child's annual income is less than $600. It is, however, necessary to communicate to the IRS by return an election to report interest annually. This is true even if the taxpayer is not otherwise required to file a return.[92] Taxpayers who have not been reporting savings bond interest annually may change to annual reporting, but are required to report both current and previously accrued interest in the year of the change.[93]

Taxpayers who report savings bond interest annually are allowed to change to the deferral method without IRS approval.[94] This is particularly useful where the decision to report interest currently was made prior to the imposition of the kiddie tax. Taxpayers who make this election are bound by it for five years.

[92] *Philip Apkin*, 86 T.C. 692 (1986).
[93] Reg. Sec. 1.454-1(a)(4), Ex. (1).
[94] Rev. Proc. 89-46, 1989-2 C.B. 597.

TOPIC REVIEW 3-3

Reporting of Income		
Type of Income	Reported On	Related Deductions Are Claimed On
Wages, salaries, tips, etc.	Form 1040	Schedule A and various other forms: moving—Form 3903; travel, transportation, etc.—Form 2106
Interest	Form 1040 (if less than $400), otherwise Schedule B	Schedule A (miscellaneous deductions if any, e.g., safe deposit box fees)
Dividends	Form 1040 (if less than $400), otherwise Schedule B	Schedule A (miscellaneous deductions if any, e.g., safe deposit box fee)
Refund of state or local income taxes	Form 1040 (instructions contain a worksheet)	Schedule A (miscellaneous deductions if any, e.g., fee paid for tax advice)
Alimony	Form 1040	Schedule A (miscellaneous deduction, if any, e.g., legal fee associated with alimony)
Business income	Schedule C or C-EZ (net income or loss is transferred to Form 1040)	Schedule C or C-EZ (e.g., depreciation, advertising, repairs)
Capital Gains	Schedule D (note: if Schedule D is not needed to report other gains or losses, capital gains dividends [from mutual funds, etc.] can be reported directly on Form 1040 and Schedule B)	Schedule D (capital losses) or Schedule A (investment expenses)
Supplemental gains	Form 4797	Form 4797 (e.g., ordinary losses)
Pensions and annuities	Form 1040 (instructions contain a worksheet)	Generally no related deductions
Rents, royalties, partnerships, S corporations, estates, trusts, etc.	Schedule E	Schedule E
Farm income	Schedule F	Schedule F
Unemployment compensation	Form 1040	Generally no related deductions
Social security benefits	Form 1040 (instructions contain a worksheet)	Generally no related deductions
Other income	Form 1040	Schedule A (miscellaneous deductions, if any)

COMPLIANCE AND PROCEDURAL CONSIDERATIONS

Additional Comment

The dollar amount of tax-exempt interest income is recorded on Form 1040, line 8b, but is not included in the tax base. The IRS likely requires the reporting of this type of income since it may affect the taxability of social security benefits.

Form 1040 lists various types of income. Some items of income (wages, tax refunds, alimony, pensions and annuities, unemployment compensation, social security benefits, and other income) are listed directly on Form 1040. Most expenses related to these items of income are deducted as miscellaneous itemized deductions on Schedule A.

Most other types of income are reported on special schedules (e.g., business income is reported on Schedule C or Schedule C-EZ (e.g., for businesses with gross receipts of $25,000 or less or total business expenses of $2,000 or less); capital gains on Schedule

D; supplemental gains on Form 4797; rents, royalties, etc. on Schedule E; and farm income on Schedule F). Related deductions are claimed on the same schedules. The net income or loss determined on these forms is transferred to Form 1040.

Dividends and interest income are listed directly on Form 1040 unless the amount of either exceeds $400. In that case, the dividends or interest are reported on Schedule B. The total is then transferred to Form 1040. In either case, the related deductions, such as a safe deposit box fee paid for storage of investment certificates, are miscellaneous itemized deductions. The miscellaneous deductions are allowable only if the total of such deductions exceeds 2% of adjusted gross income. Topic Review 3-3 summarizes the procedures for reporting income.

Example 3-43 ■

Key Point

The amount labeled as "total income" on line 23 of Form 1040 is not gross income, adjusted gross income, or taxable income.

John J. Alexander has several items of income and related deductions:

Salary	$40,000
Deductible alimony payments	6,000
Taxable interest	300
Dividends: Ford Motor Co.	150
Omaha Mutual Fund	600
($120 is a return of capital dividend and $50 is capital gain dividend)	
Rent income (depreciation, interest, repairs and other related expenses total $8,000)	11,000

■

The reporting of these items of income is illustrated on page 1 of Form 1040 (Figure 3-1) and on Schedule B of Form 1040 (Figure 3-2). Salary and interest (because the interest is less than $400) are entered directly on Form 1040. Note that on Schedule B, the capital gain distribution and the nontaxable distribution are subtracted from total dividends. Rental income would be entered on Schedule E (not illustrated), and the net income after deducting related expenses is transferred to Form 1040. Alimony received and alimony payments are reported on page 1 of Form 1040.

PROBLEM MATERIALS

DISCUSSION QUESTIONS

3-1. What phrase is found in both the Sixteenth Amendment to the Constitution and Sec. 61(a)?

3-2. Is there a single reason that explains why some items of income are taxable and others are not? What is the implication of this fact?

3-3. Contrast the accounting and economic concepts of income.

3-4. Why does the tax concept of income more closely resemble the accounting concept of income rather than the economic concept?

3-5. Explain the meaning of the term *wherewithal-to-pay* as it applies to taxation.

3-6. If a loan is repaid, the lender does not have to include the repayment in gross income. There is no exclusion in the tax law that permits taxpayers to omit such amounts from gross income. How can this be explained?

3-7. A landlord who receives prepaid rent is required to report that amount as gross income when the payment is received. Why would Congress choose to do this? What problem does this create for the taxpayer?

Form 1040

Department of the Treasury—Internal Revenue Service

U.S. Individual Income Tax Return (B) 1993

IRS Use Only—Do not write or staple in this space.

For the year Jan. 1–Dec. 31, 1993, or other tax year beginning _____ , 1993, ending _____ , 19 ___ OMB No. 1545-0074

Label

(See instructions on page 12.)

Use the IRS label. Otherwise, please print or type.

L A B E L   H E R E

Your first name and initial   Last name
John J.   Alexander

Your social security number
123 : 45 : 6789

If a joint return, spouse's first name and initial   Last name

Spouse's social security number

Home address (number and street). If you have a P.O. box, see page 12.   Apt. no.
41 Oak Street

City, town or post office, state, and ZIP code. If you have a foreign address, see page 12.
Orlando, Florida   32816

For Privacy Act and Paperwork Reduction Act Notice, see page 4.

Presidential Election Campaign
(See page 12.)

	Yes	No	Note: Checking "Yes" will not change your tax or reduce your refund.
Do you want $3 to go to this fund?		X	
If a joint return, does your spouse want $3 to go to this fund?			

Filing Status

(See page 12.)

Check only one box.

1. [X] Single
2. [ ] Married filing joint return (even if only one had income)
3. [ ] Married filing separate return. Enter spouse's social security no. above and full name here. ▶ _____
4. [ ] Head of household (with qualifying person). (See page 13.) If the qualifying person is a child but not your dependent, enter this child's name here. ▶ _____
5. [ ] Qualifying widow(er) with dependent child (year spouse died ▶ 19 ___). (See page 13.)

Exemptions

(See page 13.)

If more than six dependents, see page 14.

6a [X] **Yourself.** If your parent (or someone else) can claim you as a dependent on his or her tax return, **do not** check box 6a. But be sure to check the box on line 33b on page 2

b [ ] **Spouse**

No. of boxes checked on 6a and 6b	1

c **Dependents:**

(1) Name (first, initial, and last name)	(2) Check if under age 1	(3) If age 1 or older, dependent's social security number	(4) Dependent's relationship to you	(5) No. of months lived in your home in 1993

No. of your children on 6c who:
- lived with you
- didn't live with you due to divorce or separation (see page 15)

Dependents on 6c not entered above ___

d If your child didn't live with you but is claimed as your dependent under a pre-1985 agreement, check here ▶ [ ]

e Total number of exemptions claimed

Add numbers entered on lines above ▶ | 1 |

Income

Attach Copy B of your Forms W-2, W-2G, and 1099-R here.

If you did not get a W-2, see page 10.

If you are attaching a check or money order, put it on top of any Forms W-2, W-2G, or 1099-R.

7	Wages, salaries, tips, etc. Attach Form(s) W-2	7	40,000
8a	**Taxable** interest income (see page 16). Attach Schedule B if over $400	8a	300
b	**Tax-exempt** interest (see page 17). DON'T include on line 8a 8b		
9	Dividend income. Attach Schedule B if over $400	9	580
10	Taxable refunds, credits, or offsets of state and local income taxes (see page 17)	10	
11	Alimony received	11	
12	Business income or (loss). Attach Schedule C or C-EZ	12	
13	Capital gain or (loss). Attach Schedule D	13	
14	Capital gain distributions not reported on line 13 (see page 17)	14	50
15	Other gains or (losses). Attach Form 4797	15	
16a	Total IRA distributions 16a ___ b Taxable amount (see page 18)	16b	
17a	Total pensions and annuities 17a ___ b Taxable amount (see page 18)	17b	
18	Rental real estate, royalties, partnerships, S corporations, trusts, etc. Attach Schedule E	18	3,000
19	Farm income or (loss). Attach Schedule F	19	
20	Unemployment compensation (see page 19)	20	
21a	Social security benefits 21a ___ b Taxable amount (see page 19)	21b	
22	Other income. List type and amount—see page 20 _____	22	
23	Add the amounts in the far right column for lines 7 through 22. This is your **total income** ▶	23	43,930

Adjustments to Income

(See page 20.)

24a	Your IRA deduction (see page 20) 24a		
b	Spouse's IRA deduction (see page 20) 24b		
25	One-half of self-employment tax (see page 21) 25		
26	Self-employed health insurance deduction (see page 22) 26		
27	Keogh retirement plan and self-employed SEP deduction 27		
28	Penalty on early withdrawal of savings 28		
29	Alimony paid. Recipient's SSN ▶ 987 : 65 : 4321 29	6,000	
30	Add lines 24a through 29. These are your **total adjustments** ▶	30	6,000

Adjusted Gross Income

31	Subtract line 30 from line 23. This is your **adjusted gross income.** If this amount is less than $23,050 and a child lived with you, see page EIC-1 to find out if you can claim the "Earned Income Credit" on line 56 ▶	31	37,930

FIGURE 3-1   Form 1040 (Page 1)

Cat. No. 12598V

Form **1040** (1993)

OMB No. 1545-0074   Page **2**

Name(s) shown on Form 1040. Do not enter name and social security number if shown on other side.

John J. Alexander

Your social security number

123 : 45 : 6789

Schedule B—Interest and Dividend Income

Attachment Sequence No. **08**

Part I Interest Income (See pages 16 and B-1.)			
	Note: *If you had over $400 in taxable interest income, you must also complete Part III.*		
	Interest Income		Amount
	1 List name of payer. If any interest is from a seller-financed mortgage and the buyer used the property as a personal residence, see page B-1 and list this interest first. Also show that buyer's social security number and address ▶		
Note: If you received a Form 1099-INT, Form 1099-OID, or substitute statement from a brokerage firm, list the firm's name as the payer and enter the total interest shown on that form.	·· ·· ·· ·· ·· ·· ·· ·· ·· ·· ·· ··	**1**	
	2 Add the amounts on line 1	**2**	
	3 Excludable interest on series EE U.S. savings bonds issued after 1989 from Form 8815, line 14. You MUST attach Form 8815 to Form 1040	**3**	
	4 Subtract line 3 from line 2. Enter the result here and on Form 1040, line 8a ▶	**4**	

Part II Dividend Income (See pages 17 and B-1.)			
	Note: *If you had over $400 in gross dividends and/or other distributions on stock, you must also complete Part III.*		
	Dividend Income		Amount
	5 List name of payer. Include gross dividends and/or other distributions on stock here. Any capital gain distributions and nontaxable distributions will be deducted on lines 7 and 8 ▶ ································		
	Ford Motor Company		150 00
	Omaha Mutual Fund		600 00
Note: If you received a Form 1099-DIV or substitute statement from a brokerage firm, list the firm's name as the payer and enter the total dividends shown on that form.		**5**	

6 Add the amounts on line 5		**6**	750 00
7 Capital gain distributions. Enter here and on Schedule D* .	**7** 50 00		
8 Nontaxable distributions. (See the inst. for Form 1040, line 9.)	**8** 120 00		
9 Add lines 7 and 8		**9**	170 00
10 Subtract line 9 from line 6. Enter the result here and on Form 1040, line 9 . ▶		**10**	580 00

If you received capital gain distributions but do not need Schedule D to report any other gains or losses, see the instructions for Form 1040, lines 13 and 14.

Part III Foreign Accounts and Trusts (See page B-2.)		Yes	No
	If you had over $400 of interest or dividends OR had a foreign account or were a grantor of, or a transferor to, a foreign trust, you must complete this part.		
	11a At any time during 1993, did you have an interest in or a signature or other authority over a financial account in a foreign country, such as a bank account, securities account, or other financial account? See page B-2 for exceptions and filing requirements for Form TD F 90-22.1		X
	b If "Yes," enter the name of the foreign country ▶ ·············		
	12 Were you the grantor of, or transferor to, a foreign trust that existed during 1993, whether or not you have any beneficial interest in it? If "Yes," you may have to file Form 3520, 3520-A, or 926 .		X

For Paperwork Reduction Act Notice, see Form 1040 instructions.   **Schedule B (Form 1040) 1993**

FIGURE 3-2   Form 1040 (Schedule B)

3-8. Office space is often rented without carpet, wallcovering or windowcovering. Further, many rental agreements specify that these improvements cannot be removed by a tenant, if removal causes any damage to the property. What issue does this raise?

3-9. Does the fact that an item of income is paid in a form other than cash mean it is nontaxable? Explain.

3-10. Will an expenditure by an employer be taxable to an employee if the expenditure results in indirect economic benefit to the employee?

3-11. Explain the significance of *Lucas v. Earl* and *Helvering v. Horst.*

3-12. Under present-day tax law, community property rules are followed in allocating income between husband and wife. Is this consistent with *Lucas v. Earl?* Explain.

3-13. Ricardo owns a small unincorporated business. His 15-year-old daughter Jane works in the business on a part-time basis and was paid wages of $3,000 during the current year. Who is taxed on the child's earnings—Jane or her father? Explain.

3-14. Define the term *constructive receipt.* Explain its importance.

3-15. Explain three restrictions on the concept of constructive receipt.

3-16. When is income considered to be earned by an accrual-basis taxpayer?

3-17. a. Explain the difference between the treatment of prepaid income under the tax law and under financial accounting.
   b. Why are the two treatments so different?
   c. What problem does this treatment create for taxpayers?

3-18. Under what conditions is an accrual-basis taxpayer allowed to defer reporting amounts received in the advance of the delivery of goods?

3-19. Under what conditions is an accrual-basis taxpayer allowed to defer reporting advance payments received for services?

3-20. Is the gross income from the sale of inventory equal to the sales price of the inventory? Explain.

3-21. a. Is the interest received from government obligations taxable? Explain.
   b. What impact does the fact that some bond interest is tax exempt have on interest rates?
   c. Is an investor always better off buying tax exempt bonds? Explain.

3-22. Are improvements made by a lessee to a lessor's property included in the income of the lessor?

3-23. Explain the relationship between dividends and earnings and profits.

3-24. On what basis did the Supreme Court in *Eisner v. Macomber* decide that stock dividends are nontaxable?

3-25. What is the significance of a constructive dividend?

3-26. Explain the importance of the distinction between alimony and a property settlement.

3-27. What is an annuity? What portion of an annuity is taxable?

3-28. a. Are items of income not listed in Sec. 61 taxable? Explain.
   b. As there is no specific exclusion for unrealized income, why is it not taxable?
   c. Can income be realized even when a cash-method taxpayer does not receive cash?
   d. Does a cash basis taxpayer realize income upon the receipt of a note?

3-29. a. Briefly explain the tax benefit rule.
   b. Is a taxpayer required to report the reimbursement of a medical expense by insurance as income if the reimbursement is received in the year following the year of the expenditure?

3-30. What opportunities are available for a taxpayer to defer the recognition of certain types of prepaid income? That is, what advice could you give someone who wishes to defer the reporting of prepaid income?

3-31. Taxpayers who deduct an expense one year but recover it the next year are required to include the recovered amount in gross income. The tax benefit rule provides relief if the original deduction did not result in any tax savings. Does this rule provide relief to taxpayers who are in a higher tax bracket in the year they recover the previously deducted expense?

3-32. George, a wealthy investor, is uncertain whether he should invest in taxable or tax-exempt bonds. What tax and nontax factors should be considered?

3-33. Do you agree or disagree with the following statement: A taxpayer should not have to report income when debt is forgiven because the taxpayer receives nothing. Explain.

PROBLEMS

3-34. *Non-cash Compensation.* For each of the following items indicate whether the individual taxpayer must include any amount in gross income:
  a. York Corporation gave 100 shares of stock to each of its employees. York Corporation wanted to retain its cash for expansion, so the company transferred the stock worth $12 per share to its employees in lieu of a raise.
  b. Yellow Corporation encourages its employees to take flu shots. The company does so to reduce time off due to sickness. The company pays for the shots, which cost $20 each.
  c. Zip Corporation paid its directors $1,000 each. One director who was working in a foreign country for the entire year received the $1,000 fee, even though he did not attend any directors' meetings.

3-35. *Constructive Receipt.* Which of the following would constitute constructive receipt?
  a. A salary check received at 6:00 p.m. on December 31, after all the banks have closed.
  b. A rent check, received on December 30 by the manager of an apartment complex. The manager normally collects the rent for the owner. The owner was out of town.
  c. A paycheck received on December 29, but which was not honored by the bank because the employer's account did not have sufficient funds.
  d. A check received on December 30. The check was postdated January 2 of the following year.
  e. A check received on January 2. The check had been mailed on December 30.

3-36. *Series EE Bond Interest.* In 1990, Harry and Mary purchased Series EE Bonds, and in 1994 redeemed the bonds receiving $500 of interest and $1,500 of principal. Their income from other sources totaled $30,000. They paid tuition and fees for their dependent daughter totaling $2,200. Their daughter is a qualified student at State University.
  a. How much of the Series EE Bond interest is excludable?
  b. Assuming that the daughter received a $1,000 scholarship, how much of the interest is excludable?
  c. Assuming the daughter received the $1,000 scholarship, and that the parents' income from other sources is $67,350, how much of the interest is excludable?

3-37. *Alimony.* As a result of their divorce, Fred agrees to pay alimony to Tammy of $20,000 per year. The payments are to cease in the event of Fred's or Tammy's death or in the event of Tammy's remarriage. In addition, Tammy is to receive their residence, which cost them $100,000, but which is worth $140,000.
  a. Does the fact that Tammy receives the residence at the time of the divorce mean that there is a reduction in alimony, which will lead to Fred having to recapture an amount in the subsequent year?
  b. How will the $20,000 payments be treated by Fred and Tammy?
  c. Would recapture of the payments be necessary if payment ceased because of Tammy's remarriage?
  d. What is Tammy's basis in the residence?

3-38. *Constructive Dividend.* Brad owns a successful corporation which has substantial earnings and profits. During the year, the following payments were made by the corporation:
  a. Salary of $250,000 to Brad. Officers in other corporations performing similar services receive between $50,000 and $85,000.
  b. Rent of $25,000 to Brad. The rent is paid in connection with an office building owned by Brad and used by the corporation. Similar buildings rent for about the same amount.

c. Salary of $5,000 to Brad's daughter, who worked for the company full time during the summer and part time during the rest of the year while she attended high school.

d. Alimony of $40,000 to Brad's former wife. Although Brad was personally obligated to make the payments, he used corporation funds to make the payments.

Discuss the likelihood of these payments being treated as constructive dividends. If a payment is deemed to be a constructive dividend, indicate how such a payment will be treated.

3-39. ***Constructive Dividend.*** Which of the following would likely be a constructive dividend?
a. An unreasonable salary paid to a shareholder.
b. An unreasonable salary paid to the daughter of a shareholder.
c. A sale of a corporation's asset to a shareholder at fair market value.
d. A payment by a corporation of a shareholder's debts.
e. A payment by a corporation of a shareholder's personal expenses.

3-40. ***Prepaid Rent.*** Stan rented an office building to Clay for $3,000 per month. On December 29, 1993, Stan received a deposit of $4,000 in addition to the first and last months' rent. Occupancy began on January 2, 1994. On July 15, 1994, Clay closed his business and filed for bankruptcy. Stan had collected rent for February, March, and April on the first of each month. Stan had received May rent on May 10, but collected no payments afterwards. Stan withheld $800 from the deposit because of damage to the property and $1,500 for unpaid rent. He refunded the balance of the deposit to Clay.

What amount would Stan report as gross income for 1993? for 1994?

3-41. ***Rental Income.*** Ed owns Oak Knoll Apartments. During the year, Fred, a tenant, moved to another state. Fred paid Ed $1,000 to cancel the 2-year lease he had signed. Ed subsequently rented the unit to Wayne. Wayne paid the first and last months' rents of $800 each and a security deposit of $500. Ed also owns a building that is used as a health club. The club has signed a 15-year lease at an annual rental of $17,000. The owner of the club requested that Ed install a swimming pool on the property. Ed declined to do so. The owner of the club finally constructed the pool himself at a cost of $15,000. What amount must Ed include in gross income?

3-42. ***Gross Income.*** Joy collected $800 interest on corporate bonds and a salary of $32,000 from her employer. Joy won $100 for having the lowest golf score in her country club's golf tournament. She also won $500 in the state lottery. The ticket cost $5. Joy also stole $50 from her mother's purse when she was not looking. Which amounts are taxable?

3-43. ***Interest Income.*** Holly inherited $10,000 of City of Atlanta bonds in February. In March, she received interest of $500, and in April she sold the bonds at a $200 gain. Holly redeemed Series E U.S. savings bonds that she had purchased several years ago. The accumulated interest totaled $800. Holly received $300 of interest on bonds issued by the City of Quebec, Canada. What amount, if any, of gross income must Holly report?

3-44. ***Annuity Income.*** Tim retired during the current year at the age of 58. He purchased an annuity from American National Life Company at a cost of $40,000. The annuity pays Tim $500 per month for life.
a. Compute Tim's annual exclusion using the long method.
b. Compute Tim's annual exclusion using the shortcut method.
c. How much income will Tim report each year after reaching the age of 84?

3-45. ***Pension Income.*** On July 1, Beth turned 65 and retired from her position as a garment worker. She immediately began receiving a monthly pension for the remainder of her life of $300. Over the years she worked, Beth contributed $13,104 to the pension fund through withholding. How much must Beth report as income from the pension during the current year?

3-46. ***Social Security Benefits.*** Dan and Diana file a joint return. Dan earned $30,000 during the year before losing his job. He subsequently received unemployment compensation of $1,000. Diana received social security benefits of $5,000.
a. Determine the taxable portion of the social security benefits.
b. What is the taxable portion of the social security benefits if Dan earned $45,000 before losing his job?

3-47. *Recovery of Previously Deducted Expense.* In 1995, Fred received a $1,000 refund of state income taxes withheld from his salary during 1994. For each of the following cases, indicate whether Fred must include any portion of the refund in his 1995 gross income.
  a. Fred did not itemize during 1994.
  b. Fred does not itemize during 1995.
  c. Fred uses the accrual method for determining his deduction for state income taxes.
  d. Fred suffered a net loss during 1994 of $20,000.
  e. Fred suffered a net loss during 1995 of $20,000.
  f. Fred's itemized deductions during 1994 exceeded the standard deduction by $400.

3-48. *Social Security Benefits.* Lucia is a 69-year-old single individual who receives a taxable pension of $10,000 per year and social security benefits of $7,000. Lucia is considering the possibility of selling stock she has owned for years and using the funds to purchase a summer home. She will realize a gain of $20,000 when she sells the stock which has been paying $1,000 of dividends each year. Lucia says her brother recommended that she sell half of the stock this year and half next year because selling all of the stock at once would affect the tax treatment of her social security benefits.
  a. Compute her AGI under the assumption she sells all of the stock now after receiving $1,000 dividends from the stock.
  b. Repeat the computation under the assumption she sells only half of the stock this year and also receives $1,000 dividends from the stock.

3-49. *Recovery of Previously Deducted Expense.* As the result of unexpected surgery, Jan incurred $14,000 of medical expenses in 1994. At the end of 1994, her medical insurance had paid only $5,000. Jan anticipates that the company will eventually pay an additional $7,000 of the bill. Because her AGI is $30,000 and there is a 7.5% floor for medical deductions, Jan can deduct medical expenses over $2,250. Her other itemized deductions exceed the standard deduction.
  a. If Jan pays the balance of the $9,000 medical expenses prior to the end of the year, can she claim a deduction in 1994?
  b. If she is reimbursed $7,000 in 1995, how will the reimbursement be treated?

3-50. *Social Security Benefits.* Gary and Gail file a joint return. Gary's salary is $42,000, and they received taxable interest of $1,000. Gail received $7,000 of social security benefits. What amount, if any, of the benefits are taxable?

3-51. *Adjusted Gross Income.* Amir, who is single, retired from his job this year. He received a salary of $25,000 for the portion of the year that he worked, tax-exempt interest of $3,000, and dividends from domestic corporations of $2,700. On September 1, he began receiving monthly pension payments of $1,000 and social security payments of $600. Assume an exclusion ratio of 40% for the pension. Amir owns a duplex that he rents to others. He received rent of $12,000 and incurred $17,000 of expenses related to the duplex. He continued to actively manage the property after he retired from his job. Compute Amir's adjusted gross income.

3-52. *Court Awards and Insurance Settlements.* What amount, if any, must be included in gross income by the following taxpayers?
  a. Allen received $1,000 from his insurance company because his boat, which cost $2,000, was sunk during a storm.
  b. Barry, while walking home from work, was struck by an automobile. The driver's insurance company paid him $4,000 to reimburse him for medical expenses and $12,000 to reimburse him for pain and suffering.
  c. Collin owns Collins Construction Company. Len started Colins Construction Company and obtained a number of contracts with people who thought they were dealing with Collins Construction Company. Collin sued and collected $40,000, which was the profit that he lost because of the contracts and punitive damages of $80,000.
  d. Dick loaned his brother $2,000. Dick had to sue in order to recover the amount of the loan.
  e. Fran, an accountant, had to sue a client in order to collect her audit fee of $8,000. Would Fran's accounting method make any difference?

3-53. *Claim of Right.* USA Corporation terminated Jesse's job because sales were down, but gave him severance pay of $8,000. In the next year, after the company's business improved, USA offered to rehire Jesse *if* he would repay the earlier lump-sum severance payment. Jesse was in the 28% tax bracket in the year he was terminated, but in the 15% bracket the next year when he was rehired.

a. Is the lump-sum payment taxable to Jesse when it is received?

b. What options are available to Jesse when he repays the $8,000?

c. What options would have been available to Jesse if he had been asked to repay only $2,000?

3-54. *Tax Planning.* Bart and Kesha are in the 36% tax bracket. They are interested in reducing the taxes they pay each year. They are currently considering several alternatives. For each of the following alternatives, indicate how much tax, if any, they would save.

a. Make a gift of bonds valued at $5,000 that yield $400 per year interest to their 14-year-old daughter, who has no other income.

b. Sell the bonds from Part a rather than give them to their daughter, and buy tax-exempt bonds that pay 6%. Assume the bonds can be sold for $5,000.

c. Give $1,000 cash to a charity. Assume they itemize deductions.

d. Pay their daughter a salary of $10,000 for services rendered in their unincorporated business.

3-55. *Series EE Bond Interest.* In 1994, Ken and Lynn paid $5,000 to purchase Series EE Bonds in the name of their 11 year old son. The son has no other income, and they are in the 28% tax bracket. The taxable interest during the first year will be $400 if an election is made to accrue the interest on an annual basis.

a. Will the child owe any tax on the bond interest?

b. Does the son need to file a tax return?

c. What are the tax consequences in 1994 and subsequent years if annual gifts are made to their son?

COMPREHENSIVE PROBLEMS

3-56. Matt and Sandy reside in a community property state. Matt left home in April 1994 because of disputes with his wife Sandy. Subsequently, Matt earned $15,000. Prior to leaving home in April, Matt earned $3,000. Sandy was unaware of Matt's whereabouts or his earnings after he left home. The $3,000 earned by Matt before he left home was spent on food, housing, and other items shared by Matt and Sandy. Matt and Sandy have one child who lived with Sandy after the husband left home.

a. Is any portion of Matt's earnings after he left home taxable to Sandy?

b. What filing status is applicable to Sandy if she filed a return?

c. How much income would Sandy be required to report if she filed?

d. Is Sandy required to file?

3-57. Gary earned $57,000 as an executive. Gary, who is single, supported his half sister, who lives in a nursing home. Gary received the following interest: $400 on City of Los Angeles bonds, $200 on a money market account, and $2,100 on a loan to his brother.

Gary spent one week serving on a jury and received $50.

Gary received a refund of federal income taxes withheld during the prior year of $1,200 and a state income tax refund of $140. Gary had itemized deductions last year of $8,000.

Gary received dividends on Ace Corporation of $1,000 and on Tray Corporation of $1,400. Gary's itemized deductions equal $9,000, and withholding for federal income taxes is $11,000. Compute Gary's tax due or refund due. Use the 1994 tax rate schedules.

TAX FORM/RETURN PREPARATION PROBLEM

TurboTax **3-58.** Sally W. Emanual had the following dividends and interest during the current year:

Acorn Corporation bond—interest	$ 700
City of Boston bonds—interest	1,000
Camp Bank—interest	250
Jet Corporation stock—dividend	300
North Mutual fund—	
Capital gain distribution	100
Ordinary dividend	150
Nontaxable distribution	200
Blue Corporation stock—foreign dividend	250

Additional information pertaining to Sally Emanual includes:

Salary	$32,000
Rent income	12,000
Expenses related to rent income	14,000
Pension benefits	8,000
Alimony paid to Sally	4,000

Sally has been receiving the pension since she retired from her former job last year. Her age at the time of retirement was 52. She contributed $31,300 through withholding to the pension. Sally actively participates in the rental activity. Other relevant information includes:

Address: 430 Rumsey Place
West Falls, California 92699
Occupation: Credit manager
Social security number: 123-45-4321
Marital status: Single

Complete Sally's Schedule B and page one of her Form 1040. Assume Schedule E has already been prepared.

CASE STUDY PROBLEMS

3-59. Jim and Linda are your tax clients. They were divorced two years ago and the divorce decree stated that Jim was to make monthly payments to Linda. The court designated $300 per month as alimony and $200 per month as child support or a total of $6,000 per year. Jim has been unemployed for much of the year and paid Linda $2,000 that he said was for child support. In addition, Jim transferred title to a three year old automobile with a $4,000 FMV and basis of $7,000 in exchange for her promise not to pursue any claim she has against him for the unpaid child support and alimony. Does Linda have to report any alimony and is Jim entitled to an alimony deduction? Draft a memo for the file that discusses the tax consequences for both Jim and Linda.

3-60. John and Mary (your clients) have two small children and are looking for ways to help fund the children's college education. They have heard that Series EE bonds are a tax favored way of saving and have requested your opinion on the tax consequences. They have asked your opinion regarding the relative advantages of purchasing Series EE bonds in their names versus the children's names. John and Mary have indicated that they expect to have a high level of income in the future and that their children may receive other income sources from future inheritance.

Prepare a client memo making recommendations relative to tax consequences of Series EE bond investments for John and Mary.

CASE STUDY PROBLEM-ETHICAL ISSUES

3-61. Lee and Jane have been your firm's clients for most of the 20 years they have been married. Recently Lee came to you and said that he and Jane are obtaining a divorce, and he wants you to help him with some of the tax and financial issues that may come up during the divorce. The next day, Jane called asking you for the same assistance. What ethical issues do you see present? What possible conflicts may arise if you represent both Lee and Jane?

TAX RESEARCH PROBLEM

3-62. William owns a building that is leased to Lester's Machine Shop. Lester requests that William rewire the building for new equipment that Lester plans to purchase. The wiring would cost about $4,000, but would not increase the value of the building because its only use is in connection with the specialized equipment. Rather than lose Lester as a lessee, William agrees to forego one month's rent of $1,000 if Lester will pay for the wiring. Since Lester does not want to move, he agrees. What amount, if any, must William include in gross income?

A partial list of research sources is

- Sec. 109.
- Reg. Sec. 1.109-1.
- *CIR v. Grace H. Cunningham*, 2 AFTR 2d 5511, 58-2 USTC ¶ 9771 (9th Cir., 1958).

4

Gross Income—Exclusions

LEARNING OBJECTIVES

After studying this chapter, you should be able to

1. Explain the conditions that must exist for an item to be excluded from tax
2. Determine whether an item is income
3. Decide whether specific exclusions discussed in the chapter are available
4. Understand employment-related fringe benefit exclusion items

OBJECTIVE 1
Explain the conditions that must exist in order to exclude an item from gross income

Chapter 3 discussed specific items of income that are taxable. This chapter considers items that are excluded from gross income. Under Sec. 61(a), all items of income are taxable unless specifically excluded. Taxpayers who wish to avoid being taxed basically have two alternatives. One approach is to establish that the item is not income. If an item is not income (e.g., if it is a return of capital), it is not subject to the income tax. The second approach is to identify a specific exclusion and establish that the exclusion is applicable to the item of income.

Example 4-1 ■

Matt borrowed $10,000 from the bank. Although Matt received $10,000, it is not income because he is obligated to repay the amount borrowed. No specific statutory authority states that borrowed funds are excluded from taxation. Presumably, the fact that borrowed funds are not income is considered to be both fundamental and obvious. ■

Example 4-2 ■

Sheila enrolled in State University. The university awarded her a $1,000 tuition scholarship because of her high admission test scores and grades. Section 117 excludes such scholarships from gross income. As a result, Sheila need not report the scholarship as income. ■

Key Point

Given the sweeping definition of income, it is generally difficult to establish that an item is not income.

The term *administrative exclusion* is occasionally seen. In one sense, there are no administrative exclusions. Exclusions exist because of statute; that is, because of specific provisions in the Internal Revenue Code. The IRS has no authority to create exclusions. Yet, the IRS must interpret the meaning of the Code. A liberal interpretation of the statute by the IRS may result in a broad definition of what constitutes an exclusion, and such a broad definition may reasonably be termed an administrative exclusion.

For example, Sec. 102 excludes gifts received from gross income. The IRS has followed the practice of excluding certain welfare benefits from gross income, presumably because such benefits may be viewed as gifts.[1] The IRS could take the position that welfare benefits are not gifts. That position would no doubt be challenged in the courts.

Real World Example

Grants made to Indians by the federal government under the Indian Financing Act of 1974 to expand Indian-owned economic enterprises are excludable from gross income. Rev. Rul. 77-77, 1977-1 C.B. 11.

The term *judicial exclusions* should be considered in the same vein. Although the courts cannot create exclusions, they can interpret the statute and decide whether a particular item is covered by a statutory exclusion. Such determination may be termed a judicial exclusion.

---

[1] For example, see Rev. Rul. 57-102, 1957-1 C.B. 26, which excludes public assistance payments to blind persons from gross income.

ITEMS THAT ARE NOT INCOME

OBJECTIVE 2
Determine whether an item is income

As noted above, some items are not income and, therefore, are not subject to the income tax. In addition to amounts offset by a liability (discussed above), four other items are not considered to be income. These are:

- Unrealized income
- Self-help income
- Rental value of personal-use property
- Selling price of property (as opposed to the profit or gain earned on the sale)

Unrealized Income

Typical Misconception

It is sometimes erroneously assumed that severance pay, embezzlement proceeds, gambling winnings, hobby income, prizes, rewards, and tips are not items of income.

In *Eisner v. Macomber,* the Supreme Court held that a stock dividend cannot be taxed because the taxpayer had "received nothing that answers the definition of income within the meaning of the Sixteenth Amendment."[2] An ordinary stock dividend does not alter the existing proportionate ownership interest of any stockholder, nor does it increase the value of the individual's holdings. In effect, the court concluded that realization must occur before income is recognized. Although narrowed by subsequent legislation and litigation, ordinary stock dividends continue to be excluded from gross income even today. Perhaps more important, *Eisner v. Macomber* established realization as a criterion for the recognition of income.

Self-Help Income

Typical Misconception

When a taxpayer purchases an older house and remodels the kitchen or makes other improvements, there is a tendency to assume correctly that the taxpayer has no income from this activity, but it is often incorrectly assumed that the basis of the house can be increased by the value of the taxpayer's labor.

Although the concept of self-help income is accepted by economists, it is not sanctioned by accountants, the IRS, or the courts. Thus, if an individual painted his own residence, he would not be treated as having income. However, if a taxpayer hires someone else, the taxpayer would have to earn income, pay a tax, and use after-tax income to pay the hired painter. In either situation, the taxpayer receives the same economic benefit, but no tax is imposed when the economic benefit is derived from self-help. Taxpayers, of course, commonly perform household chores, repair their own automobiles, mow their own lawns, and perform a myriad of other self-help activities.

This should be contrasted with taxable exchanges of services. A mechanic might agree to repair a painter's automobile in exchange for the painter's promise to paint the mechanic's home. In this instance, where the parties exchange services, each party realizes income equal to the value of the services he receives. If each did his own work (i.e., the painter fixed his own automobile and the mechanic painted his own home), neither would have to report any income.

Rental Value of Personal-Use Property

Additional Comment

The tax situation of a homeowner is quite different than that of someone who lives in an apartment. The failure to include the rental value of the home as income in addition to the deduction of mortgage interest and property taxes favors homeowners.

Taxpayers are not taxed on the rental value of personally owned property. For example, taxpayers who own their own home receive the economic benefit of occupancy without being taxed on the rental value of the property. It would be very difficult to keep records and value benefits obtained from self-help and the personal

---

[2] 3 AFTR 3020, 1 USTC ¶ 32 (USSC, 1920).

use of property. For that reason, no significant effort has ever been made to tax such benefits.[3]

Selling Price of Property

If property is sold at a gain, it is the gain and not the entire sales price that is taxable. Because the basic principle is almost universally accepted, the Supreme Court has never had to rule directly on whether the entire sale proceeds could be taxed. The IRS and the courts seemed to accept the basic principle even before the rule became part of the statute.[4] The primary reason for this principle (often referred to as the "recovery of capital" principle) is that a portion of the selling price represents a return of capital to the seller.

MAJOR EXCLUSIONS

OBJECTIVE 3
Decide whether specific exclusions are available

Additional Comment

Tax expenditure estimates measure the decreases in individual and corporate income tax liabilities that result from provisions in income tax laws and regulations that provide economic incentives or tax relief to particular kinds of taxpayers.

Congress has created statutory exclusions for a variety of reasons. Nevertheless, most exclusions exist for either reasons of benevolence or for reasons of incentive. The concept of benevolence, that is, a concept of social generosity or sympathy, has prompted the government to exclude items such as

- Payments for sickness and injury (Sec. 104)
- Life insurance proceeds (Sec. 101)
- Gifts and inheritances (Sec. 102)
- Public assistance payments
- Discharge of indebtedness during bankruptcy or insolvency (Sec. 108)
- Employee death benefits (Sec. 101[b])
- Gain on sale of personal residence by taxpayers who are age 55 or older (Sec. 121)
- Partial exclusions for social security benefits (Sec. 86)

Other exclusions may be explained in terms of economic incentive, that is, the government's desire to encourage or reward a particular type of behavior.

- Awards for meritorious achievement (Sec. 74[b])
- Various employee fringe benefits (Secs. 79, 105, 106, 124, 125, 129, 132)
- Partial exclusion for scholarships (Sec. 117)
- Foreign-earned income (Sec. 911)
- Interest on state and local government obligations (Sec. 103)

Other reasons may exist for some of the exclusions listed above. For example, one reason employee death benefits (payments to the family of an employee who dies) are

---

[3] In 1928, the government tried unsuccessfully to tax the value of produce grown and consumed by a farmer (*Homer P. Morris*, 9 B.T.A. 1273 [1928]). The court stated, "To include the value of such products [would be to] in effect include in income something which Congress did not intend should be so regarded." The court did not explain how or why it reached this conclusion. In 1957, the IRS successfully disallowed the deduction of expenses incurred in raising such produce (*Robert L. Nowland v. CIR,* 51 AFTR 423, 57-1 USTC ¶ 9684 [4th Cir., 1957]).

[4] Section 202(a) of the Revenue Act of 1924 is the predecessor of current Sec. 1001(a) which describes that only the gain portion of the sale proceeds is included in gross income. S. Rept. No. 398, 68th Cong., 1st Sess., p. 10 (1924) states that Sec. 202(a) sets forth general rules to be used in the computation of gain or loss. The senate report further states that the provision "merely embodies in the law the present construction by the Department and the courts of the existing law."

excluded is to avoid confusion over whether such payments are gifts, which are nontaxable, or compensation, which is taxable. (See Chapter 3 for a discussion of tax-exempt interest and social security benefits, and Chapter 12 for the treatment of gain on the sale of a personal residence.)

Gifts and Inheritances

Congress has excluded the value of gifts received from gross income since the inception of the income tax in 1913. Section 102 excludes the value of property received during the life of the donor (**inter vivos gifts**) and transfers at death (**testamentary gifts**—bequests, devises, and inheritances).[5] The recipient of such property is taxed on the income produced by the property after the transfer.[6] It should be noted that a donor cannot avoid the income tax by making a gift of income. The donor, not the donee, is taxed on the gifted income.

Example 4-3 ∎	Stan orders a corporation that he controls to pay future dividends on the stock he personally owns to his daughter. Stan must include the dividends in gross income. Stan could avoid being taxed on future dividends by giving the stock to his daughter. ∎

It is often difficult to distinguish gifts, which are not included in the recipient's gross income, from other transfers, which are taxable. Gifts sometimes closely resemble prizes and awards.[7]

Example 4-4 ∎	Tina received a free automobile for being the 10 millionth paying guest at an amusement park. ∎

Also, some payments made to employees by employers may resemble gifts.

Example 4-5 ∎	At Christmas, Red Corporation paid $500 to each employee who had been with the company for more than 5 years. ∎

Whether a transfer is a gift depends on the intent of the donor. A donor is expected to be motivated by love, affection, kindness, sympathy, generosity, admiration, or similar emotions. In the two preceding examples, the transfers were probably made for business motives and not necessarily for donative reasons. Thus, the automobile is a taxable prize, and the amounts paid to employees represent taxable awards for services rendered, but see the discussion of Sec. 274 later in this chapter.

Life Insurance Proceeds

Life insurance proceeds paid to a beneficiary because of the insured person's death are not taxable.[8] The exclusion applies whether the proceeds are paid in a lump sum or in installments. Amounts received in excess of the face amount of the policy are usually taxable as interest.

Example 4-6 ∎	Buddy is the beneficiary of a $100,000 insurance policy on his mother's life. Upon her death, he elects to receive $13,000 per year for 10 years instead of the lump sum.

Typical Misconception

Because of confusion between the gift tax imposed on donors with the exclusion that applies to donees, it is sometimes mistakenly thought that gifts are taxable above a certain dollar amount.

Real World Example

Amounts received by a dealer from players in the operation of a gambling casino were not excludable as gifts even though impulsive generosity or superstition may be the dominant motive. The amounts were similar to tips, which are taxable. Louis R. Tomburello, 86 T.C. 540 (1986).

---

[5] Although excluded from gross income, such transfers may be subject to the gift tax or the estate tax.

[6] Reg. Sec. 1.102-1.

[7] Recall that under Sec. 74 (discussed in Chapter 3) most prizes and awards are taxable.

[8] Sec. 101(a).

He receives $10,000 per year tax free ($100,000 ÷ 10), but the remaining $3,000 per year is taxable as interest. ∎

Example 4-7 ∎

Additional Comment

The proceeds of a life insurance policy payable to named beneficiaries can be excluded from the federal estate tax when the decedent does not possess any incidents of ownership. This provision and the exclusion from gross income of life insurance proceeds underscore the favored position of life insurance.

Assume the same facts as in Example 4-6, except that Buddy elects to receive the full $100,000 face amount upon his mother's death. None of the $100,000 is taxable. ∎

The exclusion exists because life insurance benefits closely resemble inheritances, which are not taxable.

There is one exception which may result in a portion of the face amount of a life insurance policy being included in gross income.[9] In general, the life insurance exclusion is not available if the insurance policy is obtained by the beneficiary in exchange for valuable consideration from a person other than the insurance company. For example, an individual may purchase an existing life insurance policy for cash from another individual. In this situation, the exclusion for death benefits is limited to the consideration paid plus the premiums or other sums subsequently paid by the buyer.

Example 4-8 ∎

Kwame is the owner and beneficiary of a $100,000 policy on the life of his father. Kwame sells the policy to his brother Anwar for $10,000. Anwar subsequently pays premiums of $12,000. Upon his father's death, Anwar must include $78,000 ($100,000 − [$10,000 + $12,000]) in gross income. ∎

Typical Misconception

The exclusion of life insurance proceeds is available to both corporations and individuals.

The proceeds are excludable under the general exclusion for life insurance proceeds if (1) the beneficiary's basis is found by reference to the transferor's basis (as would be true in the case of a gift); or (2) if the policy is transferred to the insured, the insured's partner, a partnership that includes the insured, or a corporation in which the insured is a shareholder or officer.

Self-Study Question

A corporation acquires a life insurance policy on the president of the corporation, and the corporation is named as the beneficiary of the policy. Are the insurance premiums deductible?

Answer

No, the premiums are not deductible because any costs incurred to produce tax-exempt income are nondeductible.

Surrender of Policy Before Death. The exclusion for life insurance is available for amounts payable by reason of the death of the insured. In general, if a life insurance policy is surrendered for a lump sum before the death of the insured, the amount received is taxable to the extent it exceeds the net premiums paid.[10] Prop. Reg. Sec. 1.7702-2(c) provides, however, that an accelerated death benefit paid to a terminally ill person may be excluded from gross income. A person is considered to be terminally ill if he has an illness or physical condition that, notwithstanding appropriate medical care, is reasonably expected to result in death within 12 months. No loss is recognized if a life insurance policy is surrendered before maturity and premiums paid exceed the cash surrender value.[11]

Endowment Contracts. Endowment life insurance policies usually provide for payments upon the death of the insured. Such policies also provide for payment in the event of an alternative occurrence such as the reaching of a stated age (e.g., age 65) by the insured person. If payment is made in the event of the alternative occurrence, the excess of the amount received over the total premiums paid is included in gross income.[12] Proceeds payable in installments for life are taxed the same as other annuities.[13] If they are payable for a fixed number of years, each year's exclusion is found by dividing the contract's cost by the number of annual payments.[14]

---

[9] Sec. 101(a)(2).
[10] Sec. 72(e)(2).
[11] *London Shoe Co. v. CIR.*, 16 AFTR 1398, 35-2 USTC ¶ 9664 (2nd Cir., 1935).
[12] Sec. 72(e)(2).
[13] Sec. 72(a).
[14] Sec. 72(c)(3)(B).

Contracts that give the insured the option of receiving either a lump-sum or payments in installments are subject to special treatment. Any gain (the excess of the available lump-sum payment over premiums paid) is taxable in the year of conversion. Subsequent payments are taxable under the annuity rules (see Chapter 3). The gain recognized at the time of conversion is added to the premiums paid to establish the annuity's cost basis.

Dividends on Life Insurance and Endowment Policies. Dividends on life insurance and endowment policies are normally not taxable because they are considered to be a partial return of premiums paid. The dividends are taxable to the extent that the total dividends received exceed the total premiums paid. Also, if dividends are left with the insurance company and earn interest, the interest is taxable.

Awards for Meritorious Achievement

As was noted in Chapter 3, prizes and awards are generally taxable. An exception is applicable to awards and prizes made for religious, charitable, scientific, educational, artistic, literary, or civic achievement if the recipient

- was selected without action on his or her part to enter the contest or the proceeding,
- does not have to perform substantial future services as a condition to receiving the prize or award, and
- designates that the payor is to pay the amount of the award to either a government unit or a charitable organization.[15]

The recipient of such an award normally would owe no tax if he collected the proceeds and then contributed the proceeds to a charity. This is because the gift would qualify as a deductible charitable contribution. This rule, however, is beneficial only in situations where the taxpayer could not deduct the full amount of the award because of the limitation on the charitable contribution deduction (generally 50% of AGI; see Chapter 7) or in the case of a small award to a taxpayer who does not itemize.

Scholarships and Fellowships

Additional Comment

Athletic scholarships for fees, books, and supplies that are awarded by a university to students who are expected, but not required, to participate in a particular sport can be excludable.

Subject to certain limitations, scholarships are excluded from gross income.[16] A scholarship is an amount paid or allowed to, or for the benefit of, a student, whether an undergraduate or graduate, to aid such individual in pursuing a degree.

The exclusion for scholarships is limited to the amount of tuition, matriculation and other fees, books, supplies, and equipment. The value of services and accommodations supplied such as room, board, and laundry are not excluded. The exclusion for scholarships does not extend to salary paid for services even if all candidates for a particular degree are required to perform the services.[17]

Example 4-9 ■ Becky is awarded a $5,000 per year scholarship by State University. State University designates that $3,000 is for tuition, books, and supplies, while $2,000 is

[15] Sec. 74.

[16] Sec. 117.

[17] Scholarships may need to be reviewed to determine whether the amount constitutes compensation. A "scholarship" awarded to the winner of a televised beauty pageant by a profit-making corporation was ruled to be compensation for performing subsequent services for the corporation (Rev. Rul. 68-20, 1968-1 C.B. 55). An employer-paid "scholarship" was held to be compensation in a situation where the employee was on leave and was required to return to work after finishing the degree (*Richard E. Johnson v. Bingler,* 23 AFTR 2d 69-1212, 69-1 USTC ¶ 9348 [USSC, 1969]).

for room and board. In addition, Becky works part-time on campus and earns $4,000, which covers the rest of her room and board and other expenses. Becky is taxed on the $2,000 that is awarded for room and board and $4,000 of salary earned from her part-time job. ∎

Payments for Injury and Sickness

Under Sec. 104(a), amounts received as compensation for injury and sickness are excluded from gross income. Specifically, Sec. 104(a)(2) excludes "the amount of any damages received (whether by suit or agreement) on account of personal injury or sickness." The phrase "personal injury or sickness" not only includes awards for sickness and physical injury, but also nonphysical injury such as personal embarrassment,[18] injury to personal reputation in the community,[19] mental pain and suffering,[20] and libel.[21] Sec. 104(a) makes it clear that punitive damages are excluded only in cases involving sickness and physical injury (see Chapter 3).

As noted in Chapter 3, an award for the loss of income is normally taxable. If income is lost because of employment discrimination, is a subsequent court award reimbursing the taxpayer for the lost income taxable?

Example 4-10 ∎

After she was denied a promotion, Jane sued claiming sex discrimination. The court ordered Key Corporation, her employer, to promote Jane and pay her $36,000, an amount equal to the wages she lost because of the discrimination. ∎

Real World Example

Amounts received by an injured football player were taxable because they were not calculated with reference to the nature of the injury but were based upon the number of seasons played. Randall L. Beisler v. CIR, 59 AFTR 2d 87-964, 87-1 USTC ¶ 9620 (9th Cir., 1987).

Based on facts similar to those presented in the example above, the Supreme Court held that the personal injury exclusion was unavailable because the amount awarded was backpay.[22] As noted, punitive damages are excluded in personal injury cases only if the claim is based on sickness or physical injury.[23] Thus, additional amounts awarded to an employee intended to penalize an employer are also taxable to the employee. On the other hand, if the amount awarded was intended to compensate the discrimination victim for mental pain and suffering the award would likely be nontaxable.[24]

Furthermore, Sec. 104(a)(3) excludes from gross income amounts collected under an accident and health insurance policy purchased by the taxpayer even if the benefits are a substitute for lost income.

Example 4-11 ∎

Chuck purchased a disability income policy from an insurance company. Chuck subsequently suffered a heart attack. Under the terms of the policy, Chuck received $1,000 per month for the 5 months he was unable to work. The amounts received are not taxable, even though the payments are a substitute for the wages lost due to the illness. ∎

---

[18] *Dudley G. Seay,* 58 T.C. 32 (1972).

[19] Ibid.

[20] *Wade E. Church,* 80 T.C. 1104 (1983).

[21] Ibid.

[22] *Therese A. Burke v. U. S.,* 69 AFTR2d 92-1293, 92-1 USTC ¶ 50,254 (USSC, 1992). The *Burke* award was based on a prior version of Title VII of the federal Civil Rights Act that only permitted employment redress and awards for back pay. On the other hand, the current Civil Rights Act and the federal Age Discrimination in Employment Act (ADEA) both provide for broader awards. For example, they both provide for awards to individuals who are denied employment because of discrimination. Such amounts are not back pay as the injured individual was never employed. The Tax Court held that an ADEA award was excludable as it was sufficiently similar to a personal injury award (*Burns P. Downey,* 97 T.C. 150 (1993)). A contrary decision, however, was reached in a district court case (*Chester J. Maleszewski v. U.S.,* 72 AFTR2d 93-5172, 93-1 USTC ¶ 50,358 (D.C. N. Fla., 1993)). As a result, it is not entirely clear when discrimination awards are taxable.

[23] Sec. 104(a).

[24] *Wade E. Church,* 80 T. C. 1104 (1983).

This exclusion is not applicable if the accident and health benefits are provided by the taxpayer's employer.[25]

Example 4-12 ■

Assume the same facts as in Example 4-11 except that Chuck's employer paid the premiums on the policy. The amounts received by Chuck are taxable. ■

If the cost of the coverage is shared by the employer and the taxpayer, a portion of the benefits is taxable. For example, if the employer paid one-half of the premiums, one-half of the benefits would be taxable. The principal reason for the different tax treatment is that employer-paid coverage represents a tax-free employee fringe benefit, whereas employee-paid premiums are from after-tax dollars.

In general, the Sec. 104(a) exclusion is available whether the taxpayer is being reimbursed for out-of-pocket expenses (e.g., the cost of medical care) or the award is intended to make the taxpayer "whole as before the injury" (e.g., an award made for pain and suffering or for the loss of an arm or leg). In the case of an award intended to reimburse the taxpayer for medical expenses, it follows that the taxpayer cannot deduct the reimbursed medical expenses.[26] If the award exceeds the actual expense, it is not taxable except in the case of employer-financed accident and health insurance.[27]

State workmen's compensation laws establish fixed amounts to be paid to employees suffering specific job-related injuries. Section 104(a)(1) specifically excludes workmen's compensation from gross income, even though the payments are intended, in part, to reimburse injured workers for loss of future income.

Employee Fringe Benefits

In general, employee compensation is taxable regardless of the form it takes. Nevertheless, the tax law encourages certain types of fringe benefits by allowing an employer to deduct the cost of the benefit, by permitting the employee to exclude the benefit from gross income, or by permitting both the employer deduction and an employee exclusion. Employee fringe benefits subject to special rules include employee insurance, Sec. 132 benefits, meals and lodging, employee death benefits, dependent care, and cafeteria plans. These fringe benefits are discussed in this chapter.

Additional Comment

Many companies provide health care benefits to retired employees. However, due to mounting medical insurance bills, a rising retiree population, and a FASB rule which requires firms to recognize the associated liability, a number of companies are requiring retired workers to pick up a larger portion of their medical costs.

Employer-Paid Insurance. Employers commonly provide group insurance coverage for employees. In general, employers may deduct the premiums paid for life, health, accident, and disability insurance. Normally an employee does not have to include in gross income premiums paid on his or her behalf for health, accident, and disability insurance. Special rules applicable to life insurance premiums are discussed below.

Benefits received from medical, health, and life insurance coverage are generally excluded from an employee's gross income. Benefits received from a disability policy are normally taxable, but may qualify for the credit for the elderly and disabled (see Chapter 14). The tax treatments of employer-financed and taxpayer-financed insurance coverage are compared in Topic Review 4-1.

Additional Comment

The tax expenditure estimate associated with the exclusion of contributions by employers and self-employed individuals for medical insurance premiums and medical care for the period 1990-1994 is $205.5 billion.

In general, premiums paid by an employer on behalf of employees are deductible. Premiums paid on behalf of self-employed persons are normally not deductible. Under a temporary rule, one-fourth of the *medical* premiums attributable to the coverage of a proprietor or partner were deductible as business expenses.[28] An individual proprietor

---

[25] A limited credit is available to taxpayers who receive such benefits. See Chapter 14 for a discussion of the credit for the elderly and disabled.

[26] See Chapter 3 for a discussion of the reimbursement of an expense deducted in a preceding year.

[27] Sec. 105(a).

[28] If the law is not extended by Congress, the deduction is available only in tax years beginning before January 1, 1994.

TOPIC REVIEW 4-1

Treatment of Insurance

	Premiums Paid by	
	Employer	Taxpayer
Medical and Health Premiums	Premiums not included in employee's gross income. Premiums deductible by employer.	Premiums deductible as medical expense subject to 7.5% of AGI limitation.
Benefits	Excluded from employee's gross income except when benefits exceed actual expenses.	Excluded from gross income.
Disability Premiums	Premiums not included in employee's gross income. Premiums deductible by employer.	Not deductible.
Benefits	Included in employee's gross income. May qualify for credit for elderly and disabled.	Excluded from gross income.
Life Insurance Premiums	Included in employee's gross income (except for limited exclusion applicable to group term life insurance). Premiums deductible by employer (assuming employer is not the beneficiary).	Not deductible.
Benefits	Excluded from gross income.	Excluded from gross income.

or partner may now only deduct his own premiums as medical expenses if total medical expenses exceed 7.5% of the AGI reported on the proprietor or partner's individual return.

The Sec. 104 rules relating to accident and health insurance are more generous than those for some other types of benefits. Employers can deduct insurance premiums and employees need not report the premiums as income. This is true even if the insurance is offered only to officers and other highly compensated employees.

Some employers provide self-insured accident and health plans to employees. Under such plans the employer pays employee medical expenses directly rather than paying insurance premiums. Such plans are subject to nondiscrimination requirements. Discrimination is defined in terms of an eligibility test (whether a sufficient number of nonhighly compensated employees are covered) and benefits (whether nonhighly compensated employees receive benefits comparable to highly compensated employees).[29] Highly compensated employees include (1) the 5 highest paid officers, (2) greater than 10% shareholders, and (3) highest paid 25% of all other employees.[30] If a plan discriminates in favor of highly compensated employees, these employees must include in gross income any medical reimbursements they receive that are not available to other employees.[31]

In general, life insurance premiums paid by an employer on an employee's behalf

Key Point

The nondiscrimination requirements for self-insured accident and health plans are designed to insure that such plans do not discriminate against rank-and-file workers.

Additional Comment

The Economic Strategy Institute estimates that domestic auto producers have to pay about $400 per car to cover their health care and pension costs.

---

[29] Sec. 105(h)(2).
[30] Sec. 105(h)(5).
[31] Sec. 105(h)(1).

Typical Misconception

Since it is not difficult to forget that a cash basis taxpayer must include in income not only cash received but also the FMV of goods and services, it is not uncommon to disregard the possibility that life insurance premiums paid by an employer are includable in income.

are includable in the employee's gross income.[32] A limited exception is applicable to group term life insurance coverage. Premiums attributable to the first $50,000 of group term life insurance coverage may be excluded from an employee's gross income.[33] To qualify group term life insurance premiums for the exclusion, broad coverage of employees is required. Though somewhat different, the rules may be compared to those associated with self-insurance coverage.[34] The amount of coverage can vary between employees as long as the coverage bears a uniform relationship to each employee's compensation.

Example 4-13 ■

Data Corporation provides group term life insurance coverage for each of its full-time employees. The coverage is equal to one year's compensation. The arrangement would constitute a qualified group term life insurance plan. ■

The group term life insurance exclusion is available only for employees, whether active or retired. Thus, proprietors and partners are not employees and, therefore, the premiums paid on their behalf are not deductible.

In the case of coverage that exceeds $50,000, it is necessary to distinguish key employees from other employees. Key employees must include in gross income the greater of actual premiums attributable to the excess coverage or an amount established by the Regulations.

Example 4-14 ■

Joy, age 61, is an officer for USA Corporation. During the year, USA Corporation provides Joy with $150,000 of group term life insurance coverage. USA Corporation pays premiums of $3,000. The premiums exceed the amount provided in the Regulations. Assuming that $1,000 of the premiums are attributable to the first $50,000 of coverage, Joy may exclude $1,000 from gross income. Premiums of $2,000 attributable to the excess coverage must be included in gross income. ■

When group term coverage exceeds $50,000, employees other than key employees must include in gross income an amount established by the Regulations rather than the actual premiums. (See Table 4-1.)

Example 4-15 ■

Irene, age 61, works for USA Corporation. Irene is not a key employee. During the year, USA provides Irene with $150,000 of group term life insurance coverage. Irene must include $1,404 ([$100,000 × $1.17 × 12] ÷ $1,000) in gross income. ■

Historical Note

A limited exclusion from income for unemployment compensation was repealed in the Tax Reform Act of 1986.

Section 132 Benefits. It has become common for employers to provide employees with such diverse benefits as free parking, membership in professional organizations, or small discounts on products sold by the employer. Section 132 was added to the Code in 1984 to clarify whether certain types of benefits are taxable. Section 132 lists six types of fringe benefits which may be excluded from an employee's gross income (see Topic Review 4-2). Any costs incurred by an employer to provide the specified benefits are deductible under Sec. 162 if they meet the "ordinary and necessary" test of that section.[35] Benefits covered by Sec. 132 include

[32] If the employer is the beneficiary of the policy, the employee receives no economic benefit, and, as a result, need not include the premiums in gross income. Such premium payments would not be deductible by the employer. Subsequent benefits would not be included in the employer's gross income.

[33] Sec. 79(a).

[34] For example, the rules refer to "key employees" as opposed to highly compensated employees. The term "key employee" is somewhat narrower in scope.

[35] See Chapter 6 for a discussion of Sec. 162 and its requirements. Section 274 does provide one exception to the general rule. The costs of maintaining recreational facilities (such as swimming pools) are not deductible if the facilities are made available on a discriminatory basis (e.g., only officers may use the facilities).

TABLE 4-1   *Uniform 1-Month Group Term Premiums for $1,000 of Life Insurance Coverage*

Employee's Age	Premiums
Under 30	$0.08
30–34	0.09
35–39	0.11
40–44	0.17
45–49	0.29
50–54	0.48
55–59	0.75
60–64	1.17
65–69	2.10
70 and above	3.76

Source: Reg. Sec. 1.79-3(d)(2).

- No additional cost benefits (such as a hotel employee's use of a vacant hotel room)
- Qualified employee discounts (such as discounts on merchandise sold by the employer)
- Working condition benefits (such as membership fees in professional organizations paid by an employer)
- De minimis benefits (such as coffee provided by the employer)
- Qualified transportation fringes (such as parking subject to a $155 per month limit and an exclusion for amounts up to $60 per month for transportation benefits [i.e., transit passes, tokens, face cards, vouchers, and transportation in a commuter highway vehicle]).
- Athletic facilities (such as employer-owned tennis courts used by employees)

Discrimination is prohibited with respect to certain of the benefits. Thus, the benefits must be made available to employees in general rather than just to highly compensated employees. (See Topic Review 4-2 for specific rules.)

Employee Awards. As noted earlier, it is often difficult to distinguish between gifts and awards. The de minimis rule found in Sec. 132(e) permits employers to make small gifts such as a holiday turkey or a watch at retirement without the employee having to include the value of the gift in gross income. The employer is entitled to a deduction for the cost of such gifts.

Section 274 provides a similar rule for **employee achievement awards** and **qualified plan awards.** Such awards must be in the form of tangible personal property other than cash and must be based on safety records or length of service. Employee achievement awards are limited to $400 for any one employee during the year. Further, the awards must be presented as part of a meaningful presentation and awarded under circumstances that do not create a significant likelihood of the payment being disguised compensation. Qualified plan awards are employee achievement awards that are given under a written plan or program that does not discriminate in favor of highly compensated employees. The average cost of qualified plan awards is limited to $400, but individual awards can be as large as $1,600.

- An award for length of service cannot qualify under Sec. 274 if it is received during the employee's first 5 years of employment or if the employee has received a length of service award under Sec. 274 during the year or any of the preceding 4 years.

Additional Comment

The nondiscrimination rules do not apply to the working condition type of fringe benefit. For example, if a corporation makes bodyguards available only to key officers, the working condition fringe benefit exclusion would still apply.

Self-Study Question

Western Airlines and Central Airlines have a reciprocal agreement that permits employees of the other airline to travel for free on a standby basis. Stan, an employee of Western Airlines, takes a free flight on Central Airlines that would have cost $800. What is Stan's income?

Answer

None, reciprocal agreements with regard to no additional cost services are permitted.

TOPIC REVIEW 4-2

Summary of Sec. 132 Fringe Benefits

Section	Benefit	May Be Made Available to	Comments
132(b)	No additional cost (e.g., telephone, unused hotel rooms for hotel employees, unused airline seats for airline employees)	Employees, spouses, dependents, and retirees	The services must be of the same types that are sold to customers and in the line of business in which the employee works. Discrimination is prohibited.
132(c)	Qualified employee discounts	Employees, spouses, dependents, and retirees	Discounts on services limited to 20%. Discounts on merchandise are limited to the employer's gross profit percent. No discount is permitted on real estate, stock, or other investment type property. Discrimination is prohibited.
132(d)	Working condition (e.g., free magazines, out-placement, and memberships)	Employees	Special rules apply to tuition reductions for employees of educational institutions and to auto salesperson's demonstrator.
132(e)	De minimis (e.g., free coffee, holiday turkeys, or use of company eating facilities)	Employees	Eating facilities must be made available on a nondiscriminatory basis.
132(f)	Qualified transportation fringes (e.g., transit passes, tokens, and parking)	Employees	Limited to $155 per month for parking and $60 per month for other transportation fringes.
132(h)(5)	Recreation and athletic facilities (e.g., gyms, pools, saunas, tennis courts)	Employees, spouses, dependents, and retirees.	If discrimination is present, employer loses deduction.

- No more than 10% of an employer's eligible employees may receive an excludible safety achievement award during any year. Eligible employees are those employees whose positions involve significant safety concerns.

Example 4-16 ■   Each year USA Corporation presents length of service awards to employees who have been with the company 5, 10, 15, or 20 years. The presentations are made at a luncheon sponsored by the company and include gifts such as desk clocks, briefcases, and similar gifts, none of which cost more than $400. The awards, which qualify as employee achievement awards, are deductible by USA Corporation and are not taxable as income to USA's employees.   ■

Gifts to employees that do not qualify as employee achievement awards or qualified plan awards can be excluded by the employee only if the awards can be excluded as de minimis amounts under Sec. 132(e).

Meals and Lodging. Section 119 provides a limited exclusion for the value of meals and lodging.

- Meals provided by an employer may be excluded from an employee's gross income if they are furnished (1) on the employer's premises and (2) for the convenience of the employer.

- Lodging provided by an employer may be excluded from an employee's gross income if it is furnished (1) on the employer's premises, (2) for the convenience of the employer, and (3) the employee is required to accept the lodging as a condition of employment.

Real World Example

Many university presidents are furnished with personal residences the value of which they can generally exclude from gross income.

The requirement that meals and lodging be furnished on the premises of the employer refers to the employee's place of employment.[36] In one case, the Tax Court held that the business premises requirement was met in a situation where a hotel manager lived in a residence across the street from the hotel that he managed.[37]

The convenience of the employer test considers whether there is a substantial noncompensatory business reason for providing the meals or lodging. Thus, if the owner of an apartment complex furnishes a unit to the manager of the complex because it is necessary to have the manager present on the premises even when he is off duty, then the test is met.

Real World Example

A brewery provided houses on the business premises to officers. The value of the houses was excludable since it was important to have the officers available for the around-the-clock operations of the business. Adolph Coors Co., 1968 PH T.C. Memo ¶ 68, 256, 27 TCM 1351.

The value of lodging cannot be excluded from gross income unless the employee is required to accept the lodging as a condition of employment. This requirement is not met if the employee has a choice of accepting the lodging or receiving a cash allowance. Further, meal allowances do not qualify for the exclusion because the employer does not actually provide the meal.[38] Section 132 (discussed earlier in this chapter) provides a de minimis exception. Some employers provide "supper money" to employees who must work overtime. If such benefits are occasionally provided to employees, the amount is excludable from the employees' gross income.

Example 4-17 ■

A state highway patrol organization provides its officers with a daily meal allowance to compensate them for meals that are eaten while they are on duty. Because the officers receive cash instead of meals, the amount provided must be included in the officers' gross income. ■

Example 4-18 ■

A large corporation requires five of its employees to work overtime two evenings each year when the company takes inventory. The corporation gives each of the employees a small amount to cover the cost of the dinner for the two evenings. The amounts constitute "supper money" and are excluded from the employees' gross income. ■

Meals and Entertainment. One obvious question is whether employees who are reimbursed by their employers when they entertain customers must include the reimbursement in gross income. If they must include the reimbursement in gross income, can they deduct the cost of the entertainment and meals? Assuming conditions for deductibility (discussed in Chapter 9) are met, it is clear that only 50% of the cost of entertaining customers is deductible. What about the costs attributable to the employee?

Example 4-19 ■

Joe is a sales representative for Zero Corporation. As a part of his regular duties, Joe buys lunch for Wayne, a Zero Corporation customer. Fifty percent of the cost of

---

[36] Reg. Sec. 1.119-1(c)(1).
[37] *Jack B. Lindeman,* 60 T.C. 609 (1973).
[38] *CIR v. Robert J. Kowalski,* 40 AFTR 2d 77-6128, 77-2 USTC ¶ 9748 (USSC, 1977).

Wayne's meal is deductible by Joe if he pays for the luncheon without being reimbursed by his employer, or by the Zero Corporation if it reimburses Joe for the cost. Can Joe deduct 50% of the cost of his own meal if he pays for it and is not reimbursed? If Zero pays for the meal, must Joe include in his gross income the cost of his own lunch? ■

In 1953, the Tax Court answered the question above as follows, "The cost of meals, entertainment, and similar items for one's self . . . is ordinarily and by its very nature [a nondeductible] personal expenditure.[39] Over time this has become known as the *Sutter* rule. The *Sutter* rule has consistently been upheld by the courts.[40] The rule has been amplified to make it clear that it only applies to amounts that the taxpayer would "normally spend on himself."[41] The IRS has also stated that it will not pursue the issue except where taxpayers claim deductions for substantial amounts of personal expenses.[42] The courts, however, have not accepted this view. According to the Tax Court, personal expenses are not deductible, and the Commissioner of Internal Revenue "cannot change that basic principle by his ruling."[43] Nevertheless, the de minimis rule of the subsequently enacted Sec. 132 may cover relatively small amounts for meals and entertainment.[44]

Further, the Tax Court has extended the rule to require employees to include in income meal costs which are reimbursed by the employer.[45] It should be noted that the *Sutter* rule is not applicable to meals consumed while traveling away from home overnight or the cost of meals consumed at meetings of trade and professional associations as such meals are protected by the statute.[46]

Employee Death Benefits. On occasion an employer may make payments to the family or friends of an employee who dies. In some instances, the payments might be viewed as a gift made for reasons such as the financial need of the family, kindness, or charity. Alternatively, the amount might constitute a payment of compensation based on the past services of the deceased employee. Gifts are, of course, excluded from gross income, while compensation is taxable. The treatment of payments made to the family or other beneficiaries of the employee's estate is determined by the following rules:

- Payments for past services (such as bonuses, accrued wages, unused vacation pay) are taxable as income to the family and are deductible by the employer. The important issue is whether the employee would have received this amount had he lived. If the employer was legally obligated to make the payment at the time of the employee's death, the payments are taxable to the recipient.

- Section 101(b) provides an exclusion of up to $5,000 for payments made by an employer to the family of a deceased employee. Payments covered by Sec. 101(b) are deductible by the employer. Section 101(b) is not applicable to amounts that would have been payable to the employee had he lived. Lump-sum distributions from retirement plans, however, qualify for the exclusion even though the employee possessed a right to the benefit at the time of his death.

[39] *Richard A. Sutter,* 21 T.C. 170 (1953), at 173.
[40] The *Sutter* rule has been followed in all of the over 50 cases that have cited it.
[41] Rev. Rul. 63-144, 1963-2 C.B. 129.
[42] Ibid.
[43] *James P. Fenstermaker,* 1978 PH T. C. Memo ¶ 78,210, 37 TCM 898.
[44] Supper money is mentioned in the Committee Report for Sec. 132, but no other mention is made of meals and entertainment. One could argue that entertainment is a working condition fringe benefit. However, working condition fringe benefits are those benefits which would be deductible by the employee if paid out of pocket by the employee, and according to *Sutter,* such benefits are not deductible.
[45] *James P. Fenstermaker,* 1978 PH T. C. Memo ¶ 78,210, 37 TCM 898.
[46] Secs. 62 and 274.

- Amounts over $5,000 may either be taxable compensation or excludable gifts depending on the facts and circumstances. If the amount over $5,000 is held to be a gift, it is not deductible by the employer.[47] If the amount is taxable income to the deceased employee's family, it is deductible by the employer.

In determining whether the amount is taxable, the courts have considered such factors as whether the employer derived benefit from the payment, whether the employee had been fully compensated, and whether the payment was made to the family and not to the estate. The Supreme Court stated, "The most critical consideration [in determining whether a transfer is a gift] is the transferor's 'intention.'"[48] Though the case did not deal with death benefits, it did establish the importance of motive in determining whether a payment is a gift. Thus, the transfer should be made for reasons such as kindness, sympathy, generosity, affection, or admiration.

Key Point

The $5,000 death benefit exclusion applies to each deceased employee and not to each beneficiary.

It should be noted that it is more difficult to establish that a payment is a gift in situations where the payments are made to persons owning stock in the corporation making the payment. Such payments may be construed as constructive dividends, which are not deductible by the corporation but are taxable income to the recipients.[49]

The $5,000 exclusion is a ceiling amount for each deceased employee, and it is not increased because the deceased employee had more than one employer or because there is more than one beneficiary. If the benefits exceed $5,000 and there is more than one beneficiary, the $5,000 exclusion is allocated among the beneficiaries, regardless of their relationship to the deceased employee, based on the percentage of the total death benefits received by each person.

Example 4-20 ■

USA Corporation distributed $12,000 to a deceased employee's family. The deceased employee's widow received $6,000; his son, $3,000; and his daughter, $3,000. Because the widow received 50% of the benefits ($6,000 ÷ $12,000 = 0.50), she is entitled to an exclusion of $2,500 (0.50 × $5,000). Each child receives an exclusion of $1,250 because each child receives 25% of the benefits. The corporation is entitled to a $12,000 deduction if the additional $7,000 represents taxable compensation.

■

As noted above, lump-sum distributions from retirement plans qualify for the $5,000 exclusion, even though the employee possessed a nonforfeitable right to the benefit prior to his death. Lump-sum distributions from pension, profit-sharing, stock bonus, self-employed person retirement plans, and retirement plans established by tax-exempt organizations all qualify for the exclusion.[50]

Example 4-21 ■

Additional Comment

The $5,000 death benefit exclusion is available whether the payment is made to the deceased employee's estate, widow, or any other beneficiary.

At the time of his death, Hal had a nonforfeitable interest in his employer-financed pension plan of $10,000. The plan grants Hal's widow the right to receive a lump-sum distribution of $14,000. Hal's widow chooses the lump-sum distribution and is entitled to a death benefit exclusion of $5,000. The remaining $9,000 is taxable.

■

In some instances a beneficiary may receive an annuity rather than a lump-sum distribution. In that situation the beneficiary can exclude only amounts received in excess of the employee's nonforfeitable interest in the plan. The exclusion is equal to

---

[47] Sec. 102(c).
[48] *CIR* v. *Mose Duberstein,* 5 AFTR 2d 1626, 60-2 USTC ¶ 9515 (USSC, 1960).
[49] *Ernest L. Poyner* v. *CIR,* 9 AFTR 2d 1151, 62-1 USTC ¶ 9387 (4th Cir., 1962).
[50] Sec. 101(b)(2)(B).

the lesser of $5,000 or the difference between the present value of the annuity available to the beneficiary and the deceased employee's nonforfeitable rights at death.

Example 4-22 ■   At the time of her death, Kelly had a nonforfeitable interest in her employer's pension plan of $10,000. Kelly's husband has the option of receiving an annuity with a present value of $14,000 or a lump-sum distribution of $10,000. Kelly's husband elects to receive the annuity. His death benefit exclusion is equal to $4,000 ($14,000 − $10,000). The death benefit exclusion is added to the employee's contribution for purposes of determining the total exclusion when the individual annuity payments are received. ■

Example 4-23 ■   Assume the same facts as in Example 4-22 except that Kelly had contributed $7,000 to the pension plan during the years of her employment. Her husband is entitled to a total exclusion of $11,000 ($7,000 + $4,000). ■

Additional Comment

The $5,000 limit was placed on the exclusion for dependent care assistance programs because it was thought to be inequitable to provide an unlimited dependent care exclusion but a limited child care credit for individuals who pay their own child care expenses.

Additional Comment

The classification of an employee as highly compensated is made on the basis of the facts and circumstances of each case. Any officers and shareholders owning more than 5% of the stock are classified as highly compensated employees.

Additional Comment

About half of the large employers in the U.S. offer flexible spending accounts.

Dependent Care. **Dependent care assistance programs** are employer-financed programs that provide care for an employee's children or other dependents. The care must be of the type which, if paid by the employee, would qualify for the dependent care credit. Further, the credit is scaled down if the employee receives benefits under the employer's plan. (See Chapter 14 for a discussion of the child and dependent care rules.) An employee may exclude up to $5,000 of assistance each year ($2,500 for a married individual filing a separate return). The program cannot discriminate in favor of employees who are highly compensated or their dependents.[51]

Educational Assistance. Under educational assistance plans qualified under Sec. 127, employer paid employee educational costs. Employees excluded from gross income annual payments of up to $5,250 per year. These rules expire on December 31, 1994 and it is uncertain whether the exclusion will be extended.

Cafeteria Plans. **Cafeteria plans,** also referred to as flexible spending accounts, are plans that offer employees the option of choosing cash or statutory nontaxable fringe benefits (such as group term life insurance, medical insurance, or child care). If the employee chooses cash, the cash is taxable. However, if the employee instead chooses a statutory nontaxable fringe benefit, the value of the benefit is excluded from gross income. In other words, the fact that the employee could have chosen cash will not cause the fringe benefit to be taxed. The plan cannot discriminate in favor of highly compensated employees or their dependents or spouses.[52]

Some plans supplement wages while others are wage reduction plans. In supplemental wage plans, employer funds are used to pay fringe benefits. In the case of wage reduction plans, employees elect to receive reduced wages in exchange for the fringe benefits. In both cases, employees receive benefits without being taxed on them.

Employers frequently allow employees to use such funds to pay medical expenses. Typically, the plans supplement medical insurance, and funds are used to pay dental bills and other medical expenses not covered by regular insurance. In general, employees annually elect to set aside funds to pay medical expenses, and the employer pays the expenses using the set aside funds. One problem with the agreements is that they are binding for one year. As a result, the employee loses the funds if the actual medical expenses are less than the amount set aside. Employers, on the other hand, are obligated to pay expenses up to the agreed amount even if the full amount has not yet been withheld from the employees wages. Thus, the employer may lose money if an

[51] Sec. 129.
[52] Sec. 125.

employee terminates employment after incurring the designated amount of medical expenses but before the full amount is withheld.

Advantage of Fringe Benefits. The major advantage of taking fringe benefits (such as those descibed above) in lieu of a cash payment is the fact that employees do not have to use after-tax income to obtain the product or service.

Example 4-24 ■   Dan, an employee of Central Corporation, pays the premiums for $40,000 of life insurance coverage out of his salary which is, of course, subject to the income tax. Kay, an employee for Western Corporation, is covered by a $40,000 group term life insurance policy financed by Western Corporation. Western Corporation pays the premiums on the policy. Kay does not have to report the premiums as income. ■

Interest-Free Loans. One benefit that was often used in the past was interest-free loans to employees. The advantage of this type of transaction was diminished by the Tax Reform Act of 1984. Under present law, interest must generally be imputed on interest-free loans. (See Chapter 11 for a detailed discussion of rules applicable to interest-free loans.)

Foreign-Earned Income Exclusion

In general, the income of U.S. citizens is subject to the U.S. income tax even if the income is derived from sources outside the United States. The foreign income of U.S. citizens may also be taxed by the host country. This can lead to a substantial "double tax" on the same income. The double tax is mitigated by a **foreign tax credit.** Subject to limitations, U.S. citizens may subtract from their U.S. income tax liability the income taxes they pay to foreign countries. (See Chapter 14 for a discussion of foreign tax credit.)

In the case of foreign-earned income, individuals have available the alternative option of excluding the first $70,000 of foreign income from gross income.[53] The *exclusion* is available in lieu of the foreign tax credit. If both a husband and wife have foreign-earned income, both may claim exclusions. Community property rules are ignored in determining the amount of the exclusion. Thus, if only one spouse has foreign-earned income, only one exclusion is available. The principal reasons for the exclusion are to encourage U.S. businesses to operate in foreign countries and to hire U.S. citizens and resident aliens to manage the businesses. The hope is that such operations will improve the balance of payments. Taxpayers who elect the exclusion in one year may switch to the foreign tax credit in any subsequent year. Taxpayers who change from the exclusion to the credit may not reelect the exclusion before the sixth tax year after the tax year in which the change was made.[54] The IRS can waive the 6-year limitation in special situations (such as an individual employee changing the location of his foreign employment).

Foreign-earned income includes an individual's earnings from personal services rendered in a foreign country. The place where the services are performed controls in determining whether earned income is foreign or U.S. source income. If an individual is engaged in a trade or business in which both personal services and capital are material income- producing factors, no more than 30% of the net profits from the business may be excluded.[55] Furthermore, pensions, annuities, salary paid by the U.S. government, and deferred compensation do not qualify for the exclusion.[56]

---

[53] Sec. 911(b)(2)(A).
[54] Sec. 911(e)(2).
[55] Sec. 911(d)(2)(B).
[56] Sec. 911(b)(1)(B).

Typical Misconception

A taxpayer must be present in one or more foreign countries for 330 days during a period of 12 consecutive months, rather than 330 days during a calendar year.

To qualify for the foreign-earned income exclusion, the taxpayer must either be a bona fide resident of one or more foreign countries for an entire taxable year, or be present in one or more foreign countries for 330 days during a period of 12 consecutive months.[57] The exclusion limitation for a year must be prorated if the taxpayer is not present in, or a resident of, a foreign country or countries for the entire year.

Example 4-25 ■

Sondra is given a temporary assignment to work in foreign country T. Although Sondra does not establish a permanent residence in T, she is abroad for 330 days out of a 12-month period beginning on October 19, 1994. Thus, 73 days fall in 1994 and the rest in 1995. Sondra's exclusion for 1994 is limited to $14,000 ([73 ÷ 365] × $70,000). She may exclude $14,000 or the income she earns in foreign country T during 1994, whichever is less. ■

Additional Comment

In 1987 U.S. taxpayers excluded a total of $6.4 billion of foreign income on approximately 171,000 individual income tax returns.

Deductions directly attributable to the excluded foreign-earned income are disallowed. Expenses attributable to foreign-earned income must be allocated if foreign-earned income exceeds the exclusion. The disallowed portion is determined by multiplying the total amount of such expenses by the ratio of excluded earned income over total foreign-earned income.

Example 4-26 ■

Real World Example

A kindergarten teacher at a U.S. Air Force base in the Philippines was not entitled to the foreign-earned income exclusion because the Kindergarten School Fund from which she was paid was considered to be an instrumentality of the United States Government. Chester D. Taylor, 1971 PH T.C. Memo 30 TCM 233.

Connie earned $120,000 during 1994 while employed in a foreign country. She is entitled to an exclusion of $70,000. Connie incurred $12,000 of travel, transportation, and other deductible expenses attributable to the foreign-earned income. She may only deduct $5,000 of such expenses because $7,000 ([$70,000 ÷ $120,000] × $12,000) of the expenses are allocated to the excluded income. The $5,000 is classified as a miscellaneous itemized deduction and subject to the 2% of AGI floor associated with such deductions. ■

U.S. citizens working in foreign countries must often pay more for housing than they would pay in the United States. Therefore, an additional exclusion from gross income is available for housing costs incurred in excess of 16% of the salary paid government employees in Step 1 of grade GS-14. This GS-14 grade is used to establish a standard for taxpayers in general.

Example 4-27 ■

Wayne is employed in Tokyo, Japan, and earns a salary of $120,000. His housing costs are $32,000 for the year and are reasonable considering the high cost of living in Tokyo. Assume that 16% of the GS-14 (Step-1) salary is $10,000. Wayne can exclude $92,000 from gross income ($70,000 + $32,000 − $10,000). ■

Income from the Discharge of an Indebtedness

As noted earlier in this chapter, no income is realized when a taxpayer borrows funds because the amount borrowed is offset by a liability of an equal amount. If the debt is cancelled or forgiven, the taxpayer may have to include the cancelled amount in gross income. It is important to distinguish a debt cancellation from a gift, a bequest, or a renegotiation of the purchase price.

Example 4-28 ■

Farouk loaned his daughter $4,000 to help her purchase an automobile. Several months after she purchased the automobile, but before she repaid the $4,000, Farouk's daughter married. Farouk told his daughter that he was "tearing up" the $4,000 note as a wedding present. In this instance, the amount forgiven would constitute an excludable gift and would not be taxable as income to the daughter. ■

[57] Sec. 911(d).

Example 4-29 ■ Clay purchased an automobile from a dealer for $6,000. He paid $2,000 down and agreed to pay the balance of $4,000 over 3 years. After Clay purchased the automobile, he determined that it was defective. Clay tried to return the automobile, but the automobile dealer refused. Clay threatened to sue the dealer. To resolve the problem, the dealer offered to reduce the balance due on the purchase-money debt from $4,000 to $2,500. Clay agreed. The transaction constitutes a reduction in the purchase price of the automobile. Clay will not recognize any income, but must reduce the basis in his automobile from $6,000 to $4,500. ■

Example 4-30 ■ Blue Corporation issued bonds for $1,000 when interest rates were low. After a few years, interest rates increased and the bond price declined to $850. Blue Corporation purchased the bonds on the open market. Blue will recognize $150 of income from the discharge of indebtedness. ■

Under Sec.108(e)(4), the acquisition of indebtedness by a related party may also result in discharge of indebtedness income. Related parties include related entities such as a controlled corporation (i.e., more than 50% owned) and its shareholder and family members (spouses, parents, children and grandchildren and spouses of children and grandchildren).

Example 4-31 ■ Assume the same facts as Example 4-30 except that Blue Corporation's bonds are acquired by its sole shareholder. Blue must recognize income from the discharge of indebtedness. ■

The enforceability of a debt under state law may also determine whether the forgiveness results in income. For example, a recent case held that the forgiveness of a gambling debt was not included in gross income where the debt was unenforceable under state law.[58]

Section 61(a)(12) indicates that gross income includes income from the discharge of an indebtedness. Section 108, on the other hand, provides for the following exceptions where the discharge of an indebtedness is not taxable:

Real World Example

A taxpayer purchased and retired its own bonds. The purchase resulted in a gain because the bonds were payable in British pounds which had been devalued. The gain was excludable. Kentucky & Indiana Terminal Railroad Co. v. U.S., 13 AFTR 2d 1148, 64-1 USTC ¶ 9374 (6th Cir., 1964).

• The discharge occurs in bankruptcy.

• The discharge occurs when the taxpayer is insolvent.

These exceptions are intended to allow a "fresh start" for bankrupt and other financially troubled taxpayers. In either case, the taxpayer must reduce the following tax attributes: (1) a current net operating loss (NOL) and any NOL carryover, (2) general business tax credits[59] (both current and carryovers), (3) current capital losses and capital loss carryovers, (4) the basis of the taxpayer's property,[60] and (5) any foreign tax credit carryover. The attributes are reduced in the order listed, except that taxpayers may elect to reduce the basis of depreciable property and real property held as inventory before other attributes are reduced. Reductions are dollar for dollar except that a $1 reduction in debt results in a credit reduction of only 33⅓ cents. The effect of this reduction is to scale down current and future tax benefits by the amount of the excluded income.[61]

Additional Comment

Also excludable is the income from the cancellation of a student loan pursuant to a provision under which any part of the debt would be discharged due to working for a period of time in certain professions for a broad class of employers.

[58] *David Zarin v. CIR*, 66 AFTR 2d 90-5679, 90-2 USTC ¶ 50,530 (3rd Cir., 1990).

[59] The more significant general business tax credit items include the investment tax credit, the targeted jobs credit, the empowerment zone employment credit, the disabled access credit, the research credit, and the low-income housing credit. (See Chapter 14 for a discussion of tax credits.)

[60] The aggregate basis of property held by the taxpayer cannot be reduced below the taxpayer's aggregate liabilities.

[61] If a taxpayer is permitted to exclude a discharge of indebtedness from gross income, any carryovers of passive losses and minimum tax credits are reduced. (See Chapter 8 for the discussion of the passive loss limitation and Chapter 14 for a discussion of the minimum tax.)

Example 4-32 ■   During bankruptcy, USA Corporation's debt is reduced from $300,000 to $200,000. USA's assets are worth $220,000. USA has a NOL of $90,000, a general business credit carryover of $9,000, and depreciable property with a basis of $100,000. USA need not recognize any income from the $100,000 ($300,000 − $200,000) debt reduction. Assume that USA Corporation does not elect to reduce the basis of the depreciable property before reducing other tax attributes. USA must first reduce its $90,000 NOL to zero. Because the debt reduction is greater than the NOL, USA must also reduce the credit carryover. The balance of the debt reduction of $10,000 ($100,000 − $90,000) reduces the credit carryover by $3,333. This is because each $1 reduction in debt results in a credit reduction of 33⅓ cents.   ■

Key Point

A discharge of debt in bankruptcy does not generate income.

If a debt is reduced during bankruptcy proceedings, the taxpayer recognizes no income even if the reduction in debt exceeds the tax attributes listed above. In the case of an insolvent taxpayer, no income is recognized as long as the taxpayer is insolvent after the reduction in debt takes place. A taxpayer is insolvent if the debts owed by the taxpayer exceed the FMV of assets owned. Thus, an insolvent taxpayer reduces the tax attributes listed to the point of solvency. From that point on, any reduction in debt results in the recognition of income even if all tax attributes have not been offset.

Example 4-33 ■   Assume the same facts as in Example 4-32 except that the reduction in debt occurs as a result of negotiations with creditors rather than during bankruptcy proceedings. The reduction of USA's debts from $300,000 to $220,000 (the FMV of the assets) reduces the NOL carryover by $80,000 (from $90,000 to $10,000). The remaining $20,000 reduction of the debt (from $220,000 to $200,000) is a taxable event because it creates a positive equity (i.e., USA is solvent to the extent of $20,000 when its debt is reduced from $220,000 to $200,000). Income of $20,000 is recognized since the debt is reduced below the FMV of the assets.   ■

Section 108 also permits individuals to elect to exclude from gross income certain income realized from the discharge of qualified real property indebtedness and to reduce the basis of real property by the amount of discharged indebtedness. The rule is limited to indebtedness which is incurred or assumed in connection with the purchase or improvement of real property used in a trade or business. The reduction in basis is made at the beginning of the year following the discharge and is limited to the lesser of (1) the adjusted basis of real estate held by the taxpayer, or (2) the principal amount of the indebtedness (before the discharge) over the value of the property which is security for the debt.

Example 4-34 ■   Colin owns a building in which he operates an automobile parts store. The adjusted basis of the property at the end of the year is $240,000, the value is $150,000, and the mortgage is $225,000. The value of the property has declined because of the slow economy. Further, Colin has had difficulty making payments on the property because his business has also been slow. The mortgage holder agreed to reduce the amount of the mortgage to $175,000. Colin can elect to reduce the basis of the property by the amount of the discharge, $50,000 ($225,000 − $175,000) and to exclude such amount from gross income.   ■

As with the other Sec. 108 rules, the purpose is to provide relief for financially burdened taxpayers. In this case, the taxpayers holding business real property that has declined in value may avoid recognizing income when the lender reduces the amount of the mortgage. In one sense, this is much like a renegotiation of the purchase price of the property. However, there is no requirement that the lender be the previous owner. Loans from banks and other lenders are covered by this rule.

Exclusion For Gain From Small Business Stock

Noncorporate taxpayers may exclude up to 50% of the gain realized on the disposition of qualified small business stock issued after August 10, 1993, if the stock is held for more than five years.[62] For each issuer of qualified small business stock, there is a limit on the amount of gain that a taxpayer may exclude. The amount of gain eligible for the exclusion may not exceed the greater of $10,000,000, reduced by amounts previously excluded for gains on the company's stock, or 10 times the taxpayer's aggregate adjusted basis of the stock disposed of during the year.[63] When measuring the taxpayer's aggregate basis for the stock to determine the maximum amount of gain to exclude, the fair market value of the assets contributed to the corporation is used.

Example 4-35 ■ In 1994, Dennis contributed property with a basis of $1,000,000 and a FMV of $4,000,000 to a qualified small business corporation for all of its common stock. If he sells one-half of the stock in the year 2000 for $14,000,000, he may exclude $6,750,000 of the $13,500,000 ($14,000,000 − $500,000) realized gain. The maximum gain eligible for the exclusion is the greater of $10,000,000 or $20,000,000 (10 times the $2,000,000 basis [$4,000,000 FMV × 0.50] of the stock sold). Thus, none of the $13,500,000 realized gain is subject to the limitation. ■

A corporation may issue qualified small business stock only if the corporation is a C corporation that is not an excluded corporation with an aggregate adjusted basis of not more than $50 million of gross assets, and at least 80% of the value of its assets must be used in the active conduct of one or more qualified trades or businesses.[64]

TAX PLANNING CONSIDERATIONS

Additional Comment

A case can be made for the desirability of encouraging employers to provide health insurance and other fringe benefits. However, these provisions may contribute to increases in the cost of insurance and medical care.

Employee Fringe Benefits

The tax law encourages certain forms of fringe benefits by allowing an employer to deduct the cost of the benefit while permitting the employee to exclude the benefit from gross income. This does not represent any tax advantage to the employer because compensation, whether in the form of cash or nontaxable fringe benefits, is deductible if reasonable in amount. It is the employee who benefits from the exclusion of fringe benefits from gross income.

Example 4-35 ■ USA Company has decided to offer $20,000 of group term life insurance coverage for each of its employees at an average annual premium cost of $100 per employee. Tim, an employee of USA Corporation, is in the 15% tax bracket. Because USA is offering a nontaxable fringe benefit, Tim will owe no additional income tax. If Tim had received a salary increase of $100, he would have had to pay an additional income tax of $15 (0.15 × $100). The remaining $85 of after-tax income would

---

[62] Sec. 1202 (a).
[63] Sec. 1202 (b)(1).
[64] Secs. 1202 (d) and (e). Excluded corporations are those engaged in providing professional services (e.g., law and health), financial services (e.g., banking, and insurance), hospitality (e.g., hotels and restaurants) and mining and oil and gas production.

probably not have been sufficient to obtain the same amount of life insurance coverage. ■

Excluding fringe benefits from gross income favors employees who are subject to higher tax rates.

Example 4-36 ■   Assume the same facts as in the preceding example except that Tim is in the 36% tax rate. Tim would save $36 (0.36 × $100) of taxes by receiving the group term life insurance coverage instead of the $100 salary increase. ■

It is not always desirable for employers to offer nontaxable fringe benefits. Some employees are not interested in certain benefits. For example, in the case of married couples where both spouses are employed, it is not necessary for both employers to provide medical insurance coverage for both spouses. Alternatively, single employees may not feel the need for group term life insurance and employees with no children are uninterested in employer-provided child care.

To avoid providing fringe benefits that are unneeded or unwanted, many employers have turned to cafeteria plans. Under cafeteria plans, employees may select from a list of nontaxable fringe benefits. On the other hand, employees who so choose may elect to receive cash in lieu of some or all of the nontaxable benefits. Thus, each employee selects what he wants most. One common result is that high-tax-rate employees select the nontaxable fringe benefits, whereas other employees choose to receive cash.

Self-Help and Use of Personally Owned Property

As noted earlier in this chapter, self-help income and income derived from the use of personal property are not taxable. Thus, self-help and personal ownership of property are favored by the tax system. Taxpayers who rent their personal residences cannot deduct rental payments, but taxpayers who own their residences do not pay rent and may deduct interest and real estate taxes as itemized deductions. Thus, the tax law encourages ownership of personal residences.

Effective tax planning necessitates weighing the tax incentives with other nontax factors. Taxpayers with little accumulated funds may find it difficult to purchase a residence despite the availability of tax incentives. Taxpayers who frequently move may find that transaction costs such as real estate commissions and other closing costs are greater than the tax benefits obtained from home-ownership. Other factors such as the personal preference of the taxpayer and anticipated inflation rates must also be considered.

Self-help must be viewed in the same way. Taxpayers who are deciding whether to paint their own residences or hire someone else to do it must consider factors such as personal preference and the amount of income that could be produced if the time were spent working at an activity that produces taxable income.

COMPLIANCE AND PROCEDURAL CONSIDERATIONS

Taxpayers are not usually required to disclose excluded income on their tax returns. For example, a taxpayer who receives a tax-exempt scholarship need not disclose that

Additional Comment

Taxpayers filing Form 1040 are asked to report any tax-exempt interest income on line 8b.

income on his tax return. An exception is provided for tax-exempt interest and social security benefits which are required to be disclosed on the tax return. If a taxpayer's only income is from tax-exempt sources, the taxpayer need not file a tax return. Whether an individual must file a return is based on the amount of the individual's gross income for the year (see Chapter 2).

This chapter considers whether various fringe benefits are taxable. The rules regarding the need for an employer to withhold federal income taxes or to report a payment on an employee's Form W-2 [Statement of Income Tax Withheld on Wages] closely parallel the gross income rules. (See Chapter 14 for a discussion of these reporting requirements.) In general, if a fringe benefit is nontaxable, employers do not withhold from the benefit nor do they report the benefit on the employee's W-2 at year-end. On the other hand, if the benefit is taxable, it is subject to withholding and is reported on the employee's W-2 at year-end. Thus, employers do not withhold for nontaxable meals and lodging provided to employees[65] or a moving expense reimbursement if the expenses are deductible.[66] Similarly, no withholding is required for the following fringe benefits if they are nontaxable: scholarships and fellowships covered by Sec. 117,[67] dependent care covered by Sec. 129,[68] and miscellaneous fringes covered by Sec. 132.[69]

There are exceptions to this basic system. Certain fringe benefits are not subject to withholding even if the benefits are taxable. These include group-term life insurance coverage,[70] medical expense reimbursements,[71] and employee death benefits.[72]

Employers who are obligated to withhold from employee wages are subject to penalty if they fail to withhold, fail to provide employees with correct W-2s, or fail to correctly report the compensation and withholding information to the IRS.[73] In general, the failure to report wages and withholding to either employees or the IRS is subject to penalty generally equal to $50 per failure. The failure to withhold can result in a penalty equal to 100% of the amount that should have been withheld. The penalty can be imposed on the employer and other persons, such as officers or accountants, who are responsible for withholding.

Occasionally, employees do not want employers to withhold taxes from their wages. Officers or others who choose not to withhold from employee wages face an extremely burdensome penalty, particularly if a large number of employees are involved. Therefore, it is important that employers comply with withholding requirements. One closely related issue is whether an individual is an employee subject to withholding or an independent contractor as only employee wages are subject to withholding (see Chapter 14).

The foreign-earned income exclusion is reported on Form 2555. A simplified Form 2555-EZ (Foreign Earned Income Exclusion) may be used by taxpayers who have total foreign-earned income of $70,000 or less, are filing a calendar year return that covers a 12-month period, do not have self-employment income or business or moving expenses, and those who do not claim the foreign housing exclusion or deduction.

---

[65] Reg. Sec. 31.3401(a)-1(b)(9).
[66] Sec. 3401(a)(15).
[67] Sec. 3401(a)(20).
[68] Sec. 3401(a)(18).
[69] Sec. 3401(a)(20).
[70] Sec. 3401(a)(14).
[71] Sec. 3401(a)(19).
[72] Rev. Rul. 71-456, 1971-2 C.B. 354.
[73] Secs. 6672, 6674, and 6721 respectively.

PROBLEM MATERIALS

DISCUSSION QUESTIONS

4-1. What is meant by the terms *administrative exclusion* and *judicial exclusion*?

4-2. There is no specific statutory exclusion for welfare benefits. The IRS has, nevertheless, ruled that such benefits are not taxable. Is this within the authority of the IRS?

4-3. What is self-help income? Is it taxable? Explain.

4-4. What was the issue in the tax case *Eisner* v. *Macomber*? Why is the case important?

4-5. Most exclusions exist for one of two reasons. What are those reasons? Give examples of exclusions that exist for each of the two reasons above.

4-6. **a.** If a gift of property is made, who is taxed on income produced by the property?
b. How can interfamily gifts reduce a family's total tax liability?

4-7. **a.** What role does intent play in determining whether a transfer is a gift and therefore not subject to the income tax?
b. Are tips received by employees from customers excludable from gross income as gifts? Explain.

4-8. What is the tax significance of the face amount of a life insurance policy?

4-9. Under what circumstances are dividends on life insurance policies taxable?

4-10. What conditions must be met for an award to qualify for an exclusion under Sec. 74?

4-11. Which of the requirements for the Sec. 74 awards exclusion most severely limits its use? Does the exclusion benefit taxpayers more if they itemize their deductions or use the standard deduction?

4-12. **a.** Define the term scholarship as it is used in Sec. 117.
b. If a scholarship covers room and board, is it excludable?
c. If an employer provides a scholarship to an employee who is on leave of absence, will that scholarship be taxable?
d. Is the amount paid by a university to students for services excludable from the students' gross income?

4-13. Under what conditions would compensation received for services rendered by a student be excludable as a scholarship?

4-14. What special rules are applicable to nondegree candidates who receive scholarships?

4-15. Is the personal injury exclusion found in Sec. 104 limited to physical injury? Explain.

4-16. Answer the following questions relative to employer-financed medical and health, disability, and life insurance plans.
a. May employers deduct premiums paid on employee insurance?
b. Do employees have to include such premiums in gross income?
c. Are benefits paid to the employee included in the employee's gross income?

4-17. Special rules are applicable in situations where group term life insurance coverage exceeds $50,000. How are key employees treated in instances where coverage exceeds $50,000? How are other employees treated?

4-18. **a.** What are the six major types of fringe benefits covered by Sec. 132?
b. What tax advantage is offered relative to such benefits?
c. Are such benefits available to employees only or may the benefits also be offered to spouses, dependents, and retirees?
d. Is discrimination prohibited relative to Sec. 132 benefits?
e. What is the tax impact upon the employer and employees if an employer's plan is discriminatory?

4-19. What conditions must be met if an employee is to exclude meals and lodging furnished by an employer?

4-20. The president and vice president of USA Corporation receive benefits that are unavailable to other employees. These benefits include free parking, payment of monthly expenses in a local club, discounts on products sold by the corporation, and payment of premiums on a whole life insurance policy. Which of the benefits must be included in the gross income of the president and vice president?

4-21. Are the same fringe benefits that are available to employees also available to self-employed individuals?

4-22. Explain the *Sutter rule*.

4-23. Do amounts owed for salary by an employer to a deceased employee qualify for the $5,000 death benefit exclusion? Explain.

4-24. What types of income qualify for the foreign-earned income exclusion?

4-25. Are taxpayers who claim the foreign-earned income exclusion entitled to deduct expenses incurred in producing that income? Explain.

4-26. a. Why is it important to distinguish debt cancellation from a gift, bequest, or the renegotiation of a purchase price?
   b. What happens to the basis of an asset if the taxpayer renegotiates its purchase price?

4-27. a. Under what conditions is the discharge of indebtedness not taxable?
   b. If a father forgives a daughter's debt to him, is she required to include such amount in her gross income?

4-28. Bankrupt and insolvent taxpayers do not recognize income if debt is discharged. They must, however, reduce specified tax attributes. List these attributes in the order they must be reduced.

4-29. Are employee awards in excess of $25 taxable? Explain.

4-30. The Supreme Court recently settled the issue of whether awards for sex, race, or age discrimination are taxable. What was the fundamental issue facing the court?

4-31. Why are cafeteria plans helpful in the design of an employee benefit plan that provides nontaxable fringe benefits?

4-32. Both high income and low income employees are covered by cafeteria plans. Under cafeteria plans, all employees may select from a list of nontaxable fringe benefits or they may elect to receive cash in lieu of these benefits.
   a. Which group of employees is more likely to choose nontaxable fringe benefits in lieu of cash? Explain.
   b. Is this result desirable from a social or economic point of view? Explain.

PROBLEMS

4-33. *Self-Help Income.* In which of the following situations would the taxpayer realize taxable income?
   a. A mechanic performs work on his own automobile. The mechanic would have charged a customer $400 for doing the same work.
   b. A mechanic repairs his neighbor's automobile. In exchange, the neighbor, an accountant, agrees to prepare the mechanic's tax return. The services performed are each worth $200.
   c. A mechanic repairs his daughter's automobile without any charge.

4-34. *Excludable Gifts.* Which of the following would constitute excludable gifts?
   a. Alice appeared on a TV quiz show and received a prize of $500.
   b. Bart received $500 from his employer because he developed an idea that reduced the employer's production costs.
   c. Chuck borrowed $500 from his mother in order to finance his last year in college. Upon graduation, Chuck's mother told him he did not have to repay the $500. She intended the $500 to be a graduation present.

4-35. *Life Insurance Proceeds.* Dan is the beneficiary of a $50,000 insurance policy on the life of his mother. Upon her death, Dan has the choice of receiving either the face amount of the policy or five annual installments of $12,000 each.

   a. How much income must Dan report if he elects to receive the face of the policy?

   b. How much income must Dan report if he elects to receive the installments?

   c. Would it make any difference if the insured had been his wife instead of his mother? Explain.

4-36. *Transfer of Life Insurance.* Ed is the beneficiary of a $20,000 insurance policy on the life of his mother. Because Ed needs funds, he sells the policy to his sister, Amy, for $6,000. Amy subsequently pays premiums of $8,000.

   a. How much income must Amy report if she collects the face value of the policy upon the death of her mother?

   b. Would Amy have to report any income if her brother had given her the policy? Assume the only payment she made was $8,000 for the premiums.

4-37. *Endowment Policy.* Gary paid premiums on an endowment policy with a face value of $60,000. Prior to turning 65, Gary paid premiums totaling $24,000. Upon reaching age 65, Gary collected the face value of the policy.

   a. How much income must Gary report when he collects the face value of the policy?

   b. Assume Gary elects to receive an annuity of $4,800 per year for 15 years rather than accepting the face amount. How must income would Gary have to report each year?

   c. Would the answer be different if the $60,000 had been paid to Gary's estate upon his death at age 58?

4-38. *Insurance Policy Dividends.* Hank carries a $100,000 insurance policy on his life. Premiums paid over the years total $8,000. Dividends on the policy have totaled $6,000. Hank has left the dividends on the policy with the insurance company. During the current year, the insurance company credited $600 of interest on the accumulated dividends to Hank's account.

   a. How much income is Hank obligated to report in connection with the policy?

   b. Would it make any difference if the accumulated dividends equaled $9,000 instead of $6,000?

4-39. *Prizes and Awards.* For each of the following indicate whether the amount awarded is taxable:

   a. Irene won $100 playing bingo at her church.

   b. Jack was awarded a $100 prize for a painting he entered in a community art show.

   c. Kay was selected as coach of the year by the local school board. Kay received a $200 cash award, which was presented at the district's annual awards banquet. Awards were also presented to outstanding teachers, administrators, and students. The board selected the recipients based on its knowledge of each individual and his or her achievements.

4-40. *Scholarships.* For each of the following indicate the amount that must be included in the taxpayer's gross income:

   a. Larry was given a $1,500 tuition scholarship to attend Eastern Law School. In addition, Eastern paid Larry $4,000 per year to work part time in the campus bookstore.

   b. Marty received a $10,000 football scholarship for attending Northern University. The scholarship covered tuition, room and board, laundry, and books. Four thousand dollars of the scholarship was designated for room and board and laundry. It was understood that Marty would participate in the school's intercollegiate football program, but Marty was not required to do so.

   c. Western School of Nursing requires all third-year students to work 20 hours per week at an affiliated hospital. Each student is paid $4 per hour. Nancy, a third-year student, earned $4,000 during the year.

4-41. *Research Grants.* Otto is a biology professor who teaches at Southern University. The University awarded Otto a $2,000 grant to study the surface of the flatworm. Otto was expected to spend three months during the summer conducting the study. In addition, Otto was awarded $1,500 for supplies and typing, travel, and other incidental costs. The actual expenses totaled $1,500. How much income must Otto report?

4-42. Payments for Personal Injury. Determine which of the following may be excluded as payments for sickness and injury.

a. Pat was injured in an automobile accident. The other driver's insurance company paid him $2,000 to cover medical expenses and a compensatory amount of $4,000 for pain and suffering.

b. A newspaper article stated that Quincy had been convicted of tax evasion. Quincy, in fact, had never been accused of tax evasion. He sued and won a compensatory settlement of $4,000 from the newspaper.

c. Rob, who pays the cost of a commercial disability income policy, fell and injured his back. He was unable to work for 6 months. The insurance company paid him $1,800 per month during the time he was unable to work.

d. Steve fell and injured his knee. He was unable to work for 4 months. His employer-financed disability income policy paid Steve $1,600 per month during the time he was unable to work.

e. Ted suffered a stroke. He was unable to work for 5 months. His employer continued to pay Ted his salary of $1,700 per month during the time he was unable to work.

4-43. Employee Benefits. Ursela is employed by USA Corporation. USA Corporation provides medical and health, disability, and group term life insurance coverage for its employees. Premiums attributable to Ursela were as follows:

Medical and health	$1,800
Disability	300
Group term life (face amount is $40,000)	200

During the year, Ursela suffered a heart attack and subsequently died. Prior to her death, Ursela collected $14,000 as a reimbursement for medical expenses, and $5,000 of disability income. Upon her death, Ursela's husband collected the $40,000 face value of the life insurance policy.

a. What amount can USA Corporation deduct for premiums attibutable to Ursela?

b. How much must Ursela include in income relative to the premiums paid?

c. How much must Ursela include in income relative to the insurance benefits?

d. How much must Ursela's widower include in income?

4-44. Group-term Life Insurance. Data Corporation has four employees and provides group-term life insurance coverage for all 4 employees. Coverage is as follows:

Employee	Age	Key Employee	Coverage	Actual Premiums
Andy	62	yes	$200,000	$4,000
Bob	52	yes	40,000	700
Cindy	33	no	80,000	600
Damitria	33	no	40,000	300

a. How much may Data Corporation deduct for group-term life insurance premiums?

b. How much income must be reported by each employee?

4-45. Life Insurance Proceeds. Joe is the beneficiary of a life insurance policy taken out by his father several years ago. Joe's father died this year and Joe has the option of receiving $100,000 cash or electing to receive $14,000 per year for the remainder of his life. Joe is now 65. Joe's father paid $32,000 in premiums over the years.

a. How much must Joe include in gross income this year if he elects to accept the $100,000 face amount?

b. How much must be included in Joe's gross income if he elects to receive installment payments?

4-46. Employee Benefits. Al flies for AAA Airlines. AAA provides its employees with several fringe benefits. Al and his family are allowed to fly on a space-available basis on AAA Airline. Tickets used by Al and his family during the year are worth $2,000. AAA paid for a subscription to two magazines published for pilots. The subscriptions totaled $80. The airline paid for Al's meals and lodging while he was away from home overnight in connection with his job. Such meals and lodging cost AAA $10,000. Although Al could not eat while flying, he was allowed to drink coffee provided by the airline. The coffee was worth about $50. AAA provided Al with free parking which is valued at $100 per month. The airline treated Al and his family to a one-week all expenses paid vacation at a resort near his home. This benefit was awarded because of Al's outstanding safety record. The value of the vacation was $1,500. Which of these benefits are taxable to Al?

4-47. *Employee Benefits.* Jet Corporation is involved in the purchase and rental of several large apartment complexes. Questions have been raised about the treatment of several items pertaining to Jet Corporation and its employees. Jet Corporation employs a manager for each complex. The manager is required to occupy a unit in the complex in order to be available at all hours. The average rental value of the units is $7,800 per year. The corporation's president finds that it is beneficial to the corporation if he entertains bankers and others with whom Jet does business. He does such entertaining about once each month and the corporation pays the cost. Business is discussed at the meals. The cost for the year of such entertaining was $600, and about one-third of the cost was attributable to meals consumed by the president.

Each year as the company closes its books, the controller and certain other members of the accounting staff must work overtime. The company pays each employee "supper money" totaling $25 during this period.

The corporation's vice president is expected to travel on business-related matters to visit various properties owned by the corporation. Because of the distances involved, the vice president must stay away from home several nights. Total meals and lodging incurred while on the trips total $3,000, most of which is attributable to the vice president himself.

Which of these amounts are deductible by the corporation? Which are taxable to the employee?

4-48. *Death Benefits.* After an illness of several weeks Phil died. Although there was no legal obligation to make any payment, Phil's former employer made a payment of $15,000 to his widow. The corporation sent the widow a letter with the check indicating that the amount was being awarded in recognition of Phil's many years of loyal service.
a. Is the employer entitled to deduct the amount it paid to Phil's widow?
b. Is any portion of the amount received by Phil's widow taxable? If yes, how much?

4-49. *Death Benefits.* Determine the amount of death benefit exclusion available to the widows in each of the following:
a. The employer awarded $4,000 each to an employee's widow and son.
b. A widow elected to receive a lump-sum distribution of $26,000 from the pension plan. At the time of his death, the husband's nonforfeitable interest in the plan was $23,000.
c. A widow elected to receive an annuity with a present value of $16,000, which equals her husband's nonforfeitable interest in the plan at the time of his death. The husband during his years of employment had contributed $10,000 through withholding to the plan.

4-50. *Foreign Earned Income Exclusion.* For each of the following cases, indicate the amount of the foreign-earned income exclusion. (Disregard the effect of exemptions for certain allowances under Sec. 912.)
a. Sam, a U.S. citizen, is an assistant to the ambassador to Spain. Sam lives and works in Spain. His salary of $40,000 is paid by the U.S. government.
b. Jim, a U.S. citizen, owns an unincorporated oil drilling company that operates in Argentina, where he resides. The business is heavily dependent on equipment owned by Jim. His profit for the year totaled $100,000.
c. Ken, a U.S. citizen, works for a large Japanese corporation. Ken is employed in the United States, but must travel to Japan several times each year. During the current year he spent 60 days in Japan. This is typical of most years. His salary is $45,000.

4-51. *Foreign Earned Income Exclusion.* On January 5, Rita left the United States for Germany, where she had accepted an appointment as vice president of foreign operations. Her employer, USA Corporation, told her the assignment would last about two years. Rita decided not to establish a permanent residence in Germany because her assignment was for only two years. Her salary for the year is $210,000. Rita incurred travel, transportation, and other related expenses totaling $6,000, none of which is reimbursed.
a. What is Rita's foreign-earned income exclusion?
b. How much may she deduct for travel and transportation?

4-52. ***Discharge of Debt.*** During bankruptcy, USA Corporation debt was reduced from $780,000 to $400,000. USA Corporation's assets are valued at $500,000. USA's NOL carryover was $300,000, its general business credit carryover was $10,000, and its capital loss carryover was $100,000. The corporation owns depreciable property with a basis of $150,000.

   a. Is USA Corporation required to report any income from the discharge of its debts?

   b. Which tax attributes are reduced and by how much? Assume USA does not make any special elections when reducing its attributes.

   c. Assume USA instead elects to reduce the basis of its depreciable assets first. What would be the result?

4-53. ***Discharge of Debt.*** Old Corporation has suffered losses for several years, and its debts total $500,000 while Old's assets are only valued at $380,000. Old's creditors agree to reduce Old's debts by one-half in order to permit the corporation to continue to operate. Old's NOL carryover is $150,000, and the basis of its depreciable property is $200,000.

   a. What impact does the reduction in debt have on Old's NOL?

   b. Is Old required to report any income?

4-54. ***Court and Insurance Awards.*** Determine whether the following items represent taxable income.

   a. As the result of an age discrimination suit, Pat received a cash settlement of $40,000. One-half of the settlement represented wages lost by Pat as a result of the discrimination and the balance represented an award based on personal injury.

   b. Matt sued the local newspaper for a story that reported that he was affiliated with organized crime. The court awarded him $50,000 of libel damages.

   c. Pam was injured in an automobile accident and received $10,000 from an employer-sponsored disability policy. In addition, her employer-financed medical insurance policy reimbursed her for $15,000 of medical expenses.

4-55. ***Cafeteria Plan.*** Jangyoun is a married taxpayer with a dependent 4-year old daughter. His employer offers a flexible spending account under which he can choose to receive cash or, alternatively, choose from certain fringe benefits. These benefits include health insurance which costs $2,500 and child care which costs $2,600. Assume Jangyoun is in the 28% tax bracket.

   a. How much would Jangyoun save in taxes if he chooses to participate in the employer's health insurance plan? Assume that he does not have sufficient medical expenses to itemize his deductions.

   b. Would you recommend that Jangyoun participate in the employer's health insurance plan, if his wife's employer already provides comparable health insurance coverage for the family?

   c. Would you recommend that Jangyoun participate in the employer provided child care option if he has the alternative option of claiming a child care credit of $480.

4-56. ***Exclusion of Gain from Small Business Stock.*** Jose acquired 1,000 shares of Acorn Corporation common stock in January, 1994 by transferring property with an adjusted basis of $1,000,000 and fair market value of $4,000,000 for 100% of the stock. Acorn is a qualified small business corporation. In June 1999, Jose sells all of the Acorn Corporation common stock for $16,000,000.

   a. What is the amount of gain that may be excluded from Jose's gross income?

   b. What would your answer be if the fair market value of the Acorn stock was only $1,000,000 upon its issue in 1994?

   c. What would your answer be if the stock was sold in June 1995?

COMPREHENSIVE PROBLEM

4-57. Pat was divorced from her husband in 1987. During the current year she received alimony of $18,000 and child support of $4,000 for her 11-year old son who lives with her. Her former husband had asked her to sign an agreement giving him the dependency exemption for the child but she declined to do so. After the divorce she accepted a position as a teacher in the local school district. During the current year she received a salary of $22,000. The school district paid her medical insurance premiums of $1,900 and provided her with group term life insurance coverage of $40,000. The premiums attributable to her coverage equaled $160. During her marriage, Pat's parents loaned her $8,000 to help with the down payment on her home. Her parents told her this year that they understand her financial problems and that they were cancelling the balance on the loan, which was $5,000. They did so because they wanted to help their only daughter.

Pat received dividends from National Motor Company of $4,600 and interest on State of California bonds of $2,850.

Pat sold her personal automobile for $2,800, because she needed a larger car. The automobile had cost $8,000. She purchased a new auto for $11,000. Pat had itemized deductions of $8,600. Assume her withholding and estimated payments total $8,000. Compute her taxable income for the current year.

TAX FORM/RETURN PREPARATION PROBLEMS

4-58. A. J. Paige, social security number 111-22-3333, is the vice-president of marketing (Japan) for International Industries, Inc. (III). III is headquartered at 123 Main Street, Los Angeles, California 92601. A. J., who is single, accepted the position and became a resident of Japan on July 8th of last year. Her business address is 86 Sano, Tokyo, Japan. A. J.'s visa permits her to stay in Japan indefinitely. Her only trips to the United States in the current year were for vacations (August 2 to 16 and December 21 to 28). A. J.'s contract specifies that her appointment is to last indefinitely, but states that III is to pay her $4,000 per year to cover the cost of two vacation trips to the United States. Her salary is $140,000, out of which she pays rent on an apartment of $28,000 per year. A. J. has no family or residence in the United States. She paid an income tax in Japan of $23,500. Complete a Form 2555 for the current year.

4-59. Alice Johnson, social security number 222-23-3334, is a single mother of two children, Jack and Jill, ages 15 and 17, respectively, and is employed as a secretary by State University of Florida. She has the following items pertaining to her income tax return for the current year:

1. Received a $20,000 salary from her employer who withheld $4,000 federal income tax.
2. Received a gift of 1000 shares of Ace Corporation stock with a $100,000 FMV from her mother. She also received $4,000 of cash dividends from the Ace Corporation.
3. Received $1,000 of interest income on bonds issued by the City of Tampa.
4. Received a stock dividend (qualifying under Sec. 305) of 50 shares of Ace Corporation stock with a $5,000 FMV.
5. Alice's employer paid $2,000 of medical and health insurance premiums on her behalf.
6. Received free tuition worth $1,200 at the University under the employer's educational assistance plan.
7. Maintains a household for herself and two children and provides more than 50% of their support. In the prior year, however, she entered into an agreement with her ex-husband which provided that he is entitled to the dependency exemptions for the children.
8. Received $12,000 alimony and $6,000 child support from her ex-husband (Charlie Johnson).
9. State University provided $60,000 of group-term life insurance. Alice is 42 years old and is not a key employee.
10. Received a $1,000 cash award from her employer for being designated as the "Secretary of the Year."
11. Total itemized deductions are $7,000.

Complete Form 1040 and accompanying schedules for Alice Johnson's federal income tax return for the current year.

CASE STUDY PROBLEM

4-60. Able Corporation is a closely-held company that is engaged in the manufacture and retail sales of automotive parts. Able maintains a qualified pension plan for its employees but has not offered nontaxable fringe benefits.

You are a tax consultant for the company who has been asked to prepare suggestions for the adoption of an employee fringe benefit plan. Your discussions with the client's chief financial officer reveal the following:

1. Employees currently pay their own premiums for medical and health insurance.
2. No group-term life insurance is provided.
3. The company owns a vacant building that could easily be converted to a parking garage.
4. Many of the employees purchase automobile parts from the company's retail outlets and pay retail price.
5. The president of the corporation would like to provide a dependent care assistance program under Sec. 129 for its employees.

Required: Prepare a client memo that recommends the adoption of an employee fringe benefit program. Your recommendations should discuss the pros and cons of different types of nontaxable fringe benefits.

CASE STUDY PROBLEM—ETHICAL ISSUES

4-61. Jay Corporation owns several automobile dealerships. This year, the corporation initiated a policy of giving the top salesperson at each dealership a free vacation trip to Florida. The president believes that this is an effective sales incentive. The cost of the vacations is deductible by the corporation as compensation paid to employees, and is taxable to the recipients. Nevertheless, the president objects to both reporting the value of the vacations as income on the W-2s of the recipients and to withholding taxes from wages for the value of the trips. He feels that this undermines the effectiveness of the incentive. What are the implications of this behavior for the corporation and the president?

TAX RESEARCH PROBLEMS

4-62. For over 30 years, Tom, Steve, and Gina were partners in an accounting firm. Upon the death of Steve, the partnership made a payment to his widow of $10,000. The payment was made under the terms of the partnership agreement that had been in effect for several years. Steve's widow also received a payment of $100,000 that represented her husband's equity in the partnership. Determine whether the $10,000 received by Steve's widow qualifies for the $5,000 death benefit exclusion.

A partial list of research sources is

- Sec. 101(b).
- Reg. Sec. 1.101-2(f).
- *Mary Tighe,* 33 T.C. 557 (1959).

4-63. Kim leased an office building to USA Corporation under a 10 year lease specifying that at the end of the lease USA had to return the building to its original condition if any modifications were made. USA changed the interior of the building, and at the end of the lease USA paid Kim $30,000 instead of making the required repairs. Does Kim have to include the payment in gross income?

A partial list of research sources is

- Sec. 109.
- *Boston Fish Market Corp.,* 57 T.C. 884 (1972).
- *Sirbo Holdings Inc. v. CIR,* 31 AFTR 2d 73-1005, 73-1 USTC ¶ 9312 (2nd Cir., 1973).

4-64. As a result of a fire damaging their residence, the Taylors must stay in a motel for five weeks while their home is being restored. They pay $2,000 for the room and $500 meals. Their homeowner's policy pays $2,500 to reimburse them for the cost. They estimate that during the five week period they would normally spend $300 for meals. Is the reimbursement taxable?

A partial list of research sources is

- Sec. 123.
- Reg. Sec. 1.123-1.

5

Property Transactions— Capital Gains and Losses

LEARNING OBJECTIVES

After studying this chapter, you should be able to

1. Determine the realized gain or loss from the sale or other disposition of property
2. Determine the amount realized from the sale or other disposition of property
3. Determine the basis of property
4. Distinguish between capital assets and other assets
5. Understand how capital gains and losses affect taxable income
6. Recognize when a sale or an exchange has occurred
7. Determine the holding period for an asset when a sale or disposition occurs

Historical Note

A preferential tax rate on capital gains was included in the tax law from 1921 to 1987. A modest preferential rate was reintroduced in 1991 with capital gains for noncorporate taxpayers being subject to a maximum 28% tax rate and ordinary income being subject to a maximum tax rate of 31%. A more significant capital gains differential was created in 1993 when the highest marginal rate was increased to 39.6%.

Gross income includes "gains derived from dealings in property,"[1] and certain "losses from sale or exchange of property"[2] are allowed as deductions from gross income. All recognized gains and losses must eventually be classified as either *capital* or *ordinary*. Prior to 1987, long-term capital gains (LTCGs) generally received more favorable tax treatment than ordinary gains or short-term capital gains (STCGs). The Tax Reform Act of 1986 substantially eliminated the difference in tax treatment for capital gain income and ordinary income.

Although the Tax Reform Act of 1986 eliminated most of the preferential treatment for net capital gain income, Congress retained the distinction between capital assets and other assets in the Code. By retaining the statutory structure for capital gains, the Conference Committee Report to the 1986 Act indicated that it would be easier to facilitate reinstatement of a capital gains differential if tax rates increased.[3] As tax rates have increased, Congress has created an increase in the preferential treatment for certain taxpayers.

For tax years beginning after 1990, the maximum tax rate imposed on net capital gains (the excess of net long-term capital gains over net short-term capital losses) recognized by noncorporate taxpayers is 28%. Since the maximum tax rate is currently 39.6%, noncorporate taxpayers may benefit by having a gain classified as LTCG instead of STCG or ordinary income.

Capital losses must be offset against capital gains, and net capital losses are subjected to restrictions upon their deductibility. Thus, most taxpayers prefer to have losses classified as ordinary instead of capital.

When classifying a recognized gain or loss, three important questions must be considered:

1. What type of property has been sold or exchanged?
2. When has a sale or exchange occurred?
3. When did the holding period for the property commence?

In this chapter, these three questions are considered as well as difficulties associated with determining the basis of the property sold or exchanged and the amount of realized gains or losses.

---

[1] Sec. 61(a)(3).
[2] Sec. 62(a)(3).
[3] H. Rept. No. 99-841, 99th Cong., 2d Sess., p. II-106 (1986).

DETERMINATION OF GAIN OR LOSS

Realized Gain or Loss

To determine **realized gain** or loss, the amount realized from the sale or other disposition of property is compared with the adjusted basis of that property. A gain is realized when the amount realized is greater than the basis, and a loss is realized when the amount realized is less than the basis of the property.[4]

Example 5-1 ■

Jack sells an asset with an adjusted basis of $10,000 to Judy for $14,000. Since the amount realized is greater than the basis, Jack has a realized gain of $4,000 ($14,000 − $10,000). ■

Despite the fact that most transfers of property involve a sale, gains and losses may also be realized on certain other types of dispositions of property, such as exchanges, condemnations, casualties, thefts, bond retirements, and corporate distributions. However, generally gains and losses are not realized when property is disposed of by gift or bequest.

Example 5-2 ■

Alice owns land that is held for investment and has a basis of $20,000. The land is taken by the city by right of eminent domain, and she receives a payment of $30,000 for the land. This condemnation is treated as a sale or disposition, and Alice's realized gain is $10,000 ($30,000 − $20,000). ■

Example 5-3 ■

Two years ago Bob purchased stock of a newly formed corporation for $10,000. During the current year, he receives a $12,000 distribution, constituting a return of capital, from the corporation. This distribution is treated as a sale. Therefore, Bob has a realized gain of $2,000 ($12,000 −$10,000).[5] Bob's basis for the stock is now zero because his basis of $10,000 has been recovered. ■

For a sale or other disposition to occur, there must be an identifiable event.[6] Mere changes in the value of property are not normally recognized as a disposition for purposes of determining a realized gain or loss.

Example 5-4 ■

Angela owns Tampa Corporation stock having a $25,000 fair market value (FMV) at the end of the year. Although Angela's basis for the stock is $20,000, she does not have a realized gain for tax purposes, since there has not been a sale or other disposition of the stock. ■

Many reasons exist for not taxing unrealized gains and losses that arise due to a mere change in value. The Regulations state that "A loss is not ordinarily sustained prior to the sale or other disposition of the property, for the reason that until such sale or other disposition occurs there remains the possibility that the taxpayer may recover or recoup the adjusted basis of the property."[7] Because of administrative difficulties associated with determining FMV, disputes with the Internal Revenue Service would be greatly increased if unrealized gains were taxed and unrealized losses were allowed as deductions. In addition, payment of tax on income is generally required only when a taxpayer has the wherewithal to pay the tax (e.g., the taxpayer has received cash from the sale or other disposition of property and can therefore pay the tax on the gain).

[4] Sec. 1001(a).
[5] Reg. Sec. 1.1001-1(c)(2).
[6] Reg. Sec. 1.1001-1(c)(1).
[7] Ibid.

Amount Realized. The **amount realized** from a sale or other disposition of property is the sum of any money received plus the FMV of all other property received.[8]

Example 5-5 ■

Tony transfers land to Rita for $15,000 and a machine having a $3,000 FMV. The amount realized by Tony is $18,000 ($15,000 + $3,000). ■

OBJECTIVE 2
Determine the amount realized from the sale or other disposition of property

From a practical standpoint, the determination of FMV is a question of fact and often creates considerable controversy between taxpayers and the IRS. **Fair market value (FMV)** is "the price at which property would change hands between a willing buyer and a willing seller, neither being under any compulsion to buy or sell."[9] In some cases, the FMV of the asset given in the exchange may be easier to determine than the FMV of the property received. Therefore, the FMV of the property given may be used to measure the amount realized.[10] If a buyer assumes the seller's liability or takes the property subject to the debt, the courts have included the amount of the liability when determining the amount realized.[11]

Example 5-6 ■

Anna exchanges land subject to a liability of $20,000 for $35,000 of stock owned by Mario. Mario takes the property subject to the liability. The amount realized by Anna is $55,000 ($35,000 + $20,000 liability assumed by Mario). If Anna's adjusted basis for the land exchanged is $42,000, her realized gain is $13,000 ($55,000 amount realized − $42,000 adjusted basis). ■

In the above example, Anna receives stock with a $35,000 FMV and is relieved of a $20,000 debt. Mario's taking the property subject to the debt is equivalent to providing Anna with cash of $20,000. Thus, the amount realized by Anna is $55,000.

Generally, selling expenses such as sales commissions and advertising incurred in order to sell or dispose of the property reduce the amount realized. An exception, discussed in Chapter 11, is provided for selling expenses related to installment sales.

Example 5-7 ■

Typical Misconception

The difference between the assumption of a liability and the taking of the property subject to the debt is sometimes confusing. The latter means that the lender can satisfy the debt only by repossessing the property. In the former case, where the buyer assumes the debt, the lender can satisfy the debt by repossessing the property and by going after other assets of the buyer.

Doug sells stock of Laser Corporation, which has a cost basis of $10,000, for $17,000. Doug pays a sales commission of $300 to sell the stock. The amount realized by Doug is $16,700 ($17,000 − $300) and he has a realized gain of $6,700 ($16,700 − $10,000). ■

Adjusted Basis. The initial adjusted basis of property depends upon how the property is acquired (e.g., by purchase, gift, inheritance, and so on). For example, if property is acquired from a decedent, its basis to the estate or heir is its FMV either at the date of death or, if the alternate valuation date is elected, 6 months from the date of death. The rules for determining the adjusted basis are discussed in subsequent sections of this chapter. Once the initial basis is determined, it may be adjusted upward or downward. Capital additions (also called capital expenditures) are expenditures that add to the value or prolong the life of property or adapt the property to a new or different use.[12] Capital additions increase the basis. Capital recoveries, such as the deductions for casualty losses, cost recovery, and depreciation, reduce the basis. A property's adjusted basis can be determined by the following equation:

---

[8] Sec. 1001(b).
[9] *CIR v. Homer H. Marshman,* 5 AFTR 2d 1528, 60-2 USTC ¶ 9484 (6th Cir., 1960).
[10] *U.S. v. Thomas Crawley Davis,* 9 AFTR 2d 1625, 62-2 USTC ¶ 9509 (USSC, 1962).
[11] *Beulah B. Crane v. CIR,* 35 AFTR 776, 47-1 USTC ¶ 9217 (USSC, 1947).
[12] Reg. Sec. 1.263(a)-1(b).

Ethical Point

The taxpayer may have lost records relating to the basis of the assets acquired many years earlier. In that case, the CPA can accept estimates of the missing data made by the taxpayer.

Initial basis + Capital additions (e.g., new porch for a building) −
Capital recoveries (e.g., depreciation deduction) =Adjusted basis

Capital expenditures are distinguished from expenditures that are deductible as ordinary and necessary business expenses. For example, the cost of repairing a roof may be a deductible expense, whereas the cost of replacing a roof is a capital addition. It is sometimes difficult to determine whether an item is a capital expenditure or a business expense. Because of the preference for an immediate tax deduction, some taxpayers prefer to classify expenditures as expenses rather than as capital expenditures.

Example 5-8 ■ | Ellen pays $2,500 for a major overhaul of an automobile used in her trade or business. The $2,500 is capitalized as part of the automobile's cost rather than deducted as a repair expense.   ■

Capital recoveries reduce the adjusted basis. The most common form of capital recovery is the deduction for depreciation or cost recovery. As discussed in Chapter 10, the accelerated cost recovery system (ACRS) provides a deduction for cost recovery and applies to most property placed in service after December 31, 1980, and before 1987. A modified ACRS form of depreciation (MACRS) is mandatory for most tangible depreciable property placed in service after 1986.

Example 5-9 ■ | Jeremy paid $100,000 for equipment 2 years ago and has claimed depreciation deductions of $37,000 for the 2 years. The cost of repairs during the same period was $6,000. At the end of the 2-year period, the property's adjusted basis is $63,000 ($100,000 − $37,000). The amount spent for repairs does not affect the basis. ■

Additional Comment

In addition to depreciation, other capital recoveries that reduce the adjusted basis of property include depletion, amortization, tax-free dividends, compensation or awards for involuntary conversions, deductible casualty losses, insurance reimbursements, and cash rebates received by a purchaser.

Recovery of Basis Doctrine. The **recovery of basis doctrine** states that taxpayers are allowed to recover the basis of an asset without being taxed because such amounts are a return of capital that the taxpayer has invested in the property. If a taxpayer receives a $12,000 return of capital distribution from a corporation when the taxpayer's basis for its investment in the corporation's stock is $10,000, the first $10,000 received represents a recovery of basis and only the $2,000 excess amount is treated as a gain realized on a sale or exchange of the stock investment. In many cases, basis is recovered in the form of a deduction for depreciation, cost recovery, or a casualty loss.

Example 5-10 ■ | Colleen owns a business asset with a $40,000 basis and a $45,000 FMV. As a result of a storm, the asset is damaged, and the FMV after the casualty is $36,000. Colleen is entitled to a $9,000 casualty loss deduction ($45,000 − $36,000), and the basis of the asset is reduced from $40,000 to $31,000.   ■

Recognized Gain or Loss

Realized gain or loss represents the difference between the amount realized and the adjusted basis when a sale or exchange occurs. The amount of gain or loss that is actually reported on the tax return is referred to as the recognized gain or loss. In some instances, gain or loss is not recognized due to special provisions in the tax law (e.g., a gain or loss may be deferred or a loss may be disallowed).

Typical Misconception

It is sometimes believed that all realized gains and losses are recognized for tax purposes. Although most realized gains are recognized, some realized losses are not recognized. For example, losses on the sale or exchange of property held for personal use cannot be recognized.

Losses are generally deductible if they are (1) incurred in carrying on a trade or business (2) incurred in an activity engaged in for profit and (3) casualty and theft losses. Realized losses on the sale or exchange of assets held for personal use are not recognized for tax purposes. Therefore, a taxpayer who incurs a loss on the sale or exchange of a personal-use asset does not fully recover the basis. As explained in Chapter 8, realized losses on personal-use assets may be recognized to some extent if the property is disposed of by casualty or theft.

Example 5-11 ■

Key Point

The sale of a personal residence or other property held for personal use creates an interesting situation in that gains must be recognized but losses cannot be recognized.

Ralph purchases a personal residence for $60,000. Deductions for depreciation are not allowed because the asset is not used in a trade or business or held for the production of income. If Ralph sells the house for $55,000, the realized loss of $5,000 is not deductible, and he recovers only $55,000 of his original $60,000 basis. ■

BASIS CONSIDERATIONS

OBJECTIVE 3

Determine the basis of property

Cost of Acquired Property

With certain exceptions, the basis of property is its cost.[13] **Cost** is the amount paid for the property in cash or the FMV of other property given in the exchange.[14] Any costs of acquiring the property and preparing the property for use are included in the cost of the property.

Example 5-12 ■

Penny purchases equipment for $15,000 and pays delivery costs of $300. Installation costs of $250 are incurred. The cost of the equipment is $15,550 ($15,000 + $300 + $250). ■

Funds borrowed and used to pay for an asset are included in the cost. Obligations of the seller that are assumed by the buyer increase the asset's cost.

Example 5-13 ■

Peggy purchases an asset by paying cash of $40,000 and signs a note payable to the seller for $60,000. She also assumes a lien against the property in the amount of $2,000. Her basis for the asset is its cost of $102,000 ($40,000 + $60,000 + $2,000). ■

Uniform Capitalization Rules. Prior to 1987, taxpayers often had a degree of flexibility with respect to capitalizing or expensing certain costs. The Tax Reform Act of 1986 created one set of capitalization rules applicable to all taxpayers and all types of activities. These uniform capitalization rules for inventory are provided in Sec. 263A and discussed in Chapter 11.

Additional Comment

The sales tax is a good example of a tax that would be paid in connection with the acquisition of property.

The uniform capitalization rules also affect property other than inventory if the property is used in a taxpayer's trade or business or in an activity engaged in for profit. For tax years beginning after 1986, taxes paid or accrued in connection with the acquisition of property are included as part of the cost of the acquired property. Taxes paid or accrued in connection with the disposition of property reduce the amount realized on the disposition.[15]

Example 5-14 ■

The Compact Corporation owns and operates a funeral home. The corporation purchases a hearse for $30,000 and pays sales taxes of $1,500. The cost basis for the hearse is $31,500 ($30,000 + $1,500). ■

Capitalization of Interest. Interest on debt paid or incurred during the production period to finance production expenditures incurred to construct, build, install, manufacture, develop, or improve real or tangible personal property must be

[13] Sec. 1012.
[14] Reg. Sec. 1.1012-1(a).
[15] Sec. 164(a).

capitalized.[16] The real or tangible personal property must have "a long useful life, an estimated production period exceeding 2 years, or an estimated production period exceeding 1 year and a cost exceeding $1,000,000."[17] Property has a long useful life if it is real property or property with a class life of at least 20 years.[18] The production period starts when "production of the property begins and ends when the property is ready to be placed in service or is ready to be held for sale."[19]

Example 5-15 ■

The Indiana Corporation started construction of a $3 million motel on July 1, 1993, and borrowed an amount equal to the motel's construction costs. The motel is completed and ready for service on October 1, 1994. Interest incurred for the construction loan for the period from July 1, 1993, through October 1, 1994, is included in the motel's cost. The capitalized interest cost is depreciated over the motel's recovery period (see Chapter 10). ■

Additional Comment

If a stockholder leaves his stock with a broker in street name, the shareholder can specifically identify the shares sold by simply informing the broker which shares he wishes to sell. The date basis of the shares sold should appear on the confirmation from the broker.

Identification Problems. In most cases, the adjusted basis of property is easily identified with the property that is sold. However, problems occur when property is homogenous in nature (e.g., one investor who owns several blocks of common stock of the same corporation that are purchased on different dates at different prices). The Regulations require the taxpayer to adequately identify the particular stock that is sold or exchanged.[20] Many investors allow brokers to hold their stock in street name and thus do not make a physical transfer of securities. Such investors need to be careful to provide specific instructions to the broker as to which securities should be sold. If the stock sold or exchanged is not adequately identified, the first-in, first-out (FIFO) method must be used to identify the stock. With the FIFO method, the stock sold or exchanged is presumed to come from the first lot or lots acquired.

Example 5-16 ■

Tammy purchased 300 shares of the Acme Corporation stock during 1993:

Month Acquired	Size of Block	Basis
January	100 shares	$4,000
May	100	5,000
October	100	6,000

In March 1994 Tammy sells 120 shares of the stock for $5,160. If Tammy specifically identifies the stock sold as being all of the stock purchased in October and 20 shares purchased in May, her realized loss is $1,840. ($5,160 − [$6,000 + $1,000]). ■

Example 5-17 ■

Historical Note

If a gift was made before January 1, 1921, the basis was the FMV of the property at the time of the gift.

Assume the same facts as in Example 5-16 except that Tammy did not specifically identify the stock that is sold. In this case, the FIFO method is used, and her realized gain is $160 ($5,160 − [$4,000 + $1,000]). ■

Property Received as a Gift—Gifts After 1921

The basis of property received as a gift is generally the same as the donor's basis.[21] If the FMV of the property at time of the gift is less than the donor's basis, the donee may have to use one basis if the property is subsequently disposed of at a gain and another if the property is disposed of at a loss. As discussed later in this chapter, the basis may be increased by a portion or all of the gift tax paid because of the transfer.

---

[16] Sec. 263A(f).
[17] Sec. 263A(f)(1)(B).
[18] Sec. 263A(f)(4)(A).
[19] Sec. 263A(f)(4)(B).
[20] Reg. Sec. 1.1012-1(c)(1).
[21] Sec. 1015(a). Prior to 1921, the basis was always the donor's basis.

Current rules for determining the donee's basis for property received as a gift are a function of the relationship between the FMV of the property at the time the gift is made and the donor's basis. If the FMV is equal to or greater than the donor's basis, the donee's basis is the same as the donor's basis for all purposes. However, if the FMV is less than the donor's basis, the donee has a dual basis for the property. If the donee later transfers the property at a loss, the donee's basis is the property's FMV at the time of making the gift. However, if the donee transfers the property at a gain, the donee's basis is the same as the donor's basis.[22]

Example 5-18 ■   Kevin makes a gift of property with a basis of $350 to Janet when it has a $425 FMV. If Janet sells the property for $450, she has a realized gain of $100 ($450 − $350). If Janet sells the property for $330, she has a realized loss of $20 ($330 − $350). Since the FMV of the property at the time of the gift is more than the donor's basis, the donee's basis is $350 for determining both gain and loss.   ■

The following example illustrates the scenario when a taxpayer has a dual basis. The basis for determining a gain is different from the basis for determining a loss.

Example 5-19 ■   Chuck makes a gift of property with a basis of $600 to Maggie when the property has a $500 FMV. Maggie's basis for the property is $600 if the property is sold at a gain (i.e., for more than $600), but the basis is $500 if the property is sold at a loss (i.e., for less than $500). If the property is sold for $500 or more but not more than $600, no gain or loss is recognized.   ■

Key Point

Although unrealized losses cannot be shifted to another taxpayer, unrealized gains can be shifted.

The dual basis rules were designed to prevent tax-avoidance schemes. Taxpayers are prevented from shifting unrealized losses to another taxpayer by making gifts of such "loss"property. For example, a low-income taxpayer who owns property that has depreciated in value might transfer the property by gift to a high-income taxpayer who would receive greater tax benefit from the deduction of the loss upon the subsequent sale of the property. The loss basis rules prevent the donee from recognizing a loss on the sale of the property because the basis for loss is the lesser of the donor's basis or FMV on the date of the gift.

Key Point

No gift tax can be added to the basis of the property if the donor's basis is greater than the FMV of the property.

Effect of Gift Tax on Basis—Gifts After 1976. If the donor pays a gift tax on the transfer of property, the donee's basis may be increased. This increase only occurs if the FMV of the property exceeds the donor's basis on the date of the gift. For taxable gifts after 1976,[23] the increase in the donee's basis is equal to a pro rata portion of the gift tax that is attributable to the unrealized appreciation in the property. The amount of the addition to the donee's basis is determined as follows:[24]

$$\text{Gift tax paid} \times \frac{\text{FMV at time of the gift} - \text{Donor's basis}}{\text{FMV at time of the gift}}$$

Example 5-20 ■   During the current year, Cindy makes a gift of property with a $20,000 basis to Jessie when the property has a $30,000 FMV. Cindy pays a gift tax of $900. Jessie's basis for the property for determining both gain and loss is $20,300 ($20,000 + [0.333 × $900]).   ■

---

[22] Ibid.

[23] For gifts after September 2, 1958, and before 1977, the entire amount of the gift tax paid is added to the donee's basis. However, the basis may not exceed the property's FMV on the date of the gift.

[24] Sec. 1015(d)(6).

Example 5-21 ■   During the current year, Sally makes a gift of property with a basis of $50,000 to Troy when the property has a $40,000 FMV. Sally pays a gift tax of $1,000. Troy's basis for the property is not affected by the gift tax paid by Sally, because the FMV is less than the donor's basis at the time of the gift. Troy's basis for the property is $50,000 for purposes of determining gain and $40,000 for purposes of determining loss. ■

Property Received from a Decedent

The basis of property received from a decedent is generally the FMV of the property at the date of the decedent's death or an alternate valuation date.[25] This can result in either a step-up or step-down in basis.

Example 5-22 ■   Patrick inherits property having an $80,000 FMV on the date of the decedent's death. The decedent's basis in the property is $47,000. The executor of the estate does not elect the alternate valuation date. His basis for the property is $80,000. ■

Example 5-23 ■   Dianna inherits property having a $60,000 FMV at the date of the decedent's death. The decedent's basis in the property is $72,000. The alternate valuation date is not elected. Dianna's basis for the property is $60,000. ■

Real World Example

The alternate valuation date was typically used in valuing the estates of individuals owning large portfolios of common stocks who died shortly before the stock market crash in October 1987.

Instead of using the FMV on the date of death to determine the estate tax, the executor of the estate may elect to use the FMV on the alternate valuation date. The alternate valuation date is generally 6 months after the date of death. If the alternate valuation date is elected, the basis for all of the assets in the estate is their FMV on that date unless the property is distributed by the estate to the heirs or is sold before the alternate valuation date. If the alternate valuation date is used, property distributed or sold after the date of the decedent's death and before the alternate valuation date has a basis equal to its FMV on the date of distribution or the date it is disposed of.[26]

If the size of the estate is small enough that an estate tax return is not required, the value of the property on the alternate valuation date may not be used.[27]

Example 5-24 ■   Marilyn inherits all of the property owned by an individual who dies in April when the property has a $100,000 FMV. The value of the property 6 months later is $90,000. Because of the size of the estate, no estate tax is due. The alternate valuation date may not be used, and Marilyn's basis for the property is $100,000. ■

As noted above, the basis of the property to the estate and the heirs can be affected if the alternate valuation date is used to value the estate's assets. The alternate valuation date may be elected only if the value of the gross estate and the amount of estate tax after credits are reduced as a result of using the alternate valuation date.[28] This means that the aggregate value of the assets determined by using the alternate

[25] Sec. 1014(a).
[26] Sec. 2032(a).
[27] Rev. Rul. 56-60, 1956-1 C.B. 443. For a decedent dying after 1986, Sec. 6018(a) requires an estate tax return to be filed if the sum of the gross estate and the adjusted taxable gifts made by the decedent after December 31, 1976, exceeds $600,000.
[28] Credits available include the unified transfer tax credit and possibly credits for state death taxes, gift taxes, foreign death taxes, and the credit for taxes on prior transfers.

valuation date may be used only if the total value of the assets has decreased during the 6-month period.

Example 5-25 ■   Helmut inherits all of the property owned by an individual who dies in March when the FMV of the property amounts to $900,000. Six months after the date of death, the property has a $950,000 FMV. The property is distributed to Helmut in December. Use of the alternate valuation date is not permitted because the value of the gross estate has increased. Therefore, his basis in the property is $900,000, the FMV on the date of death.   ■

An executor may elect to use the alternate valuation date to reduce the estate taxes owed by the estate. However, the income tax basis of the property included in the estate is also reduced for the heirs who inherit the property.

Example 5-26 ■   Michelle inherits property with a $900,000 FMV at the date of the decedent's death. Since the FMV of the property on the alternate valuation date (6 months after the date of the decedent's death) is $850,000, the executor of the estate elects to use $850,000 to value the property for estate tax purposes. Michelle's basis for the property is thus $850,000 instead of $900,000.   ■

Additional Comment

With respect to the requirement that one-half of the property be included in the decedent's gross estate, it is not necessary that an estate tax return be filed, if one is not required, or that an estate tax be payable.

Community Property. If the decedent and the decedent's spouse own property under community property laws,[29] one-half of the property is included in the decedent's estate and its basis to the surviving spouse is its FMV.[30] The Code also provides that the surviving spouse's one-half share of the community property is adjusted to the FMV.[31] In effect, the surviving spouse's share of the community property is considered to have passed from the decedent.

Example 5-27 ■   Matt and Jane, a married couple, live in Texas, a community property state, and jointly own land as community property that cost $110,000. The land has an $800,000 FMV when Jane dies leaving all of her property to Matt. His basis for the entire property is $800,000.   ■

In a common law state, only one-half of the jointly owned property is included in the decedent's estate and is adjusted to its FMV. The survivor's share of the jointly held property is not adjusted.

Example 5-28 ■   Barry and Maria, a married couple, live in Iowa, a common law state, and jointly own land that cost $200,000. The property has a $700,000 FMV when Barry dies leaving all of his property to Maria. Her basis for the land is $450,000 ($100,000 + [0.50 × $700,000]).   ■

Additional Comment

It is important to estimate the FMV of property at the time that it is converted from personal use to business use.

Property Converted from Personal Use to Business Use

Frequently, taxpayers who own personal-use assets convert these assets to an income-producing use or for use in a trade or business. When this conversion occurs, the property's basis must be determined. The basis for computing depreciation is the

---

[29] Community property states are Arizona, California, Idaho, Louisiana, New Mexico, Nevada, Texas, and Washington. Effective January 1, 1986 Wisconsin adopted a marital property law that is basically the same as community property.

[30] Sec. 1014(a).

[31] Sec. 1014(b)(6).

lower of the FMV or the adjusted basis of the property at the time the asset is transferred from personal use to an income-producing use or for use in a trade or business.[32] The lower of cost or market rule is to prevent taxpayers from obtaining the benefits of depreciation to the extent that the property has declined in value during the period that it is held for personal use.

Example 5-29 ■

Real World Example

A taxpayer sold a personal residence to a purchaser, and the purchaser rented the property from the taxpayer until financing could be secured. The rental agreement was executed simultaneously with the sales agreement and was incidental to the sale. The taxpayer was not permitted to recognize any loss on the sale since the property was never converted to rental property. Henry B. Dawson, 1972 PH T.C. Memo 31 TCM 5.

Olga owns a boat that cost $2,000 and is used for personal enjoyment. At a time when the boat has a $1,400 FMV, Olga transfers the boat to her business of operating a marina. The basis for depreciation is $1,400 because the FMV is less than Olga's adjusted basis at the time of conversion to business use.

■

If the boat's FMV in Example 5-29 is more than $2,000, the basis for depreciation is $2,000, because the FMV is higher than its adjusted basis at the time the asset is transferred to business use.

If a personal-use asset is transferred to business use when its FMV is less than its adjusted basis, the basis for determining a loss on a subsequent sale or disposition of the property is its FMV on the date of the conversion to business use less any depreciation taken prior to the disposition.[33]

Example 5-30 ■

Susanna purchased a personal residence for $50,000 and subsequently converted the property to rental property. At the time of the conversion, the property had a $46,000 FMV. Assume depreciation of $20,700 has been deducted when the property is sold for $21,000. The basis of the property at the time of the sale is $25,300 ($46,000 − $20,700). Thus, her loss on the sale is $4,300 ($21,000 − $25,300).[34]

■

The rule for determining the basis, that is, lower of adjusted basis or FMV, applies only to the sale of converted property at a loss. The basis for determining gain is its adjusted basis at the time of conversion less any depreciation taken prior to the disposition.

Example 5-31 ■

Assume the same facts as in Example 5-30, except that the property is sold for $31,000 instead of $21,000. The basis of the property is $29,300 ($50,000 − $20,700) and her gain is $1,700 ($31,000 − $29,300).

■

Without the rule for determining basis of personal-use property converted to business property, taxpayers would have an incentive to convert nonbusiness assets that have declined in value to business use before selling the asset to convert nondeductible losses into deductible losses.

Example 5-32 ■

Craig owns a personal-use asset with a basis of $80,000 and a $50,000 FMV. If he sells the asset for its FMV, the $30,000 loss ($50,000 − $80,000) is not deductible because losses on the sale of personal-use assets are not deductible. If Craig converts the asset to business use and then immediately sells the asset for $50,000,

---

[32] Reg. Sec. 1.167(g)-1.
[33] Reg. Sec. 1.165-9(b)(2).
[34] Reg. Sec. 1.165-9(c), Ex. (1).

no loss is realized because the basis of the asset for purposes of determining loss is $50,000. ∎

Real World Example

A taxpayer purchased a group of lots and allocated the total cost evenly among the lots. The court, however, held that more cost should be allocated to the water-front lots than to the interior lots. Biscayne Bay Islands Co., 23 B.T.A. 731 (1931).

Allocation of Basis

When property is obtained in one transaction and portions of the property are subsequently disposed of at different times, the basis of the property is allocated to the different portions of the property. Gain or loss is computed at the time of disposal for each portion. If one purchases a 20-acre tract of land and later sells the entire tract, an allocation of basis is not needed. However if the taxpayer divides the property into smaller tracts of land for resale, the cost of the 20-acre tract must be allocated among the smaller tracts of land.

Basket Purchase. If more than one asset is acquired in a single purchase transaction (i.e., a basket purchase), the cost must be apportioned to the various assets acquired.[35] The allocation is based upon the relative FMVs of the assets.

Example 5-33 ∎ Kelly purchases a duplex for $80,000 to use as a rental property. The land has a $15,000 FMV, and the building has a $65,000 FMV. Kelly's bases for the land and the building are $15,000 and $65,000, respectively. ∎

Since no depreciation deduction is allowed for land, taxpayers tend to favor a liberal allocation of the total purchase price to the building. Appraisals or other measures of FMV may be used to make the allocation.

Common Costs. As in the case of financial accounting, common costs incurred to obtain or prepare an asset for service must be capitalized and allocated to the basis of the individual assets.

Example 5-34 ∎ Priscilla acquires three machines for $60,000, which have FMVs of $30,000, $20,000, and $10,000, respectively. Costs of delivery amount to $2,000, and costs to install the three machines amount to $1,000. The total installation and delivery costs of $3,000 are allocated to each of the three machines based upon their FMVs. The allocation of the $3,000 of common costs occurs as follows:

$$\text{Machine No. 1: } \frac{\$30,000 \text{ FMV}}{\$30,000 + \$20,000 + \$10,000} \times \$3,000 = \$1,500$$

$$\text{Machine No. 2: } \frac{\$20,000 \text{ FMV}}{\$30,000 + \$20,000 + \$10,000} \times \$3,000 = \$1,000$$

$$\text{Machine No. 3: } \frac{\$10,000 \text{ FMV}}{\$30,000 + \$20,000 + \$10,000} \times \$3,000 = \$500$$

The bases for each of the three machines are $31,500, $21,000, and $10,500, respectively. ∎

---

[35] Reg. Sec. 1.61-6(a).

Nontaxable Stock Dividends Received. If a nontaxable stock dividend is received, a portion of the basis of the stock upon which the stock dividend is received is allocated to the new shares received from the stock dividend.[36] The cost basis of the previously acquired shares is then reduced by the amount of basis that is allocated to the stock dividend shares. If the stock received as a stock dividend is the same type as the stock owned prior to the dividend, the total basis of the stock owned prior to the dividend is allocated equally to all shares now owned.

Example 5-35 ■   Wayne owns 1,000 shares of Bell Corporation common stock with a $44,000 basis. Wayne receives a nontaxable 10% common stock dividend and now owns 1,100 shares of common stock. The basis for each share of common stock is now $40 ($44,000 ÷ 1,100). ■

If the stock received as a stock dividend is not the same type as the stock owned prior to the dividend, the allocation is based on relative FMVs.[37]

Example 5-36 ■   Stacey owns 500 shares of Montana Corporation common stock with a $60,000 basis. She receives a nontaxable stock dividend payable in 50 shares of preferred stock. At time of the distribution, the common stock has a $40,000 FMV ($80 × 500 shares), and the preferred stock has a $10,000 FMV ($200 × 50 shares). After the distribution, Stacey owns 50 shares of preferred stock with a basis of $12,000 ([$10,000 ÷ $50,000] × $60,000). Thus, $12,000 of the basis of the common stock is allocated to the preferred stock, and the basis of the common stock is reduced from $60,000 to $48,000. ■

Key Point

Corporations issue stock rights to shareholders so that the shareholders will be able to maintain their same proportional ownership in the corporation. This is called the preemptive right.

Nontaxable Stock Rights Received. Stock rights represent rights to acquire shares of a specified corporation's stock at a specific exercise price when certain conditions are met. The exercise price is usually less than the market price when the stock rights are issued. Stock rights may be distributed to employees as compensation, and they are often issued to shareholders to encourage them to purchase more stock, thereby providing more capital for the corporation.

If the FMV of a nontaxable stock right received is less than 15% of the FMV of the stock, the basis of the stock right is zero unless the taxpayer elects to allocate the basis between the stock right and the stock owned prior to distribution of the stock rights.[38]

Example 5-37 ■   Tina owns 100 shares of Bear Corporation common stock with a $27,000 basis and a $50,000 FMV. She receives 100 nontaxable stock rights with a total FMV of $4,000. Since the FMV of the stock rights is less than 15% of the FMV of the stock (0.15 × $50,000 = $7,500), the basis of the stock rights is zero unless Tina elects to make an allocation. ■

Real World Example

In 1991 Time Warner, Inc. issued 0.60 of a right for each common share held. Each whole right entitled the holder to buy one common share for $80.

If in Example 5-37, Tina elects to allocate the basis of $27,000 between the stock rights and the stock, the basis of the rights is $2,000 ([$4,000 ÷ $54,000] × $27,000), and the basis of the stock is $25,000 ([$50,000 ÷ $54,000] × $27,000).

The decision to allocate the basis affects the gain or loss realized on the sale or disposition of the stock rights because the basis of the rights is zero unless an allocation is made. Furthermore, the basis of any stock acquired by exercising the rights is affected by whether or not a portion of the basis is allocated to the rights. The

[36] Sec. 307(a).
[37] Reg. Sec. 1.307-1(a).
[38] Sec. 307(b)(1).

basis of stock acquired by exercising the stock rights is the amount paid plus the basis of the stock rights exercised.

Example 5-38 ■   George receives ten stock rights as a nontaxable distribution, and no basis is allocated to the stock rights. With each stock right, George may acquire one share of stock for $20. If he exercises all ten stock rights, the new stock acquired has a basis of $200 ($20 × 10 shares). ■

Example 5-39 ■   Assume the same facts as in Example 5-38, except that George sells all ten stock rights for $135. He has a realized gain of $135 ($135 − $0 basis for the rights). ■

If the FMV of a nontaxable stock right received is equal to or greater than 15% of the FMV of the stock, the basis of the stock owned prior to the distribution must be allocated between the stock and the stock rights.

Example 5-40 ■   Helen owns 100 shares of NMO common stock with a $14,000 basis and a $30,000 FMV. She receives 100 stock rights with a total FMV of $5,000. Since the FMV of the stock rights is at least 15% of the FMV of the stock, the $14,000 basis must be allocated between the stock rights and the stock. The basis of the stock rights is $2,000 ([$5,000 ÷ $35,000] × $14,000) and the basis of the stock is $12,000 ([$30,000 ÷ $35,000] × $14,000). ■

A recipient of stock rights generally has three courses of action. The stock rights can be sold or exchanged, in which case the basis allocated to the stock rights, if any, is used to determine the gain or loss. The stock rights may be exercised, and any basis allocated to the rights is added to the purchase price of the acquired stock. The stock rights may be allowed to expire, in which case no loss is recognized, and any basis allocated to the rights is reallocated back to the stock. If the stock rights received in Example 5-40 expire without being exercised, Helen does not recognize a loss and the basis of her 100 shares of common stock is $14,000.

Property basis rules are highlighted in Topic Review 5-1.

DEFINITION OF A CAPITAL ASSET

OBJECTIVE 4
Distinguish between capital assets and other assets

Instead of defining capital assets, Sec. 1221 provides a list of properties that are not capital assets. This list includes the following:

1. Inventory or property held primarily for sale to customers in the ordinary course of a trade or business.
2. Property used in the trade or business and subject to the allowance for depreciation provided in Sec. 167 or real property used in a trade or business. (These properties are referred to as *Sec. 1231 assets* if held by the taxpayer more than one year.)
3. Accounts or notes receivable acquired in the ordinary course of a trade or business for services rendered or from the sale of property described in item 1.
4. Other assets including
   a. A letter, memorandum, or similar property held by a taxpayer for whom such property was prepared or produced.
   b. A copyright; a literary, musical, or artistic composition; a letter or memo-

TOPIC REVIEW 5-1

Property Basis Rules	
Method Acquired	Basis of the Acquired Property
1. Acquired by direct purchase	1. Basis includes the amount paid for the property, costs of preparing the property for use, and obligations of the seller that are assumed by the buyer including liens against the property.
2. Acquired as a gift. (a) FMV on the date of the gift is equal to or greater than the donor's basis	2. (a) The donee's basis is the same as the donor's basis plus a pro rata portion of the gift tax attributable to the unrealized appreciation in the property at the time of the gift.
(b) FMV on the date of the gift is less than the donor's basis	(b) The donee's gain basis is the donor's basis and the loss basis is FMV.
3. Received from a decedent (a) Alternative valuation date is not elected	3. (a) The basis is its FMV on the date of death.
(b) Alternative valuation date is elected	(b) The basis of nondistributed property is its FMV on the alternative valuation date. If the property is distributed or sold prior to this date, its basis is FMV on the date of sale or distribution.
4. Converted from personal to business use	4. The basis for a loss (as well as for depreciation) is the lesser of its adjusted basis or FMV at the date of conversion. The basis for a gain is its adjusted basis at the date of conversion.
5. Nontaxable stock dividend	5. Basis of the stock dividend shares includes a pro rata portion of the adjusted basis of the underlying shares owned.
6. Nontaxable stock right	6. If the FMV of the right is less than 15% of the FMV of the stock, the basis of the rights is zero unless an election is made. Basis of the underlying stock is allocated to the right based on the respective FMV's of the stock and the rights.

Typical Misconception

It is not uncommon in financial accounting classes to include property used in a trade or business in the definition of a capital asset. For example, factory buildings, machinery, trucks, and office buildings would be defined as capital assets. However, such items are excluded from the tax definition of a capital asset.

randum; or similar property held by a taxpayer whose personal efforts created such property or whose basis in the property for determining a gain is determined by reference to the basis of such property in the hands of one who created the property or one for whom such property was prepared or produced.

   c. A U.S. government publication held by a taxpayer who receives the publication by any means other than a purchase at the price the publication is offered for sale to the public.

   d. A U.S. government publication held by a taxpayer whose basis in the property for determining a gain is determined by reference to the basis of such property in the hands of a taxpayer in item 4c.

Example 5-41 ■

Maxine owns a building which is used in her business. Other business assets include equipment, inventory, and accounts receivable. None of the assets are classified as capital assets. ■

Chapter 13 provides an in-depth discussion of business assets such as buildings, land, and equipment. Although these items are not capital assets, Sec. 1231 provides in many cases that the gain on the sale or exchange of such an asset is eventually taxed as a long-term capital gain.

Example 5-42 ■

Eric owns an automobile that is held for personal use and also owns a copyright for a book he has written. Since the copyright is held by the taxpayer whose personal efforts created the property, it is not a capital asset. The automobile held for personal use is a capital asset. ■

By analyzing Examples 5-41 and 5-42, one can conclude that the classification of an asset is frequently determined by its use. An automobile used in a trade or business is not a capital asset but is considered to be a capital asset when it is held for personal use. Examples of assets that qualify as capital assets include a personal residence, land held for personal use, and investments in stocks and bonds.

Influence of the Courts

In *Corn Products Refining Co.,* the Supreme Court rendered a landmark decision when it determined that the sale of futures contracts related to the purchase of raw materials resulted in ordinary rather than capital gains and losses.[39] The Corn Products Company, a manufacturer of products made from grain corn, purchased futures contracts for corn to be assured of an adequate supply of raw materials. While delivery of the corn was accepted when needed for manufacturing operations, unneeded contracts were later sold. Corn Products contended that any gains or losses on the sale of the unneeded contracts should be capital gains and losses because futures contracts are customarily viewed as security investments which qualify as capital assets. The Supreme Court held that these transactions represented an integral part of the business for the purpose of protecting the company's manufacturing operations and that the gains and losses should, therefore, be ordinary in nature.

Although the *Corn Products* doctrine has been interpreted as creating a nonstatutory exception to the definition of a capital asset when the asset is purchased for business purposes, the Supreme Court ruled in the 1988 *Arkansas Best Corporation* case that the motivation for acquiring assets is irrelevant to the question of whether assets are capital assets. Arkansas Best, a bank holding company, sold shares of a bank's stock that had been acquired for the purpose of protecting its business reputation. Relying on the *Corn Products* doctrine, the company deducted the loss as

---

[39] *Corn Products Refining Co. v. CIR,* 47 AFTR 1789, 55-2 USTC ¶ 9746 (USSC, 1955).

ordinary. The Supreme Court ruled that the loss was a capital loss since the stock is within the broad definition of the term "capital asset" in Sec. 1221 and is outside the classes of property that are excluded from capital-asset status.[40] Although *Arkansas Best* apparently limits the application of *Corn Products* to hedging transactions that are an integral part of a taxpayer's system of acquiring inventory, the U.S. Claims Court ruled in 1991 that a convenience store company whose profits came largely from the sale of gasoline was entitled to an ordinary loss when it sold stock of an oil company.[41]

During the national oil shortages in the 1970s, the Circle K Corporation experienced difficulty in obtaining a sufficient supply of gasoline at competitive prices. To help avoid future shortage problems, the company purchased 12.3% of NuCorp, an oil and gas exploration company, in 1980. In 1983, Circle K sold its interest in NuCorp and realized a loss of more than $27 million.

Prior to the *Arkansas Best* case in 1988, taxpayers used the *Corn Products* case to sustain an ordinary loss deduction on the sale of corporate stock purchased by a company to obtain access to raw materials. The U.S. Claims Court ruled that *Arkansas Best* did not specifically address the case where stock is purchased to obtain inventory and concluded "that a source of supply stock purchase may qualify as a hedging transaction if it as an integral part of plaintiff's inventory purchase system."[42] Thus, the issue whether a loss is capital or ordinary continues to be litigated.

Other Code Provisions Relevant to Capital Gains and Losses

A number of Code sections provide special treatment for certain types of assets and transactions. For example, Sec. 341 converts long-term capital gain arising from the sale or exchange of stock of a collapsible corporation into ordinary income.[43] Loss on the sale or exchange of small business stock which qualifies as Sec. 1244 stock is treated as an ordinary loss rather than a capital loss to the extent of $50,000 per year ($100,000 if the taxpayer is married and files a joint return).[44]

Additional Comment

For purposes of Sec. 1236, a security is defined as any share of stock in any corporation, note, bond, debenture, or evidence of indebtedness, or any evidence of an interest in or right to subscribe to or purchase any of the foregoing.

Dealers in Securities. Normally, a security dealer's gain on the sale or exchange of securities is ordinary income. Section 1236 provides an exception for dealers in securities if the dealer clearly identifies that the property is held for investment. This act of identification must occur before the close of the day on which the security is acquired, and the security must not be held primarily for sale to customers in the ordinary course of the dealer's trade or business at any time after the close of the day of purchase.[45]

Example 5-43 ■

Allison, a dealer in securities, purchases Austin Corporation stock on April 8, 1994, and identifies the stock as being held for investment on that date. On December 21, 1994, Allison sells the stock. Any gain or loss recognized due to the sale is capital gain or loss. ■

[40] *Arkansas Best Corporation v. CIR,* 61 AFTR 2d 88-655, 88-1 USTC ¶ 9210 (USSC, 1988).

[41] *The Circle K Corporation v. U.S.,* 67 AFTR 2d 91-1055, 91-1 USTC ¶ 50,260 (Cls. Ct., 1991).

[42] Ibid.

[43] Sec. 341(a). Collapsible corporations are discussed in Chapter 6 of *Prentice Hall's Federal Taxation: Corporations, Partnerships, Estates, and Trusts* text and Chapter 18 of *Prentice Hall's Federal Taxation: Comprehensive* volume.

[44] Secs. 1244(a) and (b). (See Chapter 8 for additional discussion on small business corporation stock losses.)

[45] For securities acquired before August 14, 1981, Sec. 1236 applies only if the dealer identifies the property as being held for investment within 30 days of the date of acquisition.

Once a dealer clearly identifies a security as being held for investment, any loss on the sale or exchange of the security is treated as a capital loss.

Example 5-44 ■

Kris, a dealer in securities, purchases Boston Corporation stock and clearly identifies the stock as being held for investment on the date of purchase. Eight months later, the security is removed from the investment account and held as inventory. If the security is later sold at a gain, the gain will be an ordinary gain. However, if the stock is sold at a loss, the loss will be a capital loss. ■

Additional Comment

The conversion of an apartment building into condominiums does not qualify under Sec. 1237 even though the property has been held for five years and no substantial improvements have been made.

For tax years ending on or after December 31, 1993, securities dealers must use the mark-to-market method for their inventory of securities. Securities must be valued at fair market value at the end of each taxable year. Dealers in securities recognize gain or loss each year as if the security is sold on the last day of the tax year. Gains and losses are generally treated as ordinary rather than capital. Gains or losses due to adjustments in subsequent years or resulting from the sale of the security must be adjusted to reflect gains and losses already taken into account when determining taxable income.[46]

Example 5-45 ■

Jim Spikes, a dealer in securities and calendar year taxpayer, purchases a security for inventory on October 10, 1994, for $10,000 and sells the security for $18,000 on July 1, 1995. The security's FMV on December 31, 1994, is $15,000. Jim recognizes $5,000 of ordinary income in 1994 and $3,000 of ordinary income in 1995. ■

Real Property Subdivided for Sale. A taxpayer who engages in regular sales of real estate is considered to be a dealer, and any gain or loss recognized is ordinary gain or loss rather than capital gain or loss. A special relief provision is provided for nondealer, noncorporate taxpayers who subdivide a tract of real property into lots (two or more pieces of real property are considered to be a tract if they are contiguous).[47] Part or all of the gain on the sale of the lots may be treated as a capital gain if the following provisions of Sec. 1237 are satisfied:

- During the year of sale, the noncorporate taxpayer must not hold any other real property primarily for sale in the ordinary course of business.
- Unless the property is acquired by inheritance or devise, the lots sold must be held by the taxpayer for a period of at least 5 years.
- No substantial improvement may be made by the taxpayer while holding the lots if the improvement substantially enhances the value of the lot.[48]
- The tract or any lot may not have been previously held primarily for sale to customers in the ordinary course of the taxpayer's trade or business unless such tract at that time was covered by Sec. 1237.

The primary advantage of Sec. 1237 is that potential controversy with the IRS is avoided as to whether a taxpayer who subdivides investment property is a dealer. Section 1237 does not apply to losses. Such losses are capital losses if the property is held for investment purposes, or ordinary losses if the taxpayer is a dealer.

If the Sec. 1237 requirements are satisfied, all gain on the sale of the first five lots may be capital gain. Starting in the tax year during which the sixth lot is sold, 5% of the selling price for all lots sold in that year and succeeding years is ordinary income.[49]

---

[46] Sec. 475. The mark-to-market rule also applies to some securities that are not inventory but does not apply to any security that is held for investment and certain other transactions (see Sec. 475[b]).

[47] Secs. 1237(a) and (c).

[48] Certain improvements are not treated as substantial under Sec. 1237(b)(3) if the lot is held for at least 10 years.

[49] Sec. 1237(b).

Example 5-46 ■

Additional Comment

If a taxpayer sells any lots from a tract and does not sell any others for a period of 5 years, the remaining property is considered a new tract.

Jean subdivides a tract of land held as an investment, and all requirements of Sec. 1237 are satisfied. The lots sell for $10,000 each and have a basis of $4,000. Jean incurs no selling expenses and sells four lots in 1993 and three lots in 1994. In 1993 all of the $24,000 (4 lots × [$10,000 − $4,000]) gain is capital gain. In 1994, the year in which the sixth lot is sold, $1,500 of the gain is ordinary income (0.05 × [$10,000 × 3 lots]), and the remaining $16,500 {(3 lots × [$10,000 − $4,000]) − $1,500} gain is capital gain. ■

Example 5-47 ■

Assume the same facts as in Example 5-46, except that all seven lots are sold in 1993. The amount of ordinary income recognized is $3,500 (0.05 × [$10,000 × 7 lots]), and the remaining $38,500 {(7 lots × [$10,000 − $4,000]) − $3,500} gain is capital gain. ■

Based on Examples 5-46 and 5-47, the advantage of selling no more than five lots in the first year should be apparent. Expenditures incurred to sell or exchange the lots are also treated favorably since they are first applied against the portion of the gain that is treated as ordinary income.[50] Since selling expenses (e.g., commissions) are frequently equal to or greater than 5% of the selling price, this offset against ordinary income may result in the elimination of the ordinary income portion of the gain. Selling expenses in excess of the gain taxed as ordinary income reduce the amount realized on the sale or exchange.

Nonbusiness Bad Debt. Although the topic of bad debts is discussed in Chapter 8, it is important to note that bad debt losses from nonbusiness debts are deductible only as short-term capital losses (STCLs).[51] This treatment applies regardless of when the debt occurred. Furthermore, a nonbusiness bad debt is deductible only in the year in which the debt becomes totally worthless.[52]

Example 5-48 ■

In 1992 Alice loaned $2,000 to a friend. During the current year the friend declares bankruptcy and the debt is entirely worthless. Assuming that Alice has no other gains and losses from the sale or exchange of capital assets during the year, she deducts $2,000 in determining adjusted gross income (AGI). ■

TAX TREATMENT FOR CAPITAL GAINS AND LOSSES OF NONCORPORATE TAXPAYERS

OBJECTIVE 5
Understand how capital gains and losses affect taxable income

To recognize capital gain or loss, it is necessary to have a sale or exchange of a capital asset. Once it is determined that a capital gain or loss has been realized and is to be recognized, it is necessary to classify the gains and losses as either short-term or long-term. To be classified as a long-term capital gain (LTCG) or long-term capital loss (LTCL), the asset must be held for more than a year.[53] If the asset is held for a year or less, the gain or loss is classified as a short-term capital gain (STCG) or a short-term capital loss (STCL).

---

[50] Sec. 1237(b)(2).
[51] Sec. 166(d)(1)(B).
[52] Reg. Sec. 1.166-5(a)(2).
[53] For assets acquired after June 22, 1984, and before January 1, 1988, the holding period requirement of Sec. 1222 was more than 6 months.

Net Capital Gain

Net capital gain is defined as the excess of net long-term capital gains over net short-term capital losses.[54] To compute net capital gain, first determine all short-term capital gains, short-term capital losses, long-term capital gains, and long-term capital losses, and then net gains and losses as described below.[55]

Net Short-Term Capital Gain. If total STCGs for the tax year exceed total STCLs for that year, the excess is defined as net short-term capital gain (NSTCG).[56] As discussed later, NSTCG may be offset by net long-term capital loss (NLTCL).

Example 5-49 ■ Hal has two transactions involving the sale of capital assets during the year. As a result of those transactions, he has a STCG of $4,000 and a STCL of $3,000. Hal's NSTCG is $1,000 ($4,000 − $3,000), and his AGI increases by $1,000. His gross income increases by $4,000, and he is entitled to a $3,000 deduction for AGI. ■

Net Long-Term Capital Gain. If the total LTCGs for the tax year exceed the total LTCLs for that year, the excess is defined as net long-term capital gain (NLTCG).[57] As indicated earlier, a net capital gain exists when NLTCG exceeds net short-term capital loss (NSTCL).

Example 5-50 ■ Clay has two transactions involving the sale of capital assets during the year. As a result of the transactions, he has a LTCG of $4,000 and a LTCL of $3,000. Clay has a NLTCG and a net capital gain of $1,000. His AGI increases by $1,000. ■

Example 5-51 ■ Linda has four transactions involving the sale of capital assets during the year. As a result of the transactions, she has a STCG of $5,000, a STCL of $7,000, a LTCG of $10,000, and a LTCL of $2,000. After the initial netting of short-term and long-term gains and losses, Linda has a NSTCL of $2,000 ($7,000 − $5,000) and a NLTCG of $8,000 ($10,000 − $2,000). Since the NLTCG exceeds the NSTCL by $6,000 ($8,000 − $2,000), her net capital gain is $6,000. ■

Capital Losses

To have a capital loss, one must sell or exchange the capital asset for an amount less than its adjusted basis. As in the case of capital gains, the 1-year period is used to determine if the capital loss is short-term or long-term.

Net Short-Term Capital Loss. If total STCLs for the tax year exceed total STCGs for that year, the excess is defined as a net short-term capital loss.[58] As indicated above, the NSTCL is first offset against any NLTCG to determine the net capital gain.

If the NSTCL exceeds the NLTCG, the capital loss may be offset, in part, against other income. The NSTCL may be deducted in full (i.e., on a dollar-for-dollar basis) against a noncorporate taxpayer's ordinary income for amounts up to $3,000 in any one year.[59]

Self-Study Question

Mary sells common stock for a gain of $10,000 on December 27, 1994. The settlement date, or date that Mary will receive the proceeds from the stockbroker, is January 5, 1995. Will Mary report the gain on her 1994 or 1995 tax return?

Answer

Mary is required to report the gain in the year of the sale (1994). Losses are also recognized in the year of sale.

---

[54] Sec. 1222(11).
[55] Sec. 1222.
[56] Sec. 1222(5).
[57] Sec. 1222(7).
[58] Sec. 1222(6).
[59] Sec. 1211(b). A $1,500 limitation applies to a married individual filing a separate return.

Example 5-52 ■

Bob has gross income of $60,000 before considering capital gains and losses. If Bob has a NLTCG of $10,000 and a NSTCL of $15,000, he has $5,000 of NSTCL in excess of NLTCG and may deduct $3,000 of the losses from gross income. Assuming no other deductions for AGI, Bob's AGI is $57,000 ($60,000 − $3,000). ■

In Example 5-52, $10,000 of the NSTCL is used to offset the $10,000 of NLTCG, and $3,000 of the NSTCL in excess of the NLTCG is used to reduce ordinary income. However, $2,000 of the loss is not used. This net capital loss is carried forward for an indefinite number of years.[60] The loss retains its original character and will be treated as a STCL occurring in the subsequent year.

Example 5-53 ■

Real World Example

In 1975 an amendment was added to a tax bill in the House Ways and Means Committee that would have permitted individuals to take a three-year carry back for capital losses. When the Wall Street Journal *disclosed that the provision would provide Ross Perot with a $15 million tax break, the amendment was defeated.*

Last year, Milt had a NSTCL of $8,000 and a NLTCG of $2,600. The netting of short-term and long-term gains and losses resulted in a $5,400 excess of NSTCL over NLTCG, and $3,000 of this amount was offset against ordinary income. Milt's NSTCL carryforward is $2,400. During the current year he sells a capital asset and generates a STCG of $800. His NSTCL is $1,600 ($2,400 − $800), and the loss is offset against $1,600 of ordinary income. ■

Net Long-Term Capital Loss. If total LTCLs for the tax year exceed total LTCGs for the year, the excess is defined as net long-term capital loss. If there is both a NSTCG and a NLTCL, the NLTCL is initially offset against the NSTCG on a dollar-for-dollar basis. If the NLTCL exceeds the NLTCG, the excess is offset against ordinary income on a dollar-for-dollar basis up to $3,000 per year.[61]

Example 5-54 ■

In the current year Phyllis has a NLTCL of $3,600 and no STCG or STCL transactions. She must use the $3,600 NLTCL to offset $3,000 ordinary income. Her NLTCL carryforward is $600. ■

Example 5-55 ■

In the current year Gordon has a NLTCL of $9,000 and a NSTCG of $2,000. He must use $2,000 of the NLTCL to offset $2,000 of the NSTCG, and then use $3,000 of the $7,000 ($9,000 − $2,000) NLTCL to offset $3,000 of ordinary income. Gordon's carryforward of NLTCL is $4,000 ($9,000 − [$2,000 + $3,000]). This amount is treated as a LTCL in subsequent years. ■

If an individual has both NSTCL and NLTCL, the NSTCL is offset against ordinary income first, regardless of when the transactions occur during the year.[62]

Example 5-56 ■

In the current year Beth has a NSTCL of $2,800 and a NLTCL of $2,000. The entire NSTCL is offset initially against $2,800 of ordinary income on a dollar-for-dollar basis. Since capital losses can be offset against only $3,000 of ordinary income, $200 of NLTCL is used to offset $200 ($3,000 − $2,800) of ordinary income. The NLTCL carryover to the next year is $1,800 ($2,000 − $200). ■

Tax Treatment Before 1987. Prior to 1987, noncorporate taxpayers received a deduction from gross income equal to 60% of the taxpayer's net capital gain. There was no preferential treatment for a NSTCG.

---

[60] Sec. 1212(b) and Reg. Sec. 1.1212-1(b).
[61] Sec. 1211(b).
[62] Reg. Sec. 1.1211-1(b)(4).

Example 5-57 ∎

Self-Study Question

Would an individual taxpayer prefer to have a $1 million NLTCG in 1994 and a $1 million NLTCL in 1995, or vice versa?

Answer

The taxpayer would prefer to have the $1 million NLTCL in the first year. Under this alternative $3,000 of the NLTCL would offset ordinary income in the first year and the remainder would offset $997,000 of the $1 million NLTCG in the second year. If the $1 million dollar loss was recognized in the second year, none of it could be carried back to offset the $1 million gain recognized in the first year.

Historical Note

The provision requiring taxpayers to offset a NLTCL against ordinary income on a two-for-one basis originated when there was a 50% long-term capital gain deduction. It was thought that if only 50% of the long-term gains were taxable, then only 50% of the long-term losses should be deductible.

Example 5-58 ∎

Key Point

Only taxpayers who have a marginal tax rate of 31% or higher receive any benefit from the 28% maximum rate that applies to net capital gain.

In 1986 Bonnie had a NLTCG of $10,000 and a NSTCL of $3,000. Since Bonnie's net capital gain was $7,000 ($10,000 − $3,000), she was allowed a deduction of $4,200 (60% × $7,000). Her AGI was increased by $2,800 ($7,000 − $4,200). ∎

Preferential treatment for net capital gains was partially attributable to the desire of Congress to stimulate investment and savings. By increasing the after-tax return on investment, Congress provided additional economic incentive to engage in risky ventures such as the production of new products. The capital gain deduction also mitigates the effect of *"income bunching,"* which results when a gain earned over a long period of time is recognized in the year of sale or disposition. With progressive income tax rates, this bunching of income may create a greater tax burden than if the gain had been recognized as it accrued.

Prior to 1987, noncorporate taxpayers were required to offset a NLTCL against ordinary income on a two-for-one basis. Two dollars of NLTCL were required to offset $1 of ordinary income. A NSTCL was allowed to offset ordinary income on a dollar-for-dollar basis.

Tax Treatment After 1986. Congress repealed the special 60% deduction for capital gains in the Tax Reform Act of 1986 for 1987 and later tax years. Since the maximum marginal tax rate was reduced to 28% in 1987, Congress reasoned that it was no longer necessary to maintain preferential treatment for a net capital gain. Prior to 1987, the maximum tax rate for a net capital gain was 20%.[63] Congress retained the statutory structure for capital gains to facilitate reinstatement of a capital gains rate differential in the event that ordinary tax rates were later increased.[64]

The Tax Reform Act of 1986 provided only one significant change for the treatment of capital losses: a NLTCL may be offset against ordinary income on a dollar-for-dollar basis instead of a two-for-one basis.[65]

In the current year Betty has a NLTCL of $2,700 and no STCGs or STCLs. The entire NLTCL is offset against $2,700 of ordinary income on a dollar-for-dollar basis. ∎

Tax Treatment After 1990. For tax years beginning after 1990 and before 1993, income was taxed at three rates (i.e., 15%, 28%, 31%). For 1993 and subsequent years a 36% tax rate was added for high-income individuals with taxable income in excess of $140,000 (for married individuals filing a joint return) and $115,000 for unmarried individuals. A 39.6% effective rate is also applied in 1993 and subsequent years to taxable income in excess of $250,000 for both unmarried individuals and married individuals (filing a joint return). After 1990, the maximum marginal tax rate on net capital gain is and continues to be 28%.[66] Thus, individuals with a 31% or higher marginal tax rate benefit by having a gain classified as LTCG rather than STCG or ordinary income because the lower 28% maximum rate applies to the net capital gain. The increase in the highest tax rate from 31% to 39.6% in 1993 and subsequent years has increased the significance of the preferential treatment that is accorded to net capital gains.

---

[63] After allowing for the 60% deduction for capital gains, only 40% of the net capital gain was taxed at a rate no higher than the top marginal tax rate of 50%. Thus, the maximum effective tax rate was 20% (0.40 × 0.50). The maximum capital gain rate in 1987 was 28%. For years 1987 through 1990, the maximum marginal tax rate on both STCG and LTCG was 33%.

[64] H. Rept. No. 99-841, 99th Cong., 2d Sess., p. II-106 (1986).

[65] Sec. 1211(b).

[66] Sec. 1(h).

Example 5-59 ■ William is single with taxable income of $17,000 including $2,000 net capital gain in 1994. The marginal tax rate applicable to the net capital gain is 15%, and his tax is $2,550 (0.15 × $17,000). The 31% rate for single individuals does not apply until taxable income exceeds $55,100. ■

Example 5-60 ■ Rita is single with taxable income of $25,000 including $7,000 of net capital gain in 1994. The fact that $7,000 of taxable income is net capital gain does not result in a tax savings for Rita because her marginal tax rate is 28%. In 1994, the 31% rate for single individuals applies to taxable income over $55,100. ■

Example 5-61 ■ Gary is single with taxable income of $80,000 including $15,000 of net capital gain in 1994. The $15,000 of net capital gain would be taxed at 31% if the maximum tax rate on net capital gain was not limited to 28%. The $15,000 of net capital gain is subject to the 28% maximum capital gain rate because the 31% tax rate otherwise applies to taxable income in excess of $55,100 for single individuals in 1994. Gary's tax liability is $19,740 ($12,471 + 0.31 [$65,000 − $55,100] + 0.28 [$15,000]). ■

Example 5-62 ■ Assume the same facts as in Example 5-61 except that Gary has taxable income of $265,000 including $15,000 of net capital gain. The $15,000 of net capital gain would be taxed at 39.6% if the maximum rate on net capital gain was not 28% because a 39.6% rate applies to taxable income in excess of $250,000. The tax savings from applying the preferential 28% capital gain rate is $1,740 ($15,000 × [39.6% − 28%]). ■

TAX TREATMENT OF CAPITAL GAINS AND LOSSES—CORPORATE TAXPAYERS

Key Point

The reintroduction of a significant differential in effective tax rates between ordinary income and capital gains in 1993 may cause high-income taxpayers to modify their investment approach to emphasize capital gains rather than dividend and interest income.

Most topics covered in this chapter concerning capital gains and losses, including the classification of an asset as a capital asset, rules for determining holding periods, and the procedure for offsetting capital losses against capital gains, apply to both corporate and noncorporate taxpayers. However, a major difference is that the 28% maximum tax rate on net capital gain for noncorporate taxpayers does not apply to corporations. A second significant difference relates to the treatment of capital losses. Unlike the noncorporate taxpayer who may offset capital losses against ordinary income up to $3,000, corporations may offset capital losses only against capital gains. Corporate taxpayers may carry capital losses back to each of the 3 preceding tax years (the earliest of the 3 tax years first and then to the next 2 years) and forward for 5 years to offset capital gains in such years. When a corporate taxpayer carries a loss back to a preceding year or forward to a following year, the loss is treated as a STCL.[67]

Example 5-63 ■ The Peach Corporation has income from operations of $200,000, a NSTCG of $40,000, and a NLTCL of $56,000 during the current year. The $40,000 NSTCG is offset by $40,000 NLTCL. The remaining $16,000 of NLTCLs may not be offset against the $200,000 of other income but may be carried back 3 years and then forward 5 years to offset capital gains arising in these years. ■

Topic Review 5-2 summarizes the principal differences in the tax treatment of capital gains and losses for corporate and noncorporate taxpayers.

[67] Sec. 1212(a).

TOPIC REVIEW 5-2

Comparison of Corporate and Noncorporate Taxpayers—Capital Gains and Losses

	Noncorporate	Corporate
A statutory maximum tax rate applicable to net capital gain	Yes, 28%	No, ordinary corporate tax rates apply
Offset of net capital losses against ordinary income	Yes, up to $3,000	No
Carryback of capital losses	No	Yes, 3 years as STCLs
Carryforward of capital losses	Yes, indefinitely	Yes, 5 years as STCLs

SALE OR EXCHANGE

OBJECTIVE 6
Recognize when a sale or exchange has occurred

As previously indicated, capital gains and losses result from the sale or exchange of capital assets.[68] While Sec. 1222 does not define a sale or an exchange, a **sale** is generally considered to be a transaction where one receives cash and/or the equivalent of cash, including the assumption of one's debt. An **exchange** is a transaction where one receives a reciprocal transfer of property, as distinguished from a transaction where one receives only cash and/or a cash equivalent.[69]

Example 5-64 ■

Two years ago, Bart acquired 100 shares of Alaska Corporation common stock for $12,000 to hold as an investment. Bart sells 50 shares of the stock to Sandy for $10,000 and transfers the other 50 shares to Gail in exchange for land that has a $10,000 FMV. In each transaction, Bart realizes a $4,000 ($10,000 − $6,000) LTCG due to the sale or exchange of a capital asset. The transfer to Sandy qualifies as a sale, and the transfer to Gail qualifies as an exchange. ■

To qualify as a sale or exchange, the transaction must be bona fide. Transactions between related parties such as family members are closely scrutinized. For example, a loan to a relative may represent a disguised gift. If this is the case, a subsequent bad debt deduction due to the debt's worthlessness is disallowed. In some instances, the Code specifically states that a particular transaction or event qualifies or does not qualify for sale or exchange treatment. For example, the holder of an option who fails to exercise such an option treats the lapse of the option as a sale or exchange.[70] However, abandonment of property is generally not deemed to be a sale or an exchange.[71]

Worthless Securities

If a security which is a capital asset becomes worthless during the year, Sec. 165(g)(1) specifies that any loss is treated as a loss from the sale or exchange of a capital asset on

---

[68] Anti-conversion rules are contained in Sec. 1258 to prevent taxpayers from recharacterizing certain income on financial transactions from ordinary income to capital gain. Discussion of these rules is beyond the scope of the text.

[69] Reg. Sec. 1.1002-1(d).

[70] Sec. 1234(b) and Reg. Sec. 1.1234-1(b).

[71] Reg. Secs. 1.165-2 and 1.167(a)-8.

Additional Comment

The worthlessness of a security is treated as a sale or exchange so that the taxpayer is not forced to arrange for someone to buy the security for a token amount.

the last day of the tax year. The term includes stock, a stock option, and "a bond, debenture, note or certificate, or other evidence of indebtedness, issued by a corporation or by a government or political division thereof, with interest coupons or in registered form."[72] Whether a security has become worthless during the year is a question of fact, and the taxpayer has the burden of proof to show evidence of worthlessness.[73]

Example 5-65 ■

Charlotte purchased $40,000 of bonds issued by the Jet Corporation in March 1993. In February 1994, Jet is declared bankrupt, and its bonds are worthless. Charlotte has a LTCL of $40,000 since the bonds have become worthless and are deemed to have been sold on the last day of 1994. The more than one year holding period requirement is satisfied by the last day of 1994. ■

Real World Example

A corporation owned 76% of the stock of a Mexican company. The corporation later acquired the remaining 24% of the stock allegedly for the purpose of avoiding interference by minority shareholders. Later the corporation claimed an ordinary loss on the worthless Mexican stock since it owned at least 80% of the stock. The Court treated the loss as a capital loss since the acquisition of the remaining stock was without a business purpose. Hunter Mfg. Co., 21 T.C. 424 (1953).

Securities in Affiliated Corporations. If the security that becomes worthless is a security in a domestic affiliated corporation that is owned by a corporate taxpayer, the worthless security is not considered to be a capital asset. Thus, a corporate taxpayer's loss due to owning worthless securities in an affiliated corporation is treated as an ordinary loss. Because capital losses are of only limited benefit to corporate taxpayers, the classification of the loss as ordinary is preferable.

To qualify as an affiliated corporation, the parent corporation must own at least 80% of the voting power of all classes of stock and at least 80% of each class of nonvoting stock. The subsidiary corporation must be engaged in the active conduct of an operating business as opposed to being a passive investment company (i.e., more than 90% of its aggregate gross receipts must be from sources other than passive types of income such as royalties, dividends, and interest).[74]

Example 5-66 ■

Ace Corporation owns 80% of all classes of stock issued by the same Jet Corporation described in Example 5-65. Jet Corporation is actively engaged in an operating business and has no income from passive investments prior to being declared bankrupt. Ace's loss from its worthless stock investment is an ordinary loss instead of a capital loss because Jet is an affiliated corporation; that is, Ace owns at least 80% of all classes of Jet's stock, and more than 90% of Jet's gross receipts are from sources other than passive types of income. ■

Retirement of Debt Instruments

Generally, the collection of a debt is not a sale or an exchange. However, if a debt instrument is retired, amounts received by the holder are treated as being received in an exchange.[75] Debt instruments include bonds, debentures, notes, certificates, or other evidences of indebtedness.[76]

Example 5-67 ■

In 1989 the Rocket Corporation issued $50,000 of 5-year, interest-bearing bonds that were purchased by Elaine as an investment for $49,800. Elaine receives

[72] Sec. 165(g)(2).
[73] *Minnie K. Young v. CIR*, 28 AFTR 365, 41-2 USTC ¶ 9744 (2nd Cir., 1941).
[74] Sec. 165(g)(3).
[75] Sec. 1271(a).
[76] Sec. 1275(a).

$50,000 at maturity in 1993. Retirement of the debt instrument is an exchange, and the $200 gain is a LTCG.[77] ∎

Although Congress has provided that retirements of debt instruments are treated as exchanges, Congress is not willing to allow taxpayers to convert large amounts of potential ordinary interest income into capital gain by purchasing debt instruments at a substantial discount. As illustrated in Example 5-67, a small amount of bond discount is sometimes converted to capital gain. However, if the discount is large enough to be classified as original issue discount, the discount must be amortized and included in gross income for each day the debt instrument is held.[78] Original issue discount is defined as "the excess (if any) of the stated redemption price at maturity over the issue price.[79]

Example 5-68 ∎ | On January 1, 1994, Connie purchases $100,000 of the City Corporation's newly issued bonds for $85,000. The bonds mature in 20 years. In 1994 Connie must recognize as interest income a portion of the $15,000 of original issue discount. ∎

The original issue discount is considered to be zero if the amount of discount "is less than ¼ of 1% of the stated redemption price at maturity, multiplied by the number of complete years to maturity."[80] In Example 5-67, the $200 discount is not original issue discount since it is less than $625 (0.0025 × $50,000 × 5 years).

Example 5-69 ∎ | The Iowa Corporation issues on January 1, 1994, $500,000 of 12%, 20-year bonds for $488,000. The original issue discount is zero, since $12,000 is less than $25,000 (0.0025 × $500,000 × 20 years). ∎

Additional Comment

Two different types of bonds are sold at a discount: original issue discount (OID) bonds and market discount bonds. OID bonds are issued at a discount, whereas market discount bonds are those that have market discount resulting from a rise in interest rates subsequent to the issuance of the bonds.

Real World Example

Eastman Kodak has issued zero coupon bonds which are a type of original issue discount bonds. These bonds mature in 2011 and in late 1993 traded at 35.

Original Issue Discount—Debt Instruments Issued After July 1, 1982. The Tax Equity and Fiscal Responsibility Act of 1982 made a substantial change in the way original issue discount is recognized as ordinary income for obligations issued after July 1, 1982. Instead of spreading the original issue discount ratably over the life of the bond, amortization of the discount is based upon an interest amortization method. This method is referred to as the **constant interest rate method.** The total amount of interest income is determined by multiplying the interest yield to maturity by the adjusted issue price.[81] With this method of amortizing the discount, the amount of original issue discount amortized increases for each year the bond is held. In Example 5-68, Connie recognizes a larger amount of interest income in 1995 than in 1994 due to amortization of the original issue discount.

The daily portion of the original issue discount for any accrual period is "determined by allocating to each day in any accrual period its ratable portion to the increase during such accrual period in the adjusted issue price of the debt instrument."[82] The increase in the adjusted issue price for any accrual period is shown below.[83]

---

[77] If Rocket Corporation issued the bonds with the intention of calling the bonds before maturity, Sec. 1271(a)(2) treats the gain as ordinary income.
[78] Sec. 1272(a).
[79] Sec. 1273(a)(1).
[80] Sec. 1273(a)(3).
[81] Secs. 1272(a)(1) and (3).
[82] Sec. 1272(a)(3).
[83] Secs. 1272(a)(3)(A) and (B).

$$\text{Increase in the adjusted issue price} = \left[\begin{array}{c} \text{Adjusted issue price at the beginning of the accrual period} \end{array} \times \begin{array}{c} \text{Yield to maturity} \end{array} \right] - \begin{array}{c} \text{Interest payments during the accrual period} \end{array}$$

Example 5-70 ■

On June 30, 1994, Fred purchases a 10%, $10,000 corporate bond for $9,264. The bond is issued on June 30, 1994, and matures in 5 years. Interest is paid semiannually, and the effective yield to maturity is 12% compounded semiannually. In 1994 Fred recognizes interest income of $556, as illustrated in Table 5-1. The adjusted issue price as of January 1, 1995, is $9,320. This is the sum of the issue price plus any amounts of original issue discount includible in the income of any holder since the date of issue.[84] ■

If a debt instrument is sold or exchanged before maturity, part of the original issue discount is included in the seller's income. The amount to be included depends upon the number of days the debt instrument is owned by the seller within the accrual period.

Example 5-71 ■

Assume the same facts as in Example 5-70, except that Fred sells the corporate bond to Carolyn on February 24, 1996 (the 55th day in the accrual period). Fred must include $20 ([55 days ÷ 181 days in the accrual period] × $67) of accrued interest for the period of January 1, 1996, to February 24, 1996, in income for 1996. Fred's basis for the bond increases by $20. Thus, his basis for determining a gain or loss is $9,462 ($9,442 + $20). ■

Market Discount Bonds Purchased After April 30, 1993. The sale or exchange of a market discount bond may result in part or all of the gain being classified as ordinary income. The Revenue Reconciliation Act of 1993 substantially increased the number of bonds subject to the market discount provisions.[85] A market discount bond is a bond that is acquired in the bond market at a discount.[86] Market discount is the excess of the stated redemption price of the bond at maturity over the taxpayer's basis for such bond immediately after it is acquired.[87]

Example 5-72 ■

On January 1, 1994, Stephano purchased $100,000 of 8%, 20-year bonds for $82,000. The bonds were issued at par by the Solar Corporation two years ago on January 1. The bonds are market discount bonds. ■

Similar to original issue discount, there is a de minimis rule for determining market discount. Market discount is zero if the discount is less than ¼ of 1% of the stated redemption price of the bond at maturity multiplied by the number of complete years to maturity.[88] If Stephano had paid more than $95,500 for the Solar Corporation bonds in Example 5-72, the bonds would not be market discount bonds.[89]

---

[84] Sec. 1272(a)(4).

[85] Ordinary income treatment for accrued market discount does not apply to owners of taxable market discount bonds issued on or before July 18, 1984 if the bonds were acquired before May 1, 1993. Owners of tax-exempt bonds are not required to accrue market discount if the bonds were acquired prior to May 1, 1993 (regardless of the issue date).

[86] Sec. 1278(a) (1) (A). This topic is discussed in Chapter 17 of *Prentice Hall's Federal Taxation: Individuals* text.

[87] Sec. 1278(a) (2) (A)

[88] Sec. 1278(a) (2) (C)

[89] $100,000 × .25% × 18 years = $4,500.

TABLE 5-1   *Computation for Interest Income in Examples 5-70 and 5-71*

	Interest Received (1)	Amortization of Original Issue Discount (2)	Interest Income (3) = (1) + (2)	B's Basis for the Bond
6-30-94				$ 9,264
12-31-94	$ 500	$ 56[a]	$ 556	9,320[b]
6-30-95	500	59	559	9,379
12-31-95	500	63	563	9,442
6-30-96	500	67	567	9,509
12-31-96	500	71	571	9,580
6-30-97	500	75	575	9,655
12-31-97	500	79	579	9,734
6-30-98	500	84	584	9,818
12-31-98	500	89	589	9,907
6-30-99	500	93[c]	593	10,000
	$5,000	$736	$5,736	

[a] 6% × $9,264 − $500 = $56.
[b] $9,264 + $56 = $9,320.
[c] This figure is adjusted for rounding.

Gain realized on disposition of the market discount bond is ordinary income to the extent of the accrued market discount.[90] The ratable accrual method is used to determine the amount of the accrued market discount that is recognized as ordinary income.[91] The market discount is allocated on the basis of the number of days which the taxpayer held the bond relative to the number of days between the acquisition date and maturity date.

Example 5-73 ■ Assume the same facts as in Example 5-72 except that Stephano sells the bonds to Kimberly three years later for $86,400. $3,000 (³⁄₁₈ × $18,000) of the $4,600 ($86,400 − $82,000) gain is ordinary income and the remaining gain is LTCG. If Stephano sold the bond for more than $82,000 but less than $85,000, all of the gain is ordinary income. The entire $18,000 gain is ordinary income if the bond is held to maturity. ■

Options

The owner of an option to buy property may sell the option, exercise the option, or allow the option to expire. If the option is exercised, the amount paid for the option is added to the purchase price of the property acquired.[92]

Example 5-74 ■ On August 5, 1994, Len pays $600 for an option to acquire 100 shares of Hill Corporation common stock for $80 per share at any time prior to December 20, 1994. Len exercises the option on November 15, 1994, and pays $8,000 for the stock. Len's basis for the 100 shares of Hill is $8,600 ($8,000 + $600), and the stock's holding period begins on November 15, 1994. ■

When an option is sold or allowed to expire, a sale or exchange has occurred and gain or loss is therefore recognized.[93] The character of the underlying property

---

[90] Sec. 1276(a) (1).
[91] Sec. 1276(b) (1). A taxpayer may elect to use the constant interest rate method (see Sec. 1276(b) (2)).
[92] Rev. Rul. 58-234, 1958-1 C.B. 279.
[93] Sec. 1234(a)(2).

determines whether the gain or loss from the sale or expiration of the option is capital or ordinary in nature. If the optioned property is a capital asset, the option is treated as a capital asset and capital gain or loss is recognized on the sale or exchange.[94]

Example 5-75 ■   On March 2, 1994, Holly pays $270 for an option to acquire 100 shares of Arkansas Corporation stock for $30 per share at any time prior to December 10, 1994. As a result of an increase in the market value of the Arkansas stock, the market price of the option increases, and Holly sells the option for $600 on August 2, 1994. Since the Arkansas stock is a capital asset in the hands of Holly, the option is a capital asset and she must recognize a STCG of $330 ($600 − $270). ■

Example 5-76 ■   On October 12, 1993, Mary paid $400 for an option to acquire 100 shares of Portland Corporation stock for $50 per share at any time prior to February 19, 1994. Because the price never exceeds $50 before February 19, 1994, Mary does not exercise the option. Since the option expires, Mary recognizes a STCL of $400 in 1994. ■

Additional Comment

The Wall Street Journal publishes daily a list of all call and put options traded on the Chicago Board, the American Stock Exchange, and other exchanges where these options are traded.

Transactions in which taxpayers purchase or write options to buy (calls) are quite common today. An investor who anticipates that the market value of a stock or security (e.g., common stock) will increase during the next few months may purchase a call option instead of actually buying the stock. As indicated above, the tax treatment for the option depends upon whether the call is exercised, sold, or expires. Someone, however, must be willing to write a call on the stock. Typically an owner of the same stock will write a call option. The writer of the call receives a payment for granting the right to purchase the stock at a fixed price within a given period of time.

If the call is exercised, the writer of the call adds the amount received for the call to the sales price to determine the amount realized.[95] If the call is not exercised within the given time period and thus expires, the writer retains the amount received for the option and recognizes a STCG.[96] The gain is short-term, even if the option is written and held for a period of more than a year.

Self-Study Question

Marc writes a call option on stock owned by him and receives $800 on November 1, 1993. The value of the stock declines and the option is allowed to expire on February 15, 1994. When does Marc recognize the $800 gain?

Example 5-77 ■   Sam owns 100 shares of Madison Corporation common stock, which was purchased on May 1, 1988, for $4,000. On November 8, 1994, Sam writes a call that gives Joan, an investor, the option to purchase Sam's 100 shares of Madison stock at $60 per share any time before April 19, 1995. The current market price of Madison stock is $56 per share, and Sam receives $520 for writing the call. If the call is exercised, Sam has a LTCG of $2,520 ([$6,000 + $520] − $4,000). If the call is not exercised and expires on April 19, 1995, Sam must recognize a STCG of $520 in 1995. ■

Answer

Marc recognizes the gain in 1994 when the transaction is completed.

Example 5-78 ■   Assume the same facts as in Example 5-77, but consider instead the tax treatment for Joan, the holder of the call. If Joan exercises the call, the basis of the stock is $6,520 ($6,000 + $520). If she does not exercise the call, a STCL of $520 is recognized. If Joan sells the call, the amount received is compared with her basis in the call ($520) to compute Joan's gain or loss. ■

Patents

Key Point

A copyright held by a taxpayer whose personal efforts created it is omitted from the definition of a capital asset. However, a patent can be considered as a capital asset. In effect, the tax law could be said to favor those individuals whose efforts lead to scientific or technological advancement.

To encourage technological progress and to clarify whether a transfer of rights to a patent is capital gain or ordinary income, Congress created Sec. 1235, which allows

[94] Sec. 1234(a)(1).
[95] Rev. Rul. 58-234, 1958-1 C.B. 279.
[96] Sec. 1234(b) and Reg. Sec. 1.1234-3.

the holder of a patent to treat the gain resulting from the transfer of all substantial rights in a patent as LTCG. This tax treatment is more favorable than that accorded to producers of artistic, literary, and musical works, who receive ordinary rather than capital gain from the sale of their works. A taxpayer who recognizes LTCG from the sale of a patent may use the gain to offset capital losses or capital loss carryovers that are otherwise limited by the capital loss limitation rules.

Requirements for Capital Gain Treatment. Section 1235 provides that the transfer of all substantial rights to a patent by the holder of the patent is treated as a sale or exchange of a capital asset that has been held long term. Thus long-term capital gain is recognized on the transfer of a patent regardless of its holding period or the character of the asset. Favorable long-term capital gain treatment applies even if the transferor of the patent receives periodic payments contingent on the productivity, use, or disposition of the property transferred.[97] Section 483, which requires interest to be imputed on certain sales contracts, does not apply to the transfer of a patent in accordance with Sec. 1235.[98]

Example 5-79 ■   Clay invents a small utensil used to peel shrimp. He has a patent on the utensil and transfers all rights to the patent to a manufacturing company. Clay receives $100,000 plus 40 cents per utensil sold. Since Sec. 1235 applies, the total of the lump-sum payment and the royalty payments received less his cost basis for the patent is recognized as a LTCG.   ■

Substantial Rights. The principal requirement in Sec. 1235 is that the holder must transfer all substantial rights to the patent. The Regulations state that the circumstances of the whole transaction should be considered in determining whether all substantial rights to a patent have been transferred.[99] All substantial rights have not been transferred if the patent rights of the purchaser are limited geographically within the country of issuance or the rights are for a period less than a patent's remaining life.

Example 5-80 ■   Bruce, an inventor, transfers one of his U.S. patents on a manufacturing process to a manufacturer located in Utah. The manufacturer's rights to use the patent are limited to the state of Utah. Because the patent rights are limited to a geographical area, all of the substantial rights have not been transferred, and Sec. 1235 does not apply. Payments received for the use of the patent are royalties and taxed as ordinary income.   ■

Definition of a Holder. Long-term capital gain treatment applies only to a holder of the patent rights. For purposes of Sec. 1235, a holder is an individual whose efforts created the property or an individual who acquires the patent rights from the creator for valuable consideration before the property covered by the patent is placed in service or is utilized. Furthermore, the acquiring individual may not be related to the creator or be the creator's employer.[100]

Section 1235 may not be used by corporate taxpayers since corporations are not permitted to be classified as holders. Although a partnership is not permitted to be a holder, individual partners may qualify as holders to the extent of the partner's interest in the patent owned by the partnership.

[97] Sec. 1235(a).
[98] Sec. 483(d)(4).
[99] Reg. Sec. 1.1235-2(b).
[100] Sec. 1235(b).

Example 5-81 ■

Joy purchases a patent from Martin, whose efforts created the patent. The purchase occurs before the property is placed in service or utilized. Joy and Martin are unrelated individuals, and Joy is not Martin's employer. For purposes of Sec. 1235, both Joy and Martin qualify as holders. ■

Franchises, Trademarks, and Trade Names

Additional Comment

The scope of Sec. 1253 is very broad. A franchise "includes an agreement which gives one of the parties to the agreement the right to distribute, sell, or provide goods, services, or facilities within a specified area."

Prior to the enactment of Sec. 1253, significant uncertainty existed as to whether the transfer of a franchise, trademark, or trade name should be treated as a sale or exchange or as a licensing agreement. If the transfer is tantamount to a sale of the property, the payments received should be treated by the transferor as a return of capital and capital gain, and the transferee should be required to capitalize and amortize such payments. However, if the transfer represents a licensing agreement, the transferor should recognize ordinary income and the transferee should receive an ordinary deduction for such payments.

Section 1253, which applies to the granting of a franchise, trademark, or trade name, as well as renewals and transfers to third parties, attempts to resolve the uncertainty by stating, "A transfer of a franchise, trademark, or trade name shall not be treated as a sale or exchange of a capital asset if the transferor retains any significant power, right, or continuing interest with respect to the subject matter of the franchise, trademark, or trade name."[101]

The Code provides examples of some rights that are to be considered as a "significant power, right, or continuing interest."[102] These rights include the right to:

Real World Example

Shaquille O'Neal, the NBA star of the Orlando Magic, has obtained a trademark on his nickname "Shaq." The trademark covers nearly 200 products including athletic shoes, cake decorations, bathroom tissue, bathtub toys, kites, etc.

- Disapprove of any assignment
- Terminate the agreement at will
- Prescribe standards of quality for products, product services, and facilities
- Require the exclusive selling or advertising of the transferor's products or services
- Require the transferee to purchase substantially all of its supplies and equipment from the transferor

If the transferor does not retain any significant power, right, or continuing interest in the property, the transferor treats the transfer as a sale of the franchise and has the benefits of capital gain treatment. However, any amounts received that are contingent on the productivity, use, or disposition of such property must be treated as ordinary income by the transferor.[103]

Example 5-82 ■

Rose, who owns a franchise with a basis of $100,000, transfers the franchise to Ruth and retains no significant power, right, or continuing interest. Rose receives a $250,000 down payment when the agreement is signed and annual payments for 5 years equal to 10% of all sales in excess of $2,000,000. Rose has a capital gain of $150,000 with respect to the initial payment, but all of the payments received during the next 5 years will be ordinary income because they are contingent payments. ■

Under Sec. 1253, the transferee may deduct payments that are contingent on the productivity, use, or disposition of such property as business expenses. Generally,

---

[101] Sec. 1253(a). Section 1253(e) prevents the basic Sec. 1253 rules from applying to the transfer of a professional sports franchise.
[102] Sec. 1253(b)(2).
[103] Sec. 1253(c).

other payments are capitalized and amortized over a period of 15 years[104]. In practice, payments received for the transfer of a franchise are generally treated as ordinary income to the transferor and are deductible by the transferee because in most franchise agreements the transferor desires to maintain significant powers, rights, or continuing interests in the franchise operation. Also, in many instances the payments are, in part, predicated upon the success of the franchised business and are, therefore, established as contingent payments.

Lease Cancellation Payments

Real World Example

The taxpayer sold a building with the purchaser paying $500,000 and the lessee of the building paying $60,000 under a separate agreement to cancel the lease. The $60,000 was treated as ordinary income since no "sale or exchange" of the property occurred in return for the lessee's $60,000 payment. Gary Gurvey v. U.S., 57 AFTR 2d. 86-1062, 86-1 USTC ¶ 9260 (D.C. Ill., 1986).

A lease arrangement may be terminated before the lease period expires, and a lease cancellation payment may be made as consideration for the other party's agreement to terminate the lease. Either a lessor or a lessee may receive such a payment, since the payment is normally made by the person who wants to cancel the lease. The tax treatment may differ significantly depending on which party is the recipient.

Payments Received by Lessor. The Supreme Court has ruled that lease cancellation payments received by a lessor are treated as ordinary income on the basis that the payments represent a substitute for rent.[105] Lease cancellation payments are included in the lessor's income in the year received, even if the lessor uses an accrual method.[106]

Payments Received by Lessee. Payments received by a lessee for canceling a lease are considered to be amounts received in exchange for the lease.[107] If the lease is a capital asset, any gain or loss is a capital gain or loss.

Example 5-83 ■

Jim has a 3-year lease on a house used as his personal residence. The lessor has an opportunity to sell the house and has agreed to pay $1,000 to Jim to cancel the lease. Assuming that Jim has no basis in the lease, the gain of $1,000 is capital gain, since the lease is a capital asset. ■

HOLDING PERIOD

OBJECTIVE 7

Determine the holding period for an asset when a sale or exchange occurs

The length of time an asset is held before it is disposed of (i.e., the *holding period*) is an important factor in determining whether any gain or loss resulting from the disposition of a capital asset is treated as long-term or short-term. To be classified as a long-term capital gain or loss, the capital asset must be held more than one year.[108] To determine the holding period, the day of acquisition is excluded and the disposal date is included.[109]

If the date of disposition is the same date as the date of acquisition, but a year later, the asset is considered to have been held for only one year. If the property is held for an additional day, the holding period is more than one year.

Example 5-84 ■

Arnie purchased a capital asset on April 20, 1993, and sells the asset at a gain on April 21, 1994. The gain is classified as a LTCG. If the asset is sold on or before April 20, 1994, the gain is a STCG. ■

Additional Comment

When determining the holding period for marketable securities, it is important to use the "trade" dates and not the "settlement" dates.

---

[104] Sec. 197(a).
[105] *Walter M. Hort v. CIR,* 25 AFTR 1207, 41-1 USTC ¶ 9354 (USSC, 1941).
[106] *Farrelly-Walsh, Inc.,* 13 B.T.A. 923 (1928).
[107] Sec. 1241.
[108] Sec. 1222. A 6-month holding period was applied to property acquired after June 27, 1984, and before January 1, 1988.
[109] *H. M. Hooper,* 26 B.T.A. 758 (1932), and Rev. Rul. 70-598, 1970-2 C.B. 168.

The fact that all months do not have the same number of days is not a factor in determining the 1-year period. Acquisitions made on the last day of any month must be held until the first day of the thirteenth subsequent month in order to have been held for more than one year.

Property Received as a Gift

If a person receives property as a gift and uses the donor's basis to determine the gain or loss from a sale or exchange, the donor's holding period is added to or tacked onto the donee's holding period.[110] In other words, the donee's holding period includes the donor's holding period. If, however, the donee's basis is the FMV of the property on the date of the gift, the donee's holding period starts on the date of the gift. This situation occurs when the FMV is less than the donor's basis on the date of the gift and the property is subsequently sold at a loss.

Example 5-85 ■   Cindy receives a capital asset as a gift from Marc on July 4, 1994, when the asset has a $4,000 FMV. Marc acquired the property on April 12, 1994, for $3,400. If Cindy sells the asset after April 12, 1995, any gain or loss will be a LTCG or LTCL. Cindy's basis is the donor's cost because the FMV of the property is higher than the donor's basis on the date of the gift. Since Cindy takes Marc's basis, Marc's holding period is tacked on. ■

Example 5-86 ■   Roy receives a capital asset as a gift from Diane on September 12, 1994, when the asset has a $6,000 FMV. Diane acquired the asset on July 1, 1993, for $6,500. If the asset is sold at a gain (i.e., for more than $6,500), Roy's holding period starts on July 1, 1993, the date when Diane acquired the property, because the donor's basis of $6,500 is used by Roy to compute the gain. If the asset is sold at a loss (i.e., for less than $6,000), Roy's holding period does not start until the date of the gift—September 12, 1994—because Roy's basis is the $6,000 FMV. The FMV is used to compute the loss, because it is less than the donor's basis on the date of the gift. ■

Additional Comment

The provision permitting the holding period of property received from a decedent to be deemed to be long-term is a rule of convenience. It is not necessary to try to determine when the decedent actually acquired the property.

Property Received from a Decedent

The holding period of property received from a decedent is always deemed to be long-term. The actual time the property is held by the decedent, estate, or heirs is disregarded.[111] Therefore, the estate or heirs may sell or otherwise dispose of property immediately after the decedent's death, and the property is deemed to have been held long-term.

Example 5-87 ■   The executor of Paul's estate sells certain securities for $41,000 on September 2, 1994, which are valued in the estate at their FMV of $40,000 on June 5, 1994, the date of Paul's death. The estate has a LTCG of $1,000 because the securities are considered to have been held long term. ■

Nontaxable Exchanges

In a nontaxable exchange, the basis of the property received is determined by taking into account the basis of the property given in the exchange. If the properties are capital assets or Sec. 1231 assets, the holding period of the property received includes

[110] Sec. 1223(1) and Reg. Sec. 1.1223-1(b).
[111] Sec. 1223(11).

the holding period of the surrendered property.[112] In essence, the holding period of the property given up in a tax-free exchange is tacked on to the holding period of the property received in the exchange.

Receipt of Nontaxable Stock Dividends and Stock Rights

If a shareholder receives nontaxable stock dividends or stock rights, the holding period of the stock received as a dividend or the stock rights received includes the holding period for the stock owned by the shareholder.[113] However, if the stock rights are exercised, the holding period for the stock purchased begins with the date of exercise.[114]

Example 5-88 ■ As a result of owning Circle Corporation stock acquired 3 years ago, Paula receives nontaxable stock rights on June 5, 1994. Any gain or loss on the sale of the rights is long-term, regardless of whether any basis is allocated to the rights because the holding period of the rights includes the holding period of the stock. ■

Example 5-89 ■ Assume the same facts as in Example 5-88, except that the stock rights are exercised on August 20, 1994. The holding period for the newly acquired Circle stock begins on August 20, 1994, the date of exercise. ■

PREFERENTIAL TREATMENT FOR NET CAPITAL GAINS

Historical Note
In part the preferential treatment of net capital gains was repealed in the Tax Reform Act of 1986 because Congress believed that the reduction of individual tax rates on such forms of capital income as business profits, interest, dividends, and short-term capital gains eliminated the need for a reduced rate for net capital gains.

Preferential treatment for capital gains was first created by the Revenue Act of 1921, which became effective on January 1, 1922. Despite almost continuous controversy concerning the need for preferential treatment, some form of preferential treatment for capital gains has existed since 1922. The range of controversy concerning the need for preferential tax treatment for capital gains is wide. Some maintain that capital gains do not represent income and should not be taxed, while others maintain that capital gains are no different from any other type of income and should be taxed accordingly.[115] A few of the frequently stated arguments are discussed below.

Mobility of Capital

Without some form of preferential treatment, taxpayers who own appreciated capital assets may be unwilling to sell or exchange the asset if high tax rates exist, despite the presence of more attractive investment opportunities. In essence, the taxpayer may be "locked in" to holding an appreciated capital asset instead of shifting resources to more profitable investments.

Example 5-90 ■ Carmen owns Missouri Corporation stock with a $4,000 basis and a $20,000 FMV. She anticipates that the future after-tax annual return will be 10% on the Missouri stock and 12% on Kansas Corporation stock that has a similar level of risk.

---

[112] Sec. 1223(1).
[113] Sec. 1223(5) and Reg. Sec. 1.1223-1(e).
[114] Sec. 1223(6) and Reg. Sec. 1.1223-1(f).
[115] Walter J. Blum, "A Handy Summary of the Capital Gains Argument," *Taxes—The Tax Magazine,* 35 (April 1957), pp. 247-66.

Assume her marginal tax rate is 50% (without consideration of favorable capital gain rates or deductions). Without preferential treatment of capital gains, Carmen will have to pay a tax of $8,000 ($16,000 × 0.50) on the sale of the Missouri stock and will have only $12,000 ($20,000 − $8,000) to invest in the Kansas stock. With a 12% return, she will receive an investment return of only $1,440 ($12,000 × 0.12), as compared with $2,000 ($20,000 × 0.10) if the investment in the Missouri stock is maintained. ■

The "locked-in" effect is reduced if tax rates are lowered. The justification for eliminating the special 60% deduction for long-term capital gains after 1986 was due to a significant reduction in the top marginal tax rate applicable to ordinary income.

Mitigation of the Effects of Inflation and the Progressive Tax System

Because the tax laws do not generally reflect the effect of changes in purchasing power due to inflation, the sale or exchange of a capital asset may produce inequitable results. In fact, taxes may have to be paid even where a transaction results in an inflation-adjusted loss.

Additional Comment

The American Assembly at Columbia University in its final report on Reforming and Simplifying the Federal Tax System *issued in 1985 recommends that capital gains be taxed as ordinary income if they are adjusted for inflation.*

Example 5-91 ■

Beverly purchased a capital asset 9 years ago for $100,000. If the asset is sold today for $180,000 and the general price level has increased by 100% during the 9-year period, Beverly will have a taxable gain of $80,000, despite suffering an inflation-adjusted loss of $20,000 ($180,000 sale price − [$100,000 × 200%]). ■

With a progressive tax system, the failure to adjust for inflation creates an even greater distortion. However, it should be noted that this distortion applies to all assets, not just capital assets.

Outlook for Increased Preferential Treatment for Net Capital Gains

Additional Comment

In late 1992 some economists advocated a reduction in the tax on capital gains as a means of stimulating the economy.

During fall 1989, the House passed a bill that would have allowed a deduction equal to 30% of net capital gains until 1992. After 1991, gains due to inflation would not have been subject to tax if the capital asset was acquired after 1991 and held more than one year. However, the Senate did not include a provision in its bill for changing the tax treatment for capital gains and the Omnibus Budget Reconciliation Act of 1989 did not include provisions relating to favorable capital gain treatment.

Proponents for reinstatement of preferential treatment for capital gains cite the need to encourage capital formation to create more jobs and improve our competitive position within the global economy. Furthermore, it is anticipated that a reduction in the tax rate for capital gain income will temporarily increase tax revenue since taxpayers owning appreciated assets will be encouraged to sell. Those opposed to reintroducing preferential treatment for capital gains note the eventual decrease in revenue resulting from the lower rates and see such preferential treatment as benefiting high-income taxpayers.

Although former President George Bush advocated reinstatement of preferential capital gain treatment in the form of a deduction, Congress was unwilling to support his position. When the tax rate on ordinary income was increased by the Revenue Reconciliation Act of 1990 to 31%, Congress also provided for a 28% maximum tax rate on net capital gain recognized by noncorporate taxpayers in tax years beginning after 1990. In the Revenue Reconciliation Act of 1993, Congress did not change the tax rate on net capital gain, but the highest marginal tax rate was increased from 31% to 39.6% thus increasing the preferential treatment for some taxpayers with net capital gain. Congress did make one change that may suggest a goal of the Clinton administration to target preferential tax treatment. A new exclusion up to 50% of the gain realized on the disposition of qualified small business stock issued after August 10, 1993, is available for noncorporate taxpayers who hold qualified stock for more than five years.[116]

TAX PLANNING CONSIDERATIONS

Selection of Property to Transfer by Gift

Many tax reasons exist for making gifts of property, although the donor may incur a gift tax liability if the gift is a taxable gift.[117] Individuals may annually give property of $10,000 or less to a donee without making a taxable gift.[118]

Example 5-92 ■   Maya, who is single, owns marketable securities with a $6,200 basis and $10,000 FMV. She makes gifts of the marketable securities to Phil and cash of $10,000 to Roy. Because of the $10,000 annual exclusion per donee, Maya's gifts are not taxable gifts. ■

Example 5-93 ■   Harry, who is single, makes a gift of land with a $200,000 basis and a $930,000 FMV to Rita. Harry's taxable gift is $920,000 ($930,000 − $10,000), and he incurs a gift tax liability. ■

Individuals frequently reduce future estate taxes by making gifts. By utilizing the annual exclusion, an individual may reduce future estate taxes and avoid the gift tax.

Example 5-94 ■   Christine owns only one asset—cash of $900,000—and has no liabilities. In December of the current year, she gives $10,000 to each of her five grandchildren. Because of the $10,000 annual exclusion per donee, Christine's gifts are not taxable gifts. By making the gifts, her potential gross estate is reduced by $50,000 (5 × $10,000). ■

Additional Comment

A husband and wife can each make a $10,000 gift to their daughter enabling the daughter to receive a total of $20,000 annually without the parents incurring a gift tax.

The selection of which property to give is important if one is attempting to reduce future estate taxes. It is generally preferable to make gifts of properties that are expected to significantly increase in value during the postgift period prior to the donor's death. Any increases in value after the date of the gift are not included in the donor's gross estate.

Example 5-95 ■   In 1989 Hal owned Sun Corporation stock with a $100,000 FMV and Union Corporation stock with a $100,000 FMV. Hal expected the Sun stock to increase in value at a moderate rate and the Union stock to increase at a substantial rate. In 1989 Hal made a gift of the Union stock to Dana. Hal's taxable gift in 1989 was $90,000 ($100,000 − $10,000). Hal dies in the current year when the FMVs of the Sun and Union stocks are $180,000 and $425,000, respectively. The postgift appreciation of $325,000 ($425,000 − $100,000) is not included in Hal's gross estate. By giving the Union stock instead of the Sun stock in 1989, Hal's gross estate is smaller. ■

[116] Sec. 1202(a). (See Chapter 4 for a discussion of this topic.)
[117] For example, taxpayers may give income-producing property to a taxpayer subject to a lower tax rate, or property expected to appreciate in the future may be given away to reduce estate taxes.
[118] Sec. 2503(b).

Gifts are often made for income tax purposes to shift income to other family members who are in a lower income tax bracket than the donor.

Example 5-96 ■

In 1994 Anne has a marginal tax rate of 28% and owns Atlantic Corporation bonds, which have a $5,000 basis and $8,000 FMV. The bonds pay interest of $700 per year. If Anne gives the bonds to a dependent child, the interest income is shifted to the child. If the child has no other income, the child's taxable income is $100 ($700 − $600 standard deduction), and the child's marginal tax rate is 15%. The gift results in an annual income tax savings to the family unit of $181 ([0.28 × $700] − [0.15 × $100]). The rate of tax that is imposed may be the parent's rate (see Chapter 2) if the child is less than 14 years old and has net unearned income in excess of $1,200.

In addition to shifting the interest income, Anne has also shifted a potential gain of $3,000. The child's basis for the bonds is $5,000, since the donee takes the donor's basis when the FMV of the property at the time of the gift is greater than the donor's basis. No gain is recognized by Anne when the gift is made, and a future sale of the property by the child may be taxed at a lower income tax rate. ■

While gifts of appreciated property may generate desirable income tax benefits, it is not usually advantageous to make a gift of property which has an FMV less than its basis, due to the fact that the donee's basis for determining a loss is the FMV. The excess of the donor's basis over the FMV at the time of the gift may never generate any tax benefit for the donor or the donee. Therefore, the donor should sell the asset and make a gift of the proceeds if the loss on the sale is deductible.

Example 5-97 ■

Bob owns Red Corporation stock with an $8,000 basis and $6,000 FMV, which is held as an investment. Bob wishes to make a graduation gift of the marketable securities to Angela, although he expects her to sell the stock and purchase a car. If Angela sells the stock for $6,000, no gain or loss is recognized, since her loss basis for the stock is $6,000. In addition, no loss is recognized by Bob on the gift of the stock to Angela. Instead of giving the stock, Bob should sell it to recognize a $2,000 capital loss and then give the proceeds from the sale to Angela. ■

Self-Study Question

Doug owns shares of IBM Corporation which have a $50,000 FMV and basis of $75,000. Doug makes a deathbed telephone call to his stockbroker and sells the IBM. Assuming that Doug is in the 31% bracket and that he had no other capital gains or losses, calculate the tax savings associated with the sale.

Answer

Doug saves $930 ($3,000 × 0.31). It should be noted that the loss is limited to $3,000; if Doug dies the unused capital loss of $22,000 is lost.

The effect of gift taxes paid by the donor on the donee's basis for property received is another reason why it may be more advantageous to give appreciated property rather than property with an FMV less than its basis. A portion of the gift taxes paid as a result of giving appreciated property is added to the property's basis. However, payment of gift taxes due to the gift of property which has an FMV less than its basis does not result in an increase in the donee's basis.

Selection of Property to Transfer at Time of Death

An integral part of estate planning is the selection of property to be transferred to the heirs upon the taxpayer's death. Usually, taxpayers find it advantageous to retain highly appreciated property and transfer the property to the taxpayer's heirs since the basis of the inherited property will be increased to its FMV at the date of death (or 6 months from the date of death if the alternate valuation date is elected).

Investment and business assets that have declined in value (i.e., the FMV is less than the basis) should normally be sold prior to death to obtain an income tax deduction for the loss. If the property is not sold or otherwise disposed of prior to death, the basis of the inherited property is reduced to its FMV.

Example 5-98 ■   Paul owns two farms of similar size and quality. Each farm has a $500,000 FMV. Paul's basis for the first farm is $100,000, and his basis for the second farm is $430,000. Eventually, Paul plans for both farms to be owned by Roberta. However, he would like to transfer ownership of one farm now and retain the other farm until his death. Paul should make a gift of the second farm and transfer the first farm to Roberta upon his death because the second farm has appreciated less in value. When Paul dies and devises the first farm to Roberta, she will have a basis for the property equal to its FMV at the date of death even though Paul's basis is only $100,000. ■

COMPLIANCE AND PROCEDURAL CONSIDERATIONS

Key Point

Many taxpayers do not maintain adequate records that can be used to document the basis of their most important asset, their personal residence. For example, taxpayers can increase the basis of their residence if they have the driveway paved, add a new room or porch, etc.

Documentation of Basis

The importance of being able to determine and document the basis of assets acquired by a taxpayer cannot be overemphasized. Accurate records of asset acquisitions, dispositions, and adjustments to basis are essential. When more than one asset is acquired at the same time, the amount paid must be allocated among the assets acquired based on their relative FMVs. Subsequent adjustments to basis, such as those due to capital improvements and depreciation deductions, must be documented.

Since the basis of property can be determined by reference to another person's basis for that asset (e.g., gifts), taxpayers should be particularly aware of obtaining documentation for that basis at the time of the transfer. In the case of a gift, the taxpayer's basis may be affected by any gift tax paid by the donor. A copy of the donor's gift tax return is useful in documenting the upward adjustment to the donor's basis in determining the donee's basis.

Taxpayers who inherit property may use the decedent's federal Estate Tax Return (Form 706) to determine the FMV at the time of the decedent's death or FMV as of the alternate valuation date. However, the appraised value used for estate tax purposes is only presumptively correct for basis purposes. Although the FMVs used to determine the estate tax are typically used to determine basis, neither the taxpayer nor the IRS is barred from using an FMV for basis purposes that differs from the values used for the estate tax return.[119]

Reporting of Capital Gains and Losses on Schedule D

Capital gains and losses are reported by individuals on Schedule D, which is then attached to Form 1040. Part I is used to report short-term capital gains and losses, and Part II is used to report long-term capital gains and losses. Parts IV and V are used to list individual sales or dispositions of capital gain or loss properties if additional space is needed on parts I and II on page 1 of Schedule D. If the 28% ceiling rate on net capital gain is applicable, the taxpayer's total tax is computed on a tax worksheet that is included in the Instructions for Schedule D. The total tax is then entered on line 38 of page 2 of Form 1040.

---

[119] Rev. Rul. 54-97, 1954-1 C.B. 113 and *Achille F. Ford v. U.S.*, 5 AFTR 2d 1157, 60-1 USTC ¶ 9375 (Ct. Cls., 1960).

Capital gains due to the sale of a principal residence or due to installment sales are first reported on separate forms before being included on Schedule D. The taxpayer's share of capital gains and losses from partnerships, S corporations, and fiduciaries is reported in Parts I and II. The carryover of capital losses is also included in Parts I and II.

To improve taxpayer compliance with respect to the reporting of sales and exchanges, every person doing business as a broker is required to furnish the government with information pertaining to each customer including gross proceeds due to any sales or exchanges.[120] The Tax Reform Act of 1986 extended this requirement to real estate brokers and defined the term *real estate broker* as meaning "any of the following persons involved in a real estate transaction in the following order: the person responsible for closing the transaction, the mortgage lender, the seller's broker, or the buyer's broker."[121] The information provided by the broker to the government must be reported to each customer on Form 1099-B.[122] Taxpayers must use Schedule D to reconcile amounts shown on Form 1099-B with the taxpayer's income tax return.

PROBLEM MATERIALS

DISCUSSION QUESTIONS

5-1. What problem may exist in determining the amount realized for an investor who exchanges common stock of a publicly-traded corporation for a used building? How is the problem likely to be resolved?

5-2. In 1987 Ellen purchased a house for $60,000 to use as her personal residence. She paid $12,000 and borrowed $48,000 from the local savings and loan company. In 1989 she paid $10,000 to add a room to the house. In 1991 she paid $625 to have the house painted and $800 for built-in bookshelves. As of January 1, of the current year, she has reduced the $48,000 mortgage to $44,300. What is her basis for the house?

5-3. Vincent pays $20,000 for equipment to use in his trade or business. He pays sales tax of $800 as a result of the purchase. Must the $800 sales tax be capitalized as part of the purchase price?

5-4. Sergio owns 200 shares of Palm Corporation common stock, which were purchased during the prior year as follows: 100 shares on July 5, for $9,000; and 100 shares on October 15, for $12,000. When Sergio sells 50 shares for $8,000 on July 18 of the current year, he does not identify the particular shares sold. What is the amount and character of the gain on the sale?

5-5. On August 5 of the current year, David receives stock of Western Corporation as a gift from his grandfather, who acquired the stock on January 15, 1987. Under what conditions would David's holding period start on August 5 of the current year?

5-6. On March 15 of the current year, Carol receives land as a gift from her grandmother, who acquired the land on November 23, 1980. Under what conditions would Carol's holding period start on November 23, 1980?

5-7. Helen inherits property from her sister, who dies in January, when the property has a $450,000 FMV. Helen's basis for the property is $430,000, which reflects its FMV 6 months following the date of death. Explain how she could have a basis for the property that is less than the FMV of the property at the time of her sister's death.

[120] Sec. 6045(a).
[121] Sec. 6045(c).
[122] Sec. 6045(b).

5-8. Jim inherits property from his brother who dies in March of the current year when the property has a $980,000 FMV. This property is the only property included in his brother's gross estate and there is a taxable estate. The FMV of the property as of the alternate valuation date is $900,000.
   a. Why might the executor of the brother's estate elect to use the alternate valuation date to value the property?
   b. Why might Jim prefer the executor to use FMV at time of the death to value the property?
   c. If the marginal estate tax rate is 37% and Jim's marginal income tax rate is 28%, which value should the executor use?

5-9. Martha owns 500 shares of Columbus Corporation common stock at the beginning of the year with a basis of $82,500. During the year Columbus declares and pays a 10% nontaxable stock dividend. What is her basis for each of the 50 shares received?

5-10. Mario owns 2,000 shares of Nevada Corporation common stock at the beginning of the year. His basis for the stock is $38,880. During the year, Nevada declares and pays a stock dividend. After the dividend, Mario's basis for each share of stock owned is $18. What is the percentage dividend paid by Nevada?

5-11. A corporate taxpayer plans to build a $6 million office building during the next 18 months. How must the corporation treat the interest on debt paid or incurred during the production period?

5-12. Andy owns an appliance store where he has merchandise for sale such as refrigerators. Roger, a bachelor, owns a refrigerator, which he uses in his apartment for personal use. For which individual is the refrigerator a capital asset?

5-13. Why did the Supreme Court rule in the *Corn Products* case that a gain due to the sale of futures contracts is ordinary income instead of capital gain?

5-14. When is the gain on the sale or exchange of securities by a dealer in securities classified as capital gain?

5-15. In 1982 Florence purchased 30 acres of land. She has not used the land for business purposes nor made any substantial improvements to the property. During the current year, she subdivides the land into 15 lots and advertises the lots for sale. She sells four lots at a gain. What is the character of the gain on the sale of the four lots?

5-16. Assume the same facts as in question 5-15 and explain how the basis of each lot would be determined?

5-17. Mr. and Mrs. Smith file a joint return for the current year and have $95,000 of taxable income without considering a $10,000 net capital gain. What is their marginal tax rate for the $10,000 net capital gain?

5-18. Four years ago, Susan loaned $7,000 to her friend, Joe. During the current year, the $7,000 loan is considered to be worthless. Explain how Susan should treat the worthless debt for tax purposes.

5-19. Why did the Supreme Court rule in *Arkansas Best* that the stock of a corporation purchased by the taxpayer to protect the taxpayer's business reputation was a capital asset?

5-20. The Top Corporation, a producer of lumber, acquires 25% of the stock of the First Corporation which operates retail lumber yards. Top's primary reason for making the purchase is to obtain a potential customer. Explain how the *Corn Products* case could be used to argue that the stock of First owned by Top is not a capital asset. Explain how the *Arkansas Best* case could be used to argue that the stock of First owned by Top is a capital asset.

5-21. Ohio Corporation purchases stock of Buckeye Corporation for investment purposes and to assure a source of raw materials. If Ohio Corporation later sells the stock at a gain, is the gain taxed as ordinary income or capital gain?

5-22. Nancy and the Minor Corporation own bonds of the East Corporation. Minor Corporation owns 80% of the stock of East Corporation. East Corporation has declared bankruptcy this year, and bondholders will receive only 26% of the face value of the debt. Explain why the loss is a capital loss for Nancy but an ordinary loss for the Minor Corporation.

5-23. On January 1, of the current year, the Orange Corporation issues $500,000 of 11%, 20-year bonds for $480,000. Determine the amount of original issue discount, if any.

5-24. Today, Juanita purchases a 15-year, 7% bond of the Sunflower Corporation that was issued four years ago at par. She purchases the bond as an investment at a discount from the par value. If she sells the bonds two years from now, explain why some or all of the gain may be ordinary income.

5-25. Judy just obtained a patent on a new product she has developed. Bell Corporation wishes to market the product and will pay 12% of all future sales of the product to Judy. How can she be sure that the payments received will be treated as a long-term capital gain?

5-26. When is the transferor of a franchise unable to treat the transfer as a sale or an exchange of a capital asset?

5-27. How does a lessor treat payments received for canceling a lease?

5-28. What is the first day that an individual could sell a capital asset purchased on March 31, 1994, and have a holding period of more than a year?

5-29. Phil, a cash-basis taxpayer, sells the following marketable securities which are capital assets during 1994. Determine whether the gains or losses are long-term or short-term. Also determine the net capital gain for 1994.

Capital Asset	Basis	Date Acquired	Trade Date	Sales Price
A	$40,000	February 10, 1993	August 12, 1994	$52,000
B	20,000	December 5, 1993	May 2, 1994	17,000
C	30,000	April 9, 1992	December 10, 1994	37,400

5-30. How might the current treatment of capital losses discourage an individual investor from purchasing stock of a high-risk, start-up company?

5-31. An individual taxpayer has realized a $40,000 loss on the sale of an asset that had a holding period of eight months. Explain why the taxpayer may be indifferent as to whether the asset is a capital asset?

5-32. If Pam transfers an asset to Fred and the asset is subject to a liability that is assumed by Fred, how does Fred's assumption of the liability affect the amount realized by Pam? How does Fred's assumption of the liability affect his basis for the property?

PROBLEMS

5-33. *Amount Realized.* Tracy owns a nondepreciable capital asset that is held for investment. The asset was purchased for $150,000 six years earlier and is now subject to a $45,000 liability. During the current year, Tracy transfers the asset to Tim in exchange for $74,000 cash, and a new automobile with a $40,000 FMV that is to be used by Tracy for personal use, and Tim assumes the $45,000 liability. Determine the amount of Tracy's LTCG or LTCL.

5-34. *Basis of Property Received as a Gift.* Doug receives a duplex as a gift from his uncle. The uncle's basis for the duplex and land is $90,000. At the time of the gift, the land and building have FMVs of $40,000 and $80,000, respectively. No gift tax is paid by Doug's uncle at the time of the gift.
  a. To determine gain, what is Doug's basis for the land?
  b. To determine gain, what is Doug's basis for the building?
  c. Will the basis of the land and building be the same as in parts a and b for purposes of determining a loss?

5-35. *Sale of Property Received as a Gift.* During the current year, Stan sells a tract of land for $800,000. The property was received as a gift from Maxine on March 10, 1987, when the property had a $300,000 FMV. Maxine purchased the property on April 12, 1980, for $100,000.

At the time of the gift, Maxine paid a gift tax of $12,000. In order to sell the property, Stan paid a sales commission of $16,000.

a. What is Stan's realized gain on the sale?

b. How would your answer to part a change, if any, if the FMV of the gift property was $85,000 as of the date of the gift?

5-36. *Sale of Asset Received as a Gift.* Bud receives 200 shares of Georgia Corporation stock from his uncle on July 20, 1994, when the stock has a $45,000 FMV. The uncle pays a gift tax of $1,500. The uncle paid $30,000 for the stock on April 12, 1990.

Without considering the transactions below, Bud has AGI of $25,000 in both 1994 and 1995. No other transactions involving capital assets occur during the 2 years. Analyze each transaction below independent of the others, and determine Bud's AGI in each case.

a. He sells the stock on October 12, 1995, for $48,000.

b. He sells the stock on October 12, 1995, for $28,000.

c. He sells the stock on December 16, 1994, for $42,000.

5-37. *Basis of Property Converted from Personal Use.* Irene owns a truck costing $15,000 and used for personal activities. The truck has a $9,600 FMV when it is transferred to her business, which is operated as a sole proprietorship.

a. What is the basis of the truck for determining depreciation?

b. What is Irene's realized gain or loss if the truck is sold for $5,000 after claiming depreciation of $4,000?

5-38. *Stock Rights.* Cathy owns 100 shares of Atlanta Corporation common stock. She purchased the stock on July 25, 1986, for $4,000. On May 2 of the current year, she receives a nontaxable distribution of 100 stock rights. Each stock right has a $10 FMV, and the FMV of the Atlanta common stock is $70 per share. With each stock right, Cathy may acquire one share of Atlanta common for $68 per share. Assuming that Cathy elects to allocate basis to the stock rights, answer the following:

a. What is the basis allocated to the stock rights?

b. If she sells the stock rights on June 10 for $1,080, what are the amount and character of the recognized gain?

c. If she exercises the stock rights on May 14, what is the basis of the 100 shares purchased and when does the holding period start?

d. If she does not elect to allocate basis to the stock rights, what are the amount and character of the gain if she sells the stock rights on June 10 for $1,080?

5-39. *Real Property Subdivided for Sale.* Beth acquired only one tract of land 7 years ago as an investment. In order to sell the land at a higher price, she decides to subdivide the land into 20 lots. She pays for improvements such as clearing and leveling, but the improvements are not considered to be substantial. Each lot has a basis of $2,000, and a selling price of $6,000. Selling expenses of $480 were incurred to sell 2 lots last year. This year, 10 lots are sold, and selling expenses amount to $1,900. How much ordinary income and capital gain must be recognized in the prior and current year?

5-40. *Computing the Tax.* Donna files as a head of household in 1994 and has taxable income of $90,000 including the sale of a capital asset at a gain of $20,000. Only one asset was sold during the year and Donna does not have any capital loss carryovers.

a. What is the amount of Donna's tax liability if the gain is a LTCG?

b. What is the amount of Donna's tax liability if the gain is a STCG?

5-41. *Computing the Tax.* Wayne is single and has no dependents. Without considering his $11,000 net capital gain, his taxable income in 1994 is as follows:

AGI		$111,800
Interest on acquisition debt	$22,000	
State and local income taxes	8,000	
Charitable contributions	7,000	
Personal exemption	2,450	39,450
Taxable income		$ 72,350

    a. What is Wayne's tax liability without the net capital gain?

    b. What is Wayne's tax liability with the net capital gain?

5-42. *Computing the Sales Price.* An investor in a 28% tax bracket owns a capital asset with a $60,000 basis and a holding period of more than one year. The investor wishes to sell the asset at a price high enough so that he will have $90,000 in cash after paying the taxes. What is the minimum price which the investor could accept?

5-43. *Capital Gains and Losses.* Consider the four independent situations below for an unmarried individual, and analyze the effects of the capital gains and losses on the individual's AGI. For each case, determine AGI after considering the capital gains and losses.

	Situation 1	Situation 2	Situation 3	Situation 4
AGI (excluding property transactions)	$40,000	$50,000	$60,000	$70,000
STCG	6,000	2,000	5,000	6,000
STCL	2,000	5,000	4,000	15,000
LTCG	3,500	15,000	10,000	9,000
LTCL	2,500	4,000	12,000	4,000

5-44. *Capital Losses.* To better understand the rules for offsetting capital losses and how to treat capital losses carried forward, analyze the following data for an unmarried individual for the period 1991 through 1994. No capital loss carryforwards are included in the figures below. For each year, determine AGI and the capital losses to be carried forward to a later tax year.

	1991	1992	1993	1994
AGI (excluding property transactions)	$40,000	$50,000	$60,000	$70,000
STCG	4,000	5,000	7,000	10,000
STCL	9,000	3,000	5,000	12,000
LTCG	6,000	10,000	2,200	6,000
LTCL	5,000	21,000	1,000	9,500
AGI (including property transactions)	_____	_____	_____	_____
STCL to be carried forward	_____	_____	_____	_____
LTCL to be carried forward	_____	_____	_____	_____

5-45. *Character of Loss.* The Michigan Corporation owns 20% of the Wolverine Corporation. The Wolverine stock was acquired 8 years ago to assure Michigan of a steady supply of raw materials. Michigan also owns 30% of Spartan Corporation and 85% of Huron Corporation. Stock in both of these corporations was acquired more than 10 years ago for investment purposes. During the current year, Wolverine, Spartan, and Huron are deemed bankrupt, and the stocks are considered to be worthless. Describe how Michigan should treat its losses.

5-46. *Original Issue Discount.* On December 31, 1993, Phil purchased $20,000 of newly issued bonds of Texas Corporation for $16,568. The bonds are dated December 31, 1993. The bonds are 9%, 10-year bonds paying interest semiannually on June 30 and December 31. The bonds are priced to yield 12% compounded semiannually.

    a. What is the amount of the original issue discount?

    b. For the first semiannual period, what is the amount of the original issue discount which Phil must recognize as ordinary income?

    c. What is the total amount of interest income which Phil must recognize in 1994?

    d. What is Phil's basis for the bonds as of December 31, 1994?

    e. If the bonds were issued instead before July 2, 1982, how much of the discount is amortized each 6 months?

5-47. On January 1, 1992, Swen paid $184,000 for $200,000 of the 8%, 20-year bonds of Penn Corporation issued on January 1, 1988, at par. The bonds are held as an investment. Determine the gain and the character of the gain if the bonds are sold on January 1, 1994 for:
   a. $191,000
   b. 185,750
   c. 183,000

5-48. *Capital Gains and Losses.* During 1994, Gary receives a $50,000 salary and has no deductions for AGI. In 1993, Gary had a $5,000 STCL and no other capital losses or capital gains. Consider the following sales and determine Gary's AGI for 1993.

   • An automobile purchased in 1990 for $10,800 and held for personal use is sold for $7,000.
   • On April 10, 1994, stock held for investment is sold for $21,000. The stock was acquired on November 20, 1993, for $9,300.

5-49. *Call Options.* On February 10, 1994, Gail purchases 20 calls on Red Corporation for $250 per call. Each call represents an option to buy 100 shares of Red stock at $42 per share any time before November 25, 1994. Compute the gain or loss recognized, and determine whether the gain or loss is long-term or short-term for Gail in the following situations:
   a. The 20 calls are sold on May 15, 1994, for $310 per call.
   b. The calls are not exercised but allowed to expire.
   c. The calls are exercised on July 15, 1994, and the 2,000 shares of Red Corporation stock are sold on July 20, 1995, for $50 per share.

5-50. *Call Writing.* Dan owns 500 shares of Rocket Corporation common stock. The stock was acquired 2 years ago for $30 per share. On October 2, 1994, Dan writes 5 calls on the stock, which represent options to buy the 500 shares of Rocket at $75 per share. For each call, Dan receives $210. The calls expire on June 22, 1995. Consider the following transactions, and describe the tax treatment for Dan:
   a. The 5 calls are exercised on December 4, 1994.
   b. The calls are not exercised and allowed to expire.

5-51. *Gains and Losses and Basis.* Betty incurs the following transactions during the current year. Without considering the transactions, her 1994 AGI is $40,000. Analyze the transactions and answer the questions below:

   1. On March 10, 1994, she sells a painting for $2,000. Betty is the artist, and her basis for the painting is $50.
   2. On June 18, 1994, she receives $28,500 from the sale of stock purchased by her uncle in 1986 for $10,000, which she inherits on February 20, 1994, as a result of her uncle's death. The stock's FMV on that date is $30,000.
   3. On July 30, 1994, she sells land for $25,000 which was received as a gift from her brother on April 8, 1994, when the land's FMV was $30,000. Her brother purchased the land for $43,000 on October 12, 1987. No gift tax was paid.
   a. What is her NSTCL or NSTCG?
   b. What is her NLTCL or NLTCG?
   c. What is the effect of capital gains and losses on her AGI?
   d. What is her capital loss carryforward to 1995?

5-52. *Corporate Capital Gains and Losses.* Determine the taxable income for the Columbia Corporation for the following independent cases:

Case	*Income from Operations*	*STCG (NSTCL)*	*NLTCG (NLTCL)*
A	$110,000	$30,000	$44,000
B	100,000	(50,000)	65,000
C	80,000	(37,000)	30,000
D	90,000	(15,000)	(9,000)

5-53. *Original Issue Discount.* On January 1, 1992, Sean purchased an 8%, $100,000 corporate bond for $92,277. The bond is issued on January 1, 1993, and matures on January 1, 1998.

Interest is paid semiannually, and the effective yield to maturity is 10% compounded semiannually. On July 1, 1994, Sean sells the bond for $95,949. A schedule of interest amortization for the bond is shown in Table 5-2 above.

a. How much interest income must Sean recognize in 1993?

b. How much interest income must Sean recognize in 1994?

c. How much gain must Sean recognize in 1994 on the sale of the bond?

TABLE 5-2 *Interest Amortization for Problem 5-53*

	Interest Received (1)	Amortization of Discount (2)	Interest Income (3) = (1) + (2)
6-30-93	$4,000	$614	$4,614
12-31-93	4,000	645	4,645
6-30-94	4,000	677	4,677
12-31-94	4,000	711	4,711
6-30-95	4,000	747	4,747
12-31-95	4,000	783	4,783
6-30-96	4,000	823	4,823
12-31-96	4,000	864	4,864
6-30-97	4,000	907	4,907
12-31-97	4,000	952	4,952

5-54. *Basis and Shifting Income.* Dale purchased Blue Corporation stock 6 years ago for $1,000 as an investment. He intends to hold the stock until funds are needed to help pay for his daughter's college education. Today the stock has a $6,500 FMV and Dale decides to sell the stock and give the proceeds, less any taxes paid on the sale, to Tammy, his 18-year-old daughter. Dale's marginal tax rate is 28%, while Tammy's marginal tax rate is 15%.

a. After making the sale and paying taxes, how much cash will be given to Tammy?

b. If Dale gives the stock to Tammy and she sells the stock for $6,500, how much cash will Tammy have available for college?

5-55. *Capital Gains and Losses.* Martha has $40,000 AGI without considering the following information. During the year, she incurs a LTCL of $10,000 and has a gain of $14,000 due to the sale of a capital asset held for more than a year.

a. If the $14,000 gain is not properly classified as a LTCG (i.e., is improperly treated as an ordinary gain), determine Martha's AGI.

b. If the $14,000 gain is properly classified as a LTCG, determine her AGI.

c. If Martha has a $2,500 STCL carryover from earlier years, how would the answers to Parts a and b be affected?

5-56. *Corporate Capital Gains and Losses.* In 1989, the City Corporation sold a capital asset and incurred a $40,000 LTCL that was carried forward to subsequent years. That sale was the only sale of a capital asset that City had made until 1994 when City sells a capital asset and recognizes a STCG of $53,000. Without considering the STCG from the sale, City's taxable income is $250,000.

a. Determine the corporation's NSTCG for 1994.

b. Determine the corporation's 1994 taxable income.

c. If the sale of the asset in 1989 had occurred in 1988, determine the corporation's 1994 taxable income.

TAX FORM/RETURN PREPARATION PROBLEMS

TurboTax **5-57.** Given the following information for Jane Cole, complete Schedule D of Form 1040 through Part III.

1. Stock options, which she purchases on February 14, of the current year, for $850, expire on October 1.

2. On July 1, she sells for $1,500 her personal-use automobile acquired on March 31, 1985, for $8,000.

3. On August 16, she sells for $3,100 her stock of York Corporation purchased as an investment on February 16, for $1,600.
4. On March 15, she sells for $5,600 an antique brass bed, a gift from her grandmother on January 10, 1988, when its FMV was $1,600. The bed was purchased by her grandmother on April 2, 1979, for $1,800.
5. She has a STCL carryover of $250 from last year.

5-58. Spencer Duck (Soc. Sec. No. 277-31-7264) is single and his eight-year-old son, Mitch, lives with him nine months of the year in a rented condominium at 321 Hickory Drive in Ames, Iowa. Mitch lives with his mother, and Spencer's ex-wife, during the summer months. His mother provides more than half of Mitch's support and Spencer has agreed to allow her to claim Mitch as her dependent. Spencer has a salary of $34,000 and itemized deductions of $4,000. Taxes withheld during the year amount to $9,000. During the current year, he sold the following assets on July 14:

1. Land was sold for $35,000. The land was received as a property settlement on January 10, 1989, when the land's FMV amounted to $30,000. His ex-wife's basis for the land, purchased on January 10, 1975, was $18,600.
2. A personal-use computer was sold for $2,480 that was acquired on March 2 last year for $4,000.
3. A membership card for a prestigious country club was sold for $8,500. The card was acquired on October 10, 1985, for $6,000.
4. Marketable securities held as an investment were sold for $20,000. The securities were inherited from his uncle who died on March 10 of the current year when FMV of the securities was $21,000. The uncle purchased the securities on May 10, 1985, for $10,700.

In addition to the above sales, Spencer received a $100 refund of state income taxes paid last year. Spencer used the standard deduction last year to compute his tax liability.

Prepare Form 1040 and Schedule D for the current year.

CASE STUDY PROBLEM

5-59. As a political consultant for an aspiring politician, you have been hired to evaluate the following statements that pertain to capital gains and losses. Evaluate the statement and provide at least a one-paragraph explanation of each statement. As you prepare your answer, consider the fact that the aspiring politician does not have much knowledge about taxation.
a. The tax on capital gains is considered to be a voluntary tax.
b. The tax treatment for capital gains and losses after 1986 and before 1991 made it disadvantageous for individuals to sell or exchange capital assets as opposed to selling or exchanging assets that are not capital assets.
c. On October 22, 1986, the Tax Reform Act of 1986 was passed that eliminated the 60% of net capital gain deduction (i.e., an individual taxpayer with $10,000 of net capital gain was entitled to a $6,000 deduction when computing AGI) before January 1, 1987. Many state governments enjoyed a substantial increase in 1986 tax revenue.
d. High income taxpayers receive the most benefit from preferential treatment for capital gains.

CASE STUDY PROBLEM—ETHICAL ISSUES

5-60. Your client, Apex Corporation, entered into an agreement with an executive to purchase his personal residence at its current FMV in the event that his employment is terminated by the company during a 5-year period. The executive was terminated prior to the end of the 5-year period and Apex acquired the house for $500,000. Due to a downturn in the real estate market, a $200,000 loss was incurred by the company upon the resale of the house. The chief financial officer of Apex insists that the loss be characterized as ordinary based upon the Corn Products doctrine. Your research into this matter reveals that the weight of authority heavily favors capital loss treatment (i.e., case law based on facts which are identical to the above issue held that the loss was capital rather than ordinary). You therefore conclude that the client's position does not have a realistic possibility of being sustained administratively or judicially on its merits if challenged by the IRS. What responsibility do you have as a tax practitioner relative to preparing the client's tax return and rendering continuing tax consulting services to the client? (See the caption entitled Statements on Responsibilities in Tax Practice in Chapter 1 for a discussion of these issues.)

TAX RESEARCH PROBLEMS

5-61. Tom Williams is an equal partner in a partnership with the Kansas Corporation. Williams, an inventor, has produced a new process while working for the partnership which has been patented by the partnership. Prior to making any use of the patent, the partnership entered into a contract granting all rights to use the process for the life of the patent to the Mason Manufacturing Co.

The time between receiving the patent and entering into the contract with Mason amounted to 8 months. Mason agreed to pay 0.3% of all sales revenue generated by products produced as a result of the process. If Mason fails to make payments on a timely basis, Mason's right to use the process is forfeited and the agreement between the partnership and Mason is canceled. Will any of the proceeds collected qualify as LTCG under Sec. 1235?

A partial list of research sources is:

- Reg. Sec. 1.1235-2
- *George N. Soffron,* 35 T.C. 787 (1961)

5-62. Lynette, an outstanding basketball player, is considering the possibility of transferring the sole right to use her name to promote basketball shoes produced and sold by the NIK Corporation. NIK will pay $2 million to obtain the right to use Lynette's name for the next 40 years. NIK may use the name on the shoes and as a part of any of the company's advertisements for basketball shoes. If Lynette signs the contract and receives the $2 million payment, will she have to recognize capital gain or ordinary income?

A partial list of research sources is

- Sec. 1221.
- Rev. Rul. 65-261, 1965-2 C.B. 281.

5-63. Jack, a tenured university professor, has been a malcontent for many years at Rockport University. The university has recently offered to pay $200,000 to Jack if he will relinquish his tenure position and resign. Jack is of the opinion that tenure is an intangible capital asset and the $200,000 received for release of the tenure should be a long-term capital gain. Explain why you agree or disagree?

A partial list of research sources is

- *Harry M. Flower,* 61 T.C. 140 (1973).
- *Estelle Goldman,* 1975 PH T.C. Memo ¶ 75,138, 34 TCM 639.

5-64. Web Baker was hired three years ago by the Berry Corporation to serve as CEO for the company. As part of his employment contract, the corporation had agreed to purchase his residence at FMV in the event the company decided to fire him. Last year, Berry, unsatisfied with Web's performance fired him and purchased the residence for $350,000. Berry immediately listed the house with a real estate agency. Soon after the purchase, the real estate market in the area experienced a serious decline especially in higher-priced homes. Berry sold the house this year for $270,000 and paid selling expenses of $12,000. How should the Berry Corporation treat the $92,000 loss?

A partial list of research sources is:

- Sec. 1221.
- Rev. Rul. 82-204, 1982-2 C.B. 192.
- *Azar Nut Co. v. CIR,* 67 AFTR 2d 91-987, 91-1 USTC ¶ 50,257 (5th Cir., 1991).

6

Deductions and Losses

LEARNING OBJECTIVES

After studying this chapter, you should be able to

1. Distinguish between deductions *for* and *from* AGI
2. Explain when deductions may be taken under both the cash and accrual methods of accounting
3. Discuss the criteria for deducting business and investment expenses
4. List the substantiation requirements that must be met to deduct travel and entertainment expenses
5. Explain the tax consequences of wash sales
6. Explain the tax consequences of transactions between related parties
7. Discuss the criteria used to determine whether an activity is a hobby or a trade or business
8. Determine the tax consequences of using residential real estate for both personal use and rental purposes

This chapter discusses the requirements for the deductibility of taxpayer expenditures and losses. The general principles governing the reporting of income require the inclusion of all items of income not specifically excluded by the law. In contrast, deductions or losses are not allowed for tax purposes unless the statute specifically provides for the deduction. For example, taxpayers may take a deduction for medical expenses paid during the year because Sec. 213 provides for the deduction in the statute. This is not to say that the Internal Revenue Code has a separate provision for every type of deductible expense that a taxpayer might incur. Many expenses, although not specifically mentioned by the Code, are still deductible because they fall into a general category of deductible expenses.

One broad category of deductible expenses includes expenditures incurred in connection with profit-seeking activities. Thus, although the Code says nothing about the deductibility of expenditures for utilities or maintenance and repairs, these expenditures are deductible if incurred in a profit-motivated activity. For individuals, these deductible expenditures may be incurred either (1) in a trade or business of the taxpayer or (2) in an activity which is engaged in for the production of income. This latter category includes expenses incurred for the following:

- Production or collection of income
- Management, conservation, or maintenance of property held for the production of income
- In connection with the determination, collection, or refund of any tax[1]

Trade or business expenses are deductible under Sec. 162 of the Code, while expenses incurred for the production of income are deductible under Sec. 212. As will be discussed later, this distinction between the two general types of activities is important because it can affect both the amount and type of the deduction. Expenses incurred in both types of activities must meet additional standards of deductibility; that is, they must also be ordinary, necessary, and reasonable in the context of the activity in which they are incurred. Losses incurred in either type of activity are deductible under Sec. 165.

---

[1] Sec. 212.

The Code also provides, in general, that no deduction is allowed for any personal, living, or family expenses. However, the tax law does specifically provide for the deductibility of certain personal expenditures or losses. For example, casualty losses (subject to specific limitations) are allowed for personal-use property. Personal expenditures for certain types of interest and taxes, medical expenses, alimony, and retirement are also allowed as deductions if they meet strict requirements. These deductions and losses for personal expenditures are discussed in Chapters 7 and 8.

FOR VERSUS FROM AGI CLASSIFICATION

OBJECTIVE 1
Distinguish between deductions for and from AGI

As demonstrated in Chapter 2, the tax formula for individuals divides all allowable business, investment, or personal deductions into the following two categories:

- Deductions subtracted from gross income in order to calculate adjusted gross income (AGI) (*for* AGI deductions)
- Deductions subtracted from AGI to arrive at the amount of taxable income (*from* AGI deductions)[2]

Deductions from AGI are also known as itemized deductions. As previously explained in Chapter 2, the concept of AGI has meaning when the taxable income of individuals is being computed. It has no application to corporations.

Deductions for AGI are specifically identified in Sec. 62. All other deductions for individuals are deductions *from* AGI. The more common *for* AGI deductions include the following:

- All allowable expenses incurred in a taxpayer's trade or business, not including business expenses of an employee
- Employee business expenses that are reimbursed by the employer or paid or incurred by a qualified performing artist
- Losses from the sale or exchange of trade, business, or investment property
- Expenses attributable to the production of rent or royalty income
- Moving expenses incurred after December 31, 1993
- Contributions to certain pension, profit-sharing, or retirement plan arrangements
- Penalties paid to a bank or other savings institution because of the early withdrawal of funds from a certificate of deposit or a time savings account
- Alimony[3]
- Self-employed individuals could also deduct 25% of health insurance costs incurred for the period through December 31, 1993 as long as the individual was not eligible to participate in a subsidized health plan maintained by an employer of the taxpayer or the taxpayer's spouse.[4]

Additional Comment

The classification of deductions between "deductions for" AGI and "deductions from" AGI is not used in corporate taxation or in the taxation of estates or trusts.

Key Point

Many of the for AGI deductions are either expenses incurred in a trade or business or investment expenses or losses. Most of the deductible personal expenses are deductible "from" AGI.

---

[2] Secs. 62 and 63.

[3] Other deductions *for* AGI include (1) deductions for depreciation and depletion for life tenants and income beneficiaries of property, (2) a portion of certain lump-sum distributions from qualified pension plans, (3) reforestation expenses, (4) required repayments of supplemental unemployment compensation benefits, and jury duty pay that is remitted to an employer.

[4] Although this deduction expired on December 31, 1993, some experts believe that it may be reinstated for subsequent years. However, the deductibility of these and other insurance premiums may be dependent upon the outcome of President Clinton's health reform proposals.

• In addition, individuals who are self-employed may deduct one-half of the self-employment tax imposed on that individual for the year (see Chapter 14).

For individuals, the distinction between deductions *for* AGI and *from* AGI is critical for two reasons. First, as explained in Chapter 2, the tax formula allows individuals to deduct the greater of the standard deduction or the total of the *from* AGI deductions in arriving at taxable income. In cases where the sum of the *from* AGI deductions does not exceed the standard deduction, the benefit of these deductions is lost. Furthermore, certain itemized deductions for taxpayers with taxable income over certain levels are phased out and lost. (See Chapter 7 for a discussion of these limits.) *For* AGI deductions, on the other hand, reduce AGI (and consequently taxable income), even if the standard deduction is used in computing taxable income.

Example 6-1 ■

Brad, a single individual with no dependents, incurs $1,500 of deductible expenses during 1994 in which he earns $30,000 in gross income. If the expenses are all deductions *from* AGI, Brad's taxable income is $23,750 (i.e., Brad receives a $2,450 deduction for his personal exemption and a $3,800 standard deduction). Brad receives no direct tax benefit from the expenses, since they are not in excess of the standard deduction. However, if the expenses are all deductions *for* AGI, Brad's taxable income is $22,250. In this case, Brad receives a full tax benefit from the expenses.

		Deductions from AGI	*Deductions for AGI*
Gross income		$30,000	$30,000
Minus:	*For* AGI deductions	—0—	(1,500)
AGI		$30,000	$28,500
Minus:	Standard deduction	(3,800)	(3,800)
	Personal exemption	(2,450)	(2,450)
Taxable income		$23,750	$22,250

■

Key Point

For many individuals the benefit of a from *AGI deduction is lost completely because (1) that particular deduction is less than its applicable limit (e.g., the medical expenses are less than 7.5% of AGI) or (2) the total of the itemized deductions is less than the standard deduction. Furthermore, certain itemized deductions of taxpayers with adjusted gross income over certain levels are phased out. (See Chapter 7 for a discussion of this phaseout.)*

A second important reason for the proper classification of deductions is that AGI is used as a benchmark in establishing limits on certain deductions *from* AGI, such as medical expenses, casualty losses, charitable contributions, and miscellaneous itemized deductions. For example, an individual may deduct certain miscellaneous itemized deductions only to the extent that the sum of these deductions for the year exceeds 2% of the individual's AGI. These expenses include unreimbursed employee business expenses,[5] expenses incurred to produce investment income,[6] and the cost of tax advice and tax return preparation (see Chapter 7). Medical expenses are deductible only to the extent their total exceeds 7.5% of the individual's AGI for the year. Casualty losses on personal-use property are first reduced by $100 per casualty. After this reduction, they are deductible only to the extent they exceed 10% of the

---

[5] These expenses include unreimbursed expenditures for travel and transportation, supplies, special clothing or uniforms, union dues, and subscriptions to trade journals. Reimbursed employee expenses are deductible *for* AGI and thus, are deductible in full.

[6] These expenses include rental fees for safe deposit boxes used to hold investment property, subscriptions to investment journals, bank service charges on checking accounts used in an investment activity, and fees paid for consulting advice. Expenses incurred in an investment activity that produces either rental or royalty income are deductions *for* AGI.

individual's AGI. The deduction for charitable contributions, on the other hand, may not exceed 50% of the taxpayer's AGI. (See Chapter 7 for a discussion of these deductions and their limits.)

Example 6-2 ■ During the current year, Vivian incurs $7,000 in deductible expenses. Her gross income for the year is $60,000. Vivian is single and has no dependents. If these expenses are incurred in Vivian's business, all of the expenses are deducted *for* AGI. On the other hand, if these unreimbursed expenses are incurred by Vivian in her capacity as an employee, they are miscellaneous itemized deductions and must first be reduced by 2% of AGI. The expenses are then deducted *from* AGI, if the total of the remainder and all other itemized deductions are in excess of the standard deduction.

	Business Deductions	Employee Deductions
Gross income	$60,000	$60,000
Minus: *For* AGI deductions	(7,000)	—0—
AGI	$53,000	$60,000
Minus: Larger of standard deduction or itemized deductions	(3,800)	(5,800)[a]
Minus: Personal exemption	(2,450)	(2,450)
Taxable income	$46,750	$51,750

[a] Total miscellaneous itemized deductions of $7,000 are first reduced by 2% of AGI ($7,000 − [0.02 × $60,000]).

WHEN AN EXPENSE IS DEDUCTIBLE

OBJECTIVE 2
Explain when deductions may be taken under both the cash and accrual methods of accounting

Since taxable income is generally measured on an annual basis, the question of when a particular expense is deductible is critical. The answer to this question largely depends upon which method of accounting is being used. The most common methods include the following:

- Cash receipts and disbursements method (cash method)
- Accrual method
- Hybrid method (a combination of the cash and accrual methods where some items are accounted for on the cash method and other items are accounted for on the accrual method)[7]

Taxpayers usually use the same method for computing taxable income that they use in keeping their regular financial accounting records. The tax law does not, however, generally require conformity.[8] For example, many companies use the straight-line depreciation method for financial accounting purposes and the modified accelerated cost recovery system (MACRS) for tax purposes.

Additional Comment

Section 446(b) provides that in cases where no method of accounting has been regularly used or if the method used does not clearly reflect income, then the computation of taxable income is to be made under a method that, in the opinion of the IRS, does clearly reflect income.

---

[7] Sec. 446(c).

[8] Sec. 446(a). An exception to this general rule requires a taxpayer using the last-in, first-out (LIFO) inventory method of accounting for taxable income purposes to also use that method for financial accounting purposes.

Cash Method

Under the **cash method of accounting,** expenses are deductible when they are actually paid. As long as it is subsequently honored, payment by check is considered a cash payment in the year the check is mailed or delivered, even though it is delivered so late on the last day of the year that the payee could not have cashed it.[9] Furthermore, the use of a credit card to satisfy an obligation is considered a cash payment at the time of the charge rather than at the time the charge is paid.[10]

Example 6-3 ■

Additional Comment

If a taxpayer using the cash method pays an expense with borrowed funds, the expense is deductible when paid instead of when the loan is repaid.

Juan, a self-employed financial consultant, uses the cash method of accounting to compute his taxable income. At the end of the current year, he flies from his hometown to San Francisco to conduct a financial planning seminar. He charges the $400 airline ticket on his credit card, but does not pay the charge until it appears on the statement in January of the following year. The $400 is deductible in the current year, the year the ticket is charged, rather than in the following year when the credit card account is settled. ■

A mere promise to pay, or the issuance of a note payable, does not constitute a payment under the cash method. Thus, a charge on an open account with a creditor is not deductible until cash is actually transferred in satisfaction of the charge.

Example 6-4 ■

Additional Comment

If a check is mailed near the end of the year it is important to have evidence that the check was mailed in the year in which the deduction is claimed.

Peter, a calendar-year taxpayer, is the sole owner of a plumbing repair business. The business uses the cash method of accounting. Under an arrangement with one of his suppliers, Peter and his employees can pick up supplies at any time during the month by merely signing for them. At the end of the month, the supplier sends Peter a bill for the charges. Peter always satisfies the bill in full during the following month. In December of the current year, Peter charges $1,500 for supplies. During the same month Peter purchases a part for $250 from another supplier. Peter uses his charge card at the time of purchase. Peter must deduct the $250 during the current year. However, the $1,500 charged on the open account is deductible when paid in the following year. ■

Prepaid Expenses. In general, a capital expenditure or the prepayment of expenses by a cash method taxpayer will not result in a current deduction if the expenditure creates an asset having a useful life that extends substantially beyond the close of the tax year.[11] This can occur when a taxpayer makes expenditures for prepaid rent, services, or interest.

Example 6-5 ■

On November 1 of the current year, Twyla enters into a lease arrangement with Rashad to rent Rashad's office space for the following 36 months. By prepaying the rent for the entire 36-month period, Twyla is able to obtain a favorable monthly lease payment of $800. This prepayment creates an asset (a leasehold) whose useful life extends substantially beyond the end of the taxable year. Thus, only $1,600 ($800 × 2 months) of the total payment is deductible in the current year. The rest must be capitalized and amortized over the life of the lease. ■

---

[9] *CIR v. Estate of M. A. Bradley,* 10 AFTR 1405, 3 USTC ¶ 904 (6th Cir., 1932) and *Charles F. Kahler,* 18 T.C. 31 (1952).

[10] Rev. Rul. 78-39, 1978-1 C.B. 73. See also Rev. Rul. 80-335, 1980-2 C.B. 170, where expenses satisfied through a pay-by-phone arrangement are deductible when the financial institution actually pays the amount.

[11] Reg. Sec. 1.461-1(a).

In the case of prepaid rent, one circuit court has held that a current deduction may be taken for the entire amount of an expenditure if the period covered by the prepayment does not exceed one year.[12] Furthermore, the taxpayer must be obligated to make the prepayment.[13]

Example 6-6 ■   Assume the same facts as in Example 6-5, except that under the terms of the lease, Twyla is obligated to make three annual payments of $9,600 each. Each payment is to be made on November 1 for the subsequent 12 months. On November 1 of the current year, Twyla pays Rashad $9,600 for the first 12-month period. Since Twyla is obligated to make the prepayment and the period covered by the prepayment does not exceed one year, the entire $9,600 is deductible in the current year if the previously cited circuit court decision is followed.   ■

Prepaid Interest. Section 461(g) of the Code requires that prepaid interest expense be deducted over the period of the loan to which the interest charge is allocated. Receipt of a discounted loan does not represent prepaid interest expense. Instead, the interest is deemed to be paid as the loan is repaid.

Example 6-7 ■   During the current year, Richelle borrows $1,000 from the bank for use in her business. Richelle uses the cash method of accounting in her business. Under the terms of the loan, the bank discounts the loan by $80, paying Richelle $920. When the loan comes due in the following year, however, Richelle is to repay the full $1,000. The $80 of interest expense is not deductible until Richelle repays the loan in the following year.   ■

Real World Example

A taxpayer made an overpayment of the federal income tax in 1975. The IRS in 1979 offset the overpayment against interest the taxpayer owed to the IRS. It was held that the interest expense was deductible in 1979 rather than in 1975. Saverio Eboli, 93 T.C. 123 (1989).

Taxpayers often prepay interest in the form of points. A point is a percentage "point" of the loan amount. Thus, the payment of two points on a $100,000 loan amounts to $2,000. Generally, points paid in connection with the purchase or improvement of a principal residence are deductible when paid.[14] According to the IRS, points paid in connection with the purchase (but not the improvement) of a principal residence are automatically deductible in the year paid if the following four requirements are met:

- The closing agreement for the purchase of the residence must clearly designate the amounts as points incurred in connection with the acquisition debt. Examples include amounts designated as loan origination fees, loan discount, discount points, or points.

- The amount must be computed as a percentage of the amount borrowed. For example, a loan origination fee of two points on a $100,000 loan results in $2,000 of prepaid interest.

- The points charged must conform to the established business practice in the geographic area where the residence is located. In addition, they may not be charged in lieu of other items that normally are separately charged. These other items include appraisal fees, title fees, attorney fees, etc., and

---

[12] *Martin J. Zaninovich v. CIR*, 45 AFTR 2d 80-1442, 80-1 USTC ¶ 9342 (9th Cir., 1980).

[13] *Bonaire Development Co. v. CIR*, 50 AFTR 2d 82-5167, 82-2 USTC ¶ 9428 (9th Cir., 1982). See also *Stephen A. Keller v. CIR*, 53 AFTR 2d 84-663, 84-1 USTC ¶ 9194 (8th Cir., 1984).

[14] Sec. 461(g)(2).

- The points are paid in connection with the purchase of the taxpayer's principal residence. In addition, the loan must be secured by the residence.[15]

Although points paid for loans incurred to improve, as opposed to acquire, the taxpayer's principal residence do not fall under this safe harbor rule, they still are currently deductible if the loan is secured by the residence, the payment of points is an established business practice in the geographic area in which it is incurred, and the amount of the prepayment does not exceed the amount generally charged.

Example 6-8 ■   During the current year, Pam purchases a principal residence for $150,000, paying $50,000 down and financing the remainder with a 20-year mortgage secured by the property. Payments on the mortgage are to be made monthly. At the closing, she is required to pay three points as a loan origination fee. Since these points are paid in connection with the purchase of a principal residence, Pam may deduct $3,000 ($100,000 × 0.03) as interest expense during the current year. In addition, Pam may also deduct the interest portion of each monthly payment made during the year.   ■

Points paid to refinance a mortgage on a principal residence are not currently deductible since they are not paid in connection with the purchase or improvement of the taxpayer's residence.[16]

Example 6-9 ■   Assume the same facts as in Example 6-8, except that Pam takes out the $100,000 loan in order to refinance her home at a lower interest rate. The $3,000 prepaid interest is not currently deductible. Instead, it is to be deducted ratably over the term of the loan. Thus, Pam may deduct an additional $12.50 ($3,000 ÷ 240 payments) interest expense for each payment that comes due during the year.   ■

Since expenses are generally deductible when paid rather than when they accrue, the cash method of accounting provides some degree of flexibility to taxpayers. Thus, subject to the limitations mentioned above with regard to prepaid expenses, taxpayers may to some degree accelerate or defer deductions from one year to another by merely accelerating or deferring payment. However, there are limitations to the use of the cash method. Inventories must be accounted for under the accrual method.[17] Taxpayers who have inventories that are an income producing factor must use either the accrual method or the hybrid method. Furthermore, most C corporations (corporations that have not elected Subchapter S status), partnerships that have a C corporation as a partner, and tax shelters may not use the cash method. There are, however, exceptions to this general rule for personal service corporations, small businesses with average annual gross receipts of $5 million or less, and businesses involved in the farming and timber businesses.[18] (See Chapter 11 for a complete discussion of the different accounting methods that may be used for purposes of computing taxable income.)

---

[15] Rev. Proc. 92-12, 1992-1 C.B. 663. As explained in Chapter 7, acquisition indebtedness incurred to acquire a personal residence is limited to $1,000,000. Hence, points that are allocated to the loan principal in excess of this limit are not deductible either.

[16] Rev. Rul. 87-22, 1987-1 C.B. 146, and Rev. Proc. 87-15, 1987-1 C.B. 624. However, the Eighth Circuit has allowed a current deduction for points paid upon the refinancing of a mortgage loan because the original loan was merely a "bridge" or temporary loan until permanent financing could be arranged. See *James R. Huntsman v. CIR*, 66 AFTR 2d 90-5020, 90-2 USTC ¶ 50,340 (8th Cir., 1990).

[17] Reg. Sec. 1.446-1(c)(2).

[18] Sec. 448.

Historical Note

Although Congress began taxing income under the 16th Amendment in 1913, it was not until the Revenue Act of 1916 that the accrual method of accounting was recognized.

Accrual Method

An **accrual-method** taxpayer deducts expenses in the period in which they accrue. Generally items accrue when the **all-events test** of Reg. Sec. 1.461-1(a)(2) and the **economic performance test** of Sec. 461(h) are both met.

All-Events Test. The all-events test is met when both of the following occur:

- The existence of a liability is established; and
- The amount of the liability is determined with reasonable accuracy.

Example 6-10 ■

During the current year, Phil provides services for Louis. Louis uses the accrual method of accounting. Phil claims that Louis owes $10,000 for the services. Louis admits owing Phil $6,000 but contests the remaining $4,000. Since the amount of the liability can be accurately established only with respect to $6,000, Louis can deduct only that amount. If Louis pays the full $10,000, it can be deducted in the year of payment, even though the contested amount ($4,000) is not resolved until a subsequent taxable year.[19] If Phil loses the lawsuit and repays Louis the $4,000, Louis would include that amount in income under the tax benefit rule (see Chapter 11). ■

Because of the all-events test, reserves for estimated expenses such as warranty expenses may not be deducted until the year in which such work is actually performed.

Example 6-11 ■

Real World Example

The taxpayer was required to overhaul its aircraft engines at intervals specified by the FAA. The taxpayer wanted to accrue this expense based on the number of hours flown. However, the court found that the taxpayer had no liability unless an overhaul was performed, and held that overhaul costs were deductible when paid. World Airways, Inc. v. CIR, 41 AFTR 2d 78-323, 78-1 USTC ¶ 9149, (9th Cir., 1977).

Best Corporation uses the accrual method of accounting and is engaged in the business of painting and rustproofing automobiles. A 5-year warranty is provided for new vehicles and a 2-year warranty for used vehicles. The warranty is extended only to the person who owns the car at the time it is painted. Furthermore, in order to keep the warranty in force, the customer is required to present the vehicle to Best Corporation for inspection each year. The warranty is voided if the vehicle is involved in an accident. Even though for financial accounting purposes Best Corporation may provide a reserve for estimated warranty expenses and deduct a reasonable addition to the reserve on an annual basis, no income tax deduction is allowed until the warranty work is actually done. ■

Economic Performance Test. To be currently deductible under the accrual method, an expense must also meet an economic performance test in addition to the all-events test. Exactly when economic performance is deemed to have occurred depends upon the type of transaction. Table 6-1 contains a listing of various types of transactions that may arise and identifies when economic performance is deemed to have occurred.[20]

Example 6-12 ■

On December 20 of the current year, Chris, an accrual method of accounting taxpayer, enters into a binding contract with Pat to have Pat clean and paint the exterior of Chris's business building. Under the terms of the contract, the work is to

---

[19] Reg. Sec. 1.461-2(a)(1).
[20] Sec. 461(h)(2).

Historical Note

The economic performance test was added by Congress in the Tax Reform Act of 1984. Congress was concerned that in some situations taxpayers could deduct expenses currently, but the actual cash expenditure might not be made for several years. Taking a current deduction in such situations overstated the real cost because the time value of money was ignored.

Additional Comment

The economic performance test does not apply to accruals for estimated expenses that are specifically allowed by the Code.

be done in March of the following year. The total cost of the job is $4,000. Chris pays 10% down at the time the contract is signed. Since the job is not to be done until the following year, economic performance has not occurred in the current year, and Chris may not deduct any portion of the expense in the current year.∎

An exception is provided for recurring liabilities.[21] In other words, an expense can be treated as accrued and deducted in the current year if all of the following occur:

- The all-events test is met during the year.
- Economic performance of the item occurs within the shorter of (1) 8½ months after the close of the tax year or (2) a reasonable period after the close of the tax year.
- The expense is recurring and the taxpayer consistently treats the item as incurred in the tax year.
- Either the item is not material or the accrual of the item in the tax year results in a more proper matching against income than accruing the item in the tax year in which economic performance occurs.

This exception for recurring liabilities is available for the first four types of transactions identified in Table 6-1, but may not be used for the last type of transaction in the table.

Example 6-13 ∎ Dawn is a calendar-year, accrual method of accounting taxpayer. Every year at the end of October, Dawn enters into a contract with Sam to provide snow removal services for the parking lots at Dawn's business. This contract extends for 5 months through the end of March of the following year. Since the all-events test is met (the

TABLE 6-1 *When Economic Performance Is Deemed to Have Occurred*

Event That Gives Rise to Liability	When Economic Performance Is Deemed to Have Occurred
Another person provides the taxpayer with property or services	When the property or services are actually provided[a]
Taxpayer uses property	As the property is used[a]
Taxpayer must provide property or services to another person	As the taxpayer provides property or services to the other person[b]
Taxpayer must make payments to another, including payments for; rebates and refunds, awards or prizes, insurance or service contracts, and taxes.	As payments to the other person are made
Taxpayer must make payments to another person because of a tort, breach of contract, a violation of law, or an injury claim under a workmen's compensation act	As payments to the other person are made

[a] Economic performance may be deemed to have occurred at the earlier date of payment if the taxpayer reasonably expects the property or services to be provided within 3½ months after the payment is made. Reg. Sec. 1.461-4(d)(6)(ii).

[b] Economic performance may also occur as the taxpayer incurs costs in connection with the obligation to provide the property or services. Reg. Sec. 1.461-4(d)(4)(i).

[21] Sec. 461(h)(3).

liability is fixed), the expense recurs every year, economic performance occurs within the requisite period of time, and the item is not material, Dawn may deduct the entire expense in the year in which the contract is signed. ■

Example 6-14 ■   Under the law of State X, the lien date for real property taxes for calendar year 1994 is January 1, 1994. Three-fourths of the tax must be paid by May 1, 1995, and the remaining one-fourth must be paid by November 1, 1995. On January 1, 1994, real property taxes of $100,000 are assessed against a building that Beta Corporation owns. Beta is a calendar-year, accrual method taxpayer.

As identified in Table 6-1, economic performance occurs when the payments of the tax are made. However, since the recurring item exception applies to the payment of taxes, Beta may deduct $75,000 of the taxes in 1994 if the first payment is made by May 1, 1995. If Beta pays the remaining $25,000 after September 15, 1995 (more than 8½ months after the end of 1994) the deduction for the $25,000 is deferred until 1995 since economic performance for the $25,000 occurs in 1995.■

A special rule under Sec. 461(c) applies to real property taxes. Under this provision, instead of using the payment method or the recurring item exception a taxpayer may elect to accrue real property taxes ratably over the period to which the taxes relate. Once made, this election may not be changed without permission from the IRS.

Example 6-15 ■   Under the law of State X, the lien date for real property taxes for calendar year 1994 is January 1, 1994. The tax is payable in full on November 30, 1994. Alpha Corp. is an accrual method taxpayer that has a January 31 fiscal year-end. On January 1, 1994, real property taxes of $100,000 are assessed against a building that Alpha Corp. owns. Alpha pays the taxes on November 30, 1994. If Alpha does not make the election to use the ratable accrual method, none of the payment is deductible in Alpha's fiscal year ending January 31, 1994 because the payment date is more than 8½ months after the January 31, 1994 year-end.

On the other hand, if Alpha makes the election, it may deduct $8,333 ($100,000 × $\frac{1}{12}$) in its fiscal year that ends January 31, 1994, and $91,667 ($100,000 × $\frac{11}{12}$) in its fiscal year that ends January 31, 1995.

If the taxes are due and paid on September 30, 1994, Alpha would be better off not making the ratable accrual election. In this case, the recurring item exception applies because the payment is made within 8½ months of Alpha's 1994 fiscal year-end. Thus, if Beta does not make the election all of the $100,000 is deductible in the fiscal year ending on January 31, 1994. ■

The rules for determining when an expense is deductible are presented in Topic Review 6-1.

CRITERIA FOR DEDUCTING BUSINESS AND INVESTMENT EXPENSES

OBJECTIVE 3

Discuss the criteria for deducting business and investment expenses

For expenditures to be deductible as business or investment expenses, they must be:

- Related to a profit-motivated activity of the taxpayer (i.e., a business or investment activity rather than a personal expenditure)
- Ordinary
- Necessary

TOPIC REVIEW 6-1

When an Expense Is Deductible

Cash Method: Deductible When Paid

Payment Is Made When

- Cash or other property is transferred.
- A check is delivered or mailed.
- An item is charged on a credit card.

Note: A mere promise to pay or delivery of a note payable is not considered payment.

Prepaid Expenses

- Generally are deductible over the period covered.
- Deductible when paid if the period covered does not exceed one year.
- Generally prepaid interest is deductible over the period covered by the loan.
- Points are deductible when paid if:
—The loan is used to purchase or improve the taxpayer's principal residence.
—The loan is secured by the residence.
—Points are established business practice.
—The points are not in excess of the amount generally charged.
—For points paid to purchase a principal residence, the closing agreement must clearly designate the amounts as points and the amount must be computed as a percentage of the amount borrowed.

Accrual Method: Deductible When Accrued

In General

- The accrual method must be used for inventories.
- Accrual occurs only when both all-events test and economic performance have been met.

All-Events Test

- The existence of a liability is established and
- The amount of the liability is determined.

Economic Performance

- When economic performance is deemed to occur depends upon the transaction involved (see Table 6-1).
- May be deemed to occur in the year the all-events test is met if all of the following tests are met:
—Actual economic performance occurs within the shorter of:
    8½ months after taxable year or a reasonable period after the taxable year.
—The expense is recurring and is treated consistently from year to year.
—Either:
    The item is immaterial or
    Deducting the expense in the year the all-events test is met results in a more proper matching of income and deductions.

- Reasonable in amount
- Properly documented
- An expense of the taxpayer (not someone else's expense)

Additionally, an expenditure is not deductible if it is

- a capital expenditure
- related to tax exempt income
- illegal or in violation of public policy
- specifically disallowed by the tax law

Business or Investment Requirement

Additional Comment

A sole proprietor, when asked what his firm did, replied that they filled out tax returns and other government forms and ran a jewelry store on the side.

As previously explained, except for a relatively few personal expenses, all deductible expenditures or losses must be incurred in a profit-motivated activity. For individuals, most of these expenses are deductible either under Sec. 162 as an expense incurred in a trade or business or under Sec. 212 as an expense incurred for the production of income or for the maintenance and conservation of income-producing property. Thus, this requirement is really two-pronged: (1) a determination whether an expenditure is incurred in an activity engaged in for profit, and (2) a distinction between a trade or business and an investment activity.

Activity Engaged in for Profit. This first part of the test classifies the expense as having been incurred in either a profit-motivated activity or a personal activity.

Example 6-16 ■

Stacy is a dentist whose practice employs three full-time and four part-time employees. The business is a sole proprietorship. Stacy also employs an individual who works as a domestic worker in her personal residence. The payment of salaries to Stacy's employees in her dental practice constitutes a deductible business expense. The payment of the salary to the housekeeper is a personal expense and is not deductible. ■

Real World Example

A taxpayer attempted to deduct treasure hunting costs as a business expense, but the court concluded that there was no profit motive. The taxpayer kept no business records, the time spent was negligible and appeared to be recreational in nature, and no income was produced from the activity. William J. Hezel, 1985 PH T.C. Memo ¶ 85,010, 49 TCM 458.

Categorizing expenses can be quite difficult in some cases. For example, when does a personal activity such as the hobby of coin collecting become profit-motivated? No single objective test is available. Rather, one must examine all the facts and circumstances surrounding the activity in which the expense is incurred. The Regulations list several factors that must be examined, including the following:

- Whether the taxpayer conducts the activity in a businesslike manner
- The expertise of the taxpayer or the taxpayer's advisors
- The time and effort expended by the taxpayer in carrying on the activity
- Whether the assets used in the activity are expected to appreciate in value
- The taxpayer's success in carrying on other similar activities
- The taxpayer's history of income or losses with respect to the activity
- The amount of occasional profits, if any, that are earned
- The taxpayer's financial status
- Any elements of personal pleasure or recreation which the activity might involve[22]

Additional Comment

Many of the court cases dealing with profit motive under Sec. 183 are ranch and farm cases. In fact, Sec. 183, now titled "Activities Not Engaged In For Profit" was originally titled "Farm Losses, etc." in the Tax Reform Act of 1969.

[22] Reg. Sec. 1.183-2(b).

None of these factors is determinative. In fact, the Regulations state that other factors not listed may also be taken into consideration. Furthermore, a determination is not made by merely counting the number of factors that are present. Instead, the decision depends upon an examination of all the factors together. The IRS can, therefore, make the decision on a more subjective basis than the taxpayer might like. If the IRS asserts that an activity is a personal one (i.e., a hobby) rather than a business or investment, the burden of proof rests on the taxpayer to prove otherwise.

Example 6-17 ■

Paula, a successful businesswoman with an annual income of $200,000, enjoys raising and training quarter horses. She generally spends 5 to 6 hours each week training, showing, or racing the horses. Over the last 4 years her winnings from shows and races have amounted to $16,000. Over that same period, an additional $8,000 of income has been generated from stud fees and the sale of colts. Frequently the horses are used to take Paula's family or friends riding. In addition, Paula often participates in equestrian clinics and demonstrations for 4-H clubs and other similar groups. A high school student is employed to feed the horses each day and to clean the stalls weekly. A professional horse trainer is hired for 4 hours each week to help Paula train the horses.

In this case, several factors such as the level of earnings, the hiring of professional help, and the amount of time spent in the activity might indicate that Paula is engaged in a business. Other factors however, such as the time spent riding with family and friends, the voluntary clinics and demonstrations, and the small amount of revenue generated as compared with Paula's other income, support the position that Paula merely has a hobby of raising horses. ■

Historical Note

Before the Tax Reform Act of 1986, an activity was presumed to be one engaged in for profit if it showed a profit for any 2 years during a consecutive 5-year period.

In cases where a clear profit motive cannot be shown under the factors mentioned above, the Code provides a test whereby an activity may be presumed to be one engaged in for profit. This presumption is rebuttable (i.e., if the taxpayer meets the test, the burden of proof is upon the IRS to show that the activity *is not* profit motivated). Otherwise, the taxpayer would be required to prove that the activity *is* profit- motivated. This test is met if the activity shows a profit for any 3 years during a consecutive 5-year period. The 5-year period consists of the year in question plus the previous 4 years.[23]

Example 6-18 ■

Lorenzo, a stockbroker, enjoys raising and breeding pedigreed poodles. Although this activity is used for recreation and relaxation after work, Lorenzo periodically sells some of his poodles. Lorenzo reports $850 in income and $2,900 in expenses from the activity on his 1994 tax return. Upon auditing Lorenzo's 1994 return, the IRS disallowed the expenses in excess of the income, arguing that the activity is a hobby rather than a business or investment. If he can prove that a profit was realized from the poodle-raising operation for any 3 years from 1990 through 1994 inclusive, the presumption will be made that the poodles are raised for a profit and not for recreation. The burden of proof is then upon the IRS to show that the activity is really a hobby. If Lorenzo cannot show a profit for 3 years out of the 5-year period, he would have to rely upon the factors mentioned in the Regulations to convince the IRS and/or the courts that the activity is a business. ■

Typical Misconception

When an activity is determined to be a hobby, it is sometimes erroneously concluded that none of the hobby expenses are deductible. Section 183(b) permits the deduction of hobby losses as miscellaneous itemized deductions up to the amount of income even though the expenses are not actually incurred in connection with a business.

If the activity is determined to be a business, the taxpayer may deduct all qualified business expenses from the gross income, even if a net loss results.[24] However, if the

---

[23] Sec. 183(d). If the major part of the activity involves breeding, training, showing, or racing horses, the 5-year period is extended to a 7-year period, and a profit must be shown in only 2, rather than 3, of the years covered by that 7-year period.

[24] If the activity is a passive activity, the loss may be suspended. See Chapter 8 for a discussion of the passive loss rules.

activity is determined to be a hobby, the expenses are deductible as a miscellaneous itemized deduction but only to the extent of the gross income from the activity. A net loss may not be reported from the activity if it is a hobby. Furthermore, the expenses must be deducted in a predetermined order. (See the section entitled Special Disallowance Rules in this chapter for a discussion of these hobby loss rules.)

Example 6-19 ■

Assume the same facts as in Example 6-18, except that Lorenzo's poodle-raising activity is determined to be a business. For 1994, Lorenzo would report a net loss of $2,050 ($2,900 expenses − $850 income), assuming the loss is not incurred in a passive activity (see Chapter 8). If the activity is determined to be a hobby, however, Lorenzo may deduct only $850 of the expenses (up to the amount of the gross income) as an itemized deduction. These expenses must be deducted in a certain order. The remaining expenses are not allowed as tax deductions. ■

Trade or Business versus Investment Classification. The second part of the general profit-motive test is the determination of whether a particular activity is a trade or business of the taxpayer or is only an investment. This distinction is important for several reasons. First, a loss upon the sale of the assets used in the activity may be an ordinary loss if the activity is a trade or business.[25] If it is an investment activity, however, the loss is a capital loss.[26] Second, this distinction may control whether an expense of the activity is a deduction *for* AGI or a deduction *from* AGI. In general, expenses incurred in a trade or business are deductions *for* AGI.

Example 6-20 ■

Additional Comment

Hobby expenses are subject to the 2% of AGI limitation on miscellaneous itemized deductions. However, if the expense is one that is deductible whether or not incurred in an income producing activity, it is fully deductible.

Robin is a self-employed financial consultant. She meets daily with a variety of clients to discuss their investments. Since she must keep abreast of the latest market quotes and strategies, Robin subscribes to several trade publications, newsletters, and quote services. The expenses incurred for these services are deductions *for* AGI, since they are incurred in Robin's consulting business. ■

On the other hand, most expenses incurred in an investment activity rather than a business are miscellaneous itemized deductions *from* AGI and are deductible only to the extent they exceed 2% of AGI (see Chapter 7).[27]

Example 6-21 ■

Additional Comment

A trade or business is an activity in which there is a profit motive and where there is some type of economic activity involved. An investment activity requires a profit motive but does not require economic activity.

Steve is a wealthy attorney who invests in the stock market and keeps abreast of the latest market quotes and strategies by subscribing to several trade publications and newsletters. Steve generally spends a few hours each day studying this information and analyzing his portfolio. These subscription expenses are deductions *from* AGI since they are incurred in an investment (rather than a business) activity and do not relate to the production of rents and royalties. The deductibility of such amounts depends upon whether Steve's total miscellaneous itemized deductions exceed 2% of his AGI and whether Steve itemizes his deductions instead of using the standard deduction. ■

Finally, each year taxpayers may currently deduct up to $17,500 of tangible personal property purchased during the year for use in a trade or business, while the same expenditures must be capitalized and depreciated over several years if they are incurred in an investment activity. (See Chapter 10 for a discussion of the Sec. 179 current deduction for capital expenditures.)

---

[25] Under Sec. 1231, the exact treatment depends upon the total gains and losses from such property for the year. See Chapter 13 for a discussion of Sec. 1231.

[26] As explained in Chapter 5, the tax treatment of an ordinary loss differs significantly from the tax treatment of a capital loss.

[27] However, expenses of an investment activity that produce rents or royalties are deductions *for* AGI. See Sec. 62(a)(4).

Example 6-22 ■

Assume the same facts as in Examples 6-20 and 6-21. In addition, assume that during the current year both Robin and Steve spend $4,000 for computers to be used in their business or investment activity. Since Robin is engaged in a business, the $4,000 may be deducted under Sec. 179 in the current year. Since Steve is engaged in an investment activity rather than a business, the $4,000 must be capitalized and depreciated.

■

In spite of these important differences in treatment, the distinction between an investment activity and a trade or business is not always easily made. Neither the Code nor the Regulations provide a precise definition of what constitutes a trade or business. Some guidelines may be found in judicial law. In one of the first cases dealing with the issue, the Supreme Court stated that the carrying on of a trade or business involves "holding one's self out to others as engaged in the selling of goods or services."[28]

Later, in another case the Supreme Court emphasized the fact that one must examine all the surrounding facts and circumstances in order to determine the underlying nature of an activity. In that case, the taxpayer owned a large portfolio of stocks, bonds, and real estate. The taxpayer's holdings were so large that he rented offices and hired employees to help him manage the properties. The Court, however, regarded these activities as investment activities despite the size of the holdings and the amount of work and effort involved because the taxpayer merely kept records and collected interest and dividends from his securities.[29] Other cases, however, indicate that a taxpayer who invests in stocks and bonds may be considered to be in a business if the securities are frequently bought and sold in order to make a short-term profit on the daily swings in the market.[30]

Ordinary Expense

To be deductible, a business or investment expense must be **ordinary**. Although the Code does not provide either a definition or an application of this requirement, the Regulations under Sec. 212 indicate that for an expense to be ordinary it must be reasonable in amount and it must bear a reasonable and proximate relationship to the income-producing activity or property.[31] This means that there must be more than a remote connection between the expense and the anticipated income. It does not mean that the property must be producing income currently.

Example 6-23 ■

During the current year, Ahmed purchases a plot of land and an old vacant warehouse. Ahmed anticipates making a long-run profit from the investment because the value of the land is expected to appreciate eventually due to commercial development in the area. To help cover the costs of holding the property, Ahmed plans to rent storage space in the warehouse. During the current year, the following expenses are incurred, although Ahmed is unable to rent the warehouse:

Key Point

Whether an expense can be considered ordinary is sometimes very subjective. For example, Supreme Court Justice Cardozo in 1933 in Thomas H. Welch v. Helvering, 12 AFTR 808, 40-1 USTC ¶ 9161 (USSC, 1940) stated that, "The standard set up by the statute is not a rule of law; it is a way of life. Life in all its fullness must supply the answer to the riddle."

---

[28] *Deputy v. Pierre S. DuPont,* 23 AFTR 808, 40-1 USTC ¶ 9161 (USSC, 1940).
[29] *Eugene Higgins v. CIR,* 25 AFTR 1160, 41-1 USTC ¶ 9233 (USSC, 1941).
[30] *Walter K. Liang,* 23 T.C. 1040 (1955). See also *Ralph E. Purvis v. CIR,* 37 AFTR 2d 76-968, 76-1 USTC ¶ 9270 (9th Cir., 1976); and *Samuel B. Levin v. U.S.,* 43 AFTR 2d 79-612, 79-1 USTC ¶ 9331 (ct. Cls., 1979).
[31] Reg. Sec. 1.212-1(d).

Additional Comment

For 1988, an estimated 1.7 million individuals having self-employment income failed to file their income tax returns with the IRS. Several construction trades, including carpenters, painters, paperhangers, and plasterers, comprised the largest occupation group of self-employed nonfilers.

Expenses	Amount
Property taxes	$1,000
Interest	4,000
Insurance	800
Utilities	200

All of these expenses qualify as ordinary and are deductible under Sec. 212 because they bear a reasonable and proximate relationship to the income that Ahmed hopes to obtain, even though there is no income generated from the property during the year.[32] ∎

The Supreme Court has ruled that for an expense to be ordinary it must be customary or usual in the context of a particular industry or business community.[33] Thus, an expenditure may be ordinary in the context of one type of business, but not in the context of another.[34]

Example 6-24 ∎ For many years, Hank has been an officer in Green Corporation, which is engaged in the grain business. Green Corporation purchases its grain from various suppliers. Last year, Green Corporation went bankrupt and was relieved from having to pay off its debts to its suppliers. In the current year, Hank enters into a contract to act as a commissioned agent to purchase grain for Green Corporation. To reestablish a relationship with suppliers whom Hank knew previously, Hank decides to pay off as many of Green Corporation's debts as he can. Hank is under no legal obligation to do so. These payments made by Hank are *not* ordinary. Rather, they are extraordinary expenditures made for goodwill to establish Hank in a new trade or business, and they must be capitalized.[35] ∎

An expense may be ordinary with respect to a particular taxpayer, even though that taxpayer encounters it only once.[36]

Example 6-25 ∎ For several years, Donna has been engaged in the business of making and selling false teeth. Most of the advertisements, orders, and deliveries of the teeth are done through the mail. During the current year, the post office judged that some of the advertisements are false. As a result, a fraud order is issued under which the post office stamps "Fraudulent" on all letters addressed to Donna, and then returns them to the senders. In an unsuccessful suit to prevent the post office from continuing, Donna expends $25,000 in lawyer's fees. These fees are ordinary business expenses, since they are incurred in an action that normally or ordinarily would be taken under the circumstances.[37] ∎

The Supreme Court has also indicated that the term *ordinary* as used in this context refers to an expenditure that is currently deductible rather than an expenditure that must be capitalized.[38]

---

[32] However, they might not all be deductible in the current year because of the passive loss limitations explained in Chapter 8.
[33] *Thomas H. Welch v. Helvering,* 12 AFTR 1456, 3 USTC ¶ 1164 (USSC, 1933).
[34] *Deputy* v. *Pierre S. DuPont,* 23 AFTR 808, 40-1 USTC ¶ 9161 (USSC, 1940).
[35] *Thomas H. Welch v. Helvering,* 12 AFTR 1456, 3 USTC ¶ 1164 (USSC, 1933).
[36] *Deputy* v. *Pierre S. DuPont,* 23 AFTR 808, 40-1 USTC ¶ 9161 (USSC, 1940).
[37] *CIR* v. *S. B. Heininger,* 31 AFTR 783, 44-1 USTC ¶ 9109 (USSC, 1943).
[38] Ibid. See also *CIR v. Walter F. Tellier,* 17 AFTR 2d 633, 66-1 USTC ¶ 9319 (USSC, 1966).

Real World Example

Payments made by a corporation to an individual who was a 50% shareholder were necessary in order to prevent him from interfering in the management of the business and from damaging the corporation's reputation. Fairmont Homes, Inc., 1983 PH T.C. Memo ¶ 83,209, 45 TCM 1340.

Necessary Expense

In addition to being ordinary, a deductible investment or business expense must also be **necessary.** The Supreme Court has indicated that an expense is considered necessary if it is "appropriate and helpful" in the taxpayer's business.[39] To meet this appropriate or helpful standard, an expenditure need not be necessary in the sense that it is indispensable. Rather, the test seems to be whether a reasonable or prudent businessperson would incur the same expenditure under similar circumstances.

Example 6-26 ■

The expenditures in Example 6-24 (the payment of debts from a former business) and Example 6-25 (the payment of legal fees) are both necessary because they are appropriate and helpful in each case. However, the expenditure in Example 6-24 is not ordinary and, therefore, is not deductible. The expenditure in Example 6-25 is deductible because it meets both tests. ■

Reasonable Expense

Real World Example

Salary paid to a corporate officer, who was the son of the controlling stockholder, was found to be unreasonable in view of his age, lack of qualifications, and executive experience. Transport Manufacturing & Equipment Co. v. CIR, 26 AFTR2d 70-5556, 70-2 USTC ¶ 9627 (8th Cir., 1970).

Section 162 states that only *reasonable* amounts paid for salaries are deductible. The Regulations under Sec. 212, however, imply that for any expense to be ordinary and necessary it must be reasonable in amount.[40] Problems with meeting this standard generally arise in the context of salaries being paid to an individual who is both a shareholder and an employee in a closely held business. In a typical situation, a controlling shareholder of a corporation receives a payment, characterized as salary, that the IRS asserts is too large for the services rendered.

Example 6-27 ■

Brian, the controlling shareholder of Central Corporation, receives an annual salary of $250,000 from the corporation. Based upon several factors, such as the size of Central Corporation's total operations and a comparison of salary received by officers of comparably sized corporations, the IRS contends that Brian's salary should be no higher than $150,000. If Central successfully defends the $250,000 salary, the corporation is able to deduct the full amount as salary expense. But if the defense is not successful, the excess $100,000 is considered a dividend to the extent of earnings and profits, and no deduction is available to Central Corporation for this amount. In either event, Brian must take the full $250,000 into income. (See the section entitled Tax Planning Considerations in this chapter for a discussion of the use of a payback agreement in these situations.) ■

In an attempt to link executive compensation to productivity and business performance and to discourage a common practice of increasing executive compensation despite declines in business performance, Congress enacted tax legislation which disallows a deduction for certain employee compensation that exceeds a yearly amount of $1 million. These are amounts payable by a publicly-held corporation to the corporation's chief executive officer and its four highest compensated officers for the taxable year.[41]

The tests for determining whether an expense is deductible are highlighted in Topic Review 6-2.

Additional Comment

The determination of which costs should be considered as capital expenditures is not influenced by the property's use. For example, both the cost of a new addition to a personal residence and the cost of an improvement made to a business machine would have to be capitalized.

---

[39] *Thomas H. Welch v. Helvering,* 12 AFTR 1456, 3 USTC ¶ 1164 (USSC, 1933).

[40] Reg. Sec. 1.212-1(d). See also CIR v. *Lincoln Electric Co.,* 38 AFTR 411, 49-2 USTC ¶ 9388 (6th Cir., 1949).

[41] Sec. 162(m). Compensation based upon commissions or other performance goals is not subject to this limitation.

TOPIC REVIEW 6-2

Tests for Deductibility as a Business or Investment Expense	
Test	Application
Ordinary	1. Based on the facts and circumstances. 2. Reasonable and proximate relationship to the activity. 3. Customary or usual in context of the industry. 4. May be encountered by the taxpayer only once.
Necessary	1. Based on the facts and circumstances. 2. Appropriate and helpful. 3. Need not be indispensable. 4. Would a reasonable or prudent businessperson incur the same expense?
Reasonable	1. Based on the facts and circumstances. 2. Applies to all business and investment expenses. 3. Compensation paid to an owner-employee of a small corporation is the most frequently contested area. 4. Compensation in excess of $1 million payable by a publicly-held corporation to its key executives may not be deductible.

Capitalization Versus Expense Deduction

General Capitalization Requirements. Under Sec. 263, current deductions may not be taken for capital expenditures. Generally, expenses that add to the value of, substantially prolong the useful life of, or adapt the property to a new or different use are considered **capital expenditures** and are not currently deductible.[42] Thus, capital expenditures include the cost of acquiring or constructing buildings, machinery, equipment, furniture, and any similar property that has a useful life that extends substantially beyond the end of the tax year.[43] The cost of goodwill purchased in connection with the acquisition of the assets of a going concern is also a capital expenditure.[44]

Some capital assets, such as buildings, machinery, equipment, furniture, and fixtures, and purchased goodwill are depreciable or amortizable and may provide deductions that are spread over more than one tax year. Others, such as land, stock or partnership interests, are neither depreciable nor amortizable. With regard to these assets, the taxpayer must wait until the asset is sold or disposed of to recover the cost.

Maintenance and repair expenditures that only keep an asset in "an ordinarily efficient operating condition . . ." are deductible expenses if they do not increase the value or prolong the useful life of the asset.[45] Distinguishing between a currently

---

[42] Reg. Sec. 1.263(a)-1(b). Capital expenditures are generally subject to amortization or depreciation.

[43] Reg. Sec. 1.263(a)-2(a).

[44] Reg. Sec. 1.263(a)-2(h). See also *Indopco, Inc., v. CIR,* 69 AFTR 2d 92-694, 92-1 USTC ¶ 50,113 (USSC., 1992), where expenses incurred by a corporation that was the target of a "friendly" takeover were held to be non-deductible capital expenditures because they provided long-term benefits to the corporation. In this case, the Supreme Court held that these long-term benefits do not need to be associated with a specific identifiable asset.

[45] Reg. Sec. 1.162-4.

deductible expenditure and a capital expenditure can be difficult because expenditures for normal maintenance and repair can, at times, cost more than a capital improvement.[46] Normal maintenance and repair may also increase the value of an asset. For example, in one Tax Court case, expenditures incurred in replacing support beams and floor joists to shore up a sagging floor were held to be deductible while the cost of placing a new floor over an old one was held to be a capital expenditure.[47] It is, therefore, necessary to examine all of the facts and circumstances to determine whether the expenditures constitute part of an overall plan of improvement or a change in use of the asset.

Additional Comment

Some provisions permit taxpayers to depreciate or amortize capital expenditures over a relatively short period of time. For example, there is a rapid write-off available for pollution control facilities under Sec. 169 and for organization costs of corporations under Sec. 248.

Election to Deduct Currently. A few elections exist that allow a current deduction for certain capital expenditures. Taxpayers often prefer a current deduction over capitalizing and depreciating an asset because of the time value of money. Some expenditures that taxpayers may elect to deduct currently include:

- Cost of fertilizers incurred by farmers[48]
- Cost of soil and water conservation incurred by farmers[49]
- Intangible drilling costs incurred in drilling oil and gas wells[50]
- Costs for tertiary injectants[51]
- Costs for certain mining development projects[52]
- Costs incurred to remove architectural and transportation barriers to the handicapped and elderly[53]
- Costs for certain qualified research and development projects[54]

Taxpayers may also elect to deduct up to $17,500 each year for the purchase of qualified tangible personal property used in a trade or business. (This deduction and the deduction for qualified research and development expenditures will be examined in more detail in Chapter 10.)

Real World Example

The cost of maintenance and upkeep on unimproved and unproductive real estate does not qualify as carrying charges eligible for capitalization. Rev. Rul. 71-475, 1971-2 C.B. 304.

Capitalization of Deduction Items. The exceptions mentioned above provide a current deduction for expenditures that are normally capital in nature. Section 266 provides for the capitalization of certain expenses that normally are deductible. Section 266 is elective and applies to the following items:

- Annual property taxes, interest on a mortgage, and other carrying charges incurred on unimproved and unproductive real estate.
- Annual property taxes, interest, employment taxes, and other necessary expenses incurred for the development, improvement, or construction of real property, up to the time the development or construction is completed. For these expenses to be capitalized, the real property may be either improved or unimproved, productive or unproductive.
- Interest, and employment taxes incurred in transporting and installing personalty (as opposed to realty) up to the time when the property is first put into use by the taxpayer.

---

[46] *M. A. Stoeltzing, et al. v. CIR*, 3 AFTR 2d ¶ 1412, 59-1 USTC ¶ 9444 (3rd Cir., 1959).
[47] *Standard Fruit Product Co.*, 1949 PH T.C. Memo ¶ 49,207, 8 TCM 733.
[48] Sec. 180.
[49] Sec. 175.
[50] Sec. 263(c).
[51] Sec. 193.
[52] Sec. 616.
[53] Sec. 190.
[54] Sec. 174.

Example 6-28 ■	During 1994 and 1995, Nancy pays property taxes of $5,000 on a piece of land. During 1994 the land is vacant and unproductive. In 1995, Nancy uses the land as a parking lot, generating $7,000 in income. Nancy may elect to capitalize the taxes in 1994 because the property is both unimproved and unproductive. In 1995, however, the land is productive, and Nancy may not elect to capitalize the taxes. Since the expenses relate to the production of rental income, they are deductible *for* AGI.■

A new election to capitalize the expenses on unimproved and unproductive real estate must be made each year.

Example 6-29 ■	Assume the facts as in Example 6-28 except that the land remains unproductive during 1995. Nancy can elect to capitalize the taxes paid in 1995. However, the election need not be made for 1995 merely because it is made in 1994. ■

An election to capitalize the other expenses incurred during the development or construction period remains in effect for that year and for all subsequent years until the end of the period. However, the election may be made on each new project separately.

Example 6-30 ■	During the current year, Paul begins construction on an office building and a hotel. Paul incurs $20,000 in property taxes in constructing the office building and $12,000 in building the hotel. The election to capitalize the taxes on the office building does not bind Paul to make the same election with respect to the taxes on the hotel. ■

If a taxpayer elects to capitalize this type of expense under Sec. 266, it is added to the basis of the property to which it pertains. If the property is depreciable, a deduction is received for the expenses as the property is depreciated. Taxpayers are motivated to make this election if they have large NOL carryovers, or if they expect to be in a much higher tax rate in future years and thus feel that the benefit of the deduction is greater in the future.

Section 263A also requires certain taxpayers to capitalize certain costs into inventory instead of taking a current deduction. (See Chapters 10 and 11 for a discussion of inventories.)

Expenses Related to Exempt Income

Under Sec. 265, no deduction is allowed for any expense allocated or related to tax-exempt income. The purpose for this disallowance is to prevent a double tax benefit to the taxpayer. The following examples illustrate different types of income that are excluded from taxation and the tax consequences arising from related or allocable expenses.

Example 6-31 ■	Rich, a CPA, is self-employed. During the current year, Rich spends $1,200 for tuition, books, and fees for courses that help him meet the state's continuing education requirements. These items generally meet the requirements for deduction as education expenses. However, because Rich is a qualified veteran, he receives educational assistant payments of $1,000 from the Veterans Administration. These payments are properly excluded from Rich's taxable income. Since $1,000 of the education expenses are allocable to the exempt income, Rich's deduction is limited to $200 ($1,200 − $1,000).[55] ■

[55] Rev. Rul. 83-3, 1983-1 C.B. 72.

Example 6-32 ■

Sarah is a self-employed engineering consultant. During the current year, she wins a contract that requires her to work in a foreign country for an extended period of time. Her income attributable to her foreign work is $60,000. During the year she also incurs deductible expenses of $2,500, which are allocable to her foreign income. For the year, Sarah is entitled to exclude (subject to the applicable limits) all of her $60,000 foreign-earned income in computing her U.S. taxable income due to the availability of the foreign-earned income exclusion (discussed in Chapter 4). Since her entire $60,000 of foreign-earned income is excluded from income, Sarah may not deduct any of the $2,500 in expenses. ■

In some cases taxpayers could actually generate a positive cash flow on a transaction that is otherwise economically unsound if a deduction was allowed for an expense that is allocated or related to tax-exempt income.

Section 265 specifically disallows interest expense on debt the taxpayer incurs in order to purchase or carry tax-exempt securities.[56] Thus, the disallowance depends upon the taxpayer's intended use of the loan proceeds.[57] Intent is generally determined by an examination of all the facts and circumstances surrounding the transaction. Intent to carry the tax-exempt securities can be shown if the tax-exempt securities are used as collateral in securing a loan.[58] If an individual who holds tax-exempt securities later incurs some debt, no disallowance will occur if the debt is incurred to finance personal items (e.g., a mortgage on a personal residence).[59] If, however, the debt is incurred to finance an investment, a portion of the interest is generally disallowed.[60] Even though the interest is not incurred to carry tax-exempt securities, it still may not be deductible. For example, if interest is incurred on personal debt, it is not deductible. (See Chapter 7 for a discussion of limitations upon the deductibility of personal interest.)

Example 6-33 ■

Sam, an individual, has invested $80,000 in Gold Corporation stock, $120,000 in real estate, and $50,000 in tax-exempt municipal bonds. During the current year, Sam borrows $70,000 for the purpose of investing in a limited partnership. For the year, he pays $6,000 interest on the loan. Under these circumstances, the IRS will presume that Sam has incurred a portion of the debt in order to carry the tax-exempt securities and will disallow a portion of the deduction. Sam may overcome that presumption if he can show that he could not have sold the tax-exempt securities. According to the IRS, however, this presumption cannot be overcome if Sam can only show that the sale of the bonds would have resulted in a loss.[61] If Sam instead borrowed the money to purchase a personal residence, the IRS probably would not attempt to disallow the deduction.[62] (See Chapter 7 for a discussion of restrictions upon the deductibility of interest for personal residences.) ■

Expenditures That Are Contrary to Public Policy

Certain expenditures, even though incurred in a profit-motivated activity, may not be deductible if the payment itself is illegal or if the payment is a penalty or fine resulting

---

[56] Sec. 265(a)(2).
[57] Rev. Proc. 72-18, 1972-1 C.B. 740.
[58] *Wisconsin Cheeseman, Inc. v. U.S.*, 21 AFTR 2d 383, 68-1 USTC ¶ 9145 (7th Cir., 1968).
[59] Rev. Proc. 72-18, 1972-1 C.B. 740.
[60] Ibid.
[61] Ibid.
[62] Ibid.

Real World Example

A subcontractor involved with the construction of a new shopping mall made kickbacks to the supervisor of the primary contractor. The kickbacks were deductible since they were not illegal, and the kickbacks were also ordinary and necessary since the subcontractor would not have been able to continue to work if the kickbacks had not been made. Raymond Bertolini Trucking Co., v. CIR, 54 AFTR 2d 84-5413, 1984-2 USTC ¶ 9591 (6th Cir., 1984).

from an illegal act. These nondeductible expenses generally fall within one of the five following categories:

- Illegal payments to government officials or employees
- Other illegal payments
- Kickbacks, rebates, and bribes under Medicare and Medicaid
- Payments of fines and penalties
- Payment of treble damages under the federal antitrust laws

Bribes and Kickbacks. Under Sec. 162(c)(1), any illegal bribe or kickback made to any government official or employee is not deductible. This applies to payments made to

- Federal officials and employees
- State, local, and foreign government officials and employees
- Officials and employees of an agency of a government

Example 6-34 ■ During February of the current year, Road Corporation enters into a contract with the State of Iowa to construct a 5-mile stretch of a new highway. Under the terms of the contract, the project is to be completed by October 22 of the current year. If it is not completed and accepted by Iowa on or before that date, Road Corporation will be subject to a fine of $5,000 per day for every day after that date until the project is accepted. By October 20, the project foreman realizes that the company will not make the deadline if it complies with all the requirements imposed by the state inspector assigned to the project. To avoid the fine, the foreman arranges for the inspector to "look the other way" on several of the requirements in exchange for a payment of $8,000. Since this payment constitutes an illegal bribe to a government official, the payment is not deductible. ■

Additional Comment

Illegal price rebates made by the seller directly to the purchaser can be subtracted from gross sales to calculate gross income.

In the case of illegal payments to officials or employees of a foreign government, no deduction is allowed if the payment is unlawful under the Foreign Corrupt Practices Act of 1977. In all cases, the burden rests on the government to prove the illegality of the payment.

Illegal bribes, kickbacks, and other illegal payments made to persons other than a government official or employee are nondeductible if they are illegal under a federal law that subjects the payor to a criminal penalty or loss of the privilege of doing business. In addition, illegal payments under a state law imposing the same penalties are nondeductible if the state law is generally enforced.[63] Here, the definition of a kickback includes a payment for referring a client, patient, or customer.[64]

Example 6-35 ■ Queen Corporation is engaged in the ship repair business. It is Queen's practice to kick back approximately 10% of any repair bill to the captain and chief engineer of a foreign-owned ship. Such payments are illegal under state law and could cause Queen to lose its license. The state law is generally enforced. Queen Corporation may not take any deduction for these payments, regardless of whether Queen Corporation is prosecuted by the state.[65] ■

[63] Sec. 162(c)(2).
[64] Ibid.
[65] Reg. Sec. 1.162-18(b)(5).

The courts and the IRS have made a distinction between an illegal nondeductible kickback and an illegal rebate of the purchase price. If the rebate is made directly to the purchaser by the seller, it is considered an adjustment to the selling price and, as such, is an *exclusion* (rather than a deduction) from gross income.[66] The distinction between the two payments seems to be that the rebate is actually negotiated as part of the selling price.

Section 162(c)(3) specifically disallows a deduction for any kickback, rebate, or bribe under Medicare and Medicaid. These include payments made by physicians or suppliers and providers of goods and services who receive payment under the Social Security Act or a federally funded state plan. Unlike the other two types of payments mentioned above, these payments need not be illegal under federal or state law.

Fines and Penalties. The Code also disallows a deduction for the payment of any fine or penalty paid to a government because of the violation of a law.[67]

Example 6-36 ■

Tim owns a semitrailer truck that is used in Tim's freight-hauling business. To increase the profitability of a particular run, Tim often loads his truck in excess of the allowable weight limit. During the current year, Tim pays $600 in fines to various states because the truck is found to be overweight. Tim may not deduct the $600 in fines since the payments are made because of the violation of state law. ■

The tax law also disallows a deduction for two-thirds of any payment for damages that is made as a result of a conviction (or a guilty or no contest plea) in an action regarding a criminal violation of the federal antitrust laws.[68]

Example 6-37 ■

Ethical Point

A CPA discovers that a client had included fines and penalties in a miscellaneous expense section of a previously filed tax return. The CPA should recommend the filing of an amended return. However, the CPA is not obligated to inform the IRS, and the CPA may not do so without the client's permission, except where required by law.

During the current year, the United States files criminal and civil actions against Allen, the president of Able Corporation, and Betty, the president of Bell Corporation, for conspiring to fix and maintain prices of electrical transformers. Both Allen and Betty enter pleas of no contest, and the appropriate judgments are entered. Subsequent to this action, Circle Corporation sues both Able and Bell Corporations for treble damages of $300,000. In settlement, Able and Bell Corporations each pay Circle Corporation $75,000 in full settlement. The maximum that Able and Bell Corporations may each deduct is limited to $25,000 ($75,000 ÷ 3). ■

Expenses Relating to an Illegal Activity. Interestingly, although the payment of an illegal bribe or kickback and the payment of a fine or penalty as the result of an illegal act are both nondeductible, expenses incurred in an illegal activity are generally deductible if they are ordinary, necessary, and reasonable.[69]

Example 6-38 ■

Typical Misconception

Occasionally it is mistakenly believed that ordinary and necessary expenses incurred in carrying on an illegal activity are not deductible.

Fred owns and operates a small financial services business involved in the sale of securities and the lending of money. Fred often sells securities to customers in other states. However, since the business is not registered with the appropriate state or federal authorities, the operation of the business is illegal. During the current year, Fred incurs the following expenses:

[66] Rev. Rul. 82-149, 1982-2 C.B. 56.
[67] Sec. 162(f).
[68] Sec. 162(g).
[69] *CIR v. Neil Sullivan, et al.,* 1 AFTR 2d 1158, 58-1 USTC ¶ 9368 (USSC, 1958).

Interest	$ 20,000
Salaries	140,000
Depreciation	7,000
Printing	5,000
Bribe to employee of state securities commission	12,000
Total	$184,000

Fred's deductible expenses for the year total $172,000. The illegal payment of $12,000 to the government employee is not deductible. ∎

There is one exception to this general rule. Under Sec. 280E, expenses incurred in an illegal business of trafficking or dealing in drugs are not deductible.[70]

Legal and Accounting Fees. Legal and accounting fees are generally deductible if they are incurred in the regular conduct of a trade or business or for the production of income. Fees incurred for the determination, collection, or refund of any tax are also deductible. As mentioned previously, trade or business expenses and expenses incurred in producing rents and royalties are deductible **for** AGI. Likewise, fees paid for the determination, collection, or refund of any tax are deductible **for** AGI if they are allocable to the taxpayer's trade or business or to the production of rents and royalties. These expenses include fees paid to prepare a taxpayer's Schedule C (Profit or Loss from Business), Part I of Schedule E (Supplemental Income and Loss which is used to report rental and royalty income), and Schedule F (farm income and expenses).[71] Other tax related fees are deductible **from** AGI as miscellaneous itemized deductions, subject to the 2% of AGI limitation.

Legal fees incurred for personal purposes are not deductible. Likewise, legal fees incurred in the acquisition of property are not deductible; instead, they must be capitalized and added to the cost of the property.

Example 6-39 ∎ During the current year, Lia pays legal and accounting fees for the following:

Services rendered with regard to a contract dispute in Lia's business.	$ 8,000
Services rendered in resolving a federal tax deficiency relating to Lia's business	2,500
Tax return preparation fees:	
Allocable to preparation of Schedule C	1,600
Allocable to preparation of Schedules A and B and to the remainder of Form 1040	400
Legal fees incident to a divorce	1,200
Total	$13,700

Lia may deduct $12,100 ($8,000 + $2,500 + $1,600) **for** AGI. The legal fees incident to the divorce are personal expenses and generally are not deductible. However, a partial deduction **from** AGI as a miscellaneous itemized deduction subject to the 2% of AGI limitation could be taken to the extent that the legal fees relate to giving tax advice incident to the divorce. The remaining $400 of tax preparation fees is also deductible **from** AGI as a miscellaneous itemized deduction. ∎

---

[70] Regulation Sec. 1.61-3(a) indicates that cost of goods sold is not a deduction; rather, it is used in the computation of gross income.

[71] Rev. Rul. 92-29, 1992-1 C.B. 196.

In certain cases, legal expenses incurred in defending one's reputation or in defending against criminal charges may be deductible. In these situations, however, the legal action must have a direct relationship to the taxpayer's business or income-producing activity. In criminal proceedings, the Supreme Court has held that as long as the expenses are business expenses, they are deductible, even if the taxpayer is convicted.

Example 6-40 ■   Mario is engaged in the business of underwriting and selling securities to the public. In the current year Mario is charged and convicted on criminal charges of securities fraud. The conviction is appealed, but the conviction is upheld. Mario incurs $18,000 in attorney's fees in the unsuccessful defense. In this case, the legal expenses are directly related to Mario's business. Additionally, they are ordinary and necessary. Despite Mario's conviction, the $18,000 of attorney's fees is deductible.[72]   ■

Other Expenditures That Are Specifically Disallowed

The Code also specifically disallows deductions for certain other expenses, even though they might meet all the requirements mentioned above. These include political contributions and lobbying expenses, and, in certain situations, business start-up expenses.

Political Contributions and Lobbying Expenses.

One general category of disallowed expenses involves political contributions and lobbying expenses. Thus, no deduction is allowed for expenditures made in connection with the following:[73]

- Influencing legislation
- Participating or intervening in any political campaign of any candidate for public office
- Any attempt to influence the general public with respect to elections, legislative matters, or referendums
- Any direct communication with the President, Vice President, and certain other federal employees and officials

Historical Note
A limited credit for political contributions was repealed in the Tax Reform Act of 1986.

The law also denies a deduction for contributions to tax-exempt organizations that carry on lobbying activities if a principal purpose of the contribution is to obtain a deduction for what otherwise would have been disallowed.[74] Payments made for advertising in a convention program or any other program are also disallowed if any part of the proceeds of the publication will directly or indirectly benefit a specific political party or candidate.[75]

Lobbying expenses incurred to influence legislation on a local level are deductible if the legislation is of direct interest to the taxpayer's business. Local legislation includes actions by a legislative body of any political subdivision of a State (e.g. a city or county council), but does not include any State or Federal action. These deductible expenditures include expenses of communicating with or dues paid to an organization of which the taxpayer is a member.[76] For administrative convenience, the deduction

---

[72] *CIR v. Walter F. Tellier*, 17 AFTR 2d 633, 66-1 USTC ¶ 9319 (USSC, 1966).
[73] Sec. 162(e)(1).
[74] Sec. 162(e)(3).
[75] Sec. 276(a). Nondeductible political contributions also include payments for admission to a dinner or program where the proceeds will benefit a party or candidate, or admission to an inaugural ball, party, or concert if the activity is identified with a political party or candidate.
[76] Sec. 162(e)(2).

limit does not apply to any in-house expenditure attributable to such activities as long as the total of such expenditures for the taxable year do not exceed $2,000. In-house expenditures are expenses incurred directly by the taxpayer other than amounts paid to a professional lobbyist or dues that are allocable to lobbying. Additionally, the deduction limit does not apply to taxpayers who are engaged in the business of lobbying.[77]

Example 6-41 ■ Kate is the senior partner of a large New York law firm. During the year, she flies to Washington, D.C. to testify before a Congressional subcommittee with regard to proposed changes in the social security taxes imposed on employers. Such changes directly affect her business since they affect the amount of taxes she must pay on behalf of her employees. Kate's ordinary and necessary expenses incurred with respect to the trip are not deductible. ■

If the legislation cannot reasonably be expected to directly affect the taxpayer's trade or business, the expenses are not deductible.

Example 6-42 ■ Kate is the owner of several hotels in Chicago. The city of Chicago has proposed legislation that would increase the hotel room tax guests pay. Kate spends time researching and traveling to speak to the Chicago City Council regarding this legislation. Kate's lobbying expenses are deductible because they are used to influence legislation on the local level and are of direct interest to her business. ■

Business Investigation and Preopening Expenses. The Code also specifically disallows a current deduction for business start-up expenditures.[78] Instead, these expenses are capitalized and are subject to amortization if an election is made to amortize the start-up costs over a period of not less than 60 months starting with the month in which the taxpayer begins the new business. Start-up expenditures are specifically defined to include three general types of expenditures:

Additional Comment

Costs incurred in connection with the sale of stock or securities do not qualify as start-up costs.

- *Business investigation expenses.* These expenses are costs a taxpayer incurs in reviewing and analyzing a prospective business prior to deciding whether to acquire or create it. The key here is that the expenses are incurred prior to the actual decision. These expenses include expenditures for such things as analyses and surveys of markets, traffic patterns, products, labor supplies, and distribution facilities.[79]

- *Preopening or start-up costs.* Preopening or start-up costs are expenses that are incurred after the decision to acquire or create the business has been made but before the business activity itself has started. These costs include expenditures for (1) training employees; (2) advertising; (3) securing supplies, distributors, and potential customers; and (4) expenditures for professional services in setting up the business's books and records. These costs must be incurred by a taxpayer who (1) is not engaged in any existing business or (2) is engaged in a business that is unrelated to the business being acquired or created.

- *Expenses incurred in connection with an investment activity.* These expenses are costs incurred in connection with an investment activity that the taxpayer anticipates will become an active trade or business.[80]

---

[77] Sec. 162(e)(5).
[78] Sec. 195.
[79] S. Rept. No. 96-1036, 96th Cong., 2d Sess., p. 8 (1980).
[80] Sec. 195(c)(1)(A)(ii).

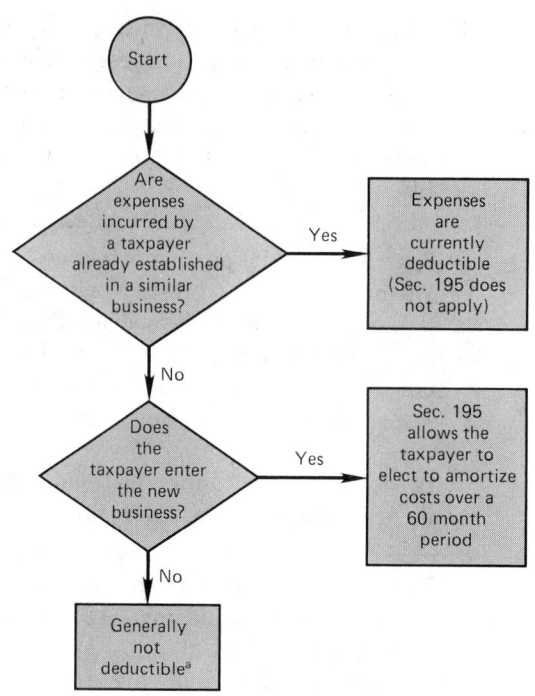

^a Rev. Rul. 57-418, 1957–2 C.B. 143; Morton Frank, 20 T.C. 511 (1953).

FIGURE 6-1 Deductibility of Business Investigation and Start-Up Costs

As defined by Sec. 195, start-up expenditures do not include these same types of expenses when they are incurred by a taxpayer who is already engaged in a business that is similar to the new one being created or acquired. In such a case, the expenditures may be deducted currently since they are incurred in the taxpayer's existing business.[81] Furthermore, expenditures for interest and taxes, which are deductible as itemized deductions under Secs. 163 and 164, are not included in the expenses that must be capitalized and amortized. Figure 6-1 summarizes these rules.

Expenses of an Entertainment Facility

Additional Comment

The cost of providing entertainment is fully deductible to the extent that it is sold by the taxpayer in a bona fide transaction. For example, the owner of a theater that sells tickets to the public can deduct depreciation on the building.

In general, expenses associated with an entertainment facility are not deductible.[82] This disallowance was imposed by Congress in an attempt to prevent taxpayers from deducting expenses incurred with respect to owning or using assets that provide an element of personal recreation for the taxpayer. Thus, no deduction is allowed for maintenance or depreciation of facilities such as hunting lodges and yachts. Yet, an employer may deduct expenses incurred for recreational, social, or similar activities and facilities that are primarily for the benefit of employees (other than highly compensated employees). The use of these facilities is not gross income to the employees under Sec. 132. (See Chapter 4 for a discussion of fringe benefits that may be excluded from the employee's gross income.) Amounts paid for membership in any club (i.e., club dues) organized for business, pleasure, recreation, or other special purpose are not deductible. These rules are discussed in greater detail in Chapter 9.

Topic Review 6-3 summarizes the restrictions on the deductibility of these items.

---

[81] S. Rept. No. 96-1036, 96th Cong., 2d Sess., p. 8 (1980).
[82] Sec. 274(a)(1)(B).

TOPIC REVIEW 6-3

Restrictions Upon the Deductibility of Certain Items	
Item	Restrictions Imposed
1. Capital Expenditures.	1. The general rule is that the expenditure is not currently deductible if its life extends beyond the end of the year. Special elections are available to currently deduct certain capital expenditures (e.g., research and experimental costs under Sec. 174; and up to $17,500 per year for acquisitions of tangible personal property used in a trade or business under Sec. 179).
2. Carrying Charges.	2. An election may be made under Sec. 266 to capitalize certain expenses that are normally deductible such as property and employment taxes, interest, and carrying charges on unimproved and unproductive real estate.
3. Expenses Related to Tax Exempt Income.	3. Expenses such as interest incurred on debt used to purchase or carry tax-exempt securities are disallowed under Sec. 265.
4. Expenditures Contrary to Public Policy.	4. Such expenditures are generally not deductible. Examples include bribes and kickbacks, fines and penalties, and expenses of an illegal activity involved with trafficking or dealing in drugs.
5. Legal and Accounting Fees.	5. Legal and accounting fees can either be *for* AGI deductible business expenses, nondeductible personal use expenditures or *from* AGI fees incurred in the determination of any tax (e.g., tax return preparation fees).
6. Political Contributions and Lobby Expenses	6. The general rule is that such items are not deductible (e.g., costs of influencing public opinion). Certain exceptions are provided (e.g., costs of appearing before local legislative bodies on topics directly related to the taxpayer's business).
7. Business Investigation and Preopening Expenses	7. The following rules are applied: a. Currently deductible if the taxpayer is already engaged in a similar business. b. Not deductible if the taxpayer is not currently engaged in a similar business and does not enter the new business. c. Amortize the expenditures over 60 months if the taxpayer enters the new business and makes an election.

PROPER SUBSTANTIATION REQUIREMENT

OBJECTIVE 4

List the substantiation requirements that must be met to deduct travel and entertainment expenses

Generally, the burden of proving the existence of a deduction or loss falls on the taxpayer. Thus, proper substantiation must be made if a taxpayer wants to deduct an expenditure or loss. Items such as receipts, cancelled checks, and paid bills documenting deductible expenditures should be retained in the event the IRS audits a return and requests proof. Occasionally, the courts will allow a deduction that is not properly substantiated by the taxpayer if it is evident that an expenditure has been made. In these cases, the amount of the deduction is estimated based on all the facts and circumstances. This procedure is known as the *Cohan* rule and derives its name from a court case in which the judge allowed a deduction for an estimated amount of certain expenses.[83] The most prudent course of action, of course, is to retain proper documentation rather than to rely upon the *Cohan* rule.

Example 6-43 ■

In April of the current year, Terry took his tax records to a CPA to have his prior year's income tax return prepared. As part of the return, the CPA attached a supplemental schedule listing all of Terry's items of income and expense. After the return was prepared and filed, Terry's records were stolen. Upon audit 2 years later, the IRS disallowed Terry's deductions because there were no records to substantiate the expenses. When the case was litigated, the court allowed deductions for an estimated amount of expenses under the *Cohan* rule because of the list that was attached to Terry's return and because the court believed that Terry had testified honestly in his own behalf.[84] ■

Historical Note

Justice Learned Hand, in permitting a deduction for unsubstantiated amounts in George M. Cohan v. CIR, 8 AFTR 10552, 2 USTC ¶ 489 (2nd Cir, 1930), wrote "absolute certainty in such matters is usually impossible and it is not necessary; the Board should make as close an approximation as it can, bearing heavily if it chooses on the taxpayer whose inexactitude is of his own making."

Additionally, the Code provides specific and more stringent record-keeping requirements for travel, entertainment, business gifts, computers, and automobiles and other vehicles used for transportation.[85] In these cases no deduction may be taken unless the taxpayer substantiates the expenditure either by an adequate record or by sufficient evidence that corroborates the taxpayer's statement.[86] This substantiation may take the form of account books, diaries, logs, receipts and paid bills, trip sheets, expense reports, and statements of witnesses.[87] The information that must be substantiated includes the following:

- Amount of the expense
- Time and place of the travel or entertainment
- Date and a description of the gift
- Business purpose of the expenditure
- Business relationship to the taxpayer of the person entertained or of the person who received the gift[88]

The *Cohan* rule may not be used for these types of expenses.[89] (See Chapter 9 for a more complete discussion regarding the deductibility of these types of expenses.)

EXPENSES AND LOSSES MUST BE INCURRED BY THE TAXPAYER

Generally, taxpayers may take a deduction only for their own losses and expenses. This requirement prevents taxpayers from engaging in manipulative schemes.

Example 6-44 ■

April and Bruce, the elderly parents of Carol, live in their own home. They have little income and Carol must help to support them. During the current year, the

---

[83] *George M. Cohan v. CIR,* 8 AFTR 10552, 2 USTC ¶ 489 (2nd Cir., 1930). Interestingly, the *Cohan* case dealt with travel and entertainment expenses. Because of the subsequent enactment of Sec. 274(d), the *Cohan* rule may not be used in order to deduct these expenses. It is still effective for other types of expenses.

[84] *Layard M. White,* 1980 PH T.C. Memo ¶ 80,582, 41 TCM 671.

[85] Secs. 274(d) and 280F(d)(4).

[86] Sec. 274(d).

[87] Temp. Reg. Sec. 1.274-5T(b).

[88] Sec. 274(d).

[89] Temp. Reg. Sec. 1.274-5T(a).

Additional Comment

When one taxpayer pays the expenses of another, neither taxpayer is entitled to the deduction.

interest and property taxes due on April and Bruce's home total $2,000. April and Bruce file a joint return. They have no other expenses that qualify as itemized deductions. Thus, April and Bruce plan to use the standard deduction, and the benefit of the $2,000 expenditure for interest and taxes will be lost. In an attempt to take advantage of a deduction that otherwise would be lost, Carol pays the interest and taxes. No deduction is allowed to Carol because these expenses are not Carol's own liability. ∎

This general rule applies to all types of expenditures, whether incurred in a trade or business, an investment activity, or a personal activity for which deductions are allowed. There is one exception: Taxpayers may take a deduction for medical expenses paid in behalf of a dependent.[90] Medical expenses also qualify as a deduction if they are paid for a person who would qualify as a dependent except for the fact that the gross income test is not met (see Chapter 2).

Example 6-45 ∎ During the current year, Dan incurs $3,400 in deductible medical expenses. Dan is not a full-time student and is not under age 19 but is otherwise supported by Tom, his father. Dan's gross income for the year is $15,000. If Tom pays Dan's medical expenses, Tom may deduct the expenses as an itemized deduction even though Tom may not take a dependency exemption for Dan. ∎

SPECIAL DISALLOWANCE RULES

In addition to the general rules of deductibility mentioned above, certain types of transactions are subject to further limitations and disallowances. These include transactions known as wash sales, transactions between related persons, gambling losses, losses associated with an activity determined to be a hobby, expenses of renting a vacation home, and expenses of an office in the taxpayer's home.

Wash Sales

OBJECTIVE 5

Explain the tax consequences of wash sales

Under Sec. 1091, losses incurred on wash sales of stock or securities are disallowed in the year of sale. For purposes of Sec. 1091, a **wash sale** occurs when

- A taxpayer realizes a loss on the sale of stock or securities, and
- "Substantially identical" stock or securities are acquired by the taxpayer within a 61-day period of time which extends from 30 days before the date of sale to 30 days after the date of sale.[91]

Thus, the purpose of the wash sale rule is to prevent taxpayers from generating artificial tax losses in situations where taxpayers do not intend to reduce their holdings in the stock or securities that are sold.

Example 6-46 ∎ Leslie realizes $10,000 in short-term capital gains (STCGs) through dealings in the stock market during the current year. Realizing that STCGs are fully includible in gross income unless they are offset against realized capital losses, Leslie analyzes

---

[90] Sec. 213(a).
[91] Here the term *acquire* includes an acquisition of the stock either by purchase or in a taxable exchange. The term "stock or securities" includes contracts or options to acquire or sell stock or securities (see Sec. 1091(a)).

her portfolio to determine whether she owns any stocks that have declined in value. She finds that the FMV of her Edison Corporation stock is only $8,000, even though it was originally purchased for $16,000. Despite this paper loss on the stock, Leslie feels that Edison Corporation is still a good investment and wants to retain the stock. If Leslie attempts to take advantage of the paper loss on the Edison stock by selling the stock she owns and repurchasing a similar number of shares of Edison stock within the 61-day period, the loss is disallowed. ∎

Typical Misconception

The wash sale rule applies only to transactions on which there are realized losses, and does not apply to transactions on which there are realized gains.

At times, taxpayers may attempt to circumvent the wash sale provisions through either a sham transaction or an indirect repurchase of the securities. If this is the case, the wash sale provisions still prevent the recognition of the loss. Thus, the Supreme Court has held that losses on sales of stock by a husband were disallowed when the stockbroker was instructed to purchase the same number of shares in the wife's name.[92]

In some instances a taxpayer may be tempted to circumvent the wash sale provisions by merely delaying the repurchase of the substantially identical stock. This tactic should work as long as a written agreement to repurchase the stock does not exist at the time of the sale or at any time within the 61-day period mandated by the Sec. 1091 wash sale provisions. If such an agreement is made, however, the courts will disallow the loss, even though the actual purchase does not occur within the 61-day period.[93]

In certain cases, losses on transactions that literally fall within the wash sale requirements above may still be recognized. For example, a taxpayer may purchase stock and then sell a portion of those shares within 30 days where the intent is merely to reduce the stock holdings. Taken together, these two transactions meet the tests of Sec. 1091. However, since the purpose of the sale is to reduce the taxpayer's holdings rather than to generate an artificial tax loss, the loss on the sale is not disallowed.[94] Section 1091 also does not apply to losses realized in the ordinary course of business by a dealer in stock or securities.

If fewer shares of stock are acquired within the 61-day period than were disposed of, only a proportionate amount of the total loss is disallowed.

Example 6-47 ∎

Henry purchased 100 shares of New Corporation common stock for $2,000 ($20 per share). Several years later, on July 2 of the current year, Henry sells all 100 shares for $1,000. On July 30 of the current year, Henry purchases 75 shares (three-fourths of the original shares) of New Corporation common stock. As a result of the reacquisition, three-fourths of the total loss ($750) is disallowed. The remaining $250 loss is recognized. ∎

Substantially Identical Stock or Securities. Only the acquisition of substantially identical stock or securities will cause a disallowance of the loss. The Code and the Regulations do not define the term *substantially identical.* Judicial and administrative rulings have held that bonds issued by the same corporation generally are not considered substantially identical if they differ in terms (e.g., interest rate and term to maturity). However, bonds of the same corporation that differ only in their maturity dates (e.g., the bonds do not come due for 16 years and mature within a few months of each other) have been held to be substantially identical.[95] The preferred stock of a

---

[92] *John P. McWilliams v. CIR,* 35 AFTR 1184, 47-1 USTC ¶ 9289 (USSC, 1947).
[93] Rev. Rul. 72-225, 1972-1 C.B. 59, and Frank Stein, 1977 PH T.C. Memo ¶ 77,241, 36 TCM 992.
[94] Rev. Rul. 56-602, 1956-2 C.B. 527.
[95] *Marie Hanlin, Executrix v. CIR,* 39-2 USTC ¶ 9783 (3d Cir., 1939).

corporation generally is not considered substantially identical to the common stock of the same corporation.[96]

Key Point
The recognition of a loss on a wash sale is only being deferred since the investor can increase the basis of the acquired stock by the disallowed loss.

Basis of Stock. If a loss is disallowed because of the wash sale provisions, the basis of the acquired stock that causes the nonrecognition is increased to reflect the disallowance. This increase means that the disallowed loss is merely postponed and will eventually be recognized either in the form of a reduced gain or an increased loss upon the subsequent sale or disposition of the stock that causes the loss disallowance. Since the amount of the increase in basis is equal to the postponed loss, the taxpayer eventually recovers the cost of the original shares of stock. If there has been more than one purchase of replacement stock and the amount of stock purchased within the 61-day period exceeds the stock that is sold, the stock that is deemed to have caused the disallowance of the loss is accounted for on a chronological basis. Thus, it is the basis of that block of stock that is increased.[97]

Example 6-48 ■

Ingrid enters into the following transactions with regard to Pacific Corporation common stock:

Date	Transaction	Amount
January 4, 1987	Purchases 600 shares	$30,000
October 2, 1994	Purchases 400 shares	10,000
October 12, 1994	Sells original 600 shares	12,000
October 20, 1994	Purchases 200 shares	5,000
October 25, 1994	Purchases 300 shares	8,400

Since Ingrid purchases more than 600 shares within the 61-day period before and after the date of sale (the purchases made on October 2, 20, and 25), the entire loss of $18,000 ($30,000 − $12,000) is postponed. The basis of the 400 shares of stock purchased on October 2 is $22,000 ($10,000 purchase price + [$18,000 disallowed loss × 0.667]). The basis of the 200 shares of stock purchased on October 20 is $11,000 ($5,000 + [$18,000 disallowed loss × 0.333]). Both of these blocks of stock have a holding period that starts on January 4, 1987.[98] The basis of the 300 shares of stock purchased on October 25 is its purchase price of $8,400. Its holding period begins on October 25. ■

Transactions Between Related Parties

OBJECTIVE 6
Explain the tax consequences of transactions between related parties

Section 267 places transactions between certain related parties under special scrutiny because of the potential for tax abuse. For example, a taxpayer could sell a piece of property at a loss to a wholly owned corporation. Without any restrictions on the deductibility of the loss, the individual could recognize the loss while still retaining effective control of the property. Under Sec. 267, current deductions may not be taken on two specific types of transactions entered into between related taxpayers. These transactions include:

---

[96] However, the IRS has held in Rev. Rul. 77-201, 1977-1 C.B. 250, that the convertible preferred stock of a corporation is substantially identical to its common stock if the preferred stock (1) has the same voting rights and is subject to the same dividend restrictions as the common stock, (2) is unrestricted as to its convertibility, and (3) sells at relatively the same price (taking into consideration the conversion ratio).

[97] The holding period of the replacement stock includes the period of time the taxpayer held the stock which was sold.

[98] An asset's holding period is important in determining whether subsequent gain or loss on the asset is long-term or short-term gain or loss. This is explained further in Chapter 5.

Additional Comment

The word "property" is not defined in Sec. 267, but it has been given a broad meaning by the IRS and the courts.

- Losses on sales of property
- Expenses that remain unpaid at the end of the obligor's tax year

Related Parties Defined. Since Sec. 267 applies to transactions between related parties, it is critical to identify who is related for purposes of this provision. Among the relationships defined as related parties under Sec. 267 are the following:

- Individuals and their families. Family is defined as an individual's (a) spouse, (b) brothers and sisters (including half-brothers and half-sisters), (c) ancestors, and (d) lineal descendants.
- An individual and a corporation in which the individual owns more than 50% of the value of the outstanding stock.
- Various relationships between grantors, beneficiaries, and fiduciaries of a trust or trusts, or between the fiduciary of a trust and a corporation if certain ownership requirements are met.
- A corporation and a partnership if the same persons own more than 50% in value of the stock of the corporation and more than 50% of the partnership.
- Two corporations if the same persons own more than 50% in value of the outstanding stock of both corporations and at least one of the corporations is an S corporation.
- Other complex relationships involving trusts, corporations and individuals.[99]

Several of these relationships depend upon an individual's ownership of a corporation. For example, if a taxpayer does not own more than 50% of a corporation's stock, the individual and the corporation are not considered to be related, and a loss on the sale of property between the two is deductible. Occasionally individuals might attempt to circumvent the related party rules by dispersing the ownership of a corporation (e.g., among close family members) while at the same time retaining economic control. To prevent these tactics, Sec. 267 contains constructive ownership rules whereby a taxpayer is deemed to own stock owned by certain other persons. These constructive ownership rules are as follows:

- Stock owned by an individual's family is treated as owned by the individual. Here the definition of family is the same as that of related parties.
- Stock owned by a corporation or partnership is treated as being owned proportionately by its shareholders or partners.[100]
- If an individual partner in a partnership owns (or is treated as owning) stock in a corporation, the individual is treated as owning any stock of that corporation owned by any other partner in the partnership. This does not occur, however, if the only stock the individual owns (or is considered as owning) is what his or her family owns.[101]
- Stock ownership that is attributed to a shareholder or partner from an entity can be reattributed to another taxpayer under any of the constructive ownership rules. However, stock ownership attributed to a taxpayer under the family or partner rules cannot be reattributed.

These rules are illustrated by the following examples:

Example 6-49 ■   Alice and Beth are equal partners in the AB Partnership. Beth owns 60% of First Corporation's stock, and Craig, Alice's husband, owns the other 40%. The

---

[99] Sec. 267(b).
[100] Stock owned by an estate or trust is also treated as owned proportionately by its beneficiaries.
[101] Reg. Sec. 1.267(c)-1(b), Exs. (2) and (3).

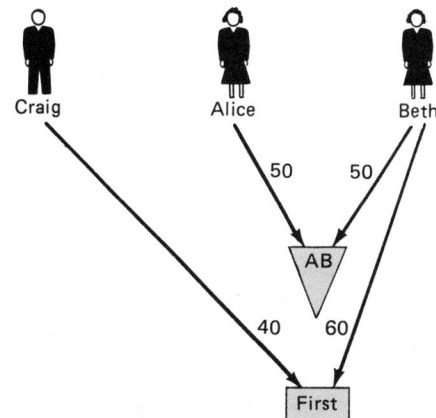

FIGURE 6-2   Illustration for Example 6-49

ownership of the partnership and the corporation is demonstrated in Figure 6-2. Under the constructive ownership rules, Alice is considered as owning Craig's 40% of the First Corporation stock. Alice is not considered as owning the First Corporation stock owned by her partner, Beth, because the only First Corporation stock Alice owns (or is considered as owning) is that owned by her husband. If Alice sells property at a loss to First Corporation, the loss is recognized because Alice does not directly or constructively own more than 50% of the First Corporation stock.   ■

Example 6-50 ■

Additional Comment

A partner will not be treated as owning the stock in a corporation owned by his partners if the only stock he owns is that which is attributed to him through the family attribution rules. However, if the partner owns directly as little as one share of the corporation stock, he will be treated as owning all of the stock owned by his partners.

Assume the same facts as in Example 6-49, except that the First Corporation stock is owned 50% by the AB Partnership and 25% each by Beth and Craig. The ownership of the partnership and the corporation is shown in Figure 6-3. In addition to Craig's 25%, Alice is considered as owning 50% of the stock owned by the AB Partnership because of her 50% ownership in AB. The other half of AB's stock ownership is attributed to her partner, Beth. However, Alice is also treated as owning the First Corporation stock which Beth owns both actually and constructively (50%). Thus, Alice is treated as owning 100% of the First Corporation stock. In this case, if Alice sells property at a loss to First Corporation, the loss will be disallowed.   ■

Disallowed Losses. If a loss is disallowed under Sec. 267, the original seller of the property receives no tax deduction. The disallowed loss has no effect on the purchaser's basis. The cost basis to the purchaser is equal to the amount paid for the property. However, partial relief is provided because on a subsequent sale of the property, the related purchaser may reduce the recognized gain by the amount of the disallowed loss. This offsetting of a subsequent gain is available only to the related person who originally purchased the property. If the disallowed loss is larger than the subsequent gain, or if the purchaser sells the property at a loss, no deduction is allowed for the unused loss. This may result in a partial disallowance of an overall economic loss for the related parties because there is no upward basis adjustment for the previously disallowed loss (as is the case for a wash sale).

Example 6-51 ■

Assume three separate situations in which Sam sells a tract of land during the current year. In each case assume that Sam purchased the land from his father, Frank, for $10,000. Frank's basis at the time of the original sale was $15,000 in each case. Thus, Frank's $5,000 loss on each land sale was disallowed.

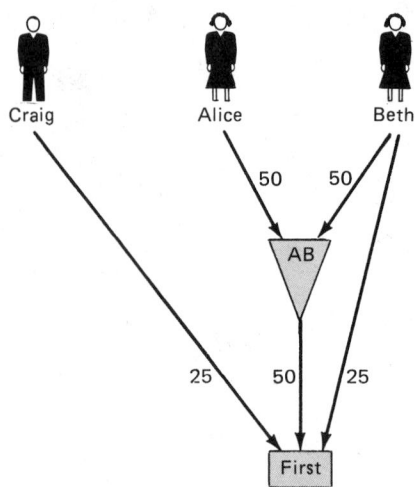

FIGURE 6-3 Illustration for Example 6-50

	Situation		
	1	2	3
Selling price	$17,000	$12,000	$ 8,000
Minus: Sam's basis	(10,000)	(10,000)	(10,000)
Sam's realized gain (loss)	$ 7,000	$ 2,000	$ (2,000)
Minus: Frank's disallowed loss (up to Sam's gain)	(5,000)	(2,000)	—0—
Sam's recognized gain (loss)	$ 2,000	—0—	($ 2,000)

Key Point

The loss disallowance rule relative to related parties is more severe when compared to the loss disallowance rule on wash sales since, in a related party transaction, it is possible to lose the tax benefit of all or a portion of the economic loss.

In situation 1, Sam and Frank together have incurred an aggregate gain of $2,000 ($17,000 − $15,000). Thus, Frank's full disallowed loss is used to reduce Sam's subsequent gain. In situation 2, the aggregate economic loss incurred by Sam and Frank is actually $3,000 ($12,000 − $15,000). However, the actual amount of the tax loss recognized for Sam and Frank is zero. In situation 3, the actual tax loss would have been $7,000 ($8,000 − $15,000) instead of $2,000 if Frank had held the land until its eventual sale. ■

A similar rule found in Sec. 707(b)(1) disallows losses between (1) a partner and a partnership in which the partner owns directly or indirectly over 50% of the partnership and (2) two partnerships in which the same persons own directly or indirectly over 50% in each partnership. The constructive ownership rules of Sec. 267 apply here in determining ownership (see Chapter 9 in *Prentice Hall's Federal Taxation: Corporations, Partnerships, Estates, and Trusts* text or Chapter 16 of the *Comprehensive* volume).

Key Point

The effect of Sec. 267 with respect to unpaid expenses is to place an accrual method taxpayer on the cash method for amounts owed to a related cash method taxpayer.

Unpaid Expenses. Section 267 also causes the obligor of any unpaid expenses to defer the deduction for those expenses until the year in which the related payee recognizes the amount as income. In effect, this rule prevents an accrual-basis taxpayer from taking a deduction for an unpaid expense in the earlier year of accrual while the related cash-basis taxpayer recognizes the payment as income in the subsequent year.

Example 6-52 ■

Michelle owns 100% of the outstanding stock of Hill Corporation. Michelle is a cash-basis taxpayer, and Hill Corporation is an accrual-basis taxpayer. Both taxpayers are calendar-year taxpayers. In a bona fide transaction, Hill borrows some funds from Michelle. By the end of the current year, $8,000 interest had accrued on the loan. However, Hill Corporation does not pay the interest to Michelle until February of the following year. Since Michelle is a cash-basis taxpayer, the interest income is reported when it is received in the following year. Although Hill is an accrual-basis taxpayer, Hill's deduction for the interest expense is deferred until it is paid in February of the following year. ∎

For purposes of these unpaid expenses, the definition of related parties in Sec. 267 is modified to include a personal-service corporation and any employee-owner.[102] A personal-service corporation is one whose principal activity is the performance of personal services that are substantially performed by employee-owners. An employee-owner is an employee who owns any of the outstanding stock of the personal-service corporation.[103]

Example 6-53 ∎	Assume the same facts as in Example 6-52, except that Michelle owns only 20% of the Hill stock and that Hill Corporation is a personal-service corporation. Even though Michelle does not own over 50% of Hill, the results are the same as in Example 6-52. ∎

For purposes of these unpaid expenses, the definition of related parties is also modified to include various relationships involving partnerships or S corporations and any person that owns (either actually or constructively) any interest in these entities.[104]

Hobby Losses

Certain activities have both profit-motivated and other attributes. In these cases it is necessary to examine all of the relevant factors to determine the tax status of the activity. The factors the IRS uses to determine whether an activity is profit-motivated were previously discussed in this chapter under the section entitled Business or Investment Requirement. If an examination of these factors is not determinative, the activity is presumed to be profit-motivated if it generates taxable income in 3 or more out of 5 consecutive years (2 out of 7 years if the activity consists mainly of breeding, training, showing, or racing horses). If this profit test is met, the burden of proof shifts, and the IRS must prove that the activity is not profit-motivated. This determination is important because, in general, a deduction is not allowed for losses incurred in an activity that is not profit-motivated. An activity that has no profit motive is likely to be a personal hobby of the taxpayer and is not a trade or business activity.

Additional Comment

Gross income from an activity not engaged in for profit is defined to include the total gains from the sale, exchange, or other disposition of property, and all other gross receipts derived from such activity. Cost of goods sold can be deducted from gross receipts to calculate gross income.

Deductible Expenses. Some hobby activities generate gross income, even though profit is not a primary motive for the activity. In such situations, Sec. 183 allows the taxpayer to deduct the expenses related to the hobby, but only to the extent of the gross income from the hobby. Furthermore, a hobby-related expense is deductible only if it would have been deductible if incurred in a trade or business or an investment activity.

---

[102] Sec. 267(a)(2).

[103] Secs. 269A(b) and 441(i)(2). In determining the ownership of an employee-owner, the constructive ownership rules of Sec. 318 as modified by Sec. 441(i)(2) are used. These rules differ substantially from the constructive ownership rules of Sec. 267.

[104] Sec. 267(e). A discussion of these modifications is beyond the scope of this book.

Example 6-54 ■   Julie, a dentist, enjoys painting in her spare time. During the current year, Julie receives $2,500 from the sale of her paintings. During that same year, she also incurs $1,700 in painting-related expenses. If these expenses were incurred in a trade or business, they would have been deductible. Julie is entitled to deduct the $1,700 in expenses up to the amount of her painting-related income of $2,500. ■

In essence, a taxpayer may deduct all the hobby-related expenses as long as there is enough gross income from the activity to cover the expenses. However, a hobby cannot generate a tax loss which is then used to offset a taxpayer's other types of income.

Example 6-55 ■   Assume the same facts as in Example 6-54, except that the expenses related to Julie's painting activities are $2,900. Julie may deduct only $2,500 of the expenses (up to the gross income generated from the activity). ■

Key Point

Expenses which cannot be deducted because the activity is a hobby are treated as personal expenditures and are lost forever.

Order of the Deductions. If the hobby expenses exceed the amount of gross income generated by the hobby, the expenses must be deducted against the gross income in the following order:

- Tier 1: Expenses that may be deducted even though they are not incurred in a trade or business (e.g., itemized deductions such as taxes, interest, and casualty losses)

- Tier 2: Other expenses of the hobby that could have been deducted if they had been incurred in a profit-motivated activity, but which do not reduce the tax basis of any of the assets used in the hobby (e.g., utilities and maintenance expenses)

- Tier 3: The expenses of the hobby that could have been deducted if incurred in a profit-motivated activity and that reduce the basis of the hobby's assets (e.g., depreciation on fixed assets used in the hobby)[105]

To the extent the expenses are taken as deductions against the gross income of the activity, they are deductions *from* AGI and are deductible if the taxpayer has itemized deductions in excess of the standard deduction.[106] The tier 1 expenses are reported in their respective sections on Schedule A of Form 1040. The tier 2 and tier 3 expenses allocated to the hobby are treated as miscellaneous itemized deductions and are, therefore, deductible only to the extent that they exceed 2% of AGI (see Chapter 7). Gross income from a hobby is reported as other income on Form 1040. If gross income is not sufficient to cover all of the tier 1 expenses, the excess expenses may also be deducted as itemized deductions on Schedule A of Form 1040 since these expenses are allowed in any event. Any remaining expenses in the other two tiers are disallowed and may not be carried over to a subsequent year.

Example 6-56 ■   As a hobby, Lynn raises various types of plants and flowers in a small greenhouse constructed specifically for that purpose. During the current year, Lynn realizes $1,000 gross income and incurs $1,150 local property taxes on the greenhouse. She also incurs an additional $300 in utilities related to the activity. If the activity was a trade or business, a total of $800 depreciation on the greenhouse could be deducted for the year. For the current year, the $1,000 gross income is included in AGI, and the full $1,150 of taxes are itemized deductions and may be deducted if Lynn has itemized deductions in excess of the standard

---

[105] Reg. Sec. 1.183-1(b).
[106] Rev. Rul. 75-14, 1975-1 C.B. 90.

deduction. No deduction is available for the $300 of utilities expense or the $800 depreciation. ∎

If depreciation expense is disallowed, it is not necessary to reduce the cost basis of the asset to the extent of the disallowance.[107]

Example 6-57 ∎ | Assume the same facts as in Example 6-56, except that the gross income is $1,700. In this case, all $1,450 ($1,150 + $300) of taxes and utilities are deductible, since the gross income exceeds that amount. In addition, Lynn can also deduct $250 ($1,700 − $1,450) of the $800 depreciation. The taxes are deductible as taxes on Schedule A of Form 1040, whereas the utilities and the depreciation are miscellaneous itemized deductions and are deductible only to the extent Lynn's total miscellaneous itemized deductions exceed 2% of AGI. The additional $550 depreciation is not deductible. However, the cost basis of the greenhouse is reduced only by the $250 depreciation that is deducted. ∎

Residential Property Used for Both Personal and Rental Purposes

OBJECTIVE 8
Determine the tax consequences of using residential real estate for both personal use and rental purposes

Because owning a second home or dwelling unit may have both personal and profit-motivated attributes, deductions for expenses related to the rental of a vacation home that is also used as a residence by the taxpayer may be disallowed or limited by Sec. 280A.

Residence Defined. For the restrictive rules of Sec. 280A to apply, the property must be a dwelling unit that qualifies as the taxpayer's residence. As used in this context, the term *dwelling unit* is quite expansive. Items such as boats and mobile homes may be considered dwelling units.[108] The determining factor is whether the property provides shelter and accommodations for eating and sleeping.[109] Thus, a mini-motorhome that contains the appropriate accommodations has been held to be a dwelling unit subject to the rules and limitations of Sec. 280A. The fact that the unit is small and cramped is disregarded.[110]

A dwelling unit is considered to be used by the taxpayer as a residence if the number of days during which the taxpayer uses the property for personal use throughout the year exceeds the greater of the following:

- 14 days or
- 10% of the number of days during the year that the property is rented at a fair rental[111]

For purposes of this test, a day of personal use includes any day that the property is used

- For personal purposes by the taxpayer or the taxpayer's family. *Family* is defined here as including a taxpayer's spouse, brothers and sisters, ancestors, and lineal descendants.[112]

Self-Study Question

What is the maximum number of days during a year that a taxpayer could use a property for personal use and not have it considered to be used as a residence?

Answer

If a property was rented for 332 days it could be used by the taxpayer for 33 days and not be considered a residence.

---

[107] Reg. Sec. 1.183-1(b).

[108] Sec. 280A(f)(1).

[109] *Ronald R. Haberkorn,* 75 T.C. 259 (1980), and *John O. Loughlin v. U.S.,* 50 AFTR 2d 82-5827, 82-2 USTC ¶ 9543 (D.C. Minn., 1982).

[110] *Ronald R. Haberkorn,* 75 T.C. 259 (1980).

[111] Sec. 280A(d)(1). In certain cases, this residence test might be met when a taxpayer uses a property as his principal residence for part of the year and rents the property for the rest of the year. This could occur, for example, when a taxpayer moves from his home and turns the old residence into a rental unit. In such a case, special rules prevent the home from being classified as a residence under Sec. 280A, thus preventing the application of the limitations.

[112] Under Sec. 280A(d)(2), a day during which the taxpayer spends substantially full time on repairs and maintenance does not count as a personal-use day.

- By any individual under a reciprocal-use arrangement.[113]
- By any individual who does not pay a fair rental for the use of the property.[114]

Despite the family-use rule, if a taxpayer rents property at a fair rental to a family member who uses the property as a principal residence, such use does not constitute personal use by the taxpayer.[115]

Example 6-58 ■

During the current year, Peggy purchases a small house as an investment and rents the property to Stan, her married son, who uses the property as his principal residence. Peggy's son pays her a fair rental for the property. Since Stan uses the property as his principal residence and also pays Peggy a fair rental for the property, Stan's personal use of the property does not constitute personal use by Peggy. Thus, the rules of Sec. 280A do not apply to limit the expenses that Peggy may deduct. ■

Key Point

A second home is going to be classified as either rental property, a residence, or some combination of the two. If it is classified as some combination of rental property and a residence, it is necessary to allocate expenses between the two categories.

Allocation of Expenses. To the extent expenses of the property relate to the taxpayer's personal use, no deduction is allowed for expenses other than for interest and taxes, which are deductible on personal residences.[116] However, expenses allocated to the rental use are deductible under Sec. 280A only to the extent of the gross income generated by the property (interest and taxes in excess of the rental income may be deducted as itemized deductions). The property may not generate a loss which is used to reduce other income of the taxpayer. Expenses that are not deductible because they exceed the gross income from the property may be carried over to the subsequent year and taken as a deduction, limited to the gross income of that year.[117] Expenses that are allocated to the rental use of the property and deducted against the gross income must be taken in the same order that the expenses under the hobby loss rules of Sec. 183 are deducted. Examples 6-56 and 6-57 illustrate these rules.

ALLOCATION FORMULA. In allocating expenses between the personal use and the rental use of the property, the following formula is used:[118]

$$\text{Rental use expenses} = \frac{\text{Number of rental days}}{\text{Total number of days used}} \times \frac{\text{Total expenses}}{\text{for the year}}$$

The denominator of the allocation fraction consists of the sum of the days the property is rented plus the days that the property is used for personal purposes. The days when the property is not used are not included in the formula.

Some courts have ruled that the allocation of interest and taxes to the rental use is to be done by taking into account the periods during the year when the property is not used. Thus, the denominator of the allocation formula would be the total number of days in the year.[119] Use of this ratio allocates less interest and taxes to the rental use,

---

[113] Sec. 280A(d)(2)(B). A reciprocal-use arrangement is one whereby another person uses the taxpayer's property in exchange for the taxpayer's use of the other person's property.

[114] Sec. 280A(d)(2)(C). Exactly what constitutes a fair rental must be determined by an examination of all the associated facts and circumstances.

[115] Sec. 280A(d)(3).

[116] No deduction is allowed for interest incurred with respect to a personal residence if the debt upon which the interest is paid is not secured by the property or the taxpayer has not chosen the property as a second residence for purposes of deducting the interest as qualified residential interest (see Chapter 7). For purposes of the discussion and examples used here, the assumption is made that the interest qualifies as qualified residential interest.

[117] Sec. 280A(c)(5)(B). The expenses that are carried over to the subsequent year are deductible to the extent of the property's gross income of that year, even though the property is not used by the taxpayer as a residence during that year.

[118] Sec. 280A(e)(1).

[119] *Dorance D. Bolton v. CIR*, 51 AFTR 2d 82-305, 82-2 USTC ¶ 9699 (9th Cir., 1982). See also *Edith G. McKinney v. CIR*, 52 AFTR 2d 83-6281, 83-2 USTC ¶ 9655 (10th Cir., 1983).

allowing more of the other expenses to be deducted against the rental income. Subject to limitations, the interest and taxes not allocated to the rental use are still deductible as itemized deductions. Example 6-59 uses the allocation formula that has been sanctioned by the courts.

Example 6-59 ■   During the current year, Joan purchases a cabin near the local ski resort. During the year, Joan and Joan's family use the cabin a total of 25 days. The cabin is also rented to out-of-state skiers for a total of 50 days during the year, generating rental income of $10,000. Joan also incurs the following expenses:

Expense	Amount
Property taxes	$1,500
Interest on mortgage	3,000
Utilities	2,000
Insurance	1,500
Security and snow removal	2,500

    Joan would have been entitled to $12,000 depreciation if the property had been entirely rental property held for investment. However, because the property is also used for personal purposes, the amount of deductions (for AGI) that Joan may take with respect to the property during the year is as follows:

Item	Calculation	Amount
Rental income		$10,000
Interest and taxes	$4,500 \times \dfrac{50}{365}$	(616)[a]
All other expenses except depreciation	$6,000 \times \dfrac{50}{75}$	(4,000)
Depreciation	$12,000 \times \dfrac{50}{75}$	(5,384)[b]
Net income from property		$—0—

[a] Under the approach favored by the IRS, $3,000 ($4,500 × 50/75) of interest and taxes would be used to offset the gross income and only $3,000 of depreciation would be deductible.
[b] If there had been sufficient gross income, Joan could have taken $8,000 depreciation. The additional $2,616 ($8,000 − $5,384) can be carried over and deducted in the subsequent year if the gross income of that year is sufficient to cover all the expenses allocable to the rental use.

Self-Study Question

Assume that a taxpayer rents his cabin to an individual who occupies it on a Saturday afternoon. Two weeks later the tenant leaves the cabin on a Saturday morning. Has the cabin been rented for fewer than 15 days?

Answer

Yes, although the tenant was on the premises for 15 calendar days, he is treated as having rented the property for only 14 days.

    In addition to the deductions above, Joan may also deduct $3,884 ($4,500 − $616) interest and taxes as itemized deductions if her total itemized deductions exceed the standard deduction and the interest is qualified residence interest (see Chapter 7). ■

Nominal Number of Rental Days. If a property qualifies as a taxpayer's residence under Sec. 280A but it is rented for less than 15 days during the year, the law takes the approach that the property is completely personal in nature. As such, no rental income is included in gross income and no expenses may be deducted. However, expenses such as interest and taxes may still be deducted as itemized deductions. (See Chapter 7 for a discussion of the limitations upon interest.)

Example 6-60 ■   Assume the same facts as in Example 6-59, except that during the year Joan's cabin is rented for only 12 days and the amount of rental income is $2,400.

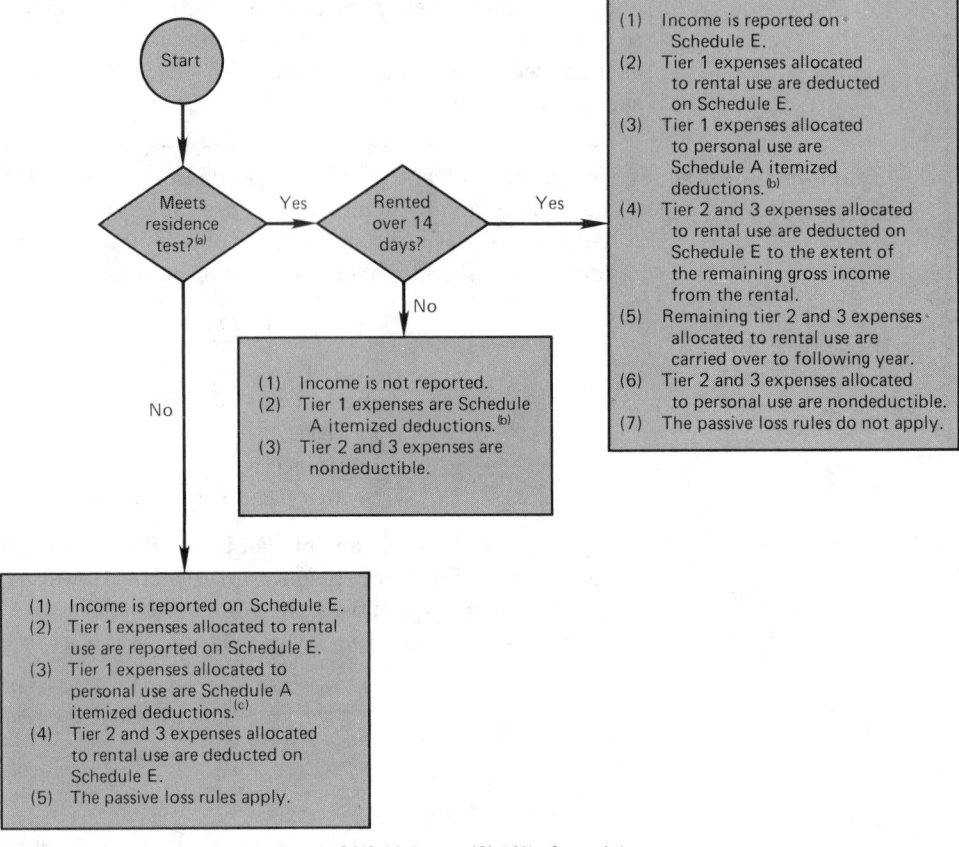

(a)   Personal use is more than the larger of (1) 14 days or (2) 10% of rental days.
(b)   In order for the interest to be deductible, it must be "qualified residence interest" (see Chapter 7).
(c)   In order for the interest to be deductible as qualified residence, the property must not have been
        rented at all during the year (see Chapter 7).

FIGURE 6-4   Section 280A: Limitation of deductions on rental of residential
property

Key Point

Assume that a taxpayer owns a beach-front condo. The taxpayer personally uses the condo for only 12 days during the year and rents the property for 35 days. Section 280A does not apply since the taxpayer has not used the property for over 14 days. However, if the taxpayer cannot demonstrate a profit motive, it may still be treated as a hobby. If so, the deductibility of the expenses allocated to the rental use is limited to the gross income generated by the property. Furthermore, the interest allocated to the personal use of the property is not deductible as qualified residential interest (see Chapter 7).

The cabin qualifies as Joan's residence since her personal use exceeds 14 days. Because the cabin is rented for less than 15 days during the year, Joan may only take itemized deductions of $4,500 for the interest and taxes. The other expenses may not be deducted. In addition, the $2,400 is not included in gross income.   ■

Nominal Number of Personal-Use Days. If a taxpayer does not have enough personal-use days during the year to qualify the property as a residence (i.e., the personal use is not more than the greater of 14 days or 10% of the rental days), the Sec. 280A rules and limitations do not apply. Under these circumstances, the property may be considered a hobby if the owner cannot demonstrate a proper profit motive. If this is the case, the hobby loss rules apply. On the other hand, if the owner demonstrates a profit motive, the property is treated as rental property. However, the expenses must still be allocated between the rental use and the personal use. The taxes allocated to the personal use are deductible as itemized deductions. Also, none of the interest allocated to the personal use is deductible because it is not qualified residence interest. (See Chapter 7 for a discussion of the deductibility of personal interest and qualified residence interest.) The tier 2 and tier 3 expenses allocated to the personal use are not deductible. The income from the property and all of the expenses allocated to the rental use are reported on Schedule E of Form 1040. As such, the expenses are *for* AGI deductions. Any net income or loss from the property is subject to the passive loss rules, which may limit the deductibility of any losses from the property (see Chapter 8).

The rules of Sec. 280A regarding the rental of property are summarized in Figure 6-4.

Expenses of an Office in the Home

Unless the taxpayer meets certain strictly imposed requirements, Sec. 280A disallows any deduction for home office expenses. In general, for a taxpayer to deduct office-in-home expenses, the office must have been regularly and exclusively used as either of the following:

- The principal place of business for a business of the taxpayer
- A place of business where the taxpayer meets or deals with clients in the normal course of business

For employees to take a deduction for home office expenses, the use must also have been for the convenience of the employer. In addition, a separate structure not attached to the taxpayer's house may qualify if regularly and exclusively used in connection with the taxpayer's business. (See Chapter 9 for a comprehensive discussion of these rules.)

TAX PLANNING CONSIDERATIONS

Hobby Losses

Additional Comment
Small or "contrived" profits to meet the presumption are generally ignored.

Ethical Point
In some cases it is difficult to ascertain whether an activity is a trade or business or a hobby. A CPA should not prepare or sign a tax return unless the CPA in good faith believes that the return takes a position that has a realistic possibility of being sustained on its merits.

Deductions for expenses incurred in a hobby activity are limited to the gross income generated by the hobby for the year. If, however, the gross income exceeds the deductions from the activity in 3 out of 5 consecutive years, the activity is presumed to be a business, and the limits on the deductibility of expenses do not apply. Thus, if possible, taxpayers should use care in timing the realization of items of income and expense. If, for example, an activity has shown a profit in only 2 out of the previous 4 years, a taxpayer may consider accelerating some of the income into the fifth year or deferring some of the expenses of the activity into the following year. Under the cash method of accounting, this can be done by delaying payment for some of the expenses or accelerating income-generating transactions. Note that meeting the 3-out-of-5-year test does not automatically ensure that the activity will be treated as a business. It merely compels the IRS to prove that the activity is *not* a business. Under these circumstances, the IRS may be less inclined to challenge the deductions.

Unreasonable Compensation

If the IRS feels that a salary payment to an officer of a corporation is excessive, it will often recharacterize the excess portion as a dividend. If that happens, the corporation is not permitted to deduct the full amount of the salary payment. To prevent a potential future disallowance, a payback or hedge agreement, which provides that the employee must return to the corporation any payment held to be excessive, may be entered into between the parties. A payback agreement must meet the following requirements to be effective:

- It must be entered into before the payment is actually made.[120]
- It must legally obligate the employee to repay the excess amount.[121]

The IRS may take the position that the existence of the payback agreement itself is evidence that the compensation is excessive.[122] This situation may be avoided if the payback agreement is included in the general corporate bylaws rather than in a specific contract with a particular employee.[123]

Timing of Deductions

Because of the time value of money, taxpayers generally prefer to deduct an expenditure as a current expense rather than capitalize it. If an expenditure is required to be capitalized, the deductions (e.g., for depreciation or amortization) are spread over several years. In addition, some capital expenditures (e.g., land or goodwill) are not subject to depreciation or amortization. In some situations, however, it may be preferable for the taxpayer to capitalize rather than expense a particular item. For example, if a taxpayer has net operating losses (NOLs) that are about to expire, a current deduction may prevent the use of these losses.[124]

In some cases it is difficult to determine whether an item should be treated as a capital expenditure or a deduction item (e.g., certain repairs may in the aggregate be treated as a capital expenditure). In addition, certain types of expenditures, such as for research and experimentation, may be either capitalized (subject to amortization) or expensed at the election of the taxpayer. Consideration should be given to the taxpayer's tax situation when this decision is made. In making this decision, taxpayers should consider NOL carryovers that might be expiring. They should also compare their current marginal tax rate with their anticipated future marginal tax rate.

COMPLIANCE AND PROCEDURAL CONSIDERATIONS

Self-Study Question

A professor in the Department of Accounting also teaches continuing education courses for the state CPA society as a sole proprietor. If the individual is a member of the state CPA society, are his or her dues deductible on Schedule C or as an itemized deduction?

Answer

Certainly, the individual would prefer to have the dues deductible on Schedule C so that they will not be subject to the 2% limit on miscellaneous itemized deductions. This question demonstrates the difficulty of classifying some deductions, and the answer likely depends on the primary reason for membership in the organization.

Proper Classification of Deductions

Individuals report trade or business expenses on Schedule C (Profit or Loss from Business or Profession). It is similar to an income statement for business-related income and expenses. The net income computed on Schedule C is then included in gross income on Form 1040. Since business-related expenses are deducted in arriving at the taxable income from the business, these expenses are deductions *for* AGI. Similar treatment is given to the deductibility of expenses attributable to the production of rental and royalty income since they are reported on Schedule E, which is an income statement. The other deductions *for* AGI have specific lines on Form

---

[120] *Vincent E. Oswald*, 49 T.C. 645 (1968); and *J. G. Pahl*, 67 T.C. 286 (1976).
[121] *Ernest H. Berger*, 37 T.C. 1026 (1962).
[122] *Charles Schneider and Co.* v. CIR, 34 AFTR 2d 74-5422, 74-2 USTC ¶ 9563 (8th Cir., 1974).
[123] *Plastics Universal Corp.*, 1979 PH T.C. Memo ¶ 79,355, 39 TCM 32.
[124] A NOL arises when business expenses exceed business income for a year. This excess can be carried to another year (back 3 years and forward 15 years) and is deducted against the income of that year. If the years to which the NOL is carried do not have enough income, the NOL is lost when the carryover period expires. See Chapter 8 for a discussion of NOLs.

Additional Comment

When the election is made to defer the determination of whether a particular activity is engaged in for profit, the statute of limitations is automatically extended for all years in the postponement period. However, the automatic extension applies only to items that might be disallowed under the hobby loss rules.

1040 itself where they are deducted.[125] All of these deductions appear before line 31 (where AGI appears) of Form 1040.

Deductions *from* AGI are reported on Schedule A, where they are totaled and then transferred to Line 34 of Form 1040.

Proper Substantiation

The burden of proving the deductibility of any expense generally rests upon the taxpayer. This has always been the case. However, in recent years Congress and the IRS have become increasingly concerned about the propriety of many deductions. In the case of travel and entertainment expenses, the Code states that no deduction may be taken for an expense that is not properly documented. This information must include (1) the amount of the expense, (2) the time and place of the travel or entertainment activity, (3) the business purpose, and (4) the business relationship of the persons entertained.

Business Versus Hobby

Self-employed individuals who claim a home office deduction on Schedule C must attach Form 8829 which is used to allocate direct and indirect expenses to the appropriate use. Form 8829 need not be filed by employees who claim home office expenses on Form 2106.

When an activity has both profit-making and personal elements associated with it, the burden is normally on the taxpayer to prove that the activity is a business. However, if a taxpayer can show that the activity has generated a profit in 3 out of 5 consecutive years, the burden of proof shifts to the IRS. Since the statute of limitations generally runs 3 years after the filing of a return for any particular year (i.e., for audit purposes the year is closed and the IRS cannot assess any tax deficiency for that year), a potential problem exists for taxpayers who want to rely on this presumption during the first year or two of an activity's life. In these cases the taxpayer may elect to defer the determination of whether the presumption applies until the fifth year of operation. The effect of this election is to keep the year in question open with respect to that activity until sufficient years have passed so that the presumptive test may be applied. If the taxpayer subsequently does not meet the presumptive test, the IRS can still assess a deficiency for that activity for the prior year, since the year is still open. This election is made by filing Form 5213 (Election to Postpone Determination as to Whether the Presumption That an Activity Is Engaged In for Profit Applies) and must be filed within 3 years after the due date for the year in which the taxpayer first engages in the activity. This form includes the following:

- Taxpayer's name, address, and identification number

- Statement declaring that the taxpayer elects to postpone the hobby versus business determination

- Description of the activity for which the election is being made[126]

In addition, the taxpayer must properly consent to an extension of the statute of limitations.[127]

---

[125] Some of these expenses, such as employee business expenses (Form 2106) and moving expenses (Form 3903), are summarized on separate forms. These separate forms, however, are not net income statements in the same sense that Schedules C and E are.

[126] Temp. Reg. Sec. 12.9.

[127] Ibid.

PROBLEM MATERIALS

DISCUSSION QUESTIONS

6-1. Why is the concept of adjusted gross income (AGI) important for individuals?

6-2. Why are deductions *for* AGI usually more advantageous than deductions *from* AGI?

6-3. Sam owns a small house that he rents out to students attending the local university. Are the expenses associated with the rental unit deductions *for* or *from* AGI?

6-4. During the year, Sara sold a capital asset at a loss of $2,000. She had held the asset as an investment. Is her deduction for this capital loss a deduction *for* or a deduction *from* AGI?

6-5. Jiro, a single individual, is an employee of Delaware Corporation. His salary is $60,000 and he has no other items of income or itemized deductions. During the year he incurs $10,000 of deductible employee business expenses. Considering only the tax consequences, which arrangement would he prefer?
  a. Keeping his salary at $60,000 and submitting for a reimbursement of the $10,000 expenses.
  b. Increasing his salary to $70,000 and paying for his own expenses without being reimbursed by his employer.

6-6. For the current year, Mario a single individual with no dependents, receives income of $55,000 and incurs deductible expenses of $9,000.
  a. What is Mario's taxable income assuming that the expenses are deductions *for* AGI.
  b. What is Mario's taxable income assuming that the expenses are deductions *from* AGI.

6-7. Under what circumstances can prepaid expenses be deducted in the year of payment by a taxpayer using the cash method of accounting?

6-8. Can a taxpayer use both the cash method and the accrual method of accounting at the same time? Explain.

6-9. Explain the concept of economic performance.

6-10. Whether the economic performance test is satisfied depends upon the type of transaction and whether the transaction is recurring.
  a. When does economic performance occur for a taxpayer who must provide property or services to another person?
  b. When does economic performance occur when another person provides the taxpayer with property or services?
  c. Explain the exception to the economic performance test for recurring liabilities.

6-11. List the factors used in determining whether an activity is profit-motivated.

6-12. If an activity does not generate a profit in 3 out of 5 consecutive years, is it automatically deemed to be a hobby? Why or why not?

6-13. Since expenses incurred in both a business and for the production of investment income are deductible, why is it important to determine in which category a particular activity falls?

6-14. What criteria must be met for a business expense to be deductible?

6-15. In order for a business expense to be deductible it must be *ordinary, necessary,* and *reasonable.* Explain what these terms mean.

6-16. What criteria must one use in distinguishing between a deductible expense and a capital expenditure?

6-17. What types of capital expenditures can a taxpayer elect to deduct currently?

6-18. What is the purpose of the disallowance for expenses related to tax-exempt income?

6-19. Under what circumstances may a taxpayer deduct an illegal bribe or kickback?

6-20. Michelle pays a CPA $400 for the preparation of her federal income tax return. Michelle's only sources of income are her salary from employment and interest and dividends from her investments.

    a. Is this a deductible expense? If so, is it a deduction *for* or *from* AGI?

    b. Assume the same facts as in Part a except that in addition to her salary and investment and dividend income, Michelle also owns a small business. Of the $400 fee paid to the CPA, $250 is for the preparation of her Schedule C (Profit or Loss from Business). How much, if any, of the $400 is a deductible expense? Identify as either *for* or *from* AGI.

6-21. Jennifer flies to her state capital to lobby the legislature to build a proposed highway that is planned to run through the area where her business is located.

    a. What part, if any, of her expenses are deductible?

    b. Would it make a difference if the proposed road was a city road rather than a state highway, and Jennifer lobbied her local government?

    c. Assume the facts in part a except that Jennifer's total expenses are $1,500. Are these expenses deductible?

6-22. What kinds of expenses are considered start-up expenditures under Sec. 195?

6-23. Why can business investigation expenditures be deducted currently by a taxpayer who is engaged in a line of business similar to the one being investigated, while the same costs must be capitalized and amortized to be deductible by a taxpayer who is not engaged in a similar business?

6-24. What documentation is required in order for a travel or entertainment expense to be deductible?

6-25. Why did Congress enact the wash sale provisions?

6-26. The wash sale rules disallow a loss in the year of sale when substantially identical stock or securities are acquired by the taxpayer within a 61-day period. What types of stock or securities are considered to be substantially identical?

6-27. Who is considered a member of a taxpayer's family under the related party transaction rules of Sec. 267?

6-28. Under the related party rules of Sec. 267, why has Congress imposed the concept of constructive ownership?

6-29. If property is sold at a loss to a related taxpayer, under what circumstances can at least partial benefit be derived from the disallowed loss?

6-30. Can a taxpayer deduct a loss incurred in an activity that is determined to be a hobby? Explain.

6-31. Under Sec. 280A, what constitutes personal use of a vacation home by the taxpayer?

6-32. Under Sec. 280A, how are expenses allocated to the rental use of a vacation home? In what order must the expenses be deducted against the gross income of the property?

6-33. Under Sec. 280A, how will a taxpayer report the income and expenses of a vacation home if it is rented out for only 12 days during the year?

PROBLEMS

6-34. *For or From AGI Deductions.* Jermaine is an attorney who is an employee of a local law firm. During the year, Jermaine incurs the following unreimbursed expenses:

Item	Amount
Bar association fees	$300
Subscriptions to professional journals	150
Travel from the office to the courthouse	200
Photocopying of the firm's law briefs	100
Taking clients to dinner	450

a. Identify which of these expenses are deductible and indicate whether they are deductions *for* or *from* AGI.

b. Would the answer to Part a change if the law firm reimburses Jermaine for these expenses?

c. Assume all of the same facts as in Part a, except that Jermaine is self-employed. Identify which of the expenses are deductible, and indicate whether they are deductions *for* or *from* AGI.

6-35. *From AGI Deductions.* During the current year, Roger, a single individual, incurred the following deductible expenses (before any limitations are applied):

Medical expenses	$5,000
Real estate taxes	2,000
Interest on a principal residence	3,000
Charitable contributions	1,500
Net personal casualty losses (already reduced by the $100 limit)	2,000
Miscellaneous itemized deductions	1,800

Roger's AGI for the current year is $60,000. What is Roger's taxable income?

6-36. *For vs. From AGI.* During the current year, Steve, a single taxpayer, reports the following items of income and expense:

Income:	
Salary	$57,000
Dividends from Alta Corporation	600
Interest income from a savings account	1,000
Rental income from a small apartment he owns	7,000
Expenses:	
Medical	3,000
Interest on a principal residence	4,000
Real property taxes on the principal residence	3,000
Charitable contributions	1,500
Casualty loss - personal	6,100
Miscellaneous itemized deductions	800
Loss from the sale of Delta Corporation stock	2,000
Expenses incurred on the rental apartment:	
Maintenance	300
Property taxes	800
Utilities	2,400
Depreciation	1,500
Insurance	600
Alimony payments	8,000

Assuming all of these items are deductible and that the amounts are before any limitations, what is Steve's taxable income for the year?

6-37. *Prepaid Expenses.* Pamela, an engineering consultant, is self-employed and uses the cash method of accounting. On November 1 of the current year, she entered into a lease to rent some office space for five years. The lease agreement states that the lease payments are $12,000 per year, payable in advance each November 1 for the following 12-month period. Under the terms of the lease Pamela is required to pay a $5,000 deposit, refundable upon the termination of the lease. On December 1 of the current year Pamela also renewed her malpractice insurance paying $18,000 for the three-year contract. On December 31 of the current year, Pamela mailed out a check for $5,000 for drafting services performed for her by an individual who lives in another city. On December 31 she also picked up $700 worth of stationary and other office supplies. Pamela has an open charge account with the office supply company which bills Pamela monthly for charges made during the year. Finally, on December 31, Pamela picked up some work that a local printing company had done for her which amounted to $1,000. She charged the $1,000 with her business credit card.

Compute the amount of Pamela's current year deductions because of these transactions.

6-38. *Prepaid Expenses.* During the current year, John and Sue, a married couple who use the cash method of accounting, purchased a principal residence. They paid $20,000 down and financed $60,000 of the purchase price with a 30-year mortgage. At the closing, they also paid $500 for an appraisal, $500 for a title search, and 1.5 points representing additional interest over the term of the loan. At the end of the year, John and Sue received a statement from the mortgage company indicating that $7,000 of their total monthly payments made during the year represents interest and $1,000 is a reduction of the principal balance.

a. What is the total amount that John and Sue may deduct in the current year arising from the purchase and ownership of their home?

b. What is the treatment of the other items that are not deductible?

6-39. *Capitalization Versus Expense.* Lavonne incurs the following expenditures on an apartment building which she owns:

Item	Amount
Replace the roof	$3,000
Repaint the exterior	1,500
Install new locks	200
Replace broken windows	150
Replace crumbling sidewalks and stairs	2,000

Discuss the proper tax treatment for these expenditures.

6-40. *Political Contributions and Lobbying Expenses.* Sam is a sole proprietor who owns several apartment complexes and office buildings. The leasing and managing of these buildings constitutes Sam's only business activity. During the current year Sam incurred the following:

- $900 in air fare and lodging incurred on a trip to Washington, D.C. The purpose of the trip was to protest proposed tax rate increases for individuals and corporations.
- $700 for renting space on billboards along the highway. The billboards express his concern regarding pending legislation that would significantly increase property taxes.
- $500 in air fare and hotel bills incurred on a trip to the state capital. The purpose of the trip was to meet with the legislative subcommittee on property taxation.
- $50 for a subscription to a political newsletter published by a national political party.
- $150 in making a presentation to the county council protesting a proposed increase in the property tax levy.

a. What is the total amount Sam may deduct because of these expenditures?

b. Assume all the same facts as in part a except that the expenses for the trip to the state capital are only $300 instead of $500. What amount may Sam deduct because of these expenditures?

6-41. *Legal and Accounting Expenses.* During the current year, Sam from Problem 6-40 incurs the following expenses. Which of these expenditures are deductible? Are they *for* or *from* AGI deductions?

a. $200 in attorney's fees for title searches on a new property that Sam has acquired.

b. $450 in legal fees in an action brought to collect back rents.

c. $500 to his CPA for the preparation of his federal income tax return. $400 is for the preparation of Schedule C (Profit or Loss from Business).

d. $300 in attorney's fees for drafting a will.

e. $250 in attorney's fees in an unsuccessful attempt to prevent the city from rezoning the area of the city where several of his office buildings are located.

6-42. *Illegal Payments.* Dave is illegally engaged in the business of purchasing and exporting firearms. Following is a list of income and expense items for the year:

Item	Amount
Sales	$500,000
Cost of goods sold	180,000
Salaries	50,000
Freight	15,000
Bribes to customs officials	20,000
Lease payments on warehouses	10,000
Interest expense	8,000

What is Dave's taxable income from the illegal business activity?

6-43. *Illegal Payments.* Assume the same facts in Problem 6-42, except that Dave's business consists of buying and selling marijuana and cocaine. What is Dave's taxable income from this illegal business activity?

6-44. *Illegal Payments.* Indicate whether Glenda can deduct the $5,000 payment in each of the following independent situations.
  a. Glenda is a supplier of medical supplies. In order to secure a large sales contract to the regional Veterans Administration Hospital, Glenda makes a gift of $5,000 to the hospital's purchasing agent. The payment is illegal under state law.
  b. Assume the same facts in Part a above, except that the payment is made to the purchasing agent of a government-owned hospital in Brazil.
  c. Assume the same facts in Part a above, except that the payment is made to the purchasing agent of a privately owned hospital in Idaho.

6-45. *Business Investigation Expenditures.* During January and February of the current year, Mario incurs $3,000 in travel, feasibility studies, and legal expenses to investigate the feasibility of opening a new entertainment gallery in one of the new suburban malls in town. Mario already owns two other entertainment galleries in other malls in town.
  a. What is the proper tax treatment of these expenses if Mario decides not to open the new gallery?
  b. What is the proper tax treatment of these expenses if Mario decides to open the new gallery?
  c. Assume the same facts except that Mario does not own any other entertainment galleries. Further assume that Mario opens the new entertainment gallery on May 1 of the current year. How much, if any, may Mario deduct in the current year?

6-46. *Business Investigation Expenditures.* Assume the same facts in Problem 6-45, except that Mario does *not* already own the other entertainment galleries.
  a. What is the proper tax treatment of these expenses if Mario does not open the new gallery?
  b. What is the proper tax treatment of these expenses if Mario decides to open the new gallery?

6-47. *Wash Sales.* Vicki owns 1,000 shares of Western Corporation common stock, which she purchased on March 8, 1990, for $12,000. On October 3, 1994, she purchases an additional 300 shares for $3,000. On October 12, 1994, she sells the original 1,000 shares for $8,500. On November 1, 1994, she purchases an additional 500 shares for $4,000.
  a. What is Vicki's recognized gain or loss as a result of the sale on October 12, 1994?
  b. What are the basis and the holding period of the stock Vicki continues to hold?
  c. How would your answers to Parts a and b change if the stock Vicki purchases during 1994 is Western nonvoting, nonconvertible, preferred stock instead of Western common stock?

6-48. *Constructive Ownership.* During the current year, Bart sells a small tract of land to Apple Corporation. The selling price is $25,000. Bart purchased the land for $35,000 four years ago. The Apple Corporation stock is owned as follows:

Owner	Percentage Ownership
Bart	10%
Bart's wife	10
Bart's brother	10
Tony (Bart's friend)	25
Bart's uncle	10
Delta Corporation	35

Delta Corporation is owned equally by Bart, Bart's brother, and Bart's uncle.
  a. What is Bart's ownership (actual and constructive) of the Apple stock?
  b. What is the amount of loss that Bart may recognize?
  c. How would your answers to parts a and b change if Bart's brother-in-law owned 10% of Apple corporation's stock instead of Bart's brother?

6-49. *Related Party Transactions.* Jack is a CPA who computes his taxable income using the cash method of accounting. King Corporation, owned equally by Jack's three children, uses the accrual method of accounting. Jack is a calendar-year taxpayer, whereas King Corporation's fiscal year ends on January 31. During 1994, Jack does some consulting work for King

Corporation for a fee of $6,000. The work is completed on December 15. For each of the following assumptions, answer the following questions: (1) During which tax year must Jack report the income? (2) During which tax year must King Corporation deduct the expense?

a. The payment to Jack is made on December 27, 1994:

b. The payment to Jack is made on January 12, 1995.

c. The payment to Jack is made on February 3, 1995.

6-50. *Related Party Transactions.* During the current year, Delta Corporation sells a tract of land for $80,000. The sale is made to Shirley, Delta Corporation's sole shareholder. Delta Corporation originally purchased the land five years earlier for $95,000.

   a. What is the amount of gain or loss that Delta Corporation will recognize on the sale during the current year?

   b. Assume that in the following year, Shirley sells the land for $85,000. (1) What is the amount of gain or loss Shirley will recognize? (2) What are the tax consequences to Delta Corporation upon the subsequent sale by Shirley?

   c. Assume that in the following year, Shirley sells the land for $70,000. What is the amount of gain or loss Shirley will recognize?

   d. Assume that in the following year, Shirley sells the land for $105,000. What is the amount of gain or loss Shirley will recognize?

6-51. *Related Party Transactions.* During the current year, James sold a mainframe computer to Byte Computer, Inc. for $50,000. James had previously used the computer in his business for two years and its adjusted basis was $90,000 on the date of sale. Byte Computer is owned by ROM Inc. and Card Corporation. ROM owns 4,000 shares of Byte while Card owns the remaining 1,000 outstanding shares. Philip, James' brother, owns 100% of ROM and three of Philip's friends own equal shares of all of the outstanding stock of Card Corporation. Two years after Byte purchases the computer, it sells the machine for $60,000 to an unrelated purchaser. Byte's adjusted basis in the computer on the date of sale is $38,000.

a. What amount of gain or loss is recognized by James?

b. What amount of gain or loss is recognized by Byte on the subsequent sale of the computer?

6-52. *Hobby Loss Presumptive Rule.* Ira is an attorney who has been engaged in raising and breeding show dogs for the past 8 years. During those years Ira has reported the following net income or loss from the activity:

Year	Net Income (Loss)
1987	$(600)
1988	(400)
1989	300
1990	(1,000)
1991	200
1992	(800)
1993	(1,100)
1994	(700)

Ira is audited for the year 1994, and the agent disallows the $700 loss. May Ira make an election for 1994 to keep the year open in anticipation of meeting the presumptive rule for the year? Why or why not?

6-53. *Hobby Losses.* Chuck, a dentist, raises prize rabbits for breeding and showing purposes. Assume that the activity is determined to be a hobby. During the year the activity generates the following items of income and expense:

Item	Amount
Sale of rabbits for breeding stock	$800
Prizes and awards	300
Property taxes on rabbit hutches	300
Feed	600
Veterinary fees	500
Depreciation on rabbit hutches	300

a. What is the total amount of deductions Chuck may take during the year with respect to the rabbit raising activities?

b. Identify which expenses may be deducted, and indicate whether they are deductions *for* or *from* AGI.

c. By what amount is the cost basis of the rabbit hutches to be reduced for the year?

6-54. *Hobby Losses.* Assume the same facts as in Problem 6-53, except that the income from the sale of rabbits is $1,200.

a. What is the total amount of deductions Chuck may take during the year with respect to the rabbit raising activities?

b. Identify which expenses may be deducted, and indicate whether they are deductions *for* or *from* AGI.

c. By what amount is the cost basis of the rabbit hutches to be reduced for the year?

6-55. *Rental of Vacation Home.* During the current year, Kim incurs the following expenses with respect to her beachfront condominium in Hawaii:

Item	Amount
Insurance	$ 500
Repairs and maintenance	700
Interest on mortgage	3,000
Property taxes	1,000
Utilities	800

In addition to the expenses listed above, Kim could have deducted a total of $8,000 depreciation if the property had been acquired only for investment purposes. During the year, Kim uses the condominium 20 days for vacation. She also rented it out for a total of 60 days during the year, generating a total gross income of $9,000.

a. What is the total amount of deductions Kim may take during the current year with respect to the condominium?

b. Identify which expenses may be deducted, and indicate whether they are deductions *for* or *from* AGI.

c. What is the effect on the basis of the condominium?

6-56. *Rental of Vacation Home.* Assume all of the same facts in Problem 6-55, except that during the year Kim rents the condominium a total of 14 days. How does Kim report the income and deductions from the property?

COMPREHENSIVE PROBLEM

6-57. Bryce, a bank official, is married and files a joint return. During the current year he engages in the following activities and transactions:

a. Being an avid fisherman, Bryce develops an expertise in tying flies. At times during the year, he is asked to conduct fly-tying demonstrations, for which he is paid a small fee. He also periodically sells flies that he makes. Income generated from these activities during the year is $2,500. The expenses for the year associated with Bryce's fly-tying activity include $125 personal property taxes on a small trailer that he uses exclusively for this purpose, $2,900 in supplies, $270 in repairs on the trailer, and $200 in gasoline from traveling to the demonstrations.

b. Bryce sells a small building lot to his brother for $30,000. Bryce purchased the lot four years ago for $35,000, hoping to make a profit.

c. Bryce enters into the following stock transactions: (None of the stock qualifies as small business stock).

Date	Transaction
March 22	Purchases 100 shares of Silver Corporation common stock for $2,800
April 5	Sells 200 shares of Gold Corporation common stock for $8,000. The stock was originally purchased two years ago for $5,000.
April 15	Sells 200 shares of Silver Corporation common stock for $5,400. The stock was originally purchased three years ago for $9,400.
May 20	Sells 100 shares of United Corporation common stock for $12,000. The stock was originally purchased five years ago for $10,000.

d. Bryce's salary for the year is $80,000. In addition to the items above, he also incurs $5,000 in other miscellaneous deductible itemized expenses.

Answer the following questions regarding Bryce's activities for the year.

1. How much in total gains and losses from the sale of property should Bryce report for the year?

2. What is the total amount of Bryce's itemized deductions for the year?

3. What is Bryce's basis in the Silver stock he continues to own?

TAX FORM/RETURN PREPARATION PROBLEMS

6-58. Carolyn Snowflake, a self-employed physician, uses the cash-method of accounting. Carolyn's social security number is 111-33-9999, her employer ID number is 12-1234567, and her business address is Suite 402A, 123 Physicians Way, Anytown, Any State 12345. Dr. Snowflake has been practicing medicine for the past 12 years. During the current year, Carolyn recorded the following items of income:

Revenue from patient visits	$200,000
Interest earned on the office checking balance	150

The following expenses were recorded on the office books:

Property taxes on the office	$3,000
Mortgage interest on the office	8,000
Depreciation on the office	3,000
Malpractice Insurance	25,000
Utilities	2,500
Office staff salaries	34,000
Rent payments on equipment	10,000
Office magazine subscriptions	100
Office supplies	16,000
Medical journals	220

Complete Schedule C of Form 1040 for the current year.

TurboTax **6-59.** Dave and Pam Brighton are married, have no children, and are filing a joint tax return in the current year. They are both managers of local retail stores. Dave and Pam, ages 38 and 37, respectively, have combined salaries of $51,000 from which $9,000 of federal income tax and $2,500 of state income tax are withheld. Dave and Pam own two homes. Their primary residence is located at 11620 N. Mount Ave., Atlanta, Georgia 22222, and their vacation home is located in Vail, Colorado. They often rent their vacation home to skiers to supplement their income. The following items are related to the Brightons' ownership of the two homes:

Item	Atlanta	Vail
Rental income	$ —	$9,000
Qualified residence interest	7,200	5,000
Property taxes	1,400	1,000
Utilities	1,000	1,300
Repairs	200	300
Depreciation	0	3,500
Advertising	0	200
Insurance	1,500	1,500

The Brightons used their Vail home 20 days during the year. They rented the vacation home 60 days during the year.

The Brightons have no other income or expense items.

Dave and Pam's social security numbers are 111-22-3333 and 444-55-6666, respectively.

File the Brightons' income tax return Form 1040, Schedules A and E using the currently available forms and rates.

TurboTax **6-60.** Burton, age 56, and Joyce Winters, age 54, are married and are filing jointly in the current year. Their social security numbers are 123-45-6789 and 987-65-4321, respectively. Burton's salary for the year is $43,000 from which $8,000 of federal income tax and $2,000 of state income tax were withheld. Joyce is the sole owner of Winter's Piano Tuning Company, a proprietorship which supplements the couple's income. Joyce reports the following income and expenses related to her business operation:

Revenues	$4,900
City business license	300
Yellow Pages—advertisement	40
Depreciation on tools	70
Supplies	300

Joyce subscribes to the following journals:

Piano Tuner's Journal	$40
Wall Street Journal	100
Money Magazine	40
Reader's Digest	50
U.S. News & World Report	40

Burton & Joyce jointly purchase stock in various corporations and make the following transactions in the current year: (None of the stock qualifies as small business stock).

Date	Transaction	Price Pd/Sold
2-15	Bought 50 shares of Lake common stock (own no other Lake stock)	$1,000
5-14	Bought 100 shares of Bass common stock (own no other Bass stock)	3,000
5-24	Sold 25 shares of Lake common stock	500
5-27	Bought 50 shares of Lake common stock	900
	Sold 50 shares of Bass common stock	1,750
7-12	Bought 100 shares of Bass common stock	2,800

During the year, Burton and Joyce receive dividend income of $200, taxable interest income of $350, make political contributions of $300, and pay $25 for use of a safety deposit box to store certain documents Joyce needs in her business.

Burton and Joyce own only one home at 237 E. 100 N., Kaysville, Ohio 11111. Their deductible mortgage interest for the year is $7,000. Burton and Joyce filed their state income tax return for the prior year in April of this year and paid an additional $400 of state income tax. In April of the current year, they also paid $180 to a CPA for preparing their federal and state income tax returns for the prior year, $100 of which was for the preparation of Joyce's Schedule C.

Burton and Joyce have no other deductions.

Prepare Burton and Joyce's tax return (Form 1040, Schedules A, C, D, and SE) for the current year.

CASE STUDY PROBLEM

6-61. John and Kathy Brown have just been audited and the IRS agent disallowed the business loss they claimed in 1992. The agent asserted that the activity was a hobby and not a business.

John and Kathy live in Rochester, NY, near Lake Ontario. Kathy is a CPA and John was formerly employed by an insurance firm. John's firm moved in 1987 and John resolved not to move to the firm's new location. Instead of seeking other employment John felt he could supplement his income by using his fishing expertise. He had been an avid fisherman for 15 years and he owned a large Chris-Craft fly-bridge which he chartered to paying parties.

In 1988 Kathy and John developed a business plan, established a bank account for the charter activities, developed a bookkeeping system, and acquired insurance to cover the boat and the passengers. John fulfilled all the requirements to receive a US Coast Guard operating license, a New York sport trolling license, and a seller's permit. These licenses and permits were necessary to legally operate a charter boat. 1988 was the first year of their activity.

John advertised in local papers and regional sport fishing magazines. He would usually have three or four half-day paying parties each week. John spent at least one day maintaining and repairing his boat. Kathy would usually accompany John on charters three or four times each year.

John's charter activity was unprofitable the first two years. In 1990, John and Kathy restructured the activity to improve profitability. The restructuring included increasing advertising, participating in outdoor shows, and negotiating small contracts with local businesses. After the restructuring, the activity provided a small profit in 1990 and 1991.

In 1992 John started working with another insurance company in the area on a full-time basis. Even though he returned to the insurance business, John would normally take two paying parties and one non-paying, promotional party each week throughout the fishing season. John's costs unexpectedly increased and he lost $8,000 in the activity during 1992. John and Kathy deducted the entire loss on Schedule C of their 1992 tax return.

Required: Prepare a memo to the Browns recommending what position they should take and why. Show the logic used in arriving at your recommendation.

CASE STUDY PROBLEM—ETHICAL ISSUES

6-62. For several years you have done the tax return for your neighbors, Scott and Cindy Snyder. Scott is a high school teacher and Cindy owns her own business. Over the years, Scott has frequently mentioned to you his love of stock car racing. For years he has spent a great deal of time after work and on weekends out at the track. He also subscribes to several automotive magazines. Unfortunately, up until this year he never has had enough money to buy his own car.

This year, however, things are different. Scott was able to purchase a car that needed a lot of fixing up. After spending a considerable amount of time and money (Scott estimates that he has spent close to $6,500 just on maintenance, repairs, and beefing the car up), the car was finally ready to race. This year Scott has entered only 3 races. In 2 of the races he didn't place. In fact, in the first race he didn't even finish. However, in the third race, he won $200 in prize money! Although Scott is excited about the money, he has boasted to you that the prize money isn't as important as the thrill of racing and winning!

When the Snyders give you their tax information for this year, Scott mentions; "Now that I've won some money from racing, we can finally write off all these expenses against our taxes."

Do you treat Scott's racing activity as a business or as a hobby? You are concerned because you know that Scott will continue in the activity whether or not he generates any more income. (See the caption entitled Statements on Responsibilities in Tax Practice in Chapter 1 for a discussion of these issues.)

TAX RESEARCH PROBLEM

6-63. Richard Penn lives in Harrisburg, PA. Richard is the president of an architectural firm. Richard has become known throughout the community for excellent work and honesty in his business dealings. Richard believes his reputation is an integral part of the success of the firm.

Oil was found recently in the area around Harrisburg and some geologists believed the reserves were large. A few well-respected business people organized Oil Company to develop a few wells. Although some oil was being extracted, the oil corporation lacked capital to develop the oil fields to their expected potential. After reading the geologists' report, Richard felt that Oil Company was a good investment; therefore, he acquired 25% of the company. A short time after Richard's acquisition, the price of foreign oil decreased sharply. The drop in foreign oil prices caused Oil Company to be unprofitable due to their high production costs. Three months later Oil Company filed bankruptcy.

The bankruptcy proceedings were reported in the local newspaper. Many of Oil Company's creditors were real estate developers that frequently engaged Richard's architectural firm to provide designs. After Oil Company declared bankruptcy the architectural firm's business noticeably decreased.

Richard felt the decline in business was related to the bankruptcy of Oil Company. Richard convinced his partner to use the accumulated earnings of the firm to repay all the creditors of Oil Company.

Richard has asked you if his firm can deduct the expenses of repaying Oil Company's creditors. After completing your research explain to Richard why the expenses are or are not deductible.

A partial list of research sources is as follows:

- Sec. 162.
- *Thomas H. Welch v. Helvering,* 12 AFTR 1456, 3 USTC ¶ 1164 (USSC, 1933).
- *William A. Thompson, Jr.,* 1983 PH T.C. Memo ¶ 83,487, 46 TCM 1109.

7 *Itemized Deductions*

LEARNING OBJECTIVES

After studying this chapter, you should be able to

1. Identify qualified medical expenses and compute the medical expense deduction
2. Determine the timing of a medical expense deduction and the effect of a reimbursement
3. Identify taxes that are deductible as itemized deductions
4. Identify different types of interest deductions
5. Compute the amount of investment interest deduction
6. Compute the deduction for qualified residence interest
7. Compute the amount of a charitable contribution deduction and identify limitations
8. Identify certain miscellaneous itemized deductions subject to the 2% of AGI limit
9. Compute total itemized deductions for a taxpayer who is subject to the itemized deduction phase-out.

As explained in Chapter 6, most deductible expenses for individuals may be classified into three general categories:

- Expenses incurred in a trade or business

- Expenses incurred for the production of income or for the determination of a tax

- Certain specified personal expenses

For individuals, all deductible expenses must also be classified as either *for* AGI or *from* AGI deductions, regardless of how the expense is categorized (see list above). *From* AGI deductions are also referred to as **itemized deductions.** This distinction is important because AGI is used as a measuring point in determining the amount of certain deductible expenses such as medical expenses, casualty losses, and miscellaneous itemized deductions. The concept of AGI has no meaning for taxpayers other than individuals. A list of the more common deductions *for* AGI is found in Chapter 6. This chapter deals with the itemized deductions for medical expenses, taxes, interest, and charitable contributions. Other itemized deductions such as unreimbursed employee business expenses, moving expenses, and casualty losses are discussed in later chapters.[1]

In arriving at taxable income, individuals may subtract from AGI the larger of the standard deduction or the sum of all itemized deductions.[2] However, as explained later in this chapter, certain itemized deductions are reduced if a taxpayer's AGI exceeds certain limits.

---

[1] Unreimbursed employee business expenses and moving expenses are explained in Chapter 9. Casualty losses are discussed in Chapter 8.

[2] Personal and dependency exemptions are also subtracted from AGI in arriving at taxable income.

MEDICAL EXPENSES

Medical expenses, which comprise one category of deductible personal expenditures, are deductible because Congress felt that excessive medical expenses might ultimately affect a taxpayer's ability to pay his or her federal income tax. However, medical expenses are deductible only to the extent they exceed 7.5% of the taxpayer's AGI. To qualify as a medical expense deduction, the expenditure must have been incurred for the medical care of a qualified individual. No deduction may be taken for medical expenses to the extent they are reimbursed (i.e., compensated for by insurance or otherwise).[3]

Qualified Individuals

Deductible medical expenses must be paid on behalf of either the taxpayer, the taxpayer's spouse, or a dependent of the taxpayer.

Taxpayer's Dependent. Medical expenses paid on behalf of a person for whom the taxpayer could take a dependency exemption except for the failure to meet the gross income or joint return tests are included in the taxpayer's medical expenses.[4]

Example 7-1 ■

In March of the current year, Jean's son, Steve, is involved in an automobile accident. Steve is 25 years old at the time of the accident and has worked full time for part of the year, earning a total of $5,000. Since he has no medical insurance and cannot pay the medical bills or support himself as a result of the accident, Jean pays Steve's medical expenses and supports him for the rest of the year. Since Jean provides over one-half of Steve's support for the year and Steve otherwise qualifies as Jean's dependent, Jean may deduct the medical expenses she pays on his behalf. Jean may not claim a dependency exemption for Steve since the gross income test is not satisfied. ■

Children of Divorced Parents. As long as one parent is entitled to the dependency exemption under Sec. 152(e), medical expenses paid on behalf of the children of divorced parents are deductible by the parent who pays the expenses. The parent taking the medical expense deduction need not be the parent who is entitled to the dependency exemption.[5]

Example 7-2 ■

Joe and Peggy are divorced during the current year. Peggy is granted custody of their daughter Carol, and she does not agree to transfer the dependency exemption to Joe. Together Joe and Peggy provide over one-half of Carol's support. Since Peggy is the custodial parent and has not released her claim to the dependency exemption for the year, she may claim a dependency exemption for Carol. During

---

[3] Sec. 213(a).

[4] Sec. 152. As explained in Chapter 2, a person qualifies as a taxpayer's dependent if (1) the taxpayer has provided over one-half of that individual's support for the year; (2) there is a proper relationship (generally a member of the taxpayer's family or household) between the taxpayer and the individual; and (3) the individual is a citizen or resident of the United States, Canada, or Mexico. To claim a dependency exemption for an individual, the individual must be the taxpayer's dependent and the following additional requirements must be satisfied: (1) The dependent must have gross income less than the exemption amount (unless he or she is a child of the taxpayer and is either under 19 years of age at the end of the year or a full-time student who has not reached the age of 24 at the close of the year), and (2) the dependent must not have filed a joint return. For 1994 the exemption amount is $2,450.

[5] Sec. 213(d)(5).

the year, Joe expends $2,500 for orthodontic work on Carol's behalf. Joe may deduct these medical expenses, even though he may not claim Carol as a dependent. ∎

Qualified Medical Expenses

OBJECTIVE 1
Identify qualified expenses and compute the medical expense deduction

The **medical expense deduction** is available only for expenditures paid for medical care. Section 213 defines *medical care* as amounts paid for:

- The diagnosis, cure, mitigation, treatment, or prevention of disease
- The purpose of affecting any structure or function of the body
- Transportation primarily for and essential to the first two items listed above
- Insurance covering all of the items listed above

Additional Comment
One cannot deduct the cost of nonprescription medicine, toothpaste, toiletries, maternity clothes, diaper service, or funeral expenses.

Diagnosis, Cure, Mitigation, Treatment, or Prevention of Disease. Although the term *medical expense* is not precisely defined, it is clear that medical expenses are deductible only if they are paid for procedures or treatments that are legal in the locality in which they are performed.[6] Routine physical and dental examinations are qualified medical expenses. However, other expenses should be ". . . confined strictly to expenses incurred primarily for the prevention or alleviation of a physical or mental defect or illness."[7] Thus, unless they are for routine physical or dental examinations, the expenditures must be incurred for the purpose of curing a specific ailment rather than being related to the general health of an individual. This determination is especially critical when the expenditures in question are for items such as vacations, weight loss programs, or programs designed to help the individual stop smoking. Such expenses may or may not be incurred for a specific ailment.

Example 7-3 ∎ | Helmut is nervous and irritable because of the pressures at work. Furthermore, he begins to suffer angina symptoms. In order to relax and "get away from it all," he takes an ocean cruise around the world. Helmut's angina symptoms ease while he is on the cruise. However, the Tax Court held that a cruise is not a proven medical necessity since Helmut's physician did not specifically prescribe it. Although the cruise was beneficial to Helmut's general health, it is not deductible.[8] ∎

Example 7-4 ∎ | Because Dave is overweight, he enrolls in a weight reduction program to improve his appearance and self-confidence. The resulting weight loss has the desired result. However, the Internal Revenue Service (IRS) ruled that the expenses are not deductible because they are related to Dave's general health.[9] ∎

Example 7-5 ∎ | Assume the same facts as in Example 7-4, except that Dave enrolls in the weight reduction program on the advice of two doctors who prescribe the program as a means of relieving his obesity, hypertension, and certain hearing problems. In a

---

[6] Reg. Sec. 1.213-1(e)(1)(ii). See also Rev. Rul. 78-325, 1978-2 C.B. 124, where amounts paid for laetrile (an illegal drug in the United States) were deductible because its use as a medicine was legal in the area where it was purchased and used.

[7] Ibid.

[8] *Daniel E. Mizl*, 1980 PH T.C. Memo ¶ 80,227, 40 TCM 552. Even if Z's physician had prescribed the trip, it still may not have been deductible.

[9] Rev. Rul. 79-151, 1979-1 C.B. 116.

private letter ruling, the IRS held that these expenses qualify as deductible medical expenditures because they are incurred for specific medical conditions.[10] ∎

Although receipt of a doctor's recommendation for incurring the cost appears to lend a great deal of weight to deductibility, it is not always sufficient. For example, the cost of dancing lessons for an emotionally disturbed child was not found deductible, even though the lessons proved to be beneficial and were recommended by a physician.[11] Likewise, a taxpayer suffering from arthritis could not deduct the cost of ballroom dance lessons, even though the lessons were recommended by a doctor.[12]

RANGE OF DEDUCTIBLE MEDICAL SERVICES. According to the Regulations, typical medical expenses include payments for a wide range of medical, dental, and other diagnostic and healing services.[13] Thus, payments to licensed or certified medical professionals such as general practitioners, obstetricians, surgeons, ophthalmologists, opticians, dentists, and orthodontists are all deductible. Furthermore, payment for medical services rendered by individuals such as chiropractors, osteopaths, and psychotherapists who may or may not be required to be licensed or certified is also deductible.[14] Acupuncture treatments are deductible if they are received for a specific medical purpose, as are payments to Christian Science practitioners.[15] Qualified medical expenses also include payment for hospital services, nursing services, laboratory fees, X-rays, artificial teeth or limbs, ambulance hire, eyeglasses, and prescribed medicines and insulin.[16] Expenditures for nonprescription medicines, drugs, vitamins, and other types of health foods that improve the individual's general health are not deductible.

In order to deduct costs incurred for schools and camps, the taxpayer must show that the facility is regularly engaged in providing medical services. Thus, the expense incurred by a taxpayer in sending his mentally handicapped son to a school that had a special curriculum for such children was found deductible. The cost of sending a child with psychiatric problems to a school specializing in certain learning disorders was also held deductible.[17] However, the cost of sending children with special medical problems to schools or camps that do not have the proper equipment, facilities, or curriculum for such problems is generally not deductible.[18]

Medical Procedures Affecting Any Function or Structure of the Body.

Deductible medical expenditures also include payments for services affecting any function or structure of the body, even though no specific illness or disease exists. Thus, expenditures for such items as physical therapy, obstetrical services, eyeglasses, dental examinations and cleaning, and hearing aids all qualify as medical expenses. Cosmetic surgery or any other similar procedure does not qualify as a medical expense unless such surgery is necessary to correct a deformity arising from a congenital

---

[10] Ltr. Rul. 8004111 (October 31, 1979).

[11] *John J. Thoene*, 33 T.C. 62 (1959).

[12] *Rose C. France v. CIR*, 50 AFTR 2d 81-5504, 1982-1 USTC ¶ 9225 (6th Cir., 1982).

[13] Reg. Sec. 1.213-1(e)(1)(ii).

[14] Rev. Rul. 63-91, 1963-1 C.B. 54. See also Ltr. Rul. 8919009 (February 6, 1989) where a pregnant woman was entitled to a deduction for the cost of childbirth classes to the extent they prepared her for the childbirth. However, the cost of the classes where she received instructions on the care of the unborn child were not qualified medical expenses.

[15] Rev. Rul. 72-593, 1972-2 C.B. 180 and IRS Special Ruling, February 2, 1943.

[16] Sec. 213(b) and Reg. Sec. 1.213-1(e)(1)(ii).

[17] Rev. Rul. 70-285, 1970-1 C.B. 52 and *Lawrence D. Greisdorf*, 54 T.C. 1684 (1970), acq. 1970-2 C.B. xix.

[18] *Devora R. Shidler*, 1971 PH T.C. Memo ¶ 71,126, 30 TCM 529. See also *John A. Dreifus*, 1977 PH T.C. Memo ¶ 77,083, 36 TCM 368, and *Dr. Ernest M. Newkirk v. U.S.*, 40 AFTR 2d 77-5114, 77-1 USTC ¶ 9452 (D.C. Ohio, 1977).

Additional Comment

In accordance with the Revenue Reconciliation Act of 1990, expenses paid for cosmetic surgery are not deductible. This would include expenses for hair removal electrolysis, hair transplants, lyposuction, and face lift operations if they do not prevent or treat an illness or disease.

Real World Example

The transportation costs of a trip to the Shrine in Lourdes, France, were not deductible since the trip was taken to obtain spiritual aid to supplement medical care and not on the suggestion of a physician. Vincent P. Ring, 23 T.C. 950 (1955).

abnormality, a personal injury resulting from an accident or trauma, or a disfiguring disease.[19] Cosmetic surgery is defined as any procedure undertaken to improve a person's appearance but which does not meaningfully promote the proper function of the body or prevent or treat an illness or disease.[20]

Transportation Essential to Medical Care. Transportation that is primarily for and essential to qualified medical care is deductible. Thus, actual out-of-pocket automobile expenditures, taxis, air fare, and other forms of transportation are all deductible if the travel is incurred for medical reasons. However, no deduction is allowed if the travel is undertaken for recreational purposes or for the general improvement of the taxpayer's health.

In lieu of the actual cost of the use of an automobile, the IRS allows a deduction of nine cents for each mile that the automobile is driven for medical reasons.[21] In addition to the standard mileage rate, the cost of tolls and parking may also be deducted.

MEALS AND LODGING EN ROUTE TO A MEDICAL FACILITY. Certain courts have held that the cost of meals and lodging while en route to a medical facility is part of travel costs incurred for medical purposes and, therefore, is deductible.[22] However, only 50% of the cost of meals may be deducted.[23] (See Chapter 9 for a discussion of the 50% disallowance rule for meals and entertainment.) The cost of meals eaten on trips that are too short to warrant a stop for meals is not deductible. Furthermore, the cost of lodging is limited to $50 per night and is deductible only if (1) the travel is primarily for and essential to medical care, (2) the medical care is provided in a licensed hospital (or a facility that is related or equivalent to a licensed hospital), and (3) there is no significant element of personal pleasure or recreation in the travel.[24] For example, in one case, a woman moved from Michigan to Florida for the winter months. This move was undertaken on the advice of her physicians in Michigan. Furthermore, her husband returned to Michigan for the winter months. Her doctors in Michigan had not referred her to any physicians in Florida, and while in Florida she only visited a doctor on two occasions. Although her move was primarily for medical care and her condition prevented any significant element of personal recreation, while in Florida she received no medical care in a licensed hospital or equivalent facility. Thus, the medical deduction was denied.[25]

The $50 limitation on lodging is imposed on a per-individual basis. Thus, if the patient is unable to travel alone, an additional $50 per night may be deducted for the lodging costs of a nurse, parent, or spouse. This limited deduction for lodging is only available if the individual is being treated by a physician in a licensed hospital or in a medical care facility that is either related to, or the equivalent of, a licensed hospital.[26]

---

[19] Sec. 213(d)(9)(A). For tax years beginning before January 1, 1991, expenditures incurred for cosmetic reasons (e.g., hair transplants) were deductible because the expenditures affected the function or structure of the body. Section 213 was amended in 1990 to restrict such deductions.

[20] Sec. 213(d)(9)(B).

[21] Rev. Proc. 92-104, 1992-2C.B.583.

[22] *Morris C. Montgomery v. CIR,* 26 AFTR 2d 70-5001, 70-2 USTC ¶ 9466 (6th Cir., 1970). See also *William L. Pfersching,* 1983 PH T.C. Memo ¶ 83,341, 46 TCM 424. The cost of lodging and meals while en route to receive medical care are deductible as transportation that is essential to medical care. The IRS has argued that the term "transportation," as opposed to "travel," excludes the cost of meals and lodging. This argument is manifest in the Regulations and in a private letter ruling (see Reg. Sec. 1.213-1(e)(1)(iv) and Ltr. Rul. 8336011). However, as indicated, at least two courts have specifically held that these expenses are deductible as medical expenses.

[23] The deductible limit of 50% of meals and entertainment is imposed by Sec. 274(n) which imposes the limit on any meals that are deductible. Prior to 1994 the deductible limit was 80%. There is some indication that the IRS may not be enforcing the limit on deductible meals incurred as a medical expense or a charitable contribution. See IRS, *Publication No. 502* [Medical and Dental Expenses], 1993, pp. 10-11, as well as the example in IRS, *Publication No. 526* [Charitable Contributions], 1993, p. 11.

[24] Sec. 213(d)(2).

[25] *Alex L. Polyak,* 94 T.C. 337 (1990).

[26] Sec. 213(d)(2). See also Rev. Rul. 58-110, 1958-1 C.B. 155, and *Leo R. Cohn,* 38 T.C. 387 (1962), *acq.* 1963-1 C.B. 4.

Example 7-6 ■ Lenea lives in a small town 50 miles from Billings, Montana. To receive treatment for a serious illness, she travels by automobile to the Mayo Clinic in Minnesota. The trip takes 3 days. The cost of the transportation, meals, and lodging incurred en route to Minnesota is deductible. ■

Example 7-7 ■ Assume the same facts as in Example 7-6, except that Lenea travels to Billings to see the doctor. Since the trip to Billings is not long enough to necessitate a meal to be eaten, no deduction is available for any meals purchased on the trip. ■

Key Point

Meals and lodging for a patient being treated on an inpatient basis are deductible.

MEALS AND LODGING WHILE AT THE MEDICAL FACILITY. The rules for deducting the cost of meals and lodging while at the medical facility differ from those for en route costs. If an individual is hospitalized and treated on an inpatient basis, the costs of meals and lodging are deductible because they are considered part of the medical treatment. If the individual is treated on an outpatient basis, however, the cost of meals is not deductible,[27] and the cost of the lodging is subject to the $50 per-person, per-night limitation.

Example 7-8 ■ Maxine's four-year old daughter, Sally, suffers from a specific medical ailment. On the advice of her local physician, Maxine takes Sally to a hospital in Houston that specializes in that type of illness. It takes 2 days to drive the 500 miles to the hospital and 2 days to return to the taxpayer's home. At the hospital, Sally is treated on an outpatient basis for 5 days. Maxine and Sally share a motel room both en route and at the hospital. In addition to the miles driven, Maxine incurs the following expenses on the trip:

Meals en route to and from the hospital:	
Maxine	$ 75
Sally	55
Motels en route to and from the hospital:	
$60 per night × 4 nights	240
Meals while in Houston:	
Maxine	95
Sally	70
Motel while at the hospital:	
$65 per night × 5 nights	325
Total	$860

Key Point

The mileage rate used in calculating the medical expense deduction is 9 cents per mile as opposed to 12 cents per mile while donating services to a charity.

Maxine may deduct the following expenses:

Mileage (1,000 miles × 0.09)	$ 90
Meals en route ($75 + $55) × 0.50	65
Motels en route	240
Motel while in Houston	325
Total	$720

Since they shared the motel, the lodging cost for each person is below the $50 per-person, per-night limitation. ■

Capital Expenditures for Medical Care. Generally, capital expenditures are not deductible for federal income tax purposes.[28] For assets used in a trade or business or held for the production of income, such costs are recovered through depreciation, cost

---

[27] *Morris C. Montgomery v. CIR,* 26 AFTR 2d 70-5001, 70-2 USTC ¶ 9466 (6th Cir., 1970).
[28] Sec. 263.

Real World Example
The cost of installing an elevator in the home upon the recommendation of a physician to help a patient with a heart condition was deductible to the extent that it did not increase the value of the home. James E. Berry v. Wiseman, *2 AFTR 2d 6015, 58-2 USTC ¶ 9870 (D.C. Okla., 1958).*

recovery, or amortization. Capital expenditures for personal medical purposes are not entitled to deductions for depreciation or amortization. However, a current deduction is available when the capital expenditure is made to acquire an asset whose primary purpose is the medical care of the taxpayer, the taxpayer's spouse, or the taxpayer's dependents. To qualify as a deduction, the expenditure must be incurred as a medical necessity for primary use by the individual in need of medical treatment, and the expenditure must be reasonable in amount. Deductible capital expenditures for medical care are classified into three categories:[29]

- Expenditures that relate only to the sick or handicapped person and not to the permanent improvement or betterment of the taxpayer's property (e.g., eyeglasses, dogs or other animals that assist the blind or the deaf, artificial teeth and limbs, wheelchairs, crutches, and portable air conditioners purchased for the sole use of a sick person)

- Expenditures that permanently improve or better the taxpayer's property as well as provide medical care (e.g., a swimming pool installed in the home of an individual suffering from arthritis)

- Expenditures incurred in removing structural barriers in the home of a physically handicapped individual[30]

This last group of expenditures includes amounts spent on the physically handicapped individual's residence for:

- Constructing entrance or exit ramps
- Widening doorways at entrances and exits
- Widening or modifying interior doorways and halls to accommodate a wheelchair
- Railings, support bars, or other modifications to bathrooms
- Lowering kitchen cabinets and equipment
- Adjusting electrical outlets and fixtures
- Installing porch lifts and other lifts (but not elevators)
- Modifying fire, smoke and other alarm systems
- Modifying stairs, doors, and areas in front of entrance and exit doorways[31]

Capital expenditures that relate only to the sick person (the first category) are fully deductible. Expenditures that improve the residence (the second category) are deductible only to the extent that the amount of the expenditure exceeds the increase in the fair market value (FMV) of the residence brought about by the capital expenditure. Expenditures incurred in removing physical barriers in the home of a physically handicapped individual (the third category) are deductible in full (i.e., the increase in the home's value is deemed to be zero). In addition, any costs of operating or maintaining the assets in all three categories are deductible as long as the medical reason for the capital expenditure continues to exist.[32]

Example 7-9 ■

During the current year, Rita is injured in an industrial accident. As a result, she suffers from a chronic disabling leg injury, which requires her to spend much time in a wheelchair. Rita's physician recommends that a swimming pool be installed in

[29] Reg. Sec. 1.213-1(e)(1)(iii) and H. Rept. No. 99-841, 99th Cong., 2d Sess. p. II-22 (1986).
[30] S. Rept. No. 99-313, 99th Cong., 2d Sess., p. 59 (1986).
[31] Rev. Rul. 87-106, 1987-2 C.B. 67.
[32] Ibid.

Real World Example

Taxpayers made nonrefundable advance payments required as a condition for an institution's future acceptance of their handicapped child for lifetime care in the event that taxpayers could not care for child. The amounts paid were deductible as expenses for medical care in the year paid. Rev. Rul. 75-303, 1975-2 C.B. 87.

her back yard and that she devote several hours each day to physical exercise. During the year, Rita makes the following expenditures:

Wheelchair	$ 500
Swimming pool	12,000
Operation and maintenance of the pool	400
Entrance ramp and door modification	3,000

A qualified appraiser estimates that the swimming pool increases the value of Rita's home by only $8,000, since most homes in the neighborhood do not have a pool. Rita's medical expenses for the year include $500 for the wheelchair, $4,000 for the swimming pool (the excess of the cost of the pool over the increase in the FMV of the home), $400 for the operation and maintenance of the pool, and $3,000 for the ramp and door modification. ■

Costs of Living in Institutions. The entire cost of in-patient hospital care, including meals and lodging, qualifies as a medical expense. However, if an individual is in an institution other than a hospital (e.g., a nursing home or a special school for the handicapped), the deductibility of the costs involved depends upon the facts of the particular case. If the principal reason for the taxpayer's presence in an institution is the need for and availability of the medical care furnished by that institution, the entire costs of meals, lodging, and other services necessary for furnishing the medical care are all qualified medical expenditures. However, if an individual is in an institution primarily for considerations other than the furnishing of medical care, only costs directly attributable to furnishing medical care are deductible. The costs of the meals, lodging, and other services are not qualified medical expenditures.[33]

Example 7-10 ■ Matt is severely mentally handicapped. Because of this condition, Matt's parents placed him in a special school which, along with providing the proper medical care and supervision, is teaching Matt certain work-related skills. The teaching of these skills is incidental to the providing of medical care. Since he is in the special school primarily for the medical care it furnishes, all costs of the institution, including the costs of meals, lodging, and special education, are qualified medical expenses. ■

Additional Comment

A taxpayer cannot deduct the 1.45% Medicare (hospital insurance benefits) tax that is withheld from wages as part of the social security tax.

Medical Insurance Premiums. Qualified medical expenses also include all premiums paid for medical insurance, including premiums paid for supplementary medical insurance for the aged under the Social Security Act.[34] In many cases, premiums are paid for insurance coverage that extends beyond mere medical care. For example, in addition to the standard medical care coverage, an insurance policy may provide coverage for loss of income or loss of life, limb, or sight. In such cases, a deduction is allowed for the medical care portion of the premium only if the cost of each type of insurance is either separately stated in the contract or is furnished to the policyholder by the insurance company in a separate statement.[35]

Example 7-11 ■ Each month Malazia pays $100 for an insurance policy under which Malazia is reimbursed for any doctor or hospital charges she incurs. In addition, the policy will pay two-thirds of her regular salary each month in the event she becomes disabled. Finally, the policy will pay her $10,000 for the loss of any limb. At the end of the year, her insurance company issues a statement that allocates two-thirds of

---

[33] Reg. Sec. 1.213-1(e)(1)(v).
[34] Sec. 213(d)(1)(C). See also Rev. Ruls. 66-216, 1966-2 C.B. 100, and 79-175, 1979-1 C.B. 117.
[35] Sec. 213(d)(6).

the premiums to the medical insurance coverage. Malazia's medical care expenditure is $800 ($100 × 12 × 0.667). ■

Prior to December 31, 1993, a self-employed individual could deduct 25% of the cost of health insurance for himself, his spouse, and dependents. This deduction was classified as a *for* AGI trade or business deduction. Taxpayers who were otherwise eligible to participate in a subsidized health plan maintained by an employer of either the taxpayer or the taxpayer's spouse were not eligible for the deduction.[36]

Amount and Timing of Deduction

OBJECTIVE 2

Determine the timing of a medical expense deduction and the effect of a reimbursement

The amount and timing of the allowable medical expense deduction are dependent upon (1) when the medical expenses are actually paid, (2) the taxpayer's AGI, and (3) whether any reimbursement is received for the medical expenses.

Timing of the Payment. In general, a deduction for medical expenses is allowed only in the year in which the expenses are actually paid. This rule applies regardless of the taxpayer's method of accounting or when the event that caused the expenditure occurs.[37] Thus, if medical care is received during the year but remains unpaid as of the end of the year, the deduction for that care is deferred until the year in which payment occurs. If the obligation is charged on a credit card, payment is deemed to have been made on the date of the charge, not on the later date when the credit card balance is paid.[38] Conversely, if medical care is prepaid, the deduction is deferred until the year the care is actually rendered unless there is a legal obligation to pay or unless the prepayment is a requirement for the receipt of the medical care.[39]

Example 7-12 ■ In December of the current year, Ed pays an orthodontist $1,200 of the estimated $3,000 for straightening his son's teeth. The work is undertaken to correct a severe overbite condition and not for cosmetic reasons. The orthodontic work will begin in January of the following year. The orthodontist requires the prepayment as a condition to the rendering of the service. Although the work will not commence until the following year, the prepayment of $1,200 is still included as a qualified medical care expenditure for the current year. ■

Limitation on Amount Deductible. As previously noted, a medical expense deduction is allowed only for those years in which the taxpayer itemizes his or her deductions and the taxpayer's expenditures for medical care exceed 7.5% of AGI.

Example 7-13 ■ During the current year, Kelly incurs qualified medical expenditures of $3,000. Her AGI for the year is $30,000. After subtracting the floor, she has $750 ($3,000 − [0.075 × $30,000]) of deductible medical expenses. These medical expenses are added to Kelly's other itemized deductions to determine if they exceed the standard deduction. ■

Self-Study Question

Why does the IRS not require that the taxpayer file an amended return when a reimbursement is received in a later year?

Answer

The administrative burden on the IRS of processing additional returns would be too great.

Medical Insurance Reimbursements. A tax deduction is only available for unreimbursed medical expenditures. It does not matter whether the reimbursement is from an insurance plan purchased from an insurance company, a medical reimbursement plan of an employer, or a payment resulting from litigation.[40]

---

[36] Sec. 162(l). In order to be eligible for this deduction, the plan also was required to cover certain employees of the self-employed business. The Revenue Reconciliation Act of 1993 retroactively extended this provision from July 1, 1992 through December 31, 1993.

[37] Reg. Sec. 1.213-1(a)(1). However, medical expenses paid within one year from the day following the taxpayer's death are treated as paid at the time they are incurred (see Sec. 213(c)).

[38] Rev. Rul. 78-38, 1978-1 C.B. 67.

[39] *Robert M. Rose v. CIR*, 26 AFTR 2d 70-5653, 70-2 USTC ¶ 9646 (5th Cir., 1970). See also Rev. Ruls. 75-302, 1975-2 C.B. 86, and 75-303, 1975-2 C.B. 87.

[40] Sec. 213(a).

If reimbursement is received in the same year the medical expenses are paid, the deduction is reduced by the amount of the reimbursement. If reimbursement is received in a year subsequent to the year of payment, the taxpayer is required to include the reimbursement in gross income for the year the payment is received to the extent that a tax benefit was derived from the deduction in the previous year. If no deduction was taken in the prior year, the reimbursement need not be reported as income. This may occur when the taxpayer's total itemized deductions do not exceed the standard deduction or when the total medical expenses do not exceed 7.5% of AGI. If a deduction was taken in the prior year, however, the taxpayer must report as income the lesser of (1) the amount of the reimbursement or (2) the amount by which the taxable income of the prior year was reduced because of medical expenses.

Example 7-14 ■

During 1994, Diane, a single taxpayer under age 65, reports the following items of income and expense:

AGI		$35,000
Total qualified medical expenses		3,500
Itemized deductions other than medical		3,000

Diane's taxable income for 1994 is calculated as follows:

AGI		$35,000
Reduction: larger of itemized deductions or standard deduction		
Medical expenses	$3,500	
Minus: 7.5% of AGI	(2,625)	875
Other itemized deductions		3,000
Total itemized deductions		$3,875
Standard deduction		$3,800	(3,875)
Personal exemption		(2,450)
Taxable income		$28,675	■

If during 1995 Diane receives a reimbursement of $1,000 for medical expenses incurred the prior year, she must include $75 ($3,875 − $3,800) in the gross income for 1995 (the amount of the tax benefit from the medical expense deduction for the prior year). This amount can be calculated by comparing the actual taxable income for 1994 with what would have been the 1994 taxable income if the reimbursement had been received that year.

AGI			$35,000
Reduction: larger of itemized deductions or standard deduction			
Medical expenses	$3,500		
Minus: Reimbursement	(1,000)		
7.5% of AGI	(2,625)		
Excess medical expenses		—0—	
Plus: Other itemized deductions		3,000	
Total itemized deductions		$3,000	
Standard deduction		$3,800	(3,800)
Personal exemption			(2,450)
Taxable income (assuming reimbursement was received in 1994)			$28,750
Minus: Actual 1994 taxable income			(28,675)
Tax benefit			$ 75

TOPIC REVIEW 7-1

Medical Expense Deduction	
Items	Deduction Rules and Limitations
1. Types of expenditures that qualify	1. (a) Expenditures for the diagnosis, cure, mitigation, treatment, or prevention of disease. (b) Transportation at 0.09 per mile and lodging limited to $50 per-night, per-person, and 50% of meals. (c) Medical insurance premiums. (d) Capital expenditures (subject to specific limitations).
2. Qualifying individuals	2. Taxpayer, spouse, dependents, and children of divorced parents even if not a dependent.
3. Amount and timing of the deduction	3. Deduct in the year paid unless prepayment is required or there is a legal obligation to pay. Medical expenses are subject to a 7.5% of AGI nondeductible limitation.
4. Treatment of insurance reimbursements	4. The deduction is reduced if the reimbursement is received in the year of payment. Reimbursements received in a subsequent year are included in gross income if tax benefit was received in the earlier year.

Topic Review 7-1 highlights the principal requirements for the medical expense deduction previously discussed.

TAXES

OBJECTIVE 3
Identify taxes that are deductible as itemized deductions

Section 164 provides taxpayers with a federal income tax deduction for specifically listed taxes that are paid or accrued during the taxable year. Generally, cash-method taxpayers are entitled to the deduction when the taxes are paid, whereas, taxpayers using the accrual method deduct taxes in the year they accrue. Other taxes are specifically listed as nondeductible. To be deductible as a tax, the assessment in question must be a tax rather than a fee or charge imposed by a government for providing specific goods or services.

Definition of a Tax

A **tax** is a mandatory assessment levied under the authority of a political entity for the purpose of raising revenue to be used for public or governmental purposes.[41] Thus, fees, assessments, or fines imposed for specific privileges or services are not deductible as taxes under Sec. 164. These nontax items include:

---

[41] Rev. Rul. 70-622, 1970-2 C.B. 41. See also Reg. Sec. 1.911-1.

Additional Comment

In 1991 the deduction for taxes represented 31.9% of the dollar amount of all itemized deductions, making it the second largest itemized deduction.

- Vehicle registration and inspection fees
- Registration tags for pets
- Toll charges for highways and bridges
- Parking meter charges
- Charges for sewer, water, and other services
- Special assessments against real estate for items such as sidewalks, lighting, and streets

However, if these nontax fees and charges are incurred in a business or income-producing activity, they may be either capitalized or deductible as ordinary and necessary business expenses or ordinary and necessary expenses incurred for the production of income.

Example 7-15 ■ During the year, Bruce's automobile license is renewed at a cost of $150. In addition, Bruce pays $300 personal property taxes on the automobile based upon its value. Bruce also incurs a total of $100 in highway toll charges. The $300 personal property tax is the only item that is deductible as a tax under Sec. 164. The license fee and the toll charges are only deductible if he uses the automobile for business or for the production of income. ■

Additional Comment

In general, only taxes imposed on the taxpayer are deductible.

Deductible Taxes

Section 164 specifically identifies the following taxes as deductible:

Key Point

All state, local, and foreign taxes paid or incurred in a trade or business or in an income-producing activity are either deductible or may be capitalized.

- State, local, and foreign real property taxes
- State and local personal property taxes if based on value
- State, local, and foreign income; war profits; and excess profits taxes
- The federal environmental tax (imposed upon corporations)
- The federal generation-skipping transfer tax on income distributions
- Other state, local, and foreign taxes that are paid or incurred in either a trade or business or an income-producing activity

Except for the environmental tax, and the generation-skipping transfer tax, all of these taxes are imposed by a governmental body other than the federal government.[42] A foreign tax includes taxes imposed by a foreign country, including any political subdivision of that country.

Federal taxes other than the ones listed generally are not deductible for federal income tax purposes. However, federal customs and excise taxes incurred in the taxpayer's business or income-producing activity are deductible as ordinary and necessary expenses under Secs. 162 or 212. Likewise, the *employer's* portion of federal social security taxes and federal and state unemployment taxes are deductible by the employer as ordinary and necessary business expenses if the employee works in the employer's business or income-producing activity.

---

[42] The environmental tax is a tax imposed by the United States on corporations with modified alternative minimum taxable income in excess of $2 million (see Sec. 59A). The generation-skipping transfer tax is imposed by the United States on certain distributions from a trust (see Sec. 2601). Furthermore, under Sec. 691(c) a taxpayer who includes income in respect of a decedent in taxable income may deduct estate tax attributable to that amount.

Nondeductible Taxes

The following taxes are not deductible under Sec. 164:

- Federal income taxes
- Federal estate, inheritance, legacy, succession, and gift taxes
- Federal import or tariff duties and excise taxes unless incurred in the taxpayer's business or for the production of income
- Employee's portion of social security and other payroll taxes
- State and local sales taxes and state inheritance, legacy, succession, and gift taxes
- Foreign income taxes if the taxpayer elects to take the taxes as a credit against his federal income tax liability
- Property taxes on real estate to the extent the taxes are treated as imposed on another taxpayer[43]

Example 7-16 ■

Self-Study Question

Would a taxpayer normally deduct foreign taxes, or would he prefer to take a foreign tax credit?

Answer

Normally the foreign tax credit is better since the dollar amount of foreign taxes can be offset directly against the U.S. tax liability.

Elaine is a U.S. citizen who works in Spain. During the current year, Elaine earns $55,000 in Spain and pays $6,000 of foreign income tax. In computing her U.S. income tax liability, she may either deduct the $6,000 in income taxes paid to Spain or take a foreign tax credit for the foreign taxes. No deduction is permitted if she makes the election to take the foreign tax credit. (See Chapter 14 for a discussion of the foreign tax credit.) This example assumes that Elaine is not eligible for the foreign-earned income exclusion under Sec. 911. ■

State and Local Income Taxes

State and local income taxes must always be taken as a deduction *from* AGI. Thus, a taxpayer does not receive any federal income tax benefit if these taxes, in addition to the other itemized deductions, do not exceed the standard deduction. Cash-basis taxpayers deduct all state and local income taxes paid or withheld during the year even if the taxes are attributable to another tax year.

Example 7-17 ■

Typical Misconception

It is not uncommon to erroneously calculate the deduction for state and local income taxes on the accrual basis for cash-basis taxpayers.

Additional Comment

Every state except Alaska, Florida, Nevada, South Dakota, Texas, Washington, and Wyoming has some type of income tax.

During 1994, Rita had $1,500 in state income taxes withheld from her salary. On April 15, 1995, Rita pays an additional $400 when she files her 1994 state income tax return. On her 1994 federal income tax return, Rita may deduct the $1,500 in state income taxes withheld from her salary as an itemized deduction. The $400 that she pays on April 15, 1995, is deductible on Rita's 1995 federal income tax return, even though the liability relates to her 1994 state income tax return. ■

If the taxpayer receives a refund of state income taxes deducted in a prior year, the refund must be included as income in the year of the refund to the extent that the taxpayer received a tax benefit from the prior deduction.[44]

Personal Property Taxes

Many state and local governments impose personal property taxes. For individuals, the key issue is whether the levy is a deductible tax under Sec. 164 or a nondeductible

---

[43] Sec. 275(a)(5). For a discussion of when and how these taxes are to be apportioned between different taxpayers, see the section of this chapter entitled Real Estate Taxes.

[44] Sec. 111.

Additional Comment

Several states impose a tax on the value of a taxpayer's investment portfolio. This is an example of a deductible intangible personal property tax.

fee. To qualify as a deductible personal property tax, the levy must meet two basic tests:

- The tax must be an ad valorem tax on personal property. In other words, the amount of the tax is determined by the property's value rather than some other measure such as a vehicle's weight or model year.
- The tax must be imposed on an annual basis, even if it is not collected annually.[45]

Example 7-18 ■

The motor vehicle tax of a particular state is imposed at the rate of 45 cents per hundredweight. Since this is not an ad valorem tax, it is not deductible as a personal property tax under Sec. 164. However, the tax is deductible as an ordinary business expense under Sec. 162 if the vehicle is used in a trade or business. ■

If a personal property tax is based partly on value and partly on some other basis, the ad valorem portion is deductible.

Example 7-19 ■

Banner County imposes a property tax of 1% of value plus 20 cents per hundredweight on all passenger automobiles. Clay's automobile has a value of $10,000 and weighs 1,500 pounds. Clay may deduct $100 ($10,000 × 0.01) under Sec. 164. The remaining $300 (1,500 × 0.20) is not deductible under Sec. 164; however, it may be deductible as an ordinary business expense if the automobile is used in his business. ■

For individuals, personal property taxes are *from* AGI deductions unless they are incurred in an individual's trade or business or for the production of rental income.

Real Estate Taxes

Additional Comment

Personal residences are the most commonly held type of real property owned by individuals.

Apportionment of Taxes. When real estate is sold during the year, the federal income tax deduction for taxes imposed upon that real estate is allocated between the seller and the purchaser based upon the amount of time each taxpayer owns the property during the real property tax year. The real property tax year may or may not coincide with the taxpayer's tax year. The apportionment, based upon the number of days each party holds the property during the real property tax year of sale, assumes that the purchaser owns the property on the date of the sale.[46] If the other party to the transaction (e.g., the buyer of the property) is liable for the payment of the tax, both cash and accrual-method taxpayers who buy or sell real estate during the year are treated as having paid, on the date of the sale, their proportionate share of the real estate taxes attributable to the property. The party that actually pays the taxes (either the buyer or the seller) deducts his share of the taxes in the year the taxes are paid unless an election is made under Sec. 461(c) to accrue the taxes. The tax consequences are not dependent upon who actually pays the real estate taxes or whether the real estate taxes are prorated under the agreement.

Example 7-20 ■

The real property tax year for Bannock County is the calendar year. Property taxes for a particular real property tax year become a lien against the property as of June 30 of that year, and the owner of the property on that date becomes liable for the tax. However, the taxes are not payable until February 28 of the subsequent year. On May 30 of the current year, Sandy, a cash-method taxpayer, sells a building to Roger, who is also a cash-method taxpayer. The real estate taxes on the property

[45] Reg. Sec. 1.164-3(c).
[46] Sec. 164(d)(1)(A).

for the current year are $1,095. Since Roger is liable for the payment of the tax, Sandy is treated as having paid $447 ($1,095 × 149/365 [the numerator of 149 is the number of days from January 1 through May 29 and the denominator is the entire real property tax year]) on the date of the sale. Roger's share of the taxes equaling $648 ($1,095 × 216/365) is deductible in the subsequent year (i.e., the year during which Roger actually pays the taxes). On the other hand, if the taxes become a lien against the property on April 1, Sandy is the owner of the building on that date and she is liable for the tax. Under these circumstances, the result is the same except that Roger may take the $648 deduction in the year of sale rather than in the year of payment. ∎

Generally, the apportionment of taxes is included as part of the sales agreement, and the amount of the taxes apportioned to each party is stated separately from the selling price of the property. However, if the agreement does not provide for an apportionment of taxes, the seller's gain or loss on the sale (and the purchaser's basis in the property) must be adjusted either upward or downward, depending upon which party actually pays the taxes. For example, a buyer who pays all of the real estate taxes has, in effect, paid the seller's portion of the taxes. The purchase price must be increased by this amount.

Example 7-21 ∎

On March 15 of the current year, William sells a tract of land to Ken for $100,000. On the date of sale, William's basis in the land is $45,000. The real estate taxes attributable to the property for the year are $2,000. The county in which the property is located uses the calendar year, and the taxes are due on February 28 of the following year. The sales agreement does not provide for apportionment of real estate taxes between the buyer and the seller.

Even though Ken pays the full amount of the taxes, $400 ($2,000 × 73/365 [the numerator is the number of days from January 1 through March 14]) is treated as having been paid by William (the seller). Only $1,600 of deductible taxes are treated as having been paid by Ken (the buyer). This, in essence, represents an increase of $400 in the selling price of the property, and William's gain on the sale is increased by that amount. In addition, Ken's basis in the property is increased by $400. ∎

Example 7-22 ∎

Assume the same facts as in Example 7-21, except that William (the seller) pays the taxes prior to the sale. Since $1,600 of the taxes actually paid by William is treated as having been paid by Ken, this represents a decrease in the selling price by that amount. Thus, William's gain on the sale and Ken's basis in the property are both decreased by $1,600. ∎

Real Property Assessments for Local Benefits. Assessments are often made against real estate for the purpose of funding local improvements. These assessments may be for such things as street improvements, sidewalks, lighting, drainage, and sewer improvements. If the tax is assessed only against the property that benefits from the improvement, it is not deductible, even though the general public may also be incidentally benefited.[47] Such assessments are capitalized as part of the property's adjusted basis.

Example 7-23 ∎

During the current year, Larry is assessed $800 for the new sidewalk and gutter the city constructed in front of his home. These local improvements are intended to

---

[47] Reg. Sec. 1.164-4. However, if the assessment against the local benefits is made for maintenance, repair, or interest charges on the benefits, the assessment is deductible. The burden of proof to show how much of the assessment is deductible falls on the taxpayer (see Sec. 164(c)(1)).

increase the beauty of the city in general. Larry may not deduct the payment because the assessment is made only against the property that is benefiting from the sidewalk. The $800 is added to the adjusted basis of his property. ∎

Real property taxes incurred on personal-use assets are deductible *from* AGI. Real property taxes incurred on business property or property held for the production of rental income are deductions *for* AGI.

Additional Comment

Congress chose to repeal the deduction for sales taxes rather than one of the other personal taxes in 1986 since a large percentage of sales tax payments were not being deducted.

General Sales Tax

Prior to 1987, Sec. 164 allowed a deduction for sales taxes. However, that deduction was eliminated by the Tax Reform Act of 1986 for 1987 and subsequent years. Instead, the sales tax is treated as part of the purchase price of the property, increasing its basis.

Self-Employment Tax

Self-employed individuals are subject to a tax on their self-employment income in lieu of the payment of a social security payroll tax on salary. The self-employment tax rate and total amount of tax are equal to the combined employee and employer social security tax (i.e., 12.4% with a ceiling of $60,600 in 1994; and no ceiling for the 2.9% additional medicare hospital insurance premium for self-employed individuals). Self-employed individuals, however, may deduct one-half of the self-employment taxes paid as a *for* AGI deduction.[48]

INTEREST

OBJECTIVE 4
Identify different types of interest deductions

Section 163(a) states simply that taxpayers may take a deduction for all interest paid or accrued within the taxable year.[49] This statement is deceptive, however, for several reasons. First, distinguishing between interest expense and a charge for services rendered may be difficult. Furthermore, the deductibility of interest incurred for certain purposes is limited or disallowed. In some cases special rules apply in determining the timing of the deduction for interest expense. Thus, the proper classification of interest expense is critical in determining the amount of interest expense deduction. These categories include:

Additional Comment

In 1991 the deduction for interest expense represented 45.4% of the total dollar amount of itemized deductions making it the largest single itemized deduction.

- active trade or business
- passive activity
- investment
- personal
- qualified residence

Key Point

A taxpayer cannot deduct interest payments made for someone else if not legally liable to make them.

Definition of Interest

Interest is defined as "compensation for the use or forbearance of money."[50] Thus, finance charges, carrying charges, loan discounts, premiums, loan origination fees, and points are all deductible as interest if they represent a cost for the use of money.

---

[48] Sec. 164(f). The ceiling for the OASDI portion of the tax was $57,600 in 1993 and a $135,000 ceiling applied to the hospital insurance portion of the tax. (See Chapter 14 for a discussion of the self-employment tax.)

[49] Sec. 163(a).

[50] *Deputy v. Pierre S. DuPont*, 23 AFTR 808, 40-1 USTC ¶ 9161 (USSC, 1940).

Charge for Services. In some instances, it is difficult to determine whether an item is interest or is a charge for services rendered (e.g., a loan processing fee).[51] For example, "points" are often charged when property is sold or purchased. A point is equal to 1% of the loan amount. Thus, two points paid on a $60,000 mortgage equal $1,200 ($60,000 × 0.02). These points may represent either (1) additional interest expense (because the stated rate of interest for the loan is lower than the current market rate of interest), or (2) service charges, such as fees for appraisals or title searches. Only the first category is interest.

Generally, prepaid interest paid in the form of points must be capitalized and amortized or deducted over the life of the loan. However, points paid on a loan incurred to purchase or improve the taxpayer's principal residence are deductible when paid if the loan is secured by the residence, the payment of points is an established business practice in the geographic area where the debt is incurred, and the points do not exceed the amount generally charged. Furthermore, the IRS has stated that if certain requirements are met the points are automatically currently deductible as interest.[52] The IRS has also indicated that points paid on VA and FHA loans are also treated as prepaid interest if they are clearly designated as points incurred in connection with the indebtedness.[53]

Example 7-24 ■

During the current year, Kevin and Donna purchase a new home for $300,000, putting $100,000 down and borrowing $200,000. At the closing, they are required to pay one and one-half points as a loan discount in connection with the loan which is secured by a mortgage against the home. The practice of charging points is an established business practice where they live.

These points represent prepaid interest on the purchase of a principal residence. Thus, in addition to the interest portion of every payment they make, Kevin and Donna may also deduct $3,000 ($200,000 × 0.015) as interest paid during the year. ■

Points paid on a loan to purchase property other than a principal residence, or for refinancing a mortgage on a principal residence must be capitalized. If the property is business, investment, or a qualified residence (the taxpayer's principal residence and one other that the taxpayer chooses) the points may be amortized or deducted over the life of the loan.[54]

In order for the points to be currently deductible, the purchaser of the principal residence (borrower) must have paid for them with unborrowed funds. Pursuant to Proposed Regulations, however, amounts provided by the borrower as down payments, escrow deposits, earnest money, or other funds are treated as paid for the points. Furthermore, as long as the borrower provides sufficient funds in these other categories, he is treated as having paid the points even if the seller has paid for them on behalf of the borrower.[55]

---

[51] The charge for services is capitalized and may be amortized and deducted over the term of the loan if it is incurred in a trade or business or for the production of income.

[52] These requirements, mentioned in Chapter 6, are: (1) The points must be paid in connection with the purchase (not the improvement) of the taxpayer's principal residence, (2) The closing agreement must clearly designate the amounts as points paid in connection with the acquisition debt, (3) The amount must be computed as a percentage of the amount borrowed, (4) The points must conform with established business practices, and (5) The loan must be secured by the residence. See Rev. Proc. 92-12, 1992-1 C.B.663.

[53] Rev. Proc. 92-12A, 1992-1 C.B. 664.

[54] Rev. Rul. 87-22, 1987-1 C.B. 146, and Rev. Proc. 87-15, 1987-1 C.B. 624. The Tax Court has held in one case that points paid on refinancing a "bridge" or temporary loan are currently deductible. *James R. Huntsman v. CIR*, 66 AFTR 2d 90-5020, 90-2 USTC ¶ 50,340 (8th Cir., 1990) rev'g 91 TC 57 (1988). However, the IRS has announced that it will not follow *Huntsman* in circuits other than the circuit in which the case was decided (IRS Action on Decision CC-1991-02, Feb. 11, 1991).

[55] Prop. Reg. Sec. 1.6050H-1(f)(3).

Bank Service Charges and Finance Charges. Bank service charges incurred on checking accounts represent nondeductible expenses for services rendered rather than interest.[56] The annual service charge on credit cards is also a charge for services rather than interest. However, finance charges on credit cards are interest.[57] Late payments charged by public utilities are interest expense because they are not incurred for any specific service.[58]

Key Point
The classification of interest expense depends on the use to which the borrowed money is put and not on the nature of the property used to secure the loan.

Classification of Interest Expense

The deductibility of interest generally depends upon the purpose for which the indebtedness is incurred since interest incurred in certain activities is subject to limitation and disallowance. For example, interest expense allocated to the taxpayer's active business is deductible in full against the business income (a deduction *for* AGI, taken on Schedule C), whereas interest expense allocated to the purchase of the taxpayer's residence is subject to the limitations applicable to that type of interest and is an itemized deduction (a deduction *from* AGI). No deduction is allowed for interest that is allocated to personal-use expenditures.

Pursuant to the Regulations, interest expense generally is allocated to the different interest expense categories by identifying the use of the borrowed money.[59] With two exceptions, what the taxpayer uses as collateral in securing the debt has no bearing on the allocation of the interest expense.[60]

Example 7-25 ■ Cathy pledges some stock and securities as collateral for a $30,000 loan. She then purchases an automobile with the proceeds of the loan. The automobile is used 100% of the time for personal use. Even though the collateral for the loan consists of investment property, the interest expense is allocated to a personal-use asset and is not deductible. ■

If the borrowed funds are deposited in a bank rather than spent immediately, the deposit is considered an investment, and the interest expense on the loan is investment interest until such time as the funds are withdrawn and expended.[61] Then the interest expense is allocated to the category for which the expenditure is made, regardless of when the interest expense for the debt is actually paid.[62] This reallocation occurs as of the date the check is written on the account as long as the check is delivered or mailed within a reasonable period of time.[63]

Example 7-26 ■ On March 1 of the current year, José borrows $100,000 and immediately deposits the funds into an account that contains no other funds. No other funds are

---

[56] *Virginia G. Edgar,* 1979 PH T.C. Memo ¶ 79,524, 39 TCM 816. If the checking account is one used in business or for an investment activity, the charge is deductible as an ordinary and necessary expense.

[57] Rev. Rul. 73-136, 1973-1 C.B. 68.

[58] Rev. Rul. 74-187, 1974-1 C.B. 48. However, interest on a credit card or interest charged by a public utility is not deductible if it is personal interest.

[59] Temp. Reg. Sec. 1.163-8T.

[60] The exceptions deal with (1) qualified residence interest attributable to home equity indebtedness and (2) loans secured by tax-exempt securities. Qualified residence interest is explained later in this chapter under the section entitled Home Equity Indebtedness. Interest expense on loans secured by tax-exempt securities is not deductible.

[61] Temp. Reg. Sec. 1.163-8T(c)(4)(i).

[62] Temp. Reg. Sec. 1.163-8T(c)(2)(ii)(A).

[63] Temp. Reg. Sec. 1.163-8T(c)(4)(iii). If during any one month several expenditures are made from an account, the taxpayer may elect to treat all the expenditures as if made on the first day of the month. This election, however, is made on each account separately and is only available for accounts where the borrowed funds are already in the account as of the first day of the month. If the funds are not in the account as of the first day of the month, the expenditures may be treated as made on the date that the borrowed funds are deposited in the account. See Temp. Reg. Sec. 1.163-8T(c)(4)(iv).

deposited into the account, and no payment is made on the loan balance. On May 1 of the current year, he withdraws $40,000 from the account and purchases a sailboat to be used for personal purposes. On July 1, José withdraws an additional $50,000 and purchases a passive activity. For the current year, the interest expense on the loan is categorized as follows: from March 1 through April 30, all of the expense is investment interest expense. 40% ($40,000/$100,000) of the interest expense attributable to the period May 1 through June 30 is classified as personal interest and the remainder is investment interest. The interest expense attributable to the period from July 1 to the end of the year is classified as 40% personal interest, 50% passive activity interest, and 10% investment interest. ■

If both borrowed and personal funds are mingled in the same account, expenditures from that account are treated as coming first from the borrowed funds.[64]

Example 7-27 ■

Key Point

The attempt to classify interest expense correctly has resulted in significant additional record-keeping costs for many taxpayers.

On April 1 of the current year, Diane borrows $30,000 and deposits it into a checking account that contains $10,000 of personal funds. On May 1 of the current year, Diane purchases a passive activity for $15,000, and on June 1 she purchases a personal automobile for $20,000. The $15,000 expended for the passive activity on May 1 is treated as coming from the borrowed funds. Thus, as of that date, one-half of the interest expense on the debt is reallocated from investment interest to passive activity interest. $15,000 of the funds expended for the personal automobile on June 1 is treated as coming from the borrowed funds, and the remaining $5,000 is treated as coming from the personal funds. Thus, as of that date, the remaining interest expense on the debt is reallocated to personal interest. ■

When a debt is repaid, the repayment is allocated to the expenditures made with that debt in the following order: (1) personal expenditures, (2) investment expenditures and passive activity expenditures other than rental real estate, (3) passive activity expenditures in rental real estate, and (4) trade or business expenditures.

Example 7-28 ■

Assume the same facts as in Example 7-27. In addition, assume that on October 31 of the current year, Diane repays $10,000 of the $30,000 debt incurred on April 1 of the current year. Even though the expenditure for the passive activity was made first, the repayment of the debt is first allocated to the expenditure for the personal automobile. Thus, beginning on November 1 of the current year, of the remaining $20,000 debt outstanding $15,000 is allocated to the passive activity and $5,000 is allocated to the expenditure for the personal automobile. ■

Active Trade or Business. Interest expense incurred in a taxpayer's active trade or business generally is fully deductible without limitation. As explained in Chapter 6, the determination of whether a particular activity constitutes a trade or business or an investment depends upon an examination of all the relevant facts and circumstances. For individuals, estates, trusts, and certain corporations, however, it is not sufficient that the interest only be incurred in the taxpayer's trade or business. In addition, the taxpayer must *materially participate* in the business. If not, the activity is considered passive, and losses from the activity (including the interest expense) are subject to the passive loss limitation rules (see Chapter 8 for a discussion of these rules). Interest incurred in an active trade or business is a deduction *for* AGI.

Passive Activity. Individuals, estates, trusts, and certain corporations that incur losses from passive activities are subject to the passive loss limitation rules explained

---

[64] Temp. Reg. Sec. 1.163-8T(c)(4)(ii). However, if an expenditure is made out of the mingled funds within 15 days from the deposit of the borrowed funds into the account, the taxpayer may designate the expenditure to which the borrowed funds are allocated.

in Chapter 8. These rules prevent taxpayers from offsetting passive activity losses against other income such as salary, interest, dividends, and income from an active business. Interest expense attributable to the passive activity is included in computing the net income or loss generated from the activity, and thus may not be deductible under these limitation rules (see Chapter 8 for a discussion of these rules).

OBJECTIVE 5
Compute the amount of investment interest deduction

Investment Interest. Since 1972, individuals and other noncorporate taxpayers have been limited on the deductibility of interest expense attributable to investments. Without this limitation, high-income taxpayers could realize significant tax savings by borrowing money to invest in assets that are appreciating in value but that produce little or no current income. This would enable the taxpayer to offset current highly taxed income with a current interest deduction, while deferring the taxable income from the investment until it is sold at a later date.[65]

Because of these concerns, the tax law limits the current deduction for investment interest expense to the taxpayer's net investment income for the taxable year.[66] Any investment interest expense disallowed as a current deduction is carried over and treated as investment interest expense incurred in the following year.

Example 7-29 ■

Additional Comment

A provision in the Revenue Reconciliation Act of 1993 eliminates net capital gain in the calculation of net investment income. Congress believed that it was inappropriate for a taxpayer to be taxed on net capital gain at a favorable 28% rate and to also be able to use that gain to deduct otherwise non-deductible investment interest against ordinary income which might otherwise be taxed at a higher rate.

In the current year, Rita earns $27,000 in net investment income and incurs $40,000 investment interest expense. Rita's interest expense deduction for the year is limited to $27,000, the amount of her net investment income.

The remaining investment interest expense of $13,000 ($40,000 − $27,000) may be carried over and deducted in a subsequent year. This carryover amount is treated as paid or accrued in the subsequent year and is subject to the disallowance rules that pertain to the subsequent year. ■

INVESTMENT INTEREST. **Investment interest** is interest expense on indebtedness properly allocable to property held for investment.[67] This includes property that generates portfolio types of income such as interest, dividends, annuities, and royalties. It does not include business interest, personal interest, qualified residence interest, or interest incurred in connection with any activity that is determined to be passive. Under Sec. 469, all rental activities are deemed to be passive (see Chapter 8 for a discussion of the passive loss limitation rules). Thus, interest incurred in owning and renting property is subject to the passive loss limitation rather than the investment interest limitation.

Example 7-30 ■

Paul owns a duplex which he rents out. The rental of the duplex is a passive activity. During the year, he incurs $7,000 in interest expense on the duplex. The $7,000 interest expense (along with the other expenses and the income from the property) is a *for* AGI deduction, but is subject to the passive loss limitation rather than the investment interest limitation. ■

Investment interest also does not include interest expense incurred to purchase or carry tax-exempt securities. This interest is not deductible at all. Without this disallowance, a taxpayer could, in certain circumstances, actually borrow funds at a higher rate of interest than the rate at which they were reinvested, while still generating a positive net cash flow because the government would be subsidizing the transaction through the interest deduction on the borrowings.

---

[65] This technique enables taxpayers to increase their capital gain income and reduce their ordinary income, since the latter is often taxed at a higher rate than the former.

[66] Sec. 163(d). Prior to 1987 the deduction was limited to the taxpayer's net investment income plus $10,000. From 1987 through 1990, the amount in excess of the taxpayer's net investment income was reduced each year by a specified percentage of the $10,000.

[67] Sec. 163(d)(3).

Additional Comment

Investment expenses are those which are deductible on the tax return, after the 2% limitation.

NET INVESTMENT INCOME. For purposes of the investment interest limitation, the term **net investment income** means the excess of the taxpayer's investment income over investment expenses.[68] Investment income is gross income from property held for investment including items such as dividends, interest, annuities, and royalties (if not earned in a trade or business).[69] Investment income also includes net gain (all gains minus all losses) on the sale of investment property, but only to the extent that the net gain exceeds the net capital gain (net long-term capital gains in excess of net short-term capital losses.)[70]

As explained in Chapter 5, net capital gain is generally taxed at a 28% maximum rate. Including net capital gain in the definition of investment income would increase the amount of deductible investment interest expense which might offset other income that is taxed at rates higher than 28%. Thus, net capital gain attributable to the disposition of property held for investment is excluded from the definition of investment income. However, net capital gain from the disposition of investment property is included in the definition to the extent the taxpayer elects to subject the gain from the disposition of investment property to the regular tax rates.[71] Gains on business and personal-use property are not included in the calculation of investment income.

Example 7-31 ∎

During the current year, Michael incurs $15,000 investment interest expense, earns $7,000 of dividends and has $3,000 interest income. He also reports the following gains and losses from the sale of stocks and bonds during the year:

Short-term capital gains	$4,000
Short-term capital losses	(3,000)
Long-term capital gains	5,000
Long-term capital losses	(2,000)

Considering all of Michael's other income and deductions for the year, assume that he has a 39.6% marginal tax rate. Michael's net capital gain is $3,000 (net long-term capital gain of $3,000 in excess of net short-term capital losses of $0). He also has a $1,000 ($4,000 − $3,000) net short-term capital gain. Thus, his net gain is $4,000 ($9,000 of total gains − $5,000 of total losses) and only $1,000 ($4,000 net gain − $3,000 net capital gain) is included in investment income. If Michael does not make an election, his investment income is $11,000 ($10,000 of dividends and interest plus $1,000 net short-term capital gain). He may deduct $11,000 of the investment interest expense in the current year. The $4,000 ($15,000 − $11,000) is carried over to the next year. The $3,000 net capital gain is subject to the 28% ceiling tax rate on net capital gain. If Michael makes the election, his investment income is $14,000 (the $3,000 net capital gain is included), and he may deduct $14,000 of the investment interest expense. Thus, only $1,000 ($15,000 − $14,000) of investment interest expense is not currently deductible and is carried over to the next year. However, his $3,000 net capital gain is subject to the 39.6% ordinary income tax rate. ∎

Investment expenses include all deductions (except interest) that are directly connected with the production of investment income.[72] These expenses include rental

---

[68] Sec. 163(d)(4)(A).
[69] Sec. 163(d)(4)(B).
[70] Ibid.
[71] Secs. 1(h) and 163(d)(4)(B).
[72] Sec. 163(d)(4)(C).

fees for safety deposit boxes, fees for investment counsel[73], and subscriptions to investment and financial planning journals. As explained later in this chapter (see the section of this chapter entitled Miscellaneous Itemized Deductions) these investment expenses are deductible only to the extent they exceed 2% of the taxpayer's AGI for the year. Only the investment expenses remaining after application of this limitation are used in computing the net investment income. Furthermore, in computing the amount of the disallowed investment expenses, the 2% of AGI limitation is applied to the noninvestment expenses first.[74] Any remaining 2% of AGI limitation is then used to reduce the noninterest investment expenses.

Example 7-32 ■   Kevin's AGI for the current year is $200,000. Included in his AGI is $175,000 salary and $25,000 of investment income. In earning the investment income, Kevin paid investment interest expense of $33,000. He also incurred the following expenditures subject to the 2% of AGI limitation:

Investment expenses:	
Subscriptions to investment journals	$ 700
Investment counseling	2,000
Safety deposit box rental	300
Noninvestment expenses:	
Unreimbursed employee business expenses	1,500
Tax return preparation fees (non-business related)	500

Kevin's investment interest expense deduction for the year is computed by first determining the deductible investment expenses (other than interest) and the net investment income.

Investment Expenses:		
Subscriptions	$ 700	
Investment counseling	2,000	
Safety deposit box rental	300	$3,000
Disallowed by the 2% Limitation:		
2% of AGI ($200,000 × 0.02)	$4,000	
Unreimbursed employee expenses	(1,500)	
Tax return preparation fees	(500)	
Investment expenses (remainder of 2% limit allocated to investment expenses)	(2,000)	(2,000)
Deductible investment expenses		$1,000
Net investment income ($25,000 − $1,000)		$24,000

The investment interest expense deduction is limited to $24,000. The remaining investment interest of $9,000 ($33,000 − $24,000) is carried over and deducted in a subsequent year (subject to the disallowance rules that pertain to the subsequent year). ■

---

[73] Not included here are commissions for the sale or purchase of investment property. A commission paid upon the purchase of property is added to the purchase price (and the basis) of the property. A commission paid upon the sale of property reduces the amount realized.

[74] H. Rept. No. 99-841, 99th Cong., 2d Sess., pp. II-153 and 154 (1986). The noninvestment expenses subject to the 2% of AGI limitation include unreimbursed employee business expenses, hobby expenses up to the income from the hobby, and tax return preparation fees.

OBJECTIVE 6
Compute the deduction for personal interest and qualified residence interest

Personal Interest. For years after 1990, no deduction is allowed for personal interest.[75] **Personal interest** is defined as all interest other than (1) interest incurred in a trade or business, (2) investment interest, (3) interest incurred in a passive activity, (4) qualified residence interest, and (5) interest incurred when paying estate taxes on installment.[76]

Example 7-33 ■

During the current year, Maya pays $1,500 interest on a loan incurred to purchase her personal-use automobile, $300 interest on her credit card, and $400 interest on a loan incurred to purchase furniture. Since all of this interest is classified as personal interest, no deduction is allowed. ■

Additional Comment

Banks and other financial institutions that have received mortgage interest from homeowners are required to report interest of $600 or more to the IRS and to the homeowners on Form 1098.

Qualified Residence Interest. Subject to certain limitations discussed below, individuals may deduct **qualified residence interest.** In order to be qualified residence interest the interest payment must be for either (1) acquisition indebtedness or (2) home equity indebtedness with respect to a qualified residence of the taxpayer.[77] In all cases the debt must be secured by the residence.[78] A qualified residence (discussed below) may consist of the taxpayer's principal residence and a second residence.

Acquisition Indebtedness. Acquisition indebtedness is any debt which is secured by the residence and is incurred in acquiring, constructing, or substantially improving the qualified residence. Debt may be treated as qualified acquisition indebtedness if the residence is acquired within 90 days before or after the date that the debt is incurred. In the case of the construction or substantial improvement of a residence, debt incurred prior to the completion of the construction or improvement can qualify as acquisition debt to the extent of construction expenditures which are made no more than 24 months prior to the date that the debt is incurred. Furthermore, debt incurred after construction is complete and within 90 days of the completion date may qualify as acquisition indebtedness to the extent of any construction expenditures made within the 24-month period ending on the date the debt is incurred.[79] As payments of principal are made on the loan, the amount of acquisition debt is reduced and cannot be increased unless the residence is substantially improved. Acquisition indebtedness may be refinanced (and therefore treated as acquisition indebtedness) to the extent that the principal amount of the refinancing does not exceed the principal amount of the acquisition debt immediately before the refinancing.

Example 7-34 ■

Kay acquired a personal residence in 1989 for $100,000 and borrowed $85,000 on a mortgage that was secured by the property. In the current year the principal balance of the mortgage has been reduced to $60,000. Kay's acquisition indebted-

---

[75] For years 1987 through 1990, a specified percentage of personal interest was deductible. These percentages were 65% in 1987, 40% in 1988, 20% in 1989, and 10% in 1990.

[76] Sec. 163(h). For this purpose, business interest does not include interest incurred in connection with the business of performing services as an employee.

[77] Sec. 163(h)(3)(A).

[78] Sec. 163(h)(3)(B). If the loan is not secured by the residence, it does not qualify. In one instance the taxpayer agreed to purchase her ex-husband's interest in their residence. The terms of the sale were $10,000 down plus an unsecured $25,000 note. In a private ruling, the IRS ruled that since the note was not secured by the residence, the interest on the note is not qualified residence interest. Thus the deductibility of the interest is subject to the personal interest deduction limitations (See Ltr. Rul. 8752010 September 18, 1987). However, if under any state or local homestead law the security interest is ineffective or unenforceable, the interest expense will still qualify as qualified residence interest. See Sec. 163(h)(4)(C). In another letter ruling the taxpayer borrowed money to purchase a residence securing the debt by pledging stock and bonds. Here also, the IRS denied the deduction because the loan was not secured by the residence. (See Ltr. Rul. 8906031 November 10, 1988)

[79] Notice 88-74, 1988-2 C.B. 385.

Real World Example
Professional basketball players, rock stars, corporate presidents, and movie stars are examples of individuals who may be affected by the $1 million limit on acquisition indebtedness.

ness in the current year is only $60,000 and cannot be increased above $60,000 (except by indebtedness incurred to substantially improve the residence). If she refinances the existing mortgage in the current year and the refinanced debt is $70,000, only $60,000 (the principal balance of the existing acquisition indebtedness) qualifies as acquisition indebtedness.   ■

LIMITATIONS ON ACQUISITION INDEBTEDNESS. Qualified acquisition indebtedness is limited to $1,000,000 ($500,000 for a married individual filing a separate return).[80] Qualified acquisition indebtedness incurred prior to October 13, 1987 (pre-October 13, 1987 indebtedness) is not subject to any limitation.[81] However, the aggregate amount of pre-October 13, 1987 indebtedness reduces the $1,000,000 limitation on the indebtedness incurred after October 13, 1987.

Additional Comment
Many banks in attempting to generate new loan business have heavily advertised the tax advantages of home equity indebtedness.

HOME EQUITY INDEBTEDNESS. Taxpayers may also deduct interest incurred on home equity indebtedness (so-called home equity loans). Subject to certain limits, home equity indebtedness is any indebtedness (other than acquisition indebtedness) that is secured by a qualified residence of the taxpayer.[82] The proceeds of the loan may be used for any purpose (including purchasing or improving a qualified residence), as long as the loan is secured by the taxpayer's qualified residence. However, home equity indebtedness is limited to the lesser of:

- the FMV of the qualified residence in excess of the acquisition indebtedness with respect to that residence, or
- $100,000 ($50,000 for a married individual filing a separate return)

The $1,000,000 limit on acquisition indebtedness and the $100,000 limit on home equity indebtedness are two separate limits. The maximum amount of indebtedness upon which a taxpayer may deduct qualified residence interest is generally limited to $1,100,000 if an individual has $100,000 or more equity in the property.

Example 7-35 ■

On April 23 of the current year, Kesha borrows $125,000 to purchase a new sailboat. The loan is secured by her personal residence. On that date, the outstanding balance on the original debt Kesha incurred to purchase the residence is $400,000 and the FMV of the residence is $900,000. The original debt is also secured by Kesha's residence. Kesha may deduct the interest paid on the $400,000 of acquisition indebtedness, plus the interest paid on $100,000 of the home equity loan. The interest on $25,000 ($125,000 − $100,000) is treated as personal interest and is, therefore, not deductible. The home equity loan is limited to the lesser of $100,000 or the FMV of the residence in excess of the outstanding acquisition indebtedness (the lesser of $100,000 or ($900,000 − $400,000)).   ■

Additional Comment
Some cynics assume that the reason for permitting the deduction of mortgage interest on two personal residences is due to the fact that most congressmen have a home in Washington and a second one in the district that they represent.

Qualified Residence. For any tax year, a taxpayer may have two qualified residences:

- Taxpayer's principal residence
- One other residence selected by the taxpayer, with regard to which the taxpayer meets the residence test of Sec. 280A(d)(1).[83]

---

[80] Sec. 163(h)(3)(B)(ii). If the acquisition indebtedness exceeds the $1,000,000 limitation, the committee reports to the Revenue Act of 1987 indicate that a reasonable method of allocation between the debt should be used in order to determine which debt exceeds the limitation. This may be done by taking debt into account in the chronological order in which it is incurred, with the most recently incurred debt treated as the debt that exceeds the limit.

[81] Sec. 163(h)(3)(D).

[82] Sec. 163(h)(3)(C).

[83] Whether a residence is a taxpayer's principal residence is dependent upon all the facts and circumstances (see Sec. 163(h)(4)(A) and Reg. Sec. 1.1034-1(c)(3)).

In order to meet this residence test, the taxpayer must have personally used the property more than the greater of (1) 14 days or (2) 10% of any rental days during the year.[84]

Example 7-36 ■   Fred owns a lakeside cabin, which he uses for vacations. He also rents the cabin out to others when he is not using it. During the year the cabin is rented at a fair rental for 90 days. Fred personally uses the cabin for a total of 22 days. Since Fred's personal use for the year (22 days) exceeds 14 days (the greater of 14 days or 9 days [10% of the rental days]), the cabin qualifies as his residence for purposes of deducting qualified residence interest for the year.   ■

In spite of the residence test, a property that has not been rented by the taxpayer at any time during the year may be selected by the taxpayer as the second residence on which qualified residence interest may be deducted.[85]

Timing of the Interest Deduction

Section 163 allows a deduction for all interest paid or accrued during the tax year. This generally means that cash-basis taxpayers deduct interest in the year it is paid, whereas accrual-basis taxpayers deduct interest as it accrues. There are, however, exceptions to this general rule.

Additional Comment

Points paid on the refinancing of an existing mortgage must be written off over the life of the new mortgage.

Prepaid Interest. If a cash-basis taxpayer prepays interest and the prepayment relates to a loan that extends beyond the end of the tax year, the payment must be capitalized and amortized over the periods to which the interest relates (i.e., the accrual method is applied to cash-basis taxpayers).[86] As previously discussed, there is one exception to this rule involving interest paid in the form of points charged in connection with the purchase or improvement of the taxpayer's principal residence. If these points represent prepaid interest, they may be deducted in the year paid.[87]

Interest Paid with Loan Proceeds. If an individual (1) borrows money from a third party rather than from the original lending institution and (2) uses the funds to make a payment on a previously outstanding loan, an interest deduction generally is allowed for the interest portion of the payment.[88] However, if the funds used to pay the interest on the first loan are borrowed from the same lender to whom the interest is due, and either (1) the purpose of the second loan is to pay the interest on the first, or (2) the borrower does not have unrestricted control of the funds, no interest deduction is available.[89]

Discounted Notes. Lending institutions often discount notes. In effect, the borrower pays the interest by repaying more money than is received when the note is signed. A cash-basis taxpayer can deduct this interest at the time the note is repaid, whereas

---

[84] Sec. 280A(d)(1). Use by (1) the taxpayer's family, as defined in Sec. 267(c)(4), (2) other individuals under a reciprocal-use arrangement, and (3) anyone when a fair rental is not charged is counted as a day of personal use by the taxpayer (see Sec. 280A(d)(2) and Chapter 6).

[85] Sec. 163(h)(4)(A)(iii).

[86] Sec. 461(g)(1).

[87] Sec. 461(g)(2). In order for the exception to apply, the home must be used to secure the loan, and the charging of points must be an established business practice in the area where the loan is granted. (See the discussion of the deductibility of points in this chapter under the heading *Definition of Interest* as well as the discussion in Chapter 6.)

[88] *H. C. Franklin v. CIR*, 50 AFTR 2d 82-5551, 82-2 USTC ¶ 9532 (5th Cir., 1982).

[89] *Newton A. Burgess*, 8 T.C. 47 (1947). See also *Norman W. Menz*, 80 T.C. 1174 (1983). The IRS has also announced that it will disallow a deduction for interest paid with funds obtained through a second loan from the same lender (see IRS News Release 83-93, July 6, 1983).

an accrual-basis taxpayer must deduct the interest as it accrues over the term of the loan.

Example 7-37 ■ On December 1, 1994, Stan borrows $1,000 from his credit union to use in his business. Under the terms of the contract, Stan actually receives $970 but is required to repay $1,000 on February 28, 1995 (3 months later). Since Stan is a cash-basis taxpayer, the full $30 interest can be deducted in 1995 only when the note is repaid. If he were an accrual-basis taxpayer, $10 ($30 × 0.333) would be deducted in 1994, and $20 ($30 × 0.667) would be deducted in 1995. ■

Interest Owed to a Related Party by an Accrual-Basis Taxpayer. One of the purposes of Sec. 267 is to require related cash-basis lenders and accrual-basis borrowers to report the results of their joint transaction in the same year. Thus, a deduction for any expense (including interest) accrued by an accrual-basis taxpayer must be deferred until the year in which it is actually paid and is reported as income by a cash-basis creditor who is related to the debtor. Section 267 also disallows losses on the sale of property between related parties. The disallowance of such losses is discussed in Chapter 6.

The relationships covered by this rule are quite extensive. Some of the more common relationships include the following:

- Members of a family (defined as an individual's brothers, sisters, spouse, ancestors, and lineal descendants)
- An individual and a C corporation in which the individual owns directly or indirectly more than 50% of the outstanding stock
- A corporation and a partnership which are both over 50% owned directly or indirectly by the same persons
- A partnership and any partner of the partnership
- An S Corporation and any shareholder of the S Corporation[90]

Example 7-38 ■ During the current year, Lisa, a cash-basis taxpayer, loans some money to her 100%-owned corporation, which uses the accrual method of accounting. As of December 31 of the current year, the corporation owes Lisa $3,000 in interest. However, because of a shortage of funds, the corporation does not actually pay the interest until February 15 of the following year. In spite of the fact that the corporation uses the accrual method of accounting, the $3,000 may not be deducted until it is actually paid to Lisa in the subsequent year. The result would be the same if the corporation were an S Corporation even if Lisa owned 50% or less of the outstanding stock. ■

Imputed Interest. Under certain circumstances, if less than an adequate rate of interest is charged, the IRS is authorized to impute an interest charge. This may cause the lender to have additional interest income and the borrower to have additional interest expense. The deductibility of this imputed interest expense also depends upon how the expense is classified (i.e. personal, investment, etc.). (See Chapter 11 for a discussion of imputed interest.)

The rules for deducting various types of interest are summarized in Topic Review 7-2.

---

[90] Secs. 267(b) and (e). The list of relationships is much more extensive than those mentioned. An S Corporation is one which meets certain requirements and has made an election to have its income taxed directly to its shareholders. A C Corporation is one which has not made an S election. (See Chapter 11 of the *Prentice Hall's Federal Taxation: Corporations, Partnerships, Estates, and Trusts* text or Chapter 22 of the *Prentice Hall's Federal Taxation: Comprehensive* text.)

TOPIC REVIEW 7-2

Deductibility of Interest Expense	
Type of Interest	Rules
1. Business	1. Deductible in full as a *for* AGI deduction.
2. Passive	2. Subject to the passive loss limits (see Chapter 8).
3. Investment	3. Deductible as an itemized deduction to the extent of the taxpayer's net investment income for the year. Any amount not deductible is carried over to subsequent years.
4. Personal	4. Not deductible.
5. Qualified residence	5. (a) Must be attributable to debt secured by the taxpayer's principal residence and one other residence selected by the taxpayer.
	(b) Interest on up to $1,000,000 of home acquisition indebtedness is deductible as an itemized deduction.
	(c) Interest on home equity debt is deductible as an itemized deduction. Home equity debt is limited to the lesser of (1) $100,000 or (2) the excess of the FMV of the residence over the home acquisition indebtedness.

CHARITABLE CONTRIBUTIONS

OBJECTIVE 7

Compute the amount of a charitable contribution deduction and identify limitations

Under Sec. 170, corporations and individuals who itemize their deductions can deduct **charitable contributions** to qualified organizations. With one exception, the deduction is taken in the year the contribution is made, regardless of the taxpayer's method of accounting. The exception deals with certain contributions made by corporations and is explained in the section of this chapter entitled Special Rules for Charitable Contributions Made by Corporations. The amount of the deduction depends upon (1) the type of charity receiving the contribution, (2) the type of property that is contributed, and (3) the applicable limitations.

Qualifying Organization

Additional Comment

In 1991 the deduction for charitable contributions represented 13.1% of the total dollar amount of itemized deductions.

To be deductible for federal income tax purposes, a contribution must be made to or for the use of a qualified organization.[91] Contributions made directly to individuals, even though they may be needy, are generally not deductible.[92] Qualified organizations include the following:[93]

---

[91] The Supreme Court has ruled that in order for a contribution to be "for the use of" a qualifying organization, the gift must be held either in a legally enforceable trust or in a similar legal arrangement. (See *U.S. v. Harold Davis,* 65 AFTR 2d 90-1051, 90-1 USTC ¶ 50,270 (USSC, 1990).)

[92] Under certain circumstances, a taxpayer may take a deduction (limited to $50 per month) for maintaining a student as a member of his household. The student (1) may not be a dependent or relative of the taxpayer, and (2) must be placed in the taxpayer's home under an arrangement with a qualifying organization (see Sec. 170(g)).

[93] Sec. 170(c).

- The United States, the District of Columbia, a state or possession of the United States, or a political subdivision of a state or possession

- A corporation, trust, community chest, fund or foundation that is created or organized under the laws of the United States, a state, possession, or the District of Columbia[94]

- A post or organization of war veterans

- A domestic fraternal society, order, or association[95]

- Certain cemetery companies

Typical Misconception

Occasionally it is erroneously believed that deductible charitable contributions can be made directly to needy individuals.

Because of the restrictions and limitations examined later in this chapter, these qualifying organizations are further classified into (1) public charities and (2) private nonoperating foundations. Different restrictions and limitations apply to each type of organization.

Public charities include:

Real World Example

The Red Cross, Boy Scouts, United Fund, Goodwill, and Indiana University are examples of public charities.

- Churches or a convention or association of churches

- Educational institutions that normally maintain a regular faculty, curriculum, and regularly enrolled students

- Organizations such as hospitals and medical schools whose principal function is medical care or medical education and research

- Government-supported organizations that exist to receive, hold, invest, and administer property for the benefit of a college or university

- Any qualified governmental unit

- Organizations that normally receive a substantial part of their support from either a governmental unit or the general public

- Certain private operating foundations[96]

Additional Comment

The list of qualifying organizations is published in a book, IRS, Publication No. 78 [Cumulative List of Organizations], 1992 that rivals the size of a big-city telephone directory.

Since several thousand organizations meet these requirements, the IRS publishes a list of many of the organizations that have applied for and received tax-exempt status.[97] Although this publication is frequently updated, an organization need not be listed in order to qualify.

Type of Property Contributed

Self-Study Question

Doug purchases an item having a FMV of $75 for $100 in a charity auction. How much can he deduct?

Answer

Doug can deduct only $25 since the cash paid must be reduced by the value of the property received.

If a contribution is made in cash, the amount of the deduction is easily determinable. However, if noncash property is donated, the amount of the contribution is not as easy to identify. In the case of noncash property, the amount of the donation is dependent upon two factors: (1) the type of property donated and (2) the type of qualifying organization (public charity or private nonoperating foundation) to whom the property is given. Furthermore, a gift of property that consists of less than the donor's entire interest in the property is not usually considered a contribution of property.

---

[94] These organizations must be organized and operated exclusively (1) for religious, charitable, scientific, literary, or educational purposes; (2) to foster national or international amateur sports competition; or (3) for the prevention of cruelty to children or animals.

[95] Furthermore, gifts to these organizations must be made by individuals and must be used exclusively for religious, charitable, scientific, literary, or educational purposes, or for the prevention of cruelty to children or animals.

[96] Sec. 170(b)(1)(E). The distinction between a private operating foundation and a private nonoperating foundation generally depends upon the way the foundation spends or distributes its income and contributions. The details of this distinction are beyond the scope of this text.

[97] IRS, *Publication No. 78* [Cumulative List of Organizations], 1993. This publication is updated and reissued annually.

Thus, for example, no charitable contribution is made when an individual donates the use of a vacation home for a charitable fund-raising auction.[98]

Contribution of Capital Gain Property. In general, the amount of a donation of capital gain property is its FMV. A property's FMV is defined as the price at which the property would change hands between a willing buyer and a willing seller, neither being under any compulsion to buy or sell and both having reasonable knowledge of relevant facts.[99] **Capital gain property** is defined as property upon which a long-term capital gain would be recognized if it were sold at its FMV on the date of the contribution.[100] If a long-term capital loss or a short-term capital gain or loss would be recognized, the property is considered to be ordinary income property for purposes of the charitable contribution deduction.

CONTRIBUTION TO A PRIVATE NONOPERATING FOUNDATION. An exception to this general rule is provided for contributions of property to private nonoperating foundations. Here the amount of the contribution is the property's FMV, reduced by the long-term capital gain that would be recognized if the property were sold at its FMV on the date of the contribution.[101] This means that generally the deductible amount of the contribution will be the property's adjusted basis.

Example 7-39 ■

Betty purchases land in 1985 for $10,000. In the current year, she contributes the land to the United Way. At the time of the contribution, the FMV of the property is $25,000. Since the land is capital gain property donated to a public charity, the amount of the contribution is $25,000 (its FMV). ■

Example 7-40 ■

Assume the same facts as in Example 7-39, except that Betty donates the land to Cherry Foundation, a private nonoperating foundation. The amount of the contribution is $10,000 ($25,000 − $15,000 long-term capital gain that would be recognized if sold). ■

UNRELATED USE PROPERTY. A second exception applies to capital gain property (which is also tangible personal property) contributed to a public charity and used by the organization for purposes unrelated to the charity's function. In such cases, the amount of the contribution deduction is equal to the property's FMV minus the long-term capital gain that would be recognized if the property were sold at its FMV.[102] This amount generally is the property's adjusted basis. Tangible property is all property that is not intangible property (e.g., property other than stock, securities, copyrights, patents, and so on). Personal property is all property other than real estate. The taxpayer is responsible for proving that the property was not put to unrelated use. However, this burden of proof is met if at the time of the contribution it is reasonable to anticipate that the property would not be put to unrelated use.[103] The immediate sale of the property by the charitable organization is considered to be a use unrelated to its tax-exempt purpose.[104]

---

[98] Sec. 170(f)(3), Reg. Sec. 1.170A-7(a)(1) and Rev. Rul. 89-51, 1989-1 C.B. 89. Note, however, that certain transfers of partial interests in property do qualify (e.g., the contribution of certain remainder interests to a trust, the transfer of a remainder interest in a personal residence or a farm, or a contribution of an undivided interest in property). These exceptions are beyond the scope of this text.

[99] Reg. Sec. 1.170A-1(c)(2).

[100] Reg. Sec. 1.170A-4(b)(2). A long-term capital gain is realized on the sale of capital assets held more than one year.

[101] Sec. 170(e)(1)(B)(ii). However, if the property donated to the private nonoperating foundation is stock listed on an established securities market and if the taxpayer does not donate more than 10% of the stock of the corporation, the amount of the contribution remains at its FMV (see Sec. 170(e)(5)).

[102] Sec. 170(e)(1)(B).

[103] Reg. Sec. 1.170A-4(b)(3)(ii).

[104] Reg. Sec. 1.170A-4(b)(3)(i).

Example 7-41 ■

Laura purchases a painting for $3,000. Several years later she contributes the painting to a local college. The FMV of the painting is $5,000 at the time the property is contributed. The painting is both tangible personal property and capital gain property. The college places the painting in the library for display and study by art students. Since the college does not use the painting for purposes unrelated to its function as an educational institution, the amount of Laura's contribution is equal to its FMV ($5,000).[105]   ■

Example 7-42 ■

Assume the same facts as in Example 7-41, except that the college sells the painting for its fair market value shortly after receiving it and uses the proceeds for educational purposes and Laura knew at the time she donated the painting that the college would sell the property. The sale of the painting constitutes an unrelated use by the college. Therefore, the amount of Laura's contribution is reduced to $3,000 ($5,000 − [$5,000 − $3,000]).   ■

Contribution of Ordinary Income Property

GENERAL RULE. If ordinary income property is contributed to a charitable organization, the deduction is equal to the property's FMV less the amount of gain that would be recognized if the property were sold at its FMV on the date of the contribution.[106] In most cases, this deduction is equal to the property's adjusted basis. This rule applies regardless of the type of charitable organization to which the property is donated.

Ordinary income property is defined as any property that would result in the recognition of ordinary income if the property were sold. Thus, ordinary income property includes inventory, works of art or manuscripts created by the taxpayer, capital assets that have been held for one year or less, and Sec. 1231 property that results in the recognition of ordinary income due to depreciation recapture.[107]

Example 7-43 ■

During the current year Bart purchases land as an investment for $10,000. Five months later he contributes the land to the United Way. At the time of the contribution the property's FMV is $15,000. The amount of Bart's contribution is $10,000 ($15,000 − [$15,000 − $10,000]) because the land has been held for one year or less.   ■

Example 7-44 ■

Paul purchased a truck a few years ago for $20,000. During the current year, Paul donates the truck previously used in his business to a local community college. At the time of the contribution, the truck's adjusted basis is $5,000 and its FMV is $8,000. Since Paul would have recognized a $3,000 gain (all ordinary income under Sec. 1245) if the truck were sold at its FMV, the amount of the contribution is $5,000 ($8,000 − $3,000), which is equal to the truck's adjusted basis.   ■

Additional Comment

An infant is defined as a minor child, an "ill" person is one who requires medical care, and a "needy" person is one who lacks the necessities of life.

DONATION OF INVENTORY BY A CORPORATION. Under certain circumstances the donation of inventory by a corporate taxpayer to certain public charities gives rise to a contribution that is valued at more than the adjusted basis of the inventory. One exception is available if the inventory is to be used by the charity solely for the care of

---

[105] Ibid.
[106] Sec. 170(e)(1).
[107] Reg. Secs. 1.170A-4(b)(1) and 1.170A-4(d). Sec. 1231 property includes property used in a trade or business that is subject to depreciation. If sold at a gain, part or all of the gain is treated as ordinary income. Any remaining gain is subject to the Sec. 1231 rules. (See Chapter 13 for an explanation of the depreciation recapture and Sec. 1231 rules.)

Real World Example

Procter & Gamble sent household products to charitable organizations in Florida to assist victims of Hurricane Andrew.

the ill, needy, or infants.[108] The other exception involves the donation of scientific equipment constructed by the taxpayer and donated to a college, university, or qualified research organization to be used for research, experimentation, or research training in the physical or biological sciences.[109] In both cases, the amount of the charitable contribution is the property's FMV, reduced by 50% of the ordinary income that would be recognized if the property were sold at its FMV. However, the amount of the contribution is limited to twice the basis of the property.[110]

Example 7-45 ■

During the current year, Able Corporation donates some of its inventory to a public charity. The charity intends to use the inventory for the care of the needy and ill. At the time of the contribution, the FMV of the inventory is $10,000. Able's basis in the inventory is $6,000. Since this transaction qualifies under the exception, the amount of Able's contribution is $8,000 ($10,000 − [0.50 × $4,000]). ■

Example 7-46 ■

Assume the same facts as in Example 7-45, except that Able's basis in the inventory is $3,000. The amount of Able's contribution (before any limitations are applied) is $6,500 ($10,000 − [0.50 × $7,000]) but the actual amount of the contribution is limited to $6,000 (2 × the $3,000 basis in the property). ■

Real World Example

The donation of blood is considered to be a personal nondeductible service.

Contribution of Services. When services are rendered to a qualified charitable organization, only the unreimbursed expenses incurred incident to the rendering of the services are deductible.[111] These items include out-of-pocket transportation expenses, the cost of lodging and 50% of the cost of meals while away from home, and the cost of a uniform without general utility that is required to be worn in performing the donated services. The out-of-pocket expenses are deductible only if they are incurred by the taxpayer who actually renders the services to the charity.[112] No deduction is allowed for traveling expenses while away from home unless there is no significant element of personal pleasure, recreation, or vacation in such travel.[113] Instead of the actual costs of operating an automobile while performing the donated services, the law permits a deduction of 12 cents per mile.[114]

Example 7-47 ■

Real World Example

The cost of newspaper advertising, paper, pencils, and other supplies purchased by volunteers in connection with their involvement in the Volunteer Income Tax Assistance Program (VITA) is deductible. Rev. Rul. 80-45, 1980-1 C.B. 54.

During the current year, Tony spends a total of 100 hours in developing an accounting system for the local council of the Boy Scouts of America. As an accountant, Tony earns $75 per hour. During the year, Tony also drives his car a total of 500 miles in performing the services for the Boy Scouts of America. If he uses the automatic mileage method to compute the amount of the charitable contribution, $60 (0.12 × 500) can be deducted. No deduction is available for the value of 100 hours of Tony's contributed services. ■

Deduction Limitations

Overall 50% Limitation. The charitable contribution deduction available for any tax year is subject to certain limitations. For individuals, the general overall limitation

---

[108] Sec. 170(e)(3). These charitable organizations are known as Sec. 501(c)(3) charities.
[109] Sec. 170(e)(4).
[110] Sec. 170(e)(3)(B).
[111] Reg. Sec. 1.170A-1(g).
[112] *U.S. v. Harold Davis,* 65 AFTR 2d 90-1051, 90-1 USTC ¶ 50,270 (USSC, 1990). In this case, the court held that funds paid directly to a church missionary to reimburse him for out-of-pocket expenses incurred incident to the rendering of charitable services were not deductible. However, such payments may, in some cases, constitute support, thereby enabling the payor to claim a dependency exemption.
[113] Sec. 170(j).
[114] Sec. 170(i).

Key Point

The charitable contribution deduction can never exceed 50% of AGI.

applicable to public charities is 50% of the taxpayer's AGI for the year.[115] Any contributions in excess of the overall limitation may be carried forward and deducted in the subsequent 5 tax years.[116] In addition, contributions of (1) capital gain property to either a public charity or a private nonoperating foundation and (2) all types of property to private nonoperating foundations may be subject to further limitation.

Key Point

The generosity of Congress in permitting individuals to use FMV is tempered by the 30% of AGI limitation.

30% Limitation. Under certain circumstances a special 30% of AGI limitation applies. Contributions of capital gain property to public charities are generally based upon the property's FMV but are subject to an overall limit of 30% of AGI instead of a 50% limit. This limit does not apply, however, in the following situations:

- Capital gain property (which is tangible personal property) donated to a public charity that does not put the property to its related use. In such cases, the amount of the contribution is scaled down by the long-term capital gain that would be recognized if the property were sold.
- The taxpayer elects to reduce the amount of the charitable contribution deduction by the long-term capital gain that would be recognized if the property were sold.

Example 7-48 ■   Joy donates a painting to the local university during a year in which she has AGI of $50,000. The painting, which cost $10,000 several years before, is valued at $30,000 at the time of the contribution. The university exhibits the painting in its art gallery. Since the painting is put to a use related to the university's purpose, the amount of her contribution is $30,000. The amount of the charitable deduction for the year, however, is limited to $15,000 (0.30 × $50,000 AGI) unless Joy elects to reduce the amount of the contribution by the long-term capital gain. ■

Example 7-49 ■   Assume the same facts as in Example 7-48, except that the university immediately sells the painting. Now the amount of Joy's contribution is $10,000 ($30,000 − $20,000 LTCG). The deduction limitation is $25,000 (0.50 × $50,000) because the 30% limitation does not apply to contributions subject to a capital gain offset. ■

The overall deduction limitation of 30% of AGI also applies to the contribution of all types of property other than capital gain property (e.g., cash and ordinary income property) to a private nonoperating foundation. However, the deductibility of certain contributions to this type of charity may be subject to even further restrictions.

Real World Example

The largest private nonoperating foundation ranked by the FMV of total assets is the Ford Foundation.

20% Limitation on Capital Gain Property Contributed to Private Nonoperating Foundations. Contributions of capital gain property to private nonoperating foundations are limited to the lesser of (1) 20% of the taxpayer's AGI or (2) 30% of the taxpayer's AGI, reduced by any contributions of capital gain property donated to a public charity.[117]

Contributions for Athletic Events. If a taxpayer makes a contribution to a college or university and in return receives the right to purchase tickets to athletic events, only 80% of the payment may be deducted.[118]

---

[115] A 10% of taxable income limitation is placed on corporate taxpayers. For purposes of this limitation, a corporation's taxable income is computed without regard to any deduction for (1) charitable contributions, (2) dividends received, (3) a net operating loss carryback, or (4) a capital loss carryback.
[116] Sec. 170(d).
[117] Sec. 170(b)(1)(D).
[118] Sec. 170(m).

Applying the Deduction Limitations. Contributions subject only to the 50% of AGI limitation are accounted for before the contributions subject to the 30% of AGI limitation.

Example 7-50 ■

During a year when Ted's AGI is $70,000, he donates $22,000 to his church and $18,000 to a private nonoperating charity. The church contribution is initially subject to the 50% limitation and is fully deductible because the $22,000 contribution is less than the limitation amount of $35,000 (0.50 × $70,000). Ted's deduction for the contribution to the private nonoperating charity (a 30% charity) is limited to $13,000 (the lesser of the following three amounts:

(1)	The actual contribution	$18,000
(2)	The remaining 50% limitation after the contribution to Ted's church ([0.50 × $70,000] − $22,000)	$13,000
(3)	30% of AGI (0.30 × $70,000)	$21,000

■

Additional Comment

If a taxpayer has contribution carryovers that are about to expire, the taxpayer should consider reducing the current year's contribution so that the carryovers can be deducted.

Application of Carryovers

As noted earlier, any contributions that exceed the 50% limitation may be carried over and deducted in the subsequent 5 years.[119] These carryovers are subject to the limitations that apply in subsequent years. Thus, carryovers may be deducted only to the extent that the limitation of the subsequent year exceeds the contributions made during that year.

These general rules also apply with regard to the special limitations. For example, if property subject to the 30% limitation is donated during the current year and the amount of the contribution exceeds the limitation, the excess may be carried over to the 5 subsequent years subject to the 30% limitation in the carryover years. In the carryover year, a deduction may be taken for the excess contribution to the extent that the 30% limitation of the subsequent year exceeds the amount of the property donated during the subsequent year subject to the 30% limitation.[120] Excess contributions of property subject to the 20% limitation may also be carried over to the subsequent 5 years.[121] This carryover is also subject to the special restrictions noted above for the 30% limitation.

Example 7-51 ■

Assume that for the years 1992 through 1994, individual Joan reports AGI and makes charitable contributions in the following amounts:

	1992	*1993*	*1994*
AGI	$40,000	$40,000	$60,000
Cash contributions subject to the 50% of AGI limitation	25,000	23,000	24,000
50% of AGI limitation	20,000	20,000	30,000

The amount of the charitable contribution deduction for each year and the order in which the deduction and carryovers are used are as follows:

---

[119] Sec. 170(d)(1).
[120] Sec. 170(b)(1)(C)(ii).
[121] Sec. 170(b)(1)(D).

	1992	*1993*	*1994*
Amount of deduction	$20,000	$20,000	$30,000
Amount of carryover			
From 1992	5,000	5,000	—0—
From 1993		3,000	2,000

Key Point

In effect, accrual basis taxpayers are placed on the cash method with respect to their charitable contributions.

Special Rules for Charitable Contributions Made by Corporations

The rules governing charitable contributions made by corporations are generally the same as those pertaining to contributions made by individuals. However, certain differences do exist.

Ethical Point

A tax practitioner should not be a party to the backdating of a Board of Director's authorization of a charitable contribution pledge so that the corporation may improperly deduct the contribution in the earlier year.

Pledges Made by Accrual-Method Corporation. Generally, deductions are only allowed for actual contributions (but not pledges) made during the tax year. This rule applies to both cash- and accrual-method taxpayers. A major exception to this general rule exists for accrual-method corporations. Such corporations may elect to claim a charitable deduction for the year in which a pledge is made as long as the actual contribution is made by the fifteenth day of the third month following the close of the year in which the pledge is made.[122]

Limitation Applicable to Corporations. Corporate charitable deductions are limited to 10% of the corporation's taxable income for the year. This amount is computed without regard to the dividends-received deduction, net operating loss or capital loss carrybacks, or any deduction for the charitable contribution itself.[123] Excess contributions may be carried forward for 5 years and are deductible only if the current year contributions are less than the current year's 10% limitation. The carryovers are used in chronological order.

Summary of Deduction Limitations

The rules governing the deduction for charitable contributions are summarized in Topic Review 7-3.

CASUALTY AND THEFT LOSSES

Generally, losses on personal-use property are not deductible. However, individuals can deduct a casualty or theft loss on personal-use property as an itemized deduction on Schedule A of Form 1040.[124] Losses on business and investment properties held for the production of rents or royalties are deductible *for* AGI. Other casualty losses on investment property are itemized deductions. These casualty losses are studied in greater depth in Chapter 8.

[122] Sec. 170(a)(2).
[123] Sec. 170(b)(2).
[124] Sec. 165(c)(3).

Deduction Rules for Charitable Contributions

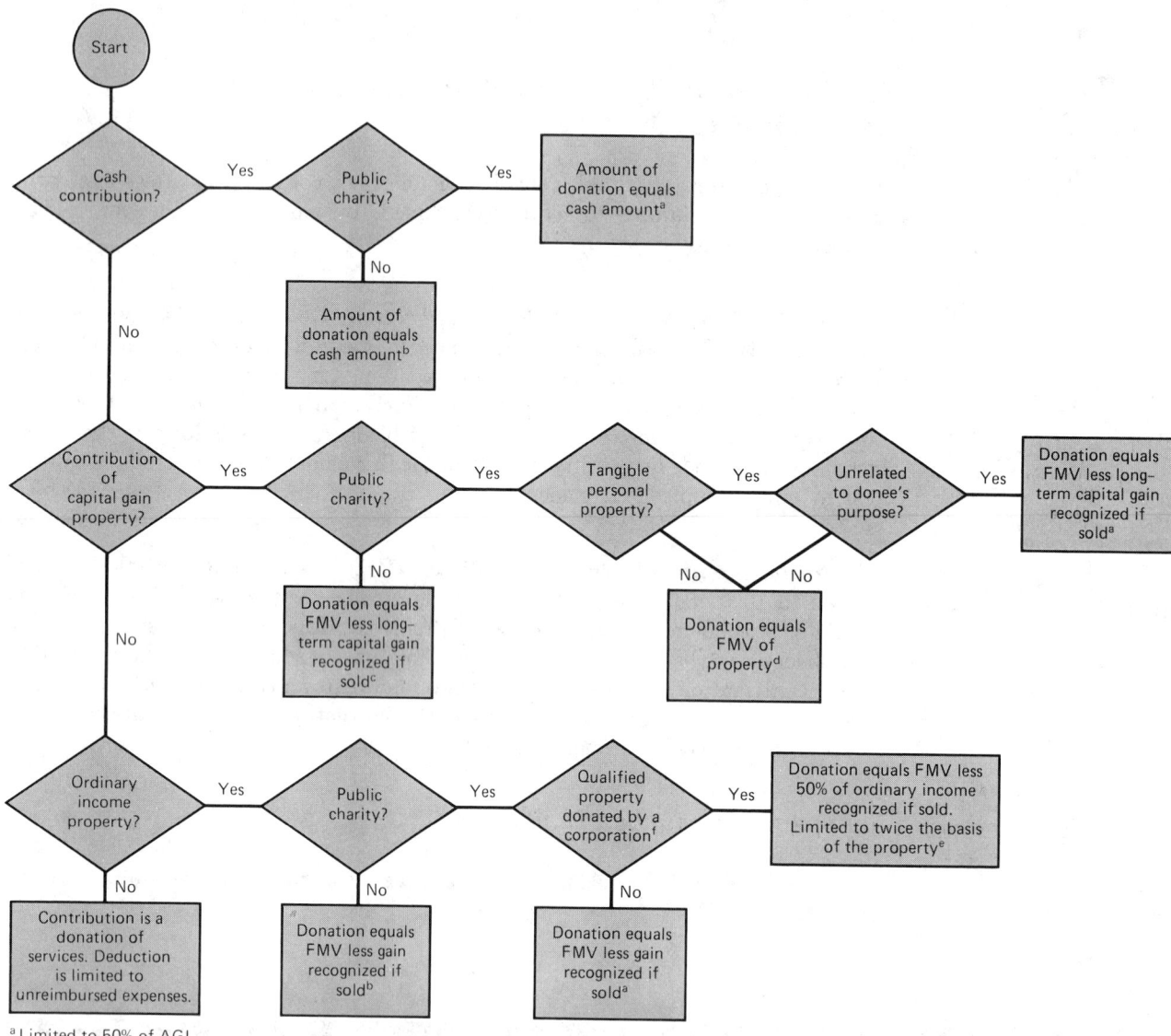

[a] Limited to 50% of AGI.

[b] Limited to lesser of (1) 30% of AGI or (2) remaining 50% of AGI after accounting for donations to public charities.

[c] Limited to lesser of (1) 20% of AGI or (2) 30% of AGI less capital gain contributions to public charities.

[d] Taxpayer may elect to scale down the amount of donation by the long-term capital gain. If the election is made, limited to 50% of AGI. If no election is made, limited to 30% of AGI.

[e] Limited to 10% of the corporation's taxable income without regard to any deduction for charitable contributions, dividends received, a net operating loss carryback or a capital loss carryback.

[f] Qualified property consists of either (1) inventory or property used in a trade or business which will be used by a Sec. 501 (c)(3) charity for the care of the ill, needy, or infants, or (2) inventory constructed by the corporation which will be used by a qualified research institution in the physical or biological sciences.

MISCELLANEOUS ITEMIZED DEDUCTIONS

Various expenses are deductible as miscellaneous itemized deductions. These deductions include employment-related expenses of employees, certain investment-related expenses, and the cost of tax advice. However, as explained in Chapter 9, generally these items are deductible only to the extent that, in the aggregate, they exceed 2% of AGI.

Certain Employee Expenses

Certain employment-related expenses of employees are also deductible as itemized deductions on Schedule A. These expenses include *unreimbursed* expenditures for travel and transportation, dues to professional organizations, costs of job hunting, items of protective clothing or uniforms not suitable for everyday wear, union dues, subscriptions to trade journals, and so on. A more detailed discussion of this topic is included in Chapter 9.

Expenses to Produce Income

Under Sec. 212, individuals may deduct expenses incurred to produce income. If these expenses arise in an activity that produces either rental or royalty income, they are deductions *for* AGI (see the explanation in Chapter 6). However, if the expenses are incurred in generating other types of investment income, they are deducted on Schedule A as itemized deductions. These investment-related expenditures include items such as rental fees for safe deposit boxes used to hold investment property, subscriptions to investment and trade journals, bank service charges on checking accounts used in an investment activity, and fees paid for consulting advice. These expenses are all subject to the 2% of AGI reduction explained in Chapter 9. Certain investment income and expenses are earned by taxpayers in mutual funds and other publicly offered regulated investment companies. These items generally flow through and are reported by the shareholders or owners of the fund. Since typically these entities simply report the net income (income minus expenses) to the owners, Sec. 67(c)(2) exempts these investment-related expenses from the 2% of AGI limitation. Other types of flow-through entities (e.g., partnerships and S corporations) must report these expenses to their owners as separately stated items so that the 2% of AGI reduction may be applied to these expenses also.

Cost of Tax Advice

Section 212 provides individuals with a deduction for expenses incurred in connection with the determination, collection, or refund of any tax, including federal, state, local, and foreign income taxes as well as estate, gift, and inheritance taxes.[125] These items include tax return preparation fees,[126] appraisal fees incurred in determining the amount of a casualty loss, certain capital improvements for a medical deduction, or the FMV of property donated to a qualified charity,[127] fees paid to an accountant for representation in a tax audit,[128] long-distance telephone calls responding to IRS

---

[125] Sec. 212(3). See also *Philip T. Sharples v. CIR,* 37 AFTR 2d 76-1223, 76-1 USTC ¶ 9356 (Ct. Cls., 1976).

[126] *Charles Crowther,* 28 T.C. 1293 (1957), *acq.* 1964-1 C.B. 4.

[127] Rev. Ruls. 58-180, 1958-1 C.B. 153, and 67-461, 1967-2 C.B. 125.

[128] *Lealand M. Blair,* 1981 PH T.C. Memo ¶ 81,634, 42 TCM 1576.

questions,[129] costs of tax return preparation materials and books,[130] and legal fees incurred in planning the tax consequences dealing with estate planning.[131] If these items are incurred in connection with the taxpayer's (1) trade or business (reported on Schedule C), (2) farm income (reported on Schedule F), or (3) an activity which produces rents or royalties (reported on Part I of Schedule E), they are *for* AGI deductions.[132] All other expenses incurred for tax advice are miscellaneous itemized deductions subject to the 2% of AGI limitation.

Fees that are not directly connected with the determination, collection, or refund of a tax, however, are personal expenses and are not deductible. Thus, legal fees incurred for drafting wills or obtaining other legal advice or incurred in tax fraud cases in connection with the filing of a fraudulent return have been found nondeductible.[133] Legal fees relating to a divorce generally are not deductible, unless they deal with tax-related items such as determining who will receive the exemption for dependent children. These fees are discussed in greater detail in Chapter 3.

REDUCTION OF CERTAIN ITEMIZED DEDUCTIONS

OBJECTIVE 9

Compute total itemized deductions for a taxpayer who is subject to the itemized deduction phase-out

Additional Comment

The reduction in itemized deductions obscures the true marginal tax rate applicable to high-income taxpayers and can be thought of as a hidden tax rate.

Because of concerns with the budget deficit, in 1990 Congress provided for a reduction in the total amount of certain itemized deductions for high income taxpayers.[134] This reduction applies only to individuals with AGI in excess of a certain threshold amount. This AGI threshold amount for 1994 is $111,800 ($55,900 for married persons filing a separate return), and will be adjusted by an inflation factor for the subsequent years. The reduction in the itemized deductions is 3% of the amount that the individual's AGI for the year exceeds the threshold amount. However, two limitations apply. First, the reduction in the itemized deductions cannot exceed 80% of the total itemized deductions other than medical expenses, investment interest, casualty losses, and wagering losses. Second, the 3% reduction is applied after taking into account the other limitations on itemized deductions (e.g., the 2% of AGI limitation on miscellaneous itemized deductions).

Example 7-52 ■

During 1994, John and Sue (a married couple filing a joint return) report AGI of $250,000. In addition, their itemized deductions consist of $10,000 charitable contributions, $4,000 real property taxes, and $8,000 state income taxes. Because their AGI exceeds $111,800, their itemized deductions for the year are limited to $17,854 ($22,000 − $4,146), computed as follows:

AGI	$250,000
Threshold	(111,800)
Excess	$138,200
Times: Reduction percentage	× 0.03
Potential reduction	$ 4,146

---

[129] Ltr. Rul. 8321042 (February 18, 1983).
[130] *Louis P. Contini,* 76 T.C. 447 (1981).
[131] *Sidney Merians,* 60 T.C. 187 (1973), *acq.* 1973-2 C.B. 2.
[132] Rev. Rul. 92-29, 1992-1 C.B. 20.
[133] Rev. Rul. 68-662, 1968-2 C.B. 69.
[134] Sec. 68. These rules were made permanent by the Revenue Reconciliation Act of 1993.

Limit to reduction:	
Charitable contributions	$ 10,000
Property taxes	4,000
State income taxes	8,000
Total	$ 22,000
Times: Limitation percentage	× 0.80
Limit	$ 17,600

Therefore, the 80% limitation does not apply because the $4,146 potential reduction is less than $17,600. Thus, John and Sue's itemized deductions for charitable contributions and taxes are reduced to $17,854 ($22,000 − $4,146).

Example 7-53 ■ Assume the same facts as Example 7-52 except that the $10,000 charitable contributions were, instead, medical expenses in excess of 7.5% of AGI and that the state income taxes were, instead, a deductible casualty loss (i.e., the amount in excess of the 10% of AGI limitation). Now John and Sue's allowable itemized deductions for the year are $18,800 ($22,000–$3,200), computed as follows:

AGI	$250,000
Threshold	(111,800)
Excess	$138,200
Times: Reduction percentage	× 0.03
Potential reduction	$ 4,146
Limit to reduction:	
Real property taxes	$ 4,000
Times: Limitation percentage	× 0.80
Limit	$ 3,200

TAX PLANNING CONSIDERATIONS

Additional Comment

Self-employed taxpayers could deduct as a business expense up to 25% of the amount paid for medical insurance prior to December 31, 1993. The balance was included with the other medical expenses. It is uncertain whether this provision will be reinstated for subsequent years.

Medical Expense Deduction

Working with the 7.5% of AGI Floor. As explained previously a deduction for medical expenses is only available to individuals to the extent those expenditures exceed 7.5% of the taxpayer's AGI for the year. Thus, many individuals find that no deduction is available, even though their medical expenses are relatively high. In these cases, some benefit may be obtained if a portion of the medical expenses can be bunched into one year. Orthodontic work, certain orthopedic treatment, noncosmetic elective surgery, and new eyeglasses are all examples of medical expenditures that may be either accelerated or delayed into a year in which other medical expenses are high or AGI is lower.

Generally, a deduction for medical expenses is allowed only in the year in which the expense is actually paid. The mere prepayment of future expenses usually will not accelerate the deduction. However, if there is a legal obligation to pay or if the prepayment is a requirement for the receipt of the medical care, a deduction is available in the earlier year of payment.[135] If the medical treatment has already been

[135] *Robert M. Rose v. CIR,* 26 AFTR 2d 70-5653, 70-2 USTC ¶ 9646 (5th Cir., 1970). See also Rev. Ruls. 75-302, 1975-2 C.B. 86, and 75-303, 1975-2 C.B. 87.

received, but the taxpayer does not have sufficient cash to pay the bill, a deduction for the current year may be preserved by either borrowing the cash to satisfy the bill or by using a credit card.

Example 7-54 ■

Key Point

Even if the medical expenses exceed 7.5% of AGI the taxpayer may not benefit from the deduction if the medical expenses in addition to the other itemized deductions do not exceed the standard deduction.

During the current year, Marty's estimated AGI is $50,000. Marty has already incurred $2,000 in medical expenses for himself and his family during the year. Since 7.5% of AGI for the year is $3,750, he receives no medical expense deduction. Marty plans to incur $2,400 in medical expenses for orthodontic work for his son next year. No other major medical expenses are anticipated, and Marty expects his AGI in the following year to remain the same. If these estimates are accurate, he will receive no medical deduction in either year. However, if the orthodontic work is started in the current year and Marty pays for the work, he will incur a total of $4,400 in medical expenses in the current year. Thus, $650 ($4,400 − $3,750) of the medical expenses may be deducted.

Mere prepayment in this case is not sufficient. Marty must have a portion of the orthodontic services performed in the earlier year. If he does not have sufficient cash to pay the bill in the current year, he could borrow the money or use a bank credit card. ■

Multiple Support Agreements. An individual may deduct medical expenses incurred for himself, his spouse, and his dependents. In cases where a multiple support agreement has been filed, the individual who is the subject of the agreement is treated as the dependent of the taxpayer who is entitled to the dependency exemption. Thus, in order to preserve the medical expense deduction, all medical expenditures for the dependent individual should be paid by the taxpayer who is entitled to the dependency exemption.

Example 7-55 ■

Amy, Bart, Clay, and Donna each provide 25% of the support of their father, Eric. Under the terms of a multiple support agreement, Bart, Clay, and Donna all agree to allow Amy to claim the dependency exemption with respect to Eric. During the year, $3,000 in medical expenses are incurred on Eric's behalf. If Amy pays these expenses, she may deduct them (subject to limitations). However, if Bart, Clay, or Donna pay these expenses, no one may claim the medical expenses as a deduction. ■

Interest Expense Deduction

A taxpayer may deduct qualified residence interest incurred on a principal residence and one other qualified residence that is selected by the taxpayer. This choice is made annually. In order for the second residence to qualify, it must have been used personally by the taxpayer for more than the greater of (1) 14 days or (2) 10% of the rental days during the year. If this test is met, however, the rental of vacation home limitations of Sec. 280A also apply. As explained in Chapter 6, these rules require the expenses to be allocated between the rental use and the personal use. The expenses allocated to the rental use are deductible only to the extent of the rental income. Of the expenses allocated to the personal use, only the taxes and interest (if the residence is selected and if the loan is secured by the residence) are deductible as itemized deductions.

If the personal use by the taxpayer does not meet the test mentioned above, the interest allocated to the personal use cannot qualify as residence interest and it becomes nondeductible personal interest. Furthermore, the rental income and expenses allocated to the rental use of the property generally are subject to the passive loss rules (see Chapter 8). Under these rules, individuals generally can deduct losses generated from a passive activity only to the extent of the individual's passive income. Certain individuals, however, may deduct up to $25,000 of losses from the rental of real estate. Thus, the two alternatives and their consequences are as follows:

1. Meet the test. No loss from the rental portion of the property may be deducted. However, the interest allocated to the personal use portion may be fully deductible as qualified residence interest.
2. Do not meet the test: The interest allocated to the personal use portion is nondeductible personal interest. However, all of the passive loss from the rental portion is deductible against passive income. Furthermore, certain individuals may deduct up to $25,000 additional passive loss.

The alternative a taxpayer chooses depends upon several factors such as (1) the amount of the taxpayer's passive income, (2) the total amount of itemized deductions, and (3) whether the loan is secured by the vacation home, etc.

Deduction for Charitable Contributions

Self-Study Question

What type of property lends itself to the "election to reduce"?

Answer

Property on which there is very little appreciation.

Election to Reduce the Amount of a Charitable Contribution. The election to reduce the contribution of capital gain property to public charities by the long-term capital gain that would be recognized if the property were sold is an annual election that applies to all capital gain property donated to public charities during the year. Because the election increases the ceiling limitation from 30% to 50%, under certain circumstances a taxpayer may actually receive a larger deduction for the year than would normally be available if the election were not made.

Example 7-56 ■

During the current year, Jane has AGI of $50,000. She donates a painting to the local university during the same year. The painting, valued at $30,000 at the time of contribution, cost her $25,000 several years before. The university displays the painting in its art museum. If Jane does not make the election, the amount of the contribution is equal to its FMV ($30,000). However, Jane's charitable contribution deduction for the year is limited to $15,000 ($50,000 × 0.30). If Jane makes the election to scale down the contribution amount, the deduction is reduced to $25,000 ($30,000 − $5,000 LTCG). The deduction limitation, however, increases to $25,000 for the year because the limitation is now based upon 50% of AGI instead of 30%. In this case, Jane will receive a larger deduction for the year by making the election. However, the cost associated with this election is the loss of $5,000 of deduction since the total deduction is reduced from $30,000 to $25,000 by making the election. ■

Many tax practitioners only make this election when preparing the taxpayer's final tax return. The election is made at this time since charitable contribution carryovers to the decedent's estate are not permitted.

Additional Comment

To help determine the FMV of contributed property, taxpayers can read IRS Publication 561 [Determining the Value of Donated Property].

Donation of Appreciated Capital Gain Property. Instead of selling substantially appreciated capital gain property and donating the cash proceeds, the property should be donated directly to charity. If property is donated in this way, the donor (1) receives a deduction equal to the FMV of the property and (2) does not recognize any gain on the disposition.

Example 7-57 ■

Colleen wishes to satisfy a pledge of $100,000 made to a local university. She owns $100,000 worth of marketable securities purchased 10 years ago for $30,000. Since the securities are marketable, the university is indifferent as to whether Colleen donates cash or the securities. Although her marginal tax rate is 31%, Colleen would be subject to a tax rate of 28% on the sale of the securities because long-term capital gains are subject to a maximum tax rate of 28%. She has enough AGI to be able to deduct the full contribution in the current year. The following chart summarizes the cash flows to Colleen under two different alternatives:

	Donate Securities	*Sell Securities and Donate Cash*
Proceeds of sale	—0—	$100,000
Tax on gain	—0—	(19,600)[a]
Cash payment to charity		(100,000)
Tax savings from the contribution deduction	$31,000[b]	31,000
Net tax benefit	$31,000	$ 11,400

[a] ($100,000 − $30,000) × 0.28 = $19,600.
[b] $100,000 × 0.31 = $31,000.

Careful planning is advised when appreciated property is contributed to a charity, however, because the untaxed appreciation may be subject to the alternative minimum tax (see Chapter 14).

In order to take a tax loss on business or investment property, a taxpayer should not donate property that has decreased in value. Rather, the property should be sold and the cash proceeds donated.

COMPLIANCE AND PRODEDURAL CONSIDERATIONS

Medical Expenses

Additional Comment

If the taxpayer incurs capital expenditures for medical care, a written recommendation should be obtained from the physician.

In certain cases, expenditures qualify as both a medical care expense and a dependent care expense (i.e., expenses for household and dependent care services that the taxpayer must pay to be gainfully employed). A taxpayer who incurs an expense that qualifies under both provisions may choose to take either (1) a medical expense deduction or (2) a tax credit under Sec. 21.[136] However, if a taxpayer takes a credit for these expenses, they are not deductible as medical expenses.

Example 7-58 ■

Joel's daughter, Debbie, is physically handicapped. As a result, Joel hires a nurse, who provides daily care while he is employed. During the year, Joel pays the nurse a total of $3,000. This amount qualifies for both the dependent care credit as well as the medical expense deduction. If Joel takes the dependent care credit, the $3,000 may not be deducted as a medical expense. Because of the limitations imposed on each, the determination of which treatment is more advantageous depends upon items such as the taxpayer's AGI, other medical expenses, and total itemized deductions. ■

[136] A credit of 30% of expenses for household and dependent care services is allowed if the dependent is under age 13 or a spouse or dependent who is mentally or physically incapable of caring for himself or herself. The credit is reduced 1% for every $2,000 (or portion thereof) of AGI over $10,000. (See the discussion on Personal Tax Credits in Chapter 14 for a more detailed explanation of the child and dependent care credit.)

Contribution of Property

When property other than cash is donated to a qualifying charity, proper determination of the property's FMV is a critical issue. Because of actual and perceived abuses in this area, the IRS often scrutinizes and, if necessary, challenges the valuation of contributed property. This is especially true of property for which no published market quotes exist. If contributions of property exceed $500, Form 8283 (see Appendix B of *Prentice Hall's Federal Taxation: Individuals* and the *Comprehensive* volume), which requires information about the type, location, holding period, basis, and FMV of the property, must be submitted with the taxpayer's return. This information must also be retained by the taxpayer. If the noncash contributions exceed $5,000, an appraisal by a qualified appraiser must be obtained,[137] and an appraisal summary, signed by the appraiser and an authorized officer of the charitable organization, must be submitted with Form 8283. Taxpayers should keep a copy of completed Form 8283 and any attachments for their records. Publicly traded securities need not be appraised. Nonpublicly traded stock must be appraised only if its value exceeds $10,000.

Charitable Contributions

Individuals report their charitable contribution deductions on Schedule A of Form 1040. Out-of-pocket expenses and contributions by cash or check are all reported on line 13. All contributions of property are included on line 14. As previously mentioned, if noncash property contributions exceed $500, Form 8283 (Noncash Charitable Contributions) must be attached to the return. The IRS has announced that a significant percentage of taxpayers are not attaching Form 8283 to their tax returns in support of their noncash contributions and that noncash contributions will be disallowed if the form is not attached.[138]

If the contribution is made in cash, the taxpayer must retain evidence of the donation by keeping a cancelled check or a receipt from the charitable organization. In the absence of a cancelled check or receipt, other reliable written records showing the charity's name and the date and amount of the contribution will be accepted.[139] If the contribution is in the form of noncash property, the taxpayer is required to maintain records containing the:

- Name and address of the charity to which the contribution was made
- Date and location of the contribution
- Description of the property
- FMV of the property
- Method of determining the property's FMV
- Signed copy of the appraisal report if an appraiser was used[140]

For charitable contributions of $250 or more made after December 31, 1993, no deduction is allowed unless the contribution is substantiated by a contemporaneous, written acknowledgment by the donee organization. Separate payments generally are treated as separate contributions for purposes of applying the $250 threshold. This acknowledgment must contain the following information:

---

[137] Reg. Sec. 1.170A-13(c). However, the requirement for an appraisal may be waived for contributions of inventory for the care of the ill, needy, or infants if the contribution is made by a closely held corporation or a personal service corporation. See Notice 89-56, 1989-1 C.B. 698.

[138] IRS Announcement 90-25, I.R.B. 1990-8, 25.

[139] Reg. Sec. 1.170A-13(a).

[140] Reg. Sec. 1.170A-13(b)(2).

Schedule A—Itemized Deductions

(Schedule B is on back)

► **Attach to Form 1040.** ► **See Instructions for Schedules A and B (Form 1040).**

OMB No. 1545-0074

1993

Attachment
Sequence No. **07**

Name(s) shown on Form 1040

Peter Smith

Your social security number

276 : 31 : 7242

Medical and Dental Expenses	**Caution:** *Do not include expenses reimbursed or paid by others.*			
	1	Medical and dental expenses (see page A-1)	1	
	2	Enter amount from Form 1040, line 32. [2]		
	3	Multiply line 2 above by 7.5% (.075)	3	
	4	Subtract line 3 from line 1. If zero or less, enter -0- . . . . . . ►	4	
Taxes You Paid (See page A-1.)	5	State and local income taxes	5	
	6	Real estate taxes (see page A-2)	6	
	7	Other taxes. List—include personal property taxes ►	7	
	8	Add lines 5 through 7 . . . . ►	8	
Interest You Paid (See page A-2.) **Note:** Personal interest is not deductible.	9a	Home mortgage interest and points reported to you on Form 1098	9a	
	b	Home mortgage interest not reported to you on Form 1098. If paid to the person from whom you bought the home, see page A-3 and show that person's name, identifying no., and address ►	9b	
	10	Points not reported to you on Form 1098. See page A-3 for special rules	10	
	11	Investment interest. If required, attach Form 4952. (See page A-3.)	11	
	12	Add lines 9a through 11 . . . . ►	12	
Gifts to Charity (See page A-3.)	**Caution:** *If you made a charitable contribution and received a benefit in return, see page A-3.*			
	13	Contributions by cash or check	13	7,730 —
	14	Other than by cash or check. If over $500, you **MUST** attach Form 8283	14	8,000 —
	15	Carryover from prior year	15	
	16	Add lines 13 through 15 . . . . ►	16	15,730 —
Casualty and Theft Losses	17	Casualty or theft loss(es). Attach Form 4684. (See page A-4.) . . . . ►	17	
Moving Expenses	18	Moving expenses. Attach Form 3903 or 3903-F. (See page A-4.) . . . . . ►	18	
Job Expenses and Most Other Miscellaneous Deductions (See page A-5 for expenses to deduct here.)	19	Unreimbursed employee expenses—job travel, union dues, job education, etc. If required, you **MUST** attach Form 2106. (See page A-4.) ►	19	
	20	Other expenses—investment, tax preparation, safe deposit box, etc. List type and amount ►	20	
	21	Add lines 19 and 20	21	
	22	Enter amount from Form 1040, line 32 [22]		
	23	Multiply line 22 above by 2% (.02)	23	
	24	Subtract line 23 from line 21. If zero or less, enter -0- . . . . ►	24	
Other Miscellaneous Deductions	25	Other—from list on page A-5. List type and amount ►	25	
Total Itemized Deductions	26	Is the amount on Form 1040, line 32, more than $108,450 (more than $54,225 if married filing separately)? • **NO.** Your deduction is not limited. Add lines 4, 8, 12, 16, 17, 18, 24, and 25 and enter the total here. Also enter on Form 1040, line 34, the **larger** of this amount or your standard deduction. • **YES.** Your deduction may be limited. See page A-5 for the amount to enter.	26	

For Paperwork Reduction Act Notice, see Form 1040 instructions.   Cat. No. 11330X   Schedule A (Form 1040) 1993

FIGURE 7-1   Partially Completed Schedule A

- The amount of cash and a description of any property contributed
- Whether or not the organization provided any goods or services in consideration for the cash or property received, including a description and good faith estimate of the value of any goods or services provided by the organization.

The acknowledgment is considered contemporaneous if it is obtained by the earlier of (1) the date the taxpayer files a return for the year in question, or (2) the extended due date for filing such return. This substantiation requirement is waived if the donee organization files a return which contains the required information.[141]

Additionally, in the case of charitable contributions made after December 31, 1993, certain disclosure requirements must be met by charitable organizations for a quid pro quo contribution in excess of $75. This $75 limit is applied separately on each transaction. A quid pro quo contribution is a transaction that is partly a contribution and partly a payment for goods and services. In order for such payments to be deductible, the donee organization must provide the donor with a written statement indicating:

- That the amount of the deduction is limited to the excess of the cash and value of the contributed property over the value of the goods and services provided by the charitable organization, and
- A good faith estimate of the value of the goods and services provided to the donor by the charitable organization.

Failure to make the required disclosure subjects the charitable organization to a $10 per contribution penalty unless the failure is due to reasonable cause. The penalty is capped at $5,000 per fund-raising event.[142]

Example 7-59 ■ During the current year, Peter Smith (Soc. Sec. No. 276-31-7242) reports AGI of $100,000. Smith also makes the following charitable contributions during the year:

1. Smith performs voluntary dental work 3 days each month in rural areas of the state. Smith drives a total of 4,000 miles on these trips during the year.
2. Smith makes the following contributions by cash or check:
   a. $750 to the city library
   b. $2,000 to the United Way
   c. $500 to a local community college
   d. $4,000 to his church
3. Smith contributes a tract of land to a small rural town. The town plans to erect a public library on the site. Smith purchased the land in 1980 for $5,000. Its appraised value at the time of the contribution is $8,000.

Smith's contributions are reported on the partially completed Schedule A shown in Figure 7-1. The out-of-pocket expenses of $480 (4,000 miles × $0.12) and the contributions by cash or check of $7,250 (library, United Way, church, and community college) are totaled and reported on line 13. The property contribution of $8,000 is separately stated on line 14. Since Smith contributes property with a value exceeding $500, Form 8283, an appraisal summary, and signed statements by the qualified appraiser and an authorized official of the organization which received the property must be attached to the return. In addition, for those donations that separately exceed $250, written acknowledgements from the donee organizations must be obtained and retained by Peter in order for the contributions to be deductible. ■

---

[141] Sec. 170(f) (8).
[142] Sec. 6115.

Additional Comment

Taxes that are incurred in the taxpayer's farming business are reported on Schedule F.

Taxes

Individuals generally report their deduction for property taxes on Schedule A of Form 1040. However, if the taxes are incurred in the taxpayer's business, they are reported on Schedule C. Taxes incurred for the production of rents and royalties are reported on Schedule E. State and local income taxes imposed on individuals are always reported on Schedule A even if the individual is self-employed.

Beginning in 1993, real estate brokers are required to report any real estate tax allocable to the purchaser of a residence. (See the discussion in this chapter regarding the allocation of real estate taxes between the seller and buyer of a residence.)[143] This information is reported by the broker on Form 1099-S (Proceeds from Real Estate Transactions).

Example 7-60 ■   During the year, Andrea incurs $1,500 in property taxes on a two-family house. Andrea lives in one unit and rents out the other. She also pays $100 in registration fees and $600 in personal property taxes on her automobile, based upon its value. Andrea uses the automobile 80% of the time in an unincorporated business. During the current year, she also pays $2,000 in state income taxes, all of which is attributable to her income of the prior year from the unincorporated business.

Since one-half of the real estate taxes are attributable to property used to produce rental income, $750 (0.50 × $1,500) is reported on Schedule E, and the remaining personal-use portion ($750) is reported on Schedule A. Since 80% of the use of the automobile is in Andrea's business, $80 (0.80 × $100) of the registration fee is deductible as a business expense on Schedule C. The remaining $20 is not deductible because the registration fee is not a tax. However, $480 (0.80 × $600) of the personal property tax on the automobile is deductible as a business expense on Schedule C. The remaining $120 is deductible as a tax on Schedule A. Finally, even though the tax is related to Andrea's business income, all $2,000 of the state income tax is reported on Schedule A. Since the state income tax is paid in the current year, it is deductible in the current year.   ■

PROBLEM MATERIALS

DISCUSSION QUESTIONS

7-1. A taxpayer may deduct medical expenses incurred on behalf of which persons?

7-2. What is the definition of medical care for purposes of the medical care deduction?

7-3. **a.** What is the definition of cosmetic surgery under the Internal Revenue Code?
b. Is the cost of cosmetic surgery deductible as a medical expense? Explain.

7-4. **a.** If a taxpayer must travel away from his or her home in order to obtain medical care, which en route costs, if any, are deductible as medical expenses?
b. Are there any limits imposed on the deductibility of these expenses?

7-5. What are the rules dealing with the deductibility of the cost of meals and lodging incurred while away from home in order to receive medical treatment as an outpatient?

7-6. **a.** Which types of capital expenditures incurred specifically for medical purposes are deductible?
b. What limitations, if any, are imposed upon the deductibility of these expenditures?

[143] Sec. 6015(4).

7-7. Bill, a plant manager, is suffering from a serious ulcer. Bill's doctor recommends that he spend three weeks fishing and hunting in the Colorado Rockies. Can Bill deduct the costs of the trip as a medical expense?

7-8. In what cases are medical insurance premiums paid by an individual not deductible as qualified medical expenses?

7-9. What is the limit placed on medical expense deductions? When can a deduction be taken for medical care? What if the medical care is prepaid?

7-10. Which taxes are specifically deductible for federal income tax purposes under Sec. 164? If a tax is not specifically listed in Sec. 164, under what circumstances may it still be deductible?

7-11. What is an ad valorem tax? If a tax that is levied on personal property is not an ad valorem tax, under what circumstances may it still be deductible?

7-12. When real estate is sold during a year, why is it necessary that the real estate taxes on the property be apportioned between the buyer and seller?

7-13. If Susan overpays her state income tax due to excess withholdings, can she deduct the entire amount in the year withheld? When Susan receives a refund from the state how must she treat that refund for tax purposes?

7-14. At times, the term *points* may be used to refer to different types of charges. Define the term and describe when points are deductible.

7-15. In which year or years are points (representing prepaid interest on a loan) deductible?

7-16. If interest expense is incurred in an unincorporated business owned by an individual, on which schedule is it deductible? (Assume that the passive loss rules do not apply).

7-17. Why does Sec. 267 impose a restriction on the deductibility of expenses accrued and payable by an accrual-method taxpayer to a related cash-method taxpayer?

7-18. a. What is the amount of the annual limitation placed on the deductibility of investment interest expense?
b. Explain how net investment income is calculated.
c. Is any disallowed interest expense for the year allowable as a deduction in another year? If so, when?

7-19. What are the different classifications of interest expense? How is the classification of the interest determined?

7-20. Explain what acquisition indebtedness and home equity indebtedness are with respect to a qualified residence of a taxpayer, and identify any limitations on the deductibility of interest expense on this indebtedness.

7-21. Explain what a qualified residence is for purposes of qualified residence interest.

7-22. Why is interest expense disallowed if it is incurred to purchase or carry tax-exempt obligations?

7-23. When is interest generally deductible for cash-method taxpayers? Explain if the general rule applies to prepaid interest, interest paid with loan proceeds, discounted notes, and personal interest. If the general rule does not apply, explain when these interest expenses are deductible.

7-24. a. For purposes of the charitable contribution deduction, what is capital gain property? Ordinary income property?
b. What is the significance of classifying property as either capital gain property or ordinary income property?

7-25. How is the *amount* of a charitable contribution of capital gain property determined if it is donated to a private nonoperating foundation? How does this determination differ if capital gain property is donated to a public charity?

7-26. Under what circumstances will the amount of a contribution of capital gain property to a public charity differ from the property's FMV?

7-27. What is the deductible standard mileage rate related to the use of an automobile for charitable purposes?

7-28. What type of services rendered to a charitable organization are deductible? What type of expenses related to these services are deductible?

7-29. May an individual who is married and files a joint return deduct any charitable contributions if the itemized deductions total only $3,000 (of which $1,000 are qualified charitable contributions)?

7-30. For individuals, what is the overall deduction limitation on charitable contributions? What is the limitation for corporations?

7-31. What are the deduction limitations imposed on the contribution of capital gain property to a public charity?

7-32. If a taxpayer's charitable contributions for any tax year exceed the deduction limitations, may the excess contributions be deducted in another year? If so, in which years may they be deducted?

7-33. How are charitable contribution deductions reported on the tax return for individuals? What reporting requirements must be met for the contribution of property?

7-34. List some of the more common miscellaneous itemized deductions and identify any limitations that are imposed on the deductibility of these items.

7-35. Certain itemized deductions of high income taxpayers must be reduced. Which itemized deductions are subject to this reduction and when does the reduction apply?

PROBLEMS

7-36. *Medical Expense Deduction.* During 1994, Liz is involved in an automobile accident and incurs the following expenditures:

Item	Amount
Doctor bills	$11,000
Hospital bills	13,000

Liz is single and has no dependents. In 1994, her salary is $30,000, and itemized deductions other than medical expenses are $1,500. During the year Liz also receives a reimbursement for medical expenses incurred in connection with the accident of $18,000 from the insurance company. What is Liz's taxable income for 1994?

7-37. *Reimbursement of Previously Deducted Medical Expenses.* Assume the same facts as in Problem 7-36. In addition, assume that in 1995, Liz receives $10,000 in a settlement of a lawsuit arising because of the automobile accident. $6,000 of the settlement is to pay Liz for the medical expenses incurred because of the accident that were not covered by insurance. What is the proper tax treatment of this $10,000 settlement?

7-38. *Medical Expense Deduction.* Dan lives in a small town in Arizona. Because of a rare blood disease, Dan is required to take special medical treatment once a month. The closest place this treatment is available to Dan is in Phoenix, 200 miles away. The treatments are provided on an outpatient basis but require him to stay overnight in Phoenix. During the year, Dan makes 12 trips to Phoenix by automobile to receive the treatment. The motel he always stays in charges $85 per night. For the year, Dan also spends a total of $250 for meals on these trips. $100 of this $250 is spent while en route to Phoenix. What is the amount of Dan's qualified medical expenses for the year?

7-39. *Medical Expense Deduction.* Kelly is divorced and has custody of Mike, Kelly's 17-year-old son. Kelly's ex-spouse has custody of their daughter, Diana. During the year, Kelly incurs $2,000 for orthodontic work for Diana to correct a severe overbite and $1,500 in unreimbursed medical expenses associated with Mike's broken leg. Kelly also pays $900 in health insurance premiums. Both Mike and Diana are covered under Kelly's medical insurance plan. In addition, Kelly incurs $400 for prescription drugs and $600 in doctor bills for himself. Kelly's AGI is $35,000. What is Kelly's medical expense deduction for the year?

7-40. *Medical Expense Deduction.* In 1994, Russ, a single taxpayer, was severely hurt in a construction accident. The accident left Russ's leg 70% paralyzed. After incurring $7,000 of medical expenses at the hospital, the doctor recommended that Russ install a jacuzzi at his home for therapy. The jacuzzi cost $8,000 to install and increased the value of his home by $5,000. He spent $300 maintaining the jacuzzi in 1994 and $500 in 1995. Russ also purchased a $500 wheelchair in 1994 but did not pay for the chair until 1995. In December 1994, Russ paid his physical therapist $4,000 for services to be performed in 1995. Russ paid $1,000 in medical insurance premiums in both 1994 and 1995. In 1995, the insurance company reimbursed Russ $5,000 for his hospital stay in 1994. His AGI for 1994 is $25,000. For 1995 his AGI is $24,000, not considering any of the above items. Russ has no other itemized deductions in either year.
a. What is the amount of his medical expense deduction in 1994?
b. What is the amount of his medical expense deduction in 1995?

7-41. *Deduction of Taxes.* During 1994, Wendy has $1,100 in state income taxes withheld from her paycheck. Additionally, on April 15, 1994, she pays $200 in state income taxes when she files her state income tax return for 1993. In 1995 when she files her 1994 state income tax return, she will owe an additional $400 for her 1994 taxes. Wendy is a single, cash-method taxpayer who has total (excluding state income taxes) itemized deductions for 1994 of $1,300. What is the amount of state income taxes Wendy may include as an itemized deduction for 1994?

7-42. *Refund of Previously Deducted Taxes.* Assume the same facts as Problem 7-41, except that Wendy receives a $600 refund of 1994's state income taxes in 1995. What is the proper tax treatment of the refund?

7-43. *Deduction of Taxes.* Dawn, a single, cash-method taxpayer, paid the following taxes in 1994: Dawn's employer withheld $5,400 for Federal income taxes, $2,000 for state income taxes, and $3,800 for FICA from her 1994 paychecks. Dawn purchased a new car and paid $600 in sales tax and $70 for the license. The car's FMV was $10,000 and weighed 3,000 pounds. The county also assessed a property tax on the car. The tax was 2% of its value and $.10 per hundredweight. The car is used 100% of the time for personal purposes. Dawn sold her house on April 15, 1994. The county's property tax on the home for 1994 is $1,850, payable on February 1, 1995. Dawn's AGI for the year is $50,000 and her other itemized deductions exclusive of taxes are $4,000.
a. What is Dawn's deduction for taxes in 1994?
b. Where on Dawn's tax return should she report her deduction for taxes?

7-44. *Apportionment of Real Estate Taxes.* On May 1 of the current year, Tanya sells a building to Brian for $100,000. Tanya's basis in the building is $60,000. The county in which the building is located has a real property tax year that ends on June 30. The taxes are payable by September 1 of that year. On September 1, Brian pays the annual property taxes of $3,000. Both Tanya and Brian are calendar-year, cash-method taxpayers.
a. What amount of real property taxes may Brian deduct in the current year?
b. What amount of real property taxes may Tanya deduct in the current year?
c. If no apportionment on the real property taxes is made in the sales agreement, what is Tanya's total selling price of the building? Brian's basis for the building?

7-45. *Classification of Interest Expense.* On January 1 of the current year, Scott borrowed $80,000 pledging the assets of his business as collateral. He immediately deposited the money in an interest bearing checking account. Scott already had $20,000 in this account. On April 1, Scott invests $75,000 in a limited real estate partnership. On July 1, he buys a new ski boat for $12,000. On August 1, he makes a $10,000 capital contribution to his unincorporated business. Scott repays $50,000 of the loan on November 30 of the current year. Classify Scott's interest expense for the year.

7-46. *Investment Interest.* During the current year, David reports interest and dividend income of $20,000, net short-term capital gains of $5,000, and net long-term capital gains of $8,000. His AGI is $100,000. His investment expenses, exclusive of interest, are $5,000. During the year

David also pays a total of $50,000 interest on debt which is incurred in his investment activities. David is married and files a joint return.

a. What is the total amount of deduction David may take with respect to his investment interest expense if he does not make a special election?

b. What is the treatment of any disallowed investment interest expense?

c. What is the total amount of deduction David may take with respect to his investment interest expense if he elects to have his net capital gain taxed at the regular marginal tax rates?

7-47. *Qualified Residence Interest.* During the current year, Tina purchases a beachfront condominium for $600,000, paying $150,000 down and taking out a $450,000 mortgage, secured by the property. At the time of the purchase, the outstanding mortgage on her principal residence is $700,000. This debt is secured by the residence and the FMV of the principal residence is $1,400,000. She purchased the principal residence in 1989. What is the amount of qualified indebtedness upon which Tina may deduct the interest payments?

7-48. *Interest Between Related Parties.* King Corporation is an accrual-method taxpayer owned 60% by Jack and 40% by Kathy. The JR Partnership is owned 75% by Jack and 25% by Ron and uses the cash-method of accounting. On January 2 of the current year, King Corporation borrows $100,000 from the JR Partnership. Interest is charged at 9%, and both interest and principal are to be paid in full on December 31 of the current year. Because of a cash-flow problem arising late in the year, however, the loan and interest are not repaid until March 31 of the following year.

a. What amount of interest expense may King Corporation deduct in the current year? In the following year?

b. Assume the same facts except that on December 30 of the current year, King Corporation borrows cash from its bank to pay off the loan. What amount of interest expense may King Corporation deduct in the current year?

7-49. *Timing of Interest Deduction.* On April 1 of the current year, Henry borrows $12,000 from the bank for a year. Since the note is discounted for the interest charge and Henry receives proceeds of $10,200, he is required to repay the face amount of the loan ($12,000) in four equal quarterly payments beginning on July 1 of the current year. Henry is a cash-method individual.

a. What is the amount of Henry's interest expense deduction in the current year with respect to this loan?

b. Assume the same facts except that the initial starting date when the repayments begin is April 1 of the following year. What is the amount of Henry's interest expense deduction in the current year?

c. Assume the same facts as in Part b, except that Henry is an accrual-method taxpayer. What is the amount of his interest expense deduction in the current year?

7-50. *Charitable Contributions—Services.* Pauline is an attorney who renders volunteer legal services to a Legal Aid Society which provides legal advice to low-income individuals. The Legal Aid Society is a qualified charitable organization. During the current year she spends a total of 200 hours in this volunteer work. Her regular billing rate is $100 per hour. In addition, she spends a total of $600 in out-of-pocket costs in providing these services. She receives no compensation and is not reimbursed for her out-of-pocket costs. What is Pauline's charitable contribution for the year because of these activities?

7-51. *Itemized Deductions.* During 1994, Doug incurs the following deductible expenses: $1,000 in state income taxes; $1,200 in local property taxes; $800 in medical expenses; and $500 in charitable contributions. He is single, has no dependents, and has $30,000 AGI for the year. What is the amount of Doug's taxable income?

7-52. *Computation of Taxable Income.* During 1994, James, a single, cash-method taxpayer incurred the following expenditures:

Qualified medical expenses	$ 8,000
Investment interest expense	16,000
Other investment activity expenses	15,000
Qualified residence interest	12,000
Interest on loan on personal auto	2,000
Charitable contributions	3,000
State income tax paid	7,000
Property taxes	4,000
Tax return preparation and consulting fees	5,000

James's income consisted of the following items:

Salary	$70,000
Interest and Dividend income	20,000
Long-term Capital gains	23,000
Long-term Capital losses	(15,000)

Compute James's taxable income for the year (assuming that an election is made to have the net capital gain taxed at the regular tax rates).

7-53. *Computation of Taxable Income.* Assume all the same facts as in problem 7-52 except that James's salary income is $100,000 instead of $70,000 and that he does not make the election. Compute James's taxable income for the year.

7-54. *Charitable Contribution Limitations.* In each of the following independent cases, determine the amount of the charitable contribution and the limitation that would apply. In each case, assume that the donee is a qualified public charity.

   a. Sharon donates a tract of land to a charitable organization. She has held the land for 7 years. Her basis in the land is $10,000 and its FMV is $40,000.

   b. Assume the same facts in Part a, except that Sharon has held the land for only 11 months and that its FMV is $23,000.

   c. Jack purchases a historical document for $50,000. He donates the historical document to a charitable organization 2 years later. The organization plans to use it for research and study. Its FMV at the time of the donation is $100,000.

   d. Assume the same facts in Part c, except that the organization plans to sell the document and put the money into an endowment fund.

   e. Valerie donates some inventory to a charitable organization. The inventory is purchased for $500 and its FMV is $1,200 at the time of the donation. She held the inventory for 7 months.

7-55. *Charitable Contributions to Private Nonoperating Foundations.* Assume the same facts as Problem 7-54, except that the qualified organization is a private nonoperating foundation. Determine the amount of the charitable contribution for Parts a through e.

7-56. *Charitable Contributions—Tax Planning.* Dean makes a pledge of $30,000 to a local college. The college is willing to accept either cash or marketable securities in fulfillment of the pledge. Dean owns stock in Ajax Corporation worth $30,000. The stock was purchased 5 years ago for $10,000. Dean's marginal tax rate is 28%. Should Dean sell the stock and then donate the cash, or should he donate the stock directly? Compute the net tax benefit from each alternative and explain the difference.

7-57. *Charitable Contribution Limitations.* During the current year, Helen donates stock worth $50,000 to her local community college. Two years ago the stock cost Helen $40,000. Her AGI for the current year is $100,000. Beginning next year, the bulk of her income will be from tax-exempt municipal securities. Thus, she is not interested in any carryover of excess charitable contribution. What is the maximum charitable contribution deduction Helen may take this year?

7-58. *Corporate Charitable Contributions.* Circle Corporation, an accrual-method taxpayer, manufactures and sells mainframe computers. In January of the current year, Circle Corporation donates a mainframe which was part of its inventory to City College. City will use the computer for physical science research. Circle's basis in the mainframe is $300,000. The computer's FMV is $650,000. On December 15 of the current year, Circle also pledged stock to the Red Cross and promised delivery of the stock by March 1 of the following year. The stock's FMV is $100,000 and Circle's adjusted basis in the stock is $50,000. Circle's taxable income (before deducting any charitable contributions) for the current year is $4,000,000.

a. What is the amount of Circle's charitable contribution for the current year?

b. How much of the contribution can Circle deduct in the current year and how much may be carried over, if any?

7-59. *Charitable Contribution Carryovers.* Bonnie's charitable contributions and AGI for the past 4 years were as follows:

	1991	1992	1993	1994
AGI	$50,000	$55,000	$58,000	$60,000
Contributions subject to the 50% limitation	40,000	29,000	25,000	10,000

What is the amount of the charitable deduction for each year and the order in which the deduction and carryovers are used?

TAX FORM/RETURN PREPARATION PROBLEMS

TurboTax **7-60.** Following is a list of information for Steven and Marcia Johnson for the current tax year. Steven and Marcia are married; have three children, Ryan, Casey and Lindsey; and live at 221 Elm St. in San Diego, California 90056. Steven is a computer programmer and Maria is a salesperson. The Johnsons' social security numbers and ages are as follows:

Name	S.S. No.	Age
Steven	215-60-1989	45
Marcia	301-60-2828	43
Ryan	713-84-5555	17
Casey	714-87-2222	14
Lindsey	430-89-1111	11

Receipts

Steven's salary	$35,000
Marcia's salary	28,000
Interest income on municipal bonds	2,000
Interest income on certificate of deposit—Universial Savings	1,400
Dividends on GM stock	600

Disbursements

Eyeglasses and exam for Ryan	300
Orthodontic work for Casey to correct a congenital defect	2,000
Medical insurance premiums	1,000
Withholding for state income taxes	3,000
Withholding for federal income taxes	6,000
State income taxes paid with last year's tax return (paid when the return was filed in the current year)	400
Property taxes on home	1,000
Property taxes on automobile	100
Interest on home	9,000
Interest on automobile	500
Interest on credit cards	100
Cash contribution to church	2,400

In addition to the above, Steven and Marcia donate some stock to their local community college. The FMV of the stock at the time of the donation is $500. They purchased the stock 3 years before for $200.

Compute Steven and Marcia's income tax liability on Form 1040 for the current year.

7-61. George and Martha Adams are married and reside at 291 Paul Revere Blvd., Boston, Massachusetts 02116. George's social security number is 222-33-4444 and Martha's is 222-34-5678. The Adamses have two children, Sherry age 23 and Sean age 19. Their social security numbers are 222-12-9876 and 222-57-6543, respectively. Sherry is single, in college and earned $8,000 during the summer. George and Martha help Sherry through school by paying for her room, board, and tuition. Sherry lives at home during the summer. Sean has a physical handicap and lives at home. He earned $2,500 addressing envelopes for a marketing firm.

George is a manager in a manufacturing plant. His salary is $80,000 from which $16,000 of federal income tax, $8,000 of state income tax, and $3,924 of social security taxes were withheld. George also pays premiums for health, disability, and life insurance. $2,000 of the premium was for health insurance, $400 for life insurance, and $250 for disability.

Martha owns Link Networks, a network consulting company. During the year, Martha's gross revenues were $12,000. She incurred the following expenses in her business:

Liability insurance	$ 500
Software rental	3,500
Journals and magazines	150
Training seminars	1,000
Supplies	800
Donations to a political campaign fund	600

George enjoys sculpting and this year he sold a few of his sculptures. His gross revenues were $1,500. He incurred the following expenses:

Studio rent expense	$1,300
Utilities	150
Clay and other supplies	400

George's father passed away during the year. George and Martha received $100,000 from the life insurance policy. Neither George nor Martha paid any of the premiums.

Martha purchased 100 shares of Kelly Co. stock on May 1, 1985 for $800. Kelly Co. was declared bankrupt during the current year.

Sean's physician recommended that he see a physical therapist to help with his disability. George paid the therapist $7,000 during the year because his insurance would not cover the bills.

George and Martha went to Atlantic City and won $4,000 at the blackjack table. The following night they lost $5,000.

George and Martha also gave $500 to their church.

During the year the Adamses had the following other income and expenses:

Real estate taxes	$1,000
Property taxes on car (determined by weight)	500
Home mortgage interest	5,000
Credit card finance charges	3,000
Tax return preparation fees ($500 is allocable to Martha's business)	1,000
Sales tax on purchases during the year	5,500
Interest from a savings account	400
Interest from City of Boston Bonds	300
Dividend from General Motors Stock	95

Prepare George and Martha's tax return Form 1040 and accompanying schedules for the current year.

CASE STUDY PROBLEM

7-62. Brian Brown, an executive at a manufacturing enterprise, comes to you on December 1 of the current year for tax advice. He has agreed to donate a small tract of land to the Rosepark Community College. The value of the land has been appraised at $53,000. Mr. Brown purchased the land 14 months ago for $50,000. Mr. Brown's estimated AGI for the current year is $100,000. He plans on retiring next year and anticipates that his AGI will fall to $30,000 for all subsequent years. He does not anticipate making any additional large charitable contributions. He understands that there are special rules dealing with charitable contributions, and wants your advice in order to get the maximum overall tax benefit from his contribution. Since the college plans on using the property, selling the land is not an alternative. You are to prepare a letter to Mr. Brown explaining the tax consequences of the different alternatives. His address is 100 East Rosebrook, Mesa, Arizona 85203. For purposes of your analysis, assume that Mr. Brown is married and files a joint return. Also assume that Mr. Brown feels that an appropriate discount rate is 10%. In your analysis, use the tax rate schedules for the current year.

CASE STUDY PROBLEM—ETHICAL ISSUES

7-63. For several years, you have prepared the tax return for Alpha Corporation, a closely-held corporation engaged in manufacturing garden tools. On February 20 of the current year, Bill Johnson, the president of Alpha Corporation, delivered to your office the files and information necessary for you to prepare Alpha's tax return for the immediately preceding tax year. Included in this information were the minutes of all meetings held by Alpha's Board of Directors during the year in question.

Then on February 27, Bill stops by your office and hands you an "addendum" to the minutes of the Director's meeting held December 15 of the tax year for which you are preparing the tax return. The addendum is dated the same day of the Director's meeting, and authorizes a charitable contribution pledge of $20,000 to the local community college. With a wink and a big smile, Bill explains that the addendum had been misplaced. In reviewing the original minutes, you find no mention about a charitable contribution pledge.

What should you do? (See the caption entitled Statements on Responsibilities in Tax Practice in Chapter 1 for a discussion of these issues.)

TAX RESEARCH PROBLEM

7-64. Last year Mr. Smith was involved in an automobile accident, severely injuring his legs. As part of a long-term rehabilitation process, his physician prescribes a daily routine of swimming. Since there is no readily available public facility nearby, Smith investigates the possibility of either building a pool in his own back yard or purchasing another home with a pool. In the current year he finds a new home with a pool and purchases it for $175,000. He then obtains some estimates and finds that it would cost approximately $20,000 to replace the pool in the home he has just purchased. He also obtains some real estate appraisals, which indicate that the existing pool only increases the value of the home by $8,000. During the current year, Smith also expends $500 in maintaining the pool and $1,800 in other medical expenses. What is the total amount of medical expenses he may claim in the current year? Smith's AGI for the year is $60,000.

A partial list of research sources is

- Sec. 213.
- Reg. Sec. 1.213-1(e)(1)(iii).
- *Richard A. Polacsek,* 1981 PH T.C. Memo ¶81,569, 42 TCM 1289.
- *Paul A. Lerew,* 1982 PH T.C. Memo ¶82,483, 44 TCM 918.
- *Jacob H. Robbins,* 1982 PH T.C. Memo ¶82,565, 44 TCM 1254.

8

Losses and Bad Debts

LEARNING OBJECTIVES

After studying this chapter, you should be able to

1. Identify transactions that may result in losses
2. Determine the proper classification for losses
3. Calculate the suspended loss from passive activities
4. Identify what constitutes a passive activity loss
5. Determine when a taxpayer has materially participated in a passive activity
6. Identify and calculate the deduction for a casualty or theft loss
7. Compute the deduction for a bad debt
8. Compute a net operating loss deduction

Additional Comment

If property is used partly for business and partly for personal use, the loss attributable to the business portion is deductible while the loss on the personal-use portion is not unless the loss was sustained in a casualty.

Taxpayers often sustain losses on property that is sold, exchanged, or otherwise disposed of. If the property on which the loss is sustained is used in a trade or business or held for investment, the tax law generally provides a deduction for these losses. The tax law also provides a limited deduction for losses on personal-use property that is either stolen or damaged in a casualty. Other losses on personal-use property (e.g. a sale of a personal residence at a loss) are not deductible. A deduction is also provided for losses that taxpayers may incur because of uncollectible business or nonbusiness debts.

This chapter discusses the rules dealing with the deductibility of these types of losses.

TRANSACTIONS THAT MAY RESULT IN LOSSES

OBJECTIVE 1
Identify transactions that may result in losses

In order for a loss on property to be deductible, it must be realized for tax purposes. Generally, *realization* occurs in a "closed transaction" evidenced by an identifiable event.

Example 8-1 ∎

Anita purchased 500 shares of Data Corporation stock for $10,000 on February 22 of the current year. By October 31 of the same year, the price of the stock declines to $8,000. Even though Anita realizes an economic loss on the stock, no realization event has occurred, and she may not deduct the $2,000 loss. However, if Anita sells the stock for $8,000 on October 31, the loss is realized for tax purposes in the current year. ∎

Key Point

Anticipated losses, including those for which reserves have been established, are not deductible.

Losses on property may arise in a variety of transactions, including

- Sale or exchange of the property
- Expropriation, seizure, confiscation, or condemnation of the property by a government
- Abandonment of the property
- Worthlessness of stock or securities
- Planned demolition of the property in order to construct other property in its place
- Destruction of the property by fire, storm, or other casualty

- Theft
- Deductible business expenses exceeding business income, giving rise to a net operating loss (NOL)

The rules dealing with the tax deductions allowable for losses incurred in each of these transactions other than casualties, thefts, and NOLs are examined in the following sections of this chapter. Casualties, thefts, and NOLs are covered in separate major headings later in the chapter.

Sale or Exchange of Property

The amount of the loss incurred in a sale or exchange of property equals the excess of the property's adjusted basis on the sale or exchange date over the amount realized for the property.[1] The amount realized for the property equals the sum of the money received plus the fair market value (FMV) of any other property received in the transaction.[2] If the property sold or exchanged is subject to a mortgage or other liability, the amount realized also includes the amount of the liability.[3] The treatment of any selling costs depends upon the type of property being sold or exchanged. If the property is inventory, the selling costs are deductible expenses in the year in which they are paid or incurred. However, if the sale involves property that is not normally held for sale by the taxpayer, the selling costs merely reduce the amount realized from the sale or exchange.[4]

> **Real World Example**
>
> *A taxpayer whose truck was repossessed was required to include in the amount realized the unpaid indebtedness on the truck. The taxpayer failed to prove that he was required to pay a portion of the indebtedness after repossession. Billie J. Ledbetter v. CIR, 61 AFTR 2d 88-638, 88-1 USTC ¶ 9183 (5th Cir., 1988).*

Example 8-2 ■

Four years ago, Louis purchased a plot of land as an investment for $50,000. Unfortunately, local economic conditions worsened after the land was purchased, and its value declined to $35,000. Becoming discouraged, Louis sells the property in the current year. At the time of the sale, the land is subject to a $10,000 mortgage. The terms of the sale are $25,000 being paid in cash with the purchaser assuming the mortgage. Louis also incurs $2,000 in sales commissions. His loss on the sale is $17,000 ($25,000 cash + $10,000 mortgage − [$2,000 selling expenses + $50,000 property's basis]). ■

Only losses incurred in the sale or exchange of property used in a trade or business or held for investment are deductible. Losses incurred in the sale or exchange of personal-use property are not deductible. Furthermore, the type of deduction that may be taken for a loss realized on the sale or exchange of business or investment property depends upon the type of property sold. For example, if the asset is a capital asset, the loss is a capital loss (see Chapter 5). If the sale is of property used in a trade or business (a Sec. 1231 asset), the type of loss depends upon the total gain or loss realized on all the taxpayer's Sec. 1231 assets sold during the year (see Chapter 13). If the sale is of inventory, the loss is an ordinary loss.

Expropriated, Seized, or Confiscated Property

A taxpayer may own property that is expropriated, seized, confiscated, or condemned by a government. In these cases, the U.S. Supreme Court has ruled that a deductible loss is incurred if the property is used in a trade or business or is held for invest-

---

[1] Sec. 1001(a).

[2] Sec. 1001(b).

[3] *Beulah B. Crane v. CIR,* 35 AFTR 776, 47-1 USTC ¶ 9217 (USSC, 1947); and Reg. Sec. 1.1001-2.

[4] The rules dealing with the amount and character of gain or loss realized upon the sale of property are examined in greater depth in Chapters 12 and 13.

ment.[5] However, the Tax Court has held that the confiscation, seizure, condemnation, or expropriation of property does not constitute a theft or a casualty. Rather, it is treated as a sale or exchange. Thus, no deductible loss arises if the seized property is personal-use property.[6] If the seized or condemned property is business or investment property, its classification depends upon the type of property. (See the section in this chapter entitled Classifying the Loss on the Taxpayer's Return.) The deduction may be taken only in the year in which the property is actually seized. It is irrelevant whether formal expropriation or nationalization occurs in a later year.[7] A gain is realized if the taxpayer receives compensation for the property in excess of its basis. Under certain circumstances this gain may be deferred. (See Chapter 12 for a discussion of the nonrecognition of gain in an involuntary conversion.)

Abandoned Property

If the taxpayer's property has become worthless or if it is not worth placing into a serviceable condition, the taxpayer may simply abandon the property. If the property still has basis, a loss is realized. Such losses are not deductible if the property is personal-use property. However, business or investment property losses are deductible. Furthermore, since the abandonment of property is not a sale or exchange, the loss is an ordinary loss.[8] The amount of the loss is the property's adjusted basis on the date of abandonment. The burden of proof to show that the property was actually abandoned rests with the taxpayer. If the property is depreciable (e.g., machinery and buildings), it must actually be physically abandoned in order for the taxpayer to take the full amount of the loss.[9]

Worthless Securities

A taxpayer may take a deduction for securities that become completely worthless during the tax year.[10] Since the deduction is only available in the year the security actually becomes worthless, a major problem for both the taxpayer and the IRS is determining the year in which the security becomes worthless. A mere decline in value is not sufficient to create a deductible loss if the stock has any recognizable value.[11] Furthermore, the sale of the stock for a nominal amount such as $1 does not necessarily establish that the stock became worthless in the year of the sale.[12] The burden of proof show (1) that the security is completely worthless and (2) that the security became worthless during the year rests with the taxpayer.

Once the year of worthlessness is determined, Sec. 165(g) provides that any loss incurred by a taxpayer is treated as a loss from the sale of a capital asset on the last day of the tax year.[13] Although this provision does not help in determining the year of worthlessness, it does establish a definite date for purposes of measuring whether the

---

[5] *U.S. v. S.S. White Dental Manufacturing Co.,* 6 AFTR 6750, 1 USTC ¶ 235 (USSC, 1927).

[6] *William J. Powers,* 36 T.C. 1191 (1961).

[7] Rev. Rul. 62-197, 1962-2 C.B. 66. See also *Estate of Frank Fuchs v. CIR,* 24 AFTR 2d 69-5077, 69-2 USTC ¶ 9505 (2nd Cir., 1969).

[8] *Industrial Cotton Mills Co., Inc.,* 43 B.T.A. 107 (1940), Acq. 1941-1 C.B. 6, and *Aetna-Standard Engineering Co.,* 15 T.C. 284 (1950).

[9] Reg. Sec. 1.167(a)-8(a)(4).

[10] For this purpose, a *security* is defined in Sec. 165(g)(2) as (1) stock in a corporation; (2) the right to subscribe for or receive a share of stock in a corporation; or (3) a bond, debenture, note, or certificate of indebtedness issued by a corporation or a government either in registered form or with interest coupons.

[11] Reg. Sec. 1.165-4(a).

[12] *O. D. Bratton v. U.S.,* 49 AFTR 386, 56-1 USTC ¶ 9431 (6th Cir., 1956).

[13] In order for this provision to apply, the security must be a capital asset in the hands of the taxpayer. Thus, if the taxpayer is a dealer in stock, Sec. 165(g) does not apply.

loss is short- or long-term.[14] In some cases, this provision causes the loss to be long-term because the time period is extended to the end of the year in which the worthlessness occurs.

Example 8-3 ■

On March 14 of the current year, Control Corporation enters into bankruptcy with no possibility for the shareholders to receive anything of value. Since the amount of Control Corporation's outstanding liabilities exceeds the FMV of its assets on that date, the stock of the corporation becomes worthless. Janet, a calendar-year taxpayer, owns 500 shares of Control's common stock, which she had purchased for $10,000 through her broker on December 12 of the prior year. Under Sec. 165(g), the loss is treated as having arisen from the sale of a capital asset on the last day of the current year. Thus, Janet incurs a $10,000 long-term capital loss because the holding period for the stock is more than one year. On the other hand, if Janet had received the stock directly from Control Corporation in exchange for either money or other property, and if certain other requirements are met, the stock may qualify as Sec. 1244 stock. Individuals who sustain losses on Sec. 1244 stock receive ordinary loss treatment rather than capital loss treatment. (See the discussion in this chapter under the heading Losses on Sec. 1244 Stock.) ■

Under certain circumstances, if the worthless securities consist of securities of an affiliated corporation that are owned by a domestic corporation, the loss is treated as having arisen from a sale of a noncapital asset. This allows the loss to be treated as an ordinary loss rather than as a capital loss.[15] For this exception to apply, the following percentage ownership requirements must be met:

- At least 80% of the voting power of all classes of the affiliated corporation's stock must be owned by the domestic corporation that is deducting the ordinary loss.[16]

- More than 90% of the affiliated corporation's gross receipts for all its taxable years must be from nonpassive income.[17]

Example 8-4 ■

Assume the same facts as in Example 8-3, except that the Control stock is owned by Valley Corporation and represents all of Control's outstanding stock. Also assume that more than 90% of Control Corporation's gross receipts are from manufacturing operations. The loss on the worthless Control stock is deductible by Valley Corporation as an ordinary loss. ■

Demolition of Property

Historical Note

For demolition costs incurred before 1984, the key question was whether or not the intent to demolish existed at the time of purchase. If the intent was to demolish, the costs had to be allocated to the land. If the intent to demolish was formed later, the costs were deductible.

At times taxpayers, intent on building their own facilities, purchase land that contains an existing structure. Taxpayers may also demolish a structure they are currently using in order to construct new facilities. In both cases, no deduction is allowed for any demolition costs or any loss sustained on account of the demolition.[18]

---

[14] Gain or loss on the sale or exchange of a capital asset is long term if the asset has been held over one year.

[15] As explained in Chapter 5, the deductibility of capital losses is of limited benefit. For corporate taxpayers, capital losses must initially be offset against capital gains of the current year, and any excess amount is not deductible but must be carried back 3 years and forward for 5 years. Individuals may offset capital losses against capital gains and any excess amount is deductible up to $3,000 per year as an offset to ordinary income. Capital losses in excess of this amount for an individual are carried forward for an indefinite period. Thus, taxpayers generally prefer losses to be considered as ordinary losses rather than capital losses.

[16] In addition, the domestic corporation must own at least 80% of all classes of any nonvoting stock.

[17] Sec. 165(g)(3). *Nonpassive income* includes all income other than royalties, rents, dividends, interest, annuities, and gains from the sale or exchange of stocks and securities.

[18] Sec. 280B.

Instead, these amounts are added to the basis of the land where the demolished structure was located.[19]

CLASSIFYING THE LOSS ON THE TAXPAYER'S TAX RETURN

OBJECTIVE 2
Determine the proper classification for losses

Key Point

The distinction between ordinary losses and capital losses is important because for individuals only $3,000 of capital losses can be offset against ordinary income each year. In addition, for individuals a 28% maximum tax rate applies to net capital gains.

If a loss is deductible, the taxpayer must determine whether the loss is an ordinary loss or a capital loss and individual taxpayers must identify the amount as either a deduction *for* or *from* AGI.

Ordinary Versus Capital Loss

Whether a deductible loss is ordinary or capital depends upon the type of property involved and the transaction in which the loss is sustained. To have a capital loss, a sale or exchange of a capital asset must occur. If both elements are not present, the deduction is an ordinary loss. In general, all assets except inventory, notes and accounts receivable, and depreciable property and land used in a trade or business (i.e., property, plant, and machinery) are classified as **capital assets.**[20]

Since a casualty is not a sale or exchange, the destruction of a capital asset by a casualty creates an ordinary rather than a capital loss.[21] Likewise, a deductible loss realized on the abandonment of property is an ordinary loss because an abandonment is not a sale or exchange. On the other hand, the seizure or condemnation of property is treated as a sale or exchange.

Example 8-5 ■

On July 24 of the current year, Jermaine sells some investment property for $75,000. The property's adjusted basis is $85,000. The investment property is a capital asset. Jermaine realizes a $10,000 ($75,000 − $85,000) capital loss. If, instead, the property had been destroyed by fire and Jermaine had received $75,000 in insurance proceeds, the $10,000 loss would have been an ordinary loss. ■

Example 8-6 ■

Assume the same facts in Example 8-5, except that the property is personal-use property. The loss resulting from the sale of the property is not deductible as a capital asset. However, since the loss resulting from the fire is a casualty loss, it is deductible as an ordinary loss (subject to limitations discussed later in this chapter). ■

Certain transactions, while not actually constituting a sale or exchange, are treated or deemed to be a sale or exchange. For example, if a security owned by an individual investor becomes worthless during the year, the loss is treated as a loss from the sale of a capital asset on the last day of the tax year, even though no sale actually occurs. Thus, the loss is a capital loss.

Section 1231 Property. Whether a loss on a particular transaction is treated as a capital loss may also depend upon the gains and losses reported from other property transactions for the tax year. For instance, under Sec. 1231, certain gains and losses are netted together. If the Sec. 1231 gains exceed the Sec. 1231 losses, both the gains and losses are treated as long-term capital gains and losses. However, if the losses equal or exceed the gains, both the gains and the losses are treated as ordinary.

---

[19] Ibid.

[20] Sec. 1221. The definition of a capital asset is more fully examined in Chapter 5.

[21] For individuals, if during the year the gains from casualties of personal-use property exceed the casualty losses on personal-use property, all the gains and losses are treated as capital. This procedure is explained later in the chapter.

Section 1231 property includes real property or depreciable property used in a trade or business that is held for more than one year. (See Chapter 13 for a discussion of the netting procedure under Sec. 1231.)

Historical Note

Section 1244 was enacted in 1958 in order to encourage investment in small business enterprises. This was the same year that the S corporation provisions were enacted.

Losses on Sec. 1244 Stock. Capital gain or loss is generally recognized upon the sale of stock or securities. An exception is provided for losses from the sale or worthlessness of small business corporation (Sec. 1244) stock. These losses are deductible as ordinary losses up to a maximum of $50,000 per tax year ($100,000 for married taxpayers filing a joint return). Any remaining loss for the year is capital loss.

To qualify the loss as ordinary under Sec. 1244, the following requirements must be met:

Additional Comment

Stock qualifying as small business corporation stock under Sec. 1244 can be either preferred or common and either voting or nonvoting.

- The stock must be owned by an individual or a partnership.[22]
- The stock must have been originally issued to the individual or to a partnership in which an individual is a partner.[23]
- The stock must be stock in a domestic (U.S.) corporation.
- The stock must have been issued for cash or property other than stock or securities. Stock issued for services rendered is not eligible for Sec. 1244 treatment.
- The corporation must not have derived over 50% of its gross receipts from passive income sources during the immediately preceding 5 tax years.[24]
- At the time the stock is issued, the amount of money and property contributed to both capital and paid-in surplus may not exceed $1 million.

Note that the last test listed above is made *at the time the stock is issued*. Thus, even though at the time of the loss the corporation has capital and paid-in surplus in excess of the $1 million, the individual may still report an ordinary loss as long as the test is met when the stock is issued.

Example 8-7 ■

During the current year, Tony, an individual and sole shareholder of First Corporation, sells all his stock in the corporation for $40,000. Tony originally incorporated First Corporation several years ago by contributing $160,000 to the capital of the corporation. First Corporation is a domestic corporation and meets all the other requirements necessary for Sec. 1244 to apply. Tony is married and files a joint return. He may take a $100,000 ordinary deduction for the year because of the loss on the sale, even though the stock is a capital asset in his hands. The remaining $20,000 loss is a long-term capital loss. If for the year Tony has no capital gains to net against the $20,000 long-term capital loss, $3,000 of the capital loss is deductible in the current year. The remaining $17,000 is carried forward to subsequent years. ■

Key Point

Casualty losses incurred on property used to produce rental or royalty income are deductible for AGI even though the property is investment property and not used in a trade or business.

Deductions for AGI Versus Deductions from AGI

Corporations may not take a deduction if capital losses exceed capital gains. However, for individuals, a net capital loss gives rise to a deduction *for* AGI. This deduction,

---

[22] A loss on stock owned by a partnership is also eligible for Sec. 1244 treatment, provided the loss incurred by the partnership flows through directly to an individual partner.

[23] Stock received in certain reorganizations of corporations in exchange for Sec. 1244 stock is also considered Sec. 1244 stock. Section 1244 does not apply to stock that the individual has received through other means such as purchase in a secondary market, exchange, gift, or inheritance.

[24] For this purpose, passive income includes royalties, rents, dividends, interest, annuities, and sales or exchanges of stocks and securities. If the corporation has not been in existence for a full 5 years, the gross receipts test is applied to the shorter period. If the corporation has not been in existence for an entire taxable year, the test is applied to the time period up to the date of the loss (see Sec. 1244(c)(2)).

limited to $3,000 per year, is available only if the capital losses exceed the capital gains. (See Chapter 5 for a discussion of capital gains and losses.)

Ordinary losses incurred on business assets, either in a sale, casualty, or other type of transaction, give rise to a deduction *for* AGI. Ordinary losses (e.g., casualty losses) incurred on investment property are usually deducted *from* AGI. However, if the investment property is used to produce rental or royalty income, the casualty loss is a deduction *for* AGI.

Example 8-8 ■   During the current year, Rita realizes a $2,000 loss on the sale of a personal-use asset, a $4,000 loss on the sale of a business asset, and a $3,000 loss on the sale of an investment asset. The $2,000 loss on the sale of the personal-use asset is not deductible for tax purposes. The $4,000 loss on the sale of the business property is a Sec. 1231 loss. Since there are no Sec. 1231 gains in the current year, the Sec. 1231 loss is deductible *for* AGI as an ordinary loss. The $3,000 loss on the sale of the investment property is netted together with Rita's other capital gain and loss transactions for the year. If her capital losses exceed her capital gains, a *for* AGI deduction of up to $3,000 may be taken. ■

Example 8-9 ■   Assume the same facts as in Example 8-8, except that the loss on the personal-use asset is realized in a casualty. The treatment of the losses on the business and investment properties remains the same as in Example 8-8. In addition, since the $2,000 loss on the personal-use property is a casualty loss, it is deductible *from* AGI, subject to the limitations discussed later in this chapter. ■

Disallowance Possibilities

Losses incurred in certain transactions and activities may be disallowed or deferred. These include

- Transfers of property to a controlled corporation in exchange for stock of the corporation (see the discussion in Chapter 2 of *Prentice Hall's Federal Taxation: Corporations, Partnerships, Estates, and Trusts* text and Chapter 15 of the *Comprehensive* volume)

- Exchanges of property for other property that is considered to be like-kind to the property given up (see the discussion in Chapter 12)

- Property sold to certain related parties (see the discussion in Chapter 6)

- Wash sale transactions (see the discussion in Chapter 6)

- Losses limited because the losses exceed the amount for which the taxpayer is at risk (see the discussion in Chapter 9 of *Prentice Hall's Federal Taxation: Corporations, Partnerships, Estates, and Trusts* text and Chapter 20 of the *Comprehensive* volume)

In addition, individuals and certain corporations may be limited on the amount of deductible losses because of the passive loss rules.

Topic Review 8-1 contains a summary of loss transactions.

PASSIVE LOSSES

In the past, taxpayers had been able to reduce their income tax liability on income from one business or investment activity with deductions, losses, and credits arising in another activity. Thus, taxpayers often invested in passive activities, called **tax**

TOPIC REVIEW 8-1

Transactions That May Result in Losses	
Type of Transaction	Result
Sale or exchange	A loss on personal-use property is not deductible. The tax treatment of a loss on business or investment property depends upon the type of property. Losses on capital assets result in capital losses. Losses on Sec. 1231 assets are subject to the Sec. 1231 netting rules discussed in Chapter 13.
Seizure or condemnation	Treated as a sale or exchange (see the above caption).
Abandonment	Not treated as a sale or exchange. No deduction is allowed for a loss on personal-use property. Ordinary loss treatment is accorded to business or investment property.
Worthless securities	Treated as a loss from the sale of the securities on the last day of the year in which the securities become worthless. This generally will result in a capital loss. However, if the requirements of Sec. 1244 are met, at least part of the loss may be treated as an ordinary loss. (See Sec. 1244 stock below.) A loss on worthless securities of an affiliated corporation results in an ordinary loss.
Demolition	No deductible loss is allowed. Instead, losses and costs of demolition are added to the basis of the land where the demolished structure was located.
Sec. 1244 stock	An ordinary loss is allowed for individuals up to $50,000 per year ($100,000 for married filing jointly). The remaining loss is capital. The stock must have been originally issued to the individual for property or cash, and the corporation must meet the requirements to be a small business corporation.

Historical Note

Before the passive activity loss limits became effective in 1987, most tax shelters were concentrated in the areas of real estate, oil and gas, equipment leasing, farming, motion pictures, timber, and research and development.

shelters, which would spin off tax deductions and credits. Many of these tax shelters were simply *passive investments* since they did not require the taxpayer's involvement or participation. In some situations, tax shelters had real economic substance other than the mere creation of tax benefits. A taxpayer's investment in this type of shelter was not based solely on the tax benefits that the activity generated. In many cases, however, tax shelters had no real economic substance other than the creation of deductions and credits that enabled taxpayers to reduce and sometimes eliminate the income tax liability from their active business activities. In an effort to prevent these perceived and real abuses, Congress enacted Sec. 469, which restricts the current use of losses and credits that arise in passive activities. These rules are effective for tax years beginning after December 31, 1986.

Computation of Passive Losses and Credits

OBJECTIVE 3
Calculate the suspended loss from passive activities

Historical Note
Because some high income taxpayers were able to reduce their taxes significantly, Congress feared that the general public was losing faith in the federal tax system. For example, in 1983 out of 260,000 tax returns reporting "total positive income" in excess of $250,000, 11% paid taxes equalling 5% or less of total positive income even though the marginal rates under the progressive system were as high as 50% at that time.

In enacting the passive loss rules, Congress did not want to prevent taxpayers from currently deducting or using losses and credits generated in active business endeavors of the taxpayer. At the same time, Congress realized that certain passive investments (such as investments that generate interest or dividend income) normally give rise to taxable income which could itself be sheltered by losses and credits that arise in other passive activities. Thus, Sec. 469 requires taxpayers to classify their income into three categories: (1) *active income* (such as wages, salaries, and active business income); (2) *portfolio (or investment) income;* and (3) *passive income*. **Portfolio income** includes dividends, interest, annuities, and royalties (and allocable expenses and interest expense) that are not derived in the ordinary course of a trade or business. Gains and losses on property which produce these types of income also are included in portfolio income if the disposition of the property does not occur in the ordinary course of business.[25] In general, losses from passive activities may not offset portfolio income or active income. Portfolio income becomes part of net investment income, which is used in computing the deduction limit for investment interest expense. (See Chapter 7 for a discussion of the investment interest expense limitation.)

Passive Income and Losses. Income and loss in the passive category are computed separately for each passive activity in which the taxpayer has invested. In general, for any tax year, losses generated in one passive activity may be used to offset income from other passive activities, but may not offset either active or portfolio income.

Example 8-10 ■

During the year, Kasi reports $100,000 of active business income, $10,000 of income from activity A, and a $15,000 loss from activity B. Both A and B are passive activities. $10,000 of the loss from activity B may offset the $10,000 of income from activity A. However, the $5,000 excess loss is not deductible in the current year, even though Kasi must report $100,000 of active business income. ■

Key Point
Excess passive activity losses are not "lost" since they can be carried over to future years.

Losses that cannot be deducted currently are carried over to subsequent years. Because of the carryover rules (explained later), if a taxpayer has invested in several passive activities, and for the year some of the activities generate income while others generate losses, the loss carried over for each loss activity is a pro rata portion of the total passive loss for the year.[26]

Example 8-11 ■

Tammy reports the following income and loss for the year:

Salary	$200,000
Loss from activity X	(40,000)
Loss from activity Y	(10,000)
Income from activity Z	30,000

[25] Sec. 469(e)(1). Gain or loss on property dispositions occuring in the ordinary course of business is either passive or active business income, depending upon the taxpayer's level of involvement (i.e., material participation) in the activity.
[26] Sec. 469(j)(4).

X, Y, and Z are all passive activities. The losses generated in activities X and Y offset the income from activity Z, but none of the salary income is offset. Thus, Tammy has a net passive loss for the year of $20,000 ($40,000 + $10,000 − $30,000), which must be carried over to subsequent years. The amount of the carryover attributable to each activity is as follows:

$$\text{Activity X:} \quad \$20,000 \times \frac{\$40,000}{\$50,000} = \$16,000$$

$$\text{Activity Y:} \quad \$20,000 \times \frac{\$10,000}{\$50,000} = \$\ 4,000 \quad \blacksquare$$

CREDITS. Credits generated in a passive activity are also limited and may be used only against the portion of the tax liability that is attributable to passive income.[27]

Example 8-12 ■

Dale invests in a passive activity. For the year, he must report $10,000 of taxable income from the passive activity. Dale's share of tax credits generated by the passive activity is $5,000. Assume Dale's precredit tax liability on all income (including the $10,000 from the passive activity) is $25,000, and his precredit tax liability on all income excluding the passive activity income is $22,000. He may use only $3,000 ($25,000 − $22,000) of the tax credits generated by the passive activity. The remaining $2,000 of tax credits is carried forward and may be used in a subsequent year against the portion of the tax liability attributable to passive activity income in that year. However, these credits may never offset any portion of the tax liability attributable to nonpassive activities. (See Chapter 14 for a discussion of credits and their carryovers.) ■

Carryovers

Passive activity losses that are disallowed as deductions for the year in which they are incurred are carried over indefinitely and treated as losses allocable to that activity in the following tax years.[28] These losses may offset passive activity income of the subsequent year, but generally may not offset other types of income.

Taxable Disposition of Interest in a Passive Activity. When a taxpayer disposes of a passive activity in a taxable transaction, the economic gain or loss generated by the activity can be computed, and the suspended losses of that activity may be deducted against the taxpayer's other income. However, the amount of the total net economic loss from the asset that is disposed of must first offset any passive income from other passive activities.[29]

Example 8-13 ■

During the current year, Pam realizes $7,000 of taxable income from activity A, $2,000 of loss from activity B, and $8,000 of taxable income from activity C. All three activities are passive activities with regard to Pam. In addition, $30,000 of passive losses from activity C are carried over from prior years. During the current year, Pam sells activity C for a $15,000 taxable gain. Pam reports salary income of $90,000 for the year. Since activity C is disposed of in a fully taxable transaction, Pam may deduct $2,000 of C's cumulative loss against the salary income:

---

[27] This amount is determined by comparing the tax liability on all income for the year with the tax liability on all income excluding the passive income.

[28] Sec. 469(b).

[29] Sec. 469(g). Income from the activity for prior years may also be taken into account in arriving at the net income from all passive activities for the year if it is necessary to prevent avoidance of the passive loss rules.

Income for the year from C	$ 8,000	
Gain from the sale of C	15,000	
Suspended losses from C	(30,000)	
Total loss from C		($7,000)
Income for the year from A	$ 7,000	
Loss for the year from B	(2,000)	5,000
Pam's deduction against salary income		$2,000

If the passive activity is sold to a related party, the suspended loss is not deductible until the related party sells the activity to a nonrelated person. The definition of related persons includes spouse, brothers and sisters, ancestors, lineal descendants, and corporations or partnerships in which the individual has a greater than 50% ownership.[30]

Although the death of a taxpayer is not a taxable disposition of the asset, some of the suspended losses may be deducted when this event occurs. The amount of the deduction allowed is the amount by which the suspended losses exceed the increase in basis of the property. These losses generally are deducted on the decedent's final income tax return. Any suspended losses up to the amount of the increase in basis are lost.[31]

Example 8-14 ■ At the time that John died during the current year, he owned passive activity property with an adjusted basis of $20,000 and a FMV of $35,000. There were $25,000 in suspended losses attributable to the property. Since the increase in the basis of the property is $15,000 ($35,000 − $20,000), $15,000 of the suspended losses are lost. However, $10,000 ($25,000 suspended losses − $15,000 increase in basis) of the suspended losses are deductible on John's final income tax return. ■

In general, the suspended losses of a passive activity become deductible only when the taxpayer completely disposes of his or her interest in the activity. However, the IRS has stated in a proposed regulation that taxpayers may treat the disposition of a substantial part of an activity as the disposition of a separate activity.[32] This treatment is only available, however, if the taxpayer can establish with reasonable certainty the amount of income, deductions, credits, and suspended losses and credits that are allocable to that part of the activity. To date there is no guidance as to what constitutes a substantial part of an activity for this purpose.

Carryovers from a Former Passive Activity. The determination of whether an activity is passive with respect to a taxpayer is made annually. Thus, an activity that previously was considered passive may not be passive with respect to the taxpayer for the current year. This is called a **former passive activity.**[33] Any loss carryover from a former passive activity is deductible against the current year's income of that activity even though the activity is not a passive activity in the current year. However, any suspended loss in excess of the activity's income for the year is still subject to the carryover limitations. Since the activity is no longer passive for the year, the current year's loss is deductible against active business income.

---

[30] Other relationships described in Secs. 267(b) and 707(b) are also considered related parties for this purpose.

[31] Sec. 469(g)(2). Generally, the basis of inherited property is its FMV on the date of death (see Chapter 5).

[32] Prop. Reg. Sec. 1.469-4(k).

[33] Sec. 469(f)(3).

Example 8-15 ■   Kris owns activity A, which, for the immediately preceding tax year, was considered a passive activity with regard to Kris. $10,000 in losses from activity A were disallowed and carried over to the current year. Because of Kris' increased involvement in activity A in the current year, it is not considered passive with regard to Kris for that year. During the current year, activity A generates a $5,000 loss. During the current year, she also has an investment in activity B, a passive activity. Her share of activity B's income is $7,000. Kris reports $60,000 in salary. Since for the current year, activity A is not a passive activity, the $5,000 current year loss is fully deductible against her salary. However, the $10,000 loss carryover from the prior year is deductible only against the $7,000 of income from passive activity B. The $3,000 ($10,000 − $7,000) excess is carried over to the subsequent year. ■

Definition of a Passive Activity

OBJECTIVE 4

Identify what constitutes a passive activity loss

The term *passive activity* includes (1) any trade or business in which the taxpayer does not materially participate, or (2) any rental activity.[34] However, items of income, deduction, gain, or loss that are subject to the limitations imposed by Sec. 280A (relating to the business use of home, and the rental of vacation homes) are not taken into account under the passive loss rules. (See Chapter 6 for a discussion of the rental of vacation homes).[35]

The definition of a passive activity is based upon two critical elements: (1) an identification of exactly what constitutes an activity, and (2) a determination of whether the taxpayer has materially participated in that activity.

Additional Comment

Tax year 1989 gave a clearer reflection of the impact of the passive loss provisions that were enacted in 1986. Net losses of limited partnerships, the type that are used as tax shelters, narrowed to $21.6 billion in 1989 from $35.5 billion in 1986.

Identification of an Activity. Identifying exactly what an activity is becomes critical for the following reasons: (1) Whether a taxpayer materially participates in an activity is determined separately for each activity. (2) Suspended losses of a passive activity are deductible when the taxpayer's ownership of the activity is completely terminated. (3) As explained in a subsequent section of this chapter, up to $25,000 of passive losses may be deducted currently if they are from rental real estate activities. Thus, losses from passive business and rental real estate activities must not be combined into one activity.

Example 8-16 ■   Wayne owns operations Y and Z. He devotes a substantial amount of time to Y, but very little to Z. If Y and Z are considered one activity, Wayne materially participates in both operations and losses from both may be deducted currently. If Y and Z are considered separate activities, Wayne does not materially participate in Z and any losses from Z must be suspended under the passive loss rules. ■

As illustrated, the way operations are combined or separated into activities can have a significant impact on the deductibility of losses that the operations may

---

[34] Secs. 469(c)(1) and (c)(2). Sec. 469(c)(6) also includes investment (production of income) activities under Sec. 212 as a passive activity. Section 469(j)(8) defines the term "rental activity" as any activity where payments are principally for the use of tangible property. Pursuant to the Regulations, there are six exceptions to this general rule. These exceptions include providing the use of tangible property where: (1) the average period of customer use is seven days or less, (2) the average period of customer use is 30 days or less and significant personal services are provided by the owner in conjunction with the use of the property, (3) extraordinary personal services are provided by the owner in conjunction with the use of the property, (4) the rental of the property is incidental to a nonrental activity of the taxpayer, (5) the property is customarily made available during defined business hours for nonexclusive use by various customers, or (6) the property is provided for use in a nonrental activity conducted by a partnership, S corporation, or joint venture in which the taxpayer owns an interest. The details of these exceptions are beyond the scope of this text. See Temp. Reg. Sec. 1.469-1T(e)(3)(ii).

[35] Sec. 469(j)(10).

generate. For tax years on or before May 10, 1992, a complex and detailed set of rules had to be applied for this purpose.[36]

For subsequent years, however, one or more operations are to be treated as a single activity only if they constitute what the new proposed regulations call an "appropriate economic unit."[37] Although this determination is made by examining all the relevant facts and circumstances, the following factors are given the greatest weight:

- Similarities and differences in the types of business
- The extent of common control
- The extent of common ownership
- The geographical location, and
- Any interdependencies between the operations (i.e. the extent to which they purchase or sell goods between themselves, have the same customers, are accounted for with a single set of books, etc.).[38]

Not all of these factors are necessary for a taxpayer to treat more than one operation as a single activity. Furthermore, a taxpayer may use any reasonable method of applying the relevant facts and circumstances in grouping the activities.[39]

Example 8-17 ■ Carla owns a significant portion of a bakery and a movie theater in two different shopping malls—one located in Baltimore and the other in Philadelphia. Depending upon other relevant facts and circumstances, a reasonable grouping of the operations may result in any of the following: ■

1. One activity involving all four operations
2. Two activities; a bakery activity and a theater activity
3. Two activities; a Baltimore activity and a Philadelphia activity
4. Four activities.[40]

Example 8-18 ■ Len is a partner in the L&B Partnership which is located in an industrial park in Ogden, Utah. L&B is engaged in a business that sells non-food items to grocery stores. Len is also a partner in the WH Partnership which owns and operates a warehouse located in the same industrial park. Most of WH's business involves warehousing goods for L&B. WH is the only warehousing business in which Len is involved. The two partnerships are under common control. Under these facts and circumstances, Len treats the two operations as a single activity.[41]

Under these proposed regulations, taxpayers apparently have some degree of flexibility in determining how different business operations are grouped into activities. However, once the activities are established, taxpayers must be consistent in grouping their activities in subsequent years unless material changes in the facts and circumstances clearly make the groupings inappropriate.[42]

In general, in identifying separate activities, rental operations may not be grouped with trade or business operations. However, the Regulations do allow a combination if either the rental operation is insubstantial in relation to the business operation, or visa versa. Unfortunately, the Regulations do not give any

---

[36] Temp. Reg. Sec. 1.469-4T.
[37] Prop. Reg. Sec. 1.469-4(c).
[38] Prop. Reg. Sec. 1.469-4(c)(2).
[39] Ibid.
[40] Prop. Reg. Sec. 1.469-4(c)(3).
[41] Ibid.
[42] Prop. Reg. Sec. 1.469-4(g).

guidance with regard to what is insubstantial.[43] Furthermore, because of the special rules dealing with real estate rental activities (explained later in this chapter), rental activities involving real estate may not be combined with rental activities involving personal property.[44]

Example 8-19 ■ Sandy owns a building in which she operates a restaurant and leases out apartments to tenants. Generally the tenants sign apartment leases of one year or longer. Of the total gross income derived from the building, 15% comes from the apartment rentals and 85% comes from the restaurant operation. If the apartment rental operation is considered insubstantial in relation to the restaurant operation, the two may be combined into one activity. If it is not insubstantial, the two operations are considered two separate activities, a business activity, and a rental real estate activity.[45]

Partnerships and S corporations (pass-through entities) are to identify their business and rental activities by applying these rules at the partnership or S corporation level and then should report the results of their operations by activity to the partners or shareholders. Each partner or shareholder must then take these activities and, using these same rules, combine them where appropriate with operations conducted either directly or through other pass-through entities.[46]

OBJECTIVE 5

Determine when a taxpayer has materially participated in a passive activity

Material Participation. Once each activity has been identified, a determination must be made as to whether the activity is passive or active with respect to the taxpayer. If the taxpayer does not materially participate in the activity, it is deemed to be a passive activity with respect to that taxpayer. Pursuant to the Regulations,[47] taxpayers are deemed to materially participate in an activity if and only if they meet one or more of the following tests:

1. The individual participates in the activity for more than 500 hours during the year.
2. The individual's participation in the activity for the year constitutes substantially all of the participation in the activity by all individuals, including individuals who do not own any interest in the activity.
3. The individual participates in the activity for more than 100 hours during the year, and that participation is more than any other individual's participation for the year (including participation by individuals who do not own any interest in the activity).
4. The individual participates in "significant participation activities" for an aggregate of more than 500 hours during the year.[48] Thus, an individual who spends over 100 hours each in several separate significant participation activities may aggregate the time spent in these activities in order to meet the 500 hour test.
5. The individual materially participated in the activity in any five years during the immediately preceding 10 taxable years. These five years need not be consecutive.

Key Point

The material participation test is not a relevant factor for taxpayers having a working interest in oil and gas property.

Additional Comment

A taxpayer may be a material participant one year and a passive investor the next year. A taxpayer must satisfy one of the material participation tests each year to be treated as a material participant.

---

[43] Prop. Reg. Sec. 1.469-4(d). For two operations situated at the same location, the old temporary regulations provided a 20% of gross income test for this purpose. The new proposed regulations do not contain any such mechanical test.

[44] Prop. Reg. Sec. 1.469-4(e).

[45] Under the old temporary regulations the two operations would have been treated as one activity.

[46] Prop. Reg. Sec. 1.469-4(j).

[47] Temp. Reg. Sec. 1.469-5T(a).

[48] A significant participation activity is a trade or business in which the individual participates for more than 100 hours during the year but for which the individual does not meet the material participation test alone (i.e., with respect to that activity, the individual does not meet one of the other material participation tests.). See: Temp. Reg. Sec. 1.469-5T(c).

6. The individual materially participated in the activity for any three years preceding the year in question, and the activity is a personal service activity.[49]

7. Taking into account all the relevant facts and circumstances, the individual participates in the activity on a regular, continuous, and substantial basis during the year.

Note that the first four tests are based upon the number of hours the taxpayer spent in the activity during the year. The fifth and sixth tests are based upon the material participation of the taxpayer in prior years and are designed to prevent taxpayers from asserting that retirement income is passive and offsetting it with passive losses from tax shelters.

Limited Partnerships. Since a limited partner's involvement in a limited partnership is restricted, the material participation test is not met and the limited partner's investment is considered to be passive.[50] However, the Code does give the Treasury Department authority to write regulations preventing taxpayers from mixing active business interests with passive interests within a limited partnership in order to circumvent the passive loss limitations.[51]

Working Interest in an Oil and Gas Property. A working interest in an oil and gas property is not a passive activity as long as the taxpayer's liability in the interest is not limited.[52] Thus, even though a taxpayer may not materially participate in the activity, the passive loss rules do not apply. This is so, even if the taxpayer holds the interest through an entity such as a partnership.

Taxpayers Subject to Passive Loss Rules

The passive loss limitation rules are applicable for

- Individuals, estates, trusts
- Any closely held C corporation
- Any personal service corporation
- Certain publicly traded partnerships

Since the income and losses of partnerships and S corporations are taxed directly to the partners and shareholders, the passive loss rules do not apply to these entities.[53] Rather, they are applied directly at the partner or shareholder level. Thus, the situation may arise where one partner or shareholder is subject to the passive loss rules while the others are not.

Additional Comment

Congress excluded a working interest in an oil or gas property from the material participation requirement in those cases where the taxpayer's liability is not limited because Congress concluded that financial risk was a more relevant standard. At the time (1986) the oil and gas industry was suffering severe hardship due to the worldwide decline in oil prices.

Key Point

The passive loss limitations do not apply to partnerships and S corporations, but they apply to partners and shareholders of S corporations.

Additional Comment

A provision in the Revenue Reconciliation Act of 1993 provided passive activity loss relief to real estate professionals by treating real estate activities in which the taxpayer "materially participates" as not subject to the passive activity loss limitation if certain eligibility requirements are satisfied.

Example 8-20 ■

Rick and Sally are both general partners in the RS Partnership. The partnership was formed a year ago with Rick contributing the ideas and expertise and Sally contributing the working capital. Rick is involved in the management and day-to-day operations of the RS Partnership, whereas Sally only occasionally meets with Rick in order to receive information and help make policy decisions.

---

[49] A personal service activity involves rendering personal services in the fields of health, law, engineering, architecture, accounting, actuarial science, performing arts, or consulting. It also includes any other trade or business in which capital is not a material income-producing factor. See: Temp. Reg. Sec. 1.469-5T(e)(2).

[50] Sec. 469(h)(2).

[51] Ibid.

[52] Sec. 469(c)(3).

[53] An S corporation is a corporation that has elected for federal income tax purposes to be treated basically like a partnership. Thus, the income or losses and separately stated items of an S corporation flow through to the shareholders and are reported on their individual tax returns.

Under these circumstances, Rick meets the material participation test with regard to the activity while Sally does not. The passive loss limitations with regard to the activities of the RS Partnership apply to Sally but not to Rick. ■

Generally, the passive loss limitation rules do not apply to regular or C corporations (as opposed to S corporations). However, in order to prevent certain individuals from avoiding the passive loss rules through the use of a regular corporation, closely held C corporations and personal service corporations are also subject to these rules.

Closely Held C Corporations. The passive loss rules apply to closely held C corporations but only on a limited basis. A **closely held C corporation** is a C corporation where more than 50% of the stock is owned by five or fewer individuals at any time during the last half of the corporation's taxable year.[54] The concern that Congress had regarding closely held C corporations was that, without this special rule, taxpayers would be motivated to transfer their investments (both portfolio investments as well as passive activities) to a C corporation where the portfolio income could be offset by the corporation's passive losses. Thus, as applied to a closely held C corporation, the passive loss rules prevent passive activity losses from offsetting portfolio income. However, a closely held C corporation's passive losses may offset its income from active business operations.[55]

Additional Comment

Since a closely held C corporation's passive losses may offset its income from active business operations, some tax professionals advise their clients to transfer their investments that generate passive losses to their profitable corporations.

Example 8-21 ■ All of the outstanding stock of Delta Corporation is owned equally by individuals Allen and Beth. During the current year, Delta generates $15,000 taxable income from its active business operations. It also earns $10,000 of interest and dividends from investments and reports a $30,000 loss from a passive activity. Since Delta is a closely held C corporation, the $15,000 of taxable income from the active business is offset by $15,000 of the passive loss. However, the $10,000 of portfolio income may not be offset. Thus, for the current year, Delta reports $10,000 of taxable income from its portfolio income and has a $15,000 passive loss carryover. ■

Personal Service Corporation. A **personal service corporation (PSC)** is a regular C corporation whose principal activity is the performance of personal services which are substantially performed by owner-employees.[56] However, a corporation is not a PSC unless more than 10% of the value of the stock is held by owner-employees.[57] In contrast with a non-PSC closely held C corporation, the passive loss limitation rules apply in their entirety.[58] Thus, passive losses of a PSC may not offset the PSC's active business income.

Material Participation by PSCs and Closely Held C Corporations. Special rules apply for determining whether closely held C corporations or PSCs materially participate in an activity. These corporations are deemed to materially participate in an activity only if one or more shareholders who own more than 50% in value of the outstanding stock materially participate in the activity. In addition, a closely held C corporation (other than a PSC) is deemed to materially participate in an activity if it meets *all* of the following tests with regard to that activity:

---

[54] Secs. 469(j)(1) and 465(a)(1)(B).
[55] Sec. 469(e)(2).
[56] Secs. 469(j)(2) and 269A(b)(1). For this purpose any employee who owns any stock of the corporation is an owner-employee. This stock ownership is determined by using the Sec. 318 constructive ownership rules as modified by Sec. 469(j)(2).
[57] Ibid.
[58] If a corporation is both a PSC and a closely held C corporation, the more restrictive rules for PSCs apply.

1. A substantial portion of the services of at least one full-time employee is in the active management of the activity.
2. A substantial portion of the services of at least three full-time nonowner employees is directly related to the activity.
3. The Sec. 162 business deductions of the activity exceed 15% of the activity's gross income for the period.[59]

Publicly Traded Partnerships

Generally, a publicly traded partnership (PTP) is treated for tax purposes as a corporation. For purposes of the passive loss rules, a PTP is defined as any partnership if interests in the partnership are either (1) traded on an established securities market, or (2) readily tradable on a secondary market.[60] If a PTP is treated for tax purposes as a corporation, the passive loss rules generally do not apply. However, PTPs that existed on December 17, 1987 are still treated as partnerships until their first tax year beginning after 1997. Since under the partnership rules the partnership's income and losses flow through to the partners, the passive loss rules apply to these existing PTPs. However, these rules are applied separately to each existing PTP.[61] Partners treat losses from a PTP as separate from any other type of income (passive, active business, or portfolio), as well as separate from any income from other PTPs. These losses can only be carried forward and be offset against income generated by that particular PTP in a subsequent year. Furthermore, the loss may not offset any portfolio income that the PTP might generate.[62] Any net income from PTPs is treated as portfolio income.

Example 8-22 ■ Mark owns interests in partnerships A and B, both of which are PTPs that existed on December 17, 1987. During the current year, Mark's share of the income from A is $2,000. Mark's share of B's loss is $1,200. B also generated some portfolio income. Mark's share of B's portfolio income is $800. The $1,200 loss from B may not offset any of B's $800 portfolio income. Furthermore, it may not offset any of the $2,000 income from A. The $2,000 income from A is treated as portfolio income. Thus, Mark reports $2,800 portfolio income and has a $1,200 suspended loss from B. In a subsequent year, Mark's share of any income from B can be offset by the $1,200 of suspended loss that is carried forward. ■

Suspended losses from a PTP may be deducted only in the year the partner disposes of his interest in the PTP.[63] No loss is recognized in the year that the PTP itself sells a passive activity.

Rental Real Estate Trade or Business

In general, rental activities are considered passive activities. However, for tax years beginning after December 31, 1993, the passive activity loss rules no longer apply to certain taxpayers that are involved in real property trades or businesses. Instead, these activities are treated as active businesses. Under the new law, a real property

---

[59] Secs. 469(h)(4) and 465(c)(7). Tests 1 and 2 must be met for the 12-month period ending on the last day of the tax year. Test 3 must be met for the tax year. Furthermore, the Sec. 404 deductions are also included in the 15% of gross income test.

[60] Sec. 469(k)(2). See Chapter 10 of *Prentice Hall's Federal Taxation: Corporations, Partnerships, Estates, and Trusts* and Chapter 21 of the *Comprehensive* volume for a definition and discussion of publicly-traded partnerships.

[61] Sec. 469(k)(1).

[62] Conf. Rept. No. 100-495, 100th Cong., 1st Sess., pp. 231-233 (1987).

[63] Ibid. at p. 289.

trade or business means any development, redevelopment, construction, reconstruction, acquisition, conversion, rental, operation, management, leasing, or brokering of real property.[64]

This exception applies to taxpayers if both the following requirements are met:

- More than one-half of the personal services performed in all trades or businesses by the taxpayer during the year must be performed in real property trades or businesses in which the taxpayer materially participates, and
- The taxpayer must perform more than 750 hours of service during the taxable year in real property trades or businesses in which the taxpayer materially participates.[65]

In meeting these tests, personal services rendered by a taxpayer in his or her capacity as an employee are not treated as performed in real property trades or businesses unless the employee owns at least five percent of the employer. Furthermore, for married taxpayers filing a joint return, the exception applies only if one of the spouses separately meets both requirements. However, the time spent in the activity by both spouses is used in determining whether or not the material participation test is met.

Example 8-23 ■   Anwar and Anya are married and file a joint return. Anwar's only job is renting and maintaining four large apartment complexes that he owns. Anwar and Anya manage the buildings themselves. During the current year, Anya spent 500 hours keeping records and corresponding with tenants. Anwar spent 700 hours during the year maintaining and repairing the apartments. Even though all of Anya and Anwar's personal services are connected with a real property trade or business in which they materially participate, this rental activity is considered passive since neither Anwar nor Anya alone spends more than 750 hours doing services related to the rental activity.   ■

In order for a closely-held C corporation to meet this rental real estate business exception, more than one-half of the gross receipts of the corporation must be derived from real property trades or businesses in which the corporation materially participates.

Any deduction allowed under the previously discussed exception for taxpayers who are involved in real property trades or businesses is not taken into consideration in determining the taxpayer's AGI for purposes of the phase-out of the $25,000 deduction available for taxpayers who actively participate in a rental real estate activity. (See the following section in this chapter for a discussion of the $25,000 active participation exception.)

Other Rental Real Estate Activities

Many rental real estate activities are not considered rental real estate businesses, and are therefore subject to the passive loss rules. However, if an individual taxpayer meets certain requirements, up to $25,000 of annual losses from these passive rental real estate activities may still be deducted against the taxpayer's other income. In order to meet this exception, an individual must do both of the following:

- *Actively* participate in the activity[66]

---

[64] Sec. 469(c)(7)(C).

[65] Sec. 469(c)(7)(B).

[66] In order for a deduction to be taken in the current year for a loss sustained in a prior year, the taxpayer must actively participate in the activity during both years. See Sec. 469(i)(1).

• Own at least 10% of the value of the activity for the entire tax year

Active Participation. *Active participation,* as opposed to material participation, can be achieved by the taxpayer without regular, continuous, and material involvement in the activity and without meeting any of the material participation tests. However, the taxpayer still must participate in the making of management decisions or arranging for others to provide services in a significant and bona fide sense.[67] This includes approving new tenants, deciding on rental terms, approving expenditures, and other similar decisions. Active participation may be achieved even if the taxpayer hires a rental agent and others provide the services.[68] In general, a limited partner is not able to participate actively in any activity of a limited partnership.

Limitation on Deduction of Rental Real Estate Loss. Rental real estate losses are first applied against other net passive income for the year and then may be used to reduce portfolio or active business income up to $25,000. The $25,000, however, is reduced by 50% of the taxpayer's AGI in excess of $100,000. For this purpose, AGI is determined without regard to any passive activity loss or to any loss allowable to taxpayers who materially participate in real property trades or businesses (e.g., a real estate developer). Thus, if a taxpayer has AGI of $150,000 or more, all of the rental real estate losses must be suspended and carried over with the taxpayer's other passive losses.

Example 8-24 ■

During the current year, Penny, a married individual who files a joint return, reports the following items of income and loss:

Salary income	$120,000
Activity A (passive)	15,000
Activity B (nonbusiness rental real estate)	(50,000)

Penny owns over 10% and actively participates in activity B. Her AGI for the year is as follows:

Salary		$120,000
Passive income from Activity A	$15,000	
Minus:		
Passive income from Activity B	(15,000)	
Minus:		
Maximum rental real estate loss	$25,000	
Reduced by phase-out:		
([$120,000 − $100,000]× 0.50)	(10,000)	
Deductible amount (but not to exceed actual loss)		(15,000)
AGI		$105,000

Penny may deduct $30,000 ($15,000 deductible amount + $15,000 as an offset to the income from Activity A) of the loss from Activity B during the year. Penny has $20,000 ($35,000 − $15,000) of suspended passive losses from activity B that are carried over to the following year. ■

The $25,000 limit applies to the sum of both deductions and credits. Thus, in order to properly apply the limit, the credits must be converted into deduction equivalents.

---

[67] S. Rept. No. 99-313, 99th Cong., 2d Sess., pp. 737-738 (1986).
[68] Ibid. However, a lessor under a net lease will probably not be deemed to achieve active participation.

A *deduction equivalent* is an amount which, if taken as a deduction, would reduce the tax liability by an amount equal to the credits. The amount of deduction equivalents can be computed by dividing the amount of the credit by the taxpayer's marginal tax rate. If the sum of the deductions and the deduction equivalents exceeds the $25,000 limit, the deductions are used first.

Example 8-25 ■ Hal owns over 10% and actively participates in activity A, which is a passive real estate rental activity. Hal's marginal tax rate is 28%, and he has AGI of less than $100,000. For the year, activity A generates a $20,000 net loss and $10,000 in tax credits. After deducting the $20,000 net loss against his active business and portfolio income, Hal has a remaining real estate deduction of $5,000 ($25,000 − $20,000). Thus, Hal may use $1,400 ($5,000 × 0.28) of the credits. The remaining $8,600 ($10,000 − $1,400) of tax credits must be carried over to subsequent years. ■

If deductions and credits exceeding the $25,000 limit arise from more than one passive activity, they must be allocated between the activities.

Example 8-26 ■ Mary has AGI of less than $100,000 and a 28% marginal tax rate. During the year she reports a $30,000 loss from activity A and a $10,000 loss from activity B. Additionally, activity A generates $5,000 of tax credits. Both activities A and B are passive real estate rental activities in which Mary actively participates and owns over 10% of each activity. The $25,000 deduction is first allocated to the losses. Since the sum of the losses ($40,000) exceeds the limit, the deductible loss must be allocated ratably between the activities as follows:

Activity A: $25,000 × $30,000 ÷ $40,000 = $18,750
Activity B: $25,000 × $10,000 ÷ $40,000 = $6,250

Activity A has an $11,250 ($30,000 − $18,750) suspended loss, and activity B has a $3,750 ($10,000 − $6,250) suspended loss. In addition, activity A has $5,000 of suspended tax credits. ■

A summary of the passive activity loss rules is presented in Topic Review 8-2.

CASUALTY AND THEFT LOSSES

OBJECTIVE 6
Identify and calculate the deduction for a casualty or theft loss

Deductions for losses on personal-use property are generally disallowed. However, a deduction is available to an individual if the loss arises from a fire, storm, shipwreck, other casualty or theft.[69] Similar losses for business and investment property are also deductible. In order for an event to qualify as a casualty, certain requirements must be met.

Casualty Defined

According to the IRS, a deductible **casualty loss** is one that has occurred in an identifiable event that was sudden, unexpected, or unusual.[70]

[69] Sec. 165(c)(3).
[70] IRS, *Publication No. 547* [Nonbusiness Disasters, Casualties, and Thefts], 1993, p. 1.

TOPIC REVIEW 8-2

Passive Losses	
Topic	Summary
Taxpayers covered	Individuals, estates, trusts, closely held C corporations, personal service corporations, certain publicly traded partnerships
Definition	Any trade or business activity in which the taxpayer does not materially participate. Includes all rental activities except for certain rental real estate activities and exceptions contained in regulations. Does not include working interests in oil and gas property.
Limitation	Passive losses are deductible against passive income, but not against active or portfolio income. Disallowed losses are carried over to subsequent years (suspended losses). Losses must be accounted for separately by activity. Activities are identified by examining the taxpayer's undertakings.
Suspended losses	Must be allocated and attributed among the passive activities that generated the losses.
Disposition of interest	Suspended losses may be deducted in the year of a taxable disposition. For inherited property, suspended losses in excess of the increase in basis may be deducted on the final return of a decedent. Losses up to the amount of the basis increase are lost.
Material participation	Must be regular, continuous, and substantial. The regulations contain 7 separate tests; 4 based on current year participation; 2 based on participation in prior years; and 1 based on facts and circumstances.
Real property trades or businesses	Passive activity loss rules do not apply to taxpayers who materially participate in real property trade or business activities constituting more than 750 hours. Additionally, more than one-half of the taxpayer's personal services must be performed in real property trades or businesses in which the taxpayer materially participates.
Rental of real estate	Individuals may deduct losses up to $25,000 against active and portfolio income if they actively particpate in the activity. This is a lesser standard than material participation, but the taxpayer must still participate in management decisions or arranging for others to provide services. The deduction phases out at a 50% rate for AGI in excess of $100,000.

Identifiable Event. Because the event which causes the loss must be *identifiable,* the act of losing or misplacing property is generally not considered a casualty.[71]

Example 8-27 ■

Key Point

In order to deduct a loss on personal-use property, it is crucial that the taxpayer establish that the loss was caused by a casualty. Otherwise, the loss is not deductible.

One day while coming home from work, Damien notices that his diamond ring is missing from his finger. He cannot remember when or where the ring might have been lost. Although he searches everywhere, the ring is not found. Since the ring is not lost as the result of an identifiable event, Damien may not deduct the loss.[72]

■

In other instances taxpayers have been able to prove that the loss of the property was the result of an identifiable event.

Example 8-28 ■

One evening Troy and his wife, Lynn, go to the theater. Troy accidentally slams the car door on Lynn's hand. The impact breaks the flanges holding the diamond in her ring. As a result, the diamond falls from the ring and is lost. In this case, a deductible casualty loss has occurred.[73]

■

Key Point

The taxpayer has the burden of proof to establish that a loss was caused by a casualty. The taxpayer should gather as much evidence as possible. Newspaper clippings, police reports, photographs, and insurance reports can be helpful in establishing the cause of the loss.

Sudden, Unexpected, or Unusual Events. According to the IRS, a *sudden event* is one that is swift, not gradual or progressive. An *unexpected event* is one that is ordinarily unanticipated and one that is not intended. An unusual event is one that is not a day-to-day occurrence and that is not typical of the activity in which the taxpayer is engaged.[74]

Thus, the IRS has ruled that a deductible casualty loss was sustained when a taxpayer went ice fishing and his automobile fell through the ice.[75] A taxpayer whose automobile was damaged as the result of an accident also sustained a deductible casualty loss.[76] However, if the accident is caused by the taxpayer's willful negligence or willful act, no deduction is allowed.[77] Damage sustained as the result of an accident in an automobile race was held nondeductible because accidents occur frequently and are not unusual events in automobile races.[78]

The following are a few examples of events that have been held to constitute a deductible casualty loss:

Additional Comment

Sudden, unexpected, or unusual events must also be accompanied by an external force. For example, a blown engine in an automobile is a sudden event but since no external force caused the event, the loss is not a casualty loss.

- Rust and water damage to furniture and carpets caused by the bursting of a water heater[79]

- Damage to the exterior paint of a residence caused by a severe, sudden, and unexpected concentration of chemical fumes in the air[80]

- Loss caused by fire (unless the taxpayer sets the fire, in which case no deduction is available)[81]

---

[71] *Emily Marx,* 13 T.C. 1099 (1949), *acq.* 1950-1 C.B. 3.

[72] *Edgar F. Stevens,* 1947 PH T.C. Memo ¶ 47,191, 6 TCM 805.

[73] *John P. White,* 48 T.C. 430 (1967), *acq.* 1969-2 C.B. xxv. In another case, the taxpayer convinced the Tax Court to allow a deduction for a lost diamond, even though the taxpayer could not remember a specific blow to the ring. In this instance, the taxpayer obtained an expert witness to testify that the flanges of the ring were strong enough and in good enough repair that the loss of the diamond had to have been caused by a sudden, unexpected blow rather than by progressive deterioration.

[74] IRS, *Publication No. 547* [Nonbusiness Disasters, Casualties, and Thefts], 1993, p. 1.

[75] Rev. Rul. 69-88, 1969-1 C.B. 58.

[76] *Willie C. Robinson,* 1984 PH T.C. Memo ¶ 84,188, 47 TCM 1510.

[77] Reg. Sec. 1.165-7(a)(3).

[78] Ltr. Rul. 8227010 (March 30, 1982).

[79] Ibid.

[80] Ibid.

[81] Ibid.

Ethical Point

A client loses his diamond ring while fishing, and wants to deduct the loss as a casualty. The CPA should not sign the tax return unless he believes that the client's position has a realistic possibility of being sustained on its merits if challenged, which is doubtful in this situation.

Real World Example

Taxpayer received a letter stating that a certain party was imprisoned in Mexico for bankruptcy. That party was alleged to have $375,000 in bills hidden in the secret compartment of a trunk checked in a customs house in the U.S. Taxpayer was told that he would be given one-third of the amount in the trunk if he went to Mexico and paid $8,300 to release the prisoner. Taxpayer went to Mexico, paid the $8,300, and later found that he had been swindled. The loss of $8,300 was a deductible theft loss. Curtis H. Muncie, 18 T.C. 849 (1952).

- Damage to a building caused by an unusually large blast at a nearby quarry[82] or a jet sonic boom[83]
- Death of trees just a few days after a sudden infestation of pine beetles[84]

The following are examples of events that have been held *not* to be a casualty:

- Water damage to the walls and ceiling of a taxpayer's personal residence as the result of the gradual deterioration of the roof[85]
- Trees dying because of gradual suffocation of the root systems[86]
- The loss of trees and shrubs because of disease[87]
- Damage to carpet and clothing caused by moths and carpet beetles[88]
- Damage to a road due to freezing, thawing, and gradual deterioration[89]
- Damage to a residence caused by the gradual sinking of the land underneath the home[90]
- Damage caused by drought since it occurs through progressive deterioration[91]
- The steady weakening of a building caused by normal wind and weather conditions[92]
- The rusting and deterioration of a water heater[93]

At times it is very difficult to determine under the particular facts whether the necessary incidents of suddenness, unexpectedness, or unusualness exist. For example, damage caused by the sudden infestation of pine beetles in some instances has been held to be a casualty,[94] while in other instances it has not constituted a casualty.[95]

Theft Defined

Under Sec. 165, a loss sustained as the result of a theft is also deductible. This includes theft of business, investment, or personal-use property. The Regulations

---

[82] *Ray Durden,* 3 T.C. 1 (1944), *acq.* 1944 C.B. 8.

[83] Rev. Rul. 60-329, 1960-2 C.B. 67.

[84] Rev. Rul. 79-174, 1979-1 C.B. 99. See also *Charles A. Smithgall v. U.S.,* 47 AFTR 2d 81-695, 81-1 USTC ¶ 9121 (D.C.-Ga., 1980). However, the IRS has ruled in Ltr. Rul. 8544001 (July 12, 1985) that no casualty loss results when the time interval between the infestation and the death of the trees was too long.

[85] *Lauren Whiting,* 1975 PH T.C. Memo ¶ 75,038, 34 TCM 241.

[86] *William R. Miller,* 1970 PH T.C. Memo ¶ 70,167, 29 TCM 741.

[87] Rev. Rul. 57-599, 1957-2 C.B. 142, *modified by* Rev. Rul. 79-174, 1979-1 C.B. 99. See also *Howard F. Burns v. U.S.,* 6 AFTR 2d 6036, 61-1 USTC ¶ 9127 (6th Cir., 1960).

[88] Rev. Rul. 55-327, 1955-1 C.B. 25. See also *J. P. Meersman v. U.S.,* 18 AFTR 2d 6152, 67-1 USTC ¶ 9125 (6th Cir., 1966).

[89] *Howard Stacey,* 1970 PH T.C. Memo ¶ 70,127, 29 TCM 542. However, the breaking up of a road over a 4-month period because of extreme weather conditions was held to be a casualty. See *Emmett J. O'Connell v. U.S.,* 29 AFTR 2d 72-596, 72-1 USTC ¶ 9312, (D.C. Cal., 1972). See also *Stephen R. Shaffer,* 1983 PH T.C. Memo ¶ 83,677, 47 TCM 285.

[90] *Henry W. Berry,* 1969 PH T.C. Memo ¶ 69,162, 28 TCM 802. See also *David McDaniel,* 1980 PH T.C. Memo ¶ 80,557, 41 TCM 563.

[91] IRS, *Publication No. 547* [Nonbusiness Disasters, Casualties, and Thefts], 1993, p. 1.

[92] Ibid.

[93] Ibid.

[94] Rev. Rul. 79-174, 1979-1 C.B. 99.

[95] *George K. Notter,* 1985 PH T.C. Memo ¶ 85,391, 50 TCM 614. A graphic illustration of the controversy that may arise when determining whether an event is a casualty can be made by comparing the following two cases. In one case the taxpayer was washing dishes. Seeing a glass of water on the windowsill, he quickly dumped the contents down the drain and turned on the garbage disposal, not realizing that his wife's rings were in the glass. Damage to the rings in this case was deemed to be a casualty (*William H. Carpenter,* 1966 PH T.C. Memo ¶ 66,228, 25 TCM 1186). In the second case, the taxpayer gathered up some tissues from the night stand and flushed them down the toilet, not knowing that his wife's rings were wrapped in one of them. This event was held not to be a casualty (*W.J. Keenan, Jr. v. Bowers,* 39 AFTR 849, 50-2 USTC ¶ 9444 (D.C.-S.C., 1950)).

state that ". . . the term "theft" shall be deemed to include, but shall not necessarily be limited to, larceny, embezzlement, and robbery."[96] A determination whether other actions also constitute theft often depends upon whether (1) criminal intent was involved and (2) the action is illegal under the state law where the action has occurred.[97] Thus, the IRS has stated that blackmail, extortion, and kidnapping for ransom may also constitute theft.[98]

Deductible Amount of Casualty Loss

The amount of a casualty loss deduction depends upon the amount of the loss sustained; any insurance or other reimbursement received; and, in the case of personal-use property, the limitations imposed under the tax law.

Measuring the Loss. In general, the amount of loss sustained in a casualty is the amount by which the property's FMV is reduced as a result of the casualty. This is measured by comparing the property's FMV immediately before and immediately after the casualty.[99] Any reduction in the FMV of the taxpayer's surrounding, but undamaged property is disregarded.

Example 8-29 ■

Additional Comment

A loss cannot be deducted unless the damaged property is owned by the taxpayer. Therefore, a taxpayer cannot deduct amounts he paid to another individual for damage he caused to the other individual's property.

Gail purchased a vacation home for $110,000. Shortly after she purchased the property, a mudslide completely destroyed several neighboring cabins. There was no damage to Gail's cabin. After the slide, an appraisal reveals that the FMV of the cabin has declined to $80,000 because of fears that other mudslides might occur. The $30,000 reduction in the FMV of the cabin does not constitute a deductible casualty loss. ■

Actual market value, not sentimental value, is used to compute the reduction in the FMV.[100] Additionally, the cost of protecting property to prevent damage from a casualty is not a deductible loss.

Example 8-30 ■

Assume the same facts as in Example 8-29, except that no mudslide occurs. Instead, lightning starts a forest fire a few miles from Gail's vacation home. To protect her property, Gail spends $3,000 to cut fire breaks around the home. However, the wind shifts and the fire is contained before reaching her property. Gail has not incurred a deductible casualty loss. ■

If the property involved in the casualty is only partially destroyed, the amount of the loss is the lesser of the reduction in the property's FMV or the taxpayer's adjusted basis in the property.[101]

Example 8-31 ■

Typical Misconception

It is sometimes thought that a taxpayer's loss should be based on the total economic loss rather than being restricted to the property's basis. It should be remembered that a taxpayer has not paid a tax on the appreciation in value, and therefore, should not be entitled to a deduction for a loss on the unrealized gain.

Troy purchased a home for $25,000 several years ago. Through the years, the value of the home appreciated until it was appraised at $125,000 in the current year. Shortly after the appraisal, a flood sweeps through the area, severely damaging Troy's home and reducing its value to $90,000. Troy does not have any flood insurance. His loss is limited to the $25,000 basis in the home even though the economic loss is $35,000 ($125,000 − $90,000). ■

[96] Reg. Sec. 1.165-8(d).
[97] Rev. Rul. 72-112, 1972-1 C.B. 60.
[98] IRS, *Publication No. 547* [Nonbusiness Disasters, Casualties, and Thefts], 1993, p. 1.
[99] Reg. Sec. 1.165-7(a)(2).
[100] IRS, *Publication No. 547* [Nonbusiness Disasters, Casualties, and Thefts], 1993, p. 2.
[101] Reg. Sec. 1.165-7(b)(1).

If business or investment property is totally destroyed in a casualty, the amount of the loss is the taxpayer's adjusted basis in the property, even if it is greater than the property's FMV.[102] However, if personal-use property is totally destroyed, the amount of the loss is limited to the lesser of (1) the reduction in the property's FMV, or (2) the property's adjusted basis.

Example 8-32 ■   A machine that Beth uses in her business is completely destoyed by fire. At the time of the fire, the adjusted basis of the machine is $5,000 and its FMV is $3,000. Because the machine is a business property, Beth's loss is $5,000. If instead the machine were a personal-use asset, the amount of the loss would be $3,000. ■

The rules concerning deductibility of losses described above are summarized as follows:

	Deduction Based on Type of Property	
Result of Casualty	*Business or Investment*	*Personal-Use*
Total destruction	Basis of property	Lesser of basis or reduction in FMV
Partial destruction	Lesser of basis or reduction in FMV	Lesser of basis or reduction in FMV

Generally, the reduction in the FMV of the property is established by an appraisal.[103] If an appraisal is difficult or impossible to obtain, the cost of the repairs may be used instead. All of the following requirements must be met before this alternative can be used:

• The repairs will bring the property back to its condition immediately prior to the casualty.

• The cost of the repairs is not excessive.

• The repairs do no more than repair the damage incurred in the casualty.

• The repairs do not increase the value of the property over its value immediately before the casualty.[104]

If more than one property is destroyed in the same casualty, the loss on each property must be calculated separately.[105] Thus, each property's basis is compared with the reduction in the FMV of that property, rather than aggregating the basis and FMV amounts for all the properties destroyed in the casualty.

Example 8-33 ■   During the current tax year, a severe windstorm uproots and destroys several large ornamental trees growing on Andy's residential property. One of the trees topples over onto Andy's car, causing substantial damage. In measuring the amount of the casualty loss, the loss on the car must be calculated separately from the loss due to the destruction of the trees.[106] ■

If the taxpayer receives insurance or any other type of recovery, the amount of the loss must be reduced by these amounts. In some cases these payments may actually

---

[102] Ibid.

[103] Reg. Sec. 1.165-7(a)(2).

[104] Ibid.

[105] Reg. Sec. 1.165-7(b)(2). For personal-use property, losses on real property and improvements to the property are computed in the aggregate. Thus, no separate basis need be apportioned to the improvements. See Reg. Secs. 1.165-7(b)(2)(ii) and 1.165-7(b)(3) Example (3).

[106] Ibid.

exceed the taxpayer's basis in the property, causing the realization of a gain. If certain requirements are met, the recognition of these gains may be deferred or excluded. (See the detailed discussion of involuntary conversions in Chapter 12.)

Limitations on Personal-Use Property

Historical Note

The reduction in the amount of a taxpayer's casualty losses by 10% of AGI became effective in 1983.

The deductibility of casualty losses on personal-use property is subject to two limitations: (1) the losses sustained in each separate casualty are reduced by $100,[107] and (2) the total amount of all net casualty losses for personal-use property is reduced by 10% of the taxpayer's AGI for the year.

Example 8-34 ■

A windstorm blows over a large tree in front of Cathy's house, damaging the house and totally destroying her automobile. After the insurance reimbursement, the loss on the house amounts to $3,000, and the loss on the automobile is $2,500. Since the losses occur in the same casualty, the total amount of the loss is reduced to $5,400 ($3,000 + $2,500 − $100). If the damage to the car was sustained in a separate event such as an automobile accident, the total amount of the casualty losses incurred by Cathy during the year would have been $5,300 ($3,000 + $2,500 − $200). This $5,300 loss is then further reduced by 10% of Cathy's AGI for the year. ■

Example 8-35 ■

As the result of a storm, Liz incurs a $4,500 casualty loss on personal-use property during the current year. She also sustains a $600 theft loss. Liz's AGI for the year is $50,000. She receives no tax deduction for the casualty and theft losses since they do not exceed the following limitations:

Key Point

Many taxpayers will not be able to deduct their casualty losses because of the $100 floor and 10% of AGI limitation.

	Storm	*Theft*	*Total*
Loss before limitations	$4,500	$600	$5,100
Minus: $100 floor	(100)	(100)	(200)
	$4,400	$500	$4,900
Minus: 10% of AGI (0.10 × $50,000)		(5,000)	
Deductible loss		—0—	■

Additional Comment

Sometimes individuals fail to file insurance claims for damage to their personal automobile for fear that their insurance rates will increase, and hoping instead to deduct the loss. Because of this limitation, no deduction is available.

As a result of these limitations, many taxpayers who sustain casualty and theft losses on personal-use property do not receive a tax deduction. Furthermore, if the property is covered by insurance, no deduction is available for a casualty loss of personal-use property unless the taxpayer timely files an insurance claim for the loss.[108] This disallowance relates only to the portion of the loss that was covered by the insurance.

Netting Casualty Gains and Losses on Personal-Use Property

Typical Misconception

The concept of a gain on a casualty is sometimes confusing. Nevertheless, if the insurance proceeds exceed the basis, a gain will result.

Casualty gains and losses incurred during the year on personal-use assets are netted against each other rather than being combined with casualty gains and losses on business and investment property.[109] For purposes of the netting process, the losses

---

[107] Sec. 165(h)(1).

[108] Sec. 165(h)(4)(E).

[109] Casualty gains and losses on business and investment property held one year or less are ordinary gains and losses. If the business or investment property has been held over one year, the gains and losses are included in the Sec. 1231 netting process, which is explained in Chapter 13.

should be reduced by any insurance reimbursements and the $100 limitation, but not the 10% of AGI floor.[110] If the gains exceed the losses for the year, all the gains and losses are treated as capital gains and losses. If the property has been held for one year or less, the gain or loss is short term. If the property has been held for more than one year, the gain or loss is long term.[111]

Example 8-36 ■

During the current year, Pat incurs the following casualty gains and losses on personal-use assets. Assets W and X are destroyed in one casualty, and asset Y is destroyed in another. Assets X and Y were acquired in the current year whereas asset W was acquired several years ago.

Asset	Reduction in FMV	Adjusted Basis	Insurance	Holding Period
W	$10,000	$3,000	$10,000	more than one year
X	4,000	5,000	2,000	less than one year
Y	2,000	3,000	–0–	less than one year

A $7,000 ($10,000 − $3,000) gain is realized on asset W since the insurance proceeds received for the asset exceed its basis. A $2,000 ($4,000 reduction in FMV − $2,000 insurance) loss is realized on asset X. Since an overall gain of $5,000 ($7,000 gain for asset W and $2,000 loss on asset X) is realized as a result of the one casualty, the loss on asset X is not reduced by the $100 limitation. A $2,000 loss is realized on asset Y. Since an overall loss of $2,000 is realized as a result of the second casualty, the $100 limitation is deducted, resulting in a $1,900 loss from that casualty. A $3,100 ($5,000 − $1,900) net gain for the year has been realized. Thus, the gain or loss on each asset is treated as a capital gain or loss. Pat must report a $7,000 long-term capital gain on asset W; a $2,000 short-term capital loss on asset X; and a $1,900 short-term capital loss on asset Y. ■

If the casualty losses on personal-use property exceed the casualty gains for the year, the net loss is further reduced by the 10% of AGI floor. If any loss remains after this reduction, the loss is reported as an itemized deduction on Schedule A of Form 1040.

Example 8-37 ■

Assume the same facts as in Example 8-36, except that the loss on asset X amounts to $12,000 and that Pat's AGI for the year is $50,000. Since a $5,000 ($12,000 loss on asset X − $7,000 gain on asset W) loss is incurred in the first casualty, it must also be reduced by the $100 limitation. For the year, Pat has incurred a total loss of $6,800 ($4,900 + $1,900) due to the destruction by casualty of personal-use property. This loss is further reduced by 10% of AGI, or $5,000 (0.10 × $50,000). Pat's deductible loss for the year is $1,800 ($6,800 − $5,000), which is reported as an itemized deduction. The result would be the same if assets W and X were destroyed in separate casualties. ■

Real World Example

In 1961, taxpayer gave two diamond rings to an acquaintance for safekeeping. In 1965 taxpayer was entitled to a casualty loss deduction after several fruitless attempts to locate the acquaintance and after reporting the matter to the police. Virginia M. Cramer, 55 T.C. 1125 (1971).

When Losses Are Deductible

In general, casualty losses must be deducted in the tax year in which the loss is sustained.[112] In the following instances, however, the casualty loss may be deducted in another year:

[110] Sec. 165(h)(3)(B).
[111] Sec. 165(h)(2)(B).
[112] Reg. Secs. 1.165-1(d)(1) and 1.165-7(a)(1).

- Theft losses
- The receipt of insurance or other reimbursements which are reasonably expected to be received in a subsequent year
- Certain disaster losses (See a subsequent section in this chapter for a discussion of this topic.)

Theft. A theft loss is deducted in the tax year in which the theft is discovered.[113] This rule is equitable and practical because a theft may not be discovered until a subsequent year.

Example 8-38 ■ Dale owns a hunting lodge in upstate New York. Sometime after his last trip to the lodge in November 1994, the lodge is broken into and several guns and paintings are stolen. The loss is discovered when Dale returns to the lodge on May 19, 1995. Dale's insurance does not cover the entire cost of the items. The loss is deductible in 1995, even though the theft may have occurred in 1994. ■

Insurance and Other Reimbursements. Any reimbursement received as compensation for a loss must be subtracted in arriving at the amount of the loss. This is necessary even when the reimbursement has not yet been received, as long as there is a reasonable prospect that it will be received in the future. Thus no deduction is allowed in the year of loss if in that year a reasonable expectation of full recovery exists.[114] If full recovery is not anticipated, a loss may be deducted in the year the casualty occurs for the estimated unrecovered amount.[115] As previously mentioned, no deduction is allowed to the extent the personal-use property is covered by insurance and the taxpayer does not file a timely insurance claim.[116]

Example 8-39 ■ In December of the current year, Andrea suffers a $10,000 casualty loss when her personal automobile is struck by a bus. Although she does not receive any reimbursement from the insurance company by December 31, there is a reasonable expectation that the full amount of the loss will be recovered. Andrea may not deduct a casualty loss in the current year. ■

Example 8-40 ■ Assume the same facts as in Example 8-39, except that Andrea reasonably anticipates that her reimbursement from the insurance company will amount to only $7,000. In this case, she may deduct $3,000 as a casualty loss in the current year. The deduction for this loss is subject to the limitations on personal-use assets. ■

If the full amount of the anticipated recovery is not received in the subsequent year, the unrecovered portion may be deducted. However, rather than filing an amended return for the year of loss, the loss is deducted in the subsequent year.[117] Thus in some cases, the income tax effects for a single casualty loss may be spread over 2 years.

Example 8-41 ■ During the current year, Javier's home is damaged by an exceptionally severe blast at a nearby stone quarry owned by Acme Corporation. Although the amount of the

---

[113] Sec. 165(e).
[114] Reg. Sec. 1.165-1(d)(2)(i).
[115] Ibid.
[116] Sec. 165(h)(4)(E).
[117] Reg. Sec. 1.165-1(d)(2)(ii).

damage is properly appraised at $20,000, Javier can reasonably anticipate a recovery of only $15,000 from Acme Corporation at the end of the current year. He does not receive any recovery from Acme during the current year. Unfortunately, in the subsequent year Acme Corporation is declared bankrupt, and Javier does not receive any reimbursement. Javier's AGI is $40,000 in the current year and $45,000 in the subsequent year. During the current year, Javier may deduct $900 ($5,000 loss reasonably anticipated in the current year − ($100 limitation + [0.10 × $40,000])). In the subsequent year, Javier may deduct an additional casualty loss of $10,500 ($15,000 additional loss − [0.10 × $45,000]). ■

If a subsequent recovery is received for a loss that is previously deducted, the reimbursement is included in income in the year of recovery. An amended return is not filed.[118] However, the amount that the taxpayer must include in income is limited to the amount of tax benefit the taxpayer received for the previous deduction.[119]

Example 8-42 ■ | During the current year, Becky's automobile sustains $5,000 in damages when it is struck by another automobile. The driver of the other automobile is at fault and is uninsured, and there is no reasonable prospect that Becky will recover any of the loss. Becky's AGI for the current year is $35,000. Becky deducts $1,400 ($5,000 loss − [$100 + $3,500]). During the subsequent year, the other driver reimburses Becky for the full amount of the damage. Since Becky received a tax benefit of only $1,400 for the loss in the year of the accident, only $1,400 must be included in gross income in the subsequent year, even though she receives a $5,000 reimbursement. Becky does not file an amended return for the year of the accident. ■

Real World Example
Losses due to Hurricane Andrew in portions of southern Florida on August 24, 1992 and portions of Louisiana on August 26, 1992, qualified as disaster losses.

Disaster Losses. Under certain circumstances, a taxpayer may elect to deduct a casualty loss in the year preceding the year in which the loss actually occurs. This election is available to taxpayers who suffer losses attributable to a disaster that occurs in an area subsequently declared by the President of the United States as a disaster area.[120] Thus, an individual can elect to deduct a disaster loss occurring in 1994 on his 1993 tax return or report it in the regular way on his 1994 return. An amended return (Form 1040X) must be filed unless the prior year's return has not been filed when the disaster occurs.

Casualty loss deduction rules are summarized in Topic Review 8-3.

BAD DEBTS

OBJECTIVE 7
Compute the deduction for a bad debt

In addition to losses on property, taxpayers may also sustain losses because of uncollectible debts. In dealing with a deduction for **bad debts,** taxpayers must address the following requirements and issues:

---

[118] Reg. Sec. 1.165-1(d)(2)(iii).
[119] Sec. 111.
[120] Sec. 165(i). Additionally, the same treatment may apply under Sec. 165 to taxpayers who live in a disaster area and who are ordered by a state or local government to move from or relocate their residence because the disaster caused the residence to be unsafe. In order to qualify for this treatment, the order to move must come from the state or local government within 120 days of the date that the President determines the area to be a disaster area. If the property destroyed in a Presidentially declared disaster area is the taxpayer's principal residence and the casualty results in a gain, a portion of the gain may be excluded if certain conditions are met (see Chapter 12).

TOPIC REVIEW 8-3

Casualty Losses	
Type of Property	Limitation and Treatment
Personal-use	1. The amount of the loss is the lesser of (a) the property's adjusted basis or (b) the reduction of the asset's FMV. This amount is reduced by any insurance reimbursement. If the insurance reimbursement exceeds the property's basis, a gain is realized. To the extent the property is insured, a claim must be filed or the loss is disallowed.
	2. The amount of loss incurred in each separate casualty event during the year is reduced by $100.
	3. All casualty gains and losses for the year are netted. If the gains exceed the losses, all gains and losses are treated as either long-term or short-term capital gains and losses, depending upon the holding period of the asset. If the losses exceed the gains, the net loss is reduced by 10% of AGI. Any remaining loss is an itemized deduction.
Business or investment	1. If the property is totally destroyed, the amount of the loss is the adjusted basis of the property. If only partially destroyed, the amount of the loss is the lesser of (a) the property's adjusted basis or (b) the reduction of the asset's FMV. This amount is reduced by any insurance reimbursement. A gain is realized if the insurance reimbursement exceeds the property's basis.
	2. For property held one year or less, the losses and gains are ordinary losses and gains. For property held over one year, the casualty gains and losses for the year are netted. The treatment depends upon the total of the taxpayer's other Sec. 1231 transactions (see Chapter 13).

Key Point

The tax provisions that deal with deductions for losses and the tax provisions that deal with the deductions for bad debts are mutually exclusive, and an amount properly deductible as a loss cannot be deducted as a bad debt or visa versa.

- A bona fide debtor-creditor relationship must exist between the taxpayer and some other person or entity.

- The taxpayer must have basis in the debt.

- The debt must actually have become worthless during the year.

- The type and timing of a bad debt deduction depend upon whether the debt is a business or nonbusiness bad debt.

- Generally, only the specific write-off method of accounting may be used in deducting the bad debt.

- A partial or complete recovery of a debt that was previously deducted may occur. In many cases a recovery of this type causes income recognition in the year of the recovery.

Bona Fide Debtor-Creditor Relationship

Only items constituting bona fide debt are eligible to be deducted as a bad debt. A **bona fide debt** is one that (1) arises from a valid and enforceable obligation to pay a fixed or determinable sum of money, and (2) results in a debtor-creditor relationship.[121]

Key Point

The fact that the debtor is a related party does not preclude deduction of a bad debt, but the taxpayer should be able to document the debt as being bona fide.

Related Party Transactions. Determining whether a bona fide loan transaction has actually taken place is especially critical when the transaction is between the taxpayer and a family member or other related party (e.g., a controlled corporation). All the facts and circumstances surrounding the transaction must be carefully examined, since a gift does not constitute a debt.[122] The taxpayer's intent is critical here. For example, if the taxpayer's intent is to provide property, cash, or services to someone else without receiving any consideration in return, a gift—not a loan—has been made. Some tests used to determine the taxpayer's intent include the following:

- Is there a note or other written instrument evidencing the obligation to repay?[123]
- Has a definite schedule of repayment been established?
- Is a reasonable rate of interest stated?
- Would a person who is unrelated to the debtor make the loan?[124]

Example 8-43 ■

During the current year Maria loaned $20,000 to her son Sam who used the money in his business. Although no written note or contract was signed, Sam orally promised to repay Maria as soon as his business became profitable. No rate of interest was stated. Unfortunately, the business failed and Sam went out of business in the subsequent year. No repayment of the loan principal or interest was ever made.

In this case, no valid debt exists, since neither an interest rate nor a repayment schedule was established. An unrelated person would not have made a loan to Sam under these conditions. In addition, Maria does not receive any consideration in return for the "loan." Since the facts indicate that the transaction is actually a gift, Maria may not claim a bad debt deduction because of Sam's failure to repay. ■

Real World Example

Taxpayer advanced $8,500 to his son-in-law who operated a livestock auction barn. Taxpayer was entitled to a bad debt deduction upon default since notations on the checks indicated that they were loans and undisputed testimony indicated that repayment was to be made within 90 days. Giffin A. Andrew, 54 T.C. 239 (1970).

Other related party transactions must also be closely examined. For example, a loan from a shareholder to a controlled corporation may actually be an additional

---

[121] Reg. Sec. 1.166-1(c).

[122] Ibid.

[123] A written note or other instrument is an evidence of a bona fide debtor-creditor relationship. However, if the note or other instrument is registered or has interest coupons and is issued by a corporation or a government, the bad debt provisions of Sec. 166 do not apply. Instead, the worthless security provisions of Sec. 165 (previously discussed) apply.

[124] *Jean C. Tyler v. Tomlinson*, 24 AFTR 2d 69-5426, 69-2 USTC ¶ 9559 (5th Cir., 1969). See also, *C. L. Hunt*, 1989 PH T.C. Memo ¶ 89,335, 57 TCM 919, where certain loans that the taxpayer made to his children were treated as bona fide loans, whereas others were treated as gifts. In that case, the children had been trading in silver futures and were required to make margin calls. Because they could not make the calls, the children's positions were involuntarily liquidated. Up to the date of the liquidation, the taxpayer had made loans to the children that were payable on demand and were subject to the prime rate of interest. These loans were evidenced by promissory notes. After the liquidation, the taxpayer continued to make loans to the children. However, these loans were not evidenced by notes. The loans up to the time of the liquidation were treated as bona fide loans while the subsequent loans were treated as gifts.

contribution to capital disguised as a loan.[125] Thus, a transfer of cash by a shareholder who owns a controlling (i.e., more than 50%) interest in the stock of a corporation may indicate a capital contribution rather than a loan. Likewise, a loan from a corporation to a controlling shareholder may actually be a disguised dividend or a salary payment.

Third Party Debt. Generally, a taxpayer may deduct a bad debt only when a debtor-creditor relationship exists. However, in some cases a taxpayer will guarantee or endorse someone else's obligation. If the taxpayer is forced to pay the third party's debt under the terms of the guarantee, the guarantor may actually be treated as the creditor. If the original debtor does not repay the taxpayer who guarantees and pays the debt, the guarantor may deduct the loss.[126] Any accrued interest that the guarantor pays may also be deductible as a bad debt. However, the interest is not deductible as interest when paid by the guarantor because it accrued on someone else's debt. Here, too, the taxpayer's intent must be examined to determine whether the guarantee and payment constitute a gift.

Example 8-44 ■   Ron is the sole shareholder and a full-time employee of Zip Corporation. In order for Zip Corporation to obtain a bank loan, Ron personally signs a guarantee that the loan would be repaid. Unfortunately, Zip Corporation defaults on the loan, and Ron is required to repay the loan. In this case, Ron signed the guarantee to preserve his job and enhance his investment in Zip Corporation. Although Ron receives no direct consideration for having signed the note, he does receive indirect consideration in the form of continued job security and protection of his investment. Since the loan guarantee was motivated by a business or investment purpose, Ron may deduct the bad debt.   ■

Example 8-45 ■   To help her son purchase a new automobile, Julie cosigns the note. She does not expect repayment if her son defaults on the note. After her son defaults on the loan payments, Julie is forced to pay the debt. Since Julie's signing of the note is not motivated by business or investment purposes (i.e., a gift has been made), she cannot deduct the payment as a bad debt.   ■

Typical Misconception

It is sometimes mistakenly assumed that a cash method taxpayer can take a bad debt deduction on a debt that arose from services rendered by the taxpayer.

Taxpayer's Basis in the Debt

For a bad debt to be deductible, the creditor must have a basis in the debt. This basis may be acquired in different ways. If a taxpayer loans money, the taxpayer's basis in the debt is the amount loaned. If the debt arises because the taxpayer provides property or services for the other party, basis is established only if the taxpayer has previously included the FMV of the property or services in income. This often depends upon the taxpayer's method of accounting. An accrual method taxpayer generally reports income in the year the services are performed or the property is provided. (See the discussion in Chapter 11.) Thus, an accrual-method taxpayer has a basis in either a note receivable or an open account receivable equal to the amount included in gross income (i.e., the FMV of the services). A cash-method taxpayer, however, reports income only in the year in which payment in the form of cash or property is received. Since a note constitutes the receipt of property, a cash-basis taxpayer reports income in the year the note is received, and therefore has a basis in

---

[125] Reg. Sec. 1.166-1(c).

[126] *Max Putman v. CIR*, 50 AFTR 502, 57-1 USTC ¶ 9200 (USSC, 1956). See also Rev. Rul. 72-505, 1972-2 C.B. 102.

the note receivable.[127] However, if no note is received and the receivable is an open account item, a cash method taxpayer reports no income until the receivable is collected. Thus, no basis is established in the receivable, and if it cannot be collected, no bad debt deduction is available.[128]

Example 8-46 ■

In October of the current year, Jim performs some legal services for Joy. Jim bills Joy for $1,000. Joy does not sign a note for the debt. As a cash-method taxpayer, Jim does not include the $1,000 in his current year's income. After repeated efforts to collect the fee, Jim discovers in June of the subsequent year that Joy has left the city and cannot be found. Thus, Jim may not deduct a bad debt for the uncollected amount in the subsequent year. If Joy had signed a note for the debt, Jim would have reported income in the current year in an amount equal to the note's FMV and could have deducted the loss when the note became uncollectible in the subsequent year. ■

Example 8-47 ■

Assume the same facts as in Example 8-46, except that Jim is an accrual-method taxpayer. Here, Jim would have reported the income in the current year and would have a bad debt deduction in the subsequent year. ■

Additional Comment

A debt may be considered worthless before it is due.

Debt Must Be Worthless

To deduct a bad debt, the taxpayer must show that the debt is worthless. This determination is made by reference to all the pertinent evidence, including the general financial condition of the debtor and whether the debt is secured by collateral.

In proving the worthlessness of a debt, a taxpayer does not need to take legal action if the surrounding circumstances indicate that legal action probably would not result in the collection of the debt. Simply showing that legal action is not warranted is sufficient proof that the debt is worthless.[129] Indications that an unsecured debt is worthless include (1) bankruptcy of the debtor,[130] (2) disappearance or death of a debtor, and (3) repeated unsuccessful attempts at collection. Furthermore, if the surrounding circumstances warrant it, a debt may be deducted as worthless even before it comes due.[131] As will be explained later in this chapter, a nonbusiness debt must be totally worthless before a deduction is allowed. However, a current deduction is allowed for a partially worthless business bad debt.

Nonbusiness Bad Debts

Key Point

It is important to make a distinction between business and nonbusiness bad debts since the tax treatment varies according to the type of debt.

The distinction between a business bad debt and a nonbusiness bad debt is important because the character of the debt determines its tax treatment. A business bad debt gives rise to an ordinary deduction, whereas a nonbusiness bad debt is treated as a short-term capital loss. All loans made by a corporation are assumed to be associated with the corporation's business; therefore, the provisions for nonbusiness bad debts do not apply to corporations.

---

[127] Reg. Sec. 1.166-1(e).
[128] For example, the IRS has held that a taxpayer may not claim a bad debt deduction for unpaid child support because there was no basis in the debt. See Rev. Rul. 93-27, I.R.B. 1993-15, 4.
[129] Reg. Sec. 1.166-2(b).
[130] Reg. Sec. 1.166-2(c).
[131] Reg. Sec. 1.166-1(c).

Definition of a Nonbusiness Bad Debt. A *nonbusiness debt* is defined as any debt other than (1) a debt created or acquired in connection with a trade or business of the taxpayer; or (2) a debt the loss from the worthlessness of which is incurred in the taxpayer's trade or business.[132] This determination depends upon an examination of the facts and circumstances surrounding the debt in question.[133]

A debt incurred in a taxpayer's business continues to be a business debt for that taxpayer even though at the time the debt goes bad the taxpayer has ceased conducting that particular business. This is situation (1) above. If another taxpayer acquires a business, any outstanding debt at the time the business is acquired continues to be business debt as long as the purchaser continues the business. This is situation (2) above. The debt is a nonbusiness debt if the person who owns the debt when it becomes worthless is not engaged in the business in which the debt is incurred either at the time the debt arose or when it becomes worthless.

Example 8-48 ■	Matt, an individual who uses the accrual method of accounting, is engaged in the grocery business. During 1994, he extends credit to Jeff on an open account. In 1995 Matt sells his business to Joan, but retains Jeff's account. Jeff's account becomes worthless in 1995. Even though Matt is no longer engaged in the grocery business at the time the debt becomes worthless, he may deduct the loss as a business bad debt in 1995.[134] ■

Example 8-49 ■	Assume the same facts as in Example 8-48, except that Joan purchases Jeff's account upon acquiring the business. Joan is entitled to a business bad debt deduction in 1995, because the debt was incurred in the trade or business in which Joan is currently engaged. ■

Example 8-50 ■	Assume the same facts as in Example 8-48, except that Matt transfers Jeff's account to Fred, his son, who is not engaged in any trade or business. When the debt becomes worthless in 1995, Fred can only deduct a nonbusiness bad debt, since the debt was not incurred in either Fred's business or a business Fred owns at the time the debt becomes worthless. ■

Typical Misconception

Assume that a taxpayer lends money to a friend to be used in the friend's business. If the friend does not repay the loan, the debt is a nonbusiness bad debt unless the taxpayer is in the business of lending money. This type of debt is occasionally improperly classified as a business debt.

Ethical Point

A tax practitioner should serve as an advocate for his client. Thus, a tax practitioner may resolve doubt in favor of the client as long as there is reasonable support for his position.

In addition, classification as a business debt requires a proximate relationship between the debt and the taxpayer's business.[135] According to the Supreme Court, this relationship exists if a business motive is the taxpayer's dominant motivation in incurring the debt. This determination must be made on a case by case basis.[136] For example, when an individual stockholder who is also an employee of the corporation loans money to the corporation, is the loan a business or nonbusiness debt? Since an employee is considered to be engaged in the business of working for a corporation, a loan made to the corporation in an attempt to protect the employment relationship may be held to be a business debt.[137] However, if the individual's dominant motive is to protect his or her stock investment, the loan is a nonbusiness debt.[138]

---

[132] Sec. 166(d)(2).
[133] Ibid.
[134] Reg. Sec. 1.166-5(d).
[135] Reg. Sec. 1.166-5(b)(2).
[136] *U.S. v. Edna Generes*, 29 AFTR 2d 72-609, 72-1 USTC ¶ 9259 (USSC, 1972).
[137] *John M. Trent v. CIR*, 7 AFTR 2d 1599, 61-2 USTC ¶ 9506 (2nd Cir., 1961). See also *Charles L. Hutchinson*, 1982 PH T.C. Memo ¶ 82,045, 43 TCM 440.
[138] *U.S. v. Edna Generes*, 29 AFTR 2d 72-609, 72-1 USTC ¶ 9259 (USSC, 1972).

Example 8-51 ■ Lisa is an individual engaged in the advertising business. If clients occasionally need additional funds to meet their cash-flow obligations, Lisa sometimes lends them money. Lisa's dominant motive for making the loans is to retain the clients. She has no ownership interests in these clients. Under these facts, if any of these loans becomes worthless, it would be considered a business bad debt.[139] ■

Example 8-52 ■ Paul, an individual, is engaged in the advertising business. Paul also has a substantial investment in a company that is his largest client. During the year, a loan that Paul made to this client becomes worthless. The issue is litigated and the court determines that because Paul's motivation in making the loan is to protect his investment in the client rather than to further his advertising business, the debt is considered to be a nonbusiness bad debt.[140] ■

Key Point

The nonbusiness bad debt of an individual is treated as a short-term capital loss regardless of how long the debt was outstanding.

Tax Treatment. Nonbusiness debts that become wholly worthless during the year are deductible by individuals as short-term capital losses.[141] The length of time the debt is outstanding has no bearing upon this treatment.

For individuals, an ordinary deduction is generally preferable to a short-term capital loss because the tax deduction attributable to net capital losses is limited to $3,000 each year. Any loss in excess of this limit is carried over to subsequent years to be included in the capital gain and loss netting process in those years (see Chapter 5).

Example 8-53 ■ During 1993, Kim loaned her friend $10,000. The friend used the funds to invest in commodities futures. The transaction had all the characteristics of a bona fide debt rather than a mere gift to a friend. Unfortunately, the commodities market prices declined, and Kim's friend incurred substantial losses. In 1994, Kim's friend declared personal bankruptcy, and Kim was unable to collect any of the loan. Kim did not recognize any other capital gains or losses during 1994. The $10,000 bad debt loss recognized in 1994 is treated as a short-term capital loss. Thus, Kim may deduct only $3,000 in 1994. The remaining $7,000 is carried over indefinitely to 1995 and subsequent years. ■

Example 8-54 ■ Assume the same facts as in Example 8-53, except that Kim also recognizes an $8,000 long-term capital gain on the sale of stock during 1994. After offsetting the net long-term gain with the short-term loss, the result is a $2,000 net short-term loss. Kim may deduct the remaining $2,000 of the nonbusiness bad debt in 1994 as a short-term capital loss. ■

Partial Worthlessness. As previously noted, no deduction is allowed for a partially worthless nonbusiness debt.[142] Thus, no deduction is allowed for a nonbusiness debt that is still partially recoverable during the year.[143]

Example 8-55 ■

Typical Misconception

"Partial worthlessness" means that a debt is still partially recoverable. The term is sometimes erroneously applied to debt where there has been a partial recovery even though there is no prospect for further recovery.

Gordon, an individual, made a $5,000, 5-year interest-bearing loan to a small company in 1990. Gordon was not in the trade or business of making commercial loans. In 1994, Gordon received word from the attorney who was appointed trustee of the company that bankruptcy proceedings have been filed. The trustee indicated that although final disposition of the case will not occur until 1995, Gordon can reasonably expect to receive only 20 cents for every $1 invested. Since this is a

---

[139] *Stuart Bart,* 21 T.C. 880 (1954), *acq.* 1954-1 C.B. 3.
[140] *Rodney B. Burton v. CIR,* 39 AFTR 2d 77-946, 77-1 USTC ¶ 9273 (6th Cir., 1977).
[141] Sec. 166(d)(1).
[142] Reg. Sec. 1.166-5(a)(2).
[143] Ibid.

nonbusiness bad debt that is still partly recoverable in 1994, Gordon may not deduct the partial loss as a short-term capital loss in 1994. ■

Example 8-56 ■   Assume the same facts as in Example 8-55, except that in 1995 Gordon receives $500 in final settlement of the loan. The remaining $4,500 is now totally worthless, and he may deduct this amount as a short-term capital loss in 1995. ■

Business Bad Debts

The tax treatment of losses from business bad debts differs substantially from the treatment of nonbusiness bad debts. As previously discussed, a business bad debt is deductible as an ordinary loss. Furthermore, a deduction may also be taken for a business debt that has become only partially worthless during the year.

Example 8-57 ■   Assume the same facts as in Examples 8-55 and 8-56, except that Gordon's loan is made for business reasons (e.g., to provide assistance to a customer in financial difficulty). Since during 1994, 80% of the loan is reasonably expected to be unrecoverable, Gordon may deduct $4,000 (0.80 × $5,000) as an ordinary loss in 1994. In 1995, when Gordon receives the $500 settlement, he may deduct an additional $500 of ordinary loss. ■

Accounting for the Business Bad Debt

Prior to 1987, two basic methods of accounting were available to account for business bad debts: (1) the specific write-off method and (2) the reserve method.[144] Except for certain specialized industries, however, only the specific write-off method may be used for tax years beginning after 1986.

Key Point

In general, only the specific write-off method of accounting for bad debts can now be used. However, a corporation or other taxpayer would likely be required to use the reserve method for financial reporting purposes.

Specific Write-Off Method. Under the **specific write-off method,** the taxpayer deducts each bad debt individually as it becomes worthless. This method is used for (1) business bad debts that are either totally or partially worthless and (2) nonbusiness bad debts that are totally worthless. However, as previously noted, no deduction is available for partially worthless nonbusiness bad debts.

In the case of a partially worthless business bad debt, only the worthless part of the debt is deductible. The taxpayer must prove to the satisfaction of the IRS the amount of the debt that has become worthless.[145]

Reserve Method. For years when the **reserve method** was available, the bad debt deduction was equal to the amount that was added to the bad debt reserve account at the end of the tax year.[146] Because the reserve method can no longer be used after 1986, the balance in the reserve account was required to be taken into income. This occurred ratably over a 4-year period starting in the first tax year that began after December 31, 1986.[147]

Recovery of Bad Debts

A taxpayer may collect a debt that was previously written off for tax purposes. As noted previously, the taxpayer must report the recovery as income in the year it is

---

[144] Reg. Sec. 1.166-1(a). This regulation does not reflect the changes enacted in the Tax Reform Act of 1986.

[145] Reg. Sec. 1.166-3(a)(2).

[146] Reg. Sec. 1.166-4(a).

[147] H. Rept. No. 99-841, 99th Cong., 2d Sess., p. II-315 (1986).

collected. The amount of the income that must be reported may depend upon the tax benefit rule discussed in Chapter 4.

Deposits in Insolvent Financial Institutions

Key Point

If the loss is treated as a casualty loss, it is subject to a $100 floor, and total net casualty losses for the year are deductible only to the extent that they exceed 10% of AGI.

At their election, qualified individuals may treat losses on deposits in qualified bankrupt or insolvent financial institutions as a personal casualty loss in the year in which the loss can be reasonably estimated. The recognized loss is the difference between the taxpayer's basis in the deposit and a reasonable estimate of the amount that will be received. This treatment allows the individual an ordinary loss deduction, but subjects the loss to the personal casualty loss limitations. In lieu of this election, qualified individuals may elect to treat these losses as if they were incurred in a transaction entered into for profit (but not connected with a trade or business). This election is available only with respect to deposits that are not insured under federal law, and is limited to $20,000 ($10,000 if married and filing separately) per institution per year. This limitation is reduced by any insurance proceeds expected to be received under state law.[148] This election also allows the individual an ordinary loss deduction but subjects the loss to the $20,000 limitation as well as the 2% of AGI floor on miscellaneous itemized deductions. If neither of these elections is made, the loss may be claimed as a nonbusiness bad debt (a capital loss) in the year of worthlessness or partial recovery, whichever comes last.

A qualified individual is any individual *except* one who

- Owns at least 1% of the outstanding stock of the financial institution
- Is an officer of the financial institution
- Is a relative of an officer or a 1% owner of the financial institution[149]

Qualified financial institutions include banks, federal or state chartered savings and loans and thrift institutions, and federal or state insured credit unions.

This election applies to all losses sustained by the individual in the same institution and cannot be revoked unless the taxpayer receives IRS permission.[150]

The treatment of business and nonbusiness bad debts is summarized in Topic Review 8-4.

NET OPERATING LOSSES

OBJECTIVE 8
Compute a net operating loss deduction

Key Point

If taxpayers were not entitled to a deduction for net operating losses, taxpayers would actually pay a tax on an amount that exceeded their economic income over a period of time. The NOL deduction permits taxpayers to offset taxable income with losses incurred in other years.

A **net operating loss (NOL)** under Sec. 172 generally involves only business income and expenses and occurs when taxable income for any year is negative because business expenses exceed business income. A deduction for this loss arises when the loss is carried to a year in which the taxpayer has taxable income and is deducted from that year's income. This is accomplished in one of two ways:

- The year's NOL is carried back and deducted from the income of a previous year. This procedure provides for a refund of some of the taxes previously paid for the prior year.
- The year's NOL is carried forward and deducted from the income of a subsequent year. This procedure provides a reduction in the taxable income of the subsequent year, thus reducing the tax liability associated with that year.

---

[148] Sec. 165(l).

[149] Sec. 165(l)(2). A *relative* is defined as a sibling, spouse, aunt, uncle, nephew, niece, ancestor, or lineal descendant.

[150] The rules dealing with this special election are found in Notice 89-28, (1989-1 C.B. 667).

TOPIC REVIEW 8-4

Bad Debts	
Type of Debt	Results
Nonbusiness	1. Deductible as a short-term capital loss.
	2. Only deductible when the debt is totally worthless.
	3. The taxpayer must have basis in the debt.
Business	1. Deductible as an ordinary loss.
	2. Except for certain specialized exceptions, the specific write-off method must be used. The reserve method is not available.
	3. May deduct partial worthlessness.
	4. Must have basis in the debt.

The NOL deduction is intended to mitigate the inequity caused by the progressive rate structure and the requirement to report income on an annual basis. This inequity arises between taxpayers whose business income fluctuates widely from year to year and those whose business income remains relatively constant.

Example 8-58 ■   Julie and Ken are both married and both file a joint return with their respective spouses. Over a two year period they both report a total of $140,000 in taxable income. However, Julie reports $70,000 of taxable income each year, while Ken reports $200,000 of taxable income in the first year and a $60,000 loss in the second year. Without the NOL provisions, Julie would report a $29,320 total tax liability for both years, whereas Ken would report a $57,305 total liability.[151]   ■

Computing the Net Operating Loss

The starting point in calculating an individual's NOL is generally taxable income. As mentioned earlier in this chapter, individuals may deduct three basic types of expenses to arrive at the amount of taxable income: (1) business-related expenses, (2) investment-related expenses, and (3) certain personal expenses. The NOL, however, generally attempts to measure only the economic loss that occurs when business expenses exceed business income. Thus, several adjustments must be made to taxable income to arrive at the amount of the NOL for any particular year.[152] These include adjustments for (1) an NOL deduction, (2) a capital loss deduction, (3) the deduction for personal exemptions, and (4) the excess of nonbusiness deductions over nonbusiness income.

Add Back Any NOL Deduction. Under certain circumstances, a deduction for an NOL arising from another tax year might have been taken in computing

---

[151] Using the 1994 tax rate schedules.
[152] In the case of a corporation, these adjustments are minor.

Additional Comment

If taxpayers were permitted to calculate the NOL for the current year by including NOL carryovers from earlier years, it would be possible to extend the carryover period beyond 15 years.

the taxable income for the current loss year. To allow this deduction to create or increase the NOL of the current loss year would provide an unwarranted benefit. Thus, taxable income for the current loss year must be increased for this deduction.[153]

Add Back Any Capital Loss Deduction. To compute taxable income, individuals may deduct up to a maximum of $3,000 capital losses in excess of capital gains in any year. Any capital loss in excess of this limit can be carried over and deducted in a subsequent tax year, subject to the same limitation. Since capital losses have their separate carryover provisions, any deduction associated with these losses must be added back to taxable income to arrive at the NOL for the current loss year. To make this adjustment, several steps must be followed:

STEP 1: A taxpayer must separate nonbusiness capital gains and losses from business capital gains and losses. The nonbusiness gains and losses are then netted, while the business gains and losses are netted separately.[154]

STEP 2: If the nonbusiness capital gains exceed the nonbusiness capital losses, the excess, along with other types of nonbusiness income, is first used to offset any nonbusiness ordinary deductions.[155] Any nonbusiness capital gain remaining is then used to offset any business capital loss in excess of the business capital gain for the year.[156]

STEP 3: If both groups of transactions result in net losses, the capital loss deduction provided by these transactions must be added back. For purposes of the NOL, no deduction is allowed for either business or nonbusiness net capital losses.[157]

STEP 4: If the taxpayer's nonbusiness capital losses exceed the nonbusiness capital gains, the losses may not be offset against the taxpayer's excess business capital gains. Allowing this offset would provide an indirect deduction for a nonbusiness economic loss.[158]

Example 8-59 ■   During the current year, Nils recognizes a short-term capital loss of $10,000 on the sale of an investment capital asset. He also recognizes a $5,000 long-term capital gain on the sale of a business capital asset. For taxable income purposes, the loss is netted against the gain, leaving a $5,000 net short-term capital loss. This loss provides a $3,000 deduction from taxable income, with the remaining $2,000 being carried forward to the following year. To compute the NOL, however, none of the $10,000 nonbusiness capital loss is deductible. Thus,

[153] Sec. 172(d)(1).
[154] Reg. Sec. 1.172-3(c).
[155] If the nonbusiness deductions exceed the nonbusiness income, the excess is added back. This adjustment is discussed later in the chapter.
[156] Reg. Sec. 1.172-3(c).
[157] Reg. Sec. 1.172-3(a)(2).
[158] Sec. 172(d)(2). Note that all deductible nonbusiness capital losses involve investment property, since capital losses on personal-use assets are not deductible in arriving at taxable income. To make the adjustment for any capital loss, the exclusion under Sec. 1202 for gains from small business stock is not allowed (see Chapter 5).

the $3,000 deduction, as well as the $5,000 loss which offset the business capital gain, must be added back. ■

Add Back the Deduction for Personal Exemptions. Since the deduction for personal and dependency exemptions is strictly a personal deduction, it must be added back to arrive at the year's NOL.[159]

Additional Comment

An excess of nonbusiness deductions over nonbusiness income cannot increase the NOL. However, an excess of nonbusiness income over nonbusiness expenses can reduce the NOL.

Add Back Excess of Nonbusiness Deductions over Nonbusiness Income. Since nonbusiness deductions do not reflect an economic loss from business, they are not deductible in arriving at the NOL. However, these deductions do offset any nonbusiness income reported during the year. Nonbusiness income includes sources of income such as dividends and interest, as well as nonbusiness capital gains in excess of nonbusiness capital losses.[160] Wages and salary, even if they are earned in part-time employment, are considered to be business income. Nonbusiness deductions include itemized deductions such as charitable contributions, medical expenses, and nonbusiness interest and taxes. Casualty losses on personal-use assets, however, are treated as business losses and are excluded from this adjustment.[161] If a taxpayer does not have itemized deductions in excess of the standard deduction, the standard deduction is used as the amount of the nonbusiness deductions.

Following are several examples demonstrating these required adjustments. In each case, assume that Nancy is a single taxpayer.

Example 8-60 ■

During 1994 Nancy, who is single, reports the following taxable income:

Gross income from business		$123,000	
Minus:	Business expenses	(147,000)	($24,000)
Plus:	Interest income		700
	Dividend income		400
AGI			($22,900)
Minus:	Greater of itemized deductions or standard deduction:		
	Interest expense	$2,000	
	Taxes	2,500	
	Casualty loss (reduced by the $100 floor)	1,000	
	Total itemized deductions	$5,500	
		or	
	Standard deduction	3,800	(5,500)
Minus:	Personal exemption		(2,450)
Taxable income			($30,850)

Nancy's NOL for the year is computed as follows:

Taxable income	($30,850)

---

[159] Sec. 172(d)(3).
[160] Reg. Sec. 1.172-3(c).
[161] Sec. 172(d)(4)(C).

Nonbusiness deductions:			
Itemized deductions		$5,500	
Minus: Casualty loss		(1,000)	$4,500
Minus: Nonbusiness income:			
Interest	$700		
Dividends	400	(1,100)	
Plus: Excess of nonbusiness deductions over nonbusiness income			3,400
Plus: Personal exemption			2,450
Net operating loss			($25,000)[a]

[a]Note that the NOL equals the total of the $24,000 net business loss and the $1,000 casualty loss.

Example 8-61 ■ During 1994 Nancy, who is single, reports the following taxable income:

Gross income from business		$123,000	
Minus: Business expenses		(147,000)	($24,000)
Plus: Interest income			700
Dividend income			400
AGI			($22,900)
Minus: Greater of itemized deductions or standard deduction:			
Interest expense		$ 2,000	
		or	
Standard deduction		3,800	(3,800)
Minus: Personal exemption			(2,450)
Taxable income			($29,150)

Nancy's NOL for the year is computed as follows:

Taxable income			($29,150)
Nonbusiness deductions:			
Standard deduction		$3,800	
Minus: Nonbusiness income:			
Interest	$700		
Dividends	400	(1,100)	
Plus: Excess of nonbusiness deductions over nonbusiness income			2,700
Plus: Personal exemption			2,450
Net operating loss			($24,000)[a]

[a]Note that the NOL equals the net business loss for the year.

Example 8-62 ■ During 1994 Nancy, who is single, reports the following taxable income:

Gross income from business		$123,000	
Minus: Business expenses		(147,000)	($24,000)
Plus: Interest income			700
Dividend income			400
Salary			6,000
Nonbusiness LTCG			4,000
AGI			($12,900)

Minus:	Greater of itemized deductions or standard deduction:			
	Interest expense	$ 2,000		
	Taxes	2,500		
	Casualty (reduced by the $100 floor)	1,000		
	Total itemized deductions	$5,500		
		or		
	Standard deduction	3,800	(5,500)	
Minus:	Personal exemption		(2,450)	
Taxable income			($20,850)	

Nancy's NOL for the year is computed as follows:

Taxable income			($20,850)
Plus:	Nonbusiness deductions:		
	Itemized deductions	$5,500	
	Reduced by: Casualty loss	(1,000)	$4,500
Minus:	Nonbusiness income:		
	Interest	$700	
	Dividends	400	
	LTCG	4,000	(5,100)
Excess of nonbusiness deductions over non-business income			—0—
Plus:	Personal exemption		2,450
Net operating loss			($18,400)[a] ∎

[a]Note that the NOL can also be calculated as follows:

Loss from business	($24,000)
Salary	6,000
Casualty loss	(1,000)
Excess of nonbusiness income ($5,100) over nonbusiness deductions ($4,500)	600
NOL	($18,400)

Carryback and Carryover Periods

Historical Note

The carryover period for an NOL was extended from 5 years to 7 years in 1976 and from 7 years to 15 years in 1981.

Under Sec. 172, an NOL is initially carried back for 3 years and is deductible as an offset to the taxable income of the carryback years. Except as noted below, the loss must be carried back first. If any loss remains, it may then be carried forward for a period of 15 years. Furthermore, in both the carryback and carryforward periods, the loss must be deducted from the years in chronological order. Thus, if an NOL is sustained in 1994, it first must be carried to 1991; then to 1992; followed by 1993, 1995, and so on until the loss is completely used. Any NOL that is not used during the carryover period expires and is of no further tax benefit.

If the NOL is carried back to a prior year, the taxpayer must file for a refund of taxes previously paid. If the NOL deduction is carried forward, it reduces the taxable income for the carryover year.

Election to Forgo Carryback Period. A taxpayer may elect not to carryback the NOL and to carry the loss forward.[162] This election, which is made with respect to the

---

[162] Sec. 172(b)(3)(C).

Additional Comment

An election to forgo the carryback period for the NOL is irrevocable.

entire carryback period, does not extend the carryforward period beyond 15 years. This allows a taxpayer some degree of flexibility in using the NOL deduction to the greatest advantage. (See the section entitled Tax Planning Considerations in this chapter for a discussion of this topic.)

Loss Carryovers from Two or More Years. At times, a taxpayer might have NOL carryovers that are incurred in 2 or more taxable years. Often these losses must be carried to the same years in the carryover period. If such is the case, the loss of the earliest year is always completely used first before deducting any of the loss incurred in a subsequent year. Because of the limited carryover period, this rule is beneficial to the taxpayer.

Recomputation of Taxable Income in the Carryover Year

When the NOL deduction is carried back to a prior year, that year's taxable income must be recomputed. Since the NOL is attributable to a taxpayer's trade or business, it is deductible *for* AGI.[163] As a result, the recomputation of taxable income for the carryback year may affect the deductible amount of certain itemized deductions since some of the deductions (e.g., the deductions for medical expenses, charitable contributions, and casualty losses) are limited or measured by reference to the taxpayer's AGI. All of these deductions except the deduction for charitable contributions must be recomputed using the reduced AGI amount.[164]

Once the tax refund for the carryback year is determined, the amount of the NOL available to be deducted in subsequent carryover years must be calculated. This is done by adjusting the recomputed income of the prior carryover year. Although certain differences exist, these adjustments are similar to those mentioned above.

The rules for computing and deducting NOLs are presented in Topic Review 8-5.

TAX PLANNING CONSIDERATIONS

Bad Debts

Key Point

If there is uncertainty as to the year in which a debt became worthless, it is possible that the issue will not be settled within the normal 3-year statute of limitations. For this reason, a taxpayer may claim a deduction for a worthless debt at any time within 7 years.

In order to deduct a bad debt, a taxpayer must show that the debt is worthless. At times the IRS might assert that the debt being written off is either not yet worthless or that it became worthless in a previous year. If the taxpayer is unable to overcome the IRS's assertion concerning the year of worthlessness, the taxpayer might be barred from filing an amended return for the prior year because of the statute of limitations.[165] Thus, taxpayers should carefully document all efforts at collection and other facts that show the debt is worthless.

As previously mentioned, a third party guarantor of a loan who is required to repay the debt may, under certain circumstances, be entitled to a bad debt deduction. The

---

[163] Sec. 62(a)(1).

[164] Reg. Sec. 1.172-5(a)(3)(ii).

[165] However, the statute of limitations for claims for a refund or credit because of a bad debt is extended from 3 years to 7 years under Sec. 6511(d)(1), thus giving the taxpayer additional time if this is the case.

TOPIC REVIEW 8-5

Net Operating Losses	
Item	Rules
Computation of NOL (adjustments to taxable income)	1. Add back any NOL deduction carried to the current year. 2. Add back any capital loss deduction. 3. Add back the deduction for personal and dependency exemptions. 4. Add back the excess of nonbusiness deductions over nonbusiness income. For this purpose, casualty losses on personal-use property are treated as business losses.
Carryover period	1. May be carried back three years and forward for fifteen years. 2. Must be carried to the carryover years in chronological order: first carried back to the third prior year, then to the second prior year, then to the first prior year, then to the first succeeding year, etc. 3. An election may be made to forgo the carryback. This does not extend the carryforward period. 4. If losses from two or more years are carried to the same year, the losses from the earliest year are completely used first.

guarantor must demonstrate that he received reasonable consideration in the form of cash or property in exchange for guaranteeing the debt.[166] If proper consideration is not received, the guarantee and subsequent payment of the loan by the guarantor is considered to be a gift rather than a loan. Reasonable consideration is also deemed to have been received if the taxpayer enters into the agreement for a good faith business purpose or in accordance with normal business practice. However, if the taxpayer guarantees the debt of a spouse or a relative, the consideration must be received in the form of cash or property.

In the case of an outright loan between related taxpayers, the lender should always make sure that proper documentation is retained to substantiate the fact that the transaction is a loan. If such documentation is not kept, the IRS may assert that the transaction is a gift.

Casualties

A deduction is allowed for stolen property, but no deduction is allowed for lost property. Thus, taxpayers should always carefully document losses of property through theft (e.g., the filing of police reports or claims with the taxpayer's insurance company). In addition, pictures and written appraisals may be helpful to prove the amount of the loss.

[166] Reg. Sec. 1.166-9(e)(1).

Additional Comment

Normally, a taxpayer would want to carry back the NOL since he or she will receive a refund in a short time period from the filing of the amended return. The carryover of the NOL involves waiting for a year or more to receive a tax benefit.

Net Operating Losses

If a net operating loss is incurred, the taxpayer should carefully analyze whether to elect to forgo the carryback period. Situations under which a taxpayer might elect to only carry the loss deduction forward include the following:

- A taxpayer might anticipate being in a higher marginal tax rate in future years than in the carryback years. If such is the case, the value of the deduction is higher in the carryforward years than in the carryback years. Consideration should be given, however, to cash flows and the time value of money (e.g., the tax benefits from a refund of taxes are immediately available only if the NOL is carried back).

- General business and other tax credits that are nonrefundable (i.e., the credits are limited to the tax liability or some percentage thereof) may be reduced or eliminated for the carryback years because these credits must be recomputed based upon the adjusted tax liability after applying the NOL carryback. (See Chaper 14 for a discussion of tax credits.)

COMPLIANCE AND PROCEDURAL CONSIDERATIONS

Casualty Losses

Key Point

In the case of a casualty loss occurring within a disaster area the taxpayer can deduct the loss on the tax return of the year prior to the loss.

If a taxpayer sustains a casualty loss in a location that the President of the United States declares a disaster area, an election may be made to deduct the loss in the year preceeding the year in which the loss occurred. This election is made by either (1) filing the return for the previous year and including the loss in that year (if the return has not already been filed), or (2) filing an amended return or claim for refund for that year.[167] The return should clearly include all the following information:

- That the election is being made
- The date of the disaster giving rise to the loss
- The city, county, and state in which the damaged property is located[168]

The election must be made before the due date of the return for the year in which the disaster actually occurs. Although the Regulations state that the election may not be revoked more than 90 days after it is made, the Tax Court has held that this part of the Regulation is invalid.[169]

Net Operating Losses

If a taxpayer carries an NOL deduction back to a prior year, a claim for refund of taxes is filed by either (1) filing an amended return on Form 1040X or (2) filing for a quick refund on Form 1045. Corporations use Form 1139. If Form 1045 is used, the IRS must act on the application for refund within 90 days from the later of (1) the date of the

---

[167] Reg. Sec. 1.165-11(e).
[168] Ibid.
[169] *Chester Matheson,* 74 T.C. 836 (1980), *acq.* 1981-2 C.B. 2.

application or (2) the last day of the month in which the return of the loss year must be filed.[170] Form 1045 must be filed within a year after the end of the year in which the NOL arose.[171] Additional information such as (1) pages 1 and 2 of Form 1040 for the year of loss, (2) a copy of the application for an extension of time to file the return for the year of loss, and (3) copies of forms or schedules for items refigured in the carryback years must be attached.[172]

A filled-in copy of the front page of Form 1045 is shown in Figure 8-1. It includes the computations relating to the information in Example 8-63.

Example 8-63 ■

For the year 1991, Larry Johnson, Soc. Sec. 123-45-6789, who is single, reports the following items of taxable income:

Net income from business				$35,000
Interest income				1,500
Dividends				1,000
AGI				$37,500
Minus:	Greater of itemized deductions or standard deduction:			
	Medical expenses	$6,000		
	Minus: 7.5% of AGI (0.075 × $37,500)	(2,813)	$3,187	
	Taxes		2,500	
	Interest on personal residence		2,500	
	Total itemized deductions		$8,187	
			or	
	Standard deduction for 1991		(3,400)	
				(8,187)
Minus:	Personal exemption for 1991			(2,150)
Taxable income				$27,163

Tax liability reported on original return[a]	$4,960

During 1994, Johnson incurred a $15,000 NOL. His tax liability for 1991 is recomputed as follows:

Net income from business				$35,000
Interest income				1,500
Dividends				1,000
NOL carryback from 1994				(15,000)
AGI				$22,500
Minus:	Greater of itemized deductions or standard deduction:			
	Medical expenses	$6,000		
	Minus: 7.5% of AGI (0.075 × $22,500)	(1,688)	$4,312	
	Taxes		2,500	
	Interest on personal residence		2,500	
	Total itemized deductions		$9,312	
			or	
	Standard deduction for 1991		(3,400)	
				(9,312)

---

[170] IRS, *Instructions for Filing Form 1045,* Revised, 1992.
[171] Ibid.
[172] Ibid.

Form **1045**

Department of the Treasury
Internal Revenue Service

Application for Tentative Refund

▶ Before you fill out this form, read the separate instructions.
▶ Do not attach to your income tax return—mail in a separate envelope.
▶ For use by individuals, estates, or trusts.

OMB No. 1545-0098

1993

Please type or print

Name	Social security or employer identification number
Larry Johnson	
Number, street, and apt. or suite no. If you have a P.O. box or a foreign address, see the instructions.	Spouse's social security number
L Street	
City, town or post office, state, and ZIP code	Telephone no. (optional)
Small Town, USA	( )

1 This application is filed to carry back:

a Net operating loss (from Schedule A, page 2, line 25) $

b Unused general business credit $

2a For the calendar year 1993, or other tax year beginning , 1993, ending , 19 .

b Date tax return was filed

c Service center where tax return was filed

3 If this application is for an unused credit created by another carryback, give year of the first carryback ▶ ....

4 If you filed a joint return (or separate return) for some, but not all, of the tax years involved in figuring the carryback, enter the years of the joint or separate returns ▶ ....

5 If social security number for carryback year is different from above, enter **a** SSN ▶ .... and **b** Year(s) ▶ ....

6 If you changed your accounting period, give date permission to change was granted ▶ ....

7 Have you filed a petition in Tax Court for the year(s) to which the carryback is to be applied? . . . . . ☐ Yes ☐ No

8 Does this carryback include a loss or credit from a tax shelter required to be registered? . . . . . . ☐ Yes ☐ No

Computation of Decrease in Tax

Note: If 1a is blank, skip lines 9 through 15.

		3rd preceding tax year ended ▶		2nd preceding tax year ended ▶		1st preceding tax year ended ▶	
		(a) Before carryback	**(b)** After carryback	**(c)** Before carryback	**(d)** After carryback	**(e)** Before carryback	**(f)** After carryback
9	Adjusted gross income from tax return or as previously adjusted	37,500	37,500				
10	Net operating loss deduction after carryback. See instructions . . .	/////	15,000	/////		/////	
11	Subtract line 10 from line 9 . . .	37,500	22,500				
12	Deductions. See instructions . . .	8,187	9,312				
13	Subtract line 12 from line 11 . . .	29,313	13,188				
14	Exemptions	2,150	2,150				
15	Taxable income. Subtract line 14 from line 13	27,163	11,038				
16	Income tax. See instructions—attach explanation	4,960	1,656				
17	General business credit						
18	Other credits. Identify						
19	Total credits. Add lines 17 and 18 .						
20	Subtract line 19 from line 16 . . .	5,105	1,656				
21	Recapture taxes						
22	Alternative minimum tax						
23	Self-employment tax						
24	Other taxes						
25	Total tax liability. Add lines 20 through 24	5,105	1,656				
26	Enter amount from line 25, cols. (b), (d), and (f)	1,656	/////	/////		/////	
27	Decrease in tax. Subtract line 26 from line 25	3,449	/////	/////		/////	
28	Overpayment of tax due to a claim of right adjustment under section 1341(b)(1)—attach computation . .						

Sign Here

Keep a copy of this application for your records.

Under penalties of perjury, I declare that I have examined this application and accompanying schedules and statements, and to the best of my knowledge and belief, they are true, correct, and complete.

Your signature	Date
▶	
Spouse's signature (if Form 1045 is filed jointly, BOTH must sign)	Date
▶	

Preparer Other Than Taxpayer	Name ▶	Date
	Address ▶	

For Paperwork Reduction Act Notice, see separate instructions.

Cat. No. 10670A

Form **1045** (1993)

FIGURE 8-1 Front Page of Form 1045 for Example 8-63

Minus: Personal exemption for 1991	(2,150)
Taxable income as recomputed	$11,038
Tax liability from original return	$4,960[a]
Minus: Recomputed tax liability	(1,656)[b]
Refund due Larry Johnson	$3,304

[a] Based on 1991 tax rate schedules.
[b] Based on 1991 tax rate schedules.

■

Worthless Securities

As explained earlier in this chapter, securities that become worthless during the taxable year are deemed to have become worthless on the last day of the year. In most cases, this treatment causes the loss to be treated as a long-term capital loss. If the loss from the worthless security is long term, it is reported in Part II of Schedule D (Form 1040) along with the taxpayer's other long-term gains and losses for the year. Short-term capital losses are reported in Part I of Schedule D.

PROBLEM MATERIALS

DISCUSSION QUESTIONS

8-1. What is the closed transaction doctrine, and why does it exist for purposes of recognizing a loss realized on holding property?

8-2. When property is disposed of, what factors influence the amount of the deductible loss?

8-3. Describe the usual tax consequences that apply to a worthless security.

8-4. Under what circumstances will a loss that is realized on a worthless security not be treated as a capital loss?

8-5. What two general requirements must be met for a transaction to result in a capital loss?

8-6. What requirements must be met for stock to be considered Sec. 1244 stock?

8-7. What tax treatment applies to gains and losses on Sec. 1244 stock?

8-8. Describe a situation where a loss on the sale of business or investment property is not currently deductible, and explain why.

8-9. a. What is a passive activity?
   b. Who is subject to the passive loss limitation rules?

8-10. a. For purposes of the passive loss rules, what is a closely held C corporation?
   b. In what way do the passive loss rules differ from the regular passive loss rules when applied to closely held C corporations?

8-11. Why is it important to identify exactly what constitutes an activity for purposes of the passive activity rules?

8-12. a. If a taxpayer is involved in several different business operations during the year, how is the determination made as to how many activities these operations constitute for purposes of the passive activity loss rules?
   b. Can a business operation and a rental operation ever be combined into one activity? Explain.

8-13. Which of the following activities are considered passive for the year? Explain. Consider each situation independently.

    a. Laura owns a rental unit which she rents out to students. The rental unit is Laura's only business and she spends approximately 875 hours per year managing, collecting the rent, advertising, and performing minor repairs. At times she must hire professionals such as plumbers to do the maintenance. Is the rental unit a passive activity with respect to Laura?

    b. Kami is a medical doctor who works four days a week in a medical practice that she and five other doctors formed. Last year she and her partners formed another partnership that owns and operates a medical lab. The lab employs ten technicians, one of whom also acts as manager. During the year Kami spent 120 hours in meetings, reviewing records, etc., for the lab. Is the lab a passive activity with respect to Kami?

    c. Assume the same facts in part b. In addition, assume that the same group of doctors have formed two other partnerships. One is a medical supply partnership. Kami spent 150 hours working for this partnership. The medical supply partnership has five full-time employees. Kami also spent 250 hours during the year working for the other partnership. This partnership specializes in providing medical services to individuals from out of town who are staying at local hotels and motels. This partnership hires two full-time and six part-time nurses. Are the lab and the two other partnerships passive activities with respect to Kami?

8-14. Explain the difference between materially participating and actively participating in an activity. When is the active participation test used?

8-15. **a.** What requirements must be met in order for a taxpayer to deduct up to $25,000 of passive losses from rental real estate activities against active and portfolio income?

    b. What requirements must be met in order for a real estate rental activity to be considered a real estate business that is not subject to the passive loss rules?

8-16. Are the suspended losses under the passive loss rules lost forever? Explain.

8-17. What tests must be met to qualify a loss as deductible under the casualty loss provisions? Discuss the application of each of these tests.

8-18. Explain how a taxable gain on property can be realized because of a casualty event such as a fire or theft. How are these gains treated?

8-19. During the current year, Bill completely destroyed his personal automobile in a one car accident. Fortunately, he was not hurt. The FMV of the automobile at the time of the accident was $8,000. Because of a previous accident as well as several driving violations, Bill is afraid that if he files a claim with his insurance company, he will become uninsurable. Instead, Bill wants to deduct the loss as a casualty loss on his tax return. His AGI for this year is $40,000, and he has other itemized deductions of $5,000. Bill is single. What is the amount of casualty loss he may deduct?

8-20. How is a theft loss treated differently from a casualty loss?

8-21. Compare and contrast the computational rules for deducting casualty losses on personal-use property with casualty losses incurred on business or investment property.

8-22. Under what circumstances may a loss arising from a casualty or theft be deducted in a year other than the year in which the loss occurs?

8-23. Is the following statement true or false?: If the amount of casualty losses sustained on personal-use property during a taxable year does not exceed 10% of the taxpayer's AGI for the year, no deduction for the losses is allowed. Explain.

8-24. For individuals, how are casualty losses on personal-use property reported on the tax return? How are casualty losses on business property reported?

8-25. Is the $100 floor on personal-use casualty losses imposed upon each individual loss item if more than one item of property is destroyed in a single casualty? Is the floor imposed before or after the casualty gains are netted against the casualty losses?

8-26. A taxpayer may take a deduction for a bad debt only when the taxpayer has a basis in that debt. Explain why this is so. Also explain how a taxpayer can establish basis in a debt.

8-27. Steve loans $50,000 to his best friend, John. John uses the money to open a pizza parlor next to the local high school. Three years later, when John still owed Steve $15,000, John closed the pizza parlor and declared bankruptcy. Discuss the appropriate tax treatment that Steve may take.

8-28. Dana is an attorney who specializes in family law. She uses the cash method of accounting and is a calendar year taxpayer. During the current year, she represented a client in a law suit, and billed the client $5,000 for her services. Although she made repeated attempts during the current and subsequent year, Dana was unable to collect the outstanding receivable. Finally in November of the subsequent year she found out that the individual has moved without leaving any forwarding address. Dana's attempts to locate the individual were futile. What is the amount of deduction that Dana may take with respect to this bad debt?

8-29. Under what circumstances may a taxpayer deduct a bad debt even though another party to the transaction is the creditor?

8-30. What is the definition of a nonbusiness debt? What is the character of the deduction for a nonbusiness bad debt?

8-31. **a.** What alternatives do individuals have in deducting a loss on a deposit in a qualifed financial institution?
   b. Explain when it might be better to elect one over the other.

8-32. May a deduction be taken for a nonbusiness debt that is partially worthless? Explain.

8-33. A taxpayer collects a debt that was previously written off as a bad debt. What tax consequences arise if the recovery is received in a subsequent tax year?

8-34. What is an NOL deduction, and why is it allowed?

8-35. List the adjustments to an individual taxpayer's negative taxable income amount which must be made in computing a NOL for the year. What is the underlying rationale for requiring these adjustments for individuals?

8-36. **a.** What is the NOL carryback and carryover period?
   b. Does a taxpayer have any choice in deciding the years to which the NOL should be carried? If so, explain the circumstances under which a taxpayer might elect not to use the regular carryback or carryover period.

8-37. Can a casualty loss on a personal-use asset create or increase an NOL? Explain.

8-38. If an NOL is carried back to a prior year, what adjustments must be made to the prior year's taxable income? What are the possible results of the adjustments?

PROBLEMS

8-39. *Sec. 1244 Losses.* During the current year Sally sells her entire interest in Central Corporation common stock for $10,000. She is the sole shareholder, and originally organized the corporation several years ago by contributing $80,000 in exchange for her stock, which qualifies as Sec. 1244 stock. Since its incorporation, Central has been involved in the manufacture of items that protect personal computers from static electricity. Unfortunately, this market is extremely competitive, and Central Corporation incurs substantial losses throughout its existence.
   a. Assuming Sally is single, what are the amount and the character of the loss recognized on the sale of the Central Corporation stock?
   b. Assuming Sally is married and files a joint return, what are the amount and the character of the loss recognized on the sale of the Central Corporation stock?
   c. How would your answer to Part a change if Sally had originally purchased the stock from another shareholder rather than organizing the corporation?
   d. How might Sally have structured the transaction in Part a to receive a greater tax advantage?

8-40. *Amount and Character of Loss Transactions.* On February 2 of the current year, Madison Corporation files for bankruptcy. At the time, it is estimated that the total FMV of its assets is $800,000, whereas the total amount of its outstanding debt amounts to $1,000,000. Madison has been engaged for several years in a gold mining operation in Montana.

a. At the time of the bankruptcy Madison is owned 100% by Barry, who purchased the stock from an investor for $300,000 several years ago. Barry is married and files a joint return. What are the amount and character of the loss sustained by Barry upon Madison's bankruptcy?

b. How would your answer to Part a change if Barry originally organized Madison Corporation capitalizing it with $300,000. Madison Corporation qualifies as a small business corporation.

c. How would your answer to Part a change if Barry were a corporation instead of an individual.

d. How would your answer to Part b change if Barry were a corporation instead of an individual.

8-41. *Character of Losses.* During the current year, Joe sold the following stocks:

Stock	Gain (Loss)	When Acquired
Acme	$6,000	5 years ago
Beta	(3,000)	3 years ago
Canary	25,000	8 years ago
Delta	(8,000)	8 months ago
Echo	2,000	3 months ago

In addition, on July 22, Joe received word that his Foxtrot, Inc. stock had gone bankrupt during the year and that Joe's entire $5,000 investment is lost. Joe purchased Foxtrot on December 5 of the prior year. All of the above corporations are large publicly-held companies. Joe asked his attorney to begin collection procedures on a $4,000 loan that was made to a friend two years ago, but the attorney informed Joe that the friend had skipped town and could not be found. Compute Joe's short-term and long-term capital gains and losses from the above transactions.

8-42. *Passive Losses.* In the current year Alice reports $150,000 of salary income, $20,000 of income from activity X, and $35,000 and $15,000 losses from activities Y and Z, respectively. All three activities are passive with respect to Alice and are purchased during the current year. What is the amount of loss that may be deducted and that must be carried over with respect to each of these activities?

8-43. *Passive Losses.* In the current year Clay reports income and losses from the following activities:

Activity X	$ 25,000
Activity Y	(10,000)
Activity Z	(20,000)
Salary	100,000

Activities X, Y, and Z are all passive with respect to Clay. $40,000 in passive losses from activity Z are carried over from the prior year. In the current year Clay sells activity Z for a taxable gain of $30,000. What is the amount of loss that Clay may deduct and that must be carried over in the current year?

8-44. *Passive Losses — Rental Real Estate.* During the current year, Irene, a married individual who files a joint return, reports the following items of income and loss:

Salary	$130,000
Activity X (passive)	10,000
Activity Y (non-trade or business rental real estate)	(30,000)
Activity Z (non-trade or business rental real estate)	(20,000)

Irene actively participates in both activities Y and Z and owns 100% of both Y and Z.

a. What is Irene's AGI for the year?

b. What is the amount of losses that may be deducted and must be carried over with respect to each activity?

8-45. *Passive Losses.* In 1993, Martha purchased two separate activities. Information regarding these activities for 1993 and 1994 is as follows:

| | 1993 | | | 1994 | |
Activity	Status	Income (Loss)	Activity	Status	Income (Loss)
A	Passive	($12,000)	A	Active	$ 5,000
B	Passive	(4,000)	B	Passive	10,000

During 1994, Martha also reports salary income of $60,000 and interest and dividend income of $10,000. Compute the amount (if any) of the suspended losses attributable to activities A and B that are carried to 1995.

8-46. *Passive Losses.* During the current year, Jim has AGI of $130,000 before taking into account any passive activity losses. He also actively participates and owns 100% of activity A which is a real estate rental activity. For the year, activity A generates a $8,000 net loss and $5,000 in tax credits. Jim is in the 31% tax bracket. What is the amount of suspended loss and credit from activity A that must be carried to subsequent years?

8-47. *Passive Losses.* In 1994, Julie, a single individual, reported the following items of income and deduction:

Salary	$120,000
Dividend income	11,000
Short-term capital gain from sales of stock	18,000
Short-term capital losses from sales of stock	(15,000)
Loss from a passive real estate activity	(18,000)
Interest expense on loan to purchase stock	(17,000)
Qualified residence interest on residence	(10,000)
Charitable contributions	(7,000)
Property taxes on residence	(3,000)
Tax return preparation fees	(2,000)
Unreimbursed employee business expenses	(3,000)

Julie owns 100% and is an active participant in the real estate activity. What is Julie's taxable income in 1994?

8-48. *Casualty Losses.* Antonio, a mechanic, owns his own auto repair business. In the current year a fire starts in his garage, destroying the following property:

Asset	Adjusted Basis	FMV Before Casualty	FMV After Casualty	Insurance Recovery
A	$15,000	$25,000	—0—	$10,000
B	7,000	10,000	$2,000	5,000
C	12,000	8,000	1,000	3,000

Assets A and B are both machines that Antonio had used in his business for several years. Asset C is Antonio's personal automobile. Because of the fire, Antonio has to close the garage for 2 weeks. He estimates $5,000 lost in income while he is closed, none of which is compensated by insurance. Antonio's AGI for the year, not including the items mentioned above, is $30,000. What are the amount and character of Antonio's deduction as a result of the items noted above?

8-49. *Theft Losses.* On December 17 of the current year, Kelly's business office safe is burglarized. The theft is discovered a few days after the burglary. $1,000 cash from the cash registers is stolen. A diamond necklace and a ring that Kelly frequently wore are also stolen. The necklace cost Kelly $1,500 many years ago, and is insured for its $5,000 FMV. Kelly purchased the ring for $1,000 just 2 weeks prior to the burglary. Unfortunately, the ring and the cash are not insured. Kelly's AGI for the year, not including the items noted above, is $60,000.

a. What is Kelly's deductible theft loss in the current year?

b. What is Kelly's deductible theft loss in the current year if the theft is not discovered until January of the following year?

8-50. *Casualty Losses—Year of Deduction.* Greg sprayed all of the landscaping around his house with a pesticide in June 1994. Shortly thereafter, all of the trees and shrubs unaccountably died. The FMV and the adjusted basis of the plants were $8,000. Later that year, the pesticide manufacturer announced a recall of the particular batch of pesticide that Greg used. It also announced a program whereby consumers would be repaid for any damage caused by the improper mixture. Greg is single and reports $30,000 AGI in 1994 and $32,000 in 1995.

a. Assume that in 1994 Greg files a claim for his losses and receives notification that payment of $8,000 will be received in 1994. Greg receives full payment for the damage in 1995. How should the loss and the reimbursement be reported?

b. How will your answer to Part a change if in 1995 the manufacturer files bankruptcy and Greg receives $2,000 in total and final payment for his claim?

c. How will your answer to Part a change if the announcement and the reimbursement do not occur until late in 1995, after Greg has already filed his tax return for 1994?

8-51. *Personal-use Casualty Losses.* In the current year Neil completely destroys his personal automobile (purchased 2 years earlier for $12,000) in a traffic accident. Fortunately none of the occupants are injured. The FMV of the car before the accident is $8,000; after the accident it is worthless. Neil receives a $5,000 settlement from the insurance company. Later in the same year his house is burglarized, and several antiques are stolen. The antiques were purchased a number of years earlier for $3,000. Their value at the time of the theft is estimated at $5,000. They are not insured. Neil's AGI for the current year is $45,000. What is the amount of Neil's deductible casualty loss in the current year, assuming the thefts are discovered in the same year?

8-52. *Casualty Losses.* During 1994, Pam incurred the following casualty losses:

Asset	FMV Before	FMV After	Basis	Insurance
Business 1	$18,000	$ 0	$15,000	$ 4,000
Business 2	25,000	10,000	8,000	3,000
Business 3	20,000	0	18,000	19,000
Personal 1	12,000	0	20,000	2,000
Personal 2	8,000	5,000	10,000	0
Personal 3	9,000	0	6,000	8,000

All of the items were destroyed in the same casualty. Before considering the casualty items, Pam reports business income of $80,000, qualified residential interest of $6,000 and property taxes on her personal residence of $2,000, and charitable contributions of $4,000. Compute Pam's taxable income for 1994.

8-53. *Business Bad Debt.* Elaine is a physician who uses the cash method of accounting for tax purposes. During the current year, Elaine bills Ralph $1,200 for office visits and outpatient surgery. Unfortunately, unknown to Elaine, Ralph moves away, leaving no payment and no fowarding address. What is the amount of Elaine's bad debt deduction with respect to Ralph's debt?

8-54. *Nonbusiness Bad Debt.* During 1991, Becky loans her brother Ken $5,000, which he intends to use to establish a small business. Since Ken has no other assets and needs cash to expand the business, the agreement provides that Ken will repay the debt if (and when) sufficient funds are generated from the business. No interest rate is agreed upon. The business is unsuccessful, and Ken is forced to file for bankruptcy in 1994. By the end of 1994, it is estimated that the creditors will receive only 20% of the amount owed. In 1995 the bankruptcy proceedings are closed, and the creditors receive 10% of the amount due on the debt. What is Becky's bad debt deduction for 1994? for 1995?

8-55. *Bad Debt Deduction.* Assume the same facts as in Problem 8-54, except that Becky and Ken are not related and that under the terms of the loan Ken agrees to repay Becky the $5,000 plus interest (at a reasonable stated rate) over a 5-year period. What is Becky's bad debt deduction for 1994? for 1995?

8-56. *Net Operating Loss Deduction.* Jeff and Julie are married and file a joint income tax return. Jeff owns an unincorporated landscaping business; Julie is employed as a bank loan officer. They have no dependents. During 1994, they report the following items of income and expense:

Revenue from landscaping business	$40,000
Expenses of landscaping business	94,000
Julie's salary	30,000
Dividends	800
LTCG on stock	2,000
Interest on personal residence	4,000
Itemized deductions for state and local taxes	5,000

a. What is Jeff and Julie's taxable income or loss for 1994?

b. What is Jeff and Julie's NOL for 1994?

8-57. ***Net Operating Loss Deduction.*** Assume the same facts as in Problem 8-56, except that in addition to the other itemized deductions Jeff and Julie suffer a $3,000 deductible casualty loss (after limitations).

a. What is Jeff and Julie's taxable income or loss for 1994?

b. What is Jeff and Julie's NOL for 1994?

8-58. ***Net Operating Loss Deduction.*** Assume the same facts as in Problem 8-56, except that instead of $5,000 itemized deductions for state and local taxes, Jeff and Julie's itemized deductions consist of a $5,000 casualty loss (after limitations).

a. What is Jeff and Julie's taxable income or loss for 1994?

b. What is Jeff and Julie's NOL for 1994?

8-59. During 1994, Kim reports the following:

Revenue from business	$ 65,000
Expenses from business	105,000

Kim also worked part time during the year, earning a salary of $12,000. She reported dividends of $1,000 and interest of $500; but she had a long-term capital loss of $5,000 on the sale of some stock she had held for investment. Her itemized deductions total $3,000.

a. What is Kim's taxable income for 1994?

b. What is Kim's NOL for 1994?

TAX FORM/RETURN PREPARATION PROBLEMS

TurboTax **8-60.** Hal and Jane Weeks are married and file a joint income tax return. Their address is 444 West Walnut Circle, Tempe, Arizona, 00000. Hal's social security number is 123-45-6789, and Jane's is 234-56-7890. Hal is employed as a steelworker, and Jane is self-employed as a financial planner. They report all of their income and expenses on the cash basis. For 1993 they report the following items of income and expense:

Gross receipts from Jane's business	$55,000
Rent on Jane's office	6,500
Receivables written off during the year (received for Jane's financial services)	900
Subscriptions to investment journals for Jane	200
Salary for Jane's secretary-receptionist	9,600
Hal's salary	40,000
Qualified medical expenses	9,000
Property taxes on their personal residence	1,500
State income tax refund received this year (the tax benefit was received in the prior year from the state income tax deduction)	600
State income taxes withheld on Hal's salary	1,200
Federal income taxes withheld on Hal's salary	7,000
Jane's estimated tax payments were	10,000
Interest paid on residence	8,000
Income tax preparation fee for the prior year's return paid this year ($400 is allocated to preparation of Schedule C)	600

Hal and Jane sold the following assets:

Asset	Acquired	Sold	Sales Price	Cost
A stock	2/15/89	3/13/93	$12,000	$ 7,000
B stock	3/2/93	7/7/93	18,000	19,000
C stock	6/8/88	4/10/93	8,000	12,000
Snowmobile	12/3/87	3/3/93	4,000	5,500

The C stock was owned by Jane and was sold to her brother. The snowmobile was used for personal recreation.

In addition to the items above, they donate Real Corporation stock to their church. The FMV of the stock on the date it is donated (7/24/93) is $5,000. It cost $2,000 when purchased on 2/12/85. Hal and Jane's residence is burglarized during the year. The burglar stole a stereo component system (FMV $2,000; cost $3,000); a diamond necklace (FMV $10,000; cost $9,000); and a painting (FMV $2,500; cost $1,500). The insurance company pays $1,000 for the stereo, $3,000 for the necklace, and $1,000 for the painting. Compute Hal and Jane's federal income tax liability, using the currently available income tax rates.

TurboTax **8-61.** Doug and Elaine Graves are married and file a joint return. Their social security numbers are 098-76-5432 and 987-65-4321. They live at 427 So. Geneva Rd., Safford, Kansas, 00001. They report their income on the cash basis. During 1993, they report the following items:

Salary	$80,000
Rental of a condominium at Vail, Co.:	
Rental income (30 days)	9,000
Interest expense	4,000
Property taxes	2,100
Maintenance	1,000
Depreciation (entire year)	6,000
Insurance	1,400
Days of personal use	16

During the year the following events also occur:

a. In 1991 Doug had loaned a friend $2,000 to help pay medical bills. During 1993 he discovers that his "friend" has skipped town.

b. On 7/15/93 Doug sells West Corporation stock for $18,000. He purchased the stock on 12/14/84 for $25,000.

c. On September 21, 1993 Elaine discovers that the penny stock of First Corp. she purchased on May 30 of the prior year is completely worthless. She paid $2,000 for the stock.

d. Rather than accept the $50 the repair person offers for their old dishwasher, they donate it to Goodwill Industries on 11/15/93. They purchased the machine for $600 on 2/2/87. The new dishwasher cost $780.

e. They purchased a new residence for $120,000. As part of the closing costs, they pay two points or $2,000 on the $100,000 mortgage, which are in the nature of interest rather than loan processing fees. This payment enables them to obtain a more favorable interest rate for the term of the loan.

f. Paid $2,700 in property taxes on their residence and $5,000 in state income taxes.

g. On 7/12/93 they donated an antique automobile to the local community college. The value of the automobile was $8,000. They purchased the automobile for $1,000 on 11/15/85 and had fixed it up themselves. They estimated they had put in approximately $5,000 worth of labor into the project. The college auctioned the car for $7,500.

h. $12,000 in federal income tax was withheld during the year.

Compute Doug and Elaine's federal income tax liability for 1993 using the currently available tax rates. Complete Form 1040 and accompanying schedules.

CASE STUDY PROBLEM

8-62. Dr. John Brown is a physician who expects to make $150,000 this year from his medical practice. In addition, Dr. Brown expects to receive $10,000 dividends and interest income.

Last year, upon the advice of a friend, Dr. Brown invested $100,000 in Limited, a limited partnership. He spends no time working for Limited. Limited's operations did not turn out exactly as planned, and Dr. Brown's share of Limited's losses last year amounted to $15,000. Dr. Brown has already been informed that his share of Limited's losses this year will be $10,000.

In January of the current year, Dr. Brown set up his own laboratory. Originally he intended to have the lab only do the work for his own practice, but other physicians in the area were impressed with the quick turn around and convenience that the lab provided, and began sending their work. This year Dr. Brown estimates that the lab will generate $30,000 of taxable income. The work in the lab is done by 2 full-time qualified laboratory technicians. A part-time bookkeeper is hired to keep the books. Dr. Brown has spent 320 hours to date establishing and managing the lab. He plans to hire another technician who will also manage the lab so that it can operate on its own.

In November, Dr. Brown calls you requesting some tax advice. Specifically, he would like to know what actions he should take before the end of the year in order to reduce his tax liability for the current year.

Write a memo to Dr. Brown, detailing your suggestions. His address is: Dr. John Brown, 444 Physician's Drive, Suite 100, Anytown, USA, 88888.

CASE STUDY PROBLEM—ETHICAL ISSUES

8-63. In preparing the tax return for one of your clients, Jack Johnson, you notice that he has listed a deduction for a large business bad debt. Jack explains that the loan was made to his corporate employer when the corporation was experiencing extreme cash flow difficulties. In fact, Jack was very concerned at the time he made the loan that the corporation would go bankrupt. This would have been extremely bad, because not only would he have lost his job, but he also would have lost the $80,000 that he had invested in the common stock of the corporation.

You know, of course, that if the loan is a business loan Jack will receive an ordinary deduction. However, if the loan is a nonbusiness debt, it becomes a short-term capital loss (and Jack can only currently deduct $3,000).

After thoroughly reviewing all of the facts you do a complete search of the relevant judicial and administrative authority. There you find that the courts are split as to whether or not under these circumstances the loan should be treated as a business or nonbusiness bad debt.

What position should you take on Jack's federal income tax return? (See the caption entitled *Statements on Responsibilities in Tax Practice* in Chapter 1 for a discussion of this issue.)

TAX RESEARCH PROBLEM

8-64. Early in 1994, Kay meets Dan through a business associate. Dan tells Kay that he is directing a business venture that purchases poorly managed restaurants in order to turn them around and make them profitable. Dan mentions that he is currently involved in acquiring a real "gold mine" but needs to raise additional cash in order to purchase it. On the strength of Dan's representations, Kay loans Dan $30,000 for the venture. An agreement is written up between Kay and Dan, wherein Dan agrees to repay Kay the entire amount over a 5-year period plus 14% interest per annum on the unpaid balance. Later in the year, however, Kay discovers that Dan had never intended to purchase the restaurant and, in fact, had used most of the money for his own benefit. Upon making this discovery, Kay sues Dan for recovery of the money, alleging that Dan falsely, fraudulently, and deceitfully represented that the money would be invested and repaid, in order to cheat and defraud Kay out of her money. Unfortunately for Kay, she is never able to recover any amount of the loan. Discuss the tax treatment that Kay may claim with regard to the loss.

A partial list of research sources is

- *Robert S. Gerstell*, 46 T.C. 161 (1966).
- *Michele Monteleone*, 34 T.C. 688 (1960).

9

Employee Expenses and Deferred Compensation

LEARNING OBJECTIVES

After studying this chapter, you should be able to

1. Determine the proper classification and deductibility of travel and transportation expenses
2. Identify deductible moving expenses and determine the amount and year of deductibility
3. Determine the proper deductible amount for entertainment expenses under the 50% disallowance rule
4. Describe the requirements for deducting education expenses
5. Determine whether the expenses of an office in home meet the requirements for deductibility and apply the gross income limitations
6. Discuss the tax treatment and requirements for various deferred compensation arrangements

This chapter discusses the tax consequences that arise from employment-related expenditures and deferred compensation for employees. **Deferred compensation** refers to methods of compensating employees based upon their current service where the benefits are deferred until future periods (e.g., a pension or incentive stock option plan). An important concept related to the deductibility of expenditures is that the nature of an expenditure determines its tax consequences. For example, automobile expenses may be deductible if the expenses are incurred in a trade or business activity or if the automobile is used by an employee in an employment-related activity. However, automobile expenses associated with personal or nonbusiness activities such as commuting are nondeductible personal expenditures. As discussed in Chapter 7, personal expenditures are not deductible unless the Internal Revenue Code specifically provides for their deductibility. Thus, personal expenditures for medical expenses, charitable contributions, certain state and local taxes, and so on are allowed as itemized deductions from one's adjusted gross income (AGI) because they are specifically authorized.

The following classification scheme illustrates how employee expenses fit within the Code's general expenditure classifications:

- Trade or business expenses that are deductible under Sec. 162 (see Chapter 6)

- Expenses related to the production of income that are deductible under Sec. 212 (e.g., operating expenses associated with the rental of an apartment house by an investor) (see Chapter 6)

- Personal-use expenditures that are either nondeductible or are deductible as itemized deductions (see Chapter 7)

- Losses that are deductible under various Code sections (e.g., casualty and theft losses, bad debts, and so on) (see Chapter 8)

- Employee expenses (Chapter 9)

- Capital expenditures that are nondeductible under Sec. 263 but may be subject to a depreciation or depletion deduction or subject to amortization (see Chapter 10)

CLASSIFICATION OF EMPLOYEE EXPENSES

Section 62(a)(2) provides that the employee may deduct reimbursed employee expenses *for* AGI. However, subject to certain limitations, unreimbursed employee expenses are generally deductible *from* AGI.[1]

Some of the more frequently encountered employee expenses discussed in this chapter include

- Travel
- Transportation
- Moving
- Entertainment
- Education
- Office in home

Key Point

The business expenses of a self-employed individual and the reimbursed business expenses of an employee are deductible for *AGI. The unreimbursed business expenses of an employee are deductible* from *AGI.*

Nature of the Employment Relationship

The nature of the employment relationship hinges upon whether an individual is classified as an employee or is engaged in a self-employed trade or business activity. Thus, a self-employed individual who incurs a trade- or business-related expenditure may deduct the expense *for* AGI under Sec. 162, and it is reported on Schedule C (or Schedule C-EZ) of Form 1040. In contrast, an individual's unreimbursed employment-related activities (e.g., travel and transportation) are deductible *from* AGI and are subject to separate tax rules and restrictions. Certain items such as moving expenses are deductible *for* AGI if they are incurred by an employee or a self-employed individual, but are nondeductible personal expenditures if an individual is not employed or is not self-employed.

Employer-Employee Relationship Defined. The Regulations provide that an employer-employee relationship generally exists where the employer has the right to control and direct the individual who provides services with regard to (1) the end result and (2) the means by which the result is accomplished.[2]

Example 9-1 ■   Carmen is a nurse who assists a group of doctors in a clinic. Carmen is under the direct supervision of the doctors and is told what procedures to perform and when to perform them. Therefore, Carmen is classified as an employee. ■

Example 9-2 ■   Carol is a live-in nurse who is paid by the patient and receives instructions from the patient's doctor regarding such items as medications and diet. Carol is directly responsible for the delivery of nursing care and is in control of the end result. Thus, Carol is self-employed. ■

Importance of Proper Classification. Proper classification is particularly important to employers because employers owe payroll taxes (e.g., the employer portion of

---

[1] Section 62(a)(15) also provides *for* AGI classification for moving expenses incurred after December 31, 1993. Prior to 1994 qualifying moving expenses were treated as itemized deductions. In addition, Sec. 62(b)(1) provides an exception for certain expenses of performing artists who perform services for two or more employers during the year, provided that (1) the expenses exceed 10% of gross income and (2) the individual's AGI does not exceed $16,000. The unreimbursed expenses are deductible *for* AGI rather than being allowed as an itemized deduction (see Sec. 62(a)(2)(B)).

[2] Reg. Sec. 31.3401(c)-1(b).

social security (FICA) taxes and unemployment taxes) for individuals who are classified as employees. Individuals may prefer to be classified as employees because the employee portion of the social security taxes (7.65% in 1994) is less than the self-employment tax rate (15.3% in 1994) on amounts up to $60,600 for the nonhospital insurance portion. The hospital insurance portion of the FICA tax continues to apply to both employees and self-employed individuals with no ceiling limitation for tax years after 1993.[3] The rate is 1.45% each for the employee and the employer, and 2.9% for self-employed individuals. Self-employed individuals receive a *for* AGI deduction for one-half of the self-employment taxes paid.

Litigation Issues and Administrative Enforcement. The IRS is currently prohibited from issuing rulings and regulations dealing with the employee-independent contractor issue. Also, the IRS may not reclassify individuals who were formerly treated as independent contractors if the taxpayer's past practice relied upon industry practices or prior IRS rulings.[4]

Substantial litigation has occurred in this area. For example, generally corporate officers are subject to corporate control and are treated as employees.[5] Corporate directors, however, are generally treated as self-employed individuals.[6]

The Code was amended in 1982 to provide clarifying rules for real estate agents and direct salespersons.[7] The law provides that such persons are not classified as employees if certain safe haven requirements are met (e.g., if substantially all of the agent's remuneration is related to sales rather than to the number of hours worked).

A 1991 Treasury Department study concluded that current law in this area is not acceptable to the business community or the IRS. Businesses would prefer certainty in the law and the elimination of inconsistent treatment of workers across industry groups while the IRS would like to equitably enforce the law.[8]

Limitations on Unreimbursed Employee Expenses

2% Nondeductible Floor. A nondeductible floor of 2% of the AGI applies to most types of unreimbursed employee expenses.[9] Unreimbursed employee expenses are combined with investment expenses (e.g., investment counseling fees and safe deposit box rentals) and other miscellaneous itemized deductions (e.g., appraisal fees for charitable contributions and fees for tax return preparation) for the purpose of computing the allowable deduction after the 2% nondeductible amount is subtracted. All of these expenses noted above are referred to as ***miscellaneous itemized deductions*** in Sec. 67.

Other unreimbursed employee expenses that are classified as miscellaneous itemized deductions include

---

[3] For years prior to 1994, a ceiling limitation ($135,000 in 1993) applied to earnings and self-employment income subject to the hospital insurance portion of the FICA tax. (See Chapter 14 for a discussion of these rules.)

[4] P.L. 95-600, Sec. 530(b), *enacted* November 6, 1978.

[5] *Galbraith & Green Inc., of Arizona v. U.S.*, 46 AFTR 2d 80-5699, 80-2 USTC ¶ 9629 (D.C.-AZ, 1980).

[6] Reg. Sec. 31.3401(c)-1(f).

[7] Sec. 3508.

[8] Dan R. Mastromarco, "The Rekindling Independent Contractor Debate," *Tax Notes*, November 4, 1991, p. 601.

[9] The 2% disallowance applies before considering the 3% scale down of total itemized deductions under Sec. 68 for upper-income individuals with AGI in excess of $111,800. See Chapter 7 for a discussion of these rules. The 2% floor does not apply to impairment-related work expenses for handicapped employees, estate tax incurred as a result of a decedent's income, amortizable bond premiums, certain expenses incurred by cooperative housing corporations, adjustments resulting from the prior inclusion of amounts in income under the claim of right doctrine, certain short sale expenses, terminated annuity payments, and gambling losses to the extent of winnings.

- The purchase cost and maintenance of special clothing (e.g., uniforms for an airline pilot)[10]
- Job-hunting expenses for seeking employment in the same trade or business (e.g., employment agency fees)[11]
- Professional journals, professional dues, union dues, small tools and supplies.

Example 9-3 ■

Self-Study Question

Before the Tax Reform Act of 1986, unreimbursed employee business expenses were not subject to the 2% nondeductible floor. Why did Congress decide to subject these expenses to this floor?

Charles, who is single, incurs $6,000 unreimbursed employee expenses in 1994. Charles also incurs $1,000 of investment counseling fees and $500 for the preparation of his 1993 tax return and pays these amounts in 1994. Charles's AGI is $100,000. The total miscellaneous itemized deductions is $7,500 ($6,000 + $1,000 + $500). Charles is limited to a $5,500 itemized deduction ($7,500 − $2,000) because of the application of the 2% nondeductible floor (0.02 × $100,000 AGI = $2,000). ■

Exceptions to the 2% Floor. Other itemized deductions such as charitable contributions, mortgage interest and real estate taxes on a principal residence are not subject to the 2% nondeductible floor.

Example 9-4 ■

Answer

Prior law required extensive record keeping with regard to items that were commonly small expenditures. These small amounts presented significant administrative and enforcement problems for the IRS. The use of a floor also takes into account the fact that some expenses are sufficiently personal in nature that they might be incurred apart from any business activities.

In the current year Carmelia, who is single, incurs $1,500 of unreimbursed employee expenses, $3,000 of charitable contributions, and $4,000 of mortgage interest and real estate taxes on her principal residence. She has no other miscellaneous itemized deductions or investment expenses, and her AGI is $100,000. The $1,500 of employee expenses are not deductible because the 2% nondeductible floor ($2,000 in this case) more than offsets the $1,500 of expenses. The $3,000 of charitable contributions and $4,000 of mortgage interest and real estate taxes are fully deductible as itemized deductions because Carmelia's itemized deductions exceed the standard deduction amount ($3,800 for a single taxpayer in 1994). The charitable contributions, mortgage interest, and real estate taxes are not subject to the 2% nondeductible floor. ■

TRAVEL EXPENSES

Deductibility of Travel Expenses

OBJECTIVE 1

Determine the proper classification and deductibility of travel and transportation expenses

The deductibility of travel expenses and the limitations, if any, placed upon the deduction depend upon (1) the nature of the expenditure and (2) whether the employee receives a reimbursement from the employer. If the taxpayer is engaged in a trade or business activity (e.g., a self-employed individual) or is engaged in an activity for the production of rental and royalty income (e.g., an owner of rental property), the travel-related expenditures are deductible *for* AGI and the 2% nondeductible floor is not applicable. If an employee is reimbursed for travel, the reimbursement is includible in gross income and the employee receives a deduction *for* AGI. Therefore, both the expense and the reimbursement are offset and neither appears on the tax return (assuming an adequate accounting is made to the employer). The 2% nondeductible floor only applies to any expenses that exceed the reimbursement. The

---

[10] Rev. Rul. 70-474, 1970-2 C.B. 34.

[11] Rev. Rul. 75-120, 1975-1 C.B. 55, as clarified by Rev. Rul. 77-16, 1977-1 C.B. 37. The expenses are deductible even if the new position is not obtained. However, job-hunting expenses are not deductible (1) if the taxpayer has been unemployed for an extended period or (2) if the employee is seeking to enter a new trade or business.

TABLE 9-1 Classification of Travel Expenses

| | | Tax Treatment | |
Situation Facts	Deductible for AGI	Deductible from AGI	Not Deductible
1. Cindy is a self-employed attorney who incurs travel expenses related to her business.	X^a		
2. Jose who lives in Dallas, is the owner of several apartment buildings in Denver. Periodically he travels to Denver to inspect and manage the properties.	X^a		
3. Clay is an employee who is required to travel to company facilities throughout the U.S. in the conduct of his management responsibilities. Clay is not reimbursed by his employer.		X^b	
4. Same as Situation 3, except that Clay is fully reimbursed by his employer.	X		
5. Colleen is a student who travels to her parents' home during the holidays.			X

^a The 2% nondeductible floor is not applicable.
^b The 2% nondeductible floor is applicable and the expenses are not deductible up to this amount.

2% floor also applies if the employee is not reimbursed for the travel. Personal travel is not deductible. Table 9-1 illustrates these tax consequences.

Definition of Travel Expenses

Travel expenses include transportation, meals, and lodging incurred in the pursuit of a trade, or business, or employment-related activity. Such expenses may not be lavish or extravagant. The term *travel expense* is more broadly defined in the Code than is the term **transportation expense.** Travel expenses include only those transportation expenses incurred when an individual is "away from home." Travel expenses also include laundry and incidental expenses.[12] If an individual is not away from home, expenses related to local transportation may, nevertheless, be deductible but are classified as transportation expenses rather than travel expenses. Transportation expenses for employees are also subject to the 2% nondeductible floor.

Additional Comment

Before 1987, travel and transportation costs were deductible for AGI whereas most other unreimbursed employee business expenses were deductible from AGI. Congress changed the law to move the travel and transportation costs to deductions from AGI to make them conform to the other business expenses. All of these expenses constitute costs of earning income.

Example 9-5 ■

Ahmed is away from home overnight on an employment-related business trip and incurs air fare and taxi fares amounting to $500. Because Ahmed is away from home, the $500 is deductible as travel expenses (subject to the limitations described above). ■

Example 9-6 ■

Charlotte uses her personal automobile to make deliveries of company products to customers in the same local area of her employer's place of business. Charlotte's automobile expenses are classified as transportation expenses (rather than travel expenses), because she was not away from home when they were incurred. ■

[12] Rev. Rul. 63-145, 1963-2 C.B. 86.

50% Disallowance of Business Meals

Business meals may be incurred as either a component of travel expense or as an entertainment activity. In both cases, the deduction is allowable but is reduced by 50%.[13] A business meal includes food and beverages. However, a portion of the total cost may be disallowed to the extent the expense is lavish or extravagant.[14] In such a situation, the 50% reduction rule is applied to the allowable portion of the business meal.

Example 9-7 ■

Historical Note

The 20% (currently 50%) disallowance of business meals (and entertainment) was enacted because Congress believed that prior law had not focused sufficiently on the personal consumption element of deductible business meal and entertainment expenses. Congress felt that taxpayers who could arrange business settings for personal consumption were unfairly receiving a federal tax subsidy for such consumption.

Craig is an employee who incurs otherwise deductible business lunch expenses of $80. $30 of the expenditure is not allowable because it is considered lavish or extravagant. Craig's allowable deduction ($50) is further reduced by 50%, thereby making his deduction $25. ■

The 50% disallowance rule does not apply to the following situations:[15]

- The full value of any meal or entertainment that is treated as compensation to the recipient.
- A business meal that qualifies as a *de minimis* fringe benefit (e.g., food and beverages provided by an employer for an annual company picnic for employees and their families) which is not taxable to the employee.
- Meal or entertainment expenses of an employee that are reimbursed by the employer. The employer (and not the employee) is limited to a business deduction for 50% of the reimbursed expenses.
- Employer-paid recreational expenses.
- Samples and promotional activities that are made available to the general public.
- Ticket costs to a sporting event and related expenses if a tax-exempt organization receives the benefits from the proceeds and substantially all work on the event is performed by nonpaid volunteers.

Example 9-8 ■

Connie incurs $400 for business meals and entertainment while traveling on a work assignment for her employer. Connie is fully reimbursed for the expenses. She includes the $400 reimbursement in gross income and may deduct $400 *for* AGI. Neither of these amounts is reported on Connie's income tax return because they are offset (assuming an adequate accounting is made to her employer). The employer is limited to a $200 business deduction ($400 − [0.50 × $400]). ■

General Qualification Requirements

To qualify as a travel expense deduction, the following requirements must be met:

- The purpose of the trip must be connected with a trade or business or be employment-related (e.g., personal vacation trips or commuting to and from a job location are nondeductible personal expenses).[16]
- The taxpayer must be away from his tax home overnight or for a sufficient duration to require resting before returning home.

---

[13] Sec. 274(n). For pre-1994 tax years the disallowance was 20%.

[14] Sec. 274(k).

[15] Sec. 274(n)(2).

[16] Travel expenses incurred in the production or collection of income are also deductible for AGI under Sec. 212(l), even though the travel is not connected with employment or with the conduct of a trade or business. See Rev. Rul. 84-113, 1984-2 C.B. 60.

Typical Misconception

There is a tendency to assume erroneously that a taxpayer's tax home is the location of the primary personal residence.

Real World Example

A Canadian hockey player residing in his team's U.S. "franchise location" was denied a travel expense deduction. The Court held that his tax home was the franchise location, and that the possibility of his being traded to another team did not constitute a temporary assignment. Garnett E. Bailey, 1984 PH T.C. Memo ¶ 84,610, 49 TCM 141.

Away-from-Tax-Home Requirement. Travel expenses are deductible if the taxpayer is temporarily away from his tax home overnight. The IRS's position is that a person's tax home is the location of his principal place of employment regardless of where the family residence is maintained. Reassignments of more than one year are treated as indefinite.[17] Work assignments for one year or less are classified as either temporary or indefinite depending upon the facts and circumstances of each case. If a person is reassigned for a temporary period, his tax home does not change, and the travel expenses are deductible. However, if the assignment is for an indefinite period, the individual's tax home shifts to the new location.

Several appeals courts have not been willing to support the IRS's position on the tax home issue.[18] The Supreme Court has reasoned that the key factor appears to be the business necessity of the travel expenses, as opposed to taxpayers choosing to locate their residence away from their employment location for personal reasons.[19]

The following factors are important to determine whether a travel expense deduction is allowed:

- Travel expenses are deductible if the individual must be away from his tax home for a temporary period (e.g., one year or less), and it is not practical or feasible for him to return to the tax home each day.

- A deduction is not permitted if an individual maintains a family residence in a distant location that requires travel to the principal place of employment because the individual is not away from his tax home (i.e., the tax home is located at the principal place of employment and the travel-related expenses are, therefore, treated as personal commuting expenses).

- A deduction should be permitted (provided the other qualification requirements are met) if the employee's living expenses are duplicated due to a change in work assignment.

- An individual who continually moves his place of abode to the same location as his frequently-changing job assignment may be denied a travel deduction because the individual is deemed to have "no tax home."[20]

Example 9-9 ■

Self-Study Question

A student accepts employment in another state during his summer vacation. Would the cost of his meals and lodging at the job location be deductible?

Answer

No, the student did not travel to the job because of the employer's business needs. Peter F. Janss v. CIR, 2 AFTR 2d. 5927, 58-2 USTC ¶ 9873 (8th Cir., 1958).

Dale is a college professor who accepts a temporary nine-month teaching assignment at another university and obtains a leave of absence from his current employer. Dale rents an apartment at the new location for himself while his family stays in the family residence. He, therefore, incurs a substantial duplication of living costs as the result of the temporary assignment. Dale's transportation to and from the two locations and at the temporary job location, as well as meals and lodging at the new location, should qualify as travel expenses because the relocation is temporary (e.g., for a period of one year or less and the nature of the assignment is not permanent). The argument for a deduction is further strengthened by the existence of duplicated living expenses and the employee's return to his permanent job at the end of the temporary assignment. The allowable travel expenses related to the meals are subject to the 50% disallowance. The total amount of travel expenses may be further reduced by the 2% nondeductible floor for miscellaneous itemized deductions.   ■

Example 9-10 ■

During the current year, Dan works as a construction worker in scattered locations through the country for short periods of time. Dan rents a room in each location

---

[17] Sec. 162(a).
[18] *Ira B. Stechel, Tax Management Portfolio No. 400 2nd* [Travel and Transportation Expenses—Deductions and Recordkeeping Requirements] (Washington, DC: Bureau of National Affairs, Inc., 1992), p. A-6.
[19] *CIR v. J.N. Flowers*, 34 AFTR 301, 46-1 USTC ¶ 9127 (USSC, 1946).
[20] Rev. Rul. 73-529, 1973-2 C.B. 37.

and moves his personal belongings to each location. Dan's travel expenses (i.e., transportation, meals and lodging, and incidental expenses) are not deductible because a new tax home is established as the result of each new job assignment. Dan is, therefore, deemed to have "no tax home" and his travel expenses are nondeductible personal expenses. ∎

Business Versus Pleasure

Travel expenses are deductible only if they are incurred in the pursuit of a trade or business activity or are related to the taxpayer's employment.[21] If the purpose for the travel is primarily personal, no deduction is permitted except for the specific expenditures that are directly related to the trade or business or employment activity.[22] In such event, all of the traveling expenses to and from the destination are treated as nondeductible personal expenditures. However, if the trip is primarily related to business or employment, all of the traveling expenses to and from the destination are deductible, and meals and lodging, local transportation, and incidental expenses are apportioned based upon the amount of cost that is allocable to each activity. In effect, an all-or-nothing approach is applied to the deductibility of traveling expenses to and from the destination depending upon the primary purpose for making the trip.

Example 9-11 ∎   Dana travels to New York on a business trip for her employer. She is not reimbursed for the travel expenses. Dana spends three days in business meetings and vacations for two days. Because the trip is primarily business, the traveling expenses to and from the destination (e.g., air fare) are fully deductible by Dana. If Dana's meals, lodging, and incidental expenses amount to $100 per day, only $300 ($100 × 3 business days) of such travel expenses is also deductible. The deductible business meal expenses are reduced by 50%, and the total amount of deductible travel expenses are subject to the nondeductible 2% floor on miscellaneous itemized deductions. A proration of the meals, lodging, and incidental expenses based upon the number of days may not be appropriate if the expenses are uneven or are directly related to either business or personal activities. For example, local transportation expenses (e.g., taxi fares) that are directly related to business meetings are deductible in full (subject to the 2% nondeductible floor limitation) with no proration being required. ∎

Example 9-12 ∎   Assume that the facts in Example 9-11 are reversed (i.e., that two days are employment-related and three days are personal). Because the trip is primarily personal, the traveling expenses to and from the destination are not deductible, and only $200 ($100 × two business days) of travel expenses related to meals, lodging, and incidental expenses are deductible (subject to the limitations previously discussed). None of the traveling expenses to and from the destination (i.e., the air fare) are deductible.

    The IRS has ruled that the incremental expenses of an additional night's lodging and an additional day's meals that are incurred to obtain "excursion" air fare rates with respect to employees whose business travel extends over Saturday night are deductible business expenses.[23] The reimbursement for these expenses is deductible by the employer (subject to the 50% disallowance for meals). The employer is not required to report the reimbursement on the employee's Form W-2 as gross income or withhold employment taxes. ∎

---

[21] Note 16 supra.
[22] Reg. Sec. 1.162-2(b)(1).
[23] Ltr. Rul. 9237014 (June 10, 1992).

Example 9-13 ■

Real World Example

A movie executive's wife accompanied him on business trips in the U.S. and abroad. She helped promote the movie company's image of a "family-type movie company." She also helped arrange his personal schedule. A deduction for her costs was allowed. As a result of the Revenue Reconciliation Act of 1993, the wife's travel costs would no longer be deductible unless she were an employee. U.S. v. Roy O. Disney, 24 AFTR 2d 69-5123, 69-2 USTC ¶ 9494 (9th Cir., 1969).

Self-Study Question

Would the cost of going on a safari in Africa be deductible if the taxpayer were in the business of selling guns?

Answer

In an actual case, the Court held that the safari expenses were not sufficiently connected to the taxpayer's gun-selling business. Therefore, the safari costs were not deductible. Vincent W. Eckel, 1974 PH T.C. Memo ¶ 74,033, 33 TCM 147.

Jesus travels to Chicago on a business trip for his employer and is reimbursed based upon an adequate accounting for all of his expenses. The trip is 100% business-related except that Jesus spends an additional nonbusiness day in Chicago to avail himself of substantial excursion fare savings from extending his trip beyond Saturday night. The lodging for the additional night and the meals for the additional day are deductible by the employer (subject to the 50% disallowance for meals) and such amounts are not reported on Jesus's Form W-2 as inclusions in gross income. ■

Stringent rules are applied if the taxpayer is accompanied by family members because of the likelihood that the trip is primarily for personal reasons. No deduction is permitted for travel expenses of a spouse or dependent (or other person accompanying the taxpayer) unless the person is an employee, the travel is for a bona fide business purpose, and the expenses would be otherwise deductible.[24]

Foreign Travel

Due to the potential for abuse, special rules apply to foreign travel and foreign convention expenses.[25] Travel expenses related to foreign conventions, seminars, or similar types of meetings are disallowed unless it can be shown that (1) the meeting is directly related to the taxpayer's trade or business (including employment) activity and (2) that it is reasonable for the meeting to be held outside of North America. In addition, complex expense allocation rules are applied to business trips made outside of the United States.[26]

Additional Limitations on Travel Expenses

Additional limitations restrict the deductibility of certain types of travel expenses, including the following:

- Travel deductions are disallowed if the expenses are deductible only as a form of education.[27] For example, a French language professor is not permitted to deduct travel expenses to France if the purpose of the trip is to maintain a general familiarity with the French language and customs.

- Travel deductions to attend a convention, seminar, or meeting are disallowed if they are related to income-producing activities coming under Sec. 212.[28]

- Deductions allowed for luxury water travel (i.e., ocean liners, cruise ships, or other forms of water transportation) are limited to twice the highest per diem amount allowable for a day of domestic travel by employees in the executive branch of the federal government.[29] These limitations do not apply to conventions, seminars, or meetings that are held on a cruise ship.

- A charitable contribution deduction is allowed for traveling expenses (including meals and lodging) only if there is no significant element of personal pleasure, recreation, or vacation in such travel (see Chapter 7).[30]

---

[24] Sec. 274(m)(3).

[25] Secs. 274(c) and (h).

[26] Reg. Sec. 1.274-4. No allocation of total expenses is made to the personal-use (nondeductible) element if an individual is away from home for seven days or less or if less than 25% of the time is devoted to personal purposes. In all other cases, all of the foreign travel expenses (including transportation costs) must be apportioned between business and personal activities based upon the relative percentage of time devoted to each activity.

[27] Sec. 274(m)(2).

[28] Sec. 274(h)(7).

[29] Sec. 274(m)(1).

[30] Sec. 170(k).

Example 9-14 ■   Danielle is an investor in real estate who attends real estate investment counseling seminars. During the current year, she incurs $4,000 travel expenses to attend the seminars. None of the travel expenses are deductible because the expenses are related to income-producing activities coming under Sec. 212.   ■

Example 9-15 ■   Dawn travels on a cruise ship to attend a business meeting in Bermuda. The round-trip cost of the cruise is $4,000, and the travel is for a period of 4 days. If the daily per diem amount is $150 for a government employee, the travel expenses related to the cruise ship are limited to $1,200 ($300 per day × 4 days travel).   ■

TRANSPORTATION EXPENSES

Additional Comment

The IRS takes the position that the hauling of equipment, tools, etc., in an automobile for business purposes does not make the commuting expenses deductible. This position is based on the Supreme Court's decision in Donald W. Fausner v. CIR, 32 AFTR 2d 73-5202, 73-2 USTC ¶ 9515 (USSC, 1973). The Court held that it was not possible to allocate the automobile expenses between nondeductible commuting expenses and deductible business expenses. However, if the taxpayer incurs additional costs, such as in renting a trailer, these additional costs are deductible.

The deductibility and classification of transportation expenses also depends upon the nature of the expenditure, as follows:

- Trade- or business-related transportation expenses are deductible *for* AGI and are not subject to specific limitations.

- Transportation expenses related to the production of rental and royalty income (e.g., an owner-investor in rental properties) are deductible *for* AGI and are not subject to specific limitations.

- Reimbursed transportation expenses are deductible *for* AGI (assuming that an adequate accounting is made to the employer).

- Unreimbursed employment-related transportation expenses are deductible *from* AGI as itemized deductions subject to the 2% nondeductible floor for miscellaneous itemized deductions.

- Commuting expenses are nondeductible personal expenses.

Definition and Classification

Transportation costs include taxi fares, automobile expenses, air fares, tolls, parking fees, and so on incurred in a trade or business or employment-related activity. Commuting costs incurred to arrive at and to return from an employee's job location are nondeductible personal expenditures regardless of the length of the trip. Transportation expenses are only treated as travel expenses if the employee meets the away-from-home requirements previously discussed. Otherwise, they are deducted separately as transportation expenses. Both unreimbursed employment-related travel and transportation expenses for employees are subject to the 2% nondeductible limitation upon miscellaneous itemized deductions. If a reimbursement were received, such expenses would be deductible *for* AGI.

Example 9-16 ■   Eurie's employer requires her to visit several customers at different locations within the metropolitan area during the course of the workday. Her transportation expenses (e.g., auto expenses, tolls, parking, and so on) are deductible as transportation expenses because they are related to providing services as an employee. If Eurie is required to travel away from home overnight, the transportation costs are included with meals and lodging and deducted as a travel expense. In either situation, the unreimbursed employment-related expenses are treated as miscellaneous itemized deductions and are subject to the 2% nondeductible floor limitation. If the expenses were reimbursed by Eurie's employer, the expenses would be deductible *for* AGI. ∎

Example 9-17 ∎ David accepts a permanent job with a company located 80 miles from his principal residence. He decides not to move to the new location. None of David's transportation costs are deductible because they are personal commuting expenses. (Note: since the job is a permanent assignment, it is for an indefinite period rather than a temporary period. If it is for a temporary period, the transportation expenses are deductible as travel expenses.) ∎

The following exceptions or unusual circumstances should be noted:

- Transportation expenses to travel from one job to another are deductible if an employee has more than one job. If the employee goes home between jobs, the deduction is the lesser of the amount spent on transportation or the cost of the transportation between jobs.[31]

- Transportation expenses from an employee's regular place of employment to a distant temporary work site are deductible.[32]

- Certain transportation expenses related to income-producing activities are deductible under Sec. 212. These expenses are deductible *for* AGI if they are related to the production of rental income or royalty income. Income-producing investment-related activities (e.g., stocks and bonds) are deductible as miscellaneous itemized deductions. Thus, allocated investment expenses to shareholders of mutual funds are deductible only as miscellaneous itemized deductions and subject to the 2% nondeductible floor.

- Transportation expenses related to medical treatment may be deductible from AGI as a medical expense (subject to the limitations upon the deductibility of medical expenses discussed in Chapter 7).

- Transportation expenses related to charitable activities may be deductible as a charitable contribution (subject to the limitations upon the deductibility of charitable contributions discussed in Chapter 7).

- If a taxpayer has a regular place of business, daily transportation expenses between home and temporary work locations (e.g., a self-employed CPA travels from home to a client's office in the same metropolitan area) qualify as deductible business expenses.[33] Unreimbursed transportation costs for an employee are deductible *from* AGI as unreimbursed employee expenses that are subject to the 2% nondeductible floor.

> **Real World Example**
>
> *The taxpayer, a surveyor, sought to deduct the cost of transportation from his home in Los Angeles County to work sites up to 67 miles away in Orange County which he considered to be beyond his principal or regular place of employment. However, the court held that the sites were within the Los Angeles metropolitan area and should be considered as commuting expenses. Edward Harris, 1980 PH T.C. Memo ¶ 80,056, 39 TCM 1126.*

Example 9-18 ∎ As shown in Figure 9-1, Dick has two jobs which are 10 miles apart. Dick lives 5 miles from the first job site and 8 miles from the second job site. If Dick drives directly from one job to the other, he may deduct the automobile costs associated with the 10-mile trip. If he goes home before driving to the second job, the deduction is limited to 10 miles, even though he actually travels 13 miles. ∎

Example 9-19 ∎ Diana owns a duplex, which she rents to tenants. She periodically drives from her place of business to this income-producing property to collect the rents and to inspect the property. The transportation expenses are deductible *for* AGI as an expense related to the production of rental income under Sec. 212. ∎

---

[31] Rev. Rul. 75-380, 1975-2 C.B. 59.
[32] Rev. Rul. 190, 1953-2 C.B. 303.
[33] Rev. Rul. 90-23, 1990-1 C.B. 28.

Example 9-20 ■

Carlos drives from home to and from various doctors' offices and hospitals for the purpose of receiving medical treatment. The transportation costs are deductible *from* AGI as medical expenses subject to the medical expense limitations (see Chapter 7). ■

Example 9-21 ■

Donna, an accountant who is employed by a CPA firm, travels from her home to an audit client located within the local metropolitan area. She is not reimbursed for her transportation costs. The transportation costs are deductible *from* AGI as unreimbursed employee expenses that are subject to the 2% nondeductible floor. If Donna were instead a self-employed CPA, her transportation expenses would be deductible *for* AGI. ■

Additional Comment

The Revenue Reconciliation Act of 1990 provided for an excise tax on the first retail sale of any passenger vehicle equal to 10% of the sales price over $30,000. The Revenue Reconciliation Act of 1993 provides that the $30,000 threshhold is indexed annually for inflation and is $32,000 for 1994. This tax is capitalized as a component of the cost basis of the automobile.

Treatment of Automobile Expenses

If detailed records of the various expenditures are maintained, an employee or self-employed person may deduct actual automobile expenses including gas, oil, repairs, depreciation, interest, license fees, insurance, and so on based on the percentage of business miles to total miles. To help reduce the burden of detailed record keeping, an alternative method, the standard mileage rate method, is available to taxpayers.

The standard mileage rate method permits a deduction based upon a standard mileage rate, which is currently 29 cents per mile. Parking and tolls are allowed as an addition to this deduction.[34] The following restrictions apply when the standard mileage rate is used:

- The standard mileage rate method cannot be used if two or more automobiles are used simultaneously for business purposes.

- If a taxpayer changes from the standard mileage rate method rate in one year to the actual expense method in a later year, the basis of the used automobile must be reduced by 12 cents per mile in 1994 (11.5 cents per mile in 1992 and 1993) for those years in which the standard mileage rate method was used.[35] The modified accelerated cost-recovery system (MACRS) rules (discussed in Chapter 10) cannot be used for computing depreciation in the year of the change and for the remaining useful life of the automobile. In such case, only the straight-line method under the alternative depreciation system (ADS) may be used (see Chapter 10).

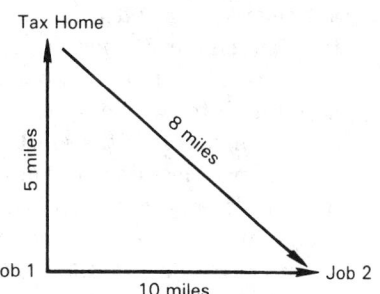

FIGURE 9-1   Illustration for Example 9-18

---

[34] Rev. Proc. 93-51, I.R.B. 1993-**42**, 30.
[35] The basis reduction was 11 cents per mile in 1989 through 1991.

- A change to the standard mileage rate method is not allowed for an automobile that was previously depreciated under the MACRS rules or where an election was made under Sec. 179 to expense part or all of the automobile's cost in the year of acquisition. (See Chapter 10 for a discussion of the Sec. 179 election.)

- The actual expense method can be used only for the business or employment-related use and is based upon the ratio of business or employment-related miles to total miles. (See Chapter 10 for a discussion of specific restrictions upon the computation of depreciation where mixed business- and personal-use automobiles are acquired.)

Example 9-22 ■ Danielle owns two automobiles which are used at the same time in her small unincorporated business. One automobile is driven by an employee of the business, and Danielle drives the other vehicle for business use. Danielle cannot use the standard mileage rate method for either automobile because both cars are used in the business simultaneously. ■

Example 9-23 ■ Doug uses the standard mileage rate method in 1993, the year the automobile is acquired for use in his unincorporated business. The automobile was used in the business for the entire year. If the actual expense method is used for 1994 and later years, the automobile's adjusted basis (for depreciation purposes) must be reduced by 11.5 cents per mile for its 1993 business usage. Thus, if the automobile originally cost $10,000 in 1993 and was used 10,000 miles for business purposes during the initial year, the adjusted basis for computing depreciation in 1994 is reduced to $8,850 ($10,000 − [0.115 × $10,000]). The remaining $8,850 basis can be depreciated using straight-line depreciation over the automobile's estimated useful life if the actual expense method is used. ■

Example 9-24 ■ Edith uses her automobile 50% of the time for business and employment-related use and 50% for personal use. These percentages are substantiated by records that document the total usage for the automobile. During 1994 Edith drives a total of 40,000 miles. If the standard mileage rate method is used, she can deduct $5,800 (0.29 × 20,000 miles) for the business and employment-related use. Additionally, Edith may deduct any business-related parking fees and tolls. ■

Additional Comment

It should be remembered that in many cases the taxpayer can choose between the automatic mileage method and calculating the actual costs of operating the car. Although the automatic mileage method has the advantage of convenience, a calculation of the actual costs might produce a larger deduction.

Reimbursed Expenses

Reimbursements of employment-related expenses by an employer or by a third party are generally included in the employee's gross income. Therefore, the law provides that the employee may deduct the related expenses in determining AGI up to the amount of the reimbursement provided that the employee has made an adequate accounting to the employer and the employee does not have the right to retain any amount in excess of the substantiated expenses.[36] This parallel or offsetting treatment was deemed necessary because the employment-related expenses would otherwise be deductible only if the employee did not use the standard deduction and then only as miscellaneous itemized deductions subject to the 2% nondeductible floor while the reimbursements are fully includible in gross income. In addition, the 3% scale down of total itemized deductions for upper-income taxpayers would reduce otherwise allowable reimbursed employee expenses if the expenses were deductible *from* AGI. (See Chapter 7 for a discussion of these rules.)

[36] Sec. 62(c).

Additional Comment

Employers are required to report on Form W-2 the amount of the reimbursement for auto expenses that exceeds the standard mileage rate. Reimbursements not in excess of the standard mileage rate are not subject to reporting.

Reporting Considerations

In most instances, an employer requires an employee to submit an adequate accounting of the expenditures to support the reimbursement request. The words "adequate accounting" mean a record (including receipts) of amounts, dates, place of expenditure, business purpose, and so on.[37] However, if an employee does not make an adequate accounting to the employer, he must submit a detailed statement on the tax return of the reimbursements and expense items. A detailed statement of all expenses and reimbursements must also be provided if the total reimbursements exceed the actual amount of travel expenses. If an adequate accounting is not made or if the employee may retain any reimbursed amounts in excess of the substantiated expenses, the expenses are deductible only as miscellaneous itemized deductions subject to the 2% nondeductible floor. Table 9-2 describes the consequences and reporting requirements for reimbursements.

Requirement to Allocate Expenses

As previously discussed, unreimbursed employee expenses are deductible as miscellaneous itemized deductions and are subject to the 2% nondeductible floor. Business meals and entertainment expenses are further limited to 50% of the otherwise deductible amount. Thus, if the employer reimbursements do not specifically identify the individual expense items (i.e., a lump-sum reimbursement amount is intended to cover a portion or all of the employee's total expenses) and the reimbursement is less than the total employee expenses, a proration of the reimbursement is required.[38]

TABLE 9-2 *Treatment of Employer Reimbursements*

Situation Facts	Tax Consequences
Eric, an employee, incurs travel expenses of $1,000 and is reimbursed $1,000 from his employer based upon an adequate accounting.	Eric may omit both the reimbursement and the travel expenses from his tax return.
Fred, an employee, incurs travel expenses of $1,000 and receives a $1,200 lump-sum reimbursement from his employer. An adequate accounting is made of the expenses to the employer, and Fred is not required to return the $200 excess amount.	Fred must include the $1,200 reimbursement in gross income and may deduct the $1,000 of travel expenses as a miscellaneous itemized deduction (subject to the 2% nondeductible floor).
Elaine, an employee, incurs travel expenses of $1,000 but is reimbursed only $800 by her employer based upon an adequate accounting of the expenses.	Elaine may deduct the $200 excess unreimbursed expense as a miscellaneous itemized deduction (subject to the 2% nondeductible floor). To the extent that the excess amount represents business meals, only 50% of such amounts are deductible. She must also submit a detailed statement of all expenses and reimbursements with her tax return despite the fact that an adequate accounting is provided to her employer. A comparable detailed statement is required for all of the situations above if an adequate accounting is not provided to the employer.

[37] Reg. Sec. 1.162-17(b)(4).
[38] Temp. Reg. Sec. 1.62-1T(e).

Example 9-25 ■

Key Point

The Tax Reform Act of 1984 imposed a "contemporaneous" records test for substantiating expenses for automobiles and certain other activities. Public outcry caused Congress to repeal this requirement in 1985. Now the business use of an automobile can be substantiated either by keeping adequate records or by sufficient corroborating evidence, oral or written.

Fred, an employee, incurs employment-related expenses of $3,000 consisting of $1,000 business meals, $1,000 local transportation, and $1,000 entertainment of customers. He receives a $1,500 reimbursement from his employer that is intended to cover all of the expenses. Of the total $1,500 unreimbursed amount ($3,000 − $1,500), $1,000 is apportioned to the $2,000 of business meals and entertainment, and $500 is allocated to the $1,000 local transportation. Only $500 of the business meals and entertainment is deductible ([$2,000 − $1,000] × 0.50) as a miscellaneous itemized deduction. The $500 of unreimbursed local transportation ($1,000 − $500) is also deductible as a miscellaneous itemized deduction subject to the 2% of AGI nondeductible floor. ■

Reimbursement of Automobile Expenses

An employee is entitled to deduct actual automobile expenses (or amounts derived under the standard mileage rate method if applicable) in excess of reimbursed amounts received from the employer. The computation is made on Form 2106 (Employee Business Expenses) and is reported on Schedule A of Form 1040.

Example 9-26 ■

Additional Comment

The kind of written record that could corroborate the business use of an automobile would include account books, diaries, logs, trip sheets, expense reports, or written statements from witnesses.

Elizabeth, who makes an adequate accounting to her employer, receives a $2,000 (20,000 miles at 10 cents per mile) reimbursement in 1994 for employment-related business miles. She incurs the following expenses related to both business and personal use:

Gas and oil	$3,900
Repairs	2,200
Depreciation	4,000ᵃ
Insurance	1,800
Parking and tolls	100
Total	$12,000

ᵃ This example assumes that depreciation is not limited by the restrictions upon automobiles that are imposed for property that is used for both business- and personal-use (see Chapter 10).

Elizabeth drives a total of 40,000 miles during the year. Thus, 50% (20,000 ÷ 40,000) of the $12,000 in automobile expenses is deductible. After subtracting the employer's $2,000 reimbursement, Elizabeth may deduct $4,000 ([$12,000 × 0.50] − $2,000) as a miscellaneous itemized deduction (subject to the 2% nondeductible floor). Alternatively, she could have claimed a deduction using the standard mileage rate method if the amount were in excess of the actual expenses. In this case the $6,000 of actual expenses exceeds the $5,850 permitted under the standard mileage rate method ([20,000 × 0.29] + $50 business related tolls). ■

MOVING EXPENSES

OBJECTIVE 2
Identify deductible moving expenses and determine the amount and year of deductibility

Moving expenses are in the nature of nondeductible personal expenditures. However, certain long-distance moves for employees and self-employed persons are deductible under Sec. 217. The underlying rationale for this deduction is that such moves are similar to business expenditures because they are frequently either employment-related job transfers or necessary to obtain employment.

Example 9-27 ■

Ken retires from his job and moves from Ohio to Arizona. His moving expenses are nondeductible personal expenditures because he is no longer employed and is not a self-employed person. ■

The following two conditions must be met for a moving expense to be deductible:

1. *Distance requirement.* The new job location must be at least 50 miles farther from the taxpayer's old residence than the old residence was from the former place of employment. If an individual has no former place of employment, the new job must be at least 50 miles from the old residence.

2. *Employment duration.* A new or transferred employee must be employed on a full-time basis at the new location for 39 weeks during the 12-month period immediately following the move. More stringent requirements must be met by self-employed persons who either work as an employee at the new location or continue to be self-employed. Such individuals are subject to a 78-week minimum work period during the first two years following the move. At least 39 of the 78 weeks must be in the first 12-month period. The Regulations provide for a waiver of the time requirements for both employees and self-employed individuals if the taxpayer becomes disabled, dies, or is involuntarily terminated (other than for willful misconduct).[39]

Additional Comment

The employment duration test insures that taxpayers cannot use temporary jobs as a pretext for deducting the cost of moving for personal reasons.

Example 9-28 ■

Ellen is employed by the Able Company in Dallas, Texas. She lives 30 miles from her place of employment in Dallas. If Ellen accepts a new job in Houston, the new job location is 270 miles from her former residence in Dallas. The 50 mile distance requirement is satisfied because the distance from her old residence to her new job in Houston (270 miles) exceeds the distance from her old residence to her old job by 240 miles (270 − 30). ■

Example 9-29 ■

Assume the same facts as in Example 9-28, except that Ellen accepts a new job in a small town outside of Dallas, which is 55 miles from her former residence. The 50 mile distance requirement is not met because the distance from her old residence to her new job only exceeds the 30-mile distance from her old residence to her old job by 25 miles (55 − 30). ■

Additional Comment

The individual need not be employed at the location that he or she is leaving. For example, a graduating college student who has not been employed for the most recent four years could deduct moving costs if the distance requirement is satisfied and if he or she has been employed at the new location for the minimum time period.

Expense Classification

Moving expenses of an employee or a self-employed individual that are incurred after December 31, 1993 are deductible *for* AGI.[40] Thus, a taxpayer may receive tax benefit from the deduction of moving expenses even if the standard deduction is used in lieu of itemizing deductions.

Definition of Moving Expenses

Direct Moving Expenses. Moving expenses may be deductible without limit as long as they are reasonable in amount and include:[41]

- The cost of moving household goods and personal effects from the former residence to the new residence.

---

[39] Reg. Sec. 1.217-2(d)(1).
[40] Sec. 62(a)(15). Under prior law, moving expenses were deductible *from* AGI as an itemized deduction (not subject to the 2% nondeductible floor).
[41] Sec. 217(b).

Key Point

The standard mileage rate for purposes of the moving expense deduction is only 9 cents per mile, compared to the 1994 standard business mileage rate of 29 cents per mile.

• The cost of traveling (including lodging but excluding meals) from the former residence to the new residence. If the trip is by personal automobile, a deduction of nine cents per mile (or actual expenses) is allowed for each automobile that is driven.[42]

The expenses of moving household goods and personal effects do not include storage charges (other than in-transit storage), penalties for breaking leases, mortgage penalties, expenses of refitting drapes, or losses on deposits and club memberships.[43]

Example 9-30 ■

Real World Example

A taxpayer incurred expenses to prepare his yacht for a trip to Florida, the location of his new residence. The Court held that the yacht did not fall into the household goods or personal effects category. Therefore, the costs were not deductible as moving expenses. William E. Aksomitas, 50 T.C. 679 (1968).

Gail, a resident of California and a college student in that state, graduates from college and accepts a new position with an accounting firm in Atlanta. Thus, Gail is an employee of the Atlanta firm. Since the move meets the distance requirement (i.e., more than 50 miles), Gail qualifies for the deduction if she also meets the 39-week time requirement. Gail incurs the following expenses pursuant to the move: moving van, $1,200; lodging enroute, $400; automobile expenses, $225 (2,500 miles × $0.09 cents per mile); and tolls and parking, $25. Assuming these expenses are reasonable, they qualify as direct moving expenses and are deductible without limitation. The cost of any meals incurred by Gail is not deductible. ■

Otherwise allowable expenses of any individual other than the taxpayer are taken into account only if the individual has both the former residence and the new residence as his principal place of abode and is a member of the taxpayer's household.

Example 9-31 ■

Assume the same facts as in Example 9-30 except that Gail's son Paul is a member of her household. Additional automobile expenses (including tolls and parking) of $250 are incurred during the move because Paul owns an automobile which is driven to the new location. The $250 of additional automobile expenses are deductible as moving expenses because Paul is a member of Gail's household and his principal place of abode includes both the former and the new residences. ■

Key Point

Indirect moving expenses are not deductible after December 31, 1993. In the Revenue Reconciliation Act of 1993 Congress eliminated the deduction for costs associated with pre-move househunting trips, temporary quarters, and selling the old residence. Congress felt that a deduction was not justified for expenses that were not directly related to the move.

Nondeductible Indirect Moving Expenses. In addition to the disallowed moving expenses previously discussed (e.g., meals en route, storage charges etc.), the following "so-called" indirect or moving-related expense items are not deductible:[44]

• House-hunting trips including meals, lodging, and transportation.
• Temporary living expenses at the new job location.
• Qualified expenses related to a sale, purchase, or lease of a residence (e.g., attorney's fees, points, or payments to a lessor to cancel a lease).

Example 9-32 ■

Assume the same facts as in Example 9-30 except that Gail incurs $1,000 of travel expenses for a house-hunting trip to the new place of employment and $500 of temporary living expenses at the new location. None of these indirectly related moving expenses are deductible because they do not meet the definition of qualified moving expenses. ■

---

[42] Rev. Proc. 93-51, I.R.B. 1993-42, 30.

[43] Reg. Sec. 1.217-2(b)(3).

[44] Prior to 1994, indirect moving expenses were deductible subject to a $1,500 limit for house-hunting trips and temporary living expenses and a $3,000 overall limitation was applied to the total amount of indirect moving expenses.

Treatment of Employer Reimbursements

Moving expense reimbursements made by an employer, either paid directly or through reimbursement, are excluded from the employee's gross income as a qualified fringe benefit under Sec. 132 to the extent that the expenses meet the requirements for deductibility (i.e., the reimbursement is for moving expenses that are otherwise deductible under Sec. 217).[45] Moving expense reimbursements are not excluded if the employee actually deducted the expenses in a prior tax year or if the expenses are otherwise not deductible under Sec. 217.[46]

Example 9-33 ■ In 1994, Ralph incurs $2,400 of otherwise deductible moving expenses related to moving household effects and traveling to his new residence. He also incurs $2,600 of nondeductible moving-related expenses (e.g., house-hunting trips and temporary living expenses). Ralph receives a $5,000 reimbursement from his employer. Out of the total reimbursement, $2,400 is excluded from gross income as a Sec. 132 fringe benefit. However, $2,600 of the reimbursement for nondeductible moving-related expenses is included in Ralph's gross income under Sec. 82. None of the $2,400 otherwise deductible moving expenses may be deducted by Paul because they were reimbursed by his employer. ■

Year of Deduction

The general rule is that moving expenses are deductible only in the year of payment. Because reimbursements may be received or an expense may be paid in the year following the year in which the move takes place, there is an exception under which cash basis taxpayers may elect to deduct moving expenses in a year following the year of the move if either of the following conditions is present:[47]

- The moving expenses are incurred and paid in one year but the reimbursement is received in a later year.
- The moving expenses are incurred in one year but are paid and the reimbursement is received in a later year.

ENTERTAINMENT EXPENSES

OBJECTIVE 3
Determine the proper deductible amount for entertainment expenses under the 50% disallowance rule

Congress has legislated specific restrictions upon the deductibility of entertainment expenses in response to widespread abuses in this area. Section 274 contains classification rules, restrictive tests, and specific recordkeeping requirements. In 1978, Sec. 274 was amended to provide restrictions upon the deductibility of entertainment facilities (e.g., country clubs and hunting lodges). The Tax Reform Act of 1986 placed additional restrictions upon the various types of entertainment expenses and applied a 20% disallowance to the otherwise allowable entertainment and business meal expenses. The Revenue Reconciliation Act of 1993 increased the disallowance of otherwise allowable entertainment and business meal expenses to 50% and provides that no deduction is permitted for all types of club dues for tax years beginning after December 31, 1993. The change was made to recognize that

---

[45] Sec. 132(a)(6).
[46] Sec. 82.
[47] Reg. Sec. 1.217-2(a)(2).

some portion of business meal and entertainment expenses may represent personal consumption.

Partial Disallowance for Meal and Entertainment Expenses

The deduction for business meals and entertainment is limited to 50% of the otherwise allowable expenses.[48] Business meals may be deductible either as travel expenses or as entertainment, depending upon the nature of the expenditure. In either case, the 50% limit applies to the cost of food and beverages including tips and taxes but is not applicable to transportation expenses incurred going to and from a business meal. Examples of entertainment expenditures that are subject to the 50% limit are

- Cover charges for admission to a nightclub
- Tickets to sporting events (limited to 50% of the face value of the ticket)
- Meals furnished by an employer to employees on the employer's premises[49]

Example 9-34 ■ Krishna, a self-employed individual, pays $40 for a business meal plus $2 sales tax and an $8 tip. The total cost of the meal is $50. Assuming that no portion of the $50 cost is deemed to be lavish or extravagant, $25 ($50 × 0.50) is deductible. ■

If an employee incurs entertainment or business meal expenses that are fully reimbursed by the employer, it is the employer rather than the employee who is limited to a deduction for 50% of the expenses. The employee merely includes the reimbursement in gross income and deducts the full amount of the entertainment or business meal expenses as a *for* AGI deduction, thus resulting in no overall tax effect to the employee.

Example 9-35 ■ Gordon incurs employment-related entertainment expenses of $1,000 and is fully reimbursed by his employer after a full accounting has been made. The employer may deduct $500 ($1,000 − [$1,000 × 0.50]) of entertainment expenses. Gordon includes the $1,000 reimbursement in gross income and is entitled to deduct $1,000 as a *for* AGI deduction. Thus there is no overall tax effect to Gordon. ■

Classification of Expenses

If an individual is engaged in a trade or business or is self-employed, allowable entertainment expenses are deductible *for* AGI. Employees, however, may deduct entertainment expenses only as a miscellaneous itemized deduction (subject to the 2% nondeductible floor) unless the expenses are reimbursed. Employee entertainment expenses are fully deductible *for* AGI to the extent that they are reimbursed by the employer, provided that the employee makes an adequate accounting to the employer and is required to pay back any unexpended amounts. Allowable expenses in excess of the employer's reimbursement are deductible *from* AGI as a miscellaneous itemized deduction.

Example 9-36 ■ Helen is a self-employed attorney who entertains clients and prospective clients. To the extent that these expenditures meet the Sec. 274 requirements, they are deductible by Helen as a *for* AGI expense on Schedule C of Form 1040 because

---

[48] Sec. 274(n). The deduction was limited to 80% for tax years prior to 1994.

[49] Section 274(n)(2)(B) provides an exception to this rule for food or beverages provided by an employer under Sec. 132 (relating to *de minimis* fringe benefits).

Helen is engaged in a trade or business activity. The entertainment expenses are subject to the 50% limit but are not subject to the 2% nondeductible floor because the entertainment is deductible when determining AGI as a trade or business expense. ∎

Example 9-37 ∎

Hal is an employee who entertains customers pursuant to his employment activities. Hal receives a lump-sum $10,000 annual reimbursement allowance for such expenses from his employer. An adequate accounting of the expenses is made to Hal's employer, and Hal must pay back any unexpended amounts. If Hal spends $12,000 for allowable entertainment expenses, $1,000 ($2,000 × 0.50) of the excess amount is deductible *from* AGI as a miscellaneous itemized deduction. Hal receives a tax benefit from these expenses only if he does not use the standard deduction, and then only to the extent that they exceed the 2% nondeductible floor. ∎

Additional Comment

Entertainment expenses will not be considered to be "directly related" if there are substantial distractions. Therefore, if a meeting takes place at a sporting event, theater, or night club, the entertainment cannot be "directly related." This type of entertainment could qualify as an "associated with" expense. An example of a "directly related" expense would be the costs related to a hospitality room at a convention.

Expense Categories. To be deductible as an entertainment expense, the expenditure must be either (1) "directly related to" the active conduct of a trade or business or (2) "associated with" the active conduct of a trade or business. Different restrictions apply to each of these categories. It should also be noted that an employee is considered to be engaged in a trade or business activity for the purpose of applying these rules.

"DIRECTLY RELATED" EXPENSES. To meet the requirements for a "directly related" **entertainment expense,** (1) some business benefit must be expected from the business conducted other than goodwill and (2) the expense must be incurred in a clear business setting (i.e., where there are no substantial distractions).[50] In other words, business in anticipation of a business benefit must actually be conducted during the entertainment period.

"ASSOCIATED WITH" EXPENSES. To qualify an expense as an **"associated with"** entertainment expenditure, the taxpayer must show a clear business purpose, such as obtaining new business or encouraging the continuation of an existing business relationship.[51] An added restriction is placed on "associated with" entertainment in that the entertainment must directly precede or follow a bona fide business discussion. This means that the entertainment generally must occur on the same day that business is discussed.[52]

Example 9-38 ∎

Holly is a lawyer who hosts a birthday party in her home. All of the guests are law partners or clients. No formal business discussions are conducted either prior to or immediately following the party. The expenditures for the birthday party are in the nature of "associated with" entertainment, but are not deductible because no business discussions are conducted. ∎

Business Meals

For the years prior to 1987, business meals (i.e., expenses for food and beverages) served in surroundings conducive to a business discussion were exempted from either of the requirements above for deductibility provided (1) a business relationship existed for the entertainment and (2) there was a reasonable expectation of business benefit.[53] Under the business meal exception (also referred to as the *quiet business*

---

[50] Reg. Secs. 1.274-2(c)(3) and (4).
[51] Reg. Sec. 1.274-2(d)(2).
[52] Reg. Sec. 1.274-2(d)(3)(ii) The Regulations also permit entertainment on the evening prior to, or on the evening of the day following, the business discussion to qualify as "directly preceding or following.".
[53] Sec. 274(e)(1).

Additional Comment

With respect to the "associated with" type of expense, there is no requirement that the business discussion last for any specified period, or that more time be devoted to business than to entertainment.

meal rule), there was no requirement that business actually be discussed before, during, or after the meal.[54]

Since 1987, however, business meals related to both travel and entertainment activities are subject to the same business-connection requirements as other types of entertainment expenses. Thus, a deduction is allowed only if the meal meets the "directly related" or "associated with" tests previously discussed. In addition, the expense must not be lavish or extravagant under the circumstances, and the taxpayer (or an employee of the taxpayer) must generally be present when the food or beverages are furnished.[55] Thus, a business meal is not currently deductible unless there is a substantial and bona fide business discussion (i.e., a discussion associated with the taxpayer's active trade or business) during, directly preceding, or immediately following the meal. This requirement does not apply to a business meal associated with travel where the taxpayer claims a deduction only for his or her own expenses.

Example 9-39 ■ Hank is a salesman for a manufacturing supply company. Hank meets Harold, a purchasing agent who is a substantial customer, for lunch during a normal business day. Business is actually conducted during the lunch, and the lunch expenses are not lavish or extravagant under the circumstances. Hank is fully reimbursed by his employer for the $30 lunch expenses after an adequate accounting of the expenses is submitted. The business meal qualifies as "directly related" entertainment because the entertainment involved the actual conduct of business where some business benefit is reasonably expected and a business discussion was conducted during the meal. Hank's employer may deduct $15 ($30 × 0.50) of entertainment expenses because the meal was not lavish or extravagant. ■

Example 9-40 ■ Assume the same facts as in Example 9-39, except that the purchasing agent is a prospective customer and no business is actually discussed either during, directly preceding, or immediately following the meal. Thus, although the business meal may otherwise qualify as "associated with" entertainment, no deduction is allowed since no business is discussed. ■

The Regulations provide that the surroundings in which food or beverages are furnished must be in an atmosphere where there are no substantial distractions to the discussion (e.g., a floor show).[56]

Example 9-41 ■ Harry is a salesman who takes a customer to a local nightclub to watch a floor show and to have a few drinks. No business is discussed either before, during, or after the entertainment. The expenses for the beverages and floor show are not deductible because neither of the business meal requirements are met (i.e., the floor show produced substantial distractions, and no business was discussed). The deduction would still be disallowed if business were actually discussed because both requirements must be met. ■

Entertainment Facilities and Club Dues

Key Point

Subject to a very few exceptions, no deduction is permitted for costs related to yachts, swimming pools, fishing camps, tennis courts, bowling alleys, vacation resorts, etc. This highly visible type of entertainment contributed to the public perception that the tax system was unfair. This explains why the current policy of not permitting a deduction for this type of facility exists.

No deduction is permitted for costs (e.g., depreciation, maintenance, repairs, and so on) related to the maintenance of facilities that are used for entertainment, amusement, or recreation. Facilities include yachts, hunting lodges, country clubs,

[54] Reg. Sec. 1.274-2(f)(2).
[55] Sec. 274(k).
[56] Reg. Sec. 1.274-2(f)(2)(i)(B).

and so on. A specific exception is provided if the entertainment facilities (e.g., a swimming pool, baseball diamond, or golf course) are provided primarily for the benefit of employees in a nondiscriminatory manner.[57]

For tax years beginning after December 31, 1993, no deduction is permitted for all types of club dues (including business, social, athletic, luncheon, and sporting clubs, as well as airline and hotel clubs).[58] Initiation fees that are paid only upon joining a club are treated as nondeductible capital expenditures. Specific business expenses (e.g., business meals and entertainment) are deductible (subject to the 50% disallowance rule) if the general requirements for a deduction are met.

Example 9-42 ■   Heidi is a self-employed CPA who entertains clients at her country club. Her club expenses include the following:

Annual dues	$4,000
Meal and entertainment charges related to business use	3,000
Personal-use charges for meals	2,500
Initiation fee	10,000
Total expenses	$19,500

None of the expenses are deductible except for 50% of the specific business expenses relating to the meals and entertainment. Thus, Heidi may deduct $1,500 ($3,000 × 0.50) *for* AGI as a business expense because she is a self-employed CPA. ■

Business Gifts

Business gifts are subject to an annual ceiling amount of $25 per donee.[59] Amounts in excess of the $25 limit per donee are disallowed. The following rules and exceptions apply to determine the business gift deduction:

- Multiple gifts to each donee are aggregated for purposes of applying the $25 per donee annual limitation. Husbands and wives and other family members are treated as a single donee.

- Husbands and wives are treated as a single taxpayer and are subject to a single $25 limit.

- Incidental costs such as gift wrapping, mailing, and delivery of gifts and certain imprinted gift items costing $4 or less are excluded.[60]

- Employee achievement awards made for length of service or safety that are under $400 are excluded.[61]

- A gift from an employee to his supervisor does not qualify as a business gift because such gifts are personal rather than business related and are, therefore, not deductible.

---

[57] Reg. Sec. 1.274-2(f)(2)(v).
[58] Sec. 274(a)(3). Under pre-1994 law a pro rata portion of club dues could be deducted if more than 50% of the use of the facility was for business purposes.
[59] Sec. 274(b)(1).
[60] Sec. 274(b)(1)(A) and Reg. Sec. 1.274-3(c).
[61] Sec. 274(j). The total limit including both qualified and nonqualified plan awards is $1,600 (see Chapter 4).

Example 9-43 ■

Real World Example

A taxpayer who had deducted the full cost of two wedding gifts, both of which were in excess of $25 apiece, was able to deduct only $25 for each gift. Jack R. Howard, 1981 PH T.C. Memo ¶ 81,250, 41 TCM 1554.

Jack, an employee, makes the following gifts during the year, none of which are reimbursed by his employer:

Jack's immediate supervisor	$20
Jack's secretary	15
Jeff (a customer of Jack's)	24
Jeff's wife (a noncustomer)	26
Gift-wrapping for the gift to Jeff	6
Total	$91

Jack's total deduction for business gifts is $46 ($15 + $25 + $6) and is classified as a miscellaneous itemized deduction subject to the 2% nondeductible floor because Jack is an employee. The $20 gift to Jack's immediate supervisor is not deductible. The gifts of $24 and $26 to Jeff and Jeff's wife must be aggregated and are limited to $25. The gift-wrapping charge is fully deductible because it is an incidental cost.

■

Limitations on Entertainment Tickets

In addition to the 50% limitation, the cost of a ticket for any entertainment activity or facility is limited to the ticket's face value.[62] Thus, the 50% limit applies to the face value of the ticket. Further restrictions are placed upon the rental of skyboxes that are leased for more than one event.[63]

Example 9-44 ■

Able Corporation acquires four tickets to a football game for $500 that are used for entertaining customers. The face amount of the tickets is only $100. Able's deduction for entertainment is initially limited to the $100 face value of the tickets. The actual deductible amount is $50 ($100 × 0.50) after applying the 50% limit on entertainment expenses.

■

EDUCATION EXPENSES

OBJECTIVE 4
Describe the requirements for deducting education expenses

Generally, education expenses are considered personal expenses and, therefore, are not deductible despite the obvious social benefits that accrue to society from the pursuit of such activities. However, certain education expenses that are necessary in the pursuit of an employment-related or trade or business activity are deductible (e.g., employees and/or self-employed individuals may need to pursue certain continuing education activities to maintain or improve their employment or professional skills). It would be inequitable if such educational expenditures were not deductible since they are incurred to produce income from employment or professional service activities. Educational expenses incurred by employees or self-employed individuals may be contrasted with scholarship and fellowship grants under Sec. 117 and educational assistance payments under Sec. 127 made by employers. Both of these latter types of payments can generally be excluded from gross income. (See Chapter 4

---

[62] Sec. 274(l)(1)(A). An exception is provided for charitable sporting events that are organized primarily to benefit a tax-exempt charitable organization if the net proceeds are contributed to the charity and nonpaid volunteers are used for substantially all the work performed. This exception does not apply to high school or college athletic events because the coaches and other officials are compensated.

[63] Sec. 274(l)(2). The cost of a skybox is disallowed to the extent that it exceeds the cost of the highest-priced nonluxury box seat tickets multiplied by the number of seats in the skybox.

TABLE 9-3   *Classification and Tax Treatment of Educational Expenses*

Situation Facts	Classification and Tax Treatment
Jeremy is a college student who is not classified as an employee and is pursuing a general course of study.	The expenses are deemed to be personal nondeductible expenditures regardless of whether Jeremy or his parents pay them.
Irene is an employee who incurs certain employment-related educational expenses including travel, transportation, tuition, books, and so on. Her expenses are not reimbursed by her employer.	If the expenses meet the two general deduction requirements, the education expenses are deductible *from* AGI as a miscellaneous itemized deduction (subject to the 2% nondeductible floor).
Jesse is an employee who receives educational assistance payments from his employer to reimburse him for certain educational expenses incurred in attending college.	Educational assistance payments up to $5,250 per year are excluded from gross income by Jesse and are deductible by the employer as trade or business expenses if the requirements of Sec. 127 are met.[64]
Jackie is a self-employed CPA who incurs education expenses including travel, transportation, books, registration fees, and so on to attend a continuing education conference.	All of the education expenses are deductible as trade or business expenses.
Jim is an employee who incurs education expenses for a continuing education course related to his employment, and the expenses are reimbursed by the employer.	The reimbursement is deductible by the employer as a trade or business expense. There is no tax effect to the employee because the education expenses are offset by the reimbursement.

Additional Comment

Attendance at a convention or professional meeting is one of the most frequently encountered deductible education expenses. Almost every profession or occupation will have its own society or association. Frequently, these organizations sponsor local, regional, or national meetings. Training sessions or other types of educational activities are normally included on the program.

for a discussion of scholarship and fellowship grants and educational assistance payments.)

Classification of Education Expenses

Depending upon the nature of the education-related activity, educational expenses may be either (1) personal and nondeductible, (2) deductible *for* AGI, (3) deductible *from* AGI (as a miscellaneous itemized deduction), or (4) reimbursed by an employer and excluded from gross income. Table 9-3 illustrates the tax consequences that are accorded to various types of education expenses depending upon the facts and circumstances and the type of expenditure for each case.

General Requirements for a Deduction

An employee may deduct expenses for education if the following requirements are met:[65]

Typical Misconception

Education costs include more than the cost of books, tuition, registration fees, and supplies. Transportation costs and travel costs are also included.

• The expenditure is incurred to maintain or improve skills required by the individual in his employment, trade, or business.

• The expenditure is incurred to meet requirements imposed by law or by the employer for retention of employment, rank, or compensation rate.

Education expenses are not deductible if the education (1) is required to meet minimum educational requirements for qualification in the taxpayer's employment,

[64] The Sec. 127 exclusion expired on June 30, 1992. The Revenue Reconciliation Act of 1993 retroactively extends the exclusion from June 30, 1992, through December 31, 1994, and includes a clarification that educational assistance payments which do not meet the requirements of Sec. 127 may nevertheless be excluded from income as a Sec. 132 working-condition fringe benefit if the requirements of this section are met.
[65] Reg. Secs. 1.162-5(a)(1) and (2).

Ethical Point

A client asks advice from his CPA as to whether certain educational expenses are deductible. The CPA should inform the client that the advice reflects professional judgment based on an existing situation. The CPA should use cautionary language to the effect that the advice is based on facts as stated and authorities that are subject to change.

trade, or business activity, or (2) qualifies the taxpayer for a new trade or business (or employment activity).[66]

The deductibility of education expenses has been a frequent source of controversy and litigation because of the uncertainty regarding the Code's requirement regarding maintaining or improving existing skills. For example, several courts have disallowed deductions to IRS agents and accountants for educational expenses incurred in obtaining a law degree, even though such training is helpful in the taxpayer's employment.[67] The courts reasoned that the taxpayers were qualifying for a new profession (i.e., the practice of law). However, the IRS has ruled that a practicing dentist may deduct educational expenses in becoming an orthodontist.[68]

Generally, a taxpayer must be employed or be self-employed to be eligible for an education expense deduction. However, some courts have permitted individuals to qualify if they are unemployed for a temporary period.[69] School teachers have generally qualified for an education expense deduction in situations where the public school system requires advanced education courses as a condition for retention of employment or renewal of a teaching certificate or where state law imposes similar requirements. However, college instructors who are working on a doctorate in a college where the Ph.D. is the minimum degree for holding a permanent position have not generally been permitted to deduct the expenditures made to obtain the degree.[70]

Example 9-45 ■

Jane is a self-employed dentist who incurs education expenses attending a continuing education conference on new techniques in her field. Such expenditures are incurred to maintain or improve her skills as a practicing dentist (a trade or business activity). All of her educational expenses are deductible *for* AGI since Jane is presently engaged in a trade or business activity. ■

Example 9-46 ■

Typical Misconception

There is sometimes a tendency to define a trade or business too narrowly. All teaching and related duties are considered to involve the same general type of work. Therefore, the following changes in duties do not constitute a new trade or business: classroom teacher to counselor, teacher to principal, teacher in one subject to teacher in another subject.

Juan is a business executive who incurs education expenses in the pursuit of an MBA degree in management. None of the expenses are reimbursed by Juan's employer. The expenses are deductible since they are incurred to maintain or improve Juan's skills as a manager and do not qualify Juan for a new trade or business. All of Juan's education expenses (e.g., travel, transportation, tuition, books, typing, and so on) are deductible *from* AGI as a miscellaneous itemized deduction (subject to the 2% nondeductible floor). ■

Example 9-47 ■

Janet is a high school teacher who is required by state law to complete a specified number of additional graduate courses to renew her provisional teaching certificate. None of the expenses are reimbursed by Janet's employer. The educational expenses are deductible *from* AGI as a miscellaneous itemized deduction (subject to the 2% nondeductible floor) because the expenditures are incurred to meet the requirements imposed by law. ■

---

[66] Reg. Secs. 1.162-5(b)(2) and (3).
[67] *Jeffry L. Weiler*, 54 T.C. 398 (1970).
[68] Rev. Rul. 74-78, 1974-1 C.B. 44.
[69] *Robert J. Picknally*, 1977 PH T.C. Memo ¶ 77,321, 36 TCM 1292. The IRS has conceded that a deduction may be warranted in periods where the cessation of business activity was for periods of a year or less (Rev. Rul. 68-591, 1968-2 C.B. 73).
[70] *Kenneth C. Davis*, 65 T.C. 1014 (1976).

Example 9-48 ■

Jean is an accountant with a public accounting firm who incurs expenses in connection with taking the CPA examination (e.g., CPA review course fees, travel, and transportation, and so on). None of the expenses are reimbursed by Jean's employer. Even though the expenditures may improve her employment-related skills, they are not deductible because they are incurred to meet the minimum educational standards for qualification in Jean's accounting position.[71] ■

Example 9-49 ■

Key Point

The deduction for travel expenses is not permitted if the travel itself is the educational activity. Therefore, a high school teacher who teaches Spanish cannot deduct expenses incurred in living in Madrid during the summer.

Joy is a tax accountant who incurs expenses to obtain a law degree. Despite the fact that the law school courses may be helpful to Joy to maintain or improve her skills as a tax practitioner, such expenses are not deductible because the taxpayer is qualifying for a new trade or business.[72] If Joy was not a degree candidate at the law school and merely took a few tax law courses for continuing education, the educational expenses would be deductible because they are incurred to maintain or improve Joy's skills as a tax specialist. In such a case, the expenses are deductible *for* AGI if Joy is self-employed and *from* AGI as a miscellaneous itemized deduction (subject to the 2% nondeductible floor) if Joy is an employee. ■

OFFICE IN HOME EXPENSES

OBJECTIVE 5

Determine whether the expenses of an office in home meet the requirements for deductibility and apply the gross income limitations

Employees or self-employed individuals who use a portion of their home for trade or business- or employment-related activities should be entitled to a deduction because of the relationship between the use of the property for trade or business- or employment-related activities. It is frequently difficult to determine whether a taxpayer is using a portion of the home such as a den for business or personal use.

Prior to 1976, some courts applied lenient standards to determine whether a deduction should be permitted. For example, some courts permitted employees to deduct office-in-home expenses even if the taxpayer's use of the facilities was not in the exclusive conduct of a trade or business activity but was merely appropriate and helpful to the taxpayer's employment activity. In 1976 the office-in-home rules were substantially restricted by the enactment of Code Sec. 280A. These restrictions were further tightened by the Tax Reform Act of 1986.

Additional Comment

Approximately 24 million individuals, or 23% of the work force, work at least part-time at home.

General Requirements for a Deduction

Employees and self-employed individuals are not permitted to deduct office-in-home expenses unless the office is used under either of the following conditions:

Real World Example

Most teachers have been denied a home office deduction because the home office is not the principal place of business. Also, most teachers cannot demonstrate that their office in the home is for the convenience of the employer since the employer typically provides an office at the school.

- The office is used exclusively on a regular basis as the principal place of business for *any* trade or business of the taxpayer.[73]
- The office is used as a place for meeting or dealing with patients, clients, or customers in the normal course of business.[74]

In addition to meeting either of these tests, an employee must further prove that the exclusive use is for the convenience of the employer. It is not enough that it is merely helpful or appropriate.

---

[71] Rev. Rul. 69-292, 1969-1 C.B. 84.

[72] Reg. Sec. 1.162-5(b)(3)(ii), Ex. (1).

[73] The exclusive use requirement does not prevent taxpayers from using a single home office for two or more businesses or require physical segregation of such activities. See *Alfred W. Hamacher*, 94 T.C. 348 (1992).

[74] Sec. 280A(c)(1).

Example 9-50 ■

Nader is a self-employed anesthesiologist who performs medical services at three hospitals none of which provide him with an office. He spends approximately two hours per day in his home office where he maintains patient records, correspondence, and performs billing procedures. The office was not used as a place for meeting with or dealing with patients, clients, or customers in the normal course of business. The Supreme Court denied a deduction in this situation because the words "principal place of business" was interpreted to mean the "most important or significant place for the business." The Court concluded that the essence of the professional service rendered by the doctor was the actual treatment in the hospitals.[75] A second factor that was considered to be important to the determination by the Supreme Court was the amount of time spent at the office relative to the total work effort. Thus, the office-in-home deduction was denied on the basis of both of these factors.

Key Point

The office-in-home deduction is only available where the office is being used for trade or business purposes. No deduction is permitted if the office is used to carry on investment activities.

Because of these strict statutory requirements, this deduction is generally restricted to (1) professionals such as attorneys, medical doctors, and accountants, and so on, who do not maintain a permanent place of business elsewhere and (2) employees who conduct a separate trade or business on a part-time basis exclusively in a portion of their personal residence. If an employee is engaged in the conduct of a separate trade or business, the allowable expenses are deductible *for* AGI as trade or business expenses. Otherwise, allowable office-in-home expenses are treated as miscellaneous itemized deductions (subject to the 2% nondeductible floor).

Example 9-51 ■

Joel, a teacher, uses his den exclusively to prepare lesson plans, grade papers, and perform other incidental tasks for his employer. Joel's employer provides office space at the school, but the den is helpful to the completion of these tasks since Joel prefers to be at home during the evening hours. No portion of the home expenditures, including depreciation, real estate taxes, mortgage interest, repairs, utilities, and so on, is deductible as employment-related business expenses because the requirements listed above are not met. In addition, the use of the den is not for "the convenience of the employer" but is merely appropriate or helpful for the employee. However, real estate taxes and mortgage interest are deductible *from* AGI if Joel itemizes his deductions. ■

Example 9-52 ■

Joan is a self-employed management consultant who maintains an office in her home. The office is used exclusively for client meetings, preparation of consulting reports, and other business-related activities. Joan's principal place of business is conducted in her home office. The office-in-home expenses are deductible *for* AGI (subject to the gross income limitations discussed below) because Joan uses the office exclusively on a regular basis as a principal place of business. Although only one of the two requirements above need to be met, Joan also meets the second requirement (i.e., to provide a place for meeting with or dealing with clients). ■

Gross Income Limitations

The total allowable office-in-home expenses may not exceed the taxpayer's gross income from the business (or rental) activity. This ceiling limitation upon otherwise qualifying office-in-home deductions is intended to prevent taxpayers from recognizing tax losses if the business (or rental) activity does not produce sufficient amounts of gross income. The allowable home office expenses (other than mortgage interest

---

[75] *CIR v. Nader E. Soliman,* 71 AFTR 2d 93-463, 93-1 USTC ¶ 50,014 (USSC, 1993).

and real estate taxes which would otherwise be deductible as itemized deductions) are limited to gross income from the business (or rental) activity less the following:

- Deductible expenses directly related to the business (or rental) activity other than office-in-home expenses.
- An allocable portion of the expenses that would otherwise be deductible as itemized deductions (e.g., mortgage interest and real estate taxes)[76]

Deductions that may be disallowed under the gross income limitation include those that are related to the use of the home as an office such as an allocable portion of depreciation, insurance, maintenance, and utilities. Operating expenses are deducted (subject to the limitation) before expenses that adjust the basis of the residence (i.e., depreciation). Unused expenses are carried forward to the succeeding taxable year whether or not the dwelling unit is used as a residence during the carryover year. The unused expenses are subject to the same gross income limitation during the carryover year.

Example 9-53 ■

Typical Misconception

Where a taxpayer is not entitled to an office-in-home deduction, the disallowed deductions are limited to depreciation, insurance, maintenance, and utilities. The taxpayer can still deduct the cost of office supplies, take a MACRS deduction on filing cabinets and other equipment, etc.

John is a self-employed attorney who maintains a qualifying office in his home. John has $40,000 of gross income from his professional practice during the current year and $34,000 of expenses that are directly related to the business (e.g., secretarial salaries, supplies, and so on). John's office-in-home expenses include $2,000 of mortgage interest and real estate taxes allocable to the office and $5,000 of other office-in-home expenses consisting of $1,000 of depreciation and $4,000 of operating expenses (i.e., maintenance, and utilities). John's business expenses (other than mortgage interest and real estate taxes) are limited to $4,000 ($40,000 gross income − [$34,000 of expenses allocable to the business + $2,000 mortgage interest and real estate taxes]). Thus, the $1,000 of depreciation is disallowed and is carried forward to a succeeding year. The carryforward amounts are subject to the same gross income limitations for the carryforward year. John's total office-in-home deductions are $6,000 ($4,000 maintenance and utilities + $2,000 mortgage interest and real estate taxes). ■

Employee expense classifications and deduction limitations are summarized in Topic Review 9-1.

DEFERRED COMPENSATION

Various types of fringe benefit plans providing favorable tax treatment are available to employees and self-employed individuals. These tax benefits were provided to stimulate savings accumulations for retirement as a supplement to the social security system. Favorable tax consequences generally include the following benefits:

OBJECTIVE 6

Discuss the tax treatment and requirements for various deferred compensation arrangements

- Deferral of taxes for employee or employer contributions to retirement plans until the individual retires or receives a distribution from the plan
- An immediate deduction for contributions to qualified retirement plans for the employer or self-employed individual
- Deferral of taxation on the income earned upon amounts contributed to the retirement plan
- Special forward income-averaging or rollover benefits for lump-sum distributions from certain retirement plans

[76] Sec. 280A(c)(5).

TOPIC REVIEW 9-1

Classification and Deductibility of Employee Expenses

Type of Expenditure	50% Disallowance	For or From AGI	Other Limitations
1. Miscellaneous itemized deductions	Applies to unreimbursed meals and entertainment	From AGI	Subject to 2% of AGI nondeductible floor.
2. Reimbursed travel expenses (adequate accounting is made)	The 50% disallowance applies to the employer for meals	For AGI	2% of AGI nondeductible floor applies only to employee expenses that exceed the reimbursement.
3. Unreimbursed travel expenses	Applies to meals portion of travel only	From AGI	Subject to the 2% of AGI nondeductible floor. Employee must be away from his tax home overnight.
4. Automobile expenses	—	From AGI	Subject to the 2% of AGI nondeductible floor. The standard mileage rate method may be used.
5. Moving expenses	Not applicable because meals are not deductible	For AGI;	Indirect moving-related expenses are not deductible.
6. Entertainment expenses	Applies to all entertainment expenses	From AGI	Subject to the 2% of AGI nondeductible floor. Club dues and initiation fees are not deductible.
7. Education expenses	Applies to meal expenses	From AGI	Qualifying expenses are subject to the 2% of AGI nondeductible floor.
8. Office-in-home	Not applicable	From AGI; If trade- or business- related, the *expenses are* for AGI	Employment-related expenses (other than real estate taxes and interest) are subject to the 2% of AGI nondeductible floor. Gross income limitations apply to allowable expenses.

The following types of *deferred compensation arrangements* are discussed here:

- Qualified pension and profit-sharing plans
- Nonqualified deferred compensation arrangements including restricted property and employee stock option plans
- Self-employed (H.R. 10) retirement plans and individual retirement accounts (IRAs)

Qualified Pension and Profit-Sharing Plans

The federal tax law provides favorable tax benefits for employers (i.e., through an immediate tax deduction for amounts contributed) and employees (i.e., through a deferral of taxes on contributions and earnings) provided the plan meets certain qualification requirements. For example, qualified plans (1) must not discriminate in

Additional Comment

The Staff of the Joint Committee on Taxation estimates the revenue loss resulting from the deferral of taxes on contributions and earnings for qualified pension and profit-sharing plans for the period from 1990 through 1994 will approximate $272.9 billion. The provision is designed to encourage employers to establish pension plans for their employees. The employer receives a deduction for the contribution, but the employee is not taxed currently. The repeal of this provision would substantially reduce the budget deficit.

favor of highly compensated individuals, (2) must be formed and operated for the exclusive benefit of employees, and (3) must meet certain vesting requirements. A distinguishing feature of a qualified plan is that the employer receives an immediate tax deduction for pension contributions. Under a nonqualified plan, the employer's deduction is generally deferred until the employee recognizes the income.

Types of Plans. Qualified plans include

- Pension plans
- Profit-sharing plans
- Stock bonus plans, including employee stock ownership plans (ESOPs)

PENSION PLANS. The features that distinguish a **qualified pension plan** include the following:

- Systematic and definite payments are made to a pension trust (without regard to profits) based upon actuarial methods.
- A pension plan may provide for incidental benefits such as disability, death, or medical insurance benefits.

A pension plan may be either contributory or noncontributory. Under a **noncontributory pension plan,** the contributions are made solely by the employer. Under a **contributory pension plan,** the employee also makes voluntary contributions that supplement those made by the employer.

Pension plans are either defined benefit plans or defined contribution plans. In a **defined contribution pension plan,** a separate account is established for each participant and fixed amounts are contributed based upon a specific formula (e.g., a specified percentage of compensation). The retirement benefits are based on the value of a participant's account (including the amount of earnings that accrue to the account) at the time of retirement rather than being established at the time the contributions are made, as is the case for a **defined benefit pension plan.**

Example 9-54 ■ Alabama Corporation establishes a qualified pension plan for its employees that provides for employer contributions equal to 8% of each participant's salary. Retirement payments to each participant are based upon the amount of accumulated benefits in the employee's account at the retirement date. The pension plan is a defined contribution plan, since the contribution rate is a fixed amount. ■

Key Point

All qualified plans can be classified into two broad categories. They are either defined contribution plans or defined benefit plans. An understanding of the distinction between these two broad categories is important since some rules will apply to one type of plan but not the other.

Defined benefit plans establish a contribution formula based upon actuarial techniques that are sufficient to fund a fixed retirement benefit amount. For example, a defined benefit plan might provide fixed retirement benefits equal to 40% of an employee's average salary for the five years prior to retirement.

A distinguishing feature of a defined benefit plan is that forfeitures of unvested amounts (e.g., due to employee resignations) must be used to reduce the employer contributions that would otherwise be made under the plan. In a defined contribution plan, however, the forfeitures related to unvested amounts may either be reallocated to the other participants in a nondiscriminatory manner or used to reduce future employer contributions.[77]

[77] Sec. 401(a)(8).

PROFIT-SHARING PLANS. A qualified profit-sharing plan may also be established by an employer in addition to, or in lieu of, a qualified pension plan arrangement. **Profit-sharing plans** include the following distinguishing features:

- A definite, predetermined formula must be used to allocate employer contributions to individual employees and to establish benefit payments. The predetermined formula need not be based upon profits.[78]

- Annual employer contributions are not required, but substantial and recurring contributions must be made to satisfy the requirement that the plan be permanent.[79]

- Employees may be given the option to receive cash that is fully taxable as current compensation or to defer taxation on employer contributions by having such amounts contributed to the profit-sharing trust.[80] Plans of this type are referred to as Sec. 401(k) plans.

- Forfeitures arising under the plan may be reallocated to the remaining participants to increase their profit-sharing benefits, provided that certain nondiscrimination requirements are met.

- Lump-sum payments made to an employee prior to retirement may be provided following a prescribed period for the vesting of such amounts.

- Incidental benefits such as disability, death, or medical insurance may also be provided in a profit-sharing arrangement.

STOCK BONUS PLAN. A **stock bonus plan** is a special type of arrangement whereby the employer's stock is contributed to the trust. The stock is allocated and subsequently distributed to the participants. Stock bonus plan requirements are similar to profit-sharing plans. An **employee stock ownership plan** (ESOP) is a qualified stock bonus plan. An ESOP is funded by a contribution of the employer's stock. This stock contribution is held for the benefit of the employees.[81] ESOPs are attractive because the employer is allowed to reduce taxable income by deducting any dividends that are paid to the participants (or their beneficiaries) in the year such amounts are paid and are taxable to the participant.[82] For employer securities acquired by the ESOP after August 4, 1989, the dividends-paid deduction is limited to dividends paid on employer stock acquired with an ESOP loan.[83]

Qualification Requirements for a Qualified Plan

Qualified pension, profit-sharing, and stock plans must meet complex qualification rules and requirements to achieve and maintain their favored qualifying status.

1. Section 401(a) requires that the plan must be for the employee's exclusive benefit. For example, the trust must follow prudent investment rules to ensure that the pension benefits will accrue for the employees' benefit.[84]

Key Point

The tax law with respect to qualified pension and profit-sharing plans is extremely complex. The student should understand that a detailed study of these provisions is beyond the scope of this text.

[78] Sec. 401(a)(27). The plan must state its intent to be either a profit-sharing or a pension plan because it might otherwise be difficult to distinguish between the two types of plans.
[79] Reg. Sec. 1.401-1(b).
[80] Sec. 401(k).
[81] Secs. 409(a) and 4975(e)(7).
[82] Sec. 404(k).
[83] Sec. 404(k)(2)(C).
[84] Rev. Rul. 73-532, 1973-2 C.B. 128.

2. The plan may not discriminate in favor of highly compensated employees.[85] Highly compensated employees generally include officers, shareholder-employees who own 5% or more of the corporation's stock, and employees who receive compensation in excess of $75,000.[86]

3. Contributions and plan benefits must bear a uniform relationship to the compensation payments made to covered employees.[87] For example, if contributions for the benefit of the participants are based upon a fixed percentage of the employee's compensation (e.g., 4%), the plan should not be disqualified despite the fact that the contributions for the highly compensated employees are greater on an actual dollar basis than those for lower paid individuals.

4. Certain coverage requirements expressed in terms of a portion of the employees that are covered by the plan must be met.

5. An employee's right to receive benefits from the employer's contributions must vest after a certain period or number of years of employment. The vesting requirement is intended to ensure that a significant percentage of employees will eventually receive retirement benefits. Employer-provided benefits must be 100% vested after 5 years of service.[88] In all cases, any employee contributions to the plan must vest immediately.

Example 9-55 ■   Ken is a participant in a noncontributory qualified pension plan that provides for no vesting until an employee completes 5 years of service. Ken terminates his employment with the company after 4 years of service. Since Ken has not met the minimum vesting requirements, he is not entitled to receive any of the employer contributions that are made on his behalf. If the plan adopted the alternative three- to seven-year vesting schedule, 40% of the employer-provided benefits would be vested at the time of his termination and would be able to provide future retirement benefits.   ■

Tax Treatment to Employees and Employers

Employer contributions to a qualified plan are immediately deductible (subject to specific limitations upon contribution amounts), and such amounts are not taxable to an employee until the pension payments are received.[89] Earnings on pension fund investments are tax-exempt to the trust. These amounts are only taxable to the employee when the pension benefits are paid. If an employee contributes to the qualified plan, such amounts are generally treated as having been made from after-tax earnings (i.e., the employee-contributed amounts are taxed to the employee when such amounts are earned).[90] Thus, when pension benefits are received, the employee's portion of the contributions is treated as a tax-free return of capital to prevent double taxation of such amounts.

---

[85] Sec. 401(a)(4).

[86] Sec. 414(q). The $75,000 amount is subject to annual indexing for inflation and was $99,000 for plan years beginning in 1994.

[87] Sec. 401(a)(5)(B).

[88] Sec. 411(a). An alternative vesting schedule may also be used which provides for 20% vesting after three years and increases by 20% per year until the employee is fully vested after seven years.

[89] Sec. 402(a)(1).

[90] Section 403(b) provides an exception to the general rule for employees of public educational organizations and certain other tax-exempt entities, whereby the amounts contributed by the employee to a tax-deferred annuity are treated as a reduction of the employee's gross income in the year the contributions are made.

Employee Retirement Payments. An employee's retirement benefits are generally taxed under the Sec. 72 annuity rules (see Chapter 3). If the plan is noncontributory (i.e., no employee contributions are made to the plan), the pension benefits are fully taxable. If the plan is contributory, each payment is treated, in part, as a tax-free return of the employee's contributions and the remainder is taxable. The excluded portion is based upon the ratio of the employee's investment in the contract to the expected return under the contract.[91] However, the total amount that may be excluded is limited to the amount of the employee's contributions to the plan.[92] If the employee dies before the entire investment in the contract is recovered, the unrecovered amount is allowed as an itemized deduction in the year of death.

Example 9-56 ■

Kevin retires in 1993 and receives annuity payments for life from his employer's qualified pension plan of $24,000 per year beginning in 1994. Kevin's investment in the contract (represented by his contributions) is $100,000, and the total expected return (based upon his life expectancy) is $300,000. The exclusion ratio is one-third, so that $8,000 ($24,000 × 0.333) is excluded from Kevin's income and $16,000 ($24,000 − $8,000) is taxable in 1994. After Kevin receives payments for 12.5 years, his investment in the contract is recovered ($8,000 × 12.5 = $100,000), and all subsequent payments are fully taxable. (See Chapter 3 for a discussion of the annuity formula and related rules.) ■

Example 9-57 ■

Assume the same facts as in Example 9-56 except that Kevin dies in 1995 after receiving pension payments for one year. Kevin's final tax return (in 1995) will include a $92,000 itemized deduction ($100,000 − $8,000). This amount represents Kevin's unrecovered investment in the contract. ■

If an employee age 59½ or older receives a lump-sum distribution from a qualified plan, a 5-year forward income-averaging technique is generally available to mitigate the effects of receiving a large amount of income in the year of the distribution (see Chapter 14 for a discussion of the forward averaging rules).[93]

Limitation on Employer Contributions. The Code places the following limitations upon the amounts that an employer may contribute to qualified pension, profit-sharing, and stock bonus plans:

- Defined contribution plan contributions are limited to the smaller of $30,000 or 25% of the employee's compensation.[94]

- Defined benefit plans are restricted to an annual benefit to an employee equal to the greater of $90,000 or 100% of the participant's average compensation for the highest three years.[95]

---

[91] Sec. 72(b)(1). Employees whose annuity starting date is before July 1, 1986, may exclude all pension benefits paid by the plan up to the amount of the employee's contributions to the plan if the pension amounts received during the first 3 years exceed the total employee contributions. Any pension benefits received thereafter are fully taxable.

[92] Sec. 72(b)(2).

[93] Sec. 402(e).

[94] Sec. 415(c). The $30,000 limit is not increased until the defined contribution limit (which is adjusted for inflation) is in excess of $120,000 (e.g., effective January 1, 1994, the adjusted dollar limitation was $118,800 so no adjustment to the $30,000 limit is currently being made). After the $120,000 amount is exceeded, the defined contribution limit is then 25% of the defined benefit limit.

[95] Sec. 415(b)(1).

Key Point

For purposes of the limitation on employer contributions, all defined contribution plans maintained by one employer are treated as a single defined contribution plan. Further, under some circumstances a group of employers can be treated as a single employer.

- An overall maximum annual employer deduction of 15% of compensation paid or accrued to plan participants is placed upon profit-sharing and stock bonus plans.[96] If an employer has more than one qualified plan (e.g., a defined benefit pension plan and a profit-sharing plan), a maximum deduction of 25% of compensation is allowed.[97]

The distinguishing features and major requirements for qualified pension and profit-sharing plans are summarized in Topic Review 9-2.

Nonqualified Plans

Nonqualified deferred compensation plans are frequently used by employers to provide incentives or supplementary retirement benefits for executives. Common forms of nonqualified plans include the following:

Key Point

Although the nonqualified plans are not subject to the same restrictions imposed upon qualified plans, they do not receive the same tax benefits as are available under qualified plans. For example, the employer may not be able to deduct amounts that are set aside or placed in an escrow account.

- An unfunded nonforfeitable promise to pay fixed amounts of compensation in future periods.[98]
- Restricted property plans involving property transfers (usually in the form of the employer-company stock), where the property transferred is subject to a substantial risk of forfeiture and is nontransferable.[99]

TOPIC REVIEW 9-2

Qualified Pension and Profit-Sharing Plans
Distinguishing Features and Major Requirements
1. Employer contributions and earnings on contributed amounts are not taxed to employees until distributed or made available. The contributions are immediately deductible by the employer.
2. Pension plans can be established as either defined contribution or defined benefit plans in which systematic and definite payments are made to a pension trust. Incidental benefits (e.g., death and disability payments) can be provided under the plan.
3. Profit-sharing plans require the use of a predetermined formula and substantial and recurring contributions must be made although annual employer contributions are not required and the contributions need not be based on profits. Section 401(k) plans can be established where employees have the option to receive cash or to have such amounts contributed to the profit-sharing trust. The employer may also establish an ESOP where the plan is funded by a contribution of the employer's stock.
4. Qualified plans must be created for the employees' exclusive benefit.
5. The plans may not discriminate in favor of highly-compensated employees.
6. Contributions and plan benefits must bear a uniform relationship to the compensation of covered employees.
7. Minimum vesting requirements must be met (e.g., 100% vesting after five years).
8. Employee benefits are taxed under the Sec. 72 annuity rules.
9. Total employer contributions to the plan are subject to specific ceiling limitations.

---

[96] Sec. 404(a)(3)(A).
[97] Sec. 404(a)(7).
[98] Rev. Rul. 60-31, 1960-1 C.B. 174.
[99] Sec. 83.

Distinguishing Characteristics of Nonqualified Plans. Nonqualified plans are not subject to the same restrictions imposed upon qualified plans (such as the nondiscrimination and vesting rules). Thus, such plans are particularly suitable for use in executive compensation planning. In general, nonqualified plans impose certain restrictions upon the outright transfer of the plan's benefits to the employee. This avoids immediate taxation under the constructive receipt doctrine which does not apply if the benefits are not yet credited, set apart, or made available so that the employee may draw upon them.[100] The employee is taxed upon the lapse of such restrictions, and the employer receives a corresponding deduction in the same year.

Unfunded Deferred Compensation Plans. **Unfunded deferred compensation plans** are frequently used to compensate highly compensated employees who desire to defer the recognition of income until future periods (e.g., a professional athlete or a business executive who receives a signing bonus may prefer to defer the recognition of income from the bonus). In general, if the promise to make the compensation payment in a future period is nonforfeitable, the agreement must not be funded (e.g., the transfer of assets to a trust for the employee's benefit) or evidenced by a negotiable note. The employer, however, may establish an *escrow account* on behalf of the employee. Such an account is used to accumulate and invest the deferred compensation amounts.[101] If the requirements for deferral are met, the employee is taxed when the compensation is actually paid or made available, and the employer receives a corresponding deduction in the same year.[102]

Example 9-58 ■

In 1994 Kelly signs an employment contract to play professional football for the Chicago Skyhawks. The contract includes a $500,000 signing bonus that is payable in five annual installments beginning in 2001. The bonus agreement is nonforfeitable and is unfunded. The Skyhawks have agreed to place sufficient amounts of money into an escrow account to fund the future payments to Kelly. None of the $500,000 bonus is deductible by the employer or taxable to Kelly when the agreement is signed in 1994. The Skyhawks do not receive a deduction for any amounts that are deposited into the escrow account during the 1994–2000 period. In 2001 Kelly receives $100,000 taxable compensation (interest, if any, that accrued and was paid to Kelly is also taxable) upon receipt of the initial payment, and the Skyhawks receive a corresponding tax deduction. ■

Restricted Property Plans. **Restricted property plans** are used to attract and retain key executives. Under such arrangements, the executive generally obtains an ownership interest (i.e., stock) in the corporation. Restricted property plans are governed by the income recognition rules contained in Sec. 83. Under these rules, the receipt of restricted property in exchange for services rendered is not taxable if the property is (1) nontransferable and (2) subject to a substantial risk of forfeiture.[103]

The employee is taxed on the compensation on the basis of the property's fair market value (FMV) (less any amount paid for the property) at the earlier of the time the property (1) is no longer subject to a substantial risk of forfeiture or (2) is transferable. The employer receives a corresponding compensation deduction at the same time the income is taxed to the employee.

---

[100] *George C. Martin,* 96 T.C. 39 (1991).
[101] Rev. Rul. 55-525, 1955-2 C.B. 543.
[102] Reg. Sec. 1.451-2(a).
[103] Regulation Sec. 1.83-3(c)(2) provides several examples of what constitutes a substantial risk of forfeiture.

Example 9-59 ■ In the current year Allied Corporation transfers 1,000 shares of its common stock to employee Karen. The FMV of the Allied Corporation stock is $10 per share on the transfer date. The restricted property agreement provides that the stock is nontransferable by Karen until the year 2000 (i.e., Karen cannot sell the stock to outsiders until year 2000). The stock is also subject to the restriction that if Karen voluntarily leaves the company prior to the year 2000, she must transfer the shares back to the company and will receive no benefit from the stock other than from the receipt of dividends. The FMV of the stock is $100 per share in year 2000 when the forfeiture and nontransferability restrictions lapse. Since the stock is both nontransferable and subject to a substantial risk of forfeiture from the issue date to year 2000, the tax consequences from the stock transfer are deferred for both Karen and Allied Corporation until the lapse of the nontransferability or forfeiture restrictions in year 2000. In year 2000 Karen must report ordinary (compensation) income of $100,000 ($100 × 1,000 shares), and Allied Corporation is entitled to a corresponding compensation deduction of the same amount. Karen is taxed currently on the dividends she receives since they are not subject to any restrictions. ■

Key Point

If an employee makes the election to be taxed immediately, he should be aware of the adverse consequences of leaving the company before the forfeiture restrictions lapse. The employee will not receive the property, and no deduction is allowed on the forfeiture.

ELECTION TO BE TAXED IMMEDIATELY. An exception which permits an employee to elect (within 30 days after the receipt of restricted property) to recognize income immediately upon receipt of the restricted property is provided in Sec. 83(b). If the election is made, the employer is entitled to a corresponding deduction at the time the income is taxed to the employee. This election was frequently made for years prior to 1987 because an eventual sale of the restricted stock at a gain resulted in favorable long-term capital gain treatment (i.e., a 60% long-term capital gain deduction was applicable to pre-1987 years). For post-1986 years, the 60% long-term capital gain deduction was eliminated, which reduced the attractiveness of the Sec. 83(b) election. The increase in marginal tax rates for high-income taxpayers from 31% to 39.6% for taxpayer's with taxable income in excess of $250,000 for 1993 and subsequent years along with the availability of a 28% maximum capital gain rate may increase the attractiveness of this election.

Example 9-60 ■ Assume the same facts as Example 9-59, except that Karen elects to recognize income on the transfer date. Karen must include $10,000 ($10 × 1,000 shares) in gross income as compensation in the current year, and Allied Corporation is entitled to a corresponding deduction in the same year. If Karen sells the stock for $100,000 in the year 2000 after the restrictions lapse, Karen reports a $90,000 ($100,000 − $10,000) long-term capital gain on the sale.[104] If Karen voluntarily leaves the company before the forfeiture restrictions lapse, no deduction is allowed when the forfeiture occurs, despite the fact that Karen is previously taxed on the stock's value on the transfer date (i.e., $10,000 of income is recognized by Karen in the current year). In such event, Allied Corporation must include $10,000 in gross income in the year of the forfeiture (i.e., the amount of the deduction that is taken in the year of the transfer to the extent of any previous tax benefit).[105] ■

Nonqualified plan features and requirements are summarized in Topic Review 9-3.

---

[104] Sec. 1223. The holding period originates on the day following the transfer date because the election to be taxed immediately was made by Karen.

[105] Reg. Sec. 1.83-6(c). A deduction would be available to Karen for any amounts that she paid for the Allied stock.

TOPIC REVIEW 9-3

Nonqualified Plans
Distinguishing Features and Major Requirements
1. The employee is taxed upon the lapse of restrictions imposed upon the availability or withdrawal of funds and the employer receives a corresponding deduction in the same year. 2. Nonqualified plans may discriminate in favor of highly compensated employees and no minimum vesting rules are required. 3. Restricted property (usually employer stock) may be offered to executives where the incidents of taxation are deferred if the property is (a) nontransferable and (b) subject to a substantial risk of forfeiture. An election may be made under Sec. 83(b) to recognize income immediately upon the receipt of the restricted property. 4. Restrictions must be imposed to avoid immediate taxation to the employee under the constructive receipt doctrine. 5. To avoid immediate taxation, restricted property plans must be both (a) nonforfeitable and (b) subject to a substantial risk of forfeiture.

Employee Stock Options

Stock option plans are used by corporate employers to attract and retain key management employees. Both stock option and restricted property arrangements using the employer's stock permit the executive to receive a proprietary interest in the corporation. Thus, an executive may identify more closely with shareholder interests and the firm's long-run profit-maximization goals. The tax law currently includes two types of stock-option arrangements. They are the incentive stock option and the nonqualified stock option.[106] Each type is treated differently for tax purposes.

Prior to the passage of the Tax Reform Act of 1986, incentive stock-option arrangements were frequently used because the employee could receive favorable long-term capital gain treatment (i.e., a 60% long-term capital gain deduction) if certain requirements were met. The nonqualified stock-option arrangement has become increasingly popular for years after 1986 because of the elimination of favorable capital gain treatment for incentive stock options for the 1987–1990 period. The enactment of a 28% maximum capital gain rate effective for 1991 and later years combined with increased marginal tax rates for high-income taxpayers effective for 1993 and subsequent years may increase the use of incentive stock option arrangements. However, an employer is more favorably treated under the nonqualified stock-option rules (i.e., the employer receives a tax deduction for the compensation related to a nonqualified stock option but does not receive a corresponding deduction if an incentive stock-option plan is adopted) and may therefore still prefer to continue to use nonqualified stock options.

Incentive Stock Option Plans.
EMPLOYER REQUIREMENTS. An **incentive stock option** (ISO) must meet the following plan or employer requirements:

- The option price must be equal to or greater than the stock's FMV on the option's grant date.
- The option must be granted within 10 years from the date the plan is adopted, and the employee must exercise the option within 10 years from the grant date.

Key Point

The incentive stock option has the disadvantage of not providing a compensation deduction for the employer. Before January 1, 1987, this negative characteristic was offset by the fact that the employee was eligible for a 60% long-term capital gain deduction. With the repeal of the long-term capital gain deduction, the incentive stock option has lost much of its appeal, although the reenactment of a maximum 28% tax rate for net long-term capital gains may help to increase the future popularity of incentive stock options.

---

[106] The incentive stock option rules are provided in Sec. 422A, whereas the rules governing nonqualified stock options are contained in Reg. Secs. 1.421-6 and 1.83-7.

- The option must be both exercisable only by the employee and nontransferable except in the event of death.
- The employee cannot own more than 10% of the voting power of the employer corporation's stock immediately prior to the option's grant date.
- The total FMV of the stock options that become exercisable to an employee in any given year may not exceed $100,000 (e.g., an employee can be granted ISOs to acquire $200,000 of stock in one year, provided that no more than $100,000 is exercisable in any given year).[107]
- Other procedural requirements must be met (e.g., shareholder approval of the plan, and so on).[108]

EMPLOYEE REQUIREMENTS. An addition to the above plan requirements, the employee must meet the following requirements:

- The employee must not dispose of the stock within two years from the option's grant date nor within one year after the option's exercise date.[109]
- The employee must be employed by the issuing company on the grant date and continue such employment until within three months prior to the exercise date.[110]

If an employee meets the requirements listed above, no tax consequences occur on the grant date or on the exercise date. However, the excess of the FMV over the option price on the exercise date is a tax preference item for purposes of the alternative minimum tax (see Chapter 14). When the employee sells the optioned stock, a long-term capital gain or loss is recognized. If the employee meets the two requirements, the employer does not receive a corresponding compensation deduction.[111] If the requirements are not met, the option is treated as a nonqualified stock option.

Example 9-61 ■   American Corporation grants an incentive stock option to Kay, an employee, on January 1, 1994. The option price is $100, and the FMV of the American stock is also $100 on the grant date. The option permits Kay to purchase 100 shares of American stock. Kay exercises the option on June 30, 1996, when the stock's FMV is $400. Kay sells the 100 shares of American stock on January 1, 1998, for $500 per share. Since Kay holds the stock for the required period (at least two years from the grant date and one year from the exercise date) and since Kay is employed by the American Corporation on the grant date and within three months prior to the exercise date, all of the requirements for an ISO have been met. No income is recognized on the grant date or on the exercise date, although $30,000 ([$400 − $100] × 100 shares) is a tax preference item for the alternative minimum tax in 1996. Kay recognizes a $40,000 ([$500 − $100] × 100 shares) long-term capital gain on the sale date in 1998. American Corporation is not entitled to a compensation deduction in 1998 or in any other year.   ■

Example 9-62 ■   Assume the same facts as Example 9-61, except that Kay disposes of the stock on August 1, 1996, thus violating the one-year holding period requirement. Kay must recognize ordinary income on the sale date equal to the spread between the option price and the exercise price, or $30,000 ([$400 − $100] × 100 shares). The

---

[107] Sec. 422A(d).
[108] Sec. 422A(b).
[109] Sec. 422A(a)(1).
[110] Sec. 422A(a)(2). Certain exceptions are provided for hardship and other special situations. See Sec. 422A(c)(9).
[111] Sec. 421(a)(2).

$30,000 spread between the FMV and the option price is no longer a tax preference item because the option ceases to qualify as an ISO. American Corporation can claim a $30,000 compensation deduction in 1996. Kay also recognizes a $10,000 ([$500 − $400 adjusted basis] × 100 shares) short-term capital gain on the sale date, which represents the appreciation of the stock from the exercise date to the sale date. The gain is short-term because the holding period from the exercise date to the sale date does not exceed one year. ∎

Nonqualified Stock Option Plans. Stock options that do not meet the plan requirements for incentive stock options are referred to as **nonqualified stock options.** The tax treatment of nonqualified stock options depends upon whether the option has a **readily ascertainable fair market value** (e.g., whether the option is traded on an established stock exchange).

READILY ASCERTAINABLE FAIR MARKET VALUE. If a nonqualified stock option has a readily ascertainable FMV (e.g., the option is traded on an established options exchange), the employee recognizes ordinary income on the grant date equal to the difference between the stock's FMV and the option's exercise price. The employer receives a compensation deduction on the grant date equal to the same amount of income that is recognized by the employee. In such case, no tax consequences occur on the date the option is exercised, and the employee recognizes capital gain or loss upon the sale or disposition of the stock.

NO READILY ASCERTAINABLE FAIR MARKET VALUE. If a nonqualified stock option has no readily ascertainable FMV, no tax consequences occur on the grant date. On the exercise date the employee recognizes ordinary income equal to the spread between the FMV of the stock and the option price, and the employer receives a corresponding compensation deduction. When the stock option is exercised, the employee's basis in the stock is equal to the option price plus the amount that is reported as ordinary income on the exercise date. Capital gain or loss is recognized upon the subsequent sale of the stock by the employee.

The alternative minimum tax does not apply to nonqualified stock options regardless of whether the option has a readily ascertainable FMV. Table 9-4 illustrates the tax consequences to employees and employers for such options.

As illustrated in Table 9-4, Kim reports a total gain of $11,000 from the option transaction under both circumstances. However, the character of her profit (i.e., ordinary income or capital gain) and the timing of the profit recognition (i.e., grant date or exercise date) depends upon whether the option's FMV is readily ascertainable.

The distinguishing features and major requirements for employee stock options are summarized in Topic Review 9-4.

Plans for Self-Employed Individuals

Self-employed individuals such as sole proprietors and partners who practice a trade or business are not classified as employees and are subject to special retirement plan rules known as **H.R. 10 plans** (also called **Keogh plans**). Retirement plans of self-employed persons are generally subject to the same contribution and benefit limitations as other qualified corporate plans. An employee who is covered under a qualified pension or profit-sharing plan for wages earned as an employee and who is also self-employed may establish an H.R. 10 plan for earned income derived from self-employment activities.

For a **defined contribution H.R. 10 plan,** a self-employed individual may contribute the smaller of $30,000 or 25% of earned income from the self-employment

TABLE 9-4 *Taxation of Nonqualified Stock Options*

Situation Facts	Readily Ascertainable FMV	No Readily Ascertainable FMV
Grant date—On January 1, 1994, Kim is granted a nonqualified stock option to purchase 100 shares of stock from Apple Corporation (Kim's employer) at $90 per share. The stock's FMV is $100 on the grant date.	Ordinary income of $1,000 is recognized ([$100 − $90] × 100 shares) by Kim. Apple Corporation receives a corresponding $1,000 compensation deduction.	No tax consequences to Kim or Apple Corporation.
Exercise date—On January 31, 1995, Kim exercises the option and acquires the 100 shares of Apple Corporation stock for the $90 option price when the FMV is $190.	No tax consequences to Kim or Apple Corporation.	Kim recognizes ordinary income of $10,000 ([$190 − $90] × 100 shares), and Apple Corporation receives a $10,000 compensation deduction.
Sale date—On February 1, 1996, Kim sells the stock for $200 per share and realizes $20,000 ($200 × 100 shares).	Kim recognizes a $10,000 ($20,000 − $10,000 basis) capital gain.[a]	Kim recognizes a $1,000 ($20,000 − $19,000 basis) long-term capital gain.[b]

[a] Kim's basis includes the amount paid for the optioned stock of $9,000 plus ordinary income of $1,000 recognized on the grant date. Kim's holding period commences on the January 1, 1994 grant date, for determining whether the gain is long-term.
[b] Kim's basis includes the $9,000 paid for the option stock plus the $10,000 ordinary income recognized on the exercise date. Kim's holding period commences on the January 31, 1995 exercise date for determining whether the gain is long-term.

activity.[112] Earned income refers to net earnings from self-employment. To compute the limitations, only $150,000 of earned income may be taken into account for any one individual.[113] For purposes of the 25% calculation, earned income is reduced by the contribution made on behalf of the self-employed individual.[114]

Example 9-63 ■   Larry is a self-employed CPA whose 1994 net earnings from his trade or business (before the H.R. 10 plan contribution but after the deduction for one-half of the self-employment taxes paid under Sec. 164(f) [see Chapter 14]) is $100,000. The 25% contribution limitation is computed as follows: $100,000 − 0.25x = x, where x equals Larry's net earned income after the contribution deduction. Thus, under this formula, Larry's net earned income is $80,000. Therefore, Larry may contribute $20,000 to the plan for 1994 ($80,000 × 0.25), since this amount is less than the $30,000 ceiling. Larry must also provide coverage for all of his eligible full-time employees under the general rules provided in the law for qualified plans (e.g., nondiscrimination, vesting, and so on).[115]   ■

Additional Comment

A Keogh plan must be created no later than the last day of your tax year.

An H.R. 10 plan must be established prior to the end of the tax year, but contributions may be made up to the due date for the tax return (including extensions). All H.R. 10 pension contributions made by a self-employed individual for employees are deductible for AGI on Schedule C. The H.R. 10 contribution for the self-employed individual is deductible *for* AGI on page 1 of Form 1040.

[112] Sec. 415(c)(1). A 15% deduction limit applies if the defined contribution plan is a profit sharing plan.
[113] Secs. 401(a)(17) and 404(1). The Revenue Reconciliation Act of 1993 reduced the ceiling amount to $150,000 to benefits accruing in plan years beginning after December 31, 1993. Under prior law, the amount was $200,000 but was inflation adjusted so that the amount for 1993 was $235,840. For years beginning after 1994 the $150,000 ceiling will be adjusted for inflation in increments of $10,000.
[114] Sec. 401(c)(2)(A)(v).
[115] Sec. 401(d).

TOPIC REVIEW 9-4

Employee Stock Options
Distinguishing Features and Major Requirements
1. For an incentive stock option (ISO) plan no tax consequences occur on the grant or the exercise date (except for the recognition of a tax preference item under the AMT provisions on the exercise date). Capital gain or loss is recognized by the employee upon the sale or exchange of the stock. No deduction is allowed to the employer.
2. ISOs and nonqualified stock options may be issued to highly compensated employees without regard to nondiscrimination rules.
3. If a nonqualified stock option has a readily ascertainable FMV, the employee recognizes ordinary income equal to the spread between the FMV of the stock and the option price on the grant date and the employer receives a corresponding deduction. If the option has no readily ascertainable FMV, income is recognized on the exercise date equal to the spread between the FMV of the stock and the option price and a corresponding deduction is available to the employer.
4. For an ISO, the option price must be equal to or greater than the FMV of the stock on the grant date; employees cannot own more than 10% of the voting power of the employer's stock; and restrictions are placed upon the total FMV of stock options that may be issued.
5. To qualify under the ISO rules, a two-year holding period from the grant date is required (and at least one year after the exercise date) and the employee must continue to be employed by the company until within three months of the exercise date.

Real World Example
The IRA savings provisions were originally enacted in 1974 to provide a tax-favored retirement savings arrangement to individuals who were not covered under a qualified plan. Beginning in 1982, Congress extended IRA availability to all taxpayers. It was hoped that the extended availability would increase the level of savings and provide a discretionary retirement savings plan that was uniformly available. However, Congress in the Tax Reform Act of 1986 restricted the availability of IRAs because there was no discernible impact on aggregate personal savings.

Individual Retirement Accounts (IRAs)

Prior to 1987, an employee or a self-employed individual could establish an IRA even though he was also covered under an employer-sponsored qualified plan or an H.R. 10 plan. The Tax Reform Act of 1986 severely curtailed the availability of deductible IRA plans for many individuals. Effective for 1987 and subsequent years, an individual may make deductible contributions equal to the lesser of $2,000 or 100% of compensation only if either of the following conditions exists:

- The individual or his spouse is not an active participant in an employer-sponsored retirement plan, including tax-sheltered annuities, government plans, simplified employee pension plans, and H.R. 10 plans.

- Individuals who are active participants in an employer-sponsored retirement plan must have an AGI equal to or below the following applicable dollar limits:[116]

- $25,000 for an unmarried individual

- $40,000 for a married couple filing a joint return

- Zero for a married individual filing separately

If the dollar limitations apply, the deductible IRA contribution amounts are phased-out on a pro-rata basis as AGI increases from $25,000 to $35,000 for unmarried taxpayers and from $40,000 to $50,000 for married taxpayers filing a joint return.[117]

---

[116] Sec. 219(g).

[117] An exception exists in Sec. 219(g)(2)(B) in that a $200 minimum deduction floor is available for individuals whose AGI is just below the phase-out range.

Example 9-64 ■   Laura is an unmarried taxpayer who is not an active participant in an employer-sponsored retirement plan (or other qualified plan). In the current year, Laura's AGI is $60,000, consisting of earned income from wages. Laura is not subject to the dollar limitations because she is not an active participant in a qualified plan, and may, therefore, contribute up to $2,000 to a deductible IRA. Laura's AGI is reduced to $58,000 ($60,000 − $2,000) if the IRA contribution is made because the amount is deductible *for* AGI. ■

Example 9-65 ■

Additional Comment

Banks, savings and loan associations, insurance companies, and stock brokerage firms make IRAs available to taxpayers. Usually, the amounts are invested in long-term savings accounts. However, self-directed plans are offered by some stock brokerage firms. In this type of IRA, the taxpayer can specify how the contributions will be invested.

Judy is a married taxpayer who is an active participant in an employer-sponsored retirement plan. Judy files a joint return with her spouse. Judy and her spouse have $46,000 of AGI, consisting of $40,000 earned income from wages and $6,000 of dividends and interest. The ceiling amount is exceeded by $6,000 ($46,000 AGI − $40,000). Thus, the maximum deductible IRA contribution is reduced by 60%. If Judy and her spouse both have earned income of more than $2,000, each may make a deductible contribution of $800 ($2,000 × 0.40). ■

If only one spouse is employed and such individual is otherwise eligible to make deductible IRA contributions, the working spouse may contribute up to $2,250, if no more than $2,000 is allocated to the working spouse's account and a joint return is filed.[118] The additional $250 spousal IRA deduction is available either if the spouse has no compensation for the year or an election is made to treat the low-income spouse as having no compensation.

Example 9-66 ■   Julie and Marc are married and file a joint return for the current year. Julie earns $20,000, and Marc earns $100 in the current year. Julie is eligible to make a deductible IRA contribution of $2,000 and may make an additional $250 contribution for Marc if an election is made to treat Marc as having earned no compensation in the current year. ■

The following significant tax rules apply to an IRA:

Additional Comment

A 1994 contribution to an IRA can be made as late as the due date for filing the 1994 return.

Key Point

Nondeductible contributions may still be advantageous since the income earned in the IRA is not subject to current taxation. However, it is important to keep track of the dollar amount of deductible and nondeductible IRA contributions so that the tax consequences of retirement payments can be determined. Some taxpayers consider the record keeping requirements to be too severe.

- Nondeductible contributions to an IRA are permitted when an individual is ineligible to make deductible contributions.[119]
- An IRA plan may be established between the end of the tax year and the due date for the tax return (not including any extensions that are permitted). Any deductible contributions made during this time period are treated as a deduction for the prior year.
- Withdrawals by a participant before age 59½ are subject to a nondeductible 10% penalty tax.[120]
- Retirement payments must begin no later than April 1 of the year following the end of the tax year in which the individual reaches age 70½. Deductible IRA contributions are fully taxable as ordinary income when the amounts are distributed. If an individual has made both deductible and nondeductible IRA contributions, all IRA contracts are treated as one contract. The annuity rules under Sec. 72 are then used to determine the taxable and nontaxable portion of the distribution. Nondeductible IRA contributions are treated as nontaxable because these amounts were contributed with after-tax dollars.

---

[118] Sec. 219(c).
[119] Sec. 408(o).
[120] Sec. 72(t). Exceptions are also provided in the event of death, disability, and for certain non-lump-sum distributions.

- A nondeductible 6% penalty tax is levied on excess contributions to an IRA.[121]

Topic Review 9-5 contains a summary of H.R. 10 and IRA plan features and requirements.

Simplified Employee Pensions

Due to the administrative complexity associated with qualified pension and profit-sharing plans, small businesses frequently establish simplified employee pension (SEP) plans for their employees. In an SEP, the employer makes contributions to IRAs of its employees.[122] The following is a summary of the tax rules which apply to an SEP:

- The employer receives an immediate tax deduction for contributions made under the plan. The annual deductible contributions for each participant are limited to the lesser of 15% of the participant's compensation (up to a ceiling of $150,000) or the dollar limitations for defined contribution plans.[123]

- Contributions are treated as being made on the last day of the tax year if they are made by the due date of the tax return (including extensions).

- Employer contributions must be nondiscriminatory.

- Participants may elect to receive cash or have the employer make contributions to the SEP (i.e., a salary reduction agreement). If an employee elects to receive cash, such amounts are immediately taxable to the recipient. Employer contributions to the SEP are excluded from gross income up to an annual inflation adjusted amount ($9,240 in 1994).[124] Such amounts are subject to taxation when the funds are withdrawn by the employee.

- Distributions from an SEP are subject to taxation based upon the IRA rules (previously discussed) including the penalty tax for premature distributions.

- A self-employed person (i.e., a partner or sole proprietor) may establish an SEP rather than using an H.R. 10 plan arrangement because of reduced administrative complexity associated with an SEP.[125]

TAX PLANNING CONSIDERATIONS

Moving Expenses

To be eligible for the moving expense deduction, the taxpayer must either be a full-time employee or self-employed. Therefore, it is important to secure full-time employment or to carry on a trade or business as a self-employed individual at the new location. Taxpayers who are approaching retirement are eligible for a moving expense deduction only if they continue to work in the new location prior to their actual retirement (e.g., 39 weeks in the 12-month period following the move).

---

[121] Sec. 4973(b).
[122] Sec. 408(k).
[123] Sec. 402(h)(2).
[124] Sec. 408(k)(6).
[125] Sec. 408(k)(7).

TOPIC REVIEW 9-5

H.R. 10 (Keogh) Plans
Distinguishing Features and Major Requirements
1. Self-employed retirement plan contribution and benefit limitations correspond to those offered to employees under the qualified pension and profit-sharing arrangements.   2. The annual contribution limit is the smaller of $30,000 or 25% of earned income.   3. An employee who is also self-employed may establish an H.R. 10 plan based upon the self-employment income.   4. H.R. 10 plan contributions are deductible *for* AGI.   5. To compute the allowable maximum H.R. 10 contribution, only $150,000 of earned income may be taken into account.   6. Self-employed individuals must cover all eligible full-time employees under the plan.   7. An H.R. 10 plan must be established before the end of the tax year but contributions may be made up to the due date for the tax return (including extensions).
Individual Retirement Accounts (IRAs)
Distinguishing Features and Major Requirements
1. Fully deductible contributions may be made only by an individual (or his spouse) who is *not* an active participant in an employer-sponsored retirement plan or by an individual (or spouse) who has AGI of $25,000 or less (or $40,000 or less for a married couple filing jointly). The deductible amounts are phased-out on a pro-rata basis as AGI increases from $25,000 to $35,000 ($40,000 to $50,000 for married taxpayers filing a joint return).   2. Contributions to an IRA can be made as late as the due date for filing the tax return (excluding extensions) (e.g., by April 17, 1995 for a deduction on the 1994 tax return for a calendar-year taxpayer).   3. Nondeductible contributions to an IRA may be made by ineligible individuals.   4. The working spouse may contribute up to $2,250 per year if only one spouse is employed provided that a maximum of $2,000 is designated to the account of the working spouse.   5. Withdrawals before age 59½ are subject to a nondeductible 10% penalty unless due to death, disability and certain non-lump-sum distributions.   6. Deductible contributions are generally limited to the lesser of $2,000 or 100% of compensation.

Example 9-67 ■   Louis decides to quit his job and return to school as a full-time graduate student. Louis incurs substantial long-distance moving expenses that would otherwise be deductible to relocate to the university where the education is to be taken. No deduction is allowed unless Louis is employed on a full-time basis or is engaged in a self-employment activity at the new location.   ■

Reimbursed Amounts. Moving expense reimbursements are frequently made in excess of the amounts allowable as a deduction. This is caused by the frequent practice of reimbursing nondeductible items (e.g., an employer may reimburse an employee for the cost of certain indirect moving expenses such as house-hunting trips which do not qualify as deductible moving expenses. This results in an increase in the employee's gross income to the extent of the excess reimbursement. From a tax planning standpoint, the employer may provide an additional payment to compensate the employee for the additional tax cost associated with the move.

Example 9-68 ■

Austin Corporation has a policy of reimbursing transferred employees for 30% of their moving reimbursement that exceeds their deductible expenses to cover the federal and state tax costs associated with the excess reimbursement. Kathy, an employee, is transferred by the company to a new job location and incurs $6,000 of deductible moving expenses and receives an $8,000 reimbursement. Austin also will make an additional payment to Kathy of $600 (0.30 × $2,000) to cover the additional federal and state income tax costs. Kathy must include the $2,600 ($2,000 + $600) of the reimbursement in gross income. ■

Maximizing Employee Travel and Transportation Expense Deductions

Corporate officers who are also key shareholders in a closely held corporation frequently incur substantial travel and transportation expenses in connection with their employment activities. Such expenditures are usually subject to close scrutiny by the IRS due to possible abuse (i.e., such reimbursements may be treated as constructive dividends if the travel or transportation is personal rather than business-related).

Typical Misconception

It is sometimes mistakenly believed that if the standard mileage rate method is used to calculate automobile costs, then no other auto costs can be deducted. In fact, interest, state and local taxes (other than gasoline taxes), parking fees, and tolls can be deducted in addition to the standard mileage rate. This maximizes the travel or transportation expense deduction. Nevertheless, the interest on the car loan of an employee is considered personal interest.

If an officer-shareholder makes frequent use of an automobile in employment-related activities, it may be desirable to have the corporation acquire the automobile and provide a company car to the employee. If the automobile is also used for personal commuting, the employee should be required to reimburse the company for the personal-use mileage. In such cases, the documentation of business and personal use is particularly important to avoid constructive dividend treatment. It is generally preferable for an employee to be fully reimbursed for travel and transportation expenses because of the 2% nondeductible floor on miscellaneous itemized deductions.

In addition, only 50% of business meals incurred as a component of travel expense or as an entertainment activity is allowed. If business meals are reimbursed by the employer, only 50% of such amounts are deductible by the employer. If the expenses are reimbursed, the employee expenses (including business meals) are fully deductible *for* AGI and are used to offset the reimbursements includible in the employee's gross income. Unreimbursed employee expenses are combined with investment expenses and other nonbusiness itemized deductions (e.g., tax return preparation fees) and are treated as miscellaneous itemized deductions. They are subject to the nondeductible 2% floor. In many instances, these expenses do not exceed 2% of AGI or an employee will use the standard deduction and will, therefore, receive limited or no tax benefit. In addition, the remaining allowable miscellaneous itemized deductions may be subject to the 3% scale down of total itemized deductions if the individual's AGI is in excess of $111,800 ($55,900 for married individuals filing separately).

Example 9-69 ■

Mark is an employee for the Bass Corporation and incurs $3,000 of travel expenses (including $1,000 in business meals) that are not reimbursed by his employer. Mark also incurs $1,000 other miscellaneous itemized deductions (e.g., safe deposit box rentals, tax return preparation fees, and professional dues and subscriptions). Mark's AGI is $100,000. Only $500 ($1,000 × 0.50) of Mark's unreimbursed business meals are deductible (before the 2% limitation is applied). Thus Mark's total travel expenses are reduced to $2,500 ($3,000 − $500). Mark's total miscellaneous itemized deductions (before the 2% limitation) are $3,500 ($2,500 travel expenses plus $1,000 other miscellaneous itemized deductions). Mark may deduct only $1,500 ($3,500 − [0.02 × $100,000]) of miscellaneous itemized deductions if he does not use the standard deduction. Since Mark's AGI is only

$100,000, his itemized deductions are not subject to the overall limitation on itemized deductions (i.e., total itemized deductions are reduced by 3% of AGI in excess of $111,800). (See Chapter 7 for a discussion of this limitation.)   ■

Providing Nontaxable Compensation to Employees

Employers should consider the tax consequences to employees when changes in fringe benefit and deferred compensation arrangements are evaluated. For example, it is preferable for an employer to pay for fringe benefit items such as group term life insurance (up to $50,000 in coverage), health and accident insurance, employee parking, and so on rather than to give cash raises of a comparable amount. Such payments are nontaxable to the employee up to certain limits, whereas a comparable salary increase is fully taxable. Both types of payments are deductible by the employer.

Consideration should also be given to increased deferred compensation benefit programs for employees, particularly highly-compensated individuals. The use of nonqualified deferred compensation plans, restricted property, and stock options result in tax deferrals and may result in the eventual recognition of capital gains that may be used to offset capital losses or that are taxed at a maximum 28% marginal tax rate.

All eligible employees should consider establishing an individual retirement account (IRA) because of the available tax deferral benefits. Even if a premature withdrawal (i.e., before age 59½ occurs), the time value of the deferred benefits for the plan contributions and the earnings may be greater than the penalty tax imposed. Employees who are not eligible to make deductible IRA contributions should consider making nondeductible contributions because the income that is earned on such accounts can be deferred until distributions are received from the IRA.

COMPLIANCE AND PROCEDURAL CONSIDERATIONS

Substantiating Travel and Entertainment Expenses

Travel and entertainment expenses are disallowed if the taxpayer does not maintain adequate records or documentary proof of the expenditures.[126] Normally, documentation includes expense statements (diary or account book) and proof of the amount, time, place, and business purpose.[127] Strict substantiation rules are enacted in the law to curb widespread abuses in the so-called expense account living practices engaged in by some taxpayers.

To make compliance easier, the IRS formulated the following administrative procedural rules:

- If an employee makes an adequate accounting of the expenditures to the employer, it is not necessary to submit a detailed statement on the employee's tax return unless the expenses exceed the reimbursements.

- The standard mileage rate may be used to compute automobile expenses in lieu of actual expenses and is reported on Form 2106.

---

[126] Sec. 274(d).
[127] Reg. Sec. 1.274-5(c)(2).

- Taxpayers may elect an optional method for computing deductions for business travel and meal expenses in lieu of using actual costs. If a per diem allowance is paid by an employer in lieu of reimbursing actual expenses; the reimbursement is deemed to be substantiated if it does not exceed a Federal per diem rate for the travel locality. In lieu of using actual expenses an employee or self-employed individual may use the applicable Federal per diem rate.[128] The taxpayer must still provide documentation of time, place, and business purpose for the expenditures.

Reporting Employee Business Expenses

Form 2106 (Employee Business Expenses) is used to report employee business expenses (see Appendix B). Part I of Form 2106 is a recap of travel and transportation expenses. Part II includes a computation of automobile expenses using either actual expenses or the standard rate mileage method. Employer reimbursements must be included in the employee's wages on Form W-2 if an adequate accounting of the expenses is not made. Employer withholding of federal income tax is also required for "nonaccountable plan" reimbursements.

Moving expenses are reported on Form 3903 (Moving Expenses) instead of Form 2106 because they are treated differently from other employee expenses (e.g., unreimbursed moving expenses are deductible *for* AGI). Expenses such as entertainment, union dues, business gifts, and education expenses are reported on Schedule A of Form 1040 as itemized deductions (see Appendix B).

Reporting Moving Expenses

Employer reimbursements for qualifying moving expenses reduce the otherwise deductible amount for the employee. Reimbursements for nondeductible moving expenses are included in gross income and should be included in total wages on the employee's Form W-2 and reported on page 1 (line 7) of Form 1040. Form 3903 should be used to compute the allowable moving expenses and should be attached to the employee's tax return (see Appendix B). Moving expenses are not subject to federal income tax withholding if it is reasonable to believe that an employee will be entitled to a deduction for such amounts. Reimbursements in excess of the deductible amounts, however, are subject to the withholding of income and social security taxes.[129]

A taxpayer may deduct moving expenses, even though the tests for qualification have not been met (e.g., the 39-week test). If the individual subsequently fails to satisfy the requirements, gross income for the subsequent year must be increased by the previous tax benefit.[130] Another alternative is to wait until the tests have been met and then file an amended return (Form 1040X–see Appendix B) for the prior year.

Reporting Office In Home Expenses

Form 8829 (Expenses for Business Use of Your Home) must be used to figure the allowable expenses for business use that are reported on Schedule C (Profit or Loss from Business) or Schedule C-EZ and the carryover of any nondeductible amounts from prior years. Form 4562 (Depreciation and Amortization) must also be used to compute depreciation on the office portion of the residence. These tax forms are reproduced in Appendix B.

---

[128] Rev. Proc. 93-50, I.R.B. 1993-42, 24.
[129] Secs. 3121(a)(11) and 3401(a)(15).
[130] Secs. 217(d)(2) and (3).

Qualification of Pension and Profit-Sharing Plans

The reporting requirements to establish and maintain a qualified pension or profit-sharing plan are too complex for this text. However, it should be noted that it is generally advisable for a taxpayer to obtain advance approval of the plan from the district director of the IRS by requesting a determination letter that all requirements for qualification have been met. A new determination letter should generally be requested when any material (e.g., substantial) modification is made to a plan. Material changes are frequently required when major tax legislation is enacted. In addition, several reports must be filed with the IRS and the U.S. Department of Labor.

PROBLEM MATERIALS

DISCUSSION QUESTIONS

9-1. Why is it important to distinguish whether an individual is an employee or an independent contractor (self-employed)?

9-2. Matt is a CPA engaged in a tax practice and has several small clients. He is also employed as a tax accountant for a major company. Matt incurs local transportation and unreimbursed travel expenses for both his business and employment activities. How does Matt report these expenses on his tax return?

9-3. Are the following expenses deductible *for* AGI or *from* AGI or nondeductible on an employee's return? Indicate whether the expenses are subject to the 2% nondeductible floor for miscellaneous itemized deductions and whether the 50% meals and entertainment deduction limit applies.
   a. Reimbursed business meals (an adequate accounting is made to the employer and any excess reimbursement must be repaid)
   b. Automobile expenses associated with commuting to and from work
   c. Legal expenses incurred to prepare the taxpayer's income tax return
   d. Unreimbursed travel and transportation expenses (including meals)
   e. Unreimbursed entertainment expenses
   f. Qualified moving expenses of an employee
   g. Education-related expenses involving tuition and books

9-4. Which of the following deduction items are subject to the 2% nondeductible floor applicable to miscellaneous itemized deductions?
   a. Investment counseling fees
   b. Fees for tax return preparation
   c. Unreimbursed professional dues for an employee
   d. Gambling losses
   e. Interest on a personal residence
   f. Unreimbursed employee travel expenses
   g. Reimbursed employee travel expenses (an adequate accounting is made to the employer and any excess reimbursement must be repaid)
   h. Safe deposit box rental expenses for an investor

9-5. In each of the following cases involving travel expenses, indicate how each item is reported on the taxpayer's tax return. Include any limitations that might impact upon its deductibility.
   a. Marilyn, who lives in Houston, owns several apartments in Denver. To supervise the management of these properties, Marilyn incurs travel expenses including air fare, lodging, and meals while traveling to and from the apartment site.
   b. Marc is an employee who incurs travel expenses as a salesman. The expenses are fully reimbursed by his employer after an adequate accounting has been made.

c. Assume the same facts as in Part b, except that the expenses are not reimbursed.

d. Kay is a self-employed attorney who incurs travel expenses (including meals) to prepare a court case in a nearby city.

9-6. Kelly is an employee who incurs $2,000 of business meal expenses in connection with business entertainment and travel, none of which are reimbursed by her employer. $500 of the business meal costs are lavish or extravagant. How much can Kelly deduct before applying the 2% nondeductible floor upon miscellaneous itemized deductions?

9-7. Latoya is a college professor who takes a nine-month leave of absence from her employment at a college in Ohio and accepts a temporary assignment at a college in Texas. Latoya leaves her spouse and six children in Ohio and incurs the following expenses in connection with the temporary assignment:

Air fare to and from the temporary assignment	$ 1,000
Living expenses in the new location (including	
meals of $1,000)	8,000
Personal clothing	1,500
Total	$10,500

a. Which (if any) of these items can Latoya deduct?

b. If Latoya quit her job in Ohio and accepted a two-year assignment with a college in Texas, which (if any) of the items listed above would be deductible?

c. Which (if any) of the expenses are deductible if Latoya is a French professor who travels to France for the purpose of maintaining a general familiarity with the French language and customs?

9-8. Larry is an investor in real estate who attends several investment counseling seminars on how to invest in real estate. In the current year, Larry incurs $4,000 of related travel expenses and registration fees. He deducts the expenses on his income tax return as a *for* AGI expense related to the production of income. Are the travel expenses and registration fees deductible? Should they be classified as *for* AGI or *from* AGI?

9-9. If an employee receives a specific monthly amount from his employer as a reimbursement for employment-related entertainment, travel, and transportation expenses, why is it necessary to allocate a portion of the total reimbursement to each expense category?

9-10. If an employee receives a reimbursement of 15 cents a mile from her employer for employment-related transportation expenses, is the employee permitted to deduct the difference between the standard mileage rate and the reimbursement rate as an unreimbursed employee expense? What other alternative is available for claiming the transportation deduction?

9-11. If an employee (or self-employed individual) uses the standard mileage rate method for the year in which an automobile is acquired, may the actual expense method be used in a subsequent year? If so, what restrictions are imposed (if any) upon depreciation methods? What adjustments to basis are required?

9-12. What reporting procedures should be followed by an employee who deducts unreimbursed employee expenses on his tax return?

9-13. What reporting procedures should be followed by an employee to report employment-related expenses on her tax return under the following conditions:

a. Expenses are less than reimbursements, and no accounting is made to the employer.

b. Expenses equal reimbursements, and an adequate accounting is made to the employer.

c. Expenses exceed reimbursements, and an adequate accounting is made to the employer.

d. Expenses are less than reimbursements. An adequate accounting is made to the employer and the employee is required to repay any excess amount.

9-14. Why were distance and time requirements legislated as conditions for eligibility for a moving expense deduction?

9-15. If moving expenses are incurred and paid in 1994 and the employee receives a reimbursement from his employer in 1995, what alternatives are available regarding the year in which these expenses can be deducted?

9-16. Does it matter whether a moving expense is incurred by an employee, a self-employed individual, or an unemployed person?

9-17. Len incurs $2,000 of allowable moving expenses in the current year and is fully reimbursed by his employer in the same year.
  a. How is the expense deduction and the reimbursement reported on Len's tax return if he uses the standard deduction?
  b. What tax consequences occur if the reimbursement is $3,000?

9-18. Why are strict recordkeeping requirements required for the deduction of entertainment expenses?

9-19. Louis incurs "directly related" entertainment expenses of $4,000, but he is reimbursed by his employer for only $3,000 after an adequate accounting is made.
  a. How are these amounts reported on Louis's tax return?
  b. What are the tax consequences if Louis is unable to provide adequate documentation of the expenditures during the course of an IRS audit of his tax return?

9-20. Latesha is a self-employed attorney who entertains clients and potential clients in her home.
  a. What requirements must be met to qualify the outlays as deductible entertainment expenses?
  b. If the expenses qualify, are they classified as "directly related" or "associated with" entertainment?

9-21. Liz is an employee who entertains customers. In the current year, Liz incurs $6,000 in business meal expenses that are connected with entertainment. Liz's expenses are not lavish or extravagant. She itemizes her deductions in the current year.
  a. If none of these expenses are reimbursed by Liz's employer, what amounts are deductible and how are they classified?
  b. How are these amounts reported by Liz and her employer if all of her expenses are reimbursed and an adequate accounting is made by Liz?

9-22. Atlantic Corporation provides a cafeteria for its employees. The meal charges are set at a sufficiently high level so that the employees are not taxed on the subsidized eating facilities. Are Atlantic's cafeteria-related costs fully deductible?

9-23. Lynn is a salesperson who entertains clients at business luncheons. A business relationship exists for the entertainment, and there is a reasonable expectation of business benefit. However, no business discussions are generally conducted prior to, during, or immediately following the course of the meals. Do the business meal expenditures qualify as entertainment expenses?

9-24. If an individual belongs to a country club and uses the facility primarily for business entertainment of customers, what portion of the club dues is deductible?

9-25. What requirements and limitations are imposed upon deducting business gifts?

9-26. Bass Corporation purchases 10 tickets to the Super Bowl in January 1994 for entertaining its customers. Due to unusually high demand, the tickets have to be purchased from scalpers for $6,000 (10 × $600). The face value of the tickets is only $900 (10 × $90). What amount is deductible by Bass in 1994?

9-27. Martin is a tax accountant who is employed by a public accounting firm. He incurs the following expenses:

CPA review course	$ 400
Law school tuition and books	4,000
Accounting continuing education course (travel, fees, and transportation, (including meals of $200)	600
Total	$5,000

Which (if any) of these expenditures qualify as deductible education expenses? How are they reported?

9-28. Why are public school teachers generally allowed a deduction for education expenses related to graduate school or advanced courses?

9-29. Discuss whether each of the following individuals is entitled to an office-in-home deduction:
  a. Maggie is a self-employed management consultant who maintains an office in her home exclusively used for client meetings and other business-related activities. Maggie has no other place of business and her office is the most significant place for her business. She has substantial income from the consulting practice.
  b. Marty is a college professor who writes research papers for academic journals in his office at home which is used exclusively for this purpose. Although Marty has an office at his place of employment, he finds it very helpful and convenient to maintain an office at home to avoid distractions from students and colleagues. Marty receives no income from the publication of the research articles for the year in question.

9-30. Compare and contrast the tax advantages accruing to employers and employees from the establishment of a qualified pension or profit-sharing plan versus a nonqualified deferred compensation arrangement (e.g., a restricted property plan).

9-31. List the features that distinguish a qualified pension plan from a qualified profit-sharing plan.

9-32. What is the difference between a defined benefit pension plan and a defined contribution pension plan?

9-33. Austin Corporation is proposing the establishment of a pension plan that will cover only those employees with salaries in excess of $70,000. No other employees are covered under comparable qualified plans. What problems (if any) do you envision regarding the plan's qualification with the IRS?

9-34. Babson Corporation is proposing the creation of a qualified profit-sharing plan for its employees. The proposed plan provides for vesting of employer contributions after 20 years because the company wants to discourage employee turnover and does not feel that short-term employees should qualify for benefits. Will this plan qualify? Why or why not?

9-35. Explain how distributions from a qualified pension plan, which are made in the form of annuity payments, are reported by an employee under the following circumstances:
  a. No employee contributions are made to the plan.
  b. The pension plan provides for matching employee contributions.

9-36. Discuss the limitations and restrictions that the Code places upon employer contributions to qualified pension and profit-sharing plans.

9-37. Why are nonqualified deferred compensation plans particularly well-suited for use in executive compensation arrangements?

9-38. If a newly formed corporation is considering going public and anticipates substantial future appreciation in its stock, would it be advisable for an executive receiving restricted property to elect to recognize income immediately under Sec. 83(b)? Contrast the tax consequences of a restricted property arrangement for both the employer and employee when this election is made versus when it is not made. Consider the effect of the subsequent lapsing of the restrictions and the employee's sale of the stock.

9-39. List and discuss the qualification requirements for an incentive stock option plan (ISO). Describe the advantages and disadvantages of ISOs compared to nonqualified stock option plans.

9-40. What difference does it make if a nonqualified stock option has a readily ascertainable FMV on the grant date or not?

9-41. Is a self-employed individual, who is also employed and covered by an employer's qualified pension plan, eligible to establish an H.R. 10 plan relative to her self-employment income?

9-42. What limitations are placed upon self-employed individuals for contributions made to defined contribution H.R. 10 plans? Must self-employed individuals cover their full-time employees if an H.R. 10 plan is established?

9-43. Would you be more favorably inclined to advise a 50-year-old individual or a 30-year-old individual to establish a deductible IRA? Why? A nondeductible IRA? Why? Consider any tax problems involved if the IRA funds are needed prior to age 59½.

9-44. Sally, age 30, has previously made deductible IRA contributions for years prior to 1987 and is no longer eligible to make deductible IRA contributions. Would you advise Sally to make nondeductible IRA contributions? Explain.

9-45. The owner of an unincorporated small business is considering whether to establish a simplified employee pension (SEP) plan for its employees.
  a. What nontax factors might make an SEP attractive as an alternative to establishing a qualified pension or profit-sharing plan?
  b. Is the owner of the small business eligible to make contributions on his behalf to the SEP?
  c. Would you advise the owner to establish a salary reduction agreement SEP? Explain.

PROBLEMS

9-46. *Employment-Related Expenses.* Matt incurs the following employment-related expenses in the current year:

Actual automobile expenses	$1,000
Moving expenses (deductible under Sec. 217)	1,000
Entertainment expenses	2,000
Travel expenses (including $500 of business meals)	2,500
Professional dues and subscriptions	500
Total	$7,000

Matt's AGI is $100,000. None of the expenses listed above are reimbursed by Matt's employer. He has no other miscellaneous itemized deductions and does not use the standard deduction.
  a. What is the amount of Matt's deduction for employment-related expenses?
  b. How are these items reported in Matt's tax return?

9-47. *Travel and Entertainment.* Monique is a self-employed manufacturer's representative who solicits business for clients and receives a commission based upon sales. She incurs the following expenditures during the current year:

Air fare and lodging while away from home overnight	$ 4,000
Business meals while traveling at which business is discussed	1,000
Local transportation costs for automobile, parking, tolls, etc.	2,000
Commuting expenses	1,000
Local entertainment of customers	2,000
Total	$10,000

  a. Which of the expenditures listed above (if any) are deductible by Monique?
  b. Are each of these items classified as *for* AGI or *from* AGI deductions?
  c. How would your answers to Parts a and b change if Monique is an employee rather than self-employed and none of the expenses are reimbursed by her employer?

9-48. *Unreimbursed Employee Expenses.* In the current year Mary incurs $2,000 of unreimbursed employment-related travel and entertainment expenses. These expenses include the following:

Air fare	$1,000
Taxi fare	100
Business meals at which business is discussed	200
Laundry	50
Lodging	150
Entertainment of customers	500
Total	$2,000

Mary also pays $1,000 of investment counseling fees and $500 of tax return preparation fees in the current year. Mary's AGI is $40,000.

a. What is the total amount of Mary's deductible expenses?

b. Are the deductible expenses classified as *for* AGI or *from* AGI?

9-49. ***Travel Expenses.*** Marilyn is a business executive who accepts a temporary out-of-town assignment for a period of ten months. Marilyn leaves her husband and children in Miami and rents an apartment in the new location during the ten-month period. Marilyn incurs the following expenses, none of which are reimbursed by her employer:

Air fare to and from the new location	$ 800
Air fare for weekend trips to visit her family	6,200
Apartment rent	7,000
Meals at the temporary location	8,500
Entertainment of customers	2,000
Total	$24,500

a. Which of the expenditures listed above (if any) are deductible by Marilyn (before any limitations are applied)?

b. Are each of these expenditures classified as *for* AGI or *from* AGI deductions?

c. If Marilyn's AGI is $60,000, what is the amount of the deduction for the expenditures?

d. Do the tax consequences change if Marilyn's assignment is for a period of more than one year and is for an indefinite period rather than a temporary period?

9-50. ***Business/Personal Travel Expenses.*** In the current year Mike's AGI is $50,000. Mike has no miscellaneous itemized deductions other than the employment-related expenses on the following list. Mike attends a professional trade association convention in Los Angeles. He spends three days at the meeting and two days vacationing before the meeting. Mike was unable to obtain excursion airfare rates despite the fact that he was on vacation immediately prior to the meeting. Mike's business related expenses, which are fully reimbursed by his employer after an adequate accounting is made, include the following:

Air fare	$ 450
Meals ($30 per day)	90
Hotel ($60 per day)	180
Entertainment of customers (business is discussed)	500
Total	$1,220

a. How much can Mike deduct for employment-related expenses?

b. How is the reimbursement reported on Mike's tax return?

c. Is the reinbursement fully deductible by Mike's employer?

9-51. ***Employment-Related Expenses and Reimbursements.*** Maxine incurs the following employment-related business expenses in the current year:

Professional dues and subscriptions	$1,000
Air fare and lodging	2,000
Local transportation for employment-related business activities	1,000
Customer entertainment (business lunches where business is discussed)	1,000
Total	$5,000

After making an adequate accounting of the expenses, Maxine receives a fixed reimbursement of $3,000 from her employer. Assume that Maxine's AGI is $50,000, she has other miscellaneous itemized deductions of $1,000, and she does not use the standard deduction.

a. What amount of the expenses are deductible by Maxine?

b. Are each of these expenditures classified as *for* AGI or *from* AGI deductions?

c. How would your answers to Parts a and b change if Maxine instead receives a $6,000 reimbursement?

9-52. *Miscellaneous Itemized Deductions.* In the current year, Melissa, a single employee whose AGI is $100,000, incurs the following expenses:

Safe deposit box rental for investments	$ 200
Tax return preparation fees	500
Moving expenses (otherwise deductible under Sec. 217)	2,000
Mortgage interest on Melissa's principal residence	12,000
Real estate taxes on Melissa's principal residence	3,000
Unreimbursed employment-related expenses (other than business meals and entertainment)	6,000
Unreimbursed employment-related expenses for business meals and entertainment (business is discussed)	400
Total	$24,100

a. What is the amount of Melissa's total miscellaneous itemized deductions (after deducting the 2% floor)?

b. What is the amount of Melissa's total itemized deductions?

c. What is the amount of Melissa's total itemized deductions if her AGI is instead $150,000?

9-53. *Auto Expenses.* Michelle is an employee who is required to use her personal automobile for employment-related business trips. During the current year Michelle drives her car 60% for business use and incurs the following total expenses:

Gas and oil	$2,000
Repairs	400
Depreciation	2,200
Insurance and license fees	1,300
Parking and tolls (business related)	100
Total	$6,000

Michelle drives 20,000 business miles during the current year and receives a reimbursement of 10 cents per mile from her employer. Assume that the 2% nondeductible floor on miscellaneous itemized deductions is not applicable and that an adequate accounting is made to Michelle's employer.

a. What amount is deductible if Michelle elects to use the standard mileage method?

b. What amount is deductible if Michelle uses the actual cost method?

9-54. *Moving Expenses.* Michael graduates from City College of New York and on February 1, 1994, accepts a position with a public accounting firm in Chicago. Michael is a resident of New York. In March, Michael travels to Chicago to locate a house and starts to work in June. He incurs the following expenses, none of which are reimbursed by the public accounting firm:

Automobile expense enroute	
(1,000 miles @ 9 cents per mile standard mileage rate)	$ 90
Cost of meals enroute	110
House-hunting trip travel expenses	1,400
Moving van rental	2,000
Commission on the sale of	
Michael's New York condominium	3,500
Points paid to acquire a mortgage on	
Michael's new residence in Chicago	1,000
Temporary living expenses for one week	
in Chicago (hotel and $100 in meals)	400
Expenses incurred in decorating the new residence	500
Total expenses	$9,000

a. What is Michael's moving expense deduction?

b. How are the deductible expenses classified on Michael's tax return?

c. How would your answer to Part a change if all of Michael's expenses are reimbursed by his employer?

9-55. *Entertainment Expenses.* Milt is a self-employed attorney who incurs the following expenses in the current year:

Business lunches for clients and prospective	
clients (Milt does not believe in conducting	
business discussions during lunch)	$ 4,000
Entertainment of professional associates in his home	
(immediately following business meetings)	2,000
Country club dues (the club is used	
exclusively for business)	2,500
Entertainment of clients and prospective clients at the country club	1,500
Total	$10,000

a. Which of the expenditures listed above (if any) are deductible by Milt?

b. Are each of these items classified as *for* AGI or *from* AGI deductions?

9-56. *Entertainment Expenses.* Beach Corporation purchases tickets to sporting events and uses them to entertain customers. In the current year Beach Corporation purchases the following tickets:

100 tickets to football games (face value of the tickets is $3,600)	$6,000
A skybox rented for six athletic events (seating capacity of the skybox	
is 30, and the highest price of a nonluxury box seat is $40)	18,000

What amount of the entertainment is deductible in the current year?

9-57. *Education Expenses.* For each of the following independent situations, determine if any of the expenditures qualify as deductible education expenses. Are the expenditures classified as *for* AGI or *from* AGI deductions?

a. Law school tuition and books for an IRS agent, $2,000.

b. Continuing professional accounting education expenses of $1,900 for a self-employed CPA travel, $1,000 (including $200 meals); registration fees, $800; books, $100.

c. MBA education expenses totaling $5,000 for a business executive of a major corporation tuition, $4,000; transportation, $800; and books, $200.

d. Tuition and books acquired for graduate education courses required under state law for a school teacher in order to renew her provisional certificate, $1,000.

e. Bar review courses for a recent law school graduate, $1,000.

9-58. *Office-in-Home.* Nancy is a self-employed artist who uses 10% of her residence as a studio. The studio portion is used exclusively for business and is frequented by customers on a regular basis. Nancy also uses her den as an office (10% of the total floor space of her home) to prepare bills and keep records. The den, however, is also used by her children as a TV room. Nancy's income from the sale of the artwork amounts to $40,000 in the current year. She also incurs $2,000 of expenses directly related to the business other than home office expenses (e.g., art supplies and selling expenses). Nancy incurs the following expenses in the current year related to her residence:

Real estate taxes	$ 2,000
Mortgage interest	5,000
Insurance	500
Depreciation	3,500
Repairs and utilities	1,000
Total	$12,000

a. Which of the expenditures above (if any) are deductible? Are they *for* AGI or *from* AGI deductions?

b. Would your answer to Part a change if Nancy's income from painting is only $2,500 for the year? What is the amount of the office-in-home deduction and the amount of the carryover (if any) of the unused deductions? (Assume that Nancy is not subject to the hobby loss restrictions.)

9-59. *Deferred Compensation Plan Requirements.* Identify whether each of the following plan features is associated with a qualified pension plan, a qualified profit-sharing plan, an employee stock ownership plan, a nonqualifed plan, or none of these plans.

a. Annual employer contributions are not required, but substantial and recurring contributions must be made based upon a predetermined formula.

b. Annual, systematic, and definite employer contributions are required without regard to profits but based upon actuarial methods.

c. Forfeitures must be used to reduce contributions that would otherwise be made under the plan.

d. The plan may discriminate in favor of highly compensated individuals.

e. The trust is funded with the contribution of employer stock, which is subsequently distributed to employees.

9-60. *Taxability of Pension Payments.* Pam is a participant in a qualified pension plan. She retires on January 1, 1994, and receives pension payments beginning in January 1994. Her pension payments, which will be received monthly for life, amount to $1,000 per month. Pam contributed $30,000 to the pension plan, and her life expectancy is 15 years from the date she starts receiving payments.

a. What gross income will Pam recognize in 1994 and each year thereafter?

b. How would your answer to Part a change if Pam did not make any contributions to the plan?

c. If Pam dies in December 1995 after receiving pension payments for two full years, what tax consequences occur in the year of death?

d. If Pam outlives her 15-year life expectancy, what amount of the pension payments are taxable in year 16 and subsequent years?

9-61. *Restricted Property.* In 1994, Bear Corporation transfers 100 shares of its stock to its employee Patrick. The stock is valued at $10 per share on the date of issue. The stock is subject to the following restrictions:

- Patrick cannot transfer the stock by sale or other disposition (except in the event of death) for a five-year period.
- The stock must be forfeited to Bear Corporation if Patrick voluntarily terminates his employment with the company within a five-year period.

In 1999, the Bear stock is worth $100 per share when the restrictions expire.

a. Assuming that no Sec. 83(b) election is made, what are the tax consequences to Patrick and Bear Corporation in 1994?

b. What are the tax consequences to Patrick and Bear Corporation if Patrick makes a valid Sec. 83(b) election in 1994?

   c. What are the tax consequences to Patrick and Bear Corporation if Patrick forfeits the stock back to the company in 1995 when the stock is worth $20 per share if an election has been made under Sec. 83(b)? What would happen if no Sec. 83(b) election has been made?

   d. What are the tax consequences to Patrick and Bear Corporation upon the lapse of the restrictions in 1999 if an election has been made under Sec. 83(b)? What would the results be if no Sec. 83(b) election has been made?

   e. What are the tax consequences to Patrick and Bear Corporation if Patrick sells the Bear stock in year 2000 for $120 per share if (1) a Sec. 83(b) election is made and (2) no Sec. 83(b) election is made?

9-62. *IRAs.* On February 15, 1994, Phong who is single and age 30, establishes an IRA and contributes $2,000 to the account. Phong's gross income is $31,000 in both 1993 and 1994. Phong is an active participant in an employer-sponsored retirement plan.

   a. What amount of the contribution is deductible? In what year is it deductible?

   b. How is the deduction (if any) reported (i.e., *for* AGI or *from* AGI)?

   c. What tax treatment is accorded to Phong if he withdraws the $2,000 contribution plus $150 of accrued interest on the IRA in 1995 due to a need for cash to pay unexpected medical bills?

   d. How would your answer to Part a change, if at all, if Phong is not an active participant in an employer-sponsored retirement plan?

   e. How would your answer to Part a change if Phong is married and files a joint return with his spouse, who has no earned income? (Assume their combined AGI is $31,000.)

9-63. *IRAs.* On February 15, 1995, Phil, a married taxpayer age 30 who files a joint return with his spouse, establishes an interspousal IRA with a $2,250 contribution. Phil's spouse earns $1,000 in 1994 from a part-time job, and their combined AGI is $40,000. Neither Phil nor his spouse is an active participant in an employer-sponsored retirement plan.

   a. What amount of the contribution is deductible?

   b. To what year does the contribution apply? (Assume that an election is made to treat Phil's spouse as having no compensation.)

   c. Is the deduction reported as *for* AGI or *from* AGI?

   d. If a portion of the contribution is nondeductible, is it possible for Phil to make a deductible and a nondeductible contribution in the same year? Explain.

   e. How would your answer to Part a change, if at all, if Phil and his spouse are active participants in an employer-sponsored retirement plan?

   f. How would your answer to Part a change if Phil and his spouse's combined AGI is $70,000 in 1994 and 1995 and Phil is an active participant in an employer-sponsored retirement plan?

9-64. *H.R. 10 Plans.* Paula is a self-employed doctor who is considering whether to establish a defined contribution H.R. 10 plan. Paula's only employee is a full-time nurse who has been employed by Paula for seven years. Paula's net earnings from self-employment (before the H.R. 10 plan contribution but after the deduction for one-half of self-employment taxes paid) is expected to be $100,000 during the current year and in future years.

   a. If the H.R. 10 plan is established, what is the maximum amount Paula can contribute for the nurse's benefit?

   b. What is the maximum amount Paula can contribute for herself and is the amount reported as a *for* AGI or *from* AGI deduction?

   c. Is Paula's nurse required to be included in the plan?

   d. What are the tax consequences if Paula makes a premature withdrawal from the plan prior to reaching age 59½?

9-65. *Stock Options.* Bell Corporation grants an incentive stock option to Peggy, an employee, on January 1, 1994, when the option price and FMV of the Bell stock is $80. Peggy receives the option to buy 10 shares of Bell stock. Peggy exercises the option and acquires the stock on April 1, 1996, when the stock's FMV is $100. Peggy, while still employed by the Bell Corporation, sells the stock on May 1, 1997, for $120 per share.

   a. What are the tax consequences to Peggy and Bell Corporation on the following dates: January 1, 1994; April 1, 1996; and May 1, 1998? (Assume all incentive stock option qualification requirements are met.)

b. How would your answer to Part a change if Peggy instead sells the Bell stock for $120 per share on May 1, 1996?

9-66. *Stock Options.* Bender Corporation grants a nonqualified stock option to Penny, an employee, on January 1, 1994, which entitled Penny to acquire 10 shares of Bender stock at $80 per share. On this date, the stock has a $100 FMV, and the option has a readily ascertainable FMV. Penny exercises the option on January 1, 1995 (when the FMV of the stock is $150), and acquires 10 shares of the stock for $80 per share. Penny later sells the Bender stock on January 1, 1997, for $200 per share.

a. What are the tax consequences to Penny and Bender Corporation on the following dates: January 1, 1994; January 1, 1995; and January 1, 1997?

b. How would your answer to Part a change if the Bender stock is instead closely held and the option has no readily ascertainable FMV?

TAX FORM/RETURN PREPARATION PROBLEMS

TurboTax **9-67.** In the current year Dennis Johnson (Soc. Sec. No. 277-33-7263) incurs the following unreimbursed employee business expenses:

Airplane and taxi fares	$ 3,000
Lodging away from home	4,000
Automobile expenses (related to 100% of the use of his personal automobile):	
Gasoline and oil	1,000
Repairs	200
Insurance	200
Depreciation	1,500
Parking and tolls (both equally allocable to business and personal use)	100
Total	$10,000

Johnson receives a $7,000 reimbursement for all of the expenses. He uses his personal automobile 80% for business use. Total business miles amount to 20,000. Johnson's AGI is $40,000, and he has no other miscellaneous itemized deductions.

a. Calculate Johnson's expense deduction using Form 2106 (Employee Business Expenses) based on actual automobile expenses and other employee business expenses.

b. Calculate Johnson's expense deduction using the standard mileage rate method and other employee business expenses. (Assume that none of the restrictions on the use of the standard mileage rate method are applicable.)

TurboTax **9-68.** George Large (Soc. Sec. No. 414-33-5688) and his wife Marge Large (Soc. Sec. No. 555-81-9495) want you to prepare their income tax return based on the following information:

George Large worked as a salesman for Toyboat, Inc. He received a salary of $50,000 ($8,000 of income taxes withheld) plus an additional $5,000 to cover his out-of-pocket expenses. George must make an adequate accounting to his employer and return any excess reimbursement. Additionally, Toyboat provides George with medical insurance worth $3,500 per year. George drove his car 20,000 miles during the year. His log indicates that 17,000 miles were for sales calls to prospective customers at the customers' offices. George uses the standard mileage rate method. George is a professional basketball fan. He purchased two season tickets for a total of $2,000. He takes a customer to every game, and they usually discuss business at the games. George also takes clients to business lunches. His log indicates that he spent $1,500 on these business meals. George also took a five-day trip to the Toyboat headquarters in Musty, Ohio. He was so well-prepared that he finished his business in three days, so he spent the other two days sightseeing. He had the following expenses during each day of his trip:

Air fare	$200
Lodging	$85/day
Meals	$50/day
Taxicabs	$20/day

Marge Large is self-employed. She repairs rubber toyboats in the basement of their home, which is 25% of the house's square footage. She had the following income and expenses:

Income from rubber toyboat repairs	$11,000
Cost of materials	5,000
Contract labor	3,500
Long-distance phone calls (business)	500

The Larges incurred other expenses:

Utility bills for the house	$2,000
Real estate taxes	2,500
Mortgage interest	4,500
Cash charitable contributions	2,500

Prepare Form 1040, Schedules A and C for Form 1040, and Form 2106 for the current year. (Assume no depreciation for this problem and that no estimated taxes were paid by the Larges.)

CASE STUDY PROBLEM

9-69. Ajax Corporation is a young high-growth company that is engaged in the manufacture and distribution of automotive parts. Its common stock has doubled in value since the company was listed on the NASDAQ exchange about two years ago. Ajax currently has a high debt/equity ratio due to the issuance of debt to finance its capital expansion needs. Despite rapid growth in assets and profitability, Ajax has severe cash flow problems and a poor working capital ratio. The company urgently needs to attract new executives to the organization and to provide financial incentives to existing top management because of recent turnover and high growth. Approximately 55% of the common stock is owned by Andrew Ajax who is the CEO and his immediate family. None of the other officers own stock in the company.

You are a tax consultant for the company who has been asked to prepare suggestions after reviewing the compensation system. Your discussions with several top management individuals reveal the following aspects of corporate strategy and philosophy:

1. The company needs to expand the equity capital base because of its concern for the high risk caused by large amounts of debt.
2. Improvement in cash flow and liquidity would enhance its stock price and enable the company to continue its high growth rate.
3. Top management feels that employee loyalty and productivity would be improved if all employees owned some stock in the company. The company currently offers a qualified pension plan to its employees and executives that provides only minimal pension benefits. No other deferred compensation or bonus arrangements are currently being offered.
4. Andrew Ajax feel that the top management group should own a substantial amount of Ajax stock to ensure that the interests of management correspond with the shareholder interests (i.e., the maximization of shareholder wealth).

The following types of compensation arrangements have been discussed:

1. Sec. 401(k) and ESOP plans for employees.
2. Encourage all employees and executives to independently fund their retirement needs over and above any social security benefits by establishing IRA and H.R. 10 plans.
3. Provide restricted property arrangements (using Ajax stock) so as to attract new top level executives and to retain existing executives.
4. Offer nonqualified and/or incentive stock options to existing and new executives.

Required: Prepare a client memo that recommends revisions to Ajax Corporation's existing compensation system for both its employee and executive groups. Your recommendations should discuss the pros and cons of different deferred compensation arrangements and should consider both tax and nontax factors.

CASE STUDY PROBLEM—ETHICAL ISSUES

9-70. Steve is part owner and manager of a small manufacturing company which makes keypads for alarm systems. The keypads are sold to several different alarm companies throughout the country. Steve must travel to several cities each year to meet with current customers and to attract new business. On his 1994 tax return, Steve tells you, his accountant, that he has spent about $5,000 during 1994 on air fare and taking his customers out to dinner to discuss business. Since he took most of his trips in the summer and fall, and it is now April of the following year, Steve cannot remember the exact time and places of the business dinners and did not retain any receipts for the cash used to pay the bills. However he remembers the names of the customers he went to see and the business topics that were discussed. As Steve's tax consultant, what is your responsibility regarding the treatment of the travel and entertainment expenses under the mandates of the AICPA's *Statements on Responsibilities in Tax Practice?* Prepare a client letter explaining to Steve the requirements under Sec. 274(d) for sufficient substantiation of travel and entertainment expenses. (See the caption entitled *Statements on Responsibilities in Tax Practice* in Chapter 1 for a discussion of these issues.)

TAX RESEARCH PROBLEM

9-71. Lou operates a small business which provides lawn maintenance services in his area. He is the sole owner of Lou's Landscaping and employs three employees. Lou rents a small warehouse in which he keeps all of his equipment but he maintains no office space in the warehouse. Since the equipment fills all of the warehouse Lou has turned an extra room in his small house into an office where he keeps a computer and all the necessary paperwork for his customers. Lou spends a few hours each day keeping his customer billings up to date, making phone calls, and performing other activities related to his business. Lou deducted $1,000 last year as home office expenses. The IRS disallowed the deduction and Lou wants to pursue the matter further. Will Lou be entitled to the deduction as an office in home expense?

A partial list of research sources include:

- Sec. 280A
- CIR v. Nader E. Soliman, 71 AFTR 2d 93-463, 93-1 USTC ¶ 50,014(USSC, 1993).

10

Depreciation, Cost Recovery, Depletion, Amortization, and Inventory Costs

LEARNING OBJECTIVES

After studying this chapter, you should be able to

1. Classify property and calculate depreciation under the pre-ACRS rules
2. Classify property and calculate cost recovery under the ACRS rules
3. Classify property and calculate depreciation under the MACRS rules
4. Apply cost and percentage depletion methods and understand the treatment for intangible drilling costs
5. Calculate amortization for intangible assets and understand the difference between amortizable and non-amortizable assets
6. Determine inventory cost and cost of goods sold under various methods

DEPRECIATION AND COST RECOVERY

Typical Misconception

It is easy to forget that the depreciation or cost-recovery system that applies to any one asset is the system that was in effect at the time that the property was placed in service. Property acquired in 1986 was not affected by the MACRS rules that became effective in 1987.

Certain asset costs incurred in connection with the conduct of a trade or business, or assets that are being held for the production of income, must be capitalized if the costs relate to future benefits. The financial accounting principal of matching expired costs with related revenues applies when capital costs are expensed in subsequent periods through depreciation, amortization, depletion, or calculation of cost of goods sold. Inventory costs, for example, are charged to cost of goods sold as expired costs in the same period that the goods are sold to customers.

Certain capital costs are neither depreciable nor amortizable under the tax law. Personal-use assets (e.g., a personal automobile or the taxpayer's personal residence) are not depreciable. In addition, no amortization or depreciation is permitted for land or internally generated goodwill.

Three separate depreciation and cost-recovery systems are currently in place because Congress completely revamped the rules in 1981 as part of the Economic Recovery Tax Act of 1981 (ERTA), and substantial revisions were also made by the Tax Reform Act of 1986. The depreciation rules contained in Sec. 167 apply to property acquired before 1981. The **accelerated cost recovery system** (ACRS) applies to assets acquired after December 31, 1980, and before 1987. For property acquired after December 31, 1986, a third set of depreciation rules—the Modified Accelerated Cost Recovery System (MACRS)—is applicable. Although the primary emphasis in this chapter is placed upon the MACRS rules, it is also important to understand the pre-ACRS rules and the ACRS rules because some assets placed in service under these rules are still in service and not yet fully depreciated.

The terms *depreciation* and *cost recovery* are used interchangeably in the text. The Sec. 167 (or pre-ACRS) and the MACRS rules under Sec. 168 refer to depreciation. However, the Sec. 168 ACRS rules referred to cost recovery. In 1981 Congress initiated the original ACRS system to provide a stimulus for private investment. Therefore, less importance was placed upon the financial accounting concept of matching costs and revenues, which is the primary theory that governed the Sec. 167 depreciation rules. The primary concern of Congress in 1981 was to allow businesses and investors to recover the cost of capitalized expenditures over a period of time that is substantially shorter than the property's economic useful life. Thus, the term *cost recovery* rather than *depreciation* was used under the ACRS system. The post-1986 MACRS rules more closely follow the concept of economic useful life. Thus, the MACRS rules refer to depreciation rather than cost recovery.

Real World Example
Harrah's Club in Reno, Nevada, restores antique autos and displays them. The restoration costs cannot be depreciated because the autos have an indefinite life as museum pieces. Harrah's Club v. U.S., 43 AFTR 2d 79-745, 81-2 USTC ¶ 9677 (Ct. Cls., 1981).

General Rules Applying to Asset Acquisitions in All Periods

Certain rules apply regardless of when an asset is acquired. For example, since neither the depreciation nor cost-recovery deductions are discretionary, certain prescribed accounting methods (e.g., straight-line or declining-balance methods) must be used on a consistent basis from year to year. Also, the basis of the property must be reduced by the amount of depreciation that should be taken even if no depreciation is claimed. These requirements effectively prevent taxpayers from not claiming a depreciation deduction during years when little or no tax benefit is derived. For example, taxpayers might prefer not to deduct any depreciation in years they have low marginal tax rates or have NOL carryovers that are about to expire.

Example 10-1 ■   Maria acquires a business building for $300,000 on January 1, 1980, and claims straight-line depreciation based on a 30-year useful life with zero salvage value under the pre-ACRS rules. The allowable depreciation is $10,000 ($300,000 ÷ 30 years), and Maria deducts this amount each year during the 1980-1992 period.[1] Maria's business deteriorates after 1992, and large NOLs are incurred in 1993 and 1994 that cannot be carried back to earlier years. Maria also anticipates that the NOL carryovers will not be utilized in the immediate future because of the unlikelihood of earning substantial amounts of taxable income during the carry-over period. Realizing that the depreciation would have little or no current tax benefit, Maria fails to claim any depreciation in 1993 and 1994. The building is sold for $200,000 on December 31, 1994. The basis of the building must be reduced by the full amount of the allowable depreciation of $150,000 ($10,000 × 15) for the 15-year period, and Maria must recognize a $50,000 gain on the sale of the building ($200,000 selling price − $150,000 adjusted basis), despite the fact that only $130,000 of depreciation was claimed during the 15-year period. ■

Conversion of Personal-Use Property. If personal-use property is either converted to business use or held for the production of income (e.g., a rental house), the property's basis for depreciation purposes is the lesser of its adjusted basis or its fair market value [FMV] $130,000 of determined as of the conversion date.[2] This lower of cost or market rule is intended to prevent taxpayers from depreciating the portion of the cost that represents a nondeductible personal loss.

Example 10-2 ■   Marty acquires a personal residence for $115,000 in 1991. In 1994 the property is converted to rental use because Marty is unable to sell the house due to a depressed local real estate market. The property's FMV is only $100,000 when it is converted to rental status in 1994. The $15,000 ($115,000 − $100,000) decline in value represents a nondeductible personal loss and is not depreciable. The depreciable basis is $100,000 (minus the portion of the property's FMV that represents land that is not depreciable). ■

---

[1] **Allowable depreciation** is the amount of depreciation permitted to be claimed under the tax law. The term *allowed depreciation* is the amount of depreciation that the taxpayer actually claims. In situations where the taxpayer has never taken depreciation, allowable is defined as the slowest possible method allowed by law (e.g., straight-line using the longest permissible recovery period). A taxpayer may file an amended tax return for the purpose of taking depreciation for all years that are not closed by the statute of limitations.

[2] Reg. Sec. 1.167(g)-1.

Pre-ACRS Depreciation (Years Prior to 1981)

OBJECTIVE 1

Classify property and calculate depreciation under the pre-ACRS rules.

Historical Note

Prior to 1954, except for the limited use of a declining-balance method, taxpayers were required to use the straight-line method.

The following depreciation methods are generally available for property that was placed in service before January 1, 1981:

- Straight-line method (SL)
- Double-declining balance method (DDB)
- 150% declining balance method (150% DB)
- Sum-of-the-years digits method (SYD)[3]

Various restrictions were placed upon the use of accelerated methods for new and used real estate (other than residential rental properties), used residential rental properties, and tangible personal property. Under the pre-ACRS rules, taxpayers could change from a declining balance method to the straight-line method without obtaining advance permission of the IRS.[4] Other changes fell under the general restrictions for changing from one accounting method to another and required approval of the IRS. Table 10-1 summarizes the methods that were permitted for pre-ACRS property.

The useful life for depreciable properties was selected based upon the individual taxpayer's prior experience and business practice regarding maintenance and asset utilization. Alternatively, taxpayers could have elected the **asset depreciation range (ADR) system,** which prescribed useful lives for various asset classes.[5]

The Code permitted taxpayers to disregard salvage value for amounts up to 10% of the basis of tangible personal property having a 3-year or longer useful life. Even though salvage value was disregarded in determining the depreciation deduction, an asset could not be depreciated below its salvage value.[6]

Example 10-3 ■

Boston Corporation acquired a business machine in 1980 (pre-ACRS period) for $20,000 with a $4,000 estimated salvage value and a 5-year useful life. Salvage value up to $2,000 (0.10 × $20,000) could be ignored in making the annual depreciation computation. However, if the estimated salvage value did not change, Boston could not deduct total depreciation in excess of $16,000 ($20,000 cost − $4,000 estimated salvage value). ■

TABLE 10-1 **Pre-ACRS Depreciation Methods**

	Tangible Personal Property (Machinery, Trucks, and so on)	Nonresidential Real Property (Commercial and Industrial Buildings, and so on)	Residential Rental Property (Apartments and so on)
New property	DDB, SYD, SL	150% DB, SL	DDB, SYD 150% DB, SL
Used property	150% DB, SL	SL	125% DB (if the estimated useful life is 20 years or more, SL)

[3] Sec. 167(b). Certain additional depreciation methods not based on the passage of time (e.g., machine hours of usage and units of production) were also available.

[4] Sec. 167(e). See Chapter 11 for a discussion of accounting methods.

[5] For example, under the ADR system the guideline life for office furniture, fixtures, and equipment was 10 years, and the taxpayer could select any life within 20% of the guideline life. Thus, the lower limit for office furniture was 8 years and the upper limit was 12 years.

[6] Sec. 167(f) and Reg. Sec. 1.167(a)-(1)(c).

An additional bonus first-year depreciation equal to 20% of the cost of new or used tangible personal property having a useful life of at least 3 years was allowed. This bonus depreciation was limited to $10,000 of cost ($20,000 if the taxpayer was married and filed a joint return). Bonus depreciation has been replaced by an election to immediately write off the first $17,500 of asset cost for certain depreciable business assets. (See the section entitled Sec. 179 Expensing Election for a discussion of this topic.)[7]

ACRS (1981) through (1986)

Additional Comment

Property is considered to be "placed in service" when it is in a condition or state of readiness and is available for a specifically assigned function. This can be important in attempting to determine the first year that a depreciation deduction is available.

The Basics. As mentioned earlier, the ACRS rules enacted in 1981 were intended to stimulate private investment, improve business productivity, simplify taxpayer compliance, and facilitate IRS administration of the tax law. ACRS provided an economic stimulus because the cost-recovery amounts were based upon accelerated methods and artificially shortened useful lives.

In 1986 Congress decided the cost-recovery system had provided too great a tax benefit. The ACRS deduction, when combined with an investment tax credit that was available for years prior to 1987, often provided a benefit greater than an immediate expensing of the asset. The MACRS system that applies to assets acquired after 1986 retains many of the original ACRS simplification features while returning to a recovery period that more nearly approaches a true economic life. This is accomplished by combining the former ADR system that was used for pre-1981 years with many of the features of the ACRS rules.

Key Point

ACRS provides a small number of depreciation classes and relatively short recovery periods.

The features present in both the ACRS and MACRS systems that contribute to simplification and fewer disputes with the IRS include the following:

- Salvage value is not considered in the computation of the cost-recovery or depreciation amount. Under prior depreciation systems, disputes between taxpayers and the IRS over the use of a proper salvage value were frequently encountered.

Historical Note

Depreciable real estate could be depreciated using a 15-year life under the ACRS rules enacted in 1981. The economic life on such property could be more than 50 years.

- Fewer asset classes are used. Most tangible personal property (e.g., machinery and equipment, trucks and autos) use a 3-year, 5-year, or 7-year recovery period. Depreciable real estate generally uses either a 15-year, 18-year, 19-year, 27½-year, 31.5-year, or 39-year recovery period, depending upon the date the asset is placed in service.

- Fewer cost-recovery methods are used and half-year mid-quarter, or mid-month conventions are built into the ACRS and MACRS tables. Initially, the tables for personal property provide for accelerated rates with an automatic change to the straight-line method when the latter method produces a greater deduction. The ACRS and MACRS tables are summarized in Appendix C.

OBJECTIVE 2

Classify property and calculate cost recovery under the ACRS rules

Classification and Recovery Rates for Tangible Personal Property. ACRS recovery property includes tangible personal and real property that is depreciable and used in a trade or business or held for the production of income (e.g., rental property held for investment).[8] Recovery property does not include personal-use assets, intangible assets (e.g., goodwill or trademarks), assets that do not decline in value, specially depreciated property (e.g., units of production method) or assets that do not have a determinable life (e.g., land and securities).

As mentioned earlier, most types of tangible personal property are classified as either 3-year property (e.g., automobiles, light-duty trucks, and research and experi-

[7] Sec. 179.
[8] Sec. 168(c)(1).

mental [R&E] equipment)[9] or 5-year property (e.g., machinery, equipment, heavy-duty trucks, furniture, and fixtures).[10] The cost-recovery rates for these recovery classes are shown in Table 10-2. The rates are based upon using the 150% declining balance method, a half-year convention, and zero salvage value.[11]

Use of the half-year convention permits taxpayers to claim the same cost recovery amount in the year of acquisition whether the property is acquired on the first or last day of the year. It also lowers the recovery percentage in the initial year. No cost-recovery deduction is permitted for tangible personal property in the year of sale or disposition.

Example 10-4 ■

Monique acquires an automobile for $10,000 and equipment for $20,000. Both properties are used in Monique's unincorporated business. The equipment is acquired and placed into service on January 1, 1986. The automobile is acquired and placed in service on December 15, 1986. No cost-recovery deductions are allowed until the asset is placed in service. The cost-recovery deduction for the automobile is based upon a 3-year recovery period and is $2,500 (0.25 × $10,000) for 1986, despite the fact that the automobile was used for less than a month during the year. The cost-recovery deduction for the equipment is based upon a 5-year recovery period and is $3,000 (0.15 × $20,000) for 1986, despite the fact that the equipment is used for the entire year. This example does not include the Sec. 179 election to expense a portion of the asset's purchase price in the year of acquisition. This and other basis adjustments are discussed in subsequent sections of the text. ■

Example 10-5 ■

Assume the same facts as in Example 10-4, except that the equipment is sold for $18,000 in 1987. No cost-recovery deduction is allowed in 1987 (the year of sale), and the property's adjusted basis for purposes of determining gain or loss is $17,000 ($20,000 cost − $3,000 cost-recovery allowance in 1986). ■

TABLE 10-2   ACRS Cost-Recovery Rates for Tangible Personal Property

Recovery Year	Recovery Classes	
	3-Year	5-Year[a]
1	25%	15%
2	38	22
3	37	21
4	—	21
5	—	21
Totals	100%	100%

[a] The percentages that are applicable to each year for 10-year property are presented in Appendix C.

---

[9] Sec. 168(c)(2). Also included is any tangible personal property with an ADR class life of 4 years or less, race horses over 2 years old, and other horses over 12 years old.

[10] Exceptions are provided for public utility equipment which uses a 10-year or 15-year class life depending upon the ADR midpoint life. Certain real property such as agricultural structures and petroleum storage facilities that are described as Sec. 1245 property are classified as 5-year recovery property.

[11] The half-year convention is an assumption that all asset acquisitions are made at the midpoint of the tax year.

Additional Comment

The effective tax rate on new capital investments is influenced by the depreciation rules. In 1983 the combination of the rapid write-off for depreciation and the investment tax credit resulted in an aggregate effective corporate tax rate of 19.4% when the highest marginal tax rate was 46%.

Classification and Recovery Rates for Real Property. The ACRS system applies to both residential and nonresidential depreciable real property used in a trade or business or held for the production of income (e.g., rental property held for investment). The recovery periods are 15, 18, or 19 years, depending upon the date the property was placed in service. Different recovery periods are used because the law was amended three times after the original enactment of ACRS in 1981. The effective dates and recovery periods are provided below:

- 15 years—real estate placed in service after 1980 and before March 16, 1984
- 18 years—real estate placed in service after March 15, 1984, and before May 9, 1985
- 19 years—real estate placed in service after May 8, 1985, through December 31, 1986
- 15 years—low-income housing placed in service after 1980 and before December 31, 1986.[12]

Additional Comment

The depreciable lives for real property are significantly longer under MACRS than the lives under ACRS. Congress, in the Tax Reform Act of 1986, made these changes with the expectation that investment in capital stock would be determined by market forces rather than by tax considerations.

The tables for real estate assume a 175% DB rate (200% DB rate for low-income housing) and automatically convert to straight-line to maximize the allowable cost-recovery amount.[13] For property placed in service after June 22, 1984, the tables assume a mid-month convention for real estate cost-recovery in the month of acquisition and in the month of disposition.[14] This means that if real property is acquired in December by a calendar-year taxpayer, only one-half month of cost recovery is allowed for the year. Eleven and one-half months cost recovery is allowed if property is disposed of in December. For the year of acquisition the partial year amount is built into the tables but the partial year amount must be computed for the year of disposition. The ACRS tables for real estate acquired prior to 1987 are reproduced in Appendix C.

Example 10-6 ■   Cable Corporation acquires a commercial office building and land for $1,000,000 on April 1, 1986. The basis amount that is allocable to the land is $300,000. Cost recovery is based upon a 19-year recovery period, and the mid-month convention is applied in the year of acquisition. The amount of cost recovery for 1986 is $45,500 (0.065 × $700,000 cost of the building). (See Table 1 on page C-25 in Appendix C.) ■

Example 10-7 ■   Assume the same facts as in Example 10-6, except that the building is sold on December 30, 1994. The cost-recovery deduction for 1994 is $29,517 (0.048 × $700,000 × [11.5 ÷ 12]). (See Table 1 on page C-25 in Appendix C.) ■

Use of the Straight-Line Method Under ACRS. Instead of using the statutory percentage methods previously described under the ACRS (pre-1987) rules, taxpayers could have elected to use the straight-line method for both tangible personal and real property. Under the straight-line method, the taxpayer could have used the same cost-recovery period or an extended period based upon the following alternatives:

- 3-year ACRS personal property—3, 5, or 12 years
- 5-year ACRS personal property—5, 12, or 25 years

---

[12] Sec. 168(b)(2).

[13] Special transitional rules are included in the Code to accommodate binding contracts to construct or acquire real estate that existed on the date of the changes in the law.

[14] Fifteen-year property and eighteen-year property placed in service after March 15, 1984, and before June 23, 1984, are subject to a full-month convention.

- 15-, 18-, or 19-year ACRS real property—basic ACRS recovery period (i.e., 15, 18, or 19 years), 35 or 45 years[15]

The following operating rules are used if the straight-line ACRS election is made for pre-1987 property:

- The half-year convention (i.e, one-half year's depreciation) is used for tangible personal property in the year the property is acquired and placed into service.[16]
- No cost recovery is permitted for personal property in the year of disposition.[17]
- The mid-month convention is used for real estate in the year of acquisition and disposition. The deduction is based on the number of months the real estate is owned during the years of acquisition and disposition.[18]
- For personal property, the straight-line election applies to all assets acquired during the year for a particular class (e.g., 3-year recovery property). The election is made on a property-by-property basis for real estate.

Example 10-8 ■

Matt acquires and places into service on December 1, 1986, a business automobile costing $10,000. Matt elects straight-line depreciation using the longest possible recovery period (12 years). Matt's cost-recovery allowance in the initial year is $417 ([$10,000 ÷ 12 years] × 0.50 year). If Matt sells the automobile in a subsequent year, no cost-recovery deduction is allowed in the year of the sale. ■

MACRS (1987 and Later Years)

OBJECTIVE 3
Classify property and calculate depreciation under the MACRS rules

Classification and Recovery Rates for Personal Property. MACRS generally follows the same rules originally provided by Congress for ACRS. However, class lives have been lengthened and depreciation methods are more rapidly accelerated.

The following classifications apply to property placed in service after December 31, 1986, under the MACRS system.[19] (Note that these classifications generally apply to personal property except for land improvements and single-purpose agricultural or horticultural structures.)

Additional Comment
The depreciable life of an automobile has been extended from 3 years to 5 years under the MACRS rules.

Key Point
Most depreciable personal property will be classified as 7-year property under MACRS.

- 3 years—ADR class life of 4 years or less including tractor units, race horses over 12 years old, and special tools.
- 5 years—ADR class life of more than 4 but less than 10 years including automobiles, light and heavy general purpose trucks, computers, and R&E equipment.
- 7 years—ADR class life of 10 years or more but less than 16 years including office furniture and equipment, horses, single-purpose agricultural or horticultural structures, and property with no ADR class life and not classified elsewhere. Most types of machinery are included in this class.
- 10 years—ADR class life of more than 16 but less than 20 years including barges, vessels, and petroleum and food processing equipment.
- 15 years—ADR class life of more than 20 but less than 25 years including billboards, service station buildings, and land improvements.
- 20 years—ADR class life of 25 or more years including utilities and sewers.

Additional Comment
The Tax Reform Act of 1986 increased the rate of acceleration on the declining-balance method from 150% to 200% for property in the 3-, 5-, 7-, and 10-year classes to compensate for the repeal of the investment tax credit.

[15] Sec. 168(b)(3). The recovery period for 10-year personal property is 10, 25, or 35 years and for 15-year personal property is 15, 35, or 45 years.
[16] Sec. 168(b)(3)(B)(iii).
[17] Sec. 168(d)(2).
[18] Sec. 168(b)(2).
[19] Secs. 168(e)(1). ADR tables are reproduced in Appendix C.

The depreciation rates for the 3-year, 5-year, and 7-year recovery classes are provided in Table 10-3. The rates in Table 10-3 are based on the 200% DB method with a conversion to straight-line when it yields a larger amount. A half-year convention is used in the year of acquisition and zero salvage value is assumed.[20]

Example 10-9 ■ Mary acquires and places into service a business machine in 1994 for $20,000. The machinery has a 7-year recovery period under the MACRS rules. The depreciation deduction for 1994 is $2,858 (0.1429 × $20,000). The rate that is applied (0.1429) is based upon the 200% DB method and assumes a half-year convention and zero salvage value. The MACRS depreciation deduction for the year of acquisition can also be computed by applying the accelerated depreciation rate (using the half-year convention) to the basis of the assets. Thus the depreciation deduction for 1994 is $2,857 ($20,000 ÷ 7 years × 200% DB × 0.50 year). Minor differences between the two calculations are due to rounding. ■

USE OF A MID-QUARTER CONVENTION. The MACRS system requires the use of a mid-quarter convention if the aggregate basis of all personal property placed in service during the last 3 months of the year exceeds 40% of the cost of all personal property placed in service during the tax year.[21] Property placed in service and disposed of during the same tax year is not taken into account.[22]

The 40% rule prevents taxpayers from using the half-year convention and thereby obtaining one-half year's depreciation in the year of acquisition when a substantial portion of the assets are acquired during the last quarter of the tax year.

Example 10-10 ■ Michael acquires 5-year recovery period personal property in 1994 and places it in service on the following schedule:

Date Placed in Service	Acquisition Cost
January 20	$100,000
April 18	200,000
November 5	300,000
Total	$600,000

Additional Comment

Caution must be exercised in situations where property may be delivered either before or after the desired quarter to be placed in service.

Self-Study Question

In Table 10-3, how has the 0.2000 first year cost recovery rate for 5-year property been calculated?

Answer

The 0.2000 rate is calculated by multiplying the double declining-balance rate of 0.4000 by 1/2 year of depreciation.

TABLE 10-3 MACRS Rates for Tangible Personal Property (using half-year convention)

Recovery Year	Recovery Classes		
	3-Year	5-Year	7-Year
1	0.3333	0.2000	0.1429
2	0.4445	0.3200	0.2449
3	0.1481	0.1920	0.1749
4	0.0741	0.1152	0.1249
5	—	0.1152	0.0893
6	—	0.0576	0.0892
7	—	—	0.0893
8	—	—	0.0446

Source: Table 1 of Rev. Proc. 87-57, 1987-2 C.B. 687.

[20] Secs. 168(b)(4) and (d).
[21] Sec. 168(d)(3).
[22] Sec. 168(d)(3)(B) and Reg. Sec. 1.168(d)-1(b)(3).

Since more than 40% of the property acquired during the year is placed in service in the last 3 months, the mid-quarter convention will apply for all property placed in service during the year. (See Tables 2, 3, and 5 of Rev. Proc. 87-57 (reproduced in Appendix C) for the percentages that are used to make this calculation.)

Property Placed in Service	Year 1 Depreciation	
January 20	$100,000 ÷ 5 years × 200% DB × [10.5 ÷ 12] =	$ 35,000[23]
April 18	200,000 ÷ 5 years × 200% DB × [7.5 ÷ 12] =	50,000
November 5	300,000 ÷ 5 years × 200% DB × [1.5 ÷ 12] =	15,000
Total	$600,000	$100,000

Note that if the half-year convention had applied in Example 10-10, $120,000 (0.2000 × $600,000) of depreciation could have been claimed. Care should be taken on asset acquisitions to prevent the application of the mid-quarter convention if larger depreciation deductions are desired. ∎

YEAR OF DISPOSITION. The MACRS system allows depreciation to be taken in the year of disposition using the same convention that applied on acquisition (e.g., half-year, mid-month, or mid-quarter convention).

Example 10-11 ∎

Assume the same facts as in Example 10-10, except that the equipment purchased on April 18 is disposed of on August 14 in the following year. The midquarter convention must be used because it is used in the year of acquisition. Thus, $37,500 of depreciation is claimed in the year of disposition ($200,000 × 0.30) × [7.5 ÷ 12]). (See Table 3 of Rev. Proc. 87-57 in Appendix C.) ∎

Example 10-12 ∎

Michelle acquires machinery in 1994 that qualifies as 7-year MACRS property and has a $100,000 basis for depreciation. The half-year convention is applied in the year of acquisition. In December 1995 the machinery is sold. Michelle's depreciation deduction in 1995 is $12,245 ($100,000 × [0.2449 × 0.50]) for the equipment (see Table 10-3). ∎

Classification and Recovery Rates for Real Property. The MACRS recovery periods that apply to real property placed in service in years after 1986 have been lengthened and include the following:

* Residential rental property—27½ years
* Nonresidential real property—39 years[24]

Depreciation must be calculated using the straight-line method.[25] A mid-month convention is used in the year of acquisition and in the year of disposition. The tables for computing depreciation for real property are located in Rev. Proc. 87-57 (Tables 6 and 7) which are reproduced in Appendix C.

[23] The percentage used in Table 2 of Rev. Proc. 87-57 (which is reproduced in Appendix C) for 5-year property placed in service in the first quarter is 0.3500. Therefore, the depreciation in year 1 for the $100,000 of property placed in service on January 20 is $35,000 (0.3500 × $100,000). The corresponding percentages in Table 3 and Table 5 for property placed in service on April 18 and November 5 are 0.2500 and 0.0500, respectively.

[24] Sec. 168(c)(1). A 31.5-year recovery period applies to property placed in service on or after January 1, 1987 and before May 13, 1993. Certain exceptions permit the continued use of the 31.5-year recovery period for binding contracts entered into before May 13, 1993, and where the construction of the property commenced prior to May 13, 1993. See Table 7A in Appendix C for the 39-year depreciation rate tables.

[25] Sec. 168(b)(3).

Real properties are divided into two categories—residential rental property and nonresidential real property. **Residential rental property** is defined as property from which at least 80% of the gross rental income is rental income from dwelling units.[26] Dwelling units include houses, apartments, and manufactured homes that are used for residential purposes but not hotels, motels, or other establishments for transient use.

Straight-Line (Method) Election Under MACRS. Instead of using the accelerated methods previously described under the MACRS rules, taxpayers may elect to use the straight-line method for tangible personal property. If the straight-line election is made, the taxpayer uses the same depreciation period or an extended period based upon the alternative depreciation system.[27]

Alternative Depreciation System. The alternative depreciation system uses the straight-line method or the 150% DB method with a half-year, mid-quarter, or mid-month convention, whichever is applicable. The ADR class life is generally used as the cost recovery period under the alternative depreciation system (see Table 8 in Rev. Proc. 87-57, which is reproduced in Appendix C, and Rev. Proc. 87-56, 1987-2 C.B. 674, which provides specific recovery periods for depreciable assets for the alternative depreciation system). However, personal property with no ADR midpoint life is assigned a 12-year life, and real property has a 40-year life. In addition, Congress provided specified lives for certain types of property under this system. The assigned recovery periods are as follows:

- 5 years—automobiles; light, general purpose trucks; qualified technological equipment; and semi-conductor manufacturing equipment
- 9½ years—computer-based telephone central office switching equipment
- 10 years—railroad track
- 12 years—personal property with no class life
- 15 years—single-purpose agricultural or horticultural structures
- 24 years—municipal waste water treatment plants and telephone distribution plants and comparable equipment used for 2-way exchange of voice and data communications
- 27½ years—low-income housing financed by tax-exempt obligations
- 40 years—nonresidential real and residential rental property and Sec. 1245 property that is real property with no useful life
- 50 years—municipal sewers

Example 10-13 ■

In December 1994, Milton acquires and places in service a business automobile costing $10,000. No other business assets are acquired by Milton during 1994. Milton elects straight-line depreciation using the shortest possible recovery period (5 years). Milton must use the mid-quarter convention because the total basis of all personal property placed in service during the last 3 months of the year exceeds 40% of the cost of all personal property placed in service during the year. Milton's depreciation allowance in the initial year is $250 ([$10,000 ÷ 5 years] × [1.5 ÷ 12 months]). If Milton sells the automobile in October 1995, depreciation in the year of disposition is $250 ([$10,000 × 0.20] × [1.5 ÷ 12 months]). ■

The alternative depreciation system is also used to compute E&P for a corporation and to compute the alternative minimum tax for both individuals and corporations (see Chapter 14).

[26] Secs. 168(e)(2)(A) and 167(j)(2)(B).
[27] Sec. 167(j)(2)(B).

TOPIC REVIEW 10-1

Comparison of ACRS and MACRS

	ACRS	MACRS
Useful lives:		
Automobiles	3 years	5 years
Computers	5 years	5 years
Office furniture and equipment	5 years	7 years
Residential rental property	15, 18, or 19 years	27.5 years
Nonresidential real property	15, 18, or 19 years	39 years
Conventions:		
Personal property	Mid-year	Mid-year or mid-quarter[a]
Real property	Mid-month[b]	Mid-month
Depreciation in year of sale:		
Personal property	No	Yes
Real property	Yes	Yes

[a] If more than 40% of personal property is placed in service during the last quarter of year.
[b] A full-month convention is used for property acquired prior to June 23, 1984.

A comparison of the ACRS and MACRS rules is presented in Topic Review 10-1.

Section 179 Expensing Election

In lieu of capitalizing the cost of new or used tangible personal business property, taxpayers may elect to expense up to $17,500 of the acquisition cost as an ordinary deduction in the year of acquisition.[28] To qualify for the deduction, the property must actually be placed into service during the year. The immediate expensing election is not applicable to real estate. The election is made on an annual basis, and the taxpayer must select the assets to which the $17,500 write-off applies. The MACRS rules apply to any amount of an asset's cost that is not expensed under Sec. 179.

Example 10-14 ∎

Tanya acquires and places into service a business machine (tangible personal property qualifying under Sec. 179) for $37,500 in July 1994. The machine has a 7-year MACRS recovery period. Tanya elects to immediately expense $17,500 of the asset's cost under Sec. 179. Tanya's basis for calculating the MACRS depreciation deduction is $20,000 ($37,500 − $17,500). Tanya's 1994 depreciation allowance is $2,858 ($20,000 × 0.1429). Tanya's total capital recovery deductions for 1994 are $20,358 ($17,500 expensed under Sec. 179 + $2,858 MACRS depreciation). ∎

The following limitations and special rules apply to the Sec. 179 election:

- The property must be purchased for use in an active trade or business as distinguished from property that is acquired for the production of income (e.g., rental personal property held by an investor does not qualify).[29]

- The property cannot be acquired from a related party under Sec. 267 or by gift or inheritance.[30]

---

[28] Sec. 179. The amount was increased from $10,000 to $17,500 for property placed in service in tax years beginning after December 31, 1992.
[29] Sec. 179(d)(1).
[30] Sec. 179(d)(2).

- The Sec. 179 tax benefits are recaptured if the property is no longer predominantly used in a trade or business (e.g., the property is converted to personal use) at any time.[31] In the year of recapture, the taxpayer is required to include in gross income the amount previously expensed reduced by the amount of depreciation that would have been allowed for the period the property was held for business use.[32]

- If the total cost of qualified property placed into service during the year is more than $200,000, the $17,500 ceiling is reduced on a dollar-for-dollar basis by the excess amount.[33] Thus, no deduction is permitted for a tax year in which $217,500 or more of Sec. 179 property is placed into service.[34]

- A second limitation on the total Sec. 179 deduction is that it cannot exceed the taxpayer's taxable income (before deducting the Sec. 179 expense) from the trade or business.[35] Any acquisition cost that is unable to be deducted because of the limitation based on taxable income is carried forward for an unlimited number of years and is added to the other amounts eligible for the Sec. 179 deduction. The carryover amount is subject to the taxable income limitation in the carryover year.

Example 10-15 ∎

Pam owns an unincorporated manufacturing business. In 1994 she purchases and places in service $212,500 of qualifying equipment for use in her business. Pam's taxable income from the business (before deducting any Sec. 179 amount) is $4,000. The $17,500 ceiling amount is initially reduced by $12,500 ($212,500 − $200,000) to reflect the fact that the qualified property placed in service during the year exceeded $200,000. The remaining $5,000 Sec. 179 deduction is further reduced by $1,000 ($5,000 − $4,000) to reflect the taxable income limitation. Pam's Sec. 179 deduction is $4,000; $1,000 is available for use as a carryover to 1995. The cost basis of the equipment for MACRS purposes is reduced by $5,000 in 1994 despite the fact that only $4,000 was immediately deductible under Sec. 179. ∎

MACRS Restrictions

Personal-Use Assets. The portion of an asset's cost that is related to personal use is not depreciable. For example, if a taxpayer owns a duplex and uses one unit as a personal residence, only the unit that is rented to tenants qualifies for depreciation. In addition, MACRS restrictions apply to certain "listed" properties including automobiles; computers and peripheral equipment; cellular telephones and other similar telecommunications equipment; and property used for entertainment, recreation, or amusement that may have been used by the taxpayer for both business and personal purposes.[36]

---

[31] Sec. 179(d)(10).
[32] Reg. Sec. 1.179-1(e).
[33] Sec. 179(b)(2).
[34] Additional tax incentives are provided under Sec. 1397A for an enterprise zone business; that is, an area specially designated by the federal government to receive special economic benefits due to factors such as high employment, etc. (See Sec. 1397B for the definition of an enterprise zone business.) First, the Sec. 179 expensing allowance of $17,500 is increased by the lesser of: (1) $20,000 or the cost of Sec. 179 property placed into service during the year that is "qualified zone property." Secondly, the $200,000 phase-out is applied by taking into account only one half of the cost of the qualified zone property that is qualified zone property.
[35] Sec. 179(b)(3). Under Reg. Sec. 1.179-2(c)(5)(iv), employees are considered to be engaged in the active conduct of the trade or business of their employment. Thus, a small business person who is also an employee may include wages and salary derived from employment in determining taxable income for purposes of this limitation. Such amounts are considered derived from the conduct of a trade or business. For an individual, taxable income is also computed without regard to the deduction for one-half of self-employment taxes paid under Sec. 164(f) (see Chapter 14).
[36] Sec. 280F(d)(4). The restrictions generally apply to property placed in service after June 18, 1984, except for cellular telephones and similar telecommunications equipment placed into service in tax years beginning after December 31, 1989.

Business-Use Assets. If a listed property's business usage is greater than 50% of its total usage, the taxpayer may use the regular MACRS tables for the business-use portion of the asset's cost. However, if the business use is 50% or less, the taxpayer must use the alternative depreciation system (e.g., 5-year straight-line cost recovery period for automobiles and computers).

Example 10-16 ■

Patrick acquires an automobile for $10,000 in June 1994. It is used 60% for business. The depreciation deduction on the business-use portion of the automobile's cost is based on the MACRS system and five-year recovery class because the automobile is predominantly used in business (i.e., more than 50%). The MACRS depreciation allowance in 1994 is $1,200 ($10,000 × 0.20 MACRS rate × 0.60 business percentage use). See Table 10-3 for the MACRS rate. ■

Example 10-17 ■

Paula acquires an automobile for $10,000 in 1994. It is used only 40% for business. Paula may claim depreciation allowances on the business portion of the automobile, only by using the alternative depreciation system. The business portion is $4,000 ($10,000 × 0.40). Paula's depreciation allowance in 1994 is $400 ([$4,000 ÷ 5 years] × 0.50) the half-year convention. If Table 8 in Rev. Proc. 87-57 (see Appendix C) were used, Paula's depreciation allowance in 1994 would also be $400 ($4,000 × 0.10). ■

Additional restrictions apply to employees who acquire listed property (e.g., an automobile, personal computer, and so on) for use in employment-related activities. In addition to the "more than 50% test," the use must be for the convenience of the employer and be required as a condition of employment.[37] Apparently this rule is interpreted very strictly by the IRS.

Example 10-18 ■

Additional Comment

An automobile for purposes of the listed property restrictions is defined as any 4-wheeled vehicle which is manufactured primarily for use on public streets and is rated at 6,000 pounds or less unloaded gross vehicle weight. At one time the Jeep Wagoneer was advertised as not being subject to the listed property limitation or luxury automobile limitation since its weight was slightly over the weight limit. Ambulances, hearses, and taxis are excluded.

Raul, a college professor, acquired a personal computer for use at home. He used the computer 60% of the time on teaching- and research-related activities associated with his job. The remaining usage was for personal activities. Raul's employer finds that it is helpful for employees to own a personal computer but does not require them to purchase a computer as a condition of employment. Raul meets the first requirement (i.e., the 60% business usage is greater than the 50% threshold). However, the second requirement for employees (that the use must be for the convenience of the employer and required as a condition of employment) is not met. Thus, no depreciation may be taken because the employment-related use is not deemed to be business use. ■

Recapture of Excess Cost-Recovery Deductions. If the MACRS rules were used and the business-use percentage decreases to 50% or less in a subsequent year, the property is subject to depreciation recapture. The depreciation deductions for all years are recomputed using the alternative depreciation system. The excess depreciation that has been taken is recaptured as ordinary income by including the excess amount in the taxpayer's gross income in the year the business-use percentage first falls to 50% or below.[38] Once the business use falls to 50% or below, the alternative depreciation system must be used for the current year and for all subsequent years, even if the business-use percentage increases to more than 50% in a subsequent year.

Example 10-19 ■

Peggy, a self-employed attorney, acquires an automobile in 1994 for $10,000. The automobile's business usage is 60% in 1994 but declines to 40% in 1995. In 1994 Peggy is eligible to use the regular MACRS depreciation rates because the business use was greater than 50%. The MACRS deduction in 1994 is $1,200 ($10,000

---

[37] Sec. 280F(d)(3). Any other property used for transportation (e.g., a pick-up truck) qualifies as listed property if the nature of the property lends itself to personal use. See Sec. 280 F(b)(4).
[38] Sec. 280F(b)(3).

cost × 0.60 business use × 0.20). The straight-line depreciation method using the five-year life specified for the alternative depreciation system and the half-year convention would have resulted in a deduction of only $600 ([$10,000 cost × 0.60 business use ÷ 5 years] × 0.50 year) in 1994. Thus, $600 ($1,200 − $600) of the previously claimed depreciation is recaptured as ordinary income in 1995. Peggy's depreciation deduction for 1995 and subsequent years is limited to the straight-line method and a 5-year recovery period. Her depreciation deduction for 1995 is $800 ([$10,000 cost × 0.40 business use] ÷ 5 years). ∎

Additional Comment

The limitations on luxury automobiles mean that the depreciation deductions are limited during the normal 5-year recovery period on business automobiles costing more than $14,400 (for 1993).

Limitations on Luxury Automobiles. Additional MACRS depreciation deduction restrictions are placed upon the purchase of so-called luxury automobiles.[39] The limitations apply even if such automobiles are used 100% of the time for business. The MACRS depreciation for automobiles placed into service in 1993 is subject to a $2,860 ceiling limitation for the first year, $4,600 for the second year, $2,750 for the third year, and $1,675 for each succeeding year in the recovery period.[40] In the years following the end of the depreciation period (e.g., in year six and subsequent years), additional depreciation up to $1,675 per year is allowed in taxable years commencing after the end of the recovery period until the business use portion of the automobile is fully depreciated. These ceilings are reduced by the percentage of personal use and also apply to amounts that are expensed under Sec. 179. The effect of these ceilings is to extend the basic MACRS depreciation period from six to seven years or longer depending upon the automobile's acquisition cost.

Example 10-20 ∎

Typical Misconception

It is sometimes mistakenly believed that the $17,500 expensing allowance can be used to boost the first-year write-off on luxury automobiles.

Phil acquires an automobile for $20,000 in 1994. The automobile is used 80% for business and 20% for personal activities during the year. Table 10-4 lists the depreciation amounts for a six-year period, assuming that the 80% business use continues for the life of the automobile and that no amount is expensed under Sec. 179. At the end of the regular six-year depreciation period, the unrecovered cost in the business use portion of the automobile may be recovered in 1999 and succeeding years at an annual rate not to exceed $1,340 ($1,675 × 0.80). ∎

Additional Comment

The amount that can be deducted for leased automobiles is also limited.

Additional Computations for Leased Luxury Automobiles. If a taxpayer leases an automobile for business purposes, the deduction for rental payments is reduced to reflect the limitations upon depreciation deductions that are imposed on owners of automobiles under Sec. 280F. If these restrictions were not applied to leased automobiles, the limitations could be avoided by leasing instead of purchasing an automobile. The leasing restriction is accomplished by requiring taxpayers to include in their gross income an "inclusion amount" which is obtained from an IRS table.[41] This amount is based upon the automobile's FMV and the tax year in which the lease commences, and is prorated for the percentage of business use and number of days used during the year.

Example 10-21 ∎

On April 1, 1993 Jim leases and places into service an automobile with a FMV of $30,500. Business use is 60%. The "inclusion amount" for the initial year of the lease (1993) from the table contained in Rev. Proc. 93-35 is $92. This amount is prorated for the number of days the automobile is leased ($275/365$) and is then multiplied by the percentage of business use (60%). Jim is entitled to deduct 60% of the lease payments but must include $42 ([$92 × $275/365$] × 60%) in his gross income for the current year. ∎

[39] Based upon current prices, these restrictions also apply to many non-luxury automobiles because price increases to automobiles have exceeded inflation adjustments made to the limitations since the law was enacted in 1986. The 1994 limitation amounts were not available when these materials were published.

[40] Sec. 280F(a)(2). The ceiling limitation for the first year includes any amounts that are immediately written off under Sec. 179. The Sec. 280F limitations restrict the deductibility of lease payments for automobiles in the same way that depreciation is restricted.

[41] Rev. Proc. 93-35, 1993-28, 51.

TABLE 10-4 *Depreciation Amounts for Example 10-20*

	MACRS Deduction Before Limitation	Ceiling Limit	Deduction Allowed
1993			
Regular calculation			
($20,000 × 0.80 × 0.20)	$3,200		
Ceiling limit			
($2,860 × 0.80)		$2,288	$2,288
1994			
Regular calculation			
($20,000 × 0.80 × 0.32)	5,120		
Ceiling limit			
($4,600 × 0.80)		3,680	3,680
1995			
Regular calculation			
($20,000 × 0.80 × 0.192)	3,072		
Ceiling limit			
($2,750 × 0.80)		2,200	2,200
1996			
Regular calculation			
($20,000 × 0.80 × 0.1152)	1,843		
Ceiling limit			
($1,675 × 0.80)		1,340	1,340
1997			
Regular calculation			
($20,000 × 0.80 × 0.1152)	1,843		
Ceiling limit			
($1,675 × 0.80)		1,340	1,340
1998			
Regular calculation			
($20,000 × 0.80 × 0.0576)	922		
Ceiling limit			
($1,675 × 0.80)		1,340	922
1999 and later years until fully depreciated			
Ceiling limit			
($1,675 × 0.80)		1,340	1,340

Special elections and restrictions are summarized in Topic Review 10-2.

DEPLETION AND INTANGIBLE DRILLING AND DEVELOPMENT COSTS

OBJECTIVE 4

Apply cost and percentage depletion methods and understand the treatment for intangible drilling costs

The exploration and development of oil and gas properties require the incurrence of the following types of expenditures:

- Payments for the mineral interest. These costs are recovered through depletion.

- Intangible drilling and development costs (e.g., labor and other operating costs to clear land, erect a derrick, and drill the well). Taxpayers elect to capitalize or immediately write off these expenditures.

- Tangible asset costs (e.g., machinery, pipe). These expenditures must be capitalized and depreciated under the MACRS rules.

TOPIC REVIEW 10-2

Special Elections and Restrictions

Section 179 Expensing Election
 Deduction—$17,500 on the purchase of new or used tangible personal business
  property used in the conduct of a trade or business.
 Limitations:
  Asset purchases—The $17,500 limit is reduced by the excess of qualified
   purchases over $200,000.
  Taxable income limitation—Limited to taxable income before the Sec. 179
   deduction.
  Basis reduction—The depreciable basis is reduced by the amount of the Sec. 179
   deduction.
  Recapture—Occurs when the asset is no longer predominantly used in a trade or
   business. The recapture amount equals the excess of the Sec. 179 expense amount
   minus the amount that would have been claimed as depreciation if no Sec. 179
   election was made.

Business Use Restriction
 Listed property—Business use must be more than 50% to use the regular
  MACRS rules. If business use is less than 50%, the alternative
  depreciation system's straight-line method must be used.
 Recapture—If business use falls below 50%, the taxpayer must recompute
  depreciation using the alternative depreciation system's straight-line method and
  recapture the difference between the prior depreciation taken and straight-line
  depreciation. The straight-line method is continued for the remaining useful life
  even if business use subsequently exceeds 50%.

Luxury Automobile Limitations for 1993
 Sum of depreciation and Sec. 179 expense limits:
1st year	$2,860
2nd year	4,600
3rd year	2,750
4th and later years	1,675

Leased Luxury Automobile Limitations
 An "inclusion amount" is added to gross income based on the automobile's FMV
  on the date placed in service to approximate the depreciation restrictions.
  Special tables that are revised annually are used to calculate the inclusion amount.

- Operating costs after the well is producing. These expenditures are immediately
  deductible under Sec. 162 when incurred.

Treatment of Intangible Drilling and Development Costs

Intangible drilling and development costs (IDCs) may either be deducted as an
expense or capitalized.[42] If the IDCs are capitalized, the amounts are added to the
property's basis for determining cost depletion, and the costs are written off through
cost depletion. An ordinary loss deduction is permitted for any such costs that have
been capitalized in connection with a nonproductive well.[43] The amount of depletion
claimed in a tax year equals the greater of the percentage depletion or cost depletion

---

[42] Sec. 263(c).
[43] Reg. Sec. 1.612-4(b).

amounts. An increase in the amount of cost depletion due to the capitalization of IDCs may produce limited or no tax benefits when percentage depletion is claimed by the taxpayer. Therefore, it is generally preferable to expense the IDCs if the percentage depletion is expected to be more than the cost depletion and is used to compute the depletion allowance.

Example 10-22 ■

Penny acquires certain rights to oil and gas property in 1994 for $1,000,000. In 1994 Penny incurs $300,000 of IDCs. If the IDCs are capitalized, the basis for cost depletion purposes is $1,300,000. Assume that the cost depletion amounts are $100,000 in 1994 if the IDCs are expensed and $130,000 if IDCs are capitalized. If the percentage depletion amount is $150,000, percentage depletion will be used because it is greater than either of the cost depletion amounts. Thus, the expensing of the IDCs permits the taxpayer to deduct the entire $300,000 of IDCs in 1994 plus $150,000 of percentage depletion. ■

Depletion Methods

Key Point

A depletion deduction is available in the case of mines, oil and gas wells, other natural resources, and timber. However, the percentage depletion method is not available in the case of timber.

Self-Study Question

Why is the percentage depletion method not available in the case of timber?

Answer

Timber is considered to be a renewable natural resource.

Depletion is calculated under the **cost depletion method** and the **percentage depletion method** for each period. The method that is used in any year is the one that results in the largest deduction. Thus, percentage depletion may be used in one year and cost depletion may be used in the following year.

Cost Depletion Method. The *cost depletion method* is similar to the units-of-production method of depreciation. The adjusted basis of the asset is divided by the estimated recoverable units to arrive at a per-unit depletion cost. This per-unit cost is then multiplied by the number of units sold to determine the cost depletion amount.[44] If percentage depletion is used in any one year because it is greater than the cost depletion amount, the property's adjusted basis for purposes of determining (1) cost depletion in the following year and (2) the gain or loss on disposition of the property is reduced by the amount of percentage depletion claimed. If the original estimate of recoverable units is subsequently determined to be incorrect, the per-unit cost depletion rate must be revised and used on a prospective basis to determine cost depletion in future years.[45] It is not proper to file an amended return for the years that the incorrect estimated unit cost was used.

Example 10-23 ■

Ralph acquires an oil and gas property interest for $100,000 in 1994. The estimate of recoverable units (i.e., barrels of oil) is 10,000. The per-unit cost depletion amount is $10 ($100,000 ÷ 10,000). If 3,000 units are produced and 2,000 units are sold in 1994, the cost depletion amount is $20,000 (2,000 units × $10 per unit). If cost depletion is used because it exceeds the percentage depletion amount, the cost basis of the property is reduced to $80,000 ($100,000 − $20,000) at the beginning of 1995. If the estimate of remaining recoverable units is revised downward from 8,000 units in 1995 (10,000 − 2,000 units sold in 1994) to 5,000 units (including the 1,000 barrels produced but not sold in 1994, the property's $80,000 adjusted basis is divided by 5,000 units to arrive at a new per-unit cost depletion amount of $16 for 1995. ■

Percentage Depletion Method. The percentage depletion method has not been available to large oil and gas producers since 1974. However, it is still available to (1) small oil and gas producers and royalty owners under a specific exemption in the law.[46]

---

[44] Sec. 612.

[45] Sec. 611(a).

[46] Sec. 613A(c). The ceiling is based upon average daily production of not more than 1,000 barrels of oil or 6 million cubic feet of natural gas.

and (2) for several types of mineral properties (e.g., coal, iron, gravel, and so on).[47] *Percentage depletion* for oil and gas properties is 15% times the gross income from the property.[48] However, it may not exceed 100% of the taxable income (before depletion is deducted).[49] Percentage depletion may not be calculated on any lease bonus, advance royalty, or other amount payable without regard to production from property.[50]

Example 10-24 ■

Historical Note

An Arab oil embargo to the United States in 1973 created a situation where oil prices increased significantly. Consequently, most domestic U.S. oil producers reported huge profits. This situation contributed to the repeal of the percentage depletion allowance for large oil and gas producers.

Key Point

The use of the percentage depletion method permits recovery of more than the cost of the property.

Carmen acquires an oil and gas property interest for $400,000 in 1994. During the year, 10,000 barrels of oil are sold for $250,000. Intangible drilling and development costs amount to $100,000 and are expensed in 1994. Other expenses are $50,000. Cost depletion is $20,000 in 1994. The computation of percentage depletion is as follows:

Gross income	$250,000
Minus: Expenses ($100,000 IDCs + $50,000 other expenses)	(150,000)
Taxable income (before depletion)	$100,000
Minus: Depletion deduction (greater of $37,500 percentage depletion or $20,000 cost depletion)	(37,500)[a]
Taxable income	$ 62,500

■

[a] Percentage depletion is the lesser of (1) percentage depletion before the limitation of $37,500 (0.15 × $250,000) or (2) the $100,000 income ceiling amount (1.00 × $100,000 taxable income before depletion).

AMORTIZATION

OBJECTIVE 5
Calculate amortization for intangible assets and understand the difference between amortizable and non-amortizable assets

An amortization deduction is permitted for certain acquired Sec. 197 intangible assets. The amortization is deducted on a ratable basis over a 15-year period beginning with the month of acquisition.[51] In general, Sec. 197 applies only to intangible assets (e.g., goodwill) that are acquired in connection with a transaction that involves the acquisition of a trade or business or a substantial portion of a trade or business. For example, Sec. 197 does not apply to an intangible asset that is internally created by the taxpayer (e.g., a patent resulting from the taxpayer's research and development lab). For example, internally created patents and copyrights both have definite and limited lives and are therefore amortizable over the defined period.[52] Additionally, Sec. 197 does not apply to intangibles that are acquired independent of an acquisition (e.g., a formula, software, or a customer list). Such intangibles are subject to amortization if a definite and limited life can be established.

Example 10-25 ■

On January 1, 1994 Central Corporation receives patent approval on an internally created process improvement. Legal costs associated with the patent are $100,000 and the patent has a legal life of 17 years. The patent has a definite and limited life and is amortizable ratably over its legal life of 17 years beginning with the month of its creation. ■

---

[47] Sec. 613. The rates vary from 5% to 22% depending upon the type of resource being mined or extracted.

[48] Under Sec. 613A(c) the statutory percentage depletion rate for marginally producing oil and gas wells is increased if the price of crude oil is less than $20 per barrel during the immediately preceding calendar year. The statutory rate is increased by 1 percentage point for each dollar below $20.

[49] The percentage limitation was 50% for years prior to 1991.

[50] Secs. 613(a) and 613A(d)(5).

[51] Sec. 197(a). The amortization rules apply to property acquired after August 13, 1993 unless an election is made to apply Sec. 197 to all property acquired after July 25, 1991.

[52] Reg. Sec. 1.167(a)-3.

Additional Comment

In the 1993 Newark Morning Ledger Co. v. U.S. case the U.S. Supreme Court held that a taxpayer could depreciate intangible assets if the asset could be valued and if it had a limited life. The case was a victory for taxpayers but promised disputes over valuation of intangibles. To eliminate potential battles, Congress in the Revenue Reconciliation Act of 1993 required a 15-year amortization of certain intangible assets such as goodwill, information base, know-how, customer lists, etc.

Definition of a Sec. 197 Intangible Asset

Sec. 197 intangibles (i.e., intangible assets which are subject to 15-year ratable amortization) include the following:[53]

- Goodwill and going concern value. Goodwill is defined as the value of a trade or business that is attributable to the expectancy of continued customer patronage. Going concern value is the added value that attaches to acquired property because it is an integral part of a going concern.[54]

- Intangible assets relating to the work force, information base, know-how, customers, suppliers, or similar items, (e.g., the portion of the purchase price of an acquired business that is attributable to an existing employment contract for a key employee may be amortized over a 15-year period). An example of an information base intangible would be a customer list. Know-how related intangibles include patents, copyrights, formulas, processes, etc.

- Licenses, permits, or other rights granted by a governmental unit or agency (e.g., the capitalized cost of acquiring a radio broadcasting license).

- Covenants not to compete. A covenant not to compete represents an agreement between a buyer and seller of a business that the seller (i.e., the selling corporation and/or its shareholders) will not compete with the buyer for a limited period. The covenant may also be limited to a geographic area.

- Franchises, trademarks, and tradenames. A franchise includes any agreement that gives one of the parties the right to distribute, sell, or provide goods, services, or facilities, within a specified area.

Example 10-26 ■

During the current year, Chicago Corporation acquires all of the net assets of Coastal Corporation for $1,000,000. The following intangible assets are included in the purchase agreement:

goodwill and going concern value	$100,000
licenses	55,000
patents	45,000
a covenant not to compete for five years	100,000

All of the intangible assets qualify under Sec. 197 and are amortizable on a ratable basis over 15 years beginning with the month of the acquisition. ■

Classification and Disposition of Intangible Assets

A Sec. 197 intangible asset is treated as depreciable property so that Sec. 1231 treatment is accorded the disposition if the intangible asset is held for more than one year.[55] Gain from the disposition of a Sec. 197 intangible is subject to depreciation recapture under Sec. 1245 (see Chapter 13).[56] A loss on the disposition of a Sec. 197 intangible asset, however, is not deductible if other intangibles acquired in the same asset acquisition of a trade or business are retained. In such case, the bases of the retained Sec. 197 intangibles are increased by the unrecognized loss.[57]

Example 10-27 ■

Assume the same facts as in Example 10-26 except that after five years the covenant not to compete expires when its adjusted basis is $66,667 ($100,000 − [0.333 × $100,000]). The loss is not deductible and the $66,667 disallowed loss is allocated to the retained Sec. 197 assets based upon their respective FMVs. ■

---

[53] Sec. 197(d).
[54] Goodwill and going concern value were not amortizable for periods prior to the enactment of Sec. 197.
[55] Secs. 1221(2) and 1221(a)(3).
[56] Sec. 1245(a)(2)(C).
[57] Sec. 197(f)(1).

Example 10-28 ■ Assume the same facts as in Example 10-26 except that after one year the patent is sold for $50,000. In the initial year, $3,000 of depreciation was deducted. The recognized gain is $8,000 ($50,000 − $42,000) and $3,000 of the gain is recaptured as ordinary income under Sec. 1245. The remaining $5,000 of gain is classified as Sec. 1231 gain. ■

Research and Experimental Expenditures

The Regulations define those items that do and do not qualify as research and experimental (R&E) expenditures.[58] These items are summarized in Table 10-5. To account for R&E expenditures, the following alternatives are available:

- Expense in the year paid or incurred
- Defer and amortize the costs as a ratable deduction over a period of 60 months or more
- Capitalize and write off the costs only when the research project is abandoned or is worthless[59]

A taxpayer must make an election to expense or defer and amortize the costs in the initial year the R&E expenditures are incurred. If no election is made, the costs must be capitalized. The taxpayer must continue to use the same accounting method for the R&E expenditures unless IRS approval to change methods is obtained.

The following points are significant regarding the computation of the deduction for R&E expenditures:

- Most taxpayers elect to expense the R&E expenditures because they prefer the immediate tax benefit.
- The deferral and amortization method is desirable if the taxpayer is currently in a low tax rate situation or expects initial NOLs during a start-up period.
- If the deferral and amortization method is used, the amortization period of 60 or more months commences with the month in which the benefits from the expenditures are first realized.
- R&E expenses include depreciation allowances related to capitalized expenditures. Thus, if the deferral and amortization method is used, depreciation

Typical Misconception

It is sometimes mistakenly believed that if a company constructs a new building to be used entirely as a research facility, the entire cost of the building can be expensed. However, the expensing election only applies to the depreciation allowances on the building.

TABLE 10-5 *Research and Experimental Expenditures*

Items That Qualify	Items That Do Not Qualify[a]
• Costs incident to the development of an experimental or pilot model, a plant process, a product, a formula, an invention.	• Expenditures for ordinary testing or inspection of materials or products for quality control purposes
• Costs associated with product improvements	• Efficiency surveys and management studies
• Costs of obtaining a patent, such as attorney fees	• Marketing research, advertising, and so on
• Research contracted to others	• Cost of acquiring another person's patent, model, production, or process
• Depreciation or cost-recovery amounts attributable to capitalized R&E items (e.g., research laboratory and equipment)	• Research incurred in connection with literary, historical, or similar projects

[a] Certain of these expenses may be deductible as trade or business expenses under Sec. 162, subject to amortization under Sec. 197, or treated as start-up expenditures under Sec. 195.

[58] Reg. Sec. 1.174-2(a)(1).
[59] Sec. 174.

allowances are deferred as part of the R&E expenditures that are amortized over a period of at least 60 months. Capital expenditures made in connection with R&E activities cannot be expensed when they are incurred merely because an election to expense R&E costs are made.

- A 20% tax credit applies to certain incremental research expenditures, even if they are immediately expensed under Sec. 174. (See Chapter 14 for a discussion of the research activities credit.)

Example 10-29 ■

In 1993 Control Corporation leases a research laboratory to develop new products and to improve existing products. Control Corporation, a calendar-year taxpayer that uses the accrual method of accounting, incurs the following expenditures during 1993:

Laboratory supplies and materials	$ 40,000
Laboratory equipment	60,000[a]
Utilities and rent	50,000
Salaries	50,000
Total expenditures	$200,000

[a] The MACRS recovery period is 5 years at a 20% rate for the initial year.

The benefits from the R&E expenditures are first realized in January 1994. If Control Corporation elects to expense the R&E expenditures, the deduction in 1993 is $152,000 ($40,000 laboratory supplies and materials + $12,000 depreciation on the equipment + $50,000 utilities and rent + $50,000 salaries). If the deferral and amortization method is elected, none of the expenditures above are deductible in 1993 because the benefits of the R&E activities are not first realized until January, 1994. If the 60-month minimum amortization period is elected, the monthly amortization commencing in January 1994 is $2,533 ($152,000 ÷ 60 months). The $48,000 ($60,000 − $12,000) of laboratory equipment cost is depreciated over the remaining MACRS recovery period beginning in 1994. ■

Special Amortization Provisions

Pollution Control Facilities. The cost of a certified pollution control facility may be amortized over a 60-month period generally beginning with the month following the completion of the facility or its acquisition date.[60] This special amortization rule, which is intended to encourage businesses to install pollution control equipment in existing facilities, is generally applicable only for pollution control equipment installed in plants that were in operation prior to 1976.

INVENTORY COSTS

OBJECTIVE 6
Determine inventory cost and cost of goods sold under various methods

Cost of goods sold is often the most significant expense claimed in determining gross income. Inventory costs and costing methods affect the determination of that cost. In many situations, the tax and financial accounting inventory rules parallel each other because of the general requirement in the tax law that inventories must conform to the

[60] Sec. 169(a). The 60-month amortization election is made by the taxpayer in lieu of using the MACRS rules. The taxpayer may also elect to begin the 60-month amortization period in the succeeding tax year.

"best accounting practice" and "clearly reflect income."[61] Other restrictions and conformity requirements also apply, as follows:

- Taxpayers must use the accrual method of accounting for purchases (accounts payable) and sales (accounts receivable) if inventories are a material, income-producing factor.
- If the last-in, first-out (LIFO) inventory method is used for tax purposes, it must generally be used for all other financial reporting purposes.[62]

Taxpayers who use LIFO for tax purposes must use the same method in their primary financial reports to shareholders and creditors. This requirement has discouraged many companies from adopting LIFO because it would cause lower amounts of net income and earnings per share to be reported for financial reporting purposes during periods of inflation. Thus, despite LIFO's potential for tax savings, approximately two-thirds of the inventories in the United States are reported under the FIFO method.[63]

The election to use LIFO is involuntarily terminated, and the taxpayer loses the benefits from the LIFO method if a taxpayer violates the conformity requirements. However, the LIFO conformity requirement has been relaxed somewhat in recent years. The Regulations now permit footnote disclosure in supplementary reports to the financial statements of the effect on net income if a method other than LIFO is used.[64] In addition, the financial income statement supplements or other reports must be clearly identified as being supplementary or explanatory.

These restrictions and conformity requirements do not mean that a method that is used and is preferable under **generally accepted accounting principles (GAAP)** will automatically be acceptable for tax purposes. The courts have generally held that the IRS has broad discretion as to whether the taxpayer's inventory method is a clear reflection of taxable income. For example, the Supreme Court held that a taxpayer could not deduct the cost of certain spare parts that were deemed to exceed normal demands, even though the inventory method was in conformity with GAAP.[65] Thus, inventory write-downs to reflect obsolescence are not generally permitted for tax purposes. The following inventory methods are unacceptable for income tax purposes:

- Deduction of a reserve for price changes or estimated depreciation (i.e., decline in value) from the value of inventories[66]
- Valuation of work in process at a nominal price
- Omission of portions of inventory
- Use of a constant price or nominal value for a normal quantity of goods in stock
- Inclusion of goods in transit in inventory
- Use of the direct costing method (i.e., treating fixed overhead costs as deductible period costs)

---

[61] Sec. 471.

[62] Sec. 472(c). Exceptions are provided for in Reg. Sec. 1.472-2(e) relating to supplementary financial reports, and so on.

[63] U.S., Treasury Department, "Tax Reform for Fairness, Simplicity, and Economic Growth," in *The Treasury Department Report to the President* (Washington DC: U.S. Government Printing Office, November 1984), vol. 2, p. 191.

[64] Reg. Sec. 1.472-2(e)(1)(i).

[65] *Thor Power Tool Co. v. CIR*, 43 AFTR 2d 79-362, 79-1 USTC ¶ 9139 (USSC, 1979).

[66] The IRS has also ruled that a home builder may not depreciate houses that are temporarily used as models and/or sales offices because depreciation is not permitted for inventories (see Rev. Rul. 90-25, 1990-1 C.B. 79). A similar rule has been applied to automobile demonstrators (see Rev. Rul. 75-538, 1975-2 C.B. 35).

- Use of the prime costing method (i.e., exclusion of both fixed and variable overhead costs from inventory and treating these costs as period costs)[67]

The last two prohibited methods are also unacceptable for GAAP reporting purposes, although some companies prepare internal reports for management use based upon these methods.

Typical Misconception

It is easy to confuse a trade discount with a cash discount.

Determination of Inventory Cost and Cost of Goods Sold

Inventory cost includes the invoice price less trade discounts. It also includes freight-in and other handling costs. The treatment of cash discounts (representing an adjustment to the purchase price for prompt payment) depends upon whether the taxpayer customarily expenses or capitalizes such amounts. Thus, cash discounts may either be charged directly to expense and excluded from the inventory or included in the inventory, providing a consistent practice is followed.[68] If the cost of goods purchased is not reduced by the amount of cash discounts received, another alternative is to credit the cash discount amounts to an income account and include such amounts in gross income.

Inventory costs include direct materials, direct labor, and manufacturing overhead based upon the full absorption costing method. With some exceptions, all indirect production costs must be included in the inventory.[69] The use of standard costing methods is acceptable if standard costs are periodically revised to reflect actual costs and if the overhead variances are not significant.[70]

Example 10-30 ■

Additional Comment

The inventory at the beginning of the year must be reduced by the cost of merchandise contributed to charitable organizations.

Additional Comment

Containers, such as kegs, cases and bottles, whether or not on hand and whether or not returnable, should be included in inventory if title to them has not passed to a buyer of the contents.

Compact Corporation uses standard costs for direct labor and material costs and omits all manufacturing overhead costs from its inventory. The total unit cost for inventory on hand at the end of the year is $4 ($2 direct material cost + $2 direct labor cost). Variable and direct overhead costs would amount to $3 per unit if the costs were capitalized as part of the inventory. Compact must value its ending inventory at $7 per unit by including the manufacturing overhead costs and must place its beginning and ending inventory amounts on the same basis, because full absorption costing procedures are required. Cost of goods sold is determined as follows:

Inventory at the beginning of the year			$ 1,000
Plus:	Merchandise purchased	$10,000	
	Labor	15,000	
	Materials and supplies	8,000	
	Overhead costs	2,000	35,000
Goods available for sale			$36,000
Minus:	Inventory at the end of the year		(2,000)
Cost of goods sold			$34,000

■

For an individual taxpayer who maintains inventory as part of his business, the cost of goods sold amount is reported on Schedule C.

---

[67] Reg. Sec. 1.471-2(f).

[68] Reg. Sec. 1.471-3(b) and Rev. Rul. 73-65, 1973-1 C.B. 216.

[69] The Tax Reform Act of 1986 enacted Code Sec. 263A, the **uniform capitalization rules,** which require certain period costs to be capitalized and included in cost of goods sold. Some of these costs include those incident to purchasing inventory, repackaging, and assembly and others incurred in processing goods, storage costs, general and administrative costs allocable to pension and profit-sharing costs, and interest expense. These rules apply only to inventories valued at cost. (See Chapter 11 for a discussion of these requirements.)

[70] Reg. Sec. 1.471-11(d)(3).

Inventory Valuation Methods

Taxpayers may value inventories based upon the cost or the **lower of cost or market (LCM)** methods. However, if the LIFO method is used, only the cost method is allowed. If the LCM method is used, each inventory item is considered separately in the calculation of the total LCM inventory amount. Once an item is reduced to market, this amount becomes the cost of the inventory item in the subsequent period. The market inventory amount usually means replacement cost (i.e., the bid price) for purchased goods or the reproduction cost for manufactured goods on the inventory date.[71] Merchandise can be written down only to the offering price, and goods that are unsalable at normal prices or are unusable due to damage, imperfections, and so on are valued at selling price less any direct cost of disposal.[72] Before the inventory can be written down to market, the goods must actually be offered for sale at the reduced price.

Example 10-31 ■ Crane Corporation has the following items in its ending inventory:

Item	Cost	Market	Lower of Cost or Market
X	$ 600	$ 650	$ 600
Y	400	350	350
Z	1,000	800	800
Total	$2,000	$1,800	$1,750

If Crane Corporation inventories its goods at cost, the inventory is valued at $2,000. If the LCM method is used, the inventory is valued at $1,750 because each item is considered separately rather than using the aggregate market value of $1,800. The method selected must be used consistently for all periods and may not be changed without IRS consent. For financial accounting purposes, it is acceptable to use the aggregate LCM method, which would result in a valuation of $1,800 and would produce a difference between the financial accounting and taxable income amounts. ■

Cost-Flow Assumptions

It is usually not feasible or practical to specifically identify each item in the inventory, although the specific identification inventory method is acceptable for tax purposes if this method is in fact is by the taxpayer. For example, an automobile dealer may use the specific identification method to value its automobile inventory. In most cases, however, a cost-flow assumption (e.g., LIFO, FIFO, or average cost) must be used to determine the cost of goods sold and the ending inventory amounts.

The use of a particular cost-flow assumption affects the determination of taxable income. The LIFO method usually results in lower taxable income during inflationary periods if inventory levels remain stable or are increasing, because the LIFO cost-flow assumption matches the most recently incurred inventory costs (and higher priced items) against sales for the period. For example, the application of a last-in, first-out assumption generally results in the ending inventory including the "oldest" inventory costs (and lowest priced items), since the most recent costs are charged to cost of goods sold.

[71] Reg. Sec. 1.471-4.
[72] Reg. Sec. 1.471-2(c).

Typical Misconception

Neither LIFO nor FIFO must be selected on the basis of the actual flow of goods.

The FIFO Method. The **FIFO method** assumes that the first goods purchased are sold to customers during the period and, therefore, these costs enter into the determination of cost of goods sold. The ending inventory consists of the last goods purchased during the year.

Example 10-32 ■

Dakota Corporation uses the FIFO inventory method and reports the following purchase and sales transactions during the current year:

- Purchases—100 units @ $12 = $1,200
- Sales—90 units @ $20 = $1,800

Dakota's beginning inventory consists of 20 units costing $10 each. Cost of goods sold consists of 90 units. Twenty of these units are deemed to have come from the beginning inventory that cost $10, and 70 units are from the purchases made in the current year that cost $12. The cost of goods sold is $1,040 ([20 units × $10] + [70 units × $12]). Ending inventory consists of the 30 most recently purchased units in the current year, which are valued at $12 per unit, or $360 (30 units × $12). ■

The LIFO Method. Under the **LIFO method,** the cost of the most recently acquired goods is charged to the cost of goods sold. Conversely, the ending inventory consists of the first items that are purchased. In a period of rapidly increasing prices, the LIFO method may result in substantial tax savings because the more recent, higher costs are charged to cost of goods sold. Taxable income is understated relative to the amount of taxable income that would have been reported under the FIFO method. However, the tax advantages of LIFO may be seriously eroded if prices decrease or if there is a reduction in the quantity of inventory resulting in a liquidation of a LIFO layer.

Example 10-33 ■

Data Corporation uses the LIFO method and reports the following purchases and sales transactions during 1994:

- Purchases—800 units @ $12 = $9,600
- Sales—750 units @ $20 = $15,000

Data's beginning inventory consists of 50 units purchased 8 years ago costing $4 each. 1994's cost of goods sold consists of 750 units. Under the LIFO method, all of the units sold are deemed to come from 1994's purchases, thereby producing a $9,000 (750 × $12) cost of goods sold amount. The ending inventory under LIFO is deemed to consist of 50 units from the beginning inventory costing $4, and a new LIFO "layer" of 50 units costing $12 from 1994's purchases, or $800 ([50 × $4] + [50 × $12]). If the FIFO inventory method had been used, cost of goods sold would consist of 50 units from the beginning inventory costing $4 each and 700 units from 1994 purchases costing $12. Under FIFO, 1994's cost of goods sold is only $8,600 (instead of the $9,000 calculated under the LIFO method). ■

Example 10-34 ■

Assume the same facts as in Example 10-33, except that Data's inventory is partially liquidated in 1995 because the units sold exceed the units purchased. Data reports the following purchase and sale transactions during 1995:

- Purchases—900 units @ $14
- Sales—1,000 units @ $20

1995's cost of goods sold under the LIFO method is determined as follows:

$$
\begin{array}{rcl}
900 \text{ units @ } \$14 &=& \$12,600 \\
50 \text{ units @ } \$12 &=& 600 \\
50 \text{ units @ } \$4 &=& 200 \\
\hline
1,000 \text{ units} & & \$13,400 \\
\end{array}
$$

Under the LIFO method, a portion of the cost of goods sold is priced using "old" costs because of the liquidation of the inventory layers, and taxable income is, therefore, increased accordingly. ∎

The following methods are available for applying LIFO:

- Specific goods method. Under this method, like-kind items are grouped into separate pools and inventory changes are measured in terms of physical units for each pool. This method frequently requires extensive record-keeping. It may also result in the liquidation of one or more inventory layers if a company (1) has several inventory pools and (2) significant differences exist between production and sales among product lines.

- Dollar-value method. This method uses dollar-value pools rather than physical unit pools, and the dollar cost for similar items are aggregated to form inventory pools. Dollar-value LIFO may be computed by using either the double-extension method, the index method, or the link-chain method. Further discussion of these methods is beyond the scope of this text.[73]

- Simplified LIFO method. The complexity of the LIFO calculation and its record-keeping requirements prevented many small businesses from adopting it until the simplified LIFO method was enacted in 1981. This method is available only to small businesses (i.e., businesses with $5 million or less average gross receipts for the 3 preceding years).[74] Under this method, inventory pools are established by general categories of items that are also contained in the producer and consumer price indexes prepared by the Bureau of Labor Statistics (BLS). The pools are then indexed for price changes by using the BLS indexes. This method is designed to allow small businesses to use LIFO without undue complexities or excessive compliance costs.

A comparison of the LIFO and FIFO methods is presented in Topic Review 10-3.

TAX PLANNING CONSIDERATIONS

Additional Comment

A taxpayer who is attempting to report a profit in three out of five years in an attempt to avoid the hobby loss rules might want to use the alternative depreciation system.

Alternative Depreciation System Under MACRS

In some instances, it may be preferable to elect to use the alternative depreciation system rather than the regular MACRS rules. For example, a taxpayer who anticipates losses during the next few years or who currently has NOL carryovers, may elect to use the alternative depreciation system, which employs the straight-line method of

---

[73] Donald E. Kieso and Jerry J. Weygandt, *Intermediate Accounting*, 7th ed. (New York: John Wiley, 1992), Ch. 8.

[74] Sec. 474(c).

TOPIC REVIEW 10-3

Comparison of LIFO and FIFO Methods

	LIFO	FIFO
Valuation methods	Only the cost method is allowed.	Either the cost method or the LCM method is allowed.
Cost-flow assumptions	The cost of the most recently acquired goods is charged to cost of goods sold.	The cost of the first goods purchased is charged to cost of goods sold.
Inventory value	Ending inventory consists of the first items that are purchased.	Ending inventory consists of the last items purchased during the year.
Effects of inflation	In periods of rising prices and stable or increasing inventories, taxable income is lower under LIFO.	If the prices of inventory components decrease, taxable income is lower under FIFO.
Special rules	LIFO must be used for financial reporting purposes if it is used for tax purposes.	If the LCM method is used, each inventory item is considered separately.

depreciation or the 150% DB method over a longer recovery period. The 150% DB cannot be used to depreciate real property but may be elected for personal property where the 200% DB method would otherwise be used.

Example 10-35 ■   Delta Corporation has substantial NOL carryovers that will expire if not used during the next few years. Delta Corporation anticipates it will not have taxable income for each of the next 7 years if the regular MACRS rules are used to depreciate its fixed asset additions. In the current year, Delta Corporation acquires new machinery and equipment at a cost of $100,000. Depreciation deductions using the MACRS rules and a 7-year recovery period are $14,290 (0.1429 × $100,000). Depreciation deductions under the straight-line method using the alternative depreciation system (a 15-year life) and the half-year convention are only $3,333 ([$100,000 ÷ 15 years] × 0.50 year). The alternative depreciation system election increases taxable income in the current year by $10,967 and allows Delta Corporation to offset additional loss carryovers (which might otherwise expire) against this income amount.   ■

Key Point

In general, the option to capitalize or to expense applies only to drilling or development expenditures having no salvage value. For example, the cost of oil well pumps, oil storage tanks, and pipe lines would not be eligible for immediate expensing.

IDCs: Capitalization Versus Expensing Election

Although most taxpayers elect to expense intangible drilling costs (IDCs), sometimes capitalization and amortization are preferable because of the effect of IDCs upon the depletion deduction.

If IDCs are expensed, taxable income from the property is reduced. This may result in a smaller percentage depletion deduction because the percentage depletion claimed is limited to 100% of pre-depletion taxable income.

Example 10-36 ■ Gross income from an oil and gas property is $500,000. Expenses of $450,000 are incurred including $200,000 of IDCs. The percentage depletion deduction (before the 100% limitation) is $75,000 (0.15 × $500,000). The percentage depletion limitation is $50,000 (1.00 × $50,000 net income before depletion). Thus, the percentage depletion that is allowed is limited to the lesser of the percentage depletion earned ($75,000) or the limitation ($50,000), or $50,000. If the IDCs are capitalized, the percentage depletion deduction limitation is $250,000 (1.00 × $250,000 net income before depletion) and the taxpayer could claim the full $75,000 of percentage depletion earned. ■

If the IDCs are capitalized, the property's basis for cost depletion purposes is increased and the IDCs are amortized as part of the cost depletion. However, if cost depletion is less than percentage depletion, the benefits from IDC amortization may be lost because percentage depletion is used.

Example 10-37 ■ Assume the same facts as in Example 10-36, except that the IDCs are capitalized and assume that cost depletion is increased from $20,000 to $45,000 due to the capitalization of the IDCs. Since percentage depletion is $75,000 and cost depletion is only $45,000, percentage depletion is used and the benefits from capitalizing IDCs (i.e., $25,000 increase in cost depletion) are lost. The election to capitalize the IDCs did result in an increase in the amount of percentage depletion from $50,000 to $75,000. ■

Structuring a Business Combination

Real World Example

A taxpayer purchased a business that owned retail franchises. It was the opinion of the IRS that the amounts paid in excess of the value of the net assets represented a nondepreciable "indivisible asset." However, the taxpayer was able to show that retail franchises have limited useful lives, and was able to amortize the excess costs. Super Food Services, Inc. v. U.S., 24 AFTR 2d 69-5309, 69-2 USTC ¶ 9558 (7th Cir., 1969).

Tax planning needs to be conducted to ensure favorable tax consequences for the acquiring company if the assets of the acquired company are purchased as part of a business combination. The sales agreement must specify the amounts that have been paid for the tangible depreciable and nondepreciable assets and the intangible assets and the reporting requirements of Sec. 1060 must be complied with. Under the requirements of Sec. 1060, both the transferor and the transferee are bound by their written agreement as to the allocation of the purchase price to individual assets unless the IRS determines that such allocation is not appropriate. The amounts paid for the tangible assets should be documented by appraisals and evidence of negotiations between the buyer and seller. Within reason, the purchaser should attempt to allocate as much of the total price to the tangible depreciable assets. The purchaser should also consider allocating part of the purchase price to depreciable Sec. 197 intangible assets such as goodwill, a covenant not to compete, patents, copyrights, licenses, and customer lists because such assets are amortizable over a 15-year period.

COMPLIANCE AND PROCEDURAL CONSIDERATIONS

IDC Election Procedures

The IDC election is made in the initial year that the expenditures are incurred. No formal statement or form is required. The expensing election is made by merely deducting the IDCs on the tax return.[75] If the costs are capitalized, cost depletion merely reflects the capitalized IDC costs.

Procedures for Changing to LIFO

The LIFO method may be adopted in the initial year that inventories are maintained by merely using the method in that year. In addition, advance approval (e.g., within 180 days following the start of the year) from the IRS is not required for an adoption of the LIFO method in the initial year that inventories are maintained on the LIFO method. However, Form 970 should be filed along with the taxpayer's tax return for the year of the change.[76] The application must include an analysis of the beginning and ending inventories.

If the former inventory is valued based upon the lower of cost or market (LCM) method, an adjustment is required to restate the beginning inventory to cost because the LCM method cannot be used under LIFO. Generally, the beginning LIFO inventory is the same as the closing inventory for the prior year, except for the required restatement of previous writedowns to market. This adjustment to the beginning inventory is permitted to be spread ratably over the year of the change and the next 2 years.[77]

Example 10-38 ■   Delaware Corporation elects to change to the LIFO inventory method for 1994. In 1993 Delaware's inventories are valued using the LCM method based upon the FIFO cost-flow assumption. The FIFO cost for the ending inventory in 1993 is $50,000, and its LCM amount is $35,000. The initial inventory for 1994 under LIFO must be restated to its cost, or $50,000. The $15,000 ($50,000 cost − $35,000 LCM value) difference is permitted to be included in taxable income over the current year and next two years. $5,000 is added to taxable income in 1994, 1995, and 1996.   ■

Reporting Cost Recovery, Depreciation, Depletion, and Amortization Deductions

If an individual is engaged in a trade or business as a sole proprietor, depreciation, cost recovery, depletion, and amortization deductions are reported on Schedule C (Profit or (Loss) from Business or Profession). Cost recovery, depreciation, and amortization are summarized on Form 4562 (Depreciation and Amortization). The totals are then carried to Schedule C. Depletion and depreciation on rental properties are reported on Schedule E instead of Schedule C if the taxpayer is an investor. Depreciation on employee business property is reported on Form 2106. Separate Form 4562s are required for each different activity.

The election to expense property under Sec. 179 is made by claiming the deduction on Part I of Form 4562. The taxpayer must specify the items of property and the portion of the cost for each asset being expensed. Form 4562 is not required of individuals and noncorporate taxpayers (including S corporations) when filing their

---

[75] Reg. Sec. 1.612-4(d).

[76] An acceptable election is considered to have been made even if Form 970 is not filed as long as all of the information required by Reg. Sec. 1.472-3(a) is provided by the taxpayer.

[77] Sec. 472(d).

1993 tax returns if the depreciation deduction is for assets, other than listed property, placed in service before 1993. In such cases, the depreciation deduction is entered directly on Form 1040 or other equivalent tax forms.

Example 10-39 ■   George Jones, Soc. Sec. No. 277-32-6542, is a building trade contractor who acquires the following properties in September, 1993:

- Specialized utility repair truck (5-year property that is not listed property under Sec. 280F(d)(4)), costing $20,000.

- Office equipment, costing $22,500. The immediate expensing election under Sec. 179 is made.

- Patent, costing $10,000 that was acquired in 1991 when it had a remaining legal life of 10 years.

- ACRS deduction for assets placed into service prior to 1987 is $2,000.

- MACRS deduction for assets placed into service prior to 1993 is $8,000.

Jones has taxable income (before the Sec. 179 deduction and the deduction for one-half of self-employment taxes paid under Sec. 164(f)) of $20,000. The cost-recovery, depreciation, and amortization amounts are reported on Form 4562 and Schedule C, respectively, and are shown in Figures 10-1 and 10-2.   ■

Additional Comment

Once the election to expense R&E expenditures has been made, it is applicable to all R&E expenditures paid or incurred in the current year and all subsequent years.

Research and Experimental Expenditures

The election to expense or to defer R&E expenditures is made by attaching a statement to the tax return for the first tax year in which the expenditures are incurred.[78] As previously discussed in the text, the capitalization method is not an election and applies only if no election is made in the initial year. Once a method has been adopted, the taxpayer is required to obtain the permission of the IRS to change to another method.

PROBLEM MATERIALS

DISCUSSION QUESTIONS

10-1. Which of the following assets are subject to either amortization, depreciation, or cost recovery?
  a. An automobile that is held for personal use
  b. Excess amounts paid in a business combination that are attributable to goodwill
  c. Excess amounts paid in a business combination that are attributable to customer lists that have a limited useful life
  d. A patent that has been created internally that has a legal life of 17 years.
  e. Land that is being held for investment purposes
  f. A covenant not to compete which is entered into by the buyer and seller of a business.

10-2. Are the ACRS or the MACRS rules in harmony with the financial accounting concept of matching costs with revenues? Explain.

10-3. Rick is a sole proprietor who has a small business that is currently operating at a loss. He would like to discontinue depreciating the fixed assets of the business for the next few years in order to

---

[78] Reg. Sec. 1.174-3(b)(1).

Form **4562**	**Depreciation and Amortization**	OMB No. 1545-0172
Department of the Treasury Internal Revenue Service (O)	**(Including Information on Listed Property)** ► See separate instructions. ► Attach this form to your return.	**1993** Attachment Sequence No. **67**

Name(s) shown on return George Jones

Identifying number 277-32-6542

Business or activity to which this form relates Building Trade Contractor

Part I Election To Expense Certain Tangible Property (Section 179) (Note: *If you have any "Listed Property," complete Part V before you complete Part I.*)

1	Maximum dollar limitation (If an enterprise zone business, see instructions.)	1	$17,500
2	Total cost of section 179 property placed in service during the tax year (see instructions)	2	42,500
3	Threshold cost of section 179 property before reduction in limitation	3	$200,000
4	Reduction in limitation. Subtract line 3 from line 2, but do not enter less than -0-	4	-0-
5	Dollar limitation for tax year. Subtract line 4 from line 1, but do not enter less than -0-. (If married filing separately, see instructions.)	5	17,500

	(a) Description of property	(b) Cost	(c) Elected cost	
6	OFFICE EQUIPMENT	22,500	22,500	

7	Listed property. Enter amount from line 26	7	
8	Total elected cost of section 179 property. Add amounts in column (c), lines 6 and 7	8	22,500
9	Tentative deduction. Enter the smaller of line 5 or line 8	9	17,500
10	Carryover of disallowed deduction from 1992 (see instructions)	10	-0-
11	Taxable income limitation. Enter the smaller of taxable income or line 5 (see instructions)	11	20,000
12	Section 179 expense deduction. Add lines 9 and 10, but do not enter more than line 11	12	17,500
13	Carryover of disallowed deduction to 1994. Add lines 9 and 10, less line 12 ►	13	

Note: *Do not use Part II or Part III below for listed property (automobiles, certain other vehicles, cellular telephones, certain computers, or property used for entertainment, recreation, or amusement). Instead, use Part V for listed property.*

Part II MACRS Depreciation For Assets Placed in Service ONLY During Your 1993 Tax Year (Do Not Include Listed Property)

(a) Classification of property	(b) Month and year placed in service	(c) Basis for depreciation (business/investment use only—see instructions)	(d) Recovery period	(e) Convention	(f) Method	(g) Depreciation deduction
14 General Depreciation System (GDS) (see instructions):						
a 3-year property						
b 5-year property		20,000	5 YR.	HALF YR	MACRS	4,000
c 7-year property						
d 10-year property						
e 15-year property						
f 20-year property						
g Residential rental property			27.5 yrs.	MM	S/L	
			27.5 yrs.	MM	S/L	
h Nonresidential real property				MM	S/L	
				MM	S/L	
15 Alternative Depreciation System (ADS) (see instructions):						
a Class life					S/L	
b 12-year			12 yrs.		S/L	
c 40-year			40 yrs.	MM	S/L	

Part III Other Depreciation (Do Not Include Listed Property)

16	GDS and ADS deductions for assets placed in service in tax years beginning before 1993 (see instructions)	16	8,000
17	Property subject to section 168(f)(1) election (see instructions)	17	
18	ACRS and other depreciation (see instructions)	18	2,000

Part IV Summary

19	Listed property. Enter amount from line 25	19	
20	**Total.** Add deductions on line 12, lines 14 and 15 in column (g), and lines 16 through 19. Enter here and on the appropriate lines of your return. (Partnerships and S corporations—see instructions)	20	31,500
21	For assets shown above and placed in service during the current year, enter the portion of the basis attributable to section 263A costs (see instructions)	21	

For Paperwork Reduction Act Notice, see page 1 of the separate instructions.   Cat. No. 12906N   Form **4562** (1993)

FIGURE 10-1   Form 4562

Part V Listed Property—Automobiles, Certain Other Vehicles, Cellular Telephones, Certain Computers, and Property Used for Entertainment, Recreation, or Amusement

*For any vehicle for which you are using the standard mileage rate or deducting lease expense, complete **only** 22a, 22b, columns (a) through (c) of Section A, all of Section B, and Section C if applicable.*

Section A—Depreciation and Other Information (Caution: *See instructions for limitations for automobiles.*)

22a Do you have evidence to support the business/investment use claimed? ☐ **Yes** ☐ **No**   **22b** If "Yes," is the evidence written? ☐ **Yes** ☐ **No**

(a) Type of property (list vehicles first)	(b) Date placed in service	(c) Business/ investment use percentage	(d) Cost or other basis	(e) Basis for depreciation (business/investment use only)	(f) Recovery period	(g) Method/ Convention	(h) Depreciation deduction	(i) Elected section 179 cost
23 Property used more than 50% in a qualified business use (see instructions):								
		%						
		%						
		%						
24 Property used 50% or less in a qualified business use (see instructions):								
		%			S/L –			////
		%			S/L –			////
		%			S/L –			////

25 Add amounts in column (h). Enter the total here and on line 19, page 1 . . . . . **25** | |////|
26 Add amounts in column (i). Enter the total here and on line 7, page 1 . . . . **26**

Section B—Information Regarding Use of Vehicles—*If you deduct expenses for vehicles:*
- *Always complete this section for vehicles used by a sole proprietor, partner, or other "more than 5% owner," or related person.*
- *If you provided vehicles to your employees, first answer the questions in Section C to see if you meet an exception to completing this section for those vehicles.*

		(a) Vehicle 1	(b) Vehicle 2	(c) Vehicle 3	(d) Vehicle 4	(e) Vehicle 5	(f) Vehicle 6
27	Total business/investment miles driven during the year (DO NOT include commuting miles)						
28	Total commuting miles driven during the year						
29	Total other personal (noncommuting) miles driven						
30	Total miles driven during the year. Add lines 27 through 29						

		Yes	No	Yes	No	Yes	No	Yes	No	Yes	No	Yes	No
31	Was the vehicle available for personal use during off-duty hours?												
32	Was the vehicle used primarily by a more than 5% owner or related person?												
33	Is another vehicle available for personal use?												

Section C—Questions for Employers Who Provide Vehicles for Use by Their Employees
Answer these questions to determine if you meet an exception to completing Section B. **Note:** *Section B must always be completed for vehicles used by sole proprietors, partners, or other more than 5% owners or related persons.*

		Yes	No
34	Do you maintain a written policy statement that prohibits all personal use of vehicles, including commuting, by your employees?		
35	Do you maintain a written policy statement that prohibits personal use of vehicles, except commuting, by your employees? (See instructions for vehicles used by corporate officers, directors, or 1% or more owners.)		
36	Do you treat all use of vehicles by employees as personal use?		
37	Do you provide more than five vehicles to your employees and retain the information received from your employees concerning the use of the vehicles?		
38	Do you meet the requirements concerning qualified automobile demonstration use (see instructions)? . .		
	Note: *If your answer to 34, 35, 36, 37, or 38 is "Yes," you need not complete Section B for the covered vehicles.*	////	////

Part VI Amortization

(a) Description of costs	(b) Date amortization begins	(c) Amortizable amount	(d) Code section	(e) Amortization period or percentage	(f) Amortization for this year
39 Amortization of costs that begins during your 1993 tax year:			////	////	////
PATENT	6-91	10,000	167	10	$1,000
40 Amortization of costs that began before 1993 . . . . **40**					
41 **Total.** Enter here and on "Other Deductions" or "Other Expenses" line of your return . . . **41**					$1,000

FIGURE 10-1 Form 4562 (Continued)

SCHEDULE C
(Form 1040)

Department of the Treasury
Internal Revenue Service   (O)

Profit or Loss From Business
(Sole Proprietorship)

▶ Partnerships, joint ventures, etc., must file Form 1065.

▶ Attach to Form 1040 or Form 1041.   ▶ See Instructions for Schedule C (Form 1040).

OMB No. 1545-0074

1993

Attachment
Sequence No. 09

Name of proprietor   *George Jones*

Social security number (SSN)   277 32 6542

A Principal business or profession, including product or service (see page C-1)   *Building Trade Contractor*

B Enter principal business code
(see page C-6) ▶ 0 8 8 5

C Business name. If no separate business name, leave blank.

D Employer ID number (EIN), if any

E Business address (including suite or room no.) ▶ *2240 88th St. Miami FL 33124*
City, town or post office, state, and ZIP code

F Accounting method: (1) ☒ Cash   (2) ☐ Accrual   (3) ☐ Other (specify) ▶ ....

G Method(s) used to value closing inventory: (1) ☐ Cost   (2) ☐ Lower of cost or market   (3) ☐ Other (attach explanation)   (4) ☐ Does not apply (if checked, skip line H)   Yes | No

H Was there any change in determining quantities, costs, or valuations between opening and closing inventory? If "Yes," attach explanation . . . . | ☒

I Did you "materially participate" in the operation of this business during 1993? If "No," see page C-2 for limit on losses. . .   ☒ |

J If you started or acquired this business during 1993, check here . . . . ▶ ☐

Part I   Income

1	Gross receipts or sales. **Caution:** *If this income was reported to you on Form W-2 and the "Statutory employee" box on that form was checked, see page C-2 and check here* . . . . ▶ ☐	**1**	
2	Returns and allowances	**2**	
3	Subtract line 2 from line 1	**3**	
4	Cost of goods sold (from line 40 on page 2)	**4**	
5	**Gross profit.** Subtract line 4 from line 3	**5**	
6	Other income, including Federal and state gasoline or fuel tax credit or refund (see page C-2) . . ▶	**6**	
7	**Gross income.** Add lines 5 and 6 . . . . ▶	**7**	

Part II   Expenses. Caution: *Do not enter expenses for business use of your home on lines 8–27. Instead, see line 30.*

8	Advertising	**8**		**19** Pension and profit-sharing plans	**19**	
9	Bad debts from sales or services (see page C-3) . .	**9**		**20** Rent or lease (see page C-4):		
				a Vehicles, machinery, and equipment .	**20a**	
10	Car and truck expenses (see page C-3)	**10**		**b** Other business property . . .	**20b**	
11	Commissions and fees. . .	**11**		**21** Repairs and maintenance . . .	**21**	
12	Depletion.	**12**		**22** Supplies (not included in Part III)	**22**	
13	Depreciation and section 179 expense deduction (not included in Part III) (see page C-3)	**13**	31,500	**23** Taxes and licenses	**23**	
				24 Travel, meals, and entertainment:		
				a Travel	**24a**	
14	Employee benefit programs (other than on line 19) . .	**14**		**b** Meals and entertainment . .		
15	Insurance (other than health) .	**15**		**c** Enter 20% of line 24b subject to limitations (see page C-4) .		
16	Interest:					
a	Mortgage (paid to banks, etc.) .	**16a**		**d** Subtract line 24c from line 24b .	**24d**	
b	Other	**16b**		**25** Utilities	**25**	
17	Legal and professional services	**17**		**26** Wages (less jobs credit) . . .	**26**	
18	Office expense	**18**		**27** Other expenses (from line 46 on page 2)	**27**	1,000

28	**Total expenses** before expenses for business use of home. Add lines 8 through 27 in columns. ▶	**28**	32,500
29	Tentative profit (loss). Subtract line 28 from line 7	**29**	
30	Expenses for business use of your home. Attach **Form 8829**	**30**	
31	**Net profit or (loss).** Subtract line 30 from line 29.		
	• If a profit, enter on **Form 1040, line 12,** and ALSO on **Schedule SE, line 2** (statutory employees, see page C-5). Fiduciaries, enter on Form 1041, line 3.	**31**	
	• If a loss, you MUST go on to line 32.		
32	If you have a loss, check the box that describes your investment in this activity (see page C-5).		
	• If you checked 32a, enter the loss on **Form 1040, line 12,** and ALSO on **Schedule SE, line 2** (statutory employees, see page C-5). Fiduciaries, enter on Form 1041, line 3.	**32a** ☐ All investment is at risk.	
	• If you checked 32b, you MUST attach **Form 6198.**	**32b** ☐ Some investment is not at risk.	

For Paperwork Reduction Act Notice, see Form 1040 instructions.   Cat. No. 11334P   Schedule C (Form 1040) 1993

FIGURE 10-2   Form 1040, Schedule C

Part III **Cost of Goods Sold** (see page C-5)

33	Inventory at beginning of year. If different from last year's closing inventory, attach explanation . .	33	
34	Purchases less cost of items withdrawn for personal use	34	
35	Cost of labor. Do not include salary paid to yourself	35	
36	Materials and supplies	36	
37	Other costs	37	
38	Add lines 33 through 37	38	
39	Inventory at end of year	39	
40	**Cost of goods sold.** Subtract line 39 from line 38. Enter the result here and on page 1, line 4 . .	40	

Part IV **Information on Your Vehicle.** Complete this part **ONLY** if you are claiming car or truck expenses on line 10 and are not required to file Form 4562 for this business.

41 When did you place your vehicle in service for business purposes? (month, day, year) ▶ .... / .... / ....

42 Of the total number of miles you drove your vehicle during 1993, enter the number of miles you used your vehicle for:

a Business .... b Commuting .... c Other ....

43 Do you (or your spouse) have another vehicle available for personal use? . . . . ☐ **Yes** ☐ **No**

44 Was your vehicle available for use during off-duty hours? . . . . ☐ **Yes** ☐ **No**

45a Do you have evidence to support your deduction? . . . . ☐ **Yes** ☐ **No**
  b If "Yes," is the evidence written? . . . . ☐ **Yes** ☐ **No**

Part V **Other Expenses.** List below business expenses not included on lines 8–26 or line 30.

PATENT AMORTIZATION	1,000
46 **Total other expenses.** Enter here and on page 1, line 27 . . . . **46**	1,000

FIGURE 10-2 Form 1040, Schedule C (Continued)

carry the deductions over to a future period. What tax consequences would result if Rick implements the plan to discontinue depreciation and then subsequently sells some of the depreciable assets?

10-4. Rita acquired a personal residence two years ago for $120,000. In the current year she purchases another residence and attempts to sell her former residence. Due to depressed housing conditions in the town where she used to live, Rita is unable to sell the house. Her former residence is now being offered for sale at $100,000 (its current FMV according to real estate appraisal experts). Rita has decided to rent the house rather than "give it away." She states that the rental for an indefinite period will permit her to write off the original $120,000 investment over its useful life and to, therefore, recoup her investment. What restrictions in the tax law may prevent her from accomplishing this objective? Explain.

10-5. Contrast and compare the ACRS and MACRS rules with the pre-ACRS rules regarding the ease of administering the tax law (e.g., mitigating disputes between taxpayers and the IRS regarding the appropriate amount of cost-recovery or depreciation deductions).

10-6. Daytona Corporation, a manufacturing corporation, acquires the following business assets in the current year:

- Furniture
- Plumbing fixtures
- Land
- Goodwill and a trademark acquired in the acquisition of a business
- Automobile
- Heavy truck
- Machinery
- Building used in manufacturing activities

a. Which of the assets above are eligible for depreciation under the MACRS rules or amortization under Sec. 197?

b. What recovery period should be used for each of the assets above that come under the MACRS rules or under Sec. 197?

10-7. Robert, a sole proprietor who uses the calendar year as his tax year, acquires a business machine on December 31, 1994, for $10,000 and sells certain business equipment on the same date for $2,000. The equipment that is sold was acquired on January 1, 1990, for $20,000. What amount (if any) of depreciation deductions should be allowed under MACRS for the newly acquired machine and for the equipment that is sold in 1994?

10-8. Is a depreciation deduction allowed under the MACRS rules for depreciable real estate (used in a business or held for investment) in the year the property is sold? If so, explain how it is calculated.

10-9. Jose is considering acquiring a new luxury automobile costing $37,500 for use in his business. The salesperson at the automobile dealership states that Jose will be entitled to both of the following tax benefits in the initial year:

- A deduction for $17,500 of the acquisition cost under Sec. 179
- A $4,000 ($20,000 × 0.20) MACRS depreciation deduction

a. Are the salesperson's assertions relative to the tax benefits accurate? Explain.

b. How would your answer to part a differ (if any) if the automobile is used only 60% for business purposes?

c. How would your answer to part a differ (if any) if Jose were to lease the automobile?

10-10. Explain why the straight-line MACRS method might be preferable to the regular MACRS method under the following circumstances:

a. Ray incurs NOLs in his business for a number of years and has NOL carryovers he would like to use.

b. Rhonda's marginal tax rate is 28% but is expected to increase to 36% in three years.

10-11. Rudy is considering whether to make the election under Sec. 179 to expense $17,500 of the acquisition cost related to certain fixed asset additions. What are the advantages that are associated with the Sec. 179 election?

10-12. Your client is a self-employed attorney who is considering the purchase of a $12,000 automobile that will be used 80% of the time for business and a $4,000 personal computer that will be used 100% of the time for business but is located in his home.

    a. What depreciation methods and recovery periods may be used under MACRS for the automobile and the personal computer?

    b. How would your answer to Part a change if your client is an employee and the computer and automobile are not required as a condition of employment?

    c. What tax consequences occur in Part a if the business use of the personal computer or the automobile decreases to 50% or less in a succeeding year? Explain.

10-13. Carmen purchases a Mercedes-Benz automobile in the current year for $50,000. Carmen plans to use the automobile exclusively in her business and boasts that she intends to recover her cost through tax benefits (i.e., MACRS depreciation allowances of $50,000 over a five-year period). What restrictions have been imposed to reduce the tax benefits from purchasing luxury automobiles for business use? Explain how these restrictions work.

10-14. Sarah enters into a three-year lease of an automobile in the current year which is used exclusively in her business. The automobile's FMV was $40,000 at the inception of the lease. Ten monthly lease payments of $600 each were made by Sarah during the current year. Is Sarah able to avoid the luxury automobile restrictions upon depreciation by leasing instead of purchasing the automobile? Explain. (The inclusion amount for Sarah's automobile under Rev. Proc. 93-35 is $143.)

10-15. Why are intangible drilling costs expensed by most taxpayers?

10-16. Simon acquires an interest in an oil property for $50,000. IDCs in the initial year are $10,000. Cost depletion is $5,000 if the IDCs are expensed and $6,000 if the costs are capitalized. Percentage depletion is $15,000 if the IDCs are expensed and $20,000 if the costs are capitalized. The difference is due to the 100% net income limitation imposed on percentage depletion. What method (i.e., immediate write-off or capitalization and amortization) should be elected for the treatment of the IDCs in the initial year?

10-17. What difference does it make whether an intangible asset is acquired in connection with (1) a business acquisition, (2) by the purchase of an individual asset (e.g., a formula), or (3) is created internally? Explain.

10-18. In January of the current year Park Corporation incurs $34,000 of legal costs associated with the obtaining of a patent that has a legal life of 17 years. Park also acquired for cash the net assets of Central Corporation on January 1, for $1,000,000. The following assets are specified in the purchase agreement:

Land	$200,000
Goodwill and going concern value	100,000
Covenant not to compete	50,000
Licenses	125,000
Customer lists	25,000
Inventory	100,000
Equipment and other tangible depreciable business assets	400,000
Total	$1,000,000

    a. What tax treatment should be accorded the intangible assets?

    b. Assuming that you were advising Park Corporation during the negotiations prior to the drafting of the purchase agreement, what suggestions would you make regarding the allocation of the total purchase price to the individual assets? How could the purchase price of individual assets be substantiated?

10-19. Why do most taxpayers prefer to expense Research and Experimental expenditures?

10-20. Dover Corporation has a 20-year-old manufacturing plant that is currently in violation of the Environmental Protection Agency regulations regarding pollutants. The company is considering whether to install certain pollution control facilities with a 15-year life at a cost of $80,000. What special tax incentive is provided in the tax laws for the installation of these devices?

10-21. Hill Corporation uses the lower of cost or market (LCM) method to value its inventory. The company accountant has advised that major write downs are now required to reflect inventory obsolescence due to an excess supply of spare parts and that a reserve should be reflected on the books of the company.

    a. Should the inventory be written down for financial reporting purposes?

    b. Is an inventory write down permitted for income tax purposes? (Assume that the write down is made so that the financial reports can reflect GAAP.)

10-22. The Indiana Corporation is considering the adoption of the LIFO inventory method for the current year. The company currently values its inventory using the lower of cost or market (LCM) method based upon the FIFO cost-flow assumption. Indiana's inventory cost at the end of the prior year is $800,000 using the FIFO method. The inventory is stated at $700,000 due to Indiana's use of the LCM method. The company wants to switch to the LIFO method because it expects substantial inflation during the next five years. However, the controller of the company states that the company would prefer to continue to use the FIFO method for financial reporting purposes because in two years the company plans to "go public" (i.e., issue stock to the public in a secondary offering).

    a. What procedures are required to change from FIFO to LIFO?

    b. What adjustment (if any) must be made to the current year's beginning inventory?

    c. Why does Indiana Corporation want to switch to LIFO for tax purposes?

    d. Can the company continue to use its existing inventory method for financial reporting to shareholders and creditors? Explain.

    e. Is it possible to issue supplementary financial statement information regarding the effect of LIFO upon reported earnings without violating the financial accounting conformity requirement? Explain.

10-23. Large Corporation uses direct costing in valuing its inventory for its internal management reports and full absorption costing for reports issued to creditors and shareholders. Which method is required for income tax purposes?

10-24. Is the lower of cost or market (LCM) method allowed if a company uses the LIFO cost-flow assumption?

10-25. Why does the LIFO method usually result in lower reported profits and taxable income during inflationary periods?

10-26. Inflation is generally measured in terms of a general purchasing power index (i.e., consumer price index). The prices of a company's inventory more closely follow the wholesale price index, which is not expected to increase in future years. Explain how these facts could affect the decision whether a company should switch to the simplified LIFO method or not.

10-27. What factors have discouraged many small companies from adopting LIFO? What special LIFO rules have encouraged more small companies to switch to LIFO for tax purposes?

10-28. In a business combination, why does the buyer generally prefer to allocate as much of the purchase price to short-lived depreciable assets, ordinary assets such as inventory, and to Sec. 197 intangible assets?

PROBLEMS

10-29. *Allowed Versus Allowable Depreciation.* Sandy acquires business machinery (which qualifies as 7-year MACRS property) on July 15, 1994, for $10,000. In 1994 Sandy claims a $1,429 depreciation deduction, but Sandy fails to claim any depreciation deduction in 1995 or 1996. The machine is sold on July 1, 1996, for $6,000.

    a. What is the adjusted basis of the machine on the sale date?

    b. How much gain or loss is recognized upon the sale of the machine?

10-30. *ACRS-Straight-Line Depreciation.* Tess acquires and places in service on November 1, 1986, a business machine costing $20,000. Tess elects straight-line depreciation using the longest possible recovery period. The machine is sold on April 1, 1994, for $18,000. (Assume that no amount is expensed under Sec. 179.)

a. What is the amount of cost-recovery deduction for 1986 through 1994?

b. What is the amount of Tess's recognized gain or loss from the sale of the machine in 1994?

10-31. ***Conversion of Personal Asset to Business Use.*** Sid purchases an automobile for personal use on January 1, 1992, for $10,000. On July 1, 1994, Sid starts a small business and begins to use the automobile exclusively in the business. The automobile's FMV on this date is $6,000. MACRS depreciation deductions are taken in 1996 based upon a five-year recovery period.

a. What is the automobile's basis for depreciation purposes when converted to business use in 1996?

b. What is Sid's depreciation deduction in 1996?

10-32. ***MACRS Depreciation.*** Small Corporation acquires and places in service the following business assets in 1994 (no other assets were placed in service during the year):

- Light truck costing $10,000 (on December 15) with a five-year MACRS recovery period
- Machinery costing $50,000 (on February 1) with a seven-year MACRS recovery period
- Land costing $60,000 (on July 1)
- Building costing $100,000 (on December 1) with a 39-year MACRS recovery period
- Equipment costing $40,000 (acquired on December 24, but not placed in service until January of the following year) with a five-year MACRS recovery period

a. What are the MACRS depreciation deductions for each asset in 1994?

b. What are the MACRS deductions for each asset in 1994 if the machinery is instead acquired on October 1, 1994?

10-33. ***MACRS Depreciation.*** Ted purchases five-year recovery period personal property costing $30,000 on April 1 of the current year, and seven-year recovery period personal property costing $40,000 on November 1 of the current year. (Assume that Ted does not elect the Sec. 179 expensing election and uses the MACRS rules.) What is the amount of the MACRS depreciation deduction for each asset in the current year?

10-34. ***Sec. 179 Expensing Election and MACRS Depreciation.*** Tish acquires and places in service a business machine with a seven-year MACRS recovery period in July 1994. The machine costs $25,000, and Tish elects to expense a portion of the asset's cost under Sec. 179. The total cost of qualifying property placed in service during the year amounts to $213,500. Tish's taxable income (before deducting the Sec. 179 amount and one-half of self-employment taxes paid) is $3,000.

a. What is the amount Tish can deduct under Sec. 179 in 1994?

b. What is the amount of MACRS depreciation deduction for the machine in 1994?

10-35. ***ACRS and MACRS Dispositions.*** Tampa Corporation disposes of the following assets in 1994:

	Date Acquired	Date Sold	Original Cost Basis	Cost-Recovery Method	Recovery Period (Years)
Truck	1/15/86	8/14/94	$ 10,000	SL-ACRS	12
Auto	1/1/92	12/1/94[a]	9,000	MACRS	5
Equipment	1/6/92	9/1/94[a]	20,000	MACRS	7
Building	4/1/86	12/15/94	100,000	ACRS	19

[a] Assume that the half-year convention was used in the year of acquisition.

What is the amount of cost-recovery or depreciation deduction for each asset in 1994?

10-36. ***Sec. 179 and MACRS Depreciation.*** Thad acquires a machine for use in his business in the current year for $27,500. The MACRS rules with a 7-year recovery period are used, and Thad elects to expense $17,500 of the acquisition cost under Sec. 179. What is the machine's basis for depreciation purposes and the depreciation deduction in its initial year?

10-37. ***Straight-Line Depreciation.*** Long Corporation has been unprofitable for several years and has substantial NOL carryovers. Therefore, the company policy has been to use the straight-line ACRS or MACRS rules for property acquisitions. The following assets are acquired or sold in 1994:

	Date Acquired	Date Sold	Original Cost Basis	Selling Price	Depreciation Method	Recovery Period (Years)
Equipment	7/1/94	—	$40,000	—	SL	7
Light trucks	7/1/86	12/1/94	30,000	$12,000	SL	12
Furniture	3/1/86	11/1/94	10,000	2,000	SL	12
Automobile	7/1/94	12/1/94	12,000	10,000	SL	5

Assume the expensing election under Sec. 179 is not made.

a. What is the depreciation deduction for each asset in 1994?

b. What amount of gain or loss is recognized on the properties sold in 1994?

10-38. *Sec. 179 and MACRS Depreciation.* Todd acquires and places in service business furniture costing $25,000 with a 7-year recovery period in April 1994. Todd elects to expense $17,500 of the acquisition cost under Sec. 179. What is the amount of the MACRS depreciation deduction for 1994?

10-39. *Mixed Personal/Business Use.* Trish, a self-employed CPA and calendar year taxpayer, acquires an automobile and a personal computer in 1994. Pertinent data include the following:

Asset	Date Acquired	Original Cost Basis	Portion of Business Usage	Sec. 179 Election
Automobile	1/1/94	$11,000	60%	No
Personal computer	7/1/94	4,000	40	No

For each asset calculate the MACRS current year depreciation deduction (assuming no change in luxury auto limits in 1994).

10-40. *Employee Listed Property.* Assume the same facts as in Problem 10-39, except that Trish is an employee and uses the automobile and personal computer on employment-related activities. Her employer does not require employees to purchase a car or a personal computer as a condition of employment. What is the amount of depreciation for each asset?

10-41. *Recapture of Depreciation Deductions Due to Personal Use.* Tammy acquires an automobile for $10,000 on July 1, 1992. She uses the automobile partially for business purposes during the 1992–1994 period. The percentage of business use is as follows: 1992, 70%; 1993, 70%; 1994, 40%. The MACRS rules with a 5-year recovery period are used in 1992 and 1993.

a. What is the amount of the MACRS depreciation deduction for 1992? 1993? 1994?

b. What is the amount of recapture of previously claimed depreciation deductions (if any) that must take place in 1994?

10-42. *Luxury Auto Limitations.* Lutz Corporation acquires a luxury automobile for use in its business on July 1, 1993, for $20,000. The Sec. 179 expensing election is not made but the company chooses to claim the maximum amount of MACRS depreciation deductions available. What is the depreciation deduction amount for 1993, 1994, 1995, and any subsequent years?

10-43. *Luxury Auto Limitations.* Tracy acquires a luxury automobile on January 1, 1993, for use 80% of the time in his business and 20% of the time for personal use. The automobile cost $30,000, and no amounts are expensed under Sec. 179. What is the depreciation amount for 1993, 1994, 1995, and any subsequent years?

10-44. *Luxury Auto Limitations—Leasing.* Troy enters into a 3-year lease of a luxury auto on January 1, 1993, for use 80% in business and 20% for personal use. The FMV of the automobile at the inception of the lease is $40,000 and 12 monthly lease payments of $600 were made in 1993. (The "inclusion amount" under Rev. Proc. 93-35 is $143.)

a. What is the amount of lease payments that are deductible in 1993?

b. What portion, if any, of the "inclusion amount" must be included in gross income in 1993?

c. How would your answers to Parts a and b change if the FMV of the auto is instead $10,000?

10-45. *Cost Depletion.* Tina acquires an oil and gas property interest for $200,000 in the current year. The following information about current year operations is supplied for purposes of computing the amount of Tina's depletion and IDC deductions:

Estimated recoverable units	20,000
Units produced	6,000
Units sold	4,000
IDCs	$20,000
Percentage depletion (after limitations)	$25,000

a. What is the cost depletion amount if the IDCs are expensed?
b. What is the cost depletion amount if the IDCs are capitalized?
c. How much depletion is deducted on the tax return?
d. Should the IDCs be capitalized or expensed? Explain.

10-46. ***Percentage Depletion.*** Tony has owned an oil and gas property for a number of years. The following information is provided about the property's operations in the current year:

Gross income	$500,000
Minus: Expenses (including IDCs of $100,000)	(300,000)
Taxable income (before depletion)	$200,000
Cost depletion (if IDCs are expensed)	$ 20,000
Cost depletion (if IDCs are capitalized)	$ 30,000

a. What is the percentage depletion amount if the IDCs are expensed?
b. What is the percentage depletion amount if the IDCs are capitalized?
c. What is the depletion deduction amount assuming that the IDCs are expensed?
d. Based on the information above, which method should be used for the IDCs? Explain.

10-47. ***Goodwill.*** On January 1 of the current year, Palm Corporation acquires the net assets of Vicki's unincorporated business for $600,000. The tangible net assets have a $300,000 book value and $400,000 FMV. The purchase agreement states that Vicki will not compete with Palm Corporation by starting a new business in the same area for a period of five years. The stated consideration received by Vicki for the covenant is $50,000. Other intangible assets included in the purchase agreement are as follows:

- Goodwill—$70,000
- Patents (12-year remaining legal life)—$30,000
- Customer list—$50,000.

a. How would Vicki's assets be recorded for tax purposes for Palm Corporation?
b. What is the amount of amortization for each of the acquired intangible assets in the current year?

10-48. ***R&E Expenditures.*** Park Corporation incurs the following costs in the initial year:

Materials and supplies for research laboratory	$ 80,000
Utilities and depreciation on research laboratory and equipment	40,000
Costs of acquiring another person's patent for a new product	20,000
Market research salaries for surveys relative to proposed new products	60,000
Labor and supplies for quality control tests	50,000
Research costs subcontracted to a local university	35,000
Total	$285,000

Park's controller states that all of these costs are qualifying R&E expenditures and that the company policy in the past has been to expense such amounts for tax purposes in the year incurred. Which of these expenditures are deductible as R&E costs under Sec. 174?

10-49. ***R&E Expenditures.*** In 1994 Phoenix Corporation acquires a new research facility and hires several scientists to develop new products. No new products are developed until 1995, although the following expenditures were incurred in 1994:

Laboratory materials	$ 40,000
Research salaries	80,000
Overhead attributable to the research facility	30,000
R&E equipment placed into service (five-year MACRS recovery period)	100,000
Total	$250,000

a. What is Phoenix Corporation's deduction for R&E expenditures in 1994 and 1995 if the expensing method is elected?

b. How would your answer to Part a change if the deferral and amortization method is elected and the amortization period is 60 months?

10-50. *Inventory Costs: LCM, Financial Accounting, and Adoption of LIFO Methods.* Red Corporation uses the LCM method to value its inventory. Cost is determined by using the FIFO cost-flow assumption. The following items are included in 1994's ending inventory:

Item	Cost	Market
X	$ 400	$300
Y	300	500
Z	300	150
Total	$1,000	$950

Red Corporation uses the aggregate market value to determine its inventory under GAAP.

a. What is the amount of Red Corporation's ending inventory for financial accounting purposes for 1994?

b. What is the amount of Red Corporation's ending inventory for tax purposes in 1994?

c. Assume Red Corporation decides to adopt the LIFO inventory method in 1995, what adjustment must be made (if any) to the beginning 1995 inventory in order to use the LIFO method?

10-51. *Inventory Costs: LCM Method.* Star Corporation uses the LCM method to value its inventory. Cost is determined by using the FIFO cost-flow assumption. The company reports the following purchases and sales in the current year:

Purchases—100 units @ $8.00	=	$ 800
Sales—120 units @ $20.00	=	$2,400

Its inventory includes the following:

Beginning Inventory—40 units @ $5.00	=	$200
Ending Inventory—20 units @ ? (market value is $9.00 per unit)		

a. What is the cost of goods sold amount for the current year?

b. What is Star's ending inventory amount?

10-52. *Inventory Costs: LIFO Method.* Small Corporation uses the LIFO inventory method. During the year Small Corporation is unable to meet its production schedules due to production problems in the plant and high product demand. Consequently, inventories decline to low levels. Inflation is rampant during the year, and the company controller states that footnote disclosure will be made in a supplementary disclosure to its financial statements to show the amount of net income under the FIFO method. Small Corporation has the following purchases, sales, and inventories during the year:

Beginning inventory—1,000 units @ $2.00 = $2,000
Purchases—1,000 units @ $20.00 = $20,000
Sales—1,800 units @ $30.00 = $54,000

a. What is the amount of Small Corporation's ending inventory and cost of goods sold?

b. Explain the effects of liquidating the LIFO layer (from the beginning inventory) upon the amount of reported earnings and taxable income.

c. Does footnote disclosure of the reported net income if the FIFO method is used constitute a violation of the financial accounting conformity requirement found in the LIFO rules?

TAX FORM/RETURN PREPARATION PROBLEMS

TurboTax **10-53.** Thom Jones (Soc. Sec. No. 277-31-7253) is an unincorporated manufacturer of widgets. He uses the LCM method to value his inventory and has the following transactions during the year:

Sales (less returns and allowances)	$800,000
Costs of goods sold	500,000
Office expenses	10,000
Depreciation and Sec. 179 deduction (see the schedule of asset transactions below)[a]	
Legal services	4,000
Salary expenses	36,000
Travel expenses	30,000
Repairs	20,000

[a] Assume that the cost of Sec. 179 property placed into service during the year is $150,000.

Mr. Jones's depreciation schedule is as follows:

Office furniture held for business use is purchased and an election is made to expense the acquisition cost under Sec. 179.	$17,500
Depreciation on recovery property:	
5-year recovery period property acquired and placed into service in 1993	6,000
7-year recovery period property acquired and placed into service in 1993	14,000
Other 12-year recovery period property using the straight-line method under the alternative depreciation system placed into service in 1993	20,000
Total depreciation allowance	$50,000

Complete Form 4562 and Schedule C of Form 1040 for Mr. Jones.

10-54. John and Ellen Brite (Soc. Sec. Nos. 265-32-1497 and 571-07-7345, respectively) own an unincorporated specialty electrical lighting retail store, Brite-On. Brite-On had the following assets on January 1, 1993:

Assets	Cost
Building purchased April 1, 1984	$100,000
Seven-year equipment purchased January 1, 1990	30,000
Inventory valued using LIFO method:	
Oldest inventory—4,000 light bulbs	$4/bulb
Newest inventory—5,000 light bulbs	5/bulb

The Brites purchased a competitor's store on March 1, 1993 for $89,000. The purchase price (without regard to the cost of land) included the following:

	FMV
Store building	$60,000
Five-year recovery period equipment	11,000
Inventory—3,000 light bulbs	6/bulb

On June 30, 1993 the Brites sold the seven-year recovery period equipment for $12,000. Brite-On leased a $30,000 car for $500/month beginning on January 1, 1993. The car is used 100% for business. Brite-On sold 8,000 light bulbs at $15/bulb during the year. Brite-On had the following revenues and additional expenses:

Service revenues	$40,000
Interest on business loans	4,000
Auto expenses (gas, oil, etc.)	3,800
Taxes and licenses	3,300
Utilities	2,800

John and Ellen also had some personal expenses:

Medical bills	$ 4,500
Real property taxes	3,800
Home mortgage interest	9,000
Charitable contributions (cash)	600

John and Ellen paid $15,000 in quarterly estimated taxes.

Additional Facts:

- Assume that an election is made under Sec. 179 to expense the cost of the 5-year equipment that was acquired in 1993.
- Rev. Proc. 93-35 requires the Brites to include $86 in their gross income due to the leased automobile restrictions.

Complete Forms 4562, 4797, and 1040—pages 1 and 2 and Schedules A and C. (Omit any self-employment tax computation.)

CASE STUDY PROBLEM

10-55. Able Corporation is a manufacturer of electrical lighting fixtures. Able is currently negotiating with Ralph Johnson, the owner of an unincorporated business, to acquire his retail electrical lighting sales business. Johnson's assets that are to be acquired include the following:

Assets	Adjusted Basis	FMV
Inventory of electrical fixtures	$30,000	$ 50,000
Store buildings	80,000	100,000
Land	40,000	100,000
Equipment—7 year recovery period	30,000	50,000
Equipment—5 year recovery period	60,000	100,000
Total	$240,000	$400,000

Mr. Johnson indicates that a total purchase price of $1,000,000 in cash is warranted for the business because of its high profitability and strategic locations and Able has agreed that the business is worth $1,000,000. Despite the fact that both parties attribute the excess payment to be for goodwill, Able would prefer that the $600,000 excess amount be designated as a 5-year covenant not to compete so that he can amortize the excess over a 5-year period.

You are a tax consultant for Able who has been asked to make recommendations as to the structuring of the purchase agreement and the amounts to be assigned to individual assets. Prepare a client memo to reflect your recommendations.

CASE STUDY PROBLEM—ETHICAL ISSUES

10-56. The Margate Corporation acquired an automobile with an acquisition cost of $30,000 for use in its business in 1991. During this time, Margate Corporation was experiencing a seasonal decline in sales. Several employees were laid off and the automobile was not immediately needed for any of the sales personnel. Instead of letting the new automobile sit in the corporate lot, the president decided to permit an officer to use the automobile for personal use. The officer used the automobile in 1992 and 1993 only. In 1994, Margate Corporation has hired you as their new CPA (tax consultant). You learn about the officer's personal use of the corporate automobile that took place for the two prior years without proper accounting of the automobile to the IRS. As Margate Corporation's tax consultant, what actions (if any) should you take regarding the proper treatment of the automobile? What are your responsibilities as a CPA regarding this matter under the rules of the AICPA's *SRTP No. 6*? (See the caption entitled *Statements on Responsibilities in Tax Practice* (SRTP) in Chapter 1 for a discussion of SRTP No. 6.)

TAX RESEARCH PROBLEM

10-57. Apple Corporation has never been audited prior to the current year. An audit is now needed from a CPA because the company is in a rapid expansion period and is planning to issue stock to the public in a secondary offering. A CPA firm has been doing preliminary evaluations of the Apple Corporation's accounts and records. One major problem involves the valuation of inventory under GAAP. Apple Corporation has been valuing its inventory under the cost method and no write downs have been made for obsolescence. A review of the inventory indicates that obsolescence and excess spare parts in the inventory are two major problems. The CPA states that for GAAP the company will be required to write down its inventory by

25% of its stated amount, or $100,000, and charge this amount against net income from operations for the current period. Otherwise, a "clean opinion" will not be rendered. The company controller asks your advice regarding the tax consequences from the obsolescence and spare parts inventory write downs for the current year and the procedures for changing to the LCM method for tax purposes. Apple Corporation is on a calendar year, and the date of your contact with the company is December 1 of the current year.

A partial list of research sources is:

- Secs. 446 and 471.
- Reg. Secs. 1.446-1(e)(3), 1.471-2 and 1.471-4.
- *American Liberty Pipe Line Co. v. CIR,* 32 AFTR 1099, 44-2 USTC ¶ 9408 (5th Cir., 1944).
- *Thor Power Tool Co. v. CIR,* 43 AFTR 2d 79-362, 79-1 USTC ¶ 9139 (USSC, 1979).

11 Accounting Periods and Methods

LEARNING OBJECTIVES

After studying this chapter, you should be able to

1. Explain the rules for adopting and changing an accounting period
2. Explain the difference between the cash and accrual methods of accounting
3. Determine whether specific costs must be included in inventory
4. Determine the amount of income to be reported from a long-term contract
5. Compute the gain to be reported from an installment sale
6. Compute the amount of imputed interest in a transaction
7. Determine the tax treatment of duplications and omissions that result from changes of accounting methods

Real World Example

The taxpayer, an immigrant from Great Britain, filed his first tax return using a fiscal year ending February 28. However, the return was placed on a calendar year because he failed to show that he kept books and records. Ian W. MacLean, 73 T.C. 1045 (1980).

An **accounting method** is a rule that is used to determine the year in which income and expenses are reported for tax purposes. The accounting methods used in computing income for tax purposes generally must be the same as those used in keeping the taxpayer's books and records. The accounting rules determine when income and expenses are reported, not whether they are reported. Although the accounting methods used by a taxpayer do not necessarily affect the amount of income reported over time, they do impact the tax burden in two ways. Selecting the appropriate accounting method can (1) accelerate deductions or defer income recognition in order to postpone the tax payment, and (2) because of the progressive tax rate structure, taxes can be saved by spreading income over several accounting periods rather than having income bunched into one period.

Example 11-1 ■

Jane, a taxpayer using the cash method of accounting, has a 28% marginal tax rate for 1994 and expects to be in a 15% marginal tax rate in 1995. Jane plans to make a charitable contribution of $1,000 in January 1995. A contribution in 1995 will reduce Jane's tax by $150 (0.15 × $1,000), whereas a contribution in 1994 will reduce Jane's tax by $280 (0.28 × $1,000). Obviously Jane may wish to accelerate the contribution in order to reduce her tax liability. ■

ACCOUNTING PERIODS

OBJECTIVE 1

Explain the rules for adopting and changing an accounting period

Taxable income is computed on the basis of the taxpayer's annual **accounting period,** which is ordinarily 12 months (either a calendar year or a fiscal year). A **fiscal year** is a 12-month period that ends on the last day of any month other than December. The tax year must coincide with the year used to keep the taxpayer's books and records. Taxpayers who do not have books (e.g., an individual with wage income) must use the calendar year.[1] A taxpayer with a seasonal business may find a fiscal year to be advantageous. During the slow season inventories may be lower and employees are available to take inventory and perform other accounting duties associated with

---

[1] Sec. 441(g).

Typical Misconception

It is sometimes mistakenly believed that a tax year can end on a day in the middle of the month.

Self-Study Question

Assume that the ABC partnership is permitted to adopt a tax year ending October 31. Alice, a partner who uses a calendar year, has $12,000 of income from ABC for the year ended October 31, 1994. How much income has Alice been able to defer?

Answer

Assuming that the income was earned ratably throughout the year Alice has deferred $2,000 of income which represents the income earned in November and December of 1993.

the year-end. The tax year is elected on the first tax return that is filed by a taxpayer and cannot be changed without consent from the IRS.[2]

A partnership must use the same tax year of the partners who own the majority of partnership income and capital. If the majority does not have the same year, the partnership must use the tax year of its principal partners (those with greater than a 5% interest in the partnership). If the principal partners do not have the same tax year, the partnership must use the calendar year.[3] An exception is made for partnerships that can establish to the satisfaction of the IRS a business purpose for having a different year.

The purpose of the rule is to prevent partners from deferring partnership income by choosing a different tax year for the partnership. For example, calendar-year partners might select a partnership year that ends on January 31. Since partnership income is considered to be earned by the partners on the last day of the partnership's tax year, reporting the profits would thus be deferred 11 months because the partnership year would end after the partner's year. (See the section entitled Required Payments and Fiscal Years in this chapter for further discussion of the calendar-year requirement.)

A similar rule generally requires S corporations and personal service corporations to adopt a calendar year unless the corporation has a business purpose for electing a fiscal year.[4] Taxpayers willing to make required payments or distributions may choose a fiscal year. (See the section entitled Required Payments and Fiscal Years in this chapter.)

An improper election to use a fiscal year automatically places the taxpayer on the calendar year.[5] Thus, if the first return is filed late because of oversight, the option to choose a fiscal year is lost.

Example 11-2 ■

City Corporation receives its charter in 1992 but does not begin operations until 1994. Tax returns are required for 1992 and 1993 as well as for 1994. Timely returns are not filed because the City's officers are unaware that returns must be filed for inactive corporations. Thus, City Corporation must use the calendar year. City Corporation must petition the IRS for approval to use a fiscal year. ■

Additional Comment

The use of a 52- to 53-week year aids in budgetary matters and statistical comparisons because a four-week period, unlike a calendar month, is a uniform, fixed period.

Taxpayers who regularly keep their books over a period that varies from 52 to 53 weeks and that always ends on the same day of the week may elect the same period for tax purposes. The year must end either (1) the last time a particular day occurs during a calendar month (e.g., the last Thursday in October) or (2) the occurrence of the particular day that is closest to the end of a calendar month (e.g., the Friday closest to the end of November).[6] Under the first alternative, the year may end as many as 6 days before the end of the month, but must end within the month. Under the second alternative, the year may end as many as 3 days before or after the end of the month.[7]

The 52- to 53-week year is especially useful to businesses with inventories. For example, a manufacturer might choose a 52- to 53-week year that ends on the last Friday in December to permit inventory to be taken over the weekend without interfering with the company's manufacturing activity. Similarly, wage accruals would be eliminated for a company with a weekly payroll if the payroll period ends on Friday.

Real World Example

Merrill Lynch & Company uses a 52 to 53 week year ending on the last Friday in December.

Although the 52- to 53-week year may actually end on a day other than the last day of the month, it is treated as ending on the last day of the calendar month for

---

[2] Reg. Sec. 1.441–1(b)(4).
[3] Sec. 706(b).
[4] Sec. 1378(a).
[5] Q.A. *Calhoun v. U.S.*, 33 AFTR 2d 74-305, 74-1 USTC ¶ 9104 (D.C. Va., 1973).
[6] Sec. 441(f).
[7] Reg. Sec. 1.441-2(a)(ii).

"effective date" changes in the tax law that would otherwise coincide with the year-end.[8]

Example 11-3 ■   Eagle Corporation has adopted a 52- to 53-week year. Eagle's tax year begins on December 29, 1994. A new rate schedule applies to tax years beginning after December 31, 1994. The new rate schedule is applicable to Eagle because, in the absence of the 52- to 53-week year, its tax period would have started on January 1, 1995. ■

Changes in the Accounting Period

Key Point

The use of a natural business year helps in the matching of revenue and expense since the business is normally in a maximum state of liquidity and the problems associated with making estimates involving uncompleted transactions are reduced to a minimum.

Once adopted, an accounting period cannot normally be changed without approval of the IRS.[9] The IRS will usually approve a change only if the taxpayer can establish a substantial business purpose for the change (i.e., changing to a natural business year).[10] A natural business year ends at or soon after the peak income earning period (e.g., the natural business year for a department store that has a seasonal holiday business may be on January 31). A business without a peak income period may not be able to establish a natural business year and may, therefore, be precluded from changing its tax year. In general, at least 25% of revenues must occur during the last 2 months of the year in order to qualify as a natural business year.

Example 11-4 ■   USA Department Store's sales reach their peak during the holiday season in December. During January the department store further reduces its inventory through storewide clearance sales. USA elects a "natural" business year-end of January 31 because its inventory levels are lowest at the end of January. ■

Real World Example

J.C. Penney, K mart, and Wal-Mart all use an accounting period ending January 31.

In a few instances IRS approval is not required to change to another accounting period.

- A newly married person may change tax years to conform to that of the other spouse so that a joint return may be filed. The election must be made in either the first or second year after the marriage date.[11]

- A change to a 52- to 53-week year that ends with reference to the same calendar month in which the former tax year ended.[12]

- A taxpayer who erroneously files tax returns using an accounting period other than that on which his books are kept is not required to obtain permission to file returns for later years based on the way the books are kept.[13]

- A corporation meeting the following specified conditions may change without IRS approval: (1) There has been no change in its accounting period within the past 10 calendar years; (2) the resulting year does not have a net operating loss (NOL); (3) the taxable income for the resulting short tax year when annualized is at least 90% of the taxable income for the preceding full tax year; and (4) there is no change in status of the corporation (such as making a S election).[14]

---

[8] Reg. Sec. 1.441–2(b).

[9] Sec. 442.

[10] Rev. Procs. 74-33, 1974-2 C.B. 489, and 87-32, 1987-2 C.B. 32.

[11] Reg. Sec. 1.442-1(e). A statement should be attached to the resulting short period return indicating that the change is being made.

[12] Reg. Sec. 1.441-2(c)(2). A statement should be attached to the first return filed under the election indicating that the change is being made.

[13] Rev. Rul. 58-256, 1958-1 C.B. 215.

[14] Reg. Sec. 1.442-1(c). A statement should be attached to the return indicating that each condition is met.

- An existing partnership can change its tax year without prior approval if the partners with a majority interest have the same tax year to which the partnership changes or if all principal partners who do not have such a tax year concurrently change to such a tax year.[15]

Additional Comment

A tax return cannot cover a period of more than 12 months except in the case of a 52- to 53-week taxable year, in which case the accounting period will exceed 12 calendar months in one out of six consecutive years.

There is one instance, however, when a change in tax years is required: A subsidiary corporation filing a consolidated return with its parent corporation must change its accounting period to conform with its parent's tax year.[16]

Application for permission to change accounting periods is made on Form 1128 (Application for Change in Accounting Period) on or before the fifteenth day of the second calendar month following the close of the resulting short period. The application must be sent to the Commissioner of the IRS, Washington, D.C.[17]

The IRS may establish certain conditions for the taxpayer to meet before it approves the change to a new tax year. For example, the IRS has ruled that if the short period that results from a change involves a NOL greater than $10,000, the taxpayer must agree to spread the loss over 6 years.[18]

Returns for Periods of Less Than 12 Months

Most income tax returns cover an accounting period of 12 months. On two occasions, however, a taxpayer's accounting period may be less than 12 months: (1) when the taxpayer's first or final return is filed and (2) when the taxpayer changes accounting periods.

Taxpayers filing an initial tax return and executors filing a taxpayer's final return or corporations filing their last return are not required to annualize the year's income nor are personal exemptions or tax credits prorated. These returns are prepared and filed, and taxes are paid as though they are returns for a 12-month period ending on the last day of the short period. An exception permits the final return of a decedent to be filed as though the decedent lived throughout the entire tax year.[19]

Example 11-5 ■ ABC Partnership, which has filed its returns on a calendar-year basis, terminates on June 30, 1994. ABC's final return is due on October 15, 1994. ■

Example 11-6 ■ Joy, a single individual who has filed her returns on a calendar-year basis, dies on June 30, 1994. Joy's final return is due on April 15, 1995. ■

Taxpayers who change from one accounting period to another must annualize their income for the resulting short period. This prevents income earned during the resulting short period from being taxed at lower rates. Income is annualized as follows:

- Determine modified taxable income. Individuals must compute their taxable income for the short period by itemizing their deductions (i.e., the standard deduction is not allowed) and personal and dependency exemptions must be prorated.[20]

[15] Reg. Sec. 1.442-1(b)(2).
[16] Reg. Sec. 1.442-1(d).
[17] Reg. Sec. 1.442-1(b)(1).
[18] Rev. Proc. 85-16, 1985-1 C.B. 517.
[19] Reg. Sec. 1.443-1(a)(2).
[20] The exemptions are prorated as follows: exemptions × (number of months in the short period ÷ 12).

- Multiply modified taxable income by the following fraction:

$$\frac{12}{\text{Number of months in short period}}$$

- Compute the tax on the resulting taxable income using the appropriate schedule.
- Multiply the resulting tax by the following fraction:

$$\frac{\text{Number of months in short period}}{12}$$

Example 11-7 ■	Pat, a single taxpayer, obtains permission to change from a calendar year to a fiscal year ending on June 30, 1994. During the six months ending June 30, 1994, Pat earns $25,000 and has $5,000 in itemized deductions.[21]

Gross Income	$25,000
Minus: Itemized deductions	(5,000)
Personal Exemption ([6 ÷ 12] × $2,450)	(1,225)
Modified taxable income	$18,775
Annualized income ([12 ÷ 6] × $18,775)	$37,550
Tax on $37,550 annualized income	7,556
Current tax ([6 ÷ 12] × $7,556)	3,778

■

Required Payments and Fiscal Years

Although taxpayers may use a fiscal year if they have an acceptable business purpose for doing so, most businesses are unable to meet the rather rigid business purpose requirements outlined by the IRS. As a result, most businesses report using the calendar year concentrating most tax work during the early months of the year. Concern over this problem led Congress to allow partnerships, S corporations, and personal service corporations (such as incorporated medical practices) to elect a taxable year that results in a tax deferral of three months or less[22] (e.g., a partnership with calendar-year partners may elect a September 30 year-end). Further, partnerships, S corporations, and personal service corporations may continue using the fiscal year they were using when the current law was passed in 1986 even if that fiscal year results in a deferral beyond three months.[23]

Additional Comment

The American Institute of Certified Public Accountants and accounting firms lobbied extensively for the provision that permits partnerships, S corporations, and personal service corporations to continue to use a fiscal year if annual required payments are made.

Electing partnerships and S corporations, however, must make annual required payments by April 15 of the following year. The purpose of the required payment is to offset the tax deferral advantage obtained when fiscal years are used.

The amount of the required payment is determined by multiplying the maximum tax rate for individuals plus 1% (i.e., 40.6% in 1994) times the previous year's taxable income times a deferral ratio.[24] The deferral ratio is equal to the number of months in the deferral period divided by the number of months in the taxable year. An adjustment is made for deductible amounts distributed to the owners during the year. If the amount due is $500 or less, no payment is required.

Example 11-8 ■	ABC Partnership begins operations on October 1, 1994. The Partnership's net income for the fiscal year ended September 30, 1995 is $100,000. ABC must make a required payment of $10,150 ($100,000 × 40.6% × ³⁄₁₂) on or before April 15, 1996. ■

[21] An alternative method to compute the tax is provided in Sec. 443(b)(2) and Reg. Sec. 1.443-1(b)(2) whereby the taxpayer can elect to compute the tax for a 12-month period beginning on the first day of the short period and then convert the tax to a short-period tax.
[22] Sec. 444(b)(1).
[23] Sec. 444(b)(3).
[24] Sec. 7519(b).

The owners of businesses making such payments do not claim a credit for the amount paid. Instead the partnership or S Corporation subtracts the previous year's required payment from the current year's required payment. If the result is negative then the entity is entitled to a refund.

Example 11-9 ■   Assume the same facts as in Example 11-8 except that ABC Partnership's required payment for the year ended September 30, 1996 is $6,000. ABC is entitled to a refund of the difference of $4,150 ($10,150 − $6,000).   ■

Personal service corporations may elect a fiscal year if they make minimum distributions to shareholders during the deferral period.[25] Personal service corporations are incorporated medical practices and other similar businesses owned by individuals who provide their services through the corporation. In general, the rules prevent a distribution pattern that creates a tax deferral. This is achieved by requiring that the deductible payments made to owners during the deferral period be at a rate no lower than during the previous fiscal year.

Example 11-10 ■   Austin is a personal service corporation of attorneys with a fiscal year ending September 30. For the year ended September 30, 1994 the company earned a profit of $480,000 before any salary payments to the owners. The entire profit, however, was paid out as wages to the owners resulting in a taxable income of zero. To avoid penalty, Austin must pay salaries to its owners of $120,000 ($480,000 × $3/12$) during the period October 1, 1994 to December 31, 1994.   ■

An option allows personal service corporations to compute the amount of the minimum distribution by using a three-year average of income and distributions.

TOPIC REVIEW 11-1

Accounting Periods and Changes

Available Years

1. Available tax years include the calendar year, a fiscal year (a year that ends on the last day of any month other than December), and a 52- to 53-week year (a year that always ends on the same day of the week).
2. A partnership must use the tax year of its partners unless the partnership can establish a satisfactory business purpose for having a different year or if the partnership makes required payments.
3. Similar rules generally require S corporations and personal service corporations to adopt a calendar year unless the corporation has a business purpose for electing a fiscal year. Taxpayers willing to make required payments or distributions may choose a fiscal year ending on September 30, October 31, or November 30.

Change in Accounting Periods

1. Once adopted, an accounting period normally cannot be changed without approval by the IRS. The IRS is more likely to approve a change to a natural business year. In general, at least 25% of revenues must occur during the last two months of the year in order to qualify as a natural business year.
2. Taxpayers who change from one accounting period to another must annualize their income for the resulting short period. This prevents income earned during the resulting short period from being taxed at lower rates.

[25] Sec. 280H(k).

OVERALL ACCOUNTING METHODS

OBJECTIVE 2
Explain the difference between cash and accrual accounting

Key Point

The Code provides the IRS with broad powers in ascertaining whether or not the taxpayer's accounting method "clearly reflects income." It entitles the IRS to more than the usual presumption of correctness.

A taxpayer's method of accounting determines the year in which income is reported and expenses are deducted. Taxable income must be computed using the method of accounting regularly employed by the taxpayer in keeping his books if that method clearly reflects income.[26] Permissible overall accounting methods are:

- Cash receipts and disbursements method (often called the *cash method of accounting*)
- Accrual method
- A combination of the first two methods, frequently called the hybrid method[27]

New taxpayers may generally choose any of the accounting methods listed above. However, the accrual method must be used for sales and cost of goods sold if inventories are an income-producing factor to the business.[28] This assumes, of course, that the chosen method clearly reflects income. The fact that an overall accounting method is used in one trade or business does not mean that the same method must be used in a second trade or business[29] or for nonbusiness income and deductions.[30]

Example 11-11 ■

Troy, a practicing CPA, also owns an appliance store. The fact that Troy uses the accrual method of reporting income from the appliance store, where inventories are an income-producing factor, does not preclude Troy from reporting income from his service-based accounting practice by using the cash method. Troy could also use the cash method for reporting nonbusiness income (such as dividends) and nonbusiness expenses (such as itemized deductions). ■

Real World Example

It has been held that the cash method of accounting can be used where inventories were inconsequential. Michael Drazen, 34 T.C. 1070 (1960).

The term *method of accounting* is used to include not only overall methods of accounting listed above but also the accounting treatment of any item.[31]

Cash Receipts and Disbursements Method

Most individuals and service businesses use the cash receipts and disbursements method of accounting. Taxpayers cannot use the cash method in a business for sales and cost of goods sold if inventories are an income-producing factor. Three other special rules apply. First, farmers in general may use the cash method even though they have inventories.[32] Second, a tax shelter cannot use the cash method, even if it does not have inventories.[33] A third rule limits the use of the cash method by C corporations and partnerships with a corporate partner.[34] C corporations and partnerships with a corporate partner may use the cash method if their average annual gross receipts for the three preceding tax years do not exceed $5 million or if the business meets the requirements associated with providing personal services (i.e., if it is owned by professionals who are using the business to provide professional

---

[26] Sec. 446.
[27] Sec. 446(c).
[28] Reg. Sec. 1.446-1(a)(4)(i).
[29] Sec. 446(d).
[30] Reg. Sec. 1.446-1(c)(1)(iv)(b).
[31] Reg. Sec. 1.446-1(a)(1). Examples of accounting methods for specific items include Sec. 174, relating to research and experimentation expenses; Sec. 451, relating to reporting income from long-term contracts; and Sec. 453, relating to reporting income from installment sales.
[32] Sec. 448(b).
[33] Sec. 448(a).
[34] Ibid.

services).[35] Thus, a law or accounting firm can use the cash basis even if its average receipts exceed $5 million.

Under the cash receipts and disbursements method of accounting, a taxpayer is required to report income for the tax year in which payments are actually or constructively received. Expenses are deducted in the year paid. Because the recognition of expense is measured by the flow of cash, a taxpayer can determine the year in which an expense is deductible by choosing when to make the payment. Individual taxpayers do not have the same opportunity to determine the year in which income is recognized, because the constructive receipt rule requires taxpayers to recognize income if a payment is available, even if actual payment has not been received. (See Chapter 3 for a discussion of constructive receipt.)

Key Point

A taxpayer using the cash method is entitled to certain deductions which do not involve current year cash disbursements, such as depreciation, depletion, and losses.

Capitalization Requirements for Cash-Method Taxpayers. Taxpayers who use the cash receipts and disbursements method are required to capitalize fixed assets and to recover the cost through depreciation or amortization. The Regulations state that prepaid expenses must be capitalized and deducted over the life of the asset if the life of the asset extends substantially beyond the end of the tax year.[36] Typically, capitalization is required only if the life of the asset extends beyond the close of the tax year following the year of payment.[37]

Example 11-12 ■

On July 1, 1994, Acme Corporation, a cash-basis, calendar-year taxpayer, pays an insurance premium of $3,000 for a policy that is effective July 1, 1994, to June 30, 1995. The full $3,000 is deductible in 1994. ■

Example 11-13 ■

Assume the same facts as in Example 11-12, except that the premium covers a 3-year period beginning July 1, 1994, and ending June 30, 1997. Acme Corporation may deduct $500 in 1994; $1,000 in 1995 and 1996; and $500 in 1997. ■

One notable exception to the one-year rule denies a deduction for prepaid interest. Cash-method taxpayers must capitalize such amounts and allocate interest over the prepayment period. A special rule allows homeowners to deduct points paid on a mortgage used to buy or improve the individual's personal residence. The payment must be an established business practice in the area and not exceed amounts generally charged for such home loans.[38] (See Chapter 7 for a discussion of the deductibility of points.)

To be deductible, a payment must be more than just a refundable deposit. A taxpayer who has an option of cancelling delivery and receiving a refund of amounts prepaid is not normally entitled to deduct the amount of the deposit.

Payments can be made either by a check that is honored in due course or by the use of a credit card.[39] Payment by credit card is considered to be the equivalent of borrowing funds to pay the expense. But a taxpayer's note is not the equivalent of cash. So, if a cash method taxpayer gives a note in payment, he cannot take the deduction until the note is paid, even if the note is secured by collateral.[40]

Accrual Method

There are two tests used to determine when an item of income must be reported or an expense deducted: the **all-events test** and the **economic performance test.**

---

[35] Secs. 448(b) and (c).
[36] Reg. Sec. 1.461-1(a)(1).
[37] *Bonaire Development Co.,* 76 T.C. 789 (1981), and *Martin J. Zaninovich v. CIR,* 45 AFTR 2d 80-1442, 80-1 USTC ¶ 9342 (9th Cir., 1980).
[38] Sec. 461(g).
[39] Rev. Rul. 78-39, 1978-1 C.B. 73.
[40] *Frank D. Quinn Exec. v. CIR,* 24 AFTR 927, 40-1 USTC ¶ 9403 (5th Cir., 1940).

Additional Comment

The phrase "reasonable accuracy" means that approximate amounts are ascertainable. Although the word "accuracy" means exactness or precision, when it is used with the word "reasonable" it implies something less than an exact amount.

All-Events Test. An accrual-method taxpayer reports an item of income when "all events" have occurred that fix the taxpayer's right to receive the item of income and when the amount of the item can be determined with reasonable accuracy.[41] Similarly, an expense is deductible when all events have occurred that establish the fact of the liability and when the amount of the expense can be determined with reasonable accuracy.[42] For deductions, the all-events test is not satisfied until economic performance has taken place.[43]

Economic Performance Test. Economic performance (of services or property to be provided to a taxpayer) occurs when the property or services are actually provided by the other party.[44]

Example 11-14 ■

The owner of a professional football team provides medical benefits for injured players through insurance coverage. Economic performance occurs over the term of the policy rather than when the team enters into a binding contract with the insurance company or during the season when the player earns the right to medical benefits. Thus, a one-year premium is deductible over the year of the insurance coverage rather than over the term of the player's contract under which the benefit is earned. ■

Similarly, if a taxpayer is obligated to provide property or services, economic performance occurs in the year the taxpayer provides the property or service.[45]

Example 11-15 ■

Assume the same facts as in Example 11-14 except that medical benefits are required under the terms of a player's contract. Also, the team decides to pay medical costs directly. Economic performance occurs as the team actually provides the benefits. Thus, the deduction is permitted only as medical care is provided. ■

Real World Example

Before the economic performance test was added to the tax law, a company engaged in strip mining coal was able to deduct the future land reclamation costs as the coal was mined since the liability was certain and the cost could be estimated. Ohio River Collieries, 77 T.C. 1369 (1981).

The requirement that economic performance take place before a deduction is allowed is waived if the following five conditions are met:

1. The all-events test, without regard to economic performance, is satisfied.
2. Economic performance occurs within a reasonable period (but in no event more than 8½ months) after the close of the tax year.
3. The item is recurring in nature, and the taxpayer consistently treats items of the same type as incurred in the tax year in which the all-events test is met.
4. The taxpayer is not a tax shelter.
5. Either the amount is not material or the earlier accrual of the item results in a better matching of income and expense.[46]

Example 11-16 ■

To promote sales, Bass Corporation (a used car sales company) offers buyers coupons for three free car washes. Bass purchases the coupons from a local car wash. The coupons must be used within 6 months after the purchase of an automobile. If Bass uses the cash method, it could deduct the cost of the coupons at the time the payment for the coupons is made to the car wash. Under the accrual method and assuming the five conditions listed above are met, Bass could deduct

---

[41] Reg. Sec. 1.451-1(a). See Chapter 3 for a discussion of the all-events test as it applies to gross income.
[42] Reg. Sec. 1.446-1(c)(1)(ii).
[43] Sec. 461(h)(1).
[44] Sec. 461(h)(2)(A).
[45] Ibid.
[46] Sec. 461(h).

Typical Misconception

It is sometimes mistakenly believed that taxpayers can deduct warranty expenses and bad debts using the allowance method instead of the direct write-off method.

the cost of the coupons as they are given to buyers (instead of having to wait until the coupons are used by the purchasers). ■

Reserves for items such as product warranty expense are commonly encountered in financial accounting. The all-events and economic performance tests prevent the use of such reserves for tax purposes. This is because the amount of such expense is not usually determinable with sufficient accuracy. Under prior law, taxpayers were permitted to use the allowance method for bad debts, but that method is no longer allowed for tax purposes.[47]

Hybrid Method

Section 446(c) permits taxpayers to use a combination of accounting methods as long as the taxpayer's income is clearly reflected. Taxpayers with inventories are required to use the accrual method to report sales and purchases. These taxpayers may use the cash method to report other items of income and expense. To assure that income is clearly reflected, certain restrictions have been placed on combining accounting methods.

Additional Comment

A taxpayer who uses the cash method in computing gross income from his business must use the cash method in computing expenses of such business.

Regulation Sec. 1.446-1(c)(1)(iv)(a) states that taxpayers who use the cash method of accounting in determining gross income from a trade or business must use the cash method for determining expenses of the same trade or business. Similarly, taxpayers who use the accrual method of accounting for expenses must use the accrual method in computing gross income from the trade or business.

The basic rules relating to accounting methods, the all-events test, and economic performance are summarized in Topic Review 11-2.

TOPIC REVIEW 11-2

Accounting Methods

Available Methods

1. Permissible overall accounting methods are the cash receipts and disbursements method, the accrual method, and the hybrid method.
2. Except for farmers, taxpayers cannot use the cash method in a business for sales and cost of goods sold if inventories are an income-producing factor. Tax shelters cannot use the cash method even if they do not have inventories. Similarly, C corporations may not use the cash method if their gross receipts in the three preceding tax years equal or exceed $5 million. An exception allows personal service corporations to use the cash method of reporting even if their receipts exceed the $5 million threshold.

All-Events Test and Economic Performance Test

1. An accrual-method taxpayer reports an item of income when "all events" have occurred that fix the taxpayer's right to receive the item of income and when the amount of the item can be determined with reasonable accuracy.
2. An expense is deductible when all events have occurred that establish that there is a liability and when the amount of the expense can be determined with reasonable accuracy. The all-events test is not satisfied until economic performance has taken place.
3. Economic performance takes place when property or services are actually provided.

[47] Section 166 permitted the allowance method prior to 1987.

INVENTORIES

Key Point

Taxpayers cannot always use inventory methods for tax purposes that conform with generally accepted accounting principles.

Manufacturing and merchandising companies are required to use the accrual method of accounting for purchases and sales of merchandise.[48] The inventory method used by a taxpayer must conform to the best accounting practice in the trade or business, and it must clearly reflect income.[49] Best accounting practices (synonymous with generally accepted accounting principles) and clear reflection of income (which is determined by the IRS) however, occasionally conflict. The Supreme Court has held that the standard of clear reflection of income prevails in a case where the two standards conflict. In the *Thor Power Tool Co.* case, the company wrote off the cost of obsolete parts even though they were kept on hand and their selling price was not reduced.[50] Regulation Sec. 1.471-4(b) states that obsolete or other slow-moving inventory cannot be written down unless the selling price is also reduced.

Although the company's practice conformed with generally accepted accounting principles, it did not, according to the Supreme Court, clearly reflect income. Hence, generally accepted accounting principles are used only when the Regulations do not specify the treatment of an item or, alternatively, when the Regulations provide more than one alternative accounting method.

Taxpayers who value inventory at cost may write down goods that are not salable at their normal price (e.g., damaged, obsolete, or shopworn goods) only after the selling price has been reduced. Items may be valued at a bona fide selling price reduced by the direct cost of disposal.[51] The option to write down this type of merchandise is available even if the taxpayers use the LIFO inventory method.

Key Point

The uniform capitalization rules, included in the Tax Reform Act of 1986, require the capitalization of significant overhead costs that previously were expensed.

Determination of Inventory Cost

Inventories may be valued at either cost or at the lower of cost or market value.[52] Taxpayers who use the LIFO inventory valuation method (discussed later in this chapter) may not use the lower of cost or market method. In the case of merchandise purchased, cost is the invoice price less trade discounts, plus freight and other handling charges.[53]

Unlike financial accounting, purchasing costs (e.g., salaries of purchasing agents), warehousing costs, packaging, and administrative costs related to these functions must be allocated between cost of goods sold and inventory. This requirement is applicable only to taxpayers whose average gross receipts for the three preceding years exceed $10 million.[54]

Ethical Point

The UNICAP rules must be followed by taxpayers. To bring a business into compliance with these rules, however, the taxpayer may need to make certain estimates. SRTP No. 4 provides that a CPA may use a client's estimates if such use is generally acceptable or if it is impractical to obtain exact data. If a change in the overhead application rate is contemplated, it may be desirable to request IRS approval.

In the case of goods manufactured by the taxpayer, cost is determined by using the Uniform Capitalization rules (UNICAP) which may be thought of as an expanded version of the full absorption costing method.[55] Thus, direct costing and prime costing are not acceptable inventory methods.[56] Direct labor and materials along with manufacturing overhead must be included in inventory. Under UNICAP, the following overhead items are included in inventory:

---

48 Reg. Sec. 1.446-1(c)(2)(i).
49 Reg. Sec. 1.471-2(a).
50 *Thor Power Tool Co. v. CIR*, 43 AFTR 2d 79-362, 79-1 USTC ¶ 9139 (USSC, 1979).
51 Reg. Sec. 1.471-2(c).
52 Ibid.
53 Reg. Sec. 1.471-3(b).
54 Sec. 263A(b)(2)(B).
55 Reg. Sec. 1.471-11(a).
56 Reg. Sec. 1.471-2(f).

Key Point

Identifying the appropriate additional overhead costs to capitalize can be confusing and extremely time consuming.

- Factory repairs and maintenance, utilities, rent, insurance, small tools, and depreciation (including the excess of tax depreciation over accounting depreciation)
- Factory administration and officers' salaries related to production
- Taxes (other than the income tax)
- Quality control and inspection
- Rework, scrap, and spoilage
- Current and past service costs of pension and profit-sharing plans
- Service support such as purchasing, payroll, and warehousing costs

Nonmanufacturing costs (e.g., advertising, selling, and research and experimental costs) are not required to be included in inventory.[57] Interest must be inventoried if the property is real property, long-lived property, or property requiring more than two years (one year in the case of property costing more than $1 million) to produce.

The main difference between full absorption costing traditionally used for financial accounting purposes and UNICAP costing required for tax purposes is that UNICAP expands the list of overhead costs to include certain indirect costs that have not always been included in overhead for financial accounting purposes. For example, for financial accounting purposes the costs of operating payroll and personnel departments have sometimes been considered sufficiently indirect or remote to justify omitting them from manufacturing overhead. This was true even though much of the effort of the payroll and personnel departments was directed toward manufacturing operations. For simplicity and other reasons, overhead costs included in inventory for financial purposes are often limited to those incurred in the factory. UNICAP requires that the costs associated with these departments must be allocated between manufacturing and nonmanufacturing functions (e.g., sales, advertising, research and experimentation).

A manufacturer may use standard costs to value inventory if any significant variance is reallocated pro rata to ending inventory and cost of goods sold.[58] Taxpayers may determine inventory costs by the following methods: specific identification method; "first-in, first-out method" (FIFO); "last-in, first-out" method (LIFO); or average cost method. A few taxpayers, such as an automobile or large appliance dealer, may find it practical to determine the specific cost of items in inventory. Most taxpayers, however, must rely on a flow of goods assumption (e.g., FIFO or LIFO). (See Chapter 10 for a more detailed discussion of inventory costs.)

LIFO Method. Many taxpayers use the LIFO cost flow assumption because, during inflationary periods, LIFO normally results in the lowest inventory value and hence the lowest taxable income. Once LIFO has been elected for tax purposes, the taxpayer's financial reports must also be prepared using LIFO.[59] This requirement to conform financial reporting frequently discourages companies from electing LIFO because lower earnings must be reported to shareholders. However, taxpayers may make footnote disclosure of the amount of net income that would have been reported under FIFO or other inventory methods.[60] Taxpayers may adopt LIFO by attaching a completed Form 970 (or by a statement acceptable to the IRS) to the return for the tax year in which the method is first used.

---

[57] Reg. Sec. 1.471-11(c)(2)(ii).
[58] Reg. Sec. 1.471-11(d)(3).
[59] Sec. 472(c).
[60] Reg. Sec. 1.472-2(e).

Record-keeping under LIFO can be cumbersome. For this reason taxpayers are permitted to determine inventories using "dollar-value" pools and government price indexes rather than by maintaining a record of actual costs.[61] Retailers use appropriate categories in the Consumer Price Index; other taxpayers use categories in the Producer Price Index. Taxpayers using the index method must divide their inventories into one or more pools (groups of similar items). Thus, a department store might create separate pools for automobile parts, appliances, clothing, furniture, and other products. Dividing inventory into pools can be critical because of the different inflation rates associated with various goods and because, if a particular pool is depleted, the taxpayer loses the right to use the lower prices associated with past layers. An important exception permits taxpayers with average annual gross receipts of $5 million or less for the current and two preceding tax years to use the **simplified LIFO method.**[62] The simplified LIFO method uses a single LIFO pool, thereby avoiding problems with multiple pools.

Example 11-17 ■

In 1994 King Department Store changes its inventory method from FIFO to LIFO. Because King's gross receipts have never exceeded $5 million, the simplified LIFO method is available. King's year-end inventories under FIFO are as follows:

1993	$100,000
1994	$130,000

Assume the 1993 price index is 120% and the 1994 index is 125%. King must convert its 1994 inventory to 1993 prices.

$$\frac{120\%}{125\%} \times \$130,000 = \$124,800$$

A base period inventory of $100,000 is established. The increase in inventory (the 1994 layer) is valued at 1994 prices.

Base inventory (1993)	$100,000
Plus: 1994 layer ([125% ÷ 120%] × [$124,800 − $100,000])	25,833
1994 ending inventory	$125,833

Assume the 1995 inventory valued under FIFO is $136,000 and the 1995 price index is 130%. The 1995 inventory is converted to 1993 prices.

$$\frac{120\%}{130\%} \times \$136,000 = \$125,538$$

The 1995 increase in inventory (the 1995 layer) is valued at 1995 prices.

Base inventory (1993)	$100,000
1994 layer	25,833
1995 layer	800[a]
1995 ending inventory	$126,633

[a] ([130% ÷ 120%] × [$125,538 − $124,800])   ■

Lower of Cost or Market Method. Inventory may be valued at the **lower of cost or market.** This option is available to all taxpayers other than those who determine cost using the LIFO method.[63] The term *market* refers to *replacement cost.* On the date an inventory is valued, the replacement cost of each item in the inventory is compared with its cost. The lower figure is used as the inventory value. The lower of

[61] Sec. 472(f).
[62] Sec. 474(c).
[63] Reg. Secs. 1.471-2(b) and (c).

cost or market method must ordinarily be applied to each separate item in the inventory.

Recall the *Thor Power Tool* case (discussed earlier in this chapter) in which the Supreme Court distinguished market value from expected selling price. **Market value** is the price at which the taxpayer can replace the goods in question. Replacement cost is used in the lower of cost or market determination. Obsolete or other slow-moving inventory can be written down below replacement cost only if the selling price has been reduced.

SPECIAL ACCOUNTING METHODS

The term *method of accounting* is used to include not only overall methods of accounting (i.e., cash, accrual, and hybrid) but also the accounting treatment of specific items. Special rules have been established for two types of transactions that cover long time spans. One rule applies to installment sales (a sale in which final payment is not received until a subsequent tax year) and a separate set of rules applies to long-term contracts (construction and similar contracts that are not completed in the same year they are started). These special rules permit taxpayers to report income from this type of transaction when they have the wherewithal to pay the tax (i.e., the year in which payment is received).

Long-Term Contracts

OBJECTIVE 4
Determine the amount of income to be reported from a long-term contract

Long-term contracts include building, installation, construction, or manufacturing contracts that are not completed in the same tax year in which they are entered into.[64] A manufacturing contract is long-term only if the contract involves the manufacture of either a unique item not normally carried in finished goods inventory or items that normally require more than 12 calendar months to complete. Contracts for services (architectural, accounting, legal, and so on) do not qualify for long-term contract treatment.[65]

Example 11-18 ∎

Diamond Corporation manufactures two planes: a small, general aviation plane that requires six months to complete and a large jet aircraft sold to airlines that requires two years to complete. Diamond carries an inventory of the small plane but manufactures the large plane to specification. Diamond can use long-term contract accounting only for the large plane. Assume Diamond also offers aircraft design assistance to the government and others who seek such services. The long-term contract method of accounting is not available for such services. ∎

Historical Note

The use of the completed contract method was severely restricted in the Tax Reform Act of 1986 because Congress found that several large corporations, particularly those with large defense contracts, had significant deferred taxes attributable to this method. Many of these companies had extremely low or negative tax rates for several years.

The accounting method selected by a taxpayer must be used for all long-term contracts in the same trade or business.[66] In general, the income and expenses associated with long-term contracts may be accounted for by using either the **percentage of completion method** or the **modified percentage of completion method.** In limited instances (explained below), taxpayers may use the **completed contract method.** Under the percentage of completion method, income from a project is reported in installments as the work progresses. Under the completed contract method, income from a project is recognized upon completion of the contract. The modified percentage of completion method is a hybrid that combines two methods (discussed below). Alternatively, taxpayers may use any other accounting method (e.g., the accrual method) that clearly reflects income.

---

[64] Reg. Sec. 1.451-3(b).
[65] Rev. Proc. 71-21, 1971-2 C.B. 549, does establish rules for service contracts that extend into the year following the receipt of payment. These rules are discussed in Chapter 3.
[66] Reg. Sec. 1.451-3(a)(1).

Additional Comment

In general, a construction contract must involve what has historically been thought of as construction which would include erecting buildings, building dams, roads, power plants, etc.

Costs Subject to Long-Term Contract Rules. Direct contract costs are subject to the long-term contract rules. Labor, materials, and overhead costs must be allocated to the contract and accounted for accordingly. Thus, under the completed contract method, such costs are capitalized and deducted from revenue in the year the contract is completed. Selling, marketing and advertising expenses, and expenses for unsuccessful bids and proposals, and research and development costs not associated with a specific contract need not be allocated to any contract and may be deducted currently.[67]

In general, administrative overhead must be allocated to long-term contracts. (See the earlier list of overhead items that must be included in inventory.) This is not required of taxpayers (other than homebuilders) using the completed contract method, but as noted below, the use of the completed contract method is limited.[68]

As previously mentioned, interest must be capitalized if the property being produced is real property, long-lived property, or property requiring more than two years (one year in the case of property costing more than $1 million) to produce. Interest costs directly attributable to a contract and those that could have been avoided if contract costs had not been incurred must be allocated to long-term contracts.[69]

Completed Contract Method. Under the completed contract method of accounting, income from a contract is reported in the taxable year in which the contract is completed. This is true without regard to whether the contract price is collected in advance, upon completion of the contract, or in installments. Costs associated with the contract are accumulated in a work-in-progress account and deducted upon completion.[70] The courts are in conflict with regard to determining when a contract is completed. Some courts have required total completion and acceptance of the contract.[71] Other courts have held the contract to have been completed when the only work remaining consists of correcting minor defects or furnishing incidental parts.[72]

The use of the completed contract method is severely restricted in two situations. The method can be used by smaller companies (those whose average gross receipts for the three preceding tax years is $10 million or less) for construction contracts that are expected to take two years or less to complete and other taxpayers for home construction contracts.[73] It cannot be used by larger companies for manufacturing, or for other long-term contracts other than construction or for construction contracts expected to last longer than 2 years.

Key Point

In general, taxpayers with long-term contracts must compute income under the percentage of completion method for contracts entered into after July 10, 1989.

Percentage of Completion Method. Under the percentage of completion method of reporting income, the taxpayer reports a percentage of the gross income from a long-term contract based on the portion of work that has been completed. The portion of the total contract price reported in a given year is determined by multiplying the total contract price by the percentage of work completed in the year. The percentage is determined by dividing current year costs by the expected total costs.[74]

Modified Percentage of Completion Method. At the beginning of a contract, it is difficult to estimate total costs. For this reason, taxpayers may elect to defer reporting

---

[67] Sec. 460(c)(4).
[68] Sec. 460(e)(1).
[69] Secs. 460(c)(3) and 263A(f).
[70] Reg. Sec. 1.451-3(d)(1).
[71] *E. E. Black Limited v. Alsup,* 45 AFTR 1345, 54-1 USTC ¶ 9340 (9th Cir., 1954), and *Thompson-King-Tate, Inc. v. U.S.,* 8 AFTR 2d 5920, 62-1 USTC ¶ 9116 (6th Cir., 1961).
[72] *Ehret-Day Co.,* 2 T.C. 25 (1943), and *Nathan Wohlfeld,* 1958 PH T.C. Memo ¶ 58,128, 17 TCM 677.
[73] Sec. 460(e).
[74] Reg. Sec. 1.451-3(c)(2).

Key Point

After a taxpayer has adopted an accounting method for long-term contracts, he or she must continue to use that method unless permission to change methods is granted.

any income from a contract until they have incurred at least 10% of the estimated total cost.[75] This is called the modified percentage of completion method. Under this method, if a contract has just been started as of the end of the year, the taxpayer does not have to estimate the profit on the contract during that year. The next year the taxpayer will report profit on all work that has been completed, including work done during the first year. Of course, this assumes that at least 10% of the work has been completed as of the end of the taxable year. If more than 10% of the costs are incurred during the first year, the modified percentage of completion method is identical to the regular percentage of completion method.

The completed contract method, the percentage of completion method, and the modified percentage of completion method are compared in Example 11-19.

Example 11-19 ■

In 1994, a contractor enters into a contract to construct a bridge for $1,400,000. At the outset, the contractor estimates that it will cost $1,200,000 to build the bridge. Actual costs in 1994 are $540,000 (45% of the $1,200,000 total estimated costs). Actual costs in 1995 are less than expected and total $600,000. The profits reported in both years of the contract are illustrated below.

	1994	1995
Completed Contract		
Revenue	-0-	$1,400,000
Costs incurred	-0-	(1,140,000)
Gross profit	-0-	$ 260,000
Percentage of Completion		
Revenue	$630,000[a]	$ 770,000[b]
Costs incurred	(540,000)	(600,000)
Gross profit	$ 90,000	$ 170,000

[a] 0.45 × $1,400,000 = $630,000
[b] $1,400,000 − $630,000 = $770,000

■

In Example 11-19, the modified percentage of completion method results in the same income being reported each year as the percentage of completion method because more than 10% of the estimated costs were incurred during the first year. Note that the completed contract method defers reporting income until the contract is completed, causing all income from the project to be reported in a single year. Thus, the tax is deferred but the taxpayer may end up being taxed at higher rates. As noted, the completed contract is available only for home construction contracts and to certain smaller contractors for projects of 2 years or less.

Look-Back Interest. Certain contracts (or portion of a contract) accounted for under either the regular or modified percentage of completion method are subject to a **look-back interest** adjustment. When a contract is completed, a computation is made to determine whether the tax paid each year during the contract is more or less than the tax that would have been paid if the actual total cost of the contract had been used rather than the estimated cost.[76] Interest is paid on any additional tax that would have been paid. The taxpayer receives interest on any additional tax that is paid.

[75] Sec. 460(a).
[76] Sec. 460(b)(3).

Look-back interest is applicable only to contracts completed more than two years after the commencement date. Further, look-back interest is only applicable if the contract price equals or exceeds either 1% of the taxpayer's average gross receipts for the 3 taxable years preceding the taxable year the contract was entered into or $1 million.[77]

Example 11-20 ■ The contractor in Example 11-19 is exempt from the look-back rule because the contract is completed within two years after the commencement date. On the other hand, if the contract took more than two years to complete, interest would be owed on the underpaid taxes for the first and subsequent contract years. The under reported income for the first year would be $33,158 [($260,000 × $540,000 ÷ $1,140,000) − $90,000]. Assuming a 35% tax bracket, the underpaid tax for the first year is $11,605. Upon completion of the contract, interest would be paid on this amount and underpaid taxes for other years. ■

Installment Sales Method

OBJECTIVE 5
Compute the gain to be reported from an installment sale

Key Point

The installment sales method allows either a cash- or an accrual-method taxpayer to spread the gain from the sale of property over the period during which payments are received.

In general, the gain or loss from the sale of property is reported in the year the property is sold. If the sales proceeds are collected in years after the sale, the taxpayer may find it difficult to pay the tax on the gain entirely in the year of sale. To reduce the burden, the tax law permits taxpayers to spread the gain from installment sales over the collection period. The installment method is applicable only to gains and is used to report income from an installment transaction unless the taxpayer elects not to use the installment method.[78] An **installment sale** is defined as any disposition of property where at least one payment is received after the close of the taxable year in which the disposition occurs.[79] The installment method is not applicable to either sales of publicly traded property (e.g., stock listed on an exchange) or sales of inventory.

Computations Under Sec. 453. Income under the installment sales method is computed as follows:

STEP 1. Compute the gross profit from the sale.

Selling price	$xx,xxx
Minus: Adjusted basis	(x,xxx)
Selling expenses	(x,xxx)
Depreciation recapture	(x,xxx)
Gross profit	$ x,xxx

Self-Study Question

A taxpayer sells 100 shares of Ford Motor Company stock for a gain of $800 on December 30, 1993. The taxpayer received the proceeds from the sale from the stockbroker on January 8, 1994. Can the taxpayer use the installment sales method?

Answer

No, the method is not applicable to sales of publicly traded property.

STEP 2. Determine the contract price.

Contract price (greater of the gross profit from above or the selling price reduced by any existing mortgage assumed or acquired by the purchaser)	$xx,xxx

STEP 3. Compute the gross profit percentage.

$$\frac{\text{Gross profit}}{\text{percentage}} = \frac{\text{Gross profit}}{\text{Contract price}} = \text{xx}\%$$

[77] Sec. 460(b)(3).
[78] Sec. 453(d).
[79] Sec. 453(b)(1).

STEP 4. Compute the gain to be reported in the year of sale.

Collections of principal received during year (exclusive of interest)	$xx,xxx
Plus: Excess mortgage (if any)[a]	x,xxx
Total	$xx,xxx
Times: Gross profit percentage	× xx%
Net gain recognized in year of sale	$ x,xxx
Plus: Depreciation recapture	x,xxx
Gain reported in year of sale	$ x,xxx

[a] (Mortgage − Basis − Selling expense − Depreciation recapture) = Excess mortgage

STEP 5. Compute the gain to be reported in subsequent years.

Collections of principal received	$ x,xxx
Times: Gross profit percent	× xx%
Gain reported in each of the subsequent years	$ x,xxx

Note that depreciation recapture (see Chapter 13) must be reported in the year of the sale even if no payment is received.[80]

Example 11-21 ■

Gina, a cash basis taxpayer, sells equipment for $200,000. The equipment originally cost $70,000, and $10,000 of MACRS depreciation has been deducted prior to the sale. The $10,000 of depreciation must be recaptured as ordinary income under Sec. 1245. The buyer assumes the existing mortgage of $50,000, pays $10,000 down, and agrees to pay $10,000 per year for 14 years plus interest at a rate acceptable to the IRS. Selling expenses are $13,000. Using the steps listed above, calculations are made as follows:

STEP 1. Compute the gross profit from the sale.

Selling price		$200,000
Minus:	Adjusted basis	(60,000)
	Selling expenses	(13,000)
	Depreciation recapture	(10,000)
Gross profit		$117,000

STEP 2. Determine the contract price.

Greater of gross profit of $117,000 or selling price minus mortgage assumed by purchaser ($150,000 = $200,000 − $50,000)	$150,000

STEP 3. Compute the gross profit percentage.

$$\frac{\text{Gross profit}}{\text{percentage}} = \frac{\text{Gross profit (\$117,000)}}{\text{Contract price (\$150,000)}} = 78\%$$

STEP 4. Compute the gain to be reported in the year of sale.

Principal received during year	$ 10,000
Plus: Excess mortgage	—0—
Total amount realized	$ 10,000
Times: Gross profit percentage	× 0.78
Gross profit	$ 7,800
Plus: Depreciation recapture	10,000
Gain reported in year of sale	$ 17,800

[80] Sec. 453(i).

STEP 5. Compute the gain to be reported in subsequent years.

Principal received	$ 10,000
Times: Gross profit percentage	× 0.78
Gain reported in each subsequent year	$ 7,800

Thus, the total gain reported is $127,000 ($17,800 + [$7,800 × 14]). This is equal to the gross profit of $117,000 (which is the amount of Sec. 1231 gain reported on the sale) plus the $10,000 of depreciation recapture. As a cash basis taxpayer Gina will report the interest income as it is collected. ■

Real World Example

When an installment obligation is assigned as collateral for a loan, the transaction is treated as a disposition of the obligation. Rev. Rul. 65-185, 1965-2 C.B. 153.

Disposition of Installment Obligations. A taxpayer who sells property on the installment basis may decide not to hold the obligation until maturity. For example, the holder may sell the obligation to a financial institution for the purpose of raising cash. Alternatively, the holder may not be able to collect the full amount of the installments because of the inability of the buyer to make payments. Thus, the holder must determine the adjusted basis of the obligation in order to compute the gain or loss realized on the disposition. The adjusted basis of an installment obligation is equal to the face amount of the obligation reduced by the gross profit that would be realized if the holder collects the face amount of the obligation. In general, this means the adjusted basis of an obligation is equal to

$$\text{Face amount} \times (100\% - \text{Gross profit percentage})$$

Example 11-22 ■

Assume the same facts as in Example 11-21 except that Gina immediately sells a single $10,000 installment to a bank for $9,700. Gina reports a gain of $7,500 computed as follows:

Selling price	$9,700
Minus: Adjusted basis of installment	(2,200)[a]
Recognized gain	$7,500

[a]$10,000 face amount × (100% − 78% gross profit percentage) = $2,200

Gina would have reported a gain of $7,800 had she decided not to sell the installment but to collect the face amount. Since the obligation is discounted by $300 ($10,000 − $9,700), the reported gain is reduced by $300. If the installment had not been sold immediately, the bank would probably also pay to Gina an amount for the accrued interest. In such a situation Gina would report the gain from the sale and the accrued interest as income. ■

Example 11-23 ■

Assume that Gina in Example 11-22 is unable to collect the final $10,000 installment because the individual who purchases the property declares bankruptcy. Gina would be entitled to a bad debt deduction of $2,200, the basis of the installment. Gina does not receive a bad debt deduction for the accrued interest because the interest has not been included in her gross income. ■

Key Point

A donor of property does not normally recognize gain, but a gift of certain installment obligations causes the recognition of gain.

Certain dispositions of installment obligations, including giving them as gifts, are taxable events.[81] The main objective of this rule is to prevent income from being shifted from one taxpayer to another. Thus, if a corporation distributes an installment obligation as a dividend or if a father gives his daughter an installment

[81] Sec. 453B(a).

obligation, gain or loss is recognized. In general, the gain or loss recognized is equal to the difference between the FMV of the obligation and its adjusted basis. In the case of a gift, the gain recognized is equal to the difference between the face of the obligation and its adjusted basis. However, certain exceptions to this rule exist. Transfers to controlled corporations under Sec. 351, certain corporate reorganizations and liquidations, transfers upon the taxpayer's death, transfers incident to divorce, distributions by partnerships, and contributions of capital to a partnership are exceptions to this rule. In these cases, the recipients of the obligations report income when the installments are collected.[82]

Repossessions of Property Sold on the Installment Basis. In general, the repossession of property sold on the installment basis is a taxable event. The gain or loss recognized is generally equal to the difference between the value of the repossessed property (reduced by any costs incurred as a result of the repossession) and the adjusted basis of any remaining installment obligations.

Example 11-24 ■ Yuji sells stock of a non-publicly traded corporation with a $7,000 adjusted basis for $10,000. Yuji receives a $1,000 down payment, and the balance of $9,000 is due the following year. In the year of the sale Yuji reports a capital gain of $300 (0.30 × $1,000) under the installment method of accounting. Yuji is unable to collect the $9,000 note, and after incurring legal fees of $500, he repossesses the stock. When Yuji repossesses the stock it is worth $8,700. The adjusted basis of the note is $6,300 (0.70 × $9,000). Yuji must report a capital gain of $1,900 ($8,700 − $500 − $6,300). The basis of the stock to Yuji is its FMV at the time it is repossessed ($8,700). ■

Section 1038 limits the amount of gain recognized from the repossession of real property. The gain recognized is limited to the lesser of (1) the gross profit in the remaining installments reduced by the costs incurred as a result of the repossession or (2) the cash and FMV of other property received from the buyer in excess of the gain previously recognized. In the case of the repossession of either real or personal property, the gain or loss retains the same character as the gain or loss on the original sale.

Example 11-25 ■ Assume the same facts as in Example 11-24, except that the property sold is land. Yuji reports a capital gain of $700, which is the lesser of $2,200 ([0.30 × $9,000]− $500) or $700 ($1,000 − $300). The basis of the land is $7,500 ($9,000 − [0.30 × $9,000] unrealized profit + $700 gain previously recognized + $500 legal fees). ■

Key Point

The installment sales method is still available for use by nondealers of personal property and real property.

Installment Sales by Dealers. Taxpayers who regularly sell personal property under an installment contract may not use the installment method.[83] In other words, dealers may not use the installment method in connection with the sale of inventory. Exceptions permit the use of the installment method for sales of residential lots, timeshares, and property used or produced in the business of farming.[84] Taxpayers who use the installment method in connection with the sale of residential lots and timeshares must, however, agree to pay interest to the government on the amount of deferred tax attributable to the use of the installment method.[85]

---

[82] Sec. 453B.
[83] Sec. 453(b)(2)(A).
[84] Sec. 453(l)(2).
[85] The interest computation is described in Sec. 453(l)(3).

Installment Sales for More Than $150,000. Special rules apply to nondealers who sell property for more than $150,000. The special rules do not apply to sales of personal use property, to sales of property used or produced in the trade or business of farming, or to sales of timeshares or residential lots.

First, if the taxpayer borrows funds using the installment obligations as security, the amount borrowed is treated as a payment received on the installment obligation.[86] This prevents the taxpayer from using the installment method to defer tax and yet obtain cash by borrowing against the installment obligation. Second, if the installment method is used, interest must be paid to the government on the deferred tax.[87] This rule, however, applies only to deferred principal payments over $5 million.[88]

Key Point

Installment sales between related parties cannot be used to defer the recognition of gain by the original owner when the related purchaser receives cash.

Installment Sales Between Related Persons. Installment sales between related persons are subject to the same rules as other installment sales except when the property is resold by the related purchaser. The primary purpose of the resale rule is to prevent the original owner from deferring gain recognition by selling the property to a related person who, in turn, resells the property.

Example 11-26 ■   Hal plans to sell land to Bob for cash, but instead sells the land to Donna (his daughter). The selling price is $200,000. Hal purchased the land for $40,000 several years earlier. Under the terms of the sale, Donna is to pay for the land over a period of 10 years. Donna immediately resells the land to Bob for $200,000. Donna owes no tax because she sells the land at her cost. In the absence of any special provision, Hal would report his gain on the sale over the 10 years he collects the sales price from Donna. This type of arrangement permits the monies from the sale to be received by the related party (Donna) (and thereby presumably reduce the risk of default) while permitting Hal to defer his taxes.   ■

Section 453(e) requires the first seller (Hal) to treat amounts received by the related person (Donna) as having been personally received. Thus, Hal in Example 11-26 would be required to report the entire gain in the year of sale. This acceleration provision is applicable only if the resale takes place within 2 years after the initial sale.

For purposes of Sec. 453(e), the term *related person* includes a spouse, children, grandchildren, and parents. Controlled corporations, partnerships, estates, and trusts are also covered.[89]

Deferred Payment Sales

The installment sale rules are not applicable to all sales involving future payments. The installment method cannot be used when the sale of property produces a loss. Also a taxpayer can elect out of the installment method when a sale results in a gain. How these transactions are reported depends on the taxpayer's accounting method. For accrual method taxpayers, the total *amount receivable* from the buyer (exclusive of interest) is treated as part of the amount realized. Thus, the entire gain or loss is reported in the year of sale. For cash method taxpayers, the FMV of the installment obligation is treated as part of the amount realized in the year of sale. The amount realized, however, cannot be considered to be less than the FMV of the property sold minus any other consideration received (e.g., cash).[90]

---

[86] Sec. 453A(d).
[87] The interest computation is described in Sec. 453A(c).
[88] Sec. 453A(b)(2)(B).
[89] Sec. 453(f).
[90] Temp. Reg. Sec. 15A.453-1(d)(2)(ii)(A).

Example 11-27 ■   USA Corporation, an accrual-method taxpayer, sells land for $100,000. USA receives $50,000 down and a $50,000 note payable in 12 months plus 14% interest. Assume the basis of the land is $80,000 and that it is a capital asset. Because of the buyer's poor credit, the value of the note is only $45,000. USA affirmatively elects not to report the installment sale on the installment method. USA reports a capital gain of $20,000 ($100,000 − $80,000). If USA collects the face of the note at maturity, no additional gain or loss is recognized. If USA sells the note for $45,000, a $5,000 capital loss is recognized.   ■

Example 11-28 ■   Assume the same facts as in Example 11-27, except that USA is a cash-method taxpayer. If the FMV of the land is $100,000 (the stated selling price), the treatment of the transaction is exactly the same as it is using the accrual method. If the FMV of the land is assumed to be $95,000 (cash received plus FMV of the note received), USA recognizes a $15,000 ($95,000 − $80,000) capital gain in the year of the sale. If USA collects the face of the note at maturity, $5,000 of ordinary income is recognized. If USA sells the note for $45,000, no gain or loss is recognized.   ■

Additional Comment

A contingent payment sale is a sale or other disposition of property in which the aggregate selling price cannot be determined by the close of the tax year in which the sale took place.

Indeterminate Market Value. In certain transactions, the value of obligations received cannot be determined. Under the Regulations, the value of obligations with an **indeterminate market value** is assumed to be no lower than the value of the property sold less the value of other property received.[91] Hence, if the value of property sold is determinable, the recognized gain equals the excess of the value of the property sold over its basis. On occasion, however, neither the value of the obligation received nor the value of property sold can be determined.

Example 11-29 ■   City Corporation sells mineral interests for an amount equal to 10% of the value of coal produced from the property. The property cost City $30,000 several years ago but has no determinable value today.   ■

Temporary regulations specify how these types of transactions are to be treated.[92] In general, the taxpayer is required to follow the installment sales rules. If the terms of the agreement specify a maximum selling price, that amount is treated as the selling price until it becomes clear that a lesser amount will be received.

Example 11-30 ■   Assume the same facts as in Example 11-29, except that the agreement specifies that the payments are not to exceed $600,000. Thus, $600,000 is treated as the selling price. The gain is assumed to be $570,000 ($600,000 − $30,000), and the gross profit percentage is 95% ($570,000 ÷ $600,000). As a result, 95% of future payments are taxable. (These calculations ignore imputed interest, which is discussed below.)   ■

If the terms of the agreement specify a fixed payment period, the adjusted basis of the property is recovered over that period.

Example 11-31 ■   Assume the same facts as in Example 11-29, except that the agreement limits the payments to 10% of the value of coal produced during a 10-year period. The $30,000 cost is allocated equally over 10 years, so that $3,000 of cost is assumed to be recovered each year. Amounts received in excess of $3,000 each year are fully taxable. (Again, imputed interest is ignored.)   ■

[91] Reg. Sec. 1.453-1(d)(3)(iii).
[92] Temp. Reg. Sec. 15A.453-1(c).

If an agreement does not specify either a fixed payment period or a maximum selling price, temporary regulations specify that the taxpayer must assume a payment period of 15 years.

Example 11-32 ■

Assume the same facts as in Example 11-29. Since neither a fixed payment period nor a maximum selling price are specified, the taxpayer must assume a payment period of 15 years. Hence, $2,000 ($30,000 ÷ 15) of cost is recovered each year. Any amount received in excess of $2,000 is fully taxable, and no loss is recognized if the amount received in any one year is less than $2,000. (Again, imputed interest is ignored.) ■

The basic rules relating to special accounting methods are summarized in Topic Review 11-3.

TOPIC REVIEW 11-3

Special Accounting Methods
Long-Term Contracts
1. Long-term contracts include building, installation, construction, or manufacturing contracts that are not completed in the same tax year in which they are entered into. A manufacturing contract is long-term only if the contract involves the manufacture of either a unique item not normally carried in inventory or an item that normally requires more than 12 calendar months to complete.
2. Long-term contracts may be reported under the regular or the modified percentage of completion method. Under both methods income is reported as work is completed, except that under the modified percentage of completion method no income is reported until at least 10% of the work is completed.
3. The completed contract method is available only for home construction contracts, for construction contracts expected to take two years or less to complete, and for use by smaller companies (those whose average gross receipts for the three preceding tax years are $10 million or less).
Installment Method
1. Under the installment method gain is reported as the sales proceeds are collected. The installment method is generally not available for sales of inventory or publicly traded property. Further, the method is available only for gains.
2. Gain is reported as sales proceeds are collected. However, both depreciation recapture and any mortgage in excess of basis must be reported in the year of sale. Gain recognition is also accelerated in certain situations if the seller borrows against the installment obligation or if a related buyer resells the property within two years.

IMPUTED INTEREST

OBJECTIVE 6
Compute the amount of imputed interest in a transaction

Before the enactment of Sec. 1274 and the amendment of Sec. 483, property could be sold on an installment basis in a contract providing for little or no interest. Instead of charging interest, the seller charged a higher price for the property. If the property sold was a capital asset, the result of the arrangement was to reduce the interest income reported by the seller and to increase the amount of favorably taxed capital gain.

Key Point

Imputed interest is important because it alters the amount of gain on the sale and causes an interest expense deduction for the buyer and interest income for the seller.

To end this tax-avoidance technique, which converted what was in reality interest income into capital gain, Sec. 1274 was enacted and Sec. 483 was substantially revised. Sections 483 and 1274 "impute" interest in a deferred payment contract where no interest or a low rate of interest is provided. Another impact of the **imputed interest** rules on sellers is to reallocate payments received between interest (which is fully taxable) and principal (only the gain portion of which is taxable). The result is often to increase the income reported in early years and decrease the income in later years. The rules are generally applicable to both buyers and sellers. In certain instances, the buyer may want interest to be imputed in order to increase his interest deduction in early years.

The following transactions are exempt from the rules:

Typical Misconception

At times it is mistakenly assumed that the imputed interest rules do not apply if the property is sold for a loss.

- Debt subject to original issue discount provisions (basically bonds issued for less than face where amortization of the discount is required under Sec. 1274, see Chapter 5)
- Sales of property for $3,000 or less
- Any sales where all of the payments are due within six months
- Sales of patents to the extent the payment is contingent on the use or disposition of the patent
- Certain carrying charges for personal property or educational services covered by Sec. 163(b) when the interest charge cannot be ascertained
- Charges for the purchase of personal-use property (purchaser only)[93]

Example 11-33 ■

Joan is involved in several transactions during the current year. No interest is stated on any of the transactions. The terms of the transactions and the applicability of the imputed interest rules are summarized below:

Transaction	*Imputation of Interest*
1. Purchases furniture costing $8,000 for her residence. Full price is payable within four months.	1. Not applicable since property is for personal use. Also, all payments are due within six months.
2. Sells a boat for $2,000. Payment is due in a year.	2. Not applicable since sales price is not more than $3,000.
3. Sells land for $100,000. Payment is due in five years.	3. Interest must be imputed since no exception is applicable.
4. Purchases a newly issued bond for $650 (face of $1,000).	4. Not applicable since transaction is subject to the original isue discount rules in Sec. 1274. Also, the price is not more than $3,000. ■

Imputed Interest Computation

In order to avoid the imputation of interest, the stated interest rate must be at least equal to 100% of the applicable federal rate (110% of the applicable federal rate in the

---

[93] Sec. 483(d). Under prior law, personal interest expense was deductible. This prevented taxpayers who purchased assets such as a personal automobile from claiming a deduction for imputed interest in the case where the stated interest rate was less than the statutory rate. Under present law, the rule will result in a lowering of the basis of a personal-use asset in order to increase any gain on the future sale of the property.

Additional Comment

The imputed interest rules do not apply if all of the installment payments are due within one year after the date of sale.

case of sale-lease back arrangements).[94] Lower rates are specified for two types of transactions: (1) If the stated principal amount for qualified debt obligations that are issued in exchange for property under Sec. 1274A does not exceed $2,800,000, the interest rate is limited to 9% compounded semiannually; and (2) the interest rate is limited to 6% compounded semiannually in the case of sales of land between related individuals (to the extent the sales price does not exceed $500,000).

The **applicable federal rate** is determined monthly and is based on the rate paid by the federal government on borrowed funds. The rate varies with the terms of the loan. Loans are divided into short-term (not over three years), mid-term (over three years but not over nine years), and long-term (over nine years).

Example 11-34 ■ Kasi sells land for $100,000 to Bill, an unrelated person. The sales price is to be paid to Kasi at the end of five years in a single installment with no stated interest. Kasi paid $60,000 for the land. Assume the current federal rate is 10%. Since the amount of the stated principal is less than $2,800,000, interest is imputed at a rate not to exceed 9% compounded semiannually. As a result, the effective rate is 9.2025% (9% compounded semiannually), and the present value factor is .64393 (1 ÷ 1.092025^5). Thus, the present value of the final payment is $64,393 (0.64393 × $100,000). Kasi reports a $4,393 ($64,393 − $60,000) gain on the sale of the land and $35,607 ($100,000 − $64,393) interest income instead of a $40,000 gain and no interest income. The buyer is treated as incurring $35,607 in interest and has a $64,393 basis in the land. Whether the interest is deductible depends on a variety of other factors (see Chapter 7). ■

Accrual of Interest

Is imputed interest reported under the cash or the accrual method? In other words, is imputed interest reported when it accrues or when it is paid? In general, imputed interest is reported as it accrues. However, there are some major exceptions, as follows:

- Sales of personal residences
- Most sales of farms for $1,000,000 or less
- Sales involving aggregate payments of $250,000 or less
- Sales of land between related persons to the extent the sales price does not exceed $500,000[95]

Additional Comment

The $2,000,000 limit on the stated principal is subject to inflation adjustments for calendar years beginning after 1989.

In addition, if the borrower and lender jointly elect, and if the stated principal does not exceed $2,000,000, accrual of interest is not required. This election is not available if the lender is an accrual-method taxpayer or a dealer with respect to the property sold or exchanged.[96]

Example 11-35 ■ Assume the same facts as in Example 11-34. Since the aggregate payments do not exceed $250,000, the transaction is exempt from the requirement that interest be accrued. As a result, Kasi reports interest income and Bill reports interest expense in the fifth year when the final payment is made on the transaction. Under the installment method, $4,393 gain on the sale is recognized in the fifth year. ■

---

[94] Different interest rates have been used in prior years.
[95] Sec. 1274(c)(4).
[96] Sec. 1274A(c).

Gift, Shareholder, and Other Loans

Imputed interest rules are not limited to installment transactions. The rules are also applicable to transactions involving related parties whose taxes are lowered as a result of low interest or interest free loans. These situations include:

- *Gift loans.*[97] For example, parents in higher tax brackets may loan money to their children without charging interest. If the children invest the borrowed money and are taxed on the income at a lower rate, the family has reduced its total tax liability in the absence of imputed interest rules.

- *Corporation shareholder loans.*[98] In the absence of imputed interest rules, taxes may be saved by a corporation that makes an interest free loan to a shareholder. If the corporation had invested the money and paid out the resulting income as a dividend, it would have first been taxed on the profit. By making the interest free loan, the corporation could, in the absence of imputed interest rules, reduce its taxes by avoiding the otherwise taxable income.

- *Compensation related loans.*[99] Employers may loan money to employees without charging interest. Without the requirement to impute interest, this could produce tax savings if the employer was unable to deduct additional compensation because of the reasonable compensation limitation or if the employee was unable to deduct the interest, say, because the borrowed funds were used to purchase personal use property.

- *Other tax avoidance loans.*[100] Any other low interest or interest free loan that produces tax savings may be subject to the imputed interest rules. For example, a club may offer its members a choice of either paying dues or making a large refundable deposit. The club can invest the money and earn interest perhaps equal to the dues. In the absence of imputed interest rules, the member avoids taxes by not having to report the income that would have been earned if the member personally invested the funds. The club is indifferent between the alternatives because both the dues and the interest income are taxable.

In general, interest is imputed on the above loans by applying the applicable federal rates discussed earlier. The resulting interest income is taxable to the lender. Whether the interest expense is deductible by the borrower is determined by applying the usual interest deduction rules (see Chapter 7).

The imputation process involves a second step. The lender is treated as returning the imputed interest to the borrower. This is necessary because the interest was not actually paid. For example, in the case of a gift loan, the lender is treated as giving the imputed interest back to the borrower. This would not normally have income tax implications, but, if the imputed interest were large enough, it could result in a gift tax. In the case of the corporation-shareholder loan, the corporation is treated as paying the imputed interest back to the shareholder as a dividend. Typically, this will not increase the corporation's tax, but it results in the recognition of dividend income to the shareholder. For compensation related loans, the second step is to impute compensation paid by the employer and received by the employee. The compensation is taxable to the employee and, if reasonable in amount, is deductible by the employer.

There are several important exceptions intended to limit the application of imputed interest in situations where tax avoidance may be immaterial. These include:

[97] Sec. 7872(c)(1)(A).
[98] Sec. 7872(c)(1)(C).
[99] Sec. 7872(c)(1)(B).
[100] Sec. 7872(c)(1)(D) and (E).

- Interest is not imputed on gift loans between two individuals totaling $10,000 or less, except when the borrowed funds are used to purchase income-producing property.[101]

- If the gift loans between two individuals total $100,000 or less, the imputed interest is limited to the borrower's "net investment income" as defined by Sec. 163(d)(4). (See Chapter 7 for a discussion of net investment income). If the net investment income is $1,000 or less, it is not necessary to impute interest.[102]

- Interest is not imputed on compensation-related and corporate shareholder loans totaling $10,000 or less.[103]

These exceptions do not apply when tax avoidance is one of the principal purposes of the loans.

Example 11-36 ■

Linda made interest free gift loans to each of her four children—Andy, Bob, Cathy, and Donna. Andy borrowed $9,000 to purchase an automobile. Bob borrowed $25,000 to buy stock. Bob's net investment income is $800. Cathy also borrowed $25,000 to buy stock, but her net investment income is $1,100. Donna borrowed $120,000 to purchase a residence, and her net investment income is $500. Tax avoidance is not a motive for any of the loans. Imputation of interest is not required for the loans to Andy or Bob. The loan to Andy is exempt because the amount is less than $10,000, and the loan to Bob is exempt because his net investment income is under $1,000. Imputation of interest is required for the loans to Cathy and Donna. In the case of Cathy, the amount of imputed interest is limited to her net investment income of $1,100. The imputed interest for Donna, however, is not limited to her net investment income because the amount of the loan is over $100,000. ■

The imputed interest rules are summarized in Topic Review 11-4.

TOPIC REVIEW 11-4

Imputed Interest

Purpose:
The imputed interest rules are intended to prevent taxpayers from reducing their taxes by charging little or no interest on installment payment transactions and loans.

Applies to:
In most cases applies to both parties, the debtor and the creditor. The result is to impute interest income to the lender and interest expense to the borrower. Several exceptions exempt small transactions from imputed interest. For example, installment sales involving payments of $3,000 or less are generally exempt as are loans of less than $10,000.

Rate:
Interest is imputed at the "applicable federal rate" if the stated interest rate is lower. The applicable federal rate is the rate the federal government pays on borrowed funds and is determined monthly. In general, the current rate at the time of the transaction is used throughout the term of the loan. The rate varies with the term of the loan. Loans are divided into short-term (not over three years), mid-term (over three years but not over nine years), and long-term (over nine years).

---

[101] Sec. 7872(c)(2).
[102] Sec. 7872(d).
[103] Sec. 7872(c)(3).

CHANGE IN ACCOUNTING METHODS

OBJECTIVE 7
Determine the tax treatment of duplications and omissions that result from changes of accounting methods

In general, a new taxpayer elects an accounting method by simply applying the selected method when computing income for the initial tax return.[104] If a particular item does not occur in the first year, the accounting method is elected the first year in which the item occurs.

Example 11-37 ■

Gordon opened a beauty shop in 1988. Because he had no inventory, no inventory method was selected. In 1994, Gordon expanded his business to offer beauty supplies to his customers. Gordon can delay electing the FIFO inventory method until 1994, the first year in which he has an inventory.   ■

Real World Example
The writedown of soil aggregate to its market value by a paving company was a change in accounting method rather than the mere correction of an accounting error. The soil aggregate was included within its election to adopt the LIFO inventory method, and the use of this method required that the soil aggregate be included at cost regardless of market value.
First National Bank of Gainesville, Trustee, 88 T.C. 1069 (1987).

In general, once an accounting method is chosen, it cannot be changed without IRS approval.[105] There are a few exceptions. For example, taxpayers may adopt the LIFO inventory method without prior IRS approval.[106] Once such methods are adopted, however, they cannot be changed without IRS approval.

As previously noted, the term *accounting method* indicates not only the overall accounting method used by the taxpayer, but also the treatment of any item of income or deduction.[107] A change of accounting methods should not be confused with the correction of an error. Errors include mathematical mistakes, posting errors, deductions of the wrong amount for an expense, omission of an item of taxable income, or incorrect computation of a credit. An error is normally corrected by filing an amended return for the tax year or years in which the error occurs. In general, there is a three-year statute of limitations on the correction of errors. After three years, the tax year is closed and changes cannot be made.[108]

Real World Example
An extension of time to file the application for change of accounting method was granted because of the death of the accountant in charge of filing the application. Rev. Rul. 79-417, 1979-2 C.B. 202.

Taxpayers wishing to change accounting methods must file Form 3115 with the IRS during the first 180 days of the tax year in which the change is made.[109] The deadline may be extended to within the first nine months if good cause can be shown for the delay. For the change to be approved, the proposed method must, in the opinion of the IRS, clearly reflect income. Permission is required even if the taxpayer has been using an erroneous method of accounting. For example, the use of prime costing to compute inventory is an erroneous accounting method because manufacturing overhead must be included in the valuation of inventories. Thus, a change from prime costing to "full absorption costing" requires the permission of the IRS, even though the method has been erroneously applied. The IRS can, however, require a taxpayer to change accounting methods if the method that has been used does not clearly reflect income, even if the taxpayer does not propose the change. The authority to require a taxpayer to adopt any accounting method necessary to clearly reflect income does not include the authority to require an arbitrary change. If the accounting methods used by a taxpayer clearly reflect income, the IRS cannot require a change to another method that would also clearly reflect income.

---

[104] Reg. Sec. 1.446-1(e)(1).
[105] Sec. 446(e).
[106] A taxpayer may adopt LIFO by merely determining year-end inventory by that method and attaching Form 970 to the tax return for the year (Reg. Sec. 1.472-3(a)).
[107] Reg. Sec. 1.446-1(e)(2)(ii)(b).
[108] Exceptions are applicable when the taxpayer omits from the return an amount of income that is over 25% of the gross income stated on the return (6 years) or where fraud occurs (no limitation).
[109] Reg. Sec. 1.446-1(e)(3).

Amount of Change

A change in accounting methods usually results in duplications or omissions of items of income or expense.

Example 11-38 ■ Bonnie, a practicing CPA, has been reporting income using the cash method. In the current year, Bonnie obtains permission to change to the accrual method. At the beginning of the current year, Bonnie has $80,000 of receivables which have not been reported in prior years. The receivables are not reported in prior years because they were not collected. Although the receivables are collected in the current year, they are not taxable because, under the accrual method, Bonnie now reports income as it is earned and the income is not earned in the current year. In this case, the income was earned in prior years.

Also, assume Bonnie has accounts payable of $15,000 at the beginning of the current year. The accounts payable have not been deducted in prior years because the expenses have not been paid. Furthermore, the accounts payable are not deductible in the current year even if they are paid. This is because the expenses are incurred in prior years. Obviously, the IRS expects to collect the tax on the $80,000 of receivables, and Bonnie is entitled to deduct the $15,000 of payables. In the absence of any special provision, both amounts would be omitted from the computation of taxable income. If the change is from the accrual method to the cash method, both amounts would be reported twice (in the year prior to the change because they had accrued and in the year of the change because they are collected or paid). Thus, a special provision is also needed for duplications. ■

Reporting the Amount of the Change

The net amount of the change must be taken into account.[110] A positive adjustment is added to income, whereas a negative adjustment is subtracted from income. This adjustment can, of course, be made in the year of the change. If the amount is small, recognizing the full amount of the net adjustment in the year of the change is both simple and equitable. Reporting a large positive adjustment in one year could push the taxpayer into a higher marginal tax bracket and result in a significant tax increase. Because the extra income is due to changing accounting methods, not increasing cash flows, the taxpayer may not have the wherewithal to pay the additional tax.

As a result, there are alternative methods that may be used to report the amount of the change. The alternative methods all have one thing in common—they spread the amount of the change over a period of more than one year. The spread may be over the current and prior tax years or the current and future tax years. The methods that are available depend on whether the change is voluntary (a change that is initiated by the taxpayer) or involuntary (a change from an unacceptable to an acceptable method that is required by the IRS).

Real World Example

A trucking company had been inventorying its used trailers at a cost of $1 per trailer. The change to a policy of inventorying the used trailers on the basis of lower of cost or market was an involuntary change from an unacceptable to an acceptable method that was required by the IRS.
Fruehauf Trailer Co., 42 T.C. 83 (1966).

Involuntary Changes. In the case of an involuntary change involving a negative adjustment or a positive adjustment of $3,000 or less, taxpayers are required to report the entire amount in the year of the change. In the case of positive adjustments over $3,000, two alternative relief provisions are available. The alternative methods allow the taxpayer to redetermine the tax on the amount of the change. If the amount so determined is lower, the taxpayer is obligated to pay only the lesser amount.

THREE-YEAR METHOD. Under the so-called three-year method, the amount of the change is divided by three. This amount is then added to the taxable income for the

---

[110] Sec. 481.

current year and each of the 2 preceding years.[111] This often produces a lower tax because the amount is taxed at lower rates.

Example 11-39 ■

In 1994 Chris is required to change from the cash to the accrual method. His taxable income for 1994 is $10,000 (not including the amount of the adjustment). The net adjustment attributable to the change is $30,000. Under the one-year method, Chris adds the amount of the change ($30,000) to his income ($10,000) and computes the tax on the total ($40,000). Because the amount of the change is positive and is more than $3,000, Chris has the option of applying the three-year method. Assume his taxable income for 1992 is $90,000 and for 1993, $100,000. Under the three-year method, Chris would compute the tax by adding $10,000 to the income for each year (1992, 1993, and 1994). The result is to compute the tax on $100,000, $110,000, and $20,000, as opposed to $90,000, $100,000, and $40,000. In this instance, the one-year method is more beneficial because the current income (and tax rates) are lower than the income (and tax rates) for the two prior years. If the reverse was true (i.e., taxable income was lower in prior years than the current year), Chris would prefer to spread the amount of the change over three years and apply the lower tax rates. ■

Self-Study Question

A corporation formed on January 1, 1993, reported taxable income of $100,000 for 1993 and $100,000 for 1994. However, the corporation expensed parts that should have been included in inventory. The cost of the parts at the end of 1993 and 1994 was $10,000 and $15,000, respectively. Reconstruct the income for 1993 and 1994.

Answer

The reconstructed taxable income is $110,000 ($100,000 + 10,000) for 1993 and $105,000 ($100,000 + 15,000 − 10,000) for 1994.

RECONSTRUCTION OF INCOME. When reconstructing income, the income for prior years is recomputed using the new method of accounting. Thus, if a taxpayer is changing from the cash to the accrual method, income is reconstructed for the prior years using the accrual method.[112] Obviously, if a taxpayer has been in existence for decades, reconstructing income can be a complicated, time-consuming procedure. Hence, this method is not often used. Amounts that cannot be assigned to a particular year (e.g., because of a lack of records) are included in the income for the year of the change.

The reconstruction of income method, like the three-year method, is a relief provision that applies if the redetermined tax is less than the tax that is computed under the three-year alternative or the regular one-year method.

In the case of changes initiated by the IRS, any portion of the adjustment that is attributable to years prior to 1954 is excluded from income.[113] This is because under pre-1954 law, duplications and omissions were not taken into account when a taxpayer changed accounting methods. If a taxpayer voluntarily initiates the change, the pre-1954 exclusion from income is not available.

Voluntary Changes. The three-year method and the reconstruction of income method are not explicitly limited to involuntary changes. Nevertheless, Rev. Proc. 84-74 specifies that in order to obtain IRS consent to change, taxpayers must agree to report the adjustment over a period not to exceed six years (not to exceed three years in the case of a change from an erroneous accounting method to a method that clearly reflects income).[114] In the case of a change spread over six years, equal portions of the change are reported in each of the six years beginning with the year of the change.

Example 11-40 ■

In 1994 Diana obtains permission to change from the accrual to the cash method of reporting income. The change results in a $45,000 negative adjustment to income. The IRS requires Diana to spread the adjustment over six years. As a result, she may deduct $7,500 in 1994 and $7,500 per year through 1999. Note that because

---

[111] Sec. 481(b)(1).
[112] Sec. 481(b)(2).
[113] Reg. Sec. 1.481-1(a)(2).
[114] 1984-2 C.B. 736.

the amount of the adjustment is spread over the current and future years, the tax savings associated with the deduction are deferred. ■

In general, the amount of the adjustment cannot be spread over a period longer than the method being changed has been used. The alternative methods for reporting the amount of a change are summarized in Topic Review 11-5.

TOPIC REVIEW 11-5

Reporting the Amount of the Change				
Section	Method of Reporting the Change	Years Involved	Conditions	Comments
481(a)	1-year	Year of change	Must be used for involuntary changes involving either a negative adjustment or a positive adjustment of $3,000 or less. Available for other changes	Simple, but can force taxpayers into higher tax rates
481(b)(1)	3-year	Year of change and two prior years	Available for involuntary changes involving positive adjustment of over $3,000	Provides relief by helping taxpayers who are in a high tax bracket in the current year
481(b)(2)	Reconstruction of income	All years involved	Available for involuntary changes involving positive adjustment of over $3,000	Involves reconstructing income for prior years using the new method (seldom used because it is difficult and time consuming)
481(c)	6-year	Year of change and up to five subsequent years	Available for voluntary changes (either positive or negative)	Sec. 481(b)(2) grants the IRS authority to determine how amounts arising from voluntary changes are to be reported. The current IRS position is that such amount should be spread over a period of no longer than six years. Desirable from the taxpayer's point of view in the case of positive adjustments because it defers tax into future.

Obtaining IRS Consent

Most changes in accounting method require IRS approval. Sec. 446(e) states that a taxpayer changing the method of accounting "on the basis of which he regularly computes his income in keeping his books" must obtain consent before computing taxable income under the new method. This implies that a taxpayer who has been computing taxable income on a method other than that used in computing book income does not need approval to conform the computation of taxable income to the method regularly used on the taxpayer's books. This conclusion is supported by Sec. 441(a), which requires that the same method of accounting be used in computing taxable income as is used in keeping the books. The alternative might be to require the taxpayer to conform his book accounting method with the tax accounting method. The answer may well be in how one defines "books." The IRS has ruled that a reconciliation of taxable income with accounting income was a part of the taxpayer's auxiliary records.[115] Hence, the taxpayer was using the same accounting method for book and tax reporting. As a result, a taxpayer who changes the method of accounting used for financial reporting may not be required to change the method of accounting used for tax reporting as long as financial income and book income are reconciled.

Real World Example

A pipeline company was required to capitalize reconditioning costs on its natural gas pipelines instead of expensing these costs. Mountain Fuel Supply Co. v. U.S., 28 AFTR 2d 71-5833, 71-2 USTC ¶ 9681 (10th Cir., 1971).

The Regulations provide that IRS consent is required to change accounting methods even when the taxpayer has been using an improper accounting method.[116] It is not clear whether the IRS, by declining to approve a change, can require a taxpayer to continue to use an improper accounting method indefinitely. Clearly, the IRS can require adjustments to prevent duplications and omissions. Further, the IRS may be able to require the taxpayer to use a proper method that is acceptable to the IRS even if the method is not the one preferred by the taxpayer. Presumably, if the first tax return for the taxpayer is still open under the statute of limitations, the taxpayer can change accounting methods by amending all prior returns and computing taxable income by using a proper accounting method.[117]

TAX PLANNING CONSIDERATIONS

Key Point

C corporations and estates have more flexibility than S corporations and partnerships in the selection of a tax year.

Accounting Periods

New corporations often routinely adopt a calendar year. Consideration should be given, however, to adopting a tax year for the initial reporting period that ends before the amount of taxable income exceeds the amount that is taxed at the lowest tax rates (e.g., when taxable income is $50,000 or less). This is less critical for a corporation suffering losses because the NOLs may be carried forward for a 15-year period.

In the past, taxpayers were able to defer income by selecting different tax years for partners and partnerships or S corporations and shareholders. Current law limits this opportunity. Nevertheless, partnerships and S corporations may adopt a tax year that differs from that of their owners if that year qualifies as a natural business year (i.e., at least 25% of revenues occur during the last two months of the year). Furthermore, deferral is possible in the case of estates, since they are not subject to similar restrictions on the choice of tax years.

[115] Rev. Rul. 58-601, 1958-2 C.B. 81.
[116] Reg. Sec. 1.446-1(e)(2)(i).
[117] Rev. Ruls. 70-539, 1970-2 C.B. 70, 75-56, 1975-1 C.B. 98, and 77-236, 1977-2 C.B. 84.

Key Point

The election to use an accounting method is made by filing the first tax return on the basis of that method.

Accounting Methods

New businesses should consider the tax implications of electing an accounting method. For example, taxpayers may benefit from the LIFO inventory method because LIFO typically reduces gross profit and defers the payment of taxes during inflationary periods. Similarly, service companies usually choose the cash method of reporting income because it permits receivables to be reported when collected rather than when the income is earned. Choosing an accounting method requires an understanding not only of the available accounting methods, but also a knowledge of the nature of the taxpayer's business. Will a specific election be to the tax advantage of the taxpayer? LIFO inventory is often recommended because, during inflationary periods, it tends to reduce inventory values and increase the cost of goods sold. In certain industries, such as the computer industry, however, costs are declining, and LIFO actually may result in a higher inventory value.

In other industries, inventories may fluctuate widely from one year to the next because of changing demand, shortages of materials, strikes, or other causes. LIFO layers may have to be depleted simply to continue business operations. This can cause one of two things to happen: (1) incurring extra record-keeping costs of LIFO for little or no benefit because the inventories are depleted before they produce significant tax deferrals or (2) depleting low-cost layers from years past, resulting in a substantial increase in taxable income in the year of occurrence.

Installment Sales

Taxpayers normally choose the installment method of reporting income from casual sales of property. By spreading the gain from a sale over more than one tax year, the taxpayer normally remains in lower tax brackets and defers the tax. A taxpayer with low current taxable income may elect not to use the installment sale method in order to take advantage of the lower current tax rates.

COMPLIANCE AND PROCEDURAL CONSIDERATIONS

Reporting Installment Sales on Form 6252

Form 6252 [Installment Sale Income] is used to report income under the installment method from sales of real property and casual sales of personal property other than inventory. Figure 11-1 illustrates how an installment sale transaction is reported. The illustration is based on Example 11-21. A separate Form 6252 is normally used for each installment sale. Form 6252 is used in the year of the sale and any year in which the taxpayer receives a payment from the sale. Taxpayers who do not wish to use the installment method may report the transaction on either Schedule D or on Form 4797.

PROBLEM MATERIALS

DISCUSSION QUESTIONS

11-1. Do accounting rules determine the amount of income to be reported by a taxpayer?

11-2. How does a taxpayer's tax accounting method impact on the amount of tax paid?

Form **6252**

Department of the Treasury
Internal Revenue Service

Installment Sale Income

▶ See separate instructions. ▶ Attach to your tax return.
▶ Use a separate form for each sale or other disposition of property on the installment method.

OMB No. 1545-0228

19**93**

Attachment
Sequence No. **79**

Name(s) shown on return   *Gina Green*

Identifying number   *123-45-6789*

1 Description of property ▶ *Equipment*

2a Date acquired (month, day, and year) ▶ *10 / 1 / 91*   b Date sold (month, day, and year) ▶ *8 / 3 / 93*

3 Was the property sold to a related party after May 14, 1980? See instructions . . . . ☐ Yes ☒ No

4 If the answer to question 3 is "Yes," was the property a marketable security? If "Yes," complete Part III. If "No," complete Part III for the year of sale and for 2 years after the year of sale. . . . . ☐ Yes ☐ No

Part I Gross Profit and Contract Price. Complete this part for the year of sale only.

5	Selling price including mortgages and other debts. Do not include interest whether stated or unstated	5	200,000
6	Mortgages and other debts the buyer assumed or took the property subject to, but not new mortgages the buyer got from a bank or other source .	6	50,000
7	Subtract line 6 from line 5	7	150,000
8	Cost or other basis of property sold	8	70,000
9	Depreciation allowed or allowable	9	10,000
10	Adjusted basis. Subtract line 9 from line 8	10	60,000
11	Commissions and other expenses of sale.	11	13,000
12	Income recapture from Form 4797, Part III. See instructions . .	12	10,000
13	Add lines 10, 11, and 12	13	83,000
14	Subtract line 13 from line 5. If zero or less, **stop here.** Do not complete the rest of this form .	14	117,000
15	If the property described on line 1 above was your main home, enter the total of lines 14 and 22 from Form 2119. Otherwise, enter -0-.	15	
16	**Gross profit.** Subtract line 15 from line 14	16	117,000
17	Subtract line 13 from line 6. If zero or less, enter -0- . .	17	0
18	**Contract price.** Add line 7 and line 17	18	150,000

Part II Installment Sale Income. Complete this part for the year of sale and any year you receive a payment or have certain debts you must treat as a payment on installment obligations.

19	Gross profit percentage. Divide line 16 by line 18. For years after the year of sale, see instructions	19	78%
20	**For year of sale only**—Enter amount from line 17 above; otherwise, enter -0-	20	
21	Payments received during year. See instructions. Do not include interest whether stated or unstated	21	10,000
22	Add lines 20 and 21	22	10,000
23	Payments received in prior years. See instructions. Do not include interest whether stated or unstated . . . . [23]		
24	**Installment sale income.** Multiply line 22 by line 19	24	7,800
25	Part of line 24 that is ordinary income under recapture rules. See instructions	25	10,000
26	Subtract line 25 from line 24. Enter here and on Schedule D or Form 4797. See instructions .	26	17,800

Part III Related Party Installment Sale Income. Do not complete if you received the final payment this tax year.

27 Name, address, and taxpayer identifying number of related party ....

28 Did the related party, during this tax year, resell or dispose of the property ("second disposition")? . . . . ☐ Yes ☐ No

29 If the answer to question 28 is "Yes," complete lines 30 through 37 below unless one of the following conditions is met. Check only the box that applies.

a ☐ The second disposition was more than 2 years after the first disposition (other than dispositions of marketable securities). If this box is checked, enter the date of disposition (month, day, year) ▶ [/ /]

b ☐ The first disposition was a sale or exchange of stock to the issuing corporation.

c ☐ The second disposition was an involuntary conversion where the threat of conversion occurred after the first disposition.

d ☐ The second disposition occurred after the death of the original seller or buyer.

e ☐ It can be established to the satisfaction of the Internal Revenue Service that tax avoidance was not a principal purpose for either of the dispositions. If this box is checked, attach an explanation. See instructions.

30	Selling price of property sold by related party	30	
31	Enter contract price from line 18 for year of first sale	31	
32	Enter the **smaller** of line 30 or line 31	32	
33	Total payments received by the end of your 1993 tax year. Add lines 22 and 23	33	
34	Subtract line 33 from line 32. If zero or less, enter -0-	34	
35	Multiply line 34 by the gross profit percentage on line 19 for year of first sale	35	
36	Part of line 35 that is ordinary income under recapture rules. See instructions	36	
37	Subtract line 36 from line 35. Enter here and on Schedule D or Form 4797. See instructions .	37	

For Paperwork Reduction Act Notice, see separate instructions.   Cat. No. 13601R   Form **6252** (1993)

FIGURE 11-1 Reporting Installment Sale Income on Form 6252 (Based on Example 11-21)

11-3. Most individuals use the calendar year as their tax year. What requirement, if any, in the tax law causes this?

11-4. Why is it desirable for a new taxpayer to select an appropriate tax year?

11-5. What restrictions apply to partnerships selecting a tax year?

11-6. Does a similar restriction apply to S corporations? Explain.

11-7. Explain the concept of a 52 to 53-week year.

11-8. How could the 52 to 53-week year prove to be beneficial? Explain.

11-9. Under what circumstances can an individual taxpayer change tax years without IRS approval?

11-10. Is there any instance in which a change in tax years is required? Explain.

11-11. a. In what situations will a tax year cover a period of less than 12 months?
  b. Under what conditions is a taxpayer required to annualize income?
  c. Does annualizing income increase or decrease the taxpayer's tax liability? Explain.

11-12. When is a final tax return due for an individual that uses a calendar year and who dies during the year?

11-13. a. Is it correct to say that businesses with inventories must use the accrual method?
  b. What other restrictions apply to taxpayers who are choosing an overall tax accounting method?
  c. Why is the cash method usually preferred to the accrual method?

11-14. a. Does the term *method of accounting* refer only to overall methods of accounting? Explain.
  b. Does a taxpayer's accounting method affect the aggregate amount of income reported over an extended time period?
  c. How can the use of an accounting method affect the total amount of tax paid over time?

11-15. a. When are expenses deductible by a cash method taxpayer?
  b. Are the rules that determine when interest is deductible by a cash method taxpayer the same as for other expenses?
  c. Is a cash method taxpayer subject to the same rules for depreciable assets as accrual method taxpayers?

11-16. Who may use the completed contract method of reporting income from long-term contracts?

11-17. When is a cash-method taxpayer allowed to deduct deposits?

11-18. What constitutes a payment in determining when a cash-basis taxpayer is entitled to deduct an expense?

11-19. What is meant by economic performance?

11-20. What conditions must be met if the economic performance test is to be waived for an accrual-method taxpayer?

11-21. When is an accrual-method taxpayer permitted to deduct estimated expenses? Explain.

11-22. What is the significance of the *Thor Power Tool Co.* decision?

11-23. a. How are overhead costs treated in determining a manufacturing company's inventory?
  b. Do retailers have a similar rule?
  c. Are these rules the same as for financial accounting? If not, explain.

11-24. What transactions are subject to the long-term contract method of reporting?

11-25. a. What conditions must be met in order to use the installment method?
  b. Why would a taxpayer elect not to use the installment method.

11-26. What is the impact of having the entire gain on an installment sale consist of ordinary income from depreciation recapture?

11-27. What impact does the gifting of an installment obligation have on the donor?

11-28. What treatment is given to an installment sale involving related persons?

11-29. What is the primary impact of the imputed interest rules on installment sales?

11-30. What is meant by applicable federal rate?

11-31. What changes in accounting method can be made without IRS approval?

11-32. **a.** Can the IRS require a taxpayer to change accounting methods?
b. If the IRS requires a change in accounting methods, how will the amount of the change be handled?

11-33. Explain the purpose of the three-year method and the income reconstruction method in computing the tax resulting from a net adjustment due to a change in accounting methods.

11-34. Why is the year 1954 significant in cases where changes in accounting methods are initiated by the IRS?

11-35. Obviously, the six-year method spreads amounts over a longer time span than the three-year method. What is another difference in these two methods of accounting for changes in accounting methods?

11-36. If a taxpayer changes the method of accounting used for financial reporting purposes, must the taxpayer also change his method of accounting for tax purposes?

PROBLEMS

11-37. ***Allowable Taxable Year.*** For each of the following cases, indicate whether the taxpayer has selected an allowable tax year in an initial year. If the year selected is not acceptable, indicate what an acceptable year would be.
a. A corporation selects a January 15 year-end.
b. A corporation selects a March 31 year-end.
c. A corporation selects a year that ends on the last Friday in March.
d. A partnership selects a year that ends on December 31 and has three equal partners whose years end on March 31, April 30, and June 30.
e. An S corporation selects a December 31 year-end.

11-38. ***Change in Accounting Period.*** In which of the following instances is a taxpayer permitted to change accounting periods without IRS approval?
a. A calendar-year taxpayer who wishes to change to a year that ends on the last Friday in December.
b. ABC Partnership has filed its tax return using a fiscal-year ending on March 31 for over 40 years. The partnership wishes to change to a calendar year-end that coincides with its partners' year-end.
c. Iowa Corporation, a newly acquired subsidiary, wishes to change its year-end to coincide with its parent.

11-39. ***Annualization.*** Each of the following cases involves a taxable year of less than 12 months. In which situations is annualization required?
a. A new corporation formed in September elects a calendar year.
b. A calendar-year individual dies on June 15.
c. Jean, who has been using a calendar year, marries Hank, a fiscal-year taxpayer. Soon after the marriage, Jean changes her tax year to coincide with her husband's tax year.
d. A calendar-year corporation liquidates on April 20.

11-40. ***Short Period Return.*** Lavanya, a single taxpayer, is a practicing accountant. She obtains permission to change her tax year from the calendar year to a year ending July 31. Her practice income for the 7 months ending July 31 is $38,000. In addition, Lavanya has $3,000 of interest income and $4,571 of itemized deductions. She is entitled to one exemption. What is her tax for the short period?

11-41. *Cash Basis Expenses.* How much of the following expenses are currently deductible by a cash-basis taxpayer?

a. Medical prescriptions costing $20 paid by credit card (medical expenses already exceed the 7.5% of AGI floor).

b. Prepaid interest (not related to points) of $200 on a residential loan.

c. Taxpayer borrows $300 from the bank to make a charitable contribution. The $300 is paid to the charitable organization prior to the end of the tax year.

d. Taxpayer gives a note to his church indicating an intent to contribute $300.

e. A calendar-year individual mails a check for $200 to his church on December 31. The check is postmarked December 31 and clears the bank on January 4.

11-42. *Economic Performance.* In light of the economic performance requirement, how much is deductible by the following accrual-basis corporate taxpayers in 1994?

a. Camp Corporation sells products with a one-year warranty. In 1994 Camp estimates that the warranty costs on products sold during the year will amount to $80,000. In 1994 Camp performs $38,000 of warranty work on products sold during 1993 and $36,000 of warranty work on products sold in 1994.

b. Data Corporation agrees to pay $10,000 per year for two years to a software developer. The developer has completed all work on the software and delivers the product to Data before the end of 1994.

c. In 1994 Palm Corporation pays $5,000 to a supplier to guarantee delivery of raw materials. The $5,000 is refundable if Palm decides not to acquire the materials.

d. In 1994 North Corporation pays a $1,000 security deposit on space it rents for a new office. In addition, North pays 1994 rent of $18,000. The security deposit is refundable if the property is returned in good condition.

11-43. *Manufacturing Inventory.* Which of the following costs must be included in inventory by a manufacturing company?

a. Raw materials

b. Advertising

c. Payroll taxes

d. Research and experimental costs

e. Factory insurance

f. Repairs to factory equipment

g. Factory utility costs

h. Factory rent

11-44. *Single Pool LIFO.* Prime Corporation begins operations in late 1994. Prime decides to use the single pool LIFO method. Year-end inventories under FIFO are as follows:

1994	$110,000
1995	134,000
1996	125,000

The price index for 1994 is 130%; for 1995, 134%; and 1996, 140%. What are 1995 and 1996 inventories?

11-45. *Installment Sale.* In 1994 Ace Construction Company sells a used crane to Go Construction Company. The crane, which cost $87,000 in 1986, sells for $80,000. Ace has deducted the entire cost of the crane under ACRS depreciation. Ace receives $20,000 down and is to receive $20,000 per year plus 10% interest for four years. Under the Sec. 1245 depreciation recapture rules, the entire gain is taxable as ordinary income. There is no applicable installment obligation. How much of the gain is taxable in 1994? 1995?

11-46. *Installment Sale.* In 1994 Fast Corporation sells land held as an investment. The land, which cost $87,000 in 1990, sells for $180,000. Fast incurs selling expenses of $12,000. The mortgage on the property at the time of the sale is $100,000. The buyer assumes the mortgage, pays $20,000 down, and agrees to pay $20,000 per year for three years plus interest at an acceptable rate to the IRS. How much of the gain is taxable in 1994? 1995?

11-47. *Installment Sale Collections.* During 1994, Bear Corporation collects $240,000 of 1994 installment sales, $150,000 of 1993 installment sales, and $40,000 of 1992 installment sales. Actual 1994 sales total $450,000. The gross profit percentage is 32% for 1994, 33% for 1993, and 35% for 1992. What gross profit must Bear report in 1994?

11-48. *Installment Sale.* On December 31, 1994, Dan sells unlisted stock with a cost of $14,000 for $20,000. Dan collects $5,000 down and is scheduled to receive $5,000 per year for three years plus interest at a rate acceptable to the IRS.

    a. How much gain must Dan recognize in 1994? Assume Dan uses the installment method to report the gain.

    b. In early January 1995, Dan sells the three installments for a total of $13,800. How much gain or loss must Dan recognize from the sale?

11-49. *Repossession.* Liz sells for $50,000 stock not listed on any exchange having a $36,000 adjusted basis. Liz receives $10,000 down and a one-year interest-bearing note for the balance. Liz is unable to collect the balance, and after incurring $1,000 in legal fees, repossesses the stock. When Liz repossesses the stock, it is worth $49,000.

    a. How much gain must Liz recognize in the year of the sale?

    b. How much gain must Liz recognize when she repossesses the stock?

    c. What is the basis of the stock after the repossession?

    d. How would your answers to Parts b and c differ if the property sold is land instead of stock?

    e. What would be the basis of the land?

11-50. *Deferred Payment Sale.* Joe sells land with a $40,000 adjusted basis for $32,000. He incurs selling expenses of $3,000. The buyers pay $8,000 down and agree to pay him $8,000 per year for 3 years plus interest at a rate acceptable to the IRS. Because of the buyers' poor credit rating, the installments are worth only $20,000 ($7,200, $6,600, and $6,200, respectively).

    a. What gain or loss is reported in the year of the sale? Assume Joe is an accrual-basis taxpayer.

    b. How would the answer to Part a change if Joe had instead been a cash-basis taxpayer? Assume the land is worth $32,000.

    c. How would your answer to Part a change if Joe had been a cash-basis taxpayer and the land is worth only $28,000?

    d. What is the tax impact of collecting the installments in Parts a through c?

11-51. *Imputed Interest.* On January 30, 1994, Amy sells land to Bob for a stated price of $200,000. The full $200,000 is payable on January 30, 1996. No interest is stated. Amy, a cash-method taxpayer, purchased the land in 1990 for $130,000.

    a. How much interest income must be reported by Amy on the sale? Assume a 9% rate compounded semiannually. The present value factor is 0.83856.

    b. In what year is the interest reported?

    c. How much gain is reported by Amy on the sale?

    d. In what year is the gain reported?

    e. What is Bob's basis in the land?

11-52. *Change of Accounting Method.* Dana owns a small retail store and is a cash-basis taxpayer. The IRS requires her to change to the accrual method in 1995. Dana's business income for 1995 is $30,000 computed on the accrual method. Her books show the following:

	December 31, 1994	December 31, 1995
Accounts receivable	$ 6,000	$ 5,300
Accounts payable	15,200	11,800
Inventory	12,000	12,400

    a. What adjustment is necessary to Dana's income?

    b. How should Dana report the adjustment?

11-53. *Required Payment.* BCD Partnership has, for many years, had a March 31 year end. The Partnership's net income for the fiscal year ended March 31, 1995 is $400,000. Because of its fiscal year, BCD has $100,000 on deposit with the IRS from 1994.

    a. How much must BCD add to the deposit?

    b. When must BCD make the addition?

    c. Will the partners receive any credit for the deposit? That is, are they permitted to treat the amount like estimated payments?

11-54. *Imputed Interest.* Lorenzo sells land to Jan, an unrelated person, for $500,000. Jan pays $200,000 down and agrees to pay the remaining $300,000 one year after the purchase. No interest is provided for in the contract of sale. Lorenzo had purchased the land for $400,000 several years earlier. Assume the applicable rate is 8% compounded semiannually and the relevant present value factor is 0.92456.

    a. What is Jan's basis in the land?

    b. How much interest income must Lorenzo report and when?

    c. How much gain must Lorenzo report from the sale?

    d. Is the installment method available to Lorenzo?

11-55. *Imputed Interest.* Jane loans $80,000 to John, her son, to permit him to purchase a principal residence. The loan principal is secured by John's residence, but the agreement does not specify any interest. The applicable federal rate for the year is 8%. John's net investment income is $800.

    a. How much interest is imputed on the loan each year?

    b. Assume that the amount of the loan is $125,000. How much interest is imputed on the loan?

    c. Is John allowed to deduct the imputed interest?

    d. What other tax implications are there for the loan?

11-56. *Long-Term Contract.* King Construction Company is engaged in a road construction contract to build a highway over a three-year period. King will receive $11,200,000 for building five miles of highway. King estimates that it will incur $10,000,000 of costs before the contract is completed. As of the end of the first year King incurred $3,000,000 of costs allocated to the contract.

    a. How much income from the contract must King report during the first year?

    b. Assume King incurs an additional $5,000,000 of costs during the second year. How much income is reported during that year?

    c. Assume that King incurs an additional $2,500,000 of costs in the third and final year of the contract. How much does King report during the third year?

    d. Will King receive or pay look-back interest? Explain.

TAX FORM/RETURN PREPARATION PROBLEM

TurboTax **11-57.** Barbara B. Kuhn (social security number 987-65-4321) purchases a fourplex on January 8, 1990 for $175,000. She allocates $25,000 of the cost to the land, and she deducts MACRS depreciation totaling $14,286. Barbara sells the fourplex on January 6, 1993, for $225,000. The buyer assumes the existing mortgage of $180,000, pays $15,000 down, and agrees to pay $15,000 per year for two years plus 12% interest. Barbara incurs selling expenses of $18,000. Complete Form 6252.

CASE STUDY PROBLEMS

11-58. Lavonne just completed medical school and residency. She plans to open her medical practice soon. She is not familiar with the intricacies of accounting methods and periods. On advice of her attorney, she plans to form a professional corporation (a form of organization permitted under the laws of most states that does not have the usual limited liability found with business corporations, but which is taxed as a corporation). She has asked you whether she should elect a fiscal year and whether she should use the cash or accrual method of reporting income. Discuss whether the options are available to her and the implications of available choices.

11-59. Don owns an office building that he purchased several years ago. He purchased the building for $400,000, allocated $280,000 of the purchase price to the structure, and over the years properly deducted $110,000 of depreciation. The depreciation will have to be recaptured as ordinary income on the sale. There is a $90,000 mortgage on the property. Don has an offer to purchase the building from an individual who says he will pay $100,000 down and $100,000 per year for five years. There is no mention of interest. As the mortgage is nonassumable, Don will pay off the mortgage using most of the down payment. Don is age 61, and proceeds from the sale along with a pension from his employer will provide for his retirement. Don plans to retire next year. He currently has a 28% marginal tax rate. Discuss the tax implications of the sale. Is there anything that Don can do to improve his situation?

CASE STUDY PROBLEM—ETHICAL ISSUES

11-60. Troy Tools manufactures over one hundred different hand tools used by mechanics, carpenters, and plumbers. Troy's cost accounting system has always been very simple. The costs allocated to inventory have included only materials, direct labor, and factory overhead. Other overhead costs such as costs of the personnel department, purchasing, payroll, computer services have never been treated as manufacturing overhead even though many of the activities of the departments relate to the manufacturing operations. You are preparing Troy's tax return for the first time and determine that the company is not following the uniform capitalization rules prescribed in the tax law. You have explained to the company's president that there is a problem, and she is reluctant to change accounting methods. She says allocating these costs to the many products the company makes will be a time-consuming and expensive process. She feels that the cost of determining the additional amounts to include in inventory under the uniform capitalization rules will probably be more than the additional tax that the company will pay. What is the appropriate way to handle this situation? (See the section entitled Statements on Responsibilities in Tax Practice in Chapter 2 for a discussion of these issues.)

TAX RESEARCH PROBLEMS

11-61. Eagle and Hill Corporations discuss the terms of a land sale in December 1994, and they agree to a price of $230,000. Eagle wants to use the installment sale method, but is not sure Hill is a reliable borrower. As a result, Eagle requires Hill to place the entire purchase price in escrow to be released in five yearly installments by the escrow agent. Is the installment method available to Eagle?

A partial list of research sources is

- Rev. Rul. 77-294, 1977-2 C.B. 173.
- Rev. Rul. 79-91, 1979-1 C.B. 179.
- *H. O. Williams v. U.S.,* 46 AFTR 1725, 55-1 USTC ¶ 9220 (5th Cir., 1955).

11-62. Texas Corporation disassembles old automobiles for the purpose of reselling their components (i.e., different types of metals, plastics, rubber, and other materials). Texas sells some of the items for scrap, but must pay to dispose of environmentally hazardous plastics and rubber. At year end, Texas Corporation has a difficult time determining the cost of the individual parts that are stacked in piles. In fact, it would be very expensive to even weigh some of the materials on hand. Texas has followed the practice of having two experienced employees estimate the weight of different stacks and then pricing them based on quotes found in trade journals. If Texas must pay to dispose of an item, it is assigned a value of zero. In other words, Texas does not value its inventory using standard FIFO or LIFO methods. Is such a practice acceptable?

A partial list of research sources is

- Reg. Secs. 1.471-2(a) and 1.471-3(d).
- *Morrie Chaitlen,* 1978 PH T.C. Memo ¶ 78,006, 37 TCM 17.
- *Justus & Parker Co.,* 13 BTA 127 (1928).

12

Property Transactions— Nontaxable Exchanges

LEARNING OBJECTIVES

After studying this chapter, you should be able to

1. Understand the tax consequences arising from a like-kind exchange
2. Determine the basis of property received in a like-kind exchange
3. Determine whether gain from an involuntary conversion may be deferred
4. Determine the basis of replacement property in an involuntary conversion
5. Determine when a gain resulting from the sale of a principal residence is deferred and the basis for replacement property
6. Determine when a gain resulting from the sale of a principal residence may be excluded

Key Point

The transactions examined in this chapter override the normal rule that provides for the recognition of realized gains and the recognition of realized losses on property used in a business or held for investment.

Taxpayers who sell or exchange property for an amount greater or less than their basis in that property have realized a gain or loss on the sale or exchange. Almost any transfer of property is treated as a sale or other disposition (see Chapter 5). Thus, unless a specific Code provision provides for nonrecognition treatment, all of the realized gain or loss must be recognized. In some cases, taxpayers may exclude or defer recognition of their realized gain.

This chapter discusses three of the most common transactions that may result in nonrecognition of a realized gain or loss:

- Like-kind exchanges under Sec. 1031 (deferred gain or loss)
- Involuntary conversions under Sec. 1033 (deferred gain)
- Sales of a personal residence under Sec. 1034 (deferred gain) or Sec. 121 (excluded gain)

Nonrecognition of gain treatment for like-kind exchanges, involuntary conversions, and the sale of a residence may be partially justified by the fact that taxpayers may lack the wherewithal to pay the tax despite the existence of a realized gain. For example, a taxpayer who realizes a gain due to an involuntary conversion may have to use the amount received to replace the converted property.

There are, however, several other types of exchanges where the gains and losses are not recognized. These include (1) a corporation's exchange of its stock for property,[1] (2) certain shareholders' transfers of property to a controlled corporation,[2] and (3) certain contributions of property by a partner to a partnership in exchange for a partnership interest.[3]

A typical requirement in a nontaxable exchange is that the taxpayer is required to maintain a continuing investment in comparable property (e.g., a building is exchanged for another building). In essence, a change in form rather than a change in substance occurs.

A transaction that is generally considered to be nontaxable may be taxable in part. In a like-kind exchange, for example, the taxpayer may also receive money or property that is not like-kind property. If non-like-kind property or money are received, the realized gain is taxable to the extent of the sum of the money and the fair market value (FMV) of the non-like-kind property received.[4]

---

[1] Secs. 118(a) and 1032.
[2] Sec. 351(a).
[3] Sec. 721(a).
[4] Sec. 1031(b).

LIKE-KIND EXCHANGES

OBJECTIVE 1
Understand the tax consequences arising from a like-kind exchange

Section 1031(a) provides that "No gain or loss shall be recognized on the exchange of property held for productive use in a trade or business or for investment if such property is exchanged solely for property of like-kind which is to be held either for productive use in a trade or business or for investment."[5]

In a **like-kind exchange,** both the property transferred and the property received must either be held for productive use in the trade or business or for investment.

Example 12-1 ■   Tom owns land used in his trade or business. He exchanges the land for other land, which is to be held for investment. No gain or loss is recognized by Tom because the exchange is a like-kind exchange.   ■

Example 12-2 ■   Dawn's automobile is held only for personal use. She exchanges the automobile, which has a $10,000 basis, for an automobile with a $12,000 FMV. A $2,000 gain is recognized since the automobile is not used in Dawn's trade or business or held for investment. The exchange is not a like-kind exchange because personal-use assets do not qualify as like-kind property.   ■

Real World Example

An exchange or trade of professional football player contracts qualifies as a like-kind exchange. Rev. Rul. 71-137, 1971-1 C.B. 104.

Additional Comment

The mandatory nonrecognition of loss under Sec. 1031 can be avoided by selling the old property in one transaction and buying the new property in a separate, unrelated transaction.

Section 1031 is not an elective provision. If the exchange qualifies as a like-kind exchange, nonrecognition of gain or loss is mandatory. To qualify for like-kind exchange treatment, a direct exchange must occur and the property exchanged must be like-kind. A taxpayer who prefers to recognize a loss on an exchange must structure the transaction to avoid having the exchange qualify as a like-kind exchange.

Like-Kind Property Defined

Character of the Property. To be a nontaxable exchange under Sec. 1031, the property exchanged must be like-kind. The Regulations specify that "the words 'like-kind' have reference to the nature or character of the property and not to its grade or quality."[6] Thus, exchanges of real property qualify even if the properties are dissimiliar.

Example 12-3 ■   Eric owns an apartment building that is held for investment. Eric exchanges the building for a warehouse to be used in his trade or business. The exchange is a like-kind exchange.   ■

Example 12-4 ■   Trail Corporation exchanges improved real estate for unimproved real estate both of which are held for investment. The exchange is a like-kind exchange.[7]   ■

Property Must Be the Same Class. An exchange is not a like-kind exchange when property of one class is exchanged for property of a different kind or class.[8] For

---

[5] Sec. 1031(a).
[6] Reg. Sec. 1.1031(a)-1(b). Section 1031(h) provides an exception for exchanges of real property located in the U.S. and real property located outside the U.S. For transfers on or after July 10, 1989 the like-kind exchange rules do not apply.
[7] Ibid.
[8] Ibid.

example, if real property is exchanged for personal property (or visa versa), no like-kind exchange occurs.[9]

Example 12-5 ∎	Fred, who owns an apartment building as an investment, exchanges the building for a farm that will be used in his business. This is an exchange of like-kind property because both the building and the farm are classified as real property and both properties are either used in business or are held for investment. ∎

Example 12-6 ∎	Gail exchanges an office building with a $400,000 adjusted basis for an airplane with a $580,000 FMV to be used in business. This is not a like-kind exchange because the office building is real property and the airplane is personal property. Gail must recognize a $180,000 ($580,000 − $400,000) gain. ∎

Example 12-7 ∎	Gary exchanges a business truck for another truck that will be used in his business. This is an exchange of like-kind property because both properties are personal property and are used in business. ∎

Property of a Like Class. Prior to the issuance of regulations in 1991, there was some uncertainty as to what kinds of personal property constitute like-kind property. The Regulations provide that personal property of a like class meets the definition of "like kind".[10]

Like class property includes depreciable tangible personal properties if the properties are either within the same General Asset Class or within the same Product Class.[11] Property within a General Asset Class consists of depreciable tangible personal property described in one of the asset classes provided in Rev. Proc. 87-56 for depreciation.[12]. Some of the General Asset Classes are as follows:

- Office furniture, fixtures, and equipment (asset class 00.11)
- Information systems such as computers and peripheral equipment (asset class 00.12)
- Automobiles, taxis (asset class 00.22)
- Buses (asset class 00.23)
- Light general purpose trucks (asset class 00.231)
- Heavy general purpose trucks (asset class 00.242)
- Vessels, barges, tugs, and similar water-transportation equipment except those used in marine construction (asset class 00.28)

For purposes of the like-kind exchange provisions, a single property may not be classified within more than one General Asset Class or within more than one Product Class. Furthermore, property within any General Asset Class may not be classified within a Product Class. A property's General Asset Class or Product Class is determined as of the exchange date.

Example 12-8 ∎	Wint transfers a personal computer used in his trade or business for a printer to be used in his trade or business. The exchange is a like-kind exchange because both properties are in the same General Asset Class (00.11). ∎

---

[9] A 30-year or longer leasehold interest in real estate is treated as real property.
[10] Reg. Sec. 1.1031(a)-2.
[11] Reg. Sec. 1.1031(a)-2(b).
[12] 1987-2 C.B. 674.

Example 12-9 ■   Renee transfers an airplane (asset class 00.21) that she uses in her trade or business for a heavy general purpose truck to use in her trade or business. The properties are not of like class since they are in different General Asset Classes. The heavy general purpose truck is in asset class 00.242. ■

Example 12-9 is taken from the regulations which further state: "Because each of the properties is within a General Asset Class, the properties may not be classified within a Product Class. The airplane and heavy general purpose truck are also not of a like kind. Therefore, the exchange does not qualify for nonrecognition of gain or loss under Sec. 1031."[13]

Property within a Product Class consists of depreciable tangible personal property listed in a 4-digit product class within Division D of the **Standard Industrial Classification (SIC)** codes set forth in the *Standard Industrial Classification Manual.*[14] The Regulations state that an exchange of a grader for a scrapper is an exchange of properties of like class because neither property is within a General Asset class and both properties are listed in the same Product Class (SIC code 3533).[15]

There are no like classes for intangible personal property, nondepreciable personal property, or personal property held for investment. To have a like-kind exchange of property held for investment, the property must be exchanged for like-kind property. To determine if an exchange of intangible personal property is a like-kind exchange, one must consider the type of right involved as well as the underlying property to which the intangible property relates. While an exchange of a copyright for a novel for a copyright on a different novel is a like-kind exchange, the exchange of a copyright on a novel for a copyright on a song is not a like-kind exchange.[16]

Additional Comment

An exchange can be a like-kind exchange for one party to the transaction, but not qualify as a like-kind exchange for the other party.

Non-Like-Kind Property Exchanges. An exchange of inventory or securities does not qualify as a like-kind exchange.[17]

Example 12-10 ■   Antonio, a dealer in farm equipment, exchanges a new combine for other property in the same General Asset Class to be used in Antonio's trade or business. Since the new combine is inventory, the exchange does not qualify as a like-kind exchange. ■

Example 12-11 ■   Nancy owns Able Corporation stock as an investment. Nancy exchanges the stock for antiques to be held as investments. This exchange is taxable because stock does not qualify as like-kind property. ■

In most cases, to qualify as a like-kind exchange of personal property, the property must be nearly identical. For example, livestock of different sexes are not like-kind property.[18] An exchange of gold bullion, held for investment for silver bullion held for investment is not a like-kind exchange. Silver and gold are intrinsically different

---

[13] Reg. Sec. 1.1031(a)-2(b)(7) Ex. 2.
[14] Reg. Sec. 1.1031(a)-2(b)(3).
[15] Reg. Sec. 1.1031(a)-2(b)(7) Ex. 3.
[16] Reg. Sec. 1.1031(a)-2(c)(1).
[17] Sec. 1031(a)(2). An exchange of stock is not a like-kind exchange. However, an exchange of stock is a nontaxable exchange if the exchange is related to a tax-free reorganization.
[18] Sec. 1031(e).

metals and primarily are used in different ways.[19] Currency exchanges are not like-kind exchanges,[20] and the exchange of a partnership interest for an interest in another partnership is not a like-kind exchange.[21]

Exchange of Securities. No gain or loss is recognized on the exchange of common stock for common stock or preferred stock for preferred stock as long as the stock is of the same corporation. However, the exchanges are not considered to be like-kind exchanges.[22] The nontaxable exchange of stock of the same corporation may be between two stockholders or a stockholder and the corporation.[23]

Example 12-12 ■	Kelly owns common stock of Best Corporation. Best issues class B common stock to Kelly in exchange for her common stock. No gain or loss is recognized, because this is an exchange of common stock for common stock in the same corporation. ■

Example 12-13 ■	Shirley owns 100 shares of Top Corporation common stock. The stock has a $40,000 adjusted basis and a $50,000 FMV. Bob owns 100 shares of Star Corporation common stock with a $50,000 FMV. If Shirley and Bob exchange their stock, the exchange is taxable, and Shirley has a $10,000 ($50,000 − $40,000) recognized gain. The exchange is neither a like-kind exchange nor an exchange of stock for stock of the same corporation. ■

A Direct Exchange Must Occur

To qualify as a like-kind exchange, a direct exchange of property must occur.[24] Thus the sale of property and the subsequent purchase of like-kind property does not qualify as a like-kind exchange unless the two transactions are interdependent.

Example 12-14 ■	Karen sells a lathe used in her business to Rashad for an amount greater than the lathe's adjusted basis. After the sale, Karen purchases another lathe from David. The gain is recognized because these two transactions do not qualify as an exchange of like-kind property. ■

A sale and a subsequent purchase may be treated as an exchange if the two transactions are interdependent. The IRS indicates that a nontaxable exchange may exist when the taxpayer sells property to a dealer and then purchases like-kind property from the same dealer.[25]

Key Point

The transfers of property in a three-party exchange must be part of a single, integrated plan. It is important that the taxpayers can show their intent to enter into a like-kind exchange even though contractual interdependence is not necessary to the finding of an exchange.

Three-Party Exchanges

The typical two-party exchange is not always practical. If both parties do not own like-kind property that meets each other's needs, a three-party exchange might be necessary. A three-party exchange is also useful when the taxpayer is willing to exchange property for like-kind property but is not willing to sell the property to a prospective buyer. The taxpayer's unwillingness to sell the property may be motivated

---

[19] Rev. Rul. 82-166, 1982-2 C.B. 190.
[20] Rev. Rul. 74-7, 1974-1 C.B. 198.
[21] Sec. 1031(a)(2).
[22] Sec. 1036(a) and Reg. Sec. 1.1036-1(a). Section 1036 applies even if voting common stock is exchanged for nonvoting stock of the same corporation.
[23] Rev. Rul. 66-248, 1966-2 C.B. 303.
[24] Sec. 1031(a).
[25] Rev. Rul. 61-119, 1961-1 C.B. 395.

by the desire to avoid an immediate tax on a gain resulting from the sale of the property. Therefore, the taxpayer may arrange to have the prospective buyer purchase property from a third party that fulfills his needs. The three-party exchange can be an effective way of allowing the taxpayer to consummate a like-kind exchange.

Example 12-15 ■	Kathy owns a farm in Nebraska, which Dick offers to purchase. Kathy is not willing to sell the farm but is willing to exchange the farm for an apartment complex in Arizona. The complex is available for sale. Dick purchases the apartment complex in Arizona from Allison and transfers it to Kathy in exchange for Kathy's farm. The farm and the apartment complex each have a $900,000 FMV. For Kathy, the transaction qualifies as a like-kind exchange because it is a direct exchange of business real property (the farm) for investment real estate (the apartment complex). For Dick and Allison, the exchange is not a like-kind exchange. ■

In the example above, the exchange is convenient for all the parties. However, it is not always this convenient to execute a three-party exchange. For example, Kathy may want to own an apartment complex in Arizona, but the property she prefers may not be currently available. In this case, a nonsimultaneous exchange may occur.

Additional Comment

The property to be received in the exchange can be identified as late as 45 days after the transfer of the property given up in the exchange.

Nonsimultaneous Exchange. As a result of the Tax Reform Act of 1984, a nonsimultaneous exchange is a like-kind exchange if the exchange is completed within a specified time period. The property to be received in the exchange must be identified within 45 days after the date of the transfer of the property relinquished in the exchange. The replacement property must be received within the earlier of (1) 180 days after the date the taxpayer transfers the property relinquished in the exchange or (2) the due date for filing a return (including extensions) for the year in which the transfer of the relinquished property occurs.[26]

Example 12-16 ■	On May 5, 1994, Joel transfers property to Lauren, who transfers cash to an escrow agent. The escrow agent is to purchase suitable like-kind property for Joel. Joel does not have actual or constructive receipt of the cash during the delayed period. To be a like-kind exchange for Joel, the suitable like-kind property must be identified by June 19, 1994 (45 days after the transfer) and Joel must receive the property by November 1, 1994 (180 days after the transfer). ■

Example 12-17 ■	Assume the same facts as Example 12-16 except that the transfer by Joel occurs on November 10, 1994. To be a like-kind exchange for Joel, the suitable like-kind property must be identified by December 25, 1994, and Joel must receive the property by April 15, 1995, unless Joel files an automatic four-month extension for the filing of his return (i.e., the due date is extended until August 15, 1995). In such a case, the property must be received no later than 180 days following the transfer of the property relinquished in the exchange, or by May 8, 1995 (i.e., 180 days after November 10, 1994). ■

Before 1984, the courts generally permitted taxpayers to engage in non-simultaneous exchanges that qualified as like-kind exchanges.[27] In the late 1960s, the

---

[26] Secs. 1031(a)(3)(A) and (B).

[27] See, for example, *James Alderson* v. *CIR,* 11 AFTR 2d 1529, 63-2 USTC ¶ 9499 (9th Cir., 1963); *Dick R. Hayden* v. *U.S.,* 50 AFTR 2d 82-5570, 82-2 USTC ¶ 9604 (D.C. Wyo., 1981) and *Bruce Starker* v. *U.S.,* 35 AFTR 2d 75-1550, 75-1 USTC ¶ 9443 (D.C. Ore., 1975).

taxpayer (Mr. T.J. Starker) and Crown Zellerbach Corporation took two years to complete an exchange. Mr. Starker deeded his interest in timberland to Crown Zellerbach on May 31, 1967, and Crown Zellerbach subsequently obtained 12 parcels of property for Mr. Starker. Except for two parcels of property transferred to Mr. Starker's daughter, the nonsimultaneous exchange was held to be tax free.[28] The effect of judicial decisions granting favorable treatment for nonsimultaneous exchanges was substantially reduced as a result of the Tax Reform Act of 1984.

Receipt of Boot

Typical Misconception

In calculating the amount of gain to be recognized when boot is received, it is important not to apply the financial accounting principles that utilize a proportionate approach.

Taxpayers who want to exchange property do not always own property of equal value. To complete the exchange, non-like-kind property or money may be given or received. Cash and non-like-kind property constitute **boot.**

Gain is recognized to the extent of the boot received. However, the amount of recognized gain is limited to the amount of the taxpayer's realized gain.[29] In effect, the realized gain serves as a ceiling for the amount of the recognized gain.

Example 12-18 ■

Mario exchanges business equipment with a $50,000 adjusted basis for $10,000 cash and business equipment with a $65,000 FMV. The realized gain is $25,000 ($75,000 − $50,000). Since the $10,000 of boot received is less than the $25,000 of realized gain, the recognized gain is $10,000. ■

Example 12-19 ■

Typical Misconception

It is possible to erroneously assume that the receipt of boot causes the recognition of loss.

Mary exchanges business equipment with a $70,000 adjusted basis for $20,000 cash and business equipment with a $65,000 FMV. Her realized gain is $15,000 ($85,000 − $70,000). Since the $20,000 of boot received is more than the $15,000 of realized gain, only $15,000 of gain is recognized. ■

The receipt of boot as part of a nontaxable exchange does not cause a realized loss to be recognized.[30]

Example 12-20 ■

Matt owns a farm with a $500,000 basis and a $420,000 FMV. Phil owns a duplex with a $300,000 FMV. Matt exchanges the farm for Phil's duplex and $120,000 cash. Matt's realized loss of $80,000 ([$300,000 + $120,000] − [$500,000]) is not recognized. Matt's basis for the duplex is $380,000 ($500,000 − $120,000). Basis considerations are discussed in a separate section of this chapter. ■

Taxing part or all of the gain when cash is received in like-kind exchanges is consistent with the wherewithal-to-pay concept. However, boot may not always be in the form of a liquid asset. If non-like-kind property other than cash is received as boot, the amount of the boot is the property's FMV.

Example 12-21 ■

Jane exchanges land held as an investment with a $70,000 basis for other land with a $100,000 FMV and a motorcycle with a $2,000 FMV. The acquired land is to be held for investment, and the motorcycle is for personal use. Personal-use property is non-like-kind property and is classified as boot. The realized gain is $32,000 ([$100,000 + $2,000] − $70,000). The amount of boot received is equal to the FMV of the motorcycle. The recognized gain is $2,000, the lesser of the amount of boot received ($2,000) or the realized gain ($32,000). ■

[28] *T. J. Starker* v. *U.S.,* 44 AFTR 2d 79-5525, 79-2 USTC ¶ 9541 (9th Cir., 1979).
[29] Sec. 1031(b).
[30] Sec. 1031(c).

Assume the same facts in Example 12-21 except that Jane uses the motorcycle in a business. The motorcycle is boot, and a $2,000 gain is still recognized because the exchange of real property for personal property is not a like-kind exchange. ■

Property Transfers Involving Liabilities. If a liability is assumed (or the property is taken "subject to" a liability), the amount of the liability is considered as money received by the taxpayer on the exchange.[31] One who assumes the debt or takes the property subject to a liability is treated as having paid cash, while the party that is relieved of the debt is treated as having received cash. If each party assumes a liability of the other party, only the net liability given or received is treated as boot.[32]

Mary exchanges land used in her business for Doug's building, which has a $450,000 FMV. Mary's basis in the land is $400,000, and the land is subject to a liability of $100,000, which Doug assumes. Mary's realized gain is $150,000 ([$450,000 + $100,000] − $400,000). Since assumption of the $100,000 liability is treated as boot, Mary recognizes a $100,000 gain. ■

Matt owns an office building with a $700,000 basis, which is subject to a liability of $200,000. Susan owns an apartment complex with a $900,000 FMV, which is subject to a $150,000 liability. Matt and Susan exchange buildings. Matt's realized gain is $250,000 ([$900,000 + $200,000] − [$700,000 + $150,000]). Matt receives boot of $50,000 ($200,000 − $150,000) and recognizes a $50,000 gain. ■

Basis of Property Received

Like-Kind Property Received. The basis of property received in a nontaxable exchange is equal to the adjusted basis of the property exchanged increased by gain recognized and reduced by any boot received or loss that is recognized on the exchange.[33]

Basis of property received in a non-taxable exchange	=	Basis of property exchanged	−	Boot received	+	Gain recognized	−	Loss recognized[34]

Chuck, who is in the business of racing horses, exchanges a racehorse with a $30,000 basis for $10,000 cash and a trotter with an $80,000 FMV. Chuck's realized gain is $60,000 ([$80,000 + $10,000] − $30,000), and $10,000 of the gain is recognized because the boot received ($10,000) is less than the realized gain ($60,000). Chuck's basis for the replacement property (i.e., the trotter) is $30,000 ($30,000 basis of property exchanged − $10,000 of boot received + $10,000 of gain recognized). ■

The basis of the like-kind property received can also be computed by subtracting the unrecognized gain from its FMV or by adding the unrecognized loss to its FMV.

---

[31] Sec. 1031(d). If a liability is assumed, the taxpayer agrees to pay the debt. If property is taken subject to the liability, the taxpayer is responsible for the debt only to the extent that the property could be used to pay the debt.

[32] Reg. Sec. 1.1031(b)-1(c).

[33] Sec. 1031(d).

[34] A loss is recognized only when the taxpayer transfers boot with a basis greater than its FMV. Transfers of non-like-kind property (i.e. boot) are discussed in a separate section of this chapter.

Chuck's $30,000 basis for the trotter in Example 12-25 may be computed by subtracting the $50,000 of unrecognized gain from the $80,000 FMV.

Example 12-26 ■

Pam, who operates a circus, exchanges an elephant with a $15,000 basis for $3,000 cash and a tiger with a $10,000 FMV. The $2,000 realized loss ([$10,000 + $3,000] − $15,000) is not recognized. Pam's basis for the replacement property (i.e., the tiger) is $12,000 ($15,000 basis of property exchanged − $3,000 boot received). ■

Key Point

The basis adjustment is the mechanism that insures that the gain or loss is being temporarily postponed rather than permanently excluded.

As indicated earlier, realized gains and losses resulting from nontaxable exchanges are deferred. This deferral is reflected in the basis of property received and is illustrated in the two preceding examples. In Example 12-25, the $50,000 ($60,000 − $10,000) unrecognized gain may be recognized when the trotter is sold or exchanged in a taxable transaction, because the basis of the replacement property is less than its FMV by the amount of the deferred gain. For example, if the trotter is sold in a taxable transaction for its $80,000 FMV, the $50,000 ($80,000 − $30,000 basis) of previously unrecognized gain would be recognized. In Example 12-26, the $2,000 unrecognized loss is reflected in the basis of the tiger. If Pam sells the tiger for its $10,000 FMV, a $2,000 loss ($10,000 − $12,000 basis) is recognized.

If more than one item of like-kind property is received, the basis is allocated among the properties in proportion to their relative FMVs on the date of the exchange.

Example 12-27 ■

Saul, who operates a zoo, exchanges a boa constrictor with a $300 basis for a python with a $400 FMV and an anaconda with a $600 FMV. The $700 realized gain ([$400 + $600] − $300) is not recognized. The total bases of the properties received is $300. This amount is allocated to the properties (i.e., the python and the anaconda) based upon their relative FMVs. Saul's basis for the python is $120 ([$400 ÷ $1,000] × $300), and the basis for the anaconda is $180 ([$600 ÷ $1,000] × $300). ■

Non-Like-Kind Property Received. The basis of non-like-kind property received is "an amount equivalent to its FMV at the date of the exchange."[35]

Example 12-28 ■

Steve exchanges a punch press with a $20,000 adjusted basis for a press brake with a $50,000 FMV and $5,000 of marketable securities. Steve's realized gain is $35,000 ([$50,000 + $5,000] − $20,000), and $5,000 of the realized gain is recognized due to the receipt of boot. Steve's basis for the marketable securities is $5,000, and the basis for the press brake is $20,000 ($20,000 basis of property exchanged − $5,000 boot received + $5,000 gain recognized). ■

Exchanges Between Related Parties

Additional Comment

The running of the two-year holding period is suspended during any period in which the property holder's risk of loss is substantially diminished.

Prior to the Revenue Reconciliation Act of 1989, related taxpayers could often utilize the like-kind exchange provisions to lower taxes since the tax basis for the property received is determined by the basis of the property exchanged. Related taxpayers could take advantage of the shift in tax basis to transfer a gain on a subsequent sale to a related party.[36] However, under current law exchanges of property between related parties are not like-kind exchanges if either party disposes of the property within two years of the exchange. Any gain resulting from the original exchange is recognized in

[35] Reg. Sec. 1.1031(d)-1(c).

[36] The definition of related parties is the same as those for Sec. 267(a) which is discussed in Chapter 6 and includes brothers, sisters, parents, children, and corporations where the taxpayer owns at least 50% in value, et. al. See Sec. 1031(f)(3).

the year of the subsequent disposition.[37] Dispositions due to death, involuntary conversion, or for non-tax avoidance purposes are disregarded.[38]

Example 12-29 ■   Melon Corporation, which is 100% owned by Linda, owns land with a basis of $200,000 that is held for investment. The land's FMV is $900,000 and Rick wants to purchase the land. Linda owns an office building with a basis of $750,000 and a FMV of $900,000. Instead of selling the land to Rick, Melon Corporation exchanges the land for Linda's office building in December, 1993. Two months later, Linda sells the land to Rick for $900,000. The exchange of the land for the office building is not a like-kind exchange since one of the related parties disposes of the property within two years of the exchange. In 1994, Melon's recognized gain on the exchange of the land is $700,000 ($900,000 − $200,000) and Linda's recognized gain on the exchange of the office building is $150,000 ($900,000 − $750,000). Since Linda's basis for the land is now $900,000, no gain is recognized on the sale of the land to Rick.   ■

If the parties in Example 12-29 were not related, a like-kind exchange occurs in 1994 and Linda's gain on the sale of the land to Rick would be $150,000 ($900,000 − $750,000). Of course, the exchange is not a like-kind exchange if Linda does not hold the land for investment or for use in her trade or business after receiving it from Melon.

Transfer of Non-Like-Kind Property

In all of the preceding examples that include a transfer of boot, the transferor (i.e., the taxpayer) received boot. If the taxpayer transfers non-like-kind property, gain or loss equal to the difference between the FMV and the adjusted basis of the non-like-kind property surrendered must be recognized.

Example 12-30 ■   Shirley exchanges land with a $30,000 basis and marketable securities with a $10,000 basis to David for land with a $60,000 FMV in a transaction that otherwise qualifies as a like-kind exchange. The FMV of the marketable securities and the land surrendered by Shirley is $14,000 and $46,000 respectively. Since the non-like-kind property that Shirley transfers has a FMV in excess of its basis, she recognizes $4,000 ($14,000 − $10,000) of gain. Shirley's basis for the land received is $44,000 ($30,000 + $10,000 + $4,000), which is the basis of both assets exchanged plus the gain recognized on the exchange.   ■

Example 12-31 ■   Paul exchanges timberland held as an investment for undeveloped land with a $200,000 FMV. Paul's basis for the timberland is $125,000. His tractor with a $6,000 basis and a $4,000 FMV is also transferred. Since the non-like-kind property (i.e., the tractor) that Paul transfers has a FMV of less than its basis, he recognizes a $2,000 ($4,000 − $6,000) loss. Paul's basis for the undeveloped land is $129,000 ($125,000 + $6,000 − $2,000).   ■

Key Point

A taxpayer who exchanges like-kind property and non-like-kind property is actually making two exchanges.

In Example 12-31, Paul recognizes a loss on the non-like-kind property that he surrenders, despite receiving property in the aggregate with a FMV in excess of the total adjusted basis of the transferred assets. Paul is actually making two exchanges. His exchange of timberland with a basis of $125,000 for undeveloped land with a $196,000 FMV is a like-kind exchange, but his exchange of the tractor with a basis of

---

[37] Sec. 1031(f)(1)(C).
[38] Sec. 1031(f)(1)(C)(2).

$6,000 for undeveloped land with a $4,000 FMV is a taxable exchange. In Example 12-32, Ed also makes two exchanges. He has a realized and recognized gain as well as a realized but unrecognized loss.

Example 12-32 ■   Ed owns equipment used in business with a $20,000 adjusted basis and a $15,000 FMV and marketable securities with a $10,000 basis and an $18,000 FMV. Ed exchanges the marketable securities and the equipment for business equipment in the same General Asset Class with a $33,000 FMV. While the net realized gain is $3,000 ($33,000 − [$20,000 + $10,000]), Ed recognizes an $8,000 gain because he has transferred non-like-kind property with a $10,000 basis and an $18,000 FMV. The $5,000 realized loss on the transfer of equipment is not recognized due to the nonrecognition of gain or loss rules of Sec. 1031. Ed's basis for the equipment received is $38,000 ($20,000 + $10,000 + $8,000). ■

Additional Comment

The holding period is relevant only when the asset is a capital asset or a Sec. 1231 asset.

Holding Period for Property Received

Like-Kind Property. The holding period of like-kind property received in a non-taxable exchange includes the holding period of the property exchanged if the like-kind property surrendered is a capital asset or an asset that is Sec. 1231 property. In essence, the holding period of the property exchanged carries over to the holding period of the like-kind property received.[39] The rule regarding the holding period carryover is consistent with the notion of a continuing investment in the underlying property that has been transferred.

Boot. The holding period for the boot property received begins the day after the date of the exchange.[40]

Example 12-33 ■   Mario owns a Van Gogh painting acquired on May 1, 1985, as an investment. He exchanges the painting on April 10, 1994, for a Picasso sculpture and marketable securities. The holding period for the sculpture begins on May 1, 1985, and the holding period for the marketable securities starts on April 11, 1994. ■

The like-kind exchange provisions are summarized in Topic Review 12-1.

INVOLUNTARY CONVERSIONS

OBJECTIVE 3
Determine whether gain from an involuntary conversion may be deferred

Key Point

Unlike the like-kind exchange provisions which are mandatory, the involuntary conversion provisions are elective with respect to gains.

Taxpayers who realize a gain due to the involuntary conversion of property may elect to defer recognition of the entire gain if qualifying replacement property is acquired within a specified time period at a cost equal to or greater than the amount realized from the involuntary conversion. No gain is recognized if the property is converted "into property similar or related in service or use to the property so converted."[41]

The opportunity provided in Sec. 1033 to defer recognition of the gain reflects the fact that the taxpayer maintains a continuing investment and may lack the wherewithal to pay the tax on the gain that would otherwise be recognized. Furthermore, the involuntary conversion is beyond the taxpayer's control.

[39] Sec. 1223(1) and Reg. Sec. 1.1223-1(a).
[40] Sec. 1223 and Reg. Sec. 1.1223-1(a).
[41] Sec. 1033(a)(1).

TOPIC REVIEW 12-1

Section 1031—Like-Kind Exchanges
1. Gains and losses are not recognized for like-kind exchanges.
2. Nonrecognition of gains and losses is mandatory if the exchange is a like-kind exchange.
3. Section 1031 applies to exchanges of property used in a trade or business or held for investment.
4. Property exchanged and received must be like-kind.
5. Subject to certain time constraints, a nonsimultaneous exchange may qualify as a like-kind exchange.
6. Some gain may be recognized if the taxpayer receives or gives non-like-kind/ property (boot) in an otherwise like-kind exchange.
7. A loss may be recognized if the taxpayer transfers non-like-kind property (boot) in an otherwise like-kind exchange.
8. The basis of property received in an exchange is the basis of the property exchanged less the boot received plus the gain recognized less any loss recognized.
9. The nonrecognized gain or loss is deferred.
10. The holding period of like-kind property received includes the holding period of the property exchanged.

Note that the gain is deferred, not excluded. The basis of the replacement property is the property's cost reduced by the amount of gain that is deferred. This is similar to the treatment of a like-kind exchange.

Example 12-34 ■

Additional Comment

Property involved in an involuntary conversion need not be used in a trade or business or held for investment to qualify for the deferral of gain.

Lenea's warehouse with a $500,000 basis is destroyed by a hurricane. She collects $650,000 from the insurance company and purchases a new warehouse for $720,000. Lenea may elect to defer recognition of the $150,000 gain ($650,000 − $500,000). If the election is made, the basis of the new warehouse is $570,000 ($720,000 − $150,000). The $150,000 gain is merely deferred rather than excluded, because an immediate sale of the replacement property at its $720,000 FMV results in a recognized gain equal to the deferred gain on the involuntarily converted property. For example, if the new warehouse is sold for $720,000, the recognized gain is $150,000 ($720,000 − $570,000). ■

Typical Misconception

Occasionally there is a failure to realize that Sec. 1033 applies only to gains and not losses.

Section 1033 does not apply to losses realized from an involuntary conversion. A taxpayer may not elect to defer recognition of a loss resulting from an involuntary conversion.

Example 12-35 ■

Barry's offshore drilling rig with an $800,000 basis is destroyed by a typhoon. He collects $700,000 from the insurance company and purchases a new drilling rig for $760,000. The $100,000 loss ($700,000 − $800,000) is recognized, and the basis of the new drilling rig is its purchase price of $760,000. ■

Involuntary Conversion Defined

Additional Comment

Typically, an involuntary conversion consists of either a casualty or a condemnation.

For Sec. 1033 to apply, property must be compulsorily or involuntarily converted into money or other property. An **involuntary conversion** may be due to theft, seizure, requisition, condemnation, or destruction of the property. The destruction of the property may be complete or partial.[42] For purposes of Sec. 1033, destruction of property does not have to meet the "suddenness" test if the cause of destruction otherwise falls within the general concept of a casualty.[43]

An involuntary conversion occurs when a governmental unit exercises its power of eminent domain to acquire the taxpayer's property without the taxpayer's consent. Furthermore, the threat or imminence of requisition or condemnation of property may permit a taxpayer to defer the recognition of gain from the sale or exchange of property under the involuntary conversion rules. Taxpayers who transfer property due to such a threat must be careful to confirm the fact that a decision to acquire their property for public use has been made.[44] Written confirmation of potential condemnation is particularly helpful.[45]

Example 12-36 ■   Bruce owns an automobile dealership near a state university campus. On a number of occasions, the president of the university has expressed an interest in acquiring Bruce's property for additional parking space. The president is not certain about the availability of funds for the purchase, and the university is reluctant to have the property condemned for its use. Based on the university's interest in the property, Bruce sells the property to the Jet Corporation. The threat or imminence of conversion does not exist merely because the property is being considered for acquisition. The sale does not constitute an involuntary conversion.[46]   ■

Threat of Condemnation. If a threat of condemnation exists and the taxpayer has reasonable grounds to believe that the property will be condemned, Sec. 1033 applies even if the taxpayer sells the property to an entity other than the governmental unit that is threatening to condemn the property.[47]

Example 12-37 ■   At its regular meeting on Tuesday night, the city commission authorized the city attorney to start the process of condemning two lots owned by Beth for use as a public park. On Wednesday afternoon, Beth sells the two lots to Marty at a gain. The sale of property to Marty is an involuntary conversion, and Beth may elect to defer recognition of the gain.   ■

Real World Example

Because of mounting losses and declining property values, a taxpayer decided to burn down his building in order to collect the fire insurance proceeds. Although the building was converted into money (insurance proceeds) as a result of its destruction, this conversion was not "involuntary" within the meaning of Sec. 1033. Rev. Rul. 82-74, 1982-1 C.B. 110.

Conversion Must Be Involuntary. The conversion must be involuntary. For example, an involuntary conversion does not occur when a taxpayer pays someone to set fire to his building.[48] An involuntary conversion does not occur when a taxpayer, who is developing a subdivision, voluntarily reserves property for a school site, which is later sold to the school district under condemnation proceedings. In this situation, to receive zoning approval for development of the subdivision, the taxpayer was required to reserve property for a school site.[49]

While the typical involuntary conversion generally results from a casualty or condemnation, Sec. 1033 provides that certain transactions involving livestock are to be treated as involuntary conversions.[50] For example, the destruction or sale of livestock because of disease is an involuntary conversion.

---

[42] Reg. Sec. 1.1033(a)-1.

[43] Rev. Rul. 59-102, 1959-1 C.B. 200.

[44] Rev. Rul. 63-221, 1963-2 C.B. 332, and *Joseph P. Balistrieri*, 1979 PH T.C. Memo ¶ 79,115, 38 TCM 526.

[45] Rev. Rul. 63-221, 1963-2 C.B. 332.

[46] *Forest City Chevrolet*, 1977 PH T.C. Memo ¶ 77,187, 36 TCM 768.

[47] Rev. Rul. 81-180, 1981-2 C.B. 161, and *Creative Solutions, Inc. v. U.S.*, 12 AFTR 2d 5229, 1963-2 USTC ¶ 9615 (5th Cir., 1963).

[48] Rev. Rul. 82-74, 1982-1 C.B. 110.

[49] Rev. Rul. 69-654, 1969-2 C.B. 162.

[50] Secs. 1033(d) and (e). If a taxpayer sells or exchanges more livestock than normal because of a drought, the sale or exchange of the excess amount is treated as an involuntary conversion. The livestock must be other than poultry and be held by the taxpayer for draft, breeding, or dairy purposes.

Tax Treatment of Gain Due to Involuntary Conversion into Boot

Gain may be deferred if the property is involuntarily converted into money or property that is not similar or related in service or use to the converted property.[51] The taxpayer must make a proper replacement of the converted property within a specific time period and elect to defer the gain.

Realized Gain. The taxpayer's realized gain is the excess of the amount received due to the involuntary conversion over the adjusted basis of the property converted. The total award or proceeds received are reduced by expenses incurred to determine the amount realized (e.g., attorney's fees incurred in connection with determining the settlement to be received from a condemnation). If the payment of the award or proceeds is delayed, any amounts paid as interest are not included in determining the amount realized.[52] Amounts received as interest on an award for property condemned are taxed as ordinary income even if the interest is paid by a state or political subdivision.[53]

Example 12-38 ■	Richard's property with a $100,000 basis is condemned by the city of Phoenix. Richard receives a $190,000 award and pays $1,000 legal expenses for representation at the condemnation proceedings and $800 for an appraisal of the property. The amount realized is $188,200 ($190,000 − [$1,000 + $800]). The gain realized is $88,200 ($188,200 − $100,000). Part or all of the realized gain may be deferred if the requirements of Sec. 1033 are satisfied and an election is made to defer the gain. ■

Additional Comment

*The gain recognized is limited to the lesser of:
(1) the gain realized, or
(2) the excess of the amount realized from the conversion over the cost of the qualified replacement property.*

Gain Recognized. To defer the entire gain, the cost of the replacement property must be equal to or greater than the amount realized from the involuntary conversion. If the replacement property is purchased for an amount less than the amount realized, that portion of the realized gain that is equal to the excess of the amount realized from the conversion over the cost of the replacement property must be recognized.[54]

Example 12-39 ■	Bob owns a restaurant with a $200,000 basis. The restaurant is destroyed by fire, and he receives $300,000 from the insurance company. Bob's realized gain is $100,000 ($300,000 − $200,000). He purchases another restaurant for $275,000. Bob may elect to defer $75,000 of the gain under Sec. 1033; $25,000 ($300,000 − $275,000) of Bob's gain must be recognized because he failed to reinvest all of the $300,000 insurance proceeds in a suitable replacement property. ■

Example 12-40 ■	Stacey owns a racehorse with a $450,000 basis which is used for breeding purposes. The racehorse is killed by lightning, and she collects $800,000 from the insurance company. Stacey's realized gain is $350,000 ($800,000 − $450,000). She purchases another racehorse for $430,000. The entire $350,000 of gain is recognized, since the cost of the replacement property is $370,000 ($800,000 − $430,000) less than the amount realized from the involuntary conversion. ■

---

[51] Sec. 1033(a)(2).
[52] *Flushingside Realty & Construction Co.*, 1943 PH T.C. Memo ¶ 43,286, 2 TCM 259.
[53] *Spencer D. Stewart* v. *CIR.*, 52 AFTR 2d 83-5885, 83-2 USTC ¶ 9573 (9th Cir., 1983).
[54] Sec. 1033(a)(2)(A).

OBJECTIVE 4

Determine the basis of replacement property in an involuntary conversion

Example 12-41 ■

Real World Example

Seven of the 18 holes of a golf course were condemned. Although 11 holes remained, it was anticipated that the course would have to be reduced to 9 holes. Therefore, $21,000 of the condemnation award was allocated to severance damages to reflect the decline in value of the two lost holes. Marco S. Marinello Associates, Inc., 1975 PH T.C. Memo ¶ 75,078, 34 TCM 392.

Example 12-42 ■

Basis of Replacement Property. If replacement property is purchased, the basis of the replacement property is its cost less any deferred gain. If the taxpayer elects to defer the gain, the holding period of the replacement property includes the holding period of the converted property.[55]

Tracy owns a yacht that is held for personal use which has a $20,000 basis. The yacht is destroyed by a storm, and Tracy collects $24,000 from the insurance company. She purchases a new yacht to be held for personal use for $35,000 and elects to defer the $4,000 ($24,000 − $20,000) gain. The basis of the new yacht is $31,000 ($35,000 − $4,000). The holding period for the new yacht includes the holding period of the yacht that was destroyed. ■

Severance Damages. If a portion of the taxpayer's property is condemned, the taxpayer may receive **severance damages** as compensation for a decline in the value of the retained property. For example, if access to the retained property becomes difficult or if the property is exposed to greater damage from flooding or erosion, its value may decline.

The IRS considers severance damages to be "analogous to the proceeds of property insurance; they represent compensation for damages to the property."[56] Amounts received as severance damages reduce the basis of the retained property, and any amount received in excess of the property's basis is treated as gain.[57]

Cindy owns a 500-acre farm with a $200 basis per acre (a total of $100,000). The state condemns 10 acres across the northwest corner of her farm to build a major highway. Cindy receives a condemnation award of $500 per acre for the 10 acres. The highway separates the farm into a 25-acre tract and a 465-acre tract. Since her ability to efficiently use the 25-acre tract for farming is reduced because of the highway, the state pays additional severance damages of $90 per acre for the 25 acres. Cindy's gain realized from the condemnation of the 10 acres is $3,000 ($5,000 − [$200 × 10 acres]). The $2,250 ($90 × 25 acres) of severance damages reduce the basis of the 25-acre tract from $5,000 ($200 × 25 acres) to $2,750 ([$200 × 25] − $2,250). The reduction in basis is applied solely to the 25 acres because of its decline in value as farmland. ■

The Sec. 1033 provisions concerning nonrecognition of gain may apply to severance damages. For instance, if severance damages are used to restore the retained property, only that portion of severance damages not spent for restoration reduces the basis of the retained property. A taxpayer who uses severance damages to purchase adjacent farmland to replace the portion of the farm condemned may utilize Sec. 1033 to defer a gain due to the receipt of the severance damages.[58]

Tax Treatment of Gain Due to an Involuntary Conversion Directly into Similar Property

Additional Comment

The direct conversion of property into similar property is encountered only infrequently.

Nonrecognition of gain is mandatory if property is involuntarily converted directly into similar property rather than money.[59] The basis of the replacement property is

---

[55] Sec. 1223(1)(A).
[56] Rev. Rul. 53-271, 1953-2 C.B. 36.
[57] Rev. Rul. 68-37, 1968-1 C.B. 359.
[58] Rev. Ruls. 69-240, 1969-1 C.B. 199, 73-35, 1973-1 C.B. 367, and 83-49, 1983-1 C.B. 191.
[59] Sec. 1033(a).

the same as the basis of the converted property, and the holding period for the converted property carries over to the replacement property.[60]

Example 12-43 ∎	Ed's farm with a $200,000 basis is condemned by the state. The state transfers other farmland with a $280,000 FMV to Ed. The $80,000 ($280,000 − $200,000) of realized gain is not recognized, and the basis of the farmland received is $200,000. Nonrecognition of gain is mandatory. Direct conversions are rarely encountered because the usual payment procedure for insurance companies and governmental agencies involves a payment of cash. ∎

Replacement Property

To qualify for nonrecognition of gain due to an involuntary conversion, the taxpayer must acquire qualified replacement property. With some exceptions, the **replacement property** must be "similar or related in service or use to the property so converted."[61]

Real World Example

The replacement of bowling alleys destroyed in a fire with a recreational billiards center did not pass the functional-use test. Rev. Rul. 76-319, 1976-2 C.B. 242.

Functional Use Test. The *functional-use test* is more restrictive than the like-kind test. To be considered similar or related in service or use, the replacement property must be functionally the same as the converted property. For example, the exchange of a business building for land used in business qualifies as a like-kind exchange. Replacing a building with land does not qualify as replacement property under the involuntary conversion rules. The building must be replaced with a building that is functionally the same as the converted building.

Example 12-44 ∎ **Real World Example** *A nursery with its trees and shrubs was condemned, and the taxpayer replaced the condemned property with land and greenhouses. The replacement was considered to have been made with like-kind property. Evert Asjes, Jr., 74 T.C. 1005 (1980).*	Julie owns a movie theater that is destroyed by fire. She uses the insurance proceeds to purchase a skating rink. The converted property has not been replaced with property that is similar or related in service or use. The election to defer gain under Sec. 1033 is not available. ∎

Replacement with Like-Kind Property. If real property held for productive use in a trade or business or for investment is condemned, a proper replacement may be made by acquiring like-kind property.[62] This exception to the functional use test applies only to real property used in a trade or business or held for investment but not to real property held as inventory.

Example 12-45 ∎	Ken owns a building used in his business that is condemned by the state to widen a highway. He uses the proceeds to purchase land to be held for investment. The land is a qualified replacement property because the condemned building is real property used in a trade or business, and the like-kind exchange rule may be applied to the condemnation. ∎

Example 12-46 ∎	Assume the same facts as in Example 12-45 except that the building is destroyed by a violent windstorm. Ken's purchase of the investment land is not qualified replacement property because the more flexible like-kind exchange rules apply only to condemnations. He must purchase property with the same functional use as the business building. ∎

[60] Sec. 1033(b).

[61] Secs. 1033(a)(2)(A) and 1033(f). The replacement of property requirement is modified when proceeds from the involuntary conversion of livestock may not be reinvested in property similar or related in use to the converted livestock because of soil contamination or other environmental contamination. Sec. 1033(f) permits the livestock to be replaced with other property, including real property, used for farming purposes.

[62] Sec. 1033(g)(1).

Taxpayer-Use Test. The *taxpayer-use test* applies to the involuntary conversion of rental property owned by an investor. This test permits greater flexibility than the functional use test. The principal requirement is that the owner-investor must lease out the replacement property that is acquired. However, the lessee is not required to use the leased property for the same functional use.[63]

Example 12-47 ■

Real World Example

Taxpayer owned land and a warehouse held for rental purposes. Upon the condemnation of this property, taxpayer invested the proceeds in a gas station on land already owned by the taxpayer which was also held for rental purposes. The taxpayer-use test applied, and the taxpayer was able to defer the gain. Rev. Rul. 71-41, 1971-1 C.B. 223.

Sally owns an apartment complex that is rented to college students. The apartment complex is destroyed by fire. She uses the insurance proceeds to purchase a medical building that is leased to physicians. This is a qualified replacement property by Sally, and the gain, if any, may be deferred if an election is made under Sec. 1033. ■

Obtaining Replacement Property

The general rule is that the taxpayer must purchase the replacement property.[64] Taxpayers may purchase replacement property indirectly by purchasing control (i.e., 80% or more of the stock) of a corporation that owns the replacement property.[65] However, this exception is not applicable to the purchase of like-kind property to replace condemned real property used in a trade or business or held for investment.[66]

Example 12-48 ■

Hank's airplane, which is used in business, is hijacked and taken to a foreign country. He uses the insurance proceeds to purchase 80% of the Fast Corporation stock. Fast Corporation owns an airplane which is qualified replacement property. The involuntary conversion requirements are satisfied if Hank elects to defer any gain realized. ■

Example 12-49 ■

Lynn's farm is condemned by the state for public use. She used the proceeds to purchase 80% of Vermont Corporation stock. Vermont Corporation owns eight parking lots. A qualified replacement property has not been obtained through the stock purchase because the farm was condemned real property. ■

Time Requirements for Replacement

Typical Misconception

The first taxable year in which any part of the gain upon the conversion is realized is the year when the insurance proceeds are received and not the year that the involuntary conversion took place.

To qualify for nonrecognition of gain treatment, the converted property must be replaced within a specified time period. The general rule is that the period begins with the date of disposition of the converted property and ends "two years after the close of the first taxable year in which any part of the gain upon the conversion is realized."[67] If the involuntary conversion is due to condemnation or requisition, or the threat of such, the replacement period begins on the date of the threat or imminence of the requisition or condemnation. The replacement period may be extended by obtaining permission from the IRS.[68]

Example 12-50 ■

On December 8, 1994, Craig's business property is destroyed by fire. Craig receives insurance proceeds in 1995 and elects to defer recognition of the gain. He must replace the property during the period starting December 8, 1994, and ending

---

[63] Rev. Rul. 64-237, 1964-2 C.B. 319.

[64] To qualify as a purchase of property or stock under Sec. 1033(a)(2)(A)(ii), the unadjusted basis of the property or stock must be its cost within the meaning of Sec. 1012 without considering the basis adjustment for the deferred gain. Property acquired by inheritance, gift, or a nontaxable exchange does not qualify as replacement property (see Reg. Sec. 1.1033(a)-2(c)(4)).

[65] Sec. 1033(a)(2)(A) and Reg. Sec. 1.1033(a)-2(c).

[66] Sec. 1033(g)(2).

[67] Sec. 1033(a)(2)(B).

[68] Sec. 1033(a)(2)(B)(ii).

December 31, 1997. The two-year time period includes 1996 and 1997 because the gain is realized when the insurance proceeds are received in 1995. ■

The replacement period is longer if the involuntary conversion is due to the condemnation of real property (excluding inventory) held for productive use in a trade or business or for investment. The replacement period ends three years after the close of the first tax year in which any part of the gain is realized.[69] This provision for a longer replacement period applies to the same type of real property which may be replaced with like-kind property.

Example 12-51 ■ | Beth owns a building used in her dry cleaning business. In 1994 the state condemns the building and awards Beth an amount greater than the adjusted basis of the building. Beth may replace the property with like-kind property, and the replacement period ends on December 31, 1997. ■

The involuntary conversion rules are summarized in Topic Review 12-2.

TOPIC REVIEW 12-2

Section 1033—Involuntary Conversions
1. Section 1033 applies only to gains, not losses.
2. Nonrecognition of gain under Section 1033 is elective. (Nonrecognition of gain is mandatory in a direct conversion, but direct conversions seldom occur.)
3. Section 1033 applies to involuntary conversions of all types of properties.
4. Some gain may be recognized if the taxpayer replaces the involuntarily converted property with property that costs less than the amount realized in the involuntary conversion.
5. The nonrecognized gain is deferred.
6. The basis of property acquired to replace the involuntarily converted property is the cost of the property less the deferred gain.
7. Property acquired to replace the involuntarily converted property generally must be functionally related property.
8. The required replacement period generally begins with the date of disposition of the converted property and ends two years after the close of the first taxable year in which any part of the gain upon the conversion is realized. (A three-year period applies to condemnations of real property used in a trade or business or held for the production of income.)

SALE OF PRINCIPAL RESIDENCE— DEFERRAL OF GAIN

OBJECTIVE 5

Determine when a gain resulting from the sale of a principal residence is deferred and the basis for replacement property

Congress uses the tax law to encourage homeownership in many ways: (1) interest on debt used to acquire a principal or second residence is deductible (see Chapter 7); (2) taxpayers can defer any gain on the sale of a principal residence if a new principal residence is acquired within 2 years of the sale date at a cost equal to or greater than

---

[69] Sec. 1033(g)(4).

Key Point

The nonrecognition of gain under Sec. 1034 only results in the deferral of gain, but if the gain can be deferred until the taxpayer becomes age 55, the deferred gain can be permanently excluded in an amount up to $125,000.

Typical Misconception

The nonrecognition of gain is mandatory and not elective, as is sometimes believed.

Key Point

A taxpayer may own two or more residences, but only one of them will qualify as the "principal" residence.

the adjusted sales price of the old principal residence;[70] and (3) taxpayers who are at least 55 years old may elect to exclude part or all of the gain from the sale of a principal residence.[71]

Section 1034(a) provides, "If property [in this section called 'old residence'] used by the taxpayer as his principal residence is sold by him and, within a period beginning two years before the date of such sale and ending two years after such date, property [in this section called 'new residence'] is purchased and used by the taxpayer as his principal residence, gain [if any] from such sale shall be recognized only to the extent that the taxpayer's adjusted sales price . . . of the old residence exceeds the taxpayer's cost of purchasing the new residence."[72]

Section 1034 applies only to gains. A loss on the sale of a personal residence is not deductible because the residence is personal-use property.[73] If Sec. 1034 applies, the nonrecognition of gain treatment is mandatory.

A gain realized on the sale of a principal residence that does not qualify under the Sec. 1034 deferral provisions or the Sec. 121 exclusion rule is treated as a capital gain because a personal residence is a capital asset.

Principal Residence Defined

For Sec. 1034 to apply, taxpayers must sell property that qualifies as their principal residence and purchase property that is used as a new principal residence. Whether property is used as the taxpayer's principal residence is determined on a case-by-case basis.[74]

Example 12-52 ∎ Len, a 40-year-old college professor, owns and occupies a house in Oklahoma. During the summer, he lives in a cabin in Idaho. After owning the cabin for eight years, Len sells it for $50,000 and realizes a gain. He purchases a new cabin in Alaska for $60,000. Gain on the sale of the cabin in Idaho must be recognized because Len's principal residence is in Oklahoma. ∎

Condominium apartments, houseboats, and housetrailers qualify as principal residences.[75] Stock held by a tenant-stockholder in a cooperative housing corporation is a principal residence if the dwelling that the taxpayer is entitled to occupy as a stockholder is used as his principal residence.[76]

Determining Whether the Property Is the Taxpayer's Principal Residence.
To qualify for the favorable tax treatment provided by Sec. 1034, both the sold and acquired residences must be the taxpayer's principal residence.[77] Controversy frequently exists as to whether a residence qualifies as the taxpayer's principal residence, and the IRS will not issue rulings or determination letters concerning whether property qualifies under Secs. 121 or 1034.[78]

---

[70] Sec. 1034. The provision for deferral of gain recognition from the sale of a personal residence was first enacted in the Revenue Act of 1951. Congress created the provision in recognition of the fact that disposition of one's residence and acquisition of another residence were often necessitated by an increase in the size of the taxpayer's family or a change in the taxpayer's place of employment. Although primarily concerned with providing relief for a forced type of sale such as the above, Congress recognized the administrative burden of confining the provision's application to specific fact situations and, therefore, extended relief to all sales of personal residences that meet certain requirements. S. Rept. No. 781, 82d Cong., 1st Sess., p. 482 (1951).

[71] Sec. 121.

[72] Sec. 1034(a).

[73] Reg. Secs. 1.165-9(a) and 1.262-1(b)(4).

[74] Reg. Sec. 1.1034-1(c)(3).

[75] Rev. Rul. 64-31, 1964-1 C.B. 300.

[76] Reg. Sec. 1.1034-1(c)(3).

[77] Sec. 1034(a) and *Anne F. Stanley,* 33 T.C. 614 (1959).

[78] Rev. Proc. 92-3, 1992-1 C.B. 561.

Property that is not being used as a principal residence when sold may have lost its character as the taxpayer's residence. A taxpayer's residence that is abandoned prior to its sale does not qualify as the taxpayer's principal residence.[79] In a case where taxpayers had not occupied their residence for more than 10 years, the court disallowed the use of Sec. 1034 to the sale of the residence. The taxpayers were in the process of remodeling the property when they received and accepted an unsolicited offer.[80]

While attempting to sell the residence, the taxpayer may rent the property to another party. This action may jeopardize the taxpayer's ability to use Sec. 1034, although temporary rental prior to the sale does not always indicate a conversion to business use.[81]

Example 12-53 ■

Key Point

A residence can be rented and retain its designation as the taxpayer's principal residence. However, the taxpayer should be able to show that he was trying to sell the property.

Additional Comment

When a residence retains its designation as the "principal residence," the taxpayer can deduct depreciation and other rental expenses during the rental period.

In December 1993, Sandy discovers that her "dream house" is available for purchase. Sandy purchases the house and immediately occupies it as her new principal residence. She lives in a college town and knows that the market for housing becomes active in the spring. She lists her vacated house for sale with a realtor and agrees to allow two college students to rent the property on a month-to-month basis. Sandy retains the right to show the house to prospective buyers while the students are tenants. In April 1994, she sells the property. Since the conversion to rental property status is temporary, the residence is still Sandy's principal residence and Sec. 1034 is applied to defer recognition of gain from the sale of the former residence. ■

If rental of the property constitutes abandonment of the residence, Sec. 1034 may not be used by the taxpayer.

Example 12-54 ■

In 1988, Sam and his spouse moved from their residence in New Orleans to a home in Mobile. After renting the house in New Orleans for six years, they sell it in 1994. Section 1034 does not apply to the sale of the residence in New Orleans.[82]

Time Requirements for Replacement of Principal Residence

Additional Comment

The taxpayer does not have to be occupying the old residence at the date of sale. The taxpayer may have already moved to a new residence and be renting the old residence temporarily before its sale.

The new principal residence must be acquired and used by the taxpayer during the period of time beginning two years before the date of sale of the old residence and ending two years after the date of sale.[83] The new residence must be used as a principal residence within this time period to avoid recognition of the gain realized on the sale of the old residence.[84] Even when failure to occupy the new residence within the required time is beyond the taxpayer's control, the benefits of Sec. 1034 will be denied.[85] However, the two year period is extended for members of the U.S. Armed Forces serving on extended active duty after the date of sale.[86]

---

[79] *William C. Stolk* v. *CIR*, 13 AFTR 2d 535, 64-1 USTC ¶ 9228 (2nd Cir., 1964).
[80] *Ann K. Demeter*, 1971 PH T.C. Memo ¶ 71,209, 30 TCM 863.
[81] Rev. Rul. 78-146, 1978-1 C.B. 260.
[82] *Rene A. Stiegler, Jr.*, 1964 PH T.C. Memo ¶ 64,057, 23 TCM 412.
[83] Sec. 1034(a).
[84] Rev. Rul. 69-434, 1969-2 C.B. 163.
[85] *Joseph T. Gelinas*, 1976 PH T.C. Memo ¶ 76,103, 35 TCM 448.
[86] Sec. 1034(h)(1). The period of time is not to extend longer than four years after the date of sale of the old residence. For sales of old residences after July 18, 1984, Sec. 1034(h)(2) provides that the extended time period is permitted by Sec. 1034(h)(2) to be as long as eight years for certain members of the armed forces. The two-year period is also extended by Sec. 1034(k) for an individual whose tax home is outside the United States after the date of the sale of the old residence.

Example 12-55 ■

Real World Example

The replacement period was not extended even when the new home that was being constructed was destroyed by fire. Rev. Rul. 75-438, 1975-2 C.B. 334.

Typical Misconception

It is easy to become confused about the opportunity of purchasing a new residence during the 2-year period prior to the sale of the old one. At times taxpayers are compelled to relocate on short notice and may not be able to sell the house at the old location before buying another residence.

After selling her home on June 10, 1992, Nancy, age 32, agrees to purchase a residence on August 5, 1992. Unfortunately, the real estate agent lacks proper authority to bind the seller, and Nancy is not able to acquire the residence. Nancy, unable to find another suitable house, signed a contract on July 2, 1993, to have a new residence constructed. Due to a strike by the carpenters' union and unusually bad weather, the house is not completed until July 25, 1994. Since Nancy does not occupy the new principal residence within two years from the date of sale, her realized gain on the sale must be recognized. ■

The new residence may be purchased by the taxpayer during the two-year period prior to the sale of the old residence. If such a purchase does occur, the purchased residence is not treated as the new residence if it is sold or otherwise disposed of before the old residence is sold.[87]

If a taxpayer acquires more than one principal residence during the two-year period after the date of sale of the old residence, only the last residence purchased qualifies as the new residence.[88] This limitation is modified in certain situations involving business transfers as discussed below.

Example 12-56 ■

Key Point

It is necessary that the taxpayer physically live in the replacement home before the expiration of the 2-year period.

Joel's principal residence is sold for $50,000 in February 1993. He realizes a gain. In September 1993, Joel purchases a principal residence for $70,000. The property is converted to rental property in March 1994 and Joel purchases another principal residence in a new neighborhood in May 1994. To determine if Joel must recognize a gain on the sale of the principal residence occurring in February 1993, the residence purchased in May 1994 is considered to be the new principal residence, since it is the last residence purchased during the two year period after the sale of the residence in February 1993. ■

Sale of More Than One Principal Residence Within a Two-Year Period

A taxpayer who sells a principal residence within a two-year period after the sale of another principal residence may not be able to defer the gain resulting from the second sale if Sec. 1034 was used to defer any part of a gain realized on the first sale.[89] This restriction prevents taxpayers from avoiding the recognition of economic gains earned from frequent sales of personal residences.

Example 12-57 ■

Gail, age 40, sells her principal residence at a profit on May 10, 1994. The gain is not recognized because she purchased a new principal residence in the same neighborhood on March 5, 1994, at a cost greater that the adjusted sales price of the residence sold on May 10, 1994. If Gail sells the residence acquired on March 5, 1994, or any other principal residence acquired during the two-year period after May 10, 1994, any gain on the sale is recognized. The gain is not deferred under Sec. 1034 unless the moves are necessitated by business (i.e., the business move exception discussed below applies). ■

The Business Move Exception. The *business move exception* recognizes that business reasons may necessitate multiple sales of personal residences within a two-year period. An employment-related move is considered to be a business reason. Thus, if

---

[87] Sec. 1034(c)(3).
[88] Sec. 1034(c)(4).
[89] Sec. 1034(d)(1).

the sale of a personal residence within two years of the sale of another personal residence is due to a work-related move, Sec. 1034 may apply to the sale. The Sec. 217(c) time and distance tests used to determine the deductibility of moving expenses must be satisfied in order to use this exception.[90] (These tests are discussed in Chapter 9.)

Example 12-58 ■ In April 1993, Helen, who lived in Texas, sold her principal residence and purchased a new principal residence. Gain on the sale was deferred under Sec. 1034. In June 1994, Helen sells the residence located in Texas for $80,000 and moves to Florida to accept a new job. Her moving expenses are deductible. In July 1994, Helen purchases a new residence in Florida for $140,000. Even though she sells more than one principal residence within a two-year period, any gain on the sale of the first replacement residence (i.e., the residence sold in June 1994) is deferred because the business move exception applies. ■

Computing the Deferred Gain and the Basis of the New Residence

No gain is recognized on the sale of a principal residence if a new principal residence is acquired at a cost equal to or greater than the adjusted sales price of the old residence. The new residence must be acquired and used as the taxpayer's personal residence during the specified two-year replacement period. If the cost of the new residence is less than the adjusted sales price of the old residence, part or all or the realized gain is recognized. The realized gain is recognized to the extent that the adjusted sales price exceeds the taxpayer's cost of purchasing the new residence.[91]

Example 12-59 ■ Judy sells her personal residence and has a $40,000 realized gain. The adjusted sales price is $94,000. She purchases a new residence two months later for $100,000. No gain is recognized because the cost of the new principal residence is greater than the adjusted sales price of the old principal residence and the other requirements of Sec. 1034 are met. ■

Example 12-60 ■ Assume the same facts in Example 12-59 except that the adjusted sales price is $105,000. Judy recognizes a $5,000 ($105,000 − $100,000) capital gain. The adjusted sales price is $5,000 more than the cost of the new principal residence, and the excess is not greater than the $40,000 of realized gain. ■

Determining the Realized Gain. Gain realized is the excess of the amount realized over the property's adjusted basis.[92] The amount realized on the sale of the property is equal to the selling price less selling expenses.[93] Selling expenses include commissions, advertising, deed preparation costs, and legal expenses incurred in connection with the sale.[94]

Example 12-61 ■ Kirby sells his personal residence, which has a $100,000 basis, to Maxine. To make the sale, Kirby pays a $7,000 sales commission and incurs $800 of legal costs. Maxine pays $30,000 cash and assumes Kirby's $90,000 mortgage. The amount realized is $112,200 ([$30,000 + $90,000] − [$7,000 + $800]). The realized gain is $12,200 ($112,200 − $100,000). ■

---

[90] Sec. 1034(d)(2).
[91] Sec. 1034(a).
[92] Reg. Sec. 1.1034-1(b)(5).
[93] Reg. Sec. 1.1034-1(b)(4).
[94] Reg. Sec. 1.1034-1(b)(4)(i).

Additional Comment

Painting, cleaning, and minor repairs are examples of fixing-up expenses.

Adjusted Sales Price. The **adjusted sales price** is the amount realized, reduced by fixing-up expenses.[95] **Fixing-up expenses** are expenses incurred to assist in the sale of the old residence. Normal repairs and painting costs are examples of fixing-up expenses. Fixing-up expenses must be incurred during the 90-day period ending on the day the taxpayer enters into a contract to sell the old residence. The expenses must be paid within 30 days after the sale. Capital expenditures are not fixing-up expenses.

Example 12-62 ■

Dale sells a personal residence with a $100,000 adjusted basis for $140,000. Selling expenses amount to $10,000. He pays $4,000 of fixing-up expenses. The amount realized is $130,000 ($140,000 − $10,000). The adjusted sales price is $126,000 ($130,000 − $4,000). The realized gain is $30,000 ($130,000 − $100,000). ■

Example 12-63 ■

Self-Study Question

How do fixing-up expenses affect the total amount of gain that a taxpayer will eventually recognize?

Answer

Fixing-up expenses may increase the amount of gain deferred but do not affect the amount of gain to be realized.

On February 10, 1994, David lists his house for sale with a broker. David pays $100 to a carpenter for minor repairs made on February 2, 1994. On April 25, 1994, he pays $6,000 to install central air conditioning. He also pays $40 to replace a broken window on May 12, 1994. David signs a contract to sell the house to Edith on June 14, 1994. Fixing-up expenses amount to $40. The $6,000 payment for central air conditioning is capitalized and increases the basis of the residence. The $100 payment to the carpenter is for work that is performed outside the 90-day period ending on the sale date (June 14, 1994). ■

Fixing-up expenses are personal in nature and do not affect the realized gain. They are considered only when determining the amount of gain to be recognized. Payment of fixing-up expenses reduces the adjusted sales price. Adjusted sales price is then compared with the cost of the new residence to determine whether any of the realized gain should be recognized.

Example 12-64 ■

Milton sells a personal residence for $90,000. The property has a $60,000 adjusted basis. Selling expenses amount to $7,000, and the realized gain is $23,000 ([$90,000 − $7,000] − $60,000). Milton purchases a new residence four months later for $70,000. Since the adjusted sales price of $83,000 ($90,000 − $7,000) is more than the $70,000 cost of the new residence, he recognizes a $13,000 ($83,000 − $70,000) gain. If Milton incurs $1,000 of fixing-up expenses, the adjusted sales price is $82,000 ($90,000 − [$7,000 + $1,000]) and the recognized gain is $12,000 ($82,000 − $70,000). Although the realized gain is not affected by the fixing-up expenses, the recognized gain is reduced from $13,000 to $12,000.■

Key Point

In computing the cost of a new residence, the taxpayer can include additional expenditures for improving the property such as the cost of remodeling a kitchen.

Cost of Replacement Residence. The cost of purchasing a new residence includes all amounts attributable to the acquisition, including partial or total construction and reconstruction and improvements constituting capital expenditures made during the replacement period.[96] The mere improvement of a residence is not considered to be a purchase of a residence.[97] Commissions and other purchasing expenses paid to acquire the new residence are included in determining the cost of the residence.[98] Capital improvements are included in determining the cost of the replacement residence only if they are incurred during the period beginning two years before the date of sale of the former residence and ending two years after that date.

[95] Reg. Sec. 1.1034-1(b).
[96] Reg. Sec. 1.1034-1(b)(7).
[97] Reg. Sec. 1.1034-1(b)(9).
[98] Reg. Sec. 1.1034-1(c)(4).

Example 12-65 ■ | On March 10, 1992, Susan purchased a lot for $15,000 to use as the site of a new residence. Construction of the new house was started on November 20, 1993, and construction is completed by April 4, 1994. Total construction costs of $70,000 (excluding the lot) are paid. On May 1, 1994, Susan's old personal residence is sold at a $20,000 gain. The adjusted sales price is $74,000. Susan recognizes a $4,000 ($74,000 − $70,000) gain. The cost of the lot was not included because it is not incurred within the replacement period (i.e., within two years prior to or after the sale of the former residence). ■

If the old principal residence is exchanged for a new principal residence, the cost of the new residence is its FMV. The value of any part of the new residence acquired by the taxpayer other than by purchase is not included in determining the taxpayer's cost of the new residence.[99] A taxpayer who inherits a residence or receives one as a gift has not made a purchase under Sec. 1034 and may not, therefore, include the value of the gift in determining the cost of the new residence.

Example 12-66 ■ | On April 10, 1994, Carol's uncle dies. She inherits her uncle's house, which has a $100,000 FMV. On May 1, 1994, Carol sells her former residence and has a $38,000 realized gain. The adjusted sales price is $75,000. Carol incurs $60,000 of reconstruction costs to modernize the inherited house and occupies the residence on July 5, 1994. Carol's cost of the new principal residence is only $60,000 because the FMV of the inherited house is excluded in determining the cost of the new residence for the purpose of determining the recognized gain under Sec. 1034. She recognizes a $15,000 ($75,000 − $60,000) gain. ■

Basis of Replacement Residence. The basis of the new residence is its cost less the unrecognized gain on the sale of the old residence.[100] As with both the provisions under like-kind exchanges and involuntary conversions, the deferred gain may be taxed at a later date. If the purchase of a new residence results in the nonrecognition of any part of a gain on the sale of an old residence, the holding period of the old residence carries over to the new residence.[101]

Example 12-67 ■ | Mark owns a personal residence with a $40,000 basis. Its holding period starts on April 10, 1980. On August 20, 1994, Mark sells the residence and has a $50,000 realized gain. The adjusted sales price is $88,000. Mark purchases and occupies a new residence on September 5, 1994. The cost of the new residence is $82,000. The recognized gain is $6,000 ($88,000 − $82,000), and the unrecognized gain is $44,000 ($50,000 − $6,000). Mark's basis in the new residence is $38,000 ($82,000 − $44,000), and its holding period begins on April 10, 1980. ■

Additional Comment

A factor that should be considered in electing to treat the condemnation of a personal residence as a voluntary sale under Sec. 1034 (in lieu of an involuntary conversion under Sec. 1033) is the replacement period. The replacement period will vary depending upon whether Sec. 1033 or Sec. 1034 applies.

Involuntary Conversion of a Principal Residence

Ordinarily, the involuntary conversion of a principal residence is governed by Sec. 1033, which was discussed earlier in this chapter. A gain due to an involuntary conversion of a personal residence may be deferred if the requirements of Sec.

---

[99] Reg. Sec. 1.1034-1(c)(4)(i).
[100] Sec. 1034(e).
[101] Sec. 1223(7).

1033 are satisfied. The functional use test must be satisfied regardless of the type of involuntary conversion. The like-kind test for replacement property may not be used since the personal residence is not used in a trade or business or held for investment.

If the gain is due to "the seizure, requisition, or condemnation of a residence, or the sale or exchange of a residence under threat or imminence thereof," the taxpayer may elect to utilize the provisions of Sec. 1034 in lieu of Sec. 1033.[102] If the involuntary conversion is a casualty, taxpayers may defer the gain only under Sec. 1033.

A loss due to a condemnation of a personal residence is not recognized. If the loss is due to a casualty, the loss is deductible and is treated like other casualty losses of nonbusiness property (see Chapter 8).

Presidentially Declared Disaster of a Principal Residence. Special treatment is provided when a taxpayer's principal residence or any of its contents is compulsorily or involuntarily converted and the residence is located in an area which is determined by the President to be in an area that warrants assistance by the Federal Government under the Disaster Relief and Emergency Assistance Act. Part of the gain resulting from the receipt of insurance proceeds is excluded and part may be deferred if the President's declaration is after August 31, 1991.[103]

No gain is recognized due to the receipt of insurance proceeds for damaged personal property located in the residence if the property was unscheduled property for the purpose of such insurance. While proceeds received for property that is not separately scheduled is excluded from gross income, other proceeds received, including those received for scheduled property, are treated as being received as a common fund for a single item of property. Separately scheduled property typically consists of items such as computers, jewelry, artwork, pianos, etc.

If insurance proceeds received due to damages to the house and separately scheduled property are used to purchase any property similar or related in service or use to the converted residence or its contents, the taxpayer may elect to defer any gain realized. Gain is recognized only to the extent that the cost of the replacement property is less than the amount of insurance funds received. The replacement period is extended to four years after the close of the first taxable year in which any part of the gain upon the conversion is realized.[104]

Example 12-68 ■ Nora's principal residence, with an adjusted basis of $70,000, was destroyed by a flood in May 1994. The area was declared by the President to be a Federal disaster area. All of the contents of her home, including a Steinway grand piano with a basis of $25,000 and a FMV of $30,000, were destroyed. Nora received the following payments from the insurance company in July 1994: $200,000 for the house, $25,000 for personal property contents with an adjusted basis of $15,000, and $30,000 for the piano that was separately scheduled property. In December 1994, Nora pays $248,000 for a new house and does not replace the piano. The $10,000 ($25,000 − $15,000) gain on the unscheduled personal property is excluded from gross income. Since she paid at least $230,000 ($200,000 + $30,000) for the replacement residence, the gain attributable to the house and the piano is deferred.

---

[102] Sec. 1034(i) and Reg. Sec. 1.1034-1(h).

[103] The Revenue Reconciliation Act of 1993 granted retroactive tax relief for taxpayers because of the mass destruction in Florida caused by Hurricane Andrew and the flooding in several midwest states which occurred in 1993.

[104] Sec. 1033(h). As noted in Chapter 8, taxpayers who suffer losses attributable to a disaster that occurs in an area subsequently declared by the President to be a disaster area may elect to deduct the loss in the year preceding the year in which the loss actually occurs.

TABLE 12-1   Comparison of Secs. 1034 and 121

	Section 1034	Section 121
Definition of principal residence	Determined on a case-by-case basis	Same as Sec. 1034
Must property have been used as a principal residence before sale?	Yes	Yes, for at least three years during the five year period ending on the date of sale
Treatment of realized gain	All or part of the gain may be deferred depending upon the relationship between the adjusted sales price of the old residence and the cost of the new principal residence	Excluded up to $125,000 ($62,500 for a married individual filing a separate return)
Availability of election	No election required because the treatment is mandatory	Election filed with tax return for year of sale
Does taxpayer need to acquire and use new residence to replace residence sold?	Yes, within a period beginning 2 years before the date of sale and ending 2 years after that date	No
Are there any restrictions on age of taxpayer?	No	Yes, must be at least 55 years of age
Are there any restrictions on number of times section may be used?	No	Yes, once a lifetime

SALE OF PRINCIPAL RESIDENCE— EXCLUDED GAIN

OBJECTIVE 6

Determine when a gain resulting from the sale of a principal residence may be excluded

Key Point

This provision is different from the like-kind exchange or the involuntary conversion in that the gain is being excluded instead of deferred.

A taxpayer may elect to exclude gain from the sale of a principal residence under Sec. 121. However, the taxpayer must be at least 55 years of age and the amount of gain excluded may not exceed $125,000. A married individual filing a separate return may not exclude more than $62,500.

As indicated in Table 12-1, significant differences exist between the deferral of gain on the sale of a principal residence under Sec. 1034 and the exclusion of gain under Sec. 121. The major difference is that an excluded gain is never subject to tax, while a deferred gain may be recognized upon the subsequent sale of the replacement residence. The basis of the replacement residence is reduced by the amount of gain deferred upon the sale of the former residence.

Requirements to Qualify for the Exclusion

To qualify for the Sec. 121 exclusion, the taxpayer must be at least 55 years of age before the date of the sale or exchange of the principal residence and must own and use the property as a principal residence for at least three years of the five year period

Key Point

In general, the IRS considers the taxpayer's age at December 31 to be his or her age for the entire year. In this case, however, the taxpayer must be age 55 at the time of sale.

ending on the date of sale.[105] "Short temporary absences such as for vacation or other seasonal absence . . . are counted as periods of use."[106]

A married couple who hold the property jointly and file a joint return meet the age, holding, and use requirements discussed above, if only one spouse satisfies them.[107] A taxpayer, age 55 or older, who inherits property from a deceased spouse may be able to exclude the gain even if the taxpayer does not satisfy the holding and use requirements. If the holding and use requirements are satisfied by the deceased spouse, these requirements are deemed to be satisfied by the surviving spouse.[108]

Example 12-69 ■

Additional Comment

To qualify for the Sec. 121 exclusion, the taxpayer must own and use the property for at least 3 years of the 5-year period ending on the date of sale. However, the ownership test and the use test do not have to be met simultaneously during the 5-year period ending on the date of sale.

Dorothy purchased a house in Iowa on April 10, 1991, and occupied it until July 1, 1992, when she accepted a six month job assignment in Alaska. While in Alaska, Dorothy rented the house to an elderly couple for five months. Dorothy returned to the house in Iowa on January 1, 1993, and sells the house, realizing a $110,000 gain on September 1, 1994. Dorothy is 55 years old and has never elected to exclude a gain under Sec. 121. The gain resulting from the sale on September 1, 1994, may be excluded because Dorothy used the house as a principal residence for at least three years of the five year period ending September 1, 1994 (i.e., the five month temporary absence is counted in the required three year period of use). Since the realized gain is less than $125,000, Dorothy may exclude the entire gain. ■

Example 12-70 ■

Clay and Kathryn live in a community property state. Kathyrn owns a residence that is separate property since it was acquired before their marriage. The house's FMV is much greater than its adjusted basis. Clay and Kathryn have occupied the house for nine years. Clay is 55 years old, but Kathryn is less than 55 years old. Kathryn wants to transfer title to the house from her sole ownership to joint ownership and then Clay and Kathryn will sell the residence shortly thereafter. None of the gain may be excluded under Sec. 121. Neither spouse meets all the requirements for an exclusion of the gain under Sec. 121. Clay has not owned the property as his principal residence for three years, and Kathryn is less than 55 years old.[109] ■

If the taxpayer sells a principal residence that is purchased as a new replacement residence under Sec. 1034, the use and ownership test period begins on the day the replacement residence is acquired.

Example 12-71 ■

In 1992, Vince sold a residence used as his principal residence for six years. Two months later, he purchased a new residence at a cost greater than the adjusted sales price for the old residence and deferred the realized gain. Vince, age 55, uses the replacement residence as a principal residence until April 10, 1994, when the residence is sold at a gain. Vince may not elect to exclude the gain under Sec. 121 because the replacement residence is not used as his principal residence for three years of the five year period ending on April 10, 1994. ■

Involuntary Conversion. For purposes of Sec. 121, the destruction, theft, seizure, requisition, or condemnation of property is treated as a sale.[110] Thus, taxpayers may

---

[105] Sec. 121(a). Section 121(d)(9) provides an exception for a taxpayer who becomes physically or mentally incapable of self-care if the property is used as a principal residence for at least one year during the 5-year period. In such case, the period that the taxpayer resides in a state-licensed facility (including a nursing home) is counted for the three-year-out-of-five-year required use requirement.

[106] Reg. Sec. 1.121-1(c).

[107] Sec. 121(d)(1)(C).

[108] Sec. 121(d)(2).

[109] Ltr. Rul. 8909020 (December 2, 1988) and Reg. Sec. 1.121-1(d) Ex. 3.

[110] Sec. 121(d)(4).

elect to exclude a gain due to the involuntary conversion of a principal residence if the use and ownership test is satisfied.

If gain due to the involuntary conversion of a principal residence is deferred under Sec. 1033, the holding period of the replacement residence includes the holding period of the converted property for purposes of satisfying the use and ownership tests of Sec. 121.[111] Thus when there is a choice, it might be preferable to defer a gain under Sec. 1033 instead of Sec. 1034.

Example 12-72 ■

Self-Study Question

Assume that Rick sells his principal residence and elects to exclude the $10,000 gain under Sec. 121. What happens to the remaining $115,000 ($125,000 − $10,000) limitation?

Answer

It is lost and has no future tax benefit for Rick.

In 1994, Gina's principal residence of 10 years was destroyed by fire. She replaced the principal residence on June 5, 1994, and elected to defer the gain under Sec. 1033.[112] After using the replacement residence as a principal residence for only two years, Gina, age 55, sells the residence at a gain. She elects to exclude the gain under Sec. 121. The use and ownership test is satisfied, since her use and ownership of the converted property is also counted towards satisfying the three-year requirement. ■

Election

The election to exclude the gain on the sale or exchange of a principal residence is a once-in-a-lifetime exclusion.[113] The election "may be made or revoked at any time before the expiration of the period for making a claim for credit or refund."[114]

A married taxpayer may elect or revoke under Sec. 121 if the taxpayer's spouse joins in such election or revocation.[115] An election by one spouse eliminates the opportunity for either spouse to make a subsequent election.

Example 12-73 ■

Roy, age 55, marries Lois, who is Jack's widow. While married, Jack and Lois sold their principal residence and elected to exclude the gain. Roy, now married to Lois, sells his principal residence of 20 years at a gain. Under Sec. 121, Roy may not elect to exclude the gain because he is married to Lois, who made a previous election with Jack. If Roy wanted to exclude the gain, he should have sold the residence before he married Lois. ■

Combination of Exclusion and Deferral Provisions

Sections 121 and 1034 apply to the same sale of a principal residence. If the realized gain exceeds $125,000, the excess amount of realized gain may be deferred under Sec. 1034. However, for Sec. 1034 to apply, the taxpayer must purchase and occupy a new principal residence during the four-year replacement period (i.e., two years prior to the sale or two years after the sale). To defer all of the remaining gain, the cost of the new residence must be equal to or greater than the adjusted sales price of the old residence. When computing the adjusted sales price, the amount realized from the sale or exchange of the residence is reduced by any gain excluded under Sec. 121.[116]

Example 12-74 ■

During the current year, Amy, age 55, sells a principal residence and purchases a new residence. The requirements for Sections 121 and 1034 are both satisfied, and Amy elects to exclude the gain. The deferral of gain under Sec. 1034 is mandatory. The following information pertains to the sale and purchase:

[111] Sec. 121(d)(8).
[112] Section 1034 does not apply when the involuntary conversion of a principal residence is due to a casualty.
[113] Sec. 121(b)(2).
[114] Sec. 121(c).
[115] Ibid.
[116] Sec. 121(d)(7).

Additional Comment

In determining the lowest price of a new residence that will result in the recognition of no gain under Sec. 1034, the adjusted selling price can be reduced by the $125,000 gain excluded under Sec. 121.

Basis of old residence	$ 60,000
Selling price of old residence	300,000
Selling expenses	18,000
Fixing-up expenses	3,000
Purchase price of new residence	150,000

The tax consequences of Amy's sale of her principal residence are as follows:

Selling price	$300,000
Minus: Selling expenses	(18,000)
Amount realized	$282,000
Minus: Adjusted basis	(60,000)
Realized gain	$222,000
Minus: Excluded gain	(125,000)
Balance of realized gain	$ 97,000
Selling price	$300,000
Minus: Selling expenses	(18,000)
Fixing-up expenses	(3,000)
Excluded gain	(125,000)
Adjusted sales price	$154,000
Adjusted sales price	$154,000
Minus: Cost of replacement residence	(150,000)
Recognized gain	$ 4,000[a]
Cost of replacement residence	$150,000
Minus: Deferred gain	
($97,000 − $4,000)	(93,000)
Basis of replacement residence	$ 57,000

[a] Limited to the balance of realized gain, or $97,000.

Section 121 allows Amy to exclude $125,000 of the $222,000 realized gain. To compute the adjusted sales price, the excluded portion of the realized gain is deducted to determine the amount realized. Thus, the adjusted sales price is the selling price less selling expenses, the excluded gain and fixing-up expenses. Since the cost of the new residence does not exceed the adjusted sales price, not all of the remaining gain of $97,000 ($222,000 − $125,000) is deferred. A $4,000 gain is recognized. The remaining $93,000 gain is deferred. The $150,000 cost of the new residence is reduced by the $93,000 deferred gain to determine the $57,000 basis for the new residence. ∎

TAX PLANNING CONSIDERATIONS

Avoiding the Like-Kind Exchange Provisions

In some cases, a taxpayer may prefer a taxable exchange to a nontaxable like-kind exchange. For instance, if the gain is taxed as a capital gain and the taxpayer has capital losses to offset the gain, the taxpayer may prefer to recognize the gain during the current year. If the gain on the exchange is recognized instead of deferred, the basis of the property received in the exchange is higher.

Example 12-75 ■   Connie owns land with a $20,000 basis. The land is held as an investment. Connie exchanges the land for a duplex with a $100,000 FMV. Since the exchange qualifies as a like-kind exchange, no gain is recognized and Connie's basis for the duplex is $20,000. If the exchange does not qualify as a like-kind exchange (e.g., the land is a personal-use asset), Connie recognizes an $80,000 capital gain. Connie's basis for the duplex is $100,000. The basis of the duplex, except for the portion allocable to land, is eligible for depreciation.   ■

If an exchange qualifies as a like-kind exchange, no loss on the exchange is recognized. A taxpayer who prefers to recognize a loss should avoid making a like-kind exchange. It may be advantageous to sell the property to recognize the loss and then purchase the replacement asset in two independent transactions. If the sale and purchase transactions are with the same party, the IRS may maintain that the like-kind exchange rules apply because the two transactions are in substance a like-kind exchange (i.e., the judicial doctrine of substance over form might be applied).

Sale of a Principal Residence

Deferral Provisions. It is unlikely that a taxpayer will ever have an incentive to avoid the mandatory tax treatment provided by Sec. 1034 because

- When the taxpayer is at least age 55, up to $125,000 of the gain may be excluded.
- A personal residence is not subject to depreciation and thus, a step-up in basis has less value as a tax benefit.
- The residence may eventually be transferred to the taxpayer's heirs as a result of the taxpayer's death and no income taxes will be paid on the unrealized appreciation as of the date of death. In addition, the heirs will receive a step-up in basis of the property to its FMV.

Identifying the Principal Residence. In view of the advantages of deferring the gain on the sale of a principal residence, a taxpayer contemplating a sale should satisfy all requirements of Sec. 1034. A taxpayer who owns and occupies more than one residence may have difficulty identifying which is the principal residence. However, the *principal residence* is defined as the one that the taxpayer occupies most of the time.[117]

Example 12-76 ■   Paula, a business consultant, owns residences in Boston and Philadelphia. She plans to sell both residences in two years and purchase a new residence in California. The Boston residence has a FMV that is $200,000 greater than its basis. The residence in Philadelphia has not appreciated. Paula's activities should be planned in a manner that will allow her to occupy the Boston residence more than the Philadelphia residence. This will enable Paula to qualify the Boston residence as her principal residence.   ■

Historical Note

The replacement period was increased for sales after July 20, 1981, from a period that began 18 months before and that ended 18 months after the sale to the current provisions.

Timing the Sale and Purchase. Since Sec. 1034 requires that the purchase and use of the new residence must occur within a period beginning two years before the date the old residence is sold and ending two years after that date, the taxpayer must consider the timing of the sale and purchase. A taxpayer who purchases a new residence before selling the old residence may lose the advantage of Sec. 1034 if it takes more than two years to sell the old residence.

---

[117] Rev. Rul. 77-298, 1977-2 C.B. 308.

To defer all of the gain, the cost of the new residence must equal or exceed the adjusted sales price of the old residence. When the cost of the new residence is determined, only those capital costs incurred during the four-year replacement period are used.

Example 12-77 ■   Eventually, Gary expects to sell his principal residence and build a new one. On March 10, 1994, Gary pays $25,000 for a lot in a new subdivision. If Gary plans to include the $25,000 as part of the cost of the new residence to defer a gain on the sale of the old residence, the old residence should be sold no later than March 10, 1996.   ■

The taxpayer may find it beneficial to postpone the sale of a principal residence if Sec. 1034 was recently used to defer the gain on the sale of a previous residence. Unless the business move exception applies, Sec. 1034 cannot be applied more than once within a two-year period.

Example 12-78 ■   On June 5, 1994, Kristie offers to purchase Tony's principal residence. Because of the attractive purchase offer, Tony is willing to sell the residence and purchase a new one. The basis of Tony's current residence was reduced by the gain deferred on the sale of Tony's previous residence on August 12, 1992. Section 1034 will not apply to the sale on June 5, 1994, because only one principal residence may be sold during the two-year period ending on August 12, 1994. To obtain the tax deferral benefit of Sec. 1034, the closing of the sale for Tony's current residence should be delayed until after August 12, 1994.   ■

Exclusion Provisions. A taxpayer who is eligible to use the $125,000 exclusion under Sec. 121 must decide whether to make the election. Careful consideration must be given to this decision since (1) the election is available only once in a person's lifetime, (2) no unused portion of the $125,000 exclusion may be used at a later date, and (3) the use of the exclusion precludes the taxpayer's spouse from using the exclusion in a subsequent year even if the spousal relationship no longer exists.

Thus, if the taxpayer has the opportunity to choose whether to either defer all of the gain under Sec. 1034 or exclude it under Sec. 121, the choice should probably be deferral. However, consideration should be given to the fact that the holding period for the use and occupancy requirement (i.e., three-year-out-of-the-five-years preceding the sale) does not carry over to the new principal residence if Sec. 1034 is used to defer the gain on the sale of the old residence.

The size of the realized gain and the likelihood of selling another principal residence at a gain are two factors that must also be considered by the taxpayer who is making the election. Despite the time value of money, a taxpayer with a small gain might not elect to exclude the gain currently if the anticipated gain on a subsequent sale of a principal residence is substantially larger than the current gain. If the taxpayer does not expect to sell another principal residence (e.g., the individual plans to rent an apartment and has no desire to be a homeowner again), the exclusion of gain provision should be elected.

As with any election provided in the Code, there is a risk that the law will change. To date, the only major change in Sec. 121 has been to increase the amount of the exclusion from $100,000 to $125,000.[118]

Property Converted to Business Use. If a residence is converted to business use at the time of the sale, it will not qualify as a principal residence.[119] A principal

---

[118] The increase to $125,000 is effective for residences sold or exchanged after July 20, 1981.
[119] Reg. Sec. 1.1034-1(a)(3)(ii).

residence converted to business use may subsequently become the taxpayer's principal residence if the business use is discontinued for a period of time.[120]

Example 12-79 ∎ Brad, a college professor, uses 20% of his residence as an office from 1970 until 1994. Brad deducted expenses related to the office portion of the residence for the years 1970 through 1975. After 1975, no deduction was allowed because Brad no longer met the eligibility requirements for an office-in-home deduction. (See Chapter 9 for a discussion of the office-in-home deduction.) If Brad sold the property before 1976, only 80% of the property would have qualified as a principal residence and 20% would be considered as business property. If he sells the residence in 1994, the entire residence is considered to be his principal residence because the business use has been discontinued. The basis of the residence is reduced by the depreciation allowed from 1970 through 1975. ∎

COMPLIANCE AND PROCEDURAL CONSIDERATIONS

Reporting of Involuntary Conversions

Additional Comment

The failure to include gain from an involuntary conversion in gross income shall be deemed to be an election even though the details are not reported.

The election to defer recognition of the gain from an involuntary conversion is made by not reporting the gain as income for the first year in which gain is realized. All details pertaining to the involuntary conversion (including those relating to the replacement of the converted property) should be reported for the taxable year or years in which any of the gain is realized.[121]

A taxpayer who elects to defer recognition of the gain but does not make a proper replacement of the property within the required period of time must file an amended return for the year or years for which the election was made. An amended return may be needed if the cost of the replacement property is less than expected at the time of the election. All details pertaining to the replacement of converted property must be reported in the year in which replacement occurs.[122]

Example 12-80 ∎ Bob's property, with a $40,000 adjusted basis, was destroyed by a storm in 1993. Bob received $45,000 insurance proceeds in 1993 and planned to purchase property similar to the converted property in 1994 at a cost of $47,000. Bob elected to defer recognition of the gain in 1993. In 1994 the replacement property is purchased for $44,500. Bob must file an amended return for 1993 and recognize a $500 ($45,000 − $44,500) gain. ∎

Additional Comment

The replacement period may be extended if special permission is obtained from the IRS.

A taxpayer who either is ineligible or does not want to defer the gain must report the gain in the usual manner. If a taxpayer does not elect to defer the gain in the year the gain is realized and the replacement period has not expired, a subsequent election may be made. In such an event, a refund claim should be filed for the tax year in which the gain was realized and previously recognized.[123]

While taxpayers who do not initially elect to defer the gain from an involuntary conversion may later make the election, the election may not subsequently be revoked. The Tax Court has ruled that the Regulations allow the filing of an amended return for a year in which the election is made only if proper replacement is not made within

---

[120] Rev. Rul. 82-26, 1982-1 C.B. 114.
[121] Reg. Sec. 1.1033(a)-2(c)(2).
[122] Ibid.
[123] Ibid.

the specified time period or the replacement is made at a cost lower than anticipated at the time of the election.[124] The IRS takes the position that taxpayers who designate qualifying property as replacement property may not later designate other qualifying property as the replacement property.[125]

Example 12-81 ∎

In 1992 Troy collected $200,000 from an insurance company as the result of the destruction of rental property with a $140,000 basis. He made the election to defer the gain realized in 1992 and attached a supporting schedule of details regarding the involuntary conversion including a designation of replacement property to be acquired in 1993. In 1993 Troy purchased the designated replacement rental property for $225,000. In 1994 Troy purchases other rental property for $400,000 and now wants to designate that property as the replacement property for the property destroyed in 1992. Troy may not designate the property acquired in 1994 as the replacement property because the rental property purchased in 1993 was already designated as such. ∎

Reporting of Sale or Exchange of a Principal Residence

Additional Comment

Form 2119 must be filed even if the sale of the residence resulted in a loss.

Form 2119 is used to report the sale or exchange of a principal residence. That form reports the date of the sale and the date the new residence is occupied. Any portion of the old and/or new residence that is not used as a principal residence is not used to determine the deferred gain. For this reason, the taxpayer must indicate whether any rooms in either residence are rented out or used for business. If a gain is recognized, the gain is reported on Schedule D of Form 1040.

Example 12-82 ∎

Amy's house, which is used as a principal residence, contains a home office. Depreciation deductions are allowed for the portion of the house used as an office. The basis of the principal residence portion of the house is $50,000 and the adjusted basis of the office is $5,000.

Amy sells the house for $80,000, and 10% of the selling price is allocated to the office portion of the house. No selling or fixing-up expenses are incurred. The gain realized on the sale of the principal residence is $22,000 ($72,000 − $50,000). The gain realized on the sale of the office portion of the house is $3,000 ($8,000 − $5,000).

Amy purchases a new residence for $100,000, and 12% of the new residence is used for an office. The $22,000 gain realized due to the sale of a principal residence is deferred since the $88,000 cost ($100,000 − [0.12 × $100,000]) allocated to the new residence exceeds the $72,000 adjusted sales price of the old residence. The $3,000 gain on the sale of the office portion of the residence is recognized. Amy's basis for the principal residence is $66,000 ($88,000 − $22,000). The basis for the office is $12,000. ∎

Form 2119 Illustrated. Part II of Form 2119, which is shown in Figure 12-1, is used to report the taxpayer's realized gain. The amount realized is $183,000, and the gain realized is $93,000.

In Part IV of Form 2119, the adjusted sales price is computed and compared with the cost of the new residence to determine the recognized gain. The excess of the realized gain over the recognized gain (i.e., the deferred gain), if any, is subtracted from the cost of the new residence to determine the adjusted basis of the new residence.

---

[124] *John McShain,* 65 T.C. 686 (1976).
[125] Rev. Rul. 83-39, 1983-1 C.B. 190.

Form **2119**

Department of the Treasury
Internal Revenue Service

Sale of Your Home

▶ Attach to Form 1040 for year of sale.

▶ See separate instructions. ▶ Please print or type.

OMB No. 1545-0072

1993

Attachment
Sequence No. **20**

Your first name and initial. If a joint return, also give spouse's name and initial.	Last name	Your social security number

| **Fill in Your Address Only If You Are Filing This Form by Itself and Not With Your Tax Return** | Present address (no., street, and apt. no., rural route, or P.O. box no. if mail is not delivered to street address) | Spouse's social security number |
| | City, town or post office, state, and ZIP code | |

Part I General Information

1	Date your former main home was sold (month, day, year) . . . . ▶	**1**	1 / 10 / 93
2	Have you bought or built a new main home?		☒ Yes ☐ No
3	Is or was any part of either main home rented out or used for business? If "Yes," see instructions . .		☐ Yes ☒ No

Part II Gain on Sale—Do not include amounts you deduct as moving expenses.

4	Selling price of home. Do not include personal property items you sold with your home . .	**4**	185,000
5	Expense of sale (see instructions)	**5**	2,000
6	Amount realized. Subtract line 5 from line 4	**6**	183,000
7	Adjusted basis of home sold (see instructions)	**7**	90,000
8	**Gain on sale.** Subtract line 7 from line 6	**8**	93,000

Is line 8 more than zero?

Yes ▶ If line 2 is "Yes," you **must** go to Part III or Part IV, whichever applies. If line 2 is "No," go to line 9.

No ▶ **Stop** and attach this form to your return.

9	If you haven't replaced your home, do you plan to do so within the **replacement period** (see instructions)? ☐ Yes ☐ No
	• If line 9 is "Yes," stop here, attach this form to your return, and see **Additional Filing Requirements** in the instructions.
	• If line 9 is "No," you **must** go to Part III or Part IV, whichever applies.

Part III One-Time Exclusion of Gain for People Age 55 or Older—By completing this part, you are electing to take the one-time exclusion (see instructions). If you are not electing to take the exclusion, go to Part IV now.

10	Who was age 55 or older on the date of sale? . . . . ☐ You ☐ Your spouse ☐ Both of you		
11	Did the person who was age 55 or older own and use the property as his or her main home for a total of at least 3 years (except for short absences) of the 5-year period before the sale? If "No," go to Part IV now . .		☐ Yes ☐ No
12	At the time of sale, who owned the home? . . . . ☐ You ☐ Your spouse ☐ Both of you		
13	Social security number of spouse at the time of sale if you had a different spouse from the one above. If you were not married at the time of sale, enter "None" . . . . ▶	**13**	
14	**Exclusion.** Enter the **smaller** of line 8 or $125,000 ($62,500 if married filing separate return). Then, go to line 15	**14**	

Part IV Adjusted Sales Price, Taxable Gain, and Adjusted Basis of New Home

15	If line 14 is blank, enter the amount from line 8. Otherwise, subtract line 14 from line 8 . .	**15**	93,000
	• If line 15 is zero, stop and attach this form to your return.		
	• If line 15 is more than zero and line 2 is "Yes," go to line 16 now.		
	• If you are reporting this sale on the installment method, stop and see the instructions.		
	• All others, stop and **enter the amount from line 15 on Schedule D, col. (g), line 4 or line 12.**		
16	Fixing-up expenses (see instructions for time limits)	**16**	-0-
17	If line 14 is blank, enter amount from line 16. Otherwise, add lines 14 and 16	**17**	93,000
18	**Adjusted sales price.** Subtract line 17 from line 6	**18**	183,000
19a	Date you moved into new home ▶ 10 / 22 / 93 **b** Cost of new home (see instructions)	**19b**	123,000
20	Subtract line 19b from line 18. If zero or less, enter -0-	**20**	60,000
21	**Taxable gain.** Enter the **smaller** of line 15 or line 20	**21**	60,000
	• If line 21 is zero, go to line 22 and attach this form to your return.		
	• If you are reporting this sale on the installment method, see the line 15 instructions and go to line 22.		
	• All others, **enter the amount from line 21 on Schedule D, col. (g), line 4 or line 12,** and go to line 22.		
22	Postponed gain. Subtract line 21 from line 15	**22**	33,000
23	**Adjusted basis of new home.** Subtract line 22 from line 19b	**23**	90,000

Sign Here Only If You Are Filing This Form by Itself and Not With Your Tax Return

Under penalties of perjury, I declare that I have examined this form, including attachments, and to the best of my knowledge and belief, it is true, correct, and complete.

Your signature	Date	Spouse's signature	Date
▶		▶	
If a joint return, both must sign.			

For Paperwork Reduction Act Notice, see separate instructions.   Cat. No. 11710J   Form **2119** (1993)

FIGURE 12-1 Form 2119

As illustrated in Part IV of Form 2119, the recognized gain is $60,000. The $183,000 adjusted sales price ($185,000 selling price − $2,000 of sales commissions) exceeds the $123,000 cost of the new residence by $60,000. The $33,000 ($93,000 − $60,000) deferred gain is subtracted from the $123,000 cost to determine the $90,000 adjusted basis of the new residence.

Part III of Form 2119 is used by taxpayers who are at least 55 years old. If the taxpayer in the illustration is eligible to elect to exclude the gain and makes the election, the $93,000 gain realized, or $125,000 if less, is reported on line 9(f). Since the gain realized is less than $125,000, no gain is recognized. Although it is not necessary to purchase a new principal residence to utilize the election, Part IV is used to report the purchase of a new residence, the possible deferral of a realized gain in excess of $125,000, and the adjusted basis of the new residence.

Additional Comment

If the personal residence was sold on the installment method, the taxpayer must also complete Form 6252 (Installment Sale Income).

New Residence Is Not Acquired in Year the Old Residence Is Sold. Often a taxpayer may sell a principal residence in one tax year and purchase a new residence in either the following tax year or the second tax year following the year of sale. If an individual plans to replace his principal residence, Form 2119 should be attached to the taxpayer's Form 1040 for the year of sale. Only lines 1 through 8 are completed, and no gain is reported on Schedule D.

If the taxpayer purchases a new residence within the replacement period at a cost greater than the adjusted sales price, the taxpayer should notify the IRS by providing a new Form 2119 for the year of sale. If the taxpayer does not purchase a new residence within the replacement period or if a new residence is purchased at a cost less than the adjusted sales price, an amended return should be filed for the year of sale.

The statute of limitations with respect to any gain due to the sale of a principal residence does not expire prior to the three-year period beginning on the day the IRS receives written notification of:

- The taxpayer's cost of the new residence used to defer any part of the gain
- The taxpayer's intention not to purchase a new residence within the replacement period
- The taxpayer's failure to purchase a new residence within the replacement period[126]

Ethical Point

Tax preparers should inform the client if there is an error in a previously filed return or if the client fails to file a required return. (See the discussion of this topic in Chapter 1 under the caption entitled Statements on Responsibilities in Tax Practice.)

Basis of Principal Residence

The normal rules for determining basis are applied when ascertaining the basis of a principal residence. The basis of property is a function of how the property is obtained (e.g., purchase, gift, inheritance, and so on).

While the basis of property purchased is usually its cost, the basis of a new principal residence is reduced by any gain deferred on the sale of the old principal residence under Sec. 1034.[127] Expenses incurred to purchase the residence (such as legal fees, commissions, survey costs, title search, and appraisal fees) are added to the basis of the residence.

The basis of the residence is increased by the cost of capital improvements. Thus, the cost of adding a room, installing an air conditioning system, finishing a basement, and landscaping are capital improvements that are added to the basis of the residence. Expenses incurred to protect the taxpayer's title in the residence are also added to the basis.[128] Prior to 1986, taxpayers were entitled to tax credits as a result of making

---

[126] Sec. 1034(j) and Reg. Sec. 1.1034-1(i).
[127] Sec. 1034(e).
[128] Reg. Sec. 1.212-1(k).

qualified energy conservation expenditures and qualified renewable energy source expenditures.[129] These expenditures were capitalized as part of the cost of the residence. The basis of the residence was reduced by the amount of any residential energy credit allowed.[130]

Example 12-83 ∎ Joe purchased a principal residence in 1980 at a cost of $100,000. As a result of the purchase, a gain of $20,000 on the sale of Joe's old principal residence was deferred. In 1983, Joe paid $900 to enlarge the patio and $100 to repair broken drainage gutters. In 1985, Joe installed storm doors and windows at a $1,500 cost and received a $225 (0.15 × $1,500) residential energy credit. In 1986, Joe added a family room to the residence at a $14,000 cost. His basis for his residence is $96,175 ($100,000 − $20,000 + $900 + $1,500 − $225 + $14,000). The basis is reduced by the deferred gain on the sale of the old residence and increased by the 3 capital expenditure items. The cost of repairing the gutters is not a capital expenditure. Since a residential energy credit was allowed due to the installation of storm doors and windows, the basis of the residence is reduced by the credit allowed. ∎

PROBLEM MATERIALS

DISCUSSION QUESTIONS

12-1. Evaluate the following statement: The underlying rationale for the nonrecognition of a gain or loss resulting from a like-kind exchange is that the exchange constitutes a liquidation of the taxpayer's investment.

12-2. Why might a taxpayer want to avoid having an exchange qualify as a like-kind exchange?

12-3. Debbie owns office equipment with a basis of $300,000 that was acquired on May 10, 1988. Debbie exchanges the equipment for other office equipment owned by Doug on July 23, 1994. Doug's equipment has a FMV of $500,000. Both Debbie and Doug use the equipment in their trade or business.
  a. What is Debbie's basis for the office equipment received in the exchange and when does the holding period start for that equipment?
  b. If Debbie and Doug are related taxpayers, explain what action could occur that would cause the exchange not to qualify as a like-kind exchange.

12-4. Kay owns equipment used in her trade or business and exchanges the equipment for other like-kind equipment and marketable securities.
  a. What is the maximum gain that Kay might be required to recognize?
  b. Will Kay's recognized gain ever exceed the FMV of the marketable securities?
  c. What is the basis of the marketable securities received?
  d. When does the holding period of the marketable securities begin?

12-5. In an otherwise like-kind exchange, the taxpayer also receives marketable securities that qualify as boot.
  a. When does the taxpayer's holding period for the marketable securities begin?
  b. What is the basis of the marketable securities?

12-6. Demetrius sells word processing equipment used in his trade or business to Edith. He then purchases new word processing equipment from Zip Corporation.
  a. Do the sale and purchase qualify as a like-kind exchange?
  b. When may a sale and a subsequent purchase be treated as a like-kind exchange?

---

[129] Sec. 23.
[130] Sec. 23(e).

12-7. When determining whether property qualifies as like-kind property, is the quality or grade of the property considered?

12-8. When will a nonsimultaneous exchange qualify as a like-kind exchange?

12-9. Will the receipt of boot in a transaction that otherwise qualifies as a like-kind exchange always cause the exchange to be at least partially taxable?

12-10. When must a taxpayer who gives boot recognize a gain or loss?

12-11. What is the justification for Sec. 1033, which allows a taxpayer to elect to defer a gain resulting from an involuntary conversion?

12-12. May a taxpayer elect under Sec. 1033 to defer the recognition of a loss resulting from an involuntary conversion?

12-13. Must property be actually condemned for the conversion of property to be classified as an involuntary conversion? Explain.

12-14. What are severance damages? What is the tax treatment for severance damages that are received if the taxpayer does not use the severance damages to restore the retained property?

12-15. When is nonrecognition of gain treatment for an involuntary conversion mandatory?

12-16. The functional use test is often used to determine if the replacement property is similar or related in service or use to the property converted. Explain the functional use test.

12-17. In what situations may a gain due to an involuntary conversion of real property be deferred if like-kind property is purchased to replace the converted property?

12-18. What is the justification for Sec. 1034, which results in nonrecognition of gain on the sale or exchange of a principal residence?

12-19. For an expense to qualify as a fixing-up expense, when must the expense be incurred? When must the expense be paid?

12-20. Which of the following statements are true?
   a. Fixing-up expenses reduce the realized gain.
   b. Capital expenditures qualify as fixing-up expenses.
   c. Fixing-up expenses reduce the amount realized to arrive at the adjusted sales price.

12-21. A taxpayer sells her principal residence on November 15, 1994, for $100,000 and realizes a gain. She purchases a new principal residence for $150,000. In which of the following independent cases will Sec. 1034 apply?
   a. The new residence is occupied on March 10, 1993.
   b. The new residence is occupied on December 2, 1996.
   c. The new residence is occupied on February 19, 1996.

12-22. Harold's principal residence has an $80,000 basis. It is involuntarily converted, and he receives $95,000 because of the conversion. Harold pays $112,000 for a new principal residence within a month after the involuntary conversion. Under what conditions may Harold use either Secs. 1033 or 1034 to defer the gain?

12-23. In the Revenue Reconciliation Act of 1993, Congress granted tax relief for certain taxpayers who suffer damage to their principal residence as a result of a disaster if the house is subsequently declared by the President to be in a disaster area. Although the law was passed in August of 1993, the favorable tax treatment applies to disasters for which a Presidential declaration is made after August 31, 1991. Why do you believe that Congress applied the law retroactively to the 1991 date?

12-24. In 1993 Diane sold her principal residence at a $40,000 gain. Since she expects to pay $150,000 for a new principal residence, and the adjusted sales price for the old residence was $146,000, Diane did not report a gain in 1993. In 1994 she purchases a new principal residence for $140,000.
   a. What is the amount of gain recognized because of the sale?
   b. Must Diane file an amended return for 1993 and recognize the gain in 1993?

12-25. Gordon sells his principal residence and defers the gain realized on the sale under Sec. 1034.
  a. Why is the basis of his new principal residence adjusted downward?
  b. Provide two reasons why the deferred gain may never be subject to tax.

12-26. What requirements must be satisfied by a taxpayer under Sec. 121 in order to be eligible for the election to exclude a gain up to $125,000 on the sale or exchange of a principal residence?

12-27. Which of the following statements are true?
  a. A new principal residence must be purchased in order to exclude a gain under Sec. 121.
  b. Sections 121 and 1034 may apply to the same sale of a principal residence.
  c. If Secs. 121 and 1034 apply to the same sale of a principal residence, the amount realized from the sale of the residence is reduced by the excluded gain to determine the adjusted sales price.

PROBLEMS

12-28. *Like-Kind Property.* Which of the following exchanges qualify as like-kind exchanges under Sec. 1031?
  a. Acme Corporation stock held for investment purposes for Mesa Corporation stock also held for investment purposes.
  b. A motel used in a trade or business for an apartment complex held for investment.
  c. A pecan orchard in Texas used in a trade or business for an orange grove in Florida used in a trade or business.
  d. A one-third interest in a general partnership for a one-fourth interest in a limited partnership.
  e. Inventory for equipment used in a trade or business.
  f. Unimproved land held as an investment for a warehouse used in a trade or business.
  g. An automobile used as a personal-use asset for marketable securities held for investment.

12-29. *Like-Kind Property.* Which of the following exchanges qualify as like-kind exchanges under Sec. 1031?
  a. A motel in Texas for a motel in Italy.
  b. An office building held for investment for an airplane to be used in the taxpayer's business.
  c. Land held for investment for marketable securities held for investment.
  d. Land held for investment for a farm to be used in the taxpayer's business.

12-30. *Like-Kind Exchange—Boot.* Determine the realized gain or loss, the recognized gain or loss, and the basis of the equipment received for the following like-kind exchanges:

Basis of Equipment Exchanged	FMV of Boot Received	FMV of Equipment Received
$40,000	$-0-	$75,000
50,000	10,000	70,000
60,000	20,000	65,000
70,000	30,000	60,000
80,000	20,000	50,000

12-31. *Like-Kind Exchange—Personal Property.* Beach Corporation owns a computer with a $40,000 adjusted basis. The computer is used in the company's trade or business. What is the realized and recognized gain or loss for each of the following independent transactions?
  a. The computer is exchanged for a used computer with a $70,000 FMV plus $8,000 cash.
  b. The computer is exchanged for a used computer with a $25,000 FMV plus $7,000 cash.
  c. The computer is exchanged for marketable securities with a $57,000 FMV.

12-32. *Like-Kind Exchange—Personal Property.* Boise Corporation exchanges a machine with a $14,000 basis for a new machine with an $18,000 FMV and $3,000 cash. The machines are used in Boise's trade or business and are in the same General Asset Class.
  a. What is Boise Corporation's recognized gain and the basis for the new machine?
  b. How would your answer to Part a change if the corporation's machine is also subject to a $6,000 liability, and the liability is assumed by the other party?

12-33. ***Like-Kind Exchange—Liabilities.*** Paul owns a building used in a trade or business with an adjusted basis of $500,000 and an $800,000 FMV. He exchanges the building for a building owned by David. David's building has a $950,000 FMV but is subject to a $150,000 liability. Paul assumes David's liability and uses David's building in his business.
a. What is Paul's realized gain?
b. What is Paul's recognized gain?
c. What is Paul's basis for the building received?

12-34. ***Like-Kind Exchange—Liabilities.*** Helmut exchanges his apartment complex for Heidi's farm, and the exchange qualifies as a like-kind exchange. Helmut's adjusted basis for the apartment complex is $600,000, and the complex is subject to a $180,000 liability. The FMV of Heidi's farm is $770,000, and the farm is subject to a $100,000 liability. Each asset is transferred subject to the liability. What is Helmut's recognized gain, and the basis of the new farm?

12-35. ***Like-Kind Exchange—Liabilities.*** Sheila owns land with a basis of $100,000 and FMV of $220,000. The land is subject to an $80,000 liability. Sheila plans to exchange the land for land owned by Tony that has a $250,000 FMV but is subject to a liability of $150,000. Sheila plans to assume Tony's debt and Tony will assume her $80,000 debt. Since the exchange is not of equal value, how much cash must Tony transfer to equalize the exchange?

12-36. ***Like-Kind Exchange—Transfer of Boot.*** Wayne exchanges unimproved land with a $40,000 basis and marketable securities with a $10,000 basis for an eight-unit apartment building having a $150,000 FMV. The land and marketable securities are held by Wayne as investments, and the apartment building is held as an investment. The marketable securities have a $25,000 FMV. What is his realized gain, recognized gain, and the basis for the apartment building?

12-37. ***Like-Kind Exchange—Related Parties.*** Bob owns a duplex used as rental property. The duplex has a basis of $86,000 and $300,000 FMV. He transfers the duplex to Cindy, his sister, in exchange for a triplex that she owns. The triplex has a basis of $279,000 and a $300,000 FMV. Two months after the exchange, Cindy sells the duplex to a business associate for $312,000.
a. What is Bob's realized and recognized gain on the exchange?
b. What is Cindy's realized and recognized gain on the exchange?

12-38. ***Like-Kind Exchange—Related Parties.*** Assume the same facts as in 12-37 except Cindy sells the duplex to a nonrelated individual more than two years after the exchange with Bob. Ignore any changes in adjusted basis due to depreciation that would have occurred after the exchange.
a. What is Bob's realized and recognized gain on the exchange?
b. What is Cindy's realized and recognized gain on the exchange?
c. What is Cindy's realized and recognized gain on the sale?

12-39. ***Involuntary Conversion.*** Duke Corporation owns an office building with a $400,000 adjusted basis. The building is destroyed by a tornado. The insurance company paid $750,000 as compensation for the loss. Eight months after the loss, Duke uses the insurance proceeds and other funds to acquire a new office building for $682,000 and machinery for one of the company's plants at a $90,000 cost. Assuming that Duke elects to defer as much of the gain as possible, what is the recognized gain, the basis for the new office building, and the basis for the machinery acquired?

12-40. ***Involuntary Conversion—Replacement Period.*** The Madison Corporation paid $3,000 for several acres of land in 1987 to use in its trade or business. The land is condemned and taken by the state in March 1994. The company receives $25,000 from the state. Whenever possible, the corporation elects to minimize taxable income. For each of the following independent cases, what is (1) the recognized gain or loss in 1994 on the conversion and (2) the tax basis of the replacement property (whenever the property is replaced)?
a. The land will not be replaced.
b. Replacement land will be purchased in July, 1995 for $22,500.
c. Replacement land will be purchased in July, 1996 for $28,500.
d. Replacement land will be purchased in July, 1997 for $23,600.

12-41. *Involuntary Conversion of Real Property.* On April 27, 1994, an office building owned by Newark Corporation, an offshore drilling company that is a calendar-year taxpayer, is destroyed by a hurricane. The basis of the office building is $700,000, and the corporation receives $910,000 from the insurance company.

   a. To defer the entire gain due to the involuntary conversion, what amount must the corporation pay for replacement property?

   b. To defer the gain due to the involuntary conversion, by what date must the corporation replace the converted property?

   c. If Newark replaces the office building by purchasing a 900,000 gallon storage tank at an $850,000 cost, may any of the gain due to the involuntary conversion be deferred?

   d. How would your answers to Parts b and c change if the office building had been condemned by the state? Explain.

12-42. *Involuntary Conversion—Different Methods of Replacement.* On September 3, 1994, Federal Corporation's warehouse is totally destroyed by fire. $800,000 of insurance proceeds are received, and the realized gain is $300,000. Whenever possible, Federal elects to defer gains. For each of the following independent situations, what is the amount of gain recognized? Explain why the gain is not deferred, if applicable.

   a. On October 23, 1994, Federal purchases a warehouse for $770,000.

   b. On February 4, 1995, Federal purchases 100% of the Park Corporation, which owns a warehouse. Federal pays $895,000 for the stock.

   c. On March 10, 1995, Federal receives a capital contribution from its majority shareholder. The shareholder transfers a warehouse to the corporation. The warehouse's FMV is $975,000. The shareholder's basis in the warehouse is $635,000.

   d. On November 20, 1996, Federal purchases an apartment complex for $900,000.

   e. On March 26, 1997, Federal purchases a warehouse for $888,000.

12-43. *Severance Damages.* Twelve years ago, Marilyn purchased two lots in an undeveloped subdivision as an investment. Each lot has a $10,000 basis and a $40,000 FMV when the city condemns one lot for use as a municipal sewage treatment plant. As a result of the condemnation, Marilyn receives $40,000 from the city. Because the value of the other lot is reduced, the city pays $7,500 severance damages. She does not plan to replace the condemned lot.

   a. What is her recognized gain due to the condemnation?

   b. What is her recognized gain from the receipt of the severance damages?

   c. What is her basis for the lot she continues to own?

12-44. *Sale of a Principal Residence.* Louis is 40 years old, single, and owns a principal residence acquired for $71,000 in 1987. During the current year he sells the residence for $90,000 and purchases a new principal residence for $78,000. In order to sell the former residence, he spends $6,100 to sell the home and $300 to fix it up.

   a. What is the realized and recognized gain from the sale of the principal residence?

   b. What is the basis of the new residence?

12-45. *Sale of a Principal Residence.* Marc, age 45, sells his personal residence in May of the current year for $70,000. He pays $5,000 in selling expenses and $600 in fixing-up expenses. He has lived in the residence since 1980, when he purchased it for $40,000. In 1984, he paid $4,000 to install central air conditioning. If Marc purchases a new principal residence in December of the current year for $62,000, what is the realized gain, recognized gain, and the basis for the new residence?

12-46. *Sale of a Principal Residence—Cost of New Residence.* Laurie sells her personal residence for $50,000 in January, 1994, and purchases a new residence in October, 1994. Her old residence has a $34,000 basis, and she incurs $1,500 fixing-up expenses to prepare the house for sale. She pays $4,000 of selling expenses. As a result of the sale, Laurie recognizes a $1,700 gain in 1994. What is the cost of the new residence?

12-47. *Sale of a Principal Residence.* In August 1994, Rob and Maria, who are married, sell their principal residence and realize a $30,000 gain. It is the first house Rob and Maria ever owned, and the adjusted sales price is $75,000. In September 1994, Rob and Maria purchase a new residence for $92,000. What is the gain recognized and the basis of the new residence?

12-48. *Definition of a Principal Residence.* Ken's parents lived with him until 1992 in a house on 23rd Street purchased by Ken in 1982 for $30,000. In 1992 Ken married Beth and moved to a rented apartment. In 1994 they purchase a house on 42nd Street for $90,000, and Ken sells the house on 23rd Street for $60,000 when his parents move into a nursing home. Ken pays $4,000 selling expenses and $1,000 fixing-up expenses. How much of the realized gain on the sale of the house on 23rd Street may be deferred?

12-49. *Sale of a Principal Residence—Rental Property.* For the last several years, Mr. and Mrs. Cockrell have rented their furnished basement to local college students. When determining their taxable income each year, they have deducted a portion of the utilities, property taxes, interest, and depreciation based on the fact that 15% of the house is used for rental purposes. The original basis of the property is $100,000, and depreciation of $4,000 has been allowed on the rental portion of the property. During the current year, Mr. and Mrs. Cockrell sell the house for $300,000. No selling expenses or fixing-up expenses are incurred. Neither individual is 55 years old or older. They plan to purchase a new principal residence and will no longer rent any portion of their house to college students.
  a. What is the amount realized on the sale of the principal residence?
  b. What is the realized gain on the sale of the principal residence?
  c. What is the amount realized on the sale of the portion of the residence not considered to be the principal residence?
  d. What is the realized gain on the sale of the portion of the residence not considered to be the principal residence?
  e. If a new principal residence is purchased for $340,000 and occupied within the next two months, what is the maximum gain that may be deferred?
  f. If Mr. and Mrs. Cockrell wish to defer all of their gain, what must be the minimum cost of the new principal residence?

12-50. *Multiple Sales of a Principal Residence.* Consider the following information for Mr. and Mrs. Di Palma:

  • On June 10, 1993, they sold their principal residence for $80,000 and incur $6,000 of selling expenses and $1,000 of fixing-up expenses. The basis of the residence, which was acquired in 1986, is $50,000.
  • On June 25, 1993, they purchased a new principal residence for $90,000 and occupied it immediately.
  • May 10, 1994, they purchase their neighbor's residence for $115,000 and occupy the residence immediately.
  • May 29, 1994, they sell the residence purchased on June 25, 1993, for $108,000. They pay $7,000 of selling expenses and $500 of fixing-up expenses.

  a. What is the realized gain on the sale of the residence in 1993 and the adjusted sales price?
  b. What is the recognized gain on the sale of the residence in 1993? Which residence is considered to be the new principal residence—the one purchased in 1993 or the one purchased in 1994?
  c. What is the realized gain on the sale of the residence in 1994?
  d. What is the recognized gain on the sale of the residence in 1994?

12-51. *Multiple Sales of a Principal Residence.* Consider the following information for Mr. and Mrs. Gomez:

  • On May 6, 1993, they sold their principal residence, acquired in 1985, for $100,000. They paid $8,000 of selling expenses and $1,500 of fixing-up expenses. Their basis in the residence was $70,000.
  • On July 2, 1993, they purchased a new principal residence for $105,000.
  • On June 9, 1994, Mr. Gomez, a bank officer, is transferred to another bank in the northern part of the state.
  • On July 1, 1994, they purchase a new principal residence for $120,000.
  • On October 6, 1994, they sell the residence which was purchased on July 2, 1993, for $118,000. They pay $10,000 of selling expenses and $1,000 of fixing-up expenses.

  a. What is the realized gain on the sale of the residence in 1993 and the adjusted sales price?

b. What is the recognized gain on the sale of the residence in 1993? Which residence is considered to be the new principal residence—the one purchased in 1993 or the one in 1994?

c. What is the realized gain on the sale of the residence in 1994 and the adjusted sales price?

d. What is the recognized gain on the sale of the residence in 1994?

12-52. *Involuntary Conversion of Principal Residence.* As a result of a hurricane, Gail's house, with an adjusted basis of $136,000, is destroyed during the current year. After viewing the damaged area, the President declares the area to be a disaster area. Gail's insurance policy specifies coverage for artwork that she has collected. She receives the following payments from the insurance company: $200,000 for the house; $26,000 for the unscheduled personal property contents with an adjusted basis of $6,000; and $50,000 for the artwork. Her basis for the artwork is $17,500. Three months after the hurricane, she purchases another residence.

a. If the purchase price of the new residence is $270,000 and she does not replace the artwork, how much of the $32,500 gain ($50,000 − $17,500) on the artwork must be recognized?

b. What amount of gain is recognized, if any, from the receipt of insurance proceeds relative to the unscheduled personal property contents?

c. Assume Gail has not purchased another residence and receives the insurance proceeds in August of the current year. How long does she have to acquire the replacement property and still be eligible to defer the gain?

12-53. *Sale of a Principal Residence—Sec. 121 Exclusion.* After owning their principal residence for 15 years, Mr. and Mrs. Hall sell their personal residence and realize a $170,000 gain. He is 77 years old, and she is 54 years old. Mr. and Mrs. Hall do not plan to purchase another residence.

a. If Mr. and Mrs. Hall file a joint return and both consent to make the election to exclude the gain under Sec. 121, what is the maximum amount of the gain that may be excluded?

b. If they file a joint return but Mrs. Hall refuses to consent to the election under Sec. 121, what is the maximum amount of the gain that may be excluded?

c. If Mrs. Hall will not consent to filing the election and Mr. Hall files a separate return, what is the maximum amount of the gain that may be excluded?

12-54. *Sale of Principal Residence—Sec. 121 Exclusion.* Russ and Sandy, who are married and file a joint return, are both more than 55 years old and are eligible to utilize Sec. 121. During the current year, they sell their old residence and purchase a new principal residence. They elect to exclude as much of the gain as possible. The following information is provided about the sale and repurchase:

Basis of old residence	$ 40,000
Selling price of residence	280,000
Selling expenses	20,000
Fixing-up expenses	3,000
Purchase price of new residence	127,000

a. What is their realized gain?

b. What is their excluded gain?

c. What is their recognized gain?

d. What is their basis for the new residence?

TAX FORM/RETURN PREPARATION PROBLEMS

12-55. On October 29, 1993, Miss Joan Seely (social security no. 123-45-6789), age 32, sells her principal residence for $150,000 cash. She purchased the residence on May 12, 1987, for $85,000. She spent $12,000 for capital improvements in 1988. To help sell the house, she pays $300 on October 2, 1993, for minor repairs made on that date. The realtor's commission amounts to $7,500. On February 3, 1994, she purchases a new principal residence for $130,000. Her old residence is never rented out or used for business, and she does not plan to rent out or use the new residence for business. None of the rooms of the old residence were rented or used for business purposes. Prepare Form 2119 for Miss Seely.

12-56. At the beginning of the current year, Donna Harp was employed as a cinematographer by Farah Movie, Inc., a motion picture company in Los Angeles, California. In June, she accepted a new job with Ocala Production in Orlando, Florida. Donna is single, age 35, and her social security number is 223-77-6793. She sold her house in California on August 10 for $300,000. She paid a $14,000 sales commission and fixing-up expenses of $500. The house was acquired on March 23, 1987, for $140,000. The house in California is the first house that she has ever owned.

The cost of transporting her household goods and personal effects from California to Orlando amounted to $2,350. To travel from California to Florida, she paid travel and lodging costs of $370 and $100 for meals. Note that for the current year (1993) moving expenses include 80% of the cost of the meals, and moving expense is an itemized deduction. In 1994 and subsequent years, none of the cost of meals qualify as moving expense and the moving expense deduction is *for* AGI.

On July 15, she purchased a house for $270,000 on 1225 Minnie Lane in Orlando. To purchase the house, she incurred a 20-year mortgage for $170,000. To obtain the loan, she paid points of $3,400. The $3,600 of property taxes for the house in Orlando were prorated with $1,950 being apportioned to the seller and $1,650 being apportioned to the buyer. In December of the current year she paid $3,600 for property taxes.

Other information related to her return:

Salary from Farah Movie, Inc.	$30,000
Salary from Ocala Production, Inc.	50,000
Federal income taxes withheld by Farah	6,000
Federal income taxes withheld by Ocala	11,000
FICA taxes withheld by Farah	2,295
FICA taxes withheld by Ocala	3,825
Interest paid for mortgage:	
Home in California	2,780
Home in Orlando	3,800
Property taxes paid in California	4,100
Sales taxes paid in California and Florida	3,125
State income taxes paid in California	2,900
Interest income from Sun National Bank	1,800

Prepare Form 1040 including Schedules A, B, and D and Forms 2119 and 3903.

12-57. Jim Sarowski, (social security no. 344-77-9255), is 70 years old and single. He received social security benefits of $16,000. He works part-time as a greeter at a local discount store and received wages of $7,300. Federal income taxes of $250 were withheld from his salary. Jim lives at Rt. 7 in Daingerfield, Texas.

In March of the current year, he purchased a duplex at 2006 Tennessee Street to use as rental property for $100,000 with 20% of the price to be allocated to land. During the current year, he had the following receipts and expenditures with respect to the duplex:

Rent receipts	$8,800
Interest paid	5,900
Property taxes	1,400
Insurance	800
Maintenance	300

Other expenditures during the current year:

Contributions to the church	$2,600
Personal property taxes	225
Sales tax	345

On July 24 of the current year, he exchanged ten acres of land for a car with a $16,500 FMV to be held for personal use. The land was purchased on November 22, 1990, for $18,000 as an investment. Because of some pollution problems in the area, the value of the land declined.

On December 1 of the current year, he sold his residence, which had been his home for 30 years, for $275,000. Sales commissions of $16,000 were paid, and the adjusted basis for his home is $110,000. He plans to rent an apartment and does not plan to purchase another home. His only other sale of a principal residence occurred 32 years ago.

Prepare Forms 1040, 2119, and 4562 and Schedules D and E.

CASE STUDY PROBLEM

12-58. The Electric Corporation, a publicly held corporation, owns land with a $1,600,000 basis that is being held for investment. The company is considering exchanging the land for two assets owned by the Quail Corporation: land with a FMV of $3,000,000 and marketable securities with a $1,000,000 FMV. Both assets will be held by the Electric Corporation for investment, although the corporation is considering the possibility of developing the land for residential use. The President of the corporation has hired you to prepare a report explaining how the exchange will affect the corporation's reported net income and its tax liability. The corporation has a tax rate of 34%.

CASE STUDY PROBLEM—ETHICAL ISSUES

12-59. Monique Srivastava, a CPA, is a self-employed tax professional who specializes in preparing tax returns for individuals and small businesses. Two weeks ago, she prepared a return for a new client, Bruce Duncan. Bruce claimed a deduction for points paid to purchase a new residence on October 24, 1994, and Monique agreed that the deduction was appropriate. Bruce did not provide any information about the sale of a residence, and Monique did not ask about a possible sale of a residence.

In a recent conversation with Tasha Short, a realtor, Monique learned that Bruce sold a residence during the summer of 1992. Given the substantial appreciation for real estate in the subdivision where Bruce's home was located, Monique estimates that the house was sold at a substantial gain.

As a normal practice, Monique always requests tax returns for at least three previous years from new clients. In reviewing the three returns, she finds that Bruce did not file Form 2119 nor report a gain on the sale of a residence in 1992. What action should Monique take? (See the caption entitled Statements on Responsibilities in Tax Practice in Chapter 1 for a discussion of this issue.)

TAX RESEARCH PROBLEMS

12-60. For the last nine years, Mr. and Mrs. Orchard, age 42 and 40, respectively, live in a residence located on eight acres. In January of the current year they sell the home and two acres of land. The purchaser of the residence does not wish to own the entire eight acres of land. In December they sell the remaining 6 acres of land to another individual for $60,000. The house and the land have never been used by the Orchards in a trade or business or held for investment. The realized gains resulting from the two sales are computed as follows:

	House and Two Acres January Sales	Eight Acres December Sale
Selling price	$140,000	$60,000
Minus: selling expenses	(8,000)	(3,000)
Amount realized	$132,000	$57,000
Minus: Basis	(80,000)	(18,000)
Realized gain	$ 52,000	$39,000

In March they purchase a new residence for $225,000. As a result of the sales described above, what is the amount of realized gain that must be recognized during the current year?

A partial list of research sources is

- Sec. 1034.
- Reg. Sec. 1.1034-1(c)(3).
- Rev. Rul. 76-541, 1976-2 C.B. 246.

12-61. George, age 68, decides to retire from farming and is considering selling his farm. The farm has a $100,000 basis and a $400,000 FMV. George's two sons are not interested in farming. Both sons have large families and would like to own houses suitable for their needs. The Iowa Corporation is willing to purchase George's farm. George's tax advisor suggests that Iowa Corporation should buy the two houses which the sons want to own for $400,000 and then exchange the houses for George's farm. After the exchange, George could make a gift of the houses to the sons.

a. If the transactions are executed as suggested by the tax advisor, George's recognized gain will be $300,000. The transaction does not qualify as a like-kind exchange. Explain why.

b. George wants the exchange to qualify as a like-kind exchange and still help his sons obtain the houses. What advice do you have for him?

A partial list of research sources is

- *Dollie H. Click,* 78 T.C. 225 (1982).
- *Fred S. Wagensen,* 74 T.C. 653 (1980).

12-62. On January 14, 1992, the Kelders sold their personal residence for $120,000 to Mr. and Mrs. Clancy. Although the Kelders did not have the house listed for sale, the Clancys fell in love with the house while driving through the neighborhood and made an offer the Kelders could not refuse. Both Kelders are less than 55 years old.

The Kelders moved to a townhouse and negotiated a renewable three-month rental agreement. In November, 1992, the Kelders were still living in the townhouse due to their inability to locate a house they wanted to buy. Finally, they decided to build a new house. They purchased a lot in December and construction was scheduled to start during the spring of 1993. However, the builder declared bankruptcy and construction of the home was not started until October 1993. The Kelders agreed to pay the new builder a $2,000 premium if the house was completed within 60 days. Because of bad weather, the house was not completed until January 10, 1994, at a total cost of $129,000. On January 11, one day prior to the Kelders' planned move into the house, the house was totally destroyed by fire. The Kelders purchased another home for $130,000 on January 23, 1994, and occupied the residence as of February 1, 1994.

May the Kelders defer the gain on the sale of the residence to the Clancys?

A partial list of resource sources is

- Rev. Rul. 75-438, 1975-2 C.B. 334.
- *Joseph T. Gelinas,* 1976 P.H. T.C. Memo 76,103, 35 TCM 448.

12-63. On March 1, 1990, Jeremy, who was 53 years old, purchased a principal residence for $90,000. He has never been married. Except for two months in 1990 when Jeremy was on vacation in Hawaii, he owned and used the house as his principal residence until January 4, 1993, when he suffered a massive stroke. He was in the hospital until February 10, 1993, when he was moved to a nursing home since he was incapable of self-care.

If he sells the house on April 12, 1994 for $160,000, may Jeremy elect to exclude the gain?

A partial list of research sources is

- Sec. 121(d)(9).
- Reg. Sec. 1.121-1(c).

13 Property Transactions— Section 1231 and Recapture

LEARNING OBJECTIVES

After studying this chapter, you should be able to

1. Identify Sec. 1231 property
2. Understand the tax treatment for Sec. 1231 transactions
3. Apply the recapture provisions of Sec. 1245
4. Apply the recapture provisions of Sec. 1250
5. Describe other recapture applications

Chapter 5 states that all recognized gains and losses must eventually be designated as either capital or ordinary. However, certain gains or losses are designated as Sec. 1231 gains or losses. Ordinary loss treatment is accorded to a net Sec. 1231 loss, which is defined as the excess of Sec. 1231 losses over Sec. 1231 gains.[1] Net Sec. 1231 gain, which is the excess of Sec. 1231 gains over Sec. 1231 losses, is treated as long-term capital gain.[2] Sec. 1231 gain is determined after any amount recaptured as ordinary income under the depreciation recapture rules is eliminated. Net Sec. 1231 gain is treated as ordinary income to the extent of nonrecaptured net Sec. 1231 losses for the preceding 5 years.[3]

HISTORY OF SEC. 1231

Key Point

If a taxpayer has gains, it is preferable to have the gains treated as capital gains; and if a taxpayer has losses, it is preferable to have the losses treated as ordinary losses. Since Sec. 1231 property receives the preferable treatment for both net gains and losses, it has been said that this property enjoys the best of both worlds.

During the depressed economy of the early and mid-1930s, business property was classified as a capital asset. Many business properties were worth less than their adjusted basis. Instead of selling business properties, taxpayers found it advantageous to retain those assets that had declined in value because they could recover the full cost as depreciation. Capital losses had only limited deductibility during this period. To encourage the mobility of capital (i.e., the replacement of business fixed assets), the Revenue Act of 1938 added business property to the list of properties not considered to be capital assets.

During the period from 1938 to 1942, gains and losses on the sale or exchange of business property were treated as ordinary gains and losses. Favorable capital gain treatment was eliminated, and taxpayers with appreciated business properties were reluctant to sell the assets because of the high tax cost. This restriction on the mobility of capital was more significant than usual because business assets had to be shifted into industries that were more heavily involved in the production of military goods. Furthermore, taxpayers were often forced to recognize ordinary gains because the government used the condemnation process to obtain business property for the war effort. In 1942 Congress created the predecessor of Sec. 1231, which allowed taxpayers to treat net gains from the sale of business property as capital gains and net losses as ordinary losses. Prior to 1987, only 40% of an individual's net capital gain might be subject to tax because of the 60% long-term capital gain deduction.

---

[1] Secs. 1231(c)(4) and (a)(2).

[2] Secs. 1231(c)(3) and (a)(1).

[3] Sec. 1231(c)(1). These rules apply for tax years beginning after December 31, 1984 and to nonrecaptured net Sec. 1231 losses for years beginning after December 31, 1981.

As explained in Chapter 5, the Tax Reform Act of 1986 eliminated the 60% long-term capital gain deduction for net long-term capital gains. Favorable long-term capital gain treatment was reinstated into the tax law in 1991 in the form of a 28% maximum tax rate applying to net capital gains for individuals. It may also be advantageous to have the gain classified as capital or Sec. 1231 if taxpayers have capital losses or capital loss carryovers because of the limitations that are imposed upon the deductibility of capital losses. Furthermore, there are other situations where it may be important for the property to be Sec. 1231 property (e.g., a contribution of appreciated property to a charitable organization).

OVERVIEW OF BASIC TAX TREATMENT FOR SEC. 1231

Typical Misconception

It is sometimes thought that each Sec. 1231 gain should be treated as a LTCG and each Sec. 1231 loss as an ordinary loss. However all Sec. 1231 gains and losses must be combined to determine if the Sec. 1231 gains and losses are LTCGs and LTCLs or ordinary gains and losses.

Net Gains

At the end of the tax year, Sec. 1231 gains are netted against Sec. 1231 losses. If the overall result is a net Sec. 1231 gain, the gains and losses are treated as long-term capital gains (LTCGs) and long-term capital losses (LTCLs).[4] For the sake of expediency, it is often stated that a net Sec. 1231 gain is treated as a LTCG. For tax years beginning after 1984, however, a portion or all of the net Sec. 1231 gain may be treated as ordinary income.

Example 13-1 ■ Dawn owns a business that has $20,000 of Sec. 1231 gains and $12,000 of Sec. 1231 losses during the current year. Since the Sec. 1231 gains exceed the Sec. 1231 losses, the gains and losses are treated as LTCGs and LTCLs. After the gains and losses are offset, there is an $8,000 net long-term capital gain (NLTCG). ■

Example 13-2 ■ Assume the same facts as in Example 13-1 except that Dawn also recognizes a $7,000 LTCG from the sale of a capital asset. After considering the $8,000, net Sec. 1231 gain, which is treated as a LTCG, Dawn has a $15,000 NLTCG ($8,000 + $7,000). ■

Net Losses

If the netting of Sec. 1231 gains and losses at the end of the year results in a net Sec. 1231 loss, the Sec. 1231 gains and losses are treated as ordinary gains and losses.[5] For expediency, it is often stated that the net Sec. 1231 loss is treated as an ordinary loss.

Example 13-3 ■ David owns an unincorporated business and has $30,000 of Sec. 1231 gains and $40,000 of Sec. 1231 losses in the current year. Since the losses exceed the gains, they are treated as ordinary losses and gains. ■

Example 13-4 ■ Assume the same facts as in Example 13-3 except that David receives a $37,000 salary as a corporate employee. David has no other income, losses, or deductions affecting his adjusted gross income (AGI). The Sec. 1231 gains and losses are treated as ordinary gains and losses, and David's AGI is $27,000 ($37,000 salary −

[4] Sec. 1231(a)(1).
[5] Sec. 1231(a)(2).

$10,000 of ordinary loss). The $40,000 of ordinary losses offsets the $30,000 of ordinary gains and $10,000 of David's salary. ■

One important advantage of Sec. 1231 is illustrated in Example 13-4. Since the Sec. 1231 gains and losses are treated as ordinary, the $10,000 net Sec. 1231 loss is fully deductible in the current year. If the gains and losses were classified as long-term capital gains and losses, David would have a $10,000 NLTCL. Only $3,000 of the $10,000 NLTCL would have been deductible against David's other income. The tax treatment for capital losses is explained in Chapter 5.

The Tax Reform Act of 1984 reduced the benefits of Sec. 1231. For tax years beginning after 1984, any net Sec. 1231 gain is ordinary gain to the extent of any nonrecaptured net Sec. 1231 losses from the previous five years.[6] In essence, net Sec. 1231 losses previously deducted as ordinary losses are recaptured by changing what would otherwise be a LTCG into ordinary income.

Additional Comment

A taxpayer's share of a Sec. 1231 loss from a partnership or S Corporation may be subject to the passive activity loss rules.

Example 13-5 ■

Historical Note

In the Tax Reform Act of 1984, Congress reduced the benefits of Sec. 1231 by requiring the recapture of any nonrecaptured net Sec. 1231 loss. This recapture is required since taxpayers have a certain amount of control over the timing of the recognition of Sec. 1231 gains or losses. Taxpayers had attempted to recognize Sec. 1231 losses in one year and Sec. 1231 gains in another year, thus avoiding the netting process.

In 1994, Craig recognizes $25,000 of Sec. 1231 gains and $15,000 of Sec. 1231 losses. In 1990, Craig reported $14,000 of Sec. 1231 losses and no Sec. 1231 gains. No other Sec. 1231 gains or losses were recognized by Craig during the 1989–1993 period. The $10,000 ($25,000 − $15,000) of net Sec. 1231 gain in 1994 is treated as ordinary income due to the $14,000 of nonrecaptured net Sec. 1231 losses. ■

To determine the amount of nonrecaptured net Sec. 1231 losses, compare the aggregate amount of net Sec. 1231 losses for the most recent preceding 5 tax years with the amount of such losses recaptured as ordinary income for those preceding tax years. The excess of the aggregate amount of net Sec. 1231 losses over the previously recaptured loss is the nonrecaptured net Sec. 1231 loss. In Example 13-5, $4,000 of nonrecaptured net Sec. 1231 losses remain which can be recaptured in 1995. In 1995, the preceding 5-year period includes 1990 through 1994.

SECTION 1231 PROPERTY

OBJECTIVE 1

Identify Sec. 1231 property

Key Point

Only property used in a trade or business is included in the definition of Sec. 1231 property. Gains and losses on property held for investment may be included only if the result of a condemnation or casualty.

Example 13-6 ■

Section 1231 Property Defined

Section 1231 property is property used in a trade or business that is real property or depreciable property held for more than one year.[7] Certain types of property do not qualify as Sec. 1231 property, even if used in a trade or business. For example, inventory is not Sec. 1231 property. Thus, a sale of inventory results in ordinary gain or loss. Publications of the U.S. Government received other than by purchase at its regular sale price; a copyright; literary, musical, or artistic compositions; letters or memorandums; or similar properties held by certain taxpayers are not classified as Sec. 1231 property.[8]

Carl, who owns a recording studio, writes a musical composition to be sold to a record company. Since the musical composition is created by the personal efforts of the taxpayer, the musical composition is not Sec. 1231 property, and the sale results in ordinary gain from the sale of an ordinary asset. ■

---

[6] Sec. 1231(c)(1).
[7] This holding period requirement coincides with the holding period requirement for LTCGs.
[8] Sec. 1231(b)(1).

Relationship to Capital Assets

Key Point

Inventory, free publications of the U.S. government, and copyrights, literary, musical or artistic compositions, etc. are not capital assets.

As noted in Chapter 5, the Code does not provide a definition of a capital asset. Instead, Sec. 1221 provides a list of noncapital assets. This list includes both depreciable property and real property used in a trade or business.[9] These properties are treated as Sec. 1231 properties if held for more than one year. Depreciable property and real property used in a trade or business and held for one year or less is neither a capital asset nor Sec. 1231 property. Any gain or loss resulting from the disposition of such an asset is ordinary.

Example 13-7 ■

The Prime Corporation owns land held as an investment and land used as an employee parking lot. The land held as an investment is a capital asset. The land used as a parking lot is real property used in a trade or business and is not a capital asset. The land used as a parking lot is a Sec. 1231 asset if held for more than one year. ■

Example 13-8 ■

Dale, a self-employed plumber, owns an automobile held for personal use and a truck used in his trade. The automobile is a capital asset because it is held for personal use. The truck is a Sec. 1231 asset if held for more than one year. As described later, a portion or all of any gain realized on the sale of the truck may be taxed as ordinary income due to the Sec. 1245 depreciation recapture provisions. ■

Natural Resources and Farming

Self-Study Question

Is the possible inclusion of timber and coal or domestic iron ore in the definition of Sec. 1231 property favorable to the taxpayers who produce these items?

Answer

Yes, it can result in income being taxed as long-term capital gain instead of ordinary income from the sale of inventory.

Congress extended Sec. 1231 treatment to transactions involving timber, coal, domestic iron ore, livestock, and land with unharvested crops. These extensions reflect Congress's concern for developing natural resources and its recognition of farming as a rather unique type of business.

Timber. Section 631 allows an election to treat the cutting of timber as a sale or exchange of such timber. To be eligible to make this election, the taxpayer must own the timber or hold the contract right on the first day of the year and for more than one year. Furthermore, the timber must be cut for sale or for use in the taxpayer's trade or business.[10]

The gain or loss is determined by comparing the timber's adjusted basis for depletion with its fair market value (FMV) on the first day of the tax year in which it is cut. If the timber is eventually sold for more or less than its FMV (determined on the first day of the year the timber is cut), the difference is ordinary gain or loss.

Example 13-9 ■

Real World Example

Christmas trees can be included in the definition of Sec. 1231 property, and this opportunity to convert ordinary income into capital gains has resulted in the use of Christmas tree tax shelters.

Vermont Corporation owns timber with a $60,000 basis for depletion. The timber, acquired 4 years ago, is cut during the current year for use in the corporation's business. The FMV of the timber on the first day of the current year is $200,000. Vermont Corporation may elect to treat the cutting of the timber as a sale or exchange and recognize a $140,000 ($200,000 − $60,000) gain. If the timber is actually sold in the following year for $210,000, $10,000 of ordinary income is recognized. ■

---

[9] Sec.1221(2).
[10] Sec. 631(a) and Reg. Sec. 1.631-1.

If the election is made to treat the cutting of timber as a sale or exchange, the timber is considered to be Sec. 1231 property.[11] Thus, the $140,000 of gain in Example 13-9 is a Sec. 1231 gain. If the taxpayer does not make the election, the character of any gain or loss depends upon whether the timber is held for sale in the ordinary course of the taxpayer's trade or business, held for investment, or held for use in a trade or business.

Coal or Domestic Iron Ore. An owner who disposes of coal (including lignite) or domestic iron ore while retaining an economic interest in it must treat the disposal as a sale.[12] The coal or iron ore is considered to be Sec. 1231 property.[13] The owner must own and retain an economic interest in the coal or iron ore in place.[14] An economic interest is owned when one acquires by investment any interest in mineral in place and seeks a return of capital from income derived from the extraction of the mineral.[15]

Additional Comment

Livestock includes cattle, hogs, horses, mules, donkeys, sheep, goats, fur-bearing animals, and other mammals, but the term excludes poultry, fish, frogs, or reptiles.

Livestock. Livestock held by the taxpayer for draft, breeding, dairy, or sporting purposes is considered to be Sec. 1231 property. However, to qualify for such treatment, cattle and horses must be held for 24 months or more from the date of acquisition and other livestock must be held for 12 months or more from the date of acquisition.[16]

Real World Example

The gain from the syndication and sale of breeding rights by horse breeders is treated as a Sec. 1231 gain.

Unharvested Crops and Land. An unharvested crop growing on land used in the trade or business is considered to be Sec. 1231 property if the crop and the land are both sold at the same time to the same person and the land is held more than one year.[17] Section 1231 does not apply to the sale or exchange of an unharvested crop if the taxpayer retains any right or option to reacquire the land.[18]

Additional Comment

The treatment of unharvested crops as a Sec. 1231 asset is largely a rule of convenience. If the taxpayer were not permitted to treat the crops in this fashion, it would be necessary to allocate the selling price between the land and crops.

If Sec. 1231 applies to the sale or exchange of an unharvested crop sold with the land, no deductions are allowed for expenses attributable to the production of the unharvested crop.[19] Instead, costs of producing the crop must be capitalized.

INVOLUNTARY CONVERSIONS

Gains and losses from involuntary conversions of property used in a trade or business generally are classified as Sec. 1231 gains and losses. Involuntary conversions of capital assets that are held in connection with a trade or business or in a transaction entered into for profit also generally qualify for Sec. 1231 treatment. The property that is involuntarily converted must be held for more than one year. Certain involuntary conversions are treated differently for income tax purposes. For example,

---

[11] Sec. 1231(b)(2) and Reg. Sec. 1.631-1(d)(4).
[12] Sec. 631(c) and Reg. Sec. 1.631-3(a)(1).
[13] Sec. 1231(b)(2) and Reg. Sec. 1.631-3(a)(2).
[14] Reg. Sec. 1.631-3(b)(4).
[15] Reg. Sec. 1.611-1(b)(1).
[16] Sec. 1231(b)(3).
[17] Sec. 1231(b)(4) and Reg. Secs. 1.1231-1(c)(5) and 1(f).
[18] Reg. Sec. 1.1231-1(f).
[19] Sec. 268 and Reg. Sec. 1.268-1.

the tax rules are different for condemnations and casualties, even though both are involuntary conversions of property.

Condemnations

Gains and losses resulting from condemnations of Sec. 1231 property and capital assets held more than one year are classified as Sec. 1231 gains and losses. As indicated above, the capital assets must be held in connection with a trade or business or with a transaction entered into for profit.[20]

Example 13-10 ∎   Kathryn owns land with a $20,000 basis and a $30,000 FMV as well as a capital asset with a $40,000 basis and a $26,000 FMV. Both assets are used in her trade or business and have been held for more than one year. As a result of the state exercising its powers of requisition or condemnation, Kathryn is required to transfer both properties to the state for cash equal to their FMVs. No other transfers of assets occur during the current year. The $10,000 gain due to condemnation of the land is a Sec. 1231 gain, and the $14,000 loss due to condemnation of the capital asset is a Sec. 1231 loss.   ∎

Typical Misconception

The inclusion of gains and losses from condemnations in the netting of the other involuntary conversions is a common error.

Other Involuntary Conversions

Gains or losses resulting from an involuntary conversion arising from fire, storm, shipwreck, other casualty, or theft are not classified as Sec. 1231 gains or losses if the recognized losses from such conversions exceed the recognized gains.[21] In such a case, the involuntary conversions are treated as ordinary gains and losses. However, if the gains from such involuntary conversions exceed the losses, both are classified as Sec. 1231 gains and losses.

Example 13-11 ∎   Jose owns equipment having a $50,000 basis and a $42,000 FMV and a building having a $30,000 basis and a $35,000 FMV which are used in Jose's trade or business. The straight-line method of depreciation is used for the building. Both assets are held for more than a year. As a result of a fire, both assets are destroyed, and Jose collects insurance proceeds equal to the assets' FMV. No other transfers of assets occur during the current year. Since the $8,000 ($42,000 − $50,000) realized loss exceeds the $5,000 ($35,000 − $30,000) realized gain, the realized loss and gain are both treated as ordinary.   ∎

PROCEDURE FOR SEC. 1231 TREATMENT

OBJECTIVE 2

Understand the tax treatment for Sec. 1231 transactions

After determining the realized gains and losses from transfers of property qualifying for Sec. 1231 treatment, it is necessary to determine if any gain must be recaptured as ordinary income under Secs. 1245 and 1250. The recaptured gain, discussed later in this chapter, is not eligible for Sec. 1231 treatment. After eliminating the gain recaptured as ordinary income, the procedure for analyzing Sec. 1231 transactions is as follows:

[20] Secs. 1231(a)(3)(A) and (4)(B).
[21] Sec. 1231(a)(4)(C).

Key Point

Gains that are recaptured under Secs. 1245 and 1250 are not eligible for Sec. 1231 treatment.

STEP 1. Determine all gains and losses resulting from casualties or thefts of Sec. 1231 property and non-personal-use capital assets held for more than one year. Gains and losses are netted and treated as Sec. 1231 gains and losses if the gains exceed the losses.

If the losses exceed the gains, both are treated as ordinary losses and gains and do not, therefore, enter into the Sec. 1231 netting procedure. Recall from Chapter 8 that business casualty losses are deductible *for* AGI, and other casualty losses are deductible *from* AGI.

STEP 2. Combine the following gains and losses to determine if Sec. 1231 gains exceed Sec. 1231 losses or vice versa:

1. Net casualty and theft gains resulting from Step 1, if any
2. Gains and losses resulting from the sale or exchange of Sec. 1231 property
3. Gains and losses resulting from the condemnation of Sec. 1231 property and non-personal-use capital assets held more than one year.

If a net Sec. 1231 loss is the result, the losses and gains are treated as ordinary losses and gains. If a net Sec. 1231 gain is the result, the gains and losses are treated as LTCGs and LTCLs. A portion or all of the capital gain may be recaptured as ordinary income as outlined in Step 3 below.

STEP 3. If a net Sec. 1231 gain is the result of Step 2, the amount of nonrecaptured net Sec. 1231 losses must be determined. Net Sec. 1231 gains to the extent of any nonrecaptured net Sec. 1231 losses are treated as ordinary income. Any net Sec. 1231 gain in excess of nonrecaptured net Sec. 1231 loss is treated as a LTCG. Nonrecaptured net Sec. 1231 losses are the excess of aggregate net Sec. 1231 losses for the preceding 5 years beginning after December 31, 1981, over losses previously recaptured as ordinary income due to the recapture provision of Sec. 1231.

Example 13-12 ■

The following gains and losses pertain to Danielle's business assets that qualify as Sec. 1231 property. Danielle does not have any nonrecaptured net Sec. 1231 losses, and the portion of gain recaptured as ordinary income due to the depreciation recapture provisions has been eliminated.

Gain due to an insurance reimbursement for fire damage	$10,000
Loss due to condemnation	19,000
Gain due to the sale of Sec. 1231 property	22,000

The $10,000 casualty gain is classified as a Sec. 1231 gain. Danielle has $32,000 ($10,000 + $22,000) of Sec. 1231 gains and a $19,000 Sec. 1231 loss. Danielle's $13,000 net Sec. 1231 gain is treated as a LTCG. No portion of the $13,000 LTCG is recaptured as ordinary income because Danielle does not have any nonrecaptured net Sec. 1231 losses during the preceding 5-year period. ■

Example 13-13 ■

Assume the same facts as in Example 13-12 except that Danielle has a $10,000 loss because of the fire instead of a $10,000 gain. The $10,000 casualty loss is an ordinary loss and not a Sec. 1231 loss. Since the loss is a business loss, it is deductible *for* AGI. Due to the $19,000 condemnation loss and the $22,000 of Sec. 1231 gain, she has a $3,000 net Sec. 1231 gain that is treated as a LTCG. ■

Example 13-14 ■   The following gains and losses recognized in 1994 pertain to Fred's business assets that were held for more than one year. The assets qualify as Sec. 1231 assets.

Gain due to an insurance reimbursement for a casualty	$15,000
Gain due to a condemnation	25,000
Loss due to the sale of Sec. 1231 property	12,000

A summary of Fred's net Sec. 1231 gains and losses for the previous 5-year period is as follows:

Year	Sec. 1231 Gain	Sec. 1231 Loss	Cumulative Nonrecaptured Net Sec. 1231 Losses (from 5 Prior Years)
1989	$ 5,000		—0—
1990		$2,000	$2,000
1991		6,000	8,000
1992	13,000		—0—
1993		9,000	9,000

The $15,000 gain due to the insurance reimbursement for a casualty is treated as a Sec. 1231 gain. The $25,000 gain from the condemnation is also a Sec. 1231 gain. Fred's net Sec. 1231 gain in 1994 is $28,000 ([$15,000 + $25,000] − $12,000). However, $9,000 of the Sec. 1231 gain is recaptured as ordinary income due to the $9,000 of nonrecaptured Sec. 1231 loss from 1993. The remaining $19,000 of net Sec. 1231 gain is a LTCG.   ■

RECAPTURE PROVISIONS OF SEC. 1245

OBJECTIVE 3

Apply the recapture provisions of Sec. 1245

In 1962 Congress enacted Sec. 1245, which substantially reduced the advantages of Sec. 1231. A gain from the disposition of Sec. 1245 property is treated as ordinary income to the extent of the total amount of depreciation (or cost-recovery) deductions allowed since January 1, 1962. The gain recaptured as ordinary income cannot exceed the amount of the realized gain.

Example 13-15 ■

Typical Misconception

It is sometimes thought that only tangible property is subject to Sec. 1245 recapture. In fact, both tangible and intangible personal property is included.

Adobe Corporation sells equipment used in its trade or business for $95,000. The equipment was acquired several years ago for $110,000 and is Sec. 1245 property.[22] The equipment's adjusted basis is reduced to $60,000 because $50,000 of depreciation was deducted. The entire $35,000 ($95,000 − $60,000) of gain is treated as ordinary income because the total amount of depreciation taken ($50,000) is greater than the $35,000 realized gain.   ■

The recapture provisions of Sec. 1245 apply to the total amount of depreciation (or cost recovery) allowed or allowable for Sec. 1245 property. It makes no difference which method of depreciation is used.[23]

Generally, the entire gain from the disposition of Sec. 1245 property is recaptured as ordinary income because the total amount of depreciation (or cost recovery) is

---

[22] Throughout this chapter, property is considered to be placed in service when it is purchased or acquired. The term Sec. 1245 property is used here to refer to either recovery property under the ACRS or MACRS rules or nonrecovery property that falls outside of the ACRS or MACRS rules.

[23] As explained later in this chapter, the method of cost recovery used determines if certain real property is treated as Sec. 1245 recovery property.

greater than the gain realized. A portion of the gain will receive Sec. 1231 treatment if the realized gain exceeds total depreciation or cost recovery.

Example 13-16 ■

Assume the same facts as in Example 13-15 except that the asset is sold for $117,000. Since the $57,000 ($117,000 − $60,000) realized gain is greater than the $50,000 of total depreciation, $50,000 of the gain is ordinary income and the remaining $7,000 is a Sec. 1231 gain. ■

Additional Comment

Section 1245 does not apply to losses because in these cases the taxpayers have taken too little depreciation rather than too much depreciation.

Purpose of Sec. 1245

The purpose of Sec. 1245 is to eliminate any advantage taxpayers would have if they were able to reduce ordinary income by deducting depreciation and subsequently receive Sec. 1231 treatment when the asset was sold. The effect of Sec. 1245 is not as significant after the Tax Reform Act of 1986, since the preferential treatment for long-term capital gain has been eliminated for corporate taxpayers. For individuals, Sec. 1245 recapture prevents net Sec. 1231 gain from being treated as net long-term capital gain and being taxed at a maximum 28% rate. An increase in the maximum tax rates for high-income individuals in 1993 and subsequent years from 31% to 36% or 39.6% has increased the importance of the Sec. 1245 recapture provisions for such individuals. The conversion of Sec. 1231 gain to Sec. 1245 ordinary income also prevents taxpayers from offsetting Sec. 1231 gains against net capital losses when offsetting capital gains do not exist.

Example 13-17 ■

During the current year, Coastal Corporation has capital losses of $50,000 and no capital gains for the current year or the preceding three years. The corporation owns equipment that was purchased several years ago for $90,000, and depreciation deductions of $48,000 have been allowed. If Coastal sells the equipment for $72,000, the entire $30,000 ($72,000 − $42,000) gain is Sec. 1245 ordinary income. Without Sec. 1245, the $30,000 gain, which is due in part to the depreciation deductions, would be a Sec. 1231 gain that could be used to offset $30,000 of the corporation's capital loss. ■

Note that Sec. 1245 does not apply to losses. If Coastal Corporation sells the equipment in Example 13-17 for $40,000, a $2,000 ($40,000 − $42,000 basis) Sec. 1231 loss would be recognized.

Key Point

On the sale of Sec. 1245 property, a portion of the gain will be treated as Sec. 1231 gain only if the property is sold for more than the original cost. This is very unlikely for factory equipment, trucks, office equipment, and other Sec. 1245 property.

Property Subject to Sec. 1245

Section 1245 applies to gains resulting from the disposition of Sec. 1245 property. Section 1245 property also includes property previously defined as Sec. 1245 recovery property. To be classified as Sec. 1245 recovery property, the property must be placed in service after 1980 and before 1987.

Key Point

Property must be depreciable or amortizable to be included in the definition of Sec. 1245 property.

Section 1245 Property. **Section 1245 property** is certain property subject to depreciation and, in some cases, amortization. The most common example of Sec. 1245 property is depreciable personal property such as equipment. Automobiles, livestock, railroad grading, and single-purpose agricultural or horticultural structures are Sec. 1245 properties.[24]

Except for certain buildings placed in service after 1980 and before 1987, buildings and structural components are not Sec. 1245 property. But tangible real property "used as an integral part of the manufacturing, production, extraction, or furnishing of transportation, communication, electrical energy, gas, water, or sewage disposal services" is Sec. 1245 property.[25]

[24] Sec. 1245(a)(3).
[25] Sec. 1245(a)(3)(B)(i).

Example 13-18 ■

Buckeye Corporation owns the following assets acquired before 1981: equipment, patent, an office building (including structural components), and land. The equipment and patent are Sec. 1245 property. The office building and the land are not Sec. 1245 property. ■

Real World Example

Pipelines, electric transmission towers, blast furnaces, greenhouses, and oil tanks are examples of real property that are included in the definition of Sec. 1245 property.

In many cases, taxpayers are allowed preferential treatment with respect to amortizing certain costs. For example, taxpayers may elect to expense up to $35,000 of the cost of making any business facility more accessible to handicapped and elderly individuals,[26] or to amortize pollution control facilities over 60 months[27] and reforestation expenditures over 84 months.[28] If taxpayers have amortized the costs of any real property under the special provisions, Sec. 1245 applies to the gain resulting from the disposition of such property.[29]

If taxpayers elect to expense certain depreciable property under Sec. 179, the amount deducted is treated as a depreciation deduction for purposes of the Sec. 1245 recapture provisions.[30]

Example 13-19 ■

Typical Misconception

The categorization of nonresidential real estate acquired during the period from 1981 to 1986, and on which an accelerated depreciation method was used, as Sec. 1250 property rather than as Sec. 1245 property is a commonly encountered error.

Compact Corporation purchased $90,000 of equipment in 1993 and elected to expense $17,500 under Sec. 179. Compact sells the equipment in 1994 for $95,000. Depreciation allowed for 1993 and 1994 is $14,500 and $11,600 respectively. The adjusted basis of the equipment on the date of sale is $46,400 ($90,000 − $17,500 − $26,100 depreciation). The realized gain is $48,600 ($95,000 − $46,400), and $43,600 ($17,500 + $26,100) of the gain is Sec. 1245 ordinary income. The remaining $5,000 is Sec. 1231 gain. ■

Application of Sec. 1245 to Certain Buildings. Most real property is not affected by Sec. 1245. However, Sec. 1245 does apply to nonresidential real estate that qualified as recovery property under the ACRS rules (i.e., placed in service after 1980 and before 1987) unless the taxpayer elected to use the straight-line method of cost recovery.[31] Section 1245 does not apply to nonresidential real estate acquired after 1986. Only straight-line depreciation may be used for nonresidential real estate acquired after 1986 (see Chapter 10).

Example 13-20 ■

Key Point

Taxpayers acquiring nonresidential real property during the period 1981 to 1986 were confronted with choosing between straight-line ACRS and ACRS using the statutory rates. In making the decision, these taxpayers should have considered the number of years that the property would be held, the estimated selling price, the present value of the additional depreciation deductions, and any preferential treatment for net capital gains.

Brad sells the following two warehouses during the current year:

	Warehouse 1	*Warehouse 2*
Year of purchase	1984	1984
Cost	$720,000	$900,000
Cost recovery—straight line ACRS	200,000	
Cost recovery—ACRS statutory rates		360,000
Adjusted basis	520,000	540,000
Selling price	700,000	800,000

Both warehouses were acquired after 1980 and qualified as recovery property. The $180,000 ($700,000 − $520,000) gain on the sale of Warehouse 1 is a Sec. 1231 gain. Section 1245 does not apply since the straight-line method of cost recovery is used. Section 1245 applies to the sale of Warehouse 2 because ACRS is used and the property is nonresidential real estate. Therefore, the $260,000 ($800,000 −

---

[26] Sec. 190.
[27] Sec. 169(a).
[28] Sec. 194(a).
[29] Sec. 1245(a)(3)(C). The Sec. 1245 rules recapture amortization deductions claimed on real property under Secs. 169, 179, 185, 188, 190, 193 and 194.
[30] Sec. 1245(a)(2)(C).
[31] Sec. 1245(a)(5), prior to being eliminated by the Tax Reform Act of 1986.

$540,000) gain is ordinary income because the $260,000 gain is less than the $360,000 total ACRS cost-recovery allowance. ∎

If the properties in Example 13-20 were acquired prior to 1981, they would not be subject to the Sec. 1245 recapture rules regardless of the method of depreciation used. However, nonresidential real estate (e.g., a warehouse) acquired prior to 1981 is subject to the Sec. 1250 recapture rules, and a portion of the gain from its disposition may be treated as ordinary income.

The Sec. 1245 recapture rules are summarized in Topic Review 13-1.

TOPIC REVIEW 13-1

Section 1245 Recapture
1. Section 1245 affects the character of the gain, not the amount of gain.
2. Section 1245 does not apply to assets sold or exchanged at a loss.
3. Section 1245 ordinary income is never more than the realized gain.
4. Section 1245 recapture applies to the total depreciation or amortization allowed or allowable.
5. Section 1245 property includes depreciable personal property.
6. Section 1245 property includes nonresidential real estate placed in service after 1980 and before 1987 under the ACRS rules **unless** the taxpayer elected to use the straight-line method of cost recovery.

RECAPTURE PROVISIONS OF SEC. 1250

OBJECTIVE 4

Apply the recapture provisions of Sec. 1250

In 1964 Sec. 1250 was enacted to extend the recapture concept to include most depreciable real property. Unlike Sec. 1245, where the recapture is based upon the total amount of depreciation (or cost recovery) allowed, Sec. 1250 applies solely to additional depreciation. **Additional depreciation,** also referred to as **excess depreciation,** is the excess of the actual amount of accelerated depreciation (or cost-recovery deductions under ACRS) over the amount of depreciation that would be deductible under the straight-line method. For property held a year or less, additional depreciation is the total amount of depreciation taken on the property.[32] Although Sec. 1250 was enacted in 1964, it is no longer necessary to consider additional depreciation for pre-1970 years.[33]

Purpose of Sec. 1250

Section 1250 has the effect of converting a portion of the Sec. 1231 gain into ordinary income when real property is sold or exchanged. The incremental benefits from using accelerated depreciation or ACRS cost recovery may be recaptured when the property is sold. Noncorporate taxpayers can avoid Sec. 1250 recapture by either (1) using the straight-line method of depreciation or cost recovery or (2) holding the Sec. 1250 property for its entire useful life or recovery period.

By applying the Sec. 1250 recapture rules solely to the additional depreciation amount instead of to the total depreciation claimed (as is the case for Sec. 1245

---

[32] Sec. 1250(b)(1).

[33] Recapture of additional depreciation allowed prior to 1970 was avoided under Sec. 1250(a)(3) if the property was held for more than 10 years.

property), real property that is not Sec. 1245 property gets more favorable treatment. Despite a number of changes making Sec. 1250 more restrictive, Sec. 1250 still affords taxpayers more favorable tax treatment than Sec. 1245.

Section 1250 Property Defined

Section 1250 property is any depreciable real property other than Sec. 1245 property and includes the following:[34]

- All other depreciable real property except nonresidential real estate that qualifies as recovery property (i.e., placed in service after 1980 and before 1987) unless the straight-line method of cost recovery is elected.
- Low-income housing
- Depreciable residential rental property

Depreciation recapture is not required on real property placed in service after 1986 because such property must be depreciated under the straight-line modified ACRS rules.[35]

Recapture Rules for Residential Rental Property

All residential rental property is Sec. 1250 property. For a building or structure to qualify as residential rental property, 80% or more of the gross rental income from the building or structure must be rental income from dwelling units. Residential rental property does not include any unit in a hotel, motel, inn, or other establishment if more than one-half of the units are used on a transient basis.[36]

For residential rental property sold or exchanged after August 1992, any additional depreciation for years prior to 1976 is not subject to recapture.[37] In essence, Sec. 1250 recapture applies only to additional depreciation allowed after 1975 if the asset is depreciable residential rental property.

Example 13-21 ■ Buddy sells an apartment complex used as residential rental property and placed in service on January 1, 1976. The cost of the apartment complex is $900,000, and the complex is sold on January 1, 1994, for $700,000. Depreciation claimed by Buddy on the property is as follows:

Time Period	Depreciation Allowed	Straight-line Depreciation	Additional Depreciation
Jan. 1, 1976-Jan. 1, 1994	$509,000	$286,000	$223,000

On the date of sale, the adjusted basis of the apartment is $391,000 ($900,000 − $509,000) and the realized gain is $309,000 ($700,000 − $391,000). All $223,000 of additional depreciation allowed is recaptured as ordinary income because the additional depreciation is less than the realized gain. The remaining $86,000 ($309,000 − $223,000) of gain is a Sec. 1231 gain. ■

---

[34] Sec. 1250(c).

[35] As explained in a subsequent section of this chapter entitled *Additional Recapture for Corporations*, corporations may have depreciation recapture under Sec. 291(a) despite the use of straight-line depreciation.

[36] Reg. Sec. 1.167(j)-3(b)(1)(i).

[37] For additional depreciation after December 31, 1969, and before January 1, 1976, the recapture percentage is 100% minus 1% for each full month over 100 months the property is held. If the residential rental property is held for at least 200 months, none of the additional depreciation is recaptured for the 1970-1975 period. Secs. 1250(a)(1)(B)(v) and (a)(2)(B)(iii).

Additional Comment

Elevators and escalators were defined as Sec. 1245 property if placed in service before 1987, but as Sec. 1250 property if placed in service after 1986.

Key Point

An apartment building is the most common type of property classified as residential real estate.

Additional Comment

If a taxpayer acquired property in December of 1975, the last month in which he or she could have additional depreciation for the 1970-1975 period ended in 1992.

Residential Rental Property That Is Recovery Property

For residential rental property that is cost-recovery property (i.e., property placed in service after 1980 and before 1987), all of the additional depreciation is recaptured as ordinary income. Additional depreciation is the excess of the ACRS deduction using the percentages provided in the ACRS tables over a hypothetical cost recovery amount based upon the straight-line ACRS method using the length of the recovery period (i.e., 15, 18, or 19 years).

Example 13-22 ■   Joel purchased depreciable residential rental property for $700,000 on January 1, 1986. The property is 19-year recovery property and accelerated cost recovery was used. Joel sells the property for $800,000 on January 1, 1994.   ■

Cost Recovery *Deductions Allowed*	Cost Recovery with *Straight-line*	Additional *Depreciation*
$376,600	$296,100	$80,500

Joel's realized gain is $476,600 ($800,000 − [$700,000 − $376,600]) and $80,500 is recaptured as Sec. 1250 ordinary income. The remaining $396,100 of gain is Sec. 1231 gain.   ■

Self Study Question

If the asset in Example 13-22 is an office building, how much ordinary income must Joel recognize?

Answer: *$343,700*

The office building is Sec. 1245 property. Joel must recognize ordinary income of $376,600 and a $100,000 Sec. 1231 gain.

Recapture Rules for Nonresidential Real Estate

Nonresidential real property is Sec. 1250 property if placed in service before 1981 or after 1986. Nonresidential real property placed in service after 1980 and before 1987 is subject to Sec. 1245 recapture if accelerated cost recovery was taken on the property.[38] Recapture may be avoided if the taxpayer elects to use the straight-line method of cost recovery[39] for nonresidential ACRS property.[40]

Example 13-23 ■   The AB partnership purchased an office building in 1981 and a warehouse in 1982. The statutory percentages provided in the ACRS table are used to determine cost-recovery deductions for the office building. The straight-line method is used to determine cost-recovery deductions for the warehouse. The office building is subject to the Sec. 1245 recapture rules, and the warehouse is Sec. 1250 property. Even though the warehouse is Sec. 1250 property, the gain realized on the sale is Sec. 1231 gain since the straight-line ACRS method was used.   ■

Pre-ACRS Nonresidential Real Estate. All additional depreciation allowed after December 31, 1969, is subject to recapture as ordinary income under Sec. 1250.[41] The recaptured amount is limited to the realized gain.

Example 13-24 ■   Wayne sells his manufacturing plant during the current year. The plant was purchased in 1972 for use in his business. Additional depreciation of $375,000 has been taken on the building. Information pertaining to the sale is as follows:

---

[38] Sec. 1245(a)(5), prior to amendment by the Tax Reform Act of 1986.

[39] The cost of 18-year recovery property may be recovered under Sec. 168(b)(3)(A) over a period of 18, 35, or 45 years.

[40] Sec. 1245(a)(5)(C), prior to being repealed by the Tax Reform Act of 1986.

[41] Secs. 1250(a)(1)(B)(v) and (a)(2)(B)(v).

	Original Cost	Total Depreciation	Adjusted Basis	Selling Price
Plant	$3,000,000	$1,400,000	$1,600,000	$2,100,000
Land	300,000		300,000	500,000

The realized gain from the sale of the plant is $500,000 ($2,100,000 − $1,600,000), and $375,000 of the gain is recaptured as ordinary income under Sec. 1250. The remaining $125,000 of gain and the $200,000 of realized gain from the sale of the land are Sec. 1231 gains. ∎

Example 13-25 ∎

Typical Misconception

It is easy to forget that the amount recaptured as ordinary income under either Sec. 1245 or Sec. 1250 can never exceed the realized gain.

Assume the same facts as in Example 13-24 except that the selling price of the plant is $1,850,000. All of the $250,000 realized gain ($1,850,000 − $1,600,000) is recaptured as ordinary income because the $375,000 of additional depreciation is greater than the $250,000 of realized gain. ∎

Recapture for ACRS Nonresidential Real Estate. Section 1245 applies to nonresidential real property placed in service after December 31, 1980, and before January 1, 1987, if the ACRS statutory rates are used to determine the cost-recovery deductions. For Sec. 1245 recovery property, all gain to the extent of the lesser of the gain realized or the cost recovery deductions claimed is ordinary income. If the straight-line method of cost recovery is elected, the property is Sec. 1250 and none of the cost-recovery deductions are recaptured under Sec. 1250.

Example 13-26 ∎

Larry owns the following two buildings that are used in his business. Both buildings qualify as recovery property under the ACRS rules. Larry uses the ACRS statutory rates to determine cost-recovery deductions for building 1 and the straight-line method for building 2.

	Original Cost	Cost-Recovery Deductions	Adjusted Basis
Building 1	$1,000,000	$420,000	$580,000
Building 2	1,000,000	300,000	700,000

If building 1 is sold for $1,200,000, the realized gain is $620,000 ($1,200,000 − $580,000). Section 1245 applies, and $420,000 is recaptured as ordinary income. The remaining $200,000 is Sec. 1231 gain. If building 2 is sold for $1,200,000, the realized gain is $500,000 ($1,200,000 − $700,000). All of the gain is Sec. 1231 gain because the straight-line cost recovery method is used and Sec. 1245 does not apply unless the ACRS statutory rates are used. ∎

Low-Income Housing

Congress has provided incentives for the construction and rehabilitation of low-income housing. For tax years after 1986, a low-income housing credit is available to owners of qualified low-income housing projects.[42]

The depreciation recapture provisions of Sec. 1250 also favor low-income housing. The recapture percentage applied to the amount of additional depreciation allowed for low-income housing after 1975 is 100% less one percentage point for each full month the property is held for more than 100 months.[43] If the low-income housing unit is held for 16 years and 8 months, none of the additional depreciation is subject to

---

[42] Sec. 42.
[43] Secs. 1250(a)(1)(B)(i), (ii), (iii), and (iv).

recapture as ordinary income. To illustrate the more favorable treatment provided in Sec. 1250 for low-income housing, consider Example 13-27.

Example 13-27 ■

On January 1, 1980, Priscilla acquired two apartment buildings for $3,000,000 each. Building 1 qualifies as low-income housing, and building 2 is residential rental property but not low-income housing. Accelerated depreciation is used for both buildings, and $300,000 in additional depreciation has been deducted with respect to each building. Each building is sold on January 1, 1994, for $2,650,000.

Apartment Building	Cost	Total Depreciation	Adjusted Basis
Building 1	$3,000,000	$1,000,000	$2,000,000
Building 2	3,000,000	1,000,000	2,000,000

Gain realized from the sale of each apartment building is $650,000 ($2,650,000 − $2,000,000). While 100% of the additional depreciation for building 2 is recaptured as ordinary income under Sec. 1250, only 32% of the additional depreciation for building 1 is recaptured as ordinary income. The low-income housing unit has been held for 168 months. For the first 100 months, the recapture percentage is 100%. Then the recapture percentage decreases by 1% each month for the next 68 months. $96,000 (0.32 × $300,000 additional depreciation) of the $650,000 gain realized from the sale of building 1 is recaptured as ordinary income. The remaining $554,000 ($650,000 − $96,000) of gain is Sec. 1231 gain. Of the $650,000 gain realized from the sale of building 2, $300,000 is recaptured as ordinary income and $350,000 is Sec. 1231 gain. ■

The Sec. 1250 recapture rules for noncorporate taxpayers are summarized in Topic Review 13-2.

TOPIC REVIEW 13-2

Section 1250 Recapture for Noncorporate Taxpayers
1. Section 1250 affects the character of the gain, not the amount of gain.
2. Section 1250 does not apply to assets sold or exchanged at a loss.
3. Section 1250 ordinary income is never more than the realized gain.
4. Section 1250 ordinary income is never more than the *additional* depreciation allowed. (Note, that this statement is not true for corporate taxpayers.)
5. Section 1250 property includes depreciable real property unless the real property is nonresidential real estate placed in service in 1980 and before 1987 under the ACRS rules and the straight-line method is not elected.
6. Section 1250 ordinary income does not exist if the straight-line method of depreciation is used. (Note that this statement is not true for corporate taxpayers.)

ADDITIONAL RECAPTURE FOR CORPORATIONS

Key Point

Section 291 has no effect on Sec. 1245 property since gain is already recaptured to the extent of all depreciation.

Corporations are subject to additional recapture rules under Sec. 291 if depreciable real estate is sold or otherwise disposed of. This recapture is in addition to the normal recapture rules under Sec. 1250. The additional ordinary income that is recaptured effectively reduces the amount of the Sec. 1231 gain.

The additional recapture amount under Sec. 291 is equal to 20% of the difference between the amount that would be recaptured under Sec. 1245 and the actual recapture amount under Sec. 1250.[44]

Example 13-28 ■

Additional Comment

Corporations are subject to an additional 20% depreciation recapture rule under Sec. 291 on sales of Sec. 1250 property.

In 1980 Orlando Corporation purchased an office building for $500,000 for use in its trade or business. The building is sold during the current year for $480,000. Total depreciation allowed for the building is $170,000. Total depreciation of $125,000 would have been allowed if the straight-line method of depreciation was used. The property's adjusted basis is $330,000 ($500,000 − $170,000), and the realized gain is $150,000 ($480,000 − $330,000). Under Sec. 1250, the ordinary income recaptured amount is equal to 100% of the additional depreciation, which is $45,000 ($170,000 − $125,000). Under Sec. 1245, the ordinary income recapture amount would be $150,000. The amount of Sec. 1250 ordinary income under Sec. 291 is $21,000 (0.20 × [$150,000 − $45,000]). To summarize, the total amount recaptured as Sec. 1250 ordinary income is $66,000 ($45,000 + $21,000), and the Sec. 1231 gain is $84,000 ($150,000 − $66,000). ■

Example 13-29 ■

Pacific Corporation purchased an office building in 1981 for $800,000 for use in its trade or business. The building is sold during the current year for $850,000. Pacific elected to use the straight-line method of cost recovery and $320,000 cost-recovery deductions have been allowed. The realized gain is $370,000 ($850,000 − $480,000). Since the straight-line method was elected, none of the gain is ordinary income under Sec. 1250. If the building were instead Sec. 1245 recovery property, $320,000 of the gain would be treated as ordinary income. The amount of Sec. 1250 ordinary income under Sec. 291 is $64,000 (0.20 × [$320,000 − $0]). The remaining $306,000 ($370,000 − $64,000) gain is Sec. 1231 gain. ■

RECAPTURE PROVISIONS—OTHER APPLICATIONS

OBJECTIVE 5
Describe other recapture applications

The Secs. 1245 and 1250 recapture provisions take precedence over other provisions of the tax law.[45] Unless an exception or limitation is specifically stated in Secs. 1245 or 1250, gain is recognized under Secs. 1245 or 1250 despite the existence of provisions elsewhere in the Code that allow nonrecognition of gain.[46]

Gifts of Property Subject to Recapture

A gift of appreciated depreciable property does not result in the recapture of depreciation or cost-recovery deductions under Secs. 1245 or 1250.[47] The donee must consider the recapture potential when disposing of the property. The recapture amount for the donee is computed by including the recaptured amount attributable to the donor.[48]

[44] Sec. 291(a)(1).
[45] Secs. 1245(d) and 1250(i).
[46] Reg. Secs. 1.1245-6(a) and 1.1250-1(c)(1).
[47] Secs. 1245(b)(1) and 1250(d)(1).
[48] Reg. Secs. 1.1245-2(a)(4) and 1.1250-2(d).

Example 13-30 ■   Danielle makes a gift of equipment with an $8,200 FMV to Helmut. Danielle paid $10,000 for the equipment and deducted $4,000 of depreciation before making the gift. Danielle does not have to recapture any depreciation when making the gift. Helmut's basis for the equipment is $6,000, and the potential depreciation recapture carries over to Helmut.   ■

Example 13-31 ■   Assume the same facts as in Example 13-30 except that Helmut uses the equipment in a trade or business, deducts $1,500 of depreciation, and sells the equipment for $7,100. When determining the amount of depreciation subject to recapture, Helmut must consider the depreciation allowed to Danielle. The entire $2,600 ($7,100 − [$6,000 − $1,500]) of gain is recaptured as ordinary income since it is less than the $5,500 of depreciation claimed.   ■

Key Point

Death is one of the few ways to avoid the recapture provisions.

Transfer of Property Subject to Recapture at Death

The transfer of appreciated property at death does not cause a recapture of depreciation deductions to the decedent's estate under Secs. 1245 or 1250.[49] In addition, recapture potential does not carry over to the person who receives the property from the decedent.

Example 13-32 ■   Nancy dies while owning a building with a $900,000 FMV. The building is Sec. 1245 property acquired in 1982 for $800,000, and upon which cost-recovery deductions of $680,000 have been claimed. Pam inherits the building from Nancy. Pam's basis for the building is $900,000, and the $680,000 of cost-recovery deductions are not recaptured. If Pam immediately sells the building, there is no depreciation recapture attributable to the $680,000 of cost-recovery deductions taken by the decedent.   ■

Charitable Contributions

As discussed in Chapter 7, the deduction for a charitable contribution of ordinary income property is generally limited to its adjusted basis (i.e., the amount of the contribution deduction is equal to the FMV of the property less the amount of gain that would not have been LTCG [or Sec. 1231 gain] if the contributed property had been sold by the taxpayer at its FMV).[50] Thus, the contribution deduction for recapture property is generally scaled down to reflect the ordinary income that would be recognized if the property was sold rather than contributed to the charity.

Example 13-33 ■

Additional Comment

If the FMV of the organ in Example 13-33 is $11,000, the charitable contribution deduction is limited to $3,000, the $11,000 FMV less $8,000. If the organ was sold for $11,000, $8,000 of the gain would be ordinary income.

   Ralph makes a gift of an organ to a church. The organ is used in Ralph's trade or business and has a $6,300 FMV. Ralph paid $10,000 for the organ, and $8,000 depreciation has been claimed. If the organ was sold for its $6,300 FMV, the realized and recognized gain would be $4,300 ($6,300 − $2,000) and all of the gain would be ordinary income due to the recapture of depreciation under Sec. 1245. The charitable contribution deduction is limited to $2,000 ($6,300 − $4,300), since none of the $4,300 gain would be taxed as a LTCG if the organ were sold.   ■

Like-Kind Exchanges

A taxpayer who receives boot (i.e., non-like-kind property) in a transaction that otherwise qualifies as a like-kind exchange recognizes gain equal to the lesser of the

---

[49] Secs. 1245(b)(2) and 1250(d)(2).
[50] Sec. 170(e)(1)(A).

realized gain or the amount of boot received.[51] If the property is Sec. 1245 or 1250 property, the gain is first considered to be ordinary income up to the maximum amount of the gain that is subject to the recapture provisions.

Example 13-34 ■

Virginia owns a duplex which is residential rental property. The duplex cost $300,000 in 1979 and has a $140,000 adjusted basis. Additional depreciation of $22,000 has been deducted. Virginia exchanges the duplex for a four-unit apartment building with a $250,000 FMV and $25,000 in cash. Gain realized on the exchange is $135,000 ($250,000 + $25,000 − $140,000), and the recognized gain is $25,000. Gain recognized is the lesser of the $25,000 boot received or the $135,000 of gain realized. Since additional depreciation is recaptured as ordinary income under Sec. 1250, $22,000 of the gain is ordinary income and $3,000 of the gain is Sec. 1231 gain. ■

If gain is not recognized in a like-kind exchange, the recapture potential carries over to the replacement property (i.e., any recapture potential associated with the property exchanged attaches to the property received in the exchange).[52]

Example 13-35 ■

Melissa owns a Chevrolet pickup truck used in business that cost $10,000 and has a $6,000 adjusted basis due to $4,000 in depreciation deductions that she has claimed. The truck is exchanged for a Ford pickup truck with a $9,000 FMV. The Ford truck is used in Melissa's trade or business. Melissa does not recognize any portion of the $3,000 realized gain because the exchange qualifies as a like-kind exchange and no boot is received. Her basis for the Ford truck is $6,000 (i.e., a substituted basis).

After deducting $2,000 of depreciation, Melissa sells the Ford truck for $7,300. All of the recognized gain of $3,300 ($7,300 − $4,000) is ordinary income. The depreciation recapture amount under Sec. 1245 is equal to the total $6,000 in depreciation (including $4,000 on the Chevrolet pickup truck).[53] The amount of ordinary income realized is limited to the $3,300 of recognized gain. ■

Involuntary Conversions

If an involuntary conversion of Sec. 1245 property occurs and all or a portion of the gain is not recognized,[54] the amount of gain that is considered to be Sec. 1245 ordinary income is limited. Ordinary income under Sec. 1245 may not exceed the sum of: (1) the recognized gain and (2) the FMV of acquired property that is not Sec. 1245 property but is qualifying property under Sec. 1033.[55] A similar provision exists for the involuntary conversion of Sec. 1250 property.[56]

Example 13-36 ■

Joan owns an office building with a $600,000 adjusted basis. The building was originally purchased in 1978, and additional depreciation amounted to $60,000. The building is destroyed by fire, and she receives insurance proceeds of $800,000. Joan purchases another office building for $750,000 and elects to defer as much of

---

[51] Like-kind exchanges involving the receipt of boot are discussed in Chapter 12.

[52] Reg. Sec. 1.1245-2(c)(4).

[53] Reg. Sec. 1.1245-2(a)(4).

[54] As discussed in Chapter 12, one may elect to defer recognition of the gain if the Sec. 1033 requirements are satisfied.

[55] Sec. 1245(b)(4) and Reg. Sec. 1.1245-4(d)(1).

[56] Sec. 1250(d)(4) and Reg. Sec. 1.1250-3(d).

the gain as possible. Joan must recognize $50,000 of the $200,000 ($800,000 − $600,000) realized gain since the cost of the replacement property is $50,000 ($800,000 − $750,000) less than the insurance proceeds. The amount of ordinary income under Sec. 1250 is limited to $50,000 since Sec. 1250 property is purchased to replace the Sec. 1250 property destroyed by the fire. ∎

Installment Sales

As discussed in Chapter 11, gain resulting from an installment sale is generally recognized as payments are received. Thus, the gain may be spread over more than one accounting period. An installment sale of depreciable property may result in all of the recaptured gain being taxed in the year of the sale.[57] Recapture income is "the aggregate amount which would be treated as ordinary income under Sec. 1245 or 1250 for the taxable year of the disposition if all payments to be received were received in the taxable year of disposition."[58] Recapture income must be recognized in the year of sale, even if no payments are received.

Example 13-37 ∎

Key Point

In the case of an installment sale of Sec. 1245 or 1250 property, it is possible to report a large taxable gain even though the taxpayer has not yet received the cash to pay the tax on such gain.

Pat owns equipment with a $100,000 acquisition cost and a $50,000 adjusted basis. Depreciation of $50,000 has been allowed. In 1994, Pat sells the property for $30,000 cash and a $60,000 10-year interest-bearing note. The realized gain is $40,000 ($90,000 − $50,000), and the recapture income amount is $40,000 (the lesser of total depreciation deductions of $50,000 or the $40,000 of realized gain). The $40,000 of gain is all recognized as ordinary income in 1994, despite the fact that the transaction qualifies as an installment sale and only $30,000 cash is received in the year of sale. ∎

If the gain realized from the installment sale exceeds the recapture income, the excess gain is reported under the installment method.[59] The amount of recapture income recognized is added to the adjusted basis to determine the gross profit ratio.

Example 13-38 ∎

Bob owns an office building acquired for $700,000 in 1986 and subject to the Sec. 1245 recapture rules. After claiming $120,000 of cost recovery deductions, Bob sells the building to Judy in 1994 for $1,000,000. Bob receives $200,000 in cash and an $800,000 interest-bearing note. The note is to be paid with annual principal payments of $100,000 beginning in 1995. The total amount of realized gain is $420,000 ($1,000,000 − $580,000). In 1994 Bob recognizes $120,000 of Sec. 1245 ordinary income. The gross profit ratio is determined by adding $120,000 recapture income to the $580,000 basis. The gross profit ratio is 30% ([$1,000,000 − $700,000] ÷ $1,000,000). In addition to recognizing $120,000 of ordinary income, Bob recognizes $60,000 (0.30 × $200,000) Sec. 1231 gain in 1993 because a $200,000 cash down payment was received in the year of the sale. In 1995 and in each subsequent year, $30,000 (0.30 × $100,000) of Sec. 1231 gain is recognized as the cash payments on the principal are received. ∎

---

[57] Sec. 453(i)(1).
[58] Sec. 453(i)(2).
[59] Sec. 453(i)(1)(B).

Section 179 Expensing Election

In lieu of capitalizing the cost of new or used tangible personal business property, taxpayers may elect to expense up to $17,500 of the acquisition cost[60] (see Chapter 10). If the property is subsequently converted to nonbusiness use, previous tax benefits derived from the immediate expensing election must be recaptured and added to the taxpayer's gross income in the year of the conversion.[61] The recaptured amount equals the difference between the amount expensed under Sec. 179 and the total depreciation that would otherwise have been claimed for the period of business use.

Example 13-39 ■ Joel purchased business equipment in 1993 for $17,500 and elected to expense the entire amount under Sec. 179. In 1994, he converts the equipment to nonbusiness use. Depreciation of $3,500 (0.20 × $17,500) based upon a 5-year recovery period under the MACRS rules would have been allowed during the period the equipment was held for business use. Joel must include $14,000 ($17,500 − $3,500) in his gross income for 1994. This amount represents the previous tax benefit obtained from the immediate expensing election. ■

Key Point

There is no recapture of conservation or land clearing costs if the farm land has been held for at least 10 years.

Conservation and Land Clearing Expenditures

Taxpayers engaged in the business of farming may deduct expenditures paid or incurred during the taxable year for soil and water conservation or the prevention of erosion. The expenditures must be made with respect to land used in farming and would be capital expenditures except for this provision.[62] Farmers could also elect to expense expenditures paid or incurred prior to 1986 for the purpose of clearing land to make it suitable for use in farming.[63]

The deductions for conservation and land clearing expenditures may be partially or fully recaptured as ordinary income if the farmland is disposed of before the land is held for ten years.[64] The amount of deductions recaptured as ordinary income under Sec. 1252 is a percentage of the aggregate deductions allowed for conservation and land clearing expenditures. The amount of ordinary income recognized under Sec. 1252 is limited to the lesser of the taxpayer's realized gain or the applicable recapture percentage times the total conservation and land clearing expenditures.

The recapture percentage is 100% if the farmland is disposed of within five years after the date it is acquired. The percentage declines by 20 percentage points for each additional year the property is held. If the land is disposed of after being held for ten years or more, none of the expenses are recaptured.[65]

Example 13-40 ■ Paula owns farm land with a $400,000 basis. She has deducted $50,000 for conservation and land clearing expenses. After farming the land for 6 years and 5 months, Paula sells the land for $520,000. The realized gain is $120,000 ($520,000 − $400,000), and the recapture percentage is 60%, since the farm land is disposed of within the seventh year after it was acquired. The amount of ordinary income due to recapture under Sec. 1252 is $30,000, the lesser of the $120,000 realized gain or the $30,000 (0.60 × $50,000) recapture amount. ■

[60] Secs. 179(a) and (b)(1).
[61] Sec. 179(d)(10) and Reg. Sec. 1.179-1(e).
[62] Sec. 175(a).
[63] Sec. 182(a), prior to its repeal.
[64] Sec. 1252(a)(1).
[65] Sec. 1252(a)(3).

Additional Comment
Intangible drilling and development costs represent the major cost of operations and can provide investors with working interests in oil and gas properties with a first-year write-off of substantially all of their investment.

Intangible Drilling Costs and Depletion

Taxpayers may elect to either expense or capitalize intangible drilling and development costs (IDC).[66] If the election to expense is not made, the costs are capitalized and recovered through additional cost depletion deductions. Intangible drilling and development costs include "all expenditures made by an operator for wages, fuel, repairs, hauling, supplies, etc., incident to and necessary for the drilling of wells and the preparation of wells for the production of oil or gas."[67]

Part or all of the gain from the sale of oil and gas properties may be recaptured as ordinary income due to the recapture of the IDC deduction and the deduction for depletion. However, the amount of ordinary income recognized from the recapture of IDC and depletion is limited to the gain realized from the disposition of the property.[68]

Example 13-41 ■   In 1987 Marty purchased undeveloped property for the purpose of drilling for oil and gas. Intangible drilling and development costs of $400,000 were paid in 1987. Marty elected to expense the IDC. During the current year, Marty sells the property and realizes a $900,000 gain. $300,000 of cost depletion was allowed. Marty must recognize $700,000 of ordinary income because of the recapture of IDC ($400,000) and the recapture of depletion ($300,000). The remaining $200,000 ($900,000 − $700,000) gain is Sec. 1231 gain. ■

Example 13-42 ■   In 1988 Tina acquired oil and gas properties for $700,000. During 1988, she elected to expense $200,000 of IDC. Total depletion allowed was $80,000. During the current year, Tina sells the property for $840,000 and realizes a $220,000 ($840,000 − [$700,000 − $80,000]) gain. The amount of ordinary income due to recapture is $220,000, since both IDC and depletion must be recaptured only to the extent of the gain. ■

Gain on Sale of Depreciable Property Between Related Parties

All of the gain recognized on the sale or exchange of property between related parties is ordinary income if the property is subject to depreciation in the hands of the transferee (i.e., the person who purchases the property). The sale or exchange may be direct or indirect.[69]

Example 13-43 ■   Phil owns a building with a $500,000 adjusted basis and $800,000 FMV. The building, which cost $700,000, is used in his business, and the straight-line method of depreciation is used. $200,000 of depreciation deductions were allowed. If the building is sold to Phil's 100%-owned corporation for $800,000, the $300,000 realized gain ($800,000 − $500,000) is treated as ordinary income under Sec. 1239, since the property is subject to depreciation in the hands of the transferee and the corporation and Phil are related parties. ■

---

[66] Sec. 263(c).
[67] Reg. Sec. 1.612-4(a).
[68] Sec. 1254(a)(1).
[69] Sec. 1239(a).

A sale or exchange of property could be subject to depreciation recapture under either Secs. 1245 or 1250 as well as the Sec. 1239 related party rules. If so, recapture under Secs. 1245 or 1250 is considered before recapture under Sec. 1239.[70]

Example 13-44 ■

Assume the same facts as in Example 13-43 except that Phil sells equipment to the corporation instead of a building. All of the $300,000 realized gain is treated as ordinary income. The recapture amount under Sec. 1245 is $200,000, and Sec. 1239 applies to the remaining $100,000 gain. ■

Real World Example

A taxpayer sold a secret formula for typing correction fluid to a corporation that was a related party. The gain on the sale was treated as a capital gain and not as ordinary income under Sec. 1239 since the secret formula was not depreciable. Bette C. Graham v. U.S., 43 AFTR 2d 79-1013, 79-1 USTC ¶ 9274 (D.C. Tx., 1979).

Purpose of Sec. 1239. Without Sec. 1239, a taxpayer would be able to transfer appreciated depreciable property to a related party and recognize a Sec. 1231 gain on the sale. Net Sec. 1231 gain is treated as LTCG. The related purchaser of the property would receive a step-up in the depreciation basis of the property to its FMV and be able to claim a larger amount of depreciation. In Example 13-43, Phil might prefer to recognize a $300,000 Sec. 1231 gain if the 100%-owned corporation was able to obtain a step-up in the property's basis to $800,000. Since Sec. 1239 applies, Phil must recognize $300,000 of ordinary income rather than Sec. 1231 gain. This rule prevents an individual taxpayer from receiving favorable Sec. 1231 gain treatment and prevents all taxpayers having large capital loss carryovers from using a related party to recognize a Sec. 1231 or capital gain which can be offset against their capital losses.

Related Parties. A person is related (1) to any corporation if the individual owns (directly or indirectly) more than 50% of the value of the outstanding stock and (2) to any partnership in which the person has a capital or profits interest of more than 50%.[71] Constructive ownership rules apply when determining whether the person owns more than 50% of the corporation or has more than a 50% interest in the partnership. Thus, an individual is considered to own stock that is owned by other family members and related entities (e.g., corporations, partnerships, estates, and trusts).

Example 13-45 ■

Tony sells a truck, which he has used for nonbusiness purposes, to the Able Corporation for $15,000. The adjusted basis of the truck is $12,000 on the date of the sale.

Tony owns 60% of the Able stock, and his spouse owns the remaining 40% of the Able stock. Tony and Able are related parties since Tony is deemed to own all of the Able stock under the constructive ownership rules and $3,000 of ordinary income must be recognized under Sec. 1239 unless the overriding recapture rules of Sec. 1245 apply. ■

A person is related to any trust in which such a person or the person's spouse is a beneficiary.[72] Section 1239 also applies to a sale or exchange of depreciable property between two corporations if the same individual owns more than 50% of each corporation.[73]

---

[70] Reg. Sec. 1.1245-6(f).
[71] Sec. 1239(c).
[72] Sec. 1239(b)(2).
[73] Rev. Rul. 79-157, 1979-1 C.B. 281.

TAX PLANNING CONSIDERATIONS

For noncorporate taxpayers, net Sec. 1231 gains are generally preferable to ordinary gains because of the 28% maximum tax rate that is applicable to net capital gain. For corporate taxpayers, however, after 1986, it usually does not make any difference whether a gain is classified as Sec. 1231 or as ordinary.

Example 13-46 ■ Western Corporation sells equipment for $400,000 during the current year. The equipment originally cost $500,000 and has a $350,000 adjusted basis after deducting depreciation. The corporation has no other gains and losses during the year or any capital loss carryovers from previous years. For Western Corporation, it does not make any difference whether the gain is Sec. 1245 ordinary income or Sec. 1231 gain. The effect on the corporation's taxable income and tax liability is the same regardless of how the gain is classified. ■

The avoidance of the recapture provisions is important to both corporate and noncorporate taxpayers if capital loss carryovers exist. For example, if Western Corporation has a capital loss carryforward of $40,000 in Example 13-46, the corporation's taxable income is increased by $10,000 ($50,000 − $40,000) if the $50,000 gain is Sec. 1231 gain. However, since the gain is Sec. 1245 ordinary income, the corporation's taxable income is increased by $50,000. The $40,000 capital loss carryforward is not deductible unless it can be offset by a capital gain or a net Sec. 1231 gain.

Avoiding the Recapture Provisions

In view of the pervasiveness of the recapture provisions discussed in this chapter, recapture is difficult to avoid. In some cases, recapture can be avoided by holding the property a specific length of time before disposing of it (e.g., the recapture of conservation and land clearing expenses can be avoided by holding the farm land for at least ten years).[74] Contributing appreciated property to a qualified charitable organization cannot be used to circumvent the recapture provisions because in such case the amount of the charitable contribution is reduced by the amount of the gain that would not be a LTCG if the property was sold by the taxpayer.[75]

Although it is often difficult to avoid the recapture provisions, taxpayers may dispose of the property and defer recapture if the disposition is a nontaxable exchange. In a like-kind exchange where no boot is received, the recapture potential is carried over to the property received in the exchange. In a tax-free incorporation under Sec. 351, the recapture potential is transferred to the corporation receiving the recapture property. Recapture may also be avoided in situations involving a transfer of property to a partnership in exchange for a partnership interest.

Proper timing of the asset's disposition may be advantageous. Disposition may be delayed until the taxpayer's tax rate is low or the property can be sold in the same year that the taxpayer has a NOL that is about to expire.

The recapture potential may be shifted to other taxpayers by making a gift of property subject to recapture. The recapture potential remains with the property and must be considered when the donee disposes of the property.

[74] Sec. 1252(a)(1).
[75] Sec. 170(e)(1)(A).

Residential Rental Property. Noncorporate taxpayers can avoid the recapture provisions for residential rental property by using the straight-line method of depreciation.[76] The recapture provisions do not apply to residential rental property acquired after 1986 because only the straight-line depreciation method may be used. Recapture can also be avoided if the asset is fully depreciated at the date of disposal since no additional depreciation or cost recovery exists.

Example 13-47 ■

Vincent owns a building used as residential rental property. The building was purchased before 1981 and is not ACRS recovery property. Vincent could avoid depreciation recapture at the time of disposing of the asset by using the straight-line method of depreciation. If Vincent uses an accelerated method of depreciation, recapture is avoided if the disposition does not occur until the asset is fully depreciated. ■

Example 13-48 ■

Assume the same facts as in Example 13-47 except that Vincent purchased the building after 1980 and before 1987 and the building is ACRS recovery property. Vincent could avoid recapturing cost recovery deductions at the time of disposing of the asset by using the straight-line method of cost recovery. If Vincent uses the accelerated method of cost recovery and disposes of the residential rental property at a gain, recapture cannot be avoided unless the asset's cost is fully recovered (i.e., no additional cost recovery exists). ■

Key Point

For noncorporate taxpayers, there is no recapture on either residential or nonresidential real property placed in service after 1986 since the property can be depreciated only by using the straight-line method.

Nonresidential Real Property. For noncorporate taxpayers, the Sec. 1250 recapture provisions do not apply to nonresidential real property acquired after 1986 because only the straight-line method may be used. However, to avoid recapture on the disposition of appreciated nonresidential real property acquired after 1980 and prior to 1987 noncorporate taxpayers must use the straight-line method of depreciation. Nonresidential real property acquired before 1987, which is recovery property subject to ACRS, is subject to the Sec. 1245 recapture rules unless the straight-line method is used. If the accelerated method of cost recovery is used, recapture cannot be avoided by waiting until the asset's cost is fully recovered before disposing of the asset.

Example 13-49 ■

Christine purchased an office building in 1986 for $225,000 for use in her business. The property is ACRS recovery property, and she uses the accelerated method to compute the cost-recovery deductions. Cost-recovery deductions taken prior to the sale of the building amount to $100,000. If she sells the building for $250,000, $100,000 of the $125,000 ($250,000 − $125,000) realized gain is recaptured as ordinary income under Sec. 1245. The remaining gain of $25,000 is Sec. 1231 gain. Recapture could have been avoided if Christine had instead used the straight-line method of cost recovery. If the straight-line method were used instead, she would report a smaller realized gain, all of which is Sec. 1231 gain. ■

Example 13-50 ■

Bryce purchased an office building in 1986 for $300,000 for use in his trade or business. The property is 19-year recovery property, and he used the accelerated method of cost recovery. If Bryce sells the building for $250,000 after all of the cost has been recovered (i.e., the adjusted basis is zero), the realized gain of $250,000 is recaptured as ordinary income under Sec. 1245 without regard to

[76] Corporate taxpayers must consider Sec. 291(a). (See the section entitled Additional Recapture For Corporations in this chapter.)

the amount of additional depreciation that has been claimed with respect to the property. ■

Transfer Property at Death. One of the most effective ways to avoid the recapture provisions is to transfer the property at death. No recapture occurs at the time of the transfer, and the basis of property received from a decedent is generally the FMV of the property at the date of the decedent's death.[77] The property's recapture potential does not carry over to the beneficiary as in the case of a gift made to a donee.

COMPLIANCE AND PROCEDURAL CONSIDERATIONS

Additional Comment

Form 4797 has three major parts. In completing this form one should normally begin with Part III on page 2 where the recapture is calculated. Note that the total amount recaptured from line 33 is carried forward to Part II where it is combined with other ordinary gains and losses. Any unrecaptured gain from line 34 is carried forward to Part I where it is netted with other Sec. 1231 gains and losses.

Form 4797, Supplemental Schedule of Gains and Losses, is used to report gains and losses from sales or exchanges of assets used in a trade or business (see Figures 13-1 through 13-3). The form is also used to report gains or losses resulting from involuntary conversions, other than casualties or thefts, of property used in the trade or business and capital assets held more than a year. If gains or losses due to casualties or thefts of property used in a trade or business or property held to produce income are recognized, they are reported on Form 4684, Casualties and Thefts (see Figure 13-4). If such casualties or thefts occur, Form 4684 is prepared either before or at the same time as Form 4797.

Reporting Sec. 1231 Gains and Losses on Form 4797

Part I of Form 4797, which is reproduced in Figure 13-1, is used to report gains and losses resulting from

- The sale or exchange of Sec. 1231 property
- An involuntary conversion, other than a casualty or theft, of Sec. 1231 property
- An involuntary conversion, other than a casualty or theft, of capital assets held more than one year and used to produce income.

As indicated on lines 3 through 6 in Part I of Form 4797, gains and losses recorded on other forms and in Part III of Form 4797 are reported in Part I. The netting of Sec. 1231 gains and losses occurs in Part I of Form 4797. If Sec. 1231 gains exceed Sec. 1231 losses, the net gain is reported on line 8 and then recorded on Schedule D, unless the taxpayer has nonrecaptured net Sec. 1231 losses from prior years. Net Sec. 1231 gain to the extent of any nonrecaptured net Sec. 1231 losses, as reported on line 9, is ordinary and is reported on line 13 of Part II. If Sec. 1231 losses exceed Sec. 1231 gains, the loss is reported on line 8 and on line 12 of Part II. Part II of Form 4797 which is reproduced in Figure 13-2 is used to report ordinary gains and losses.

Ordinary gains and losses recognized including those recorded on other forms and in Parts I and III of Form 4797 are reported on lines 11 through 18 in Part II of Form 4797.

---

[77] Sec. 1014(a).

Form **4797**

Department of the Treasury
Internal Revenue Service (O)

Sales of Business Property
(Also Involuntary Conversions and Recapture Amounts Under Sections 179 and 280F(b)(2))
▶ Attach to your tax return. ▶ See separate instructions.

OMB No. 1545-0184

1993

Attachment
Sequence No. **27**

Name(s) shown on return	Identifying number

1 Enter here the gross proceeds from the sale or exchange of real estate reported to you for 1993 on Form(s) 1099-S (or a substitute statement) that you will be including on line 2, 11, or 22 . . . . | **1** |

Part I Sales or Exchanges of Property Used in a Trade or Business and Involuntary Conversions From Other Than Casualty or Theft—Property Held More Than 1 Year

(a) Description of property	(b) Date acquired (mo., day, yr.)	(c) Date sold (mo., day, yr.)	(d) Gross sales price	(e) Depreciation allowed or allowable since acquisition	(f) Cost or other basis, plus improvements and expense of sale	(g) LOSS ((f) minus the sum of (d) and (e))	(h) GAIN ((d) plus (e) minus (f))
2							

3 Gain, if any, from Form 4684, line 39 . . . . | **3** |
4 Section 1231 gain from installment sales from Form 6252, line 26 or 37 . . . . . . | **4** |
5 Section 1231 gain or (loss) from like-kind exchanges from Form 8824 . . . . . . | **5** |
6 Gain, if any, from line 34, from other than casualty or theft . . . . | **6** | | 2,000 |
7 Add lines 2 through 6 in columns (g) and (h). . . . . | **7** ( ) | 2,000 |

8 Combine columns (g) and (h) of line 7. Enter gain or (loss) here, and on the appropriate line as follows: . . . . | **8** |

Partnerships—Enter the gain or (loss) on Form 1065, Schedule K, line 6. Skip lines 9, 10, 12, and 13 below.

S corporations—Report the gain or (loss) following the instructions for Form 1120S, Schedule K, lines 5 and 6. Skip lines 9, 10, 12, and 13 below, unless line 8 is a gain and the S corporation is subject to the capital gains tax.

All others—If line 8 is zero or a loss, enter the amount on line 12 below and skip lines 9 and 10. If line 8 is a gain and you did not have any prior year section 1231 losses, or they were recaptured in an earlier year, enter the gain as a long-term capital gain on Schedule D and skip lines 9, 10, and 13 below.

9 Nonrecaptured net section 1231 losses from prior years (see instructions) . . . . | **9** |
10 Subtract line 9 from line 8. If zero or less, enter -0-. Also enter on the appropriate line as follows (see instructions): | **10** |

S corporations—Enter this amount (if more than zero) on Schedule D (Form 1120S), line 13, and skip lines 12 and 13 below.

All others—If line 10 is zero, enter the amount from line 8 on line 13 below. If line 10 is more than zero, enter the amount from line 9 on line 13 below, and enter the amount from line 10 as a long-term capital gain on Schedule D.

FIGURE 13-1 Part I of Form 4797

Part II Ordinary Gains and Losses

11 Ordinary gains and losses not included on lines 12 through 18 (include property held 1 year or less):

12 Loss, if any, from line 8 . . . . | **12** |
13 Gain, if any, from line 8, or amount from line 9 if applicable . . . . | **13** |
14 Gain, if any, from line 33 . . . . | **14** | 3,000 |
15 Net gain or (loss) from Form 4684, lines 31 and 38a . . . . | **15** |
16 Ordinary gain from installment sales from Form 6252, line 25 or 36 . . . . . | **16** |
17 Ordinary gain or (loss) from like-kind exchanges from Form 8824 . . . . . . | **17** |
18 Recapture of section 179 expense deduction for partners and S corporation shareholders from property dispositions by partnerships and S corporations (see instructions) . . . . . | **18** |
19 Add lines 11 through 18 in columns (g) and (h). . . . . | **19** ( ) | 3,000 |

20 Combine columns (g) and (h) of line 19. Enter gain or (loss) here, and on the appropriate line as follows: . . . | **20** |
a For all except individual returns: Enter the gain or (loss) from line 20 on the return being filed.
b For individual returns:
  (1) If the loss on line 12 includes a loss from Form 4684, line 35, column (b)(ii), enter that part of the loss here and on line 20 of Schedule A (Form 1040). Identify as from "Form 4797, line 20b(1)." See instructions . . . . | **20b(1)** |
  (2) Redetermine the gain or (loss) on line 20, excluding the loss, if any, on line 20b(1). Enter here and on Form 1040, line 15 . . | **20b(2)** | 3,000 |

For Paperwork Reduction Act Notice, see page 1 of separate instructions.   Cat. No. 13086I   Form **4797** (1993)

FIGURE 13-2 Part II of Form 4797

Part III   Gain From Disposition of Property Under Sections 1245, 1250, 1252, 1254, and 1255

21	(a) Description of section 1245, 1250, 1252, 1254, or 1255 property:		(b) Date acquired (mo., day, yr.)	(c) Date sold (mo., day, yr.)
A	*EQUIPMENT*		3-10-91	4-30-93
B				
C				
D				

	Relate lines 21A through 21D to these columns ▶		Property A	Property B	Property C	Property D
22	Gross sales price (**Note:** *See line 1 before completing.*)	22	20,000			
23	Cost or other basis plus expense of sale	23	18,000			
24	Depreciation (or depletion) allowed or allowable	24	3,000			
25	Adjusted basis. Subtract line 24 from line 23	25	15,000			
26	Total gain. Subtract line 25 from line 22	26	5,000			
27	**If section 1245 property:**					
a	Depreciation allowed or allowable from line 24	27a	3,000			
b	Enter the **smaller** of line 26 or 27a	27b	3,000			
28	**If section 1250 property:** If straight line depreciation was used, enter -0- on line 28g, except for a corporation subject to section 291.					
a	Additional depreciation after 1975 (see instructions)	28a				
b	Applicable percentage multiplied by the **smaller** of line 26 or line 28a (see instructions)	28b				
c	Subtract line 28a from line 26. If residential rental property or line 26 is not more than line 28a, skip lines 28d and 28e	28c				
d	Additional depreciation after 1969 and before 1976	28d				
e	Enter the **smaller** of line 28c or 28d	28e				
f	Section 291 amount (corporations only)	28f				
g	Add lines 28b, 28e, and 28f	28g				
29	**If section 1252 property:** Skip this section if you did not dispose of farmland or if this form is being completed for a partnership.					
a	Soil, water, and land clearing expenses	29a				
b	Line 29a multiplied by applicable percentage (see instructions)	29b				
c	Enter the **smaller** of line 26 or 29b	29c				
30	**If section 1254 property:**					
a	Intangible drilling and development costs, expenditures for development of mines and other natural deposits, and mining exploration costs (see instructions)	30a				
b	Enter the **smaller** of line 26 or 30a	30b				
31	**If section 1255 property:**					
a	Applicable percentage of payments excluded from income under section 126 (see instructions)	31a				
b	Enter the **smaller** of line 26 or 31a	31b				

Summary of Part III Gains. Complete property columns A through D, through line 31b before going to line 32.

32	Total gains for all properties. Add columns A through D, line 26	32	5,000
33	Add columns A through D, lines 27b, 28g, 29c, 30b, and 31b. Enter here and on line 14	33	3,000
34	Subtract line 33 from line 32. Enter the portion from casualty or theft on Form 4684, line 33. Enter the portion from other than casualty or theft on Form 4797, line 6	34	2,000

Part IV   Recapture Amounts Under Sections 179 and 280F(b)(2) When Business Use Drops to 50% or Less
               See instructions for Part IV.

			(a) Section 179	(b) Section 280F(b)(2)
35	Section 179 expense deduction or depreciation allowable in prior years	35		
36	Recomputed depreciation (see instructions)	36		
37	Recapture amount. Subtract line 36 from line 35. See instructions for where to report	37		

FIGURE 13-3   Part III of Form 4797

Name(s) shown on tax return. Do not enter name and identifying number if shown on other side. | **Identifying number**

SECTION B—Business and Income-Producing Property (Use this section to report casualties and thefts of property used in a trade or business or for income-producing purposes.)

Part I   Casualty or Theft Gain or Loss (Use a separate Part I for each casualty or theft.)

19   Description of properties (show type, location, and date acquired for each):

Property **A** ....

Property **B** ....

Property **C** ....

Property **D** ....

Properties (Use a separate column for each property lost or damaged from one casualty or theft.)

		A	B	C	D
20	Cost or adjusted basis of each property				
21	Insurance or other reimbursement (whether or not you filed a claim). See the instructions for line 3. **Note:** *If line 20 is more than line 21, skip line 22.*				
22	Gain from casualty or theft. If line 21 is **more than** line 20, enter the difference here and on line 29 or line 34, column (**c**), except as provided in the instructions for line 33. Also, skip lines 23 through 27 for that column. See the instructions for line 4 if line 21 includes insurance or other reimbursement you did not claim, or you received payment for your loss in a later tax year				
23	Fair market value **before** casualty or theft				
24	Fair market value **after** casualty or theft				
25	Subtract line 24 from line 23				
26	Enter the **smaller** of line 20 or line 25				
	Note: *If the property was totally destroyed by casualty or lost from theft, enter on line 26 the amount from line 20.*				
27	Subtract line 21 from line 26. If zero or less, enter -0-				

28   Casualty or theft loss. Add the amounts on line 27. Enter the total here and on line 29 **or** line 34 (see instructions). | **28** |

Part II   Summary of Gains and Losses (from separate Parts I)

(a) Identify casualty or theft	**(b)** Losses from casualties or thefts		**(c)** Gains from casualties or thefts includible in income
	(i) Trade, business, rental or royalty property	*(ii)* Income-producing property	

Casualty or Theft of Property Held One Year or Less

29		( )	( )	
		( )	( )	
30	Totals. Add the amounts on line 29 **30**	( )	( )	

31   Combine line 30, columns (b)(i) and (c). Enter the net gain or (loss) here and on Form 4797, line 15. If Form 4797 is not otherwise required, see instructions | **31** |

32   Enter the amount from line 30, column (b)(ii) here and on Schedule A (Form 1040), line 20. Partnerships, S corporations, estates and trusts, see instructions | **32** |

Casualty or Theft of Property Held More Than One Year

33   Casualty or theft gains from Form 4797, line 34 | **33** |

| **34** | | (   ) | (   ) | |
| | | (   ) | (   ) | |

35   Total losses. Add amounts on line 34, columns (b)(i) and (b)(ii)   **35** | (   ) | (   ) |

36   Total gains. Add lines 33 and 34, column (c) | **36** |

37   Add amounts on line 35, columns (b)(i) and (b)(ii) | **37** |

38   If the loss on line 37 is **more than** the gain on line 36:

  a   Combine line 35, column (b)(i) and line 36, and enter the net gain or (loss) here. Partnerships and S corporations see the note below. All others enter this amount on Form 4797, line 15. If Form 4797 is not otherwise required, see instructions | **38a** |

  b   Enter the amount from line 35, column (b)(ii) here. Partnerships and S corporations see the note below. Individuals enter this amount on Schedule A (Form 1040), line 20. Estates and trusts, enter on the "Other deductions" line of your tax return | **38b** |

39   If the loss on line 37 is **equal to** or **less than** the gain on line 36, combine these lines and enter here. Partnerships, see the note below. All others, enter this amount on Form 4797, line 3 | **39** |

  Note: *Partnerships, enter the amount from line 38a, 38b, or line 39 on Form 1065, Schedule K, line 7. S corporations, enter the amount from line 38a or 38b on Form 1120S, Schedule K, line 6.*

FIGURE 13-4   Section B of Form 4684

Reporting Gains Recaptured as Ordinary Income on Form 4797

Part III of Form 4797, reproduced in Figure 13-2, is used to determine and report ordinary income due to the recapture provisions of Secs. 1245, 1250, 1252, 1254, and 1255. Part III is completed before Parts I and II. To illustrate the use of Part III, assume an individual sells equipment used in a trade or business for $20,000 on April 30, 1993. The equipment cost $18,000 on March 10, 1991, and depreciation deductions of $3,000 were allowed. The $5,000 ($20,000 − $15,000) total gain is reported on line 26. The $3,000 of depreciation allowed is reported on lines 27(a) and (b). On line 32, total gains resulting from the sale of all properties ($5,000 in this illustration) reported in Part III are combined. The total amount of ordinary income due to the recapture provisions ($3,000 in this illustration) is reported on line 33 and then reported as ordinary income on line 14 in Part II. The excess of the gain over the amount of ordinary income is reported on line 34. The portion of this gain not due to casualty or theft ($2,000 in this illustration) is a Sec. 1231 gain and is reported on line 6 of Part I of Form 4797. If any of the gain is due to casualty or theft, that portion of the gain is reported on Section B of Form 4684.

Reporting Casualty or Theft Gain or Loss on Form 4684

Section A of Form 4684 is used to report gains and losses resulting from a casualty or theft of personal-use property. These gains and losses are not Sec. 1231 transactions. Thus Sec. A of Form 4684 is not discussed in this chapter.

Section B of Form 4684, which is reproduced in Figure 13-4, is used to report gains and losses resulting from a casualty or theft of property used in a trade or business or held for the production of income. Note that a separate Part I is used for each different casualty or theft. Gains are reported on line 22, and losses are reported on line 28. For properties held a year or less, the gains and losses are reported on lines 29 through 32 of Part II. These gains and losses are either recorded as ordinary gains and losses on line 15 of Part II of Form 4797 or as itemized deductions on Schedule A of Form 1040.

For properties held more than a year, the gains and losses are reported on lines 33 and 34. If gains exceed losses, the net gain is reported on line 39 and then on line 3 of Part I of Form 4797 (i.e., the gains and losses are treated as Sec. 1231 gains and losses). If the losses exceed the gains, all or part of the gains and losses are reported as ordinary in Part II of Form 4797 and/or on Schedule A of Form 1040.

PROBLEM MATERIALS

DISCUSSION QUESTIONS

13-1. Explain how the gain on the sale or exchange of land could be classified as either ordinary income, a Sec. 1231 gain, or a LTCG, depending upon the facts and circumstances.

13-2. Why were taxpayers reluctant to sell appreciated business property during the period from 1938 to 1942? What effect did this reluctance have on the tax law?

13-3. Alice owns timber, purchased in 1989, with an adjusted basis of $50,000. The timber is cut for use in her furniture business on October 1, 1994, when the FMV of the timber is $200,000. The FMV of the timber on January 1, 1994, is $190,000. May Alice treat any of the gain as Sec. 1231 gain? If so, how much?

13-4. Under certain conditions, the gain earned from the sale of an unharvested crop is treated as Sec. 1231 gain. Must the unharvested crop be held for more than one year to obtain the favorable Sec. 1231 treatment?

13-5. Explain how the gain from an involuntary conversion of business property held more than one year is taxed if the involuntary conversion is the result of a condemnation. Explain the tax treatment if the involuntary conversion is due to a casualty.

13-6. When is livestock considered to be Sec. 1231 property?

13-7. When is a net Sec. 1231 gain treated as ordinary income?

13-8. Why is it unlikely that gains due to the sale of equipment will be treated as Sec. 1231 gains?

13-9. Hank sells equipment used in a trade or business for $25,000. The equipment costs $30,000 and has an adjusted basis of $25,500. Why is it important to know the holding period?

13-10. Jackie purchases equipment during the current year for $800,000 that has a seven-year MACRS recovery period. She expects to sell the property after three years. Jackie anticipates that her marginal tax rate in the year of sale will be significantly higher than her current marginal tax rate. Why might it be advantageous for her to use the straight-line method of depreciation?

13-11. Karen purchased a computer in 1992 for $4,500 to use exclusively in her trade or business. She expensed the entire cost of the computer under Sec. 179 and sells the computer during the current year for $1,622. What is the amount and character of her recognized gain?

13-12. Sheila owns a motel that is used in a trade or business. If she sells the motel, the gain will be Sec. 1245 ordinary income. During what period of time was the motel placed into service?

13-13. What types of assets are subject to depreciation recapture under Sec. 1250?

13-14. How may a taxpayer avoid having additional depreciation?

13-15. Marty sells his fully depreciated building at a gain to an unrelated party. The building is purchased before 1981. Is any of the gain taxed as ordinary income?

13-16. Which of the following assets (assume all assets have a holding period of more than one year) do not qualify as Sec. 1231 property: inventory, a pig held for breeding, land used as a parking lot for customers, and marketable securities?

13-17. When is an office building subject to the depreciation recapture rules of Sec. 1245?

13-18. Does a building that is 60% rented for residential use and 40% for commercial use qualify as residential rental property?

13-19. Roger owns an apartment complex with a FMV of $2 million. If he sells the apartment complex, $700,000 of the gain is ordinary income. If he dies before selling the apartment complex and his estate sells the property for $2 million, how much ordinary income must the estate recognize?

13-20. Rashad owns a duplex that is used 100% as residential rental property. Under what conditions, if any, will any gain that he recognizes be Sec. 1245 ordinary income?

13-21. Are the recapture provisions for low-income housing more or less favorable than the recapture provisions for other residential rental property?

13-22. Why may a corporation recognize a greater amount of ordinary income due to the sale of Sec. 1250 property than a noncorporate taxpayer?

13-23. Assume a taxpayer sells equipment used in a trade or business for a gain that is less than the depreciation allowed. If the taxpayer is a corporation, will a greater amount of Sec. 1245 income be recognized than if the taxpayer is an individual? Explain.

13-24. Dale owns business equipment with a $100,000 FMV and an adjusted basis of $60,000. The property was originally acquired for $150,000. Which one of the following transactions would result in recognition of $40,000 ordinary income by Dale due to the depreciation recapture rules of Sec. 1245?
a. He makes a gift of the property to a daughter.

    b. He contributes the property to a qualified charitable organization.

    c. He disposes of the equipment in an installment sale and receives $10,000 cash in the year of sale.

13-25. Carlos owns an office building with a $700,000 acquisition cost, a $250,000 adjusted basis, and a $500,000 FMV. The office building was acquired before 1981, and additional depreciation amounts to $110,000. Carlos makes a gift of the building to a charitable organization. What is the amount of his charitable contribution deduction?

13-26. Ted owns a warehouse that cost $650,000 in 1984 and is subject to depreciation recapture under Sec. 1245. The warehouse, which has an adjusted basis of $500,000, is destroyed by a tornado and Ted receives $600,000 from the insurance company. Within 9 months, he pays $680,000 for a new warehouse and an election is made to defer the gain under Sec. 1033. What are the amount and character of Ted's recognized gain?

13-27. Richard, a farmer, who elected to expense the cost of clearing land in 1985 to make it suitable for farming, may have to recapture a portion of the expenses as ordinary income if he sells the land. In order to avoid recapture of any portion of those expenses, how long must Richard hold the farmland?

13-28. When a taxpayer disposes of oil, gas, or geothermal property, part or all of the gain may be recaptured as ordinary income. Explain how the recapture amount is determined for oil and gas and geothermal properties.

13-29. William owns two appreciated assets, land and a building, which have been used in his trade or business for several years. The straight-line method of depreciation is used for the building. If he sells the two assets to his 100%-owned corporation, will William have to recognize any ordinary income? Explain.

PROBLEMS

13-30. *Sec. 1231, 1245, and 1250 Transactions.* All assets listed below have been held for more than one year. Which assets might be classified as Sec. 1231, Sec. 1245, or Sec. 1250 property? An asset may be classified as more than one type of property.

    a. Land on which a factory is located

    b. Equipment used in the factory

    c. Raw materials inventory

    d. Patent purchased to allow use of a manufacturing process

    e. Land held primarily for sale

    f. Factory building acquired in 1986 (the straight-line ACRS recovery method is used)

13-31. *Sec. 1231 Gains and Losses.* Consider the following independent cases for Vivian, and determine the amount of Vivian's AGI if her AGI is $40,000, without considering the gains and losses below. Assume she has no unrecaptured net Sec. 1231 losses at the beginning of the year.

	Case a	Case b	Case c	Case d
Sec. 1231 gain	$15,000	$10,000	$20,000	$ 5,000
Sec. 1231 loss	5,000	18,000	25,000	12,000
LTCG	—0—	—0—	4,000	—0—
LTCL	—0—	—0—	—0—	4,200

13-32. *Sec. 1231 Transactions.* Which of the following transactions or events is treated as a Sec. 1231 gain or loss? Assume all assets are held for more than one year.

    a. Theft of uninsured diamond ring, with an $800 basis and a $1,000 FMV.

    b. Gain due to condemnation of land used in business.

    c. Loss on the sale of a warehouse.

    d. Gain on the sale of equipment. The gain recognized amounts to $4,000 and the depreciation deductions allowed amount to $10,000.

13-33. *Capital Loss Versus Sec. 1231 Loss.* Vicki has an AGI of $70,000 without considering the sale of a nondepreciable asset for $28,000. The asset was acquired 6 years ago and has an adjusted basis of $39,000. She has no other sales or exchanges. Determine her AGI for the following independent situations:

a. The asset is a capital asset.

b. The asset is Sec. 1231 property.

13-34. *Ordinary Income Versus Sec. 1231 Gain.* At the beginning of 1994, Silver Corporation has a $95,000 capital loss carryforward from 1993. During 1994, the corporation sells land, held for 4 years, and realizes a $80,000 gain. Silver has no unrecaptured Sec. 1231 losses, and it made no other sales during the current year. Determine the amount of capital loss carryforward that Silver can use in 1994 if:

a. The land is Sec. 1231 property.

b. The land is not a capital asset or Sec. 1231 property.

13-35. *Sec. 1231 Transactions.* During the current year, Sean's office building is destroyed by fire. After collecting the insurance proceeds, Sean has a $50,000 recognized gain. The building was acquired in 1978, and the straight-line method of depreciation has been used. He does not plan to acquire a replacement building. Consider the following independent cases and determine his net capital gain. For each case, include the $50,000 casualty gain described above.

a. Land used in his trade or business and held more than a year is condemned by the state. The recognized gain is $60,000.

b. Assume the same facts as in Case a, except the condemnation results in a $60,000 loss.

c. An apartment building used as residential rental property and held more than one year is destroyed by a sudden, unexpected mudslide. The building is not insured, and the loss amounts to $200,000.

13-36. *Nonrecaptured Net Sec. 1231 Losses.* Consider the following summary of Sec. 1231 gains and losses recognized by Janet during the period 1989–1994. If Janet has no capital gains and losses during the 6-year period, determine her net capital gain for each year.

	Sec. 1231 Gains	Sec. 1231 Losses
1989	$9,000	$ 7,000
1990	20,000	24,000
1991	12,000	20,000
1992	9,000	5,000
1993	25,000	12,000
1994	10,000	17,000

13-37. *Sec. 1245.* The Pear Corporation owns equipment with a $300,000 adjusted basis. The equipment was purchased six years ago for $700,000. If Pear sells the equipment for the selling prices given in the three independent cases below, what is the amount and character of Pear's recognized gain or loss?

Case	Selling Price
a	$415,000
b	725,000
c	260,000

13-38. *Sec. 1245.* Elizabeth owns equipment that cost $300,000 and has an adjusted basis of $125,000. If the straight-line method of depreciation had been used, the adjusted basis would be $180,000.

a. What is the maximum selling price that she could sell the equipment for without having to recognize Sec. 1245 ordinary income?

b. If she sold the equipment and had to recognize $42,000 of Sec. 1245 ordinary income, what was the selling price?

13-39. *Secs. 1231, 1245, and 1250.* Betty is in the business of breeding and racing horses. Consider the following transactions that occur during the year:

- A building with an adjusted basis of $300,000 is destroyed by fire. Insurance proceeds of $500,000 are received, but Betty does not plan to replace the building. The building was built 12 years ago at a cost of $430,000 and straight-line depreciation has been used. The building was used to provide lodging for her employees.

- Four acres of the farm are condemned by the state to widen the highway and Betty receives $50,000. The adjusted basis of the four acres is $15,000 and the land was inherited from her Mother 15 years ago. She does not plan to purchase additional land.
- A racehorse purchased four years ago for $200,000 was sold for $550,000. Total depreciation allowed using the straight-line method amounts to $160,000.
- Equipment purchased three years ago for $200,000 is exchanged for $100,000 of IBM common stock. The adjusted basis of the equipment is $120,000. If straight-line depreciation had been used, the adjusted basis would be $152,000.
- A pony, with an adjusted basis of $20,000 and FMV of $35,000, that her daughter uses only for personal use is injured while attempting a jump. Because of the injury, the uninsured pony has to be destroyed by a veterinarian.

  a. What amount of Sec. 1245 ordinary income must be recognized?
  b. What amount of Sec. 1250 ordinary income must be recognized?
  c. Will the loss resulting from the destruction of her daughter's pony be used to determine net Sec. 1231 gains or losses?
  d. After all of the netting of gains or losses is completed, will the gain resulting from the involuntary conversion of the building be treated as LTCG?
  e. What is the amount of the net Sec. 1231 gain or loss?

13-40. *Sale of Business and Personal-use Property.* Arnie, a college student, purchased a new truck in 1992 for $6,000. He used the truck 70% of the time as a distributor for the local newspaper and 30% of the time for personal use. The truck has a 5-year recovery period, and he claimed depreciation deductions of $840 in 1992 and $1,344 in 1993. Arnie sells the truck on June 20, 1994, for $3,000.
  a. What is the amount of allowable depreciation in 1994?
  b. What are the amount and character of Arnie's realized and recognized gain or loss?

13-41. *Like-kind Exchange of Sec. 1245 Property.* General Corporation owns equipment costing $40,000 in 1987 and currently having a $22,000 adjusted basis. General exchanges the equipment for other equipment with a $35,000 FMV and marketable securities with a $15,000 FMV. Determine the following:
  a. Realized gain
  b. Recognized gain
  c. Gain treated as ordinary income
  d. Gain treated as Sec. 1231 gain
  e. Basis of marketable securities received
  f. Basis of equipment received

13-42. *Purpose of Sec. 1245.* Assume the year is 1986 and noncorporate taxpayers are allowed to deduct 60% of net capital gains to determine their AGI. Martin owns equipment used in his trade or business that was purchased in 1979 for $200,000. Allowed depreciation deductions amount to $160,000. Martin sells the equipment in 1986 for $110,000. No other sales or exchanges are made in 1986 or the preceding 5 years.
  a. Determine the increase in Martin's 1986 AGI as a result of the sale if Sec. 1245 did not exist.
  b. Given that Sec. 1245 does exist, what is the increase in his AGI as a result of the sale?
  c. How would your answers to parts a and b change if the sale date is 1994?

13-43. *Secs. 1231 and 1250.* Charles owns an office building and land that are used in his trade or business. The office building and land were acquired in 1978 for $800,000 and $100,000, respectively. During the current year, the properties are sold for $900,000 with 20% of the selling price being allocated to the land. The assets as shown on the taxpayer's books prior to their sale are as follows:

Building	$800,000	
Accumulated depreciation	185,000[a]	$615,000
Land		100,000

[a] If the straight-line method of depreciation had been used, the accumulated depreciation would be $120,000.

a. What is recognized gain due to the sale of the building?

b. What is the character of the recognized gain due to the sale of the building?

c. What are the recognized gain and character of the gain due to the sale of the land?

d. If the taxpayer is a corporation, how will the answers to Parts a-c change? Explain.

13-44. *Sec. 1250.* Maggie owns a motel that is operated as a trade or business adjacent to an interstate highway. The motel was purchased in March 1965 for $2,000,000, and she used an accelerated method of depreciation. The motel is sold during the current year for $975,000. The adjusted basis of the motel is $600,000. Additional depreciation is deducted as follows:

	Additional Depreciation
March 1965 to January 1, 1970	$ 95,000
January 1, 1970 to current date	205,000

a. What is the amount of realized gain?

b. What is the amount, if any, of ordinary income that Maggie must recognize as a result of the additional depreciation deducted prior to January 1, 1970?

c. What is the amount of ordinary income that must be recognized by Maggie as a result of selling the motel?

13-45. *Sec. 1250.* Ken purchased an office building on January 1, 1980, for $360,000 (40-year life and a $32,000 salvage value) and he elected to use the sum-of-the-years'digits method of depreciation. The building is sold on January 1, 1994, for $340,000. Given the following depreciation schedule for the asset, what is the amount of gain recognized and the character of the gain?

Year	Depreciation
1980	$ 16,000
1981	15,600
1982	15,200
1983	14,800
1984	14,400
1985	14,000
1986	13,600
1987	13,200
1988	12,800
1989	12,400
1990	12,000
1991	11,600
1992	11,200
1993	10,800
	$187,600

13-46. *Sec. 1250.* Assume the same facts as Problem 13-45 except that the taxpayer is a corporation instead of an individual. What is the amount and character of the corporation's recognized gain or loss?

13-47. *Sec. 1250 Residential Rental Property.* Assume the same facts as Problem 13-45 except that the building is an apartment complex that qualifies as residential rental property. What is the amount and character of Ken's recognized gain or loss?

13-48. *Sec. 1250 Residential Rental Property.* Assume the same facts as in Problem 13-46 except that the building is an apartment complex that qualifies as residential rental property. What is the amount and character of the corporation's recognized gain or loss?

13-49. *Sec. 1250 Residential Rental Property.* Jesse owns a duplex which he uses as residential rental property. The duplex cost $100,000 nine years ago, and 10% of the cost was allocated to the land. Total cost-recovery deductions allowed amount to $36,000. The statutory percentages were used to compute cost-recovery deductions. If the straight-line method of cost recovery was used instead, $25,000 of cost-recovery deductions would have been allowed.

a. What is the amount of recognized gain and the character of the gain if Jesse sells the duplex for $125,000?

b. What is the amount of recognized gain in the year of sale and the character of the gain if Jesse sells the property under the installment sale method? Terms of the installment sale are as follows: $25,000 in the year of sale and a $100,000 note to be paid in four annual payments. The note is an interest-bearing note at the market rate of interest.

13-50. *Sec. 1250.* Rosemary owns an office building that cost $500,000 and has an adjusted basis of $190,000. If the straight-line method of depreciation had been used, the adjusted basis would be $260,000.

a. What is the maximum selling price that she could sell the building for without having to recognize Sec. 1250 ordinary income?

b. If she sold the building and had to recognize $45,000 of Sec. 1250 ordinary income, what was the selling price?

13-51. *Recapture of Soil and Water Conservation Expenditures.* Bob owns farm land with a $600,000 basis, and he elects to expense $100,000 of expenditures incurred for soil and water conservation purposes. After farming for 7 years and 4 months, Bob sells the farm land for $825,000.

a. What is the amount of the recognized gain and the character of the gain?

b. What is the amount of recognized gain and the character of the gain if the farm land is sold for $615,000?

13-52. *Recapture of Intangible Drilling Costs.* Jeremy purchased undeveloped oil and gas property in 1987 and paid $300,000 for intangible drilling and development costs. He elected to expense the intangible drilling and development costs in 1987. During the current year, Jeremy sells the property which has an $800,000 adjusted basis for $900,000. What is the amount of gain treated as ordinary income under Sec. 1254 because of the election to expense intangible drilling and development costs?

13-53. *Recapture of Intangible Drilling Costs and Depletion.* In 1988, Jack purchased undeveloped oil and gas property for $900,000 and paid $170,000 for intangible drilling and development costs. He elected to expense the intangible drilling and development costs. During the current year he sells the property for $950,000 when the property's adjusted basis is $700,000. Depletion of $200,000 was allowed on the property.

a. What is the realized gain and how much of the gain is ordinary income?

b. For Jack to have a Sec. 1231 gain, the selling price must exceed what amount?

13-54. *Related Party Transactions.* Ed operates a storage business as a sole proprietorship and owns the following assets acquired in 1977:

Warehouse	$400,000	
Minus: Accumulated depreciation (straight-line method)	(100,000)	
Adjusted basis		$300,000
Land		75,000

The FMV of the warehouse and the land is $500,000 and $200,000, respectively. Ed owns 75% of the stock of the Crane Corporation. If he sells the two assets to Crane at a price equal to the FMV of the assets, determine the following:

a. Recognized gain due to sale of the building and character of the gain.

b. Recognized gain due to the sale of the land and character of the gain.

13-55. *Timing of Sec. 1231 Transactions.* Russ has never recognized any Sec. 1231 gains or losses. In December 1994, Russ is considering the sale of two Sec. 1231 assets. The sale of one asset will result in a $20,000 Sec. 1231 gain, while the sale of the other asset will result in a $20,000 Sec. 1231 loss. Russ has no other capital or Sec. 1231 gains and losses in 1994 and does not expect to have any other capital or Sec. 1231 gains and losses in 1994. He is aware that it might be advantageous to recognize the Sec. 1231 gain and the Sec. 1231 loss in different tax years. However, he does not know if he should recognize the Sec. 1231 gain in 1994 and the Sec. 1231 loss in 1995 or visa versa. His marginal tax rate for each year is expected to be 31%. Advise the taxpayer with respect to these two alternatives:

a. Recognize the $20,000 Sec. 1231 loss in 1994 and the $20,000 Sec. 1231 gain in 1995.

b. Recognize the $20,000 Sec. 1231 gain in 1994 and the $20,000 Sec. 1231 loss in 1995.

13-56. *Timing of Sec. 1231 Transaction.* Holly has recognized a $9,000 STCL. She has no other recognized capital gains and losses in 1994. She is considering the sale of a Sec. 1231 asset at a $5,000 gain in 1994. She had not recognized any Sec. 1231 losses during the previous 5 years and does not expect to have any other Sec. 1231 transactions in 1993. Her marginal tax rate for 1994 is 31%. What is the amount of increase in her 1994 taxes if Holly recognizes the $5,000 Sec. 1231 gain in 1994?

TAX FORM/RETURN PREPARATION PROBLEMS

TurboTax **13-57.** Mr. Buckner, Soc. Sec. No. 267-31-7251, sells an apartment building during the current year for $1,750,000. The building was purchased on January 1, 1978, for $2,000,000. An accelerated method of depreciation has been used, and depreciation of $880,000 has been taken. If the straight-line method of depreciation had been used, depreciation of $600,000 would have been allowed. The figures given above do not include the purchase price or the selling price of the land. Mr. Buckner's adjusted basis for the land is $200,000, and the sales price is $300,000. Mr. Buckner, who owns and operates a taxi business, sells one of the automobiles for $1,800. The automobile's adjusted basis is zero, and the original cost is $5,000. The automobile was purchased on April 25, 1988. Mr. Buckner has no other gains and losses during the year, and nonrecaptured net Sec. 1231 losses amount to zero. Prepare Form 4797 for the current year.

13-58. Julie Hernandez is single and has no dependents. She operates a dairy farm and her social security number is 510-88-6387. She lives at 1325 Vermont Street in Costa, Florida. Consider the following information for her tax return for the current year:

- Schedule C was prepared by her accountant and the net profit from the dairy operations for the current year is $48,000.
- Itemized deductions amount to $3,185.
- Dividend income amounts to $280.
- State income tax refund received during the year is $125. She did not itemize her deductions last year.
- In June, a burglar broke into her house and stole the following two assets which were acquired in 1979:

	Basis	FMV	Insurance Proceeds Received
Painting	$2,000	$10,000	$9,000
Sculpture	1,700	1,500	0

The following assets used in her trade or business were sold during the year:

	Acquisition Date	Original Cost	Depreciation to Date of Sale	Date of Sale	Selling Price
Tractor	June 10, 1980	$25,000	$25,000	Oct. 20	$ 8,300
Barn	May 23, 1980	90,000	36,000[1]	May 13	87,000
Land	May 23, 1980	15,000	-0-	May 13	27,000
Cows	Sept. 7, 1987	20,000	13,000	Nov. 8	21,000

[1] $25,000 if the straight-line method had been used.

In August, three acres of the farm were taken by the state under the right of eminent domain for the purpose of building a highway. The basis of the three acres is $1,500 and the state paid the FMV, $22,000, on February 10. The farm was purchased on August 12, 1968.

Nonrecaptured net Section 1231 losses from the five most recent tax years preceding the current year amount to $7,000. Estimated taxes paid during the year amount to $38,200.

Prepare Forms 1040, 4684, 4797, Schedule D, and a Schedule D Tax Worksheet in the Instructions to Form 1040 for the current year. (Do not consider self-employment taxes discussed in Chapter 14.)

CASE STUDY PROBLEM

13-59. Your client Kent Earl owns a bowling alley and has indicated that he wants to sell the business for $1,000,000 and purchase a minor league baseball franchise. His business consists of the following tangible assets:

	Acquisition Date	Original Cost	Adjusted Basis
Equipment	1984	$600,000	$150,000
Building	1978	900,000	400,000[1]
Land	1978	100,000	100,000
Inventory	Current year	50,000	50,000

[1] $480,000 if straight-line depreciation had been used.

Since you have another client, Tom Quick, who is interested in purchasing a business, you informed Tom of Kent's interest in selling. Tom wants to purchase the bowling alley, and the price sounds right to him. The bowling alley business has been very profitable in the last few years because Kent has developed a loyal group of customers by promoting bowling leagues during the week days and a special Saturday afternoon session for children in the elementary school grades. Kent and Tom have come to you and want to know how the transaction should be handled for the best tax results. You know, of course, that the $1,000,000 purchase price will have to be allocated among the assets and it will be necessary to estimate the FMV of all assets. Since FMV is often subjective, Kent and Tom recognize that some flexibility might exist in allocating the purchase price. For example, it might be just as easy to justify a FMV of $300,000 or $325,000 for the equipment.

1. What advice do you have for Kent with respect to the allocation (i.e., should he be interested in allocating more to some assets than others)? Explain the reasoning for your advice.
2. Would your advice to Kent be different if he had a large amount of capital losses and no nonrecaptured net Sec. 1231 losses?
3. What advice do you have for Tom with respect to the allocation (i.e., should he be interested in allocating more of the purchase price to some assets than to others)? Explain the reasoning for your advice.
4. What advantages might result from having Kent sign an agreement not to compete (i.e., operate a bowling alley)?
5. Should you have a concern about the ethical implications of advising both Kent and Tom?

CASE STUDY PROBLEM—ETHICAL ISSUES

13-60. Assume the same facts as in Case Study Problem 13-59 except you have the following market values as a result of an appraisal:

Equipment	$ 250,000
Building	500,000
Land	140,000
Inventory	110,000
Total	$1,000,000

Tom insists that $150,000 of the purchase price should be allocated to inventory and $100,000 should be allocated to land. He refuses to complete the purchase unless the allocation is made as he requests. What action should you take with respect to Tom's request? (See Chapter 10 for a discussion of valuation issues in the purchase and sale of a business.)

TAX RESEARCH PROBLEM

13-61. Berkeley Corporation has a policy of furnishing new automobiles to the athletic department of the local university. The automobiles are used for short periods of time by the extremely popular head basketball coach. When the automobiles are returned to Berkeley Corporation, they are sold to regular customers. The owner of Berkeley Corporation maintains that any such cars held for more than one year should qualify as Sec. 1231 property. Do you agree?

A partial list of research sources is

• Rev. Rul. 75-538, 1975-2 C.B. 34.

14

Special Tax Computation Methods, Payment of Tax, and Tax Credits

LEARNING OBJECTIVES

After studying this chapter, you should be able to

1. Calculate the alternative minimum tax
2. Apply the forward averaging calculation to lump-sum distributions
3. Describe what constitutes self-employment income and compute the self-employment tax
4. Understand the mechanics of the federal withholding tax system and the requirements for making estimated tax payments
5. Describe the various business and personal tax credits

Chapter 2 discussed the basic tax computation for individuals using the tax table and tax rate schedules. This chapter considers special methods for computing the tax in unusual circumstances. Some of these methods—for example, a forward averaging technique—are available to mitigate the tax effects of bunching large amounts of income (such as lump-sum distributions from qualified pension plans) in a single year. Other methods, such as the alternative minimum tax and the self-employment tax, result in additional taxes.

This chapter also discusses the methods for payment of an individual's tax liability, including the pay-as-you-go withholding rules and the estimated tax payment requirements. The chapter concludes with a discussion of the various credits available to reduce the final tax liability.

ALTERNATIVE MINIMUM TAX

OBJECTIVE 1
Calculate the alternative minimum tax

The minimum tax provisions were originally enacted in 1969 in response to a Treasury Department study that indicated that some taxpayers with substantial amounts of economic income were able to avoid paying any federal income tax because of claiming deductions for tax preference items. Originally, this tax upon individuals was referred to as an **add-on minimum tax** because it was added to the taxpayer's income tax liability. The amount of the tax was 10% times the taxpayer's tax preferences in excess of a $30,000 statutory exemption.

The present **alternative minimum tax (AMT)** applies to individuals and estates and trusts only if it exceeds the taxpayer's regular income tax liability.[1] Most taxpayers are not subject to the AMT because they do not have substantial tax preferences, and a liberal exemption amount (i.e., $45,000 for married individuals filing a joint return and $33,750 for single individuals) is provided to reduce the minimum tax base.

Example 14-1 ■   Ricardo and Sue are married and file a joint return for 1994 with taxable income of $30,000 and $12,000 of tax preferences and other adjustments. Their alternative minimum taxable income (AMTI) is $42,000 ($30,000 + $12,000), but the alternative minimum tax base is zero because of the $45,000 exemption. Thus, their tax liability is based upon the regular tax computation and no AMT liability is owed.   ■

[1] Corporations are also subject to an alternative minimum tax under Sec. 55 calculated at a 20% rate. This topic is discussed in Chapter 5 of *Prentice Hall's Federal Taxation: Corporations, Partnerships, Estates, and Trusts* text and in Chapter 16 of the *Comprehensive* volume.

Additional Comment

Some tax advisors recommend accelerating income into a year in which the taxpayer is subject to the AMT since the income will be taxed at a 26% or a 28% rate rather than a possibly higher rate in a later year.

Computational Aspects

The formula for computing the alternative minimum tax for the tax year is to apply a two-tiered graduated rate schedule (i.e., a 26% rate applies to the first $175,000 of the tax base and a 28% rate applies to amounts in excess of $175,000). The tax base consists of the following items:[2]

Taxable income

Plus: Tax preference items[3]

Plus: Personal and dependency exemptions

The standard deduction if the taxpayer does not itemize

Plus or minus: Certain other adjustments required because different rules are used for calculating the alternative minimum taxable income as compared with taxable income (e.g., special limitations on certain itemized deductions)

Alternative minimum taxable income (AMTI)

Minus: Exemption amount ($45,000 for a married couple filing a joint return and surviving spouses, $33,750 for single individuals, and $22,500 for a married individual filing separately). The exemption amount is reduced by 25% of AMTI in excess of $150,000 for a married couple filing a joint return and surviving spouses, $112,500 for single individuals, and $75,000 for a married individual filing separately.[4]

Alternative minimum tax base

Times: Tax Rate

Equals: Tentative minimum tax

Minus: Regular tax

Equals: Alternative minimum tax

Example 14-2 ■

Key Point

For purposes of the alternative minimum tax, no deduction is allowed for personal exemptions or the standard deduction.

Rita, a single taxpayer, has a regular tax liability of $39,427 and taxable income of $138,300, a positive adjustment due to limitations on itemized deductions of $30,000, and tax preferences of $40,000 in 1994. Rita's alternative minimum tax for 1994 is calculated as follows:

Taxable income		$138,300
Plus:	Tax preferences	40,000
Plus:	Personal exemption	2,450
Plus:	Adjustments related to itemized deductions	30,000
Alternative minimum taxable income		$210,750
Minus:	Exemption	(9,188)[a]
Alternative minimum tax base		$201,562
Tax rate on initial $175,000		× 0.26
Tax on initial $175,000		$ 45,500
Tax base in excess of $175,000		$ 26,562
Tax rate on excess amount		× 0.28
Tax on excess amount		$ 7,437

[2] Sec. 55(b)(1).

[3] Sec. 57.

[4] Sec. 55(d)(3).

Tentative minimum tax ($45,500 + $7,437) $ 52,937[b]
Minus: Regular tax   (39,427)

Alternative minimum tax $ 13,510[c]

Rita will pay a total of $52,937 ($39,427 regular tax + $13,510 AMT).

[a] $33,750 − (0.25 × [$210,750 − $112,500]).
[b] Section 55(c) generally prevents individuals from using tax credits to reduce the AMT except for the foreign tax credit, which cannot offset more than 90% of the tentative minimum tax.
[c] The AMT is simply an acceleration of the payment of income tax. When an AMT liability is paid, a minimum tax credit is available to offset future regular income tax liabilities. ■

Tax Preference Items

Historical Note

In 1986 the alternative minimum tax generated tax revenue of $6.7 billion, but now this tax produces less than $1 billion annually in tax revenue. The decline can be attributed to the Tax Reform Act of 1986 that eliminated many preferentially treated items.

Tax preferences are provisions in the Code granting favorable treatment to taxpayers. For example, accelerated depreciation allowed for real property placed in service prior to 1987 is a tax preference item. (See Chapter 10 for a discussion of ACRS depreciation.) To compute the tax base for the AMT, the tax preferences designated in Sec. 57 must be added to taxable income. Some of the most common tax preference items include the following:[5]

- Excess of accelerated depreciation (or ACRS cost recovery) claimed over a hypothetical straight-line depreciation amount for real property placed in service before 1987 computed on an item-by-item basis.
- Tax-exempt interest on certain private activity bonds.[6]

It should be noted, however, that not all items receiving preferential treatment are tax preference items. For example, most municipal bond interest income is exempt from federal income tax but is not a tax preference item. Only tax-exempt interest on private activity bonds (e.g., bonds issued by a municipality to fund certain nongovernmental activities like an industrial park) issued after August 7, 1986 are subject to the AMT.

Example 14-3 ■

Additional Comment

In the Revenue Reconciliation Act of 1993 Congress created a two-tier alternative minimum tax schedule in order to make the individual income tax system more progressive.

Richard, a single taxpayer, has the following tax preference items for the current year:

- $15,000 ACRS cost-recovery deduction on real property placed in service prior to 1987 and held for investment. The straight-line ACRS deduction would have been $10,000.
- $10,000 of tax-exempt interest on private activity bonds.

Richard's total tax preferences are $15,000, consisting of $5,000 excess cost recovery deductions and $10,000 tax-exempt interest on the private activity bonds. ■

AMT Adjustments

As previously discussed, AMTI equals taxable income as modified by certain adjustments and increased by tax preference items. AMT adjustments represent either itemized deductions that are not allowed in computing AMTI or timing

---

[5] Sec. 57. Another tax preference item added in 1993 which does not have immediate application is an exclusion of up to 50% of gain from the disposition of small business stock issued after August 10, 1993 and held for more than five years. (See Chapter 5.)
[6] Sec. 57(a)(5).

differences relating to the deferral of income or the acceleration of deductions under the regular tax rules. These adjustments generally increase the AMT tax base, although the netting of timing differences may result in an overall reduction of the AMT tax base when the timing differences reverse. Some of the more important adjustments are included below.

Additional Comment

In the Revenue Reconciliation Act of 1993 Congress repealed the AMT preference for donated appreciated capital gain property. Congress felt that the repeal would induce additional charitable giving.

Limitation on Itemized Deductions. Only certain itemized deductions are allowed in computing AMTI. Additionally, the standard deduction is not allowed if an individual does not itemize deductions.[7] The following items are deductible for AMT purposes:

- Casualty and theft losses in excess of 10% of AGI
- Charitable contributions (but not in excess of the 20%, 30%, and 50% limitation amounts)
- Medical expenses in excess of 10% of AGI (a 7.5% ceiling applies to the regular tax computation)
- Qualified housing interest and certain other interest up to the amount of qualified net investment income included in the AMT base
- Estate tax deduction on income in respect of a decedent
- Gambling losses

Some of the more significant itemized deductions that are not deductible for the AMT include miscellaneous itemized deductions (e.g., unreimbursed employee expenses), state, and local and foreign income taxes, and real and personal property taxes. The 3% disallowance rule for itemized deductions of high-income taxpayers does not apply to the AMT.

Example 14-4 ■

Robin, a single taxpayer, has the following itemized deductions in 1994:

Personal casualty loss in excess of 10% of AGI	$12,000
Charitable contributions	4,000
Medical expenses in excess of 7.5% of AGI ($10,000 actual expenses − $7,500)	2,500
Mortgage interest on Robin's personal residence	19,200
Real estate taxes	4,000
State income taxes	6,000

Robin's AGI is $100,000, taxable income is $50,000, and she has $20,000 of tax preferences. Robin's AMT adjustments for disallowed itemized deductions include (1) $2,500 of medical expenses, because the 10% limitation for AMT purposes eliminates the medical expense deduction ($10,000 − [0.10 × $100,000 AGI] = $0) and (2) $10,000 of real estate and state income taxes ($4,000 + $6,000). Thus, Robin's total AMT adjustment for disallowed itemized deductions is $12,500 ($2,500 + $10,000). Robin's AMTI is $84,950 ($50,000 taxable income + $20,000 tax preferences + $12,500 disallowed itemized deductions + her $2,450 personal exemption). ■

AMT Adjustments Due to Timing Differences. Other adjustments are required when the rules for calculating taxable income permit the taxpayer to temporarily defer the recognition of income or to accelerate deductions. This temporary benefit is caused by applying different accounting methods that result in timing differences

---

[7] Sec. 56(b)(1)(E).

when income or expenses are recognized. When an AMT liability is paid, an AMT tax credit is available to reduce the taxpayer's regular tax liability in subsequent years.[8] The most common AMT adjustments for individuals that represent timing differences include:

Key Point

The 40-year life that is used to calculate the AMT adjustment for real property placed in service after 1986 causes taxpayers to maintain two separate depreciation schedules.

- For real property placed in service after 1986, the difference between the MACRS depreciation claimed and a hypothetical straight-line depreciation amount calculated using a 40-year life (see Chapter 10 for a discussion of the alternative depreciation system).

- For personal property placed in service after 1986, the difference between the MACRS deduction and the amount determined by using the 150% declining balance method (i.e., the amount computed under the alternative depreciation system) with a switch to the straight-line method.

- For research and experimental (R&E) expenditures, the difference between the amount expensed and the deduction that would have been allowed if the expenditures were capitalized and amortized over a 10-year period.[9]

Example 14-5 ∎

Rob has the following AMT adjustments caused by timing differences in the current year:

- Depreciation on residential rental real property costing $100,000 and placed in service in January of the current year is $3,485 based upon the straight-line method and a 27½-year recovery period under the MACRS rules. The depreciation for AMT purposes is $2,396 based upon the straight-line method and a 40-year recovery period under the alternative depreciation system. Thus, the positive AMT adjustment is $1,089 ($3,485 − $2,396).

- Depreciation on an automobile used in business costing $10,000 and placed in service in the current year is $2,000 based upon the MACRS rules (i.e., 200% DB method, a half-year convention and a 5-year recovery period). The depreciation for AMT purposes is $1,500 based upon the alternative depreciation system (i.e., 150% DB method, half-year convention and a 5-year recovery period). Thus, the positive AMT adjustment is $500 ($2,000 − $1,500).

Additional Comment

For corporate taxpayers only, there is a 0.12% environmental tax imposed on the excess of the corporation's modified alternative minimum taxable income over $2 million.

- R&E expenditures amounting to $50,000 are expensed in the current year. The R&E deduction would be $5,000 ($50,000 ÷ 10 years) if the expenditures are capitalized and amortized over a 10-year period. Thus, the positive AMT adjustment is $45,000 ($50,000 − $5,000).

Rob's total positive AMT adjustment to his taxable income to arrive at AMTI is $46,589 ($1,089 + $500 + $45,000). ∎

Summary Illustration of the AMT Computation

The AMT tax formula is illustrated in the following example:

Example 14-6 ∎

Roger and Kate are married and file a joint return. They have the following items (including $25,000 in tax preference items from interest income earned on private activity bonds) that are used to compute taxable income in 1994:

---

[8] Sec. 53. The AMT credit may be carried forward indefinitely against the regular tax liability but is limited to the excess of the taxpayer's regular tax (reduced by nonrefundable credits) over the tentative minimum tax for the year. Detailed discussion of the rules for computing the AMT credit is beyond the scope of the text.

[9] Sec. 56(a).

Additional Comment

Some tax advisors recommend that cash basis taxpayers prepay their local property taxes or state income taxes before the end of the year in order to reduce the current year's tax liability. However, if the taxpayer is subject to the AMT, this is not a valid strategy.

Gross income:

Salary		$ 60,000
Dividends and interest		10,000
Business income		30,000[a]
AGI		$100,000
Minus: Itemized deductions:		
State and local property taxes	$10,000	
Mortgage interest on their personal residence	12,000	
Charitable contributions	3,000	(25,000)
Minus: Personal and dependency exemptions ($2,450 × 2)		(4,900)
Taxable income		$ 70,100

[a] MACRS depreciation deductions of $70,000 on personal property placed in service after 1986 were claimed in arriving at business income. Only $50,000 of depreciation would be claimed under the alternative depreciation system.

Roger's AMT is computed as follows:

Taxable income		$ 70,100
Plus: Tax preferences		25,000
Personal and dependency exemptions		4,900
AMT adjustments:		
Excess depreciation	$20,000	
State and local property taxes	10,000	30,000
AMTI		$130,000
Minus: AMT exemption		(45,000)
Tax base		$85,000
Times: Tax rate on amounts up to $175,000		× 0.26
Tentative minimum tax		$22,100
Minus: Regular tax		(14,688)
Alternative minimum tax		$ 7,412 ∎

The total tax liability for Roger and Kate is $22,100 ($14,688 + $7,412). An AMT credit in the amount of $7,412 is available to be carried over to 1995 and later years and offset any regular tax that is owed.

FORWARD AVERAGING

OBJECTIVE 2
Apply the forward averaging calculation to lump-sum distributions

Forward averaging was initially enacted in 1974. It was intended to provide relief for individuals who must report a portion of a lump-sum distribution from a qualified pension or profit-sharing plan as ordinary income. The averaging device mitigates the adverse effects of our progressive tax rate structure that result when there is a "bunching" of substantial amounts of income into a single year. Prior to 1974, the entire taxable portion of a lump-sum distribution was taxed as a long-term capital gain. For years prior to 1992, transitional rules were provided for individuals who attained the age of 50 before January 1, 1986. Such individuals could elect capital gain treatment (taxed at a 20% rate) for a portion of the lump-sum distribution. Additionally, the ordinary income portion of the lump-sum distribution was subject to a ten-year forward averaging convention. These rules are no longer applicable.

Historical Note

A tax calculation known as "income averaging," which permitted taxpayers to reduce their income tax in peak income years by averaging income over a 4-year period, was repealed in the Tax Reform Act of 1986.

Under current law, a five-year forward averaging convention is available if an individual is a participant in a qualified pension or profit-sharing plan for at least five years and receives a lump-sum distribution from the plan.[10] The forward averaging provisions are generally available with respect to a single lump-sum distribution received on or after an individual reaches age 59½.[11] The tax attributable to the distribution is computed separately from the regular tax calculation on the taxpayer's other taxable income.

Determining the Taxable Amount of the Distribution

The taxable amount of the distribution is determined as follows:

Additional Comment

A distribution from an IRA does not qualify for five-year forward averaging.

Distribution from a qualified pension or profit-sharing plan	$xxx
Minus:	
Employee contributions	(xx)
Unrealized appreciation on the employee's stock	(xx)
Minimum distribution allowance	(xx)
Taxable amount	$ xx

The taxable amount is then taxed at the taxpayer's regular tax rates or by using the forward averaging rules.

The following nontaxable amounts are subtracted from the total lump-sum distribution:

- *Employee contributions.* Employee contributions are treated as a tax-free return of capital because they were taxable to the employee when they were initially contributed to the qualified plan.

- *Unrealized appreciation on employer securities distributed as part of the lump-sum distribution.* Any appreciation accruing during the period the stock is held by the pension or profit-sharing trust is not taxed to the employee until the underlying securities are sold. The stock's basis in the employee's hands is its basis when the stock is contributed to the trust.

- *Minimum distribution allowance.* This amount is the lesser of (1) $10,000 or (2) one-half of the taxable amount of the lump-sum distribution. This amount is reduced by 20% of the taxable amount that is in excess of $20,000.[12] This allowance provides relief for taxpayers receiving small lump-sum distributions (i.e., because the 20% offsetting reduction generally reduces the minimum distribution allowance to zero for larger distributions).

Example 14-7 ∎   Rashad retires at the end of the current year at age 65 and receives a $120,000 lump-sum distribution in cash and employer securities from his employer's qualified profit-sharing plan. The distribution includes $10,000 of Rashad's contributions and $30,000 of unrealized appreciation on the employer's stock. Rashad has been a participant in the plan for 30 years. The taxable portion of the distribution is computed as follows:

[10] Sec. 402(e).
[11] Sec. 402(e)(4)(B).
[12] Sec. 402(e)(1)(C).

Total distribution to Rashad		$120,000
Minus:		
Employee contributions		(10,000)
Unrealized appreciation on the employer's stock		(30,000)
Taxable amount (before minimum distribution allowance)		$ 80,000
Minus: Minimum distribution allowance:		
One-half of the $80,000 taxable amount (subject to a $10,000 ceiling)	$10,000	
Minus: 0.20 × ($80,000 taxable amount − $20,000 statutory exemption)	(12,000)	—0—
Taxable amount		$ 80,000 ∎

Computing the Tax

The tax on the lump-sum distribution is determined by using the five-year averaging rules as follows:

1. Determine one-fifth of the taxable amount.
2. Compute the tax on the amount obtained in step 1 by using the current rate schedule for single taxpayers.
3. Multiply the amount obtained in step 2 by 5.

Example 14-8 ∎ Assume the same facts as in Example 14-7. The tax on the distribution is computed as follows:

One-fifth of the taxable amount ($80,000 × 0.20)	$16,000
Tax on $16,000 (using single taxpayer rates for the current year)	$ 2,400
Times: 5	× 5
Tax on distribution	$12,000

∎

Key Point

A taxpayer can use 5-year averaging only once and must have reached age 59½.

The average rate of tax on the lump-sum distribution in Example 14-8 is only 15% ($12,000 ÷ $80,000). This low rate is achieved because the individual's other taxable income is not included in the tax calculation. Otherwise, the application of the progressive tax rate structure would tax the distribution at higher rates if the individual has other taxable income in the year the lump-sum distribution is received. For example, an individual who has a 39.6% marginal tax rate in the year the lump-sum distribution is received would incur additional regular tax of $31,680 (0.396 × $80,000) if the five-year forward averaging rules were not available. The tax savings from using the forward averaging rules in Example 14-8 are $19,680 ($31,680 − $12,000).

SELF-EMPLOYMENT TAX

Most individuals are classified as employees and are not subject to the self-employment tax. Employees are covered under the Federal Insurance Contributions Act (FICA) through the payment of payroll taxes. The employer must withhold the

Ethical Point

An employer is required to have a reasonable basis for treating a worker as an independent contractor or meet the general common law rules for determining whether an employer-employee relationship exists. Otherwise, the employer will be liable for federal and state income tax withholding, FICA and FUTA taxes, interest, and penalties associated with the misclassification.

Historical Note

The ceiling amount on income from self-employment was $7,800 in 1971.

employee's share of the FICA tax and to provide a matching amount. Employees are not subject to an additional employment tax upon the filing of their federal income tax return.

The self-employment tax is imposed to finance social security coverage for self-employed individuals. Thus, the distinction between whether an individual is performing services as an independent contractor (i.e., a self-employed individual) or as an employee is important because no employer FICA contribution is required if the payee is deemed to have independent contractor status. Independent contractors are subject to self-employment tax on the amount of net earnings from the self-employment activity. Employees who have a small business in addition to their regular employment (e.g., an accountant who is an employee for a large corporation and also prepares tax returns as a consultant) may also be subject to the self-employment tax in addition to the FICA tax.

Computing the Tax

Individuals having net earnings from self-employment of $400 or more are subject to the self-employment tax.[13] The FICA tax imposed on both wages and self-employment income includes a 6.2% (12.4% for self-employed individuals) tax for the old-age, survivors and disability insurance (OASDI) component up to a $60,600 ceiling amount in 1994 ($57,600 in 1993). The second component of the FICA tax is a 1.45% (2.9% for self-employed individuals) tax for the hospital insurance (HI) portion. No ceiling amount applies to self-employment income received after 1993. A $135,000 ceiling applied in 1993. For employee wages the 6.2 and 1.45 percentages (totaling 7.65%) must be matched by the employer.

One-half of the self-employment tax that is imposed is allowed as a *for* AGI business deduction and is reported on page 1 of Form 1040.[14] Net earnings from self-employment is determined by multiplying self-employment income by 0.9235 (which is equivalent to multiplying the total earnings by .0765 and subtracting the result) to compute the amount that is subject to self-employment tax.

Example 14-9 ■

Rose has $80,000 of earnings from self-employment in 1994. Her net earnings from self-employment is $73,880 ($80,000 × 0.9235). The OASDI portion of the tax is $7,514 ($60,600 × 0.124). The amount of self-employment income that is subject to the hospital insurance portion of the tax is $73,880 and the HI tax is $2,143 ($73,880 × 0.029). Thus, the total self-employment tax reported on Schedule SE is $9,657. Rose also receives a *for* AGI tax deduction of $4,829 ($9,657 × 0.50) which is reported on page 1 of Form 1040. ■

Additional Comment

The Revenue Reconciliation Act of 1993 eliminated the wage cap on the hospital insurance component of wages. Although presented as a tax increase for high-income individuals, it will also increase the tax burden for employers of high-income individuals.

If an individual is an employee and also has income from self-employment, the tax base for computing the self-employment tax is reduced by the wages that are subject to the self-employment tax. The self-employment tax base for the OASDI component is equal to the lesser of the primary ceiling ($60,600 in 1994) reduced by the FICA wages or the self-employment income multiplied by 0.9235.

Example 14-10 ■

Sandy receives wages of $35,000 in 1994 that are subject to FICA tax. In addition, Sandy has a small consulting practice that generates $10,000 of net earnings from self-employment. The tentative tax base for computing the self-employment tax is $9,235 ($10,000 × 0.9235). Thus, the tax base for computing the OASDI portion of the tax is the lesser of $9,235 net earnings from self-employment or $25,600 ($60,600 ceiling − $35,000 FICA wages). Sandy's self-employment tax for the OASDI portion is $1,145 ($9,235 × 0.124) and the HI component is $268 ($9,235 × 0.029) The total amount of self-employment tax is therefore, $1,413 ($1,145 + $268) and Sandy also receives a *for* AGI deduction of $707 ($1,413 × 0.50) which is reported on page 1 of Form 1040. ■

[13] Sec. 6017.
[14] Sec. 164(f).

Example 14-11 ■

Assume the same facts as in Example 14-10 except that Sandy's wages are instead $100,000. Sandy's taxable self-employment income for the OASDI portion of the tax is zero because her FICA wages exceed the $60,600 primary ceiling amount. However, she is subject to self-employment tax with respect to the HI portion. The tax base for the HI portion is $9,235 ($10,000 self-employment earnings × 0.9235) because no ceiling amount is applicable. The HI portion of the self-employment tax is $268 ($9,235 × 0.029) and Sandy also receives a *for* AGI deduction for $134 ($268 × 0.50). ■

Key Point

In the case of married taxpayers filing joint returns, it is important on Schedule SE of Form 1040 to fill in the name and social security number of the spouse with the self-employment income. This information is used to establish benefit eligibility.

What Constitutes Self-Employment Income

Individuals who carry on a trade or business as a proprietor or partnership render services as independent contractors and are, therefore, subject to the self-employment tax. If an individual has two separate self-employment activities, the *net* earnings from each activity are aggregated. However, where a husband and wife file a joint return and both have self-employment income, the self-employment tax must be computed separately.[15]

Example 14-12 ■

Russ and Ruth are married and file a joint return. Russ has $13,000 net earnings from a consulting business and a $4,000 net loss from a retail store that is operated as a sole proprietorship. Ruth has wages of $50,000 from her employer that are subject to FICA taxes. Russ's taxable self-employment earnings are $8,312 ($9,000 × 0.9235). No reduction in the self-employment tax base is allowed for Ruth's wages as an employee because Ruth is not self-employed and the tax is computed separately for Russ and Ruth. ■

Among the items that constitute earnings that are subject to the self-employment tax are:

• Net earnings from a sole proprietorship
• Director's fees[16]
• Taxable research grants
• Distributive share of partnership income plus guaranteed payments from the partnership

The self-employment tax is computed on Schedule SE of Form 1040 (see Appendix B). The rules for computing the self-employment tax are summarized in Topic Review 14-1.

TOPIC REVIEW 14-1

Self-Employment Tax Summary
• The self-employment tax is imposed on self-employment income over $400.
• The tax base for computing the self-employment tax is the amount of self-employment income multiplied by 0.9235 and this amount is reduced by any wages that are subject to FICA taxes.
• A $60,600 ceiling applies to the old age survivors and disability (OASDI) portion. However, no ceiling applies to the hospital insurance (HI) portion of the tax.
• Self-employment tax is computed separately for married individuals filing joint returns.
• One-half of the self-employment tax that is imposed is allowed as a business deduction *for* AGI.
• The self-employment tax rate is 15.3% which includes 12.4% for the OASDI portion and 2.9% for the hospital insurance (HI) portion.

[15] Reg. Sec. 1.6017-1(b).
[16] Rev. Rul. 57-246, 1957-1 C.B. 338.

PAYMENT OF TAXES

OBJECTIVE 4

Understand the mechanics of the federal withholding tax system and the requirements for making estimated tax payments.

Real World Example

A teacher claimed a credit for social security taxes that had been withheld from his salary. He believed that the social security tax was illegally withheld since he did not authorize the collection of the tax. The Tax Court held that the social security tax is mandatory for designated employees and does not allow a person to elect not to contribute. Richard L. Feldman, 1967 PH T.C. Memo ¶ 67,091, 26 TCM 444.

The IRS collects federal income taxes either through withholding upon wages or quarterly estimated tax payments. If the withholdings and estimated taxes are less than the amount of tax, the taxpayer must pay the balance of the tax due when the tax return is filed. If there has been an overpayment of tax, the taxpayer may either request a refund or may choose to apply the overpayment to the following year's quarterly estimated taxes.

Substantial penalties are imposed if an employer fails to withhold federal income tax and pay such amounts to the IRS.[17] In addition, a taxpayer may be subject to a nondeductible penalty upon an underpayment of estimated tax.[18]

Withholding of Taxes

An employer must withhold federal income taxes and FICA taxes from an employee's wages. No withholdings are required if an employer-employee relationship does not exist (e.g., if the individual who performs the services is an independent contractor).[19] Generally, unless a specific exemption is provided under the Code, withholding is required upon all forms of remuneration paid to an employee. Thus, salaries, fees, bonuses, dismissal payments, commissions, vacation pay, and taxable fringe benefits are subject to withholding.[20] Special rules are provided for the following:

- *More than one employer during the same year.* Each employer must withhold FICA and federal income tax without regard to the fact that the employee has more than one employer. This requirement may result in an overwithholding of FICA tax if the ceiling amount on the OASDI portion of the tax is exceeded. In the event of an overwithholding of taxes, the employee may credit the excess amount as an additional payment of tax on line 58a on page 2 of Form 1040 (see Appendix B). However, the excess FICA contributions related to the matching employer contributions are not refundable or creditable against the tax liabilities of either employer.

- *Exemptions for certain employment activities.* Certain employees such as agricultural laborers, ministers, domestic servants, newspaper carriers under age 18, and tips of less than $20 per month are exempt from income tax withholding. Note, however, that the earnings of such individuals are fully taxable and that an employer may be liable for FICA tax payments on these earnings.[21]

- *Exemptions for certain fringe benefits.* Fringe benefits such as moving expense reimbursements, payments under a self-insured medical reimbursement plan, meals and lodging, travel expense reimbursements, payments under a qualified educational assistance program, and so on, are not subject to withholding if it is

---

[17] Sec. 3403. Employers are liable for payment of the full amount of withholdings that must be withheld and paid to the IRS. In addition, responsible individuals (e.g., corporate officers, directors, consultants, and so on) may be held personally liable for payment of the tax. (See *Renate Schiff v. U.S.,* 69 AFTR 2d 92-804, 92-1 USTC ¶ 50,248 (D.C. NV, 1992), *Ted E. Tsouprake v. U.S.,* 69 AFTR 2d 92-821, 92-1 USTC ¶ 50,249 (D.C. FL, 1992), and *Ralph M. Guito, Jr. v. U.S.,* 67 AFTR 2d 91-1066, 92-1 USTC ¶ 50,231 (D.C. FL, 1991).

[18] Sec. 6654. The Revenue Reconciliation Act of 1993 permits high-income taxpayers who are subject to the 36% and 39.6% tax rates in 1993 to elect to pay any additional 1993 taxes due to the higher rates in three non-interest bearing annual installments, the first of which must be paid on or before the due date for filing the 1993 return. Form 8841 (Deferral of Additional 1993 Taxes) must be filed with the 1993 tax return.

[19] Reg. Sec. 31.3401(c)-1(c).

[20] Reg. Sec. 31.3401(a)-1(a)(2).

[21] Reg. Sec. 31.3401(a)-(4)(b)(1). An employer is liable for FICA tax payments for domestic servants and agricultural labor if $50 or more is paid to an individual in any one quarter.

reasonable to believe that an employee can deduct the item or the item is nontaxable. Any excess reimbursements are subject to withholding.[22] For example, the portion of moving expenses that is not deductible by an employee (e.g., nondeductible indirect moving expenses) is subject to withholding.

- *Backup Withholding.* Backup withholding rules were enacted to prevent abusive noncompliance situations. Taxpayers who give false information to avoid backup withholding are subject to both civil and criminal penalties.[23] A 31% withholding rate is required on most types of payments that are reported on Form 1099 (e.g., interest, dividends, royalties, and so on) under the following circumstances:
  - The taxpayer does not provide the payor with the taxpayer identification number in the required manner.
  - The taxpayer is required to certify that he is not subject to backup withholding but fails to do so.
  - The IRS notifies the payor that the taxpayer gave an incorrect taxpayer identification number.
  - The IRS notifies the payor that the taxpayer has failed to report the item of income on his return.[24]

- *Special rules for lump-sum pension plan or annuity payments.* Federal income tax withholding is mandatory for such payments unless the individual elects to have no tax withheld.[25] These requirements are intended to (1) increase the level of taxpayer compliance and (2) alleviate the need for retired persons to pay quarterly estimated taxes, which would otherwise be necessary to avoid an underpayment penalty.

If the pension payments are periodic (i.e., received as an annuity), the withholding is figured using the same procedures that are used for salary and wages. The retiree merely fills out a withholding certificate (Form W-4P). If this form is not filled out, the withholding is based upon the tables for a married individual claiming three withholding allowances.[26] A 10% withholding rate is generally used for nonperiodic payments (e.g., lump-sum distributions). Withheld amounts are based upon the taxable portion of a pension payment.[27]

Example 14-13 ■ Roy, a married taxpayer with four dependents, retires in the current year and receives taxable pension income from a qualified pension plan of $600 per month. He also receives a lump-sum distribution of $50,000 from a qualified profit-sharing plan. The trustees of both plans notify Roy that amounts will be withheld unless he elects not to have any amount withheld. If Roy elects not to have any taxes withheld, he may be required to make quarterly estimated tax payments to the extent that the pension payments are taxable to avoid an underpayment penalty. If Roy does not make an election and files two withholding certificates, regular withholding procedures will apply to the periodic pension payments and a 10% withholding rate will apply to the lump-sum distribution. ■

Historical Note

The withholding of federal income taxes by employers began during World War II.

Withholding Allowances and Methods. Every employee must file an employee's withholding allowance certificate (Form W-4), which lists the employee's marital status and number of withholding allowances and becomes the basic source of input for the computation of the amount to be withheld. If an employee's circumstances change (e.g., a married taxpayer is divorced or the amount of allowances claimed is

[22] Temp. Reg. Sec. 31.3401(a)-1T.
[23] Sec. 6682.
[24] Sec. 3406.
[25] Sec. 3405. Withholding is imposed at a 20% rate on any distribution eligible for tax deferral rollover treatment (e.g., a distribution from a qualified pension plan to an IRA) unless the funds are transferred directly to the eligible plan (see Sec. 3405(c)). The percentage withholding rate on supplemental wage payments (i.e., bonuses, commissions, overtime pay, etc.) was increased from 20% to 28% for payments made after December 31, 1993.
[26] Sec. 3405(a)(4).
[27] Pension payments are subject to tax under the Sec. 72 annuity rules (see Chapter 3).

reduced), an amended Form W-4 must be filed within 10 days. In general, the employee's Form W-4 is not sent to the IRS unless (1) the number of withholding allowances exceeds 10 or (2) an employee claims an exemption from withholding when his earnings are more than $200 per week.[28] This procedure is intended to prevent employees from avoiding the withholding of income tax on amounts that are otherwise due.

The following procedural rules apply to withholding:

- A $500 civil penalty is imposed for filing false statements (e.g., claiming excessive numbers of withholding allowances).[29]

- An employee may claim an exempt status on Form W-4 if he has no income tax liability in the prior year and anticipates none in the current year. High school or college students with jobs earning amounts less than the minimum dollar amount required to file a tax return should take advantage of this exemption. Otherwise, it may be necessary to file a return to obtain a tax refund in the following year. In such a case, the student has, in effect, made an interest-free loan to the government.

- Income tax withholding tables result in a lower amount being withheld if the taxpayer is married.

- An individual may request that additional amounts be withheld if it is anticipated that taxes will be owed at the end of the year and the person does not want to make quarterly estimated payments. It is also possible to claim fewer withholding allowances in order to increase the amount withheld.

- Each additional withholding allowance that is claimed reduces the amount withheld.

Withholding allowances on Form W-4 may be claimed for the same number of personal and dependency exemptions that will be taken on the employee's tax return for the year. An additional special withholding allowance that reflects the standard deduction may be claimed by a taxpayer who has one job or, if married, has a spouse who is unemployed.[30] Additional withholding allowances may be claimed if an individual has an unusually large amount of deductions from adjusted gross income, alimony deductions, or tax credits. Tables and a worksheet are provided to compute the amount of the additional withholding allowances.[31]

Real World Example

It has been held that the employer's withholding of federal income taxes is not an improper taking of property without due process in violation of the Fifth Amendment. Michael O. Campbell v. Amax Coal Co., 610 F.2d 701, 45 AFTR2d 80-564, 80-1 USTC ¶ 9185 (10th Cir., 1980).

Example 14-14 ■   Sam and Sally are married and have three dependent children. They file a joint return. Sally is not employed, and Sam does not claim additional withholding allowances for unusually large deductions or tax credits. Sam may claim six allowances (two personal exemptions [for Sam and Sally]) plus three dependency exemptions plus one special withholding allowance to reflect the standard deduction). The special allowance is available because Sam's spouse is not employed and Sam has only one job. ■

Computation of Federal Income Tax Withheld. The computation of the amount to be withheld is made by using wage bracket tables or by an optional percentage method of withholding. Both methods produce approximately the same results. Wage bracket tables are available for daily, weekly, biweekly, and monthly payroll periods. Separate tables are used for single (including heads-of-household) and married individuals. The wage bracket table for married persons using a monthly payroll period for wages from $0 through $3,239.99 is reproduced in Figure 14-1.

---

[28] Reg. Sec. 31.3402(f)(2)-1. A $500 civil penalty may be imposed when a taxpayer claims withholding allowances based on false information (see Sec. 6682).

[29] Sec. 6682(a).

[30] Sec. 3402(f)(1)(E).

[31] Married taxpayers who are both employed may allocate withholding allowances as they see fit as long as the same allowance is not claimed more than once.

MARRIED Persons—MONTHLY Payroll Period

(For Wages Paid in 1994)

If the wages are—		And the number of withholding allowances claimed is—										
At least	But less than	0	1	2	3	4	5	6	7	8	9	10
		The amount of income tax to be withheld is—										
$0	$540	$0	$0	$0	$0	$0	$0	$0	$0	$0	$0	$0
540	560	3	0	0	0	0	0	0	0	0	0	0
560	580	6	0	0	0	0	0	0	0	0	0	0
580	600	9	0	0	0	0	0	0	0	0	0	0
600	640	14	0	0	0	0	0	0	0	0	0	0
640	680	20	0	0	0	0	0	0	0	0	0	0
680	720	26	0	0	0	0	0	0	0	0	0	0
720	760	32	1	0	0	0	0	0	0	0	0	0
760	800	38	7	0	0	0	0	0	0	0	0	0
800	840	44	13	0	0	0	0	0	0	0	0	0
840	880	50	19	0	0	0	0	0	0	0	0	0
880	920	56	25	0	0	0	0	0	0	0	0	0
920	960	62	31	0	0	0	0	0	0	0	0	0
960	1,000	68	37	6	0	0	0	0	0	0	0	0
1,000	1,040	74	43	12	0	0	0	0	0	0	0	0
1,040	1,080	80	49	18	0	0	0	0	0	0	0	0
1,080	1,120	86	55	24	0	0	0	0	0	0	0	0
1,120	1,160	92	61	30	0	0	0	0	0	0	0	0
1,160	1,200	98	67	36	6	0	0	0	0	0	0	0
1,200	1,240	104	73	42	12	0	0	0	0	0	0	0
1,240	1,280	110	79	48	18	0	0	0	0	0	0	0
1,280	1,320	116	85	54	24	0	0	0	0	0	0	0
1,320	1,360	122	91	60	30	0	0	0	0	0	0	0
1,360	1,400	128	97	66	36	5	0	0	0	0	0	0
1,400	1,440	134	103	72	42	11	0	0	0	0	0	0
1,440	1,480	140	109	78	48	17	0	0	0	0	0	0
1,480	1,520	146	115	84	54	23	0	0	0	0	0	0
1,520	1,560	152	121	90	60	29	0	0	0	0	0	0
1,560	1,600	158	127	96	66	35	5	0	0	0	0	0
1,600	1,640	164	133	102	72	41	11	0	0	0	0	0
1,640	1,680	170	139	108	78	47	17	0	0	0	0	0
1,680	1,720	176	145	114	84	53	23	0	0	0	0	0
1,720	1,760	182	151	120	90	59	29	0	0	0	0	0
1,760	1,800	188	157	126	96	65	35	4	0	0	0	0
1,800	1,840	194	163	132	102	71	41	10	0	0	0	0
1,840	1,880	200	169	138	108	77	47	16	0	0	0	0
1,880	1,920	206	175	144	114	83	53	22	0	0	0	0
1,920	1,960	212	181	150	120	89	59	28	0	0	0	0
1,960	2,000	218	187	156	126	95	65	34	3	0	0	0
2,000	2,040	224	193	162	132	101	71	40	9	0	0	0
2,040	2,080	230	199	168	138	107	77	46	15	0	0	0
2,080	2,120	236	205	174	144	113	83	52	21	0	0	0
2,120	2,160	242	211	180	150	119	89	58	27	0	0	0
2,160	2,200	248	217	186	156	125	95	64	33	3	0	0
2,200	2,240	254	223	192	162	131	101	70	39	9	0	0
2,240	2,280	260	229	198	168	137	107	76	45	15	0	0
2,280	2,320	266	235	204	174	143	113	82	51	21	0	0
2,320	2,360	272	241	210	180	149	119	88	57	27	0	0
2,360	2,400	278	247	216	186	155	125	94	63	33	2	0
2,400	2,440	284	253	222	192	161	131	100	69	39	8	0
2,440	2,480	290	259	228	198	167	137	106	75	45	14	0
2,480	2,520	296	265	234	204	173	143	112	81	51	20	0
2,520	2,560	302	271	240	210	179	149	118	87	57	26	0
2,560	2,600	308	277	246	216	185	155	124	93	63	32	1
2,600	2,640	314	283	252	222	191	161	130	99	69	38	7
2,640	2,680	320	289	258	228	197	167	136	105	75	44	13
2,680	2,720	326	295	264	234	203	173	142	111	81	50	19
2,720	2,760	332	301	270	240	209	179	148	117	87	56	25
2,760	2,800	338	307	276	246	215	185	154	123	93	62	31
2,800	2,840	344	313	282	252	221	191	160	129	99	68	37
2,840	2,880	350	319	288	258	227	197	166	135	105	74	43
2,880	2,920	356	325	294	264	233	203	172	141	111	80	49
2,920	2,960	362	331	300	270	239	209	178	147	117	86	55
2,960	3,000	368	337	306	276	245	215	184	153	123	92	61
3,000	3,040	374	343	312	282	251	221	190	159	129	98	67
3,040	3,080	380	349	318	288	257	227	196	165	135	104	73
3,080	3,120	386	355	324	294	263	233	202	171	141	110	79
3,120	3,160	392	361	330	300	269	239	208	177	147	116	85
3,160	3,200	398	367	336	306	275	245	214	183	153	122	91
3,200	3,240	404	373	342	312	281	251	220	189	159	128	97

FIGURE 14-1   Monthly Payroll Period—Married Persons

Example 14-15 ■   Henry is married and claims six withholding allowances. His monthly salary is $2,500. The federal income tax withheld using the wage bracket table in Figure 14-1 is $112.

                                                              ■

Estimated Tax Payments

Additional Comment

The IRS does not mail reminder statements for the required quarterly estimated payments.

Certain types of income are not subject to withholding (e.g., investment income, rents, income from self-employment, capital gains, and so on). Taxpayers who earn this type of income must make quarterly estimated tax payments.

    The purpose of the estimated tax system is to ensure that all taxpayers have paid enough tax by the end of the tax year to cover their tax liability. Thus, estimated tax payments may also be required if insufficient tax is being withheld from an individual's salary, pension, or other income (although many taxpayers prefer to file an amended Form W-4 instead and request additional withholding amounts or reduce the number of withholding allowances). The amount of estimated tax is the taxpayer's tax liability (including self-employment tax and alternative minimum tax) reduced by withholdings, tax credits, and any excess FICA amounts.[32]

Required Estimated Tax Payments. For calendar-year individuals, required quarterly payments are due by April 15, June 15, September 15 of the current year, and January 15 of the following year. The estimated tax payments should be the lesser of the following amounts to avoid the imposition of a penalty on the underpaid amount:

Additional Comment

Red Skelton on the IRS: "I get even with them. I send in an estimated tax form, but I don't sign it. If I've got to guess what I'm making, let them guess who's making it.

- 90% of the tax shown on the return for the current year

- 100% of the tax liability shown on the return for the prior year (110% for taxpayers whose AGI on the prior year's return exceeded $150,000)[33]

- 90% of the tax shown on the return for the current year computed on an annualized basis

In addition, no penalty is imposed if (1) the estimated tax for the current year is less than $500 or (2) the individual has no tax liability for the prior year.[34]

    It should be noted that no penalty is imposed for failure to file quarterly estimated tax payments, even though the Code includes specific filing requirements. A penalty is imposed only if (1) the taxpayer fails to meet the minimum payment requirements or (2) one of the previously mentioned exceptions does not apply.

Example 14-16 ■   Sarah does not make quarterly estimated tax payments for 1994, even though she has a substantial amount of income not subject to withholding. Her actual tax liability (including self-employment taxes and the alternative minimum tax) for 1994 is $10,000. Withholdings from her salary are $7,000. She pays the $3,000 balance due to the IRS with the filing of the return on April 3, 1995. Sarah's tax liability for 1993 was only $6,000. There is no penalty for failure to file the quarterly estimated tax. In addition, Sarah is not subject to the underpayment of estimated tax penalty because she meets one or more of the exceptions relating to the minimum payment requirement. Although the first exception is not met because her $7,000 of withholdings (plus zero estimated tax payments) is less than 90% of her $10,000 tax liability for 1994 ($7,000 ÷ $10,000 = 70%), she meets the

---

[32] Excess FICA payments will occur if an employee has more than one employer during the year and the total FICA payments exceed in the aggregate the ceiling on FICA taxes.

[33] Sec. 6654(d). The 110% safe harbor exception for high-income taxpayers applies for tax years after 1993. Under prior law, taxpayers were prevented from using the 100%-of-prior-year's-tax safe harbor if their modified AGI exceeded $75,000 and exceeded their prior year's AGI by more than $40,000.

[34] Sec. 6654(e).

second exception because the $7,000 of withholdings is more than 100% of her $6,000 tax liability for 1993. If Sarah's AGI for 1993 was in excess of $150,000, the second exception safe harbor amount would be 110% (instead of 100%) of the prior year's tax or $6,600 ($6,000 × 1.10). Since the $7,000 of withholding is more than 110% of her $6,000 tax liability, Sarah would also meet the second exception and would not be subject to the underpayment penalty. ■

Form 2210 (see Appendix B) should be completed and submitted with the tax return if a possible underpayment of tax is indicated. This form is used to determine whether one of the exceptions is applicable and, if not, to compute the amount of the underpayment penalty.

Typical Misconception

The underpayment penalty for estimated payments is computed separately for each quarter. It is sometimes mistakenly believed that estimated payments can be made anytime during the year.

Application of the Underpayment Penalty. The penalty for underpayment of estimated tax is not deductible as interest even though the rate is based upon the federal short-term rate plus three percentage points as determined on a quarterly basis.[35] The underpayment penalty is computed separately for each quarter, and a penalty is imposed if the estimated taxes paid and income tax withheld by the quarterly payment date are less than 25% of the required minimum annual payment.[36] Withholdings for the year are spread evenly to each quarterly payment date regardless of when such amounts are withheld. If the required minimum payment is not made for a quarter, the penalty is imposed on the difference between the total amount of estimated tax payments and withholdings and the lesser of one-quarter of 90% of the tax liability shown on the return for the current year or one-quarter of 100% of the tax shown on the return for the preceding year.

Example 14-17 ■

Stan makes estimated tax payments for 1994 as follows:

April 15, 1994	$2,000
June 15, 1994	1,000
September 15, 1994	1,000
January 15, 1995	1,000
Total	$5,000

Additional Comment

Tax withheld by an employer is considered to have been evenly paid throughout the year. Therefore, a taxpayer who has made insufficient estimated payments may be able to correct the situation by having greater amounts withheld from wages late in the year.

In addition, Stan has $4,000 withheld from his salary during 1994. His actual tax liabilities for 1993 and 1994 are $15,000 and $16,000, respectively. (Assume that the income annualization exception does not apply because Stan's income is earned evenly throughout 1994.) Stan is subject to the underpayment penalty because his minimum required payment under the 90% test is $14,400 (0.90 × $16,000). In addition, the minimum payment under the 100% test is not met because his $9,000 of total payments (withholdings of $4,000 plus estimated tax payments of $5,000) do not equal or exceed his $15,000 tax liability for the prior year. The penalty is applied to the difference between the amount of estimated tax and withholdings for each quarter and one-fourth of 90% of the actual 1994 tax liability because the amount computed under the 90% test ($14,400) is less than the amount computed under the 100% test ($15,000). Thus, $3,600 ($16,000 × 0.90 × 0.25) should have been paid each quarter, and only $3,000 ($2,000 + $1,000 withheld) was actually paid in the first quarter, resulting in an underpayment of $600. The underpayment for each of the last three quarters is $1,600 ($3,600 − $2,000), and the penalty is applied to the underpayments from the date the

---

[35] Secs. 6621(a)(2) and (b). The rate was 7% for the period October 1, 1992, through September 30, 1993.

[36] One exception to this rule applies if a taxpayer's income is not earned evenly throughout the year and the income annualization exception results in a lower required payment.

TOPIC REVIEW 14-2

Withholding Taxes and Estimated Payments

	Withholding of Taxes	
	FICA	Income Tax
• When to withhold	All employee earnings up to $60,600 (in 1994) per employer. No ceiling applies to the hospital insurance portion of the FICA tax.	All employee wages. salaries, fees, bonuses, commissions, taxable fringe benefits, and so on.[a]
• Amount to withhold	7.65% of FICA wages including 1.45% for the hospital insurance portion of the tax. 1.45% for amounts in excess of $60,600 is withheld from the employee's earnings.	Determined by using withholding tables or the percentage method based on an individual's filing status and number of exemptions.

[a]Exceptions are provided for certain nontaxable fringe benefits.

Estimated Tax Payments

- To avoid an underpayment penalty, the estimated tax payments and withholdings for the year must be equal to or exceed any one of the following:
  a. 90% of the tax shown on the return for the current year.
  b. 100% of the tax liability shown on the return for the prior year (110% if AGI for the prior year exceeds $150,000).
  c. 90% of the tax shown on the return for the current year computed on an annualized basis.
- The underpayment penalty is not deductible for tax purposes.
- Form 2210 should be completed and submitted with the tax return if an underpayment is indicated.

payment is due to the earlier of the dates the underpayment is paid or the 15th day of the fourth month following the close of the tax year. ∎

Topic Review 14-2 summarizes the withholding tax and estimated payment requirements.

TAX CREDITS

OBJECTIVE 5
Describe the various business and personal tax credits

Historical Note
The political contributions credit was repealed in the Tax Reform Act of 1986.

Use and Importance of Tax Credits

Tax credits are often used to implement tax policy objectives. For example, tax credits are provided to increase employment, encourage energy conservation and Research and Experimental activities, encourage certain socially desired activities, and provide tax relief for low-income taxpayers and working couples with dependent children. Tax credits are also used to mitigate the effects of double taxation on income from foreign countries. Topic Review 14-3 includes a summary of selected tax credits and the rationale for their inclusion in the tax law. Note that most tax credits are nonrefundable (e.g., the credit amount is not paid to the taxpayer if no tax is otherwise due). The principal refundable credits include taxes withheld on wages and the earned income credit.

Value of a Credit versus a Deduction

One of the reasons tax credits have become so popular is that the benefits from a tax credit are the same for all taxpayers regardless of their marginal tax rate. In contrast, the tax benefits accruing from a tax deduction are greater for high-income taxpayers.

Example 14-18 ■ If Tasha's marginal tax rate is 15%, a deduction of $100 produces a tax benefit of $15 ($100 × 0.15). If Sean's marginal tax rate is 28%, a $100 deduction produces a tax benefit of $28 ($100 × 0.28). However, a tax credit provides the same benefit to both Tasha and Sean. ■

Limitation on General Business Credit

Additional Comment

The total amount of tax credits claimed by individual taxpayers increased by 11.4% in 1991.

The tax credits commonly available to businesses are grouped into a special credit category called the **general business credit.** The more significant items included in the general business credit are the investment tax credit, targeted jobs credit, research credit, low-income housing credit, empowerment zone employment credit, and the disabled access credit.[37] These business credits are combined for the purpose of computing an overall dollar limitation upon their utilization because these credits are not refundable. The general business credit may not exceed the "net income tax" minus the greater of (1) the tentative minimum tax or (2) 25% of the "net regular tax liability" above $25,000.[38]

Additional Comment

The general business credit fell from $4.8 billion in 1985 to $0.5 billion in 1991. The decrease is attributable to the phasing out in 1986 of the major component of the general business credit, the investment tax credit.

Nonrefundable personal tax credits are allowed against the taxpayer's tax liability before all other credits up to the amount of the taxpayer's tax liability for the year.[39] Certain other business tax credits (items 2, 3, and 4 below) are also nonrefundable and are offset against the taxpayer's tax liability before the general business credit is deducted. These credits are used after the personal tax credits are deducted but before the general business credit. Nonrefundable credits are deducted against the taxpayer's tax liability in the following order of priority:

1. Personal tax credits
2. Foreign tax credit
3. Drug testing credit
4. Nonconventional source fuel credit
5. General business credit

Example 14-19 ■ Steve's general business tax credit includes a $40,000 research credit and a $10,000 targeted jobs credit. Steve's regular tax liability (before credits) is $45,000, and his tentative minimum tax is $10,000. Nonrefundable tax credits also include a $2,000 child and dependent care credit (a nonrefundable personal tax credit) and a $1,000

---

[37] Sec. 38. Also included in the general business credit is the alcohol fuels credit, enhanced oil recovery credit, renewable electricity production credit, Indian employment credit, and the employer social security credit for employee tips. For property placed into service after 1990, the investment tax credit has been reconstituted as the sum of the following three components: (1) the rehabilitation credit (2) the business energy credit, and (3) the reforestation credit.

[38] Sec. 38(c). The term "net income tax" is the sum of the regular tax plus the alternative minimum tax reduced by other nonrefundable credits. The term "net regular tax liability" means the regular tax liability reduced by nonrefundable credits.

[39] Nonrefundable personal tax credits include the child and dependent care credit, credit for the elderly, and the residential mortgage interest credit. For the purpose of deducting these credits, the tax liability does not include special taxes such as the alternative mimimum tax. Refundable personal tax credits include the earned income credit and federal income taxes withheld (including quarterly estimated taxes). In such case an individual may receive a tax refund from the IRS equal to the amount of the credit even if no tax is owed.

TOPIC REVIEW 14-3

Summary of Selected Tax Credits

Tax Credit Item	Rationale
Investment tax credit	To encourage new private investment, which stimulates the economy and employment
Rehabilitation expenditure credit	To encourage the rehabilitation of older buildings including certified historic structures
Business energy credits	To encourage energy conservation measures and the use of fuel other than petroleum
Foreign tax credit	To mitigate the effects of double taxation on foreign source income
Research credit	To encourage research and development activities to enhance our technological base
Targeted jobs credit	To encourage employers to hire unemployed individuals from disadvantaged groups
Child and dependent care credit	To provide equitable relief for parents and other individuals who are employed and who must incur expenses for household and dependent care services
Earned income credit, supplemental young child credit, and supplemental health insurance credit	To provide special tax breaks for certain low-income individuals who have earned income (e.g., salary and wages) and dependent children or other incapacitated individuals living in the household
Tax credit for the elderly	To provide tax relief for elderly taxpayers who are not substantially covered by the social security system
Residential mortgage interest credit	To encourage qualified first-time home buyers to purchase a principal residence (this credit is not discussed in the text due to its limited applicability)
Low-income housing credit	To encourage construction, rehabilitation, and ownership of qualified low-income housing projects (this credit is not discussed in the text due to its limited applicability)
Qualified electrical vehicles credit	To encourage energy conservation (this credit is not discussed in the text due to its limited applicability)
Disabled access credit	To encourage small business to provide access for disabled persons
Empowerment zone employment credit	To reduce the level of unemployment in distressed urban and rural areas.

foreign tax credit. Steve's dollar limitation on the general business tax credit is initially limited by the amount of net income tax of $42,000 ($45,000 regular tax minus $3,000 other nonrefundable credits). This amount is reduced by the $10,000 tentative minimum tax because this amount is greater than $4,250 (0.25 × [$45,000 regular tax − $3,000 nonrefundable credits − $25,000]) net regular tax ceiling. Thus, the limitation upon the $50,000 of general business tax credits ($40,000 + $10,000) is $32,000 ($42,000 − $10,000). ∎

Carryback and Carryover of Unused Credits

Initially, unused general business tax credits are carried back 3 years. Any remaining unused credits are then carried forward for 15 years.[40] The entire amount of unused credit is first carried to the earliest year.

Example 14-20 ∎   Eagle Corporation has unused business tax credits of $50,000 in 1994. The following is a schedule showing the utilization of credits in the carryback years:

---

[40] Sec. 39(a)(1).

Additional Comment

A provision in Sec. 6411 permits a quick refund of taxes resulting from the carryback of an unused general business credit. An individual uses Form 1045 to file for the quick refund.

	Credits Earned in Carryback Year	*Credit Limitation in Carryback Year*	*Carryback Applied*
1991	$40,000	$60,000	$20,000
1992	70,000	70,000	—0—
1993	30,000	50,000	20,000

Eagle Corporation carries back $20,000 of its unused general business tax credit to 1991 and an additional $20,000 to 1993. The tax liability for the carryback years is recomputed, and Eagle files amended tax returns in order to obtain a refund of the taxes paid in 1991 and 1993. The remaining $10,000 of unused credit is carried forward to 1994 and the 14 succeeding years. ■

During the carryover years, the unused credits from prior years are first applied (commencing with the earliest carryover year) before the current year credits that are earned are used (i.e., a first-in, first-out [FIFO] method is applied). This method permits the utilization of credits from the earliest of the carryover years and may prevent such carryovers from expiring.

Example 14-21 ■ Eastern Corporation has unused general business tax credits of $10,000 in 1993 that are carried forward to 1994. Eastern earns $5,000 of additional credits in 1994 and has a $12,000 limitation. The $12,000 of credits that are utilized consist of the $10,000 carryover from 1993 and $2,000 from 1994. The remaining $3,000 ($5,000 − $2,000) of 1994 credits are carried forward to 1995. ■

FOREIGN TAX CREDIT

Key Point

The foreign tax credit is available only on income, war profits, and excess profits taxes or taxes paid in lieu of such taxes. It is sometimes difficult to determine whether a particular foreign tax falls into the qualifying category.

U.S. citizens, resident aliens, and U.S. corporations are subject to U.S. taxation on their worldwide income.[41] To reduce double taxation, the tax law provides a foreign tax credit for income taxes paid or accrued to a foreign country or a U.S. possession.[42]

Taxpayers may elect to take a deduction for the taxes paid or accrued in lieu of a foreign tax credit.[43] In general, the foreign tax credit results in greater tax benefit because (as previously discussed) a credit is fully offset against the tax liability, while a deduction merely reduces taxable income.

Computation of Allowable Credit

Additional Comment

In 1992, 875,000 individual taxpayers claimed foreign tax credits totaling $1.71 billion.

The **foreign tax credit** amount equals the lesser of the foreign taxes paid or accrued in the tax year or the portion of the U.S. income tax liability attributable to the income earned in all foreign countries.[44] This limitation, which restricts the claiming of foreign tax credit if the effective foreign tax rate on the foreign earnings exceeds the effective U.S. tax rate on these earnings, may result in double taxation if the unused credit cannot be used as a carryback or carryover (see discussion under the next heading). The foreign tax credit limitation is based upon the following formula:

---

[41] Certain exceptions are provided by treaty agreements between the United States and foreign countries whereby certain types of foreign source income may be exempt from taxation in the foreign country.

[42] Under Sec. 911, U.S. citizens and resident aliens may elect to exclude from gross income up to $70,000 of foreign-earned income and certain "housing cost amounts." The foreign taxes that are attributable to the excluded income cannot be taken as a credit. (See Chapter 4 for a discussion of these exclusions.)

[43] Sec. 164(a)(3).

[44] Sec. 904.

$$\frac{\text{Foreign source taxable income}}{\text{Worldwide taxable income}} \times \begin{array}{c} \text{U.S. income tax} \\ \text{before credits} \end{array} = \begin{array}{c} \text{Foreign tax credit} \\ \text{limitation} \end{array}$$

Example 14-22 ■

Self-Study Question

When would a taxpayer be advised to elect to take a deduction for foreign taxes in lieu of the foreign tax credit?

Answer

If a taxpayer has foreign source taxable income from one country and an equal loss from another foreign country, the foreign tax credit limitation will be zero since the "net" foreign source taxable income is zero. Since none of the taxes paid in the foreign country in which taxable income was produced can be claimed as a credit, the taxpayer may choose to deduct them unless the credits are carried back or forward to future years.

Edison Corporation has $200,000 U.S. source taxable income and $100,000 of foreign source taxable income from countries A and B. Total worldwide taxable income is $300,000 ($200,000 + $100,000). Countries A and B levy a total of $40,000 in foreign taxes upon the foreign source taxable income (i.e., a 40% effective tax rate). The U.S. tax before credits is $100,250 on the $300,000 of taxable income. Using the formula given above, the overall foreign tax credit limitation is computed as follows:[45]

$$\frac{\$100,000}{\$300,000} \times \$100,250 = \$33,417$$

Because the foreign tax payments ($40,000) exceed the U.S. tax attributable to the foreign source income ($33,417), the limitation applies. Thus, $6,583 ($40,000 − $33,417) of foreign tax credit cannot be used in the current year. ■

Treatment of Unused Credits

Unused foreign tax credits are carried back 2 years and then forward for 5 years to years where the limitation is not exceeded (i.e., the foreign tax payment is lower than the U.S. taxes attributable to the foreign source income in the carryback or carryover years).[46] The unused credits are lost if they are not used by the end of the 5-year carryover period.

CREDIT FOR INCREASING RESEARCH ACTIVITIES

Historical Note

The research credit was enacted in 1981 because Congress was concerned about the substantial relative decline in total U.S. expenditures for research and development.

Additional Comment

The Joint Committee on Taxation has estimated that the credit for increasing research activities will result in lost tax revenues of $4.0 billion for the 5-year period 1992–1996.

The tax law provides a twofold means of encouraging research and experimental activities: (1) Research and experimental expenditures may be either deducted immediately or capitalized and amortized over a period of 60 months or more under Sec. 174 (see Chapter 6 for a discussion of these rules); and (2) a 20% tax credit for increasing qualified research expenses as well as a 20% credit for basic research payments is available under the tax law.[47] The research credit is equal to the sum of (1) 20% of the excess of qualified research expenses over the base amount and (2) a separately determined 20% basic research payments credit (discussed in a following section).

The "base amount" is defined as the product of (1) the fixed-base percentage, and (2) the taxpayer's average annual gross receipts for the four tax years prior to the current (credit) year. All taxpayers are limited to a minimum base amount that may not be less than 50% of the qualified research expenses for the current (credit) year.[48]

---

[45] Certain types of income may have a separate foreign tax credit limitation. These types of income include passive income, high withholding tax interest, financial services income, shipping income, dividends from noncontrolled foreign (Sec. 902) corporations, dividends from Domestic International Sales Corporations (DISCs), and foreign trade income from a Foreign Sales Corporation.

[46] Sec. 904(c).

[47] Sec. 41(a). The research credit was scheduled to expire after 1991 but was initially extended through June 30, 1992. The credit was extended retroactively from July 1, 1992 through June 30, 1995 and was amended by the Revenue Reconciliation Act of 1993.

[48] Sec. 41(c)(2).

The "fixed-base percentage" is the ratio that the taxpayer's total qualified research expenses for the 1984–1988 period bears to its total gross receipts for the same period (subject to a maximum ratio of 0.16).[49]

Example 14-23 ■ Able Corporation incurs $200,000 of qualified research expenses in the current calendar year. Able's fixed-base percentage (i.e., the ratio of total qualified research expenses over total gross receipts for the 1984–1988 period) is 0.15. This ratio is used in the computation of the base amount because it is less than the maximum ratio of 0.16. Average annual gross receipts for the four years prior to the current (credit) year amount to $600,000. The base amount is $90,000 (0.15 × $600,000) before considering the 50% minimum base amount. The base amount is adjusted upward from $90,000 to $100,000 (0.50 × $200,000 qualified research expenses) because the minimum base amount exceeds the calculated amount for the current year. Thus, the credit for increasing research activities (without regard for the basic research payments credit) is $20,000 (0.20 × [$200,000 − $100,000]). ■

Additional Comment

The objective of the basic research payments credit is to provide an incentive to corporations to contract with universities to conduct research on projects that do not possess immediate commercial applications.

Basic Research Payments Credit

Corporations that fund basic research for the advancement of scientific knowledge without a specific commercial objective qualify for a 20% credit for such expenses if two conditions are met: (1) The payments must be made in cash under a written agreement, and (2) the research must be performed or controlled by a university, college, or other nonprofit scientific research organization.[50] Expenditures that qualify for the basic research credit do not enter into the computation of the credit for increasing research expenses.

The amount available for the credit is equal to the qualifying basic research payments less certain statutory reductions.[51] The amount of any statutory reduction is available for use as a contract research expense in calculating the credit for increasing research expenses discussed above.

Example 14-24 ■ Hill Corporation makes $100,000 of qualified basic research payments in the current year. The required statutory reductions total $30,000. The research credit for Hill Corporation related to basic research payments is $14,000 (0.20 × [$100,000 − $30,000]). The $30,000 reduction is available for use as a contract research expense in calculating the research credit for incremental research expenses. ■

Limitations and Treatment of Unused Credits

The deduction for research and experimental expenditures under Sec. 174 is reduced by the full amount of the amount of the research credit. A taxpayer may make an election to avoid reducing the deduction. In such case, the research credit is reduced by the product of (1) 50% of the credit and (2) the maximum corporate tax rate. Research and experimental expenditures that are capitalized must also be reduced by the full amount of the research credit.

---

[49] Sec. 41(c)(3). Special rules are provided for so called start-up companies (i.e., those companies with fewer than three tax years beginning after December 31, 1983, and before January 1, 1989 in which the taxpayer has both gross receipts and qualified research expenses). In such case, a start-up company's fixed-base percentage is 3% for each of its first five tax years after 1993. After five years the percentage is determined by using the ratio of research expenses to gross receipts for specific preceding years.

[50] Sec. 41(e).

[51] The statutory reductions are related to the corporation's incremental qualified research expenses and nondesignated university contributions (e.g., any decrease in nonresearch university contributions is compared with the corporation's contributions that were made during a fixed base period).

Example 14-25 ■	Island Corporation deducts $100,000 of research expenditures under Sec. 174 in the current year and claims a $40,000 research credit. No election is made to avoid reducing the Sec. 174 deduction. Island can deduct only $60,000 ($100,000 − $40,000) of research expenses. ■

The research credit (whether based on increasing research and experimental expenses or basic research payments) is one of the items included in the general business credit. Thus, both the limitations based on the taxpayer's tax liability and the carryback and carryover rules described below in Sec. 38 apply to the research credits.

TARGETED JOBS CREDIT

The targeted jobs credit is intended to reduce unemployment for individuals who are usually economically disadvantaged (e.g., economically disadvantaged youths, certain Vietnam-era veterans, ex-convicts, handicapped individuals, and so on).[52] The credit is 40% of up to $6,000 of qualified first-year wages paid or incurred for each individual that is hired.[53] The Tax Reform Act of 1986 added minimum employment periods to the requirements.[54] To qualify for the credit, the employer must obtain a certification from a local jobs service office of a state employment security agency which states that the unemployed individual is a qualified member of a targeted group on or before the day work is commenced for the employer. A major disadvantage associated with the targeted jobs credit is that the employer's deduction for wages must be reduced by the amount of the credit.[55]

Additional Comment

The employer must receive or request the certification in writing no later than the employee's first day of work.

Example 14-26 ■	Jet Corporation hires two economically disadvantaged Vietnam War-era veterans in the current year. Both individuals are properly certified by the state agency prior to being hired. One of the individuals is paid $8,000 of wages during the year, and the second individual is paid $4,000. The amount of wages eligible for the targeted jobs credit is $10,000 ($6,000 ceiling limit for the first employee plus $4,000 actual wages paid to the second employee). The credit is $4,000 (0.40 × $10,000). Jet Corporation must reduce its $12,000 deduction for wages paid to the two individuals by $4,000 in the current year. ■

Additional Comment

The targeted jobs credit was permanently extended by the Revenue Reconciliation Act of 1993, since Congress thought that the credit provides a useful incentive for hiring disadvantaged individuals. Originally, the credit was scheduled to expire as of June 30, 1992.

The targeted jobs credit is one of the items included in the general business credit. Thus, the limitation is based on the taxpayer's tax liability, and the carryback and carryover of excess credits are governed by the Sec. 38 rules.

EMPOWERMENT ZONE EMPLOYMENT CREDIT

The empowerment zone employment credit is an attempt to provide economic revitalization of distressed urban and rural areas. Empowerment zones and enterprise communities that have a condition of pervasive poverty, unemployment, and general

---

[52] Sec. 51(d).

[53] Sec. 51(b)(3). A comparable jobs credit is also available for qualified summer youth employees aged 18 through 22 under Sec. 51(d)(12) for youths that are members of economically disadvantaged families. In such case, the maximum wages that are eligible for the credit are $3,000 per employee for any 90-day period between May 1 and September 15, and the credit rate is 40%. The targeted jobs credit expired on June 30, 1992. However, the credit has been retroactively extended for individuals who began work after June 30, 1992 through December 31, 1994.

[54] No wages are taken into account unless the individual is employed at least 90 days or at least 120 hours. Qualified summer youth employees must be employed at least 14 days or 20 hours for their wages to be taken into account.

[55] Sec. 280(C)(a).

distress are to be designated by the Secretary of Housing and Urban Development and by the Secretary of Agriculture in 1994 and 1995.

Employers are eligible for a 20% tax credit on the first $15,000 of wages per employee including training and educational costs paid to full- and part-time employees who are residents of an empowerment zone providing that the employer's trade or business and the employee's principal place of abode is within the empowerment zone.[56]

Qualified wages do not include wages taken into account for purposes of the targeted jobs credit (discussed above).[57] As in the case for the targeted jobs credit, the empowerment zone employment credit is one of the items included in the general business credit and the employer's deduction for wages is also reduced by the amount of the credit.

Example 14-27 ■   Ace Corporation is located in a designated empowerment zone and employs two eligible individuals who reside in the empowerment zone. One of the individuals is paid $12,000 in wages (plus $4,000 of training expenses are incurred for the employee) and the second employee is paid $10,000 in wages. The credit is $5,000 ($25,000 × 0.20). Ace Corporation must reduce its deduction for wages by $5,000 (the credit amount for the year). ■

DISABLED ACCESS CREDIT

A nonrefundable tax credit is available to eligible small businesses for expenditures incurred to make existing business facilities accessible to disabled individuals. Eligible access expenditures include payments for the purpose of removing architectural, communication, physical or transportation barriers that prevent a business from being accessible or usable by disabled individuals. Expenditures made in connection with new construction are not eligible for the credit. The disabled access credit is equal to 50 percent of eligible expenditures that exceed $250 but do not exceed $10,250.[58] Thus, the annual credit limitation is $5,000. The basis of the property is reduced by the allowable credit. An eligible small business is any business that either (1) had gross receipts of $1 million or less in the preceding year or (2) in the case of a business failing the first test had no more than 30 full-time employees in the preceding year and makes a timely election to claim the credit.

Example 14-28 ■   Crane Corporation had 14 employees during the preceding tax year and $2 million of gross receipts. During the current year, Crane installed concrete access ramps at a total cost of $14,000. Crane is an eligible small business because the company had 30 or fewer full-time employees during the preceding year even though its gross receipts exceed the threshold amount (i.e., $1 million or less). The credit is limited to $5,000 ($10,000 × 0.50). The depreciable basis of the property is reduced by the amount of the credit to $9,000 ($14,000 − $5,000). ■

The disabled access credit is also one of the items included in the general business credit. Thus, the limitation is based on the taxpayer's tax liability, and the carryback and carryover of excess credits are governed by the Sec. 38 rules.

[56] Sec. 1396.
[57] Sec. 1396(c)(3)(A).
[58] Sec. 44.

TAX CREDIT FOR REHABILITATION EXPENDITURES

Real World Example

Taxpayers incurred substantial rehabilitation expenditures on an old factory building, but the tax credit was not allowed since the taxpayers did not use the straight-line depreciation method. Frank DeMarco, *87 T.C. 518 (1986).*

Congress has provided incentives for the rehabilitation of older industrial and commercial buildings and certified historic structures. The following special rules and qualification requirements apply:

- The credit is 10% for structures that were originally placed in service before 1936 and 20% for certified historic structures.[59]

- The credit applies only to trade or business property and property held for investment that is depreciable. Residential rental property does not qualify unless the building is a certified historic structure.

- At least 75% of the external walls, including at least 50% utilization of external walls, and at least 75% of the building's internal structural framework, must remain in place.[60]

- Straight-line depreciation generally must be used with the applicable Sec. 168 recovery periods with respect to rehabilitation expenditures. The regular MACRS depreciation rules apply to the portion of the property's basis that is not eligible for the credit.[61]

- The basis of the property for depreciation is reduced by the full amount of the credit taken.[62]

- The rehabilitation expenditures must exceed the greater of the property's adjusted basis or $5,000.[63]

- The rehabilitation credit is recaptured at a rate of 20% per year if there is an early disposition of the property.[64]

Example 14-29 ■ During the current year, Ted rehabilitates a certified historic structure used in his business at a cost of $40,000. The adjusted basis of the certified historic structure is $38,000 at the time the property is rehabilitated. The property qualifies for the rehabilitation credit because

- It is used in Ted's trade or business and is depreciable

- The property is a certified historic structure

- The amount of the expenditure exceeds the greater of the property's $38,000 adjusted basis or the $5,000 statutory minimum.

The credit is $8,000 (0.20 × $40,000). The basis of the rehabilitation expenditures for depreciation purposes is reduced by the full amount of the credit to $32,000 ($40,000 − $8,000). If the property is disposed of after one year, $1,600 of the credit (0.20 × $8,000) is earned and $6,400 ($8,000 − $1,600) is recaptured. ■

---

[59] Secs. 47(a)(1) and (2). A certified historic structure must be certified by the Department of Treasury and must be located in a registered historic district or listed in the *National Register.*
[60] Sec. 47(c)(1)(A). The percentage requirements for rehabilitation do not apply to a certified historic structure.
[61] Sec. 47(c)(2)(B)(i).
[62] Sec. 50(c)(1).
[63] Sec. 47(c)(1)(C)(i).
[64] Sec. 50(a)(1)(B).

BUSINESS ENERGY CREDITS

To encourage energy conservation measures, additional credits are available to businesses that invest in energy conserving properties (e.g., solar and geothermal property).[65] The business energy credit is 10%. The construction, reconstruction, or erection of the property must be completed by the taxpayer and its original use must commence with the taxpayer. This credit is subject to the same limitations upon deductibility and carryback and carryover rules as other general business credits.[66]

PERSONAL TAX CREDITS

Personal nonrefundable credits include the child and dependent care credit and credit for the elderly and disabled. These credits are allowed as an offset against an individual's tax liability before all other credits (e.g., the general business credit and the foreign tax credit) are deducted. The earned income credit for certain low-income individuals is refundable (e.g., an individual may receive a tax refund from the IRS equal to the amount of the credit even if no tax is owed). Most tax credits for individuals have been enacted for social welfare rather than economic reasons.

Additional Comment

The dollar amount of the child and dependent care credit amounted to $2.5 billion in 1991.

Child and Dependent Care Credit

The child and dependent care credit provides relief for taxpayers who incur child and dependent care expenses because of employment activities.[67] Thus, if one spouse performs household and child care tasks and is not employed, these services are not taxed. If, however, the nonemployed spouse obtains a job and must, therefore, incur child or dependent care expenses, the earnings from employment are included in gross income. The child and dependent care expenses are not deductible, however. Instead, a limited tax credit is provided. To qualify for the credit, an individual must meet two requirements: (1) Employment-related expenses (i.e., qualifying child or dependent care expenses) must be incurred to enable the taxpayer to be gainfully employed,[68] and (2) the taxpayer must maintain a household for a dependent under age 13 or an incapacitated dependent or spouse.[69]

Example 14-30 ■

Tim and Tina are married and have two children under age 13. They incur child care expenses (e.g., a housekeeper and nurse) to enable Tina to pursue nonemployment-related social activities. The child care expenditures are not eligible for the child and dependent care credit, even though the expenses would otherwise qualify (i.e., they are proper child care expenses and the children are under age 13), because Tina is not employed or attending school as a full-time student. ■

Additional Comment

Qualifying child care expenses include amounts spent to send a child to nursery school or kindergarten, but not first grade.

Qualifying Employment-Related Expenses. Eligible expenses include amounts spent for housekeeping, nursing, cooking, baby-sitting, and so on in the taxpayer's home. If the child or dependent care is provided outside the home by a dependent care facility (e.g., a day care facility), the amounts will generally qualify only if the dependent care facility provides care for more than six individuals. Employment-related expenses do not include amounts paid for services outside of the taxpayer's

[65] Sec. 48(a)(2). This credit has been permanently extended by the Energy Tax Act of 1992.
[66] As previously discussed, these business credits are combined for the purpose of computing the taxpayer's limitation. Unused general business tax credits are carried back 3 years and forward 15 years.
[67] Sec. 21.
[68] Secs. 21(a)(1) and (b)(2)(A).
[69] Secs. 21(b)(1) and (e)(1). Maintaining a household means that the individual (or the individual and spouse if married) must provide over one-half of the cost of maintaining the home. Married individuals must generally file a joint return to obtain the credit.

household at a camp where the qualifying individual stays over night.[70] In addition, amounts paid for services outside of the taxpayer's household (e.g., adult day care) that are spent for the care of an incapacitated dependent or spouse qualify only if the individual lives in the taxpayer's home for at least 8 hours a day.[71]

Example 14-31 ■

Tony is divorced and has two children under age 13. He is employed and incurs child care expenses at a preschool nursery for one of the children. He also has a live-in nanny who provides housekeeping services and a gardener to care for his yard. The expenditures for the nursery and the live-in nanny qualify since these services constitute eligible household services and care of a qualifying individual. However, the payments to the gardener do not constitute qualifying household services. ■

The following special rules also apply:

Additional Comment

According to the Census Bureau, 58.4% of married women with preschoolers worked in the paid labor force in 1989, up from 35% in 1977.

- Payments to a relative qualify unless the relative is a dependent or a child (under age 19) of the taxpayer.[72]
- The maximum child and dependent care expenses cannot exceed the individual's earned income.[73] For married individuals, the limitation is applied to the earned income of the spouse with the smaller amount of earned income.
- A spouse who either is a full-time student or is incapacitated is deemed to have earned income of $200 per month.[74] The amount is increased to $400 per month if there are two or more qualifying individuals (e.g., children under age 13) in the household.
- The ceiling amount on qualifying child and dependent care expenses is $2,400 for one qualifying individual and $4,800 for two or more individuals.[75] These ceilings are reduced by the aggregate amount excludable from gross income due to the exclusion under Sec. 129 relating to dependent care assistance programs.

Example 14-32 ■

Troy and Tracy are married and incur qualifying child care expenses of $4,000 to take care of their two children ages 1 and 3. Tracy's earned income is $20,000, and Troy's earned income from a part-time job is $3,000. The limitation on qualifying child care expenses is $3,000. The earned income limitation applies because Troy's earned income ($3,000) is less than the child care expenses ($4,000) and is also less than the overall limitation on such expenses for an individual with two qualifying children ($4,800). Therefore, the amount of eligible child-care expenses is limited to $3,000. ■

Key Point

The percentage used to calculate the credit varies from 20% to 30% depending upon the taxpayer's AGI.

Computation of the Credit Rate and Amount. The credit is 30% of the qualifying expenses (after the ceiling limitations of $2,400 or $4,800 have been applied).[76] However, the credit rate is reduced by one percentage point for each $2,000 (or fraction thereof) of adjusted gross income (AGI) in excess of $10,000. The minimum credit (20%) is applied once a taxpayer's AGI is in excess of $28,000.

Example 14-33 ■

Vincent and Vicki are married, file a joint return, and have three children under age 13. Vincent and Vicki's employment-related earnings are $25,000 and $10,000, respectively. Their AGI is $35,000. They incur $8,000 of child care expenses during

---

[70] Sec. 21(b)(2)(A)(ii).
[71] Sec. 21(b)(2)(B)(ii).
[72] Sec. 21(e)(6).
[73] Sec. 21(d).
[74] Sec. 21(d)(2). To qualify as a full-time student, the individual must enroll in an educational institution on a full-time basis for at least 5 calendar months of the year (Reg. Sec. 1.44A-2(b)(3)(B)(ii).
[75] Sec. 21(c).
[76] Sec. 21(a)(2).

the current year. The eligible child care expenses are limited to $4,800, because Vincent and Vicki have more than one child who is qualified and this limitation is less than Vicki's earned income or the actual expenses incurred. Since their AGI is in excess of $28,000, the minimum 20% credit rate is applicable. The child and dependent care credit is $960 (0.20 × $4,800). ∎

Dependent Care Assistance. An employee may exclude amounts up to $5,000 from gross income for dependent care assistance payments made by the individual's employer and provided to the employee.[77] The exclusion amount is limited to the earned income of the employee (or in the case of a married taxpayer, the lesser of the employee's earned income or the earned income of the spouse). To avoid a double benefit, the otherwise eligible expenses for purposes of computing the child and dependent care credit are reduced by the amount of assistance that is excluded from gross income.[78]

Example 14-34 ∎	Assume the same facts as in Example 14-33 except that Vincent was reimbursed $4,000 by his employer under a qualified dependent care assistance program and this amount was excluded from gross income. The earned income limitation does not apply because both Vincent and Vicki have employment-related earnings in excess of $4,000. Thus, the eligible child care expenses are reduced to $800 ($4,800 − $4,000) and the child care credit is $160 (0.20 × $800). ∎

Additional Comment

The earned income credit was claimed on 12.8 million tax returns in 1991 and amounted to $7.6 billion.

Earned Income Credit

The earned income credit is refundable (i.e., the individual receives a refund of tax even though no tax is due or paid). As such, the earned income credit is a special type of "negative income tax" or welfare benefit for certain low-income families. The credit is based upon earned income that includes wages, salaries, tips, and other employee compensation plus net earnings from self-employment.

Eligibility Rules. The credit is available to individuals with qualifying children and to certain individuals without children if the earned income and AGI thresholds are met.[79] The earned income credit applies to married individuals only if a joint return is filed.[80] Individuals without children are eligible only if the following requirements are met:

Key Point

The Revenue Reconciliation Act of 1993 dramatically increased the benefits available from the earned income credit which follows President Clinton's campaign promise to provide tax relief to the working poor.

- The individual's principal place of abode is in the United States for more than one-half of the tax year.

- The individual (or spouse if married) is at least age 25 and not more than age 64 at the end of the tax year.

- The individual is not a dependent of another taxpayer for the tax year.[81]

Computation of the Credit Amount. The earned income credit percentages and the maximum amount of earned income used to compute the credit for 1994 are summarized in Table 14-1. The basic percentage rate and the maximum amount of earned income used to compute the credit depend upon the number of qualifying

---

[77] Sec. 129. (See Chapter 4 for a discussion of the requirements for exclusion.)

[78] Sec. 21(c).

[79] Sec. 32(c). A qualifying child must be the taxpayer's child, stepchild, foster child, or a descendent of the taxpayer's child. The child must share the same principal place of abode with the taxpayer for more than one-half of the tax year and the child must be less than age 19 or be a full-time student under age 24 or be permanently and totally disabled.

[80] Sec. 32(c)(1)(A).

[81] Sec. 32(d).

TABLE 14-1 Earned Income Credit Table

Number of Qualifying Children	Basic Percentage	Maximum Amount of Earned Income to Compute Credit	Maximum Tentative Credit
None	7.65%	$4,000	$ 306
One	26.3%	7,750	2,038
Two or more	30.0%	8,425	2,528

children (from none to two or more). The maximum allowable credit is then reduced by a phase-out percentage (see Table 14-2).[82]

TABLE 14-2 Earned Income Credit Phase-out Table

Number of Qualifying Children	Phase-out Begins at[a]	Phase-out Percentage
None	$ 5,000	7.65%
One	11,000	15.98%
Two or more	11,000	17.68%

[a]Larger of AGI or earned income.

Example 14-35 ■

Vivian is eligible for the earned income credit and has one qualifying child. In the current year she has $10,360 of earned income from wages and $2,000 of alimony. Vivian's AGI is, therefore, $12,360 ($10,360 wages + $2,000 alimony). The tentative credit is $2,038 (0.263 × the first $7,750 of earned income). This amount is reduced by $217 (0.1598 × [$12,360 − $11,000]).[83] The allowable credit is therefore $1,821 ($2,038 − $217), and this amount is partially or fully refundable to Vivian if she owes less than $1,821 in taxes.   ■

Tax Credit for the Elderly

A limited, personal, nonrefundable credit is provided for certain low-income elderly individuals who have attained age 65 before the end of the tax year and individuals who retired because of a permanent and total disability who receive insubstantial social security benefits. Most elderly taxpayers are ineligible for the credit because they receive social security benefits in excess of the ceiling limitations that apply to the credit (e.g., an initial amount of $5,000 per year for a single taxpayer) or they have AGI amounts in excess of the limitations, which effectively reduces or eliminates the allowable credit.

The maximum credit is 15% times an initial amount of $5,000 ($7,500 for married individuals filing jointly if both spouses are 65 or older).[84] This initial amount is reduced by[85]

• Social security, railroad retirement, or Veterans Administration pension or annuity benefits that are excluded from gross income

---

[82] The percentages are liberalized in 1995 and 1996 and are adjusted for inflation after 1994.

[83] Sec. 32(b)(1). $12,360 is used in the formula because AGI of $12,360 is greater than $10,360 of earned income.

[84] Sec. 22(c)(2). The initial ceiling amount is $5,000 if one spouse filing a joint return is less than age 65 and the limitation is $3,750 for a married individual filing a separate return. Unless married individuals are living apart for the entire year, they must file a joint return in order to obtain the credit.

[85] Secs. 22(c)(3) and (d).

- One-half of AGI in excess of $7,500 for a single individual ($10,000 for married taxpayers filing a joint return).[86] All types of taxable income items are included in AGI (e.g., salaries, taxable pension and taxable FICA benefits, investment income, and so on).

Example 14-36 ■ Wayne and Tammy are both 65 years old and file a joint return. They have AGI of $11,000 and receive nontaxable social security payments of $3,000 during the current year. The tax credit for the elderly is computed as follows:

Initial ceiling amount			$7,500
Minus:	Nontaxable social security	$3,000	
	One-half of AGI in excess of $10,000		
	(0.50 × [$11,000 − $10,000])	500	(3,500)
Total credit base			$4,000
Times: Rate			× 0.15
Tax credit			$ 600

The $600 credit is allowed only to the extent that Wayne and Tammy's total personal tax credits do not exceed the actual tax due before credits. ■

TAX PLANNING CONSIDERATIONS

Key Point

The alternative minimum tax can be avoided or its impact lessened by various tax strategies.

Avoiding the Alternative Minimum Tax

Taxpayers with substantial amounts of tax preference items and a corresponding low regular tax liability may be subject to the AMT. These taxpayers need to engage in tax planning in order to minimize or avoid the AMT. Because a liberal exemption is provided for most individuals (i.e., $45,000 for married individuals filing a joint return and $33,750 for single taxpayers and heads-of-households), the timing of certain income and deduction items may result in the full utilization of the exemption in each year. For example, planning to avoid the AMT may be accomplished by delaying the payment of certain itemized deductions (e.g., state and local taxes) that reduce the regular income tax but do not reduce the AMT. A cash method of accounting taxpayer who defers the payment of state income taxes into the following year triggers an increase in the regular tax for the current year. This increase can eliminate the AMT liability. However, it is necessary to consider the tax effects for both the current and following years because state income taxes are deductible for purposes of the regular tax calculation when the payment is made in the following year. This reduction may affect the AMT calculation in such a year and increase the amount of tax that is owed.

Certain tax-exempt investments generate additional tax preferences for the investor such as interest on private activity bonds. Before such investments are acquired, an investor should determine the impact upon his/her AMT.

Avoiding the Underpayment Penalty for Estimated Tax

Many taxpayers find it difficult to estimate their taxes for the purposes of making quarterly estimated payments and are uncertain whether their withholdings and estimated tax will equal or exceed 90% or more of their actual tax liability for the year.

---

[86] The AGI ceiling is $5,000 for married individuals filing a separate return. To obtain the credit, however, a separate return can be filed only if both spouses live apart for the entire tax year.

A frequently used planning technique to avoid a possible underpayment tax penalty is to make estimated tax payments and withholdings in an amount that is at least 100% of the actual tax liability for the prior year, thereby meeting one of the exceptions that prevents the underpayment penalty from being imposed.

Example 14-37 ■

Yong expects his federal income tax withholdings to be $14,000 for the current year and estimates that his income tax liability will be $24,000. Last year Yong's actual federal income taxes were $20,000. If estimated taxes of at least $6,000 are paid during the year, Yong's estimated taxes plus withholding will be at least 100% of his prior year's tax liability ($14,000 + $6,000 = $20,000), and no underpayment penalty is due despite the fact that there is a $4,000 ($24,000 − $20,000) underpayment of the actual tax liability. If Yong's AGI was in excess of $150,000 for the prior year, his estimated taxes plus withholding must be at least 110% of his prior year's tax liability or $22,000 (1.10 × $20,000) to avoid the underpayment penalty. Thus, his estimated tax payments must be at least $8,000. ■

Cash-Flow Considerations

Key Point

A taxpayer should avoid making estimated payments that are in excess of the actual tax liability since the taxpayer is making an interest-free loan to the IRS. Nevertheless, many taxpayers deliberately have excess amounts withheld from their wages or make excessive estimated payments in order to receive a refund. These taxpayers view this strategy as a forced saving plan.

Assuming that the underpayment penalty can be avoided, it is generally preferable to have an underpayment of tax to the government at the time for filing the return rather than to receive a refund resulting from an overpayment of tax. No interest is paid on a refund if the IRS pays the refund within 45 days from the later of the due date of the return or its filing date.[87] In addition, the IRS has, in effect, received an interest-free loan from the taxpayer during the period such overpayment is made. To avoid an overpayment, a taxpayer may file an amended W-4 form and claim additional withholding allowances if the requirements are met (e.g., the taxpayer has unusually large itemized deductions, tax credits, alimony payments, and so on).

If an individual anticipates that his estimated tax payments and withholdings are insufficient to avoid the underpayment penalty, it may be preferable to increase the amounts that are withheld prior to the end of the tax year (e.g., the amounts that are withheld in the fourth quarter) to avoid the penalty rather than to increase the estimated tax payments. This technique may be advantageous because the penalty is calculated upon a quarterly basis, and the withholdings are spread evenly over the year, despite the fact that such increased amounts of withholding are paid near the end of the year. The end result is cash-flow savings to the taxpayer. Another alternative means to avoid the underpayment penalty is to accelerate certain deductions (e.g., real estate taxes on a personal residence), by paying such amounts prior to the end of the tax year. Additionally, otherwise deductible contributions to an IRA made between the end of the tax year and the due date for the tax return may be treated as a deduction for the prior year thereby avoiding the underpayment penalty (see Chapter 9).

Utilization of General Business Tax Credits

Business tax credits (e.g., the disabled access credit and the targeted jobs credit) are combined for the purpose of computing an overall limitation based upon the taxpayer's tax liability. Also, an individual's personal tax credits (e.g., the child and dependent care credit) are deducted from the tax liability before the limitations are applied to the foreign tax credit and the general business tax credit. Therefore, it is necessary to consider the priority and interrelated aspects of these credits to ensure that a particular credit will be fully utilized.

---

[87] Sec. 6611(e).

Foreign Tax Credits and Exclusion

Individuals who accept foreign job assignments should consider the federal income tax implications, because U.S. citizens are subject to U.S. tax on their worldwide income. Assuming that certain requirements and limitations are met, an individual may elect to take either a foreign tax credit or a foreign-earned income exclusion of $70,000 with respect to salaries, allowances, and other forms of earned income that is earned while on extended non-U.S. assignments.[88] Any taxes that are paid or accrued with respect to the excluded income are not available as a foreign tax credit. In general, the exclusion is preferable if the effective foreign tax rate is less than the effective U.S. tax rate because the foreign tax credit that can be claimed does not equal the gross U.S. tax that is owed on the income. If the foreign tax rate on the earned income exceeds the U.S. tax rate, U.S. taxpayers ordinarily elect not to use the exclusion. Instead, the "excess" tax credits on earned income are used to offset the U.S. taxes owed on other types of foreign income. Detailed coverage of foreign tax credits and the exclusion is contained in Chapter 15 of the *Prentice Hall's Federal Taxation: Corporations, Partnerships, Estates and Trusts* text and in Chapter 14 of the *Comprehensive* volume.

Child and Dependent Care Credit

Additional Comment

If the employer provides a child care assistance plan, the taxpayer may lose the benefit of the child and dependent care credit because it is necessary to reduce the amount of expenses eligible for the credit dollar-for-dollar by the amount excluded from gross income under the employer's child care plan.

The child and dependent care credit is increasingly important because a greater percentage of both spouses are now in the labor force. Nonworking spouses who are considering employment should evaluate the tax consequences arising from the child and dependent care credit.

It should be noted that certain child and dependent care expenses may qualify as a medical expense (e.g., nursing care for a disabled dependent). It is, therefore, necessary to compare the marginal tax benefit from the additional child and dependent care credit with the marginal tax benefit from the additional medical expense deduction to determine if the credit is worth more than the deduction. Expenditures in excess of the child and dependent care ceiling amounts (e.g., $2,400 for one child or dependent and $4,800 for two or more children or dependents) may also qualify as medical expenses.

Example 14-38 ■

Real World Example

Many taxpayers do not comply with the tax law when they hire individuals to care for their children. Zoe Baird withdrew as attorney general nominee when it was disclosed that she had hired illegal aliens to care for her children and had failed to withhold the FICA tax from the employee's wages and to pay the employer's FICA tax.

Stacey, a single taxpayer, maintains a household for an incapacitated dependent parent and two children under age 13. Stacey has AGI from alimony of $20,000 and could earn an additional $15,000 working as a secretary. To enable Stacey to be employed, assume that she would incur $4,000 of eligible child care expenses for the children and an additional $4,000 of nursing expenses for the care of her disabled parent. Before considering the tax effects, Stacey's net increase in income from being employed would only be $7,000 ($15,000 earnings − $8,000 of child and dependent care expenses). The tax credit for child and dependent care expenses is $960 ($4,800 × 0.20). The rate is scaled down from 30% to 20% because Stacey's AGI is $35,000 (i.e., the credit rate is reduced by one percentage point for each $2,000 of AGI in excess of $10,000 until it reaches 20% when AGI exceeds $28,000). A portion of the qualified nursing care expenses (i.e., $8,000 − $4,800 = $3,200) that is not used as child and dependent care expenditures may be deducted as medical expenses if they are in excess of the 7.5% (of AGI) nondeductible medical expense floor. If Stacey itemizes her deductions and has other medical expenses equal to or greater than 7.5% of AGI and has an average tax rate of 20%, the value of the additional medical deductions is $640 (0.20 × $3,200). Stacey's additional net cash flows from working are only $4,453, consisting of the following:

---

[88] Sec. 911(a). The foreign income exclusion requirements are discussed in Chapter 4.

Gross earnings from employment		$15,000
Minus:	Federal income tax on earnings ($15,000 × 0.20)	(3,000)[a]
	Actual child and dependent care expenses	(8,000)
	FICA taxes (0.765 × $15,000)	(1,147)
Plus:	Child and dependent care credit	960
	Medical expense tax benefit	640
Cash flow from employment		$ 4,453

[a] A 20% average tax rate was used because more than one tax rate is used to compute Stacey's tax liability.

Consideration should also be given to additional incremental work-related expenditures (e.g., clothing, meals, and commuting expenses) that are not deductible. The income tax and cash flow consequences arising from an employee assistance program should also be considered if a plan is offered to employees. ■

COMPLIANCE AND PROCEDURAL CONSIDERATIONS

Additional Comment

The Revenue Reconciliation Act of 1993 raised the AMT rate from 24% to 26% on the first $175,000 of AMTI in excess of the exemption amount and 28% on amounts in excess of $175,000. Because the rate on net capital gains was capped at 28%, taxpayers whose income is primarily from net capital gains are more likely to fall into an AMT position.

Alternative Minimum Tax Filing Procedures

Form 6251 is used by individuals to compute the AMT, and corporations must use Form 4626 (see Appendix B). Form 6251 must be completed and attached to an individual's tax return in any of the following situations:

- An AMT tax liability actually exists
- The taxpayer has tax credits that are limited by the tentative minimum tax
- The AMT base exceeds the exemption amounts and an individual has AMT adjustment or tax preference items

IRS Publication 909 contains detailed information regarding filing considerations for individuals.

Five-Year Forward Averaging on Lump-Sum Distributions

It is possible to defer recognition of income tax on a lump-sum distribution if the lump-sum amount is rolled over into an individual retirement account (IRA). The transfer must be made within 60 days from the distribution date.[89] If an individual elects to roll over only part of the lump-sum distribution, the portion of the distribution that is not invested in an IRA is taxed as ordinary income without the benefit of any long-term capital gain or forward averaging treatment. Also, if the entire amount is transferred to an IRA, the tax benefit associated with a lump-sum distribution (i.e., 5-year forward averaging) is lost when the funds are withdrawn from the IRA.

Forward averaging is computed on Form 4972, which must be attached to Form 1040 (see Appendix B). Individuals who receive a lump-sum distribution should receive a Form 1099-R from the employer or trustee of the pension plan. This form describes the tax consequences arising from the lump-sum distribution.

---

[89] Sec. 402(a)(5)(C). Withholding of federal income taxes at a 20% rate can be avoided if a direct trustee-to-trustee transfer is elected by the taxpayer.

Withholding and Estimated Tax

Taxpayers who have income taxes withheld from wages, pensions, and so on should receive a Form W-2 (or Form 1099-R for pensions) by January 31. These forms should be attached to the tax return to substantiate the amount of the withholdings. If the form is incorrect, the taxpayer should request a corrected form from the payor.

If an individual makes quarterly estimated tax payments, Form 1040A or Form 1040EZ may not be used. Married individuals may make either joint estimated tax payments or separate estimated tax payments. If joint estimated tax payments are made and the married individuals subsequently file separate returns (e.g., in the case of a divorce that is pending or a divorce completed prior to the end of the year), the joint estimated tax payments are divided in proportion to each spouse's individual tax if no agreement is reached concerning an appropriate division.

Example 14-39 ■   Allen and Alice make joint estimated tax payments during 1994 of $10,000. Allen and Alice are separated in February 1995, and Alice refuses to file a joint return with Allen. Allen's tax liability for 1994 on his separate return is $20,000, and Alice's tax liability on her separate return is $5,000. Alice is entitled to claim $2,000 of the estimated tax payments to her return ([$5,000 ÷ $25,000] × $10,000). The remaining $8,000 is apportioned to Allen. ■

General Business Tax Credits

The computation of the business energy credit is made on Form 3468. Individuals must transfer the totals to page 2 of Form 1040. Form 3800 must be filed if any other general business credits are claimed.

Personal Tax Credits

Key Point

The earned income credit is available even in cases where the taxpayer has no tax liability.

Personal tax credits, including the credit for child and dependent care expenses and credit for the elderly, are reported on page 2 of Form 1040. These credits are deducted from the taxpayer's tax liability before other credits. The credits section on page 2 of Form 1040 limits the deduction for personal tax credits to the amount of the tax due. Form 2441 (see Appendix B) must be filed to claim the child and dependent care credit. Taxpayers who claim the child and dependent care credit must also include the care provider's name, address, and taxpayer identification number on their tax return. If the caregiver will not provide the required information, the taxpayer has the option to supply the name and address of the caregiver on Form 2441 and attach a statement explaining that the caregiver has refused to provide his identification number (TIN). Schedule R of Form 1040 (see Appendix B) is filed to claim the credit for the elderly. An elderly individual may elect to have the IRS compute the tax and the amount of the tax credit.[90]

The earned income credit is refundable to an individual even if no tax is owed. The IRS will automatically compute the credit amount. However, tax tables to assist in the process are included in IRS instructions to Forms 1040 and 1040A. Schedule EIC of Form 1040 (see Appendix B) is used to compute the credit if Form 1040 is used. Schedule 4 is used for Form 1040A. If an individual expects to be eligible for the earned income credit, he can obtain advance payments of the credit amount by filing Form W-5 (an Earned Income Credit Advance Payment Certificate) with his employer, who will increase the employee's pay by the amount of the credit. Individuals who receive advance payments must file Form 1040 or Form 1040A to obtain the credit even if they are not required to file a tax return. Taxpayers who are eligible for the earned income credit can not use Form 1040-EZ (see Appendix B).

The foreign tax credit for individuals is computed on Form 1116 (see Appendix B). The foreign tax credit amount so determined is entered on page 2 of Form 1040.

---

[90] Sec. 6014. (See Form 1040 instructions for more reporting details.)

PROBLEM MATERIALS

DISCUSSION QUESTIONS

14-1. Why are most taxpayers not subject to the alternative minimum tax (AMT)?

14-2. Does the AMT apply if an individual's tax liability as computed under the AMT rules is less than his regular tax amount?

14-3. Which of the following are tax preference items for purposes of computing the individual AMT?
a. Net long-term capital gain
b. Excess depreciation for real property placed in service before 1987
c. Straight-line depreciation on residential real estate acquired in 1992
d. Appreciated element for charitable contributions of capital gain real property

14-4. Which of the following are individual AMT adjustments?
a. Itemized deductions that are not allowed in computing AMTI
b. Excess of MACRS depreciation over depreciation computed under the alternative depreciation system for real property placed in service after 1986.
c. Excess of MACRS depreciation over depreciation computed under the alternative depreciation system for personal property placed in service after 1986
d. Tax-exempt interest earned on State of Michigan general revenue bonds.

14-5. Which of the following itemized deductions are deductible when computing the alternative minimum tax for individuals?
a. Charitable contributions
b. Mortgage interest on a personal residence
c. State and local income taxes
d. Interest related to an investment in undeveloped land where the individual has no investment income
e. Medical expenses amounting to 8% of AGI

14-6. If a single (flat rate) tax were enacted, would the forward averaging rules be needed? Why or why not?

14-7. Under what conditions is 5-year forward averaging available to an individual receiving a pension distribution?

14-8. Tasha receives a lump-sum distribution from her employer's qualified profit-sharing plan in the current year. The distribution includes $130,000 cash and stock of the employer corporation. $20,000 of the total amount represents Tasha's voluntary contributions. The stock has a $50,000 basis to the employer and an $70,000 FMV. What is the taxable amount of the lump-sum distribution?

14-9. Why are most individuals not subject to the self-employment tax?

14-10. Tony, who is single and 58 years of age, is considering early retirement. He currently has $60,000 salary and $50,000 of profits from a consulting business. What advice would you give Tony relative to the need to make social security tax payments if he retires and continues to be actively engaged as a consultant during his retirement years?

14-11. Theresa is a college professor who wants to work for a consulting firm during the summer months. She will be working on special projects involving firm professional development programs. What advantages might accrue to the consulting firm if the engagement is set up as a consulting arrangement rather than as an employment contract?

14-12. Ted and Tina are both self-employed and file a joint return in 1994. Ted has self-employment income of $20,000 and receives a $30,000 salary from his employer. Tina's self-employment income is $10,000.
a. How much self-employment tax is due for Ted and Tina on a joint return?
b. How much, (if any) of the self-employment tax payments may be deducted on Ted and Tina's income tax return?

14-13. If an employer fails to withhold federal income taxes and FICA taxes on wages and/or fails to make payment to the IRS, what adverse tax consequences may result? May corporate officers or other corporate officials be held responsible for the underpayment?

14-14. Jet Corporation reimburses Tracy, an employee, for certain moving expenses. The reimbursement is $6,000. However, only $4,000 is deductible on Tracy's income tax return. Should Jet Corporation withhold federal income tax upon the reimbursed amounts? If so, how much?

14-15. When Vicki retires during the current year, she will receive a monthly pension of $800 and a fully taxable lump-sum distribution of $50,000 from her employer's qualified profit-sharing plan. She does not want the trustee of either plan to withhold any federal income tax because she expects that it will be difficult for her to live on the pension income and the investment income from the lump-sum distribution.
a. What procedures should Vicki follow if she does not want the trustees to withhold on the periodic pension payments or the lump-sum distribution?
b. What are the possible tax consequences that might occur if Vicki does not file estimated tax payments?
c. What percentage rate is used to determine the amount withheld from periodic pension payments and lump-sum distributions?

14-16. Although Virginia is entitled to five personal and dependency exemptions, she claims only one withholding allowance on Form W-4.
a. Is it permissible to claim fewer allowances than an individual is entitled to?
b. Why would an individual claim fewer allowances?

14-17. Mario is a college student who had no income tax liability in the prior year and expects to have no tax liability for the current year.
a. What steps should Mario take to avoid having amounts being withheld from his summer employment wages?
b. What are the cash-flow implications to Mario if the employer withholds federal income taxes?

14-18. What is backup withholding? What is its purpose?

14-19. Under what circumstances may an individual claim additional withholding allowances on Form W-4?

14-20. In April 1994, Vincent anticipates that his actual tax liability for 1994 will be $12,000 and that the federal income taxes withheld from his salary will be $11,600. His actual federal income tax liability for 1993 is $8,000 and his AGI for 1993 was not in excess of $150,000.
a. Is Vincent required to make estimated tax payments in 1994?
b. If no estimated tax payments are made, will Vincent be subject to an underpayment penalty if the actual tax liability for 1994 is $12,000? Why or why not?
c. Will Vincent be subject to an underpayment penalty if his actual tax liability for 1994 is instead $25,000?

14-21. What tax planning strategy can you suggest to avoid the penalty for underpayment of estimated tax for an individual who has increasing levels of income each year and is uncertain regarding the amount of his estimated taxable income for any given year?

14-22. From a cash-flow perspective, why is it generally preferable to have an underpayment of tax (assuming there is no underpayment penalty imposed) rather than an overpayment of tax?

14-23. Why do many taxpayers intentionally overpay their tax through withholdings so as to obtain a tax refund?

14-24. Discuss the underlying rationale for the following tax credit items:
a. Foreign tax credit
b. Research credit
c. Business energy credit
d. Targeted jobs credit
e. Child and dependent care credit
f. Earned income credit
g. Tax credit for the elderly
h. Low-income housing credit

    i. Disabled access credit

    j. Empowerment zone employment credit

14-25. If Congress is considering a tax credit or deduction as an incentive to encourage certain activities, is a $40 tax credit more valuable than a $200 tax deduction for a taxpayer with a 15% marginal rate? A 28% marginal rate?

14-26. What are the more significant tax credit items included in the computation of the general business tax credit?

14-27. Discuss the limitations that have been imposed upon the claiming of the general business tax credit including the following:
    a. Overall ceiling limitation based upon the tax liability
    b. Priority of general business and personal credits
    c. Carryback and carryover of unused credits (including the application of the FIFO method).

14-28. Wayne is considering a foreign assignment for two years. He will earn approximately $70,000 in the foreign country and will be eligible for the foreign tax credit and/or the earned income exclusion. The effective tax rate on Wayne's earnings if fully taxable under U.S. law would be 30%. The effective tax rate for the foreign salary is 20% under the foreign country's laws.
    a. Discuss in general terms the computation of the foreign tax credit and its limitation.
    b. Would Wayne be better off electing the foreign tax credit or the earned income exclusion? Explain.

14-29. Discuss the following aspects relative to the research and experimental tax credit:
    a. Computation of the credit and its base amount
    b. Reduction in the Sec. 174 deduction amount.
    c. The consequences of electing not to reduce the Sec. 174 deduction

14-30. King Corporation is expanding its business and is planning to hire four additional employees at an annual labor cost of $12,000 each. What will the tax consequences be if King hires employees who are eligible for the targeted jobs credit?

14-31. Queen Corporation has been in business since 1979. During the preceding year the company had 25 full-time employees and gross receipts of $8,000,000. During the current year Queen spent $10,000 to install access ramps for disabled individuals. Is Queen Corporation eligible for the disabled access credit? If so, compute its amount and the basis reduction, if any, for the depreciable property.

14-32. Discuss the special tax rules that apply to the tax credit for rehabilitation expenditures including the following:
    a. Types of eligible expenditures
    b. Applicable tax credit rates
    c. Restrictions upon depreciation methods
    d. Calculation of basis for expenditures
    e. Potential recapture of the credit

14-33. What types of business property qualify for the business energy credit?

14-34. What is the underlying reason for enactment of most of the personal tax credits?

14-35. Discuss the difference between a refundable tax credit and a nonrefundable tax credit. Give at least one example of each type of credit.

14-36. If an individual is unemployed and has no earned income, is it possible to receive a child and dependent care credit for otherwise qualifying child and dependent care expenses? Explain.

14-37. What is the maximum child and dependent care credit that is available to an individual who has at least $4,800 of qualifying child care expenses and two or more qualifying children or incapacitated dependents?

14-38. Vivian is a single taxpayer with two children who qualify for the child and dependent care credit. She incurred $5,000 of qualifying child care expenses during the current year. She also received $3,000 in reimbursements from her employer from a qualified employee dependent care assistance program. What is the maximum child and dependent care credit that is available to Vivian?

14-39. Alice is a single taxpayer who is 37 years old with two qualifying children ages 3 and 6. She receives $2,500 alimony and $8,000 of wages and has $10,500 of AGI. Is Alice eligible for the earned income credit? If so, is it possible for her to receive advance payments of the credit amounts rather than receiving a tax refund when the tax return is filed?

14-40. Why are most elderly people unable to qualify for the tax credit for the elderly?

PROBLEMS

14-41. *AMT Computation.* William, a married taxpayer who files a joint return with his spouse, reports the following items in the current year:

Taxable income	$50,000
Tax preferences	50,000
AMT adjustments related to itemized deductions	30,000
Regular tax liability	12,000

a. What is the amount of William's AMT liability in the current year?
b. What is the amount of William's AMT liability in the current year if he is instead a single taxpayer?
c. What is the amount of William's alternative minimum tax liability if he files a joint return and his AMT adjustments are $60,000 instead of $30,000?

14-42. *AMT Computation.* Jose, a single taxpayer without any dependents, reports the following items in the current year:

Taxable income	$130,000
Tax preferences	40,000
AMT adjustments related to itemized deductions	30,000
Regular tax liability	36,440

What is the amount of Jose's AMT in the current year?

14-43. *AMT Tax Preferences.* Allison, a single taxpayer, reports the following items on her federal income tax return in the current year:

Excess depreciation on real property placed in service in 1986	$ 20,000
Excess depreciation on personal property placed in service in 1992	10,000
Net long-term capital gain	20,000
Charitable contribution of capital gain real property having a $100,000 FMV and a $70,000 basis	30,000
Tax-exempt municipal bond interest (private activity bonds)	30,000

What is the amount of Allison's tax preferences for purposes of computing the AMT in the current year?

14-44. *AMT Adjustments and Computation of Tax.* Allen, a single taxpayer, reports the following items on his current year federal income tax return:

Adjusted gross income	$75,000
Taxable income	30,000
Regular tax liability	6,000
Tax preferences	25,000
Itemized deductions including:	
Charitable contributions	7,500
Medical expenses (before AGI floor)	10,000
Mortgage interest on personal residence	10,000
State income taxes	5,000
Real estate taxes	8,000

a. What is the amount of Allen's AMT adjustments related to the itemized deductions?
b. What is Allen's alternative minimum tax liability for the current year?

14-45. *5-Year Forward Averaging.* Antonio, a married taxpayer who files a joint return, retires at the end of the current year and receives a lump-sum distribution of $60,000 from his employer's noncontributory qualified pension plan. Antonio's other taxable income in the current year is $30,000. What is the amount of tax on the distribution using five-year forward averaging?

14-46. *Self-Employment Tax.* In the current year Amelia receives wages of $30,000 and net earnings from a small unincorporated business of $50,000. What is the amount of Amelia's self-employment tax and *for* AGI deduction for her self-employment tax (if any) on her income tax return?

14-47. *Self-Employment Tax.* Arnie and Angela are married and file a joint return in the current year. Arnie is a partner in a public accounting firm. His share of the partnership's income in the current year is $40,000, and he receives guaranteed payments of $30,000. Angela receives wages of $50,000 from a large corporation. What is each taxpayer's self-employment tax amount?

14-48. *Self-Employment Tax.* Anita, a single taxpayer, reports the following items for the current year:

Salary (subject to withholding)	$20,000
Director's fees	10,000
Consulting fees	10,000
Expenses related to consulting practice	(15,000)

  a. What is the amount of Anita's self-employment tax?
  b. How would your answer to Part a change if Anita's salary is instead $70,000?

14-49. *Penalties for Nonpayment of Withholding and FICA Taxes.* Lake Corporation has some severe cash-flow problems. You are the company's financial and tax consultant. The treasurer of the company has informed you that the company has failed to make FICA and federal income tax withholding payments for both the employer and employee contributions to the IRS for a period of approximately six months.
  a. What advice can you give to the company treasurer regarding the nonpayment of taxes?
  b. Can the liability for payment of the taxes extend to parties other than the corporation? Explain.

14-50. *Exemptions from Withholding.* Which of the following categories of individuals or income are exempt from the federal withholding tax requirements?
  a. Domestic servants
  b. Independent contractors
  c. Newspaper carriers over age 18
  d. Bonuses
  e. Commissions
  f. Vacation pay
  g. Tips under $20 per month from a single employer
  h. Nontaxable fringe benefits
  i. Pensions

14-51. *Withholding Exemptions.* Barry is a college student who is employed as a waiter during the summer months. He earns approximately $1,500 during the summer and estimates that he will not be required to file a tax return and will have no federal income tax liability. Last year, however, he made $6,000 and was required to file a return and pay $400 in taxes. Barry is single and is supported by his parents. He has no dependents and does not have any other sources of income or deductions.
  a. Is Barry permitted to claim an exempt status on Form W-4 for withholding purposes?
  b. Is it possible for Barry to claim more than one exemption on Form W-4 (e.g., additional withholding allowances and/or the standard deduction allowance) to minimize the amount withheld? Explain.

14-52. *Witholding Allowances.* Bart's spouse is not employed. They plan to file a joint return. Bart obtains a new job and is asked to fill out a form W-4. His monthly gross earnings will be $3,000. Bart, who has four dependent children, can claim three additional withholding allowances because he is obligated to pay substantial alimony to his ex-wife.
  a. What is the correct number of withholding allowances that may be claimed on form W-4?
  b. What is the amount of federal income tax to be withheld using the wage bracket tables (in Figure 14-1)?
  c. What disclosure procedures will be required by Bart's employer if Bart claims more than 10 allowances?

14-53. *Estimated Tax Requirements.* Anna does not make quarterly estimated tax payments even though she has substantial amounts of income that are not subject to withholding. Last year Anna's tax liability was $18,000. This year Anna's actual tax liability is $30,000, although only $18,200 was withheld from her salary. Anna's AGI for the prior year was not in excess of $150,000.

   a. Is Anna subject to the underpayment penalty? Why?

   b. If Anna's withholdings were only $15,000, would she be subject to the underpayment penalty? Why?

   c. If Anna is subject to an underpayment penalty, can she deduct this amount as interest? Explain.

14-54. *Estimated Tax Underpayment Penalty.* Anne's estimated tax payments for the current year are $8,000. Her withholdings amount to $12,000. Anne's actual tax liability for the current year and for the prior year are $25,000 and $19,000, respectively. Her income is earned evenly throughout the year in the current year. Anne's AGI for the prior year was $160,000. Is Anne subject to the underpayment penalty? Explain.

14-55. *Computation of Tax Credits.* Becky's tentative tax credits for the current year include the following:

Targeted jobs credit	$ 1,000
Child and dependent care credit	960
Research credit	14,000
Business energy credit	600
Total	$16,560

Becky's regular tax liability before credits is $14,000. There is no alternative minimum tax liability.

   a. What is the amount of allowable personal tax credits?

   b. What is the amount of allowable business tax credits?

   c. What treatment is accorded to the unused tax credits for the current year?

14-56. *Business Tax Credit Carrybacks and Carryovers.* In 1994 Large Corporation, which was incorporated in 1988, has an unused general business tax credit of $40,000 in 1991. The following schedule shows the amount of business tax credits earned and used for the period 1988–1994:

	Credits Earned During the Year	Credit Limitation for the Carryback or Carryover Year
1988	$40,000	$40,000
1989	30,000	40,000
1990	25,000	25,000
1991	60,000	20,000
1992	20,000	22,000
1993	15,000	20,000
1994	15,000	15,000

The excess credits for 1991 were carried back to 1988, the initial year of operation.

   a. How much of the unused 1991 credit is used in the carryback period?

   b. What is the amount of the unused credit that is carried foward? In what years are the credits utilized?

   c. What is the amount of the general business credit carryovers to 1995? Identify the tax years in which the credit carryovers are earned.

14-57. *Foreign Tax Credit.* Laser Corporation has a foreign office which conducts business in France. Laser pays foreign taxes of $40,000 on foreign source taxable income of $100,000. Its U.S. source taxable income is $200,000, and the total U.S. tax liability (before reductions for the foreign tax credit) is $100,250. What is Laser's foreign tax credit?

14-58. *Targeted Jobs Credit.* Last Corporation hires two economically disadvantaged youths (qualified for the targeted jobs credit) in August of the current year. Each employee receives $8,000 wages in the current year. Salaries and wages paid to other employees in the current year are $50,000. Last Corporation has a regular tax liability of $50,000 in the current year before deducting its tax credits assuming the appropriate deduction is claimed for the youths' salaries. Its tentative minimum tax is $10,000. Business tax credits other than the targeted jobs credit amount to $50,000 in the current year.

a. What is Last Corporation's tentative jobs credit (before limitations) in the current year?

b. What is Last Corporation's total general business credit that is utilized in the current year? What amount is available for carryover or carryback?

c. What is Last Corporation's deduction for salaries and wages paid in the current year?

14-59. *Empowerment Zone Employment Credit.* Acorn Corporation operates its business in an empowerment zone and John, one of its employees, lives in the zone. In the current year John received $12,000 in wages. In addition, Acorn incurred $4,000 of training expenses related to John's employment.

a. What is Acorn Corporation's tentative empowerment zone credit (before any limitations on the general business credit are considered)?

b. What is Acorn Corporation's deduction for wages paid in the current year?

14-60. *Rehabilitation Tax Credit.* Bob acquires a certified historic structure to be used as an office for his business in the current year. He pays $20,000 for the building (exclusive of the land) and spends $40,000 for renovation costs.

a. What is the rehabilitation tax credit (before limitations)?

b. What depreciation method(s) must be used for the property?

c. What is the basis of the building for MACRS purposes?

14-61. *Child and Dependent Care Credit.* In each of the following independent situations, determine the amount of the child and dependent care tax credit. (Assume that both taxpayers are employed.)

a. Brad and Bonnie are married and file a joint return. Brad and Bonnie have earned income of $40,000 and $14,000, respectively. Their combined AGI is $52,000. They have two children ages 10 and 12 and employ a live-in nanny at an annual cost of $9,000.

b. Assume the same facts as in Part a, except that Brad and Bonnie employ Bonnie's mother as the live-in nanny. Bonnie's mother is not claimed as a dependent by her children.

c. Bruce is divorced and has two children ages 10 and 16. He has AGI and earned income of $27,000. Bruce incurs qualifying child care expenses of $8,000 during the year which were incurred equally for both children. Bruce's employer maintains an employee dependent care assistance program. $1,000 was paid to Bruce from this program and excluded from Bruce's gross income.

d. Buddy and Candice are married and file a joint return. Their combined AGI is $50,000. Buddy earns $46,000, and Candice's salary from a part-time job is $4,000. They incur $5,000 of qualifying child care expenses for a day-care facility for their two children ages 2 and 4.

14-62. *Earned Income Credit.* Carolyn has a dependent child, age 6, who lived with her for the entire year. She has earned income of $9,000 of wages and $4,000 of alimony in the current year. Her AGI is $13,000.

a. What is Carolyn's tentative earned income credit (before the phase-out reduction is applied)?

b. What is Carolyn's allowable earned income credit?

c. If Carolyn has no income tax liability (before the earned income credit is subtracted), is she entitled to a tax refund in the current year?

14-63. *Earned Income Credit.* Jose is single with no qualifying children. He has $7,000 of wages during the current year and is otherwise eligible for the earned income credit. Jose has $1,000 of interest income and no *for* AGI deductions. His AGI is $8,000.

a. What is Jose's tentative earned income credit (before the phaseout reduction is applied?

b. What is Jose's allowable earned income credit?

c. If Jose has no income tax liability (before the earned income credit is subtracted), is he entitled to a refund for the current year?

14-64. *Tax Credit for the Elderly.* Caroline, age 66 and single, receives the following income items for the current year:

Social security payments	$ 3,000
Fully taxable pension	4,000
Dividend and interest income	4,500
Total	$11,500

Caroline's tax liability (before credits) is $300 in the current year.
   a. What is Caroline's tentative tax credit for the elderly (before the tax liability limitation is applied) in the current year?
   b. What is the amount of Caroline's allowable tax credit for the elderly in the current year?

COMPREHENSIVE PROBLEM

14-65. Chuck's tax file reveals the following information for the current year:

Salary		$35,000
Net income from consulting (before deducting one-half of self-employment taxes paid)		30,000
Net loss from an unincorporated business		(10,000)
Itemized deductions:		
State and local taxes	$6,000	
Mortgage interest on personal residence	8,000	
Contributions	2,000	
Medical expenses (actual)	2,000	18,000
Credit for child and dependent care		500
General business tax credits		500
Estimated taxes paid and withholdings from salary		7,500
Actual income tax liability for the current year (after credits)		10,000
Actual income tax liability for the prior year		7,000
AGI for the prior year		60,000
Personal and dependency exemptions		4
Filing Status: Married filing jointly		

   a. Is Chuck subject to the self-employment tax? If so, compute the amount of self-employment tax liability and the amount of self-employment taxes that may be deducted on Chuck's income tax return.
   b. Is Chuck subject to the estimated income tax underpayment penalty? Explain.

TAX FORM/RETURN PREPARATION PROBLEMS

TurboTax **14-66.** Warren (Soc. Sec. No. 123-45-6789) and Alice (Soc. Sec. No. 987-65-4321) Williams have the following tax credits for the current year:

General business credits	$12,140
Child and dependent care credit	960
Total	$13,100

Warren and Alice Williams have two children, 5 and 7, and incur $5,000 of qualifying child care expenses ($2,500 for day care and $2,500 for a nurse). Each spouse had earned income of $25,000 and their AGI is $50,000. Their regular tax liability (before credits) is $20,000. Disregard any limitations that might be imposed by the tentative minimum tax.
   Complete Form 2441 and the Tax Credits section on page 2 of Form 1040.

TurboTax **14-67.** Harold Milton (Soc. Sec. No. 574-45-5477) is single. He had the following income and deductions for the current year:

Salary	$77,000	Charitable contributions	27,000
Interest income	12,000	State income taxes	8,000
Dividend income	3,000	Mortgage interest expense	19,000
IRA contribution	2,000	Interest expense on car loan	3,000
Tax-exempt interest		Real estate taxes	2,000
from private activity		Miscellaneous deductions	
bonds issued in 1990	24,000	subject to the 2% AGI floor)	7,000
		Income taxes withheld	9,000

Complete Form 1040, Schedule A, and Form 6251.

CASE STUDY PROBLEM

14-68. Barbara was divorced in 1991. However, the final property settlement and determination of alimony payments was not made until February, 1994 because of extended litigation. Barbara received a $20,000 payment of back alimony in March 1994 and will receive monthly alimony payments of $2,000 for the period April through December, 1994. In 1993, Barbara's income consisted of $15,000 salary and $2,000 of taxable interest income. She uses the standard deduction and has no dependents. In 1993 Barbara's tax liability was $1,900. She expects to continue working at an annual salary of $15,000 and have $2,000 of interest income in 1994. Her monthly alimony payments of $2,000 are also expected to continue for an indefinite period.

In April, 1994 Barbara requests your advice regarding the payment of quarterly estimated taxes for 1994. Prepare a memo to your client that discusses these requirements including the possible payment of any penalties and nontax issues such as cash-flow and investment income decisions.

CASE STUDY PROBLEM—ETHICAL ISSUES

14-69. Chips-R-Us is a computer technology corporation which designs hardware and software for use in large businesses. The corporation regularly pays individuals to install programs and give advice to different companies who buy their software. In the current year, Simone, a computer expert, was sent to a customer of Chips-R-Us by the corporation to perform computer services. Simone is not a regular employee of the corporation and the corporation did not train Simone for the task. Simone keeps track of the time spent on the job at the customer and reports to the corporation, who pays Simone for her services. The corporation specifies the work to be done for their client. The corporation can also replace Simone with another individual if her work is not satisfactory to them. Chips-R-Us treats Simone as an independent contractor for employment tax purposes. In the current year the IRS challenges the corporation that it has failed to remit FICA taxes and income taxes withheld in respect to Simone's employment. Chips-R-Us refuses to pay the amount stating that it is not required to do so because Simone is not an employee of the corporation. What will be the likely outcome of the IRS's decision concerning the status of Simone as an employee v. independent contractor? Who may be liable for payment of the employment taxes, interest, and penalties to the government and what ethical responsibilities should be followed in the remittance of taxes on behalf of an employee?

TAX RESEARCH PROBLEM

14-70. Lean Corporation was incorporated in 1981 by Bruce Smith who has served as an officer and member of the Board of Directors. Carl Jones has served as the secretary-treasurer of the company as a convenience to his friend Bruce Smith. He acted as a part-time bookkeeper but did not run the everyday business affairs and paid only the bills he was instructed to pay. Carl was an authorized signatory for the corporate bank accounts but had no final control over expenditures.

Beginning in the last quarter of 1993, the company failed to pay all of the taxes withheld from employees and the employer's share of FICA taxes to the IRS. Despite this delinquency, the corporation continued to pay other creditors, including its employees, in preference to the IRS.

In January 1994, Lean Corporation entered into an installment agreement with the IRS to keep current on its withholding taxes and to make payments on the past due balance until paid in full. The company subsequently defaulted on the agreement in April 1994. During this period, Bruce Smith was serving as chief financial officer and was a member of the Board of Directors. He had the authority to make policy decisions. He was responsible for negotiating the installment agreement with the IRS and the decision to default on the agreement.

Who is liable for the penalty for the nonpayment of the payroll tax withholdings?

A partial list of research sources is

- Sec. 6672.
- *Ernest W. Carlson v. U.S.,* 67 AFTR 2d 91-1104, 91-1 USTC ¶ 50,262 (D.C. UT, 1991).

15 Partnerships and S Corporations

LEARNING OBJECTIVES

After studying this chapter, you should be able to

1. Determine the tax implications of a partnership formation
2. Determine the operating rules for partnerships
3. Understand the tax implications (to the partnership and its partners) of distributions to partners
4. Understand the requirements for S corporation status
5. Discuss the operating rules for S corporations
6. Describe the tax treatment of an S corporation's shareholders

Additional Comment

The number of partnership tax returns has declined from 1,713,600 in 1985 to 1,554,000 in 1990.

Additional Comment

Almost all of the states in the United States have either created limited liability companies (LLCs) or are taking action to do so. The best known is the Wyoming Limited Liability Company. The LLCs represent a special type of company that has limited liability and flow-through (partnership) status for tax purposes. The use of LLCs has increased significantly in recent years.

A business may be organized and operated as a sole proprietorship, regular or C corporation, S corporation, or partnership. The choice of organization form is frequently influenced by nontax considerations. Many large businesses use the corporate form because of the need to raise equity capital from the public. The corporate form of organization offers limited liability to the shareholders for the payment of corporate debts and enables the corporation to raise substantial funds from investors.

Small businesses and professional service organizations are frequently organized as sole proprietorships. This form of organization is relatively uncomplicated because it is not necessary to operate the business as a separate legal entity. For income tax purposes, a sole proprietor merely includes the business income and expenses on Schedule C of Form 1040, and the income is taxed to the individual proprietor.

Many small closely held businesses incorporate and elect to be taxed as an S corporation because of both general business considerations (e.g., limited liability protection) and income tax considerations. The partnership form of organization is popular among professional service organizations (e.g., lawyers, certified public accountants, and doctors) and in specialized industries such as real estate and oil and gas.

Chapter 15 provides an introduction to the taxation of partnerships and S corporations. C corporations are discussed in Chapter 16. The S corporation, while a corporate entity, is discussed in Chapter 15 because of the similarity of its tax provisions to the partnership tax provisions.

TAXATION OF PARTNERSHIPS

Key Point

The partnership form of business lies between the well-defined ownership arrangements of corporations and other profit-motivated arrangements where the participants have separate or individual financial interests.

Partnerships are generally treated as a conduit rather than as a separate taxable entity.[1] Income, deduction, loss, and credit items flow through to the individual partners, who report such amounts on their own returns. The partnership merely files an annual information return on Form 1065 [U.S. Partnership Return of Income] (see Appendix B), which summarizes certain financial information such as partnership ordinary income or loss and separately stated items of income, deductions, losses, and credits that flow through to the partners.

---

[1] Although a partnership is not taxed under federal income tax law, the Internal Revenue Code treats a partnership as a separate entity for purposes of determining its tax year and accounting methods and making other elections.

Thus, a partnership is treated as a conduit (i.e., income, deduction, loss, and credit items flow through and are reported by the individual partner). On the other hand, a **C corporation** is treated as a separate taxable entity. Thus, if a C corporation has taxable income, a separate tax is paid at the corporate level. If the income is subsequently distributed to shareholders as a dividend, a second tax is levied at the shareholder level. As noted above, C corporations are the subject of Chapter 16.

S corporations (named after Subchapter S in the Code where their rules can be found) are corporations that have elected to be subject to taxation under the special rules contained in the Code. Basically, S corporations are treated as a conduit under rules similar to the taxation of partnerships. The ordinary income of an S corporation and other separately stated items pass through to its shareholders, even if the income is *not* distributed in the form of a dividend. The S corporation is generally not subject to tax, although a Form 1120S (U.S. Income Tax Return for an S Corporation) tax return must be filed.[2] Form 1120S is included in Appendix B.

In some circumstances, the nontax attributes related to the corporate form of organization (e.g., limited liability or ability to attract external sources of financing) may be highly desirable in selecting a particular form of business organization. The S corporation form was enacted to provide neutrality in the tax law by permitting the retention of nontax corporate attributes following incorporation while using tax rules similar to the partnership form of doing business.

Example 15-1 ■ Andy and Barry operate as the AB Partnership and are considering the incorporation of their business. Currently the partnership generates annual business income of approximately $50,000. Andy and Barry are equal partners. Thus, $25,000 of income flows through and is taxed to each Andy and Barry on their individual returns. If an S corporation election is made and Andy and Barry each own 50% of the corporation's stock, there will be no change in the tax consequences to Andy and Barry, and the S corporation will not incur a tax liability. If, however, an S corporation election is not made, the corporation will incur taxes on the business income (less any salary payments made to Andy and Barry), and no tax consequences will arise to Andy and Barry from the earning of the business income, except to the extent that such amounts are paid in the form of salary or dividends. ■

Formation of a Partnership

When a partnership is formed, the partners frequently contribute properties (e.g., money, business equipment, inventory previously used in a proprietorship) and/or services to the partnership. In exchange for these properties and/or services, the partners receive a capital and/or profits interest in the partnership. For each partner a **partnership interest** is in the nature of an investment security similar to corporate stock (i.e., a capital asset).

Section 721: Nonrecognition Rules. Section 721 prevents the recognition of gain or loss upon either (1) the transfer of properties in exchange for a partnership interest or (2) subsequent transfers of property by the partners in exchange for a pro rata increase in their partnership interests. The depreciation recapture provisions of Secs. 1245 and 1250 do not come into play if no gain is recognized under Sec. 721. If this

---

[2] An S corporation may be subject to a built-in gains tax under Sec. 1374 and the excess passive income tax under Sec. 1375 if certain requirements are met. These requirements are discussed more fully later in this chapter.

rule was not part of the Code, gain on a transfer of appreciated properties would be recognized and the partners might not have sufficient liquidity (e.g., cash) to pay the tax.

The following exceptions to the Sec. 721 nonrecognition rules should be noted:

- The Sec. 721 nonrecognition of gain or loss rules do not apply unless a partnership interest is received.[3]

Example 15-2 ■

Key Point

Neither the Code nor the regulations defines the kind of property that qualifies for the nonrecognition provisions. However, the word "property" has been interpreted very broadly by the courts.

Arnie sells inventory held by his proprietorship with a $10,000 FMV and a $9,000 adjusted basis to the ABC Partnership in exchange for $10,000 cash. Arnie holds a one-third capital and profits interest in the partnership. The transaction is treated as a sale or exchange of property, and a $1,000 gain is recognized. Section 721 does not apply since the transaction was not a contribution to the partnership's capital.

- If a partner contributes services that have been rendered (or are to be rendered) instead of cash or property in exchange for an unrestricted partnership interest that includes both a profits interest and a capital interest, the fair market value (FMV) of the services is subject to tax as compensation to the contributing partner because services do not qualify as property.[4] ■

Example 15-3 ■

Typical Misconception

It is frequently assumed that the transfer of accounts receivable to a partnership will be treated as a contribution of services and be subject to immediate taxation. No income will be recognized, however, until the receivables are collected. At that time the income will be assigned to the partner who contributed the receivables.

Anna agrees to provide legal services necessary to the creation of the ABC Partnership in exchange for a 20% interest in the capital and profits of the partnership. If the FMV of the services is $10,000, Anna has ordinary income equal to this amount upon the receipt of the partnership interest. ■

It is clear that a service partner who receives an unrestricted interest in the partnership capital is subject to immediate taxation on the value of the capital interest because its FMV is determinable. However, some uncertainty exists if a partner provides current or future services in exchange solely for an interest in the future partnership profits. Litigation in this area has held that if a profits interest is received for past services, the service provider is taxed upon the receipt of the interest if the interest has a determinable FMV.[5] However, a recent U.S. Court of Appeals case, which reversed the Tax Court, held that the profits interest was speculative and was, therefore, without value upon its receipt.[6] In Rev. Proc. 93-27, the IRS held that the receipt of a profits interest for services will not be treated as a taxable event unless the profits interest is in the form of a substantially certain and predictable stream of income; the partner disposes of the profits interest within two years; or the profits interest is a limited partnership interest in a publicly traded partnership.[7]

Key Point

The substituted basis of the partnership interest is consistent with the nonrecognition of gain or loss.

- Gain may be recognized by the contributing partner if liabilities that are transferred to the partnership would result in a negative basis for the partner's interest in the partnership.[8]

- Gain is recognized if property is transferred to a partnership that would be treated as an investment company if the partnership were incorporated under Sec. 351.[9]

---

[3] Reg. Sec. 1.721-1(a). An exception is provided if the partners make ratable contributions of property where no additional interests are received. In such case, the contributions do not trigger the recognition of gain.

[4] Reg. Sec. 1.721-1(b)(1).

[5] *Sol Diamond, v. CIR*, 33 AFTR 2d 74-852, 74-1 USTC ¶ 9306 (7th Cir., 1974).

[6] *William G. Campbell, v. CIR*, 59 AFTR 2d 87-917, 91-2 USTC ¶ 50,420 (8th Cir., 1991).

[7] Rev. Proc. 93-27, I.R.B. 1993-24, 63.

[8] The recognized gain is equal to the negative basis that would otherwise result under Sec. 752. See Example 15-7 and the discussion of the partnership basis rules.

[9] Sec. 721(b). The partnership is considered to be an investment company if 80% or more of the transferred assets (exclusive of cash and nonconvertible debt obligations) consists of marketable stocks or securities. This restriction prevents investors from diversifying their portfolios by creating a partnership through a tax-free transfer of securities in exchange for a partnership interest.

Basis of a Partnership Interest. Section 722 provides a substituted basis rule for determining the basis of a partnership interest if the Sec. 721 nonrecognition rules apply. Disregarding the effect of any liabilities, the basis of the partnership interest to the contributing partner equals the sum of money contributed plus the adjusted basis of the property transferred to the partnership.

Example 15-4 ■   Allen contributes property (e.g., business equipment) having a $10,000 FMV and a $4,000 adjusted basis to the ABC Partnership in exchange for a 30% interest in the capital and profits. The basis of Allen's partnership interest is $4,000 (a substituted basis), since no gain or loss is recognized under Sec. 721. No gain is recognized even if the business equipment is subject to depreciation recapture under Sec. 1245. ■

If a contributing partner renders services to the partnership in exchange for a partnership interest, the contributing partner's basis equals the amount of income recognized from the rendering of the services (i.e., the FMV of the services).[10] The FMV basis is permitted because the partner recognizes ordinary income equal to the FMV of the services.

Example 15-5 ■   Angela contributes property having a $10,000 FMV and a $4,000 adjusted basis and renders services valued at $10,000 in exchange for a 60% interest in the capital and profits of the ABC Partnership. Section 721 prevents the gain from being recognized on the transfer of the properties. However, Angela recognizes $10,000 of ordinary income (i.e., the FMV of the services rendered). Thus, the basis of Angela's partnership interest equals $14,000 ($4,000 adjusted basis of the property plus the $10,000 FMV of the services). ■

SECTION 752 BASIS ADJUSTMENT. A partner's basis for their partnership interest includes the partner's ratable share of the partnership liabilities as well as the basis attributable to any property and services contributed to the partnership. If a partner contributes property subject to a liability (e.g., a building is transferred to the partnership and the mortgage is assumed by the partnership) or if the partnership assumes any of the contributing partner's liabilities, the following basis adjustments are made under Sec. 752:

- The excess of (1) the decrease in a contributing partner's liabilities resulting from the transfer of the liabilities to the partnership over (2) the amount of the partnership liabilities assumed by the contributing partner is treated as a distribution of money to the contributing partner from the partnership. The basis of a partnership interest is reduced by distributions to the partner. (See the section entitled Partnership Distributions starting on page 15-15 for a discussion of the tax treatment for money or property distributions made to partners.) Thus, the contributing partner's basis in the partnership interest is decreased by this amount.

- The noncontributing partners increase the basis of their partnership interests equal to their share of the partnership liabilities that were transferred to the partnership by the contributing partner.

Self-Study Question

Bob, a partner in an equal 3-person partnership, had a $10,000 basis before the partnership borrowed $300,000 to purchase a building. What is Bob's basis after the loan is made?

Answer

It is increased from $10,000 to $110,000. This characteristic could result in the partner being allocated losses greater than his cash investment.

Example 15-6 ■   Brad contributes a building having a $90,000 FMV and a $80,000 adjusted basis which is subject to a $60,000 mortgage in exchange for a one-third interest in the BCD Partnership. The partnership owes no other liabilities. Following the contribution, Brad, Carol, and Dale share profits and losses equally and each has a one-third interest in partnership capital. Brad's basis in his partnership interest in calculated as follows:

[10] Reg. Sec. 1.722-1.

Adjusted basis of the building transferred	$80,000
Plus: Brad's share of the mortgage transferred	
to the partnership ($60,000 × 0.333)	20,000
Minus: Decrease in Brad's individual liabilities	(60,000)
Brad's basis in his partnership interest	$40,000

Both Carol and Dale increase their basis in the partnership interest by the increase in their respective shares of the partnership liabilities of $20,000 ($60,000 × 0.333). This adjustment is required because a partner's basis in the partnership interest includes the partner's share of any partnership liabilities. ∎

Under the general rules of Sec. 752, a partner's basis in the partnership interest is increased by a partner's share of any changes in the partnership's liabilities during the year. For example, if the total partnership liabilities (including accounts and notes payable, mortgages, bank loans, etc.) increases during the year from $100,000 to $200,000, the basis of a partner with a 50% interest in the partnership increases by $50,000 ($100,000 increase in liabilities × 0.50).

NEGATIVE BASIS RULE. The basis of a partnership interest cannot be a negative number. Therefore, Sec. 731 requires the recognition of gain in situations where a negative basis would otherwise occur.

Example 15-7 ∎   Becky transfers property having a $100,000 FMV and a $20,000 adjusted basis, which is subject to a $60,000 mortgage in exchange for a one-third interest in the BCD Partnership. The partnership owes no other liabilities. Becky, Cindy, and Dan share profits and losses equally, and each has a one-third interest in partnership capital. The $60,000 reduction in Becky's individual liabilities is treated as a distribution of money under Sec. 752. Gain must be recognized to the extent that the distribution exceeds Becky's $40,000 basis for the partnership interest, or $20,000. Becky's basis in the partnership interest is zero after the distribution.

Adjusted basis of property transferred	$20,000
Plus: Becky's share of the mortgage transferred to the	
partnership ($60,000 × 0.333)	20,000
Minus: Decrease in Becky's individual liabilities	(60,000)
Tentative basis of Becky's partnership interest	($20,000)
Plus: Gain recognized by Becky (to the extent of negative basis)	20,000
Becky's basis in the partnership interest	$—0—

∎

Holding Period for a Partnership Interest. If cash is the partner's sole contribution to the partnership in exchange for a partnership interest, the holding period begins on the date the interest is acquired. If property is contributed, the holding period for the partnership interest generally includes the holding period of the contributed property. However, if the contributed property is other than a capital asset or Sec. 1231 asset (e.g., inventory), the holding period begins on the date the partnership interest is acquired.[11]

Example 15-8 ∎   In the current year, Johanna contributes business machinery (a Sec. 1231 asset) to the JK Partnership in exchange for a partnership interest. The machinery was originally acquired by Johanna in 1990. Because the machinery is Sec. 1231

[11] Reg. Sec. 1.1223-1(a).

property, Johanna's holding period for her partnership interest begins in 1990 (the date the machinery was acquired). ■

Additional Comment

When property that has been held for personal use is contributed to a partnership, the basis is equal to the lesser of the FMV or the adjusted basis of the property.

Basis of Partnership Assets. Section 723 provides a carryover basis rule for property contributed to the partnership. In general, the partnership's basis in the property is the same as that of the transferor partner, even if gain is recognized by the contributing partner.[12] If this rule was not in effect, the partners could increase the basis of their property for depreciation and subsequent sale purposes by merely contributing appreciated properties to a partnership. Since the carryover basis rules apply, the holding period of the property includes the period the property was held by the contributing partner.[13]

Example 15-9 ■

In the current year, Carlos contributes equipment with a $6,000 adjusted basis and an $8,000 FMV to the CDE Partnership and receives a one-third capital and profits interest in the partnership. The equipment was acquired by Carlos in 1990. CDE's basis for the equipment is $6,000, its adjusted basis in the hands of the contributing partner. No gain is recognized due to the operation of the nonrecognition of gain or loss rules under Sec. 721. The partnership's basis for the equipment would remain $6,000, even if gain were recognized on the transfer due to the operation of the rules applicable to liabilities that were illustrated in Example 15-7. CDE's holding period for the equipment commences in 1990 and includes Carlos' holding period for the property. ■

Financial Accounting Considerations. Under generally accepted accounting principles (GAAP), the carryover basis and nonrecognition of gain rules used in taxation are not applied. For example, if property is contributed to a partnership, its basis and the partner's capital account are recorded at an amount equal to the contributed property's FMV. This results in a difference between the tax and financial accounting bases of the contributed assets and capital account balances in the partnership records.

Example 15-10 ■

Key Point

For many items, the partnership will be required to maintain records for tax purposes, and a separate set of records for financial accounting purposes.

Anwar contributes cash of $30,000 and Beth contributes land having a $30,000 FMV and a $20,000 adjusted basis to the AB Partnership. Each partner receives a 50% interest in the partnership profits and capital. For financial accounting purposes, the land and Beth's capital account are recorded at $30,000. For tax purposes, Beth's capital account and the basis of the land to the partnership are $20,000 due to the operation of the Sec. 723 carryover basis rules. No gain or loss is recorded for financial accounting purposes if the land is later sold by the partnership for $30,000. However, a $10,000 gain is reported under the tax rules because the land's adjusted basis for tax purposes is only $20,000. The $10,000 pre-contribution gain is allocated to Anwar. (See the section entitled Special Allocations on page 15-9 for a discussion of the treatment of pre-contribution gains and losses.) ■

The nonrecognition of gain or loss and basis rules under Sec. 721 are highlighted in Topic Review 15-1.

Organizational and Syndication Fees. The costs of organizing a partnership are not immediately deductible but must be capitalized by the partnership and amortized over a period of not less than 60 months beginning with the month in which the

---

[12] An exception is provided if the partnership is considered to be an investment company under Sec. 721(b). In this case, the partnership receives a basis increase for the property equal to the amount of the recognized gain.

[13] Sec. 1223(2) and Reg. Sec. 1.723-1.

TOPIC REVIEW 15-1

Section 721 Formations—Nonrecognition of Gain or Loss Rules

1. A transfer of properties in exchange for a partnership interest or pro rata increase in a partnership interest is required for nonrecognition of gain or loss treatment.
2. The depreciation recapture rules do not apply to contributed properties unless a gain is recognized, but the recapture potential carries over to the partnership.
3. An individual's basis in partnership interest is adjusted for the following:
   a. Cash contributed to the partnership
   b. Adjusted basis of noncash property contributed
   c. FMV of services contributed
   d. Sec. 752 adjustment for liabilities
   e. Gain recognized under Sec. 731 due to negative basis
4. The partnership's basis in the transferred properties carries over from the transferor partners.
5. The partnership's holding period for the transferred properties includes the contributing partner's holding period.
6. The nonrecognition of gain or loss rules do not apply to services contributed. The contributing partner's basis in the partnership interest is increased by the amount of income recognized from the rendering of the services.

---

partnership begins business.[14] **Organizational expenses** include legal and accounting fees incident to the organization of the partnership, filing fees, etc.[15]

Expenses attributable to the syndication of a partnership must be capitalized by the partnership and are *not* amortizable.[16] **Syndication fees** are expenses incurred to promote and market partnership interests (usually associated with tax-sheltered limited partnership interests). Examples of nondeductible syndication fees include brokerage and registration fees, legal fees of the underwriter and issuer, and printing costs associated with the prospectus and promotional materials.

Partnership Operations

OBJECTIVE 2
Determine the operating rules for partnerships

Additional Comment

A number of states impose an income tax on each nonresident partner's share of income produced by the partnership in that state. This can cause a partner to file several state income tax returns where a partnership conducts business in those states.

The primary purpose for the partnership tax return (Form 1065) is to provide information regarding the measurement and reporting of the income, deduction, loss and credit items that pass through to the individual partners. Certain separately stated items (e.g., capital gains and losses, charitable contributions, and Sec. 1231 gains and losses) are segregated and passed through to individual partners without losing their identity. It is necessary to identify such items because their tax effect depends upon the partner's particular tax situation. These items are reported on Schedules K and K-1 of the partnership return. Schedule K reports tax information for the entire partnership while a separate schedule K-1 is prepared and summarizes the results for each partner (see Appendix B).

Items that do not have special tax effect (e.g., salaries and wages and depreciation recapture) are netted at the partnership level and are reported on page 1 of Form 1065. The netting of such items results in the reporting of partnership ordinary income or ordinary loss, which is then apportioned to the individual partners depending upon the profit and loss sharing ratios that are contained in the partnership agreement.

---

[14] Secs. 709(a) and (b)(1). An election to amortize organization costs must be made by the partnership by attaching a statement to the partnership's tax return that includes the month in which it begins in business (Reg. Sec. 1.709-1(c)).

[15] Reg. Sec. 1.709-2(a).

[16] Reg. Sec. 1.709-2(b).

TABLE 15-1 *Segregation of Ordinary Income and Separately Stated Items*

	Separately Stated Items (Schedules K and K-1)	Partnership Ordinary Income (or Loss) (Page 1 of Form 1065)
Sales minus cost of goods sold		X
Salaries and wages		X
Guaranteed payments to partners[a]	X	X
Taxes, bad debts, repairs		X
Charitable contributions	X	
Tax preference items	X	
Investment interest income and expense	X	
Foreign income taxes paid or accrued	X	
Specially allocated items of income, deductions, and so on, that differ from the general profit and loss allocation ratios	X	
Tax-exempt interest income	X	
Capital gains and losses	X	
Tax credits	X	
Recapture of depreciation under Secs. 1245 and 1250		X
Sec. 1231 gains or losses	X	

[a] Guaranteed payments are included in both columns because they are deductible by the partnership to arrive at partnership ordinary income (or loss) and are reported separately and are taxable to the partner who receives the payment.

Table 15-1 contains a list of commonly encountered separately stated items and items that comprise partnership ordinary income or loss.[17]

Special Allocations

Additional Comment

In general, the partnership income or loss is allocated according to the provisions of the partnership agreement, and the partnership agreement can be amended anytime up to the due date for filing the partnership return.

Section 704 generally permits partners wide latitude to decide how the income, deductions, losses, and credit items are to be allocated among the individual partners. Special allocations are unique to partnerships and permit flexible arrangements among the partners for sharing specific items of income and loss. A partner's distributive share of such items is generally determined by the partnership agreement.[18] However, the ability to make special allocations resulting in a shift of tax benefits among individual partners is subject to certain restrictions. For example, the special allocation must have "substantial economic effect" (e.g., it cannot be a tax sham).[19] In addition, the Code provides that a special allocation must be made for property contributed by the partners when determining the allocation of the depreciation deductions and the amount of gain or loss recognized when the property is eventually sold or exchanged by the partnership.[20] Essentially, the allocation of the depreciation deductions and the amount of recognized gain or loss must take into account the difference between the partnership's basis for the contributed property and the property's FMV at the time of the contribution.

[17] The actual *taxable income* (or *loss*) is not computed on the partnership tax return. Instead, the reporting of partnership income (or loss) involves a two-step approach. Items that have special tax effects upon the individual partners are reported separately on Schedules K and K-1. Other items (i.e., ordinary income and expenses) that do not have special tax effects are reported as part of the partnership's ordinary income (or loss) on page 1 of Form 1065.

[18] Sec. 704(a).

[19] Sec. 704(b).

[20] Sec. 704(c).

Example 15-11 ■

Additional Comment

Regulation Sec. 1.704-1, which deals with the definition of "substantial economic effect," contains approximately 60 pages and is extremely complex.

Clay and Dana form an equal partnership five years ago. Clay contributed cash of $100,000, and Dana contributed land having a $60,000 adjusted basis and a $100,000 FMV. The partnership's basis for the land is $60,000 (Dana's basis) because no gain or loss is recognized by Dana on the transfer. If the land is sold by the partnership in the current year for $110,000, $50,000 ($110,000 − $60,000) of gain is recognized. If a special allocation of the gain was not required, $25,000 of the gain would be allocated to each Clay and Dana based upon their equal profit and loss sharing ratios. The special allocation rules require $45,000 of the gain to be allocated to Dana ($40,000 unrealized appreciation accruing prior to the transfer of the property to the partnership plus $5,000, which is one-half of the postcontribution appreciation). The remaining $5,000 of the postcontribution gain is allocated to Clay ([$110,000 − $100,000] × 0.50). ■

Allocation of Partnership Income, Deductions, Losses, and Credits to Partners

Key Point

The varying interest rule applies to any partner who sells or exchanges less than his entire interest, or whose interest is reduced either by the entry of a new partner who purchases his interest directly from the partnership, by partial liquidation, by gift, or otherwise.

If there is a change in any partner's interest in the partnership during the year (e.g., due to the sale of a partnership interest or the entry of a new partner who contributes property to the partnership in exchange for an interest), all of the partners are required to determine their distributive share of the partnership income, deductions, losses, and credits according to their varying interests in the partnership during the year.[21] Retroactive allocations (e.g., of deductions or losses) to new partners who are admitted prior to the end of the partnership's tax year are not allowed.

Example 15-12 ■

Colleen and Dan are equal partners in the CDE Partnership, which uses the calendar year as its tax year. On December 1, 1994, Ed contributes $50,000 cash for a one-third interest in the partnership's profits and losses and capital. The partnership reports a $9,000 ordinary loss for the 1994 tax year ending on December 31, 1994. The partners must report their shares of the partnership loss based upon their varying interests. A daily allocation of the loss (assuming all months have 30 days) takes place as follows:[22]

Partner		Loss Allocation
Colleen	½ × $9,000 × ¹¹⁄₁₂	$4,125
	⅓ × $9,000 × ¹⁄₁₂	250
		$4,375
Dan	Same as Colleen	4,375
Ed	⅓ × $9,000 × ¹⁄₁₂	250
		$9,000

Ed's loss is limited to his ratable share of the loss incurred after his entry into the partnership, or $250. This result occurs even if the partnership agreement provides that Ed would receive one-third of all losses for the entire year. ■

Basis Adjustments for Operating Items

Key Point

Although the basis of corporate stock is not likely to change over time, the basis of a partnership interest is subject to annual adjustment.

Under Sec. 705, each partnership interest is adjusted to reflect the partner's share of income and deduction items. This basis adjustment is necessary because the items of

---

[21] Sec. 706(d)(1).

[22] Regulation Sec. 1.706-1(c)(2) provides for alternative allocation methods. The partners may elect to use the interim closing method as an alternative to the pro rata method that was used in Example 15-12. Section 706(d)(2) further requires cash method of accounting partnerships to allocate certain cash-basis items such as interest and taxes over the period that the expenses accrue. These complex allocations are discussed in Chapter 9 of *Prentice Hall's Federal Taxation: Corporations, Partnerships, Estates, and Trusts* text.

income and deduction are subject to taxation on a current basis, regardless of whether a distribution is made to the partners. In addition, each partner's basis in the partnership interest is adjusted for capital contributions, withdrawals, and changes in liabilities that occur during the year. Each partner's basis is increased by the partner's distributive share of the following items: (1) ordinary income of the partnership and (2) separately stated income and gain items of the partnership. The basis of the partnership interest is increased whether the income is taxable to the partners or is tax-exempt.[23]

The partner's basis is decreased (but not below zero) by partnership distributions and by the partner's distributive share of the following items: (1) ordinary loss of the partnership; (2) separately stated loss and deduction items of the partnership (e.g., charitable contributions made by the partnership); and (3) expenditures that are nondeductible in computing partnership ordinary income or loss.

Example 15-13 ■

David and Edith form a partnership in the current year with an equal sharing of profits and losses. No special allocations are provided for in the partnership agreement. The following transactions occur during the year that affect David's basis in his partnership interest:

• David contributes land having a $60,000 basis and a $100,000 FMV in exchange for the initial partnership interest.

• The partnership liabilities increase from zero to $100,000 by the end of the tax year.

• The partnership earns $50,000 of ordinary income.

• The partnership earns $5,000 of tax-exempt interest income.

• The partnership incurs $10,000 of capital losses.

• David withdraws $20,000 in cash from the partnership.

• The partnership makes a $15,000 charitable contribution.

David's year-end basis is determined as follows:

Capital contribution of land	$60,000
Plus:	
Share of the increase in partnership liabilities ($100,000 × 0.50)	50,000
Share of ordinary income ($50,000 × 0.50)	25,000
Share of tax-exempt interest income ($5,000 × 0.50)	2,500
Minus:	
Share of capital losses ($10,000 × 0.50)	(5,000)
Withdrawals by David	(20,000)
Share of charitable contributions ($15,000 × 0.50)	(7,500)
David's basis at the end of the current year	$105,000

■

Limitations on Losses and Restoration of Basis

Section 704(d) limits a partner's distributive share of the partnership's ordinary loss and any separately stated losses and deductions that are passed through to the adjusted basis of his partnership interest as determined at the end of the partnership's

---

[23] If the partnership includes oil and gas properties, an increase in basis is made for the excess of percentage depletion claimed over the basis of the property subject to depletion, and a reduction in basis is made for the depletion deduction claimed under Sec. 611.

tax year.[24] The positive adjustments referred to in Example 15-13 are made before the limitation upon the deductibility of losses and deductions is considered. If the loss limitation rule did not apply, the partner's interest could have a negative basis. Any unused losses and deductions are carried over indefinitely and are allowed in subsequent years where the partner again has a positive basis in the partnership interest.

Example 15-14 ■

Ellen, who has a 50% profits and loss interest in the EF Partnership, has a $10,000 basis in her partnership interest at the end of 1994 (before deducting her share of losses). The EF Partnership incurs a $50,000 ordinary loss in 1994. Ellen's share of the loss is $25,000 ($50,000 × 0.50), but only $10,000 is deductible in 1994. The remaining $15,000 of the loss is carried over to 1995. Ellen's basis in her partnership interest is zero at the end of 1994.   ■

Example 15-15 ■

Assume the same facts as in Example 15-14, except that in 1995 Ellen's share of partnership liabilities increases by $5,000; Ellen's share of the 1995 ordinary income is $5,000; and Ellen makes a $5,000 additional capital contribution. Since Ellen's basis is increased by $15,000 due to the three items, the $15,000 loss carryover from 1994 is fully deductible in 1995. Ellen's basis is also zero at the end of 1995. A zero tax basis for a partnership interest does not necessarily mean that the interest is worthless. All that has happened is that the tax losses have reduced the basis to zero. The FMV of the partnership's net assets or their financial accounting basis may be substantial.   ■

The special allocation and basis rules are summarized in Topic Review 15-2.

Typical Misconception
Since the passive activity loss limitation does not apply to partnerships, it is sometimes concluded that these limitations are not important in partnership taxation. However, these provisions do apply at the partner level if the partner is a limited partner or is not materially participating.

Limitations on Passive Losses. Before the Tax Reform Act of 1986, many taxpayers invested in tax shelters. **Tax shelters** are passive investments designed to decrease an individual's taxes by producing paper losses to offset the individual's earned income. The Tax Reform Act of 1986 implemented new tax laws that severely curtail the benefits of tax shelters. The Revenue Act of 1987 placed further restrictions upon publicly traded partnerships (see Chapters 8 and 17).

The cornerstone of the attack on tax shelters is a provision that restricts the ability of taxpayers to shelter earned income with losses arising from "passive" activities. An activity is *passive* if it involves the conduct of a trade or business and the taxpayer does not "materially participate." An interest in a limited partnership is by definition always a passive activity. The disallowed passive losses can be carried forward and used to offset future income from passive activities.

The passive loss limitation rules apply to individuals estates, trusts, partnerships, S corporations, closely-held C corporations, and personal service corporations. (See Chapter 8 for a detailed discussion of these rules.)

Transactions Between a Partner and the Partnership

It is not uncommon for a partner to independently engage in transactions with the partnership. For example, a partner may sell property to the partnership rather than make a capital contribution of such property. In such transactions, the partner is

---

[24] Two other rules also restrict the deductibility of losses. The at-risk rules contained in Sec. 465 limit loss deductions to the partner's at-risk basis. In addition, Sec. 469 contains passive activity loss rules that disallow virtually all net passive activity losses. These restrictions are discussed in Chapter 8 of this text and in Chapter 9 of *Prentice Hall's Federal Taxation: Corporations, Partnerships, Estates, and Trusts* text.

TOPIC REVIEW 15-2

Allocation Rules and Basis Adjustments

1. When property is contributed to a partnership under Sec. 721, any unrecognized gain or loss is subsequently required to be allocated to the contributing partner when the property is sold by the partnership.

2. Partnership income, deductions, losses and credits are allocated to individual partners on a daily basis based on each partner's interest in the partnership.

3. Special allocations of income, gains, deductions, losses, and credits are permitted as long as they have substantial economic effect.

4. Basis in the partnership interest is increased by the partner's share of ordinary income, separately stated income items and tax-exempt income. Basis is reduced by a partner's share of ordinary loss, separately stated deductions and losses, and nondeductible expenditures. Basis is also adjusted for capital contributions, withdrawals, and changes in the liabilities of the partnership. Basis cannot be decreased below zero.

5. Ordinary losses and separately stated items that would reduce a partner's basis below zero are carried over indefinitely until the partner has a positive basis for the partnership interest.

generally treated as an outside independent party.[25] Thus, gain or loss is recognized on the sale of property by a partner to the partnership, and the partnership receives a cost basis equal to the amount of consideration paid in the exchange transaction. Since the partner and the partnership are not truly independent parties, abuse of this provision is possible. For example, the partners might want to recognize paper losses by selling certain assets at a loss to the partnership while still retaining those assets in the partnership. Alternatively, it may be desirable to sell certain depreciable business assets (Sec. 1231 properties) at a gain that will be taxed to the partner at favorable capital gains rates while the partnership could receive a step-up in the basis of its assets (for depreciation purposes) equal to their FMV. Because this type of potential abuse exists, Sec. 707(b) was enacted to forestall such abuses. It disallows losses and provides ordinary income (rather than as a capital gain) treatment under the following circumstances:

Additional Comment

Defining a partner's interest in profits and capital is not always an easy matter. These determinations can become difficult if a partner has varying interests in different types of income.

- Losses are disallowed on sales or exchanges between a partner and the partnership if the partner owns (directly or indirectly) more than a 50% interest in the partnership capital or profits.[26] A loss is also disallowed if there is a sale or exchange of property between two partnerships in which the same persons own more than a 50% interest in the capital or profits. The Sec. 267 constructive ownership rules are applied to determine whether the more than 50% test is met. Under Sec. 267, constructive ownership takes place between related parties including family members, an individual and his controlled (more than 50% owned) corporation, and a partnership, trust, or estate and its partners or beneficiaries. If the purchaser (i.e., the partner or the partnership) of the property later sells the asset to an outsider, the gain recognized is reduced by the loss that was previously disallowed.

---

[25] Sec. 707(a). A transfer of property in exchange for a partnership interest which is usually tax-free under Sec. 721 may be treated as a taxable sale or exchange if the transfer is followed by a distribution to the contributing partner and the facts and circumstances indicate that the contribution is more properly characterized as a disguised sale (see Sec. 707(a)(2) and Reg. Sec. 1.707-3).

[26] Sec. 707(b)(1).

• Gains are treated as ordinary income (rather than as a capital gain) if the partner owns (directly or indirectly) more than a 50% interest in the partnership's capital or profits interests and the asset that is exchanged is not a capital asset in the transferee's hands.[27]

Example 15-16 ■   Ira has a 60% interest in the profits and capital of the HI Partnership. Ira sells a building with a $100,000 adjusted basis to the partnership for its $60,000 FMV. The $40,000 ($60,000 − $100,000) loss is not recognized, and the basis of the building to the partnership is $60,000, because Ira owns more than 50% of the partnership's profits and capital interests. If the partnership later sells the property to an outsider for $110,000, only $10,000 of gain is recognized because the $50,000 ($110,000 − $60,000) gain is reduced by the $40,000 previously disallowed loss. To simplify the example, the effect of subsequent depreciation deductions upon the basis of the property were ignored. ■

Example 15-17 ■   Helen has a 90% interest in the profits and capital of the HI Partnership. Helen sells a building (used in her business) with a $50,000 adjusted basis to the HI Partnership for $100,000. The building is held for business use by the HI Partnership. Straight-line depreciation was used by Helen. If the building was sold to an outsider for $100,000, Helen would recognize $50,000 of Sec. 1231 gain. No depreciation recapture would be recognized if a sale were made to an outsider because straight-line depreciation was used to depreciate the building. Net Sec. 1231 gain is treated as capital gain, so that the taxpayer may use the gain to offset capital losses. Because the sale is made to a partnership in which Helen owns more than 50% of the profits or capital interests, and the building is not a capital asset in the hands of the partnership, Helen's $50,000 gain is treated as ordinary income. The basis of the building to the HI Partnership is $100,000. ■

Real World Example

A guaranteed payment made to a partner for organizing and syndicating the partnership was in the nature of a capital expenditure and not deductible to the partnership despite the fact that the payment was taxable to the recipient. Sydney Kimmelman, *72 T.C. 294 (1979).*

Guaranteed Payments. Despite the fact that a partner does not qualify as an employee of the partnership for tax purposes, the partnership agreement may provide for fixed salary payments that are *not* based on partnership income. Generally, such payments are deductible by the partnership as guaranteed payments to arrive at the partnership's ordinary income. They are includible in the partner's income in the tax year that they are received. Guaranteed payments can also be made in lieu of interest payments on the amount of the partner's capital investment.[28] Such payments are also deductible by the partnership to arrive at the partnership's ordinary income and are includible in the partner's income.

Example 15-18 ■   José owns a 40% interest in the capital and profits of the JKL Partnership. The partnership agreement provides that José is to receive a fixed salary of $20,000 and 10% interest on his average capital balance. No other guaranteed payments are made to the other partners. If the average capital balance is $50,000, $5,000 (0.10 × $50,000) of interest would be paid as a guaranteed payment. If partnership ordinary income is $10,000 before deducting the guaranteed payments, the partnership ordinary loss is $15,000 ($10,000 income less $25,000 of guaranteed payments to José). José reports $25,000 of ordinary income for the year consisting of the $20,000 salary and the $5,000 interest. José also reports a $6,000 ($15,000 × 0.40) ordinary loss. The other partners report a $9,000 ($15,000 × 0.60) ordinary loss. ■

---

[27] Gains are also converted to ordinary income if the sale is between two partnerships where the same persons owns directly or indirectly more than 50% of the capital or profits interests. In determining the 50% ownership rule, the constructive ownership rules found in Sec. 267 are also used.

[28] Sec. 707(c).

Partnership Distributions

OBJECTIVE 3

Understand the tax implications (to the partnership and its partners) of distributions to partners

A distribution of cash or property from the partnership to a partner is generally treated as a tax-free return of capital. This treatment closely parallels the tax-free consequences resulting from a capital contribution of property made in exchange for a partnership interest under Sec. 721.

A distribution may result in a reduction of a partner's capital interest in the partnership. This type of distribution is referred to as a **nonliquidating distribution.** The partnership may desire to liquidate a partner's entire interest due to retirement, death, or other business reasons. Such distributions are referred to as **liquidating distributions.** In such cases, the liquidating distribution is generally treated as a sale or exchange of the partnership interest. It may result in a capital gain being recognized with respect to the liquidated partner's interest.

Due to the complex nature of this topic, this chapter includes only an abbreviated coverage of these materials and the discussion of liquidating distributions is omitted. Comprehensive coverage of these topics is included in Chapter 10 of the *Prentice Hall's Federal Taxation: Corporations, Partnerships, Estates, and Trusts* text.

Key Point

The FMV of distributed property is irrelevant in determining the tax consequences.

Nonliquidating Distributions. The general rule is that no gain or loss is recognized by the partner or the partnership if the partnership makes a distribution of money or other property to the partner.[29] Such a distribution, which is known as a nonliquidating distribution, is generally treated as a tax-free return of capital (i.e., a reduction in the partner's capital interest in the partnership). An exception is provided if the amount of money, including a partner's release from a liability that is treated as a money distribution, received by the partner exceeds the partner's basis for the partnership interest.[30] Gain (but not loss) is recognized to the extent of the otherwise negative basis that would have resulted from the distribution. If property other than money (e.g., land, machinery, and so on) is distributed to the partner, the basis of the partnership interest is reduced by the adjusted basis of the distributed assets. As previously mentioned, no gain or loss is recognized by the partnership or by the distributee partner even if the adjusted basis of the distributed property is greater than the partner's basis in his partnership interest. In such case the basis of the property to the partner is reduced to reflect the difference between the basis of the property and the basis of the partnership interest. If distributions of both money and property are made, the money distribution is initially applied as a reduction to the basis of the partnership interest before any adjustment is made for the property distribution.

Self-Study Question

Carl, a partner with a $10,000 basis in the ABC Partnership, receives property having a FMV of $20,000 and a basis of $8,000 in a nonliquidating distribution. How much gain is recognized by Carl?

Answer

None; gain is usually recognized only when the amount of cash distributed exceeds the basis of the partnership interest.

Example 15-19 ■

Jane receives a nonliquidating distribution of $10,000 in money from the JK Partnership. At the distribution date, Jane's basis in her partnership interest is $8,000. $8,000 of the $10,000 distribution is a tax-free return of capital, which reduces Jane's basis to zero. The remaining $2,000 represents capital gain from the disposition of the partnership interest.[31] ■

Example 15-20 ■

Jeff receives a nonliquidating distribution of land having a $6,000 adjusted basis and a $10,000 FMV from the JK Partnership. When the distribution is made,

[29] Secs. 731(a) and (b). An exception is provided in Sec. 704(c)(1)(B) for distributions of appreciated property that were contributed by a partner where the property is distributed within five years of the contribution. In such event, gain is recognized by the contributing partner equal to the amount of gain that would have been recognized had the property been sold at its FMV.

[30] Sec. 731(a)(1). Exceptions are also provided if there are unrealized receivables and inventory items referred to as Sec. 751 assets which remain in the partnership or are distributed to the partner. In such instances, the partnership and/or the partner may recognize gain on the distribution.

[31] A portion of this gain may be converted to ordinary income if Jane's share of any Sec. 751 assets (i.e., unrealized receivables and substantially appreciated inventory items) held by the partnership changes as a result of the cash distribution.

TOPIC REVIEW 15-3

Nonliquidating Distributions

1. No gain or loss is generally recognized by the partner or the partnership when a nonliquidating distribution of money or property is made. Gain is recognized by a partner who receives a money distribution which exceeds his basis for the partnership interest.

2. The basis of the partnership interest is reduced (but not below zero) by the adjusted basis of the distributed property. Basis is first reduced by any money that is distributed or deemed distributed as a result of a partner's release from a partnership liability.

3. If money is distributed or deemed distributed from a partner's release of liabilities, no gain or loss is recognized to the extent that the distribution does not exceed the partner's basis in his partnership interest. Any excess amount distributed results in a capital gain to the partner who receives the distribution.

4. If distributions of both money and property are made, the money distribution is initially applied as a reduction to the partner's basis in his partnership interest. No gain or loss is generally recognized by either the partner or the partnership.

   a. If property (other than money) having a total basis in excess of a partner's remaining basis in his partnership interest is distributed, the partner's basis in the property distributed is limited to his remaining basis in the partnership interest, and his basis in the partnership interest is reduced to zero. This remaining basis in the partnership interest is allocated to the individual properties that are distributed.

   b. If property (other than money) having a total basis that is less than the partner's remaining basis in his partnership interest is distributed, the partnership's basis in the property distributed carries over to the partner's books and a corresponding reduction is made to the partner's basis in the partnership interest.

Jeff's basis in his partnership interest is $8,000. No gain or loss is recognized by either Jeff or the JK Partnership when the distribution is made. Jeff's basis in the partnership interest is reduced by $6,000 (the adjusted basis of the property distributed). Jeff's basis in his partnership interest is $2,000 ($8,000 − $6,000) following the distribution. His basis in the land is $6,000. ∎

Example 15-21 ∎ Jean receives a nonliquidating distribution of $5,000 in money and land having a $6,000 adjusted basis and a $10,000 FMV from the JK Partnership. When the distribution is made, Jean's basis in her partnership interest is $8,000. Her basis is initially reduced by the $5,000 money distribution to reflect its tax-free return of capital treatment. The remaining $3,000 basis for the partnership interest is allocated to the land, and no gain or loss is recognized by either Jean or the JK Partnership. Jean's basis for her partnership interest is zero after the distribution. ∎

Topic Review 15-3 summarizes the gain or loss recognition rules relating to nonliquidating distributions.

Sale of a Partnership Interest

Recognition of Gain or Loss. A partnership interest is a capital asset similar to a corporate security. It may be sold or exchanged as existing partners retire or withdraw from the business. The remaining partners may acquire the selling partner's interest, or the interest may be sold to an outsider.

Additional Comment

A sale of a partnership interest will be treated as a sale even though the sale results in the termination of the partnership. For example, if one partner in a two-man partnership sells his interest to the other partner, the transaction is treated as a sale.

Capital gain or loss generally arises from the sale of a partnership interest because the interest is a capital asset in the hands of the selling partner. Thus, in some instances a partnership is viewed as an entity separate and distinct from the partners. However, in some circumstances a partner is considered to own a proportionate interest in each partnership asset (i.e., the partnership is viewed as a conduit), and this results in part capital gain and part ordinary income treatment.

Under the general rules of Sec. 741, gain or loss is measured by the difference between the amount realized and the selling partner's adjusted basis in the partnership interest. The amount realized includes the partner's share of partnership liabilities that he is released from as a result of the sale. The basis of the partnership interest is also adjusted by the selling partner's distributive share of partnership income or loss which must be computed up to the sale date.

Example 15-22 ■ On October 1 Jesse sells his interest in the JK Partnership to Paula, an outsider, for $150,000 cash plus the release from $30,000 of partnership liabilities. Jesse's basis in his partnership interest is $74,000 before taking into account his distributive share of partnership income for the period ending on the sale date and his share of the increase in partnership liabilities. For the current year Jesse's share of the partnership income for the period up to the date of sale is $20,000, and his share of the increase in partnership liabilities is $6,000. Jesse's basis in his partnership interest is $100,000 ($74,000 basis on January 1 + $20,000 share of partnership income + $6,000 share of the increase in partnership liabilities). The amount realized on the sale is $180,000 ($150,000 selling price + $30,000 liabilities). Thus Jesse's recognized gain on the sale is $80,000, which is capital gain unless ordinary income is triggered under Sec. 751. (See Example 15-24 for a discussion of Sec. 751.) ■

Section 751 Ordinary Income Treatment. Ordinary income rather than capital gains treatment may result under Sec. 751 if a partnership has unrealized receivables or substantially appreciated inventory at the time that a partnership interest is sold or a nonliquidating or liquidating distribution of money or property is made to a partner. This overriding (recapture) rule is intended to prevent a partner from converting ordinary income into capital gain by selling or liquidating the partnership interest. A sale of Sec. 751 assets by the partnership results in ordinary income, which would eventually flow through to the partners. The principal Sec. 751 assets include the following:

- Substantially appreciated inventory[32]
- Accounts receivable of a cash method of accounting partnership that generally have a zero basis
- Section 1245 and 1250 depreciation recapture potential (i.e., amounts that would be recaptured as ordinary income if Sec. 1245 or 1250 properties are sold by the partnership)

Example 15-23 ■ Joy's basis in her partnership interest is $100,000, and the amount realized on its sale is $180,000. The cash method of accounting partnership has accounts receivable with a zero basis and a $30,000 FMV. Joy's share of these receivables is $10,000. Thus, $10,000 of the amount realized on the sale of the partnership interest is deemed to be attributed to the sale of Joy's share of the accounts receivable. Because the receivables have a zero basis and a $10,000 FMV, the entire $10,000 ($10,000 − $0) is ordinary income to Joy. The remaining $70,000 ($170,000 − $100,000) of gain derived from the sale of Joy's partnership interest is a capital gain. ■

---

[32] Inventory is substantially appreciated if its FMV exceeds 120% of its adjusted basis.

Additional Comment

The Sec. 754 election can be both an opportunity and a trap since both positive and negative basis adjustments are required.

Optional Basis Adjustments

Section 754 provides an election for new and existing partners which permits a basis adjustment of the assets of a continuing partnership when a partnership interest is sold or exchanged or when certain nonliquidating or liquidating distributions take place. This election, which is made at the partnership level, is intended to prevent any inequities that might arise because the basis of the partnership assets are not adjusted under the general partnership tax accounting rules. The election is binding for all future years unless the IRS consents to a revocation of the election.

Example 15-24 ■

Key Point

Record keeping and administrative problems can increase substantially if the Sec. 754 election is made.

Jim acquires Antonio's one-third partnership interest in the ABC Partnership for $40,000. The balance sheet of the partnership on the sale date includes the following:

	Adjusted Basis	FMV
Assets:		
Cash	$20,000	$ 20,000
Accounts receivable	10,000	10,000
Inventory	15,000	20,000
Depreciable assets	15,000	85,000
Total	$60,000	$135,000
Liabilities	$15,000	$ 15,000
Capital:		
Antonio	15,000	40,000
Beth	15,000	40,000
Carmen	15,000	40,000
Total	$60,000	$135,000

Jim's basis adjustment equals the difference between his basis for the partnership interest of $45,000 ($40,000 amount paid + $5,000 of ABC's liabilities assumed by Jim) and his $20,000 ($60,000 × 0.333) basis in the underlying partnership assets. Thus, if the optional basis adjustment is made with respect to the sale or a previous election is in effect on the sale date, Jim may step-up the basis of his share of the partnership assets from $20,000 to $45,000. ■

In Example 15-24, the election would be favorable solely to Jim because his share of the appreciated partnership assets (inventories and depreciable assets) would be stepped up by $25,000, based on the relative amounts of appreciation for each asset.[33] Jim would then be entitled to additional amounts of depreciation on the increased value of his share of the depreciable assets. In addition, Jim would receive an increased basis for calculating gain on the sale of the inventory. If this election were not in effect and the inventory was sold, Jim would report $1,667 (0.333 × $5,000) gain from the sale of his one-third interest in the inventory even though he paid $6,667 (0.333 × $20,000) for such interest.

Once the election is in effect, its application may be detrimental because a downward adjustment is required if the amount paid for a partnership interest is less than the book value of the net assets (i.e., the assets have declined rather than appreciated in value). The complexities of the basis adjustment rules relative to partnership distributions and sales of an interest to existing partners are discussed in Chapter 10 of the *Prentice Hall's Federal Taxation: Corporations, Partnerships, Estates, and Trusts* text.

---

[33] Section 755 provides rules for allocating the basis adjustment amount to the assets based upon the amount of unrealized appreciation or depreciation in value for each asset class.

PARTNERSHIP ELECTIONS

Tax Year Restrictions

When a partnership's tax year ends, each partner's distributive share of the partnership income (including guaranteed payments) is reported on each individual's Form 1040 (or Form 1120 for corporate partners). Thus, if the partnership's tax year ends on January 31, 1994, and the partners report on a calendar-year basis ending December 31, 1993, none of the partnership income for 1993 is reported on the partners' federal income tax returns until 1994. This results in an effective 11-month deferral of income.

Example 15-25 ■   Kim is admitted to the ABC Partnership on April 1, 1993. Kim is a calendar-year taxpayer who was previously employed by the partnership from January 1, 1993, until her admission to the partnership on April 1, 1993. Kim's earnings as an employee for the 3-month period are $8,000. She receives monthly drawings from her capital account of $3,000 for the last 9 months of the year that represent her share of the partnership income for the year ending on January 31, 1994. ABC's tax year ends on January 31, 1994, and Kim's distributive share of the partnership income for the period April 1, 1993, through January 31, 1994, is $60,000. Because partner drawings are treated as made on the last day of the partnership's tax year (January 31, 1994) and the partnership tax year ends after December 31, 1993, Kim's income for 1993 is only $8,000 (her salary as an employee for the first 3 months of 1993). Kim's $60,000 share of the partnership income for the year ending January 31, 1994, is reported on her 1994 tax return. ■

To prevent or minimize opportunities for the deferral of partnership income, Sec. 706 provides the following restrictions on the selection of a tax year by the partners and the partnership:

- A partnership is generally required to use the tax year of the one or more partners who own a majority interest (more than 50%) in partnership profits and capital. This majority interest tax year rule is generally determined on the first day of the partnership's existing tax year.

- If partners owning a majority of the partnership profits and capital do not have the same tax year, the partnership is required to use the same tax year as all of its principal partners or the tax year to which the principal partners are changing (a **principal partner** is a partner owning 5% or more of partnership profits or capital).

- If the principal partners do not have the same tax year and no majority of its partners have the same tax year, the partnership is required to use the tax year which allows the "least aggregate deferral." (See Chapter 9 of the *Prentice Hall's Federal Taxation: Corporations, Partnerships, Estates, and Trusts* text for a detailed discussion of this requirement.)

Example 15-26 ■   ABC Partnership has one corporate partner, Ace Corporation, with a fiscal year-end of March 31. Ace Corporation owns 25% of the capital and profits of the ABC Partnership. The other partners are all individuals with a calendar year for tax purposes, none of whom owns 5% or more of the capital or profits of the ABC Partnership. ABC Partnership must use a calendar year for tax purposes (the tax year of the partners who own a majority interest). ■

There are two exceptions to the rules given above. First, a partnership with all calendar-year partners can adopt or change to a fiscal year if it can convince the IRS that a business purpose exists for the choice. For example, if the partnership owns a ski resort, it could probably make a good case for closing the partnership tax year on May 31, shortly after the ski season has ended, rather than December 31, which is in the middle of the ski season. However, the IRS must agree that there is a valid business purpose for using the fiscal year.

The second exception allows a partnership to adopt or change to a fiscal year-end if 25% or more of the business's gross receipts in the year are recognized in the last 2 months of the fiscal year, and this must have been the case for 3 consecutive 12-month periods. The net effect of these rules is to restrict any deferral opportunities for partnerships in choosing their year-end. A partnership which does not have a peak income-earning period must use a calendar year as its tax year unless it qualifies under one of the other rules.

The Tax Reform Act of 1986 required most fiscal year partnerships to switch to a calendar year. However, the Revenue Act of 1987 relaxed these restrictions by allowing a fiscal year partnership to elect to retain either the tax year used in 1986 or use a tax year that results in a deferral of the lesser of the current deferral period or three months.[34]

A partnership may continue to use the same fiscal year that was in effect during 1986 even if the fiscal year results in a deferral of over 3 months.[35] However, to continue to use the same fiscal year or to elect a fiscal year that results in a deferral of three months or less, a partnership must make a formal election and must make annual required payments which are a substitute for the tax owed on the deferred income.[36] (See Chapter 11 of this text and Chapter 9 of the *Prentice Hall's Federal Taxation, Corporations, Partnerships, Estates and Trusts* text for a detailed discussion of this topic.)

Cash Method of Accounting Restrictions

The tax laws generally allow a partnership to elect, with its first tax return, any method of accounting that clearly reflects income. Unlike with the tax year election, partnerships may elect any accounting method without regard to the methods employed by its partners. The two most commonly used methods are the cash method and the accrual method. Under the *cash method,* income is reported as received and expenses are reported when actually paid. Under the *accrual method,* income is reported when earned, even if the cash has not yet been received. Similarly, expenses are reported when incurred and not when actually paid.

Whenever Congress considers new tax legislation, they usually discuss the fact that the cash method does not always reflect the economic realities of a business. However, they concede that the cash method is much simpler to use than the accrual method. Because of its simplicity, the cash method is still an option but it has been restricted by Congress.

Partnerships that have a C corporation for a partner and that have average gross receipts of over $5,000,000 during the prior three tax years are not allowed to use the cash method of accounting.[37] Tax shelters, no matter what their size, may not use the cash method under any circumstances. (See Chapter 17 for a further discussion of tax-sheltered investments and Chapter 11 for a discussion of allowable accounting methods.)

---

[34] Secs. 444(a) and (b).
[35] Sec. 444(b)(3).
[36] Sec. 444(c).
[37] Sec. 448(a)(2). Section 448(b) provides exceptions for farming businesses and certain qualified personal service corporations.

TAXATION OF S CORPORATIONS

When the tax law initially sanctioned Subchapter S corporations in 1958, they were a hybrid form of organization. While certain partnership tax attributes were present in the S corporation law, many of the regular corporation tax rules continued to apply. In addition, the initial Subchapter S corporation rules were overly restrictive regarding qualification, election, and revocation of election requirements.

The Subchapter S corporation rules were substantially overhauled in 1982, resulting in a new designation—S corporations. Taxation of S corporations now more closely parallels the tax rules that apply to partnerships.

Qualification Requirements

OBJECTIVE 4
Understand the requirements for S corporation status

To qualify as an S corporation, a business must meet the definition of a "small business corporation."[38] To meet the definition of a small business corporation, the corporation

- Must be a domestic (or U.S.) corporation rather than a foreign corporation
- Must not be an ineligible (or special tax status) corporation
- Cannot be a member of an affiliated group of corporations[39]
- Must not have more than 35 shareholders
- Must have only individuals (other than nonresident aliens), estates, and certain kinds of trusts as shareholders
- Must issue only one class of stock

Typical Misconception

It is sometimes assumed that S corporations are subject to dollar limitations on the amount of sales, paid-in capital, or profits. In fact, there are no such limits and it is possible that an S corporation could have $1 or $2 billion of sales.

All of the above requirements must be met in order for the initial election to be made. Once an election is made, the requirements must be met on every day of each tax year that the S corporation election is in effect.

Additional Comment

The limitation of 35 shareholders corresponds to the private placement exemption under federal securities law.

Thirty-Five Shareholder Limitation. The 35 shareholder limitation is intended to restrict S corporation status principally to small, closely held corporations. Note, however, that there is no restriction upon the amount of an S corporation's assets or income. However, most large, publicly traded corporations have more than 35 shareholders and are not, therefore, eligible for S corporation treatment.

Under the 35 shareholder limitation, the termination occurs on the day preceding the date of the terminating event even if the defect is corrected prior to the end of the tax year. Special rules, however, permit the S corporation election to continue if an inadvertent termination occurs (i.e., the IRS must agree that the termination was inadvertent) and the taxpayer takes the necessary steps to restore its small business corporation status.[40]

The following operating rules apply to S corporations:

- A husband and wife (each owning stock individually or jointly) are treated as one shareholder.[41] This might create problems if a divorce results in a severance of the stock where both individuals continue their ownership interests because two shareholders rather than one shareholder result from the divorce.

---

[38] Sec. 1361(b)(1).

[39] An S corporation cannot generally own 80% or more of the stock of another corporation. Section 1361(c)(6) permits the ownership of stock of an inactive corporation as long as the affiliate has not begun business and has not produced gross income during the years in question. Corporations that maintain a special federal income tax status (e.g., financial institutions, U.S. possessions corporations, and Domestic International Sales Corporations) are also ineligible corporations.

[40] Sec. 1362(f).

[41] Sec. 1361(c)(1).

- If one spouse dies, the estate of the deceased spouse is not counted as an additional shareholder. Thus, the death of a spouse does not create problems if the estate distributes the stock to the surviving spouse. However, additional shareholders are created if the stock is distributed to heirs who do not already own any stock in the S corporation.

Example 15-27 ■

Self-Study Question

At any one time, how many different individuals could be shareholders in a single S corporation?

Answer

There could be as many as 70 shareholders in the case of 35 married couples.

Adobe Corporation, a qualifying S corporation, has 35 shareholders, including Brad and Bonnie, who are married and who are counted as one shareholder. Brad dies and his stock is willed to his two children, who do not already own stock in Adobe. Prior to the distribution of the stock from the estate, the estate and Bonnie are counted as one shareholder, and the S corporation remains qualified under the 35 shareholder limitation. The S corporation is disqualified when the stock is distributed to the two children, because the S corporation then has 36 shareholders. ■

Type of Shareholder Restrictions. A qualifying shareholder must be an individual (other than a nonresident alien), estate, or qualifying trusts (i.e., voting trusts, Sec. 678 grantor trusts, and qualified Subchapter S trusts).[42] Thus, a C corporation or a partnership may *not* own stock in the S corporation. If a C corporation or partnership were permitted to own stock, the 35 shareholder limitation could easily be avoided through indirect ownership of the S corporation stock by another corporation or partnership.

One Class of Stock Restriction. An S corporation can have only one class of stock outstanding. These shares of stock must have identical rights to share in the profits and the assets of the corporation. Note that both voting and nonvoting common stock can be issued without violating this requirement because differences in voting rights are ignored in classifying stock. This requirement is intended to simplify the tax problems that otherwise result from determining the shareholders who should be subject to tax from the corporate income flowing through to its shareholders.

The requirement for one class of stock has been particularly troublesome for taxpayers because if an S corporation is thinly capitalized (i.e., significant amounts of debt exist in the capital structure), the debt may in fact be equity and represent a second class of stock. In an attempt to reduce the uncertainty regarding the second class of stock issue, a safe-harbor rule was added in 1982. This rule provides that straight debt shall not be treated as a second class of stock if it meets the safe harbor requirements.[43] To qualify as straight debt, the interest rate cannot be contingent on profits, the debt cannot be convertible into stock, and the creditor must be a person who is otherwise eligible to be an S corporation shareholder.[44]

The Treasury Department has issued final regulations providing that a corporation is treated as having only one class of stock if all outstanding shares of stock confer identical rights to distribution and liquidation proceeds. This test is determined based on the corporate charter, articles of incorporation, bylaws, applicable state law, and any binding agreements relating to distribution or liquidation proceeds.[45] The Regulations provide certain safe harbors or exceptions for ordinary business arrangements entered into by S corporations and their shareholders (e.g., buy-sell or stock redemption agreements and most call options conferred with the stock are disregarded for purposes of determining whether a corporation has more than one class of stock).

---

[42] Secs. 1361(c)(2) and (d). See Chapter 11 of the *Prentice Hall's Federal Taxation: Corporations, Partnerships, Estates, and Trusts* text for a discussion of these trusts.

[43] Sec. 1361(c)(5).

[44] The interest rate may, however, vary with the prime rate or a similar factor unrelated to the debtor corporation.

[45] Reg. Sec. 1.1361-1(l).

Example 15-28 ■ Dale is the sole owner of an S corporation. For estate tax planning purposes, Dale desires to make gifts of certain shares of the corporation's stock to his children while still retaining control over the company. S corporation common stock with limited or no voting rights may be issued to Dale, who subsequently makes gifts of this stock to his children without disqualifying the S corporation status. ■

Election Requirements

All of the shareholders who own stock on the date the S corporation election is filed must consent to the election to be taxed as an S corporation.[46] The election and consent are filed with the IRS on Form 2553 (Election by a Small Business Corporation). If the stock is jointly owned, both joint owners must sign the consent form. The consent of a minor shareholder can be made by the minor or by the legal or natural guardian. If the stock is gifted under the Uniform Gifts to Minors Act, the custodian may file the consent form if he is the minor's legal or natural guardian. Persons who are shareholders during any part of the tax year preceding the date the election is made must consent to the election even though they are not shareholders on the election date.[47] It would be unfair to require less than 100% consent of the shareholders owning stock prior to the election date because the consequences of the election are that income will flow through and be taxed to all persons who are shareholders at any time during the tax year if the election is made.

A corporation may make the election in the tax year preceding the election year or on or before the fifteenth day of the third month of the election year. An election after the fifteenth day of the third month of the election year is treated as made for the next tax year.

Example 15-29 ■ Circle Corporation is a C corporation that uses the calendar year as its tax year. To file an S corporation election for 1994, the election may be filed anytime in 1993 or during the period that starts on January 1, 1994, and ends on March 15, 1994. If Circle Corporation makes the election on March 31, 1994, the corporation remains a C corporation in 1994 and becomes an S corporation in 1995. Once an S corporation election is made, it remains in effect until the S corporation status is either voluntarily or involuntarily revoked. ■

Termination Conditions

Revocation of S Corporation Status. An S corporation election may be terminated either voluntarily by the shareholders or involuntarily if the corporation fails to continue to meet the requirements for a small business corporation (e.g., if on any day in any year the S corporation has more than 35 shareholders or a second class of stock is issued). Voluntary revocation is permitted if consents are obtained from individuals who own more than 50% of the corporation's stock.[48]

GENERAL EFFECTIVE DATE. Under the general rules, a revocation is effective for the entire tax year if a statement is filed by the corporation on or before the fifteenth day of the third month of the tax year. If the revocation is filed after this date (e.g., after March 15 for a calendar-year S corporation), the effective date is the first day of the next tax year.

Example 15-30 ■ Individuals who own more than 50% of the stock of a qualifying calendar-year S corporation consent to a voluntary revocation statement filed by the corporation on

Additional Comment

Because of the new higher individual income tax rates in the Revenue Reconciliation Act of 1993, the S corporation election and continued status may be less favorable than under prior law.

Key Point

An election to be taxed as an S corporation becomes effective only as of the beginning of a tax year, but a termination can become effective before the end of the normal tax year.

---

[46] Sec. 1362(a)(2).
[47] Sec. 1362(b)(2).
[48] Sec. 1362(d)(1)(B).

March 12, 1994. Because the revocation is filed in the first 2½ months of the corporation's tax year, the corporation is taxed as a C corporation for all of 1994. If the consent is not filed until March 18, 1994, the corporation continues to be taxed as an S corporation during 1994 and its special tax status is revoked for 1995. ■

SPECIFIED TERMINATION DATE. An exception is provided when the corporation and its shareholders specify a prospective termination date. In this case the revocation takes effect as of the specified date. If a prospective date is specified that is other than the first day of a tax year, the revocation results in a short tax year for the final S corporation return and a short tax year for the initial C corporation return. In such a case, the income or loss is allocated among the two short years on a prorated daily basis.

Example 15-31 ■   Assume the same facts as in Example 15-30, except that a prospective termination date of July 1, 1994, is specified. The termination is effective as of this date regardless of whether the consent is filed before or after March 15. Thus, an S corporation short-period return is filed for the period January 1, through June 30, 1994, and a C corporation short-period return is filed for the period July 1 through December 31, 1994. The income or loss is prorated to each return on a daily basis.[49]   ■

Involuntary Revocations and Inadvertant Terminations. An S corporation may involuntarily lose its special tax status and revert to a C corporation if it fails to meet the small business corporation requirements or if it has excessive amounts of passive (investment) income for each year in a three-year period (i.e., more than 25% of gross receipts).[50] However, if the IRS deems that the termination was inadvertant, and the S corporation or its shareholders take the necessary steps within a reasonable time period to restore its small business corporation status, the S corporation status is considered to have been continuously in effect.[51]

Example 15-32 ■   A calendar-year S corporation adds a thirty-sixth shareholder on June 4, 1994. The S corporation status terminates on June 3, 1994. A short-period S corporation return is filed for the period January 1, 1994, through June 3, 1994, and a C corporation return is filed for the period from June 4, 1994, through December 31, 1994. Income or loss is prorated to the two tax returns on a daily basis.   ■

Example 15-33 ■   Assume the same facts as in Example 15-32 except that the termination is deemed to be inadvertant and the violation of the thirty-five shareholder requirement is corrected within a reasonable time period. The S corporation status is considered to have been continuously in effect and no C corporation return is required.   ■

The S corporation qualification, election, and termination rules are summarized in Topic Review 15-4.

---

[49] Sec. 1362(e)(1). The first day of the C corporation tax year is the day on which the revocation occurs. A special election may be made to use the interim closing method (i.e., the books are closed as of the termination date) if all persons who are shareholders during the S corporation tax year consent to this method.

[50] The passive income restrictions apply solely to S corporations that were previously taxed as C corporations in pre-election years and have accumulated Subchapter C earnings and profits from those years on the last day of 3 consecutive S corporation tax years. Thus, a corporation that elects S corporation status in its initial tax year is not subject to the restrictions. If the restrictions apply and the S corporation has passive income in excess of 25% of its gross receipts for 3 consecutive years, the S corporation election is automatically terminated at the beginning of the fourth year. In addition, a penalty tax equal to 35% of the corporation's excess net passive income is imposed during each year of the 3-year period.

[51] Sec. 1362(f).

TOPIC REVIEW 15-4

S Corporation Qualification, Election, and Termination Rules

Qualification requirements:

- An S corporation must be a domestic corporation.
- A maximum of 35 shareholders; a husband and wife count as one shareholder, and each beneficiary of a qualifying trust is a separate shareholder.
- Only individuals (citizens or resident aliens), estates, and certain kinds of trusts can be shareholders. No corporate or partnership shareholders are permitted.
- Only one class of stock may be issued and outstanding.
- An S corporation may not be a member of an affiliated group of corporations and certain corporations that maintain special tax statuses are ineligible.

Election requirements:

- All shareholders on the S election date must consent and the corporation must file Form 2553. The S election and consent form must be filed on or before the fifteenth day of the third month of the election year.

Termination rules:

- To effect a voluntary revocation, consent must be obtained from individuals who own more than 50% of the S corporation's stock. The revocation is effective for the entire year if it is made on or before the fifteenth day of the third month of the tax year. Otherwise, the termination is effective the first day of the next tax year unless a prospective termination date is specified.
- An involuntary revocation takes place if the S corporation fails to meet any of the small business corporation requirements (e.g., more than 35 shareholders) or it has excessive amounts of passive investment income in a 3-year period (i.e., more than 25% of gross receipts are passive investment income) and it has Subchapter C earnings and profits at the end of each of the three tax years. If the involuntary termination is deemed to be inadvertent, the S corporation status is considered to have been continuously in effect.

S Corporation Operations

OBJECTIVE 5
Discuss the operating rules for S corporations

Income, gain, loss, deduction, and credit items pass through to the S corporation shareholders in a manner similar to the partnership rules. A two-stage process is employed. It is first necessary to identify separately stated items that do not lose their identity as they are reported on the shareholder's tax returns. Such items are reported on Schedule K (see Appendix B) of Form 1120S. Some of the more frequently encountered separately stated items include:

- Short-term and long-term capital gains and losses
- Sec. 1231 gains and losses
- Charitable contributions
- Credits
- Interest on investment indebtedness (see Chapter 7 for a discussion of this item)
- Tax preference items
- Foreign taxes paid or accrued
- Dividend and other portfolio income

Additional Comment

Some states do not recognize the S corporation election for state income tax purposes which will result in the payment of state income taxes by the S corporation.

Additional Comment

An extensive list of additional separately stated items can be found in Reg. Sec. 1.702-1.

(See Table 15-1 for the treatment of comparable items for a partnership.) These separately stated items must be eliminated from the computation of ordinary income (or loss) because each item affects the tax returns of the various shareholders differently, depending upon their particular tax situation. The residual income or loss amount (i.e., the amount remaining after removing the separately stated items) represents the S corporation's ordinary income (or loss) which passes through to the shareholders as of the last day of the S corporation's tax year.[52]

The tax treatment of particular S corporation items is similar to that for C corporations. S corporations are entitled to amortize organizational expenditures over a period of at least 60 months under the general corporate taxation rules. However, S corporations are not entitled to other corporate deductions such as the 70% or 80% dividends-received deduction under Sec. 243 or the net operating loss deduction permitted under Sec. 172, because dividends and net operating losses are passed directly through to the S corporation's shareholders.

Example 15-34 ■

Ajax Corporation, an electing S corporation owned equally by Linda and Hal, reports the following operating results for the current year:

Sales	$10,000
Minus: Cost of goods sold	(2,000)
Gross profit	$8,000
Long-term capital gains	3,000
Total income	$11,000
Minus: Administrative expenses	(500)
Repairs	(500)
Sec. 1231 losses	(1,000)
Charitable contributions	(1,000)
Net income per books	$ 8,000

The individual items are reported on the S corporation tax return as follows:

	Ordinary Income (Page 1 of Form 1120S)	Separately Stated Items (Schedules K and K-1)
Sales	$10,000	
Long-term capital gains		$ 3,000
Cost of goods sold	(2,000)	
Administrative expenses	(500)	
Repairs	(500)	
Sec. 1231 losses		(1,000)
Charitable contributions		(1,000)
	$ 7,000	

Linda and Hal each report $3,500 of ordinary income plus 50% of each separately stated item on their individual tax returns. ■

Income, gains, losses, deductions, credits, and other separately stated items are allocated to the shareholders based on the number of shares of stock owned on each day of the S corporation's tax year. Thus, if the S corporation stock is disposed of

[52] Sec. 1363.

during the year, the ordinary income (or loss) and the separately stated items are allocated on a daily basis to the seller and purchaser of the stock.[53]

Example 15-35 ■   Assume the same facts as in Example 15-34, except that Linda sells her stock to Marc on the 181st day of the tax year. Income through the day preceding the date of the transfer is allocated to Linda. Only $1,726 (0.50 × [180 ÷ 365] × $7,000) of the ordinary income and a similar portion of each separately stated item would be reported by Linda. The ordinary income and separately stated items attributable to Linda's one-half interest for the remainder of the year are reported by Marc. The sale does not effect Hal's reporting of his share of the income.   ■

Basis Adjustments to S Corporation Stock

A shareholder's original basis for the S corporation stock is generally either (1) the amount paid for the stock or (2) a substituted basis from a nontaxable transaction (e.g., a Sec. 351 tax-free incorporation transaction).[54] Adjustments are subsequently made for ordinary income (or loss) and separately stated items that flow through to the shareholders, additional capital contributions, and distributions to the shareholders.[55]

Example 15-36 ■   Juan acquires 100 shares of Allied Corporation stock during the current year for $40,000. Allied Corporation is a qualifying calendar-year S corporation. Juan's share of Allied's current year ordinary income is $10,000. In addition, his share of the separately stated items includes $4,000 of long-term capital gains and $2,000 of Sec. 1231 losses. Allied Corporation also distributes $5,000 cash to Juan on November 9. Juan's basis in the S corporation stock at December 31 is computed as follows:

Original purchase cost		$40,000
Plus:	Share of ordinary income	10,000
	Share of long-term capital gains	4,000
Minus:	Share of Sec. 1231 losses	(2,000)
	Cash distribution to Juan	(5,000)
Basis of stock at December 31		$47,000

■

The logic behind these basis adjustments can be explained by differentiating between the conduit and entity concepts. For example, C corporations are taxable as separate entities. Thus, corporate earnings are taxed at the corporate level, and no adjustments are, therefore, made to a shareholder's C corporation stock basis when amounts are earned by the corporation. The S corporation's shareholders would be subject to double taxation if the basis adjustments were not allowed, because all corporate earnings (distributed and undistributed) flow through and are taxed to the individual shareholders on an annual basis.

Example 15-37 ■   Mary is the sole shareholder of Apple Corporation, an electing S corporation. Mary originally contributed $100,000 to the newly formed company. The funds were used

[53] If a special election is made under Sec. 1377(a)(2), the income is allocated according to the accounting methods employed by the S corporation (instead of on a daily basis) when a shareholder terminates his interest during the tax year.

[54] The death or gift tax basis rules may also be used to determine the initial basis for S corporation stock.

[55] Sec. 1367.

to acquire various corporate assets. During the next 10 years, the corporation earned $900,000 of ordinary income and reinvested these earnings in corporate assets. After 10 years the stock is sold for $1,000,000 (its tax basis). Mary's gain on the sale of her stock is as follows:

	Basis Adjustments Provided for under the Tax Law	If No Basis Adjustments Were Permitted
Selling price of the stock	$1,000,000	$1,000,000
Minus: Original capital contribution	(100,000)	(100,000)
Share of ordinary income (taxed to Mary)	(900,000)	
Adjusted basis	($1,000,000)	($ 100,000)
Gain on sale	$ —0—	$ 900,000

The $900,000 of earnings would be taxed twice to Mary if the positive basis adjustments were not permitted under the S corporation rules. With a C corporation, the $900,000 of earnings would be taxed at the corporate level and not to Mary. However, Mary would have an eventual capital gain of $900,000 upon the sale of her stock at the end of the ten-year period. ■

S Corporation Losses and Limitations

OBJECTIVE 6

Describe the tax treatment of an S corporation's shareholders

Limitations on Loss Deductions. When a loss is reportable, the ordinary loss and any separately stated loss and deduction items of an S corporation are allocated among the shareholders based on the number of shares of stock owned on each day of the S corporation's tax year.[56] The last day of the S corporation's tax year determines when the shareholders report the loss.[57] (See page 15-31 for a discussion of tax year restrictions applicable to an S corporation.)

Example 15-38 ■

Adobe Corporation is an S corporation whose tax year ends on January 31, 1994. All of its shareholders report their taxes on a calendar year. Adobe reports a $100,000 ordinary loss for the 12-month period ending on January 31, 1994. This loss is reported by the shareholders on their calendar-year 1994 returns. ■

Real World Example

A shareholder's unsecured demand promissory note to the corporation that remained unpaid at the end of the corporation's tax year did not create basis against which losses would pass through. Rev. Rul. 81-187, 1981-2 C.B. 167.

A shareholder's deduction for ordinary losses and separately stated items cannot exceed his basis for the S corporation stock plus the basis for any shareholder loans made to the S corporation.[58] The following rules are applied when determining the deductibility of ordinary loss and separately-stated loss items:

• A positive basis adjustment is made for any ordinary income or separately stated income or gain items accruing during the year to the stock before the ordinary losses and separately stated loss and deduction items are used to reduce basis. However, losses pass through to shareholders before distributions, or other deduction and loss items incurred during the year are taken into account.[59]

---

[56] Sec. 1366(a)(1).

[57] The same rule is applied for the reporting of ordinary income and separately stated income and gain items.

[58] Sec. 1366(d)(1). The deductible loss is treated as a deduction for AGI on an individual shareholder's return. S corporation shareholders are also subject to special limitations on losses and deductions that are passed through by the S corporation (e.g., at-risk limitations under Sec. 465 and passive activity losses under Sec. 469 (see Chapter 11 of the *Prentice Hall's Federal Taxation: Corporations, Partnerships, Estates, & Trusts* text for a discussion of these additional limitations and the discussion on page 15-29 of this text.)

[59] Secs. 1366(d)(1)(A) and 1367(a)(2).

- The shareholder's loss pass-through is first used to reduce the basis of the shareholder's stock to zero.

- Any excess loss pass-through is then applied against the basis of the shareholder's loans to the corporation until the loan basis is reduced to zero.

- Any remaining loss pass-through is carried over by each shareholder and is deductible in a subsequent year when the shareholder again has basis in his stock or debt. The carryover period is indefinite but does not transfer to another taxpayer if the shareholder disposes of all of his stock or the shareholder dies. Furthermore, if the S corporation election is terminated, the loss must be utilized against any basis for the former S corporation's stock by the end of a 1-year post-termination transition period.

Typical Misconception

It is sometimes mistakenly thought that the carryover period for any unused losses is limited to 5 or 15 years. The carryover period is indefinite.

Example 15-39 ■

Matt owns 20% of the stock of an electing S corporation. His basis in the stock is $20,000 at the end of 1994 after adjustments are made for separately stated income and gain items. Matt also loans the S corporation $10,000. The S corporation incurs a $200,000 ordinary loss in 1994. Matt's share of the ordinary loss is $40,000 (0.20 × $200,000). Matt's deduction and carryover of the unused loss are as follows:

Basis in stock	$20,000
Minus: Ordinary loss applied against stock basis	(20,000)
Basis in stock after ordinary loss absorption	—0—
Basis in loan	$10,000
Minus: Ordinary loss applied against loan basis	(10,000)
Basis in loan after ordinary loss absorption	—0—
Share of ordinary loss	$40,000
Minus: Deduction in 1994 ($20,000 + $10,000)	(30,000)
Carryover of ordinary loss to 1995	$10,000

■

If a shareholder's basis is insufficient to absorb the entire amount of ordinary loss (and separately-stated loss and deduction items), the flow-through of each item is determined on a pro rata basis. For example, if a shareholder's basis is $5,000 and he has a $6,000 ordinary loss and a $4,000 capital loss, his total deduction is limited to $5,000. This consists of a $3,000 ([$6,000 ÷ $10,000] × $5,000) ordinary loss and a $2,000 ([$4,000 ÷ $10,000] × $5,000) capital loss. He also has a $3,000 ordinary loss and a $2,000 capital loss carryover.

Restoration of Basis. If a shareholder's basis in a loan made to the S corporation is reduced due to the utilization of a loss deduction, subsequent increases in basis due to income reported by the S corporation in a future year are initially applied to increase the basis of the loan until the basis reduction is fully restored. Any excess positive adjustment is then applied to increase the basis of the shareholder's stock.

Example 15-40 ■

Assume the same facts as in Example 15-39, except that in 1995 the S corporation's ordinary income is $140,000. Matt's share of the income is $28,000 (0.20 × $140,000). The $28,000 of income earned in 1995 permits Matt to deduct the $10,000 ordinary loss carryover from 1994. Next the basis of the loan is restored to its original $10,000 amount. Finally, the basis of Matt's stock is increased to $8,000 ($28,000 − [$10,000 + $10,000]). ■

If the loan basis is not fully restored, gain results when the loan is repaid. If the loan is in the form of a note, the repayment results in a capital gain being recognized because the note constitutes a capital asset.[60] However, ordinary income results if the loan is an unsecured advance.[61]

Passive Activity Loss Limitations. S corporations are subject to the passive activity loss limitations in the same manner as partnerships. Losses that are passed through to a shareholder who does not materially participate in the S corporation's business may not be deducted against that shareholder's other earned income or against portfolio income (e.g., dividends and interest). Such passive losses can only offset other passive activity income. S corporation shareholders who materially participate (i.e., participate on a regular, continuous, and substantial basis) can avoid the passive activity loss limitations. (See Chapter 8 for a detailed discussion of the passive activity loss limitations rules.)

The basic tax rules for S corporation shareholders are summarized in Topic Review 15-5.

Other S Corporation Considerations

Key Point

Another important difference between partnerships and S corporations involves the tax consequences of property distributions. An S corporation recognizes gain if it distributes appreciated property to its shareholders, but a partnership would not recognize gain.

Distributions of Cash and Property to Shareholders. A money or property distribution made by an S corporation to its shareholders is treated as a return of capital if the S corporation has no accumulated earnings and profits from pre-S corporation years.[62] As such, the money or FMV of the property distributed reduces the basis of the shareholders' S corporation stock. If distributions are made in excess of the shareholders' basis, the excess is treated as a capital gain.[63]

TOPIC REVIEW 15-5

Basic Tax Rules for S Corporation Shareholders
1. Reportable ordinary losses and separately stated loss and deduction items are allocated to shareholders on a per share per day basis.
2. The last day of the S corporation's tax year determines the year in which the shareholders report their share of income, gain, deductions, losses, credits, and other separately stated items.
3. Basis cannot be reduced below zero. A positive basis adjustment is made for any ordinary income or separately stated income or gain items before ordinary losses, separately stated loss and deduction items, and distributions are used to reduce basis.
4. Losses are initially used to reduce the shareholder's stock basis to zero. Any excess losses are then used to reduce the basis of shareholder loans.
5. Unused losses are suspended and carried over until the shareholder again has basis to absorb the losses.
6. Positive basis adjustments in subsequent years are initially applied to increase the shareholder's loan basis until fully restored. Any additional positive basis adjustments increase the basis of the shareholder's S corporation stock.

[60] Rev. Rul. 64-162, 1964-1 C.B. 304.

[61] Rev. Rul. 68-537, 1968-2 C.B. 372.

[62] The tax consequences of property distributions to shareholders are discussed in Chapter 11 of the *Prentice Hall's Federal Taxation: Corporations, Partnerships, Estates, and Trusts* text.

[63] Sec. 1368(b). The S corporation can also have an accumulated earnings and profits balance from a pre-1983 S corporation tax year or a tax year in which it was taxed as a C corporation. The tax consequences of a distribution made by an S corporation having an accumulated earnings and profits balance are more complex. These rules are beyond the scope of this text but are discussed in Chapter 11 of the *Prentice Hall's Federal Taxation: Corporations, Partnerships, Estates, and Trusts* text.

Gain is recognized by an S corporation if it distributes appreciated property to its shareholders.[64] The distribution is treated as if the property was sold to the shareholders at its FMV. The gain is then passed through to the shareholders whose basis for the property is its FMV.

Example 15-41 ■ Austin Corporation, an electing S corporation, distributes land (a capital asset) to its shareholders. The land has a $10,000 basis and a $90,000 FMV. An $80,000 capital gain is recognized by the S corporation and is passed through to its shareholders. The basis of the land to the shareholders is $90,000 (its FMV). ■

Tax Year Restrictions. The restrictions on S corporation tax years are similar to those that apply to partnerships. Thus, S corporations are required to use a calendar year unless a business purpose (i.e., a natural business year) can be established for choosing a fiscal year-end.[65] These year-end restrictions were enacted in 1986 to conform the S corporation rules with the partnership provisions and to prevent the deferral of the corporate income that is passed through to the shareholders for a period of up to 11 months (e.g., if a January 31 fiscal year-end was permitted under the tax law). Existing fiscal year S corporations may also continue to use the same fiscal year in effect in 1986 or use a tax year that results in a deferral of three months or less if an election is made to make annual required payments (see Chapter 11).

Additional Comment

For purposes of calculating which shareholders own more than 2% of the outstanding stock, the Sec. 318 attribution rules are applied.

Treatment of Fringe Benefits. Prior to 1983, S corporations and their shareholders received certain tax benefits that were more favorable than partnerships and sole proprietorships because owner-managers were treated as employees and were thus eligible for tax-favored corporate fringe benefits. Now, however, S corporation shareholders who own more than 2% of the outstanding stock are not eligible for tax-free corporate employee fringe benefits including the following:

- The group term life insurance exclusion under Sec. 79 for premiums paid for up to $50,000 coverage.

- The exclusion from income for premiums paid for accident and health insurance and medical reimbursement plans under Secs. 105 and 106.[66]

- The exclusion under Sec. 119 for meals and lodging furnished for the convenience of the employer

- The $5,000 death benefit exclusion under Sec. 101(b)

Example 15-42 ■ Bass Corporation is an electing S corporation. Health insurance and group term life insurance premiums are paid by the corporation for its employee-owner group, all of whom own more than 2% of the Bass stock. The premiums are included in the gross income of the owner-employees and are deductible by the S corporation. ■

Corporate Tax on Built-in Gains. A corporate tax on built-in gains applies only if the election to be taxed as an S corporation is made after 1986. However, the built-in gains tax does not generally apply to a corporation that has always been taxed as an S corporation.[67] When the Tax Reform Act of 1986 was being written, Congress was

---

[64] Sec. 311(b).

[65] Sec. 1378(b).

[66] Rev. Rul. 91-26, 1991-1 C.B. 184. The IRS ruled that amounts paid on behalf of partners and more-than-2% shareholder-employees for accident and health premiums that are related to services rendered are treated like guaranteed payments—that is, the amounts are deductible by both a partnership and an S corporation and are included in the partner's or shareholder's gross income.

[67] Sec. 1374(c). The built-in gains tax can also apply if an S corporation acquires assets in a tax-free transaction from a C corporation. These rules are discussed in greater detail in Chapter 11 of the *Prentice Hall's Federal Taxation: Corporations, Partnerships, Estates, and Trusts* text.

worried that C corporations would elect to be taxed as S corporations to avoid the new corporate rules that imposed a tax upon liquidating and nonliquidating distributions of appreciated property. Therefore, Congress imposed a new tax applying to asset dispositions made by an S corporation that was previously a C corporation. The tax is imposed on the net built-in gains that exists on the date the S corporation election becomes effective.[68] A built-in gain exists if the FMV of an asset is greater than its adjusted basis on the first day the S corporation election is effective. If an asset with a built-in gain is sold or exchanged within the 10-year period beginning on the effective date for the election, the built-in gain is taxed to the S corporation. The recognized built-in gain for the year is reduced by the recognized built-in loss for that year.[69]

The tax is imposed at a 35% rate times the lesser of the following: (1) the corporation's net built-in gains (recognized built-in gains minus built-in losses) for the tax year, or (2) the amount which would be its taxable income if it were a C corporation. Any net built-in gain that is not subject to tax because of the taxable income limitation is carried over to subsequent tax years. Any appreciation on the asset that occurs after conversion from a C corporation to an S corporation is subject to the regular S corporation pass-through rules, but is not taxed under the built-in gains tax. Any asset not held on the first day of the S corporation election period is also exempt from the built-in gains tax. The built-in gain tax that is paid by the S corporation ratably reduces the income or separately stated income items that trigger the tax.

Example 15-43 ■ Beach Corporation, an accrual method of accounting taxpayer incorporated in 1989, elects to be taxed as an S corporation on January 1, 1994, effective for 1994. On January 1, 1994, Beach has land with a $50,000 basis and a $200,000 FMV. There are no built-in losses when the S corporation election is made. If the land is sold before January 1, 2004, the built-in gains tax will be imposed on the $150,000 ($200,000 − $50,000) built-in gain as of January 1, 1994. If the land is sold in 1994 for $225,000, Beach Corporation reports a total gain of $175,000 ($225,000 − $50,000). The $150,000 is subject to the built-in gains tax, and the other $25,000 of post-conversion appreciation is subject to the regular S corporation pass-through rules and is not subject to the built-in gains tax. ■

Tax on Excess Net Passive Income. The excess net passive income tax is levied when (1) an S corporation has passive investment income for the tax year that exceeds 25% of its gross receipts and (2) at the close of the tax year the S corporation has Subchapter C E&P. The excess net passive income tax equals the S corporation's excess net passive income times the highest corporate tax rate (35% for 1994).[70]

The special tax reduces (on a pro rata basis) the passive income items that are passed through to shareholders.

Example 15-44 ■ Acorn Corporation made an S corporation last year after having been a C corporation for several years. Acorn has C corporation E&P at the end of the current year. During the current year Acorn's excess net passive income is $10,000. The excess net passive income tax is $3,500 ($10,000 × 0.35). The tax reduces (on a pro rata basis) the passive income items (e.g., dividends and interest) that are passed through to shareholders. ■

---

[68] Sec. 1374(a).

[69] A recognized built-in loss is any loss recognized on an asset disposition occurring during the recognition period unless an S corporation can establish that (1) the asset was not held by the S corporation as of the beginning of the first day of the first tax year to which the S corporation applies, or (2) the recognized loss exceeds the excess of the property's adjusted basis over its FMV on such day (see Sec. 1374(d)(4)).

[70] Sec. 1375(a). These rules are discussed in greater detail in Chapter 11 of the *Prentice Hall's Federal Taxation: Corporations, Partnerships, Estates, & Trusts* text.

TAX PLANNING CONSIDERATIONS

Utilization of Net Operating Losses

Frequently, the decision to select a particular form of business organization involves both tax and nontax issues. For example, the corporate form may be preferred due to the availability of nontax attributes such as limited liability, the relative freedom to transfer ownership interests, and the ability to raise outside equity capital.

In many instances, however, the tax attributes are predominant and the partnership or S corporation form may be preferred. If net operating losses (NOLs) are anticipated in the initial years of operation, the partnership form may be preferred to either the C corporation or the S corporation form of organization. In a C corporation, the operating losses are of no direct benefit to the shareholders and may be of no benefit if sufficient profits are not available in future years to offset the NOL carryovers.[71] In a partnership, the losses pass through to the partners up to the amount of their basis for the partnership interest. The basis of a partner's interest includes his share of the liabilities of the partnership (including accounts payable, notes payable, mortgages, etc.). This difference in basis rules between a partnership and an S corporation frequently results in the utilization of losses that would not otherwise be deductible for an S corporation due to the restrictions placed upon negative basis. In contrast, an S corporation's ability to pass through losses is limited to the shareholder's basis in the stock and any shareholder loans. Other S corporation liabilities are not included in determining the shareholder's loss limitation.

Example 15-45 ■ Mary and Marty are considering whether to operate a new business venture as a C corporation, S corporation, or a partnership. Mary and Marty plan to invest a total of $50,000 of equity and raise an additional $50,000 from outside creditors (e.g., accounts payable, mortgage, etc.). Initial losses are expected amounting to $20,000 per year for 5 years. If a C corporation is used, none of the corporate losses are deductible (i.e., the corporation has loss carryovers of $100,000 after the 5-year period). If an S corporation is formed, Mary and Marty will be able to deduct only $50,000 due to the exclusion of general corporate debt from determining the basis for the shareholder's investment. The remaining $50,000 loss will be carried forward indefinitely unless the shareholders choose to lend $50,000 of additional funds to the corporation (instead of borrowing these amounts from outside creditors) or make $50,000 of additional capital contributions. If a partnership is formed, Mary and Marty will be able to deduct the full $100,000 of losses because their basis includes the partnership's liabilities. Assuming Mary and Marty have sufficient other sources of income to absorb the losses, the value of these additional deductions in the first 5 years favors the partnership form of organization. ■

Self-Study Question

Under what conditions would capital be considered to be a material income-producing factor?

Answer

Capital is normally a material income-producing factor where the business requires substantial inventories, or a substantial investment in plant and equipment.

Comparison of Other Tax Attributes

Table 15-2 includes a comparison of tax attributes (other than losses that were previously discussed) for partnerships, S corporations, and C corporations.

Income Shifting Among Family Members

Subject to gift tax rules and restrictions, an attractive tax planning strategy is to shift income from higher tax bracket family members to children or others who are subject

---

[71] In a corporation, NOLs are carried back 3 years and forward 15 years. In a newly formed corporation, the carryback rules do not apply.

TABLE 15-2 *Comparison of Tax Attributes for Three Major Entity Forms*

	Partnership	S Corporation	C Corporation
Choice of tax year	Restricted to the tax year of the majority partners, principal partners or the least aggregate deferral year; A fiscal year may also be used if a business purpose (i.e., a natural business year) can be established. Fiscal year partnerships may continue to use their pre-1987 tax year or use a fiscal year that results in an income deferral of the lesser of the current deferral period or three months if an election is made to make required payments.	Restricted to a calendar year or a fiscal year that is identical to the same year of its shareholders who own a majority of the stock. Fiscal year restrictions similar to partnerships apply to S corporations.	No restrictions, except for personal service corporations
Tax rates	Individual progressive rates apply to noncorporate partners at 15%, 28%, 31%, 36%, or 39.6% depending on the income levels of the partners.	Individual tax rates apply; the S corporation can be taxed on built-in gains, and excess net passive income	Stair-step progressive rates from 15% to 34% on the first $10 million of taxable income and 35% above $10 million. The reduced tax rates are recaptured by using two surtaxes.
Double taxation	No double taxation because income, gain, deductions, losses, credits, etc. pass through to the partners	Same as for partnerships	Income taxed to the corporation when earned; a second tax is levied on dividends if the earnings are distributed to the shareholders
Ownership restrictions	None	35 shareholders; only individuals, estates, and certain trusts allowed	None
Treatment of special items (e.g., capital gains and losses, tax credits, tax preferences)	Conduit treatment is applied; each partner reports his individual share of such items	Same as for partnerships except for built-in gains tax and excess net passive income tax; not subject to the corporate alternative minimum tax	Corporations are subject to different rules regarding capital gains and losses, distributions to shareholders, corporate alternative minimum tax, etc.
Fringe benefits	Partners are not employees and not eligible for tax-free corporate fringe benefits (e.g., group term life insurance); accident and health insurance premiums paid by the partnership are treated as guaranteed payments to the partners.	Same as for partnerships for shareholders owning more than 2% of the stock	Corporate fringe benefits available as exclusions for employees and deductible by the corporation

Self-Study Question

Paul owns a business that produces $50,000 of annual profits. If the business were incorporated, it could justify the retention of all of its earnings and pay little or no dividends. Paul also has $100,000 of taxable income from other sources. Should Paul organize the business as an S corporation or as a C corporation?

Answer

Although there could be many factors involved, it is important to point out that Paul's income from the business could be taxed at a 39.6% rate if it is an S corporation. The rate of taxation on a C corporation is 15% on the first $50,000 of taxable income. Double taxation would result, however, if the profits were withdrawn as a dividend.

to lower tax rates. In an S corporation, parents may gift nonvoting common stock to their children age 14 and older (subject to the gift tax rules and restrictions). Thus, a portion of the S corporation income is taxed to the children even though the parents retain all voting rights for the corporate stock. A partnership interest may also be gifted to other family members. However, the IRS will not generally recognize the family member as a partner in a partnership where capital is a material income-producing factor unless the individual is the "real" owner of the interest and has dominion and control over it. In a service partnership (e.g., an accounting firm), the family member must provide vital or substantial services. If property is given to a child under age 14, the child's unearned income in excess of $1,200) is taxed at the parents' higher tax rate. Therefore, if S corporation stock or a partnership interest is given to a child under age 14, the child's share of the income from the S corporation or the partnership will generally be taxed to the child at the parents' highest marginal tax rate. Essentially, the tax planning technique of income shifting from higher tax bracket family members to children under age 14 no longer exists. These rules do not apply to children age 14 and older (see Chapter 2).

With an S corporation or a partnership, it is possible to employ family members (e.g., children) as employees. Thus, income may be shifted to the lower tax bracket family members. The under-age-14 rules discussed previously have no effect on earned income, even if derived from a parent's business. In a partnership and an S corporation, the IRS will reallocate income to reflect the realities of the value of the services and capital contributions if reasonable salaries are not paid.[72]

Example 15-46 ■

Paul, the sole owner of an electing S corporation, gifts 20% of the corporation's stock to his children age 14 and older. The S corporation's ordinary income is $100,000 after deducting a $10,000 salary paid to Paul. If a reasonable salary for Paul's services is $50,000, the IRS may reduce ordinary income to $60,000 ($100,000 − $40,000) and increase Paul's taxable compensation to $50,000. Thus, the share of income which passes through to the children is reduced from $20,000 (0.20 × $100,000) to $12,000 (0.20 × $60,000). ■

COMPLIANCE AND PROCEDURAL CONSIDERATIONS

Additional Comment

Most partnerships that have more than 10 partners must select a partner to serve as the tax matters partner. This partner will be in charge of administrative matters in the event of a partnership audit.

Partnership Filing Requirements and Elections

Partnerships must file Form 1065 on or before the fifteenth day of the fourth month following the close of the tax year (by April 15 for a calendar-year partnership). The IRS can allow reasonable extensions of time up to 6 months, although initial extensions are usually limited to 60 days. Penalties are imposed for failure to file a timely or complete partnership return.

Real World Example

Since a partnership reported its capital gain on a sale in one tax year rather than on the installment basis, the partners could not use the installment method since this is a partnership election. George Rothenberg, 48 T.C. 369 (1967).

Partnership Elections. Most elections affecting the computation of partnership income are made by the partnership. They include

- Selection of a tax year
- Selection of an overall accounting method
- Inventory valuation method
- Depreciation methods

[72] Secs. 1366(e) and 704(e).

- Amortization method for organization expenses
- Optional basis adjustments under Sec. 754

If an election must be made at the partnership level, it is binding on all partners.

Certain elections are made by each individual partner. The most-often encountered election is the election to take a credit or deduction for foreign income taxes.

Reporting Partnership Items on Form 1065

The partnership ordinary income and deduction items are reported on page 1 of Form 1065 (see Appendix B). Schedule K is used to summarize all of the partner's share of separately stated items (e.g., capital gains and losses, tax credits, and charitable contributions). Schedule K also includes guaranteed payments made to partners and the ordinary income or loss, even though both items are reported on page 1. A separate Schedule K-1 is then prepared for each partner. The Schedule K-1 represents *each* partner's share of the Schedule K items, depending upon the agreed ratio for sharing income, deduction, loss, and credit items. This schedule then becomes the primary input for the preparation of each partner's federal income tax return.

A partnership is also required to prepare a balance sheet (Schedule L) similar to the one reported on a C corporation return and a reconciliation of income per books with income per tax (Schedule M-1) and an analysis of capital accounts (Schedule M-2).

Optional Basis Adjustment Election under Sec. 754

Additional Comment

Section 754 is a lot like marriage—it is easier to get into than to get out of. The election may be revoked only with the approval of the District Director, and no application for revocation shall be approved when the purpose is primarily to avoid stepping down the basis of partnership assets.

A basis adjustment election under Sec. 754 is usually desirable for an incoming partner whose partnership interest cost more than the tax book value of his share of the partnership's assets. The excess amount is added to the new partner's basis for his interest in the partnership's assets. If a Sec. 754 election was made in a prior year, the election continues in effect and automatically applies to the current year. However, if the election was not previously made, all of the partners must agree to make the election because it is made at the partnership (rather than at the individual partner) level.

A Sec. 754 election may have adverse effects in subsequent years if the amount paid for a partnership interest is less than the book value of the partnership assets because a reduction in the basis of the partnership's assets is required. Also, if a liquidating distribution is made to a partner and results in a recognized loss, similar adverse tax consequences result from an existing Sec. 754 election. Therefore, before a sale is consummated, an incoming partner should attempt to obtain assurances from the remaining partners that the partnership will agree to make the election in the current year if the election is not already in effect. The election is made by attaching a statement to a timely filed tax return for the year the transaction occurs. A retroactive election cannot be made for prior years.[73]

S Corporation Filing Requirements and Accounting Method Elections

An S corporation must file its corporate tax return not later than the fifteenth day of the third month following the end of the tax year.[74] The S corporation reports its results on Form 1120 S (U.S. Income Tax Return for an S Corporation). Form 1120 S is included in Appendix B. An S corporation is allowed an automatic 6-month extension of time for filing its tax return by filing Form 7004 (Application for Automatic Extension of Time to File U.S. Corporation Income Tax Return) that is also included in Appendix B.

---

[73] Reg. Sec. 1.754-1(b).
[74] Sec. 6072(b).

The accounting method elections used to compute ordinary income or loss and the separately stated items are made by the S corporation rather than individual shareholders. As with a partnership, these elections are made independent of the accounting method elections made by its shareholders.

Reporting S Corporation Items on Form 1120S

Page 1 of Form 1120S is used to summarize the ordinary income and deduction items for the S corporation. If any tax is due at the corporate level due to the excess net passive income tax under Sec. 1375 or the built-in gains tax under Sec. 1374, such amounts are reported on page 1 of the return. Schedule K lists the separately stated items and the ordinary income or loss for the S corporation. A Schedule K-1 is then prepared for each shareholder reflecting their share of the ordinary income (loss) and separately stated items. The Schedule K-1 becomes the basis for preparing each shareholder's federal income tax return. The S corporation is also required to prepare a balance sheet (Schedule L) similar to the one reported on a C corporation return and a reconciliation of income per books with income (or loss) per tax (Schedule M-1).

PROBLEM MATERIALS

DISCUSSION QUESTIONS

15-1. Distinguish between the partnership, S corporation, and C corporation forms of organization regarding the following:
  a. Incidence of taxation upon the business income of the organization
  b. Taxation of distributions to owners
  c. Application of the conduit and separate entity concepts of taxation

15-2. Paula transfers the following assets to a partnership:
  a. Land with a $60,000 adjusted basis and a $100,000 FMV is exchanged for a 20% interest in partnership capital and profits
  b. A machine with a $50,000 adjusted basis and a $40,000 FMV. The partnership signs a note for $40,000 as consideration for the exchange.
  Explain whether gain or loss is recognized by Paula for either of these transactions and the reason for any difference in tax treatment.

15-3. Peggy agrees to act as a broker to arrange debt financing for the PQR Partnership. In exchange, the PQR Partnership offers the following alternative forms of compensation for the brokerage services rendered by Peggy:
  a. Peggy would receive a 25% interest in the partnership capital and profits having a $50,000 value.
  b. Peggy would receive a 20% interest in partnership profits only for the duration of the partnership. The interest in future profits has no readily determinable FMV.
  Discuss the tax implications to Peggy under each alternative.

15-4. In the current year, Penny contributes machinery (a Sec. 1231 property) that was acquired five years earlier and that has a $50,000 adjusted basis and an $80,000 FMV to a partnership in exchange for a partnership interest. What is Penny's basis and holding period for the partnership interest? Explain the reasons for the application of this rule in the tax law.

15-5. How is Mario's basis in his partnership interest affected by the following changes in partnership liabilities (assuming that he has a 50% interest in the partnership capital and profits)?
  a. Mario contributes a building with a $70,000 basis subject to a $50,000 mortgage which is assumed by the partnership.
  b. The partnership's accounts payable increase by $50,000 during the tax year.
  c. The partnership pays off a $50,000 bank note which was outstanding for several years.

15-6. What are the tax consequences to a partner who contributes both assets and liabilities to a partnership that has already incurred accounts payable and a mortgage? What happens if the liabilities are in excess of the basis of the assets transferred?

15-7. Why are certain special partnership income and deduction items (e.g., capital gains and losses, charitable contributions, etc.) reported separately on the Schedule K rather than being included in the determination of ordinary income on page 1 of Form 1065?

15-8. What inequities might result if partners were not required to make special allocations for pre-contribution gains and losses when a contribution of noncash properties is made to the partnership?

15-9. Indicate whether a partner's basis in the partnership interest increases (+), decreases (−) or is not affected (0) by the partner's share of the following operating items:
a. Ordinary income
b. Ordinary loss
c. Tax-exempt income
d. Capital losses
e. Charitable contributions made by the partnership
f. Distributions of property to the partners

15-10. Phyllis owns a 30% capital and profits interest in the PQR Partnership and has a $20,000 basis in her partnership interest (before adjustments are made for Phyllis's share of income or loss from the partnership). During the current year, the PQR Partnership reports a $100,000 ordinary loss and no change in partnership liabilities and Phyllis materially participates in the business.
a. What amount of the loss is deductible by Phyllis in the current year?
b. What is Phyllis's basis in her partnership interest at the end of the current year?
c. What happens to Phyllis's unused ordinary loss (if any)?

15-11. Ralph sells an asset to the RST Partnership at a loss. In which of the following situations is the loss recognized?
a. Ralph owns a 20% direct interest in the partnership, and his son also owns a 20% interest.
b. Ralph owns a 35% direct interest in the partnership, and his daughter also owns a 35% interest.
c. Ralph owns a 35% direct interest in the partnership, and his 100%-owned corporation also owns a 35% interest.

15-12. Jose owns a 60% capital and profits interest in the JKL Partnership. What are the amount and character of the recognized gain or loss in each of the following situations?
a. Jose sells a security (e.g., common stock) with a $1,000 adjusted basis and a $2,000 FMV to the partnership.
b. Jose sells a parcel of land held for investment with a $10,000 adjusted basis and a $20,000 FMV to the partnership.
c. Jose sells a building used in his business with a $100,000 adjusted basis and a $60,000 FMV to the partnership.

15-13. Ursula is a new partner who is to receive a 20% capital and profits interest in the UVW Partnership. The partnership's ordinary income before any guaranteed payments are made is $100,000. Ursula would prefer to receive her share of the partnership profits in the form of a guaranteed payment (rather than a percentage of the profits) because she needs a minimum level of income. What difference does it make to Ursula and to the other partners if Ursula receives a $20,000 guaranteed payment or a 20% interest in partnership profits?

15-14. Explain the circumstances that cause a partner to recognize gain or loss if money or other property is distributed in a nonliquidating partnership distribution.

15-15. Explain why a partner who sells his interest in the partnership for cash must include his share of the partnership liabilities in the amount realized from the sale.

15-16. What are the tax consequences to a partner who sells his partnership interest if the partnership has Sec. 751 assets (i.e., unrealized receivables or substantially appreciated inventory)?

15-17. What inequity might result if an incoming partner purchases a partnership interest for an amount in excess of their share of the book and tax basis of the partnership's net assets? Assume that no basis adjustment election is made under Sec. 754.

15-18. What are the tax consequences to an S corporation and to its shareholders if one of the requirements for a small business corporation is not met at some point in a tax year?

15-19. What are the major advantages and disadvantages of being an S corporation instead of a C corporation? Being a partnership instead of a C corporation?

15-20. An S corporation issues straight debt obligations to its shareholders. Is it possible for the debt to be treated as a second class of stock, which would terminate the S corporation election? Explain.

15-21. Andrew sells his Ajax Corporation stock to Angela on March 1. On March 15, Ajax Corporation elects to be taxed as an S corporation for the current year. Which shareholder(s) must consent to the election? Why?

15-22. An S corporation's shareholder wants to voluntarily revoke the S corporation election. What percentage of stock interests must agree to the revocation? When is the revocation first effective?

15-23. Under what conditions may an S corporation involuntarily lose its special tax status and revert to a C corporation? What remedies are available if the S corporation termination is deemed to be inadvertant?

15-24. Indicate whether the following items are reported on the tax return of an S corporation as part of ordinary income (or loss) or as a separately stated item:
   a. Repairs
   b. Long-term capital gains
   c. Short-term capital losses
   d. Sec. 1231 gains
   e. Tax credits
   f. Tax preference items

15-25. Explain why the basis of S corporation stock is reduced by the stockholder's share of the ordinary loss.

15-26. Anne's basis in her S corporation stock on January 1, 1994 is $10,000. On March 1, 1994, Anne also lends the corporation $8,000. Her share of the S corporation's ordinary loss for 1994 (which has not yet ended) is expected to be $28,000. Anne's marginal tax rate is expected to be 15% in 1994. She expects that her marginal tax rate will increase to 31% in 1995. Substantial profits are anticipated for the S corporation in 1995. Advise Anne regarding the deductibility of her share of the losses and the desirability of making additional capital contributions in either year.

15-27. Allied Corporation, an electing S corporation, is considering making a distribution of land (acquired three years earlier and held for investment) having a $60,000 adjusted basis and a $120,000 FMV to its sole shareholder. Explain the tax consequences to the corporation and to the shareholder if the land is distributed.

15-28. Barry and Bart are considering whether to start a new manufacturing business. Alternative forms of business organization being considered include operating as a partnership, an S corporation, or a C corporation. Barry and Bart are calendar-year taxpayers but would like to use a January 31 year-end for the business and to, therefore, obtain an 11-month deferral of the income. Discuss the implications, restrictions, etc. of operating under each alternative form of business organization being considered.

15-29. Assume the same facts as in Problem 15-28, except that Barry and Bart are instead considering the treatment of fringe benefits. Barry and Bart want to provide group term life insurance and accident and health insurance for themselves and their employees and plan to make the premium payments from business funds. Explain any restrictions that apply to each form of business organization.

15-30. Explain the circumstances when an S corporation is subject to taxation at the corporate level.

PROBLEMS

15-31. *Formation of a Partnership.* Becky, Beth, and Bob form the BBB Partnership and all of the partners have an equal share in the partnership capital, profits, and losses. Becky contributes cash of $100,000; Beth contributes land (acquired five years earlier and held for business use) with a $50,000 adjusted basis and a $100,000 FMV; and Bob contributes legal and brokerage services with a $100,000 value.

a. What are the amount and character of the gain or loss Beth must recognize on the land transfer to the partnership?

b. What are the amount and character of the income Bob must recognize due to the services he performed?

c. What is the basis of each individual's partnership interest?

d. Beth sells her partnership interest 4 months after it is acquired and recognizes a capital gain. Is the gain long-term or short-term? Explain.

15-32. *Formation of a Partnership.* Bonnie, Carlos, and Dale form the BCD Partnership, and all of the partners have an equal share in the capital, profits, and losses. Bonnie contributes land and a building with a $50,000 adjusted basis and a $200,000 FMV that is subject to a $100,000 mortgage assumed by the partnership. Carlos contributes cash of $100,000, and Dale contributes land (a capital asset) with a $200,000 adjusted basis and a $100,000 FMV. The building originally cost $200,000. Straight-line depreciation in the amount of $150,000 has been claimed on the building. Disregard the value of the land that was contributed by Bonnie. All assets have been held for more than one year.

a. What are the amount and character of Bonnie's recognized gain or loss on the transfer?

b. What is Bonnie's basis in her partnership interest?

c. What is Carlos's basis in his partnership interest?

d. What are the amount and character of Dale's recognized gain or loss on the transfer?

e. What is Dale's basis in his partnership interest?

f. What is the basis of the contributed properties to the BCD Partnership?

15-33. *Formation of a Partnership.* In the current year, Dana transfers to the DE Partnership land and a building having a $20,000 adjusted basis and an $80,000 FMV that is subject to a $70,000 mortgage. The building cost $100,000 when it was acquired by Dana in 1970 and has been depreciated using the straight-line method in the amount of $80,000. Dana receives a one-half interest in the partnership capital, profits, and losses. Disregard the value of any land that was contributed by Dana.

a. What are the amount and character of Dana's recognized gain or loss on the transfer?

b. What is Dana's basis in her partnership interest?

c. When does Dana's holding period for the partnership interest commence?

d. What is the basis of the contributed properties to the DE Partnership?

15-34. *Formation of a Partnership.* Dan contributes $10,000 to the newly formed DEF Partnership for a 10% interest in the partnership capital, profits, and losses. No liabilities are transferred to the partnership by any of the partners. During the partnership's first year, DEF borrows $100,000 from a bank and is liable for accounts payable amounting to $100,000 at the end of its tax year. The DEF Partnership incurs a $400,000 ordinary loss during the year.

a. How much of the ordinary loss is deductible by Dan on his individual return?

b. What is Dan's basis in his partnership interest at the end of the year?

c. How much of the loss (if any) is carried over to future years?

15-35. *Formation of a Partnership.* David contributes machinery having a $6,000 adjusted basis and a $10,000 FMV to the DE Partnership in exchange for a one-half interest in the capital, profits, and losses. Eric contributes furniture and fixtures with a $14,000 adjusted basis and a $10,000 FMV in exchange for his one-half interest in the partnership. Both properties were originally acquired three years earlier by David and Eric, and the transfers were made in the current year.

a. What are the amount and character of the gain or loss David and Eric must recognize on the transfers?

b. What are the bases of the properties to the DE Partnership?

c. When does the partnership's holding period commence for both properties?

d. How should the properties be recorded on the partnership's books under generally accepted accounting principles?

15-36. *Expenses of Forming a Partnership.* The ABC Partnership, a calendar-year entity, is formed on July 1 of the current year, and incurs the following expenditures on the date the partnership is formed:

Legal fees incident to the organization of the partnership	$3,000
Printing costs associated with the syndication of the partnership	6,000
Brokerage fees associated with underwriting efforts to sell limited partnership interests	5,000

    a. What is the appropriate tax treatment (i.e., capitalization, capitalization subject to amortization, or immediate expensing) for each of these items?

    b. How much amortization should be deducted for the current year?

15-37. *Pass Through of Income and Separately Stated Items.* Damien and Donna are partners in the DD Partnership. They share capital, profits, and losses equally. The partnership reports the following items on its Schedule K during the current year:

Ordinary loss	$10,000
Long-term capital gains	40,000
Guaranteed payments to Donna	20,000
Research and experimentation credit	4,000
Tax preferences	6,000

Damien's basis in his partnership interest is $80,000 at the beginning of the current year.
The DD Partnership liabilities increased by $20,000 during the current year.

    a. What amounts should be reported by Damien on his individual tax return as a result of the DD Partnership's activities?

    b. What is Damien's basis in his partnership interest after the adjustments are made for the Schedule K items?

15-38. *Special Allocations.* Ed contributes land (a capital asset) having an $80,000 adjusted basis and a $100,000 FMV and Gail contributes $100,000 cash to the EG Partnership. Ed and Gail each receive 50% interests in the partnership capital, profits, and losses. Two years later the partnership sells the land (still a capital asset) for $110,000. What are the amount and character of the EG Partnership's gain or loss? How much of EG's gain or loss is allocated to Ed? To Gail?

15-39. *Partnership Losses.* Alice and Bruce are equal partners in the calendar-year AB Partnership. On December 1 of the current year, Carl is admitted to the partnership by making a $100,000 cash contribution in exchange for a one-third interest in the partnership capital, profits, and losses. Alice and Bruce's partnership interests are each reduced to one-third. The partnership agreement is amended to provide that Carl will receive a retroactive allocation of one-third of all partnership profits and losses that are incurred for the entire year. The AB Partnership reports a $90,000 ordinary loss for the tax year ending on December 31. How much of the partnership's loss is allocated to Alice, Bruce, and Carl?

15-40. *Basis of a Partnership Interest.* Anita has a one-half interest in the profits, losses, and capital of the AB Partnership. Anita's basis in her interest at the beginning of the current year is $50,000. During the year the following events occur:

- Partnership liabilities increase by $50,000.
- Ordinary income of $60,000 is earned.
- Capital losses of $20,000 are incurred.
- Tax-exempt interest of $10,000 is earned.
- Anita withdraws $20,000 in cash.
- Anita contributes land having a $40,000 adjusted basis and a $100,000 FMV as an additional capital contribution without increasing her interest in AB's capital, profits (or losses).

What is Anita's basis in his partnership interest at the end of the current year?

15-41. *Partnership Losses and Basis.* Ken has a one-half interest in the profits, losses, and capital of the KL Partnership. His basis in the partnership interest at the end of 1994 (before deducting his share of the partnership losses) is $40,000. Ken also has a $50,000 loan to the partnership that is outstanding at the end of 1994. His share of the partnership's ordinary loss in 1994 is $180,000. In 1995, Ken makes a $50,000 additional capital contribution and the partnership's ordinary income is $100,000. Assume that there is no change in Ken's interest in the partnership as a result of the capital contribution.

a. How much ordinary loss can Ken deduct in 1994?

b. What is Ken's basis in his partnership interest at the end of 1994?

c. How much ordinary income or loss does Ken report in 1995?

d. What is Ken's basis in his partnership interest at the end of 1995?

15-42. *Transactions Between the Partners and the Partnership.* Kevin has a 30% interest in the capital, profits, and losses of the KLM Partnership. Louis (Kevin's son) also has a 30% interest in the capital, profits, and losses. The remaining 40% interest in capital, profits, and losses is owned by an individual unrelated to either Kevin or Louis. Kevin sells the following assets to the partnership during the year:

- Common stock having a $10,000 basis and a $20,000 FMV and selling price.
- Land having a $100,000 adjusted basis and a $60,000 FMV and selling price.
- Machine having a $50,000 adjusted basis and a $70,000 FMV and selling price. The original cost of the machine was $60,000, and $10,000 in MACRS depreciation allowances has been taken.

a. What are the amount and character of Kevin's recognized gain or loss on the sale of the common stock? the land? the machine?

b. What gain or loss would be recognized by the partnership if it sells the land 2 years later for $90,000?

15-43. *Guaranteed Payments.* Laura and Mark are equal partners in the LM Partnership. Laura receives a $30,000 guaranteed payment in the current year and withdraws $20,000 of her partnership capital in cash. Partnership ordinary income is $100,000 for the current year. What amounts must be included in Laura's income for the current year?

15-44. *Nonliquidating Distributions.* Lynn's basis in her partnership interest is $10,000 when she receives a nonliquidating distribution of $5,000 cash and land having a $6,000 adjusted basis and a $12,000 FMV.

a. What are the amount and character of the gain Lynn must recognize on the distribution?

b. What is Lynn's basis in the land?

c. What is Lynn's basis in his partnership interest after the distribution?

15-45. *Sale of a Partnership Interest.* The balance sheet of the ABC Partnership at November 30 of the current year is as follows:

	Adjusted Basis	FMV
Assets:		
Cash	$ 10,000	$ 10,000
Accounts receivable	20,000	20,000
Inventory	15,000	16,000
Land, buildings, and machinery	60,000	74,000[a]
Total	$105,000	$120,000
Liabilities and Capital:		
Accounts payable	$ 5,000	$ 5,000
Notes payable	10,000	10,000
Allen's Capital—⅓	30,000	35,000
Beth's Capital—⅓	30,000	35,000
Candace's Capital—⅓	30,000	35,000
Total	$105,000	$120,000

[a] Assume that $6,000 would be recaptured as ordinary income under Secs. 1245 and 1250 if the assets are sold.

All partners share equally in the profits, losses, and capital. Allen sells his partnership interest to an outsider on November 30 for $35,000. Allen's share of the partnership income for the eleven-month period ending on November 30 is $3,000, and his basis in the partnership interest is $38,000 (which includes Allen's share of the income and change in partnership liabilities for the period ending on November 30.

    a. What amount is realized by Allen on the sale?

    b. What are the amount and character of the gain or loss Allen must recognize on the sale?

15-46. *Reporting Partnership Income.* Rita, a calendar-year taxpayer, is an employee of the RST Partnership, which has an April 30 year-end. Rita is paid a salary of $3,000 per month for the period from January 1 to April 30, 1994. On May 1, she is admitted to the partnership and receives monthly drawings of $3,000 for the 12-month period ending on April 30, 1995. The drawings reflect her approximate share of the partnership income for the period from May 1, 1994, to April 30, 1995. On April 30, 1995, it is determined that Rita's share of the partnership ordinary income is $40,000.

    a. What amount of income is reported by Rita on her 1994 individual tax return?

    b. What amount of income is reported by Rita on her 1995 individual tax return?

15-47. *S Corporation Terminations.* Which of the following events will cause a termination of the S corporation election? When is the termination effective? (Assume that all other requirements for an S corporation election are met and that the termination is not inadvertant.)

    a. Best Corporation has 35 qualifying S corporation shareholders. Sam dies on October 13 and his stock is held by the estate at the end of the year.

    b. Assume the same facts as in Part a, except that the estate distributes the stock to Sam's child prior to the end of the tax year. Sam's child did not previously own any Best stock.

    c. Best Corporation issues nonvoting common stock to Susan's two children during the current year.

    d. Shareholders Susan, Ted, and Tim, who own 60% of the Best stock, file an election on October 1 to terminate the election as of this date.

15-48. *S Corporation Ordinary Income and Separately Stated Items.* The income statement for the Central Corporation, an electing S corporation, reflects the following:

Sales	$200,000
Cost of goods sold	(60,000)
Repair expense	(5,000)
Depreciation expense	(10,000)
Salary expense	(30,000)
Long-term capital losses	(10,000)
Charitable contributions	(5,000)
Sec. 1231 losses	(8,000)
Net income per books	$ 72,000

    a. What is Central's ordinary income (or loss) for the year?

    b. Which of the items above appear as separately stated items on the Schedule K?

    c. Carol owns 50% of Central's stock, having a $50,000 basis (before any of the items above are taken into account). What is Carol's adjusted basis for her stock after all adjustments are made for Carol's share of Central's ordinary income or loss and separately stated items?

15-49. *Basis of S Corporation Stock.* Cathy is a 50% shareholder of the City Corporation. City is an electing (calendar-year) S corporation. Cathy acquires her stock on January 1 of the current year for $50,000. In the current year, City reports the following results of operations, cash distributions, and salary payments:

Ordinary income allocable to Cathy	$30,000
Salary payments to Cathy	40,000
Long-term capital losses allocable to Cathy	5,000
Cash distributions to Cathy	10,000

    a. What is Cathy's basis in her stock at the end of the current year?

    b. What amounts should be included in Cathy's individual tax return for the current year?

15-50. *S Corporation Losses and Stock Basis.* Chris owns one-third of the stock of the Coastal Corporation, an electing S corporation and materially participates in the business. Coastal uses the calendar year as its tax year. On January 1 of the current year, Chris's basis in the stock is $25,000, and he has a $10,000 loan outstanding to the corporation. In the current year, Coastal Corporation reports a $180,000 ordinary loss.

a. What amount of loss can Chris deduct on his individual tax return?

b. What is Chris's basis in his stock and loan at December 31?

c. How much of the loss is carried forward to subsequent years?

15-51. *S Corporation Basis for Stock and Loans.* Because of earlier losses, Cindy has a zero basis in her S corporation stock and a zero basis in her $10,000 loan to the corporation. During the current year, Cindy acquires additional shares of the S corporation stock for $8,000, and her share of the S corporation income is $7,000.

a. What is Cindy's basis in her loan and stock on December 31?

b. What are the tax consequences to Cindy if her loan (secured by a note) is repaid in full on January 1 of the following year?

15-52. *S Corporation Distributions and Basis of Property.* Compact Corporation, an electing S corporation, distributes land used in its business to Clay, its sole shareholder. The land has an $80,000 adjusted basis and a $100,000 FMV. Clay's basis in the Compact stock which includes his share of ordinary income and separately stated items for the current year (other than any gains or losses recognized because of the distribution) is $150,000. Compact has always been an S corporation.

a. What are the tax consequences of the distribution to Compact Corporation and Clay?

b. What is the basis of the land to Clay?

15-53. *S Corporation Distributions and Basis of Stock.* Control Corporation distributes $10,000 cash to shareholder Craig whose basis in his stock is $8,000. Control Corporation is an electing S corporation and has always been an S corporation.

a. What are the tax consequences of the distribution (i.e., amount and character of income or gain to Control Corporation and Craig)?

b. What is Craig's basis in his stock immediately after the distribution?

15-54. *S Corporation Fringe Benefits.* Copper Corporation is formed in 1983 and immediately elects to be taxed as an S corporation. In 1994, the corporation pays the following insurance premiums for its employees:

Group-term life insurance for shareholder-employees all of whom own more than 2% of the stock	$3,000
Accident and health insurance premiums for shareholder-employees all of whom own more than 2% of the stock	5,000
Accident, health, and group term life insurance premiums for employees who are not shareholders	2,000

a. What tax consequences result from payment of the insurance premiums by Copper Corporation?

b. What are the tax consequences to the shareholder-employees and to the non-shareholder employees?

15-55. *S Corporation Built-in Gains Tax.* Delta Corporation made an S corporation election on January 1 of the current year. It had been a C corporation prior to the election since 1981. The corporation has the following operating results during the current year:

Ordinary income	$200,000
Long-term capital gains	130,000

The adjusted basis and FMV of the capital assets that were held on January 1 and sold during the current year were $200,000 and $300,000, respectively, as of the January 1 election date.

a. Is the Delta Corporation subject to the built-in gains tax under Sec. 1374? Explain.

b. What is the amount of corporate tax liability on the built-in gain (if applicable)?

c. How would your answers to Parts a and b change if Delta Corporation instead elected to be taxed as an S corporation as of December 31, 1986?

TAX FORM/RETURN PREPARATION PROBLEMS

15-56. The XYZ Partnership reports the following items during the current year:

Sales	$200,000
Cost of goods sold	100,000
Dividends	10,000
Salaries to employees	20,000
Guaranteed payments to partners	30,000
Net long-term capital gain	15,000
Net short-term capital gain	5,000
Repairs	3,000
MACRS depreciation	8,000
Charitable contributions	2,000
Research and experimentation credit	3,000
Payments to an IRA account for partners	4,000
Partner withdrawals	8,000

Compute ordinary income (or loss) by completing page 1 of Form 1065 and the Schedule K (Partners' Shares of Income, Credits, Deductions, etc.).

15-57. The Eagle Corporation, an electing S corporation, reports the following items during the current year:

Sales	$200,000
Cost of goods sold	100,000
Dividends	10,000
Officer salaries	20,000
Net short-term capital gain	2,000
Net long-term capital loss	1,000
Repairs	10,000
Depreciation	5,000
Sec. 1231 losses	15,000
Charitable contributions	8,000
Research and experimentation credit	4,000

Compute ordinary income (or loss) by completing page 1 of Form 1120S and Schedule K (Shareholders' Share of Income, Credits, Deductions, etc.).

CASE STUDY PROBLEM

15-58. Peggy, Phil, and Ralph each have unincorporated accounting practices and they wish to pool their resources and operate as a single business entity. Peggy owns a building that has appreciated in value since she purchased it eight years ago. They intend to use this building for their office. Other than the building, the other assets that they have are office and computer equipment and furniture, none of which is worth more than book value. They all have substantial outstanding accounts receivable with a zero basis because each individual uses the cash method of accounting. Each individual has substantial amounts of portfolio income (i.e., dividends and interest). Under the plan, accounts payable with a zero basis from the unincorporated accounting practices would be transferred to the new entity.

Each accountant has two or three employees each. They all agree that it is important to provide benefits to their employees such as group health insurance, group term life insurance and a retirement plan of some kind. Additionally, they wish to have their staff participate in the profits of the company and have some form of equity interest in the company.

Peggy, Phil, and Ralph use different computerized accounting and billing systems. They also have different documentation requirements for their client files. The computerized accounting records, billing records and client files will all have to be consolidated from three systems to one system. The conversion will take place over a period of time. For this reason, they anticipate losses for the first tax year.

Peggy, Phil, and Ralph have agreed that they want to operate as a conduit-type entity because they wish to avoid double taxation and they want to use the losses from the first year immediately. They have come to you for advice. Write a client memo comparing the pros and cons of operating the accounting practice as a partnership and an S corporation.

CASE STUDY PROBLEM—ETHICAL ISSUES

15-59. Dan is the owner of an S corporation which currently has 35 shareholders. In March of the current year, Dan sold some of his S corporation stock to each of his two adult children. In August, Dan redeemed the stock he sold because he is in the midst of a divorce and was, therefore, fearful of the consequences associated with giving voting rights of his business to his children. Dan informs you, his tax consultant, of the sale of stock and subsequent redemption. You explain to Dan that by selling the stock he created 37 shareholders between the months of March and August and that the S corporation election had been terminated on the day preceding the date the corporation had more than 35 shareholders. Dan tells you that there is no reason to inform the IRS of the termination because he bought back the stock within the year and the IRS would probably not discover the event. What are your responsibilities as a CPA under the SRTP rules as mandated by the AICPA concerning the S election termination? (See the caption entitled *Statements on Responsibilities in Tax Practice* in Chapter 1 for a discussion of these issues.) What advice can you offer Dan concerning reinstatement of the S election under the rules for inadvertent terminations?

TAX RESEARCH PROBLEMS

15-60. Sandee is an employee of the Beach Group, an organization active in the Florida real estate industry. Sandee performs the task of finding real estate properties on Miami Beach and subsequently organizing partnerships to acquire and finance the properties. Sandee was particularly interested in one building in the Art Deco district that was to be purchased and renovated. She gathered interested investors who formed the Deco Partnership, consisting of two general partners and several limited partners. In exchange for her services in organizing the partnership, Sandee received a 3% limited partnership interest in the profits of the Deco Partnership. As part of the agreement, the profits interest was only transferable at the discretion of the general partners. Based on the uncertainty in the South Florida real estate industry at the time, the partners could not estimate whether profits or losses would be generated when the renovation was completed in three years. Based on these facts, will Sandee's receipt of the limited partnership interest be a taxable event?

A partial list of research sources include:

- Sec. 721.
- Reg. Sec. 1.721-1(a).
- *William G. Campbell v. CIR,* 68 AFTR 2d 91-5425, 91-2 USTC ¶ 50,420 (8th Cir., 1991).
- *Sol Diamond v. CIR,* 33 AFTR 2d 74-852, 74-1 USTC ¶ 9306 (7th Cir., 1974).
- Rev. Proc. 93-27, I.R.B. 1993-24, 63.

15-61. Chuck, Cindy, and Clay are the three equal owners of common stock in the Able Corporation incorporated in the current year. Able elects to be taxed as an S Corporation starting in its initial year. Chuck, Cindy, and Clay each contributed $10,000 cash to Able Corporation in exchange for their common stock. Able borrows $60,000 from a bank which was personally guaranteed by Chuck, Cindy, and Clay. In the current year, Able Corporation suffers a $90,000 ordinary loss. How much of the loss will be deductible by Chuck, Cindy, and Clay? (Assume that the at-risk and passive activity loss limitation rules do not apply).

A partial list of research sources is

- Sec. 1366(d)(1).
- *Estate of Daniel Leavitt v. CIR,* 63 AFTR 2d 89-1437, 89-1 USTC ¶ 9332 (4th Cir., 1989).
- *Edward M. Selfe v. U.S.,* 57 AFTR 2d 86-464, 86-1 USTC ¶ 9115 (11th Cir., 1986).

16

Corporations

LEARNING OBJECTIVES

After studying this chapter, you should be able to

1. Describe the corporate form and its characteristics
2. Calculate the corporate income tax liability and explain specific tax rules
3. Discuss the nonrecognition of gain or loss rules for corporate formations
4. Understand the significance of earnings and profits
5. Describe the consequences of distributions and stock redemptions
6. Understand the consequences of a corporate liquidation to shareholders and the liquidating corporation

Additional Comment

In 1990 there were 3.7 million corporation income tax returns filed of which 1.9 million reported taxable income.

The purpose of this chapter is to provide an introduction to the complex tax provisions which apply to C corporations. Detailed coverage of these rules is reserved for the companion volume to the text entitled *Prentice Hall's Federal Taxation: Corporations, Partnerships, Estates, and Trusts.*

A C corporation is a separate taxpaying entity. Thus, its income is subject to an initial tax at the corporate level. Its shareholders are subject to a second tax if dividends are paid from the corporation's earnings and profits. C corporations are also subject to numerous tax provisions that do not apply to unincorporated businesses or S corporations.

CORPORATE TAX STRUCTURE COMPARED WITH OTHER FORMS OF BUSINESS ORGANIZATIONS

OBJECTIVE 1

Describe the corporate form and its characteristics

Business activities may be conducted in corporate form, or a small business may choose to operate as a sole proprietorship. Two or more proprietors may decide to combine their businesses and form a partnership or incorporate their businesses. If the business is operated in corporate form, the S corporation election may be a desirable alternative. Table 16-1 summarizes the general attributes for each particular form of business organization. (See Chapter 15 for a detailed discussion of partnerships and S corporations.)

DEFINITION OF A CORPORATION

A business that is incorporated under state law may, nevertheless, be disregarded under the federal income tax law if the corporation does not possess more corporate characteristics than noncorporate characteristics. Conversely, a partnership may be treated as a corporation for federal income tax purposes if it possesses a predominance of corporate attributes.

TABLE 16-1 General Tax Structure—Alternative Forms of Business Organizations

Attributes	Sole Proprietorship	Partnership	S Corporation	C Corporation
Application of the separate entity versus the conduit (flow-through) concepts	Conduit: The individual who owns the proprietorship reports all items of income, expense, loss and credit on his individual return.	Modified conduit: The partners report their distributive share of partnership ordinary income and separately stated items on their individual returns. Most elections, such as depreciation methods, accounting period and methods, are made at the partnership level.	Modified conduit: Similar to the partnership form of organization. However, the S corporation may be subject to tax at the corporate level on excess net passive income and built-in gains under special circumstances.	Entity: The corporation is treated as a separate taxpaying entity. If income is distributed to shareholders as a dividend, the shareholders are subject to a second tax levy on such amounts.
Income tax rates	Tax rates applicable to individuals of 15%, 28%, and 31% are levied on the income from the business.	Same as a sole proprietorship for partners who are individuals.	Same as a sole proprietorship except for situations where a special corporate tax applies to the S corporation.	15% on the first $50,000; 25% from $50,000 to $75,000; 34% from $75,000 to $10 million. A 5 percentage point surtax (39% rate) applies to taxable income from $100,000 to $335,000. A 35% rate applies to taxable income in excess of $10 million. A 3 percentage point surtax (38% rate) applies to taxable income from $15 million to $18,333,333. A flat 35% rate applies to corporations with taxable income in excess of $18,333,333. Personal service corporations are subject to a 35% rate on all amounts of taxable income.

TABLE 16-1 *General Tax Structure—Alternative Forms of Business Organizations (cont'd)*

Attributes	Sole Proprietorship	Partnership	S Corporation	C Corporation
Nontax factors	A sole proprietor has noncorporate attributes such as unlimited liability for business debts, management continuity problems, and difficulty raising outside capital.	Partnerships have non-corporate attributes such as unlimited liability, management continuity problems, and restrictions upon the transfer of partnership interests. It may be difficult to raise additional external capital unless additional general or limited partners are admitted.	S corporations have the same attributes as C corporations (e.g., continuity of life, centralized management, limited liability, and free transferability of interests). Problems may arise if the state income tax law does not recognize the conduit form of taxation and taxes the S corporation as a C corporation.	Corporations possess certain attributes referred to in the S corporation discussion which may outweigh the disadvantages of double taxation under the corporate tax structure. The corporate form may be a greater administrative burden than a proprietorship or a partnership, however, due to additional record-keeping and tax compliance requirements.
Employment-related tax considerations	A sole proprietor is not considered an employee of the business and must pay self-employment taxes on the earnings from the business. Corporate fringe benefits such as group term life insurance are not available.	Same as a sole proprietor.	Corporate fringe benefits are generally not available to S corporation shareholders owning more than 2% of the stock. S corporation shareholders may be treated as employees, however, for social security tax purposes if a salary is paid.	An owner-employee may be treated as an employee for social security tax and corporate fringe benefit purposes. The corporate qualified pension and profit-sharing benefits available to owner-employees are comparable to the plan benefits for self-employed individuals (e.g., partners and sole proprietors).

Additional Comment

Under the Revenue Act of 1987, most publicly traded partnerships are taxed as corporations unless they were in existence on December 17, 1987, in which case they will not be taxed as corporations until 1998.

In the majority of incorporated or unincorporated business situations, the IRS does not attempt to disregard or collapse the existing corporate or unincorporated business structure. Principally, problems have arisen when the IRS has attempted to tax personal-service corporations (e.g., an incorporated medical practice) as partnerships and when the IRS has attempted to treat the limited partnership as a corporation.[1]

The Regulations list the following corporate characteristics:

- Associates (i.e., shareholders or partners)
- A joint profit motive
- Continuity of life
- Centralization of management
- Limited liability for the entity's debts
- Free transferability of ownership interests[2]

An unincorporated business will not be reclassified as an association and thus taxable as a corporation unless it possesses more corporate than noncorporate characteristics. Since the first two characteristics are common to both corporations and partnerships, a partnership must possess at least three out of the last four corporate characteristics to be reclassified as an association (i.e., to be taxable as a corporation).

Example 16-1 ■ The XYZ Limited Partnership has an agreement providing that the partners may not transfer their partnership interests to another without prior approval of the partnership. The partnership agreement also provides restrictions upon the continuity of life of the partnership if the general partner either dies or retires. Restrictions upon the transfer of partnership interests and continuity of life for the partnership are consistent with being a partnership. Thus, even if the last two corporate characteristics (centralized management and limited liability) are present, the partnership is not reclassified as an association (taxable as a corporation) because at least three of the four corporate characteristics must exist in the partnership for such a reclassification to occur. ■

SIMILARITIES AND DIFFERENCES BETWEEN CORPORATIONS AND INDIVIDUALS

Key Point

Many of the provisions relating to the determination of business income previously examined in this book apply to corporations as well as individuals.

Similarities

The computation of taxable income for a C corporation is similar to the computation of taxable income for an unincorporated business operating as a sole proprietorship. For example, corporations are permitted to deduct ordinary and necessary business expenses under Sec. 162 and may exclude items such as tax-exempt interest and life insurance proceeds from gross income. Corporations are also allowed to deduct

---

[1] *U.S. v. Arthur R. Kintner*, 46 AFTR 995, 54-2 USTC ¶ 9626 (9th Cir., 1954).
[2] Reg. Sec. 301.7701-2(a)(1).

interest, depreciation, and other business-related expenses in a manner similar to unincorporated taxpayers.

Differences

One of the principal differences in computing taxable income for a corporation compared with an individual is that personal, consumption-type expenditures and exemptions apply solely to individuals. Certain specific differences should be noted before discussing the corporate provisions in greater detail:

- A corporation may not deduct personal-use expenditures. Therefore, the term *adjusted gross income* (AGI) only applies to individuals.
- A corporation is not permitted to use the standard deduction or deduct personal and dependency exemptions.
- Corporations receive a dividends-received deduction of 70%, 80%, or 100% for qualifying dividends under Sec. 243; whereas individuals are taxed on their total dividends with no exclusion or deduction.
- Corporate charitable contributions are limited in any given year to 10% of taxable income (with certain adjustments described more fully on page 16-20 of this chapter), whereas individual contributions are limited to generally 50% of AGI.

COMPUTATION OF TAX

Computation of Taxable Income

OBJECTIVE 2
Calculate the corporate income tax liability and explain specific tax rules

Table 16-2 illustrates the computation of taxable income for a C corporation.

Computation of Regular Tax

The corporate tax rates reflect a stair-step pattern of progression. The corporate tax rates are as follows:[3]

If Taxable Income Is:			Of the
Over . . .	But Not Over . . .	The Tax Is:	Amount Over . . .
$0	$50,000	15%	$0
50,000	75,000	$7,500 + 25%	50,000
75,000	100,000	13,750 + 34%	75,000
100,000	335,000	22,250 + 39%	100,000
335,000	10,000,000	113,900 + 34%	335,000
10,000,000	15,000,000	3,400,000 + 35%	10,000,000
15,000,000	18,333,333	5,150,000 + 38%	15,000,000
18,333,333		6,416,667 + 35%	18,333,333

Example 16-2 ■ Able Corporation's taxable income for the current year is $100,000. Its regular tax liability is computed as follows:

[3] Sec. 11(b)(1).

Historical Note

The corporate tax rates were lowered from a maximum rate of 46% to 34% schedule in the Tax Reform Act of 1986 to promote economic growth by increasing the rate of return on investment.

TABLE 16-2   Computation of Corporate Taxable Income

Sales	$600,000
Minus: Cost of goods sold	(300,000)
Gross profit	$300,000
Plus: Other income	
Dividends from 25% owned corporation	$100,000
Interest	10,000
Net capital gain	90,000
Gross income	$500,000
Minus: Deductions:	
Salaries	$ 80,000
Repairs	20,000
Bad debts	30,000
Taxes	10,000
Contributions (subject to the 10% corporate limitations discussed on page 16-20)	5,000
Depreciation	20,000
Pension and profit-sharing contributions	35,000
Total deductions	$200,000
Taxable income before special deductions	$300,000
Minus: Special deductions:	
Net operating loss deduction	(15,000[a])
Dividends-received deduction	(80,000[b])
Taxable income	$205,000

[a] This amount represents an NOL carryover from a prior year.
[b] $0.80 \times \$100,000 = \$80,000$ dividends-received deduction.

$$
\begin{array}{lcr}
0.15 \times \$50,000 & = & \$ 7,500 \\
0.25 \times \$25,000 & = & 6,250 \\
0.34 \times \$25,000 & = & 8,500 \\
\text{Total tax} & & \$22,250
\end{array}
$$

The total tax due on the $100,000 of taxable income is $22,250. This amount is $11,750 less than the tax due if the 34% rate was applied to the entire $100,000 of taxable income ($34,000 − $22,250). ■

The benefits of the lower tax rates on the first $75,000 of taxable income are completely eliminated for corporations with taxable income in excess of $335,000. An additional surtax of 5 percentage points is imposed on taxable income from $100,000 to $335,000 to recapture the $11,750 ($235,000 × 0.05 = $11,750) tax savings. Therefore, corporations with taxable income in excess of $335,000 up to $10,000,000 pay a 34% flat rate of tax.

Example 16-3 ■   Ajax Corporation's taxable income for the current year is $335,000. Its tax liability is computed as follows:

Additional Comment

Most states in the U.S. also impose an income tax. In 1991 Connecticut had the highest marginal corporate state income tax rate of 13.8%.

$$
\begin{array}{lcr}
0.15 \times \$\ 50,000 & = & \$\ \ 7,500 \\
0.25 \times \$\ 25,000 & = & 6,250 \\
0.34 \times \$260,000 & = & 88,400 \\
0.05 \times \$235,000 & = & 11,750 \\
\text{Total tax} & & \$113,900
\end{array}
$$

The $113,900 tax liability is 34% times $335,000 of taxable income. Thus, the benefit of the lower rates on the first $75,000 of taxable income is completely phased-out at $335,000 of taxable income. ∎

A 35% rate applies to taxable income in excess of $10 million. An additional 3 percentage point surtax (or a 38% rate) is imposed on taxable income from $15 million to $18,333,333 which eliminates the benefits of the lower 34% rate on taxable income up to $10 million once taxable income equals or exceeds $18,333,333. Thus, a flat 35% rate applies to corporations with taxable income in excess of $18,333,333.

Example 16-4 ∎

Key Point

The corporation income tax is essentially a flat tax for larger corporations.

Ajax Corporation's taxable income for the current year is $18,333,333. Its tax liability is computed as follows:

0.34 × $10,000,000	=	$3,400,000
0.35 × $5,000,000	=	1,750,000
0.38 × $3,333,333	=	1,266,667
Total tax		$6,416,667[a]

[a]At $18,333,333 of taxable income a flat 35% rate again applies (0.35 × $18,333,333 = $6,416,667). ∎

Special Rule for Certain Personal Service Corporations. Personal service corporations are denied the benefits of the corporate graduated rates.[4] Thus, a flat rate of 35% is imposed upon a personal service corporation that performs services in the fields of health, law, engineering, architecture, accounting, actuarial science, performing arts, or consulting where substantially all of the stock is held by employees or retired employees, or by their estates.

Computation of Corporate Alternative Minimum Tax (AMT)

Key Point

The AMT is designed to insure that no corporation with substantial economic income can use exclusions, deductions and credits to avoid significant tax liability.

The corporate alternative minimum tax (AMT) is similar to that applicable to individuals (see Chapter 14 for a discussion of the AMT for individuals). The objective of the AMT is to ensure that corporations with substantial economic income pay a minimum amount of federal income tax. If a corporation's AMT liability is greater than its regular tax liability, the excess amount is payable in addition to the regular tax.[5]

The corporate AMT is 20% of alternative minimum taxable income (AMTI) less an exemption amount.[6] The exemption amount for corporations is $40,000 reduced by 25% of the excess of AMTI over $150,000.

Example 16-5 ∎

Additional Comment

It should be noted that accelerated depreciation on real property was permitted to achieve certain economic objectives, but this provision can become counterproductive when the result is to avoid taxes.

Allied Corporation has $200,000 of AMTI before the exemption. The $40,000 exemption is reduced by $12,500 (0.25 × [$200,000 − $150,000]). Thus, the tax base for the AMT is $172,500 ($200,000 − $27,500). Note that when AMTI reaches $310,000, the $40,000 exemption is eliminated. ∎

Computation of AMTI. AMTI is equal to taxable income modified by certain adjustments and increased by tax preference items. Tax preferences are items that receive preferential tax treatment. Like with the individual AMT these tax preference

---

[4] Sec. 11(b)(2).
[5] Sec. 55(a).
[6] Secs. 55(b)(1) and (d)(2).

items are *added* to taxable income to compute AMTI. Tax preferences are computed separately for each item of property. The most common tax preference item is the excess of accelerated depreciation over straight-line depreciation for real property placed in service before 1987.[7]

AMT ADJUSTMENTS. AMT adjustments are timing differences relating to the deferral of income or the acceleration of deductions. These adjustments generally increase the AMT tax base, although the netting of the timing differences may result in an overall reduction of the AMT tax base when the timing differences reverse. (See Chapter 14 for a detailed discussion of this topic.) The most common AMT adjustments include

Additional Comment

Most, but not all, tax preferences are included in AMTI. For example, the preference relating to the expensing of research and experimentation expenditures is omitted from AMTI.

- For real property placed in service after 1986, the difference between tax depreciation claimed and a hypothetical straight-line depreciation amount claimed under the alternative depreciation system using a 40-year life (see Chapter 10 for a discussion of the alternative depreciation system).

- For personal property placed in service after 1986, the difference between the MACRS depreciation deduction and the amount determined by using the 150% declining balance method under the alternative depreciation system.

- 75% of the excess of the adjusted current earnings over AMTI (before this adjustment and the alternative tax NOL deduction but after all other adjustments and tax preference items).[8]

Example 16-6 ■   Beach Corporation's adjusted current earnings is $1,400,000 while its AMTI (before the adjustment amount) is $400,000. The AMT adjustment is $750,000 (0.75 × [$1,400,000 − $400,000]). Thus, its AMTI is $1,150,000 ($400,000 + $750,000).   ■

Example 16-7 ■   Camp Corporation has taxable income of $100,000. Camp Corporation's tax preference items and adjustments total $200,000. Its regular tax liability is $22,250. Camp Corporation has AMTI of $300,000 ($100,000 + $200,000) before the statutory exemption. Since Camp Corporation has AMTI in excess of $150,000, the $40,000 exemption is reduced by $37,500 ([$300,000 − $150,000] × 0.25 = $37,500) to $2,500 ($40,000 − $37,500). The tax base for the AMT is $297,500 ($300,000 − $2,500). The tentative minimum tax is $59,500 ($297,500 × 0.20). The $59,500 tentative minimum tax amount is greater than the $22,250 regular tax amount. Thus, Camp Corporation's total tax liability is $59,500 ($22,250 regular tax + $37,250 AMT).   ■

Ethical Issue

Because of the subjective nature of the accumulated earnings tax, a corporation is not required to voluntarily pay the tax or to inform the IRS that an accumulated earnings tax problem exists. The responsibility is upon the IRS to audit the taxpayer's return and to allege that the penalty tax should be imposed. The personal holding company tax, on the other hand, is a self-assessed tax and a Schedule PH should be filed with the Form 1120 in any year the corporation is a personal holding company.

Special Taxes

The following two penalty taxes are imposed to avoid otherwise abusive practices: the accumulated earnings tax and the personal holding company tax. The computation of both these penalty taxes involves a complex array of rules that are discussed in detail in the companion volume to this text entitled *Prentice Hall's Federal Taxation: Corporations, Partnerships, Estates, and Trusts*. Here, we only present an overview of these complex subjects.

---

[7] Sec. 57(a)(6).

[8] Sec. 56(g). The term adjusted current earnings is a concept based on the traditional earnings and profits definition found in Sec. 312. (See Chapter 5 of the *Prentice Hall's Federal Taxation: Corporations, Partnerships, Estates and Trusts* text for a detailed discussion of this AMT adjustment.)

Accumulated Earnings Tax. The intent of the **accumulated earnings tax** is to discourage companies from retaining excessive amounts of earnings if the funds are invested in assets that are unrelated to business needs (i.e., a company may avoid the penalty tax if its earnings are reinvested in operating-type assets). If this tax was not imposed, closely held corporations would be inclined not to pay dividends to their shareholders (thereby avoiding a double tax on the earnings). The retained earnings could then be reinvested in passive investments.

Reasonable needs of the business include

- Reasonably anticipated needs for expanding the business and plant replacement
- Acquiring the assets or stock (other than portfolio investments) of another business
- Providing working capital for the business
- Retiring debts
- Making investments or loans to suppliers or customers[9]

The accumulated earnings tax is not imposed if a company has retained its earnings to provide for a bona fide expansion of its business and if its expansion plans are definite rather than vague or indefinite. The accumulated earnings tax is generally imposed on closely held corporations. However, the tax may be imposed on a publicly held company if effective control is in the hands of a few related shareholders.[10]

COMPUTATION OF ACCUMULATED EARNINGS TAX. The accumulated earnings tax is imposed upon a corporation's accumulated taxable income for a particular year. The accumulated earnings tax rate is 39.6%.[11] Accumulated taxable income is computed as follows:[12]

> Taxable income
> Plus: Dividends-received deduction
>   Net operating loss deduction
> Minus: Net capital losses
>   Net long-term capital gains over net short-term capital
>   losses (less federal income tax on such net gains)
>   Federal income tax liability
>   Charitable contributions in excess of the 10% limit
>   Deductions for dividends paid or deemed paid[13]
> Accumulated earnings credit
> Accumulated taxable income

The accumulated earnings credit equals the greater of the following: (1) $250,000 minus the accumulated earnings and profits at the beginning of the year,[14] or (2) the amount of earnings and profits for the tax year retained for the reasonable needs of

---

[9] Sec. 537(a)(1).

[10] Sec. 532(c) and *Golconda Mining Corp. v. CIR,* 35 AFTR 2d 75-336, 74-2 USTC ¶ 9845 (9th Cir., 1974).

[11] Sec. 531. The rate was increased from 28% to 39.6% for taxable years beginning on or after January 1, 1993 to correspond with the increased top rate for individuals.

[12] Sec. 535(b).

[13] Sec. 561. The deduction for dividends paid includes dividends actually paid during the tax year and consent dividends (e.g., a hypothetical dividend) where the shareholders agree to be taxed on such amounts. Under Sec. 563, dividends paid during the first 2½ months following the end of the tax year are considered as paid during the last day of the preceding tax year.

[14] The $250,000 credit amount is reduced to $150,000 for certain service corporations engaged in the field of health. law, engineering, architecture, accounting, actuarial science, performing arts, or consulting.

the business (minus the amount of the corporation's net capital gain for the year reduced by the taxes paid on such gains). Reasonable needs of the business as determined at the end of the tax year are reduced by the amount of accumulated earnings and profits at the beginning of the year. Thus, only the amount of earnings and profits (net of capital gains) retained to meet the reasonable increase in needs can be claimed as a credit.

Example 16-8 ■ Compact Corporation has taxable income of $100,000 in the current year. Compact's federal income tax liability is $22,250, and $10,000 in dividends are paid to its shareholders. Compact claims a dividends-received deduction of $80,000 on $100,000 of dividend income. There are no other adjustments to income (e.g., capital gains or losses, charitable contributions, and so forth). Accumulated earnings and profits at the beginning of the year retained for the reasonable needs of the business are $200,000, and Compact Corporation's reasonable needs of the business at the end of the year amount to $220,000. The accumulated taxable income and the accumulated earnings credit are computed as follows:

Additional Comment

The personal holding company tax is imposed on the basis of mechanical criteria, whereas the accumulated earnings tax uses the subjective standard of purpose to avoid the tax on shareholders.

Taxable income	$100,000
Plus: Dividends-received deduction	80,000
Minus: Federal income tax liability	(22,250)
Dividends paid deduction	(10,000)
Accumulated earnings credit—the greater of (1) $250,000 (statutory exemption) − $200,000 (accumulated E&P at the beginning of the year), or $50,000; or (2) earnings retained for the increased reasonable needs of the business $220,000 − $200,000, or $20,000	(50,000)
Accumulated taxable income	$ 97,750

The accumulated earnings tax is $38,709 (0.396 × $97,750). ■

Personal Holding Company Tax. A company must meet both of the following tests to be classified as a **personal holding company**:

1. More than 50% of the value of the outstanding stock must be owned by five or fewer individuals at some time during the last 6 months of the tax year.
2. 60% or more of the adjusted ordinary gross income must be personal holding company income (e.g., dividends, interest, and rental income if certain tests are met).[15]

Most closely held companies find it difficult to avoid personal holding company status by failing to meet the 50% stock ownership test because of the application of the family stock attribution rules contained in Sec. 544. For example, 20 family members (e.g., spouses, children, and grandchildren) owning stock in a family corporation count as only 1 shareholder for purposes of applying the "50% and 5 or fewer shareholders" test.

The personal holding company tax is intended to prevent closely held companies from converting an operating company into a nonoperating investment company by reinvesting substantial amounts of earnings into passive investments (e.g., stocks and bonds of other companies). The primary purpose of the personal holding company tax is to force a company to distribute its earnings to shareholders as dividends if the earnings and profits are not invested in operating assets. This tax is imposed even if

---

[15] Sec. 542(a).

there is no tax-avoidance motive, whereas the element of intent to avoid tax on dividend distributions must be present under the accumulated earnings tax provisions.[16] However, both penalty taxes cannot be imposed in the same year.[17] In many instances, a corporation that is gradually converting itself into a nonoperating company by reinvesting its earnings in passive investments will have an accumulated earnings tax problem before being subjected to the personal holding company tax. However, this is not always the case. For example, a newly formed company that is temporarily investing surplus funds in nonoperating assets may be classified as a personal holding company while the $250,000 accumulated earnings credit will temporarily shield the same company from the accumulated earnings tax.

Additional Comment

A personal holding company is required to file Schedule PH, Form 1120.

COMPUTATION OF PERSONAL HOLDING COMPANY TAX. The **personal holding company tax** is 39.6% times the undistributed personal holding company income. Various adjustments are made to taxable income to arrive at the tax base. These adjustments are similar to those for the accumulated earnings tax and are illustrated in Example 16-9.

Example 16-9 ■

Point to Stress

The personal holding company tax, like the accumulated earnings tax, can be avoided by the payment of a large enough dividend or by making an S corporation election. The S corporation prevents the corporation from being classified as a personal holding company for the years the S corporation election is in effect.

Crane Corporation has only four shareholders who in total own more than 50% of the value of the stock at all times during the current year. In addition, 60% or more of the adjusted ordinary gross income is personal holding company income. Therefore, Crane is classified as a personal holding company for the current year because the stock ownership and the income tests are met. Crane receives a $25,000 dividend for which a $20,000 dividends-received deduction is claimed and pays $18,750 of dividends to shareholders. Crane has $200,000 taxable income and a $61,250 regular federal income tax liability.

The personal holding company tax for Crane Corporation is computed as follows:

Taxable income	$200,000
Adjustments:	
Federal income tax liability	(61,250)
Dividends-received deduction	20,000
Dividends-paid deduction[18]	(18,750)
Undistributed personal holding company income	$140,000
Times: Personal holding company tax rate	× 0.396
Personal holding company tax	$ 55,440

Crane's total federal tax liability is $116,690 ($61,250 + $55,440). The $55,440 personal holding company tax may be avoided if Crane pays the undistributed personal holding company income amount to its shareholders as a deficiency dividend under Sec. 547. ■

A comparison of the accumulated earnings tax and personal holding company tax rules is presented in Topic Review 16-1.

Additional Comment

Section 1561(a) requires the apportionment not only of the lower tax rates but also of the $250,000 accumulated earnings credit and the $40,000 exemption for the alternative minimum tax.

---

[16] Sec. 532(a).
[17] Sec. 532(b)(1).
[18] Secs. 547 and 561. The dividends-paid deduction is available for dividends paid during the tax year, dividends paid within 2½ months following the end of the tax year (subject to certain limitations), consent dividends, and dividends paid within 90 days following a determination that a personal holding company tax liability is owed (i.e., deficiency dividends). Deficiency dividends are not allowed for purposes of computing the accumulated earnings tax.

Computation of Tax for Controlled Groups

Operating a single business as two or more separately incorporated businesses controlled by the same shareholders might result in a substantial tax advantage because of the lower corporate tax rates that apply to taxable income amounts up to $10 million. Under Sec. 1561(a), however, a **controlled group** must apportion the lower tax rates among the group members as if only one corporation is in existence. An equal apportionment to each member is required unless all of the controlled group's members consent to an unequal allocation of such amounts. This eliminates the potential for abuse.

Example 16-10 ■ West and East Corporations are members of a controlled group. West and East each have taxable income of $100,000. Assuming that an equal apportionment of the reduced tax rate brackets is made, the tax liability for each company is computed as follows:

	Corporation	
	West	East
Tax on initial $50,000 of taxable income apportioned equally to West and East (0.15 × $25,000)	$ 3,750	$ 3,750
Tax on next $25,000 apportioned equally to West and East (0.25 × $12,500)	3,125	3,125
Tax on next $25,000 apportioned equally to West and East (0.34 × $12,500)	4,250	4,250
Tax on remaining $50,000 of taxable income for each corporation (0.39 × $50,000)	19,500	19,500
Tax on $100,000 taxable income for each corporation	$30,625	$30,625

Each corporation has only $37,500 ($25,000 + $12,500) of income taxed at the 15% and 25% rates. The next $12,500 of income is taxed at a 34% rate. The remaining $50,000 of income is taxed at a 39% rate thus resulting in a total tax of $61,250. No change in the total tax liability for the two corporations would result in this situation if an unequal allocation of the benefits of the 15% and 25% rates occurred. An unequal allocation in this example would produce a tax savings for the two corporations if one corporation reported less than $37,500 of taxable income and the other corporation reported taxable income in excess of $37,500. Without these apportionment rules, each corporation's tax liability would be $22,250 [(0.15 × $50,000 + (0.25 × $25,000) + (0.34 × $25,000)], or a total of $44,500. ■

If taxable income of the controlled group is in excess of $15 million, a comparable recapture needs to occur to reflect the lower 34% rate applying to taxable income up to $10 million.

Brother-Sister Corporations. A controlled corporate group may consist of parent-subsidiary corporations, brother-sister corporations, or a combination of the two called a combined group of corporations (see Chapter 3 of the *Prentice Hall's Federal Taxation: Corporations, Partnerships, Estates and Trusts* volume for a discussion of

TOPIC REVIEW 16-1

Comparison of Penalty Taxes		
Item	Accumulated Earnings Tax—Sec. 531	Personal Holding Company Tax—Sec. 541
1. Reason for imposing the penalty tax.	To discourage companies from retaining excessive amounts of earnings if the funds are invested in nonoperating assets. A primary purpose is to force dividend payments of excess earnings.	To prevent closely held companies from converting an operating company into a passive investment company. A primary purpose is to force dividend payments of passive income.
2. Nature of the tax formula.	The tax base is taxable income plus or minus certain adjustments. The tax computation is inherently subjective because the accumulated earnings credit (which frequently reduces the tax base to zero) is based on the retention of earnings for the reasonable needs of the business which is a subjective determination.	The determination of whether a corporation is a personal holding company and the computation of the penalty tax is largely a mechanical process. Once it is determined that the corporation is a PHC, the tax base is taxable income plus or minus certain adjustments.
3. Computation of tax.	Adjustments are made to taxable income including such items as the dividends-received deduction, the dividends-paid deduction, the federal income tax liability and the accumulated earnings credit (see Example 16-8). The tax is 39.6% of accumulated taxable income.	Adjustments such as the dividends-received deduction, dividends-paid deduction, and the federal income tax liability are made to taxable income to arrive at undistributed PHC income (see Example 16-9). The tax rate is 39.6% of undistributed PHC income.

combined groups.) A **brother-sister controlled group** exists if the following conditions are met:

- Five or fewer persons (individuals, estates, or trusts) own at least 80% of the voting power or value of all classes of stock of each corporation.[19]
- There is common ownership of more than 50% of the total voting power or value of all classes of stock. The stock is counted for this test only to the extent that each shareholder owns an identical interest in each corporation.[20]

Example 16-11 ■ The single class of outstanding stock of East, Fast, and General Corporations is owned by Amir, Beth, Carol, Dawn, and Edith as shown below.

[19] The 80% test is met if 80% or more of the total combined voting power of all classes of voting stock *or* at least 80% of the total value of all classes of stock of each corporation is held by five or fewer persons on December 31. To be counted for the 80% test, a shareholder must own stock in each corporation of the brother-sister controlled group.

[20] Sec. 1563(a)(2).

	Corporation			
Individuals	East	Fast	General	Identical Interest
Amir	40%	20%	20%	20%
Beth	30	30	60	30
Carol	10	40	10	10
Dawn	10	10	—	—
Edith	10	—	10	—
Total	100%	100%	100%	60%

The 80% test is met because five or fewer individuals own at least 80% of the East, Fast, and General stock. This test is met because Amir, Beth, and Carol own 80% of the East stock, and 90% of the Fast and General stock. Dawn and Edith are not included for purposes of the 80% test because they do not have ownership in each of the three corporations. The 50% test is also met because there is more than 50% common ownership. For the purposes of the 50% test, the stock ownership of Dawn and Edith is not counted because they do not own shares in each of the three corporations. For example, if Dawn owned at least 10% of the General stock, the common ownership would increase from 60% to 70%. ■

Parent-Subsidiary Controlled Groups. A **parent-subsidiary controlled group** exists if the following conditions are met:

- A common parent corporation must own at least 80% of the stock of at least one subsidiary corporation.[21]
- At least 80% of the stock of each other component member of the controlled group must be owned by other members of the controlled group.

Example 16-12 ■ Federal Corporation owns 100% of the stock of First Corporation and 30% of the stock of Giant Corporation. First Corporation also owns 50% of the stock of Giant Corporation. Each corporation has only one class of stock outstanding. Federal Corporation is the common parent corporation of the controlled group by owning at least 80% of the First stock. Giant Corporation is also a member of the controlled group, since at least 80% of the Giant stock is owned by members of the controlled group (Federal and First own 30% + 50%). The parent-subsidiary controlled group consists of Federal, First, and Giant Corporations. ■

Typical Misconception

A brother-sister controlled group is not eligible to file a consolidated return. It is sometimes erroneously assumed that a brother-sister corporation can file a consolidated return since it is one type of a controlled corporate group.

Consolidated Returns

Corporations that are members of a parent-subsidiary affiliated group are eligible to file a consolidated tax return if an election is made under the consolidated return regulations. Parent-subsidiary controlled groups are generally eligible to file a consolidated tax return, although the eligibility requirements for an affiliated group and a controlled group are slightly different (see Chapter 8 of the *Prentice Hall's Federal Taxation: Corporations, Partnerships, Estates, and Trusts* text for a detailed discussion of the requirements for filing a consolidated tax return).

[21] Sec. 1563(a)(1). A parent-subsidiary controlled group is a group of two or more corporations where one corporation (the parent corporation) owns directly at least 80% of the voting power of all classes of voting stock, or 80% of the total value of all classes of stock of a second corporation (the subsidiary corporation). There can be more than one subsidiary corporation in the group. If the parent corporation, the subsidiary corporation, or any other members of the controlled group in total own at least 80% of the voting power of all classes of voting stock, or 80% of the total value of all classes of stock of a corporation, the corporation is included in the parent-subsidiary controlled group.

The consolidated tax return is based upon the theory that the affiliated group constitutes a single entity. Thus, consolidated return elimination entries are made for intercompany dividends and gains and losses on intercompany sales transactions. In addition, losses of one group member may be offset by profits of other group members. Once the election is made, it is difficult to terminate because IRS permission must be obtained to discontinue filing on a consolidated basis.[22]

SPECIFIC RULES APPLICABLE TO CORPORATIONS

Capital Gains and Losses

The rules for the netting of long- and short-term capital gains and losses, the treatment of Sec. 1231 (i.e., business fixed assets) gains and losses, and the long-term capital gain and loss holding periods are the same for both corporations and individuals. The netting process consists of the following procedural rules:

- Long-term capital gains (LTCGs) are netted against long-term capital losses (LTCLs).
- Short-term capital gains (STCGs) are netted against short-term capital losses (STCLs).
- A net long-term capital gain (NLTCG) is then offset against a net short-term capital loss (NSTCL).
- A net long-term capital loss (NLTCL) is then offset against a net short-term capital gain (NSTCG).
- If a corporation reports both a NLTCG and a NSTCG after the netting procedure is completed, both the NSTCG and the NLTCG are taxed at the same rates as ordinary income.
- NSTCGs are netted against NLTCLs and any excess amount is taxed at the same rates as ordinary income.
- NLTCLs and NSTCLs cannot be deducted from ordinary income.

Example 16-13 ■   Gulf Corporation has the following capital gains and losses during the current year:

LTCG	$15,000
LTCL	5,000
STCG	3,000
STCL	8,000

Gulf Corporation has a NLTCG of $10,000 and a NSTCL of $5,000. The NLTCG is then offset against the NSTCL, resulting in a $5,000 NLTCG that is fully includible in gross income as a capital gain and taxed at the same rates as ordinary income.   ■

Example 16-14 ■   High Corporation has the following capital gains and losses during the current year:

[22] Reg. Sec. 1.1502-75(c).

LTCG	$15,000
LTCL	5,000
STCG	10,000
STCL	8,000

High Corporation has a NLTCG of $10,000 and a NSTCG of $2,000. The $2,000 NSTCG and the $10,000 NLTCG are fully includible in gross income as capital gains and are taxed at the same rates as ordinary income. ■

Example 16-15 ■ Huge Corporation has the following capital gains and losses during 1994:

LTCG	$ 5,000
LTCL	15,000
STCG	8,000
STCL	10,000

Huge Corporation has a $10,000 NLTCL and a $2,000 NSTCL. Neither loss is deductible in computing its 1994 taxable income. ■

Corporate Capital Loss Limitations. Neither a NLTCL nor a NSTCL is deductible in the year it is incurred. Instead, they are subject to a 3-year carryback and 5-year carryover as an offset against capital gains for those years.[23] For corporations, both the NSTCL and the NLTCL are treated as STCLs for purposes of the carryback and carryover rules. The corporate capital loss limitations and carryback-carryover rules differ from the rules that apply to noncorporate taxpayers (see the discussion in Chapter 5).[24]

Example 16-16 ■ Assume the same facts as in Example 16-15. The $10,000 NLTCL and the $2,000 NSTCL are not deductible in 1994. The $12,000 ($10,000 + $2,000) total loss is carried back initially to 1991 as a NSTCL. If the net capital gains (first short-term and then long-term) in the carryback years (1991 through 1993) are insufficient to absorb the $12,000 STCL carryback from 1994, the excess is carried over for up to 5 years (1995 through 1999). ■

Self-Study Question

What are the major differences between the capital gain and loss taxation of individuals and corporations?

Answer

First, an individual can offset $3,000 of capital losses against ordinary income. Second, an individual has an indefinite carryover instead of a 3-year carryback and a 5-year carryover. Third, all corporate capital loss carrybacks and carryovers are treated as STCLs. A 28% maximum tax rate applies to net capital gain (i.e., the excess of net long-term capital gain over net short-term capital loss) for noncorporate taxpayers in 1991 and subsequent years.

Dividends-Received Deduction

Corporations are eligible to deduct 80% of dividends received from a domestic corporation if the recipient corporation owns 20% or more of the voting power and value of the stock of the issuing corporation.[25] If a corporation owns less than 20% of the stock of the distributing corporation, the dividends-received deduction is 70%.[26] The percentage increases to 100% if the dividend is received from a related corporation.[27] This seemingly liberal deduction was intended to mitigate the effects of triple taxation that would otherwise apply if one corporation paid dividends to

---

[23] Secs. 1211(a) and 1212(a).

[24] Noncorporate taxpayers (e.g., individuals) can deduct up to $3,000 of net capital losses against ordinary income. Unused capital losses are carried over (but not carried back) for an indefinite period and retain their character as long- or short-term capital losses.

[25] Sec. 243(c).

[26] Sec. 243(a)(1).

[27] Secs. 243(a)(3) and (b)(1). The 100% dividends-received deduction is available for members of an affiliated group. In general, the requirements for the 100% dividends-received deduction are the same as the eligibility requirements for filing a consolidated tax return. A common parent corporation must own at least 80% of the total voting power of all classes of voting stock and at least 80% of the value of the outstanding stock of at least one member of the affiliated group. In addition, the common parent and other group members must own at least 80% of the voting stock and 80% of the value of the outstanding stock of the other affilated group members. See Sec. 1504(a).

another corporate shareholder, which in turn distributed such amounts to its shareholders.

The dividends-received deduction is subject to limitations that may reduce the deduction amount. These limitations are initially applied to the dividends that are eligible for the 80% deduction. A separate limitation computation is then applied to the dividends that are eligible for the 70% deduction.[28] For this purpose the amount of taxable income is reduced by the total amount of dividends received from the 20% owned corporations before computing the 70% deduction.

The 80% and 70% **dividends-received deduction** are subject to the following limitations:

- The dividends-received deduction is limited to 80% (or 70%) of taxable income (computed without regard to the net operating loss (NOL) deduction, the dividends-received deduction, and capital loss carrybacks to the current year).

- The limitation based on 80% (or 70%) of taxable income does not apply if the corporation has a NOL for the year after deducting the dividends-received deduction under the general rules.

- The dividends-received deduction is not available if the stock is held for 45 days or less.[29]

Example 16-17 ■

King Corporation has the following income and expense items during the current year:

Net income from operations	$ 50,000
Dividend income from 20% (or more) owned corporations	200,000

The dividends-received deduction under the general rule is $160,000 (0.80 × $200,000 dividends). The deduction limitation is $200,000 (0.80 × $250,000 taxable income before the dividends-received deduction). Since the limitation ($200,000) is greater than the dividends-received deduction computed under the general rule ($160,000), the full dividends-received deduction of $160,000 is allowed. A second limitation based upon the 70% dividends-received deduction does not apply because all of the dividends were from 20% (or more) owned corporations. ■

Example 16-18 ■

Assume the same facts as in Example 16-17, except that there is $10,000 net loss from operations. The dividends-received deduction under the general rule is $160,000 (0.80 × $200,000 dividends). The limitation under the general rule based upon taxable income before the dividends-received deduction is $152,000 (0.80 × $190,000). A NOL does not result after deducting the entire 80% dividends-received deduction computed under the general rule as shown below:

Net loss from operations	$ (10,000)
Plus: Dividends received	200,000
Minus: Dividends-received deduction (0.80 × $200,000)	(160,000)
Taxable income as computed under the general rule	$ 30,000

---

[28] Sec. 246(b)(3).
[29] Secs. 246(b) and (c). A 90-day period applies to certain preferred stock dividends. Similar disallowance rules apply when the corporation has entered into a short sale of the stock before the dividends are received.

Since the dividends-received deduction is limited to $152,000 (0.80 × $190,000 taxable income before deducting the dividends-received deduction), the actual taxable income for the year is $38,000 ($190,000 − $152,000). ■

Example 16-19 ■   Assume the same facts as in Example 16-18, except that the loss from operations is $50,000. The dividends-received deduction under the general rule is $160,000 (0.80 × $200,000 dividends). The limitation is $120,000 (0.80 × $150,000 taxable income before the dividends-received deduction). The limitation does not apply, however, because a $10,000 NOL results after the dividends-received deduction (computed using the general rule) is subtracted ($50,000 net loss from operations + $200,000 dividends received − $160,000 dividends-received deduction = $10,000 NOL). Therefore, the full $160,000 dividends-received deduction is allowed. ■

Example 16-20 ■   Lean Corporation acquires Madison Corporation stock on June 1. Madison Corporation pays a cash dividend of $100,000 to Lean on June 15. On July 1, Lean sells the Madison stock. The dividends-received deduction is not allowed because Lean does not hold the Madison stock for the required 45-day holding period. ■

Typical Misconception

It is possible to mistakenly believe that the dividends-received deduction should be eliminated in the calculation of the NOL.

Net Operating Losses

The computation of a corporate **net operating loss** does not involve making adjustments for nonbusiness deductions and capital gains and losses as is required for individuals (see Chapter 8 for a discussion of these adjustments for individuals).[30] Thus, the corporate rules are fairly straightforward. The primary adjustment that is required in computing the corporate NOL is the dividends-received deduction.

Example 16-21 ■   Maine Corporation's NOL is computed from the following income and deduction items:

Operating income	$ 400,000
Plus: Dividends	300,000
Gross income	$ 700,000
Minus: Business operating expenses	(600,000)
Dividends-received deduction (0.80 × $300,000)	(240,000)
NOL	$(140,000)

NOLs are carried back three years (beginning with the earliest tax year).[31] Any excess amounts are carried forward up to 15 years to offset taxable income in those years. ■

An election may be made not to carryback an NOL to an earlier tax year in order to carry the unused loss forward.[32] For example, if the corporation has taxable income of less than $75,000 in the carryback year(s) that was, therefore, subject to tax rates less than 34% (i.e., 15% or 25%), the tax benefit may be of limited value because the NOL carryback offsets income that is taxed at these lower rates. The NOL might be more valuable if the carryback is forgone and the NOL is used as a carryover where the marginal tax rate may be as high as 35%. However, a mitigating factor is that the

---

[30] Sec. 172(d).
[31] Sec. 172(b).
[32] Sec. 172(b)(3)(C).

realization of the tax savings is deferred while a carryback produces tax savings currently.[33]

Charitable Contributions

Some of the rules governing charitable contributions for individuals also apply to corporations (e.g., the restriction imposed upon contributions of ordinary income property, which is discussed in Chapter 7).[34] The following rules apply solely to corporations:

Additional Comment

Taxable income for purposes of determining the charitable contribution limit is calculated without regard to NOL and capital loss carrybacks, but carryovers are reflected in calculating taxable income.

- Accrual-basis corporations may accrue a contribution deduction in the year preceding payment if (1) the payment is authorized by the board of directors prior to the end of the tax year and (2) the contribution is actually made within 2½ months following the end of the tax year.[35] Under the general rule, a payment must actually be made before a contribution deduction is allowed.
- Corporate charitable contributions are limited to 10% of taxable income (computed without regard to the charitable contribution deduction, NOL and capital loss carrybacks, or the dividends-received deduction).[36]
- Unused contributions are carried forward 5 years.[37]

Example 16-22 ■

Additional Comment

In 1990 charitable contributions deducted by corporations totaled $4.8 billion.

The board of directors of Melon Corporation, an accrual method of accounting taxpayer that uses the calendar year as its tax year, authorizes a $10,000 donation to a qualified charity on December 28, 1994. The payment is actually made on March 15, 1995. The company may claim the $10,000 contribution in 1994, despite the fact that the payment is not made until 1995 because the payment is authorized by the board of directors prior to the end of the year and the payment was made within 2½ months following the end of the year. If the payment is not made within the 2½ month period, the contribution is deductible only in the year of payment. ■

Example 16-23 ■

During 1994, Mesa Corporation reports the following results:

Taxable income (after deducting the dividends-received deduction and charitable contributions)	$100,000
Dividends-received deduction	10,000
Charitable contributions	20,000

To compute the charitable contribution limitation, the charitable contributions and dividends-received deduction are added to the taxable income. Thus, the limitation on contributions is $13,000 ([$100,000 + $10,000 + $20,000] × 0.10) The $7,000 ($20,000 − $13,000) of unused contributions can be carried forward for five years. ■

Example 16-24 ■

Assume that the same facts as in Example 16-23 for 1994 also apply to 1995, except that taxable income (after deducting the dividends-received deduction and charitable contributions) is $190,000, and the contribution limitation is therefore $22,000

---

[33] A NOL carryover does, however, effect the amount of estimated tax payments in the initial carryover year.

[34] Special rules are also provided in Sec. 170(e)(3) for corporate taxpayers who donate inventory and business property to certain public charities where the donee uses the property for the care of the ill, the needy, or infants. Section 170(e)(4) also provides special rules for corporate contributions of scientific property used for research.

[35] Sec. 170(a)(2).

[36] Sec. 170(b)(2).

[37] Sec. 170(d)(2). In the carryover year the current year's contributions are deducted first in applying the 10% limitation. Any unused limitation amounts are then applied to contribution carryovers from the earliest year.

([\$190,000 + \$10,000 + \$20,000] × 0.10). The \$20,000 charitable contribution amount from 1995 is initially applied against the \$22,000 limitation, thereby leaving a \$2,000 unused charitable contribution limitation. \$2,000 of the carryover from 1994 is used against this limitation, leaving a \$5,000 carryover from 1994, which can be used in tax years 1996 through 1999. ■

For a summary of the capital gain and loss, dividends-received deduction, net operating loss, and charitable contribution deduction rules for corporations, see Topic Review 16-2.

Compensation Deduction Limitation for Publicly Held Corporations

A publicly held corporation is denied a deduction for compensation paid to its chief executive officer and its four highest compensated officers if the compensation amount for any individual exceeds \$1 million per year.[38] Includible compensation includes both cash and noncash benefits. The following types of compensation are not taken into account for purposes of the \$1 million limitation:

- Remuneration payable on a commission basis
- Compensation based on individual performance goals (if approved by certain outside directors and shareholders)
- Payments to a qualified retirement plan
- Tax free employee benefits (such as employer-provided health benefits and Sec. 132 fringe benefits)
- Remuneration payable under pre-February 17, 1993 binding contracts

Example 16-25 ■   Acorn Corporation is a publicly held company listed on the New York Stock Exchange. During the current year, its chief executive officer, Rodney, receives the following compensation from the corporation: salary, \$1,200,000; commissions based on sales generated by Rodney, \$400,000; payments to a qualified pension plan, \$25,000; tax free fringe benefits, \$10,000. The commissions, payments to the qualified pension plan, and the fringe benefits are not subject to the \$1 million annual deduction limitation for Rodney's compensation. Thus, \$200,000 (\$1,200,000 − \$1,000,000) of Rodney's salary is not deductible by Acorn Corporation. The \$200,000 nondeductible amount is includible in Rodney's gross income as additional compensation or as a constructive dividend depending upon the circumstances. ■

TRANSFERS OF PROPERTY TO CONTROLLED CORPORATIONS

OBJECTIVE 3
Discuss the nonrecognition of gain or loss rules for corporate formations

Section 351 permits the shareholders of a corporation to defer recognition of gain or loss on the transfer of assets to the corporation. The transfer of properties may either be made when a new corporation is formed or may reflect additional capital contributions to an existing corporation. Without Sec. 351, it would be difficult for a sole proprietorship or a partnership to adopt the corporate form of organization because the transfer of appreciated properties would constitute a taxable transaction resulting in a recognized gain.

---

[38] Sec. 162 (m). A publicly held corporation is any corporation issuing any class of securities required to be registered under Section 12 of the Securities Exchange Act of 1934. The Conference Committee Report indicates that this is generally a corporation listed on a national securities exchange, or which has at least \$5 million or more of assets and 500 or more shareholders.

TOPIC REVIEW 16-2

Summary of Capital Gain and Loss, Dividends-Received Deduction, Net Operating Loss Deduction, Charitable Contribution Deduction, and Compensation Deduction Limitation Rules for Corporations

---

1. If a net loss results after netting long-term and short-term capital losses, no amount can be deducted from ordinary income. Instead, net capital losses are carried back three years and forward five years as STCLs.

2. The corporate net capital gain does not receive favorable tax treatment. The maximum 28% tax rate for net capital gains applies only to individuals.

3. The dividends-received deduction for corporate shareholders is 80% if 20% or more of the stock is owned and 70% if less than 20% is owned by the corporate investor. A 100% dividends-received deduction is available for dividends from affiliated group members.

4. The dividends-received deduction is limited to 80% (or 70% as the case may be) of taxable income (after adjustments are made for the NOL deduction, the dividends-received deduction, and capital loss carrybacks) unless the corporate shareholder has an NOL after deducting the full amount of the dividends-received deduction.

5. NOLs are carried back three years (beginning with the earliest year) and forward 15 years.

6. Accrual-basis corporate donors may accrue a contribution deduction at the end of the tax year if authorized by the board of directors and paid within 2½ months following the end of the tax year.

7. Contributions are limited to 10% of the taxable income (with certain adjustments).

8. Unused charitable contributions are carried forward five years.

9. Publicly held corporations are denied a deduction for compensation payments in excess of $1 million to certain key executives.

Section 351 Nonrecognition Requirements

Typical Misconception

The nonrecognition provisions of Sec. 351 are mandatory rather than elective.

The postponement of gain or loss under Sec. 351 can be justified because realization has not occurred. The assets have merely been transferred to a corporation that is controlled by the transferors. In addition, the transferors do not have the wherewithal to pay the tax on the gains that would otherwise be recognized because the shareholders receive only stock of the transferee (controlled) corporation, rather than cash or liquid assets.[39] Section 351 also prevents the recognition of artificial losses on transfers of property that have declined in value.

Gain or loss is not recognized if the following conditions are met:

- Property (other than services) is transferred to the corporation solely in exchange for stock of the transferor corporation.[40]

- Immediately after the exchange, the transferor-shareholders must be in control (i.e., 80% stock ownership) of the transferee corporation.[41]

---

[39] Sec. 351(a).

[40] Section 351(d) provides that services do not qualify as property. Thus, if an individual transfers services in exchange for stock, the individual is not counted as a transferor for purposes of meeting the 80% control requirement, unless the individual also transfers substantial other properties. In any event, the transfer of services results in ordinary income being recognized by the transferor equal to the FMV of the services rendered.

[41] Sec. 368(c). Control means the ownership of at least 80% of the total combined voting power of all classes of stock and at least 80% of the total number of shares of each other class of stock.

Additional Comment

The nonrecognition provisions even apply to accounts receivable.

- If property or money (other than stock in the transferee corporation) is received by the transferor, gain (but not loss) is recognized to the extent of the lesser of the boot received (i.e., money plus the FMV of other property received) or the realized gain.[42] In such a case, gain is also recognized under Sec. 311(b) by the corporation that transfers appreciated property (other than its own stock) to the transferor-shareholders.[43]

- Depreciation recapture does not apply to a transfer coming under Sec. 351, unless gain is recognized by the transferor.[44]

Example 16-26 ■

Carlos and Fred decide to combine their sole proprietorships by forming the Miami Corporation. Carlos transfers land and a building having a $50,000 adjusted basis and a $100,000 FMV to the corporation in exchange for 40% of the Miami stock. Fred transfers equipment with a $60,000 adjusted basis and a $150,000 FMV to the corporation in exchange for 60% of the Miami stock. No gain or loss is recognized by Carlos or Fred because the requirements of Sec. 351 are met. Carlos and Fred receive stock of Miami Corporation, which is controlled by Carlos and Fred (owning at least 80% of the single class of stock) immediately after the exchange. Gain is not recognized by Carlos or Fred because no property is received by the transferors other than Miami Corporation stock. The depreciation recapture potential on the building and equipment carries over to the controlled corporation. ■

Example 16-27 ■

Gail and Gary form Michigan Corporation. Gail transfers inventory with a $50,000 adjusted basis and a $100,000 FMV to Michigan Corporation in exchange for 50% of the stock and $20,000 cash. The cash funds represent borrowings by Michigan Corporation from a bank. Gary transfers equipment with a $150,000 adjusted basis and a $100,000 FMV in exchange for 50% of the stock and a Michigan corporation ten-year note valued at $20,000. Section 351 applies to the exchange because the requirements of Sec. 351 are met (i.e., property is transferred by transferors who control at least 80% of the stock of the corporation immediately after the exchange). However, $20,000 of ordinary income (the lesser of Gail's $50,000 realized gain [$100,000 − $50,000] or $20,000 boot received) is recognized by Gail upon the receipt of boot. Gary's realized loss is $50,000 ($100,000 − $50,000). No loss is recognized by Gary, even though he also receives boot of $20,000. ■

Basis Considerations

If Sec. 351 is applicable, substituted basis rules apply to the stock received by the transferors and carryover basis rules apply to the basis of the property in the hands of the transferee corporation. The basis formula for the transferor's stock is as follows:

Additional Comment

When different classes of stock are received in a Sec. 351 exchange, the available basis must be allocated to the different classes in proportion to their relative FMVs when received.

Basis of the property transferred to the corporation
Plus: Any gain recognized by the transferors
            on the exchange (e.g., due to boot received)
Minus: Amount of money received (including any liabilities
            transferred to the corporation) plus the FMV of any
            nonmoney boot property received

Basis of the stock received[45]

---

[42] Sec. 351(b).
[43] Sec. 351(f).
[44] Secs. 1245(b)(3) and 1250(d)(3). The depreciation recapture potential is recognized if the assets are subsequently sold or disposed of by the corporation.
[45] Sec. 358(a).

The basis amount is allocated to the stock according to its relative FMVs. The boot property takes a basis equal to its FMV.

Example 16-28 ■

George and Gina form New Corporation. George transfers land and a building with a $50,000 adjusted basis and a $100,000 FMV in exchange for 50% of the New stock. Gina transfers equipment with a $120,000 adjusted basis and a $100,000 FMV for 50% of the New stock. No gain or loss is recognized because of the application of Sec. 351. Therefore, George's basis in the New stock is $50,000, and Gina's basis in the New stock is $120,000. George has a $50,000 deferred gain ($100,000 − $50,000), which is reflected as a reduction in the basis of his stock from its $100,000 FMV. If George sells his stock for its FMV, the $50,000 deferred gain is recognized ($100,000 − $50,000 adjusted basis in the stock). Gina's $20,000 ($100,000 − $120,000) deferred loss is reflected as an increase in the basis of her stock. Thus, if Gina sells her stock for its $100,000 FMV, the $20,000 deferred loss would be recognized ($100,000 − $120,000 adjusted basis in the stock). ■

Property Received by Transferee Corporation. The carryover basis rules apply to the basis of property received by the transferee corporation. The basis of property received by the transferee corporation is computed as follows:

> Basis of property in the transferor's hands
> Plus: Gain recognized by the transferor
> _____
> Basis of property in the transferee corporation's hands[46]

Example 16-29 ■

North Corporation receives property having a $60,000 adjusted basis in the transferor's hands and a $100,000 FMV in an exchange qualifying under Sec. 351. Assume that a $10,000 gain is recognized by the transferor because boot (e.g., cash) is received from the transferee corporation. North Corporation's basis of the property is $70,000 ($60,000 adjusted basis in the hands of the transferor + $10,000 gain recognized by the transferor). ■

Typical Misconception

When a corporation assumes a shareholder's liabilities and no gain is recognized, it is easy to mistakenly assume that the basis of the shareholder's stock is not reduced by the amount of liabilities assumed.

Treatment of Liabilities

Nonrecognition of Gain. Section 357(a) permits the assumption of liabilities by the transferee corporation (or the corporation may take the property subject to the liability) without the recognition of gain under the boot rules previously discussed. Thus, under the general rule, no gain is recognized by the shareholders if liabilities are transferred to a controlled corporation. The shareholders, however, must reduce their stock basis by the amount of the liabilities assumed or acquired. This rule is logical because if an individual transfers net assets of $10,000 (i.e., gross assets of $100,000 and liabilities of $90,000), the amount of the contribution to capital is only $10,000, despite the fact that $100,000 in assets are transferred. Thus, the shareholder has been relieved from an individual debt obligation.

Example 16-30 ■

Ira transfers land with an $80,000 adjusted basis and a $100,000 FMV to a corporation in exchange for 100% of its stock having a $60,000 FMV in a transaction otherwise qualifying under Sec. 351. The property is subject to a $40,000 liability that is acquired by the corporation. None of Ira's $20,000 ([$60,000 + $40,000] − $80,000) gain is recognized. However, the basis of Ira's stock is only $40,000 ($80,000 adjusted basis for the land − $40,000 in liabilities acquired by the corporation). ■

[46] Sec. 362(a).

Exceptions. There are two exceptions in which the transfer of liabilities results in the recognition of gain. The first exception relates to the nature of the exchange. If the principal purpose for the assumption of the liabilities is tax avoidance or if the transaction does not have a bona fide business purpose, all of the transferor's liabilities assumed or acquired by the transferee corporation are treated as boot and gain is recognized.[47] If the shareholder mortgages the property immediately prior to the Sec. 351 exchange and transfers the property and the liability to the corporation, it is likely that the transaction will lack a bona fide business purpose if the mortgaged funds are used for personal purposes.

Example 16-31 ■ Helen transfers land and a building with a $70,000 adjusted basis and a $100,000 FMV to the Orlando Corporation in exchange for 100% of its stock in a transaction otherwise qualifying under Sec. 351. Shortly before the transfer, Helen obtains a $60,000 mortgage on the property and uses the funds to pay off personal debts. If the $60,000 mortgage is assumed by the corporation, the liability is treated as boot by Helen, resulting in a $30,000 recognized gain. Gain is recognized to the extent of the lesser of the $30,000 ($100,000 − $70,000) gain realized or the $60,000 of boot deemed to have been received when the corporation assumed the liability. ■

Real World Example

Customer deposits representing obligations to perform future services were considered to be liabilities. Since these liabilities exceeded the basis of the assets transferred to the corporation, gain was recognized. William P. Orr, 78 T.C. 1059 (1982).

A second exception applies where the total liabilities assumed or acquired by the corporation from a transferor are in excess of the adjusted basis of the transferor's transferred assets.[48] Gain is recognized by the transferor to the extent the liabilities transferred exceed the total adjusted basis of the property transferred. If this rule was not in effect, the shareholder would have a negative basis in the stock that is received in the exchange. In addition, gain is recognized because the transferor has received a net economic benefit equal to the excess of the liabilities assumed over the adjusted basis of the transferred assets.

Example 16-32 ■ Jack transfers assets with a $60,000 adjusted basis and a $100,000 FMV, along with $80,000 of liabilities that are assumed by the transferee corporation in a transaction otherwise qualifying under Sec. 351. A $20,000 gain is recognized to the extent the liabilities assumed by the corporation exceed the basis of the assets transferred ($80,000 − $60,000). If the gain was not recognized, Jack's basis for his stock would be a negative $20,000 ($60,000 − $80,000). Jack's net economic benefit from the exchange is also $20,000 ($80,000 liabilities assumed by the corporation − $60,000 adjusted basis of assets transferred). Jack's basis in the stock received is zero ($60,000 adjusted basis of assets + $20,000 gain recognized − $80,000 liabilities assumed). Since Jack's realized gain is $40,000 and $20,000 of the gain is recognized, $20,000 of the gain is deferred. ■

Character of Gain Recognized

If gain is recognized in a Sec. 351 exchange (e.g., due to the receipt of boot) by the transferor-shareholders, its character is determined by the nature of the asset and how it was used by the transferor. If the transferred asset is Sec. 1231 property (e.g., land or machinery used in the transferor's business), the gain is Sec. 1231 gain, except for any gain that is recaptured under the depreciation recapture rules. If the asset is something other than a capital asset or a Sec. 1231 asset (e.g., inventory), the recognized gain is ordinary income. Income recognized from tranferred capital assets is treated as a capital gain.

[47] Sec. 357(b).
[48] Sec. 357(c). Accounts receivable and accounts payable with a zero basis for a cash- or hybrid-basis transferor are disregarded for purposes of applying the Sec. 357(c) rules. See Sec. 357(c)(3).

TOPIC REVIEW 16-3

Sec. 351 Requirements, Gain Recognition Rules, and Basis Rules

1. To qualify for nonrecognition treatment under Sec. 351, there must be an exchange of property solely for stock and the transferor-shareholders must be in control (i.e., 80% stock ownership) of the corporation immediately after the exchange.
2. Nonqualifying property (e.g., cash or debt obligations of the transferee corporation) received by the transferors is treated as boot received.
3. Gain is recognized by the transferors to the extent of the lesser of the boot received or the realized gain.
4. Generally, no gain is recognized by the transferor-shareholders if liabilities are transferred to a controlled corporation. Exceptions to the nonrecognition of gain rule apply if (1) the principal purpose of the liability transfer is tax avoidance or if there is no bona fide business purpose or (2) if the total liabilities assumed or acquired by the corporation are in excess of the transferor's adjusted basis for the assets.
5. Substituted basis rules apply to the stock received by the transferors and carryover basis rules apply to contributed property in the hands of the transferee corporation.

The general requirements relating to the transfer of property to controlled corporations are summarized in Topic Review 16-3.

CAPITALIZATION OF THE CORPORATION

A corporation may be capitalized with both equity securities and long-term debt that are issued to the shareholders even though the issuance of debt no longer qualifies for nonrecognition of gain treatment under Sec. 351. The following advantages accrue from the issuance of debt in the capital structure:

- The interest payments on the debt are deductible by the corporation, whereas dividends are not deductible.

- Redemptions of stock may result in dividend income treatment to the shareholders unless certain requirements are met (see page 16-30) whereas a repayment of debt is a tax-free return of capital.

As previously mentioned, if the corporation is too thinly capitalized (e.g., excessive amounts of debt are issued relative to the amount of equity capital), the IRS will attempt to recharacterize the debt as equity and deny an interest deduction to the corporation. Generally, the courts have characterized an instrument solely as debt or equity. Section 385 now provides that an instrument having significant debt and equity characteristics may be treated as part debt and part equity.[49] The Treasury Department at one time issued Regulations providing safe-harbor rules and debt-equity ratio limits to determine the character of an instrument. The Regulations were so complex and controversial that they were withdrawn leaving taxpayers with no guidance other than from judicial decisions and Sec. 385 itself. Section 385 provides the following guidelines (or factors) for determining whether the debt is recharacterized as equity:

Typical Misconception

The thin capitalization issue is primarily a problem in the case of closely held corporations where the stockholders are also the ones holding the debt, and is not normally a problem for large publicly held corporations.

---

[49] Section 385(a) as amended by the Revenue Reconciliation Act of 1989 provides for part-debt and part-equity treatment on a nonretroactive basis pending the issuance of Treasury Regulations. To date these regulations have not been issued.

- The legal form of the instrument and actual adherence to its terms—For example, if (1) a reasonable interest rate is stated and interest is currently being paid and (2) a definite maturity date is stated and the notes are actually repaid when due, the evidence supports the taxpayer's contention that the instrument is, in fact, debt.

- Excessive debt-equity ratio—The courts have not prescribed any exact mathematical formula, although it is usually assumed that a debt-equity ratio that does not exceed 3 to 1 is likely to be acceptable.[50]

Key Point

The main advantages of debt are the deductibility of interest and the fact that the repayment of debt is not a taxable transaction.

- Proportionality of debt and the shareholder's equity interests—If the shareholders own the same percentage of the debt as their percentage of common stock, there is a greater likelihood that the debt is a disguised form of equity.

- Convertibility of the debt into stock of the corporation or contingent interest payments that are based upon corporate earnings—These features are more likely to be found in equity rather than in debt instruments.

The issuing corporation is required to characterize the interest as debt or stock. The holders (i.e., shareholders or debtholders) are prohibited from treating the interest inconsistently with the issuer's characterization unless they disclose the inconsistent treatment on their tax returns. The issuer's characterization is not binding on the IRS.

Example 16-33 ■

Palm Corporation is formed with $90,000 of debt consisting of 3-year shareholder notes and $10,000 of common stock. Individual notes of $30,000 are issued to each shareholder, Hank, Harold, and Antonio, who also own equal interests in the common stock. The interest payments are contingent upon the earnings of the company and the notes were not repaid at maturity. All of the factors above (i.e., high debt-equity ratio, proportionality of debt and equity interests, contingent interest payments, and the failure to observe the legal form of the obligation) indicate that the debt likely will be reclassified by the IRS as equity. If the debt is treated as equity on audit, the interest payments are not deductible by the corporation over the life of the debt and any repayments of debt are treated as a stock redemption and may represent dividends to the shareholders. ■

EARNINGS AND PROFITS

OBJECTIVE 4

Understand the significance of earnings and profits

Calculation of Earnings and Profits

Earnings and profits (E&P) is a measure of a corporation's economic ability to pay a dividend from its current and accumulated earnings without an impairment of capital. If there is no earnings and profits, a distribution represents a tax-free return of capital rather than a taxable dividend.

E&P is a tax term that is similar to the term *retained earnings* in financial accounting, although numerous differences exist between the two accounts.[51] For example, the issuance of a stock dividend usually results in a reduction of retained earnings but does not affect the E&P balance.

[50] Boris I. Bittker and James S. Eustice, *Federal Income Taxation of Corporations and Shareholders* (Boston: Warren, Gorham and Lamont, 1994), p. 4-35.

[51] The calculation of E&P has taken on added significance for 1990 and subsequent years because its definition is a factor in computing the adjusted current earnings used to calculate the AMT adjustment for the corporate alternative minimum tax.

Current E&P is calculated by making various adjustments to the corporation's taxable income, indicating the corporation's ability to pay a dividend. The computation of current E&P and the addition to accumulated E&P is illustrated as follows:

Taxable income

Plus: Income excluded from taxable income:
Tax-exempt interest income
Life insurance proceeds where the corporation is the beneficiary
Recoveries of bad debts and other deductions from which the corporation received no tax benefit
Federal income tax refunds from prior years

Plus: Income deferred to a later year when computing taxable income:
Deferred gain on installment sales

Plus or minus: Adjustments for items that must be recomputed:
Income on long-term contracts must be based on percentage of completion method rather than completed contract method
Excess of accelerated depreciation over straight-line depreciation
Excess of ACRS depreciation deductions claimed over straight-line ACRS calculation using an extended recovery period
Depreciation on personalty and realty must be based on:
The straight-line method for property other than MACRS or ACRS property
A straight-line ACRS calculation with an extended recovery period for ACRS property
The alternative depreciation system for MACRS property[52]
Excess of percentage depletion claimed over cost depletion

Plus: Deductions not allowed in computing E&P:
Dividends-received deduction
NOL carryovers, charitable contribution carryovers, and capital loss carryovers used in the current year

Minus: Expenses and losses not deductible in computing taxable income:
Federal income taxes
Life insurance premiums where the corporation is the beneficiary
Excess capital losses that are not deductible
Excess charitable contributions that are not deductible
Expenses related to production of tax-exempt income
Nondeductible losses on sales to related parties
Nondeductible penalties and fines
Nondeductible political contributions

Current E&P (or E&P deficit)
Minus: Distributions to shareholders

Addition to accumulated E&P (if any)

Example 16-34 ■ Park Corporation has the following taxable income and adjustments to its current E&P:

---

[52] Sec. 312(k)(3). For property placed in service after 1986, the alternative depreciation system is used to compute depreciation for E&P purposes. Depreciation is computed by using the straight-line method with a 5-year life for qualified technological equipment, automobiles, and light trucks; 12-year life for other personal property; and 40-year life for all real property.

Key Point

Several items that cannot be deducted in computing taxable income may be deducted in computing E&P.

Taxable income	$100,000
Plus:	
Tax-exempt bond interest	2,000
Key officer life insurance proceeds (nontaxable)	10,000
Dividends-received deduction (special deduction)	20,000
MACRS depreciation in excess of ADS depreciation	18,000
Percentage depletion in excess of cost depletion	10,000
	$160,000
Minus:	
Federal income tax liability	(22,250)
Capital losses (in excess of capital gains)	(5,000)
Key officer life insurance premiums (not deductible because the corporation is the beneficiary)	(2,000)
Charitable contributions (in excess of the 10% limitation)	(3,000)
Disallowed expense (e.g., penalties and fines)	(5,000)
Current E&P	$122,750
Minus: Cash dividends	(5,000)
Addition to accumulated E&P	$117,750

Real World Example

A corporation made a distribution to a stockholder in a year in which the corporation had available current E&P. However, there was an E&P deficit on the books of the company throughout the year resulting from a large negative balance in accumulated E&P at the beginning of the year. The court found the distribution to be taxable to the extent of the current E&P. Stanley V. Waldheim v. CIR, 51 AFTR 231, 57-1 USTC ¶ 9663 (7th Cir., 1957).

Current Versus Accumulated E&P

It is necessary to distinguish between current and accumulated E&P, because Sec. 316 provides specific tracing rules to determine whether a distribution is taxable as a dividend. For example, a distribution to shareholders is deemed to be made first out of current E&P, and therefore results in a taxable dividend even if there is a deficit in accumulated E&P. Accumulated E&P represents the total of all prior years' undistributed current E&P amounts as of the first day of the tax year. Distributions are deemed to be made out of accumulated E&P only after the current E&P (if any) is exhausted.

Example 16-35 ■ Pacific Corporation, a calendar-year taxpayer, has a $100,000 accumulated E&P deficit as of January 1. It reports $30,000 of current E&P. A $40,000 distribution is made to the shareholders. $30,000 of the distribution is a taxable dividend to the extent of the current E&P balance. $10,000 of the distribution is a tax-free return of capital (to the extent Pacific's shareholders have the requisite basis in their stock) because there is an accumulated E&P deficit. ■

If a shareholder's basis is reduced to zero due to a tax-free return of capital distribution, any excess amounts received are treated as a gain from the sale or exchange of the stock. Usually such amounts are taxed as a capital gain.

Current E&P is allocated on a pro rata basis to the distributions made during the year if the current E&P is less than the total amount distributed. However, accumulated E&P is allocated to the distributions in a chronological order.

Example 16-36 ■ Peach Corporation, a calendar-year taxpayer, has three shareholders who own their stock for all of the current year. Current E&P is $30,000, and accumulated E&P on January 1, is $10,000. Distributions of $30,000 each (totaling $60,000) are made on June 1, and December 1. The distributions are applied to the current and accumulated E&P accounts as follows:

	June 1 Distribution	*December 1 Distribution*
From current E&P[a]	$15,000	$15,000
From accumulated E&P	10,000	-0-
Tax-free return of capital	5,000	15,000
Total distribution	$30,000	$30,000

[a] $\dfrac{\$30,000}{\$60,000} \times \$30,000$

The impact of the allocation upon the tax treatment for individual shareholders is significant if new shareholders are added during the year or if there are sales of outstanding stock during the year. ∎

If there is a current E&P deficit and a positive accumulated E&P balance, both the current and accumulated E&P are netted on the date of the distribution.[53] The current E&P deficit for the year is prorated on a daily basis unless a nonratable allocation can be shown to be more appropriate.

Example 16-37 ∎ Prime Corporation, a calendar-year taxpayer, has a positive accumulated E&P balance of $100,000 and a $50,000 current E&P deficit. Prime makes a $30,000 distribution to its shareholders on June 30. The total E&P balance is $75,000 ($100,000 accumulated E&P − [0.50 × $50,000 current E&P deficit]) as of June 30, because the loss is allocated ratably during the year (i.e., 6 months out of 12 months, assuming that all months have 30 days), unless the corporation can show that a nonratable allocation is more appropriate. Therefore, the $30,000 distribution is fully taxable as a dividend. ∎

PROPERTY DISTRIBUTIONS

OBJECTIVE 5

Describe the consequences of distributions and stock redemptions

Tax Consequences to the Shareholders

Occasionally, a corporation distributes property (i.e., assets other than its stock or stock rights) instead of money to its shareholders. If property is distributed to the shareholders, the distributed amount

- Equals the FMV of the property.
- Is treated as a taxable dividend if there is sufficient E&P.
- Is reduced by the amount of distributed liabilities. In addition, the basis of the dividend property is equal to its FMV (without any reduction for any liabilities that are distributed).

Example 16-38 ∎ Red Corporation distributes land and a building having a $50,000 adjusted basis and a $100,000 FMV to its sole shareholder, Irene. Red has current and accumulated E&P of more than $60,000. The property is also subject to a $40,000 mortgage, which is assumed by Irene. The amount of the distribution to Irene is $60,000 ($100,000 FMV of the property − $40,000 liability). Irene has a $60,000

---

[53] Reg. Sec. 1.316-2(b).

Real World Example

A distribution of $20 Double Eagle gold coins was considered to be a property distribution rather than a distribution of money because the gold coins were withdrawn from circulation and had numismatic value. Warren C. Cordner v. U.S., 49 AFTR 2d 82-1353, 82-1 USTC ¶ 9275 (9th Cir., 1982).

taxable dividend because there is sufficient E&P. Irene's basis in the real estate is $100,000, its FMV. ∎

Tax Consequences to the Distributing Corporation

The general rule is that no gain or loss is recognized by a corporation that distributes property to its shareholders.[54] However, if a corporation distributes appreciated property to its shareholders, it is treated as if the corporation sold the property to the shareholder for its FMV immediately before the distribution and recognized any realized gain.[55]

Example 16-39 ∎

Key Point

A corporation usually recognizes gain on the distribution of appreciated property, but does not recognize losses on the distribution of property that has declined in value.

Rocket Corporation distributed land having a $50,000 adjusted basis and a $60,000 FMV to its shareholders. Rocket Corporation must recognize $10,000 ($60,000 − $50,000) of gain on the distribution of the appreciated property. ∎

If the property distributed is subject to a liability in excess of its basis, the FMV of such property, for purposes of determining the gain on the distribution, is treated as not being less than the amount of the liability.[56]

Example 16-40 ∎

Assume the same facts as in Example 16-39 except that Rocket Corporation also transfers a $70,000 liability to its shareholders. Rocket must recognize a $20,000 ($70,000–$50,000) gain on the distribution because the property's FMV is deemed to be no less than the amount of the liability. ∎

STOCK REDEMPTIONS

Two possible tax consequences can result when a corporation repurchases its outstanding stock from a shareholder:

Key Point

If all stock redemptions were treated as exchanges, it would be simple for individual stockholders in closely held corporations to recognize a capital gain on a redemption rather than ordinary (dividend) income.

- The redemption is treated as a taxable dividend (to the extent of E&P)
- The redemption is treated as an exchange of the stock, generally resulting in capital gain or loss treatment by the shareholder.

The dividend income rule prevents corporations from paying disguised dividends in the form of a stock redemption. For example, the corporation might redeem 10% of its sole shareholder's stock rather than pay a cash dividend to the shareholder. After the redemption, the shareholder (1) continues to own all of the outstanding stock, (2) has retained the same amount of control over the corporation, and (3) has received a substantial distribution of money or other property.

The tax advantage of capital gain treatment that is accorded to a stock redemption (compared with ordinary income treatment for dividends) is significant because individual shareholders are subject to a 28% maximum tax rate on their net capital gain. In addition, the exchange treatment is preferable if the shareholders have unused capital losses or capital loss carryovers that would otherwise be of limited tax benefit (e.g., capital losses for individuals are deductible against ordinary income up to $3,000 in any tax year and any excess is carried over). An additional advantage to the exchange treatment is that it permits the shareholders a tax-free recovery of their investment in the stock. A tax-free recovery of the shareholder's stock basis is not permitted if the distribution is a dividend.

---

[54] Sec. 311(a).
[55] Sec. 311(b).
[56] Secs. 311(b)(2) and 336(b).

Determining Whether a Redemption Is a Dividend or Capital Gain

Under Sec. 302, a redemption is treated as an exchange subject to capital gain or loss treatment if any of the following conditions or tests are met:

- The redemption is not essentially equivalent to a dividend.[57]
- The redemption is substantially disproportionate with respect to the shareholder's interest after the redemption is completed.[58]
- The redemption results in a complete termination of the shareholder's interest.[59]
- The redemption is made in partial liquidation of the corporation.[60]
- The redemption occurs in order to pay the funeral and administration expenses and death taxes of a deceased shareholder.[61]
- The redemption occurs when the stock is purchased by a related corporation, the sale is deemed to be a redemption, and one of the preceding five conditions or tests is met.[62]

Substantially Disproportionate Rule. If a distribution is substantially disproportionate, or if there is a complete termination of the shareholder's interest, capital gain or loss (rather than dividend income treatment results) because the shareholder or shareholders have significantly reduced the percentage of stock owned in the corporation or have completely disposed of the stock. Constructive stock ownership rules are generally applied to determine whether a redemption is disproportionate or is a complete termination of the shareholder's interest.[63] **Constructive stock ownership** means that the redeeming shareholder is deemed to own the stock of certain related parties (e.g., family members, partnerships, and corporations in which an ownership interest is held, and trusts and estates in which a beneficial interest is held).

To qualify as a substantially disproportionate redemption, the following tests must be met immediately after the redemption:

- The shareholder must own less than 80% of his former percentage interest in the voting stock (including stock held by related parties).
- The shareholder must also own less than 80% of his former percentage interest in the common (voting and nonvoting) stock (including stock held by related parties).
- The shareholder must own less than 50% of the voting stock (including stock held by related parties).

Jane owns 60 shares of Slow Corporation's single class of stock, and her mother owns 20 additional shares of Slow stock. 100 shares of the stock are outstanding. Slow Corporation redeems 30 shares of Jane's stock for $100,000. Jane's percentage interest before the redemption is 80% ([60 + 20 shares] ÷ 100 shares).

[57] Sec. 302(b)(1). This rule has been applied in limited situations to the redemption of preferred and common stock. Relief has been granted where the redeemed shareholder's voting control, right to share in current earnings, and rights to receive corporate assets upon liquidation has been significantly reduced. Ordinarily this occurs when a shareholder's majority interest is converted to a minority (less than 50%) interest, or a minority interest is reduced. The use of Sec. 302(b)(1) has been restricted by the Supreme Court (in *U.S. v. Maclin P. Davis*, 25 AFTR 2d 70-827, 70-1 USTC ¶ 9289 [USSC, 1970]).
[58] Sec. 302(b)(2).
[59] Sec. 302(b)(3).
[60] Sec. 302(b)(4).
[61] Sec. 303(a).
[62] Sec. 304(a).
[63] Sec. 318.

Real World Example
All of a father's stock in a corporation was redeemed, and his children were the remaining shareholders. Then the father entered into a long-term contract with the corporation to perform consulting and advisory services. The contract represented an "interest in the corporation" and the family attribution rules were not waived. Rev. Rul. 70-104, 1970-1 C.B. 66.

Immediately after the redemption, Jane's percentage interest is 71.4% ([30 + 20 shares] ÷ 70 shares). To meet the 80% test, Jane's interest must be less than 64% (80% × 80%). Therefore, Jane does not meet the 80% test. Also, Jane does not meet the 50% test because she does not own less than 50% of the Slow stock after the redemption. Both tests must be met to qualify as a substantially disproportionate redemption. Therefore, the $100,000 received is treated as a dividend and is taxable to Jane to the extent of Slow's E&P balance. The adjusted basis of the shares that were redeemed is added to Jane's basis in her remaining shares. ■

Complete Termination. Under Sec. 302(b)(3), a complete termination of a shareholder's stock interest qualifies for capital gain treatment. At first glance, it appears that this rule is redundant because the substantially disproportionate redemption rule should also apply to a redemption that results in a complete termination of a shareholder's interest. However, this is not the case because a special rule permits a waiver of the constructive ownership rules for family members if there is a complete termination. The constructive ownership rules are waived in a complete termination if the former shareholder files an agreement with the IRS that he will have no interest other than a creditor interest in the corporation for a period of 10 years.[64]

Example 16-42 ■

Assume the same facts as in Example 16-41 except that Slow Corporation redeems the 60 shares held by Jane for $200,000, and Jane's basis for her shares is $90,000. The constructive stock ownership rules are waived if Jane agrees not to acquire any interest in Slow Corporation for a period of 10 years. Therefore, Jane's interest is completely terminated, and the redemption is treated as a sale of stock qualifying for capital gain treatment. Jane has a capital gain of $110,000 ($200,000 − $90,000). If the waiver is not obtained, the substantially disproportionate tests under Sec. 302(b)(2) are applied to determine if the redemption qualifies as a sale or exchange. Jane would be considered to own 50% of the stock (20 shares owned ÷ 40 outstanding shares) immediately after the redemption and the substantially disproportionate redemption test would not be met. The redemption does not qualify as a complete termination because Jane is deemed to own her mother's stock unless a waiver of the constructive ownership rules is obtained. Thus, the redemption would be treated as a dividend to Jane unless a waiver is obtained so that the complete termination rules will apply or the distribution is "not essentially equivalent" to a dividend under Sec. 302(b)(1). ■

Redemption Provisions for Specialized Situations

The Code contains the following redemption rules to cover specialized situations:

- Section 302(b)(4) provides sale or exchange (rather than dividend income) treatment for noncorporate shareholder redemptions in a partial liquidation. To qualify, the distribution must be "not essentially equivalent" to a dividend to the distributing corporation, or the distribution must be made pursuant to the termination of an active trade or business.[65]
- Section 303 permits the executor of an estate or a beneficiary to redeem stock in a closely held corporation, whereby the redemption is treated as a sale or

---

[64] Sec. 302(c)(2). The former shareholder cannot serve as an officer, director, or employee for at least 10 years and must notify the IRS if additional stock is acquired (other than by bequest or inheritance). If such stock is acquired, it usually causes the redemption to be taxed as a dividend.

[65] Sec. 302(e). The distributions must be made pursuant to a plan and must occur within the same tax year in which the plan is adopted or within the next succeeding tax year. Immediately after the distribution, the distributing corporation must be actively engaged in the conduct of at least one qualified trade or business.

exchange (rather than as dividend income) provided the value of the closely held stock included in the estate is in excess of 35% of the value of the gross estate (reduced by deductions for debts, funeral and administration expenses and losses deductible under Secs. 2053 and 2054).[66] The redemption amount is limited to the death taxes imposed and the amount of funeral and administration expenses deductible under Sec. 2053.[67]

- Section 306 (known as the **preferred stock bailout** provision) prevents shareholders who receive nontaxable preferred stock dividends from receiving capital gain treatment upon the sale or redemption of the preferred stock. The sale of the preferred stock usually results in ordinary income to the shareholder; the redemption of the preferred stock is treated as dividend income (provided sufficient E&P is present).[68] (See Chapter 4 of the *Prentice Hall's Federal Taxation: Corporations, Partnerships, Estates, and Trusts* text for detailed coverage of these other redemption provisions including redemptions through the use of related corporations under Sec. 304 that are not discussed in this text.)

CORPORATE DISTRIBUTIONS IN COMPLETE LIQUIDATION

OBJECTIVE 6

Understand the consequences of a corporate liquidation to shareholders and the liquidating corporation

Typical Misconception

It is sometimes assumed that the liquidation of a corporation is always associated with the discontinuance of business activities. Sometimes the business is operated as a partnership or sole proprietorship after the liquidation.

Sometimes it is desirable to terminate a corporation's existence. A complete liquidation is similar to a stock redemption, except that all (rather than a portion) of the stock is redeemed. In a complete liquidation, the assets are either (1) distributed in kind to the shareholders in exchange for their stock or (2) sold and converted to cash, which is then distributed to the shareholders in exchange for their stock. The corporation is then usually dissolved under state law.

Surprisingly, the reasons for a complete termination are not always associated with unprofitable operations. For example, a highly successful closely held company may have management continuity problems because the key officer-shareholder group is approaching retirement age, or it may also be desirable as a matter of organizational management policy for a parent corporation to liquidate a subsidiary and continue its operations as a separate division.

Tax Consequences to the Liquidating Corporation

Distribution of Assets. The liquidating corporation recognizes gains and losses on distributions of property. A corporation that makes the liquidating distribution is treated as if it had sold the assets for their FMV to the shareholders immediately before the distribution. If the distributed property is subject to a liability, the FMV of the property is treated as being not less than the amount of the liability.[69]

Example 16-43 ■

Pursuant to a complete liquidation, Southern Corporation distributes the following assets to its shareholders:

- Inventory—$10,000 basis, $20,000 FMV

- Land held as an investment—$5,000 basis, $30,000 FMV, subject to a liability of $40,000

- Marketable securities—$20,000 basis, $15,000 FMV

[66] Sec. 303(b)(2). Special rules apply to stock owned in two or more corporations. See Sec. 303(b)(2)(B).

[67] Secs. 303(a)(1) and (2).

[68] Secs. 306(a)(1) and (2).

[69] Sec. 336(b).

Additional Comment

Before the Tax Reform Act of 1986, a corporation in liquidation generally recognized no gain or loss on distributions of property to shareholders. Congress changed this policy since the prior law created distortions in business behavior since a liquidating distribution was given preferential tax treatment over a nonliquidating distribution. Also, the rule tended to undermine the imposition of the corporate income tax.

Key Point

Losses on the distribution of property to related persons can be recognized if the distribution is pro rata.

Southern Corporation recognizes: $10,000 ($20,000 − $10,000) of ordinary income on the distribution of the inventory; $35,000 ($40,000 − $5,000) of capital gain on the distribution of the land; and $5,000 ($15,000 − $20,000) of capital loss on the distribution of the marketable securities. ∎

Sale of Assets. The tax consequences for an asset sale closely parallel a liquidating distribution. For example, if a corporation sells its assets pursuant to a complete liquidation and then distributes money to its shareholders, all gain or loss realized on the sale of the assets is recognized by the corporation.

Limitation on Loss Recognition. Under the general rule, both gains and losses are recognized on liquidations. When the liquidation rules were being revised by the Tax Reform Act of 1986, it was felt that taxpayers might attempt to recognize losses in inappropriate situations or inflate losses actually sustained. Therefore, special limitations are provided for the recognition of losses in certain situations.

The recognition of losses is restricted in related party situations.[70] A corporation and a shareholder are related parties if the shareholder's direct and constructive ownership is more than 50% in value of the corporation's outstanding stock. Generally, losses cannot be recognized on the distribution of property to a related person if the property (1) is not distributed pro rata to all shareholders or (2) consists of "disqualified property."[71] Disqualified property is property acquired by the liquidating corporation in certain types of tax-free transfers (i.e., a Sec. 351 transaction or a capital contribution) from the shareholders during the 5-year period preceding the distribution.

Example 16-44 ∎

Star Corporation's stock is owned equally by three sisters who are related parties under Sec. 267 because they own more than 50% of the corporation's outstanding stock. One year before Star Corporation is liquidated, the three shareholders transfer property having a $100,000 basis and a $40,000 FMV to Star Corporation in return for additional Star stock in a transaction that qualifies under Sec. 351. In liquidation, Star Corporation transfers the property having a $100,000 basis and a $40,000 FMV to the three related shareholders. Star cannot recognize the $60,000 ($40,000 − $100,000) realized loss, since this is a related party situation where disqualified property is being distributed. ∎

Section 336(d)(2) contains a special rule for carryover basis transactions where the principal purpose of the transfer and a subsequent sale or distribution of the property is to recognize a loss for the liquidating corporation. The prohibited purpose of shifting losses will be presumed to exist if the transfer occurs after the date two years before the date that a plan of complete liquidation is adopted. In such a case the adjusted basis of the transferred property for loss purposes only is reduced by the built-in loss (i.e., the excess of the adjusted basis of the property immediately after its acquisition by the corporation over its FMV).

Tax Attribute Carryovers. The tax attributes (e.g., NOL carryovers, earnings and profits, capital loss carryovers, and tax credits) disappear when the liquidation is completed.

Key Point

An appraisal may be necessary to determine the FMV of distributed assets.

Tax Consequences to the Shareholders

The general rule for complete liquidations is that the shareholders are deemed to have sold their stock to the corporation in exchange for money or other property.[72] If the

---

[70] Related party situations are those covered by Sec. 267.
[71] Sec. 336(d).
[72] Sec. 331(a)(1).

stock is a capital asset, capital gain or loss is recognized equal to the difference between the money plus the FMV of the other property distributed to the shareholder and the adjusted basis of the shareholder's stock.[73] The basis of the property that is received is its FMV on the distribution date.[74]

Example 16-45 ■

Sun Corporation makes a liquidating distribution of land with a $70,000 adjusted basis and a $100,000 FMV to shareholder John, who surrenders his Sun stock to the corporation. Joan, another shareholder, receives cash of $100,000 for her shares. John's adjusted basis in the Sun stock is $40,000. Joan's adjusted basis is $120,000. John recognizes a $60,000 capital gain ($100,000 − $40,000), while Joan has a $20,000 capital loss ($120,000 − $100,000). The tax basis of the land received by John is $100,000 (the land's FMV on the distribution date).　■

Section 332: Liquidation of a Subsidiary Corporation

Gain and Loss Considerations. There is an exception to the general rule that gain or loss is recognized in a liquidating distribution. This exception applies to the liquidation of a subsidiary corporation into its parent corporation. No gain or loss is recognized by either the parent or the subsidiary corporations if a parent corporation liquidates an 80%-owned subsidiary corporation.[75] In a Sec. 332 liquidation, the subsidiary corporation is usually dissolved and the assets and liabilities are transferred to the parent corporation. Section 332 nonrecognition rules are mandatory (rather than elective) if their requirements are satisfied.

Key Point

Section 351 permits a parent corporation to incorporate a subsidiary corporation tax free. Section 332 permits a parent to liquidate a subsidiary without incurring adverse tax results where the subsidiary's property has significantly appreciated in value.

The subsidiary corporation is required to do either of the following:[76]

- Distribute all its property to the parent corporation in complete redemption of its stock within a single tax year.

- Make a series of liquidating distributions resulting in a complete liquidation over a 3-year period that commences with the close of the tax year in which the first liquidating distribution is made.

If there is a minority interest being liquidated also, the general liquidation rules apply, and gain (but not loss) is recognized by the subsidiary corporation on property distributed to a minority shareholder. The liquidation will also be taxable to the minority shareholders with gain or loss being recognized under the general liquidation rules outlined above.

Key Point

A parent corporation that has a basis for its subsidiary's stock greater than the tax basis of its share of the subsidiary's net assets may lose the tax benefit of the economic loss if the subsidiary is liquidated.

Basis Considerations. The basis of the subsidiary's assets carry over to the parent corporation, and the adjusted basis of the parent corporation's interest in the subsidiary stock disappears.[77] This carryover basis rule may create certain inequities because the parent corporation may have paid an amount for the subsidiary stock that is greater (or less) than the tax basis of the parent corporation's share of the subsidiary's net assets.

Example 16-46 ■

Tampa Corporation acquires 100% of Top Corporation's stock in 1990 for $100,000. In 1994, Top is liquidated, and assets having a $50,000 tax basis are

---

[73] Certain losses on small business stock receive ordinary loss treatment if the requirements of Sec. 1244 are met (see Chapter 8).

[74] Sec. 334(a).

[75] Secs. 332 and 337. Pursuant to Sec. 1504(a)(2), eighty percent ownership means the parent corporation must own at least 80% of the total combined voting power of all classes of stock and at least 80% of the total value of all classes of stock.

[76] Secs. 332(b)(2) and (3). See Rev. Rul. 71-326, 1971-2C.B. 177 which holds that the distributions must occur within a single tax year which does not have to be the same tax year in which the plan is adopted.

[77] Sec. 334(b)(1).

transferred to Tampa Corporation. Under the general rule, Tampa's $100,000 stock basis disappears, and the basis of Top's assets is only $50,000 on Tampa's books. ∎

If these carryover basis rules apply, the parent corporation inherits the tax attributes of the subsidiary.[78] For example, NOL and capital loss carryovers and the E&P balance of the liquidated subsidiary carry over to the parent corporation. Under the carryover basis rules of Sec. 334(b)(1), the subsidiary does not recognize any depreciation or investment tax credit recapture. This recapture potential carries over to the parent corporation.

The complete liquidation rules under Secs. 331 and 332 are summarized in Topic Review 16-4.

TAX PLANNING CONSIDERATIONS

Key Point

Reasonableness of a salary payment is a question of fact to be determined for each case. There is no formula that can be used to determine a reasonable amount.

Dividend Policy

Dividends that are paid from E&P are (1) fully taxable to shareholders and (2) not deductible by the corporation. Thus, in a closely-held corporation where there is no separation of ownership and management, it may be desirable to increase salaries or rental payments to owner-shareholders rather than to increase dividends. Despite the fact that the increased salary or rental payments are also taxable to the shareholders, these payments are deductible as business expenses as long as the amounts are not unreasonable.

Example 16-47 ∎ Mario and Nancy are equal owners of the Texas Corporation, which is highly profitable and has substantial E&P. Mario and Nancy are the key officers and are paid a salary of $100,000 each. A reasonable salary for each would be $150,000. If it is desirable to increase cash distributions to the owners, additional salary payments of $50,000 should be made to both Mario and Nancy (rather than increasing the dividend payments by the same amount) because the salary payments are deductible by the corporation, whereas the dividend payments are not. The salary payments result in only a single level of taxation, while the dividend payments result in double taxation. Consideration should also be given to payroll taxes because the additional $50,000 compensation may subject the employer and the officers to additional payroll taxes (e.g., the hospitalization portion of the FICA tax). ∎

Utilization of Losses

Net operating losses and capital losses may be of limited benefit due to the loss carryover limitations (i.e., NOL carryovers are limited to 15 years and net capital losses expire after 5 years). Therefore, attempts should be made to trigger the recognition of additional amounts of ordinary income and/or capital gains to utilize any expiring carryovers. The sale of appreciated business assets results in the recognition of Sec. 1231 gain that may be used to offset capital loss carryovers, because net Sec. 1231 gains receive capital gain treatment. The sale or disposition of assets may also result in the recognition of ordinary income because of the depreciation recapture rules. This ordinary income may be offset against the expiring NOLs.

[78] Sec. 381.

TOPIC REVIEW 16-4

Distributions in Complete Liquidation

Sec. 331 Liquidation— General Liquidation Rules	Liquidating Corporation	Shareholders
Recognition of gain or loss	Gain or loss is generally recognized equal to the difference between the FMV of property distributed and its adjusted basis.	Gain or loss is recognized equal to the difference between the sum of the money and the FMV of the other property received and the basis of the shareholder's stock in the liquidating corporation.
Exception to the gain or loss rule	Generally, losses are not recognized on certain distributions of property to related persons, or property acquired in a carryover basis transaction where the principal purpose was tax avoidance.	Not applicable.
Basis considerations	Not applicable.	The basis of property received is its FMV.
Tax attributes	The tax attributes (e.g., NOL carryovers and E&P) disappear when the liquidation is completed.	Not applicable.

Sec. 332 Liquidation— Subsidiary Corporation	Parent Corporation	Subsidiary Corporation
General requirements	Sec. 332 is mandatory. The parent corporation must own at least 80% of the subsidiary corporation's stock.	The subsidiary corporation is dissolved and its assets and liabilities are transferred to the parent corporation.
Recognition of gain or loss	No gain or loss is recognized. An exception is provided for distributions to minority shareholders.	No gain or loss is recognized on the transfer of assets to the parent. Gain but not loss is recognized on distributions to minority shareholders.
Basis considerations	The basis of the subsidiary's assets carryover from the subsidiary's books.	Not applicable.
Tax attributes	The tax attributes (e.g., NOL carryovers and E&P) carry over to the parent corporation.	Not applicable.

If net operating losses or capital losses are anticipated during a business's start-up phase, an S corporation election may be desirable because the losses can be used by the shareholders. The S corporation election may be terminated when the corporation becomes profitable. (See Chapter 15 for a discussion of S corporations.)

Charitable Contributions

Many owners of closely held corporations prefer to make charitable donations through their controlled corporation rather than as individuals because of the deductibility of the contributions by the corporation. Otherwise, to fund the contributed amounts, it would be necessary for the controlled corporation to make nondeductible dividend payments to the shareholders.

Even though corporate contributions in excess of the 10% limitation may be carried forward 5 years, it is generally undesirable for a corporation to have excess contributions because they may be unable to utilize such amounts during the carryover years. An accrual-basis corporation sometimes can avoid making excess contributions by accruing contributions if (1) an accrual equal to or less than the limitation amount is authorized by the board of directors before the end of the tax year and (2) the payment is made to the charities within 2½ months following the end of the tax year.

Dividends-Received Deduction

Under the general rule in Sec. 243, corporate shareholders are eligible to deduct 80% (or 70%) of dividends received. However, this deduction is limited to 80% (or 70%) of taxable income unless the corporation is in an NOL position (after the dividends-received deduction is computed under the general rule). Thus, a substantial scale-down of the dividends-received deduction may result if taxable income (other than the dividend income) is negative and if the final result is a small amount of taxable income instead of an NOL. Therefore, if the limitation is expected to apply, the corporation should either (1) accelerate deductions into the current year or (2) postpone the recognition of income to a later year. Either action can result in the recognition of an NOL that prevents the limitation on the dividends-received deduction from applying. (See Examples 16-18 and 16-19.)

COMPLIANCE AND PROCEDURAL CONSIDERATIONS

Filing Requirements

Form 1120 (U.S. Corporation Income Tax Return) must be filed even if the corporation is only in existence for part of the year. The basic return is supplemented with a separate Schedule D to report capital gains and losses. In addition, Form 4626 (Alternative Minimum Tax—Corporations) must be filed even if no alternative minimum tax is due (see Appendix B for sample Forms 1120, 1120—Schedule D, and 4626). Certain (small) corporations are eligible to file a simplified Form 1120-A (U.S. Corporation Short-Form Income Tax Return) if their gross receipts, total income, or total assets are less than $500,000. (See Appendix B for a sample Form 1120-A.) The Form 1120-A may not be filed in certain instances (e.g., the corporation is in the process of being liquidated or is a member of a controlled group).

Key Point

The due date for paying the final estimated tax installment is one month earlier than for individuals.

The regular filing due date for the corporate return is the fifteenth day of the third month following the end of the tax year (e.g., March 15 for calendar-year corporations). An automatic 6-month extension can be obtained by filing Form 7004 (Application for Automatic Extension of Time to File Corporation Income Tax Return) which is included in Appendix B. If an extension is obtained, the full amount of the estimated tax due must be paid on or before the due date of the return (e.g., March 15 for calendar-year corporations).

Quarterly estimated tax payments must be made on the fifteenth day of the fourth, sixth, ninth, and twelfth months of the tax year. In general, the estimated tax payments must be the lesser of (1) 100% of the corporation's tax liability for the current year or (2) 100% of the tax shown on the preceding year's return.[79] However, a corporation may not base the installment payments of estimated tax on the preceding year's tax liability if that liability was $0.[80] The corporation is subject to a nondeductible underpayment penalty on the underpayment to the extent that the amount paid by one of the four payment dates is less than the portion of the smaller of 100% of the tax due for the current year or 100% of the tax due for the preceding year that is owed by the corporation on such date.

Schedule M-1 and M-2 Reconciliations

Schedule M-1 is used to reconcile financial accounting net income with taxable income. A completed Schedule M-1 based upon the following adjustments is shown in Figure 16-1:

Net income per books	$100,000
Plus:	
Federal income tax liability	3,000
Net capital losses	2,000
Nondeductible premiums on key officers' life insurance	4,000
Minus:	
Tax-exempt interest	(9,000)
Excess of tax depreciation over financial accounting depreciation	(75,000)
Taxable income (before special deductions)	$ 25,000

Schedule M-2 reconciles the beginning of the year balance in retained earnings (for financial accounting purposes) with the balance in the account at the end of the year. This reconciliation helps to explain changes in the balance sheet which are reported on Schedule L or to account for items of income, gain, or loss that are taken directly to retained earnings without being reported as part of net income. A completed Schedule M-2 based upon the above facts which include a $140,000 balance for retained earnings on January 1, $100,000 of net income for financial accounting, and the payment of a $40,000 cash dividend is shown in Figure 16-2.

Key Point

The due date for filing the corporate tax return is one month earlier than the due date for individual returns.

[79] The percentage of the corporation's current year tax liability was 97% in 1993. Exceptions are provided for (1) large corporations and (2) corporations that earn their income unevenly during the tax year. Large corporations—those corporations with taxable income of more than $1 million in any of the 3 preceding tax years—must make quarterly estimated tax payments based on 100% of the tax shown on their current year return, although they are permitted to make their first quarter payment based on 100% of the preceding year's tax liability (Sec. 6654[d]). Section 6655(e) permits corporations to use an annualized income installment or seasonally adjusted installment if it is less than the normally required installment (Sec. 6655[e]).

[80] Rev. Rul. 92-54 1992-2 C.B. 320.

Schedule M-1	Reconciliation of Income (Loss) per Books With Income per Return (See instructions.)				
1	Net income (loss) per books	100,000	7	Income recorded on books this year not included on this return (itemize):	
2	Federal income tax	3,000		Tax-exempt interest $ 9,000	
3	Excess of capital losses over capital gains .	2,000			
4	Income subject to tax not recorded on books this year (itemize):				9,000
5	Expenses recorded on books this year not deducted on this return (itemize):		8	Deductions on this return not charged against book income this year (itemize):	
a	Depreciation . . . . . $		a	Depreciation . . . . . $ 75,000	
b	Contributions carryover $		b	Contributions carryover $	
c	Travel and entertainment $				
	Premiums on Life Insurance	4,000	9	Add lines 7 and 8	75,000
6	Add lines 1 through 5	109,000	10	Income (line 28, page 1)—line 6 less line 9	84,000
					25,000

FIGURE 16-1 Form 1120, Schedule M-1

Schedule M-2	Analysis of Unappropriated Retained Earnings per Books (Line 25, Schedule L)				
1	Balance at beginning of year	140,000	5	Distributions: a Cash	40,000
2	Net income (loss) per books	100,000		b Stock	
3	Other increases (itemize):			c Property	
			6	Other decreases (itemize):	
			7	Add lines 5 and 6	40,000
4	Add lines 1, 2, and 3	240,000	8	Balance at end of year (line 4 less line 7)	200,000

FIGURE 16-2 Form 1120, Schedule M-2

Maintenance of Records for E&P

Companies are not required to compute E&P on the tax return. Therefore, many companies do not maintain adequate records for this account. Detailed records of items that comprise current and accumulated E&P should be maintained because the statute of limitations remains open indefinitely on this determination and the taxpayer has the burden of proof. Thus, if the IRS determines that a company has current or accumulated E&P and treats a distribution as a taxable dividend rather than a tax-free return of capital, the taxpayer must show that the IRS determination is erroneous.

Form 5452 (Corporate Report of Nondividend Distributions) must be filed by a corporation that makes a return of capital distribution. This form requires a computation of earnings and profits for the tax year and a schedule of differences between taxable income and the earnings and profits. A year-by-year computation of accumulated earnings and profits is also required.

PROBLEM MATERIALS

DISCUSSION QUESTIONS

16-1. Allen is the sole proprietor of a highly profitable business. He asks your advice regarding the incorporation of the business and the possible election of S corporation treatment. Discuss the tax and nontax factors that should be considered and prepare a list of questions that you should raise with Allen regarding his personal and business situation.

16-2. Anya is considering whether to become a limited partner in a real estate limited partnership by making an investment of $10,000. The limited partnership will generate substantial operating losses for the first 5 years.

    a. What are the tax consequences to Anya if the partnership is deemed to be an association (taxable as a corporation)?

    b. How many of the corporate characteristics must the partnership possess to be reclassified as an association?

16-3. Able Corporation has $40,000 of taxable income (excluding property transactions). A $20,000 NLTCG is recognized from the property transactions. How is the $20,000 NLTCG taxed?

16-4. Apple Corporation's annual taxable income is currently $600,000 and is expected to continue at this level for several years. The company's chief financial officer indicates that a proposed investment in new assets is expected to increase taxable income by $100,000 but will result in an increase in after-tax income of only $61,000 because the corporation's marginal tax rate is 39%.

    a. Is the chief financial officer correct that the corporation's marginal tax rate is 39%? Explain.

    b. Would your answer to Part a change if Apple's taxable income (before making the investment) is only $100,000?

    c. Would your answer to Part a change if Apple's taxable income (before making the investment) is $15 million?

16-5. Ace Corporation's taxable income is $20,000, and its tax preferences and positive adjustments for alternative minimum tax purposes are $100,000.

    a. Is the corporation subject to the corporate alternative minimum tax?

    b. What reporting requirements must be satisfied for the preparation of the corporation's tax return?

16-6. Acme Corporation is a highly profitable closely held corporation that has never paid a dividend. During the past 5 years, earnings of $200,000 per year have been retained in the business. All of the earnings have been reinvested in operating assets to finance an expansion of the business. Is the corporation subject to possible attack by the IRS regarding the imposition of the accumulated earnings tax because no dividends have been paid?

16-7. How is it possible for a newly formed corporation to be subject to the personal holding company tax but be exempt from the accumulated earnings tax?

16-8. Why are controlled groups of corporations required to apportion the lower tax rates applicable to taxable income up to $75,000 among the group members?

16-9. Acorn Corporation has a NSTCG of $5,000 and a NLTCL of $9,000 in 1994. In 1993, Acorn Corporation has a NLTCG of $3,000. No other capital gains or losses are reported in prior tax years.

    a. Do the NSTCG and NLTCL have to be offset in 1994?

    b. Is any portion of the NLTCL deductible in 1994?

    c. What loss carryback or carryforward rules should be applied to any unused capital losses incurred in 1994?

16-10. If a corporation has net Sec. 1231 (business assets) losses and net long-term capital gains, are the gains and losses netted against each other? What difference does it make if the items are netted or treated separately?

16-11. How is it possible for a corporation to derive only limited tax benefit from its dividends-received deduction?

16-12. Under what circumstances might a corporation elect not to carry back a NOL to one of the three carryback years?

16-13. What requirements must be met for an accrual-basis corporation to deduct a charitable contribution in a year prior to its payment?

16-14. Acorn Corporation is publicly traded on the American Stock Exchange. Its chief executive officer, Carl, currently receives an annual salary of $1 million. The Board of Directors is considering an increase in his compensation level by $200,000.

    a. What are the income tax consequences to Acorn if Carl's salary is increased to $1,200,000?

    b. What alternatives might be considered to increase Carl's annual compensation that would produce more favorable tax consequences for Acorn Corporation?

16-15. Andy, Barry, and Carmen form a new corporation by transferring properties from their sole proprietorships in exchange for all of the Adobe Corporation stock. Describe the effect of the following events on the taxability of the exchange transaction:

    a. Andy transfers assets with a $30,000 adjusted basis and a $38,000 FMV in exchange for $28,000 of Adobe stock and $10,000 cash.

    b. Barry transfers assets with a $50,000 adjusted basis and a $100,000 FMV in exchange for $40,000 of Adobe stock and Barry's liabilities of $60,000 being assumed by the corporation.

    c. Carmen transfers assets (including $10,000 cash) with a $50,000 adjusted basis and a $60,000 FMV in exchange for Adobe stock and $20,000 of ten-year Adobe notes.

16-16. Discuss the underlying rationale for the nonrecognition of gain or loss in a Sec. 351 transaction.

16-17. Cathy receives 40% of Allied Corporation stock and an Allied demand note of $50,000 in a transaction otherwise qualifying for nonrecognition of gain or loss under Sec. 351. Cathy transfers assets with a $60,000 adjusted basis and an $80,000 FMV in exchange for $30,000 of Allied stock and the $50,000 demand note. How is the demand note treated for purposes of Sec. 351?

16-18. Explain why the basis of property that is contributed to a corporation in a Sec. 351 exchange is not equal to its FMV on the date of the exchange. Is the basis of the property to the corporation adjusted if a gain is recognized by the transferor?

16-19. Carmen transfers land and a building having a $60,000 adjusted basis and a $100,000 FMV to the Bass Corporation in a transaction qualifying under Sec. 351. Immediately prior to the exchange, Carmen takes out a $50,000 mortgage on the property. The mortgage is assumed by the corporation, and the mortgage proceeds are used by Carmen to remodel her personal residence. What are the likely tax consequences of the asset transfer?

16-20. Damien, Eric, and Fred are forming a new corporation. Each individual will contribute $100,000 of property and receive a one-third ownership interest. The plan is for each individual to receive $10,000 of common stock and a $90,000 20-year corporate note bearing an 8% annual interest rate.

    a. What are the advantages of capitalizing the corporation with a high percentage of debt?

    b. What are the income tax complications to Damien, Eric, and Fred if they transfer appreciated properties to the newly formed corporation in a transaction that qualifies under Sec. 351?

    c. List the factors that are used to determine whether an instrument is debt or equity.

    d. What are the tax consequences if the notes are subsequently recharacterized as equity upon an audit of the corporation by the IRS?

16-21. Due to severe financial difficulties Big Corporation has not paid a dividend to its shareholders for several years. Big has a $300,000 accumulated E&P deficit on January 1, 1994 but has sufficient liquidity to resume dividend payments. Current E&P is expected to be $10,000 in 1994 and $50,000 for 1995 and subsequent years.

    a. What are the income tax consequences for the shareholders if a $50,000 cash distribution is made in 1994?

    b. What are the income tax consequences for the shareholders if the $50,000 distribution is delayed until January, 1995?

16-22. Best Corporation has a $100,000 accumulated E&P deficit and $50,000 of current E&P. A $60,000 cash distribution is made to shareholders in the current year. How much, if any, of the distribution is taxable to the shareholders?

16-23. Blue Corporation distributes a one-half interest in land to each of its two shareholders—Gail and Central Corporation. The land has a $50,000 adjusted basis and a $200,000 FMV. Blue Corporation has E&P of $400,000.

    a. What are the amount of the dividend and basis of the land to Gail and Central Corporation?

    b. What is the gain recognized on the distribution by Blue Corporation?

   c. What are the tax consequences to Gail and Central Corporation if Blue Corporation instead has a deficit in both accumulated and current E&P? (Assume that Gail's stock basis is $80,000 and that Central Corporation's stock basis is $120,000).

16-24. Why is it generally preferable to structure the redemption of a shareholder's stock so that it meets the mechanical tests in Sec. 302(b)(2) (substantially disproportionate) or Sec. 302(b)(3) (complete termination), rather than to rely upon Sec. 302(b)(1) (not essentially equivalent to a dividend)?

16-25. If the Sec. 302(b)(3) (complete termination of a shareholder's interest) requirements are met, shouldn't the Sec. 302(b)(2) (substantially disproportionate redemption) requirements also be met? What is the major difference between these two provisions?

16-26. Explain the tax consequences to a liquidating corporation and its shareholders of each of the following independent situations.
   a. City Corporation adopts a plan of liquidation, sells its assets and makes a final $500,000 cash liquidating distribution to its sole shareholder in redemption of her stock. The sale of City's assets results in a $70,000 recognized loss. The shareholder's basis in her stock is $300,000.
   b. Coastal Corporation distributes all of its assets having a $400,000 adjusted basis and a $500,000 FMV to its sole shareholder in complete liquidation of his stock. The shareholder's basis in his Coastal stock is $200,000.

16-27. Why is it generally preferable to increase salaries or rental payments to employee-shareholders in a closely held corporation rather than to increase dividends?

PROBLEMS

16-28. *Corporate Tax Rates.* In December of the current year, Colorado Corporation is considering the sale of certain corporate assets that would result in the recognition of a $50,000 LTCG. The company comptroller estimates that the taxable income for the current year will be $60,000 (before considering the LTCG). It is estimated that taxable income for the following year will be $200,000 (before considering the LTCG).
   a. What is Colorado Corporation's tax liability if the assets are sold in the current year?
   b. What is Colorado Corporation's tax liability if the assets are sold in the following year?
   c. Should the assets be sold in the current year or in the following year? Explain.

16-29. *Corporate Tax Rates.* Ajax Corporation's taxable income for the current year is $20 million.
   a. What is Ajax Corporation's regular tax liability?
   b. What is Ajax's regular tax liability if taxable income is $10 million?
   c. What is Ajax's regular tax liability if taxable income is only $335,000?

16-30. *Alternative Minimum Tax* Columbus Corporation reports the following results for the current year:

Taxable income	$100,000
Regular tax liability	22,250
Tax preferences	60,000
Positive AMT adjustments	40,000

   a. What is Columbus Corporation's alternative minimum taxable income?
   b. What is Columbus Corporation's tentative minimum tax and alternative minimum tax liability?

16-31. *Alternative Minimum Tax.* Compact Corporation reports the following results for the current year:

Taxable income	$400,000
Adjusted current earnings	600,000
Tax preferences	80,000

   a. What is Compact Corporation's alternative minimum taxable income?
   b. What is Compact Corporation's regular tax liability?
   c. What is Compact Corporation's tentative minimum tax and alternative minimum tax liability?

16-32. *Tax Preferences and AMT Adjustments.* During the course of an audit of the Control Corporation, you have been assigned to review the company's 1994 tax accrual (e.g., provision for federal income taxes and the related liability). The following information is made available for your review:

- Taxable income for regular income tax purposes is $100,000.
- Tax depreciation on real estate placed in service in 1989 is $90,000. Straight-line depreciation with a 40-year life would have been $50,000.
- Accelerated depreciation on real estate placed in service in 1986 is $2,000,000. Straight-line depreciation would have been $1,900,000.
- Adjusted current earnings is $340,000.

a. What is the total amount of Control Corporation's tax preferences and AMT adjustments for the current year?

b. What is Control Corporation's alternative minimum tax liability?

16-33. *Accumulated Earnings Tax.* Crane Corporation, a manufacturer of widgets, is being audited by the IRS to ascertain whether the company is subject to the accumulated earnings tax in the current year. Crane reported the following results during the year:

Taxable income	$150,000
Federal income taxes	41,750
Dividends-received deduction	85,000
Dividends paid on June 1	20,000

The accumulated E&P balance on January 1 was $180,000, and the company can justify the retention of $80,000 of current earnings to meet its reasonable needs.

a. What is Crane Corporation's accumulated taxable income?

b. What is Crane Corporation's accumulated earnings tax liability?

16-34. *Personal Holding Company Tax.* Delta Corporation has been gradually converting its operating business into an investment company because its retained earnings have been invested in passive investments. The company is owned by three shareholders, and more than 60% of its income is personal holding company income. George, the president of Delta Corporation, however, feels that personal holding company status should not be detrimental because the company has paid dividends to its shareholders for several years and should, therefore, not be liable for any penalty tax.

Delta reports the following results for the current year:

Taxable income	$25,000
Federal income tax liability	3,750
Dividends paid	3,000
Dividends-received deduction	81,750

What is the Delta Corporation's personal holding company tax liability for the current year?

16-35. *Controlled Group.* Eagle and East Corporations are members of a controlled group. Eagle's taxable income is $50,000, and East's taxable income is $75,000.

a. What is the total federal income tax liability for Eagle and East Corporations?

b. What is the total federal income tax liability for Eagle and East Corporations if they are not members of a controlled group?

16-36. *Capital Gains and Losses.* First Corporation has the following capital gains and losses in the current year:

LTCG	$10,000
LTCL	4,000
STCG	8,000
STCL	20,000

Taxable income (exclusive of the capital gains and losses) is $30,000.

a. What is First Corporation's capital gain or loss position?

b. What is First Corporation's taxable income for the current year?

c. Explain the tax treatment for any unused capital losses.

16-37. *Capital Loss Carrybacks and Carryovers.* Federal Corporation has the following net capital losses in 1994:

STCL	$ 80,000
LTCL	120,000

NLTCGs were incurred in 1991 through 1993 as follows:

1991	$20,000
1992	20,000
1993	60,000

a. What are the amount and character of the capital loss carryback to 1991 through 1993?
b. What treatment should be accorded to any unused capital losses after the carryback rules are applied?
c. What is the character of any unused capital loss carryovers?

16-38. *Dividends-Received Deduction.* During the current year, Florida Corporation reports the following results:

Net income from operations	$100,000
Dividend income from a 20%-owned corporation (qualifying for the dividends-received deduction)	200,000

a. What is Florida Corporation's dividends-received deduction?
b. How would your answer to Part a change if Florida Corporation instead reports a $20,000 loss from operations?
c. How would your answer to Part a change if the dividend income is instead from a 10%-owned corporation?

16-39. *Dividends-Received Deduction.* During the current year Maine Corporation reports the following results:

Net income (loss) from operations	($20,000)
Dividend income from a 10%-owned corporation (qualifying for the dividends-received deduction)	200,000

a. What is Maine Corporation's dividends-received deduction?
b. How would your answer to Part a change if Maine Corporation's dividend income is from a 20%-owned corporation and net income from operations is instead $100,000?

16-40. *Net Operating Losses.* General Corporation reports the following results for its second tax year:

Gross operating income	$300,000
Business operating expenses	500,000
Dividend income from a 20%-owned corporation	100,000
Dividends-received deduction	80,000

a. What is General Corporation's NOL for the current year?
b. What is the disposition of the NOL if General Corporation reports a $40,000 profit in its first tax year on which federal income taxes of $6,000 were paid and no special elections were made?
c. What is the best disposition of the NOL if General Corporation anticipates taxable income of $500,000 in the following year?

16-41. *Charitable Contributions.* On May 15, 1994 the board of directors of the Georgia Corporation authorizes a $40,000 donation to a qualified charity. The $40,000 payment was made to the charity on December 1, 1994. No other charitable contributions were made during the year. During 1994, Georgia Corporation reports the following results:

Taxable income (after deducting the dividends-received deduction and charitable contributions)	$200,000
Dividends-received deduction	10,000

a. What amount of charitable contributions are deductible in 1994?

b. How are any unused contributions treated?

c. How would your answer to Part a change, if at all, if Georgia incurs a $30,000 capital loss in 1995 that is carried back to 1994?

16-42. *Corporate Formation.* Jack, Karen, Latoya, and Marc transfer the following properties to Giant Corporation (an existing corporation) which is owned equally by the transferors in the current year.

- Jack transfers land and a building with a $60,000 adjusted basis and a $100,000 FMV for 25% of the Giant stock having an $80,000 FMV and $20,000 of marketable securities having an adjusted basis of $15,000 to Giant Corporation.
- Karen transfers equipment with a $120,000 adjusted basis and a $100,000 FMV for 25% of the Giant stock having an $80,000 FMV and a $20,000 20-year Giant Corporation note.
- Latoya transfers inventory with a $70,000 adjusted basis and a $100,000 FMV for 25% of the Giant stock having an $80,000 FMV and $20,000 cash.
- Marc transfers land with an $80,000 adjusted basis and a $100,000 FMV, subject to a $20,000 mortgage, which is assumed by Giant Corporation, for 25% of the Giant stock having an $80,000 FMV.

a. How much gain or loss is recognized by Jack? What is Jack's basis in the Giant stock and the marketable securities? What is Giant's basis in the land and building?

b. How much gain or loss is recognized by Karen? What is Karen's basis in the Giant stock and note, and Giant's basis in the equipment?

c. How much gain or loss is recognized by Latoya? What is Latoya's basis in the Giant stock? What is Giant's basis in the inventory?

d. How much gain or loss is recognized by Marc? What is Marc's basis in the Giant stock? What is Giant's basis in the land?

e. How much gain or loss, if any, is recognized by Giant Corporation from the distribution of its assets to the shareholders?

16-43. *Corporate Formation.* Gold Corporation receives land from Marty in a transaction qualifying for nonrecognition of gain or loss under Sec. 351. Marty's basis in the land was $80,000. The FMV of the land is $200,000. Marty receives $20,000 cash and 80% of the Gold stock. Mary transfers a building with a $50,000 adjusted basis and a $200,000 FMV to Gold in exchange for $200,000 of Gold Corporation's debt obligations. Marty and Mary are unrelated individuals, and Mary acquired the remaining 20% of the Gold stock for $45,000. Mary recognizes a $150,000 gain because Mary received debt obligations of Gold in addition to the Gold stock.

a. What is the basis of the land to Gold Corporation?

b. What is the basis of the building to Gold Corporation?

c. Under what circumstances might it be preferable for Sec. 351 *not* to apply?

16-44. *Corporate Formations—Transfer of Liabilities.* Matt transfers land with a $600,000 adjusted basis and a $1,000,000 FMV to Hill Corporation in a transaction that otherwise qualifies under Sec. 351. The land is subject to an $800,000 mortgage, which is assumed by the Hill Corporation. Matt receives 100% of the Hill stock.

a. What are the amount and character of the gain or loss (if any) recognized by Matt?

b. What is Matt's basis in the Hill stock?

c. What is Hill's basis in the land?

16-45. *Debt/Equity.* Huge Corporation is formed in 1989 by Joe and Joy with an initial total capitalization of $500,000. Joe receives $80,000 of Huge stock and a $100,000, 12% 15-year Huge Corporation note. Joy receives $20,000 of Huge stock and a $300,000 12% 15-year Huge Corporation note. During the next 5 years, the interest payments are made when due, and the corporation retains earnings of $500,000 that are reinvested in the corporation to finance operating needs. The company is audited by the IRS in the current year, and the agent maintains that the debt should be reclassified as equity and that the interest payments on the notes should be treated as dividends.

a. List the factors which should be taken into consideration in determining whether debt should be reclassified as equity.

b. Present the arguments the taxpayer should make to the agent why the debt should not be reclassified as equity.

16-46. *Earnings and Profits.* During the current year, Nevada Corporation distributed $100,000 in dividends to its sole shareholder. Because the corporation has a $300,000 accumulated earnings and profits deficit at the beginning of the current year and only $10,000 of taxable income in the current year, Nevada's controller feels that the distribution should be treated as a tax-free return of capital to the shareholder. Your investigation reveals the following items that may impact upon the computation of current E&P:

Federal income tax liability	$ 1,500
Dividends-received deduction	60,000
MACRS depreciation deductions in excess of	
alternative depreciation system depreciation for E&P purposes	40,000
Excess charitable contributions	9,000

  a. What is Nevada Corporation's current E&P?
  b. How much (if any) of the $100,000 distribution is taxable as a dividend to the sole shareholder?
  c. What is the amount of Nevada Corporation's accumulated E&P on the last day of the current year?

16-47. *Earnings and Profits.* North Corporation has $200,000 of accumulated E&P at the beginning of the current year. North made cash distributions of $300,000 during the current year to its shareholders. The company's operating results on the last day of the current year are as follows:

Taxable income	$100,000
Tax-exempt bond interest	10,000
Dividends-received deduction	7,000
Federal income tax liability	22,250
Net capital losses	5,000

  a. What is North Corporation's current E&P?
  b. How much of the $300,000 distribution is taxable as a dividend?
  c. What is North Corporation's accumulated E&P balance at the end of the current year?

16-48. *Earnings and Profits.* Ohio Corporation has an accumulated E&P balance of $40,000 at the beginning of the current year and a $75,000 current E&P deficit. A $60,000 cash distribution is made to its sole shareholder on April 30. The shareholder's tax basis in her Ohio stock is $15,000.
  a. What amount of the $60,000 distribution is taxable as a dividend (assume that all months have 30 days and that a ratable allocation of the deficit is used)?
  b. What are the amount and character of any nondividend amounts that are received by the shareholder?

16-49. *Property Distributions.* Old Corporation has a severe liquidity shortage but desires to maintain its existing dividend payment policy. Therefore, Old distributes land that was being held as an investment to its two shareholders. The land has a $30,000 adjusted basis and a $100,000 FMV. Old Corporation has E&P of $300,000. Nancy receives 50% of the land, and Palm Corporation receives the remaining 50%.
  a. What amount of the distribution is taxable to Nancy and Palm Corporation?
  b. What is the basis of the property to Nancy and Palm Corporation?
  c. What are the income tax consequences of the distribution to Old Corporation?

16-50. *Property Distributions.* Park Corporation distributes equipment with a $60,000 adjusted basis and a $70,000 FMV as a nonliquidating distribution to Pam. The equipment is subject to a $40,000 mortgage note assumed by Pam. Park Corporation has $300,000 of E&P.
  a. How much gain (if any) is recognized by Park Corporation on the distribution of the equipment?
  b. What amount of the distribution is taxable as a dividend to Pam?
  c. What is Pam's basis in the equipment?

16-51. *Stock Redemptions.* Private Corporation redeems some of its stock from Jane, a major shareholder in the company. Before the redemption Jane owns 50 of the 100 outstanding shares and her daughter Jill owns 40 shares. The remaining 10 shares are owned by unrelated individuals. Private Corporation redeems 40 of Jane's shares having a $200,000 basis for $600,000. Private Corporation has $900,000 of current and accumulated E&P. Jane's basis in her remaining 10 shares of Private Corporation stock is $50,000.

a. What are the tax consequences of the redemption to Jane, assuming that Sec. 302(b)(1) does not apply?

b. What is the basis of Jane's remaining 10 shares of Private stock after her 40 shares are redeemed?

16-52. *Stock Redemption.* Prime Corporation redeems some of its stock from two of its shareholders on the same date. Frank and Sam own 50 and 20 shares, respectively, of the 100 shares outstanding prior to the redemption. The remaining 30 shares are owned by unrelated individuals. Prime redeems 10 of Frank's shares having a $15,000 basis for $50,000. All of Sam's shares having a $30,000 basis are redeemed for $100,000. Frank and Sam are father and son. Sam files an agreement with the IRS that he will have no interest other than a creditor interest in the corporation for a period of 10 years. Prime Corporation has current and accumulated E&P totaling $200,000.

a. What are the tax consequences of the redemption to Frank and Sam, assuming that Sec. 302(b)(1) does not apply?

b. What are the tax consequences of the redemption to Sam if he does not file an agreement with the IRS to waive the family attribution rules or if he violates the agreement during the 10-year period?

16-53. *Corporate Liquidation.* Queen Corporation adopts a plan of complete liquidation on January 1 of the current year. The assets listed below are sold by the corporation during the current year, and this is followed by the payment of Queen's liabilities and a single liquidating distribution of $1,200,000 cash on December 12 of the current year to Ahmed (Queen's sole shareholder). Ahmed has a $400,000 basis for his Queen stock.

- Inventory costing $600,000 is sold to customers for $1,000,000.
- Depreciable fixed assets with a $2,000,000 adjusted basis are sold for $3,000,000. Depreciation recapture under Sec. 1245 is $800,000.
- Land with a $4,000,000 adjusted basis is sold for $5,000,000.

a. What are the tax consequences to Queen Corporation of the liquidation?

b. What are the tax consequences to Ahmed of receiving the liquidating distribution?

16-54. *Tax Consequences of a Corporate Liquidation.* King Corporation is owned 75% by Lynn and 25% by Mark. Lynn and Mark have $135,000 and $60,000 bases in their stock, respectively. A plan of liquidation is adopted by King Corporation on February 1, and Lynn receives the following property as a liquidating distribution on March 12: money, $40,000; land, $140,000 FMV; and Blue Corporation securities, $30,000 FMV. The land is subject to a $15,000 mortgage. The land and securities (both capital assets) have adjusted bases of $50,000 and $70,000, respectively, in King Corporation's hands. The securities were purchased eight years ago by King Corporation. After payment of all liabilities, Mark receives $10,000 FMV of Blue Corporation securities and $55,000 in cash as a liquidating distribution.

a. What is the amount and character of King Corporation's recognized gain or loss on the liquidating distribution?

b. What is the amount and character of Lynn and Mark's recognized gains or losses?

c. What are the bases of the land and securities in Lynn's hands?

16-55. *Corporate Liquidation.* Tampa Corporation acquires 100% of Union Corporation's stock on July 1, 1990, for $1,000,000. On the date of liquidation the tax basis and FMV of Union Corporation's assets are $700,000 and $2,000,000, respectively. Union Corporation also has $100,000 of liabilities outstanding and E&P of $100,000 on the date of liquidation. In August, 1994, Tampa liquidates Union Corporation and continues to operate it as a division.

a. How much gain or loss is recognized by Union Corporation as a result of the liquidation?

b. What is Tampa's basis for Union Corporation's assets?

c. What tax attributes of Union Corporation are carried over to Tampa Corporation?

TAX FORM/RETURN PREPARATION PROBLEMS

16-56. Zane Corporation's financial accounting balance sheet as of the end of the current year is as follows:

Cash	$ 50,000
Accounts receivable	30,000
Land	20,000
Buildings (net of $30,000 accumulated depreciation)	100,000
Equipment (net of $50,000 accumulated depreciation)	150,000
Total assets	$350,000
Accounts payable	$ 50,000
Mortgage payable	50,000
Capital stock	100,000
Retained earnings	150,000*
Total liabilities and stockholders' equity	$350,000

* The retained earnings balance at the beginning of the current year was $120,000.

Zane Corporation reports the following financial accounting operating results for the current year:

Sales	$500,000
Minus: Costs of goods sold	(300,000)
Gross profit	$200,000
Dividend income (from 20%-owned domestic corporations)	100,000
Net long-term capital gains	100,000
Total income	$400,000

Expenses:	
Salaries (including officer's salaries of $30,000)	$ 80,000
Repairs	20,000
Bad debts	30,000
State and local taxes	50,000
Contributions	60,000
Depreciation (straight-line for financial accounting purposes)	40,000
Total expenses (before federal income tax expense)	$280,000
Operating profit	$120,000
Minus: Provision for federal income taxes	(40,000)
Net income	$ 80,000

In addition, the following items should be taken into account in the preparation of the Form 1120:

Current year estimated tax payments	$20,000
Depreciation (MACRS for tax purposes)	60,000
Dividends-received deduction (20%-owned corporations)	80,000

Prepare Form 1120 (U.S. Corporation Income Tax Return) for Zane Corporation. (Disregard balance sheet amounts other than retained earnings at the beginning of the year.)

16-57. Huge Corporation has the following balance sheet information at the beginning and end of the current year:

	Beginning of Year	End of Year
Cash	$ 40,000	$ 50,000
Accounts receivable	23,000	21,500
Inventories	26,000	53,000
Marketable securities	30,000	30,000
Investment in 100% owned subsidiary	100,000	115,000
Depreciable assets	100,000	100,000
Accumulated depreciation	(20,000)	(30,000)
Total assets	$299,000	$339,500
Accounts payable	$ 50,000	$ 60,000
Short-term loans	20,000	35,000
Mortgage	80,000	79,000
Common stock	1,000	1,000
Additional paid-in capital	49,000	49,000
Retained earnings	99,000	115,500
Total liabilities and stockholders' equity	$299,000	$339,500

Huge Corporation had the following income and expense items for the year:

Sales	$665,000
Purchases	525,000
Dividend income from 100% owned subsidiary	30,000
Dividend income from less than 20%-owned corporations	10,000
Salaries (including officers' salaries of $20,000)	80,000
Repairs	12,000
Contributions	60,000
State and local taxes	7,500
Interest	11,000
MACRS depreciation (financial accounting depreciation is $10,000)	17,490
Federal income tax expense	10,000

In addition, Huge Corporation reported an NOL carryover of $12,000 from the preceding year and made estimated tax payments of $10,000.

Prepare Form 1120 (U.S. Corporation Income Tax Return) for Huge Corporation.

CASE STUDY PROBLEM

16-58. Frank, Paul, and Sam are considering whether to merge their respective unincorporated businesses and create a C corporation. Frank would transfer land and a building with a $50,000 adjusted basis and $100,000 FMV to the corporation in exchange for $100,000 of common stock in the newly-formed FPS Corporation. Paul would transfer inventory with an adjusted basis of $60,000 and $100,000 FMV to FPS Corporation for $50,000 of FPS stock and $50,000 of FPS ten-year notes. Sam will contribute equipment with an adjusted basis of $80,000 and $60,000 FMV and legal services relative to the creation of the business with a $40,000 FMV in exchange for $100,000 of FPS stock.

Prepare a client memo that details the tax consequences of the transaction to the newly formed corporation and to Frank, Paul, and Sam if the transaction is carried out as it is proposed.

CASE STUDY PROBLEM—ETHICAL ISSUES

16-59. Scott, Steve, and Sean own 100% of the outstanding stock of Sofa Corporation for all of 1994. Sofa Corporation, a manufacturer of custom-made sofas, has never paid a dividend to its shareholders preferring to retain earnings for working capital, capital additions, and marketable security investments. Scott and Steve would like to borrow money from Sofa before the end of the year because Scott is planning to open a florist shop as an additional business and Steve needs a loan to pay off personal debts. For these reasons Sofa Corporation will not pay a dividend in the current year. However, the company plans to start paying dividends in 1995. Sofa has accumulated earnings and profits in excess of $250,000. As Sofa's tax consultant, you inform the shareholders of the possibility that the company will be subject to the accumulated earnings tax. The shareholders ask you if they should inform the IRS, voluntarily pay the tax, or just wait to be audited by the IRS.

a. What advice would you give the shareholders relative to the reporting of the potential accumulated earnings tax problem to the IRS and or the payment of the tax? (See the caption entitled Statements on Responsibilities in Tax Practice in Chapter 1.)

b. What advice would you give to the shareholders if the corporation reported low operating profits from its sofa-making activities and met the requirements for a personal holding company during the current year?

TAX RESEARCH PROBLEM

16-60. Ted is the sole shareholder of Zero Corporation. Prior to his retirement from the company, he transfers 100 shares of Zero stock by gift to his son. A few months later Ted sells the remaining 1,900 shares to Zero Corporation for $2,000,000. The company has E&P of more than $2,000,000. Ted's basis for his 2,000 shares prior to the two transfers was $80,000. Ted then files for a waiver of the attribution rules under Sec. 318 and treats the redemption of Zero stock as a long-term capital gain. He also signs a consulting contract with the company that provides him with consulting income of $5,000 per month for five years. The IRS audits Ted's return and argues that the redemption should be treated as a dividend under Sec. 301. Have the requirements for Sec. 302(c)(2) been met which would permit a waiver of the family attribution rules?

A partial list of research sources is

- Secs. 302(c)(2) and (b)(3).
- Reg. Sec. 1.302-4.
- *William M. Lynch, v. CIR,* 58 AFTR 2d 86-5970, 86-2 USTC ¶ 9731 (9th Cir., 1986).

17

Tax Considerations for Investors

LEARNING OBJECTIVES

After studying this chapter, you should be able to

1. Understand the importance of nontax considerations for investor decisions
2. Understand the tax restrictions upon limited partnerships
3. Describe the tax considerations for investments in equity securities
4. Understand the tax consequences associated with fixed-income securities
5. Describe the tax rules for purchasers and writers of call options
6. Calculate and classify gains or losses from short sale transactions
7. Understand the tax and nontax implications for employment-related investments

This chapter covers the tax and nontax consequences arising from the following types of investments:

- Tax-sheltered investments
- Tax-exempt securities
- Equity and fixed-income investments
- Options and short sales
- Employment-related investments

Detailed tax provisions for investments were discussed in prior chapters of the text. Thus, this chapter builds upon the student's prior understanding of the detailed tax rules.

Tax specialists are frequently asked to advise clients about the desirability of a particular investment (e.g., the tax specialist may be asked to review a prospectus for a limited partnership real estate investment and to comment upon its financial and tax aspects). It is, therefore, necessary to have a basic awareness and understanding of both the tax and nontax aspects associated with these types of investments.

Example 17-1 ■ Jesse is a tax specialist for a public accounting firm. One of his clients mentions that he is considering an investment in a real estate limited partnership and asks Jesse to review the financial and tax information contained in the prospectus. The prospectus contains general business and financial information about the investment including background information regarding the economic viability of the project, a description of the real estate properties, a description of the relationship of the general partner to the limited partners, and so on. The prospectus also includes projections of the cash flows that are expected over a period of years, a tax opinion as to the likely tax consequences to the limited partners, and a detailed discussion of the income tax consequences (e.g., whether the partnership will be treated as a partnership for tax purposes, capitalization versus expensing of certain start-up costs, depreciation methods to be used, the basis of limited partnership interests due to borrowings, and limitations upon the deductibility of losses).

Jesse's responsibility is to review the prospectus and make specific recommendations to the client. ■

The role of the tax specialist is not to promote a specific investment or to make the investment decision for the client. The ultimate decision whether to invest in the partnership is the client's responsibility.

IMPORTANT TAX AND NONTAX CONSIDERATIONS

OBJECTIVE 1

Understand the importance of nontax considerations for investor decisions

Many investors and some investment advisors (e.g., brokers and promoters of real estate and oil and gas investments) tend to place undue emphasis upon an investment's tax consequences. Although both income tax and gift and estate tax consequences impact upon the rate of return on an investment, the basic determinants of the investor's *return on investment* (*ROI*) should be related to its economic viability. Thus, the following factors should be considered:

- *Cash flows.* Tax consequences affect the cash flows from an investment (e.g., tax depreciation reduces tax payments arising from profits that are generated by the investment). However, the basic determinants of cash flow are from the revenues and expenses associated with the investment.

- *Liquidity.* Certain investments are more liquid than others (e.g., limited partnership investments in real estate and oil and gas are usually not liquid because an established active market may not exist to dispose of such investments).[1]

- *Risk.* Certain ventures (e.g., a proposed stock offering in a newly formed, small closely held corporation) have a higher risk factor than others. Higher-risk investments should generally be avoided unless the anticipated investment returns are commensurate with the risk.

Real World Example

Some universities will not invest endowment funds in companies doing business in South Africa.

- *Ethical or moral and personal considerations.* Some investors may object to investments in a tobacco company on ethical or moral grounds. Others may avoid certain investments if they require an extensive amount of personal involvement (e.g., property management activity in a real estate investment).

- *Uncertain tax consequences and compliance costs.* Some investors may be averse to investments that result in uncertain income tax consequences or increased compliance costs. For example, an investment in a limited partnership may generate additional tax preferences or AMT adjustments that may subject the investor to the alternative minimum tax. (See Chapter 14 for a discussion of this topic.) In addition, any losses from limited partnership investments may be limited by the passive activity limitation rules. (See Chapter 8 for a discussion of this topic.) It may then be necessary to maintain additional tax records, and increased tax costs may result (e.g., increased tax return preparation fees).

Example 17-2 ■

Kesha is a wealthy investor who is considering whether to purchase a real estate limited partnership interest. According to the prospectus, the investment is expected to earn a 12% rate of return on an after-tax basis; there will be no active

---

[1] In general, a limited partnership interest is not a liquid investment because there is no established market for these interests. Master limited partnership interests have been established that provide for increased liquidity because the interests are traded on a stock exchange and secondary exchange markets have been created for the sale of some limited partnership interests. (See the section entitled Publicly Traded Limited Partnerships in this chapter for a discussion of master limited partnerships.)

market for the limited partnership interests; and there is substantial risk associated with the economic projections due to uncertainty regarding occupancy and rental rates that can be charged to tenants. The investment is expected to produce AMT adjustments (e.g., depreciation) that will be passed through to the limited and general partners. Although profitable operations are anticipated, any tax losses and credits resulting from the investment may be of limited benefit to the investors because of the passive activity limitation rules. The at-risk rules and basis limitations may also limit the deductibility of tax losses. An investment advisor informs Kesha that the promoter, who will also serve as the general partner, is relatively inexperienced, and there is some question regarding his ability to manage the partnership operations. Based upon this information, Kesha decides to invest in common stock of a growth company that is actively traded on a major stock exchange, even though the current investment dividend yield is only 2%. ∎

Return on Investment Considerations

Investment analysts generally use the **internal rate of return** (*IRR*) or the **net present value** (*NPV*) method to determine the anticipated return on investment. Both of these methods incorporate discounting techniques that apply discount factors to reflect the time value of future cash flows from the investment. Under the IRR method, the computation equates the positive future cash flows with the cost of the investment. The NPV method uses a fixed discount rate to compute the net present value of the future cash flows.[2] The relative attractiveness of investment alternatives can be evaluated under either approach. The rate of return is readily determinable for certain types of investments. For example, if an investor acquires a taxable bond in the open market, the yield to maturity will be available and is determined through the use of annuity tables. In a real estate or oil and gas investment, the prospectus may include a forecast of future cash flows and projections of return on investment to the investor. However, tax specialists and investors should be aware that such forecasts may be biased and unreliable.

Impact of Income Taxes upon Return on Investment

Additional Comment

The impact of income taxes on the calculation of return on investment has diminished since the Tax Reform Act of 1986. In earlier years the rate of return was increased by tax credits and substantial tax writeoffs. Syndicators are now promoting limited partnerships that offer positive cash flow, appreciation potential, and diversification.

An investor should evaluate a prospective investment by taking the tax effects into account (e.g., a municipal or state government bond may be more attractive than a corporate bond of comparable risk if the tax exemption provided for the interest income earned from the state or local government bond is taken into consideration). One way to perform a comparative analysis is to compute the effective before-tax equivalent yield for the tax-exempt bond by dividing the investment yield by 1 minus the investor's marginal tax rate.

Example 17-3 ∎

Joel, who has a 36% marginal tax rate, is considering whether to invest in a corporate bond that has an 8% current investment yield or a comparable tax-exempt municipal bond that has a 6% current investment yield. To compare the two bond yields, it is helpful to convert the tax-exempt bond yield to an equivalent before-tax yield. It is, therefore, necessary to divide the after-tax yield of the tax-exempt bond (6%) by 0.64 (1 − 0.36) to arrive at an 9.4% equivalent before-tax yield. The 9.4% before-tax yield from the tax-exempt bond compares favorably with the 8% comparable yield from the taxable bond. ∎

---

[2] For a detailed discussion of how to compute ROI, see a basic text in managerial finance or accounting such as Charles T. Horngren and George Foster, *Cost Accounting—A Managerial Emphasis,* 8th ed. (Englewood Cliffs, NJ: Prentice Hall, 1994).

LIMITED PARTNERSHIP INVESTMENTS

OBJECTIVE 2

Understand the tax restrictions upon limited partnerships

Additional Comment

In 1991 the IRS received 1.6 million partnership tax returns, of which over half were classified as finance, insurance, and real estate partnerships.

Limited partnership investments are commonly used to finance real estate, oil and gas, and farming activities (e.g., cattle feeding and breeding, citrus and almond groves, and so on). Prior to the passage of the Tax Reform Act of 1986, limited partnership investments were extremely popular among investors due to their so-called tax-shelter benefits.

Most of these tax-sheltered investments provided a temporary tax deferral because investors were permitted to deduct their share of the partnership losses that were typically recognized during the initial years (e.g., operating losses resulting from the use of accelerated depreciation and artificially shortened useful lives, and higher expenses arising from deducting interest charges and certain front-end charges [e.g., commissions]).[3] Certain tax benefits that have been available to investors in a limited partnership interest represent a permanent reduction in taxes. For example, for years prior to 1986, the investment tax credit was frequently earned in a tax shelter (e.g., a limited partnership engaged in equipment leasing), and the benefits were passed through to the investors. The Tax Reform Act of 1986 eliminated the investment tax credit generally for years after 1985, and enacted passive activity limitation rules which place restrictions upon the investor's ability to deduct passive losses and use tax credits.

A third advantage of most pre-1987 tax shelters was the favorable 60% long-term capital gain deduction allowed upon the sale of the limited partnership interest or the pass-through of long-term capital gains from the sale or disposition of appreciated partnership assets. Favorable net long-term capital gain treatment is available on a lesser scale through the enactment of a 28% maximum tax rate on net capital gains.[4]

Real estate ventures in particular used limited partnerships to attract investment capital. Investors are able to receive favorable tax benefits from the direct pass-through of losses (subject to the restrictions upon the deductibility of passive activity losses). Investors also expect long-run appreciation in real estate property values and the opportunity to use financial leverage in the form of nonrecourse debt to enhance their investment returns.

Restrictions upon Income Tax Advantages

Most of the income tax advantages that were previously associated with tax-sheltered investments were eliminated by the Tax Reform Act of 1986, including the following:

- The passive activity loss rules prevent investors from obtaining temporary deferral benefits through an immediate deduction of losses by restricting the limited partners from deducting operating losses and using tax credits after 1986.[5] Passive losses (and deduction equivalent tax credits) offset passive activity income earned from other passive activities in the year incurred. Excess losses and tax credits from a taxpayer's passive activities are suspended and are carried forward to reduce any passive activity income that is earned in future years. Suspended loss carryovers and tax credits are also allowed when the investor sells or otherwise disposes of the passive activity in a fully taxable transaction during a future period.[6]

---

[3] Front-end charges or "loading charges" refer to brokerage commissions, professional and management fees, syndication costs, registration fees, and so forth. Some of these costs are paid from the proceeds of the initial investment, while other fees continue over the life of the partnership and reduce cash flows to the investor. Some loading charges such as syndication costs and brokerage fees are not currently deductible for tax purposes.

[4] Sec. 1(h).

[5] Sec. 469.

[6] Sec. 469(g).

Key Point

The active participation test for certain real estate investors represents a less stringent test than the material participation test that is used for other passive activities.

Additional Comment

In 1991, 4.0 million individual income tax returns reported rental net income, and 5.0 million individual returns reported rental net losses.

- The passive loss rules contain a limited exception for certain actively participating real estate investors.[7] Active participation includes approval of rental terms, selection of tenants, and making decisions regarding repairs, and so on, although an investor may use a rental agent or a property manager. Active participation does not require continuous and substantial involvement. Although rental activities are treated as passive activities under the general rule, up to $25,000 of annual real estate losses and deduction equivalent credits may be used to offset other types of income (e.g., earned income from salaries and dividends and interest) if the investor actively participates in the business activity in both the year the deduction arose and in the year it is deducted. To qualify for the $25,000 immediate deduction (or deduction equivalent), an investor must own at least a 10% interest in the real estate property for the entire year or for the period of time that the interest is held if it is acquired during the year.[8] The $25,000 deduction is phased-out for investors with AGI of more than $100,000. The $25,000 deduction is reduced by 50% of the investor's AGI in excess of $100,000, so that the deduction is completely eliminated when AGI is $150,000. A loss that is disallowed because of the phase-out is treated as a passive activity loss. A limited partner in a real estate partnership does not qualify for the $25,000 immediate loss deduction, because a limited partner does not actively participate in the partnership's business activities.

Example 17-4 ■ In the current year Joy acquires an apartment house as an investment and incurs a $30,000 operating loss during the initial year. She has no other passive activity income or loss. Her AGI is $80,000 before the inclusion of the $30,000 loss. A rental agent and property manager help in the operation, but Joy personally approves tenants and rental terms and makes decisions regarding repairs and capital improvements to the property. $25,000 of the real estate loss is deductible because Joy is an active participant in the real estate activity and her AGI does not exceed $100,000. The remaining $5,000 loss ($30,000 − $25,000) is treated as a suspended passive activity loss and is carried forward to future periods.

If Joy had purchased a limited partnership interest in a real estate partnership instead of acquiring the property, the losses would probably not qualify for the $25,000 exception because a limited partner is usually not an active participant in the activity. ■

The passive activity loss limitation rules do not apply to individuals and closely held C corporations that are involved in real property trades or businesses provided that certain requirements are met. To meet these requirements, (1) more than one-half of the personal services performed in trades or businesses by the taxpayer must be performed in real property trades or businesses in which the taxpayer materially participates, and (2) the taxpayer must perform more than 750 hours of service in real property trades or businesses in which the taxpayer materially participates.[9] The term "real property trades or business" means any development, redevelopment, construction, reconstruction, acquisition, conversion, rental, operation, management, leasing, or brokering of real property.[10] In general, a limited partner in a real estate activity is not eligible under these exclusion rules.

Example 17-5 ■ In the current year John is an unincorporated developer who is in the business of constructing and leasing commercial shopping centers. The business incurs a

---

[7] Sec. 469(i).
[8] Sec. 469(i)(6).
[9] Sec. 469(c)(7)(B).
[10] Sec. 469(c)(7)(C).

$120,000 operating loss during the year. John devotes 100% of his personal services (more than one-half) to the business and he works 2,000 hours during the year (more than 750 hours). John materially participates in the real estate development business and is therefore excluded from the passive activity loss limitations. He may, therefore, deduct the $130,000 loss as a loss from his trade or business in the current year. ∎

- The investment tax credit has been repealed generally for years after 1985.

- The favorable 60% long-term capital gain deduction for individuals is no longer applicable for years after 1986, although a 28% maximum tax rate is in effect for 1991 and subsequent years.

- The at-risk rules, which limit the deduction of losses in certain situations (e.g., investors in highly leveraged limited partnerships that use nonrecourse debt financing), have been extended to real estate activities.[11] To prevent the application of the at-risk rules for real estate activities, it is necessary to use qualified nonrecourse financing (e.g., the nonrecourse loan must be obtained from a bank, savings and loan, insurance company, pension trust, and so on). The loan is generally not at risk if it is obtained from a related party or from the seller of the property to the partnership.

- The alternative minimum tax (AMT) rules for individuals have become more restrictive and may discourage high-income investors from investing in activities that generate tax preferences and AMT adjustments.[12]

Example 17-6 ∎ In the current year, a limited partnership is formed to acquire and operate a commercial office building. The limited partnership's objective is to hold the property for 10 years, obtain the tax benefits from owning the real estate, and then to liquidate the partnership. The partnership raises $6,000,000 from the sale of limited partnership interests and $4,000,000 from a nonrecourse mortgage on the property (i.e., the limited partners have no obligation to repay the debt in the event of default). A nonrecourse loan, which is qualified nonrecourse financing, is obtained from an insurance company. This prevents the application of the at-risk rules, which would otherwise prevent the limited partners from deducting partnership losses in excess of their original capital investment ($6,000,000).

It is anticipated that tax losses will be incurred and passed through to the limited partners during the first four years because of high interest charges, lower-than-normal occupancy rates during the first few years, incurrence of certain front-end costs, and the use of MACRS depreciation. The office building is expected to appreciate in value, and a substantial capital gain is anticipated because the adjusted basis of the office building will be substantially reduced due to the use of MACRS depreciation. In this situation,

- The partnership losses that are passed through to the limited partners are not restricted by the at-risk rules because qualified nonrecourse financing is used.

- Each of the partners may use his share of the partnership losses only to the extent of his taxable income from other passive activities. The losses may not be used to offset portfolio income (e.g., dividends and interest) or earned income (e.g., salaries and wages). Any unused losses are suspended and carried forward to years in which the investor has taxable income from passive activities or in the year that the limited partnership interest is sold or otherwise disposed of in a taxable transaction.

---

[11] Sec. 465(c).
[12] Sec. 55. (See Chapter 14 for a discussion of the AMT rules.)

- The partner's share of depreciation (in excess of alternative depreciation system depreciation) on the office building is an adjustment item for AMT purposes.

- The eventual gain on the sale of the office building may be used to offset any remaining suspended losses from the investment and is taxed at a maximum 28% net long-term capital gain rate. ■

Publicly Traded Limited Partnerships

Publicly traded "master limited partnership interests" are actively traded on stock exchanges or are readily tradable on a secondary market. In the 1980s many master limited partnerships were formed by a spinoff of assets from a company to its shareholders or by the merging of several private partnerships whereby the interests were exchanged for publicly traded units.

The Revenue Act of 1987 severely curtailed the formation of newly formed publicly traded partnerships after December 17, 1987, because such partnerships are generally treated for tax purposes as a corporation. Publicly traded partnerships that have 90% or more of their gross income from interest, dividends, real property rents, and income and gain from the exploration, development, mining, production, transportation, or marketing of any mineral or natural resource are exempt from the law that requires publicly traded partnerships to be taxed as corporations.[13] Any losses from nonexempt publicly traded partnerships (created after December 17, 1987) cannot be passed through to the partners.

Publicly traded partnerships that existed on December 17, 1987 are still treated as partnerships until their first tax year beginning after 1997.[14] The passive activity loss limitation rules apply to existing publicly traded partnerships except that these restrictions have been tightened. Partnerships losses from existing publicly traded partnerships (i.e., those in existence as of December 17, 1987) can only be carried forward and offset against taxable income earned by the same publicly traded partnership interest in a subsequent year. Such losses cannot be offset against the investor's portfolio income or other types of passive activity income for the year that the losses are incurred (see Chapter 8).

Example 17-7 ■

Julie owns a limited partnership interest in the JKL Limited Partnership that is publicly traded on the New York Stock Exchange. JKL has been a publicly traded partnership since before December 17, 1987. Julie's share of the partnership's ordinary loss for 1994 is $20,000. Julie has $10,000 of taxable income from other passive activities in the current year and $25,000 of portfolio income (i.e., dividends and interest). Julie's $20,000 loss from the JKL Limited Partnership is not deductible in 1994 and can only be used to offset future income from JKL in 1995 and subsequent years. The loss cannot be used to offset Julie's other passive activity income or her portfolio income. ■

Oil and Gas Limited Partnerships

Limited partnership interests in oil and gas drilling funds are popular with investors because of their tax advantages and potential for economic gain. The tax advantages and economic gain potential associated with oil and gas investments include the following:

- The tax deduction for expensing intangible drilling costs.

- The tax deduction for percentage depletion.

[13] Sec. 7704(a).
[14] Sec. 7704(c)(1).

• Eventual realization of economic profit from the sale or liquidation of the investment as a long-term capital gain.

Percentage Depletion Deduction. The depletion amount can be computed by using either the cost or percentage depletion methods depending upon which method produces the larger deduction. (See Chapter 10 for a discussion of depletion methods.) The percentage depletion deduction is generally available for most investors in oil and gas limited partnerships under the exception for independent producers and royalty owners (i.e., percentage depletion is available if daily production of oil does not exceed 1,000 barrels).[15] Percentage depletion is no longer available to major producers. However, most of the drilling of oil and gas in the United States is conducted by small independent producers whose financing is raised, in part, from investors in oil and gas limited partnerships.

In most cases, percentage depletion is used because it is greater than cost depletion. Percentage depletion is based upon gross income and, unlike cost depletion, is not limited to the property's cost basis. Thus, if a well is productive, an investor may recover depletion deductions in excess of the property's cost basis. The availability of percentage depletion is a major advantage to investors because deductions that are based upon percentage depletion can be passed through to the limited partners.

RESTRICTIONS ON THE DEDUCTION. The percentage depletion rate for oil and gas is generally 15% and is subject to the following restrictions:[16]

• The amount claimed may not exceed 100% of the taxable income from the property (computed without regard to the percentage depletion allowance). (See Chapter 10 for the details regarding the computation of percentage depletion.)

• The deduction cannot exceed 65% of a taxpayer's taxable income, computed without regard to the percentage depletion allowance.[17]

• Percentage depletion cannot be claimed for lease bonuses, advance royalties, or other amounts that are payable without regard to production.[18]

Example 17-8 ■

John owns a limited partnership interest in an oil and gas drilling fund. John's basis for cost depletion is now zero because depletion allowances in prior years (based upon percentage depletion) have reduced the property's basis to zero. John's share of percentage depletion is $10,000, and his taxable income from the property (before depletion is deducted) is $30,000. John has taxable income (before depletion) in total of $100,000. The 100% limitation does not apply because the percentage depletion ($10,000) is less than the taxable income ($30,000) from the property. The 65% limitation does not apply because the percentage depletion ($10,000) is less than 65% of John's $100,000 taxable income (0.65 × $100,000 = $65,000). John is able to deduct $10,000 of percentage depletion (subject to the possible application of the passive loss limitation rules) despite the fact that his cost basis is zero. ■

Intangible Drilling Costs (IDCs). The IDC deduction represents the intangible costs of drilling productive wells that would ordinarily be required to be capitalized. (See Chapter 10 for a discussion on IDCs and the Glossary in Appendix D for a definition of the term.)

The tax law permits an immediate deduction for such costs, although the taxpayer has the option of capitalizing the IDCs as an addition to the property's basis for cost

[15] Sec. 613A(c).
[16] The statutory percentage depletion rate for marginally producing oil and gas wells may exceed 15% in certain circumstances. See Chapter 10 for a discussion of these rules.
[17] Sec. 613A(d).
[18] Sec. 613A(d)(5).

depletion. IDCs on nonproductive wells are deducted as incurred. IDCs represent a significant tax benefit during the initial period of the investment and are generally allocated to the limited partners. Investors generally prefer to expense IDCs due to their preference for an immediate deduction (i.e., the time value of deferring income tax payments). In addition, since percentage depletion is generally used, the benefit from capitalizing IDCs (i.e., the increase in the cost depletion amount) may be of limited or no benefit.

Example 17-9 ■

Karen invests $10,000 in an oil and gas limited partnership interest. Karen's share of the IDCs is $3,000 in the first year. Percentage depletion is $2,000, and cost depletion (without regard to the capitalization of IDCs) is only $1,000. Assume that if the partnership elects to capitalize IDCs, Karen's cost depletion amount would increase from $1,000 to $1,500. Ignoring the effects of the 100% and 65% limitations upon the amount of percentage depletion claimed, an immediate write-off of the IDCs is more advantageous due to the $3,000 IDC deduction and the $2,000 percentage depletion deduction. If the IDCs are capitalized, the cost depletion is only $1,500.   ■

Disadvantages of Oil and Gas Investments. The potential tax disadvantages of an oil and gas investment include the following:

- Ordinary income may be recognized from the recapture of IDCs and previous depletion allowances upon the disposition of the investment.

- Under Sec. 465, the at-risk rules apply to oil and gas investments and may restrict both the use of nonrecourse financing and the advantages of financial leverage.

- If an investor does not materially participate in the oil and gas activity, losses or credits may not be currently deductible because of the passive activity limitation rules. Passive losses from the oil and gas activity can only be used to offset an investor's passive activity income from other passive activities. Any excess loss amounts are carried forward and used to offset net passive activity income in a subsequent year or are deductible in the year that the passive loss activity is sold or otherwise disposed of in a taxable transaction.

Additional Comment

In 1990, 38,602 oil and gas partnership tax returns were filed showing net income of $2.0 billion.

TAXATION OF EQUITY INVESTMENTS

OBJECTIVE 3

Describe the tax considerations for investments in equity securities

The tax law generally favors the issuance of fixed-income obligations as opposed to equity securities because dividends are not deductible by the corporate payor, whereas interest payments are fully deductible. Both dividends and interest are fully taxable to individual investors. A form of triple taxation of dividends may result if a corporation pays dividends to a corporate shareholder, who then distributes the income in the form of dividends to its individual shareholders (i.e., the income is taxed to both corporations and to the individual shareholders). The dividends-received deduction for corporate shareholders provides partial relief to mitigate these harsh results (see page 17-11 and Chapter 16).

The nondeductibility of dividends encourages closely held corporations to finance their capital needs by borrowing from shareholders rather than by selling additional stock. Shareholders in closely held companies may make only minimal contributions of equity capital before lending the additional monies that are needed. However, if the shareholders' debt holdings and the percentage of stock ownership are proportional and the debt is excessive, the IRS is empowered under the tax law to disallow the interest deductions and treat the debt as additional stock.[19] Furthermore, any retirements of the debt may be treated as a stock redemption and therefore taxable as a dividend.[20]

Kay, Kelly, and Ken form Able Corporation with a total capital contribution of $100,000 consisting of $90,000 of Able bonds and $10,000 of Able common stock. If the debt and stock are owned proportionately by the shareholders (e.g., Kay, Kelly, and Ken each own one-third of the stock and one-third of the debt), the IRS may attempt to treat the debt as equity and disallow the interest deductions to the corporation.

■

Corporate shareholders receive partial relief from the effects of double (or triple) taxation through the receipt of a 70% or 80% dividends-received deduction.[21] Certain restrictions are placed upon the dividends-received deduction if borrowed funds are used to acquire the stock or if the stock is held for a period of 45 days or less. Also, the shareholder's basis of the stock may be reduced by the nontaxable amount of the dividend (i.e., 70% or 80%) if the dividend is deemed to be extraordinary. (See Chapter 16 for a discussion of the dividends-received deduction available to corporate shareholders.) The deduction is 100% if the dividends are received from a member of an affiliated corporate group.

The availability of the dividends-received deduction may influence the investment strategy of a corporate investor. For example, excess corporate funds may be invested in common or preferred stock rather than in fixed-income securities to take advantage of the tax benefits from the dividends-received deduction.

Example 17-11 ■

Acme Corporation has excess funds of $10,000, which are to be invested in either 7% bonds or preferred stock of a domestic corporation that is currently yielding 6%. Assume that Acme's marginal tax rate (including both federal and state taxes) is 40%. The interest income of $700 and the dividend income of $600 (consisting of four quarterly dividend payments) are fully includible in gross income. However, Acme receives a $420 ($600 × 0.70) dividends-received deduction on the preferred stock. Acme's after-tax yield from the debentures would be only 4.2% ([$700 − $280 tax] ÷ $10,000), whereas the after-tax yield from the preferred stock is 5.28% ([$600 − $72 tax] ÷ $10,000).

■

If a closely held corporation invests an excessive amount of its retained earnings in fixed-income or equity securities instead of paying dividends to its shareholders, the corporation may be subject to a penalty tax (i.e., the accumulated earnings tax or the personal holding company tax).[22] (See Chapter 16 for a detailed discussion on these penalty taxes.)

Taxation of Stock Dividends

The receipt of a stock dividend is usually nontaxable to the shareholder.[23] However, an exception exists if the shareholder has the option to receive cash in lieu of stock or if certain disproportionate distributions occur and the relative interest of one class of shareholders increases.[24] These exceptions are rarely encountered in practice because

[19] Sec. 385. This topic is discussed more fully in Chapter 16.
[20] Secs. 301 and 302.
[21] Sec. 243(a). For corporations that own less than 20% of the value and voting stock of the distributing corporation the dividends-received deduction is 70%. The percentage is 80% if the ownership interest is 20% to 80%. The dividends-received deduction is 100% if the ownership interest is 80% or more.
[22] Secs. 531 and 541.
[23] Sec. 305(a).
[24] Sec. 305(b).

most companies want to make a tax-free distribution of stock to their shareholders.

Stock dividends are nontaxable because the shareholder has not realized anything of value as a result of the distribution (i.e., the shareholder has proportionately more shares of stock worth proportionately less per share). No corporate assets are distributed, and the shareholder's percentage interest in the assets and earnings does not change. Therefore, the shareholder's basis for the stock is merely allocated on a proportionate basis to (1) the stock dividend shares and (2) the shares held by the investor prior to the dividend distribution.

Example 17-12 ■   Larry owns 1,000 shares of Ajax Corporation's single class of stock having a $10,000 basis, or $10 per share. Ajax pays a 20% stock dividend to its shareholders. Before the issuance of the stock dividend, 10,000 shares of Ajax stock are outstanding. After the stock is distributed, 12,000 shares are outstanding. Larry owns 10% of the company both before the stock dividend (1,000 ÷ 10,000 = 0.10) and after the stock dividend (1,200 ÷ 12,000 = 0.10). Larry's total basis for the 1,200 shares is $10,000. The dividend reduces Larry's per-share basis to $8.33 ($10,000 ÷ 1,200 shares). ■

Some investors mistakenly believe that a stock dividend is equivalent to a cash dividend. Such is not the case, however, because when a stock dividend is paid, the corporation's earnings per share decrease proportionately to the percentage increase in common stock. Thus, the price of each share of stock decreases proportionately unless there is an increase in the price-earnings ratio.

Example 17-13 ■   Assume the same facts as in Example 17-12, except for the following additional facts: The net earnings of the Ajax stock before the 20% stock dividend are $10,000, or $1 ($10,000 ÷ 10,000 shares) per share. The stock is selling at 15 times the amount of earnings, or $15.00 ($1.00 × 15) per share. After the stock dividend, the net earnings remain $10,000, or $0.833 ($10,000 ÷ 12,000 shares) per share. If the stock continues to sell at 15 times the amount of earnings, Larry's shares are worth $15,000 before the stock dividend (1,000 shares × $1.00 × 15) and $15,000 after the stock dividend (1,200 shares × $0.833 × 15). ■

Classification of Gains and Losses

Investors in equity securities generally receive capital gain or loss treatment upon the sale or other disposition of the property, because stock that is held by an investor is generally classified as a capital asset. If the holding period is more than a year, the gain or loss is classified as long-term. Short-term capital gains do not receive favorable tax treatment for either individual or corporate taxpayers.

Capital Gains Tax. The highest tax rate for individuals is currently 39.6% and a 28% maximum rate applies to net capital gains (i.e., the excess of net long-term capital gains over net short-term capital losses). Currently, net short-term capital gains do not receive preferential capital gain treatment. In 1993 and subsequent years, the highest tax rate was increased from 31% to 39.6% for individuals with taxable income in excess of $250,000. A 36% rate also applies to married taxpayers with taxable income in excess of $140,000 ($115,000 for unmarried individuals, and $127,500 for heads of households). Thus, the effective spread between the 28% maximum rate applicable to net capital gains and the ordinary income rates has widened. This change should favor equity investments in high-growth low-dividend payout stocks which are more likely to reward investors with stock appreciation and long-term capital gains upon the disposition of the stock.

Capital Losses. The capital loss limitation rules may prevent an investor from deducting the entire amount of a capital loss in the year the loss is recognized. Under current law, net long-term and net short-term capital losses are fully deductible up to the $3,000 ceiling amount. Unused net capital losses are carried forward for an indefinite period. Therefore, ordinary losses are usually preferable to capital losses because they are not subject to these restrictions. (See Chapter 5 for a discussion of the capital loss limitation rules.)

Example 17-14 ■	In the current year Latoya, whose marginal tax rate is 39.6%, has a $10,000 net long-term capital gain. Her tax on the net long-term capital gain is $2,800 ($10,000 × 0.28) because the net long-term capital gain is subject to a maximum 28% rate. If Latoya's marginal tax rate is 15%, her tax on the net long-term capital gain would be $1,500 ($10,000 × 0.15) because the 28% maximum capital gain rate does not apply. If, instead, Latoya had a $10,000 net long-term capital loss in the current year, $3,000 of the net long-term capital loss would be deductible as an offset to ordinary income and provides a tax benefit at a 39.6% rate, while $7,000 would be carried forward as a long-term capital loss for an indefinite period. ■
Example 17-15 ■	Assume the same facts as in Example 17-14 except that Latoya's capital gains and losses are short term instead of long-term. In the first case, a $10,000 net short-term capital gain is fully includible in gross income and is taxed at Latoya's 39.6% marginal tax rate. In the second case, a $10,000 net short-term capital loss results in a $3,000 deduction against ordinary income and $7,000 being carried forward as a short-term capital loss for an indefinite period. ■

Return of Capital Distributions

In some situations, investors may be able to exclude a portion or all of a corporate distribution from gross income. A distribution is taxable to the shareholder as a dividend only to the extent that the corporation has current or accumulated earnings and profits.[25] Distributions are treated as a tax-free return of capital if they are made when the corporation does not have any earnings and profits or if they are in excess of its earnings and profits.

If an investor receives a return of capital distribution, the basis of the stock is reduced (but not below zero) by the amount of the distribution. Any distributions that are received after the basis of the stock has been reduced to zero are generally treated as capital gain. The distributing corporation must notify investors that all or a portion of the distributions represent a tax-free return of capital. This notification is accomplished by sending a Form 1099-DIV to the shareholders.

Example 17-16 ■	Allied Corporation has a deficit in accumulated earnings and profits and no current earnings and profits. The corporation has sufficient cash flow, however, to make a cash distribution to its shareholders. Louis, who has a $6,000 basis for his Allied stock (a capital asset), receives an $8,000 distribution from Allied. The distribution is treated as a tax-free return of capital until the basis of Louis's stock is reduced to zero. Additional amounts that are received are taxed as gain from the sale or exchange of the stock. The basis of Louis's stock is first reduced to zero, and Louis must recognize a $2,000 capital gain ($8,000 distribution − $6,000 basis reduction). Form 1099-DIV states that the distribution is not a dividend but the shareholder must determine if the distribution is a tax-free return of capital and/or capital gain. ■

---

[25] Sec. 316. See Chapter 16 for a discussion of earnings and profits for a corporation.

Capital gain or loss is generally recognized upon the sale of stock or securities. An exception is provided for losses from the sale or worthlessness of small business corporation (Sec. 1244) stock. These losses are deductible as ordinary losses up to a maximum of $50,000 per year ($100,000 for married taxpayer's filing a joint return). (See Chapter 8 for a discussion of the Sec. 1244 requirements.)

The Revenue Reconciliation Act of 1993 added additional incentives for investments in stocks of small businesses. Noncorporate taxpayers may exclude up to 50% of the gain realized on the disposition of qualified small business stock issued after August 10, 1993, if the stock is held for more than five years. (See Chapter 4 for a discussion of what constitutes qualified small business stock and limitations upon the exclusion.)

TAXATION OF FIXED-INCOME INVESTMENTS

OBJECTIVE 4
Understand the tax consequences associated with fixed-income securities

If a fixed-income investment (e.g., a bond) is issued at par to an investor who holds the bonds until maturity, no gain or loss is recognized at maturity. However, if a previously issued bond is acquired from another investor in the bond market, gain or loss is generally recognized upon the sale of the security or its redemption at maturity.[26]

As discussed in the next section, investors are often able to purchase bonds in the market at a discount because a change in interest rates affects the value of outstanding bonds. For example, if interest rates increase, the prices of outstanding bonds decrease because investors are no longer willing to pay the same price for outstanding bonds that offer a below-market interest rate.

Example 17-17 ■

Bonds with a coupon rate of 7% are issued at par in 1994. In 1995 the market interest rate for comparable bonds increases from 7% to 8%. The price of the bond issued at par in 1994 will decrease by an amount that is sufficient to enable a purchaser of the bond to earn an 8% equivalent yield to maturity. The yield to a purchaser of the bond includes the 7% coupon rate of interest plus the gain on the market discount that is realized upon the maturity of the bond. ■

Ethical Point

A CPA has an ethical responsibility to make sure that a proper position has been taken with regard to whether a gain is treated as ordinary or capital.

Market Discount Bonds

If a taxable or tax-exempt bond is acquired in the market at a discount, investors are generally required to treat any subsequent gain upon the disposition (or receipt of the proceeds at maturity) of the bond as ordinary income to the extent of accrued market discount.[27] The difference between the bond's cost basis and its redemption value at maturity must be amortized over the remaining life of the bond for purposes of computing the ordinary income portion of the gain.[28] The distinction between ordinary income and long-term capital gain treatment is important for 1993 and later years because the highest tax rate for investors on ordinary income is 39.6% whereas a

---

[26] Gain or loss is not recognized if the bond is purchased and sold or redeemed at the same amount (e.g., at par).

[27] Secs. 1276(a) and (b). Ordinary income treatment for accrued market discount does not apply to owners of taxable market discount bonds issued on or before July 18, 1984 if the bonds were acquired before May 1, 1993. Owners of tax-exempt bonds are not required to accrue market discount if the bonds were acquired prior to May 1, 1993 (regardless of the issue date).

[28] Sec. 1278(a)(2)(C). Market discount is zero if the discount is less than one-quarter of 1% of the stated redemption price multiplied by the number of years to maturity.

28% maximum rate applies to long-term capital gains. The distinction is also significant if the investor has unused capital losses or capital loss carryovers that would otherwise not be currently deductible due to the capital loss limitation rules.

For taxable bonds, market discount need not be accrued on an annual basis, although the investor may elect to do so.[29] If the election is made, the basis in the bond is increased by the amount that is included in gross income. The payment of tax is deferred on the accrued market discount if this election is not made. The requirement to accrue market discount merely converts capital gain into ordinary income upon the sale or disposition (or redemption) of the bonds but does not accelerate the period for recognizing income.

Key Point

In the normal case a taxpayer would not accelerate income by electing to accrue market discount on an annual basis. He might elect to do so when he has unused investment expenses, however.

Example 17-18 ■

Marc purchases for $800 on January 1, 1992, a $1,000 taxable bond issued at par in 1991. The bond matures on January 1, 1996 (4 years from the date the bond is acquired by Marc). On January 1, 1994, Marc sells the bond for $950. His recognized gain is $150 ($950 − $800), of which $100 represents accrued market discount ([2 years ÷ 4 years] × $200) that is reported as ordinary income. The remainder of the gain ($50) is long-term capital gain. No accrual of the $200 market discount is required for the period the bond is held by Marc (i.e., 1992 and 1993), unless he makes the appropriate election. ■

Original Issue Discount and Zero Coupon Bonds

Bonds are usually issued at a price that approximates their par value since the established interest rate equals the current market rate for comparable bonds. In some situations, however, corporate borrowers issue a bond at a coupon rate that is either zero (i.e., **zero coupon bonds**) or substantially less than the current market rate. Original issue discount bonds may result because the bonds must be offered at a substantial discount from par to attract investors. The discount from par value is needed to offset the lower than market interest rate that is being offered to investors. Zero coupon bonds are quite popular because they offer significant cash-flow advantages to corporate borrowers since no cash outlay for interest is required until the bonds mature.

Investors are generally required to accrue the original issue discount ratably over the life of the bond (the straight-line method). However, if the bond is issued after July 1, 1982, the yield-to-maturity (or constant-rate) method must be used.[30] Thus, investors must recognize interest income from the accrual of original issue discount on a current basis, even though the interest payments are based upon the lower coupon rate (or in the case of a zero coupon bond, there are no periodic interest payments). The requirement to pay tax on a current basis without the receipt of interest payments may create cash-flow problems for some investors.

Self-Study Question

Would a zero coupon bond or a bond that makes semiannual interest payments equal to 8% of the face value of the bond be more subject to price fluctuation as interest rates rise or fall?

Answer

The zero coupon bond is subject to more severe price changes since its value is based solely on the present value of the maturity amount.

Example 17-19 ■

Key Point

Zero coupon bonds are a popular investment in self-directed IRA accounts and other tax-sheltered investment accounts since the interest income from the accrual of the discount is not subject to current taxation.

Maria purchases for $636 on December 31, 1994, a $1,000 zero coupon bond. The bond matures on December 31, 1998 (4 years from the date the bond is issued). The current market yield for the bond is 8%. Because the bond is issued after July 1, 1982, the yield-to-maturity (or constant-rate) method must be used to accrue the original issue discount over the life of the bond. Maria is required to recognize interest income on a current basis equal to the accrued discount amount, and her basis for the bond is increased by the amount of income that is recognized. The tax consequences are illustrated below.

[29] Sec. 1278(b).
[30] Sec. 1272.

Year	Beginning of Year Basis for the Bond	Amortized Original Issue Discount and Interest Income	End of Year Basis of the Bond
1994	—	—	$ 735
1995	$735	$ 59[a]	794
1996	794	64	858
1997	858	68	926
1998	927	74	1,000

[a] 0.08 current market yield × $735 = $59

Maria does not receive any cash from the investment to pay the tax on the interest until the $1,000 principal amount is paid at maturity. The money needed to pay these taxes must come from Maria's other income or investments. No gain or loss is recognized by Maria when the bond is redeemed at maturity. ∎

Deferred Investment Annuities

Deferred annuities offer investors the opportunity to defer the recognition of income until the funds are withdrawn. Funds are typically contributed to an insurance company, which invests the amounts in fixed-income securities. The annuity starting date may be several years after the investment is made so that a long-term income deferral is possible. Quite often, the annuity is not started until after the investor has retired, when the monies can be taxed at a reduced rate.

If any distribution or loans are made by the insurance company to the investor prior to the starting date of the annuity, the investor must recognize ordinary income (rather than a return of the investor's capital investment) to the extent that the cash value of the contract exceeds the investment in the contract.[31] Annuity payments made after the annuity starting date are taxed under the normal annuity rules (see Chapter 3).

Deferred annuities are particularly attractive for high-income taxpayers who are 10 to 15 years away from retirement and who anticipate a need for additional retirement income. One disadvantage of the deferred annuity is that the investor cannot have full control over future investments made by the insurance company, although the annuity may provide for a guaranteed rate of interest in the early years.[32]

Example 17-20 ∎ Mark, age 60, is planning to retire at age 70 and needs additional retirement income to supplement his pension and social security. He expects to have a 36% marginal tax rate during the 10-year deferral period and a 15% marginal tax rate during his retirement years. Mark invests $100,000 in a deferred investment annuity. After 10 years, the principal plus accumulated untaxed income amounts to $200,000, and Mark begins to collect an annuity for life of $30,000 per year. Assume that Mark's life expectancy at the annuity starting date is 10 years. The amount that is treated as a tax-free return of capital is computed as follows:

$$\frac{\$100,000 \text{ Investment in contract}}{\$300,000 \ (\$30,000 \times 10 \text{ years}) \text{ Expected proceeds}} = 1/3$$

Thus, two-thirds of each $30,000 annuity payment is taxable as ordinary income. If Mark receives a $10,000 distribution 2 years prior to the annuity starting date, the distribution is taxable as ordinary income as long as the cash

Additional Comment

In computing the investment in the contract, any additional premium for double indemnity or disability benefits is not to be included.

[31] Secs. 72(e)(3) and (4).

[32] Rev. Rul. 77-85, 1977-1 C.B. 12. The IRS has also ruled that an investor is currently taxed on income earned from a wraparound annuity contract. See Rev. Ruls. 80-274, 1980-2 C.B. 27, and 81-225, 1981-2 C.B. 12.

value of the annuity is at least $10,000 greater than Mark's $100,000 investment in the contract. ∎

If the annuity starting date is before January 1, 1987, the exclusion ratio continues to apply to the annuity payments even if the annuitant lives beyond his life expectancy. However, for annuity contracts starting after December 31, 1986, the amount of the exclusion is limited to the unrecovered investment in the contract.[33] After an annuitant's investment in the contract is recovered, all future amounts received are fully taxable. If the annuitant dies before he has recovered his investment in the contract, the unrecovered amount is allowed as an itemized deduction in the year of death.[34]

Example 17-21 ∎

Assume the same facts as in Example 17-20, and that the annuity starting date is after December 31, 1986. The exclusion ratio is applied for 10 years until Mark has recovered his investment in the contract, and $10,000 is excludible from income each year during this period. The $30,000 annuity payments are fully taxable to Mark in year 11 and subsequent years after Mark has outlived his life expectancy. If Mark dies after receiving annuity payments for 9 years, $10,000 is deductible as an itemized deduction on Mark's final income tax return in the year of death because he has recovered only $90,000 of his $100,000 investment in the contract (0.333 × $30,000 × 9 years). ∎

Certificates of Deposit and Treasury Bills

Certificates of Deposit. Investors that use the cash method of accounting are permitted to defer the recognition of income on short-term (i.e., maturities of one year or less) **certificates of deposit** (*CDs*) if the interest (1) is not credited to the investor's account and (2) the principal amount cannot be withdrawn immediately without penalty for early withdrawal.[35] Generally, interest income on CDs can be deferred because this type of obligation meets these two criteria. However, the interest income must be recognized in the year the CD matures or in the year of redemption. Income must also be recognized currently if the investor uses the accrual method of accounting.

Self-Study Question

The rate of interest on U.S. Treasury bills is quoted as a percentage discount on the maturity amount. Is the actual yield higher or lower than this discount rate?

Answer

The actual yield would be calculated on the cost. Since the cost is less than the maturity amount, the actual yield is greater than the discount rate.

Treasury Bills. **U.S. Treasury bills** are short-term obligations (e.g., 90 days to maturity) that are issued at a discount from the maturity amount. The difference between the issue price and the maturity amount represents the interest income. Cash method of accounting investors are not required to accrue the interest income, although they may elect to do so.[36] It is usually preferable not to accrue interest because the investor is able to obtain a tax deferral until the Treasury bills mature in the subsequent year.

If a Treasury bill is sold prior to its maturity, the portion of the difference between the issue price and the selling price that represents an accrued discount is taxed as ordinary income.[37] The remainder is treated as a short-term capital gain or loss.

Example 17-22 ∎

Martha, a cash method of accounting investor, acquires a newly issued 3-month Treasury bill for $9,700 ($10,000 maturity value). After holding the investment for a month, Martha sells the Treasury bill for $9,825. $100 (0.333 × $300 discount) of

---

[33] Sec. 72(b)(2).
[34] Sec. 72(b)(3).
[35] Rev. Rul. 82-113, 1982-1 C.B. 78.
[36] Sec. 454(a). Accrual method of accounting taxpayers must accrue the interest on short-term U.S. government obligations.
[37] Sec. 1271(a)(3).

the gain represents interest income. The remaining $25 ($9,825 − [$9,700 + $100]) of gain is short-term capital gain that accrued because of a decline in the market interest rate. ∎

Tax-Exempt Securities

Private Activity Bonds. Bonds that are issued by state and local government units are generally exempt from the federal income tax.[38] The interest earned on certain private activity bonds issued after August 7, 1986, is not tax-exempt for federal income tax purposes under the regular tax computation.[39] **Private activity bonds** are obligations issued by state or local governments to finance nongovernmental activities (e.g., a sports arena or an industrial park). Certain private activity bonds are tax-exempt in computing the regular tax, but the interest is a tax preference item for the alternative minimum tax (e.g., tax-exempt interest on nonessential function bonds issued after August 7, 1986).[40]

The effective pretax interest rate on private activity bonds that are taxable or subject to the alternative minimum tax should be higher than those of fully tax-exempt bonds of comparable quality. Thus, investors should consider whether the higher pretax yield is sufficient to offset any increased federal tax liability incurred under the regular tax or alternative minimum tax calculations.

Change in Tax-Exempt Status. Some investors have expressed concern that outstanding state and municipal bonds may lose their current tax-exempt status. Several legislative proposals to eliminate or restrict the bonds' tax-exempt status have been introduced. The changes enacted by the Tax Reform Act of 1986 also reflect this trend. Investors should note, however, that the 1986 Act changes merely restrict the issuance of certain types of tax-exempt bonds. They do not apply retroactively. The net effect may be (1) a decreased supply of existing tax-exempt bonds and (2) increased prices that would be beneficial to holders of existing tax-exempt bonds.

Accrual of Original Issue Discount. The rules for accruing original issue discount on tax-exempt bonds are the same as for taxable bonds, except that the accrued portion of the discount is not taxable. In other words, investors merely increase the adjusted basis of the bond by the amount of the accrued original issue discount.

Accrual of Market Discount. Tax-exempt obligations are subject to the previously discussed accrual of market discount requirements for taxable bonds.[41] Therefore, if an existing tax-exempt bond is acquired in the bond market at a discount on or after May 1, 1993, any subsequent gain upon its sale, disposition, or maturity is ordinary income to the extent of the accrued market discount and any remaining amount is capital gain.

Additional Comment

Tax-exempt interest on state or local government obligations has to be shown on Federal income tax returns even though it usually is not subject to Federal taxation.

Additional Comment

In 1991 more than 4.1 million people reported $44 billion in tax-exempt interest. Nearly half of the tax-exempt interest was reported on returns with adjusted gross income of $100,000 or more.

Example 17-23 ∎ Paul acquires a tax-exempt bond for $800 in the bond market in 1994. The bond was issued at par, and has four years to maturity. After 2 years, he sells the bond for $950. Although no federal income tax is owed on the interest, Paul must recognize $150 ($950 − $800) gain when the bond is sold: $100 (2 years ÷ 4 years × $200 market discount) of the gain is ordinary income and $50 ($150 − $100) is capital gain. ∎

---

[38] Sec. 103.
[39] Secs. 103(b)(1) and 141.
[40] Sec. 57(a)(5).
[41] Sec. 1278(a)(1)(B).

Tax-Exempt Mutual Funds and Unit Investment Trusts. Currently, many tax-exempt bonds are marketed through tax-exempt bond mutual funds or unit investment trusts. Such mutual funds and unit trusts usually provide reduced risk and a higher degree of liquidity because they are diversified. Thus, a tax-exempt mutual fund may offer to redeem the investor's units at the fund's current net asset value, and the sponsor of a unit trust (e.g., a securities firm) may establish a market for the trust units so that investors may readily dispose of their investment. In addition, some municipal bond trusts provide private insurance against failure to pay interest and principal, although this insurance does not protect the investor against a decline in market price.

Taxation of Social Security Payments. Elderly taxpayers who receive both tax-exempt interest and social security benefits may be taxed on a portion (up to 85%) of their social security benefits because tax-exempt interest is includible in the calculation of their modified AGI. (See Chapter 3 for a discussion of the rules for computing the taxable portion of the social security payments.)

Additional Comment

Some tax-exempt mutual funds invest only in bonds issued within a particular state. These bonds are called "double tax-exempt" since a unit holder in the mutual fund would pay neither federal nor state income taxes.

Effect of State Income Taxes. Even though state and municipal bond interest may be exempt from federal income taxation, the interest may be subject to state income taxes. Most states tax interest income derived from bonds that are issued by another state or an out-of-state local government unit. However, an exemption is generally provided for bonds that are issued by either the state imposing the income tax or a local government unit from within the state. In addition, interest on obligations of the Federal government (e.g., U.S. Treasury bills) is not subject to state income tax.

State income taxes should be taken into account by investors. The attractiveness of in-state and out-of-state municipal bond yields should be compared with the after-tax yields of taxable securities.

Example 17-24 ■

Maxine is considering whether to invest in (1) a tax-exempt bond issued in her state of residence that is exempt from both federal and state income taxes or (2) a tax-exempt bond issued by another state. Maxine's marginal state income tax rate is 10%. Both the in- and out-of-state bonds have a 7% yield on a before-tax basis. However, a comparison of the after-tax yield reveals that the in-state bond is more attractive to Maxine because the out-of-state bond yields only 6.3% (7% − [0.10 × 7%]), whereas the in-state yield remains at 7% because no state income tax is owed. ■

The following section of this chapter discusses the tax consequences for equity investments including call options and short sale transactions.

CALL OPTIONS

OBJECTIVE 5
Describe the tax rules for purchasers and writers of call options

Instead of actually making an investment in a stock, an investor may acquire an option (also known as a *call*) to buy the stock at a fixed price (e.g., $50 per share) for a specified period of time (e.g., 6 months). There are two major advantages to purchasing a call instead of making an outright purchase of the stock:

1. The investor's risk of loss is reduced because several calls may be purchased in a broad range of companies each for a relatively small call premium. If the stock price remains constant or declines while the call is outstanding, the investor can allow the call to expire, and the only loss to the purchaser is the premium that is paid for the call. Nevertheless, the purchase of call options is generally considered to be of high risk and a speculative investment.

TOPIC REVIEW 17-1

Taxation of Fixed-Income Investments

Investment Type	Income Recognition	Character of Gain or Loss
Market discount bonds	Accrual of market discount is not mandatory but an election may be made.	Gain on sale, disposition, or maturity is generally treated as ordinary income to the extent of the accrued market discount. The remaining gain or loss is capital gain or loss. An exception is provided for taxable market discount bonds issued on or before July 18, 1984 if the bonds were acquired before May 1, 1993.
Original issue discount bonds	Accrual of original issue discount as ordinary income is required ratably over the life of the bond. Basis of the bond is increased by the amount of accrued interest.	Gain or loss on disposition is capital gain or loss. No gain or loss is recognized if the bond is held to maturity.
Deferred investment annuities	An exclusion ratio is used to compute the tax-free return of capital portion of the annuity payments. After the investment in the contract is recovered, all future amounts are taxable. Premature death results in a deduction in the year of death equal to the unrecovered investment in the contract.	No gain or loss is generally recognized.
Certificates of deposit	Income recognition is generally deferred for cash basis taxpayers until maturity or redemption for CDs having a duration of one year or less. Accrual of interest is mandatory for accrual basis taxpayers.	Interest income is recognized in the year of maturity or redemption.
U.S. Treasury bills	Accrual of interest income is not mandatory for cash basis taxpayers but may be elected. Accrual of interest is mandatory for accrual basis taxpayers.	If held to maturity, the difference between the issue price and maturity amount is interest income. If sold prior to maturity, the accrued discount portion is ordinary interest income and the residual profit amount is short-term capital gain or loss.
Tax-exempt securities	Interest is generally tax exempt. However, any gain or loss upon the disposition of tax-exempt securities is taxable. Certain private activity bond interest is taxable under the regular tax and/or subject to the alternative minimum tax.	Gain or loss on the disposition of tax-exempt bonds is generally capital gain or loss. Any gain due to accrued market discount for bonds acquired on or after May 1, 1993 (regardless of issue date) is treated as ordinary income to the extent of the accrued market discount.

Real World Example

In late 1993, one could have purchased an option to buy 100 shares of Federal Express at $70 per share for $175. At that time the market price of Federal Express was $65.37 and the option was to expire in January, 1994.

2. If the stock price increases substantially during the exercise period, the investor can sell the call to another investor and earn a profit (see Example 17-25). In such an exchange, the original investor's only cost is the call premium. Alternatively, the investor may exercise the call and acquire the stock. Exercising the call, however, requires a greater capital investment (i.e., the purchase price of the stock) than merely trading in calls.

Example 17-25 ■

Michael acquires an option to buy 100 shares of Atlantic stock for $6,200 (or $62 per share) for a 6-month period. The current market price for 100 shares of the Atlantic stock is $5,500. Michael pays a call premium of $500 to the writer of the call. The Atlantic stock price increases to $80 per share during the next three months, and Michael sells the call option in the options market for $1,800 ([$80 − $62] × 100). Michael's basis for the option is $500, and his profit from the transaction is $1,300 ($1,800 − $500). This represents a 260% return on the investment, even though the percentage increase in the stock value is only 45.4% ($2,500 increase in value ÷ $5,500 investment cost). ■

Purchaser's Tax Consequences

A call option on a stock or other security is a capital asset because the underlying property into which the option is converted (i.e., the stock) is a capital asset. Thus, the call premium is viewed as a capital expenditure. The tax treatment depends upon whether the option lapses, is sold, or is exercised. The tax consequences are not determined until the option is sold, exercised, or permitted to lapse.

Additional Comment

A call option represents the right to purchase a certain amount of stock at a certain price within a stipulated time period. A put option represents the right to sell a certain amount of stock at a certain price within a stipulated time period.

Call Option Lapses. If the price of the stock does not increase during the exercise period, the purchaser of the call may fail to exercise the option, thus permitting it to expire. The lapse of the call is treated as a sale or exchange.[42] Thus, a capital loss is recognized by the purchaser of the call.

Call Option Is Sold. It is very common for the investor to sell the call rather than to permit it to expire or to exercise the call. After all, the intent of most purchasers of call options is to speculate on short-term changes in the price of the underlying stock. A long-term investment in the stock is generally not a goal. Call options are regularly traded on the Chicago Board Options Exchange and on other option exchanges.

If the call option is sold, the difference between the selling price and the call premium is a capital gain or loss. For exchange-traded options, the capital gain or loss is usually short-term, because call options are generally written for a period that is shorter than the required holding period for long-term capital gain or loss.

Call Option Is Exercised. If the call is exercised, the premium is added to the investor's basis for the stock that is acquired. The stock's holding period begins on the day after the day on which the call is exercised.

Example 17-26 ■

Pam purchases 3 separate call options for the stock of Austin, Blue, and Camp Corporations. The option period is 6 months in each case, and each option permits Pam to acquire 100 shares of the Austin, Blue, and Camp stock for a $10 per share price. Pam pays a $100 call premium for each call.

• The call option for the Austin stock expires. Pam recognizes a $100 short-term capital loss.

[42] Sec. 1234A(1).

- The call option on the Blue stock is exercised. Pam acquires the stock for its $1,000 ($10 × 100) option price. Her cost basis in the Blue stock is $1,100 ($1,000 + $100), and its holding period begins on the day following the exercise date.

- The call option on the Camp stock is sold after 2 months for $300. Pam recognizes a $200 ($300 − $100) short-term capital gain. ∎

If an investor has net long-term capital losses from other securities transactions, the recognition of short-term capital gains from completed call option transactions may be used to offset these long-term losses. This offset may be desirable because short-term capital gains are includible in ordinary income in full, whereas a net long-term capital loss is subject to a $3,000 overall ceiling per year.

Writer's Tax Consequences

The writer of a call option is an investor who agrees to sell a fixed number of shares of stock (usually 100 per call) at a fixed price for a given period (e.g., 6 months). Generally, the investor who writes the call owns the underlying stock at the time the call is written. Naked calls (i.e., calls that are written when the underlying stock is not owned) are riskier. For example, if the call is exercised, the call writer must deliver the stock to the purchaser to close out the option. If the call in question is a naked call, the call writer will have to purchase the stock at a price that is higher than its exercise price.

Economic Consequences. Option writing is generally considered to be a conservative investment strategy. It entails the following economic consequences:

- In a period of declining prices the investor receives a stream of income in the form of call premiums. This offsets part or all of the decline in value of the underlying stock held by the writer.

- In a period of rapidly increasing stock prices, the writer of the call forgoes some of the appreciation because the stock must be sold at a fixed price during the option period. Some economic benefit accrues to the writer of the call in this situation since (1) the option price is initially established at a price that is higher than the market value of the stock at the date the option is written, and (2) a call premium is received for writing the option.

Tax Consequences. The following events create tax consequences for call writers:

- The call expires unexercised.
- The call is exercised.
- The writer of the call closes out his position by purchasing a call on the same stock during the option period.[43]

CALL EXPIRES UNEXERCISED. No income is recognized when the call premium is received. If the price of the stock does not increase to or above its exercise price, the option expires unexercised. In such a case, the writer recognizes a short-term capital gain equal to the amount of the call premium received for writing the call.[44] Recognition of gain from the expiration of call options may be a tax planning opportunity for investors who have offsetting capital losses or capital loss carryforwards.

---

[43] See Rev. Rul. 78-182, 1978-1 C.B. 265, for a detailed discussion of holders and writers of calls, puts, and straddle options.

[44] Sec. 1234(b)(1).

CALL IS EXERCISED. If the call is exercised (e.g., due to an increase in the stock price), the call premium is added to the proceeds from the sale of the stock delivered by the option writer. Any capital gain or loss that is recognized is long- or short-term, depending upon the holding period of the underlying stock that is used to close the sale.

CLOSING TRANSACTIONS. A call writer may terminate his call position by purchasing an identical call option in a closing transaction.[45] Here, any gain or loss is short-term and is equal to the difference between the call premium received for writing the call and the premium that is paid to purchase the call in the closing transaction.

Example 17-27 ■

Pat owns 100 shares of the stock of Adobe, Bell, and Cable Corporations and receives call premiums of $300 ($100 for each call) for writing calls on the three stocks. The calls permit each of the three 100-share blocks of stock to be purchased for $1,000. Pat's basis for each stock is $800. The price of the Adobe stock increases above the $1,000 exercise price, and the holder of the call exercises his right to acquire the Adobe stock. Pat recognizes a $300 ([$1,000 proceeds + $100 call premium] − $800 cost basis) capital gain on the sale of the Adobe stock. This gain is long-term if Pat's holding period for the Adobe stock delivered is more than one year. The price of the Bell stock does not increase above the $1,000 exercise price, and the option expires unexercised. Pat recognizes a $100 short-term capital gain equal to the amount of the call premium received upon the expiration of the call. Pat decides to close out his call position on the Cable stock because it has increased in price and he anticipates further price appreciation in the stock before the option expires. Pat acquires an identical call option on the Cable stock for $250. A $150 ($250 − $100) short-term capital loss is recognized by Pat on closing the transaction. ■

The tax consequences for call options are summarized in Topic Review 17-2.

SHORT SALE TRANSACTIONS

OBJECTIVE 6
Calculate and classify gains or losses from short sale transactions

Additional Comment

Each month the New York Stock Exchange will disclose the number of shares sold short for each listed company.

A *short sale* is essentially a speculative activity whereby an investor anticipates that the price of a stock, commodity future, or other investment medium will decline in value. The objective is to make a profit from a decline in the value of the security by selling it at its current price and repurchasing the same security at a future date at a lower price. In short sales, however, the investor does not own the security that is sold. Instead, he merely borrows the security from a broker (i.e., the broker sells the security that is held by the brokerage firm in a fiduciary capacity). Under the short sale contract, the short seller is obligated to cover the short sale in the future by purchasing identical securities in the market, or by delivering securities that are already owned, to replace the borrowed securities. If cash dividends are paid on the borrowed stock prior to the close of the short sale, the short seller is obligated to repay the lender a compensating amount.

Tax Consequences

The basic tax rules applicable to short sales are discussed in Chapter 5. Here, these general rules are highlighted, and the investment and tax planning strategies

---

[45] The purchase of an identical call (i.e., an option to acquire the same underlying stock with the same expiration period and terms) closes out the call writer's position because the written call and the purchased call are cancelled.

TOPIC REVIEW 17-2

Tax Consequences for Call Options		
Transaction	Purchaser of Call	Writer of Call
Option is written or purchased.	None	None
Option is sold or a similar option is purchased in a closing transaction.	The difference between the selling price and the premium is short-term capital gain or loss.	The difference between the call premium received and the amount paid to purchase the option is short-term capital gain or loss.
Option is exercised.	The call premium is added to the basis of the acquired stock and no gain or loss is recognized.	The call premium received is added to the sales proceeds and capital gain or loss is recognized.
Option lapses.	Short-term capital loss is recognized equal to the amount of the call premium paid.	Short-term capital gain is recognized equal to the call premium received.

involving short sales are discussed. The general rules for determining the timing and character of the gain or loss from short sale transactions include the following:

- No gain or loss is recognized until the short sale is closed.[46]

- If substantially identical property (e.g., stock) has been held for a year or less prior to the short sale, or if substantially identical property is acquired after the short sale is entered into, the gain or loss recognized upon the closing of the short sale is short-term.[47]

- If substantially identical property has been held for more than a year prior to the short sale, any loss recognized on closing the short sale is long-term.[48] A gain on the sale is long-term if stock that has been held for more than one year is used to close the short position.

- The holding period of the stock that is actually used to close the short sale transaction does not determine whether the gain is short- or long-term.

These rules were originally enacted to prevent investors from artificially converting short-term capital gain into long-term capital gain or long-term capital loss into short-term capital loss by entering into a short sale. Under the current rules, net capital gain (i.e., the excess of net long-term capital gain over net short-term capital loss) is subject to a 28% maximum rate and both net long- and short-term capital losses are fully deductible against an individual's ordinary income up to $3,000. The spread between the 28% maximum rate on net capital gains and ordinary income has widened in 1993 and subsequent years thus making the rules relating to short sales once again of greater importance to investors.

Typical Misconception

It is difficult to understand how you can sell something that you do not own. In a short sale, the investor borrows the stock from a broker. The broker typically obtains the stock from other customers who have left their stock with the broker in "street name." The broker will ask the customers to sign an agreement that permits the broker to lend the stock to short sellers.

---

[46] Reg. Sec. 1.1233-1(a)(1).
[47] Sec. 1233(b).
[48] Sec. 1233(d).

Treatment of Dividend Payments

Dividend payments on borrowed stock must be repaid by the short seller to the lender. If a repayment were not required, the lender would not receive a dividend because the stock was previously sold by his broker.

The payment generally represents an itemized deduction *from* AGI for the short seller if the short sale is held open for at least 46 days after the date of the short sale.[49] If the short position is closed within 45 days, however, the payment made in lieu of the dividend must be capitalized as part of the short seller's basis in the stock that is used to close the short sale. It is generally preferable to receive a deduction *from* AGI (if the taxpayer's deductions are itemized), rather than to capitalize such amounts if the short sale transaction results in a capital loss.

Capitalization merely increases the loss amount that may be of limited benefit due to the capital loss limitations. If a deduction *from* AGI is allowed because the short sale is held open for at least 46 days, the investor can use the short-term capital gain from the short sale to offset long-term capital losses or capital loss carryovers, and the itemized deduction will be allowed in full. If the short sale results in a short-term capital gain, the investor who itemizes his deductions is generally indifferent as to whether the dividend payment is capitalized or is allowed as a deduction *from* AGI. In this case, the capitalization treatment merely reduces the short-term capital gain recognized upon the short sale, and the short-term capital gain is fully includible in gross income.

Example 17-28 ■ Phil acquires 100 shares of Florida Corporation stock on July 10 for $5,000. On October 1, he enters into a short sale of the stock when it is selling for $7,000. On November 15, Florida Corporation pays a $100 cash dividend. Phil must pay $100 to the lender of the stock. If Phil closes the short sale within 45 days after October 1, (the date of the short sale) the $100 is not deductible and must be added to the basis of the Florida stock that is used to close the short sale. If Phil does not close until 46 days after the date of the short sale (on or after November 16th), the $100 payment is a deduction *from* AGI. If Phil uses the previously acquired stock to close the short sale on December 1, a short-term capital gain of $2,000 ($7,000 selling price − $5,000 basis) is recognized. This gain may be used to offset other capital losses or capital loss carryovers, as well as the $100 itemized deduction. ■

Deferral of Gain on Sale of Stock

Additional Comment

Short sales are frequently used in arbitrage transactions by professional traders.

Despite the previously discussed restrictions, certain tax advantages may accrue to investors who engage in short sales. For example, a short sale "against the box" may be used to defer the recognition of gain on appreciated securities until the short sale is closed in the subsequent year. (The investment term *against the box* is used to describe a short sale transaction where the investor actually owns the underlying stock that is being sold short.) Thus, instead of selling the appreciated securities and recognizing a gain in the current year, an investor can enter into a short sale and freeze his economic position. For example, an increase in the future price of the stock results in an economic gain from the "long" position in the stock that will be offset by a comparable loss in the "short" position due to the short sale. If the securities are held for more than 1 year prior to the short sale, any gain recognized upon the closing of the short sale by the delivery of the appreciated securities in the following year is long-term capital gain.

[49] Sec. 263(h)(1).

Example 17-29 ■   Paula acquires 100 shares of Compact stock in 1987 for $5,000. In November 1993, the stock is worth $25,000. Paula would like to sell the stock because of her uncertainty about its future investment potential. However, Paula would prefer to defer recognition of the gain until 1994, because (1) she expects to be in a lower tax bracket in that year and (2) she has already recognized $3,000 of capital losses in 1993 which would otherwise be deductible against her ordinary income. Paula enters into a short sale of the stock for $25,000 in November 1993 and closes the short sale in January 1994 by delivering the appreciated Compact stock. Paula recognizes a $20,000 ($25,000 selling price − $5,000 basis) long-term capital gain when the short sale is closed in 1994.   ■

EMPLOYMENT-RELATED INVESTMENTS

OBJECTIVE 7
Understand the tax and nontax implications for employment-related investments

Investments in company-sponsored retirement plans and other retirement funding arrangements (e.g., IRAs) represent a significant portion of the total net worth and savings of many individuals. (See Chapter 9 for a discussion of retirement plan arrangements.) This section highlights the tax planning and investment-related aspects of such plans.

Individual Retirement Accounts

An individual may establish an IRA and make contributions that are deductible *for* AGI only if one of the following two conditions exists:

Additional Comment

Individuals who can make deductible contributions to an IRA can continue to do so until they reach age 70½.

- Neither the individual nor his spouse are active participants in an employer-sponsored retirement plan (including tax-sheltered annuities, government plans, simplified employee pension plans, and H.R. 10 plans).

Additional Comment

The number of returns with IRA deductions dropped by 69.0% from 15.5 million for 1986 to 4.7 million for 1991 because the eligibility requirements for a deductible IRA were severely restricted by Congress for 1987 and subsequent years.

- Other individuals are eligible to make deductible IRA contributions if their AGI is equal to or less than $25,000 for a single individual or $40,000 for a married couple filing a joint return.[50] Individuals who are not participants in an employer-sponsored retirement plan are not subject to the dollar limitations. The deductible IRA contributions are phased-out on a pro rata basis between $25,000 and $35,000 for single individuals and between $40,000 and $50,000 for married individuals.

Eligible individuals may contribute up to $2,000 per year ($2,250 for married taxpayers filing a joint return where one spouse does not have any earned income). If both spouses work, each may establish an IRA and contribute a maximum of $2,000 to each account.[51] Many individuals who are covered under employer-sponsored qualified pension plans or profit-sharing plans (or H.R. 10 plans for self-employed persons) view the IRA as a supplement to their existing retirement savings program. Annual contributions are not required, and contributions for the current period may be made after the end of the tax year if they are made prior to the due date for the tax return (excluding extensions). This timing benefit permits an individual who is eligible to make deductible IRA contributions to assess his tax position prior to the

[50] The applicable dollar amount for a married individual filing a separate return is zero (see Sec. 219(g)(3)(B)(iii)).
[51] Sec. 219(b). The allowable amount is the lesser of $2,000 or the compensation includible in the individual's gross income for the year.

due date of the return and to make a deductible IRA contribution for the prior year. A deduction for the post-year-end contribution may permit an individual to avoid a penalty on the underpayment of tax for the prior year.

Nondeductible Contributions. Individuals who are not eligible to make deductible contributions (e.g., high-income taxpayers who are participants in an employer-sponsored retirement plan) can make nondeductible IRA contributions.[52] The advantage of such contributions is that the earnings on the amounts contributed are not subject to taxation until the funds are withdrawn. Investors should be aware, however, that the withdrawal of nondeductible contributions may also result in the taxation of IRA contributions that were deducted in prior years (i.e., many individuals who were previously eligible to make deductible contributions for years prior to 1987 are no longer eligible to make deductible IRA contributions for 1987 and subsequent years).

The withdrawal of nondeductible IRA contributions does not result in taxable income, because the individual did not receive a tax deduction when the IRA contributions were made. However, if an individual has made both deductible and nondeductible IRA contributions in prior years, all of the IRA contracts are treated as one contract. The annuity rules under Sec. 72 are then used to determine the taxable and nontaxable portions of the distribution. This allocation procedure results in the recognition of gross income to the extent of the amount of deductible IRA contributions in the IRA contract. The taxable portion of a withdrawal from an IRA is also subject to an additional 10% penalty if the amounts are withdrawn before the taxpayer is 59½ years old unless the amounts are withdrawn due to death, disability, or if the withdrawals are made in the form of a life annuity.[53]

Example 17-30 ■   Richard makes $8,000 in deductible IRA contributions for the period 1983 through 1986 and a $2,000 nondeductible contribution in 1987. No contributions are made in 1988 through 1993. In 1994 he withdraws $2,000. Richard's investment in the contract is $2,000, and the return of capital recovery ratio is 20% ($2,000 ÷ $10,000). Thus, only $400 (0.20 × $2,000) is deemed to be a tax-free return of the nondeductible IRA contribution, and $1,600 ($2,000 − $400) is taxable. The 10% penalty on premature withdrawals may also apply to the $1,600 taxable portion of the distribution if Richard is not at least age 59½ or if one of the other exceptions does not apply (e.g., the amounts are withdrawn due to Richard's death or disability). ■

Funding Sources. Several investment vehicles are available for IRAs. These include banks, savings and loans, mutual fund accounts with brokerage firms, and annuity contracts from insurance companies. If an IRA is established with a bank or savings and loan association, the funds are generally invested in long-term certificates of deposit. Greater diversity is generally permitted if the funds are contributed to a mutual fund because both fixed-income securities, equity securities, and real estate investments may be used.

Tax Advantages of Deductible IRAs. The principal tax advantages of a deductible IRA include the following:

* A deferral of tax on the investment income that is earned on the contributed amounts until the funds are withdrawn.

* An immediate tax deduction *for* AGI when the funds are contributed.

Additional Comment

Many brokerage firms make available to customers an IRA account known as a self-directed account. It is similar to a regular brokerage account where the customer leaves the stock with the brokerage firm in street name. The advantage of the self-directed account is that the taxpayer can make decisions as to which specific securities are to be purchased and sold.

[52] Sec. 408(o).
[53] Sec. 72(t).

- A withdrawal of funds during retirement years when the individual is in a lower tax bracket.

Example 17-31 ■ Jason makes $20,000 of deductible IRA contributions for the period of 1984 through 1993. The funds are invested in certificates of deposit by a local bank. Jason's IRA account is worth $30,000 upon his retirement in 1994 representing $20,000 of deductible contributions and $10,000 of untaxed accumulated earnings. In 1994, Jason has a marginal tax rate of 15% and withdraws $2,500 from the IRA account. The entire $2,500 is included in Jason's gross income because the IRA contributions were deductible when made and the accumulated earnings have not been taxed. His tax on the distribution is only $375 (0.15 × $2,500) because Jason has a low marginal tax rate during his retirement years. ■

Additional Comment

Failure to take the required minimum distribution for taxpayers who have reached age 70½ results in a severe penalty amounting to 50% of the difference between the minimum required distribution and the amount actually withdrawn.

Withdrawals from an IRA. IRAs are essentially nonliquid investments because of the restrictions upon withdrawal. As previously discussed, withdrawals of deductible IRA contributions prior to age 59½ are not only subject to tax as ordinary income but may also be subject to a nondeductible 10% penalty. Younger individuals may find these provisions particularly burdensome due to the need for liquidity. However, the time value associated with the tax deferral may outweigh the tax detriment, even if the funds are prematurely withdrawn and the 10% penalty is incurred. Distributions from an IRA must begin no later than April 1 following the calendar year in which the taxpayer reaches age 70½.

IRA Rollovers. Funds may be rolled over from one IRA to another without incurring the 10% penalty for premature withdrawal. In addition, a lump-sum distribution from a qualified plan may be transferred to an IRA within 60 days to avoid tax on the lump-sum distribution.[54] These rollover features permit investors (1) to defer paying tax on lump-sum distributions from qualified plans and (2) to avoid penalties that are associated with IRA plans while retaining the flexibility to consolidate numerous retirement accounts into a single IRA.

Simplified Employee Pensions

Small businesses frequently establish simplified employee pension (SEP) plans for their employees to avoid the administrative complexities associated with the establishment of a qualified pension or profit-sharing plan. In an SEP, the employer makes contributions to the individual IRAs of its employees.[55] The employer receives an immediate deduction for contributions made under the plan. The annual deductible contributions for each participant are limited to 15% of compensation (up to a ceiling of $150,000) or the dollar limitations for defined contribution plans.[56]

Participants may elect to receive cash or have the employer make contributions to the SEP. If an employee elects to receive cash, the amounts are immediately taxable whereas employees who elect to have the employer make contributions to the SEP (up to $9,240 in 1994) are not subject to tax at ordinary income rates until the funds are withdrawn.[57]

Example 17-32 ■ Ace Corporation has an SEP plan that allows employees to receive cash equal to 6% of their salary (up to a maximum of $9,000) or to have the employer contribute an equivalent amount to an individual IRA account for the employee. John, whose

---

[54] Sec. 402(a)(5).
[55] Sec. 408(k). These IRA accounts are not subject to the previously discussed restrictions associated with regular IRA contributions under Sec. 219.
[56] Sec. 402 (h)(2).
[57] Sec. 408 (k)(6).

salary is $50,000, elects to receive $3,000 (0.06 × $50,000) in cash. This amount is immediately taxable to John and is deductible by Ace Corporation when the cash payment is made. Larry, whose salary is $60,000, elects to have his employer make a $3,600 (0.06 × $60,000) contribution to an individual IRA account on his behalf. The $3,600 contribution is deductible by Ace but is not included in Larry's gross income until the funds are withdrawn from the IRA. ∎

Cash or Deferred Compensation Arrangements

Additional Comment

Although a person is not subject to the federal income tax on the money contributed to a Sec. 401(k) plan, this amount is still subject to the Social Security tax in the year earned.

Section 401(k) plans are generally used to supplement a company's regular qualified pension and profit-sharing plans. Under such plans, employees can elect to receive either cash or an equivalent contribution to the company's profit-sharing plan.[58] Such plans typically contain a salary reduction feature that permits the employee to either reduce his amount of taxable compensation or to forgo a salary increase.

The maximum annual amount that an employee may elect to defer from tax is currently $9,240.[59] However, employers may make additional contributions to the plan subject to the overall limitations imposed upon qualified plans (i.e., generally 25% of compensation, or $30,000).

Section 401(k) plans have two major disadvantages:

Additional Comment

Most Sec. 401(k) plans offer a menu of investment choices with employees being able to select stock market investments, fixed-income investments, or the company stock fund.

1. The plan is prohibited from discriminating in favor of highly compensated individuals.[60]
2. Employees may withdraw their deferred contributions in the event of separation from service, death, disability or hardship before they are age 59½, but the withdrawals are generally subject to a 10% penalty.[61]

Example 17-33 ∎

Duke Corporation has a Sec. 401(k) plan in effect that allows employees to elect to receive cash equal to 5% of their salary or to contribute an equivalent amount to the company's profit-sharing plan. Ted, whose salary is $50,000, elects to receive $2,500 (0.05 × $50,000) cash. Sam, whose salary is also $50,000, elects to have additional contributions of $2,500 made by the company on his behalf to the profit-sharing plan. The deferral amount is less than the overall ceiling that exists for Sec. 401(k) plans. Sam enters into a salary reduction agreement with his employer. Ted receives a salary of $50,000 (which includes the $2,500 cash), and the entire amount is taxable to Ted. Sam is not subject to taxation on the $2,500, and his gross income (reported on Form W-2) is reduced to $47,500. ∎

Employees should consider the following additional income tax and economic considerations before making an election:

- All amounts that are contributed to the plan are fully vested.

- The amounts that are contributed under Sec. 401(k) do not cause a decline in the employee's other retirement benefits under the company's regular pension or profit-sharing plans.

- The amounts received from the Sec. 401(k) plan are generally taxed under the annuity rules and result in ordinary income upon their receipt during retirement years, because the employee has no investment in the contract (e.g., all

---

[58] Sec. 401(k)(2).
[59] Sec. 402(g)(1). This amount is adjusted annually for inflation.
[60] Sec. 401(k)(3).
[61] Secs. 401(k)(2)(B) and 72(t). Certain exceptions apply to: distributions to individuals age 55 or older that are made after separation from service; payments made in the form of a life annuity; payments made due to death or disability; the payment of medical expenses; and withdrawals pursuant to a domestic relations order.

contributions are made with pretax dollars, so that the amounts are considered the same as employer contributions).

- Employees should weigh the benefits of current income against the opportunity to shelter income from taxation and provide additional savings for retirement. (The tax on contributions to the plan and the earnings on the contributed amounts are deferred until the funds are withdrawn by the employee.)

- Section 401(k) plans are particularly attractive to (1) elderly employees having high income levels who need supplemental retirement income and (2) those taxpayers having a low preference for current consumption.

Tax-Deferred Annuities

Employees of educational institutions and certain tax-exempt organizations may provide for retirement benefits through the purchase of tax-deferred annuity contracts.[62] The tax on both the employer contributions and the employee contributions (which are made indirectly by the employer through a salary reduction agreement) is deferred until the funds are withdrawn. The investment earnings on the annuity contracts are also deferred.

Example 17-34 ■

Self-Study Question

An employee can make a $9,500 annual contribution to a tax-deferred annuity. How much will accumulate over 15 years if the funds are invested at a return of 8%?

Answer

The annuity contract would have a value of approximately $258,000. This amount would be subject to taxation when withdrawn.

Key Point

The maximum ceiling limitation of $9,500 for tax deferred annuities is much greater than the $2,000 maximum limitation for IRAs.

Kris is employed as a professor by Chicago University at an annual salary of $50,000. The University makes a contribution equal to 10% of her salary to a tax-sheltered annuity program, and Kris contributes 5% under a salary reduction agreement with her employer. Neither the employer's contribution of $5,000 (0.10 × $50,000) nor Kris's contribution of $2,500 (0.05 × $50,000) is included in her gross income reported on Form W-2. Kris's gross income is $47,500 ($50,000 − $2,500). ■

The employer may invest the funds in annuity contracts with an insurance company or the funds may be contributed to a mutual fund if certain requirements are met.[63] The funds are typically invested in fixed-income securities, equity securities, or a combination of both investment forms depending upon the investment choice that is made by the individual employee.

Tax Consequences. The following tax features should be noted:

- The total amount that may be excluded from an employee's gross income is limited to the greater of $9,500 or the ceiling limitations that apply to Sec. 401(k) plans.[64] In addition, overall limitations are imposed upon both employer and employee contributions.[65] If the overall limitations are not exceeded, an employee may make additional tax-deferred contributions to a supplemental retirement annuity (SRA) up to the maximum ceiling allowance. Thus, additional amounts of an employee's salary may be excluded from his gross income under a supplemental retirement annuity arrangement.

---

[62] Sec. 403(b).
[63] Sec. 403(b)(7)(A). No amounts may be paid or made available before the employee dies, separates from service, becomes disabled, or encounters financial hardship.
[64] Sec. 402(g)(4).
[65] Sec. 403(b)(2). The exclusion is 20% of the employee's reduced compensation times the number of years of service less the amounts contributed by the employer and excluded from income in prior years. This exclusion is further limited by Sec. 415 where the maximum annual contribution is the lesser of 25% of the employee's compensation or $30,000.

- Distributions from a tax-deferred annuity are fully taxable as ordinary income.
- A 10% penalty is imposed on distributions that are paid prior to age 59½, although certain exceptions are provided for: separation from service after age 55, death, disability, and withdrawals made in the form of a life annuity.[66]

Nontax Consequences. The following nontax features should be considered:

- Employer contributions generally vest immediately or after a 1-year period. Employee contributions made under the salary reduction arrangement vest immediately.
- An employee generally has considerable flexibility regarding whether the funds are invested in fixed-income or equity securities or a combination of each. If a mutual fund or annuity contract is used, the funds usually may be moved (at the election of the employee) from a fixed-income fund to an equity fund or vice versa.
- Distribution options (e.g., whether a lump-sum election can be made) vary depending upon the investment vehicle selected. Tax-deferred annuity contracts usually preclude a lump-sum distribution upon the termination of employment, whereas most mutual funds permit a lump-sum withdrawal of the funds under such a circumstance.

Restricted Property Arrangements

Restricted property plans are frequently offered either as a recruiting incentive or as a means to retain key employees. Such plans, which often discriminate in favor of highly compensated employees, typically provide a restricted stock agreement involving stock in the employer company. The stock is generally subject to a substantial risk of forfeiture and is nontransferable.[67] For example, the terms of the agreement may prevent the executive from transferring the stock to another person by sale or disposition (except by death) for a period of years. In addition, the forfeiture restriction may require the executive to forfeit the stock back to the company if he voluntarily resigns from the company within a prescribed period of time. These restrictions are required to prevent the executive from recognizing income immediately in an amount equal to the FMV of the property received (less any amounts that are paid for the stock).

Income Tax Consequences. There are two primary advantages of restricted property plans: (1) the deferral of compensation by the executive, (2) the ability of the employer to discriminate in favor of highly compensated employees, and (3) the employer receives a corresponding salary expense deduction when the amounts are taxed as ordinary income to the executive. The executive is taxed on the compensation (ordinary income) when either the forfeitability or nontransferability restrictions lapse. The amount of compensation that is recognized when the restrictions lapse is equal to the FMV of the property received (less any amount that is paid for the property).

Section 83(b) Election. Section 83(b) provides an exception whereby an executive may elect (within 30 days from the grant date) to recognize ordinary income equal to the property's FMV (less any amount that is paid for the property) upon its receipt.

---

[66] Secs. 72(t)(1) and 4974(c)(3).
[67] Sec. 83.

This election was particularly attractive prior to the elimination of the 60% long-term capital gain deduction in 1986. Its popularity may increase somewhat in the future due to the enactment of a 28% maximum tax rate on net capital gains in 1991 and the increase in the highest tax rate on ordinary income from 31% to 39.6% effective for 1993 and subsequent years. The Sec. 83(b) election may also have merit if an employee has substantial unused capital loss carryovers or anticipates significant amounts of capital losses in future periods. However, the nondeductibility by the employer of amounts that are recognized as capital gain by the employee makes the Sec. 83(b) election less attractive to the employer as a means of compensating executives. If a Sec. 83(b) election is made, the appreciation element is taxed as a capital gain to the employee and is not deductible by the employer when the stock (or other property) is sold.

Example 17-35 ■ City Corporation is closely held and its stock has an FMV of $1 per share. A public offering is anticipated to raise substantial amounts of additional capital for a planned expansion of the company. It is anticipated that the stock will be worth $50 per share after 5 years. City hires a key executive from a competitor and offers him a substantial salary plus a restricted stock plan whereby he will receive 10,000 shares of City stock at no cost. The stock is nontransferable and is subject to a substantial risk of forfeiture for a 5-year period. If the newly hired executive makes the Sec. 83(b) election to be taxed immediately, he will recognize ordinary taxable income of $10,000 (10,000 shares × $1) in the initial year and long-term capital gain of $490,000 ($500,000 − $10,000) if the stock is sold for $50 per share after the restrictions lapse in the sixth year. City receives a $10,000 deduction for compensation in the initial year but no deduction for the $490,000 appreciation element that is recognized by the executive when the stock is sold. ■

Example 17-36 ■ Assume the same facts as in Example 17-35 except that the FMV of the stock decreases to 50 cents per share at the end of the 5-year period. The tax consequences of making the election are unfavorable to the executive. A sale of the stock by the executive in the sixth year results in a capital loss of $5,000 ($10,000 cost basis − $5,000 selling price), while the executive is initially required to recognize ordinary income of $10,000 in the year the stock is received. ■

Example 17-37 ■ Assume the same facts as in Example 17-35, except that the executive does not elect to recognize income currently under Sec. 83(b). He must recognize ordinary income of $500,000 (10,000 shares × $50) in the sixth year when the restrictions lapse. City receives a $500,000 deduction for compensation in the same year. ■

Investment Considerations. An executive who receives restricted stock from his employer should recognize that the investment is not liquid (due to restrictions upon transfer and forfeiture). In addition, substantial risk may be involved because the executive's investment portfolio may not be adequately diversified (i.e., it may consist almost solely of stock of the employer corporation). The executive may also incur substantial personal risk by virtue of his employment contract with the company. The combined employment and investment risks may discourage an executive from accepting a job offer with a new or speculative company, especially if the restricted stock plan is intended to "buy-out" the executive's unvested pension plan contributions from his current employer. If an election is made under Sec. 83(b) to recognize income currently, the executive may have cash-flow difficulties because the immediate payment of tax must come from the executive's liquid funds or salary.

Employment-related compensation arrangements are summarized in Topic Review 17-3.

Employment-Related Investments

Type	Major Tax Considerations	Financial Considerations
Individual retirement accounts	Contributions made by eligible individuals are deductible up to $2,000 per year per individual but but not in excess of the individual's compensation ($2,250 for a married individual with a spouse who has no earned income). Many individuals are not eligible to make tax deductible contributions because they are either active participants in an employer-sponsored retirement plan or have AGI in excess of the phase-out limits. Non-deductible IRA contributions may be made by ineligible individuals. An employer may also establish an SEP for its employees where contributions are made to individual IRA accounts.	IRA funding sources include banks, savings and loans, mutual funds, annuity contracts, etc. Investments may be made in fixed income obligations, stocks, and annuities as well as in real estate. Earnings on the funds are tax deferred until the amounts are withdrawn during retirement years.
Cash or deferred compensation arrangements— Sec. 401(k) plans	A $9,240 (in 1994) ceiling is imposed upon annual deductible contributions to the plan. A salary reduction feature permits the employee to reduce his taxable compensation by the amount of the contribution. Nondiscrimination requirements are imposed and penalties are imposed for early withdrawal.	Sec. 401(k) plans are generally used to supplement a company's existing qualified plans. Employees can elect to receive either cash or an employer contribution on their behalf to the plan. Sec. 401(k) plans are particularly attractive for elderly employees who have a low preference for current consumption.
Tax-deferred annuities— Sec. 403(b)	Provides retirement benefits for employees of educational institutions and certain tax-exempt organizations. A salary reduction agreement permits the employee to reduce his taxable earnings by the amount of the employee contribution. The tax on employer contributions and investment earnings is also deferred until withdrawals are made during retirement.	Contributions are typically invested in annuity contracts with an insurance company or contributed to a mutual fund. Investments may be made in fixed income securities, stocks, or real estate. Employer contributions generally vest immediately or after one year.
Restricted property arrangments— Sec. 83	Restricted property plans may discriminate in favor of highly compensated employees. Property transferred to employees must be subject to both a substantial risk of forfeiture and be non-transferrable. When the restrictions lapse the employee is taxed (as ordinary income) on the FMV of the property and the employer receives a corresponding deduction. A Sec. 83(b) election may be made to be taxed immediately upon the FMV of the transferred property on the grant date.	Restricted property arrangements do not provide liquidity and diversification for executives. Such plans are frequently used to attract new key executives to the business and to retain top management personnel.

TAX PLANNING CONSIDERATIONS

The emphasis in this chapter has been upon tax planning and nontax considerations for investor decisions. This section presents an overview of the use of computer software applications in tax planning and analytical techniques used to evaluate a real estate investment.

Use of Personal Computers in Tax Planning

Additional Comment

Personal computers equipped with a modem can now also access tax data bases such as LEXIS (see Chapter 1).

The widespread availability and use of microcomputers by practicing accountants has greatly expanded the role of computer applications to tax planning situations. Various commercially prepared spreadsheet programs such as Lotus 1-2-3 are available for use on personal computers. In addition, many large public accounting firms have developed tax planning computer software to assist with tax planning applications involving complex mechanical computations.

The increased complexity of the tax law has undoubtedly increased the need for computer applications. In many cases, it is extremely difficult and time consuming to analyze the tax effects of a proposed tax plan using the conventional, non-computerized approach.

Example 17-38 ■

Tony, a client, is considering whether to make an investment in commercial real estate to be financed with borrowed funds. Tax considerations include the implications, if any, of the investment interest deduction limitation, the possible application of the alternative minimum tax, limitations on the deductibility of losses due to the passive activity loss rules, and the calculation of tax benefits including the capital gain that is expected to be recognized upon the disposition of the investment. For this purpose it is necessary to project cash flows and use discounting techniques to determine after-tax ROI and internal rate of return projections.

Some other examples of computer applications of tax planning problems include the following:

- Cash-flow calculations of the internal rate of return and/or net present value for investment alternatives.

- Analyses of oil and gas, real estate, and equipment leasing tax-sheltered investments which report annual cash flows and taxable income for the partnership and the individual partners. (These programs will also compute the amount of tax preference items, after-tax rate of return on the investment, and so on.)

- Year-end tax planning models for executives that project the tax effects for proposed changes in an individual's investment portfolio. The tax and cash-flow effects can be projected using various decision alternatives. ■

Sample Analysis of a Real Estate Investment

In January 1994, Tracy, a wealthy client who has a 36% marginal tax rate, acquires an apartment building for investment. Tracy is actively involved in the management of the real estate properties, although she plans to hire a custodian and a property manager. The purchase price of the property is $500,000, and a $400,000 mortgage with a 10% annual interest rate is obtained. The mortgage provides for no payment on principal for 5 years. It is anticipated that the property will be sold for $600,000 after 5 years because of general inflation in real estate in the local area. A projection of the cash flows and tax consequences is presented in Tables 17-1 and 17-2.

TABLE 17-1   Tracy's Tax Consequences

	1994	1995	1996	1997	1998
Rental income	$60,000	$63,000	$66,000	$69,000	$ 72,000
Interest expense	(40,000)	(40,000)	(40,000)	(40,000)	(40,000)
MACRS depreciation[a]	(13,750)	(13,750)	(13,750)	(13,750)	(13,750)
Deductible points paid to acquire the mortgage	(8,000)	—0—	—0—	—0—	—0—
Operating expenses[b]	(18,250)	(19,250)	(20,250)	(21,250)	(22,250)
Decrease in taxable income (from operations)	($20,000)	($10,000)	($ 8,000)	($ 6,000)	($ 4,000)
Gain on sale of apartment[c]	—0—	—0—	—0—	—0—	168,750
Decrease or increase in taxable income	($20,000)	($10,000)	($ 8,000)	($ 6,000)	$164,750
Times: Marginal tax rate	× 0.36	× 0.36	× 0.36	× 0.36	× 0.28
Tax (benefits) or costs	($ 7,200)	($ 3,600)	($2,880)	($ 2,160)	$ 46,130

[a] Residential real estate is depreciable using the straight-line method and a 27½-year recovery period. It is assumed that the property's basis for depreciation is $378,125. The remaining basis was assigned to the land. To simplify the analysis, a full year's depreciation was taken in the initial year.
[b] Operating expenses include real estate taxes, salaries, maintenance, insurance, etc.
[c] The gain is computed by subtracting the adjusted basis of $431,250 ($500,000 − $68,750 depreciation deduction) from the $600,000 estimated sales price.

The analysis in Table 17-2 reveals that Tracy can expect to receive a return on her investment of somewhat more than 13% if the assumptions are correct. The most critical assumption is that the property will appreciate in value during the 5-year period from $500,000 to $600,000. To simplify the calculations, we have ignored the disallowance of itemized deductions, any suspended real estate losses under the passive activity loss limitation rules, the application of the alternative minimum tax, state income taxes, and the phase-out of personal exemptions.

TABLE 17-2   Cash Flows from Tracy's Investment

	1994	1995	1996	1997	1998
Rental income	$60,000	$63,000	$66,000	$69,000	$ 72,000
Interest	(40,000)	(40,000)	(40,000)	(40,000)	(40,000)
Points paid to acquire mortgage	(8,000)	—0—	—0—	—0—	—0—
Operating expenses	(18,250)	(19,250)	(20,250)	(21,250)	(22,250)
Positive (negative) cash flow from operations before taxes	($ 6,250)	$ 3,750	$ 5,750	$ 7,750	$ 9,750
Tax benefits (costs) from the investment Table 17–1	7,200	3,600	2,880	2,160	(46,130)
Cash flow from the sale of real estate	—0—	—0—	—0—	—0—	200,000[a]
Net cash flow to Tracy	$ 950	$ 7,350	$ 8,630	$ 9,910	$163,620
Present value discount factor at 13%	0.885	0.783	0.693	0.613	0.542
Present value of cash flows	$841	$ 5,755	$ 5,981	$ 6,075	$ 88,682

Cumulative present value of cash flows	$107,334
Minus: Investment cost (down payment)	(100,000)
Net present value	$ 7,334

[a] $600,000 selling price − $400,000 repayment of mortgage = $200,000.

TABLE 17-3   **Reporting Investment Items**

Income, Deduction, or Credit Items	Reporting Location
Rents, royalties, and income or loss from partnerships	Schedule E
Interest and dividend income	Schedule B or page 1 of Form 1040 (if less than indicated amounts)
Pension and annuity income	Page 1 of Form 1040
Capital gains and losses	Schedule D
Investment-related expenses (e.g., safe deposit box rental, investment periodicals, and so on)	Schedule A (Miscellaneous Itemized Deductions)
IRA deductions	Page 1 of Form 1040 and Form 8606

COMPLIANCE AND PROCEDURAL CONSIDERATIONS

Reporting of Investment Income and Taxpayer Compliance

Table 17-3 is a summary of where income, expenses, and credit items should be reported by investors on Form 1040. Table 17-4 summarizes the results of government estimates which indicate surprisingly low taxpayer voluntary compliance rates for some types of income.[68]

Additional Comment

The IRS defines the gross tax gap as the amount of income tax owed for a given year but not voluntarily paid. The gap is comprised of unpaid income taxes on legally earned individual and corporate income.

The relatively high compliance percentages for pensions and annuities, interest and dividends reported in Table 17-4 may be due to the requirement that a payor must report the income payments to the IRS on an information return (Form 1099). The high percentage compliance for wages and salaries may be accounted for by the requirement that such amounts be reported to the IRS on Form W-2. The somewhat lower percentage for capital gains may be due to the fact that not all capital asset transactions are reported to the IRS. Investors must include a reconciliation of all Form 1099-Bs that are sent to the IRS on brokerage transactions with the capital

TABLE 17-4   **Estimates of Taxpayer Compliance**

Type of Income	Voluntary Reporting Percentage
Wages and salaries	99.5%
Interest	96.0
Dividends	91.1
Alimony	71.0
Capital gains	90.8
Pensions and annuities	98.3
Partnerships	77.5
Small business corporations	65.4
Rents and royalties	83.5
Non-farm sole proprietors	41.4
Self-employment taxes	50.3

[68] U.S., Department of the Treasury, Internal Revenue Service Research Division Publication No. 1415, [*Income Tax Compliance Research: Supporting Appendices to Pub. 7285*] (Washington, DC: U. S. Government Printing Office), July, 1988.

gains and losses that are reported in Part VII of Schedule D, Form 1040. However, the IRS is unable to verify the amount of capital gain that is reported without conducting an audit of the taxpayer's return.

The IRS also reported that the number of personal dependents claimed on tax returns declined from 76.7 million in 1986 to 69.7 million in 1987 resulting in increased tax revenues of $2.8 billion. The decrease is deemed attributable to a 1987 requirement that taxpayers list the social security numbers of their dependents age five and over. The age requirements were reduced to age 2 or over in 1990 and age 1 or over in 1991 and subsequent years.

PROBLEM MATERIALS

DISCUSSION QUESTIONS

17-1. Why is it important for a tax specialist to have a basic awareness of nontax aspects of investments such as cash-flow, economic risk, and return on investment considerations?

17-2. Explain the ways in which income taxes affect the amount of the cash flows that are generated from a real estate investment.

17-3. A client who is considering investing in a real estate limited partnership investment has asked for your advice regarding the tax and financial considerations. What tax and nontax factors should be considered in your analysis and recommendations?

17-4. Raul is a wealthy taxpayer who is in the 36% marginal federal tax bracket. During the current year his father dies, and he receives a distribution from the estate amounting to $100,000. The following two investment alternatives are being considered: taxable bonds yielding 8% and tax-free municipal bonds (of similar quality to the taxable bonds) yielding 6%.
a. Compare the two alternatives in terms of a before-tax equivalent yield.
b. How would your answer to Part a change if Raul's marginal tax rate *is* only 15%?

17-5. Why do many types of tax shelters generate losses during the initial years of the investment?

17-6. What impact has the elimination of the 60% long-term capital gain deduction in 1986 had upon the attractiveness of limited partnership investments? Is it likely that the enactment of a 28% maximum rate on net capital gains and the increase in the highest tax rates will stimulate future investments in limited partnerships?

17-7. You are discussing the merits of a limited partnership real estate tax shelter with a friend of yours. Your friend indicates that she "can't lose" from the investment because the tax benefits in the first two years are substantial and that she will be able to deduct the losses against both earned income and portfolio income (e.g., dividends and interest). Your friend has no other taxable income from passive activities and the activity does not constitute a real estate trade or business.
a. What incorrect assumptions has your friend made regarding the nature of the deductions from the real estate tax shelter?
b. What tax treatment will be accorded the tax losses during the initial years?

17-8. In the current year an investor purchases real estate investments. Losses are incurred during the initial year. What amount of loss is currently deductible under each of the following independent situations?
a. Rita purchases a limited partnership interest in a real estate activity, and her share of the partnership's loss is $20,000. Rita has no other income from passive activities.
b. Rob purchases an apartment building as an investment and is an active participant in the real estate activity. The business loss is $35,000, and Rob's adjusted gross income is $90,000.
c. Assume the same facts as Part b, except that Rob's adjusted gross income is $150,000.

17-9. John, a client of your accounting firm, inquires whether his new real estate investment and management activities are subject to the passive activity loss limitations. John devotes approximately 900 hours annually to such endeavors. Are the passive activity loss limitation rules applied to individuals who are engaged in a real estate trade or business in which the individual performs more than 750 hours of service in the trade or business and where more than one-half of the personal services performed by the taxpayer are performed in real estate trades or businesses in which the individual materially participates? What would your answer be if the real estate trade or business is conducted by a closely-held corporation?

17-10. Are the at-risk rules applied to real estate activities where nonrecourse financing is obtained from a bank?

17-11. Robin owns a limited partnership interest in a "master limited partnership" that was acquired in 1986. During the 1986–1993 period Robin's share of the partnership's losses was $40,000. These losses have been suspended and carried forward to the current year. In 1994, Robin has portfolio income (e.g., dividends and interest) of $60,000 and her share of the taxable income from the master limited partnership is $30,000.

    a. How much, if any of the $40,000 suspended loss may be used to offset Robin's taxable income in the current year?

    b. What would your answer to Part a be if the master limited partnership was formed in 1988?

17-12. Describe the two principal tax advantages that are associated with oil and gas tax-sheltered investments.

17-13. Ahmed, a wealthy client, is considering whether to invest in an oil and gas limited partnership. He currently has approximately $50,000 annual income from other passive investments and $80,000 of dividend and interest income. It is anticipated that the proposed oil and gas passive investment will produce tax losses of $20,000 for each of the first two years.

    a. What are the likely tax consequences if Ahmed acquires the oil and gas limited partnership investment?

    b. What tax disadvantages are associated with oil and gas limited partnership investments?

17-14. During the current year, the controller of the Able Corporation informs you that the company has generated excess funds from operations and is undecided whether to invest these amounts in preferred stock or long-term debenture bonds. The company has never paid a dividend to its shareholders and has substantial current and accumulated earnings and profits. What income tax factors should be considered?

17-15. Would an investor prefer to receive a taxable stock dividend or an equivalent cash dividend? Why?

17-16. George, age 40, is a wealthy investor whose marginal tax rate is 39.6%. He is considering the following stock investments:

    • Ajax Corporation, a high growth company which does not currently pay cash dividends because of the need to retain substantial earnings for future expansion of its operations. Above-average price appreciation for its stock is anticipated.

    • Georgia Corporation, a public utility that currently distributes most of its earnings to its shareholders. The utility rates charged to customers are highly regulated and Georgia's growth in earnings and dividends has been minimal.

    a. Which of the two investments is preferable for George? Explain.

    b. Would your answer be different if George is age 70 and has a 15% marginal tax rate?

17-17. A $1,000 corporate bond is acquired at a $200 discount in the secondary bond market. The bond was originally issued in 1990 at par. When the bond is acquired, 10 years remained until its maturity. The investor does not elect to accrue the market discount. What are the tax consequences arising from each of the following situations?

    a. The bond is held for the entire year.

    b. The bond is held for 5 years and is sold for $900.

    c. Assume the same facts as part b except that the bond is sold for $950.

    d. Would your answer to parts a through c change if the bond is a tax-exempt municipal obligation which was acquired in June, 1994?

17-18. Is it possible for an investor to convert ordinary interest income into long-term capital gain by investing in original issue discount or zero coupon bonds? Explain.

17-19. Why are deferred annuities particularly attractive for high-income individuals who are 10 to 15 years from retirement?

17-20. Rose, a cash method of accounting taxpayer using a calendar tax year, acquires a 1-year $10,000 certificate of deposit (CD) on July 1, 1994. Interest is not paid or credited to Rose's account until the CD matures on June 30, 1995. Substantial penalty is required for early withdrawal. The interest rate on the CD is 10%, but Rose would incur a $300 penalty if the certificate is redeemed on December 31, 1994. How much interest income must Rose report in 1994?

17-21. Ruth is a wealthy widow (in the 36% marginal tax bracket) who is considering a certain change to her investment portfolio. She currently owns $300,000 worth of tax-exempt state and local bonds with a $300,000 basis that are yielding 6%. Ruth is concerned that the value of these bonds may decline in the future if the tax law is changed to eliminate the tax exemption for state and local bonds. Ruth proposes the following two alternatives and asks your advice about which one to follow: (disregard the possible effects of a phase-out of personal and dependency exemptions and itemized deductions for high income individuals.)

   a. Sell the tax-exempt bonds and reinvest the proceeds in an insured tax-exempt unitrust bond fund that yields 5.5%.

   b. Sell the tax-exempt bonds and acquire 8% taxable bonds.

17-22. Why is option writing considered a conservative investment strategy? Why is the purchase of call options usually considered to be a speculative investment?

17-23. In February 1995, Sam finds that his withholding and quarterly estimated payments are insufficient and that he may be subject to a penalty for underpayment of income tax for 1994 unless corrective actions are taken. Sam has established an IRA account in prior years but has not yet made a contribution in 1994. He is eligible to make deductible IRA contributions in 1994. What corrective actions might be taken to avoid the underpayment penalty?

17-24. What is the principal tax advantage associated with making nondeductible contributions to an IRA? Are there any disadvantages? Explain.

17-25. What tax and nontax advantages are associated with the establishment of a simplified employee pension (SEP) plan to the employer and to the employees?

17-26. Ace Corporation has a Sec. 401(k) cash or deferred compensation arrangement for its employees. Some of the employees have elected to receive cash, while others have entered into salary reduction agreements with the company.

   a. What are the tax consequences for employees who elect to receive cash?

   b. Explain the tax consequences for employees who decide to enter into a salary reduction agreement with regard to the following aspects of the plan:

   - The effect upon taxable income for any year that the agreement is in effect
   - Vesting of employee contributions
   - The effect of making contributions to the plan upon the employee's other retirement plan contributions
   - The possibility of making an early withdrawal of funds
   - The taxability of distributions to employees

17-27. Sean, age 56, has been employed as a professor in a state university for the past 25 years. The university has made contributions amounting to 10% of his salary, with matching contributions being made by Sean toward the purchase of shares in a tax-deferred mutual fund under Sec. 403(b). These contracts are currently worth $350,000. Sean has lived modestly during the past 25 years and now wants to quit his job and "enjoy life."

   a. What are the tax consequences if Sean terminates his employment in 1994 and receives a $350,000 lump-sum distribution?

   b. What are the tax consequences if Sean receives a yearly annuity of $30,000 starting in 1994 based upon his remaining life expectancy of 20 years?

17-28. Explain the advantages and disadvantages of a Sec. 83(b) election for both an executive and an employer with regard to a restricted property arrangement. Is the election generally advisable? Explain.

17-29. Under what circumstances might a tax-sheltered limited partnership investment that produces losses during the initial years be attractive to an investor?

17-30. Explain why taxpayer compliance regarding the reporting of capital gains is lower than the reporting percentage for wages and salaries.

17-31. Explain why the use of personal computer software to solve tax problems has become important in tax planning.

PROBLEMS

17-32. *Comparison of Equivalent Pretax Investment Yield.* Sharon, an investor with a 15% marginal tax rate, and Stan, an investor with a 31% marginal tax rate, are considering the following alternative investments:

- A fully taxable bond, with a maturity value of $1,000 and a yield to maturity of 8%, that can be acquired for $900. The bond was originally issued at par in 1990.
- A tax-exempt municipal bond with a yield to maturity of 6% that can be acquired at par. The original issue price and maturity value of the bond are $1,000.

a. What are the pretax equivalent yields on the tax-exempt municipal bond for Sharon and Stan?

b. Which investor would obtain the greatest tax benefit from the tax-exempt bond?

c. What are the tax consequences in the year of maturity if a taxable bond that was issued in 1990 is acquired in June, 1994 for $900 and an investor receives $1,000 when the bonds mature?

17-33. *Limited Partnership Investments.* In 1994, Sheryl invests $10,000 in a limited partnership interest in a real estate tax shelter. In the initial year, Sheryl's share of the partnership losses is $40,000. Sheryl has no other passive activity income or losses. The partnership completes the financing of the venture by arranging a $900,000 nonrecourse debt with a savings and loan association, and Sheryl's share of the nonrecourse debt is $90,000. On January 1, 1995, Sheryl disposes of her limited partnership interest in a taxable transaction and recognizes a $25,000 gain.

a. Do the at-risk rules apply to limit the amount of losses that are deductible by Sheryl? Explain.

b. What amount, if any, of loss is deductible by Sheryl in 1994?

c. How are any unused losses treated?

d. What amount of loss may Sheryl deduct in 1995?

17-34. *Real Estate Investments.* In the current year Ira acquires a two-family house as an investment for $200,000. The property is rented to tenants during the year. However, due to depreciation, real estate taxes, interest, and high initial repairs and maintenance, a $30,000 operating loss is incurred during the current year. Ira has no other passive activity income or loss. Ira's AGI (before deducting the loss) in the current year is $90,000. Ira actively participates in the management of the real estate.

a. What amount of loss, if any, is deductible by Ira in the current year?

b. How are unused losses, if any, treated?

c. What amount of loss is deductible if Ira has $50,000 of income from other passive activity investments?

d. What amount of loss, if any, is deductible if Ira's adjusted gross income is $130,000?

e. What amount of loss, if any, would be deductible if Ira had acquired a real estate limited partnership interest instead of the two-family house?

17-35. *Oil and Gas Investments.* Are the following statements true or false? If a statement is false, explain why.

a. The percentage depletion deduction is generally not available to large oil companies.

b. Percentage depletion may be taken even if the basis for cost depletion purposes is zero.

c. The percentage depletion rate for oil and gas properties is 15%, but the amount of percentage depletion cannot exceed 65% of the taxable income from the property.

d. If IDCs are capitalized, the costs may be amortized over a period of 60 months or more and are allowable in addition to the deduction for percentage depletion.

17-36. *Debt/Equity Restrictions.* The Acme Corporation is organized in the current year by Ted, Tim, and Tony. A total of $900,000 capital is needed to begin operations. Ted, Tim, and Tony will own an equal percentage of the equity capital. Three alternative methods of obtaining the needed capital have been proposed:

- Ted, Tim, and Tony would each contribute $300,000 to purchase all of the Acme common stock.
- Ted, Tim, and Tony would each contribute $300,000 to purchase $100,000 of Acme common stock and $200,000 of Acme Corporation long-term bonds that yield 8% to maturity.
- Ted, Tim, and Tony would each contribute $50,000 to purchase one-third of the Acme common stock. Tony would then contribute an additional $750,000 in exchange for the 8% Acme Corporation long-term bonds.

a. Which of the three alternatives might be attacked by the IRS? Why?

b. Assuming that the interest deduction is allowed, which alternatives are preferable for the Acme Corporation?

17-37. *Dividends-Received Deduction.* The Acorn Corporation has excess funds of $100,000 that are invested in marketable fixed-income securities yielding 8%. Assume that the company is not subject to the accumulated earnings or personal holding company penalty taxes and has a 34% marginal tax rate. The company's investment advisor recommends a sale of the fixed-income securities (whose cost approximates their FMV) and reinvestment of the proceeds in 8% noncumulative preferred stock in a large publicly traded company.

a. What is the amount of after-tax benefit that would result to Acorn if the investment switch is made (ignore any transaction costs)?

b. What nontax factors might impact upon the investment decision?

17-38. *Nontaxable Stock Dividends.* Lucia owns 100 shares of Adobe Corporation common stock with a $1,000 basis and $2,000 FMV. The company has 1,000 shares of common stock outstanding and financial accounting net income of $2,000. The Adobe stock is selling for ten times its earnings in the stock market. Adobe issues a 20% nontaxable stock dividend to all of its shareholders. The company's earnings and price-earnings multiple in the stock market do not change after the stock dividend is issued.

a. What is Lucia's tax basis in the Adobe shares immediately after the stock dividend is issued?

b. What is the amount of Adobe's earnings per share before and after the stock dividend?

c. What is the per-share price of the stock after the stock dividend?

d. What is the total value of Lucia's shares before and after the stock dividend?

e. Is there justification for the tax treatment of the stock dividend? Explain.

17-39. *Capital Gains and Losses—Timing.* Vicki sells some of her stock in 1994 and recognizes a $10,000 long-term capital gain because her broker suggested that a sale in 1994 is preferable to one in 1993 due to income tax considerations. Vicki's marginal tax rate is 31% in 1993 and 15% in 1994. Assume that Vicki has no other capital gains or losses in prior years.

a. What amount of tax is due in 1994?

b. What amount of tax would be due if Vicki sells the stock and recognizes a $10,000 long-term capital gain in 1993 instead of 1994?

c. If the sale results in a $10,000 long-term capital loss (instead of a $10,000 long-term capital gain), would a sale of the stock in 1994 be preferable to a sale in 1993? Explain.

17-40. *Return of Capital Distributions.* Wayne is an investor who receives a $1,000 cash distribution in 1994 from the Allied Corporation. Allied Corporation has an accumulated earnings and profits deficit at the beginning of 1994 and no current earnings and profits for 1994. Wayne's tax basis for the Allied stock, which he has held for several years, is $400.

a. How much of the distribution is taxable to Wayne?

b. What is the character of any income or gain that is recognized by Wayne?

c. What is Wayne's basis for the Allied stock at the end of 1994?

17-41. *Market Discount.* In the current year Amy acquires a taxable bond for $800. The bond was issued at par value in 1990 and has a maturity value of $1,000 in 10 years. The bond is sold for $1,100 after being held for 5 years.

    a. What is the amount of discount that must be accrued as interest income in the current year?

    b. What is the amount and character of the gain or loss that must be recognized on the sale of the bond after 5 years? (Assume that Amy does not elect to accrue the market discount.)

    c. Assume the same facts except that the bond is an original issue discount bond and was issued to Amy in the current year. What is the amount of discount that must be accrued as interest income?

17-42. *Deferred Annuities.* Andy invests $100,000 in a deferred investment annuity on December 31, 1982, with an insurance company which guarantees a minimum fixed annual return of 10% for the 1983–1993 period. In 1983 the insurance company reports that interest income of $12,000 is earned by Andy's investment annuity. In 1986 the insurance company pays a $4,000 distribution to Andy. The annuity starting date is 1994, and Andy receives annuity payments of $20,000 in 1994. His life expectancy is 20 years in 1994.

    a. How much interest income (if any) is taxable to Andy in 1983? In 1986? (Assume that the cash value of the contract is always substantially in excess of Andy's investment in the contract.)

    b. How much income is recognized by Andy in 1994 when the annuity payments begin?

    c. How much income is recognized (after Andy outlives his life expectancy) in year 2014 (the 21st year of the annuity)?

17-43. *Purchase of Call Options.* Angela acquires a call option on Ajax Corporation stock which expires in 6 months. The option entitles Angela to acquire 100 shares of the Ajax stock for $8,000. Angela pays a call premium of $200 to the writer of the call. What are the income tax consequences of the investment to Angela and the writer of the call for each of the following independent situations:

    a. The value of the Ajax stock does not increase, and the option expires unexercised after 6 months.

    b. The value of the Ajax stock increases to $9,000, and Angela exercises her option and acquires the Ajax stock for $8,000.

    c. The value of the Ajax stock increases, and Angela sells the option for $700 after 3 months.

17-44. *Writing Call Options.* Anna acquires 100 shares of Apple stock in 1986 for $10,000. On August 1, 1994, she writes an option that entitles the purchaser to acquire her Apple stock during a 6-month period for $20,000. Anna receives a call premium of $2,000 for writing the call at a time when the Apple stock is worth $22,000. Explain the income tax consequences of writing a call for each of the following situations:

    a. The call has not been exercised and is still outstanding on December 31, 1994.

    b. The call is exercised on November 1, 1994, and Anna receives $20,000 for her stock that is worth $30,000 on the exercise date.

    c. The call is not exercised and lapses in 1995. (Answer this question for both 1994 and 1995.)

17-45. *Short Sales.* Bart acquires 100 shares of the Austin Corporation common stock for $5,000 in 1987. The stock increases in value to $20,000 by December 1994. Bart would like to sell the stock in order to realize his profit but does not want to recognize the gain until 1995. Bart sells his Austin Corporation stock short in December 1994 for $20,000. He closes the short position in January 1995 by delivering the 100 shares of Austin stock acquired in 1987.

    a. What are the tax consequences from the short sale (if any) in 1994?

    b. What is the amount and character of the gain or loss recognized upon the closing of the short sale in January 1995?

17-46. *Individual Retirement Accounts.* Kathy, who is single, is employed by a company that does not offer a qualified pension or profit-sharing plan for its employees. In 1994, her AGI is $30,000. Kathy has not previously established an IRA. In February, 1995 she requests your advice relative to the establishment of an IRA.

    a. Is Kathy eligible to establish a deductible IRA?

    b. If so, what is the maximum allowable deduction that can be claimed if Kathy makes a contribution in February, 1995?

    c. In what tax year may the deduction be claimed?

17-47. *Sec. 401(k) Plans.* Bass Corporation has recently established a Sec. 401(k) cash or deferred compensation plan for its employees. Brad and Bob both have a salary of $60,000 and are scheduled to receive $2,000 raises in the near future. Brad needs cash to pay for needed personal expenses and elects to receive his raise in the form of cash. Bob, however, is anxious to defer as much tax as possible and provide additional funds for retirement, so he enters into a salary reduction plan with the company and elects to defer the $2,000 salary increase.

a. What gross income amounts will be reported by Brad and Bob after receiving their raises?

b. What are the income tax consequences to Bob if the funds are withdrawn in the form of a lump-sum distribution following his retirement?

c. What are the income tax consequences to Bob if the funds are withdrawn as a life annuity during his retirement years?

17-48. *Tax Deferred Annuities.* Columbus University currently offers retirement benefits to employees through the purchase of tax-deferred annuity contracts. The University makes a contribution equal to 10% of an employee's salary and employees are required to contribute 5% under a salary reduction agreement. Karen's annual salary at the university is $60,000.

a. What amount of salary will be reported as taxable income by Karen if she enters into a salary reduction agreement and 5% of her salary is contributed?

b. Is the employer portion of the retirement plan contribution subject to immediate taxation to Karen?

c. What restrictions are imposed if Karen receives distributions from the retirement plan prior to age 59½?

d. What portion of the post-retirement distributions are taxable and how is such income taxed when received by Karen during her retirement years?

17-49. *Restricted Property.* Beach Corporation offers to give at no cost 1,000 of its shares of common stock with a FMV of $100,000 to Chris, an executive with a competitor, as an inducement for him to join the company. The shares would be subject to a substantial risk of forfeiture for five years (i.e., Chris would be required to transfer the stock back to the company during the 5-year period if he voluntarily resigns from his job). The stock is also nontransferable by Chris except by his death.

a. What are the amount and character of the gain recognized by Chris in the year of grant?

b. What is the amount and character of the gain recognized by Chris if he makes a Sec. 83(b) election in the year of the grant?

c. Is Beach Corporation entitled to a tax deduction in Parts a or b? Explain.

d. If the stock increases in value to $400,000 in the year that the restrictions lapse, what are the amount and character of the income that is recognized by Chris if a Sec. 83(b) election is made in the year of the grant? If a Sec. 83(b) election is not made?

COMPREHENSIVE PROBLEM

17-50. James Johnson, an investor, reports the following items of income, loss, and deduction in the current year:

Salary	$60,000
Safe deposit box rent	25
Wall Street Journal subscription	115
Miami Herald subscription	70
Excess of deductions over rental income from a two-family house	4,000
Dividend income	3,000
Contribution to an IRA account	2,000
Net short-term capital losses	6,000
Net long-term capital gains	15,000
Net loss from a real estate limited partnership (acquired in the current year)	10,000

What is Johnson's AGI, taxable income, and tax liability for the current year, assuming the following additional facts:

- Johnson is single and has no dependents.
- Johnson's other itemized deductions include cash or check contributions to his church of $10,000. He does not have any miscellaneous itemized deductions other than those specified above.
- Johnson is not subject to the alternative minimum tax.
- Johnson actively participates in the two-family house rental activity.

TAX FORM/RETURN PREPARATION PROBLEMS

17-51. Assuming the same items of income, loss, and deductions as in Problem 17-50, describe where each item should be reported on Johnson's tax return (including any tax forms which are also needed).

TurboTax **17-52.** Assuming the same facts as Problem 17-50, prepare Johnson's Form 1040 (including any supplementary tax forms and schedules that are needed).

CASE STUDY PROBLEM

17-53. Wayne, who is 35-years old and single, is not eligible to participate in an employer-sponsored retirement plan and is now considering whether to establish an Individual Retirement Account (IRA). Wayne's AGI is $25,000; he has a high preference for current personal consumption (e.g., sports cars and a bachelor pad) and has no investment savings.

Prepare a memo to your client (Wayne) that outlines the IRA eligibility requirements, alternative funding possibilities, the tax consequences, and any nontax factors that you deem important.

CASE STUDY PROBLEM—ETHICAL ISSUES

17-54. Your client, Kerry, purchased a $1,000 bond in the market in 1988 as an investment. The bond was issued in 1986. She paid $600 for the bond which has now matured in 1994, the current year. Kerry made no election to amortize the bond discount on an annual basis. Kerry has incurred some long-term capital losses from the sale of other investments during the current year. She would like to report a long-term capital gain of $400 from the bond and use her capital losses to offset the gain from the bond. What should you tell your client concerning the treatment of gain from the bond as a long-term capital gain? What is your responsibility as Kerry's CPA regarding treatment of the gain? (See the caption entitled *Statements on Responsibilities in Tax Practice* in Chapter 1 for a discussion of these issues.)

TAX RESEARCH PROBLEM

17-55. Ted invests $40,000 in a real estate tax shelter during 1987 and obtains a limited partnership interest. The partnership borrows $1,000,000 with a qualified nonrecourse mortgage. Ted's share of the debt is $100,000. The real estate venture is largely unsuccessful and generates tax losses (due to depreciation, interest, and operating losses) of $100,000 for Ted during the 1987–1993 period. Ted deducts all of these losses on his tax return for the entire period because he had other passive activity income equal to the loss amounts. Ted's limited partnership interest is virtually worthless by 1994, so he sells the interest for $1,000 and claims a $39,000 long-term capital loss. Ted's share of the partnership's nonrecourse liabilities on the date of the sale is still $100,000.

Upon audit by the IRS, the agent agrees that Ted's basis in the partnership interest is $40,000 ($40,000 original cash contribution + $100,000 share of the partnership liabilities − $100,000 share of partnership losses). However, according to the IRS, the amount realized from the sale of the partnership interest is $101,000 ($1,000 selling price + $100,000 share of the partnership liabilities). Ted believes that the amount realized for his partnership interest should not include his share of the nonrecourse liabilities because the $600,000 value of the real estate was less than the $1,000,000 of nonrecourse debt, and the limited partners would not suffer any economic detriment in the event of default on the debt. Which position should prevail—the IRS's or Ted's?

A partial list of research sources is

- *Beulah B. Crane v. CIR*, 35 AFTR 776, 47-1 USTC ¶ 9217 (USSC, 1947).
- *CIR v. John F. Tufts*, 51 AFTR 2d 83-1132, 83-1 USTC ¶ 9328 (USSC, 1983).

APPENDIX

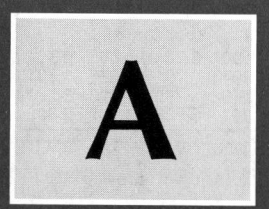

1993 Tax Table and Rate Schedules

1993 Tax Table

Use if your taxable income is less than $100,000. If $100,000 or more, use the Tax Rate Schedules.

Example. Mr. and Mrs. Brown are filing a joint return. Their taxable income on line 37 of Form 1040 is $25,300. First, they find the $25,300–25,350 income line. Next, they find the column for married filing jointly and read down the column. The amount shown where the income line and filing status column meet is $3,799. This is the tax amount they must enter on line 38 of their Form 1040.

Sample Table

At least	But less than	Single	Married filing jointly	Married filing separately	Head of a household
			Your tax is—		
25,200	25,250	4,190	3,784	4,665	3,784
25,250	25,300	4,204	3,791	4,679	3,791
25,300	25,350	4,218	(3,799)	4,693	3,799
25,350	25,400	4,232	3,806	4,707	3,806

If line 37 (taxable income) is—		And you are—				If line 37 (taxable income) is—		And you are—				If line 37 (taxable income) is—		And you are—			
At least	But less than	Single	Married filing jointly *	Married filing separately *	Head of a household	At least	But less than	Single	Married filing jointly *	Married filing separately *	Head of a household	At least	But less than	Single	Married filing jointly *	Married filing separately *	Head of a household
		Your tax is—						**Your tax is—**						**Your tax is—**			
0	5	0	0	0	0	1,300	1,325	197	197	197	197	2,700	2,725	407	407	407	407
5	15	2	2	2	2	1,325	1,350	201	201	201	201	2,725	2,750	411	411	411	411
15	25	3	3	3	3	1,350	1,375	204	204	204	204	2,750	2,775	414	414	414	414
25	50	6	6	6	6	1,375	1,400	208	208	208	208	2,775	2,800	418	418	418	418
50	75	9	9	9	9	1,400	1,425	212	212	212	212	2,800	2,825	422	422	422	422
75	100	13	13	13	13	1,425	1,450	216	216	216	216	2,825	2,850	426	426	426	426
100	125	17	17	17	17	1,450	1,475	219	219	219	219	2,850	2,875	429	429	429	429
125	150	21	21	21	21	1,475	1,500	223	223	223	223	2,875	2,900	433	433	433	433
150	175	24	24	24	24	1,500	1,525	227	227	227	227	2,900	2,925	437	437	437	437
175	200	28	28	28	28	1,525	1,550	231	231	231	231	2,925	2,950	441	441	441	441
200	225	32	32	32	32	1,550	1,575	234	234	234	234	2,950	2,975	444	444	444	444
225	250	36	36	36	36	1,575	1,600	238	238	238	238	2,975	3,000	448	448	448	448
250	275	39	39	39	39	1,600	1,625	242	242	242	242						
275	300	43	43	43	43	1,625	1,650	246	246	246	246	**3,000**					
300	325	47	47	47	47	1,650	1,675	249	249	249	249	3,000	3,050	454	454	454	454
325	350	51	51	51	51	1,675	1,700	253	253	253	253	3,050	3,100	461	461	461	461
350	375	54	54	54	54	1,700	1,725	257	257	257	257	3,100	3,150	469	469	469	469
375	400	58	58	58	58	1,725	1,750	261	261	261	261	3,150	3,200	476	476	476	476
400	425	62	62	62	62	1,750	1,775	264	264	264	264	3,200	3,250	484	484	484	484
425	450	66	66	66	66	1,775	1,800	268	268	268	268	3,250	3,300	491	491	491	491
450	475	69	69	69	69	1,800	1,825	272	272	272	272	3,300	3,350	499	499	499	499
475	500	73	73	73	73	1,825	1,850	276	276	276	276	3,350	3,400	506	506	506	506
500	525	77	77	77	77	1,850	1,875	279	279	279	279	3,400	3,450	514	514	514	514
525	550	81	81	81	81	1,875	1,900	283	283	283	283	3,450	3,500	521	521	521	521
550	575	84	84	84	84	1,900	1,925	287	287	287	287	3,500	3,550	529	529	529	529
575	600	88	88	88	88	1,925	1,950	291	291	291	291	3,550	3,600	536	536	536	536
600	625	92	92	92	92	1,950	1,975	294	294	294	294	3,600	3,650	544	544	544	544
625	650	96	96	96	96	1,975	2,000	298	298	298	298	3,650	3,700	551	551	551	551
650	675	99	99	99	99							3,700	3,750	559	559	559	559
675	700	103	103	103	103	**2,000**						3,750	3,800	566	566	566	566
700	725	107	107	107	107	2,000	2,025	302	302	302	302	3,800	3,850	574	574	574	574
725	750	111	111	111	111	2,025	2,050	306	306	306	306	3,850	3,900	581	581	581	581
750	775	114	114	114	114	2,050	2,075	309	309	309	309	3,900	3,950	589	589	589	589
775	800	118	118	118	118	2,075	2,100	313	313	313	313	3,950	4,000	596	596	596	596
800	825	122	122	122	122	2,100	2,125	317	317	317	317						
825	850	126	126	126	126	2,125	2,150	321	321	321	321	**4,000**					
850	875	129	129	129	129	2,150	2,175	324	324	324	324						
875	900	133	133	133	133	2,175	2,200	328	328	328	328	4,000	4,050	604	604	604	604
900	925	137	137	137	137	2,200	2,225	332	332	332	332	4,050	4,100	611	611	611	611
925	950	141	141	141	141	2,225	2,250	336	336	336	336	4,100	4,150	619	619	619	619
950	975	144	144	144	144	2,250	2,275	339	339	339	339	4,150	4,200	626	626	626	626
975	1,000	148	148	148	148	2,275	2,300	343	343	343	343	4,200	4,250	634	634	634	634
						2,300	2,325	347	347	347	347	4,250	4,300	641	641	641	641
1,000						2,325	2,350	351	351	351	351	4,300	4,350	649	649	649	649
						2,350	2,375	354	354	354	354	4,350	4,400	656	656	656	656
1,000	1,025	152	152	152	152	2,375	2,400	358	358	358	358	4,400	4,450	664	664	664	664
1,025	1,050	156	156	156	156	2,400	2,425	362	362	362	362	4,450	4,500	671	671	671	671
1,050	1,075	159	159	159	159	2,425	2,450	366	366	366	366	4,500	4,550	679	679	679	679
1,075	1,100	163	163	163	163	2,450	2,475	369	369	369	369	4,550	4,600	686	686	686	686
1,100	1,125	167	167	167	167	2,475	2,500	373	373	373	373	4,600	4,650	694	694	694	694
1,125	1,150	171	171	171	171	2,500	2,525	377	377	377	377	4,650	4,700	701	701	701	701
1,150	1,175	174	174	174	174	2,525	2,550	381	381	381	381	4,700	4,750	709	709	709	709
1,175	1,200	178	178	178	178	2,550	2,575	384	384	384	384	4,750	4,800	716	716	716	716
1,200	1,225	182	182	182	182	2,575	2,600	388	388	388	388	4,800	4,850	724	724	724	724
1,225	1,250	186	186	186	186	2,600	2,625	392	392	392	392	4,850	4,900	731	731	731	731
1,250	1,275	189	189	189	189	2,625	2,650	396	396	396	396	4,900	4,950	739	739	739	739
1,275	1,300	193	193	193	193	2,650	2,675	399	399	399	399	4,950	5,000	746	746	746	746
						2,675	2,700	403	403	403	403						

Continued on next page

* This column must also be used by a qualifying widow(er).

1993 Tax Table—*Continued*

If line 37 (taxable income) is—		And you are—			
At least	But less than	Single	Married filing jointly *	Married filing separately	Head of a house-hold
		Your tax is—			

5,000

At least	But less than	Single	MFJ*	MFS	HoH
5,000	5,050	754	754	754	754
5,050	5,100	761	761	761	761
5,100	5,150	769	769	769	769
5,150	5,200	776	776	776	776
5,200	5,250	784	784	784	784
5,250	5,300	791	791	791	791
5,300	5,350	799	799	799	799
5,350	5,400	806	806	806	806
5,400	5,450	814	814	814	814
5,450	5,500	821	821	821	821
5,500	5,550	829	829	829	829
5,550	5,600	836	836	836	836
5,600	5,650	844	844	844	844
5,650	5,700	851	851	851	851
5,700	5,750	859	859	859	859
5,750	5,800	866	866	866	866
5,800	5,850	874	874	874	874
5,850	5,900	881	881	881	881
5,900	5,950	889	889	889	889
5,950	6,000	896	896	896	896

6,000

At least	But less than	Single	MFJ*	MFS	HoH
6,000	6,050	904	904	904	904
6,050	6,100	911	911	911	911
6,100	6,150	919	919	919	919
6,150	6,200	926	926	926	926
6,200	6,250	934	934	934	934
6,250	6,300	941	941	941	941
6,300	6,350	949	949	949	949
6,350	6,400	956	956	956	956
6,400	6,450	964	964	964	964
6,450	6,500	971	971	971	971
6,500	6,550	979	979	979	979
6,550	6,600	986	986	986	986
6,600	6,650	994	994	994	994
6,650	6,700	1,001	1,001	1,001	1,001
6,700	6,750	1,009	1,009	1,009	1,009
6,750	6,800	1,016	1,016	1,016	1,016
6,800	6,850	1,024	1,024	1,024	1,024
6,850	6,900	1,031	1,031	1,031	1,031
6,900	6,950	1,039	1,039	1,039	1,039
6,950	7,000	1,046	1,046	1,046	1,046

7,000

At least	But less than	Single	MFJ*	MFS	HoH
7,000	7,050	1,054	1,054	1,054	1,054
7,050	7,100	1,061	1,061	1,061	1,061
7,100	7,150	1,069	1,069	1,069	1,069
7,150	7,200	1,076	1,076	1,076	1,076
7,200	7,250	1,084	1,084	1,084	1,084
7,250	7,300	1,091	1,091	1,091	1,091
7,300	7,350	1,099	1,099	1,099	1,099
7,350	7,400	1,106	1,106	1,106	1,106
7,400	7,450	1,114	1,114	1,114	1,114
7,450	7,500	1,121	1,121	1,121	1,121
7,500	7,550	1,129	1,129	1,129	1,129
7,550	7,600	1,136	1,136	1,136	1,136
7,600	7,650	1,144	1,144	1,144	1,144
7,650	7,700	1,151	1,151	1,151	1,151
7,700	7,750	1,159	1,159	1,159	1,159
7,750	7,800	1,166	1,166	1,166	1,166
7,800	7,850	1,174	1,174	1,174	1,174
7,850	7,900	1,181	1,181	1,181	1,181
7,900	7,950	1,189	1,189	1,189	1,189
7,950	8,000	1,196	1,196	1,196	1,196

8,000

At least	But less than	Single	MFJ*	MFS	HoH
8,000	8,050	1,204	1,204	1,204	1,204
8,050	8,100	1,211	1,211	1,211	1,211
8,100	8,150	1,219	1,219	1,219	1,219
8,150	8,200	1,226	1,226	1,226	1,226
8,200	8,250	1,234	1,234	1,234	1,234
8,250	8,300	1,241	1,241	1,241	1,241
8,300	8,350	1,249	1,249	1,249	1,249
8,350	8,400	1,256	1,256	1,256	1,256
8,400	8,450	1,264	1,264	1,264	1,264
8,450	8,500	1,271	1,271	1,271	1,271
8,500	8,550	1,279	1,279	1,279	1,279
8,550	8,600	1,286	1,286	1,286	1,286
8,600	8,650	1,294	1,294	1,294	1,294
8,650	8,700	1,301	1,301	1,301	1,301
8,700	8,750	1,309	1,309	1,309	1,309
8,750	8,800	1,316	1,316	1,316	1,316
8,800	8,850	1,324	1,324	1,324	1,324
8,850	8,900	1,331	1,331	1,331	1,331
8,900	8,950	1,339	1,339	1,339	1,339
8,950	9,000	1,346	1,346	1,346	1,346

9,000

At least	But less than	Single	MFJ*	MFS	HoH
9,000	9,050	1,354	1,354	1,354	1,354
9,050	9,100	1,361	1,361	1,361	1,361
9,100	9,150	1,369	1,369	1,369	1,369
9,150	9,200	1,376	1,376	1,376	1,376
9,200	9,250	1,384	1,384	1,384	1,384
9,250	9,300	1,391	1,391	1,391	1,391
9,300	9,350	1,399	1,399	1,399	1,399
9,350	9,400	1,406	1,406	1,406	1,406
9,400	9,450	1,414	1,414	1,414	1,414
9,450	9,500	1,421	1,421	1,421	1,421
9,500	9,550	1,429	1,429	1,429	1,429
9,550	9,600	1,436	1,436	1,436	1,436
9,600	9,650	1,444	1,444	1,444	1,444
9,650	9,700	1,451	1,451	1,451	1,451
9,700	9,750	1,459	1,459	1,459	1,459
9,750	9,800	1,466	1,466	1,466	1,466
9,800	9,850	1,474	1,474	1,474	1,474
9,850	9,900	1,481	1,481	1,481	1,481
9,900	9,950	1,489	1,489	1,489	1,489
9,950	10,000	1,496	1,496	1,496	1,496

10,000

At least	But less than	Single	MFJ*	MFS	HoH
10,000	10,050	1,504	1,504	1,504	1,504
10,050	10,100	1,511	1,511	1,511	1,511
10,100	10,150	1,519	1,519	1,519	1,519
10,150	10,200	1,526	1,526	1,526	1,526
10,200	10,250	1,534	1,534	1,534	1,534
10,250	10,300	1,541	1,541	1,541	1,541
10,300	10,350	1,549	1,549	1,549	1,549
10,350	10,400	1,556	1,556	1,556	1,556
10,400	10,450	1,564	1,564	1,564	1,564
10,450	10,500	1,571	1,571	1,571	1,571
10,500	10,550	1,579	1,579	1,579	1,579
10,550	10,600	1,586	1,586	1,586	1,586
10,600	10,650	1,594	1,594	1,594	1,594
10,650	10,700	1,601	1,601	1,601	1,601
10,700	10,750	1,609	1,609	1,609	1,609
10,750	10,800	1,616	1,616	1,616	1,616
10,800	10,850	1,624	1,624	1,624	1,624
10,850	10,900	1,631	1,631	1,631	1,631
10,900	10,950	1,639	1,639	1,639	1,639
10,950	11,000	1,646	1,646	1,646	1,646

11,000

At least	But less than	Single	MFJ*	MFS	HoH
11,000	11,050	1,654	1,654	1,654	1,654
11,050	11,100	1,661	1,661	1,661	1,661
11,100	11,150	1,669	1,669	1,669	1,669
11,150	11,200	1,676	1,676	1,676	1,676
11,200	11,250	1,684	1,684	1,684	1,684
11,250	11,300	1,691	1,691	1,691	1,691
11,300	11,350	1,699	1,699	1,699	1,699
11,350	11,400	1,706	1,706	1,706	1,706
11,400	11,450	1,714	1,714	1,714	1,714
11,450	11,500	1,721	1,721	1,721	1,721
11,500	11,550	1,729	1,729	1,729	1,729
11,550	11,600	1,736	1,736	1,736	1,736
11,600	11,650	1,744	1,744	1,744	1,744
11,650	11,700	1,751	1,751	1,751	1,751
11,700	11,750	1,759	1,759	1,759	1,759
11,750	11,800	1,766	1,766	1,766	1,766
11,800	11,850	1,774	1,774	1,774	1,774
11,850	11,900	1,781	1,781	1,781	1,781
11,900	11,950	1,789	1,789	1,789	1,789
11,950	12,000	1,796	1,796	1,796	1,796

12,000

At least	But less than	Single	MFJ*	MFS	HoH
12,000	12,050	1,804	1,804	1,804	1,804
12,050	12,100	1,811	1,811	1,811	1,811
12,100	12,150	1,819	1,819	1,819	1,819
12,150	12,200	1,826	1,826	1,826	1,826
12,200	12,250	1,834	1,834	1,834	1,834
12,250	12,300	1,841	1,841	1,841	1,841
12,300	12,350	1,849	1,849	1,849	1,849
12,350	12,400	1,856	1,856	1,856	1,856
12,400	12,450	1,864	1,864	1,864	1,864
12,450	12,500	1,871	1,871	1,871	1,871
12,500	12,550	1,879	1,879	1,879	1,879
12,550	12,600	1,886	1,886	1,886	1,886
12,600	12,650	1,894	1,894	1,894	1,894
12,650	12,700	1,901	1,901	1,901	1,901
12,700	12,750	1,909	1,909	1,909	1,909
12,750	12,800	1,916	1,916	1,916	1,916
12,800	12,850	1,924	1,924	1,924	1,924
12,850	12,900	1,931	1,931	1,931	1,931
12,900	12,950	1,939	1,939	1,939	1,939
12,950	13,000	1,946	1,946	1,946	1,946

13,000

At least	But less than	Single	MFJ*	MFS	HoH
13,000	13,050	1,954	1,954	1,954	1,954
13,050	13,100	1,961	1,961	1,961	1,961
13,100	13,150	1,969	1,969	1,969	1,969
13,150	13,200	1,976	1,976	1,976	1,976
13,200	13,250	1,984	1,984	1,984	1,984
13,250	13,300	1,991	1,991	1,991	1,991
13,300	13,350	1,999	1,999	1,999	1,999
13,350	13,400	2,006	2,006	2,006	2,006
13,400	13,450	2,014	2,014	2,014	2,014
13,450	13,500	2,021	2,021	2,021	2,021
13,500	13,550	2,029	2,029	2,029	2,029
13,550	13,600	2,036	2,036	2,036	2,036
13,600	13,650	2,044	2,044	2,044	2,044
13,650	13,700	2,051	2,051	2,051	2,051
13,700	13,750	2,059	2,059	2,059	2,059
13,750	13,800	2,066	2,066	2,066	2,066
13,800	13,850	2,074	2,074	2,074	2,074
13,850	13,900	2,081	2,081	2,081	2,081
13,900	13,950	2,089	2,089	2,089	2,089
13,950	14,000	2,096	2,096	2,096	2,096

* This column must also be used by a qualifying widow(er).

Continued on next page

1993 Tax Table—Continued

14,000 / 15,000 / 16,000

If line 37 (taxable income) is—		And you are—			
At least	But less than	Single	Married filing jointly *	Married filing separately	Head of a household
		Your tax is—			
14,000					
14,000	14,050	2,104	2,104	2,104	2,104
14,050	14,100	2,111	2,111	2,111	2,111
14,100	14,150	2,119	2,119	2,119	2,119
14,150	14,200	2,126	2,126	2,126	2,126
14,200	14,250	2,134	2,134	2,134	2,134
14,250	14,300	2,141	2,141	2,141	2,141
14,300	14,350	2,149	2,149	2,149	2,149
14,350	14,400	2,156	2,156	2,156	2,156
14,400	14,450	2,164	2,164	2,164	2,164
14,450	14,500	2,171	2,171	2,171	2,171
14,500	14,550	2,179	2,179	2,179	2,179
14,550	14,600	2,186	2,186	2,186	2,186
14,600	14,650	2,194	2,194	2,194	2,194
14,650	14,700	2,201	2,201	2,201	2,201
14,700	14,750	2,209	2,209	2,209	2,209
14,750	14,800	2,216	2,216	2,216	2,216
14,800	14,850	2,224	2,224	2,224	2,224
14,850	14,900	2,231	2,231	2,231	2,231
14,900	14,950	2,239	2,239	2,239	2,239
14,950	15,000	2,246	2,246	2,246	2,246
15,000					
15,000	15,050	2,254	2,254	2,254	2,254
15,050	15,100	2,261	2,261	2,261	2,261
15,100	15,150	2,269	2,269	2,269	2,269
15,150	15,200	2,276	2,276	2,276	2,276
15,200	15,250	2,284	2,284	2,284	2,284
15,250	15,300	2,291	2,291	2,291	2,291
15,300	15,350	2,299	2,299	2,299	2,299
15,350	15,400	2,306	2,306	2,306	2,306
15,400	15,450	2,314	2,314	2,314	2,314
15,450	15,500	2,321	2,321	2,321	2,321
15,500	15,550	2,329	2,329	2,329	2,329
15,550	15,600	2,336	2,336	2,336	2,336
15,600	15,650	2,344	2,344	2,344	2,344
15,650	15,700	2,351	2,351	2,351	2,351
15,700	15,750	2,359	2,359	2,359	2,359
15,750	15,800	2,366	2,366	2,366	2,366
15,800	15,850	2,374	2,374	2,374	2,374
15,850	15,900	2,381	2,381	2,381	2,381
15,900	15,950	2,389	2,389	2,389	2,389
15,950	16,000	2,396	2,396	2,396	2,396
16,000					
16,000	16,050	2,404	2,404	2,404	2,404
16,050	16,100	2,411	2,411	2,411	2,411
16,100	16,150	2,419	2,419	2,419	2,419
16,150	16,200	2,426	2,426	2,426	2,426
16,200	16,250	2,434	2,434	2,434	2,434
16,250	16,300	2,441	2,441	2,441	2,441
16,300	16,350	2,449	2,449	2,449	2,449
16,350	16,400	2,456	2,456	2,456	2,456
16,400	16,450	2,464	2,464	2,464	2,464
16,450	16,500	2,471	2,471	2,471	2,471
16,500	16,550	2,479	2,479	2,479	2,479
16,550	16,600	2,486	2,486	2,486	2,486
16,600	16,650	2,494	2,494	2,494	2,494
16,650	16,700	2,501	2,501	2,501	2,501
16,700	16,750	2,509	2,509	2,509	2,509
16,750	16,800	2,516	2,516	2,516	2,516
16,800	16,850	2,524	2,524	2,524	2,524
16,850	16,900	2,531	2,531	2,531	2,531
16,900	16,950	2,539	2,539	2,539	2,539
16,950	17,000	2,546	2,546	2,546	2,546

17,000 / 18,000 / 19,000

If line 37 (taxable income) is—		And you are—			
At least	But less than	Single	Married filing jointly *	Married filing separately	Head of a household
		Your tax is—			
17,000					
17,000	17,050	2,554	2,554	2,554	2,554
17,050	17,100	2,561	2,561	2,561	2,561
17,100	17,150	2,569	2,569	2,569	2,569
17,150	17,200	2,576	2,576	2,576	2,576
17,200	17,250	2,584	2,584	2,584	2,584
17,250	17,300	2,591	2,591	2,591	2,591
17,300	17,350	2,599	2,599	2,599	2,599
17,350	17,400	2,606	2,606	2,606	2,606
17,400	17,450	2,614	2,614	2,614	2,614
17,450	17,500	2,621	2,621	2,621	2,621
17,500	17,550	2,629	2,629	2,629	2,629
17,550	17,600	2,636	2,636	2,636	2,636
17,600	17,650	2,644	2,644	2,644	2,644
17,650	17,700	2,651	2,651	2,651	2,651
17,700	17,750	2,659	2,659	2,659	2,659
17,750	17,800	2,666	2,666	2,666	2,666
17,800	17,850	2,674	2,674	2,674	2,674
17,850	17,900	2,681	2,681	2,681	2,681
17,900	17,950	2,689	2,689	2,689	2,689
17,950	18,000	2,696	2,696	2,696	2,696
18,000					
18,000	18,050	2,704	2,704	2,704	2,704
18,050	18,100	2,711	2,711	2,711	2,711
18,100	18,150	2,719	2,719	2,719	2,719
18,150	18,200	2,726	2,726	2,726	2,726
18,200	18,250	2,734	2,734	2,734	2,734
18,250	18,300	2,741	2,741	2,741	2,741
18,300	18,350	2,749	2,749	2,749	2,749
18,350	18,400	2,756	2,756	2,756	2,756
18,400	18,450	2,764	2,764	2,764	2,764
18,450	18,500	2,771	2,771	2,775	2,771
18,500	18,550	2,779	2,779	2,789	2,779
18,550	18,600	2,786	2,786	2,803	2,786
18,600	18,650	2,794	2,794	2,817	2,794
18,650	18,700	2,801	2,801	2,831	2,801
18,700	18,750	2,809	2,809	2,845	2,809
18,750	18,800	2,816	2,816	2,859	2,816
18,800	18,850	2,824	2,824	2,873	2,824
18,850	18,900	2,831	2,831	2,887	2,831
18,900	18,950	2,839	2,839	2,901	2,839
18,950	19,000	2,846	2,846	2,915	2,846
19,000					
19,000	19,050	2,854	2,854	2,929	2,854
19,050	19,100	2,861	2,861	2,943	2,861
19,100	19,150	2,869	2,869	2,957	2,869
19,150	19,200	2,876	2,876	2,971	2,876
19,200	19,250	2,884	2,884	2,985	2,884
19,250	19,300	2,891	2,891	2,999	2,891
19,300	19,350	2,899	2,899	3,013	2,899
19,350	19,400	2,906	2,906	3,027	2,906
19,400	19,450	2,914	2,914	3,041	2,914
19,450	19,500	2,921	2,921	3,055	2,921
19,500	19,550	2,929	2,929	3,069	2,929
19,550	19,600	2,936	2,936	3,083	2,936
19,600	19,650	2,944	2,944	3,097	2,944
19,650	19,700	2,951	2,951	3,111	2,951
19,700	19,750	2,959	2,959	3,125	2,959
19,750	19,800	2,966	2,966	3,139	2,966
19,800	19,850	2,974	2,974	3,153	2,974
19,850	19,900	2,981	2,981	3,167	2,981
19,900	19,950	2,989	2,989	3,181	2,989
19,950	20,000	2,996	2,996	3,195	2,996

20,000 / 21,000 / 22,000

If line 37 (taxable income) is—		And you are—			
At least	But less than	Single	Married filing jointly *	Married filing separately	Head of a household
		Your tax is—			
20,000					
20,000	20,050	3,004	3,004	3,209	3,004
20,050	20,100	3,011	3,011	3,223	3,011
20,100	20,150	3,019	3,019	3,237	3,019
20,150	20,200	3,026	3,026	3,251	3,026
20,200	20,250	3,034	3,034	3,265	3,034
20,250	20,300	3,041	3,041	3,279	3,041
20,300	20,350	3,049	3,049	3,293	3,049
20,350	20,400	3,056	3,056	3,307	3,056
20,400	20,450	3,064	3,064	3,321	3,064
20,450	20,500	3,071	3,071	3,335	3,071
20,500	20,550	3,079	3,079	3,349	3,079
20,550	20,600	3,086	3,086	3,363	3,086
20,600	20,650	3,094	3,094	3,377	3,094
20,650	20,700	3,101	3,101	3,391	3,101
20,700	20,750	3,109	3,109	3,405	3,109
20,750	20,800	3,116	3,116	3,419	3,116
20,800	20,850	3,124	3,124	3,433	3,124
20,850	20,900	3,131	3,131	3,447	3,131
20,900	20,950	3,139	3,139	3,461	3,139
20,950	21,000	3,146	3,146	3,475	3,146
21,000					
21,000	21,050	3,154	3,154	3,489	3,154
21,050	21,100	3,161	3,161	3,503	3,161
21,100	21,150	3,169	3,169	3,517	3,169
21,150	21,200	3,176	3,176	3,531	3,176
21,200	21,250	3,184	3,184	3,545	3,184
21,250	21,300	3,191	3,191	3,559	3,191
21,300	21,350	3,199	3,199	3,573	3,199
21,350	21,400	3,206	3,206	3,587	3,206
21,400	21,450	3,214	3,214	3,601	3,214
21,450	21,500	3,221	3,221	3,615	3,221
21,500	21,550	3,229	3,229	3,629	3,229
21,550	21,600	3,236	3,236	3,643	3,236
21,600	21,650	3,244	3,244	3,657	3,244
21,650	21,700	3,251	3,251	3,671	3,251
21,700	21,750	3,259	3,259	3,685	3,259
21,750	21,800	3,266	3,266	3,699	3,266
21,800	21,850	3,274	3,274	3,713	3,274
21,850	21,900	3,281	3,281	3,727	3,281
21,900	21,950	3,289	3,289	3,741	3,289
21,950	22,000	3,296	3,296	3,755	3,296
22,000					
22,000	22,050	3,304	3,304	3,769	3,304
22,050	22,100	3,311	3,311	3,783	3,311
22,100	22,150	3,322	3,319	3,797	3,319
22,150	22,200	3,336	3,326	3,811	3,326
22,200	22,250	3,350	3,334	3,825	3,334
22,250	22,300	3,364	3,341	3,839	3,341
22,300	22,350	3,378	3,349	3,853	3,349
22,350	22,400	3,392	3,356	3,867	3,356
22,400	22,450	3,406	3,364	3,881	3,364
22,450	22,500	3,420	3,371	3,895	3,371
22,500	22,550	3,434	3,379	3,909	3,379
22,550	22,600	3,448	3,386	3,923	3,386
22,600	22,650	3,462	3,394	3,937	3,394
22,650	22,700	3,476	3,401	3,951	3,401
22,700	22,750	3,490	3,409	3,965	3,409
22,750	22,800	3,504	3,416	3,979	3,416
22,800	22,850	3,518	3,424	3,993	3,424
22,850	22,900	3,532	3,431	4,007	3,431
22,900	22,950	3,546	3,439	4,021	3,439
22,950	23,000	3,560	3,446	4,035	3,446

* This column must also be used by a qualifying widow(er).

Continued on next page

1993 Tax Table—*Continued*

23,000 – 25,000

At least	But less than	Single	Married filing jointly *	Married filing separately	Head of a household
23,000					
23,000	23,050	3,574	3,454	4,049	3,454
23,050	23,100	3,588	3,461	4,063	3,461
23,100	23,150	3,602	3,469	4,077	3,469
23,150	23,200	3,616	3,476	4,091	3,476
23,200	23,250	3,630	3,484	4,105	3,484
23,250	23,300	3,644	3,491	4,119	3,491
23,300	23,350	3,658	3,499	4,133	3,499
23,350	23,400	3,672	3,506	4,147	3,506
23,400	23,450	3,686	3,514	4,161	3,514
23,450	23,500	3,700	3,521	4,175	3,521
23,500	23,550	3,714	3,529	4,189	3,529
23,550	23,600	3,728	3,536	4,203	3,536
23,600	23,650	3,742	3,544	4,217	3,544
23,650	23,700	3,756	3,551	4,231	3,551
23,700	23,750	3,770	3,559	4,245	3,559
23,750	23,800	3,784	3,566	4,259	3,566
23,800	23,850	3,798	3,574	4,273	3,574
23,850	23,900	3,812	3,581	4,287	3,581
23,900	23,950	3,826	3,589	4,301	3,589
23,950	24,000	3,840	3,596	4,315	3,596
24,000					
24,000	24,050	3,854	3,604	4,329	3,604
24,050	24,100	3,868	3,611	4,343	3,611
24,100	24,150	3,882	3,619	4,357	3,619
24,150	24,200	3,896	3,626	4,371	3,626
24,200	24,250	3,910	3,634	4,385	3,634
24,250	24,300	3,924	3,641	4,399	3,641
24,300	24,350	3,938	3,649	4,413	3,649
24,350	24,400	3,952	3,656	4,427	3,656
24,400	24,450	3,966	3,664	4,441	3,664
24,450	24,500	3,980	3,671	4,455	3,671
24,500	24,550	3,994	3,679	4,469	3,679
24,550	24,600	4,008	3,686	4,483	3,686
24,600	24,650	4,022	3,694	4,497	3,694
24,650	24,700	4,036	3,701	4,511	3,701
24,700	24,750	4,050	3,709	4,525	3,709
24,750	24,800	4,064	3,716	4,539	3,716
24,800	24,850	4,078	3,724	4,553	3,724
24,850	24,900	4,092	3,731	4,567	3,731
24,900	24,950	4,106	3,739	4,581	3,739
24,950	25,000	4,120	3,746	4,595	3,746
25,000					
25,000	25,050	4,134	3,754	4,609	3,754
25,050	25,100	4,148	3,761	4,623	3,761
25,100	25,150	4,162	3,769	4,637	3,769
25,150	25,200	4,176	3,776	4,651	3,776
25,200	25,250	4,190	3,784	4,665	3,784
25,250	25,300	4,204	3,791	4,679	3,791
25,300	25,350	4,218	3,799	4,693	3,799
25,350	25,400	4,232	3,806	4,707	3,806
25,400	25,450	4,246	3,814	4,721	3,814
25,450	25,500	4,260	3,821	4,735	3,821
25,500	25,550	4,274	3,829	4,749	3,829
25,550	25,600	4,288	3,836	4,763	3,836
25,600	25,650	4,302	3,844	4,777	3,844
25,650	25,700	4,316	3,851	4,791	3,851
25,700	25,750	4,330	3,859	4,805	3,859
25,750	25,800	4,344	3,866	4,819	3,866
25,800	25,850	4,358	3,874	4,833	3,874
25,850	25,900	4,372	3,881	4,847	3,881
25,900	25,950	4,386	3,889	4,861	3,889
25,950	26,000	4,400	3,896	4,875	3,896

26,000 – 28,000

At least	But less than	Single	Married filing jointly *	Married filing separately	Head of a household
26,000					
26,000	26,050	4,414	3,904	4,889	3,904
26,050	26,100	4,428	3,911	4,903	3,911
26,100	26,150	4,442	3,919	4,917	3,919
26,150	26,200	4,456	3,926	4,931	3,926
26,200	26,250	4,470	3,934	4,945	3,934
26,250	26,300	4,484	3,941	4,959	3,941
26,300	26,350	4,498	3,949	4,973	3,949
26,350	26,400	4,512	3,956	4,987	3,956
26,400	26,450	4,526	3,964	5,001	3,964
26,450	26,500	4,540	3,971	5,015	3,971
26,500	26,550	4,554	3,979	5,029	3,979
26,550	26,600	4,568	3,986	5,043	3,986
26,600	26,650	4,582	3,994	5,057	3,994
26,650	26,700	4,596	4,001	5,071	4,001
26,700	26,750	4,610	4,009	5,085	4,009
26,750	26,800	4,624	4,016	5,099	4,016
26,800	26,850	4,638	4,024	5,113	4,024
26,850	26,900	4,652	4,031	5,127	4,031
26,900	26,950	4,666	4,039	5,141	4,039
26,950	27,000	4,680	4,046	5,155	4,046
27,000					
27,000	27,050	4,694	4,054	5,169	4,054
27,050	27,100	4,708	4,061	5,183	4,061
27,100	27,150	4,722	4,069	5,197	4,069
27,150	27,200	4,736	4,076	5,211	4,076
27,200	27,250	4,750	4,084	5,225	4,084
27,250	27,300	4,764	4,091	5,239	4,091
27,300	27,350	4,778	4,099	5,253	4,099
27,350	27,400	4,792	4,106	5,267	4,106
27,400	27,450	4,806	4,114	5,281	4,114
27,450	27,500	4,820	4,121	5,295	4,121
27,500	27,550	4,834	4,129	5,309	4,129
27,550	27,600	4,848	4,136	5,323	4,136
27,600	27,650	4,862	4,144	5,337	4,144
27,650	27,700	4,876	4,151	5,351	4,151
27,700	27,750	4,890	4,159	5,365	4,159
27,750	27,800	4,904	4,166	5,379	4,166
27,800	27,850	4,918	4,174	5,393	4,174
27,850	27,900	4,932	4,181	5,407	4,181
27,900	27,950	4,946	4,189	5,421	4,189
27,950	28,000	4,960	4,196	5,435	4,196
28,000					
28,000	28,050	4,974	4,204	5,449	4,204
28,050	28,100	4,988	4,211	5,463	4,211
28,100	28,150	5,002	4,219	5,477	4,219
28,150	28,200	5,016	4,226	5,491	4,226
28,200	28,250	5,030	4,234	5,505	4,234
28,250	28,300	5,044	4,241	5,519	4,241
28,300	28,350	5,058	4,249	5,533	4,249
28,350	28,400	5,072	4,256	5,547	4,256
28,400	28,450	5,086	4,264	5,561	4,264
28,450	28,500	5,100	4,271	5,575	4,271
28,500	28,550	5,114	4,279	5,589	4,279
28,550	28,600	5,128	4,286	5,603	4,286
28,600	28,650	5,142	4,294	5,617	4,294
28,650	28,700	5,156	4,301	5,631	4,301
28,700	28,750	5,170	4,309	5,645	4,309
28,750	28,800	5,184	4,316	5,659	4,316
28,800	28,850	5,198	4,324	5,673	4,324
28,850	28,900	5,212	4,331	5,687	4,331
28,900	28,950	5,226	4,339	5,701	4,339
28,950	29,000	5,240	4,346	5,715	4,346

29,000 – 31,000

At least	But less than	Single	Married filing jointly *	Married filing separately	Head of a household
29,000					
29,000	29,050	5,254	4,354	5,729	4,354
29,050	29,100	5,268	4,361	5,743	4,361
29,100	29,150	5,282	4,369	5,757	4,369
29,150	29,200	5,296	4,376	5,771	4,376
29,200	29,250	5,310	4,384	5,785	4,384
29,250	29,300	5,324	4,391	5,799	4,391
29,300	29,350	5,338	4,399	5,813	4,399
29,350	29,400	5,352	4,406	5,827	4,406
29,400	29,450	5,366	4,414	5,841	4,414
29,450	29,500	5,380	4,421	5,855	4,421
29,500	29,550	5,394	4,429	5,869	4,429
29,550	29,600	5,408	4,436	5,883	4,436
29,600	29,650	5,422	4,444	5,897	4,447
29,650	29,700	5,436	4,451	5,911	4,461
29,700	29,750	5,450	4,459	5,925	4,475
29,750	29,800	5,464	4,466	5,939	4,489
29,800	29,850	5,478	4,474	5,953	4,503
29,850	29,900	5,492	4,481	5,967	4,517
29,900	29,950	5,506	4,489	5,981	4,531
29,950	30,000	5,520	4,496	5,995	4,545
30,000					
30,000	30,050	5,534	4,504	6,009	4,559
30,050	30,100	5,548	4,511	6,023	4,573
30,100	30,150	5,562	4,519	6,037	4,587
30,150	30,200	5,576	4,526	6,051	4,601
30,200	30,250	5,590	4,534	6,065	4,615
30,250	30,300	5,604	4,541	6,079	4,629
30,300	30,350	5,618	4,549	6,093	4,643
30,350	30,400	5,632	4,556	6,107	4,657
30,400	30,450	5,646	4,564	6,121	4,671
30,450	30,500	5,660	4,571	6,135	4,685
30,500	30,550	5,674	4,579	6,149	4,699
30,550	30,600	5,688	4,586	6,163	4,713
30,600	30,650	5,702	4,594	6,177	4,727
30,650	30,700	5,716	4,601	6,191	4,741
30,700	30,750	5,730	4,609	6,205	4,755
30,750	30,800	5,744	4,616	6,219	4,769
30,800	30,850	5,758	4,624	6,233	4,783
30,850	30,900	5,772	4,631	6,247	4,797
30,900	30,950	5,786	4,639	6,261	4,811
30,950	31,000	5,800	4,646	6,275	4,825
31,000					
31,000	31,050	5,814	4,654	6,289	4,839
31,050	31,100	5,828	4,661	6,303	4,853
31,100	31,150	5,842	4,669	6,317	4,867
31,150	31,200	5,856	4,676	6,331	4,881
31,200	31,250	5,870	4,684	6,345	4,895
31,250	31,300	5,884	4,691	6,359	4,909
31,300	31,350	5,898	4,699	6,373	4,923
31,350	31,400	5,912	4,706	6,387	4,937
31,400	31,450	5,926	4,714	6,401	4,951
31,450	31,500	5,940	4,721	6,415	4,965
31,500	31,550	5,954	4,729	6,429	4,979
31,550	31,600	5,968	4,736	6,443	4,993
31,600	31,650	5,982	4,744	6,457	5,007
31,650	31,700	5,996	4,751	6,471	5,021
31,700	31,750	6,010	4,759	6,485	5,035
31,750	31,800	6,024	4,766	6,499	5,049
31,800	31,850	6,038	4,774	6,513	5,063
31,850	31,900	6,052	4,781	6,527	5,077
31,900	31,950	6,066	4,789	6,541	5,091
31,950	32,000	6,080	4,796	6,555	5,105

* This column must also be used by a qualifying widow(er).

Continued on next page

1993 Tax Table—*Continued*

If line 37 (taxable income) is—		And you are—			
At least	But less than	Single	Married filing jointly *	Married filing separately	Head of a household
		Your tax is—			

32,000

At least	But less than	Single	MFJ	MFS	HoH
32,000	32,050	6,094	4,804	6,569	5,119
32,050	32,100	6,108	4,811	6,583	5,133
32,100	32,150	6,122	4,819	6,597	5,147
32,150	32,200	6,136	4,826	6,611	5,161
32,200	32,250	6,150	4,834	6,625	5,175
32,250	32,300	6,164	4,841	6,639	5,189
32,300	32,350	6,178	4,849	6,653	5,203
32,350	32,400	6,192	4,856	6,667	5,217
32,400	32,450	6,206	4,864	6,681	5,231
32,450	32,500	6,220	4,871	6,695	5,245
32,500	32,550	6,234	4,879	6,709	5,259
32,550	32,600	6,248	4,886	6,723	5,273
32,600	32,650	6,262	4,894	6,737	5,287
32,650	32,700	6,276	4,901	6,751	5,301
32,700	32,750	6,290	4,909	6,765	5,315
32,750	32,800	6,304	4,916	6,779	5,329
32,800	32,850	6,318	4,924	6,793	5,343
32,850	32,900	6,332	4,931	6,807	5,357
32,900	32,950	6,346	4,939	6,821	5,371
32,950	33,000	6,360	4,946	6,835	5,385

33,000

At least	But less than	Single	MFJ	MFS	HoH
33,000	33,050	6,374	4,954	6,849	5,399
33,050	33,100	6,388	4,961	6,863	5,413
33,100	33,150	6,402	4,969	6,877	5,427
33,150	33,200	6,416	4,976	6,891	5,441
33,200	33,250	6,430	4,984	6,905	5,455
33,250	33,300	6,444	4,991	6,919	5,469
33,300	33,350	6,458	4,999	6,933	5,483
33,350	33,400	6,472	5,006	6,947	5,497
33,400	33,450	6,486	5,014	6,961	5,511
33,450	33,500	6,500	5,021	6,975	5,525
33,500	33,550	6,514	5,029	6,989	5,539
33,550	33,600	6,528	5,036	7,003	5,553
33,600	33,650	6,542	5,044	7,017	5,567
33,650	33,700	6,556	5,051	7,031	5,581
33,700	33,750	6,570	5,059	7,045	5,595
33,750	33,800	6,584	5,066	7,059	5,609
33,800	33,850	6,598	5,074	7,073	5,623
33,850	33,900	6,612	5,081	7,087	5,637
33,900	33,950	6,626	5,089	7,101	5,651
33,950	34,000	6,640	5,096	7,115	5,665

34,000

At least	But less than	Single	MFJ	MFS	HoH
34,000	34,050	6,654	5,104	7,129	5,679
34,050	34,100	6,668	5,111	7,143	5,693
34,100	34,150	6,682	5,119	7,157	5,707
34,150	34,200	6,696	5,126	7,171	5,721
34,200	34,250	6,710	5,134	7,185	5,735
34,250	34,300	6,724	5,141	7,199	5,749
34,300	34,350	6,738	5,149	7,213	5,763
34,350	34,400	6,752	5,156	7,227	5,777
34,400	34,450	6,766	5,164	7,241	5,791
34,450	34,500	6,780	5,171	7,255	5,805
34,500	34,550	6,794	5,179	7,269	5,819
34,550	34,600	6,808	5,186	7,283	5,833
34,600	34,650	6,822	5,194	7,297	5,847
34,650	34,700	6,836	5,201	7,311	5,861
34,700	34,750	6,850	5,209	7,325	5,875
34,750	34,800	6,864	5,216	7,339	5,889
34,800	34,850	6,878	5,224	7,353	5,903
34,850	34,900	6,892	5,231	7,367	5,917
34,900	34,950	6,906	5,239	7,381	5,931
34,950	35,000	6,920	5,246	7,395	5,945

35,000

At least	But less than	Single	MFJ	MFS	HoH
35,000	35,050	6,934	5,254	7,409	5,959
35,050	35,100	6,948	5,261	7,423	5,973
35,100	35,150	6,962	5,269	7,437	5,987
35,150	35,200	6,976	5,276	7,451	6,001
35,200	35,250	6,990	5,284	7,465	6,015
35,250	35,300	7,004	5,291	7,479	6,029
35,300	35,350	7,018	5,299	7,493	6,043
35,350	35,400	7,032	5,306	7,507	6,057
35,400	35,450	7,046	5,314	7,521	6,071
35,450	35,500	7,060	5,321	7,535	6,085
35,500	35,550	7,074	5,329	7,549	6,099
35,550	35,600	7,088	5,336	7,563	6,113
35,600	35,650	7,102	5,344	7,577	6,127
35,650	35,700	7,116	5,351	7,591	6,141
35,700	35,750	7,130	5,359	7,605	6,155
35,750	35,800	7,144	5,366	7,619	6,169
35,800	35,850	7,158	5,374	7,633	6,183
35,850	35,900	7,172	5,381	7,647	6,197
35,900	35,950	7,186	5,389	7,661	6,211
35,950	36,000	7,200	5,396	7,675	6,225

36,000

At least	But less than	Single	MFJ	MFS	HoH
36,000	36,050	7,214	5,404	7,689	6,239
36,050	36,100	7,228	5,411	7,703	6,253
36,100	36,150	7,242	5,419	7,717	6,267
36,150	36,200	7,256	5,426	7,731	6,281
36,200	36,250	7,270	5,434	7,745	6,295
36,250	36,300	7,284	5,441	7,759	6,309
36,300	36,350	7,298	5,449	7,773	6,323
36,350	36,400	7,312	5,456	7,787	6,337
36,400	36,450	7,326	5,464	7,801	6,351
36,450	36,500	7,340	5,471	7,815	6,365
36,500	36,550	7,354	5,479	7,829	6,379
36,550	36,600	7,368	5,486	7,843	6,393
36,600	36,650	7,382	5,494	7,857	6,407
36,650	36,700	7,396	5,501	7,871	6,421
36,700	36,750	7,410	5,509	7,885	6,435
36,750	36,800	7,424	5,516	7,899	6,449
36,800	36,850	7,438	5,524	7,913	6,463
36,850	36,900	7,452	5,531	7,927	6,477
36,900	36,950	7,466	5,542	7,941	6,491
36,950	37,000	7,480	5,556	7,955	6,505

37,000

At least	But less than	Single	MFJ	MFS	HoH
37,000	37,050	7,494	5,570	7,969	6,519
37,050	37,100	7,508	5,584	7,983	6,533
37,100	37,150	7,522	5,598	7,997	6,547
37,150	37,200	7,536	5,612	8,011	6,561
37,200	37,250	7,550	5,626	8,025	6,575
37,250	37,300	7,564	5,640	8,039	6,589
37,300	37,350	7,578	5,654	8,053	6,603
37,350	37,400	7,592	5,668	8,067	6,617
37,400	37,450	7,606	5,682	8,081	6,631
37,450	37,500	7,620	5,696	8,095	6,645
37,500	37,550	7,634	5,710	8,109	6,659
37,550	37,600	7,648	5,724	8,123	6,673
37,600	37,650	7,662	5,738	8,137	6,687
37,650	37,700	7,676	5,752	8,151	6,701
37,700	37,750	7,690	5,766	8,165	6,715
37,750	37,800	7,704	5,780	8,179	6,729
37,800	37,850	7,718	5,794	8,193	6,743
37,850	37,900	7,732	5,808	8,207	6,757
37,900	37,950	7,746	5,822	8,221	6,771
37,950	38,000	7,760	5,836	8,235	6,785

38,000

At least	But less than	Single	MFJ	MFS	HoH
38,000	38,050	7,774	5,850	8,249	6,799
38,050	38,100	7,788	5,864	8,263	6,813
38,100	38,150	7,802	5,878	8,277	6,827
38,150	38,200	7,816	5,892	8,291	6,841
38,200	38,250	7,830	5,906	8,305	6,855
38,250	38,300	7,844	5,920	8,319	6,869
38,300	38,350	7,858	5,934	8,333	6,883
38,350	38,400	7,872	5,948	8,347	6,897
38,400	38,450	7,886	5,962	8,361	6,911
38,450	38,500	7,900	5,976	8,375	6,925
38,500	38,550	7,914	5,990	8,389	6,939
38,550	38,600	7,928	6,004	8,403	6,953
38,600	38,650	7,942	6,018	8,417	6,967
38,650	38,700	7,956	6,032	8,431	6,981
38,700	38,750	7,970	6,046	8,445	6,995
38,750	38,800	7,984	6,060	8,459	7,009
38,800	38,850	7,998	6,074	8,473	7,023
38,850	38,900	8,012	6,088	8,487	7,037
38,900	38,950	8,026	6,102	8,501	7,051
38,950	39,000	8,040	6,116	8,515	7,065

39,000

At least	But less than	Single	MFJ	MFS	HoH
39,000	39,050	8,054	6,130	8,529	7,079
39,050	39,100	8,068	6,144	8,543	7,093
39,100	39,150	8,082	6,158	8,557	7,107
39,150	39,200	8,096	6,172	8,571	7,121
39,200	39,250	8,110	6,186	8,585	7,135
39,250	39,300	8,124	6,200	8,599	7,149
39,300	39,350	8,138	6,214	8,613	7,163
39,350	39,400	8,152	6,228	8,627	7,177
39,400	39,450	8,166	6,242	8,641	7,191
39,450	39,500	8,180	6,256	8,655	7,205
39,500	39,550	8,194	6,270	8,669	7,219
39,550	39,600	8,208	6,284	8,683	7,233
39,600	39,650	8,222	6,298	8,697	7,247
39,650	39,700	8,236	6,312	8,711	7,261
39,700	39,750	8,250	6,326	8,725	7,275
39,750	39,800	8,264	6,340	8,739	7,289
39,800	39,850	8,278	6,354	8,753	7,303
39,850	39,900	8,292	6,368	8,767	7,317
39,900	39,950	8,306	6,382	8,781	7,331
39,950	40,000	8,320	6,396	8,795	7,345

40,000

At least	But less than	Single	MFJ	MFS	HoH
40,000	40,050	8,334	6,410	8,809	7,359
40,050	40,100	8,348	6,424	8,823	7,373
40,100	40,150	8,362	6,438	8,837	7,387
40,150	40,200	8,376	6,452	8,851	7,401
40,200	40,250	8,390	6,466	8,865	7,415
40,250	40,300	8,404	6,480	8,879	7,429
40,300	40,350	8,418	6,494	8,893	7,443
40,350	40,400	8,432	6,508	8,907	7,457
40,400	40,450	8,446	6,522	8,921	7,471
40,450	40,500	8,460	6,536	8,935	7,485
40,500	40,550	8,474	6,550	8,949	7,499
40,550	40,600	8,488	6,564	8,963	7,513
40,600	40,650	8,502	6,578	8,977	7,527
40,650	40,700	8,516	6,592	8,991	7,541
40,700	40,750	8,530	6,606	9,005	7,555
40,750	40,800	8,544	6,620	9,019	7,569
40,800	40,850	8,558	6,634	9,033	7,583
40,850	40,900	8,572	6,648	9,047	7,597
40,900	40,950	8,586	6,662	9,061	7,611
40,950	41,000	8,600	6,676	9,075	7,625

* This column must also be used by a qualifying widow(er).

Continued on next page

1993 Tax Table—*Continued*

If line 37 (taxable income) is—		And you are—				If line 37 (taxable income) is—		And you are—				If line 37 (taxable income) is—		And you are—			
At least	But less than	Single	Married filing jointly *	Married filing sepa-rately	Head of a house-hold	At least	But less than	Single	Married filing jointly *	Married filing sepa-rately	Head of a house-hold	At least	But less than	Single	Married filing jointly *	Married filing sepa-rately	Head of a house-hold
		Your tax is—						Your tax is—						Your tax is—			
41,000						**44,000**						**47,000**					
41,000	41,050	8,614	6,690	9,089	7,639	44,000	44,050	9,454	7,530	9,929	8,479	47,000	47,050	10,294	8,370	10,842	9,319
41,050	41,100	8,628	6,704	9,103	7,653	44,050	44,100	9,468	7,544	9,943	8,493	47,050	47,100	10,308	8,384	10,858	9,333
41,100	41,150	8,642	6,718	9,117	7,667	44,100	44,150	9,482	7,558	9,957	8,507	47,100	47,150	10,322	8,398	10,873	9,347
41,150	41,200	8,656	6,732	9,131	7,681	44,150	44,200	9,496	7,572	9,971	8,521	47,150	47,200	10,336	8,412	10,889	9,361
41,200	41,250	8,670	6,746	9,145	7,695	44,200	44,250	9,510	7,586	9,985	8,535	47,200	47,250	10,350	8,426	10,904	9,375
41,250	41,300	8,684	6,760	9,159	7,709	44,250	44,300	9,524	7,600	9,999	8,549	47,250	47,300	10,364	8,440	10,920	9,389
41,300	41,350	8,698	6,774	9,173	7,723	44,300	44,350	9,538	7,614	10,013	8,563	47,300	47,350	10,378	8,454	10,935	9,403
41,350	41,400	8,712	6,788	9,187	7,737	44,350	44,400	9,552	7,628	10,027	8,577	47,350	47,400	10,392	8,468	10,951	9,417
41,400	41,450	8,726	6,802	9,201	7,751	44,400	44,450	9,566	7,642	10,041	8,591	47,400	47,450	10,406	8,482	10,966	9,431
41,450	41,500	8,740	6,816	9,215	7,765	44,450	44,500	9,580	7,656	10,055	8,605	47,450	47,500	10,420	8,496	10,982	9,445
41,500	41,550	8,754	6,830	9,229	7,779	44,500	44,550	9,594	7,670	10,069	8,619	47,500	47,550	10,434	8,510	10,997	9,459
41,550	41,600	8,768	6,844	9,243	7,793	44,550	44,600	9,608	7,684	10,083	8,633	47,550	47,600	10,448	8,524	11,013	9,473
41,600	41,650	8,782	6,858	9,257	7,807	44,600	44,650	9,622	7,698	10,098	8,647	47,600	47,650	10,462	8,538	11,028	9,487
41,650	41,700	8,796	6,872	9,271	7,821	44,650	44,700	9,636	7,712	10,114	8,661	47,650	47,700	10,476	8,552	11,044	9,501
41,700	41,750	8,810	6,886	9,285	7,835	44,700	44,750	9,650	7,726	10,129	8,675	47,700	47,750	10,490	8,566	11,059	9,515
41,750	41,800	8,824	6,900	9,299	7,849	44,750	44,800	9,664	7,740	10,145	8,689	47,750	47,800	10,504	8,580	11,075	9,529
41,800	41,850	8,838	6,914	9,313	7,863	44,800	44,850	9,678	7,754	10,160	8,703	47,800	47,850	10,518	8,594	11,090	9,543
41,850	41,900	8,852	6,928	9,327	7,877	44,850	44,900	9,692	7,768	10,176	8,717	47,850	47,900	10,532	8,608	11,106	9,557
41,900	41,950	8,866	6,942	9,341	7,891	44,900	44,950	9,706	7,782	10,191	8,731	47,900	47,950	10,546	8,622	11,121	9,571
41,950	42,000	8,880	6,956	9,355	7,905	44,950	45,000	9,720	7,796	10,207	8,745	47,950	48,000	10,560	8,636	11,137	9,585
42,000						**45,000**						**48,000**					
42,000	42,050	8,894	6,970	9,369	7,919	45,000	45,050	9,734	7,810	10,222	8,759	48,000	48,050	10,574	8,650	11,152	9,599
42,050	42,100	8,908	6,984	9,383	7,933	45,050	45,100	9,748	7,824	10,238	8,773	48,050	48,100	10,588	8,664	11,168	9,613
42,100	42,150	8,922	6,998	9,397	7,947	45,100	45,150	9,762	7,838	10,253	8,787	48,100	48,150	10,602	8,678	11,183	9,627
42,150	42,200	8,936	7,012	9,411	7,961	45,150	45,200	9,776	7,852	10,269	8,801	48,150	48,200	10,616	8,692	11,199	9,641
42,200	42,250	8,950	7,026	9,425	7,975	45,200	45,250	9,790	7,866	10,284	8,815	48,200	48,250	10,630	8,706	11,214	9,655
42,250	42,300	8,964	7,040	9,439	7,989	45,250	45,300	9,804	7,880	10,300	8,829	48,250	48,300	10,644	8,720	11,230	9,669
42,300	42,350	8,978	7,054	9,453	8,003	45,300	45,350	9,818	7,894	10,315	8,843	48,300	48,350	10,658	8,734	11,245	9,683
42,350	42,400	8,992	7,068	9,467	8,017	45,350	45,400	9,832	7,908	10,331	8,857	48,350	48,400	10,672	8,748	11,261	9,697
42,400	42,450	9,006	7,082	9,481	8,031	45,400	45,450	9,846	7,922	10,346	8,871	48,400	48,450	10,686	8,762	11,276	9,711
42,450	42,500	9,020	7,096	9,495	8,045	45,450	45,500	9,860	7,936	10,362	8,885	48,450	48,500	10,700	8,776	11,292	9,725
42,500	42,550	9,034	7,110	9,509	8,059	45,500	45,550	9,874	7,950	10,377	8,899	48,500	48,550	10,714	8,790	11,307	9,739
42,550	42,600	9,048	7,124	9,523	8,073	45,550	45,600	9,888	7,964	10,393	8,913	48,550	48,600	10,728	8,804	11,323	9,753
42,600	42,650	9,062	7,138	9,537	8,087	45,600	45,650	9,902	7,978	10,408	8,927	48,600	48,650	10,742	8,818	11,338	9,767
42,650	42,700	9,076	7,152	9,551	8,101	45,650	45,700	9,916	7,992	10,424	8,941	48,650	48,700	10,756	8,832	11,354	9,781
42,700	42,750	9,090	7,166	9,565	8,115	45,700	45,750	9,930	8,006	10,439	8,955	48,700	48,750	10,770	8,846	11,369	9,795
42,750	42,800	9,104	7,180	9,579	8,129	45,750	45,800	9,944	8,020	10,455	8,969	48,750	48,800	10,784	8,860	11,385	9,809
42,800	42,850	9,118	7,194	9,593	8,143	45,800	45,850	9,958	8,034	10,470	8,983	48,800	48,850	10,798	8,874	11,400	9,823
42,850	42,900	9,132	7,208	9,607	8,157	45,850	45,900	9,972	8,048	10,486	8,997	48,850	48,900	10,812	8,888	11,416	9,837
42,900	42,950	9,146	7,222	9,621	8,171	45,900	45,950	9,986	8,062	10,501	9,011	48,900	48,950	10,826	8,902	11,431	9,851
42,950	43,000	9,160	7,236	9,635	8,185	45,950	46,000	10,000	8,076	10,517	9,025	48,950	49,000	10,840	8,916	11,447	9,865
43,000						**46,000**						**49,000**					
43,000	43,050	9,174	7,250	9,649	8,199	46,000	46,050	10,014	8,090	10,532	9,039	49,000	49,050	10,854	8,930	11,462	9,879
43,050	43,100	9,188	7,264	9,663	8,213	46,050	46,100	10,028	8,104	10,548	9,053	49,050	49,100	10,868	8,944	11,478	9,893
43,100	43,150	9,202	7,278	9,677	8,227	46,100	46,150	10,042	8,118	10,563	9,067	49,100	49,150	10,882	8,958	11,493	9,907
43,150	43,200	9,216	7,292	9,691	8,241	46,150	46,200	10,056	8,132	10,579	9,081	49,150	49,200	10,896	8,972	11,509	9,921
43,200	43,250	9,230	7,306	9,705	8,255	46,200	46,250	10,070	8,146	10,594	9,095	49,200	49,250	10,910	8,986	11,524	9,935
43,250	43,300	9,244	7,320	9,719	8,269	46,250	46,300	10,084	8,160	10,610	9,109	49,250	49,300	10,924	9,000	11,540	9,949
43,300	43,350	9,258	7,334	9,733	8,283	46,300	46,350	10,098	8,174	10,625	9,123	49,300	49,350	10,938	9,014	11,555	9,963
43,350	43,400	9,272	7,348	9,747	8,297	46,350	46,400	10,112	8,188	10,641	9,137	49,350	49,400	10,952	9,028	11,571	9,977
43,400	43,450	9,286	7,362	9,761	8,311	46,400	46,450	10,126	8,202	10,656	9,151	49,400	49,450	10,966	9,042	11,586	9,991
43,450	43,500	9,300	7,376	9,775	8,325	46,450	46,500	10,140	8,216	10,672	9,165	49,450	49,500	10,980	9,056	11,602	10,005
43,500	43,550	9,314	7,390	9,789	8,339	46,500	46,550	10,154	8,230	10,687	9,179	49,500	49,550	10,994	9,070	11,617	10,019
43,550	43,600	9,328	7,404	9,803	8,353	46,550	46,600	10,168	8,244	10,703	9,193	49,550	49,600	11,008	9,084	11,633	10,033
43,600	43,650	9,342	7,418	9,817	8,367	46,600	46,650	10,182	8,258	10,718	9,207	49,600	49,650	11,022	9,098	11,648	10,047
43,650	43,700	9,356	7,432	9,831	8,381	46,650	46,700	10,196	8,272	10,734	9,221	49,650	49,700	11,036	9,112	11,664	10,061
43,700	43,750	9,370	7,446	9,845	8,395	46,700	46,750	10,210	8,286	10,749	9,235	49,700	49,750	11,050	9,126	11,679	10,075
43,750	43,800	9,384	7,460	9,859	8,409	46,750	46,800	10,224	8,300	10,765	9,249	49,750	49,800	11,064	9,140	11,695	10,089
43,800	43,850	9,398	7,474	9,873	8,423	46,800	46,850	10,238	8,314	10,780	9,263	49,800	49,850	11,078	9,154	11,710	10,103
43,850	43,900	9,412	7,488	9,887	8,437	46,850	46,900	10,252	8,328	10,796	9,277	49,850	49,900	11,092	9,168	11,726	10,117
43,900	43,950	9,426	7,502	9,901	8,451	46,900	46,950	10,266	8,342	10,811	9,291	49,900	49,950	11,106	9,182	11,741	10,131
43,950	44,000	9,440	7,516	9,915	8,465	46,950	47,000	10,280	8,356	10,827	9,305	49,950	50,000	11,120	9,196	11,757	10,145

* This column must also be used by a qualifying widow(er).

Continued on next page

1993 Tax Table—Continued

If line 37 (taxable income) is—		And you are—				If line 37 (taxable income) is—		And you are—				If line 37 (taxable income) is—		And you are—			
At least	But less than	Single	Married filing jointly *	Married filing separately	Head of a household	At least	But less than	Single	Married filing jointly *	Married filing separately	Head of a household	At least	But less than	Single	Married filing jointly *	Married filing separately	Head of a household
		Your tax is—						Your tax is—						Your tax is—			
50,000						**53,000**						**56,000**					
50,000	50,050	11,134	9,210	11,772	10,159	53,000	53,050	11,974	10,050	12,702	10,999	56,000	56,050	12,890	10,890	13,632	11,839
50,050	50,100	11,148	9,224	11,788	10,173	53,050	53,100	11,988	10,064	12,718	11,013	56,050	56,100	12,905	10,904	13,648	11,853
50,100	50,150	11,162	9,238	11,803	10,187	53,100	53,150	12,002	10,078	12,733	11,027	56,100	56,150	12,921	10,918	13,663	11,867
50,150	50,200	11,176	9,252	11,819	10,201	53,150	53,200	12,016	10,092	12,749	11,041	56,150	56,200	12,936	10,932	13,679	11,881
50,200	50,250	11,190	9,266	11,834	10,215	53,200	53,250	12,030	10,106	12,764	11,055	56,200	56,250	12,952	10,946	13,694	11,895
50,250	50,300	11,204	9,280	11,850	10,229	53,250	53,300	12,044	10,120	12,780	11,069	56,250	56,300	12,967	10,960	13,710	11,909
50,300	50,350	11,218	9,294	11,865	10,243	53,300	53,350	12,058	10,134	12,795	11,083	56,300	56,350	12,983	10,974	13,725	11,923
50,350	50,400	11,232	9,308	11,881	10,257	53,350	53,400	12,072	10,148	12,811	11,097	56,350	56,400	12,998	10,988	13,741	11,937
50,400	50,450	11,246	9,322	11,896	10,271	53,400	53,450	12,086	10,162	12,826	11,111	56,400	56,450	13,014	11,002	13,756	11,951
50,450	50,500	11,260	9,336	11,912	10,285	53,450	53,500	12,100	10,176	12,842	11,125	56,450	56,500	13,029	11,016	13,772	11,965
50,500	50,550	11,274	9,350	11,927	10,299	53,500	53,550	12,115	10,190	12,857	11,139	56,500	56,550	13,045	11,030	13,787	11,979
50,550	50,600	11,288	9,364	11,943	10,313	53,550	53,600	12,130	10,204	12,873	11,153	56,550	56,600	13,060	11,044	13,803	11,993
50,600	50,650	11,302	9,378	11,958	10,327	53,600	53,650	12,146	10,218	12,888	11,167	56,600	56,650	13,076	11,058	13,818	12,007
50,650	50,700	11,316	9,392	11,974	10,341	53,650	53,700	12,161	10,232	12,904	11,181	56,650	56,700	13,091	11,072	13,834	12,021
50,700	50,750	11,330	9,406	11,989	10,355	53,700	53,750	12,177	10,246	12,919	11,195	56,700	56,750	13,107	11,086	13,849	12,035
50,750	50,800	11,344	9,420	12,005	10,369	53,750	53,800	12,192	10,260	12,935	11,209	56,750	56,800	13,122	11,100	13,865	12,049
50,800	50,850	11,358	9,434	12,020	10,383	53,800	53,850	12,208	10,274	12,950	11,223	56,800	56,850	13,138	11,114	13,880	12,063
50,850	50,900	11,372	9,448	12,036	10,397	53,850	53,900	12,223	10,288	12,966	11,237	56,850	56,900	13,153	11,128	13,896	12,077
50,900	50,950	11,386	9,462	12,051	10,411	53,900	53,950	12,239	10,302	12,981	11,251	56,900	56,950	13,169	11,142	13,911	12,091
50,950	51,000	11,400	9,476	12,067	10,425	53,950	54,000	12,254	10,316	12,997	11,265	56,950	57,000	13,184	11,156	13,927	12,105
51,000						**54,000**						**57,000**					
51,000	51,050	11,414	9,490	12,082	10,439	54,000	54,050	12,270	10,330	13,012	11,279	57,000	57,050	13,200	11,170	13,942	12,119
51,050	51,100	11,428	9,504	12,098	10,453	54,050	54,100	12,285	10,344	13,028	11,293	57,050	57,100	13,215	11,184	13,958	12,133
51,100	51,150	11,442	9,518	12,113	10,467	54,100	54,150	12,301	10,358	13,043	11,307	57,100	57,150	13,231	11,198	13,973	12,147
51,150	51,200	11,456	9,532	12,129	10,481	54,150	54,200	12,316	10,372	13,059	11,321	57,150	57,200	13,246	11,212	13,989	12,161
51,200	51,250	11,470	9,546	12,144	10,495	54,200	54,250	12,332	10,386	13,074	11,335	57,200	57,250	13,262	11,226	14,004	12,175
51,250	51,300	11,484	9,560	12,160	10,509	54,250	54,300	12,347	10,400	13,090	11,349	57,250	57,300	13,277	11,240	14,020	12,189
51,300	51,350	11,498	9,574	12,175	10,523	54,300	54,350	12,363	10,414	13,105	11,363	57,300	57,350	13,293	11,254	14,035	12,203
51,350	51,400	11,512	9,588	12,191	10,537	54,350	54,400	12,378	10,428	13,121	11,377	57,350	57,400	13,308	11,268	14,051	12,217
51,400	51,450	11,526	9,602	12,206	10,551	54,400	54,450	12,394	10,442	13,136	11,391	57,400	57,450	13,324	11,282	14,066	12,231
51,450	51,500	11,540	9,616	12,222	10,565	54,450	54,500	12,409	10,456	13,152	11,405	57,450	57,500	13,339	11,296	14,082	12,245
51,500	51,550	11,554	9,630	12,237	10,579	54,500	54,550	12,425	10,470	13,167	11,419	57,500	57,550	13,355	11,310	14,097	12,259
51,550	51,600	11,568	9,644	12,253	10,593	54,550	54,600	12,440	10,484	13,183	11,433	57,550	57,600	13,370	11,324	14,113	12,273
51,600	51,650	11,582	9,658	12,268	10,607	54,600	54,650	12,456	10,498	13,198	11,447	57,600	57,650	13,386	11,338	14,128	12,287
51,650	51,700	11,596	9,672	12,284	10,621	54,650	54,700	12,471	10,512	13,214	11,461	57,650	57,700	13,401	11,352	14,144	12,301
51,700	51,750	11,610	9,686	12,299	10,635	54,700	54,750	12,487	10,526	13,229	11,475	57,700	57,750	13,417	11,366	14,159	12,315
51,750	51,800	11,624	9,700	12,315	10,649	54,750	54,800	12,502	10,540	13,245	11,489	57,750	57,800	13,432	11,380	14,175	12,329
51,800	51,850	11,638	9,714	12,330	10,663	54,800	54,850	12,518	10,554	13,260	11,503	57,800	57,850	13,448	11,394	14,190	12,343
51,850	51,900	11,652	9,728	12,346	10,677	54,850	54,900	12,533	10,568	13,276	11,517	57,850	57,900	13,463	11,408	14,206	12,357
51,900	51,950	11,666	9,742	12,361	10,691	54,900	54,950	12,549	10,582	13,291	11,531	57,900	57,950	13,479	11,422	14,221	12,371
51,950	52,000	11,680	9,756	12,377	10,705	54,950	55,000	12,564	10,596	13,307	11,545	57,950	58,000	13,494	11,436	14,237	12,385
52,000						**55,000**						**58,000**					
52,000	52,050	11,694	9,770	12,392	10,719	55,000	55,050	12,580	10,610	13,322	11,559	58,000	58,050	13,510	11,450	14,252	12,399
52,050	52,100	11,708	9,784	12,408	10,733	55,050	55,100	12,595	10,624	13,338	11,573	58,050	58,100	13,525	11,464	14,268	12,413
52,100	52,150	11,722	9,798	12,423	10,747	55,100	55,150	12,611	10,638	13,353	11,587	58,100	58,150	13,541	11,478	14,283	12,427
52,150	52,200	11,736	9,812	12,439	10,761	55,150	55,200	12,626	10,652	13,369	11,601	58,150	58,200	13,556	11,492	14,299	12,441
52,200	52,250	11,750	9,826	12,454	10,775	55,200	55,250	12,642	10,666	13,384	11,615	58,200	58,250	13,572	11,506	14,314	12,455
52,250	52,300	11,764	9,840	12,470	10,789	55,250	55,300	12,657	10,680	13,400	11,629	58,250	58,300	13,587	11,520	14,330	12,469
52,300	52,350	11,778	9,854	12,485	10,803	55,300	55,350	12,673	10,694	13,415	11,643	58,300	58,350	13,603	11,534	14,345	12,483
52,350	52,400	11,792	9,868	12,501	10,817	55,350	55,400	12,688	10,708	13,431	11,657	58,350	58,400	13,618	11,548	14,361	12,497
52,400	52,450	11,806	9,882	12,516	10,831	55,400	55,450	12,704	10,722	13,446	11,671	58,400	58,450	13,634	11,562	14,376	12,511
52,450	52,500	11,820	9,896	12,532	10,845	55,450	55,500	12,719	10,736	13,462	11,685	58,450	58,500	13,649	11,576	14,392	12,525
52,500	52,550	11,834	9,910	12,547	10,859	55,500	55,550	12,735	10,750	13,477	11,699	58,500	58,550	13,665	11,590	14,407	12,539
52,550	52,600	11,848	9,924	12,563	10,873	55,550	55,600	12,750	10,764	13,493	11,713	58,550	58,600	13,680	11,604	14,423	12,553
52,600	52,650	11,862	9,938	12,578	10,887	55,600	55,650	12,766	10,778	13,508	11,727	58,600	58,650	13,696	11,618	14,438	12,567
52,650	52,700	11,876	9,952	12,594	10,901	55,650	55,700	12,781	10,792	13,524	11,741	58,650	58,700	13,711	11,632	14,454	12,581
52,700	52,750	11,890	9,966	12,609	10,915	55,700	55,750	12,797	10,806	13,539	11,755	58,700	58,750	13,727	11,646	14,469	12,595
52,750	52,800	11,904	9,980	12,625	10,929	55,750	55,800	12,812	10,820	13,555	11,769	58,750	58,800	13,742	11,660	14,485	12,609
52,800	52,850	11,918	9,994	12,640	10,943	55,800	55,850	12,828	10,834	13,570	11,783	58,800	58,850	13,758	11,674	14,500	12,623
52,850	52,900	11,932	10,008	12,656	10,957	55,850	55,900	12,843	10,848	13,586	11,797	58,850	58,900	13,773	11,688	14,516	12,637
52,900	52,950	11,946	10,022	12,671	10,971	55,900	55,950	12,859	10,862	13,601	11,811	58,900	58,950	13,789	11,702	14,531	12,651
52,950	53,000	11,960	10,036	12,687	10,985	55,950	56,000	12,874	10,876	13,617	11,825	58,950	59,000	13,804	11,716	14,547	12,665

* This column must also be used by a qualifying widow(er).

Continued on next page

1993 Tax Table—*Continued*

If line 37 (taxable income) is—		And you are—				If line 37 (taxable income) is—		And you are—				If line 37 (taxable income) is—		And you are—			
At least	But less than	Single	Married filing jointly *	Married filing separately	Head of a household	At least	But less than	Single	Married filing jointly *	Married filing separately	Head of a household	At least	But less than	Single	Married filing jointly *	Married filing separately	Head of a household
		Your tax is—						Your tax is—						Your tax is—			
59,000						**62,000**						**65,000**					
59,000	59,050	13,820	11,730	14,562	12,679	62,000	62,050	14,750	12,570	15,492	13,519	65,000	65,050	15,680	13,410	16,422	14,359
59,050	59,100	13,835	11,744	14,578	12,693	62,050	62,100	14,765	12,584	15,508	13,533	65,050	65,100	15,695	13,424	16,438	14,373
59,100	59,150	13,851	11,758	14,593	12,707	62,100	62,150	14,781	12,598	15,523	13,547	65,100	65,150	15,711	13,438	16,453	14,387
59,150	59,200	13,866	11,772	14,609	12,721	62,150	62,200	14,796	12,612	15,539	13,561	65,150	65,200	15,726	13,452	16,469	14,401
59,200	59,250	13,882	11,786	14,624	12,735	62,200	62,250	14,812	12,626	15,554	13,575	65,200	65,250	15,742	13,466	16,484	14,415
59,250	59,300	13,897	11,800	14,640	12,749	62,250	62,300	14,827	12,640	15,570	13,589	65,250	65,300	15,757	13,480	16,500	14,429
59,300	59,350	13,913	11,814	14,655	12,763	62,300	62,350	14,843	12,654	15,585	13,603	65,300	65,350	15,773	13,494	16,515	14,443
59,350	59,400	13,928	11,828	14,671	12,777	62,350	62,400	14,858	12,668	15,601	13,617	65,350	65,400	15,788	13,508	16,531	14,457
59,400	59,450	13,944	11,842	14,686	12,791	62,400	62,450	14,874	12,682	15,616	13,631	65,400	65,450	15,804	13,522	16,546	14,471
59,450	59,500	13,959	11,856	14,702	12,805	62,450	62,500	14,889	12,696	15,632	13,645	65,450	65,500	15,819	13,536	16,562	14,485
59,500	59,550	13,975	11,870	14,717	12,819	62,500	62,550	14,905	12,710	15,647	13,659	65,500	65,550	15,835	13,550	16,577	14,499
59,550	59,600	13,990	11,884	14,733	12,833	62,550	62,600	14,920	12,724	15,663	13,673	65,550	65,600	15,850	13,564	16,593	14,513
59,600	59,650	14,006	11,898	14,748	12,847	62,600	62,650	14,936	12,738	15,678	13,687	65,600	65,650	15,866	13,578	16,608	14,527
59,650	59,700	14,021	11,912	14,764	12,861	62,650	62,700	14,951	12,752	15,694	13,701	65,650	65,700	15,881	13,592	16,624	14,541
59,700	59,750	14,037	11,926	14,779	12,875	62,700	62,750	14,967	12,766	15,709	13,715	65,700	65,750	15,897	13,606	16,639	14,555
59,750	59,800	14,052	11,940	14,795	12,889	62,750	62,800	14,982	12,780	15,725	13,729	65,750	65,800	15,912	13,620	16,655	14,569
59,800	59,850	14,068	11,954	14,810	12,903	62,800	62,850	14,998	12,794	15,740	13,743	65,800	65,850	15,928	13,634	16,670	14,583
59,850	59,900	14,083	11,968	14,826	12,917	62,850	62,900	15,013	12,808	15,756	13,757	65,850	65,900	15,943	13,648	16,686	14,597
59,900	59,950	14,099	11,982	14,841	12,931	62,900	62,950	15,029	12,822	15,771	13,771	65,900	65,950	15,959	13,662	16,701	14,611
59,950	60,000	14,114	11,996	14,857	12,945	62,950	63,000	15,044	12,836	15,787	13,785	65,950	66,000	15,974	13,676	16,717	14,625
60,000						**63,000**						**66,000**					
60,000	60,050	14,130	12,010	14,872	12,959	63,000	63,050	15,060	12,850	15,802	13,799	66,000	66,050	15,990	13,690	16,732	14,639
60,050	60,100	14,145	12,024	14,888	12,973	63,050	63,100	15,075	12,864	15,818	13,813	66,050	66,100	16,005	13,704	16,748	14,653
60,100	60,150	14,161	12,038	14,903	12,987	63,100	63,150	15,091	12,878	15,833	13,827	66,100	66,150	16,021	13,718	16,763	14,667
60,150	60,200	14,176	12,052	14,919	13,001	63,150	63,200	15,106	12,892	15,849	13,841	66,150	66,200	16,036	13,732	16,779	14,681
60,200	60,250	14,192	12,066	14,934	13,015	63,200	63,250	15,122	12,906	15,864	13,855	66,200	66,250	16,052	13,746	16,794	14,695
60,250	60,300	14,207	12,080	14,950	13,029	63,250	63,300	15,137	12,920	15,880	13,869	66,250	66,300	16,067	13,760	16,810	14,709
60,300	60,350	14,223	12,094	14,965	13,043	63,300	63,350	15,153	12,934	15,895	13,883	66,300	66,350	16,083	13,774	16,825	14,723
60,350	60,400	14,238	12,108	14,981	13,057	63,350	63,400	15,168	12,948	15,911	13,897	66,350	66,400	16,098	13,788	16,841	14,737
60,400	60,450	14,254	12,122	14,996	13,071	63,400	63,450	15,184	12,962	15,926	13,911	66,400	66,450	16,114	13,802	16,856	14,751
60,450	60,500	14,269	12,136	15,012	13,085	63,450	63,500	15,199	12,976	15,942	13,925	66,450	66,500	16,129	13,816	16,872	14,765
60,500	60,550	14,285	12,150	15,027	13,099	63,500	63,550	15,215	12,990	15,957	13,939	66,500	66,550	16,145	13,830	16,887	14,779
60,550	60,600	14,300	12,164	15,043	13,113	63,550	63,600	15,230	13,004	15,973	13,953	66,550	66,600	16,160	13,844	16,903	14,793
60,600	60,650	14,316	12,178	15,058	13,127	63,600	63,650	15,246	13,018	15,988	13,967	66,600	66,650	16,176	13,858	16,918	14,807
60,650	60,700	14,331	12,192	15,074	13,141	63,650	63,700	15,261	13,032	16,004	13,981	66,650	66,700	16,191	13,872	16,934	14,821
60,700	60,750	14,347	12,206	15,089	13,155	63,700	63,750	15,277	13,046	16,019	13,995	66,700	66,750	16,207	13,886	16,949	14,835
60,750	60,800	14,362	12,220	15,105	13,169	63,750	63,800	15,292	13,060	16,035	14,009	66,750	66,800	16,222	13,900	16,965	14,849
60,800	60,850	14,378	12,234	15,120	13,183	63,800	63,850	15,308	13,074	16,050	14,023	66,800	66,850	16,238	13,914	16,980	14,863
60,850	60,900	14,393	12,248	15,136	13,197	63,850	63,900	15,323	13,088	16,066	14,037	66,850	66,900	16,253	13,928	16,996	14,877
60,900	60,950	14,409	12,262	15,151	13,211	63,900	63,950	15,339	13,102	16,081	14,051	66,900	66,950	16,269	13,942	17,011	14,891
60,950	61,000	14,424	12,276	15,167	13,225	63,950	64,000	15,354	13,116	16,097	14,065	66,950	67,000	16,284	13,956	17,027	14,905
61,000						**64,000**						**67,000**					
61,000	61,050	14,440	12,290	15,182	13,239	64,000	64,050	15,370	13,130	16,112	14,079	67,000	67,050	16,300	13,970	17,042	14,919
61,050	61,100	14,455	12,304	15,198	13,253	64,050	64,100	15,385	13,144	16,128	14,093	67,050	67,100	16,315	13,984	17,058	14,933
61,100	61,150	14,471	12,318	15,213	13,267	64,100	64,150	15,401	13,158	16,143	14,107	67,100	67,150	16,331	13,998	17,073	14,947
61,150	61,200	14,486	12,332	15,229	13,281	64,150	64,200	15,416	13,172	16,159	14,121	67,150	67,200	16,346	14,012	17,089	14,961
61,200	61,250	14,502	12,346	15,244	13,295	64,200	64,250	15,432	13,186	16,174	14,135	67,200	67,250	16,362	14,026	17,104	14,975
61,250	61,300	14,517	12,360	15,260	13,309	64,250	64,300	15,447	13,200	16,190	14,149	67,250	67,300	16,377	14,040	17,120	14,989
61,300	61,350	14,533	12,374	15,275	13,323	64,300	64,350	15,463	13,214	16,205	14,163	67,300	67,350	16,393	14,054	17,135	15,003
61,350	61,400	14,548	12,388	15,291	13,337	64,350	64,400	15,478	13,228	16,221	14,177	67,350	67,400	16,408	14,068	17,151	15,017
61,400	61,450	14,564	12,402	15,306	13,351	64,400	64,450	15,494	13,242	16,236	14,191	67,400	67,450	16,424	14,082	17,166	15,031
61,450	61,500	14,579	12,416	15,322	13,365	64,450	64,500	15,509	13,256	16,252	14,205	67,450	67,500	16,439	14,096	17,182	15,045
61,500	61,550	14,595	12,430	15,337	13,379	64,500	64,550	15,525	13,270	16,267	14,219	67,500	67,550	16,455	14,110	17,197	15,059
61,550	61,600	14,610	12,444	15,353	13,393	64,550	64,600	15,540	13,284	16,283	14,233	67,550	67,600	16,470	14,124	17,213	15,073
61,600	61,650	14,626	12,458	15,368	13,407	64,600	64,650	15,556	13,298	16,298	14,247	67,600	67,650	16,486	14,138	17,228	15,087
61,650	61,700	14,641	12,472	15,384	13,421	64,650	64,700	15,571	13,312	16,314	14,261	67,650	67,700	16,501	14,152	17,244	15,101
61,700	61,750	14,657	12,486	15,399	13,435	64,700	64,750	15,587	13,326	16,329	14,275	67,700	67,750	16,517	14,166	17,259	15,115
61,750	61,800	14,672	12,500	15,415	13,449	64,750	64,800	15,602	13,340	16,345	14,289	67,750	67,800	16,532	14,180	17,275	15,129
61,800	61,850	14,688	12,514	15,430	13,463	64,800	64,850	15,618	13,354	16,360	14,303	67,800	67,850	16,548	14,194	17,290	15,143
61,850	61,900	14,703	12,528	15,446	13,477	64,850	64,900	15,633	13,368	16,376	14,317	67,850	67,900	16,563	14,208	17,306	15,157
61,900	61,950	14,719	12,542	15,461	13,491	64,900	64,950	15,649	13,382	16,391	14,331	67,900	67,950	16,579	14,222	17,321	15,171
61,950	62,000	14,734	12,556	15,477	13,505	64,950	65,000	15,664	13,396	16,407	14,345	67,950	68,000	16,594	14,236	17,337	15,185

* This column must also be used by a qualifying widow(er).

Continued on next page

1993 Tax Table—*Continued*

If line 37 (taxable income) is—		And you are—			
At least	But less than	Single	Married filing jointly *	Married filing separately	Head of a household
		Your tax is—			

68,000

At least	But less than	Single	MFJ *	MFS	HoH
68,000	68,050	16,610	14,250	17,352	15,199
68,050	68,100	16,625	14,264	17,368	15,213
68,100	68,150	16,641	14,278	17,383	15,227
68,150	68,200	16,656	14,292	17,399	15,241
68,200	68,250	16,672	14,306	17,414	15,255
68,250	68,300	16,687	14,320	17,430	15,269
68,300	68,350	16,703	14,334	17,445	15,283
68,350	68,400	16,718	14,348	17,461	15,297
68,400	68,450	16,734	14,362	17,476	15,311
68,450	68,500	16,749	14,376	17,492	15,325
68,500	68,550	16,765	14,390	17,507	15,339
68,550	68,600	16,780	14,404	17,523	15,353
68,600	68,650	16,796	14,418	17,538	15,367
68,650	68,700	16,811	14,432	17,554	15,381
68,700	68,750	16,827	14,446	17,569	15,395
68,750	68,800	16,842	14,460	17,585	15,409
68,800	68,850	16,858	14,474	17,600	15,423
68,850	68,900	16,873	14,488	17,616	15,437
68,900	68,950	16,889	14,502	17,631	15,451
68,950	69,000	16,904	14,516	17,647	15,465

69,000

At least	But less than	Single	MFJ *	MFS	HoH
69,000	69,050	16,920	14,530	17,662	15,479
69,050	69,100	16,935	14,544	17,678	15,493
69,100	69,150	16,951	14,558	17,693	15,507
69,150	69,200	16,966	14,572	17,709	15,521
69,200	69,250	16,982	14,586	17,724	15,535
69,250	69,300	16,997	14,600	17,740	15,549
69,300	69,350	17,013	14,614	17,755	15,563
69,350	69,400	17,028	14,628	17,771	15,577
69,400	69,450	17,044	14,642	17,786	15,591
69,450	69,500	17,059	14,656	17,802	15,605
69,500	69,550	17,075	14,670	17,817	15,619
69,550	69,600	17,090	14,684	17,833	15,633
69,600	69,650	17,106	14,698	17,848	15,647
69,650	69,700	17,121	14,712	17,864	15,661
69,700	69,750	17,137	14,726	17,879	15,675
69,750	69,800	17,152	14,740	17,895	15,689
69,800	69,850	17,168	14,754	17,910	15,703
69,850	69,900	17,183	14,768	17,926	15,717
69,900	69,950	17,199	14,782	17,941	15,731
69,950	70,000	17,214	14,796	17,957	15,745

70,000

At least	But less than	Single	MFJ *	MFS	HoH
70,000	70,050	17,230	14,810	17,973	15,759
70,050	70,100	17,245	14,824	17,991	15,773
70,100	70,150	17,261	14,838	18,009	15,787
70,150	70,200	17,276	14,852	18,027	15,801
70,200	70,250	17,292	14,866	18,045	15,815
70,250	70,300	17,307	14,880	18,063	15,829
70,300	70,350	17,323	14,894	18,081	15,843
70,350	70,400	17,338	14,908	18,099	15,857
70,400	70,450	17,354	14,922	18,117	15,871
70,450	70,500	17,369	14,936	18,135	15,885
70,500	70,550	17,385	14,950	18,153	15,899
70,550	70,600	17,400	14,964	18,171	15,913
70,600	70,650	17,416	14,978	18,189	15,927
70,650	70,700	17,431	14,992	18,207	15,941
70,700	70,750	17,447	15,006	18,225	15,955
70,750	70,800	17,462	15,020	18,243	15,969
70,800	70,850	17,478	15,034	18,261	15,983
70,850	70,900	17,493	15,048	18,279	15,997
70,900	70,950	17,509	15,062	18,297	16,011
70,950	71,000	17,524	15,076	18,315	16,025

71,000

At least	But less than	Single	MFJ *	MFS	HoH
71,000	71,050	17,540	15,090	18,333	16,039
71,050	71,100	17,555	15,104	18,351	16,053
71,100	71,150	17,571	15,118	18,369	16,067
71,150	71,200	17,586	15,132	18,387	16,081
71,200	71,250	17,602	15,146	18,405	16,095
71,250	71,300	17,617	15,160	18,423	16,109
71,300	71,350	17,633	15,174	18,441	16,123
71,350	71,400	17,648	15,188	18,459	16,137
71,400	71,450	17,664	15,202	18,477	16,151
71,450	71,500	17,679	15,216	18,495	16,165
71,500	71,550	17,695	15,230	18,513	16,179
71,550	71,600	17,710	15,244	18,531	16,193
71,600	71,650	17,726	15,258	18,549	16,207
71,650	71,700	17,741	15,272	18,567	16,221
71,700	71,750	17,757	15,286	18,585	16,235
71,750	71,800	17,772	15,300	18,603	16,249
71,800	71,850	17,788	15,314	18,621	16,263
71,850	71,900	17,803	15,328	18,639	16,277
71,900	71,950	17,819	15,342	18,657	16,291
71,950	72,000	17,834	15,356	18,675	16,305

72,000

At least	But less than	Single	MFJ *	MFS	HoH
72,000	72,050	17,850	15,370	18,693	16,319
72,050	72,100	17,865	15,384	18,711	16,333
72,100	72,150	17,881	15,398	18,729	16,347
72,150	72,200	17,896	15,412	18,747	16,361
72,200	72,250	17,912	15,426	18,765	16,375
72,250	72,300	17,927	15,440	18,783	16,389
72,300	72,350	17,943	15,454	18,801	16,403
72,350	72,400	17,958	15,468	18,819	16,417
72,400	72,450	17,974	15,482	18,837	16,431
72,450	72,500	17,989	15,496	18,855	16,445
72,500	72,550	18,005	15,510	18,873	16,459
72,550	72,600	18,020	15,524	18,891	16,473
72,600	72,650	18,036	15,538	18,909	16,487
72,650	72,700	18,051	15,552	18,927	16,501
72,700	72,750	18,067	15,566	18,945	16,515
72,750	72,800	18,082	15,580	18,963	16,529
72,800	72,850	18,098	15,594	18,981	16,543
72,850	72,900	18,113	15,608	18,999	16,557
72,900	72,950	18,129	15,622	19,017	16,571
72,950	73,000	18,144	15,636	19,035	16,585

73,000

At least	But less than	Single	MFJ *	MFS	HoH
73,000	73,050	18,160	15,650	19,053	16,599
73,050	73,100	18,175	15,664	19,071	16,613
73,100	73,150	18,191	15,678	19,089	16,627
73,150	73,200	18,206	15,692	19,107	16,641
73,200	73,250	18,222	15,706	19,125	16,655
73,250	73,300	18,237	15,720	19,143	16,669
73,300	73,350	18,253	15,734	19,161	16,683
73,350	73,400	18,268	15,748	19,179	16,697
73,400	73,450	18,284	15,762	19,197	16,711
73,450	73,500	18,299	15,776	19,215	16,725
73,500	73,550	18,315	15,790	19,233	16,739
73,550	73,600	18,330	15,804	19,251	16,753
73,600	73,650	18,346	15,818	19,269	16,767
73,650	73,700	18,361	15,832	19,287	16,781
73,700	73,750	18,377	15,846	19,305	16,795
73,750	73,800	18,392	15,860	19,323	16,809
73,800	73,850	18,408	15,874	19,341	16,823
73,850	73,900	18,423	15,888	19,359	16,837
73,900	73,950	18,439	15,902	19,377	16,851
73,950	74,000	18,454	15,916	19,395	16,865

74,000

At least	But less than	Single	MFJ *	MFS	HoH
74,000	74,050	18,470	15,930	19,413	16,879
74,050	74,100	18,485	15,944	19,431	16,893
74,100	74,150	18,501	15,958	19,449	16,907
74,150	74,200	18,516	15,972	19,467	16,921
74,200	74,250	18,532	15,986	19,485	16,935
74,250	74,300	18,547	16,000	19,503	16,949
74,300	74,350	18,563	16,014	19,521	16,963
74,350	74,400	18,578	16,028	19,539	16,977
74,400	74,450	18,594	16,042	19,557	16,991
74,450	74,500	18,609	16,056	19,575	17,005
74,500	74,550	18,625	16,070	19,593	17,019
74,550	74,600	18,640	16,084	19,611	17,033
74,600	74,650	18,656	16,098	19,629	17,047
74,650	74,700	18,671	16,112	19,647	17,061
74,700	74,750	18,687	16,126	19,665	17,075
74,750	74,800	18,702	16,140	19,683	17,089
74,800	74,850	18,718	16,154	19,701	17,103
74,850	74,900	18,733	16,168	19,719	17,117
74,900	74,950	18,749	16,182	19,737	17,131
74,950	75,000	18,764	16,196	19,755	17,145

75,000

At least	But less than	Single	MFJ *	MFS	HoH
75,000	75,050	18,780	16,210	19,773	17,159
75,050	75,100	18,795	16,224	19,791	17,173
75,100	75,150	18,811	16,238	19,809	17,187
75,150	75,200	18,826	16,252	19,827	17,201
75,200	75,250	18,842	16,266	19,845	17,215
75,250	75,300	18,857	16,280	19,863	17,229
75,300	75,350	18,873	16,294	19,881	17,243
75,350	75,400	18,888	16,308	19,899	17,257
75,400	75,450	18,904	16,322	19,917	17,271
75,450	75,500	18,919	16,336	19,935	17,285
75,500	75,550	18,935	16,350	19,953	17,299
75,550	75,600	18,950	16,364	19,971	17,313
75,600	75,650	18,966	16,378	19,989	17,327
75,650	75,700	18,981	16,392	20,007	17,341
75,700	75,750	18,997	16,406	20,025	17,355
75,750	75,800	19,012	16,420	20,043	17,369
75,800	75,850	19,028	16,434	20,061	17,383
75,850	75,900	19,043	16,448	20,079	17,397
75,900	75,950	19,059	16,462	20,097	17,411
75,950	76,000	19,074	16,476	20,115	17,425

76,000

At least	But less than	Single	MFJ *	MFS	HoH
76,000	76,050	19,090	16,490	20,133	17,439
76,050	76,100	19,105	16,504	20,151	17,453
76,100	76,150	19,121	16,518	20,169	17,467
76,150	76,200	19,136	16,532	20,187	17,481
76,200	76,250	19,152	16,546	20,205	17,495
76,250	76,300	19,167	16,560	20,223	17,509
76,300	76,350	19,183	16,574	20,241	17,523
76,350	76,400	19,198	16,588	20,259	17,537
76,400	76,450	19,214	16,602	20,277	17,552
76,450	76,500	19,229	16,616	20,295	17,567
76,500	76,550	19,245	16,630	20,313	17,583
76,550	76,600	19,260	16,644	20,331	17,598
76,600	76,650	19,276	16,658	20,349	17,614
76,650	76,700	19,291	16,672	20,367	17,629
76,700	76,750	19,307	16,686	20,385	17,645
76,750	76,800	19,322	16,700	20,403	17,660
76,800	76,850	19,338	16,714	20,421	17,676
76,850	76,900	19,353	16,728	20,439	17,691
76,900	76,950	19,369	16,742	20,457	17,707
76,950	77,000	19,384	16,756	20,475	17,722

* This column must also be used by a qualifying widow(er).

Continued on next page

1993 Tax Table—*Continued*

77,000

At least	But less than	Single	Married filing jointly *	Married filing separately	Head of a household
77,000	77,050	19,400	16,770	20,493	17,738
77,050	77,100	19,415	16,784	20,511	17,753
77,100	77,150	19,431	16,798	20,529	17,769
77,150	77,200	19,446	16,812	20,547	17,784
77,200	77,250	19,462	16,826	20,565	17,800
77,250	77,300	19,477	16,840	20,583	17,815
77,300	77,350	19,493	16,854	20,601	17,831
77,350	77,400	19,508	16,868	20,619	17,846
77,400	77,450	19,524	16,882	20,637	17,862
77,450	77,500	19,539	16,896	20,655	17,877
77,500	77,550	19,555	16,910	20,673	17,893
77,550	77,600	19,570	16,924	20,691	17,908
77,600	77,650	19,586	16,938	20,709	17,924
77,650	77,700	19,601	16,952	20,727	17,939
77,700	77,750	19,617	16,966	20,745	17,955
77,750	77,800	19,632	16,980	20,763	17,970
77,800	77,850	19,648	16,994	20,781	17,986
77,850	77,900	19,663	17,008	20,799	18,001
77,900	77,950	19,679	17,022	20,817	18,017
77,950	78,000	19,694	17,036	20,835	18,032

78,000

At least	But less than	Single	Married filing jointly *	Married filing separately	Head of a household
78,000	78,050	19,710	17,050	20,853	18,048
78,050	78,100	19,725	17,064	20,871	18,063
78,100	78,150	19,741	17,078	20,889	18,079
78,150	78,200	19,756	17,092	20,907	18,094
78,200	78,250	19,772	17,106	20,925	18,110
78,250	78,300	19,787	17,120	20,943	18,125
78,300	78,350	19,803	17,134	20,961	18,141
78,350	78,400	19,818	17,148	20,979	18,156
78,400	78,450	19,834	17,162	20,997	18,172
78,450	78,500	19,849	17,176	21,015	18,187
78,500	78,550	19,865	17,190	21,033	18,203
78,550	78,600	19,880	17,204	21,051	18,218
78,600	78,650	19,896	17,218	21,069	18,234
78,650	78,700	19,911	17,232	21,087	18,249
78,700	78,750	19,927	17,246	21,105	18,265
78,750	78,800	19,942	17,260	21,123	18,280
78,800	78,850	19,958	17,274	21,141	18,296
78,850	78,900	19,973	17,288	21,159	18,311
78,900	78,950	19,989	17,302	21,177	18,327
78,950	79,000	20,004	17,316	21,195	18,342

79,000

At least	But less than	Single	Married filing jointly *	Married filing separately	Head of a household
79,000	79,050	20,020	17,330	21,213	18,358
79,050	79,100	20,035	17,344	21,231	18,373
79,100	79,150	20,051	17,358	21,249	18,389
79,150	79,200	20,066	17,372	21,267	18,404
79,200	79,250	20,082	17,386	21,285	18,420
79,250	79,300	20,097	17,400	21,303	18,435
79,300	79,350	20,113	17,414	21,321	18,451
79,350	79,400	20,128	17,428	21,339	18,466
79,400	79,450	20,144	17,442	21,357	18,482
79,450	79,500	20,159	17,456	21,375	18,497
79,500	79,550	20,175	17,470	21,393	18,513
79,550	79,600	20,190	17,484	21,411	18,528
79,600	79,650	20,206	17,498	21,429	18,544
79,650	79,700	20,221	17,512	21,447	18,559
79,700	79,750	20,237	17,526	21,465	18,575
79,750	79,800	20,252	17,540	21,483	18,590
79,800	79,850	20,268	17,554	21,501	18,606
79,850	79,900	20,283	17,568	21,519	18,621
79,900	79,950	20,299	17,582	21,537	18,637
79,950	80,000	20,314	17,596	21,555	18,652

80,000

At least	But less than	Single	Married filing jointly *	Married filing separately	Head of a household
80,000	80,050	20,330	17,610	21,573	18,668
80,050	80,100	20,345	17,624	21,591	18,683
80,100	80,150	20,361	17,638	21,609	18,699
80,150	80,200	20,376	17,652	21,627	18,714
80,200	80,250	20,392	17,666	21,645	18,730
80,250	80,300	20,407	17,680	21,663	18,745
80,300	80,350	20,423	17,694	21,681	18,761
80,350	80,400	20,438	17,708	21,699	18,776
80,400	80,450	20,454	17,722	21,717	18,792
80,450	80,500	20,469	17,736	21,735	18,807
80,500	80,550	20,485	17,750	21,753	18,823
80,550	80,600	20,500	17,764	21,771	18,838
80,600	80,650	20,516	17,778	21,789	18,854
80,650	80,700	20,531	17,792	21,807	18,869
80,700	80,750	20,547	17,806	21,825	18,885
80,750	80,800	20,562	17,820	21,843	18,900
80,800	80,850	20,578	17,834	21,861	18,916
80,850	80,900	20,593	17,848	21,879	18,931
80,900	80,950	20,609	17,862	21,897	18,947
80,950	81,000	20,624	17,876	21,915	18,962

81,000

At least	But less than	Single	Married filing jointly *	Married filing separately	Head of a household
81,000	81,050	20,640	17,890	21,933	18,978
81,050	81,100	20,655	17,904	21,951	18,993
81,100	81,150	20,671	17,918	21,969	19,009
81,150	81,200	20,686	17,932	21,987	19,024
81,200	81,250	20,702	17,946	22,005	19,040
81,250	81,300	20,717	17,960	22,023	19,055
81,300	81,350	20,733	17,974	22,041	19,071
81,350	81,400	20,748	17,988	22,059	19,086
81,400	81,450	20,764	18,002	22,077	19,102
81,450	81,500	20,779	18,016	22,095	19,117
81,500	81,550	20,795	18,030	22,113	19,133
81,550	81,600	20,810	18,044	22,131	19,148
81,600	81,650	20,826	18,058	22,149	19,164
81,650	81,700	20,841	18,072	22,167	19,179
81,700	81,750	20,857	18,086	22,185	19,195
81,750	81,800	20,872	18,100	22,203	19,210
81,800	81,850	20,888	18,114	22,221	19,226
81,850	81,900	20,903	18,128	22,239	19,241
81,900	81,950	20,919	18,142	22,257	19,257
81,950	82,000	20,934	18,156	22,275	19,272

82,000

At least	But less than	Single	Married filing jointly *	Married filing separately	Head of a household
82,000	82,050	20,950	18,170	22,293	19,288
82,050	82,100	20,965	18,184	22,311	19,303
82,100	82,150	20,981	18,198	22,329	19,319
82,150	82,200	20,996	18,212	22,347	19,334
82,200	82,250	21,012	18,226	22,365	19,350
82,250	82,300	21,027	18,240	22,383	19,365
82,300	82,350	21,043	18,254	22,401	19,381
82,350	82,400	21,058	18,268	22,419	19,396
82,400	82,450	21,074	18,282	22,437	19,412
82,450	82,500	21,089	18,296	22,455	19,427
82,500	82,550	21,105	18,310	22,473	19,443
82,550	82,600	21,120	18,324	22,491	19,458
82,600	82,650	21,136	18,338	22,509	19,474
82,650	82,700	21,151	18,352	22,527	19,489
82,700	82,750	21,167	18,366	22,545	19,505
82,750	82,800	21,182	18,380	22,563	19,520
82,800	82,850	21,198	18,394	22,581	19,536
82,850	82,900	21,213	18,408	22,599	19,551
82,900	82,950	21,229	18,422	22,617	19,567
82,950	83,000	21,244	18,436	22,635	19,582

83,000

At least	But less than	Single	Married filing jointly *	Married filing separately	Head of a household
83,000	83,050	21,260	18,450	22,653	19,598
83,050	83,100	21,275	18,464	22,671	19,613
83,100	83,150	21,291	18,478	22,689	19,629
83,150	83,200	21,306	18,492	22,707	19,644
83,200	83,250	21,322	18,506	22,725	19,660
83,250	83,300	21,337	18,520	22,743	19,675
83,300	83,350	21,353	18,534	22,761	19,691
83,350	83,400	21,368	18,548	22,779	19,706
83,400	83,450	21,384	18,562	22,797	19,722
83,450	83,500	21,399	18,576	22,815	19,737
83,500	83,550	21,415	18,590	22,833	19,753
83,550	83,600	21,430	18,604	22,851	19,768
83,600	83,650	21,446	18,618	22,869	19,784
83,650	83,700	21,461	18,632	22,887	19,799
83,700	83,750	21,477	18,646	22,905	19,815
83,750	83,800	21,492	18,660	22,923	19,830
83,800	83,850	21,508	18,674	22,941	19,846
83,850	83,900	21,523	18,688	22,959	19,861
83,900	83,950	21,539	18,702	22,977	19,877
83,950	84,000	21,554	18,716	22,995	19,892

84,000

At least	But less than	Single	Married filing jointly *	Married filing separately	Head of a household
84,000	84,050	21,570	18,730	23,013	19,908
84,050	84,100	21,585	18,744	23,031	19,923
84,100	84,150	21,601	18,758	23,049	19,939
84,150	84,200	21,616	18,772	23,067	19,954
84,200	84,250	21,632	18,786	23,085	19,970
84,250	84,300	21,647	18,800	23,103	19,985
84,300	84,350	21,663	18,814	23,121	20,001
84,350	84,400	21,678	18,828	23,139	20,016
84,400	84,450	21,694	18,842	23,157	20,032
84,450	84,500	21,709	18,856	23,175	20,047
84,500	84,550	21,725	18,870	23,193	20,063
84,550	84,600	21,740	18,884	23,211	20,078
84,600	84,650	21,756	18,898	23,229	20,094
84,650	84,700	21,771	18,912	23,247	20,109
84,700	84,750	21,787	18,926	23,265	20,125
84,750	84,800	21,802	18,940	23,283	20,140
84,800	84,850	21,818	18,954	23,301	20,156
84,850	84,900	21,833	18,968	23,319	20,171
84,900	84,950	21,849	18,982	23,337	20,187
84,950	85,000	21,864	18,996	23,355	20,202

85,000

At least	But less than	Single	Married filing jointly *	Married filing separately	Head of a household
85,000	85,050	21,880	19,010	23,373	20,218
85,050	85,100	21,895	19,024	23,391	20,233
85,100	85,150	21,911	19,038	23,409	20,249
85,150	85,200	21,926	19,052	23,427	20,264
85,200	85,250	21,942	19,066	23,445	20,280
85,250	85,300	21,957	19,080	23,463	20,295
85,300	85,350	21,973	19,094	23,481	20,311
85,350	85,400	21,988	19,108	23,499	20,326
85,400	85,450	22,004	19,122	23,517	20,342
85,450	85,500	22,019	19,136	23,535	20,357
85,500	85,550	22,035	19,150	23,553	20,373
85,550	85,600	22,050	19,164	23,571	20,388
85,600	85,650	22,066	19,178	23,589	20,404
85,650	85,700	22,081	19,192	23,607	20,419
85,700	85,750	22,097	19,206	23,625	20,435
85,750	85,800	22,112	19,220	23,643	20,450
85,800	85,850	22,128	19,234	23,661	20,466
85,850	85,900	22,143	19,248	23,679	20,481
85,900	85,950	22,159	19,262	23,697	20,497
85,950	86,000	22,174	19,276	23,715	20,512

* This column must also be used by a qualifying widow(er).

Continued on next page

1993 Tax Table—*Continued*

If line 37 (taxable income) is—		And you are—				If line 37 (taxable income) is—		And you are—				If line 37 (taxable income) is—		And you are—			
At least	But less than	Single	Married filing jointly *	Married filing separately	Head of a household	At least	But less than	Single	Married filing jointly *	Married filing separately	Head of a household	At least	But less than	Single	Married filing jointly *	Married filing separately	Head of a household
		Your tax is—						Your tax is—						Your tax is—			
86,000						**89,000**						**92,000**					
86,000	86,050	22,190	19,290	23,733	20,528	89,000	89,050	23,120	20,130	24,813	21,458	92,000	92,050	24,050	21,056	25,893	22,388
86,050	86,100	22,205	19,304	23,751	20,543	89,050	89,100	23,135	20,144	24,831	21,473	92,050	92,100	24,065	21,072	25,911	22,403
86,100	86,150	22,221	19,318	23,769	20,559	89,100	89,150	23,151	20,158	24,849	21,489	92,100	92,150	24,081	21,087	25,929	22,419
86,150	86,200	22,236	19,332	23,787	20,574	89,150	89,200	23,166	20,173	24,867	21,504	92,150	92,200	24,096	21,103	25,947	22,434
86,200	86,250	22,252	19,346	23,805	20,590	89,200	89,250	23,182	20,188	24,885	21,520	92,200	92,250	24,112	21,118	25,965	22,450
86,250	86,300	22,267	19,360	23,823	20,605	89,250	89,300	23,197	20,204	24,903	21,535	92,250	92,300	24,127	21,134	25,983	22,465
86,300	86,350	22,283	19,374	23,841	20,621	89,300	89,350	23,213	20,219	24,921	21,551	92,300	92,350	24,143	21,149	26,001	22,481
86,350	86,400	22,298	19,388	23,859	20,636	89,350	89,400	23,228	20,235	24,939	21,566	92,350	92,400	24,158	21,165	26,019	22,496
86,400	86,450	22,314	19,402	23,877	20,652	89,400	89,450	23,244	20,250	24,957	21,582	92,400	92,450	24,174	21,180	26,037	22,512
86,450	86,500	22,329	19,416	23,895	20,667	89,450	89,500	23,259	20,266	24,975	21,597	92,450	92,500	24,189	21,196	26,055	22,527
86,500	86,550	22,345	19,430	23,913	20,683	89,500	89,550	23,275	20,281	24,993	21,613	92,500	92,550	24,205	21,211	26,073	22,543
86,550	86,600	22,360	19,444	23,931	20,698	89,550	89,600	23,290	20,297	25,011	21,628	92,550	92,600	24,220	21,227	26,091	22,558
86,600	86,650	22,376	19,458	23,949	20,714	89,600	89,650	23,306	20,312	25,029	21,644	92,600	92,650	24,236	21,242	26,109	22,574
86,650	86,700	22,391	19,472	23,967	20,729	89,650	89,700	23,321	20,328	25,047	21,659	92,650	92,700	24,251	21,258	26,127	22,589
86,700	86,750	22,407	19,486	23,985	20,745	89,700	89,750	23,337	20,343	25,065	21,675	92,700	92,750	24,267	21,273	26,145	22,605
86,750	86,800	22,422	19,500	24,003	20,760	89,750	89,800	23,352	20,359	25,083	21,690	92,750	92,800	24,282	21,289	26,163	22,620
86,800	86,850	22,438	19,514	24,021	20,776	89,800	89,850	23,368	20,374	25,101	21,706	92,800	92,850	24,298	21,304	26,181	22,636
86,850	86,900	22,453	19,528	24,039	20,791	89,850	89,900	23,383	20,390	25,119	21,721	92,850	92,900	24,313	21,320	26,199	22,651
86,900	86,950	22,469	19,542	24,057	20,807	89,900	89,950	23,399	20,405	25,137	21,737	92,900	92,950	24,329	21,335	26,217	22,667
86,950	87,000	22,484	19,556	24,075	20,822	89,950	90,000	23,414	20,421	25,155	21,752	92,950	93,000	24,344	21,351	26,235	22,682
87,000						**90,000**						**93,000**					
87,000	87,050	22,500	19,570	24,093	20,838	90,000	90,050	23,430	20,436	25,173	21,768	93,000	93,050	24,360	21,366	26,253	22,698
87,050	87,100	22,515	19,584	24,111	20,853	90,050	90,100	23,445	20,452	25,191	21,783	93,050	93,100	24,375	21,382	26,271	22,713
87,100	87,150	22,531	19,598	24,129	20,869	90,100	90,150	23,461	20,467	25,209	21,799	93,100	93,150	24,391	21,397	26,289	22,729
87,150	87,200	22,546	19,612	24,147	20,884	90,150	90,200	23,476	20,483	25,227	21,814	93,150	93,200	24,406	21,413	26,307	22,744
87,200	87,250	22,562	19,626	24,165	20,900	90,200	90,250	23,492	20,498	25,245	21,830	93,200	93,250	24,422	21,428	26,325	22,760
87,250	87,300	22,577	19,640	24,183	20,915	90,250	90,300	23,507	20,514	25,263	21,845	93,250	93,300	24,437	21,444	26,343	22,775
87,300	87,350	22,593	19,654	24,201	20,931	90,300	90,350	23,523	20,529	25,281	21,861	93,300	93,350	24,453	21,459	26,361	22,791
87,350	87,400	22,608	19,668	24,219	20,946	90,350	90,400	23,538	20,545	25,299	21,876	93,350	93,400	24,468	21,475	26,379	22,806
87,400	87,450	22,624	19,682	24,237	20,962	90,400	90,450	23,554	20,560	25,317	21,892	93,400	93,450	24,484	21,490	26,397	22,822
87,450	87,500	22,639	19,696	24,255	20,977	90,450	90,500	23,569	20,576	25,335	21,907	93,450	93,500	24,499	21,506	26,415	22,837
87,500	87,550	22,655	19,710	24,273	20,993	90,500	90,550	23,585	20,591	25,353	21,923	93,500	93,550	24,515	21,521	26,433	22,853
87,550	87,600	22,670	19,724	24,291	21,008	90,550	90,600	23,600	20,607	25,371	21,938	93,550	93,600	24,530	21,537	26,451	22,868
87,600	87,650	22,686	19,738	24,309	21,024	90,600	90,650	23,616	20,622	25,389	21,954	93,600	93,650	24,546	21,552	26,469	22,884
87,650	87,700	22,701	19,752	24,327	21,039	90,650	90,700	23,631	20,638	25,407	21,969	93,650	93,700	24,561	21,568	26,487	22,899
87,700	87,750	22,717	19,766	24,345	21,055	90,700	90,750	23,647	20,653	25,425	21,985	93,700	93,750	24,577	21,583	26,505	22,915
87,750	87,800	22,732	19,780	24,363	21,070	90,750	90,800	23,662	20,669	25,443	22,000	93,750	93,800	24,592	21,599	26,523	22,930
87,800	87,850	22,748	19,794	24,381	21,086	90,800	90,850	23,678	20,684	25,461	22,016	93,800	93,850	24,608	21,614	26,541	22,946
87,850	87,900	22,763	19,808	24,399	21,101	90,850	90,900	23,693	20,700	25,479	22,031	93,850	93,900	24,623	21,630	26,559	22,961
87,900	87,950	22,779	19,822	24,417	21,117	90,900	90,950	23,709	20,715	25,497	22,047	93,900	93,950	24,639	21,645	26,577	22,977
87,950	88,000	22,794	19,836	24,435	21,132	90,950	91,000	23,724	20,731	25,515	22,062	93,950	94,000	24,654	21,661	26,595	22,992
88,000						**91,000**						**94,000**					
88,000	88,050	22,810	19,850	24,453	21,148	91,000	91,050	23,740	20,746	25,533	22,078	94,000	94,050	24,670	21,676	26,613	23,008
88,050	88,100	22,825	19,864	24,471	21,163	91,050	91,100	23,755	20,762	25,551	22,093	94,050	94,100	24,685	21,692	26,631	23,023
88,100	88,150	22,841	19,878	24,489	21,179	91,100	91,150	23,771	20,777	25,569	22,109	94,100	94,150	24,701	21,707	26,649	23,039
88,150	88,200	22,856	19,892	24,507	21,194	91,150	91,200	23,786	20,793	25,587	22,124	94,150	94,200	24,716	21,723	26,667	23,054
88,200	88,250	22,872	19,906	24,525	21,210	91,200	91,250	23,802	20,808	25,605	22,140	94,200	94,250	24,732	21,738	26,685	23,070
88,250	88,300	22,887	19,920	24,543	21,225	91,250	91,300	23,817	20,824	25,623	22,155	94,250	94,300	24,747	21,754	26,703	23,085
88,300	88,350	22,903	19,934	24,561	21,241	91,300	91,350	23,833	20,839	25,641	22,171	94,300	94,350	24,763	21,769	26,721	23,101
88,350	88,400	22,918	19,948	24,579	21,256	91,350	91,400	23,848	20,855	25,659	22,186	94,350	94,400	24,778	21,785	26,739	23,116
88,400	88,450	22,934	19,962	24,597	21,272	91,400	91,450	23,864	20,870	25,677	22,202	94,400	94,450	24,794	21,800	26,757	23,132
88,450	88,500	22,949	19,976	24,615	21,287	91,450	91,500	23,879	20,886	25,695	22,217	94,450	94,500	24,809	21,816	26,775	23,147
88,500	88,550	22,965	19,990	24,633	21,303	91,500	91,550	23,895	20,901	25,713	22,233	94,500	94,550	24,825	21,831	26,793	23,163
88,550	88,600	22,980	20,004	24,651	21,318	91,550	91,600	23,910	20,917	25,731	22,248	94,550	94,600	24,840	21,847	26,811	23,178
88,600	88,650	22,996	20,018	24,669	21,334	91,600	91,650	23,926	20,932	25,749	22,264	94,600	94,650	24,856	21,862	26,829	23,194
88,650	88,700	23,011	20,032	24,687	21,349	91,650	91,700	23,941	20,948	25,767	22,279	94,650	94,700	24,871	21,878	26,847	23,209
88,700	88,750	23,027	20,046	24,705	21,365	91,700	91,750	23,957	20,963	25,785	22,295	94,700	94,750	24,887	21,893	26,865	23,225
88,750	88,800	23,042	20,060	24,723	21,380	91,750	91,800	23,972	20,979	25,803	22,310	94,750	94,800	24,902	21,909	26,883	23,240
88,800	88,850	23,058	20,074	24,741	21,396	91,800	91,850	23,988	20,994	25,821	22,326	94,800	94,850	24,918	21,924	26,901	23,256
88,850	88,900	23,073	20,088	24,759	21,411	91,850	91,900	24,003	21,010	25,839	22,341	94,850	94,900	24,933	21,940	26,919	23,271
88,900	88,950	23,089	20,102	24,777	21,427	91,900	91,950	24,019	21,025	25,857	22,357	94,900	94,950	24,949	21,955	26,937	23,287
88,950	89,000	23,104	20,116	24,795	21,442	91,950	92,000	24,034	21,041	25,875	22,372	94,950	95,000	24,964	21,971	26,955	23,302

* This column must also be used by a qualifying widow(er).

Continued on next page

1993 Tax Table—*Continued*

If line 37 (taxable income) is—		And you are—				If line 37 (taxable income) is—		And you are—			
At least	But less than	Single	Married filing jointly *	Married filing separately	Head of a household	At least	But less than	Single	Married filing jointly *	Married filing separately	Head of a household
		Your tax is—						Your tax is—			

95,000

95,000	95,050	24,980	21,986	26,973	23,318
95,050	95,100	24,995	22,002	26,991	23,333
95,100	95,150	25,011	22,017	27,009	23,349
95,150	95,200	25,026	22,033	27,027	23,364
95,200	95,250	25,042	22,048	27,045	23,380
95,250	95,300	25,057	22,064	27,063	23,395
95,300	95,350	25,073	22,079	27,081	23,411
95,350	95,400	25,088	22,095	27,099	23,426
95,400	95,450	25,104	22,110	27,117	23,442
95,450	95,500	25,119	22,126	27,135	23,457
95,500	95,550	25,135	22,141	27,153	23,473
95,550	95,600	25,150	22,157	27,171	23,488
95,600	95,650	25,166	22,172	27,189	23,504
95,650	95,700	25,181	22,188	27,207	23,519
95,700	95,750	25,197	22,203	27,225	23,535
95,750	95,800	25,212	22,219	27,243	23,550
95,800	95,850	25,228	22,234	27,261	23,566
95,850	95,900	25,243	22,250	27,279	23,581
95,900	95,950	25,259	22,265	27,297	23,597
95,950	96,000	25,274	22,281	27,315	23,612

96,000

96,000	96,050	25,290	22,296	27,333	23,628
96,050	96,100	25,305	22,312	27,351	23,643
96,100	96,150	25,321	22,327	27,369	23,659
96,150	96,200	25,336	22,343	27,387	23,674
96,200	96,250	25,352	22,358	27,405	23,690
96,250	96,300	25,367	22,374	27,423	23,705
96,300	96,350	25,383	22,389	27,441	23,721
96,350	96,400	25,398	22,405	27,459	23,736
96,400	96,450	25,414	22,420	27,477	23,752
96,450	96,500	25,429	22,436	27,495	23,767
96,500	96,550	25,445	22,451	27,513	23,783
96,550	96,600	25,460	22,467	27,531	23,798
96,600	96,650	25,476	22,482	27,549	23,814
96,650	96,700	25,491	22,498	27,567	23,829
96,700	96,750	25,507	22,513	27,585	23,845
96,750	96,800	25,522	22,529	27,603	23,860
96,800	96,850	25,538	22,544	27,621	23,876
96,850	96,900	25,553	22,560	27,639	23,891
96,900	96,950	25,569	22,575	27,657	23,907
96,950	97,000	25,584	22,591	27,675	23,922

97,000

97,000	97,050	25,600	22,606	27,693	23,938
97,050	97,100	25,615	22,622	27,711	23,953
97,100	97,150	25,631	22,637	27,729	23,969
97,150	97,200	25,646	22,653	27,747	23,984
97,200	97,250	25,662	22,668	27,765	24,000
97,250	97,300	25,677	22,684	27,783	24,015
97,300	97,350	25,693	22,699	27,801	24,031
97,350	97,400	25,708	22,715	27,819	24,046
97,400	97,450	25,724	22,730	27,837	24,062
97,450	97,500	25,739	22,746	27,855	24,077
97,500	97,550	25,755	22,761	27,873	24,093
97,550	97,600	25,770	22,777	27,891	24,108
97,600	97,650	25,786	22,792	27,909	24,124
97,650	97,700	25,801	22,808	27,927	24,139
97,700	97,750	25,817	22,823	27,945	24,155
97,750	97,800	25,832	22,839	27,963	24,170
97,800	97,850	25,848	22,854	27,981	24,186
97,850	97,900	25,863	22,870	27,999	24,201
97,900	97,950	25,879	22,885	28,017	24,217
97,950	98,000	25,894	22,901	28,035	24,232

98,000

98,000	98,050	25,910	22,916	28,053	24,248
98,050	98,100	25,925	22,932	28,071	24,263
98,100	98,150	25,941	22,947	28,089	24,279
98,150	98,200	25,956	22,963	28,107	24,294
98,200	98,250	25,972	22,978	28,125	24,310
98,250	98,300	25,987	22,994	28,143	24,325
98,300	98,350	26,003	23,009	28,161	24,341
98,350	98,400	26,018	23,025	28,179	24,356
98,400	98,450	26,034	23,040	28,197	24,372
98,450	98,500	26,049	23,056	28,215	24,387
98,500	98,550	26,065	23,071	28,233	24,403
98,550	98,600	26,080	23,087	28,251	24,418
98,600	98,650	26,096	23,102	28,269	24,434
98,650	98,700	26,111	23,118	28,287	24,449
98,700	98,750	26,127	23,133	28,305	24,465
98,750	98,800	26,142	23,149	28,323	24,480
98,800	98,850	26,158	23,164	28,341	24,496
98,850	98,900	26,173	23,180	28,359	24,511
98,900	98,950	26,189	23,195	28,377	24,527
98,950	99,000	26,204	23,211	28,395	24,542

99,000

99,000	99,050	26,220	23,226	28,413	24,558
99,050	99,100	26,235	23,242	28,431	24,573
99,100	99,150	26,251	23,257	28,449	24,589
99,150	99,200	26,266	23,273	28,467	24,604
99,200	99,250	26,282	23,288	28,485	24,620
99,250	99,300	26,297	23,304	28,503	24,635
99,300	99,350	26,313	23,319	28,521	24,651
99,350	99,400	26,328	23,335	28,539	24,666
99,400	99,450	26,344	23,350	28,557	24,682
99,450	99,500	26,359	23,366	28,575	24,697
99,500	99,550	26,375	23,381	28,593	24,713
99,550	99,600	26,390	23,397	28,611	24,728
99,600	99,650	26,406	23,412	28,629	24,744
99,650	99,700	26,421	23,428	28,647	24,759
99,700	99,750	26,437	23,443	28,665	24,775
99,750	99,800	26,452	23,459	28,683	24,790
99,800	99,850	26,468	23,474	28,701	24,806
99,850	99,900	26,483	23,490	28,719	24,821
99,900	99,950	26,499	23,505	28,737	24,837
99,950	100,000	26,514	23,521	28,755	24,852

$100,000 or over — use Tax Rate Schedules

* This column must also be used by a qualifying widow(er).

1993 Tax Rate Schedules

Caution: *Use **only** if your taxable income (Form 1040, line 37) is $100,000 or more. If less, use the **Tax Table**. Even though you cannot use the tax rate schedules below if your taxable income is less than $100,000, all levels of taxable income are shown so taxpayers can see the tax rate that applies to each level.*

Schedule X—Use if your filing status is **Single**

If the amount on Form 1040, line 37, is: Over—	But not over—	Enter on Form 1040, line 38	of the amount over—
$0	$22,100	.... 15%	$0
22,100	53,500	$3,315.00 + 28%	22,100
53,500	115,000	12,107.00 + 31%	53,500
115,000	250,000	31,172.00 + 36%	115,000
250,000	....	79,772.00 + 39.6%	250,000

Schedule Y-1—Use if your filing status is **Married filing jointly** or **Qualifying widow(er)**

If the amount on Form 1040, line 37, is: Over—	But not over—	Enter on Form 1040, line 38	of the amount over—
$0	$36,900	.... 15%	$0
36,900	89,150	$5,535.00 + 28%	36,900
89,150	140,000	20,165.00 + 31%	89,150
140,000	250,000	35,928.50 + 36%	140,000
250,000	....	75,528.50 + 39.6%	250,000

Schedule Y-2—Use if your filing status is **Married filing separately**

If the amount on Form 1040, line 37, is: Over—	But not over—	Enter on Form 1040, line 38	of the amount over—
$0	$18,450	.... 15%	$0
18,450	44,575	$2,767.50 + 28%	18,450
44,575	70,000	10,082.50 + 31%	44,575
70,000	125,000	17,964.25 + 36%	70,000
125,000	....	37,764.25 + 39.6%	125,000

Schedule Z—Use if your filing status is **Head of household**

If the amount on Form 1040, line 37, is: Over—	But not over—	Enter on Form 1040, line 38	of the amount over—
$0	$29,600	.... 15%	$0
29,600	76,400	$4,440.00 + 28%	29,600
76,400	127,500	17,544.00 + 31%	76,400
127,500	250,000	33,385.00 + 36%	127,500
250,000	....	77,485.00 + 39.6%	250,000

TABLE A—Basic Credit
1993 Earned Income Credit

Caution: This is **not** a tax table.

To find your basic credit: First, read down the "At least — But less than" columns and find the line that includes the amount you entered on line 7 or line 9 of Schedule EIC. Next, read across to the column that includes the number of qualifying children you listed on Schedule EIC. Then, enter the credit from that column on Schedule EIC, line 8 or line 10, whichever applies.

If the amount on Schedule EIC, line 7 or line 9, is— At least	But less than	One child	Two children	If the amount on Schedule EIC, line 7 or line 9, is— At least	But less than	One child	Two children	If the amount on Schedule EIC, line 7 or line 9, is— At least	But less than	One child	Two children	If the amount on Schedule EIC, line 7 or line 9, is— At least	But less than	One child	Two children
$1	$50	$5	$5	2,800	2,850	523	551	5,600	5,650	1,041	1,097	12,800	12,850	1,351	1,424
50	100	14	15	2,850	2,900	532	561	5,650	5,700	1,050	1,107	12,850	12,900	1,345	1,417
100	150	23	24	2,900	2,950	541	570	5,700	5,750	1,059	1,116	12,900	12,950	1,338	1,410
150	200	32	34	2,950	3,000	550	580	5,750	5,800	1,068	1,126	12,950	13,000	1,331	1,403
200	250	42	44	3,000	3,050	560	590	5,800	5,850	1,078	1,136	13,000	13,050	1,325	1,396
250	300	51	54	3,050	3,100	569	600	5,850	5,900	1,087	1,146	13,050	13,100	1,318	1,389
300	350	60	63	3,100	3,150	578	609	5,900	5,950	1,096	1,155	13,100	13,150	1,312	1,382
350	400	69	73	3,150	3,200	587	619	5,950	6,000	1,105	1,165	13,150	13,200	1,305	1,375
400	450	79	83	3,200	3,250	597	629	6,000	6,050	1,115	1,175	13,200	13,250	1,298	1,368
450	500	88	93	3,250	3,300	606	639	6,050	6,100	1,124	1,185	13,250	13,300	1,292	1,362
500	550	97	102	3,300	3,350	615	648	6,100	6,150	1,133	1,194	13,300	13,350	1,285	1,355
550	600	106	112	3,350	3,400	624	658	6,150	6,200	1,142	1,204	13,350	13,400	1,279	1,348
600	650	116	122	3,400	3,450	634	668	6,200	6,250	1,152	1,214	13,400	13,450	1,272	1,341
650	700	125	132	3,450	3,500	643	678	6,250	6,300	1,161	1,224	13,450	13,500	1,265	1,334
700	750	134	141	3,500	3,550	652	687	6,300	6,350	1,170	1,233	13,500	13,550	1,259	1,327
750	800	143	151	3,550	3,600	661	697	6,350	6,400	1,179	1,243	13,550	13,600	1,252	1,320
800	850	153	161	3,600	3,650	671	707	6,400	6,450	1,189	1,253	13,600	13,650	1,246	1,313
850	900	162	171	3,650	3,700	680	717	6,450	6,500	1,198	1,263	13,650	13,700	1,239	1,306
900	950	171	180	3,700	3,750	689	726	6,500	6,550	1,207	1,272	13,700	13,750	1,232	1,299
950	1,000	180	190	3,750	3,800	698	736	6,550	6,600	1,216	1,282	13,750	13,800	1,226	1,292
1,000	1,050	190	200	3,800	3,850	708	746	6,600	6,650	1,226	1,292	13,800	13,850	1,219	1,285
1,050	1,100	199	210	3,850	3,900	717	756	6,650	6,700	1,235	1,302	13,850	13,900	1,212	1,278
1,100	1,150	208	219	3,900	3,950	726	765	6,700	6,750	1,244	1,311	13,900	13,950	1,206	1,271
1,150	1,200	217	229	3,950	4,000	735	775	6,750	6,800	1,253	1,321	13,950	14,000	1,199	1,264
1,200	1,250	227	239	4,000	4,050	745	785	6,800	6,850	1,263	1,331	14,000	14,050	1,193	1,257
1,250	1,300	236	249	4,050	4,100	754	795	6,850	6,900	1,272	1,341	14,050	14,100	1,186	1,250
1,300	1,350	245	258	4,100	4,150	763	804	6,900	6,950	1,281	1,350	14,100	14,150	1,179	1,243
1,350	1,400	254	268	4,150	4,200	772	814	6,950	7,000	1,290	1,360	14,150	14,200	1,173	1,236
1,400	1,450	264	278	4,200	4,250	782	824	7,000	7,050	1,300	1,370	14,200	14,250	1,166	1,229
1,450	1,500	273	288	4,250	4,300	791	834	7,050	7,100	1,309	1,380	14,250	14,300	1,160	1,222
1,500	1,550	282	297	4,300	4,350	800	843	7,100	7,150	1,318	1,389	14,300	14,350	1,153	1,215
1,550	1,600	291	307	4,350	4,400	809	853	7,150	7,200	1,327	1,399	14,350	14,400	1,146	1,208
1,600	1,650	301	317	4,400	4,450	819	863	7,200	7,250	1,337	1,409	14,400	14,450	1,140	1,201
1,650	1,700	310	327	4,450	4,500	828	873	7,250	7,300	1,346	1,419	14,450	14,500	1,133	1,194
1,700	1,750	319	336	4,500	4,550	837	882	7,300	7,350	1,355	1,428	14,500	14,550	1,127	1,187
1,750	1,800	328	346	4,550	4,600	846	892	7,350	7,400	1,364	1,438	14,550	14,600	1,120	1,180
1,800	1,850	338	356	4,600	4,650	856	902	7,400	7,450	1,374	1,448	14,600	14,650	1,113	1,173
1,850	1,900	347	366	4,650	4,700	865	912	7,450	7,500	1,383	1,458	14,650	14,700	1,107	1,166
1,900	1,950	356	375	4,700	4,750	874	921	7,500	7,550	1,392	1,467	14,700	14,750	1,100	1,160
1,950	2,000	365	385	4,750	4,800	883	931	7,550	7,600	1,401	1,477	14,750	14,800	1,094	1,153
2,000	2,050	375	395	4,800	4,850	893	941	7,600	7,650	1,411	1,487	14,800	14,850	1,087	1,146
2,050	2,100	384	405	4,850	4,900	902	951	7,650	7,700	1,420	1,497	14,850	14,900	1,080	1,139
2,100	2,150	393	414	4,900	4,950	911	960	7,700	7,750	1,429	1,506	14,900	14,950	1,074	1,132
2,150	2,200	402	424	4,950	5,000	920	970	7,750	12,200	1,434	1,511	14,950	15,000	1,067	1,125
2,200	2,250	412	434	5,000	5,050	930	980	12,200	12,250	1,430	1,508	15,000	15,050	1,061	1,118
2,250	2,300	421	444	5,050	5,100	939	990	12,250	12,300	1,424	1,501	15,050	15,100	1,054	1,111
2,300	2,350	430	453	5,100	5,150	948	999	12,300	12,350	1,417	1,494	15,100	15,150	1,047	1,104
2,350	2,400	439	463	5,150	5,200	957	1,009	12,350	12,400	1,411	1,487	15,150	15,200	1,041	1,097
2,400	2,450	449	473	5,200	5,250	967	1,019	12,400	12,450	1,404	1,480	15,200	15,250	1,034	1,090
2,450	2,500	458	483	5,250	5,300	976	1,029	12,450	12,500	1,397	1,473	15,250	15,300	1,028	1,083
2,500	2,550	467	492	5,300	5,350	985	1,038	12,500	12,550	1,391	1,466	15,300	15,350	1,021	1,076
2,550	2,600	476	502	5,350	5,400	994	1,048	12,550	12,600	1,384	1,459	15,350	15,400	1,014	1,069
2,600	2,650	486	512	5,400	5,450	1,004	1,058	12,600	12,650	1,378	1,452				
2,650	2,700	495	522	5,450	5,500	1,013	1,068	12,650	12,700	1,371	1,445				
2,700	2,750	504	531	5,500	5,550	1,022	1,077	12,700	12,750	1,364	1,438				
2,750	2,800	513	541	5,550	5,600	1,031	1,087	12,750	12,800	1,358	1,431				

(This table continues on next page)

1993 Earned Income Credit TABLE A—Basic Credit Continued

If the amount on Schedule EIC, line 7 or line 9, is—		And you listed—		If the amount on Schedule EIC, line 7 or line 9, is—		And you listed—		If the amount on Schedule EIC, line 7 or line 9, is—		And you listed—	
		One child	Two children			One child	Two children			One child	Two children
At least	But less than	Your basic credit is—		At least	But less than	Your basic credit is—		At least	But less than	Your basic credit is—	
15,400	15,450	1,008	1,062	18,400	18,450	611	644	21,400	21,450	215	226
15,450	15,500	1,001	1,055	18,450	18,500	605	637	21,450	21,500	209	219
15,500	15,550	995	1,048	18,500	18,550	598	630	21,500	21,550	202	212
15,550	15,600	988	1,041	18,550	18,600	592	623	21,550	21,600	195	205
15,600	15,650	981	1,034	18,600	18,650	585	616	21,600	21,650	189	198
15,650	15,700	975	1,027	18,650	18,700	578	609	21,650	21,700	182	191
15,700	15,750	968	1,020	18,700	18,750	572	602	21,700	21,750	175	184
15,750	15,800	961	1,013	18,750	18,800	565	595	21,750	21,800	169	177
15,800	15,850	955	1,006	18,800	18,850	559	588	21,800	21,850	162	170
15,850	15,900	948	999	18,850	18,900	552	581	21,850	21,900	156	164
15,900	15,950	942	992	18,900	18,950	545	574	21,900	21,950	149	157
15,950	16,000	935	985	18,950	19,000	539	567	21,950	22,000	142	150
16,000	16,050	928	978	19,000	19,050	532	561	22,000	22,050	136	143
16,050	16,100	922	971	19,050	19,100	526	554	22,050	22,100	129	136
16,100	16,150	915	964	19,100	19,150	519	547	22,100	22,150	123	129
16,150	16,200	909	958	19,150	19,200	512	540	22,150	22,200	116	122
16,200	16,250	902	951	19,200	19,250	506	533	22,200	22,250	109	115
16,250	16,300	895	944	19,250	19,300	499	526	22,250	22,300	103	108
16,300	16,350	889	937	19,300	19,350	493	519	22,300	22,350	96	101
16,350	16,400	882	930	19,350	19,400	486	512	22,350	22,400	90	94
16,400	16,450	876	923	19,400	19,450	479	505	22,400	22,450	83	87
16,450	16,500	869	916	19,450	19,500	473	498	22,450	22,500	76	80
16,500	16,550	862	909	19,500	19,550	466	491	22,500	22,550	70	73
16,550	16,600	856	902	19,550	19,600	460	484	22,550	22,600	63	66
16,600	16,650	849	895	19,600	19,650	453	477	22,600	22,650	57	59
16,650	16,700	843	888	19,650	19,700	446	470	22,650	22,700	50	52
16,700	16,750	836	881	19,700	19,750	440	463	22,700	22,750	43	45
16,750	16,800	829	874	19,750	19,800	433	456	22,750	22,800	37	38
16,800	16,850	823	867	19,800	19,850	426	449	22,800	22,850	30	31
16,850	16,900	816	860	19,850	19,900	420	442	22,850	22,900	24	24
16,900	16,950	810	853	19,900	19,950	413	435	22,900	22,950	17	17
16,950	17,000	803	846	19,950	20,000	407	428	22,950	23,000	10	10
17,000	17,050	796	839	20,000	20,050	400	421	23,000	23,050	4	3
17,050	17,100	790	832	20,050	20,100	393	414				
17,100	17,150	783	825	20,100	20,150	387	407				
17,150	17,200	777	818	20,150	20,200	380	400				
17,200	17,250	770	811	20,200	20,250	374	393				
17,250	17,300	763	804	20,250	20,300	367	386				
17,300	17,350	757	797	20,300	20,350	360	379				
17,350	17,400	750	790	20,350	20,400	354	372				
17,400	17,450	744	783	20,400	20,450	347	366				
17,450	17,500	737	776	20,450	20,500	341	359				
17,500	17,550	730	769	20,500	20,550	334	352				
17,550	17,600	724	763	20,550	20,600	327	345				
17,600	17,650	717	756	20,600	20,650	321	338				
17,650	17,700	711	749	20,650	20,700	314	331				
17,700	17,750	704	742	20,700	20,750	308	324				
17,750	17,800	697	735	20,750	20,800	301	317				
17,800	17,850	691	728	20,800	20,850	294	310				
17,850	17,900	684	721	20,850	20,900	288	303				
17,900	17,950	677	714	20,900	20,950	281	296				
17,950	18,000	671	707	20,950	21,000	275	289				
18,000	18,050	664	700	21,000	21,050	268	282				
18,050	18,100	658	693	21,050	21,100	261	275				
18,100	18,150	651	686	21,100	21,150	255	268				
18,150	18,200	644	679	21,150	21,200	248	261				
18,200	18,250	638	672	21,200	21,250	242	254				
18,250	18,300	631	665	21,250	21,300	235	247				
18,300	18,350	625	658	21,300	21,350	228	240				
18,350	18,400	618	651	21,350	21,400	222	233				

$23,050 or more—you may not take the credit

TABLE B—Health Insurance Credit

1993 Earned Income Credit

Caution: This is not a tax table.

To find your health insurance credit: First, read down the "At least—But less than" columns and find the line that includes the amount you entered on line 7 or line 9 of Schedule EIC. Next, read across and find the credit. Then, enter the credit on Schedule EIC, line 12 or line 13, whichever applies.

If the amount on Schedule EIC, line 7 or line 9, is— At least	But less than	Your health insurance credit is—
$1	$50	$2
50	100	5
100	150	8
150	200	11
200	250	14
250	300	17
300	350	20
350	400	23
400	450	26
450	500	29
500	550	32
550	600	35
600	650	38
650	700	41
700	750	44
750	800	47
800	850	50
850	900	53
900	950	56
950	1,000	59
1,000	1,050	62
1,050	1,100	65
1,100	1,150	68
1,150	1,200	71
1,200	1,250	74
1,250	1,300	77
1,300	1,350	80
1,350	1,400	83
1,400	1,450	86
1,450	1,500	89
1,500	1,550	92
1,550	1,600	95
1,600	1,650	98
1,650	1,700	101
1,700	1,750	104
1,750	1,800	107
1,800	1,850	110
1,850	1,900	113
1,900	1,950	116
1,950	2,000	119
2,000	2,050	122
2,050	2,100	125
2,100	2,150	128
2,150	2,200	131
2,200	2,250	134
2,250	2,300	137
2,300	2,350	140
2,350	2,400	143
2,400	2,450	146
2,450	2,500	149
2,500	2,550	152
2,550	2,600	155
2,600	2,650	158
2,650	2,700	161
2,700	2,750	164
2,750	2,800	167
2,800	2,850	170
2,850	2,900	173
2,900	2,950	176
2,950	3,000	179
3,000	3,050	182
3,050	3,100	185
3,100	3,150	188
3,150	3,200	191
3,200	3,250	194
3,250	3,300	197
3,300	3,350	200
3,350	3,400	203
3,400	3,450	206
3,450	3,500	209
3,500	3,550	212
3,550	3,600	215
3,600	3,650	218
3,650	3,700	221
3,700	3,750	224
3,750	3,800	227
3,800	3,850	230
3,850	3,900	233
3,900	3,950	236
3,950	4,000	239
4,000	4,050	242
4,050	4,100	245
4,100	4,150	248
4,150	4,200	251
4,200	4,250	254
4,250	4,300	257
4,300	4,350	260
4,350	4,400	263
4,400	4,450	266
4,450	4,500	269
4,500	4,550	272
4,550	4,600	275
4,600	4,650	278
4,650	4,700	281
4,700	4,750	284
4,750	4,800	287
4,800	4,850	290
4,850	4,900	293
4,900	4,950	296
4,950	5,000	299
5,000	5,050	302
5,050	5,100	305
5,100	5,150	308
5,150	5,200	311
5,200	5,250	314
5,250	5,300	317
5,300	5,350	320
5,350	5,400	323
5,400	5,450	326
5,450	5,500	329
5,500	5,550	332
5,550	5,600	335
5,600	5,650	338
5,650	5,700	341
5,700	5,750	344
5,750	5,800	347
5,800	5,850	350
5,850	5,900	353
5,900	5,950	356
5,950	6,000	359
6,000	6,050	362
6,050	6,100	365
6,100	6,150	368
6,150	6,200	371
6,200	6,250	374
6,250	6,300	377
6,300	6,350	380
6,350	6,400	383
6,400	6,450	386
6,450	6,500	389
6,500	6,550	392
6,550	6,600	395
6,600	6,650	398
6,650	6,700	401
6,700	6,750	404
6,750	6,800	407
6,800	6,850	410
6,850	6,900	413
6,900	6,950	416
6,950	7,000	419
7,000	7,050	422
7,050	7,100	425
7,100	7,150	428
7,150	7,200	431
7,200	7,250	434
7,250	7,300	437
7,300	7,350	440
7,350	7,400	443
7,400	7,450	446
7,450	7,500	449
7,500	7,550	452
7,550	7,600	455
7,600	7,650	458
7,650	7,700	461
7,700	7,750	464
7,750	12,200	465
12,200	12,250	464
12,250	12,300	462
12,300	12,350	460
12,350	12,400	458
12,400	12,450	455
12,450	12,500	453
12,500	12,550	451
12,550	12,600	449
12,600	12,650	447
12,650	12,700	445
12,700	12,750	443
12,750	12,800	440
12,800	12,850	438
12,850	12,900	436
12,900	12,950	434
12,950	13,000	432
13,000	13,050	430
13,050	13,100	428
13,100	13,150	425
13,150	13,200	423
13,200	13,250	421
13,250	13,300	419
13,300	13,350	417
13,350	13,400	415
13,400	13,450	413
13,450	13,500	410
13,500	13,550	408
13,550	13,600	406
13,600	13,650	404
13,650	13,700	402
13,700	13,750	400
13,750	13,800	398
13,800	13,850	395
13,850	13,900	393
13,900	13,950	391
13,950	14,000	389
14,000	14,050	387
14,050	14,100	385
14,100	14,150	383
14,150	14,200	380
14,200	14,250	378
14,250	14,300	376
14,300	14,350	374
14,350	14,400	372
14,400	14,450	370
14,450	14,500	368
14,500	14,550	365
14,550	14,600	363
14,600	14,650	361
14,650	14,700	359
14,700	14,750	357
14,750	14,800	355
14,800	14,850	353
14,850	14,900	350
14,900	14,950	348
14,950	15,000	346
15,000	15,050	344
15,050	15,100	342
15,100	15,150	340
15,150	15,200	338
15,200	15,250	335
15,250	15,300	333
15,300	15,350	331
15,350	15,400	329
15,400	15,450	327
15,450	15,500	325
15,500	15,550	323
15,550	15,600	320
15,600	15,650	318
15,650	15,700	316
15,700	15,750	314
15,750	15,800	312
15,800	15,850	310
15,850	15,900	308
15,900	15,950	305
15,950	16,000	303
16,000	16,050	301
16,050	16,100	299
16,100	16,150	297
16,150	16,200	295
16,200	16,250	293
16,250	16,300	290
16,300	16,350	288
16,350	16,400	286
16,400	16,450	284
16,450	16,500	282
16,500	16,550	280
16,550	16,600	278
16,600	16,650	275
16,650	16,700	273
16,700	16,750	271
16,750	16,800	269
16,800	16,850	267
16,850	16,900	265
16,900	16,950	263
16,950	17,000	260
17,000	17,050	258
17,050	17,100	256
17,100	17,150	254
17,150	17,200	252
17,200	17,250	250
17,250	17,300	248
17,300	17,350	245
17,350	17,400	243
17,400	17,450	241
17,450	17,500	239
17,500	17,550	237
17,550	17,600	235
17,600	17,650	233
17,650	17,700	230
17,700	17,750	228
17,750	17,800	226
17,800	17,850	224
17,850	17,900	222
17,900	17,950	220
17,950	18,000	218
18,000	18,050	215
18,050	18,100	213
18,100	18,150	211
18,150	18,200	209
18,200	18,250	207
18,250	18,300	205
18,300	18,350	203
18,350	18,400	200
18,400	18,450	198
18,450	18,500	196
18,500	18,550	194
18,550	18,600	192
18,600	18,650	190
18,650	18,700	188
18,700	18,750	185
18,750	18,800	183
18,800	18,850	181
18,850	18,900	179
18,900	18,950	177
18,950	19,000	175
19,000	19,050	173
19,050	19,100	170
19,100	19,150	168
19,150	19,200	166
19,200	19,250	164
19,250	19,300	162
19,300	19,350	160
19,350	19,400	158
19,400	19,450	155
19,450	19,500	153
19,500	19,550	151
19,550	19,600	149
19,600	19,650	147
19,650	19,700	145
19,700	19,750	143
19,750	19,800	140
19,800	19,850	138
19,850	19,900	136
19,900	19,950	134
19,950	20,000	132
20,000	20,050	130
20,050	20,100	128
20,100	20,150	125
20,150	20,200	123
20,200	20,250	121
20,250	20,300	119
20,300	20,350	117
20,350	20,400	115
20,400	20,450	113
20,450	20,500	110
20,500	20,550	108
20,550	20,600	106
20,600	20,650	104
20,650	20,700	102
20,700	20,750	100
20,750	20,800	98
20,800	20,850	95
20,850	20,900	93
20,900	20,950	91
20,950	21,000	89
21,000	21,050	87
21,050	21,100	85
21,100	21,150	83
21,150	21,200	80
21,200	21,250	78
21,250	21,300	76
21,300	21,350	74
21,350	21,400	72
21,400	21,450	70
21,450	21,500	68
21,500	21,550	65
21,550	21,600	63
21,600	21,650	61
21,650	21,700	59
21,700	21,750	57
21,750	21,800	55
21,800	21,850	53
21,850	21,900	50
21,900	21,950	48
21,950	22,000	46
22,000	22,050	44
22,050	22,100	42
22,100	22,150	40
22,150	22,200	38
22,200	22,250	35
22,250	22,300	33
22,300	22,350	31
22,350	22,400	29
22,400	22,450	27
22,450	22,500	25
22,500	22,550	23
22,550	22,600	20
22,600	22,650	18
22,650	22,700	16
22,700	22,750	14
22,750	22,800	12
22,800	22,850	10
22,850	22,900	8
22,900	22,950	5
22,950	23,000	3
23,000	23,050	1

$23,050 or more—you may not take the credit

TABLE C—Extra Credit for Child Born in 1993

1993 Earned Income Credit

Caution: This is **not** a tax table.

To find your extra credit for a child born in 1993: First, read down the "At least—But less than" columns and find the line that includes the amount you entered on line 7 or line 9 of Schedule EIC. Next, read across and find the credit. Then, enter the credit on Schedule EIC, line 17 or line 18, whichever applies.

At least	But less than	Your credit for a child born in 1993 is—
$1	$50	$1
50	100	4
100	150	6
150	200	9
200	250	11
250	300	14
300	350	16
350	400	19
400	450	21
450	500	24
500	550	26
550	600	29
600	650	31
650	700	34
700	750	36
750	800	39
800	850	41
850	900	44
900	950	46
950	1,000	49
1,000	1,050	51
1,050	1,100	54
1,100	1,150	56
1,150	1,200	59
1,200	1,250	61
1,250	1,300	64
1,300	1,350	66
1,350	1,400	69
1,400	1,450	71
1,450	1,500	74
1,500	1,550	76
1,550	1,600	79
1,600	1,650	81
1,650	1,700	84
1,700	1,750	86
1,750	1,800	89
1,800	1,850	91
1,850	1,900	94
1,900	1,950	96
1,950	2,000	99
2,000	2,050	101
2,050	2,100	104
2,100	2,150	106
2,150	2,200	109
2,200	2,250	111
2,250	2,300	114
2,300	2,350	116
2,350	2,400	119
2,400	2,450	121
2,450	2,500	124
2,500	2,550	126
2,550	2,600	129
2,600	2,650	131
2,650	2,700	134
2,700	2,750	136
2,750	2,800	139
2,800	2,850	141
2,850	2,900	144
2,900	2,950	146
2,950	3,000	149
3,000	3,050	151
3,050	3,100	154
3,100	3,150	156
3,150	3,200	159
3,200	3,250	161
3,250	3,300	164
3,300	3,350	166
3,350	3,400	169
3,400	3,450	171
3,450	3,500	174
3,500	3,550	176
3,550	3,600	179
3,600	3,650	181
3,650	3,700	184
3,700	3,750	186
3,750	3,800	189

At least	But less than	Your credit for a child born in 1993 is—
3,800	3,850	191
3,850	3,900	194
3,900	3,950	196
3,950	4,000	199
4,000	4,050	201
4,050	4,100	204
4,100	4,150	206
4,150	4,200	209
4,200	4,250	211
4,250	4,300	214
4,300	4,350	216
4,350	4,400	219
4,400	4,450	221
4,450	4,500	224
4,500	4,550	226
4,550	4,600	229
4,600	4,650	231
4,650	4,700	234
4,700	4,750	236
4,750	4,800	239
4,800	4,850	241
4,850	4,900	244
4,900	4,950	246
4,950	5,000	249
5,000	5,050	251
5,050	5,100	254
5,100	5,150	256
5,150	5,200	259
5,200	5,250	261
5,250	5,300	264
5,300	5,350	266
5,350	5,400	269
5,400	5,450	271
5,450	5,500	274
5,500	5,550	276
5,550	5,600	279
5,600	5,650	281
5,650	5,700	284
5,700	5,750	286
5,750	5,800	289
5,800	5,850	291
5,850	5,900	294
5,900	5,950	296
5,950	6,000	299
6,000	6,050	301
6,050	6,100	304
6,100	6,150	306
6,150	6,200	309
6,200	6,250	311
6,250	6,300	314
6,300	6,350	316
6,350	6,400	319
6,400	6,450	321
6,450	6,500	324
6,500	6,550	326
6,550	6,600	329
6,600	6,650	331
6,650	6,700	334
6,700	6,750	336
6,750	6,800	339
6,800	6,850	341
6,850	6,900	344
6,900	6,950	346
6,950	7,000	349
7,000	7,050	351
7,050	7,100	354
7,100	7,150	356
7,150	7,200	359
7,200	7,250	361
7,250	7,300	364
7,300	7,350	366
7,350	7,400	369
7,400	7,450	371
7,450	7,500	374
7,500	7,550	376
7,550	7,600	379

At least	But less than	Your credit for a child born in 1993 is—
7,600	7,650	381
7,650	7,700	384
7,700	7,750	386
7,750	12,200	388
12,200	12,250	387
12,250	12,300	385
12,300	12,350	383
12,350	12,400	381
12,400	12,450	379
12,450	12,500	378
12,500	12,550	376
12,550	12,600	374
12,600	12,650	372
12,650	12,700	371
12,700	12,750	369
12,750	12,800	367
12,800	12,850	365
12,850	12,900	363
12,900	12,950	362
12,950	13,000	360
13,000	13,050	358
13,050	13,100	356
13,100	13,150	354
13,150	13,200	353
13,200	13,250	351
13,250	13,300	349
13,300	13,350	347
13,350	13,400	346
13,400	13,450	344
13,450	13,500	342
13,500	13,550	340
13,550	13,600	338
13,600	13,650	337
13,650	13,700	335
13,700	13,750	333
13,750	13,800	331
13,800	13,850	329
13,850	13,900	328
13,900	13,950	326
13,950	14,000	324
14,000	14,050	322
14,050	14,100	321
14,100	14,150	319
14,150	14,200	317
14,200	14,250	315
14,250	14,300	313
14,300	14,350	312
14,350	14,400	310
14,400	14,450	308
14,450	14,500	306
14,500	14,550	304
14,550	14,600	303
14,600	14,650	301
14,650	14,700	299
14,700	14,750	297
14,750	14,800	296
14,800	14,850	294
14,850	14,900	292
14,900	14,950	290
14,950	15,000	288
15,000	15,050	287
15,050	15,100	285
15,100	15,150	283
15,150	15,200	281
15,200	15,250	280
15,250	15,300	278
15,300	15,350	276
15,350	15,400	274
15,400	15,450	272
15,450	15,500	271
15,500	15,550	269
15,550	15,600	267
15,600	15,650	265
15,650	15,700	263
15,700	15,750	262
15,750	15,800	260

At least	But less than	Your credit for a child born in 1993 is—
15,800	15,850	258
15,850	15,900	256
15,900	15,950	255
15,950	16,000	253
16,000	16,050	251
16,050	16,100	249
16,100	16,150	247
16,150	16,200	246
16,200	16,250	244
16,250	16,300	242
16,300	16,350	240
16,350	16,400	238
16,400	16,450	237
16,450	16,500	235
16,500	16,550	233
16,550	16,600	231
16,600	16,650	230
16,650	16,700	228
16,700	16,750	226
16,750	16,800	224
16,800	16,850	222
16,850	16,900	221
16,900	16,950	219
16,950	17,000	217
17,000	17,050	215
17,050	17,100	213
17,100	17,150	212
17,150	17,200	210
17,200	17,250	208
17,250	17,300	206
17,300	17,350	205
17,350	17,400	203
17,400	17,450	201
17,450	17,500	199
17,500	17,550	197
17,550	17,600	196
17,600	17,650	194
17,650	17,700	192
17,700	17,750	190
17,750	17,800	188
17,800	17,850	187
17,850	17,900	185
17,900	17,950	183
17,950	18,000	181
18,000	18,050	180
18,050	18,100	178
18,100	18,150	176
18,150	18,200	174
18,200	18,250	172
18,250	18,300	171
18,300	18,350	169
18,350	18,400	167
18,400	18,450	165
18,450	18,500	163
18,500	18,550	162
18,550	18,600	160
18,600	18,650	158
18,650	18,700	156
18,700	18,750	155
18,750	18,800	153
18,800	18,850	151
18,850	18,900	149
18,900	18,950	147
18,950	19,000	146
19,000	19,050	144
19,050	19,100	142
19,100	19,150	140
19,150	19,200	138
19,200	19,250	137
19,250	19,300	135
19,300	19,350	133
19,350	19,400	131
19,400	19,450	130
19,450	19,500	128
19,500	19,550	126
19,550	19,600	124

At least	But less than	Your credit for a child born in 1993 is—
19,600	19,650	122
19,650	19,700	121
19,700	19,750	119
19,750	19,800	117
19,800	19,850	115
19,850	19,900	114
19,900	19,950	112
19,950	20,000	110
20,000	20,050	108
20,050	20,100	106
20,100	20,150	105
20,150	20,200	103
20,200	20,250	101
20,250	20,300	99
20,300	20,350	97
20,350	20,400	96
20,400	20,450	94
20,450	20,500	92
20,500	20,550	90
20,550	20,600	89
20,600	20,650	87
20,650	20,700	85
20,700	20,750	83
20,750	20,800	81
20,800	20,850	80
20,850	20,900	78
20,900	20,950	76
20,950	21,000	74
21,000	21,050	72
21,050	21,100	71
21,100	21,150	69
21,150	21,200	67
21,200	21,250	65
21,250	21,300	64
21,300	21,350	62
21,350	21,400	60
21,400	21,450	58
21,450	21,500	56
21,500	21,550	55
21,550	21,600	53
21,600	21,650	51
21,650	21,700	49
21,700	21,750	47
21,750	21,800	46
21,800	21,850	44
21,850	21,900	42
21,900	21,950	40
21,950	22,000	39
22,000	22,050	37
22,050	22,100	35
22,100	22,150	33
22,150	22,200	31
22,200	22,250	30
22,250	22,300	28
22,300	22,350	26
22,350	22,400	24
22,400	22,450	22
22,450	22,500	21
22,500	22,550	19
22,550	22,600	17
22,600	22,650	15
22,650	22,700	14
22,700	22,750	12
22,750	22,800	10
22,800	22,850	8
22,850	22,900	6
22,900	22,950	5
22,950	23,000	3
23,000	23,050	1

$23,050 or more—you may not take the credit

APPENDIX

B *Tax Forms*

Form **1040** Department of the Treasury—Internal Revenue Service

U.S. Individual Income Tax Return (B) 1993

IRS Use Only—Do not write or staple in this space.

For the year Jan. 1–Dec. 31, 1993, or other tax year beginning _____, 1993, ending _____, 19 _____ | OMB No. 1545-0074

Label

(See instructions on page 12.)

Use the IRS label. Otherwise, please print or type.

L A B E L   H E R E

Your first name and initial | Last name | Your social security number

If a joint return, spouse's first name and initial | Last name | Spouse's social security number

Home address (number and street). If you have a P.O. box, see page 12. | Apt. no. | **For Privacy Act and Paperwork Reduction Act Notice, see page 4.**

City, town or post office, state, and ZIP code. If you have a foreign address, see page 12.

Presidential Election Campaign (See page 12.) ▶

Do you want $3 to go to this fund? . . . .

If a joint return, does your spouse want $3 to go to this fund? . . . .

Yes | No | **Note:** *Checking "Yes" will not change your tax or reduce your refund.*

Filing Status

(See page 12.)

Check only one box.

1 ☐ Single

2 ☐ Married filing joint return (even if only one had income)

3 ☐ Married filing separate return. Enter spouse's social security no. above and full name here. ▶ _____

4 ☐ Head of household (with qualifying person). (See page 13.) If the qualifying person is a child but not your dependent, enter this child's name here. ▶ _____

5 ☐ Qualifying widow(er) with dependent child (year spouse died ▶ 19 ___). (See page 13.)

Exemptions

(See page 13.)

If more than six dependents, see page 14.

6a ☐ **Yourself.** If your parent (or someone else) can claim you as a dependent on his or her tax return, **do not** check box 6a. But be sure to check the box on line 33b on page 2 .

b ☐ **Spouse** . . . .

No. of boxes checked on 6a and 6b _____

c **Dependents:**

(1) Name (first, initial, and last name)	(2) Check if under age 1	(3) If age 1 or older, dependent's social security number	(4) Dependent's relationship to you	(5) No. of months lived in your home in 1993

No. of your children on 6c who:

• lived with you _____

• didn't live with you due to divorce or separation (see page 15) _____

Dependents on 6c not entered above _____

d If your child didn't live with you but is claimed as your dependent under a pre-1985 agreement, check here ▶ ☐

e Total number of exemptions claimed . . . .

Add numbers entered on lines above ▶ ☐

Income

Attach Copy B of your Forms W-2, W-2G, and 1099-R here.

If you did not get a W-2, see page 10.

If you are attaching a check or money order, put it on top of any Forms W-2, W-2G, or 1099-R.

7 Wages, salaries, tips, etc. Attach Form(s) W-2 . . . . | 7 |

8a **Taxable** interest income (see page 16). Attach Schedule B if over $400 . . . . . | 8a |

b **Tax-exempt** interest (see page 17). DON'T include on line 8a | 8b | |

9 Dividend income. Attach Schedule B if over $400 . . . . | 9 |

10 Taxable refunds, credits, or offsets of state and local income taxes (see page 17) . . | 10 |

11 Alimony received . . . . | 11 |

12 Business income or (loss). Attach Schedule C or C-EZ . . . . . . | 12 |

13 Capital gain or (loss). Attach Schedule D . . . . | 13 |

14 Capital gain distributions not reported on line 13 (see page 17) . . . . | 14 |

15 Other gains or (losses). Attach Form 4797 . . . . | 15 |

16a Total IRA distributions . | 16a | | b Taxable amount (see page 18) | 16b |

17a Total pensions and annuities | 17a | | b Taxable amount (see page 18) | 17b |

18 Rental real estate, royalties, partnerships, S corporations, trusts, etc. Attach Schedule E | 18 |

19 Farm income or (loss). Attach Schedule F . . . . | 19 |

20 Unemployment compensation (see page 19) . . . . | 20 |

21a Social security benefits | 21a | | b Taxable amount (see page 19) | 21b |

22 Other income. List type and amount—see page 20 .... | 22 |

23 Add the amounts in the far right column for lines 7 through 22. This is your **total income** ▶ | 23 |

Adjustments to Income

(See page 20.)

24a Your IRA deduction (see page 20) . . . . | 24a | |

b Spouse's IRA deduction (see page 20) . . . . . . | 24b | |

25 One-half of self-employment tax (see page 21) . . . | 25 | |

26 Self-employed health insurance deduction (see page 22) | 26 | |

27 Keogh retirement plan and self-employed SEP deduction | 27 | |

28 Penalty on early withdrawal of savings . . . . . | 28 | |

29 Alimony paid. Recipient's SSN ▶ _____ | 29 | |

30 Add lines 24a through 29. These are your **total adjustments** . . . . ▶ | 30 |

Adjusted Gross Income

31 Subtract line 30 from line 23. This is your **adjusted gross income.** *If this amount is less than $23,050 and a child lived with you, see page EIC-1 to find out if you can claim the "Earned Income Credit" on line 56* . . . . ▶ | 31 |

Form 1040 (1993)   Page **2**

Tax Compu- tation	**32**	Amount from line 31 (adjusted gross income)		**32**	

33a Check if: ☐ **You** were 65 or older, ☐ Blind; ☐ **Spouse** was 65 or older, ☐ Blind.
Add the number of boxes checked above and enter the total here . . . . ▶ **33a** ☐

b If your parent (or someone else) can claim you as a dependent, check here . . ▶ **33b** ☐

c If you are married filing separately and your spouse itemizes deductions or
you are a dual-status alien, see page 24 and check here . . . . . . ▶ **33c** ☐

(See page 23.)

34 Enter the larger of your:
  Itemized deductions from Schedule A, line 26, **OR**
  Standard deduction shown below for your filing status. **But if you checked
  any box on line 33a or b,** go to page 24 to find your standard deduction.
  If you checked **box 33c,** your standard deduction is zero.
  • Single—$3,700   • Head of household—$5,450
  • Married filing jointly or Qualifying widow(er)—$6,200
  • Married filing separately—$3,100 | **34** |

35 Subtract line 34 from line 32 . . . . | **35** |

36 If line 32 is $81,350 or less, multiply $2,350 by the total number of exemptions claimed on
line 6e. If line 32 is over $81,350, see the worksheet on page 25 for the amount to enter . | **36** |

If you want the IRS to figure your tax, see page 24.

37 **Taxable income.** Subtract line 36 from line 35. If line 36 is more than line 35, enter -0- . | **37** |

38 Tax. Check if from **a** ☐ Tax Table, **b** ☐ Tax Rate Schedules, **c** ☐ Schedule D Tax Work-
sheet, or **d** ☐ Form 8615 (see page 25). Amount from Form(s) 8814 ▶ **e** _____ | **38** |

39 Additional taxes (see page 25). Check if from **a** ☐ Form 4970 **b** ☐ Form 4972 . . . | **39** |

40 Add lines 38 and 39 . . . . ▶ | **40** |

Credits

(See page 25.)

41 Credit for child and dependent care expenses. Attach Form 2441	**41**
42 Credit for the elderly or the disabled. Attach Schedule R . .	**42**
43 Foreign tax credit. Attach Form 1116	**43**
44 Other credits (see page 26). Check if from **a** ☐ Form 3800 **b** ☐ Form 8396 **c** ☐ Form 8801 **d** ☐ Form (specify) _____	**44**

45 Add lines 41 through 44 . . . . | **45** |

46 Subtract line 45 from line 40. If line 45 is more than line 40, enter -0- . . . . . . ▶ | **46** |

Other Taxes

47 Self-employment tax. Attach Schedule SE. Also, see line 25 . . . . | **47** |

48 Alternative minimum tax. Attach Form 6251 . . . . | **48** |

49 Recapture taxes (see page 26). Check if from **a** ☐ Form 4255 **b** ☐ Form 8611 **c** ☐ Form 8828 | **49** |

50 Social security and Medicare tax on tip income not reported to employer. Attach Form 4137 . | **50** |

51 Tax on qualified retirement plans, including IRAs. If required, attach Form 5329 . . . . | **51** |

52 Advance earned income credit payments from Form W-2 . . . . | **52** |

53 Add lines 46 through 52. This is your **total tax** . . . . ▶ | **53** |

Payments

Attach Forms W-2, W-2G, and 1099-R on the front.

54 Federal income tax withheld. If any is from Form(s) 1099, check ▶ ☐	**54**
55 1993 estimated tax payments and amount applied from 1992 return .	**55**
56 **Earned income credit.** Attach Schedule EIC	**56**
57 Amount paid with Form 4868 (extension request)	**57**
58a Excess social security, Medicare, and RRTA tax withheld (see page 28) .	**58a**
b Deferral of additional 1993 taxes. Attach Form 8841	**58b**
59 Other payments (see page 28). Check if from **a** ☐ Form 2439 **b** ☐ Form 4136	**59**

60 Add lines 54 through 59. These are your **total payments** . . . . ▶ | **60** |

Refund or Amount You Owe

61 If line 60 is more than line 53, subtract line 53 from line 60. This is the amount you **OVERPAID**. ▶ | **61** |

62 Amount of line 61 you want **REFUNDED TO YOU**. . . . . ▶ | **62** |

63 Amount of line 61 you want **APPLIED TO YOUR 1994 ESTIMATED TAX** ▶ **63**

64 If line 53 is more than line 60, subtract line 60 from line 53. This is the **AMOUNT YOU OWE**.
For details on how to pay, including what to write on your payment, see page 29 . . . | **64** |

65 Estimated tax penalty (see page 29). Also include on line 64 **65**

Sign Here

Keep a copy of this return for your records.

Under penalties of perjury, I declare that I have examined this return and accompanying schedules and statements, and to the best of my knowledge and belief, they are true, correct, and complete. Declaration of preparer (other than taxpayer) is based on all information of which preparer has any knowledge.

▶ Your signature	Date	Your occupation
▶ Spouse's signature. If a joint return, BOTH must sign.	Date	Spouse's occupation

Paid Preparer's Use Only

Preparer's signature ▶	Date	Check if self-employed ☐	Preparer's social security no.
Firm's name (or yours if self-employed) and address ▶		E.I. No.	
		ZIP code	

SCHEDULES A&B
(Form 1040)

Department of the Treasury
Internal Revenue Service (O)

Schedule A—Itemized Deductions

(Schedule B is on back)

▶ Attach to Form 1040. ▶ See Instructions for Schedules A and B (Form 1040).

OMB No. 1545-0074

1993

Attachment
Sequence No. **07**

Name(s) shown on Form 1040

Your social security number

Medical and Dental Expenses	**Caution:** *Do not include expenses reimbursed or paid by others.*		
	1 Medical and dental expenses (see page A-1)	**1**	
	2 Enter amount from Form 1040, line 32 . ⌊ **2** ⌋		
	3 Multiply line 2 above by 7.5% (.075)	**3**	
	4 Subtract line 3 from line 1. If zero or less, enter -0- . . . . ▶	**4**	
Taxes You Paid (See page A-1.)	**5** State and local income taxes	**5**	
	6 Real estate taxes (see page A-2)	**6**	
	7 Other taxes. List—include personal property taxes ▶	**7**	
	8 Add lines 5 through 7 . . . . ▶	**8**	
Interest You Paid (See page A-2.)	**9a** Home mortgage interest and points reported to you on Form 1098	**9a**	
	b Home mortgage interest not reported to you on Form 1098. If paid to the person from whom you bought the home, see page A-3 and show that person's name, identifying no., and address ▶		
Note: Personal interest is not deductible.		**9b**	
	10 Points not reported to you on Form 1098. See page A-3 for special rules	**10**	
	11 Investment interest. If required, attach Form 4952. (See page A-3.)	**11**	
	12 Add lines 9a through 11 . . . . ▶	**12**	
Gifts to Charity (See page A-3.)	**Caution:** *If you made a charitable contribution and received a benefit in return, see page A-3.*		
	13 Contributions by cash or check	**13**	
	14 Other than by cash or check. If over $500, you **MUST** attach Form 8283	**14**	
	15 Carryover from prior year	**15**	
	16 Add lines 13 through 15 . . . . ▶	**16**	
Casualty and Theft Losses	**17** Casualty or theft loss(es). Attach Form 4684. (See page A-4.) . . . . . . ▶	**17**	
Moving Expenses	**18** Moving expenses. Attach Form 3903 or 3903-F. (See page A-4.) . . . . . ▶	**18**	
Job Expenses and Most Other Miscellaneous Deductions (See page A-5 for expenses to deduct here.)	**19** Unreimbursed employee expenses—job travel, union dues, job education, etc. If required, you **MUST** attach Form 2106. (See page A-4.) ▶	**19**	
	20 Other expenses—investment, tax preparation, safe deposit box, etc. List type and amount ▶	**20**	
	21 Add lines 19 and 20	**21**	
	22 Enter amount from Form 1040, line 32 . ⌊ **22** ⌋		
	23 Multiply line 22 above by 2% (.02)	**23**	
	24 Subtract line 23 from line 21. If zero or less, enter -0- . . . . ▶	**24**	
Other Miscellaneous Deductions	**25** Other—from list on page A-5. List type and amount ▶		
		25	
Total Itemized Deductions	**26** Is the amount on Form 1040, line 32, more than $108,450 (more than $54,225 if married filing separately)?		
	● **NO.** Your deduction is not limited. Add lines 4, 8, 12, 16, 17, 18, 24, and 25 and enter the total here. Also enter on Form 1040, line 34, the **larger** of this amount or your standard deduction. ⎫⎬ ▶	**26**	
	● **YES.** Your deduction may be limited. See page A-5 for the amount to enter. ⎭		

For Paperwork Reduction Act Notice, see Form 1040 instructions.   Cat. No. 11330X   **Schedule A (Form 1040) 1993**

Schedules A&B (Form 1040) 1993

OMB No. 1545-0074   Page **2**

Name(s) shown on Form 1040. Do not enter name and social security number if shown on other side.

Your social security number

Schedule B—Interest and Dividend Income

Attachment
Sequence No. **08**

Part I **Interest** **Income** (See pages 16 and B-1.) **Note:** If you received a Form 1099-INT, Form 1099-OID, or substitute statement from a brokerage firm, list the firm's name as the payer and enter the total interest shown on that form.	**Note:** *If you had over $400 in taxable interest income, you must also complete Part III.*	
	Interest Income	Amount
	1 List name of payer. If any interest is from a seller-financed mortgage and the buyer used the property as a personal residence, see page B-1 and list this interest first. Also show that buyer's social security number and address ▶	**1**
	2 Add the amounts on line 1	**2**
	3 Excludable interest on series EE U.S. savings bonds issued after 1989 from Form 8815, line 14. You MUST attach Form 8815 to Form 1040	**3**
	4 Subtract line 3 from line 2. Enter the result here and on Form 1040, line 8a ▶	**4**

Part II **Dividend** **Income** (See pages 17 and B-1.) **Note:** If you received a Form 1099-DIV or substitute statement from a brokerage firm, list the firm's name as the payer and enter the total dividends shown on that form.	**Note:** *If you had over $400 in gross dividends and/or other distributions on stock, you must also complete Part III.*	
	Dividend Income	Amount
	5 List name of payer. Include gross dividends and/or other distributions on stock here. Any capital gain distributions and nontaxable distributions will be deducted on lines 7 and 8 ▶	**5**
	6 Add the amounts on line 5	**6**
	7 Capital gain distributions. Enter here and on Schedule D* . **7**	
	8 Nontaxable distributions. (See the inst. for Form 1040, line 9.) **8**	
	9 Add lines 7 and 8	**9**
	10 Subtract line 9 from line 6. Enter the result here and on Form 1040, line 9 . ▶	**10**
	If you received capital gain distributions but do not need Schedule D to report any other gains or losses, see the instructions for Form 1040, lines 13 and 14.	

Part III **Foreign** **Accounts** **and** **Trusts** (See page B-2.)	If you had over $400 of interest or dividends OR had a foreign account or were a grantor of, or a transferor to, a foreign trust, you must complete this part.	**Yes**	**No**
	11a At any time during 1993, did you have an interest in or a signature or other authority over a financial account in a foreign country, such as a bank account, securities account, or other financial account? See page B-2 for exceptions and filing requirements for Form TD F 90-22.1		
	b If "Yes," enter the name of the foreign country ▶		
	12 Were you the grantor of, or transferor to, a foreign trust that existed during 1993, whether or not you have any beneficial interest in it? If "Yes," you may have to file Form 3520, 3520-A, or 926 .		

For Paperwork Reduction Act Notice, see Form 1040 instructions.

Schedule B (Form 1040) 1993

SCHEDULE C
(Form 1040)

Department of the Treasury
Internal Revenue Service (O)

Profit or Loss From Business
(Sole Proprietorship)
▶ Partnerships, joint ventures, etc., must file Form 1065.
▶ Attach to Form 1040 or Form 1041. ▶ See Instructions for Schedule C (Form 1040).

OMB No. 1545-0074

1993

Attachment
Sequence No. **09**

Name of proprietor | Social security number (SSN)

| A | Principal business or profession, including product or service (see page C-1) | B Enter principal business code |
| | | (see page C-6) ▶ |

| C | Business name. If no separate business name, leave blank. | D Employer ID number (EIN), if any |

E Business address (including suite or room no.) ▶
City, town or post office, state, and ZIP code

F Accounting method: (1) ☐ Cash (2) ☐ Accrual (3) ☐ Other (specify) ▶

G Method(s) used to value closing inventory: (1) ☐ Cost (2) ☐ Lower of cost or market (3) ☐ Other (attach explanation) (4) ☐ Does not apply (if checked, skip line H) | Yes | No

H Was there any change in determining quantities, costs, or valuations between opening and closing inventory? If "Yes," attach explanation . . . .

I Did you "materially participate" in the operation of this business during 1993? If "No," see page C-2 for limit on losses. . . .

J If you started or acquired this business during 1993, check here . . . . ▶ ☐

Part I Income

1	Gross receipts or sales. **Caution:** *If this income was reported to you on Form W-2 and the "Statutory employee" box on that form was checked, see page C-2 and check here* . . . . . ▶ ☐	1	
2	Returns and allowances	2	
3	Subtract line 2 from line 1	3	
4	Cost of goods sold (from line 40 on page 2)	4	
5	**Gross profit.** Subtract line 4 from line 3	5	
6	Other income, including Federal and state gasoline or fuel tax credit or refund (see page C-2) . . .	6	
7	**Gross income.** Add lines 5 and 6 . . . . ▶	7	

Part II Expenses. Caution: *Do not* enter expenses for business use of your home on lines 8–27. Instead, see line 30.

8	Advertising	8			19	Pension and profit-sharing plans	19	
9	Bad debts from sales or services (see page C-3) . .	9			20	Rent or lease (see page C-4):		
10	Car and truck expenses (see page C-3)	10			a	Vehicles, machinery, and equipment .	20a	
11	Commissions and fees. . .	11			b	Other business property . .	20b	
12	Depletion.	12			21	Repairs and maintenance . .	21	
13	Depreciation and section 179 expense deduction (not included in Part III) (see page C-3) . .	13			22	Supplies (not included in Part III) .	22	
					23	Taxes and licenses	23	
14	Employee benefit programs (other than on line 19) . . .	14			24	Travel, meals, and entertainment:		
15	Insurance (other than health) .	15			a	Travel	24a	
16	Interest:				b	Meals and entertainment .		
a	Mortgage (paid to banks, etc.) .	16a			c	Enter 20% of line 24b subject to limitations (see page C-4) .		
b	Other	16b			d	Subtract line 24c from line 24b .	24d	
17	Legal and professional services	17			25	Utilities	25	
					26	Wages (less jobs credit) . .	26	
18	Office expense	18			27	Other expenses (from line 46 on page 2)	27	

28	**Total expenses** before expenses for business use of home. Add lines 8 through 27 in columns. . ▶	28	
29	Tentative profit (loss). Subtract line 28 from line 7	29	
30	Expenses for business use of your home. Attach **Form 8829**	30	
31	**Net profit or (loss).** Subtract line 30 from line 29.		
	• If a profit, enter on **Form 1040, line 12,** and ALSO on **Schedule SE, line 2** (statutory employees, see page C-5). Fiduciaries, enter on Form 1041, line 3.	31	
	• If a loss, you MUST go on to line 32.		
32	If you have a loss, check the box that describes your investment in this activity (see page C-5).		
	• If you checked 32a, enter the loss on **Form 1040, line 12,** and ALSO on **Schedule SE, line 2** (statutory employees, see page C-5). Fiduciaries, enter on Form 1041, line 3.	32a ☐ All investment is at risk.	
	• If you checked 32b, you MUST attach **Form 6198.**	32b ☐ Some investment is not at risk.	

For Paperwork Reduction Act Notice, see Form 1040 instructions. | Cat. No. 11334P | Schedule C (Form 1040) 1993

Part III	Cost of Goods Sold (see page C-5)				

33	Inventory at beginning of year. If different from last year's closing inventory, attach explanation . .	33			
34	Purchases less cost of items withdrawn for personal use	34			
35	Cost of labor. Do not include salary paid to yourself	35			
36	Materials and supplies	36			
37	Other costs	37			
38	Add lines 33 through 37	38			
39	Inventory at end of year	39			
40	**Cost of goods sold.** Subtract line 39 from line 38. Enter the result here and on page 1, line 4 . .	40			

Part IV	Information on Your Vehicle. Complete this part **ONLY** if you are claiming car or truck expenses on line 10 and are not required to file Form 4562 for this business.

41   When did you place your vehicle in service for business purposes? (month, day, year) ▶ .... / .... / ....

42   Of the total number of miles you drove your vehicle during 1993, enter the number of miles you used your vehicle for:

a   Business ....   b Commuting ....   c Other ....

43   Do you (or your spouse) have another vehicle available for personal use? . . . . ☐ Yes   ☐ No

44   Was your vehicle available for use during off-duty hours? . . . . ☐ Yes   ☐ No

45a   Do you have evidence to support your deduction? . . . . ☐ Yes   ☐ No
  b   If "Yes," is the evidence written? . . . . ☐ Yes   ☐ No

Part V	Other Expenses. List below business expenses not included on lines 8–26 or line 30.

....			
....			
....			
....			
....			
....			
....			
....			
....			
46 **Total other expenses.** Enter here and on page 1, line 27	46		

SCHEDULE C-EZ
(Form 1040)

Department of the Treasury
Internal Revenue Service (X)

Net Profit From Business

(Sole Proprietorship)

▶ Partnerships, joint ventures, etc., must file Form 1065.
▶ **Attach to Form 1040 or Form 1041.** ▶ **See instructions on back.**

OMB No. 1545-0074

1993

Attachment
Sequence No. **09A**

Name of proprietor | Social security number (SSN)

Part I   **General Information**

You May Use This Form If You:

- Had gross receipts from your business of $25,000 or less.
- Had business expenses of $2,000 or less.
- Use the cash method of accounting.
- Did not have an inventory at any time during the year.
- Did not have a net loss from your business.
- Had only one business as a sole proprietor.

And You:

- Had no employees during the year.
- Are not required to file **Form 4562,** Depreciation and Amortization, for this business. See the instructions for Schedule C, line 13, on page C-3 to find out if you must file.
- Do not deduct expenses for business use of your home.
- Do not have prior year unallowed passive activity losses from this business.

A   Principal business or profession, including product or service | **B**   Enter principal business code (see page C-6) ▶

C   Business name. If no separate business name, leave blank. | **D**   Employer ID number (EIN), if any

E   Business address (including suite or room no.). Address not required if same as on Form 1040, page 1.

City, town or post office, state, and ZIP code

Part II   **Figure Your Net Profit**

1   **Gross receipts.** If more than $25,000, you **must** use Schedule C.
Caution: *If this income was reported to you on Form W-2 and the "Statutory employee" box on that form was checked, see* **Statutory Employees** *in the instructions for Schedule C, line 1, on page C-2 and check here* . . . . ▶ ☐ | **1** |

2   **Total expenses.** If more than $2,000, you **must** use Schedule C. See instructions . . . . . | **2** |

3   **Net profit.** Subtract line 2 from line 1. Enter on **Form 1040, line 12,** and ALSO on **Schedule SE, line 2.** (Statutory employees **do not** report this amount on Schedule SE, line 2. Fiduciaries, enter on Form 1041, line 3.) If less than zero, you **must** use Schedule C . . . . | **3** |

Part III   **Information on Your Vehicle.** Complete this part **ONLY** if you are claiming car or truck expenses on line 2.

4   When did you place your vehicle in service for business purposes? (month, day, year) ▶ ..... / ..... / ......

5   Of the total number of miles you drove your vehicle during 1993, enter the number of miles you used your vehicle for:

a   Business ....   **b**   Commuting ....   **c**   Other ....

6   Do you (or your spouse) have another vehicle available for personal use? . . . . ☐ **Yes**   ☐ **No**

7   Was your vehicle available for use during off-duty hours? . . . . ☐ **Yes**   ☐ **No**

8a   Do you have evidence to support your deduction? . . . . ☐ **Yes**   ☐ **No**

b   If "Yes," is the evidence written? . . . . ☐ **Yes**   ☐ **No**

For Paperwork Reduction Act Notice, see Form 1040 instructions.   Cat. No. 14374D   **Schedule C-EZ (Form 1040) 1993**

Instructions

You may use Schedule C-EZ instead of Schedule C if you operated a business or practiced a profession as a sole proprietorship and you have met all the requirements listed in Part I of the form.

Line A

Describe the business or professional activity that provided your principal source of income reported on line 1. Give the general field or activity and the type of product or service.

Line B

Enter on this line the four-digit code that identifies your principal business or professional activity. See page C-6 for the list of codes.

Line D

You need an employer identification number (EIN) only if you had a Keogh plan or were required to file an employment, excise, fiduciary, or alcohol, tobacco, and firearms tax return. If you need an EIN, file **Form SS-4,** Application for Employer Identification Number. If you don't have an EIN, leave line D blank. **Do not** enter your SSN.

Line E

Enter your business address. Show a street address instead of a box number. Include the suite or room number, if any.

Line 1—Gross Receipts

Enter gross receipts from your trade or business. Be sure to include any amount you received in your trade or business that was reported on Form(s) 1099-MISC. You must show all items of taxable income actually or constructively received during the year (in cash, property, or services). Income is constructively received when it is credited to your account or set aside for you to use. Do not offset this amount by any losses.

Line 2—Total Expenses

Enter the total amount of all deductible business expenses you actually paid during the year. Examples of these expenses include advertising, car and truck expenses, commissions and fees, insurance, interest, legal and professional services, office expense, rent or lease expenses, repairs and maintenance, supplies, taxes, travel, 80% of business meals and entertainment, and utilities (including telephone). For details, see the instructions for Schedule C, Parts II and V, on pages C-3 through C-5.

If you claim car or truck expenses, be sure to complete Part III.

SCHEDULE D
(Form 1040)

Department of the Treasury
Internal Revenue Service (O)

Capital Gains and Losses

▶ Attach to Form 1040.   ▶ See Instructions for Schedule D (Form 1040).

▶ Use lines 20 and 22 for more space to list transactions for lines 1 and 9.

OMB No. 1545-0074

1993

Attachment
Sequence No. **12**

Name(s) shown on Form 1040

Your social security number

Part I Short-Term Capital Gains and Losses—Assets Held One Year or Less

(a) Description of property (Example: 100 sh. XYZ Co.)	(b) Date acquired (Mo., day, yr.)	(c) Date sold (Mo., day, yr.)	(d) Sales price (see page D-3)	(e) Cost or other basis (see page D-3)	(f) LOSS If (e) is more than (d), subtract (d) from (e)	(g) GAIN If (d) is more than (e), subtract (e) from (d)
1						

2 Enter your short-term totals, if any, from line 21 . . . . | **2** |

3 **Total short-term sales price amounts.** Add column (d) of lines 1 and 2 . . . | **3** |

4 Short-term gain from Forms 2119 and 6252, and short-term gain or (loss) from Forms 4684, 6781, and 8824 . . . . . . | **4** |

5 Net short-term gain or (loss) from partnerships, S corporations, and fiduciaries from Schedule(s) K-1 . . . . | **5** |

6 Short-term capital loss carryover from 1992 Schedule D, line 38 . . . . | **6** |

7 Add lines 1, 2, and 4 through 6, in columns (f) and (g) . . . . | **7** ( ) |

8 **Net short-term capital gain or (loss).** Combine columns (f) and (g) of line 7 . . . . | **8** |

Part II Long-Term Capital Gains and Losses—Assets Held More Than One Year

9						

10 Enter your long-term totals, if any, from line 23 . . . . | **10** |

11 **Total long-term sales price amounts.** Add column (d) of lines 9 and 10 . . . | **11** |

12 Gain from Form 4797; long-term gain from Forms 2119, 2439, and 6252; and long-term gain or (loss) from Forms 4684, 6781, and 8824 . . . . | **12** |

13 Net long-term gain or (loss) from partnerships, S corporations, and fiduciaries from Schedule(s) K-1 . . . . | **13** |

14 Capital gain distributions . . . . | **14** |

15 Long-term capital loss carryover from 1992 Schedule D, line 45 . . . . | **15** |

16 Add lines 9, 10, and 12 through 15, in columns (f) and (g) . . . . . . | **16** ( ) |

17 **Net long-term capital gain or (loss).** Combine columns (f) and (g) of line 16 . . . . . . | **17** |

Part III Summary of Parts I and II

18 Combine lines 8 and 17. If a loss, go to line 19. If a gain, enter the gain on Form 1040, line 13.
Note: *If both lines 17 and 18 are gains, see the **Schedule D Tax Worksheet** on page D-4* . . | **18** |

19 If line 18 is a (loss), enter here and as a (loss) on Form 1040, line 13, the **smaller** of these losses:
   a The (loss) on line 18; **or**
   b ($3,000) or, if married filing separately, ($1,500) . . . . | **19** ( ) |

Note: *See the **Capital Loss Carryover Worksheet** on page D-4 if the loss on line 18 exceeds the loss on line 19 **or** if Form 1040, line 35, is a loss.*

For Paperwork Reduction Act Notice, see Form 1040 instructions.   Cat. No. 11338H   **Schedule D (Form 1040) 1993**

Schedule D (Form 1040) 1993   Attachment Sequence No. **12**   Page **2**

Name(s) shown on Form 1040. Do not enter name and social security number if shown on other side.   **Your social security number**

Part IV Short-Term Capital Gains and Losses—Assets Held One Year or Less *(Continuation of Part I)*

(a) Description of property (Example: 100 sh. XYZ Co.)	(b) Date acquired (Mo., day, yr.)	(c) Date sold (Mo., day, yr.)	(d) Sales price (see page D-3)	(e) Cost or other basis (see page D-3)	(f) LOSS If (e) is more than (d), subtract (d) from (e)	(g) GAIN If (d) is more than (e), subtract (e) from (d)
20						
21 Short-term totals. Add columns (d), (f), and (g) of line 20. Enter here and on line 2 . **21**						

Part V Long-Term Capital Gains and Losses—Assets Held More Than One Year *(Continuation of Part II)*

22						
23 Long-term totals. Add columns (d), (f), and (g) of line 22. Enter here and on line 10 . **23**						

Part III

Line 18

The maximum tax rate on net capital gain (the smaller of line 17 or 18 of Schedule D) that you did not elect to treat as investment income on Form 4952, line 4e, is 28%. If both lines 17 and 18 are gains, and Form 1040, line 37, is over $89,150 ($53,500 if single; $76,400 if head of household; $44,575 if married filing separately), use the **Schedule D Tax Worksheet** on this page to figure your tax; otherwise, use the Tax Table or Tax Rate Schedules, whichever applies.

Line 19

If line 18 is a (loss), enter on line 19 and as a (loss) on Form 1040, line 13, the **smaller** of these losses: **(a)** the (loss) on line 18; **or (b)** ($3,000) or, if your filing status is married filing separately, ($1,500). For example, if the (loss) on line 18 is ($1,000), you would enter ($1,000) on Form 1040, line 13, because that is the smaller loss.

If the loss on line 19 is a smaller loss than the loss on line 18, **or** Form 1040, line 35, is a loss, use the **Capital Loss Carryover Worksheet** on this page to figure your short-term and long-term capital loss carryovers to 1994. You will need these amounts to complete your 1994 Schedule D, so be sure to keep the worksheet for your records.

Schedule D Tax Worksheet (keep for your records)

Use this worksheet to figure your tax **only** if both lines 17 and 18 of Schedule D are gains, **and:**

Your filing status is:	AND	Form 1040, line 37, is over:	Your filing status is:	AND	Form 1040, line 37, is over:
Single		$53,500	Married filing separately		$44,575
Married filing jointly or qualifying widow(er)		$89,150	Head of household		$76,400

1. Enter the amount from Form 1040, line 37 . . . . **1.** _____
2. **Net capital gain.** Enter the **smaller** of Schedule D, line 17 or line 18 . . . . **2.** _____
3. If you are filing Form 4952, enter the amount from Form 4952, line 4e . . . . **3.** _____
4. Subtract line 3 from line 2. If zero or less, stop here; you cannot use this worksheet to figure your tax. Instead, use the Tax Table or Tax Rate Schedules, whichever applies . . . . . . **4.** _____
5. Subtract line 4 from line 1 . . . . **5.** _____
6. Enter: $22,100 if single; $36,900 if married filing jointly or qualifying widow(er); $18,450 if married filing separately; or $29,600 if head of household . . . . **6.** _____
7. Enter the **greater** of line 5 or line 6 . . . . **7.** _____
8. Subtract line 7 from line 1 . . . . **8.** _____
9. Figure the tax on the amount on line 7. Use the Tax Table or Tax Rate Schedules, whichever applies . . . . . . **9.** _____
10. Multiply line 8 by 28% (.28) . . . . **10.** _____
11. Add lines 9 and 10 . . . . **11.** _____
12. Figure the tax on the amount on line 1. Use the Tax Table or Tax Rate Schedules, whichever applies . . . . . . **12.** _____
13. **Tax.** Enter the **smaller** of line 11 or line 12 here and on Form 1040, line 38. Check the box for Schedule D Tax Worksheet . **13.** _____

Capital Loss Carryover Worksheet (keep for your records)

Use this worksheet to figure your capital loss carryovers from 1993 to 1994 if Schedule D, line 19, is a loss and **(a)** that loss is a smaller loss than the loss on Schedule D, line 18, **or (b)** Form 1040, line 35, is a loss.

1. Enter the amount from Form 1040, line 35. If a loss, enclose the amount in parentheses . . . . **1.** _____
2. Enter the loss from Schedule D, line 19, as a positive amount **2.** _____
3. Combine lines 1 and 2. If zero or less, enter -0- . . . . **3.** _____
4. Enter the **smaller** of line 2 or line 3 . . . . **4.** _____
   Note: *If line 8 of Schedule D is a loss, go to line 5; otherwise, skip lines 5 through 9.*
5. Enter the loss from Schedule D, line 8, as a positive amount **5.** _____
6. Enter the gain, if any, from Schedule D, line 17 . . . . **6.** _____
7. Enter the amount from line 4 . . . . . **7.** _____
8. Add lines 6 and 7 . . . . **8.** _____
9. **Short-term capital loss carryover to 1994.** Subtract line 8 from line 5. If zero or less, enter -0- . . . . **9.** _____
   Note: *If line 17 of Schedule D is a loss, go to line 10; otherwise, skip lines 10 through 14.*
10. Enter the loss from Schedule D, line 17, as a positive amount **10.** _____
11. Enter the gain, if any, from Schedule D, line 8 . . . . **11.** _____
12. Subtract line 5 from line 4. If zero or less, enter -0- . . . . **12.** _____
13. Add lines 11 and 12 . . . . **13.** _____
14. **Long-term capital loss carryover to 1994.** Subtract line 13 from line 10. If zero or less, enter -0- . . . . **14.** _____

SCHEDULE E (Form 1040) Department of the Treasury Internal Revenue Service (O)	**Supplemental Income and Loss** (From rental real estate, royalties, partnerships, S corporations, estates, trusts, REMICs, etc.) ▶ **Attach to Form 1040 or Form 1041.** ▶ **See Instructions for Schedule E (Form 1040).**	OMB No. 1545-0074 19**93** Attachment Sequence No. **13**

Name(s) shown on return	Your social security number

Part I — Income or Loss From Rental Real Estate and Royalties

Note: *Report income and expenses from your business of renting personal property on* **Schedule C** *or* **C-EZ** *(see page E-1). Report farm rental income or loss from* **Form 4835** *on page 2, line 39.*

1	Show the kind and location of each **rental real estate property:**	2	For each rental real estate property listed on line 1, did you or your family use it for personal purposes for more than the greater of 14 days or 10% of the total days rented at fair rental value during the tax year? (See page E-1.)		Yes	No
A			A			
B			B			
C			C			

Income:			Properties			Totals (Add columns A, B, and C.)	
			A	B	C		
3	Rents received	3				3	
4	Royalties received	4				4	
Expenses:							
5	Advertising	5					
6	Auto and travel (see page E-2)	6					
7	Cleaning and maintenance	7					
8	Commissions	8					
9	Insurance	9					
10	Legal and other professional fees	10					
11	Management fees	11					
12	Mortgage interest paid to banks, etc. (see page E-2)	12				12	
13	Other interest	13					
14	Repairs	14					
15	Supplies	15					
16	Taxes	16					
17	Utilities	17					
18	Other (list) ▶	18					
19	Add lines 5 through 18	19				19	
20	Depreciation expense or depletion (see page E-2)	20				20	
21	Total expenses. Add lines 19 and 20	21					
22	Income or (loss) from rental real estate or royalty properties. Subtract line 21 from line 3 (rents) or line 4 (royalties). If the result is a (loss), see page E-2 to find out if you must file **Form 6198**	22					
23	Deductible rental real estate loss. **Caution:** *Your rental real estate loss on line 22 may be limited. See page E-3 to find out if you must file* **Form 8582**	23	( )	( )	( )		
24	**Income.** Add positive amounts shown on line 22. **Do not** include any losses					24	
25	**Losses.** Add royalty losses from line 22 and rental real estate losses from line 23. Enter the total losses here					25	( )
26	Total rental real estate and royalty income or (loss). Combine lines 24 and 25. Enter the result here. If Parts II, III, IV, and line 39 on page 2 do not apply to you, also enter this amount on Form 1040, line 18. Otherwise, include this amount in the total on line 40 on page 2					26	

For Paperwork Reduction Act Notice, see Form 1040 instructions.   Cat. No. 11344L   **Schedule E (Form 1040) 1993**

Schedule E (Form 1040) 1993 — Attachment Sequence No. **13** — Page **2**

Name(s) shown on return. Do not enter name and social security number if shown on other side.	Your social security number

Note: *If you report amounts from farming or fishing on Schedule E, you must enter your gross income from those activities on line 41 below.*

Part II — Income or Loss From Partnerships and S Corporations

If you report a loss from an at-risk activity, you MUST check either column **(e)** or **(f)** of line 27 to describe your investment in the activity. See page E-4. If you check column **(f)**, you must attach **Form 6198**.

27	(a) Name	(b) Enter P for partnership; S for S corporation	(c) Check if foreign partnership	(d) Employer identification number	Investment At Risk?	
					(e) All is at risk	(f) Some is not at risk
A						
B						
C						
D						
E						

	Passive Income and Loss		Nonpassive Income and Loss		
	(g) Passive loss allowed (attach Form 8582 if required)	(h) Passive income from Schedule K–1	(i) Nonpassive loss from Schedule K–1	(j) Section 179 expense deduction from Form 4562	(k) Nonpassive income from Schedule K–1
A					
B					
C					
D					
E					
28a Totals					
b Totals					

29	Add columns (h) and (k) of line 28a	29	
30	Add columns (g), (i), and (j) of line 28b	30	( )
31	Total partnership and S corporation income or (loss). Combine lines 29 and 30. Enter the result here and include in the total on line 40 below	31	

Part III — Income or Loss From Estates and Trusts

32	(a) Name	(b) Employer identification number
A		
B		
C		

	Passive Income and Loss		Nonpassive Income and Loss	
	(c) Passive deduction or loss allowed (attach Form 8582 if required)	(d) Passive income from Schedule K–1	(e) Deduction or loss from Schedule K–1	(f) Other income from Schedule K–1
A				
B				
C				
33a Totals				
b Totals				

34	Add columns (d) and (f) of line 33a	34	
35	Add columns (c) and (e) of line 33b	35	( )
36	Total estate and trust income or (loss). Combine lines 34 and 35. Enter the result here and include in the total on line 40 below	36	

Part IV — Income or Loss From Real Estate Mortgage Investment Conduits (REMICs)—Residual Holder

37	(a) Name	(b) Employer identification number	(c) Excess inclusion from Schedules Q, line 2c (see page E-4)	(d) Taxable income (net loss) from Schedules Q, line 1b	(e) Income from Schedules Q, line 3b

38	Combine columns (d) and (e) only. Enter the result here and include in the total on line 40 below	38	

Part V — Summary

39	Net farm rental income or (loss) from **Form 4835**. Also, complete line 41 below	39	
40	TOTAL income or (loss). Combine lines 26, 31, 36, 38, and 39. Enter the result here and on Form 1040, line 18 . . . . ▶	40	
41	**Reconciliation of Farming and Fishing Income:** Enter your **gross** farming and fishing income reported in Parts II and III and on line 39 (see page E-4)	41	

SCHEDULE EIC	Earned Income Credit	OMB No. 1545-0074

SCHEDULE EIC
(Form 1040A or 1040)

Department of the Treasury
Internal Revenue Service   (B)

Earned Income Credit

▶ **Attach to Form 1040A or 1040.**

▶ **See Instructions for Schedule EIC.**

OMB No. 1545-0074

19**93**

Attachment
Sequence No. **43**

Name(s) shown on return

Your social security number

Want the IRS to figure the credit for you? Just fill in this page. We'll do the rest.

General Information

To take
this credit

- You **must** have worked and earned **less** than $23,050, **and**
- Your adjusted gross income (Form 1040A, line 16, or Form 1040, line 31) **must** be **less** than $23,050, **and**
- Your filing status can be any status **except** married filing a separate return, **and**
- You **must** have at least one qualifying child (see boxes below), **and**
- You **cannot** be a qualifying child yourself.

A **qualifying child** is a child who:

is your:		**was (at the end of 1993):**		**who:**
son daughter adopted child grandchild stepchild or foster child	**A N D**	under age 19 or under age 24 and a full-time student or any age and permanently and totally disabled	**A N D**	lived with you in the U.S. for more than half of 1993* (or all of 1993 if a foster child*)

*If the child didn't live with you for the required time (for example, was born in 1993), see the **Exception** on page 64 (1040A) or page EIC-2 (1040).

Do you have at least one qualifying child?	**No**	You **cannot** take the credit. Enter "NO" next to line 28c of Form 1040A (or line 56 of Form 1040).
	Yes	Go to line 1. But if the child was married or is also a qualifying child of another person (other than your spouse if filing a joint return), first see page 64 (1040A) or page EIC-2 (1040).

Information About Your Qualifying Child or Children

If more than two qualifying children, see page 65 (1040A) or page EIC-2 (1040). **1(a)** Child's name (first, initial, and last name)	**(b)** Child's year of birth	For a child born **before 1975**, check if child was—		**(e)** If child was born **before 1993**, enter the child's social security number	**(f)** Child's relationship to you (for example, son, grandchild, etc.)	**(g)** Number of months child lived with you in the U.S. in 1993
		(c) a student **under age 24** at end of 1993	**(d)** disabled (see booklet)			
	19					
	19					

Caution: *If a child you listed above was born in 1993 **and** you chose to claim the credit or exclusion for child care expenses for this child on **Schedule 2** (Form 1040A) or **Form 2441** (Form 1040), check here* . . . . ▶ ☐

Do you want the IRS to figure the credit for you?	**Yes**	Fill in lines 2 and 3; **and** enter the amount from Form 1040A, line 16, or Form 1040, line 31, here.	$
	No	Go to page 2 on the back now.	

Other Information

2 Enter any **nontaxable earned income** (see page 65 (1040A) or page EIC-2 (1040)) such as military housing and subsistence or contributions to a 401(k) plan. Also, list type and amount here. ▶ . . . . | **2** |

3 Enter the total amount you paid in 1993 for health insurance that covered at least one qualifying child. See instructions . . . . | **3** |

If you want the IRS to figure the credit for you:	**S T O P**	**Attach this schedule to your return.** • If filing **Form 1040A**, print "EIC" on the line next to line 28c. • If filing **Form 1040**, print "EIC" on the dotted line next to line 56.

For Paperwork Reduction Act Notice, see Form 1040A or 1040 instructions.   Cat. No. 14636S   **Schedule EIC (Form 1040A or 1040) 1993**

Figure Your Basic Credit

4   Enter the amount from line 7 of Form 1040A or Form 1040. If you received a taxable scholarship or fellowship grant, see instructions . . . . | **4** |

5   Enter any **nontaxable earned income** (see page 65 (1040A) or page EIC-2 (1040)) such as military housing and subsistence or contributions to a 401(k) plan. Also, list type and amount here. ▶ ....
.... | **5** |

6   **Form 1040 Filers Only:** If you were self-employed **or** used Sch. C or C-EZ as a statutory employee, enter the amount from the worksheet on page EIC-3 . . . . | **6** |

7   **Earned income.** Add lines 4, 5, and 6. If $23,050 or more, you **cannot** take the credit. Enter "NO" next to line 28c of Form 1040A (or line 56 of Form 1040) . . . . ▶ | **7** |

8   Use **line 7** above to find your credit in **TABLE A** on pages **69 and 70** (1040A) or pages **EIC-4 and 5** (1040). Enter here . . . . | **8** |

9   **Adjusted gross income.** Enter the amount from Form 1040A, line 16, or Form 1040, line 31 ▶ | **9** |

10 **Is line 9 $12,200 or more?**

   YES. Use **line 9** to find your credit in **TABLE A** on pages **69 and 70** (1040A) or pages **EIC-4 and 5** (1040). Enter here . . . . . | **10** |
   NO. Go to line 11.

11 **Basic credit:**
   • If you answered "YES" to line 10, enter the **smaller** of line 8 or line 10.
   • If you answered "NO" to line 10, enter the amount from line 8. } . . . . | **11** |

   Next: To take the health insurance credit, fill in lines 12–16. To take the extra credit for a child born in 1993, fill in lines 17–19. Otherwise, go to line 20 now.

Figure Your Health Insurance Credit

12 Use **line 7** above to find your credit in **TABLE B** on page **71** (1040A) or page **EIC-6** (1040). Enter here . . . . | **12** |

13 **Is line 9 above $12,200 or more?**

   YES. Use **line 9** to find your credit in **TABLE B** on page **71** (1040A) or page **EIC-6** (1040). Enter here. . . . . | **13** |
   NO. Go to line 14.

14 • If you answered "YES" to line 13, enter the **smaller** of line 12 or line 13.
   • If you answered "NO" to line 13, enter the amount from line 12. } | **14** |

15 Enter the total amount you paid in 1993 for health insurance that covered at least one qualifying child. See instructions . . . . . | **15** |

16 **Health insurance credit.** Enter the **smaller** of line 14 or line 15 . . . . | **16** |

Figure Your Extra Credit for Child Born in 1993

   Take this credit **only** if you did not take the credit or exclusion for child care expenses on **Schedule 2** or **Form 2441** for the same child.

   TIP: You can take **both** the **basic credit** and the **extra credit** for your child born in 1993.

17 Use **line 7** above to find your credit in **TABLE C** on page **72** (1040A) or page **EIC-7** (1040). Enter here . . . . | **17** |

18 **Is line 9 above $12,200 or more?**

   YES. Use **line 9** to find your credit in **TABLE C** on page **72** (1040A) or page **EIC-7** (1040). Enter here . . . . | **18** |
   NO. Go to line 19.

19 **Extra credit for child born in 1993:**
   • If you answered "YES" to line 18, enter the **smaller** of line 17 or line 18.
   • If you answered "NO" to line 18, enter the amount from line 17. } . . . . | **19** |

Figure Your Total Earned Income Credit

20 Add lines 11, 16, and 19. Enter the total here and on Form 1040A, line 28c (or on Form 1040, line 56). This is your **total earned income credit** . . . . ▶ | **20** |

   TIP: Do you want the earned income credit added to your take-home pay in 1994? To see if you qualify, get **Form W-5** from your employer or by calling the IRS at 1-800-829-3676.

Schedule R
(Form 1040)

Department of the Treasury
Internal Revenue Service   (O)

Credit for the Elderly or the Disabled

► **Attach to Form 1040.**   ► **See separate instructions for Schedule R.**

OMB No. 1545-0074

19**93**

Attachment
Sequence No. **16**

Name(s) shown on Form 1040

Your social security number

You may be able to use Schedule R to reduce your tax if by the end of 1993:

● You were age 65 or older, **OR** ● You were under age 65, you retired on **permanent and total** disability, and you received taxable disability income.

But you must also meet other tests. See the separate instructions for Schedule R.

Note: *In most cases, the IRS can figure the credit for you. See page 25 of the Form 1040 instructions.*

Part I	**Check the Box for Your Filing Status and Age**

If your filing status is:	And by the end of 1993:	Check only one box:
Single, Head of household, or Qualifying widow(er) with dependent child	**1** You were 65 or older **1**	☐
	2 You were under 65 and you retired on permanent and total disability . . . **2**	☐
Married filing a joint return	**3** Both spouses were 65 or older **3**	☐
	4 Both spouses were under 65, but only one spouse retired on permanent and total disability **4**	☐
	5 Both spouses were under 65, and both retired on permanent and total disability **5**	☐
	6 One spouse was 65 or older, and the other spouse was under 65 and retired on permanent and total disability **6**	☐
	7 One spouse was 65 or older, and the other spouse was under 65 and **NOT** retired on permanent and total disability **7**	☐
Married filing a separate return	**8** You were 65 or older and you lived apart from your spouse for all of 1993 . . **8**	☐
	9 You were under 65, you retired on permanent and total disability, and you lived apart from your spouse for all of 1993 . . . . **9**	☐

If you checked box 1, 3, 7, or 8, skip Part II and complete Part III on the back. All others, complete Parts II and III.

Part II	**Statement of Permanent and Total Disability** (Complete **only** if you checked box 2, 4, 5, 6, or 9 above.)

IF: 1 You filed a physician's statement for this disability for 1983 or an earlier year, or you filed a statement for tax years after 1983 and your physician signed line B on the statement, **AND**

   2 Due to your continued disabled condition, you were unable to engage in any substantial gainful activity in 1993, check this box . . . . ► ☐

● If you checked this box, you do not have to file another statement for 1993.
● If you **did not** check this box, have your physician complete the following statement.

Physician's Statement (See instructions at bottom of page 2.)

I certify that _____
                                         Name of disabled person

was permanently and totally disabled on January 1, 1976, or January 1, 1977, **OR** was permanently and totally disabled on the date he or she retired. If retired after December 31, 1976, enter the date retired. ► _____

Physician: Sign your name on **either** line A or B below.

A The disability has lasted or can be expected to last continuously for at least a year . . . . _____

Physician's signature	Date

B There is no reasonable probability that the disabled condition will ever improve . . . . . _____

Physician's signature	Date

Physician's name	Physician's address

For Paperwork Reduction Act Notice, see Form 1040 instructions.   Cat. No. 11359K   **Schedule R (Form 1040) 1993**

Part III   **Figure Your Credit**

10 If you checked (in Part I):   **Enter:**

Box 1, 2, 4, or 7 . . . . $5,000

Box 3, 5, or 6 . . . . $7,500 } **10**

Box 8 or 9 . . . . $3,750

     Caution: *If you checked box 2, 4, 5, 6, or 9 in Part I, you* **MUST** *complete line 11 below. All others, skip line 11 and enter the amount from line 10 on line 12.*

11 If you checked:

- Box 6 in Part I, add $5,000 to the taxable disability income of the spouse who was under age 65. Enter the total.

- Box 2, 4, or 9 in Part I, enter your taxable disability income. } . . . **11**

- Box 5 in Part I, add your taxable disability income to your spouse's taxable disability income. Enter the total.

     TIP: For more details on what to include on line 11, see the instructions.

12 • If you completed line 11, look at lines 10 and 11. Enter the **smaller** of the two amounts. } . . . **12**

     • All others, enter the amount from line 10.

13 Enter the following pensions, annuities, or disability income that you (and your spouse if filing a joint return) received in 1993:

a Nontaxable part of social security benefits, and Nontaxable part of railroad retirement benefits treated as } . . . **13a** social security. See instructions.

b Nontaxable veterans' pensions, and Any other pension, annuity, or disability benefit that is } . . . **13b** excluded from income under any other provision of law. See instructions.

c Add lines 13a and 13b. (Even though these income items are not taxable, they **must** be included here to figure your credit.) If you did not receive any of the types of nontaxable income listed on line 13a or 13b, enter -0- on line 13c **13c**

14 Enter the amount from Form 1040, line 32 **14**

15 If you checked (in Part I):   **Enter:**

Box 1 or 2 . . . . $7,500

Box 3, 4, 5, 6, or 7 . . . . $10,000 } **15**

Box 8 or 9 . . . . . . $5,000

16 Subtract line 15 from line 14. If line 15 is more than line 14, enter -0- **16**

17 Divide line 16 above by 2 . . . . **17**

18 Add lines 13c and 17 . . . . **18**

19 Subtract line 18 from line 12. If line 18 is more than line 12, stop here; you **cannot** take the credit. Otherwise, go to line 21 . . . . **19**

20 Decimal amount used to figure the credit . . . . **20**   × .15

21 Multiply line 19 above by the decimal amount (.15) on line 20. Enter the result here and on Form 1040, line 42. **Caution:** *If you file Schedule C, C-EZ, D, E, or F (Form 1040), your credit may be limited. See the instructions for line 21 for the amount of credit you can claim* **21**

Instructions for Physician's Statement

Taxpayer

If you retired after December 31, 1976, enter the date you retired in the space provided in Part II.

Physician

A person is permanently and totally disabled if **both** of the following apply:

    1. He or she cannot engage in any substantial gainful activity because of a physical or mental condition, and

2. A physician determines that the disability has lasted or can be expected to last continuously for at least a year or can lead to death.

SCHEDULE SE	Self-Employment Tax	OMB No. 1545-0074
(Form 1040)	▶ See Instructions for Schedule SE (Form 1040).	**1993**
Department of the Treasury Internal Revenue Service (O)	▶ Attach to Form 1040.	Attachment Sequence No. **17**

Name of person with **self-employment** income (as shown on Form 1040)	Social security number of person with **self-employment** income ▶	

Who Must File Schedule SE

You must file Schedule SE if:

- Your wages (and tips) subject to social security AND Medicare tax (or railroad retirement tax) were less than $135,000; **AND**
- Your net earnings from self-employment from other than church employee income (line 4 of Short Schedule SE or line 4c of Long Schedule SE) were $400 or more; **OR**
- You had church employee income of $108.28 or more. Income from services you performed as a minister or a member of a religious order **is not** church employee income. See page SE-1.

Note: *Even if you have a loss or a small amount of income from self-employment, it may be to your benefit to file Schedule SE and use either "optional method" in Part II of Long Schedule SE. See page SE-3.*

Exception. If your only self-employment income was from earnings as a minister, member of a religious order, or Christian Science practitioner, **AND** you filed Form 4361 and received IRS approval not to be taxed on those earnings, **DO NOT** file Schedule SE. Instead, write "Exempt–Form 4361" on Form 1040, line 47.

May I Use Short Schedule SE or MUST I Use Long Schedule SE?

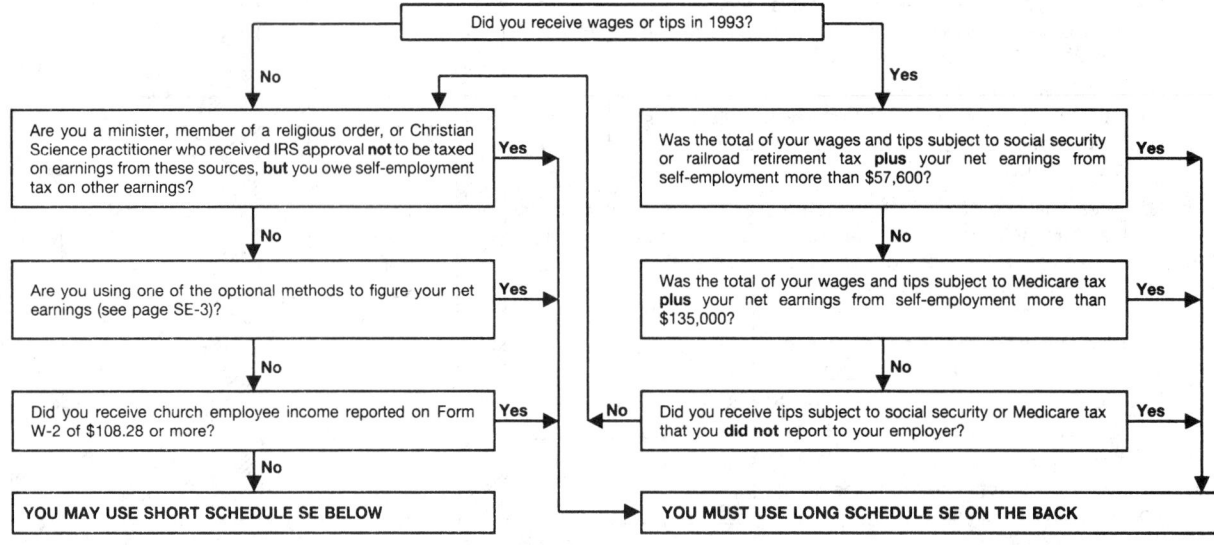

Section A—Short Schedule SE. Caution: *Read above to see if you can use Short Schedule SE.*

1	Net farm profit or (loss) from Schedule F, line 36, and farm partnerships, Schedule K-1 (Form 1065), line 15a	**1**
2	Net profit or (loss) from Schedule C, line 31; Schedule C-EZ, line 3; and Schedule K-1 (Form 1065), line 15a (other than farming). Ministers and members of religious orders see page SE-1 for amounts to report on this line. See page SE-2 for other income to report	**2**
3	Combine lines 1 and 2	**3**
4	**Net earnings from self-employment.** Multiply line 3 by 92.35% (.9235). If less than $400, **do not** file this schedule; you do not owe self-employment tax . . . . ▶	**4**
5	**Self-employment tax.** If the amount on line 4 is: • $57,600 or less, multiply line 4 by 15.3% (.153) and enter the result. • More than $57,600 but less than $135,000, multiply the amount in excess of $57,600 by 2.9% (.029). Then, add $8,812.80 to the result and enter the total. • $135,000 or more, enter $11,057.40. Also enter on **Form 1040, line 47. (Important:** You are allowed a deduction for **one-half** of this amount. Multiply line 5 by 50% (.5) and enter the result on **Form 1040, line 25.)**	**5**

For Paperwork Reduction Act Notice, see Form 1040 instructions.   Cat. No. 11358Z   **Schedule SE (Form 1040) 1993**

Name of person with **self-employment** income (as shown on Form 1040)	Social security number of person with **self-employment** income ▶	: :

Section B—Long Schedule SE

Part I   Self-Employment Tax

Note: *If your only income subject to self-employment tax is church employee income, skip lines 1 through 4b. Enter -0- on line 4c and go to line 5a. Income from services you performed as a minister or a member of a religious order is **not** church employee income. See page SE-1.*

A   If you are a minister, member of a religious order, or Christian Science practitioner **AND** you filed Form 4361, but you had $400 or more of **other** net earnings from self-employment, check here and continue with Part I . . . . . . ▶ ☐

1	Net farm profit or (loss) from Schedule F, line 36, and farm partnerships, Schedule K-1 (Form 1065), line 15a. **Note:** *Skip this line if you use the farm optional method. See page SE-3* . .	**1**	
2	Net profit or (loss) from Schedule C, line 31; Schedule C-EZ, line 3; and Schedule K-1 (Form 1065), line 15a (other than farming). Ministers and members of religious orders see page SE-1 for amounts to report on this line. See page SE-2 for other income to report. **Note:** *Skip this line if you use the nonfarm optional method. See page SE-3*	**2**	
3	Combine lines 1 and 2	**3**	
4a	If line 3 is more than zero, multiply line 3 by 92.35% (.9235). Otherwise, enter amount from line 3	**4a**	
b	If you elected one or both of the optional methods, enter the total of lines 17 and 19 here . .	**4b**	
c	Combine lines 4a and 4b. If less than $400, **do not** file this schedule; you do not owe self-employment tax. **Exception.** If less than $400 and you had church employee income, enter -0- and continue . ▶	**4c**	
5a	Enter your church employee income from Form W-2. **Caution:** *See page SE-1 for definition of church employee income* **5a**		
b	Multiply line 5a by 92.35% (.9235). If less than $100, enter -0-	**5b**	
6	**Net earnings from self-employment.** Add lines 4c and 5b	**6**	
7	Maximum amount of combined wages and self-employment earnings subject to social security tax or the 6.2% portion of the 7.65% railroad retirement (tier 1) tax for 1993	**7**	57,600 00
8a	Total social security wages and tips (from Form(s) W-2) and railroad retirement (tier 1) compensation **8a**		
b	Unreported tips subject to social security tax (from Form 4137, line 9) **8b**		
c	Add lines 8a and 8b	**8c**	
9	Subtract line 8c from line 7. If zero or less, enter -0- here and on line 10 and go to line 12a ▶	**9**	
10	Multiply the **smaller** of line 6 or line 9 by 12.4% (.124)	**10**	
11	Maximum amount of combined wages and self-employment earnings subject to Medicare tax or the 1.45% portion of the 7.65% railroad retirement (tier 1) tax for 1993	**11**	135,000 00
12a	Total Medicare wages and tips (from Form(s) W-2) and railroad retirement (tier 1) compensation **12a**		
b	Unreported tips subject to Medicare tax (from Form 4137, line 14) . **12b**		
c	Add lines 12a and 12b	**12c**	
13	Subtract line 12c from line 11. If zero or less, enter -0- here and on line 14 and go to line 15 .	**13**	
14	Multiply the **smaller** of line 6 or line 13 by 2.9% (.029)	**14**	
15	**Self-employment tax.** Add lines 10 and 14. Enter here and on **Form 1040, line 47. (Important:** You are allowed a deduction for **one-half** of this amount. Multiply line 15 by 50% (.5) and enter the result on **Form 1040, line 25.)**	**15**	

Part II   Optional Methods To Figure Net Earnings (See page SE-3.)

Farm Optional Method. You may use this method **only** if **(a)** Your gross farm income[1] was not more than $2,400 **or (b)** Your gross farm income[1] was more than $2,400 and your net farm profits[2] were less than $1,733.

16	Maximum income for optional methods	**16**	1,600 00
17	Enter the **smaller** of: two-thirds (⅔) of gross farm income[1] (not less than zero) or $1,600. Also, include this amount on line 4b above	**17**	

Nonfarm Optional Method. You may use this method **only** if **(a)** Your net nonfarm profits[3] were less than $1,733 and also less than 72.189% of your gross nonfarm income,[4] **and (b)** You had net earnings from self-employment of at least $400 in 2 of the prior 3 years. **Caution:** *You may use this method no more than five times.*

18	Subtract line 17 from line 16	**18**	
19	Enter the **smaller** of: two-thirds (⅔) of gross nonfarm income[4] (not less than zero) **or** the amount on line 18. Also, include this amount on line 4b above	**19**	

[1] From Schedule F, line 11, and Schedule K-1 (Form 1065), line 15b.   [3] From Schedule C, line 31; Schedule C-EZ, line 3; and Schedule K-1 (Form 1065), line 15a.
[2] From Schedule F, line 36, and Schedule K-1 (Form 1065), line 15a.   [4] From Schedule C, line 7; Schedule C-EZ, line 1; and Schedule K-1 (Form 1065), line 15c.

Form **1040-ES**

Department of the Treasury
Internal Revenue Service

Estimated Tax for Individuals

This package is primarily for first-time filers of estimated tax.

OMB No. 1545-0087

1993

Paperwork Reduction Act Notice

We ask for the information on the payment vouchers to carry out the Internal Revenue laws of the United States. You are required to give us the information. We need it to ensure that you are complying with these laws and to allow us to figure and collect the right amount of tax.

The time needed to complete the worksheets and prepare and file the payment vouchers will vary depending on individual circumstances. The estimated average time is: **Recordkeeping,** 1 hr., 19 min.; **Learning about the law,** 19 min.; **Preparing the worksheets and payment vouchers,** 53 min.; **Copying, assembling, and sending the payment voucher to the IRS,** 10 min. If you have comments concerning the accuracy of these time estimates or suggestions for making this package easier, we would be happy to hear from you. You can write to both the **Internal Revenue Service,** Washington, DC 20224, Attention: IRS Reports Clearance Officer, T:FP; and the **Office of Management and Budget,** Paperwork Reduction Project (1545-0087), Washington, DC 20503. **DO NOT** send the payment vouchers to either of these offices. Instead, see **Where To File Your Payment Voucher** on page 5.

Purpose of This Package

Use this package to figure and pay your estimated tax. Estimated tax is the method used to pay tax on income that is not subject to withholding; for example, earnings from self-employment, interest, dividends, rents, alimony, unemployment compensation, etc.

This package is primarily for first-time filers who are or may be subject to paying estimated tax. This package can also be used if you did not receive or have lost your preprinted 1040-ES package. The estimated tax worksheet on page 3 will help you figure the correct amount to pay. The vouchers in this package are for crediting your estimated tax payments to your account correctly. Use the **Record of Estimated Tax Payments** on page 5 to keep track of the payments you have made and the number and amount of your remaining payments.

After we receive your first payment voucher from this package, we will mail you a preprinted 1040-ES package with your name, address, and social security number on each payment voucher. Use the preprinted vouchers when you receive them to make your **remaining** estimated tax payments for the year. This will speed processing, reduce processing costs, and reduce the chance of errors.

Do not use the vouchers in this package to notify the IRS of a **change of address.** If you have a new address, get **Form 8822,** Change of Address, by calling 1-800-TAX-FORM (1-800-829-3676). Send the completed form to the Internal Revenue Service Center where you filed your last tax return. The Service Center will update your record and send you new preprinted payment vouchers.

Note: *Continue to use your old preprinted payment vouchers to make payments of estimated tax until you receive the new package of preprinted payment vouchers.*

Who Must Make Estimated Tax Payments

In most cases, you must make estimated tax payments if you expect to owe, after subtracting your withholding and credits, at least $500 in tax for 1993, and you expect your withholding and credits to be less than the **smaller** of:

● 90% of the tax shown on your 1993 tax return, or

● 100% of the tax shown on your 1992 tax return (the return must cover all 12 months).

Caution: If 100% of your 1992 tax is the **smaller** of the two amounts, see **Limit on Use of Prior Year's Tax** on this page for special rules that may apply to you.

Generally, you do not have to pay estimated tax if you were a U.S. citizen or resident alien for all of 1992 and you had no tax liability for the full 12-month 1992 tax year.

The estimated tax rules apply to:

● U.S. citizens and residents,

● Residents of Puerto Rico, the Virgin Islands, Guam, the Commonwealth of the Northern Mariana Islands, and American Samoa, and

● Nonresident aliens (use Form 1040-ES (NR)).

If you also receive salaries and wages, you can avoid having to make estimated tax payments by asking your employer to take more tax out of your earnings. To do this, file a new **Form W-4,** Employee's Withholding Allowance Certificate, with your employer.

Caution: You may not make joint estimated tax payments if you or your spouse is a nonresident alien, you are separated under a decree of divorce or separate maintenance, or you and your spouse have different tax years.

Limit on Use of Prior Year's Tax. Some individuals (other than farmers and fishermen) with income over a certain amount must make a special computation to figure their estimated tax payments. Although these individuals may use 100% of their 1992 tax to figure the amount of their first payment, they may not be able to use that amount to figure their remaining payments. To see if this special computation applies to you, first fill in the **1993 Estimated Tax Worksheet** on page 3 through line 14b. Then, answer the questions below. But if you answer NO to any question, stop and read the instructions below question 3.

1. Did you make any estimated tax payments for 1992, 1991, or 1990, **OR** were you charged an estimated tax penalty for any of those years? (If either applies, answer "Yes.") . . . . □ **Yes** □ **No**

2. Is your 1993 adjusted gross income (AGI) on line 1 of the worksheet more than $75,000 ($37,500 if married filing separately)? . . . . □ **Yes** □ **No**

3. Do you expect your 1993 **modified AGI** (defined below) to exceed your 1992 actual AGI by more than $40,000 ($20,000 if married filing separately)? . . . . . . □ **Yes** □ **No**

If you answered NO to any of the questions above, you don't have to make the special computation. Instead, fill in the rest of the worksheet on page 3.

If you answered YES to all three of the questions above, you must make the special computation. Do not fill in the rest of the worksheet on page 3. Instead, use the **1993 Estimated Tax Worksheet Limiting Use of Prior Year's Tax** in Pub. 505 to figure all your estimated tax payments. That worksheet uses 100% of your 1992 tax to figure your first payment.

Modified AGI for this purpose means AGI figured without including any gain from the sale or exchange of your main home or gain from a casualty, theft, condemnation, or other involuntary conversion required to be shown on your 1993 return. Partners, and shareholders in an S corporation, must include their income, gains and losses (other than from the disposition of their interests in a partnership or S corporation), and deductions for 1992 from the partnership or S corporation instead of the amounts for 1993. But this rule does not apply to general partners, partners who owned at least a 10% capital or profit interest in the partnership, or shareholders who owned at least 10% of the stock (vote or value) of the S corporation.

Additional Information You May Need

Most of the information you will need can be found in:
  Pub. 505, Tax Withholding and Estimated Tax
Other available information:
  Pub. 553, Highlights of 1992 Tax Changes
  Instructions for the 1992 Form 1040 or 1040A
For forms and publications, call 1-800-TAX-FORM (1-800-829-3676). For assistance, call 1-800-829-1040.

Cat. No. 11340T

(Continued on page 2)

Tax Law Changes Effective for 1993

Use your 1992 tax return as a guide in figuring your 1993 estimated tax, but be sure to consider the changes noted in this section. For more information on the following provisions and other changes that may affect your 1993 estimated tax, see Pub. 553.

Qualified Electric Vehicle Credit. A tax credit equal to 10% of the cost of a qualified new electric vehicle, or $4,000, whichever is less, is available for each vehicle placed in service after June 30, 1993.

Deduction for Clean-Fuel Vehicle Property. A deduction is available for qualified clean-fuel vehicle property placed in service after June 30, 1993. Qualified clean-fuel vehicle property includes the engine (and its related fuel storage, delivery, and exhaust systems) of a new vehicle that uses a clean-burning fuel. New retrofit parts and components used to convert a vehicle to operate on a clean-burning fuel are also qualified clean-fuel vehicle property. To qualify, the vehicle must be made for use on public roads and have at least 4 wheels. Clean-burning fuels are natural gas, liquefied natural gas, liquefied petroleum (LP) gas, hydrogen, electricity, and fuels containing at least 85% alcohol (including methanol or ethanol) or ether. The deduction is generally limited to $2,000 for each vehicle. A higher limit applies to certain trucks, vans, and buses.

Repeal of Certain Tax Preferences Relating to Oil and Gas Production. Starting in 1993, the alternative minimum tax preference for oil and gas depletion is repealed for independent producers and royalty owners. Also, beginning in 1993, for taxpayers other than integrated oil companies, the tax preference item for intangible drilling costs of oil and gas wells will no longer apply, except to the extent this change causes alternative minimum taxable income (with certain adjustments) to be reduced by more than 30%. In addition, the energy preference adjustment has been eliminated.

Travel Expenses. Travel expenses paid or incurred after 1992 in connection with employment away from home are not deductible if that period of employment exceeds 1 year. Such employment is not considered temporary.

Standard Deduction for 1993. If you do not itemize your deductions, you may take the 1993 standard deduction listed below:

Filing Status	Standard Deduction
Married filing jointly or Qualifying widow(er)	$6,200
Head of household	$5,450
Single	$3,700
Married filing separately	$3,100

Caution: If you can be claimed as a dependent on another person's 1993 return, your standard deduction is the greater of $600 or your earned income, up to the standard deduction amount.

An additional amount is added to the standard deduction if:

1. You are an unmarried individual (single or head of household) and are:

65 or older or blind	$900
65 or older and blind	$1,800

2. You are a married individual (filing jointly or separately) or a qualifying widow(er) and are:

65 or older or blind	$700
65 or older and blind	$1,400
Both spouses 65 or older	$1,400 *
Both spouses 65 or older and blind	$2,800 *

* If married filing separately, these amounts apply only if you can claim an exemption for your spouse.

To Figure Your Estimated Tax Use

- The **1993 Estimated Tax Worksheet** on page 3
- The instructions on page 4 for the worksheet on page 3
- The **1993 Tax Rate Schedules** below
- Your 1992 tax return as a guide

See the 1992 Instructions for Form 1040 or 1040A for information on figuring your income, deductions, and credits, including the taxable amount of social security benefits.

If you receive your income unevenly throughout the year, for example, you operate your business on a seasonal basis, you may be able to lower or eliminate the amount of your required estimated tax payment for one or more periods by using the annualized income installment method. See Pub. 505 for details.

To amend or correct your estimated tax, see **Amending Estimated Tax Payments** on page 4.

1993 Tax Rate Schedules

Caution: *Do not use these Tax Rate Schedules to figure your 1992 taxes. Use only to figure your 1993 estimated taxes.*

Single—Schedule X

If line 5 is: Over—	But not over—	The tax is:	of the amount over—
$0	$22,100	. . . . 15%	$0
22,100	53,500	$3,315.00 + 28%	22,100
53,500	. . . .	12,107.00 + 31%	53,500

Head of household—Schedule Z

If line 5 is: Over—	But not over—	The tax is:	of the amount over—
$0	$29,600	. . . . 15%	$0
29,600	76,400	$4,440.00 + 28%	29,600
76,400	. . . .	17,544.00 + 31%	76,400

Married filing jointly or Qualifying widow(er)—Schedule Y-1

If line 5 is: Over—	But not over—	The tax is:	of the amount over—
$0	$36,900	. . . . 15%	$0
36,900	89,150	$5,535.00 + 28%	36,900
89,150	. . . .	20,165.00 + 31%	89,150

Married filing separately—Schedule Y-2

If line 5 is: Over—	But not over—	The tax is:	of the amount over—
$0	$18,450	. . . . 15%	$0
18,450	44,575	$2,767.50 + 28%	18,450
44,575	. . . .	10,082.50 + 31%	44,575

1993 Estimated Tax Worksheet (keep for your records)

1	Enter amount of adjusted gross income you expect in 1993	**1**	
2	• If you plan to itemize deductions, enter the estimated total of your itemized deductions. **Caution:** If line 1 above is over $108,450 ($54,225 if married filing separately), your deduction may be reduced. See Pub. 505 for details. • If you do not plan to itemize deductions, see **Standard Deduction for 1993** on page 2, and enter your standard deduction here.	**2**	
3	Subtract line 2 from line 1	**3**	
4	Exemptions. Multiply $2,350 by the number of personal exemptions. If you can be claimed as a dependent on another person's 1993 return, your personal exemption is not allowed. **Caution:** If line 1 above is over $162,700 ($135,600 if head of household; $108,450 if single; $81,350 if married filing separately), get Pub. 505 to figure the amount to enter	**4**	
5	Subtract line 4 from line 3	**5**	
6	**Tax.** Figure your tax on the amount on line 5 by using the 1993 Tax Rate Schedules on page 2. DO NOT use the Tax Table or the Tax Rate Schedules in the 1992 Form 1040 or Form 1040A instructions. **Caution:** If you have a net capital gain and line 5 is over $89,150 ($76,400 if head of household; $53,500 if single; $44,575 if married filing separately), get Pub. 505 to figure the tax	**6**	
7	Additional taxes (see line 7 instructions)	**7**	
8	Add lines 6 and 7	**8**	
9	Credits (see line 9 instructions). Do not include any income tax withholding on this line . . .	**9**	
10	Subtract line 9 from line 8. Enter the result, but not less than zero	**10**	
11	Self-employment tax. Estimate of 1993 net earnings from self-employment $.................; if **$57,600 or less,** multiply the amount by .153; if **more than $57,600,** see line 11 instructions for the amount to enter. **Caution:** If you also have wages subject to social security or Medicare tax, get Pub. 505 to figure the amount to enter	**11**	
12	Other taxes (see line 12 instructions)	**12**	
13a	Add lines 10 through 12	**13a**	
b	Earned income credit and credit from **Form 4136**	**13b**	
c	Subtract line 13b from line 13a. Enter the result, but not less than zero. **THIS IS YOUR TOTAL 1993 ESTIMATED TAX** . . . . ▶	**13c**	

14a	Multiply line 13c by 90% (66⅔% for farmers and fishermen) . . .	**14a**			
b	Enter 100% of the tax shown on your 1992 tax return	**14b**			
	Caution: If 14b is **smaller** than 14a **and** line 1 above is over $75,000 ($37,500 if married filing separately), stop here and see **Limit on Use of Prior Year's Tax** on page 1 before continuing.				
c	Enter the **smaller** of line 14a or 14b. **THIS IS YOUR REQUIRED ANNUAL PAYMENT TO AVOID A PENALTY** . . . . ▶			**14c**	
	Caution: Generally, if you do not prepay at least the amount on line 14c, you may owe a penalty for not paying enough estimated tax. To avoid a penalty, make sure your estimate on line 13c is as accurate as possible. Even if you pay the required annual payment, you may still owe tax when you file your return. If you prefer, you may pay the amount shown on line 13c. For more details, get Pub. 505.				
15	Income tax withheld and estimated to be withheld during 1993 (including income tax withholding on pensions, annuities, certain deferred income, etc.)			**15**	
16	Subtract line 15 from line 14c. (**Note:** *If zero or less, or line 13c minus line 15 is less than $500, stop here. You are not required to make estimated tax payments.*)			**16**	
17	If the first payment you are required to make is due April 15, 1993, enter ¼ of line 16 (minus any 1992 overpayment that you are applying to this installment) here and on your payment voucher(s)			**17**	

Instructions for Worksheet on Page 3

Line 1—If you are self-employed, be sure to take into account the deduction for one-half of your self-employment tax.

Line 7—Additional Taxes. Enter the additional taxes from **Form 4970,** Tax on Accumulation Distribution of Trusts, or **Form 4972,** Tax on Lump-Sum Distributions.

Line 9—Credits. See the 1992 Form 1040, lines 41 through 45, or Form 1040A, lines 24a and 24b, and the related instructions.

Line 11—Self-Employment Tax. If you and your spouse make joint estimated tax payments and you both have self-employment income, figure the self-employment tax for each of you separately. Enter the total on line 11. When figuring your estimate of 1993 net earnings from self-employment, be sure to use only 92.35% of your total net profit from self-employment.

If your estimate of 1993 net earnings from self-employment is more than $57,600 but less than $135,000, multiply the amount in excess of $57,600 by .029. Add $8,812.80 to the result and enter the total on line 11. If your estimate of 1993 net earnings from self-employment is $135,000 or more, enter $11,057.40 on line 11.

Line 12—Other Taxes. Enter any other taxes, such as tax on early distributions (Form 5329, Part II, only), and alternative minimum tax. Do not include any recapture of Federal mortgage subsidy. For details, see the 1992 Instructions for Form 1040, line 49. You do not have to include social security and Medicare tax on tip income not reported to your employer or uncollected employee social security and Medicare or RRTA tax on tips or group-term life insurance.

Payment Due Dates

Use one of the following charts to determine your payment due dates. Payments are due by the dates indicated whether or not you are outside the United States and Puerto Rico.

You may have a large change in income, deductions, additional taxes, or credits during the year that may require you to make estimated tax payments. If you meet the requirement to make estimated tax payments after March 31, use Chart B. Otherwise, use Chart A to determine the payment due dates.

Whether you have steady or unexpected income, you do not have to make the payment due January 18, 1994, if you:

• File your 1993 Form 1040 or 1040A by January 31, 1994, and

• Pay the entire balance due with the return.

Chart A—Individuals With Steady Income. You may pay all of your estimated tax by April 15, 1993, or in four equal amounts by the dates below.

Estimated payments due by:

1st Payment	April 15, 1993
2nd Payment	June 15, 1993
3rd Payment	Sept. 15, 1993
4th Payment	Jan. 18, 1994

Chart B—Individuals With Unexpected Income. Use the amount on line 16 of the estimated tax worksheet, minus any 1992 overpayment that was applied to 1993, for the estimated tax due.

If the requirement to pay estimated tax is met after:	Payment date is:	Of the estimated tax due, pay:
Mar. 31 and before June 1 .	June 15, 1993 . . .	1/2
May 31 and before Sept. 1 .	Sept. 15, 1993 . . .	3/4
Aug. 31	Jan. 18, 1994 . . .	all

Farmers and Fishermen. If at least two-thirds of your gross income for 1992 or 1993 is from farming or fishing, you may do one of the following:

• Pay all of your estimated tax by January 18, 1994, or

• File your 1993 Form 1040 by March 1, 1994, and pay the total tax due. In this case, 1993 estimated payments are not required.

Fiscal Year Filers. You are on a fiscal year if your 12-month tax period ends on any day except December 31. Due dates for fiscal year filers are the 15th day of the 4th, 6th, and 9th months for your current fiscal year and the 1st month of the following fiscal year. If any payment date falls on a Saturday, Sunday, or legal holiday, use the next working day.

Amending Estimated Tax Payments

To change or amend your estimated payments, first refigure your estimated tax using the worksheet on page 3. From your new estimated tax, subtract any amount of 1992 tax overpayment credited to 1993 and any estimated payments made to date. Make your remaining payments using the instructions for **Payment Due Dates** on this page.

When a Penalty is Applied

In some cases, you may owe a penalty when you file your return. The penalty is imposed on each underpayment for the number of days it remains unpaid. A penalty may be applied if you did not pay enough estimated tax or you did not make the payments on time or in the required amount. A penalty may apply even if you have an overpayment on your tax return.

The penalty may be waived under certain conditions. See Pub. 505 for details.

How To Complete and Use the Payment Voucher

There is a separate voucher for each due date. Please be sure you use the voucher with the correct due date shown in the upper right corner. Complete and send in the voucher **only** if you are making a payment. To complete your voucher:

• Type or print your name, address, and social security number in the space provided on the voucher. If filing a joint voucher, also enter your spouse's name and social security number.

• Enter only the amount you are sending in on the payment line of the voucher. When making payments of estimated tax, be sure to take into account any 1992 overpayment that you choose to credit against your 1993 tax, but do not include the overpayment amount on this line.

• Enclose your payment, making the check or money order payable to: "Internal Revenue Service" (not "IRS").

• Do not staple or attach your payment to the voucher.

• Write your social security number and "1993 Form 1040-ES" on your check or money order.

• Mail your payment voucher to the address shown on page 5 for the place where you live.

• Fill in the **Record of Estimated Tax Payments** on page 5 for your files.

If you changed your name and made estimated tax payments using your old name, attach a statement to the front of your 1993 Form 1040 or 1040A. List all of the estimated tax payments you and your spouse made for 1993, the address where you made the payments, and the name(s) and social security number(s) under which you made the payments.

Record of Estimated Tax Payments (see page 4 for correct payment due dates)

Payment number	(a) Date	(b) Amount paid	(c) 1992 overpayment credit applied	(d) Total amount paid and credited (add (b) and (c))
1				
2				
3				
4				
Total . . . . . ▶				

Where To File Your Payment Voucher

Mail your payment voucher to the Internal Revenue Service at the address shown below for the place where you live. **Do not** mail your tax return to this address. Also, do not mail your estimated tax payments to the address shown in the Form 1040 or 1040A instructions.

Note: *For proper delivery of your estimated tax payment, you must include the P.O. box number, if any, in the address.*

If you live in: ▼	Use this address: ▼
New Jersey, New York (New York City and counties of Nassau, Rockland, Suffolk, and Westchester)	P.O. Box 162 Newark, NJ 07101-0162
New York (all other counties), Connecticut, Maine, Massachusetts, New Hampshire, Rhode Island, Vermont	P.O. Box 371999 Pittsburgh, PA 15250-7999
Delaware, District of Columbia, Maryland, Pennsylvania, Virginia	P.O. Box 839 Newark, NJ 07101-0839
Florida, Georgia, South Carolina	P.O. Box 970004 St. Louis, MO 63197-0004
Indiana, Kentucky, Michigan, Ohio, West Virginia	P.O. Box 7422 Chicago, IL 60680-7422

Alabama, Arkansas, Louisiana, Mississippi, North Carolina, Tennessee	P.O. Box 371300M Pittsburgh, PA 15250-7300
Illinois, Iowa, Minnesota, Missouri, Wisconsin	P.O. Box 6413 Chicago, IL 60680-6413
Kansas, New Mexico, Oklahoma, Texas	P.O. Box 970001 St. Louis, MO 63197-0001
Alaska, Arizona, California (counties of Alpine, Amador, Butte, Calaveras, Colusa, Contra Costa, Del Norte, El Dorado, Glenn, Humboldt, Lake, Lassen, Marin, Mendocino, Modoc, Napa, Nevada, Placer, Plumas, Sacramento, San Joaquin, Shasta, Sierra, Siskiyou, Solano, Sonoma, Sutter, Tehama, Trinity, Yolo, and Yuba), Colorado, Idaho, Montana, Nebraska, Nevada, North Dakota, Oregon, South Dakota, Utah, Washington, Wyoming	P.O. Box 510000 San Francisco, CA 94151-5100
California (all other counties), Hawaii	P.O. Bcx 54030 Los Angeles, CA 90054-0030
American Samoa	P.O. Box 839 Newark, NJ 07101-0839

Guam	Commissioner of Revenue and Taxation 855 West Marine Drive Agana, GU 96910
The Commonwealth of the Northern Mariana Islands	P.O. Box 839 Newark, NJ 07101-0839
Puerto Rico (or if excluding income under section 933)	P.O. Box 839 Newark, NJ 07101-0839
Virgin Islands: Nonpermanent residents	P.O. Box 839 Newark, NJ 07101-0839
Permanent residents*	V.I. Bureau of Internal Revenue Lockharts Garden No. 1A Charlotte Amalie St. Thomas, VI 00802

* You must prepare separate vouchers for estimated income tax and self-employment tax payments. Send the income tax vouchers to the V.I. address and the self-employment tax vouchers to the address for V.I. nonpermanent residents shown above.

All A.P.O. and F.P.O. addresses	P.O. Box 839 Newark, NJ 07101-0839
Foreign country: U.S. citizens and those filing Form 2555, Form 2555-EZ, or Form 4563	P.O. Box 839 Newark, NJ 07101-0839

- **Tear off here** -

Form **1040-ES** | **1993 Payment Voucher 4**

Department of the Treasury
Internal Revenue Service

OMB No. 1545-0087

Calendar year—Due Jan. 18, 1994

Return this voucher with check or money order payable to the **"Internal Revenue Service."** Please write your social security number and "1993 Form 1040-ES" on your check or money order. Please do not send cash. Enclose, but do not staple or attach, your payment with this voucher. File only if you are making a payment of estimated tax.

Amount of payment	Please type or print	Your first name and initial	Your last name	Your social security number
		If joint payment, complete for spouse		
		Spouse's first name and initial	Spouse's last name	Spouse's social security number
$ _ _ _ _ _ _		Address (number, street, and apt. no.)		
		City, state, and ZIP code		

For Paperwork Reduction Act Notice, see instructions on page 1.

Form **1040-ES**
Department of the Treasury
Internal Revenue Service

1993
Payment
Voucher 3

OMB No. 1545-0087

Calendar year—Due Sept. 15, 1993

Return this voucher with check or money order payable to the **"Internal Revenue Service."** Please write your social security number and "1993 Form 1040-ES" on your check or money order. Please do not send cash. Enclose, but do not staple or attach, your payment with this voucher. File only if you are making a payment of estimated tax.

Amount of payment

$----------------

Please type or print

Your first name and initial	Your last name	Your social security number
If joint payment, complete for spouse		
Spouse's first name and initial	Spouse's last name	Spouse's social security number
Address (number, street, and apt. no.)		
City, state, and ZIP code		

For Paperwork Reduction Act Notice, see instructions on page 1.

- - - - - - - - - - - - **Tear off here** - - - - - - - - - - - -

Form **1040-ES**
Department of the Treasury
Internal Revenue Service

1993
Payment
Voucher 2

OMB No. 1545-0087

Calendar year—Due June 15, 1993

Return this voucher with check or money order payable to the **"Internal Revenue Service."** Please write your social security number and "1993 Form 1040-ES" on your check or money order. Please do not send cash. Enclose, but do not staple or attach, your payment with this voucher. File only if you are making a payment of estimated tax.

Amount of payment

$----------------

Please type or print

Your first name and initial	Your last name	Your social security number
If joint payment, complete for spouse		
Spouse's first name and initial	Spouse's last name	Spouse's social security number
Address (number, street, and apt. no.)		
City, state, and ZIP code		

For Paperwork Reduction Act Notice, see instructions on page 1.

- - - - - - - - - - - - **Tear off here** - - - - - - - - - - - -

Form **1040-ES**
Department of the Treasury
Internal Revenue Service

1993
Payment
Voucher 1

OMB No. 1545-0087

Calendar year—Due April 15, 1993

Return this voucher with check or money order payable to the **"Internal Revenue Service."** Please write your social security number and "1993 Form 1040-ES" on your check or money order. Please do not send cash. Enclose, but do not staple or attach, your payment with this voucher. File only if you are making a payment of estimated tax.

Amount of payment

$----------------

Please type or print

Your first name and initial	Your last name	Your social security number
If joint payment, complete for spouse		
Spouse's first name and initial	Spouse's last name	Spouse's social security number
Address (number, street, and apt. no.)		
City, state, and ZIP code		

For Paperwork Reduction Act Notice, see instructions on page 1.

Form **1040A**

Department of the Treasury—Internal Revenue Service

U.S. Individual Income Tax Return (B)   **1993**   IRS Use Only—Do not write or staple in this space.

OMB No. 1545-0085

Label
(See page 15.)

Use the IRS label. Otherwise, please print or type.

L A B E L   H E R E

Your first name and initial   Last name

If a joint return, spouse's first name and initial   Last name

Home address (number and street). If you have a P.O. box, see page 16.   Apt. no.

City, town or post office, state, and ZIP code. If you have a foreign address, see page 16.

Your social security number

Spouse's social security number

For Privacy Act and Paperwork Reduction Act Notice, see page 4.

Presidential Election Campaign Fund (See page 16.)   Yes   No

Do you want $3 to go to this fund? . . . .

If a joint return, does your spouse want $3 to go to this fund?

Note: *Checking "Yes" will not change your tax or reduce your refund.*

Check the box for your filing status
(See page 16.)

Check only one box.

1 ☐ Single

2 ☐ Married filing joint return (even if only one had income)

3 ☐ Married filing separate return. Enter spouse's social security number above and full name here. ▶ _____

4 ☐ Head of household (with qualifying person). (See page 17.) If the qualifying person is a child but not your dependent, enter this child's name here. ▶ _____

5 ☐ Qualifying widow(er) with dependent child (year spouse died ▶ 19___). (See page 18.)

Figure your exemptions
(See page 19.)

If more than seven dependents, see page 22.

6a ☐ **Yourself.** If your parent (or someone else) can claim you as a dependent on his or her tax return, **do not** check box 6a. But be sure to check the box on line 18b on page 2.

b ☐ **Spouse**

c **Dependents:**

(1) Name (first, initial, and last name)	(2) Check if under age 1	(3) If age 1 or older, dependent's social security number	(4) Dependent's relationship to you	(5) No. of months lived in your home in 1993

d If your child didn't live with you but is claimed as your dependent under a pre-1985 agreement, check here . . . . ▶ ☐

e Total number of exemptions claimed.

No. of boxes checked on 6a and 6b _____

No. of your children on 6c who:
• lived with you _____
• didn't live with you due to divorce or separation (see page 22) _____

Dependents on 6c not entered above _____

Add numbers entered on lines above ☐

Figure your total income

Attach Copy B of your Forms W-2 and 1099-R here.

If you didn't get a W-2, see page 24.

If you are attaching a check or money order, put it on top of any Forms W-2 or 1099-R.

7 Wages, salaries, tips, etc. This should be shown in box 1 of your W-2 form(s). Attach Form(s) W-2.   7

8a **Taxable** interest income (see page 25). If over $400, also complete and attach Schedule 1, Part I.   8a

b **Tax-exempt** interest. DO NOT include on line 8a.   8b

9 Dividends. If over $400, also complete and attach Schedule 1, Part II.   9

10a Total IRA distributions.   10a   **10b** Taxable amount (see page 26).   10b

11a Total pensions and annuities.   11a   **11b** Taxable amount (see page 26).   11b

12 Unemployment compensation (see page 30).   12

13a Social security benefits.   13a   **13b** Taxable amount (see page 30).   13b

14 Add lines 7 through 13b (far right column). This is your **total income.** ▶   14

Figure your adjusted gross income

15a Your IRA deduction (see page 32).   15a

b Spouse's IRA deduction (see page 32).   15b

c Add lines 15a and 15b. These are your **total adjustments.**   15c

16 Subtract line 15c from line 14. This is your **adjusted gross income.** If less than $23,050 and a child lived with you, see page 63 to find out if you can claim the "Earned income credit" on line 28c. ▶   16

Cat. No. 12603D

■ 1993 Form 1040A page 2

Name(s) shown on page 1	Your social security number

Figure your standard deduction, exemption amount, and taxable income

17	Enter the amount from line 16.		17	

18a Check if: ☐ **You** were 65 or older   ☐ Blind   ☐ **Spouse** was 65 or older   ☐ Blind   **Enter number of boxes checked ▶** 18a ☐

b If your parent (or someone else) can claim you as a dependent, check here . . . . ▶ 18b ☐

c If you are married filing separately and your spouse files Form 1040 and itemizes deductions, see page 36 and check here ▶ 18c ☐

19 Enter the **standard deduction** shown below for your filing status. **But if you checked any box on line 18a or b,** go to page 36 to find your standard deduction. **If you checked box 18c,** enter -0-.

- Single—$3,700   • Head of household—$5,450
- Married filing jointly or Qualifying widow(er)—$6,200
- Married filing separately—$3,100

19

20	Subtract line 19 from line 17. If line 19 is more than line 17, enter -0-.	20	
21	Multiply $2,350 by the total number of exemptions claimed on line 6e.	21	
22	Subtract line 21 from line 20. If line 21 is more than line 20, enter -0-. This is your **taxable income.** ▶	22	

Figure your tax, credits, and payments

If you want the IRS to figure your tax, see the instructions for line 22 on page 37.

23 Find the tax on the amount on line 22. Check if from: ☐ Tax Table (pages 50–55) or   ☐ Form 8615 (see page 38).   23

24a Credit for child and dependent care expenses. Complete and attach Schedule 2.   24a

b Credit for the elderly or the disabled. Complete and attach Schedule 3.   24b

c Add lines 24a and 24b. These are your **total credits.**   24c

25	Subtract line 24c from line 23. If line 24c is more than line 23, enter -0-.	25	
26	Advance earned income credit payments from Form W-2.	26	
27	Add lines 25 and 26. This is your **total tax.** ▶	27	

28a Total Federal income tax withheld. If any tax is from Form(s) 1099, check here. ▶ ☐   28a

b 1993 estimated tax payments and amount applied from 1992 return.   28b

c **Earned income credit.** Complete and attach Schedule EIC.   28c

d Add lines 28a, 28b, and 28c. These are your **total payments.** ▶ 28d

Figure your refund or amount you owe

29	If line 28d is more than line 27, subtract line 27 from line 28d. This is the amount you **overpaid.**	29	
30	Amount of line 29 you want **refunded to you.**	30	
31	Amount of line 29 you want **applied to your 1994 estimated tax.**	31	
32	If line 27 is more than line 28d, subtract line 28d from line 27. This is the **amount you owe.** For details on how to pay, including what to write on your payment, see page 42.	32	
33	Estimated tax penalty (see page 43). Also, include on line 32.	33	

Sign your return

Keep a copy of this return for your records.

Under penalties of perjury, I declare that I have examined this return and accompanying schedules and statements, and to the best of my knowledge and belief, they are true, correct, and accurately list all amounts and sources of income I received during the tax year. Declaration of preparer (other than the taxpayer) is based on all information of which the preparer has any knowledge.

Your signature	Date	Your occupation
Spouse's signature. If joint return, BOTH must sign.	Date	Spouse's occupation

Paid preparer's use only

Preparer's signature ▶	Date	Check if self-employed ☐	Preparer's social security no.
Firm's name (or yours if self-employed) and address ▶		E.I. No.	
		ZIP code	

1993 Form 1040A page 2

Schedule 1

(Form 1040A)

Department of the Treasury—Internal Revenue Service

**Interest and Dividend Income
for Form 1040A Filers** (B)

1993

OMB No. 1545-0085

Name(s) shown on Form 1040A

Your social security number

Part I

**Interest
income**

(See pages 25
and 56.)

Note: *If you received a Form 1099–INT, Form 1099–OID, or substitute statement from a
brokerage firm, enter the firm's name and the total interest shown on that form.*

		Amount	
1	List name of payer. If any interest is from a seller-financed mortgage and the buyer used the property as a personal residence, see page 56 and list this interest first. Also, show that buyer's social security number and address.		
		1	
2	Add the amounts on line 1.	2	
3	Excludable interest on series EE U.S. savings bonds issued after 1989 from Form 8815, line 14. You MUST attach Form 8815 to Form 1040A.	3	
4	Subtract line 3 from line 2. Enter the result here and on Form 1040A, line 8a.	4	

Part II

**Dividend
income**

(See pages 25
and 57.)

Note: *If you received a Form 1099–DIV or substitute statement from a brokerage firm, enter the
firm's name and the total dividends shown on that form.*

		Amount	
5	List name of payer		
		5	
6	Add the amounts on line 5. Enter the total here and on Form 1040A, line 9.	6	

For Paperwork Reduction Act Notice, see Form 1040A instructions.   Cat. No. 12605Z   **1993 Schedule 1 (Form 1040A) page 1**

Schedule 2
(Form 1040A)

Department of the Treasury—Internal Revenue Service

**Child and Dependent Care
Expenses for Form 1040A Filers** (B)   **1993**

OMB No. 1545-0085

Name(s) shown on Form 1040A

Your social security number

You need to understand the following terms to complete this schedule: **Dependent care benefits, Earned income, Qualified expenses,** and **Qualifying person(s).** See **Important terms** on page 58. Also, if you had a child born in 1993 and line 17 of Form 1040A is less than $23,050, see **A change to note** on page 59.

Part I

Persons or organizations who provided the care

You MUST complete this part.

	(a) Care provider's name	**(b)** Address (number, street, apt. no., city, state, and ZIP code)	**(c)** Identifying number (SSN or EIN)	**(d)** Amount paid (see page 61)
1				

(If you need more space, use the bottom of page 2.)

2 Add the amounts in column (d) of line 1.   2

3 Enter the number of **qualifying persons** cared for in 1993 . . . ▶ ☐

Did you receive **dependent care benefits?**	**NO** ──────▶ Complete only Part II below.
	YES ──────▶ Complete Part III on the back now.

Part II

Credit for child and dependent care expenses

4 Enter the amount of **qualified expenses** you incurred and paid in 1993. DO NOT enter more than $2,400 for one qualifying person or $4,800 for two or more persons. If you completed Part III, enter the amount from line 25.   4

5 Enter YOUR **earned income.**   5

6 If married filing a joint return, enter YOUR SPOUSE'S earned income (if student or disabled, see page 61); **all others,** enter the amount from line 5.   6

7 Enter the **smallest** of line 4, 5, or 6.   7

8 Enter the amount from Form 1040A, line 17.   8

9 Enter on line 9 the decimal amount shown below that applies to the amount on line 8.

If line 8 is—		Decimal amount is	If line 8 is—		Decimal amount is
Over	**But not over**		**Over**	**But not over**	
$0	10,000	.30	$20,000	22,000	.24
10,000	12,000	.29	22,000	24,000	.23
12,000	14,000	.28	24,000	26,000	.22
14,000	16,000	.27	26,000	28,000	.21
16,000	18,000	.26	28,000	No limit	.20
18,000	20,000	.25			

9   × .

10 Multiply **line 7** by the decimal amount on line 9. Enter the result. Then, see page 61 for the amount of credit to enter on Form 1040A, line 24a.   10 =

Caution: *If you paid $50 or more in a calendar quarter to a person who worked in your home, you must file an employment tax return. Get* **Form 942** *for details.*

For Paperwork Reduction Act Notice, see Form 1040A instructions.   Cat. No. 12608G   **1993 Schedule 2 (Form 1040A) page 1**

Name(s) shown on page 1	Your social security number

Part III

Dependent care benefits

Complete this part **only** if you received these benefits.

11 Enter the total amount of **dependent care benefits** you received for 1993. This amount should be shown in box 10 of your W-2 form(s). DO NOT include amounts that were reported to you as wages in box 1 of Form(s) W-2. **11**

12 Enter the amount forfeited, if any. See page 62. **12**

13 Subtract line 12 from line 11. **13**

14 Enter the total amount of **qualified expenses** incurred in 1993 for the care of the qualifying person(s). **14**

15 Enter the **smaller** of line 13 or 14. **15**

16 Enter YOUR **earned income.** **16**

17 If married filing a joint return, enter YOUR SPOUSE'S earned income (if student or disabled, see the line 6 instructions); if married filing a separate return, see the instructions for the amount to enter; **all others,** enter the amount from line 16. **17**

18 Enter the **smallest** of line 15, 16, or 17. **18**

19 **Excluded benefits.** Enter here the **smaller** of the following:
● The amount from line 18, or
● $5,000 ($2,500 if married filing a separate return **and** you were required to enter your spouse's earned income on line 17). **19**

20 **Taxable benefits.** Subtract line 19 from line 13. Also, include this amount on Form 1040A, line 7. In the space to the left of line 7, write "DCB." **20**

To claim the child and dependent care credit, complete lines 21–25 below, and lines 4–10 on the front of this schedule.

21 Enter the amount of qualified expenses you incurred and paid in 1993. DO NOT include on this line any excluded benefits shown on line 19. **21**

22 Enter $2,400 ($4,800 if two or more qualifying persons). **22**

23 Enter the amount from line 19. **23**

24 Subtract line 23 from line 22. If zero or less, **STOP.** You cannot take the credit. **Exception.** If you paid 1992 expenses in 1993, see the line 10 instructions. **24**

25 Enter the **smaller** of line 21 or 24 here **and** on line 4 on the front of this schedule. **25**

Schedule 3
(Form 1040A)

Department of the Treasury—Internal Revenue Service

Credit for the Elderly or the Disabled
for Form 1040A Filers (M)

1993

OMB No. 1545-0085

Name(s) shown on Form 1040A

Your social security number

You may be able to use Schedule 3 to reduce your tax if by the end of 1993:

- You were age 65 or older, **OR**
- You were under age 65, you retired on **permanent and total** disability, and you received taxable disability income.

But you must also meet other tests. See the separate instructions for Schedule 3.

Note: *In most cases, the IRS can figure the credit for you. See page 38 of the Form 1040A instructions.*

Part I	**If your filing status is:**	**And by the end of 1993:**	**Check only one box:**
Check the box for your filing status and age	Single, Head of household, or Qualifying widow(er) with dependent child	**1** You were 65 or older	1 ☐
		2 You were under 65 and you retired on permanent and total disability	2 ☐
	Married filing a joint return	**3** Both spouses were 65 or older	3 ☐
		4 Both spouses were under 65, but only one spouse retired on permanent and total disability	4 ☐
		5 Both spouses were under 65, and both retired on permanent and total disability	5 ☐
		6 One spouse was 65 or older, and the other spouse was under 65 and retired on permanent and total disability	6 ☐
		7 One spouse was 65 or older, and the other spouse was under 65 and **NOT** retired on permanent and total disability	7 ☐
	Married filing a separate return	**8** You were 65 or older and you lived apart from your spouse for all of 1993	8 ☐
		9 You were under 65, you retired on permanent and total disability, and you lived apart from your spouse for all of 1993	9 ☐

If you checked box 1, 3, 7, or 8, skip Part II and complete Part III on the back. All others, complete Parts II and III.

Part II

Statement of permanent and total disability

Complete this part **only** if you checked box 2, 4, 5, 6, or 9 above.

IF: 1 You filed a physician's statement for this disability for 1983 or an earlier year, or you filed a statement for tax years after 1983 and your physician signed line B on the statement, **AND**

2 Due to your continued disabled condition, you were unable to engage in any substantial gainful activity in 1993, check this box ▶ ☐

- If you checked this box, you do not have to file another statement for 1993.
- If you **did not** check this box, have your physician complete the following statement:

Physician's statement (See instructions at bottom of page 2.)

I certify that _____
Name of disabled person

was permanently and totally disabled on January 1, 1976, or January 1, 1977, **OR** was permanently and totally disabled on the date he or she retired. If retired after December 31, 1976, enter the date retired ▶ _____

Physician: Sign your name on **either** line A or B below.

A The disability has lasted or can be expected to last continuously for at least a year ....

B There is no reasonable probability that the disabled condition will ever improve ....

Physician's signature	Date
Physician's signature	Date

Physician's name	Physician's address

For Paperwork Reduction Act Notice, see Form 1040A instructions.

Cat. No. 12064K

1993 Schedule 3 (Form 1040A) page 1

1993 Schedule 3 (Form 1040A) page 2

Name(s) shown on page 1	Your social security number

Part III
Figure your credit

10 If you checked (in Part I):   **Enter:**

Box 1, 2, 4, or 7 . . . . $5,000

Box 3, 5, or 6 . . . . $7,500

Box 8 or 9 . . . . $3,750   **10**

     Caution: *If you checked box 2, 4, 5, 6, or 9 in Part I, you* **MUST** *complete line 11 below. All others, skip line 11 and enter the amount from line 10 on line 12.*

11   ● If you checked box 6 in Part I, add $5,000 to the taxable disability income of the spouse who was under age 65. Enter the total.

     ● If you checked box 2, 4, or 9 in Part I, enter your taxable disability income.

     ● If you checked box 5 in Part I, add your taxable disability income to your spouse's taxable disability income. Enter the total.

     TIP: For more details on what to include on line 11, see the instructions.   **11**

12   ● If you completed line 11, look at lines 10 and 11. Enter the **smaller** of the two amounts.

     ● All others, enter the amount from line 10.   **12**

13 Enter the following pensions, annuities, or disability income that you (and your spouse if filing a joint return) received in 1993:

   a Nontaxable part of social security benefits, and

     Nontaxable part of railroad retirement benefits treated as social security. See instructions.   **13a**

   b Nontaxable veterans' pensions and any other pension, annuity, or disability benefit that is excluded from income under any other provision of law. See instructions.   **13b**

   c Add lines 13a and 13b. (Even though these income items are not taxable, they **must** be included here to figure your credit.) If you did not receive any of the types of nontaxable income listed on line 13a or 13b, enter -0- on line 13c.   **13c**

14 Enter the amount from Form 1040A, line 17.   **14**

15 **If you checked (in Part I):**   **Enter:**

Box 1 or 2 . . . . $7,500

Box 3, 4, 5, 6, or 7 . . . . $10,000

Box 8 or 9 . . . . $5,000   **15**

16 Subtract line 15 from line 14. If line 15 is more than line 14, enter -0-.   **16**

17 Divide line 16 above by 2.   **17**

18 Add lines 13c and 17.   **18**

19 Subtract line 18 from line 12. If line 18 is more than line 12, stop here; you **cannot** take the credit. Otherwise, go to line 21.   **19**

20 Decimal amount used to figure the credit.   **20**   × .15

21 Multiply line 19 above by the decimal amount (.15) on line 20. Enter the result here and on Form 1040A, line 24b.   **21**

Instructions for physician's statement

Taxpayer.—If you retired after December 31, 1976, enter the date you retired in the space provided in Part II.

Physician.—A person is permanently and totally disabled if **both** of the following apply:

1. He or she cannot engage in any substantial gainful activity because of a physical or mental condition, and

2. A physician determines that the disability has lasted or can be expected to last continuously for at least a year or can lead to death.

Form
1040EZ

Department of the Treasury—Internal Revenue Service

Income Tax Return for Single and Joint Filers With No Dependents (B) 1993

OMB No. 1545-0675

Use the IRS label
(See page 10.)
Otherwise, please print.

L A B E L H E R E

Print your name (first, initial, last)

If a joint return, print spouse's name (first, initial, last)

Home address (number and street). If you have a P.O. box, see page 11.   Apt. no.

City, town or post office, state and ZIP code. If you have a foreign address, see page 11.

Your social security number

Spouse's social security number

See instructions on back and in Form 1040EZ booklet.

Presidential Election Campaign
(See page 11.)

Note: *Checking "Yes" will not change your tax or reduce your refund.*
Do you want $3 to go to this fund? ▶
If a joint return, does your spouse want $3 to go to this fund? ▶

Yes   No

Dollars   Cents

Filing status

1 ☐ Single   ☐ Married filing joint return
(even if only one had income)

Report your income

Attach Copy B of Form(s) W-2 here.
Attach any tax payment on top of Form(s) W-2.

Note: *You must check Yes or No.*

2 Total wages, salaries, and tips. This should be shown in box 1 of your W-2 form(s). Attach your W-2 form(s).   2

3 Taxable interest income of $400 or less. If the total is over $400, you cannot use Form 1040EZ.   3

4 Add lines 2 and 3. This is your **adjusted gross income.**   4

5 Can your parents (or someone else) claim you on their return?
☐ **Yes.** Do worksheet on back; enter amount from line G here.
☐ **No.** If **single,** enter 6,050.00. If **married,** enter 10,900.00. For an explanation of these amounts, see back of form.   5

6 Subtract line 5 from line 4. If line 5 is larger than line 4, enter 0. This is your **taxable income.**   6

Figure your tax

7 Enter your Federal income tax withheld from box 2 of your W-2 form(s).   7

8 **Tax.** Look at line 6 above. Use the amount on **line 6** to find your tax in the tax table on pages 24–28 of the booklet. Then, enter the tax from the table on this line.   8

Refund or amount you owe

9 If line 7 is larger than line 8, subtract line 8 from line 7. This is your **refund.**   9

10 If line 8 is larger than line 7, subtract line 7 from line 8. This is the **amount you owe.** For details on how to pay, including what to write on your payment, see page 16.   10

Sign your return

Keep a copy of this form for your records.

I have read this return. Under penalties of perjury, I declare that to the best of my knowledge and belief, the return is true, correct, and accurately lists all amounts and sources of income I received during the tax year.

Your signature

Spouse's signature if joint return

Date   Your occupation   Date   Spouse's occupation

For IRS Use Only — Please do not write in boxes below.

1993   Instructions for Form 1040EZ

Use this form if	• Your filing status is single or married filing jointly. • You do not claim any dependents. • You had **only** wages, salaries, tips, and taxable scholarship or fellowship grants, and your taxable interest income was $400 or less. **But** if you earned tips, including allocated tips, that are not included in box 5 and box 7 of your W-2, you may not be able to use Form 1040EZ. See page 13. • You did not receive any advance earned income credit payments. • You (and your spouse if married) were under 65 on January 1, 1994, and not blind at the end of 1993. • Your taxable income (line 6) is less than $50,000. **Caution:** *If married and either you or your spouse had total wages of over $57,600, you may not be able to use this form. See page 6.* If you are not sure about your filing status, see page 12. If you have questions about dependents, call Tele-Tax (see page 22) and listen to topic 354. If you **can't use this form,** call Tele-Tax (see page 22) and listen to topic 352.

Use this form if

• Your filing status is single or married filing jointly.

• You do not claim any dependents.

• You had **only** wages, salaries, tips, and taxable scholarship or fellowship grants, and your taxable interest income was $400 or less. **But** if you earned tips, including allocated tips, that are not included in box 5 and box 7 of your W-2, you may not be able to use Form 1040EZ. See page 13.

• You did not receive any advance earned income credit payments.

• You (and your spouse if married) were under 65 on January 1, 1994, and not blind at the end of 1993.

• Your taxable income (line 6) is less than $50,000.

Caution: *If married and either you or your spouse had total wages of over $57,600, you may not be able to use this form. See page 6.*

If you are not sure about your filing status, see page 12. If you have questions about dependents, call Tele-Tax (see page 22) and listen to topic 354. If you **can't use this form,** call Tele-Tax (see page 22) and listen to topic 352.

Filling in your return

Because this form is read by a machine, please print your numbers inside the boxes like this:

9 8 7 6 5 4 3 2 1 0   Do not type your numbers. Do not use dollar signs.

Most people can fill in the form by following the instructions on the front. But you will have to use the booklet if you received a scholarship or fellowship grant or tax-exempt interest income, such as on municipal bonds. Also, use the booklet if you received a Form 1099-INT showing income tax withheld (backup withholding).

Remember, you must report all wages, salaries, and tips even if you don't get a W-2 form from your employer. You must also report all your taxable interest income, including interest from banks, savings and loans, credit unions, etc., even if you don't get a Form 1099-INT.

If you paid someone to prepare your return, see page 17.

Worksheet for dependents who checked "Yes" on line 5

Use this worksheet to figure the amount to enter on line 5 if someone can claim you (or your spouse if married) as a dependent, even if that person chooses not to do so. To find out if someone can claim you as a dependent, call Tele-Tax (see page 22) and listen to topic 354.

A. Enter the amount from line 2 on the front.   A. _____

B. Minimum standard deduction.   B. _____ 600.00

C. Enter the LARGER of line A or line B here.   C. _____

D. Maximum standard deduction. If single, enter 3,700.00; if married, enter 6,200.00.   D. _____

E. Enter the SMALLER of line C or line D here. This is your standard deduction.   E. _____

F. Exemption amount.
  • If single, enter 0.
  • If married and both you and your spouse can be claimed as dependents, enter 0.
  • If married and only one of you can be claimed as a dependent, enter 2,350.00.   F. _____

G. Add lines E and F. Enter the total here and on line 5 on the front.   G. _____

If you checked "No" on line 5 because no one can claim you (or your spouse if married) as a dependent, enter on line 5 the amount shown below that applies to you.

• Single, enter 6,050.00. This is the total of your standard deduction (3,700.00) and personal exemption (2,350.00).

• Married, enter 10,900.00. This is the total of your standard deduction (6,200.00), exemption for yourself (2,350.00), and exemption for your spouse (2,350.00).

Avoid mistakes

Please see page 17 of the Form 1040EZ booklet for a list of common mistakes to avoid that will help you make sure your form is filled in correctly.

Mailing your return

Mail your return by **April 15, 1994.** Use the envelope that came with your booklet. If you don't have that envelope, see page 29 for the address to use.

Form 1040X
(Rev. October 1992)

Department of the Treasury—Internal Revenue Service

Amended U.S. Individual Income Tax Return
▶ See separate instructions.

OMB No. 1545-0091
Expires 10-31-94

This return is for calendar year ▶ 19   , OR fiscal year ended ▶.   , 19   .

Please print or type

Your first name and initial	Last name	Your social security number
If a joint return, spouse's first name and initial	Last name	Spouse's social security number
Home address (number and street). If you have a P.O. box, see instructions.	Apt. no.	Telephone number (optional) ( )
City, town or post office, state, and ZIP code. If you have a foreign address, see instructions.		For Paperwork Reduction Act Notice, see page 1 of separate instructions.

Enter name and address as shown on original return. If same as above, write "Same." If changing from separate to joint return, enter names and addresses from original returns.

A Service center where original return was filed

B Has original return been changed or audited by the IRS?   ☐ Yes ☐ No
If "No," have you been notified that it will be? . . . . ☐ Yes ☐ No
If "Yes," identify the IRS office ▶

C Are you amending your return to include any item (loss, credit, deduction, other tax benefit, or income) relating to a tax shelter required to be registered? . . . . ☐ Yes ☐ No
If "Yes," you must attach **Form 8271,** Investor Reporting of Tax Shelter Registration Number.

D Filing status claimed. **Note:** *You cannot change from joint to separate returns after the due date has passed.*

On original return ▶ ☐ Single ☐ Married filing joint return ☐ Married filing separate return ☐ Head of household ☐ Qualifying widow(er)
On this return ▶ ☐ Single ☐ Married filing joint return ☐ Married filing separate return ☐ Head of household ☐ Qualifying widow(er)

Income and Deductions (see instructions) Caution: *Be sure to complete Part II on page 2.*		A. As originally reported or as adjusted (see instructions)	B. Net change—Increase or (Decrease)—explain on page 2	C. Correct amount
1 Total income	1			
2 Adjustments to income	2			
3 Adjusted gross income. Subtract line 2 from line 1 . .	3			
4 Itemized deductions or standard deduction	4			
5 Subtract line 4 from line 3	5			
6 Exemptions. If changing, fill in Parts I and II on page 2 . .	6			
7 Taxable income. Subtract line 6 from line 5	7			
8 Tax (see instructions). Method used in col. C	8			
9 Credits (see instructions)	9			
10 Subtract line 9 from line 8. Enter the result but not less than zero .	10			
11 Other taxes (such as self-employment tax, alternative minimum tax, etc.)	11			
12 Total tax. Add lines 10 and 11	12			
13 Federal income tax withheld and excess social security, Medicare, and RRTA taxes withheld. If changing, see instructions	13			
14 Estimated tax payments	14			
15 Earned income credit	15			
16 Credits for Federal tax paid on fuels, regulated investment company, etc.	16			

Tax Liability

Payments

17 Amount paid with Form 4868, Form 2688, or Form 2350 (application for extension of time to file) .	17	
18 Amount paid with original return plus additional tax paid after it was filed	18	
19 Add lines 13 through 18 in column C	19	

Refund or Amount You Owe

20 Overpayment, if any, as shown on original return or as previously adjusted by the IRS . . .	20	
21 Subtract line 20 from line 19 (see instructions) .	21	
22 **AMOUNT YOU OWE.** If line 12, column C, is more than line 21, enter the difference and see instructions .	22	
23 **REFUND** to be received. If line 12, column C, is less than line 21, enter the difference . . .	23	

Sign Here

Keep a copy of this return for your records.

Under penalties of perjury, I declare that I have filed an original return and that I have examined this amended return, including accompanying schedules and statements, and to the best of my knowledge and belief, this amended return is true, correct, and complete. Declaration of preparer (other than taxpayer) is based on all information of which the preparer has any knowledge.

▶ Your signature   Date   ▶ Spouse's signature. If a joint return, BOTH must sign.   Date

Paid Preparer's Use Only

Preparer's signature ▶	Date	Check if self-employed ☐	Preparer's social security no.
Firm's name (or yours if self-employed) and address ▶		E.I. No.	
		ZIP code	

Cat. No. 11360L

Form **1040X** (Rev. 10-92)

Form 1040X (Rev. 10-92)   Page **2**

Part I	Exemptions. See Form 1040 or Form 1040A instructions.		A. Number originally reported	B. Net change	C. Correct number
	If you are not changing your exemptions, do not complete this part. If claiming more exemptions, complete lines 24–30 and, if applicable, line 31. If claiming fewer exemptions, complete lines 24–29.				

			A. Number originally reported	B. Net change	C. Correct number
24	Yourself and spouse	**24**			
	Caution: *If your parents (or someone else) can claim you as a dependent (even if they chose not to), you cannot claim an exemption for yourself.*				
25	Your dependent children who lived with you	**25**			
26	Your dependent children who did not live with you due to divorce or separation	**26**			
27	Other dependents	**27**			
28	Total number of exemptions. Add lines 24 through 27	**28**			
29	**For tax year 1992,** if the amount on page 1, line 3, is more than $78,950, see the instructions. Otherwise, multiply $2,300 by the number of exemptions claimed on line 28. **For tax year 1991,** if the amount on page 1, line 3, is more than $75,000, see the instructions. Otherwise, multiply $2,150 by the number of exemptions claimed on line 28. **For tax year 1990,** use $2,050; **for tax year 1989,** use $2,000. Enter the result here and on page 1, line 6	**29**			

30 Dependents (children and other) not claimed on original return:

(a) Dependent's name (first, initial, and last name)	(b) Check if under age 1 (under age 2 if a 1989 or 1990 return)	(c) If age 1 or older (age 2 or older if a 1989 or 1990 return), enter dependent's social security number	(d) Dependent's relationship to you	(e) No. of months lived in your home	
					No. of your children on line 30 who lived with you ▶ ☐
					No. of your children on line 30 who **didn't** live with you due to divorce or separation (see instructions) ▶ ☐
					No. of other dependents listed on line 30 . . . ▶ ☐

31 If your child listed on line 30 didn't live with you but is claimed as your dependent under a pre-1985 agreement, check here . . . . ▶ ☐

Part II	Explanation of Changes to Income, Deductions, and Credits

Enter the line number from page 1 for each item you are changing and give the reason for each change. Attach all supporting forms and schedules for items changed. If you don't, your Form 1040X may be returned. Be sure to include your name and social security number on any attachments.

If the change pertains to a net operating loss carryback or a general business credit carryback, attach the schedule or form that shows the year in which the loss or credit occurred. See instructions. Also, check here . . . . ▶ ☐

_____

_____

_____

_____

_____

_____

_____

_____

Part III	Presidential Election Campaign Fund

Checking below will not increase your tax or reduce your refund.

If you did not previously want to have $1 go to the fund but now want to, check here . . . . ▶ ☐
If a joint return and your spouse did not previously want to have $1 go to the fund but now wants to, check here . . ▶ ☐

Form **1045**

Department of the Treasury
Internal Revenue Service

Application for Tentative Refund

▶ Before you fill out this form, read the separate instructions.
▶ Do not attach to your income tax return—mail in a separate envelope.
▶ For use by individuals, estates, or trusts.

OMB No. 1545-0098

1993

Please type or print

Name	Social security or employer identification number
Number, street, and apt. or suite no. If you have a P.O. box or a foreign address, see the instructions.	**Spouse's social security number**
City, town or post office, state, and ZIP code	Telephone no. (optional) ( )

1 This application is filed to carry back:

a Net operating loss (from Schedule A, page 2, line 25) $

b Unused general business credit $

2a For the calendar year 1993, or other tax year
beginning , 1993, ending , 19

b Date tax return was filed

c Service center where tax return was filed

3 If this application is for an unused credit created by another carryback, give year of the first carryback ▶ ....

4 If you filed a joint return (or separate return) for some, but not all of the tax years involved in figuring the carryback, enter the years of the joint or separate returns ▶ ....

5 If social security number for carryback year is different from above, enter **a** SSN ▶ ....and **b** Year(s) ▶ ....

6 If you changed your accounting period, give date permission to change was granted ▶ ....

7 Have you filed a petition in Tax Court for the year(s) to which the carryback is to be applied? . . . . . ☐ Yes ☐ No

8 Does this carryback include a loss or credit from a tax shelter required to be registered? . . . . ☐ Yes ☐ No

Computation of Decrease in Tax *Note: If 1a is blank, skip lines 9 through 15.*	3rd preceding tax year ended ▶		2nd preceding tax year ended ▶		1st preceding tax year ended ▶	
	(a) Before carryback	**(b)** After carryback	**(c)** Before carryback	**(d)** After carryback	**(e)** Before carryback	**(f)** After carryback
9 Adjusted gross income from tax return or as previously adjusted						
10 Net operating loss deduction after carryback. See instructions . . .	▨		▨		▨	
11 Subtract line 10 from line 9 . . .						
12 Deductions. See instructions . . .						
13 Subtract line 12 from line 11 . . .						
14 Exemptions						
15 Taxable income. Subtract line 14 from line 13						
16 Income tax. See instructions—attach explanation						
17 General business credit						
18 Other credits. Identify						
19 Total credits. Add lines 17 and 18 .						
20 Subtract line 19 from line 16 . . .						
21 Recapture taxes						
22 Alternative minimum tax						
23 Self-employment tax						
24 Other taxes						
25 Total tax liability. Add lines 20 through 24						
26 Enter amount from line 25, cols. (b), (d), and (f)	▨		▨		▨	
27 Decrease in tax. Subtract line 26 from line 25	▨		▨		▨	
28 Overpayment of tax due to a claim of right adjustment under section 1341(b)(1)—attach computation . .						

Sign Here

Keep a copy of this application for your records.

Under penalties of perjury, I declare that I have examined this application and accompanying schedules and statements, and to the best of my knowledge and belief, they are true, correct, and complete.

Your signature	Date
Spouse's signature (if Form 1045 is filed jointly, BOTH must sign)	Date

Preparer Other Than Taxpayer	Name ▶	Date
	Address ▶	

For Paperwork Reduction Act Notice, see separate instructions.   Cat. No. 10670A   Form **1045** (1993)

Schedule A—Net Operating Loss (NOL). See instructions.

1	Adjusted gross income from 1993 Form 1040, line 32. Estates and trusts, skip lines 1 and 2 . .	**1**
2	Deductions (individuals only):	
a	Enter amount from your 1993 Form 1040, line 34	**2a**
b	Enter your deduction for exemptions from 1993 Form 1040, line 36 . .	**2b**
c	Add lines 2a and 2b	**2c** ( )
3	Combine lines 1 and 2c. Estates and trusts, enter your taxable income	**3**

Note: *If line 3 is zero or more, do not complete rest of schedule. You **do not** have a net operating loss.*

Adjustments:

4	Deduction for exemptions from line 2b above. Estates and trusts, enter exemption amount from your tax return	**4**
5	Total nonbusiness capital losses before limitation. Enter as a positive number . . .	**5**
6	Total nonbusiness capital gains	**6**
7	If line 5 is more than line 6, enter difference; otherwise, enter -0-.	**7**
8	If line 6 is more than line 5, enter difference; otherwise, enter -0-.	**8**
9	Nonbusiness deductions. See instructions . .	**9**
10	Nonbusiness income other than capital gains. See instructions	**10**
11	Add lines 8 and 10	**11**
12	If line 9 is more than line 11, enter difference; otherwise, enter -0-	**12**
13	If line 11 is more than line 9, enter difference; otherwise, enter -0-. Do not enter more than line 8	**13**
14	Total business capital losses before limitation. Enter as a positive number	**14**
15	Total business capital gains	**15**
16	Add lines 13 and 15	**16**
17	If line 14 is more than line 16, enter difference; otherwise, enter -0-.	**17**
18	Add lines 7 and 17	**18**
19	Enter the loss, if any, from line 18 of Schedule D (Form 1040). (Estates and trusts, enter the loss, if any, from line 17, column (c), of Schedule D (Form 1041).) Enter as a positive number. If you do not have a loss on that line, skip lines 19 through 21 and enter on line 22 the amount from line 18	**19**
20	Enter the loss from line 19 of Schedule D (Form 1040). (Estates and trusts, enter the loss from line 18 of Schedule D (Form 1041).) Enter as a positive number	**20**
21	Subtract line 20 from line 19	**21**
22	Subtract line 21 from line 18	**22**
23	Net operating loss deduction for losses from other years. Enter as a positive number	**23**
24	Add lines 4, 12, 22, and 23	**24**
25	**Net operating loss.** Combine lines 3 and 24. If the combined amount is less than zero, enter it here and on page 1, line 1a. If the combined amount is zero or more, you **do not** have a net operating loss	**25**

Schedule B—Net Operating Loss Carryover. See instructions.

Complete one column **before** going to the next column.	(a) 3rd preceding tax year ended ▶	(b) 2nd preceding tax year ended ▶	(c) 1st preceding tax year ended ▶
1 **Net operating loss deduction.** In column (a), enter as a positive number the net operating loss from Schedule A, line 25. In columns (b) and (c), enter amounts from line 8 below, columns (a) and (b), respectively			
2 Taxable income from tax return (or as previously adjusted) before 1993 NOL carryback. (For individuals, if line 37 of Form 1040 is zero, subtract line 36 (Form 1040) from line 35 (Form 1040), and enter the difference as a negative number			
3 Net capital loss deduction from Sch. D (Form 1040) (line 20 of 1992 Sch. D, line 18 of 1991 Sch. D, line 19 of 1990 Sch. D), or from Sch. D (Form 1041), line 18. Enter as a positive number			
4 Adjustments to adjusted gross income. See instructions			
5 Adjustment to itemized deductions. See instructions			
6 Deduction for exemptions from tax return (or as previously adjusted). Estates and trusts, enter your exemption amount			
7 Modified taxable income. Combine lines 2 through 6. If zero or less, enter -0-			
8 **Net operating loss carryover.** Subtract line 7 from line 1. If zero or less, enter -0-. See instructions . .			

Adjustment to Itemized Deductions (Individuals Only)

Complete lines 9 through 33 **ONLY** *if*, for any of the 3 preceding years, you itemized deductions and line 3 above has an entry other than zero.

9 Adjusted gross income per return (or as previously adjusted) before 1993 NOL carryback.			
10 Add lines 3 and 4 above			
11 Modified adjusted gross income. Add lines 9 and 10			
12 Medical expenses from Sch. A (Form 1040), line 1.			
13 Multiply line 11 by .075			
14 Subtract line 13 from line 12. If zero or less, enter -0-			
15 Medical expenses from Sch. A (Form 1040), line 4 (or as previously adjusted)			
16 Subtract line 14 from line 15 . . .			

Schedule B—Net Operating Loss Carryover *(Continued)*

Complete one column **before** going to the next column.	(a) 3rd preceding tax year ended ▶	(b) 2nd preceding tax year ended ▶	(c) 1st preceding tax year ended ▶
17 Modified adjusted gross income from line 11			
18 Enter as a positive number any NOL carryback from a year before 1993 that was deducted in figuring line 9 on page 3			
19 Add lines 17 and 18			
20 Refigure your charitable contributions using line 19 as your adjusted gross income. See instructions			
21 Charitable contributions from Sch. A (Form 1040), line 16 (line 17 of 1990 Sch. A (Form 1040))			
22 Subtract line 20 from line 21 . . .			
23 Casualty and theft losses from Form 4684, line 16			
24 Multiply line 11 by .10			
25 Subtract line 24 from line 23. If zero or less, enter -0-			
26 Casualty and theft losses from Form 4684, line 18 (or as previously adjusted).			
27 Subtract line 25 from line 26 . . .			
28 Miscellaneous itemized deductions from Sch. A (Form 1040), line 21 (line 22 of 1990 Sch. A (Form 1040)) . .			
29 Multiply line 11 by .02			
30 Subtract line 29 from line 28. If zero or less, enter -0-			
31 Miscellaneous itemized deductions from Sch. A (Form 1040), line 24 (line 25 of 1990 Sch. A (Form 1040)) (or as previously adjusted)			
32 Subtract line 30 from line 31 . . .			
33 Combine lines 16, 22, 27, and 32. If the NOL is carried to 1991 or 1992 and line 11 is more than $100,000 for 1991 ($50,000 if married filing separately), or more than $105,250 for 1992 ($52,625 if married filing separately), complete the worksheet on page 4 of the instructions. Otherwise, enter the amount from this line on line 5 (page 3)			

Form **1065**

Department of the Treasury
Internal Revenue Service

U.S. Partnership Return of Income

For calendar year 1993, or tax year beginning .... , 1993, and ending .... , 19 ..... .
▶ See separate instructions.

OMB No. 1545-0099

1993

A Principal business activity	**Use the IRS label. Otherwise, please print or type.**	Name of partnership	**D** Employer identification number
B Principal product or service		Number, street, and room or suite no. (If a P.O. box, see page 9 of the instructions.)	**E** Date business started
C Business code number		City or town, state, and ZIP code	**F** Total assets (see **Specific Instructions**) $

G Check applicable boxes: **(1)** ☐ Initial return **(2)** ☐ Final return **(3)** ☐ Change in address **(4)** ☐ Amended return
H Check accounting method: **(1)** ☐ Cash **(2)** ☐ Accrual **(3)** ☐ Other (specify) ▶ ....
I Number of Schedules K-1. Attach one for each person who was a partner at any time during the tax year ▶ ....

*Caution: Include **only** trade or business income and expenses on lines 1a through 22 below. See the instructions for more information.*

Income

1a Gross receipts or sales	1a		
b Less returns and allowances	1b		**1c**
2 Cost of goods sold (Schedule A, line 8)			**2**
3 Gross profit. Subtract line 2 from line 1c			**3**
4 Ordinary income (loss) from other partnerships and fiduciaries *(attach schedule)*			**4**
5 Net farm profit (loss) *(attach Schedule F (Form 1040))*			**5**
6 Net gain (loss) from Form 4797, Part II, line 20			**6**
7 Other income (loss) (see instructions) *(attach schedule)*			**7**
8 **Total income (loss).** Combine lines 3 through 7			**8**

Deductions (see instructions for limitations)

9a Salaries and wages (other than to partners)	9a		
b Less employment credits	9b		**9c**
10 Guaranteed payments to partners			**10**
11 Repairs and maintenance			**11**
12 Bad debts			**12**
13 Rent			**13**
14 Taxes and licenses			**14**
15 Interest			**15**
16a Depreciation (see instructions)	16a		
b Less depreciation reported on Schedule A and elsewhere on return	16b		**16c**
17 Depletion **(Do not deduct oil and gas depletion.)**			**17**
18 Retirement plans, etc.			**18**
19 Employee benefit programs			**19**
20 Other deductions *(attach schedule)*			**20**
21 **Total deductions.** Add the amounts shown in the far right column for lines 9c through 20			**21**
22 **Ordinary income (loss)** from trade or business activities. Subtract line 21 from line 8			**22**

Please Sign Here

Under penalties of perjury, I declare that I have examined this return, including accompanying schedules and statements, and to the best of my knowledge and belief, it is true, correct, and complete. Declaration of preparer (other than general partner) is based on all information of which preparer has any knowledge.

▶ Signature of general partner _____ ▶ Date _____

Paid Preparer's Use Only

Preparer's signature ▶	Date	Check if self-employed ▶ ☐	Preparer's social security no.
Firm's name (or yours if self-employed) and address ▶		E.I. No. ▶	
		ZIP code ▶	

For Paperwork Reduction Act Notice, see page 1 of separate instructions. Cat. No. 11390Z Form **1065** (1993)

Form 1065 (1993)   Page **2**

Schedule A	Cost of Goods Sold

1	Inventory at beginning of year	1	
2	Purchases less cost of items withdrawn for personal use	2	
3	Cost of labor	3	
4	Additional section 263A costs (see instructions) *(attach schedule)*	4	
5	Other costs *(attach schedule)*	5	
6	**Total.** Add lines 1 through 5	6	
7	Inventory at end of year	7	
8	**Cost of goods sold.** Subtract line 7 from line 6. Enter here and on page 1, line 2	8	

9a Check all methods used for valuing closing inventory:

   (i) ☐ Cost

   (ii) ☐ Lower of cost or market as described in Regulations section 1.471-4

   (iii) ☐ Writedown of "subnormal" goods as described in Regulations section 1.471-2(c)

   (iv) ☐ Other (specify method used and attach explanation) ▶ ....

   b Check this box if the LIFO inventory method was adopted this tax year for any goods *(if checked, attach Form 970)* . . ▶ ☐

   c Do the rules of section 263A (for property produced or acquired for resale) apply to the partnership? . . ☐ **Yes** ☐ **No**

   d Was there any change in determining quantities, cost, or valuations between opening and closing inventory? ☐ **Yes** ☐ **No**
   If "Yes," attach explanation.

Schedule B	Other Information

		Yes	No
1	What type of entity is filing this return? Check the applicable box ▶ ☐ General partnership ☐ Limited partnership ☐ Limited liability company		
2	Are any partners in this partnership also partnerships?		
3	Is this partnership a partner in another partnership?		
4	Is this partnership subject to the consolidated audit procedures of sections 6221 through 6233? If "Yes," see **Designation of Tax Matters Partner** below		
5	Does this partnership meet **ALL THREE** of the following requirements?		
a	The partnership's total receipts for the tax year were less than $250,000;		
b	The partnership's total assets at the end of the tax year were less than $600,000; **AND**		
c	Schedules K-1 are filed with the return and furnished to the partners on or before the due date (including extensions) for the partnership return. If "Yes," the partnership is not required to complete Schedules L, M-1, and M-2; Item F on page 1 of Form 1065; or Item J on Schedule K-1		
6	Does this partnership have any foreign partners?		
7	Is this partnership a publicly traded partnership as defined in section 469(k)(2)?		
8	Has this partnership filed, or is it required to file, **Form 8264,** Application for Registration of a Tax Shelter? . .		
9	At any time during calendar year 1993, did the partnership have an interest in or a signature or other authority over a financial account in a foreign country (such as a bank account, securities account, or other financial account)? (See the instructions for exceptions and filing requirements for form TD F 90-22.1.) If "Yes," enter the name of the foreign country. ▶		
10	Was the partnership the grantor of, or transferor to, a foreign trust that existed during the current tax year, whether or not the partnership or any partner has any beneficial interest in it? If "Yes," you may have to file Forms 3520, 3520-A, or 926		
11	Was there a distribution of property or a transfer (e.g., by sale or death) of a partnership interest during the tax year? If "Yes," you may elect to adjust the basis of the partnership's assets under section 754 by attaching the statement described on page 5 of the instructions under **Elections Made By the Partnership**		

Designation of Tax Matters Partner (See instructions.)

Enter below the general partner designated as the tax matters partner (TMP) for the tax year of this return:

Name of designated TMP ▶		Identifying number of TMP ▶	
Address of designated TMP ▶			

Form 1065 (1993)
Page **3**

Schedule K	Partners' Shares of Income, Credits, Deductions, etc.		
	(a) Distributive share items		**(b) Total amount**

Income (Loss)	**1** Ordinary income (loss) from trade or business activities (page 1, line 22)		**1**	
	2 Net income (loss) from rental real estate activities *(attach Form 8825)*		**2**	
	3a Gross income from other rental activities	**3a**		
	b Expenses from other rental activities *(attach schedule)*	**3b**		
	c Net income (loss) from other rental activities. Subtract line 3b from line 3a		**3c**	
	4 Portfolio income (loss) (see instructions): **a** Interest income		**4a**	
	b Dividend income		**4b**	
	c Royalty income		**4c**	
	d Net short-term capital gain (loss) *(attach Schedule D (Form 1065))*		**4d**	
	e Net long-term capital gain (loss) *(attach Schedule D (Form 1065))*		**4e**	
	f Other portfolio income (loss) *(attach schedule)*		**4f**	
	5 Guaranteed payments to partners		**5**	
	6 Net gain (loss) under section 1231 (other than due to casualty or theft) *(attach Form 4797)*		**6**	
	7 Other income (loss) *(attach schedule)*		**7**	
Deductions	**8** Charitable contributions (see instructions) *(attach schedule)*		**8**	
	9 Section 179 expense deduction *(attach Form 4562)*		**9**	
	10 Deductions related to portfolio income (see instructions) (itemize)		**10**	
	11 Other deductions *(attach schedule)*		**11**	
Investment Interest	**12a** Interest expense on investment debts		**12a**	
	b (1) Investment income included on lines 4a, 4b, 4c, and 4f above		**12b(1)**	
	(2) Investment expenses included on line 10 above		**12b(2)**	
Credits	**13a** Credit for income tax withheld		**13a**	
	b Low-income housing credit (see instructions):			
	(1) From partnerships to which section 42(j)(5) applies for property placed in service before 1990		**13b(1)**	
	(2) Other than on line 13b(1) for property placed in service before 1990		**13b(2)**	
	(3) From partnerships to which section 42(j)(5) applies for property placed in service after 1989		**13b(3)**	
	(4) Other than on line 13b(3) for property placed in service after 1989		**13b(4)**	
	c Qualified rehabilitation expenditures related to rental real estate activities *(attach Form 3468)*		**13c**	
	d Credits (other than credits shown on lines 13b and 13c) related to rental real estate activities (see instructions)		**13d**	
	e Credits related to other rental activities (see instructions)		**13e**	
	14 Other credits (see instructions)		**14**	
Self-Employment	**15a** Net earnings (loss) from self-employment		**15a**	
	b Gross farming or fishing income		**15b**	
	c Gross nonfarm income		**15c**	
Adjustments and Tax Preference Items	**16a** Depreciation adjustment on property placed in service after 1986		**16a**	
	b Adjusted gain or loss		**16b**	
	c Depletion (other than oil and gas)		**16c**	
	d (1) Gross income from oil, gas, and geothermal properties		**16d(1)**	
	(2) Deductions allocable to oil, gas, and geothermal properties		**16d(2)**	
	e Other adjustments and tax preference items *(attach schedule)*		**16e**	
Foreign Taxes	**17a** Type of income ▶ .... **b** Foreign country or U.S. possession ▶			
	c Total gross income from sources outside the United States *(attach schedule)*.		**17c**	
	d Total applicable deductions and losses *(attach schedule)*		**17d**	
	e Total foreign taxes (check one): ▶ ☐ Paid ☐ Accrued		**17e**	
	f Reduction in taxes available for credit *(attach schedule)*		**17f**	
	g Other foreign tax information *(attach schedule)*		**17g**	
Other	**18a** Total expenditures to which a section 59(e) election may apply		**18a**	
	b Type of expenditures ▶..........			
	19 Tax-exempt interest income		**19**	
	20 Other tax-exempt income		**20**	
	21 Nondeductible expenses		**21**	
	22 Other items and amounts required to be reported separately to partners (see instructions) *(attach schedule)*			
Analysis	**23a** Income (loss). Combine lines 1 through 7 in column (b). From the result, subtract the sum of lines 8 through 12a, 17e, and 18a		**23a**	

	b Analysis by type of partner:	**(a)** Corporate	**(b) Individual**		**(c)** Partnership	**(d)** Exempt organization	**(e)** Nominee/Other
			i. Active	ii. Passive			
	(1) General partners						
	(2) Limited partners						

Note: *If Question 5 of Schedule B is answered "Yes," the partnership is not required to complete Schedules L, M-1, and M-2.*

Schedule L   Balance Sheets

Assets	Beginning of tax year		End of tax year	
	(a)	(b)	(c)	(d)
1 Cash				
2a Trade notes and accounts receivable				
b Less allowance for bad debts				
3 Inventories				
4 U.S. government obligations				
5 Tax-exempt securities				
6 Other current assets (attach schedule)				
7 Mortgage and real estate loans				
8 Other investments (attach schedule)				
9a Buildings and other depreciable assets				
b Less accumulated depreciation				
10a Depletable assets				
b Less accumulated depletion				
11 Land (net of any amortization)				
12a Intangible assets (amortizable only)				
b Less accumulated amortization				
13 Other assets (attach schedule)				
14 **Total** assets				
Liabilities and Capital				
15 Accounts payable				
16 Mortgages, notes, bonds payable in less than 1 year				
17 Other current liabilities (attach schedule)				
18 All nonrecourse loans				
19 Mortgages, notes, bonds payable in 1 year or more				
20 Other liabilities (attach schedule)				
21 Partners' capital accounts				
22 **Total** liabilities and capital				

Schedule M-1   Reconciliation of Income (Loss) per Books With Income (Loss) per Return (see instructions)

1 Net income (loss) per books		6 Income recorded on books this year not included on Schedule K, lines 1 through 7 (itemize):	
2 Income included on Schedule K, lines 1 through 4, 6, and 7, not recorded on books this year (itemize):		a Tax-exempt interest $	
		....	
3 Guaranteed payments (other than health insurance)		7 Deductions included on Schedule K, lines 1 through 12a, 17e, and 18a, not charged against book income this year (itemize):	
4 Expenses recorded on books this year not included on Schedule K, lines 1 through 12a, 17e, and 18a (itemize):		a Depreciation $	
a Depreciation $		....	
b Travel and entertainment $		....	
....		8 Add lines 6 and 7	
....		9 Income (loss) (Schedule K, line 23a). Subtract line 8 from line 5	
5 Add lines 1 through 4			

Schedule M-2   Analysis of Partners' Capital Accounts

1 Balance at beginning of year		6 Distributions: a Cash	
2 Capital contributed during year		b Property	
3 Net income (loss) per books		7 Other decreases (itemize):	
4 Other increases (itemize):		....	
....		....	
....		8 Add lines 6 and 7	
5 Add lines 1 through 4		9 Balance at end of year. Subtract line 8 from line 5	

SCHEDULE D (Form 1065) Department of the Treasury Internal Revenue Service	Capital Gains and Losses ► Attach to Form 1065.	OMB No. 1545-0099 19**93**

Name of partnership	Employer identification number

Part I Short-Term Capital Gains and Losses—Assets Held 1 Year or Less

(a) Description of property (e.g., 100 shares 7% preferred of "Z" Co.)	(b) Date acquired (month, day, year)	(c) Date sold (month, day, year)	(d) Sales price (see instructions)	(e) Cost or other basis (see instructions)	(f) Gain (loss) ((d) minus (e))
1					

2	Short-term capital gain from installment sales from Form 6252, line 26 or 37	**2**	
3	Short-term capital gain (loss) from like-kind exchanges from Form 8824	**3**	
4	Partnership's share of net short-term capital gain (loss), including specially allocated short-term capital gains (losses), from other partnerships and from fiduciaries	**4**	
5	Net short-term capital gain (loss). Combine lines 1 through 4. Enter here and on Form 1065, Schedule K, line 4d or 7	**5**	

Part II Long-Term Capital Gains and Losses—Assets Held More Than 1 Year

6					

7	Long-term capital gain from installment sales from Form 6252, line 26 or 37	**7**	
8	Long-term capital gain (loss) from like-kind exchanges from Form 8824	**8**	
9	Partnership's share of net long-term capital gain (loss), including specially allocated long-term capital gains (losses), from other partnerships and from fiduciaries	**9**	
10	Capital gain distributions	**10**	
11	Net long-term capital gain (loss). Combine lines 6 through 10. Enter here and on Form 1065, Schedule K, line 4e or 7	**11**	

General Instructions

Section references are to the Internal Revenue Code.

Purpose of Schedule

Use Schedule D (Form 1065) to report sales or exchanges of capital assets, capital gain distributions, and nonbusiness bad debts. Do not report on Schedule D capital gains (losses) specially allocated to any partners.

Enter capital gains (losses) specially allocated to the partnership as a partner in other partnerships and from fiduciaries on Schedule D, line 4 or 9, whichever applies. Enter capital gains (losses) of the partnership that are specially allocated to partners directly on line 4d, 4e, or 7 of Schedules K and K-1, whichever applies. See **How Income Is Shared Among Partners** in the Instructions for Form 1065 for more information.

To report sales or exchanges of property other than capital assets, including the sale or exchange of property used in a trade or business and involuntary conversions (other than casualties and thefts), get **Form 4797**, Sales of Business Property, and related instructions. If property is involuntarily converted because of a casualty or theft, use **Form 4684,** Casualties and Thefts.

For amounts received from an installment sale, the holding period rule in effect in the year of sale will determine the treatment of the amounts received as long-term or short-term capital gain.

Report every sale or exchange of property in detail, even if there is no gain or loss.

For more information, get **Pub. 544,** Sales and Other Dispositions of Assets.

What Are Capital Assets?

Each item of property the partnership held (whether or not connected with its trade or business) is a capital asset **except:**

1. Assets that can be inventoried or property held mainly for sale to customers.

2. Depreciable or real property used in the trade or business.

3. Certain copyrights; literary, musical, or artistic compositions; letters or memorandums; or similar property.

4. Accounts or notes receivable acquired in the ordinary course of trade or business for services rendered or from the sale of property described in **1** above.

5. U.S. Government publications, including the Congressional Record, that the partnership received from the government, other than by purchase at the normal sales price, or that the partnership got from another taxpayer who had received it in a similar way, if the partnership's basis is determined by reference to the previous owner.

Items for Special Treatment and Special Cases

The following items may require special treatment:

• Transactions by a securities dealer.

• Bonds and other debt instruments.

• Certain real estate subdivided for sale that may be considered a capital asset.

• Gain on the sale of depreciable property to a more than 50%-owned entity, or to a trust in which the partnership is a beneficiary, is treated as ordinary gain.

• Liquidating distributions from a corporation. Get **Pub. 550,** Investment Income and Expenses.

• Gain on disposition of stock in an Interest-Charge Domestic International Sales Corporation or a Foreign Sales Corporation.

For Paperwork Reduction Act Notice, see page 1 of the Instructions for Form 1065.   Cat. No. 11393G   **Schedule D (Form 1065) 1993**

- Gain or loss on options to buy or sell, including closing transactions.

- Transfer of property to a foreign corporation as paid-in surplus or as a contribution to capital, or to a foreign trust or partnership.

- Transfer of property to a partnership that would be treated as an investment company if the partnership were incorporated.

- Transfer of property to a political organization if the fair market value of the property exceeds the partnership's adjusted basis in such property.

- Any loss on the disposition of converted wetland or highly erodible cropland that is first used for farming after March 1, 1986, is reported as a long-term capital loss on Schedule D, but any gain on such a disposition is reported as ordinary income on Form 4797. See section 1257 for details.

- Conversion of a general partnership interest into a limited partnership interest in the same partnership. See Rev. Rul. 84-52, 1984-1 C.B. 157.

- Transfer of partnership assets and liabilities to a newly formed corporation in exchange for all of its stock. See Rev. Rul. 84-111, 1984-2 C.B. 88.

- Contribution of limited partnership interests in exchange for limited partnership interests in another partnership. See Rev. Rul. 84-115, 1984-2 C.B. 118.

- Disposition of foreign investment in a U.S. real property interest. See section 897.

- Any loss from a sale or exchange of property between the partnership and certain related persons is not allowed, except for distributions in complete liquidation of a corporation. See sections 267 and 707(b) for details.

- Any loss from securities that are capital assets that become worthless during the year is treated as a loss from the sale or exchange of a capital asset on the last day of the tax year.

- Gain from the sale or exchange of stock in a collapsible corporation is not a capital gain. See section 341.

- A nonbusiness bad debt must be treated as a short-term capital loss and can be deducted only in the year the debt becomes totally worthless. For each bad debt, enter the name of the debtor and "schedule attached" in column (a) of line 1 and the amount of the bad debt as a loss in column (f). Also attach a statement of facts to support each bad debt deduction.

- Any loss from a wash sale of stock or securities (including contracts or options to acquire or sell stock or securities) cannot be deducted unless the partnership is a dealer in stock or securities and the loss was sustained in a transaction made in the ordinary course of the partnership's trade or business. A wash sale occurs if the partnership acquires (by purchase or exchange), or has a contract or option to acquire, substantially identical stock or securities within 30 days before or after the date of the sale or exchange. See section 1091 for more information.

- Gains and losses from section 1256 contracts and straddles are reported on **Form 6781,** Gains and Losses From Section 1256 Contracts and Straddles.

If there are limited partners, see section 1256(e)(4) for the limitation on losses from hedging transactions.

- Gains from the sale of property (other than publicly traded stock or securities) for which any payment is to be received in a tax year after the year of sale must be reported using the installment method on **Form 6252,** Installment Sale Income, unless the partnership elects to report the entire gain in the year of sale. The partnership should also use Form 6252 if it received a payment this year from a sale made in an earlier year on the installment method.

If the partnership wants to elect out of the installment method for installment gain that **is not** specially allocated among the partners, it must report the full amount of the gain on a timely filed return (including extensions).

If the partnership wants to elect out of the installment method for installment gain that **is** specially allocated among the partners, it must do the following on a timely filed return (including extensions):

1. For a **short-term capital gain,** report the full amount of the gain on Schedule K, line 4d or 7.

For a **long-term capital gain,** report the full amount of the gain on Schedule K, line 4e or 7.

2. Enter each partner's share of the full amount of the gain on Schedule K-1, line 4d, 4e, or 7, whichever applies.

- An exchange of business or investment property for property of a like kind is reported on **Form 8824,** Like-Kind Exchanges.

Specific Instructions

Columns (b) and (c)—Date Acquired and Date Sold

Use the trade dates for date acquired and date sold for stocks and bonds traded on an exchange or over-the-counter market.

Column (d)—Sales Price

Enter in this column either the gross sales price or the net sales price from the sale. On sales of stocks and bonds, report the gross amount as reported to the partnership by the partnership's broker on **Form 1099-B,** Proceeds From Broker and Barter Exchange Transactions, or similar statement. However, if the broker advised the partnership that gross proceeds (gross sales price) less commissions and option premiums were reported to the IRS, enter that net amount in column (d).

Column (e)—Cost or Other Basis

In general, the cost or other basis is the cost of the property plus purchase commissions and improvements and minus depreciation, amortization, and depletion. If the partnership got the property in a tax-free exchange, involuntary conversion, or wash sale of stock, it may not be able to use the actual cash cost as the basis. If the partnership does not use cash cost, attach an explanation of the basis.

When selling stock, adjust the basis by subtracting all the stock-related nontaxable distributions received before the sale. This includes nontaxable distributions from utility company stock and mutual funds. Also adjust the basis for any stock splits or stock dividends.

If a charitable contribution deduction is passed through to a partner because of a sale of property to a charitable organization, the adjusted basis for determining gain from the sale is an amount that has the same ratio to the adjusted basis as the amount realized has to the fair market value.

See section 852(f) for the treatment of certain load charges incurred in acquiring stock in a mutual fund with a reinvestment right.

If the gross sales price is reported in column (d), increase the cost or other basis by any expense of sale such as broker's fee, commission, or option premium before making an entry in column (e).

For more information, get **Pub. 551,** Basis of Assets.

Lines 4 and 9—Capital Gains and Losses From Other Partnerships and Fiduciaries

See the Schedule K-1 or other information supplied to you by the other partnership or fiduciary.

Line 10—Capital Gain Distributions

On line 10, report as capital gain distributions **(a)** capital gain dividends and **(b)** the partnership's share of undistributed capital gains from a regulated investment company. Report the partnership's share of taxes paid on undistributed capital gains by a regulated investment company on Schedule K, line 22, and Schedule K-1, line 23.

SCHEDULE K-1
(Form 1065)
Department of the Treasury
Internal Revenue Service

Partner's Share of Income, Credits, Deductions, etc.

▶ See separate instructions.

For calendar year 1993 or tax year beginning _____ , 1993, and ending _____ , 19 ___

OMB No. 1545-0099

1993

Partner's identifying number ▶

Partnership's identifying number ▶

Partner's name, address, and ZIP code

Partnership's name, address, and ZIP code

A This partner is a ☐ general partner ☐ limited partner
☐ limited liability company member

B What type of entity is this partner? ▶ ....

C Is this partner a ☐ domestic or a ☐ foreign partner?

D Enter partner's percentage of:
| | (i) Before change or termination | (ii) End of year |
Profit sharing . . . . % . . . . . %
Loss sharing . . . . % . . . . . %
Ownership of capital . . . . % . . . . . %

E IRS Center where partnership filed return:

F Partner's share of liabilities (see instructions):
Nonrecourse . . . . $ ....
Qualified nonrecourse financing . $ ....
Other . . . . $ ....

G Tax shelter registration number . ▶ ....

H Check here if this partnership is a publicly traded partnership as defined in section 469(k)(2) . . . . ☐

I Check applicable boxes: **(1)** ☐ Final K-1 **(2)** ☐ Amended K-1

J Analysis of partner's capital account:

(a) Capital account at beginning of year	(b) Capital contributed during year	(c) Partner's share of lines 3, 4, and 7, Form 1065, Schedule M-2	(d) Withdrawals and distributions	(e) Capital account at end of year (combine columns (a) through (d))
			( )	

	(a) Distributive share item		(b) Amount	(c) 1040 filers enter the amount in column (b) on:
Income (Loss)	**1** Ordinary income (loss) from trade or business activities . . .	**1**		See Partner's Instructions for Schedule K-1 (Form 1065).
	2 Net income (loss) from rental real estate activities	**2**		
	3 Net income (loss) from other rental activities	**3**		
	4 Portfolio income (loss):			
	a Interest	**4a**		Sch. B, Part I, line 1
	b Dividends	**4b**		Sch. B, Part II, line 5
	c Royalties	**4c**		Sch. E, Part I, line 4
	d Net short-term capital gain (loss)	**4d**		Sch. D, line 5, col. (f) or (g)
	e Net long-term capital gain (loss)	**4e**		Sch. D, line 13, col. (f) or (g)
	f Other portfolio income (loss) *(attach schedule)*	**4f**		Enter on applicable line of your return.
	5 Guaranteed payments to partner	**5**		See Partner's Instructions for Schedule K-1 (Form 1065).
	6 Net gain (loss) under section 1231 (other than due to casualty or theft)	**6**		
	7 Other income (loss) *(attach schedule)*	**7**		Enter on applicable line of your return.
Deductions	**8** Charitable contributions (see instructions) *(attach schedule)* . .	**8**		Sch. A, line 13 or 14
	9 Section 179 expense deduction	**9**		See Partner's Instructions for Schedule K-1 (Form 1065).
	10 Deductions related to portfolio income *(attach schedule)* . . .	**10**		
	11 Other deductions *(attach schedule)*	**11**		
Investment Interest	**12a** Interest expense on investment debts	**12a**		Form 4952, line 1
	b **(1)** Investment income included on lines 4a, 4b, 4c, and 4f above	**b(1)**		See Partner's Instructions for Schedule K-1 (Form 1065).
	(2) Investment expenses included on line 10 above	**b(2)**		
Credits	**13a** Credit for income tax withheld	**13a**		See Partner's Instructions for Schedule K-1 (Form 1065).
	b Low-income housing credit:			
	(1) From section 42(j)(5) partnerships for property placed in service before 1990	**b(1)**		
	(2) Other than on line 13b(1) for property placed in service before 1990	**b(2)**		Form 8586, line 5
	(3) From section 42(j)(5) partnerships for property placed in service after 1989	**b(3)**		
	(4) Other than on line 13b(3) for property placed in service after 1989	**b(4)**		
	c Qualified rehabilitation expenditures related to rental real estate activities (see instructions)	**13c**		
	d Credits (other than credits shown on lines 13b and 13c) related to rental real estate activities (see instructions)	**13d**		See Partner's Instructions for Schedule K-1 (Form 1065).
	e Credits related to other rental activities (see instructions) . . .	**13e**		
	14 Other credits (see instructions)	**14**		

For Paperwork Reduction Act Notice, see Instructions for Form 1065.

Cat. No. 11394R

Schedule K-1 (Form 1065) 1993

	(a) Distributive share item		(b) Amount	(c) 1040 filers enter the amount in column (b) on:
Self-employment	**15a** Net earnings (loss) from self-employment	**15a**		Sch. SE, Section A or B
	b Gross farming or fishing income.	**15b**		See Partner's Instructions for Schedule K-1 (Form 1065).
	c Gross nonfarm income.	**15c**		
Adjustments and Tax Preference Items	**16a** Depreciation adjustment on property placed in service after 1986	**16a**		See Partner's Instructions for Schedule K-1 (Form 1065) and Instructions for Form 6251.
	b Adjusted gain or loss	**16b**		
	c Depletion (other than oil and gas)	**16c**		
	d (1) Gross income from oil, gas, and geothermal properties . .	**d(1)**		
	(2) Deductions allocable to oil, gas, and geothermal properties	**d(2)**		
	e Other adjustments and tax preference items *(attach schedule)*	**16e**		
Foreign Taxes	**17a** Type of income ▶			Form 1116, check boxes
	b Name of foreign country or U.S. possession ▶			
	c Total gross income from sources outside the United States *(attach schedule)*	**17c**		Form 1116, Part I
	d Total applicable deductions and losses *(attach schedule)* . . .	**17d**		
	e Total foreign taxes (check one): ▶ ☐ Paid ☐ Accrued . . .	**17e**		Form 1116, Part II
	f Reduction in taxes available for credit *(attach schedule)* . . .	**17f**		Form 1116, Part III
	g Other foreign tax information *(attach schedule)*	**17g**		See Instructions for Form 1116.
Other	**18a** Total expenditures to which a section 59(e) election may apply	**18a**		See Partner's Instructions for Schedule K-1 (Form 1065).
	b Type of expenditures ▶			
	19 Tax-exempt interest income	**19**		Form 1040, line 8b
	20 Other tax-exempt income.	**20**		See Partner's Instructions for Schedule K-1 (Form 1065).
	21 Nondeductible expenses	**21**		
	22 Recapture of low-income housing credit:			
	a From section 42(j)(5) partnerships	**22a**		Form 8611, line 8
	b Other than on line 22a.	**22b**		
Supplemental Information	**23** Supplemental information required to be reported separately to each partner *(attach additional schedules if more space is needed):*			

Form **1116**	**Foreign Tax Credit**	OMB No. 1545-0121
Department of the Treasury Internal Revenue Service	(Individual, Fiduciary, or Nonresident Alien Individual) ▶ Attach to Form 1040, 1040NR, 1041, or 990-T. ▶ See separate instructions.	19**93** Attachment Sequence No. **19**

Name	Identifying number as shown on page 1 of your tax return

Report all amounts in U.S. dollars except where specified in Part II. Use a separate Form 1116 for each category of income listed below. Check only **one** *box. Before you check a box, read* **Categories of Income** *on page 3 of the instructions. Complete this form for credit for taxes on:*

a ☐ Passive income

b ☐ High withholding tax interest

c ☐ Financial services income

d ☐ Shipping income

e ☐ Dividends from a DISC or former DISC

f ☐ Certain distributions from a foreign sales corporation (FSC) or former FSC

g ☐ Lump-sum distributions (see instructions before completing form)

h ☐ General limitation income—all other income from sources outside the United States (including income from sources within U.S. possessions)

i Resident of (name of country) ▶

Note: *If you paid taxes to one foreign country or U.S. possession, use column A in Part I and line A in Part II. If you paid taxes to* **more than one** *foreign country or U.S. possession, use a separate column and line for each country or possession. However, see the exception under* **A Change To Note** *on page 1 of the Instructions.*

Part I   Taxable Income or Loss From Sources Outside the United States for Separate Category Checked Above

		Foreign Country or U.S. Possession			Total
		A	**B**	**C**	(Add cols. A, B, and C.)
j	Enter the name of the foreign country or U.S. possession . . . . ▶				
1	Gross income from sources within country shown above and of the type checked above. See instructions:				**1**
	Applicable deductions and losses. (See instructions.):				
2	Expenses directly allocable to the income on line 1 (attach schedule)				
3	Pro rata share of other deductions not directly allocable:				
a	Certain itemized deductions or standard deduction. See instructions				
b	Other deductions (attach schedule)				
c	Add lines 3a and 3b				
d	Gross foreign source income. See instructions .				
e	Gross income from all sources. See instructions				
f	Divide line 3d by line 3e				
g	Multiply line 3c by line 3f				
4	Pro rata share of interest expense. See instructions:				
a	Home mortgage interest from line 5 of the worksheet on page 6 of the instructions . . .				
b	Other interest expense				
5	Losses from foreign sources				
6	Add lines 2, 3g, 4a, 4b, and 5				**6**
7	Subtract line 6 from line 1. Enter the result here and on line 14. . . . . ▶				**7**

Part II   Foreign Taxes Paid or Accrued (See instructions.)

Country	Credit is claimed for taxes (you must check one) **(k)** ☐ Paid **(l)** ☐ Accrued	Foreign taxes paid or accrued								
		In foreign currency				In U.S. dollars				
		Taxes withheld at source on:			**(q)** Other foreign taxes paid or accrued	Taxes withheld at source on:			**(u)** Other foreign taxes paid or accrued	**(v)** Total foreign taxes paid or accrued (add cols. (r) through (u))
	(m) Date paid or accrued	**(n)** Dividends	**(o)** Rents and royalties	**(p)** Interest		**(r)** Dividends	**(s)** Rents and royalties	**(t)** Interest		
A										
B										
C										

8   Add lines A through C, column (v). Enter the total here and on line 9 . . . . ▶   **8**

For Paperwork Reduction Act Notice, see page 1 of separate instructions.	Cat. No. 11440U	Form **1116** (1993)

Part III   Figuring the Credit

9	Enter amount from line 8. This is the total foreign taxes paid or accrued for the category of income checked above Part I	**9**	
10	Carryback or carryover (attach detailed computation)	**10**	
11	Add lines 9 and 10	**11**	
12	Reduction in foreign taxes. See instructions	**12**	
13	Subtract line 12 from line 11. This is the total amount of foreign taxes available for credit	**13**	
14	Enter amount from line 7. This is your taxable income or (loss) from sources outside the United States (before adjustments) for the category of income checked above Part I. See instructions . . .	**14**	
15	Adjustments to line 14. See instructions	**15**	
16	Combine the amounts on lines 14 and 15. This is your net foreign source taxable income. (If the result is zero or less, you have no foreign tax credit for the category of income you checked above Part I. Skip lines 17 through 21.)	**16**	
17	**Individuals:** Enter amount from Form 1040, line 35. If you are a nonresident alien, enter amount from Form 1040NR, line 34. **Estates and trusts:** Enter your taxable income without the deduction for your exemption	**17**	
	Caution: *If you figured your tax using the maximum tax rate on capital gains, see instructions.*		
18	Divide line 16 by line 17. If line 16 is more than line 17, enter the figure "1"	**18**	
19	**Individuals:** Enter amount from Form 1040, line 40, **less** any amounts on Form 1040, lines 41, 42, and any mortgage interest credit (from Form 8396) on line 44. If you are a nonresident alien, enter amount from Form 1040NR, line 39, less any amount on Form 1040NR, line 40 and any mortgage interest credit (from Form 8396) on line 42. **Estates and trusts:** Enter amount from Form 1041, Schedule G, line 1c, or Form 990-T, line 37. .	**19**	
20	Multiply line 19 by line 18 (maximum amount of credit)	**20**	
21	Enter the amount from line 13 or line 20, whichever is smaller. (If this is the only Form 1116 you are completing, skip lines 22 through 29 and enter this amount on line 30. Otherwise, complete the appropriate lines in Part IV.) . . . . ▶	**21**	

Part IV   Summary of Credits From Separate Parts III (See instructions.)

22	Credit for taxes on passive income	**22**	
23	Credit for taxes on high withholding tax interest	**23**	
24	Credit for taxes on financial services income	**24**	
25	Credit for taxes on shipping income	**25**	
26	Credit for taxes on dividends from a DISC or former DISC	**26**	
27	Credit for taxes on certain distributions from a FSC or former FSC .	**27**	
28	Credit for taxes on lump-sum distributions	**28**	
29	Credit for taxes on general limitation income (all other income from sources outside the United States)	**29**	
30	Add lines 22 through 29.	**30**	
31	Reduction of credit for international boycott operations. See instructions for line 12	**31**	
32	Subtract line 31 from line 30. This is your foreign tax credit. Enter here and on Form 1040, line 43; Form 1040NR, line 41; Form 1041, Schedule G, line 2a; or Form 990-T, line 38a. . . . . . . ▶	**32**	

✪ *Printed on recycled paper*

Form **1120**	**U.S. Corporation Income Tax Return**	OMB No. 1545-0123
Department of the Treasury Internal Revenue Service	For calendar year 1993 or tax year beginning .... , 1993, ending .... , 19 ... ▶ **Instructions are separate. See page 1 for Paperwork Reduction Act Notice.**	19**93**

A Check if a:	Use IRS label. Other-wise, please print or type.	Name		**B** Employer identification number
1 Consolidated return (attach Form 851) ☐				
2 Personal holding co. (attach Sch. PH) ☐		Number, street, and room or suite no. (If a P.O. box, see page 7 of instructions.)		**C** Date incorporated
3 Personal service corp. (as defined in Temporary Regs. sec. 1.441-4T— see instructions)		City or town, state, and ZIP code		**D** Total assets (see Specific Instructions)

E Check applicable boxes: (1) ☐ Initial return (2) ☐ Final return (3) ☐ Change of address $

Income	**1a** Gross receipts or sales [ ] **b** Less returns and allowances [ ] **c** Bal ▶	**1c**		
	2 Cost of goods sold (Schedule A, line 8)	**2**		
	3 Gross profit. Subtract line 2 from line 1c	**3**		
	4 Dividends (Schedule C, line 19)	**4**		
	5 Interest	**5**		
	6 Gross rents	**6**		
	7 Gross royalties	**7**		
	8 Capital gain net income (attach Schedule D (Form 1120))	**8**		
	9 Net gain or (loss) from Form 4797, Part II, line 20 (attach Form 4797)	**9**		
	10 Other income (see instructions—attach schedule)	**10**		
	11 **Total income.** Add lines 3 through 10 ▶	**11**		
Deductions (See instructions for limitations on deductions.)	**12** Compensation of officers (Schedule E, line 4)	**12**		
	13a Salaries and wages [ ] **b** Less employment credits [ ] **c** Bal ▶	**13c**		
	14 Repairs and maintenance	**14**		
	15 Bad debts	**15**		
	16 Rents	**16**		
	17 Taxes and licenses	**17**		
	18 Interest	**18**		
	19 Charitable contributions (see instructions for 10% limitation)	**19**		
	20 Depreciation (attach Form 4562) **20** [ ]			
	21 Less depreciation claimed on Schedule A and elsewhere on return **21a** [ ]	**21b**		
	22 Depletion	**22**		
	23 Advertising	**23**		
	24 Pension, profit-sharing, etc., plans	**24**		
	25 Employee benefit programs	**25**		
	26 Other deductions (attach schedule)	**26**		
	27 **Total deductions.** Add lines 12 through 26 ▶	**27**		
	28 Taxable income before net operating loss deduction and special deductions. Subtract line 27 from line 11	**28**		
	29 **Less: a** Net operating loss deduction (see instructions) **29a** [ ]			
	b Special deductions (Schedule C, line 20) **29b** [ ]	**29c**		
Tax and Payments	**30** **Taxable income.** Subtract line 29c from line 28	**30**		
	31 **Total tax** (Schedule J, line 10)	**31**		
	32 **Payments: a** 1992 overpayment credited to 1993 **32a** [ ]			
	b 1993 estimated tax payments **32b** [ ]			
	c Less 1993 refund applied for on Form 4466 **32c** ( ) **d** Bal ▶ **32d** [ ]			
	e Tax deposited with Form 7004 **32e** [ ]			
	f Credit from regulated investment companies (attach Form 2439) **32f** [ ]			
	g Credit for Federal tax on fuels (attach Form 4136). See instructions **32g** [ ]	**32h**		
	33 Estimated tax penalty (see instructions). Check if Form 2220 is attached ▶ ☐	**33**		
	34 **Tax due.** If line 32h is smaller than the total of lines 31 and 33, enter amount owed	**34**		
	35 **Overpayment.** If line 32h is larger than the total of lines 31 and 33, enter amount overpaid	**35**		
	36 Enter amount of line 35 you want: **Credited to 1994 estimated tax** ▶ Refunded ▶	**36**		

Please Sign Here	Under penalties of perjury, I declare that I have examined this return, including accompanying schedules and statements, and to the best of my knowledge and belief, it is true, correct, and complete. Declaration of preparer (other than taxpayer) is based on all information of which preparer has any knowledge.
	▶ Signature of officer Date ▶ Title

Paid Preparer's Use Only	Preparer's signature ▶	Date	Check if self-employed ☐	Preparer's social security number
	Firm's name (or yours if self-employed) and address ▶		E.I. No. ▶	
			ZIP code ▶	

Cat. No. 11450Q

Form 1120 (1993)   Page **2**

Schedule A   Cost of Goods Sold (See instructions.)

1	Inventory at beginning of year	1		
2	Purchases	2		
3	Cost of labor	3		
4	Additional section 263A costs (attach schedule)	4		
5	Other costs (attach schedule)	5		
6	**Total.** Add lines 1 through 5	6		
7	Inventory at end of year	7		
8	**Cost of goods sold.** Subtract line 7 from line 6. Enter here and on page 1, line 2	8		

9a Check all methods used for valuing closing inventory:

☐ Cost   ☐ Lower of cost or market as described in Regulations section 1.471-4

☐ Writedown of subnormal goods as described in Regulations section 1.471-2(c)

☐ Other (Specify method used and attach explanation.) ▶ --

b Check if the LIFO inventory method was adopted this tax year for any goods (if checked, attach Form 970) . . . . . . ▶ ☐

c If the LIFO inventory method was used for this tax year, enter percentage (or amounts) of closing
inventory computed under LIFO 9c

d Do the rules of section 263A (for property produced or acquired for resale) apply to the corporation? . . . . . ☐ Yes   ☐ No

e Was there any change in determining quantities, cost, or valuations between opening and closing inventory? If "Yes,"
attach explanation . . . . ☐ Yes   ☐ No

Schedule C   Dividends and Special Deductions (See instructions.)

		(a) Dividends received	(b) %	(c) Special deductions (a) × (b)
1	Dividends from less-than-20%-owned domestic corporations that are subject to the 70% deduction (other than debt-financed stock)		70	
2	Dividends from 20%-or-more-owned domestic corporations that are subject to the 80% deduction (other than debt-financed stock)		80	
3	Dividends on debt-financed stock of domestic and foreign corporations (section 246A)		see instructions	
4	Dividends on certain preferred stock of less-than-20%-owned public utilities		42	
5	Dividends on certain preferred stock of 20%-or-more-owned public utilities		48	
6	Dividends from less-than-20%-owned foreign corporations and certain FSCs that are subject to the 70% deduction		70	
7	Dividends from 20%-or-more-owned foreign corporations and certain FSCs that are subject to the 80% deduction		80	
8	Dividends from wholly owned foreign subsidiaries subject to the 100% deduction (section 245(b))		100	
9	**Total.** Add lines 1 through 8. See instructions for limitation			
10	Dividends from domestic corporations received by a small business investment company operating under the Small Business Investment Act of 1958		100	
11	Dividends from certain FSCs that are subject to the 100% deduction (section 245(c)(1))		100	
12	Dividends from affiliated group members subject to the 100% deduction (section 243(a)(3))		100	
13	Other dividends from foreign corporations not included on lines 3, 6, 7, 8, or 11			
14	Income from controlled foreign corporations under subpart F (attach Form(s) 5471)			
15	Foreign dividend gross-up (section 78)			
16	IC-DISC and former DISC dividends not included on lines 1, 2, or 3 (section 246(d))			
17	Other dividends			
18	Deduction for dividends paid on certain preferred stock of public utilities (see instructions)			
19	**Total dividends.** Add lines 1 through 17. Enter here and on line 4, page 1 ▶			

20 **Total special deductions.** Add lines 9, 10, 11, 12, and 18. Enter here and on line 29b, page 1 . . . . . . ▶

Schedule E   Compensation of Officers (See instructions for line 12, page 1.)

Complete Schedule E only if total receipts (line 1a plus lines 4 through 10 on page 1, Form 1120) are $500,000 or more.

(a) Name of officer	(b) Social security number	(c) Percent of time devoted to business	Percent of corporation stock owned		(f) Amount of compensation
			(d) Common	(e) Preferred	
1		%	%	%	
		%	%	%	
		%	%	%	
		%	%	%	
		%	%	%	

2 Total compensation of officers . . . .

3 Compensation of officers claimed on Schedule A and elsewhere on return . . . .

4 Subtract line 3 from line 2. Enter the result here and on line 12, page 1 . . . .

Form 1120 (1993)   Page **4**

Schedule L	Balance Sheets	Beginning of tax year		End of tax year	
	Assets	**(a)**	**(b)**	**(c)**	**(d)**
1	Cash				
2a	Trade notes and accounts receivable				
b	Less allowance for bad debts	( )		( )	
3	Inventories				
4	U.S. government obligations				
5	Tax-exempt securities (see instructions)				
6	Other current assets (attach schedule)				
7	Loans to stockholders				
8	Mortgage and real estate loans				
9	Other investments (attach schedule)				
10a	Buildings and other depreciable assets				
b	Less accumulated depreciation	( )		( )	
11a	Depletable assets				
b	Less accumulated depletion	( )		( )	
12	Land (net of any amortization)				
13a	Intangible assets (amortizable only)				
b	Less accumulated amortization	( )		( )	
14	Other assets (attach schedule)				
15	Total assets				
	Liabilities and Stockholders' Equity				
16	Accounts payable				
17	Mortgages, notes, bonds payable in less than 1 year				
18	Other current liabilities (attach schedule)				
19	Loans from stockholders				
20	Mortgages, notes, bonds payable in 1 year or more				
21	Other liabilities (attach schedule)				
22	Capital stock: **a** Preferred stock				
	b Common stock				
23	Paid-in or capital surplus				
24	Retained earnings—Appropriated (attach schedule)				
25	Retained earnings—Unappropriated				
26	Less cost of treasury stock		( )		( )
27	Total liabilities and stockholders' equity				

Note: *You are not required to complete Schedules M-1 and M-2 below if the total assets on line 15, column (d) of Schedule L are less than $25,000.*

Schedule M-1	**Reconciliation of Income (Loss) per Books With Income per Return** (See instructions.)

1	Net income (loss) per books		7	Income recorded on books this year not included on this return (itemize):	
2	Federal income tax			Tax-exempt interest $	
3	Excess of capital losses over capital gains			....	
4	Income subject to tax not recorded on books this year (itemize):		8	Deductions on this return not charged against book income this year (itemize):	
	....		a	Depreciation . . . . $	
5	Expenses recorded on books this year not deducted on this return (itemize):		b	Contributions carryover $	
a	Depreciation . . . . $			....	
b	Contributions carryover $			....	
c	Travel and entertainment $				
	....		9	Add lines 7 and 8	
6	Add lines 1 through 5		10	Income (line 28, page 1)—line 6 less line 9	

Schedule M-2	**Analysis of Unappropriated Retained Earnings per Books (Line 25, Schedule L)**

1	Balance at beginning of year		5	Distributions: **a** Cash	
2	Net income (loss) per books			**b** Stock	
3	Other increases (itemize):			**c** Property	
	....		6	Other decreases (itemize):	
	....			....	
	....		7	Add lines 5 and 6	
4	Add lines 1, 2, and 3		8	Balance at end of year (line 4 less line 7)	

Form 1120 (1993)   Page **3**

Schedule J   Tax Computation (See instructions.)

1   Check if the corporation is a member of a controlled group (see sections 1561 and 1563) . . . . ▶ ☐

2a If the box on line 1 is checked, enter the corporation's share of the $50,000, $25,000, and $9,925,000 taxable income brackets (in that order):

(1) ☐ $_____|____| (2) ☐ $_____|____| (3) ☐ $_____|____|

b   Enter the corporation's share of:

(1) additional 5% tax (not more than $11,750)   ☐ $_____|____|

(2) additional 3% tax (not more than $100,000) ☐ $_____|____|

3   Income tax. Check this box if the corporation is a qualified personal service corporation as defined in section 448(d)(2) (see instructions on page 15). . . . . ▶ ☐ | **3** |

4a Foreign tax credit (attach Form 1118) . . . . | **4a** |

b   Possessions tax credit (attach Form 5735) . . . . | **4b** |

c   Orphan drug credit (attach Form 6765) . . . . | **4c** |

d   Check: ☐ Nonconventional source fuel credit ☐ QEV credit (attach Form 8834) | **4d** |

e   General business credit. Enter here and check which forms are attached:

☐ Form 3800 ☐ Form 3468 ☐ Form 5884 ☐ Form 6478 ☐ Form 6765

☐ Form 8586 ☐ Form 8830 ☐ Form 8826 ☐ Form 8835 . . . . . | **4e** |

f   Credit for prior year minimum tax (attach Form 8827) . . . . | **4f** |

5   **Total credits.** Add lines 4a through 4f . . . . | **5** |

6   Subtract line 5 from line 3 . . . . | **6** |

7   Personal holding company tax (attach Schedule PH (Form 1120)) . . . . | **7** |

8   Recapture taxes. Check if from: ☐ Form 4255 ☐ Form 8611 . . . . | **8** |

9a Alternative minimum tax (attach Form 4626) . . . . | **9a** |

b   Environmental tax (attach Form 4626) . . . . | **9b** |

10 **Total tax.** Add lines 6 through 9b. Enter here and on line 31, page 1 . . . . | **10** |

Schedule K   Other Information (See pages 17 and 18 of instructions.)

		Yes	No

1   Check method of accounting: **a** ☐ Cash   **b** ☐ Accrual   **c** ☐ Other (specify) ▶ ....

2   Refer to page 19 of the instructions and state the principal:

a   Business activity code no. ▶ ....

b   Business activity ▶ ....

c   Product or service ▶ ....

3   Did the corporation at the end of the tax year own, directly or indirectly, 50% or more of the voting stock of a domestic corporation? (For rules of attribution, see section 267(c).) . . . .

If "Yes," attach a schedule showing: (a) name and identifying number, (b) percentage owned, and (c) taxable income or (loss) before NOL and special deductions of such corporation for the tax year ending with or within your tax year.

4   Is the corporation a subsidiary in an affiliated group or a parent-subsidiary controlled group?

If "Yes," enter employer identification number and name of the parent corporation ▶ ....
....

5   Did any individual, partnership, corporation, estate or trust at the end of the tax year own, directly or indirectly, 50% or more of the corporation's voting stock? (For rules of attribution, see section 267(c).) . . . . . .

If "Yes," attach a schedule showing name and identifying number. (Do not include any information already entered in **4** above.) Enter percentage owned ▶.................

6   During this tax year, did the corporation pay dividends (other than stock dividends and distributions in exchange for stock) in excess of the corporation's current and accumulated earnings and profits? (See secs. 301 and 316.) . . . .

If "Yes," file Form 5452. If this is a consolidated return, answer here for the parent corporation and on **Form 851,** Affiliations Schedule, for each subsidiary.

7   Was the corporation a U.S. shareholder of any controlled foreign corporation? (See sections 951 and 957.) . . .

If "Yes," attach Form 5471 for each such corporation. Enter number of Forms 5471 attached ▶.................

8   At any time during the 1993 calendar year, did the corporation have an interest in or a signature or other authority over a financial account in a foreign country (such as a bank account, securities account, or other financial account)? .

If "Yes," the corporation may have to file Form TD F 90-22.1. If "Yes," enter name of foreign country ▶ ....

9   Was the corporation the grantor of, or transferor to, a foreign trust that existed during the current tax year, whether or not the corporation has any beneficial interest in it? If "Yes," the corporation may have to file Forms 926, 3520, or 3520-A

10 Did one foreign person at any time during the tax year own, directly or indirectly, at least 25% of: **(a)** the total voting power of all classes of stock of the corporation entitled to vote, or **(b)** the total value of all classes of stock of the corporation? If "Yes,"

a   Enter percentage owned ▶.................

b   Enter owner's country ▶.................

c   The corporation may have to file Form 5472. Enter number of Forms 5472 attached ▶.................

11 Check this box if the corporation issued publicly offered debt instruments with original issue discount . ▶ ☐

If so, the corporation may have to file Form 8281.

12 Enter the amount of tax-exempt interest received or accrued during the tax year ▶ $ ....

13 If there were 35 or fewer shareholders at the end of the tax year, enter the number ▶.................

14 If the corporation has an NOL for the tax year and is electing to forego the carryback period, check here ▶ ☐

15 Enter the available NOL carryover from prior tax years (Do not reduce it by any deduction on line 29a.) ▶ $

SCHEDULE D
(Form 1120)

Department of the Treasury
Internal Revenue Service

Capital Gains and Losses

To be filed with Forms 1120, 1120-A, 1120-DF, 1120-IC-DISC,
1120-F, 1120-FSC, 1120-H, 1120-L, 1120-ND, 1120-PC, 1120-POL,
1120-REIT, 1120-RIC, 990-C, and certain Forms 990-T

OMB No. 1545-0123

1993

Name | Employer identification number

Part I — Short-Term Capital Gains and Losses—Assets Held 1 Year or Less

(a) Kind of property and description (Example, 100 shares of "Z" Co.)	(b) Date acquired (mo., day, yr.)	(c) Date sold (mo., day, yr.)	(d) Gross sales price	(e) Cost or other basis, plus expense of sale	(f) Gain or (loss) ((d) less (e))
1					

2 Short-term capital gain from installment sales from Form 6252, line 26 or 37	**2**	
3 Short-term gain or (loss) from like-kind exchanges from Form 8824	**3**	
4 Unused capital loss carryover (attach computation)	**4**	( )
5 Net short-term capital gain or (loss). (Combine lines 1 through 4.)	**5**	

Part II — Long-Term Capital Gains and Losses—Assets Held More Than 1 Year

(a)	(b)	(c)	(d)	(e)	(f)
6					

7 Enter gain from Form 4797, line 8 or 10	**7**	
8 Long-term capital gain from installment sales from Form 6252, line 26 or 37	**8**	
9 Long-term gain or (loss) from like-kind exchanges from Form 8824	**9**	
10 Net long-term capital gain or (loss). (Combine lines 6 through 9.)	**10**	

Part III — Summary of Parts I and II

11 Enter excess of net short-term capital gain (line 5) over net long-term capital loss (line 10).	**11**	
12 Net capital gain. Enter excess of net long-term capital gain (line 10) over net short-term capital loss (line 5)	**12**	
13 Add lines 11 and 12. Enter here and on Form 1120, page 1, line 8, or the proper line on other returns.	**13**	

Note: *If losses exceed gains, see instructions on capital losses for explanation of capital loss carrybacks.*

Instructions

Section references are to the Internal Revenue Code.

Changes To Note

The Revenue Reconciliation Act of 1993 made the following changes to the tax law:

● Effective for bonds purchased after April 30, 1993, gain on tax-exempt obligations or other market discount bonds issued on or before July 18, 1984, is treated as ordinary income (instead of capital gain) to the extent of the accrued market discount. See Act section 13206.

● A corporation that sells publicly traded securities at a gain after August 9, 1993, may elect to postpone all or part of the gain if the seller buys stock or a partnership interest in a specialized small business investment company (SSBIC) during the 60-day period that begins on the date the securities are sold.

An SSBIC is any partnership or corporation licensed by the Small Business Administration

under section 301(d) of the Small Business Investment Act of 1958. The corporation must recognize gain on the sale to the extent the proceeds from the sale exceed the cost of the SSBIC stock or partnership interest purchased during the 60-day period that began on the date of the sale (and not previously taken into account). The gain a corporation may postpone each tax year is limited to the lesser of: (a) $250,000 or (b) $1 million, reduced by the gain previously excluded under these provisions. The basis of the SSBIC stock or partnership interest is reduced by any postponed gain.

To make the election to postpone gain, complete line 1 or line 6, whichever applies, showing the entire gain realized in column (f). Directly below the line on which the gain is reported, enter "SSBIC Rollover" in column (a). Enter the amount of the postponed gain (in parentheses) in column (f). Also, attach a schedule showing (a) how you figured the postponed gain, (b) the name of the SSBIC in which you purchased common stock or a partnership interest, (c) the date of that

purchase, and (d) the new basis in that SSBIC stock or partnership interest.

For details, see new section 1044.

Purpose of Schedule

Schedule D is used to report sales and exchanges of capital assets for tax years beginning in 1993.

Sales or exchanges of property other than capital assets are reported on **Form 4797,** Sales of Business Property. A sale or exchange of property includes property used in a trade or business; involuntary conversions (other than casualties or thefts); gain from the disposition of oil, gas, or geothermal property; and the section 291 adjustment to section 1250 gains. See the instructions for Form 4797 for more information.

If property is involuntarily converted because of a casualty or theft, use **Form 4684,** Casualties and Thefts.

Parts I and II

Generally, a corporation must report sales and exchanges even though there is no gain or loss. No loss is allowed for a wash sale of stock or securities (including contracts or options to acquire or sell stock or securities) or from a transaction between related persons. See sections 1091 and 267 for details and exceptions.

Use Part I to report the sale or exchange of capital assets held 1 year or less. Use Part II to report the sale or exchange of capital assets held more than 1 year.

What Is a Capital Asset?—Each item of property the corporation held (whether or not connected with its trade or business) is a capital asset except:

1. Assets that can be inventoried or property held mainly for sale to customers.

2. Depreciable or real property used in the trade or business.

3. Certain copyrights; literary, musical, or artistic compositions; letters or memorandums; or similar property.

4. Accounts or notes receivable acquired in the ordinary course of trade or business for services rendered or from the sale of property described in 1 above.

5. A U.S. Government publication (including the Congressional Record) received from the Government or any of its agencies in a manner other than buying it at the price offered for public sale, which is held by a taxpayer who received the publication or by a second taxpayer in whose hands the basis of the publication is determined, for purposes of determining gain from a sale or exchange, by referring to its basis in the hands of the first taxpayer.

Capital losses.—Capital losses are allowed only to the extent of capital gains. A net capital loss may be carried back 3 years and forward 5 years as a short-term capital loss. Carry back a capital loss to the extent it does not increase or produce a net operating loss in the tax year to which it is carried. Foreign expropriation capital losses may not be carried back, but may be carried forward 10 years. A net capital loss for a regulated investment company may be carried forward 8 years.

Special Rules for the Treatment of Certain Gains and Losses

Note: *For more information, get Pub. 544, Sales and Other Dispositions of Assets, and Pub. 542, Tax Information on Corporations.*

● **Like-kind exchanges.**—An exchange of business or investment property for property of a like kind is reported on **Form 8824,** Like-Kind Exchanges.

● **At-risk limitations (section 465).**—If the corporation sold or exchanged a capital asset used in an activity to which the at-risk rules apply, combine the gain or loss on the sale or exchange with the profit or loss from the activity. If the result is a net loss, complete **Form 6198,** At-Risk Limitations. Report any gain from the capital asset on Schedule D and on Form 6198.

● **Gains and losses from passive activities.**—A closely held or personal service corporation that has a gain or loss that relates to a passive activity (section 469) may be required to complete **Form 8810,**

Corporate Passive Activity Loss and Credit Limitations, before completing Schedule D. A Schedule D loss may be limited under the passive activity rules. See Form 8810 for more detailed information.

● **Gain on distributions of appreciated property.**—Generally, gain (but not loss) is recognized on a nonliquidating distribution of appreciated property to the extent that the property's fair market value exceeds its adjusted basis. See section 311 for more information.

● **Gain or loss on distribution of property in complete liquidation.**— Generally, gain or loss is recognized on property distributed in a complete liquidation. Treat the property as if it had been sold at its fair market value. An exception to this rule applies for liquidations of certain subsidiaries. See sections 336 and 337 for more information and other exceptions to the general rules.

● **Gains and losses on section 1256 contracts and straddles.**—Use Form 6781, Gains and Losses From Section 1256 Contracts and Straddles, to report these gains and losses.

● **Gain or loss on certain short-term Federal, state, and municipal obligations.**—Such obligations are treated as capital assets in determining gain or loss. On any gain realized, a portion is treated as ordinary income and the balance as a short-term capital gain. See section 1271.

● **Gain from installment sales.**—Use Form 6252, Installment Sale Income, to report a gain from the casual sale of real or personal property (other than inventory) if payments will be received in more than 1 tax year. See the instructions below for how to elect out of the installment method. Also use Form 6252 if a payment is received this year from a sale made in an earlier year on the installment method.

To elect out of the installment method, report the full amount of the gain with a timely filed return (including extensions).

The installment method may not be used for sales of stock or securities (or certain other property described in the regulations) traded on an established securities market. See section 453(k).

● **Gain or loss on an option to buy or sell property.**—See sections 1032 and 1234 for the rules that apply to a purchaser or grantor of an option.

● **Gain or loss from a short sale of property.**—Report the gain or loss to the extent that the property used to close the short sale is considered a capital asset in the hands of the taxpayer.

● **Gains and losses of foreign corporations from the disposition of investment in U.S. real property.**— Foreign corporations are required to report gains and losses from the disposition of U.S. real property interests. See section 897 for details.

● **Gains on certain insurance property.**— Form 1120-L filers with gains on property held on December 31, 1958, and certain substituted property acquired after 1958 should see section 818(c).

● **Gain or loss from shares purchased in a regulated investment company (RIC).**—In some cases, the load charge (advance charge for sales fees) incurred to purchase shares in a RIC may not be allowed when figuring the basis for gain or loss on the disposition of the shares. See section 852(f) if the shares were disposed of within 90 days of purchase, and the load charge on stock subsequently acquired in that RIC (or another RIC) was reduced because of a reinvestment right.

● **Loss from the sale or exchange of capital assets of an insurance company taxable under section 831.**—Under the provisions of section 834(c)(6), capital losses of a casualty insurance company are deductible to the extent that the assets were sold to meet abnormal insurance losses or to provide for the payment of dividend and similar distributions to policyholders.

● **Loss from securities that are capital assets that become worthless during the year.**—Except for securities held by a bank, treat the loss as a capital loss as of the last day of the tax year. (See section 582 for the rules on the treatment of securities held by a bank.)

● **Disposition of market discount bonds.**— See section 1276 for rules on the disposition of market discount bonds.

● **Capital gain distributions.**—Report capital gain distributions paid by mutual funds as long-term capital gains on line 6 regardless of how long the corporation owned stock in the fund.

● **Sale or acquisition of assets.**—If the corporation acquired or disposed of assets that constitute a business, it may be required to file Form 8594, Asset Acquisition Statement.

Determining the Cost or Other Basis of Property

In determining gain or loss, the basis of property will generally be its cost. See section 1012 and the related regulations. Exceptions to the general rule are provided in sections in subchapters C, K, O, and P of the Code. For example, if the corporation acquired the property by dividend, liquidation of a corporation, transfer from a shareholder, reorganization, bequest, contribution or gift, tax-free exchange, involuntary conversion, certain asset acquisitions, or wash sale of stock, see sections 301 (or 1059), 334, 362 (or 358), 1014, 1015, 1031, 1033, 1060, and 1091, respectively. Attach an explanation if the corporation uses a basis other than actual cash cost of the property.

If the corporation is allowed a charitable contribution deduction because it sold property to a charitable organization, figure the adjusted basis for determining gain from the sale by dividing the amount realized by the fair market value and multiplying that result by the adjusted basis.

Form **1120-A**

Department of the Treasury
Internal Revenue Service

U.S. Corporation Short-Form Income Tax Return

See separate instructions to make sure the corporation qualifies to file Form 1120-A.
For calendar year 1993 or tax year beginning ...., 1993, ending............., 19.....

OMB No. 1545-0890

1993

A Check this box if the corp. is a personal service corp. (as defined in Temporary Regs. section 1.441-4T—see instructions) ▶ ☐

Use IRS label. Otherwise, please print or type.

Name

Number, street, and room or suite no. (If a P.O. box, see page 7 of instructions.)

City or town, state, and ZIP code

B Employer identification number

C Date incorporated

D Total assets (see Specific Instructions)
$

E Check applicable boxes: **(1)** ☐ Initial return **(2)** ☐ Change of address

F Check method of accounting: **(1)** ☐ Cash **(2)** ☐ Accrual **(3)** ☐ Other (specify) . . ▶

Income

1a Gross receipts or sales	**b** Less returns and allowances	**c** Balance ▶ **1c**
2 Cost of goods sold (see instructions)		**2**
3 Gross profit. Subtract line 2 from line 1c		**3**
4 Domestic corporation dividends subject to the 70% deduction		**4**
5 Interest		**5**
6 Gross rents		**6**
7 Gross royalties		**7**
8 Capital gain net income (attach Schedule D (Form 1120))		**8**
9 Net gain or (loss) from Form 4797, Part II, line 20 (attach Form 4797) . .		**9**
10 Other income (see instructions)		**10**
11 **Total income.** Add lines 3 through 10 . . . . ▶		**11**

Deductions

(See instructions for limitations on deductions.)

12 Compensation of officers (see instructions)		**12**
13a Salaries and wages	**b** Less employment credits	**c** Bal ▶ **13c**
14 Repairs and maintenance		**14**
15 Bad debts		**15**
16 Rents		**16**
17 Taxes and licenses		**17**
18 Interest		**18**
19 Charitable contributions (see instructions for 10% limitation)		**19**
20 Depreciation (attach Form 4562) **20**		
21 Less depreciation claimed elsewhere on return **21a**		**21b**
22 Other deductions (attach schedule)		**22**
23 **Total deductions.** Add lines 12 through 22 . . . . ▶		**23**
24 Taxable income before net operating loss deduction and special deductions. Subtract line 23 from line 11		**24**
25 **Less: a** Net operating loss deduction (see instructions) **25a**		
b Special deductions (see instructions) **25b**		**25c**

Tax and Payments

26 **Taxable income.** Subtract line 25c from line 24		**26**
27 **Total tax** (from page 2, Part I, line 7)		**27**
28 **Payments:**		
a 1992 overpayment credited to 1993 **28a**		
b 1993 estimated tax payments . **28b**		
c Less 1993 refund applied for on Form 4466 **28c** ( ) Bal ▶ **28d**		
e Tax deposited with Form 7004 . . . . . **28e**		
f Credit from regulated investment companies (attach Form 2439) . **28f**		
g Credit for Federal tax on fuels (attach Form 4136). See instructions **28g**		
h **Total payments.** Add lines 28d through 28g		**28h**
29 Estimated tax penalty (see instructions). Check if Form 2220 is attached . . . ▶ ☐		**29**
30 **Tax due.** If line 28h is smaller than the total of lines 27 and 29, enter amount owed . .		**30**
31 **Overpayment.** If line 28h is larger than the total of lines 27 and 29, enter amount overpaid . .		**31**
32 Enter amount of line 31 you want: **Credited to 1994 estimated tax** ▶	Refunded ▶	**32**

Please Sign Here

Under penalties of perjury, I declare that I have examined this return, including accompanying schedules and statements, and to the best of my knowledge and belief, it is true, correct, and complete. Declaration of preparer (other than taxpayer) is based on all information of which preparer has any knowledge.

▶ _____ Signature of officer   Date   ▶ _____ Title

Paid Preparer's Use Only

Preparer's signature ▶	Date	Check if self-employed ▶ ☐	Preparer's social security number
Firm's name (or yours if self-employed) and address ▶		E.I. No. ▶	
		ZIP code ▶	

For Paperwork Reduction Act Notice, see page 1 of the instructions.   Cat. No. 11456E   Form **1120-A** (1993)

Part I Tax Computation (See instructions.)

1	Income tax. Check this box if the corporation is a qualified personal service corporation as defined in section 448(d)(2) (see instructions on page 15) . . . . ▶ ☐	1
2a	General business credit. Check if from: ☐ Form 3800 ☐ Form 3468 ☐ Form 5884 ☐ Form 6478 ☐ Form 6765 ☐ Form 8586 ☐ Form 8830 ☐ Form 8826 ☐ Form 8835 **2a**	
b	Credit for prior year minimum tax (attach Form 8827) **2b**	
3	**Total credits.** Add lines 2a and 2b	3
4	Subtract line 3 from line 1	4
5	Recapture taxes. Check if from: ☐ Form 4255 ☐ Form 8611	5
6	Alternative minimum tax (attach Form 4626)	6
7	**Total tax.** Add lines 4 through 6. Enter here and on line 27, page 1	7

Part II Other Information (See instructions.)

1 Refer to page 19 of the instructions and state the principal:
  a Business activity code no. ▶ . . . .
  b Business activity ▶ . . . .
  c Product or service ▶ . . . .

2 Did any individual, partnership, estate, or trust at the end of the tax year own, directly or indirectly, 50% or more of the corporation's voting stock? (For rules of attribution, see section 267(c).) . . . . ☐ Yes ☐ No

If "Yes," attach a schedule showing name and identifying number.

3 Enter the amount of tax-exempt interest received or accrued during the tax year . . . . ▶ $|

4 Enter amount of cash distributions and the book value of property (other than cash) distributions made in this tax year . . . . ▶ $|

5a If an amount is entered on line 2, page 1, see the worksheet on page 13 for amounts to enter below:
  (1) Purchases . . . .
  (2) Additional sec. 263A costs (see instructions—attach schedule) .
  (3) Other costs (attach schedule)

b Do the rules of section 263A (for property produced or acquired for resale) apply to the corporation? . . . . . . ☐ Yes ☐ No

6 At any time during the 1993 calendar year, did the corporation have an interest in or a signature or other authority over a financial account in a foreign country (such as a bank account, securities account, or other financial account)? If "Yes," the corporation may have to file Form TD F 90-22.1 . . . . ☐ Yes ☐ No
If "Yes," enter the name of the foreign country ▶ . . . .

Part III Balance Sheets

		(a) Beginning of tax year		(b) End of tax year	
Assets					
1	Cash				
2a	Trade notes and accounts receivable				
b	Less allowance for bad debts	(	)	(	)
3	Inventories				
4	U.S. government obligations				
5	Tax-exempt securities (see instructions) . .				
6	Other current assets (attach schedule)				
7	Loans to stockholders				
8	Mortgage and real estate loans				
9a	Depreciable, depletable, and intangible assets . .				
b	Less accumulated depreciation, depletion, and amortization	(	)	(	)
10	Land (net of any amortization)				
11	Other assets (attach schedule)				
12	Total assets				
Liabilities and Stockholders' Equity					
13	Accounts payable				
14	Other current liabilities (attach schedule) . . .				
15	Loans from stockholders				
16	Mortgages, notes, bonds payable				
17	Other liabilities (attach schedule)				
18	Capital stock (preferred and common stock) . . .				
19	Paid-in or capital surplus				
20	Retained earnings				
21	Less cost of treasury stock	(	)	(	)
22	Total liabilities and stockholders' equity . . .				

Part IV Reconciliation of Income (Loss) per Books With Income per Return (You are not required to complete Part IV if the total assets on line 12, column (b), Part III are less than $25,000.)

1	Net income (loss) per books	
2	Federal income tax	
3	Excess of capital losses over capital gains . .	
4	Income subject to tax not recorded on books this year (itemize)	
5	Expenses recorded on books this year not deducted on this return (itemize)	
6	Income recorded on books this year not included on this return (itemize)	
7	Deductions on this return not charged against book income this year (itemize)	
8	Income (line 24, page 1). Enter the sum of lines 1 through 5 less the sum of lines 6 and 7 . . .	

Form **1120S**

Department of the Treasury
Internal Revenue Service

U.S. Income Tax Return for an S Corporation

▶ **Do not file this form unless the corporation has timely filed
Form 2553 to elect to be an S corporation.**
▶ **See separate instructions.**

OMB No. 1545-0130

1993

For calendar year 1993, or tax year beginning .... , 1993, and ending .... , 19 .....

A Date of election as an S corporation	Use IRS label. Otherwise, please print or type.	Name		C Employer identification number
		Number, street, and room or suite no. (If a P.O. box, see page 9 of the instructions.)		D Date incorporated
B Business code no. (see Specific Instructions)		City or town, state, and ZIP code		E Total assets (see Specific Instructions) $

F Check applicable boxes: (1) ☐ Initial return   (2) ☐ Final return   (3) ☐ Change in address   (4) ☐ Amended return
G Check this box if this S corporation is subject to the consolidated audit procedures of sections 6241 through 6245 (see instructions before checking this box) . ▶ ☐
H Enter number of shareholders in the corporation at end of the tax year .... ▶

Caution: *Include only trade or business income and expenses on lines 1a through 21. See the instructions for more information.*

Income

1a Gross receipts or sales	**b** Less returns and allowances	**c** Bal ▶	**1c**
2 Cost of goods sold (Schedule A, line 8)			**2**
3 Gross profit. Subtract line 2 from line 1c			**3**
4 Net gain (loss) from Form 4797, Part II, line 20 *(attach Form 4797)*			**4**
5 Other income (loss) (see instructions) *(attach schedule)*			**5**
6 **Total income (loss).** Combine lines 3 through 5 . . . . . . ▶			**6**

Deductions (See instructions for limitations.)

7 Compensation of officers		**7**
8a Salaries and wages	**b** Less employment credits	**c** Bal ▶ **8c**
9 Repairs and maintenance.		**9**
10 Bad debts		**10**
11 Rents		**11**
12 Taxes and licenses.		**12**
13 Interest		**13**
14a Depreciation (see instructions)	**14a**	
b Depreciation claimed on Schedule A and elsewhere on return .	**14b**	
c Subtract line 14b from line 14a		**14c**
15 Depletion **(Do not deduct oil and gas depletion.)**		**15**
16 Advertising		**16**
17 Pension, profit-sharing, etc., plans		**17**
18 Employee benefit programs		**18**
19 Other deductions (see instructions) *(attach schedule)*		**19**
20 **Total deductions.** Add lines 7 through 19 . . . . ▶		**20**
21 Ordinary income (loss) from trade or business activities. Subtract line 20 from line 6		**21**

Tax and Payments

22 **Tax: a** Excess net passive income tax *(attach schedule)*. . .	**22a**		
b Tax from Schedule D (Form 1120S)	**22b**		
c Add lines 22a and 22b (see instructions for additional taxes) . .			**22c**
23 **Payments: a** 1993 estimated tax payments.	**23a**		
b Tax deposited with Form 7004	**23b**		
c Credit for Federal tax paid on fuels *(attach Form 4136)* . . .	**23c**		
d Add lines 23a through 23c			**23d**
24 Estimated tax penalty (see instructions). Check if Form 2220 is attached. . . . . . ▶ ☐			**24**
25 **Tax due.** If the total of lines 22c and 24 is larger than line 23d, enter amount owed. See instructions for depositary method of payment . . . . ▶			**25**
26 **Overpayment.** If line 23d is larger than the total of lines 22c and 24, enter amount overpaid ▶			**26**
27 Enter amount of line 26 you want: **Credited to 1994 estimated tax** ▶	**Refunded** ▶		**27**

Please Sign Here

Under penalties of perjury, I declare that I have examined this return, including accompanying schedules and statements, and to the best of my knowledge and belief, it is true, correct, and complete. Declaration of preparer (other than taxpayer) is based on all information of which preparer has any knowledge.

▶ _____   _____   ▶ _____
Signature of officer   Date   Title

Paid Preparer's Use Only

Preparer's signature ▶	Date	Check if self-employed ▶ ☐	Preparer's social security number
Firm's name (or yours if self-employed) and address ▶		E.I. No. ▶	
		ZIP code ▶	

For Paperwork Reduction Act Notice, see page 1 of separate instructions.   Cat. No. 11510H   Form **1120S** (1993)

Form 1120S (1993)   Page **2**

| Schedule A | **Cost of Goods Sold** (See instructions.) |

1	Inventory at beginning of year	1		
2	Purchases	2		
3	Cost of labor	3		
4	Additional section 263A costs (see instructions) *(attach schedule)*	4		
5	Other costs *(attach schedule)*	5		
6	**Total.** Add lines 1 through 5	6		
7	Inventory at end of year	7		
8	**Cost of goods sold.** Subtract line 7 from line 6. Enter here and on page 1, line 2	8		

9a Check all methods used for valuing closing inventory:

   (i) ☐ Cost

   (ii) ☐ Lower of cost or market as described in Regulations section 1.471-4

   (iii) ☐ Writedown of "subnormal" goods as described in Regulations section 1.471-2(c)

   (iv) ☐ Other (specify method used and attach explanation) ▶ ....

  b Check if the LIFO inventory method was adopted this tax year for any goods *(if checked, attach Form 970)* . . . . . . ▶ ☐

  c If the LIFO inventory method was used for this tax year, enter percentage (or amounts) of closing inventory computed under LIFO . . . . | 9c | | |

  d Do the rules of section 263A (for property produced or acquired for resale) apply to the corporation? . . . . ☐ Yes ☐ No

  e Was there any change in determining quantities, cost, or valuations between opening and closing inventory? . . . ☐ Yes ☐ No
    If "Yes," attach explanation.

| Schedule B | **Other Information** |

		Yes	No
1	Check method of accounting: **(a)** ☐ Cash **(b)** ☐ Accrual **(c)** ☐ Other (specify) ▶		
2	Refer to the list in the instructions and state the corporation's principal: **(a)** Business activity ▶ .... **(b)** Product or service ▶		
3	Did the corporation at the end of the tax year own, directly or indirectly, 50% or more of the voting stock of a domestic corporation? (For rules of attribution, see section 267(c).) If "Yes," attach a schedule showing: **(a)** name, address, and employer identification number and **(b)** percentage owned.		
4	Was the corporation a member of a controlled group subject to the provisions of section 1561?		
5	At any time during calendar year 1993, did the corporation have an interest in or a signature or other authority over a financial account in a foreign country (such as a bank account, securities account, or other financial account)? (See instructions for exceptions and filing requirements for Form TD F 90-22.1.) If "Yes," enter the name of the foreign country ▶		
6	Was the corporation the grantor of, or transferor to, a foreign trust that existed during the current tax year, whether or not the corporation has any beneficial interest in it? If "Yes," the corporation may have to file Forms 3520, 3520-A, or 926		
7	Check this box if the corporation has filed or is required to file **Form 8264,** Application for Registration of a Tax Shelter . . . . ▶ ☐		
8	Check this box if the corporation issued publicly offered debt instruments with original issue discount . . ▶ ☐ If so, the corporation may have to file **Form 8281,** Information Return for Publicly Offered Original Issue Discount Instruments.		
9	If the corporation: **(a)** filed its election to be an S corporation after 1986, **(b)** was a C corporation before it elected to be an S corporation **or** the corporation acquired an asset with a basis determined by reference to its basis (or the basis of any other property) in the hands of a C corporation, and **(c)** has net unrealized built-in gain (defined in section 1374(d)(1)) in excess of the net recognized built-in gain from prior years, enter the net unrealized built-in gain reduced by net recognized built-in gain from prior years (see instructions) . . . . . . ▶ $		
10	Check this box if the corporation had subchapter C earnings and profits at the close of the tax year (see instructions) . . . . ▶ ☐		

Designation of Tax Matters Person (See instructions.)

Enter below the shareholder designated as the tax matters person (TMP) for the tax year of this return:

Name of designated TMP ▶		Identifying number of TMP ▶	

Address of designated TMP ▶	

Form 1120S (1993) Page **3**

Schedule K — Shareholders' Shares of Income, Credits, Deductions, etc.

	(a) Pro rata share items		(b) Total amount
Income (Loss)	**1** Ordinary income (loss) from trade or business activities (page 1, line 21)	**1**	
	2 Net income (loss) from rental real estate activities *(attach Form 8825)*	**2**	
	3a Gross income from other rental activities **3a**		
	b Expenses from other rental activities *(attach schedule)*. **3b**		
	c Net income (loss) from other rental activities. Subtract line 3b from line 3a	**3c**	
	4 Portfolio income (loss):		
	a Interest income	**4a**	
	b Dividend income	**4b**	
	c Royalty income	**4c**	
	d Net short-term capital gain (loss) *(attach Schedule D (Form 1120S))*	**4d**	
	e Net long-term capital gain (loss) *(attach Schedule D (Form 1120S))*	**4e**	
	f Other portfolio income (loss) *(attach schedule)*	**4f**	
	5 Net gain (loss) under section 1231 (other than due to casualty or theft) *(attach Form 4797)*	**5**	
	6 Other income (loss) *(attach schedule)*	**6**	
Deductions	**7** Charitable contributions (see instructions) *(attach schedule)*	**7**	
	8 Section 179 expense deduction *(attach Form 4562)*	**8**	
	9 Deductions related to portfolio income (loss) (see instructions) (itemize)	**9**	
	10 Other deductions *(attach schedule)*	**10**	
Investment Interest	**11a** Interest expense on investment debts	**11a**	
	b (1) Investment income included on lines 4a, 4b, 4c, and 4f above	**11b(1)**	
	(2) Investment expenses included on line 9 above	**11b(2)**	
Credits	**12a** Credit for alcohol used as a fuel *(attach Form 6478)*	**12a**	
	b Low-income housing credit (see instructions):		
	(1) From partnerships to which section 42(j)(5) applies for property placed in service before 1990	**12b(1)**	
	(2) Other than on line 12b(1) for property placed in service before 1990.	**12b(2)**	
	(3) From partnerships to which section 42(j)(5) applies for property placed in service after 1989	**12b(3)**	
	(4) Other than on line 12b(3) for property placed in service after 1989	**12b(4)**	
	c Qualified rehabilitation expenditures related to rental real estate activities *(attach Form 3468)*	**12c**	
	d Credits (other than credits shown on lines 12b and 12c) related to rental real estate activities (see instructions).	**12d**	
	e Credits related to other rental activities (see instructions)	**12e**	
	13 Other credits (see instructions)	**13**	
Adjustments and Tax Preference Items	**14a** Depreciation adjustment on property placed in service after 1986	**14a**	
	b Adjusted gain or loss	**14b**	
	c Depletion (other than oil and gas)	**14c**	
	d (1) Gross income from oil, gas, or geothermal properties	**14d(1)**	
	(2) Deductions allocable to oil, gas, or geothermal properties	**14d(2)**	
	e Other adjustments and tax preference items *(attach schedule)*	**14e**	
Foreign Taxes	**15a** Type of income ▶		
	b Name of foreign country or U.S. possession ▶		
	c Total gross income from sources outside the United States *(attach schedule)*	**15c**	
	d Total applicable deductions and losses *(attach schedule)*	**15d**	
	e Total foreign taxes (check one): ▶ ☐ Paid ☐ Accrued	**15e**	
	f Reduction in taxes available for credit *(attach schedule)*	**15f**	
	g Other foreign tax information *(attach schedule)*	**15g**	
Other	**16a** Total expenditures to which a section 59(e) election may apply	**16a**	
	b Type of expenditures ▶		
	17 Tax-exempt interest income	**17**	
	18 Other tax-exempt income	**18**	
	19 Nondeductible expenses	**19**	
	20 Total property distributions (including cash) other than dividends reported on line 22 below	**20**	
	21 Other items and amounts required to be reported separately to shareholders (see instructions) *(attach schedule)*		
	22 Total dividend distributions paid from accumulated earnings and profits	**22**	
	23 **Income (loss).** (Required only if Schedule M-1 must be completed.) Combine lines 1 through 6 in column (b). From the result, subtract the sum of lines 7 through 11a, 15e, and 16a	**23**	

Form 1120S (1993)

Schedule L	Balance Sheets	Beginning of tax year		End of tax year	
	Assets	(a)	(b)	(c)	(d)
1	Cash				
2a	Trade notes and accounts receivable				
b	Less allowance for bad debts				
3	Inventories				
4	U.S. Government obligations				
5	Tax-exempt securities				
6	Other current assets (attach schedule)				
7	Loans to shareholders				
8	Mortgage and real estate loans				
9	Other investments (attach schedule)				
10a	Buildings and other depreciable assets				
b	Less accumulated depreciation				
11a	Depletable assets				
b	Less accumulated depletion				
12	Land (net of any amortization)				
13a	Intangible assets (amortizable only)				
b	Less accumulated amortization				
14	Other assets (attach schedule)				
15	Total assets				
	Liabilities and Shareholders' Equity				
16	Accounts payable				
17	Mortgages, notes, bonds payable in less than 1 year				
18	Other current liabilities (attach schedule)				
19	Loans from shareholders				
20	Mortgages, notes, bonds payable in 1 year or more				
21	Other liabilities (attach schedule)				
22	Capital stock				
23	Paid-in or capital surplus				
24	Retained earnings				
25	Less cost of treasury stock		( )		( )
26	Total liabilities and shareholders' equity				

Schedule M-1 — Reconciliation of Income (Loss) per Books With Income (Loss) per Return (You are not required to complete this schedule if the total assets on line 15, column (d), of Schedule L are less than $25,000.)

1	Net income (loss) per books		5 Income recorded on books this year not included on Schedule K, lines 1 through 6 (itemize):	
2	Income included on Schedule K, lines 1 through 6, not recorded on books this year (itemize):		a Tax-exempt interest $	
	....		....	
3	Expenses recorded on books this year not included on Schedule K, lines 1 through 11a, 15e, and 16a (itemize):		6 Deductions included on Schedule K, lines 1 through 11a, 15e, and 16a, not charged against book income this year (itemize):	
a	Depreciation $		a Depreciation $	
b	Travel and entertainment $		....	
	....			
	....		7 Add lines 5 and 6	
4	Add lines 1 through 3		8 Income (loss) (Schedule K, line 23). Line 4 less line 7	

Schedule M-2 — Analysis of Accumulated Adjustments Account, Other Adjustments Account, and Shareholders' Undistributed Taxable Income Previously Taxed (See instructions.)

		(a) Accumulated adjustments account	(b) Other adjustments account	(c) Shareholders' undistributed taxable income previously taxed
1	Balance at beginning of tax year			
2	Ordinary income from page 1, line 21			
3	Other additions			
4	Loss from page 1, line 21	( )		
5	Other reductions	( )	( )	
6	Combine lines 1 through 5			
7	Distributions other than dividend distributions			
8	Balance at end of tax year. Subtract line 7 from line 6			

SCHEDULE D
(Form 1120S)

Department of the Treasury
Internal Revenue Service

Capital Gains and Losses and Built-In Gains

▶ Attach to Form 1120S.

▶ See separate instructions.

OMB No. 1545-0130

1993

Name	Employer identification number

Part I — Short-Term Capital Gains and Losses—Assets Held One Year or Less

(a) Kind of property and description (Example, 100 shares of "Z" Co.)	(b) Date acquired (mo., day, yr.)	(c) Date sold (mo., day, yr.)	(d) Gross sales price	(e) Cost or other basis, plus expense of sale	(f) Gain or (loss) ((d) less (e))
1					

2 Short-term capital gain from installment sales from Form 6252, line 26 or 37	**2**	
3 Short-term capital gain or (loss) from like-kind exchanges from Form 8824	**3**	
4 Combine lines 1 through 3 and enter here	**4**	
5 Tax on short-term capital gain included on line 31 below.	**5**	
6 **Net short-term capital gain or (loss).** Subtract line 5 from line 4. Enter here and on Form 1120S, Schedule K, line 4d or line 6	**6**	

Part II — Long-Term Capital Gains and Losses—Assets Held More Than One Year

7					

8 Long-term capital gain from installment sales from Form 6252, line 26 or 37	**8**	
9 Long-term capital gain or (loss) from like-kind exchanges from Form 8824.	**9**	
10 Combine lines 7 through 9 and enter here	**10**	
11 Tax on long-term capital gain included on lines 23 and 31 below	**11**	
12 **Net long-term capital gain or (loss).** Subtract line 11 from line 10. Enter here and on Form 1120S, Schedule K, line 4e or line 6	**12**	

Part III — Capital Gains Tax (See instructions before completing this part.)

13 Enter section 1231 gain from Form 4797, line 10	**13**	
14 Net long-term capital gain or (loss)—Combine lines 10 and 13	**14**	
Note: If the corporation is liable for the excess net passive income tax (Form 1120S, page 1, line 22a) or the built-in gains tax (Part IV below), see the line 15 instructions before completing line 15.		
15 Net capital gain. Enter excess of net long-term capital gain (line 14) over net short-term capital loss (line 4) .	**15**	
16 Statutory minimum	**16**	$25,000
17 Subtract line 16 from line 15	**17**	
18 Enter 34% of line 17	**18**	
19 Taxable income (see instructions and attach computation schedule)	**19**	
20 Enter tax on line 19 amount (see instructions and attach computation schedule)	**20**	
21 Net capital gain from substituted basis property (see instructions and attach computation schedule) . . .	**21**	
22 Enter 35% of line 21	**22**	
23 **Tax.** Enter the smallest of line 18, 20, or 22 here and on Form 1120S, page 1, line 22b	**23**	

Part IV — Built-In Gains Tax (See instructions before completing this part.)

24 Excess of recognized built-in gains over recognized built-in losses (see instructions and attach computation schedule)	**24**	
25 Taxable income (see instructions and attach computation schedule)	**25**	
26 Net recognized built-in gain. Enter smaller of line 24 or line 25 (see instructions)	**26**	
27 Section 1374(b)(2) deduction	**27**	
28 Subtract line 27 from line 26. (If zero or less, enter -0- here and on line 31.)	**28**	
29 Enter 35% of line 28	**29**	
30 Business credit and minimum tax credit carryforwards under section 1374(b)(3) from C corporation years	**30**	
31 **Tax.** Subtract line 30 from line 29 (if zero or less, enter -0-). Enter here and on Form 1120S, page 1, line 22b	**31**	

For Paperwork Reduction Act Notice, see page 1 of Instructions for Form 1120S.   Cat. No. 11516V   **Schedule D (Form 1120S) 1993**

SCHEDULE K-1 (Form 1120S)	**Shareholder's Share of Income, Credits, Deductions, etc.**	OMB No. 1545-0130
Department of the Treasury Internal Revenue Service	▶ See separate instructions. For calendar year 1993 or tax year beginning _____ , 1993, and ending _____ , 19 ___	**1993**

Shareholder's identifying number ▶	Corporation's identifying number ▶
Shareholder's name, address, and ZIP code	Corporation's name, address, and ZIP code

A Shareholder's percentage of stock ownership for tax year (see Instructions for Schedule K-1) . . . . ▶ _____ %

B Internal Revenue Service Center where corporation filed its return ▶ ....

C Tax shelter registration number (see Instructions for Schedule K-1) . . . . ▶ ....

D Check applicable boxes: **(1)** ☐ Final K-1 **(2)** ☐ Amended K-1

		(a) Pro rata share items		(b) Amount	(c) Form 1040 filers enter the amount in column (b) on:
Income (Loss)	1	Ordinary income (loss) from trade or business activities . . .	1		See Shareholder's Instructions for Schedule K-1 (Form 1120S).
	2	Net income (loss) from rental real estate activities	2		
	3	Net income (loss) from other rental activities	3		
	4	Portfolio income (loss):			
	a	Interest	4a		Sch. B, Part I, line 1
	b	Dividends	4b		Sch. B, Part II, line 5
	c	Royalties	4c		Sch. E, Part I, line 4
	d	Net short-term capital gain (loss)	4d		Sch. D, line 5, col. (f) or (g)
	e	Net long-term capital gain (loss)	4e		Sch. D, line 13, col. (f) or (g)
	f	Other portfolio income (loss) *(attach schedule)*	4f		(Enter on applicable line of your return.)
	5	Net gain (loss) under section 1231 (other than due to casualty or theft)	5		See Shareholder's Instructions for Schedule K-1 (Form 1120S)
	6	Other income (loss) *(attach schedule)*	6		(Enter on applicable line of your return.)
Deductions	7	Charitable contributions (see instructions) *(attach schedule)* . .	7		Sch. A, line 13 or 14
	8	Section 179 expense deduction	8		See Shareholder's Instructions for Schedule K-1 (Form 1120S)
	9	Deductions related to portfolio income (loss) *(attach schedule)*	9		
	10	Other deductions *(attach schedule)*	10		
Investment Interest	11a	Interest expense on investment debts	11a		Form 4952, line 1
	b	**(1)** Investment income included on lines 4a, 4b, 4c, and 4f above	b(1)		See Shareholder's Instructions for Schedule K-1 (Form 1120S).
		(2) Investment expenses included on line 9 above	b(2)		
Credits	12a	Credit for alcohol used as fuel	12a		Form 6478, line 10
	b	Low-income housing credit:			
		(1) From section 42(j)(5) partnerships for property placed in service before 1990	b(1)		
		(2) Other than on line 12b(1) for property placed in service before 1990	b(2)		Form 8586, line 5
		(3) From section 42(j)(5) partnerships for property placed in service after 1989	b(3)		
		(4) Other than on line 12b(3) for property placed in service after 1989	b(4)		
	c	Qualified rehabilitation expenditures related to rental real estate activities (see instructions)	12c		
	d	Credits (other than credits shown on lines 12b and 12c) related to rental real estate activities (see instructions)	12d		See Shareholder's Instructions for Schedule K-1 (Form 1120S).
	e	Credits related to other rental activities (see instructions) . . .	12e		
	13	Other credits (see instructions)	13		
Adjustments and Tax Preference Items	14a	Depreciation adjustment on property placed in service after 1986	14a		See Shareholder's Instructions for Schedule K-1 (Form 1120S) and Instructions for Form 6251
	b	Adjusted gain or loss	14b		
	c	Depletion (other than oil and gas)	14c		
	d	**(1)** Gross income from oil, gas, or geothermal properties . . .	d(1)		
		(2) Deductions allocable to oil, gas, or geothermal properties .	d(2)		
	e	Other adjustments and tax preference items *(attach schedule)*	14e		

For Paperwork Reduction Act Notice, see page 1 of Instructions for Form 1120S.   Cat. No. 11520D   **Schedule K-1 (Form 1120S) 1993**

		(a) Pro rata share items	(b) Amount	(c) Form 1040 filers enter the amount in column (b) on:
Foreign Taxes	**15a**	Type of income ▶		Form 1116, Check boxes
	b	Name of foreign country or U.S. possession ▶		
	c	Total gross income from sources outside the United States *(attach schedule)*	15c	Form 1116, Part I
	d	Total applicable deductions and losses *(attach schedule)* . . .	15d	
	e	Total foreign taxes (check one): ▶ ☐ Paid ☐ Accrued . .	15e	Form 1116, Part II
	f	Reduction in taxes available for credit *(attach schedule)* . . .	15f	Form 1116, Part III
	g	Other foreign tax information *(attach schedule)*	15g	See Instructions for Form 1116
Other	**16a**	Total expenditures to which a section 59(e) election may apply	16a	See Shareholder's Instructions for Schedule K-1 (Form 1120S).
	b	Type of expenditures ▶		
	17	Tax-exempt interest income	17	Form 1040, line 8b
	18	Other tax-exempt income	18	
	19	Nondeductible expenses	19	See Shareholder's Instructions for Schedule K-1 (Form 1120S).
	20	Property distributions (including cash) other than dividend distributions reported to you on Form 1099-DIV	20	
	21	Amount of loan repayments for "Loans From Shareholders" . .	21	
	22	Recapture of low-income housing credit:		
	a	From section 42(j)(5) partnerships	22a	Form 8611, line 8
	b	Other than on line 22a	22b	

Supplemental Information	**23**	Supplemental information required to be reported separately to each shareholder *(attach additional schedules if more space is needed)*:

Form **1120-W** (WORKSHEET) Department of the Treasury Internal Revenue Service	**Corporation Estimated Tax** For calendar year 1994, or tax year beginning .... , 1994, and ending .... , 19 ..... **(Keep for the corporation's records—Do *Not* Send to the Internal Revenue Service)**	OMB No. 1545-0975 **1994**

1	Taxable income expected in the tax year	1	
	Qualified personal service corporations (defined in the instructions): Skip lines 2 through 13 and go to line 14.		
2	Enter the smaller of line 1 or $50,000 (members of a controlled group, see instructions) . . .	2	
3	Subtract line 2 from line 1	3	
4	Enter the smaller of line 3 or $25,000 (members of a controlled group, see instructions) . . .	4	
5	Subtract line 4 from line 3	5	
6	Enter the smaller of line 5 or $9,925,000 (members of a controlled group, see instructions) . .	6	
7	Subtract line 6 from line 5	7	
8	Multiply line 2 by 15%	8	
9	Multiply line 4 by 25%	9	
10	Multiply line 6 by 34%	10	
11	Multiply line 7 by 35%	11	
12	If line 1 is greater than $100,000, enter the smaller of 5% of the excess over $100,000 or $11,750. Otherwise, enter -0- (members of a controlled group, see instructions)	12	
13	If line 1 is greater than $15 million, enter the smaller of 3% of the excess over $15 million or $100,000. Otherwise, enter -0- (members of a controlled group, see instructions)	13	
14	**Total.** Add lines 8 through 13 (**Qualified personal service corporations:** Multiply line 1 by 35%.)	14	
15	Estimated tax credits (see instructions)	15	
16	Subtract line 15 from line 14	16	
17	Recapture of: **a** Investment credit, and **b** Low-income housing credit	17	
18a	Alternative minimum tax (see instructions)	18a	
b	Environmental tax (see instructions)	18b	
19	**Total.** Add lines 16 through 18b	19	
20	Credit for Federal tax paid on fuels (see instructions)	20	
21	Subtract line 20 from line 19. **Note:** *If the result is less than $500, the corporation is not required to make estimated tax payments.*	21	
22a	Enter the tax shown on the corporation's 1993 tax return. **CAUTION: See instructions before completing this line**	22a	
b	**Required annual payment.** Enter the smaller of line 21 or line 22a. If the corporation is required to skip line 22a, enter the amount from line 21 on line 22b	22b	

		(a)	(b)	(c)	(d)
23	**Installment due dates** (see instructions) . . . . ▶ **23**				
24	**Required installments.** Enter 25% of line 22b in columns **(a)** through **(d)** unless **a** or **b** below applies to the corporation. Subtract any 1993 overpayment being credited to 1994 estimated tax. (See instructions.)				
a	**Annualized income installment method and/or adjusted seasonal installment method.** Complete Schedule A and enter the amounts from line 41 in each column of line 24. (See instructions.)				
b	**"Large corporations."** See the instructions for the amount to enter in each column of line 24 . **24**				

For Paperwork Reduction Act Notice, see the instructions on page 4.   Cat. No. 11525G   Form **1120-W** (1994)

Schedule A	**Required Installments Using the Annualized Income Installment Method and/or the Adjusted Seasonal Installment Method Under Section 6655(e).** (See the instructions for Schedule A.)

Part I—Annualized Income Installment Method		**(a)**	**(b)**	**(c)**	**(d)**
			Period		
1	Annualization periods (see instructions).	1	First ____ months	First ____ months	First ____ months	First ____ months
2	Enter taxable income for each period.	2				
3	Annualization amounts (see instructions).	3				
4	Multiply line 2 by line 3.	4				
5	Figure the tax on the amount in each column on line 4 by following the same steps used to figure the tax for line 14, page 1 of Form 1120-W.	5				
6	Enter other taxes for each payment period (see instructions).	6				
7	Total tax. Add lines 5 and 6.	7				
8	For each period, enter the same type of credits as allowed on lines 15 and 20, page 1 of Form 1120-W (see instructions).	8				
9	Total tax after credits. Subtract line 8 from line 7. If zero or less, enter -0-.	9				
10	Applicable percentage.	10	25%	50%	75%	100%
11	Multiply line 9 by line 10.	11				
12	Add the amounts in all preceding columns of line 41 (see instructions).	12	////			
13	Subtract line 12 from line 11. If zero or less, enter -0-.	13				

Part II—Adjusted Seasonal Installment Method *(Use this method only if the base period percentage for any 6 consecutive months is at least 70%.)*		**(a)**	**(b)**	**(c)**	**(d)**
			Period		
14	Enter taxable income for the following periods:	14	First 3 months	First 5 months	First 8 months	First 11 months
	a Tax year beginning in 1991	14a				
	b Tax year beginning in 1992	14b				
	c Tax year beginning in 1993	14c				
15	Enter taxable income for each period for the tax year beginning in 1994.	15				
16	Enter taxable income for the following periods:	16	First 4 months	First 6 months	First 9 months	Entire year
	a Tax year beginning in 1991	16a				
	b Tax year beginning in 1992	16b				
	c Tax year beginning in 1993	16c				
17	Divide the amount in each column on line 14a by the amount in column (d) on line 16a.	17				
18	Divide the amount in each column on line 14b by the amount in column (d) on line 16b.	18				
19	Divide the amount in each column on line 14c by the amount in column (d) on line 16c.	19				

			(a)	(b)	(c)	(d)
				Period		
			First 4 months	First 6 months	First 9 months	Entire year
20	Add lines 17 through 19.	20				
21	Divide line 20 by 3.	21				
22	Divide line 15 by line 21.	22				
23	Figure the tax on the amount on line 22 by following the same steps used to figure the tax for line 14, page 1 of Form 1120-W.	23				
24	Divide the amount in columns (a) through (c) on line 16a by the amount in column (d) on line 16a.	24				
25	Divide the amount in columns (a) through (c) on line 16b by the amount in column (d) on line 16b.	25				
26	Divide the amount in columns (a) through (c) on line 16c by the amount in column (d) on line 16c.	26				
27	Add lines 24 through 26.	27				
28	Divide line 27 by 3.	28				
29	Multiply the amount in columns (a) through (c) of line 23 by the amount in the corresponding column of line 28. In column (d), enter the amount from line 23, column (d).	29				
30	Enter other taxes for each payment period (see instructions).	30				
31	Total tax. Add lines 29 and 30.	31				
32	For each period, enter the same type of credits as allowed on lines 15 and 20, page 1 of Form 1120-W (see instructions).	32				
33	Total tax after credits. Subtract line 32 from line 31. If zero or less, enter -0-.	33				
34	Add the amounts in all preceding columns of line 41 (see instructions).	34				
35	Subtract line 34 from line 33. If zero or less, enter -0-.	35				

Part III—Required Installments

			1st installment	2nd installment	3rd installment	4th installment
36	If only one of the above parts is completed, enter the amount in each column from line 13 or line 35. If both parts are completed, enter the **smaller** of the amounts in each column from line 13 or line 35.	36				
37	Divide line 22b, page 1 of Form 1120-W, by 4 and enter the result in each column. (**Note:** *"Large corporations," see instructions for line 24b on page 5 for the amount to enter.*)	37				
38	Enter the amount from line 40 for the preceding column.	38				
39	Add lines 37 and 38.	39				
40	If line 39 is more than line 36, subtract line 36 from line 39. Otherwise, enter -0-.	40				
41	**Required installments.** Enter the **smaller** of line 36 or line 39 here and on line 24, page 1 of Form 1120-W.	41				

General Instructions

Section references are to the Internal Revenue Code unless otherwise noted.

Paperwork Reduction Act Notice.—Use of this form is optional. It is provided to aid the corporation in determining its tax liability.

The time needed to complete this form will vary depending on individual circumstances. The estimated average time is:

Form	Recordkeeping	Learning about the law or the form	Preparing the form
1120-W	7 hr., 39 min.	1 hr., 23 min.	1 hr., 34 min.
1120-W, Sch. A (Pt. I)	11 hr., 14 min.	6 min.	17 min.
1120-W, Sch. A (Pt. II)	23 hr., 26 min.	....	23 min.
1120-W, Sch. A (Pt. III)	5 hr., 16 min.	....	5 min.

If you have comments concerning the accuracy of these time estimates or suggestions for making this form more simple, we would be happy to hear from you. You can write to both the **Internal Revenue Service,** Attention: Reports Clearance Officer, PC:FP, Washington, DC 20224; and the **Office of Management and Budget,** Paperwork Reduction Project (1545-0975), Washington, DC 20503. **DO NOT** send the tax form to either of these offices. Instead, keep the form for your records.

Changes To Note.—Form 1120-W has been revised to reflect changes made by the Revenue Reconciliation Act of 1993 (the Act). The Act increases the maximum corporate tax rate to 35% for corporations with taxable income over $10 million. Corporations with taxable income over $15 million are subject to an additional tax of 3% of the excess over $15 million, or $100,000, whichever is smaller.

In addition, the Act increases the amount of estimated tax payments that a corporation must make. For tax years beginning after 1993, the estimated tax payments are increased from 97% to 100% of the corporation's current tax year liability. This change applies regardless of whether the corporation uses the regular installment method, the annualized income installment method, or the adjusted seasonal installment method. The Act does not change the rule that allows a small corporation to pay 100% of last year's liability. In addition, a "large corporation" may continue to base its first required installment on 100% of the prior year's tax liability.

Also for tax years beginning after 1993, the Act modifies the rules for income annualization for corporate estimated tax purposes. A corporation now has 3 sets of periods over which it may annualize income.

Standard Option. This option requires the payments to be figured over the first 3 months for the 1st installment, the first 3 months for the 2nd installment, the first 6 months for the 3rd installment, and the first 9 months for the 4th installment.

Option 1. This option requires the payments to be figured over the first 2 months for the 1st installment, the first 4 months for the 2nd installment, the first 7 months for the 3rd installment, and the first 10 months for the 4th installment.

Option 2. This option requires the payments to be figured over the first 3 months for the 1st installment, the first 5 months for the 2nd installment, the first 8 months for the 3rd installment, and the first 11 months for the 4th installment.

Note: *If Option 1 or Option 2 is used, the corporation must make an election by filing* **Form 8842,** *Election To Use Different Annualization Periods for Corporate Estimated Tax, on or before the due date of the corporation's first required installment payment.*

Who Must Make Estimated Tax Payments.—Generally, a corporation must make installment payments of estimated tax if it expects its estimated tax (income tax less credits) to be $500 or more. S corporations must also make estimated tax payments for certain taxes. See the instructions for **Form 1120S,** U.S. Income Tax Return for an S Corporation, to figure the estimated tax payments of an S corporation.

In addition, tax-exempt corporations filing **Form 990-T,** Exempt Organization Business Income Tax Return, must make estimated tax payments for their unrelated business income tax. Tax-exempt corporations use **Form 990-W,** Estimated Tax on Unrelated Business Taxable Income for Tax-Exempt Organizations, to figure their estimated tax.

When To Make Estimated Tax Payments.—For a calendar or fiscal year corporation, the payments are due by the 15th day of the 4th, 6th, 9th, and 12th months of the tax year. If the regular due date falls on a Saturday, Sunday, or legal holiday, the payment is due on the next business day.

Underpayment of Estimated Tax.—A corporation that does not pay estimated tax when due may be charged an underpayment penalty for the period of underpayment (section 6655), using the underpayment rate determined under section 6621.

Overpayment of Estimated Tax.—A corporation that has overpaid its estimated tax may apply for a quick refund if the overpayment is at least 10% of its expected income tax liability for the tax year, **and** at least $500.

To apply for a quick refund, file **Form 4466,** Corporation Application for Quick Refund of Overpayment of Estimated Tax, before the 16th day of the 3rd month after the end of the tax year, but before the corporation files its income tax return. Do not file Form 4466 before the end of the corporation's tax year.

Depositary Method of Tax Payment.—Deposit corporation income tax payments and estimated tax payments with **Form 8109,** Federal Tax Deposit Coupon. Do not send deposits directly to an IRS office. Mail or deliver the completed Form 8109 with the payment to a qualified depositary for Federal taxes or to the Federal Reserve bank (FRB) servicing the corporation's geographic area. Make checks or money orders payable to that depositary or FRB.

To help ensure proper crediting, write the corporation's employer identification number, the tax period to which the deposit applies, and "Form 1120" on the check or money order. Be sure to darken the "1120" box on the coupon. These records of deposits will be sent to the IRS.

A penalty may be imposed if the deposits are mailed or delivered to an IRS office rather than to an authorized depositary or FRB.

For more information on deposits, see the instructions in the coupon booklet (Form 8109) and **Pub. 583,** Taxpayers Starting a Business.

Amended Estimated Tax.—If after the corporation figures and deposits estimated tax, it finds that its tax liability for the year is much more or less than originally estimated because its economic condition has changed, it may have to refigure its required installments. If earlier installments were underpaid, the corporation may owe a penalty for underpayment of estimated tax.

An immediate "catch-up" payment should be made to reduce the amount of any penalty resulting from the underpayment of any earlier installments, whether caused by a change in estimate, failure to make a deposit, or a mistake.

Specific Instructions

Line 1—Qualified personal service corporations.—A qualified personal service corporation is taxed at a flat rate of 35% on taxable income. A corporation is a qualified personal service corporation if it meets both of the following tests:
(1) substantially all of the corporation's activities involve the performance of services in the fields of health, law,

engineering, architecture, accounting, actuarial science, performing arts, or consulting, and **(2)** at least 95% of the corporation's stock, by value, is owned, directly or indirectly, by **(a)** employees performing the services, **(b)** retired employees who had performed the services listed above, **(c)** any estate of an employee or retiree described above, or **(d)** any person who acquired the stock of the corporation as a result of the death of an employee or retiree (but only for the 2-year period beginning on the date of the employee's or retiree's death). See Temporary Regulations section 1.448-1T(e) for details.

Lines 2, 4, and 6.—Members of a controlled group enter on line 2 the smaller of the amount on line 1 or their share of the $50,000 amount. On line 4, members of a controlled group enter the smaller of the amount on line 3 or their share of the $25,000 amount. On line 6, members of a controlled group enter the smaller of the amount on line 5 or their share of the $9,925,000 amount.

If no apportionment plan is adopted, the members of the controlled group must divide the amount in each taxable income bracket equally among themselves. For example, Controlled Group AB consists of Corporation A and Corporation B. They do not elect an apportionment plan. Therefore, both Corporation A and Corporation B are entitled to $25,000 (one-half of $50,000) in the $50,000 taxable income bracket, $12,500 (one-half of $25,000) in the $25,000 taxable income bracket, and $4,962,500 (one-half of $9,925,000) in the $9,925,000 taxable income bracket.

Members of a controlled group may elect an unequal apportionment plan and divide the taxable income brackets as they wish. There is no need for consistency between taxable income brackets. For example, if Controlled Group AB above elects an unequal apportionment plan, any member of the controlled group may be entitled to all, some, or none of the $50,000 amount in the first taxable income bracket, as long as the total for all members of the controlled group is not more than $50,000. Similarly, any member may be entitled to all, some, or none of the $25,000 amount in the second taxable income bracket (or the $9,925,000 amount in the third taxable income bracket) as long as the total for all members of the controlled group is not more than $25,000 in the second taxable income bracket (or $9,925,000 in the third taxable income bracket).

Line 12.—Members of a controlled group of corporations are treated as one corporation for purposes of figuring the additional 5% tax that must be paid by corporations with taxable income in excess of $100,000. If the additional tax applies, each member of the controlled group will pay that tax based on the part of the amount that is used in each taxable income bracket to reduce that member's tax. See section 1561(a). Each member of the group must enter on line 12 its share of the smaller of 5% of the excess over $100,000, or $11,750.

Line 13.—If the additional 3% tax applies, each member of the controlled group must enter on line 13 its share of the smaller of 3% of the excess over $15 million, or $100,000. See **Line 12** above.

Line 15.—The estimated tax credits include the sum of any credits against tax provided by Part IV of Subchapter A of Chapter 1 (except the credits shown on line 20).

Line 18a.—Alternative minimum tax is generally the excess of tentative minimum tax for the tax year over the regular tax for the tax year. See section 55 for definitions of tentative minimum tax and regular tax. A limited amount of the foreign tax credit may be used to offset the minimum tax. See sections 55 through 59 for more information on alternative minimum tax.

Line 18b.—The environmental tax is 0.12% of the excess of modified alternative minimum taxable income for the tax year over $2 million. See section 59A and **Pub. 542,** Tax Information on Corporations, for more information.

Line 20.—Complete **Form 4136,** Credit for Federal Tax Paid on Fuels, if the corporation qualifies to take the credit. Include on line 20 any credit the corporation is claiming under section 4682(g)(3) for tax on ozone-depleting chemicals used in the manufacture of rigid foam insulation. Also include any credit under section 4682(g)(4) for taxes paid on chemicals used for sterilizing medical instruments and as propellants in metered-dose inhalers.

Line 22a.—Figure the corporation's 1993 tax in the same manner that line 21 of this worksheet was determined, using the taxes and credits from the 1993 tax return. If a return was not filed for the 1993 tax year showing a liability for at least some amount of tax, or if the 1993 tax year was for less than 12 months, do not complete line 22a. Instead, skip line 22a and enter the amount from line 21 on line 22b. "Large corporations" see the instructions for line 24b below.

Line 23.—**Calendar year taxpayers:** Enter 4-15-94, 6-15-94, 9-15-94, and 12-15-94, respectively, in columns (a) through (d).

Fiscal year taxpayers: Enter the 15th day of the 4th, 6th, 9th, and 12th months of your tax year in columns (a) through (d). If the regular due date falls on a Saturday, Sunday, or legal holiday, substitute the next business day.

Line 24.—Payments of estimated tax should take into account any 1993 overpayment that the corporation chose to credit against its 1994 tax. Any overpayment will be applied to the first installment, unless the corporation notifies the IRS that the overpayment should be applied against another installment.

Line 24a—Annualized income installment method and/or adjusted seasonal installment method.—If the corporation's income is expected to vary during the year because, for example, it operates its business on a seasonal basis, it may be able to lower the amount of one or more required installments by using the annualized income installment method and/or the adjusted seasonal installment method. For example, a ski shop, which receives most of its income during the winter months, may be able to benefit from using one or both of these methods in figuring one or more of its required installments.

To use one or both of these methods to figure one or more required installments, use Schedule A on pages 2 and 3. If Schedule A is used for any payment date, it must be used for all payment due dates. To arrive at the amount of each required installment, Schedule A automatically selects the smallest of **(a)** the annualized income installment, **(b)** the adjusted seasonal installment (if applicable), or **(c)** the regular installment under section 6655(d) (increased by any reduction recapture under section 6655(e)(1)(B)).

Line 24b—Large corporations.—A "large corporation" is a corporation that had, or its predecessor had, taxable income of $1 million or more for any of the 3 tax years immediately preceding the 1994 tax year. For this purpose, taxable income is modified to exclude net operating loss or capital loss carrybacks or carryovers. Members of a controlled group, as defined in section 1563, must divide the $1 million amount among themselves according to rules similar to those in section 1561.

If the annualized income installment method or adjusted seasonal installment method is not used, follow the instructions below to figure the amounts to enter on line 24. (If the annualized income installment method and/or the adjusted seasonal installment method are used, these instructions apply to line 37 of Schedule A.)

If line 21 is smaller than line 22a: Enter 25% of line 21 in columns (a) through (d) of line 24.

If line 22a is smaller than line 21: Enter 25% of line 22a in column (a) of line 24. In column (b), determine the amount to enter as follows:

1. Subtract line 22a from line 21,

2. Add the result to the amount on line 21, and

3. Multiply the result in **2** above by 25% and enter the result in column (b).

Enter 25% of line 21 in columns (c) and (d).

Schedule A

If only the annualized income installment method (Part I) is used, complete Parts I and III of Schedule A. If only the adjusted seasonal installment method (Part II) is used, complete Parts II and III of Schedule A. If both methods are used, complete all three parts of Schedule A. Enter in each column on line 24 of page 1 the amounts from the corresponding column of line 41 of Schedule A.

Caution: *If Schedule A is used, do not figure any required installment until after the end of the month preceding the due date for that installment.*

Part I—Annualized Income Installment Method

Note: See **Changes To Note** on page 4.

Line 1—Annualization periods.—Enter in the space on line 1, columns (a) through (d), respectively, the annualization period that the corporation is using. **Caution:** *Use Option 1 or Option 2 only if the corporation elected to do so by filing Form 8842, on or before the due date of the first required installment payment.*

Standard option—Enter "3" in column (a), "3" in column (b), "6" in column (c), and "9" in column (d).

Option 1—Enter "2" in column (a), "4" in column (b), "7" in column (c), and "10" in column (d).

Option 2—Enter "3" in column (a), "5" in column (b), "8" in column (c), and "11" in column (d).

Line 3—Annualization amounts.—Enter the annualization amount for the option used on line 1 above.

Standard option—Enter "4" in column (a), "4" in column (b), "2" in column (c), and "1.33333" in column (d).

Option 1—Enter "6" in column (a), "3" in column (b), "1.71429" in column (c), and "1.2" in column (d).

Option 2—Enter "4" in column (a), "2.4" in column (b), "1.5" in column (c), and "1.09091" in column (d).

Line 6.—Enter the taxes the corporation owed because of events that occurred during the months shown in the headings used to figure annualized taxable income. Include the same taxes used to figure line 19 of Form 1120-W.

Compute the alternative minimum tax and environmental tax by figuring alternative minimum taxable income and modified alternative minimum taxable income based on the corporation's income and deductions during the months shown in the column headings used to figure annualized taxable income. Multiply the alternative minimum taxable income and modified alternative minimum taxable income by the annualization amounts used to figure annualized taxable income (line 3) before subtracting the exemption amounts (see sections 55(d) and 59A(a)(2)).

Line 8.—Enter the credits the corporation is entitled to because of events that occurred during the months shown in the column headings used to figure annualized taxable income.

Line 12.—Before completing line 12 in columns (b) through (d), complete line 13; Part II (if applicable); and lines 36 through 41, in each of the preceding columns. For example, complete line 13, lines 14 through 35 (if using the adjusted seasonal installment method), and lines 36 through 41, in column (a) before completing line 12 in column (b).

Part II—Adjusted Seasonal Installment Method

Do not complete this part unless the corporation's base period percentage for any 6 consecutive months of the tax year equals or exceeds 70%. Base period percentage for any period of 6 consecutive months is the average of the three percentages figured by dividing the taxable income for the corresponding 6-consecutive-month period in each of the 3 preceding tax years by the taxable income for each of their respective tax years.

Example. An amusement park that has a calendar year as its tax year receives the largest part of its taxable income during the 6-month period from May through October. To compute its base period percentage for the period May through October 1994, it must figure its taxable income for the period May through October in each of the years 1991, 1992, and 1993. The taxable income for each May through October period is then divided by the total taxable income for the tax year in which the period is included, resulting in the following quotients: .69 for May through October 1991, .74 for May through October 1992, and .67 for May through October 1993. Since the average of .69, .74, and .67 is .70, the base period percentage for May through October 1994 is 70%. Therefore, the amusement park qualifies for the adjusted seasonal installment method.

Line 30.—Enter any other taxes the corporation owed because of events that occurred during the months shown in the column headings above line 14 of Part II. Include the same taxes used to figure line 19 of Form 1120-W.

Compute the alternative minimum tax and environmental tax by figuring alternative minimum taxable income and modified alternative minimum taxable income based on the corporation's income and deductions during the months shown in the column headings above line 14 of Part II. Divide the alternative minimum taxable income and modified alternative minimum taxable income by the amounts shown on line 21 before subtracting the exemption amounts (see sections 55(d) and 59A(a)(2)). For columns (a) through (c) only, multiply the alternative minimum tax and environmental tax by the amounts shown on line 28.

Line 32.—Enter the credits to which the corporation is entitled because of events that occurred during the months shown in the column headings above line 14 of Part II.

Line 34.—Before completing line 34 in columns (b) through (d), complete lines 35 through 41 in each of the preceding columns. For example, complete lines 35 through 41 in column (a) before completing line 34 in column (b).

Form **1120X**
(Rev. May 1991)
Department of the Treasury
Internal Revenue Service

Amended U.S. Corporation Income Tax Return

OMB No. 1545-0132
Expires 4-30-94

For tax year ending in ▶ ....
(Enter month and year)

Please Type or Print

Name	Employer identification number
Number, street, and room or suite no. (If a P.O. box, see instructions.)	
City or town, state, and ZIP code	Telephone number (optional) ( )

Enter name and address used on original return (If same as above, write "Same.")

Internal Revenue Service Center
where original return was filed ▶

Fill in Applicable Items and Use Part II To Explain Any Changes

Part I Income and Deductions	(a) As originally reported or as adjusted (see Specific Instructions)	(b) Net change (increase or decrease— explain in Part II)	(c) Correct amount
1 Total income (Form 1120 or 1120-A, line 11)			
2 Total deductions (total of lines 27 and 29c, Form 1120, or lines 23 and 25c, Form 1120-A)			
3 Taxable income. Subtract line 2 from line 1			
4 Tax (Form 1120, line 31, or Form 1120-A, line 27) . . .			

Payments and Credits

5a Estimated tax payments. Include overpayment in prior year allowed as a credit			
b Amount of refund applied for on Form 4466			
c Subtract line 5b from line 5a			
6 Tax deposited with Form 7004 (see instructions) . . .			
7 Credit from regulated investment companies			
8 Credit for Federal tax on fuels			
9 Other payment or refundable credit (specify) ▶			
10 Tax deposited or paid with (or after) the filing of the original return			
11 Add lines 5c through 10, column (c)			
12 Overpayment, if any, as shown on original return or as later adjusted			
13 Subtract line 12 from line 11			

Tax Due or Refund

14 **Tax due.** Subtract line 13 from line 4, column (c). Make check payable to "Internal Revenue Service" (see instructions) . . . . ▶	
15 **Refund.** Subtract line 4, column (c), from line 13 . . . . ▶	

Please Sign Here

Under penalties of perjury, I declare that I have filed an original return and that I have examined this amended return, including accompanying schedules and statements, and to the best of my knowledge and belief, this amended return is true, correct, and complete. Declaration of preparer (other than taxpayer) is based on all information of which preparer has any knowledge.

▶ _____ ▶ _____ ▶ _____
Signature of officer | Date | Title

Paid Preparer's Use Only	Preparer's signature ▶	Date	Check if self-employed ▶ ☐	Preparer's social security no.
	Firm's name (or yours if self-employed) and address ▶		E.I. No. ▶	
			ZIP code ▶	

For Paperwork Reduction Act Notice, see instructions on back.
Cat. No. 11530Z
Form **1120X** (Rev. 5-91)

Form 1120X (Rev. 5-91)   Page **2**

Part II **Explanation of Changes to Income, Deductions, Credits, etc.** Enter the line number from page 1 for the items you are changing, and give the reason for each change. **Show any computation in detail. Attach additional sheets if necessary.**

If the change is due to a net operating loss carryback, a capital loss carryback, or a general business credit carryback (see **Carryback Claims,** below), check here . . . . ▶ ☐

General Instructions

(Section references are to the Internal Revenue Code.)

Paperwork Reduction Act Notice

We ask for the information on this form to carry out the Internal Revenue laws of the United States. You are required to give us this information. We need it to ensure that you are complying with these laws and to allow us to figure and collect the right amount of tax.

The time needed to complete and file this form will vary depending on individual circumstances. The estimated average time is:

Recordkeeping . . . . . 11 hr., 14 min.
**Learning about the law
or the form** . . . . 40 min.
Preparing the form . . . . 1 hr., 49 min.
**Copying, assembling, and
sending the form to IRS** . . . . 16 min.

If you have comments concerning the accuracy of these time estimates or suggestions for making this form more simple, we would be happy to hear from you. You can write to both the **Internal Revenue Service,** Washington, DC 20224, Attention: IRS Reports Clearance Officer, T:FP; and the **Office of Management and Budget,** Paperwork Reduction Project (1545-0132), Washington, DC 20503. DO NOT send the tax form to either of these offices. Instead, see **Where To File** below.

Purpose of Form.—Use Form 1120X to correct **Form 1120,** U.S. Corporation Income Tax Return, or **Form 1120-A,** U.S. Corporation Short-Form Income Tax Return, as you originally filed it or as it was later adjusted by an amended return, a claim for refund, or an examination. Please note that it often takes 3 to 4 months to process Form 1120X.

Do not use Form 1120X to apply for a tentative refund or a quick refund of estimated tax. Use the following forms instead:

• **Form 4466,** Corporation Application for Quick Refund of Overpayment of Estimated Tax. For a quick refund of estimated tax, file Form 4466 within 2½ months after the end of the tax year and before the corporation files its tax return.

• **Form 1139,** Corporation Application for Tentative Refund. For a tentative refund due to the carryback of a net operating loss, a net capital loss, unused credits, or overpaid tax resulting from a claim-of-right adjustment under section 1341(b)(1), file Form 1139. You may use Form 1139 only if one year or less has passed since the tax year in which the carryback or adjustment occurred. For additional information on net operating losses and a worksheet to help figure the corporation's net operating loss deduction in a carryback year, see **Pub. 536,** Net Operating Losses.

When To File.—File Form 1120X only after the corporation has filed its original return. Generally, Form 1120X must be filed within 3 years after the date the original return was due or 3 years after the date the corporation filed it, whichever is later. A Form 1120X based on a net operating loss carryback, a capital loss carryback, or a general business credit carryback, generally must be filed within 3 years after the due date of the return for the tax year of the net operating loss, capital loss, or unused credit. Other claims for refund must be filed within 3 years after the date the original return was due, 3 years after the date the corporation filed it, or 2 years after the date the tax was paid, whichever is later.

What To Attach.—If the change you are making involves an item of income, deduction, or credit, that the corporation income tax return (or its instructions) requires the corporation to support with a schedule, statement, or form, attach the appropriate schedule, statement, or form to Form 1120X.

Tax Shelters. If you are amending your return to include any item (loss, credit, deduction, other tax benefit, or income) relating to a tax shelter required to be registered, you must attach **Form 8271,** Investor Reporting of Tax Shelter Registration Number.

Carryback Claims. If Form 1120X is used as a carryback claim, attach copies of Form 1120 (pages 1 and 3) or Form 1120-A (pages 1 and 2), for both the year the loss or credit originated and for the carryback year. Also attach any other forms, schedules, or statements that are necessary to support the claim. At the top of these attachments, write "Copy Only—Do Not Process."

Information on Income, Deductions, Tax Computation, etc.—See the instructions for Forms 1120 and 1120-A for the year you are amending for information about the taxability of certain types of income, the allowability of certain expenses as deductions from income, computation of tax, etc.

Note: *Deductions for such items as charitable contributions and the dividends-received deduction may have to be refigured because of changes made to items of income or expense.*

Where To File.—Mail this form to the Internal Revenue Service Center where the corporation filed its original return.

Specific Instructions

Tax Year.—In the space above the employer identification number, enter the ending month and year of the calendar or fiscal year for the tax return you are amending.

P.O. Box.—If the post office does not deliver mail to the street address and the corporation has a P.O. box, show the P.O. box number instead of the street address.

Column (a)

Enter the amounts from your return as originally filed or as you later amended it. If

your return was changed or audited by IRS, enter the amounts as adjusted.

Column (b)

Enter the net increase or net decrease for each line you are changing. Use parentheses around all amounts that are decreases. Explain the increase or decrease in Part II.

Column (c)

Lines 1 and 2.—Add the increase in column (b) to the amount in column (a) or subtract the column (b) decrease from column (a). Enter the result in column (c). For any item not changed, enter the amount from column (a) in column (c).

Line 4.—Figure the new amount of tax using the taxable income on line 3, column (c). Use Schedule J, Form 1120, or Part I, Form 1120-A, of the original return to make the necessary tax computation.

Line 6.—Enter the amount of tax deposited with **Form 7004,** Application for Automatic Extension of Time To File Corporation Income Tax Return.

Line 12—Overpayment.—Enter the amount from the "Overpayment" line of the original return, even if the corporation chose to credit all or part of this amount to the next year's estimated tax. This amount must be considered in preparing Form 1120X since any refund due from the original return will be refunded separately (or credited to estimated tax) from any additional refund claimed on Form 1120X.

Line 14—Tax due.—Make the check payable to "Internal Revenue Service" for the amount shown on line 14 and attach it to this form. Do not use the depositary method of payment.

Line 15—Refund.—If the corporation is entitled to a refund larger than the amount claimed on the original return, line 15 will show only the additional amount of refund. This additional amount will be refunded separately from the amount claimed on the original return.

Signature.—The return must be signed and dated by the president, vice president, treasurer, assistant treasurer, chief accounting officer, or any other corporate officer (such as tax officer) authorized to sign. A receiver, trustee, or assignee must sign and date any return required to be filed on behalf of a corporation.

If a corporate officer filled in Form 1120X, the Paid Preparer's space should remain blank. If someone prepares Form 1120X and does not charge the corporation, that person should not sign the return. Certain others who prepare Form 1120X should not sign. See the instructions for Forms 1120 and 1120-A for more information.

Note: *IRS will figure any interest due and will either include it in the refund or bill the corporation for the interest.*

Form **2106**

Department of the Treasury
Internal Revenue Service   (O)

Employee Business Expenses

▶ See separate instructions.

▶ Attach to Form 1040.

OMB No. 1545-0139

1993

Attachment
Sequence No. **54**

Your name	Social security number	Occupation in which expenses were incurred

Part I   Employee Business Expenses and Reimbursements

STEP 1   Enter Your Expenses

		Column A — Other Than Meals and Entertainment	Column B — Meals and Entertainment
1	Vehicle expense from line 22 or line 29	1	
2	Parking fees, tolls, and transportation, including train, bus, etc., that **did not** involve overnight travel	2	
3	Travel expense while away from home overnight, including lodging, airplane, car rental, etc. **Do not** include meals and entertainment	3	
4	Business expenses not included on lines 1 through 3. **Do not** include meals and entertainment	4	
5	Meals and entertainment expenses (see instructions)	5	
6	**Total expenses.** In Column A, add lines 1 through 4 and enter the result. In Column B, enter the amount from line 5	6	

Note: *If you were not reimbursed for any expenses in Step 1, skip line 7 and enter the amount from line 6 on line 8.*

STEP 2   Enter Amounts Your Employer Gave You for Expenses Listed in STEP 1

7	Enter amounts your employer gave you that were **not** reported to you in box 1 of Form W-2. Include any amount reported under code "L" in box 13 of your Form W-2 (see instructions) . . .	7	

STEP 3   Figure Expenses To Deduct on Schedule A (Form 1040)

8	Subtract line 7 from line 6	8	
	Note: *If **both columns** of line 8 are zero, **stop here.** If Column A is less than zero, report the amount as income on Form 1040, line 7, and enter -0- on line 10, Column A.*		
9	Enter 20% (.20) of line 8, Column B	9	
10	In Column A, enter the amount from line 8. In Column B, subtract line 9 from line 8	10	
11	Add the amounts on line 10 of both columns and enter the total here. **Also, enter the total on Schedule A (Form 1040), line 19.** (Qualified performing artists and individuals with disabilities, see the instructions for special rules on where to enter the total.) . . . . . ▶	11	

For Paperwork Reduction Act Notice, see instructions.   Cat. No. 11700N   Form **2106** (1993)

Form 2106 (1993)   Page **2**

Part II   Vehicle Expenses (See instructions to find out which sections to complete.)

Section A.—General Information

			(a) Vehicle 1	**(b)** Vehicle 2
12	Enter the date vehicle was placed in service	12	/ /	/ /
13	Total miles vehicle was driven during 1993	13	miles	miles
14	Business miles included on line 13	14	miles	miles
15	Percent of business use. Divide line 14 by line 13	15	%	%
16	Average daily round trip commuting distance	16	miles	miles
17	Commuting miles included on line 13	17	miles	miles
18	Other personal miles. Add lines 14 and 17 and subtract the total from line 13.	18	miles	miles

19   Do you (or your spouse) have another vehicle available for personal purposes? . . . . ☐ Yes ☐ No

20   If your employer provided you with a vehicle, is personal use during off duty hours permitted? ☐ Yes ☐ No ☐ Not applicable

21a   Do you have evidence to support your deduction? . . . . ☐ Yes ☐ No

21b   If "Yes," is the evidence written? . . . . ☐ Yes ☐ No

Section B.—Standard Mileage Rate (Use this section only if you own the vehicle.)

22	Multiply line 14 by 28¢ (.28). Enter the result here and on line 1. (Rural mail carriers, see instructions).	22	

Section C.—Actual Expenses

			(a) Vehicle 1		**(b)** Vehicle 2	
23	Gasoline, oil, repairs, vehicle insurance, etc.	23				
24a	Vehicle rentals	24a				
b	Inclusion amount (see instructions)	24b				
c	Subtract line 24b from line 24a	24c				
25	Value of employer-provided vehicle (applies only if 100% of annual lease value was included on Form W-2—see instructions)	25				
26	Add lines 23, 24c, and 25 . .	26				
27	Multiply line 26 by the percentage on line 15 . . .	27				
28	Depreciation. Enter amount from line 38 below	28				
29	Add lines 27 and 28. Enter total here and on line 1.	29				

Section D.—Depreciation of Vehicles (Use this section only if you own the vehicle.)

			(a) Vehicle 1		**(b)** Vehicle 2	
30	Enter cost or other basis (see instructions)	30				
31	Enter amount of section 179 deduction (see instructions) .	31				
32	Multiply line 30 by line 15 (see instructions if you elected the section 179 deduction) . . .	32				
33	Enter depreciation method and percentage (see instructions) .	33				
34	Multiply line 32 by the percentage on line 33 (see instructions) . .	34				
35	Add lines 31 and 34	35				
36	Enter the limitation amount from the table in the line 36 instructions	36				
37	Multiply line 36 by the percentage on line 15 . . .	37				
38	Enter the **smaller** of line 35 or line 37. Also, enter this amount on line 28 above	38				

Form **2119**	**Sale of Your Home**	OMB No. 1545-0072
	▶ **Attach to Form 1040 for year of sale.**	**19**93
Department of the Treasury Internal Revenue Service	▶ **See separate instructions.** ▶ **Please print or type.**	Attachment Sequence No. **20**

Your first name and initial. If a joint return, also give spouse's name and initial.	Last name	**Your social security number**

Fill in Your Address Only If You Are Filing This Form by Itself and Not With Your Tax Return	Present address (no., street, and apt. no., rural route, or P.O. box no. if mail is not delivered to street address)	**Spouse's social security number**
	City, town or post office, state, and ZIP code	

Part I General Information

1. Date your former main home was sold (month, day, year) . . . . ▶ **1** __/__/__
2. Have you bought or built a new main home? . . . . ☐ Yes ☐ No
3. Is or was any part of either main home rented out or used for business? If "Yes," see instructions . . ☐ Yes ☐ No

Part II Gain on Sale—Do not include amounts you deduct as moving expenses.

4. Selling price of home. Do not include personal property items you sold with your home . . **4**
5. Expense of sale (see instructions) **5**
6. Amount realized. Subtract line 5 from line 4 . . . . **6**
7. Adjusted basis of home sold (see instructions) **7**
8. **Gain on sale.** Subtract line 7 from line 6 . . . . **8**

Is line 8 more than zero?	— Yes ▶	If line 2 is "Yes," you **must** go to Part III or Part IV, whichever applies. If line 2 is "No," go to line 9.
	— No ▶	**Stop** and attach this form to your return.

9. If you haven't replaced your home, do you plan to do so within the **replacement period** (see instructions)? ☐ Yes ☐ No
   - If line 9 is "Yes," stop here, attach this form to your return, and see **Additional Filing Requirements** in the instructions.
   - If line 9 is "No," you **must** go to Part III or Part IV, whichever applies.

Part III One-Time Exclusion of Gain for People Age 55 or Older—By completing this part, you are electing to take the one-time exclusion (see instructions). If you are not electing to take the exclusion, go to Part IV now.

10. Who was age 55 or older on the date of sale? . . . . ☐ You ☐ Your spouse ☐ Both of you
11. Did the person who was age 55 or older own and use the property as his or her main home for a total of at least 3 years (except for short absences) of the 5-year period before the sale? If "No," go to Part IV now . . ☐ Yes ☐ No
12. At the time of sale, who owned the home? . . . . ☐ You ☐ Your spouse ☐ Both of you
13. Social security number of spouse at the time of sale if you had a different spouse from the one above. If you were not married at the time of sale, enter "None" . . . . . . ▶ **13**
14. **Exclusion.** Enter the **smaller** of line 8 or $125,000 ($62,500 if married filing separate return). Then, go to line 15 . . . . . **14**

Part IV Adjusted Sales Price, Taxable Gain, and Adjusted Basis of New Home

15. If line 14 is blank, enter the amount from line 8. Otherwise, subtract line 14 from line 8 . . **15**
    - If line 15 is zero, stop and attach this form to your return.
    - If line 15 is more than zero and line 2 is "Yes," go to line 16 now.
    - If you are reporting this sale on the installment method, stop and see the instructions.
    - All others, stop and **enter the amount from line 15 on Schedule D, col. (g), line 4 or line 12.**
16. Fixing-up expenses (see instructions for time limits) **16**
17. If line 14 is blank, enter amount from line 16. Otherwise, add lines 14 and 16 . . . . . **17**
18. **Adjusted sales price.** Subtract line 17 from line 6 . . . . **18**
19a. Date you moved into new home ▶ __/__/__ **b** Cost of new home (see instructions) **19b**
20. Subtract line 19b from line 18. If zero or less, enter -0- **20**
21. **Taxable gain.** Enter the **smaller** of line 15 or line 20 . . . . **21**
    - If line 21 is zero, go to line 22 and attach this form to your return.
    - If you are reporting this sale on the installment method, see the line 15 instructions and go to line 22.
    - All others, **enter the amount from line 21 on Schedule D, col. (g), line 4 or line 12,** and go to line 22.
22. Postponed gain. Subtract line 21 from line 15 . . . . **22**
23. **Adjusted basis of new home.** Subtract line 22 from line 19b **23**

Sign Here Only If You Are Filing This Form by Itself and Not With Your Tax Return	Under penalties of perjury, I declare that I have examined this form, including attachments, and to the best of my knowledge and belief, it is true, correct, and complete.	
	Your signature ▶ _____ Date _____	Spouse's signature ▶ _____ Date _____
	If a joint return, both must sign.	

For Paperwork Reduction Act Notice, see separate instructions.   Cat. No. 11710J   Form **2119** (1993)

Form **2120**
(Rev. May 1991)

Department of the Treasury
Internal Revenue Service

Multiple Support Declaration

▶ **Attach to Form 1040 or Form 1040A.**

OMB No. 1545-0071
Expires 5-31-94

Attachment
Sequence No. **50**

Name of taxpayer claiming person as a dependent	Social security number

During the calendar year 19 _____ , I paid over 10% of the support of

_____
(Name of person)

I could have claimed this person as a dependent except that I did not pay over 50% of his or her support. I understand that this person is being claimed as a dependent on the income tax return of

_____
(Name)

_____
(Address)

I agree not to claim this person as a dependent on my Federal income tax return for any tax year that began in this calendar year.

_____
(Your signature)

_____
(Your social security number)

_____
(Date)

_____
(Address)

Instructions

Paperwork Reduction Act Notice

We ask for the information on this form to carry out the Internal Revenue laws of the United States. You are required to give us the information. We need it to ensure that you are complying with these laws and to allow us to figure and collect the right amount of tax.

The time needed to complete and file this form will vary depending on individual circumstances. The estimated average time is: **Recordkeeping, 7 minutes; Learning about the law or the form, 2 minutes; Preparing the form, 7 minutes; Copying, assembling, and sending the form to the IRS, 10 minutes.**

If you have comments concerning the accuracy of these time estimates or suggestions for making this form more simple, we would be happy to hear from you. You can write to both the IRS and the Office of Management and Budget at the addresses listed in the instructions of the tax return with which this form is filed.

Purpose

When two or more individuals together pay over 50% of another person's support, Form 2120 is used to allow one of them to claim the person as a dependent for tax purposes.

General Information

To claim someone as a dependent, you must pay over 50% of that person's living expenses (support). However, sometimes no one individual pays over 50%; but two or more together provide over 50% of the support. If each individual could have claimed the person as a dependent except for the 50% support rule, then one individual, but only one, can still claim the dependent.

All of those who paid over 10% of the support should decide who will claim the person as a dependent. If you are chosen, you can claim the dependent only if

● You paid over 10% of the support, AND

● All others who paid over 10% agree not to claim the person as a dependent.

How To File

The individuals who agree not to claim the person as a dependent do so by each signing a Form 2120. They give the signed forms to the one who does claim the person as a dependent.

If you are the one who claims the person as a dependent, you must attach all Forms 2120 from the others to YOUR return. Be sure to enter your name and social security number at the top of each Form 2120. In addition, you must meet all of the other rules for claiming dependents. See **Pub. 501,** Exemptions, Standard Deduction, and Filing Information.

Cat. No. 11712F

Form **2120** (Rev. 5-91)

Form **2210**

Department of the Treasury
Internal Revenue Service

Underpayment of
Estimated Tax by Individuals and Fiduciaries
► See separate instructions.
► Attach to Form 1040, Form 1040A, Form 1040NR, or Form 1041.

OMB No. 1545-0140

19**93**

Attachment
Sequence No. **06**

Name(s) shown on tax return	Identifying number

Note: *In most cases, you* **do not** *need to file Form 2210. The IRS will figure any penalty you owe and send you a bill. File Form 2210* **only** *if one or more boxes in Part I apply to you. If you do not need to file Form 2210, you still may use it to figure your penalty. Enter the amount from line 20 or line 32 on the penalty line of your return, but do not attach Form 2210.*

Part I **Reasons For Filing**—If 1a, b, c, or d below applies to you, you may be able to lower or eliminate your penalty. But you MUST check the boxes that apply and file Form 2210 with your tax return. If 1e or f below applies to you, check that box and file Form 2210 with your tax return.

1 Check whichever boxes apply (if none apply, see the **Note** above):

a ☐ You request a **waiver.** In certain circumstances, the IRS will waive all or part of the penalty. See the instructions for **Waiver of Penalty.**

b ☐ You use the **annualized income installment method.** If your income varied during the year, this method may reduce the amount of one or more required installments. See the **Instructions for Schedule B.**

c ☐ You had Federal income tax withheld from wages and you treat it as paid for estimated tax purposes when it was **actually** withheld instead of in equal amounts on the payment due dates. See the instructions for line 22.

d ☐ **(1)** You made estimated tax payments for 1990, 1991, or 1992 (or were charged an estimated tax penalty for any of those years), **AND**

(2) Your adjusted gross income (AGI) is more than $75,000 (more than $37,500 if married filing separately), **AND**

(3) Your 1993 **modified** AGI exceeds your 1992 AGI by more than $40,000 (more than $20,000 if married filing separately), **AND**

(4) Your 2nd, 3rd, or 4th required installment (column (b), (c), or (d) of line 21) is based on **either** your 1992 tax **or** 90% of your 1993 **modified** tax.

See the **Instructions for Schedule A** for more information.

e ☐ Conditions (1), (2), and (4) (but not condition (3)) in box 1d apply to you, and your 1993 AGI exceeds your 1992 AGI by more than $40,000 (more than $20,000 if married filing separately). If you check this box, you must also attach a computation of your 1993 modified AGI.

f ☐ One or more of your required installments (line 21) are based on your 1992 tax and you filed or are filing a joint return for either 1992 or 1993 but not for both years.

Part II **All Filers Must Complete This Part**

2	Enter your 1993 tax after credits (see instructions)	**2**	
3	Other taxes (see instructions)	**3**	
4	Add lines 2 and 3	**4**	
5	Earned income credit **5**		
6	Credit for Federal tax paid on fuels **6**		
7	Add lines 5 and 6	**7**	
8	Current year tax. Subtract line 7 from line 4	**8**	
9	Multiply line 8 by 90% (.90) **9**		
10	Withholding taxes. **Do not** include any estimated tax payments on this line (see instructions) .	**10**	
11	Subtract line 10 from line 8. If less than $500, stop here; **do not** complete or file this form. You do not owe the penalty	**11**	
12	Tax shown on your prior year (1992) return. (**Caution:** *See instructions.*)	**12**	
13	Enter the **smaller** of line 9 or line 12 (see instructions)	**13**	

Part III **Short Method (Caution:** *Read the instructions to see if you can use the short method. If you checked box* **1b, c,** *or* **d** *in Part I, skip this part and go to Part IV.)*

14	Enter the amount, if any, from line 10 above **14**		
15	Enter the total amount, if any, of estimated tax payments you made **15**		
16	Add lines 14 and 15	**16**	
17	**Total underpayment for year.** Subtract line 16 from line 13. If zero or less, stop here; you do not owe the penalty. Do not file Form 2210 unless you checked box 1e or f above	**17**	
18	Multiply line 17 by .04655	**18**	
19	• If the amount on line 17 was paid **on or after** 4/15/94, enter -0-.		
	• If the amount on line 17 was paid **before** 4/15/94, make the following computation to find the amount to enter on line 19.		
	Amount on line 17 × Number of days paid before 4/15/94 × .00019	**19**	
20	**PENALTY.** Subtract line 19 from line 18. Enter the result here and on Form 1040, line 65; Form 1040A, line 33; Form 1040NR, line 66; or Form 1041, line 26 . . . . ►	**20**	

For Paperwork Reduction Act Notice, see page 1 of separate instructions.   Cat. No. 11744P   Form **2210** (1993)

Form 2210 (1993)

Part IV Regular Method (See the instructions if you are filing Form 1040NR.)

Section A—Figure Your Underpayment

		Payment Due Dates			
		(a) 4/15/93	(b) 6/15/93	(c) 9/15/93	(d) 1/15/94
21	**Required installments.** If box 1b applies, enter the amounts from Schedule B, line 26. If you must use Schedule A to figure your penalty (and box 1b does not apply), enter the amounts from Schedule A, line 5, 8, or 19, whichever applies. All others, enter ¼ of line 13, Form 2210, in each column	**21**			
22	Estimated tax paid and tax withheld (see instructions). For column (a) only, also enter the amount from line 22 on line 26. If line 22 is equal to or more than line 21 for all payment periods, stop here; you do not owe the penalty. Do not file Form 2210 unless you checked a box in Part I	**22**			
	Complete lines 23 through 29 of one column before going to the next column.				
23	Enter amount, if any, from line 29 of previous column	**23**			
24	Add lines 22 and 23	**24**			
25	Add amounts on lines 27 and 28 of the previous column	**25**			
26	Subtract line 25 from line 24. If zero or less, enter -0-. For column (a) only, enter the amount from line 22 .	**26**			
27	If the amount on line 26 is zero, subtract line 24 from line 25. Otherwise, enter -0-	**27**			
28	**Underpayment.** If line 21 is equal to or more than line 26, subtract line 26 from line 21. Then go to line 23 of next column. Otherwise, go to line 29 . . ▶	**28**			
29	Overpayment. If line 26 is more than line 21, subtract line 21 from line 26. Then go to line 23 of next column	**29**			

Section B—Figure the Penalty (Complete lines 30 and 31 of one column before going to the next column.)

			4/15/93	6/15/93	9/15/93	1/15/94
30	Number of days FROM the date shown above line 30 TO the date the amount on line 28 was paid **or** 4/15/94, whichever is earlier	**30**	*Days:*	*Days:*	*Days:*	*Days:*
31	$\dfrac{\text{Underpayment on line 28 (see instructions)} \times \frac{\text{Number of days on line 30}}{365} \times .07}{}$ ▶	**31**	$	$	$	$
32	**PENALTY.** Add the amounts in each column of line 31. Enter the total here and on Form 1040, line 65; Form 1040A, line 33; Form 1040NR, line 66; or Form 1041, line 26 . . . . ▶	**32**	$			

Form 2210 (1993)   Page **3**

Schedule A—Required Installments for Taxpayers Affected by Limitation on Prior Year's Tax (see instructions)

Part I Installments Based on Limitation on Prior Year's Tax		(a) 1st installment	(b) 2nd installment	(c) 3rd installment	(d) 4th installment
1	Divide line 12, Form 2210 by four (4) and enter the result in each column	1				
2	In each column, enter 22.5% of your 1993 modified tax (see instructions)	2				
3	Enter the larger of line 1 or line 2	3				
4	Divide line 9, Form 2210 by four (4) and enter the result in each column	4				
5	Enter the smaller of line 3 or line 4. If **both** line 2 and line 4 are larger than line 1, go to line 6. Otherwise, skip lines 6-19 and enter these amounts on line 21, Form 2210 (or on line 22 of Schedule B, if applicable) . . . . *Complete line 7 in column (a) before going to line 6 in column (b).*	5				
6	Enter the amount from column (a), line 7	6	/////		/////	/////
7	Subtract line 1 from line 5	7		/////	/////	/////
8	In column (a), enter the amount from line 1. In column (b), add lines 5 and 6. In columns (c) and (d), enter the amount from line 5. If you are using Part II below, go to line 9. Otherwise, skip Part II and enter these amounts on line 21, Form 2210 (or on line 22 of Schedule B, if applicable)	8				

Part II Installments Based on Annualization Exception (see instructions)					
Estates and trusts, **do not** use the period ending dates shown to the right. Instead, use the following: 2/28/93, 4/30/93, 7/31/93, and 11/30/93.		(a) 1/1/93 - 3/31/93	(b) 1/1/93 - 5/31/93	(c) 1/1/93 - 8/31/93	(d) 1/1/93 - 12/31/93
9	Enter your modified AGI for each period shown above line 9 (see instructions)	9	/////			
10	Annualization amounts. (Estates and trusts, **do not** use the amounts shown to the right. Instead, use 3, 1.71429, and 1.09091.) . . .	10	/////	2.4	1.5	1
11	**Annualized modified AGI.** Multiply line 9 by line 10	11	/////			
12	Enter your 1992 AGI as shown on your return in each column . .	12	/////			
13	Subtract line 12 from line 11. If less than zero, enter -0-	13	/////			
14	Enter your AGI for each period shown above line 9 (see instructions)	14	/////			
15	**Annualized AGI.** Multiply line 14 by line 10	15	/////			
16	In column (a), enter the amount from line 1. In columns (b)-(d), enter the amount from line 5 **if:** ● Line 13 is more than $40,000 (more than $20,000 if married filing separately), **and** ● Line 15 is more than $75,000 (more than $37,500 if married filing separately). Otherwise, enter the amount from line 1	16				
17	Subtract line 16 from line 5 . . . . *Complete lines 18 and 19 in one column before going to the next column.*	17				
18	If you entered -0- on line 17, add the amounts on line 17 of all preceding columns. From the result, subtract the total of the amounts on line 18 of all preceding columns and enter the result. Otherwise, enter -0-	18	/////			
19	In column (a), enter the amount from line 16. In columns (b) through (d), add lines 16 and 18. Enter here and on line 21, Form 2210 (or on line 22 of Schedule B, if applicable)	19				

Form 2210 (1993)   Page **4**

Schedule B—Annualized Income Installment Method (see instructions)

Estates and trusts, **do not** use the period ending dates shown to the right. Instead, use the following: 2/28/93, 4/30/93, 7/31/93, and 11/30/93.

		(a) 1/1/93 - 3/31/93	(b) 1/1/93 - 5/31/93	(c) 1/1/93 - 8/31/93	(d) 1/1/93 - 12/31/93

Part I   **Annualized Income Installments**   Caution: *Complete lines 20–26 of one column before going to the next column.*

		(a)	(b)	(c)	(d)
1	Enter your adjusted gross income for each period (see instructions). (Estates and trusts, enter your taxable income without your exemption for each period.) **1**				
2	Annualization amounts. (Estates and trusts, see instructions.) . . **2**	4	2.4	1.5	1
3	Annualized income. Multiply line 1 by line 2 . . . . **3**				
4	Enter your itemized deductions for the period shown in each column. If you do not itemize, enter -0- and skip to line 7. (Estates and trusts, enter -0-, skip to line 9, and enter the amount from line 3 on line 9.) **4**				
5	Annualization amounts **5**	4	2.4	1.5	1
6	Multiply line 4 by line 5 (see instructions if line 3 is more than $54,225) **6**				
7	In each column, enter the full amount of your standard deduction from Form 1040, line 34; or Form 1040A, line 19 (Form 1040NR filers, enter -0-) **7**				
8	Enter line 6 or line 7, whichever is **larger** **8**				
9	Subtract line 8 from line 3 . . . . **9**				
10	In each column, multiply $2,350 by the total number of exemptions claimed (see instructions if line 3 is more than $81,350). (Estates and trusts and Form 1040NR filers, enter the exemption amount shown on your tax return.) **10**				
11	Subtract line 10 from line 9 . . . . **11**				
12	Figure your tax on the amount on line 11 (see instructions) . . . **12**				
13	Form 1040 filers only, enter your self-employment tax from line 40 below **13**				
14	Enter other taxes for each payment period (see instructions) . . **14**				
15	Total tax. Add lines 12, 13, and 14 . . . . **15**				
16	For each period, enter the same type of credits as allowed on Form 2210, lines 2, 5, and 6 (see instructions) **16**				
17	Subtract line 16 from line 15. If zero or less, enter -0- **17**				
18	Applicable percentage **18**	22.5%	45%	67.5%	90%
19	Multiply line 17 by line 18 . . . . **19**				
20	Add the amounts in all preceding columns of line 26 . . . . **20**	//////			
21	Subtract line 20 from line 19. If zero or less, enter -0- **21**				
22	If you are required to use Schedule A, enter the amounts from Schedule A, line 5, 8, or 19, whichever applies. Otherwise, enter ¼ of line 13, Form 2210, in each column **22**				
23	Enter amount from line 25 of the preceding column of this schedule **23**	//////			
24	Add lines 22 and 23 and enter the total **24**				
25	Subtract line 21 from line 24. If zero or less, enter -0- **25**				//////
26	Enter the **smaller** of line 21 or line 24 here and on Form 2210, line 21 ▶ **26**				

Part II   **Annualized Self-Employment Tax**

		(a)	(b)	(c)	(d)
27a	Net earnings from self-employment for the period (see instructions) **27a**				
b	Annualization amounts **27b**	4	2.4	1.5	1
c	Multiply line 27a by line 27b **27c**				
28	Social security tax limit **28**	$57,600	$57,600	$57,600	$57,600
29	Enter actual wages subject to social security tax or the 6.2% portion of the 7.65% railroad retirement (tier 1) tax **29**				
30	Annualization amounts **30**	4	2.4	1.5	1
31	Multiply line 29 by line 30 . . . . **31**				
32	Subtract line 31 from line 28. If zero or less, enter -0- **32**				
33	Multiply the smaller of line 27c or line 32 by .124 . . . . . . **33**				
34	Medicare tax limit **34**	$135,000	$135,000	$135,000	$135,000
35	Enter actual wages subject to Medicare tax or the 1.45% portion of the 7.65% railroad retirement (tier 1) tax **35**				
36	Annualization amounts **36**	4	2.4	1.5	1
37	Multiply line 35 by line 36 . . . . **37**				
38	Subtract line 37 from line 34. If zero or less, enter -0- **38**				
39	Multiply the smaller of line 27c or line 38 by .029 . . . . . . **39**				
40	Add lines 33 and 39. Enter the result here and on line 13 above ▶ **40**				

Form **2220**

Department of the Treasury
Internal Revenue Service

Underpayment of Estimated Tax by Corporations

▶ See separate instructions.

▶ Attach to the corporation's tax return.

OMB No. 1545-0142

1993

Name	Employer identification number

Note: *In most cases, the IRS will figure the penalty and the corporation will not have to complete this form. See the instructions for more information.*

Part I Figuring the Underpayment

1	Total tax (see instructions)	**1**

2a	Personal holding company tax included on line 1 (Schedule PH (Form 1120), line 26).	**2a**	
b	Interest due under the look-back method of section 460(b)(2) for completed long-term contracts included on line 1	**2b**	
c	Credit for Federal tax paid on fuels (see instructions)	**2c**	

d	**Total.** Add lines 2a through 2c	**2d**

3   Subtract line 2d from line 1. If the result is less than $500, **do not** complete or file this form. The corporation does not owe the penalty   **3**

| 4a | Multiply line 3 by 97% | **4a** | |
| b | Tax shown on the corporation's 1992 income tax return. *(CAUTION: See instructions before completing this line.)* | **4b** | |

c   Enter the **smaller** of line 4a or line 4b. If the corporation is required to skip line 4b, enter the amount from line 4a on line 4c   **4c**

		(a)	(b)	(c)	(d)
5	**Installment due dates.** Enter in columns (a) through (d) the 15th day of the 4th, 6th, 9th, and 12th months of the corporation's tax year ▶				
6	**Required installments.** Enter 25% of line 4c in columns (a) through (d) unless **a** or **b** below applies to the corporation.				
a	**Annualized income installment method and/or the adjusted seasonal installment method:** If the corporation uses one or both of these methods, complete the worksheet in the instructions and enter on line 6 the amounts from line 45 of the worksheet. Also check this box ▶ ☐ and attach a copy of the worksheet.				
b	**"Large corporations:"** Check this box ▶ ☐ and see the instructions for the amount to enter in each column of line 6				
7	Estimated tax paid or credited for each period (see instructions). For column (a) only, enter the amount from line 7 on line 11				
	Complete lines 8 through 14 of one column before going to the next column.				
8	Enter amount, if any, from line 14 of the preceding column				
9	Add lines 7 and 8				
10	Add amounts on lines 12 and 13 of the preceding column.				
11	Subtract line 10 from line 9. If zero or less, enter -0-. For column (a) only, enter the amount from line 7				
12	If the amount on line 11 is zero, subtract line 9 from line 10. Otherwise, enter -0-				
13	**Underpayment.** If line 11 is less than or equal to line 6, subtract line 11 from line 6. Then go to line 8 of the next column. Otherwise, go to line 14 (see instructions)				
14	**Overpayment.** If line 6 is less than line 11, subtract line 6 from line 11. Then go to line 8 of the next column				

Complete Part II on the back of this form to figure the penalty. If there are no entries on line 13, no penalty is owed.

For Paperwork Reduction Act Notice, see page 1 of instructions.

Cat. No. 11746L

Form **2220** (1993)

Form 2220 (1993)   Page **2**

Part II Figuring the Penalty

		(a)	(b)	(c)	(d)
15 Enter the date of payment or the 15th day of the 3rd month after the close of the tax year, whichever is earlier (see instructions). *(Form 990-PF and Form 990-T filers:* Use 5th month instead of 3rd month.)	**15**				
16 Number of days from due date of installment on line 5 to the date shown on line 15	**16**				
17 Number of days on line 16 after 4/15/93 and before 4/1/94 .	**17**				
18 Number of days on line 16 after 3/31/94 and before 7/1/94 .	**18**				
19 Number of days on line 16 after 6/30/94 and before 10/1/94.	**19**				
20 Number of days on line 16 after 9/30/94 and before 1/1/95 .	**20**				
21 Number of days on line 16 after 12/31/94 and before 2/16/95	**21**				
22 Underpayment on line 13 × $\frac{\text{Number of days on line 17}}{365}$ × 7% . .	**22**	$	$	$	$
23 Underpayment on line 13 × $\frac{\text{Number of days on line 18}}{365}$ × *% . .	**23**	$	$	$	$
24 Underpayment on line 13 × $\frac{\text{Number of days on line 19}}{365}$ × *% . .	**24**	$	$	$	$
25 Underpayment on line 13 × $\frac{\text{Number of days on line 20}}{365}$ × *% . .	**25**	$	$	$	$
26 Underpayment on line 13 × $\frac{\text{Number of days on line 21}}{365}$ × *% . .	**26**	$	$	$	$
27 Add lines 22 through 26	**27**	$	$	$	$

28 PENALTY. Add columns (a) through (d), line 27. Enter here and on line 33, Form 1120; line 29, Form 1120-A; or comparable line for other income tax returns . . . . | **28** | $

*If the corporation's tax year ends after December 31, 1993, see the Instructions for lines 23 through 26.

Form **2441**

Department of the Treasury
Internal Revenue Service   (O)

Child and Dependent Care Expenses

▶ **Attach to Form 1040.**

▶ **See separate instructions.**

OMB No. 1545-0068

1993

Attachment
Sequence No. **21**

Name(s) shown on Form 1040

Your social security number

You need to understand the following terms to complete this form: **Dependent Care Benefits, Earned Income, Qualified Expenses, and Qualifying Person(s). See Important Terms** on page 1 of the Form 2441 instructions. Also, if you had a child born in 1993 and line 32 of Form 1040 is less than $23,050, see **A Change To Note** on page 2 of the instructions.

Part I **Persons or Organizations Who Provided the Care—You must complete this part.**
(If you need more space, use the bottom of page 2.)

1	**(a)** Care provider's name	**(b)** Address (number, street, apt. no., city, state, and ZIP code)	**(c)** Identifying number (SSN or EIN)	**(d)** Amount paid (see instructions)

2 Add the amounts in column (d) of line 1 . . . . **2**

3 Enter the number of **qualifying persons** cared for in 1993 . . . . ▶

| Did you receive **dependent care benefits?** | — **NO** ——▶ Complete only Part II below. |
| | — **YES** ——▶ Complete Part III on the back now. |

Part II **Credit for Child and Dependent Care Expenses**

4 Enter the amount of **qualified expenses** you incurred and paid in 1993. DO NOT enter more than $2,400 for one qualifying person or $4,800 for two or more persons. If you completed Part III, enter the amount from line 25 . . . . **4**

5 Enter YOUR **earned income** **5**

6 If married filing a joint return, enter YOUR SPOUSE'S earned income (if student or disabled, see instructions); **all others,** enter the amount from line 5 . . . . **6**

7 Enter the **smallest** of line 4, 5, or 6 . . . . **7**

8 Enter the amount from Form 1040, line 32 . . . . **8**

9 Enter on line 9 the decimal amount shown below that applies to the amount on line 8

If line 8 is—		Decimal amount is	If line 8 is—		Decimal amount is
Over	But not over		Over	But not over	
$0—10,000		.30	$20,000—22,000		.24
10,000—12,000		.29	22,000—24,000		.23
12,000—14,000		.28	24,000—26,000		.22
14,000—16,000		.27	26,000—28,000		.21
16,000—18,000		.26	28,000—No limit		.20
18,000—20,000		.25			

9 × .

10 Multiply **line 7** by the decimal amount on line 9. Enter the result. Then, see the instructions for the amount of credit to enter on Form 1040, line 41 . . . . **10**

Caution: *If you paid $50 or more in a calendar quarter to a person who worked in your home, you must file an employment tax return. Get **Form 942** for details.*

For Paperwork Reduction Act Notice, see separate instructions.   Cat. No. 11862M   Form **2441** (1993)

Form 2441 (1993)   Page **2**

Part III **Dependent Care Benefits**—Complete this part **only** if you received these benefits.

11 Enter the total amount of **dependent care benefits** you received for 1993. This amount should be shown in box 10 of your W-2 form(s). DO NOT include amounts that were reported to you as wages in box 1 of Form(s) W-2 . . . . | **11**

12 Enter the amount forfeited, if any. See the instructions . . . . | **12**

13 Subtract line 12 from line 11 . . . . | **13**

14 Enter the total amount of **qualified expenses** incurred in 1993 for the care of the qualifying person(s) . . . . | **14**

15 Enter the **smaller** of line 13 or 14 . . . . | **15**

16 Enter YOUR **earned income** . . . . | **16**

17 If married filing a joint return, enter YOUR SPOUSE'S earned income (if student or disabled, see the line 6 instructions); if married filing a separate return, see the instructions for the amount to enter; **all others,** enter the amount from line 16 . . | **17**

18 Enter the **smallest** of line 15, 16, or 17. . . . . | **18**

19 **Excluded benefits.** Enter here the **smaller** of the following:

• The amount from line 18, or
• $5,000 ($2,500 if married filing a separate return **and** you were required to enter your spouse's earned income on line 17). | **19**

20 **Taxable benefits.** Subtract line 19 from line 13. Also, include this amount on Form 1040, line 7. On the dotted line next to line 7, write "DCB" . . . . | **20**

To claim the child and dependent care credit, complete
lines 21–25 below, and lines 4–10 on the front of this form.

21 Enter the amount of qualified expenses you incurred and paid in 1993. DO NOT include on this line any excluded benefits shown on line 19 . . . . | **21**

22 Enter $2,400 ($4,800 if two or more qualifying persons) . . . | **22**

23 Enter the amount from line 19 . . . . | **23**

24 Subtract line 23 from line 22. If zero or less, **STOP**. You cannot take the credit. **Exception.** If you paid 1992 expenses in 1993, see the line 10 instructions . . . . | **24**

25 Enter the **smaller** of line 21 or 24 here **and** on line 4 on the front of this form . . . . . | **25**

Form **2555**	**Foreign Earned Income**	OMB No. 1545-0067

Department of the Treasury
Internal Revenue Service

▶ See separate instructions.   ▶ Attach to front of Form 1040.

1993

Attachment
Sequence No. **34**

For Use by U.S. Citizens and Resident Aliens Only

Name shown on Form 1040	Your social security number

Part I   General Information

1   Your foreign address (including country)   **2** Your occupation

3   Employer's name ▶ ....

4a Employer's U.S. address ▶ ....

b   Employer's foreign address ▶ ....

5   Employer is (check ▶   **a** ☐ A foreign entity   **b** ☐ A U.S. company   **c** ☐ Self
any that apply):   **d** ☐ A foreign affiliate of a U.S. company   **e** ☐ Other (specify) ▶ ....

6a If, after 1981, you filed Form 2555 to claim either of the exclusions or Form 2555-EZ to claim the foreign earned income
exclusion, enter the last year you filed the form. ▶ ....

b   If you did not file Form 2555 or 2555-EZ after 1981 to claim either of the exclusions, check here ▶ ☐ and go to line 7 now.

c   Have you ever revoked either of the exclusions?   .   .   .   .   ☐ Yes ☐ No

d   If you answered "Yes," enter the type of exclusion and the tax year for which the revocation was effective. ▶ ....

7   Of what country are you a citizen/national? ▶ ....

8a Did you maintain a separate foreign residence for your family because of adverse living conditions at your
tax home? See **Second foreign household** on page 3 of the instructions .   .   .   .   ☐ Yes ☐ No

b   If "Yes," enter city and country of the separate foreign residence. Also, enter the number of days during your tax year that
you maintained a second household at that address. ▶ ....

9   List your tax home(s) during your tax year and date(s) established. ▶ ....

**Next, complete either Part II or Part III. If an item does not apply, write "NA." If you do not give
the information asked for, any exclusion or deduction you claim may be disallowed.**

Part II   Taxpayers Qualifying Under Bona Fide Residence Test (See page 2 of the instructions.)

10 Date bona fide residence began ▶ ...., and ended ▶ ....

11 Kind of living quarters in foreign country ▶ **a** ☐ Purchased house **b** ☐ Rented house or apartment **c** ☐ Rented room
d ☐ Quarters furnished by employer

12a Did any of your family live with you abroad during any part of the tax year?.   .   .   .   .   ☐ Yes ☐ No

b   If "Yes," who and for what period? ▶ ....

13a Have you submitted a statement to the authorities of the foreign country where you claim bona fide residence
that you are not a resident of that country? (See instructions.) .   .   .   .   ☐ Yes ☐ No

b   Are you required to pay income tax to the country where you claim bona fide residence? (See instructions.) ☐ Yes ☐ No

**If you answered "Yes" to 13a and "No" to 13b, you do not qualify as a bona fide resident. Do not complete the rest of
Part II.**

14 If you were present in the United States or its possessions during the tax year, complete columns **(a)-(d)** below. **Do not** include
the income from column **(d)** in Part IV, but report it on Form 1040.

(a) Date arrived in U.S.	**(b)** Date left U.S.	**(c)** Number of days in U.S. on business	**(d)** Income earned in U.S. on business (attach computation)	**(a)** Date arrived in U.S.	**(b)** Date left U.S.	**(c)** Number of days in U.S. on business	**(d)** Income earned in U.S. on business (attach computation)

15a List any contractual terms or other conditions relating to the length of your employment abroad. ▶ ....
....

b   Enter the type of visa under which you entered the foreign country. ▶ ....

c   Did your visa limit the length of your stay or employment in a foreign country? If "Yes," attach explanation ☐ Yes ☐ No

d   Did you maintain a home in the United States while living abroad?.   .   .   .   .   ☐ Yes ☐ No

e   If "Yes," enter address of your home, whether it was rented, the names of the occupants, and their relationship
to you. ▶ ....

For Paperwork Reduction Act Notice, see page 1 of separate instructions.   Cat. No. 11900P   Form **2555** (1993)

Form 2555 (1993)   Page **2**

Part III   Taxpayers Qualifying Under Physical Presence Test (See page 2 of the instructions.)

16 The physical presence test is based on the 12-month period from ▶ .... through ▶ ....

17 Enter your principal country of employment during your tax year. ▶ ....

18 If you traveled abroad during the 12-month period entered on line 16, complete columns **(a)-(f)** below. Exclude travel between foreign countries that did not involve travel on or over international waters, or in or over the United States, for 24 hours or more. If you have no travel to report during the period, enter "Physically present in a foreign country or countries for the entire 12-month period." **Do not** include the income from column **(f)** below in Part IV, but report it on Form 1040.

(a) Name of country (including U.S.)	(b) Date arrived	(c) Date left	(d) Full days present in country	(e) Number of days in U.S. on business	(f) Income earned in U.S. on business (attach computation)

Part IV   All Taxpayers

Note: *Enter on lines 19 through 23 all income, including noncash income, you earned and actually or constructively received during your 1993 tax year for services you performed in a foreign country. If any of the foreign earned income received this tax year was earned in a prior tax year, or will be earned in a later tax year (such as a bonus), see the instructions. **Do not** include income from line 14, column **(d),** or line 18, column **(f).** Report amounts in U.S. dollars, using the exchange rates in effect when you actually or constructively received the income.*

If you are a cash basis taxpayer, report on Form 1040 all income you received in 1993, no matter when you performed the service.

1993 Foreign Earned Income		**Amount (in U.S. dollars)**
19 Total wages, salaries, bonuses, commissions, etc..	**19**	
20 Allowable share of income for personal services performed (see instructions):		
a In a business (including farming) or profession	**20a**	
b In a partnership. List partnership's name and address and type of income. ▶	**20b**	
21 Noncash income (market value of property or facilities furnished by employer—attach statement showing how it was determined):		
a Home (lodging)	**21a**	
b Meals	**21b**	
c Car	**21c**	
d Other property or facilities. List type and amount. ▶	**21d**	
22 Allowances, reimbursements, or expenses paid on your behalf for services you performed:		
a Cost of living and overseas differential	**22a**	
b Family	**22b**	
c Education	**22c**	
d Home leave	**22d**	
e Quarters	**22e**	
f For any other purpose. List type and amount. ▶	**22f**	
g Add lines 22a through 22f	**22g**	
23 Other foreign earned income. List type and amount. ▶	**23**	
24 Add lines 19 through 21d, line 22g, and line 23	**24**	
25 Total amount of meals and lodging included on line 24 that is excludable (see instructions)	**25**	
26 Subtract line 25 from line 24. Enter the result here and on line 27 on page 3. This is your **foreign earned income** ▶	**26**	

Part V   **All Taxpayers**

27	Enter the amount from line 26	**27**	

   • If you choose to claim the housing exclusion or are claiming the housing deduction, complete
     Part VI.
   • All others, go to Part VII.

Part VI   **For Taxpayers Claiming the Housing Exclusion AND/OR Deduction**

28	Qualified housing expenses for the tax year (see instructions)	**28**	
29	Number of days in your qualifying period that fall within your 1993 tax year (see instructions) **29**		
30	Multiply $23.94 by the number of days on line 29. Enter the result but do not enter more than $8,737.00	**30**	
31	Subtract line 30 from line 28. If zero or less, do not complete the rest of Part VI or any of Part IX	**31**	
32	Enter employer-provided amounts (see instructions) **32**		
33	Divide line 32 by line 27. Enter the result as a decimal (to two places), but do not enter more than "1.00"	**33**	× .
34	**Housing exclusion.** Multiply line 31 by line 33. Enter the result but do not enter more than the amount on line 32. Also, complete Part VIII . . . . ▶	**34**	

   Note: *The housing deduction is figured in Part IX. If you choose to claim the foreign earned income exclusion, complete Parts VII and VIII before Part IX.*

Part VII   **For Taxpayers Claiming the Foreign Earned Income Exclusion**

35	Maximum foreign earned income exclusion	**35**	$70,000 00
36	• If you completed Part VI, enter the number from line 29. • All others, enter the number of days in your qualifying period that fall within your 1993 tax year (see the instructions for line 29). **36**		
37	• If line 36 and the number of days in your 1993 tax year (usually 365) are the same, enter "1.00." • Otherwise, divide line 36 by the number of days in your 1993 tax year and enter the result as a decimal (to two places).	**37**	× .
38	Multiply line 35 by line 37	**38**	
39	Subtract line 34 from line 27	**39**	
40	**Foreign earned income exclusion.** Enter the **smaller** of line 38 or line 39. Also, complete Part VIII ▶	**40**	

Part VIII   **For Taxpayers Claiming the Housing Exclusion, Foreign Earned Income Exclusion, or Both**

41	Add lines 34 and 40	**41**	
42	Deductions allowed in figuring your adjusted gross income (Form 1040, line 31) that are allocable to the excluded income. See instructions and attach computation	**42**	
43	Subtract line 42 from line 41. Enter the result here and in parentheses on Form 1040, line 22. Next to the amount write "Form 2555." On Form 1040, subtract this amount from your income to arrive at total income on Form 1040, line 23. . . . . ▶	**43**	

Part IX   **For Taxpayers Claiming the Housing Deduction—**Complete this part only if (a) line 31 is more than line 34 and (b) line 27 is more than line 41.

44	Subtract line 34 from line 31	**44**	
45	Subtract line 41 from line 27	**45**	
46	Enter the **smaller** of line 44 or line 45	**46**	

   Note: *If line 45 is **more than** line 46 and you couldn't deduct all of your 1992 housing deduction because of the 1992 limit, use the worksheet on page 4 of the instructions to figure the amount to enter on line 47. Otherwise, go to line 48.*

47	Housing deduction carryover from 1992 (from worksheet on page 4 of the instructions)	**47**	
48	**Housing deduction.** Add lines 46 and 47. Enter the total here and on Form 1040 to the left of line 30. Next to the amount on Form 1040, write "Form 2555." Add it to the total adjustments reported on that line . . . . ▶	**48**	

Form **2555-EZ**

Department of the Treasury
Internal Revenue Service

Foreign Earned Income Exclusion

▶ **See separate instructions.**   ▶ **Attach to front of Form 1040.**

OMB No. 1545-1326

1993

Attachment
Sequence No. **34A**

Name shown on Form 1040

Your social security number

You May Use This Form If You:	• Are a U.S. citizen or a resident alien. • Earned wages/salaries in a foreign country. • Had total foreign earned income of $70,000 or less. • Are filing a calendar year return that covers a 12-month period.	**And You:** • Do not have self-employment income. • Do not have business/moving expenses. • Do not claim the foreign housing exclusion or deduction.

Part I **Tests To See If You Can Take the Foreign Earned Income Exclusion**

1 **Bona Fide Residence Test**

a Were you a bona fide resident of a foreign country or countries for a period that includes an entire tax year (see page 2 of the instructions)? . . . . ☐ Yes ☐ No
   • If you answered "Yes," you meet this test. Fill in line 1b and then go to line 3.
   • If you answered "No," you **do not** meet this test. Go to line 2 to see if you meet the Physical Presence Test.

b Enter the date your bona fide residence began ▶ _____ , and ended (see instructions) ▶ _____ .

2 **Physical Presence Test**

a Were you physically present in a foreign country or countries for at least 330 full days during—
   { 1993, **or**
   { any other period of 12 months in a row starting or ending in 1993? } . . . . ☐ Yes ☐ No

   • If you answered "Yes," you meet this test. Fill in line 2b and then go to line 3.
   • If you answered "No," you **do not** meet this test. You **cannot** take the exclusion unless you meet the Bona Fide Residence Test above.

b The physical presence test is based on the 12-month period from ▶ _____ through ▶ _____ .

3 **Tax Home Test.** Was your tax home in a foreign country or countries throughout your period of bona fide residence or physical presence, whichever applies?. . . . . ☐ Yes ☐ No
   • If you answered "Yes," you can take the exclusion. Complete Part II below and then go to page 2.
   • If you answered "No," you **cannot** take the exclusion. **Do not** file this form.

Part II **General Information**

4 Your foreign address (including country)

5 Your occupation

6 Employer's name

7 Employer's U.S. address (including ZIP code)

8 Employer's foreign address

9 Employer is (check any that apply):
a A U.S. business . . . . ☐
b A foreign business . . . . ☐
c Other (specify) ▶ _____ ☐
10a If you filed Form 2555 or 2555-EZ after 1981, enter the last year you filed the form. ▶ _____
   b If you did not file Form 2555 or 2555-EZ after 1981, check here ▶ ☐   and go to line 11a now.
   c Have you ever revoked the foreign earned income exclusion? . . . . ☐ Yes ☐ No
   d If you answered "Yes," enter the tax year for which the revocation was effective. ▶ _____
11a List your tax home(s) during 1993 and date(s) established. ▶ _____

   b Of what country are you a citizen/national? ▶

For Paperwork Reduction Act Notice, see page 1 of separate instructions.   Cat. No. 13272W   Form **2555-EZ** (1993)

Form 2555-EZ (1993)   Page **2**

Part III   Days Present in the United States—Complete this part if you were present in the United States or its possessions in 1993.

12 (a) Date arrived in U.S.	(b) Date left U.S.	(c) Number of days in U.S. on business	(d) Income earned in U.S. on business (attach computation)

Part IV   Figure Your Foreign Earned Income Exclusion

13	Maximum foreign earned income exclusion	**13**	$70,000	00
14	Enter the number of days in your qualifying period that fall within 1993 . **14**		
15	• If you entered 365 days on line 14, enter "1.00" here. • Otherwise, divide line 14 by 365 and enter the result here as a decimal (to two places). } · ·	**15**	×
16	Multiply line 13 by line 15	**16**	
17	Enter, in U.S. dollars, the total foreign earned income you earned and received in 1993 (see instructions). Be sure to include this amount on Form 1040, line 7	**17**	
18	**Foreign earned income exclusion.** Enter the **smaller** of line 16 or line 17 here and in parentheses on **Form 1040, line 22.** Next to the amount write **"2555-EZ."** On Form 1040, subtract this amount from your income to arrive at total income on **Form 1040, line 23** . . . . . . ▶	**18**	

Form **3903**

Department of the Treasury
Internal Revenue Service

Moving Expenses

▶ **Attach to Form 1040.**

▶ **See separate instructions.**

OMB No. 1545-0062

1993

Attachment
Sequence No. **62**

Name(s) shown on Form 1040	Your social security number

Caution: *If you are a member of the armed forces, see the instructions before completing this form.*

1	Enter the number of miles from your **old home** to your **new workplace**	**1**	
2	Enter the number of miles from your **old home** to your **old workplace**	**2**	
3	Subtract line 2 from line 1. Enter the result but not less than zero . . . . ▶	**3**	

If line 3 is 35 or more miles, complete the rest of this form. Also, see **Time Test** in the instructions. If line 3 is less than 35 miles, you may not deduct your moving expenses.

Part I Moving Expenses

Note: *Any payments your employer made for any part of your move (including the value of any services furnished in kind) should be included on your W-2 form. Report that amount on **Form 1040, line 7**. See **Reimbursements** in the instructions.*

Section A—Transportation of Household Goods

4	Transportation and storage for household goods and personal effects	**4**	

Section B—Expenses of Moving From Old To New Home

5	Travel and lodging **not** including meals	**5**		
6	Total meals	**6**		
7	Multiply line 6 by 80% (.80)	**7**		
8	Add lines 5 and 7	**8**		

Section C—Pre-move Househunting Expenses and Temporary Quarters
(for any 30 days in a row after getting your job)

9	Pre-move travel and lodging **not** including meals	**9**		
10	Temporary quarters expenses **not** including meals	**10**		
11	Total meal expenses for both pre-move househunting and temporary quarters	**11**		
12	Multiply line 11 by 80% (.80)	**12**		
13	Add lines 9, 10, and 12	**13**		

Section D—Qualified Real Estate Expenses

14	Expenses of (check one) **a** ☐ selling or exchanging your old home, or ⎫ **b** ☐ if renting, settling an unexpired lease. ⎭	**14**	
15	Expenses of (check one) **a** ☐ buying your new home, or ⎫ **b** ☐ if renting, getting a new lease. ⎭	**15**	

Part II Dollar Limits and Moving Expense Deduction

Note: *If you and your spouse moved to separate homes, see the instructions.*

16	Enter the **smaller** of: • The amount on line 13, or • $1,500 ($750 if married filing a separate return and at the end of ⎫ 1993 you lived with your spouse who also started work in 1993). ⎭	**16**	
17	Add lines 14, 15, and 16	**17**	
18	Enter the **smaller** of: • The amount on line 17, or • $3,000 ($1,500 if married filing a separate return and at the end ⎫ of 1993 you lived with your spouse who also started work in 1993). ⎭	**18**	
19	Add lines 4, 8, and 18. Enter the total here and on Schedule A, line 18. This is your **moving expense** deduction . . . . ▶	**19**	

For Paperwork Reduction Act Notice, see separate instructions.   Cat. No. 12490K   Form **3903** (1993)

Form **4562**	**Depreciation and Amortization**	OMB No. 1545-0172
Department of the Treasury Internal Revenue Service (O)	**(Including Information on Listed Property)** ► See separate instructions. ► Attach this form to your return.	**1993** Attachment Sequence No. **67**

Name(s) shown on return	Identifying number

Business or activity to which this form relates

Part I Election To Expense Certain Tangible Property (Section 179) (Note: *If you have any "Listed Property," complete Part V before you complete Part I.*)

1	Maximum dollar limitation (If an enterprise zone business, see instructions.)	**1**	$17,500
2	Total cost of section 179 property placed in service during the tax year (see instructions)	**2**	
3	Threshold cost of section 179 property before reduction in limitation	**3**	$200,000
4	Reduction in limitation. Subtract line 3 from line 2, but do not enter less than -0-	**4**	
5	Dollar limitation for tax year. Subtract line 4 from line 1, but do not enter less than -0-. (If married filing separately, see instructions.)	**5**	

(a) Description of property	(b) Cost	(c) Elected cost	
6			

7	Listed property. Enter amount from line 26.	**7**	
8	Total elected cost of section 179 property. Add amounts in column (c), lines 6 and 7	**8**	
9	Tentative deduction. Enter the smaller of line 5 or line 8	**9**	
10	Carryover of disallowed deduction from 1992 (see instructions)	**10**	
11	Taxable income limitation. Enter the smaller of taxable income or line 5 (see instructions)	**11**	
12	Section 179 expense deduction. Add lines 9 and 10, but do not enter more than line 11	**12**	
13	Carryover of disallowed deduction to 1994. Add lines 9 and 10, less line 12 ►	**13**	

Note: *Do not use Part II or Part III below for listed property (automobiles, certain other vehicles, cellular telephones, certain computers, or property used for entertainment, recreation, or amusement). Instead, use Part V for listed property.*

Part II MACRS Depreciation For Assets Placed in Service ONLY During Your 1993 Tax Year (Do Not Include Listed Property)

(a) Classification of property	(b) Month and year placed in service	(c) Basis for depreciation (business/investment use only—see instructions)	(d) Recovery period	(e) Convention	(f) Method	(g) Depreciation deduction
14 General Depreciation System (GDS) (see instructions):						
a 3-year property						
b 5-year property						
c 7-year property						
d 10-year property						
e 15-year property						
f 20-year property						
g Residential rental property			27.5 yrs.	MM	S/L	
			27.5 yrs.	MM	S/L	
h Nonresidential real property				MM	S/L	
				MM	S/L	
15 Alternative Depreciation System (ADS) (see instructions):						
a Class life					S/L	
b 12-year			12 yrs.		S/L	
c 40-year			40 yrs.	MM	S/L	

Part III Other Depreciation (Do Not Include Listed Property)

16	GDS and ADS deductions for assets placed in service in tax years beginning before 1993 (see instructions)	**16**	
17	Property subject to section 168(f)(1) election (see instructions)	**17**	
18	ACRS and other depreciation (see instructions)	**18**	

Part IV Summary

19	Listed property. Enter amount from line 25.	**19**	
20	**Total.** Add deductions on line 12, lines 14 and 15 in column (g), and lines 16 through 19. Enter here and on the appropriate lines of your return. (Partnerships and S corporations—see instructions)	**20**	
21	For assets shown above and placed in service during the current year, enter the portion of the basis attributable to section 263A costs (see instructions)	**21**	

For Paperwork Reduction Act Notice, see page 1 of the separate instructions.   Cat. No. 12906N   Form **4562** (1993)

Form 4562 (1993)

Page **2**

Part V — Listed Property—Automobiles, Certain Other Vehicles, Cellular Telephones, Certain Computers, and Property Used for Entertainment, Recreation, or Amusement

*For any vehicle for which you are using the standard mileage rate or deducting lease expense, complete **only** 22a, 22b, columns (a) through (c) of Section A, all of Section B, and Section C if applicable.*

Section A—Depreciation and Other Information (Caution: *See instructions for limitations for automobiles.*)

22a Do you have evidence to support the business/investment use claimed? ☐ **Yes** ☐ **No**   **22b** If "Yes," is the evidence written? ☐ **Yes** ☐ **No**

(a) Type of property (list vehicles first)	(b) Date placed in service	(c) Business/ investment use percentage	(d) Cost or other basis	(e) Basis for depreciation (business/investment use only)	(f) Recovery period	(g) Method/ Convention	(h) Depreciation deduction	(i) Elected section 179 cost
23 Property used more than 50% in a qualified business use (see instructions):								
		%						
		%						
		%						
24 Property used 50% or less in a qualified business use (see instructions):								
		%				S/L –		
		%				S/L –		
		%				S/L –		

25 Add amounts in column (h). Enter the total here and on line 19, page 1 . . . . . . **25**

26 Add amounts in column (i). Enter the total here and on line 7, page 1 . . . . **26**

Section B—Information Regarding Use of Vehicles—*If you deduct expenses for vehicles:*

• *Always complete this section for vehicles used by a sole proprietor, partner, or other "more than 5% owner," or related person.*
• *If you provided vehicles to your employees, first answer the questions in Section C to see if you meet an exception to completing this section for those vehicles.*

	(a) Vehicle 1		(b) Vehicle 2		(c) Vehicle 3		(d) Vehicle 4		(e) Vehicle 5		(f) Vehicle 6	
27 Total business/investment miles driven during the year (DO NOT include commuting miles)												
28 Total commuting miles driven during the year												
29 Total other personal (noncommuting) miles driven												
30 Total miles driven during the year. Add lines 27 through 29												
	Yes	No	Yes	No	Yes	No	Yes	No	Yes	No	Yes	No
31 Was the vehicle available for personal use during off-duty hours?												
32 Was the vehicle used primarily by a more than 5% owner or related person?												
33 Is another vehicle available for personal use?												

Section C—Questions for Employers Who Provide Vehicles for Use by Their Employees

Answer these questions to determine if you meet an exception to completing Section B. **Note:** *Section B must always be completed for vehicles used by sole proprietors, partners, or other more than 5% owners or related persons.*

	Yes	No
34 Do you maintain a written policy statement that prohibits all personal use of vehicles, including commuting, by your employees?		
35 Do you maintain a written policy statement that prohibits personal use of vehicles, except commuting, by your employees? (See instructions for vehicles used by corporate officers, directors, or 1% or more owners.)		
36 Do you treat all use of vehicles by employees as personal use?		
37 Do you provide more than five vehicles to your employees and retain the information received from your employees concerning the use of the vehicles?		
38 Do you meet the requirements concerning qualified automobile demonstration use (see instructions)? . .		

Note: *If your answer to 34, 35, 36, 37, or 38 is "Yes," you need not complete Section B for the covered vehicles.*

Part VI — Amortization

(a) Description of costs	(b) Date amortization begins	(c) Amortizable amount	(d) Code section	(e) Amortization period or percentage	(f) Amortization for this year
39 Amortization of costs that begins during your 1993 tax year:					

40 Amortization of costs that began before 1993 . . . . **40**

41 Total. Enter here and on "Other Deductions" or "Other Expenses" line of your return . . . **41**

Form **4626**

Department of the Treasury
Internal Revenue Service

Alternative Minimum Tax—Corporations
(including environmental tax)
▶ See separate instructions.
▶ Attach to the corporation's tax return.

OMB No. 1545-0175

1993

Name | Employer identification number

1	Taxable income or (loss) before net operating loss deduction. (**Important:** See instructions if the corporation is subject to the environmental tax.)	**1**	
2	**Adjustments:**		
a	Depreciation of tangible property placed in service after 1986	**2a**	
b	Amortization of certified pollution control facilities placed in service after 1986.	**2b**	
c	Amortization of mining exploration and development costs paid or incurred after 1986 .	**2c**	
d	Amortization of circulation expenditures paid or incurred after 1986 (personal holding companies only)	**2d**	
e	Basis adjustments in determining gain or loss from sale or exchange of property .	**2e**	
f	Long-term contracts entered into after February 28, 1986.	**2f**	
g	Installment sales of certain property	**2g**	
h	Merchant marine capital construction funds	**2h**	
i	Section 833(b) deduction (Blue Cross, Blue Shield, and similar type organizations only) .	**2i**	
j	Tax shelter farm activities (personal service corporations only)	**2j**	
k	Passive activities (closely held corporations and personal service corporations only)	**2k**	
l	Certain loss limitations	**2l**	
m	Other adjustments	**2m**	
n	Combine lines 2a through 2m	**2n**	
3	**Tax preference items:**		
a	Depletion	**3a**	
b	Tax-exempt interest from private activity bonds issued after August 7, 1986	**3b**	
c	Charitable contributions	**3c**	
d	Intangible drilling costs	**3d**	
e	Reserves for losses on bad debts of financial institutions	**3e**	
f	Accelerated depreciation of real property placed in service before 1987 . . .	**3f**	
g	Accelerated depreciation of leased personal property placed in service before 1987 (personal holding companies only).	**3g**	
h	Add lines 3a through 3g	**3h**	
4	Preadjustment alternative minimum taxable income (AMTI). Combine lines 1, 2n, and 3h	**4**	
5	**Adjusted current earnings (ACE) adjustment:**		
a	Enter the corporation's ACE from line 10 of the worksheet on page 8 of the instructions	**5a**	
b	Subtract line 4 from line 5a. If line 4 exceeds line 5a, enter the difference as a negative number (see instructions for examples)	**5b**	
c	Multiply line 5b by 75% and enter the result as a positive number	**5c**	
d	Enter the excess, if any, of the corporation's total increases in AMTI from prior year ACE adjustments over its total reductions in AMTI from prior year ACE adjustments (see instructions). **Note:** *You **must** enter an amount on line 5d (even if line 5b is positive)*	**5d**	
e	ACE adjustment: ● If you entered a positive number or zero on line 5b, enter the amount from line 5c on line 5e as a positive amount. ● If you entered a negative number on line 5b, enter the smaller of line 5c or line 5d on line 5e as a negative amount.	**5e**	
6	Combine lines 4 and 5e. If zero or less, stop here (the corporation is not subject to the alternative minimum tax).	**6**	
7	Alternative tax net operating loss deduction (see instructions)	**7**	
8	**Alternative minimum taxable income.** Subtract line 7 from line 6.	**8**	

For Paperwork Reduction Act Notice, see separate instructions.   Cat. No. 12955I   Form **4626** (1993)

9	Enter the amount from line 8 (alternative minimum taxable income)		**9**
10	**Exemption phase-out computation** (if line 9 is $310,000 or more, skip lines 10a and 10b and enter -0- on line 10c):		
a	Subtract $150,000 from line 9 (if you are completing this line for a member of a controlled group of corporations, see instructions). If the result is zero or less, enter -0-	**10a**	
b	Multiply line 10a by 25%	**10b**	
c	Exemption. Subtract line 10b from $40,000 (if you are completing this line for a member of a controlled group of corporations, see instructions). If the result is zero or less, enter -0-		**10c**
11	Subtract line 10c from line 9. If the result is zero or less, enter -0-		**11**
12	Multiply line 11 by 20%		**12**
13	Alternative minimum tax foreign tax credit. (See instructions for limitations.)		**13**
14	Tentative minimum tax. Subtract line 13 from line 12		**14**
15	Regular tax liability before all credits except the foreign tax credit and possessions tax credit . . .		**15**
16	**Alternative minimum tax.** Subtract line 15 from line 14. If the result is zero or less, enter -0-. Also enter the result on the line provided on the corporation's income tax return (e.g., if you are filing Form 1120 for 1993, enter this amount on line 9a, Schedule J)		**16**
17	**Environmental tax.** Subtract $2,000,000 from line 6 (computed without regard to the corporation's environmental tax deduction) and multiply the excess, if any, by 0.12% (.0012). Enter the result here and on the line provided on the corporation's income tax return (e.g., if you are filing Form 1120 for 1993, enter this amount on line 9b, Schedule J). If you are completing this line for a member of a controlled group of corporations, see instructions.		**17**

Form **4684**

Department of the Treasury
Internal Revenue Service

Casualties and Thefts

▶ See separate instructions.
▶ Attach to your tax return.
▶ Use a separate Form 4684 for each different casualty or theft.

OMB No. 1545-0177

19 93

Attachment
Sequence No. **26**

Name(s) shown on tax return

Identifying number

SECTION A—Personal Use Property (Use this section to report casualties and thefts of property **not** used in a trade or business or for income-producing purposes.)

1 Description of properties (show type, location, and date acquired for each):

Property **A** ....

Property **B** ....

Property **C** ....

Property **D** ....

		Properties (Use a separate column for each property lost or damaged from one casualty or theft.)			
		A	**B**	**C**	**D**
2	Cost or other basis of each property **2**				
3	Insurance or other reimbursement (whether or not you filed a claim). See instructions . . . . . **3** **Note:** *If line 2 is **more than** line 3, skip line 4.*				
4	Gain from casualty or theft. If line 3 is **more than** line 2, enter the difference here and skip lines 5 through 9 for that column. See instructions if line 3 includes insurance or other reimbursement you did not claim, or you received payment for your loss in a later tax year **4**				
5	Fair market value **before** casualty or theft . . . **5**				
6	Fair market value **after** casualty or theft **6**				
7	Subtract line 6 from line 5 . . . . **7**				
8	Enter the **smaller** of line 2 or line 7 . . . . . **8**				
9	Subtract line 3 from line 8. If zero or less, enter -0- **9**				

10	Casualty or theft loss. Add the amounts on line 9. Enter the total	**10**	
11	Enter the amount from line 10 or $100, whichever is **smaller**	**11**	
12	Subtract line 11 from line 10 . . . . **Caution:** *Use only one Form 4684 for lines 13 through 18.*	**12**	
13	Add the amounts on line 12 of all Forms 4684	**13**	
14	Combine the amounts from line 4 of all Forms 4684	**14**	
15	• If line 14 is **more than** line 13, enter the difference here and on Schedule D. Do not complete the rest of this section (see instructions).		
	• If line 14 is **less than** line 13, enter -0- here and continue with the form.	**15**	
	• If line 14 is **equal to** line 13, enter -0- here. Do not complete the rest of this section.		
16	If line 14 is **less than** line 13, enter the difference	**16**	
17	Enter 10% of your adjusted gross income (Form 1040, line 32). Estates and trusts, see instructions	**17**	
18	Subtract line 17 from line 16. If zero or less, enter -0-. Also enter result on Schedule A (Form 1040), line 17. Estates and trusts, enter on the "Other deductions" line of your tax return	**18**	

For Paperwork Reduction Act Notice, see page 1 of separate instructions.   Cat. No. 12997O   Form **4684** (1993)

Form 4684 (1993)   Attachment Sequence No. **26**   Page **2**

Name(s) shown on tax return. Do not enter name and identifying number if shown on other side.	**Identifying number**

SECTION B—Business and Income-Producing Property (Use this section to report casualties and thefts of property used in a trade or business or for income-producing purposes.)

Part I   **Casualty or Theft Gain or Loss** (Use a separate Part I for each casualty or theft.)

19   Description of properties (show type, location, and date acquired for each):

Property **A** ....

Property **B** ....

Property **C** ....

Property **D** ....

Properties (Use a separate column for each property lost or damaged from one casualty or theft.)

		A	B	C	D
20	Cost or adjusted basis of each property				
21	Insurance or other reimbursement (whether or not you filed a claim). See the instructions for line 3 **Note:** *If line 20 is* **more than** *line 21, skip line 22.*				
22	Gain from casualty or theft. If line 21 is **more than** line 20, enter the difference here and on line 29 or line 34, column **(c)**, except as provided in the instructions for line 33. Also, skip lines 23 through 27 for that column. See the instructions for line 4 if line 21 includes insurance or other reimbursement you did not claim, or you received payment for your loss in a later tax year				
23	Fair market value **before** casualty or theft . . .				
24	Fair market value **after** casualty or theft				
25	Subtract line 24 from line 23				
26	Enter the **smaller** of line 20 or line 25				
	Note: *If the property was totally destroyed by casualty or lost from theft, enter on line 26 the amount from line 20.*				
27	Subtract line 21 from line 26. If zero or less, enter -0-				
28	Casualty or theft loss. Add the amounts on line 27. Enter the total here and on line 29 **or** line 34 (see instructions).	**28**			

Part II   **Summary of Gains and Losses** (from separate Parts I)

(a) Identify casualty or theft	**(b)** Losses from casualties or thefts		**(c)** Gains from casualties or thefts includible in income
	(i) Trade, business, rental or royalty property	*(ii)* Income-producing property	

Casualty or Theft of Property Held One Year or Less

29		( )	( )	
		( )	( )	
30	Totals. Add the amounts on line 29 . . . . **30**	( )	( )	

31   Combine line 30, columns (b)(i) and (c). Enter the net gain or (loss) here and on Form 4797, line 15. If Form 4797 is not otherwise required, see instructions **31**

32   Enter the amount from line 30, column (b)(ii) here and on Schedule A (Form 1040), line 20. Partnerships, S corporations, estates and trusts, see instructions **32**

Casualty or Theft of Property Held More Than One Year

33	Casualty or theft gains from Form 4797, line 34	**33**	
34			
		( ) ( )	
		( ) ( )	
35	Total losses. Add amounts on line 34, columns (b)(i) and (b)(ii) . . . **35** ( ) ( )		
36	Total gains. Add lines 33 and 34, column (c)	**36**	
37	Add amounts on line 35, columns (b)(i) and (b)(ii)	**37**	

38   If the loss on line 37 is **more than** the gain on line 36:

a   Combine line 35, column (b)(i) and line 36, and enter the net gain or (loss) here. Partnerships and S corporations see the note below. All others enter this amount on Form 4797, line 15. If Form 4797 is not otherwise required, see instructions **38a**

b   Enter the amount from line 35, column (b)(ii) here. Partnerships and S corporations see the note below. Individuals enter this amount on Schedule A (Form 1040), line 20. Estates and trusts, enter on the "Other deductions" line of your tax return   **38b**

39   If the loss on line 37 is **equal to** or **less than** the gain on line 36, combine these lines and enter here. Partnerships, see the note below. All others, enter this amount on Form 4797, line 3 . . . .   **39**

Note: *Partnerships, enter the amount from line 38a, 38b, or line 39 on Form 1065, Schedule K, line 7. S corporations, enter the amount from line 38a or 38b on Form 1120S, Schedule K, line 6.*

Form **4797**	**Sales of Business Property**	OMB No. 1545-0184
Department of the Treasury Internal Revenue Service (O)	(Also Involuntary Conversions and Recapture Amounts Under Sections 179 and 280F(b)(2)) ▶ **Attach to your tax return.** ▶ **See separate instructions.**	**1993** Attachment Sequence No. **27**

Name(s) shown on return	Identifying number

1 Enter here the gross proceeds from the sale or exchange of real estate reported to you for 1993 on Form(s) 1099-S (or a substitute statement) that you will be including on line 2, 11, or 22 . . . . **1**

Part I **Sales or Exchanges of Property Used in a Trade or Business and Involuntary Conversions From Other Than Casualty or Theft—Property Held More Than 1 Year**

(a) Description of property	**(b)** Date acquired (mo., day, yr.)	**(c)** Date sold (mo., day, yr.)	**(d)** Gross sales price	**(e)** Depreciation allowed or allowable since acquisition	**(f)** Cost or other basis, plus improvements and expense of sale	**(g)** LOSS ((f) minus the sum of (d) and (e))	**(h)** GAIN ((d) plus (e) minus (f))
2							

3 Gain, if any, from Form 4684, line 39 . . . . **3**

4 Section 1231 gain from installment sales from Form 6252, line 26 or 37 . . . . . **4**

5 Section 1231 gain or (loss) from like-kind exchanges from Form 8824 . . . . . . **5**

6 Gain, if any, from line 34, from other than casualty or theft **6**

7 Add lines 2 through 6 in columns (g) and (h) . . . . **7** ( )

8 Combine columns (g) and (h) of line 7. Enter gain or (loss) here, and on the appropriate line as follows: **8**

> **Partnerships**—Enter the gain or (loss) on Form 1065, Schedule K, line 6. Skip lines 9, 10, 12, and 13 below.
>
> **S corporations**—Report the gain or (loss) following the instructions for Form 1120S, Schedule K, lines 5 and 6. Skip lines 9, 10, 12, and 13 below, unless line 8 is a gain and the S corporation is subject to the capital gains tax.
>
> **All others**—If line 8 is zero or a loss, enter the amount on line 12 below and skip lines 9 and 10. If line 8 is a gain and you did not have any prior year section 1231 losses, or they were recaptured in an earlier year, enter the gain as a long-term capital gain on Schedule D and skip lines 9, 10, and 13 below.

9 Nonrecaptured net section 1231 losses from prior years (see instructions) **9**

10 Subtract line 9 from line 8. If zero or less, enter -0-. Also enter on the appropriate line as follows (see instructions): **10**

> **S corporations**—Enter this amount (if more than zero) on Schedule D (Form 1120S), line 13, and skip lines 12 and 13 below.
>
> **All others**—If line 10 is zero, enter the amount from line 8 on line 13 below. If line 10 is more than zero, enter the amount from line 9 on line 13 below, and enter the amount from line 10 as a long-term capital gain on Schedule D.

Part II **Ordinary Gains and Losses**

11 Ordinary gains and losses not included on lines 12 through 18 (include property held 1 year or less):

12 Loss, if any, from line 8 . . . . **12**

13 Gain, if any, from line 8, or amount from line 9 if applicable **13**

14 Gain, if any, from line 33 . . . . **14**

15 Net gain or (loss) from Form 4684, lines 31 and 38a **15**

16 Ordinary gain from installment sales from Form 6252, line 25 or 36 . . . . . . **16**

17 Ordinary gain or (loss) from like-kind exchanges from Form 8824 . . . . . . **17**

18 Recapture of section 179 expense deduction for partners and S corporation shareholders from property dispositions by partnerships and S corporations (see instructions) **18**

19 Add lines 11 through 18 in columns (g) and (h) . . . . **19** ( )

20 Combine columns (g) and (h) of line 19. Enter gain or (loss) here, and on the appropriate line as follows: . . . **20**

  a For all except individual returns: Enter the gain or (loss) from line 20 on the return being filed.

  b For individual returns:

  (1) If the loss on line 12 includes a loss from Form 4684, line 35, column (b)(ii), enter that part of the loss here and on line 20 of Schedule A (Form 1040). Identify as from "Form 4797, line 20b(1)." See instructions . . . . **20b(1)**

  (2) Redetermine the gain or (loss) on line 20, excluding the loss, if any, on line 20b(1). Enter here and on Form 1040, line 15 . **20b(2)**

For Paperwork Reduction Act Notice, see page 1 of separate instructions.   Cat. No. 13086I   Form **4797** (1993)

Form 4797 (1993)   Page **2**

Part III Gain From Disposition of Property Under Sections 1245, 1250, 1252, 1254, and 1255

21	(a) Description of section 1245, 1250, 1252, 1254, or 1255 property:	(b) Date acquired (mo., day, yr.)	(c) Date sold (mo., day, yr.)
A			
B			
C			
D			

	Relate lines 21A through 21D to these columns ▶		Property A	Property B	Property C	Property D
22	Gross sales price (**Note:** *See line 1 before completing.*)	22				
23	Cost or other basis plus expense of sale	23				
24	Depreciation (or depletion) allowed or allowable	24				
25	Adjusted basis. Subtract line 24 from line 23	25				
26	Total gain. Subtract line 25 from line 22	26				
27	**If section 1245 property:**					
a	Depreciation allowed or allowable from line 24	27a				
b	Enter the **smaller** of line 26 or 27a	27b				
28	**If section 1250 property:** If straight line depreciation was used, enter -0- on line 28g, except for a corporation subject to section 291.					
a	Additional depreciation after 1975 (see instructions)	28a				
b	Applicable percentage multiplied by the **smaller** of line 26 or line 28a (see instructions)	28b				
c	Subtract line 28a from line 26. If residential rental property or line 26 is not more than line 28a, skip lines 28d and 28e	28c				
d	Additional depreciation after 1969 and before 1976	28d				
e	Enter the **smaller** of line 28c or 28d	28e				
f	Section 291 amount (corporations only)	28f				
g	Add lines 28b, 28e, and 28f	28g				
29	**If section 1252 property:** Skip this section if you did not dispose of farmland or if this form is being completed for a partnership.					
a	Soil, water, and land clearing expenses	29a				
b	Line 29a multiplied by applicable percentage (see instructions)	29b				
c	Enter the **smaller** of line 26 or 29b	29c				
30	**If section 1254 property:**					
a	Intangible drilling and development costs, expenditures for development of mines and other natural deposits, and mining exploration costs (see instructions)	30a				
b	Enter the **smaller** of line 26 or 30a	30b				
31	**If section 1255 property:**					
a	Applicable percentage of payments excluded from income under section 126 (see instructions)	31a				
b	Enter the **smaller** of line 26 or 31a	31b				

Summary of Part III Gains. Complete property columns A through D, through line 31b before going to line 32.

32	Total gains for all properties. Add columns A through D, line 26	32	
33	Add columns A through D, lines 27b, 28g, 29c, 30b, and 31b. Enter here and on line 14	33	
34	Subtract line 33 from line 32. Enter the portion from casualty or theft on Form 4684, line 33. Enter the portion from other than casualty or theft on Form 4797, line 6	34	

Part IV Recapture Amounts Under Sections 179 and 280F(b)(2) When Business Use Drops to 50% or Less
See instructions for Part IV.

			(a) Section 179	(b) Section 280F(b)(2)
35	Section 179 expense deduction or depreciation allowable in prior years	35		
36	Recomputed depreciation (see instructions)	36		
37	Recapture amount. Subtract line 36 from line 35. See instructions for where to report	37		

Form **4868**

Department of the Treasury
Internal Revenue Service

Application for Automatic Extension of Time
To File U.S. Individual Income Tax Return
▶ This is not an extension of time to pay your tax.
▶ See separate instructions.

OMB No. 1545-0188

19**93**

Please Type or Print	Your first name and initial	Last name	Your social security number
	If a joint return, spouse's first name and initial	Last name	Spouse's social security number
	Home address (number, street, and apt. no. or rural route). If you have a P.O. box, see the instructions.		
	City, town or post office, state, and ZIP code		

I request an automatic 4-month extension of time to August 15, 1994, to file Form 1040EZ, Form 1040A, or Form 1040 for the calendar year 1993 or to _____ , 19 ____ , for the fiscal tax year ending _____ , 19 ____ .

Part I   Individual Income Tax—You must complete this part.

1   **Total tax liability for 1993.** This is the amount you expect to enter on Form 1040EZ, line 8; Form 1040A, line 27; or Form 1040, line 53. If you expect this amount to be zero, enter -0-.   **1**

    Caution: *You MUST enter an amount on line 1 or your extension will be denied. You can estimate this amount, but be as exact as you can with the information you have. If we later find that your estimate was not reasonable, the extension will be null and void.*

2   **Total payments for 1993.** This is the amount you expect to enter on Form 1040EZ, line 7; Form 1040A, line 28d; or Form 1040, line 60 . . . .   **2**

3   **BALANCE DUE.** Subtract line 2 from line 1. If line 2 is more than line 1, enter -0-. For details on how to pay, including what to write on your payment, see the instructions . . . . . ▶   **3**

Part II   Gift or Generation-Skipping Transfer (GST) Tax—Complete this part if you expect to owe either tax.

Caution: *Do not include income tax on lines 5a and 5b. See the instructions.*

4   If you or your spouse plan to file a gift tax return (Form 709 or 709-A) for 1993, generally due by April 15, 1994, see the instructions and check here . . .   Yourself ▶ ☐   Spouse ▶ ☐

5a   Enter the amount of gift or GST tax **you** are paying with this form **5a**

  b   Enter the amount of gift or GST tax **your spouse** is paying with this form **5b**

Signature and Verification

Under penalties of perjury, I declare that I have examined this form, including accompanying schedules and statements, and to the best of my knowledge and belief, it is true, correct, and complete; and, if prepared by someone other than the taxpayer, that I am authorized to prepare this form.

▶ _____   _____   ▶ _____   _____
    Your signature   Date   Spouse's signature, if filing jointly   Date

▶ _____   _____
    Preparer's signature (other than taxpayer)   Date

If you want correspondence regarding this extension to be sent to you at an address other than that shown above or to an agent acting for you, please enter the name of the agent and/or the address where it should be sent.

Please Type or Print	Name
	Number and street (include suite, room, or apt. no.) or P.O. box number if mail is not delivered to street address
	City, town or post office, state, and ZIP code

For Paperwork Reduction Act Notice, see separate instructions.   Cat. No. 13141W   Form **4868** (1993)

Form **4952**

Department of the Treasury
Internal Revenue Service

Investment Interest Expense Deduction

▶ **Attach to your tax return.**

OMB No. 1545-0191

19**93**

Attachment
Sequence No. **12A**

Name(s) shown on return

Identifying number

Part I — Total Investment Interest Expense

1	Investment interest expense paid or accrued in 1993. See instructions	**1**
2	Disallowed investment interest expense from 1992 Form 4952, line 5	**2**
3	**Total investment interest expense.** Add lines 1 and 2	**3**

Part II — Net Investment Income

4a	Gross income from property held for investment (excluding any net gain from the disposition of property held for investment)		**4a**
b	Net gain from the disposition of property held for investment . . .	**4b**	
c	Net capital gain from the disposition of property held for investment	**4c**	
d	Subtract line 4c from line 4b. If zero or less, enter -0-		**4d**
e	Enter all or part of the amount on line 4c that you elect to include in investment income. Do not enter more than the amount on line 4b. See instructions . . . . ▶		**4e**
f	Investment income. Add lines 4a, 4d, and 4e. See instructions		**4f**
5	Investment expenses. See instructions		**5**
6	**Net investment income.** Subtract line 5 from line 4f. If zero or less, enter -0-		**6**

Part III — Investment Interest Expense Deduction

7	Disallowed investment interest expense to be carried forward to 1994. Subtract line 6 from line 3. If zero or less, enter -0-	**7**
8	**Investment interest expense deduction.** Enter the smaller of line 3 or 6. See instructions . .	**8**

Paperwork Reduction Act Notice

We ask for the information on this form to carry out the Internal Revenue laws of the United States. You are required to give us the information. We need it to ensure that you are complying with these laws and to allow us to figure and collect the right amount of tax.

The time needed to complete and file this form will vary depending on individual circumstances. The estimated average time is:

Recordkeeping	13 min.
Learning about the law or the form	15 min.
Preparing the form	21 min.
Copying, assembling, and sending the form to the IRS . .	10 min.

If you have comments concerning the accuracy of these time estimates or suggestions for making this form more simple, we would be happy to hear from you. You can write to both the IRS and the Office of Management and Budget at the addresses listed in the instructions for the tax return with which this form is filed.

General Instructions

Section references are to the Internal Revenue Code unless otherwise noted.

A Change To Note

Beginning in 1993, for purposes of computing your investment interest expense deduction, net capital gain from the disposition of property held for investment is excluded from investment income. However, you may elect to include in your investment income all or

part of the net capital gain from the disposition of property held for investment if you also reduce the amount of net capital gain eligible for the 28% maximum capital gains rate by the same amount. See the instructions for line 4e on page 2.

Purpose of Form

Interest expense paid by an individual, estate, or a trust on a loan that is allocable to property held for investment may not be fully deductible in the current year. Form 4952 is used to figure the amount of investment interest expense deductible for the current year and the amount, if any, to carry forward to future years.

For more details, get **Pub. 550,** Investment Income and Expenses.

Form **4952** (1993)

Who Must File

If you are an individual, estate, or a trust, and you claim a deduction for investment interest expense, you must complete and attach Form 4952 to your tax return, unless **all** of the following apply:

- Your only investment income was from interest or dividends,

- You have no other deductible expenses connected with the production of interest or dividends,

- Your investment interest expense is not more than your investment income, and

- You have no carryovers of investment interest expense from 1992.

Allocation of Interest Expense Under Temporary Regulations Section 1.163-8T

If you paid or accrued interest on a loan and you used the proceeds of the loan for more than one purpose, you may have to allocate the interest paid. This is necessary because of the different rules that apply to investment interest, personal interest, trade or business interest, home mortgage interest, and passive activity interest. See Pub. 550.

Specific Instructions

Part I—Total Investment Interest Expense

Line 1

Enter the investment interest paid or accrued during the tax year, regardless of when the indebtedness was incurred. Investment interest is interest paid or accrued on a loan (or part of a loan) that is allocable to property held for investment (as defined below).

Be sure to include investment interest expense reported to you on Schedule K-1 from a partnership or an S corporation. Include amortization of bond premium on taxable bonds purchased after October 22, 1986, but before January 1, 1988, unless you elected to offset amortizable bond premium against the interest payments on the bond. A taxable bond is a bond on which the interest is includible in gross income.

Investment interest expense does not include the following:

- Home mortgage interest.

- Interest expense that is properly allocable to a passive activity. A passive activity is any business activity in which you **do not** materially participate and any rental activity regardless of participation. See the separate instructions for **Form 8582,** Passive Activity Loss Limitations, for the material participation tests and the definition of "rental activity."

- Any interest expense that is capitalized, such as construction interest subject to section 263A.

- Interest expense related to tax-exempt interest income under section 265.

Property held for investment.—Property held for investment includes property that produces income (unless derived in the ordinary course of a trade or business) from interest, dividends, annuities, or royalties; and gains from the disposition of property that produces those types of income or is held for investment. However, it does not include an interest in a passive activity.

Property held for investment also includes an interest in an activity of conducting a trade or business in which you did not materially participate and that is not a passive activity. For example, a working interest in an oil or gas property that is not a passive activity is property held for investment if you did not materially participate in the activity.

Part II—Net Investment Income

Line 4a

Gross income from property held for investment to be entered on line 4a includes income (unless derived in the ordinary course of a trade or business) from:

- Interest,

- Dividends (except Alaska Permanent Fund dividends),

- Annuities, and

- Royalties.

If you are filing **Form 8814,** Parents' Election To Report Child's Interest and Dividends, part or all of your child's income may be included on line 4a. See Form 8814 for details.

Also, include on line 4a net income from the following passive activities:

- Rental of substantially nondepreciable property,

- Equity-financed lending activities, and

- Acquisition of certain interests in a pass-through entity licensing intangible property.

See Regulations section 1.469-2(f)(10) for details.

Net passive income from a passive activity of a publicly traded partnership (as defined in section 469(k)(2)) is also included in investment income. See Notice 88-75, 1988-2 C.B. 386, for details.

Include investment income reported to you on Schedule K-1 from a partnership or an S corporation. Also include net investment income from an estate or a trust.

Do not include on line 4a any net gain from the disposition of property held for investment. Instead, enter this amount on line 4b.

Line 4b

Net gain from the disposition of property held for investment is the excess, if any, of total gains over total losses from the disposition of property held for investment. When figuring this amount, be sure to include capital gain distributions from mutual funds.

Line 4c

Net capital gain from the disposition of property held for investment is the excess, if any, of net long-term capital gain over net short-term capital loss from the disposition of property held for investment. When figuring this amount, be sure to include capital gain distributions from mutual funds.

Line 4e

Enter all or part of the amount on line 4c, but not more than the amount on line 4b, that you choose to include in investment income. If you make an entry on line 4e and you are using the **Schedule D Tax Worksheet** on page D-4 of the Form 1040 instructions (or Part VI of Schedule D (Form 1041)), you must also reduce the amount of net capital gain eligible for the 28% maximum capital gains

rate by the amount on this line. Therefore, you should consider the effect on your tax using the maximum capital gains rate before making an entry on this line.

Line 5

Investment expenses are your allowed deductions, other than interest expense, directly connected with the production of investment income. For example, depreciation or depletion allowed on assets that produce investment income is an investment expense.

Be sure to include investment expenses reported to you on Schedule K-1 from a partnership or an S corporation.

Investment expenses do not include any deductions taken into account in determining your income or loss from a passive activity.

If you have investment expenses that are included as a miscellaneous itemized deduction on Schedule A (Form 1040), line 20, you may not have to use all of the amount for purposes of Form 4952, line 5. The 2% adjusted gross income limitation on Schedule A may reduce the amount.

To figure the amount to use, compare the amount of the investment expenses included on Schedule A, line 20, with the total miscellaneous expenses on Schedule A, line 24. The smaller of the investment expenses included on line 20 or the total of line 24 is the amount to use to figure the investment expenses from Schedule A for line 5.

Example. Assume Schedule A, line 20, includes investment expenses of $3,000, and line 24 is $1,300 after the 2% adjusted gross income limitation. Investment expenses from Schedule A of $1,300 are used to figure the amount of investment expenses for line 5. If investment expenses of $800 were included on line 20 and line 24 was $1,300, investment expenses from Schedule A of $800 would be used.

Part III—Investment Interest Expense Deduction

Line 8

This is the amount you may deduct as investment interest expense.

Individuals.—Enter the amount from line 8 on Schedule A (Form 1040), line 11, even if all or part of it is attributable to a partnership or an S corporation. However, if any portion of this amount is attributable to royalties, enter that part of the interest expense on Schedule E (Form 1040).

Estates and trusts.—Enter the amount from line 8 on Form 1041, line 10.

Form 6198.—If any portion of the deductible investment interest expense is attributable to an activity for which you are not at risk, you must also use **Form 6198,** At-Risk Limitations, to figure your deductible investment interest expense. Enter the portion attributable to the at-risk activity on Form 6198, line 4. Reduce Form 4952, line 8, by the amount entered on Form 6198. See Form 6198 and its instructions for more details, especially the instructions for line 4 of that form.

Alternative minimum tax.—Deductible interest expense is an adjustment for alternative minimum tax purposes. Get **Form 6251,** Alternative Minimum Tax—Individuals, or Form 1041, Schedule H, for estates and trusts.

Form **4972**	**Tax on Lump-Sum Distributions**	OMB No. 1545-0193

Form **4972**

Department of the Treasury
Internal Revenue Service

Tax on Lump-Sum Distributions
(Use This Form Only for Lump-Sum Distributions From
Qualified Retirement Plans)
▶ **Attach to Form 1040 or Form 1041.** ▶ **See separate instructions.**

OMB No. 1545-0193

1993

Attachment
Sequence No. **28**

Name of recipient of distribution

Identifying number

Part I	Complete this part to see if you qualify to use Form 4972.		Yes	No
1	Did you roll over any part of the distribution? If "Yes," do not complete the rest of this form	**1**		
2	Was the retirement plan participant born before 1936? If "No," do not complete the rest of this form	**2**		
3	Was this a lump-sum distribution from a qualified pension, profit-sharing, or stock bonus plan? (See **Distributions That Qualify for the 20% Capital Gain Election or for 5- or 10-Year Averaging** in the instructions.) If "No," do not complete the rest of this form	**3**		
4	Was the participant in the plan for at least 5 years before the year of the distribution?	**4**		
5	Was this distribution paid to you as a beneficiary of a plan participant who died?	**5**		
	If you answered "No" to both questions 4 **and** 5, do not complete the rest of this form.			
6	Was the plan participant:			
a	An employee who received the distribution because he or she quit, retired, was laid off, or was fired?	**6a**		
b	Self-employed or an owner-employee who became permanently and totally disabled before the distribution?	**6b**		
c	Age 59½ or older at the time of the distribution?	**6c**		
	If you answered "No" to question 5 and **all** parts of question 6, do not complete the rest of this form.			
7	Did you use Form 4972 in a prior year for any distribution received after 1986 for the same plan participant, including yourself, for whom the 1993 distribution was made? If "Yes," do not complete the rest of this form	**7**		

If you qualify to use this form, you may choose to use Part II, Part III, or Part IV; **or** Part II and Part III; **or** Part II and Part IV.

Part II	Complete this part to choose the 20% capital gain election. (See instructions.)		
8	Capital gain part from box 3 of Form 1099-R. (See instructions.)	**8**	
9	Multiply line 8 by 20% (.20) and enter here. If you do not choose to use Part III or Part IV, also enter the amount on Form 1040, line 39, or Form 1041, Schedule G, line 1b	**9**	

Part III	Complete this part to choose the 5-year averaging method. (See instructions.)		
10	Ordinary income from Form 1099-R, box 2a minus box 3. If you did not complete Part II, enter the taxable amount from box 2a of Form 1099-R. (See instructions.)	**10**	
11	Death benefit exclusion. (See instructions.)	**11**	
12	Total taxable amount—Subtract line 11 from line 10	**12**	
13	Current actuarial value of annuity, if applicable (from Form 1099-R, box 8)	**13**	
14	Adjusted total taxable amount—Add lines 12 and 13. If this amount is $70,000 or more, skip lines 15 through 18, and enter this amount on line 19	**14**	
15	Multiply line 14 by 50% (.50), but **do not** enter more than $10,000 .	**15**	
16	Subtract $20,000 from line 14. If line 14 is $20,000 or less, enter -0-	**16**	
17	Multiply line 16 by 20% (.20)	**17**	
18	Minimum distribution allowance—Subtract line 17 from line 15	**18**	
19	Subtract line 18 from line 14	**19**	
20	Federal estate tax attributable to lump-sum distribution. Do not deduct on Form 1040 or Form 1041 the amount attributable to the ordinary income entered on line 10. (See instructions.)	**20**	
21	Subtract line 20 from line 19	**21**	
22	Multiply line 21 by 20% (.20)	**22**	
23	Tax on amount on line 22. See the Tax Rate Schedule for the 5-Year Method in the instructions	**23**	
24	Multiply line 23 by five (5). If line 13 is blank, skip lines 25 through 30, and enter this amount on line 31	**24**	
25	Divide line 13 by line 14 and enter the result as a decimal. (See instructions.)	**25**	× .
26	Multiply line 18 by the decimal amount on line 25	**26**	
27	Subtract line 26 from line 13	**27**	
28	Multiply line 27 by 20% (.20)	**28**	
29	Tax on amount on line 28. See the Tax Rate Schedule for the 5-Year Method in the instructions	**29**	
30	Multiply line 29 by five (5)	**30**	
31	Subtract line 30 from line 24. (Multiple recipients, see instructions.)	**31**	
32	Tax on lump-sum distribution—Add Part II, line 9, and Part III, line 31. Enter on Form 1040, line 39, or Form 1041, Schedule G, line 1b ▶	**32**	

For Paperwork Reduction Act Notice, see separate instructions. Cat. No. 13187U Form **4972** (1993)

Part IV   **Complete this part to choose the 10-year averaging method.** (See instructions.)

33	Ordinary income part from Form 1099-R, box 2a minus box 3. If you did not complete Part II, enter the taxable amount from box 2a of Form 1099-R. (See instructions.)	33	
34	Death benefit exclusion. (See instructions.)	34	
35	Total taxable amount—Subtract line 34 from line 33	35	
36	Current actuarial value of annuity, if applicable (from Form 1099-R, box 8)	36	
37	Adjusted total taxable amount—Add lines 35 and 36. If this amount is $70,000 or more, skip lines 38 through 41, and enter this amount on line 42	37	
38	Multiply line 37 by 50% (.50), but **do not** enter more than $10,000 .	38		
39	Subtract $20,000 from line 37. If line 37 is $20,000 or less, enter -0-	39		
40	Multiply line 39 by 20% (.20)	40		
41	Minimum distribution allowance—Subtract line 40 from line 38	41	
42	Subtract line 41 from line 37	42	
43	Federal estate tax attributable to lump-sum distribution. Do not deduct on Form 1040 or Form 1041 the amount attributable to the ordinary income entered on line 33. (See instructions.) . .	43	
44	Subtract line 43 from line 42	44	
45	Multiply line 44 by 10% (.10)	45	
46	Tax on amount on line 45. See the Tax Rate Schedule for the 10-Year Method in the instructions	46	
47	Multiply line 46 by ten (10). If line 36 is blank, skip lines 48 through 53, and enter this amount on line 54	47	
48	Divide line 36 by line 37 and enter the result as a decimal. (See instructions.)	48	× .
49	Multiply line 41 by the decimal amount on line 48	49	
50	Subtract line 49 from line 36	50	
51	Multiply line 50 by 10% (.10)	51	
52	Tax on amount on line 51. See the Tax Rate Schedule for the 10-Year Method in the instructions	52	
53	Multiply line 52 by ten (10)	53	
54	Subtract line 53 from line 47. (Multiple recipients, see instructions.)	54	
55	Tax on lump-sum distribution—Add Part II, line 9, and Part IV, line 54. Enter on Form 1040, line 39, or Form 1041, Schedule G, line 1b . . . . ▶	55	

Form **6251**

Department of the Treasury
Internal Revenue Service (O)

Alternative Minimum Tax—Individuals

▶ See separate instructions.

▶ Attach to Form 1040 or Form 1040NR.

OMB No. 1545-0227

1993

Attachment
Sequence No. **32**

Name(s) shown on Form 1040

Your social security number

Part I Adjustments and Preferences

1	If you itemized deductions on Schedule A (Form 1040), go to line 2. If you did not itemize deductions, enter your standard deduction from Form 1040, line 34, and skip to line 6	1
2	Medical and dental expenses. See instructions	2
3	Taxes. Enter the amount from Schedule A, line 8	3
4	Certain interest on a home mortgage not used to buy, build, or improve your home	4
5	Miscellaneous itemized deductions. Enter the amount from Schedule A, line 24	5
6	Refund of taxes. Enter any tax refund from Form 1040, line 10 or 22	6 ( )
7	Investment interest. Enter difference between regular tax and AMT deduction	7
8	Post-1986 depreciation. Enter difference between regular tax and AMT depreciation	8
9	Adjusted gain or loss. Enter difference between AMT and regular tax gain or loss	9
10	Incentive stock options. Enter excess of AMT income over regular tax income	10
11	Passive activities. Enter difference between AMT and regular tax income or loss	11
12	Beneficiaries of estates and trusts. Enter the amount from Schedule K-1 (Form 1041), line 8	12
13	Tax-exempt interest from private activity bonds issued after 8/7/86	13

14 Other. Enter the amount, if any, for each item and enter the total on line 14.

a	Charitable contributions	g	Long-term contracts	
b	Circulation expenditures	h	Loss limitations	
c	Depletion	i	Mining costs	
d	Depreciation (pre-1987)	j	Pollution control facilities	
e	Installment sales	k	Research and experimental	
f	Intangible drilling costs	l	Tax shelter farm activities	
		m	Related adjustments	14

15	**Total Adjustments and Preferences.** Combine lines 1 through 14 ▶	15

Part II Alternative Minimum Taxable Income

16	Enter the amount from **Form 1040, line 35.** If less than zero, enter as a (loss) ▶	16
17	Net operating loss deduction, if any, from Form 1040, line 22. Enter as a positive amount	17
18	If Form 1040, line 32, is over $108,450 (over $54,225 if married filing separately), enter your itemized deductions limitation, if any, from line 9 of the worksheet for Schedule A, line 26	18 ( )
19	Combine lines 15 through 18 ▶	19
20	Alternative tax net operating loss deduction. See instructions	20
21	**Alternative Minimum Taxable Income.** Subtract line 20 from line 19. (If married filing separately and line 21 is more than $165,000, see instructions.) ▶	21

Part III Exemption Amount and Alternative Minimum Tax

22 **Exemption Amount.** (If this form is for a child under age 14, see instructions.)

If your filing status is:	And line 21 is not over:	Enter on line 22:	
Single or head of household	$112,500	$33,750	
Married filing jointly or qualifying widow(er)	150,000	45,000	22
Married filing separately	75,000	22,500	

If line 21 is **over** the amount shown above for your filing status, see instructions.

23	Subtract line 22 from line 21. If zero or less, enter -0- here and on lines 26 and 28 ▶	23
24	If line 23 is $175,000 or less ($87,500 or less if married filing separately), multiply line 23 by 26% (.26). Otherwise, see instructions	24
25	Alternative minimum tax foreign tax credit. See instructions	25
26	Tentative minimum tax. Subtract line 25 from line 24 ▶	26
27	Enter your tax from Form 1040, line 38 (plus any amount from Form 4970 included on Form 1040, line 39), minus any foreign tax credit from Form 1040, line 43	27
28	**Alternative Minimum Tax.** (If this form is for a child under age 14, see instructions.) Subtract line 27 from line 26. If zero or less, enter -0-. Enter here and on Form 1040, line 48 ▶	28

For Paperwork Reduction Act Notice, see separate instructions.   Cat. No. 13600G   Form **6251** (1993)

Form **6252**	**Installment Sale Income**	OMB No. 1545-0228
Department of the Treasury Internal Revenue Service	▶ See separate instructions. ▶ Attach to your tax return. ▶ Use a separate form for each sale or other disposition of property on the installment method.	**1993** Attachment Sequence No. **79**

Name(s) shown on return	Identifying number

1 Description of property ▶ ....

2a Date acquired (month, day, and year) ▶ |___/___/___| **b** Date sold (month, day, and year) ▶ |___/___/___|

3 Was the property sold to a related party after May 14, 1980? See instructions . . . . ☐ Yes ☐ No

4 If the answer to question 3 is "Yes," was the property a marketable security? If "Yes," complete Part III. If "No," complete Part III for the year of sale and for 2 years after the year of sale. . . . . ☐ Yes ☐ No

Part I **Gross Profit and Contract Price.** Complete this part for the year of sale only.

5	Selling price including mortgages and other debts. Do not include interest whether stated or unstated	**5**	
6	Mortgages and other debts the buyer assumed or took the property subject to, but not new mortgages the buyer got from a bank or other source .	**6**	
7	Subtract line 6 from line 5	**7**	
8	Cost or other basis of property sold	**8**	
9	Depreciation allowed or allowable	**9**	
10	Adjusted basis. Subtract line 9 from line 8	**10**	
11	Commissions and other expenses of sale.	**11**	
12	Income recapture from Form 4797, Part III. See instructions . .	**12**	
13	Add lines 10, 11, and 12	**13**	
14	Subtract line 13 from line 5. If zero or less, **stop here.** Do not complete the rest of this form .	**14**	
15	If the property described on line 1 above was your main home, enter the total of lines 14 and 22 from Form 2119. Otherwise, enter -0-.	**15**	
16	**Gross profit.** Subtract line 15 from line 14	**16**	
17	Subtract line 13 from line 6. If zero or less, enter -0- . .	**17**	
18	**Contract price.** Add line 7 and line 17	**18**	

Part II **Installment Sale Income.** Complete this part for the year of sale and any year you receive a payment or have certain debts you must treat as a payment on installment obligations.

19	Gross profit percentage. Divide line 16 by line 18. For years after the year of sale, see instructions	**19**	
20	**For year of sale only—**Enter amount from line 17 above; otherwise, enter -0-	**20**	
21	Payments received during year. See instructions. Do not include interest whether stated or unstated	**21**	
22	Add lines 20 and 21	**22**	
23	Payments received in prior years. See instructions. Do not include interest whether stated or unstated. **23**		
24	**Installment sale income.** Multiply line 22 by line 19	**24**	
25	Part of line 24 that is ordinary income under recapture rules. See instructions	**25**	
26	Subtract line 25 from line 24. Enter here and on Schedule D or Form 4797. See instructions .	**26**	

Part III **Related Party Installment Sale Income.** Do not complete if you received the final payment this tax year.

27 Name, address, and taxpayer identifying number of related party ....

....

28 Did the related party, during this tax year, resell or dispose of the property ("second disposition")? . . . . ☐ Yes ☐ No

29 **If the answer to question 28 is "Yes," complete lines 30 through 37 below unless one of the following conditions is met. Check only the box that applies.**

a ☐ The second disposition was more than 2 years after the first disposition (other than dispositions of marketable securities). If this box is checked, enter the date of disposition (month, day, year) ▶ |___/___/___|

b ☐ The first disposition was a sale or exchange of stock to the issuing corporation.

c ☐ The second disposition was an involuntary conversion where the threat of conversion occurred after the first disposition.

d ☐ The second disposition occurred after the death of the original seller or buyer.

e ☐ It can be established to the satisfaction of the Internal Revenue Service that tax avoidance was not a principal purpose for either of the dispositions. If this box is checked, attach an explanation. See instructions.

30	Selling price of property sold by related party	**30**	
31	Enter contract price from line 18 for year of first sale	**31**	
32	Enter the **smaller** of line 30 or line 31	**32**	
33	Total payments received by the end of your 1993 tax year. Add lines 22 and 23	**33**	
34	Subtract line 33 from line 32. If zero or less, enter -0-	**34**	
35	Multiply line 34 by the gross profit percentage on line 19 for year of first sale	**35**	
36	Part of line 35 that is ordinary income under recapture rules. See instructions	**36**	
37	Subtract line 36 from line 35. Enter here and on Schedule D or Form 4797. See instructions .	**37**	

For Paperwork Reduction Act Notice, see separate instructions.   Cat. No. 13601R   Form **6252** (1993)

Form **7004**
(Rev. October 1991)

Department of the Treasury
Internal Revenue Service

Application for Automatic Extension of Time To File Corporation Income Tax Return

OMB No. 1545-0233
Expires 10-31-94

Name of corporation

Employer identification number

Number, street, and room or suite no. (If a P.O. box, see instructions.)

City or town, state, and ZIP code

Check type of return to be filed:

☐ Form 1120	☐ Form 1120F	☐ Form 1120L	☐ Form 1120-POL	☐ Form 1120S
☐ Form 1120-A	☐ Form 1120-FSC	☐ Form 1120-ND	☐ Form 1120-REIT	☐ Form 990-C
☐ Form 1120-DF	☐ Form 1120-H	☐ Form 1120-PC	☐ Form 1120-RIC	☐ Form 990-T

Form 1120F filers: Check here if you do not have an office or place of business in the United States . . . . ▶ ☐

1a I request an automatic 6-month extension of time until ...., 19......, to file the income tax return of the corporation named above for ▶ ☐ calendar year 19...... or ▶ ☐ tax year beginning ...., 19......, and ending ...., 19...... .

b If this tax year is for less than 12 months, check reason:
☐ Initial return   ☐ Final return   ☐ Change in accounting period   ☐ Consolidated return to be filed

2 If this application also covers subsidiaries to be included in a consolidated return, complete the following:

Name and address of each member of the affiliated group	Employer identification number	Tax period

3	Tentative tax (see instructions).		**3**	
4	**Credits:**			
a	Overpayment credited from prior year.	**4a**		
b	Estimated tax payments for the tax year.	**4b**		
c	Less refund for the tax year applied for on Form 4466	**4c** ( ) Bal ▶	**4d**	
e	Credit from regulated investment companies		**4e**	
f	Credit for Federal tax on fuels		**4f**	
5	Total. Add lines 4d through 4f		**5**	
6	**Balance due.** Subtract line 5 from line 3. **Deposit this amount with a Federal Tax Deposit (FTD) Coupon** (see instructions)		**6**	

Signature.—Under penalties of perjury, I declare that I have been authorized by the above-named corporation to make this application, and to the best of my knowledge and belief, the statements made are true, correct, and complete.

....
(Signature of officer or agent)

....
(Title)

....
(Date)

For Paperwork Reduction Act Notice, see instructions.   Cat. No. 13804A   Form **7004** (Rev. 10-91)

General Instructions

(Section references are to the Internal Revenue Code unless otherwise noted.)

Paperwork Reduction Act Notice.— We ask for the information on this form to carry out the Internal Revenue laws of the United States. You are required to give us the information. We need it to ensure that you are complying with these laws and to allow us to figure and collect the right amount of tax.

The time needed to complete and file this form will vary depending on individual circumstances. The estimated average time is:

Recordkeeping . . . . . 5 hr., 30 min.

Learning about the law or form . . . . 46 min.

Preparing the form . . 1 hr., 49 min.

Copying, assembling, and sending the form to the IRS . . . . 16 min.

If you have comments concerning the accuracy of these time estimates or suggestions for making this form more simple, we would be happy to hear from you. You can write to both the **Internal Revenue Service,** Washington, DC 20224, Attention: IRS Reports Clearance Officer, T:FP; and the **Office of Management and Budget,** Paperwork Reduction Project (1545-0233), Washington, DC 20503. **DO NOT** send the tax form to either of these offices. Instead, see **When and Where To File** below.

Purpose of Form.—Form 7004, Application for Automatic Extension of Time To File Corporation Income Tax Return, is used by a corporation to request a 6-month extension of time to file its income tax return.

The extension will be granted if you complete this form properly, file it, and pay any balance due on line 6 by the due date for the return for which the extension applies.

Note: *Certain filers of Form 990-T (section 401(a) or 408(a) trust) or Form 1120-ND (section 4951 taxes) should use* **Form 2758,** *Application for Extension of Time To File Certain Excise, Income, Information, and Other Returns, to request an extension.*

When and Where To File.—File Form 7004 by the due date of the return with the Internal Revenue Service Center where the corporation will file the return.

Foreign corporations with an office or place of business in the United States and other corporations qualifying for an automatic 3-month extension under Regulations section 1.6081-5 should not file Form 7004 unless they are unable to file their returns within the 3-month extended period. If additional time is needed, Form 7004 should be filed by the 15th day of the 3rd month following the close of the tax year to obtain a 6-month extension.

Foreign corporations that do not have an office or place of business in the United States should file Form 7004 by the 15th day of the 6th month following the close of the tax year.

Payment of Tax.—Form 7004 does not extend the time for payment of tax.

Foreign corporations that do not have an office or place of business in the United States may pay the tax by check or money order, made payable to the Internal Revenue Service.

Foreign corporations with an office or place of business in the United States and domestic corporations must deposit all income tax payments with a **Form 8109,** Federal Tax Deposit Coupon.

Note: *On all payments, write the corporation's employer identification number, the type of tax, and the tax year to which the payment applies.*

Penalty for Not Paying Tax.—The penalty for late payment of taxes is usually ½ of 1% of the unpaid tax for each month or part of a month the tax is unpaid. The penalty cannot exceed 25% of the amount due. The penalty may also apply to any additional tax not paid within 10 days of the date of the notice and demand for payment.

If you are allowed an extension of time to file, you will not be charged a late payment penalty if **(a)** the tax shown on line 3 (or the amount of tax paid by the regular due date of the return) is at least 90% of the tax shown on line 31 of Form 1120, or the comparable line on other returns, and **(b)** you pay the balance due shown on the return by the extended due date.

Termination of Extension.—The IRS may terminate the automatic extension at any time by mailing a notice of termination to the corporation or to the person who requested the extension. The notice will be mailed at least 10 days before the termination date given in the notice.

Specific Instructions

Address.—Include the suite, room, or other unit number after the street address. If the Post Office does not deliver mail to the street address and the corporation has a P.O. box, show the P.O. box number instead of the street address.

Line 1b—Short tax year.—If you checked the box for change in accounting period, you must have applied for approval to change your tax year unless certain conditions have been met. See **Form 1128,** Application To Adopt, Change, or Retain a Tax Year, and **Pub. 538,** Accounting Periods and Methods, for details.

Line 2—Affiliated group members.— Enter the name and address, employer identification number, and tax period for each member of the affiliated group. Generally, all members of an affiliated group must have the same tax period. However, if a group member is required to file a separate return for a short period, and an extension of time to file is being requested, a separate Form 7004 must be filed for that period. See Regulations section 1.1502-76 for details.

Line 3—Tentative tax.—Enter the tentative amount of total tax for the year, reduced by any nonrefundable credits against the tax. This will usually be the tax shown on Form 1120, line 31, or the comparable line from other returns.

Line 6—Balance due.—This is the amount of tax you are required to deposit.

Note: *Except for certain foreign corporations described under* **Payment of Tax,** *make all deposits with a Federal depository bank.* **Do not** *include your payment with Form 7004.*

If the corporation expects to have a net operating loss carryback, the corporation may reduce the amount to be deposited to the extent of the overpayment resulting from the carryback, providing all other prior year tax liabilities have been fully paid and a **Form 1138,** Extension of Time for Payment of Taxes by a Corporation Expecting a Net Operating Loss Carryback, accompanies Form 7004. See Rev. Rul. 82-47, 1982-1 C.B. 201 for details.

Interest will be charged on any part of the final tax due not shown on line 6. The interest is figured from the original due date of the return to the date of payment.

Signature.—The person authorized by the corporation should sign the Form 7004. This person may be:

1. An officer of the corporation;

2. A duly authorized agent holding a power of attorney;

3. A person currently enrolled to practice before the IRS; or

4. An attorney or certified public accountant qualified to practice before the IRS.

Form **8283**
(Rev. November 1992)

Department of the Treasury
Internal Revenue Service

Noncash Charitable Contributions

▶ Attach to your tax return if the total deduction claimed
for all property contributed exceeds $500.

▶ See separate instructions.

OMB No. 1545-0908
Expires 11-30-95

Attachment
Sequence No. **55**

Name(s) shown on your income tax return

Identifying number

Note: *Figure the amount of your contribution deduction before completing this form. See your tax return instructions.*

Section A—Include in this section **only** items (or groups of similar items) for which you claimed a deduction of $5,000 or less per item or group, and certain publicly traded securities (see instructions).

Part I   **Information on Donated Property**—If you need more space, attach a statement.

1	(a) Name and address of the donee organization	(b) Description of donated property
A		
B		
C		
D		
E		

Note: *If the amount you claimed as a deduction for an item is $500 or less, you do not have to complete columns (d), (e), and (f).*

	(c) Date of the contribution	(d) Date acquired by donor (mo., yr.)	(e) How acquired by donor	(f) Donor's cost or adjusted basis	(g) Fair market value	(h) Method used to determine the fair market value
A						
B						
C						
D						
E						

Part II   **Other Information**—If you gave less than an entire interest in property listed in Part I, complete lines 2a–2e. If restrictions were attached to a contribution listed in Part I, complete lines 3a–3c.

2   If less than the entire interest in the property is contributed during the year, complete the following:

a   Enter letter from Part I that identifies the property _____. If Part II applies to more than one property, attach a separate statement.

b   Total amount claimed as a deduction for the property listed in Part I: **(1)** For this tax year _____
(2) For any prior tax years _____.

c   Name and address of each organization to which any such contribution was made in a prior year (complete only if different than the donee organization above).

Name of charitable organization (donee)

Address (number, street, and room or suite no.)

City or town, state, and ZIP code

d   For tangible property, enter the place where the property is located or kept _____

e   Name of any person, other than the donee organization, having actual possession of the property _____

3   If conditions were attached to any contribution listed in Part I, answer the following questions and attach the required statement (see instructions):

		Yes	No
a	Is there a restriction, either temporary or permanent, on the donee's right to use or dispose of the donated property?		
b	Did you give to anyone (other than the donee organization or another organization participating with the donee organization in cooperative fundraising) the right to the income from the donated property or to the possession of the property, including the right to vote donated securities, to acquire the property by purchase or otherwise, or to designate the person having such income, possession, or right to acquire?		
c	Is there a restriction limiting the donated property for a particular use?		

For Paperwork Reduction Act Notice, see separate instructions.   Cat. No. 62299J   Form **8283** (Rev. 11-92)

Form 8283 (Rev. 11-92)
Page **2**

Name(s) shown on your income tax return	Identifying number

Section B—Appraisal Summary—Include in this section only items (or groups of similar items) for which you claimed a deduction of more than $5,000 per item or group. Report contributions of certain publicly traded securities only in Section A.

If you donated art, you may have to attach the complete appraisal. See the **Note** in Part I below.

Part I Information on Donated Property—To be completed by the taxpayer and/or appraiser.

4 Check type of property:
- ☐ Art* (contribution of $20,000 or more)
- ☐ Art* (contribution of less than $20,000)
- ☐ Real Estate
- ☐ Coin Collections
- ☐ Gems/Jewelry
- ☐ Books
- ☐ Stamp Collections
- ☐ Other

*Art includes paintings, sculptures, watercolors, prints, drawings, ceramics, antique furniture, decorative arts, textiles, carpets, silver, rare manuscripts, historical memorabilia, and other similar objects.

Note: *If your total art contribution deduction was $20,000 or more, you must attach a complete copy of the signed appraisal. See instructions.*

5	(a) Description of donated property (if you need more space, attach a separate statement)	(b) If tangible property was donated, give a brief summary of the overall physical condition at the time of the gift	(c) Appraised fair market value
A			
B			
C			
D			

	(d) Date acquired by donor (mo., yr.)	(e) How acquired by donor	(f) Donor's cost or adjusted basis	(g) For bargain sales, enter amount received	(h) Amount claimed as a deduction	(i) Average trading price of securities
A						
B						
C						
D						

Part II Taxpayer (Donor) Statement—List each item included in Part I above that is separately identified in the appraisal as having a value of $500 or less. See instructions.

I declare that the following item(s) included in Part I above has to the best of my knowledge and belief an appraised value of not more than $500 (per item). Enter identifying letter from Part I and describe the specific item: _____

Signature of taxpayer (donor) ▶   Date ▶

Part III Certification of Appraiser

I declare that I am not the donor, the donee, a party to the transaction in which the donor acquired the property, employed by, married to, or related to any of the foregoing persons, or an appraiser regularly used by any of the foregoing persons and who does not perform a majority of appraisals during the taxable year for other persons.

Also, I declare that I hold myself out to the public as an appraiser or perform appraisals on a regular basis; and that because of my qualifications as described in the appraisal, I am qualified to make appraisals of the type of property being valued. I certify that the appraisal fees were not based upon a percentage of the appraised property value. Furthermore, I understand that a false or fraudulent overstatement of the property value as described in the qualified appraisal or this appraisal summary may subject me to the civil penalty under section 6701(a) (aiding and abetting the understatement of tax liability). I affirm that I have not been barred from presenting evidence or testimony by the Director of Practice.

Sign Here
Signature ▶   Title ▶   Date of appraisal ▶

Business address (including room or suite no.)	Identifying number

City or town, state, and ZIP code

Part IV Donee Acknowledgment—To be completed by the charitable organization.

This charitable organization acknowledges that it is a qualified organization under section 170(c) and that it received the donated property as described in Section B, Part I, above on _____
(Date)

Furthermore, this organization affirms that in the event it sells, exchanges, or otherwise disposes of the property (or any portion thereof) within 2 years after the date of receipt, it will file an information return (**Form 8282,** Donee Information Return) with the IRS and furnish the donor a copy of that return. This acknowledgment does not represent concurrence in the claimed fair market value.

Name of charitable organization (donee)	Employer identification number
Address (number, street, and room or suite no.)	City or town, state, and ZIP code

Authorized signature	Title	Date

Form **8332**
(Rev. March 1993)

Department of the Treasury
Internal Revenue Service

Release of Claim to Exemption
for Child of Divorced or Separated Parents

ATTACH to noncustodial parent's return each year exemption claimed.

OMB No. 1545-0915
Expires 3-31-96

Attachment
Sequence No. **51**

Name(s) of parent claiming exemption

Social security number

Part I	**Release of Claim to Exemption for Current Year**

I agree not to claim an exemption for_____

Name(s) of child (or children)

for the tax year 19_____ .

_____
Signature of parent releasing claim to exemption

_____
Social security number

_____
Date

If you choose not to claim an exemption for this child (or children) for future tax years, complete Part II.

Part II	**Release of Claim to Exemption for Future Years** *(If completed, see **Noncustodial Parent** below.)*

I agree not to claim an exemption for_____

Name(s) of child (or children)

for the tax year(s)_____ .

(Specify. See instructions.)

_____
Signature of parent releasing claim to exemption

_____
Social security number

_____
Date

General Instructions

Paperwork Reduction Act Notice.—We ask for the information on this form to carry out the Internal Revenue laws of the United States. You are required to give us the information. We need it to ensure that you are complying with these laws and to allow us to figure and collect the right amount of tax.

The time needed to complete and file this form will vary depending on individual circumstances. The estimated average time is: **Recordkeeping,** 7 min.; **Learning about the law or the form,** 5 min.; **Preparing the form,** 7 min.; and **Copying, assembling, and sending the form to the IRS,** 14 min.

If you have comments concerning the accuracy of these time estimates or suggestions for making this form more simple, we would be happy to hear from you. You can write to both the IRS and the Office of Management and Budget at the addresses listed in the instructions for the return with which this form is filed.

Purpose of Form.—If you are a **custodial parent,** you may use this form to release your claim to your child's exemption. To do so, complete this form and give it to the **noncustodial parent** who will claim the child's exemption. Then, the noncustodial parent must attach this form or a similar statement to his or her tax return each year the exemption is claimed.

You are the **custodial parent** if you had custody of the child for most of the year. You are the **noncustodial parent** if you had custody for a shorter period of time or did not have custody at all.

Instead of using this form, you (the custodial parent) may use a similar

statement as long as it contains the same information required by this form.

Children of Divorced or Separated Parents.—Special rules apply to determine if the support test is met for children of parents who are divorced or legally separated under a decree of divorce or separate maintenance or separated under a written separation agreement. The rules also apply to children of parents who did not live together at any time during the last 6 months of the year, even if they do not have a separation agreement.

The general rule is that the custodial parent is treated as having provided over half of the child's support if:

1. The child received over half of his or her total support for the year from both of the parents, **AND**

2. The child was in the custody of one or both of his or her parents for more than half of the year.

Note: *Public assistance payments, such as Aid to Families with Dependent Children, are not support provided by the parents.*

If both **1** and **2** above apply, and the other four dependency tests in the instructions for Form 1040 or Form 1040A are also met, the custodial parent can claim the child's exemption.

Exception. The general rule does not apply if **any** of the following applies:

● The custodial parent agrees not to claim the child's exemption by signing this form or similar statement. The noncustodial parent **must** attach this form or similar statement to his or her tax return for the tax year. See **Custodial Parent** later.

● The child is treated as having received over half of his or her total support from a

person under a multiple support agreement (**Form 2120,** Multiple Support Declaration).

● A pre-1985 divorce decree or written separation agreement states that the noncustodial parent can claim the child as a dependent. But the noncustodial parent must provide at least $600 for the child's support during the year. The noncustodial parent must also check the box on line 6d of Form 1040 or Form 1040A. This rule does not apply if the decree or agreement was changed after 1984 to say that the noncustodial parent cannot claim the child as a dependent.

Additional Information.—For more details, get **Pub. 504,** Divorced or Separated Individuals.

Specific Instructions

Custodial Parent.—You may agree to release your claim to the child's exemption for the current tax year or for future years, or both.

● Complete **Part I** if you agree to release your claim to the child's exemption for the current tax year.

● Complete **Part II** if you agree to release your claim to the child's exemption for any or all future years. If you do, write the specific future year(s) or "all future years" in the space provided in Part II.

Noncustodial Parent.—Attach Form 8332 or a similar statement to your tax return for the tax year in which you claim the child's exemption. You may claim the exemption **only** if the other four dependency tests in the Form 1040 or Form 1040A instructions are met.

Note: *If the custodial parent completed Part II, you **must** attach a copy of this form to your tax return for each future year in which you claim the exemption.*

Cat. No. 13910F

Form **8332** (Rev. 3-93)

Form **8582**	**Passive Activity Loss Limitations**	OMB No. 1545-1008

Department of the Treasury
Internal Revenue Service

▶ See separate instructions.

▶ Attach to Form 1040 or Form 1041.

1993

Attachment
Sequence No. **88**

Name(s) shown on return

Identifying number

Part I **1993 Passive Activity Loss**

Caution: *See the instructions for Worksheets 1 and 2 on page 7 before completing Part I.*

Rental Real Estate Activities With Active Participation (For the definition of active participation see **Active Participation in a Rental Real Estate Activity** on page 3 of the instructions.)

1a Activities with net income (from Worksheet 1, column (a)) . . .	**1a**	
b Activities with net loss (from Worksheet 1, column (b))	**1b** ( )	
c Prior year unallowed losses (from Worksheet 1, column (c)) . .	**1c** ( )	
d Combine lines 1a, 1b, and 1c	**1d**	

All Other Passive Activities

2a Activities with net income (from Worksheet 2, column (a)) . . .	**2a**	
b Activities with net loss (from Worksheet 2, column (b))	**2b** ( )	
c Prior year unallowed losses (from Worksheet 2, column (c)) . .	**2c** ( )	
d Combine lines 2a, 2b, and 2c	**2d**	

3 Combine lines 1d and 2d. If the result is net income or zero, see the instructions for line 3. If this line and line 1d are losses, go to line 4. Otherwise, enter -0- on line 9 and go to line 10 . | **3** |

Part II **Special Allowance for Rental Real Estate With Active Participation**

Note: *Enter all numbers in Part II as positive amounts. (See instructions on page 7 for examples.)*

4 Enter the **smaller** of the loss on line 1d or the loss on line 3	**4**	
5 Enter $150,000. If married filing separately, see the instructions .	**5**	
6 Enter modified adjusted gross income, but not less than zero (see instructions)	**6**	

Note: *If line 6 is equal to or greater than line 5, skip lines 7 and 8, enter -0- on line 9, and then go to line 10. Otherwise, go to line 7.*

7 Subtract line 6 from line 5	**7**	
8 Multiply line 7 by 50% (.5). **Do not** enter more than $25,000. If married filing separately, see instructions	**8**	
9 Enter the **smaller** of line 4 or line 8	**9**	

Part III **Total Losses Allowed**

10 Add the income, if any, on lines 1a and 2a and enter the total	**10**	
11 **Total losses allowed from all passive activities for 1993.** Add lines 9 and 10. See the instructions to find out how to report the losses on your tax return	**11**	

For Paperwork Reduction Act Notice, see separate instructions. Cat. No. 63704F Form **8582** (1993)

Form 8582 (1993)   Page **2**

Caution: *The worksheets are not required to be filed with your tax return and may be detached before filing Form 8582. Keep a copy of the worksheets for your records.*

Worksheet 1—For Form 8582, Lines 1a, 1b, and 1c (See instructions on page 7.)

Name of activity	Current year		Prior year	Overall gain or loss	
	(a) Net income (line 1a)	**(b) Net loss (line 1b)**	**(c) Unallowed loss (line 1c)**	**(d) Gain**	**(e) Loss**
Total. Enter on Form 8582, lines 1a, 1b, and 1c . . . . ▶					

Worksheet 2—For Form 8582, Lines 2a, 2b, and 2c (See instructions on page 7.)

Name of activity	Current year		Prior year	Overall gain or loss	
	(a) Net income (line 2a)	**(b) Net loss (line 2b)**	**(c) Unallowed loss (line 2c)**	**(d) Gain**	**(e) Loss**
Total. Enter on Form 8582, lines 2a, 2b, and 2c . . . . ▶					

Worksheet 3—Use this worksheet if an amount is shown on Form 8582, line 9 (See instructions on page 8.)

Name of activity	Form or schedule to be reported on	(a) Loss (See instructions.)	(b) Ratio (See instructions.)	(c) Special allowance (See instructions.)	(d) Subtract column (c) from column (a) (See instructions.)
Total . . . . ▶			1.00		

Worksheet 4—Allocation of Unallowed Losses (See instructions on page 8.)

Name of activity	Form or schedule to be reported on	(a) Loss (See instructions.)	(b) Ratio (See instructions.)	(c) Unallowed loss (See instructions.)
Total . . . . ▶			1.00	

Worksheet 5—Allowed Losses (See instructions on page 8.)

Name of activity	Form or schedule to be reported on	(a) Loss (See instructions.)	(b) Unallowed loss (See instructions.)	(c) Allowed loss (See instructions.)
Total . . . . ▶				

Worksheet 6—Activities With Losses Reported on Two or More Different Forms or Schedules (See instructions on page 8.)

Name of Activity:	(a) (See instr.)	(b) (See instr.)	(c) Ratio (See instr.)	(d) Unallowed loss (See instr.)	(e) Allowed loss (See instr.)
Form or Schedule To Be Reported on:					
1a Net loss plus prior year unallowed loss from form or schedule . ▶					
b Net income from form or schedule . . . . ▶					
c Subtract line 1b from line 1a. If zero or less, enter -0- . . . . ▶					
Form or Schedule To Be Reported on:					
1a Net loss plus prior year unallowed loss from form or schedule . ▶					
b Net income from form or schedule . . . . ▶					
c Subtract line 1b from line 1a. If zero or less, enter -0- . . . . ▶					
Form or Schedule To Be Reported on:					
1a Net loss plus prior year unallowed loss from form or schedule . ▶					
b Net income from form or schedule . . . . ▶					
c Subtract line 1b from line 1a. If zero or less, enter -0- . . . . ▶					
Total . . . . ▶		1.00			

Form **8582-CR**

Department of the Treasury
Internal Revenue Service

Passive Activity Credit Limitations

▶ See separate instructions.

▶ Attach to Form 1040 or 1041.

OMB No. 1545-1034

1993

Attachment
Sequence No. **88a**

Name(s) shown on return

Identifying number

Part I **1993 Passive Activity Credits**

Caution: *If you have credits from a publicly traded partnership, see **Publicly Traded Partnerships (PTPs)** on page 14 of the instructions.*

Credits From Rental Real Estate Activities With Active Participation (Other Than Rehabilitation Credits and Low-Income Housing Credits) (See Lines 1a through 1c on page 9 of the instructions.)

1a Credits from Worksheet 1, column (a)	**1a**	
b Prior year unallowed credits from Worksheet 1, column (b)	**1b**	
c Add lines 1a and 1b.	**1c**	

Rehabilitation Credits from Rental Real Estate Activities and Low-Income Housing Credits for Property Placed in Service Before 1990 (or From Pass-Through Interests Acquired Before 1990) (See Lines 2a through 2c on page 9 of the instructions.)

2a Credits from Worksheet 2, column (a)	**2a**	
b Prior year unallowed credits from Worksheet 2, column (b)	**2b**	
c Add lines 2a and 2b.	**2c**	

Low-Income Housing Credits for Property Placed in Service After 1989 (See Lines 3a through 3c on page 9 of the instructions.)

3a Credits from Worksheet 3, column (a)	**3a**	
b Prior year unallowed credits from Worksheet 3, column (b)	**3b**	
c Add lines 3a and 3b.	**3c**	

All Other Passive Activity Credits (See Lines 4a through 4c on page 9 of the instructions.)

4a Credits from Worksheet 4, column (a)	**4a**	
b Prior year unallowed credits from Worksheet 4, column (b)	**4b**	
c Add lines 4a and 4b.	**4c**	
5 Add lines 1c, 2c, 3c, and 4c	**5**	
6 Enter the tax attributable to net passive income (see instructions)	**6**	
7 Subtract line 6 from line 5. If line 6 is more than or equal to line 5, enter -0- and see the instructions	**7**	

Part II **Special Allowance for Rental Real Estate Activities With Active Participation**

Note: *Complete Part II if you have an amount on line 1c. Otherwise, go to Part III.*

8 Enter the smaller of line 1c or line 7		**8**	
9 Enter $150,000. If married filing separately, see instructions . . .	**9**		
10 Enter modified adjusted gross income, but not less than zero (see instructions). If line 10 is equal to or greater than line 9, skip lines 11 through 15 and enter -0- on line 16	**10**		
11 Subtract line 10 from line 9	**11**		
12 Multiply line 11 by 50% (.5). Do not enter more than $25,000. If married filing separately, see instructions	**12**		
13 Enter the amount, if any, from line 9 of Form 8582	**13**		
14 Subtract line 13 from line 12	**14**		
15 Enter the tax attributable to the amount on line 14 (see instructions)		**15**	
16 Enter the smaller of line 8 or line 15		**16**	

For Paperwork Reduction Act Notice, see separate instructions.

Cat. No. 64641R

Form **8582-CR** (1993)

Part III **Special Allowance for Rehabilitation Credits From Rental Real Estate Activities and Low-Income Housing Credits for Property Placed in Service Before 1990 (or From Pass-Through Interests Acquired Before 1990)**
Note: Complete Part III if you have an amount on line 2c. Otherwise, go to Part IV.

17 Enter the amount from line 7	**17**	
18 Enter the amount from line 16	**18**	
19 Subtract line 18 from line 17. If zero, enter -0- here and on lines 30 and 36, and then go to Part V	**19**	
20 Enter the smaller of line 2c or line 19	**20**	
21 Enter $250,000. If married filing separately, see instructions. (See instructions to see if you can skip lines 21 through 26.)	**21**	
22 Enter modified adjusted gross income, but not less than zero. (See instructions for Part II, line 10.) If line 22 is equal to or greater than line 21, skip lines 23 through 29, and enter -0- on line 30	**22**	
23 Subtract line 22 from line 21	**23**	
24 Multiply line 23 by 50% (.5). Do not enter more than $25,000. If married filing separately, see instructions	**24**	
25 Enter the amount, if any, from line 9 of Form 8582	**25**	
26 Subtract line 25 from line 24	**26**	
27 Enter the tax attributable to the amount on line 26 (see instructions) .	**27**	
28 Enter the amount, if any, from line 18	**28**	
29 Subtract line 28 from line 27	**29**	
30 Enter the smaller of line 20 or line 29	**30**	

Part IV **Special Allowance for Low-Income Housing Credits for Property Placed in Service After 1989**
Note: Complete Part IV if you have an amount on line 3c. Otherwise, go to Part V.

31 If you completed Part III, enter the amount from line 19. Otherwise, subtract line 16 from line 7 .	**31**	
32 Enter the amount from line 30	**32**	
33 Subtract line 32 from line 31. If zero, enter -0- here and on line 36	**33**	
34 Enter the smaller of line 3c or line 33	**34**	
35 Tax attributable to the remaining special allowance (see instructions)	**35**	
36 Enter the smaller of line 34 or line 35	**36**	

Part V **Passive Activity Credit Allowed**

37 **Passive Activity Credit Allowed.** Add lines 6, 16, 30, and 36. If you have any credits from a publicly traded partnership, see **Publicly Traded Partnerships (PTPs)** on page 14 of the instructions . . . . *Note: Use Worksheets 5 through 9, whichever apply, to allocate the allowed and unallowed credits if you have credits from more than one passive activity. Also use the worksheets if you must allocate the credits because they are reported on different forms.*	**37**	

Form **8594**
(Rev. January 1993)
Department of the Treasury
Internal Revenue Service

Asset Acquisition Statement
Under Section 1060
▶ **Attach to your Federal income tax return.**

OMB No. 1545-1021
Expires 2-29-96

Attachment
Sequence No. **61**

Name as shown on return	Identification number as shown on return

Check the box that identifies you: ☐ Buyer ☐ Seller

Part I General Information—To be completed by all filers

1 Name of other party to the transaction | Other party's identification number

Address (number, street, and room or suite no.)

City, state, and ZIP code

2 Date of sale | **3** Total sales price

Part II Assets Transferred—To be completed by all filers of an original statement

4 Assets	Aggregate Fair Market Value (Actual Amount for Class I)	Allocation of Sales Price
Class I	$	$
Class II	$	$
Class III	$	$
Class IV		$
Total		$

5 Did the buyer and seller provide for an allocation of the sales price in the sales contract or in another written document signed by both parties? . . . . ☐ Yes ☐ No
If "Yes," are the aggregate fair market values listed for each of asset Classes I, II, and III the amounts agreed upon in your sales contract or in a separate written document? . . . . ☐ Yes ☐ No

6 In connection with the purchase of the group of assets, did the buyer also purchase a license or a covenant not to compete, or enter into a lease agreement, employment contract, management contract, or similar arrangement with the seller (or managers, directors, owners, or employees of the seller)? . . . . ☐ Yes ☐ No
If "Yes," specify (a) the type of agreement, and (b) the maximum amount of consideration (not including interest) paid or to be paid under the agreement. See the instructions for line 6.

For Paperwork Reduction Act Notice, see instructions. | Cat. No. 63768Z | Form **8594** (Rev. 1-93)

Form 8594 (Rev. 1-93) Page **2**

| Part III | Class III, Intangible Amortizable Assets Only—Complete if applicable. The amounts shown below also must be included under Class III assets in Part II. Attach additional sheets if more space is needed. |

Assets	Fair Market Value	Useful Life	Allocation of Sales Price
	$		$
	$		$
	$		$
	$		$
	$		$
	$		$
	$		$
	$		$
	$		$

| Part IV | Supplemental Statement—To be completed only if amending an original statement or previously filed supplemental statement because of an increase or decrease in consideration. |

7 Assets	Allocation of Sales Price as Previously Reported	Increase or (Decrease)	Redetermined Allocation of Sales Price
Class I	$	$	$
Class II	$	$	$
Class III	$	$	$
Class IV	$	$	$
Total	$		$

8 Reason(s) for increase or decrease. Attach additional sheets if more space is needed.

9 Tax year and tax return form number with which the original Form 8594 and any supplemental statements were filed.

Form **8606**

Department of the Treasury
Internal Revenue Service

Nondeductible IRAs
(Contributions, Distributions, and Basis)
▶ **Please see What Records Must I Keep? below.**
▶ **Attach to Form 1040, Form 1040A, or Form 1040NR.**

OMB No. 1545-1007

1993

Attachment
Sequence No. **47**

Name. If married, file a separate Form 8606 for each spouse. See instructions.

Your social security number

Fill in Your Address Only If You Are Filing This Form by Itself and Not With Your Tax Return ▷

Home address (number and street, or P.O. box if mail is not delivered to your home)

Apt. no.

City, town or post office, state, and ZIP code

Contributions, Nontaxable Distributions, and Basis

1	Enter your IRA contributions for 1993 that you choose to be nondeductible. Include those made during 1/1/94–4/15/94 that were for 1993. See instructions	**1**
2	Enter your total IRA basis for 1992 and earlier years. See instructions	**2**
3	Add lines 1 and 2	**3**

Did you receive any IRA distributions (withdrawals) in 1993?
→ No → Enter the amount from line 3 on line 12. Then, **stop and read When and Where To File** on page 2.
→ Yes → Go to line 4.

4	Enter only those contributions included on line 1 that were made during 1/1/94–4/15/94. This amount will be the same as line 1 if all of your nondeductible contributions for 1993 were made in 1994 by 4/15/94. See instructions	**4**
5	Subtract line 4 from line 3	**5**
6	Enter the total value of **ALL** your IRAs as of 12/31/93 plus any outstanding rollovers. See instructions	**6**
7	Enter the total IRA distributions received during 1993. Do not include amounts rolled over before 1/1/94. See instructions	**7**
8	Add lines 6 and 7 . . . . **8**	
9	Divide line 5 by line 8 and enter the result as a decimal (to at least two places). Do not enter more than "1.00" . . . . **9** × .	
10	Multiply line 7 by line 9. This is the amount of your **nontaxable distributions for 1993**	**10**
11	Subtract line 10 from line 5. This is the **basis in your IRA(s) as of 12/31/93**	**11**
12	Add lines 4 and 11. This is your **total IRA basis for 1993 and earlier years**	**12**

Taxable Distributions for 1993

13	Subtract line 10 from line 7. Enter the result here and on Form 1040, line 16b; Form 1040A, line 10b; or Form 1040NR, line 17b, whichever applies	**13**

Sign Here Only If You Are Filing This Form by Itself and Not With Your Tax Return

Under penalties of perjury, I declare that I have examined this form, including accompanying attachments, and to the best of my knowledge and belief, it is true, correct, and complete.

▶ Your signature

▶ Date

General Instructions

Paperwork Reduction Act Notice.—We ask for the information on this form to carry out the Internal Revenue laws of the United States. You are required to give us the information. We need it to ensure that you are complying with these laws and to allow us to figure and collect the right amount of tax.

The time needed to complete and file this form will vary depending on individual circumstances. The estimated average time is: **Recordkeeping,** 26 min.; **Learning about the law or the form,** 7 min.; **Preparing the form,** 22 min.; and **Copying, assembling, and sending the form to the IRS,** 20 min.

If you have comments concerning the accuracy of these time estimates or suggestions for making this form more simple, we would be happy to hear from

you. You can write to both the IRS and the Office of Management and Budget at the addresses listed in the Instructions for Form 1040, Form 1040A, or Form 1040NR.

Purpose of Form

Use Form 8606 to report your IRA contributions that you choose to be nondeductible. For example, if you cannot deduct all of your contributions because of the income limits for IRAs, you may want to make nondeductible contributions.

Also use Form 8606 to figure the basis in your IRA(s) and the taxable part of any distributions you received in 1993 if you have ever made nondeductible contributions.

Your **basis** is the total of all your nondeductible IRA contributions minus the total of all nontaxable IRA distributions received. It is to your advantage to keep

track of your basis because it is used to figure the nontaxable part of future distributions.

Note: *To figure your deductible IRA contributions, use the Instructions for Form 1040 or Form 1040A, whichever applies.*

Who Must File

You must file Form 8606 for 1993 if:

• You made nondeductible contributions to your IRA for 1993, **or**

• You received IRA distributions in 1993 **and** you have ever made nondeductible contributions to any of your IRAs.

What Records Must I Keep?

To verify the nontaxable part of distributions from your IRA, keep a copy of this form together with copies of the following forms and records until all distributions are made from your IRA(s):

Cat.No. 63966F

Form **8606** (1993)

• Page 1 of Forms 1040 (or Forms 1040A or Forms 1040NR) filed for each year you make a nondeductible contribution.

• Forms 5498 or similar statements received each year showing contributions you made.

• Forms 5498 or similar statements you received showing the value of your IRA(s) for each year you received a distribution.

• Forms 1099-R and W-2P received for each year you received a distribution.

When and Where To File

Attach Form 8606 to your 1993 Form 1040, Form 1040A, or Form 1040NR.

If you are required to file Form 8606 but do not have to file an income tax return because you do not meet the requirements for filing a return, you still **must** file Form 8606 with the Internal Revenue Service at the same time and place you would be required to file Form 1040, Form 1040A, or Form 1040NR.

Penalty for Not Filing

If you are required to file Form 8606 but do not do so, you will have to pay a $50 penalty for each failure to file this form unless you can show reasonable cause.

Penalty for Overstatement

If you overstate your nondeductible contributions for any tax year, you must pay a $100 penalty for each overstatement unless it was due to reasonable cause.

Additional Information

For more details on nondeductible contributions, IRA basis, and distributions, get **Pub. 590,** Individual Retirement Arrangements (IRAs).

Amending Form 8606

After you file your return, you may change a nondeductible contribution made on a prior year's return to a deductible contribution or vice versa. To do this, complete a new Form 8606 showing the revised information and attach it to **Form 1040X,** Amended U.S. Individual Income Tax Return. Send both of these forms to the Internal Revenue Service Center shown in the Form 1040X instructions for your area.

Specific Instructions

Section references are to the Internal Revenue Code.

Note: *If you received an IRA distribution in 1993 and you also made IRA contributions for 1993 that may not be fully deductible because of the income limits, you need to make a special computation before completing this form. For details, including how to complete Form 8606, see Tax Treatment of Distributions in Chapter 6 of Pub. 590.*

Name and Social Security Number

If you file a joint return on Form 1040 or Form 1040A, enter the name and social security number of the spouse whose IRA information is shown.

Line 1

If you used IRA Worksheet 2 in the Form 1040 or Form 1040A instructions, include the following on line 1 of Form 8606:

• The amount shown on line 10 of IRA Worksheet 2 (Form 1040) or line 8 of IRA Worksheet 2 (Form 1040A) that you choose to make nondeductible.

• The part, if any, of the amount shown on line 9 of IRA Worksheet 2 (Form 1040) or line 7 of IRA Worksheet 2 (Form 1040A) that you choose to make nondeductible. You cannot take a deduction for the part included on line 1.

Note: *Enter any nondeductible contributions for your* **nonworking spouse** *from the appropriate lines of IRA Worksheet 2 on line 1 of your spouse's* **separate** *Form 8606.*

If none of your contributions are deductible, you may choose to make up to $2,000 (but not more than your earned income) of your contributions nondeductible. Enter on line 1 of Form 8606 your contributions that you choose to make nondeductible.

If contributions were also made to your nonworking spouse's IRA, you may choose to make nondeductible contributions up to $2,250 (but not more than your earned income). Enter on line 1 of your Form 8606 the total nondeductible contributions you are making to your IRA. Enter the balance on line 1 of your nonworking spouse's Form 8606. Do not enter more than $2,000 on either your or your spouse's Form 8606. Also, the total of the two amounts cannot be more than $2,250.

If you used IRA Worksheet 1 in the Form 1040 or Form 1040A instructions but choose not to deduct the full amount shown on line 3 of that worksheet, subtract the amount you are deducting from the amount on line 3. Enter the result on line 1 of your Form 8606.

If contributions were made to your nonworking spouse's IRA but you choose not to deduct the full amount shown on line 8 of IRA Worksheet 1, subtract the amount you are deducting for your nonworking spouse from the amount on line 8. Enter the result on line 1 of your nonworking spouse's Form 8606.

Line 2

If this is the first year you are required to file Form 8606, enter zero. If you filed a Form 8606 for any year **after 1988,** enter the amount from line 14 of the **last** Form 8606 you filed. Otherwise, enter the total of the amounts from lines 7 and 16 of your **1988** Form 8606. Or, if you didn't file a 1988 Form 8606, enter the total of the amounts from lines 4 and 13 of your **1987** Form 8606.

Line 4

If you made contributions in 1993 and 1994 that are for 1993, you may choose to

apply the contributions made in 1993 first to nondeductible contributions and then to deductible contributions, or vice versa. But the amount on line 1 minus the amount on line 4 cannot be more than the IRA contributions you actually made in 1993.

Example. You made contributions of $1,000 in 1993, and $1,000 in 1994. $1,500 of your contributions are deductible and $500 are nondeductible. You choose $500 of your contribution in 1993 to be nondeductible. In this case, the $500 would be entered on line 1, but not on line 4, and would become part of your basis for 1993.

Line 5

Although the 1993 IRA contributions you made during 1/1/94–4/15/94 (line 4) can be treated as nondeductible for purposes of line 1, they are not included in your basis for purposes of figuring the nontaxable part of any distributions you received in 1993. This is why you subtract line 4 from line 3.

Line 6

Enter the total value of **ALL** your IRAs as of 12/31/93 **plus** any outstanding rollovers. You should receive a statement by 1/31/94 for each IRA account showing the value on 12/31/93. A **rollover** is a tax-free distribution from one IRA that is contributed to another IRA. The rollover must be completed within 60 days of receiving the distribution from the first IRA. An **outstanding rollover** is any amount distributed to you from one IRA within 60 days of the end of 1993 (between Nov. 2 and Dec. 31) that you did not roll over to another IRA by 12/31/93, but that you roll over to another IRA in 1994 within the normal 60-day rollover period.

Line 7

Do not include on line 7:

• Distributions received in 1993 and rolled over to another IRA by 12/31/93,

• Outstanding rollovers included on line 6,

• Contributions under section 408(d)(4) returned to you on or before the due date of the return, or

• Excess contributions under section 408(d)(5) returned to you after the due date of the return.

Line 11

This is the total of your nondeductible IRA contributions made in 1993 and earlier years minus the total of any nontaxable IRA distributions received in those years.

Line 12

This is the total of your IRA basis as of 12/31/93 and any nondeductible IRA contributions for 1993 that you made in 1994 by 4/15/94.

This amount will be used on Form 8606 in future years if you make nondeductible IRA contributions or receive distributions.

Form **8615**

Department of the Treasury
Internal Revenue Service

**Tax for Children Under Age 14
Who Have Investment Income of More Than $1,200**
▶ See instructions below and on back.
▶ Attach ONLY to the child's Form 1040, Form 1040A, or Form 1040NR.

OMB No. 1545-0998

19**93**

Attachment
Sequence No. **33**

Child's name shown on return

Child's social security number

A Parent's name (first, initial, and last). **Caution:** See instructions on back before completing.

B Parent's social security number

C Parent's filing status (check one):

☐ Single ☐ Married filing jointly ☐ Married filing separately ☐ Head of household ☐ Qualifying widow(er)

	Step 1 Figure child's net investment income	
1	Enter child's investment income, such as taxable interest and dividend income. See instructions. If this amount is $1,200 or less, **stop here;** do not file this form	**1**
2	If the child DID NOT itemize deductions on Schedule A (Form 1040 or Form 1040NR), enter $1,200. If the child ITEMIZED deductions, see instructions	**2**
3	Subtract line 2 from line 1. If the result is zero or less, **stop here;** do not complete the rest of this form but ATTACH it to the child's return	**3**
4	Enter child's **taxable** income from Form 1040, line 37; Form 1040A, line 22; or Form 1040NR, line 36	**4**
5	Enter the **smaller** of line 3 or line 4 here ▶	**5**

Step 2   Figure tentative tax based on the tax rate of the parent listed on line A

6	Enter parent's **taxable** income from Form 1040, line 37; Form 1040A, line 22; Form 1040EZ, line 6; or Form 1040NR, line 36. If the parent transferred property to a trust, see instructions	**6**
7	Enter the total net investment income, if any, from Forms 8615, line 5, of ALL OTHER children of the parent identified above. **Do not** include the amount from line 5 above	**7**
8	Add lines 5, 6, and 7	**8**
9	Tax on line 8 based on the **parent's** filing status. See instructions. If from Schedule D Tax Worksheet, enter amount from line 4 of that worksheet here ▶ _____	**9**
10	Enter parent's tax from Form 1040, line 38; Form 1040A, line 23; Form 1040EZ, line 8; or Form 1040NR, line 37. If from Schedule D Tax Worksheet, enter amount from line 4 of that worksheet here ▶ _____	**10**
11	Subtract line 10 from line 9. If line 7 is blank, enter on line 13 the amount from line 11; skip lines 12a and 12b	**11**
12a	Add lines 5 and 7 . . . . **12a**	
b	Divide line 5 by line 12a. Enter the result as a decimal (rounded to two places)	**12b** ✕ .
13	Multiply line 11 by line 12b ▶	**13**

Step 3   Figure child's tax—If lines 4 and 5 above are the same, go to line 16 now.

14	Subtract line 5 from line 4 . . . . **14**	
15	Tax on line 14 based on the **child's** filing status. See instructions. If from Schedule D Tax Worksheet, enter amount from line 4 of that worksheet here ▶ _____	**15**
16	Add lines 13 and 15	**16**
17	Tax on line 4 based on the **child's** filing status. See instructions. If from Schedule D Tax Worksheet, check here . . . . ▶ ☐	**17**
18	Enter the **larger** of line 16 or line 17 here and on Form 1040, line 38; Form 1040A, line 23; or Form 1040NR, line 37. Be sure to check the box for "Form 8615" even if line 17 is more than line 16 . ▶	**18**

General Instructions

A Change To Note.—If line 8 of Form 8615 is over $70,000 (over $140,000 if the parent's filing status is married filing jointly or qualifying widow(er)), the election to defer additional 1993 taxes may apply to the child. Get **Form 8841,** Deferral of Additional 1993 Taxes, for details. If the election is made, Form 1040A **cannot** be filed for the child.

Purpose of Form.—For children under age 14, investment income over $1,200 is taxed at the parent's rate if the parent's rate is higher than the child's rate. If the child's investment income is more than $1,200, use this form to figure the child's tax.

Investment Income.—As used on this form, "investment income" includes all taxable income other than earned income as defined on page 2. It includes income such as taxable interest, dividends, capital gains, rents, royalties, etc. It also includes pension and annuity income and income (other than earned income) received as the beneficiary of a trust.

Who Must File.—Generally, Form 8615 must be filed for any child who was under age 14 on January 1, 1994, had more than $1,200 of investment income, and is required to file a tax return. If neither parent was alive on December 31, 1993, do not use Form 8615.

Instead, figure the child's tax in the normal manner.

Note: *The parent may be able to elect to report the child's interest and dividends on his or her return. If the parent makes this election, the child will not have to file a return or Form 8615. For more details, see the instructions for Form 1040 or Form 1040A, or get* **Form 8814,** *Parents' Election To Report Child's Interest and Dividends.*

Additional Information.—For more details, get **Pub. 929,** Tax Rules for Children and Dependents.

Incomplete Information for Parent.—If the parent's taxable income or filing status or the net investment income of

For Paperwork Reduction Act Notice, see back of form.   Cat. No. 64113U   Form **8615** (1993)

the parent's other children is not known by the due date of the child's return, reasonable estimates may be used. Write "Estimated" on the appropriate line(s) of Form 8615. For more details, see Pub. 929.

Amended Return.—If after the child's return is filed, the parent's taxable income is changed or the net investment income of any of the parent's other children is changed, the child's tax must be refigured using the adjusted amounts. If the child's tax is changed as a result of the adjustment(s), file **Form 1040X,** Amended U.S. Individual Income Tax Return, to correct the child's tax.

Alternative Minimum Tax.—A child whose tax is figured on Form 8615 may owe the alternative minimum tax. For details, get **Form 6251,** Alternative Minimum Tax—Individuals, and its instructions.

Line Instructions

Section references are to the Internal Revenue Code.

Lines A and B.—If the child's parents were married to each other and filed a joint return, enter the name and social security number (SSN) of the parent who is listed first on the joint return. For example, if the father's name is listed first on the return and his SSN is entered in the block labeled "Your social security number," enter his name on line A and his SSN on line B.

If the parents were married but filed separate returns, enter the name and SSN of the parent who had the **higher** taxable income. If you do not know which parent had the higher taxable income, see Pub. 929.

If the parents were unmarried, treated as unmarried for Federal income tax purposes, or separated either by a divorce or separate maintenance decree, enter the name and SSN of the parent who had custody of the child for most of the year (the custodial parent).

Exception. If the custodial parent remarried and filed a joint return with his or her new spouse, enter the name and SSN of the person listed first on the joint return, even if that person is not the child's parent. If the custodial parent and his or her new spouse filed separate returns, enter the name and SSN of the person with the **higher** taxable income, even if that person is not the child's parent.

Note: *If the parents were unmarried but lived together during the year with the child, enter the name and SSN of the parent who had the* **higher** *taxable income.*

Line 1.—If the child had no earned income (defined later), enter the child's adjusted gross income from Form 1040, line 32; Form 1040A, line 17; or Form 1040NR, line 32.

If the child had earned income, use the following worksheet to figure the amount to enter on line 1. But if the child files **Form 2555,** Foreign Earned Income, or **Form 2555-EZ,** Foreign Earned Income Exclusion, has a net loss from self-employment, or claims a net operating loss deduction, **do not** use the worksheet below. Instead, use the worksheet in Pub. 929 to figure the amount to enter on line 1.

Worksheet (keep a copy for your records)

1. Enter the amount from the child's Form 1040, line 23; Form 1040A, line 14; or Form 1040NR, line 24, whichever applies . . . _____

2. Enter the child's **earned income** (defined below) plus any deduction the child claims on Form 1040, line 28, or Form 1040NR, line 28, whichever applies _____

3. Subtract line 2 from line 1. Enter the result here and on Form 8615, line 1 . . _____

Earned income includes wages, tips, and other payments received for personal services performed. Generally, earned income is the total of the amounts reported on Form 1040, lines 7, 12, and 19; Form 1040A, line 7; or Form 1040NR, lines 8, 13, and 20.

Line 2.—If the child itemized deductions, enter on line 2 the **greater** of:

● $600 plus the portion of the amount on Schedule A (Form 1040), line 26, or Schedule A (Form 1040NR), line 17, that is directly connected with the production of the investment income on Form 8615, line 1; **OR**

● $1,200.

Line 6.—If the parent's taxable income is less than zero, enter zero on line 6. If the parent filed a joint return, enter the taxable income shown on that return even if the parent's spouse is not the child's parent. If the parent transferred property to a trust which sold or exchanged property during the year at a gain, include any gain that was taxed to the trust under section 644 in the amount entered on line 6. Enter "Section 644" and the amount to the right of the line 6 entry. Also, see the instructions for line 10.

Line 9.—Figure the tax using the Tax Table, Tax Rate Schedules, or the Schedule D Tax Worksheet, whichever applies. If any net capital gain is included on lines 5, 6, and/or 7, the tax on the amount on line 8 may be less if the Schedule D Tax Worksheet can be used to figure the tax. See Pub. 929 for details on how to figure the net capital gain included on line 8 and how to complete the worksheet. The Schedule D Tax Worksheet should be used to figure the tax if:

the parent's filing status is:	AND	the amount on Form 8615, line 8, is over:
● Single		$53,500
● Married filing jointly or Qualifying widow(er)		$89,150
● Married filing separately		$44,575
● Head of household		$76,400

If the Schedule D Tax Worksheet is used to figure the tax, enter on Form 8615, line 9, the amount from line 13 of that worksheet. Also, enter the amount from line 4 of that worksheet in the space next to line 9 of Form 8615.

Line 10.—If the parent filed a joint return, enter the tax shown on that return even if the parent's spouse is not the child's parent. If the parent filed Form 8814, enter "Form 8814" and the total tax from line 8 of Form(s) 8814 in the space next to line 10 of Form 8615.

If line 6 includes any gain taxed to a trust under section 644, add the tax imposed under section 644(a)(2)(A) to the tax shown on the parent's return. Enter the total on line 10 instead of the tax from the parent's return. Also, enter "Section 644" next to line 10.

Line 15.—Figure the tax using the Tax Table, Tax Rate Schedule X, or the Schedule D Tax Worksheet, whichever applies. If line 14 is more than $53,500 and includes any net capital gain, the tax may be less if the Schedule D Tax Worksheet is used to figure the tax. See Pub. 929 for details on how to figure the net capital gain included on line 14 and how to complete the worksheet.

Line 17.—Figure the tax as if these rules did not apply. For example, if the child files Schedule D and can use the Schedule D Tax Worksheet to figure his or her tax, complete that worksheet.

Paperwork Reduction Act Notice.—We ask for the information on this form to carry out the Internal Revenue laws of the United States. You are required to give us the information. We need it to ensure that you are complying with these laws and to allow us to figure and collect the right amount of tax.

The time needed to complete and file this form will vary depending on individual circumstances. The estimated average time is: **Recordkeeping,** 13 min.; **Learning about the law or the form,** 12 min.; **Preparing the form,** 45 min.; and **Copying, assembling, and sending the form to the IRS,** 17 min.

If you have comments concerning the accuracy of these time estimates or suggestions for making this form more simple, we would be happy to hear from you. You can write to both the IRS and the Office of Management and Budget at the addresses listed in the instructions of the tax return with which this form is filed.

Form **8829**

Department of the Treasury
Internal Revenue Service   (O)

Expenses for Business Use of Your Home

▶ File only with Schedule C (Form 1040). Use a separate Form 8829 for each home you used for business during the year.

▶ **See separate instructions.**

OMB No. 1545-1266

1993

Attachment
Sequence No. **66**

Name(s) of proprietor(s)

Your social security number

Part I	**Part of Your Home Used for Business**		
1	Area used regularly and exclusively for business, regularly for day care, or for inventory storage. See instructions	1	
2	Total area of home	2	
3	Divide line 1 by line 2. Enter the result as a percentage	3	%

- For day-care facilities not used exclusively for business, also complete lines 4–6.
- All others, skip lines 4–6 and enter the amount from line 3 on line 7.

4	Multiply days used for day care during year by hours used per day .	4	hr.	
5	Total hours available for use during the year (365 days × 24 hours). See instructions	5	8,760 hr.	
6	Divide line 4 by line 5. Enter the result as a decimal amount	6	.	
7	Business percentage. For day-care facilities not used exclusively for business, multiply line 6 by line 3 (enter the result as a percentage). All others, enter the amount from line 3 . . . . . ▶	7		%

Part II	**Figure Your Allowable Deduction**			
8	Enter the amount from Schedule C, line 29, **plus** any net gain or (loss) derived from the business use of your home and shown on Schedule D or Form 4797. If more than one place of business, see instructions		8	

See instructions for columns (a) and (b) before completing lines 9–20.

		(a) Direct expenses	(b) Indirect expenses		
9	Casualty losses. See instructions	9			
10	Deductible mortgage interest. See instructions .	10			
11	Real estate taxes. See instructions	11			
12	Add lines 9, 10, and 11.	12			
13	Multiply line 12, column (b) by line 7		13		
14	Add line 12, column (a) and line 13			14	
15	Subtract line 14 from line 8. If zero or less, enter -0- .			15	
16	Excess mortgage interest. See instructions . .	16			
17	Insurance	17			
18	Repairs and maintenance	18			
19	Utilities	19			
20	Other expenses. See instructions	20			
21	Add lines 16 through 20	21			
22	Multiply line 21, column (b) by line 7		22		
23	Carryover of operating expenses from 1992 Form 8829, line 41 . .		23		
24	Add line 21 in column (a), line 22, and line 23			24	
25	Allowable operating expenses. Enter the **smaller** of line 15 or line 24			25	
26	Limit on excess casualty losses and depreciation. Subtract line 25 from line 15			26	
27	Excess casualty losses. See instructions	27			
28	Depreciation of your home from Part III below	28			
29	Carryover of excess casualty losses and depreciation from 1992 Form 8829, line 42	29			
30	Add lines 27 through 29			30	
31	Allowable excess casualty losses and depreciation. Enter the **smaller** of line 26 or line 30 .			31	
32	Add lines 14, 25, and 31			32	
33	Casualty loss portion, if any, from lines 14 and 31. Carry amount to **Form 4684**, Section B . .			33	
34	Allowable expenses for business use of your home. Subtract line 33 from line 32. Enter here and on Schedule C, line 30. If your home was used for more than one business, see instructions ▶			34	

Part III	**Depreciation of Your Home**		
35	Enter the **smaller** of your home's adjusted basis or its fair market value. See instructions . .	35	
36	Value of land included on line 35	36	
37	Basis of building. Subtract line 36 from line 35	37	
38	Business basis of building. Multiply line 37 by line 7	38	
39	Depreciation percentage. See instructions	39	%
40	Depreciation allowable. Multiply line 38 by line 39. Enter here and on line 28 above. See instructions	40	

Part IV	**Carryover of Unallowed Expenses to 1994**		
41	Operating expenses. Subtract line 25 from line 24. If less than zero, enter -0-	41	
42	Excess casualty losses and depreciation. Subtract line 31 from line 30. If less than zero, enter -0- .	42	

For Paperwork Reduction Act Notice, see page 1 of separate instructions.   Cat. No. 13232M   Form **8829** (1993)

Form **8841**	**Deferral of Additional 1993 Taxes**	OMB No. 1545-1405
Department of the Treasury Internal Revenue Service	▶ See separate instructions. ▶ Attach to Form 1040 or Form 1040NR.	**19**93 Attachment Sequence No. **99**

Name(s) shown on Form 1040	Social security number

Part I   Modified Regular Tax

1	Enter your taxable income from Form 1040, line 37	**1**	
2	Figure the tax on the amount on line 1 using the tax computation in the instructions for this line	**2**	
3	Enter any amount from Form 4970 included on Form 1040, line 39	**3**	
4	If you completed Part III of Form 4972, refigure Part III using the tax computation in the instructions for this line and include the refigured amount from line 32 here. If you completed Part II or IV of Form 4972, also include the amounts you originally entered on lines 9 and 55	**4**	
5	**Modified regular tax.** Add lines 2 through 4 above and enter the result. If Form 1040, line 45, is zero, go to Part III. Otherwise, go to Part II	**5**	

Part II   Modified Credits

6	**Modified credits.** Complete the worksheet in the instructions to figure your modified credits. Enter the amount from line 21 of that worksheet	**6**	

Part III   Modified Other Taxes

7	Subtract the amount on line 6, if any, from line 5		**7**	
8	Add Form 1040, lines 47, 49 through 52, and any write-in entries included on line 53 . . .		**8**	
9	Enter the amount from Form 6251, line 26. You must complete Form 6251 through line 26 to figure the amount to enter on this line . .	**9**		
10	If Form 1040, line 45, is zero, enter the sum of lines 2 and 3. Otherwise, subtract the amount from line 6 of the worksheet in the instructions, if any, from the sum of lines 2 and 3 and enter the result	**10**		
11	Subtract line 10 from line 9. If zero or less, enter -0-. (If this form is for a child under age 14, see instructions.)		**11**	
12	**Modified total tax.** Add lines 7, 8, and 11		**12**	

Part IV   Deferral of Additional 1993 Taxes

13	Enter the amount from Form 1040, line 53	**13**		
14	Enter the amount from line 12	**14**		
15	Subtract line 14 from line 13. If zero or less, stop here; you do not have any additional 1993 taxes to defer		**15**	
16	**Deferral of additional 1993 taxes.** Enter ⅔ of line 15 here and on Form 1040, line 58b. See instructions		**16**	

For Paperwork Reduction Act Notice, see separate instructions.   Cat. No. 15994L   Form **8841** (1993)

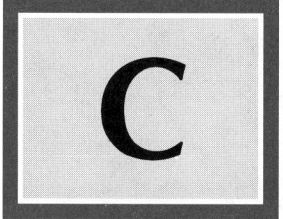

MACRS and ACRS Tables

ACRS, MACRS and ADS Depreciation Methods Summary

System	Characteristics	Depreciation Method		Rev. Proc. 87-57 Table No.	
		MACRS	ADS	MACRS	ADS
MACRS & ADS	Personal Property:				
	1. Accounting Convention	Half-year or mid-quarter	Half-year or mid-quarter		
	2. Life and Method				
	a. 3-year, 5-year, 7-year, 10-year	200% DB or elect straight-line	150% DB or elect straight-line	1, 2, 3, 4, 5, 8	8, 14[a]
	b. 15-year, 20-year	150% DB or elect straight-line	150% DB or elect straight-line[b]	1, 2, 3, 4, 5, 8	8, 14[a]
	Real Property:				
	1. Accounting Convention	Mid-month	Mid-month		
	2. Life and Method				
	a. Residential rental property	27.5 years, straight-line	40 years straight-line	6	13
	b. Nonresidential real property	39 years, straight-line[c]	40 years straight-line	7A	13

	Characteristics	ACRS
ACRS	Personal Property	
	1. Accounting Convention	Half-year
	2. Life and Method	
	a. 3-year, 5-year, 10-year, 15-year	150% DB or elect straight-line[d]
	Real Property	
	1. Accounting Convention	First of month or Mid-month[e]
	2. Life	
	a. 15-year property	Placed in service after 12/31/80 and before 3/16/84
	b. 18-year property	Placed in service after 3/15/84 and before 6/23/84
	c. 19-year property	Placed in service after 6/22/84
	3. Method	
	a. All but low-income housing	175% DB or elect straight-line
	b. Low-income housing property	200% DB or elect straight-line

[a] The mid-quarter tables are available in Rev. Proc. 87-57, but are not reproduced here.

[b] Special recovery periods are assigned certain MACRS properties under the alternative depreciation system.

[c] A 31.5 year recovery period applied to nonresidential real property placed in service under the MACRS rules prior to May 13, 1993. (See Table 7 of Rev. Proc. 87-57).

[d] Special recovery periods are required or able to be elected for personalty and realty for which a straight-line ACRS election is made. These recovery periods can be as long as 45 years.

[e] The first-of-the-month convention is used with 15-year property and 18-year real property placed in service before June 23, 1984. The mid-month convention is used with 18-year real property placed in service after June 22, 1984 and 19-year real property.

Rev. Proc. 87-57—MACRS Rules

Table 1

General Depreciation System
Applicable Depreciation Method: 200 or 150 Percent
Declining Balance Switching to Straight Line
Applicable Recovery Periods: 3, 5, 7, 10, 15, 20 Years
Applicable Convention: Half-year

If the Recovery Year Is:	and the Recovery Period Is:					
	3-Year	*5-Year*	*7-Year*	*10-Year*	*15-Year*	*20-Year*
	the Depreciation Rate Is:					
1	33.33	20.00	14.29	10.00	5.00	3.750
2	44.45	32.00	24.49	18.00	9.50	7.219
3	14.81	19.20	17.49	14.40	8.55	6.677
4	7.41	11.52	12.49	11.52	7.70	6.177
5		11.52	8.93	9.22	6.93	5.713
6		5.76	8.92	7.37	6.23	5.285
7			8.93	6.55	5.90	4.888
8			4.46	6.55	5.90	4.522
9				6.56	5.91	4.462
10				6.55	5.90	4.461
11				3.28	5.91	4.462
12					5.90	4.461
13					5.91	4.462
14					5.90	4.461
15					5.91	4.462
16					2.95	4.461
17						4.462
18						4.461
19						4.462
20						4.461
21						2.231

Rev. Proc. 87-57 cont.

Table 14
General Depreciation System
Applicable Depreciation Method: 200 or 150 Percent
Declining Balance Switching to Straight Line
Applicable Recovery Periods: 3, 5, 7, 10, 15, 20 Years
Applicable Convention: Mid-quarter (property placed in service in first quarter)

If the Recovery Year is:	and the Recovery Period Is					
	3-Year	5-Year	7-Year	10-Year	15-Year	20-Year
	the Depreciation Rate Is:					
1	58.33	35.00	25.00	17.50	8.75	6.563
2	27.78	26.00	21.43	16.50	9.13	7.000
3	12.35	15.60	15.31	13.20	8.21	6.482
4	1.54	11.01	10.93	10.56	7.39	5.996
5		11.01	8.74	8.45	6.65	5.546
6		1.38	8.74	6.76	5.99	5.130
7			8.75	6.55	5.90	4.746
8			1.09	6.55	5.91	4.459
9				6.56	5.90	4.459
10				6.55	5.91	4.459
11				0.82	5.90	4.459
12					5.91	4.460
13					5.90	4.459
14					5.91	4.460
15					5.90	4.459
16					0.74	4.460
17						4.459
18						4.460
19						4.459
20						4.460
21						0.557

Table 3

General Depreciation System
Applicable Depreciation Method: 200 or 150 Percent
Declining Balance Switching to Straight Line
Applicable Recovery Periods: 3, 5, 7, 10, 15, 20 Years
Applicable Convention: Mid-quarter (property placed in
service in second quarter)

If the Recovery Year Is:	|		and the Recovery Period Is:			
	3-Year	5-Year	7-Year	10-Year	15-Year	20-Year
	the Depreciation Rate Is:					
1	41.67	25.00	17.85	12.50	6.25	4.688
2	38.89	30.00	23.47	17.50	9.38	7.148
3	14.14	18.00	16.76	14.00	8.44	6.612
4	5.30	11.37	11.97	11.20	7.59	6.116
5		11.37	8.87	8.96	6.83	5.658
6		4.26	8.87	7.17	6.15	5.233
7			8.87	6.55	5.91	4.841
8			3.33	6.55	5.90	4.478
9				6.56	5.91	4.463
10				6.55	5.90	4.463
11				2.46	5.91	4.463
12					5.90	4.463
13					5.91	4.463
14					5.90	4.463
15					5.91	4.462
16					2.21	4.463
17						4.462
18						4.463
19						4.462
20						4.463
21						1.673

Table 4

General Depreciation System
Applicable Depreciation Method: 200 or 150 Percent
Declining Balance Switching to Straight Line
Applicable Recovery Periods: 3, 5, 7, 10, 15, 20 Years
Applicable Convention: Mid-quarter (property placed in
service in third quarter)

If the Recovery Year Is:	3-Year	5-Year	7-Year	10-Year	15-Year	20-Year
			the Depreciation Rate Is:			
1	25.00	15.00	10.71	7.50	3.75	2.813
2	50.00	34.00	25.51	18.50	9.63	7.289
3	16.67	20.40	18.22	14.80	8.66	6.742
4	8.33	12.24	13.02	11.84	7.80	6.237
5		11.30	9.30	9.47	7.02	5.769
6		7.06	8.85	7.58	6.31	5.336
7			8.86	6.55	5.90	4.936
8			5.53	6.55	5.90	4.566
9				6.56	5.91	4.460
10				6.55	5.90	4.460
11				4.10	5.91	4.460
12					5.90	4.460
13					5.91	4.461
14					5.90	4.460
15					5.91	4.461
16					3.69	4.460
17						4.461
18						4.460
19						4.461
20						4.460
21						2.788

Rev. Proc. 87-57 cont.

Table 5

General Depreciation System
Applicable Depreciation Method: 200 or 150 Percent
Declining Balance Switching to Straight Line
Applicable Recovery Periods: 3, 5, 7, 10, 15, 20 Years
Applicable Convention: Mid-quarter (Property placed in
service in fourth quarter)

If the Recovery Year Is:	and the Recovery Period Is:					
	3-Year	5-Year	7-Year	10-Year	15-Year	20-Year
	the Depreciation Rate Is:					
1	8.33	5.00	3.57	2.50	1.25	0.938
2	61.11	38.00	27.55	19.50	9.88	7.430
3	20.37	22.80	19.68	15.60	8.89	6.872
4	10.19	13.68	14.06	12.48	8.00	6.357
5		10.94	10.04	9.98	7.20	5.880
6		9.58	8.73	7.99	6.48	5.439
7			8.73	6.55	5.90	5.031
8			7.64	6.55	5.90	4.654
9				6.56	5.90	4.458
10				6.55	5.91	4.458
11				5.74	5.90	4.458
12					5.91	4.458
13					5.90	4.458
14					5.91	4.458
15					5.90	4.458
16					5.17	4.458
17						4.458
18						4.459
19						4.458
20						4.459
21						3.901

Rev. Proc. 87-57 cont.

Table 6

General Depreciation System
Applicable Depreciation Method: Straight Line
Applicable Recovery Period: 27.5 Years
Applicable Convention: Mid-month

If the Recovery Year Is:	And the Month in the First Recovery Year the Property Is Placed in Service Is:											
	1	2	3	4	5	6	7	8	9	10	11	12
	the Depreciation Rate Is:											
1	3.485	3.182	2.879	2.576	2.273	1.970	1.667	1.364	1.061	0.758	0.455	0.152
2	3.636	3.636	3.636	3.636	3.636	3.636	3.636	3.636	3.636	3.636	3.636	3.636
3	3.636	3.636	3.636	3.636	3.636	3.636	3.636	3.636	3.636	3.636	3.636	3.636
4	3.636	3.636	3.636	3.636	3.636	3.636	3.636	3.636	3.636	3.636	3.636	3.636
5	3.636	3.636	3.636	3.636	3.636	3.636	3.636	3.636	3.636	3.636	3.636	3.636
6	3.636	3.636	3.636	3.636	3.636	3.636	3.636	3.636	3.636	3.636	3.636	3.636
7	3.636	3.636	3.636	3.636	3.636	3.636	3.636	3.636	3.636	3.636	3.636	3.636
8	3.636	3.636	3.636	3.636	3.636	3.636	3.636	3.636	3.636	3.636	3.636	3.636
9	3.636	3.636	3.636	3.636	3.636	3.636	3.636	3.636	3.636	3.636	3.636	3.636
10	3.637	3.637	3.637	3.637	3.637	3.637	3.636	3.636	3.636	3.636	3.636	3.636
11	3.636	3.636	3.636	3.636	3.636	3.636	3.637	3.637	3.637	3.637	3.637	3.637
12	3.637	3.637	3.637	3.637	3.637	3.637	3.636	3.636	3.636	3.636	3.636	3.636
13	3.636	3.636	3.636	3.636	3.636	3.636	3.637	3.637	3.637	3.637	3.637	3.637
14	3.637	3.637	3.637	3.637	3.637	3.637	3.636	3.636	3.636	3.636	3.636	3.636
15	3.636	3.636	3.636	3.636	3.636	3.636	3.637	3.637	3.637	3.637	3.637	3.637
16	3.637	3.637	3.637	3.637	3.637	3.637	3.636	3.636	3.636	3.636	3.636	3.636
17	3.636	3.636	3.636	3.636	3.636	3.636	3.637	3.637	3.637	3.637	3.637	3.637
18	3.637	3.637	3.637	3.637	3.637	3.637	3.636	3.636	3.636	3.636	3.636	3.636
19	3.636	3.636	3.636	3.636	3.636	3.636	3.637	3.637	3.637	3.637	3.637	3.637
20	3.637	3.637	3.637	3.637	3.637	3.637	3.636	3.636	3.636	3.636	3.636	3.636
21	3.636	3.636	3.636	3.636	3.636	3.636	3.637	3.637	3.637	3.637	3.637	3.637
22	3.637	3.637	3.637	3.637	3.637	3.637	3.636	3.636	3.636	3.636	3.636	3.636
23	3.636	3.636	3.636	3.636	3.636	3.636	3.637	3.637	3.637	3.637	3.637	3.637
24	3.637	3.637	3.637	3.637	3.637	3.637	3.636	3.636	3.636	3.636	3.636	3.636
25	3.636	3.636	3.636	3.636	3.636	3.636	3.637	3.637	3.637	3.637	3.637	3.637
26	3.637	3.637	3.637	3.637	3.637	3.637	3.636	3.636	3.636	3.636	3.636	3.636
27	3.636	3.636	3.636	3.636	3.636	3.636	3.637	3.637	3.637	3.637	3.637	3.637
28	1.970	2.273	2.576	2.879	3.182	3.485	3.636	3.636	3.636	3.636	3.636	3.636
29	0.000	0.000	0.000	0.000	0.000	0.000	0.152	0.455	0.758	1.061	1.364	1.667

Rev. Proc. 87-57 cont.

Table 7
General Depreciation System
Applicable Depreciation Method: Straight Line
Applicable Recovery Period: 31.5 Years
Applicable Convention: Mid-month

If the Recovery Year is:	And the Month in the First Recovery Year the Property Is Placed in Service Is:											
	1	2	3	4	5	6	7	8	9	10	11	12
	the Depreciation Rate Is:											
1	3.042	2.778	2.513	2.249	1.984	1.720	1.455	1.190	0.926	0.661	0.397	0.132
2	3.175	3.175	3.175	3.175	3.175	3.175	3.175	3.175	3.175	3.175	3.175	3.175
3	3.175	3.175	3.175	3.175	3.175	3.175	3.175	3.175	3.175	3.175	3.175	3.175
4	3.175	3.175	3.175	3.175	3.175	3.175	3.175	3.175	3.175	3.175	3.175	3.175
5	3.175	3.175	3.175	3.175	3.175	3.175	3.175	3.175	3.175	3.175	3.175	3.175
6	3.175	3.175	3.175	3.175	3.175	3.175	3.175	3.175	3.175	3.175	3.175	3.175
7	3.175	3.175	3.175	3.175	3.175	3.175	3.175	3.175	3.175	3.175	3.175	3.175
8	3.175	3.174	3.175	3.174	3.175	3.174	3.175	3.175	3.175	3.175	3.175	3.175
9	3.174	3.175	3.174	3.175	3.174	3.175	3.174	3.175	3.174	3.175	3.174	3.175
10	3.175	3.174	3.175	3.174	3.175	3.174	3.175	3.174	3.175	3.174	3.175	3.174
11	3.174	3.175	3.174	3.175	3.174	3.175	3.174	3.175	3.174	3.175	3.174	3.175
12	3.175	3.174	3.175	3.174	3.175	3.174	3.175	3.174	3.175	3.174	3.175	3.174
13	3.174	3.175	3.174	3.175	3.174	3.175	3.174	3.175	3.174	3.175	3.174	3.175
14	3.175	3.174	3.175	3.174	3.175	3.174	3.175	3.174	3.175	3.174	3.175	3.174
15	3.174	3.175	3.174	3.175	3.174	3.175	3.174	3.175	3.174	3.175	3.174	3.175
16	3.175	3.174	3.175	3.174	3.175	3.174	3.175	3.174	3.175	3.174	3.175	3.174
17	3.174	3.175	3.174	3.175	3.174	3.175	3.174	3.175	3.174	3.175	3.174	3.175
18	3.175	3.174	3.175	3.174	3.175	3.174	3.175	3.174	3.175	3.174	3.175	3.174
19	3.174	3.175	3.174	3.175	3.174	3.175	3.174	3.175	3.174	3.175	3.174	3.175
20	3.175	3.174	3.175	3.174	3.175	3.174	3.175	3.174	3.175	3.174	3.175	3.174
21	3.174	3.175	3.174	3.175	3.174	3.175	3.174	3.175	3.174	3.175	3.174	3.175
22	3.175	3.174	3.175	3.174	3.175	3.174	3.175	3.174	3.175	3.174	3.175	3.174
23	3.174	3.175	3.174	3.175	3.174	3.175	3.174	3.175	3.174	3.175	3.174	3.175
24	3.175	3.174	3.175	3.174	3.175	3.174	3.175	3.174	3.175	3.174	3.175	3.174
25	3.174	3.175	3.174	3.175	3.174	3.175	3.174	3.175	3.174	3.175	3.174	3.175
26	3.175	3.174	3.175	3.174	3.175	3.174	3.175	3.174	3.175	3.174	3.175	3.174
27	3.174	3.175	3.174	3.175	3.174	3.175	3.174	3.175	3.174	3.175	3.174	3.175
28	3.175	3.174	3.175	3.174	3.175	3.174	3.175	3.174	3.175	3.174	3.175	3.174
29	3.174	3.175	3.174	3.175	3.174	3.175	3.174	3.175	3.174	3.175	3.174	3.175
30	3.175	3.174	3.175	3.174	3.175	3.174	3.175	3.174	3.175	3.174	3.175	3.174
31	3.174	3.175	3.174	3.175	3.174	3.175	3.174	3.175	3.174	3.175	3.174	3.175
32	1.720	1.984	2.249	2.513	2.778	3.042	3.175	3.174	3.175	3.174	3.175	3.174
33	0.000	0.000	0.000	0.000	0.000	0.000	0.132	0.397	0.661	0.926	1.190	1.455

Table 7A
General Depreciation System
Applicable Depreciation Method: Straight Line
Applicable Recovery Period: 39 years
And the Month in the First Recovery Year the Property is Placed in Service

If the Recovery Year is:	the Depreciation Rate Is:											
	1	2	3	4	5	6	7	8	9	10	11	12
1	2.461	2.247	2.033	1.819	1.605	1.391	1.177	0.963	0.749	0.535	0.321	0.107
2-39	2.564	2.564	2.564	2.564	2.564	2.564	2.564	2.564	2.564	2.564	2.564	2.564
40	0.107	0.321	0.535	0.749	0.963	1.177	1.391	1.605	1.819	2.033	2.247	2.461

Source: IRS Publication No. 534 [Depreciation]

Rev. Proc. 87-57 cont.

Table 8
General and Alternative Depreciation Systems
Applicable Depreciation Method: Straight Line
Applicable Recovery Periods: 2.5—50 years
Applicable Convention: Half-Year

If the Recovery Year Is:	and the Recovery Period Is:														
	the Depreciation Rate Is:														
	2.5	3.0	3.5	4.0	4.5	5.0	5.5	6.0	6.5	7.0	7.5	8.0	8.5	9.0	9.5
1	20.00	16.67	14.29	12.50	11.11	10.00	9.09	8.33	7.69	7.14	6.67	6.25	5.88	5.56	5.26
2	40.00	33.33	28.57	25.00	22.22	20.00	18.18	16.67	15.39	14.29	13.33	12.50	11.77	11.11	10.53
3	40.00	33.33	28.57	25.00	22.22	20.00	18.18	16.67	15.38	14.29	13.33	12.50	11.76	11.11	10.53
4		16.67	28.57	25.00	22.23	20.00	18.18	16.67	15.39	14.28	13.33	12.50	11.77	11.11	10.53
5				12.50	22.22	20.00	18.19	16.66	15.38	14.29	13.34	12.50	11.76	11.11	10.52
6						10.00	18.18	16.67	15.39	14.28	13.33	12.50	11.77	11.11	10.53
7								8.33	15.38	14.29	13.34	12.50	11.76	11.11	10.52
8										7.14	13.33	12.50	11.77	11.11	10.53
9												6.25	11.76	11.11	10.52
10														5.56	10.53

If the
Recovery
Year Is:

and the Recovery Period Is:

the Depreciation Rate Is:

Recovery Year	10.0	10.5	11.0	11.5	12.0	12.5	13.0	13.5	14.0	14.5	15.0	15.5	16.0	16.5	17.0
1	5.00	4.76	4.55	4.35	4.17	4.00	3.85	3.70	3.57	3.45	3.33	3.23	3.13	3.03	2.94
2	10.00	9.52	9.09	8.70	8.33	8.00	7.69	7.41	7.14	6.90	6.67	6.45	6.25	6.06	5.88
3	10.00	9.52	9.09	8.70	8.33	8.00	7.69	7.41	7.14	6.90	6.67	6.45	6.25	6.06	5.88
4	10.00	9.53	9.09	8.69	8.33	8.00	7.69	7.41	7.14	6.90	6.67	6.45	6.25	6.06	5.88
5	10.00	9.52	9.09	8.70	8.33	8.00	7.69	7.41	7.14	6.90	6.67	6.45	6.25	6.06	5.88
6	10.00	9.53	9.09	8.69	8.33	8.00	7.69	7.41	7.14	6.89	6.67	6.45	6.25	6.06	5.88
7	10.00	9.52	9.09	8.70	8.34	8.00	7.69	7.41	7.14	6.90	6.67	6.45	6.25	6.06	5.88
8	10.00	9.53	9.09	8.69	8.33	8.00	7.69	7.41	7.15	6.89	6.66	6.45	6.25	6.06	5.88
9	10.00	9.52	9.09	8.70	8.34	8.00	7.69	7.41	7.14	6.90	6.67	6.45	6.25	6.06	5.88
10	10.00	9.53	9.09	8.69	8.33	8.00	7.70	7.40	7.15	6.89	6.66	6.45	6.25	6.06	5.88
11	5.00	9.52	9.09	8.70	8.34	8.00	7.69	7.41	7.14	6.90	6.67	6.45	6.25	6.06	5.89
12			4.55	8.69	8.33	8.00	7.70	7.40	7.15	6.89	6.66	6.45	6.25	6.06	5.88
13					4.17	4.00	7.69	7.41	7.14	6.90	6.67	6.45	6.25	6.06	5.88
14							3.85	7.40	7.15	6.89	6.66	6.46	6.25	6.06	5.89
15									3.57	6.90	6.67	6.45	6.25	6.06	5.88
16											3.33	6.46	6.25	6.06	5.89
17													3.12	6.07	5.89
18															2.94

If the Recovery Year Is:	and the Recovery Period Is: the Depreciation Rate Is:														
	17.5	18.0	18.5	19.0	19.5	20.0	20.5	21.0	21.5	22.0	22.5	23.0	23.5	24.0	24.5
1	2.86	2.78	2.70	2.63	2.56	2.500	2.439	2.381	2.326	2.273	2.222	2.174	2.128	2.083	2.041
2	5.71	5.56	5.41	5.26	5.13	5.000	4.878	4.762	4.651	4.545	4.444	4.348	4.255	4.167	4.082
3	5.71	5.56	5.41	5.26	5.13	5.000	4.878	4.762	4.651	4.545	4.444	4.348	4.255	4.167	4.082
4	5.71	5.55	5.41	5.26	5.13	5.000	4.878	4.762	4.651	4.545	4.445	4.348	4.255	4.167	4.082
5	5.72	5.56	5.40	5.26	5.13	5.000	4.878	4.762	4.651	4.546	4.444	4.348	4.255	4.167	4.082
6	5.71	5.55	5.41	5.26	5.13	5.000	4.878	4.762	4.651	4.545	4.445	4.348	4.255	4.167	4.082
7	5.72	5.56	5.40	5.26	5.13	5.000	4.878	4.762	4.651	4.546	4.444	4.348	4.255	4.167	4.082
8	5.71	5.55	5.41	5.26	5.13	5.000	4.878	4.762	4.651	4.545	4.445	4.348	4.255	4.167	4.082
9	5.72	5.56	5.40	5.27	5.13	5.000	4.878	4.762	4.651	4.546	4.444	4.348	4.255	4.167	4.081
10	5.71	5.55	5.41	5.26	5.13	5.000	4.878	4.762	4.651	4.545	4.445	4.348	4.255	4.167	4.082
11	5.72	5.56	5.40	5.27	5.13	5.000	4.878	4.762	4.651	4.546	4.444	4.348	4.256	4.166	4.081
12	5.71	5.55	5.41	5.26	5.13	5.000	4.878	4.762	4.651	4.545	4.445	4.348	4.255	4.167	4.082
13	5.72	5.56	5.40	5.27	5.13	5.000	4.878	4.762	4.651	4.546	4.444	4.348	4.256	4.166	4.081
14	5.71	5.55	5.41	5.26	5.13	5.000	4.878	4.762	4.651	4.545	4.445	4.348	4.255	4.167	4.082
15	5.72	5.56	5.40	5.27	5.13	5.000	4.878	4.762	4.651	4.546	4.444	4.348	4.256	4.166	4.081
16	5.71	5.55	5.41	5.26	5.13	5.000	4.878	4.762	4.651	4.545	4.445	4.348	4.255	4.167	4.082
17	5.72	5.56	5.40	5.27	5.13	5.000	4.878	4.762	4.652	5.546	4.444	4.347	4.256	4.166	4.081
18	5.71	5.55	5.41	5.26	5.12	5.000	4.878	4.762	4.651	4.545	4.445	4.348	4.255	4.167	4.082
19		2.78	5.40	5.27	5.13	5.000	4.879	4.762	4.652	4.546	4.444	4.347	4.256	4.166	4.081
20				2.63	5.12	5.000	4.878	4.762	4.651	4.545	4.445	4.348	4.255	4.167	4.082
21						2.500	4.878	4.762	4.651	4.546	4.444	4.348	4.256	4.166	4.081
22							2.500	2.381	4.651	4.545	4.445	4.348	4.255	4.167	4.082
23									2.273	4.444	4.348	4.256	4.166	4.081
24										2.174	4.255	4.167	4.082		
25												2.083	4.081		

and the Recovery Period Is:

the Depreciation Rate Is:

Recovery Year	25.0	25.5	26.0	26.5	27.0	27.5	28.0	28.5	29.0	29.5	30.0	30.5	31.0	31.5	32.0
1	2.000	1.961	1.923	1.887	1.852	1.818	1.786	1.754	1.724	1.695	1.667	1.639	1.613	1.587	1.563
2	4.000	3.922	3.846	3.774	3.704	3.636	3.571	3.509	3.448	3.390	3.333	3.279	3.226	3.175	3.125
3	4.000	3.922	3.846	3.774	3.704	3.636	3.571	3.509	3.448	3.390	3.333	3.279	3.226	3.175	3.125
4	4.000	3.922	3.846	3.774	3.704	3.636	3.571	3.509	3.448	3.390	3.333	3.279	3.226	3.175	3.125
5	4.000	3.922	3.846	3.774	3.704	3.636	3.571	3.509	3.448	3.390	3.333	3.279	3.226	3.175	3.125
6	4.000	3.921	3.846	3.774	3.704	3.636	3.572	3.509	3.448	3.390	3.333	3.279	3.226	3.175	3.125
7	4.000	3.922	3.846	3.774	3.704	3.636	3.571	3.509	3.448	3.390	3.333	3.279	3.226	3.175	3.125
8	4.000	3.921	3.846	3.773	3.704	3.636	3.572	3.509	3.448	3.390	3.333	3.279	3.226	3.175	3.125
9	4.000	3.922	3.846	3.774	3.704	3.637	3.571	3.509	3.448	3.390	3.333	3.279	3.226	3.174	3.125
10	4.000	3.921	3.846	3.773	3.704	3.636	3.572	3.509	3.448	3.390	3.333	3.279	3.226	3.175	3.125
11	4.000	3.922	3.846	3.774	3.704	3.637	3.571	3.509	3.448	3.390	3.333	3.279	3.226	3.174	3.125
12	4.000	3.921	3.846	3.773	3.704	3.636	3.572	3.509	3.448	3.390	3.333	3.279	3.226	3.175	3.125
13	4.000	3.922	3.846	3.774	3.703	3.637	3.571	3.509	3.448	3.390	3.334	3.279	3.226	3.174	3.125
14	4.000	3.921	3.846	3.773	3.704	3.636	3.572	3.509	3.448	3.390	3.333	3.279	3.226	3.175	3.125
15	4.000	3.922	3.846	3.774	3.703	3.637	3.571	3.509	3.449	3.390	3.334	3.279	3.226	3.174	3.125
16	4.000	3.921	3.846	3.773	3.704	3.636	3.572	3.509	3.448	3.390	3.333	3.279	3.226	3.175	3.125
17	4.000	3.922	3.846	3.774	3.703	3.637	3.571	3.509	3.449	3.390	3.334	3.279	3.226	3.174	3.125
18	4.000	3.921	3.846	3.773	3.704	3.636	3.572	3.508	3.448	3.390	3.333	3.279	3.226	3.175	3.125
19	4.000	3.922	3.846	3.774	3.703	3.637	3.571	3.509	3.449	3.390	3.334	3.278	3.226	3.174	3.125
20	4.000	3.921	3.847	3.773	3.704	3.636	3.572	3.508	3.448	3.390	3.333	3.279	3.226	3.175	3.125
21	4.000	3.922	3.846	3.774	3.703	3.637	3.571	3.509	3.449	3.389	3.334	3.278	3.225	3.174	3.125
22	4.000	3.921	3.847	3.773	3.704	3.636	3.572	3.508	3.448	3.390	3.333	3.279	3.226	3.175	3.125
23	4.000	3.922	3.846	3.774	3.703	3.637	3.571	3.509	3.449	3.389	3.334	3.278	3.225	3.174	3.125
24	4.000	3.921	3.847	3.773	3.704	3.636	3.572	3.508	3.448	3.390	3.333	3.279	3.226	3.175	3.125
25	4.000	3.922	3.846	3.774	3.703	3.637	3.571	3.509	3.449	3.389	3.334	3.278	3.226	3.174	3.125
26	2.000	3.921	3.846	3.773	3.704	3.636	3.572	3.508	3.448	3.390	3.333	3.279	3.226	3.175	3.125
27			1.923	3.774	3.703	3.637	3.571	3.509	3.449	3.389	3.334	3.278	3.225	3.174	3.125
28					1.852	3.636	3.572	3.508	3.448	3.390	3.333	3.279	3.226	3.175	3.125
29							1.786	3.509	3.449	3.389	3.334	3.278	3.225	3.174	3.125
30									1.724	3.390	3.333	3.279	3.226	3.175	3.125
31											1.667	3.278	3.225	3.175	3.125
32													1.613	3.174	3.125
33															1.562

and the Recovery Period is:

the Depreciation Rate Is:

Year	32.5	33.0	33.5	34.0	34.5	35.0	35.5	36.0	36.5	37.0	37.5	38.0	38.5	39.0	39.5
1	1.538	1.515	1.493	1.471	1.449	1.429	1.408	1.389	1.370	1.351	1.333	1.316	1.299	1.282	1.266
2	3.077	3.030	2.985	2.941	2.899	2.857	2.817	2.778	2.740	2.703	2.667	2.632	2.597	2.564	2.532
3	3.077	3.030	2.985	2.941	2.899	2.857	2.817	2.778	2.740	2.703	2.667	2.632	2.597	2.564	2.532
4	3.077	3.030	2.985	2.941	2.899	2.857	2.817	2.778	2.740	2.703	2.667	2.632	2.597	2.564	2.532
5	3.077	3.030	2.985	2.941	2.899	2.857	2.817	2.778	2.740	2.703	2.667	2.632	2.597	2.564	2.532
6	3.077	3.030	2.985	2.941	2.899	2.857	2.817	2.778	2.740	2.703	2.667	2.632	2.597	2.564	2.532
7	3.077	3.030	2.985	2.941	2.898	2.857	2.817	2.778	2.740	2.703	2.667	2.632	2.597	2.564	2.532
8	3.077	3.030	2.985	2.941	2.899	2.857	2.817	2.778	2.740	2.703	2.667	2.632	2.597	2.564	2.532
9	3.077	3.030	2.985	2.941	2.898	2.857	2.817	2.778	2.740	2.703	2.667	2.632	2.597	2.564	2.532
10	3.077	3.030	2.985	2.941	2.899	2.857	2.817	2.778	2.740	2.703	2.667	2.632	2.597	2.564	2.532
11	3.077	3.030	2.985	2.941	2.898	2.857	2.817	2.778	2.740	2.703	2.667	2.632	2.597	2.564	2.532
12	3.077	3.030	2.985	2.941	2.899	2.857	2.817	2.778	2.740	2.703	2.667	2.632	2.598	2.564	2.532
13	3.077	3.030	2.985	2.941	2.898	2.857	2.817	2.778	2.740	2.703	2.667	2.632	2.597	2.564	2.532
14	3.077	3.030	2.985	2.941	2.899	2.857	2.817	2.778	2.740	2.703	2.667	2.632	2.598	2.564	2.531
15	3.077	3.031	2.985	2.941	2.898	2.857	2.817	2.778	2.740	2.703	2.666	2.632	2.597	2.564	2.532
16	3.077	3.030	2.985	2.941	2.899	2.857	2.817	2.778	2.740	2.703	2.667	2.632	2.598	2.564	2.531
17	3.077	3.031	2.985	2.941	2.898	2.857	2.817	2.778	2.740	2.703	2.666	2.632	2.597	2.564	2.532
18	3.077	3.030	2.985	2.941	2.899	2.857	2.817	2.778	2.740	2.703	2.667	2.632	2.598	2.564	2.531
19	3.077	3.031	2.985	2.941	2.898	2.857	2.817	2.778	2.739	2.702	2.666	2.631	2.597	2.564	2.532
20	3.077	3.030	2.985	2.941	2.898	2.857	2.817	2.778	2.740	2.703	2.667	2.632	2.598	2.564	2.531
21	3.077	3.031	2.985	2.941	2.899	2.857	2.817	2.778	2.739	2.702	2.666	2.631	2.597	2.564	2.532
22	3.077	3.030	2.985	2.941	2.898	2.857	2.817	2.777	2.740	2.703	2.667	2.632	2.598	2.564	2.531
23	3.077	3.031	2.985	2.941	2.899	2.857	2.817	2.778	2.739	2.703	2.666	2.631	2.597	2.564	2.532
24	3.077	3.030	2.985	2.941	2.898	2.857	2.817	2.777	2.740	2.702	2.667	2.632	2.598	2.564	2.531
25	3.077	3.031	2.985	2.942	2.899	2.857	2.817	2.778	2.739	2.703	2.666	2.632	2.597	2.564	2.532
26	3.077	3.030	2.985	2.941	2.898	2.857	2.817	2.777	2.740	2.702	2.667	2.631	2.598	2.564	2.531
27	3.077	3.031	2.985	2.942	2.899	2.857	2.817	2.778	2.739	2.703	2.666	2.632	2.597	2.564	2.532
28	3.077	3.030	2.985	2.941	2.898	2.858	2.817	2.777	2.740	2.702	2.667	2.631	2.598	2.564	2.531
29	3.077	3.031	2.985	2.942	2.899	2.857	2.817	2.778	2.739	2.703	2.666	2.632	2.597	2.564	2.532
30	3.077	3.030	2.985	2.941	2.898	2.858	2.817	2.777	2.740	2.702	2.667	2.631	2.598	2.564	2.531
31	3.076	3.031	2.986	2.942	2.899	2.857	2.817	2.778	2.739	2.703	2.666	2.632	2.597	2.564	2.532
32	3.077	3.030	2.985	2.941	2.898	2.858	2.816	2.777	2.740	2.702	2.667	2.631	2.598	2.564	2.531
33	3.076	3.031	2.986	2.942	2.899	2.857	2.817	2.778	2.739	2.703	2.666	2.632	2.597	2.565	2.532
34		1.515	2.985	2.941	2.898	2.857	2.816	2.778	2.740	2.702	2.667	2.631	2.598	2.564	2.531
35			1.493	1.471	2.899	2.857	2.817	2.778	2.739	2.703	2.666	2.632	2.597	2.565	2.532
36					1.449	1.429	2.816	2.778	2.740	2.702	2.667	2.631	2.598	2.564	2.531
37							1.408	1.389	2.739	2.703	2.666	2.632	2.597	2.565	2.532
38									1.370	1.351	2.667	2.631	2.598	2.564	2.531
39											1.333	1.316	2.597	2.565	2.532
40													1.316	1.282	2.531

and the Recovery Period Is:

the Depreciation Rate Is:

	40.0	40.5	41.0	41.5	42.0	42.5	43.0	43.5	44.0	44.5	45.0	45.5	46.0	46.5	47.0
1	1.250	1.235	1.220	1.205	1.190	1.176	1.163	1.149	1.136	1.124	1.111	1.099	1.087	1.075	1.064
2	2.500	2.469	2.439	2.410	2.381	2.353	2.326	2.299	2.273	2.247	2.222	2.198	2.174	2.151	2.128
3	2.500	2.469	2.439	2.410	2.381	2.353	2.326	2.299	2.273	2.247	2.222	2.198	2.174	2.151	2.128
4	2.500	2.469	2.439	2.410	2.381	2.353	2.326	2.299	2.273	2.247	2.222	2.198	2.174	2.151	2.128
5	2.500	2.469	2.439	2.410	2.381	2.353	2.326	2.299	2.273	2.247	2.222	2.198	2.174	2.151	2.128
6	2.500	2.469	2.439	2.410	2.381	2.353	2.326	2.299	2.273	2.247	2.222	2.198	2.174	2.150	2.128
7	2.500	2.469	2.439	2.410	2.381	2.353	3.326	2.299	2.273	2.247	2.222	2.198	2.174	2.151	2.128
8	2.500	2.469	2.439	2.410	2.381	2.353	2.326	2.299	2.273	2.247	2.222	2.198	2.174	2.150	2.128
9	2.500	2.469	2.439	2.410	2.381	2.353	2.325	2.299	2.273	2.247	2.222	2.198	2.174	2.151	2.128
10	2.500	2.469	2.439	2.410	2.381	2.353	2.326	2.299	2.273	2.247	2.222	2.198	2.174	2.150	2.128
11	2.500	2.469	2.439	2.410	2.381	2.353	2.325	2.299	2.273	2.247	2.222	2.198	2.174	2.151	2.128
12	2.500	2.469	2.439	2.410	2.381	2.353	2.326	2.299	2.273	2.247	2.222	2.198	2.174	2.150	2.128
13	2.500	2.469	2.439	2.409	2.381	2.353	2.325	2.299	2.273	2.247	2.222	2.198	2.174	2.151	2.128
14	2.500	2.469	2.439	2.410	2.381	2.353	2.326	2.299	2.273	2.247	2.222	2.198	2.174	2.151	2.128
15	2.500	2.469	2.439	2.409	2.381	2.353	2.325	2.299	2.273	2.247	2.222	2.198	2.174	2.150	2.128
16	2.500	2.469	2.439	2.410	2.381	2.353	2.326	2.299	2.273	2.247	2.222	2.198	2.174	2.151	2.128
17	2.500	2.469	2.439	2.409	2.381	2.353	2.325	2.299	2.273	2.247	2.222	2.198	2.174	2.150	2.127
18	2.500	2.469	2.439	2.410	2.381	2.353	2.326	2.299	2.273	2.247	2.222	2.198	2.174	2.151	2.128
19	2.500	2.469	2.439	2.409	2.381	2.353	2.325	2.299	2.273	2.247	2.222	2.198	2.174	2.150	2.127
20	2.500	2.469	2.439	2.410	2.381	2.353	2.326	2.299	2.273	2.247	2.222	2.198	2.174	2.151	2.128
21	2.500	2.469	2.439	2.409	2.381	2.353	2.325	2.299	2.273	2.247	2.222	2.198	2.174	2.150	2.127
22	2.500	2.469	2.439	2.410	2.381	2.353	2.326	2.299	2.273	2.247	2.222	2.198	2.174	2.151	2.128
23	2.500	2.469	2.439	2.409	2.381	2.353	2.325	2.299	2.272	2.247	2.222	2.198	2.174	2.150	2.127
24	2.500	2.469	2.439	2.409	2.381	2.353	2.326	2.299	2.273	2.247	2.222	2.198	2.174	2.151	2.128

25	2.500	2.469	2.439	2.410	2.381	2.353	2.325	2.299	2.272	2.247	2.222	2.198	2.174	2.150	2.127
26	2.500	2.469	2.439	2.409	2.381	2.353	2.326	2.299	2.273	2.247	2.222	2.198	2.174	2.151	2.128
27	2.500	2.469	2.439	2.410	2.381	2.353	2.325	2.299	2.272	2.247	2.223	2.198	2.174	2.150	2.127
28	2.500	2.469	2.439	2.409	2.381	2.353	2.326	2.299	2.273	2.247	2.222	2.198	2.174	2.151	2.128
29	2.500	2.469	2.439	2.410	2.381	2.353	2.325	2.299	2.272	2.247	2.223	2.198	2.174	2.150	2.127
30	2.500	2.469	2.439	2.409	2.381	2.353	2.326	2.299	2.273	2.248	2.222	2.197	2.174	2.151	2.128
31	2.500	2.469	2.439	2.410	2.381	2.353	2.325	2.299	2.272	2.247	2.223	2.198	2.174	2.150	2.127
32	2.500	2.469	2.439	2.409	2.381	2.353	2.326	2.299	2.273	2.248	2.222	2.197	2.174	2.151	2.128
33	2.500	2.470	2.439	2.410	2.381	2.353	2.325	2.298	2.272	2.247	2.223	2.198	2.174	2.150	2.127
34	2.500	2.470	2.439	2.409	2.381	2.353	2.326	2.299	2.273	2.248	2.222	2.197	2.174	2.151	2.128
35	2.500	2.469	2.439	2.410	2.381	2.353	2.325	2.298	2.272	2.247	2.223	2.198	2.174	2.150	2.127
36	2.500	2.470	2.139	2.409	2.381	2.353	2.326	2.299	2.273	2.248	2.222	2.197	2.174	2.151	2.128
37	2.500	2.469	2.439	2.410	2.381	2.353	2.325	2.298	2.272	2.247	2.223	2.198	2.174	2.150	2.127
38	2.500	2.470	2.439	2.409	2.381	2.353	2.326	2.299	2.273	2.248	2.222	2.197	2.174	2.151	2.128
39	2.500	2.469	2.439	2.410	2.381	2.353	2.325	2.298	2.272	2.247	2.223	2.198	2.174	2.150	2.127
40	2.500	2.470	2.439	2.409	2.381	2.353	2.326	2.299	2.273	2.248	2.222	2.197	2.174	2.151	2.128
41	1.250	2.469	2.439	2.409	2.381	2.353	2.325	2.298	2.272	2.247	2.223	2.198	2.173	2.150	2.127
42			1.220	2.409	2.381	2.353	2.326	2.299	2.273	2.248	2.223	2.198	2.174	2.150	2.128
43					1.190	2.352	2.325	2.298	2.272	2.247	2.223	2.198	2.174	2.150	2.127
44							1.163	2.299	2.273	2.248	2.223	2.198	2.174	2.151	2.128
45									1.136	2.247	2.223	2.197	2.174	2.150	2.127
46											1.111	2.198	2.174	2.151	2.128
47													1.087	2.150	2.127
48															1.064

If the Recovery Year Is:	and the Recovery Period Is:					
	47.5	48.0	48.5	49.0	49.5	50.0
	the Depreciation Rate Is:					
1	1.053	1.042	1.031	1.020	1.010	1.000
2	2.105	2.083	2.062	2.041	2.020	2.000
3	2.105	2.083	2.062	2.041	2.020	2.000
4	2.105	2.083	2.062	2.041	2.020	2.000
5	2.105	2.083	2.062	2.041	2.020	2.000
6	2.105	2.083	2.062	2.041	2.020	2.000
7	2.105	2.083	2.062	2.041	2.020	2.000
8	2.105	2.083	2.062	2.041	2.020	2.000
9	2.105	2.083	2.062	2.041	2.020	2.000
10	2.105	2.083	2.062	2.041	2.020	2.000
11	2.105	2.083	2.062	2.041	2.020	2.000
12	2.105	2.083	2.062	2.041	2.020	2.000
13	2.105	2.083	2.062	2.041	2.020	2.000
14	2.105	2.083	2.062	2.041	2.020	2.000
15	2.105	2.083	2.062	2.041	2.020	2.000
16	2.105	2.083	2.062	2.041	2.020	2.000
17	2.105	2.083	2.062	2.041	2.020	2.000
18	2.105	2.083	2.062	2.041	2.020	2.000
19	2.105	2.084	2.062	2.041	2.020	2.000
20	2.105	2.083	2.062	2.041	2.020	2.000
21	2.105	2.084	2.062	2.041	2.020	2.000
22	2.105	2.083	2.062	2.041	2.020	2.000
23	2.105	2.084	2.062	2.041	2.020	2.000
24	2.105	2.083	2.062	2.041	2.020	2.000
25	2.105	2.084	2.062	2.041	2.020	2.000
26	2.106	2.083	2.062	2.041	2.020	2.000
27	2.105	2.084	2.062	2.041	2.020	2.000
28	2.106	2.083	2.062	2.041	2.020	2.000
29	2.105	2.084	2.062	2.041	2.020	2.000
30	2.106	2.083	2.062	2.041	2.020	2.000
31	2.105	2.084	2.062	2.041	2.021	2.000
32	2.106	2.083	2.062	2.041	2.020	2.000
33	2.105	2.084	2.062	2.041	2.021	2.000
34	2.106	2.083	2.062	2.040	2.020	2.000
35	2.105	2.084	2.062	2.041	2.021	2.000
36	2.106	2.083	2.062	2.040	2.020	2.000
37	2.105	2.084	2.061	2.041	2.021	2.000
38	2.106	2.083	2.062	2.040	2.020	2.000
39	2.105	2.084	2.061	2.041	2.021	2.000
40	2.106	2.083	2.062	2.040	2.020	2.000
41	2.105	2.084	2.061	2.041	2.021	2.000
42	2.106	2.083	2.062	2.040	2.020	2.000
43	2.105	2.084	2.061	2.041	2.021	2.000
44	2.106	2.083	2.062	2.040	2.020	2.000
45	2.105	2.084	2.061	2.041	2.021	2.000
46	2.106	2.083	2.062	2.040	2.020	2.000
47	2.105	2.084	2.061	2.041	2.021	2.000
48	2.106	2.083	2.062	2.040	2.020	2.000
49		1.042	2.061	2.041	2.021	2.000
50				1.020	2.020	2.000
51						1.000

Table 13
Alternative Depreciation System
Applicable Depreciation Method: Straight Line
Applicable Recovery Period: 40 years
Applicable Convention: Mid-month

If the
Recovery
Year is:

And the Month in the First Recovery Year
the Property is Placed in Service is:

the Depreciation Rate Is:

Recovery Year	1	2	3	4	5	6	7	8	9	10	11	12
1	2.396	2.188	1.979	1.771	1.563	1.354	1.146	0.938	0.729	0.521	0.313	0.104
2 to 40	2.500	2.500	2.500	2.500	2.500	2.500	2.500	2.500	2.500	2.500	2.500	2.500
41	0.104	0.312	0.521	0.729	0.937	1.146	1.354	1.562	1.771	1.979	2.187	2.396

Table 14
General and Alternative Depreciation System
Applicable Depreciation Method: 150 Percent Declining Balance
Switching to Straight Line
Applicable Recovery Periods: 2.5 — 50 years
Applicable Convention: Half-year

If the Recovery Year is: and the Recovery Period is: — the Depreciation Rate Is:

Recovery Year	2.5	3.0	3.5	4.0	4.5	5.0	5.5	6.0	6.5	7.0	7.5	8.0	8.5	9.0	9.5
1	30.00	25.00	21.43	18.75	16.67	15.00	13.64	12.50	11.54	10.71	10.00	9.38	8.82	8.33	7.89
2	42.00	37.50	33.67	30.47	27.78	25.50	23.55	21.88	20.41	19.13	18.00	16.99	16.09	15.28	14.54
3	28.00	25.00	22.45	20.31	18.52	17.85	17.13	16.41	15.70	15.03	14.40	13.81	13.25	12.73	12.25
4		12.50	22.45	20.31	18.52	16.66	15.23	14.06	13.09	12.25	11.52	11.22	10.91	10.61	10.31
5				10.16	18.51	16.66	15.23	14.06	13.09	12.25	11.52	10.80	10.19	9.65	9.17
6						8.33	15.22	14.06	13.09	12.25	11.52	10.80	10.19	9.64	9.17
7								7.03	13.08	12.25	11.52	10.80	10.19	9.65	9.17
8										6.13	11.52	10.80	10.18	9.64	9.17
9												5.40	10.18	9.65	9.17
10														4.82	9.16

If the Recovery Year is: and the Recovery Period is: — the Depreciation Rate Is:

Recovery Year	10.0	10.5	11.0	11.5	12.0	12.5	13.0	13.5	14.0	14.5	15.0	15.5	16.0	16.5	17.0
1	7.50	7.14	6.82	6.52	6.25	6.00	5.77	5.56	5.36	5.17	5.00	4.84	4.69	4.55	4.41
2	13.88	13.27	12.71	12.19	11.72	11.28	10.87	10.49	10.14	9.81	9.50	9.21	8.94	8.68	8.43
3	11.79	11.37	10.97	10.60	10.25	9.93	9.62	9.33	9.05	8.80	8.55	8.32	8.10	7.89	7.69
4	10.02	9.75	9.48	9.22	8.97	8.73	8.51	8.29	8.08	7.88	7.70	7.51	7.34	7.17	7.01
5	8.74	8.35	8.18	8.02	7.85	7.69	7.53	7.37	7.22	7.07	6.93	6.79	6.65	6.52	6.39
6	8.74	8.35	7.98	7.64	7.33	7.05	6.79	6.55	6.44	6.34	6.23	6.13	6.03	5.93	5.83
7	8.74	8.35	7.97	7.64	7.33	7.05	6.79	6.55	6.32	6.10	5.90	5.72	5.55	5.39	5.32
8	8.74	8.35	7.98	7.63	7.33	7.05	6.79	6.55	6.32	6.10	5.90	5.72	5.55	5.39	5.23
9	8.74	8.36	7.97	7.64	7.33	7.04	6.79	6.55	6.32	6.10	5.91	5.72	5.55	5.39	5.23
10	8.74	8.35	7.98	7.63	7.33	7.05	6.79	6.55	6.32	6.11	5.90	5.72	5.55	5.39	5.23
11	4.37	8.36	7.97	7.64	7.32	7.04	6.79	6.55	6.32	6.10	5.91	5.72	5.55	5.38	5.23
12			3.99	7.63	7.33	7.05	6.78	6.55	6.32	6.11	5.90	5.72	5.54	5.39	5.23
13					3.66	7.04	6.79	6.56	6.32	6.10	5.91	5.72	5.55	5.38	5.23
14							3.39	6.55	6.31	6.11	5.90	5.72	5.54	5.39	5.23
15									3.16	6.10	5.91	5.72	5.55	5.38	5.23
16											2.95	5.72	5.54	5.39	5.23
17													2.77	5.38	5.23
18															2.62

and the Recovery Period is:

the Depreciation Rate Is:

	17.5	18.0	18.5	19.0	19.5	20.0	20.5	21.0	21.5	22.0	22.5	23.0	23.5	24.0	24.5
1	4.29	4.17	4.05	3.95	3.85	3.750	3.659	3.571	3.488	3.409	3.333	3.261	3.191	3.125	3.061
2	8.20	7.99	7.78	7.58	7.40	7.219	7.049	6.888	6.733	6.586	6.444	6.309	6.179	6.055	5.935
3	7.50	7.32	7.15	6.98	6.83	6.677	6.534	6.396	6.264	6.137	6.015	5.898	5.785	5.676	5.572
4	6.86	6.71	6.57	6.43	6.30	6.177	6.055	5.939	5.827	5.718	5.614	5.513	5.416	5.322	5.231
5	6.27	6.15	6.04	5.93	5.82	5.713	5.612	5.515	5.420	5.328	5.240	5.153	5.070	4.989	4.910
6	5.73	5.64	5.55	5.46	5.37	5.285	5.202	5.121	5.042	4.965	4.890	4.817	4.746	4.677	4.610
7	5.24	5.17	5.10	5.03	4.96	4.888	4.821	4.755	4.690	4.627	4.564	4.503	4.443	4.385	4.327
8	5.08	4.94	4.81	4.69	4.57	4.522	4.468	4.415	4.363	4.311	4.260	4.210	4.160	4.111	4.062
9	5.08	4.94	4.81	4.69	4.58	4.462	4.354	4.252	4.155	4.063	3.976	3.935	3.894	3.854	3.814
10	5.08	4.94	4.81	4.69	4.57	4.461	4.354	4.252	4.155	4.063	3.976	3.890	3.808	3.729	3.655
11	5.08	4.94	4.81	4.69	4.58	4.462	4.354	4.252	4.155	4.063	3.976	3.890	3.808	3.729	3.655
12	5.08	4.94	4.82	4.69	4.57	4.461	4.354	4.252	4.155	4.063	3.976	3.890	3.808	3.729	3.655
13	5.09	4.95	4.81	4.69	4.58	4.462	4.354	4.252	4.155	4.064	3.976	3.890	3.808	3.730	3.655
14	5.08	4.94	4.82	4.69	4.57	4.461	4.354	4.252	4.155	4.063	3.976	3.890	3.808	3.729	3.655
15	5.09	4.95	4.81	4.69	4.58	4.462	4.354	4.252	4.155	4.064	3.976	3.890	3.808	3.730	3.655
16	5.08	4.94	4.82	4.69	4.57	4.461	4.354	4.252	4.155	4.063	3.976	3.890	3.808	3.729	3.655
17	5.09	4.95	4.81	4.69	4.58	4.462	4.354	4.252	4.155	4.064	3.976	3.889	3.808	3.730	3.655
18	5.08	2.47	4.82	4.70	4.57	4.461	4.354	4.252	4.156	4.063	3.976	3.890	3.807	3.729	3.655
19				4.69	4.58	4.462	4.353	4.251	4.155	4.064	3.976	3.889	3.808	3.730	3.655
20				2.35	4.57	4.461	4.354	4.252	4.156	4.063	3.976	3.890	3.807	3.729	3.655
21						2.231	4.353	4.251	4.155	4.064	3.976	3.889	3.808	3.730	3.655
22								2.126	4.156	4.063	3.976	3.890	3.807	3.729	3.655
23										2.032		1.945	3.808	3.730	3.655
24													3.807	3.729	3.654
25														1.865	3.654

If the Recovery Year is:	and the Recovery Period is: the Depreciation Rate Is:														
	25.0	25.5	26.0	26.5	27.0	27.5	28.0	28.5	29.0	29.5	30.0	30.5	31.0	31.5	32.0
1	3.000	2.941	2.885	2.830	2.778	2.727	2.679	2.632	2.586	2.542	2.500	2.459	2.419	2.381	2.344
2	5.820	5.709	5.603	5.500	5.401	5.306	5.214	5.125	5.039	4.955	4.875	4.797	4.722	4.649	4.578
3	5.471	5.374	5.280	5.189	5.101	5.016	4.934	4.855	4.778	4.704	4.631	4.561	4.493	4.427	4.363
4	5.143	5.057	4.975	4.895	4.818	4.743	4.670	4.599	4.531	4.464	4.400	4.337	4.276	4.216	4.159
5	4.834	4.760	4.688	4.618	4.550	4.484	4.420	4.357	4.297	4.237	4.180	4.124	4.069	4.016	3.964
6	4.544	4.480	4.417	4.357	4.297	4.239	4.183	4.128	4.074	4.022	3.971	3.921	3.872	3.824	3.778
7	4.271	4.216	4.163	4.110	4.059	4.008	3.959	3.911	3.864	3.817	3.772	3.728	3.685	3.642	3.601
8	4.015	3.968	3.922	3.877	3.833	3.790	3.747	3.705	3.664	3.623	3.584	3.545	3.506	3.469	3.432
9	3.774	3.735	3.696	3.658	3.620	3.583	3.546	3.510	3.474	3.439	3.404	3.370	3.337	3.304	3.271
10	3.584	3.515	3.483	3.451	3.419	3.387	3.356	3.325	3.294	3.264	3.234	3.204	3.175	3.146	3.118
11	3.583	3.515	3.448	3.383	3.321	3.262	3.205	3.150	3.124	3.098	3.072	3.047	3.022	2.996	2.971
12	3.584	3.515	3.448	3.383	3.321	3.262	3.205	3.150	3.096	3.044	2.994	2.945	2.899	2.854	2.832
13	3.583	3.515	3.448	3.383	3.321	3.262	3.205	3.150	3.096	3.044	2.994	2.945	2.899	2.854	2.809
14	3.584	3.515	3.448	3.383	3.321	3.262	3.205	3.150	3.096	3.044	2.994	2.945	2.899	2.854	2.809
15	3.583	3.515	3.448	3.383	3.321	3.262	3.205	3.150	3.096	3.044	2.994	2.945	2.899	2.854	2.809
16	3.584	3.515	3.448	3.383	3.322	3.262	3.205	3.150	3.096	3.044	2.994	2.945	2.899	2.854	2.809
17	3.583	3.515	3.448	3.383	3.321	3.262	3.205	3.150	3.096	3.044	2.994	2.945	2.899	2.854	2.809
18	3.584	3.516	3.448	3.383	3.322	3.262	3.205	3.150	3.096	3.044	2.994	2.946	2.899	2.854	2.809
19	3.583	3.515	3.448	3.383	3.321	3.262	3.205	3.150	3.096	3.044	2.994	2.945	2.899	2.854	2.809
20	3.584	3.516	3.447	3.384	3.322	3.262	3.205	3.150	3.096	3.044	2.993	2.946	2.899	2.854	2.809
21	3.583	3.515	3.448	3.383	3.321	3.262	3.205	3.150	3.096	3.044	2.994	2.945	2.899	2.854	2.809
22	3.584	3.516	3.447	3.384	3.322	3.262	3.205	3.150	3.096	3.044	2.993	2.946	2.898	2.854	2.809
23	3.583	3.515	3.448	3.383	3.321	3.262	3.205	3.150	3.096	3.044	2.994	2.945	2.899	2.854	2.809
24	3.584	3.516	3.447	3.384	3.322	3.262	3.205	3.151	3.096	3.044	2.993	2.946	2.898	2.854	2.810
25	3.583	3.515	3.448	3.383	3.321	3.262	3.205	3.150	3.096	3.044	2.994	2.945	2.899	2.853	2.809
26	1.792	3.516	3.447	3.384	3.322	3.262	3.205	3.151	3.096	3.044	2.993	2.946	2.898	2.854	2.810
27			1.724	3.383	3.321	3.262	3.205	3.150	3.096	3.044	2.994	2.945	2.899	2.853	2.809
28					1.661	3.263	3.205	3.151	3.096	3.044	2.993	2.946	2.898	2.853	2.810
29							1.602	3.150	3.095	3.044	2.994	2.945	2.899	2.854	2.809
30									1.548	3.043	2.993	2.946	2.899	2.853	2.810
31											1.497	2.945	2.899	2.854	2.809
32													1.449	2.853	2.810
33															1.405

If the Recovery Year is:

and the Recovery Period is:

the Depreciation Rate Is:

If the Recovery Year is:	32.5	33.0	33.5	34.0	34.5	35.0	35.5	36.0	36.5	37.0	37.5	38.0	38.5	39.0	39.5
1	2.308	2.273	2.239	2.206	2.174	2.143	2.113	2.083	2.055	2.027	2.000	1.974	1.948	1.923	1.899
2	4.509	4.442	4.377	4.314	4.253	4.194	4.136	4.080	4.025	3.972	3.920	3.869	3.820	3.772	3.725
3	4.301	4.240	4.181	4.124	4.068	4.014	3.961	3.910	3.860	3.811	3.763	3.717	3.671	3.627	3.584
4	4.102	4.048	3.994	3.942	3.892	3.842	3.794	3.747	3.701	3.656	3.613	3.570	3.528	3.488	3.448
5	3.913	3.864	3.815	3.768	3.722	3.677	3.634	3.591	3.549	3.508	3.468	3.429	3.391	3.353	3.317
6	3.732	3.688	3.645	3.602	3.560	3.520	3.480	3.441	3.403	3.366	3.329	3.294	3.259	3.225	3.191
7	3.560	3.520	3.481	3.443	3.406	3.369	3.333	3.298	3.263	3.229	3.196	3.164	3.132	3.100	3.070
8	3.396	3.360	3.325	3.291	3.258	3.225	3.192	3.160	3.129	3.099	3.068	3.039	3.010	2.981	2.953
9	3.239	3.208	3.177	3.146	3.116	3.086	3.057	3.029	3.001	2.973	2.946	2.919	2.893	2.867	2.841
10	3.090	3.062	3.034	3.007	2.980	2.954	2.928	2.903	2.877	2.852	2.828	2.804	2.780	2.756	2.733
11	2.947	2.923	2.898	2.875	2.851	2.828	2.804	2.782	2.759	2.737	2.715	2.693	2.671	2.650	2.629
12	2.811	2.790	2.769	2.748	2.727	2.706	2.686	2.666	2.646	2.626	2.606	2.587	2.567	2.548	2.529
13	2.766	2.725	2.685	2.646	2.608	2.590	2.572	2.555	2.537	2.519	2.502	2.485	2.467	2.450	2.433
14	2.766	2.725	2.685	2.646	2.608	2.571	2.535	2.500	2.466	2.434	2.402	2.386	2.371	2.356	2.341
15	2.766	2.725	2.685	2.646	2.608	2.571	2.535	2.500	2.466	2.434	2.402	2.370	2.340	2.310	2.281
16	2.766	2.725	2.685	2.646	2.608	2.571	2.535	2.500	2.466	2.434	2.402	2.370	2.340	2.310	2.281
17	2.766	2.725	2.685	2.646	2.608	2.571	2.535	2.500	2.467	2.434	2.402	2.370	2.340	2.310	2.281
18	2.766	2.725	2.685	2.646	2.608	2.571	2.535	2.500	2.466	2.434	2.402	2.370	2.340	2.310	2.281
19	2.766	2.725	2.685	2.646	2.609	2.571	2.535	2.500	2.467	2.434	2.402	2.370	2.340	2.310	2.281
20	2.766	2.725	2.685	2.646	2.608	2.571	2.535	2.500	2.466	2.434	2.402	2.370	2.340	2.310	2.281
21	2.766	2.725	2.685	2.646	2.608	2.571	2.535	2.500	2.467	2.434	2.402	2.370	2.340	2.310	2.281
22	2.767	2.725	2.685	2.646	2.609	2.571	2.535	2.500	2.466	2.434	2.402	2.370	2.340	2.310	2.281
23	2.766	2.725	2.685	2.646	2.608	2.571	2.535	2.500	2.467	2.433	2.402	2.370	2.340	2.310	2.281
24	2.767	2.724	2.685	2.646	2.609	2.571	2.535	2.500	2.466	2.434	2.402	2.370	2.340	2.310	2.281
25	2.766	2.725	2.685	2.646	2.608	2.571	2.535	2.500	2.467	2.433	2.402	2.370	2.340	2.310	2.281
26	2.767	2.724	2.685	2.646	2.609	2.571	2.535	2.500	2.466	2.434	2.402	2.370	2.339	2.310	2.281
27	2.766	2.725	2.684	2.646	2.608	2.571	2.536	2.500	2.467	2.433	2.402	2.370	2.339	2.310	2.281
28	2.767	2.724	2.685	2.646	2.609	2.572	2.535	2.501	2.466	2.434	2.402	2.370	2.340	2.310	2.281
29	2.766	2.725	2.684	2.646	2.608	2.571	2.536	2.500	2.467	2.433	2.402	2.370	2.339	2.310	2.281
30	2.767	2.724	2.685	2.646	2.609	2.572	2.535	2.501	2.466	2.434	2.402	2.371	2.340	2.310	2.281
31	2.766	2.725	2.684	2.646	2.608	2.571	2.536	2.500	2.467	2.433	2.401	2.370	2.339	2.310	2.281
32	2.767	2.724	2.685	2.646	2.609	2.572	2.535	2.501	2.466	2.434	2.402	2.371	2.340	2.310	2.281
33	2.766	2.725	2.684	2.646	2.608	2.571	2.536	2.500	2.467	2.433	2.404	2.370	2.339	2.310	2.281
34	2.766	1.362	2.685	2.645	2.609	2.572	2.535	2.501	2.466	2.434	2.402	2.371	2.340	2.310	2.281
35			2.685	1.323	2.608	2.571	2.535	2.500	2.467	2.433	2.401	2.370	2.339	2.310	2.281
36					2.608	1.286	2.535	2.500	2.466	2.434	2.402	2.370	2.340	2.310	2.281
37							2.535	1.250	2.467	2.433	2.401	2.370	2.339	2.310	2.281
38									2.467	1.217	2.402	2.371	2.340	2.310	2.281
39											2.402	1.185	2.339	2.309	2.282
40													2.339	1.155	2.281

If the
Recovery
Year is:

and the Recovery Period is:

the Depreciation Rate Is:

Year	40.0	40.5	41.0	41.5	42.0	42.5	43.0	43.5	44.0	44.5	45.0	45.5	46.0	46.5	47.0
1	1.875	1.852	1.829	1.807	1.786	1.765	1.744	1.724	1.705	1.685	1.667	1.648	1.630	1.613	1.596
2	3.680	3.635	3.592	3.549	3.508	3.467	3.428	3.389	3.351	3.314	3.278	3.242	3.208	3.174	3.141
3	3.542	3.500	3.460	3.421	3.382	3.345	3.308	3.272	3.237	3.202	3.169	3.135	3.103	3.071	3.040
4	3.409	3.371	3.334	3.297	3.262	3.227	3.193	3.159	3.126	3.094	3.063	3.032	3.002	2.972	2.943
5	3.281	3.246	3.212	3.178	3.145	3.113	3.081	3.050	3.020	2.990	2.961	2.932	2.904	2.876	2.849
6	3.158	3.126	3.094	3.063	3.033	3.003	2.974	2.945	2.917	2.889	2.862	2.836	2.809	2.784	2.758
7	3.040	3.010	2.981	2.952	2.924	2.897	2.870	2.843	2.817	2.792	2.767	2.742	2.718	2.694	2.670
8	2.926	2.899	2.872	2.846	2.820	2.795	2.770	2.745	2.721	2.698	2.674	2.652	2.629	2.607	2.585
9	2.816	2.791	2.767	2.743	2.719	2.696	2.673	2.651	2.629	2.607	2.585	2.564	2.543	2.523	2.503
10	2.710	2.688	2.666	2.644	2.622	2.601	2.580	2.559	2.539	2.519	2.499	2.480	2.460	2.441	2.423
11	2.609	2.588	2.568	2.548	2.529	2.509	2.490	2.471	2.452	2.434	2.416	2.398	2.380	2.363	2.345
12	2.511	2.492	2.474	2.456	2.438	2.421	2.403	2.386	2.369	2.352	2.335	2.319	2.303	2.287	2.271
13	2.417	2.400	2.384	2.367	2.351	2.335	2.319	2.304	2.288	2.273	2.257	2.242	2.228	2.213	2.198
14	2.326	2.311	2.296	2.282	2.267	2.253	2.238	2.224	2.210	2.196	2.182	2.169	2.155	2.141	2.128
15	2.253	2.226	2.212	2.199	2.186	2.173	2.160	2.148	2.135	2.122	2.110	2.097	2.085	2.072	2.060
16	2.253	2.226	2.198	2.172	2.146	2.121	2.097	2.073	2.062	2.051	2.039	2.028	2.017	2.055	1.994
17	2.253	2.226	2.198	2.172	2.146	2.121	2.097	2.073	2.050	2.027	2.005	1.983	1.962	1.941	1.931
18	2.253	2.226	2.198	2.172	2.147	2.121	2.097	2.073	2.050	2.027	2.005	1.983	1.961	1.941	1.920
19	2.253	2.226	2.199	2.172	2.146	2.121	2.097	2.073	2.050	2.027	2.005	1.983	1.962	1.941	1.920
20	2.253	2.226	2.198	2.172	2.147	2.121	2.097	2.074	2.050	2.027	2.005	1.983	1.961	1.941	1.920
21	2.253	2.225	2.199	2.172	2.146	2.122	2.097	2.073	2.050	2.027	2.005	1.983	1.962	1.941	1.920
22	2.253	2.226	2.198	2.172	2.147	2.121	2.097	2.074	2.050	2.027	2.005	1.983	1.961	1.941	1.920
23	2.253	2.225	2.199	2.172	2.146	2.122	2.097	2.073	2.050	2.027	2.005	1.983	1.962	1.941	1.920
24	2.253	2.226	2.198	2.172	2.147	2.121	2.097	2.074	2.050	2.027	2.004	1.983	1.961	1.941	1.920

25.	2.253	2.225	2.199	2.172	2.146	2.122	2.097	2.074	2.050	2.027	2.005	1.983	1.962	1.941	1.920
26.	2.253	2.226	2.198	2.172	2.147	2.121	2.097	2.073	2.050	2.027	2.004	1.983	1.961	1.941	1.920
27.	2.253	2.225	2.199	2.172	2.146	2.122	2.097	2.074	2.050	2.027	2.005	1.983	1.962	1.941	1.920
28.	2.253	2.226	2.198	2.172	2.147	2.121	2.097	2.073	2.050	2.027	2.004	1.983	1.961	1.941	1.920
29.	2.253	2.225	2.199	2.172	2.146	2.122	2.097	2.074	2.050	2.027	2.005	1.983	1.962	1.941	1.920
30.	2.253	2.226	2.198	2.172	2.147	2.121	2.097	2.073	2.050	2.027	2.004	1.983	1.961	1.941	1.920
31.	2.253	2.225	2.199	2.172	2.146	2.122	2.097	2.074	2.050	2.027	2.005	1.983	1.962	1.941	1.920
32.	2.253	2.225	2.198	2.172	2.147	2.121	2.097	2.073	2.050	2.027	2.004	1.983	1.961	1.941	1.920
33.	2.252	2.226	2.199	2.172	2.146	2.122	2.097	2.074	2.050	2.027	2.005	1.983	1.962	1.941	1.920
34.	2.253	2.225	2.198	2.172	2.147	2.121	2.097	2.073	2.050	2.027	2.004	1.983	1.961	1.940	1.920
35.	2.252	2.226	2.199	2.173	2.146	2.122	2.097	2.074	2.050	2.027	2.005	1.983	1.962	1.941	1.920
36.	2.253	2.225	2.198	2.172	2.147	2.121	2.098	2.073	2.050	2.027	2.004	1.982	1.961	1.940	1.920
37.	2.252	2.226	2.199	2.173	2.146	2.122	2.097	2.074	2.050	2.027	2.005	1.983	1.962	1.941	1.920
38.	2.253	2.225	2.198	2.172	2.147	2.121	2.098	2.073	2.050	2.027	2.004	1.982	1.961	1.940	1.920
39.	2.252	2.226	2.199	2.173	2.146	2.122	2.097	2.074	2.050	2.027	2.005	1.983	1.962	1.941	1.921
40.	2.253	2.225	2.198	2.172	2.147	2.121	2.098	2.073	2.049	2.027	2.004	1.982	1.961	1.940	1.920
41.	1.126	2.226	2.199	2.173	2.146	2.122	2.097	2.074	2.050	2.027	2.005	1.983	1.962	1.941	1.921
42.			1.099	2.172	2.147	2.121	2.098	2.073	2.049	2.027	2.004	1.982	1.961	1.940	1.920
43.					1.073	2.122	2.097	2.074	2.050	2.027	2.005	1.983	1.962	1.941	1.921
44.							1.049	2.073	2.049	2.027	2.004	1.982	1.961	1.940	1.920
45.									1.025	2.027	2.005	1.983	1.962	1.941	1.921
46.										2.026	1.002	1.982	1.961	1.940	1.920
47.												0.981	1.962	1.941	1.921
48.															0.960

If the Recovery Year is: **and the Recovery Period is:**

	47.5	48.0	48.5	49.0	49.5	50.0
	the Depreciation Rate Is:					
1	1.579	1.563	1.546	1.531	1.515	1.500
2	3.108	3.076	3.045	3.014	2.984	2.955
3	3.010	2.980	2.951	2.922	2.894	2.866
4	2.915	2.887	2.860	2.833	2.806	2.780
5	2.823	2.797	2.771	2.746	2.721	2.697
6	2.734	2.709	2.685	2.662	2.639	2.616
7	2.647	2.625	2.602	2.580	2.559	2.538
8	2.564	2.543	2.522	2.501	2.481	2.461
9	2.483	2.463	2.444	2.425	2.406	2.388
10	2.404	2.386	2.368	2.351	2.333	2.316
11	2.328	2.312	2.295	2.279	2.262	2.246
12	2.255	2.239	2.224	2.209	2.194	2.179
13	2.184	2.169	2.155	2.141	2.127	2.114
14	2.115	2.102	2.089	2.076	2.063	2.050
15	2.048	2.036	2.024	2.012	2.000	1.989
16	1.983	1.972	1.961	1.951	1.940	1.929
17	1.921	1.911	1.901	1.891	1.881	1.871
18	1.900	1.880	1.861	1.842	1.824	1.815
19	1.900	1.880	1.861	1.842	1.824	1.806
20	1.900	1.880	1.861	1.842	1.824	1.806
21	1.900	1.880	1.861	1.842	1.824	1.806
22	1.900	1.880	1.861	1.842	1.824	1.806
23	1.900	1.880	1.861	1.842	1.824	1.806
24	1.900	1.880	1.861	1.842	1.824	1.806
25	1.900	1.880	1.861	1.842	1.824	1.806
26	1.900	1.880	1.861	1.842	1.824	1.806
27	1.900	1.880	1.861	1.842	1.824	1.806
28	1.900	1.880	1.861	1.842	1.824	1.806
29	1.900	1.880	1.861	1.843	1.824	1.806
30	1.900	1.881	1.861	1.842	1.824	1.806
31	1.900	1.880	1.861	1.843	1.824	1.806
32	1.900	1.881	1.861	1.842	1.824	1.806
33	1.900	1.880	1.861	1.843	1.824	1.806
34	1.900	1.881	1.861	1.842	1.824	1.806
35	1.900	1.880	1.861	1.843	1.824	1.806
36	1.900	1.881	1.861	1.842	1.824	1.806
37	1.900	1.880	1.861	1.843	1.824	1.806
38	1.900	1.881	1.861	1.842	1.824	1.806
39	1.900	1.880	1.861	1.843	1.824	1.806
40	1.900	1.881	1.862	1.842	1.824	1.806
41	1.900	1.880	1.861	1.843	1.824	1.806
42	1.900	1.881	1.862	1.842	1.824	1.805
43	1.900	1.880	1.861	1.843	1.824	1.806
44	1.900	1.881	1.862	1.842	1.824	1.805
45	1.900	1.880	1.861	1.843	1.825	1.806
46	1.900	1.881	1.862	1.842	1.824	1.805
47	1.900	1.880	1.861	1.843	1.825	1.806
48	1.899	1.881	1.862	1.842	1.824	1.805
49		0.940	1.861	1.843	1.825	1.806
50				0.921	1.824	1.805
51						0.903

ACRS Cost-Recovery Rates for Tangible Personal Property

Recovery Year	Recovery Classes	
	3-Year	5-Year[a]
1	25%	15%
2	38	22
3	37	21
4	—	21
5	—	21
Totals	100%	100%

[a] The percentages that are applicable to each year for 10-year property are year 1, 8%; year 2, 14%; year 3, 12%; years 4 through 6, 10%; and years 7 through 10, 9%. The percentages that apply to 15-year property are year 1, 5%; year 2, 10%; year 3, 9%; year 4, 8%; years 5 and 6, 7%; and years 7 through 15, 6%.

ACRS Cost Recovery Tables for 19-Year Real Property

Table 1
19-Year Property (19-Year 175% Declining Balance)
(Assuming Mid-Month Convention)

If the Recovery Year is:	and the Month in the First Recovery Year the Property Is Placed in Service Is:											
	1	2	3	4	5	6	7	8	9	10	11	12
	the Depreciation Rate Is:											
1	8.8	8.1	7.3	6.5	5.8	5.0	4.2	3.5	2.7	1.9	1.1	0.4
2	8.4	8.5	8.5	8.6	8.7	8.8	8.8	8.9	9.0	9.0	9.1	9.2
3	7.6	7.7	7.7	7.8	7.9	7.9	8.0	8.1	8.1	8.2	8.3	8.3
4	6.9	7.0	7.0	7.1	7.1	7.2	7.3	7.3	7.4	7.4	7.5	7.6
5	6.3	6.3	6.4	6.4	6.5	6.5	6.6	6.6	6.7	6.8	6.8	6.9
6	5.7	5.7	5.8	5.9	5.9	5.9	6.0	6.0	6.1	6.1	6.2	6.2
7	5.2	5.2	5.3	5.3	5.3	5.4	5.4	5.5	5.5	5.6	5.6	5.6
8	4.7	4.7	4.8	4.8	4.8	4.9	4.9	5.0	5.0	5.1	5.1	5.1
9	4.2	4.3	4.3	4.4	4.4	4.5	4.5	4.5	4.5	4.6	4.6	4.7
10	4.2	4.2	4.2	4.2	4.2	4.2	4.2	4.2	4.2	4.2	4.2	4.2
11	4.2	4.2	4.2	4.2	4.2	4.2	4.2	4.2	4.2	4.2	4.2	4.2
12	4.2	4.2	4.2	4.2	4.2	4.2	4.2	4.2	4.2	4.2	4.2	4.2
13	4.2	4.2	4.2	4.2	4.2	4.2	4.2	4.2	4.2	4.2	4.2	4.2
14	4.2	4.2	4.2	4.2	4.2	4.2	4.2	4.2	4.2	4.2	4.2	4.2
15	4.2	4.2	4.2	4.2	4.2	4.2	4.2	4.2	4.2	4.2	4.2	4.2
16	4.2	4.2	4.2	4.2	4.2	4.2	4.2	4.2	4.2	4.2	4.2	4.2
17	4.2	4.2	4.2	4.2	4.2	4.2	4.2	4.2	4.2	4.2	4.2	4.2
18	4.2	4.2	4.2	4.2	4.2	4.2	4.2	4.2	4.2	4.2	4.2	4.2
19	4.2	4.2	4.2	4.2	4.2	4.2	4.2	4.2	4.2	4.2	4.2	4.2
20	0.2	0.5	0.9	1.2	1.6	1.9	2.3	2.6	3.0	3.3	3.7	4.0

ACRS Cost Recovery Tables for 18-Year Real Property

Table 1

**18-Year Real Property Placed in Service
after 3-15-84 and before 5-9-85
(18-Year 175% Declining Balance)
(Assuming Mid-Month Convention)**

If the Recovery Year Is:	and the Month in the First Recovery Year the Property Is Placed in Service Is:											
	1	2	3	4	5	6	7	8	9	10	11	12
	The applicable percentage is:											
1	9	9	8	7	6	5	4	4	3	2	1	0.4
2	9	9	9	9	9	9	9	9	9	10	10	10.0
3	8	8	8	8	8	8	8	8	9	9	9	9.0
4	7	7	7	7	7	8	8	8	8	8	8	8.0
5	7	7	7	7	7	7	7	7	7	7	7	7.0
6	6	6	6	6	6	6	6	6	6	6	6	6.0
7	5	5	5	5	6	6	6	6	6	6	6	6.0
8	5	5	5	5	5	5	5	5	5	5	5	5.0
9	5	5	5	5	5	5	5	5	5	5	5	5.0
10	5	5	5	5	5	5	5	5	5	5	5	5.0
11	5	5	5	5	5	5	5	5	5	5	5	5.0
12	5	5	5	5	5	5	5	5	5	5	5	5.0
13	4	4	4	5	4	4	5	4	4	4	5	5.0
14	4	4	4	4	4	4	4	4	4	4	4	4.0
15	4	4	4	4	4	4	4	4	4	4	4	4.0
16	4	4	4	4	4	4	4	4	4	4	4	4.0
17	4	4	4	4	4	4	4	4	4	4	4	4.0
18	4	3	4	4	4	4	4	4	4	4	4	4.0
19		1	1	1	2	2	2	3	3	3	3	3.6

ACRS Cost Recovery Table for 15-Year Real Property

1. All Real Estate (Except Low-Income Housing)

If the Recovery Year Is:	(Use the Column for the Month in the First Year the Property Is Placed in Service)											
	1	2	3	4	5	6	7	8	9	10	11	12
	The applicable percentage is:											
1	12	11	10	9	8	7	6	5	4	3	2	1
2	10	10	11	11	11	11	11	11	11	11	11	12
3	9	9	9	9	10	10	10	10	10	10	10	10
4	8	8	8	8	8	8	9	9	9	9	9	9
5	7	7	7	7	7	7	8	8	8	8	8	8
6	6	6	6	6	7	7	7	7	7	7	7	7
7	6	6	6	6	6	6	6	6	6	6	6	6
8	6	6	6	6	6	6	5	6	6	6	6	6
9	6	6	6	6	5	6	5	5	5	6	6	6
10	5	6	5	6	5	5	5	5	5	5	6	5
11	5	5	5	5	5	5	5	5	5	5	5	5
12	5	5	5	5	5	5	5	5	5	5	5	5
13	5	5	5	5	5	5	5	5	5	5	5	5
14	5	5	5	5	5	5	5	5	5	5	5	5
15	5	5	5	5	5	5	5	5	5	5	5	5
16	—	—	1	1	2	2	3	3	4	4	4	5

2. Low-Income Housing

If the Recovery Year Is:	(Use the Column for the Month in the First Year the Property Is Placed in Service)											
	1	2	3	4	5	6	7	8	9	10	11	12
	The applicable percentage is:											
1	13	12	11	10	9	8	7	6	4	3	2	1
2	12	12	12	12	12	12	12	13	13	13	13	13
3	10	10	10	10	11	11	11	11	11	11	11	11
4	9	9	9	9	9	9	9	9	10	10	10	10
5	8	8	8	8	8	8	8	8	8	8	8	9
6	7	7	7	7	7	7	7	7	7	7	7	7
7	6	6	6	6	6	6	6	6	6	6	6	6
8	5	5	5	5	5	5	5	5	5	5	6	6
9	5	5	5	5	5	5	5	5	5	5	5	5
10	5	5	5	5	5	5	5	5	5	5	5	5
11	4	5	5	5	5	5	5	5	5	5	5	5
12	4	4	4	5	4	5	5	5	5	5	5	5
13	4	4	4	4	4	4	5	4	5	5	5	5
14	4	4	4	4	4	4	4	4	4	5	4	4
15	4	4	4	4	4	4	4	4	4	4	4	4
16	—	—	1	1	2	2	2	3	3	3	4	4

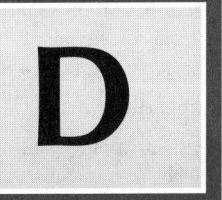

Glossary

Accelerated Cost Recovery System (ACRS) Established by ERTA in 1981, the ACRS provides an accelerated depreciation and shorter cost-recovery period for real and personal property. The Tax Reform Act of 1986 changed the previously allowed depreciation tables and assigned recovery periods that approach the asset's true economic life. The current depreciation system is referred to as MACRS.

Accounting method The method of determining the taxable year in which income and expenses are reported for tax purposes. Generally, the same method must be used for tax purposes as is used for keeping books and records. The accounting treatment used for any item of income or expense and of specific items (e.g., installment sales and contracts) is included in this term. See also each specific accounting method.

Accounting period The period of time, usually 12 months, used by taxpayers to compute their taxable income. Taxpayers who do not keep records must use a calendar year. Taxpayers who do keep books and records may choose between a calendar year or a fiscal year. The accounting period election is made on the taxpayer's first filed return and cannot be changed without IRS consent. The accounting period may be less than 12 months if it is the taxpayer's first or final return or if the taxpayer is changing accounting periods. Certain restrictions upon the use of a fiscal year apply to partnerships, S corporations, and personal service corporations.

Accrual method of accounting Accounting method under which income is reported and expenses are deducted when (1) all events have occurred that fix the taxpayer's right to receive the income and (2) the amount of the item can be determined with reasonable accuracy. Taxpayers with inventories to report must use this method to report sales and purchases.

Accumulated earnings tax This penalty tax is intended to discourage companies from retaining excessive amounts of earnings if the funds are invested in earnings that are unrelated to the business's needs. The current tax rate is 39.6%.

Acquiescence policy IRS policy of announcing whether it agrees or disagrees with a regular Tax Court decision. Such statements are not issued for every case.

ACRS See Accelerated Cost Recovery System.

Active income Income that is produced by the taxpayer's involvement or participation—wages, salaries, and other business income—is considered active income. It is the opposite of passive income.

Additional depreciation The excess of the actual amount of accelerated depreciation (or cost-recovery deductions under ACRS) over the amount of depreciation that would be deductible under the straight-line method. Such depreciation applies to Section 1250 depreciable real property acquired prior to 1987.

Adjusted current earnings An AMT adjustment item for corporations used to compute the Alternative Minimum Tax. The term is a concept based on the traditional earnings and profits definition found in Sec. 312.

Adjusted gross income (AGI) A measure of taxable income that falls between gross income and taxable income. It is the income amount that is used as the basis for calculating the floor or the ceiling for numerous other tax computations.

Adjusted sales price The amount realized from the sale of a residence less any fixing-up expenses.

AGI See Adjusted gross income.

Alimony Payments made pursuant to divorce or separation or written agreement between spouses subject to conditions specified in the tax law. Alimony payments (as contrasted to property settlements) are deductible for AGI by the payor and are included in the gross income of the recipient.

All events test Rule holding that an accrual basis taxpayer must report an item of income (1) when all events have occurred that fix the taxpayer's right to receive the item of income and (2) when the amount of the item can be determined with reasonable accuracy. This test is not satisfied until economic performance has taken place.

Alternative minimum tax (AMT) Applies to individuals, corporations, and estates and trusts only if it exceeds the taxpayer's regular tax liability. Most taxpayers are not subject to this tax.

Amount realized The amount realized equals the sum of money plus the fair market value of all other property received from the sale or other disposition of the property less any selling expenses (e.g., commissions, advertising, deed preparation costs, and legal expenses) incurred in connection with the sale.

AMT See Alternative Minimum Tax.

Annual accounting period See Accounting period.

Annuity A series of regular payments that will continue for either a fixed period of time or until the death of the recipient. Pensions are usually paid in this way.

Applicable federal rate The rate determined monthly by the federal government which is based on the rate paid by the government on borrowed funds. The rate varies with the term of the loan. Thus, short-term loans are for a period of under 3 years, mid-term loans are for over 3 years and under 9 years, and long-term loans are for over 9 years.

Asset depreciation range (ADR) system of depreciation Depreciation method allowed for property placed in service before January 1, 1981. This method prescribed useful lives for various classes of assets.

Average tax rate The taxpayer's total tax liability divided by the amount of his taxable income.

Backup withholding A modified withholding system intended to prevent abusive noncompliance situations.

Bad debt Bona fide debt that is uncollectible because it is worthless. Such debts are further characterized as "business bad debts," which give rise to an ordinary deduction, and "nonbusiness bad debts," which are treated as a short-term capital loss. A determination of whether a debt is worthless is made by reference to all the pertinent evidence (e.g., the debtor's general financial condition and whether the debt is secured by collateral). Such debts are deductible subject to certain requirements.

Bona fide debt A debt that (1) arises from a valid and enforceable obligation to pay a fixed or determinable sum of money and (2) results in a debtor-creditor relationship.

Boot Cash and nonlike-kind property given to complete an exchange of like-kind property where the property exchanged is not of equal value. Gain on the exchange is limited to the amount of boot received.

Brother-sister controlled group This type of corporation exists if (1) 5 or fewer individuals, estates, or trusts own at least 80% of the stock of each corporation and (2) there is common ownership of at least 50% of the total value of all classes of the stock. Each shareholder must own an interest in each corporation.

Business bad debt See Bad debt.

Cafeteria plan Employer-financed plan that offers employees the option of choosing cash or statutory nontaxable fringe benefits (other than scholarships, fellowships, and Sec. 132 benefits such as discounts on merchandise). Such plans may not discriminate in favor of highly compensated individuals or their dependents or spouses.

Capital addition See Capital expenditure.

Capital asset This category of assets includes all assets except inventory, notes and accounts receivable, and depreciable property or land used in a trade or business (e.g., property, plant, and machinery).

Capital expenditure An expenditure that adds to the value of, substantially prolongs the useful life of, or adapts the property to a new or different use qualifies as a capital expenditure.

Capital gain Gain realized on the sale or exchange of a capital asset.

Capital gain dividend A distribution by a regulated investment company (i.e., a mutual fund) of capital gains realized from the sale of investments in the fund. Such dividends also include undistributed capital gains allocated to the shareholders.

Capital gain property Property that is contributed to a public charity upon which a long-term capital gain would be recognized if that property was sold at its fair market value.

Capital loss Loss realized on the sale or exchange of a capital asset.

Capital recovery A capital recovery amount is a deduction for depreciation or cost recovery. It is a factor in the determination of a property's adjusted basis.

Cash method of accounting Accounting method that requires the taxpayer to report income for the taxable year in which payments are actually or constructively received. Expenses are reported in the year they are paid. Most individuals and service businesses (i.e., businesses without inventories) use this method.

Cash receipts and disbursements method of accounting See Cash method of accounting.

Casualty loss Loss that arises from an identifiable event that was sudden, unexpected, or unusual (e.g., fire, storm, shipwreck, other casualty, or theft). Within certain limitations, individuals may deduct such losses from AGI. Business casualty losses are deductible for AGI.

C Corporation Form of business entity that is taxed as a separate tax-paying entity. Its income is subject to an initial tax at the corporate level. Its shareholders are subject to a second tax when dividends are paid from the corporation's earnings and profits. Under certain conditions, S corporation status may be elected for tax purposes. C corporations are sometimes referred to as "regular corporations."

CD See Certificate of deposit.

Certificate of deposit (CD) An investment vehicle that earns interest as of a specific maturity date (e.g., one year). Generally, there is a penalty if the investor withdraws the principal amount before the maturity date.

Charitable contribution deduction Contributions of money or property made to qualified organizations (i.e., public charities and private nonoperating foundations) may be deducted from AGI. The amount of the deduction depends upon (1) the type of charity receiving the contribution, (2) the type of property contributed, and (3) other limitations mandated by the tax law. See also Unrelated use property.

Closed-fact situation Situation or transaction that has already occurred.

Closely held C corporation For purposes of the at risk rules, a closely held C corporation is defined as a corporation where more than 50% of the stock is owned by 5 or fewer individuals at any time during the last half of the corporation's taxable year. These individuals may or may not be members of the same family.

Combined controlled group A group of three or more corporations which are members of a parent-subsidiary or brother-sister controlled group. At least one of these corporations must be the parent of a parent-subsidiary controlled group and a member of a brother-sister controlled group.

Community income In any of the 8 community property states, such income consists of the income from the personal efforts, investments, etc. of either spouse. Community income belongs equally to both spouses.

Compensation Payment for personal services. Salaries, wages, fees, commissions, tips, bonuses, and specialized forms of compensation such as director's fees and jury's fees fall into this category. However, certain fringe benefits and some foreign-earned income are not taxed.

Completed contract method of accounting Accounting method for long-term contracts undertaken by smaller companies. Income from the contract is reported in the taxable year in which the contract is completed. The completed contract method is limited to construction contracts undertaken by smaller companies.

Constant interest rate method Used to amortize the original issue discount ratably over the life of the bond, this method determines the amount of interest income by multiplying the interest yield to maturity by the adjusted issue price.

Constructive dividend Distribution that is intended to result in a deduction to the corporation. For example, excessive salary payments to shareholder-employees may be recharacterized as nondeductible dividends to the corporation to the extent that such amounts are not reasonable. The excess amount may be treated as dividend income to the shareholder-employees rather than as compensation provided that certain conditions are met.

Constructive receipt doctrine Rule holding that cash method taxpayers cannot turn their backs on the receipt of income if the funds are unqualifiedly made available.

Constructive stock ownership Shares that are indirectly or deemed to be owned by another shareholder due to related party situations.

Contributory pension plan A qualified pension plan to which employees make voluntary contributions.

Controlled group A controlled group is two or more separately incorporated businesses owned by the same individuals or entities. Such groups may consist of parent-subsidiary corporations, brother-sister corporations, or a combination of both (combined group).

Cost The amount paid for property in cash or the fair market value of the property given in exchange. The costs of acquiring the property and preparing it for use are included in the cost of the property.

Cost depletion method Calculation of the depletion of an asset (e.g., oil and gas properties) under which the asset's adjusted basis is divided by the estimated recoverable units to arrive at a per-unit depletion. This amount is then multiplied by the number of units sold to determine the cost depletion. This method may be alternated with the percentage depletion method as long as the calculation takes that into account.

Current year's exclusion The amount of the annuity payment that is excluded from gross income. This amount is determined by multiplying the exclusion ratio by the amount received during the year.

Customs duties A federal excise tax on imported goods.

Deductions for AGI Expenses one would see on an income statement prepared for financial accounting purposes, for example, compensation paid to employees, repairs to business property, and depreciation expenses. Certain nonbusiness deductions (e.g., alimony payments, moving expenses, and deductible payments to an individual retirement account (IRA) are also deductible for AGI.

Deductions from AGI Generally, deductions are allowed for certain personal expenses such as medical deductions and charitable contributions which are referred to as itemized deductions. Alternatively, individuals may deduct the standard deduction. Personal and dependency deductions are also deductions from AGI.

Deferred compensation Methods of compensating employees based upon their current service where the benefits are deferred until future periods (e.g., a pension plan).

Deferred contribution H.R. 10 plan A special retirement plan for self-employed individuals where a separate account is maintained for the individual and fixed amounts are contributed based upon a specific percentage-of-compensation formula. The retirement benefits are based on the value of the self-employed individual's account at the time of retirement.

Defined benefit pension plan Qualified pension plan which establishes a contribution formula based upon actuarial techniques that are intended to fund a fixed retirement benefit amount. Thus, the amount that will be available at the time of retirement is determined when the contributions are made.

Defined contribution pension plan Qualified pension plan under which a separate account is maintained for each participant and fixed amounts are contributed based upon a specific percentage-of-compensation formula. The retirement benefits are based on the value of the participant's account at the time of retirement.

Dependent care assistance program Employer-financed programs that provide care for an employee's children or other dependents. An employee may exclude up to $5,000 from gross income although the ceiling amount (i.e., $2,400 or $4,800) on the child care credit is reduced by the amount of assistance that is excluded from gross income.

DIF See Discriminate Function System.

Discriminate Function System (DIF) System used by the IRS to select individual returns for audit. This system is intended to identify those tax returns which are most likely to contain errors.

Dividends-received deduction This deduction attempts to mitigate the triple taxation that would occur if one corporation paid dividends to a corporate shareholder who, in turn, distributed such amounts to its individual shareholders. Certain restrictions and limitations apply to this deduction.

E&P See Earnings and profits.

Earnings and profits (E&P) A measure of the corporation's ability to pay a dividend from its current and accumulated earnings without an impairment of capital.

Economic performance test Economic performance occurs when the property or services to be provided are actually delivered.

Education expense Subject to certain limitations and restrictions, education expenses are deductible if they are incurred (1) to improve or maintain the individual's existing skills or (2) to meet requirements that are requisite to continued employment or meet the requirements of state law.

Effective tax rate The taxpayer's total tax liability divided by his total economic income.

Employee achievement award Award given under circumstances that does not create a likelihood that it is really disguised compensation. It must be in the form of

tangible personal property (other than cash) and be valued at no more than $400.

Employee stock ownership plan (ESOP) A qualified stock bonus plan or combined stock bonus plan and money purchase pension plan. ESOP's are funded by contributions of the employer's stock which are held for the employees' benefit.

Employment taxes Social security (FICA) and federal and state unemployment compensation taxes.

Entertainment expense Entertainment expenses (e.g., business meals) that are either directly related to or associated with the active conduct of a trade or business are deductible within certain limitations and restrictions. Directly related expenses are those that (1) derive a business benefit other than goodwill and (2) are incurred in a clear business setting. Expenses that are associated with the business are those that show a clear business purpose (e.g., obtaining new business) and occur on the same day the business is discussed.

ESOP See Employee stock ownership plan.

Estate tax Part of the federal unified transfer tax system, this tax is based upon the total property transfers an individual makes during his lifetime and at death.

Excess depreciation See Additional depreciation.

Exchange A transaction in which one receives a reciprocal transfer of property rather than cash and/or a cash equivalent.

Excise taxes Federal tax on alcohol, gasoline, telephone usage, oil and gas production, etc. State and local governments may impose similar taxes on goods and services.

Exclusion Any item of income that the tax law says is not taxable.

Exclusion ratio The portion of the annuity payment that is excluded from taxation. This amount equals the investment in the contract (its cost) divided by the expected return from the annuity.

Expected return The amount which a taxpayer can expect to receive from an annuity. It is determined by multiplying the amount of the annuity's annual payment by the expected return multiple.

Expected return multiple The number of years that the annuity is expected to continue. This amount may be a stated term or for the remainder of the taxpayer's life.

Fair market value (FMV) This amount is the price at which property would change hands between a willing buyer and a willing seller where neither party is under any compulsion to buy or sell.

Federal estate tax See estate tax.

Federal Insurance Contributions Act See FICA.

Federal Unemployment Tax Act See FUTA.

FICA Tax withheld through the payment of payroll taxes, FICA is intended to finance social security benefits for individuals who are not self-employed. Employees and employers contribute matching amounts until a federally-set annual earnings ceiling is reached. At that time, no further contributions need be met for that year. Self-employed individuals are subject to self-employment tax and currently receive a *for* AGI income tax deduction equal to 50% of their self-employment tax payments.

Field audit procedure Audit procedure generally used by the IRS for corporations or individuals engaged in a trade or business and conducted at either the taxpayer's place of business or his tax advisor's office. Generally, several items on the tax return are examined.

FIFO method of inventory valuation This flow of cost method assumes that the first goods purchased will be the first goods sold. Thus, the ending inventory consists of the last goods purchased.

Fiscal year An annual accounting period that ends on the last day of any month other than December. A fiscal year may be elected by taxpayers that keep books and records, such as businesses.

Fixing-up expenses Expenses incurred to assist in the sale of a residence (e.g., normal repairs and painting costs). Capital expenditures do not qualify as fixing-up expenses.

Flat tax See Proportional tax.

Foreign-earned income An individual's earnings from personal services rendered in a foreign country.

Foreign tax credit Tax credit given to mitigate the possibility of double taxation faced by U.S. taxpayers earning foreign income.

Former passive activity An activity that was formerly considered passive, but which is not considered to be passive with respect to the taxpayer for the current year.

Franchise tax State tax levy sometimes based upon a weighted average formula consisting of net worth, income, and sales.

FUTA Federal and state unemployment compensation tax.

GAAP See Generally accepted accounting principles.

Gain realized This amount is equal to the excess of the amount realized from the sale of the property over the property's adjusted basis.

General business credit Special credit category consisting of tax credits commonly available to businesses. The more significant credit items are (1) the investment tax credit, (2) the targeted jobs credit, (3) the research credit, (4) the low-income housing credit, (5) the empowerment zone employment credit, (6) the disabled access credit.

Generally accepted accounting principles (GAAP) The accounting principles that govern the preparation of financial reports to shareholders. GAAP does not apply to the tax treatment unless the method clearly reflects income. It is used only when the regulations do not specify the treatment of an item or when the regulations provide more than one alternative accounting method.

Gift tax A tax that is imposed upon the donor for transfers that are not supported by full and adequate consideration. A $10,000 annual exclusion is allowed per donee.

Gross income All income received in cash, property, or services, from whatever source derived and from which the taxpayer derives a direct economic benefit.

Gross tax For income tax purposes, the amount determined by multiplying taxable income by the appropriate tax rate(s). The gross tax may also be found in the appropriate tax table for the taxpayer's filing status.

Holding period The length of time an asset is held before it is disposed of. This period is used to determine whether the gain or loss is long- or short-term.

H.R. 10 Plan Special retirement plan rules applicable to self-employed individuals. Such plans are often referred to as "Keogh plans."

Hybrid method of accounting Accounting method that combines the cash and accrual methods. Under this method, taxpayers can report sales and purchases under the accrual method and other income and expense items under the cash method. See also the cash method of accounting and the accrual method of accounting.

IDCs See Intangible drilling and development costs.

Imputed interest rule This rule reallocates the payments received in an installment sale between interest (fully taxable) and principal (only gain is taxable). To avoid this, the stated interest rate must equal at least 100% of the applicable federal rate as determined monthly according to the rate paid by the government on borrowed funds.

Incentive stock option plan (ISO) Stock option plan that allows executives to receive a proprietary interest in the corporation. The option to participate in this type of plan must be exercised according to certain requirements and must follow certain procedures.

Income The economic concept of income measures the amount an individual can consume during a period and remain as well off at the end of the period as at the beginning. The accounting concept of income is a measure of the income that is realized in a transaction. The tax concept of income is close to the accounting concept. It includes both taxable and nontaxable income from any source. However, it does not include a return of capital.

Indeterminate market value If the market value of the property in question cannot be determined by the usual methods, the "open transaction" doctrine may be applied and the tax consequences may be deferred until the transaction is closed. Alternatively, the property may be valued by using the fair market value of the property that is given in the exchange (e.g., the value of the services rendered).

Individual retirement account (IRA) Contribution for AGI that is deductible if (1) neither the taxpayer nor his spouse are active participants in an employer-sponsored retirement plan or (2) certain income limitations are met. Taxpayers who do not meet these requirements may make nondeductible IRA contributions.

Information Release An administrative pronouncement concerning an issue the IRS thinks the general public will be interested in. Such releases are issued in lay terms.

Innocent spouse rule Rule that exempts a spouse from penalty of from liability for the tax if such spouse had no knowledge of nor reason to know about an item of community income.

Installment sale Any disposition of property which involves receiving at least one payment after the close of the taxable year in which the sale occurs.

Installment sale method of accounting Taxpayers may use this method of accounting to reduce the tax burden from gains on the sale of property paid for in installments. Under this method, payment of the tax is deferred until the sale proceeds are collected. This method is not applicable to sales of publicly traded property or to losses.

Intangible drilling and development costs (IDCs) Expenditures made by an operator for wages, fuel, repairs, hauling supplies, and so forth, incident to and necessary for the preparation and drilling of oil and gas wells.

Interest The cost charged by a lender for the use of money. For example, finance charges, loan discounts, premiums, loan origination fees, and points paid by a buyer to obtain a mortgage loan are all interest expenses. The deductibility of the expense depends upon the purpose for which the indebtedness was incurred.

Internal Rate of Return (IRR) Method of determining the anticipated return on an investment. This method equates the investment's positive future cash flows with the cost of the investment.

Internal Revenue Code The primary legislative source and authority for tax research, planning, and compliance activities.

Internal Revenue Service (IRS) The branch of the Treasury Department that is responsible for administering the federal tax law.

Interpretative Regulations Treasury Regulations that serve to broadly interpret the provisions of the Internal Revenue Code.

Inter vivos gifts Gifts made during the donor's life-time.

Investment expenses All deductions other than interest that are directly connected with the production of investment income.

Investment income Gross income from property held for investment and any net gain attributable to the disposition of such property. See also Net investment income.

Investment interest Interest expense on indebtedness incurred to purchase or carry property held for investment (e.g., income from interest, dividends, annuities, and royalties). Interest expenses incurred from passive activities are not subject to the investment interest limitations and interest incurred to purchase or carry tax-exempt securities is not deductible. Interest incurred from passive activities is subject to the passive activity loss limitation rules.

Involuntary conversion Such a conversion occurs when property is compulsorily converted into money or other property due to theft, seizure, requisition, condemnation, or partial or complete destruction. For example, an involuntary conversion occurs when the government exercises its right of eminent domain.

IRA See Individual retirement account.

IRC See Internal Revenue Code.

IRR See Internal rate of return.

IRS See Internal Revenue Service.

ISO See Incentive stock option.

Itemized deductions Also known as "deductions from AGI," these personal expenditures are allowable for such items as medical expenses, state and local taxes, charitable contributions, unreimbursed employee business expenses, interest on a personal residence, and casualty and theft losses. There are specific requirements for and limitations on the deductibility of each of these items. In addition, only those taxpayers whose total itemized deductions exceed the standard deduction amount can itemize their deductions. In general, the total itemized deductions for an individual is reduced by 3% of AGI in excess of $111,800 ($55,900 for married individuals filing a separate return).

Joint income Income from jointly-held property.

Keogh plan Retirement plan for self-employed individuals. This type of plan is also known as an "H.R. 10 plan."

LCM See Lower of cost or market method of inventory valuation.

Legislative Regulations Treasury Regulations issued at the mandate of the Internal Revenue Code. Legislative regulations have a higher degree of authority than interpretative regulations.

Letter Ruling Letter rulings originate from the IRS at the taxpayer's request. They describe how the IRS will treat a proposed transaction. It is only binding on the person requesting the ruling providing the taxpayer completes the transaction as proposed in the ruling. Those of general interest are published as Revenue Rulings.

LIFO method of inventory valuation This method assumes a last-in, first out flow of cost. It results in the lowest taxable income during periods of inflation because it shows the lowest inventory value. Price indexes are used for the valuation. The information in these indexes is grouped into groups (pools) of similar items. See also Simplified LIFO method.

Like-kind exchange A direct exchange of like-kind property. The transferred property and the received property must be held for productive use either (1) in a trade or business or (2) as an investment. Nonrecognition of gain or loss is mandatory. Certain like-kind exchanges between related parties are restricted if either party disposes of the property within 2 years of the exchange.

Like-kind property Property with a similar nature and character. This term does not refer to either the grade or quality of the property.

Liquidating distribution A distribution that liquidates a partner's entire partnership interest due to retirement, death, or other business reason. Such distributions result in a capital gain or loss to the partner whose interest is liquidated. In a corporate liquidation, the liquidating corporation generally recognizes gains and losses on the distribution of the properties and its shareholders recognize capital gain or loss on the surrender of their stock.

Long-term capital gain (LTCG) Gain realized on the sale or exchange of a capital asset held longer than one year.

Long-term capital loss (LTCL) Loss realized on the sale or exchange of a capital asset held longer than one year.

Long-term contracts Building, manufacturing, installation, and construction contracts that are not completed in the same taxable year in which they are entered into. Service contracts do not qualify as long-term contracts. See also Completed contract method of accounting.

Look-back interest Interest that is assessed on any additional tax that would have been paid if the actual total cost of the contract was used to calculate the tax rather than the estimated cost. Thus, it is applicable to any contract of portion of a contract that is accounted for under either the hybrid or percentage of completion method of accounting.

Lower of cost or market method (LCM) of inventory valuation The valuation method is available to all taxpayers other than those using LIFO valuation. It is applied to each separate item in the inventory.

Marginal tax rate The tax that is applied to an incremental amount of taxable income that is added to the tax base. This rate can be used to measure the tax effect of a proposed transaction. Currently, the highest marginal tax rate for individuals is 39.6%.

Market value This term refers to replacement cost under the lower of cost or market inventory method. That is, it is the price at which the taxpayer can replace the goods in question. See also Fair market value.

Medical expense deduction Unreimbursed medical expenses incurred for medical procedures or treatments that are (1) legal in the locality in which they are performed and (2) incurred for the purpose of alleviating a physical or mental defect or illness that affects the body's structure or function are deductible from AGI. Out-of-pocket travel costs incurred while en route to a medical facility, certain capital expenditures affecting the sick person, premiums for medical insurance, and in-patient hospital care are also deductible. Certain restrictions and limitations apply to this deduction.

Memorandum decision Decision issued by the Tax Court. They deal with factual variations on matters which were decided in earlier cases.

Method of accounting See Accounting method.

Miscellaneous itemized deductions Certain unreimbursed employee expenses (e.g., required uniforms, travel, entertainment, and so on) fall into this category. Miscellaneous itemized deductions also include certain investment expenses, appraisal fees for charitable contributions and fees for tax return preparation. The nature of the deduction depends on whether the taxpayer is an employee or a self-employed individual.

Modified percentage of completion method A variation of the regular percentage of completion method where an election may be made to defer reporting profit from a long-term contract until at least 10% of the estimated total cost has been incurred.

Moving expense Expenses incurred in relation to employment-related job transfers.

Necessary expense Expense that is deductible because it is appropriate and helpful in the taxpayer's business. Such expenses must also qualify as ordinary.

Net investment income The excess of the taxpayer's investment income over his investment expenses. See also Investment income.

Net operating loss (NOL) A net operating loss occurs when business expenses exceed business income for any taxable year. Such losses may be carried back 3 years or carried forward 15 years to a year in which the taxpayer has taxable income. Loss must be carried back first and must be deducted from years in chronological order.

Net Present Value (NPV) Method used by investment analysts to determine the anticipated return on an investment. This method uses a fixed discount rate to compute the net present value of future cash flows.

NOL See Net operating loss.

Nonbusiness bad debt See Bad debt.

Noncontributory pension plan Only the employer makes contributions to this type of pension plan.

Nonliquidating distribution Distribution that reduces but does not eliminate, a partner's partnership interest. Such distributions are generally treated as tax-free returns of capital.

Nonpassive income All income other than royalties, rents, dividends, interest, annuities, and gains from the sale or exchange of stocks and securities.

Nonqualified deferred compensation plan Type of plan used by employer to provide incentives or supplementary retirement benefits for executives. Such plans are not subject to the nondiscrimination and vesting rules.

Nonqualified stock option Stock option that does not meet the requirements for an incentive stock option.

Nonrefundable credit Allowances, such as the dependent child care credit, that have been created for various social, economic, and political reasons. The tax credits in this category do not result from payments made to the government in advance. Thus, they can be deducted from the tax, but they are not payable to the taxpayer in situations where the credit exceeds the tax.

NPV See Net Present Value

Office audit procedure IRS audit of a specific item on an individual's tax return. An office audit takes place at the IRS branch office.

Open-fact situation A situation that has not yet occurred. That is, one for which the facts and events are still controllable and can be planned for.

Ordinary expense An expense that is deductible because it is reasonable in amount and bears a reasonable and proximate relationship to the income-producing activity or property.

Ordinary income property For purposes of the charitable contribution deduction, any property that would result in the recognition of ordinary income if the property were sold. Such property includes inventory, works of art or manuscripts created by the taxpayer, capital assets that have been held for one year or less, and Section 1231 property that results in ordinary income due to depreciation recapture.

Organizational expenditures The amortizable legal, accounting, filing, and other fees incidental to organizing a partnership or a corporation.

Parent-subsidiary controlled group To qualify, a common parent must own at least 80% of the stock of at least one subsidiary corporation and at least 80% of each other component member of the controlled group must be owned by other members of the controlled group.

Partnership Syndicate, group pool, joint venture, or other unincorporated organization which carries on a business or financial operation or venture.

Partnership interest The capital and/or profits interest in a partnership received in exchange for a contribution of properties or services (e.g., money or business equipment). The nature of a partnership interest is similar to that of corporate stock.

Passive activity To define what constitutes a passive activity for the purpose of applying the passive loss rules, it is necessary to (1) identify what constitutes an activity and (2) determine whether the taxpayer has materially participated in the activity. Temp. Reg. Sec. 1.469-4T contains detailed rules for making these determinations.

Passive income Income from an activity that does not require the taxpayer's material involvement or participation. Thus, income from tax shelters and rental activities fall into the category.

Passive loss Loss generated from a passive activity. Such losses are computed separately. They may be used to offset income from other passive activities, but may not be used to offset either active or portfolio income.

Percentage depletion method Depletion method for assets such as oil and gas that is equal to a specified percentage times the gross income from the property but which may not exceed 100% of the taxable income before depletion is deducted. Lease bonuses, advance royalties, and other amounts payable without regard to production may not be included in the calcualtion. This method is only available to small oil and gas producers and royalty owners and for certain mineral properties.

Percentage of completion method of accounting Accounting method generally used for long-term contracts under which income is reported in proportion to the amount of work that has been completed in a given year.

Personal exemption A deduction in an amount mandated by Congress. The amount for 1994 is $2,450. For years after 1989 the amount is adjusted for increases in the cost of living. An additional exemption is allowed for each individual who is a dependent. Personal and dependency exemptions are phased out for high income taxpayers.

Personal holding company (PHC) A closely held corporation (1) that is owned by 5 or fewer shareholders who own more than 50% of the corporation's outstanding stock at any time during the last half of its taxable year and (2) whose PHC income equals at least 60% of the corporation's adjusted gross income for the tax year.

Certain corporations (e.g., S corporations) are exempt from this definition.

Personal holding company tax This tax is equal to 39.6% of the undistributed personal holding company income. It is intended to prevent closely held companies from converting an operating company into a nonoperating investment company.

Personal interest All interest other than active business interest, investment interest, interest incurred in a passive activity, qualified residence interest, and interest incurred when paying the estate tax on an installment basis. Personal interest is currently treated as a nondeductible personal expenditure. See also Interest.

Personal service corporation (PSC) A regular C corporation whose principal activity is the performance of personal services that are substantially performed by owner-employees who own more than 10% of the value of the corporation's stock.

PHC See Personal holding company.

Portfolio income Dividends, interest, annuities, and royalties not derived in the ordinary course of business. Gains and losses on property that produces portfolio income are included in such income.

Preferred stock bailout A provision mandated by Sec. 306 which prevents shareholders who receive nontaxable preferred stock dividends from receiving capital gain treatment upon the sale or redemption of the preferred stock.

Primary cite The highest level official reporter which reports a particular case is called the primary cite.

Principal partner A partner owning 5% or more of the partnership profits and capital interests.

Principal residence The residence that the taxpayer occupies most of the time.

Private activity bond Obligation issued by a state of local government to finance nongovernmental activities (e.g., a sports arena).

Private Letter Ruling See Letter Ruling

Profit-sharing plan A qualified defined benefit plan which may be established in lieu of or in addition to a qualified pension plan. Contributions to a profit-sharing plan are usually based upon profits. Incidental benefits may or may not be included. In addition, the plan must meet certain requirements concerning determination of the amount and timing of the employer's contribution, how the employee wants to receive the employer's contribution, vesting, and forfeitures.

Progressive tax Tax that increases as the taxpayer's taxable income increases. The U.S. income tax is an example of a progressive tax.

Property settlement The division of property between spouses upon their separation or divorce.

Property tax Federal, state, or local tax levied on real and/or personal property (e.g., securities, a personal automobile).

Proportional tax A method of taxation under which the tax rate is the same for all taxpayers regardless of their income. State and local sales taxes are examples of this form of tax.

Proposed Regulations Issued following changes in the tax law. May or may not be amended after hearings are conducted and comments received. Proposed regulations are not binding on taxpayers.

PSC See Personal service corporation.

Qualified pension plan Pension plan that includes (1) systematic and definite payments made to a pension trust based upon actuarial methods and (2) usually provides for incidental benefits such as disability, or medical insurance benefits.

Qualified plan award Employee achievement awards given under a written plan or program that does not discriminate in favor of highly compensated employees. Such awards must be in the form of tangible personal property other than cash and be worth no more than $1,600.

Qualified residence interest Interest on an indebtedness which is secured by the taxpayer's qualified residence when it is paid or accrued. A taxpayer may have two qualified residences: a principal residence and a residence that he has personally used more than the greater of 14 days or 10% of the rental days during the year.

Readily ascertainable fair market value The fair market value of nonqualified stock options can be readily ascertained where the option is traded on an established options exchange.

Recapture provision A provision requiring recapture of earlier alimony payments as ordinary income by the payor if the payments decline sharply in either the second or third year.

Recovery of basis doctrine Rule that allows taxpayers to recover the basis of an asset without being taxed. Such amounts are considered a return of capital.

Refundable credit See Tax credit.

Regressive tax A form of taxation under which the tax rate decreases as the tax base (e.g., income) increases.

Regular corporation See C corporation.

Regular decision Tax Court decision that is issued on a particular issue for the first time.

Replacement cost See Market value.

Replacement property Property that is acquired to replace converted property in order to retain nonrecognition of gain status. Such property must generally be functionally the same as the converted property. For example, a business machine must be replaced with a similar business machine. There are exceptions to this rule: The taxpayer-use test applies to the involuntary conversion of rental property owned by an investor; condemnations of real property held for business or investment use may be replaced by like-kind property.

Reserve method Accounting method where a bad debt reserve is created. Additions to the reserve are made at year-end for expected uncollectible accounts based upon the taxpayer's experience rate. Reductions in the reserve are made when an account receivable became a bad debt.

Residential rental property Property from which at least 80% of the gross rental income is rental from dwelling units. Residential units include manufactured homes that are used for rental purposes, but not hotels, motels, or other establishments for transient use.

Restricted property plan Such plans are used to attract and retain key executives by giving them an ownership interest in the corporation. The income recognition rules contained in Sec. 83 govern this type of plan.

Revenue Amounts received by the taxpayer from any source. It includes both taxable and nontaxable amounts and items that are a return of capital. Although closely related to income or gross income, differences between these items do exist.

Revenue Procedure Issued by the national office of the IRS, Revenue Procedures reflect the IRS' position on compliance relating to tax preparation issues. Revenue Procedures, which are published in the Cumulative Bulletin, have less weight than Treasury Regulations.

Revenue Ruling Issued by the national office of the IRS, Revenue Rulings reflect the IRS's interpretation of a narrow tax issue. Revenue Rulings, which are published in the Cumulative Bulletin, have less weight than the Treasury Regulations.

Royalties Ordinary income arising from amounts paid for the right to use property that belongs to another and is transferred for valuable consideration (e.g., a patent right where substantially all rights are transferred).

Sale A transaction where one receives cash and/or the equivalent of cash, including the assumption of debt, in exchange for an asset.

Sales tax State or local tax on purchases. Generally, food items and medicines are exempt from such tax.

S corporation Small business corporations may elect S corporation status if they meet the 35-shareholder limitation, the type of shareholder restrictions, and the one class of stock restriction. Taxation of such corporations parallels the tax rules that apply to partnerships.

Secondary cite Citation to secondary source (i.e., unofficial reporter).

Section 401(k) plan Type of plan that is often used to supplement a company's regular qualified pension and profit-sharing plan. Such plans, which generally contain a salary reduction feature, permit the employer to receive either cash or an equivalent contribution to the company's profit-sharing plan. The amount of the contribution is limited.

Section 1231 asset Real or depreciable property that is (1) held for more than one year and (2) used in a trade or business. Certain property, such as inventory, U.S. government publications, copyrights, literary, musical, or artistic compositions, and letters, are excluded from this definition.

Section 1245 property Certain property subject to depreciation and, in some cases, amortization. Depreciable personal property such as equipment is Section 1245 property. However, most real property is not.

Section 1250 property Any real property that (1) is not Section 1245 property and (2) is subject to a depreciation allowance.

Security A long-term debt obligation. Long-term is generally defined as 10 years or more.

Separate property All property that is owned before marriage and any gifts or inheritances acquired after marriage are separate property. This distinction depends on the state of residence. However, it is possible even in community property states.

Severance damages Compensation for a decline in the value of the property remaining after part of the taxpayer's property is condemned. The IRS considers such damages analogous to the proceeds from property insurance.

Shifting income The process of transferring income from one family member to another. Methods for shifting income include gifts of stock or bonds to family members who are in lower tax brackets.

Short-term capital gain (STCG) Gain realized on the sale or exchange of a capital asset held for one year or less.

Short-term capital loss (STCL) Loss realized on the sale or exchange of a capital asset held for one year or less.

Simplified LIFO method This method of inventory valuation allows taxpayers to use a single LIFO pool rather than multiple pools. See also LIFO method.

Small cases procedure When $10,000 or less is in question for a particular year, the taxpayer may opt to have the case heard by a special commissioner rather than the regular Tax Court. The decision of the commissioner cannot be appealed.

Social security benefits These benefits include (1) the basic monthly retirement and disability benefits paid under social security and (2) tier-one railroad retirement benefits.

Sole proprietorship Form of business entity owned by an individual who reports all items of income, expense, on his individual return on Schedule C.

Specific write-off method of accounting Method of accounting used for bad debts. Under this method, the taxpayer deducts each bad debt individually as it becomes worthless. This is the only allowable accounting method for bad debts arising after 1986.

Splitting income The process of creating additional taxable entities, especially corporations, in order to reduce an individual's effective tax rate.

Standard deduction A floor amount set by Congress to simplify the tax computation. It is used by taxpayers who do not have enough deductions to itemize. The amount of the deduction varies according to the taxpayer's filing status, age, and vision. Taxpayers who use this standard deduction are not required to keep records.

State corporate income tax See Franchise tax.

Statements on Responsibilities in Tax Practice (SRTP) Ethical guidelines of the AICPA-Federal Tax Division for CPAs to promote high standards of tax practice.

Stock bonus plan A special type of defined benefit plan under which the employer's stock is contributed to a trust. The stock is then allocated and distributed to the participants. See also Employee stock ownership plan.

Stock dividend A dividend paid in the form of stock in the corporation issuing the dividend.

Stock option plan This category includes incentive stock options and nonqualified stock option arrangements. Such plans are used to attract and retain key employees.

Substance-over-form doctrine Judicial weighing of a transaction's economic substance more heavily than its legal form.

Surviving spouse A special filing status available to widows and widowers who file a joint return for the year his or her spouse dies and for the following two years. The surviving spouse may not have remarried, must be a U.S. citizen or resident, have qualified to file a joint return for the year, and must have at least one dependent child living at home during the year.

Syndication fees The nonamortizable fees (e.g., brokerage and registration fees) incurred to promote and market partnership interests. Such fees are generally associated with tax-sheltered limited partnership interests.

Tax A mandatory assessment levied under the authority of a political entity for the purpose of raising revenue to be used for public or governmental purposes. Such taxes may be levied by the federal, state, or local government.

Taxable income For individuals, taxable income is adjusted gross income reduced by deductions from adjusted gross income.

Tax benefit rule Recovery of an amount in a subsequent year that produced a tax benefit in a prior year and is thus taxable to the recipient.

Tax credit Amount that can be deducted from the gross tax to arrive at the net tax due or refund due. Prepaid amounts, that is, amounts paid to the government during the year, are tax credits. Such prepaid amounts are often referred to as "refundable credits."

Tax law The tax law is comprised of the Internal Revenue Code, administrative and judicial interpretations, and the committee reports issued by the Congressional committees involved in the legislative process.

Taxpayer Compliance Measurement Program (TCMP) A stratified random sample used to select tax returns for audit. The program is intended to test the extent to which taxpayers are in compliance with the law.

Tax research Search for the best possible solution to a problem involving either a proposed or completed transaction.

Tax shelter Passive activity which may lack economic substance other than creating tax deductions and credits that enable taxpayers to reduce or eliminate the income tax liability from their regular business activities. Section 469 restricts the current use of deductions and credits arising from passive activities.

Tax year See Accounting period.

TCMP See Taxpayer Compliance Measurement Program.

Technical Advice Memorandum Such memoranda are administrative interpretations issued in the form of letter ruling. Taxpayers may request them if they need guidance about the tax treatment of complicated technical matters which are being audited.

Temporary Regulations Temporary Regulations are Treasury Regulations that are issued to provide guidance for taxpayers pending the issuance of the final regulations. They are binding upon taxpayers. Temporary Regulations are also required to be issued as proposed regulations and must expire within three years.

Testamentary gift Transfer of property made at the death of the donor (i.e., bequests, devises, and inheritances).

Theft loss Loss of business, investment, or personal-use property due to crimes such as, but not limited to, larceny, embezzlement, robbery, extortion, blackmail, or kidnapping for ransom. Such losses are deductible from AGI, subject to certain limitations.

Total economic income The amount of the taxpayer's income, including exclusions and deductions from the tax base (e.g., tax-exempt bonds), is categorized as total economic income.

Transportation expense The deductibility of this type of expense depends upon whether it is trade- or business-related, whether it is related to the production of income, whether the expense is employment related and therefore subject to the 2% nondeductible floor for miscellaneous itemized deductions. Commuting expenses are nondeductible. See also Travel expense.

Travel expense Such expenses include transportation, meals, and lodging incurred in the pursuit of a trade, business, or employment-related activity. There are limitations and restrictions on the deductibility of these expenses. See also Transportation expense.

Treasury bill Short-term (i.e., 90-day) obligation that is issued by the government at a discount from the maturity amount. The difference between the issue price and the maturity amount represents the interest income.

Treasury Regulation The principal administrative source of the federal tax law, these Regulations reflect the Treasury and the IRS's interpretation of the Internal Revenue Code. They may be either legislative or interpretative and they may be issued in either proposed, temporary, or final form.

Unfunded deferred compensation plan This type of plan is used for highly-compensated employees who wish to defer the recognition of income until future periods. Funding is generally accomplished through an escrow account for the employee's benefit.

Uniform Capitalization rules (UNICAP) The requirements under the tax law for determining inventory cost. Under UNICAP certain indirect overhead costs are required to be included in inventory for tax purposes which are generally not included for financial accounting.

Unrelated use property Capital gain property which is also tangible personal property and which is contributed to a public charity for a use that is unrelated to the charity's function. The contribution deduction (from AGI) for such property is equal to the property's fair market value minus the capital gain that would be recognized if the property was sold at that value.

Unreported decision District Court decisions that are not officially reported in the Federal Supplement. Such decisions may be reported in secondary reporters that report only tax-related cases.

U.S. Treasury Bill See Treasury bill.

Wash sale A wash sale results when the taxpayer (1) sells stock or securities and (2) purchases substantially identical stock or securities within the 61-day period extending from 30 days before the date of sale to 30 days after the date of sale.

Wealth transfer tax A tax imposed upon the value of property transferred during one's lifetime (i.e., a gift tax) or upon the death of the transferor (i.e., an estate tax). The tax is imposed upon the transferor of property or upon the estate.

Zero coupon bond Bond that is issued at a cost that is substantially less than the current market rate because no interest payments are made. The original issue discount (OID) must be amortized over the term of the bond by investors using the constant rate method. Such bonds offer cash-flow advantages to corporate issuers since no cash outlay for interest is required until the bonds mature.

E

Index of Code Sections

Index of Government Promulgations

Index of Court Cases

Subject Index

1994 *Tax Rate Schedules*

ESTATES AND TRUSTS

If Taxable Income Is:		The Tax Is:	
Over—	But Not Over—		Of the Amount Over—
$0	$1,500	15%	$0
1,500	3,600	$225 + 28%	1,500
3,600	5,500	813 + 31%	3,600
5,500	7,500	1,402 + 36%	5,500
7,500		2,122 + 39.6%	7,500

CORPORATIONS

If Taxable Income Is:		The Tax Is:	
Over—	But Not Over—		Of the Amount Over—
$0	$50,000	15%	$0
50,000	75,000	$7,500 + 25%	50,000
75,000	100,000	13,750 + 34%	75,000
100,000	335,000	22,250 + 39%	100,000
335,000	10,000,000	113,900 + 34%	335,000
10,000,000	15,000,000	3,400,000 + 35%	10,000,000
15,000,000	18,333,333	5,150,000 + 38%	15,000,000
18,333,333		6,416,667 + 35%	18,333,333

UNIFIED CREDIT AMOUNT FOR ESTATE AND GIFT TAX

Year of Gift/ Year of Death	Amount of Credit	Exemption Equivalent
January through June, 1977	$6,000	$30,000
July through December, 1977	30,000	120,666
1978	34,000	134,000
1979	38,000	147,333
1980	42,500	161,563
1981	47,000	175,625
1982	62,800	225,000
1983	79,300	275,000
1984	96,300	325,000
1985	121,800	400,000
1986	155,800	500,000
1987 and later years	192,800	600,000